A
History of China

A
History of China

Wolfram Eberhard

UNIVERSITY OF CALIFORNIA PRESS
Berkeley and Los Angeles

'Chinas Geschichte' first published in Switzerland 1948
Translated by E. W. Dickes

English edition first published 1950
Second edition (revised by the author
and reset) 1960

Third edition (revised and enlarged)
published in the United States 1969

This fourth edition (revised by the author
and reset) first published in the United States 1977
by The University of California Press
Berkeley and Los Angeles, California

First Paperback Edition, 1977
Copyright © Wolfram Eberhard 1977

Library of Congress Catalog Card Number 76-7758
ISBN 0-520-03268-3

2 3 4 5 6 7 8 9

Printed in the United States of America

To My Wife

CONTENTS

Chapter V: MILITARY RULE
(250–200 B.C.)

Chapter VI: THE EARLY GENTRY SOCIETY
(200 B.C.–A.D. 250)

Chapter VII: THE EPOCH OF THE FIRST
DIVISION OF CHINA (A.D. 220–580)   109

(A) THE THREE KINGDOMS (A.D. 220–265)

(B) THE WESTERN CHIN DYNASTY (A.D. 265–317)

(C) THE ALIEN EMPIRES IN NORTH CHINA, DOWN
TO THE TOBA (A.D. 317–385)

(D) THE TOBA EMPIRE IN NORTH CHINA (A.D. 385–550)

(E) SUCCESSION STATES OF THE TOBA (A.D. 550–580): NORTHERN CH'I DYNASTY, NORTHERN CHOU DYNASTY

(F) THE SOUTHERN EMPIRES

Chapter VIII: CLIMAX AND DOWNFALL OF THE IMPERIAL GENTRY (A.D. 580–950) 169

(A) THE SUI DYNASTY (A.D. 580–618)

(B) THE T'ANG DYNASTY (A.D. 618–906)

(C) THE SECOND DIVISION OF CHINA: THE FIVE DYNASTIES (A.D. 906–960)

Chapter IX: MODERN TIMES   205

(A) GENERAL CHARACTERISTICS

(B) PERIOD OF MODERATE ABSOLUTISM

(1) The Northern Sung dynasty

(2) The Liao (Kitan) dynasty in the north (937–1125)

(3) The Hsi-Hsia state in the north (1038–1227)

(4) The empire of the Southern Sung dynasty (1127–1279)

ILLUSTRATIONS

MAPS

INTRODUCTION

Histories of China have to be rewritten from time to time, and so I have attempted to rewrite some parts of my own History of China. There are several reasons for this. First, our knowledge of China's history has changed. Many new excavations have been made and many new studies have been produced which have corrected our former views. Perhaps we should admit that it is a bad moment to bring out a History of China, because many of the new excavations have not yet been described and analysed fully; many new texts have been found, but we do not have them yet in our hands and the necessary philological work on them is not yet done; many other documents will undoubtedly be found in the next years. Thus, in a couple of years, yet another 'revision' will be necessary.

Second, we have changed. Changes in our own society have raised new questions and made us aware of new problems. A scholar, even a historian who studies Chinese history, is necessarily influenced by these new trends; he looks at his Chinese data in a way which differs from the way he studied the data formerly. To give a simple example only: when the position of women in our society is discussed daily and often passionately, the writer is naturally stimulated to look into the question: what was and what is the position of women in Chinese society? Or, when we discuss the problems of ecology in our society, we are stimulated to find out what attitudes Chinese had towards their environment.

Finally, the greater the role becomes which China plays in the world, the greater their pride in their achievements tends to become; the deeper roots Marxist-Maoist thinking develops, the more will publications from the People's Republic be permeated by nationalist and Maoist thoughts. And the more will our own public be influenced by publications which consciously or unconsciously incorporate such traits. I admit, nobody is completely without bias, but it may be important to attempt to show an interpretation of Chinese history which tries to avoid the 'official' bias. Of course, both sides agree that the basic sources of Chinese history contain biases. It has been realized that the sources on which reliance has always been placed were not objective, but deliberately and emphatically represented a particular philosophy. The reports on the emperors and ministers of the earliest period are not historical at all, but served as examples of ideas of social policy or as glorifications of particular noble families. Myths such as we find to this day among China's neighbours were made into history; gods were made men and linked together by long family trees. We have been able to touch on all these things only briefly, and have had to dispense with any account of the complicated processes that have taken place here.

The official dynastic histories apply to the course of Chinese history the criterion of Confucian ethics; for them history is a text-book of ethics, designed to show by means of examples how the man of high character should behave or not behave. Practically all our written sources were produced by men of the upper class and represent the social and political values these men had. These historians and chroniclers were not much interested in and often not well informed about the great majority of the people. We have, thus, to try to go deeper and to extract the historic truth from these records. This is a tremendous task in which scholars from all countries are engaged, but, to this day, we are far from having really worked through every period of Chinese history; there are long periods on which scarcely any work has yet been done. Thus the picture we are able to give today has no finality about it and will need many modifications.

The present work is intended for the general reader and not for the specialist. It attempts to pay more attention to social and cultural developments than to purely political history; to try to find out how the 'common man' lived and not only how the leaders lived. I have also been concerned not to leave out of account China's relations with her neighbours. Now that we have a better knowledge of China's neighbours, the Turks, Mongols, Tibetans, Tunguses, Thai, not confined to the narratives of Chinese, who always speak only of 'barbarians', we are better able to realize how closely China has been associated with her neighbours from the first day of her history to the present time; how greatly she is indebted to them, and how much she has given them. We no longer see China as a great civilization surrounded by barbarians, but we study the Chinese coming to terms with their neighbours, who had civilizations of quite different types but nevertheless developed ones.

These special stresses make, I think, this book different from others, and try to make the reader see the Chinese people in a different light. I have to admit that even in such a limited field as Chinese social-cultural history, almost innumerable studies have appeared in recent years in all languages of the world that it is impossible to be fully 'up-to-date'. Perhaps a group of scholars, each specializing in a limited period of history, might have been able to overcome this weakness, but in all collective works on China that I know, unity of thought and method is missing.

It is usual to split up Chinese history under the various dynasties that have ruled China or parts thereof. The beginning or end of a dynasty does not always indicate the beginning or the end of a definite period of China's social or cultural development. We have tried to break China's history down into the three large periods— 'Antiquity', 'The Middle Ages', and 'Modern Times'. This does not mean that we compare these periods with periods of the same name in Western history although, naturally, we find some similarities with the development of society and culture in the West. Every attempt towards periodization is to some degree arbitrary: the beginning and end of the Middle Ages, for instance, cannot be fixed to a year, because development is a continuous process. To some degree any periodization is a matter of convenience, and it should be accepted as such.

Chinese words are transcribed according to the Wade-Giles system with the exception of names for which already a popular way of transcription exists (such as Peking). Place names are written without hyphen, if they remain readable.

W.E.

CHAPTER ONE

Prehistory

1 Sources for the earliest history

Until recently we were dependent for the beginnings of Chinese history on the written Chinese tradition. According to these sources China's history began either about 4000 B.C. or about 2700 B.C. with a succession of wise emperors who 'invented' the elements of a civilization, such as clothing, the preparation of food, marriage, and a state system; they instructed their people in these things, and so brought China, as early as in the third millennium B.C., to an astonishingly high cultural level. However, all we know of the origin of civilizations makes this of itself entirely improbable; no other civilization in the world originated in any such way. As time went on, Chinese historians found more and more to say about primeval times. All these narratives were collected in the great imperial history that appeared at the beginning of the Manchu epoch. The older historical sources make no mention of any rulers before 2200 B.C., no mention even of their names. The names of earlier rulers first appear in documents of about 400 B.C.; the deeds attributed to them and the dates assigned to them often do not appear until much later.

Modern research has not only demonstrated that all these accounts are inventions of a much later period, but has also shown *why* such narratives were composed. We will discuss this later at the appropriate moment, but briefly mention that on the one hand these accounts can be seen as an attempt of Chinese philosophers to explain the development of culture and society and to use them to legitimize the system of government that existed in their time. On the other hand, the accounts served to legitimize the aspirations and actions of particular persons or groups of persons.

Furthermore, we can now state with certainty that all historical data which were given in written documents for times down to about 1000 B.C. are false. They are the result of astronomical-astrological calculations, made by specialists of later times who pursued their own special political aims by doing these calculations. To this day,

1

we do not have written sources which are earlier than c. 1300 B.C., but we have reason to say that persons and activities mentioned in sources written after that time and said to have lived before it, really did live and seem to have done certain actions, perhaps up to the time shortly before 2000 B.C. There is, however, no reason to accept anything that is said in later sources about periods before 2000 B.C. as 'historical'. Strictly speaking, then, a history of China should not begin before the time for which written documentation exists. During the last 50 years, numerous excavations have been made on the territory of the People's Republic of China, but to call the cultures which have been found, 'Chinese' is just about as logical as to call the people of Mohenjo Dharo 'Pakistani'. We now know definitely, though not all the evidence has been published, that on the territory of China people of different cultures and even of different races lived. We also know that in present-day China people of different cultures live as minorities, though 'racially' most of them are not different from 'Chinese', and we know that the people who now call themselves 'Chinese' do not all have all the same racial origins—in whichever way we may define this controversial term 'race'. The matter is not a matter of race or language and not a matter of territory. We should speak of 'Chinese' from the moment that we can find a group of people under an organized government, a form of 'state' that regards itself as a group with a common culture and as different from other groups. From at least 1000 B.C. on, we find a clear term which the Chinese used for themselves and which excluded others. As the state of that time was a clear continuation of an earlier state, we can speak of 'Chinese' probably from about 1500 B.C. on. What is before this time should be called 'pre-Chinese' and we can study this period only by means of archaeology and comparative ethnology. However, both methods tend to give different results.

2 The earliest periods

For the earliest period, we have nothing but a few excavations. Actually, we cannot expect very many traces of the first man, as there were probably only a few small hordes in some places of the Far East. The main settlement which we know consists of caves in Chou-k'ou-tien, south of Peking. Here lived the so-called 'Peking Man'. He is vastly different from the men of today, and forms a special branch of the human race, closely allied to the Pithecanthropus of Java. The formation of later races of mankind from these types has not yet been traced, if it occurred at all.

The Peking Man lived in caves; no doubt he was a hunter, already in possession of very simple stone implements and also of the art of making fire. As none of the skeletons so far found is complete, it is

2

assumed that he buried certain bones of the dead in different places from the rest. This burial custom, which is found among primitive peoples in other parts of the world, suggests the conclusion that the Peking Man already had religious notions. We have no knowledge yet of the length of time the Peking Man may have inhabited the Far East. His first traces are attributed to a million years ago, and he may have flourished in 500,000 B.C.

The first remnants of the Peking Man were already found in the 1920s. Only in recent years, remnants of this race were found also in other parts of northern China.

In a later phase of the Pleistocene remnants of a different human race, perhaps related to the Neanderthal race of Europe and Western Asia, have recently been discovered, and the more developed stone scrapers and other implements show some relation to Aurignacian and Moustérian tools of the West. However, it is still much too early to state whether such similarities are the result of transmission or of pure chance.

Finally, in the last part of the Pleistocene, a modern race of Homo sapiens is found in China, first in the upper levels of the Chou-k'ou-tien caves, then in other parts of China; with him appear still further refined and specialized stone tools. Archaeologists are of the opinion that this Far Eastern race may be the ancestor of the Mongoloid races of the northern Far East, but at the same time also the ancestor of a Negroid Oceanic race. Such dark-skinned races are found in parts of the Malay peninsula and the Philippines, as well as in New Guinea. And there are literary allusions in Chinese texts suggesting that a dark-skinned race may once have lived in historical periods in some parts of south China.

Possibly, this new race, which certainly is the ancestor of still existing races, may have developed in the Far East from an earlier Neanderthal race, which again could have developed from the Peking Man race. In any case, none of these earlier human beings has survived anywhere. With the beginning of the 'recent period' of geological time, the separation of the Mongoloid and the Negroid race seems to have taken place. Yet the skeletal remains found in An-yang and dating somewhat before the year 1000 B.C. seem to indicate that, at least at that time, still other races may have lived in the area of China.

At the beginning of this 'recent period' we find in the Ordos area and north of it a microlithic culture, i.e. a culture in which stone implements of very small size, but well made, were used; similar cultures have also been discovered in the West. At probably the same time, a distinct mesolithic culture appears in the area of the south of China, roughly the area around Canton and west of it. It seems that these people were largely fishers living along the rivers and the coast. It is here that the earliest remnants of a simple, cord-marked pottery have been found. The use of cord indicates that fibres were used, and it is likely that these fishermen already made a kind of barkcloth by beating fibres from trees into a vegetable felt. This is perhaps one of the most important human inventions, as it may have led to the invention of felt among animal breeders and to the invention of paper and printing many, many centuries later. And it may be that in this southern culture, the first experiments with the cultivation of plants were made. Rice, the staple food of the Chinese, seems to have been cultivated somewhere in South-East Asia; some archaeologists believe in Thailand, others seem to prefer south China. As far as we know, the population of both areas was closely related. Similarly, the cultivation of taro and yam must have begun in the same area.

It is different, however, with those plants which are still typical for the north. It is more generally assumed that wheat and millet came to the Far East from the West, the 'Fertile crescent' or even the eastern parts of Africa. Together with these plants came cattle and sheep.

3 The eight basic cultures

The principal drawback of archaeology is that what can be excavated is only a small, select section of the total culture of a society. Occasionally, we can draw conclusions from the findings on the religion and the social organization of the people. Thus, even in areas in which archaeologists have done very much work, it often remains impossible and usually questionable to assign to a specific layer that the archaeologists have established, a specific culture which is known from historical accounts to have lived in that same area. Because of the selectivity of archaeological findings, cultures seem to be very much alike over large areas in which numerous different types of societies may have existed. If later archaeologists were to excavate sites of our present time, and if they did not find written documents, they might easily conclude that there was a unified culture all over the world, because they would find the same automobiles, airplanes, radios and televisions everywhere. Here, historical ethnology may come to help. By carefully mapping the distribution of elements of material and non-material culture, by using legends and other traditions, and by tracing the distribution of still existing 'local cultures' as far back as possible, it seems possible to establish that in the area which is now China, a considerable number of different, local cultures existed, each developing along its own lines, but finally all contributing in different degrees to the formation of what we then begin to

4

call 'Chinese culture'. We will mention only the most important local cultures.

(a) The north-east culture, centred in the present provinces of Hopei (in which Peking lies), Shantung, and southern Manchuria. The people of this culture were ancestors of the Tunguses, probably mixed with an element that is contained in the present-day Paleo-Siberian tribes. These men were mainly hunters, but probably soon developed a little primitive agriculture and made coarse, thick pottery with certain basic forms which were long preserved in subsequent Chinese pottery (for instance, a type of the so-called tripods). Later, pig-breeding became typical of this culture.

(b) The northern culture existed to the west of that culture, in the region of the present Chinese province of Shansi and in the province of Jehol in Inner Mongolia. These people had been hunters, but then became pastoral nomads, depending mainly on cattle. The people of this culture were the tribes later known as Mongols, the so-called proto-Mongols. Anthropologically they belonged, like the Tunguses, to the Mongol race.

(c) The people of the culture farther west, the north-west culture, were not Mongols. They, too, were originally hunters, and later became a pastoral people, with a not inconsiderable agriculture (especially growing wheat and millet). The typical animal of this group soon became the horse. The horse seems to be the last of the great animals to be domesticated, and the date of its first occurrence in domesticated form in the Far East is not yet determined, but we can assume that by 2500 B.C. this group was already in possession of horses. The horse has always been a 'luxury', a valuable animal which needed special care. For their economic needs, these tribes depended on other animals, probably sheep, goats, and cattle. The centres of this culture, so far as can be ascertained from Chinese sources, were the present provinces of Shensi and Kansu, but mainly only the plains. The people of this culture were most probably ancestors of the later Turkish peoples. It is not suggested, of course, that the original home of the Turks lay in the region of the Chinese provinces of Shensi and Kansu; one gains the impression, however, that this was a border region of the Turkish expansion; the Chinese documents concerning that period do not suffice to establish the centre of the Turkish territory. Recent linguistic research has made it likely that Turkic, Mongolic, and Tungusic languages are to some degree related and may have developed from one single type of language; it seems also that the Korean language is related to these languages, while Japanese may have more complex origins, though still be related to Korean and through it to the Altaic languages.

(d) In the west, in the present provinces of Szechwan and in all the mountain regions of the provinces of Kansu and Shensi, lived the ancestors of the Tibetan peoples as another separate culture. They were shepherds, generally wandering with their flocks of sheep and goats on the mountain heights.

(e) In the south we meet with four further cultures. One is very primitive, the Liao culture, the peoples of which are the Austro-asiatics already mentioned. These are peoples who never developed beyond the stage of primitive hunters, some of whom were not even acquainted with the bow and arrow. Farther east is the Yao culture, an early Austronesian culture, the people of which also lived in the mountains, some as collectors and hunters, some going over to a simple type of agriculture (denshiring). They mingled later with the last great culture of the south, the Thai culture, distinguished by agriculture. The people lived in the valleys and mainly cultivated rice. The centre of this Thai culture may have been in the present provinces of Kuangtung and Kuangsi. Today, their descendants form the principal components of the Thai in Thailand, the Shan in Burma and the Lao in Laos. Their immigration into the areas of the Shan States of Burma and into Thailand took place only in quite recent historical periods, probably not much earlier than A.D. 1000.

Finally there arose from the mixture of the Yao with the Thai culture, at a rather later time, the Yüeh culture, another early Austronesian culture, which then spread over wide regions of Indonesia, and of which the axe of rectangular section became typical. Linguistically, the languages of the Tibetans (to which minorities in China proper, like the Lolo, belong) are related to the Chinese language. The Thai languages are even closer relatives of the Chinese, while the languages of the Yao and Yüeh seem to have been related to the languages of Indonesia and the South Pacific. The Liao may have relatives in Mon and Kmer cultures of South-East Asia.

Thus, to sum up, we may say that, quite roughly, in the middle of the third millennium we meet in the north and west of present-day China with a number of herdsmen cultures. In the south there were a number of agrarian cultures, of which the Thai was the most powerful, becoming of most importance to the later China. We must assume that these cultures were as yet undifferentiated in their social composition, that is to say that as yet there was no distinct social stratification, but at most beginnings of class-formation, especially among the nomad herdsmen. This picture of prehistoric cultures, each of which is a contributor in its own way to the later 'Chinese' culture, is much more detailed than the picture gained from archaeology alone, but is, in my opinion, not in contradiction to the results of archaeology. Doubtless further research will clarify and correct this reconstruction of the last period of Chinese prehistory.

6

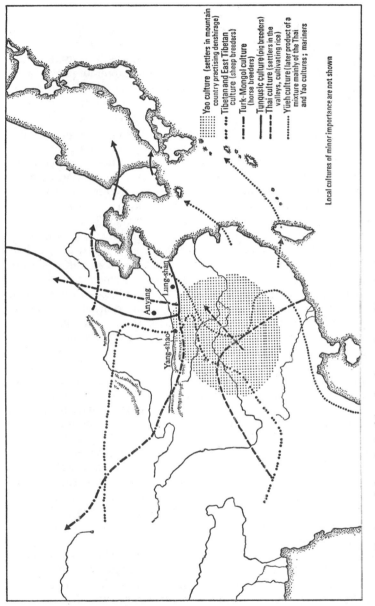

Yao culture (settlers in mountain country practising denshirage)

Tibetan and East Tibetan culture (sheep breeders)

Turk-Mongol culture (horse breeders)

Tungusic culture (pig breeders)

Thai culture (settlers in the valleys, cultivating rice)

Yüeh culture (later product of a mixture mainly of the Thai and Yao cultures; mariners)

Local cultures of minor importance are not shown

Anyang

Lung-shan

Yang-shao

MAP 1   *Regions of the principal local cultures in prehistoric times*

4 *The Yang-shao culture*

The various cultures here described gradually penetrated one another, especially at points where they met. Such a process does not yield a simple total of the cultural elements involved; any new combination produces entirely different conditions with corresponding new results which, in turn, represent the characteristics of the culture that supervenes. We can no longer follow this process of penetration in detail; it need not by any means have been always warlike. Conquest of one group by another was only one way of mutual cultural penetration. In other cases, a group which occupied the higher altitudes and practised hunting or slash-and-burn agriculture came into closer contacts with another group in the valleys which practised some form of higher agriculture; frequently, such contacts resulted in particular forms of division of labour in a unified and often stratified new form of society. Recent and present developments in South-East Asia present a number of examples for such changes. Increase of population is certainly one of the most important elements which lead to these developments. The result, as a rule, was a stratified society being made up of at least one privileged and one ruled stratum. Thus there came into existence around 2000 B.C. some new cultures, which are well known archaeologically. The most important of these are the Yang-shao culture in the west and the Lung-shan culture in the east. Our knowledge of both these cultures is of quite recent date and there are many enigmas still to be cleared up.

The Yang-shao culture takes its name from a prehistoric settlement in the west of the present province of Honan, where Swedish investigators discovered it. Typical of this culture is its wonderfully fine pottery, apparently used as gifts to the dead. It is painted in three colours, white, red, and black. The patterns are all stylized, designs copied from nature being rare. This pottery is still handmade; the potter's wheel is a later invention. Together with this fine pottery, a common grey pottery was still used, and some scholars think that the painted pottery may be a development from earlier cord- or mat-marked pottery. Others have pointed out that the designs on the painted pottery have close parallels with pottery found in Iran (Anau) and other sites in western Asia. Doubtless some ethnocentrism has entered the debate here: Western scholars seem to have a tendency to derive Chinese culture from the West, while many Chinese scholars have tried to show that Yang-shao culture developed in the nuclear area of old China and spread later to the West. They claim that the earliest Yang-shao remains come from south Shansi, west Honan, east and central Shensi, and that the findings in west Shensi and Kansu are of a later period. This may be correct, but does not

8

exclude the possibility that Yang-shao has at some time also received stimuli from western Asia. The more we know, the more we can see that Near and Far East were never as independent from one another as we formerly have thought. Certain it is, however, that the Yang-shao people lived only on the western highlands of China, along river terraces and along small basins. They did not live in the eastern great plains of China. The distribution of this culture is similar to that of the reconstructed Tibetan culture, though we certainly cannot regard Yang-shao as a 'proto-Tibetan' culture. Though they kept sheep and goats, and some cattle, their main animals were the pig and the dog. Much of their food still came from hunting and fishing, but they were already farmers who cultivated millet and wheat—and both, as we have noted, come from the West. Earlier scholars believed that they also cultivated rice, but this seems still to be doubtful. They seem to have used hemp for clothing, but there is an indication that they already produced some kind of silk from the cocoons of one variety of the silkworm. Until late in history, silk has been the typical invention of the Chinese which made them famous already in the times of the Roman Empire.

The tools of the Yang-shao people were already highly specialized; we can distinguish agricultural tools such as hoe, spade, digging stick, sickle and grain grinders, from tools used for carpentry and from weapons. Their stone tools were polished.

They lived in compact villages—a settlement type which remained typical until the present. However, it seems that the villages often shifted, perhaps in connection with their slash-and-burn agriculture which made periodic migrations necessary. The villages seem to exhibit some planning. Often, the cemetery was in the north of the village, and their pottery kilns were also outside the settlement. Houses were made of stamped clay (adobe), often semi-subterranean and mainly rectangular or square; however, round buildings were found as well as fully subterranean storage buildings. In a later period, Chinese archaeologists have claimed to have found 'long houses', in which more than one family lived, each in a compartment with its fire-place. As in Marxist theory 'communal settlement' plays an important role, such interpretations have to be taken with some scepticism. Such long houses still exist in parts of South-East Asia and Indonesia.

5 *The Lung-shan culture*

The Lung-shan culture, characterized by a black, fine pottery, often already made on the wheel, was discovered shortly before the Second World War. It is a culture of the east and of the plains. The discussion of its relation to Yang-shao and to the later historical cultures is again not free from elements of ideological speculation. As the eastern plains have always been regarded by Chinese historians as a part of the nuclear area of Chinese culture—it is the area in which China's greatest thinkers were born—a 'two culture' theory was hypothesized: Yang-shao and Lung-shan were both contemporary, each one independent of the other. The more recent consensus seems to be that Lung-shan is slightly later than Yang-shao. Some Western scholars, agreeing with this, tried to derive the Lung-shan culture again from a later period of West Asian cultures. In fact, there is a black pottery of quite similar type widely spread over Turkey and Iran. Chinese scholars, on the other hand, have tried to derive the Lung-shan culture from the Yang-shao culture. In favour of the first hypothesis speaks the fact that many Yang-shao vessels have forms which we know from the West, while Lung-shan vessels are clearly prototypes of vessels which later became typical of 'Chinese' pottery.

Lung-shan is certainly more highly developed than Yang-shao. Their villages were more permanent and were surrounded by mud walls; they seem to have had a higher agriculture with permanent use of the same fields. They had scapulimancy, i.e. used animal bones for the purpose of fortune-telling. Such and other characteristics have induced some scholars to assume that the people of the Lung-shan culture had already a social organization with some stratification, a beginning of the formation of social classes.

Most important for the Lung-shan culture is that it seems to have quickly spread over wide parts of the Far East, from Manchuria in the north to Canton and Taiwan. It is today possible to isolate several 'local cultures' of the Lung-shan type, and it may well be possible in the future to identify some of these local cultures with those hypothesized by the ethno-historic method. There is as yet no unanimity among scholars as to the age of Yang-shao and Lung-shan. It may perhaps be adequate to say that Lung-shan existed, perhaps even in different local forms, around 2000 B.C. Then, Yang-shao must have existed before 2400 B.C., but perhaps even a good deal earlier.

6   The first petty states in Shansi

At the time in which, according to archaeological research, the painted pottery flourished in west China, Chinese historical tradition has it that the model rulers Yao, Shun, and Yü ruled the empire. What we know about them comes from sources which were written not much before 400 B.C., and the traditional dates (Yao 2333–2234; Shun 2233–2184; Yü 2183–2177 B.C.) are found in much later sources still and are clearly the result of astrological calculations. These men became the models of good kings: it is said that Yao

10

ceded the throne when he was old to a simple man, Shun, and not to his son; Shun supposedly did the same, while Yü tried to act the same way but 'people' wanted him to establish his son as successor, and from then on hereditary rule became established. All three are credited with acts which benefited mankind, especially Yü, who controlled a large flood by designing channels for the waters. It has been possible to show that these 'actions' in part are euhemerized myths, in part constructions of philosophers who wanted to explain the origins of society and culture. Much more creditable is another, equally late and questionable source which states that Shun made war against Yao and killed him, and that Yü acted similarly. The only conclusion which we may perhaps draw from all these texts is that sometime around 2000 B.C. small statelets may have existed in the area of the southern part of today's province of Shansi, similar to many such statelets of Chinese and of non-Chinese that still existed down to the middle of the first millennium B.C.

Perhaps the creation of statelets coincides with the next great cultural progress: bronze seems to appear in traces within the later Yang-shao culture about 1800 B.C. By about 1400 B.C. it had become very widespread and technically very well developed. As the forms of the oldest weapons and their ornamentation show similarities with weapons from north Central Asia and as also mythology seems to indicate that the bronze came from the north into China, some scholars assume that bronze was brought to the Far East either through the agency of peoples living north of China, perhaps people related to the later Turkish tribes, or by individual clans or families which migrated from customer to customer, as we meet them later in Turkish and Central Asian tradition. These tribes or clans, in turn, could have learned the technique from some Near Eastern society, as bronze was used there much earlier than in central and east Asia. Other scholars believe that bronze was independently discovered in the area of north China and spread from there to the areas north of China. The bronze vessels which made their appearance about 1450 B.C. seem to be a direct development from earlier pottery, while their ornamentation seems to be largely derived from earlier wood-carving of southern style. This is not astonishing as there were few deposits of tin and copper in north China, while in the south, an area at that time inhabited mainly by Thai tribes, both metals were plentiful, so that a trade from the south to the north must soon have set in.

It is at this time that Chinese tradition has its first 'dynasty', the Hsia, which is said to have been founded by Yü. The traditional date for the Hsia dynasty (2176–1725 B.C.) is certainly false. What the late sources say about this period cannot be accepted as historical, though there seems to be an indication that some kind of dynasty may have existed. Archaeology has to this time not yet been able to find incontestable traces of the Hsia, in spite of numerous excavation attempts in the supposed centres of this dynasty.

CHAPTER TWO

The Emergence of Feudalism (c. 1600–1028 B.C.)

1 *Period, origin, material culture*

With the Shang dynasty, we come at last into the realm of history, though we still do not have reliable data for its duration. It can now be proved that the traditional date for the end of the dynasty (1112 B.C.) is wrong and the result of calculations. Therefore, the traditional year for its beginning (1751 B.C.) must also be wrong. We have lists of the Shang kings and excavated documents have proved that these lists are by and large correct. But in spite of these documents we still cannot say how long individual kings ruled and from when to when. While the written texts do not say much about Shang culture, numerous excavations show that the Shang civilization was a complex one with elements that clearly come from the Lung-shan culture, and others which seem to come from Yang-shao. The inscriptions on bone which have been found show that the Shang had quite a number of towns, some of which have tentatively been identified with excavation sites. These excavations seem to prove one point in the later documents, namely that the Shang changed their capital several times in the course of the dynasty. While it is still disputed that the place where the overwhelming number of inscriptions were found, a place near the present city of An-yang in Hopei province, really was the capital of the Shang shortly before the end of the dynasty, the important fact for us is that settlements enclosed by walls which first were found in the Lung-shan period now became the norm. Down to modern times, the walled city the symbol of Chinese rule and the seat of local or central government. The walls of one of the earliest cities seem to have had an average height of 10 metres and an average width of 20 metres, so that the wall of over 7,000 metres required the moving of almost 3 million cubic metres of soil. It has been calculated that such a structure would need 10,000 workers who worked for 18 years continuously. These calculations are rough ones, but indicate that only a society with stratification and a centralized government could have produced them.

Before the Second World War, only one site of Shang culture was excavated, the city of Yin, near An-yang. With new excavations made after 1950, we know much more and can now say that the earliest site with a clearly 'Shang culture' is near Yen-shih, between Lo-yang and Cheng-chou in Honan province. Tradition has it that the first Shang ruler lived in Po, and Po has, by some scholars, been identified with the area of Yen-shih. Here several different sites have been found, but not all of them have been excavated. Important is, that excavations found below the Shang level a Lung-shan level and below that a Yang-shao level. We should also keep in mind that Yen-shih is geographically at the beginning of the plains, where Lung-shan people touched Yang-shao people. The Yen-shih people did not yet have a script, though some of their incisions on pots may be symbols of some early script. They used stone, shells and bone for their implements, and had some bronze implements. This seems to be the earliest occurrence of metal in the Far East, much later than in the Near East.

The next important Shang settlement is very close to the present Cheng-chou. It may have been the city of Ao, reported in Shang texts. It seems that inside the city walls, only the upper class lived and was buried, so that the city can be regarded as an administrative centre. The commoners seem to have lived outside the walls. Later Chinese cities often have two walls: one enclosing the administrative centre or the imperial palaces, the larger one enclosing the area in which the ordinary people lived. Ao was already surrounded by a rectangular wall, the 'ideal' form of the Chinese city to the recent past. Inside the walls remnants of large buildings were found, perhaps remnants of a palace. Even the earlier Yen-shih may have had a palace-like building, it is assumed. In both places there are indications that some of the corpses found may have been victims of human sacrifice.

The city of Yin near An-yang, is by far the greatest Shang settlement and belongs to a later period. Here, the first written documents were found. Yin seems to have had a wall, too, although it is largely destroyed. Inside the walls was a complex which is regarded as a palace area, surrounded by houses which seem to have been houses of palace artisans, while the houses of others were more on the outside. The rectangular houses were built in a style still found in Chinese houses, except that their front did not always face south as is now the general rule. The Shang buried their kings in large, subterranean, cross-shaped tombs outside the city, and many imple-

14

ments, animals and human sacrifices were buried together with them. The custom of large burial mounds, which later became typical of the Chou dynasty, did not yet exist.

The Shang had sculptures in stone, an art which later more or less completely disappeared and which was resuscitated only in post-Christian times under the influence of Indian Buddhism. Yet Shang culture cannot well be called a 'megalithic' culture. Bronze implements and especially bronze vessels were now developed to a degree that has rarely been reached again in China or any other early civilization of the world. The implements were made by specialists whose 'trade marks' we often can see on the vessels. The bronze weapons have some similarity to weapons from central north Asia and are often ornamented in the so-called 'animal style' which was used among all the nomad peoples between the Ordos region and Siberia to Iran in the West until the beginning of the Christian era. But whether this 'animal style' was first developed by the Shang and from there spread towards the West or whether the process went the other way, is still unclear. Thus far, we cannot prove that the Chinese learned metallurgy and the earliest style of decoration of weapons from the West. Certainly, the famous bronze vessels show a decoration which is more closely related to the south than to the West.

There can be no doubt that the bronze vessels were used for religious service and not for everyday life. For everyday use there were earthenware vessels. Even in the middle of the first millennium B.C., bronze was exceedingly dear, as we know from the records of prices. China has always suffered from scarcity of metal. For that reason metal was accumulated as capital, entailing a further rise in prices; when prices had reached a sufficient height, the stocks were thrown on the market and prices fell again. Later, when there was a metal coinage, this cycle of inflation and deflation became still clearer. The metal coinage was of its full nominal value, so that it was possible to coin money by melting down bronze implements. As the money in circulation was increased in this way, the value of the currency fell. Then it paid to turn coin into metal implements. This once more reduced the money in circulation and increased the value of the remaining coinage. Thus through the whole course of Chinese history the scarcity of metal and insufficiency of production of metal continually produced extensive fluctuations of the stocks and the value of metal, amounting virtually to an economic law in China. Consequently metal implements were never universally in use, and vessels were usually of earthenware, with the further result of the early invention of porcelain. Porcelain vessels have many of the qualities of metal ones, but are cheaper.

The earthenware vessels used in this period are in many cases already very near to porcelain: there was a pottery of a brilliant white, lacking only the glaze which would have made it into porcelain. Patterns were stamped on the surface, often resembling the patterns on bronze articles. This ware was used only for formal, ceremonial purposes. For daily use there was also a perfectly simple grey pottery.

The houses and palaces which have been excavated were made of adobe, but in contrast to earlier periods, the houses were built on stamped-earth foundations, a technique that has remained typically Chinese. Of course, we should assume that in addition to these more solid houses, much of the population lived in simple huts of which no remnants remained. Similar to the ancient cities of India, like Harappa, the palace area seems to have had a system of water ditches, probably for drainage.

The area under more or less organized Shang control comprised towards the end of the dynasty the present provinces of Honan, western Shantung, southern Hopei, central and south Shansi, east Shensi, parts of Kiangsu and Anhui. We can only roughly estimate the size of the population of the Shang state. Late texts say that at the time of the annihilation of the dynasty, some 3·1 million free men and 1·1 million serfs were captured by the conquerors; this would indicate a population of at least some 4–5 millions. This seems a possible number, if we consider that an inscription of the tenth century B.C. which reports about an ordinary war against a small and unimportant western neighbour, speaks of 13,081 free men and 4,812 serfs taken as prisoners.

Inscriptions mention many neighbours of the Shang with whom they were in a more or less continuous state of war. Many of these neighbours can now be identified. We know that Shansi at that time was inhabited by Ch'iang tribes, belonging to the Tibetan culture, as well as by Ti tribes, belonging to the northern culture, and by Hsien-yün and other tribes, belonging to the north-western culture; the centre of the Ch'iang tribes was more in the south-west of Shansi and in Shensi. Some of these tribes definitely once formed a part of the earlier Hsia state. The identification of the eastern neighbours of the Shang presents more difficulties. We might regard them as representatives of the Tungus cultures, Thai tribes, or descendants of early states of the Lung-shan cultures. We should not think that all these neighbours were primitives. On the contrary, we should assume that they, too, had societies which could be regarded as states, similar to those early pre-Chinese statelets which we discussed above.

As in earlier time, the Shang Chinese used fibres of plants, and their nobility even silk, woven in intricate designs, for their clothing. They kept cattle, pigs, dogs, chickens, but in the later Shang period, horse-breeding becomes more and more evident. Some authors believe that the art of riding was already known in late Shang times, although it was certainly not yet so highly developed that cavalry units could be used in war. With horse-breeding the two-wheeled light war-chariot makes its appearance. The wheel was already known in earlier times in the form of the potter's wheel. Recent excavations have brought to light burials in which up to eighteen chariots with two or four horses were found together with the owners of the chariots. The cart is not a Chinese invention but came from the north, possibly from Turkish peoples. It has been contended that it was connected with the war-chariot of the Near East: shortly before the Shang period there had been vast upheavals in western Asia, mainly in connection with the expansion of peoples who spoke Indo-European languages (Hittites, etc.) and who became successful through the use of quick, light, two-wheeled war-chariots. It is possible, but cannot be proved, that the war-chariot spread through Central Asia in connection with the spread of such Indo-European-speaking groups or by the intermediary of Turkish tribes. We have some reasons to believe that the first Indo-European-speaking groups arrived in the Far East in the middle of the second millennium B.C. Some authors even connect the Hsia with these groups. In any case, the maximal distribution of these people seems to have been to the western borders of the Shang state. As in western Asia, a Shang-time chariot was manned by three men: the warrior who was a nobleman, his driver, and his servant who handed him arrows or other weapons when needed. There developed a quite close relationship between the nobleman and his chariot-driver. The chariot was a valuable object, manufactured by specialists; horses were always expensive and rare in China, and in many periods of Chinese history horses were directly imported from nomadic tribes in the north or west. One of the main sports of the noblemen in this period, in addition to warfare, was hunting. The Shang had their special hunting grounds south of the mountains which surround Shansi province, along the slopes of the T'ai-hang mountain range, and south to the shores of the Yellow river. Here, there were still forests and swamps in Shang time, and boars, deer, buffaloes and other animals, as well as occasional rhinoceros and elephants, were hunted. None of these wild animals were used as a sacrifice; all sacrificial animals, such as cattle, pigs, etc., were domesticated animals.

2 Writing and religion

Not only the material but also the intellectual level attained in the Shang period was very high. We meet for the first time with writing—much later than in the Middle East and in India. Chinese scholars have succeeded in deciphering some of the documents discovered, so that we are able to learn a great deal from them. The writing is a rudimentary form of the present-day Chinese script, and like it is a pictorial writing, but also makes use, as today, of phonetic signs. There were, however, a good many characters that no longer exist, and many now used are absent. There were already more than 3,000 characters in use of which some 1,000 can now be read. (Today newspapers use some 3,000 characters; scholars have command of up to 8,000; the whole of Chinese literature, ancient and modern, comprises some 50,000 characters.) With these 3,000 characters the Chinese of the Shang period were able to express themselves well.

The still existing fragments of writing of this period are found almost exclusively on tortoiseshells or on other bony surfaces, and they represent oracles. Thus, we have to keep in mind, that these texts cannot give us a full picture of their literature, not even of their vocabulary and grammar. Shang bronzes have usually only a very few characters, and often these are still illegible. As the old Chinese script is not based on the sounds of the words, we do not know how it was pronounced. To the present time, Chinese characters can be pronounced in different ways, according to dialects, even according to languages, i.e. Korean, Vietnamese, and Japanese formerly were written down with Chinese characters, though pronounced according to the Korean, Vietnamese, or Japanese languages. Thus, we cannot definitely say that the language of the Shang was the same as that of their successors, although most scholars assume that it was.

In spite of the limited scope of the oracle texts and the fact that almost all of them were found near An-yang and belong to the late Shang period, most of what we know about Shang society comes from these texts. But as the oracles were taken for the ruler, our knowledge of the culture of the common people remains limited.

Characteristic of Shang religion is the ancestral cult which is the forerunner of the ancestral worship typical of the Chinese to recent days. Deceased rulers and even ministers were given sacrifices at fixed dates and, apparently, they were regarded as intermediaries between their descendants and the highest deity, Shang Ti. Even the deceased mothers of the rulers received sacrifices. In addition to the worship of the royal ancestors, the Shang knew many nature deities, especially deities of fertility. There was no systematized pantheon, different deities being revered in each locality, often under the most varied names. These various deities were, however, similar in character, and later it often occurred that many of them were combined by the priests into a single god. The composite deities thus formed were officially worshipped. Their primeval forms lived on, however, especially in the villages, many centuries longer than the Shang

18

dynasty. The sacrifices associated with them became popular festivals, and so these gods or their successors were saved from oblivion.

The Shang, as well as later Chinese, seem not to have had much interest in speculating about the origins of the world and mankind. It seems that Shang Ti was conceived as a male, living above and guiding all growth and birth, while the earth, also worshipped, was a kind of mother goddess who bore the plants and animals procreated by Shang Ti. It is likely that some myths which later sources report already existed in some parts of the Shang realm. Thus, we hear in a local myth that the two main deities were conceived as a married couple who later were parted by one of their children. The husband went to heaven, and the rain is the male seed that creates life on earth. In other regions it was supposed that in the beginning of the world there was a world-egg, out of which a primeval god came, whose body was represented by the earth: his hair formed the plants, and his limbs the mountains, and valleys. Every considerable mountain was also itself a god and, similarly, the river god, the thunder god, cloud, lightning, and wind gods, and many others were worshipped.

In order to promote the fertility of the earth, it was believed that sacrifices must be offered to the gods. Consequently, in the Shang realm and the regions surrounding it there were many sorts of human sacrifices; often the victims were prisoners of war. One gains the impression that many wars were conducted not as wars of conquest but only for the purpose of capturing prisoners, although the area under Shang control gradually increased towards the west and the south-east, a fact demonstrating the interest in conquest. In some regions men lurked in the spring for people from other villages; they slew them, sacrificed them to the earth, and distributed portions of the flesh of the sacrifice to the various owners of fields, who buried them. At a later time all human sacrifices were prohibited, but we have reports down to the eleventh century A.D., and even later, that such sacrifices were offered secretly in certain regions of central China. In other regions a great boat festival was held in the spring, to which many crews came crowded in long narrow boats. At least one of the boats had to capsize; the people who were thus drowned were a sacrifice to the deities of fertility. This festival has maintained its fundamental character to this day, in spite of various changes. The same is true of other festivals, customs, and conceptions, vestiges of which are contained at least in folklore.

The main problem in understanding Shang religion and even the religion of much later periods of Chinese history is that we find on their sacrificial bronzes numerous figures which are doubtless supernatural beings but which cannot be identified with deities mentioned in texts. It seems that texts mention, with few exceptions, only deities which were officially recognized and worshipped, while representations on bronzes and later on walls of buildings depict some of the popular deities.

There are some indications that the Shang had some star-worship. Certainly, they observed celestial phenomena and developed some elements of later astrology and geomancy. Their calendar was basically oriented according to the moon, but as they also had intercalatory months, they must have known that twelve moon cycles do not amount to one full cycle of the year. Thus, their calendar was already a luni-solar one, a calendar which tried to achieve a synchronism between the two luminaries. However, attempts to establish the exact form of their calendar and to interpret the dates given in Shang oracle texts in terms of our chronology have not yet been successful. As the tombs of Shang noblemen show some orientation (the heads are turned to the north), they also must have had some beliefs which we later find systematized in Chinese geomancy and astrology.

3 Early feudalism

At the head of the Shang state was a king, posthumously called a 'Ti', the same word as in the name of the supreme god. We have found on bones the names of all the rulers of this dynasty and even some of their pre-dynastic ancestors. These names can be brought into agreement with lists of rulers found in the ancient Chinese literature. The ruler seems to have been a high priest, too; and around him were many other priests. We know some of them now so well from the inscriptions that their biographies could be written. The priests as a special class, disappear later in Chinese society and are replaced by scribes.

Perhaps the best way to describe Chinese society at this time is to say that with the exception of the ruler, there were no free men: nobody was free, but the higher a person was in the social scheme, the more freedom he had. Around the king, in the capital, there were 'ch'en', officials who served the ruler personally, as well as scribes and military officials. We hear of different and often quite specialized ranks and have to assume that there was some bureaucracy, though we do not know whether there was already a true bureaucratic system with promotions and demotions according to merit and/or seniority. It seems clear, however, that important posts were in the hands of members of a nobility, lesser ones were manned by commoners. Characteristic of the nobility was the use of vehicles. Commoners did not have war-chariots; we do not know whether they were even allowed to own horses. The war-chariot was the decisive weapon and remained so until late Chou time.

The basic army organization was in units of one hundred men which were combined as 'right', 'left' and 'central' units into an army of 300 men. But it seems that the central power did not extend very far. In the more distant parts of the realm were more or less independent lords, who recognized the ruler only as their supreme lord and religious leader. The main obligations of these lords were to send tributes of grain, to participate with their soldiers in the wars, to send tortoiseshells to the capital to be used there for oracles, and to send occasionally cattle and horses. There were some thirty such dependent states. Although we do not know much about the general population, we know that in most parts of the Shang state, the society was patriarchal, patrilinear, and patrilocal. The Shang kings seem to have had a complicated system of succession as well as of marriage. After the death of the ruler his brothers followed him on the throne, the older brothers first. After the death of all brothers, the sons of the elder or younger brothers became rulers. We do not know, however, whether a difference was made between sons of main and of secondary wives. Nor does it seem that the sons of the oldest brother were preferred to the sons of younger brothers. The main wives were, according to one recent study, selected according to a kind of moiety system, somewhat similar to marriage regulations among Australian aborigines. We do not know whether such a system was limited to the royal clan, to the whole upper class, or to the whole population. Until very recent times, different Chinese groups had different systems regulating the selection of the partner, coexisting at the same time. It has been said that Shang society had traces of an earlier matrilinear system. Certainly, the nobility had no matrilinear marriage rules, but it seems possible that matrilinear and matrilocal societies existed in some parts of the Shang state. Below the nobility, we find large numbers of dependent people. Modern Chinese scholars frequently call them 'slaves' and like to speak of a 'slave society'. If this means that the economy was based on the labour of a slave class, it is certainly not true. However, there certainly were slaves, i.e. people who had no social rights and were regarded as pieces of property. But we cannot prove that their labour was the basis of Shang economy. The majority of people were certainly farmers, and they were not 'free'; it seems that the Shang rulers claimed the right over the land these farmers used, and they imposed certain obligations, mainly forced labour, upon these farmers. Thus, we might call them 'serfs'. Some serfs were in hereditary group dependence upon some noble families and working on land which the noble families regarded as theirs. Families of artisans and craftsmen also were hereditary servants of noble families—a type of social organization which has its parallels in ancient Japan and in later India and other parts of the world. The independent states around the Shang state also had serfs. When the Shang captured neighbouring states, they resettled the captured foreign aristocracy by attaching them as a group to their own noblemen. The captured serfs remained under their masters and shared their fate. The same system was later practised by the Chou after their conquest of the Shang state.

The conquests of late Shang added more territory to the realm than could be coped with by the primitive communications of the time. When the last ruler of Shang made his big war which lasted 260 days against the tribes in the south-east, rebellions broke out which led to the end of the dynasty, about 1028 B.C. according to the new chronology (1122 B.C. old chronology).

CHAPTER THREE

Mature Feudalism (c. 1028–500 B.C.)

1 *Cultural origin of the Chou and end of the Shang dynasty*

Many of the countries against which the Shang fought should probably be regarded as statelets, and some of them may already have
ruled in cities. Among these, apparently, were the ancestors of the
Chou who at first lived in central Shensi, an area which even in much
later times was the home of many non-Chinese tribes. According to
their tradition, they were forced to leave their homes due to the
pressure of tribes, which may have belonged to the Turkish ethnic
groups, though it is also possible that the movement of the Chou was
connected with pressures from Indo-European tribes. There are some
indications that the ruling house of Chou may have been related to
the Turkish ethnic group, while their population consisted mainly
of Tibetan tribes. Whether the Chou language contained elements of
these languages is not yet clear. Certainly the language of the Chou
is the ancestor of what we now call the Chinese language.

The culture of the Chou before their conquest is still little known,
but it seems to be closely related to that of the earlier Yang-shao.
They certainly had bronze weapons which differed in shape from
those of the Shang; they had the war-chariot, and the horse seems to
have played a much greater role among them than among the Shang.
Their eastward migration, however, brought them within the zone
of the Shang culture, by which they were strongly influenced, so that
the Chou culture lost more and more of its original character and
increasingly resembled the Shang culture. The Chou were also
brought into the political sphere of the Shang, as shown by the fact
that marriages took place between the ruling houses of Shang and
Chou, until the Chou state became nominally dependent on the
Shang state in the form of a dependency with special prerogatives.
Meanwhile the power of the Chou state steadily grew, while that
of the Shang state diminished more and more through the disloyalty
of its feudatories and through wars in the east. Finally, about 1028

B.C., the Chou ruler, named Wu Wang ('the martial king'), crossed his eastern frontier and pushed into central Honan. His army was formed by an alliance between various tribes, in the same way as happened again and again in the building up of the armies of the rulers of the steppes. Wu Wang forced a passage across the Yellow river and annihilated the Shang army. He pursued its vestiges as far as the capital, captured the last emperor of the Shang, and killed him. Thus was the Chou dynasty founded, and with it we begin the actual history of China. The Chou brought to the Shang culture elements of Turkish and also Tibetan culture, which were needed for the release of such forces as could create a new empire and maintain it through thousands of years as a cultural and, generally, also a political unit.

2 Chou feudalism

In contrast to Marxist scholars, who tend to call feudal any society in which a class of landowners who at the same time also exercised political power, controlled a class of farmers and often also a class of slaves, we define feudalism as a system of government of agrarian societies in which we find a hereditary upper class which in itself is stratified, and in which some sovereign rights are given to lower members of the upper class, the nobility, in exchange for services to the highest members of that class. These services are mainly military services, but also can be others. The relation between the 'vassals' and the 'lord' are contractual and renewable each time at the time of the death of either partner. Below this class of aristocrats, we have one or several classes, constituting the majority of the population, and consisting always of farmers, often also of artisan classes and of slaves. There are different ways by which such a feudal society can be formed; the case of the Chou is a very common one: a case of 'super-stratification', in which a conquering federation puts itself over an already stratified society. The Chou conquering power consisted of members of the clan to which the future rulers belonged, clans which were related to them by marriage, and clans which had joined them or had been forced to join them already before the time of the war of conquest. The conquerors were regarded as an alien minority, so that they had to march out and spread over the whole country. Moreover, the allied tribal chieftains expected to be rewarded. The territory to be governed was enormous, but the communications in northern China at that time were similar to those still existing not long ago in southern China—narrow foot-paths from one settlement to another. It is very difficult to build roads in the loess of northern China; and the war-chariots that required roads had only just been introduced. Under such conditions, the simplest way of administering the empire was to establish garrisons of the invading tribes in the various parts of the country under the command of their chieftains. Thus separate regions of the country were distributed as fiefs. If a former subject of the Shang surrendered betimes with the territory under his rule, or if there was one who could not be overcome by force, the Chou recognized him as a feudal lord.

We find in the early Chou time the typical signs of true feudalism: fiefs were given in a ceremony in which symbolically a piece of earth was handed over to the new fiefholder, and his instalment, his rights and obligations were inscribed in a 'charter'. Most of the fiefholders were members of the Chou ruling family or members of the clan to which this family belonged; other fiefs were given to heads of the allied tribes. The fiefholder (feudal lord) regarded the land of his fief, as far as he and his clan actually used it, as 'clan' land; parts of this land he gave to members of his own branch-clan for their use without transferring rights of property, thus creating new sub-fiefs and sub-lords. In much later times the concept of landed property of a family developed, and the whole concept of 'clan' disappeared. By 500 B.C., most feudal lords had retained only a dim memory that they originally belonged to the Chi clan of the Chou or to one of the few other original clans, and their so-called sub-lords felt themselves as members of independent noble families. Slowly, then, the family names of later China began to develop, but it took many centuries until, at the time of the Han Dynasty, all citizens (slaves excluded) had accepted family names. Then, conversely, families grew again into new clans.

Thus we have this picture of the early Chou state: the imperial central power established in Shensi, near the present Sian; supposedly over a thousand feudal states, great and small, often consisting only of a small garrison, or sometimes a more considerable one, with the former chieftain as feudal lord over it. Around these garrisons the old population lived on, in the north the Shang population, farther east and south various other peoples and cultures. The conquerors' garrisons were like islands in a sea. Most of them formed new towns, walled, with a rectangular plan and central crossroads, similar to the European towns subsequently formed out of Roman encampments. This town plan has been preserved to the present day.

This upper class in the garrisons formed the nobility; it was sharply divided from the indigenous population around the towns. The conquerors called the population 'the black-haired people', and themselves 'the hundred families'. The rest of the town populations consisted often of urban Shang people: Shang noble families together with their bondsmen and serfs had been given to Chou fiefholders. Such forced resettlements of whole populations have remained

25

typical even for much later periods. By this method new cities were provided with urban, refined people and, most important, with skilled craftsmen and businessmen who assisted in building the cities and in keeping them alive. Some scholars believe that many resettled Shang urbanites either were or became businessmen; incidentally, the same word 'Shang' means 'merchant', up to the present time. The people of the Shang capital lived on and even attempted a revolt in collaboration with some Chou people. The Chou rulers suppressed this revolt, and then transferred a large part of this population to Loyang. They were settled there in a separate community, and vestiges of the Shang population were still to be found there in the fifth century A.D.: they were entirely impoverished potters, still making vessels in the old style.

3 Fusion of Chou and Shang

The conquerors brought with them, for their own purposes to begin with, their rigid patriarchate in the family system and their cult of Heaven (t'ien), in which the worship of sun and stars took the principal place; a religion most closely related to that of the Turkish peoples. Some of the Shang popular deities, however, were admitted into the official Heaven-worship. Popular deities became 'feudal lords' under the Heaven-god. Earlier conceptions of the soul were also admitted into the Chou religion: the human body housed two souls, the personality-soul and the life-soul. Death meant the separation of the souls from the body, the life-soul also slowly dying. The personality-soul, however, could move about freely and lived as long as there were people who remembered it and kept it from hunger by means of sacrifices. The Chou systematized this idea and made it into the ancestor-worship that has endured down to the present time.

The Chou officially abolished human sacrifices, especially since, as former pastoralists, they knew of better means of employing prisoners of war than did the more agrarian Shang. The Chou used Shang and other slaves as domestic servants for their numerous nobility, and Shang serfs as farm labourers on their estates. They seem to have regarded the land under their control as 'state land' and all farmers as 'serfs'. Thus, the following, still rather hypothetical, picture of the land system of the early Chou time emerges: around the walled towns of the feudal lords and sub-lords, always in the plains, was 'state land' which produced millet and more and more wheat. Cultivation was still largely 'shifting', so that the serfs in groups cultivated more or less standardized plots for a year or more and then shifted to other plots. During the growing season they lived in huts on the fields; during the winter in the towns in adobe houses.

In this manner the yearly life cycle was divided into two different periods. The produce of the serfs supplied the lords, their dependants and the farmers themselves. Whenever the lord found it necessary, the serfs had to perform also other services for the lord, most of all, military services in case of war, where they accompanied the war-chariots of the lords. Farther away from the towns were the villages of the 'natives', nominally also subjects of the lord. In most parts of eastern China, these, too, were agriculturists. They acknowledged their dependence by sending 'gifts' to the lord in the town. Later these gifts became institutionalized and turned into a form of tax. The lord's serfs, on the other hand, tended to settle near the fields in villages of their own because, with growing urban population, the distances from the town to many of the fields became too great. It was also at this time of new settlements that a more intensive cultivation with a fallow system began. At latest from the sixth century B.C. on, the distinctions between both land systems became unclear; and the pure serf-cultivation, called by the old texts the 'well-field system' because eight cultivating families used one common well, disappeared in practice.

The actual structure of early Chou administration is difficult to ascertain. The 'Duke of Chou', brother of the first ruler, Wu Wang, later regent during the minority of Wu Wang's son, and certainly one of the most influential persons of this time, was the alleged creator of the book 'Chou-li' which contains a detailed table of the bureaucracy of the country. The 'Chou-li' is certainly written down more than 800 years after the beginning of the Chou and gives an ideal picture of a bureaucratic state. But the study of Chou bronze texts has shown that the Chou had indeed a bureaucracy which was highly developed and complex. Some offices were fully feudal, i.e. officers were granted sovereign rights over certain pieces of land and the population living on it; others were given special offices near the capital or at the court and had income from these offices. Other officers around the ruler were comparable to personal servants, and still others had to have professional knowledge and training, such as the court scribes. We must assume that the majority of them came from the ranks of the nobility; upward social mobility seems to have developed only in a later period.

The Chou capital, at Sian, was a twin city. In one part lived the master-race of the Chou with the imperial court, in the other the subjugated population. At the same time, as previously mentioned, the Chou built a second capital, Loyang, in the present province of Honan. Loyang was just in the middle of the new state, and for the purposes of Heaven-worship it was regarded as the centre of the universe, where it was essential that the emperor should reside.

Loyang was another twin city: in one part were the rulers' administrative buildings, in the other the transferred population of the Shang capital, probably artisans for the most part. The valuable artisans seem all to have been taken over from the Shang, for the bronze vessels of the early Chou age are virtually identical with those of the Shang age. The shapes of the houses also remained unaltered, and probably also the clothing, though the Chou brought with them the novelties of felt and woollen fabrics, old possessions of their earlier period. The only fundamental material change was in the form of the graves: in the Shang age house-like tombs were built underground; now great tumuli were constructed in the fashion preferred by all steppe peoples.

One professional class was severely hit by the changed circumstances—the Shang priesthood. The Chou had no priests. As with the peoples of the steppes, the head of the family himself performed the religious rites. Beyond this there were only shamans for certain purposes of magic. And very soon Heaven-worship was combined with the family system, the ruler being declared to be the Son of Heaven; the mutual relations within the family were thus extended to the religious relations with the deity. If, however, the god of Heaven is the father of the ruler, the ruler as his son himself offers sacrifice, and so the priest becomes superfluous. Thus the priests became 'unemployed'. Some of them changed their profession. They were the only people who could read and write, and as an administrative system was necessary they obtained employment as scribes. Others withdrew to their villages and became village priests. They organized the religious festivals in the village, carried out the ceremonies connected with family events, and even conducted the exorcism of evil spirits with shamanistic dances; they took charge, in short, of everything connected with customary observances and morality. The Chou lords were great respecters of propriety. The Shang culture had, indeed, been a high one with an ancient and highly developed moral system, and the Chou as rough conquerors must have been impressed by the ancient forms and tried to imitate them. In addition, they had in their religion of Heaven a conception of the existence of mutual relations between Heaven and Earth: all that went on in the skies had an influence on earth, and vice versa. Thus, if any ceremony was 'wrongly' performed, it had an evil effect on Heaven—there would be no rain, or the cold weather would arrive too soon, or some such misfortune would come. It was therefore of great importance that everything should be done 'correctly'. Hence the Chou rulers were glad to call in the old priests as performers of ceremonies and teachers of morality similar to the ancient Indian rulers who needed the Brahmans for the correct performance of all rites. There thus came into existence in the early Chou empire a new social group, later called 'scholars', men who were not regarded as belonging to the lower class represented by the subjugated population but were not included in the nobility; men who were not productively employed but belonged to a sort of independent profession. They became of very great importance in later centuries.

In the first centuries of the Chou dynasty the ruling house steadily lost power. Some of the emperors proved weak, or were killed at war; above all, the empire was too big and its administration too slow-moving. The feudal lords and nobles were occupied with their own problems in securing the submission of the surrounding villages to their garrisons and in governing them; they soon paid little attention to the distant central authority. In addition to this, the situation at the centre of the empire was more difficult than that of its feudal states farther east. The settlements around the garrisons in the east were inhabited by agrarian tribes, but the subjugated population around the centre at Sian was made up of nomadic tribes of Turks and Mongols together with semi-nomadic Tibetans. Sian lies in the valley of the river Wei; the riverside country certainly had belonged, though perhaps only insecurely, to the Shang empire and was specially well adapted to agriculture; but its periphery—mountains in the south, steppes in the north—was inhabited (until a late period, to some extent to the present day) by nomads, who had also been subjugated by the Chou. The Chou themselves were by no means strong, as they had been only a small tribe and their strength had depended on auxiliary tribes, which had now spread over the country as the new nobility and lived far from the Chou. The Chou emperors had thus to hold in check the subjugated but warlike tribes of Turks and Mongols who lived quite close to their capital. In the first centuries of the dynasty they were more or less successful, for the feudal lords still sent auxiliary forces. In time, however, these became fewer and fewer, because the feudal lords pursued their own policy; and the Chou were compelled to fight their own battles against tribes that continually rose against them, raiding and pillaging their towns. Campaigns abroad also fell mainly on the shoulders of the Chou, as their capital lay near the frontier.

It must not be simply assumed, as is often done by the Chinese and some of the European historians, that the Turkish and Mongolian tribes were so savage or so pugnacious that they continually waged war just for the love of it. The problem is much deeper, and to fail to recognize this is to fail to understand Chinese history down to the Middle Ages. The conquering Chou established their garrisons everywhere, and these garrisons were surrounded by the quarters of artisans and by the villages of peasants, a process that ate into the pasturage of the Turkish and Mongolian nomads. Some of the nomadic tribes living between garrisons withdrew, to escape from the growing pressure, mainly into the province of Shansi, where the influence of the Chou was weak and they were not numerous; some of the nomad chiefs lost their lives in battle, and some learned from the Chou lords and turned themselves into petty rulers. We will have to discuss these processes again later. Within the area in which the Chou ruled over people who had been farmers for a long time, a kind of symbiosis developed in these first centuries of Chou rule between the urban aristocrats and the country-people. The rulers of the towns took over from the general population almost the whole vocabulary of the language which from now on we may call 'Chinese'. They naturally took over elements of the material civilization. The subjugated population had, meanwhile, to adjust itself to its lords. In the organism that thus developed, with its unified economic system, the conquerors became an aristocratic ruling class, and the subjugated population became a lower class, with varied elements but mainly a peasantry. From now on we may call this society 'Chinese'; it has endured to the middle of the twentieth century. Most later essential societal changes are the result of internal development and not of aggression from without.

4 *Limitation of the imperial power*

In 771 B.C. an alliance of northern feudal states had attacked the ruler in his western capital; in a battle close to the city they had overcome and killed him. This campaign appears to have set in motion considerable groups from various tribes, so that almost the whole province of Shensi was lost. With the aid of some feudal lords who had remained loyal, a Chou prince was rescued and conducted eastward to the second capital, Loyang, which until then had never been the ruler's actual place of residence. In this rescue a lesser feudal prince, ruler of the feudal state of Ch'in, specially distinguished himself. Soon afterwards this prince, whose domain had lain close to that of the ruler, reconquered a great part of the lost territory, and thereafter regarded it as his own fief. The Ch'in family resided in the same capital in which the Chou had lived in the past, and five hundred years later we shall meet with them again as the dynasty that succeeded the Chou. The period that now begins, is called 'Eastern Chou', and its first part, to 481 B.C., is the 'Spring and Autumn' period, called after an annalistic history on which Confucius worked.

The new ruler, resident now in Loyang, was foredoomed to impotence. He was now in the centre of the country, and less exposed to large-scale enemy attacks; but his actual rule extended little beyond the town itself and its immediate environment. Moreover, attacks did not entirely cease; several times parts of the indigenous population living between the Chou towns rose against the towns, even in the centre of the country.

Now that the emperor had no territory that could be the basis of a strong rule and, moreover, because he owed his position to the feudal lords and was thus under an obligation to them, he ruled no longer as the chief of the feudal lords but as a sort of sanctified overlord; and this was the position of all his successors. A situation was formed that may be compared with that of Japan down to the middle of the nineteenth century. The ruler was a symbol rather than an exerciser of power. There had to be a supreme ruler because, in the worship of Heaven which was recognized by all the feudal lords, the supreme sacrifices could only be offered by the Son of Heaven in person. There could not be a number of sons of heaven because there were not a number of heavens. The imperial sacrifices secured that all should be in order in the country, and that the necessary equilibrium between Heaven and Earth should be maintained. For in the religion of Heaven there was a close parallelism between Heaven and Earth, and every omission of a sacrifice, or failure to offer it in due form, brought down a reaction from Heaven. For these religious reasons a central ruler was a necessity for the feudal lords. They needed him also for practical reasons. In the course of centuries the personal relationship between the various feudal lords had ceased. Their original kinship and united struggles had long been forgotten. When the various feudal lords proceeded to subjugate the territories at a distance from their towns, in order to turn their city states into genuine territorial states, they came into conflict with each other. In the course of these struggles for power many of the small fiefs were simply destroyed. It may fairly be said that not until the eighth and seventh centuries B.C. did the old garrison towns become real states. In these circumstances the struggles between the feudal states called urgently for an arbiter, to settle simple cases, and in more difficult cases either to try to induce other feudal lords to intervene or to give sanction to the new situation. These were the only governing functions of the ruler from the time of the transfer to the second capital.

5 Changes in the relative strength of the feudal states

In these disturbed times China also made changes in her outer frontiers. When we speak of frontiers in this connection, we must take little account of the European conception of a frontier. No frontier in that sense existed in China until her conflict with the European powers. In the dogma of the Chinese religion of Heaven, all the countries of the world were subject to the Chinese emperor, the Son of Heaven. Thus there could be no such thing as other independent states. In practice the dependence of various regions on the ruler naturally varied: near the centre, that is to say near the ruler's place of residence, it was most pronounced; then it gradually diminished in the direction of the periphery. The feudal lords of the inner territories were already rather less subordinated than at the centre, and those at a greater distance scarcely at all; at a still greater distance were territories whose chieftains regarded themselves as independent, subject only in certain respects to Chinese overlordship. In such a system it is difficult to speak of frontiers. In practice there was, of course, a sort of frontier, where the influence of the outer feudal lords ceased to exist. The development of the original feudal towns into feudal states with factual sovereignty over their territories proceeded, of course, not only in the interior of China but also on its borders, where the feudal territories had the advantage of more unrestricted opportunities of expansion; thus they became more and more powerful.

Along the northern borders, the difference between 'Chinese' lords and 'non-Chinese' rulers also became blurred. Statelets which in the early years of the Chou certainly were ruled by non-Chinese and inhabited largely by non-Chinese, slowly became more and more 'Chinese' by adopting institutions of their neighbours, the feudal lords, and probably also by immigration of Chinese into their area.

In the south (that is to say, in the south of the Chou empire, in the present central China) the garrisons that founded feudal states were relatively small and widely separated; consequently their cultural system was largely absorbed into that of the aboriginal population, so that they developed into feudal states with a character of their own. Three of these attained special importance—(1) Ch'u, in the neighbourhood and north of the present Hankow; (2) Wu, near the present Nanking; and (3) Yüeh, near the present Hangchow. In 704 B.C. the feudal prince of Wu proclaimed himself 'Wang'. 'Wang', however, was the title of the ruler of the Chou dynasty. This meant that Wu broke away from the old Chou religion of Heaven, according to which there could be only one ruler (*wang*) in the world. Though Chinese sources always regard these southerners as 'barbarians', i.e. as people with no civilization, archaeology has shown us that this was not at all the case. The south-eastern part of China developed cultures of its own, probably derived from the Lung-shan culture. A geometrical style of pottery becomes typical of the lower Yangtze area. But soon we find here the use of bronze and iron, and according to some scholars, the first iron cultures of China originated here. At our middle Chou period, archaeology confirms well what we can learn from Chou texts: mixed and side by side with these native

32

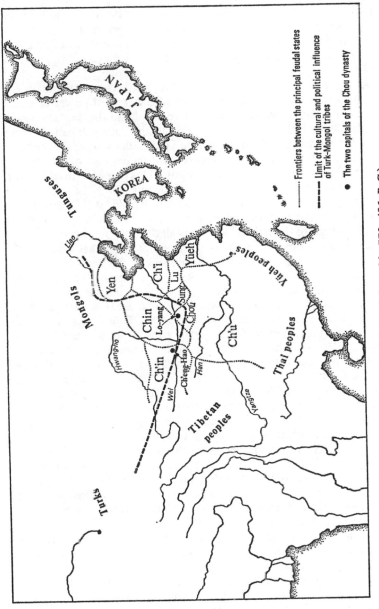

MAP 2 *The principal feudal states in the feudal epoch (roughly 770–481 B.C.)*

········· Frontiers between the principal feudal states

╌╌╌ Limit of the cultural and political influence
     of Turk-Mongol tribes

● The two capitals of the Chou dynasty

southern cultures we find definite traces of Shang and mainly of Chou culture, indicating that settlers from the north, feudal lords of the Chou, had begun to settle in the south together with their own men, amidst local people. Similarly, the western province of Szechwan developed, as archaeology tells us, two local cultures which seem to have been derived from an earlier neolithic one.

At the beginning of the seventh century it became customary for the ruler to unite with the feudal lord who was most powerful at the time. This feudal lord became a dictator, and had the military power in his hands, like the shoguns in nineteenth-century Japan. If there was a disturbance of the peace, he settled the matter by military means. The first of these dictators was the feudal lord of the state of Ch'i, in the present province of Shantung. This feudal state had grown considerably through the conquest of the outer end of the peninsula of Shantung, which until then had been independent. Moreover, and this was of the utmost importance, the state of Ch'i was a trade centre. Much of the bronze, and later all the iron, for use in northern China came from the south by road and in ships that went up the rivers to Ch'i, where it was distributed among the various regions of the north, north-east, and north-west. In addition to this, through its command of portions of the coast, Ch'i had the means of producing salt, with which it met the needs of great areas of eastern China. It was also in Ch'i that money was first used. Thus Ch'i soon became a place of great luxury, far surpassing the court of the Chou, and Ch'i also became the centre of the most developed civilization.

After the feudal lord of Ch'i, supported by the wealth and power of his feudal state, became dictator, he had to struggle not only against other feudal lords, but also many times against risings among the most various parts of the population, and especially against the nomad tribes in the southern part of the present province of Shansi. In the seventh century not only Ch'i but the other feudal states had expanded. The regions in which the nomad tribes were able to move had grown steadily smaller, and the feudal lords now set to work to bring the nomads of their country under their direct rule. The greatest conflict of this period was the attack in 660 B.C. against the feudal state of Wei, in northern Honan. The nomad tribes seem this time to have been proto-Mongols; they made a direct attack on the garrison town and actually conquered it. The remnant of the urban population, no more than 730 in number, had to flee southward. It is clear from this incident that nomads were still living in the middle of China, within the territory of the feudal states, and that they were still decidedly strong, though no longer in a position to get rid entirely of the feudal lords of the Chou.

The period of the dictators came to an end after about a century, because it was found that none of the feudal states was any longer strong enough to exercise control over all the others. These others formed alliances against which the dictator was powerless. Thus this period passed into the next, which the Chinese call the period of the Contending States (403–221 B.C.).

6   Confucius and the Chinese basic values

After this outline of the political history we must consider the intellectual development of this period. The centuries between 500 and 280 B.C. are certainly the period in which we find the greatest variety of ideas, many of which remained decisive down to almost the present day. It is symbolic that Mao Tse-tung has recently called for the fight against Confucius and the praise of Shih Huang-ti, though both men have been dead for more than two thousand years.

We saw how the priests of the earlier dynasty of the Shang developed into the group of so-called 'scholars'. When the Chou ruler, after the move to the second capital, had lost virtually all but his religious authority, these 'scholars' gained increased influence. They were the specialists in traditional morals, in sacrifices, and in the organization of festivals. The continually increasing ritualism at the court of the Chou called for more and more of these men. The various feudal lords also attracted these scholars to their side, employed them as tutors for their children, and entrusted them with the conduct of sacrifices and festivals.

China's best-known philosopher, Confucius (Chinese: K'ung Tzŭ), was one of these scholars. He was born in 551 B.C. in the feudal state Lu in the present province of Shantung. In Lu and its neighbouring state Sung, institutions of the Shang had remained strong and traces of Shang culture can be seen in Confucius's political and ethical ideas. He acquired the knowledge which a scholar had to possess, and then taught in the families of nobles, also helping in the administration of their properties. He made several attempts to obtain advancement, either in vain or with only a short term of employment ending in dismissal. Thus his career was a continuing pilgrimage from one noble to another, from one feudal lord to another, accompanied by a few young men, sons of scholars, who were partly his pupils and partly his servants. Many of these disciples seem to have been 'illegitimate' sons of noblemen, i.e. sons of concubines, and Confucius's own family seems to have been of the same origin. In the strongly patriarchal and patrilinear system of the Chou and the developing primogeniture, children of secondary wives had a lower social status. Ultimately Confucius gave up his wanderings, settled in his home town of Lu, and there taught his disciples until his death in 479 B.C.

Such was briefly the life of Confucius. His enemies claim that he was a political intriguer, inciting the feudal lords against each other in the course of his wanderings from one state to another, with the intention of somewhere coming into power himself. There may, indeed, be some truth in that.

Confucius's importance lies in the fact that he systematized a body of ideas, not of his own creation, and communicated it to a circle of disciples. His teachings were later set down in writing and formed, right down to the twentieth century, the moral code of the upper classes of China. Confucius was fully conscious of his membership in a social class whose existence was tied to that of the feudal lords. With their disappearance, his type of scholar would become superfluous. The common people, the lower class, was in his view in an entirely subordinate position. Thus his moral teaching is a code for the ruling class. Accordingly it retains almost unaltered the elements of the old cult of Heaven, following the old tradition inherited from the northern peoples. For him Heaven is not an arbitrarily governing divine tyrant, but the embodiment of a system of legality. Heaven does not act independently, but follows a universal law, the so-called 'Tao'. Just as sun, moon, and stars move in the heavens in accordance with law, so man should conduct himself on earth in accord with the universal law, not against it. The ruler should not actively intervene in day-to-day policy, but should only act by setting an example, like Heaven; he should observe the established ceremonies, and offer all sacrifices in accordance with the rites, and then all else will go well in the world. The individual, too, should be guided exactly in his life by the prescriptions of the rites, so that harmony with the law of the universe may be established.

Today, we see this stress on harmony as one of the basic values of Chinese civilization. Harmony is seen as the principle of the cosmic order, therefore also as the principle of human social organization. It presupposes the subordination of the individual under the community; the will to give up freedom, the highest value of Western, European cultures, in favour of the security which the community has to offer when harmony is established. More and more we see that there is a contradiction between freedom and security; man cannot have both at the same time. Chinese society and its philosophers by stressing harmony instead of conflict, elected security.

A second idea of the Confucian system came also from the old conceptions of the Chou conquerors, and thus originally from the northern peoples. This is the patriarchal idea, according to which the family is the cell of society, and at the head of the family stands the eldest male adult as a sort of patriarch. The state is simply an extension of the family, 'state', of course, meaning simply the class of the feudal lords (the 'chün-tzǔ'). And the organization of the family is also that of the world of the gods. Within the family there are a number of ties, all of them, however, one-sided: that of father to son (the son having to obey the father); that of husband to wife (the wife had fewer rights); that of elder to younger brother. An extension of these is the association of friend with friend, which is conceived as an association between an elder and a younger brother. The final link, and the only one extending beyond the family and uniting it with the state, is the association of the ruler with the subject, a replica of that between father and son. The ruler in turn is in the position of son to Heaven. Thus in Confucianism the cult of Heaven, the family system, and the state are welded into unity.

The 'five relations', enumerated above, exhibit a second basic value of Chinese society: no two persons are equal. Inequality is expressed by three criteria. The person who is older has more rights than the younger one; the male person has more rights than the female; the person in higher rank has more rights. This basic inequality of people is, of course, the opposite to the idea of the 'brother' in Christianity and to the principle of democracy and equality in the West. But, as China's history shows, a well-functioning society can be built on this principle. There is almost no possibility that two persons who meet have any doubt as to how they have to deal with the other person and how this other person expects to be treated. A great number of conflicts and stresses in our society have their origin in the fact that it is very difficult for us to find out how the person with whom we interact expects to be treated—just think of the problems American fathers have with their children, or the heads of bureaucracies with their employees. By determining the status of each person within the state, frictions could be reduced. Existing vagueness was prevented by precise rules of etiquette. Every step, every action was prescribed (to some degree as in our books of etiquette, though these were never 'official'), and whoever followed these rules experienced no frictions and could expect to live in harmony. We might want to explain these first two basic values as a consequence of the compact way of settlement of the Chinese. With very few exceptions, Chinese never lived in open settlements, always in compact villages. They were compact, because Chinese settled along valleys, avoiding as far as possible the hills. Their fields were in these valleys, and the more space a settlement took, the less land for production was available, because fields could not be too far from the settlement, otherwise they would be exposed to attacks and thefts and their cultivation would cost too much time and labour. In a compact settlement, with the lightly built Chinese houses which, in early times, had no windows, later windows of paper, and which have no solid inner walls, every

37

and any sound can be heard by everybody who is in the house, and also by everybody who passes by or lives in the next houses. With no 'rules of behaviour' incessant friction would occur. The individual had to restrain himself and be quiet. Down to the present time, one of the basic rules is that one should not talk 'empty talk', not talk about what is not one's own business.

So far as we have described it above, the teaching of Confucius was a further development of the old cult of Heaven. Through bitter experience, however, Confucius had come to realize that nothing could be done with the ruling house as it existed in his day. So shadowy a figure as the Chou ruler of that time could not fulfil what Confucius required of the 'Son of Heaven'. But the opinions of students of Confucius's actual ideas differ. Some say that in the only book in which he personally had a hand, the so-called 'Annals of Spring and Autumn', he intended to set out his conception of the character of a true emperor; others say that in that book he showed how he would himself have acted as emperor, and that he was only awaiting an opportunity to make himself emperor. He was called indeed, at a later time, the 'uncrowned ruler'. In any case, the 'Annals of Spring and Autumn' seem to be simply a dry work of annals, giving the history of his native state of Lu on the basis of the older documents available to him. In his text, however, Confucius made small changes by means of which he expressed criticism or recognition; in this way he indirectly made known how in his view a ruler should act or should not act. He did not shrink from falsifying history, as can today be demonstrated. Thus on one occasion a ruler had to flee from a feudal prince, which in Confucius's view was impossible behaviour for the ruler; accordingly he wrote instead that the ruler went on a hunting expedition. Elsewhere he tells of an eclipse of the sun on a certain day, on which in fact there was no eclipse. By writing of an eclipse he meant to criticize the way a ruler had acted, for the sun symbolized the ruler, and the eclipse meant that the ruler had not been guided by divine illumination.

Rendered alert by this experience, we are able to see and to show that most of the other later official works of history follow the example of the 'Annals of Spring and Autumn' in containing things that have been deliberately falsified. This is especially so in the work called 'T'ung-chien kang-mu', which was the source of the history of the Chinese empire translated into French by de Mailla. History, for Confucius, and down to the present time, is not an objective science, but an educational tool: history can tell us how to behave in a specific situation, by studying how others, before us, have acted in similar situations. Good history should make clear the values of society, and, if necessary, criticize the unworthy in clear terms. To the present time, the newspapers of the People's Republic call the leaders of the Republic of China 'bandits' and vice versa: they know very well, that these men are not real bandits, but they want to express that they violate moral standards which they (each of them differently) have set up and want to defend.

Apart from Confucius's criticism of the inadequate capacity of the emperor of his day, there is discernible, though only in the form of cryptic hints, a fundamentally important progressive idea. It is that a nobleman (chün-tzŭ) should not be a member of the ruling élite by right of birth alone, but should be a man of superior moral qualities. From Confucius on, 'chün-tzŭ' came to mean 'a gentleman'. Consequently, a country should not be ruled by a dynasty based on inheritance through birth, but by members of the nobility who show outstanding moral qualification for rulership. That is to say, the rule should pass from the worthiest to the worthiest, the successor first passing through a period of probation as a minister of state. In an unscrupulous falsification of the tradition, Confucius declared that this principle was followed in early times. It is probably safe to assume that Confucius had in view here an eventual justification of claims to rulership of his own.

Thus Confucius undoubtedly had ideas of reform, but he did not interfere with the foundations of feudalism. For the rest, his system consists only of a social order and a moral teaching. Metaphysics, logic, epistemology, i.e. branches of philosophy which played so great a part in the West, are of no interest to him. Nor can he be described as the founder of a religion; for the cult of Heaven of which he speaks and which he takes over existed in the same form before his day. He is merely the man who first systematized those notions. He had no successes in his lifetime and gained no recognition; nor did his disciples or their disciples gain any general recognition; his work did not become of importance until some three hundred years after his death, when in the second century B.C. his teaching was adjusted to the new social conditions: out of a moral system for the decaying feudal society of the past centuries developed the ethic of the rising social order of the gentry. The gentry (in much the same way as the European bourgeoisie) continually claimed that there should be access for every civilized citizen to the highest places in the social pyramid, and the rules of Confucianism became binding on every member of society if he were to be considered a gentleman. Only then did Confucianism begin to develop into the imposing system that dominated China almost down to the present day. Confucianism did not become a religion. The Jesuit missionaries in the sixteenth and seventeenth centuries came to that conviction and stated that the cult of the ancestors which is commonly associated with Confucianism as one of its important rituals, is not a cult to deified beings. To some degree, we could call Confucianism a 'community religion' if we compare it with such customs of ours, as to stand up when the national anthem is played, to erect war memorials and decorate them with flowers, to give precedence to older people or people of high rank in the government, and many other things by which we show our sense of belonging. A similar but much more conscious and much more powerful part was played by Confucianism in the life of the average Chinese, though he was not necessarily knowledgeable in the field of philosophical ideas. We may feel that the rules to which he was subjected were pedantic; but there was no limit to their effectiveness: they reduced to a minimum the friction that always occurs when great masses of people live close together; they gave Chinese society the strength through which it has endured; they gave security to its individuals. China's first real social crisis after the collapse of feudalism, that is to say, after the fourth or third century B.C., began only in the present century with the collapse of the social order of the gentry and the breakdown of the family system.

Confucius as a personality remains obscure to us, in spite of all studies. It is remarkable that the man who paid so much attention to the family, came from a family that was unusual, to say the least; apparently had little contact with his wife, and had only one son who hardly was as he would have expected. But these bits of information do not suffice to reconstruct Confucius as a man.

7 Lao Tzŭ

In eighteenth-century Europe Confucius was the only Chinese philosopher held in regard; in the last hundred years, the years of Europe's internal crisis, the philosopher Lao Tzŭ steadily advanced in repute, so that his book was translated almost a hundred times into various European languages. According to the general view among the Chinese, Lao Tzŭ was an older contemporary of Confucius; recent Chinese and Western research (A. Waley; H. H. Dubs) has contested this view and places Lao Tzŭ in the latter part of the fourth century B.C., or even later. Virtually nothing at all is known about his life; the oldest biography of Lao Tzŭ, written about 100 B.C., says that he lived as an official at the ruler's court, and one day, became tired of the life of an official and withdrew from the capital to his estate, where he died in old age. This, too, may be legendary, but it fits well into the picture given to us by Lao Tzŭ's teaching and by the life of his later followers. From the second century A.D., that is to say at least four hundred years after his death, there are legends of his migrating to the far west. Still later narratives tell of his going to Turkestan (where a temple was actually built in his honour in the

Medieval period); according to other sources he travelled as far as India or Sogdiana (Samarkand and Bokhara), where according to some accounts he was the teacher or forerunner of Buddha, and according to others of Mani, the founder of Manichaeism. For all this there is not a vestige of documentary evidence.

Lao Tzŭ's ideas are contained in a small book, the 'Tao Tê Ching', the 'Book of the World Law and its Power'. The book is written in quite simple language, at times in rhyme, but the sense vague and ambiguous. We now believe that it is an abstract of a full book, parts of which have recently been discovered. With its help, we may arrive at a better understanding of Lao Tzŭ's teachings.

Lao Tzŭ's teaching is essentially an effort to bring man's life on earth into harmony with the life and law of the universe (Tao). This was also Confucius's purpose. But while Confucius set out to attain that purpose in a somewhat rationalistic way, by laying down a number of rules of human conduct, Lao Tzŭ tries to attain his ideal by an intuitive, emotional method. Lao Tzŭ is always described as a mystic, but perhaps this is not entirely appropriate; it must be borne in mind that in his time the Chinese language, spoken and written, still had great difficulties in the expression of ideas. In reading Lao Tzŭ's book we feel that he is trying to express something for which the language of his day was inadequate; and what he wanted to express belonged to the emotional, not the intellectual, side of the human character, so that any perfectly clear expression of it in words was entirely impossible. It must be borne in mind that the Chinese language lacks definite word categories like substantive, adjective, adverb, or verb; any word can be used now in one category and now in another, with a few exceptions; thus the understanding of a combination like 'white horse' formed a difficult logical problem for the thinker of the fourth century B.C.: did it mean 'white' plus 'horse'? Or was 'white horse' no longer a horse at all but something quite different?

Confucius's way of bringing human life into harmony with the life of the universe was to be a process of assimilating Man as a social being, Man in his social environment, to Nature, and of so maintaining his activity within the bounds of the community. Lao Tzŭ pursues another path, the path for those who feel disappointed with life in the community. A Taoist, as a follower of Lao Tzŭ is called, withdraws from social life, and carries out none of the rites and ceremonies which a man of the upper class should observe throughout the day. He lives in self-imposed seclusion, in an elaborate primitivity which is often described in moving terms that are almost convincing of actual 'primitivity'. Far from the city, surrounded by Nature, the Taoist lives his own life, together with a few friends and his servants, entirely according to his nature. His own nature, like everything else, represents for him a part of the Tao, and the task of the individual consists in the most complete adherence to the Tao that is conceivable, as far as possible performing no act that runs counter to the Tao. This is the main element of Lao Tzŭ's doctrine, the doctrine of *wu-wei*, 'passive achievement'.

Lao Tzŭ seems to have thought that this doctrine could be applied to the life of the state. He assumed that an ideal life in society was possible if everyone followed his own nature entirely and no artificial restrictions were imposed. Thus he writes:

> The more the people are forbidden to do this and that, the poorer will they be. The more sharp weapons the people possess, the more will darkness and bewilderment spread through the land. The more craft and cunning men have, the more useless and pernicious contraptions will they invent. The more laws and edicts are imposed, the more thieves and bandits there will be. 'If I work through Non-action,' says the Sage, 'the people will transform themselves.'

('The Way of Acceptance', a new version of Lao Tzŭ's 'Tao Tê Ching', by Hermon Ould (Dakers, 1946), Ch. 57.) Thus according to Lao Tzŭ, who takes the existence of a monarchy for granted, the ruler must treat his subjects as follows:

> By emptying their hearts of desire and their minds of envy, and by filling their stomachs with what they need; by reducing their ambitions and by strengthening their bones and sinews; by striving to keep them without the knowledge of what is evil and without cravings. Thus are the crafty ones given no scope for tempting interference. For it is by Non-action that the Sage governs, and nothing is really left uncontrolled. ('The Way of Acceptance', Ch. 3.)

Lao Tzŭ did not live to learn that such rule of good government would be followed by only one sort of rulers—dictators; and as a matter of fact the 'Legalist theory' which provided the philosophic basis for dictatorship in the third century B.C. was attributable to Lao Tzŭ. He was not thinking, however, of dictatorship; he was an individualistic anarchist, believing that if there were no active government all men would be happy. Then everyone could attain unity with Nature for himself. Thus we find in Lao Tzŭ, and later in all other Taoists, a scornful repudiation of all social and official obligations. An answer that became famous was given by the Taoist Chuang Tzŭ (see below) when it was proposed to confer high office in the state on him (the story may or may not be true, but it is typical of Taoist thought): 'I have heard,' he replied, 'that in Ch'u there is a tortoise sacred to the gods. It has now been dead for 3,000 years, and the king keeps it in a shrine with silken cloths, and gives it shelter in the halls of a temple. Which do you think that tortoise would prefer— to be dead and have its vestigial bones so honoured, or to be still alive and dragging its tail after it in the mud?' The officials replied: 'No doubt it would prefer to be alive and dragging its tail after it in the mud.' Then spoke Chuang Tzŭ: 'Begone! I, too, would rather drag my tail after me in the mud!' (Chuang Tzŭ 17, 10.)

The true Taoist withdraws also from his family. Typical of this is another story, surely apocryphal, from Chuang Tzŭ (Ch. 3, 3). At the death of Lao Tzŭ a disciple went to the family and expressed his sympathy quite briefly and formally. The other disciples were astonished, and asked his reason. He said: 'Yes, at first I thought that he was our man, but he is not. When I went to grieve, the old men were bewailing him as though they were bewailing a son, and the young wept as though they were mourning a mother. To bind them so closely to himself, he must have spoken words which he should not have spoken, and wept tears which he should not have wept. That, however, is a falling away from the heavenly nature.'

Lao Tzŭ's teaching, like that of Confucius, cannot be described as religion; like Confucius's, it is a sort of social philosophy, but of irrationalistic character. Thus it was quite possible, and later it became the rule, for one and the same person to be both Confucian and Taoist. As an official and as the head of his family, a man would think and act as a Confucian; as a private individual, when he had retired far from the city to live in his country mansion (often modestly described as a cave or a thatched hut), or when he had been dismissed from his post or suffered some other trouble, he would feel and think as a Taoist. In order to live as a Taoist it was necessary, of course, to possess such an estate, to which a man could retire with his servants, and where he could live without himself doing manual work. This difference between the Confucian and the Taoist found a place in the works of many Chinese poets. I take the following quotation from an essay by the statesman and poet Ts'ao Chih, of the end of the second century A.D.:

Master Mysticus lived in deep seclusion on a mountain in the wilderness; he had withdrawn as in flight from the world, desiring to purify his spirit and give rest to his heart. He despised official activity, and no longer maintained any relations with the world; he sought quiet and freedom from care, in order in this way to attain everlasting life. He did nothing but

43

send his thoughts wandering between sky and clouds, and consequently there was nothing worldly that could attract and tempt him.

When Mr Rationalist heard of this man, he desired to visit him, in order to persuade him to alter his views. He harnessed four horses, who could quickly traverse the plain, and entered his light fast carriage. He drove through the plain, leaving behind him the ruins of abandoned settlements; he entered the boundless wilderness, and finally reached the dwelling of Master Mysticus. Here there was a waterfall on one side, and on the other were high crags; at the back a stream flowed deep down in its bed, and in front was an odorous wood. The master wore a white doeskin cap and a striped fox-pelt. He came forward from a cave buried in the mountain, leaned against the tall crag, and enjoyed the prospect of wild nature. His ideas floated on the breezes, and he looked as if the wide spaces of the heavens and the countries of the earth were too narrow for him; as if he was going to fly but had not yet left the ground; as if he had already spread his wings but wanted to wait a moment. Mr. Rationalist climbed up with the aid of vine shoots, reached the top of the crag, and stepped up to him, saying very respectfully:

'I have heard that a man of nobility does not flee from society, but seeks to gain fame; a man of wisdom does not swim against the current, but seeks to earn repute. You, however, despise the achievements of civilization and culture; you have no regard for the splendour of philanthropy and justice; you squander your powers here in the wilderness and neglect ordered relations between man. . . .'

Frequently Master Mysticus and Mr. Rationalist were united in a single person. Thus, Shih Ch'ung wrote in an essay on himself:

In my youth I had great ambition and wanted to stand out above the multitude. Thus it happened that at a little over twenty years of age I was already a court official; I remained in the service for twenty-five years. When I was fifty I had to give up my post because of an unfortunate occurrence. . . . The older I became, the more I appreciated the freedom I had acquired; and as I loved forest and plain, I retired to my villa. When I built this villa, a long embankment formed the boundary behind it; in front the prospect extended over a clear canal; all around grew countless cypresses, and flowing water meandered round the house. There were pools there, and outlook towers; I bred birds and fishes. In my harem there were always good

1 Painted pottery from Kansu: Neolithic.
(In the collection of the Museum für Völkerkunde, Berlin.)

2 Ancient bronze tripod found at An-yang.
(From G. Ecke, 'Frühe chinesische Bronzen aus der
Sammlung Oskar Trautmann', Peking, 1939, plate 3.)

musicians who played dance tunes. When I went out I enjoyed nature or hunted birds and fished. When I came home, I enjoyed playing the lute or reading; I also liked to concoct an elixir of life and to take breathing exercises [both Taoist practices], because I did not want to die, but wanted one day to lift myself to the skies, like an immortal genius. Suddenly I was drawn back into the official career, and became once more one of the dignitaries of the Emperor.

Thus Lao Tzŭ's individualist and anarchist doctrine was not suited to form the basis of a general Chinese social order, and its employment in support of dictatorship was certainly not in the spirit of Lao Tzŭ. Throughout history, however, Taoism of the type that the 'Tao Tê Ching' seems to propose remained the philosophic attitude of individuals of the highest circle of society; its real doctrine never became popularly accepted; for the strong feeling for nature that distinguishes the Chinese, and their reluctance to interfere in the sanctified order of nature by technical and other deliberate acts, was not actually a result of Lao Tzŭ's teaching, but one of the fundamentals from which his ideas started. But there appeared a religious system which claims to derive from Lao Tzŭ and which still exists today. We call it sometimes 'Vulgar Taoism' or 'Folk religion'. It is not clear whether it existed at the time of Lao Tzŭ or originated later. We believe that it contains many elements of an old folk religion of which hardly any traces were preserved in our sources. We will come back to this 'Taoism'. Here, it suffices that in the writings of their thinkers, Lao Tzŭ's book is interpreted as a religious text, given a different meaning and purpose. In this system, some thinkers were true mystics; others, more practical, tried to prolong their life by sexual techniques and by control of the breath and the diet; still others tried to develop an elixir of life and became alchemists. In all these schools, the 'Tao Tê Ching' was the basic book; all interpreted it in their way.

If the date assigned to Lao Tzŭ by present-day research (the fourth instead of the sixth century B.C.) is correct, he was more or less contemporary with Chuang Tzŭ, who was probably the most gifted poet among the Chinese philosophers. At the time of his writing, there was not yet a single 'real' book, except more or less annalistic books of history. So his book consists of short essays which exhibit a wealth of fresh metaphors and similes which nobody before him had thought of, and a wealth also of thoughts of a different kind, some even reminding us strongly of Indian thought, and, as we will see, it is not impossible that elements of Indian thought reached China around or before 400 B.C.

From Lao Tzŭ and Chuang Tzŭ a thin thread extends as far as the fourth century A.D.: Huai-nan Tzŭ, Chung-ch'ang T'ung, Yüan Chi (210–263), Liu Ling (221–300), and T'ao Ch'ien (365–427), are some of the most eminent names of Taoist philosophers. After that the stream of original thought dried up, and we rarely find a new idea among the late Taoists. These gentlemen living on their estates had acquired a new means of expressing their inmost feelings: they wrote poetry and, above all, painted. Their poems and paintings contain in a different form what Lao Tzŭ had tried to express with the inadequate means of the language of his day. Thus Lao Tzŭ's teaching has had the strongest influence to this day in this field, and has inspired creative work which is among the finest achievements of mankind.

CHAPTER FOUR

The Dissolution
of the Feudal System
(c. 500–250 B.C.)

1 *Social and military changes*

The period following that of the Chou dictatorships is known as that of the Contending States (480–222 B.C.). Out of over a thousand states, fourteen remained, of which, in the period that now followed, one after another disappeared, until only one remained. This period is the fullest, or one of the fullest, of strife in all Chinese history. The various feudal states had lost all sense of allegiance to the ruler, and acted in entire independence. It is a pure fiction to speak of a Chinese state in this period; the emperor had no more power than the ruler of the Holy Roman Empire in the late medieval period of Europe, and the so-called 'feudal states' of China can be directly compared with the developing national states of Europe. A comparison of this period with late medieval Europe is, indeed, of highest interest. If we adopt a political system of periodization, we might say that around 400 B.C. the unified feudal state of the first period of Antiquity had ceased to exist and that 'national states' had emerged which took a development in the direction of the national states of medieval Europe, although formally, the feudal system continued and the national states still retained many feudal traits.

As none of these states was strong enough to control and subjugate the rest, alliances were formed. The most favoured union was the north-south axis; it struggled against an east-west league. The alliances were not stable but broke up again and again through bribery or intrigue, which produced new combinations. We must confine ourselves to mentioning the most important of the events that took place behind this military façade.

Through the continual struggles more and more feudal lords lost their lands; and not only they, but the families of the nobles dependent on them, who had received so-called sub-fiefs. Some of the landless nobles perished; some offered their services to the remaining feudal lords as soldiers or advisers. Thus in this period we meet with a large number of migratory politicians who became competitors of the wandering scholars. Both these groups recommended to their lord ways and means of gaining victory over the other feudal lords, so as to become sole ruler. In order to carry out their plans the advisers claimed the rank of a Minister or Chancellor.

The main literary source for this period is the 'Plans of the Contending States' ('Chan Kuo Ts'ê'), a book which is not so much a book of history as a kind of early novel which reports the clever tricks and schemes of these advisers. Thus, though certainly many events did not take place exactly as the book says, the spirit behind these events seems to be caught very well.

Realistic though these advisers and their lords were in their thinking, they did not dare to trample openly on the old tradition. The emperor was indeed a completely powerless figurehead, but he belonged nevertheless, according to tradition, to a family of divine origin, which had obtained its office not merely by the exercise of force but through a 'divine mandate'. Whether or not the lords believed in this 'mandate', rulers and pretenders always in history have tried to establish their 'legitimacy'. Accordingly, if one of the feudal lords thought of putting forward a claim to the imperial throne, he felt compelled to demonstrate that his family was just as much of divine origin as the emperor's, and perhaps of remoter origin. In this matter the travelling 'scholars' rendered valuable service as manufacturers of genealogical trees. Each of the old noble families already had its family tree, as an indispensable requisite for the sacrifices to ancestors. But in some cases this tree began as a branch of that of the imperial family: this was the case of the feudal lords who were of imperial descent and whose ancestors had been granted fiefs after the conquest of the country. Others, however, had for their first ancestor a local deity long worshipped in the family's home country, such as the ancient agrarian god Huang Ti, or the bovine god Shen Nung. Here the 'scholars' stepped in, turning the local deities into human beings and 'emperors'. This suddenly gave the noble family concerned an imperial origin. Finally, order was brought into this collection of ancient emperors. They were arranged and connected with each other in 'dynasties' or in some other 'historical' form. Thus at a stroke Huang Ti, who about 450 B.C. had been a local god in the region of southern Shansi, became the forefather of almost all the noble families, including that of the imperial house of the Chou. Needless to say, there would be discrepancies between the family trees constructed by the various scholars for their lords, and later, when this problem had lost its political importance, the commentators laboured for centuries on the elaboration of an impeccable system of 'ancient emperors'—and to this day there are sinologists who continue to present these humanized gods as historical personalities.

In the earlier wars fought between the nobles they were themselves the actual combatants, accompanied only by their retinue. As the struggles for power grew in severity, each noble hired such mercenaries as he could, for instance the landless nobles just mentioned. Very soon it became the custom to arm peasants and send them to the wars. This substantially increased the armies. The numbers of soldiers who were killed in particular battles may have been greatly exaggerated (in a single battle in 260 B.C., for instance, the number who lost their lives was put at 450,000, a quite impossible figure); but there must have been armies of several thousand men, perhaps as many as 10,000. The population had grown considerably by that time.

The armies of the earlier period consisted mainly of the nobles in their war-chariots; each chariot surrounded by the retinue of the nobleman. Now came large troops of commoners as infantry as well, drawn from the peasant population. To these, cavalry were first added in the fifth century B.C., by the northern state of Chao (in the present Shansi), following the example of its Turkish and Mongol neighbours. The general theory among ethnologists is that the horse was first harnessed to a chariot, and that riding came much later; but it is my opinion that effective horse-breeding was impossible without mastering the art of riding on a horse. However, it seems that cavalry could be used in war only after the domestication of horses had progressed and the riders had been trained in disciplined, co-ordinated action on horseback while being able to shoot accurately with the bow from the back of a galloping horse, especially shooting to the rear. In any case, its cavalry gave the feudal state of Chao a military advantage for a short time. Soon the other northern states copied it one after another—especially Ch'in, in north-west China. The introduction of cavalry brought a change in clothing all over China, for the former long skirt-like garb could not be worn on horseback. Trousers and the riding-cap were introduced from the north.

The new technique of war made it important for every state to possess as many soldiers as possible, and where it could to reduce the enemy's numbers. One result of this was that wars became much more sanguinary; another was that men in other countries were induced to immigrate and settle as peasants, so that the taxes they paid should provide the means for further recruitment of soldiers. In the state of Ch'in, especially, the practice soon started of using the whole of the peasantry simultaneously as a rough soldiery. Hence that state was particularly anxious to attract peasants in large numbers.

2 *Economic changes*

In the course of the wars much land of former noblemen had become free. Often the former serfs had then silently become landowners. Others had started to cultivate land in the area inhabited by the indigenous population and regarded this land, which they themselves had made fertile, as their private family property.

The natives probably in most parts of what was China at that time, still used digging sticks and other light tools. Chinese used a plough, drawn by an animal, and even before the cultivation of rice and irrigation had become widely accepted, fields had to be relatively level and rectangular. Thus, each new development of land needed much investment in labour. There was, in spite of the growth of the population, still much cultivable land available. Victorious feudal lords induced farmers to come to their territory and to cultivate the wasteland. This is a period of great migrations, internal and external. It seems that from this period on not only merchants but also farmers began to migrate southwards into the area of the present provinces of Kwangtung and Kwangsi and as far as Tonking.

As long as the idea that all land belonged to the great clans of the Chou prevailed, sale of land was inconceivable; but when individual family heads acquired land or cultivated new land, they regarded it as their natural right to dispose of the land as they wished. From now on until the end of the medieval period, the family head as representative of the family could sell or buy land. However, the land belonged to the family and not to him as a person. This development was favoured by the spread of money. In time land in general became an asset with a market value and could be bought and sold.

Another important change can be seen from this time on. Under the feudal system of the Chou strict primogeniture among the nobility existed: the fief went to the oldest son by the main wife. The younger sons were given independent pieces of land with its inhabitants as new, secondary fiefs. With the increase in population there was no more such land that could be set up as a new fief. From now on, primogeniture was retained in the field of ritual and religion down to the present time: only the oldest son of the main wife represents the family in the ancestor worship ceremonies; only the oldest son of the emperor could become his successor. But the landed property from now on was equally divided among all sons. Occasionally the oldest son was given some extra land to enable him to pay the expenses for the family ancestral worship. Mobile property, on the other side, was not so strictly regulated and often the oldest son was given preferential treatment in the inheritance. Daughters did not inherit land. Until recently, daughters were regarded as a kind of trust: their parents raised them for their husbands, and the husband had to repay to the parents the cost which was involved in raising the girl from birth to the moment of her marriage. Thus, the family of the groom had to pay a 'bridal gift', and the bride's family did not have to let her inherit parts of the family property.

The technique of cultivation underwent some significant changes. There seems to have been a plough, made of wood, which in use was drawn by one or two persons, together with a 'pull-spade'. From this time on, the animal-drawn plough seems to have become more common and it was often strengthened by an iron plough-share. Iron sickles, too, became common. A fallow system was introduced so that cultivation became more intensive. Manuring of fields was already known in Shang time. It seems that the consumption of meat decreased from this period on: less mutton and beef were eaten. Pig and dog became the main sources of meat, and higher consumption of beans made up for the loss of proteins. All this indicates a strong population increase. We have no statistics for this period, but by 400 B.C. it is conceivable that the population under the control of the various individual states comprised something around 25 million. The eastern plains emerge more and more as centres of production.

Iron, which now became quite common, was produced apparently in south China and also in Shansi. The blacksmiths of this time were able to produce cast as well as wrought iron which indicates that they must have had well-constructed furnaces and bellows in order to reach the necessary temperatures. Firing material was obviously at this period still charcoal; the use of coal seems to have come up somewhat later, and it is quite likely that the Chinese already at a relatively early time were able to transform coal into coke with a technique similar to that by which they produced charcoal. In any case, it seems to be clear that Chinese could handle iron and soon steel at a time much earlier than Western countries.

The raw materials for bronze came mainly from the south. We know now that Chinese made bronze mirrors already in the Shang time, but from our period on, mirrors become pieces of art, decorated with numerous symbolic figures. Swords of bronze appear already before our period, but belt hooks are new and indicate some change in clothing. The bronze vessels of the period of the Warring States replace the highly stylized animals and mythical beings by vivid scenes of battle, by wrestling matches, or other representations from daily life. This indicates that their use was no longer limited to ritual ceremonies, though bronze still was too expensive to be used in ordinary households.

The increased use of metal and the invention of metal coins greatly stimulated trade. Money normally was of copper and remained so until modern times; the value of the coin always was supposed to correspond to the metal value of the coin. Thus, a considerable capital in the form of copper coin took up a good deal of room and was not easy to conceal. If anyone had much money, everyone in his village knew it. No one dared to hoard to any extent for fear of attracting bandits and creating lasting insecurity. On the other hand the merchants wanted to attain the standard of living which the nobles, the landowners, used to have. Thus they began to invest their money in land. This was all the easier for them since it often happened that one of the lesser nobles or a peasant fell deeply into debt to a merchant and found himself compelled to give up his land in payment of the debt.

Soon the merchants took over another function. So long as there had been many small feudal states, and the feudal lords had created lesser lords with small fiefs, it had been a simple matter for the taxes to be collected, in the form of grain, from the peasants through the agents of the lesser lords. Now that there were only a few great states in existence, the old system was no longer effectual. This gave the merchants their opportunity. The rulers of the various states entrusted the merchants with the collection of taxes, and this had great advantages for the ruler: he could obtain part of the taxes at once, as the merchant usually had grain in stock, or was himself a landowner and could make advances at any time. Through having to pay the taxes to the merchant, the village population became dependent on him. Thus the merchants developed into the first administrative officials in the provinces.

In connection with the growth of business, the cities kept on growing. It is estimated that at the beginning of the third century, the city of Lin-chin, near the present Chi-nan in Shantung, had a population of 210,000 persons. Each of its walls had a length of 4,000 metres; thus, it was even somewhat larger than the famous city of Lo-yang, capital of China during the Later Han dynasty, in the second century A.D. Several other cities of this period have been recently excavated and must have had populations far above 10,000 persons. There were two types of cities: the rectangular, planned city of the Chou conquerors, a seat of administration; and the irregularly shaped city which grew out of a market place and became only later an administrative centre. We do not know much about the organization and administration of these cities, but they seem to have had considerable independence because some of them issued their own city coins.

From this period on, one can study the expansion of Chinese

settlement into areas of indigenous, non-Chinese societies by the spread of cities A settlement became a 'city' (*ch'eng*) when it became the seat of an administration, and its outer symbol was its city wall. Normally, farmers did not live in cities. It was the aristocracy, its dependants, and a part of the craftsmen who had to work for the aristocracy that were the urbanites. We know, however, from neolithic times on that certain industries were usually outside the cities, mainly brick-making and metal founding. This has given rise to the theory that originally the cities were primarily cult centres to which the upper class which conducted the cult, became attached. The surrounding villages, specialized in farming or crafts, came to the city as their religious centre and their market; only at a subsequent period did the villages coalesce with the cult centre into a city. In general, this does not seem to be the best explanation for the Chinese type of urban development. We should regard the specialized rural settlements as outposts of the cities, where craftsmen were socially like Indian craft castes tied to the city aristocracy and had to work for their masters. True farm villages, on the other hand, did not at first have specialized craftsmen, as the farmer could produce most of what he needed and could get the rest on the markets. It seems that only at a later period, villages also usually contained some men who produced some of the tools the farmers needed.

When these cities grew, the food produced in the neighbourhood of the towns no longer sufficed for their inhabitants. This led to the building of roads, which also facilitated the transport of supplies for great armies. These roads mainly radiated from the centre of consumption into the surrounding country, and they were less in use for communication between one administrative centre and another. For long journeys the rivers were of more importance, since transport by wagon was always expensive owing to the shortage of draught animals. Thus we see in this period the first important construction of canals and a development of communications. With the canal construction was connected the construction of irrigation and drainage systems, which further promoted agricultural production. The cities were places in which great luxury often developed; music, dance, and other refinements were cultivated. We know that already at the time of Confucius the lords who invited other lords or ambassadors from other lords to their cities for the conclusion of treaties, entertained such guests not only with big dinners, but also had female dancers and musicians at hand, who, if we interpret Confucius's reaction correctly, influenced the guests by their charms. Similarly, the parties which the merchants gave and during which they discussed business, were enlivened by the presence of prostitutes. It is said that a statesman before the time of Confucius in the state of Ch'i opened the first houses of prostitution and drew profits from taxes imposed on these houses. We get the impression that the inmates of these houses were wives and daughters of convicted and executed criminals as well as prisoners of war while other unfortunate females were employed in state spinning and weaving factories and produced the technically superior silks of the time.

The life of the commoners in these cities was regulated by laws; the first codes are mentioned in 536 B.C. By the end of the fourth century B.C. a large body of criminal law existed, supposedly collected by Li K'uei, which became the foundation of all later Chinese law. It is interesting to remark that the use of minted coins as well as the formulation of laws begins in China later, but not much later than in the Near East, as recent research seems to have shown that the so-called codes of Sumer and Babylon were not applied by judges to actual cases, but in fact they were regarded as guidelines only.

So far nothing has been said in these chapters about China's foreign policy. Since the central ruling house was completely powerless, and the feudal lords were virtually independent rulers, little can be said, of course, about any 'Chinese' foreign policy. Some statelets which had existed in the North, along the zone in which farming was possible but marginal, had meanwhile been absorbed into the larger states of this time and fights with tribes of non-Chinese inside and outside the states continued. The important new development comes around 300 B.C. when, for the first time, a number of tribes of Turkish and/or Mongol type concluded a federation which took 'Hsiung-nu' as its name; the names of individual tribes at that time is not known, only later such names begin to be recorded. It is known that these northern peoples had mastered the technique of horseback warfare and were far ahead of the Chinese, although the Chinese imitated their methods. The peasants of China, as they penetrated farther and farther north, had to be protected by their rulers against the northern peoples, and since the rulers needed their armed forces for their struggles within China, a beginning was made with the building of frontier walls, to prevent sudden raids of the northern peoples against the peasant settlements. Thus came into existence the early forms of the 'Great Wall of China'. This provided for the first time a visible frontier between Chinese and non-Chinese. Along this frontier, just as by the walls of towns, great markets were held at which Chinese peasants bartered their produce to non-Chinese nomads. Both partners in this trade became accustomed to it and drew very substantial profits from it. We even know the names of several great horse-dealers who bought horses from the nomads and sold them within China.

3 *Cultural changes*

Together with the economic and social changes in this period, there came cultural changes. New ideas sprang up in exuberance, as would seem entirely natural, because in times of change and crisis men always come forward to offer solutions for pressing problems. We shall refer here only briefly to the principal philosophers of the period.

Mencius (c. 372–289 B.C.) and Hsün Tzŭ (c. 298–238 B.C.) both belonged to the so-called 'scholars', and both lived in the present Shantung, that is to say, in eastern China. Both elaborated the ideas of Confucius, but neither of them achieved personal success. Mencius (Meng Tzŭ) recognized that the removal of the ruling house of the Chou no longer presented any difficulty. The difficult question for him was when a change of ruler would be justified. And how could it be ascertained whom Heaven had destined as successor if the existing dynasty was brought down? Mencius replied that the voice of the 'people', that is to say of the upper class and its following, would declare the right man, and that this man would then be Heaven's nominee. This theory persisted throughout the history of China, but never led to the emergence of democracy. Every rebel claimed that Heaven had destined him to be the new legitimate ruler. If he was successful, he was right; if not, he was simply an impostor who deserved his death.

Hsün Tzŭ's chief importance lies in the fact that he recognized that the 'laws' of nature are unchanging but that man's fate is determined not by nature alone but, in addition, by his own activities. Man's nature is basically bad, but by working on himself within the framework of society, he can change his nature and can develop. Thus, Hsün Tzŭ's philosophy contains a dynamic element, fit for a dynamic period of history.

In the strongest contrast to these thinkers was the school of Mo Ti (at some time between 479 and 381 B.C.). The Confucian school held fast to the old feudal order of society, and was only ready to agree to a few superficial changes. The school of Mo Ti proposed to alter the fundamental principles of society. Family ethics must no longer be retained; the principles of family love must be extended to the whole upper class, which Mo Ti called the 'people'. One must love another member of the upper class just as much as one's own father. Then the friction between individuals and between states would cease. Instead of families, large groups of people friendly to one another must be created. Further one should live frugally and not expend endless money on effete rites, as the Confucianists demanded. The expenditure on weddings and funerals under the Confucianist ritual consumed so much money that many families

55

fell into debt and, if they were unable to pay off the debt, sank from the upper into the lower class. In order to maintain the upper class, therefore, there must be more frugality. Mo Ti's teaching won great influence. He and his successors surrounded themselves with a private army of supporters which was rigidly organized and which could be brought into action at any time as its leader wished. Thus the Mohists came forward everywhere with an approach entirely different from that of the isolated Confucians. When the Mohists offered their assistance to a ruler, they brought with them a group of technical and military experts who had been trained on the same principles. In consequence of its great influence this teaching was naturally hotly opposed by the Confucianists.

We see clearly in Mo Ti's and his followers' ideas the influence of the changed times. His principle of 'universal love' reflects the breakdown of the clans and the general weakening of family bonds which had taken place. His ideal of social organization resembles organizations of merchants and craftsmen which we know only from later periods. His stress upon frugality, too, reflects a line of thought which is typical of businessmen. The rationality which can also be seen in his metaphysical ideas and which has induced modern Chinese scholars to call him an early materialist is fitting to an age in which a developing money economy and expanding trade required a cool, logical approach to the affairs of this world.

A similar mentality can be seen in another school which appeared from the fifth century B.C. on, the 'dialecticians'. Here are a number of names to mention: the most important are Kung-sun Lung and Hui Tzŭ, who are comparable with the ancient Greek dialecticians and Sophists. They saw their main task in the development of logic. Since, as we have mentioned, many 'scholars' journeyed from one princely court to another, and other people came forward, each recommending his own method to the prince for the increase of his power, it was of great importance to be able to talk convincingly, so as to defeat a rival in a duel of words on logical grounds.

Unquestionably, however, the most important school of this period was that of the so-called Legalists, whose most famous representative was Shang Yang (or Shang Tzŭ, died 338 B.C.). The supporters of this school came principally from old princely families that had lost their feudal possessions, and not from among the so-called scholars. They were people belonging to the upper class who possessed political experience and now offered their knowledge to other princes who still reigned. These men had entirely given up the old conservative traditions of Confucianism; they were the first to make their peace with the new social order. They recognized that little or nothing remained of the old upper class of feudal lords and their following.

The last of the feudal lords collected around the heads of the last remaining princely courts, or lived quietly on the estates that still remained to them. Such a class, with its moral and economic strength broken, could no longer lead. The Legalists recognized, therefore, only the ruler and next to him, as the really active and responsible man, the chancellor; under these there were to be only the common people, consisting of the richer and poorer peasants; the people's duty was to live and work for the ruler, and to carry out without question whatever orders they received. They were not to discuss or think, but to obey. The chancellor was to draft laws which came automatically into operation. The ruler himself was to have nothing to do with the government or with the application of the laws. He was only a symbol, a representative of the equally inactive Heaven. Clearly these theories were much the best suited to the conditions of the break-up of feudalism about 300 B.C. Thus they were first adopted by the state in which the old idea of the feudal state had been least developed, the state of Ch'in, in which alien peoples were most strongly represented. Shang Yang became the actual organizer of the state of Ch'in. His ideas were further developed by Han Fei Tzŭ (died 233 B.C.). The mentality which speaks out of his writings has closest similarity to the famous Indian Arthashastra which originated slightly earlier; both books exhibit a 'Machiavellian' spirit. It must be observed that these theories had little or nothing to do with the ideas of the old cult of Heaven or with family allegiance; on the other hand, the soldierly element, with the notion of obedience, was well suited to the militarized peoples of the west. The population of Ch'in, organized throughout on these principles, was then in a position to remove one opponent after another. In the middle of the third century B.C. the greater part of the China of that time was already in the hands of Ch'in, and in 256 B.C. the last emperor of the Chou dynasty was compelled, in his complete impotence, to abdicate in favour of the ruler of Ch'in.

Apart from these more or less political speculations, there came into existence in this period, by no mere chance, a school of thought which never succeeded in fully developing in China, concerned with natural science and comparable with the Greek natural philosophy. We have already several times pointed to parallels between Chinese and Indian thoughts. Such similarities may be the result of mere coincidence. But recent findings in Central Asia indicate that direct connections between India, Persia, and China may have started at a time much earlier than we had formerly thought. Sogdian merchants who later played a great role in commercial contacts might have been active already from 400 B.C. on and might have been the transmitters of new ideas. The most important philosopher of this school was

Tsou Yen (flourished between 320 and 295 B.C.); he, as so many other Chinese philosophers of this time, was a native of Shantung, and the ports of the Shantung coast may well have been ports of entrance of new ideas from western Asia as were the roads through the Sinkiang basin into western China. Tsou Yen's basic ideas had their root in earlier Chinese speculations: the doctrine that all that exists is to be explained by the positive, creative, or the negative, passive action (Yang and Yin) of the five 'elements', wood, fire, earth, metal, and water (Wu hsing). But Tsou Yen also considered the form of the world, and was the first to put forward the theory that the world consists not of a single continent with China in the middle of it, but of nine continents. The names of these continents sound like Indian names, and his idea of a central world-mountain may well have come from India. The 'scholars' of his time were quite unable to appreciate this beginning of science, which actually led to the contention of this school, in the first century B.C., that the earth was of spherical shape. Tsou Yen himself was ridiculed as a dreamer; but very soon, when the idea of the reciprocal destruction of the 'elements' was applied, perhaps by Tsou Yen himself, to politics, namely when, in connection with the astronomical calculations much cultivated by this school and through the identification of dynasties with the five elements, the attempt was made to explain and to calculate the duration and the supersession of dynasties, strong pressure began to be brought to bear against this school. For hundreds of years its books were distributed and read only in secret, and many of its members were executed as revolutionaries. Thus, this school, instead of becoming the nucleus of a school of natural science, was driven underground.

The secret societies which started to arise clearly from the first century B.C. on, but which may have been in existence earlier, adopted the politico–scientific ideas of Tsou Yen's school. Such secret societies have existed in China down to the present time. They all contained a strong religious, but heterodox element which can often be traced back to influences from a foreign religion. In times of peace they were centres of a true, emotional religiosity. In times of stress, a 'messianic' element tended to become prominent: the world is bad and degenerating; morality and a just social order have decayed, but the coming of a saviour is close; the saviour will bring a new, fair order and destroy those who are wicked. Tsou Yen's philosophy seemed to allow them to calculate when this new order would start; later secret societies contained ideas from Iranian Mazdaism, Manichaeism and Buddhism, mixed with traits from the popular religions and often couched in terms taken from the Taoists. The members of such societies were, typically, ordinary farmers who here found an emotional outlet for their frustrations in daily life. In times of stress, members of the leading élite often but not always established contacts with these societies, took over their leadership and led them to open rebellion.

The fate of Tsou Yen's school did not mean that the Chinese did not develop in the field of sciences. At about Tsou Yen's lifetime, the first mathematical handbook was written. From these books it is obvious that the interest of the government in calculating the exact size cf fields, the content of measures for grain, and other fiscal problems stimulated work in this field, just as astronomy developed from the interest of the government in the fixation of the calendar. Science kept on developing in other fields, too, but mainly as a hobby of scholars and in the shops of craftsmen, if it did not have importance for the administration and especially taxation and budget calculations.

CHAPTER FIVE

Military Rule
(250–200 B.C.)

1 *Towards the unitary state*

In 256 B.C. the last ruler of the Chou dynasty abdicated in favour of the feudal lord of the state of Ch'in. Some people place the beginning of the Ch'in dynasty in that year, 256 B.C.; others prefer the date 221 B.C., because it was only in that year that the remaining feudal states came to their end and Ch'in really ruled all China.

The territories of the state of Ch'in, the present Shensi and eastern Kansu, were from a geographical point of view transit regions, closed off in the north by steppes and deserts and in the south by almost impassable mountains. Only between these barriers, along the rivers Wei (in Shensi) and T'ao (in Kansu), is there a rich cultivable zone which is also the only means of transit from east to west. All traffic from and to Central Asia had to take this route. It is believed that strong relations with Central Asia allowed the state of Ch'in to make big profits from such 'foreign trade'. We have reasons to believe that traders from a foreign country had first to offer their merchandise to the ruler, and could sell only what was left over to the populace. The population was growing through immigration from the east which the government encouraged. This growing population with its increasing means of production, especially the great new irrigation systems, provided a welcome field for trade which was also furthered by the roads, though these were actually built for military purposes.

The state of Ch'in had never been so closely associated with the feudal communities of the rest of China as the other feudal states. A great part of its population, including the ruling class, was not purely Chinese but contained an admixture of Turks and Tibetans. The other Chinese even called Ch'in a 'barbarian state', and the foreign influence was, indeed, unceasing. This was a favourable soil for the overcoming of feudalism, and the process was furthered by the factors mentioned in the preceding chapter, which were leading to a change in the social structure of China. Especially the recruitment of the whole population, including the peasantry, for war was entirely in the interest of the influential nomad fighting peoples within the state. About 250 B.C., Ch'in was not only one of the economically strongest among the feudal states, but had already made an end of its own feudal system.

Every feudal system harbours some seeds of a bureaucratic system of administration: feudal lords have their personal servants who are not recruited from the nobility, but who by their easy access to the lord can easily gain importance. They may, for instance, be put in charge of estates, workshops, and other properties of the lord and thus acquire experience in administration and an efficiency which are obviously of advantage to the lord. When Chinese lords of the preceding period, with the help of their sub-lords of the nobility, made wars, they tended to put the newly conquered areas not into the hands of newly enfeoffed noblemen, but to keep them as their property and to put their administration into the hands of efficient servants; these were the first bureaucratic officials. Thus, in the course of the later Chou period, a bureaucratic system of administration had begun to develop, and terms like 'district' or 'prefecture' began to appear, indicating that areas under a bureaucratic administration existed beside and inside areas under feudal rule. This process had gone furthest in Ch'in and was sponsored by the representatives of the Legalist School, which was best adapted to the new economic and social situation.

A son of one of the concubines of the penultimate feudal ruler of Ch'in was living as a hostage in the neighbouring state of Chao, in what is now northern Shansi. There he made the acquaintance of an unusual man, the merchant Lü Pu-wei, a man of education. Lü Pu-wei persuaded the feudal ruler of Ch'in to declare this son his successor. He also sold a girl to the prince to be his wife, and the son of this marriage was to be the famous and notorious Shih Huang-ti. Lü Pu-wei came with his protégé to Ch'in, where he became his Prime Minister, and after the prince's death in 247 B.C. Lü Pu-wei became the regent for his young son Shih Huang-ti (then called Cheng). For the first time in Chinese history a merchant, a commoner, had reached one of the highest positions in the state. It is not known what sort of trade Lü Pu-wei had carried on, but probably he dealt in horses, the principal export of the state of Chao. As horses were an absolute necessity for the armies of that time, it is easy to imagine that a horse-dealer might gain great political influence.

Soon after Shih Huang-ti's accession Lü Pu-wei was dismissed, and a new group of advisers, strong supporters of the Legalist school, came into power. These new men began an active policy of conquest instead of the peaceful course which Lü Pu-wei had pursued. One campaign followed another in the years from 230 to 222, until all the feudal states had been conquered, annexed, and brought under Shih Huang-ti's rule.

2 Centralization in every field

The main task of the now gigantic realm was the organization of administration. One of the first acts after the conquest of the other feudal states was to deport all the ruling families and other important nobles to the capital of Ch'in; they were thus deprived of the basis of their power, and their land could be sold. These upper-class families supplied to the capital a class of consumers of luxury goods which attracted craftsmen and businessmen and changed the character of the capital from that of a provincial town to a centre of arts and crafts. It was decided to set up the uniform system of administration throughout the realm, which had already been successfully introduced in Ch'in: the realm was split up into provinces and the provinces into prefectures; and an official was placed in charge of each province or prefecture. Originally the prefectures in Ch'in had been placed directly under the central administration, with an official, often a merchant, being responsible for the collection of taxes; the provinces, on the other hand, formed a sort of military command area, especially in the newly conquered frontier territories. With the growing militarization of Ch'in, greater importance was assigned to the provinces, and the prefectures were made subordinate to them. Thus the officials of the provinces were originally army officers but now, in the reorganization of the whole realm, the distinction between civil and military administration was abolished. At the head of the province were a civil and also a military governor, and both were supervised by a controller directly responsible to the emperor. Since there was naturally a continual struggle for power between these three officials, none of them was supreme and none could develop into a sort of independent lord. In this system we can see the essence of the later Chinese administration.

Owing to the centuries of division into independent feudal states, the various parts of the country had developed differently. Each province spoke a different dialect which also contained many words borrowed from the language of the indigenous population; and as these earlier populations sometimes belonged to different races with different languages, in each state different words had found their way into the Chinese dialects. This caused divergences not only in the spoken but in the written language, and even in the characters in use for writing. There were two possibilities: one could write a word from such a local language or dialect by using a word which in the language of the court had a definite meaning, and a sound similar to the local one. This is a technique used down to the present time if Cantonese want to write local dialect or slang words. Or one could invent new characters, not existing in standard Chinese. We have found documents written in this way which are only partially understandable today. There exist to this day dictionaries in which the borrowed words of that time are indicated, and keys to the various old forms of writing also exist. Thus difficulties arose if, for instance, a man from the old territory of Ch'in was to be transferred as an official to the east: he could not properly understand the language and could not read the borrowed words, if he could read at all! For a large number of the officials of that time, especially the officers who became military governors, were certainly unable to read. The government therefore ordered that the language of the whole country should be unified, and that a definite style of writing should be generally adopted. The words to be used were set out in lists, so that the first lexicography came into existence simply through the needs of practical administration, as had happened much earlier in Babylonia. From Ch'in times on, all characters found on Chinese documents are easily readable, because they are written in the standardized script, and all words used are found in dictionaries. We know now that all classical texts of pre-Ch'in time as we have them today, have been rewritten in this standardized script in the second century B.C.: we do not know which words they actually contained at the time when they were composed, nor how these words were actually pronounced, a fact which makes the reconstruction of Chinese language before Ch'in very difficult.

The next requirement for the carrying on of the administration was the unification of weights and measures and, a surprising thing to us, of the gauge of the tracks for wagons. In the various feudal states there had been different weights and measures in use, and this had led to great difficulties in the centralization of the collection of taxes. The centre of administration, that is to say the new capital of Ch'in, had grown through the transfer of nobles and through the enormous size of the administrative staff into a thickly populated city with very large requirements of food. The fields of the former state of Ch'in alone could not feed the city; and the grain supplied in payment of taxation had to be brought in from far around, partly by cart. The only roads then existing consisted of deep cart-tracks. If the axles were not of the same length for all carts, the roads were simply unusable for many of them. Accordingly a fixed length was laid down for axles. The advocates of all these reforms were also their beneficiaries, the merchants.

The first principle of the Legalist school, a principle which had been applied in Ch'in and which was to be extended to the whole realm, was that of the training of the population in discipline and obedience, so that it should become a convenient tool in the hands of the officials. This requirement was best met by a people composed as far as possible only of industrious, uneducated, and tax-paying peasants. Scholars and philosophers were not wanted, in so far as they were not directly engaged in work commissioned by the state. The Confucianist writings came under special attack because they kept alive the memory of the old feudal conditions, preaching the ethic of the old feudal class which had just been destroyed and must not be allowed to rise again if the state was not to suffer fresh dissolution or if the central administration was not to be weakened. In 213 B.C. there took place the great holocaust of books which destroyed the Confucianist writings with the exception of one copy of each work for the State Library. Books on practical subjects were not affected. In the fighting at the end of the Ch'in dynasty the State Library was burnt down, so that many of the old works have only come down to us in an imperfect state and with doubtful accuracy. Some of the damage which Chinese literature suffered from this persecution, may be remedied in the near future: recently, some texts were found in tombs which may allow us to reconstruct some important texts. One of the most important ones is the 'Art of War' by Sun Tzŭ ('Sun Tzŭ ping-fa'), a book still used by leaders of the present regime. We know now that our text is a combination of two, originally independent books. Tradition, written down later by Confucianists, also reports that the emperor buried alive hundreds of famous scholars. This may not really be true, but it may give us to think that in 1974 the present regime fought a campaign against Confucius and in favour of Shih Huang-ti. At a time when writing was not very widely spread, and where books consisted of bundles of bamboo slips, it was easy to confiscate all books; it also was easy to bring scholars to silence, but the real loss to Chinese culture arose from the fact that the new generation was little interested in the Confucianist literature, so that when, fifty years later, the effort was made to restore some texts from the oral tradition, there no longer existed any scholars who really knew them by heart, as had been customary in the past.

In 221 B.C. Shih Huang-ti had become emperor of all China. The judgements passed on him vary greatly: the official Chinese historiography rejects him entirely—naturally, for he tried to exterminate Confucianism, while every later historian was himself a Confucian. As with other prominent figures in Chinese history, his real personality remains unknown to us. It is interesting to see that this great military organizer was, on the other hand, a mystic. He built a palace which was constructed according to astronomical and magical principles. His tomb, later, was a copy of the universe. He believed that far away in the eastern ocean there was an island of the immortals and he sent an expedition to this island, which never returned. The emissaries, most of whom were young boys, probably drowned. Others think that they may have reached Japan. He believed that he was the first emperor of a series of ten thousand emperors of his own dynasty (Shih Huang-ti means 'first emperor'), though his empire like that of other dictators came to an end already under his successor. The basic principles of his administration had been laid down long before his time by the philosophers of the Legalist school, and were given effect by his Chancellor Li Ssŭ. Li Ssŭ was the really great personality of that period. The Legalists taught that the ruler must do as little as possible himself. His Ministers were there to act for him. He himself was to be regarded as a symbol of Heaven. In that capacity Shih Huang-ti undertook periodical journeys into the various parts of the empire, less for any practical purpose of inspection than for purposes of public worship. They corresponded to the course of the sun, and this indicates that Shih Huang-ti had adopted a notion derived from the older northern culture. Within the palace the emperor continually changed his residential quarters, probably not only from fear of assassination but also for astral reasons.

We cannot expect that this period brought forth a blossoming of literature. However, one aspect should be mentioned. Some time before Shih Huang-ti's time there lived in the state of Ch'u a member of the upper class, Ch'ü Yüan, who, according to tradition, was an adviser of his king. When the king did not listen to the advice he left the court and in despair threw himself into a river and drowned. Before his death he wrote a long poem in which he expressed his mood, the 'Li-sao', regarded as a poem with political undertones, although some Chinese scholars think it was a poem praising homosexuality. There are other poems attributed to him, and today he is praised as the first great poet of China, at least the first one whose name is known to us. The style of his poems, often called 'elegies', soon became a court style, used by poets who glorified their rulers and their actions in a flowery, very rich and complex, but beautiful language, very different from that kind of poetry which was incorporated into songs sung by female entertainers and dancers at the courts. We do not know whether this style of the 'elegy' was already used at the court of Shih Huang-ti, though we know that Ch'ü's descendants were among those upper class families which were deported by the emperor and resettled near the capital.

3 Frontier defence. Internal collapse

When the empire had been unified by the destruction of the feudal states, the central government became responsible for the protection of the frontiers from attack from without. In the south there were only peoples in a very low state of civilization, who could offer no serious menace to the Chinese. The trading colonies that gradually extended to Canton and still farther south served as Chinese administrative centres for provinces and prefectures, with small but adequate armies of their own, so that in case of need they could defend themselves. In the north the position was much more difficult. In addition to their conquest within China, the rulers of Ch'in had pushed their frontier far to the north. The nomad tribes had been pressed back and deprived of their best pasturage, namely the Ordos region. Here, the new tribal federation of the Hsiung-nu got its first leader known by name to us, T'ou-man. This first realm of the Hsiung-nu was not yet extensive, but its ambitious and warlike attitude made it a danger to Ch'in. It was therefore decided to maintain a large permanent army in the north. In addition to this, the frontier walls already existing in the mountains were rebuilt and made into a single great system. Thus came into existence in 214 B.C., out of the blood and sweat of countless pressed labourers, the famous Great Wall. Down to the present, folk ballads still sing about the cruel emperor and the sufferings of the people. The Great Wall as we can admire it today, is not the old one of Shih Huang-ti. In the course of centuries and again not many years ago, the wall was again and again repaired, first because it still served as a military bastion, today because it became a symbol of China and an attraction for tourists who do not think of the thousands who died there. Plate 5 shows a part of the wall as it was in 1935. Since then it has been repaired again.

On one of his periodical journeys the emperor fell ill and died. His death was the signal for the rising of many rebellious elements. Nobles rose in order to regain power and influence: generals rose because they objected to the permanent pressure from the central administration and their supervision by controllers; men of the people rose as popular leaders because the people were more tormented than ever, doing forced labour, generally at a distance from their homes. Within a few months there were six different rebellions and six different 'rulers'.

A court intrigue caused the death of the young and apparently capable heir to the throne. He was replaced by an adolescent who was controlled by eunuchs. Assassinations became the order of the day; the young heir to the throne was removed in this way and replaced by another young prince. But as early as 206 B.C. one of the rebels, Liu Chi (also called Liu Pang), entered the capital and dethroned the nominal emperor. Liu Chi at first had to retreat and was involved in hard fighting with a rival, but gradually he succeeded in gaining the upper hand and defeated not only his rival but also the other eighteen states that had been set up anew in China in those years. This brought an end to a military dictatorship and became the beginning of a new period of Chinese social history.

CHAPTER SIX

The Early Gentry Society (200 B.C.–A.D. 250)

1 *Development of the gentry-state*

In 206 B.C. Liu Chi assumed the title of Emperor and gave his dynasty the name of the Han Dynasty. After his death he was given as emperor the name of Kao Tsu. (From then on, every emperor was given after his death an official name as emperor, under which he appears in the Chinese sources. We have adopted the original or the official name according to which of the two has come into the more general use in Western books.) The period of the Han dynasty may be described as the beginning of the Chinese Middle Ages, while that of the Ch'in dynasty represents the transition from antiquity to the Middle Ages; for under the Han dynasty we meet in China with a new form of state, the 'gentry state'. The feudalism of ancient times has come definitely to its end.

In recent times, Chinese have adopted the name of the new dynasty to designate 'the Chinese race' (Han-jen) in distinction from minority ethnic groups inside the political frontiers of China. Our name 'China' may come from the Ch'in dynasty's name, though this is contested, and seems to have spread from India to the Mediterranean and Europe.

Emperor Kao Tsu came from eastern China, from a lowly family. He was the leader of a small band of soldiers who mutinied against the government because they had to fear punishment for neglect of orders. Other, similar groups, joined him. After his destruction of his strongest rival, the removal of the kings who had made themselves independent in the last years of the Ch'in dynasty was a relatively easy task for the new autocrat, although these struggles occupied the greater part of his reign. A much more difficult question, however, faced him: How was the empire to be governed? Kao Tsu's old friends and fellow-countrymen, who had helped him into power, had been rewarded by appointment as generals or high officials. Gradually he got rid of those who had been his best comrades, as so many upstart rulers have done before and after him in every country in the world. An emperor does not like to be reminded of a very humble past, and he is liable also to fear the rivalry of men who formerly were his equals. It is evident that little attention was paid to theories of administration; policy was determined mainly by practical considerations. Kao Tsu allowed many laws and regulations to remain in force, including the prohibition of Confucianist writings. On the other hand, he reverted to the allocation of fiefs, though not to old noble families but to his relatives and some of his closest adherents, generally men of inferior social standing. Thus a mixed administration came into being: part of the empire was governed by new feudal princes, and another part split up into provinces and prefectures and placed directly under the central power through its officials.

But whence came the officials? Kao Tsu and his supporters, as farmers from eastern China, looked down upon the trading population to which farmers always regard themselves as superior. The merchants were ignored as potential officials although they had often enough held official appointments under the former dynasty. The second group from which officials had been drawn under the Ch'in was that of the army officers, but their military functions had now, of course, fallen to Kao Tsu's soldiers. The emperor had little faith, however, in the loyalty of officers, even of his own, and apart from that he would have had first to create a new administrative organization for them. Accordingly he turned to another class which had come into existence, the class which we like to call 'gentry' in spite of important differences between the Chinese gentry and the English gentry.

The term 'gentry' has no direct parallel in Chinese texts; the later terms 'shen-shih' and 'chin-shen' do not quite cover this concept. The basic unit of the gentry class are families, not individuals. Such families often derive their origin from branches of the Chou nobility. But other gentry families were of different and more recent origin in respect to land ownership. Some late Chou and Ch'in officials of non-noble origin had become wealthy and had acquired land; the same was true for wealthy merchants and finally, some non-noble farmers who were successful in one or another way, bought additional land reaching the size of large holdings. All 'gentry' families owned substantial estates in the provinces which they leased to tenants on a kind of contract basis. The tenants, therefore, cannot be called 'serfs' although their factual position often was not different from the position of serfs. The rents of these tenants, usually about half the gross produce, are the basis of the livelihood of the gentry. One part of a gentry family normally lives in the country on a small home farm in order to be able to collect the rents. If the family can acquire more land and if this new land is too far away from the home farm to make collection of rents easy, a new home farm is set up under the control of another branch of the family. But the original home remains to be regarded as the real family centre.

In a typical gentry family, another branch of the family is in the capital or in a provincial administrative centre in official positions. These officials at the same time are the most highly educated members of the family and are often called the 'literati'. There are also always individual family members who are not interested in official careers or who failed in their careers and live as free 'literati' either in the big cities or on the home farms. It seems, to judge from much later sources, that the families assisted their most able members to enter the official careers, while those individuals who were less able were used in the administration of the farms, This system in combination with the strong familism of the Chinese, gave a double security to the gentry families. If difficulties arose in the estates either by attacks of bandits or by war or other catastrophes, the family members in official positions could use their influence and power to restore the property in the provinces. If, on the other hand, the family members in official positions lost their positions or even their lives by displeasing the court, the home branch could always find ways to remain untouched and could, in a generation or two, recruit new members and regain power and influence in the government. Thus, as families, the gentry was secure, although failures could occur to individuals. There are many gentry families who remained in the ruling élite for many centuries, some over more than a thousand years, weathering all vicissitudes of life. Some authors believe that Chinese leading families generally pass through a three- or four-generation cycle: a family member by his official position is able to acquire much land, and his family moves upward. He is able to give the best education and other facilities to his sons who lead a good life. But either these sons or the grandsons are spoiled and lazy; they begin to lose their property and status. The family moves downward, until in the fourth or fifth generation a new rise begins. Actual study of families seems to indicate that this is not true. The main branch of the family retains its position over centuries, if necessary by adopting intelligent children into the family from another branch. Of course, individuals within the main branch may turn out to be failures. Some of the other branch families, created by less able family members and often endowed with the less desirable pieces of landed property, may start on a lower level and not be able to move up again.

This system developed several typical traits. First, it is clear from

70

the above that a gentry family should be interested in having a fair number of children. The more sons they have, the more positions of power the family can occupy and thus, the more secure it will be; the more daughters they have, the more 'political' marriages they can conclude, i.e. marriages with sons of other gentry families in positions of influence. Therefore, gentry families in China tend to be, on the average, larger than ordinary families, while in our Western countries the leading families usually were smaller than the lower-class families. This means that gentry families produced more children than was necessary to replenish the available leading positions; or, looking at this from the other side, gentry families, by their higher standard of living were able to keep more children alive, than the lower-class families. Down to this century, an average mother had nine pregnancies, but fewer than four children grew up to maturity. If a group produces more children than are needed to fill the positions which their parents had, necessarily some family members had to get into lower positions and had to lose status. In view of this situation it was very difficult for lower-class families to achieve access into this gentry group. In European countries the leading élite did not quite replenish their ranks in the next generation, so that there was always some chance for the lower classes to move up into leading ranks. The gentry society was, therefore, a comparably stable society with little upward social mobility but with some downward mobility. As a whole and for reasons of gentry self-interest, the gentry stood for stability and against change.

Second, if a gentry family had no sons and, therefore, felt forced to adopt a boy in order to continue the position and tradition of the family, they adopted only sons from one of the other branches of the family with the same family name, because any son of another family might later turn against the adopting family and return to his native family. This rule has, in general, continued to the present time, though the middle and lower classes developed some other devices because they could not always find a suitable nephew. Third, down to the present time, biographies of Chinese do not mention the place where the person actually was born. This is not important. Important is the place where the family home, the country seat is. Thus, when we hear that a man comes from Nanking, this does not mean that he was born there; in fact, he may never have been there in his life.

Fourth, because the gentry preferred 'political marriages', the position of women was relatively high. Behind them was the power and wealth of their own family, and if the husband needed their support, he had to treat his wife well. Thus, women in the early gentry period play an important role in society. They could remarry, when widowed, could participate in ceremonies, and we know of some women who were poetesses, and one even who was a historian in a semi-official position.

The gentry members in the bureaucracy collaborated closely with one another because they were tied together by bonds of blood or marriage. It was easy for them to find good tutors for their children, because a pupil owed a debt of gratitude to his teacher and a child from a gentry family could later on nicely repay this debt; often, these teachers themselves were members of other gentry families. It was easy for sons of the gentry to get into official positions, because the people who had to recommend them for office were often related to them or knew the position of their family. In Han time, local officials had the duty to recommend young able men; if these men turned out to be good, the officials were rewarded, if not they were blamed or even punished. An official took less of a chance, if he recommended a son of an influential family, and he obliged such a candidate so that he could later count on his help if he himself should come into difficulties. When, towards the end of the second century B.C., a kind of examination system was introduced, this attitude was not basically changed.

The country branch of the family by the fact that it controlled large tracts of land, supplied also the logical tax collectors: they had the standing and power required for this job. Even if they were appointed in areas other than their home country (a rule which later was usually applied), they knew the gentry families of the other district or were related to them and got their support by appointing their members as their assistants.

Gentry society continued from Kao Tsu's time to the early twentieth century, but it went through a number of phases of development and changed considerably in time. We will later outline some of the most important changes. In general the number of politically leading gentry families was around one hundred (texts often speak of 'the hundred families' in this time) and they were concentrated in the capital; the most important home seats of these families in Han time were close to the capital and east of it or in the plains of eastern China, at that time the main centre of grain production.

Recently, Chinese historians have tended to describe this social system as an exploitatory one; earlier historians took a different view. They saw that a large society needs administrators who cannot be expected to earn their living by producing material goods. They need leisure time to develop new ideas. They may live in luxury, but this demand for luxury goods after all was responsible for all that we and present-day Chinese admire in Chinese culture and art. No agrarian society in history which did not have a well-defined upper class has developed into a higher society. Only an agro-industrial society of modern type has perhaps different possibilities. But Chinese thinkers recognized always that privileges also include obligations, and have always criticized and condemned men who did not live up to their obligations.

2 Situation of the Hsiung-nu empire; its relation to the Han empire. Incorporation of south China

In the time of the Ch'in dynasty there had already come into unpleasant prominence north of the Chinese frontier the tribal union, then relatively small, of the Hsiung-nu. Since then, the Hsiung-nu empire had destroyed the federation of Yüeh-chih tribes in the west, partly in the western sections of the present province of Kansu, and incorporated their people into their own federation. Some of the Yüeh-chih tribes seem to have been of Indo-European language stock. The Hsiung-nu also had conquered the less-well-organized eastern pastoral tribes, the Tung-hu and thus had become a formidable power. Everything goes to show that it had close relations with the territories of northern China. Many Chinese seem to have migrated to the Hsiung-nu empire, where they were welcome as artisans and probably also as farmers; but above all they were needed for the staffing of a new state administration. The scriveners in the newly introduced state secretariat were Chinese and wrote Chinese, for at that time the Hsiung-nu apparently had no written language. There were Chinese serving as administrators and court officials, and even as instructors in the army administration, teaching the art of warfare, against non-nomads. But what was the purpose of all this? Mao Tun, the second ruler of the Hsiung-nu, and his first successors undoubtedly intended ultimately to conquer China, exactly as many other northern peoples after them planned to do, and a few of them did. The main purpose of this was always to bring large numbers of peasants under the rule of the nomad rulers and so to solve, once for all, the problem of the provision of additional winter food. Everything that was needed, and everything that seemed to be worth trying to get as they grew more civilized, would thus be obtained better and more regularly than by raids or by tedious commercial negotiations. But if China was to be conquered and ruled there must exist a state organization of equal authority to hers; the Hsiung-nu ruler must himself come forward as Son of Heaven and develop a court ceremonial similar to that of a Chinese emperor. Thus the basis of the organization of the Hsiung-nu state lay in its rivalry with the neighbouring China; but the details naturally corresponded to the special nature of the Hsiung-nu social system. The young Hsiung-nu feudal state differed from the ancient Chinese feudal state not only in depending on a nomad economy with only supplementary agriculture, but also in possessing, in addition to a whole class of nobility and another of commoners, a stratum of slavery to be analysed further below. Similar to the Chou state, the Hsiung-nu state contained, especially around the ruler, an element of court bureaucracy which, however, never developed far enough to replace the basically feudal character of administration.

Thus Kao Tsu was faced in Mao Tun not with a mere nomad chieftain but with the most dangerous of enemies, and Kao Tsu's policy had to be directed to preventing any interference of the Hsiung-nu in north Chinese affairs, and above all to preventing alliances between Hsiung-nu and Chinese. Hsiung-nu alone, with their technique of horsemen's warfare, would scarcely have been equal to the permanent conquest of the fortified towns of the north and the Great Wall, although they controlled a population which may have been in excess of 2,000,000 people. But they might have succeeded with Chinese aid. Actually a Chinese opponent of Kao Tsu had already come to terms with Mao Tun, and in 200 B.C. Kao Tsu was very near suffering disaster in northern Shansi, as a result of which China would have come under the rule of the Hsiung-nu. But it did not come to that, and Mao Tun made no further attempt, although the opportunity came several times. Apparently the policy adopted by his court was not imperialistic but national, in the un-corrupted sense of the word. It was realized that a country so thickly populated as China could only be administered from a centre within China. The Hsiung-nu would thus have had to abandon their home territory and rule in China itself. That would have meant abandoning the flocks, abandoning nomad life, and turning into Chinese. The main supporters of the national policy, the first principle of which was loyalty to the old ways of life, seem to have been the tribal chief-tains. Mao Tun fell in with their view, and the Hsiung-nu maintained their state as long as they adhered to that principle—for some seven hundred years. Other nomad peoples, Toba, Mongols, and Manchus, followed the opposite policy, and before long they were caught in the mechanism of the much more highly developed Chinese economy and culture, and each of them disappeared from the political scene in the course of a century or so.

The national line of policy of the Hsiung-nu did not at all mean an end of hostilities and raids on Chinese territory, so that Kao Tsu declared himself ready to give the Hsiung-nu the foodstuffs and clothing materials they needed if they would make an end of their raids. A treaty to this effect was concluded, and sealed by the mar-riage of a Chinese princess with Mao Tun. This was the first inter-national treaty in the Far East between two independent powers mutually recognized as equals, and the forms of international diplomacy developed in this time remained the standard forms for the next thousand years. The agreement was renewed at the accession of each new ruler, but was never adhered to entirely by either side. The needs of the Hsiung-nu increased with the expansion of their empire and the growing luxury of their court; the Chinese, on the other hand, wanted to give as little as possible, and no doubt they did all they could to cheat the Hsiung-nu. Even the princesses they sent were never real daughters of the emperor. Thus, in spite of the treaties the Hsiung-nu raids went on. With China's progressive consolidation, the voluntary immigration of Chinese into the Hsiung-nu empire came to an end, and the Hsiung-nu actually began to kidnap Chinese subjects. These were the main features of the relations between Chinese and Hsiung-nu almost until 100 B.C.

In the extreme south, around the present-day Canton, another independent empire had been formed in the years of transition, under the leadership of a Chinese. The narrow basis of this realm was no doubt provided by the trading colonies, but the indigenous population of Yüeh tribes was not sufficiently organized for the building up of a state that could have maintained itself against China. Kao Tsu sent a diplomatic mission to the ruler of this state, and invited him to place himself under Chinese suzerainty (196 B.C.). The ruler realized that he could offer no serious resistance, while the existing circumstances guaranteed him virtual independence and he yielded to Kao Tsu without a struggle.

3 Brief feudal reaction. Consolidation of the gentry

Kao Tsu died in 195 B.C. From then to 179 the actual ruler was his widow, the empress Lü, while children were officially styled emperors. The empress tried to remove all members of her husband's family, the Liu, and to replace them with members of the Lü family. She met, however, with strong resistance from the remnants of the Liu family and their supporters who already in many cases belonged to the new gentry and controlled much of the land.

Chinese historians have depicted empress Lü in the darkest colours, and after her the two other women who rose to the highest power. Their objection was not only that the 'son of heaven' should be a man, but also that the empresses naturally had to try to remove the family of their husbands from power and put their own family in. This, in the view of the historians, violated the principle of legitimacy. Thus, we do not know whether empress Lü was as wicked as the texts show her.

On the death of the empress her opponents rose, under the leadership of Kao Tsu's family. Every member of the empress's family was exterminated, and a son of Kao Tsu, known later under the name of

Wen Ti (Emperor Wen), came to the throne. He reigned from 179 to 157 B.C. Under him there were still many fiefs, but with the limitation which the emperor Kao Tsu had laid down shortly before his death: only members of the imperial family should receive fiefs, to which the title of King was attached. Thus all the more important fiefs were in the hands of the imperial family, though this did not mean that rivalries came to an end.

On the whole, Wen Ti's period of rule passed in comparative peace. For the first time since the beginning of Chinese history, great areas of continuous territory were under unified rule, without unending internal warfare such as had existed under Shih Huang-ti and Kao Tsu. The creation of so extensive a region of peace produced great economic advance. The burdens that had lain on the peasant population were reduced, especially since under Wen Ti the court was very frugal. The population grew and cultivated fresh land, so that production increased. This may not all be the consequence of peace and good government. Recent research seems to indicate that China experienced a period of warmer weather from the late second century B.C. on to the third or fourth century A.D.

Already in the early years of the Eastern Chou dynasty local rulers had begun to interfere with the economy by manipulating taxes and money. Now, we enter a period in which economics were seriously studied. One of the important economic moves of emperor Wen was the abandonment of restrictions on the minting of copper coin, in order to prevent deflation through insufficiency of payment media. As a consequence more taxes were brought in, partly in kind, partly in coin, and this increased the power of the central government. The new gentry streamed into the towns, their standard of living rose, and they made themselves more and more into a class apart from the general population. As people free from material cares, they were able to devote themselves to scholarship. They went back to the old writings and studied them once more. They began to identify themselves with the nobles of feudal times. A member of the gentry also wanted to be a gentleman, and the Confucian books gave them the directions. We have to assume that in this period of early Han time there were small Confucian schools in which specialists in the books taught a selected group of pupils. On the other hand, we know that already in the time before the Han, there was a kind of examination for applicants for state jobs. Probably, such examinations consisted mainly of tests as to whether the men could read and write. Now, the Confucian schools also became training grounds for future government officials, for men who could read and write and who also knew the rules of social grace and behaviour. Around 100 B.C. a kind of official examination system arose, a system which underwent many

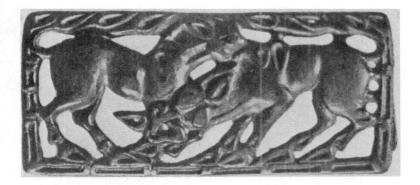

3 Bronze plaque representing two horses fighting each other
Ordos region, animal style.
(From V. Griessmaier, 'Sammlung Baron Eduard von der
Heydt', Vienna, 1936, illustration No. 6.)

4 Hunting scene: detail from the reliefs in the tombs
at Wu-liang-tz'u.
(From a rubbing in the author's possession.)

5 Part of the 'Great Wall'.
(Photo Eberhard.)

changes, but remained in operation in principle until 1904. The object of examinations was not to test job qualification or job efficiency but command of the ideals of the gentry and knowledge of the literature inculcating them. A man trained in this way would be able to analyse every problem and to find the right solution; if not, he could ask his advisers, hear their arguments and then make his decisions. We find a similar concept in the early English civil service system which trained 'gentlemen' and not 'specialists' or 'technicians', and again today in the People's Republic, we see this in the discussion about 'Red' versus 'Expert'.

In theory this path to training of character and to admission to the state service was open to every 'respectable' citizen. Of the traditional four 'classes' of Chinese society, only the first two officials, (*shih*) and farmers (*nung*) were always regarded as fully 'respectable' (*liang-min*). Members of the other two classes, artisans (*kung*) and merchants (*shang*), were under numerous restrictions. Below these were classes of 'lowly people' (*chien-min*) and below these the slaves which were not part of society proper. The privileges and obligations of these categories were soon legally fixed. In practice, during the first thousand years of the existence of the examination system no peasant had a chance to become an official by means of the examinations. In the Han period, special state schools were created for the sons of officials, who, thus, had an easier start than others. It is interesting to note that there were, again and again, complaints about the low level of instruction in these schools. Nevertheless, through these schools all sons of officials, whatever their capacity or lack of capacity, could become officials in their turn. In spite of its weaknesses, the system had its good side. It inoculated a class of people with ideals that were unquestionably of high ethical value. The Confucian moral system gave a Chinese official or any member of the gentry a spiritual attitude and an outward bearing which in their best representatives has always commanded respect, an integrity that has always preserved its possessors, and in consequence Chinese society as a whole, from moral collapse, from spiritual nihilism, and has thus contributed to the preservation of Chinese cultural values in spite of all foreign conquerors.

In the time of Wen Ti and especially of his successors, the revival at court of the Confucianist ritual and of the earlier Heaven-worship proceeded steadily. The sacrifices supposed to have been performed in ancient times, the ritual supposed to have been prescribed for the emperor in the past, all this was reintroduced. Obviously much of it was spurious: much of the old texts had been lost, and when fragments were found they were arbitrarily completed. Moreover, the old writing was difficult to read and difficult to understand; thus various things were read into the texts without justification. The new Confucians who came forward as experts in the moral code were very different men from their predecessors; above all, like all their contemporaries, they were strongly influenced by the astrological speculations developed in the late Chou and Ch'in times.

Wen Ti's reign had brought economic advance and prosperity; intellectually it had been a period of renaissance, but like every such period it did not simply resuscitate what was old, but filled the ancient moulds with an entirely new content. This is seen most clearly in the field of law. In the time of the Legalists the first steps had been taken in the codification of the criminal law. They clearly intended these laws to serve equally for all classes of the people. The Ch'in code which was supposedly Li K'uei's code, was used in the Han period, and was extensively elaborated by Hsiao Ho (died 193 B.C.) and others. This code consisted of two volumes of the chief laws for grave cases, one of mixed laws for the less serious cases, and six volumes on the imposition of penalties. In the Han period 'decisions' were added, so that about A.D. 200 the code had grown to 26,272 paragraphs with over 17,000,000 words. The collection then consisted of 960 volumes. This colossal code has been continually revised, abbreviated, or expanded, and under its last name of 'Collected Statutes of the Manchu Dynasty' it retained its validity down to the present century.

Alongside this collection there was another book that came to be regarded and used as a book of precedences. The great Confucianist philosopher Tung Chung-shu (179–104 B.C.), a firm supporter of the ideology of the new gentry class, declared that the classic Confucianist writings, and especially the book 'Ch'un-ch'iu', 'Annals of Spring and Autumn', attributed to Confucius himself, were essentially books of legal decisions. They contained 'cases' and Confucius's decisions of them. Consequently any case at law that might arise could be decided by analogy with the cases contained in 'Annals of Spring and Autumn'. Only an educated person, of course, a member of the gentry, could claim that his action should be judged by the decisions of Confucius and not by the code compiled for the common people, for Confucius had expressly stated that his rules were intended only for the upper class. Thus, right down to modern times an educated person could be judged under regulations different from those applicable to the common people, or if judged on the basis of the laws, he had to expect a special treatment. The principle of the 'equality before the law' which the Legalists had advocated and which fitted well into the absolutistic, totalitarian system of the Ch'in, had been attacked by the feudal nobility at that time and was attacked by the new gentry of the Han time. Legalist thinking remained an important undercurrent for many centuries to come, but application of the equalitarian principle was from now on never seriously considered.

This 'double law' does not a priori mean that officials could get away with crimes for which the others were harshly punished, though in fact that often happened. We can also find many cases in which officials were exposed to 'double jeopardy', comparable to the disciplinary courts for officials in the old German system and the special treatment of party officials in one-party systems. The offender was first judged according to Confucian rules, and this could mean that he was judged to be unfit and deprived of his status. Afterwards, he was again judged according to criminal law.

Discussing Chinese written law, we should always keep in mind that it was basically criminal and administrative law. Large areas which fall into civil law, or trade law were never codified. Cases of this type were solved by processes of arbitration or mediation between the partners or, more often, between the families involved.

Against the growing influence of the officials belonging to the gentry there came a last reaction. It came as a reply to the attempt of a representative of the gentry to deprive the feudal princes of the whole of their power. In the time of Wen Ti's successor a number of feudal kings formed an alliance against the emperor, and even invited the Hsiung-nu to join them. The Hsiung-nu did not do so, because they saw that the rising had no prospect of success, and it was quelled. After that the feudal princes were steadily deprived of rights. They were divided into two classes, and only privileged ones were permitted to live in the capital, the others being required to remain in their domains. At first, the area was controlled by a 'minister' of the prince an official of the state; later the area remained under normal administration and the feudal prince kept only an empty title; the tax income of a certain number of families of an area was assigned to him and transmitted to him by normal administrative channels. Often, the number of assigned families was fictional in that actual income was from far fewer families. This system differs from the Near Eastern system in which also no actual enfeoffment took place, but where deserving men were granted the right to collect themselves the taxes of a certain area with certain numbers of families.

Soon after this the whole government was given the shape which it continued to have until A.D. 220, and which formed the point of departure for all later forms of government. At the head of the state was the emperor, in theory the holder of absolute power in the state restricted only by his responsibility towards 'Heaven', i.e. he had to follow and to enforce the basic rules of morality, otherwise 'Heaven' would withdraw its 'mandate', the legitimation of the emperor's rule, and would indicate this withdrawal by sending natural catastrophes. Time and again we find emperors publicly accusing themselves for their faults when such catastrophes occurred; and to draw the emperor's attention to actual or made-up calamities or celestial irregularities was one way to criticize an emperor and to force him to change his behaviour. There are two other indications which show that Chinese emperors—excepting a few individual cases—at least in the first ten centuries of gentry society were not despots: it can be proved that in some fields the responsibility for governmental action did not lie with the emperor but with some of his ministers. Second, the emperor was bound by the law code: he could not change it nor abolish it. We know of cases in which the ruler disregarded the code, but then tried to 'defend' his arbitrary action. Each new dynasty developed a new law code, usually changing only details of the punishment, not the basic regulations. Rulers could issue additional 'regulations', but these, too, had to be in the spirit of the general code and the existing moral norms. This situation has some similarity to the situation in Muslim countries. At the ruler's side were three counsellors who had, however, no active functions. The real conduct of policy lay in the hands of the 'chancellor', or of one of the 'nine ministers'. Unlike the practice with which we are familiar in the West, the activities of the ministries (one of them being the court secretariat) were concerned primarily with the imperial palace. As, however, the court secretariat (*Shang-shu*), one of the nine ministries, was at the same time a sort of imperial statistical office, in which all economic, financial, and military statistical material was assembled, decisions on issues of critical importance for the whole country could and did come from it. The court, through the Ministry of Supplies, operated mines and workshops in the provinces and organized the labour service for public constructions. The court also controlled centrally the conscription for the general military service. Beside the ministries there was an extensive administration of the capital with its military guards. The various parts of the country, including the lands given as fiefs to princes, had a local administration, entirely independent of the central government and more or less elaborated according to their size. The regional administration was loosely associated with the central government through a sort of ministry of the interior, and similarly the Chinese representatives in the protectorates, that is to say the foreign states which had submitted to Chinese 'protective' overlordship, were loosely united with a sort of foreign ministry in the central government. When a rising or a local war broke out, that was the affair of the officer of the region concerned. If the regional troops were insufficient, those of the adjoining regions were drawn upon; if even these were insufficient, a real 'state of war' came into being; that is to say, the emperor appointed eight generals-in-chief, mobilized the imperial troops, and intervened. This imperial army then had authority over the regional and feudal troops, the troops of the protectorates, the guards of the capital, and those of the imperial palace. At the end of the war the imperial army was demobilized and the generals-in-chief were transferred to other posts.

In all this there gradually developed a division into civil and military administration. A number of regions would make up a province with a military governor, who was in a sense the representative of the imperial army, and who was supposed to come into activity only in the event of war.

This administration of the Han period lacked the tight organization that would make precise functioning possible. On the other hand, an extremely important institution had already come into existence in a primitive form. As central statistical authority, the court secretariat had a special position within the ministries and supervised the administration of the other offices. Thus there existed alongside the executive a means of independent supervision of it, and the resulting rivalry enabled the emperor or the chancellor to detect and eliminate irregularities. Later, in the system of the T'ang period (A.D. 618–906), this institution developed into an independent censorship, and the system was given a new form as a 'State and Court Secretariat', in which the whole executive was comprised and unified. Towards the end of the T'ang period the permanent state of war necessitated the permanent commissioning of the imperial generals-in-chief and of the military governors, and as a result there came into existence a 'Privy Council of State', which gradually took over functions of the executive. The system of administration in the Han and in the T'ang period is shown in the following table:

Han epoch	T'ang epoch
1. Emperor	1. Emperor
2. Three counsellors to the emperor (with no active functions)	2. Three counsellors and three assistants (with no active functions)
3. Eight supreme generals (only appointed in time of war)	3. Generals and governors-general (only appointed in time of war: but in practice continuously in office)
4. ———	4. (a) State secretariat 　　(1) Central secretariat 　　(2) Secretariat of the Crown 　　(3) Secretariat of the Palace and imperial historical commission

Han epoch	T'ang epoch
	(b) Emperor's secretariat
	(1) Private archives
	(2) Court adjutants' office
	(3) Harem administration
5. Court administration (Ministries)	5. Court administration (Ministries)
(1) Ministry for state sacrifices	(1) Ministry for state sacrifices
(2) Ministry for imperial coaches and horses	(2) Ministry for imperial coaches and horses
(3) Ministry for justice at court	(3) Ministry for justice at court
(4) Ministry for receptions	(4) Ministry for receptions (i.e. foreign affairs)
(5) Ministry for ancestors' temples	(5) Ministry for ancestors' temples
(6) Ministry for supplies to the court	(6) Ministry for supplies to the court
(7) Ministry for the harem	(7) Economic and financial Ministry
(8) Ministry for the palace guards	(8) Ministry for the payment of salaries
(9) Ministry for the court (state secretariat)	(9) Ministry for armament and magazines
6. Administration of the capital:	6. Administration of the capital:
(1) Crown prince's palace	(1) Crown prince's palace
(2) Security service for the capital	(2) Palace guards and guards' office
(3) Capital administration:	(3) Arms production department
(a) Guards of the capital	
(b) Guards of the city gates	
(c) Building department	
	(4) Labour service department
	(5) Building department
	(6) Transport department
	(7) Department for education (of sons of officials!)
7. Ministry of the Interior (Provincial administration)	7. Ministry of the Interior (Provincial administration)
8. Foreign Ministry	8. ————————————————
	9. Censorship (Audit council)

There is no denying that according to our standard this whole system was still elementary and 'personal', that is to say, attached to the emperor's person—though it should not be overlooked that we ourselves are not yet far from a similar phase of development. To this day the titles of not a few of the highest officers of state—the Lord Privy Seal, for instance—recall that in the past their offices were conceived as concerned purely with the personal service of the monarch. In one point, however, the Han administrative set-up was quite modern: it already had a clear separation between the emperor's private treasury and the state treasury; laws determined which of the two received certain taxes and which had to make certain payments. This separation, which in Europe occurred not until the late Middle Ages, in China was abolished at the end of the Han dynasty.

The picture changes considerably to the advantage of the Chinese as soon as we consider the provincial administration. The governor of a province, and each of his district officers or prefects, had a staff often of more than a hundred officials. These officials were drawn from the province or prefecture and from the personal friends of the administrator, and they were appointed by the governor or the prefect. The staff was made up of officials responsible for communications with the central or provincial administration (private secretary, controller, finance officer), and a group of officials who carried on the actual local administration. There were departments for transport, finance, education, justice, medicine (hygiene), economic and military affairs, market control, and presents (which had to be made to the higher officials at the New Year and on other occasions). In addition to these offices, organized in a quite modern style, there was an office for advising the governor and another for drafting official documents and letters.

The interesting feature of this system is that the provincial administration was de facto independent of the central administration, and that the governor and even his prefects could rule like kings in their regions, appointing and discharging as they chose. This was a vestige of feudalism, but on the other hand it was a healthy check against excessive centralization. It is thanks to this system that even the collapse of the central power or the cutting off of a part of the empire did not bring the collapse of the country. In a remote frontier town like Tunhuang, on the border of Sinkiang, the life of the local Chinese went on undisturbed whether communication with the capital was maintained or was broken through invasions by foreigners.

Governors or other local officials (such as magistrates) were liable to be transferred from time to time. Many dynasties had certain normal periods of service. The local official was, therefore, unable in times of order to accumulate sufficient power to become a threat to the central government. On the other hand, being a stranger in his district, he could not rely on local people. Thus, he brought with him his own trusted friends, and in addition hired local people who knew the local situation and could help the official to collect the taxes he had to forward to the capital. By having such a staff which was antagonistic to one another, a good official had some ways to check upon them and to retain personal power.

In theory, the officials of the various offices or Ministries were appointed under the state examination system, but they had no special professional training; only for the more important subordinate posts were there specialists, such as jurists, physicians, and so on. A change came towards the end of the T'ang period, when a Department of Commerce and Monopolies was set up; only specialists were appointed to it, and it was placed directly under the emperor. Except for this, any official could be transferred from any ministry to any other without regard to his experience. Thus, professionalization and professional careers are a relatively late development. Within the central administration the officials were classified according to ranks, defined by salary classification. Most Chinese administrations had nine ranks, generally subdivided into eighteen ranks, and promotion meant a rise in rank. The official lists of the state system never do give us a full list of all ranks. There were always some ranks lower than the official ones; men in these classes were not regarded as members of the privileged class. Often men were assigned a specific rank and an appropriate title. Men could have concurrently numerous titles. This then did not necessarily mean that they exercised several different jobs; they may have had only one job, while the other titles expressed rank. And rank did not only mean salary, but also the right to appear at court and to have a specific place assigned in official ceremonies. We have in Western administrations similar posts which have no function but give rank; and the court ceremonials at the remaining kingdoms are regulated by the level of the rank the officials have, not by the title of their jobs.

4 Central Asia policy. End of the Hsiung-nu empire

In the two decades between 160 and 140 B.C. there had been further trouble with the Hsiung-nu, though there was no large-scale fighting. There was a fundamental change of policy under the next emperor, Wu (or Wu Ti, 141–86 B.C.). The Chinese entered for the first time upon an active policy against the Hsiung-nu. There seem to have been several reasons for this policy, and several objectives. The raids of the Hsiung-nu from the Ordos region and from northern Shansi had shown themselves to be a direct menace to the capital and to its extremely important hinterland. Northern Shansi is mountainous, with deep ravines. A considerable army on horseback could penetrate some distance to the south before attracting attention. Northern Shensi and the Ordos region are steppe country, in which there were few Chinese settlements and through which an army of horsemen could advance very quickly. It was therefore determined to push back the Hsiung-nu far enough to remove this threat. It was also of importance to break the power of the Hsiung-nu in the province of Kansu, and to separate them as far as possible from the Tibetans living in that region, to prevent any union of those two dangerous adversaries. A third point of importance was the safeguarding of caravan routes. The state, and especially the capital, had grown rich through Wen Ti's policy. Goods streamed into the capital from all quarters. Commerce with Central Asia had particularly increased, bringing the products of the Middle East to China. The caravan routes passed through western Shensi and Kansu to Sinkiang, but at that time the Hsiung-nu dominated the approaches to Sinkiang and were in a position to divert the trade to themselves or cut it off. The commerce brought profit not only to the caravan traders, most of whom were probably foreigners, but to the officials in the provinces and prefectures through which the routes passed. Thus the officials in western China were interested in the trade routes being brought under direct control, so that the caravans could arrive regularly and be immune from robbery. Finally, the Chinese government may well have regarded it as little to its honour to be still paying dues to the Hsiung-nu and sending princesses to their rulers, now that China was incomparably wealthier and stronger than at the time when that policy of appeasement had begun.

The first active step taken was to try, in 133 B.C., to capture the head of the Hsiung-nu state, who was called a *shan-yü*; but the *shan-yü* saw through the plan and escaped. There followed a period of continuous fighting until 119 B.C. The Chinese made countless attacks, without lasting success. But the Hsiung-nu were weakened, one sign of this being that there were dissensions after the death of the *shan-yü* Chün-ch'en, and in 127 B.C. his son went over to the Chinese. Finally the Chinese altered their tactics, advancing in 119 B.C. with a strong army of cavalry, which suffered enormous losses but inflicted serious loss on the Hsiung-nu. After that the Hsiung-nu withdrew farther to the north, and the Chinese settled peasants in the important region of Kansu.

Meanwhile, in 125 B.C., the famous Chang Ch'ien had returned. He had been sent in 138 to conclude an alliance with the Yüeh-chih against the Hsiung-nu. The Yüeh-chih had formerly been neighbours of the Hsiung-nu as far as the Ala Shan region, but owing to defeat by the Hsiung-nu their remnants had migrated to western Turkestan (i.e. roughly what is now Soviet Central Asia). Chang Ch'ien had followed them. Politically he had had no success, but he brought back accurate information about the countries in the far west, concerning which nothing had been known beyond the vague reports of merchants. Now it was learnt whence the foreign goods came and whither the Chinese goods went. Chang Ch'ien's reports (which are one of the principal sources for the history of Central Asia at that remote time) strengthened the desire to enter into direct and assured commercial relations with those distant countries. The government

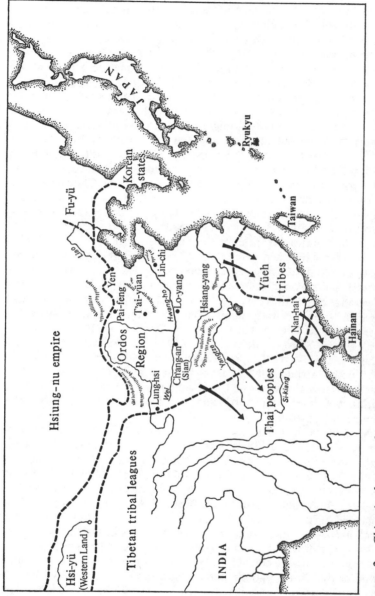

MAP 3 *China in the struggle with the Huns or Hsiung-nu (roughly 128–100 B.C.)*

Hsi-yü
(Western Land)

Tibetan tribal leagues

Hsiung-nu empire

Ordos
Region

Lung-hsi
Wei

Chang-an
(Sian)

Pai-feng
Yen
Tai-yüan
Hwang-ho
Lin-chi
Lo-yang
Hsiang-yang
Yangtze

Fu-yü
Liao

Korean
states

JAPAN

Ryukyu

Taiwan

Yüeh
tribes

Nan-hai

Hainan

Thai peoples

Si-kiang

INDIA

evidently thought of getting this commerce into its own hands. The way to do this was to impose 'tribute' on the countries concerned. The idea was that the missions bringing the annual 'tribute' would be a sort of state bartering commission. The state laid under tribute must supply specified goods at its own cost, and received in return Chinese produce, the value of which was to be roughly equal to the 'tribute'. Thus Chang Ch'ien's reports had the result that, after the first successes against the Hsiung-nu, there was increased interest in a central Asian policy. The greatest military success were the campaigns of General Li Kuang-li to Ferghana in 104 and 102 B.C. The result of the campaigns was to bring under tribute all the small states in the Tarim basin and some of the states of western Turkestan. From now on not only foreign consumer goods came freely into China, but with them a great number of other things, notably plants such as grape, peach, pomegranate.

In 108 B.C. the western part of Korea was also conquered. At this time, Korea was no more a primitive country. Korean tradition claims that a sage of the end of Shang time left China and migrated to Korea, becoming the culture hero of the country. This is probably a myth, but it is true that Korea had a population closely related to that which at the time lived in the area of Peking, while the other, northern, parts of the country were inhabited by relatives of Tungus tribes and the southern tip by relatives of the Ryukyu and perhaps even people related to those in Taiwan and the Philippines. There were several small states in Korea, when the Chinese attacked. The attack gave the Chinese control over trade with the Japanese islands. Although the conquest represented a peril to the eastern flank of the Hsiung-nu, it did not by any means mean that they were conquered. The Hsiung-nu while weakened evaded the Chinese pressure, but in 104 B.C. and again in 91 they inflicted defeats on the Chinese. The Hsiung-nu were indirectly threatened by Chinese foreign policy, for the Chinese concluded an alliance with old enemies of the Hsiung-nu, the Wu-sun, in the north of the Tarim basin. This made the Tarim basin secure for the Chinese, and threatened the Hsiung-nu with a new danger in their rear. Finally the Chinese did all they could through intrigue, espionage, and sabotage to promote disunity and disorder within the Hsiung-nu, though it cannot be seen from the Chinese accounts how far the Chinese were responsible for the actual conflicts and the continual changes of *shan-yü*. One of the most interesting documents of Han literature is an essay, attributed to Chia I, but probably written later, in which in detail a whole strategy of propaganda and sabotage was outlined. It is not the earliest text of this type, but the first one in which techniques of mass persuasion applied to enemies were described. Hostilities against the

Hsiung-nu continued incessantly, after the death of Wu Ti, under his successor, so that the Hsiung-nu were further weakened. In consequence of this it was possible to rouse against them other tribes who until then had been dependent on them—the Ting-ling in the north and the Wu-huan in the east. The internal difficulties of the Hsiung-nu increased further.

Wu Ti's active policy had not been directed only against the Hsiung-nu. After heavy fighting he brought southern China, with the region round Canton, and the south-eastern coast, firmly under Chinese dominion—in this case again on account of trade interests. No doubt there were already considerable colonies of foreign merchants in Canton and other coastal towns, trading in Indian and Middle East goods. The traders seem often to have been Sogdians. We believe that the knowledge of glass and glassmaking came from the Mediterranean (Egypt?) via Canton to China, and Roman coins were found in Vietnam and South China.

The southern wars gave Wu Ti the control of the revenues from this commerce. He tried several times to advance through Yünnan in order to secure a better land route to India, but these attempts failed. Nevertheless, Chinese influence became stronger in the south-west.

In spite of his long rule, Wu Ti did not leave an adult heir, as the crown prince was executed, with many other persons, shortly before Wu Ti's death. The crown prince had been implicated in an alleged attempt by a large group of people to remove the emperor by various sorts of magic. It is difficult to determine today what lay behind this affair; probably it was a struggle between two cliques of the gentry. Thus a regency council had to be set up for the young heir to the throne; it included a member of a Hsiung-nu tribe. The actual government was in the hands of a general and his clique until the death of the heir to the throne and the beginning of his successor's reign.

At this time came the end of the Hsiung-nu empire—a foreign event of the utmost importance. As a result of the continual disastrous wars against the Chinese, in which not only many men but, especially, large quantities of cattle fell into Chinese hands, the livelihood of the Hsiung-nu was seriously threatened; their troubles were increased by plagues and by a few severe winters. To these troubles were added political difficulties, including unsettled questions in regard to the succession to the throne. The result of all this was that the Hsiung-nu could no longer offer effective military resistance to the Chinese. There were a number of *shan-yü* ruling contemporaneously as rivals, and one of them had to yield to the Chinese in 58 B.C.; in 51 he came as a vassal to the Chinese court. The collapse of the Hsiung-nu empire was complete. After 58 B.C.

the Chinese were freed from all danger from that quarter and were able, for a time, to impose their authority in Central Asia.

5 *Impoverishment. Cliques. End of the dynasty*

In other respects the Chinese were not doing as well as might have been assumed. The wars carried on by Wu Ti and his successors had been ruinous. The maintenance of large armies of occupation in the new regions also meant a permanent drain on the national funds. There was a special need for horses, for the people of the steppes could only be fought by means of cavalry. As the Hsiung-nu were supplying no horses, and the campaigns were not producing horses enough as booty, the peasants had to rear horses for the government. Additional horses were bought at very high prices, and apart from this the general financing of the wars necessitated increased taxation of the peasants, a burden on agriculture no less serious than was the enrolment of many peasants for military service. Finally, the new external trade did not by any means bring the economic advantages that had been hoped for. The tribute missions brought tribute but, to begin with, this meant an obligation to give presents in return; moreover, these missions had to be fed and housed in the capital, often for months, as the official receptions took place only on New Year's Day. Their maintenance entailed much expense, and meanwhile the members of the missions traded privately with the inhabitants and the merchants of the capital, buying things they needed and selling things they had brought in addition to the tribute. The tribute itself consisted mainly of 'precious articles', which meant strange or rare things of no practical value. The emperor made use of them as elements of personal luxury, or made presents of some of them to deserving officials. The gifts offered by the Chinese in return consisted mainly of silk. Silk was received by the government as a part of the tax payments and formed an important element of the revenue of the state. It now went abroad without bringing in any corresponding return. The private trade carried on by the members of the missions was equally unserviceable to the Chinese. It, too, took from them goods of economic value, silk and gold, which went abroad in exchange for luxury articles of little or no economic importance, such as glass, precious stones, or luxury horses, which in no way benefited the general population. Thus in this last century B.C. China's economic situation deteriorated. The peasants, more heavily taxed than ever, were impoverished, and yet the exchequer became not fuller but emptier, so that gold began even to be no longer available for payments. Wu Ti was aware of the situation and called different groups together to discuss the problems of economics. Under the name 'Discussions on Salt and Iron' ('Yen-t'ieh-lun') the gist of these talks is preserved and shows that one group under the leadership of Sang Hung-yang (143–80 B.C.) was business-oriented and thinking in economic terms, while their opponents, mainly Confucianists, regarded the situation mainly as a moral crisis. Sang proposed an 'equable transportation' and a 'standardization' system and favoured other state monopolies and controls; these ideas were taken up later and continued to be discussed, again and again.

Already under Wu Ti there had been signs of a development which now appeared constantly in Chinese history. Among the new gentry, families entered into alliances with each other, sealed their mutual allegiance by matrimonial unions, and so formed large cliques. Each clique made it its concern to get the most important government positions into its hands, so that it should itself control the government. Under Wu Ti, for example, almost all the important generals had belonged to a certain clique, which remained dominant under his two successors. Two of the chief means of attaining power were for such a clique to give the emperor a girl from its own ranks or any other beautiful girl. Such gifts were nothing unusual in the course of Chinese history. Governors as well as other important persons always felt obliged to present gifts to the emperor when they came to court, and from later texts we know that the parents of daughters in whole provinces trembled for fear that their daughter might be ordered to be presented to the ruler. It could mean glory, if the emperor ever spent a night with her and if she bore him a son, but it normally meant misery and loneliness. But if she gained the emperor's favour, if not love, she could (and felt morally forced to) bring as many of her relatives or of the family members of the man who presented her to the court, into office as she could. The eunuchs at court who watched over the harem and served the emperor personally, came usually from the poorer classes; they, too, were often presented to the emperor by the members of the great cliques, and could gain great influence because they could see the emperor in private. Some of the Han eunuchs were even homosexual lovers of the ruler.

The chief influence of the cliques lay, however, in the selection of officials. It is not surprising that the officials recommended only sons of people in their own clique—their family or its closest associates. On top of all this, the examiners were in most cases themselves members of the same families to which the provincial officials belonged. Thus it was made doubly certain that only those candidates who were to the liking of the dominant group among the gentry should pass.

Surrounded by these cliques, the emperors easily became powerless figureheads. At times energetic rulers were able to play off various cliques against each other, and so to acquire personal power;

but the weaker emperors found themselves entirely in the hands of cliques. Not a few emperors in China were removed by cliques which they had attempted to resist; and various dynasties were brought to their end by the cliques; this was the fate of the Han dynasty.

The beginning of its fall came with the activities of the widow of the emperor Yüan Ti. She virtually ruled in the name of her eighteen-year-old son, the emperor Ch'eng Ti (32–7 B.C.), and placed all her brothers, and also her nephew, Wang Mang, in the principal government posts. They succeeded at first in either removing the strongest of the other cliques or bringing them into dependence. Within the Wang family the nephew Wang Mang steadily advanced, securing direct supporters even in some branches of the imperial family; these personages declared their readiness to join him in removing the existing line of the imperial house. When Ch'eng Ti died without issue, a young nephew of his (Ai Ti, 6–1 B.C.) was placed on the throne by Wang Mang, and during this period the power of the Wangs and their allies grew further, until all their opponents had been removed and the influence of the imperial family very greatly reduced. When Ai Ti died, Wang Mang placed an eight-year-old boy on the throne, himself acting as regent; four years later the boy fell ill and died, probably with Wang Mang's aid. Wang Mang now chose a one-year-old baby, but soon after he felt that the time had come for officially assuming the rulership. In A.D. 8 he dethroned the baby, ostensibly at Heaven's command, and declared himself emperor and first of the Hsin ('new') dynasty. All the members of the old imperial family in the capital were removed from office and degraded to commoners, with the exception of those who had already been supporting Wang Mang. Only those members who held unimportant posts at a distance remained untouched.

Wang Mang's 'usurpation' is unusual from two points of view. First, he paid great attention to public opinion and induced large masses of the population to write petitions to the court asking the Han ruler to abdicate; he even fabricated 'heavenly omina' in his own favour and against the Han dynasty in order to get wide support even from intellectuals. Second, he inaugurated a formal abdication ceremony, culminating in the transfer of the imperial seal to himself. This ceremony became standard for the next centuries. The seal was made of a precious stone, once presented to the Ch'in dynasty ruler before he ascended the throne. From now on, the possessor of this seal was the legitimate ruler.

6   *The pseudo-socialistic dictatorship. Revolt of the 'Red Eyebrows'*
Wang Mang's dynasty lasted only from A.D. 9 to 23; but it was one of the most stirring periods of Chinese history. It is difficult to

evaluate Wang Mang, because all we know about him stems from sources hostile towards him. Yet we gain the impression that some of his innovations, such as the legalization of enthronement through the transfer of the seal, the changes in the administration of provinces and in the bureaucratic set-up in the capital, and even some of his economic measures, were so highly regarded that they were retained or reintroduced, although this happened in some instances centuries later and without mentioning Wang Mang's name. But most of his policies and actions were certainly neither accepted nor acceptable. He made use of every conceivable resource in order to secure power to his clique. As far as possible he avoided using open force, and resorted to a high-level propaganda. Confucianism, the philosophic basis of the power of the gentry, served him as a bait; he made use of the so-called 'old character school' for his purposes. When, after the holocaust of books, it was desired to collect the ancient classics again, texts were found under strange circumstances in the walls of Confucius's house; they were written in an archaic script. The people who occupied themselves with these books were called the old character school. The texts came under suspicion; most scholars had little belief in their genuineness. Wang Mang, however, and his creatures energetically supported the cult of these ancient writings. The texts were edited and issued, and in the process, as can now be seen, certain things were smuggled into them that fitted in well with Wang Mang's intentions. He even had other texts reissued with falsifications. He now represented himself in all his actions as a man who did with the utmost precision the things which the books reported of rulers or ministers of ancient times. As regent he had declared that his model was the brother of the first emperor of the Chou dynasty; as emperor he took for his exemplar one of the mythical emperors of ancient China; of his new laws he claimed that they were simply revivals of decrees of the golden age. In all this he appealed to the authority of literature that had been tampered with to suit his aims. Actually, such laws had never before been customary; either Wang Mang completely misinterpreted passages in an ancient text to suit his purpose, or he had dicta that suited him smuggled into the text. There can be no question that Wang Mang and his accomplices began by deliberately falsifying and deceiving. However, as time went on, he probably began to believe in his own frauds.

Wang Mang's great series of certain laws has brought him the name of 'the first Socialist on the throne of China'. But closer consideration reveals that these measures, ostensibly and especially aimed at the good of the poor, were in reality devised simply in order to fill the imperial exchequer and to consolidate the imperial power.

When we read of the turning over of great landed estates to the state, do we not imagine that we are faced with a modern land reform? But this applied only to the wealthiest of all the landowners, who were to be deprived in this way of their power. The prohibition of private slave-owning had a similar purpose, the state reserving to itself the right to keep slaves. We know that still in later times the state, i.e. the ruler, could give state male and female slaves to persons he favoured. Landless farmers were supposed to receive land to till, at the expense of expropriated landlords. As far as we can see, this was never seriously attempted. To help the farmers, a system of state credits for peasants was set up, but the aim of this measure seems to have been to increase the revenue, in spite of supposedly reduced interest rates. The peasants had never been in a position to pay back their private debts together with the usurious interest, but there were at least opportunities of coming to terms with a private usurer, whereas the state proved a merciless creditor. It could dispossess the peasant, and either turn his property into a state farm, convey it to another owner, or make the peasant a state slave. Thus this measure worked against the interest of the peasants, as did the state monopoly of the exploitation of mountains and lakes. 'Mountains and lakes' meant the uncultivated land around settlements, the 'village commons', where people collected firewood or went fishing. They now had to pay money for fishing rights and for the right to collect wood, money for the emperor's exchequer. The same purpose lay behind the wine, salt, and iron tool monopolies. Enormous revenues came to the state from the monopoly of minting coin, when old metal coin of full value was called in and exchanged for debased coin. Another modern-sounding institution, that of the 'equalization offices', was supposed to buy cheap goods in times of plenty in order to sell them to the people in times of scarcity at similarly low prices, so preventing want and also preventing excessive price fluctuations. In actual fact these state offices formed a new source of profit, buying cheaply and selling as dearly as possible.

Thus the character of these laws was in no way socialistic; nor, however, did they provide an El Dorado for the state finances, for Wang Mang's officials turned all the laws to their private advantage. The revenues rarely reached the capital; they vanished into the pockets of subordinate officials. We have reasons to assume that members of the clique which was related or connected with the Han dynasty were still in power in the provinces and thus in a position to sabotage the new laws. But Wang Mang had great need of money, because he attached importance to display and because he was planning a new war. He aimed at the final destruction of the Hsiung-nu, so that access to Central Asia should no longer be precarious and it

93

should thus be possible to reduce the expense of the military administration of Central Asia. The war would also distract popular attention from the troubles at home. By way of preparation for war, Wang Mang sent a mission to the Hsiung-nu with dishonouring proposals, including changes in the name of the Hsiung-nu and in the title of the *shan-yü*. The name Hsiung-nu was to be given the insulting change of Hsiang-nu, meaning 'subjugated slaves'. The result was that risings of the Hsiung-nu took place, whereupon Wang Mang commanded that the whole of their country should be partitioned among fifteen *shan-yü* and declared the country to be a Chinese province. Since this declaration had no practical result, it robbed Wang Mang of the increased prestige he had sought and only further infuriated the Hsiung-nu. Wang Mang concentrated a vast army on the frontier. Meanwhile he lost the whole of the possessions in Central Asia. We have no way of knowing why Wang Mang made these moves. It seems to be possible to assume that already at that time he had lost contact with reality.

Before Wang Mang's campaign against the Hsiung-nu could begin, the difficulties at home grew steadily worse. In A.D. 12 Wang Mang felt obliged to abrogate all his reform legislation. There were continual risings, which culminated in A.D. 18 in a great popular insurrection, a genuine revolutionary rising of the peasants, whose distress had grown beyond bearing through Wang Mang's ill-judged measures. The rebels called themselves 'Red Eyebrows'; they had painted their eyebrows red by way of a badge and in order to bind their members indissolubly to their movement. The nucleus of this rising was a secret society. Such secret societies are usually harmless, but may, in emergency situations, become an immensely effective instrument in the hands of the rural population. The secret societies then organize the peasants, in order to achieve a forcible settlement of the matter in dispute. Occasionally, however, the movement grows far beyond its leaders' original objective and becomes a popular movement directed against the whole establishment. Like other similar movements in later times, this one finally failed. Their own leaders did not have the ability to unite masses of people with different backgrounds. In some popular rebellions, members of the old upper class joined the rebels and took over the command—but then, though chances for success became greater, after the victory a new regime was set up which was not different from the old one, perhaps less corrupt.

Vast swarms of peasants marched to the capital, killing all officials and people of position on their way. The troops sent against them by Wang Mang either went over to the Red Eyebrows or copied them, plundering wherever they could and killing officials. Owing to the appalling mass murders and the fighting, the forces placed by Wang Mang along the frontier against the Hsiung-nu received no reinforcements and, instead of attacking the Hsiung-nu, themselves went over to plundering, so that ultimately the army simply disintegrated. Fortunately for China, the *shan-yü* of the time did not take advantage of his opportunity, perhaps because his position within the Hsiung-nu empire was too insecure.

Scarcely had the popular rising begun when descendants of the deposed Han dynasty appeared and tried to secure the support of the upper class. They came forward as fighters against the usurper Wang Mang and as defenders of the old social order against the revolutionary masses. The armies which these Han princes were able to collect were no better than those of the other sides. They, too, consisted of poor and hungry peasants, whose aim was to get money or goods by robbery; they, too, plundered and murdered more than they fought.

However, one prince by the name of Liu Hsiu gradually gained the upper hand. The basis of his power was the district of Nanyang in Honan, one of the wealthiest agricultural centres of China at that time and also the centre of iron and steel production. The big landowners, the gentry of Nanyang, joined him, and the prince's party conquered the capital. Wang Mang, placing entire faith in his sanctity, did not flee; he sat in his robes in the throne-room and recited the ancient writings, convinced that he would overcome his adversaries by the power of his words. But a soldier cut off his head (A.D. 22). The skull was kept for two hundred years in the imperial treasury. The fighting, nevertheless, went on. Various branches of the prince's party fought one another, and all of them fought the Red Eyebrows. In those years millions of men came to their end. Finally, in A.D. 24, Liu Hsiu prevailed, becoming the first emperor of the second Han dynasty, also called the Later Han dynasty; his name as emperor was Kuang-wu Ti (A.D. 25–57).

7 Reaction and restoration: the Later Han dynasty

Within the country the period that followed was one of reaction and restoration. The massacres of the preceding years had so reduced the population that there was land enough for the peasants who remained alive. Moreover, their lords and the money-lenders of the towns were generally no longer alive, so that many peasants had become free of debt. The government was transferred from Sian to Loyang, in the present province of Honan. This brought the capital nearer to the great wheat-producing regions, so that the transport of grain and other taxes in kind to the capital was cheapened. Soon this cleared foundation was covered by a new stratum, a very sparse one, of great landowners who were supporters and members of the new imperial house, largely descendants of the landowners of the earlier Han period. At first they were not much in evidence, but they gained power more and more rapidly. In spite of this, the first half-century of the Later Han period was one of good conditions on the land and economic recovery.

8 Hsiung-nu policy

In foreign policy the first period of the Later Han dynasty was one of extraordinary success, both in the extreme south and in the question of the Hsiung-nu. During the period of Wang Mang's rule and the fighting connected with it, there had been extensive migration to the south and south-west. Considerable regions of Chinese settlement had come into existence in Yünnan and even in Annam and Tonking, and a series of campaigns under General Ma Yüan (14 B.C.–A.D. 49) now added these regions to the territory of the empire. These wars were carried on with relatively small forces, as previously in the Canton region, the natives being unable to offer serious resistance owing to their inferiority in equipment and civilization. The hot climate, however, to which the Chinese soldiers were unused, was hard for them to endure.

The Hsiung-nu, in spite of internal difficulties, had regained considerable influence in Sinkiang during the reign of Wang Mang. But the king of the city state of Yarkand had increased his power by shrewdly playing off Chinese and Hsiung-nu against each other, so that before long he was able to attack the Hsiung-nu. The small states in Sinkiang, however, regarded the overlordship of the distant China as preferable to that of Yarkand or the Hsiung-nu both of whom, being nearer, were able to bring their power more effectively into play. Accordingly many of the small states appealed for Chinese aid. Kuang-wu Ti met this appeal with a blank refusal, implying that order had only just been restored in China and that he now simply had not the resources for a campaign in Sinkiang. Thus, the king of Yarkand was able to extend his power over the remainder of the small states of Sinkiang, since the Hsiung-nu had been obliged to withdraw. Kuang-wu Ti had had several frontier wars with the Hsiung-nu without any decisive result. But in the years around A.D. 45 the Hsiung-nu had suffered several severe droughts and also great plagues of locusts, so that they had lost a large part of their cattle. They were no longer able to assert themselves in Sinkiang and at the same time to fight the Chinese in the south and the Hsien-pi and the Wu-huan in the east. These two peoples, apparently largely of Mongol origin, had been subject in the past to Hsiung-nu overlordship. They had spread steadily in the territories bordering Manchuria and Mongolia, beyond the eastern frontier of the Hsiung-nu empire. Living there in relative peace and at the same time in possession of very fertile pasturage, these two peoples had grown in strength. And since the great political collapse of 58 B.C. the Hsiung-nu had not only lost their best pasturage in the north of the provinces of Shensi and Shansi, but had largely grown used to living in co-operation with the Chinese. They had become much more accustomed to trade with China, exchanging animals for textiles and grain, than to warfare, so that in the end they were defeated by the Hsien-pi and Wu-huan, who had held to the older form of purely war-like nomad life. Weakened by famine and by the wars against Wu-huan and Hsien-pi, the Hsiung-nu split into two, one section withdrawing to the north.

The southern Hsiung-nu were compelled to submit to the Chinese in order to gain security from their other enemies. Thus the Chinese were able to gain a great success without moving a finger: the Hsiung-nu, who for centuries had shown themselves again and again to be the most dangerous enemies of China, were reduced to political insignificance. About a hundred years earlier the Hsiung-nu empire had suffered defeat; now half of what remained of it became part of the Chinese state. Its place was taken by the Hsien-pi and Wu-huan, but at first they were of much less importance.

In spite of the partition, the northern Hsiung-nu attempted in the years between A.D. 60 and 70 to regain a sphere of influence in Sinkiang; this seemed the easier for them since the king of Yarkand had been captured and murdered, and Sinkiang was more or less in a state of confusion. The Chinese did their utmost to play off the northern against the southern Hsiung-nu and to maintain a political balance of power in the west and north. So long as there were a number of small states in Sinkiang, of which at least some were friendly to China, Chinese trade caravans suffered relatively little disturbance on their journeys. Independent states in Sinkiang had proved more profitable for trade than when a large army of occupation had to be maintained there. When, however, there appeared to be the danger of a new union of the two parts of the Hsiung-nu as a restoration of a large empire also comprising all Sinkiang, the Chinese trading monopoly was endangered. Any great power would secure the best goods for itself, and there would be no good business remaining for China.

For these reasons a great Chinese campaign was undertaken against Central Asia in A.D. 73 under Tou Ku. Mainly owing to the ability of the Chinese deputy commander Pan Ch'ao, the whole of Sinkiang was quickly conquered. Meanwhile the emperor Ming Ti (A.D. 58–75) had died, and under the new emperor Chang Ti (76–88) the 'isolationist' party gained the upper hand against the clique of Tou Ku and Pan Ch'ao: the danger of the restoration of a Hsiung-nu empire, the isolationists contended, no longer existed; Central Asia should be left to itself; the small states would favour trade with China of their own accord. Meanwhile, a considerable part of Sinkiang had fallen away from China, for Chang Ti sent neither money nor troops to hold the conquered territories. Pan Ch'ao nevertheless remained in Sinkiang (at Kashgar and Khotan) where he held on amid countless difficulties. Although he reported (A.D. 78) that the troops could feed themselves and needed neither supplies nor money from home, no reinforcements of any importance were sent; only a few hundred or perhaps a thousand men, mostly released criminals, reached him. Not until A.D. 89 did the Pan Ch'ao clique return to power when the mother of the young emperor Ho Ti (89–105) took over the government during his minority; she was a member of the family of Tou Ku. She was interested in bringing to a successful conclusion the enterprise which had been started by members of her family and its followers. In addition, it can be shown that a number of other members of the 'war party' had direct interests in the west, mainly in the form of landed estates. Accordingly, a campaign was started in 89 under her brother against the northern Hsiung-nu, and it decided the fate of Sinkiang in China's favour. Sinkiang remained firmly in Chinese possession until the death of Pan Ch'ao in 102. Shortly afterwards heavy fighting broke out again: the Tanguts advanced from the south in an attempt to cut off Chinese access to Sinkiang. The Chinese drove back the Tanguts (a political unit related to the Tibetans) and maintained their hold on Sinkiang, though no longer absolutely.

9 Economic situation. Rebellion of the 'Yellow Turbans'. Collapse of the Han dynasty

The economic results of the Sinkiang trade in this period were not so unfavourable as in the earlier Han period. The army of occupation was incomparably smaller, and under Pan Ch'ao's policy the soldiers were fed and paid in Sinkiang itself, so that the cost to China remained small. Moreover, the drain on the national income was no longer serious because, in the intervening period, regular Chinese settlements had been planted at the eastern borders of Sinkiang including Chinese merchants, so that the trade no longer remained entirely in the hands of foreigners.

In spite of the economic consolidation at the beginning of the Later Han dynasty, and in spite of the more balanced trade, the political situation within China steadily worsened from A.D. 80 onwards. Although the class of great landowners was small, a number of cliques formed within it, and their mutual struggle for power soon went beyond the limits of court intrigue. New actors now came upon the state, namely the eunuchs. With the economic improvement there had been a general increase in the luxury at the court of the Han emperors, and the court steadily increased in size. The many hundred wives and concubines in the palace made necessary a great army of eunuchs. As they had the ear of the emperor and so could influence him, the eunuchs formed an important political factor. For a time the main struggle was between the group of eunuchs and the group of scholars. The eunuchs served a particular clique to which some of the emperor's wives belonged. The scholars, that is to say the ministers, together with members of the ministries and the administrative staff, served the interests of another clique. The struggles grew more and more sanguinary in the middle of the second century A.D. It soon proved that the group with the firmest hold in the provinces had the advantage, because it was not easy to control the provinces from a distance. The result was that, from about A.D. 150, events at court steadily lost importance, the lead being taken by the generals commanding the provincial troops. It would carry us too far to give the details of all these struggles. The provincial generals were at first Ts'ao Ts'ao, Lü Pu, Yüan Shao, and Sun Ts'ê; later came Liu Pei. All were striving to gain control of the government, and all were engaged in mutual hostilities from about 180 onwards. Each general was also trying to get the emperor into his hands. Several times the last emperor of the Later Han dynasty, Hsien Ti (190–220), was captured by one or another of the generals. As the successful general was usually unable to maintain his hold on the capital, he dragged the poor emperor with him from place to place until he finally had to give him up to another general. The point of this chase after the emperor was that according to the idea introduced earlier by Wang Mang the first ruler of a new dynasty had to receive the imperial seals from the last emperor of the previous dynasty. The last emperor must abdicate in proper form. Accordingly, each general had to get possession of the emperor to begin with. in order at the proper time to take over the seals.

By about A.D. 200 the new conditions had more or less crystallized. There remained only three great parties. The most powerful was that of Ts'ao Ts'ao, who controlled the north and was able to keep permanent hold of the emperor. In the west, in the province of Szechwan, Liu Pei had established himself, and in the south-east Sun Ts'ê's brother.

But we must not limit our view to these generals' struggles. At this time there were two other series of events of equal importance with those. The incessant struggles of the cliques against each other

99

continued at the expense of the people, who had to fight them, whose harvests were confiscated and whose houses were destroyed. Orderly government broke down, and a new popular movement broke out, that of the so-called 'Yellow Turbans'. This was the first of the two important events. This popular movement had a characteristic which from now on became typical of many such uprisings. The intellectual leaders of the movement, Chang Ling and others, were members of a particular religious sect. This sect was, it seems, influenced by Iranian Mazdaism on the one side and by certain ideas from Lao Tzŭ on the other side; and these influences were superimposed on popular rural as well as, perhaps, local tribal religious beliefs. The sect had roots along the coastal settlements of Eastern China, where it seems to have gained the support of the peasantry and their local priests. These priests of the people were opposed to the representatives of the official religion, that is to say the officials drawn from the gentry. In small towns and villages the temples of the gods of the fruits of the field, of the soil, and so on, were administered by authorized local officials, and these officials also carried out the prescribed sacrifices and were thus integrated into the 'state cult'. As we have many edicts of the Han period which order the destruction of what the texts call 'wild temples', i.e. unauthorized temples, we may conclude that we had a situation which continued until this century. People had their own cults. Souls of people who had died without descendants, animals which seemed to have shown extraordinary powers, even trees and stones could develop into deities who were cared for by men and occasionally women, whom we for convenience usually call shamans. These priests built small places of worship which sometimes developed into regular temples and took care of the deities which, in turn, answered prayers, healed the sick, gave children to unfertile women. The educated regarded such cults as pure superstition; the gentry watched them and when they felt that the cult developed too strongly and might become a centre of power and unrest, they had the temples destroyed. In times of weak government this was not always done, and suffering peasants flocked ever more to them, regarding their unauthorized priests as their natural leaders against the gentry and against gentry forms of religion. One branch, probably the main branch of this movement, developed a stronghold in eastern Szechwan province, where its members succeeded to create a state of their own which retained its independence for a while. It is the only group which developed real religious communities in which men and women participated, extensive welfare schemes existed and class differences were discouraged. It had a real church organization with dioceses, communal friendship meals and a confession ritual: in short, real piety developed as it could not develop in the official religions. After the annihilation of this state, remnants of the organization can be traced through several centuries, mainly in central and south China. At least one later religious-political movement can be directly traced back to the Yellow Turbans. There is also the possibility that this movement grew up from a common religious background which we later call in Tibet the Bhon religion and in Burma the Nat religion and find under other names in south China. We also must mention that books belonging to such societies are rarely preserved; the government did all it could to destroy them. But the 'Book of the Great Peace' ('T'ai-p'ing ch:ng') of the Yellow Turbans is, at least in fragments, preserved and has later been used by other societies.

The rising of the Yellow Turbans began in 184; all parties, cliques and generals alike, were equally afraid of them, since these were a threat to the gentry as such, and so to all parties. Consequently a combined army of considerable size was got together and sent against the rebels. The Yellow Turbans were beaten.

During these struggles it became evident that Ts'ao Ts'ao with his troops had become the strongest of all the generals. His troops seem to have consisted not of Chinese soldiers alone, but also of Hsiung-nu. It is understandable that the annals say nothing about this, and it can only be inferred. It appears that in order to reinforce their armies the generals recruited not only Chinese but foreigners. The generals operating in the region of the present-day Peking had soldiers of the Wu-huan and Hsien-pi, and even of the Ting-ling; Liu Pei, in the west, made use of Tanguts, and Ts'ao Ts'ao clearly went farthest of all in this direction; he seems to have been responsible for settling nineteen tribes of Hsiung-nu in the Chinese province of Shansi between 180 and 200, in return for their armed aid. In this way Ts'ao Ts'ao gained permanent power in the empire by means of these troops, so that immediately after his death his son Ts'ao P'i, with the support of powerful allied families, was able to force the emperor to abdicate and to found a new dynasty, the Wei dynasty (A.D. 220).

This meant, however, that a part of China which for several centuries had been Chinese was given up to the Hsiung-nu. This was not, of course, what Ts'ao Ts'ao had intended; he had given the Hsiung-nu some area of pasturage in Shansi with the idea that they should be controlled and administered by the officials of the surrounding district. His plan had been similar to what the Chinese had often done with success: aliens were admitted into the territory of the empire in a body, but then the influence of the surrounding administrative centres was steadily extended over them, until the immigrants completely lost their own nationality and became

Chinese. The nineteen tribes of Hsiung-nu, however, were much too numerous, and after the prolonged struggles in China the provincial administration proved much too weak to be able to carry out the plan. Thus there came into existence here, within China, a small Hsiung-nu realm ruled by several *shan-yü*. This was the second major development, and it became of the utmost importance to the history of the next four centuries.

10   *Culture, literature, and art*

After so much politics, we have to come back to discussing culture. One of the typical fields of culture of the Han seems to be directly in connection with the political development. With the emergence of a unified China under a ruler like Wu Ti, who came closer than others before him to make himself an all-powerful autocrat, the thinkers made attempts to unify the social world with the cosmos. Steps in this direction go back to the time of Tsou Yen, but Han thinkers went much farther still. On the basis of the theory of the 'five elements' each dynasty was assigned a specific number; the numbers again were associated with the five directions (four directions and centre), the directions with the five colours and with the basic tones of the five-tone scale. This then meant, for instance, that each dynasty developed its own ceremonial music based on the appropriate scale; the court dresses had the appropriate colour; the calendar was based on this number, as were all the measures. When Wang Mang set up his own regime, he changed everything to the new 'element' which, for instance, has the consequence that the calendar of his dynasty was not as exact as that of the Han dynasty. 'Progress' was subordinated to 'ideology'. Of course, the human body, too, was dominated by the five elements, the seasons expressed the elements, so that Chinese medicine of the time was dominated by these ideas, so that the 'science' of geomancy developed which attempted to calculate the good and bad luck of the living or their descendants from the position of tombs and houses in nature. While we tend to regard geomancy as a pseudo-science it cannot be denied that in practice many buildings are ecologically ideally placed, even down to our century. As the five elements also corresponded to the five planets, attempts were made to bring their movements in harmony with the social world. This had its influence on the one hand on the development of astronomy but also on the development of astrology. In its basic assumptions Chinese astrology shows parallels to Mesopotamian and Western astrology, but it is certainly an independent development. In both systems we find a zodiac, though the Chinese one is a cycle of twelve animals which also dominate a cycle of twelve years and give each year its special character. For all such developments this period has sometimes been called an age of magic and superstition, but we would hardly join in such an evaluation. In any case, the books on astrology and geomancy, and also the basic medical texts were written down, if not composed, during the Han time. At least the medical books are still today regarded as 'classics' of Chinese medicine. In Han time also the fundamental text on arithmetics was written down. Here, we can clearly see how mathematics was needed on the one hand to measure exactly the size of fields, so as to make land transactions and taxation easy, and on the other hand to develop rock-throwing machines which could shoot exactly at distant aims.

Excavations have brought forth bamboo slips with texts from military stations along China's north-western borders. They show us that indeed military conscription was relatively effective, so that soldiers from almost all parts of China were moved to the frontiers, but that they often remained there much longer than they should have. We see that the army had registers about their soldiers, describing them. We know that there were population registers and we have reasons to believe that the first reported census made between A.D. 1–2 was relatively accurate. It gave a population of over 57 million. From then on to the present, we have census reports. Some were incomplete, others complete; but none of them counted all citizens. Some censuses left out non-taxpayers, others minorities or other groups. In spite of this, with some skill, our demographers can get valuable information from these documents, such as the age of marriage, the number of children who survived the first years of life, the life expectancy of persons over fourteen, and the density of population in different areas. The Han also had information about food production and calculated the average food consumption of an adult, the cost of transportation of food; we even have calculations of how much labour had to be used for a certain building project and how much this would cost.

One point these materials clearly show: there were now many people who could read and write and do arithmetic. The spread of writing brought forth the development of encyclopaedias. Encyclopaedias convey knowledge in an easily grasped and easily found form. The first compilation of this sort dates from the third century B.C. It was the work of Lü Pu-wei, the merchant who was prime minister and regent during the minority of Shih Huang-ti. It contains general information concerning ceremonies, customs, historic events, and other things the knowledge of which was part of a general education. Soon afterwards other encyclopaedias appeared, of which the best known is the 'Book of the Mountains and Seas' ('Shan Hai Ching'). This book, arranged according to regions of the world, contains everything known at the time about geography, natural philosophy, and the animal and plant world, and also about popular myths. This tendency to systemization is shown also in the historical works. The famous 'Shih Chi', one of our main sources for Chinese history, is the first historical work of the modern type, that is to say, built up on a definite plan, and it was also the model for all later official historiography. Its author, Ssǔ-ma Ch'ien (born 135 B.C.), and his father, made use of the material in the state archives and of private documents, old historical and philosophical books, inscriptions, and the results of their own travels. The philosophical and historical books of earlier times (with the exception of those of the nature of chronicles) consisted merely of brief essays or sayings, attributed to thinkers. The 'Shih Chi' is a compendium of a mass of source-material. The documents were abbreviated, but the text of the extracts was altered as little as possible, so that the general result retains in a sense the value of an original source. In its arrangement the 'Shih Chi' became a model for all later historians: the first part is in the form of annals, and there follow tables concerning the occupants of official posts and fiefs, and then biographies of various important personalities, though the type of the comprehensive biography did not appear till later. We miss in those biographies which the history books contain a stress on the individual characteristics of the person. The biography describes him (or her) in his (or her) role in society and evaluates actions in terms of Confucian morality. We do not learn how they looked, what their personal life was, often not even whether they had daughters and one or more than one wife. They remain figures to us, not warm human beings. But Chinese history did not want to imitate individuals—this was left to the novels. The 'Shih Chi' also, like later historical works, contains many monographs dealing with particular fields of knowledge, such as astronomy, the calendar, music, economics, official dress at court, and much else. The whole type of construction differs fundamentally from such works as those of Thucydides or Herodotus. The Chinese historical works have the advantage that the section of annals gives at once the events of a particular year, the monographs describe the development of a particular field of knowledge, and the biographical section offers information concerning particular personalities. The mental attitude is that of the gentry: shortly after the time of Ssǔ-ma Ch'ien an historical department was founded, in which members of the gentry worked as historians upon the documents prepared by representatives of the gentry in the various government offices.

In addition to encyclopaedias and historical works, many books of philosophy were written in the Han period, but most of them offer no fundamentally new ideas and only three of them are of importance. One is the work of Tung Chung-shu, already mentioned. The second is a book by Liu An called 'Huai-nan Tzŭ'. Prince Liu himself with Taoism and allied problems, gathered scholars of different schools, and carried on discussion Many of his writings are lost, but enough is extant to s was one of the earliest Chinese alchemists.

When we hear of alchemy or read books about it we should always keep in mind that many of these books can also be read as books of sex; in a similar way, books on the art of war, too, can be read as books on sexual relations. The first real sex book was probably also written in Han time, the 'Book of the Plain Girl' ('Su Nü Ching'), is still printed today and contains valuable observations and advice.

The third important book of the Han period was the 'Lun Hêng' ('Critique of Opinions') of Wang Ch'ung (born A.D. 27). Wang Ch'ung advocated rational thinking and tried to pave the way for a free natural science, in continuation of the beginnings which the natural philosophers of the later Chou period had made. The book analyses reports in ancient literature and customs of daily life, and shows how much they were influenced by superstition and by ignorance of the facts of nature. It had little impact in its time, but has recently been highly praised by Chinese scholars; to us it is also a rich source of beliefs and attitudes.

There were great literary innovations in the field of poetry. The splendour and elegance at the new imperial court of the Han dynasty attracted many poets who sang the praises of the emperor and his court and were given official posts and dignities. These praises were in the form of grandiloquent, overloaded poetry, full of strange similes and allusions, but with little real feeling. This style of describing poetry ultimately has its source in the poetry of Ch'ü Yüan and his successors. Indeed, the luxury of the court was overwhelming. The palaces of the emperor had galleries with paintings of heroes of history. In addition to the main palace, the rulers had their hunting parks (the word which we use to describe the 'paradise' originally meant 'emperor's hunting preserve') which were stocked with rare animals sent by local governors or foreign ambassadors—and in line with more than two millennia of history, an American president coming to Communist China like the tribute-bringing kings of old, brought a rare animal to the ruler of the country.

In the tombs have been found reliefs whose technique is generally intermediate between simple outline engraving and intaglio. The lining-in is most frequently executed in scratched lines. The representations, mostly in strips placed one above another, are of lively historical scenes, scenes from the life of the dead, great ritual ceremonies, or adventurous scenes from mythology. Bronze vessels have representations in inlaid gold and silver, mostly of animals. The most important documents of the painting of the Han period have also been found in tombs. We see especially ladies and gentlemen of society, with richly ornamented, elegant, expensive clothing that is very reminiscent of the clothing customary to this day in Japan. We also see fantastic beings or deities which in only a very few cases can be identified with the beasts and demons in the 'Shan Hai Ching'. However, when recently in a magnificent tomb a corpse was found completely clothed in a dress made of jade plates, sewn togther with gold wire, it was found that actually such a custom had been mentioned in a book of the Han period, but the reference had been neglected, probably because it sounded too unbelievable. Jade is a very hard mineral and it takes an enormous amount of time to shape a single plate, not to speak of a whole dress.

The tombs also revealed numerous vessels made of lacquer—a typically Chinese material to the present time. Lacquer caskets and bowls show artistic representations of human figures and scenes which, in some cases, we knew from literary works. We see here the court parties in which women enlivened the meal with music and dancing. These women, mostly slaves from southern China, introduced at the court southern Chinese forms of song and poem, which were soon adopted and elaborated by poets. Poems and dance songs were composed which belonged to the finest that Chinese poetry can show—full of natural feeling, simple in language, moving in content. Other scenes show us jugglers and acrobats. As these performances were called 'Hunnic plays', we have reason to assume that they were inspired by Central Asian or western Asian performances; if not the performers themselves were in some cases foreigners. Some scholars have been tempted to regard some of the scenes on the walls of Han tombs as showing theatre plays, not real life scenes. If this does not mean that there must be a standard text, spoken or sung to be called a 'theatre' play, it is quite possible that mimic religious plays were known and were early forms of the later Chinese theatres.

In Han time, Chinese still used to sit and to sleep on mats on the floor; however, the first kind of bed, a wooden frame with a network of strings, is mentioned, as well as a kind of light chair. The still typical north Chinese 'oven-bed', a brick or mud platform which could be heated from below, was probably a Korean invention and spread to China proper only later.

We know that in Han time silk was used as a writing material at court, and some of the painting was also on silk, but almost nothing has yet been found of it. Paper had meanwhile been invented in the second century A.D., according to tradition, but most likely earlier. At first fibres of textiles were used in a technique similar to that used in making bark-cloth and felt. Later bamboo fibres became the common material. Ink, made of the soot of specific wood, seems to have been known already in the beginning of history, and the brush, too, seems to be very old.

The persons who painted the walls of tombs or of palaces were regarded as craftsmen, because they did not belong to the gentry, though we would call many of their products works of art. In Han time, representations of human beings, probably even true portraits, were common When painting became also an occupation of the gentry and then an 'art', the human being begins to fade more and more into the background, though it never fully disappeared. The gentry painted as a social pastime, just as they assembled together for poetry, discussion, or performances of song and dance; they painted as an aesthetic pleasure and rarely as a means of earning. We find philosophic ideas or greetings, emotions, and experiences represented by paintings—paintings with fanciful or ideal landscapes; paintings representing the life and environment of the cultured class in idealized form, never naturalistic either in fact or in intention. Until recently t was an indispensable condition in the Chinese view that an artist must be 'cultured' and be a member of the gentry—distinguished, unoccupied, wealthy. A man who was paid for his work, for instance for a portrait for the ancestral cult, was until late time regarded as a craftsman, not as an artist. Yet these, 'craftsmen' have produced in Han time and even earlier, many works which, in our view, undoubtedly belong to the realm of art.

In contrast to ancient Greece, sculpture did not count as 'art'; it was a craft only. We mentioned that the Shang produced sculptures, but then we do not know much about sculpture until the coming of Buddhism, and certainly for a long time Buddhist sculptures, even if made by Chinese craftsmen, were artistically determined by rules developed in India.

We mentioned above a possible influence of Mazdaism, an Iranian religion developed probably at the time of Confucius, characterized by a strong dualism, which is expressed as an unending fight of the forces of the light against those of the dark, of good against evil. We find in Han time a set of seven planets, i.e. the old five together with sun and moon—the set of names which in the West became the names of the seven days of the week. Later texts even mention the foreign words for the Iranian days of the week. But the Chinese never accepted our concept of a week. There is also a set of nine planets which originated in the West, the seven enlarged by two imagined counterparts to the moon; as nine is an important number in Chinese numerical speculation (the square of three, which is a male number), this cycle got some distribution in China.

107

More important than Mazdaism and Manichaeism, which developed centuries after the end of Han, was Buddhism. According to Chinese legend, it came to China in A.D. 65, as a consequence of a dream of emperor Ming. According to our present knowledge, Buddhism entered China from the south coast and through Central Asia at latest in the first century B.C.; it came with foreign merchants from India or Central Asia. According to Indian customs, Brahmans, the Hindu caste providing all Hindu priests, could not leave their their homes. As merchants on their trips, which lasted often several years, did not want to go without religious services, they turned to Buddhist priests as well as to priests of Near Eastern religions. These priests were not prevented from travelling and used this opportunity for missionary purposes. Thus, for a long time after the first arrival of Buddhists, the Buddhist priests in China were foreigners who served foreign merchant colonies. Buddhism brought something to China which was new. Chinese philosophers had never speculated about the origin of mankind and about man's fate on earth. There had been among the people a vague belief that the souls of dead people would gather somewhere around mountains; that some souls could change into dangerous, evil demons and ghosts, others into gods. Buddhism brought the new idea that our present fate is conditioned by acts done by ourselves in a previous existence, and that our present actions influence our next reincarnation. In a period of unrest and misery, as the second century A.D. was, Buddhism attracted members of the lower classes into its arms, while the parts of Indian science which these monks brought with them from India aroused some interest in certain educated circles. Buddhism, therefore, undeniably exercised an influence at the end of the Han dynasty, although no Chinese were priests and few, if any, gentry members were adherents of the religious teachings.

With the end of the Han period a further epoch of Chinese history comes to its close. The Han period was that of the final completion and consolidation of the social order of the gentry. The period that followed was that of the conflicts of the Chinese with the populations on their northern borders.

6 Sun Ch'üan, ruler of Wu.
(From a painting by Yen Li-pen, c. 640-680.)

7 General view of the Buddhist cave-temples of Yün-kang. In the foreground, the present village; in the background, the rampart.

(Photo H. Hammer-Morrisson.)

CHAPTER SEVEN

The Epoch of the First Division of China (A.D. 220–580)

(A) THE THREE KINGDOMS (A.D. 220–265)

1 *Social, intellectual, and economic problems during the first division*
The end of the Han period was followed by the three and a half centuries of the first division of China into several kingdoms, each with its own dynasty. In fact, once before during the period of the Contending States, China had been divided into a number of states, but at least in theory they had been subject to the Chou dynasty, and none of the contending states had made the claim to be the legitimate ruler of all China. In this period of the 'first division' several states claimed to be legitimate rulers, and later Chinese historians tried to decide which of these had 'more right' to this claim. At the outset (220–280) there were three kingdoms (Wei, Wu, Shu Han); then came an unstable reunion during twenty-seven years (280–307) under the rule of the Western Chin. This was followed by a still sharper division between north and south: while a wave of non-Chinese nomad dynasties poured over the north, in the south one Chinese clique after another seized power, so that dynasty followed dynasty until finally, in 580, a united China came again into existence, adopting the culture of the north and the traditions of the gentry.

In some ways, the period from 220 to 580 can be compared with the period of the coincidentally synchronous breakdown of the Roman Empire: in both cases there was no great increase in population, although in China perhaps no over-all decrease in population as in the Roman Empire; decrease occurred, however, in the population of the great Chinese cities, especially of the capital; furthermore we witness, in both empires, a disorganization of the monetary system, i.e. in China the reversal to a predominance of natural economy after almost 400 years of an economy in which prices were calculated in terms of money. As in the West, gold disappears almost completely. It is possible, though not too likely, that much of China's gold went into the gilding of millions of large and small Buddha statues; it seems more likely that it left China and the Roman Empire as well and came together in Central Asia or India.

Yet this period cannot be simply dismissed as a transition period, as was usually done by the older European works on China. The social order of the gentry, whose birth and development inside China we followed, had for the first time to defend itself against views and systems entirely opposed to it; for the Turkish and Mongol peoples who ruled northern China brought with them their traditions of a feudal nobility with privileges of birth and all that they implied. Thus this period, socially regarded, is especially that of the struggle between the Chinese gentry and the northern nobility, the gentry being excluded at first as a direct political factor in the northern and more important part of China. In the south the gentry continued in the old style with a constant struggle between cliques, the only difference being that the class assumed a sort of 'colonial' character through the formation of gigantic estates and through association with the merchant class.

To throw light on the scale of events, we need to have figures of population. There are no figures for the years around A.D. 220, and we must make do with those of 140; but in order to show the relative strength of the three states it is the ratio between the figures that matters. In 140 the regions which later belonged to Wei had roughly 29,000,000 inhabitants; those later belonging to Wu had 11,700,000; those which belonged later to Shu Han had a bare 7,500,000. (The figures take no account of the non-Chinese native population, which was not yet included in the taxation lists.) The Hsiung-nu formed only a small part of the population, as there were only the nineteen tribes which had abandoned one of the parts, already reduced, of the Hsiung-nu empire. The whole Hsiung-nu empire may never have counted more than some 3,000,000. At the time when the population of what became the Wei territory totalled 29,000,000 the capital with its immediate environment had over a million inhabitants. The figure is exclusive of most of the officials and soldiers, as these were taxable in their homes and so were counted there. It is clear that this was a disproportionate concentration round the capital.

It was at this time that both south and north China felt the influence of Buddhism, which until A.D. 220 had no more real effect on China than had, for instance, the penetration of European civilization between 1580 and 1842. Buddhism offered new notions, new ideals, foreign science, and many other elements of culture, with which the old Chinese philosophy and science had to contend. At the same time there came with Buddhism the first direct knowledge of the great civilized countries west of China. Until then China had regarded herself as the only existing civilized country, and all other countries had been regarded as barbaric, for a civilized country was then taken to mean a country with urban industrial crafts and agriculture. In our present period, however, China's relations with the Middle East and with southern Asia were so close that the existence of civilized countries outside China had to be admitted. Consequently, when alien dynasties ruled in northern China and a new high civilization came into existence there, it was impossible to speak of its rulers as barbarians any longer. Even the theory that the Chinese emperor was the Son of Heaven and enthroned at the centre of the world was no longer tenable. Thus a vast widening of China's intellectual horizon took place.

Economically, our present period witnessed an adjustment in south China between the Chinese way of life, which had penetrated from the north, and that of the natives of the south. Large groups of Chinese had to turn over from wheat culture in dry fields to rice culture in wet fields, and from field culture to market gardening. In north China the conflict went on between Chinese agriculture and the cattle breeding of Central Asia. Was the will of the ruler to prevail and north China to become a country of pasturage, or was the country to keep to the agrarian tradition of the people under this rule? Only by attention to this problem shall we be in a position to explain why the rule of the Turkish peoples did not last, why these peoples were gradually absorbed and disappeared.

2 Status of the two southern kingdoms

When the last emperor of the Han period had to abdicate in favour of Ts'ao P'i and the Wei dynasty began, China was in no way a unified realm. Almost immediately, in 221, two other army commanders, who had long been independent, declared themselves emperors. In the south-west of China, in the present province of Szechwan, the Shu Han dynasty was founded in this way, and in the south-east, in the region of the present Nanking, the Wu dynasty.

The situation of the southern kingdom of Shu Han (221–263) corresponded more or less to that of the Chungking regime in the Second World War. West of it the high Tibetan mountains towered up; there was very little reason to fear any major attack from that direction. In the north and east the realm was also protected by difficult mountain country. The south lay relatively open, but at that time there were few Chinese living there, only natives with a relatively low civilization. The kingdom could only be seriously attacked from two corners—through the north-west, where there was a negotiable plateau, between the Ch'in-ling mountains in the north and the Tibetan mountains in the west, a plateau inhabited by fairly highly developed Tibetan tribes; and secondly through the south-east corner, where it would be possible to penetrate up the Yangtze. There was in fact incessant fighting at both these dangerous corners.

Economically, Shu Han was not in a bad position. The country had long been part of the Chinese wheat lands, and had a fairly large Chinese peasant population in the well-irrigated plain of Ch'engtu. There was also a wealthy merchant class, supplying grain to the surrounding mountain peoples and buying medicaments and other profitable Tibetan products. And there were trade routes from here through the present province of Yünnan to India.

Shu Han's difficulty was that its population was not large enough to be able to stand against the northern state of Wei; moreover, it was difficult to carry out an offensive from Shu Han, though the country could defend itself well. The first attempt to find a remedy was a campaign against the native tribes of the present Yünnan. The purpose of this was to secure man-power for the army and also slaves for sale; for the south-west had for centuries been a main source for traffic in slaves. Finally it was hoped to gain control over the trade to India. All these things were intended to strengthen Shu Han internally, but in spite of certain military successes they produced no practical result, as the Chinese were unable in the long run to endure the climate or to hold out against the guerrilla tactics of the natives. Shu Han tried to buy the assistance of the Tibetans and with their aid to carry out a decisive attack on Wei, whose dynastic legitimacy was not recognized by Shu Han. The ruler of Shu Han claimed to be a member of the imperial family of the deposed Han dynasty, and therefore to be the rightful, legitimate ruler over China. His descent, however, was a little doubtful, and in any case it depended on a link far back in the past. Against this the Wei of the north declared that the last ruler of the Han dynasty had handed over to them with all due form the seals of the state and therewith the imperial prerogative. The controversy was of no great practical importance, but it played a big part in the Chinese Confucianist school until the twelfth century, and contributed largely to a revision of the old conceptions of legitimacy.

The political plans of Shu Han were well considered and far-seeing. They were evolved by the premier, a man from Shantung named Chu-ko Liang; but the ruler died in 226 and his successor was still a child. Chu-ko Liang lived only for a further eight years, and after his death in 234 the decline of Shu Han began. Its political leaders no longer had a sense of what was possible. Thus Wei inflicted several defeats on Shu Han, and finally subjugated it in 263.

The situation of the state of Wu was much less favourable than that of Shu Han, though this second southern kingdom lasted from

221 to 280. Its country consisted of marshy plains or mountains with narrow valleys. Here Thai peoples had long cultivated their rice, while in the mountains Yao tribes lived by hunting and by simple agriculture. Peasants immigrating from the north found that their wheat and pulse did not thrive here, and they had to gain familiarity with rice cultivation. They were also compelled to give up their sheep and cattle and in their place to breed pigs and water buffaloes, as was done by the former inhabitants of the country. The lower class of the population was mainly non-Chinese; above it was an upper class of Chinese, at first relatively small, consisting of officials, soldiers, and merchants in towns and administrative centres. The country was poor, and its only important economic asset was the trade in metals, timber, and other southern products; soon there came also a growing overseas trade with India and the Middle East, bringing revenues to the state in so far as the goods were re-exported from Wu to the north.

Wu never attempted to conquer the whole of China, but endeavoured to consolidate its own difficult territory with a view to building up a state on a firm foundation. In general, Wu played mainly a passive part in the incessant struggles between the three kingdoms, though it was active in diplomacy. The Wu kingdom entered into relations with a man who in 232 had gained control of the present South Manchuria and shortly afterwards assumed the title of king. This new ruler of 'Yen', as he called his kingdom had determined to attack the Wei dynasty, and hoped, by putting pressure on it in association with Wu, to overrun Wei from north and south. Wei answered this plan very effectively by recourse to diplomacy and it began by making Wu believe that Wu had reason to fear an attack from its western neighbour Shu Han. A mission was also dispatched from Wei to negotiate with Japan. Japan was then emerging from its stone age and introducing metals; there were countless small principalities and states, of which the state of Yamato, then ruled by a queen, was the most powerful. Recently a debate has arisen: traditional sources claim that Yamato already at this time had control over a piece of southern Korea; others believe that a massive emigration from this part of Korea turned to Japan, and that, for some time the emigrants retained contact with the motherland. In any case, Wei offered Yamato the prospect of gaining the whole of Korea if it would turn against the state of Yen in south Manchuria. Wu, too, had turned to Japan, but the negotiations came to nothing, since Wu, as an ally of Yen, had nothing to offer. The queen of Yamato accordingly sent a mission to Wei; she had already decided in favour of that state. Thus Wei was able to embark on war against Yen, which it annihilated in 237. This wrecked Wu's diplomatic projects, and no more was heard of any ambitious plans of the kingdom of Wu.

113

The two southern states had a common characteristic: both were condottiere states, not built up from their own population but conquered by generals from the north and ruled for a time by those generals and their northern troops. Natives gradually entered these northern armies and reduced their percentage of northerners, but a gulf remained between the native population, including its gentry, and the alien military rulers. This reduced the striking power of the southern states.

On the other hand, this period had its positive element. For the first time there was an emperor in south China, with all the organization that implied. A capital full of officials, eunuchs, and all the satellites of an imperial court provided incentives to economic advance, because it represented a huge market. The peasants around it were able to increase their sales and grew prosperous. The increased demand resulted in an increase of tillage and a thriving trade. Soon the transport problem had to be faced, as had happened long ago in the north, and new means of transport, especially ships, were provided, and new trade routes opened which were to last far longer than the three kingdoms; on the other hand, the costs of transport involved fresh taxation burdens for the population. The skilled staff needed for the business of administration came into the new capital from the surrounding districts, for the conquerors and new rulers of the territory of the two southern dynasties had brought with them from the north only uneducated soldiers and almost equally uneducated officers. The influx of scholars and administrators into the chief cities produced cultural and economic centres in the south, a circumstance of great importance to China's later development.

3 The northern state of Wei

The situation in the north, in the state of Wei (220–265) was anything but rosy. Wei ruled what at that time were the most important and richest regions of China, the plain of Shensi in the west and the great plain east of Loyang, the two most thickly populated areas of China. But the events at the end of the Han period had inflicted great economic injury on the country. The southern and south-western parts of the Han empire had been lost, and though parts of Central Asia still gave allegiance to Wei, these, as in the past, were economically more of a burden than an asset, because they called for incessant expenditure. At least the trade caravans were able to travel undisturbed from and to China through Sinkiang. Moreover, the Wei kingdom, although much smaller than the empire of the Han, maintained a completely staffed court at great expense, because the rulers, claiming to rule the whole of China, felt bound to display more magnificence than the rulers of the southern dynasties. They had also to reward the nineteen tribes of the Hsiung-nu in the north for their military aid, not only with cessions of land but with payments of money. Finally, they would not disarm but maintained great armies for the continual fighting against the southern states. The Wei dynasty did not succeed, however, in closely subordinating the various army commanders to the central government. Thus the commanders, in collusion with groups of the gentry, were able to enrich themselves and to secure regional power. The inadequate strength of the central government of Wei was further undermined by the rivalries among the dominant gentry. The imperial family (Ts'ao P'i, who reigned from 220 to 226, had taken as emperor the name of Wen Ti) was descended from one of the groups of great landowners that had formed in the later Han period. The nucleus of that group was a family named Ts'ui, of which there is mention from the Han period onward and which maintained its power down to the tenth century; but it remained in the background and at first held entirely aloof from direct intervention in high policy. Another family belonging to this group was the Hsia-hou family which was closely united to the family of Wen Ti by adoption; and very soon there was also the Ssŭ-ma family. Quite naturally Wen Ti, as soon as he came into power, made provision for the members of these powerful families, for only thanks to their support had he been able to ascend the throne and to maintain his hold on the throne. Thus we find many members of the Hsia-hou and Ssŭ-ma families in government positions. The Ssŭ-ma family especially showed great activity, and at the end of Wen Ti's reign their power had so grown that a certain Ssŭ-ma I was in control of the government, while the new emperor Ming Ti (227–233) was completely powerless. This virtually sealed the fate of the Wei dynasty, so far as the dynastic family was concerned. The next emperor was installed and deposed by the Ssŭ-ma family; dissensions arose within the ruling family, leading to members of the family assassinating one another. In 264 a member of the Ssŭ-ma family declared himself king; when he died and was succeeded by his son Ssŭ-ma Yen, the latter, in 265, staged a formal act of renunciation of the throne of the Wei dynasty and made himself the first ruler of the new Chin dynasty. There is nothing to gain by detailing all the intrigues that led up to this event: they all took place in the immediate environment of the court and in no way affected the people, except that every item of expenditure, including all the bribery, had to come out of the taxes paid by the people.

With such a situation at court, with the bad economic situation in the country, and with the continual fighting against the two southern states, there could be no question of any far-reaching foreign

115

policy. Parts of eastern Sinkiang still showed some measure of allegiance to Wei, but only because at the time it had no stronger opponent. The Hsiung-nu beyond the frontier were suffering from a period of depression which was at the same time a period of reconstruction. It seems that some of their tribes went farther to the west, joined other tribes there and reappeared in western Asia and Europe as the feared Huns. Thus, the western Huns and the eastern Hsiung-nu seem to some, as yet undetermined, degree to be related. Other Hsiung-nu tribes were beginning slowly to form a new unit, together with Mongol tribes, the Juan-juan; but at this time, the new federation was still politically unimportant. We see here a typical process: after the breakdown of a tribal federation, the remaining tribes or fragments of tribes, join other tribal groups and form a new federation under a new name—thus, we often cannot easily recognize them in the new conglomerate. The nineteen tribes within north China held more and more closely together as militarily organized nomads, but did not yet represent a military power and remained loyal to the Wei. The only important element of trouble seems to have been furnished by the Hsien-pi tribes, who had joined with Wu-huan tribes and apparently also with vestiges of the Hsiung-nu in eastern Mongolia, and who made numerous raids over the frontier into the Wei empire. The state of Yen, in southern Manchuria, had already been destroyed by Wei in 238 thanks to Wei's good relations with Japan. Loose diplomatic relations were maintained with Japan in the period that followed; in that period many elements of Chinese civilization found their way into Japan and there, together with settlers from many parts of China, helped to transform the culture of ancient Japan.

This period is not a time of flourishing literature and art. On the contrary, we find here for the first time an intelligentsia which turned away from working with the government. Groups of scholars came together for what is called 'clean discussion' (ch'ing-t'an), consisting of short verbal exchanges or 'bons mots', brilliant remarks, sometimes combined with philosophical insights, often with exercises in logic. These men were no more imbued with Confucian ethics, often knew philosophical Taoism well, and, slightly later, Buddhism too. Their products, collected in part in the famous 'Shih-shuo hsin-yü', are not great or deep, but give us better insight into the spirit of the time and the character of the intelligentsia than any document from earlier time gives. The movement seems to have begun already before A.D. 200, though Wang Pi (226–249) is regarded as their leader. Wang Pi was also one of the important commentators of the book of Lao Tzǔ. Others went further and rejected social life as it was defined for the governing class completely. We hear of men who were drunk all the time, others who walked around in the nude—considering the modesty of Chinese at all times, an extreme act of rejection. Some scholars are of the belief that this was a real period of drug use, though they have not been able to tell us which drug was used. Chinese knew the effects of hemp (which is related to marijuana); opium and its derivates, however, were not yet known.

(B) THE WESTERN CHIN DYNASTY (A.D. 265–317)

1 Internal situation in the Chin empire

The change of dynasty in the state of Wei did not bring any turn in China's internal history. Ssŭ-ma Yen, who as emperor was called Wu Ti (265–289), had come to the throne with the aid of his clique and his extraordinarily large and widely ramified family. To these he had to give offices as reward. There began at court once more the same spectacle as in the past, except that princes of the new imperial family now played a greater part than under the Wei dynasty, whose ruling house had consisted of a small family. It was now customary, in spite of the abolition of the feudal system, for the imperial princes to receive large regions to administer, the fiscal revenues of which represented their income. The princes were not, however, to exercise full authority in the style of the former feudal lords: their courts were full of imperial control officials. In the event of war it was their duty to come forward, like other governors, with an army in support of the central government. The various Chin princes succeeded, however, in making other governors, beyond the frontiers of their regions, dependent on them. Also, they collected armies of their own independently of the central government and used those armies to pursue personal policies. The members of the families allied with the ruling house, for their part, did all they could to extend their own power. Thus the first ruler of the dynasty was tossed to and fro between the conflicting interests and was himself powerless. But though intrigue was piled on intrigue, the ruler who, of course, himself had come to the head of the state by means of intrigues, was more watchful than the rulers of the Wei dynasty had been, and by shrewd counter-measures he repeatedly succeeded in playing off one party against another, so that the dynasty remained in power. Numerous widespread and furious risings nevertheless took place, usually led by princes. Thus during this period the history of the dynasty was of an extraordinarily dismal character.

In spite of this, the Chin troops succeeded in overthrowing the second southern state, that of Wu (A.D. 280), and in so restoring the unity of the empire, the Shu Han realm having been already conquered by the Wei. After the destruction of Wu there remained no external enemy that represented a potential danger, so that a general disarmament was decreed (280) in order to restore a healthy economic and financial situation. This disarmament applied, of course, to the troops directly under the orders of the dynasty, namely the troops of the court and the capital and the imperial troops in the provinces. Disarmament could not, however, be carried out in the princes' regions, as the princes declared that they needed personal guards. The dismissal of the troops was accompanied by a decree ordering the surrender of arms. It may be assumed that the government proposed to mint money with the metal of the weapons surrendered, for coin (the old coin of the Wei dynasty) had become very scarce; as we indicated previously, money had largely been replaced by goods so that, for instance, grain and silks were used for the payment of salaries. China, from c. A.D. 200 on until the eighth century, remained in a period of such partial 'natural economy'.

Naturally the decree for the surrender of weapons remained a dead-letter. The discharged soldiers kept their weapons at first and then preferred to sell them. A large part of them was acquired by the Hsiung-nu and the Hsien-pi in the north of China; apparently they usually gave up land in return. In this way many Chinese soldiers, though not all by any means, went as peasants to the regions in the north of China and beyond the frontier. They were glad to do so, for the Hsiung-nu and the Hsien-pi had not the efficient administration and rigid tax collection of the Chinese; and above all, they had no great landowners who could have organized the collection of taxes. For their part, the Hsiung-nu and the Hsien-pi had no reason to regret this immigration of peasants, who could provide them with the farm produce they needed. And at the same time they were receiving from them large quantities of the most modern weapons.

This ineffective disarmament was undoubtedly the most pregnant event of the period of the Western Chin dynasty. The measure was intended to save the cost of maintaining the soldiers and to bring them back to the land as peasants (and taxpayers); but the discharged men were not given land by the government. The disarmament achieved nothing, not even the desired increase in the money in circulation; what did happen was that the central government lost all practical power, while the military strength both of the dangerous princes within the country and also of the frontier people was increased. The results of these mistaken measures became evident at once and compelled the government to arm anew.

2 *Effect on the frontier peoples*
Four groups of frontier peoples drew more or less advantage from the demobilization law—the people of the Toba, the Tibetans, and

the Hsien-pi in the north, and the nineteen tribes of the Hsiung-nu within the frontiers of the empire. In the course of time all sorts of complicated relations developed among those ascending peoples as well as between them and the Chinese.

The Toba (T'o-po, Tabgaç) formed a small group in the north of the present province of Shansi, north of the city of Tat'ungfu, and they were about to develop their small state. They were probably of Turkish origin, but had absorbed many tribes of the older Hsiung-nu and the Hsien-pi. In considering the ethnic relationships of all these northern peoples we must rid ourselves of our present-day notions of national unity. Among the Toba there were many Turkish tribes, but also Mongols, and probably a Tungus tribe, as well as perhaps others whom we cannot yet analyse. These tribes may even have spoken different languages, much as later not only Mongol but also Turkish was spoken in the Mongol empire. The political units they formed were tribal unions, not national states.

Such a union or federation can be conceived of, structurally, as a cone. At the top point of the cone there was the person of the ruler of the federation. He was a member of the leading family or clan of the leading tribe (the two top layers of the cone). If we speak of the Toba as of Turkish stock, we mean that according to our present knowledge, their leading tribe (a) spoke a language belonging to the Turkish language family and (b) exhibited a pattern of culture which belonged to the type described above in Chapter One as 'north-western Culture'. The next layer of the cone represented the 'inner circle of tribes', i.e. such tribes as had joined with the leading tribe at an early moment. The leading family of the leading tribe often took their wives from the leading families of the 'inner tribes', and these leaders served as advisers and councillors to the leader of the federation. The next lower layer consisted of the 'outer tribes', i.e. tribes which had joined the federation only later, often under strong pressure; their number was always much larger than the number of the 'inner tribes', but their political influence was much weaker. Every layer below that of the 'outer tribes' was regarded as inferior and more or less 'unfree'. There was many a tribe which, as a tribe, had to serve a free tribe; and there were others who, as tribes, had to serve the whole federation. In addition, there were individuals who had quit or had been forced to quit their tribe or their home and had joined the federation leader as his personal 'bondsmen'; further, there were individual slaves and, finally, there were the large masses of agriculturists who had been conquered by the federation. When such a federation was dissolved, by defeat or inner dissent, individual tribes or groups of tribes could join a new federation or could resume independent life.

Typically, such federations exhibited two tendencies. In the case of the Hsiung-nu we indicated previously that the leader of the federation repeatedly attempted to build up a kind of bureaucratic system, using his bondsmen as a nucleus. A second tendency was to replace the original tribal leaders by members of the family of the federation leader. If this initial step, usually first taken when 'outer tribes' were incorporated, was successful, a reorganization was attempted: instead of using tribal units in war, military units on the basis of 'Groups of Hundred', 'Groups of Thousand', etc., were created and the original tribes were dissolved into military regiments. In the course of time, and especially at the time of the dissolution of a federation, these military units had gained social coherence and appeared to be tribes again; we are probably correct in assuming that all 'tribes' which we find from this time on were already 'secondary' tribes of this type. A secondary tribe often took its name from its leader, but it could also revive an earlier 'primary tribe' name.

The Toba, whom we will soon discuss in detail, represented a good example of this 'cone' structure of pastoral society. Also the Hsiung-nu of this time seem to have had a similar structure. Incidentally, we will from now on call the Hsiung-nu 'Huns' because Chinese sources begin to call them 'Hu', a term which also had a more general meaning (all non-Chinese in the north and west of China) as well as a more special meaning (non-Chinese in Central Asia and India).

The Tibetans fell apart into two sub-groups, the Ch'iang and the Ti. Both names appeared repeatedly as political conceptions, but the Tibetans, like all other state-forming groups of peoples, sheltered in their realms countless alien elements. In the course of the third and second centuries B.C. the group of the Ti, mainly living in the territory of the present Szechwan, had mixed extensively with remains of the Yüeh-chih; the others, the Ch'iang, were northern Tibetans or so-called Tanguts; that is to say, they contained Turkish and Mongol elements. In A.D. 296 there began a great rising of the Ti, whose leader Ch'i Wan-nien took on the title emperor. The Ch'iang rose with them, but it was not until later, from 312, that they pursued an independent policy. The Ti State, however, though it had a second emperor, very soon lost importance, so that we shall be occupied solely with the Ch'iang.

As the tribal structure of Tibetan groups was always weak and as leadership developed among them only in times of war, their states always show a military rather than a tribal structure, and the continuation of these states depended strongly upon the personal qualities of their leaders. Incidentally, Tibetans fundamentally were sheep-breeders and not horse-breeders and, therefore, they always showed inclination to incorporate infantry into their armies. Thus, Tibetan states differed strongly from the aristocratically organized 'Turkish' states as well as from the tribal, non-aristocratic 'Mongol' states of that period.

The Hsien-pi, according to our present knowledge, were under 'Mongol' leadership, i.e. we believe that the language of the leading group belonged to the family of Mongolian languages and that their culture belonged to the type described above as 'northern culture'. They had, in addition, a strong admixture of Hunnic tribes. Throughout the period during which they played a part in history, they never succeeded in forming any great political unit, in strong contrast to the Huns, who excelled in state formation. The separate groups of the Hsien-pi pursued a policy of their own; very frequently Hsien-pi fought each other, and they never submitted to a common leadership. Thus their history is entirely that of small groups. As early as the Wei period there had been small-scale conflicts with the Hsien-pi tribes, and at times the tribes had had some success. The campaigns of the Hsien-pi against north China now increased, and in the course of them the various tribes formed firmer groupings, among which the Mu-jung tribes played a leading part. In 281, the year after the demobilization law, this group marched south into China, and occupied the region round Peking. After fierce fighting, in which the Mu-jung section suffered heavy losses, a treaty was signed in 289, under which the Mu-jung tribe of the Hsien-pi recognized Chinese overlordship. The Mu-jung were driven to this step mainly because they had been continually attacked from southern Manchuria by another Hsien-pi tribe, the Yü-wen, the tribe most closely related to them. The Mu-jung made use of the period of their so-called subjection to organize their community in north China.

South of the Toba were the nineteen tribes of the Hsiung-nu or Huns, as we are now calling them. Their leader in A.D. 287, Liu Yüan, was one of the principal personages of this period. His name is purely Chinese, but he was descended from the Hun *shan-yü*, from the family and line of Mao Tun. His membership of that long-famous noble line and old ruling family of Huns gave him a prestige which he increased by his great organizing ability.

3 Struggles for the throne

We shall return to Liu Yüan later; we must now cast another glance at the official court of the Chin. In that court a family named Yang had become very powerful, a daughter of this family having become empress. When, however, the emperor died, the wife of the new emperor Hui Ti (290–306) secured the assassination of the old empress Yang and of her whole family. Thus began the rule at court of the Chia family. In 299 the Chia family got rid of the heir to the throne, to whom they objected, assassinating this prince and another one. This event became the signal for large-scale activity on the part of the princes, each of whom was supported by particular groups of families. The princes had not complied with the disarmament law of 280 and so had become militarily supreme. The generals newly appointed in the course of the imperial rearmament at once entered into alliance with the princes, and thus were quite unreliable as officers of the government. Both the generals and the princes entered into agreements with the frontier peoples to assure their aid in the struggle for power. The most popular of these auxiliaries were the Hsien-pi, who were fighting for one of the princes whose territory lay in the east. Since the Toba were the natural enemies of the Hsien-pi, who were continually contesting their hold on their territory, the Toba were always on the opposite side to that supported by the Hsien-pi, so that they now supported generals who were ostensibly loyal to the government. The Huns, too, negotiated with several generals and princes and received tempting offers. Above all, all the frontier peoples were now militarily well equipped, continually receiving new war material from the Chinese who from time to time were co-operating with them.

In A.D. 300 Prince Lun assassinated the empress Chia and removed her group. In 301 he made himself emperor, but in the same year he was killed by the prince of Ch'i. This prince was killed in 302 by the prince of Ch'ang-sha, who in turn was killed in 303 by the prince of Tung-hai. The prince of Ho-chien rose in 302 and was killed in 306; the prince of Ch'engtu rose in 303, conquered the capital in 305, and then, in 306, was himself removed. I mention all these names and dates only to show the disunion within the ruling groups.

4 Migration of Chinese

All these struggles raged round the capital, for each of the princes wanted to secure full power and to become emperor. Thus the border regions remained relatively undisturbed. Their population suffered much less from the warfare than the unfortunate people in the neighbourhood of the central government. For this reason there took place a mass migration of Chinese from the centre of the empire to its periphery. This process, together with the shifting of the frontier peoples, is one of the most important events of that epoch. A great number of Chinese migrated especially into the present province of Kansu, where a governor who had originally been sent there to fight the Hsien-pi had created a sort of paradise by his good administration and maintenance of peace. The territory ruled by this Chinese, first as governor and then in increasing independence, was surrounded by Hsien-pi, Tibetans, and other peoples, but thanks to the great immigration of Chinese and to its situation on the main caravan route to Sinkiang, it was able to hold its own, to expand, and to become prosperous.

Other groups of Chinese peasants migrated southward into the territories of the former state of Wu. A Chinese prince of the house of the Chin was ruling there, in the present Nanking. His purpose was to organize that territory, and then to intervene in the struggles of the other princes. We shall meet him again at the beginning of the Hun rule over north China in 317, as founder and emperor of the first south Chinese dynasty, which was at once involved in the usual internal and external struggles. For the moment, however, the southern region was relatively at peace, and was accordingly attracting settlers.

Finally, many Chinese migrated northward, into the territories of the frontier peoples, not only of the Hsien-pi but especially of the Huns. These alien peoples, although in the official Chinese view they were still barbarians, at least maintained peace in the territories they ruled, and they left in peace the peasants and craftsmen who came to them, even while their own armies were involved in fighting inside China. Not only peasants and craftsmen came to the north but more and more educated persons. Members of families of the gentry that had suffered from the fighting, people who had lost their influence in China, were welcomed by the Huns and appointed teachers and political advisers of the Hun nobility.

5 Victory of the Huns. The Hun Han dynasty
(later renamed the Earlier Chao dynasty)

With its self-confidence thus increased, the Hun council of nobles declared that in future the Huns should no longer fight now for one and now for another Chinese general or prince. They had promised loyalty to the Chinese emperor, but not to any prince. No one doubted that the Chinese emperor was a complete nonentity and no longer played any part in the struggle for power. It was evident that the murders would continue until one of the generals or princes overcame the rest and made himself emperor. Why should not the Huns have the same right? Why should not they join in this struggle for the Chinese imperial throne?

There were two arguments against this course, one of which was already out of date. The Chinese had for many centuries set down the Huns as uncultured barbarians; but the inferiority complex thus engendered in the Huns had virtually been overcome, because in the course of time their upper class had deliberately acquired a Chinese education and so ranked culturally with the Chinese. Thus the ruler

Liu Yüan, for example, had enjoyed a good Chinese education and was able to read all the classical texts. The second argument was provided by the rigid conceptions of legitimacy to which the Turkish-Hunnic aristocratic society adhered. The Huns asked themselves: 'Have we, as aliens, any right to become emperors and rulers in China, when we are not descended from an old Chinese family?' On this point Liu Yüan and his advisers found a good answer. They called Liu Yüan's dynasty the 'Han dynasty', and so linked it with the most famous of all the Chinese dynasties, pointing to the pact which their ancestor Mao Tun had concluded five hundred years earlier with the first emperor of the Han dynasty and which had described the two states as 'brethren'. They further recalled the fact that the rulers of the Huns were closely related to the Chinese ruling family, because Mao Tun and his successors had married Chinese princesses. Finally, Liu Yüan's Chinese family name, Liu, had also been the family name of the rulers of the Han dynasty. Accordingly the Han Lius came forward not as aliens but as the rightful successors in continuation of the Han dynasty, as legitimate heirs to the Chinese imperial throne on the strength of relationship and of treaties.

Thus the Hun Liu Yüan had no intention of restoring the old empire of Mao Tun, the empire of the nomads; he intended to become emperor of China, emperor of a country of farmers. In this lay the fundamental difference between the earlier Hun empire and this new one. The question whether the Huns should join in the struggle for the Chinese imperial throne was therefore decided among the Huns themselves in 304 in the affirmative, by the founding of the 'Hun Han dynasty'. All that remained was the practical question of how to hold out with their small army of 50,000 men if serious opposition should be offered to the 'barbarians'.

Meanwhile Liu Yüan provided himself with court ceremonial on the Chinese model, in a capital which, after several changes, was established at P'ing-ch'êng in southern Shansi. He attracted more and more of the Chinese gentry, who were glad to come to this still rather barbaric but well-organized court. In 309 the first attack was made on the Chinese capital, Loyang. Liu Yüan died in the following year, and in 311, under his successor Liu Ts'ung (310–318), the attack was renewed and Loyang fell. The Chin emperor, Huai Ti, was captured and kept a prisoner in P'ing-ch'êng until in 313 a conspiracy in his favour was brought to light in the Hun empire, and he and all his supporters were killed. Meanwhile the Chinese clique of the Chin dynasty had hastened to make a prince emperor in the second capital, Ch'ang-an (Min Ti, 313–316) while the princes' struggles for the throne continued. Nobody troubled about the fate of the unfortunate emperor in his capital. He received no reinforcements, so that he was helpless in face of the next attack of the Huns, and in 316 he was compelled to surrender like his predecessor. Now the Hun Han dynasty held both capitals, which meant virtually the whole of the western part of north China, and the so-called 'Western Chin dynasty' thus came to its end. Its princes and generals and many of its gentry became landless and homeless and had to flee into the south.

(C) THE ALIEN EMPIRES IN NORTH CHINA, DOWN TO THE TOBA (A.D. 317–385)

1 *The Later Chao dynasty in eastern north China (Hun; 329–352)* At this time the eastern part of north China was entirely in the hands of Shih Lo, a former follower of Liu Yüan Shih Lo had escaped from slavery in China and had risen to be a military leader among de-tribalized Huns. In 310 he had not only undertaken a great campaign right across China to the south, but had slaughtered more than 100,000 Chinese, including forty-eight princes of the Chin dynasty, who had formed a vast burial procession for a prince. This achieve-ment added considerably to Shih Lo's power, and his relations with Liu Ts'ung, already tense, became still more so. Liu Yüan had tried to organize the Hun state on the Chinese model, intending in this way to gain efficient control of China; Shih Lo rejected Chinese methods, and held to the old warrior-nomad tradition, making raids with the aid of nomad fighters. He did not contemplate holding the territories of central and southern China which he had conquered; he withdrew, and in the two years 314–315 he contented himself with bringing considerable expanses in north-eastern China, especially territories of the Hsien-pi, under his direct rule, as a base for further raids. Many Huns in Liu Ts'ung's dominion found Shih Lo's method of rule more to their taste than living in a state ruled by officials, and they went over to Shih Lo and joined him in breaking entirely with Liu Ts'ung. There was a further motive for this: in states founded by nomads, with a federation of tribes as their basis, the personal qualities of the ruler played an important part. The chiefs of the various tribes would not give unqualified allegiance to the son of a dead ruler unless the son was a strong personality or gave promise of becoming one. Failing that, there would be independence move-ments. Liu Ts'ung did not possess the indisputable charisma of his predecessor Liu Yüan; and the Huns looked with contempt on his court splendour, which could only have been justified if he had con-quered all China. Liu Ts'ung had no such ambition; nor had his successor Liu Yao (319–329), who gave the Hun Han dynasty retro-actively, from its start with Liu Yüan, the new name of 'Earlier Chao

dynasty' (304–320). Many tribes then went over to Shih Lo, and the remainder of Liu Yao's empire was reduced to a precarious existence. In 329 the whole of it was annexed by Shih Lo.

Although Shih Lo had long been much more powerful than the emperors of the 'Earlier Chao dynasty', until their removal he had not ventured to assume the title of emperor. The reason for this seems to have lain in the conceptions of nobility held by the Turkish peoples in general and the Huns in particular, according to which only those could become *shan-yü* (or, later, emperor) who could show descent from the Tu-ku tribe, the rightful *shan-yü* stock. In accordance with this conception, all later Hun dynasties deliberately disowned Shih Lo. For Shih Lo, after his destruction of Liu Yao, no longer hesitated: ex-slave as he was, and descended from one of the non-noble stocks of the Huns, he made himself emperor of the 'Later Chao dynasty' (329–352).

Shih Lo was a forceful army commander, but he was a man without statesmanship, and without the culture of his day. He had no Chinese education; he hated the Chinese and would have been glad to make north China a grazing ground for his nomad tribes of Huns. Accordingly he had no desire to rule all China. The part already subjugated, embracing the whole of north China with the exception of the present province of Kansu, sufficed for his purpose.

The governor of that province was a loyal subject of the Chinese Chin dynasty, a man famous for his good administration, and himself a Chinese. After the execution of the Chin emperor Huai Ti by the Huns in 313, he regarded himself as no longer bound to the central government; he made himself independent and founded the 'Earlier Liang dynasty', which was to last until 376. This mainly Chinese realm was not very large, although it had admitted a broad stream of Chinese emigrants from the dissolving Chin empire; but economically the Liang realm was very prosperous, so that it was able to extend its influence as far as Central Asia. During the earlier struggles Central Asia had been virtually in isolation, but now new contacts began to be established. Many traders from Central Asia set up branches in Liang. In the capital there were whole quarters inhabited only by aliens from western and eastern Central Asia and from India. With the traders came Buddhist monks; trade and Buddhism seemed to be closely associated everywhere. In the trading centres monasteries were installed in the form of blocks of houses within strong walls that successfully resisted many an attack. Consequently the Buddhists were able to serve as bankers for the merchants, who deposited their money in the monasteries, which made a charge for its custody; the merchants also warehoused their goods in the monasteries. Sometimes the process was reversed, a trade centre being formed around an existing monastery. In this case the monastery also served as a hostel for the merchants. Economically this Chinese state in Kansu was much more like a Sinkiang city state that lived by commerce than the agrarian states of the Far East, although agriculture was also pursued under the Earlier Liang.

From this trip to the remote west we will return first to the Hun capital. From 329 onward Shih Lo possessed a wide empire, but an unstable one. He himself felt at all times insecure, because the Huns regarded him, on account of his humble origin, as a 'revolutionary'. He exterminated every member of the Liu family, that is to say the old *shan-yü* family, of whom he could get hold, in order to remove any possible pretender to the throne; but he could not count on the loyalty of the Hun and other Turkish tribes under his rule. During this period not a few Huns went over to the small realm of the Toba; other Hun tribes withdrew entirely from the political scene and lived with their herds as nomad tribes in Shansi and in the Ordos region. The general insecurity undermined the strength of Shih Lo's empire. He died in 333, and there came to the throne, after a short interregnum, another personality of a certain greatness, Shih Hu (334–349). He transferred the capital to the city of Yeh, in northern Honan, where the rulers of the Wei dynasty had reigned. There are many accounts of the magnificence of the court of Yeh. Foreigners, especially Buddhist monks, played a greater part there than Chinese. On the one hand, it was not easy for Shih Hu to gain the active support of the educated Chinese gentry after the murders of Shih Lo and, on the other hand, Shih Hu seems to have understood that foreigners without family and without other relations to the native population, but with special skills, are the most reliable and loyal servants of a ruler. Indeed, his administration seems to have been good, but the regime remained completely parasitic, with no support of the masses or the gentry. After Shih Hu's death there were fearful combats between his sons; ultimately a member of an entirely different family of Hun origin seized power, but was destroyed in 352 by the Hsien-pi, bringing to an end the Later Chao dynasty.

2 *Earlier Yen dynasty in the north-east (proto-Mongol; 352–370),*
and the Earlier Ch'in dynasty in all north China (Tibetan; 351–394)
In the north, proto-Mongol Hsien-pi tribes had again made themselves independent; in the past they had been subjects of Liu Yüan and then of Shih Lo. A man belonging to one of these tribes, the tribe of the Mu-jung, became the leader of a league of tribes, and in 337 founded the state of Yen. This proto-Mongol state of the Mu-jung, which the historians call the 'Earlier Yen' state, conquered parts of southern Manchuria and also the state of Kao-li in Korea,

and there began then an immigration of Hsien-pi into Korea, which became noticeable at a later date. The conquest of Korea, which was still, as in the past, a Japanese market and was very wealthy, enormously strengthened the state of Yen. Not until a little later, when Japan's trade relations were diverted to central China, did Korea's importance begin to diminish. Although this 'Earlier Yen dynasty' of the Mu-jung officially entered on the heritage of the Huns, and its regime was therefore dated only from 352 (until 370), it failed either to subjugate the whole realm of the 'Later Chao' or effectively to strengthen the state it had acquired. This old Hun territory had suffered economically from the anti-agrarian nomad tendency of the last of the Hun emperors; and unremunerative wars against the Chinese in the south had done nothing to improve its position. In addition to this, the realm of the Toba was dangerously gaining strength on the flank of the new empire. But the most dangerous enemy was in the west, on former Hun soil, in the province of Shensi —Tibetans, who finally came forward once more with claims to dominance. These were Tibetans of the P'u family, which later changed its name to Fu. The head of the family had worked his way up as a leader of Tibetan auxiliaries under the 'Later Chao', gaining more and more power and following. When under that dynasty the death of Shih Hu marked the beginning of general dissolution, he gathered his Tibetans around him in the west, declared himself independent of the Huns, and made himself emperor of the 'Earlier Ch'in dynasty' (351–394). He died in 355, and was followed after a short interregnum by Fu Chien (357–385), who was unquestionably one of the most important figures of the fourth century. This Tibetan empire ultimately defeated the 'Earlier Yen dynasty' and annexed the realm of the Mu-jung. Thus the Mu-jung Hsien-pi came under the dominion of the Tibetans; they were distributed among a number of places as garrisons or mounted troops.

The empire of the Tibetans was organized quite differently from the empires of the Huns and the Hsien-pi tribes. The Tibetan organization was purely military and had nothing to do with tribal structure. This had its advantages, for the leader of such a formation had no need to take account of tribal chieftains; he was answerable to no one and possessed considerable personal power. Nor was there any need for him to be of noble rank or descended from an old family. The Tibetan ruler Fu Chien organized all his troops, including the non-Tibetans, on this system, without regard to tribal membership.

Fu Chien's state showed another innovation: the armies of the Huns and the Hsien-pi had consisted entirely of cavalry, for the nomads of the north were, of course, horsemen; to fight on foot was in their eyes not only contrary to custom but contemptible. So long as a state consisted only of a league of tribes, it was simply out of the question to transform part of the army into infantry. Fu Chien, however, with his military organization that paid no attention to the tribal element, created an infantry in addition to the great cavalry units, recruiting for it large numbers of Chinese. The infantry proved extremely valuable, especially in the fighting in the plains of north China and in laying siege to fortified towns. Fu Chien thus very quickly achieved military predominance over the neighbouring states. As we have seen already, he annexed the 'Earlier Yen' realm of the proto-Mongols (370), but he also annihilated the Chinese 'Earlier Liang' realm (376) and in the same year the small Turkish Toba realm. This made him supreme over all north China and stronger than any alien ruler before him. He had in his possession both the ancient capitals, Ch'ang-an and Loyang; the whole of the rich agricultural regions of north China belonged to him; he also controlled the routes to Sinkiang. He himself had had a Chinese education, and he attracted Chinese to his court; he protected the Buddhists; and he tried in every way to make the whole country culturally Chinese. As soon as Fu Chien had all north China in his power, as Liu Yüan and his Huns had done before him, he resolved, like Liu Yüan, to make every effort to gain the mastery over all China, to become emperor of China. Liu Yüan's successors had not had the capacity for which such a venture called; Fu Chien was to fail in it for other reasons. Yet, from a military point of view, his chances were not bad. He had far more soldiers under his command than the Chinese 'Eastern Chin dynasty' which ruled the south, and his troops were undoubtedly better. In the time of the founder of the Tibetan dynasty, the southern empire had been utterly defeated by his troops (354), and the south Chinese were no stronger now.

Against them the north had these assets: the possession of the best northern tillage, the control of the trade routes, and 'Chinese' culture and administration. At the time, however, these represented only potentialities and not tangible realities. It would have taken ten to twenty years to restore the capacities of the north after its devastation in many wars, to reorganize commerce, and to set up a really reliable administration, and thus to interlock the various elements and consolidate the various tribes. But as early as 383 Fu Chien started his great campaign against the south, with an army of something like a million men. At first the advance went well. The horsemen from the north, however, were men of the mountain country, and in the soggy plains of the Yangtze region, cut up by hundreds of water-courses and canals, they suffered from climatic and natural conditions to which they were unaccustomed. Their main strength

129

was still in cavalry; and they came to grief. The supplies and reinforcements for the vast army failed to arrive in time; units did not reach the appointed places at the appointed dates. The southern troops under the supreme command of Hsieh Hsüan, far inferior in numbers and militarily of no great efficiency, made surprise attacks on isolated units before these were in regular formation. Some they defeated, others they bribed; they spread false reports. Fu Chien's army was seized with widespread panic, so that he was compelled to retreat in haste. As he did so it became evident that his empire had no inner stability: in a very short time it fell into fragments. The south Chinese had played no direct part in this, for in spite of their victory they were not strong enough to advance far to the north.

3 The fragmentation of north China

The first to fall away from the Tibetan ruler was a noble of the Mu-jung, a member of the ruling family of the 'Earlier Yen dynasty', who withdrew during the actual fighting to pursue a policy of his own. With the vestiges of the Hsien-pi who followed him, mostly cavalry, he fought his way northwards into the old homeland of the Hsien-pi and there, in central Hopei, founded the 'Later Yen dynasty' (384–409), himself reigning for twelve years. In the remaining thirteen years of the existence of that dynasty there were no fewer than five rulers, the last of them a member of another family. The history of this Hsien-pi dynasty, as of its predecessor, is an unedifying succession of intrigues; no serious effort was made to build up a true state.

In the same year 384 there was founded, under several other Mu-jung princes of the ruling family of the 'Earlier Yen dynasty', the 'Western Yen dynasty' (384–394). Its nucleus was nothing more than a detachment of troops of the Hsien-pi which had been thrown by Fu Chien into the west of his empire, in Shensi, in the neighbourhood of the old capital Ch'ang-an. There its commanders, on learning the news of Fu Chien's collapse, declared their independence. In western China, however, far removed from all liaison with the main body of the Hsien-pi, they were unable to establish themselves, and when they tried to fight their way to the north-east they were dispersed, so that they failed entirely to form an actual state.

There was a third attempt in 384 to form a state in north China. A Tibetan who had joined Fu Chien with his followers declared himself independent when Fu Chien came back, a beaten man, to Shensi. He caused Fu Chien and almost the whole of his family to be assassinated, occupied the capital, Ch'ang-an, and actually entered into the heritage of Fu Chien. This Tibetan dynasty is known as the 'Later Ch'in dynasty' (384–417). It was certainly the strongest of those founded in 384, but it still failed to dominate any considerable part of China and remained of local importance, mainly confined to the present province of Shensi. Fu Chien's empire nominally had three further rulers, but they did not exert the slightest influence on events.

With the collapse of the state founded by Fu Chien, the tribes of Hsien-pi who had left their homeland in the third century and migrated to the Ordos region proceeded to form their own state: a man of the Hsien-pi tribe of the Ch'i-fu founded the so-called 'Western Ch'in dynasty' (385–431). Like the other Hsien-pi states, this one was of weak construction, resting on the military strength of a few tribes and failing to attain a really secure basis. Its territory lay in the east of the present province of Kansu, and so controlled the eastern end of the western Asian caravan route, which might have been a source of wealth if the Ch'i-fu had succeeded in attracting commerce by discreet treatment and in imposing taxation on it. Instead of this the bulk of the long-distance traffic passed through the Ordos region, a little farther north, avoiding the Ch'i-fu state, which seemed to the merchants to be too insecure. The Ch'i-fu depended mainly on cattle-breeding in the remote mountain country in the south of their territory, a region that gave them relative security from attack; on the other hand, this made them unable to exercise any influence on the course of political events in western China.

Mention must be made of one more state that rose from the ruins of Fu Chien's empire. It lay in the far west of China, in the western part of the present province of Kansu, and was really a continuation of the Chinese 'Earlier Liang' realm, which had been annexed ten years earlier (376) by Fu Chien. A year before his great march to the south, Fu Chien had sent the Tibetan Lü Kuang into the 'Earlier Liang' region in order to gain influence over Sinkiang. As mentioned previously, after the great Hun rulers Fu Chien was the first to make a deliberate attempt to secure cultural and political overlordship over the whole of China. Although himself a Tibetan, he never succumbed to the temptation of pursuing a 'Tibetan' policy; like an entirely legitimate ruler of China, he was concerned to prevent the northern peoples along the frontier from uniting with the Tibetan peoples of the west for political ends. The possession of Sinkiang would avert that danger, which had shown signs of becoming imminent of late: some tribes of the Hsien-pi had migrated as far as the high mountains of Tibet and had imposed themselves as a ruling class on the still very primitive Tibetans living there. From this symbiosis there began to be formed a new people, the so-called T'u-yü-hun, a hybridization of Mongol and Tibetan stock with a slight Turkish admixture. Lü Kuang had had success in Sinkiang; he had brought

131

considerable portions of eastern Sinkiang under Fu Chien's sovereignty and administered those regions almost independently. When the news came of Fu Chien's end, he declared himself an independent ruler, of the 'Later Liang' dynasty (386–403). Strictly speaking, this was simply a trading State, like the city-states of Central Asia: its basis was the transit traffic that brought it prosperity. For commerce brought good profit to the small states that lay right across the caravan route, whereas it was of doubtful benefit, as we know, to agrarian China as a whole, because the luxury goods which it supplied to the court were paid for out of the production of the general population.

This 'Later Liang' realm was inhabited not only by a few Tibetans and many Chinese, but also by Hsien-pi and Huns. These heterogeneous elements with their divergent cultures failed in the long run to hold together in this long but extremely narrow strip of territory, which was almost incapable of military defence. As early as 397 a group of Huns in the central section of the country made themselves independent, assuming the name of the 'Northern Liang' (397–439). These Huns quickly conquered other parts of the 'Later Liang' realm, which then fell entirely to pieces. Chinese again founded a state, 'West Liang' (400–421) in western Kansu, and the Hsien-pi founded 'South Liang' (379–414) in eastern Kansu. Thus the 'Later Liang' fell into three parts, more or less differing ethnically, though they could not be described as ethnically unadulterated states.

4 Sociological analysis of the two great alien empires

The two great empires of north China at the time of its division had been founded by non-Chinese—the first by the Hun Liu Yüan, the second by the Tibetan Fu Chien. Both rulers went to work on the same principle of trying to build up truly 'Chinese' empires, but the traditions of Huns and Tibetans differed, and the two experiments turned out differently. Both failed, but not for the same reasons and not with the same results. The Hun Liu Yüan was the ruler of a league of feudal tribes, which was expected to take its place as an upper class above the unchanged Chinese agricultural population with its system of officials and gentry. But Liu Yüan's successors were national reactionaries who stood for the maintenance of the nomad life against that new plan of transition to a feudal class of urban nobles ruling an agrarian population. Liu Yüan's more far-seeing policy was abandoned, with the result that the Huns were no longer in a position to rule an immense agrarian territory, and the empire soon disintegrated. For the various Hun tribes this failure meant falling back into political insignificance, but they were able to maintain their national character and existence.

Fu Chien, as a Tibetan, was a militarist and soldier, in accordance with the past of the Tibetans. Under him were grouped Tibetans without tribal chieftains; the great mass of Chinese; and dispersed remnants of tribes of Huns, Hsien-pi, and others. His organization was militaristic and, outside the military sphere, a militaristic bureaucracy. The Chinese gentry, so far as they still existed, preferred to work with him rather than with the feudalist Huns. These gentry probably supported Fu Chien's southern campaign, for, in consequence of the wide ramifications of their families, it was to their interest that China should form a single economic unit. They were, of course, equally ready to work with another group, one of southern Chinese, to attain the same end by other means, if those means should prove more advantageous: thus the gentry were not a reliable asset, but were always ready to break faith. Among other things, Fu Chien's southern campaign was wrecked by that faithlessness. When an essentially military state suffers military defeat, it can only go to pieces. This explains the disintegration of that great empire within a single year into so many diminutive states, as already described.

5 *Sociological analysis of the petty states*

The states that took the place of Fu Chien's empire, those many diminutive states (the Chinese speak of the period of the Sixteen Kingdoms), may be divided from the economic point of view into two groups—trading states and warrior states; sociologically they also fall into two groups, tribal states and military states.

The small states in the west, in Kansu (the Later Liang and the Western, Northern, and Southern Liang), were trading states: they lived on the earnings of transit trade with Sinkiang. The eastern states were warrior states, in which an army commander ruled by means of an armed group of non-Chinese and exploited an agricultural population. It is only logical that such states should be short-lived, as in fact they all were.

Sociologically regarded, during this period only the Southern and Northern Liang were still tribal states. In addition to these came the young Toba realm, which began in 385 but of which mention has not yet been made. The basis of that state was the tribe, not the family or the individual; after its political disintegration the separate tribes remained in existence. The other states of the east, however, were military states, made up of individuals with no tribal allegiance but subject to a military commandant. But where there is no tribal association, after the political downfall of a state founded by ethnic groups, those groups sooner or later disappear as such. We see this in the years immediately following Fu Chien's collapse: the

Tibetan ethnic group to which he himself belonged disappeared entirely from the historical scene. The two Tibetan groups that outlasted him, also forming military states and not tribal states, similarly came to an end shortly afterwards for all time. The Hsien-pi groups in the various fragments of the empire, with the exception of the petty states in Kansu, also continued only as tribal fragments led by a few old ruling families. They, too, after brief and undistinguished military rule, came to an end; they disappeared so completely that thereafter we no longer find the term Hsien-pi in history. Not that they had been exterminated. When the social structure and its corresponding economic form fall to pieces, there remain only two alternatives for its individuals. Either they must go over to a new form, which in China could only mean that they became Chinese; many Hsien-pi in this way became Chinese in the decades following 384. Or, could retain their old way of living in association with another stock of similar formation; this, too, happened in many cases. Both these courses, however, meant the end of the Hsien-pi as an independent ethnic unit. We must keep this process and its reasons in view if we are to understand how a great people can disappear once and for all.

The Huns, too, so powerful in the past, were suddenly scarcely to be found any longer. Among the many petty states there were many Hsien-pi kingdoms, but only a single, quite small Hun state, that of the Northern Liang. The disappearance of the Huns was, however, only apparent; at this time they remained in the Ordos region and in Shansi as separate nomad tribes with no integrating political organization; their time had still to come.

6 Culture and religion

According to the prevalent Chinese view, nothing of importance was achieved during this period in north China in the intellectual sphere; there was no culture in the north, only in the south. This is natural: for a Confucian this period, the fourth century, was one of degeneracy in north China, for no one came into prominence as a celebrated Confucian. Nothing else could be expected, for in the north the gentry, which had been the class that maintained Confucianism since the Han period, had largely been destroyed; from political leadership especially it had been shut out during the periods of alien rule. Nor could we expect to find Taoists in the true sense, that is to say followers of the teaching of Lao Tzŭ, for these, too, had been dependent since the Han period on the gentry. Until the fourth century, these too had remained the dominant philosophies.

What could take their place? The alien rulers had left little behind them. Most of them had been unable to write Chinese, and in so far

134

as they were warriors they had no interest in literature or in political philosophy, for they were men of action. As far as we know, none of these foreigners as yet had developed a script of their own. We have, naturally, also to keep in mind that what has been written about the culture of the northern foreigners, was written by basically hostile Chinese for whom the tribal rulers, even if they lived in a luxury prepared for them by their Chinese employees and slaves, remained 'barbarians'. Few songs and poems of theirs remain extant in translations from their language into Chinese, but these preserve a strong alien flavour in their mental attitude and in their diction. They are the songs of fighting men, songs that were sung on horseback, songs of war and its sufferings. These songs have nothing of the excessive formalism and aestheticism of the Chinese, but give expression to simple emotions in unpolished language with a direct appeal. The epic of the Turkish peoples had clearly been developed already, but Chinese sources do not mention it. We find songs which we call 'ballads'. We have many early ballads which are clearly Chinese, but should assume that the tribal rulers, too, had ballads of their own. With very few exceptions, Chinese scholars found ballads 'vulgar' and did not write them down for us. Even today, there are still in all parts of China traditional ballads, often written down in local dialect, yet just as with genuine folk songs, nobody—except a small group of Chinese and foreign folklorists—seems to be interested in them.

The actual literature, however, and the philosophy of this period are Buddhist. How can we explain that Buddhism had gained such influence? If we look into the Buddhist canon as it exists now, compiled many centuries after our period, we see many elements of Buddhism which Chinese must have detested. A real Buddhist is a monk, and a monk must 'leave the family' and live in the artificial family of his monastery. To leave one's family is still one of the most serious breaches of filial piety, China's highest ethical ideal to this century. A real Buddhist must give up sex, and Buddhist texts designed for the layman, describe sexual life in most disgusting terms. For Chinese, sex life was a natural part of life, necessary in order to preserve the family. When a Chinese saw a statue of Buddha, modelled after Indian standards of beauty, laid down in Buddhist texts, they found the figure extremely ugly and strange; they abhorred Buddha's dress which, leaving one shoulder open, was regarded as immodest. Numerous Buddhist texts and sects, spreading in these and the following centuries, preached that our world is irreal, the result of our imaginations, an idea which for the down-to-earth Chinese has remained strange to this day. Finally, the idea of sin and punishment was strange. But it had some attraction to the lower classes.

135

This doctrine was in a certain sense revolutionary: it declared that all the high officials and superiors who treated the people so unjustly and who so exploited them, would in their next reincarnation be born in poor circumstances or into inferior rank and would have to suffer punishment for all their ill deeds. The poor who had to suffer undeserved evils would be born in their next life into high rank and would have a good time. This doctrine brought a ray of light, a promise, to the country people who had suffered so much since the later Han period of the second century A.D. Of course, the doctrine was also utilized by the élite: people who are poor are suffering the just punishment for sins committed in a prior existence.

But Buddhism still had other attractions for the unsophisticated 'common man'. Chinese ancestral worship had no way to take care of people who died without children, who died far away from their home, of children or daughters who died before maturity or marriage. These beings could change into demons and become a menace to the people. Buddhists, many of whom in the first centuries were foreigners, were a different breed, they lived in a pseudo-family and thus, could take others into their houses, errant souls. They would provide masses for them and pacify them. They were also outside the Chinese circle of purity and pollution, so they could handle the dead, the corpses. Thus, to the present time, Buddhism has functioned as an institution which filled a hole in Chinese beliefs and rituals of the lower classes. These men and women knew very little of philosophical Buddhism, or even of ordinary texts. To the present time, only a few sections of some texts are generally known and recited. Ritual is more important than the word.

The merchants made use of the Buddhist monasteries as banks and warehouses. Thus they, too, were well inclined towards Buddhism and gave money and land for its temples. The temples were able to settle peasants on this land as their tenants. In those times a temple was a more reliable landlord than an individual alien, and the poorer peasants readily became temple tenants; this increased their inclination towards Buddhism.

The Indian, Sogdian, and Sinkiang monks were readily allowed to settle by the alien rulers of China, who had no national prejudice against other aliens. The monks were educated men and brought some useful knowledge from abroad. Educated Chinese were scarcely to be found, for the gentry retired to their estates, which they protected as well as they could from their alien ruler. So long as the gentry had no prospect of regaining control of the threads of political life that extended throughout China, they were not prepared to provide a class of officials and scholars for the anti-Confucian foreigners, who showed interest only in fighting and trading. Thus educated persons were needed at the courts of the alien rulers, and Buddhists were therefore engaged. These foreign Buddhists had all the important Buddhist writings translated into Chinese, and so made use of their influence at court for religious propaganda.

Big translation bureaux were set up for the preparation of these translations into Chinese, in which many copyists simultaneously took down from dictation a translation made by a 'master' with the aid of a few native helpers. The translations were not literal but were paraphrases, most of them greatly reduced in length, glosses were introduced when the translator thought fit for political or doctrinal reasons, or when he thought that in this way he could better adapt the texts to Chinese feeling.

This does not mean that every text was translated from Indian languages; especially in the later period many works appeared which came not from India but from Sogdia or Sinkiang, or had even been written in China by Sogdians or other natives of Sinkiang, and were then translated into Chinese. In Sinkiang, Khotan in particular became a centre of Buddhist culture. Buddhism was influenced by vestiges of indigenous cults, so that Khotan developed a special religious atmosphere of its own; deities were honoured there (for instance, the king of Heaven of the northerners) to whom little regard was paid elsewhere. This 'Khotan Buddhism' had special influence on the Buddhist Turkish peoples.

Buddhism, quite apart from the special case of 'Khotan Buddhism', underwent extensive modification on its way across Central Asia. Its main Indian form (Hinayana) was a purely individualistic religion of salvation without a God—related in this respect to genuine Taoism —and based on a concept of two classes of people: the monks who could achieve salvation and, second, the masses who fed the monks but could not achieve salvation. This religion did not gain a footing in China; only traces of it can be found in some Buddhistic sects in China. Mahayana Buddhism, on the other hand, developed into a true popular religion of salvation. It did not interfere with the indigenous deities and did not discountenance life in human society; it did not recommend Nirvana at once, but placed before it a hereafter with all the joys worth striving for. In this form Buddhism was certain of success in Asia. On its way from India to China it divided into countless separate streams, each characterized by a particular book. We commonly speak of Buddhist 'sects' which is a wrong term. There are philosophical differences between Buddhist sects in China, but the important point is that each Master teaches 'his' text to his disciples; when a priest is asked about his qualifications, he will give the name of his Master and his Master's Masters and transmit this wisdom, this book, to an endless chain of Masters. He would not regard a school which reads a different book with a different philosophy as 'heretic'.

The Chinese state cult, the cult of Heaven saturated with Confucianism, was another living form of religion. The alien rulers, in turn, had brought their own mixture of worship of Heaven and shamanism. Their worship of Heaven was their official 'representative' religion; their shamanism the private religion of the individual in his daily life. The alien rulers, accordingly, showed interest in the Chinese shamans as well as in shamanistic aspects of Mahayana Buddhism.

Here was an area of conflict. The folk religion which we have mentioned in an earlier chapter also contained many elements which we would call shamanistic. The folk priests resented the competition of Buddhist priests who also could work miracles. Moreover, the Buddhists, when they had to translate strange Indian terms into Chinese, had extensively used Taoist terminology, so that in the eyes of the less sophisticated, both religions were similar. The foreign rulers have often exploited this antagonism: they called in priests of both religions and let them compete in the production of miracles or simply in scholarly discussions. Some of these discussions (contained in the 'Hung-ming-chi') belong to the most fascinating pieces of early Chinese literature, such as for instance the discussion as to whether a soul exists or not. We can compare such courtly 'diversions' with similar disputes arranged by rulers in India and the West, and in all these cases, the defeated party could lose more than just an argument.

(D) THE TOBA EMPIRE IN NORTH CHINA (A.D. 385–550)

1   *The rise of the Toba state*

On the collapse of Fu Chien's empire one more state made its appearance; it has not yet been dealt with, although it was the most important one. This was the empire of the Toba, in the north of the present province of Shansi. Fu Chien had brought down the small old Toba state in 376, but had not entirely destroyed it. Its territory was partitioned, and part was placed under the administration of a Hun: in view of the old rivalry between Toba and Huns, this seemed to Fu Chien to be the best way of preventing any revival of the Toba. However, a descendant of the old ruling family of the Toba succeeded, with the aid of related families, in regaining power and forming a small new kingdom. Very soon many tribes which still lived in north China and which had not been broken up into military units, joined him. Of these there were ultimately 119, including many Hun tribes from Shansi and also many Hsien-pi tribes.

Thus the question who the Toba were is not easy to answer. The leading tribe itself had migrated southward in the third century from the frontier territory between northern Mongolia and northern Manchuria. After this migration the first Toba state, the so-called Tai state, was formed (338–376); not much is known about it. The tribes that, from 385 after the break-up of the Tibetan empire, grouped themselves round this ruling tribe, were both Turkish and Mongol; but from the culture and language of the Toba we think that the Turkish element seems to have been stronger than the Mongolian.

Thus the new Toba kingdom was a tribal state, not a military state. But the tribes were no longer the same as in the time of Liu Yüan a hundred years earlier. Their total population must have been quite small; we must assume that they were but the remains of 119 tribes rather than 119 full-sized tribes. Only part of them were still living the old nomad life; others had become used to living alongside Chinese peasants and had assumed leadership among the peasants. These Toba now faced a difficult situation. The country was arid and mountainous and did not yield much agricultural produce. For the many people who had come into the Toba state from all parts of the former empire of Fu Chien, to say nothing of the needs of a capital and a court which since the time of Liu Yüan had been regarded as the indispensable entourage of a ruler who claimed imperial rank, the local production of the Chinese peasants was not enough. All the government officials, who were Chinese, and all the slaves and eunuchs needed grain to eat. Attempts were made to settle more Chinese peasants round the new capital, but without success; something had to be done. It appeared necessary to embark on a campaign to conquer the fertile plain of eastern China. In the course of a number of battles the Hsien-pi of the 'Later Yen' were annihilated and eastern China conquered (409).

Now a new question arose: what should be done with all those people? Nomads used to enslave their prisoners and use them for watching their flocks. Some tribal chieftains had adopted the practice of establishing captives on their tribal territory as peasants. There was an opportunity now to subject the millions of Chinese captives to servitude to the various tribal chieftains in the usual way. But those captives who were peasants could not be taken away from their fields without robbing the country of its food; therefore it would have been necessary to spread the tribes over the whole of eastern China, and this would have added immensely to the strength of the various tribes and would have greatly weakened the central power. Furthermore almost all Chinese officials at the court had come originally from the territories just conquered. They had come from there about a hundred years earlier and still had all their relatives in the east. If the eastern territories had been placed under the rule of separate tribes, and the tribes had been distributed in this way, the gentry in those territories would have been destroyed and reduced to the position of enslaved peasants. The Chinese officials accordingly persuaded the Toba emperor not to place the new territories under the tribes, but to leave them to be administered by officials of the central administration. These officials must have a firm footing in their territory, for only they could extract from the peasants the grain required for the support of the capital. Consequently the Toba government did not enslave the Chinese in the eastern territory, but made the local gentry into government officials, instructing them to collect as much grain as possible for the capital. This Chinese local gentry worked in close collaboration with the Chinese officials at court, a fact which determined the whole fate of the Toba empire.

The Hsien-pi of the newly conquered east no longer belonged to any tribe, but only to military units. They were transferred as soldiers to the Toba court and placed directly under the government, which was thus notably strengthened, especially as the millions of peasants under their Chinese officials were also directly responsible to the central administration. The government now proceeded to convert also its own Toba tribes into military formations. The tribal men of noble rank were brought to the court as military officers, and so were separated from the common tribesmen and the slaves who had to remain with the herds. This change, which robbed the tribes of all means of independent action, was not carried out without bloodshed. There were revolts of tribal chieftains which were ruthlessly suppressed. The central government had triumphed, but it realized that more reliance could be placed on Chinese than on its own people, who were used to independence. Thus the Toba were glad to employ more and more Chinese, and the Chinese pressed more and more into the administration. In this process the differing social organizations of Toba and Chinese played an important part. The Chinese have patriarchal families with often hundreds of members. When a member of a family obtains a good position, he is obliged to make provision for the other members of his family and to secure good positions for them too; and not only the members of his own family but those of allied families and of families related to it by marriage. In contrast the Toba had a patriarchal nuclear family system; as nomad warriors with no fixed abode, they were unable to form extended family groups. Among them the individual was much more independent; each one tried to do his best for himself. No Toba thought of collecting a large clique around himself; everybody should be the artificer of his own fortune. Thus, when a Chinese obtained an

8 Detail from the Buddhist cave-reliefs of Lung-men.
(From a rubbing in the author's possession.)

9 Statue of Mi-lo (Maitreya, the next future Buddha), in the 'Great Buddha Temple' at Chengting (Hopei).

(Photo H. Hammer-Morrisson.)

official post, he was followed by countless others; but when a Toba had a position he remained alone, and so the sinification of the Toba empire went on incessantly.

2 The Hun kingdom of the Hsia (407–431)

At the rebuilding of the Toba empire, however, a good many Hun tribes withdrew westward into the Ordos region beyond the reach of the Toba, and there they formed the Hun 'Hsia' kingdom. Its ruler, Ho-lien P'o-p'o, belonged to the family of Mao Tun and originally, like Liu Yüan, bore the sinified family name Liu; but he altered this to a Hun name, taking the family name of Ho-lien. This one fact alone demonstrates that the Hsia rejected Chinese culture and were nationalistic Hun. Thus there were now two realms in north China, one undergoing progressive sinification, the other falling back to the old traditions of the Huns.

3 Rise of the Toba to a great power

The present province of Szechwan, in the west, had belonged to Fu Chien's empire. At the break-up of the Tibetan state, that province passed to the southern Chinese empire and gave the southern Chinese access, though it was very difficult access, to the caravan route leading to Central Asia. The small states in Kansu, which dominated the route, now passed on the traffic along two routes, one northward to the Toba and the other alien states in north China, the other through north-west Szechwan to south China. In this way the Kansu states were strengthened both economically and politically, for they were able to direct the commerce either to the northern states or to south China as suited them. When the south Chinese saw the break-up of Fu Chien's empire into numberless fragments, Liu Yü, who was then all-powerful at the south Chinese court, made an attempt to conquer the whole of western China. A great army was sent from south China into the province of Shensi, where the Tibetan empire of the 'Later Ch'in' was situated. The Ch'in appealed to the Toba for help, but the Toba were themselves too hotly engaged to be able to spare troops. They also considered that south China would be unable to maintain these conquests, and that they themselves would find them later an easy prey. Thus in 417 the state of 'Later Ch'in' received a mortal blow from the south Chinese army. Large numbers of the upper class fled to the Toba. As had been foreseen, the south Chinese were unable to maintain their hold over the conquered territory, and it was annexed with ease by the Hun Ho-lien P'o-p'o. But why not by the Toba?

Towards the end of the fourth century, vestiges of Hun, Hsien-pi, and other tribes had united in Mongolia to form the new people of

141

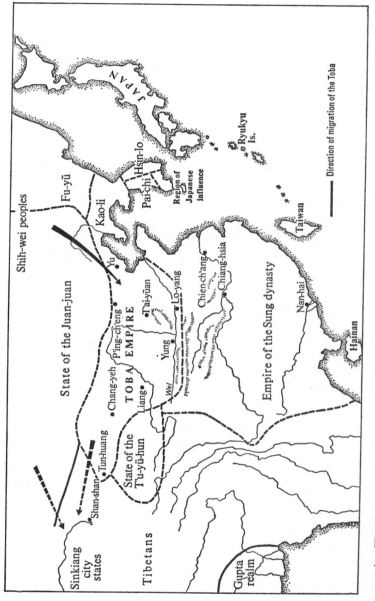

MAP 4   *The Toba empire (about A.D. 500)*

the Juan-juan (also called Ju-juan or Jou-jan). Scholars disagree as to whether the Juan-juan were Turks or Mongols; European investigators believe them to have been identical with the Avars who appeared in the Near East in 558 and later in Europe, and are inclined, on the strength of a few vestiges of their language, to regard them as Mongols. Investigations concerning the various tribes, however, show that among the Juan-juan there were both Mongol and Turkish tribes, and that the question cannot be decided in favour of either group. Some of the tribes belonging to the Juan-juan had formerly lived in China. Others had lived farther north or west and came into the history of the Far East now for the first time.

This Juan-juan people threatened the Toba in the rear, from the north. It made raids into the Toba empire for the same reasons for which the Huns in the past had raided agrarian China; for agriculture had made considerable progress in the Toba empire. Consequently, before the Toba could attempt to expand southward, the Juan-juan peril must be removed. This was done in the end, after a long series of hard and not always successful struggles. That was why the Toba had played no part in the fighting against south China, and had been unable to take immediate advantage of that fighting.

After 429 the Juan-juan peril no longer existed and in the years that followed the whole of the small states of the west were destroyed, one after another, by the Toba—the 'Hsia kingdom' in 431, bringing down with it the 'Western Ch'in', and the 'Northern Liang' in 439. The non-Chinese elements of the population of those countries were moved northward and served the Toba as soldiers: the Chinese also, especially the remains of the Kansu 'Western Liang' state (conquered in 420), were enslaved, and some of them transferred to the north. Here again, however, the influence of the Chinese gentry made itself felt after a short time. As we know, the Chinese of 'Western Liang' in Kansu had originally migrated there from eastern China. Their eastern relatives who had come under Toba rule through the conquest of eastern China and who through their family connections with Chinese officials of the Toba empire had found safety, brought their influence to bear on behalf of the Chinese of Kansu, so that several families regained office and social standing.

Their expansion into Kansu gave the Toba control of the commerce with Sinkiang, and there are many mentions of tribute missions to the Toba court in the years that followed, some even from India. The Toba also spread in the east. And finally there was fighting with south China (430–431), which brought to the Toba empire a large part of the province of Honan with the old capital, Loyang. Thus about 440 the Toba must be described as the most powerful state in the Far East, ruling the whole of north China.

4 *Economic and social conditions*

The internal changes of which there had only been indications in the first period of the Toba empire now proceeded at an accelerated pace. There were many different factors at work. The whole of the civil administration had gradually passed into Chinese hands, the Toba retaining only the military administration. But the wars in the south called for the services of specialists in fortification and in infantry warfare, who were only to be found among the Chinese. The growing influence of the Chinese was further promoted by the fact that many Toba families were exterminated in the revolts of the tribal chieftains, and others were wiped out in the many battles. Thus the Toba lost ground also in the military administration.

The wars down to A.D. 440 had been large-scale wars of conquest, lightning campaigns that had brought in a great deal of booty. With their loot the Toba developed great magnificence and luxury. The campaigns that followed were hard and long-drawn-out struggles, especially against south China, where there was no booty, because the enemy retired so slowly that they could take everything with them. The Toba therefore began to be impoverished, because plunder was the main source of their wealth. In addition to this, their herds gradually deteriorated, for less and less use was made of them; for instance, horses were little required for the campaign against south China, and there was next to no fighting in the north. In contrast with the impoverishment of the Toba, the Chinese gentry grew not only more powerful but more wealthy.

The Toba seem to have tried to prevent this development by introducing the famous 'land equalization system' (*chün-t'ien*), one of their most important innovations. We must admit, however, that already before the Toba period, attempts had been made to give 'land to the tiller'. The direct purposes of this measure were to resettle uprooted farm population; to prevent further migrations of farmers; and to raise production and taxes. The founder of this system was Li An-shih, member of a Toba family and later husband of an imperial princess. The plan was basically accepted in 477, put into action in 485, and remained the land law until c. 750. Every man and every woman had a right to receive a certain amount of land for their lifetime. After their death, the land was redistributed. In addition to this 'personal land' there was so-called 'mulberry land' on which farmers could plant mulberries for silk production; but they also could plant other crops under the trees. This land could be inherited from father to son and was not redistributed. Incidentally we know many similar regulations for trees in the Near East and Central Asia. As the tax was levied upon the personal land in form of grain, and

on the tree land in form of silk, this regulation stimulated the cultivation of diversified crops on the tree land which then was not taxable.
The basic idea behind this law was, that all land belonged to the state,
a concept for which the Toba could point to the ancient Chou but
which also fitted well for a dynasty of conquest. The new *chün-t'ien*
system required a complete land and population survey which was
done in the next years. We know from much later census fragments
that the government tried to enforce this equalization law, but did
not always succeed; we read statements such as 'X has so and so
much land; he has a claim on so and so much land and, therefore,
has to get so and so much'; but there are no records that X ever
received the land due to him.

One consequence of the new land law was a legal fixation of the
social classes. Already during Han time (and perhaps even earlier)
a distinction had been made between 'free burghers' (*liang-min*) and
'commoners' (*chien-min*). This distinction had continued as informal
tradition until, now, it became a legal concept. Only 'burghers', i.e.
gentry and free farmers, were real citizens with all rights of a free
man. The 'commoners' were completely or partly unfree and fell
under several heads. Ranking as the lowest class were the real slaves
(*nu*), divided into state and private slaves. By law, slaves were regarded as pieces of property, not as members of human society.
They were, however, forced to marry and thus, as a class, were probably reproducing at a rate similar to that of the normal population,
while slaves in Europe reproduced at a lower rate than the population.
The next higher class were serfs (*fan-hu*), hereditary state servants,
usually descendants of state slaves. They were obliged to work three
months during the year for the state and were paid for this service.
They were not registered in their place of residence but under the
control of the Ministry of Agriculture which distributed them to
other offices, but did not use them for farm work. Similar in status
to them were the private bondsmen (*pu-ch'ü*), hereditarily attached to
gentry families. These serfs received only 50 per cent of the land
which a free burgher received under the land law. Higher than these
were the service families (*tsa-hu*), who were registered in their place
of residence, but had to perform certain services; here we find 'tomb
families' who cared for the imperial tombs, 'shepherd families', postal
families, kiln families, soothsayer families, medical families, and
musician families. Each of these categories of commoners had its
own laws, each had to marry within the category. No intermarriage
or adoption was allowed. It is interesting to observe that a similar
fixation of the social status of citizens occurred in the Roman Empire
from c. A.D. 300 on.

Thus in the years between 440 and 490 there were great changes not only in the economic but in the social sphere. The Toba declined in number and influence. Many of them married into rich families of the Chinese gentry and regarded themselves as no longer belonging to the Toba. In the course of time the court was completely sinified.

The Chinese at the court now formed the leading element, and they tried to persuade the emperor to claim dominion over all China, at least in theory, by installing his capital in Loyang, the old centre of China. This transfer had the advantage for them personally that the territories in which their properties were situated were close to that capital, so that the grain they produced found a ready market. And it was indeed no longer possible to rule the great Toba empire, now covering the whole of north China from north Shansi. The administrative staff was so great that the transport system was no longer able to bring in sufficient food. For the present capital did not lie on a navigable river, and all the grain had to be carted, an expensive and unsafe mode of transport. Ultimately, in 493–4, the Chinese gentry officials secured the transfer of the capital to Loyang. In the years 490 to 499 the Toba emperor Wen Ti (471–499) took further decisive steps required by the stage reached in internal development. All aliens were prohibited from using their own language in public life. Chinese became the official language. Chinese clothing and customs also become general. The system of administration which had largely followed a pattern developed by the Wei dynasty in the early third century, was changed and took a form which became the model for the T'ang dynasty in the seventh century. It is important to note that in this period, for the first time, an office for religious affairs was created which dealt mainly with Buddhistic monasteries. While after the Toba such a special office for religious affairs disappeared again, this idea was taken up later by Japan when Japan accepted a Chinese-type of administration.

Owing to his bringing up, the emperor no longer regarded himself as Toba but as Chinese; he adopted the Chinese culture, acting as he was bound to do if he meant to be no longer an alien ruler in North China. Already he regarded himself as emperor of all China, so that the south Chinese empire was looked upon as a rebel state that had to be conquered. While, however, he succeeded in everything else, the campaign against the south failed except for some local successes.

The transfer of the capital to Loyang was a blow to the Toba nobles. Their herds became valueless, for animal products could not be carried over the long distance to the new capital. In Loyang the Toba nobles found themselves parted from their tribes, living in an unaccustomed climate and with nothing to do, for all important posts were occupied by Chinese. The government refused to allow them to return to the north. Those who did not become Chinese by finding their way into Chinese families grew visibly poorer and poorer.

It is understandable that in this period of constant warfare and of great movements, the examination system by which the best qualified men should be selected for state service did not function. In the third century, a new system was developed which continued to be used for centuries, especially under the Toba. The government at first set up a system of nine ranks for families. Each family of the upper class was classified and a definite rank was assigned to them. According to that rank, the family members could move into one of the (usually) nine official ranks, i.e. the positions in the administration. The basic idea behind this was, that some families had a higher level of culture (or of social status) and were, therefore, automatically qualified. This system eliminated the recommendation system of the Han period. It led to the development of a strong feeling for family genealogy: each high-class family tried to keep their genealogy up, so that their claims to positions could not be doubted; they were proud of their status and preferred marriages between families of equal rank. The Toba nobility, of course, could easily be fitted into this system, and as conquerors, they occupied the top ranks. It seems that this system was also introduced into Japan; the complicated rank system of Japanese upper-class families of the seventh century is most easily explained, it seems, by reference to the Toba system. In fact, it seems that many traits in Japanese society and culture which were regarded as loans from the T'ang dynasty, were in fact loans from the Toba. Perhaps the Japanese rulers, whom the real Chinese always regarded as 'barbarians' felt closer to the Toba who also were 'barbarians'.

5 *Victory and retreat of Buddhism*

What we said in regard to the religious position of the other alien peoples applied also to the Toba, As soon, however, as their empire grew, they, too, needed an 'official' religion of their own. For a few years they had continued their old sacrifices to Heaven; then another course opened to them. The Toba, together with many Chinese living in the Toba empire, were all captured by Buddhism, and especially by its shamanist element. One element in their preference of Buddhism was certainly the fact that Buddhism accepted all foreigners alike—both the Toba and the Chinese were 'foreign' converts to an essentially Indian religion; whereas the Confucianist Chinese always made the non-Chinese feel that in spite of all their attempts they were still 'barbarians' and that only real Chinese could be real Confucianists.

Second, it can be assumed that the Toba rulers by fostering Buddhism intended to break the power of the Chinese gentry. A few centuries later, Buddhism was accepted by the Tibetan kings to break the power of the native nobility, by the Japanese to break the power of a federation of noble clans, and still later by the Burmese kings for the same reason. The acceptance of Buddhism by rulers in the Far East always meant also an attempt to create a more autocratic, absolutistic regime. Mahayana Buddhism, as an ideal, desired a society without clear-cut classes under one enlightened ruler; in such a society all believers could strive to attain the ultimate goal of salvation.

Throughout the early period of Buddhism in the Far East, the question had been discussed of what should be the relations between the Buddhist monks and the emperor, whether they were subject to him or not. This was connected, of course, with the fact that to the early fourth century the Buddhist monks were foreigners who, in the view prevalent in the Far East, owed only a limited allegiance to the ruler of the land. The Buddhist monks at the Toba court now submitted to the emperor, regarding him as a reincarnation of Buddha. Thus the emperor became protector of Buddhism and a sort of god. This combination was a good substitute for the old Chinese theory that the emperor was the Son of Heaven; it increased the prestige and the splendour of the dynasty. At the same time the old shamanism was legitimized under a Buddhist reinterpretation. Thus Buddhism became a sort of official religion. The emperor appointed a Buddhist monk as head of the Buddhist state church, and through this 'Pope' he conveyed endowments on a large scale to the church. T'an-yao, head of the state church since 460, induced the state to attach state slaves, i.e. enslaved family members of criminals, and their families to state temples. They were supposed to work on temple land and to produce for the upkeep of the temples and monasteries. Thus, the institution of 'temples slaves' was created, an institution which existed in South Asia and Burma for a long time, and which greatly strengthened the economic position of Buddhism.

Like all Turkish peoples, the Toba possessed a myth according to which their ancestors came into the world from a sacred grotto. The Buddhists took advantage of this conception to construct, with money from the emperor, the vast and famous cave-temple of Yün-kang, in northern Shansi. If we come from the bare plains into the green river valley, we may see to this day hundreds of caves cut out of the steep cliffs of the river bank. Here monks lived in their cells, worshipping the deities of whom they had thousands of busts and reliefs sculptured in stone, some of more than life-size, some diminutive. The majestic impression made today by the figures does not correspond to their original effect, for they were covered with a layer of coloured stucco.

We know only few names of the artists and craftsmen who made these objects. Probably some at least were foreigners from Sinkiang, for in spite of the predominantly Chinese character of these sculptures, some of them are reminiscent of works in Sinkiang and even in the Near East. In the past the influences of the Near East on the Far East—influences traced back in the last resort to Greece—were greatly exaggerated; it was believed that Greek art, carried through Alexander's campaign as far as the present Afghanistan, degenerated there in the hands of Indian imitators (the so-called Gandhara art) and ultimately passed on in more and more distorted forms to China. Actually, however, some eight hundred years lay between Alexander's campaign and the Toba period sculptures at Yün-kang and, owing to the different cultural development, the contents of the Greek and the Toba-period art were entirely different. We may say, therefore, that suggestions came from the centre of the Greco-Bactrian culture (in the present Afghanistan) and were worked out by the Toba artists; old forms were filled with a new content, and the elements in the reliefs of Yün-kang that seem to us to be non-Chinese were the result of this synthesis of Western inspiration and Turkish initiative. It is interesting to observe that all steppe rulers showed special interest in sculpture and, as a rule, in architecture; after the Toba period, sculpture flourished in China in the T'ang period, the period of strong cultural influence from Turkish peoples, and there was a further advance of sculpture and of the cave-dwellers' worship in the period of the 'Five Dynasties' (906–960; three of these dynasties were Turkish) and in the Mongol period.

But not all Buddhists joined the 'Church', just as not all Taoists had joined the Church of Chang Ling's Taoism. Some Buddhists remained unorganized in the small towns and villages and suffered oppression from the central Church. These village Buddhist monks soon became instigators of a considerable series of attempts at revolution. Their Buddhism was of the so-called 'Maitreya school', which promised the appearance on earth of a new Buddha who would do away with all suffering and introduce a Gold Age. The Chinese peasantry, exploited by the gentry, came to the support of these monks whose Messianism gave the poor a hope in this world. The nomad tribes also, abandoned by their nobles in the capital and wandering in poverty with their now worthless herds, joined these monks. We know of many revolts of Hun and Toba tribes in this period, revolts that had a religious appearance but in reality were simply the result of the extreme impoverishment of these remaining tribes.

In addition to these conflicts between state and popular Buddhism, clashes between Buddhists and representatives of organized

Taoism occurred. Such fights, however, reflected more the power struggle between cliques than between religious groups. The most famous incident was the action against the Buddhists in 446 which brought destruction to many temples and monasteries and death to many monks. Here, a mighty Chinese gentry faction under the leadership of the Ts'ui family had united with the Taoist leader K'ou Ch'ien-chih against another faction under the leadership of the crown prince.

With the growing influence of the Chinese gentry, however, Confucianism gained ground again, until with the transfer of the capital to Loyang it gained a complete victory, taking the place of Buddhism and becoming once more as in the past the official religion of the state. This process shows us once more how closely the social order of the gentry was associated with Confucianism.

(E) SUCCESSION STATES OF THE TOBA (A.D. 550–580): NORTHERN CH'I DYNASTY, NORTHERN CHOU DYNASTY

1 *Reasons for the splitting of the Toba empire*

Events now pursued their logical course. The contrast between the central power, now become entirely Chinese, and the remains of the tribes who were with their herds mainly in Shansi and the Ordos region and were hopelessly impoverished, grew more and more acute. From 530 onward the risings became more and more formidable. A few Toba who still remained with their old tribes placed themselves at the head of the rebels and conquered not only the whole of Shansi but also the capital, where there was a great massacre of Chinese and pro-Chinese Toba. The rebels were driven back; in this a man of the Kao family distinguished himself, and all the Chinese and pro-Chinese gathered round him. The Kao family, which may have been originally a Hsien-pi family, had its estates in eastern China and so was closely associated with the eastern Chinese gentry, who were the actual rulers of the Toba State. In 534 this group took the impotent emperor of their own creation to the city of Yeh in the east, where he reigned *de jure* for a further sixteen years. Then he was deposed, and Kao Yang made himself the first emperor of the Northern Ch'i dynasty (550–577).

The national Toba group, on the other hand, found another man of the imperial family and established him in the west. After a short time this puppet was removed from the throne and a man of the Yü-wen family made himself emperor, founding the 'Northern Chou dynasty' (557–580). The Hsien-pi family of Yü-wen was a branch of the Hsien-pi, but was closely connected with the Huns and probably

150

of Turkish origin. All the still existing remains of Toba tribes who had eluded sinification moved into this western empire.

The splitting of the Toba empire into these two separate realms was the result of the policy embarked on at the foundation of the empire. Once the tribal chieftains and nobles had been separated from their tribes and organized militarily, it was inevitable that the two elements should have different social destinies. The nobles could not hold their own against the Chinese; if they were not actually eliminated in one way or another, they disappeared into Chinese families. The rest, the people of the tribe, became destitute and were driven to revolt. The northern peoples had been unable to perpetuate either their tribal or their military organization, and the Toba had been equally unsuccessful in their attempt to perpetuate the two forms of organization alongside each other.

These social processes are of particular importance because the ethnic disappearance of the northern peoples in China had nothing to do with any racial inferiority or with any particular power of assimilation; it was a natural process resulting from the different economic, social, and cultural organizations of the northern peoples and the Chinese.

2 *Appearance of the (Gök) Turks*

The Toba had liberated themselves early in the fifth century from the Juan-juan peril. None of the fighting that followed was of any great importance. The Toba resorted to the old means of defence against nomads—they built great walls. Apart from that, after their move southward to Loyang, their new capital, they were no longer greatly interested in their northern territories. When the Toba empire split into the Ch'i and the Northern Chou, the remaining Juan-juan entered into treaties first with one realm and then with the other: each realm wanted to secure the help of the Juan-juan against the other.

Meanwhile there came unexpectedly to the fore in the north a people grouped round a nucleus tribe of Huns, the tribal union of the 'T'u-chüeh', that is to say the Gök Turks, who began to pursue a policy of their own under their khan. In 546 they sent a mission to the western empire, then in the making, of the Northern Chou, and created the first bonds with it, following which the Northern Chou became allies of the Turks. The eastern empire, Ch'i, accordingly made terms with the Juan-juan, but in 552 the latter suffered a crushing defeat at the hands of the Turks, their former vassals. The remains of the Juan-juan either fled to the Ch'i state or went reluctantly into the land of the Chou. Soon there was friction between the Juan-juan and the Ch'i, and in 555 the Juan-juan in that state were annihilated. In response to pressure from the Turks, the Juan-juan in the western empire of the Northern Chou were delivered up to them and killed in the same year. The Juan-juan then disappeared from the history of the Far East. They broke up into their several tribes, some of which were admitted into the Turks' tribal league. A few years later the Turks also annihilated the Ephthalites, who had been allied with the Juan-juan; this made the Turks the dominant power in Central Asia. The Ephthalites (Yet-ha, Haytal) were a mixed group which contained elements of the old Yüeh-chih and spoke an Indo-European language. Some scholars regard them as a branch of the Tocharians of Central Asia. One menace to the northern states of China had disappeared—that of the Juan-juan. Their place was taken by a much more dangerous power, the Turks.

3   The Northern Ch'i dynasty; the Northern Chou dynasty

In consequence of this development the main task of the Northern Chou state consisted in the attempt to come to some settlement with its powerful Turkish neighbours, and meanwhile to gain what it could from shrewd negotiations with its other neighbours. By means of intrigues and diplomacy it intervened with some success in the struggles in south China. One of the pretenders to the throne was given protection; he was installed in the present Hanko was a quasi-feudal lord depending on Chou, and there he founded the 'Later Liang dynasty' (555–587). In this way Chou had brought the bulk of south China under its control without itself making any real contribution to that result.

Unlike the Chinese state of Ch'i, Chou followed the old Toba tradition. Old customs were revived, such as the old sacrifice to Heaven and the lifting of the emperor on to a carpet at his accession to the throne; family names that had been sinified were turned into Toba names again, and even Chinese were given Toba names; but in spite of this the inner cohesion had been destroyed. After two centuries it was no longer possible to go back to the old nomad, tribal life. There were also too many Chinese in the country, with whom close bonds had been forged which, in spite of all attempts, could not be broken. Consequently there was no choice but to organize a state essentially similar to that of the great Toba empire.

There is just as little of importance that can be said of the internal politics of the Ch'i dynasty. The rulers of that dynasty were thoroughly repulsive figures, with no positive achievements of any sort to their credit. Confucianism had been restored in accordance with the Chinese character of the state. It was a bad time for Buddhists, and especially for the followers of the popularized Taoism. In spite of this, about A.D. 555 great new Buddhist cave-temples were created in Lung-men, near Loyang, in imitation of the famous temples of Yün-kang.

The fighting with the western empire, the Northern Chou state, still continued, and Ch'i was seldom successful. In 563 Chou made preparations for a decisive blow against Ch'i, but suffered defeat because the Turks, who had promised aid, gave none and shortly afterwards began campaigns of their own against Ch'i. In 571 Ch'i had some success in the west against Chou, but then it lost parts of its territory to the south Chinese empire, and finally in 576–7 it was defeated by Chou in a great counter-offensive. Thus for some three years all north China was once more under a single rule, though of nothing approaching the strength of the Toba at the height of their power. For in all these campaigns the Turks had played an important part, and at the end they annexed further territory in the north of Ch'i, so that their power extended far into the east.

Meanwhile intrigue followed intrigue at the court of Chou; the mutual assassinations within the ruling group were as incessant as in the last years of the great Toba empire, until the real power passed from the emperor and his Toba entourage to a Chinese family, the Yang. Yang Chien's daughter was the wife of a Chou emperor; his son was married to a girl of the Hun family Tu-ku; her sister was the wife of the father of the Chou emperor. Amid this tangled relationship in the imperial house it is not surprising that Yang Chien should attain great power. The Tu-ku were a very old family of the Hun nobility, originally the name belonged to the Hun house from which the *shan-yü* had to be descended. This family still observed the traditions of the Hun rulers, and relationship with it was regarded as an honour even by the Chinese. Through their centuries of association with aristocratically organized foreign peoples, some of the notions of nobility had taken root among the Chinese gentry; to be related with old ruling houses was a welcome means of evidencing or securing a position of special distinction among the gentry. Yang Chien gained useful prestige from his family connections. After the leading Chinese cliques had regained predominance in the Chou empire, much as had happened before in the Toba empire, Yang Chien's position was strong enough to enable him to massacre the members of the imperial family and then, in 581, to declare himself emperor. Thus began the Sui dynasty, the first dynasty that was once more to rule all China.

But what had happened to the Toba? With the ending of the Chou empire they disappeared for all time, just as the Juan-juan had done a little earlier. So far as the tribes did not entirely disintegrate, the people of the tribes seem during the last years of Toba and Chou to have joined Turkish and other tribes. In any case, nothing more is heard of them as a people, and they themselves lived on under the name of the tribe that led the new tribal league.

Most of the Toba nobility, on the other hand, became Chinese. This process can be closely followed in the Chinese annals. The tribes that had disintegrated in the time of the Toba empire broke up into families of which some adopted the name of the tribe as their family name, while others chose Chinese family names. During the centuries that followed, in some cases indeed down to modern times, these families continue to appear, often playing an important part in Chinese history.

(F) THE SOUTHERN EMPIRES

1 *Economic and social situation in the south*
During the 260 years of alien rule in north China, the picture of south China also was full of change. When in 317 the Huns had destroyed the Chinese Chin dynasty in the north, a Chin prince who normally would not have become heir to the throne declared himself, under the name Yüan Ti, the first emperor of the 'Eastern Chin dynasty' (317–419). The capital of this new southern empire adjoined the present Nanking. Countless members of the Chinese gentry had fled from the Huns at that time and had come into the southern empire. They had not done so out of loyalty to the Chinese dynasty or out of national feeling, but because they saw little prospect of attaining rank and influence at the courts of the alien rulers, and because it was to be feared that the aliens would turn the fields into pasturage, and also that they would make an end of the economic and monetary system which the gentry had evolved for their own benefit.

But the south was, of course, not uninhabited. There were already two groups living there—the old autochthonous population, consisting of Yao, Tai and Yüeh, and the earlier Chinese immigrants from the north, who had mainly arrived in the time of the Three Kingdoms, at the beginning of the third century A.D. The countless new immigrants now came into sharp conflict with the old-established earlier immigrants. Each group looked down on the other and abused it. The two immigrant groups in particular not only spoke different dialects but had developed differently in respect to manners and customs. A look for example at Taiwan in the first years after 1948 will certainly help in an understanding of this situation: analogous tensions developed between the new refugees, the old Chinese immigrants, and the native Taiwanese population. But let us return to the southern empires.

The two immigrant groups also differed economically and socially: the old immigrants were firmly established on the large properties they had acquired, and dominated their tenants, who were largely autochthones; or they had engaged in large-scale commerce. In any case, they possessed capital, and more capital than was usually possessed by the gentry of the north. Some of the new immigrants, on the other hand, were military people. They came with empty hands, and they had no land. They hoped that the government would give them positions in the military administration and so provide them with means; they tried to gain possession of the government and to exclude the old settlers as far as possible. The tension was increased by the effect of the influx of Chinese in bringing more land into cultivation, thus producing a boom period such as is produced by the opening up of colonial land. Everyone was in a hurry to grab as much land as possible. There was yet a further difference between the two groups of Chinese: the old settlers had long lost touch with the remainder of their families in the north. For them, south China was the home; here were the temples of their ancestors. Their economic interests lay in the south. We also can assume that many families had intermarried with the indigenous population. For the wealthier among them, it was easy to get a beautiful native girl as a concubine, because they were able to pay a higher bridal price than the native man could pay. For the poorer ones, sometimes marriage with an indigenous woman was the only way to find an acceptable wife—the bridal price was always lower than that for a Chinese wife. Such intermarriages created ties between both groups which often turned out to be economically profitable for the Chinese. The new immigrants had left part of their families in the north under alien rule. Their interests still lay to some extent in the north. They were working for the reconquest of the north by military means; at times individuals or groups returned to the north, while others persuaded the rest of their relatives to come south. It would be wrong to suppose that there was no inter-communication between the two parts into which China had fallen. As soon as the Chinese gentry were able to regain any footing in the territories under alien rule, the official relations, often those of belligerency, proceeded alongside unofficial intercourse between individual families and family groupings, and these latter were, as a rule, in no way belligerent.

The lower stratum in the south consisted mainly of the remains of the original non-Chinese population, particularly in border and southern territories which had been newly annexed from time to time. In the centre of the southern state the way of life of the non-Chinese was very quickly assimilated to that of the Chinese, so that the aborigines were soon indistinguishable from Chinese. The remaining part of the lower class consisted of Chinese peasants. This whole lower section of the population rarely took any active and

155

visible part in politics, except at times in the form of great popular risings.

Until the third century, the south had been of no great economic importance, in spite of the good climate and the extraordinary fertility of the Yangtze valley. The country had been too thinly settled, and the indigenous population had not become adapted to organized trade. After the move southward of the Chin dynasty the many immigrants had made the country of the lower Yangtze more thickly populated, but not over-populated. The top-heavy court with more than the necessary number of officials (because there was still hope for a reconquest of the north which would mean many new jobs for administrators) was a great consumer; prices went up and stimulated local rice production. The estates of the southern gentry yielded more than before, and naturally much more than the small properties of the gentry in the north where, moreover, the climate is far less favourable. Thus the southern landowners were able to acquire great wealth, which ultimately made itself felt in the capital.

One very important development was characteristic in this period in the south, although it also occurred in the north. Already in pre-Han times, some rulers had gardens with fruit trees. The Han emperors had large hunting parks which were systematically stocked with rare animals; they also had gardens and hot-houses for the production of vegetables for the court. These 'gardens' (*yüan*) were often called 'manors' (*pieh-yeh*) and consisted of fruit plantations with luxurious buildings. We hear soon of water-cooled houses for the gentry, of artificial ponds for pleasure and fish breeding, artificial water-courses, artificial mountains, bamboo groves, and parks with parrots, ducks, and large animals. Here, the wealthy gentry of both north and south, relaxed from government work, surrounded by their friends and by women. These manors grew up in the hills, on the 'village commons' where formerly the villagers had collected their firewood and had grazed their animals. Thus, the village commons begin to disappear. The original farmland was taxed, because it produced one of the two products subject to taxation, namely grain or mulberry leaves for silk production. But the village common had been and remained tax-free because it did not produce taxable things. While land-holdings on the farmland were legally restricted in their size, the 'gardens' were unrestricted. Around A.D. 500 the ruler allowed high officials to have manors of three hundred *mou* size, while in the north a family consisting of husband and wife and children below fifteen years of age were allowed a farm of sixty *mou* only; but we hear of manors which were many times larger than the allowed size of three hundred. These manors began to play an important economic role, too: they were cultivated by tenants and pro-

156

duced fish, vegetables, fruit and bamboo for the market, thus they gave more income than ordinary rice or wheat land.

With the creation of manors the total amount of land under cultivation increased, though not the amount of grain-producing land. We gain the impression that from about the third century A.D. on to the eleventh century the intensity of cultivation was generally lower than in the period before.

The period from c. A.D. 300 on also seems to be the time of the second change in Chinese dietary habits. The first change occurred probably between 400 and 100 B.C. when the meat-eating Chinese reduced their meat intake greatly, gave up eating beef and mutton and changed over to some pork and dog meat. This first change was the result of increase of population and decrease of available land for pasturage. Cattle breeding in China was then reduced to the minimum of one cow or water-buffalo per farm for ploughing. Wheat was the main staple for the masses of the people. Between A.D. 300 and 600 rice became the main staple in the southern states although, theoretically, wheat could have been grown and some wheat probably was grown in the south. The vitamin and protein deficiencies which this change from wheat to rice brought forth, were made up by higher consumption of vegetables, especially beans, and partially also by eating of fish and sea food. In the north, rice became the staple food of the upper class, while wheat remained the main food of the lower classes. However, new forms of preparation of wheat, such as dumplings of different types, were introduced. The foreign rulers consumed more meat and milk products. Chinese never in their history used milk, except during periods of foreign rule, when milk products like yoghurt were sometimes used. It seems that to this day, many Chinese lack the enzyme which is necessary for an adult in order to digest milk. A change seems to be beginning now, when the consumption of ice-cream has greatly increased and when children are given milk after the weaning period and into adolescence. In most cases, the enzyme then continues to be produced. This trait, which has often been regarded as a genetic particularity seems, after all, to be socially conditioned.

2 Struggles between cliques under the Eastern Chin dynasty (A.D. 317–419)

The officials immigrating from the north regarded the south as colonial country, and so as more or less uncivilized. They went into its provinces in order to get rich as quickly as possible, and they had no desire to live there for long: they had the same dislike of a provincial existence as had the families of the big landowners. Thus as a rule the bulk of the families remained in the capital, close to the court. Thither the products accumulated in the provinces were sent, and they found a ready sale, as the capital was also a great and long-established trading centre with a rich merchant class. Thus in the capital there was every conceivable luxury and every refinement of civilization. The people of the gentry class, who were maintained in the capital by relatives serving in the provinces as governors or senior officers, themselves held offices at court, though these gave them little to do. They had time at their disposal, and made use of it—in much worse intrigues than ever before, but also in music and poetry and in the social life of the harems. There is no question at all that the highest refinement of the civilization of the Far East between the fourth and the sixth century was to be found in south China, but the accompaniments of this over-refinement were terrible.

We cannot enter into all the intrigues recorded at this time. The details are, indeed, historically unimportant. They were concerned only with the affairs of the court and its entourage. Not a single ruler of the Eastern Chin dynasty possessed personal or political qualities of any importance. The rulers' power was extremely limited because, with the exception of the founder of the state, Yüan Ti, who had come rather earlier, they belonged to the group of the new immigrants, and so had no firm footing and were therefore caught at once in the net of the newly regrouping gentry class.

To the present time, cliques have existed, but as the period of the southern dynasties is perhaps the period of Chinese history in which cliques were best developed and most powerful, it may be the place to discuss briefly their structure. Basically, they consist of members of two classes. Their leaders are of the gentry. One strong family with a material background and an intelligent head, begins to form his clique. He does this once by contracting marriages for his sons and daughters. The sons have to get brides from other families who the father thinks will join him in the struggle for power and who are already of importance or wealth. The daughters are given to families who are already close to the leader. If possible and necessary, several marriage bonds with these families are created in order to fasten the ties. These families then form the 'inner circle' of the forming clique. They, in turn, have already marriage relations with a circle of other families, and they may be induced to join the clique. The next step then is, to bring as many sons, cousins, nephews and in-laws into position in the government. We can assume that at the time of the formation of the clique, the leading family at least, already had several members in the government. An important move then is to give the emperor a daughter, or if there is no suitable one available, to give him a girl from a lower-class family, which in turn depends upon the gentry family, as concubine. These women bring into the palace their servants, and these again may act as spies, reporting on the activities of the emperor and other officials; they may also directly influence the emperor. And if they gained the favour of the ruler and had a son from him, their influence would be very strong. The lower-class members of the clique consisted of bondsmen, servants, advisers, teachers of the leading families. They could contact persons of the same status within the families belonging to the clique, but could also do more secret jobs, such as offer bribes to influential persons whose favours were needed; they could, if necessary, kill enemies of the clique. They had, in general, to do the 'dirty jobs' for their masters. The aim of all these cliques was to gain power, if possible supreme power, and to keep power. The wider the network of a clique was, the safer it was; if a political move failed, they could still save at least the lives of most of their members, and always some part of their wealth, so that a resuscitation in the future was possible, if the other members of the clique remained faithful. Within the clique, there were, of course, also fights for power, and such fights could break up the clique. Thus, not all cliques had a long life.

In later centuries, the constitution of cliques changed: not all members were related to one another or tied to one another by intrigues which they had started in common. Now, clique members could be persons who had been together in school, or persons who lived in the same hometown and had properties in the same area. It seems that these changes made the later cliques less long-living and more changeable.

When today Chinese discuss politics, they still regard the cliques as the most important factor and first try to find out who belongs to which clique and what are his ties to the leader of the clique. From this basis they try to analyse their political moves. That means, they do not pay much attention to the proclaimed ideological or other goals of those in power or aiming at power, in contrast to Western observers who take the proclamations much more seriously and tend to believe that political actions were taken because of an ideological, economic or other goal which is to be realized in the future.

The emperor Yüan Ti lived to see the first great rising. This rising (under Wang Tun) started in the region of the present Hankow, a region that today is one of the most important in China; it was already a centre of special activity. To it lead all the trade routes from the western provinces of Szechwan and Kweichow and from the central provinces of Hupei, Hunan, and Kiangsi. Normally the traffic from those provinces comes down the Yangtze, and thus in practice this region is united with that of the lower Yangtze, the environment of Nanking, so that Hankow might just as well have been the capital as Nanking. For this reason, in the period with which we are now concerned the region of the present Hankow was several times the place of origin of great risings whose aim was to gain control of the whole of the southern empire.

Wang Tun had grown rich and powerful in this region; he also had near relatives at the imperial court; so he was able to march against the capital. The emperor in his weakness was ready to abdicate but died before that stage was reached. His son, however, defeated Wang Tun with the aid of General Yü Liang (A.D. 323). Yü Liang was the empress's brother; he, too, came from a northern family. Yüan Ti's successor also died early, and the young son of Yü Liang's sister came to the throne as Emperor Ch'eng (326–342); his mother ruled as regent, but Yü Liang carried on the actual business of government. Against this clique rose Su Chün, another member of the northern gentry, who had made himself leader of a bandit gang in A.D. 300 but had then been given a military command by the dynasty. In 328 he captured the capital and kidnapped the emperor, but then fell before the counterthrust of the Yü Liang party. The domination of Yü Liang's clique continued after the death of the twenty-one-year-old emperor. His twenty-year-old brother was set in his place; he, too, died two years later, and his two-year-old son became emperor (Mu Ti, 345–361).

Meanwhile this clique was reinforced by the very important Huan family. This family came from the same city as the imperial house and was a very old gentry family of that city. One of the family attained a high post through personal friendship with Yü Liang: on his death his son Huan Wen came into special prominence as military commander.

Huan Wen, like Wang Tun and others before him, tried to secure a firm foundation for his power, once more in the west. In 347 he reconquered Szechwan and deposed the local dynasty. Following this, Huan Wen and the Yü family undertook several joint campaigns against northern states—the first reaction of the south against the north, which in the past had always been the aggressor. The first fighting took place directly to the north, where the collapse of the 'Later Chao' seemed to make intervention easy. The main objective was the regaining of the regions of eastern Honan, northern Anhwei and Kiangsu, in which were the family seats of Huan's and the emperor's families, as well as that of the Hsieh family which also formed an important group in the court clique. The purpose of the northern campaigns was not, of course, merely to defend private interests of court cliques: the northern frontier was the weak spot of the southern empire, for its plains could easily be overrun. It was then observed that the new 'Earlier Ch'in' state was trying to spread from the north-west eastward into this plain, and Ch'in was attacked in an attempt to gain a more favourable frontier territory. These expeditions brought no important practical benefit to the south; and they were not embarked on with full force, because there was only the one court clique at the back of them, and that not whole-heartedly, since it was too much taken up with the politics of the court.

Huan Wen's power steadily grew in the period that followed. He sent his brothers and relatives to administer the regions along the upper Yangtze, those fertile regions were the basis of his power. In 371 he deposed the reigning emperor and appointed in his place a frail old prince who died a year later, as required, and was replaced by a child. The time had now come when Huan Wen might have ascended the throne himself, but he died. None of his family could assemble as much power as Huan Wen had done. The equality of strength of the Huan and the Hsieh saved the dynasty for a time.

In 383 came the great assault of the Tibetan Fu Chien against the south. As we know, the defence was carried out more by the methods of diplomacy and intrigue than by military means, and it led to the disaster in the north already described. The successes of the southern state especially strengthened the Hsieh family, whose generals had come to the fore. The emperor (Hsiao Wu Ti, 373–396), who had come to the throne as a child, played no part in events at any time during his reign. He occupied himself occasionally with Buddhism, and otherwise only with women and wine. He was followed by his five-year-old son. At this time there were some changes in the court clique. In the Huan family Huan Hsüan, a son of Huan Wen, came especially into prominence. He parted from the Hsieh family, which had been closest to the emperor, and united with the Wang (the empress's) and Yin families. The Wang, an old Shansi family, had already provided two empresses, and was therefore strongly represented at court. The Yin had worked at first with the Hsieh, especially as the two families came from the same region, but afterwards the Yin went over to Huan Hsüan. At first this new clique had success, but later one of its generals, Liu Lao-chih, went over to the Hsieh clique, and its power declined. Wang Kung was killed, and Yin Chung-k'an fell away from Huan Hsüan and was killed by him in 399. Huan Hsüan himself, however, held his own in the regions loyal to him. Liu Lao-chih had originally belonged to the Hsieh clique, and his family came from a region not far from that of the Hsieh. He was very ambitious, however, and always took the side which seemed most to his own interest. For a time he joined Huan Hsüan; then he went over to the Hsieh, and finally returned to Huan Hsüan in 402 when the latter reached the height of his power. At that moment Liu Lao-chih was responsible for the defence of the capital from Huan Hsüan, but instead he passed over to him. Thus Huan Hsüan conquered the capital, deposed the emperor, and began a dynasty of his own. Then came the reaction, led by an earlier subordinate of Liu Lao-chih, Liu Yü. It may be assumed that these two army commanders were in some way related, though the two branches of their family must have been long separated. Liu Yü had distinguished himself especially in the suppression of a great popular rising which, around the year 400, had brought wide stretches of Chinese territory under the rebels' power, beginning with the southern coast. This rising was the first in the south. It was led by members of a secret society which was a direct continuation of the 'Yellow Turbans' of the latter part of the second century A.D. and of organized church-Taoism. The whole course of this rising of the exploited and ill-treated lower classes was very similar to that of the popular rising of the 'Yellow Turbans'. The movement spread as far as the neighbourhood of Canton, but in the end it was suppressed, mainly by Liu Yü.

Through these achievements Liu Yü's military power and political influence steadily increased; he became the exponent of all the cliques working against the Huan clique. He arranged for his supporters to dispose of Huan Hsüan's chief collaborators; and then, in 404, he himself marched on the capital. Huan Hsüan had to flee, and in his flight he was killed in the upper Yangtze region. The emperor was restored to his throne, but he had as little to say as ever, for the real power was Liu Yü's.

Before making himself emperor, Liu Yü began his great northern campaign, aimed at the conquest of the whole of western China. The Toba had promised to remain neutral, and in 415 he was able to conquer the 'Later Ch'in' in Shensi. The first aim of this campaign was to make more accessible the trade routes to Central Asia, which up to now had led through the difficult mountain passes of Szechwan; to this end treaties of alliance had been concluded with the states in Kansu against the 'Later Ch'in'. In the second place, this war was intended to increase Liu Yü's military strength to such an extent that the imperial crown would be assured to him; and finally he hoped to cut the claws of pro-Huan Hsüan elements in the 'Later Ch'in' kingdom who, for the sake of the link with Sinkiang, had designs on Szechwan.

3 The Liu-Sung dynasty (A.D. 420–478) and the Southern Ch'i dynasty (479–501)

After his successes in 416–417 in Shensi, Liu Yü returned to the capital, and shortly after he lost the chief fruits of his victory to Ho-lien P'o-p'o, the Hun ruler in the north, while Liu Yü himself was occupied with the killing of the emperor (419) and the installation of a puppet. In 420 the puppet had to abdicate and Liu Yü became emperor. He called his dynasty the Sung dynasty, but to distinguish it from another and more famous Sung dynasty of later time his dynasty is also called the Liu-Sung dynasty.

The struggles and intrigues of cliques against each other continued as before. We shall pass quickly over this period after a glance at the nature of these internal struggles.

Part of the old imperial family and its following fled northwards from Liu Yü and surrendered to the Toba. There they agitated for a campaign of vengeance against south China, and they were supported at the court of the Toba by many families of the gentry with landed interests in the south. Thus long-continued fighting started between Sung and Toba, concerned mainly with the domains of the deposed imperial family and its following. This fighting brought little success to south China, and about 450 it produced among the Toba an economic and social crisis that brought the wars to a temporary close. In this pause the Sung turned to the extreme south, and tried to gain influence there and in Annam. The merchant class and the gentry families of the capital who were allied with it were those chiefly interested in this expansion.

About 450 began the Toba policy of shifting the central government to the region of the Yellow river, to Loyang; for this purpose the frontier had to be pushed farther south. Their great campaign brought the Toba in 450 down to the Yangtze. The Sung suffered a heavy defeat; they had to pay tribute, and the Toba annexed parts of their northern territory.

The Sung emperors who followed were as impotent as their predecessors and personally much more repulsive. Nothing happened at court but drinking, licentiousness, and continual murders.

From 460 onward there were a number of important risings of princes; in some of them the Toba had a hand. They hoped by supporting one or another of the pretenders to gain overlordship over the whole of the southern empire. In these struggles in the south the Hsiao family, thanks mainly to General Hsiao Tao-ch'eng, steadily gained in power, especially as the family was united by marriage with the imperial house. In 477 Hsiao Tao-ch'eng finally had the emperor killed by an accomplice, the son of a shamaness; he set a boy on the throne and made himself regent. Very soon after this the boy emperor and all the members of the imperial family were murdered, and Hsiao Tao-ch'eng created the 'Southern Ch'i' dynasty (479–501). Once more the remaining followers of the deposed dynasty fled northward to the Toba, and at once fighting between Toba and the south began again.

This fighting ended with a victory for the Toba and with the final establishment of the Toba in the new capital of Loyang. South China was heavily defeated again and again, but never finally conquered. There were intervals of peace. In the years between 480 and 490 there was less disorder in the south, at all events in internal affairs. Princes were more often appointed to governorships, and the influence of the cliques was thus weakened. In spite of this, a stable regime was not built up, and in 494 a prince rose against the youthful emperor. This prince, with the help of his clique including the Ch'en family, which later attained importance, won the day, murdered the emperor, and became emperor himself. All that is recorded about him is that he fought unsuccessfully against the Toba, and that he had the whole of his own family killed out of fear that one of its members might act exactly as he had done. After his death there were conflicts between the emperor's few remaining relatives; in these the Toba again had a hand. The victor was a person named Hsiao Yen; he removed the reigning emperor in the usual way and made himself emperor. Although he belonged to the imperial family, he altered the name of the dynasty, and reigned from 502 as the first emperor of the 'Liang dynasty'.

4 The Liang dynasty (A.D. 503–556)

The fighting with the Toba continued until 515. As a rule the Toba were the more successful, not least through the aid of princes of the deposed 'Southern Ch'i dynasty' and their followers. Wars began also in the west, where the Toba tried to cut off the access of the Liang to the caravan routes to Sinkiang. In 507, however, the Toba suffered an important defeat. The southern states had tried at all times to work with the Kansu states against the northern states; the Toba now followed suit and allied themselves with a large group of native chieftains of the south, whom they incited to move against the Liang. This produced great native unrest, especially in the provinces by the upper Yangtze. The natives, who were steadily pushed back by the Chinese peasants, were reduced to migrating into the mountain country or to working for the Chinese in semi-servile conditions; and they were ready for revolt and very glad to work with the Toba. The result of this unrest was not decisive, but it greatly reduced the strength of the regions along the upper Yangtze. Thus the main strength of the southern state was more than ever confined to the Nanking region.

The first emperor of the Liang dynasty, who assumed the name Wu Ti (502–549), became well known in the Western world owing to his love of literature and of Buddhism. After he had come to the throne with the aid of his followers, he took no further interest in politics; he left that to his court clique. From now on, however, the political initiative really belonged to the north. At this time there began in the Toba empire the risings of tribal leaders against the government which we have fully described above. One of these leaders, Hou Ching, who had become powerful as a military leader in the north, tried in 547 to conclude a private alliance with the Liang to strengthen his own position. At the same time the ruler of the northern state of the 'Northern Ch'i', then in process of formation, himself wanted to negotiate an alliance with the Liang, in order to be able to get rid of Hou Ching. There was indecision in Liang. Hou Ching, who had been getting into difficulties, now negotiated with a dissatisfied prince in Liang, invaded the country in 548 with the prince's aid, captured the capital in 549, and killed Emperor Wu. Hou Ching now staged the usual spectacle: he put a puppet on the imperial throne, deposed him eighteen months later and made himself emperor.

This man of the Toba on the throne of south China was unable, however, to maintain his position; he had not sufficient backing. He was at war with the new rulers in the northern empire, and his own army, which was not very large, melted away; above all, he proceeded with excessive harshness against the helpers who had gained access for him to the Liang, and thereafter he failed to secure a following from among the leading cliques at court. In 552 he was driven out by a Chinese army led by one of the princes and was killed.

The new emperor had been a prince in the upper Yangtze region, and his closest associates were engaged there. They did not want to move to the distant capital, Nanking, because their private financial interests would have suffered. The emperor therefore remained in the city now called Hankow. He left the eastern territory in the hands of two powerful generals, one of whom belonged to the Ch'en family, which he no longer had the strength to remove. In this situation the generals in the east made themselves independent, and this naturally produced tension at once between the east and the west of the Liang empire; this tension was now exploited by the leaders of the Chou state then in the making in the north. On the invitation of a clique in the south and with its support, the Chou invaded the present province of Hupei and in 555 captured the Liang emperor's capital. They were now able to achieve their old ambition: a prince of the Chou dynasty was installed as a feudatory of the north, reigning until 587 in the present Hankow. He was permitted to call his quasi-feudal territory a kingdom and his dynasty, as we know already, the 'Later Liang dynasty'.

5   *The Ch'en dynasty (A.D. 557–588) and its ending by the Sui*
The more important of the independent generals in the east, Ch'en Pa-hsien, installed a shadow emperor, forced him to abdicate, and

made himself emperor. The Ch'en dynasty which thus began was even feebler than the preceding dynasties. Its territory was confined to the lower Yangtze valley. Once more cliques and rival pretenders were at work and prevented any sort of constructive home policy. Abroad, certain advantages were gained in north China over the Northern Ch'i dynasty, but none of any great importance.

Meanwhile in the north, Yang Chien had brought into power the Chinese Sui dynasty. It began by liquidating the quasi-feudal state of the 'Later Liang'. Then followed, in 588–589, the conquest of the Ch'en empire, almost without any serious resistance. This brought all China once more under united rule, and a period of 360 years of division was ended.

6 Cultural achievements of the south

For nearly three hundred years the southern empire had witnessed unceasing struggles between powerful cliques, making impossible any peaceful development within the country. Culturally, however, the period was rich in achievement. The court and the palaces of wealthy members of the gentry attracted scholars and poets, and the gentry themselves had time for artistic occupations. A large number of the best-known Chinese poets appeared in this period, and their works plainly reflect the conditions of that time: they are poems for the small circle of scholars among the gentry and for cultured patrons, spiced with quotations and allusions, elaborate in metre and construction, masterpieces of aesthetic sensitivity—but unintelligible except to highly educated members of the aristocracy. The works were of the most artificial type, far removed from all natural feeling.

An exception is T'ao Ch'ien (T'ao Yüan-ming, 372?–427), who retreated to his villa after a rather unsuccessful career and composed poems which are simple and full of a real appreciation of landscape and nature. Modern historians of literature praise him highly as a precursor of modern poetry. He is also credited with a collection of short stories about miraculous or curious happenings, the continuation of an earlier similar collection by Kan Pao. Such collections, which later became more and more common, are valuable sources of folk traditions and beliefs, for the Chinese reader they serve as entertainment. Some collections of this period have a Buddhist tinge and tell of ghosts who take revenge for wrongs they had suffered during their human life, and of the punishment of others for sins committed. As in all Chinese literature, the moral tone is strong, but they still provided a diversion, as we today may feel when reading a detective story. In this period, there was a feverish activity of Buddhists in translating holy texts from Indian or Central Asian sources. Some of these texts were highly sophisticated and brought to China the fundamentals of the Indian system of logic and philology. Others had a different purpose. The so-called 'Jataka' are entertaining stories, usually stories of the past in which Buddha and/or some of his disciples in an earlier incarnation play the main role. These stories, too, are moralistic, but highly entertaining, because they introduced into China famous folktales and fables of India.

As in other Buddhist countries, the stories were used by monks to make their sermons more interesting or to illuminate a moral rule by a story. It is very interesting that many animal tales—for which India is famous—came to China, but in the course of time were eliminated again, so that today China has few animal tales, i.e. tales in which animals interact with other animals (not with humans). The reason for this seems to be that for a Chinese animals cannot talk; thus, such stories are untrue, and one should not tell children lies. If an animal talks to a man, the animal then is not a real animal but a ghost or spirit, and ghosts and spirits are believed to exist and to be able to speak in human language.

Ideologically, the gentry of the south was still Confucian, in the sense that they claimed to adhere to the rules of behaviour that were expected, and that they performed the ceremonies prescribed. But they were much more fascinated by Buddhism. While the so-called 'Mahayana' schools of Buddhism were most widely spread, in the south 'Hinayana' schools flourished, and a special importance was gained by the meditative schools which we later call with the Japanese name of Zen (Chinese: Ch'an). These meditative schools were close ideologically to the original Taoism, highly individualistic, not interested in society or life in society, only in the perfection of the self and the attainment of higher levels of insight.

Others took to the more common schools and tried to make up for their evil deeds by rich gifts to the monasteries. Many emperors in this period, especially Wu Ti of the Liang dynasty, inclined to Buddhism. Wu Ti turned to it especially in his old age, when he was shut out entirely from the tasks of a ruler and was no longer satisfied with the usual pleasures of the court. Several times he instituted Buddhist ceremonies of purification on a large scale in the hope of so securing forgiveness for the many murders he had committed.

Music, too, was never so assiduously cultivated as at this time. But the old Chinese music disappeared in the south as in the north, where dancing troupes and women musicians in the Sodgian commercial colonies of the province of Kansu established the music of Central Asia. Here in the south, native courtesans brought the aboriginal, non-Chinese music to the court; Chinese poets wrote songs in Chinese for this music, and so the old Chinese music became unfashionable and was forgotten.

Although, as we have mentioned, houses of prostitution existed, the gentry did not visit them and—during many periods of China's history—were not allowed to visit them. Instead, they bought courtesans from slave markets or houses of prostitution and kept them not as concubines but as house entertainers to enliven their parties.

Principal dynasties of north and south China

North and south

Western Chin dynasty (A.D. 265–317)

North		South	
1. Earlier Chao (Hsiung-nu)	304–329	1. Eastern Chin (Chinese)	
2. Later Chao (Hsiung-nu)	328–329		317–419
3. Earlier Ch'in (Tibetans)	351–394		
4. Later Ch'in (Tibetans)	384–417		
5. Western Ch'in (Hsiung-nu)			
	385–431		
6. Earlier Yen (Hsien-pi)	352–370		
7. Later Yen (Hsien-pi)	384–409		
8. Western Yen (Hsien-pi)	384–395		
9. Southern Yen (Hsien-pi)	398–410		
10. Northern Yen (Hsien-pi)	409–436		
11. Tai (Toba)	338–376		
12. Earlier Liang (Chinese)	313–376		
13. Northern Liang (Hsiung-nu)			
	397–439		
14. Western Lian (Chinese?)	400–421		
15. Later Liang (Tibetans)	386–403		
16. Southern Liang (Hsien-pi)	379–414		
17. Hsia (Hsiung-nu)	407–431		
18. Toba (Turks)	385–550		
		2. Liu-Sung	420–478
		3. Southern Ch'i	479–501
19. Northern Ch'i (Chinese?)	550–576	4. Liang	502–556
20. Northern Chou (Toba)	557–579	5. Ch'en	557–588
21. Sui (Chinese)	580–618	6. Sui	580–618

CHAPTER EIGHT

Climax and Downfall of the Imperial Gentry (A.D. 580–950)

These 370 years brings us to the most glorious period of China's history, the time when China reached its greatest extension before the eighteenth century, when China became known to the Western world as a centre of civilization. To this day, Chinese in some parts of the world still call themselves 'T'ang-jen', people of the T'ang (dynasty). This is at the same time the climax of gentry society. The rule of northern tribal federations with their strong ideas of aristocracy and nobility, had its influence upon the Chinese gentry and we will see this in the following chapters. But after three hundred years of glory, a new world began to emerge, in which the gentry as we knew it disintegrated and disappeared to make room for a gentry of different type and a different society. It is always somewhat arbitrary to cut history into periods, and the last seventy or so years of this period can be and have been regarded as the period of the emergence of the new society or as the end of the old one.

(A) THE SUI DYNASTY (A.D. 580–618)

1 *Internal situation in the newly unified empire*

The last of the northern dynasties, the Northern Chou, had been brought to an end by Yang Chien: rapid campaigns had made an end of the remaining petty states, and thus the Sui dynasty had come into power. China, reunited after 360 years, was again under Chinese rule. This event brought about a new epoch in the history of the Far East. But the happenings of 360 years could not be wiped out by a change of dynasty. The short Sui period can only be described as a period of transition to unified forms.

In the last resort the union of the various parts of China proceeded from the north. The north had always, beyond question, been militarily superior, because its ruling class had consisted of warlike peoples. Yet it was not a northerner who had united China but a Chinese who was closely related to the northern peoples. His wife, the jealous empress, was from the Tu-ku family, the noble family from which tribal leaders had come again and again. The rule, however, of the actual northern peoples was at an end. The start of the Sui dynasty, while the Chou still held the north, was evidence, just like the emergence in the north-east some thirty years earlier of the Northern Ch'i dynasty, that the Chinese gentry with their land-owning basis had gained the upper hand over the warrior nomads.

The Chinese gentry had not come unchanged out of that struggle. Culturally they had taken over many things from the foreigners, beginning with music and the style of their clothing, in which they had entirely adopted the northern pattern, and including other ele-ments of daily life. Among the gentry were now many formerly alien families who had gradually become entirely Chinese. On the other hand, the foreigners' feudal outlook had influenced the gentry, so that a sense of distinctions of rank had developed among them. There were Chinese families who regarded themselves as superior to the rest, just as had been the case among the northern peoples, and who married only among themselves or with the ruling house and not with ordinary families of the gentry. They paid great attention to their genealogies, had the state keep records of them and insisted that the dynastic histories mentioned their families and their main family members. Lists of prominent gentry families were set up which mentioned the home of each clan, so that pretenders could easily be detected. Genealogies, all over the world, are documents to the glory of a family; they are not strictly honest. Misbegotten sons were omitted—daughters and wives seldom mentioned at all; if a family member was punished for a crime and banished, the fact was either not mentioned or couched in special, unclear language. Yet, for the research in Chinese social history, they are, if used with caution, one of the most important 'unofficial', i.e. not government-sponsored, sources. The rules of giving personal names were changed so that it became possible to identify a person's genealogical position within the family. At the same time the contempt of the military underwent modification; the gentry were even ready to take over high military posts, and also to profit by them.

The new Sui empire found itself faced with many difficulties. Dur-ing the three and a half centuries of division, north and south had developed in different ways. They no longer spoke the same language in everyday life (we distinguish to this day between a Nanking and Peking 'High Chinese', to say nothing of dialects). The social and economic structures were very different in the two parts of the country. How could unity be restored in these things?

Then there was the problem of population. The north-eastern plain had always been thickly populated; it had early come under Toba rule and had been able to develop further. The region round the old northern capital Ch'ang-an, on the other hand, had suffered greatly from the struggles before the Toba period and had never entirely recovered. Meanwhile, in the south the population had greatly increased in the region north of Nanking, while the regions south of the Yangtze and the upper Yangtze valley were more thinly peopled. The real south, i.e. the modern provinces of Fukien, Kwangtung and Kwangsi, was still underdeveloped, mainly because of the malaria there. In the matter of population the north unquestionably remained prominent.

The founder of the Sui dynasty, known by his reign name of Wen Ti (589–604), came from the west, close to Ch'ang-an. There he and his following had their extensive domains. Owing to the scanty population there and the resulting shortage of agricultural labourers, these properties were very much less productive than the small properties in the north-east. This state of things was well known in the south, and it was expected, with good reason, that the government would try to transfer parts of the population to the north-west, in order to settle a peasantry round the capital for the support of its greatly increasing staff of officials, and to satisfy the gentry of the region. This produced several revolts in the south.

As an old soldier who had long been a subject of the Toba, Wen Ti had no great understanding of theory: he was a practical man. He was anti-intellectual and emotionally attached to Buddhism; he opposed Confucianism for emotional reasons and believed that it could give him no serviceable officials of the sort he wanted. He demanded from his officials the same obedience and sense of duty as from his soldiers; and he was above all thrifty, almost miserly, because he realized that the finances of his state could only be brought into order by the greatest exertions. The budget had to be drawn up for the vast territory of the empire without any possibility of saying in advance whether the revenues would come in and whether the transport of dues to the capital would function.

This cautious calculation was entirely justified, but it aroused great opposition. Both east and south were used to a much better style of living; yet the gentry of both regions were now required to cut down their consumption. On top of this they were excluded from the conduct of political affairs. In the past, under the Northern Ch'i empire in the north-east and under the Ch'en empire in the south, there had been thousands of positions at court in which the whole of the gentry could find accommodation of some kind. Now the central government was far in the west, and other people were its administrators.

171

In the past the gentry had had a profitable and easily accessible market for their produce in the neighbouring capital; now the capital was far away, entailing long-distance transport at heavy risk with little profit.

The dissatisfied circles of the gentry in the north-east and in the south incited Prince Kuang to rebellion. The prince and his followers murdered the emperor and set aside the heir-apparent; and Kuang came to the throne, assuming the name of Yang Ti. His first act was to transfer the capital back to the east, to Loyang, close to the grain-producing regions. His second achievement was to order the construction of great canals, to facilitate the transport of grain to the capital and to provide a valuable new market for the producers in the north-east and the south. It was at this time that the first fore-runner of the famous 'Imperial Canal' was constructed, the canal that connects the Yangtze with the Yellow river. Small canals, connecting various streams, had long been in existence, so that it was possible to travel from north to south by water, but these canals were not deep enough or broad enough to take large freight barges. There are records of lighters of 500 and even 800 tons capacity! These are dimensions unheard of in the West in those times. In addition to a serviceable canal to the south, Yang Ti made another that went north almost to the present Peking.

Hand in hand with these successes of the north-eastern and southern gentry went strong support for Confucianism, and a reorganization of the Confucian examination system. As a rule, however, the examinations were a mere formality; the various governors were ordered each to send annually to the capital three men with the required education, for whose quality they were held personally responsible; merchants and artisans were expressly excluded.

2 *Relations with the Turks and with Korea*

In foreign affairs an extraordinarily fortunate situation for the Sui dynasty had come into existence. The T'u-chüeh, the Turks, much the strongest people of the north, had given support now to one and now to another of the northern kingdoms, and this, together with their many armed incursions, had made them the dominant political factor in the north. But in the first year of the Sui period (581) they split into two sections, so that the Sui had hopes of gaining influence over them. At first both sections of the Turks had entered into alliance with China, but this was not a sufficient safeguard for the Sui, for one of the Turkish khans was surrounded by Toba who had fled from the vanished state of the Northern Chou, and who now tried to induce the Turks to undertake a campaign for the reconquest of north China. The leader of this agitation was a princess of the Yü-

172

10 Ladies of the court: clay models which accompanied the dead
person to the grave. T'ang period.
(In the collection of the Museum für Völkerkunde, Berlin.)

11 Distinguished founder: a temple banner found
at Khotcho, Sinkiang.
(Museum für Völkerkunde, Berlin, No. 1B 4524,
illustration B 408.)

wen family, the ruling family of the Northern Chou. The Chinese fought the Turks several times; but much more effective results were gained by their diplomatic missions, which incited the eastern against the western Turks and vice versa, and also incited the Turks against the Toba clique. In the end one of the sections of Turks accepted Chinese overlordship, and some tribes of the other section were brought over to the Chinese side; so, fresh disunion was sown among the Turks.

Under the emperor Yang Ti, P'ei Chü carried this policy further. He induced the Tölös tribes to attack the T'u-yü-hun, and then himself attacked the latter, so destroying their power. The T'u-yü-hun were a people living in the extreme north of Tibet, under a ruling class apparently of Hsien-pi origin; the people were largely Tibetan. The purpose of the conquest of the T'u-yü-hun was to safeguard access to Central Asia. An effective Central Asia policy was, however, impossible so long as the Turks were still a formidable power. Accordingly, the intrigues that aimed at keeping the two sections of Turks apart were continued. In 615 came a decisive counter-attack from the Turks. Their khan, Shih-pi, made a surprise assault on the emperor himself, with all his following, in the Ordos region, and succeeded in surrounding them. They were in just the same desperate situation as when, eight centuries earlier, the Chinese emperor had been beleaguered by Mao Tun. But the Chinese again saved themselves by a trick. The young Chinese commander, Li Shih-min, succeeded in giving the Turks the impression that large reinforcements were on the way; a Chinese princess who was with the Turks spread the rumour that the Turks were to be attacked by another tribe—and Shih-pi raised the siege, although the Chinese had been entirely defeated.

In the Sui period the Chinese were faced with a further problem. Korea or, rather, the most important of three states in Korea, had generally been on friendly terms with the southern state during the period of China's division, and for this reason had been more or less protected from its north Chinese neighbours. After the unification of China, Korea had reason for seeking an alliance with the Turks, in order to secure a new counterweight against China.

A Turco-Korean alliance would have meant for China a sort of encirclement that might have grave consequences. The alliance might be extended to Japan, who had certain interests in Korea. Accordingly the Chinese determined to attack Korea, though at the same time negotiations were set on foot. The fighting, which lasted throughout the Sui period, involved technical difficulties, as it called for combined land and sea attacks; in general it brought little success.

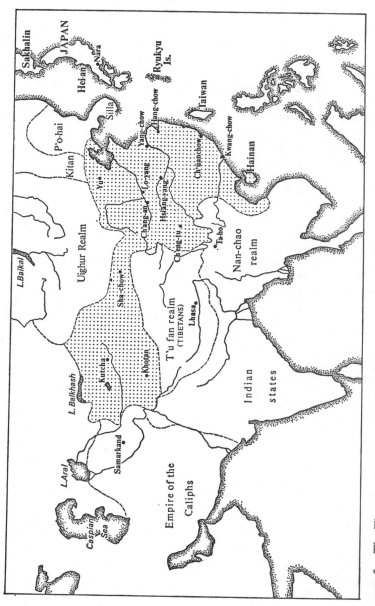

MAP 5 *The T'ang realm (about A.D. 750)*

3   Reasons for collapse

The continual warfare entailed great expense, and so did the intrigues, because they depended for their success on bribery. Still more expensive were the great canal works. In addition to this, the emperor Yang Ti, unlike his father, was very extravagant. He built enormous palaces and undertook long journeys throughout the empire with an immense following. All this wrecked the prosperity which his father had built up and had tried to safeguard. The only productive expenditure was that on the canals, and they could not begin to pay in so short a period. The emperor's continual journeys were due, no doubt, in part simply to the pursuit of pleasure, though they were probably intended at the same time to hinder risings and to give the emperor direct control over every part of the country. But the empire was too large and too complex for its administration to be possible in the midst of journeying. The whole of the chancellery had to accompany the emperor, and all the transport necessary for the feeding of the emperor and his government had continually to be diverted to wherever he happened to be staying. Later Chinese historians regard these travels as mere amusement trips made by an emperor whose main interest was in sexual adventures. A whole novel, written around 1600 is devoted to this aspect of Yang Ti's life, and the end of his dynasty is attributed to it. We are not sure whether he was really such a playboy or whether the breakdown of the Sui was not caused by his attempt to create a new type of administration. In any case, the gentry, who at first had so strongly supported the emperor and had been able to obtain anything they wanted from him, now began to desert him and set up pretenders. From 615 onward, after the defeat at the hands of the Turks, rising broke out everywhere. The emperor had to establish his government in the south, where he felt safer. There, however, in 618, he was assassinated by conspirators led by Toba of the Yü-wen family. Everywhere now independent governments sprang up, and for five years China was split up into countless petty states.

(B) THE T'ANG DYNASTY (A.D. 618–906)

1   Reforms and decentralization

The hero of the Turkish siege, Li Shih-min, had allied himself with the Turks in 615–616. There were special reasons for his ability to do this. In his family it had been a regular custom to marry women belonging to Toba families, so that he naturally enjoyed the confidence of the Toba party among the Turks. There are various theories as to the origin of his family, the Li. The family itself claimed to be

175

descended from the ruling family of the Western Liang. It is doubtful whether that family was purely Chinese, and in any case Li Shih-min's descent from it is a matter of doubt. It is possible that his family was a sinified Toba family, or at least came from a Toba region. There was again a marriage with a woman from the Tu-ku family.

Li Shih-min continued the policy which had been pursued since the beginning of the Sui dynasty by the members of the deposed Toba ruling family of the Northern Chou—the policy of collaboration with the Turks in the effort to remove the Sui. The nominal leadership in the rising that now began lay in the hands of Li Shih-min's father, Li Yüan; in practice Li Shih-min saw to everything. At the end of 617 he was outside the first capital of the Sui, Ch'ang-an, with a Turkish army that had come to his aid on the strength of the treaty of alliance. After capturing Ch'ang-an he installed a puppet emperor there, a grandson of Yang Ti. In 618 the puppet was dethroned and Li Yüan, the father, was made emperor, in the T'ang dynasty. Internal fighting went on until 623, and only then was the whole empire brought under the rule of the T'ang.

Great reforms then began. A new land law aimed at equalizing ownership, so that as far as possible all peasants should own the same amount of land and the formation of large estates be prevented. The law aimed also at protecting the peasants from the loss of their land. The law was, however, nothing but a modification of the Toba land law (*chün-t'ien*), and it was hoped that now it would provide a sound and solid economic foundation for the empire. Census reports, found in Tun-huang, note the amount of land an individual family should receive, and, in many cases, how much they actually did receive. We may then conclude that the measures were in fact effective, though few farmers seem to have received as much as they were legally entitled to. Soon, however, loopholes in the laws began to influence the situation: members of the gentry who were connected with the imperial house were given a privileged position; then officials were excluded from the prohibition of leasing, so that there continued to be tenant farmers in addition to the independent peasants. Moreover, the temples enjoyed special treatment, and were also exempted from taxation. All these exceptions brought grist to the mills of the gentry, and so did the failure to carry into effect many of the provisions of the law. Before long a new gentry had been formed, consisting of the old gentry together with those who had directly aided the emperor's ascent to the throne. From the beginning of the eighth century there were repeated complaints that peasants were 'disappearing'. In at least some cases, the gentry by direct pressure or by giving credit to farmers and, when they could not repay the debt, taking over their land and treating them as tenants, succeeded in controlling much more land than they were entitled to. Due to the privileged position of the gentry in regard to taxation, the revenue sank in proportion as the number of independent peasants decreased. One of the reasons for the flight of farmers may have been the corvée laws connected with the 'equal land' system: small families were much less affected by the corvée obligation than larger families with many sons. It may be, therefore, that large families or at least sons of the sons in large families moved away in order to escape these obligations. In order to prevent irregularities, the T'ang renewed the old *pao-chia* system, as a part of a general reform of the administration in 624. In this system groups of five families were collectively responsible for the payment of taxes, the corvée, for crimes committed by individuals within one group, and for loans from state agencies. Such a system is attested for pre-Christian times already; it was reactivated in the eleventh century and again from time to time, down to the present.

Thus the system of land equalization soon broke down and was abolished officially around A.D. 780. But the classification of citizens into different classes, first legalized under the Toba, was retained and even more refined.

As early as in the Han period there had been a dual administration—the civil and, independent of it, the military administration. One and the same area would belong to a particular administrative prefecture (*caün*) and at the same time to a particular military prefecture (*chou*). This dual organization had persisted during the Toba period and, at first, remained unchanged in the beginning of the T'ang.

The backbone of the military power in the seventh century was the militia, 574 units of an average of a thousand men, recruited from the general farming population for short-term service: one month in five in the areas close to the capital. These men formed a part of the emperor's protection and were under the command of members of the Shensi gentry. This system, which had its direct parallels in the Han time and evolved out of a Toba system, broke down when short offensive wars were no longer fought. The sixteen units of imperial guards were staffed with young sons of the gentry who were stationed in the most delicate parts of the palaces. The emperor T'ai-Tsung had his personal bodyguard, a part of his own army of conquest, consisting of his former bondsmen (*pu-ch'ü*). The ranks of the Army of conquest were later filled by descendants of the original soldiers and by orphans.

In the provinces, the armies of the military prefectures gradually lost their importance when wars became longer and militiamen proved insufficient. Many of the soldiers here were convicts and

177

exiles. It is interesting to note that the title of the commander of these armies, *tu-tu*, in the fourth century meant a commander in the church-Taoist organization; it was used by the Toba and from the seventh century on became widely accepted as a title among the Uighurs, Tibetans, Sogdians, Turks and Khotanese.

The wars of conquest which the T'ang conducted led to the creation of frontier armies with permanent commanders and a corresponding weakening of the prefectural armies and the militia (from 678 on). A similar institution had existed among the Toba, but they had greatly reduced these armies after 500. The commanders of these new T'ang armies soon became more important than the civil administrators, because they commanded a number of districts making up a whole province. This assured a better functioning of the military machine, but put the governors-general in a position to pursue a policy of their own, even against the central government. In addition to this, the financial administration of their commands was put under them, whereas in the past it had been in the hands of the civil administration of the various provinces. The civil administration was also reorganized (see the table on pages 81–2).

Towards the end of the T'ang period the state secretariat was set up in two parts: it was in possession of all information about the economic and political affairs of the empire, and it made the actual decisions. Moreover, a number of technical departments had been created—in all, a system that might compare favourably with European systems of the eighteenth century. At the end of the T'ang period there was added to this system a section for economic affairs, working quite independently of it and directly under the emperor; it was staffed entirely with economic or financial experts, while for the staffing of the other departments no special qualification was demanded besides the passing of the state examinations. In addition to these, at the end of the T'ang period a new department was in preparation, a sort of Privy Council, a mainly military organization, probably intended to control the generals (section 3 of the table on page 81), just as the state secretariat controlled the civil officials. The Privy Council became more and more important in the tenth century and especially in the Mongol epoch. Its absence in the early T'ang period gave the military governors much too great freedom, ultimately with baneful results.

We now have to look into the social stratification of the upper class. There was a 'super-gentry', divided into four regional groups which were often in competition with one another. First, the Lung-hsi gentry, from the area of the present province of Kansu. The imperial house of T'ang came from this group, as had the Sui house. This gentry was highly mixed with non-Chinese, Toba and Turkish elements and therefore was looked down upon by the Shantung gentry which, together with the Kiangsu gentry regarded themselves as the banner-carriers of old Chinese traditions. It is, for instance, the Ts'ui family which expressed the attitude that a marriage with the imperial house was a mismarriage. The fourth gentry group consisted of remnants of Toba and Turkish tribal leaders who had, in time, been assimilated and become 'Chinese'. Their influence tended to diminish with time.

Below this 'super-gentry' there was a provincial gentry, locally important, but only rarely able to play a role at the capital. The gentry created lists, comparable to the European 'Gotha calendar' in which, area by area, the gentry families were enumerated as a guide for marriages.

For the relatives of the emperor, moves into positions of great power were easiest. Members of the super-gentry could get into office simply as being sons of officials (the so-called 'yin' privilege), others had to pass one state examination. The road to success was through state schools. Two of the three state schools took only sons of officials, the third one occasionally also took some others. Prefectural officials could 'recommend' able men, but only if these men already belonged to gentry families of power did they have a chance to get into office. Men who came from provincial gentry families and passed the examination usually got into advisory jobs, advising the emperor on questions of ethics, after a career in low prefectural administrative positions. They could also, without taking an examination, move into one of the nine ranks of clerical jobs at the court, and after ten years of service take an examination and become regular officials of low rank with little hope of advancement. Similarly, they could enter the imperial guards, and after ten years take an examination and then become low regular officials in the civil administration.

Thus, the posts of political importance were taken almost exclusively by the members of the super-gentry, the clerical and military jobs usually by members of the provincial gentry. For men from ordinary families, the only chance was to enter the armies of frontier generals in the hope of being promoted by them.

During the seventh century the reforms of A.D. 624 worked well. The administration showed energy, and taxes flowed in. In the middle of the eighth century the annual budget of the state included the following items: over a million tons of grain for the consumption of the capital and the palace and for salaries of civil and military officials; twenty-seven million pieces of textiles, also for the consumption of capital and palace and army, and for supplementary purchases of grain; two million strings of money (a string nominally held a thousand copper coins) for salaries and for the army. This

179

was much more than the state budget of the Han period. The population of the empire had also increased; it seems to have amounted to some fifty million. The capital grew enormously, at times containing two million people. Ch'ang-an, before its destruction in 881 had 110 wards. Each ward, like a ghetto, was surrounded by a wall with gates; at night the gates were closed. There was a special prostitution quarter, not too far from the centre of the city. Members of the gentry often secretly went there, though it was not allowed, and ate and drank and played games with the ladies. Many of China's best poets created their poems there in the company of ladies and friends. Typically, a Chinese poet does not write poems at home, in his studio, but in a group in which one member may propose a theme and a rhyme pattern. Then each member of the party may add a line or two; or each may create a whole poem, parallel to that of his predecessor. The ladies also were famous musicians and dancers, many of them from Central Asia, with their own local dances and their own music. Among the many imports of musical instruments and tunes, the import of the bow for string instruments at the end of the T'ang time is important because it changed the style of music. If the guests of the amusement quarter wanted to have more than just entertainment, they ordered the ladies to their houses. Of course, many of the more official parties took place in the houses of the gentry and entertainers were invited to enliven these parties. For those who retired from the bustle of the capital to work on their estates and to enjoy the society of their friends, there was time to occupy themselves with Taoism and Buddhism, especially meditative Buddhism. Everyone, of course, was Confucian, as was fitting for a member of the gentry, but Confucianism was so taken for granted that it was not discussed. It was the basis of morality for the gentry, but held no problems. It no longer contained anything of interest.

In addition to the actual capital, Ch'ang-an, there was the second capital, Loyang, in no way inferior to the other in importance; and the great towns in the south also played their part as commercial and cultural centres that had developed in the 360 years of division between north and south. There the local gentry gathered to lead a cultivated life, though not quite in the grand style of the capital. If an official was transferred to the Yangtze, it no longer amounted to a punishment as in the past; he would not meet only uneducated people, but a society resembling that of the capital. The institution of governors-general further promoted this decentralization: the governor-general surrounded himself with a little court of his own, drawn from the local gentry and the local intelligentsia. This placed the whole edifice of the empire on a much broader foundation, with lasting results.

2   Turkish policy

The foreign policy of this first period of the T'ang, lasting until about 690, was mainly concerned with the Turks and Sinkiang. There were still two Turkish realms in the Far East, both of considerable strength but in keen rivalry with each other. The T'ang had come into power with the aid of the eastern Turks, but they admitted the leader of the western Turks to their court; he had been at Ch'ang-an in the time of the Sui. He was murdered, however, by Chinese at the instigation of the eastern Turks. The next khan of the eastern Turks nevertheless turned against the T'ang, and gave his support to a still surviving pretender to the throne representing the Sui dynasty; the khan contended that the old alliance of the eastern Turks had been with the Sui and not with the T'ang. The T'ang therefore tried to come to terms once more with the western Turks, who had been affronted by the assassination; but the negotiations came to nothing in face of an approach made by the eastern Turks to the western, and of the distrust of the Chinese with which all the Turks were filled. About 624 there were strong Turkish invasions, carried right up to the capital. Suddenly, however, for reasons not disclosed by the Chinese sources, the Turks withdrew, and the T'ang were able to conclude a fairly honourable peace. This was the time of the maximum power of the eastern Turks. Soon afterwards disturbances broke out (627), under the leadership of Turkish Uighurs and their allies. The Chinese took advantage of these disturbances, and in a great campaign in 629–630 succeeded in overthrowing the eastern Turks; the khan was taken to the imperial court in Ch'ang-an, and the Chinese emperor made himself 'Heavenly Khan' of the Turks. In spite of the protest of many of the ministers, who pointed to the result of the settlement policy of the Later Han dynasty, the eastern Turks were settled in the bend of the upper Hwang-ho and placed more or less under the protectorate of two governors-general. Their leaders were admitted into the Chinese army, and the sons of their nobles lived at the imperial court. No doubt it was hoped in this way to turn the Turks into Chinese, as had been done with the Toba, though for entirely different reasons. More than a million Turks were settled in this way, and some of them actually became Chinese later and gained important posts.

In general, however, this in no way broke the power of the Turks. The great Turkish empire, which extended as far as Byzantium, continued to exist. The Chinese success had done no more than safeguard the frontier from a direct menace and frustrate the efforts of the supporters of the Sui dynasty and the Toba dynasty, who had been living among the eastern Turks and had built on them. The power of the western Turks remained a lasting menace to China, especially if they should succeed in co-operating with the Tibetans. After the annihilation of the T'u-yü-hun by the Sui at the very beginning of the seventh century, a new political unit had formed in northern Tibet, the T'u-fan, who also seem to have had an upper class of Turks and Mongols and a Tibetan lower class. Just as in the Han period, Chinese policy was bound to be directed to preventing a union between Turks and Tibetans. This, together with commercial interests, seems to have been the political motive of the Chinese Central Asian policy under the T'ang.

3 Conquest of Central Asia and Korea. Summit of power

The Central Asian wars began in 639 with an attack on the city-state of Kao-ch'ang (Khocho). This state had been on more or less friendly terms with north China since the Toba period, and it had succeeded again and again in preserving a certain independence from the Turks. Now, however, Kao-ch'ang had to submit to the western Turks, whose power was constantly increasing. China made that submission a pretext for war. By 640 the whole basin of Sinkiang was brought under Chinese dominance. The whole campaign was really directed against the western Turks, to whom Sinkiang had become subject. The western Turks had been crippled by two internal events, to the advantage of the Chinese: there had been a tribal rising, and then came the rebellion and the rise of the Uighurs (640–650). These events belong to Turkish history, and we shall confine ourselves here to their effects on Chinese history. The Chinese were able to rely on the Uighurs; above all, they were furnished by the Tölös Turks with a large army, with which they turned once more against Sinkiang in 647–648, and now definitely established their rule there.

The active spirit at the beginning of the T'ang rule had not been the emperor but his son Li Shih-min, who was not, however, named as heir to the throne because he was not the eldest son. The result of this was tension between Li Shih-min and his father and brothers, especially the heir to the throne. When the brothers learned that Li Shih-min was claiming the succession, they conspired against him, and in 626, at the very moment when the western Turks had made a rapid incursion and were once more threatening the Chinese capital, there came an armed collision between the brothers, in which Li Shih-min was the victor. The brothers and their families were exterminated, the father compelled to abdicate, and Li Shih-min became emperor, assuming the name T'ai Tsung (627–649). His reign marked the zenith of the power of China and of the T'ang dynasty. Their inner struggles and the Chinese penetration of Central Asia had weakened the position of the Turks; the reorganization of the administration and of the system of taxation, the improved transport resulting from the canals constructed under the Sui, and the useful results of the creation of great administrative areas under strong military control, had brought China inner stability and in consequence external power and prestige. The reputation which she then obtained as the most powerful state of the Far East endured when her inner stability had begun to deteriorate. Thus in 638 the Sassanid ruler Jedzgerd sent a mission to China asking for her help against the Arabs. Three further missions came at intervals of a good many years. The Chinese declined, however, to send a military expedition to such a distance; they merely conferred on the ruler the title of a Chinese governor; this was of little help against the Arabs, and in 675 the last ruler, Peruz, fled to the Chinese court.

The last years of T'ai Tsung's reign were filled with a great war against Korea, which represented a continuation of the plans of the Sui emperor Yang Ti. This time Korea came firmly into Chinese possession. In 661, under T'ai Tsung's son, the Korean fighting was resumed, this time against Japanese who were defending their interests in Korea. This was the period of great Japanese enthusiasm for China. The Chinese system of administration was copied, and Buddhism was adopted, together with every possible element of Chinese culture. This meant increased trade with Japan, bringing in large profits to China, and so the Korean middleman was to be eliminated.

T'ai Tsung's son, Kao Tsung (650–683), merely carried to a conclusion what had been begun. Externally China's prestige continued at its zenith. The caravans streamed into China from western and Central Asia, bringing great quantities of luxury goods. At this time, however, the foreign colonies were not confined to the capital but were installed in all the important trading ports and inland trade centres. The whole country was covered by a commercial network; foreign merchants who had come overland to China met others who had come by sea. The foreigners set up their own counting-houses and warehouses; whole quarters of the capital were inhabited entirely by foreigners who lived as if they were in their own country. They brought with them their own religions: Manichaeism, Mazdaism, and Nestorian Christianity. The first Jews came into China, apparently as dealers in fabrics, and the first Arabian Mohammedans made their appearance. In China the foreigners bought silkstuffs and collected everything of value that they could find, especially precious metals. Culturally this influx of foreigners enriched China; economically, as in earlier periods, it did not; its disadvantages were only compensated for a time by the very beneficial results of the trade with Japan, and this benefit did not last long.

The pressure of the western Turks had been greatly weakened in this period, especially as their attention had been diverted to the west, where the advance of Islam and of the Arabs was a new menace for them. On the other hand, from 650 onward the Tibetans gained immensely in power, and pushed from the south into the Tarim basin. In 678 they inflicted a heavy defeat on the Chinese, and it cost the T'ang decades of diplomatic effort before they attained, in 699, their aim of breaking up the Tibetans' realm and destroying their power. In the last year of Kao Tsung's reign, 683, came the first of the wars of liberation of the northern Turks, known until then as the western Turks, against the Chinese.

4   The reign of the empress Wu: Buddhism and capitalism

With the end of Kao Tsung's reign began the decline of the T'ang regime. Most of the historians attribute it to a woman, the later empress Wu. She had been a concubine of T'ai Tsung, and after his death had become a Buddhist nun—a frequent custom of the time—until Kao Tsung fell in love with her and made her a concubine of his own. In the end he actually divorced the empress and made the concubine empress (655). She gained more and more influence, being placed on a par with the emperor and soon entirely eliminating him in practice; in 680 she removed the rightful heir to the throne and put her own son in his place; after Kao Tsung's death in 683 she became regent for her son. Soon afterwards she dethroned him in favour of his twenty-two-year-old brother; in 690 she deposed him too and made herself empress in the 'Chou dynasty' (690–701). This officially ended the T'ang dynasty.

Matters, however, were not so simple as this might suggest. For otherwise on the empress's deposition there would not have been a mass of supporters moving heaven and earth to treat the new empress Wei (705–712) in the same fashion. There is every reason to suppose that behind the empress Wu there was a group opposing the ruling clique.

Communist Chinese historians like to praise her. First, as a woman; indeed, during the T'ang time, as a survival of Toba times, women were freer than in almost the next thousand years; they took part in official parties, accompanied their men on hunting expeditions. Second, Empress Wu is credited with progressive ideas. It is said that she stressed examinations and thus brought new men from families other than the super-gentry into the government. This seems to be incorrect. During her rule fewer examinations than before were held. The real point seems to have been a power struggle. In spite of everything, the T'ang government clique was very pro-Turkish, and many Turks and members of Toba families had government posts

184

and, above all, important military commands. No campaign of that period was undertaken without Turkish auxiliaries. The fear seems to have been left in some quarters that this T'ang group might pursue a military policy hostile to the gentry. The T'ang group had its roots mainly in western China; thus the eastern Chinese gentry were inclined to be hostile to it. The first act of the empress Wu had been to transfer the capital to Loyang in the east. Thus, she tried to rely upon the co-operation of the eastern gentry which since the Northern Chou and Sui dynasties had been out of power. There were differences in education and outlook between both groups which continued long after the death of the empress. In addition, the eastern gentry, who supported the empress Wu and later the empress Wei, were closely associated with the foreign merchants of western Asia and the Buddhist organizations to which they adhered. In gratitude for help from the Buddhists, the empress Wu endowed them with enormous sums of money, and tried to make Buddhism a sort of state religion. A similar development had taken place in the Toba and also in the Sui period. Like these earlier rulers, the empress Wu seems to have aimed at combining spiritual leadership with her position as ruler of the empire.

In this epoch Buddhism helped to create the first beginnings of capitalism. In connection with the growing foreign trade, the monasteries grew in importance as repositories of capital; the temples bought more and more land, became more and more wealthy, and so gained increasing influence over economic affairs. They accumulated large quantities of metal, which they stored in the form of bronze figures of Buddha, and with these stocks they exercised controlling influence over the money market. There is a constant succession of records of the total weight of the bronze figures, as an indication of the money value they represented. It is interesting to observe that temples and monasteries also acquired shops and had rental income from them. They further operated many mills, as did the owners of private estates (now called *chuang*) and thus controlled the price of flour, and polished rice.

The cultural influence of Buddhism found expression in new and improved translations of countless texts, and in the passage of pilgrims along the caravan routes, helped by the merchants, as far as western Asia and India, like the famous Hsüan-tsang. Translations were made not only from Indian or other languages into Chinese, but also, for instance, from Chinese into the Uighur and other Turkish tongues, and into Tibetan, Korean, and Japanese.

The attitude of the Turks can only be understood when we realize that the background of events during the time of empress Wu was formed by the activities of groups of the eastern Chinese gentry. The

185

northern Turks, who since 630 had been under Chinese overlordship, had fought many wars of liberation against the Chinese; and through the conquest of neighbouring Turks they had gradually become once more, in the decade-and-a-half after the death of Kao Tsung, a great Turkish realm. In 698 the Turkish khan, at the height of his power, demanded a Chinese prince for his daughter—not, as had been usual in the past, a princess for his son. His intention, no doubt, was to conquer China with the prince's aid, to remove the empress Wu, and to restore the T'ang dynasty—but under Turkish overlordship! Thus, when the empress Wu sent a member of her own family, the khan rejected him and demanded the restoration of the deposed T'ang emperor. To enforce this demand, he embarked on a great campaign against China. In this the Turks must have been able to rely on the support of a strong group inside China, for before the Turkish attack became dangerous the empress Wu recalled the deposed emperor, at first as 'heir to the throne'; thus she yielded to the khan's principal demand.

In spite of this, the Turkish attacks did not cease. After a series of imbroglios within the country in which a group under the leadership of the powerful Ts'ui gentry family had liquidated the supporters of the empress Wu shortly before her death, a T'ang prince finally succeeded in killing empress Wei and her clique. At first, his father ascended the throne, but was soon persuaded to abdicate in favour of his son, now called emperor Hsüan Tsung (713–755), just as the first ruler of the T'ang dynasty had done. The practice of abdicating —in contradiction with the Chinese concept of the ruler as Son of Heaven and the duties of a son towards his father—seems to have impressed Japan where similar steps later became quite common. With Hsüan Tsung there began now a period of forty-five years, which the Chinese describe as the second blossoming of T'ang culture, a period that became famous especially for its painting and litera-ture.

5 Second blossoming of T'ang culture

The T'ang literature shows the co-operation of many favourable factors. The ancient Chinese classical style of official reports and decrees which the Toba had already revived, now led to the clear prose style of the essayists, of whom Han Yü (768–825) and Liu Tsung-yüan (747–796) call for special mention. But entirely new forms of sentences make their appearance in prose writing, with new pictures and similes brought from India through the medium of the Buddhist translations. Poetry was also enriched by the simple songs that spread in the north under Turkish influence, and by southern influences. The great poets of the T'ang period adopted the rules of

186

form laid down by the poetic art of the south in the fifth century; but while at that time the writing of poetry was a learned pastime, precious and formalistic, the T'ang poets brought to it genuine feeling. Widespread fame came to Li T'ai-po (701–762) and Tu Fu (712–770); in China two poets almost equal to these two in popularity were Po Chü-i (772–846) and Yüan Chen (779–831), who in their works kept as close as possible to the vernacular.

New forms of poetry rarely made their appearance in the T'ang period, but the existing forms were brought to the highest perfection. Not until the very end of the T'ang period did there appear the form of a 'free' versification, with lines of no fixed length. This form came from the indigenous folk-songs of south-western China, and was spread through the agency of the *filles de joie* in the houses. Before long it became the custom to string such songs together in a continuous series—the first step towards opera. For these song sequences were sung by way of accompaniment to the theatrical productions. Thus the Chinese theatre, with its union with music, should rather be called opera, although it offers a sort of pantomimic show. What amounted to a court conservatoire trained actors and musicians as early as in the T'ang period for this court opera. These actors and musicians were selected from the best-looking 'commoners', but they soon tended to become a special caste with a legal status just below that of 'burghers'.

The short-story, too, developed in T'ang times further by taking up episodes of normal life, rather than stressing the supernatural. Thus, the first short-stories of lightly erotic character, depicting love affairs, began to appear. Many of these short-stories later became the texts for operas down to the sixteenth century.

In plastic art there are fine sculptures in stone and bronze, and we have also technically excellent fabrics, the finest of lacquer, and remains of artistic buildings; but the principal achievement of the T'ang period lies undoubtedly in the field of painting. As in poetry, in painting there are strong traces of alien influences; even before the T'ang period, the painter Hsieh Ho laid down the six fundamental laws of painting, in all probability drawn from Indian practice. Foreigners were continually brought into China as decorators of Buddhist temples, since the Chinese could not know at first how the new gods had to be presented. The Chinese regarded these painters as craftsmen, but admired their skill and their technique and learned from them.

The most famous Chinese painter of the T'ang period is Wu Tao-tzŭ, who was also the painter most strongly influenced by Central Asian works. As a pious Buddhist he painted pictures for temples among others. Among the landscape painters, Wang Wei (721–729) ranks first; he was also a famous poet and aimed at uniting poem and painting into an integral whole. With him begins the great tradition of Chinese landscape painting, which attained its zenith later, in the Sung epoch.

Porcelain had been invented in China long ago. There was as yet none of the white porcelain that is preferred today; the inside was a brownish-yellow; but on the whole it was already technically and artistically of a very high quality. Since porcelain was at first produced only for the requirements of the court and of high dignitaries —mostly in state factories—a few centuries later the T'ang porcelain had become a great rarity. But in the centuries that followed, porcelain became an important new article of Chinese export. The Chinese prisoners taken by the Arabs in the great battle of Samarkand (751), the first clash between the world of Islam and China, brought to the West the knowledge of Chinese culture, of several Chinese crafts, of the art of papermaking, and also of porcelain.

The emperor Hsüan Tsung gave active encouragement to all things artistic. Poets and painters contributed to the elegance of his magnificent court ceremonial. As time went on he showed less and less interest in public affairs, and grew increasingly inclined to Taoism and mysticism in general—an outcome of the fact that the conduct of matters of state was gradually taken out of his hands. On the whole, however, Buddhism was pushed into the background in favour of a rather formalistic Confucianism, as a reaction against the unusual privileges that had been accorded to the Buddhists in the past fifteen years under the empress Wu.

6 Revolt of a military governor

At the beginning of Hsüan Tsung's reign the capital had been in the east at Loyang; then it was transferred once more to Ch'ang-an in the west due to pressure of the western gentry. The emperor soon came under the influence of the unscrupulous but capable and energetic Li Lin-fu, a distant relative of the ruler. Li was a virtual dictator at the court from 736 to 752, who had first advanced in power by helping the concubine Wu, a relative of the famous empress Wu, and by continually playing the eastern against the western gentry. After the death of the concubine Wu, he procured for the emperor a new concubine named Yang, of a western family. This woman, usually called 'Concubine Yang' (Yang Kui-fei), became the heroine of countless state-plays and stories and even films; all the misfortunes that marked the end of Hsüan Tsung's reign were attributed solely to her. This is incorrect, as she was but a link in the chain of influences that played upon the emperor. Naturally she found important official posts for her brothers and all her relatives; but more important than these was a military governor named An Lu-shan (703–757). His mother was a Turkish shamaness, his father a foreigner, probably of Sogdian origin. An Lu-shan succeeded in gaining favour with the Li clique, which hoped to make use of him for its own ends. Chinese sources describe him as a prodigy of evil, and it will be very difficult today to gain a true picture of his personality. In any case, he was certainly a very capable military officer. His rise started from a victory over the Kitan in 744. He spent some time establishing relations with the court and then went back to resume operations against the Kitan. He made so much of the Kitan peril that he was permitted a larger army than usual, and he had command of 150,000 troops in the neighbourhood of Peking. Meanwhile Li Lin-fu died. He had sponsored An as a counterbalance against the western gentry. When now, within the clique of Li Lin-fu, the Yang family tried to seize power, they turned against An Lu-shan. But he marched against the capital, Ch'ang-an, with 200,000 men; on his way he conquered Loyang and made himself emperor (756: Yen dynasty). T'ang troops were sent against him under the leadership of the Chinese Kuo Tzŭ-i, a Kitan commander, and a Turk, Ko-shu Han.

The first two generals had considerable success, but Ko-shu Han, whose task was to prevent access to the western capital, was quickly defeated and taken prisoner. The emperor fled betimes, and An Lu-shan captured Ch'ang-an. The emperor now abdicated; his son, emperor Su Tsung (756–762), also fled, though not with him into Szechwan, but into north-western Shensi. There he defended himself against An Lu-shan and his capable general Shih Ssŭ-ming (himself a Turk), and sought aid in Central Asia. A small Arab troop came from the caliph Abu-Jafar, and also small bands from Sinkiang; of more importance was the arrival of Uighur cavalry in substantial strength. At the end of 757 there was a great battle in the neighbourhood of the capital, in which An Lu-shan was defeated by the Uighurs; shortly afterwards he was murdered by one of his eunuchs. His followers fled; Loyang was captured and looted by the Uighurs. The victors further received in payment from the T'ang government 10,000 rolls of silk with a promise of 20,000 rolls a year; the Uighur khan was given a daughter of the emperor as his wife. An Lu-shan's general, the Turk Shih Ssŭ-ming, entered into An Lu-shan's heritage, and dominated so large a part of eastern China that the Chinese once more made use of the Uighurs to bring him down. The commanders in the fighting against Shih Ssŭ-ming this time were once more Kuo Tzŭ-i and the Kitan general, together with P'u-ku Huai-en, a member of a Tölös family that had long been living in China. At first Shih Ssŭ-ming was victorious, and he won back Loyang, but then he was murdered by his own son, and only by taking advantage of the disturbances that now arose were the government troops able to quell the dangerous rising.

In all this, two things seem interesting and important. To begin with, An Lu-shan had been a military governor. His rising showed that while this new office, with its great command of power, was of value in attacking external enemies, it became dangerous, especially if the central power was weak, the moment there were no external enemies of any importance. An Lu-shan's rising was the first of many similar ones in the later T'ang period. The gentry of eastern China had shown themselves entirely ready to support An Lu-shan against the government, because they had hoped to gain advantage as in the past from a realm with its centre once more in the east. In the second place, the important part played by aliens in events within China calls for notice: not only were the rebels An Lu-shan and Shih Ssŭ-ming non-Chinese, but so also were most of the generals opposed to them. But they regarded themselves as Chinese, not as members of another national group. The Turkish Uighurs brought in to help against them were fighting actually against Turks, though they regarded those Turks as Chinese. We must not bring to the circumstances of those times the present-day notions with regard to national feeling.

7 The role of the Uighurs. Confiscation of the capital of the monasteries

This rising and its sequels broke the power of the dynasty, and also of the empire. The extremely sanguinary wars had brought fearful suffering upon the population. During the years of the rising, no taxes came in from the greater part of the empire, but great sums had to be paid to the peoples who had lent aid to the empire. And the looting by government troops and by the auxiliaries injured the population as much as the war itself did.

When the emperor Su Tsung died, in 762, Tengri, the khan of the Uighurs, decided to make himself ruler over China. The events of the preceding years had shown him that China alone was entirely defenceless. Part of the court clique supported him, and only by the intervention of P'u-ku Huai-en, who was related to Tengri by marriage, was his plan frustrated. Naturally there were countless intrigues against P'u-ku Huai-en. He entered into alliance with the Tibetan T'u-fan, and in this way the union of Turks and Tibetans, always feared by the Chinese, had come into existence. In 763 the Tibetans captured and burned down the western capital, while P'u-ku Huai-en with the Uighurs advanced from the north. Undoubtedly this campaign would have been successful, giving an entirely different turn to China's destiny, if P'u-ku Huai-en had not died in 765 and the Chinese under Kuo Tzŭ-i had not succeeded in breaking up the alliance. The Uighurs now came over into an alliance with the Chinese, and the two allies fell upon the Tibetans and robbed them of their booty. China was saved once more.

Friendship with the Uighurs had to be paid for this time even more dearly. They crowded into the capital and compelled the Chinese to buy horses, in payment for which they demanded enormous quantities of silkstuffs. They behaved in the capital like lords, and expected to be maintained at the expense of the government. The system of military governors was adhered to in spite of the country's experience of them, while the difficult situation throughout the empire, and especially along the western and northern frontiers, facing the Tibetans and the more and more powerful Kitan, made it necessary to keep considerable numbers of soldiers permanently with the colours. This made the military governors stronger and stronger; ultimately they no longer remitted any taxes to the central government, but spent them mainly on their armies. Thus from 750 onward the empire consisted of an impotent central government and powerful military governors, who handed on their positions to their sons as a further proof of their independence. When in 781 the government proposed to interfere with the inheriting of the posts, there was a great new rising, which in 783 again extended as far as the capital; in 784 the T'ang government at last succeeded in overcoming it. A compromise was arrived at between the government and the governors, but it in no way improved the situation. Life became more and more difficult for the central government. In 780, the 'equal land' system was finally officially given up and with it a tax system which was based upon the idea that every citizen had the same amount of land and, therefore, paid the same amount of taxes. The new system tried to equalize the tax burden and the corvée obligation, but not the land. This change may indicate a step towards greater freedom for private enterprise. Yet it did not benefit the government, as most of the tax income was retained by the governors and was used for their armies and their own court.

In the capital, eunuchs ruled in the interests of various cliques. Several emperors fell victim to them or to the drinking of 'elixirs of long life'.

Abroad, the Chinese lost their dominion over Sinkiang, for which Uighurs and Tibetans competed. There is nothing to gain from any full description of events at court. The struggle between cliques soon became a struggle between eunuchs and literati, in much the same way as at the end of the second Han dynasty. Trade steadily diminished, and the state became impoverished because no taxes were coming in and great armies had to be maintained, though they did not even obey the government.

Events that exerted on the internal situation an influence not to be belittled were the break-up of the Uighurs (from 832 onward) the appearance of the Sha-t'o, and almost at the same time, the dissolution of the Tibetan empire (from 842). Many other foreigners had placed themselves under the Uighurs living in China, in order to be able to do business under the political protection of the Uighur embassy, but the Uighurs no longer counted, and the T'ang government decided to seize the capital sums which these foreigners had accumulated. It was hoped in this way especially to remedy the financial troubles of the moment, which were partly due to a shortage of metal for minting. As the trading capital was still placed with the temples as banks, the government attacked the religion of the Uighurs, Manichaeism, and also the religions of the other foreigners, Mazdaism, Nestorianism, and apparently also Islam. In 843 alien religions were prohibited; aliens were also ordered to dress like Chinese. This gave them the status of Chinese citizens and no longer of foreigners, so that Chinese justice had a hold over them. That this law abolishing foreign religions was aimed solely at the foreigners' capital is shown by the proceedings at the same time against Buddhism which had long become a completely Chinese Church. Four thousand, six hundred Buddhist temples, 40,000 shrines and monasteries were secularized, and all statues were required to be melted down and delivered to the government, even those in private possession. Two hundred and sixty thousand, five hundred monks were to become ordinary citizens once more. Until then monks had been free of taxation, as had millions of acres of land belonging to the temples and leased to tenants or some 150,000 temple slaves.

Thus the edict of 843 must not be described as concerned with religion at all times, down to the present, Chinese governments looked with suspicion at any organization other than the family (the basis of Chinese society to 1949), because such an organization could become a centre of power and thus a threat. In this case, the persecution was also a measure of compulsion aimed at filling the government coffers. All the property of foreigners and a large part of the property of the Buddhist Church came into the hands of the government. The law was not applied to Taoism, because the ruling gentry of the time were, as so often before, Confucianist and at the same time interested in applied Taoism. As early as 846 there came a reaction: with the new emperor, Confucians came into power who were at the same time Buddhists and who now evicted some of the Taoists. From this time one may observe closer co-operation between Confucianism and Buddhism; not only with meditative Buddhism (Zen) as at the beginning of the T'ang epoch and earlier, but with the main branch of Buddhism, monastery Buddhism (Vinaya). From now onward the Buddhist doctrines of transmigration and retribution, which had been really directed against the gentry and in favour of the common people, were turned into an instrument serving the gentry: everyone who was unfortunate in this life must show such amenability to the government and the gentry that he would have a chance of a better existence at least in the next life. Thus the revolutionary Buddhist doctrine of retribution became a reactionary doctrine that was of great service to the gentry. One of the Buddhist Confucians in whose works this revised version makes its appearance most clearly was Niu Seng-yu, who was at once summoned back to court in 846 by the new emperor. Three new large Buddhist sects came into existence in the T'ang period. One of them, the school of the Pure Land (*Ching-t'u tsung*) since 641 required of its mainly lower-class adherents only the permanent invocation of the Buddha Amitabha who would secure them a place in the 'Western Paradise' —a place without social classes and economic troubles. The cult of Maitreya, which was always more revolutionary, receded for a while.

8   First successful peasant revolt. Collapse of the empire

The chief sufferers from the continual warfare of the military governors, the sanguinary struggles between the cliques, and the universal impoverishment which all this fighting produced, were, of course, the common people. The Chinese annals are filled with records of popular risings, but not one of these had attained any wide extent, for want of organization. In 860 began the first great popular rising, a revolt caused by famine in the province of Chekiang. Government troops suppressed it with bloodshed. Further popular risings followed. In 874 began a great rising in the south of the present province of Hopei, the chief agrarian region.

The rising was led by a peasant, Wang Hsien-chih, together with Huang Ch'ao, a salt merchant, who had fallen into poverty and had joined the hungry peasants, forming a fighting group of his own. It is important to note that Huang was well educated. It is said that he failed in the state examination. Huang is not the first merchant who became rebel. An Lu-shan, too, had been a businessman for a while. It was pointed out that trade had greatly developed in the T'ang period; of the lower Yangtze region people it was said that 'they were so much interested in business that they paid no attention to agriculture'. Yet merchants were subject to many humiliating conditions. They could not enter the examinations, except by illegal means. In various periods, from the Han time on, they had to wear special dress. Thus, a law from c. A.D. 300 required them to wear a white turban on which name and type of business was written, and to wear one white and one black shoe, but we have reasons to doubt that

193

these discriminatory measures were enforced. They were subject to various taxes, but were either not allowed to own land, or were allotted less land than ordinary citizens. Thus they could not easily invest in land, the safest investment at that time. Finally, the government occasionally resorted to the method which was often used in the Near East: when in 782 the emperor ran out of money, he requested the merchants of the capital to 'loan' him a large sum—a request which in fact was a special tax.

Wang and Huang both proved good organizers of the peasant masses, and in a short time they had captured the whole of eastern China, without the military governors being able to do anything against them, for the provincial troops were more inclined to show sympathy to the peasant armies than to fight them. The terrified government issued an order to arm the people of the other parts of the country against the rebels; naturally this helped the rebels more than the government, since the peasants thus armed went over to the rebels. Finally Wang was offered a high office. But Huang urged him not to betray his own people, and Wang declined the offer. In the end the government, with the aid of the troops of the Turkish and Sogdian Sha-t'o, defeated Wang and beheaded him (878). Huang Ch'ao now moved into the south-east and the south, where in 879 he captured and burned down Canton; according to an Arab source, over 120,000 foreign merchants lost their lives in addition to the Chinese. From Canton Huang Ch'ao returned to the north, laden with loot from that wealthy commercial city. His advance was held up again by the Sha-t'o troops; he turned away to the lower Yangtze, and from there marched north again. At the end of 880 he captured the eastern capital. The emperor fled from the western capital, Ch'ang-an, into Szechwan, and Huang Ch'ao now captured with ease the western capital as well, and removed every member of the ruling family on whom he could lay hands. He then made himself emperor, in a Ch'i dynasty. It was the first time that a peasant rising had succeeded against the gentry.

There was still, however, the greatest disorder in the empire. There were other peasant armies on the move, armies that had deserted their governors and were fighting for themselves; finally, there were still a few supporters of the imperial house and, above all, the Sha-t'o, who had a competent commander with the sinified name of Li K'o-yung. The Sha-t'o, who had remained loyal to the government, revolted the moment the government had been overthrown. They ran the risk, however, of defeat at the hands of an alien army of the Chinese government's, commanded by an Uighur, and they therefore fled to the Tatars. In spite of this, the Chinese entered again into relations with the Sha-t'o, as without them there could be no possibility of getting rid of Huang Ch'ao. At the end of 881 Li K'o-yung fell upon the capital; there was a fearful battle. Huang Ch'ao was able to hold out, but a further attack was made in 883 and he was defeated and forced to flee; in 884 he was killed by the Sha-t'o.

This popular rising, which had only been overcome with the aid of foreign troops, brought the end of the T'ang dynasty. In 885 the T'ang emperor was able to return to the capital, but the only question now was whether China should be ruled by the Sha-t'o under Li K'o-yung or by some other military commander. In a short time Chu Ch'üan-chung, a former follower of Huang Ch'ao, proved to be the strongest of the commanders. In 890 open war began between the two leaders. Li K'o-yung was based on Shansi; Chu Ch'üan-chung had control of the plains in the east. Meanwhile the governors of Szechwan in the west and Chekiang in the south-east made themselves independent. Both declared themselves kings or emperors and set up dynasties of their own (from 895).

Within the capital, the emperor was threatened several times by revolts, so that he had to flee and place himself in the hands of Li K'o-yung as the only leader on whose loyalty he could count. Soon after this, however, the emperor fell into the hands of Chu Ch'üan-chung, who killed the whole entourage of the emperor, particularly the eunuchs; after a time he had the emperor himself killed, set a puppet—as had become customary—on the throne, and at the beginning of 907 took over the rule from him, becoming emperor in the 'Later Liang dynasty'.

That was the end of the T'ang dynasty, at the beginning of which China had risen to unprecedented power. Its downfall had been brought about by the military governors, who had built up their power and had become independent hereditary satraps, exploiting the people for their own purposes, and by their continual mutual struggles undermining the economic structure of the empire. In addition to this, the empire had been weakened first by its foreign trade and then by the dependence on foreigners, especially Turks, into which it had fallen owing to internal conditions. A large part of the national income had gone abroad. Such is the explanation of the great popular risings which ultimately brought the dynasty to its end.

(C) THE SECOND DIVISION OF CHINA: THE FIVE DYNASTIES (A.D. 906–960)

1 *Political situation in the tenth century*

The Chinese call the period from 906 to 960 the 'period of the Five Dynasties' (*Wu Tai*). This is not quite accurate. It is true that there were five dynasties in rapid succession in north China; but at the same time there were ten other dynasties in south China. The ten southern dynasties, however, are regarded by Chinese historians as not legitimate. The south was much better off with its illegitimate dynasties than the north with the legitimate ones. The dynasties in the south (we may dispense with giving their names) were the realms of some of the military governors so often mentioned above. These governors had already become independent at the end of the T'ang epoch; they declared themselves kings or emperors and ruled particular provinces in the south, the chief of which covered the territory of the present provinces of Szechwan, Kwangtung and Chekiang. In these territories there was comparative peace and economic prosperity, since they were able to control their own affairs and were no longer dependent on a corrupt central government. They also made great cultural progress, and they did not lose their importance later when they were annexed in the period of the Sung dynasty.

As an example of these states one may mention the small state of Ch'u in the present province of Hunan. Here, Ma Yin, a former carpenter (died 931), had made himself a king. He controlled some of the main trade routes, set up a clean administration, bought up all merchandise which the merchants brought, but allowed them to export only local products, mainly tea, iron and lead. This regulation gave him a personal income of several millions every year, and in addition fostered the exploitation of the natural resources of this hitherto retarded area.

2 Monopolistic trade in south China. Printing and paper money in the north

The prosperity of the small states of south China was largely due to the growth of trade, especially the tea trade. The habit of drinking tea seems to have been an ancient Tibetan custom, which spread to south-eastern China in the third century A.D. Since then there had been two main centres of production, Szechwan and south-eastern China. Until the eleventh century, Szechwan had remained the leading producer, and tea had been drunk in the Tibetan fashion, mixed with flour, salt, and ginger. It then began to be drunk without admixture. In the T'ang epoch tea drinking spread all over China, and there sprang up a class of wholesalers who bought the tea from the peasants, accumulated stocks, and distributed them. From 783 date the first attempts of the state to monopolize the tea trade and to make it a source of revenue; but it failed in an attempt to make the cultivation a state monopoly. A tea commissariat was accordingly set up to buy the tea from the producers and supply it to traders in possession of a state licence. There naturally developed then a pernicious collaboration between state officials and the wholesalers.

The latter soon eliminated the small traders, so that they themselves secured all the profit; official support was secured by bribery. The state and the wholesalers alike were keenly interested in the prevention of tea smuggling, which was strictly prohibited.

The position was much the same with regard to salt. We have here for the first time the association of officials with wholesalers or even with a monopoly trade. This was of the utmost importance in all later times. Monopoly progressed most rapidly in Szechwan, where there had always been a numerous commercial community. In the period of political fragmentation Szechwan, as the principal tea-producing region and at the same time an important producer of salt, was much better off than any other part of China. Salt in Szechwan was largely produced by, technically, very interesting salt wells which had existed there since around the first century B.C. The importance of salt will be understood if we remember that a grown-up person in China uses an average of twelve pounds of salt per year. The salt tax was the top budget item around A.D. 900.

South-eastern China was also the chief centre of porcelain production, although china clay is found also in north China. The use of porcelain spread more and more widely. The first translucent porcelain made its appearance, and porcelain became an important article of commerce both within the country and for export. Already the Muslim rulers of Baghdad around 800 used imported Chinese porcelain, and by the end of the fourteenth century porcelain was known in Eastern Africa. Exports to South-East Asia and Indonesia, and also to Japan gained more and more importance in later centuries. Manufacture of high quality porcelain calls for considerable amounts of capital investment and working capital; small manufacturers produce too many second-rate pieces; thus we have here the first beginnings of an industry that developed industrial towns such as Ching-tê, in which the majority of the population were workers and merchants, with some 10,000 families alone producing porcelain. Yet, for many centuries to come, the state controlled the production and even the design of porcelain and appropriated most of the production for use at court or as gifts.

The third important new development to be mentioned was that of printing, which since c. 770 was known in the form of wood-block printing. The first reference to a printed book dated from 835, and the most important event in this field was the first printing of the Classics by the orders of Feng Tao (882–954) around 940. The first attempts to use movable type in China occurred around 1045, although this invention did not get general acceptance in China. It was more commonly used in Korea from the thirteenth century on and revolutionized Europe from 1538 on. It seems that from the middle of the twentieth century on, the West, too, shows a tendency to come back to the printing of whole pages, but replacing the wood blocks by photographic plates or other means. In the Far East, just as in Europe, the invention of printing had far-reaching consequences. Books, which until then had been very dear, because they had had to be produced by copyists, could not be produced cheaply and in quantity. It became possible for a scholar to accumulate a library of his own and to work in a wide field, where earlier he had been confined to a few books or even a single text. The results were the spread of education, beginning with reading and writing, among wider groups, and the broadening of education: a large number of texts were read and compared, and no longer only a few. Private libraries came into existence, so that the imperial libraries were no longer the only ones. Publishing soon grew in extent, and in private enterprise works were printed that were not so serious and politically important as the classic books of the past. Thus a new type of literature, the literature of entertainment, could come into existence. Not all these consequences showed themselves at once; some made their first appearance later, in the Sung period.

A fourth important innovation, this time in north China, was the introduction of prototypes of paper money. The Chinese copper 'cash' was difficult or expensive to transport, simply because of its weight. It thus presented great obstacles to trade. Occasionally a region with an adverse balance of trade would lose all its copper money, with the result of a local deflation. From time to time, iron money was introduced in such deficit areas; it had for the first time been used in Szechwan for a short time in the first century B.C., and was there extensively used in the tenth century. In the history of business and trade, this iron money was an important step. For the first time, China had a medium of exchange which did not have the value which the metal of the coin itself had. The drawback was, that iron money was still relatively heavy. Paper money is an even more important step in the direction of symbolic money. So long as there was an orderly administration, the government could send money, though at considerable cost; but if the administration was not functioning well, the deflation continued. For this reason some provinces prohibited the export of copper money from their territory at the end of the eighth century. As the provinces were in the hands of military governors, the central government could do next to nothing to prevent this. On the other hand, the prohibition automatically made an end of all external trade. The merchants accordingly began to prepare deposit certificates, and in this way to set up a sort of transfer system. Soon these deposit certificates entered into circulation as a sort of medium of payment at first again in Szechwan, and gradually this led to a banking system and the linking of wholesale trade with it. This made possible a much greater volume of trade. Towards the end of the T'ang period the government began to issue deposit certificates of its own: the merchant deposited his copper money with a government agency, receiving in exchange a certificate which he could put into circulation like money. Meanwhile the government could put out the deposited money at interest, or throw it into general circulation. The government's deposit certificates were now printed. They were the predecessors of the paper money used from the time of the Sung.

3 Political history of the Five Dynasties

The southern states were a factor not to be ignored in the calculations of the northern dynasties. Although the southern kingdoms were involved in a confusion of mutual hostilities, any one of them might come to the fore as the ally of Turks or other northern powers. The capital of the first of the five northern dynasties (once more a Liang dynasty, but not to be confused with the Liang dynasty of the south in the sixth century) was, moreover, quite close to the territories of the southern dynasties, close to the site of the present K'aifeng, in the fertile plain of eastern China with its good means of transport. Militarily the town could not be held, for its one and only defence was the Yellow river. The founder of this Later Liang dynasty, Chu Ch'üan-chung (906), was himself an eastern Chinese and, as will be remembered, a past supporter of the revolutionary Huang Ch'ao, but he had then gone over to the T'ang and had gained high military rank.

His northern frontier remained still more insecure than the southern, for Chu Ch'üan-chung did not succeed in destroying the Turkish general Li K'o-yung; on the contrary, the latter continually widened the range of his power. Fortunately he, too, had an enemy at his back—the Kitan (or Khitan), whose ruler had made himself emperor in 916, and so staked a claim to reign over all China. The first Kitan emperor held a middle course between Chu and Li, and so was able to establish and expand his empire in peace. The striking power of his empire, which from 937 onward was officially called the Liao empire, grew steadily, because the old tribal league of the Kitan was transformed into a centrally commanded military organization.

To these dangers from abroad threatening the Later Liang state internal troubles were added. Chu Ch'üan-chung's dynasty was one of the three Chinese dynasties that have ever come to power through a popular rising. He himself was of peasant origin, and so were a large part of his subordinates and helpers. Many of them had originally been independent peasant leaders; others had been under Huang

199

Ch'ao. All of them were opposed to the gentry, and the great slaughter of the gentry of the capital, shortly before the beginning of Chu's rule, had been welcomed by Chu and his followers. The gentry therefore would not co-operate with Chu and preferred to join the Turk Li K'o-yung. But Chu could not confidently rely on his old comrades. They were jealous of his success in gaining the place they all coveted, and were ready to join in any independent enterprise as opportunity offered. All of them, moreover, as soon as they were given any administrative post, busied themselves with the acquisition of money and wealth as quickly as possible. These abuses not only ate into the revenues of the state but actually produced a common front between the peasantry and the remnants of the gentry against the upstarts.

In 917, after Li K'o-yung's death, the Sha-t'o beat off an attack from the Kitan, and so were safe for a time from the northern menace. They then marched against the Liang state, where a crisis had been produced in 912 after the murder of Chu Ch'üan-chung by one of his sons. The Liang generals saw no reason why they should fight for the dynasty, and all of them went over to the enemy. Thus the 'Later T'ang dynasty' (923–936) came into power in north China, under the son of Li K'o-yung.

The dominant element at this time was quite clearly the Chinese gentry, especially in western and central China. The Sha-t'o themselves must have been extraordinarily few in number, probably little more than 100,000 men. Most of them, moreover, were politically passive, being simple soldiers. Only the ruling family and its following played any active part, together with a few families related to it by marriage. The whole state was regarded by the Sha-t'o rulers as a sort of family enterprise, members of the family being placed in the most important positions. As there were not enough of them, they adopted into the family large numbers of aliens of all nationalities. Military posts were given to faithful members of Li K'o-yung's or his successor's bodyguard, and also to domestic servants and other clients of the family. Thus, while in the Later Liang state elements from the peasantry had risen in the world, some of these neo-gentry reaching the top of the social pyramid in the centuries that followed, in the Sha-t'o state some of its warriors, drawn from the most various peoples, entered the gentry class through their personal relations with the ruler. But in spite of all this the bulk of the officials came once more from the Chinese. These educated Chinese not only succeeded in winning over the rulers themselves to the Chinese cultural ideal, but persuaded them to adopt laws that substantially restricted the privileges of the Sha-t'o and brought advantages only to the Chinese gentry. Consequently all the Chinese historians are

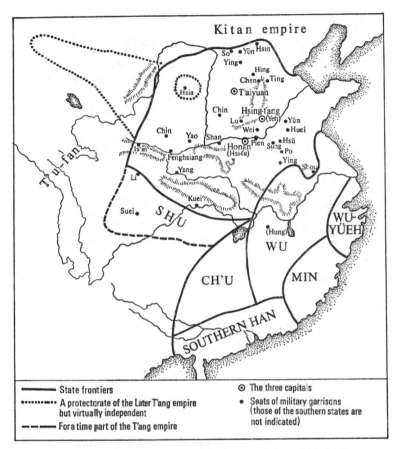

MAP 6   *The state of the Later T'ang dynasty (A.D. 923–935)*

enthusiastic about the 'Later T'ang', and especially about the emperor Ming Ti, who reigned from 927 onward, after the assassination of his predecessor. They also abused the Liang because they were against the gentry.

In 936 the Later T'ang dynasty gave place to the Later Chin dynasty (936–946), but this involved no change in the structure of the empire. The change of dynasty meant no more than that instead of the son following the father the son-in-law had ascended the throne. It was of more importance that the son-in-law, the Sha-t'o Turk Shih Ching-t'ang, succeeded in doing this by allying himself with the Kitan and ceding to them some of the northern provinces. The youthful successor, however, of the first ruler of this dynasty was soon made to realize that the Kitan regarded the founding of his dynasty as no more than a transition stage on the way to their annexation of the whole of north China. The old Sha-t'o nobles, who had not been sinified in the slightest, suggested a preventive war; the actual court group, strongly sinified, hesitated, but ultimately were unable to avoid war. The war was very quickly decided by several governors in eastern China going over to the Kitan, who had promised them the imperial title. In the course of 946–947 the Kitan occupied the capital and almost the whole of the country. In 947 the Kitan ruler proclaimed himself emperor of the Kitan and the Chinese.

The Chinese gentry seem to have accepted this situation because a Kitan emperor was just as acceptable to them as a Sha-t'o emperor; but the Sha-t'o were not prepared to submit to the Kitan regime, because under it they would have lost their position of privilege. At the head of this opposition group stood the Sha-t'o general Liu Chih-yüan, who founded the 'Later Han dynasty' (947–950). He was able to hold out against the Kitan only because in 947 the Kitan emperor died and his son had to leave China and retreat to the north; fighting had broken out between the empress dowager, who had some Chinese support, and the young heir to the throne. The new Turkish dynasty, however, was unable to withstand the internal Chinese resistance. Its founder died in 948, and his son, owing to his youth, was entirely in the hands of a court clique. In his effort to free himself from the tutelage of this group he made a miscalculation, for the men on whom he thought he could depend were largely supporters of the clique. So he lost his throne and his life, and a Chinese general, Kuo Wei, took his place, founding the 'Later Chou dynasty' (951–959).

A feature of importance was that in the years of the short-lived 'Later Han dynasty' a tendency showed itself among the Chinese military leaders to work with the states in the south. The increase in the political influence of the south was due to its economic advance while the north was reduced to economic chaos by the continual heavy fighting, and by the complete irresponsibility of the Sha-t'o ruler in financial matters: several times in this period the whole of the money in the state treasury was handed out to soldiers to prevent them from going over to some enemy or other. On the other hand, there was a tendency in the south for the many neighbouring states to amalgamate, and as this process took place close to the frontier of north China the northern states could not passively look on. During the 'Later Han' period there were wars and risings, which continued in the time of the 'Later Chou'.

On the whole, the few years of the rule of the second emperor of the 'Later Chou' (954–958) form a bright spot in those dismal fifty-five years. Sociologically regarded, that dynasty formed merely a transition stage on the way to the Sung dynasty that now followed: the Chinese gentry ruled under the leadership of an upstart who had risen from the ranks, and they ruled in accordance with the old principles of gentry rule. The Sha-t'o, who had formed the three preceding dynasties, had been so reduced that they were now a tiny minority and no longer counted. This minority had only been able to maintain its position through the special social conditions created by the 'Later Liang' dynasty: the Liang, who had come from the lower classes of the population, had driven the gentry into the arms of the Sha-t'o Turks. As soon as the upstarts, in so far as they had not fallen again or been exterminated, had more or less assimilated themselves to the old gentry, and on the other hand the leaders of the Sha-t'o had become numerically too weak, there was a possi-bility of resuming the old form of rule.

There had been certain changes in this period. The north-west of China, the region of the old capital Ch'ang-an, had been so ruined by the fighting that had gone on mainly there and farther north, that it was eliminated as a centre of power for a hundred years to come: it had been largely depopulated. The north was under the rule of the Kitan: its trade, which in the past had been with the Huang-ho basin, was now perforce diverted to Peking, which soon became the main centre of the power of the Kitan. The south, par-ticularly the lower Yangtze region and the province of Szechwan, had made economic progress, at least in comparison with the north; consequently it had gained in political importance.

One other event of this time has to be mentioned: the great persecu-tion of Buddhism in 955, but not only because 30,336 temples and monasteries were secularized and only some 2,700 with 61,200 monks were left. Although the immediate reason for this action seems to have been that too many men entered the monasteries in order to avoid being taken as soldiers, the effect of the law of 955 was that from now on the Buddhists were put under regulations which clarified once and for ever their position within the framework of a society which had as its aim to define clearly the status of each individual within each social class. Private persons were no more allowed to erect temples and monasteries. The number of temples per district was legally fixed. A person could become a monk only if the head of the family gave its permission. He had to be over fifteen years of age and had to know by heart at least one hundred pages of texts. The state took over the control of the ordinations which could be performed only after a successful examination. Each year a list of all monks had to be submitted to the government in two copies. Monks had to carry six identification cards with them, one of which was the ordination diploma for which a fee had to be paid to the government (already since 755). The diploma was, in the eleventh century, issued by the Bureau of Sacrifices, but the money was collected by the Ministry of Agriculture. It can be regarded as a payment in lieu of land tax. The price was in the eleventh century 130 strings, which represented the value of a small farm or the value of some 17,000 litres of grain. The price of the diploma went up to 220 strings in 1101, and the then government sold 30,000 diplomas per year in order to get still more cash. But as diplomas could be traded, a black market developed, on which they were sold for as little as twenty strings.

12 Ancient tiled pagoda at Chengting (Hopei).
(Photo H. Hammer-Morrisson.)

13 Horse-training. Painting by Li Lung-mien. Late Sung period.
(Manchu Imperial House Collection.)

CHAPTER NINE

Modern Times

(A) GENERAL CHARACTERISTICS

Any division into periods is arbitrary as changes do not happen from one year to the next. The first beginnings of the changes which led to the 'Modern Times' actually can be seen from the end of An Lushan's rebellion on, from c. A.D. 780 on. The period of the 'Five Dynasties' can be regarded as the end of the 'Middle Ages' or with about just as much justification, the beginning of a new age. In any case, the changes which went on in all parts of China, in all the different local governments, were very radical and deep-going, and only around A.D. 1000 was the transformation more or less completed.

If we want to characterize the 'Modern Times' by one concept, we would have to call this epoch the time of the emergence of a middle class, and it will be remembered that the growth of the middle class in Europe was also the decisive change between the Middle Ages and Modern Times in Europe. The parallelism should, however, not be overdone. The gentry continued to play a role in China during the Modern Times, much more than the aristocracy did in Europe. The middle class did not ever really get into power during the whole period. And yet, if we had no documents about China after the year 1300, we would probably have concluded that China entered the 'industrial age' shortly after that date. Probably we would also have predicted the development of a clear capitalistic system. It did not happen, and the reasons for this are not yet fully clear; different explanations have been proposed.

While we will discuss the individual developments later in some detail, a few words about the changes in general might be given already here. The wars which followed Huang Ch'ao's rebellion greatly affected the ruling gentry. A number of families were so strongly affected that they lost their importance and disappeared. Commoners from the followers of Huang Ch'ao or other armies succeeded in getting into power, acquiring property and entering the ranks of the gentry. At about A.D. 1000 almost half of the gentry families were new families of low origin. The state, often ruled by men who had just moved up, was no more interested in the aristocratic manners of the old gentry families, especially no more interested in their genealogies. When conditions began to improve after A.D. 1000, and when the new families felt themselves as real gentry families, they tried to set up a mechanism to protect the status of their families. In the eleventh century private genealogies began to be more generally kept, and such genealogies have often been preserved to the present day. Their function was on the one side to avoid mistakes in the ancestral worship by forgetting to honour one ancestor or by putting his ancestral tablet in a wrong place. Another function was that any claim against the clan could be checked. Clans set up rules of behaviour and procedure to regulate all affairs of the clan and its branches without the necessity of asking the state to interfere in case of conflict. Many such 'clan rules' exist in China and also in Japan, which took over this innovation. Clans often set apart special pieces of land as clan land; the income of this land was to be used to secure a minimum of support for every clan member and his own family, so that no member ever could fall into utter poverty. Clan schools which were run by income from special pieces of clan land were established to guarantee an education for the members of the clan, again in order to make sure that the clan would remain a part of the élite. Many clans set up special marriage rules for clan members, and after some time cross-cousin marriages between two or three families were legally allowed; such marriages tended to fasten bonds between clans and to prevent the loss of property by marriage. While on the one hand, a new 'clan consciousness' grew up among the gentry families in order to secure their power, tax and corvée legislation, especially in the eleventh century, induced many families to split up into small families.

It can be shown that over the next centuries, the power of the family head increased. He was now regarded as owner of the property, not only mere administrator of family property. He got power over the life and death of his children. The increase of power went together with a change of position of the ruler. The period of transition (until c. A.D. 1000) was followed by a period of 'moderate absolutism' (until 1278) in which emperors as persons played a greater role than before, and some emperors, such as Shen Tsung (in 1071), even declared that they regarded the welfare of the masses as more important than the profit of the gentry. After 1278, however, the personal influence of the emperors grew further towards absolutism and at times became pure despotism.

Individuals, especially family heads, gained more freedom in

'Modern Times'. Not only the period of transition, but also the following period was a time of much greater social mobility than existed in the Middle Ages. By various legal and/or illegal means people could move up into positions of power and wealth: we know of many merchants who succeeded in being allowed to enter the state examinations and thus got access to jobs in the administration. Large, influential gentry families in the capital protected sons from less important families and thus gave them a chance to move into the gentry. Thus, these families built up a clientele of lesser gentry families which assisted them and upon the loyalty of which they could count. The gentry can from now on be divided into two parts. First, there was a 'big gentry' which consisted of much fewer families than in earlier times and which directed the policy in the capital; and second, there was a 'small gentry' which was operating mainly in the provincial cities, directing local affairs and bound by ties of loyalty to big gentry families. Gentry cliques now extended into the provinces and it often became possible to identify a clique with a geographical area, which, however, usually did not indicate particularistic tendencies.

Individual freedom did not show itself only in greater social mobility. The restrictions which, for instance, had made the craftsmen and artisans almost into serfs, were gradually lifted. From the early sixteenth century on, craftsmen were free and no longer subject to forced labour services for the state. Only in the first decades of the eighteenth century did the 'outcast' groups acquire the status of citizens. Such 'outcasts' were small ethnic groups, living as minorities in areas now fully colonized by Chinese and performing 'dishonourable' professions, such as prostitution and music. Slavery, too, faded out slowly over the centuries. However, some of the larger ethnic groups living in areas where they still were the majority, remained under restrictions to the twentieth century.

To return to the craftsmen: most of them down to the nineteenth century still had their shops in one lane or street and lived above their shops, as they had done in the earlier period. But from now on, they began to organize in guilds of an essentially religious character, as similar guilds in other parts of Asia at the same time also did. They provided welfare services for their members, made some attempts towards standardization of products and prices, imposed taxes upon their members, kept their streets clean and tried to regulate salaries. Apprentices were initiated in a kind of semi-religious ceremony, and often meetings took place in temples. No guild, however, connected people of the same craft living in different cities. Thus, they did not achieve political power. Furthermore, each trade had its own guild; in Peking in the nineteenth century there existed over 420 different guilds. Thus, guilds failed to achieve political influence even within individual cities.

Probably at the same time, regional associations, the so-called *huikuan* originated. Such associations united people from one city or one area who lived in another city. People of different trades, but mainly businessmen, came together under elected chiefs and councillors. Sometimes, such regional associations could function as pressure groups, especially as they were usually financially stronger than the guilds. They often owned city property or farmland. Not all merchants, however, were so organized. Although merchants remained under humiliating restrictions as to the colour and material of their dress and the prohibition to ride a horse, they could more often circumvent such restrictions and in general had much more freedom in this epoch.

Trade, including overseas trade, developed greatly from now on. Soon we find in the coastal ports a special office which handled custom and registration affairs, supplied interpreters for foreigners, received them officially and gave good-bye dinners when they left. Down to the thirteenth century, most of this overseas trade was still in the hands of foreigners, mainly Indians. Entrepreneurs hired ships, if they were not ship-owners, hired trained merchants who in turn hired sailors mainly from the South-East Asian countries, and sold their own merchandise as well as took goods on commission. Wealthy Chinese families invested money in such foreign enterprises and in some cases even gave their daughters in marriage to foreigners in order to profit from this business.

While there was thus more freedom for men of the ranks below the gentry than ever before, there was a severe restriction of the freedom of women—all women. This may be a consequence of the greater powers of the family heads at this time. Remarriage of widows was now regarded as immoral: a widow had belonged to her husband in life, she still belonged to him or at least to his family after his death and could not simply go away and join another family. Women, with the exception of courtesans and musicians, could normally no more participate in parties. And, again with the exception of a small ethnic group, women did no more participate in the actual work on the land: their place was in the house where they were supposed to spin, weave, cook, and take care of the children.

We also see an emergence of industry from the eleventh century on. We find men who were running almost monopolistic enterprises, such as preparing charcoal for iron production and producing iron and steel at the same time; some of these men had several factories, operating under hired and qualified managers with more than 500 labourers. We find beginnings of a labour legislation and the first strikes (A.D. 782 the first strike of merchants in the capital; 1601 first strike of textile workers).

Some of these labourers were so-called 'vagrants', farmers who had secretly left their land or their landlord's land for various reasons, and had shifted to other regions where they did not register and thus did not pay taxes. Entrepreneurs liked to hire them for industries outside the towns where supervision by the government was not so strong; naturally, these 'vagrants' were completely at the mercy of their employers.

Since c. 780 the economy can again be called a money economy; more and more taxes were imposed in form of money instead of in kind. This pressure forced farmers out of the land and into the cities in order to earn there the cash they needed for their tax payments. These men provided the labour force for industries, and this in turn led to the strong growth of the cities, especially in central China where trade and industries developed most.

Wealthy people not only invested in industrial enterprises, but also began to make heavy investments in agriculture in the vicinity of cities in order to increase production and thus income. We find men who drained lakes in order to create fields below the water level for easy irrigation; others made floating fields on lakes and avoided land tax payments; still others combined pig and fish breeding in one operation.

The introduction of money economy and money taxes led to a need for more coinage. As metal was scarce and minting very expensive, iron coins were introduced, silver became more and more common as a means of exchange, and paper money was issued. As the relative value of these moneys changed with supply and demand, speculation became a flourishing business which led to further enrichment of people in business. Even the government became more money-minded: costs of operations and even of wars were carefully calculated in order to achieve savings; financial specialists were appointed by the government, just as clans appointed such men for the efficient administration of their clan properties.

Yet no real capitalism or industrialism developed until towards the end of this epoch, although at the end of the twelfth century almost all conditions for such a development seemed to be given.

(B) PERIOD OF MODERATE ABSOLUTISM

(1) The Northern Sung dynasty

1 *Southward expansion*

The founder of the Sung dynasty, Chao K'uang-yin (ruled 960–974), came of a Chinese military family living to the south of Peking.

He advanced from general to emperor, and so differed in no way from the emperors who had preceded him. But his dynasty did not disappear as quickly as the others; for this there were several reasons. To begin with, there was the simple fact that he remained alive longer than the other founders of dynasties, and so was able to place his rule on a firmer foundation. But in addition to this he followed a new course, which in certain ways smoothed matters for him and for his successors, in foreign policy.

This Sung dynasty, as Chao K'uang-yin named it, no longer turned against the northern peoples, particularly the Kitan, but against the south. This was not exactly an heroic policy: the north of China remained in the hands of the Kitan. There were frequent clashes, but no real effort was made to destroy the Kitan, whose dynasty was now called 'Liao'. The second emperor of the Sung was actually heavily defeated several times by the Kitan. But they, for their part, made no attempt to conquer the whole of China, especially since the task would have become more and more burdensome the farther south the Sung expanded. And very soon there were other reasons why the Kitan should refrain from turning their whole strength against the Chinese.

As we said, the Sung turned at once against the states in the south. Some of the many small southern states had made substantial economic and cultural advance, but militarily they were not strong. Chao K'uang-yin (named as emperor T'ai Tsu) attacked them in succession. Most of them fell very quickly and without any heavy fighting, especially since the Sung dealt mildly with the defeated rulers and their following. The gentry and the merchants in these small states could not but realize the advantages of a widened and well-ordered economic field, and they were therefore entirely in favour of the annexation of their country so soon as it proved to be tolerable. And the Sung empire could only endure and gain strength if it had control of the regions along the Yangtze and around Canton, with their great economic resources. The process of absorbing the small states in the south continued until 980. Before it was ended, the Sung tried to extend their influence in the south beyond the Chinese border, and secured a sort of protectorate over parts of North Vietnam (973). This sphere of influence was politically insignificant and not directly of any economic importance; but it fulfilled for the Sung the same functions which colonial territories fulfilled for Europeans, serving as a field of operation for the commercial class, who imported raw materials from it—mainly, it is true, luxury articles such as special sorts of wood, perfumes, ivory, and so on—and exported Chinese manufactures. As the power of the empire grew, this zone of influence extended as far as Indonesia: the process had begun in the T'ang period. The trade with the south had not the deleterious effects of the trade with Central Asia. There was no sale of refined metals, and none of fabrics, as the natives produced their own textiles which sufficed for their needs. And the export of porcelain brought no economic injury to China, but the reverse.

This Sung policy was entirely in the interest of the gentry and of the trading community which was now closely connected with them. Undoubtedly it strengthened China. The policy of non-intervention in the north was endurable even when peace with the Kitan had to be bought by the payment of an annual tribute. From 1004 onward, 100,000 ounces of silver and 200,000 bales of silk were paid annually to the Kitan, amounting in value to about 270,000 strings of cash, each of 1,000 coins. The state budget amounted to some 20,000,000 strings of cash. In 1038 the payments amounted to 500,000 strings, but the budget was by then much larger. One is liable to get a false impression when reading of these big payments if one does not take into account what percentage they formed of the total revenues of the state. The tribute to the Kitan amounted to less than 2 per cent of the revenue, while the expenditure on the army accounted for 25 per cent of the budget. It cost much less to pay tribute than to maintain large armies and go to war. Financial considerations played a great part during the Sung epoch. The taxation revenue of the empire rose rapidly after the pacification of the south; soon after the beginning of the dynasty the state budget was double that of the T'ang. If the state expenditure in the eleventh century had not continually grown through the increase in military expenditure—in spite of everything! —there would have come a period of great prosperity in the empire.

2 Administration and army. Inflation

The Sung emperor, like the rulers of the transition period, had gained the throne by his personal abilities as military leader; in fact, he had been made emperor by his soldiers as had happened to so many emperors in later Imperial Rome. For the next 300 years we observe a change in the position of the emperor. On the one hand, if he was active and intelligent enough, he exercised much more personal influence than the rulers of the Middle Ages. On the other hand, at the same time, the emperors were much closer to their ministers as before. We hear of ministers who patted the ruler on the shoulders when they retired from an audience; another one fell asleep on the emperor's knee and was not punished for this familiarity. The emperor was called *kuan-chia* (Administrator) and even called himself so. And in the early twelfth century an emperor stated 'I do not regard the empire as my personal property; my job is to guide the people.' Financially-minded as the Sung dynasty was, the cost of

211

the operation of the palace was calculated, so that the emperor had a budget: in 1068 the salaries of all officials in the capital amounted to 40,000 strings of money per month, the armies 100,000, and the emperor's ordinary monthly budget was 70,000 strings. For festivals, imperial birthdays, weddings and burials extra allowances were made. Thus, the Sung rulers may be called 'moderate absolutists' and not despots.

One of the first acts of the new Sung emperor, in 963, was a fundamental reorganization of the administration of the country. The old system of a civil administration and a military administration independent of it was brought to an end and the whole administration of the country placed in the hands of civil officials. The gentry welcomed this measure and gave it full support, because it enabled the influence of the gentry to grow and removed the fear of competition from the military, some of whom did not belong by birth to the gentry. The generals by whose aid the empire had been created were put on pension, or transferred to civil employment, as quickly as possible. The army was demobilized, and this measure was bound up with the settlement of peasants in the regions which war had depopulated, or on new land. Soon after this the revenue noticeably increased. Above all, the army was placed directly under the central administration, and the system of military governors was thus brought to an end. The soldiers became mercenaries of the state, whereas in the past there had been conscription. In 975 the army had numbered only 378,000, and its cost had not been insupportable. Although the numbers increased greatly, reaching 912,000 in 1017 and 1,259,000 in 1045, this implied no increase in military strength; for men who had once been soldiers remained with the army even when they were too old for service. Moreover, the soldiers grew more and more exacting; when detachments were transferred to another region, for instance, the soldiers would not carry their baggage; an army of porters had to be assembled. The soldiers also refused to go to regions remote from their homes until they were given extra pay. Such allowances gradually became customary, and so the military expenditure grew by leaps and bounds without any corresponding increase in the striking power of the army.

The government was soon unable to meet the whole cost of the army out of taxation revenue. The attempt was made to cover the expenditure by coining fresh money. In connection with the increase in commercial capital described above, and the consequent beginning of an industry, China's metal production had greatly increased. In 1050 thirteen times as much silver, eight times as much copper, and fourteen times as much iron was produced as in 800. It is estimated that the production per year was perhaps around 2,120,000 tons. In part, this was made possible by the extensive use of coal instead of the predominant use of charcoal in earlier periods. Iron money remained in use in Szechwan and parts of Hunan, but copper remained the main currency. The cost of minting, however, amounted in China to about 75 per cent and often over 100 per cent of the value of the money coined.

To meet the increasing expenditure, an unexampled quantity of new money was put into circulation. The state budget increased from 22,200,000 in A.D. 1000 to 150,800,000 in 1021. The Kitan state coined a great deal of silver, and some of the tribute was paid to it in silver. The greatly increased production of silver led to its being put into circulation in China itself. And this provided a new field of speculation, through the variations in the rates for silver and for copper. Speculation was also possible with the deposit certificates, which were issued in quantities by the state from the beginning of the eleventh century, and to which the first true paper money was soon added. The paper money and the certificates were redeemable at a definite date, but at a reduction of at least 3 per cent of their value; this, too, yielded a certain revenue to the state.

The inflation that resulted from all these measures brought profit to the big merchants in spite of the fact that they had to supply directly or indirectly all non-agricultural taxes (in 1160 some 40,000,000 strings annually), especially the salt tax (50 per cent), wine tax (36 per cent), tea tax (7 per cent) and customs (7 per cent). Although the official economic thinking remained Confucian, i.e. anti-business and pro-agrarian, we find in this time insight in price laws, for instance, that peace times and/or decrease of population induce deflation. The government had always attempted to manipulate the prices by inter-ference. Already in much earlier times, again and again, attempts had been made to lower the prices by the so-called 'ever-normal granaries' of the government which threw grain on the market when prices were too high and bought grain when prices were low. But now, in addition to such measures, we also find others which exhibit a deeper insight: in a period of starvation the scholar and official Fan Chung-yen, instead of officially reducing grain prices, raised the prices in his district considerably. Although the population got angry, merchants started to import large amounts of grain; as soon as this happened, Fan (himself a big landowner) reduced the price again. Similar results were achieved by others by just stimulating merchants to import grain into deficit areas.

It was in land that the newly formed capital was invested. Thus we see in the Sung period, and especially in the eleventh century, the greatest accumulation of estates that there had ever been up to then in China.

Many of these estates came into origin as gifts of the emperor to individuals or to temples, others were created on hillsides on land which belonged to the villages. From this time on, the rest of the village commons in China proper disappeared. Villagers could no longer use the top-soil of the hills as fertilizer, or the trees as firewood and building material. In addition, the hillside estates diverted the water of springs and creeks, thus damaging severely the irrigation works of the villagers in the plains. The estates (*chuang*) were controlled by appointed managers who often became hereditary managers. There is still a controversy as to what the tenants were. Some say they were serfs, while others regard them as tenants in the narrower definition of the word. Unfortunately, Chinese at the time had no clear terminology, and we probably have to assume that combinations of all kinds existed. Some tenants were probably the non-registered migrants, of whom we spoke above. As such, they depended upon the managers who could always denounce them to the authorities, which would lead to punishment, because nobody was allowed to leave his home without officially changing his registration. If such restriction of movement were typical of tenants only, we could properly call them serfs, but other citizens were under the same restrictions, officials excepted. Other scholars think that some tenants were freed slaves. It all depends upon the explanation of the term *k'o-hu* (guest families). As officials had 'office land' as source of income, and as the state had state land, we should probably assume that such land was tilled by tenants who were not allowed to leave, because officials were transferred quite often and would have a hard time to find new tenants every time they were transferred to a new post. The problem arises that our documents are often tendentious. Some make overstatements for political reasons, others talk about exceptional and regional situations, and the interpreters often have their own biases. Only in-depth studies of small areas over longer periods of time can be of help, and such studies are under way in Japan and the West. Certainly, there was not only a great diversity of rural labour organization, but also of farming itself. In Sung times, many tanks to store water for irrigation purposes were built; sluices to regulate the flow were built. We even hear that in addition to the treadmills and other implements to lift water into the fields, some windmills were in use. On the other hand, some farmers surrounded low-lying land by dykes and had fields below the water level ('polders', as they are called in Holland), while still others raised the level by excavating a part of their land, thus creating fields safe of floods, and ponds in which they could raise fish.

To return to the estates: some of them operated their own mills and even textile factories with non-registered weavers. It seems that in course of time, many such estates later became villages (recogniz-able by the syllable -*chuang* at the end of the village name) which were, from the beginning, not merely farming villages but also had some 'industries' in the village, in contrast to villages in other parts of Asia where villages house only farmers and no other professionals,

A new development in this period were the 'clan estates' (*i-chuang*). created by Fan Chung-yen (989–1052) in 1048. The incomes of these clan estates were used for the benefit of the whole clan, were con-trolled by clan-appointed managers and had tax-free status, guaran-teed by the government which regarded them as welfare institutions. Technically, they might better be called corporations because they were similar in structure to some of our industrial corporations. Under the Chinese economic system, large-scale landowning always proved socially and politically injurious. Up to very recent times the peasant who rented his land paid 40–50 per cent of the produce to the landowner, who was responsible for payment of the normal land tax. The landlord, however, had always found means of evading payment. As each district had to yield a definite amount of taxation, the more the big landowners succeeded in evading payment the more had to be paid by the independent small farmers. These independent peasants could then either 'give' their land to the big landowner and pay rent to him, thus escaping from the attentions of the tax-officer, or simply leave the district and secretly enter another one where they were not registered. In either case the government lost taxes.

All this made itself felt especially in the south with its great estates of tax-evading landowners. Here the remaining small peasant-owners had to pay the new taxes or to become tenants of the landowners and lose their property, though some of them may have managed to sur-vive by becoming part-tenant and part-owners. Still others seem to have managed by going into commercial farming or fruit-culture, fish-breeding, or doing labour services in transport business. The diversification of rural life is a typical trait of the Sung time. The agricultural boom which took place in spite of the pressure of taxa-tion may, perhaps, at least in part be an effect of a new period of warmer climate (900–1100?).

Furthermore, we find now a significant difference between the northern and the southern parts of the Sung empire. The north was still suffering from the war-devastation of the tenth century. As the landlords were always the first sufferers from popular uprisings as well as from war, they had disappeared, leaving their former tenants as free peasants. From this period on, we have enough data to observe a social 'law': as the capital was the largest consumer, especially of high-priced products such as vegetables which could not be trans-ported over long distances, the gentry always tried to control the

215

land around the capital. Here, we find the highest concentration of landlords and tenants. Production in this inner circle shifted at least partly from rice and wheat to mulberry trees for silk, and vegetables grown under the trees. These urban demands resulted in the growth of an 'industrial' quarter on the outskirts of the capital, in which especially silk for the upper classes was produced. The next circle also contained many landlords, but production was more in staple foods such as wheat and rice which could be transported. Exploitation in this second circle was not much less than in the first circle, because of less close supervision by the authorities. In the third circle we find independent subsistence farmers. Some provincial capitals, especially in Szechwan, exhibited a similar pattern of circles. With each shift of the capital, a complete reorganization appeared: landlords and officials gave up their properties, cultivation changed, and a new system of circles began to form around the new capital. We find, therefore, the grotesque result that the thinly populated province of Shensi in the north-west yielded about a quarter of the total revenues of the state: it had no large landowners, no wealthy gentry, with their evasion of taxation, only a mass of newly settled small peasants' holdings. For this reason the government was particularly interested in that province, and closely watched the political changes in its neighbourhood. In 990 a man belonging to a sinified Toba family, living on the border of Shensi, had made himself king with the support of remnants of Toba tribes. In 1034 came severe fighting, and in 1038 the king proclaimed himself emperor, in the Hsia dynasty, and threatened the whole of north-western China. Tribute was now also paid to this state (250,000 strings), but the fight against it continued, to save that important province.

These were the main events in internal and external affairs during the Sung period until 1068. It will be seen that foreign affairs were of much less importance than developments in the country.

3 Reforms and welfare schemes

The situation just described was bound to produce a reaction. In spite of the inflationary measures the revenue fell, partly in consequence of the tax evasions of the great landowners. It fell from 150,000,000 in 1021 to 116,000,000 in 1065. Expenditure did not fall, and there was a constant succession of budget deficits. The young emperor Shen Tsung (1068–1085) became convinced that the policy followed by the ruling clique of officials and gentry was bad, and he gave his adhesion to a small group led by Wang An-shih (1021–1086). The ruling gentry clique represented especially the interests of the large tea producers and merchants in Szechwan and Kiangsi. It advocated a policy of laissez-faire in trade: it held that

216

everything would adjust itself. Wang An-shih himself came from Kiangsi and was therefore supported at first by the government clique, within which the Kiangsi group was trying to gain predominance over the Szechwan group. But Wang An-shih came from a poor family, as did his supporters, for whom he quickly secured posts. They represented the interests of the small landholders and the small dealers. This group succeeded in gaining power, and in carrying out a number of reforms, all directed against the monopolist merchants. Credits for small peasants were introduced, and officials were given bigger salaries, in order to make them independent and to recruit officials who were not big landowners. The army was greatly reduced, and in addition to the paid soldiery a national militia was created. Special attention was paid to the province of Shensi, whose conditions were taken more or less as a model.

It seems that one consequence of Wang's reforms was a strong fall in the prices, i.e. a deflation; therefore, as soon as the first decrees were issued, the large owners and the merchants who were allied to them, offered furious opposition. A group of officials and landlords who still had large properties in the vicinity of Loyang—at that time a quiet cultural centre—also joined them. Even some of Wang An-shih's former adherents came out against him. After a few years the emperor was no longer able to retain Wang An-shih and had to abandon the new policy. How really political interests were here at issue may be seen from the fact that for many of the new decrees which were not directly concerned with economic affairs, such, for instance, as the reform of the examination system, Wang An-shih was strongly attacked though his opponents had themselves advocated them in the past and had no practical objection to offer to them. The contest, however, between the two groups was not over. The monopolistic landowners and their merchants had the upper hand from 1086 to 1102, but then the advocates of the policy represented by Wang again came into power for a short time. They had but little success to show, as they did not remain in power long enough and, owing to the strong opposition, they were never able to make their control really effective.

Basically, both groups were against allowing the developing middle class and especially the merchants to gain too much freedom, and whatever freedom they in fact gained, came through extra-legal or illegal practices. A proverb of the time said 'People hate their ruler as animals hate the net (of the hunter).' The basic laws of medieval times which had attempted to create stable social classes remained: down to the eighteenth century there were slaves, different classes of serfs, 'commoners', and free burghers. Craftsmen remained under work obligation. Merchants were second-class people. Each class had to wear dresses of special colour and material, so that the social status of a person, even if he were not an official and thus recognizable by his insignia, was immediately clear when one saw him. The houses of different classes differed from one another by the type of tiles, the decorations of the doors and gates; the size of the main reception room of the house was prescribed and was kept small for all non-officials; and even size and form of the tombs was prescribed in detail for each class. Once a person had a certain privilege, he and his descendants, even if they had lost their position in the bureaucracy, retained their elevated status in the community. All burghers were admitted to the examinations and thus there was a certain social mobility allowed within the leading class of the society, and a new 'small gentry' emerged. There is no doubt that in the Sung states (as opposed to the northern Liao and later Chin states) examinations became more and more the ladder to success. But this broadening of the basis of the 'upper class' also meant that in general, the power of the central gentry, i.e. those families whose members were in offices around the court, diminished, and in the countryside the dominant element now became the 'small gentry', whose status depended in part of the political situation at court, in part on the local situation: local fights between gentry families as well as severe floods or droughts could severely affect them. There was now a feeling of insecurity within the gentry. The eleventh and twelfth centuries were periods of extensive social legislation in order to give the lower classes some degree of security and thus prevent them from attempting to upset the status quo. In addition to the 'ever-normal granaries' of the state, 'social granaries' were revived, into which all farmers of a village had to deliver grain for periods of need. In 1098 a bureau for housing and care was created which created homes for the old and destitute; 1102 a bureau for medical care sent state doctors to homes and hospitals as well as to private homes to care for poor patients; from 1104 a bureau of burials took charge of the costs of burials of poor persons. Doctors as craftsmen were under corvée obligation and could easily be ordered by the state. Buddhist priests sometimes also took charge of medical care, burial costs and hospitalization. The state gave them premiums if they did good work. The Ministry of Civil Affairs made the surveys of cases and costs, while the Ministry of Finances paid the costs. We hear of state orphanages in 1247, a free pharmacy in 1248, state hospitals were reorganized in 1143. In 1167 the government gave low-interest loans to poor persons and (from 1159 on) sold cheap grain from state granaries. Fire protection services in large cities were organized. Finally, from 1141 on, the government opened up to twenty-three geisha houses for the entertainment of soldiers who were far from home in the capital and had no possibility for other amusements. Public baths had existed already some centuries ago; now Buddhist temples opened public baths as a social service.

Social services for the officials were also extended. Already from the eighth century on, offices were closed every tenth day and during holidays, a total of almost eighty days per year. Even criminals got some leave and exiles had the right of a home leave once every three years. The pensions for retired officials after the age of seventy which amounted to 50 per cent of the salary from the eighth century on, were again raised, though widows did not receive benefits.

All these data, however, should be treated with care: we really do not know how often free medicines were distributed, how many state hospitals there were, how they functioned and who actually was accepted as a patient. The same is the case with the above-mentioned 'sumptuary laws': to some degree, they were operating, but to what degree?

4 Cultural situation (philosophy, religion, literature, painting)

Culturally the eleventh century was the most active period China had so far experienced, apart from the fourth century B.C. As a consequence of the immensely increased number of educated people resulting from the invention of printing, circles of scholars and private schools set up by scholars were scattered all over the country. The various philosophical schools differed in their political attitude and in the choice of literary models with which they were politically in sympathy. Thus Wang An-shih and his followers preferred the rigid classic style of Han Yü (768–825) who lived in the T'ang period and had also been an opponent of the monopolistic tendencies of pre-capitalism. For the Wang An-shih group formed itself into a school with a philosophy of its own and with its own commentaries on the classics. As the representative of the small merchants and the small landholders, this school advocated policies of state control and specialized in the study and annotation of classical books which seemed to favour their ideas.

But the Wang An-shih school was unable to hold its own against the school that stood for monopolist trade capitalism, the new philosophy described as Neo-Confucianism or the Sung school. Here Confucianism and Buddhism were for the first time in a fruitful dialogue. In the last centuries, Buddhistic ideas had penetrated all of Chinese culture: the slaughtering of animals and the executions of criminals were allowed only on certain days, in accordance with Buddhist rules. Formerly, monks and nuns had to greet the emperor as all citizens had to do; now they were exempt from this rule. On the other hand, the first Sung emperor was willing to throw himself

219

to the earth in front of the Buddha statues, but he was told he did not have to do it because he was the 'Buddha of the present time' and thus equal to the God. Buddhist priests participated in the celebrations on the emperor's birthday, and emperors from time to time gave free meals to large crowds of monks. Buddhist thought entered the field of justice: in Sung time we hear complaints that judges did not apply the laws and showed laxity, because they hoped to gain religious merit by sparing the lives of criminals. We have seen how the main current of Buddhism had changed from a revolutionary to a reactionary doctrine. The new gentry of the eleventh century adopted a number of elements of this reactionary Buddhism and incorporated them in the Confucianist system. This brought into Confucianism a metaphysic which it had lacked in the past, greatly extending its influence on the people and at the same time taking the wind out of the sails of Buddhism. The gentry never again placed themselves on the side of the Buddhist Church as they had done in the T'ang period. When they got tired of Confucianism, they interested themselves in Taoism or the politically innocent, escapist, meditative Buddhism.

Men like Chou Tun-i (1017–1073) and Chang Tsai (1020–1077) developed a cosmological theory which could measure up with Buddhistic cosmology and metaphysics. But perhaps more important was the attempt of the Neo-Confucianists to explain the problem of evil. Confucius and his followers had believed that every person could perfect himself by overcoming the evil in him. As the good persons should be the élite and rule the others, theoretically everybody who was a member of human society, could move up and become a leader. It was commonly assumed that human nature is good or indifferent, and that human feelings are evil and have to be tamed and educated. When in Han time, with the establishment of the gentry society and its social classes, the idea that any person could move up to become a leader if he only perfected himself, appeared to be too unrealistic, the theory of different grades of men was formed which found its clearest formulation by Han Yü: some people have a good, others a neutral, and still others a bad nature; therefore, not everybody can become a leader. The Neo-Confucianists, especially Ch'eng Hao (1032–1085) and Ch'eng I (1033–1107), tried to find the reasons for this inequality. According to them, nature is neutral; but physical form originates with the combination of Matter with Spiritual Force (*ch'i*). This combination produces individuals in whom there is a lack of balance or harmony. Man should try to transform physical form and recover original nature. The creative force by which such a transformation is possible is *jen*, love, the creative, life-giving quality of nature itself.

It should be remarked that Neo-Confucianism accepts an inequality of men, as early Confucianism did; and that *jen*, benevolence, i.e. humane behaviour of one of a higher status towards one in a lower status, in its practical application has to be channelled by *li*, the system of rules of behaviour. The *li*, however, always started from the idea of a stratified class society. Chu Hsi (1130–1200), the famous scholar and systematizer of Neo-Confucian thoughts, brought out rules of behaviour for those burghers who did not belong to the gentry and could not, therefore, be expected to perform all *li*; his 'simplified *li*' exercised a great influence not only upon contemporary China, but also upon Korea and Annam and there strengthened a hitherto looser patriarchal, patrilinear family system. By taking texts in the Classics seriously the freedom of women was now severely limited. Women began to disappear from the fields, from the streets and from social parties. They had to be virgins on the day of the wedding and were not supposed to marry again after divorce (by their husband) or after the husband's death. Still, we know of a good number of famous men in the eleventh century who married divorced women and did not seem to be against marrying a widow. However, the rules became more and more strict down to the nineteenth century.

The Neo-Confucianists also compiled great analytical works of history and encyclopaedias whose authority continued for many centuries. They interpreted in these works all history in accordance with their outlook; they issued new commentaries on all the classics in order to spread interpretations that served their purposes. In the field of commentary this school of thought was given perfect expression by Chu Hsi, who also wrote one of the chief historical works. Chu Hsi's commentaries became standard works for centuries, until the beginning of the twentieth century. Yet, although Chu became the symbol of conservatism, he was quite interested in science, and in this field he had an open eye for changes.

The Sung period is so important because it is also the time of the greatest development of Chinese science and technology. Many new theories, but also many practical new inventions were made. Medicine made substantial progress. About 1145 the first autopsy was made, on the body of a south Chinese captive. Sung medicine seems to be the highpoint of traditional Chinese medicine; afterwards, few developments of importance are noticeable. Most important was the attempt to bring medical knowledge about the human body, pharmacology, and general philosophy into one system, to unify in this area, too, the cosmos, nature, and man. We should keep in mind, that before the Sung, Chinese doctors did not know how organs which were called 'liver', 'heart', etc., looked and where they were located in the body. It is important to observe that in Sung time detailed standards of professional ethics were laid down; the first attempts in this direction of a 'Hippocratic oath' were made in the sixth century. Further, it is interesting sociologically that Sung doctors were of the opinion that the bodies of upper-class people were finer than those of ordinary persons, and both classes of men should be treated differently and by different doctors. This is an application of the doctrine of the inequality of men, stressed so much in the eleventh century.

Another important field of development in Sung time was law. We find here for the first time theoretical discussions and legal rules concerning the interrogation of defendants, the right to appeal, the training of judges, the evaluation of testimony. If these rules were really applied in practical life, the judicial system of China can only be called very progressive and modern, if compared to Europe at the same time.

The Wang An-shih school of political philosophy had opponents also in the field of literary style, the so-called Shu Group (Shu means the present province of Szechwan), whose leaders were the famous Three Sus. The greatest of the three was Su Shih or Su Tung-p'o (1036–1101); the others were his father, Su Hsün, and his brother, Su Che. It is characteristic of these Shu poets, and also of the Kiangsi school associated with them, that they made as much use as they could of the vernacular. It had not been usual to introduce the phrases of everyday life into poetry, but Su Tung-p'o made use of the most everyday expressions, without diminishing his artistic effectiveness by so doing; on the contrary, the result was to give his poems much more genuine feeling than those of other poets. These poets were in harmony with the writings of the T'ang period poet Po Chü-i (772–846) and were supported, like Neo-Confucianism, by representatives of trade capitalism. Politically, in their conservatism they were sharply opposed to the Wang An-shih group. Midway between the two stood the so-called Loyang School, whose greatest leaders were the historian and poet Ssŭ-ma Kuang (1019–1086) and the philosopher-poet Shao Yung (1011–1077).

In addition to its poems, the Sung literature was famous for the so-called *pi-chi* or miscellaneous notes. These consist of short notes of the most various sort, notes on literature, art, politics, archaeology, all mixed together. The *pi-chi* are a treasure-house for the history of the culture of the time; they contain many details, often of importance, about China's neighbouring peoples. They were intended to serve as suggestions for learned conversation when scholars came together; they aimed at showing how wide was a scholar's knowledge. To this group we must add the accounts of travel, of which some of great value dating from the Sung period are still extant; they contain information of the greatest importance about the early Mongols and also about Sinkiang and south China.

Mainly through the *pi-chi* literature of the Sung period, we learn more about the folk literature and art. We hear that there were story-tellers, professionals who told their long stories for cash reward on the market places, as their descendants in this century still did. To judge from some titles we can assume that many of these stories were based upon official histories or travel accounts, but changed by the story-tellers into folk language and adorned with thrilling episodes and details. Thus, the story-tellers formed long stories which later were written down and became the early forms of novels. They also told ballads, performed shadow-plays and marionette plays. The shadow-play seems to have a long history in China, though we cannot believe a story according to which it was known already in the second century B.C. Marionette plays existed in two forms; in one, the figures were moved by strings from above; in the other by sticks moved from below. The figures which were manipulated by putting the hand into the body of the figure, the so-called 'bag plays', seem to be of later origin and have only a local distribution.

While these men performed in the open, behind screens or on temporary platforms, the upper class already could enjoy real theatre plays; some of these Sung period plays are still preserved today. There developed several local styles, which will be mentioned later. Another entertainment of the upper class was the dance. Here, some foreign influence remains, as in T'ang time. According to one theory, one style of dance consisted of dancing delicate patterns on carpets, according to the designs on the carpet. As the designs were small in size, the dancers danced on the tip of their toes, and this led to the development, it is said, of the custom of foot-binding, famous in China to the beginning of this century. It is certain that the custom at first developed at the court and later trickled down to the lower classes, so that it was finally widely spread even among the poor. The very painful custom, by which the foot was so deformed that the women could walk only with difficulty, kept women in the house and prevented their moving around or doing physical labour. Some Chinese men openly confessed that this custom made faithful and obedient wives. It is interesting that this custom was connected with an erotic cult of the foot; as soon as the custom disappeared the Chinese foot lost its erotic appeal.

Foreign influence played a role also in the music of the time. From Sung on, the seven-tone scale becomes dominant, displacing the old Chinese five-tone scale. The use of notation systems becomes more general.

All these performers: musicians, dancers, and actors belonged to the outcasts: they were regarded as the lowest members of society, allowed only to marry within their caste, excluded from other professions and from state service. Yet, the customers often were very attached to them, and rumours about sexual or homosexual relations circulated then as later.

While the Sung period was of perfection in all fields of art, painting undoubtedly gained its highest development in this time. We find now two main streams in painting: some painters preferred the decorative, pompous, but realistic approach, with great attention to detail. Men who belonged to this school of painting often were active court officials or painted for the court and for other representative purposes. One of the most famous among them, Li Lung-mien (c. 1040–1106), for instance painted the different breeds of horses in the imperial stables. He was also famous for his Buddhistic figures. Another school regarded painting as an intimate, personal expression. They tried to paint inner realities and not outer forms. They, too, were educated, but they did not paint for anybody. They painted in their country houses when they felt in the mood for expression. Their paintings did not stress details, but tried to give the spirit of a landscape, for in this field they excelled most. Best known of them is Mi Fei (c. 1051–1107), a painter as well as a calligrapher, art collector, and art critic. Typically, his paintings were not much liked by the emperor Hui Tsung (ruled 1101–1125) who was one of the greatest art collectors and whose catalogue of his collection became very famous. He created the Painting Academy, an institution which mainly gave official recognition to painters in form of titles which gave the painter access to and status at court. Ma Yüan (c. 1190–1224), member of a whole painter's family, and Hsia Kui (c. 1180–1230) continued the more 'impressionistic' tradition. Already in Sung time, however, many painters could and did paint in different styles, 'copying', i.e. painting in the way of T'ang painters, in order to express their changing emotions by changed styles, a fact which often makes the dating of Chinese paintings very difficult.

Finally, art craft has left us famous porcelains of the Sung period. The most characteristic production of that time is the green porcelain known as 'Celadon'. It consists usually of a rather solid paste, less like porcelain than stoneware, covered with a green glaze; decoration is incised, not painted, under the glaze. In the Sung period, however, came the first pure white porcelain with incised ornamentation under the glaze, and also with painting on the glaze. Not until near the end of the Sung period did the blue and white porcelain begin (blue painting on a white ground). The cobalt needed for this came from Asia Minor. In exchange for the cobalt, Chinese porcelain went to Asia Minor. This trade did not, however, grow greatly until the Mongol epoch; later really substantial orders were placed in China, the Chinese executing the patterns wanted in the West.

5 *Military collapse*

In foreign affairs the whole eleventh century was a period of diplomatic manoeuvring, with every possible effort to avoid war. There was long-continued fighting with the Kitan, and at times also with the Turco-Tibetan Hsia, but diplomacy carried the day: tribute was paid to both enemies, and the effort was made to stir up the Kitan against the Hsia and vice versa; the other parties also intrigued in like fashion. In 1110 the situation seemed to improve for the Sung in this game, as a new enemy appeared in the rear of the Liao (Kitan), the Tungusic Juchên (Jurchen), who in the past had been more or less subject to the Kitan. In 1114 the Juchên made themselves independent and became a political factor. The Kitan were crippled, and it became an easy matter to attack them. But this pleasant situation did not last long. The Juchên conquered Peking, and in 1125 the Kitan empire was destroyed; but in the same year the Juchên marched against the Sung. In 1126 they captured the Sung capital; the emperor and his art-loving father, who had retired a little earlier, were taken prisoner, and the Northern Sung dynasty was at an end. The report of the transport of the emperor towards the north is one of the most touching of Chinese literature. At first, he was still treated with some respect and allowed to keep some of his concubines, servants and maids in acceptable quarters. Step by step, everything was taken away from him, and in the end he died in a miserable hut, alone, totally degraded.

The collapse came so quickly because the whole edifice of security between the Kitan and the Sung was based on a policy of balance and of diplomacy. Neither state was armed in any way, and so both collapsed at the first assault from a military power.

(2) The Liao (Kitan) dynasty in the north (937–1125)

1 *Social structure. Claim to the Chinese imperial throne*

The Kitan, a league of tribes under the leadership of a Mongol tribe, had grown steadily stronger in north-eastern Mongolia during the T'ang epoch. They had gained the allegiance of many tribes in the west and also in Korea and Manchuria, and in the end, about A.D. 900, had become the dominant power in the north. The process of growth of this nomad power was the same as that of other nomad states, such as the Toba state, and therefore need not be described again in any detail here. When the T'ang dynasty was deposed, the Kitan were among the claimants to the Chinese throne, feeling fully justified in their claim as the strongest power in the Far East. Owing to the strength of the Sha-t'o, who themselves claimed leadership in China, the expansion of the Kitan empire slowed down. In the many battles the Kitan suffered several setbacks. They also had enemies in the rear, a state named Po-hai, ruled by Tunguses, in northern Korea, and the new Korean state of Kao-li, which liberated itself from Chinese overlordship in 919.

In 927 the Kitan finally destroyed Po-hai. This brought many Tungus tribes, including the Jurchen (Juchên), under Kitan dominance. Then, in 936, the Kitan gained the allegiance of the Turkish general Shih Ching-t'ang, and he was set on the Chinese throne as a feudatory of the Kitan. It was hoped now to secure dominance over China, and accordingly the Mongol name of the dynasty was altered to 'Liao dynasty' in 937, indicating the claim to the Chinese throne. Considerable regions of north China came at once under the direct rule of the Liao. As a whole, however, the plan failed: the feudatory Shih Ching-t'ang tried to make himself independent; Chinese fought the Liao; and the Chinese sceptre soon came back into the hands of a Sha-t'o dynasty (947). This ended the plans of the Liao to conquer the whole of China.

For this there were several reasons. A nomad people was again ruling the agrarian regions of north China. This time the representatives of the ruling class remained military commanders, and at the same time retained their herds of horses. As early as 1100 they had well over 10,000 herds, each of more than a thousand animals. The army commanders had been awarded large regions which they themselves had conquered. They collected the taxes in these regions, and passed on to the state only the yield of the wine tax. On the other hand, in order to feed the armies, in which there were now many Chinese soldiers, the frontier regions were settled, the soldiers working as peasants in times of peace, and peasants being required to contribute to the support of the army. Both processes increased the interest of the Kitan ruling class in the maintenance of peace. That class was growing rich, and preferred living on the income from its properties or settlements to going to war, which had become a more and more serious matter after the founding of the great Sung empire, and was bound to be less remunerative. The herds of horses were a further excellent source of income, for they could be sold to the Sung, who had no good horses. Then, from 1004 onward, came the tribute payments from China, strengthening the interest in the maintenance of peace. Thus great wealth accumulated in Peking, the capital of the Liao; in this wealth the whole Kitan ruling class participated, but the tribes in the north, owing to their remoteness, had no share in it. In 988 the Chinese began negotiations, as a move in their diplomacy, with the ruler of the later realm of the Hsia; in 990 the Kitan also negotiated with him, and they soon became a third partner in the diplomatic game. Delegations were continually going from one to another of the three realms, and they were joined by trade missions. Agreement was soon reached on frontier questions, on armament, on questions of demobilization, on the demilitarization of particular regions, and so on, for the last thing anyone wanted was to fight.

Then came the rising of the tribes of the north. They had remained military tribes; of all the wealth nothing reached them, and they were given no military employment, so that they had no hope of improving their position. The leadership was assumed by the tribe of the Juchên (1114). In a campaign of unprecedented rapidity they captured Peking, and the Liao dynasty was ended (1125), a year earlier, as we know, than the end of the Sung.

2   The state of the Kara-Kitai

A small troop of Liao, under the command of a member of the ruling family, fled into the west. They were pursued without cessation, but they succeeded in fighting their way through. After a few years of nomad life in the mountains of northern Sinkiang, they were able to gain the collaboration of a few more tribes, and with them they then invaded western Sinkiang. There they founded the 'Western Liao' state, or, as the western sources call it, the 'Kara-Kitai' state, with its capital at Balasagun. This state must not be regarded as a purely Kitan state. The Kitan formed only a very thin stratum, and the real power was in the hands of autochthonous Turkish tribes, to whom the Kitan soon became entirely assimilated in culture. Thus the history of this state belongs to that of western Asia, especially as the relations of the Kara-Kitai with the Far East were entirely broken off. In 1211 the state was finally destroyed.

(3)   The Hsi-Hsia state in the north (1038–1227)

1   Continuation of Toba traditions

After the end of the Toba state in north China in 550, some tribes of the Toba, including members of the ruling tribe with the tribal name Toba, withdrew to the borderland between Tibet and China, where they ruled over Tibetan and Tangut tribes. At the beginning of the T'ang dynasty this tribe of Toba joined the T'ang. The tribal leader received in return, as a distinction, the family name of the T'ang dynasty, Li. His dependence on China was, however, only nominal and soon came entirely to an end. In the tenth century the tribe gained in strength. It is typical of the long continuance of old tribal traditions that a leader of the tribe in the tenth century married a woman belonging to the family to which the khans of the Hsiung-nu and all Turkish ruling houses had belonged since 200 B.C. With the rise of the Kitan in the north and of the Tibetan state in the south, the tribe decided to seek the friendship of China. Its first mission, in 982, was well received. Presents were sent to the chieftain of the tribe, he was helped against his enemies, and he was given the status of a feudatory of the Sung; in 988 the family name of the Sung, Chao, was conferred on him. Then the Kitan took a hand. They over-trumped the Sung by proclaiming the tribal chieftain king of Hsia (990). Now the small state became interesting. It was pampered by Liao and Sung in the effort to win it over or to keep its friendship. The state grew; in 1031 its ruler resumed the old family name of the Toba, thus proclaiming his intention to continue the Toba empire; in 1034 he definitely parted from the Sung, and in 1038 he proclaimed himself emperor in the Hsia dynasty, or, as the Chinese generally called it, the 'Hsi-Hsia', which means the Western Hsia. This name, too, had associations with the old Hun tradition; it recalled the state of Ho-lien P'o-p'o in the early fifth century. The state soon covered the present province of Kansu, small parts of the adjoining Tibetan territory, and parts of the Ordos region. It attacked the province of Shensi, but the Chinese and the Liao attached the greatest importance to that territory. Thus that was the scene of most of the fighting.

The Hsia state had a ruling group of Toba, but these Toba had become Tibetanized. The language of the country was Tibetan; the customs were those of the Tanguts. A script was devised, in imitation of the Chinese script. Only in recent years has it begun to be studied.

In 1125, when the Tungusic Juchên destroyed the Liao, the Hsia also lost large territories in the east of their country, especially the province of Shensi, which they had conquered; but they were still able to hold their own. Their political importance to China, however, vanished, since they were now divided from southern China and as partners were no longer of the same value to it. Not until the Mongols became a power did the Hsia recover some of their importance; but they were among the first victims of the Mongols: in 1209 they had to submit to them, and in 1227, the year of the death of Genghiz Khan, they were annihilated.

This section on the northern, non-Chinese dynasties, reports almost exclusively about the rulers and their fights. What about the people? Most of what we know about the Kitan and Juchên is written by Chinese; the Hsi-Hsia had their own script which is still not yet wholly deciphered, and Chinese do not report much about them. We hear of terrible suffering of the population under the 'barbarians', but we should be careful in assigning such statements great weight, as they are written by the enemy, the Chinese. The overwhelming majority of the population in these states, perhaps with the exception of Hsi-Hsia, was Chinese. Some of the Chinese upper class collaborated with the foreign rulers, some continued to compose essays and poems in almost the same style and content as their Sung colleagues. There is some indication that the lot of the common man was not much worse than on the other side. We know that under the Chin (Juchên) a new sect of Taoism (Cheng-i sect) developed to importance, a sect which still exists and supplies many of the priests who administer masses for the population in times of need or of death. Parallel to this, a Tantric sect of Buddhism gained more importance, although it had entered China, possibly from the area of Bengal, already in T'ang time. Tantric Buddhism, often called magic Buddhism, stresses the use of 'mantra', magic formulae; it also harbours a secret sub-sect which combines meditative techniques with sexual practices.

(4) The empire of the Southern Sung dynasty (1127–1279)

1 *Foundation*

In the disaster of 1126, when the Juchên captured the Sung capital and destroyed the Sung empire, a brother of the captive emperor escaped. He made himself emperor in Nanking and founded the 'Southern Sung' dynasty, whose capital was soon shifted to the present Hangchow. The foundation of the new dynasty was a relatively easy matter, and the new state was much more solid than the southern kingdoms of 800 years earlier, for the south had already been economically supreme, and the great families that had ruled the state were virtually all from the south. The loss of the north, i.e. the area north of the Yellow river and of parts of Kiangsu, was of no importance to this governing group and meant no loss of estates to it. Thus the transition from the Northern to the Southern Sung was not of fundamental importance. Consequently the Juchên had no chance of success when they arranged for Liu Yü, who came of a northern Chinese family of small peasants and had become an official to be proclaimed emperor in the 'Ch'i' dynasty in 1130. They hoped that this puppet might attract the southern Chinese, but seven years later they dropped him.

Many southern Chinese families today trace their genealogy back to the year in which the capital K'ai-feng fell to the Liao (Kitan), saying that their family originally was a northern one, but decided to leave when the 'barbarians' came. Especially the Hakka (K'o-chia), a fairly large minority in the present province of Kuangtung, southern Fukien, Taiwan and in the South-East Asian settlements of Chinese claim to be the 'original' Chinese, stemming from the home province of China, Honan. They assert that their dialect is closest to the old Chinese language, but their claims are quite doubtful and some scholars today believe that we have here a case which has numerous other parallels in China: a minority, in order to free itself from discrimination, claims to be in fact Chinese and not a minority. These scholars think it is possible that the Hakka are fully sinicized Yao. However, we can say with certainty that the twelfth and thirteenth centuries with their upheavals were periods in which many Chinese migrated into the south. There is hardly any Chinese family in the provinces of Fukien or Kuangtung and Kuangsi which can retrace its genealogy as a southern family beyond this period.

2 *Internal situation*

Perhaps we should here throw some light on the internal organization of the Sung, especially the rural administration. It has been estimated that the population of Southern Sung in the early twelfth century was somewhere between 30 and 50 million. These were ruled by a bureaucracy which was probably not much over 12,000 men. Of these 8,000 were in the capital, around the emperor. The country was divided into 170 larger units with an average of eight officials; these units controlled 800 districts (*hsien*) with, at most, three officials each. This was the whole staff of the administration on the government payroll, except, of course, the army.

In each district was a staff of clerks, scribes, gaolers; normally between 100 and 150 men. In certain periods, many of them were salaried, and this meant a heavy load on the payroll; in other periods they received no salary and we can assume that they had sufficient income from unofficial and/or illegal sources, because many of these posts became hereditary. Below the district were the villages with unpaid staff. Neither the district clerks and employees nor the village officials had the right to move up into the regular career. The village headman, *li-chang*, nominally a chief of a hundred households, was selected out of 'better' rural families and ordered to serve for a limited time, usually three years. Then another family's head took over. He had to collect taxes and was assisted by a 'household chief'. He also had one scribe to keep the records, and three 'elders' and 'stalwart men' who were responsible for law and order, the upkeep of roads and the building of bridges. This system, by which a very large state is governed by a small bureaucratic élite, assisted by small bureaucrats and helped by unpaid village workers lasted, with some changes, basically to the end of the monarchy. It was developed in Northern Sung time, and not much changed in Southern Sung. So, the countryside was not affected by the loss of the north.

Only the policy of diplomacy could not be pursued at once, as the Juchên were bellicose at first and would not negotiate. There were therefore several battles at the outset (in 1131 and 1134), in which the Chinese were actually the more successful, but not decisively. The Sung military group was faced as early as in 1131 with furious opposition from the greater gentry, led by Ch'in K'ui, one of the largest landowners of all. His estates were around Nanking, and so in the deployment region and the region from which most of the soldiers had to be drawn for the defensive struggle. Ch'in K'ui secured the assassination of the leader of the military party, General Yo Fei, in 1141, and was able to conclude peace with the Juchên. To this day, numerous Chinese operas show Ch'in K'ui as the model of a traitor, while a long, famous folk novel praises Yo Fei as the ideal patriot, and in many places on the mainland and in Taiwan temples were erected in his honour.

The Sung had to accept the status of vassals and to pay annual tribute to the Juchên. This was the situation that best pleased the greater gentry. They paid hardly any taxes (in many districts the greater gentry directly owned more than 30 per cent of the land, in addition to which they had indirect interests in the soil), and they were now free from the war peril that ate into their revenues. The tribute amounted only to 500,000 strings of cash.

In 1165 it was agreed between the Sung and the Juchên to regard each other as states with equal rights. It is interesting to note here that in the treaties during the Han time with the Hsiung-nu, the two countries called one another brothers—with the Chinese ruler as the older and thus privileged brother; but the treaties since the T'ang time with northern powers and with Tibetans used the terms father-in-law and son-in-law. The foreign power was the 'father-in-law', i.e. the elder and, therefore, in a certain way the more privileged; the Chinese were the 'son-in-law', the representative of the paternal lineage and, therefore, in another respect also the more privileged! In spite of such agreements with the Juchên, fighting continued, but it was mainly of the character of frontier engagements. Not until 1204 did the military party, led by Han T'o-wei, regain power; it resolved upon an active policy against the north. In preparation for this a military reform was carried out. The campaign proved a disastrous failure, as a result of which large territories in the north were lost. The Sung sued for peace; Han T'o-wei's head was cut off and sent to the Juchên. In this way peace was restored in 1208. The old treaty relationship was now resumed, but the relations between the two states

remained tense. Meanwhile the Sung observed with malicious pleasure how the Mongols were growing steadily stronger, first destroying the Hsia state and then aiming the first heavy blows against the
Juchên. In the end the Sung entered into alliance with the Mongols
(1233) and joined them in attacking the Juchên, thus hastening the
end of the Juchên state.

The Sung now faced the Mongols, and were defenceless against
them. All the buffer states had gone. The Sung were quite without
adequate military defence. They hoped to stave off the Mongols in
the same way as they had met the Kitan and the Juchên. This time,
however, they misjudged the situation. In the great operations begun
by the Mongols in 1273 the Sung were defeated over and over again.
In 1276 their capital was taken by the Mongols and the emperor was
made prisoner. For three years longer there was a Sung emperor, in
flight from the Mongols, until the last emperor perished near Macao
in south China.

3   *Cultural situation; reasons for the collapse*
The Southern Sung period was again one of flourishing culture.
The imperial court was entirely in the power of the important families; several times the emperors, who personally do not deserve individual mention, were compelled to abdicate. They then lived on with
a court of their own, devoting themselves to pleasure in much the
same way as the 'reigning' emperor. Round them was a countless
swarm of poets and artists. Never was there a time so rich in poets,
though hardly one of them was in any way outstanding. The poets,
unlike those of earlier times, belonged to the lesser gentry who were
suffering from the prevailing inflation. Salaries bore no relation to
prices. Food was not dear, but the things which a man of the upper
class ought to have were far out of reach: a big house cost 2,000
strings of cash, a concubine 800 strings. Thus the lesser gentry and
the intelligentsia all lived on their patrons among the greater gentry
—with the result that they were entirely shut out of politics. This
explains why the literature of the time is so unpolitical, and also why
scarcely any philosophical works appeared. The writers took refuge
more and more in romanticism and flight from realities.

The greater gentry, on the other hand, led a very elegant life,
building themselves magnificent palaces in the capital. They also
speculated in every direction. They speculated in land, in money,
and above all in the paper money that was coming more and more
into use. In 1166 the paper circulation exceeded the value of
10,000,000 strings!

It seems that after 1127 a good number of farmers had left Honan
and the Yellow river plains when the Juchên conquered these places

and showed little interest in fostering agriculture; more left the border areas of Southern Sung because of permanent war threat. Many of these lived as tenants on the farms of the gentry between Nanking and Hangchow. By this time, the influence of the wealthy rural families had grown, because they succeeded in becoming appointed as village officers or even as Superior Guard Officers. These latter were the leaders of the local militia, but also functioned as local police, could influence the tax registers and therefore control the tax assessments of individual families. If they did not want to take over the office, they could appoint replacements, poorer villagers who did the work for them. As the village officers and Superior Guard Officers had obligations which included expenses, such as supplying food and lodging for travelling government officials, poorer rural families would not try to get appointed. Thus, the power of wealthy landowners and rural gentry increased in this period. There are some indications that wealthier merchants also became interested in the farmers. They began to give loans to poor farmers whose wives would then weave textiles, which the merchant would accept in the autumn as repayment of the loan. This is an early form of the putting-out system of later times.

The increase of the power of the wealthy landowners and of their control over tenants and free farmers soon became a serious problem for the finances of the state. At this stage, Chia Ssŭ-tao drafted a reform law. Chia had come to the court through his sister becoming the emperor's concubine, but he himself belonged to the lesser gentry. His proposal was that state funds should be applied to the purchase of land in the possession of the greater gentry over and above a fixed maximum. Peasants were to be settled on this land, and its yield was to belong to the state, which would be able to use it to meet military expenditure. In this way the country's military strength was to be restored. Chia's influence lasted just ten years, until 1275. He began putting the law into effect in the region south of Nanking, where the principal estates of the greater gentry were then situated. He brought upon himself, of course, the mortal hatred of the greater gentry, and paid for his action with his life. The emperor, in entering upon this policy, no doubt had hoped to recover some of his power, but the greater gentry brought him down. The gentry now openly played into the hands of the approaching Mongols, so hastening the final collapse of the Sung. The peasants and the lesser gentry would have fought the Mongols if it had been possible; but the greater gentry enthusiastically went over to the Mongols, hoping to save their property and so their influence by quickly joining the enemy. On a long view they had not judged badly. The Mongols removed the members of the gentry from all political posts, but left them their estates; and before long the greater gentry reappeared in political life. And when, later, the Mongol empire in China was brought down by a popular rising, the greater gentry showed themselves to be the most faithful allies of the Mongols!

(5) The empire of the Juchên in the north (1115–1234)

1 *Rapid expansion from northern Korea to the Yangtze*
The Juchên in the past had been only a small league of Tungus tribes, whose name is preserved in that of the present Tungus tribe of the Jurchen, which came under the domination of the Kitan after the collapse of the state of Po-hai in northern Korea. We have already briefly mentioned the reasons for their rise. After their first successes against the Kitan (1114), their chieftain at once proclaimed himself emperor (1115), giving his dynasty the name 'Chin' (The Golden). The Chin quickly continued their victorious progress. In 1125 the Kitan empire was destroyed. It will be remembered that the Sung were at once attacked, although they had recently been allied with the Chin against the Kitan. In 1126 the Sung capital was taken. The Chin invasions were pushed farther south, and in 1130 the Yangtze was crossed. But the Chin did not hold the whole of these conquests. Their empire was not yet consolidated. Their partial withdrawal closed the first phase of the Chin empire.

But a few years after this maximum expansion, a withdrawal began which went on much more quickly than usual in such cases. The reasons were to be found both in external and in internal politics. The Juchên had gained great agrarian regions in a rapid march of conquest. Once more, great cities with a huge urban population and immense wealth had fallen to alien conquerors. Now the Juchên wanted to enjoy this wealth as the Kitan had done before them. All the Juchên people counted as citizens of the highest class; they were free from taxation and only liable to military service. They were entitled to take possession of as much cultivable land as they wanted; this they did, and they took not only the 'state domains' actually granted to them but also peasant properties, so that Chinese free peasants had to be contented with the remaining, poorer land, unless they became tenants on Juchên estates. A united front was therefore formed between all Chinese, both peasants and landowning gentry, against the Chin, such as it had not been possible to form against the Kitan. This made an important contribution later to the rapid collapse of the Chin empire.

The Chin who had thus come into possession of the cultivable land and at the same time of the wealth of the towns, began a sort of competition with each other for the best winnings, especially after

234

the government had returned to the old Sung capital, Pien-liang (now K'aifeng, in eastern Honan). Serious crises developed in their own ranks. In 1149 the ruler was assassinated by his chancellor (a member of the imperial family), who in turn was murdered in 1161. The Chin thus failed to attain what had been secured by all earlier conquerors, a reconciliation of the various elements of the population and the collaboration of at least one group of the defeated Chinese.

2 Start of the Mongol empire

The cessation of fighting against the Sung brought no real advantage in external affairs, though the tribute payments appealed to the greed of the rulers and were therefore welcomed. There could be no question of further campaigns against the south, for the Hsia empire in the west had not been destroyed, though some of its territory had been annexed; and a new peril soon made its appearance in the rear of the Chin. When in the tenth century the Sha-t'o had had to withdraw from their dominating position in China, because of their great loss of numbers and consequently of strength, they went back into Mongolia and there united with the Ta-tan (Tatars), among whom a new small league of tribes had formed towards the end of the eleventh century, consisting mainly of Mongols and Turks. In 1139 one of the chieftains of the Juchên rebelled and entered into negotiations with the south Chinese. He was killed, but his sons and his whole tribe then rebelled and went into Mongolia, where they made common cause with the Mongols. The Chin pursued them, and fought against them and against the Mongols, but without success. Accordingly negotiations were begun, and a promise was given to deliver meat and grain every year and to cede twenty-seven military strongholds. A high title was conferred on the tribal leader of the Mongols, in the hope of gaining his favour. He declined it, however, and in 1147 assumed the title of emperor of the 'greater Mongol empire'. This was the beginning of the power of the Mongols, who remained thereafter a dangerous enemy of the Chin in the north, until in 1189 Genghiz Khan became their leader and made the Mongols the greatest power of Central Asia. In any case, the Chin had reason to fear the Mongols from 1147 onward, and therefore were the more inclined to leave the Sung in peace.

In 1210 the Mongols began the first assault against the Chin, the moment they had conquered the Hsia. In the years 1215–1217 the Mongols took the military key-positions from the Chin. After that there could be no serious defence of the Chin empire. There came a respite only because the Mongols had turned against the West. But in 1234 the empire finally fell to the Mongols.

Many of the Chin entered the service of the Mongols, and with their permission returned to Manchuria; there they fell back to the cultural level of a warlike nomad people. Not until the sixteenth century did these Tunguses recover, reorganize, and appear again in history this time under the name of Manchus.

The north Chinese under Chin rule did not regard the Mongols as enemies of their country, but were ready at once to collaborate with them. The Mongols were even more friendly to them than to the south Chinese, and treated them rather better.

14 Aborigines of South China, of the 'Black Miao'
tribe, at a festival. Water-colour drawing of the
eighteenth century.

(Collection of the Museum für Völkerkunde, Berlin,
No. ID 8756, 68.)

15 Pavilion on the 'Coal Hill' at Peking, in which
the last Ming emperor committed suicide.

(Photo Eberhard.)

CHAPTER TEN

The Period of Absolutism

(A) THE MONGOL EPOCH (1280–1368)

1 *Beginning of new foreign rules*

During more than half of the second period of 'Modern Times' which now began, China was under alien rule. Of the 631 years from 1280 to 1911, China was under national rulers for 276 years and under alien rule for 355. The alien rulers were first the Mongols, and later the Tungus Manchus. It is interesting to note that the alien rulers in the earlier period came mainly from the north-west, and only in modern times did peoples from the north-east rule over China. This was due in part to the fact that only peoples who had attained a certain level of civilization were capable of dominance. In antiquity and the Middle Ages, eastern Mongolia and Manchuria were at a relatively low level of civilization, from which they emerged only gradually through permanent contact with other nomad peoples, especially Turks. We are dealing here, of course, only with the Mongol epoch in China and not with the great Mongol empire, so that we need not enter further into these questions.

Yet another point is characteristic: the Mongols were the first alien people to rule the whole of China; the Manchus, who appeared in the seventeenth century, were the second and last. All alien peoples before these two ruled only parts of China. Why was it that the Mongols were able to be so much more successful than their predecessors? In the first place the Mongol political league was numerically stronger than those of the earlier alien peoples; second, the military organization and technical equipment of the Mongols were exceptionally advanced for their day. It must be borne in mind, for instance, that during their many years of war against the Sung dynasty in south China the Mongols already made use of small cannon in laying siege to towns. We have no exact knowledge of the number of Mongols who invaded and occupied China, but it is estimated that there were more than a million Mongols living in China. Not all of them, of course, were really Mongols! The name covered Turks, Tunguses, and others.

The name Meng-ku (Mongol) is found in sources much earlier than the thirteenth century; apparently, this was the name of a tribe, once belonging to the Shih-wei tribal federation. Early Western sources often call the Mongols 'Tatars', which is not quite correct, though the Tatar federation was, as far as we know, speaking a Mongol language, the Mongols as a political unit had broken off from the Tatars and formed their own federation. Among the auxiliaries of the Mongols were Uighurs, men from Central Asia and the Middle East, and even Europeans. When the Mongols attacked China they had the advantage of all the arts and crafts and all the new technical advances of Western and Central Asia. At their court, we even find some European technicians. They also had learned much from the Chinese, for instance the use of firearms. Thus, they were technically more advanced than earlier conquerors of China had been.

2 'Nationality legislation'

It was only after the Hsia empire in north China, and then the empire of the Juchên, had been destroyed by the Mongols, and only after long and remarkably modern tactical preparation, that the Mongols conquered south China, the empire of the Sung dynasty. They were now faced with the problem of ruling their great new empire, with a population of certainly more than sixty million (always omitting the western parts of the Mongol empire). The conqueror of that empire, Kublai, himself recognized that China could not be treated in quite the same way as the Mongol's previous conquests; he therefore separated the empire in China from the rest of the Mongol empire. Mongol China became an independent realm within the Mongol empire, a sort of dominion. The Mongol rulers were well aware that in spite of their numerical strength they were still only a minority in China, and this implied certain dangers. They therefore elaborated a 'nationality legislation', the first of its kind in the Far East. The purpose of this legislation was, of course, to be the protection of the Mongols. The population of conquered China was divided into four groups—(1) Mongols, themselves falling into four sub-groups (the oldest Mongol tribes, the White Tatars, the Black Tatars, the Wild Tatars); (2) Central Asian auxiliaries (Naimans, Uighurs, and various other Turkish people, Tanguts, and so on); (3) north Chinese; (4) south Chinese. The Mongols formed the privileged ruling class. They remained militarily organized, and were distributed in garrisons over all the big towns of China as soldiers, maintained by the state. All the higher government posts were reserved for them, so that they also formed the heads of the official staffs. The auxiliary peoples were also admitted into the government service; they, too, had privileges, but were not all soldiers but in many cases merchants, who used their privileged position to promote business. Not a few of these merchants were Uighurs and Mohammedans; many Uighurs were also employed as clerks, as the Mongols were very often unable to read and write Chinese, and the government offices were bilingual, working in Mongolian and Chinese. The clever Uighurs quickly learned enough of both languages for official purposes, and made themselves indispensable assistants to the Mongols. Persian, the main language of administration in the western parts of the Mongol empire besides Uighuric, also was a lingua franca among the new rulers of China.

In the Mongol legislation the south Chinese had the lowest status, and virtually no rights. Intermarriage with them was prohibited. The Chinese were not allowed to carry arms. For a time they were forbidden even to learn the Mongol or other foreign languages. In this way they were to be prevented from gaining official positions and playing any political part. Their ignorance of the languages of northern, central, and western Asia also prevented them from engaging in commerce like the foreign merchants, and every possible difficulty was put in the way of their travelling for commercial purposes. On the other hand, foreigners were, of course, able to learn Chinese, and so to gain a footing in Chinese internal trade.

Through legislation of this type the Mongols tried to build up and to safeguard their domination over China. Yet their success did not last a hundred years.

3 *Military position*

In foreign affairs the Mongol epoch was for China something of a breathing space, for the great wars of the Mongols took place at a remote distance from China and without any Chinese participation. Only a few concluding wars were fought under Kublai in the Far East. The first was his war against Japan (1281): it ended in complete failure, the fleet being destroyed by a storm. In this campaign the Chinese furnished ships and also soldiers. The subjection of Japan would have been in the interest of the Chinese, as it would have opened a market which had been almost closed against them in the Sung period. Mongol wars followed in the south. In 1282 began the war against Burma; in 1284 Annam and Cambodia were conquered; in 1292 a campaign was started against Java. It proved impossible to hold Java, but almost the whole of South-East Asia came under Mongol rule, to the satisfaction of the Chinese, for South-East Asia had already been one of the principal export markets in the Sung period. After that, however, there was virtually no more warfare, apart from small campaigns against rebellious tribes. The

Mongol soldiers now lived on their pay in their garrisons, with nothing to do. The old campaigners died and were followed by their sons, brought up also as soldiers; but these young Mongols were born in China, had seen nothing of war, and learned of the soldiers' trade either nothing or very little; so that after about 1320 serious things happened. An army nominally 1,000 strong was sent against a group of barely fifty bandits and failed to defeat them. Most of the 1,000 soldiers no longer knew how to use their weapons, and many did not even join the force. Such incidents occurred again and again.

4 *Social situation*

The results, however, of conditions within the country were of much more importance than events abroad. The Mongols made Peking their capital as was entirely natural, for Peking was near their home-land Mongolia. The emperor and his entourage could return to Mongolia in the summer, when China became too hot or too humid for them; and from Peking they were able to maintain contact with the rest of the Mongol empire. But as the city had become the capital of a vast empire, an enormous staff of officials had to be housed there, consisting of persons of many different nationalities. The emperor naturally wanted to have a magnificent capital, a city really worthy of so vast an empire. As the many wars had brought in vast booty, there was money for the building of great palaces, of a size and magnificence never before seen in China. They were built by Chinese forced labour, and to this end men had to be brought from all over the empire—poor peasants, whose fields went out of cultivation while they were held in bondage far away. If they ever returned home, they were destitute and had lost their land. The rich gentry, on the other hand, were able to buy immunity from forced labour. The great increase in the population of Peking (the huge court with its enormous expenditure, the mass of officials, the great merchant community, largely foreigners, and the many servile labourers), necessitated vast supplies of food. Now, as mentioned in earlier chapters, since the time of the Later T'ang the region round Nanking had become the main centre of production in China, and the Chinese population had gone over more and more to the consumption of rice instead of millet or wheat. As rice could not be grown economically in the north, practically the whole of the food supplies for the capital had to be brought from the south. The transport system taken over by the Mongols had not been created for long-distance traffic of this sort. The capital of the Sung had lain in the main centre of production. Consequently, a great fleet had suddenly to be built, canals and rivers had to be regulated, and some new canals excavated. This again called for a vast quantity of forced labour, often brought from afar to the points at which it was needed. The Chinese peasants had been exploited by the large landowners. The Mongols had not removed these landowners, as the Chinese gentry had gone over to their side. The Mongols had deprived them of their political power, but had left them their estates, the basis of their power. In past changes of dynasty the gentry had either maintained their position or been replaced by a new gentry: the total number of their class had remained virtually unchanged. Now, however, in addition to the original gentry there were about a million Mongols, for whose maintenance the peasants had also to provide, and their standard of maintenance was high. This was a great increase in the burdens of the peasantry.

Two other elements further pressed on the peasants in the Mongol epoch—organized religion and the traders. The upper classes among the Chinese had in general little interest in religion, but the Mongols, owing to their historical development, were very religious. Some of them and some of their allies were Buddhists, some were still shamanists. The Chinese Buddhists and the representatives of popular Taoism approached the Mongols and the foreign Buddhist monks trying to enlist the interest of the Mongols and their allies. The old shamanism was unable to compete with the higher religions, and the Mongols in China became Buddhist or interested themselves in popular Taoism. They showed their interest especially by the endowment of temples and monasteries. The temples were given great estates, and the peasants on those estates became temple servants. The land belonging to the temples was free from taxation.

We have as yet no exact statistics of the Mongol epoch, only approximations. These set the total area under cultivation at some six million *ch'ing* (a *ch'ing* is the ideal size of the farm worked by a peasant family, but it was rarely held in practice); the population amounted to fourteen or fifteen million families. Of this total tillage some 170,000 *ch'ing* were allotted to the temples; that is to say, the farms for some 400,000 peasant families were taken from the peasants and no longer paid taxes to the state. The peasants, however, had to make payments to the temples. Some 200,000 *ch'ing* with some 450,000 peasant families were turned into military settlements; that is to say, these peasants had to work for the needs of the army. Their taxes went not to the state but to the army. Moreover, in the event of war they had to render service to the army. In addition to this, all higher officials received official properties, the yield of which represented part payment of their salaries. Then, Mongol nobles and dignitaries received considerable grants of land, which was taken away from the free peasants; the peasants had then to work their farms as tenants and to pay dues to their landlords, no longer to the state. Finally, especially in north China, many peasants were entirely dispossessed, and their land was turned into pasturage for the Mongol's horses; the peasants themselves were put to forced labour. All this meant an enormous diminution in the number of free peasants and thus of taxpayers. As the state was involved in more expenditure than in the past owing to the large number of Mongols who were its virtual pensioners, the taxes had to be continually increased. Meanwhile the many peasants working as tenants of the great landlords, the temples, and the Mongol nobles were entirely at their mercy. In this period, a second migration of farmers into the southern provinces, mainly Fukien and Kwangtung, took place; it had its main source in the lower Yangtze valley. A few gentry families whose relatives had accompanied the Sung emperor on their flight to the south, also settled with their followers in the Canton basin.

The many merchants from abroad, especially those belonging to the peoples allied to the Mongols, also had in every respect a privileged position in China. They were free of taxation, free to travel all over the country, and received privileged treatment in the use of means of transport. They were thus able to accumulate great wealth, most of which went out of China to their own country. Chinese merchants fell more and more into dependence on the foreign merchants; the only field of action really remaining to them was the local trade within China and the trade with South-East Asia, where the Chinese had the advantage of knowing the language.

The impoverishment of China began with the flow abroad of her metallic currency. To make up for this loss, the government was compelled to issue great quantities of paper money, which very quickly depreciated, because after a few years the government would no longer accept the money at its face value, so that the population could place no faith in it. The depreciation further impoverished the people.

Thus we have in the Mongol epoch in China the imposing picture of a commerce made possible with every country from Europe to the Pacific; this, however, led to the impoverishment of China. We also see the raising of mighty temples and monumental buildings, but this again only contributed to the denudation of the country. The Mongol epoch was thus one of continual and rapid impoverishment in China, simultaneously with a great display of magnificence. The enthusiastic descriptions of the Mongol empire in China offered by travellers from the Near East or from Europe, such as Marco Polo, give an entirely false picture: as foreigners they had a privileged position, living in the cities and seeing nothing of the situation of the general population. It seems to be certain that Marco Polo, in spite of his long stay in China, never learned to speak Chinese. His statement that he had a high administrative post in China may not be true, according to some scholars who even doubt that he saw as many parts of China as he claimed to have seen. If we read his reports, we are again and again amazed about what he did not write about, though he must have observed it: for instance, he does not seem to have appreciated Chinese painting and had no understanding of the complexities of Chinese religion.

5 Cultural developments

During the Mongol epoch a large number of the Chinese scholars withdrew from official life. They lived in retirement among their friends, and devoted themselves mainly to the pursuit of poetry, which had been elaborated in the Southern Sung epoch, without themselves arriving at any important innovations in form. Their poems were built up meticulously on the rules laid down by the various schools; they were routine productions rather than the outcome of any true poetic inspiration. In the realm of prose the best achievements were the 'miscellaneous notes' already mentioned, collections of learned essays. The foreigners who wrote in Chinese during this epoch are credited with no better achievements by the Chinese historians of literature. Chief of them were a statesman named Yeh-lü Ch'u-ts'ai, a Kitan in the service of the Mongols; and a Mongol named T'o-t'o (Tokto). The former accompanied Genghiz Khan in his great campaign against western Sinkiang, and left a very interesting account of his journeys, together with many poems about Samarkand and Sinkiang. His other works were mainly letters and poems addressed to friends. They differ in no way in style from the Chinese literary works of the time, and are neither better nor worse than those works. He shows strong traces of Taoist influence, as do other contemporary writers. We know that Genghiz Khan was more or less inclined to Taoism, and admitted a Taoist monk to his camp (1221–1224). This man's account of his travels has also been preserved, and with the numerous European accounts of Central Asia written at this time it forms an important source. The Mongol Tokto was the head of an historical commission that issued the annals of the Sung dynasty, the Kitan, and the Juchên dynasty. The annals of the Sung dynasty became the largest of all the historical works, but they were fiercely attacked from the first by Chinese critics on account of their style and their hasty composition, and, together with the annals of the Mongol dynasty, they are regarded as the worst of the annals preserved. Tokto himself is less to blame for this than the circumstance that he was compelled to work in great haste, and had not time to put into order the overwhelming mass of his material.

The greatest literary achievements, however, of the Mongol period belong beyond question to the theatre (or, rather, opera). The emperors were great theatre-goers, and the wealthy private families were also enthusiasts, so that gradually people of education devoted themselves to writing librettos for the operas, where in the past this work had been left to others. Most of the authors of these librettos remained unknown: they used pseudonyms, partly because playwriting was not an occuption that befitted a scholar, and partly because in these works they criticized the conditions of their day. These works are divided in regard to style into two groups, those of the 'southern' and the 'northern' drama; these are distinguished from each other in musical construction and in their intellectual attitude: in general the northern works are more heroic and the southern more sentimental, though there are exceptions. The most famous northern works of the Mongol epoch are 'P'i-p'a-chi' ('The Story of a Lute'), written about 1356, probably by Kao Ming, and 'Chao-shih ku-erh-chi' ('The Story of the Orphan of Chao'), a work that enthralled Voltaire, who made a paraphrase of it; its author was the otherwise unknown Chi Chün-hsiang. One of the most famous of the southern dramas is 'Hsi-hsiang-chi' ('The Romance of the Western Chamber'), by Wang Shih-fu and Kuan Han-ch'ing. Kuan lived under the Juchên dynasty as a physician, and then among the Mongols. He is said to have written fifty-eight dramas, many of which are still preserved. Kuan (c. 1220–1307) was highly praised during one period of the present regime and was called the Chinese Shakespeare. A newly composed opera depicted him as a populist, a friend of the common man. The Yüan drama introduced a new language into Chinese literature: a highly colloquial, northern dialect with a number of Mongolisms. A southern style of opera, which also began to emerge in this period, differs in language as well as in the music. Perhaps we should remark here that in Chinese operas the music is not newly composed for each opera, but each style of opera uses a number of standard melodies which the audience knows, just as they usually also know the content of the action. What is admired is mainly the art of acting and singing, and here, the actor in spite of being bound by tradition, can show his individuality.

In the fine arts, foreign influence made itself felt during the Mongol epoch much more than in literature. This was due in part to the Mongol rulers' predilection for the Lamaism that was widespread in their homeland. Lamaism is a special form of Buddhism which developed in Tibet, where remnants of the old national Tibetan cult (Bon) were fused with Buddhism into a distinctive religion. During the rise of the Mongols this religion, which closely resembled the shamanism of the ancient Mongols, spread in Mongolia, and through the Mongols it made great progress in China, where it had been insignificant until their time. Religious sculpture especially came entirely under Tibetan influence (particularly that of the sculptor Aniko, who came from Nepal, where he was born in 1244). This influence was noticeable in the Chinese sculptor Liu Yüan; after him it became stronger and stronger, lasting until the Manchu epoch.

In architecture, too, Indian and Tibetan influence was felt in this period. The Tibetan pagodas came into special prominence alongside the previously known form of pagoda, which has many storeys, growing smaller as they go upward; these towers originally contained relics of Buddha and his disciples. The Tibetan pagoda has not this division into storeys, and its lower part is much larger in circumference, and often round. To this day Peking is rich in pagodas in the Tibetan style.

The Mongols also developed in China the art of carpet-knotting, which to this day is found only in north China in the zone of northern influence. There were carpets before these, but they were mainly of felt. The knotted carpets were produced in imperial workshops—only, of course, for the Mongols, who were used to carpets. A further development probably also due to west Asian influence was that of cloisonné technique in China in this period.

Painting, on the other hand, remained free from alien influence, with the exception of the craft painting for the temples. The most famous painters of the Mongol epoch were Chao Mêng-fu (also called Chao Chung-mu, 1254–1322), a relative of the deposed imperial family of the Sung dynasty, and Ni Tsan (1301–1374).

In the fields of technology, we observe some further developments. We now find that the use of machines using water power became more widely spread. There were silk-reeling machines already in Sung time, but in 1313 we hear about a machine with 32 spindles, driven by water. But otherwise, the great developments now come to a standstill. China did not move into the industrial age. This surprising fact has been explained in different ways. Recently a cold period lasting from about A.D. 1200 to 1400 has been made responsible for the standstill, and it is said that between the end of the twelfth and the end of the fourteenth century the population of China decreased and only after 1400 began to go up regularly to the end of the sixteenth century. M. Elvin has proposed the theory of a 'high level equilibrium' which is tempting but needs further research. In briefest form, this theory explains that at around 1300 Chinese technology had developed to a point where industrialization comparable to the 'industrial revolution' in Europe in the eighteenth century was possible. It did not take place because the intensive agriculture of China could keep many more people alive than European agriculture, so that there was always an over-supply of human labour which made the use of machines uneconomical. Thus technology had no chance to develop to a level which made cheap mass production possible and competitive; everywhere, the earliest machines were somewhat quicker and more efficient than human labour, but required too much investment to be competitive. Others have made another observation which is not incompatible with Elvin's theory. The men who developed these machines were, for the most part, members of the gentry or 'leisure class' who took an interest in the crafts or the farmers. They worked together with craftsmen who built for them the machines they had invented. They even had these machines working on their properties, but they really did not need extra income; they had enough secure income. On the other hand, the craftsmen were not yet free and remained until the fifteenth century tied to the government, forced to do labour services. They were hardly in a position in which they could accumulate enough capital to set up their own workshops or machine factories.

There is no doubt that not only in the field of technology, but also in applied sciences, like medicine, the period of great progress was over with the Yüan, and new impulses came only in the late sixteenth and the seventeenth centuries. At this time, the best explanation seems to be to accept Elvin's explanation and the other explanation together with the impact of a foreign rule, i.e. to take internal as well as external reasons to explain the standstill.

6 Popular revolts

Possibly due to the cold period, possibly due to Mongol exploitation of farmers, or due to both factors, popular risings began early in the Mongol dynasty. The first popular rising came in 1325. Statistics of 1329 show that there were then some 7,600,000 persons in the empire who were starving; as this was only the figure of the officially admitted sufferers, the figure may have been higher. In any case, seven-and-a-half million were a substantial percentage of the total population. The risings that now came incessantly were led by men of the lower orders—a cloth-seller, a fisherman, a peasant, a salt smuggler, the son of a soldier serving a sentence, an office messenger, and so on. They never attacked the Mongols as aliens, but always the rich in general, whether Chinese or foreign. Wherever they came, they killed all the rich and distributed their money and possessions.

As already mentioned, the Mongol garrisons were unable to cope with these risings. But how was it that the Mongol rule did not collapse until some forty years later? The Mongols parried the risings by raising loans from the rich and using the money to recruit volunteers to fight the rebels. The state revenues would not have sufficed for these payments, and the item was not one that could be included in the military budget. What was of much more importance was that the gentry themselves recruited volunteers and fought the rebels on their own account, without the authority or the support of the government. Thus it was the Chinese gentry, in their fear of being killed by the insurgents, who fought them and so bolstered up the Mongol rule.

In 1351 the dykes along the Yellow river burst. The dykes had to be reconstructed and further measures of conservancy undertaken. To this end the government impressed 170,000 men. Following this action, great new revolts broke out. Everywhere in Honan, Kiangsu, and Shantung, the regions from which the labourers were summoned, revolutionary groups were formed, some of them amounting to 100,000 men. Some groups had a religious tinge; others declared their intention to restore the emperors of the Sung dynasty. Before long great parts of central China were wrested from the hands of the government. The government recognized the menace to its existence, but resorted to contradictory measures. In 1352 southern Chinese were permitted to take over certain official positions. In this way it was hoped to gain the full support of the gentry, who had a certain interest in combating the rebel movements. On the other hand, the government tightened up its nationality laws. All the old segregation laws were brought back into force, with the result that in a few years the aim of the rebels became no longer merely the expulsion of the rich but also the expulsion of the Mongols: a social movement thus became a national one. A second element contributed to the change in the character of the popular rising. The rebels captured many towns. Some of these towns refused to fight and negotiated terms of submission. In these cases the rebels did not murder the whole of the gentry, but took some of them into their service. The gentry did not agree to this out of sympathy with the rebels, but simply in order to save their own lives. Once they had taken the step, however, they could not go back; they had no alternative but to remain on the side of the rebels.

In 1352 Kuo Tzŭ-hsing rose in southern Honan. Kuo was the son of a wandering soothsayer and a blind beggar-woman. He had success; his group gained control of a considerable area around his home. There was no longer any serious resistance from the Mongols, for at this time the whole of eastern China was in full revolt. In 1353 Kuo was joined by a man named Chu Yüan-chang, the son of a small peasant, probably a tenant farmer. Chu's parents and all his relatives had died from a plague, leaving him destitute. He had first entered a monastery and become a monk. This was a favourite resource—and has been almost to the present day—for poor sons of peasants who were threatened with starvation. As a monk he had gone about begging, until in 1353 he returned to his home and collected a group, mostly men from his own village, sons of peasants and young fellows who had already been peasant leaders. Monks were often peasant leaders. They were trusted because they promised divine aid, and because they were usually rather better educated than the rest of the peasants. Chu at first also had contacts with a secret society, a branch of the White Lotus Society which several times in the course of Chinese history has been the nucleus of rebellious movements. Chu took his small group, which identified itself by a red turban and a red banner, to Kuo, who received him gladly, entered into alliance with him, and in sign of friendship gave him his daughter in marriage. In 1355 Kuo died, and Chu took over his army, now many thousands strong. In his campaigns against towns in eastern China, Chu succeeded in winning over some capable members of the gentry. One was the chairman of a committee that yielded a town to Chu; another was a scholar whose family had always been opposed to the Mongols, and who had himself suffered injustice several times in his official career, so that he was glad to join Chu out of hatred of the Mongols.

These men gained great influence over Chu, and persuaded him to give up attacking rich individuals, and instead to establish an assured control over large parts of the country. He would then, they pointed out, be permanently enriched, while otherwise he would only be in funds at the moment of the plundering of a town. They set before him strategic plans with that aim. Through their counsel Chu changed from the leader of a popular rising into a fighter against the dynasty. Of all the peasant leaders he was now the only one pursuing a definite aim. He marched first against Nanking, the great city of central China, and captured it with ease. He then crossed the Yangtze, and conquered the rich provinces of the south-east. He was a rebel who no longer slaughtered the rich or plundered the towns, and the whole of the gentry with all their followers came over to him en masse. The armies of volunteers went over to Chu, and the whole edifice of the dynasty collapsed.

The years 1355–1368 were full of small battles. After his conquest of the whole of the south, Chu went north. In 1368 his generals captured Peking almost without a blow. The Mongol ruler fled on horseback with his immediate entourage into the north of China, and soon after into Mongolia. The Mongol dynasty had been brought down, almost without resistance. The Mongols in the isolated garrisons marched northward wherever they could. A few surrendered to the Chinese and were used in southern China as professional soldiers, though they were always regarded with suspicion.

The only serious resistance offered came from the regions in which other Chinese popular leaders had established themselves, especially the remote provinces in the west and south-west, which had a different social structure and had been relatively little affected by the Mongol regime.

Thus the collapse of the Mongols came for the following reasons: (1) They had not succeeded in maintaining their armed strength or that of their allies during the period of peace that followed Kublai's conquest. The Mongol soldiers had become effeminate through their life of idleness in the towns. (2) The attempt to rule the empire through Mongols or other aliens, and to exclude the Chinese gentry entirely from the administration, failed through insufficient knowledge of the sources of revenue and through the abuses due to the favoured treatment of aliens. The whole country, and especially the peasantry, was completely impoverished and so driven into revolt. (3) There was also a psychological reason. In the middle of the fourteenth century it was obvious to the Mongols that their hold over China was growing more and more precarious, and that there was little to be got out of the impoverished country: they seem in consequence to have lost interest in the troublesome task of maintaining their rule, preferring, in so far as they had not already entirely degenerated, to return to their old home in the north. It is important to bear in mind these reasons for the collapse of the Mongols, so that we may compare them later with the reasons for the collapse of the Manchus.

No mention need be made here of the names of the Mongol rulers in China after Kublai. After his death in 1294, grandsons and great-grandsons of his followed each other in rapid succession on the throne; not one of them was of any personal significance. Their life was spent in intriguing against one another. In part, these intrigues had to do with the conditions of the whole Mongol empire, especially with the homeland of the Mongols. Some cliques wanted to strengthen their hold over Mongolia, others tried to rely upon Chinese collaborators and make their rule over China more 'Chinese', accepting more and more typically Chinese techniques of governing.

(B) CHINESE ABSOLUTISM (1368–1644)

1 *Popular rebellion*

The many popular risings during the latter half of the period of Mongol rule in China were all of a purely economic and social character, and at first they were not directed at all against the Mongols as representatives of an alien people. Conditions in the fourteenth century were harsh. In addition to the factors already mentioned, the common man suffered from inflation because of the emission of more and more paper money which was not convertible. Overseas trade along the coast had more or less stopped, and even the grain transports from central to north China could not go by sea any more because of increasing danger from pirates. Canal transport was costly, slow and required a large labour force. Chu Yüan-chang's revolt is one of many that started, but only three times in Chinese history has a man of the peasantry become emperor and founder of a dynasty. The first of these three men founded the Han dynasty; the second founded the first of the so-called 'Five Dynasties' in the tenth century; Chu was the third.

We have a tendency to see in peasant revolts revolutionary movements, i.e. movements which attempt to change the social and governmental system. Perhaps the revolt of Wang Tsê (1047–1048), celebrated in a folk novel and mentioned in at least five theatre plays, was a true revolutionary rebellion; smaller rebellions before and after him sometimes had revolutionary elements, often in messianic guise. Chu, in the beginning does not seem to have had an ideology. When he came into power, however, some revolutionary ideas appeared, perhaps because of his collaboration with a secret society, characterized by red flags and red scarves. But soon after his movement was joined by the gentry what had been a revolutionary movement became a struggle for the substitution of one dynasty for another without interfering with the existing social system. However, the fights against the Mongols and the tightening of the Mongol nationality laws as a reaction, developed among the Chinese a feeling of nationalism. This feeling should not be confounded with the very old feeling of Chinese as a culturally superior group according to which, at least in theory though rarely in practice, every person who assimilated Chinese cultural values and traits was a 'Chinese'. The roots of nationalism seem to lie in the Southern Sung period, growing up in the course of contacts with the Juchên and Mongols; but the discriminatory laws of the Mongols greatly fostered this feeling. From now on, it was regarded a shame to serve a foreigner as official, even if he was a ruler of China.

2   Wars against Mongols and Japanese

It had been easy to drive the Mongols out of China, though apparently a considerable number of individual Mongols, disguising themselves as Chinese, seem to have remained in China. There is even a tradition that some small caste-like groups in central China are assimilated Mongols, depressed to the status of outcasts. As a political unit, however, the Mongols were never really beaten in their own country. On the contrary, they seem to have regained

strength after their withdrawal from China: they reorganized themselves and were soon capable of counterthrusts, while Chinese
offensives had as a rule very little success, and at all events no
decisive success. In the course of time, however, the Chinese gained
a certain influence over Sinkiang, but it was never absolute, always
challenged. After the Mongol empire had fallen to pieces, small states
came into existence in Sinkiang, for a long time with varying fortunes; the most important one during the Ming epoch was that of
Hami, until in 1473 it was occupied by the city-state of Turfan. At
this time China actively intervened in the policy of Sinkiang in a
number of combats with the Mongols. As the situation changed
from time to time, these city-states united more or less closely
with China or fell away from her altogether. In this period, however, Sinkiang was of no military or economic importance to
China.

In the time of the Ming there also began in the east and south
the plague of Japanese piracy. Japanese contacts with the coastal
provinces of China (Kiangsu, Chêkiang and Fukien) had a very
long history: pilgrims from Japan often went to these places in order
to study Buddhism in the famous monasteries of central China;
businessmen sold at high prices Japanese swords and other Japanese products here and bought Chinese products; they also tried to
get Chinese copper coins which had a higher value in Japan. Chinese
merchants co-operated with Japanese merchants and also with
pirates in the guise of merchants. Some Chinese, who were or felt
persecuted by the government, became pirates themselves. This
trade-piracy had started already at the end of the Sung dynasty,
when Japanese navigation had become superior to Korean shipping
which had in earlier times dominated the eastern seaboard. These
conditions may even have been one of the reasons why the Mongols
tried to subdue Japan. As early as 1387 the Chinese had to begin the
building of fortifications along the eastern and southern coasts of
the country. The Japanese attacks now often took the character of
organized raids: a small, fast-sailing flotilla would land in a bay, as
far as possible without attracting notice; the soldiers would march
against the nearest town, generally overcoming it, looting, and withdrawing. The defensive measures adopted from time to time during
the Ming epoch were of little avail, as it was impossible effectively
to garrison the whole coast. Some of the coastal settlements were
transferred inland, to prevent the Chinese from co-operating with
the Japanese, and to give the Japanese so long a march inland as to
allow time for defensive measures. The Japanese pirates prevented
the creation of a Chinese navy in this period by their continual
threats to the coastal cities in which the shipyards lay. Not until

much later, at a time of unrest in Japan in 1467, was there any peace from the Japanese pirates.

The Japanese attacks were especially embarrassing for the Chinese government for one other reason. Large armies had to be kept all along China's northern border, from Manchuria to Central Asia. Food supplies could not be collected in north China which did not have enough surpluses. Canal transportation from central China was not reliable, as the canals did not always have enough water and were often clogged by hundreds of ships. And even if canals were used, grain still had to be transported by land from the end of the canals to the frontier. The Ming government, therefore, had organized an overseas flotilla of grain ships which brought grain from central China directly to the front in Liao-tung and Manchuria. And these ships, vitally important, were so often attacked by the pirates that this plan later had to be given up again.

These activities along the coast led the Chinese to the belief that basically all foreigners who came by ships were 'barbarians'; when towards the end of the Ming epoch the Japanese were replaced by Europeans who did not behave much differently and were also pirate-merchants, the nations of Western Europe, too, were regarded as 'barbarians' and were looked upon with great suspicion. On the other side, continental powers, even if they were enemies, had long been regarded as 'states', sometimes even as equals. Therefore, when at a much later time the Chinese came into contact with Russians, their attitude towards them was similar to that which they had taken towards other Asian continental powers.

3 Social legislation within the existing order

At the time when Chu Yüan-chang conquered Peking, in 1368, becoming the recognized emperor of China (Ming dynasty), it seemed as though he would remain a revolutionary in spite of everything. His first laws were directed against the rich. Many of the rich were compelled to migrate to the capital, Nanking, thus losing their land and the power based on it. Land was redistributed among poor peasants; new land registers were also compiled, in order to prevent the rich from evading taxation. The number of monks living in idleness was cut down and precisely determined; the possessions of the temples were reduced, land exempted from taxation being thus made taxable—all this, incidentally, although Chu had himself been a monk! These laws might have paved the way to social harmony and removed the worst of the poverty of the Mongol epoch. But all this was frustrated in the very first years of Chu's reign. The laws were only half carried into effect or not at all, especially in the hinterland of the present Shanghai. That region had been conquered by Chu at the very beginning of the Ming epoch; in it lived the wealthy land-owners who had already been paying the bulk of the taxes under the Mongols. The emperor depended on this wealthy class for the financing of his great armies, and so could not be too hard on it.

Chu Yüan-chang and his entourage were also unable to free themselves from some of the ideas of the Mongol epoch. Neither Chu, nor anybody else before and long after him, discussed the possibility of a form of government other than that of a monarchy. The first ever to discuss this question, although very timidly, was Huang Tsung-hsi (1610–1695), at the end of the Ming dynasty. Chu's conception of an emperor was that of an absolute monarch, master over life and death of his subjects; it was formed by the Mongol emperors with their magnificence and the huge expenditure of their life in Peking; Chu was oblivious of the fact that Peking had been the capital of a vast empire embracing almost the whole of Asia, and expenses could well be higher than for a capital only of China. It did not occur to Chu and his supporters that they could have done without imperial state and splendour; on the contrary, they felt compelled to display it. The splendour of Peking, which we still admire today, is largely the result of the building activities in early Ming time, after the change of the capital from Nanking to Peking. Another sign of Chu's tendency to imitate the Mongol rulers were his grants: he conferred great land grants on all his relatives, friends, and supporters; he would give to a single person land sufficient for 20,000 peasant families; he ordered the payments of state pensions to members of the imperial family, just as the Mongols had done, and the total of these pension payments was often higher than the revenue of the region involved. For the capital alone over eight million *shih* of grain had to be provided in payment of pensions—that is to say, more than 160,000 tons! These pension payments were in themselves a heavy burden on the state; not only that, but they formed a difficult transport problem! We have no close figure of the total population at the beginning of the Ming epoch; about 1500 it is estimated to have been 53,280,000, and this population had to provide some 266,000,000 *shih* in taxes. At the beginning of the Ming epoch the population and revenue must, however, have been smaller.

The laws against the merchants and the restrictions under which the craftsmen worked remained under Chu essentially as they had been before, and changed only in the sixteenth century. But now the few remaining foreign merchants lost their privileged status and also fell under these laws, and their influence quickly diminished. All craftsmen, a total of some 300,000 men with families, were still registered and had to serve the government in the capital for three

253

months once every three years; others had to serve ten days per month, if they lived close by. They were a hereditary caste as were the professional soldiers, and not allowed to change their occupation except by special imperial permission. When a craftsman or soldier died, another family member had to replace him; therefore, families of craftsmen were not allowed to separate into small nuclear families, in which there might not always be a suitable male. Yet, in an empire as large as that of the Ming, this system did not work too well: craftsmen lost too much time in travelling and often succeeded in running away while travelling. Therefore, from 1505 on, they had to pay a tax instead of working for the government, and from then on the craftsmen became relatively free.

4   Colonization and agricultural developments

As already mentioned, the Ming had to keep a large army along the northern frontiers. But they also had to keep armies in south China, especially in Yünnan. Here, the Mongol invasions of Burma and Thailand had brought unrest among the tribes, especially the Shan. The Ming did not hold Burma but kept it in a loose dependency as a 'tributary nation'. In order to supply armies so far away from all agricultural surplus centres, the Ming resorted to the old system of 'military colonies' which seems to have been invented in the second century B.C. and is still used even today (in Sinkiang). Soldiers were settled in camps called *ying*, and therefore there are so many place names ending with *ying* in the outlying areas of China. They worked as state farmers and accumulated surpluses which were used in case of war in which these same farmers turned soldiers again. Many criminals were sent to these state farms, too. This system, especially in south China, transformed territories formerly inhabited by native tribes or uninhabited, into solidly Chinese areas. In addition to these military colonies, a steady stream of settlers from central China and the coast continued to move into Kwangtung and Hunan provinces. They felt protected by the army against attacks by natives. Yet Ming texts are full of reports on major and minor clashes with the natives, from Kiangsi and Fukien to Kwangtung and Kwanghsi.

But the production of military colonies was still not enough to feed the armies, and the government in Chu's time resorted to a new design. It promised to give merchants who transported grain from central China to the borders, government salt certificates. Upon the receipt, the merchants could acquire a certain amount of salt and sell it with high profits. Soon, these merchants began to invest some of their capital in local land which was naturally cheap. They then attracted farmers from their home countries as tenants. The rent of the tenants, paid in form of grain, was then sold to the army, and the merchant's gains increased. Tenants could easily be found: the density of population in the Yangtze plains had further increased since the Sung time. This system of merchant colonization did not last long, because soon, in order to curb the profits of the merchants, money was given instead of salt certificates, and the merchants lost interest in grain transports. Thus, grain prices along the frontiers rose and the effectiveness of the armies was diminished.

Although the history of Chinese agriculture is as yet only partially known, a number of changes in this field, which began to show up from Sung time on, seem to have produced an 'agricultural revolution' in Ming time. We have already mentioned the Sung attempts to increase production near the big cities by deep-lying fields, cultivation on and in lakes. At the same time, there was an increase in cultivation of mountain slopes by terracing and by distributing water over the terraces in balanced systems. New irrigation machines, especially the so-called Persian wheel, were introduced in the Ming time. Perhaps the most important innovation, however, was the introduction of rice from Indo-China's kingdom Champa in 1012 into Fukien from where it soon spread. This rice had three advantages over ordinary Chinese rice: it was drought-resistant and could, therefore, be planted in areas with poor or even no irrigation. It had a great productivity, and it could be sown very early in the year. At first it had the disadvantage that it had a vegetation period of a hundred days. But soon, the Chinese developed a quick-growing Champa rice, and the speediest varieties took only sixty days from transplantation into the fields to the harvest. This made it possible to grow two rice harvests instead of only one, and more than doubled the production. Rice varieties which grew again after being cut and produced a second, but very much smaller harvest, disappeared from now on. Furthermore, fish were kept in the ricefields and produced not only food for the farmers but also fertilized the fields, so that continuous cultivation of ricefields without any decrease in fertility became possible. Incidentally, fish control the malaria mosquitoes; although the Chinese did not know this fact, large areas in south China which had formerly been avoided by Chinese because of malaria, gradually became inhabitable. Some enterpreneurs raised baby fish in hatcheries and sold them commercially.

The importance of alternating crops was also discovered and from now on, the old system of fallow cultivation was given up and continuous cultivation with, in some areas, even more than one harvest per field per year, was introduced even in wheat-growing areas. Considering that under the fallow system from one-half to one-third of all fields remained uncultivated each year, the increase in production under the new system must have been tremendous.

255

We believe that the population revolution which in China started about 1550, was the result of this earlier agrarian revolution. From the eighteenth century on we get reports of depletion of fields due to wrong application of the new system.

Another plant deeply affected Chinese agriculture: cotton. It is often forgotten that, from very early times, the Chinese in the south had used kapok and similar cotton-like fibres, and that all the time cocoons of different kinds of worms had been used for silk. Real cotton probably came from Bengal over South-East Asia first to the coastal provinces of China and spread quickly into Fukien and Kwangtung in Sung time.

On the other side, cotton reached China through Central Asia, and already in the thirteenth century we find it in Shensi in north-western China. Farmers in the north could in many places grow cotton in summer and wheat in winter, and cotton was a high-priced product. They ginned the cotton with iron rods; a mechanical cotton gin was not introduced until later. The raw cotton was sold to merchants who transported it into the industrial centre of the time, the Yangtze valley, and who re-exported cotton cloth to the north. Raw cotton, loosened by the string of the bow (a method which was known since Sung), could now in the north also be used for quilts and padded winter garments.

5 Commercial and industrial developments

Intensivation and modernization of agriculture led to strong population increases especially in the Yangtze valley from Sung time on. Thus, in this area commerce and industry also developed most quickly. Urbanization was greatest here. Nanking, the new Ming capital, grew tremendously because of the presence of the court and administration, and even when later the capital was moved, Nanking continued to remain the cultural capital of China. The urban population needed textiles and food. From Ming time on, fashions changed quickly as soon as government regulations which determined colour and material of the dress of each social class were relaxed or as soon as they could be circumvented by bribery or ingenious devices. Now, only factories could produce the amounts which the consumers wanted. We hear of many men who started out with one loom and later ended up with over forty looms, employing many weavers. Shanghai began to emerge as a centre of cotton cloth production. A system of middle-men developed who bought raw cotton and raw silk from the producers and sold it to factories.

Consumption in the Yangtze cities raised the value of the land around the cities. The small farmers who were squeezed out migrated to the south. Absentee landlords in cities relied partly on migratory, seasonal labour supplied by small farmers from Chêkiang who came to the Yangtze area after they had finished their own harvest. More and more, vegetables and mulberries or cotton were planted in the vicinity of the cities. As rice prices went up quickly a large organization of rice merchants grew up. They ran large ships up to Hankow where they bought rice which was brought down from Hunan in river boats by smaller merchants. The small merchants again made contracts with the local gentry who bought as much rice from the producers as they could and sold it to these grain merchants. Thus, local grain prices went up and we hear of cases where the local population attacked the grain boats in order to prevent the depletion of local markets.

While there always had been markets, from Sung time on, China became dotted with a network of markets of different types. There were markets in the cities, often comparable to the Near Eastern bazaars, and markets along the borders for trade with foreigners, both types strongly controlled by the government. But there were also farmers' markets, often called 'malaria markets' because they were held on alternate days (like the attacks by malaria tertiana). Such markets were often outside the villages ('mountain markets') and served as an exchange for the products of local villagers, but itinerant pedlars came to these places, too, and sold city-made textiles or iron implements. There were, separately, cattle and horse markets, held at times when it suited the farmers best. Finally, there were temple fairs, held on the birthday of the god of the temple. Here, more luxury articles were sold; scholars often found here valuable paintings or rare books, ordinary citizens bought toys and sweets for their children.

Grain, collected from farmers by agents or sent in by farmers, came to the cities and specialized big grain merchants. Their centre in central China soon became the district of Hui-chou, in particular Hsin-an, a city on the borders of Anhui and Chêkiang. When the grain transportation to the frontiers came to an end in early Ming time, the Hsin-an merchants specialized first in silver trade. Later in Ming time, they spread their activities all over China and often monopolized the salt, silver, rice, cotton, silk or tea businesses. In the sixteenth century they had well-established contacts with smugglers on the Fukien coast and brought foreign goods into the interior. Their home was also close to the main centres of porcelain production in Kiangsi which was exported overseas and to the urban centres. The demand for porcelain had increased so much that state factories could not fulfil it. The state factories seem often to have suffered from a lack of labour: indented artisans were imported from other

257

provinces and later sent back on state expenses or were taken away from other state industries. Thus, private porcelain factories began to develop, and in connection with quickly changing fashions a great diversification of porcelain occurred.

One other industry should also be mentioned. With the development of printing, which will be discussed below, the paper industry was greatly stimulated. The state also needed special types of paper for the paper currency. Printing and book selling became a profitable business, and with the application of block print to textiles (probably first used in Sung time) another new field of commercial activity was opened.

As already mentioned, silver in form of bars had been increasingly used as currency in Sung time. The yearly government production of silver was about 10,000 kg. Mongol currency was actually based upon silver. The Ming, however, reverted to copper as basic unit, in addition to the use of paper money. This encouraged the use of silver for speculative purposes.

The development of business changed the face of cities. From Sung time on, the division of cities into wards with gates which were closed during the night, began to break down. Ming cities had no more wards. Business was no more restricted to official markets but grew up in all parts of the cities. The individual trades were no more necessarily all in one street. Shops did not have to close at sunset. The guilds developed and in some cases were able to exercise locally some influence upon the officials.

The increasing development of markets led to several other changes. We observe, for instance, a growing specialization and division of labour, so that, for instance, cloth was no more produced from the raw cotton to the finished product by one worker, but spinning, weaving and dyeing were done by different specialists, often in different cities.

In the countryside, too, the social organization became more and more complex. It seems, according to recent research, that the Hsin-an merchants have originated from landowner families who first went for diversification of cultivation, in order to protect themselves against catastrophies. They then invested in land in places outside; then they either had tenants working the land or bought up products of farmers and became merchants in the first place. Such merchant families had a stability, often over centuries, like the old gentry families and can be compared to the urban patricians in Europe.

From this period, we have enough contracts between landowners and tenants to see that, basically the relationship was contractual, so that, technically, we cannot call the producers 'serfs' any more.

Some tenants, though, could not leave the land and had servile obligations, such as to take care of the master's estate when he was away on business, or to take care of the master's family tombs. But at the same time, the master had to supply them with a house, had to give them gifts at the festivals, and often also gave them tools. Some landowners gave their tenants the housemaids as wives, thus saving the tenants from an expense which equalled a year's income. The tenant could pawn his land; he also could own land, and there were many farm labourers on one-year contracts, as well as free tenants who could move away or try to get a different piece of land from another landowner. There are cases in which a tenant, in order to get a wife, moved to the wife's family and served her family, in one case as long as twenty-two years—reminding us of the Old Testament and Jacob's service at Laban's house.

But there were also still slaves, apparently mainly criminals who were given to officials to work on their land. They were hereditary slaves and could not move. Thus, we observe a great complexity and diversity in Ming time.

6 Changing times

There appears in Ming times a different outlook on society and life. The old attitude is still found. For instance:

> Somebody gave to Lü Meng-cheng [Sung time] a mirror which could reflect 200 *li* afar. Lü said, his face was small, he needed no big mirror ('Ch'iu-yü-wan sui-pi', ch. 5).

Or:

> Formerly, women's work was with hemp, linen, and silk. They wove it and made yarn, and their product was solid and heavy, so that it did last a long time. In later times, women worked on stitching and embroidering; the product was light and easily spoiled. In the morning it was a splendid bed cover or dress; in the evening it was already thrown away. A waste of energy and of money, as it could not be worse ('Leng-lu tsa-chih', ch. 2).

This was a typical attitude against progress and change and in favour of frugality. At the base of it was what G. Foster called the concept of the 'limited good'. Now we find different opinions for the first time:

> Customs change from the simple to the vulgar, and this is irreversible, like the flowing of rivers downstream. From old times on, this was regretted. Our Sung-chiang [a city not far from Shanghai] was always known for its extravagant and artful, haughty customs. There was no more chance for a return

259

to simple life. But from the Chia-ching [1522–1566] and Lung-ch'ing [1567–1572] times on, the big houses, the honoured families indulged in extravagance, went towards sinfulness. . . . Every day unusual new things come up, every year there are hundreds of new things. Shepherd boys and village oldsters are competing to become 'rats' (i.e. oppressive officials), and rural women and country ladies change into seducing foxes ('Yün-chien chü-mu ch'ao', Ch. 2).

This author then gives a long list of changes. He regrets some of these changes. Thus he remarks that the rules for dress were made to 'clarify the fine distinctions between men and women, between high and low' and then says: 'When slaves compete for glorious (appearance), it will be difficult for them to become decent; if women copy the whores, it will be difficult for them to be decent.' He observes that formerly there were no shoe shops in town, but since 1573 male shoemakers began to make shoes. Shoes became lighter and finer. 'Slaves and masters use the same types now. This is the worst of all customs.' The forms and colours of hats changed rapidly, as did women's hair fashions. New brands of wine, new dishes were introduced. Since 1567 there were boatsmen at the gates of the city and excursions with parties on board became fashionable. 'Recently, wives and daughters of "small people" [i.e. rural landowners], as soon as they can get out, immediately call themselves sales-women. They buy and sell gold and pearl head-dresses . . . and also indulge in prostitution.' Such a sales-woman rented herself out to a doctor who had no son and gave birth to a son for him. She became famous and the wealthy houses competed in inviting her. She later also sold sex drugs, and sex implements and became wealthy. Finally, the author complains about juvenile delinquency, another innovation, especially after 1580. These gangs divided the city up among the individual gangs, cheated country-people who wanted to sell merchandise in town, and blackmailed them. He even reports mob actions against officials. Thus, we may say that the changes in the sixteenth century were so quick and obvious that scholars observed them and got worried. It is only in the nineteenth century that some authors begin to regard the changes as a progress:

The use of *shih* [boys representing a dead ancestor] in funeral sacrifices; the use of human sacrifices for the dead; the use of cousins [of the wife] as concubines; the mutilating punishments by the courts; the divorce of women because of disabling diseases or barrenness: all these things occurred in the old time and have now disappeared. In such cases, the new is better than the old [custom] ('Leng-lu tsa-shih', Ch. 7).

And another author of the nineteenth century remarks that, apparently, even the gods change their customs: formerly, every man wore square boots, not pointed boots, now, deities appear in modern, pointed boots!

What I want to point out here is that great changes occurred during the lifetime of a person from Ming times on; that the thinkers wondered about them. Some regard them as bad, but unavoidable, others still long for the past. Only in the nineteenth century do some of them regard some changes as a progress towards a better society. Perhaps even more important is the growing social mobility, which, of course, the old gentry disliked.

7 Growth of the small gentry

There were still other factors which made for social mobility. With the spread of book printing, all kinds of books became easily accessible, including reprints of examination papers. Even businessmen and farmers increasingly learned to read and to write, and many people now could prepare themselves for the examinations. Attendance, however, at the examinations cost a good deal. The candidate had to travel to the local or provincial capital, and for the higher examinations to the capital of the country; he had to live there for several months and, as a rule, had to bribe the examiners or at least to gain the favour of influential people. There were many cases of candidates becoming destitute. Most of them were heavily in debt when at last they gained a position. They naturally set to work at once to pay their debts out of their salary, and to accumulate fresh capital to meet future emergencies. The salaries of officials were, however, so small that it was impossible to make ends meet; and at the same time every official was liable with his own capital for the receipt in full of the taxes for the collection of which he was responsible. Consequently every official began at once to collect more taxes than were really due, so as to be able to cover any deficits, and also to cover his own cost of living—including not only the repayment of his debts but the acquisition of capital or land so as to rise in the social scale. The old gentry had been rich landowners, and had had no need to exploit the peasants on such a scale.

The Chinese empire was greater than it had been before the Mongol epoch, and the population was also greater, so that more officials were needed. Thus in the Ming epoch there began a certain democratization, larger sections of the population having the opportunity of gaining government positions.

The new 'small gentry' did not consist of great families like the original gentry. When, therefore, people of that class wanted to play a political part in the central government, or to gain a position there, they had either to get into close touch with one of the families of the gentry, or to try to approach the emperor directly. In the immediate entourage of the emperor, however, were the eunuchs. Some members of the new class had themselves castrated after they had passed their state examination. Originally eunuchs were forbidden to acquire education. But soon the Ming emperors used the eunuchs as a tool to counteract the power of gentry cliques and thus to strengthen their personal power. When, later, eunuchs controlled appointments to government posts, long-established practices of bureaucratic administration were eliminated and the court, i.e. the emperor and his tools, the eunuchs, could create a rule by way of arbitrary decisions, a despotic rule. For such purposes, eunuchs had to have education, and these new educated eunuchs, when they had once secured a position, were able to gain great influence in the immediate entourage of the emperor; later such educated eunuchs were preferred, especially as many offices were created which were only filled by eunuchs and for which educated eunuchs were needed. Whole departments of eunuchs came into existence at court, and these were soon made use of for confidential business of the emperor's outside the palace.

These eunuchs worked, of course, in the interest of their families. On the other hand, they were very ready to accept large bribes from the gentry for placing the desires of people of the gentry before the emperor and gaining his consent. Thus the eunuchs generally accumulated great wealth, which they shared with their small gentry relatives. The rise of the small gentry class was therefore connected with the increased influence of the eunuchs at court.

8 *Literature, art, crafts*

The growth of the small gentry which had its stronghold in the provincial towns and cities, as well as the rise of the merchant class and the liberation of the artisans, are reflected in the new literature of Ming time. While the Mongols had developed the theatre, the novel may be regarded as the typical Ming creation. Its precursors were the stories of story-tellers centuries ago. The novels pretended to be stories of story-tellers: they were cut into chapters, not according to logical principles, but the cuts were made at the most interesting places, to induce the reader to read further on—just as the story-teller stopped at the interesting place, collected money, and then continued. Like the stories, the novels were interspersed with poems, some of which were summaries of the content of the chapter and served as a kind of memory-aid to the teller, other poems gave descriptions of nature or of human emotions, interrupting the more factual stories. But, most important, the novels were written in everyday language, not in the language of the gentry. To this day every

Chinese knows and reads with enthusiasm 'Shui-hu-chuan' ('The Story of the River Bank'), probably written about 1550 by Wang Tao-k'un, in which the ruling class was first described in its decay. Against it are held up as ideals representatives of the middle class in the guise of the gentleman brigand. Every Chinese also knows the great satirical novel 'Hsi-yu-chi' ('The Westward Journey'), by Feng Mêng-lung (1574–1645), in which ironical treatment is meted out to all religions and sects against a mythological background, with a freedom that would not have been possible earlier. The characters are not presented as individuals but as representatives of human types: the intellectual, the hedonist, the pious man, and the simpleton, are drawn with incomparable skill, with their merits and defects. A third famous novel is 'San-kuo yen-i' ('The Tale of the Three Kingdoms'), by Lo Kuan-chung. Just as the European middle class read with avidity the romances of chivalry, so the comfortable class in China was enthusiastic over romanticized pictures of the struggle of the gentry in the third century. 'The Tale of the Three Kingdoms' became the model for countless historical novels of its own and subsequent periods. Later, mainly in the sixteenth century, the sensational and erotic novel developed, most of all in Nanking. It has deeply influenced Japanese writers, but was mercilessly suppressed by the Chinese gentry which resented the frivolity of this wealthy and luxurious urban class of middle or small gentry families who associated with rich merchants, actors, artists and musicians. Censorship of printed books had started almost with the beginning of book printing as a private enterprise: to the famous historian, anti-Buddhist and conservative Ou-yang Hsiu (1007–1072), the enemy of Wang An-shih, belongs the sad glory of having developed the first censorship rules. Since Ming time, it became a permanent feature of Chinese governments.

The best known of the erotic novels is the 'Chin-p'ing-mei', which is still forbidden by the Communists as well as by the Nationalists, except in expurgated versions. Similarly, there is only one German translation which is not expurgated, but the objectionable sections are not in the commercial edition and have to be ordered separately; other translators used Latin at the same places. Much less 'erotic' and closer to the form of an historical novel is the 'Amorous adventures of Yang Ti, emperor of Sui' ('Sui Yang Ti yen-shih'), which does not yet exist in a translation but would deserve one. It might be pointed out that many novels were printed in Hui-chou, the commercial centre of the time.

The short story which formerly served the entertainment of the educated only and which was, therefore, written in classical Chinese, now also became a literary form appreciated by the middle classes.

The collection 'Chin-ku ch'i-kuan' ('Strange Stories of New Times and Old'), compiled by Feng Mêng-lung, is the best known of these collections in vernacular Chinese.

Little original work was done in the Ming epoch in the fields generally regarded as 'literature' by educated Chinese, those of poetry and the essay. There are some admirable essays, but these are only isolated examples out of thousands. So also with poetry: the poets of the gentry, united in 'clubs', chose the poets of the Sung epoch as their models to emulate.

The Chinese drama made further progress in the Ming epoch. Many of the finest Chinese dramas were written under the Ming; they are still produced again and again to this day. The most famous dramatists of the Ming epoch are Wang Shih-chen (1526–1590) and T'ang Hsien-tsu (1556–1617). T'ang wrote the well-known drama 'Mu-tan-t'ing' ('The Peony Pavilion'), one of the finest love-stories of Chinese literature, full of romance and remote from all reality. This is true also of the other dramas by T'ang, especially his 'Four Dreams', a series of four plays. In them a man lives in dream through many years of his future life, with the result that he realizes the worthlessness of life and decides to become a monk.

Together with the development of the drama (or, rather, the opera) in the Ming epoch went an important endeavour in the modernization of music, the attempt to create a 'well-tempered scale' made in 1584 by Chu Tsai-yü. This solved in China a problem which was not tackled till later in Europe. The first Chinese theorists of music who occupied themselves with this problem were Ching Fang (77–37 B.C.) and Ho Ch'êng-t'ien (A.D. 370–447).

In the Mongol epoch, most of the Chinese painters had lived in central China; this remained so in the Ming epoch. Of the many painters of the Ming epoch, all held in high esteem in China, mention must be made especially of Ch'iu Ying (c. 1525), T'ang Yin (1470–1523), and Tung Ch'i-ch'ang (1555–1636). Ch'iu Ying painted in the Academic Style, indicating every detail, however small, and showing preference for a turquoise-green ground. T'ang Yin was the painter of elegant women; Tung became famous especially as a calligraphist and a theoretician of the art of painting; a textbook of the art was written by him.

Just as puppet plays and shadow plays are the 'opera of the common man' and took a new development in Ming time, the wood-cut and block-printing developed largely as a cheap substitute of real paintings. The new urbanites wanted to have paintings of the masters and found in the wood-cut which soon became a multi-colour print a cheap mass medium. Block-printing in colours, developed in the Yangtze valley, was adopted by Japan and found its highest refinement there. But the Ming are also famous for their monumental architecture which largely followed Mongol patterns. Among the most famous examples is the famous Great Wall which had been in dilapidation and was rebuilt; the great city walls of Peking; and large parts of the palaces of Peking, begun in the Mongol epoch. It was at this time that the official style which we may observe to this day in north China was developed, the style employed everywhere. Nationalist China on the mainland and in Taiwan transformed this style into concrete.

In the Ming epoch the porcelain with blue decoration on a white ground became general; the first examples, from the famous kilns in Ching-te-chen, in the province of Kiangsi, were relatively coarse, but in the fifteenth century the production was much finer. In the sixteenth century the quality deteriorated, owing to the disuse of the cobalt from the Middle East (perhaps from Persia) in favour of Sumatra cobalt, which did not yield the same brilliant colour. In the Ming epoch there also appeared the first brilliant red colour, a product of iron, and a start was then made with three-colour porcelain (with lead glaze) or five-colour (enamel). The many porcelains exported to western Asia and Europe first influenced European ceramics (Delft), and then were imitated in Europe (Böttger); the early European porcelains long showed Chinese influence (the so-called onion pattern, blue on a white ground). In addition to the porcelain of the Ming epoch, of which the finest specimens are in the palace at Istanbul, especially famous are the lacquers (carved lacquer, lacquer painting, gold lacquer) of the Ming epoch and the cloisonné work of the same period. These are closely associated with the contemporary work in Japan.

Finally a few words about religious developments in Ming time. It seems that the present religious situation came to full development during Ming, after early beginnings, probably in Sung time. By this I mean that now each Chinese uses three systems for the main problems he has to deal with, paralleling the division of the world into three spheres: the upper world, our world, and the netherworld. These three worlds are symbolized by three kinds of buildings: temples for the deities of the upper world—they are 'clean'; houses in this world for humans—they are clean as well as polluted; tombs for the ghosts in the netherworld—they are polluted. Taoist priests can deal with the deities above; they have to be unpolluted and keep the temples clean. Buddhist priests can handle the ghosts and the dead, because being chaste and living outside the world of family and state in their monasteries they cannot be polluted. The cult in the house is often regarded as Confucianist. In the house, the ancestors above are honoured, because their *hun* soul is thought to be above;

at the tomb of an ancestor the dead are honoured as helpful spirits, and in the house the family lives and reproduces.

This is a predominantly 'cultic' approach, the approach that the common man has to religion. And thus, cultic Buddhism from Ming time on interests mainly the common man. There is a kind of revival of populist Buddhist sects in Ming, but philosophical Buddhism does not show much development. A great number of so-called *shan-shu* (books which should turn you to the Good) appears now in which the consequences of sinful actions are described and people are admonished to avoid falling into sin. This may be some reaction against the loosening of society as described above. It also shows that the common man was expected to act morally not because he is afraid of shame (external), but of sin (internalized feeling).

9 *Politics at court*

After the founding of the dynasty by Chu Yüan-chang, important questions had to be dealt with apart from the social legislation. What was to be done, for instance, with Chu's helpers? Chu, like many revolutionaries before and after him, recognized that these people had been serviceable in the years of struggle but could no longer remain useful. He got rid of them by the simple device of setting one against another so that they murdered one another. In the first decades of his rule the dangerous cliques of gentry had formed again, and were engaged in mutual struggles. The most formidable clique was led by Hu Wei-yung. Hu was a man of the gentry of Chu's old homeland, and one of his oldest supporters. Hu and his relations controlled the country after 1370, until in 1380 Chu succeeded in beheading Hu and exterminating his clique. New cliques formed before long and were exterminated in turn.

Chu had founded Nanking in the years of revolution, and he made it his capital. In so doing he met the wishes of the rich grain producers of the Yangtze delta. But the north was the most threatened part of his empire, so that troops had to be permanently stationed there in considerable strength. Thus Peking, where Chu placed one of his sons as 'king', was a post of exceptional importance.

In Chu Yüan-chang's last years (he was named T'ai Tsu as emperor) difficulties arose in regard to the dynasty. The heir to the throne died in 1391; and when the emperor himself died in 1398, the son of the late heir-apparent was installed as emperor (Hui Ti, 1399–1402). This choice had the support of some of the influential Confucian gentry families of the south. But a protest against his enthronement came from the other son of Chu Yüan-chang, who as king in Peking had hoped to become emperor. With his strong army this prince, Ch'eng Tsu, marched south and captured Nanking, where the palaces were burnt down. There was a great massacre of supporters of the young emperor, and the victor made himself emperor (better known under his reign name, Yung-lo). As he had established himself in Peking, he transferred the capital to Peking, where it remained throughout the Ming epoch. Nanking became a sort of subsidiary capital.

This transfer of the capital to the north, as the result of the victory of the military party and Buddhists allied to them, produced a new element of instability: the north was of military importance, but the Yangtze region remained the economic centre of the country. The interests of the gentry of the Yangtze region were injured by the transfer. The first Ming emperor had taken care to make his court resemble the court of the Mongol rulers, but on the whole had exercised relative economy. Yung-lo (1403–1424), however, lived in the actual palaces of the Mongol rulers, and all the luxury of the Mongol epoch was revived. This made the reign of Yung-lo the most magnificent period of the Ming epoch, but beneath the surface decay had begun. Typical of the unmitigated absolutism which developed now, was the word of one of the emperor's political and military advisers, significantly a Buddhist monk: 'I know the way of heaven. Why discuss the hearts of the people?'

10 *Navy. Southward expansion*

After the collapse of Mongol rule in Indo-China, partly through the simple withdrawal of the Mongols, and partly through attacks from various Chinese generals, there were independence movements in south-west China and Indo-China. In 1393 wars broke out in Annam. Yung-lo considered that the time had come to annex these regions to China and so to open a new field for Chinese trade, which was suffering continual disturbance from the Japanese. He sent armies to Yünnan and Indo-China; at the same time he had a fleet built by one of his eunuchs, Cheng Ho. The fleet was successfully protected from attack by the Japanese. Cheng Ho, who had promoted the plan and also carried it out, began in 1405 his famous mission to Indo-China, which had been envisaged as giving at least moral support to the land operations, but was also intended to renew trade connections with Indo-China, where they had been interrupted by the collapse of Mongol rule. This was the first of several expeditions by which Chinese ships ultimately reached the east coast of Africa and Arabia. Cheng Ho was a member of a Chinese Muslim family, so that he was an ideal person to contact the holy cities of Islam. This may give us one of the possible explanations for these very expensive expeditions: they could have been an attempt by the Chinese to counteract the occupation of large parts of the Near East by Timur (died in 1406). We know that Timur actually had planned to attack China and preparations came to a standstill with his death. If the Chinese could have interested the Muslims of the Near East in a collaboration with China, this would have made an attack against China very dangerous for Timur. The death of Timur and the breakdown of his empire eliminated this danger and reopened Central Asia for trade with China. Soon, trade missions from the kingdom of Shahruk in north Iran were able to come to China (the famous mission of 1409–1411).

Chinese and other scholars have often regarded these expeditions as either an outgrowth of the interest of the Yung-lo emperor in rare luxury goods, or merely as a 'friendship mission'. However, the fleet of Cheng Ho was loaded with soldiers and weapons, sufficient to overwhelm the small South-East Asian kingdoms into submission. In at least one case, Cheng Ho directly interfered in the politics of a south Asian kingdom and deported its ruler, setting up a puppet regime. It seems more likely that further expeditions were stopped after the death of Timur and the re-establishment of caravan trade. The cost of supplying the great fleet was certainly in no relation to the material advantages. A final reason for ending the expeditions may have been that the fleet would have had to be permanently guarded against the Japanese, as it had been stationed not in south China but in the Yangtze region. As early as 1411 the canals had been repaired, and from 1415 onward all the traffic of the country went by the canals, so evading the Japanese peril. This ended the short chapter of Chinese naval history.

These travels of Cheng Ho seem to have had two, more cultural, results: a large number of fairy-tales from the Middle East were brought to China, or at all events reached China at that time. The Chinese, being a realistically minded people, have produced relatively few fairy-tales of their own. The bulk of their finest fairy-tales was brought by Buddhist monks, in the course of the first millennium A.D., from India by way of Central Asia. The Buddhists made use of them to render their sermons more interesting and impressive. As time went on, these stories, spread all over China, modified in harmony with the spirit of the people and adapted to the Chinese environment. Only the fables failed to strike root in China: the matter-of-fact Chinese was not interested in animals that talked and behaved to each other like human beings. In addition, however, to these early fairly-tales, there was another group of stories that did not spread throughout China, but were found only in the southeastern coastal provinces. These came from the Middle East, especially from Persia. The fairy-tales of Indian origin spread not only to Central Asia but at the same time to Persia, where they found a very

268

16 The imperial summer palace of the Manchu rulers, at Jehol.
(Photo H. Hammer-Morrisson.)

17 Tower on the city wall of Peking.
(Photo H. Hammer-Morrisson.)

congenial soil. The Persians made radical changes in the stories and gave them the form in which they came to Europe by various routes—through North Africa to Spain and France; through Constantinople, Venice, or Genoa to France; through Russian Central Asia to Russia, Finland, and Sweden; through Turkey and the Balkans to Hungary and Germany. Thus the stories found a European home. And this same Persian form was carried by sea in Cheng Ho's time to south China. Thus we have the strange experience of finding some of our own finest fairy-tales in almost the same form in south China. Another result of these travels was a great increase of the knowledge of the Western world. Chinese now had some general knowledge of the shape of Africa and heard details about countries of the Mediterranean. It has recently been asserted that the Koreans received information of the same quality through Central Asian contacts which, we may guess, the Chinese also could have received.

11 Struggles between cliques

Yung-lo's successor died early. Under the latter's son, the emperor Hsüan Tsung (1426–1435; reign name Hsüan-tê), fixed numbers of candidates were assigned for the state examinations. It had been found that almost the whole of the gentry in the Yangtze region sat at the examinations; and that at these examinations their representatives made sure, through their mutual relations, that only their members should pass, so that the candidates from the north were virtually excluded. The important military clique in the north protested against this, and a compromise was arrived at: at every examination one-third of the candidates must come from the north and two-thirds from the south. This system lasted for a long time, and led to many disputes.

At his death Hsüan Tsung left the empire to his eight-year-old son Ying Tsung (1436–1449 and 1456–1464), who was entirely in the hands of the Yang clique, which was associated with his grandmother. Soon, however, another clique, led by the eunuch Wang Chen, gained the upper hand at court. The Mongols were very active at this time, and made several raids on the province of Shansi; Wang Chen proposed a great campaign against them, and in this campaign he took with him the young emperor, who had reached his twenty-first birthday in 1449. The emperor had grown up in the palace and knew nothing of the world outside; he was therefore glad to go with Wang Chen; but that eunuch had also lived in the palace and also knew nothing of the world, and in particular of war. Consequently he failed in the organization of reinforcements for his army, some 100,000 strong; after a few brief engagements the Oirat-Mongol prince Esen had the imperial army surrounded and the emperor a prisoner. The eunuch Wang Chen came to his end, and his clique, of course, no longer counted. The Mongols had no intention of killing the emperor; they proposed to hold him to ransom, at a high price. The various cliques at court cared little, however, about their ruler. After the fall of the Wang clique there were two others, of which one, that of General Yü, became particularly powerful, as he had been able to repel a Mongol attack on Peking. Yü proclaimed a new emperor—not the captive emperor's son, a baby, but his brother, who became the emperor Ching Tsung. Yü Ch'ien (1398–1457) is celebrated in many operas as a patriot; there were temples devoted to his memory. Wang Chen, on the other hand, became the symbol of a traitor. The Yang clique insisted on the rights of the imperial baby. From all this the Mongols saw that the Chinese were not inclined to spend a lot of money on their imperial captive. Accordingly they made an enormous reduction in the ransom demanded, and more or less forced the Chinese to take back their former emperor. The Mongols hoped that this would at least produce political disturbances by which they might profit, once the old emperor was back in Peking. And this did soon happen. At first the ransomed emperor was pushed out of sight into a palace, and Ching Tsung continued to reign. But in 1456 Ching Tsung fell ill, and a successor to him had to be chosen. The Yü clique wanted to have the son of Ching Tsung; the Yang clique wanted the son of the deposed emperor Ying Tsung. No agreement was reached, so that in the end a third clique, led by the soldier Shih Heng, who had helped to defend Peking against the Mongols, found its opportunity, and by a coup d'état reinstated the deposed emperor Ying Tsung.

This was not done out of love for the emperor, but because Shih Heng hoped that under the rule of the completely incompetent Ying Tsung he could best carry out a plan of his own, to set up his own dynasty. It is not so easy, however, to carry a conspiracy to success when there are several rival parties, each of which is ready to betray any of the others. Shih Heng's plan became known before long, and he himself was beheaded (1460).

The next forty years were filled with struggles between cliques, which steadily grew in ferocity, particularly since a special office, a sort of secret police headquarters, was set up in the palace, with functions which it extended beyond the palace, with the result that many people were arrested and disappeared. This office was set up by the eunuchs and the clique at their back, and was the first dictatorial organ created in the course of a development towards despotism that made steady progress in these years.

In 1505 Wu Tsung came to the throne, an inexperienced youth of fifteen who was entirely controlled by the eunuchs who had brought him up. The leader of the eunuchs was Liu Chin, who had the support of a group of people of the gentry and the middle class. Liu Chin succeeded within a year in getting rid of the eunuchs at court who belonged to other cliques and were working against him. After that he proceeded to establish his power. He secured in entirely official form the emperor's permission for him to issue all commands himself; the emperor devoted himself only to his pleasures, and care was taken that they should keep him sufficiently occupied to have no chance to notice what was going on in the country. The first important decree issued by Liu Chin resulted in the removal from office or the punishment or murder of over three hundred prominent persons, the leaders of the cliques opposed to him. He filled their posts with his own supporters, until all the higher posts in every department were in the hands of members of his group. He collected large sums of money which he quite openly extracted from the provinces as a special tax for his own benefit. When later his house was searched there were found 240,000 bars and 57,800 pieces of gold (a bar was equivalent of ten pieces), 791,800 ounces and 5,000,000 bars of silver (a bar was five ounces), three bushels of precious stones, two gold cuirasses, 3,000 gold rings, and much else—of a total value exceeding the annual budget of the state! The treasure was to have been used to finance a revolt planned by Liu Chin and his supporters.

Among the people whom Liu Chin had punished were several members of the former clique of the Yang, and also the philosopher Wang Yang-ming (1473–1529), who later became so famous, a member of the Wang family which was allied to the Yang. In 1510 the Yang won over one of the eunuchs in the palace and so became acquainted with Liu Chin's plans. When a revolt broke out in western China, this eunuch (whose political allegiance was, of course, unknown to Liu Chin) secured appointment as army commander. With the army intended for the crushing of the revolt, Liu Chin's palace was attacked when he was asleep, and he and all his supporters were arrested. Thus the other group came into power in the palace, including the philosopher Wang Yang-ming. Liu Chin's rule had done great harm to the country, as enormous taxation had been expended for the private benefit of his clique. On top of this had been the young emperor's extravagance: his latest pleasures had been the building of palaces and the carrying out of military games; he constantly assumed new military titles and was burning to go to war.

12 Risings

The emperor might have had a good opportunity for fighting, for his misrule had resulted in a great popular rising which began in the west, in Szechwan, and then spread to the east. As always, the rising was joined by some ruined scholars, and the movement, which

271

had at first been directed against the gentry as such, was turned into a movement against the government of the moment. No longer were all the wealthy and all officials murdered, but only those who did not join the movement. In 1512 the rebels were finally overcome, not so much by any military capacity of the government armies as through the loss of the rebels' fleet of boats in a typhoon.

In 1517 a new favourite of the emperor's induced him to make a great tour in the north, to which the favourite belonged. The tour and the hunting greatly pleased the emperor, so that he continued his journeying. This was the year in which the Portuguese Fernão Pires de Andrade landed in Canton—the first modern European to enter China.

In 1518 Wang Yang-ming, the philosopher general, crushed a rising in Kiangsi. The rising had been the outcome of years of unrest, which had had two causes: local risings of the sort we described above, and loss for the gentry due to the transfer of the capital. The province of Kiangsi was a part of the Yangtze region, and the great landowners there had lived on the profit from their supplies to Nanking. When the capital was moved to Peking, their takings fell. They placed themselves under a prince who lived in Nanking. This prince regarded Wang Yang-ming's move into Kiangsi as a threat to him, and so rose openly against the government and supported the Kiangsi gentry. Wang Yang-ming defeated him, and so came into the highest favour with the incompetent emperor. When peace had been restored in Nanking, the emperor dressed himself up as an army commander, marched south, and made a triumphal entry into Nanking.

One other aspect of Wang Yang-ming's expeditions has not yet been studied: he crushed also the so-called salt-merchant rebels in the southernmost part of Kiangsi and adjoining Kwangtung. These merchants-turned-rebels had dominated a small area, off and on since the eleventh century. At this moment, they seem to have had connections with the rich inland merchants of Hsin-an and perhaps also with foreigners. Information is still too scanty to give more details, but a local movement as persistent as this one deserves attention.

We know, however, that Wang fought against the minorities in south China and his war also has to be seen as a part of the great drive towards subjugation and 'assimilation' of minorities into the Chinese state.

Wang Yang-ming became acquainted as early as 1519 with the first European rifles, imported by the Portuguese who had landed in 1517. (The Chinese then called them Fu-lang-chi, meaning Franks. Wang was the first Chinese who spoke of the 'Franks'.) The Chinese had already had mortars which hurled stones, as early as the second century A.D. In the seventh or eighth century their mortars had sent stones of a couple of hundredweights some four hundred yards. There is mention in the eleventh century of cannon which apparently shot with a charge of a sort of gunpowder. The Mongols were already using true cannon in their sieges. In the early years of the Ming, the Chinese armies also had bombs and muskets. This was at a time when the armies of Ming had more than three million soldiers. This number was, however, much reduced in the fourteenth century.

In 1519, the first Portuguese were presented to the Chinese emperor in Nanking, where they were entertained for about a year in a hostel, a certain Lin Hsün learned about their rifles and copied them for Wang Yang-ming. In general, however, the Chinese had no respect for the Europeans, whom they described as 'bandits' who had expelled the lawful king of Malacca and had now come to China as its representatives. Later they were regarded as a sort of Japanese, because they, too, practised piracy.

13   Machiavellism

All main schools of Chinese philosophy were still based on Confucius. Wang Yang-ming's philosophy also followed Confucius, but he liberated himself from the Neo-Confucian tendency as represented by Chu Hsi, which started in the Sung epoch and continued to rule in China in his time and after him; he introduced into Confucian philosophy the conception of 'intuition'. He regarded intuition as the decisive philosophic experience; only through intuition could man come to true knowledge. This idea shows an element of meditative Buddhism along lines which the philosopher Lu Hsiang-shan (1139–1192) had first developed, while classical Neo-Confucianism was more an integration of monastic Buddhism into Confucianism. Lu had felt himself close to Wang An-shih (1021–1086), and this whole school, representing the small gentry of the Yangtze area, was called the southern or the Lin-ch'uan school, Lin-ch'uan in Kiangsi being Wang An-shih's home. During the Mongol period, a Taoist group, the Cheng-i-chiao (Correct Unity Sect) had developed in Lin-ch'uan and had accepted some of the Lin-ch'uan school's ideas. Originally, this group was a continuation of Chang Ling's church Taoism. Through the Cheng-i adherents, the southern school had gained political influence on the despotic Mongol rulers. The despotic Yung-lo emperor had favoured the monk Tao-yen (c. 1338–1418) who had also Taoist training and proposed a philosophy which also stressed intuition. He was, incidentally, in charge of the compilation of the largest encyclopaedia ever written, the 'Yung-lo ta-tien', commissioned by the Yung-lo emperor.

Wang Yang-ming followed the Lin-ch'uan tradition. The introduction of the conception of intuition, a highly subjective conception, into the system of a practical state philosophy like Confucianism could not but lead in the practice of the statesman to machiavellism. The statesman who followed the teaching of Wang Yang-ming had the opportunity of justifying whatever he did by his intuition.

Wang Yang-ming failed to gain acceptance for his philosophy. His disciples also failed to establish his doctrine in China, because it served the interests of an individual despot against those of the gentry as a class, and the middle class, which might have formed a counterweight against them, was not yet politically ripe for the seizure of the opportunity here offered to it. In Japan, however, Wang's doctrine gained many followers, because it admirably served the dictatorial state system which had developed in that country. Incidentally, Chiang Kai-shek in those years in which he showed rightist tendencies, also became interested in Wang Yang-ming.

14   Foreign relations in the sixteenth century

The feeble emperor Wu Tsung died in 1521, after an ineffective reign, without leaving an heir. The clique then in power at court looked among the possible pretenders for the one who seemed least likely to do anything, and their choice fell on the fifteen-year-old Shih Tsung, who was made emperor. The forty-five years of his reign were filled in home affairs with intrigues between the cliques at court, with growing distress in the country, and with revolts on a larger and larger scale. Abroad there were wars with Annam, increasing raids by the Japanese, and, above all, long-continued fighting against the famous Mongol ruler Anda (1529–1567), from 1549 onward. At one time Anda reached Peking and laid siege to it. Anda's raids went as far south as Szechwan and Shansi. The emperor, who had no knowledge of affairs, and to whom Anda had been represented as a petty bandit, was utterly dismayed and ready to do whatever Anda asked; in the end he was dissuaded from this, and an agreement was arrived at with Anda for state-controlled markets to be set up along the frontier, where the Mongols could dispose of their goods against Chinese goods on very favourable terms. After further difficulties lasting many years, a compromise was arrived at: the Mongols were earning good profits from the markets, and in 1571 Anda accepted a Chinese title. On the Chinese side, this Mongol trade, which continued in rather different form in the Manchu epoch, led to the formation of a local merchant class in the frontier province of Shansi, with great experience in credit business; later the first Chinese bankers came almost entirely from this quarter.

After a brief interregnum there came once more to the throne a ten-year-old boy, the emperor Shen Tsung (reign name Wan-li; 1573–

1619). He, too, was entirely under the influence of various cliques, at first that of his tutor, the scholar Chang Chü-chan. Then, another man, Yen Sung, became the most influential, and at the same time harmful figure in politics. Recently, Yen Sung came into the limelight in connection with Hai Jui (1514–1587). Hai seems to have been an honest official and judge, praised in classical operas as much as his enemy Yen was cursed. At the beginning of the so-called 'Cultural Revolution' a newly written drama praised Hai as a model of a member of the upper class who was not, as the others, corrupt and did not harm his people. The author was attacked and, to some degree, the outbreak of the Cultural Revolution was caused by this drama.

At about the time of the death of Anda, we hear for the first time of a new people. In 1581 there had been unrest in southern Manchuria. The Mongolian tribal federation of the Tümet attacked China, and there resulted collisions not only with the Chinese but between the different tribes living there. In southern and central Manchuria were remnants of the Tungus Juchên. The Mongols had subjugated the Juchên, but the latter had virtually become independent after the collapse of Mongol rule over China. They had formed several tribal alliances, but in 1581–1583 these fought each other, so that one of the alliances to all intents was destroyed. The Chinese intervened as mediators in these struggles, and drew a demarcation line between the territories of the various Tungus tribes. All this is only worth mention because it was from these tribes that there developed the tribal league of the Manchus, who were then to rule China for some three hundred years.

In 1592 the Japanese invaded Korea. This was their first real effort to set foot on the continent, a purely imperialistic move. Korea, as a Chinese vassal, appealed for Chinese aid. At first the Chinese army had no success, but in 1598 the Japanese were forced to abandon Korea. They revenged themselves by intensifying their raids on the coast of central China; they often massacred whole towns, and burned down the looted houses. The fighting in Korea had its influence on the Tungus tribes: as they were not directly involved, it contributed to their further strengthening.

The East India Company was founded in 1600. At this time, while the English were trying to establish themselves in India, the Chinese tried to gain increased influence in the south by wars in Annam, Burma, and Thailand (1594–1604). These wars were for China colonial wars, similar to the colonial fighting by the British in India. But there began to be defined already at that time in the south of Asia, the outlines of the states as they exist at the present time.

In 1601 the first European, the Jesuit Matteo Ricci, succeeded in gaining access to the Chinese court, through the agency of a eunuch.

He made some presents, and the Chinese regarded his visit as a mission from Europe bringing tribute. Ricci was therefore permitted to remain in Peking. He was an astronomer and was able to demonstrate to his Chinese colleagues the latest achievements of European astronomy. In 1613, after Ricci's death, the Jesuits and some Chinese whom they had converted were commissioned to reform the Chinese calendar. In the time of the Mongols, Arabs had been at work in Peking as astronomers, and their influence had continued under the Ming until the Europeans came. By his astronomical labours Ricci won a place of honour in Chinese literature; he is the European most often mentioned. Only Western scholars regarded the Jesuit astronomers as 'harmful', because they did not spread the new Copernican concepts among the Chinese, supposedly because of the danger which these ideas harboured for Christian doctrine. It may be fair to say that they were not yet convinced that the new system was superior and better founded than theirs.

The missionary work was less effective. The missionaries penetrated by the old trade routes from Canton and Macao into the province of Kiangsi and then into Nanking. Kiangsi and Nanking were their chief centres. They soon realized that missionary activity that began in the lower strata would have no success; it was necessary to work from above, beginning with the emperor, and then, they hoped, the whole country could be converted to Christianity. When later the emperors of the Ming dynasty were expelled and fugitives in south China, one of the pretenders to the throne was actually converted—but it was politically too late. The missionaries had, moreover, mistaken ideas as to the nature of Chinese religion; we know today that a universal adoption of Christianity in China would have been impossible even if an emperor had personally adopted that foreign faith: there were emperors who had been interested in Buddhism or in Taoism, but that had been their private affair and had never prevented them, as heads of the state, from promoting the religious system which politically was the most expedient—that is to say, usually Confucianism. What we have said here in regard to the Christian mission at the Ming court is applicable also to the missionaries at the court of the first Manchu emperors, in the seventeenth century. Early in the eighteenth century missionary activity was prohibited—not for religious but for political reasons, and only under the pressure of the Capitulations in the nineteenth century were the missionaries enabled to resume their labours.

15   *External and internal perils*
Towards the end of the reign of Wan-li, about 1620, the danger that threatened the empire became more and more evident. The Manchus

complained, no doubt with justice, of excesses on the part of Chinese officials; the friction constantly increased, and the Manchus began to attack the Chinese cities in Manchuria. in 1616, after his first considerable successes, their leader Nurhachu assumed the imperial title; the name of the dynasty was Tai Ch'ing (interpreted as 'The great clarity', but probably a transliteration of a Manchurian word meaning 'hero'). In 1618, the year in which the Thirty Years War started in Europe, the Manchus conquered the greater part of Manchuria, and in 1621 their capital was Liaoyang, then the largest town in Manchuria.

But the Manchu menace was far from being the only one. On the south-east coast Cheng Ch'eng-kung (in European sources usually Coxinga), the son of a Chinese merchant and a Japanese mother, made himself independent; later, with his family, he dominated Taiwan and fought many battles with the Dutch and Spaniards there. In western China there came a great popular rising, in which some of the natives joined, and which spread through a large part of the southern provinces. This rising was particularly sanguinary, and when it was ultimately crushed by the Manchus the province of Szechwan, formerly so populous, was almost depopulated, so that it had later to be resettled. And in the provinces of Shantung in the east there came another great rising, also very sanguinary, that of the secret society of the 'White Lotus'. We have already pointed out that these risings of secret societies were always a sign of intolerable conditions among the peasantry. This was now the case once more. All the elements of danger which we mentioned at the outset of this chapter began during this period, between 1610 and 1640, to develop to the full.

Then there were the conditions in the capital itself. The struggles between cliques came to a climax. On the death of Shen Tsung (or Wan-li; 1573–1619), he was succeeded by his son, who died scarcely a month later, and then by his sixteen-year-old grandson. The grandson had been from his earliest youth under the influence of a eunuch, Wei Chung-hsien, who had castrated himself. With the emperor's wet-nurse and other people, mostly of the middle class, this man formed a powerful group. The moment the new emperor ascended the throne, Wei was all-powerful. He began by murdering every eunuch who did not belong to his clique, and then murdered the rest of his opponents. Meanwhile the gentry had concluded among themselves a defensive alliance that was a sort of party; this party was called the Tung-lin Academy. It was confined to literati among the gentry, and included in particular the literati who had failed to make their way at court, and who lived on their estates in central China and were trying to gain power themselves. This group was opposed to

277

Wei Chung-hsien, who ruthlessly had every discoverable member murdered. The remainder went into hiding and organized themselves secretly under another name. As the new emperor had no son, the attempt was made to foist a son upon him; at his death in 1627, eight women of the harem were suddenly found to be pregnant! He was succeeded by his brother, who was one of the opponents of Wei Chung-hsien and, with the aid of the opposing clique, was able to bring him to his end. The new emperor tried to restore order at court and in the capital by means of political and economic decrees, but in spite of his good intentions and his unquestionable capacity he was unable to cope with the universal confusion. There was insurrection in every part of the country. The gentry, organized in their 'Academies', and secretly at work in the provinces, no longer supported the government; the central power no longer had adequate revenues, so that it was unable to pay the armies that should have marched against all the rebels and also against external enemies. It was clear that the dynasty was approaching its end, and the only uncertainty was as to its successor. The various insurgents negotiated or fought with each other; generals loyal to the government won occasional successes against the rebels; other generals went over to the rebels or to the Manchus. The two most successful leaders of bands were Li Tzŭ-ch'êng and Chang Hsien-chung. Li came from the province of Shensi; he had come to the fore during a disastrous famine in his country. The years around 1640 brought several widespread droughts in north China, a natural phenomenon that was repeated in the nineteenth century, when unrest again ensued. Chang Hsien-chung returned for a time to the support of the government, but later established himself in western China. It was typical, however, of all these insurgents that none of them had any great objective in view. They wanted to get enough to eat for themselves and their followers; they wanted to enrich themselves by conquest; but they were incapable of building up an ordered and new administration. Li ultimately made himself 'king' in the province of Shensi and called his dynasty 'Shun', but this made no difference: there was no distribution of land among the peasants serving in Li's army; no plan was set into operation for the collection of taxes; not one of the pressing problems was faced.

Meanwhile the Manchus were gaining support. Almost all the Mongol princes voluntarily joined them and took part in the raids into north China. In 1637 the united Manchus and Mongols conquered Korea. Their power steadily grew. What the insurgents in China failed to achieve, the Manchus achieved with the aid of their Chinese advisers: they created a new military organization, the 'Banner Organization'. The men fit for service were distributed among eight 'banners', and these banners became the basis of the

Manchu state administration. By this device the Manchus emerged from the stage of tribal union, just as before them Turks and other northern peoples had several times abandoned the traditional authority of a hierarchy of tribal leaders, a system of ruling families, in favour of the authority, based on efficiency, of military leaders. At the same time the Manchus set up a central government with special ministries on the Chinese model. In 1638 the Manchus appeared before Peking, but they retired once more. Manchu armies even reached the province of Shantung. They were hampered by the death at the critical moment of the Manchu ruler Abahai (1626–1643). His son Fu Lin was not entirely normal and was barely six years old; there was a regency of princes, the most prominent among them being Prince Dorgon.

Meanwhile Li Tzŭ-ch'êng broke through to Peking. The city had a strong garrison, but owing to the disorganization of the government the different commanders were working against each other; and the soldiers had no fighting spirit because they had had no pay for a long time. Thus the city fell, on 24 April 1644, and the last Ming emperor killed himself. A prince was proclaimed emperor; he fled through western and southern China, continually trying to make a stand, but it was too late; without the support of the gentry he had no resource, and ultimately, in 1659, he was compelled to flee into Burma.

Thus Li Tzŭ-ch'êng was now emperor. It should have been his task rapidly to build up a government, and to take up arms against the other rebels and against the Manchus. He had a good chance. His revolt was not a revolt of uneducated peasants. Peasants were his soldiers, but most of them were forced to join him. The core of his armies were professional bandits and disgruntled soldiers. But early in his rising, numerous gentry members had joined him or found themselves forced to join him. Among those who joined him of their own free will were officials who had been exiled, banished, or demoted by the government. We would think that such men would not again try to get into an official post and take the risk to suffer again a similar, often very cruel punishment after a few years. We would also think that the new government would not accept them, if they thought that these officials had deserved their punishment by the former dynasty. This has always been different in China and still is different today. Whenever we study the life history of an official, we see his career going upward for a time; but then comes a fall; the great majority of high officials at least once in their life had to suffer severe beatings, exile, or other punishments, and often solely because of the intrigues of an opposing faction, or because of an advice which did not please the ruler. Almost all of these men, as soon as they could, again served the ruler and their career began to turn upward. Very few of them felt so dishonoured and shamed that they never again served. Li Tzŭ-ch'êng got some of these proud men. When he was emperor, they were given important posts. Other officials changed their loyalty and were willing to go over to Li. Still others preferred to commit suicide instead of serving two masters. Thus, Li was in a position to build up a qualified staff. However, he, too, had no money. The treasury was empty. Requisitions and forced 'gifts' did not bring in enough cash. So his troops began to loot and to kill; Li got more and more suspicious of all those who had joined him only recently.

A rule of terror began. Li behaved in such a way that he was unable to gain any support from the existing officials in the capital; and as there was no one among his former supporters who had any positive, constructive ideas, just nothing was done.

This, however, improved the chances of all the other aspirants to the imperial throne. General Wu San-kui, who was defending the frontiers against the Manchus, thought that in the existing conditions he could easily occupy the capital and take revenge for the emperor who had been forced to commit suicide, as well as his own father who had been tortured to death. But when he moved south the Manchu threatened him from the north, so that he was forced to negotiate with the Manchu Prince Dorgon, to form an alliance with the Manchus. With them he entered Peking on 6 June 1644. Li Tzŭ-ch'êng quickly looted the city, burned down whatever he could, and fled into the west, continually pursued by Wu San-kui. In the end he was abandoned by all his supporters and killed by peasants. The Manchus, however, had no intention of leaving Wu San-kui in power: they established themselves in Peking, and Wu became their general.

(C) THE MANCHU DYNASTY (1644–1911)

1 Installation of Manchus

The Manchus had gained the mastery over China owing rather to China's internal situation than to their military superiority. How was it that the dynasty could endure for so long, although the Manchus were not numerous, although the first Manchu ruler (Fu Lin, known under the rule name Shun-chih; 1644–1662) was a psychopathic youth, although there were princes of the Ming dynasty ruling in south China, and although there were strong groups of rebels all over the country? The Manchus were aliens; at that time the national feeling of the Chinese had already been awakened; aliens were despised. In addition to this, the Manchus demanded that as a sign of their subjection the Chinese should wear pigtails and assume Manchurian clothing (law of 1645). Such laws could not but offend national pride. Moreover, marriages between Manchus and Chinese were prohibited, and a dual government was set up, with Manchus always alongside Chinese in every office, the Manchus being of course in the superior position. The Manchu soldiers were distributed in military garrisons among the great cities, and were paid state pensions, which had to be provided by taxation. They were the master race, and had no need to work. Manchus did not have to attend the difficult state examinations which the Chinese had to pass in order to gain an appointment. How was it that in spite of all this the Manchus were able to establish themselves?

The conquering Manchu generals first went south from eastern China, and in 1645 captured Nanking, where a Ming prince had ruled. The region round Nanking was the economic centre of China. Soon the Manchus were in the adjoining southern provinces, and thus they conquered the whole of the territory of the landowning gentry, who after the events of the beginning of the seventeenth century had no longer trusted the Ming rulers. The Ming prince in Nanking was just as incapable, and surrounded by just as evil a clique, as the Ming emperors of the past. The gentry were not inclined to defend him. A considerable section of the gentry were reduced to utter despair; they had no desire to support the Ming any longer; in their own interest they could not support the rebel leaders; and they regarded the Manchus as just a particular sort of 'rebels'. Interpreting the refusal of some Sung ministers to serve the foreign Mongols as an act of loyalty, it was now regarded as shameful to desert a dynasty when it came to an end and to serve the new ruler, even if the new regime promised to be better. Many thousands of officials, scholars, and great landowners committed suicide. Many books, often really moving and tragic, are filled with the story of their lives. Some of them tried to form insurgent bands with their peasants and went into the mountains, but they were unable to maintain themselves there. The great bulk of the élite soon brought themselves to collaborate with the conquerors when they were offered tolerable conditions. In the end the Manchus did not interfere in the ownership of land in central China.

At the time when in Europe Louis XIV was reigning, the Thirty Years War was coming to an end, and Cromwell was carrying out his reforms in England, the Manchus conquered the whole of China. Chang Hsien-chung and Li Tzǔ-ch'êng were the first to fall; Coxinga lasted a little longer and was even able to plunder Nanking in 1659, but in 1661 he had to retire to Formosa (Taiwan). Wu San-kui, who meanwhile had conquered western China, saw that the situation was becoming difficult for him. His task was to drive out the last Ming pretenders for the Manchus. As he had already been opposed to the Ming in 1644, and as the Ming no longer had any following among the gentry, he could not suddenly work with them against the Manchus. He therefore handed over to the Manchus the last Ming prince, whom the Burmese had delivered up to him in 1661. Wu San-kui's only possible allies against the Manchus were the gentry. But in the west, where he was in power, the gentry counted for nothing; they had in any case been weaker in the west, and they had been decimated by the insurrection of Chang Hsien-chung. Thus Wu San-kui was compelled to try to push eastward, in order to unite with the gentry of the Yangtze region against the Manchus. The Manchus guessed Wu San-kui's plan, and in 1673, after every effort at accommodation had failed, open war came. Wu San-kui made himself emperor, and the Manchus marched against him. Meanwhile, the Chinese gentry of the Yangtze region had come to terms with the Manchus, and they gave Wu San-kui no help. He vegetated in the south-west, a region too poor to maintain an army that could conquer all China, and too small to enable him to last indefinitely as an independent power. He was able to hold his own until his death, although, with the loss of the support of the gentry, he had had no prospect of final success. Not until 1681 was his successor, his grandson Wu Shih-fan, defeated. The end of the rule of Wu San-kui and his successor (1683) marked the end of the national governments of China; the whole country was now under alien domination, for the simple reason that all the opponents of the Manchus had failed. Only the Manchus were accredited with the ability to bring order out of the universal confusion, so that there was clearly no alternative but to put up with the many insults and humiliations they inflicted—with the result that the national feeling that had just been aroused died away, except, it seems, in some secret societies.

In the first phase of the Manchu conquest the gentry had refused to support either the Ming princes or Wu San-kui, or any of the rebels, or the Manchus themselves. A second phase began about twenty years after the capture of Peking, when the Manchus won over the gentry by desisting from any interference with the ownership of land, and by the use of Manchu troops to clear away the 'rebels' who were hostile to the gentry. A reputable government was then set up in Peking, free from eunuchs and from all the old cliques; in their place the government looked for Chinese scholars for its administrative posts. Literati and scholars streamed into Peking, especially members of the 'Academies' that still existed in secret, men who had been the chief sufferers from the conditions at the end of the Ming epoch. The young emperor Sheng Tsu (1663–1722; K'ang-hsi is the name by which his rule was known, not his name) was keenly interested in Chinese culture and gave privileged treatment to the scholars of the gentry who came forward. A rapid recovery quite clearly took place. The disturbances of the years that had passed had got rid of the worst enemies of the people, the formidable rival cliques and the individuals lusting for power; the gentry had become more cautious in their behaviour to the peasants; and bribery had been largely stamped out. Finally, the empire had been greatly expanded. All these things helped to stabilize the regime of the Manchus.

2   Decline in the eighteenth century

The improvement continued until the middle of the eighteenth century. About the time of the French Revolution there began a continuous decline, slow at first and then gathering speed. The European works on China offer various reasons for this: the many foreign wars (to which we shall refer later) of the emperor, known by the name of his ruling period, Ch'ien-lung, his craze for building, and the irruption of the Europeans into Chinese trade. In the eighteenth century the court surrounded itself with great splendour, and countless palaces and other luxurious buildings were erected, but it must be borne in mind that so great an empire as the China of that day possessed very considerable financial strength, and could support this luxury. The wars were certainly not inexpensive, as they took place along the Russian frontier and entailed expenditure on the transport of reinforcements and supplies; the wars against Sinkiang and Tibet were carried on with relatively small forces. This expenditure should not have been beyond the resources of an ordered budget. Interestingly enough, the period between 1640 and 1840 belongs to those periods for which scholarly interest has begun only recently. Western scholars have been too much interested in the impact of Western economy and culture or in the military events. Chinese scholars thus far have shown a prejudice against the Manchu dynasty and were mainly interested in the study of anti-Manchu movements and the downfall of the dynasty. On the other hand, the documentary material for this period is extremely extensive, and many years of work are necessary to reach any general conclusions even in one single field. The following remarks should, therefore, be taken as very tentative and preliminary, and they are, naturally, fragmentary.

The decline of the Manchu dynasty began at a time when the European trade was still insignificant, and not as late as after 1842, when China had had to submit to the foreign capitulations. These cannot have been the true cause of the decline. Above all, the decline was not so noticeable in the state of the Exchequer as in a general impoverishment of China. The number of really wealthy persons among the gentry diminished, but the middle class, that is to say the people who had education but little money and property, grew steadily in number.

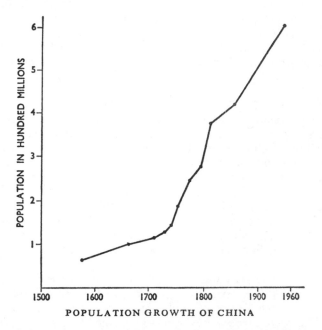

POPULATION GROWTH OF CHINA

One of the deeper reasons for the decline of the Manchu dynasty seems to lie in the enormous increase in the population. Here are a few Chinese statistics:

Year	Population			
1578 (before the Manchus)	10,621,463 families or	60,692,856 individuals		
1662	19,203,233	,,	100,000,000	,,	*
1710	23,311,236	,,	116,000,000	,,	*
1729	25,480,498	,,	127,000,000	,,	*
1741			143,411,559	,,	
1754			184,504,493	,,	
1778			242,965,618	,,	
1796			275,662,414	,,	
1814			374,601,132	,,	
1850			414,493,899	,,	
(1953)			(601,938,035 | ,,)	*

*Approximately

284

It may be objected that these figures are incorrect and exaggerated. Undoubtedly they contain errors. But the first figure (for 1578) of some sixty millions is in close agreement with all other figures of early times; the figure for 1850 seems high, but cannot be far wrong, for even after the great T'ai P'ing Rebellion of 1851, which, together with its after-effects, cost the lives of countless millions, all statisticians of today estimate the population of China at more than four hundred millions. If we enter these data together with the census of 1953 into a chart (see p. 284), a fairly smooth curve emerges; the special features are that already before the end of the Ming the population was increasing and, second, that the high rate of increase in the population began with the long period of internal peace since about 1700. From that time onward, all China's wars were fought at so great a distance from China proper that the population was not directly affected. Moreover, in the seventeenth and eighteenth centuries the government saw to the maintenance of the river dykes so that the worst inundations were prevented. Thus there were not so many of the floods which had often cost the lives of many million people in China; and there were no internal wars, with their heavy cost in lives.

But while the population increased, the tillage failed to increase in the needed proportion. I have, unfortunately, no statistics for all periods; but the general tendency is shown by the following table:

Date	Cultivated area in *mou*	*mou* per person
1578	701,397,600	11·6
1662	531,135,800	
1719	663,113,200	
1729	878,176,000	6·1
(1953)	(1,627,930,000)	(2·7)

Six *mou* are about one acre. In 1578, there were 66 *mou* land per family of the total population. This was close to the figures regarded as ideal by Chinese early economists for the producing family (100 *mou*) considering the fact that about 80 per cent of all families at that time were producers. By 1729 it was only 35 *mou* per family, i.e. the land had to produce almost twice as much as before. We have shown that the agricultural developments in the Ming time greatly increased the productivity of the land. This then, obviously, resulted in an increase of population. But by the middle of the eighteenth century, assuming that production doubled since the sixteenth century, population pressure was again as heavy as it had been then. And after

c. 1750, population pressure continued to build up to the present time.

Internal colonization continued during the Manchu time; there was a continuous but slow flow of people into Kwangsi, Kweichou, Yünnan, accompanied by periodic uprisings of the native, non-Chinese, population which lost their land to Chinese settlers. In spite of laws which prohibited emigration, Chinese also moved into South-East Asia. Chinese settlement in Manchuria was allowed only in the last years of the Manchus. But such internal colonization or emigration could alleviate the pressure only in some areas, while it continued to build up in others.

In Europe as well as in Japan, we find a strong population increase; in Europe at almost the same time as in China. But before population pressure became too serious in Europe or Japan, industry developed and absorbed the excess population. Thus, farms did not decrease too much in size. Too small farms are always and in many ways uneconomical. With the development of industries, the percentage of farm population decreased. In China, however, the farm population was still as high as 73·3 per cent of the total population in 1932 and the percentage rose to 81 per cent in 1950.

European farmers could produce more once the American plants, such as corn and potato, were introduced, plants with a higher yield per acre and at the same time plants which could utilize soils of lower quality. Corn came to China, too; and potato was not superior (in south China) to the indigenous sweet potatoes and yams. Thus, the new plants from the New World did not help China much.

In the first years of Manchu rule, we hear of serfs' rebellions in the areas of highest intensity of farming, Kiangsu, Kiangsi and Kwangtung. It seems that this is the beginning of a new trend. Many absentee landowners seem to find that it is difficult to get rent from serfs in villages, even with the help of managers. Investment in land is no longer the best investment, though still the safest. There seems to be a shift away from keeping bonded tenants, at least in the most developed areas, and towards pawnbroking, as a method of getting much more money out of the pocket of the farmer. Thus, bonded tenantship became changed into free tenantship. The relaxation of the landowners over their dependants and their move into towns seems also to have led to the emergence of organizations in villages, such as youth crop protection associations, dyke protection, canal cleaning and repair associations, i.e. many of the necessary activities were now taken over by farmers and tenants themselves. The farmers also had better access to the numerous markets, even markets in towns, and could sell there their farm products as well as the products of home industries. They were now better informed about price oscillations and could attempt, to some degree, to manipulate the market.

Thus, we cannot say that the level of living of the farmers went down in comparison to the level of living of city people. Rather, there was a slow, general downward trend, expressed, it seems, in a lowering of the life expectancy among all classes.

From the middle of the seventeenth century on, commercial activities, especially along the coast, continued to increase and we find gentry families who equip sons who were unwilling or not capable to study and to enter the ranks of the officials, but who were too unruly to sit in villages and collect the rent from the tenants of the family, with money to enter business. The newly settled areas of Kwangtung and Kwangsi were ideal places for them: here they could sell Chinese products to the native tribes or to the new settlers at high prices. Some of these men introduced new techniques from the old provinces of China into the 'colonial' areas and set up dye factories, textile factories, etc., in the new towns of the south. The new products replaced the hand-made textiles of the minorities and induced them to become more and more dependent upon the Chinese merchants who also brought good Chinese wine. We find a development among the minorities which has many parallels in other colonial areas: with the breakdown of the native culture and economy, the men become addicted to alcohol and lose first their money, then their land, finally their daughters to the colonial masters.

But the greatest stimulus for these commercial activities was foreign, European trade. American silver which had flooded Europe in the sixteenth century, began to flow into China from the beginning of the seventeenth century on. The influx was stopped not until between 1661 and 1684 when the government again prohibited coastal shipping and removed coastal settlements into the interior in order to stop piracy along the coasts of Fukien and independence movements on Formosa (Taiwan). But even during these twenty-three years, the price of silver was so low that home production was given up because it did not pay off. In the eighteenth century, silver again continued to enter China, while silk and tea were exported. This demand led to a strong rise in the prices of silk and tea, and benefited the merchants. When, from the late eighteenth century on, opium began to be imported, the silver left China again. The merchants profited this time from the opium trade, but farmers had to suffer: the price of silver went up, and taxes had to be paid in silver, while farm products were sold for copper. By 1835, the ounce of silver had a value of 2,000 copper coins instead of one thousand before 1800. High gains in commerce prevented investment in industries, because they would give lower and later profits than commerce.

At the latest in the eighteenth century, Chinese banks began to develop. Most famous were the bankers of Shansi, but Ningpo banks, too, were important. These banks are a good example of the commercial attitude that had developed: the bankers did not employ family members (which, according to the familistic attitude, they were supposed to do), but non-related men, to operate the branch offices. The families of these men lived as a kind of hostage in the head office, and the employee was personally responsible for any business losses he incurred. Similarly, the guards whom the bankers hired to transport cash from one place to another were not related to the boss. Thus, we have enough indications to say that capital was available for the development of industries. It is true that the government and the gentry tried to get into any larger business, either to control the business which then took the form of a joint private-government operation, or in order to draw income from co-operation with a businessman who, on the other side, got 'protection' against extortion from other officials. Such operations could not be fully successful, especially because the officials were not technical experts and often prevented the development of an enterprise by their political interference. Still, modern research is of the opinion that none of these factors was decisive, that there was an 'entrepreneurial spirit', but that perhaps the size of the industrial enterprises (except the state-operated ones) was too small to really lead to industrial development.

3 *Expansion in Central Asia; the first state treaty*

The rise of the Manchu dynasty actually began under the K'ang-hsi rule (1663–1722). The emperor had three tasks. The first was the removal of the last supporters of the Ming dynasty and of the generals, such as Wu San-kui, who had tried to make themselves independent. This necessitated a long series of campaigns, most of them in the south-west or south of China; these scarcely affected the population of China proper. In 1683 Formosa (Taiwan) was occupied and the last of the local rulers was defeated. It was shown above that the situation of all these leaders became hopeless as soon as the Manchus had occupied the rich Yangtze region and the intelligentsia and the gentry of that region had gone over to them.

A quite different type of insurgent commander was the Mongol prince Galdan. He, too, planned to make himself independent of Manchu overlordship. At first the Mongols had readily supported the Manchus, when the latter were making raids into China and there was plenty of booty. Now, however, the Manchus, under the influence of the Chinese gentry whom they brought, and could not but bring, to their court, were rapidly becoming Chinese in respect to culture. Even in the time of K'ang-hsi the Manchus began to forget Manchurian; they brought tutors to court to teach the young

Manchus Chinese. Later even the emperors did not understand Manchurian! As a result of this process, the Mongols became alienated from the Manchurians, and the situation began once more to be the same as at the time of the Ming rulers. Thus Galdan tried to found an independent Mongol realm, free from Chinese influence.

The Manchus could not permit this, as such a realm would have threatened the flank of their homeland, Manchuria, and would have attracted those Manchus who objected to sinification. Between 1690 and 1696 there were battles, in which the emperor actually took part in person. Galdan was defeated. In 1715, however, there were new disturbances, this time in western Mongolia. Tsewang Rabdan, whom the Chinese had made khan of the Ölöt, rose against the Chinese. The wars that followed, extending far into Sinkiang and also involving its Turkish population together with the Dzungars, ended with the Chinese conquest of the whole of Mongolia and of Sinkiang. As Tsewang Rabdan had tried to extend his power as far as Tibet, a campaign was undertaken also into Tibet, Lhasa was occupied, a new Dalai Lama was installed there as supreme ruler, and Tibet was made into a protectorate. Since then Tibet, Sinkiang and Inner Mongolia have remained to this day under Chinese colonial rule.

This penetration of the Chinese into Central Asia took place just at the time when the Russians were enormously expanding their empire in Asia, and this formed the third problem for the Manchus. In 1650 the Russians had established a fort by the river Amur. The Manchus regarded the Amur (which they called the 'River of the Black Dragon') as part of their own territory, and in 1685 they destroyed the Russian settlement. After this there were negotiations, which culminated in 1689 in the Treaty of Nerchinsk. This treaty was the first concluded by the Chinese state with a European power. Jesuit missionaries played a part in the negotiations as interpreters. Owing to the difficulties of translation the text of the treaty, in Chinese, Russian, and Manchurian, contained some obscurities, particularly in regard to the frontier line. Accordingly, in 1727 the Russians asked for a revision of the old treaty. The Chinese emperor, whose rule name was Yung-cheng, arranged for the negotiations to be carried on at the frontier, in the town of Kyakhta, in Mongolia, where after long discussions a new treaty was concluded. Under this treaty the Russians received permission to set up a legation and a commercial agency in Peking, and also to maintain a church. This was the beginning of the foreign capitulations. The present Chinese regime regards the treaties dealing with the Amur region and with the western parts of Sinkiang as unfair, and even before the revolution armed conflicts had begun; they still continue. The Chinese expected the Russians to cancel the treaties which they regard as 'unequal'.

On the other hand, the Chinese saw nothing extraordinary in granting the Russians quarters for their legation in Peking and other privileges, such as having their own churches. For some fifteen centuries all the 'barbarians' who had to bring tribute had been given houses in the capital, where their envoys could wait until the emperor would receive them—usually on New Year's Day. The custom had sprung up at the reception of the Huns. Moreover, permission had always been given for envoys to be accompanied by a few merchants, who during the envoy's stay did a certain amount of business. Furthermore the time had been when the Uighurs were permitted to set up a temple of their own. At the time of the permission given to the Russians to set up a 'legation', a similar office was set up (in 1729) for 'Uighur' peoples (meaning Mohammedans), again under the control of an office, called the Office for Regulation of Barbarians. The Mohammedan office was placed under two Mohammedan leaders who lived in Peking. The Europeans, however, had quite different ideas about a 'legation', and about the significance of permission to trade. They regarded this as the opening of diplomatic relations between states on terms of equality, and the carrying on of trade as a special privilege, a sort of capitulation. This reciprocal misunderstanding produced in the nineteenth century a number of serious political conflicts. The Europeans charged the Chinese with breach of treaties, failure to meet their obligations, and other such things, while the Chinese considered that they had acted with perfect correctness.

4 *Culture*

In this K'ang-hsi period culture began to flourish again. The emperor had attracted the gentry, and so the intelligentsia, to his court because his Manchus could not alone have administered the enormous empire; and he showed great interest in Chinese culture, and himself delved deeply into it. Following his example, many young Manchus also began to study Chinese and soon we find Manchu scholars and poets who were in no way inferior to Chinese. To increase his knowledge of China, the emperor had many works compiled, especially works of an encyclopaedic character. The encyclopaedias enabled information to be rapidly gained on all sorts of subjects, and thus were just what an interested ruler needed, especially when, as a foreigner, he was not in a position to gain really thorough instruction in things Chinese. The Chinese encyclopaedias of the seventeenth and especially of the eighteenth century were thus the outcome of the initiative of the Manchurian emperor, and were compiled for his information; they were, of course, inspired by the great Ming time encyclopaedia, the 'Yung-lo ta-tien', but this work was never printed and remained accessible only to the court, while the Manchu encyclopaedias were printed and copies were found in many parts of the country. However, they were not a part of a movement to spread knowledge among the people, like the French encyclopaedias of the eighteenth century. For this latter purpose the gigantic encyclopaedias of the Manchus, each of which fills several bookcases, were much too expensive and were printed in much too limited editions. The compilations began with the great geographical encyclopaedia of Ku Yen-wu (1613–1682), and attained their climax in the gigantic eighteenth-century encyclopaedia 'T'u-shu chi-ch'eng', scientifically impeccable in the accuracy of its references to sources. Here were already the beginnings of the 'Archaeological school', built up in the course of the eighteenth century. This school was usually called 'Han school' because the adherents went back to the commentaries of the classical texts written in Han time and discarded the orthodox explanations of Chu Hsi's school of Sung time. Later, its most prominent leader was Tai Chen (1723–1777). Tai was greatly interested in technology and science; he can be regarded as the first philosopher who exhibited an empirical, scientific way of thinking. Late nineteenth and early twentieth century Chinese scholarship is greatly obliged to him.

The most famous literary works of the Manchu epoch belong once more to the field which Chinese do not regard as that of true literature—the novel, the short story, and the drama. Poetry did exist, but it kept to the old paths and had few fresh ideas. All the various forms of the Sung period were made use of. The essayists, too, offered nothing new, though their number was legion. One of the best known is Yüan Mei (1716–1797), who was also the author of the collection of short stories 'Tse-pu-yü' ('The Master Did Not Tell'), which is regarded very highly by the Chinese. Yüan Mei, a kind of 'eccentric', deserves mention also because he tried to attract young daughters of the upper class to become his students, in spite of his somewhat doubtful reputation. The volume of short-stories entitled 'Liao-chai chih-i' ('Strange Stories from a Chinese Studio') by P'u Sung-ling (1640–1715?) is world-famous and has been translated into many languages. The collection is important for the folklorist because P'u was interested in folk beliefs. Both collections are distinguished by their simple but elegant style. The short story was popular among the greater gentry; it abandoned the popular style it had had in the Ming epoch, and adopted the polished language of scholars.

The Manchu epoch has left to us what is by general consent the finest novel in Chinese literature, 'Hung-lou-meng' ('The Dream of the Red Chamber'), by Ts'ao Hsüeh-ch'in, who died in 1763. It describes the downfall of a rich and powerful family from the highest rank of the gentry, and the decadent son's love of a young and emotional lady of the highest circles. The story is clothed in a mystical garb that does something to soften its tragic ending. Western readers appreciate this novel mainly because it is the only classical novel in which individual characters are clearly depicted, and in which emotions are openly expressed. This was and remained unusual, because to the present time, Chinese do not like to express their emotions openly. Down to the nineteenth century, the novel was from time to time forbidden, and parents were warned not to let their children read it. Even at the present time, surveys indicate that, though almost all young Chinese have read it, many regard it as a decadent book which is depressing and therefore has no moral value.

The interesting novel 'Ju-lin wai-shih' ('Private Reports from the Life of Scholars'), by Wu Ching-tzŭ (1701–1754), is a mordant criticism of Confucianism with its rigid formalism, of the social system, and of the examination system. Social criticism is the theme of many novels. The most modern in spirit of the works of this period is perhaps the treatment of feminism in the novel 'Ching-hua-yüan', by Li Yu-chên (d. 1830), which demanded equal rights for men and women, long before any Western influence could be felt. In particular, the novel is against the custom of foot-binding. Some of its economic and social proposals were later taken over by the T'ai P'ing, and at that time, too, the movement against foot-binding took roots and eventually led to its end.

In the nineteenth century, novels which describe the more intimate aspects of Chinese social life come forth. There are depictions of marital happiness, but also descriptions of the life of prostitutes in Shanghai (in the novel 'Hai-shang-hua lieh-chuan'), a novel from the end of the nineteenth century which—and this is another important novelty—was written in Shanghai dialect, not in the usual half-colloquial style of other novels. Somewhat later (published in 1907) is the most intimate story of a big Cantonese merchant, describing in detail the ways by which he made his fortunes, the corruption in the highest places, and the operation of a household with numerous concubines ('Erh-shih-tsai Fan-hua-meng').

The drama developed quickly in the Manchu epoch, particularly in quantity, especially since the emperors greatly appreciated the theatre. A catalogue of plays compiled in 1781 contains 1,013 titles! Some of these dramas were of unprecedented length. One of them was played in 26 parts containing 240 acts; a performance took two years to complete! Probably the finest dramas of the Manchu epoch are those of Li Yü (born 1611), who also became the first of the Chinese dramatic critics. What he had to say about the art of the theatre, and about aesthetics in general, is still worth reading.

About the middle of the nineteenth century the influence of Europe became more and more marked. Translation began with Yen Fu (1853–1921), who translated the first philosophical and scientific books and books on social questions and made his compatriots acquainted with Western thought. At the same time Lin Shu (1852–1924) translated the first Western short stories and novels. With these two began the new style, which was soon elaborated by Liang Ch'i-ch'ao, a collaborator of Sun Yat-sen's, and by others, and which ultimately produced the 'literary revolution' of 1917. Translation has continued to this day; almost every book of outstanding importance in world literature is translated within a few months of its appearance, and on the average these translations are of a fairly high level.

Particularly fine work was produced in the field of porcelain in the Manchu epoch. In 1680 the famous kilns in the province of Kiangsi were reopened, and porcelain that is among the most artistically perfect in the world was fired in them. Among the new colours were especially green shades (one group is known as 'famille verte'), and also black and yellow compositions. Monochrome porcelain also developed further, including very fine dark blue, brilliant red (called 'ox-blood'), and white. In the eighteenth century, however, there began an unmistakable decline, which has continued to this day, although there are still a few craftsmen and a few kilns that produce outstanding work (usually attempts to imitate old models), often in small factories.

In painting, European influence soon shows itself. The best-known example of this is Lang Shih-ning, an Italian missionary whose original name was Giuseppe Castiglione (1688–1766); he began to work in China in 1715. He learned the Chinese method of painting, but introduced a number of technical tricks of European painters, especially the Western way of depicting perspective. Many of these innovations were taken over by the official court painters: the painting of the scholars who lived in seclusion remained uninfluenced. Dutch flower-painting also had some influence in China as early as the eighteenth century.

The missionaries played an important part at court. The first Manchu emperors were as generous in this matter as the Mongols had been, and allowed the foreigners to work in peace. They showed special interest in the European science introduced by the missionaries; they had less sympathy for their religious message. The missionaries, for their part, sent to Europe enthusiastic accounts of the wonderful conditions in China, and so helped to popularize the idea that was being formed in Europe of an 'enlightened', a constitutional, monarchy. The leaders of the Enlightenment read these reports with enthusiasm, with the result that they had an influence on the French Revolution. Confucius was found particularly attractive, and was regarded as a forerunner of the Enlightenment. The philosopher Leibniz (1646–1716) was informed by the writings of the Jesuits of Chinese ideas, and it seems that the 'I-ching' ('Book of Changes') in which he detected a binary counting system, influenced his own development of a binary system—the system which is now basic for all computer work.

The missionaries gained a reputation at court as 'scientists', and in this they were of service both to China and to Europe. The behaviour of the European merchants who followed the missions, spreading gradually in growing numbers along the coasts of China, was not by any means so irreproachable. The Chinese were certainly justified when they declared that European ships often made landings on the coast and simply looted, just as the Japanese had done before them. Reports of this came to the court, and captured foreigners described themselves as 'Christians' and also seemed to have some connection with the missionaries living at court. When, additionally, quarrels between Jesuits and Franciscans broke out concerning the character of the Chinese ancestral cult (honouring the ancestors or venerating them?), the Yung-cheng emperor (1723–1736; his name as emperor was Shih Tsung) regarded the missionaries as a part of a secret organization and forbade their activities.

5 Relations with the outer world

During the Yung-cheng period, when Chinese population increases were very quick, long fights against the minorities in south-west China took place, but at the beginning of the Ch'ien-lung period (1736–1796), fighting started again in Sinkiang. Mongols, now called Kalmuks, defeated by the Chinese, had migrated to the Ili region, where after heavy fighting they gained supremacy over some of the Kazaks and other Turkish peoples living there and in western Sinkiang. Some Kazak tribes went over to the Russians, and in 1735 the Russian colonialists founded the town of Orenburg in the western Kazak region. The Kalmuks fought the Chinese without cessation until, in 1739, they entered into an agreement under which they ceded half their territory to Manchu China, retaining only the Ili region. The Kalmuks subsequently reunited with other sections of the Kazaks against the Chinese. In 1754 peace was again concluded with China, but it was followed by raids on both sides, so that the Manchus determined to enter on a great campaign against the Ili region. This ended with a decisive victory for the Chinese (1755). In the years that followed, however, the Chinese began to be afraid that the various Kazak tribes might unite in order to occupy the territory of the Kalmuks, which was almost unpopulated owing to the mass slaughter of Kalmuks by the Chinese. Unrest began among the Mohammedans throughout the neighbouring western Sinkiang, and the same Chinese generals who had fought the Kalmuks marched into Sinkiang and captured the Mohammedan city states of Uch, Kashgar, and Yarkand.

The reinforcements for these campaigns, and for the garrisons which in the following decades were stationed in the Ili region and in the west of Sinkiang, marched along the road from Peking that leads northward through Mongolia to the far distant Uliassutai and Kobdo. The cost of transport for one *shih* (about 66 lb.) amounted to 120 pieces of silver. In 1781 certain economies were introduced, but between 1781 and 1791 over 30,000 tons, making some 8 tons a day, were transported to that region. The cost of transport for supplies alone amounted in the course of time to the not inconsiderable sum of 120,000,000 pieces of silver. In addition to this there was the cost of the transported goods and of the pay of soldiers and of the administration. These figures apply to the period of occupation, of relative peace: during the actual wars of conquest the expenditure was naturally far higher. Thus these campaigns, though I do not think they brought actual economic ruin to China, were nevertheless a costly enterprise, and one which produced little positive advantage.

In addition to this, these wars brought China into conflict with the European colonial powers. In the years during which the Chinese armies were fighting in the Ili region, the Russians were putting out their feelers in that direction, and the Chinese annals show plainly how the Russians intervened in the fighting with the Kalmuks and Kazaks. The Ili region remained thereafter a bone of contention between China and Russia, until it finally went to Russia, bit by bit, between 1847 and 1881. The present Chinese government still regards the Ili area as a part of China which should be returned to China.

The Kalmuks and Kazaks played a special part in Russo-Chinese relations. The Chinese had sent a mission to the Kalmuks farthest west, by the lower Volga, and had entered into relations with them, as early as 1714. As Russian pressure on the Volga region continually grew, these Kalmuks (mainly the Turgut tribe), who had lived there since 1630, decided to return into Chinese territory (1771). During this enormously difficult migration, almost entirely through hostile territory, a large number of the Turgut perished; 85,000, however, reached the Ili region, where they were settled by the Chinese on the lands of the eastern Kalmuks, who had been largely exterminated.

In the south, too, the Chinese came into direct touch with the European powers. In 1757 the English occupied Calcutta, and in 1766 the province of Bengal. In 1767 a Manchu general, Ming Jui, who had been victorious in the fighting for Sinkiang, marched against Burma, which was made a dependency once more in 1769. And in 1790–1791 the Chinese conquered Nepal, south of Tibet, because Nepalese had made two attacks on Tibet. Thus English and Chinese political interests came here into contact.

For the Ch'ien-lung period's many wars of conquest there seem to have been two main reasons. The first was the need for security. The Mongols had to be overthrown because otherwise the homeland of the Manchus was menaced; in order to make sure of the suppression of the eastern Mongols, the western Mongols (Kalmuks) had to be overthrown; to make them harmless, Sinkiang and the Ili region had to be conquered; Tibet was needed for the security of Sinkiang and Mongolia—and so on. Vast territories, however, were conquered in this process which were of no economic value, and most of which actually cost a great deal of money and brought nothing in. They were conquered simply for security. That advantage had been gained: an aggressor would have to cross great areas of unproductive territory, with difficult conditions for reinforcements, before he could actually reach China. In the second place, the Chinese may actually have noticed the efforts that were being made by the European powers, especially Russia and England, to divide Asia among themselves, and accordingly they made sure of their own good share.

6 Decline; revolts

The period of Ch'ien-lung is that of the greatest expansion of the Chinese empire, also that of the greatest under the Manchu regime. But there began at the same time to be signs of internal decline. If we are to fix a particular year for this, perhaps it should be the year 1774, in which came the first great popular rising, in the province of Shantung. In 1775 there came another popular rising, in Honan—that of the 'Society of the White Lotus'. This society, which had long existed as a secret organization and had played a part in the Ming epoch, had been reorganized by a man named Liu Sung. Liu Sung was captured and was condemned to penal servitude. His followers, however, regrouped themselves, particularly in the province of Anhui. These risings seem to have been stimulated by local excesses of administrators or landlords, but began to become dangerous because of their connection with a sect which was widely spread over China and had an internal organization and leaders. Under such conditions, local uprisings of farmers can become dangerous. As the anger of the population was naturally directed also against the idle Manchus of the cities, who lived on their state pensions, did no work, and behaved as a ruling class, the government saw in these movements a nationalist spirit, and took drastic steps against them. The popular leaders now altered their programme, and acclaimed a supposed descendant from the Ming dynasty as the future emperor. Government troops caught the leader of the 'White Lotus' agitation, but he succeeded in escaping. In the regions through which the society had spread, there then began a sort of Inquisition, of exceptional ferocity. Six provinces were affected, and in and around the single city of Wuch'ang in four months more than 20,000 people were beheaded. The cost of the rising to the government ran into millions. In answer to this oppression, the popular leaders tightened their organization and marched north-west from the western provinces of which they had gained control. The rising was suppressed only by a very big military operation, and not until 1802. There had been very heavy fighting between 1793 and 1802—just when in Europe, in the French Revolution, another oppressed population won its freedom.

The Ch'ien-lung emperor abdicated on New Year's Day, 1795, after ruling for sixty years. He died in 1799. His successor was Jen Tsung (1796–1821; reign name: Chia-ch'ing). In the course of his reign the rising of the 'White Lotus' was suppressed, but in 1813 there began a new rising, this time in north China—again that of a secret organization, the 'Society of Heaven's Law'. One of its leaders bribed some eunuchs, and penetrated with a group of followers into the palace; he threw himself upon the emperor, who was only saved through the intervention of his son. At the same time the rising spread in the provinces. Once more the government succeeded in suppressing it and capturing the leaders. But the memory of these risings was kept alive among the Chinese people. For the government failed to realize that the actual cause of the risings was the general impoverishment, and saw in them a nationalist movement, thus actually arousing a national consciousness, stronger than in the Ming epoch, among the middle and lower classes of the people, together with hatred of the Manchus. They were held responsible for every evil suffered, regardless of the fact that similar evils had existed earlier.

7 European imperialism in the Far East

With the Tao-kuang period (1821–1850) began a new period in Chinese history which came to an end only in 1911.

In foreign affairs these ninety years were marked by the steadily growing influence of the Western powers, aimed at turning China into a colony. Culturally this period was that of the gradual infiltration of Western civilization into the Far East; it was recognized in China that it was necessary to learn from the West. In home affairs we see the collapse of the dynasty and the destruction of the unity of the empire; of four great civil wars, one almost brought the dynasty to its end. North and south China, the coastal area and the interior, developed in different ways.

Great Britain had made several attempts to improve her trade relations with China, but the mission of 1793 had no success, and that of 1816 also failed. English merchants, like all foreign merchants, were only permitted to settle in a small area adjoining Canton and at Macao, and were only permitted to trade with a particular group of monopolists, known as the 'Hong'. The Hong had to pay taxes to the state, but they had a wonderful opportunity of enriching themselves. The Europeans were entirely at their mercy, for they were not allowed to travel inland, and they were not allowed to try to negotiate with other merchants, to secure lower prices by competition.

The Europeans concentrated especially on the purchase of silk and tea; but what could they import into China? The higher the price of the goods and the smaller the cargo space involved, the better were the chances of profit for the merchants. It proved, however, that European woollens or luxury goods could not be sold; the Chinese would probably have been glad to buy food, but transport was too expensive to permit profitable business. Thus a new article was soon discovered—opium, carried from India to China: the price was high and the cargo space involved was very small. The Chinese were familiar with opium, under its Near-Eastern name, *afyûn* (*a-fu-yung*), probably since Sung times. In Ming time, the emperor received 200 pounds for himself and 100 for the empress from Thailand, but from the eighteenth century on, opium arrived in China from the coast. At the time of Ch'ien-lung, the court received between 200 and 1,000 crates from the Portuguese. In 1729, the government confiscated 34 pounds in the storeroom of a merchant in Chang-chou (Fukien). Thus, opium is not a drug, recently imported into China, but has a long history in China. The problem, which to my knowledge is not yet satisfactorily explained is, why opium smoking suddenly became a fashion in China and took proportions which threatened public health. Was it perhaps that only from the late eighteenth century on, opium was smoked and not taken internally only? In any case, from 1800 onward opium became more and more the chief article of trade, especially for the English, who were able to bring it conveniently from India. The opium trade resulted in certain groups of merchants being inordinately enriched; a great deal of Chinese money went abroad. The government became apprehensive and sent Lin Tsê-hsü as its commissioner to Canton. In 1839 he prohibited the opium trade and burned the chests of opium found in British possession. The British view was that to tolerate the Chinese action might mean the destruction of British trade in the Far East and that, on the other hand, it might be possible by active intervention to compel the Chinese to open other ports to European trade and to shake off the monopoly of the Canton merchants. In 1840 British ships-of-war appeared off the south-eastern coast of China and bombarded it. In 1841 the Chinese opened negotiations and dismissed Lin Tsê-hsü. As the Chinese concessions were regarded as inadequate, hostilities continued; the British entered the Yangtze estuary and threatened Nanking. In this first armed conflict with the West, China found herself defenceless owing to her lack of a navy, and it was also found that the European weapons were far superior to those of the Chinese. In 1842 China was compelled to capitulate: under the Treaty of Nanking Hong Kong was ceded to Great Britain, a war indemnity was paid, certain ports were thrown open to European trade, and the monopoly was brought to an end. A great deal of opium came, however, into China through smuggling—regrettably, for the state lost the customs revenue!

Opium cultivation in China became widely spread; in 1934, 7 per cent of the farmland in Yünnan was planted with opium, in spite of strict regulations against its cultivation and use. In the borderland between Yünnan and Burma, opium cultivation existed until the present time.

The treaty introduced the period of the capitulations. It contained the dangerous clause which added most to China's misfortunes—the Most Favoured Nation clause, providing that if China granted any privilege to any other state, that privilege should also automatically be granted to Great Britain. In connection with this treaty it was agreed that the Chinese customs should be supervised by European consuls; and a trade treaty was granted. Similar treaties followed in 1844 with France and the United States. The missionaries returned; until 1860, however, they were only permitted to work in the treaty ports. Shanghai was thrown open in 1843, and developed with extraordinary rapidity from a town to a city of a million and a centre of world-wide importance.

The terms of the Nanking Treaty were not observed by either side; both evaded them. In order to facilitate the smuggling, the British had permitted certain Chinese junks to fly the British flag. This also enabled these vessels to be protected by British ships-of-war from pirates, which at that time were very numerous off the southern coast owing to the economic depression. The Chinese, for their part, placed every possible obstacle in the way of the British. In 1856 the Chinese held up a ship sailing under the British flag, pulled down its flag, and arrested the crew on suspicion of smuggling. In connection with this and other events, Britain decided to go to war. Thus began the 'Lorcha War' of 1857, in which France joined for the sake of the booty to be expected. Britain had just ended the Crimean War, and was engaged in heavy fighting against the Moguls in India. Consequently only a small force of a few thousand men could be landed in China; Canton, however, was bombarded, and also the forts of Tientsin. There still seemed no prospect of gaining the desired objectives by negotiation, and in 1860 a new expedition was fitted out, this time some 20,000 strong. The troops landed at Tientsin and marched on Peking; the emperor fled to Jehol and did not return; he died in 1861. The new Treaty of Tientsin (1860) provided for (a) the opening of further ports to European traders; (b) the cession of Kowloon, the strip of land lying opposite Hong Kong; (c) the establishment of a British legation in Peking; (d) freedom of navigation along the Yangtze; (e) permission for British subjects to purchase land in China; (f) the British to be subject to their own consular courts and not to the Chinese courts; (g) missionary activity to be permitted throughout the country. In addition to this, the commercial treaty was revised, the opium trade was permitted once more, and a war indemnity was to be paid by China. In the eyes of Europe, Britain had now succeeded in turning China not actually into a colony, but at all events into a semi-colony; China must be expected soon to share the fate of India. China, however, with her very different conceptions of intercourse between states, did not realize the full import of these terms; some of them were regarded as concessions on unimportant points, which there was no harm in granting to the trading 'barbarians', as had been done in the past; some were regarded as simple injustices, which at a given moment could be swept away by administrative action.

But the result of this European penetration was that China's balance of trade was adverse, and became more and more so, as under the commercial treaties she could neither stop the importation of European goods nor set a duty on them; and on the other hand she could not compel foreigners to buy Chinese goods. The efflux of silver brought general impoverishment to China, widespread financial stringency to the state, and continuous financial crises and inflation. China had never had much liquid capital, and she was soon compelled to take up foreign loans in order to pay her debts. At that time internal loans were out of the question (the first internal loan was floated in 1894): the population did not even know what a state loan meant; consequently the loans had to be issued abroad. This, however, entailed the giving of securities, generally in the form of economic privileges. Under the Most Favoured Nation clause, however, these privileges had then to be granted to other states which had made no loans to China. Clearly a vicious spiral, which in the end could only bring disaster.

The only exception to the general impoverishment, in which not only the peasants but the old upper classes were involved, was a certain section of the trading community and the middle class, which had grown rich in its dealings with the Europeans. These people now accumulated capital, became Europeanized with their staffs, acquired land from the impoverished gentry, and sent their sons abroad to foreign universities, and learned European capitalist methods. This class was, of course, to be found mainly in the treaty ports in the south and in their environs. The south, as far north as Shanghai, became more modern and more advanced; the north made no advance. In the south, European ways of thought were learnt, and Chinese and European theories were compared. Criticism began. The first revolutionary societies were formed in this atmosphere in the south.

8   Risings in Sinkiang and within China:
the T'ai-p'ing Rebellion

But the emperor Hsüan Tsung (reign name Tao-kuang), a man in poor health though not without ability, had much graver anxieties than those caused by the Europeans. He did not yet fully realize the seriousness of the European peril.

In Sinkiang, where Turkish Mohammedans lived under Chinese rule, conditions were far from being as the Chinese desired. The Chinese, a fundamentally rationalistic people, regarded religion as a purely political matter, and accordingly required every citizen to take part in the official form of worship. Subject to that, he might privately belong to any other religion. To a Mohammedan, this was impossible and intolerable. The Mohammedans were only ready to practise their own religion, and absolutely refused to take part in any other. The Chinese also tried to apply to Sinkiang in other matters the same legislation that applied to all China, but this proved irreconcilable with the demands made by Islam on its followers. All this produced continual unrest.

Sinkiang had had a feudal system of government with a number of feudal lords (*beg*), who tried to maintain their influence and who had the support of the Mohammedan population. The Chinese had come to Sinkiang as soldiers and officials, to administer the country. They regarded themselves as lords of the land and occupied themselves with the extraction of taxes. Most of the officials were also associated with the Chinese merchants who travelled throughout Central Asia and as far as Siberia. The conflicts implicit in this situation produced great Mohammedan risings in the nineteenth century. The first came in 1825–1827; in 1845 a second rising flamed up, and thirty years later these revolts led to the temporary loss of the whole of Sinkiang.

In 1848, native unrest began in the province of Hunan, as a result

of the growing pressure of the Chinese settlers on the native population; in the same year there was unrest farther south, in the province
of Kwangsi, this time in connection with the influence of the Europeans. The leader was a quite simple man of Hakka blood, Hung
Hsiu-ch'üan (born 1814), who gathered impoverished Hakka peasants
round him as every peasant leader had done in the past. Very often
the nucleus of these peasant movements had been a secret society
with a particular religious tinge; this time the peasant revolutionaries
came forward as at the same time the preachers of a new religion of
their own. Hung had heard of Christianity from missionaries (1837),
and he mixed Christian ideas with those of ancient China and proclaimed to his followers a doctrine that promised the Kingdom of
God on earth. He called himself 'Christ's younger brother', and his
kingdom was to be called *T'ai P'ing* ('Supreme Peace'). He made his
first comrades, charcoal makers, local doctors, pedlars and farmers,
into kings, and made himself emperor. The movement, like many
before it, was religious as well as social, and it produced a great
response from the peasants. The programme of the T'ai P'ing, in
some points influenced by Christian ideas but more so by traditional
Chinese thought, was in many points revolutionary: (a) all property
was communal property; (b) land was classified into categories
according to its fertility and equally distributed among men and
women. Every producer kept of the produce as much as he and his
family needed and delivered the rest into the communal granary; (c)
administration and tax systems were revised; (d) women were given
equal rights: they fought together with men in the army and had
access to official position. They had to marry, but monogamy was
requested; (e) the use of opium, tobacco and alcohol was prohibited,
prostitution was illegal; (f) foreigners were regarded as equals,
capitulations that the Manchus had accepted were not recognized. A
large part of the officials, and particularly of the soldiers sent against
the revolutionaries, were Manchus, and consequently the movement
very soon became a nationalist movement, much as the popular movement at the end of the Mongol epoch had done. Hung made rapid
progress; in 1852 he captured Hankow, and in 1853 Nanking, the
important centre in the east. With clear political insight he made
Nanking his capital. In this he returned to the old traditions of the
beginning of the Ming epoch, no doubt expecting in this way to
attract support from the eastern Chinese gentry, who had no liking
for a capital far away in the north. He made a parade of adhesion to
the ancient Chinese tradition: his followers cut off their pigtails and
allowed their hair to grow as in the past.

He did not succeed, however, in carrying his reforms from the
stage of sporadic action to a systematic reorganization of the country,

and he also failed to enlist the elements needed for this as for all other administrative work, so that the good start soon degenerated into a terrorist regime.

Hung's followers pressed on from Nanking, and in 1853–1855 they advanced nearly to Tientsin; but they failed to capture Peking itself.

The new T'ai P'ing state faced the Europeans with big problems. Should they work with it or against it? The T'ai P'ing always insisted that they were Christians; the missionaries hoped now to have the opportunity of converting all China to Christianity. The T'ai P'ing treated the missionaries well but did not let them operate. After long hesitation and much vacillation, however, the Europeans placed themselves on the side of the Manchus. Not out of any belief that the T'ai P'ing movement was without justification, but because they had concluded treaties with the Manchu government and given loans to it, of which nothing would have remained if the Manchus had fallen; because they preferred the weak Manchu government to a strong T'ai P'ing government; and because they disliked the socialistic element in many of the measures adopted by the T'ai P'ing.

At first it seemed as if the Manchus would be able to cope unaided with the T'ai P'ing, but the same thing happened as at the end of the Mongol rule: the imperial armies, consisting of the 'banners' of the Manchus, the Mongols, and some Chinese had lost their military skill in the long years of peace; they had lost their old fighting spirit and were glad to be able to live in peace on their state pensions. Now three men came to the fore—a Mongol named Seng-ko-lin-ch'in, a man of great personal bravery, who defended the interests of the Manchu rulers; and two Chinese, Tsêng Kuo-fan (1811–1892) and Li Hung-chang (1823–1901), who were in the service of the Manchus but used their position simply to further the interests of the gentry. The Mongol saved Peking from capture by the T'ai P'ing. The two Chinese were living in central China, and there they recruited, Li at his own expense and Tsêng out of the resources at his disposal as a provincial governor, a sort of militia, consisting of peasants out to protect their homes from destruction by the peasants of the T'ai P'ing. Thus the peasants of central China, all suffering from impoverishment, were divided into two groups, one following the T'ai P'ing, the other following Tsêng Kuo-fan. Tsêng's army, too, might be described as a 'national' army, because Tsêng was not fighting for the interests of the Manchus. Thus the peasants could choose between two sides, between the T'ai P'ing and Tsêng Kuo-fan. Although Tsêng represented the gentry and was thus not the man of the simple common people, peasants fought in masses on his side, for he paid better, and especially more regularly. Tsêng, being a good strategist, won successes and gained adherents. Thus by 1856 the T'ai

303

P'ing were pressed back on Nanking and some of the towns round it; in 1864 Nanking was captured.

While in the central provinces the T'ai P'ing rebellion was raging, China was suffering grave setbacks owing to the Lorcha War of 1856; and there were also great and serious risings in other parts of the country. In 1855 the Yellow river had changed its course, entering the sea once more at Tientsin, to the great loss of the regions of Honan and Anhui. In these two central provinces the peasant rising of the so-called 'Nien Fei' had begun, but it only became formidable after 1855, owing to the increasing misery of the peasants. This purely peasant revolt was not suppressed by the Manchu government until 1868, after many collisions. Then, however, there began the so-called 'Mohammedan risings'. Here there are, in all, five movements to distinguish: (1) the Mohammedan rising in Kansu (1864–1865); (2) the Salar movement in Shensi; (3) the Mohammedan revolt in Yünnan (1855–1873); (4) the rising in Kansu (1895); (5) the rebellion of Yakub Beg in Sinkiang (from 1866 onward).

While we are fairly well informed about the other popular risings of this period, the Mohammedan revolts have not yet been well studied. We know from unofficial accounts that these risings were suppressed with great brutality. To this day there are many Mohammedans in, for instance. Yünnan, but the revolt there is said to have cost a million lives. The figures all rest on very rough estimates: in Kansu the population is said to have fallen from fifteen million to one million; the Sinkiang revolt is said to have cost ten million lives. There are no reliable statistics; but it is understandable that at that time the population of China must have fallen considerably, especially if we bear in mind the equally ferocious suppression of the risings of the T'ai P'ing and the Nien Fei within China, and smaller risings of which we have made no mention.

The Mohammedan risings were not elements of a general Mohammedan revolt, but separate events only incidentally connected with each other. The risings had different causes. An important factor was the general distress in China. In addition to this, owing to the national feeling which had been aroused in so unfortunate a way, the Chinese felt a revulsion against non-Chinese, such as the Salars, who were of Turkish race. Here there were always possibilities of friction, which might have been removed with a little consideration but which swelled to importance through the tactless behaviour of Chinese officials. Finally there came divisions among the Mohammedans of China which led to fighting between themselves.

All these risings were marked by two characteristics. They had no general political aim such as the founding of a great and universal Islamic state. Separate states were founded, but they were too small to endure; they would have needed the protection of great states. But they were not moved by any pan-Islamic idea. Second, they all took place on Chinese soil, and all the Mohammedans involved, except in the rising of the Salars, were Chinese. These Chinese who became Mohammedans are called Dungans. The Dungans are, of course, no longer pure Chinese, because Chinese who have gone over to Islam readily form mixed marriages with Islamic non-Chinese, that is to say with Turks and Mongols.

The revolt, however, of Yakub Beg in Sinkiang had a quite different character. Yakub Beg (his Chinese name was An Chi-yeh) had risen to the Chinese governorship when he made himself ruler of Kashgar. In 1866 he began to try to make himself independent of Chinese control. He conquered Ili, and then in a rapid campaign made himself master of all Sinkiang.

His state had a much better prospect of endurance than the other Mohammedan states. He had full control of it from 1874. Sinkiang was connected with China only by the few routes that led between the desert and the Tibetan mountains. The state was supported against China by Russia, which was continually pressing eastward, and in the south by Great Britain, which was pressing towards Tibet. Farther west was the great Ottoman empire; the attempt to gain direct contact with it was not hopeless in itself, and this was recognized at Istanbul. Missions went to and fro, and Turkish officers came to Yakub Beg and organized his army; Yakub Beg recognized the Turkish sultan as Khalif. He also concluded treaties with Russia and Great Britain. But in spite of all this he was unable to maintain his hold of Sinkiang. In 1877 the famous Chinese general Tso Tsung-t'ang (1812–1885), who had fought against the T'ai P'ing and also against the Mohammedans in Kansu, marched into Sinkiang and ended Yakub Beg's rule.

Yakub was defeated, however, not so much by Chinese superiority as by a combination of circumstances. In order to build up his kingdom he was compelled to impose heavy taxation, and this made him unpopular with his own followers: they had had to pay taxes under the Chinese, but the Chinese collection had been much less rigorous than that of Yakub Beg. It was technically impossible for the Ottoman empire to give him any aid, even had its internal situation permitted it. Britain and Russia would probably have been glad to see a weakening of the Chinese hold over Sinkiang, but they did not want a strong new state there, once they had found that neither of them could control the country while it was in Yakub Beg's hands. In 1881 Russia occupied the Ili region, Yakub's first conquest. In the end the two great powers considered it better for Sinkiang to return officially into the hands of the weakened China, hoping that in practice they would be able to bring Sinkiang more and more under their control. Consequently, when in 1880, three years after the removal of Yakub Beg, China sent a mission to Russia with the request for the return of the Ili region to her, Russia gave way, and the Treaty of Ili was concluded, ending for the time the Russian penetration of Sinkiang. In 1882 the Manchu government raised the conquered area to a 'new frontier' (Sinkiang) with a special administration.

This process of colonial penetration of Sinkiang continued. Until the end of the First World War there was no fundamental change in the situation in the country, owing to the rivalry between Great Britain and Russia. But after 1920 a period began in which Sinkiang became almost independent, under a number of rulers of parts of the country. Then, from 1928 onward, a more and more thorough penetration by Russia began, so that by 1940 Sinkiang could almost be called a Soviet Republic. The Second World War diverted Russian attention to the West, and at the same time compelled the Chinese to retreat into the interior from the Japanese, so that by 1943 the country was more firmly held by the Chinese government than it had been for seventy years. After the creation of the People's Democracy a directed immigration into Sinkiang began, in connection with the development of oil fields and of many new industries in the border area between Sinkiang and China proper. Roads and air communications opened Sinkiang. Yet, the differences between immigrant Chinese and local Muslim Turks continue to play a role.

9   Collision with Japan; further capitulations

The reign of Wen Tsung (reign name Hsien-feng 1851–1861) was marked throughout by the T'ai P'ing and other rebellions and by wars with the Europeans, and that of Mu Tsung (reign name T'ung-chih: 1862–1874) by the great Mohammedan disturbances. There began also a conflict with Japan which lasted until 1945. Mu Tsung came to the throne as a child of five, and never played a part of his own. It had been the general rule for princes to serve as regents for minors on the imperial throne, but this time the princes concerned won such notoriety through their intrigues that the Peking court circles decided to entrust the regency to two concubines of the late emperor. One of these, called Tzŭ Hsi (born 1835), of the Manchu tribe of the Yehe-Nara, quickly gained the upper hand. The empress Tzŭ Hsi was one of the strongest personalities of the later nineteenth century who played an active part in Chinese political life. She played a more active part than any emperor had played for many decades.

Meanwhile great changes had taken place in Japan. The restoration of the Meiji had ended the age of feudalism, at least on the surface. Japan rapidly became Westernized, and at the same time entered on an imperialist policy. Her aims from 1868 onward were clear, and remained unaltered until the end of the Second World War: she was to be surrounded by a wide girdle of territories under Japanese domination, in order to prevent the approach of any enemy to the Japanese homeland. This girdle was divided into several zones—(1) the inner zone with the Kurile Islands, Sakhalin, Korea, the Ryukyu archipelago, and Taiwan; (2) the outer zone with the Marianne, Philippine, and Caroline Islands, eastern China, Manchuria, and eastern Siberia; (3) the third zone, not clearly defined, including especially the Netherlands Indies, Indo-China, and the whole of China, a zone of undefined extent. The outward form of this subjugated region was to be that of the Greater Japanese Empire, described as the Imperium of the Yellow Race (the main ideas were contained in the Tanaka Memorandum 1927 and in the Tada Interview of 1936). Round Japan, moreover, a girdle was to be created of producers of raw materials and purchasers of manufactures, to provide Japanese industry with a market. Japan had sent a delegation of amity to China as early as 1869, and a first Sino-Japanese treaty was signed in 1871; from then on, Japan began to carry out her imperialistic plans. In 1874 she attacked the Ryukyu islands and Formosa (Taiwan) on the pretext that some Japanese had been murdered there. Under the treaty of 1874 Japan withdrew once more, only demanding a substantial indemnity; but in 1876, in violation of the treaty and without a declaration of war, she annexed the Ryukyu Islands. These islands (one of which is in Japanese called Okinawa) were since centuries in a loose dependency with China, while, on the other hand, they paid tribute to some lords in Kyushu. The population of the islands has a culture and social structure of its own, and their language differs from standard Japanese. They felt discriminated against by the Japanese and gained after the Second World War some kind of independence while under American occupation; finally, however, Japan reassumed its control over the islands. In 1876 began the Japanese penetration into Korea; by 1885 she had reached the stage of a declaration that Korea was a joint sphere of interest of China and Japan; until then China's protectorate over Korea had been unchallenged. At the same time (1876) Great Britain had secured further capitulations in the Chefoo Convention; in 1862 France had acquired Cochin China, in 1864 Cambodia, in 1874 Tongking, and in 1883 Annam. This led in 1884 to war between France and China, in which the French did not by any means gain an indubitable victory; but the Treaty of Tientsin left them with their acquisitions.

Meanwhile, at the beginning of 1875, the young Chinese emperor died of smallpox, without issue. Under the influence of the two empresses, who still remained regents, a cousin of the dead emperor, the three-year-old prince Tsai T'ien was chosen as emperor Tê Tsung (reign name Kuang-hsü: 1875–1909). He came of age in 1889 and took over the government of the country. The empress Tzǔ Hsi retired, but did not really relinquish the reins.

In 1894 the Sino-Japanese War broke out over Korea, as an outcome of the undefined position that had existed since 1885 owing to the imperialistic policy of the Japanese. China had created a North China squadron, but this was all that can be regarded as Chinese preparation for the long-expected war. The governor-general of Chihli (now Hopei—the province in which Peking is situated), Li Hung-chang, was a general who had done good service, but he lost the war, and at Shimonoseki (1895) he had to sign a treaty on very harsh terms, in which China relinquished her protectorate over Korea and lost Taiwan. The intervention of France, Germany, and Russia compelled Japan to content herself with these acquisitions, abandoning her demand for South Manchuria. Korea and Formosa (Taiwan) became colonies, Taiwan first, Korea later, and remained so until the end of the Second World War.

10   Russia in Manchuria

After the Crimean War, Russia had turned her attention once more to the East. There had been hostilities with China over eastern Siberia, which were brought to an end in 1858 by the Treaty of Aigun, under which China ceded certain territories in northern Manchuria. This made possible the founding of Vladivostok in 1860. Russia received Sakhalin from Japan in 1875 in exchange for the Kurile Islands. She received from China the important Port Arthur as a leased territory, and then tried to secure the whole of south Manchuria. This brought Japan's policy of expansion into conflict with Russia's plans in the Far East. Russia wanted Manchuria in order to be able to pursue a policy in the Pacific; but Japan herself planned to march into Manchuria from Korea, of which she already had possession. This imperialist rivalry made war inevitable: Russia lost the war; under the Treaty of Portsmouth in 1905 Russia gave Japan the main railway through Manchuria, with adjoining territory. Thus Manchuria became Japan's sphere of influence and was lost to the Manchus without their being consulted in any way. The Japanese penetration of Manchuria then proceeded stage by stage, not without occasional setbacks, until she had occupied the whole of Manchuria from 1932 to 1945. After the end of the Second World War, Manchuria was returned to China, with certain reservations in favour of the Soviet Union, which were later revoked. Japan also got half of the island of Sakhalin (Japanese: Karafuto), which it had to return back to the Soviet Union after the defeat of 1945.

11 *Reform and reaction: the Boxer Rising*

China had lost the war with Japan because she was entirely without modern armament. While Japan went to work at once with all her energy to emulate Western industrialization, the ruling class in China had shown a marked repugnance to any modernization; and the centre of this conservatism was the dowager empress Tzŭ Hsi. She was a woman of strong personality, but too uneducated—in the modern sense—to be able to realize that modernization was an absolute necessity for China if it was to remain an independent state. The empress failed to realize that the Europeans were fundamentally different from the neighbouring tribes or the pirates of the past; she had not the capacity to acquire a general grasp of the realities of world politics. She felt instinctively that Europeanization would wreck the foundations of the power of the Manchus and the gentry, and would bring another class, the middle class and the merchants, into power. She has often been blamed for not thinking of the possibility that China might become a colony of one or several Western countries; with hindsight, we have today to admit that such a development could not have been successful.

There were reasonable men, however, who had seen the necessity of reform—especially Li Hung-chang, who has already been mentioned. In 1896 he went on a mission to Moscow, and then toured Europe. The reformers were, however, divided into two groups. One group advocated the acquisition of a certain amount of technical knowledge from abroad and its introduction by slow reforms, without altering the social structure of the state or the composition of the government. The others held that the state needed fundamental changes, and that superficial loans from Europe were not enough. According to the dominant sociological theory until about 1960, the introduction only of Western technology and technical knowledge could not have succeeded. Today, we are much more cautious in our judgement. We now know of numerous examples where social changes came long after successful technical changes. The failure in the war with Japan made the general desire for reform more and more insistent not only in the country but in Peking. Until now Japan had been despised as a barbarian state; now Japan had won! The Europeans had been despised; now they were all cutting bits out of China for themselves, extracting from the government one privilege after another, and quite openly dividing China into 'spheres of interest', obviously as the prelude to annexation of the whole country.

In Europe at that time the question was being discussed over and over again, why Japan had so quickly succeeded in making herself a modern power, and why China was not succeeding in doing so; the Japanese were praised for their capacity and the Chinese blamed for their lassitude. Both in Europe and in Chinese circles it was overlooked that there were fundamental differences between both societies. When Japan modernized under the Meiji regime, the old upper class co-operated fully with the government out of fear that otherwise Japan would be unable to preserve its integrity. Thus, the upper class remained intact and led the modernization, willing even to give up numerous of its privileges. In China, nobody seriously feared the loss of independence of the country. Further, there was a cleft between the ruling dynasty, the Manchu conquerors, and the Chinese élite, and the tension between the two absorbed the energy that should have gone into modernization. The leaders of China remained, except for small attempts, inactive and when modernization later began, it was not carried through by the élite. Additionally, Japan had a developed middle class, the merchants, who entered into a symbiosis with the feudal lords. Thus, changes initiated by Japan's élite, were taken up and sponsored by the middle class. China's middle class of merchants was weak. It was not a willing partner of the disunited élite. It had still to gain the strength to liberate itself before it could become the support for a capitalistic state. And the gentry were still strong enough to maintain their dominance and so to prevent a radical reconstruction; all they would agree to were a few reforms during the so-called 'T'ung-chih reforms' or 'Self-strengthening Movement' (1861–1895).

In 1895 and in 1898 a scholar, K'ang Yo-wei (1858–1927), who was admitted into the presence of the emperor, submitted to him memoranda in which he called for radical reform. K'ang was a scholar who belonged to the empiricist school of philosophy of the early Manchu period, the so-called Han school. He was a man of strong and persuasive personality, and had such an influence on the emperor that in 1898 the emperor issued several edicts ordering the fundamental reorganization of education, law, trade, communications and the army. These laws were not at all bad in themselves; they would have paved the way for a liberalization of Chinese society. But they aroused the utmost hatred in the conservative gentry and also in the moderate reformers among the gentry. K'ang Yo-wei and his followers, to whom a number of well-known modern scholars belonged, had strong support in south China. We have already mentioned that owing to the increased penetration of European goods and ideas, south China had become more progressive than the north; this had added to the tension already existing for other reasons between north and south. In foreign policy the north was more favourable to Russia and radically opposed to Japan and Great Britain; the south was in favour of co-operation with Britain and Japan, in order to learn from those two states how reform could be carried through. In the north the men of the south were suspected of being anti-Manchu and revolutionary in feeling. This was to some extent true, though K'ang Yo-wei and his friends, among them the publicist Liang Ch'i-ch'ao (1873–1929), were as yet largely unconscious of it.

When the empress Tzŭ Hsi saw that the emperor was actually thinking about reforms, she went to work with lightning speed. Very soon the reformers had to flee; those who failed to make good their escape were arrested and executed. The emperor was made a prisoner in a palace near Peking, and remained a captive until his death; the empress resumed her regency on his behalf. The period of reforms lasted only for a few months of 1898. A leading part in the extermination of the reformers was played by troops from Kansu under the command of a Mohammedan, Tung Fu-hsiang. General Yüan Shih-k'ai, who was then stationed at Tientsin in command of 7,000 troops with modern equipment, the only ones in China, could have removed the empress and protected the reformers; but he was already pursuing a personal policy, and thought it safer to give the reformers no help.

There now began, from 1898, a reactionary rule of the dowager empress. But China's general situation permitted no breathing-space. In 1900 came the so-called Boxer Rising, a new popular movement against the gentry and the Manchus similar to the many that had preceded it. The Peking government succeeded, however, in negotiations that brought the movement into the service of the government and directed it against the foreigners. This removed the danger to the government and at the same time helped it against the hated foreigners. But incidents resulted which the Peking government had not anticipated. An international army was sent to China, and marched from Tientsin against Peking, to liberate the besieged European legations and to punish the government. The Europeans captured Peking (1900); the dowager empress and her prisoner, the emperor, had to flee; some of the palaces were looted. The peace treaty that followed exacted further concessions from China to the Europeans and enormous war indemnities, the payment of which continued into the 1940s, though most of the states placed the money at China's disposal for educational purposes. When in 1902 the dowager empress returned to Peking and put the emperor back into his palace-prison, she was forced by what had happened to realize that at all events a certain measure of reform was necessary. The reforms, however, which she decreed, mainly in 1904, were very modest and were never fully carried out. They were only intended to make an impression on the

311

outer world and to appease the continually growing body of supporters of the reform party, especially numerous in south China. The
south remained, nevertheless, a focus of hostility to the Manchus.
After his failure in 1898, K'ang Yo-wei went to Europe, and no
longer played any important political part. His place was soon taken
by a young Chinese physician who had been living abroad. Sun Yat-
sen (1866–1925), who turned the reform party into a middle-class
revolutionary party.

12 *End of the dynasty*

Meanwhile the dowager empress held her own. General Yüan Shih-
k'ai, who had played so dubious a part in 1898, was not impeccably
loyal to her, and remained unreliable. He was beyond challenge the
strongest man in the country, for he possessed the only modern
army; but he was still biding his time.

In 1908 the dowager empress fell ill; she was seventy-four years
old. When she felt that her end was near, she seems to have had the
captive emperor Tê Tsung assassinated (at 5 p.m. on 14 November);
she herself died next day (15 November, 2 p.m.): she was evidently
determined that this man, whom she had ill-treated and oppressed
all his life, should not regain independence. As Tê Tsung had no
children, she nominated on the day of her death the two-year-old
prince P'u Yi as emperor (reign name Hsüan-t'ung, 1909–1911).

The empress Tzŭ Hsi is still regarded as responsible for the sufferings that China had to suffer for about half a century, and popular
stories about her abound in description of her misdeeds. Together
with the Empress Lü in the early Han time, and the Empress Wu in
T'ang time, she became the symbol of evil: what would become of a
country under the rule of a woman. This may well be one of the
reasons why still so few women are in high positions and recognized
as capable in the People's China.

The fact that another child was to reign and a new regency to act
for him, together with all the failures in home and foreign policy,
brought further strength to the revolutionary party. The government
believed that it could only maintain itself if it allowed Yüan Shih-
k'ai, the commander of the modern troops, to come to power. The
chief regent, however, worked against Yüan Shih-k'ai and dismissed
him at the beginning of 1909; Yüan's supporters remained at their
posts. Yüan himself now entered into relations with the revolutionaries, whose centre was Canton, and whose undisputed leader was
now Sun Yat-sen. At this time Sun and his supporters had already
made attempts at revolution, but without success, as his following
was as yet too small. It consisted mainly of young intellectuals who
had been educated in Europe and America; the great mass of the

Chinese people remained unconvinced: the common people could not understand the new ideals, and the middle class did not entirely trust the young intellectuals.

The state of China in 1911 was as lamentable as could be: the European states, Russia, America, and Japan regarded China as a field for their own plans, and in their calculations paid scarcely any attention to the Chinese government. Foreign capital was penetrating everywhere in the form of loans or railway and other enterprises. If it had not been the mutual rivalries of the powers, China would long ago have been annexed by one of them. The government needed a great deal of money for the payment of the war indemnities, and for carrying out the few reforms at last decided on. In order to get money from the provinces, it had to permit the viceroys even more freedom than they already possessed. The result was a spectacle altogether resembling that of the end of the T'ang dynasty, about A.D. 900: the various governors were trying to make themselves independent. In addition to this there was the revolutionary movement in the south.

The government made some concession to the progressives, by providing the first beginnings of parliamentary rule. In 1910 a national assembly was convoked. It had a Lower House with representatives of the provinces (provincial diets were also set up), and an Upper House, in which sat representatives of the imperial house, the nobility, the gentry, and also the protectorates. The members of the Upper House were all nominated by the regent. It very soon proved that the members of the Lower House, mainly representatives of the provincial gentry, had a much more practical outlook than the routineers of Peking. Thus the Lower House grew in importance, a fact which, of course, brought grist to the mills of the revolutionary movement.

In 1910 the first risings directed actually against the regency took place, in the province of Hunan. In 1911 the 'railway disturbances' broke out in western China as a reply of the railway shareholders in the province of Szechwan to the government decree of nationalization of all the railways. The modernist students, most of whom were sons of merchants who owned railway shares, supported the movement, and the government was unable to control them. At the same time a great anti-Manchu revolution began in Wuch'ang, one of the cities of which Wuhan, on the Yangtze, now consists. The revolution was the result of government action against a group of terrorists. Its leader was an officer named Li Yüan-hung. The Manchus soon had some success in this quarter, but the other provincial governors now rose in rapid succession, repudiated the Manchus, and declared themselves independent. Most of the Manchu garrisons in the provinces were murdered. The governors remained at the head of their troops in their provinces, and for the moment made common cause with the revolutionaries, from whom they meant to break free at the first opportunity. The Manchus themselves failed at first to realize the gravity of the revolutionary movement; they then fell into panic-stricken desperation. As a last resource, Yüan Shih-k'ai was recalled (10 November 1911) and made prime minister.

Yüan's excellent troops were loyal to his person, and he could have made use of them in fighting on behalf of the dynasty. But a victory would have brought no personal gain to him; for his personal plans he considered that the anti-Manchu side provided the springboard he needed. The revolutionaries, for their part, had no choice but to win over Yüan Shih-k'ai for the sake of his troops, since they were not themselves strong enough to get rid of the Manchus, or even to wrest concessions from them, so long as the Manchus were defended by Yüan's army. Thus Yüan and the revolutionaries were forced into each other's arms. He then began negotiations with them, explaining to the imperial house that the dynasty could only be saved by con-cessions. The revolutionaries—apart from their desire to neutralize the prime minister and general, if not to bring him over to their side—were also readier than ever to negotiate, because they were short of money and unable to obtain loans from abroad, and because they could not themselves gain control of the individual governors. The negotiations, which had been carried on at Shanghai, were broken off on 18 December 1911, because the revolutionaries demanded a republic, but the imperial house was only ready to grant a constitu-tional monarchy.

Meanwhile the revolutionaries set up a provisional government at Nanking (29 December 1911), with Sun Yat-sen as president and Li Yüan-hung as vice-president. Yüan Shih-k'ai now declared to the imperial house that the monarchy could no longer be defended, as his troops were too unreliable, and he induced the Manchu govern-ment to issue an edict on 12 February 1912, in which they renounced the throne of China and declared the Republic to be the constitu-tional form of state. The young emperor of the Hsüan-t'ung period, after the Japanese conquest of Manchuria in 1931, was installed there. He was, however, entirely without power during the melan-choly years of his nominal rule, which lasted until 1945.

In 1912 the Manchu dynasty came in reality to its end. On the news of the abdication of the imperial house, Sun Yat-sen resigned in Nanking, and recommended Yüan Shih-k'ai as president.

CHAPTER ELEVEN

The Republic (1912–1948)

1 *Social and intellectual position*

In order to understand the period that now followed, let us first consider the social and intellectual position in China in the period between 1911 and 1927. The Manchu dynasty was no longer there, nor were there any remaining real supporters of the old dynasty. The gentry, however, still existed. Alongside it was a still numerically small middle class, with little political education or enlightenment.

The political interests of these two groups were obviously in conflict. But after 1912 there had been big changes. The gentry were largely in a process of decomposition. They still possessed the basis of their existence, their land, but the land was falling in value, as there were now other opportunities of capital investment, such as export-import, shareholding in foreign enterprises, or industrial undertakings. It is important to note, however, that there was not much fluid capital at their disposal. In addition to this, cheaper rice and other foodstuffs were streaming from abroad into China, bringing the prices for Chinese foodstuffs down to the world market prices, another painful business blow to the gentry. Silk had to meet the competition of Japanese silk and especially of rayon; the Chinese silk was of very unequal quality and sold with difficulty. On the other hand, through the influence of the Western capitalistic system, which was penetrating more and more into China, land itself became 'capital', an object of speculation for people with capital; its value no longer depended entirely on the rents it could yield but, under certain circumstances, on quite other things—the construction of railways or public buildings, and so on. These changes impoverished and demoralized the gentry, who in the course of the past century had grown fewer in number. The gentry were not in a position to take part fully in the capitalist manipulations, because they had never possessed much capital; their wealth had lain entirely in their land, and the income from their rents was consumed quite unproductively in luxurious living.

Moreover, the class solidarity of the gentry was dissolving. In the past, politics had been carried on by cliques of gentry families, with the emperor at their head as an unchangeable institution. This edifice had now lost its summit; the struggles between cliques still went on, but entirely without the control which the emperor's power had after all exercised, as a sort of regulative element in the play of forces among the gentry. The arena for this competition had been the court. After the destruction of the arena, the field of play lost its boundaries: the struggles between cliques no longer had a definite objective; the only objective left was the maintenance or securing of any and every hold on power. Under the new conditions cliques or individuals among the gentry could only ally themselves with the possessors of military power, the generals or governors. In this last stage the struggle between rival groups turned into a rivalry between individuals. Family ties began to weaken and other ties, such as between school mates, or origin from the same village or town, became more important than they had been before. For the securing of the aim in view any means were considered justifiable. Never was there such bribery and corruption among the officials as in the years after 1912. This period, until 1927, may therefore be described as a period of dissolution and destruction of the social system of the gentry.

Over against this dying class of the gentry stood, broadly speaking, a tripartite opposition. To begin with, there was the new middle class, divided and without clear political ideas; anti-dynastic of course, but undecided especially as to the attitude it should adopt towards the peasants who, to this day, form over 80 per cent of the Chinese population. The middle class consisted mainly of traders and bankers, whose aim was the introduction of Western capitalism in association with foreign powers. There were also young students who were often the sons of old gentry families and had been sent abroad for study with grants given them by their friends and relatives in the government; or sons of businessmen sent away by their fathers. These students not always accepted the ideas of their fathers; they were influenced by the ideologies of the West, Marxist or non-Marxist, and often created clubs or groups in the University cities of Europe, the United States, and Japan. In 1906 there were about 30,000 students in Japan alone. Such groups of people who had studied together or passed examinations together, had already begun to play a role in politics in the nineteenth century. Now, the influence of such organizations of usually informal character increased. Against the returned students who often had difficulties in adjustment, stood the students at Chinese universities, especially the National University in Peking (Peita). They represented people of the same origin, but of the lower strata of the gentry or of business; they were more nationalistic and politically active and often less influenced by Western ideologies.

In the second place, there was a relatively very small genuine proletariat, the product of the first activities of big capitalists in China, found mainly in Shanghai. Third and finally, there was a gigantic peasantry, uninterested in politics and mostly uneducated, but ready to give unthinking allegiance to anyone who promised to make an end of the conditions in the matter of rents and taxes, conditions that were growing steadily worse with the decay of the gentry. These peasants were thinking of popular risings on the pattern of all the risings in the history of China—attacks on the towns and the killing of the hated landowners, officials, and money-lenders, that is to say, of the gentry.

Such was the picture of the middle class and those who were ready to support it, a group with widely divergent interests, held together only by its opposition to the gentry system and the monarchy. It could not but be extremely difficult, if not impossible, to achieve political success with such a group. Sun Yat-sen (1866–1925), the 'Father of the Republic', accordingly laid down three stages of progress in his many works, of which the best-known are 'San-min chu-i' ('The Three Principles of the People'), and 'Chien-kuo fang-lüeh' ('Plans for the Building up of the Realm'). The three phases of development through which republican China was to pass were: the phase of struggle against the old system, the phase of educative rule, and the phase of truly democratic government. The phase of educative rule was to be a sort of authoritarian system with a democratic content, under which the people should be familiarized with democracy and enabled to grow politically ripe for true democracy.

Difficult as was the internal situation from the social point of view, it was no less difficult in economic respects. China had recognized that she must at least adopt Western technical and industrial progress in order to continue to exist as an independent state. But the building up of industry demanded large sums of money. The existing Chinese banks were quite incapable of providing the capital needed; but the acceptance of capital from abroad led at once, every time, to further political capitulations. The gentry, who had no cash worth the mention, were violently opposed to the capitalization of their properties, and were in favour of continuing as far as possible to work the soil in the old style. Quite apart from all this, all over the country there were generals, the so-called 'warlords', who had come from the ranks of the gentry, and who collected the whole of the financial resources of their region for the support of their private armies. Investors had little confidence in the republican government so long as they could not tell whether the government would decide in favour of its right or of its left wing.

No less complicated was the intellectual situation at this time. Confucianism, and the whole of the old culture and morality bound up with it, was unacceptable to the middle-class element. In the first place, Confucianism rejected the principle, required at least in theory by the middle class, of the equality of all people; second, the Confucian great-family system was irreconcilable with middle-class individualism, quite apart from the fact that the Confucian form of state could only be a monarchy. Every attempt to bolster up Confucianism in practice or theory was bound to fail and did fail. Even the gentry could scarcely offer any real defence of the Confucian system any longer. With Confucianism went the moral standards especially of the upper classes of society. Philosophical Taoism was out of the question as a substitute, because of its anarchistic and egocentric character. Consequently, in these years, part of the gentry turned to Buddhism and part to Christianity. Some of the middle class who had come under European influence also turned to Christianity, regarding it as a part of the European civilization they had to adopt. Others adhered to modern philosophic systems such as pragmatism and positivism. Marxist doctrines spread rapidly.

Education was secularized. Great efforts were made to develop modern schools, though the work of development was continually hindered by the incessant political unrest. Only at the universities, which became foci of republican and progressive opinion, was any positive achievement possible. Many students and professors were active in politics, organizing demonstrations and strikes. They pursued a strong national policy, often also socialistic. At the same time real scientific work was done; many young scholars of outstanding ability were trained at the Chinese universities, often better than the students who went abroad. There is a permanent disagreement between these two groups of young men with a modern education: the students who return from abroad claim to be better educated, but in reality they often have only a very superficial knowledge of things modern and none at all of China, her history, and her special circumstances. The students of the Chinese universities have been much better instructed in all the things that concern China, and most of them are in no way behind the returned students in the modern sciences. They are therefore a much more serviceable element.

The intellectual modernization of China goes under the name of the 'Movement of May Fourth', because on 4 May 1919, students of the National University in Peking demonstrated against the government and their pro-Japanese adherents. When the police attacked the students and jailed some, more demonstrations and student strikes and finally a general boycott of Japanese imports were the consequence. In these protest actions, professors such as Ts'ai Yüanp'ei (1876–1940), later president of the Academia Sinica, took an active part. The forces which had now been mobilized, rallied around the journal 'New Youth' ('Hsin Ch'ing-nien'), created in 1915 by Ch'en Tu-hsiu (1879–1942). The journal was progressive, against the monarchy, Confucius, and the old traditions. Ch'en Tu-hsiu who put himself strongly behind the students, was more radical than other contributors but at first favoured Western democracy and Western science; he was influenced mainly by John Dewey who was guest professor in Peking in 1919–1920. Similarly tending towards liberalism in politics and Dewey's ideas in the field of philosophy were others, mainly Hu Shih. Finally, some reformers criticized conservatism purely on the basis of Chinese thought. Hu Shih (1892–1962) gained greatest acclaim by his proposal for a 'literary revolution', published in the 'New Youth' in 1917. This revolution was the logically necessary application of the political revolution to the field of education. The new 'vernacular' replaced the old 'classical' literary language. The language of the classical works is so remote from the language of daily life that no uneducated person can understand it. A command of it requires a full knowledge of all the ancient literature, entailing decades of study. The gentry had elaborated this style of speech for themselves and their dependants; it was their monopoly; nobody who did not belong to the gentry and had not attended its schools could take part in literary or in administrative life. The literary revolution introduced the language of daily life, the language of the people, into literature: newspapers, novels, scientific treatises, translations, appeared in the vernacular, and could thus be understood by anyone who could read and write, even if he had no Confucianist education.

It may be said that the literary revolution has achieved its main objects. As a consequence of it, a great quantity of new literature has been published. Not only is every important new book that appears in the West published in translation within a few months, but modern novels and short stories and poems have been written, some of them of high literary value.

At the same time as this revolution there took place another fundamental change in the language. It was necessary to take over a vast number of new scientific and technical terms. As Chinese, owing to the character of its script, is unable to write foreign words accurately and can do no more than provide a rather rough paraphrase, the practice was started of expressing new ideas by newly formed native words. Thus modern Chinese has very few foreign words, and yet it has all the new ideas. For example, a telegram is a 'lightning-letter'; a wireless telegram is a 'not-have-wire-lightning-communication'; a fountain-pen is a 'self-flow-ink-water-brush'; a typewriter is a 'strike-letter-machine'. Most of these neologisms are identical in the modern languages of China and Japan.

There had been several proposals in recent decades to do away with the Chinese characters and to introduce an alphabet in their place. They have all proved to be unsatisfactory so far, because the character of the Chinese language, as it is at this moment, is unsuited to an alphabetical script. They would also destroy China's cultural unity: there are many dialects in China that differ so greatly from each other that, for instance, a man from Canton cannot understand a man from Shanghai. If Chinese were written with letters, the result would be a Canton literature and another literature confined to Shanghai, and China would break up into a number of areas with different languages. The old Chinese writing is independent of pronunciation. A Cantonese and a Pekingese can read each other's newspapers without difficulty. They pronounce the words quite differently, but the meaning is unaltered. Even a Japanese can understand a Chinese newspaper without special study of Chinese, and a Chinese with a little preparation can read a Japanese newspaper without understanding a single word of Japanese.

The aim of modern education in China is to work towards the establishment of 'High Chinese', the former official (Mandarin) language, throughout the country, and to set limits to the use of the various dialects. Once this has been done, it will be possible to proceed to a radical reform of the script without running the risk of political separatist movements, which are always liable to spring up, and also without leading, through the adoption of various dialects as the basis of separate literatures, to the break-up of China's cultural unity. In the last years, the unification of the spoken language has made great progress. Yet, alphabetic script is used only in cases in which illiterate adults have to be enabled in a short time to read very simple information. More attention is given to a simplification of the script as it is; Japanese had started this some forty years earlier. Unfortunately, the new Chinese abbreviated forms of characters are not always identical with long-established Japanese forms, and are not developed in such a systematic form as would make learning of Chinese characters easier.

2   First period of the Republic: The warlords

The situation of the Republic after its foundation was far from hopeful. Republican feeling existed only among the very small groups of students who had modern education, and a few traders, in other words, among the 'middle class'. And even in the revolutionary party to which these groups belonged there were the most various conceptions of the form of republican state to be aimed at. The left wing of the party, mainly intellectuals and manual workers, had in view more or less vague socialistic institutions; the liberals, for instance the traders, thought of a liberal democracy, more or less on the American pattern; and the nationalists merely wanted the removal of the alien Manchu rule. The three groups had come together for the practical reason that only so could they get rid of the dynasty. They gave allegiance to Sun Yat-sen as their leader. He succeeded in mobilizing the enthusiasm of continually widening circles for action, not only by the integrity of his aims but also because he was able to present the new socialistic ideology in an alluring form. The anti-republican gentry, however, whose power was not yet entirely broken, took a stand against the party. The generals who had gone over to the republicans had not the slightest intention of founding a republic, but only wanted to get rid of the rule of the Manchus and to step into their place. This was true also of Yüan Shih-k'ai, who in his heart was entirely on the side of the gentry, although the European press especially had always energetically defended him. In character and capacity he stood far above the other generals, but he was no republican.

Thus the first period of the Republic, until 1927, was marked by incessant attempts by individual generals to make themselves independent. The Government could not depend on its soldiers, and so was impotent. The first risings of military units began at the outset of 1912. The governors and generals who wanted to make themselves independent sabotaged every decree of the central government; especially they sent it no money from the provinces and also refused to give their assent to foreign loans. The province of Canton, the actual birthplace of the republican movement and the focus of radicalism, declared itself in 1912 an independent republic.

Within the Peking government matters soon came to a climax. Yüan Shih-k'ai and his supporters represented the conservative view, with the unexpressed but obvious aim of setting up a new imperial house and continuing the old gentry system. Most of the members of the parliament came, however, from the middle class and were opposed to any reaction of this sort. One of their leaders was murdered, and the blame was thrown upon Yüan Shih-k'ai; there then came, in the middle of 1912, a new revolution, in which the radicals made themselves independent and tried to gain control of south China. But Yüan Shih-k'ai commanded better troops and won the day. At the end of October 1912 he was elected, against the opposition, as president of China, and the new state was recognized by foreign countries.

China's internal difficulties reacted on the border states, in which the European powers were keenly interested. The powers considered that the time had come to begin the definitive partition of China. Thus there were long negotiations and also hostilities between China and Tibet, which was supported by Great Britain. The British demanded the complete separation of Tibet from China, but the Chinese rejected this (1912); the rejection was supported by a boycott of British goods. In the end the Tibet question was left undecided. Tibet remained until recent years a Chinese dependency with a good deal of internal freedom. The Second World War and the Chinese retreat into the interior brought many Chinese settlers into Eastern Tibet which was then separated from Tibet proper and made a Chinese province (Hsi-k'ang) in which the native Khamba will soon be a minority. The communist regime soon after its establishment conquered Tibet (1950) and has tried to change the character of its society and its system of government which led to the unsuccessful attempt of the Tibetans to throw off Chinese rule (1959) and the flight of the Dalai Lama to India. The construction of highways, air and missile bases and military occupation have thus tied Tibet closer to China than ever since early Manchu times.

In Outer Mongolia Russian interests predominated. In 1911 there were diplomatic incidents in connection with the Mongolian question. At the end of 1911 the Hutuktu of Urga declared himself independent, and the Chinese were expelled from the country. A secret treaty was concluded in 1912 with Russia, under which Russia recognized the independence of Outer Mongolia, but was accorded an important part as adviser and helper in the development of the country. In 1913 a Russo-Chinese treaty was concluded, under which the autonomy of Outer Mongolia was recognized, but Mongolia became a part of the Chinese realm. After the Russian revolution had begun, revolution was carried also into Mongolia. The country suffered all the horrors of the struggles between White Russians (General Ungern-Sternberg) and the Reds; there were also Chinese attempts at intervention, though without success, until in the end Mongolia became a Soviet Republic. Hemmed in on all sides by China and the Soviet Union, with no access to the sea, the small country had to manoeuvre between its two big neighbours. Since the establishment of the People's Republic and especially since the crisis between China and the Soviet Union, Outer Mongolia has moved closer to the Soviet Union as the—at the moment—less dangerous side. China did not quickly recognize Mongolia's independence, and in his work 'China's Destiny' (1944) Chiang Kai-shek insisted that China's aim remained the recovery of the frontiers of 1840, which means among other things the recovery of Outer Mongolia. In spite of this, after the Second World War Chiang Kai-shek had to renounce de jure all rights in Outer Mongolia. Inner Mongolia was always united to China much more closely; only for a time during the war with Japan did the Japanese maintain there a puppet government. The disappearance of this government went almost unnoticed.

At the time when Russian penetration into Mongolia began, Japan had entered upon a similar course in Manchuria, which she regarded as her 'sphere of influence'. On the outbreak of the First World War Japan occupied the former German-leased territory of Tsingtao, at the extremity of the province of Shantung, and from that point she occupied the railways of the province. Her plan was to make the whole province a protectorate; Shantung is rich in coal and especially in metals. Japan's plans were revealed in the notorious 'Twenty-one Demands' (1915). Against the furious opposition especially of the students of Peking, Yüan Shih-k'ai's government accepted the greater part of these demands. In negotiations with Great Britain, in which Japan took advantage of the British commitments in Europe, Japan had to be conceded the predominant position in the Far East.

Meanwhile Yüan Shih-k'ai had made all preparations for turning the Republic once more into an empire, in which he would be emperor; the empire was to be based once more on the gentry group. In 1914 he secured an amendment of the constitution under which the governing power was to be entirely in the hands of the president; at the end of 1914 he secured his appointment as president for life, and on 12 December 1915 he induced the parliament to resolve that he should become emperor.

This naturally aroused the resentment of the republicans, but it also annoyed the generals belonging to the gentry, who had had the same ambition. Thus there were disturbances, especially in the south, where Sun Yat-sen with his followers agitated for a democratic republic. The foreign powers recognized that a divided China would be much easier to penetrate and annex than a united China, and accordingly opposed Yüan Shih-k'ai. Before he could ascend the throne, he died suddenly (June 1916)—and this terminated the first attempt to re-establish monarchy.

Yüan was succeeded as president by Li Yüan-hung. Meanwhile five provinces had declared themselves independent. Foreign pressure on China steadily grew. She was forced to declare war on Germany, and though this made no practical difference to the war, it enabled the European powers to penetrate further into China. Difficulties grew to such an extent in 1917 that a dictatorship was set up and soon after an interlude, the recall of the Manchus and the reinstatement of the deposed emperor (1st–8th July 1917).

This led to various risings of generals, each aiming simply at the satisfaction of his thirst for personal power. Ultimately the victorious group of generals, headed by Tuan Ch'i-jui, secured the election of Fêng Kuo-chang in place of the retiring president. Fêng was succeeded at the end of 1918 by Hsü Shih-ch'ang, who held office until 1922. Hsü, as a former ward of the emperor, was a typical representative of the gentry, and was opposed to all republican reforms.

The south held aloof from these northern governments. In Canton an opposition government was set up, formed mainly of followers of Sun Yat-sen; the Peking government was unable to remove the Canton government. But the Peking government and its president scarcely counted any longer even in the north. All that counted were the generals, the most prominent of whom were: (1) Chang Tso-lin, who had control of Manchuria and had made certain terms with Japan, but who was ultimately murdered by the Japanese (1928); (2) Wu P'ei-fu, who held north China; (3) the so-called 'Christian general', Fêng Yü-hsiang, and (4) Ts'ao K'un, who became president in 1923.

At the end of the First World War Japan had a hold over China amounting almost to military control of the country. China did not sign the Treaty of Versailles, because she considered that she had been duped by Japan, since Japan had driven the Germans out of China but had not returned the liberated territory to the Chinese. In 1921 peace was concluded with Germany, the German privileges being abolished. The same applied to Austria. Russia, immediately after the setting up of the Soviet government, had renounced all her rights under the capitulations. The present regime is of the opinion that the Soviet Union also should have returned to China the land which they had forced the Manchu to give up. The Russian view is that these outlying territories had been conquered by China's foreign rulers, not by the Chinese. But still, this was the first step in the gradual rescinding of the capitulations; the last of them went only in 1943, as a consequence of the difficult situation of the Europeans and Americans in the Pacific produced by the Second World War.

At the end of the First World War the foreign powers revised their attitude towards China. The idea of territorial partitioning of the country was replaced by an attempt at financial exploitation; military friction between the Western powers and Japan was in this way to be minimized. Financial control was to be exercised by an international banking consortium (1920). It was necessary for political reasons that this committee should be joined by Japan. After her Twenty-one Demands, however, Japan was hated throughout China. During the World War she had given loans to the various governments and rebels, and in this way had secured one privilege after another. Consequently China declined the banking consortium. She tried to secure capital from her own resources; but in the existing political situation and the acute economic depression internal loans had no success.

324

In an agreement between the United States and Japan in 1917, the United States, in consequence of the war, had had to give their assent to special rights for Japan in China. After the war the international conference at Washington (November 1921–February 1922) tried to set narrower limits to Japan's influence over China, and also to redetermine the relative strength in the Pacific of the four great powers (America, Britain, France, Japan). After the failure of the banking plan this was the last means of preventing military conflicts between the powers in the Far East. This brought some relief to China, as Japan had to yield for the time to the pressure of the Western powers.

The years that followed until 1927 were those of the complete collapse of the political power of the Peking government—years of entire dissolution. In the south Sun Yat-sen had been elected generalissimo in 1921. In 1924 he was re-elected with a mandate for a campaign against the north. In January 1924 there also met in Canton the first general congress of the Kuomintang ('People's Party') with 165 delegates. The party, which had, in 1929, 653,000 members, or roughly 0·15 per cent of the population, is the continuation of the Komintang ('Revolutionary Party') founded by Sun Yat-sen, which as a middle-class party had worked for the removal of the dynasty. The new Kuomintang was more socialistic, as is shown by its admission of Communists and the stress laid upon land reform.

The Communist party had been created under Soviet stimulation in July 1921. Twelve men came together in a school in the protected French concession of Shanghai. The party had two wings. The Peking wing was created by Li Ta-chao. Li was a librarian at the Peking University who in 1918 created a society which in 1919 openly became a 'Marxist Research Society'. He was soon joined by a student, Ch'ü Chiu-pai, and a young library assistant, Mao Tsê-tung. Ch'en Tu-hsiu founded in 1920 in Shanghai the Marxist Study Society. Ch'en held on to the Western Communist programme which said that a revolution would have to be led by the urban proletariat—though, at that time, only Shanghai had some 'proletariat'. Li, who was executed in 1927, found that without the peasants, the majority of all Chinese, no revolution could succeed, an idea which his pupil Mao later accepted. At the time of the constitution of the KMT, Sun Yat-sen was advised by two Russian Communists, Borodin, adviser for party organization, and Galen, adviser for military affairs. Both men together with some forty other Russians, reorganized the southern armies which now came under the leadership of Chiang Kai-shek (1866–1975). Due to the presence of the Russian advisers, the KMT accepted co-operation with Communists, a co-operation which was resented by both sides and did not last long.

At the end of 1924 Sun Yat-sen with some of his followers went to Peking, to discuss the possibility of a reunion between north and south on the basis of the programme of the People's Party. There, however, he died on 12 March 1925 before any definite results had been attained; there was no prospect of achieving anything by the negotiations, and the south broke them off. But the death of Sun Yat-sen had been followed after a time by tension within the party between its right and left wings. Sun's successor, Hu Han-min (died 1936), represented the more rightist wing, but Chiang soon emerged as the true leader, based upon his new, modernized army which he trained in the military academy at Whampoa, near Canton.

The People's Party of the south and its governments, at that time fairly radical in politics, were disliked by the foreign powers; only Japan supported them for a time, owing to the anti-British feeling of the south Chinese and in order to further her purpose of maintaining disunion in China. The first serious collision with the outer world came on 30 May 1925, when British soldiers shot at a crowd demonstrating in Shanghai. This produced a widespread boycott of British goods in Canton and in British Hong Kong, inflicting a great loss on British trade with China and bringing considerable advantages in consequence to Japanese trade and shipping: from the time of this boycott began the Japanese grip on Chinese coastwise shipping.

The second party congress was held in Canton in 1926. Chiang Kai-shek already played a prominent part. The People's Party, under Chiang Kai-shek and with the support of the Communists, began the great campaign against the north (27 July 1926). At first it had good success: the various provincial governors and generals and the Peking government were played off against each other, and in a short time one leader after another was defeated. The Yangtze was reached, and in 1926 the southern government moved to Hankow. All over the southern provinces there now came a genuine rising of the masses of the people, mainly the result of Communist propaganda and of the government's promise to give land to the peasants, to set limits to the big estates, and to bring order into the taxation. In spite of its Communist element, at the beginning of 1927 the southern government was essentially one of the middle class and the peasantry, with a socialistic tendency.

3 Second period of the Republic: Nationalist China

With the continued success of the northern campaign, and with Chiang Kai-shek's southern army at the gates of Shanghai (21 March 1927), a decision had to be taken. Should the left wing be allowed to gain the upper hand, and the great capitalists of Shanghai be expropriated as it was proposed to expropriate the gentry? Or should the right wing prevail, an alliance be concluded with the capitalists, and limits be set to the expropriation of landed estates? Chiang Kai-shek, through his marriage with Sun Yat-sen's wife's sister, had become allied with one of the greatest banking families. In the days of the siege of Shanghai, Chiang, together with his closest colleagues (with the exception of Hu Han-min and Wang Ching-wei, a leftist leader who will be mentioned later), decided on the second alternative. Shanghai came into his hands without a struggle, and the capital of the Shanghai financiers, and soon foreign capital as well, was placed at his disposal, so that he was able to pay his troops and finance his administration. At the same time the Russian advisers were dismissed or executed. The Communists in Shanghai, on Russian advice, did not rise against Chiang, when he approached the city, which made his victory much easier. On the other hand, Chiang's army did not trust the Communists, so that the dismissal of the advisers and actions against Communists within the army was also possible.

The decision arrived at by Chiang Kai-shek and his friends did not remain unopposed, and he parted from the 'left group' (1927) which formed a rival government in Hankow, while Chiang Kai-shek made Nanking the seat of his government (April 1927). The choice of Nanking as the new capital pleased both the industrialists and the agrarians: the great bulk of China's young industries lay in the Yangtze region, and that region was still the principal one for agricultural produce; the landowners of the region were also in a better position with the great market of the capital in their neighbourhood. In this situation, Chiang could not alienate the landowners by a radical land reform. He needed the industrialists and the capital which was safely in Shanghai. Now, the Nanking government succeeded in carrying its dealings with the northern generals to a point at which they were largely out-manoeuvred and became ready for some sort of collaboration (1928). There were now five supreme commanders—Chiang Kai-shek, Fêng Yü-hsiang (the 'Christian general'), Yen Hsi-shan, the governor of Shansi, Chang Tso-lin (killed 4 June 1928, and replaced by his son Chang Hsüeh-liang), and the Muslim Li Chung-yen. Naturally this was not a permanent solution; not only did Chiang Kai-shek's four rivals try to free themselves from his ever-growing influence and to gain full power themselves, but various groups under military leadership rose again and again, even in the home of the Republic, Canton itself. These struggles, which were carried on more by means of diplomacy and bribery than at arms, lasted until 1936. Chiang Kai-shek, as by far the most skilful player in this game, and at the same time the man who had the support of the foreign governments and of the financiers of Shanghai, gained the victory. However, there still was no peace. Since 1934, the

Communists emerged a real danger in central China, and from 1928 on, Japan's attitude towards a unified China became more and more threatening. We will discuss the developments in central China later and first focus on the foreign interventions.

In April 1928, Japan landed troops in Shanghai, apparently in order to weaken Chiang's power, and to strengthen Chang Tso-lin who tended towards Japan. When, however, after fighting in Shantung (3 May 1928), Chang seemed to dissociate himself from Japan, he was killed in a railway accident which was, according to rumours, arranged by Japanese. During the next three years, the Japanese who had, as we have heard, control over the South Manchurian Railway and adjacent territory, tried to strengthen their position in Manchuria, and finally, in 1931, took it over. At that time, Nanking was helpless, since Manchuria was only loosely associated with Nanking, and its governor, Chang Hsüeh-liang, had tried to remain independent of it. Thus Manchuria was lost almost without a blow. On the other hand, the fighting with Japan that broke out soon afterwards in Shanghai brought credit to the young Nanking army, though owing to its numerical inferiority it was unsuccessful. China protested to the League of Nations against its loss of Manchuria. The League sent a commission (the Lytton Commission), which condemned Japan's action, but nothing further happened, and China indignantly broke away from her association with the Western powers (1932–1933). In view of the tense European situation (the beginning of the Hitler era in Germany, and the Italian plans of expansion), the Western powers did not want to fight Japan on China's behalf, and without that nothing more could be done. They pursued, indeed, a policy of playing off Japan against China, in order to keep those two powers occupied with each other, and so to divert Japan from Indo-China and the Pacific.

China had thus to be prepared for being involved one day in a great war with Japan. Chiang Kai-shek wanted to postpone war as long as possible. He wanted time to establish his power more thoroughly within the country, and to strengthen his army. In regard to external relations, the great powers would have to decide their attitude sooner or later. America could not be expected to take up a clear attitude: she was for peace and commerce, and she made greater profits out of her relations with Japan than with China; she sent supplies to both (until 1941). On the other hand, Britain and France were more and more turning away from Japan, and Russo-Japanese relations were at all times tense. Japan tried to emerge from her isolation by joining the 'axis powers', Germany and Italy (1936); but it was still doubtful whether the Western powers would proceed with Russia, and therefore against Japan, or with the Axis, and therefore in alliance with Japan.

Japan for her part considered that if she was to raise the standard of living of her large population and to remain a world power, she must bring into being her 'Greater East Asia', so as to have the needed raw material resources and export markets in the event of a collision with the Western powers; in addition to this, she needed a security girdle as extensive as possible in case of a conflict with Russia. In any case, 'Greater East Asia' must be secured before the European conflict should break out.

4 The Sino-Japanese war (1937–1945)

Accordingly, from 1933 onward Japan followed up her conquest of Manchuria. A military, rather unsuccessful intervention by the Japanese army in January 1932 was followed on 9 March by the declaration of Manchukuo, as an independent state under Japanese control. The Japanese made the last Manchu emperor, P'uYi, 'emperor' of this puppet state in March 1934, probably hoping that the glory of an emperor could attract Chinese to desert Chiang. Already in 1933, Japanese armies had moved close to Peking, and the result of this was that the whole area north of Peking became a demilitarized zone, under a semi-dependent government. Japan also began to exercise pressure on inner Mongolia and succeeded, by means of an immense system of smuggling, currency manipulation, and propaganda, in bringing a number of Mongol princes over to her side

The signal for the outbreak of war was an 'incident' by the Marco Polo Bridge, south of Peking (7 July 1937). The Japanese government profited by a quite unimportant incident, undoubtedly provoked by the Japanese, in order to extend its dominion a little further. China still hesitated; there were negotiations. Japan brought up reinforcements and put forward demands which China could not be expected to be ready to fulfil. Japan then occupied Peking and Tientsin and wide regions between them and south of them. The Chinese soldiers stationed there withdrew almost without striking a blow, but formed up again and began to offer resistance. In order to facilitate the planned occupation of north China, including the province of Shantung, Japan decided on a diversionary campaign against Shanghai. The Nanking government sent its best troops to the new front, and held it for nearly three months against superior forces; but meanwhile the Japanese steadily advanced in north China. On 9 November Nanking fell into their hands, followed by a mass massacre. By the beginning of January 1938, the province of Shantung had also been conquered.

Chiang Kai-shek and his government fled to Ch'ung-ch'ing (Chungking), the most important commercial and financial centre of the interior after Hankow, which was soon threatened by the Japanese fleet. By means of a number of landings the Japanese soon conquered the whole coast of China, so cutting off all supplies to the country; against hard fighting in some places they pushed inland along the railways and conquered the whole eastern half of China, the richest and most highly developed part of the country. Chiang Kai-shek had the support only of the agriculturally rich province of Szechwan, and of the scarcely developed provinces surrounding it. Here there was as yet no industry. Everything in the way of machinery and supplies that could be transported from the hastily dismantled factories was carried westward. Students and professors went west with all the contents of their universities, and worked on in small villages under very difficult conditions—one of the most memorable achievements of this war for China. But all this was by no means enough for waging a defensive war against Japan. Even the famous Burma Road could not save China.

By 1940–1941 Japan had attained her war aim: China was no longer a dangerous adversary. She was still able to engage in small-scale fighting, but could no longer secure any decisive result. Puppet governments were set up in Peking, Canton, and Nanking, and the Japanese waited for these governments gradually to induce supporters of Chiang Kai-shek to come over to their side. Most was expected of Wang Ching-wei, who headed the new Nanking government. He was one of the oldest followers of Sun Yat-sen, and was regarded as a democrat with leftist tendencies. In 1925, after Sun Yat-sen's death, he had been for a time the head of the Nanking government, and for a short time in 1930 he had led a government in Peking that was opposed to Chiang Kai-shek. Beyond any question Wang still had many followers, including some in the highest circles at Chungking, men of eastern China who considered that collaboration with Japan, especially in the economic field, offered good prospects. Japan paid lip service to this policy: there was talk of sister peoples, which could help each other and supply each other's needs. There was propaganda for a new 'Greater East Asian' philosophy, *Wang-tao*, in accordance with which all the peoples of the East could live together in peace under a thinly disguised dictatorship. What actually happened was that everywhere Japanese capitalists established themselves in the former Chinese industrial plants, bought up land and securities, and exploited the country for the conduct of their war.

After the great initial successes of Hitlerite Germany in 1939–1941, Japan became convinced that the time had come for a decisive blow against the positions of the Western European powers and the United States in the Far East. Lightning blows were struck at Hong Kong and Singapore, at French Indo-China, and at the Netherlands

East Indies. The American navy seemed to have been eliminated by the attack on Pearl Harbor (December 1941), and one group of islands after another fell into the hands of the Japanese. Japan was at the gates of India and Australia. Russia was carrying on a desperate defensive struggle against the Axis, and there was no reason to expect any intervention from her in the Far East. Greater East Asia seemed assured against every danger.

The situation of Chiang Kai-shek's Chungking government seemed hopeless. Even the Burma Road was cut, and supplies could only be sent by air; there was shortage of everything. With immense energy small industries were begun all over western China, often organized as co-operatives; roads and railways were built—but with such resources would it ever be possible to throw the Japanese into the sea? Everything depended on holding out until a new page was turned in Europe. Infinitely slow seemed the progress of the first gleams of hope—the steady front in Burma, the reconquest of the first groups of islands; the first bomb attacks on Japan itself. Even in May 1945, with the war ended in Europe, there seemed no sign of its ending in the Far East. Then came the atom bomb, bringing the collapse of Japan; the Japanese armies receded from China, and suddenly China was free, mistress once more in her own country as she had not been for decades.

Before we have to come back to events of the War, it might be useful to throw a look at the non-political developments of this period between 1927 and 1945.

Until the time of the 'Manchurian incident' (1931), the Nanking government steadily grew in strength. It gained the confidence of the Western powers, who proposed to make use of it in opposition to Japan's policy of expansion in the Pacific sphere. On the strength of this favourable situation in its foreign relations, the Nanking government succeeded in getting rid of one after another of the capitulations. Above all, the administration of the 'Maritime Customs', that is to say of the collection of duties on imports and exports, was brought under the control of the Chinese government (1927): until then it had been under foreign control. Now that China could act with more freedom in the matter of tariffs, the government had greater financial resources, and through this and other measures it became financially more independent of the provinces. It succeeded in building up a small but modern army, loyal to the government and superior to the still existing provincial armies. This army gained its military experience in skirmishes with the Communists and the remaining generals and later fought gallantly the Japanese invaders. The financial situation, however, deteriorated quickly during the War, because large parts of China were not under the control of

331

the Nationalists, and the cost of the War climbed higher and higher.

On the literary front, many writers began to publish in the 1920s and 1930s who now are recognized as representatives of China's modern literature. Some of these writers were leftists, after a start along liberal lines, such as Lu Hsün (1881–1936) whose 'Diary of a Madman' and 'True Story of Ah O' have gained general acclaim. Mao Tun's (1898–   ) 'Twilight', a novel about life in Shanghai, is equally well known. On the other side of the liberal writers, we should mention Lao Shê (1898–   ), whose 'Ricksha Boy' found many readers even in the West, Pa Chin (1904–   ), a more romantic writer, and Lin Yü-t'ang. Lin is probably best known in the West for those of his works in which he wanted to show the West what China was and is, and how we should look at China. But Lin has also ventured into other fields, such as the project of a large, modern Chinese–English dictionary, which was recently published, or his translations of Chinese classics and literary masterpieces into English.

CHAPTER TWELVE

Present-day China

(A) THE GROWTH OF COMMUNISM

In order to understand today's China, we have to go back in time to report events which were cut short or left out of our earlier discussion in order to present them in the context of this chapter.

Although Socialism and Communism had been known in China long ago, this line of development of Western philosophy had interested Chinese intellectuals much less than liberalistic, democratic Western ideas. It was widely believed that Communism had no real prospects for China, as a dictatorship of the proletariat seemed to be relevant only in a highly industrialized and not in an agrarian society. Thus, in its beginning the 'Movement of May Fourth' of 1919 had Western ideological traits but was not communistic. This changed with the success of Communism in Russia and with the theoretical writings of Lenin. Here it was shown that Communist theories could be applied to a country similar to China in its level of development.

Thus, we may regard the 'Movement of May Fourth' as the critical point at which the division began which finally ended with the establishment of the People's Democratic Republic. We mentioned already that the Communist Party (CCP) was founded in Shanghai in 1921. As in all Communist movements, the leaders were members of the middle class and well-educated men who deserted their own class, made themselves fighters for the proletariat, and worked for the destruction of the other classes. The leaders who emerged in the first years after the founding of the CCP came in part from the Peking group, and from the Shanghai group, but also from Chinese who had been students in Europe: Chou En-lai and Li Li-san learned about Communism when they were students in Paris; Chu Tê in Germany.

When Chiang Kai-shek entered Shanghai and tried to exterminate the Communists, some leaders could escape to the interior. Mao Tsê-tung moved close to his home and took a position which is described well in the classic novel 'Shui-hu-chuan' which he knows so well and quotes often: he settled on the Chin-kang shan, a mountain area

333

between the provinces of Hunan and Kiangsi, i.e. an area in which the powers of either province were weak and where by clever moves any danger from one province could be avoided by moving into the adjacent one. Like the heroes of the novel. Mao collected men around him and made his first, unsuccessful rising in September 1927. Chu Tê and Ch'en Yi attempted a coup in Kiangsi, which also failed. The rest of the party assembled in Hankow, replaced Ch'en Tu-hsiu by the pro-Soviet Li Li-san (until 1930).

The years following the débâcle of 1927 are years of political 'soul-searching' in China as well as in the Soviet Union. The main question was: why was the attempt to establish a socialist regime in China a failure? The tactic which Chinese Communists, operating together with Chiang's armies, and supported by the Russian advisers, adopted had been developed on the basis of classical Marxist-Leninist doctrine, which assumed that a socialist revolution has to be carried by the urban proletariat. This was the tactic which had brought Communism in the Soviet Union to success, it was said. The other side, the ideological leader of which was K. A. Wittfogel, was of the opinion that the failure had been caused by the application of a strategy which was based upon European economy and society; however, China's society was an 'Oriental society', based not on rain agriculture, but on irrigation agriculture. In such a society, revolutionary tactics and strategy have to be different, and the fight has to be carried out by a group other than the urban proletariat, at least in the beginnings. Within the Chinese CCP, Ch'en Tu-hsiu was the representative of the 'classical' theory; it would be wrong to call Li Ta-chao the representative of the theory of 'Oriental Society', because these ideas became known in China more widely only after 1927, but Li was of the opinion that for a revolution the collaboration of the peasantry was essential.

In the Hankow talks, the Soviet side got the victory and Mao's opinions were rejected. Yet Mao gained some successes in Kiangsi and P'eng Te-huei emerged as one of his best military leaders. Thus, a small Communist republic was proclaimed on 7 November 1931 in Kiangsi.

Chiang tried to consolidate China, as we have seen, and naturally, the elimination of Communism was one of his aims. Between 1930 and 1934, he launched five campaigns against Kiangsi. At first, he was not successful, partly because the 19th Route Army which had fought the Japanese in Shanghai (1932) upon its return to Fukien turned itself into a 'People's Revolutionary Army' and took up contacts with the Kiangsi regime. From 1934 on, however, the new strategy which Chiang, with his German advisers developed, forced the Communists to give up Kiangsi. On 15 October 1934, they decided to move. It is said that over 100,000 men started out their 'legendary' Long March through all of west China, often through areas inhabited by minorities, always on the flight before Chiang's and other armies, troubled by dissensions within the Party. It is during these years that Chou En-lai emerged as the military and political leader. In December 1936 the marchers settled in Yen-an (Yenan) in Shensi province; only some 30,000 made it. It is here, in an area which was remote, poor, and not yet under the control of Chiang's forces, Mao Tsê-tung came up as the leader of the CCP. The Party took up some contacts with Chang Hsüeh-liang, the son of Chang Tso-lin, who had control over Manchuria (Chinese term: 'Eastern Three Provinces', later and today 'North East'), who was afraid of Chiang's strength. On 12 December 1936 his men succeeded in kidnapping Chiang and in extorting some concessions from him. This was the time when a Japanese attack was in the air, and a proposal for a 'United Front' was made.

When the Japanese began their war with the Marco Polo Bridge 'incident' (7 July 1937), Chiang's forces were fully engaged, while Mao's CCP began to organize guerrilla units behind the Japanese forces and to strengthen his own territory which was not yet threatened by the Japanese. In the summer of 1938. Mao again committed himself to collaborate with the KMT, however, the situation remained the same: neither party trusted the other. Thus, many troops which could well have been used to fight the Japanese had to be kept in waiting.

As everywhere, the attack by Hitler upon the Soviet Union produced great changes in Communist parties. Suddenly, the Soviet Union, which now had to assume that Japan would attack Russia once it had sufficiently subdued China, shifted from an interest in the Communist Yenan group to the Chiang government and supplied it with material assistance, as the United States did. The United States, deeply involved in the fight against the Japanese and against Hitler, had an interest in persuading the KMT to co-operate with the CCP and made, through General Stillwell, attempts to form a United Front. Like so many democratic countries, they did not understand that for Communists a 'United Front' of any kind is a strategic movement at the time of relative weakness, to lull the enemy in security, to get its men inside the other side and to move into important or key positions so that later they can take the organization over; reading of Lenin would have given insight into this strategy.

When the War in Europe was over and the defeat of Japan expected, the Soviet Union entered the war against Japan (8 August 1945) by occupying Manchuria, Jehol and Chahar. They looted Manchuria, the most industrialized part of China, and were also able to supply the CCP with the weapons they took from the Japanese. This enabled the CCP to move into Manchuria and parts of north China, by accepting Japanese surrender, until Chiang by agreement with the Japanese succeeded in having the Japanese surrender to his armies.

The Soviet Union offered Chiang (14 August 1945) a treaty of friendship, but under the condition that they were given special privileges in Manchuria, similar to those imperial Russia had had until 1904. However, they promised to evacuate Manchuria as quickly as possible.

In the face of the Yenan government's moves, Chiang had to ask the United States to assist him in airlifting troops from west China to the east. Thus, his troops could occupy the great cities of the east when the Japanese surrendered. On 2 August 1945, Chiang made an attempt to reach an agreement with Mao in Chungking, but any agreement was now impossible. When the Soviets retreated from Manchuria, they let the CCP move in and prevented as much as they could the move of Chiang's troops into Manchuria. Again, General Marshall's mission in late 1945 attempted to induce the KMT and the CCP to form an integrated National Army, to convoke a political conference and a cease-fire. Fighting began soon, as negotiations were, as predictable, unsuccessful. In the first phase Chiang's troops were successful; in March 1947, they even entered Yenan. Finally, Chiang could move large numbers of his troops into Manchuria, where he was opposed by Lin Piao. Lin, well equipped with Japanese arms, defeated him, so that Chiang lost his best troops. With this defeat, general demoralization began. September 1948, Ch'en Yi occupied Shantung. Then came in late 1948 the decisive battle near Hsü-chou, which ended with defections from Chiang and therefore, a defeat. On 23 January 1949 Peking fell; on 24 April Nanking; and by 1 October 1949, all of China's mainland was in the hand of the Communist regime.

The end of Chiang on the mainland was not simply a military defeat. When the Nationalist government took over the administration, it lacked popular support in the areas liberated from the Japanese. Farmers who had been given land by the Communists, or who had been promised it, were afraid that their former landlords, whether they had remained to collaborate with the Japanese or had fled to west China, would regain control of the land. Workers hoped for new social legislation and rights. Businessmen and industrialists were faced with destroyed factories, worn-out or antiquated equipment, and an unchecked inflation which induced them to shift their accounts into foreign banks or to favour short-term gains rather than long-term investments. As in all countries which have suffered from a long war and an occupation, the youth believed that the old regime had been to blame, and saw promise and hope on the political left. And, finally, the Nationalist soldiers, most of whom had been separated for years from their homes and families, were not willing to fight other Chinese in the civil war now well under way; they wanted to go home and start a new life. The Communists, however, were now well organized militarily and were constantly strengthened by deserters from the KMT.

(B) NATIONALIST CHINA IN TAIWAN

The Nationalist government retreated to Taiwan (Formosa) with those soldiers who remained loyal. This island was returned to China after the defeat of Japan, though final disposition of its status had not yet been determined.

Taiwan's original population had been made up of more than a dozen tribes who are probably distant relatives of tribes in the Philippines. These are Taiwan's 'aborigines', altogether about 200,000 people in 1948.

At about the time of the Sung dynasty, Chinese began to establish outposts on the island; these developed into regular agricultural settlements towards the end of the Ming dynasty. Immigration increased in the eighteenth and especially the nineteenth centuries. These Chinese immigrants and their descendants are the 'Taiwanese', Taiwan's main population of about 8 million people as of 1948.

Taiwan was at first a part of the province of Fukien, whence most of its Chinese settlers came; there was also a minority of Hakka, Chinese from Kuangtung province. When Taiwan was ceded to Japan, it was still a colonial area with much lawlessness and disorder, but with a number of flourishing towns and a growing population. The Japanese, who sent administrators but no settlers, established law and order, protected the aborigines from land-hungry Chinese settlers, and attempted to abolish headhunting by the aborigines and to raise the cultural level in general. They built a road and railway system and strongly stressed the production of sugar cane and rice. During the Second World War, the island suffered from air attacks and from the inability of the Japanese to protect its industries.

After Chiang Kai-shek and the remainder of his army and of his government officials arrived in Taiwan, they were followed by others fleeing from the Communist regime, mainly from Chekiang, Kiangsu, and the northern provinces of the mainland. Eventually, there were on Taiwan about two million of these 'mainlanders', as they have sometimes been called.

When the Chinese Nationalists took over from the Japanese, they

337

assumed all the leading positions in the government. The Taiwanese nationals who had opposed the Japanese were disappointed; for their part, the Nationalists felt threatened because of their minority position. The next years, up to 1952, were characterized by bloody confrontations. Tensions persisted for many years, but have lessened since about 1960.

The new government of Taiwan resembled China's pre-war government under Chiang Kai-shek. First, to maintain his claim to the legitimate rule of all of China, Chiang retained—and controlled through his party, the KMT—his former government organization, complete with cabinet ministers, administrators, and elected parliament, under the name 'Central Government of China'. Second, the actual government of Taiwan, which he considered one of China's provinces, was organized as the 'Provincial Government of Taiwan', whose leading positions were at first in the hands of KMT mainlanders. There have since been regular elections for the provincial assembly, for local government councils and boards, and for various provincial and local positions. Third, the military forces were organized under the leadership and command of mainlanders. And finally, the education system was set up in accordance with former mainland practices by mainland specialists. However, evolutionary changes soon occurred.

The government's aim was to make Mandarin Chinese the language of all Chinese in Taiwan, as it had been in mainland China long before the War, and to weaken the Taiwanese dialects. Soon almost every child had a minimum of six years of education (increased in 1968 to nine years), with Mandarin Chinese as the medium of instruction. In the beginning few Taiwanese qualified as teachers because, under Japanese rule, Japanese had been the medium of instruction. As the children of Taiwanese and mainland families went to school together, the Taiwanese children quickly learned Mandarin, while most mainland children became familiar with the Taiwan dialect. For the generation in school today, the difference between mainlander and Taiwanese has lost its importance. At the same time, more teachers of Taiwanese origin, but with modern training, have begun to fill first the ranks of elementary, later of high-school, and now even of university, instructors, so that the end of mainland predominance in the educational system is foreseeable.

The country is still ruled by the KMT, but although at first hardly any Taiwanese belonged to the Party, many of the elective jobs and almost all positions in the provincial government are at present in the hands of Taiwanese independents, or KMT members, more of whom are continuously entering the central government as well. Because military service is compulsory, the majority of common

338

soldiers are Taiwanese: as career officers grow older and their sons show little interest in an army career, more Taiwan-Chinese are occupying higher army positions. Foreign policy and major political decisions still lie in the hands of mainland Chinese, but economic power, once monopolized by them, is now held by Taiwan-Chinese.

This shift gained impetus with the end of American economic aid. which had tied local businessmen to American industry and thus worked to the advantage of mainland Chinese, for these had contacts in the United States, whereas the Taiwan-Chinese had contacts only in Japan. After the termination of American economic aid, Taiwanese trade with Japan, the Philippines, and Korea grew in importance and with it the economic strength of Taiwan-Chinese businessmen. After 1964, Taiwan became a strong competitor of Hong Kong and Japan in some export industries, such as electronics and textiles. We can regard Taiwan from 1964 on as occupying the 'take-off' stage, to use Rostow's terminology—a stage of rapid development of new, principally light and consumer, industries. There has been a rapid rise of industrial towns around the major cities, and there are already many factories in the countryside, even in some villages. Electrification is essentially completed, and heavy industries, such as fertilizer and assembly plants and oil refineries, now exist.

This rapid industrialization was accompanied by an unusually fast development of agriculture. A land-reform programme limited land ownership, reduced rents, and redistributed formerly Japanese-owned land. This was the programme that the Nationalist government had attempted unsuccessfully to enforce in liberated China after the Pacific War. It is well known that the abolition of landlordism and the distribution of land to small farmers do not in themselves improve or enlarge production. The Joint Council on Rural Reconstruction, on which American advisers worked with Chinese specialists to devise a system comparable to American agricultural extension services but possessing elements of community development, introduced better seeds, more and better fertilizers, and numerous other innovations which the farmers quickly adopted, with the result that the island became self-supporting, in spite of a steadily growing population (16 million in 1974).

At the same time, the government succeeded in stabilizing the currency and in eliminating corruption, thus re-establishing public confidence and security. Good incomes from farming as well as from industries were invested on the island instead of flowing into foreign banks. In addition, the population had enough surplus money to buy the products of the new domestic industries as these appeared. Thus, the industrialization of Taiwan may be called 'industrialization without tears', without the suffering, that is, of proletarian masses who produce objects which they cannot afford for themselves. Today, even lower middle-class families have television consoles which cost the equivalent of US $300; they own electric fans and radios; they are buying Taiwan-produced refrigerators and air conditioners; and more and more think of buying Taiwan-assembled cars. They encourage their children to finish high school and to attend college if at all possible; competition for admission is very strong in spite of the continuous building of new schools and universities. Education to the level of the B.A. is of good quality, but for some graduate study students are still sent abroad. Taiwan complains about the 'brain drain', as about 93 per cent of its students who go overseas do not return, but it has more than sufficient trained manpower to continue its development, and in any case there would not be enough jobs available if all the students returned.

When Chiang Kai-shek died (5 April 1975), Taiwan had changed from an underdeveloped colony into the country with the second-highest standard of living in Asia. His son Chiang Ching-kuo became leader of the KMT and remained premier, the office he had held in the last years of his father's life. With Chiang died the last of the four great men of the Second World War, and at the same time ended a period of world history. For the first time, a group of small countries which produce an essential raw material, oil, could cause a serious depression among the industrialized countries (1973); for the first time, America lost a war (Vietnam) which it could not win after the decision was made not to invade North Vietnam; public pressure forced a withdrawal (1973). America gave up its role in South-East Asia which caused the breakdown of Vietnam, Cambodia and Laos (1975), and the creation of three new Communist states. This will change the total power relation in the Far East and South-East Asia and initiate a new period. Of all countries which might be affected by these changes, Taiwan is the one which is most united, but also one of the smallest.

(C) PEOPLE'S REPUBLIC OF CHINA (1949–   )

1   *General remarks*

Perhaps a historian should not write about anything that is still ongoing or less than a hundred years old, and leave the field to a political scientist. Writing about a controlled society is even more dangerous. We cannot freely travel and freely speak to the common man. If we can speak to a political leader we know that he says what he wants us to believe; and if a common man talks to us, he, too, would say what he is supposed to say or what he wants us to believe. We can read those books, pamphlets, and papers which the regime lets out, i.e. certainly not all existing publications; we can listen to some radio and television emissions, but they are sent out for specific purposes. History in a controlled socialist society is not a field of scholarship, but a piece of political education, subjected to constant rewriting when political conditions change. Many specialists try to decipher the messages contained in these materials, but the results are never reliable. From this results the fact that those who study a totalitarian regime often are the victims of propaganda. Or, they see and know the truth but do not dare to write it, because it would make it impossible for them to get an entry visa next time. This is aggravated by the credulity and ignorance of many Americans: they hear words like 'democracy' and think of American democracy; they think Chinese react in the same way as we do and interpret what they see as we would interpret information in our countries. Many of the visitors of today's China have seen China during the War, in its worst time, and, compared to that, they are greatly impressed with the changes; but had they travelled in China before 1937, they would have a different impression. Others talk about mainland China without having seen Taiwan: this would give them some possibility of evaluation. Thus, I do not think it is possible for any of us to write an accurate and objective history of the last thirty years of China; all we can do is to try.

Let us first discuss a few general points The quick development of the People's Republic is not astonishing. Both Taiwan and mainland China have developed extremely quickly. The reasons do not seem to lie solely in the form of government, for the preconditions for a 'take-off' existed in China as early as the 1920s, if not earlier. That is, the quick development of China could have started forty years ago but was prevented, primarily for political reasons. One of the main preconditions for quick development is that a large part of the population is inured to hard and repetitive work. The Chinese farmer was accustomed to such work; he put more time and energy into his land than any other farmer. He and his fellows were the industrial workers of the future: reliable, hard-working, tractable, intelligent. To train them was easy, and absenteeism was never a serious problem, as it is in other developing nations. Another pre-condition is the existence of sufficient trained people to manage industry. Forty years ago China had enough such men to start modernization; foreign assistance would have been necessary in some fields, but only briefly.

Another requirement (at least in the period before radio and television) is general literacy. Meaningful statistical data on literacy in China before 1937 are lacking. Some authors remark that before 1800 probably all upper-class sons and most daughters were educated, and that men in the middle and even in the lower classes often had

341

some degree of literacy. In this context 'educated' means that these persons could read classical poetry and essays written in literary Chinese, which was not the language of daily conversation. 'Literacy', however, might mean only that a person could read and write some 600 characters, enough to conduct a business and to read simple stories. Although newspapers today have a stock of about 6,000 characters, only some 600 characters are commonly used, and a farmer or worker can manage well with a knowledge of about 100 characters. Statements to the effect that in 1935 some 70 per cent of all men and 95 per cent of all women were illiterate cannot include all those millions who could read what they had to read in their professions; probably not even those who could read some 600 characters. There are sufficient data to establish that the literacy programme of the KMT had penetrated the countryside and had reached even outlying villages before 1940.

The transportation system in China before the war was not highly developed, but numerous railroads connecting the main industrial centres did exist, and bus and truck services connected small towns with the larger centres. What were missing in the pre-war years were laws to protect the investor, efficient credit facilities, an insurance system supported by law, and a modern tax structure. In addition, the monetary system was inflation-prone. Although sufficient capital probably could have been mobilized within the country, the available resources went into military construction and preparation.

The failure to capitalize on existing means of development before the War resulted from the chronic unrest caused by warlordism, revolutionaries and foreign invaders, which occupied the energies of the Nationalist government from its establishment to its fall. Once a stable government free from internal troubles arose, national development, whether private or socialist, could proceed at a rapid pace.

Thus, the development of Communist China is not a miracle, possible only because of its form of government. What is unusual about Communist China is the fact that it is the only nation possessing a highly developed culture of its own to have jettisoned it in favour of a foreign one. What missionaries had dreamed of for centuries and knew they would never accomplish, Mao Tsê-tung achieved; he imposed an ideology created by Europeans and understandable only in the context of central Europe in the nineteenth century. We speak of 'Maoism' today, and admittedly, in a few points, Maoism differs from Russian Communism as developed by Lenin and Stalin. But the steps which were taken in China to develop the new society are much too similar to those taken in the Soviet Union to enable us to regard Maoism as a completely different system. Confrontations between China and the Soviet Union show again and again that China believes that its form of Communism is the correct one and that China should be the leader of the Communist world, not Russia, which has 'deviated'.

This may change over time. One school of analysts believes that the friction between Soviet Russia and Communist China indicates that China's Communism has become Chinese These men point out that Communist Chinese practices are often direct continuations of earlier Chinese practices, customs, and attitudes. And they predict that this trend will continue, resulting in a form of socialism or communism distinctly different from that found in any other country. Another school, however, believes that Communism precedes 'Sinism', and that the regime will slowly eliminate traits which once were typical of China and replace them with institutions developed out of Marxist thinking. In any case, for the present, we believe that in present-day China many traits are preserved which were developed in the old time but can be easily integrated in so far as they contribute to the stability of the system. Later we will discuss some of these traits.

2 Political development

After the foundation of the 'People's Democratic Republic' on 1 October 1948, a government was created which was modelled after the Soviet system. It did, in the beginning, recognize the existence of other, small, parties which never had any say in politics, and recognized four classes of people: workers, farmers, small and big capitalists, all under the 'democratic dictatorship under the leadership of the CCP', as Russia had in the early years. Executive, legislative, and judicial powers were in the hands of the Central People's Government Council, which had 71 members and Mao Tsê-tung as chairman. The actual work was done by a State Administrative Council, somewhat comparable to a cabinet, responsible to the Government Council or to Mao. The country remained subdivided into provinces and districts. A new constitution was proclaimed in 1954 which created an All China People's Congress which laid down the general line of politics. Below this was a Party Congress, inside which there was the Central Committee, appointed for a five-year period. The actual political decisions were made here. The constitution established two classes of citizens: men and women over 18 were full citizens; people regarded as landlords and as counter-revolutionaries were excluded. The CCP, which in 1949 already had, it is said, 4·5 million members, was the élite of the citizens. It should be mentioned that to this day even the descendants of the outcasts are outcasts and do not have the same rights as other citizens.

In order to solidify the regime, the great land reform was begun in

343

June 1950, following in its steps very closely the Russian model. The first step was the elimination of those people who were declared to be landlords. If we think of landlords as men who own hundreds of acres and had these worked by tenants, we are mistaken. In comparison to Western farms, even 'big' landlords had little land. The CCP had already, during their Kiangsi period, difficulties in establishing whom they wanted to define as landlord and as 'rich peasant'. The land situation was so complicated that in one case almost half of those persons who first had been regarded as landlords or rich peasants had to be reclassified as ordinary farmers, because some farmers owned some land and rented more land; some used hired labour only in some seasons and not permanently, some had become relatively rich recently through their own labour, and so on. In general, according to estimates, four-fifths of the land was operated by owners in north China, three-fifths in central China, and one-half in south China. Landlordism was not as extensive as had been asserted. The cost of this land reform and the elimination of other enemies in human lives is not known. However, the most conservative estimates mention two million.

As in Soviet Russia, this land reform, which gave land to those who work on the land, was followed by taking the land away from them in the drive towards collectivization, at first the establishment of co-operative farms (1953–1957). The last step then began in 1958 with the establishment of communes and collectivization. Some 26,000 communes were created, each one made up of thirty former co-operatives; each commune with a population of about 25,000 people. The communes were units which included farmers as well as rural industries. It may well be that the original aim of this was to enable each such unit to continue to offer resistance in case of a war and a breakdown of central organization. The famous creation of the 'backyard furnaces', which produced high-cost iron of low quality, seems to have had a similar purpose: to teach citizens how to produce iron for armaments in case of war and enemy occupation, when only guerrilla resistance would be possible. In the same year, aggressive actions against offshore, Nationalist-held islands increased. China may have believed that war with the United States was imminent. To this day, no analysis of the communes is possible. Several scholars assert that the lowest units within the communes are the old, village- and kinship-based groupings, now centrally directed and obliged to follow the plans laid out by the government. Even so, the 'Great Leap Forward' of 1958 brought on a serious crisis, as the Russian advisers had predicted. The years 1961–1964 provided a needed respite from the failures of the Great Leap. Farmers regained limited rights to income from private efforts, and improved farm techniques such as better seed and the use of fertilizer began to produce results. China can now feed her population in normal years.

It should be mentioned that at the same time that rural communes were established, urban communes, too, began to appear. These, however, seem to be not much more than a further attempt at control of what formerly were block and city quarter organizations.

Soon after the establishment of the Peking regime, a pact of friendship and alliance with the Soviet Union was concluded (February 1950), and Soviet specialists and civil and military products poured into China to speed its development. China had to pay for this assistance as well as for the loans it received from Russia, but the application of Russian experience, often involving the duplication of whole factories, was successful. In a few years, China developed its heavy industry, just as Russia had done. It should not be forgotten that Manchuria, as well as other parts of China, had had modern heavy industries long before 1949. The Manchurian factories ceased production because, when the Russians invaded Manchuria at the end of the war, they removed the machinery to Russia.

Similar to Soviet Russia, China developed its five-year plans; the first one only actually began in 1955 and stressed, after the initial work of reconstruction of the damages of revolution, the building of heavy industries. This work was connected with a change of higher instruction. The government stressed training in the technical fields, in order to have sufficient competent technicians; similar to the practice in the Soviet Union, the young men and women were given a relatively brief and specialized training which meant that the manpower needs could quickly be eliminated. There has been great progress since 1955 and China astonished the world when it exploded its first atomic bomb (1966), built with the help of American-trained scientists. We know now that the building of atomic bombs is relatively easy. However, it requires a great investment in means and trained manpower, and the question has been raised whether the propaganda value of the bomb was so great. Other projects had to be postponed which probably were more urgent. Was it done to impress the world with the war potential of a young socialist country? Or was it in response to Soviet threats?

Today, problems in industry still continue. China has discovered oil, mainly in the innermost provinces of Sinkiang, Shensi and Kansu; only the oil from Hei-lung-kiang in northern Manchuria is relatively close to big industrial centres. Offshore oil drilling is planned and the outlook is good, but China has already begun to export oil, to get needed foreign exchange as well as to impress the oil-hungry nations of Asia; yet in spite of stepped-up production, China's production is not yet sufficient (estimated 70 million tons for 1974) to supply its petro-chemical industries, especially fertilizer factories, its agriculture (machines), and its transportation problems (cars, trucks). There are still problems with iron and steel, after the dismal failure of the 'backyard furnaces' which produced at a high cost in fuel and labour very low-quality iron. By 1974, it is estimated, China produced about 400 million tons of coal, an increase of 6 per cent over 1973, but the needs are growing much quicker than the supply.

As in the Soviet Union, the stress upon heavy and military industry together with the farm policy produced strains which found their expression in the so-called 'Hundred Flowers' movement (1956). This event has been explained in different ways. One explanation is that Mao Tsê-tung envisaged that China would rapidly industrialize, and that for this aim China would need all of China's human resources, and that he, therefore, wanted to liberalize the restrictions posed upon non-Party members, so that different opinions could be brought forth and that, at the same time a bureaucratization of the Party could be prevented by the influx of new blood. The other explanation which, to me, seems to be more likely, is that by permitting discussions, the Party could find out who was not in agreement with the Party line and could eliminate such persons. In any case, the outpour of opposition seems to have frightened the leaders and the 'Hundred Flowers' were stopped. The years of 1956–1957 are also the years in which in the Soviet Union the de-Stalinization began and unrest in Eastern Europe developed. Mao and his group remained closer to the Stalin line and the personality cult which was criticized so strongly in the Soviet Union became even stronger in China in the form of a cult of Mao. On the other side, the first measures against bureaucratization of the Party which are to be seen in these years and which grew strongly in the 1960s indicate a position much closer to Trotsky than to Stalin. Perhaps the most important element behind all these 'ideological' speculations is what has always been behind political changes in China: the fight for ultimate power between two cliques.

Certainly, not only the pro-Stalin attitude of Mao, but also the 'deviation' of China in creating communes at a state which, according to the Soviets was premature, and the attempt of China to build up military and atomic strength, was a strain upon the Soviet–Chinese relations. The Russian advisers left and Russian assistance stopped around 1960. From then on, tensions between the two Communist countries began to increase. The Chinese believed that the Soviet Union might try to destroy China's developing atomic industry. There were also numerous clashes of a military character along the northernmost frontier: the Chinese claimed some islands in the frontier river which the Soviets regarded as theirs. And finally, there was a considerable flight of the Turkish (Uighur) inhabitants of Sinkiang into the adjacent areas of the Soviet Union where they had tribal relatives and where the standard of living was a good deal higher, combined with an influx of cadres trained in the Soviet Union which were supposed to incite Sinkiang to rebellion. All these developments which became more and more large-scale in the 1960s forced both countries to keep large armies, fully war-equipped, along the almost endless frontiers (most important in 1969).

This, combined with bad harvests which the government attributed to inclement climate but which seem to have mainly been caused by the commune policy, made the years between 1957 and 1962 years of crisis. The first big outward sign of crisis was the Lu-shan Conference in August 1959 of the Central Committee. Defence Minister P'eng Tê-huai, just returned from Moscow, spoke up against Mao's policies. Mao and his faction were strong enough to swing the situation by dismissing P'eng and replacing him by Lin Piao as new Minister of Defence. The more radical party of Mao decided in favour of 'red' against 'expert' in the discussion whether a Communist should in the first place be a good Communist and only in the second place a good specialist, or whether at this stage of development the most important problem was to mobilize and utilize as many experts as were available and look at ideology only in the second place. Only in the field of agriculture, the Conference made some concessions in the form of temporary relaxations, so that farm production would increase again. The other result of the Conference was that Liu Shao-ch'i emerged as Chairman of the Republic. He had been Vice-Chairman since 1949. Mao did not lose prestige, on the contrary, the cult of Mao was stepped up, but he did lose direct political control. It seems that the developments of 1965 and 1966 are an attempt of Mao to regain full political control.

Major political changes are often in totalitarian societies initiated by outwardly unimportant events. Wu Han, deputy major of Peking, had written in 1961 a play about an official in the Ming time who, supposedly, fought for the right of the common man and opposed the emperor, Hai Jui (1514–1587). This was nothing extraordinary, as Hai Jui was the hero of at least eight classical plays. In late 1965 he published 'Hai Jui dismissed from Office', and this work was strongly attacked by Yao Wen-yüan in Shanghai at the same time that Mao was staying in Shanghai. The 'theoretical question' with Hai Jui was whether a member of the former upper class, the élite, could under any circumstances be regarded as a 'good' man, or, in application to the present, whether an outcast member of Communist society could under any circumstances turn out to be a friend of the people. The criticism was regarded as an attack of the Mao clique against Liu Shao-ch'i to whose clique Wu Han belonged. This event became the forerunner of the so-called 'Great Socialist Cultural Revolution' which officially began on 18 April 1966. The term 'cultural' should not be taken in the common meaning. The first action was that all universities and most schools were closed and remained closed for more than a year, at a time when China needed trained manpower most urgently and quickly. During the course of the 'Cultural Revolution' numerous cultural treasures of China were destroyed. The term seems to mean that a different group of people would come into power and change China's political culture. In fact, Mao mobilized China's youngsters against Liu Shao-ch'i and his clique. The so-called 'Red Guards' rose up everywhere in the country, a sign that the movement was well prepared, and masses stormed offices of Party officials as well as houses of officials and other persons disliked by the regime; they attacked professors and dishonoured Party leaders. Masses of them streamed through the country up to Peking. Much more so than during the 'Hundred Flowers' movement, the young radicals went overboard, alienated even the friends of Mao and threatened to become a danger to all the over-aged party leaders, so that, finally, the army had to interfere and to restore some order again. The worst was over in the autumn of 1967, when a few schools began to open again, but fights, especially in provincial centres, continued until late 1968. By that time, Mao was in full control and had gained a decisive victory over Liu Shao-ch'i who from then on disappeared from the political horizon. With him went Chu Tê, the man who had created the Red Army (People's Liberation Army). Lin Piao became the First Vice-Chairman of the Central Committee, that is, he became the second most powerful man in the regime and the designated successor of Mao. With him rose Ch'en Po-ta and Chiang Ch'ing, Mao's third wife. Chiang had been an actress and film heroine before the Revolution and after a life full of changes had felt forced to leave Shanghai and the film world and joined the Communist camp in Yenan, where she became the lover and later the wife of Mao. The Party Congress of April 1969 made these changes official; it was the first congress since 1958.

In 1971, Lin Piao (born 1908) died in a plane crash in Outer Mongolia. The background of this event is still not quite clear. It is said that Lin tried to assume the highest power and control with the help of parts of the military in the areas of Central China; that his plans, however, were betrayed by his own daughter, so that the revolt could not start, Lin had to escape, and was either shot down or crashed on his flight to Soviet Russia. As Lin had been designated to become Mao's successor, major reshuffling was necessary. This was finalized in the People's Congress of 13–17 January 1974, in Peking. The result was a kind of compromise. Chou En-lai (age 76), of weak health, was elected as Premier. Chou is certainly the most able living politician of China and regarded as a moderate man, though close to Mao. His friend Yeh Chien-ying, Party Vice-Chairman, became Minister of Defence.

But the new government included Teng Hsiao-p'ing (age 70), who became the most senior of the Vice-Premiers. Teng was one of the most prominent victims of the 'Cultural Revolution'. Chu Tê (age 88) was also rehabilitated and became Chairman of the National People's Congress. On the other, radical, side, only Chang Chun-chiao of the Shanghai group, became a Vice-Premier, and Mrs Chiang Ch'ing is now only a member of the Central Politburo. Mao received new powers and, most important, the control of the army. Many regard this cabinet as a 'patchwork' to prepare for the moment when Mao as well as Chou En-lai will disappear (Chou died 1975). It is impossible to predict what then will come. Certainly, the tension between the radical (Mao) and the 'revisionist' (former Liu Shao-ch'i) cliques is still as strong as before.

3 *Foreign relations*

In contrast to the opinion of many western scholars who, like Western politicians, have swallowed the Confucian myth of the peaceful Chinese, China has a long military tradition. The most popular folk novels and theatre plays glorify war and military heroes. The backbone of the People's Republic is the army which consists of a central military élite and five other élite groups which emerged as the 'People's Liberation Army' during the revolutionary wars. Within these army groups exist tensions and rivalries. More important, however, are the tensions which are created by the existence of two power groups within each army: the unit commanders and the political commissars—a copy of the Soviet system of the early revolutionary period. The third partner in these rivalries are the civil party administrators whose role is similar to the civil administrators in imperial China. These tensions played a decisive role in the liquidation of the 'Red Guards' during the 'Cultural Revolution' and in the 1975 Party Congress.

However, thus far, the army has been successful not only in the preservation of the regime in the country, but also in conflicts on and beyond its frontiers.

China's military strength was first demonstrated in the Korean War when Chinese armies entered Korea (October 1950). Their successes contributed to the prestige of the Peking regime at home and abroad, but while South Korea retained its independence, North Korea came under Soviet and not under Chinese influence.

349

In the same year, China invaded and conquered Tibet. Tibet, under Manchu rule until 1911, had achieved a certain degree of independence thereafter: no republican Chinese regime ever ruled Lhasa. The military conquest of Tibet is regarded by many as an act of Chinese imperialism, or colonialism, as the Tibetans certainly did not want to belong to China or be forced to change their traditional form of government. Having regarded themselves as subjects of the Manchu but not of the Chinese, they rose against the Communist rulers in March 1959, but without success.

Chinese control of Tibet, involving the construction of numerous roads, airstrips, and military installations, as well as differences concerning the international border, led in 1959 to conflicts with India. It seems today that the military conflicts, in which India was the loser, were started by India rather than by China. It is true that the borders between China and India were uncertain and looked different depending on whether one used Manchu or Indian maps. But looking at the recent consolidation of India's grip over Kashmir, its domination of Sikkim, its action in Bengal, we see a clear pattern into which the conflict with China fits well.

China's other border problem was with Burma. Early in 1960 the two countries concluded a border agreement which ended disputes dating from British colonial times. But as Burma's policy oscillates between different forms of Socialism, at the moment apparently China seems to be more interested in influencing the outcome of these internal tensions.

Very early in its existence Communist China assumed control of Sinkiang, Chinese Central Asia, a large area originally inhabited by Turkish and Mongolian tribes and states, later conquered by the Manchu, and then integrated into China in the early nineteenth century. The Communist action was to be expected, although after the Revolution of 1911 Chinese rule over this area had been erratic, and during the Pacific War some Soviet-inspired hope had existed that Sinkiang might gain independence, following the example of Outer Mongolia, another country which had been attached to the Manchu until 1911 and which, with Russian assistance, had gained its independence from China. Sinkiang is of great importance to Communist China as the site of large sources of oil and of atomic industries and testing grounds. The government has stimulated and often forced Chinese immigration into Sinkiang, so that the erstwhile Turkish and Mongolian majorities have become minorities, envious of their ethnic brothers in Soviet Central Asia who now enjoy a much higher standard of living and more freedom.

Inner Mongolia had a brief dream of independence under Japanese protection during the War. But the majority of the population was

Chinese, and already before the Pacific War, the country had been divided into three Chinese provinces, of which the Chinese Communists gained control without delay.

In general, when the Chinese Communists discuss territorial claims, they appear to seek the restoration of borders that China claimed in the eighteenth century. Thus, they make occasional remarks about the Ili area and parts of Eastern Siberia, which the Manchu either lost to the Russians or claimed as their territory. North Vietnam is probably aware that Imperial China exercised political rights over Tongking and Annam (the present-day North and part of South Vietnam). China does not seem to have participated in the Vietnam War with its army, but has supplied the North Vietnamese with military equipment and advisers, as did the Soviet Union. The whole Asian situation should be seen in world perspective. Clearly, the Korean War was the beginning of the decline of American power; in fact, it was a war which the United States lost. The war in Vietnam, Cambodia and Laos was also lost: the United States succeeded in their 'Peace with honour' only in being allowed to bring their troops out of the area, while the war continued uninterrupted. Thus, while the United States faded out of Asia like Great Britain had during and right after the Second World War, the real question is now whether China or the Soviet Union should take over. The countries of South-East Asia are in a difficult situation: China is a close neighbour, and it is always the best policy to be allied with the power which is in the rear of the neighbour, which in this case would be the Soviet Union. But will they be able to sustain their factual independence with the assistance of distant Russia? Or will they end up with a nominal independence?

China's South Asia policy was, to this date, not fully successful. One result of the war with India was that China came closer to Pakistan, but on the other side, India turned towards the Soviet Union, which supported it in the interference in East Pakistan and the creation of Bangladesh. China's attempts to gain influence in the Near East, too, were not successful, and the African situation is still too unclear: both countries try to gain influence but none has yet shown much success.

These tensions between the two powers show up clearly in the international party meetings. Here, the split with the Russian Communist Party deepened strongly during the meetings of 1966 and 1969. The Russian party could neither reintegrate the Chinese party into the old framework, nor prevent China's influence over Communist parties in countries thus far aligned with the Soviet Union who became interested in China. The Chinese Party regards itself as the true successor of the Communist Party after the decease of

Stalin, and brands the Soviet Party as being revisionist. China has also indicated that it is the true representative of the Third World, or in other words, of the non-white world, and pointed to the fact that the Soviet Union and its Eastern European colonies are, after all, heirs of white supremacy.

President Nixon's first China visit (1972) was an attempt to exploit the tensions and achieve a solution of some kind in South-East Asia, and, finally, to open trade with Communist China. For China, this visit was one of its easiest and greatest successes. Nixon's visit was seen as a 'tributary mission' of the old time: a foreign power sends its ruler to show its submission to China, by bringing rare animals and other 'products of the country' to China and asking for favours. No other measure could have strengthened the prestige of China inside the country more than this one. The visit could have taken place at a neutral location, or the conference in Warsaw which had been held for many years could have been stepped up or been transferred to a neutral place if the main aim had been to increase contacts and trade. Thus far, the trade relations are unimportant and depend fully on the political aims of China which can step them up or stop them at will. The United States also had to indicate its readiness to sell out Taiwan, a process which is now under way, in order to get trade promises. China finally could use the 'friendship' with the United States to exercise some pressure upon the Soviet Union. There cannot be any doubt, however, that China still regards the United States as a main enemy, and that the United States will not at all succeed in playing the Soviets against China and vice versa: in the ultimate case, both countries would go together against the common enemy.

A further result of the Nixon visit was the acceptance of China into the United Nations and the rejection of, what would seem natural, the recognition of Taiwan as a member of the United Nations, though with a status different from its former one. China has always openly declared that it does not agree with the principles of the United Nations, but can now use this platform to propagate its ideas and aims.

Another line of Chinese foreign policy is similar to policies of Fascist Italy and Nazi Germany: the attempt to make use of ethnic minorities as a political tool. The events in Indonesia which ended with a complete failure and the death of a great number of Indonesian Chinese, and the attempts to influence Chinese-Americans, which have thus far not been successful either, are examples. Many overseas Chinese who have been invited to visit China have not returned with enthusiasm for the new China, but have kept quiet in order not to endanger their relatives inside China and so as not to make a second visit to their families impossible. Like other countries under a dictatorial regime, China does not allow its citizens to leave the country; exceptions are made only in special cases, mainly with old people who are unable to work productively. As the only way by which ethnic Chinese can secretly leave the country is Hong Kong, and as Hong Kong, already overcrowded, is not happy to receive more people, while China tries to prevent illegal emigration, the number of emigrants is a kind of thermometer of the internal situation. The high point of illegal emigration was in 1962 (165,000 persons). After 1962, the numbers decreased, to increase again steadily from 1967 on. The estimated number in 1974 was 70,000. We have no data on the number of inhabitants of Sinkiang leaving for the Soviet Union.

4 Social developments

Chinese leaders realize that an improved level of living is difficult to attain while the birth rate remains high. They have hesitated to adopt a family-planning policy, which would fly in the face of Marxist doctrine, although for a short period family planning was openly recommended. Their most efficient method of limiting the birth rate has been to recommend postponement of marriage. Birth control pills are available, and to women who have already two children, sterilization is mentioned in case of a third child. We have, however, no statistical data on average age at marriage, extent of use of family-planning devices and number of actual sterilizations. It is said that the average life expectancy, supposedly 53 years in 1949, has gone up to over 70 years. In Taiwan during the War and under Japanese rule, life expectancy for men was 41, for women 45·7 years (1950); it is now 65·5 for men and 71 for women (end of 1974); the Taiwanese data seem quite reliable. The total population of China has been variously estimated between 600 and 800 million. The 1953 census was, as research could show, based on some sample census results and an extrapolation of earlier, also unreliable census data from the pre-revolutionary time.

China has also claimed to have eradicated infectious diseases; thus, no cases of syphilis were reported in 1974. Not knowing to what degree all these data may be true, it seems that the Chinese government has made attempts on the one hand to limit great population increases and on the other hand to increase general health by mainly preventive methods. In the field of medicine there were indeed only few 'Western' doctors available, i.e. doctors with a training in Western medicine. There were, however, many 'Chinese' doctors in the country, i.e. persons with a more or less formal training in the classical Chinese medical techniques. Before the Revolution, there was a considerable tension between the two groups. The new regime employed both types on an equal level, requiring the Western doctors to learn the basics of Chinese medicine, and vice versa. This had the result that there were more doctors at hand; that the competition among both kinds disappeared, and that in the time period in which a Chinese chemical industry was not yet able to supply sufficient Western drugs, Chinese herb medicines could be used. In order to educate a greater number of doctors, the general medical training was reduced to three years. In addition large numbers of so-called 'barefoot doctors' were trained in very short training periods. These men and women correspond roughly to our nurse's helpers; they can treat the most common and not too serious illnesses and are supposed to transfer the patients to the fully trained doctors in complex cases. This is probably the most realistic policy if the aim of the government is to create very quickly a medical organization which can combat efficiently infectious diseases and thus create socialized medical care. Acupuncture, which existed in China for more than two thousand years but was more or less given up when Western medical knowledge came to China, has been taken up again and some amazing successes have been reported, though the cases which were in the press could not be regarded as scientifically supervised so as to exclude suggestion or even the use of additional medicines. Yet much research has been stimulated all over the world.

China had a developed educational system before the Revolution, as indicated above. The level of universities was remarkably high. The War interrupted this development. The new regime tried to build up higher education with, as far as possible, students only from the lower classes, excluding descendants of the old upper class from higher education. Great stress was laid upon the ideological indoctrination of students. With the Cultural Revolution all universities were closed. The new system which is now accepted has shortened college training to three years only. Only such men and women are allowed to study who have been working in factories or rural communes and are recommended by the local party leaders as politically reliable. This, naturally, brings a special type of student to the colleges, often persons who have little ability and no great interest in acquiring scientific and scholarly training. We read about a movement to eliminate all examinations and to stress only political worth. In general, the universities have taken the function they have in the Soviet Union: they are training schools for teachers and the professors have to give the students standardized information. There are no research scholars as in Western universities. What we would regard as graduate work goes on in academies in which a few selected students work under the direct guidance of recognized scholars and political educators as in the Soviet Union. There is no knowledge yet of whether this system can produce the great number of highly specialized scientists which a developing country needs. Moreover, the students who have finished college are normally sent back to the rural and often outlying parts of China, supposedly to bring their knowledge to the farmers and workers and, in co-operation with them, to develop the countryside. We have numerous reports that the students resent this very much, and there is no doubt that they will have hardly any opportunity to increase their knowledge and keep abreast of new progress in their fields.

One field of social change which has been praised very much by the People's Republic is the 'liberation' of women. In fact, the marriage law of April 1950 was one of the few new laws which were introduced. As in the Soviet Union, much of the legal procedure is still based on hearings before groups of reliable citizens, of arbitration or mediation in the absence of law codes. Now, Nationalist China earlier created a modern and liberal marriage law; moreover, women were never the slaves that they have sometimes been painted. In many parts of China, long before the Pacific War, women worked in the fields with their husbands. Elsewhere they worked in secondary agricultural industries (weaving, preparation of food conserves, home industries, and even textile factories) and provided supplementary income for their families. All that 'liberation' in 1950 really meant was that women had to work a full day as their husbands did, and had, in addition, to do housework and care for their children much as before. The new marriage law did, indeed, make both partners equal; it also made it easier for men to divorce their wives, political incompatibility becoming a ground for divorce.

The ideological justification for a new marriage law was the desirability of destroying the traditional Chinese family and its economic basis because a close family, and all the more an extended family or a clan, could obviously serve as a centre of resistance. Land collectivization and the nationalization of business destroyed the economic basis of families. The 'liberation' of women brought them out of the house and made it possible for the government to exploit dissension between husband and wife, thereby increasing its control over the family. Finally, the new education system, which indoctrinated all children from nursery to the end of college, separated children from parents, thus undermining parental control and enabling the state to intimidate parents by encouraging their children to denounce their 'deviations'. Sporadic efforts to dissolve the family completely by separating women from men in communes—recalling an attempt made almost a century earlier by the T'ai P'ing—were unsuccessful.

The central problem facing China or any nation that modernizes and industrializes in the twentieth century can be simply stated.

Nineteenth-century industry needed large masses of workers which only the rural areas could supply; and, with the development of farming methods, the countryside could afford to send its youth to the cities. Twentieth-century industry, on the other hand, needs technicians and highly qualified personnel, often with college degrees, but few unskilled workers. China has traditionally employed human labour and did not make use of inventions which could have freed human labour, as we saw above. Now, it needs modern industries very urgently and quickly, especially in order to preserve its military preparedness and to produce the fertilizers that are necessary to raise the production of food per acre, so that it can safely feed its population. As the new industries need relatively few people and as cities already are crowded, the government attempts to prevent a further influx into the cities and to keep people in the countryside. Not only students, but many others have been removed from cities and forced to settle in villages. As every citizen is registered and needs food coupons (grain, cloth and cooking oil are still rationed), it is difficult to circumvent such orders. But if more and more people have to be kept in farming occupations, it will be very difficult to raise the general standard of living, especially as the farmers know that life in the cities is more interesting and offers a higher standard of living. The Soviet Union is faced with a similar problem, but at least it has much land which is practically empty and at least parts of it still can be taken under cultivation. This is not the case in China; within its present territory, there is very little empty land, and even little under-used land. The foreign press has often given the fantastically low prices of goods such as bicycles, motorcycles or watches, but compared to the average urban worker's income, to buy a bicycle means the expense of three months' salary; a motorcycle costs eight months' salary, and a watch, two months'.

Another related problem is that China can hardly afford to build a network of highways that eat up much productive land, and to tear down large parts of the cities to make room for broad streets. This means that China will have to develop a system of transportation different from that of Western countries, even if it can produce enough oil.

Finally, a word about the minorities in China. The government has recognized 54 ethnic groups as minorities and has given them a status very similar to that given to minorities in the Soviet Union. Some of the minorities are millions strong, such as the Tibetans; others are small tribal units. There has been some effort to bring the small units —with all their own dialects or languages—together into more or less artificial larger units, but the general line of policy is the same as in the Soviet Union. Children in elementary schools receive lectures in their own languages, but the textbooks are in Chinese, and higher education is fully in Chinese. Large numbers of settlers as well as 'instructors' have been sent into the minority areas, and when we hear that these areas have a large increase in population, larger than the purely Chinese areas, it means that the Chinese population is quickly increasing so that soon in most of these minority areas, the native population will numerically be a minority, while at the time of the creation of the 'autonomous' areas, they were still the majority in these areas. Under the guidance of Party workers, the old élite in these areas has been eliminated, as among the Chinese, and in the Minority Institute in Peking new, reliable Party cadres are trained. The Institute, in addition, prepares some dictionaries of the native languages, collects some local legends, local music and dances in order to keep up the appearance in conformity with Lenin's slogan 'Nationalist in form, socialist in content'.

5 Cultural developments

According to Marxian doctrine, culture and art are 'superstructures' and have to be shaped in accordance to the economic structure. This created a number of problems which we cannot expect to see solved within a decade or two. After the establishment of the People's Republic of China and during the period of strong Russian influence, experiments with 'socialist realism' in literature and art were made. This trend was given up when the friendship broke up, but the new literature is stylistically not basically different from the old socialist realism. The new literature wants to show the 'typical', not the exceptional or individual. The hero has to be the Communist hero of the time of the Long March, the Japanese War, the War against the KMT, or the Korean War. He and his followers are always heroic, fight happily to death, do acts of unheard-of heroism, protect equally heroic women and always come from the 'people'. Love and sex do not play a role in their lives. Their enemies are always ugly, mean, and even if they are courageous, they are in the end always defeated. If the hero fights until his own death, he dies for the glory of the Party, not for his own glory. In some cases, he ends his life with his own hands, when no other way is seen, but he never surrenders. He willingly sacrifices his wife and even his son for the Party and its victory. He is often shown in a heroic landscape, mountain cliffs are all over, and they have to be climbed: the hero struggles against and defeats nature. In some novels, minorities play a role; they always co-operate with the Chinese Communist Party against their own traditional leaders who co-operate with the bad old Chinese leaders.

Thus, novels do not, with few exceptions, depict heroes of history.

The past is always dark and black, while the future looms bright. All this means that the new literature is repetitive and limited, yet we have to keep in mind that with the exception of the early years of this century, literature was always regarded as a tool of education. Thus, the new literature wants to show models which the population should admire and imitate. An interesting point here is the stress upon the fight against nature at a time when the world turns more and more towards an ecological view. Pre-modern China was very ecology-conscious, expressed in the stress laid upon geomancy: man should try to fit himself into nature, should adjust to and not destroy nature. China here adheres more to Western Marxism which praised the power of man to make nature his servant. Similarly to the expression of this attitude in literature, we observe in photographs and paintings the proud chimneys of factories, pouring their pollution into nature, in contrast to classical Chinese art which showed only the vapours of virginal nature in which man is a small, insignificant element.

Art and poetry were, in pre-modern China, two upper-class activities. We can hardly name one painting which shows ordinary men or women doing ordinary work. When farmers, fishermen, or woodcutters are depicted, they seem to be leisurely working, while often a scholar looks benignly at their activities. The new regime, in agreement with Marxist doctrine, stimulated the ordinary man to paint, and wanted to have paintings which show people hard at work, producing something that is of social or simply practical use. Thus, we find the new paintings are more like posters, realistic, didactic; and if these paintings show some traces of old Chinese painting traditions, they seem to be almost as outlandish as if they were painted by a Western poster-designer who tries to paint in the 'Chinese style'. In contrast to the traditional paintings, they want to be clear, easy to understand, in harmony with socialist thought; I must confess that I never found a satisfactory way to explain the paintings of Sung, Ming and Ch'ing as expressions of a gentry ideology, though certainly, the more one studied their every single detail, the more one was impressed by the hidden meanings and allusions. For the educated viewer this was still the case with most of the works of China's most famous modern and modernistic painter, Ch'i Pai-shih, and the honours given him by the new regime seem to be given mainly because he was one of the few modern painters who was known and loved by foreign art lovers.

It is equally difficult to detect an ideology in Chinese poems: they, too, are technical masterpieces, following numerous complex rules of construction, and are full of allusions and quotations, rather than vehicles for the expression of very personal emotions. Recently, Tu

Fu, the T'ang poet, received praise because he describes in many poems the sufferings of the common man in the time of unrest and revolt in which the poet lived and under which he, personally, also suffered. Yet, no person without a full classical education can understand his poems and their hidden meanings. The new regime took two approaches towards the poem. First, they stimulated the common man to make poems; many thousands of such 'worker-poems' have been published and praised. This was done in order to give the ordinary man the belief that the making of poems is something he, too, can do, and not only the members of the old upper class. The other approach was to collect and to publish folk songs and folk poems, especially those in which the exploitation of the farmer by the landlord is described. These songs and poems were presented as models of real poetry. Folklorists have difficulties in deciding whether such 'poems of protest' were real folk poems or how many of them were; because many of the poems made by living workers and farmers were also published as 'folk poems', because these persons were 'folk'.

The strong interest in folklore—which also has its parallels in the Soviet Union—decreased from about 1960 on; after all, most existing and loved folk songs were simply love songs, romantic and not heroic, and, therefore, not educational and not in harmony with the new spirit. The same is true with folk tales and more so with fairy tales. And in most of the great number of jokes and jests, the scoundrel and the butt of the joke is not the landlord or the monk, but the stupid daughter-in-law or her equally stupid husband. We pointed out already that China's classical opera is also an art form which resists transformation into a revolutionary art. Attempts to collect and then to perform folk operas, which existed in all parts of China, were not satisfactory. Thus, we now see ballets or musicals in which some American traits, but many Russian traditions are obvious. Gone are the elegant sword dances of the warriors and the fleeting, flowing steps of the heroines, replaced by Russian interpretations of old Viennese traditions. The few operas which the new regime recognizes, like 'The East is Red', which was also made into a film, emulate the same virtues that the new novels show; some are made on the basis of novels. Pure dance performances of 'Chinese folk dances' bring dances of minorities, a fact which is not always clearly stated.

Thus, in the field of art there are problems which derive from an attempt to translate abstract Marxian art theory into practical life. Soviet Russia had made similar attempts, and after more than fifty years an 'underground art' begins to emerge which tries to liberate itself from stifling control. It can be expected that in the long run the same development will appear in China.

Finally, the field of religion has to be mentioned. Naturally, a socialist regime has to regard religion as superstition and as a super-structure resulting from an earlier economic system. Thus, most Taoist and Buddhist temples as well as Christian churches have been closed or destroyed; monks and nuns have been returned to 'productive life'. Foreign visitors are shown some temples and some monks or nuns; to judge from pictures and films, the temples were reorganized and filled with figures which normally do not belong together in one temple or on one altar. Monks and nuns are usually old and unable to work; some of them who have been interviewed inside or outside China were clearly rather uneducated in their field.

Instead of religious processions, temple fairs, and other religious events, political processions, demonstrations, and celebrations have been performed, in a conscious attempt to change the mind of the citizen.

When saying all this, we should not forget that religion as well as theatre, play, and literature were always in imperial China controlled and censored by the emperor's officials: they were stimulated only when the regime believed that some educational or political aim could be achieved by permitting them. Thus, the ideology has changed, and techniques of control have been improved, but the general attitude is very similar.

6 Concluding observations

We have in the preceding sections always attempted to show to what degree modern Communist China is following the line of old Chinese tradition, i.e. to what degree it still is 'China'; but we also tried to indicate to what degree it is 'Western' in the sense that the official doctrine, Maoism, is a child of German and Russian parents. Our observations can best be summarized by a look at the present 'Anti-Confucius, anti-Lin Piao' campaign (1974–1975). Confucius is the symbol of Chinese social and cultural values of the old time. With his name the basic values of Chinese society are connected. All these values are class-based values; only one of them can easily be accepted by the present regime. For Confucius, the family was the unit of society; and the family was hierarchically ordered. Some family members had more power and more rights than others. The present government attempts to replace the family by the Party. Though nominally egalitarian, the Party, too, is hierarchically organized. But the main difference between family and Party is that the family is tied together by bonds of blood and emotion, bonds which, ideally can never be untied. The Party is tied together by political activity, and the bonds do not remain the same under all conditions. Many members have been thrown out of the Party or lost their status in the Party.

The second Confucian value is loyalty to the 'son of heaven'—to the emperor who, in theory at least, represented heaven and the order of Nature. This value has been transferred to loyalty to the Party and its leader, because to transfer it to the nation could possibly give impetus to the rise of nationalism; nationalism is undesirable for an organization which claims to represent all the oppressed in the world.

The only Confucian value which could easily be accepted and used is the belief in education and the role of the leader as educator.

Confucius is also a symbol of 'civil culture', a man who never did make war or advocated war. More symptomatic than the fight against Confucius is the praise for Shih Huang-ti, the all-time symbol of war against the independent states of the late Chou time, and the dictator who burned the books of morality and killed their makers, the educated. It sounds incongruous that Lin Piao, the military man, is put together with Confucius; but if we see Shih Huang-ti on the other side, it may mean that Lin is identified with a 'revisionist' soft line, and that Mao wants to promote the strong line of permanent revolution.

The future development of the People's Republic still cannot be guessed. We see developments, see a certain raising of the standard of living, but cannot foresee how the internal situation will look even in a few years from today. Similarly, we cannot predict the future of the Republic of China on Taiwan. Its economic development is amazing, but its fate does not lie in the hands of these 16 million people.

Notes and References

The following notes and references are intended to help the interested reader. They draw his attention to some more specialized literature in English, and occasionally in French and German. They also indicate for the more advanced reader the sources for some of the interpretations of historical events. As such sources are most often written in Chinese or Japanese and, therefore, inaccessible to most readers, only brief hints and not full bibliographical data are given. The specialists know the names and can easily find details in the standard bibliographies. The general reader will profit most from the bibliography on Chinese history published each year in the 'Journal of Asian Studies'. These Notes do not mention the original Chinese sources which are the factual basis of this book.

Chapter 1
Section 2
The best analysis of the results of archaeology in China is Chang Kwang-chih, 'The Archaeology of Ancient China', revised edition, New Haven, 1968.

Section 3
This discussion is mainly based upon my 'Kultur und Siedlung der Rand-völker Chinas', Leiden, 1942; 'Die Lokalkulturen des Nordens und Westens', Leiden, 1942; 'The Local Cultures of South and East China', Leiden, 1968. See also H. J. Wiens, 'China's March toward the Tropics', Hamden, 1954.

Sections 4, 5 and 6
I have made use of Chang Kwang-chih's book, the main excavation reports, and my own ethno-historical studies (see section 3).

Chapter 2
Section 1
The first and for a long time best study of the Shang period was H. G. Creel's 'The Birth of China', London, 1936. For the archaeological remains, Chang Kwang-chih is now the best analyst. For the dating and the social structure of the Shang I have made use of unpublished studies by

David N. Keightley (his Ph.D. dissertation 'Public Work in Ancient China: a Study of Forced Labour in the Shang and Western Chou', Columbia University, 1969, and several public lectures and personal discussions). Once these studies are completed and published, many of our old concepts will have to be changed.

Section 2

New insights can be expected from the forthcoming studies by D. N. Keightley. I have made use of my own studies ('Local Cultures', see above) and Chang Kwang-chih's book (see above).

Section 3

Again, Keightley's studies will probably necessitate revisions in this section. A general discussion of theories dealing with Chinese feudalism is given by D. Bodde, Feudalism in China in R. Coulborn, 'Feudalism in History', Princeton, 1956. For the origins of the Chinese city and its development, Paul Wheatley, 'The Pivot of the Four Corners', Edinburgh, 1970 is most stimulating because Wheatley has tried to develop a general theory of the ancient city.

Chapter 3
Sections 1 and 2

A different view of the basic character of Chou culture and development, especially concerning the use of horses in warfare and possible Western connections, is presented by Magdalene von Dewall, 'Pferd und Wagen als Kulturgut im frühen China', Hamburg, 1964. My own theory of feudalism is in 'Conquerors and Rulers', second edition, Leiden, 1965.

Section 3

The best discussion on 'shifting cultivation' is found in K. J. Pelzer, 'Population and Land Utilization', New York, 1941.

Sections 4 and 5

Important is H. G. Creel, 'The Origins of Statecraft in China', vol. 1: 'The Western Chou Empire', Chicago, 1970.

Sections 6 and 7

Here, I have made use of my own studies in 'Moral and Social Values of the Chinese', Taipei, 1971. These should be compared with studies like those of D. J. Munro, 'The Concept of Man in Early China', Stanford, 1969; Noah E. Fehl, 'Rites and Propriety in Literature and Life', Hong Kong, 1971; W. Eichhorn, 'Chinese Civilization', New York, 1969, and others. Discussion of the basic values of the Chinese, from ancient to modern times has given rise to numerous, often stimulating studies. I may refer here to Lily Abegg, 'Mind of Asia', New York, 1952 as one fairly extreme study, and to Li Yih-yüan (ed.), 'Symposium on the Character of the Chinese', Taipei, 1972, which takes a different approach. The stimulating book by Wolfgang Bauer, 'China und die Hoffnung auf Glück', Munich, 1971, studies diachronically the Chinese ideas about the good life. There is as yet, in my opinion, no satisfactory study on Lao Tzŭ and Chuang Tzŭ.

Chapter 4
Sections 1 and 2

The book by J. Prusek, 'Chinese Statelets and the Northern Barbarians in the Period 1400–300 B.C.', New York, 1971, is very helpful, though I do not agree with Prusek in many questions. For many special questions of settlement and clans G. Haloun's Contributions to the History of Clan Settlement in Ancient China in 'Asia Major', vol. 1, Leipzig, 1924, is still the best study. Perhaps even more important is his short article Die Rekonstruktion der chinesischen Urgeschichte durch die Chinesen in 'Japanisch-deutsche Zeitschrift für Wissenschaft und Technik', no. 3, of 7 July 1925. For all discussions about the development of Chinese science and technology, J. Needham's 'Science and Civilization in China', Cambridge, 1954–? (not yet completed), is indispensable, though a certain caution should be preserved in questions of interpretation. The separate study 'Clerks and Craftsmen in China and the West', Cambridge, 1970, is more important for the later periods of Chinese technology, but contains the same bias as the main work.

In several places in this book, I have referred to the possible influence of climatic changes upon the development of culture. I have relied upon G. Jenkins, A Note on Climatic Cycles and the Rise of Chinggis Khan, 'Central Asiatic Journal', vol. 18, 1974, pp. 217–26. Jenkins is familiar with other recent studies on this subject.

Section 3

There is no satisfactory, modern study of Chinese philosophy of this time. We often still use Fung Yu-lan's, 'History of Chinese Philosophy' (trans. by D. Bodde), Princeton, 1952. Charles A. Moore (ed.), 'The Chinese Mind, Essentials of Chinese Philosophy and Culture', Honolulu, 1967, is not satisfactory. Stimulating is H. G. Creel, 'What is Taoism?', Chicago, 1970.

Chapter 5
Sections 1, 2 and 3

The immediately earlier period is critically studied by J. I. Crump, 'Chan-Kuo Ts'e', Oxford, 1970; his interpretation gives new insight, and his translation of the text is the first one yet. For the Ch'in history, we still have to refer to D. Bodde's 'China's First Unifier', Leiden, 1938, and his 'Statesman, Patriot, and General in Ancient China', New Haven, 1940. From this period on, the impressive 'Geschichte des chinesischen Reiches', Berlin, 1930 (5 vols) by Otto Franke is still usable and for the medieval period still the best one; the earlier sections are now too antiquated. For the study of social changes in the time down to the Ch'in dynasty look into Hsu Cho-yün, 'Ancient China in Transition', Stanford, 1956.

Chapter 6
Section 1

The definition of 'gentry' is based on research which is discussed in my 'Social Mobility in Traditional China', Leiden, 1962. Other scholars use the term in a different sense as those men who have passed the imperial examinations and therefore achieved special status. In my definition, the gentry is a class in the Marxist sense and not in the contemporary American sense; moreover, the basic unit of the gentry is not the individual but his family.

Sections 2 and 4

There is still no modern, satisfactory study of the Hsiung-nu and their relations to the Chinese. W. M. MacGovern, 'The Early Empires of Central Asia', Chapel Hill, 1939, is very much out of date. A general survey of Central Asian societies is given by Lawrence Krader, 'Peoples of Central Asia', The Hague, 1963. Discussions on nomadism and on settlement of nomads can be found in W. Irons and N. Dyson-Hudson (eds), 'Perspectives on Nomadism', International Studies in Sociology and Social Anthropology, vol. 13, 1972, and Rolf Herzog, 'Sesshaftwerden von Nomaden', Köln, 1963. The process of interaction between Central Asian nomadic states and Chinese is studied in my 'Conquerors and Rulers', Leiden, 1965.

Sections 3 and 5

The basic historical texts are translated by H. H. Dubs, 'The History of the Former Han Dynasty', Baltimore, 1938. An extensive study of Han history and society in perhaps as much as 18 volumes is planned; thus far only the first volume is published: Ch'ü T'ung-tsu, 'Han Social Structure', Seattle, 1971. The best study of life in Han time is M. Loewe, 'Everyday Life in Early Imperial China', London, 1968. On Chinese bureaucracy see F. Balazs, 'Chinese Civilization and Bureaucracy', New Haven, 1964. For a theoretical discussion of pre-modern empires see S. N. Eisenstadt, 'The Political Systems of Empires: The Rise and Fall of the Historical Bureaucratic Societies', Glencoe, 1963. The concepts of K. A. Wittfogel, 'Oriental Despotism', New Haven, 1957, differ strongly from my own and those of Eisenstadt.

Sections 6, 7 and 8

H. Bielenstein, 'The Restoration of the Han Dynasty', Stockholm, 1953, is still the most detailed and careful study. An important study of Han China's foreign relations is Ying-shih Yü, 'Trade and Expansion in Han China', Berkeley, 1967.

Section 9

The religious book used by the Yellow Turbans and influential in later times has been studied by W. Eichhorn, in 'Mitteilungen des Instituts für Orientforschung', Berlin, 1954, vol. 2, no. 2, pp. 326 ff.

Section 10

The book of Wang Ch'ung has been translated by Alfred Forke, 'Lun Hêng, Philosophical Essays of Wang Ch'ung', Shanghai and London, 1907, continued in 'Mitteilungen des Seminars für orientalische Sprachen', Supplements 10 and 14 (1906–11). For alchemy see J. R. Ware (trans.),

'Alchemy, Medicine, and Religion in the China of A.D. 320', Cambridge, 1966. For the history of Buddhism in China, E. Zürcher, 'The Buddhist Conquest of China', is the best study. A. F. Wright, 'Buddhism in Chinese History', Stanford, 1959 discusses the general importance of Buddhism for China's culture.

Chapter 7

The political history of this whole period is best described in O. Franke's 'Geschichte des chinesischen Reiches', vol. 2, Berlin, 1936. For the Toba period see my 'Das Toba-Reich Nordchinas', Leiden, 1949. For Chinese–Central Asian relations see O. Lattimore, 'Inner Asian Frontiers of China', New York, 1951. A. C. Soper discusses the secular arts of this period in his 'Textual Evidence for the Secular Arts of China in the Period from Liu Sung through Sui', Ascona, 1967.

Chapter 8
Part A

For the creation of the Sui see A. F. Wright, The Formation of Sui Ideology in J. K. Fairbank (ed.), 'Chinese Thought and Institutions', Chicago, 1957, pp. 71–104. For the foundation of the T'ang see W. Bingham, 'The Founding of the T'ang Dynasty', Baltimore, 1941. On genealogies in general see my 'Social Mobility in Traditional China', Leiden, 1962; Chow Yung-teh, 'Social Mobility in China', New York, 1966, presents a strongly different view. On the principles of name-giving in China see the interesting study by Wolfgang Bauer, 'Der chinesische Personenname', Wiesbaden, 1959.

Part B

For an understanding of T'ang administration the book by D. C. Twitchett, 'Financial Administration under the T'ang Dynasty', New York, 1963, is indispensable. Among the many important works by Lien-sheng Yang, his 'Les Aspects économiques des travaux publics dans la Chine imperiale', Paris, 1964, is of special interest. R. Hartwell's A Cycle of Economic Change in Imperial China: Coal and Iron in North-east China, 750–1350, in 'Journal of the Economic and Social History of the Orient', vol. 10, 1967, pp. 102–59 is the first study marking a new approach to Chinese economic history. For the analysis of the Chinese upper class in this and the preceding period, David G. Johnson has made highly important studies. I have used his Ph.D. dissertation 'The Medieval Chinese Oligarchy', Department of History, University of California, Berkeley, 1970. The publication of a revised form of this thesis can be expected soon. Johnson has revised and refined some of my own studies and those of my Japanese colleagues. While Chinese official historiography has always treated the Empress Wu as a bad ruler, the novel 'Flowers in a Mirror' ('Ching-hua yüan') gives a completely different picture of her, representing the new interpretation of a novelist of the early nineteenth century. Some material for this chapter is found in my 'Moral and Social Values of the Chinese', Taipei, 1971, and in the 'Settlement and Social Change in Asia', Hong Kong, 1967.

Part C

This chapter is mainly based upon my own studies, which will soon (1976) be reprinted in a volume 'China und seine westlichen Nachbarn', Darmstadt.

Chapter 9
Parts A and B

Our evaluation of the Sung period will probably change in the next years, due to a multitude of work under way. Some indication of what is done can be found in the 'Sung Studies Newsletter'. For the Sung and the following periods important is the new theory developed by Mark Elvin, 'The Pattern of the Chinese Past', Stanford, 1974 (see also R. Myers's review in the 'Journal of Asian Studies', vol. 33, February 1974). Elvin has translated also Shiba Yoshinobu's 'Commerce and Society in Sung China', Ann Arbor, 1970, a book which summarizes much of the research done by Japanese specialists. See also Laurence J. C. Ma, 'Commerical Development and Urban Change in Sung China', Ann Arbor, 1971. Ma uses more Chinese publications. For aspects of the political history, a Marxist interpretation by G. Lewin, 'Die ersten 50 Jahre der Song Dynastie', Berlin, 1973, is interesting; for diplomatic history the article by Herbert Franke, Treaties between Sung and Chin in 'Sung Studies', series 1, History, 1970, pp. 55–84, is important.

For the development of science in this period see U. Libbrecht, 'Chinese Mathematics in the 13th Century', MIT East Asian Studies, 1973; further see J. Needham's above-cited great book and Shigeru Nakayama and N. Sivin, 'Chinese Science, Explorations of an Ancient Tradition', MIT Press, Cambridge, 1973.

For administration see Johanna Menzel (ed.), 'The Chinese Civil Service. Career Open to Talent?', Boston, 1963, and B. E. McKnight, 'Village and Bureaucracy in Southern Sung China', Chicago, 1971. For folk poetry, I have used P. Pelliot, 'Airs de Touen-huang' (Mission P. Pelliot, II), Paris, 1972. Social life is excellently described by J. Gernet, 'Daily Life in China on the Eve of Mongol Invasion', Stanford, 1970. A detailed geographical study of the city of Hangchou by I. d'Argencé is, unfortunately, not yet published.

We should mention here some studies on the intimate life of the time, such as G. Schlegel, 'La Prostitution en Chine', Rouen, 1886, still not yet replaceable by a more modern study; R. Des Rotours, 'Courtisanes Chinoises à la fin des T'ang', Paris, 1968, Howard S. Levy, 'Chinese Foot-binding. The History of a Curious Custom', New York, 1966, Cheng Wou-chan, 'Érotologie de la Chine', Paris, 1963, and the classic in this field, R. H. van Gulik, 'Sexual Life in Ancient China', Leiden, 1961.

For the development of Chinese pharmacology and medicine the studies by P. U. Unschuld should be consulted, mainly his 'Pen-ts'ao, 2000 Jahre traditionelle pharmazeutische Literatur Chinas', Munich, 1973.

Chapter 10
Part A

For aspects of the economy during the Mongol period see Herbert Franke, 'Geld und Wirtschaft in China unter der Mongolen-Herrschaft', Leipzig,

1949 and Franz Schurman, 'Economic Structure of the Yüan Dynasty', Cambridge, 1956. The study on the Mongol postal system by Peter Olbricht, 'Das Postwesen in China unter der Mongolenherrschaft', Göttingen, 1954, is still important. P. Pelliot's 'Notes on Marco Polo', Paris, 1963, 2 vols, is a treasury of information concerning the cultural history of the period, and L. Olschki's 'Marco Polo's Asia', Berkeley, 1960, brings Marco Polo into the focus of European and Asian relations. The complex development among the Mongol rulers is shown by John W. Dardess, 'Conquerors and Confucians. Aspects of Political Change in Late Yüan China', New York, 1973.

Part B

For the developments in the field of philosophy in Ming time see W. Th. DeBary, 'Self and Society in Ming Thought', New York, 1970. On law and treatment of law cases in the last centuries of traditional China see D. Bodde and C. Morris, 'Law in Imperial China', Cambridge, 1967. A brief summary of the government structure is given by C. Hucker, 'The Traditional Chinese State in Ming Time,' New York, 1969. On schools and education see T. Grimm, 'Erziehung und Politik im konfuzianischen China der Ming-Zeit', Hamburg, 1960.

For China at the time of the early Christian missionaries see C. J. Gallagher, 'China in the 16th century', New York, 1953. For the last years of the Ming Dynasty I have made use of an unpublished manuscript by Fred Wakeman on the 'Shun Dynasty', and James B. Parsons, 'Peasant Rebellions of the Late Ming Dynasty', Tucson, 1970. A study on the merchants of the Hsin-an area by Harriet Zurndorfer will soon be completed; some of my remarks are influenced by discussions with her. Two books by Ho Ping-ti are of great value for questions of social mobility and of demography: 'The Ladder of Success in Imperial China', New York, 1962, and 'Studies on the Population of China, 1368–1953', Cambridge, 1959.

China's expansion during this time and the maritime policy are discussed by C. P. Fitzgerald, 'The Southern Expansion of the Chinese People', London, 1972, and Bodo Wiethoff, 'Die chinesische Seeverbotspolitik und der private Überseehandel von 1368 bis 1567', Hamburg, 1963.

The most recent study on eunuchs is by Taisuke Mitamura, 'Chinese Eunuchs, the Structure of Intimate Politics', Rutland, 1970. Although strongly biased, the following studies on sexual life and aberrations contain much material for this and later periods: Herbert D. Lamson, 'Social Pathology in China', Shanghai, 1935, and J. J. Matignon, 'La Chine hermétique', Paris, 1936. Michel Beurdeley, 'Chinese Erotic Art', Tokyo, 1969, is a serious study. On folk literature see now W. C. Idema, 'Chinese Vernacular Fiction', Leiden, 1974, and Cornelia Töpelmann's 'Shan-ko von Feng Meng-lung', Wiesbaden, 1973, brings translations of some Ming time folk poems. The study by Andrew Boyd, 'Chinese Architecture and Town Planning, 1500 B.C. to A.D. 1911', London, 1962, is disappointing, as is W. Speiser, 'Baukunst des Ostens. Von der Zeitenwende bis zum 19. Jahrhundert', Essen, 1963.

Part C

On General Chinese world concepts of the time see J. K. Fairbank (ed.), 'The Chinese World Order. Traditional China's Foreign Relations', Cambridge, 1968, and J. R. Levenson, 'Confucian China and its Modern Fate', Berkeley, 1968. A general history of the last century is found in Immanuel C. Y. Hsu, 'The Rise of Modern China', New York, 1970. A new light on the relations between England and China as well as India is given by Dilip K. Basu, 'A Comparative Study of Calcutta and Canton, 1800–1840', unpublished Ph.D. thesis, Berkeley, 1975.

The mechanisms of government are studied by Silas H. L. Wu, 'Communications and Imperial Control in China', Cambridge, 1970, and Th. A. Metzger, 'The Internal Organization of Ch'ing Bureaucracy: Legal, Normative, and Communication Aspects', Cambridge, 1973. On rural organization see K. Ch. Hsiao, 'Rural China: Imperial Control in the 19th Century', Seattle, 1960. On the economic situation of the government officials see Chung-li Chang, 'The Income of the Chinese Gentry', Seattle, 1962. The most important recent studies on the economy which have greatly modified our concepts are W. E. Wilmott (ed.), 'Economic Organization in Chinese Society', Stanford, 1972; Ramon H. Myers, 'The Chinese Peasant Economy: Agricultural Development in Hopei and Shantung 1890–1949', Cambridge, 1970; Evelyn S. Rawski, 'Agricultural Change and the Peasant Economy of South China', Cambridge, 1972; A. Feuerwerker, 'The Chinese Economy, ca. 1870–1911', Ann Arbor, 1969. W. Skinner's Marketing and Social Structure in Rural China, 'Journal of Asian Studies', vol. 24, 1964–5, is an application of theories developed in connection with Europe and will have to be modified, but is still the best available study. On the Chinese city see W. Skinner and M. Elvin, 'The Chinese Cities between the Two Worlds', Stanford, 1974. Still the only study on the settlement forms of villages is the Ph.D. thesis by H. D. Scholz, 'Die Formen der ländlichen Siedlung in China', Bonn, 1949 (unpublished). Two older studies should be mentioned: Heinrich Schmidthenner, 'Chinesische Landschaften und Städte', Stuttgart, 1925 and F. Gutkind, 'Revolution of Environment', London, 1946. Schmidthenner, but especially Gutkind, brings (on pp. 190–333) the ecological viewpoint which now has become so popular.

For the T'ai P'ing Rebellion, the best recent book is by Jen Yu-wen, 'The Taiping Revolutionary Movement', New Haven, 1973. On recent attitudes towards non-Chinese minorities see Henry G. Schwarz, 'Chinese Policies Towards Minorities', Western Washington State College, 1971.

For the position of women in pre-modern China see F. Ayscough, 'Chinese Women, Yesterday and Today', Boston, 1937; this should be compared with the two modern studies by Margery Wolf, 'Women and the Family in Rural Taiwan', Stanford, 1972, and Marilyn B. Young (ed.), 'Women in China', Ann Arbor, 1973. Ms Young's book treats mainly the situation in the People's Republic.

On Chinese religion, the book by C. K. Yang, 'Religion in Chinese Society', Berkeley, 1962, is too much of an adaptation of Max Weber's ideas to China; the new study by P. C. Baity, 'Religion in a Chinese Town',

369

Taipei, 1975 gives a very new approach, which to some degree is also apparent in Arthur P. Wolf (ed.), 'Religion and Ritual in Chinese Society', Stanford, 1974. For Buddhism see especially Holmes Welch, 'The Practice of Chinese Buddhism, 1900–1950', Cambridge, 1967. Concerning the practice and teachings of modern Taoists see Michael Saso, 'Taoism and the Rite of Cosmic Renewal', Washington State Univ. Press, 1972, and another forthcoming book by Saso.

Among the many socially interesting novels of the nineteenth century, 'Flowers in the Mirror', trans. by Lin Tai-yi, Berkeley, 1965; 'The Scholars' ('Ju-lin wai-shih') by Wu Ching-tzu, Peking, 1957, and the 'Chapters from a Floating Life' by Shen Fu, trans. by Lin Yutang, Boston, 1937, should be mentioned: 'Flowers' because of its modern attitude towards women and its criticism of existing society; 'Scholars' as a biting criticism of corruption, and 'Floating Life' as the best, most intimate and tender description of marital life. Many books on the Chinese opera are now available. For practical use, L. C. Arlington and H. Acton, 'Famous Chinese Plays', Peking, 1937, reprint 1963, is the best. See also A. C. Scott, 'The Classical Theatre of China', London, 1957.

The first study of Chinese psychiatry should perhaps be mentioned here. It is by G. Schaltenbrand, Psychiatrie in Peking, 'Zeitschr. f. d. gesamte Neurologie und Psychiatrie', vol. 137, 1931, no. 1, pp. 169–232; modern research dealing with this field has tended to forget this contribution.

Chapter 11

Out of the enormous mass of publications about China since 1911, only a few studies should be mentioned here, such as F. Wakeman, 'History and Will. Philosophical Perspectives of Mao Tse-tung's Thought', New Haven, 1974, because of his different approach; James P. Harrison, 'The Communists and Chinese Peasant Rebellions. A Study in the Rewriting of Chinese History', New York, 1969. Because of the new opinion concerning the character of peasant rebellions, Chiang Ch'ing (Mrs Mao), 'On the Revolution of the Peking Opera', Peking, 1968, because of the Party line concerning the classical opera and its substitute. G. V. H. Moseley, 'The Consolidation of the South China Frontier', Berkeley, 1973, because of the description of minority policy. M. J. Meijer, 'Marriage Law and Policy in the Chinese People's Republic', Hong Kong, 1971, as the first study of the new 'liberation' of women, and Wu Yüan-li, 'An Economic Survey of Communist China', New York, 1956, as one of many studies on the state of economy.

INDEX

371

THE ROUGH GUIDE TO

Japan

This sixth edition updated by

Sophie Branscombe, Neil Maclean, Sally McLaren, Roger Norum and Martin Zatko

roughguides.com

Contents

Introduction to

Japan

There's no place quite like Japan. The very quintessence of Eastern culture, it has long excited the imagination of the West, with a great many of its joys etched indelibly into the minds of folk who live oceans away. Sushi and sake, anime and manga, samurai, ninja and the bullet train: everyone knows something of this island nation's culture, but there's far more to discover beyond these highly enjoyable stereotypes. Prepare to be pleasantly disorientated.

"Land of contrasts" may be the world's laziest travel cliché, but those who visit Japan find themselves constantly surprised at the easy co-existence between the country's **past and present**. Go shopping for cutting-edge fashions in the neon-soaked Tokyo pleasure grounds of Shinjuku and Shibuya, and it won't be long before you stumble upon a Buddhist temple or Shintō shrine, or perhaps even a clanging *matsuri* ceremony. Head to the **countryside**, and you may well see the oddly pleasing spectacle of a high-speed train reflected in the waters of emerald-green rice paddies.

Seeing the ancient and contemporary waltzing around hand in hand may appear incongruous, but it's important to remember the reasons behind it – few other countries have ever changed so fast in so short a period of time. **Industrialized** at lightning speed in the late nineteenth century, Japan shed its feudal trappings to become the most powerful and outwardly aggressive country in Asia in a matter of decades. After defeat in World War II, the nation transformed itself from atom-bomb victim to **economic giant**, the envy of the world. Having weathered a decade-long recession from the mid-1990s, Japan is now relishing its **"soft power"** status as the world's pre-eminent purveyor of pop culture, with the visual mediums of anime and manga leading the way.

The **"bubble years"** of 1980s Japan are still keeping many Western visitors away: the sky-high prices of those times still evoke fears that visiting Japan will prove hideously expensive. The truth is that it's no more costly to travel around than Western Europe or

ABOVE RICE PADDY, IWATE PREFECTURE **RIGHT** BULLET TRAIN, TOKYO the USA, and in many ways a fair bit cheaper. Hotel rooms can be on the small side but are often reasonably priced, and food is so cheap that many travelers find themselves eating out three times a day. Public transport in Japan's cities is surprisingly good value, while recent price-cutting means that airline tickets now rival the famed bargain rail passes as a means to get to far-flung corners of the country.

In the **cities**, you'll first be struck by the mass of people. These hyperactive metropolises are the places to catch the latest trend, the hippest fashions and must-have gadgets before they hit the rest of the world. It's not all about modernity, however: Tokyo, Kyoto, Osaka and Kanazawa, for example, also provide the best opportunities to view traditional performance arts, such as kabuki and nō plays, as well as a wealth of Japanese visual arts in major museums. **Outside the cities**, there's a vast range of travel options, from the UNESCO World Heritage-listed Shiretoko National Park in Hokkaidō to the balmy subtropical islands of Okinawa.

It's not all perfect, however. The Japanese are experts at focusing on detail (the exquisite wrapping of gifts and the mouthwatering presentation of food are just two examples) but often miss the broader picture. Rampant development and sometimes appalling pollution are difficult to square with a country also renowned for cleanliness and appreciation of nature. Part of the problem is that **natural cataclysms**, such as earthquakes and typhoons, regularly hit Japan, so few people expect things to last for long anyway. And there's no denying the pernicious impact of **mass tourism**, with ranks of gift shops, ugly hotels and crowds often ruining potentially idyllic spots.

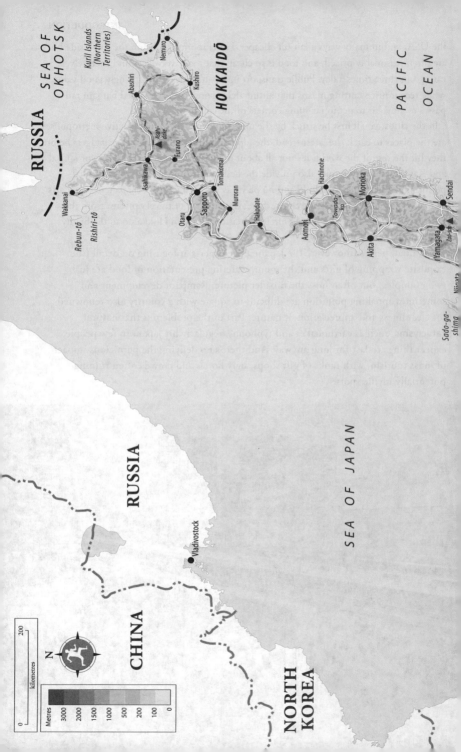

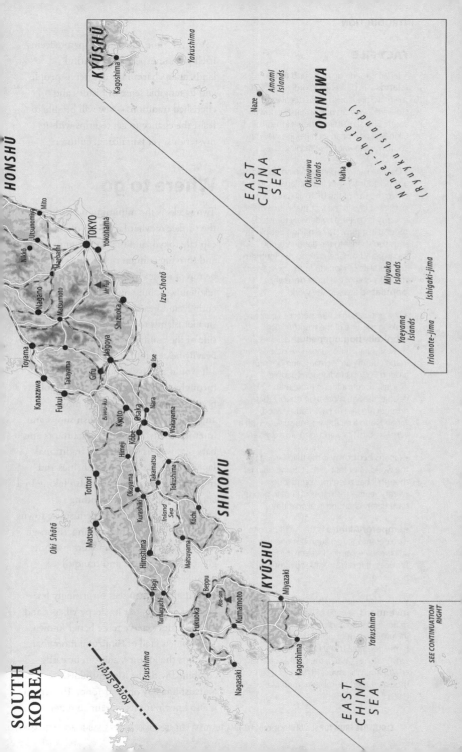

SOUTH KOREA

HONSHŪ

KYŪSHŪ

Mito
Utsunomiya
Nikkō
Maebashi
TOKYO
Yokohama
Nagano
Matsumoto
Shizuoka
Mt Fuji
Nagoya
Toyama
Takayama
Kanazawa
Gifu
Fukui
Biwa-ko
Kyōto
Nara
Ōsaka
Kōbe
Wakayama
Himeji
Tottori
Okayama
Takamatsu
Kurashiki
Tokushima
Matsue
Hiroshima
Matsuyama
Inland Sea
Kōchi
Hagi
Yamaguchi
Beppu
Fukuoka
Aso-san
Kumamoto
Nagasaki
Kagoshima
Miyazaki

SHIKOKU

KYŪSHŪ

Oki-Shotō

Tsushima

Korea Strait

Izu-Shotō

Ise

EAST CHINA SEA

Yakushima

SEE CONTINUATION RIGHT

KYŪSHŪ

Kagoshima

Yakushima

EAST CHINA SEA

Naze
Amami Islands

OKINAWA

Okinawa Islands
Naha

Nansei-shotō (Ryūkyū Islands)

Miyako Islands

Ishigaki-jima

Yaeyama Islands
Iriomote-jima

FACT FILE

• Japan is made up of around **6800 islands** – in descending order of size, the main five are Honshū, the mainland; Hokkaidō, way up north; Kyūshū, down south; Shikoku, sitting under Honshū; and Okinawa, part of an archipelago way out southwest, towards the tropics.

• Despite many Japanese telling you what a small country they live in, Japan is in fact twice the size of the UK. This sense of smallness lays in the fact that much of the country is covered by densely forested mountains; some 127.6 million people are thus squished into the flat quarter of Japan's land surface, making the southern coastal plain of Honshū from Tokyo down to Osaka one of the most **densely populated** areas in the world.

• The population is 98.5 percent Japanese, making this one of the world's most **ethnically homogeneous** societies. The most significant non-Japanese group living in the country are Koreans, numbering around 900,000. Indigenous people officially account for no more than 100,000 people, though more than double that number are said to have native blood. Japan is also a rapidly ageing society, with a very low birth rate and long life expectancy.

• Japan's **economy** is the third largest in the world, after that of the US and China, though it has been moribund for over twenty years – the prices of certain goods have barely changed in all that time.

• **Emperor Akihito** is the head of state. It's a ceremonial position but one that is still greatly respected – even if a fair number of locals struggle to remember his name.

• Japan is famed for its many post-war **inventions**, several of which have had major impacts on global society. These include: instant noodles (1958); high-speed rail travel (1964); quartz wristwatches (1967); the pocket calculator (1970); the Walkman (1979); and a certain moustachioed plumber named Mario (1981).

And yet, time and again, Japan redeems itself with unexpectedly beautiful landscapes, charmingly courteous people and its tangible sense of history and cherished traditions – few will be able to resist the chance to get to grips with its mysterious, yet tantalizing, culture.

Where to go

Two weeks is the minimum needed to skim the surface of what Japan can offer. The capital, Tokyo, and the former imperial city and thriving cultural centre of Kyoto, will be top of most visitors' itineraries, and justifiably so, but you could avoid the cities entirely and head to the mountains or smaller islands to discover an alternative side of the country, away from the most heavily beaten tourist tracks.

It would be easy enough to spend a fortnight just in **Tokyo**. The metropolis is home to some of the world's most ambitious architecture, stylish shops and internationally celebrated restaurants and bars – as well as glimpses of traditional Japan at scores of temples, shrines and imperial gardens. Consider also taking in a couple of the city's surrounding attractions, in particular the historic towns of **Nikkō**, home to the amazing Tōshō-gū shrine complex, and **Kamakura**, with its giant Buddha statue and tranquil woodland walks.

Northern Honshū sees surprisingly few overseas visitors, but its sleepy villages and relaxed cities deserve to be better known. The Golden Hall of **Hiraizumi** more than warrants the journey, and can be easily combined with the islet-sprinkled **Matsushima Bay** or rural **Tōno**. The region is also known for its vibrant **summer**

GETTING YOUR NOODLE ON

Eating is undoubtedly one of the highlights of travelling in Japan – a fair chunk of domestic tourism is geared this way, with locals heading all over the country in order to sample subtle nuances of taste. No food lends itself to regionalism quite as well as the humble **noodle**, with the three main styles – ramen (wheat noodles in broth), udon (thick wheat noodles) and soba (buckwheat noodles) – served in umpteen different ways across the land. Here are a few particularly delicious recommendations:

Hakata ramen Fukuoka's signature dish: made with pork bone broth, many deem it the country's tastiest variety of ramen. For added atmosphere, slurp it down in a street-side *yatai* stall (see box, p.684).

Hōtō If you're in the Fuji Five Lakes area, try this hearty, udon-based dish (see p.198) served with a range of filling ingredients including sweet pumpkin, duck and even bear.

Midorio OK, this delicious pesto-and-cheese ramen isn't exactly traditional, but it's certainly emblematic of Japan's ever-continuing noodle science experiment.

Sapporo ramen Ramen varieties come on a sliding scale between *kotteri* (rich) and *assari* (light). This northern variety is as *kotteri* as they come – a miso-based beast served with a blob of rapidly melting butter.

Sara udon The port city of Nagasaki (p.691) has a long history of international trade, and this Cantonese import is one of the best extant results of its long-standing connections with China: crispy fried noodles that slowly mop up the delicious gravy under which they are served.

Sōki soba Okinawa's take on noodles is simple but truly delicious and quite possibly life extending (see box, p.757): yellow strands of soba, served with broth and a couple of hunks of pork rib.

Zaru soba Served on a bamboo mat, with a cold sauce for dipping, *zaru soba* isn't a regional dish. However, it's best accompanied by freshly grated *wasabi*, and as such the best place to head for it is Shūzenji (p.212) on the Izu peninsula, where much of Japan's *wasabi* is grown.

ABOVE SŌKI SOBA

festivals, notably those at Sendai, Aomori, Hirosaki and Akita, and for its sacred mountains, including **Dewa-sanzan**, home to a sect of ascetic mountain priests, and the eerie, remote wastelands of **Osore-zan**.

Further north, across the Tsugaru Straits, **Hokkaidō** is Japan's final frontier, with many national parks including the outstanding **Daisetsu-zan**, offering excellent hiking trails over mountain peaks and through soaring rock gorges. The lovely far northern islands of **Rebun-tō** and **Rishiri-tō** are ideal summer escapes. Hokkaidō's most historic city is **Hakodate**, with its late nineteenth-century wooden houses and churches built by expat traders, while its modern capital, **Sapporo**, is home to the raging nightlife centre of Suskino and the original Sapporo Brewery. Winter is a fantastic time to visit, when you can catch Sapporo's amazing Snow Festival and go skiing at some of Japan's top resorts, such as **Niseko**.

Skiing, mountaineering and soaking in hot springs are part of the culture of **Central Honshū**, an area dominated by the magnificent Japan Alps. **Nagano**, home to the atmospheric temple of pilgrimage, Zenkō-ji, and the old castle town of **Matsumoto** can be used as a starting point for exploring the region. Highlights include the tiny mountain resort of **Kamikōchi** and the immaculately preserved Edo-era villages of **Tsumago** and **Magome**, linked by a short hike along the remains of a 300-year-old stone-paved road. **Takayama** deservedly draws many visitors to its handsome streets lined with merchant houses and temples, built by generations of skilled carpenters. In the remote neighbouring valleys, you'll find the rare thatched houses of **Ogimachi**, **Suganuma** and **Ainokura**, remnants of a fast-disappearing rural Japan.

On the Sea of Japan coast, the historic city of **Kanazawa** is home to Kenroku-en, one of Japan's best gardens, and the stunning 21st Century Museum of Contemporary Art, Kanazawa. **Nagoya**, on the heavily industrialized southern coast, is a more manageable city than Tokyo or Osaka, and has much to recommend it, including the fine Tokugawa Art Museum and many great places to eat. The efficient new airport nearby also makes the city a good alternative entry point. From Nagoya, it's a short hop to the pretty castle towns of **Inuyama** and **Gifu**, the latter holding summer displays of the ancient skill of *ukai*, or cormorant fishing.

South of the Japan Alps, the **Kansai** plains are scattered with ancient temples, shrines and the remnants of imperial cities. **Kyoto**, custodian of Japan's traditional culture, is home to its most refined cuisine, classy ryokan, glorious gardens, and magnificent temples and palaces. Nearby **Nara** is a more manageable size but no slouch when it comes to venerable monuments, notably the great bronze Buddha of Tōdai-ji and Hōryū-ji's unrivalled collection of early Japanese statuary. The surrounding region contains a number of still-thriving religious foundations, such as the highly atmospheric temples of **Hiei-zan** and **Kōya-san**, the revered Shintō shrine **Ise-jingū**, and the beautiful countryside pilgrimage routes of the UNESCO World Heritage-listed Kumano region.

Not all of Kansai is so rarefied, though. The slightly unconventional metropolis of **Osaka** has an easy-going atmosphere and boisterous nightlife, alongside several interesting sights. Further west, the port of **Kōbe** offers a gentler cosmopolitan feel, while **Himeji** is home to Japan's most fabulous castle, as well as some impressive modern gardens and buildings.

For obvious reasons, **Hiroshima** is the most visited location in **Western Honshū**. On the way there, pause at **Okayama** to stroll around one of Japan's top three gardens, Kōraku-en, and the appealingly preserved Edo-era town of **Kurashiki**. The beauty of the Inland Sea, dotted with thousands of islands, is best appreciated from the idyllic fishing village of **Tomonoura**, the port of **Onomichi** and the relaxed islands of **Nao-shima**, **Ikuchi-jima** and **Miyajima**.

Crossing to the San-in coast, the castle town of **Hagi** retains some handsome samurai houses and atmospheric temples, only surpassed by even more enchanting **Tsuwano**, further inland. One of Japan's most venerable shrines, **Izumo Taisha**, lies roughly midway along the coast, near the lake- and seaside city of **Matsue**, home to the region's only original fort.

Shikoku is the location for Japan's most famous pilgrimage (a walking tour around 88 Buddhist temples), but also offers dramatic scenery in the **Iya valley** and along its rugged coastline. The island's largest city, Matsuyama, has an imperious castle and the splendidly ornate Dōgo Onsen Honkan – one of Japan's best hot springs. There's also the lovely garden Ritsurin-kōen in **Takamatsu** and the ancient Shintō shrine at **Kotohira**.

The southernmost of Japan's four main islands, **Kyūshū** is probably best known for **Nagasaki**, an attractive and cosmopolitan city that has overcome its terrible wartime history. Hikers and onsen enthusiasts should head up into the central highlands, where **Aso-san**'s smouldering peak dominates the world's largest volcanic crater, or to the more southerly meadows of **Ebino Kōgen**. So much hot water gushes out of the ground in **Beppu**, on the east coast, that it's known as Japan's hot-spring capital. **Fukuoka**, on the other hand, takes pride in its innovative modern architecture and an exceptionally lively entertainment district.

Okinawa comprises more than a hundred islands stretching in a great arc to within sight of Taiwan. An independent kingdom until the early seventeenth century, traces of the island's distinctive, separate culture still survive. The beautifully reconstructed former royal palace dominates the capital city, **Naha**, but the best of the region lies on its remoter islands. This is where you'll find Japan's most stunning white-sand beaches and its best diving, particularly around the subtropical islands of **Ishigaki**, **Taketomi** and **Iriomote**.

When to go

Average temperature and weather patterns vary enormously across Japan. The main influences on Honshū's climate are the mountains and surrounding warm seas, which bring plenty of rain and, in the colder months, snow. **Winter** weather differs greatly, however, between the western Sea of Japan and the Pacific coasts, the former suffering cold winds and heavy snow while the latter tends towards dry, clear winter days. Regular heavy snowfalls in the mountains provide ideal conditions for skiers.

OPPOSITE CAPSULE HOTEL, TOKYO

ON THE HUNT FOR CONTEMPORARY JAPAN

Japan has something of a reputation for being a bit off the wall when it comes to contemporary culture: Takeshi's Castle, tentacle-porn anime, Yoko Ono and Haruki Murakami have a lot to answer for, though they're by no means the end of the story. Here are a few examples of some uniquely Japanese things to enjoy during your stay:

Capsule hotels (see p.42 and p.130) No, it's not like sleeping in a coffin. But yes, the rooms at capsule hotels are pretty darn small, and there's no more characteristic Japanese sleeping experience – including ryokan.

Game centres Bash the hell out of the world's weirdest arcade machines in one of the game centres strewn liberally across the land – you'll even find them in minor towns.

Izakaya (see p.47 You can't beat having a drink at an *izakaya*. Japan's own answer to the pub, these venues can be just as garrulous as a London boozer. While you're draining your beer, sake, shōchū or cocktail, glance around at the bar snacks everyone's wolfing down – it's almost impossible to resist joining in.

Oddball cafés Most big Japanese cities have a couple of interesting options for caffeine addicts: have your coffee served by costumed girls at a maid café (see box, p.143), in the midst of thousands of comic books at a manga *kissaten* (see p.141) or surrounded by purring felines at a cat café.

Pachinko parlours (see p.399) Perhaps the world's most boring form of gambling, these glorified pinball arcades are still worth having a gawp at, or even just a listen to – peek in the door, and you'll be amazed by the gigantic din that crashes out. Dare to step inside, and prepare to be visually assaulted by rows of TV panels and LED bulbs, all being glared at by silent, seemingly joyless gamers – something quite intriguing to foreigners.

Standing restaurants (see p.48) Eat like a horse, standing up at one of the thousands of noodle bars dotted around Japan's cities.

Sumo (see p.56) Three times a year, the sumō circus rolls into Tokyo; even if your visit doesn't coincide with a tournament, at any time of year you'll be able to see giant, *yukata*-clad *rikishi* making their way to and from the many "stables" of Ryōgoku district.

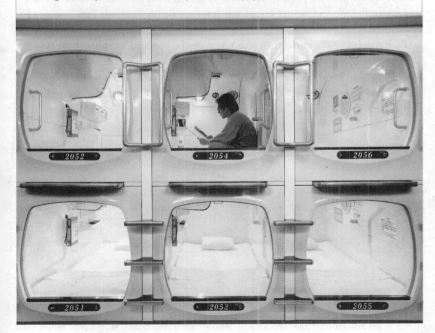

AVERAGE DAILY TEMPERATURES AND MONTHLY RAINFALL

	Jan	Feb	Mar	Apr	May	Jun	Jul	Aug	Sep	Oct	Nov	Dec
AKITA												
Max/Min °C	2/-5	3/-5	6/-2	13/4	18/8	23/14	26/18	28/19	24/15	18/8	11/3	4/-2
rainfall mm	142	104	104	105	112	127	198	188	211	188	191	178
KŌCHI												
Max/Min °C	12/4	12/4	15/7	19/12	22/17	24/19	28/24	29/25	28/22	23/17	19/12	14/7
rainfall mm	64	142	160	188	244	323	257	213	323	279	175	107
NAGASAKI												
Max/Min °C	9/2	10/2	14/5	19/10	23/14	26/18	29/23	31/23	27/20	22/14	17/9	12/4
rainfall mm	71	84	125	185	170	312	257	175	249	114	94	81
SAPPORO												
Max/Min °C	2/-10	2/-10	6/-7	13/-1	18/3	21/10	24/16	26/18	22/12	17/6	11/-1	5/-6
rainfall mm	25	43	61	84	102	160	188	155	160	147	56	38
TOKYO												
Max/Min °C	10/1	10/1	13/4	18/10	23/15	25/18	29/22	31/24	27/20	21/14	17/8	12/3
rainfall mm	110	155	228	254	244	305	254	203	279	228	162	96

Despite frequent showers, **spring** is one of the most pleasant times to visit Japan, when the weather reports chart the steady progress of the cherry blossom from warm Kyūshū in March to colder Hokkaidō around May. A rainy season (*tsuyu*) in June ushers in the swamp-like heat of **summer**; if you don't like tropical conditions, head for the cooler hills or the northern reaches of the country. A bout of typhoons and more rain in September precede **autumn**, which lasts from October to late November; this is Japan's most spectacular season, when the maple trees explode into a range of brilliant colours.

Also worth bearing in mind when planning your visit are Japan's **national holidays**. During such periods, including the days around New Year, the "Golden Week" break of April 29 to May 5 and the Obon holiday of mid-August, the nation is on the move, making it difficult to secure last-minute transport and hotel bookings. Avoid travelling during these dates, or make your arrangements well in advance.

OPPOSITE FROM TOP TEA-PICKING, UJI; 21ST CENTURY MUSEUM OF CONTEMPORARY ART, KANAZAWA; HANAMI, KYOTO

Author picks

On their journeys across Japan, our authors have seen unforgettable sights and eaten wonderful food; they've risen to great alpine heights, drummed to an ancient beat and felt the sand beneath their toes at astoundingly beautiful beaches. Here are some of their personal highlights:

Tea-picking The finest green tea in Japan has been cultivated on the low rolling hills of Wazuka-chō, near Uji, since the thirteenth century (see p.460).

Loveliest beach Iriomote-jima is one of Okinawa's most beautiful islands; for a real getting-away-from-it-all feeling, head to Funauki (see p.787), a cute village only accessible by ferry.

Shibuya Shinjuku may be Tokyo's most famous district, but Shibuya (see p.116) is just as captivating – a zany, teeming scene blanketed with neon by night.

Spectacular views The views of the Seto Ōhashi bridge and the Inland Sea from Washū-zan (see p.555) are some of Japan's most spectacular.

Feel the beat Learn from Taiko masters with a high-energy drumming workshop on Sado-ga-shima (see p.279).

Stunning art Kanazawa's 21st Century Museum of Contemporary Art (see p.381) is a suitably cutting-edge space to celebrate playful, ambitious and surprising modern art.

Cross the roof of Japan The Tateyama-Kurobe Alpine Route (see p.379) combines buses, funiculars and cable-cars to whisk you over the Japan Alps, with spectacular mountain views.

Hanami Clouds of pink blossom offset by perfect blue skies or night-time lanterns – cherry-blossom viewing offers not just communion with nature but an excuse to party (see p.55).

A ryokan meal Indulge in course upon course of exquisitely presented dishes, each more tasty than the next; a feast for the eyes and the stomach (see p.43).

Our author recommendations don't end here. We've flagged up our favourite places – a perfectly sited hotel, an atmospheric café, a special restaurant – throughout the guide, highlighted with the ★ symbol.

29

things not to miss

It's not possible to see everything that Japan has to offer in one trip – and we don't suggest you try. What follows, in no particular order, is a selective and subjective taste of the country's highlights: impressive museums, tranquil gardens, lively festivals, awe-inspiring temples and much more. All entries are colour coded to the corresponding chapter and have a page reference to take you straight into the Guide.

1

1 **KYOTO**
Page 408
The capital of Japan for a thousand years, endowed with an almost overwhelming legacy of temples, palaces and gardens, and also home to the country's richest traditional culture and most refined cuisine.

2 **YAKUSHIMA**
Page 745
Commune with millenium-old cedar trees in Kirishima-Yaku National Park, a UNESCO World Heritage Site.

3 **KŌYA-SAN**
Page 507
Mingle with monks and pilgrims on one of Japan's holiest mountains, home to over a hundred monasteries.

4 **EARTH CELEBRATION**
Page 279
Vibrant international world music festival, hosted by the drumming group Kodō on the lovely island of Sado-ga-shima.

10

11 KAMIKŌCHI
Page 361
This busy but pretty mountain village preserves a Shangri-la atmosphere and serves as the gateway to the Northern Alps.

12 OGIMACHI
Page 375
Discover the distinctive *gasshō-zukuri* houses, whose steep-sided thatched roofs are said to recall two hands joined in prayer.

13 NIKKŌ
Page 164
This pilgrim town is home to the fabulously over-the-top Tōshō-gū shrine, one of Japan's most sumptuous buildings.

14 HIROSHIMA
Page 566
Pay your respects to the A-bomb's victims in the city of Hiroshima, impressively reborn from the ashes of World War II.

15 KABUKIZA
Page 87
This is the best place to enjoy kabuki, the most dramatic of traditional Japanese performing arts.

16 SUMO
Page 56
Watch the titanic, ritualized clashes of Japan's sporting giants.

17 NARA
Page 470
The ancient former capital is home to the Buddhist temple of Tōdai-ji.

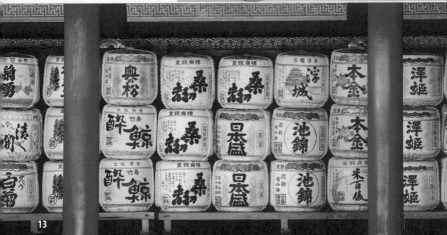

14

15

16

17

21

22

24 MATSUMOTO CASTLE
Page 358

This magnificent building, known as "Crow Castle", due to its menacing dark exterior, is Japan's oldest existing wooden castle.

25 NAHA FISH MARKET
Page 761

The fish section of Naha's delightful market area is a truly spectacular sight – a whole rainbow of seafood to choose from and have cooked for you.

26 AWA ODORI
Page 635

Dance through the streets at the country's biggest Obon bash, held in Tokushima, Shikoku.

27 TOKYO'S ART SCENE
Page 108

Tokyo remains the most important art city in Asia – hit the Roppongi Art Triangle to see why.

28 KAISEKI-RYŌRI
Page 48

Indulge yourself with a meal of *kaiseki-ryōri*, Japan's haute cuisine, comprised of a selection of beautifully prepared morsels made from the finest seasonal ingredients.

29 ONSEN
Page 61

Take a dip at a top onsen resort town, such as Dōgo or Sukayu Onsen, or experience the exquisite warmth of a rotemburo (outdoor bath) as the snow falls.

24

25

26

27

28

29

Itineraries

Japan may not be terribly large, but there's enough historic, natural and contemporary sights to keep you busy for months on end. Most visitors hit Tokyo and Kyoto, the capitals past and present, but the further you get from the beaten track, the more rewarding the experience. These itineraries head all over Japan's varied landscapes, and give at least an idea of what this fascinating country is all about.

THE FULL MONTY

Hitting most of Japan's main sights, this itinerary loosely follows the old Tōkaidō route that linked Tokyo with Kyoto, then moves further west to within a short ferry ride of the Korean peninsula.

❶ Tokyo Japan's wonderful capital needs no introduction – the only question is what to do with your time there, which will never be quite enough. **See p.76**

❷ Mount Fuji This emblematic volcanic cone, just west of Tokyo, is climbable through the summer, but visible from the Shinkansen trains all year round. **See p.197**

❸ Kyoto Contrary to the expectations of many visitors, Japan's vaunted ancient ex-capital is actually a large, modern city, albeit one brimming with compelling historical gems. **See p.408**

❹ Nara Just south of Kyoto, Nara is a far more natural-feeling place – witness the deer merrily grazing around the temples and shrines. **See p.470**

❺ Naoshima Take a detour from the mainland route to this small island, home to swathes of fantastic modern art. **See p.627**

❻ Hiroshima The name of this city is etched quite firmly into the world's conscience. Dark

tourism it may be, but the gutted Hypocenter is a stark reminder of those tragic times. **See p.566**

❼ Fukuoka Way out west, this is perhaps the friendliest city in the land – its characteristic *yatai* stalls make perfect places in which to bond with ramen-slurping locals over a few glasses of sake. **See p.678**

WORLD HERITAGE TOUR

Japan boasts thirteen cultural and four natural World Heritage Sites; focusing your visit on the country's ancient wonders alone could keep you well occupied for a good ten days or more.

❶ Nikkō One of Japan's most relaxed cities, where a clutch of dreamy temples lurk in the mountainous forests around the fabulously preposterous Heritage-listed Tōshō-gū complex. **See p.164**

❷ Shirakawa-gō and Gokayama The lovingly preserved villages of Shirakawa-gō and Gokayama, with their distinctive A-frame houses, give a glimpse of Japanese rural life centuries ago. **See p.374**

❸ Kyoto Having functioned as capital for around one millennium, it's no surprise that over two dozen places in Kyoto have been

ABOVE FROM LEFT OTARU CANALS, HOKKAIDŌ; GEISHAS IN GION DISTRICT, KYOTO protected as World Heritage sites; whatever you do, don't miss the phenomenal Kiyomizu-dera temple. See p.408

④ Miyajima Close to Hiroshima, this is one of Japan's most famed attractions – a vermillion-red *torii* rising elegantly from the sea. See p.573

⑤ Nara This historic city has eight sites showcasing the early development of Buddhism, as well as a Shintō shrine, a primeval forest, a park and a palace. See p.470

⑥ Shuri Castle If you make it as far as Okinawa, don't miss this castle, a fantastic relic of the Ryūkyū Kingdom that once ruled this gorgeous island chain. See p.759

TŌHOKU–HOKKAIDŌ

You could easily spend a couple of weeks winding your way up Honshū's northern tip, full of rich heritage and timeless agricultural scenes, before making your way over into the unspoilt,

wild landscape of Hokkaido, Japan's most northernmost island which bursts with natural phenomena and wildlife.

① Sendai Stroll the tree-lined streets of the city and take day-trips to the Yamadera temple complex and the scenic bay of Matsushima. See p.228

② Dewa-sanzan Spend a few days hiking up this extinct volcano along the pilgrims route taken by the Yamabushi ascetic mountain hermits. See p.265

③ Tōno Valley Cycle through the rural landscape of this flat valley and envelop yourself in the mysterious folk tales embedded in the region's ancient shrines and rock carvings. See p.240

④ Aomori Stop in at Honshū's northernmost city and take excursions to the eerie landscape of Shimokita Hantō, populated by wandering souls, and Towada-ko, for a hike around a volcanic lake. See p.249

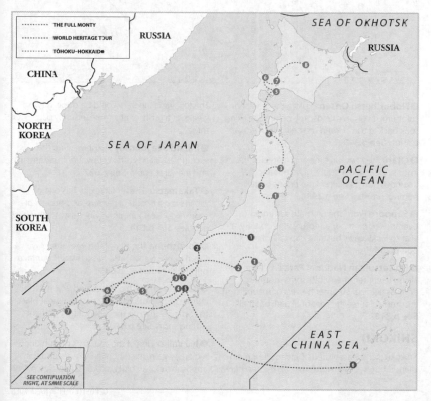

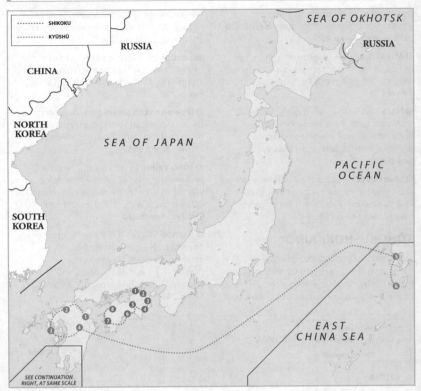

❺ Noboribetsu Onsen Explore the smoking, sulphurous volcanic landscape before a relaxing soak back at the inn and the delights of ryokan cuisine. **See p.313**

❻ Otaru Step back in time and marvel at the imposing Meiji-era public buildings and luxurious homes built on the profits of the herring industry. **See p.298**

❼ Sapporo From the ultimate summer evenings to or snow sculptures in February, a visit to Hokkaidō's bustling capital is a must. See p.288

❽ Daisetsu-zan National Park Excellent skiing in winter, cherry blossoms in spring, endless fields of summer flowers or magnificent autumn colours – this national park has it all. See p.318

SHIKOKU

Shikoku is the least visited of Japan's four main islands, but it is well worth making the trip here.

The following itinerary could be done in two weeks, at a push, or at a more leisurely pace over three.

❶ Inland Sea journey Naoshima and the exciting art islands offer captivating modern art and friendly people. **See p.627**

❷ Takamatsu. This amiable city has one of Japan's most beautiful gardens and dozens of *sanuki udon* restaurants serving tasty thick white noodles. **See p.614**.

❸ Tokushima The city of the energetic Awa Odori dance festival also has a historic *bunraku* puppet theatre. **See p.635**

❹ Kaifu Thanks to big waves and warm Pacific currents, Shikoku's eastern coast is a great place to come if you're on the lookout for excellent surfing spots. **See p.640**

❺ Iya Valley One of the country's most hidden regions, with rustic mountain villages and the atmosphere of an older, slower Japan. **See p.642**

OPPOSITE DEER IN NARA-KŌEN

❻ Kōchi The hometown of Sakamoto Ryōma, one of Japan's most revered samurai heroes, the densely populated city of Kōchi has a lively night food market. **See p.646**

❼ Uwajima Visit a sex museum and watch a bloodless bullfighting match in this quiet, unassuming town. **See p.654**

❽ Matsuyama Check out the magnificent ancient castle and historic hot spring of Dōgo Onsen in Shikoku's largest city. **See p.662**

KYŪSHŪ

You could forget Tokyo and Kyoto entirely and still get a pretty accurate impression of Japan by visiting its third-largest island, home to active volcanoes, great food, friendly locals and hot springs aplenty.

❶ Beppu This is one of Japan's foremost hot-spring resorts. A small, pleasingly retro place where steam billows from the streets; there are even a couple of onsens hiding away in the forested hills above town. **See p.718**

❷ Fukuoka Start your trip in the island's main city, where you can expect tasty meals, boisterous nightlife and a thoroughly enjoyable vibe. **See p.687**

❸ Nagasaki Like Hiroshima, this city has rebounded with phenomenal gusto from the atomic blasts that left the place in tatters. Head on a trip to intriguing Battleship Island – a Bond-villain set so otherworldly that it didn't even need to be touched up for the film. **See p.691**

❹ Aso This giant volcanic crater, with sulphurous steam still shooting out from the peaks at its centre, is an easily accessible place in which to get a handle on rural Japan. **See p.710**

❺ Kagoshima Interested in seeing a volcano explode? Sakurajima erupts several times a day, just across the bay from this unique city. **See p.734**

❻ Yakushima The inspiration behind certain Studio Ghibli cartoons, the richly forested highlands on this pristine island feature trees so old, nobody has yet been able to verify their age. **See p.745**

VENDING MACHINE SELLING CANNED NOODLES, TOKYO

Basics

Getting there

Tokyo's Narita International Airport (see p.125), Osaka's Kansai International Airport (see p.493) and Centrair (see p.396) near Nagoya are the main international flight gateways, while Tokyo's Haneda Airport (see p.125) has recently expanded and now offers a wider range of international connections.

Airfares are highest around the Golden Week holiday period at the beginning of May, and the Obon festival in mid-August, as well as at Christmas and New Year, when seats are at a premium. Prices drop during the "shoulder" seasons – April to June and September to October – with the best deals in the low season, January to March and November to December (excluding Christmas and New Year).

Flights from the UK and Ireland

ANA, British Airways, Japan Airlines and Virgin fly nonstop from **London** to Tokyo, with the trip taking about twelve hours. Return **fares** start from around £550, but since you can find occasional special deals for as low as £400, it pays to shop around. There are no direct flights from **Dublin**; if you fly via London, expect to pay in the region of €800.

Flights from the US and Canada

A number of airlines fly nonstop from **the US and Canada** to Tokyo, Osaka and Nagoya, including Air Canada, ANA, American Airlines, Japan Airlines and United; there are connections from virtually every US regional airport. Flying time is around fifteen hours from New York, thirteen hours from Chicago and ten hours from Los Angeles. Low-season return **fares** to Tokyo start at around US$1000 from Chicago or New York; US$800 from Los Angeles; and Can$1200 from Vancouver.

Flights from Australia, New Zealand and South Africa

Qantas, Japan Airlines and Air New Zealand operate nonstop flights to Tokyo from **Australia and New Zealand**. Flying time is around ten hours from Australia and twelve hours from New Zealand. Return **fares** from Australia to Tokyo are often under Aus$1000 with Jetstar, who fly from Cairns, Darwin and the Gold Coast. From New Zealand, direct routings will cost at least NZ$2000, though again

you can lop a far bit from this by flying indirectly with Jetstar.

Flying from **South Africa**, you'll be routed through Southeast Asia or the Middle East. Promotional fares can be as cheap as R8000, though you're more likely to be paying in the region of R11,000 and above.

Flights from other Asian countries

If you're already in Asia, it can be quite cheap to fly to Japan with low-cost regional carriers. **Air Asia** (Wairasia.com) have flights from Kuala Lumpur to Osaka, Nagoya and Tokyo; **Cebu Pacific** (Wcebupacificair.com) head from Manila to the same destinations; **Eastar Jet** (Weastarjet.com) and **Jeju Air** (Wjejuair.net) go to Tokyo from Seoul; and **Scoot** (Wflyscoot.com) scoot into Tokyo from Singapore and Taipei. Japanese operations include **Peach** (Wflypeach.com), who operate flights from Hong Kong, Seoul, Busan, Taipei and Kaohsiung; and **Vanilla Air** (Wvanilla-air.com), who offer flights from Seoul and Taipei.

Train and ferry

Adventurous travellers can take advantage of a number of alternative routes to Japan from Europe and Asia via **train and ferry**. There are three long-distance train journeys – the Trans-Siberian, Trans-Mongolian and Trans-Manchurian – all of which will put you on the right side of Asia for a hop across to Japan. The shortest ferry route is on the hydrofoil between Busan in South Korea and Fukuoka (Hakata port) on Japan's southern island of Kyūshū.

The Trans-Siberian train and getting there from Russia

The classic overland adventure route to or from Japan is via the **Trans-Siberian** train, a seven-night journey from Moscow to Vladivostok on Russia's far-eastern coast. The cost of a one-way ticket in a four-berth sleeper compartment between **Moscow** and **Vladivostok** is around £470/US$770/Aus$845, on top of which you'll need to factor in costs for visas, hotels etc along the way. You'll end up saving a lot of money if you arrange your own visa and buy tickets within Russia; however, to avoid some of the inevitable hassles (tickets often sell out in summer, for example), most choose to go through an agent. The same advice goes for the **Trans-Manchurian** train, which heads from Moscow down through northern China and terminates in Beijing, and the

A BETTER KIND OF TRAVEL

At Rough Guides we are passionately committed to travel. We believe it helps us understand the world we live in and the people we share it with – and of course tourism is vital to many developing economies. But the scale of modern tourism has also damaged some places irreparably, and climate change is accelerated by most forms of transport, especially flying. All Rough Guides' flights are carbon-offset, and every year we donate money to a variety of environmental charities.

Trans-Mongolian, which runs from Moscow via Mongolia to Beijing. You can then take a train to Shanghai and pick up a ferry to Japan (see below).

Vladivostok Air (Ⓦ vladivostokavia.ru) and S7 (Ⓦ s7.ru) offer connections from Vladivostok to Narita. If you're absolutely insistent on continuing your journey overland, you can take a weekly **ferry** to the Japanese port of Sakaiminato, near Matsue. These head via the Korean city of Donghae, where there's a nine-hour stopover (you'll be able to get off, though Donghae is not the nicest place to hang around), and take 43 hours in total. The cheapest tickets cost ¥22,000 one-way; see the DBS site (Ⓦ dbsferry.com) for more details. For those planning to return from Japan to Europe on this route, start by arranging your **visa** at the Russian Embassy in Tokyo (see p.160) or the Osaka consulate (see p.505).

The shortest journey from Russia to Japan is on the ferry service (May–Oct) from **Korsakov** on the Siberian island of Sakhalin to Wakkanai in Hokkaidō (see p.322).

Ferries from China and South Korea

Both the Shanghai Ferry Company (Ⓣ 06 6243 6345, Ⓦ shanghai-ferry.co.jp) and Japan–China International Ferry Co (Ⓣ 06 6536 6541, Ⓦ www .shinganjin.com) ply the **Shanghai–Osaka** route (48hr; from ¥22,000); the latter heads from **Kōbe** on alternate weeks. Conditions on board are good, the berths are clean and comfortable, and facilities include swimming pools, restaurants and even discos. Orient Ferry (Ⓣ 0832 32 6615, Ⓦ orientferry.co.jp) has services between **Qingdao** and **Shimonoseki** (40hr; ¥19,000).

There are daily ferry and hydrofoil services from **Busan** in South Korea to **Fukuoka** (see p.682) and Shimonoseki (see p.582).

Airlines, agents and operators

Contact details for airlines in the listings below are given selectively, reflecting the territories from which they offer flights to Japan.

AIRLINES

Air Canada Ⓦ aircanada.ca.
Air France Ⓦ airfrance.com.
Air New Zealand Ⓦ airnewzealand.com.
All Nippon Airways (ANA) Ⓦ ana.co.jp.
American Airlines Ⓦ aa.com.
British Airways Ⓦ britishairways.com.
Cathay Pacific Ⓦ cathaypacific.com.
Delta Ⓦ delta.com.
Japan Airlines (JAL) Ⓦ jal.com.
KLM Royal Dutch Airlines Ⓦ klm.com.
Korean Airlines Ⓦ koreanair.com.
Lufthansa Ⓦ lufthansa.com.
Malaysia Airlines Ⓦ malaysiaairlines.com.
Northwest Airlines Ⓦ nwa.com.
Qantas Ⓦ qantas.com.au.
Singapore Airlines Ⓦ singaporeair.com.
Thai Airways International Ⓦ thaiair.com.
United Airlines Ⓦ united.com.
Virgin Atlantic Ⓦ virgin-atlantic.com.

AGENTS AND OPERATORS

Artisans of Leisure US Ⓣ 1 800 214 8144, Ⓦ artisansofleisure .com. Luxury private tours including ones focused on food, art and gardens.
AWL Pitt Australia Ⓣ 02 9264 7384, Ⓦ japanpackage.com.au. Sydney-based agent offering a variety of Japan packages, and Japan Rail passes.
AWL Travel UK Ⓣ 020 7222 1144, Ⓦ awlt.com. UK-based Japan specialist.
Baumann Travel US Ⓣ 914 419 8470, Ⓦ baumanntravel.com. Arts and cultural tours, covering themes such as Japanese gardens and cuisine.
Deep Powder Tours Australia Ⓣ 02 9525 9774, Ⓦ deeppowdertours.com. Ski trips to Niseko, and other Japanese resorts.
Elite Orient Tours US & Canada Ⓣ 1 800 668 8100 or 416 977 3026, Ⓦ elitetours.com. Canada-based company specializing in Japan.
HIS Travel Japan Australia Ⓣ 02 9267 3333, New Zealand Ⓣ 09 336 1336; Ⓦ traveljapan.com.au. Flights, packages and customized itineraries are available from this long-established specialist.
IACE Travel US Ⓣ 1 866 735 4223, Ⓦ iace-usa.com. US-based Japan specialist with many packages and themed tours to Tokyo.
Inside Japan UK Ⓣ 0117 314 4620, Ⓦ insidejapantours.com. Great range of well-designed small-group, self-guided and fully tailored trips, ranging from Tokyo stopovers to climbing Mount Fuji.

Into Japan UK ☎ 01865 841 443, ⓦ intojapan.co.uk. Upmarket tours from a reliable operator; they only run a couple of off-the-peg ones each year, with most opting for tailored itineraries.

Japan Journeys UK ☎ 020 7756 5267, ⓦ japanjourneys.co.uk. Tokyo options include an anime and manga-themed tour.

Japan Package Tours Australia ☎ 03 9909 7212, ⓦ japanpackagetours.com.au. Fully escorted and self-guided tours, tailor-made itineraries, accommodation packages and rail passes.

Japan Travel Bureau (JTB) US ☎ 1 877 798 9808, ⓦ www.jtbusa.com; Canada ☎ 416 367 5824, ⓦ jtb.ca; Australia ☎ 1300 739 330, ⓦ japantravel.com.au. As well as the usual options, they handle Sunrise Tours (see box, p.35) taking in the capital and surrounding region.

Japan Travel Centre UK ☎ 020 7611 0150, ⓦ japantravel.co.uk. Offers flights, accommodation packages, Japan Rail passes and guided tours.

Kintetsu International Express US ☎ 1 800 422 348, ⓦ japanforyou.com. A good variety of trips on offer, covering everything from architecture to onsen.

Magical Japan UK ☎ 0161 443 7332, ⓦ magicaljapan.co.uk. Their guided tours all offer at least three days in and around Tokyo; customized packages possible.

Mitsui Travel Australia ☎ 02 9262 2720, ⓦ mitsuitravel.com.au. Options include a three-night onsen tour to Tokyo and Hakone.

Quest Japan Japan ☎ 03 5226 1169, ⓦ hikejapan.com. Small-group hiking tours. Itineraries include some unusual destinations such as the volcanoes of Kyūshū and the island Yakushima

Oka Tours Japan ☎ 0422 266644, ⓦ okatours.com. Cycling tours, both moderate and challenging in terms of terrain covered, on Sado Island, Niigata and the Izu peninsula.

Oku Japan UK ☎ 020 7099 6147, ⓦ okujapan.com. Broad range of escorted small-group tours, many including Tokyo.

Travel Japan by H.I.S. Australia ☎ 02 9267 0333, New Zealand ☎ 09 335 1336; ⓦ traveljapan.com.au. Provides everything from flights to Tokyo to packages and customized itineraries.

ViaJapan! UK ☎ 020 7484 3323, ⓦ viajapan.co.uk. UK-based arm of major Japanese travel company H.I.S., offering flights, packages and rail passes.

Wright Way Travel US ☎ 708 848 1976, ⓦ wrightwaytravel.org. Annual tour to Japan (usually in the spring) focusing on the work and legacy of architect Frank Lloyd Wright.

Getting around

The time of year is an important factor to consider when arranging your transport around Japan. Peak travelling seasons are the few days either side of New Year, the Golden Week holidays of late April and early May, and the mid-August Obon holiday (see p.55). During these times, the whole of Japan can seem on the move, with trains, planes and ferries packed to the gills and roads clogged with traffic. Book well in advance and be prepared to pay higher fares on flights, as all discounts are suspended during peak periods.

Domestic **travel agencies**, such as JTB, can book all types of transport and are also useful sources for checking travel schedules. The staff in these agencies have access to the **jikokuhyō timetable**, an incredible source of information, updated monthly, on virtually every form of public transport in Japan. There's always a *jikokuhyō* available for consultation at stations, and most hotels have a copy too. If you're going to travel around Japan a lot, get hold of a JR English timetable for all the Shinkansen and many major express train services, available from JNTO offices in Japan and abroad and at major train stations. Also incredibly useful is the **Hyperdia Timetable** (ⓦ hyperdia.com), an online resource providing a whole range of travel options, including transfers by air, bus, train and ferry between almost any two points in Japan.

By train

The vast majority of services on Japan's brilliant rail network are operated by the six regional **JR (Japan Railways)** companies: JR Hokkaidō (ⓦ www .jrhokkaido.co.jp), JR East (ⓦ www.jreast.co.jp), JR Central (ⓦ english.jr-central.co.jp), JR West (ⓦ www .westjr.co.jp), JR Shikoku (ⓦ jr-shikoku.co.jp) and JR Kyūshū (ⓦ www.jr-kyushu.co.jp). JR is run as a single company as far as buying tickets is concerned. Smaller rail companies, including Hankyū, Kintetsu, Meitetsu, Odakyū and Tōbu, are based in the major cities and surrounding areas, but in the vast majority of Japan it's JR services that you'll be using.

Individual **tickets** can be pricey, especially for the fastest trains, but many discount tickets and **rail passes** are available to cut the cost. If you plan to travel extensively by train, the various Japan Rail passes provide the best overall deal (see p.35), while the discount tour packages by the Japan Travel Bureau's Sunrise Tours arm (see box, p.35) are also

---

LEFT LUGGAGE

You'll usually only find **left-luggage offices** at the largest train stations in big cities, though all train stations, many subway stations, department stores and shopping centres have **coin lockers** where you can stash your bags. These come in a range of sizes, charging from ¥300 to ¥600 for a day's storage.

excellent value. If you have lots of time, and are travelling during the main student holiday periods, the **Seishun Jūhachi-kippu** (see p.36) is also an excellent buy.

Shinkansen

For many visitors, riding the **Shinkansen** (新幹線) is an eagerly anticipated part of a trip to Japan. Often referred to as the "Bullet Train" because of the smooth, rounded design of the earliest locomotives, you'll barely notice the speed of these smooth-running beasts, which purr along some lines at a whopping 320kph. They are also frighteningly punctual – two seconds late on the platform and you'll be waving goodbye to the back end of the train – and reliable: only the severest weather conditions or earthquakes stop the Shinkansen.

There are six main Shinkansen lines. The busiest route is the **Tōkaidō–Sanyō** line, which runs south from Tokyo through Nagoya, Kyoto, Osaka and Hiroshima, terminating at Hakata Station in Fukuoka (the Tōkaidō line runs from Tokyo to Shin-Osaka Station, while the Sanyō line continues from there to Fukuoka).

The **Tōhoku line** is the main northern route, passing through Sendai and terminating at Shin-Aomori; an extension through the Seikan Tunnel to Hakodate will open in 2016. The **Akita line** runs from Tokyo to Akita on the north coast, while the **Yamagata line** to Shinjō, in the middle of the Tōhoku region, splits off west from the Tōhoku line at Fukushima; these are both "mini-Shinkansen" services, and are not as fast as the regular ones.

The **Jōetsu line** heads north from Tokyo, tunnelling through the mountains to Niigata along the Sea of Japan coast, with the **Nagano line** (also known as the Hokuriku line) branching off west at Takasaki to end at Nagano; an extension to Kanazawa will open in 2015. Lastly, the **Kyūshū line** connects Kagoshima with Hakata.

To travel by Shinkansen, you'll pay a hefty **surcharge** on top of the basic fare for a regular train. Three types of Shinkansen services are available: the *Kodama* (こだま), which stops at all stations; the *Hikari* (ひかり), which stops only at major stations; and the *Nozomi* (のぞみ; available on the Tōkaidō–Sanyō line only), the fastest service, for which you'll have to pay an extra fee (and which you're not allowed to take if you're travelling on most types of rail pass). If you're travelling from Tokyo to Fukuoka, the *Nozomi* shaves an hour off the six-hour journey on the *Hikari*, but for shorter hops to Nagoya, Kyoto or Osaka, the time saved isn't generally worth the extra expense.

On the train, there are announcements and electronic signs in English telling you which stations are coming up. Get to the door in good time before the train arrives, as you'll generally only have a few seconds in which to disembark before the train shoots off again.

Other trains

Aside from the Shinkansen, the fastest services are **limited express** (*tokkyū*; 特急) trains, their misleading name deriving from the fact that they make a limited number of stops. Like Shinkansen, you have to pay a surcharge to travel on them, and there are separate classes of reserved and non-reserved seats (see box, p.36). Less common are the **express** trains (*kyūkō*; 急行), which also only stop at larger stations but carry a lower surcharge. Oddly, the **rapid** trains (*kaisoku*; 快速) are slower still, making more stops than express ones, but with no surcharge. **Ordinary** trains (*futsū*; 普通) are local services stopping at all stations, and usually limited to routes under 100km.

The above categories of train and surcharges apply to all JR services, and to some, but not all, private rail routes. To further confuse matters, you may find that if you're travelling on a JR train on one of the more remote branch lines, you may be charged an additional fare due to part of the old JR network having been sold off to another operating company.

EATING AND DRINKING ON TRAINS AND AT STATIONS

On long-distance trains there'll almost always be a **trolley**, laden with overpriced drinks and snacks, being pushed down the aisle. You're generally better off both financially and in culinary terms packing your own picnic for the train, but useful fallbacks are the station **noodle stands** and the **ekiben**, a contraction of *eki* (station) and bentō (boxed meal). At the station noodle stalls, you can get warming bowls of freshly made hot noodles, usually soba or the thicker udon, for under ¥500. *Ekiben*, often featuring tenuous local-speciality foods, are sold both on and off the trains and come in a wide range of permutations. If you have time, pop into a convenience or department store close to the station for a more keenly priced selection of bentō.

SUNRISE TOURS

There are several **great-value deals** only available to overseas visitors on tourist visas offered by **Sunrise Tours**, a division of the Japan Travel Bureau. For example, for ¥25,300, Sunrise offers a two-day, one-night unaccompanied trip to Kyoto from Tokyo with reserved seats on the Shinkansen and a night's accommodation at a reasonable tourist hotel in Kyoto; for slightly more you can upgrade the hotel and go on the faster *Nozomi* trains. This is cheaper than the cost of a return Shinkansen ticket to Kyoto alone. The package is also flexible: you can stay longer than one night in Kyoto and return on any train you like (on a pre-specified day) as long as you cancel your return-seat reservation and take your chances in the unreserved section of the train (see box, p.36). There are **Shinkansen tours** starting in Osaka, Kyoto and Nagoya, too; for the latest details see ⓦjtb.co.jp.

There are only a handful of overnight **sleeper trains** – the main services are from Tokyo and Osaka to Aomori and Sapporo; if you have a Japan Rail Pass and want a berth for the night, you'll have to pay the berth charge (couchette cabin sleeping four to six ¥6000–10,000; private double or single room ¥6000–38,000 depending on the class of cabin), plus the surcharge for the express or limited express service. A few overnight trains have reclining seats, which JR Pass holders can use without paying a surcharge. Reservations are necessary.

There are several **SL (steam locomotive)** services across the country, which run from spring through to autumn, mainly on weekends and holidays. These leisurely trains, with lovingly restored engines and carriages, have proved a huge hit with tourists, and you'd be well advised to book in advance. Among the more popular routes are the Senmō line between Kushiro and Shibecha, along with the SL Fuyu-no-Shitsugen-gō service in winter, the Yamaguchi line between Ogōri and Tsuwano in Western Honshū (see p.595); and the Mōka line from Shimodate to Motegi via Mashiko in Tochigi-ken.

Buying tickets

JR **tickets** can be bought at any JR station and at many travel agencies. At major city stations, there will be a **fare map** in English beside the vending machine. Otherwise, if you're buying your ticket from the ticket counter, it's a good idea to have written down on a piece of paper the date and time you wish to travel, your destination, the number of tickets you want and whether you'll need smoking or non-smoking seats. A fallback is to buy the minimum fare ticket from the vending machine and pay any surcharges on or when leaving the train – though this may sound dodgy, it's completely kosher, and locals often do this too.

To make **advance reservations** for *tokkyū* and Shinkansen trains, or to buy special types of tickets, you'll generally need to go to the green window, or "*midori-no-madoguchi*" – sales counters marked by a green logo. In order to swap your exchange voucher for a Japan Rail Pass, you'll have to go to a designated ticket office; they're listed in the booklet you'll receive with your rail pass voucher and on the rail pass website.

Japan Rail passes

If you plan to make just one long-distance train journey, such as Tokyo to Kyoto one way, a **Japan Rail Pass** (ⓦjapanrailpass.net) will not be good value. In all other cases it will be, and you should invest in one before you arrive, since the full Japan Rail Pass can only be bought *outside* Japan (other types of passes can bought inside the country, however). For unfettered flexibility, the comprehensive Japan Rail Pass is the way to go, while regional Japan Rail Passes are good deals if they fit with your travel itinerary. All the prices quoted below are for ordinary rail passes (Green Car passes cost more; see box p.36), and note that you will have to be travelling on a tourist visa to buy any of them.

The traditional **Japan Rail Pass** allows travel on virtually all JR services throughout Japan, including buses and ferries, and is valid for seven (¥28,300), fourteen (¥45,100) or twenty-one (¥57,700) consecutive days. The major service for which it is not valid is the *Nozomi* Shinkansen (see opposite); if you're caught on one of these, even unwittingly you'll be liable for the full fare for the trip. As with all JR tickets, children aged between 6 and 11 years inclusive pay half-price, while those under 6 travel free.

The **JR East Pass** (ⓦwww.jreast.co.jp) covers all JR East services, including the Shinkansen; five days' consecutive use costs is ¥22,000. **JR West** offers a couple of local travel passes (see p.466, p.489 and p.54) while both **JR Hokkaidō and JR Kyūshū** (see p.288 and p.678) offer passes for their respective networks.

TRAIN CLASSES AND RESERVATIONS

On Shinkansen trains and JR *tokkyū* (limited express) and *kyūkō* (express) services, there's a choice of ordinary (*futsū-sha*; 普通車) carriages or more expensive first-class **Green Car** (*guriin-sha* ; グリーン車) carriages, where seats are two abreast either side of the aisle (as opposed to three). There may be a choice between **smoking** (*kitsuen*; 喫煙), and **non-smoking** (*kin'en*; 禁煙) cars; these days, many services are either entirely non-smoking or have smoking cabins in between certain carriages. On *Nozomi* Shinkansen, it's also possible to buy **standing-only tickets** for a small discount.

Each train also has both reserved (*shitei-seki*; 指定席), and unreserved (*jiyū-seki*; 自由席) sections. **Seat reservations** cost between ¥300 and ¥500, depending on the season; they are free if you have a rail pass. You cannot sit in the reserved section of a train without a reservation, even if it's empty and the unreserved section full, although you can buy a reservation ticket from the train conductor.

If you don't have a reservation, aim to get to the station early, locate your platform and stand in line at the marked section for the unreserved carriages; ask the platform attendants for *jiyū-seki*, and they'll point the way. If you have a reservation, platform signs will also direct you where to stand, so that you're beside the right door when the train pulls in.

If you buy any of these passes abroad, the cost in your own currency will depend on the exchange rate at the time of purchase – you might be able to save a little money by **shopping around** between agents offering the pass, because they don't all use the same exchange rate. You'll be given an exchange voucher which must be swapped for a pass in Japan **within three months**. Once issued, the dates on the pass cannot be changed. Exchanges can only be made at designated JR stations; you'll be issued with a list of locations when you buy your pass. Again, note that passes can only be issued if you're travelling on a **temporary visitor visa**; JR staff are very strict about this, and you'll be asked to show your passport when you present your exchange voucher for the pass or when you buy a pass directly in Japan. Also, note that if you lose your pass, it will not be replaced, so take good care of it.

Rail Pass holders can get a **discount**, typically around 10 percent, at all JR Group Hotels; check the

list in the information booklet provided when you buy your pass.

Other discount tickets

The **Seishun Jūhachi-kippu** (青春18きっぷ; ⓦ jreast.co.jp/e/pass/seishun18.html) is available to everyone regardless of age, but only valid during school vacations. These are roughly March 1 to April 10, July 20 to September 10, and December 10 to January 20; all are sold from ten days before these windows until ten days before they close. For ¥11,500 you get five day-tickets that can be used to travel anywhere in Japan, as long as you take only the slow *futsū* and *kaisoku* trains. The tickets can also be split and used individually by different people. If you're not in a hurry, this ticket can be the **biggest bargain** on the whole of Japan's rail system: you can, for example, use one of the day-tickets to travel from Tokyo to Nagasaki – it'll take almost 24 hours, but cost the equivalent of ¥2300. The tickets are also handy for touring a local area in a day, since you can get on and off trains as many times as you wish within 24 hours.

Kaisūken (回数券) are usually four or more one-way tickets to the same destination. These work out substantially cheaper than buying the tickets individually, and as such are good for groups travelling to the same destination. Among other places they are available on the limited express services from Tokyo to Matsumoto and Nagano-ken.

Furii kippu (フリー切符) excursion-type tickets are available for various areas of Japan, usually with unlimited use of local transport for a specified period of time. The **Hakone Furii Pass**

TRAVEL INFORMATION SERVICE

JR East Infoline (daily 10am–6pm; ☎050 2016 1603) is an information service in English, Chinese and Korean dealing with all train enquiries nationwide. Train bookings cannot be made on this service, but they will be able to tell you about the **fastest route** between any two points on the system and where to make a seat reservation.

(see box, p.205), offered by the Odakyū railway company, covering routes from Tokyo to the lakeland area of Hakone, is particularly good value. If you plan to travel in one area, it's always worth asking the JR East Infoline (see box opposite) or the tourist information offices if there are any other special tickets that could be of use.

By plane

The big two **domestic airlines** are All Nippon Airways (ANA; W ana.co.jp) and Japan Airlines (JAL; W jal.co.jp). Both carriers offer substantial **discounts** for advance bookings, with an extra discount if the booking is made entirely online. There's little difference between the two as far as prices and quality of service are concerned.

Local low-cost airlines have ballooned of late, providing much-needed competition to the rail; these include **Skymark** (W skymark.co.jp), with cut-price routes between various major airports; **Solaseed Air** (W skynetasia.co.jp), who operate routes to and from their hubs of Haneda and Naha; **Peach** (W flypeach.com), who reach numerous destinations from their Osaka hub; and **Jetstar** (W jetstar.com), who offer services from Tokyo and Osaka.

If you're not using a rail pass (see p.35), low-cost and discounted plane fares are well worth considering. For example, to travel by train to Sapporo from Tokyo costs ¥22,780 and takes the better part of a day, compared with a discounted plane fare which can fall to as low as ¥9000 for a journey of an hour and a half. Discounts are generally not available during the peak travelling seasons.

Both JAL and ANA offer **discount flight passes** to overseas visitors, which are definitely worth considering if you plan to make several plane trips. JAL (W jal.co.jp/yokosojapan) offers the **oneworld Yokoso** and the **Welcome to Japan** passes: the former, only available to those using oneworld carriers to fly into Japan (including JAL, BA and Qantas), allows you to make up to five flights at ¥10,500 per sector; the latter, available to anyone regardless of which airline used, allows two flights for ¥27,300, three for ¥40,950, four for ¥54,600 and five for ¥68,250. ANA (W ana.co.jp) offers the similar **Star Alliance Japan Airpass** with up to five flights available on each pass at ¥10,500 per flight; and the **Visit Japan** fare with two to five flights available from ¥13,000 per flight. These fares are excellent value if you plan to visit far-flung destinations, such as the islands of Okinawa. These tickets are not available during peak travelling seasons

such as July and August and the New Year and Golden Week holidays.

By bus

Japan has a comprehensive system of **long-distance buses** (*chōkyori basu*; 長距離バス), including **night buses** (*yakō basu*; 夜行バス) between major cities. Fares are always cheaper than the fastest trains, but the buses are usually slower and can get caught up in traffic, even on the expressways (Japan's fastest roads), especially during peak travel periods. Most bus journeys start and finish next to or near the main train station. For journeys over two hours, there is usually at least one rest stop.

Willer Express (W willerexpress.com) is one of the largest long-distance bus operators and offers some great deals. A seven-hour overnight service from Tokyo to Kyoto, for example, can cost as little as ¥2160; by way of comparison, the Shinkansen costs ¥13,710, and takes 2hr 40min. There are hundreds of small bus companies operating different routes, so for full details of current services, timetables and costs make enquiries with **local tourist information offices**. Buses come into their own in the more rural parts of Japan where there are few or no trains. With a handful of exceptions (mentioned in the Guide), you don't need to book tickets or such services but can pay on the bus. JR runs a number of buses, some of which are covered by the various rail passes. Other private bus companies may also offer bus passes to certain regions; again, check with local tourist offices for any deals.

CABLE-CARS AND ROPEWAYS

It's worth noting a linguistic distinction that applies to the transport at several of Japan's mountain resorts. What is known in the West as a cable-car (a capsule suspended from a cable going up a mountain) is called a **ropeway** in Japan, while the term "**cable-car**" means a funicular or rack-and-pinion railway.

By ferry

One of the most pleasant ways of travelling around this island nation is by **ferry**. Overnight journeys between Honshū and Hokkaidō in the north, and Kyūshū and Shikoku in the south, are highly recommended. If you can't spare the time, try a short hop, say to one of the islands of the Inland Sea, or from Niigata to Sado-ga-shima.

On the **overnight ferries**, the cheapest fares, which entitle you to a sleeping space on the floor of a large room with up to a hundred other passengers, can be a bargain compared with train and plane fares to the same destinations. For example, the overnight ferry fare from Ōarai, two hours north of Tokyo, to Tomakomai, around an hour south of Sapporo on Hokkaidō, can be as low as ¥8500. Even if you pay extra for a bed in a shared or private berth, it's still cheaper than the train, and you'll have a very comfortable cruise as part of the bargain; see ⓦsunflower.co.jp for details. Ferries are also an excellent way of transporting a bicycle or motorbike (though you'll pay a small supplement for these); many also take cars.

Ferry **schedules** are subject to seasonal changes and also vary according to the weather, so for current details of times and prices, it's best to consult the local tourist information office.

By car

While it would be foolhardy to rent a car to get around Japan's big cities, **driving** is often the best way to tour the country's less populated and off-the-beaten-track areas. Japanese roads are of a very high standard, with the vast majority of signs on main routes being in *rōmaji* as well as Japanese script. Although you'll have to pay tolls to travel on the expressways (reckon on around ¥30 per kilometre), many other perfectly good roads are free; regular petrol averages around ¥140 a litre. For a group of people, renting a car to tour a rural area over a couple of days can work out much better

value than taking buses. It's often possible to rent cars for less than a day, too, for short trips.

There are **car rental** counters at all the major airports and train stations. The main Japanese companies include Mazda Rent-a-car (ⓦmazda-rentacar.co.jp); Nippon Rent-a-car (ⓦnipponrentacar.co.jp); Nissan Rent-a-car (ⓦnissan-rentacar.com); and Toyota Rent-a-car (ⓦrent.toyota.co.jp). Budget, Hertz and National also have rental operations across Japan (although not as widely spread). For local car rental firms' contact numbers, see the "Arrival and departure" or "Getting around" sections in the relevant area accounts, or consult the car rental company websites. **Rates**, which vary little between companies and usually include unlimited mileage, start from around ¥6500 for the first 24 hours for the smallest type of car (seating four people), plus ¥1000 insurance. During the peak seasons of Golden Week, Obon and New Year, rates for all cars tend to increase.

Most cars come with a **GPS** (Global Positioning Satellite) navigation system. It's sometimes possible to get an English-language version CD to work with the GPS – ask for this when you book. Input the telephone number for a location (the number of the hotel you're staying at or a museum you want to visit, for example) and the GPS system will plot the course for you.

Since you're unlikely to want to drive in any of the cities, the best rental **deals** are often through **Eki Rent-a-Car** (ⓦwww.ekiren.co.jp), which gives a discounted rate by combining the rental with a train ticket to the most convenient station for the area you wish to explore. Eki-Rent-a-Car's offices are close to stations, as are often those of other major car rental firms.

To rent a car you must have an **international driver's licence** based on the 1949 Geneva Convention (some international licences are not valid, including those issued in France, Germany and Switzerland), as well as your national licence. Officially, if you have a French, German or Swiss licence (regular or international) you are supposed to get an official Japanese translation of the licence – contact your local Japanese embassy for further info. You may get lucky and find a car rental firm that doesn't know or ignores this rule, but don't count on it. If you've been in Japan for more than six months, you'll need to apply for a Japanese licence.

Driving is on the **left**, the same as in Britain, Ireland, Australia, South Africa and most of Southeast Asia, and international traffic signals are used. The bilingual *Japan Road Atlas* (¥2890), published by Shōbunsha, includes many helpful notes, such as the dates when some roads close during winter. If you're a member of an automobile association at home, the chances are that you'll qualify for reciprocal rights with the Japan Auto Federation (W jaf.or.jp), which publishes the English-language *Rules of the Road* book, detailing Japan's driving code.

The top **speed limit** in Japan is 80kph, which applies only on expressways, though drivers frequently exceed this and are rarely stopped by police. In cities, the limit is 40kph. There are always car parks close to main train stations; at some, your vehicle will be loaded onto a rotating conveyor belt and whisked off to its parking spot. Reckon on ¥500 per hour for a central city car park and ¥300 per hour elsewhere. If you manage to locate a parking meter, take great care not to overstay the time paid for (usually around ¥300/hour); some have mechanisms to trap cars, which will only be released once the fine has been paid directly into the meter (typically ¥10,000–15,000).

In rural areas, parking is not so much of a problem and is rarely charged.

If you've drunk any **alcohol** at all, even the smallest amount, don't drive – its illegal, as well as dumb, and if you're caught by the police you'll be in big trouble, as will anyone sharing the vehicle with you (drunk or otherwise).

By bike

Although you're unlikely to want to **cycle** around the often traffic-clogged streets of Japan's main cities, a bike is a great way to get from A to B in the smaller towns and countryside, allowing you to see plenty en route. Cycle touring is a very popular activity with students over the long summer vacation. Hokkaidō, in particular, is a cyclist's dream, with excellent roads through often stunning scenery and a network of basic but ultra-cheap cyclists' accommodation.

JAPANESE ADDRESSES

Japanese **addresses** are, frankly, a little bit ridiculous – when it's impossible to find the building you're looking for even when you're standing right in front of it, it's clear that there are some major system failures. This stems from the fact that few roads have names; instead, city districts are split into **numbered blocks**, on which the numbers themselves are usually not visible.

A typical address starts with the largest administrative district, the **ken** (prefecture), accompanied by a seven-digit postcode – for example, Nagasaki-ken 850-0072. The four exceptions are Tōkyo-*to* (metropolis), Kyoto-*fu* and Ōsaka-*fu* (urban prefectures), and Hokkaidō – all independent administrative areas at the same level as the *ken*, also followed by a seven-digit code. Next comes the **shi** (city) or, in the country, the **gun** (county) or **mura** (village). The largest cities are then subdivided into **ku** (wards), followed by **chō** (districts), then **chōme** (local neighbourhoods), blocks and, finally, **individual buildings**.

If a building has a name and/or holds several different businesses or homes on different floors, you'll find the **floor number** generally listed according to the US fashion with the first floor (1F) being the ground floor and the second floor (2F) being the first floor above ground. B1F, B2F and so on, stands for the floors below ground level. Some addresses, where the block is entirely taken up by one building, will only have two numerals. If an address has four numerals, the first one is for a separate business within a certain part of the building.

Japanese addresses are written in reverse order from the Western system. However, when written in English, they usually follow the Western order; this is the system we adopt in the Guide. For example the address 2F Maru Bldg, 2-12-7 Kitano-chō, Chūō-ku, Kōbe-shi identifies the second floor of the Maru Building which is building number 7, somewhere on block 12 of number 2 *chōme* in Kitano district, in Chūō ward of Kōbe city. Buildings may bear a small metal tag with their number (eg 2-12-7, or just 12-7), while lampposts often have a bigger plaque with the district name in *kanji* and the block reference (eg 2-12). Note that the same address can also be written 12-7 Kitano-chō 2-chōme, Chūō-ku.

Though the system's not too difficult in theory, actually **locating an address** on the ground can be frustrating. The consolation is that even Japanese people find it tough. The best strategy is to have the address written down, preferably in Japanese, and then get to the nearest train or bus station. Once in the neighbourhood, start asking; local police boxes (*kōban*) are a good bet and have detailed maps of their own areas. If all else fails, don't be afraid to phone – often someone will come to meet you.

In many places, you can **rent bikes** from outlets beside or near the train station; some towns even have free bikes – enquire at the tourist office. Youth hostels often rent out bikes, too, usually at the most competitive rates. You can buy a brand-new bike in Japan for under ¥20,000 but you wouldn't want to use it for anything more than getting around town; for sturdy touring and mountain bikes, hunt out a specialist bike shop or bring your own. Although repair shops can be found nationwide, for foreign models it's best to bring essential spare parts with you. And despite Japan's low crime rate, a small but significant section of the Japanese public treats bikes as common property; if you don't want to lose it, make sure your bike is well chained whenever you leave it.

If you plan to take your bike on a train or bus, ensure you have a bike bag in which to parcel it up; on trains, you're also supposed to pay a special **bike transport supplement** of ¥270 (ask for a *temawarihin kippu*), though ticket inspectors may not always check.

If you're planning a serious cycling tour, an excellent investment is *Cycling Japan* by Brian Harrell, a handy practical guide detailing many touring routes around the country. There's also useful cycling information on the following sites: Ⓦjapancycling.org, Ⓦkancycling.com and Ⓦoutdoorjapan.com. If you're up for a two-month pedal from Hokkaidō to Kyūshū, see the website for Bicycling for Everyone's Earth (BEE; Ⓦbeejapan.org).

Hitching

There's always a risk associated with **hitching**. That said, Japan is one of the safest and easiest places in the world to hitch a ride, and in some rural areas it's just about the only way of getting around without your own transport. It's also a fantastic way to meet locals, who are often only too happy to go kilometres out of their way to give you a lift just for the novelty value (impecunious students apart, hitching is very rare in Japan), or the opportunity it provides to practise English or another foreign language.

As long as you don't look too scruffy, you'll seldom be waiting long for a ride; as is the case anywhere, it's best to pick your standing point wisely (somewhere cars can see you and stop safely, and are likely to be heading your way). It's a good idea to write your intended destination in large *kanji* characters on a piece of card to hold up. Note that in Japan, convenience stores are a godsend; almost all have decent maps of the surrounding area, toilets and spare cardboard boxes which you can tear up and scrawl your destination on. Carry a stock of small gifts you can leave as a thank you; postcards, sweets and small cuddly toys are usually popular. Will Ferguson's *A Hitch hiker's Guide to Japan* and his entertaining travel narrative *Hokkaidō Highway Blues* (see p.837) are useful reference books.

Accommodation

It's wise to reserve at least your first few nights' accommodation before arrival, especially at the cheaper hostels and minshuku (family-run B&B-style inns) in Tokyo and Kyoto, where budget places are scarce. If you do arrive without a reservation, make use of the free accommodation booking services in Narita and Kansai International airports (see p.125 and p.498).

Once in Japan, book one or two days ahead to ensure that your selected targets aren't full. Outside peak season, however, you'll rarely be stuck for accommodation. Around major **train stations** there's usually a clutch of business hotels and a **tourist information desk** – the majority will make a booking for you.

Most large- and medium-sized hotels in big cities have English-speaking receptionists who'll take a booking over the phone. The cheaper and more rural the place, however, the more likely you are to have to **speak in Japanese**, or a mix of Japanese and English. Don't be put off: armed with the right phrases (see Language, p.839), and speaking slowly and clearly, you should be able to make yourself understood – many of the terms you'll need are actually English words pronounced in a Japanese way. If you're having difficulty, the staff at your current accommodation may be able to help. Booking online is an option, with the advantage that you'll often get a slightly lower room rate; major chains and places that receive a lot of foreign guests generally have an English-language page.

ROUGH GUIDE ACCOMMODATION PRICES

Unless stated otherwise, **prices** in this guide for all types of lodging are quoted per night for the cheapest double room in high season.

Almost without exception, **security** is not a problem, though it's never sensible to leave valuables lying around in your room. In hostels, it's advisable to use lockers, if provided, or leave important items at the reception desk. Standards of **service** and **cleanliness** vary according to the type of establishment, but are usually more than adequate. Check-in is generally between 3pm and 7pm, and check-out by 10am.

While credit cards are becoming more widely accepted, in many cases **payment** is still expected in cash. In hostels and many cheaper business hotels, you'll be expected to pay when you check in.

While all hotel rates must include eight-percent consumption **tax**, there are a couple of other taxes to look out for. Most top-end hotels add a service charge of ten to fifteen percent, while in Tokyo the Metropolitan Government levies a tax of ¥100 per person per night in rooms that cost over ¥10,000 per person per night (or ¥200 if the room costs over ¥15,000); check to make sure if these are included in the published room rate. In hot-spring resorts, there's a small onsen tax (usually ¥150), though again this may already be included in the rates. And it's always worth asking when booking if there are any deals, usually referred to as "plans", such as special weekend rates at business hotels

Tipping is not necessary, nor expected, in Japan. The only exception is at high-class Japanese ryokan, where it's good form to leave ¥2000 for the room attendant – put the money in an envelope and hand it over discreetly at the end of your stay.

Online accommodation resources

There are a number of general booking and information sites, the best of which are listed below.

ACCOMMODATION WEBSITES

Ikyū Ⓦ ikyu.com. Japanese-only site offering heavily discounted rooms at nearly one thousand top-class hotels and ryokan.

Japan Hotel Association Ⓦ j-hotel.or.jp. Covering most major cities, though the hotels tend to be part of big, expensive chains. Lots of information provided.

Japan Hotel Net Ⓦ japanhotel.net. Offering a good range of accommodation nationwide, with a special section on ski resorts. Lots of information, including photos.

JAPANiCAN Ⓦ japanican.com. Good deals on around four thousand hotels, ryokan and tours across the country.

Japan Ryokan Association Ⓦ ryokan.or.jp. Around 1200 ryokan and hotels offering Japanese-style accommodation, many of them with onsen baths. Links take you to the relevant homepage, and there's plenty of background information about staying in ryokan.

JAPANESE SCRIPT

To help you find your way around, we've included **Japanese script** for all place names and for sights, hotels, restaurants, cafés, bars and shops. Where the English name for a point of interest is very different from its Japanese name, we've also provided the *rōmaji*, so that you can easily pronounce the Japanese.

Japanese Guest Houses Ⓦ japaneseguesthouses.com. Over 550 ryokan – from humble to grand – across the country. Also offer cultural tours in Kyoto.

Japanese Inn Group Ⓦ japaneseinngroup.com. A long-established association of about eighty good-value ryokan and minshuku.

The Ryokan Collection Ⓦ ryokancollection.com. Book one of 29 specially selected top ryokan, grouped in six locations across Japan.

Travel Rakuten Ⓦ travel.rakuten.co.jp/en. Pick of the local booking sights with great discounts on published rates and the broadest selection of properties.

Hotels

Most Western-style **hotel** rooms have en-suite bathrooms, TV, phone and air conditioning as standard; there's usually high-speed internet access too, sometimes through LAN only if there's no wi-fi. Don't expect a lot of character, however, especially among the older and cheaper business hotels, although things are slowly beginning to improve and even relatively inexpensive chains are now smartening up their act.

Rates for a double or twin room range from an average of ¥30,000 at a top-flight hotel, to ¥15,000–20,000 for a smartish establishment, which will usually have a restaurant and room service. At the lowest level, a room in a basic hotel with minimal amenities will cost ¥5000–10,000. Charges are almost always on a per-room basis and usually exclude meals, though breakfast may occasionally be included. **Single room** rates usually range from just over half to three-quarters the price of a double. Most hotels offer non-smoking rooms and some have "ladies' floors".

Business hotels

Modest **business hotels** constitute the bulk of the middle and lower price brackets. Primarily designed for those travelling on business and usually clustered around train stations, they are perfect if all you want is a place to crash out, though at the cheapest places you may find just a box with a tiny bed, a desk and a chair crammed into the smallest possible space. While the majority of rooms are single, most places have a few twins, doubles or "semi-doubles" – a large single bed which takes two at a squeeze. Squeeze is also the operative word for the aptly named "unit baths", which business hotels specialize in; these moulded plastic units contain a shower, bathtub, toilet and washbasin but leave little room for manoeuvre. That said, some business hotels are relatively smart and there are a number of reliable chains including *Tōyoko Inn* (Ⓦtoyoko-inn .com), which has scores of hotels across the country, offering a simple breakfast and free internet connections in their room rates. More upmarket are *Washington Hotels* (Ⓦwh-rsv.com/english) and the *Solare* group (Ⓦsolarehotels.com), which encompasses *Chisun* business hotels and the smarter *Loisir* and *Solare Collection* chains. Some have smoking and non-smoking floors.

Capsule hotels

Catering mainly for commuters – often in various states of inebriation – who have missed their last train home are **capsule hotels**; you'll find them mostly near major stations. Inside are rows of tube-like rooms, roughly 2m long, 1m high and 1m wide; despite their "coffin-like" reputation, they can feel surprisingly comfy, with a mattress, bedding, phone, alarm and TV built into the plastic surrounds. The "door" consists of a flimsy curtain, which won't keep out the loudest snores, and they are definitely not designed for claustrophobics. However, they're relatively cheap at ¥2500–4000 per night, and fun to try at least once, though the majority are for men only. You can't stay in the hotel during the day – not that you'd want to – but you can leave luggage in their lockers. Check-in usually starts around 4pm and often involves buying a ticket from a vending machine in the lobby. Rates generally include a *yukata* (cotton dressing gown), towel and toothbrush set, and many establishments have onsen-like communal bathing facilities. Kyoto and Osaka offer a couple of stylish modern takes on the capsule hotel that are worth trying (see p.441 and p.501), while recent years have seen a few **cabin hotels** enter the market. These are just like the capsules, but with a tiny bit of attached space for you to stand, and occasionally an internet-ready computer terminal to boot.

Love hotels

Love hotels – where you can rent rooms by the hour – are another quintessential Japanese experience. Generally located in entertainment districts, they are immediately recognizable from the sign outside quoting prices for "rest" or "stay", and many sport ornate exteriors. Some can be quite sophisticated: the main market is young people or married couples taking a break from crowded apartments. All kinds of tastes can be indulged at love hotels, with rotating beds in mirror-lined rooms now decidedly passé in comparison with some of the fantasy creations on offer. Some rooms even come equipped with video cameras so you can take home a souvenir DVD of your stay. You usually choose your room from a back-lit display indicating those still available, and then negotiate with a cashier lurking behind a tiny window (eye-to-eye contact is avoided to preserve privacy). Though "rest" rates are high (from about ¥5000 for 2hr), the price of an overnight stay can cost the same as a business hotel (roughly ¥8000–10,000), although you usually can't check in until around 10pm. To learn more about love hotels buy the photo book *Love Hotels* by Ed Jacob (Ⓦquirkyjapan.or.tv/lovehotelbookintro.htm).

Japanese-style accommodation

A night in a traditional Japanese inn, or **ryokan**, is one of the highlights of a visit to Japan. The best charge five-star hotel rates, but there are plenty where you can enjoy the full experience at affordable prices. Cheaper are **minshuku**, family-run guesthouses, and the larger government-owned **kokuminshukusha** (people's lodges) located in national parks and resort areas. In addition, some temples and shrines offer simple accommodation, or you can arrange to stay with a Japanese family through the **homestay** programme.

It's advisable to **reserve** at least a day ahead and essential if you want to eat in. Though a few don't take foreigners, mainly through fear of language problems and cultural faux pas, you'll find plenty that do listed in the Guide chapters. JNTO also publishes useful lists of ryokan and distributes brochures of the *Japanese Inn Group* (see p.41), which specializes in inexpensive, foreigner-friendly accommodation.

Ryokan

Rooms in a typical **ryokan** are generally furnished with just a low table and floor cushions sitting on pale green rice-straw matting (tatami) and a hanging scroll – nowadays alongside a TV and phone – decorating the alcove (tokonoma) on one wall. Though you'll increasingly find a toilet and washbasin in the room, baths are generally communal. The rules of ryokan etiquette (see box opposite) may seem daunting, but overall these are great places to stay.

STAYING IN JAPANESE-STYLE ACCOMMODATION

Whenever you're staying in Japanese-style accommodation, you'll be expected to check in early – between 3pm and 6pm – and to follow local custom from the moment you arrive.

Just inside the front door, there's usually a row of **slippers** for you to change into, but remember to slip them off when walking on the tatami. The **bedding** is stored behind sliding doors in your room during the day and only laid out in the evening. In top-class ryokan this is done for you, but elsewhere be prepared to tackle your own. There'll be a mattress (which goes straight on the tatami) with a sheet to put over it, a soft quilt to sleep under, and a pillow stuffed with rice husks.

Most places provide a **yukata**, a loose cotton robe tied with a belt, and a short jacket (tanzen) in cold weather. The yukata can be worn in bed, during meals, when going to the bathroom and even outside – in resort areas many Japanese holiday-makers take an evening stroll in their yukata and wooden sandals (geta; also supplied by the ryokan). Wrap the left side of the yukata over the right; the opposite is used to dress the dead.

The traditional Japanese **bath** (furo) has its own set of rules (see p.61). It's customary to bathe in the evenings. In ryokan, there are usually separate bathrooms for men (男) and women (女), but elsewhere there will either be designated times for males and females, or you'll simply have to wait until it's vacant – it's perfectly acceptable for couples and families to bathe together, though there's not usually a lot of space.

Evening **meals** tend to be early, at 6pm or 7pm. Smarter ryokan generally serve meals in your room, while communal dining is the norm in cheaper places. **At night**, the doors are locked pretty early, so check before going out – they may let you have a key.

Room rates vary according to the season, the grade of room, the quality of meal you opt for and the number of people in a room; prices almost always include breakfast and an evening meal. Rates are usually quoted per person and calculated on the basis of two people sharing. One person staying in a room will pay slightly more than the advertised per-person price; three people sharing a room, slightly less. On average, a night in a basic ryokan will cost between ¥8000 and ¥10,000 per head, while a classier establishment, perhaps with meals served in the room, will cost up to ¥20,000. Top-rank ryokan with exquisite meals and the most attentive service imaginable can cost upwards of ¥50,000 per person.

At cheaper ryokan, it's possible to ask for a room without **meals**, though this is frowned on at the more traditional places and, anyway, the delicious multicourse meals are often very good value. If you find miso soup, cold fish and rice a bit hard to tackle in the morning, you might want to opt for a Western breakfast, if available.

Minshuku and kokuminshukusha

There's a fine line between the cheapest ryokan and a **minshuku**. In general, minshuku are smaller and less formal than ryokan: more like staying in a private home, with varying degrees of comfort and cleanliness. All rooms will be Japanese-style, with communal bathrooms and dining areas. A night in a minshuku will cost from around ¥4500 per person excluding meals, or from ¥6000 with two meals; rates are calculated in the same way as for ryokan.

In country areas and popular resorts, you'll also find homely guesthouses called **pensions** –a word borrowed from the French. Though the accommodation and meals are Western-style, these are really minshuku in disguise. They're family-run – generally by young couples escaping city life – and specialize in hearty home cooking. Rates average around ¥8000 per head, including dinner and breakfast.

In the national parks, onsen resorts and other popular tourist spots, minshuku and pensions are supplemented by large, government-run **kokuminshukusha**, which cater to family groups and tour parties. They're often quite isolated and difficult to get to without your own transport. The average cost of a night's accommodation is around ¥8000 per person, including two meals.

Temples and shrines

A few Buddhist **temples** and Shinto **shrines** take in regular guests for a small fee, and some belong to the Japanese Inn Group (see p.41) or the Japan Youth Hostels association (see p.44). By far the best places to experience temple life are at the Buddhist retreat of Kōya-san (see p.507) and in Kyoto's temple lodges (see p.442).

Though the accommodation is inevitably basic, the food can be superb, especially in temple lodgings (*shukubō*), where the monks serve up delicious vegetarian cuisine (*shōjin ryōri*). In many temples, you'll also be welcome to attend the early-morning prayer ceremonies. Prices vary between ¥4000 and ¥10,000 per person, with no meals or perhaps just breakfast at lower rates.

Hostels

Japan has over four hundred **hostels** spread throughout the country, offering cheap accommodation. The majority of hostels are well run, clean and welcoming, with the best housed in wonderful old farmhouses or temples, often in great locations.

There are two main types of hostel in Japan. Increasing in number every year are private establishments, which tend to be far friendlier affairs than those run by the government or Japan Youth Hostels (JYH; ❿jyh.or.jp), which is affiliated to Hostelling International (HI; ❿hihostels.com). The JYH hostels generally impose a six-night maximum stay, evening curfews and a raft of regulations. **Membership** cards are not required at government or private hostels, but all JYH ask for a current Youth Hostel card. Non-members have to buy a "welcome stamp" (¥600) each time they stay at a JYH hostel; six stamps within a twelve-month period entitles you to the Hostelling International card. JNTO offices abroad and around Japan stock a free **map** that gives contact details of all JYH hostels.

The average **price** of hostel accommodation ranges from around ¥2000 per person for a dorm bed up to ¥5500 for a private room; this means that once you've included meals, a night at a private room in a hostel may work out only slightly less expensive than staying at a minshuku, or a night at a business hotel. Rates at some hostels increase during peak holiday periods.

It's essential to make **reservations** well in advance for the big-city hostels and during school vacations: namely, New Year, March, around Golden Week (late April to mid-May), and in July and August. At other times, it's a good idea to book ahead, since hostels in prime tourist spots are always busy; some close for a day or two in the off season, and others for the whole winter. If you want an evening meal, you also need to let them know a day in advance. Hostel accommodation normally consists of either dormitory bunks or shared Japanese-style tatami rooms, with communal bathrooms and dining areas. An increasing number also have private or family rooms, but these tend to fill up quickly. **Bedding** is provided. The majority of hostels have **laundry** facilities and internet access; wi-fi is usually a given these days and almost always free, though there's occasionally a small charge for using the hostel's own computer terminals.

At the JYH and government hostels, optional **meals** are sometimes offered; these vary in quality, though can be pretty good value. Dinner will generally be Japanese-style, while breakfast frequently includes bread, jam and coffee, sometimes as part of a buffet. Some hostels have a basic kitchen.

Check-in is generally between 3pm and 8pm; you sometimes have to vacate the building during the day (usually by 10am at JYH hostels).

Camping and mountain huts

There are thousands of **campsites** (*kyampu-jō*) scattered throughout Japan, with prices ranging from nothing up to ¥5000 or more to pitch a tent. In some places, you'll also pay an entry fee of a few hundred yen per person, plus charges for water and cooking gas. In general, facilities are pretty basic compared with American or European sites; many have no hot water, for example, and the camp shop may stock nothing but Pot-Noodles. Most sites open during the summer months, when they're packed out with students and school parties.

JNTO publishes lists of selected campsites, or ask at local tourist offices. If you haven't got your own

---

HOMESTAY PROGRAMMES & WWOOF

Homestay **programmes** are a wonderful way of getting to know Japan – contact any of the local tourism associations and international exchange foundations listed in this book to see if any programmes are operating in the area you plan to visit.

It's also possible to arrange to stay at one of nearly four hundred or so organic farms and other rural properties around Japan through **WWOOF** (Willing Workers on Organic Farms; ❿wwoof.org). Bed and board is provided for free in return for work on the farm; see Living in Japan (see p.70) for more details. This is a great way to really experience how country folk live away from the big cities and the beaten tourist path. To get a list of host farms, you have to take out an annual membership, though a few examples are posted on the Japanese site (❿wwoofjapan.com).

JAPAN'S CHEAPEST SLEEPS

The cheapest places to stay in Japan are not sleazy love motels, capsule hotel pods or (Okinawa aside) youth hostel dormitories. No, to really hit the bottom of the barrel you have to head to an **internet café**, where you can get a night's sleep for under ¥1500. Those thinking that such places cannot count as accommodation would be wrong – while most have "regular" computer terminals lining open corridors, many have terminals in tiny, walled-off cubicles, often with a choice between a soft, reclinable chair and a cushioned floor (the latter being particularly comfortable). Many also have shower facilities (usually ¥100), snack counters, and free soft-drink vending machines. Indeed, many Japanese actually live semi-permanently in these places, if they can't afford rent elsewhere – they're known locally as the "cyber-homeless". Drawbacks include occasional loud snorers, and neighbouring couples making the most of some rare, if imperfect, privacy. You'll find such establishments in almost any large city in Japan; at some, you'll need to pay a one-off membership fee of around ¥300.

---

tent, you can often hire everything on site or rent simple cabins from around ¥2500 – check before you get there. The best sites are in national parks and can be both time-consuming and costly to get to unless you have your own transport. Sleeping rough in national parks is banned, but elsewhere in the countryside **camping wild** is tolerated. However, it's advisable to choose an inconspicuous spot – don't put your tent up till dusk and leave early in the morning. Pitch too early or wake too late, and don't be too surprised if worried locals alert the local police to your presence (though as long as you've got your passport handy you should be fine).

In the main hiking areas, you'll find a good network of **mountain huts** (*yama-goya*). These range from basic shelters to much fancier places with wardens and meals. Huts get pretty crowded in summer and during student holidays; count on at least ¥5000 per head, including two meals. Many places will also provide a picnic lunch. You can get information about mountain huts from local tourist offices.

Long-term accommodation

There's plenty of long-term **rental accommodation** available in Japan, making it a relatively easy and affordable country in which to set up home.

Newcomers who arrive without a job, or are not on some sort of expat package that includes accommodation, usually start off in what's known as a **gaijin house** (foreigner house). Located in Tokyo, Kyoto and other cities with large foreign populations, these are shared apartments with a communal kitchen and bathroom, ranging from total fleapits to the almost luxurious. They're usually rented by the month, though if there's space, weekly or even nightly rates may be available. You'll find *gaijin* houses advertised in the English-language press, or simply ask around. Monthly rates

for a shared apartment in Tokyo start at ¥30,000–40,000 per person if you share a room, and ¥50,000–60,000 for your own room. A deposit may also be required.

The alternative is a **private apartment**. These are usually rented out by real estate companies, though you'll also find places advertised in the media. Unfortunately, some landlords simply refuse to rent to non-Japanese. Some rental agencies specialize in dealing with foreigners, or you could ask a Japanese friend or colleague to act as an intermediary. When you've found a place, be prepared to pay a deposit of one to two months' rent in addition to the first month's rent, key money (usually one or two months' non-refundable rent when you move in) and a month's rent in commission to the agent. You may also be asked to provide information about your financial situation and find someone – generally a Japanese national – to act as a guarantor. The basic monthly rental in Tokyo starts at ¥50,000–60,000 per month for a one-room box, and upwards of ¥100,000 for somewhere more comfortable with a separate kitchen and bathroom.

Food and drink

One of the great pleasures of a trip to Japan is exploring the full and exotic range of Japanese food and drink. While dishes such as sushi and tempura are common the world over these days, there are hundreds of other types of local cuisine that may provide new and delicious discoveries. Regional specialities abound, and form a major part of the domestic travel scene: many locals seemingly holiday to different parts of the country for culinary reasons alone.

It's hard to blame them, for many Japanese recipes embody a subtlety of flavour and mixture of texture rarely found in other cuisines, and the presentation is often so exquisite that it feels an insult to the chef to eat what has been so painstakingly crafted.

Picking at delicate morsels with chopsticks is only one small part of the dining experience. It's far more common to find Japanese tucking into robust and cheap dishes such as hearty bowls of **ramen noodles** or the comforting concoction **karē raisu** (curry rice) as well as burgers and fried chicken from ubiquitous Western-style fast-food outlets. All the major cities have an extensive range of restaurants serving Western and other Asian dishes, with Tokyo, Kyoto and Osaka in particular being major destinations for foodies.

Eating out needn't cost the earth. Lunch is always the best-value meal of the day, seldom costing more than ¥2000. If you fuel up well for lunch, a cheap bowl of noodles for dinner could carry you through the night.

Meals

Breakfast is generally served from around 7am to 9am at most hotels, ryokan and minshuku. At the top end and mid-range places you'll generally have a choice between a Western-style breakfast or a traditional meal consisting of miso soup, grilled fish, pickles and rice; at the cheaper minshuku and ryokan, only a Japanese-style meal will be available. Western-style breakfasts, when available, sometimes resemble what you might eat at home, but most commonly involve wedges of thick white tasteless bread and some form of eggs and salad. Most cafés also have a "morning-service" menu which means *kōhii* and *tōsuto* (coffee and toast).

Restaurants generally open for **lunch** around 11.30am and finish serving at 2pm. Lacklustre sandwiches are best passed over in favour of a full meal at a restaurant; set menus (called *teishoku*) are always on offer and usually cost ¥600–1200 for a couple of courses, often with a drink.

Teishoku are sometimes available at night, when you may also come across **course menus**, which involve a series of courses and are priced according to the number of courses and quality of ingredients used. At any time of day, you can snack in stand-up noodle bars – often found around train stations – and from revolving conveyor belts at cheap sushi shops.

Dinner, the main meal of the day, is typically served from 6pm to around 9pm. The major cities are about the only option for late-night dining. In a traditional Japanese meal, you'll usually be served all your courses at the same time, but at more formal places, rice and soup are always served last. You are most likely to finish your meal with a piece of seasonal **fruit**, such as melon, orange, persimmon or *nashi* (a crisp type of pear), or an ice cream (if it's green, it will be flavoured with *matcha* tea).

At **tea ceremonies** (see box, p.52), small, intensely sweet *wagashi* are served – these prettily decorated sweetmeats are usually made of pounded rice, red azuki beans or chestnuts. *Wagashi* can also be bought from specialist shops and department stores and make lovely gifts.

Where to eat and drink

A *shokudō* is a kind of canteen that serves a range of traditional and generally inexpensive dishes. Usually found near train and subway stations and in busy shopping districts, *shokudō* can be identified by the displays of plastic meals in their windows. Other restaurants (*resutoran*) usually serve just one type of food, for example sushi and sashimi (*sushi-ya*), or yakitori (*yakitori-ya*), or specialize in a particular style of cooking, such as *kaiseki* (haute cuisine) or *teppanyaki*, where food is prepared on a steel griddle, either by diners themselves or a chef.

All over Japan, but particularly in city suburbs, you'll find bright and breezy **family restaurants**, such as *Royal Host* and *Jonathan's*, American-style operations specifically geared to family dining and serving Western and Japanese dishes. The food at these places can be on the bland side, but is invariably keenly priced. They also have menus illustrated with photographs to make ordering easy. If you can't decide what to eat, head for the restaurant floors of major **department stores**, where you'll find a collection of Japanese and Western operations, often outlets of reputable local restaurants. Many will have plastic food displays in their front windows and daily special menus.

Western and other ethnic food restaurants proliferate in the cities, and it's seldom a problem finding popular **foreign cuisines** such as Italian (*Itaria-ryōri*), French (*Furansu-ryōri*), Korean (*Kankoku-ryōri*), Chinese (*Chūgoku-ryōri* or *Chūka-ryōri*) or Thai (*Tai-ryōri*) food. However, the recipes are often adapted to suit Japanese tastes, which can mean less spicy dishes than you may be used to.

Coffee shops (*kissaten*) are something of an institution in Japan, often designed to act as a lounge

BENTŌ: THE JAPANESE PACKED LUNCH

Every day, millions of Japanese trot off to school or work with a **bentō** stashed in their satchel or briefcase. Bentō are boxed **lunches** which are either made at home or bought from shops all over Japan. Traditional bentō include rice, pickles, grilled fish or meat and vegetables. There are thousands of permutations depending on the season and the location in Japan, with some of the best being available from department stores, where there's always a model or picture to show you what's inside the box. At their most elaborate, in classy restaurants, bentō come in beautiful multilayered lacquered boxes, each compartment containing some exquisite culinary creation. Among housewives, it's become something of a competitive sport and art form to create fun designs out of the bentō ingredients for their children's lunch. Empty bentō boxes in a huge range of designs are sold in the household section of department stores and make lovely souvenirs.

or business meeting place for patrons starved of space at home or the office. Others have weird designs or specialize in certain things, such as jazz or comic books. In such places, a speciality coffee or tea will usually set you back ¥500 or more. There are also plenty of cheap and cheerful operations like *Doutor* and *Starbucks*, serving drinks and snacks at reasonable prices; search these places out for a cheap breakfast or a quick bite.

The liveliest places to **drink** are izakaya, pub-type restaurants which also serve an extensive menu of mainly small dishes. Traditional *izakaya* are rather rustic-looking, although in the cities you'll come across more modern, trendy operations aimed at the youth market. One type of traditional *izakaya* is the *robatayaki*, which serves charcoal-grilled food. Most *izakaya* open around 6pm and shut down around midnight, if not later; there'll usually be a cover charge of ¥200–500 per person. From mid-June to late August, outdoor **beer gardens** – some attached to existing restaurants and izakayas, other stand-alone operations – flourish across Japan's main cities and towns; look out for the fairy lights on the roofs of buildings, or in street-level gardens and plazas.

Regular bars, or **nomiya**, often consist of little more than a short counter and a table, and are run by a *mamc-san* if female, or *papa-san* or master if male. Prices at most *nomiya* tend to be high and, although you're less likely to be ripped off if you speak some Japanese, it's no guarantee. All such bars operate a **bottle keep** system for regulars to stash a bottle of drink with their name on it behind the bar. It's generally best to go to such bars with a regular, since they tend to operate like mini-clubs, with non-regulars being given the cold shoulder. *Nomiya* stay open to the early hours, provided there are customers. A variation on the *nomiya* is the *tachinomiya*, or standing bar, which are usually cheaper and more casual. Some specialize in selling

premium wines or sake, and they often serve good food alongside the drinks.

Some bars also have cover charges (for which you'll usually get some small snack with your drink), although there's plenty of choice among those that don't, so always check before buying your drink. Bars specializing in **karaoke** aren't difficult to spot (see box p.146); if you decide to join in, there's usually a small fee to pay and songs with English lyrics to choose from. Some places also do all-you-can-drink specials, which usually work out cheaper if you'll be having three or more drinks; two hours of singing and drinking will set you back ¥2000–3000 per head.

Ordering and etiquette

On walking into most restaurants in Japan, you'll be greeted by the word *irasshaimase* ("welcome"). Indicate with your fingers how many places are needed. After being seated you'll be handed an *oshibori*, a damp, folded hand towel, usually steaming hot, but sometimes offered refreshingly cold in summer. A chilled glass of water (*mizu*) will also usually be brought automatically.

To help you decipher the menu, there's a basic glossary of essential words and phrases at the end of this book (see p.839). It's always worth asking if an English menu is available. If a restaurant has a plastic food window display, get up from your seat and use it to point out to your waiter or waitress what you want. If all else fails, look round at what your fellow diners are eating and point out what you fancy. Remember that the *teishoku* (set meal) or *kōsu* (course) meals offer the best value. The word *Baikingu* (written in katakana and standing for "Viking") means a help-yourself buffet.

Don't stick **chopsticks** (*hashi*) upright in your rice – though it is an allusion to death, for most Japanese it simply just looks wrong (remember that the West

KAISEKI-RYŌRI: JAPANESE HAUTE CUISINE

Japan's finest style of cooking, **kaiseki-ryōri**, comprises a series of small, carefully balanced and expertly presented dishes. Described by renowned Kyoto chef Murata Yoshihiro as "eating the seasons", this style of cooking began as an accompaniment to the tea ceremony and still retains the meticulous design of that elegant ritual. At the best *kaiseki-ryōri* restaurants, the **atmosphere** of the room in which the meal is served is just as important as the food, which will invariably reflect the best of the season's produce; you'll sit on tatami, a scroll decorated with calligraphy will hang in the *tokonoma* (alcove) and a waitress in kimono will serve each course on beautiful china and lacquerware. For such a sublime experience you should expect to pay ¥10,000 or more for dinner, although a lunchtime *kaiseki* bentō (see box, p.47) is a more affordable option, typically costing around ¥5000.

has its own odd table rules too). Also, never cross your chopsticks when you put them on the table, or use them to point at things. When it comes to eating soupy noodles, it's considered good form to slurp them up noisily; it's also fine to bring the bowl to your lips and drink directly from it.

When you want the **bill**, say okanjō o kudasai; the usual form is to pay at the till on the way out, not by leaving money on the table. There's no need to leave a tip, but it's polite to say gochisō-sama deshita ("That was delicious!") to the waiter or chef. Only the most upmarket Western restaurants and top hotels will add a service charge (typically ten percent).

Sushi, sashimi and seafood

Many non-Japanese falsely assume that all **sushi** is fish, but the name actually refers to the way the rice is prepared with vinegar, and you can also get sushi dishes with egg or vegetables. Fish and seafood are, of course, essential and traditional elements of Japanese cuisine, and range from the seaweed used in *miso-shiru* (soup) to the slices of tuna, salmon and squid laid across the slabs of sushi rice. Slices of raw fish and seafood on their own are called **sashimi**.

In a traditional **sushi-ya**, each plate is freshly made by a team of chefs working in full view of the customers. If you're not sure of the different types to order, point at the trays on show in the glass chiller cabinets at the counter, or go for the *nigiri-zushi mori-awase*, six or seven different types of fish and seafood on fingers of sushi rice. Other types of sushi include *maki-zushi*, rolled in a sheet of crisp seaweed, and *chirashi-zushi*, a layer of rice topped with fish, vegetables and cooked egg.

While a meal at a reputable *sushi-ya* can hit ¥5000 (or even more at a high-class joint), there are still some excellent places serving lunch sets for ¥600 and up. At **kaiten-zushi** shops, where you choose whatever sushi dish you want from the continually replenished conveyor belt, the bill will depend upon how much you order: anything from ¥600–3000 per person. In *kaiten-zushi*, plates are colour-coded according to how much they cost, and are totted up at the end for the total cost of the meal. If you can't see what you want, you can ask the chefs to make it for you. Green tea is free, and you can usually order beer or sake.

To try **fugu**, or blowfish, go to a specialist fish restaurant, which can be easily identified by the picture or model of a balloon-like fish outside. *Fugu's* reputation derives from its potential to be fatally poisonous rather than its bland, rubbery taste. The actual risk of dropping dead at the counter is virtually nil – at least from *fugu* poisoning – and you're more likely to keel over at the bill, which (cheaper, farmed *fugu* apart) will be in the ¥10,000 per-person bracket. *Fugu* is often served as part of a set-course menu including raw slivers of fish (sashimi) and a stew made from other parts of the fish served with rice.

A more affordable and tasty seafood speciality is **unagi**, or eel, typically basted with a thick sauce of soy and sake, sizzled over charcoal and served on a bed of rice. This dish is particularly popular in summer, when it's believed to provide strength in the face of sweltering heat.

Noodles

The three main types of **noodle** are soba, udon and ramen. **Soba** are thin noodles made of brown buckwheat flour. If the noodles are green, they've been made with green-tea powder.

There are two main styles of serving soba: hot and cold. It comes in a clear broth, often with added ingredients such as tofu, vegetables and chicken. Cold noodles piled on a bamboo-screen bed, with a cold sauce for dipping (which can be flavoured with chopped spring onions, seaweed flakes and *wasabi* – grated green horseradish paste) are called *zaru-soba* or *mori-soba*. In more traditional restaurants, you'll also be served a flask of the hot water (*soba-yu*) to cook the noodles, which is added to the dipping sauce to make a soup drink once you've finished the soba.

In most soba restaurants, **udon** will also be on the menu. These chunkier noodles are made with plain wheat flour and are served in the same hot or cold styles as soba. In **yakisoba** and **yakiudon** dishes the noodles are fried, often in a thick soy sauce, along with seaweed flakes, meat and vegetables.

Ramen, or yellow wheat-flour noodles, were originally imported from China but have now become part and parcel of Japanese cuisine. They're usually served in big bowls in three varieties: miso (flavoured with fermented bean paste), *shio* (a salty soup) or *shōyu* (a broth made with soy sauce). The dish is often finished off with a range of garnishes including seaweed, bamboo shoots, pink and white swirls of fish paste, and pork slices. You can usually spice it up with condiments such as minced garlic or a red pepper mixture at your table. Wherever you eat ramen, you can also usually get **gyōza**, fried half-moon-shaped dumplings filled with pork or seafood, to accompany them.

Rice dishes

A traditional meal isn't considered finished until a bowl of rice has been eaten. This Japanese staple also forms the basis of the alcoholic drink sake, as well as **mochi**, a chewy dough made from pounded glutinous rice (usually prepared and eaten during festivals such as New Year).

Rice is an integral part of several cheap snack-type dishes. **Onigiri** are palm-sized triangles of rice with a filling of soy, tuna, salmon roe, or sour *umeboshi* (pickled plum), all wrapped up in a sheet of crisp *nori* (seaweed). They can be bought at convenience stores for ¥100–150 each, and are ingeniously packaged so that the *nori* stays crisp until the *onigiri* is unwrapped. **Donburi** is a bowl of rice with various toppings, such as chicken and egg (*oyako-don*, literally "parent and child"), strips of stewed beef (*gyū-don*) or *katsu-don*, which come with a *tonkatsu* (see below) pork cutlet.

A perennially popular Japanese comfort food is **curry rice** (*karē raisu* in *rōmaji*). Only mildly spicy, this bears little relation to the Indian dish: what goes into the sludgy brown sauce that makes up the curry is a mystery, and you'll probably search in vain for evidence of any beef or chicken in the

so-called *biifu karē* and *chikin karē*. The better concoctions are very tasty and invariably cheap.

Meat dishes

Meat is an uncommon part of traditional Japanese cuisine, but in the last century dishes using beef, pork and chicken have become a major part of the national diet. Burger outlets are ubiquitous, and expensive steak restaurants, serving up dishes like **sukiyaki** (thin beef slices cooked in a soy, sugar and sake broth) and **shabu-shabu** (beef and vegetable slices cooked at the table in a light broth and dipped in various sauces), are popular treats.

Like *sukiyaki* and *shabu-shabu*, **nabe** (the name refers to the cooking pot) stews are prepared at the table over a gas or charcoal burner by diners who throw a range of raw ingredients (meat or fish along with vegetables) into the pot to cook. As things cook, they're fished out, and the last thing to be immersed is usually some type of noodle. *Chanko-nabe* is the famous chuck-it-all-in stew used to beef up sumo wrestlers.

Other popular meat dishes include **tonkatsu**, breadcrumb-covered slabs of pork, crisply fried and usually served on a bed of shredded cabbage with a brown, semi-sweet sauce; and **yakitori**, delicious skewers of grilled chicken (and sometimes other meats and vegetables). At the cheapest *yakitori-ya*, you'll pay for each skewer individually, typically around ¥100 per stick. **Kushiage** is a combination of *tonkatsu* and *yakitori* dishes, where skewers of meat, seafood and vegetables are coated in bread-crumbs and deep-fried.

Vegetarian dishes

Despite being the home of macrobiotic cooking, **vegetarianism** isn't a widely practised or fully understood concept in Japan. You might ask for a vegetarian (*saishoku*) dish in a restaurant and still be served something with meat or fish in it. If you're a committed vegetarian, things to watch out for include *dashi* stock, which contains *bonito* (dried tuna), and omelettes, which may contain chicken stock. To get a truly vegetarian meal, you will have to be patient and prepared to spell out exactly what you do and do not eat when you order. **Vege-Navi** (W vege-navi.jp) lists many vegetarian, vegan and macrobiotic options across the country.

If you're willing to turn a blind eye to occasionally eating meat, fish or animal fats by mistake, then tuck in because Japan has bequeathed some marvellous vegetarian foods to the world. Top of

DINING ON THE CHEAP

Japan isn't exactly paradise for budget travellers, but as far as food goes, there are some very good ways to stretch your yen. Many head straight to chain **convenience stores** such as 7-Eleven, AM/PM and Lawson, which sell snacks and drinks round the clock. Not quite as numerous, but found in every city district, **supermarkets** sell bananas, sandwich fodder and other regular backpacker staples, as well as super-cheap fresh noodles; note that in the hours before closing (9–11pm), they tend to lop off up to half of the price of sushi and other bento sets.

If you want to eat out, try a **standing noodle bar**; a bowl of soba or udon will cost from ¥290, though it can be tricky to operate the Japanese-only ticket machines. However, the real value is to be had at local **fast-food chains**, almost all of which supply English-language menus. All of the following can be found several times over in every single city; just ask around.

CoCo Ichiban-ya CoCo壱番屋 A quirky curry chain that allows you to piece together your meal. First, choose the type of stock you desire, then the amount of rice you want (up to 900g), then your desired level of spice (level one barely registers a hit; level ten provides a veritable spice-gasm). Then you come to the fun add-your-ingredients part: choices include beef, okra, scrambled egg, cheese, *tonkatsu*, *nattō* and a whole lot more. It'll end up costing ¥600–1100. Daily 8am–4am.

Matsu-ya 松屋 Fronted by yellow, Japanese-only signs with red and blue blobs on them, this chain specializes in cheap curry (from ¥330) and *gyudon* (beef on rice, ¥280). They

chuck in a steaming-hot bowl of miso soup with whatever you order. Daily 24hr.

Saizeriya Budget Italian food, often surprisingly good; their tasty *doria* (rice gratin) will fill a hole for ¥299, pasta dishes and small pizzas can be had from ¥399, or have a fried burger-and-egg set for ¥399. The wine prices are also ridiculous: ¥100 per glass, or an astonishingly cheap ¥1050 for a 1.5-litre (ie double-size) bottle. Daily 8am–midnight (often later).

★**Yoshinoya** 吉野家 You can't miss the bright-orange signs marking branches of the nation's favourite fast-food chain, famed for its cheap, tasty bowls of *gyudon* from just ¥280. Daily 24hr.

the list is **tofu**, compacted cakes of soya-bean curd, which comes in two main varieties, *momengoshi-dōfu* (cotton tofu), so called because of its fluffy texture, and the smoother, more fragile *kinugoshi-dōfu* (silk tofu). Buddhist cuisine, *shōjin-ryōri*, concocts whole menus based around different types of tofu dishes; although they can be expensive, it's worth searching out the specialist restaurants serving this type of food, particularly in major temple cities, such as Kyoto, Nara and Nagano. Note, though, that the most popular tofu dish you'll come across in restaurants – *hiya yakko*, a small slab of chilled tofu topped with grated ginger, spring onions and soy sauce – is usually sprinkled with *bonito* flakes.

Miso (fermented bean paste) is another crucial ingredient of Japanese cooking, used in virtually every meal, if only in the soup *miso-shiru*. It often serves as a flavouring in vegetable dishes, and comes in two main varieties: the light *shiro-miso*, and the darker, stronger-tasting *aka-miso*.

Most Japanese assume that no foreigners are able to stomach the nation's favourite breakfast snack: **nattō**, a sticky, stringy treat made with fermented beans. Its strong taste, pungent aroma and unfamiliar texture can be off-putting to Western palates, and many young Japanese hate

the stuff; it's worth trying at least once, though, and is usually served in little tubs at breakfast, to be mixed with mustard and soy sauce and eaten with rice. Hawaiian Japanese eat it with raw tuna – you can do likewise by picking the components up at any supermarket, then mixing them together.

Other Japanese dishes

Said to have been introduced to Japan in the sixteenth century by Portuguese traders, **tempura** are lightly battered pieces of seafood and vegetables. Tempura are dipped in a bowl of light sauce (*ten-tsuyu*) mixed with grated *daikon* radish and sometimes ginger. At specialist tempura restaurants, you'll generally order the *teishoku* set meal, which includes whole prawns, squid, aubergines, mushrooms and the aromatic leaf *shiso*.

Oden is a warming dish, usually served in winter but available at other times too – it tastes much more delicious than it looks. Large chunks of food, usually on skewers, are simmered in a thin broth, and often served from portable carts (*yatai*) on street corners or in convenience stores from beside the till. The main ingredients are blocks of tofu, *daikon* (a giant radish), *konnyaku* (a hard jelly made from a root vegetable), *konbu* (seaweed), hard-boiled eggs and fish cakes. All are best eaten with a smear of fiery English-style mustard.

Japan's equivalent of the pizza is **okonomiyaki**, a fun, cheap meal that you can often assemble yourself. A pancake batter is used to bind shredded cabbage and other vegetables with either seafood or meat. If it's a DIY restaurant, you'll mix the individual ingredients and cook them on a griddle in the middle of the table. Otherwise, you can sit at the kitchen counter watching the chefs at work. Once cooked, *okonomiyaki* is coated in a sweet brown sauce and/or mayonnaise and dusted off with dried seaweed and flakes of *bonito*, which twist and curl in the rising heat – looking almost alive, they're as mesmerizing as any lava lamp. At most *okonomiyaki* restaurants, you can also get fried noodles (*yakisoba*). In addition, *okonomiyaki*, along with its near-cousin **takoyaki** (battered balls of octopus), are often served from *yatai* carts at street festivals.

Authentic Western restaurants are now commonplace across Japan, but there is also a hybrid style of cooking known as **yōshoku** ("Western food") that developed during the Meiji era early in the twentieth century. Often served in *shokudō*, *yōshoku* dishes include omelettes with rice (*omu-raisu*), deep-fried potato croquettes (*korokke*) and hamburger steaks (*hanbāgu*) doused in a thick sauce. The contemporary version of *yōshoku* is **mukokuseki** or "no-nationality" cuisine, a mishmash of world cooking styles usually found in *izakaya*.

Drinks

The Japanese are enthusiastic social drinkers. It's not uncommon to see totally inebriated people slumped in the street, though on the whole drunkenness rarely leads to violence.

If you want a **non-alcoholic** drink, you'll never be far from a coffee shop (*kissaten*) or a *jidō hambaiki* (vending machine), where you can get a vast range of canned drinks, both hot and cold; note that canned coffee, and even some of the tea, is often very sweet. Soft drinks from machines typically cost ¥120 and up; hot drinks are identified by a red stripe under the display, cold drinks by a blue one. Vending machines selling beer, sake and other alcoholic drinks are rare these days: those that still exist shut down at 11pm, the same time as liquor stores. Most 24-hour convenience stores sell alcohol around the clock; look for the *kanji* for alcohol (酒) outside.

Sake

Legend has it that the ancient deities brewed Japan's most famous alcoholic beverage – **sake**, also known as *nihonshu*– from the first rice of the new year. Although often referred to as rice wine, the drink, which comes in thousands of different brands, is actually brewed, and as such more closely related to beer (which long ago surpassed sake as Japan's most popular alcoholic drink).

Made either in sweet (*amakuchi*) or dry (*karakuchi*) varieties, sake is graded as *tokkyū* (superior), *ikkyū* (first) and *nikyū* (second), although this is mainly for tax purposes; if you're after the best quality, connoisseurs recommend going for *ginjō-zukuri* (or *ginjō-zō*), the most expensive and rare of the *junmai-shu* pure rice sake. Some types of sake are cloudier and less refined than others, and there's also the very sweet, milky and usually non-alcoholic *amazake*, often served at temple festivals and at shrines over New Year.

In restaurants and *izakaya* you'll be served sake in a small flask (*tokkuri*) so you can pour your own serving or share it with someone else. You will also be given the choice of drinking your sake warm (*atsukan*) or cold (*reishu*). The latter is usually the preferred way to enable you to taste the wine's complex flavours properly; never drink premium sake warm. When served cold, sake is sometimes presented and drunk out of a small wooden box (*masu*) with a smidger of salt on the rim to counter the slightly sweet taste. Glasses are traditionally filled right to the brim and are sometimes placed on a saucer or in a *masu* to catch any overflow; they're generally small servings because, with an alcohol content of fifteen percent or more, sake is a strong drink – and it goes to your

---

DRINKING ETIQUETTE

If you're out **drinking** with Japanese friends, always pour your colleagues' drinks, but never your own; they'll take care of that. In fact, you'll find your glass being topped up after every couple of sips. The usual way to make a **toast** in Japanese is "*kampai*".

In many bars, you'll be served a small snack or a plate of nuts (*otōshi*) with your first drink, whether you've asked for it or not; this typically accounts for a cover charge being added to the bill. It's fine to get blind drunk and misbehave with your colleagues at night, but it's very bad form to talk about it in the cold light of day.

head even more quickly if drunk warm. For more on sake, check out ⓦsake-world.com.

Beer

American brewer William Copeland set up Japan's first brewery in Yokohama in 1870 to serve **beer** to fellow expats streaming into the country in the wake of the Meiji Restoration. Back then, the Japanese had to be bribed to drink it, but these days they need no such encouragement, knocking back a whopping 6.11 billion litres of beer and "beer-like beverages" (see below) a year. Copeland's brewery eventually became Kirin, one of the nation's big-four brewers along with Asahi, Sapporo and Suntory. All turn out a range of lagers and ale-type beers (often called black beer), as well as half-and-half concoctions. There are also low-malt beers called *happoshu*, and no-malt varieties called *daisan-no-biiru*, which have proved very popular of late because of their lower price (the higher the malt content, the higher the government tax), even if they generally taste insipid.

Standard-size cans of beer cost around ¥200 from a shop or vending machine, while bottles (*bin-biiru*) served in restaurants and bars usually start at ¥500. Draught beer (*nama-biiru*) is often available and, in beer halls, will be served in a *jokki* (mug-like glass), which comes in three different sizes: *dai* (big), *chū* (medium) and *shō* (small).

Microbrew craft beers from around Japan (sometimes called *ji-biiru* – "regional beer") are becoming more popular and many have way more character than found in the products of the big four. For more information on the craft beer scene, there's the bilingual free magazine *The Japan Beer Times* (ⓦjapanbeertimes.com) and the blog *Beer in Japan* (ⓦbeerinjapan.com).

Shōchū

Generally with a higher alcohol content than sake, **shōchū** is a distilled white spirit made from rice, barley, sweet potato or several other ingredients. You can get an idea of its potency (usually 15–25 percent, though sometimes higher) by its nickname: white lightning. Shōchū is typically mixed with a soft drink into a *sawā* (as in lemon-sour) or a *chūhai* highball cocktail, although purists favour enjoying the drink straight, or with ice. There's something of a shōchū boom currently going on in Japan, and the best brands are very drinkable and served like sake (see p.739). The cheap stuff, however, can give you a wicked hangover.

Western alcoholic drinks

The Japanese love **whisky**, with the top brewers producing several respectable brands, often served

---

THE WAY OF TEA

Tea was introduced to Japan from China in the ninth century and was popularized by Zen Buddhist monks, who appreciated its caffeine kick during their long meditation sessions. Gradually, tea-drinking developed into a formal ritual known as *cha-no-yu*, or the "way of tea", whose purpose is to heighten the senses within a contemplative atmosphere. The most important aspect of the **tea ceremony** is the etiquette with which it is performed. Central to this is the selfless manner in which the host serves the tea and the humble manner in which the guests accept it.

The spirit of *wabi*, sometimes described as "rustic simplicity", pervades the Japanese tea ceremony. The traditional teahouse is positioned in a suitably understated garden, and naturalness is emphasized in all aspects of its architecture: in the unpainted wooden surfaces, the thatched roof, tatami-covered floors and the sliding-screen doors (*fusuma*) which open directly onto the garden. Colour and ostentation are avoided. Instead, the alcove, or *tokonoma*, becomes the focal point for a single object of adornment, a simple flower arrangement or a seasonal hanging scroll.

The utensils themselves also contribute to the mood of refined ritual. The roughcast tea bowls are admired for the accidental effects produced by the firing of the pottery, while the water containers, tea caddies and bamboo ladles and whisks are prized for their rustic simplicity. The guiding light behind it all was the great tea-master **Sen no Rikyū** (1521–91), whose "worship of the imperfect" has had an indelible influence on Japanese aesthetics.

Having set the tone with the choice of implements and ornamentation, the host whisks powdered green tea (*matcha*) into a thick, frothy brew and presents it to each guest in turn. They take the bowl in both hands, turn it clockwise (so the decoration on the front of the bowl is facing away) and drink it down in three slow sips. It's then customary to admire the bowl while nibbling on a dainty sweetmeat (*wagashi*), which counteracts the tea's bitter taste.

THE MODERN WAY OF FOOD

Flick through the channels of your TV in Japan, and it won't be long before you hit your first **food programme**. As well as showing off the delights of Japanese cuisine, these can be rather hilarious to watch, for they all follow the same tried-and-trusted format. First of all, footage will be shown of the food being prepared, to multiple coos from the presenters (and canned ones from the studio audience). Once the food is ready, the camera zooms in on a morsel being slowly teased apart (more cooing), and then on it being held aloft with a shaky pair of chopsticks (yet more cooing). Then comes the first taste; the camera zooms in on the recipient who, predictably self-conscious, is left with only two options: **oishii** and **umai**, which both mean "delicious!".

Nobody now knows if this is life imitating art or the other way around, but Japanese almost always do this with the first bite of a meal. It'll be expected of you, too, and with sudden silence and all eyes on you there's only one thing to say… "*oishii.*"

with water and ice and called *mizu-wari*. In contrast, Japanese **wine** (*wain*), often very sweet, is a less successful product, or least to Western palates. Imported wines, however, are widely sold – not only are they becoming cheaper, but there is now a better choice and higher quality available in both shops and restaurants; most convenience stores sell bottles from ¥500.

Tea, coffee and soft drinks

Unless you're in a specialist *kissaten*, most of the time when you order coffee in Japan you'll get a blend (*burendo*), a medium-strength drink that is generally served black and comes in a choice of hot (*hotto*) or iced (*aisu*). If you want milk, ask for *miruku-kōhii* (milky coffee) or *kafe-ōre* (café au lait).

You can also get regular **black tea** in all coffee shops, served either with milk, lemon or iced. If you want the slightly bitter Japanese **green tea**, *ocha* ("honourable tea"), you'll usually have to go to a traditional teahouse. Green teas, which are always served in small cups and drunk plain, are graded according to their quality. *Bancha*, the cheapest, is for everyday drinking and, in its roasted form, is used to make the smoky *hōjicha*, or mixed with popped brown rice for the nutty *genmaicha*. Medium-grade *sencha* is served in upmarket restaurants or to favoured guests, while top-ranking, slightly sweet *gyokuro* (dewdrop) is reserved for special occasions. Other types of tea you may come across are *ūron-cha* (Oolong tea), a refreshing Chinese-style brew, and *mugicha*, made from roasted barley.

As well as the international brand-name **soft drinks** and fruit juices, there are many other soft drinks unique to Japan. You'll probably want to try *Pocari Sweat*, *Post Water* or *Calpis* for the name on the can alone.

The media

For those who can read Japanese, there are scores of daily newspapers and hundreds of magazines covering almost every subject. In the big cities, English newspapers and magazines are readily available, while on TV and radio there are some programmes presented in English or with an alternative English soundtrack, such as the main news bulletins on NHK. Throughout this guide we list websites wherever useful (some will be in Japanese only).

Newspapers and magazines

Japan's top paper, the *Yomiuri Shimbun*, sells almost fourteen million copies daily (combining its morning and evening editions), making it the most widely read **newspaper** in the world. Lagging behind by about two million copies a day is the *Asahi Shimbun*, seen as the intellectual's paper, with the other three national dailies, the *Mainichi Shimbun*, the right-wing *Sankei Shimbun* and the business paper the *Nihon Keizai Shimbun*, also selling respectable numbers.

The **English-language daily** newspaper you'll most commonly find on newsstands is *The Japan Times* (W japantimes.co.jp). It has comprehensive coverage of national and international news, as well as occasionally interesting features, some culled from the world's media: it's also great for updates when there's a sumo tournament on. Other English newspapers include *The International New York Times*, formerly the *International Herald Tribune* and published in conjunction with the English-language version of the major Japanese newspaper *Asahi Shimbun*; the *Daily Yomiuri* (W www.yomiuri .co.jp); and the Japan edition of the *Financial Times*.

DATES IN JAPAN

According to the Japanese system of **numbering years**, which starts afresh with each change of emperor, 2014 is the twenty-sixth year of Heisei – Heisei being the official name of Emperor Akihito's reign. Upon his death, the number will reset to 1 for the first year of his successor's reign. This shouldn't cause you too many problems, since the "regular" calendar is more visible, though prepare for some initially confusing dates on train passes, hotel receipts and the like.

It's also important to note that Japanese dates run **year-month-day**: going from big to small, just like the time on your digital watch – it actually makes a lot of sense.

The free weekly Tokyo listings **magazine** *Metropolis* (Ⓦ metropolis.co.jp) is packed with interesting features, reviews, and listings of film, music and other events. *Japanzine* (Ⓦ seekjapan.jp), a free monthly published in Nagoya but also available in Kyoto, Osaka and Tokyo, is worth searching out. The twice-yearly publication *KIE* (Kateigaho International Edition; ¥1260; Ⓦ int.kateigaho.com) is a gorgeous glossy magazine which covers cultural matters, with many travel features and in-depth profiles of areas of Tokyo and other parts of Japan. Other widely available English-language magazines include *Time* and *The Economist*.

Bookstores such as Kinokuniya and Maruzen stock extensive ranges of imported and local magazines. For those who are studying Japanese, or even just trying to pick up a bit of the language during your stay, the bilingual magazine *Hiragana Times* is good.

Radio

You can listen to FM **radio** in Japan the regular way (though you'll need a radio built for the local market, as the 76–90 MHz FM spectrum here is unique to Japan) or via the internet, where you're likely to hear more interesting music on stations such as **Samurai FM** (Ⓦ samurai.fm), which links up DJs in London and Tokyo. There's also **Radio JapanOnline**, which streams programmes in eighteen languages from NHK Japan's national broadcaster (see below).

Television

The state broadcaster, NHK (Ⓦ nhk.or.jp), has two non-digital TV channels (NHK and NHK Educational). Many TV sets can access a bilingual soundtrack, and thus it's possible to tune into English-language commentary for NHK's nightly 7pm news; films and imported TV shows on both NHK and the commercial channels are also sometimes broadcast with an alternative English soundtrack. **Digital**, **satellite** and **cable** channels available in all top-end hotels include BBC World, CNN and MTV.

Festivals

Don't miss attending a festival (matsuri) if one happens during your visit – it will be a highlight of your stay in Japan. The more important events are listed below.

In recent years, several **non-Japanese festivals** have caught on, with a few adaptations for local tastes. Women give men gifts of chocolate on **Valentine's Day** (February 14), while on **White Day** (March 14) men get their turn to give the object of their affection more chocolate (white, of course). Later on in the year, **Pocky Day** (November 11) is an even more overtly commercial day, even by Japanese standards – people give their loved ones boxes of Pocky, sweet breadsticks whose skinny nature vaguely resembles the date (eleven-eleven). **Christmas** is also an almost totally commercial event in Japan. Christmas Eve, rather than New Year, is *the* time to party and a big occasion for romance – you'll be hard-pressed to find a table at any fancy restaurant or a room in the top hotels.

Major festivals and public holidays

Note that if any of the following public holidays fall on a Sunday, then the following Monday is also a holiday.

JANUARY

Ganjitsu (or Gantan) Jan 1. On the first day of the year, everyone heads for the shrines and temples to pray for good fortune. Public holiday.

Yamayaki Jan 15. The slopes of Wakakusa-yama, Nara, are set alight during a grass-burning ceremony.

Seijin-no-hi (Adults' Day) Second Mon in Jan. Twenty-year olds celebrate their entry into adulthood by visiting their local shrine. Many women dress in sumptuous kimono. Public holiday.

FEBRUARY

Setsubun Feb 3 or 4. On the last day of winter by the lunar calendar, people scatter lucky beans round their homes and at shrines or temples to drive out evil and welcome in the year's good luck. In Nara, the event is marked by a huge lantern festival on Feb 3.

Yuki Matsuri Feb 5–11. Sapporo's famous snow festival features giant snow sculptures.

MARCH

Hina Matsuri (Doll Festival) March 3. Families with young girls display beautiful dolls (*hina ningyō*) representing the emperor, empress and their courtiers dressed in ancient costume. Department stores, hotels and museums often put on special displays at this time.

Cherry-blossom festivals Late March to early May. With the arrival of spring in late March, a pink tide of cherry blossom washes north from Kyūshū, travels up Honshū during the month of April and peters out in Hokkaidō in early May. There are cherry-blossom festivals, and the sake flows at blossom-viewing (*hanami*) parties.

APRIL

Hana Matsuri April 8. The Buddha's birthday is celebrated at all temples with parades or quieter celebrations, during which a small statue of Buddha is sprinkled with sweet tea.

Takayama Matsuri April 14–15. Parade of ornate festival floats (*yatai*), some carrying mechanical marionettes.

MAY

Kodomo-no-hi (Children's Day) May 5. The original Boys' Day now includes all children, as families fly carp banners, symbolizing strength and perseverance, outside their homes. Public holiday.

Aoi Matsuri (Hollyhock Festival) May 15. Costume parade through the streets of Kyoto, with ceremonies to ward off storms and earthquakes.

Kanda Matsuri Mid-May. One of Tokyo's top three *matsuri*, taking place in odd-numbered years at Kanda Myōjin, during which people in Heian-period costume escort eighty gilded *mikoshi* through the streets.

Tōshō-gū Grand Matsuri May 17. Nikkō's most important festival, featuring a parade of over a thousand costumed participants and horseback archery to commemorate the burial of Shogun Tokugawa Ieyasu in 1617. There's a smaller-scale repeat performance on October 17.

Sanja Matsuri Third weekend in May. Tokyo's most boisterous festival takes place in Asakusa. Over a hundred *mikoshi* are jostled through the streets, accompanied by lion dancers, geisha and musicians.

JUNE

Otaue June 14. Ceremonial planting of rice seedlings according to time-honoured techniques at Osaka's Sumiyoshi Taisha shrine, accompanied by dance and song performances.

Sannō Matsuri Mid-June. In even-numbered years the last of Tokyo's big three *matsuri* (after Kanda and Sanja) takes place, focusing on colourful processions of *mikoshi* through Akasaka.

JULY

Hakata Yamagasa July 1–15. Fukuoka's main festival culminates in a 5km race, with participants carrying or pulling heavy *mikoshi*, while spectators douse them with water.

Tanabata Matsuri (Star Festival) July 7. According to legend, the only day in the year when the astral lovers, Vega and Altair, can meet across the Milky Way. Poems and prayers are hung on bamboo poles outside houses.

Gion Matsuri July 17. Kyoto's month-long festival focuses around a parade of huge floats hung with rich silks and paper lanterns.

Hanabi Taikai Last Sat in July. The most spectacular of Japan's many summer firework displays takes place in Tokyo, on the Sumida River near Asakusa. Some cities also hold displays in early Aug.

AUGUST

Nebuta and Neputa Matsuri Aug 1–7. Aomori and Hirosaki hold competing summer festivals, with parades of illuminated paper-covered figures.

Tanabata Matsuri Aug 6–8. Sendai's famous Star Festival (see above) is held a month after everyone else, so the lovers get another chance.

Obon (Festival of Souls) Aug 13–15, or July 13–15 in some areas. Families gather around the ancestral graves to welcome back the spirits of the dead and honour them with special Bon-Odori dances on the final night.

MUSIC FESTIVALS

Late July and August in Japan is the time for **rock and popular music festivals**. One of the best is the **Earth Celebration** on Sado-ga-shima (see box, p.279), where the famed Kodō drummers collaborate with guests from the world music scene. If you want to catch up on the latest in Japanese rock and pop then schedule your visit to coincide with the most established event, as far as foreign bands are concerned, **Fuji Rock** (w fujirockfestival.com). This huge three-day event hosts a wide range of top-name acts covering musical genres from dance and electronica to jazz and blues, on multiple stages. It takes place at Naeba Ski Resort in Niigata prefecture, easily accessible from Tokyo via Shinkansen. It's possible to visit for a day, camp or stay in the hotels that in winter cater to the ski crowd.

Attracting an audience of well over 100,000 and simpler to get to is **Summer Sonic** (w summersonic.com), a two-day event held in Chiba, just across the Edo-gawa from Tokyo. This festival showcases a good mix of both local and overseas bands and has both indoor and outdoor performances.

Rock in Japan (w rijfes.jp), focusing on domestic bands, is usually held in August at Hitachi Seaside Park, north of Tokyo in Ibaraki-ken (accessible from Ueno Station).

Awa Odori Aug 12–15. The most famous *Bonodori* takes place in Tokushima, when up to eighty thousand dancers take to the streets.

SEPTEMBER

Yabusame Sept 16. Spectacular displays of horseback archery (*yabusame*) by riders in samurai armour at Tsurugaoka Hachimangū shrine in Kamakura.

OCTOBER

Okunchi Matsuri Oct 7–9. Shinto rites mingle with Chinese- and European-inspired festivities to create Nagasaki's premier celebration, incorporating dragon dances and floats in the shape of Chinese and Dutch ships.

Kawagoe Grand Matsuri Oct 14–15. One of the liveliest festivals in the Tokyo area, involving some 25 ornate floats and hundreds of costumed revellers.

Jidai Matsuri Oct 22. Kyoto's famous, if rather sedate, costume parade vies with the more exciting **Kurama Matsuri**, a night-time fire festival which takes place in a village near Kyoto.

NOVEMBER

Shichi-go-san Nov 15. Children aged 3, 5 and 7 don traditional garb to visit their local shrine.

DECEMBER

Ōmisoka Dec 31. Just before midnight on the last day of the year, temple bells ring out 108 times (the number of human frailties according to Buddhist thinking), while people all over the country gather at major shrines to honour the gods with the first shrine visit of the year (*hatsumōde*).

Sports and outdoor activities

Big believers in team spirit, the Japanese embrace many sports with almost religious fervour. Baseball, football and even mixed martial arts are all far more popular than home-grown sumo. Martial arts, such as aikido, judo and karate, all traditionally associated with Japan, have a much lower profile than you might expect. Tokyo, with its many dōjō (practice halls), is the best place in the country in which to view or learn these ancient sports. Tokyo's TICs (see p.130) have a full list of dōjō that allow visitors to watch practice sessions for free.

Popular **outdoor activities** include **skiing**, **hiking** and **mountain climbing**. The Tokyo-based International Adventurers Club (IAC; Ⓦ iac-tokyo .org) and Outdoor Club Japan (Ⓦ outdoorclubjapan .com), and the International Outdoor Club (IOC;

Ⓦ iockansai.com) in the Kansai region provide informal opportunities to explore the countryside in the company of like-minded people. The bilingual, bimonthly magazine *Outdoor Japan* (Ⓦ outdoorjapan.com) is also a mine of useful information.

Baseball

Baseball first came to Japan in the 1870s, but it wasn't until 1934 that the first professional teams were formed. Now Japan is *yakyū* (baseball) crazy, and if you're in the country from April to the end of October, during the baseball season, consider watching a professional match. Even if you're not a fan, the buzzing atmosphere and audience enthusiasm can be infectious – Osaka's Hanshin Tigers are famed for their boisterous fans (and consistently underperforming team).

In addition to the two professional leagues, **Central** and **Pacific**, each with six teams, there's the equally (if not more) popular **All-Japan High School Baseball Championship**. You might be able to catch one of the local play-offs before the main tournament, which is held each summer at Kōshien Stadium near Osaka.

In the professional leagues, the teams are sponsored by big businesses, a fact immediately apparent from their names, such as the Yakult Swallows (named after a food company) and Yomiuri Giants (this time a newspaper conglomerate). The victors from the Central and Pacific leagues go on to battle it out for the supreme title in the seven-match Japan Series every autumn. **Tickets** for all games are available from the stadia or at advance ticket booths. They start at ¥1500 and go on sale on the Friday two weeks prior to a game. For more information on Japan's pro-baseball leagues, check out the official professional league site (Ⓦ npb.or.jp), and the fan-site Baseball Guru (Ⓦ baseballguru.com).

Sumo

There's something fascinating about Japan's national sport **sumo**, even though the titanic clashes between the enormous, near-naked wrestlers can be blindingly brief. The age-old pomp and ceremony that surrounds sumo – from the design of the *dohyō* (the ring in which bouts take place) to the wrestler's slicked-back topknot – give the sport a gravitas completely absent from Western wrestling. The sport's aura is enhanced by the majestic size of the wrestlers

A SHORT HISTORY OF SUMO

Accounts of **sumo** bouts (*basho*) are related in Japan's oldest annals dating back around two thousand years when it was a Shinto rite connected with praying for a good harvest. By the Edo period, sumo had developed into a spectator sport, and really hit its stride in the post-World War II period when *basho* started to be televised. The old religious trappings remain, though: the *gyōji* (referee) wears robes similar to those of a Shinto priest and above the *dohyō* hangs a thatched roof like those found at shrines.

Sumo **tournaments** take place on odd-numbered months, running for fifteen days (see box, p.58). The day starts at 9pm with the amateur divisions, before the stadium starts to fill up around 3pm for the professional ranks. These guys fight every day; if they win eight or more they go up the rankings, if they lose eight or more they go down, and whoever gets the most wins in the top division wins the trophy. At the very top of the tree is the *yokozuna* level; there can be more than one of these fighters (sometimes as many as four) but it may come as a surprise to learn that, at the time of writing, there had not been a Japanese "Grand Champion" since 2003.

The foreign appropriation of sumo started with Konishiki (aka the "dump truck") and Akebono, who both hailed from Hawaii, and Musashimaru from American Samoa; in recent years, Mongolian Yokozuna Asashōryū (a naughty boy forced into premature retirement), Hakuhō (regarded by some as the best in history) and Harumafuji have swept the board. the only other tournament winners being the Bulgarian Kotoōshū and the blond-haired and blue-eyed Baruto, from Estonia (now retired).

themselves: the average weight is around 140kg, but they can be much larger – Konishiki, one of the sumo stars of the 1990s, for example, weighed a scale-busting 272kg.

At the start of a bout, the two *rikishi* (wrestlers) wade into the ring, wearing only *mawashi* aprons, which are essentially giant jockstraps. Salt is tossed to purify the ring, and then the *rikishi* hunker down and indulge in the time-honoured ritual of psyching each other out with menacing stares. When ready, each *rikishi* attempts to throw his opponent to the ground or out of the ring using one or more of 82 legitimate techniques. The first to touch the ground with any part of his body other than his feet, or to step out of the *dohyō*, loses

Despite their formidable girth, top *rikishi* enjoy the media status of supermodels, their social calendars being documented obsessively by the media. When not fighting in tournaments, groups of *rikishi* live and train together at their *heya* (stables), the youngest wrestlers acting pretty much as the menial slaves of their older, more experienced, colleagues. If you make an advance appointment, it's possible to visit some *heya* to observe the early-morning practice sessions; contact the Tokyo TICs see p.130) for details. For all you could want to know and more on the current scene, plus how to buy tickets, check out the official website of sumo's governing body, Nihon Sumo Kyōkai, at ⓦsumo.or.jp.

Football (soccer)

Generally referred to as **soccer** in Japan, the sport was introduced here in 1873 by an Englishman: Lieutenant Commander Douglas of the Royal Navy. However, it wasn't until Japan's first professional soccer league, the **J-League** (ⓦj-league.or.jp), was launched in 1993 that the sport captured the public's imagination. Following on from the success of the 2002 World Cup, hosted jointly by Japan and Korea, the sport is now a huge crowd puller.

Games are played between March and October, with a break in August. Eighteen clubs play in the top J1 league, and 22 in the J2; all participate in the JL Yamazaki Nabisco Cup. There is a host of other cups and contests including the JOMO Cup, in which fans pick their dream teams from among all the J-League players.

Martial arts

Japan has bequeathed to the world several forms of **martial** fisticuffs, and many visit to learn or hone one of the forms. If you'd like to do likewise, it's usually best to start by contacting the relevant federation in your home country; in Tokyo, however, there are a few particularly foreigner-friendly associations (see p.159)

The martial art most closely associated with Japan s **judo,** a self-defence technique that developed out of the Edo-era fighting schools of Jūjutsu. Then

THE ANNUAL SUMO TOURNAMENTS

The must-see **annual sumo tournaments** are held at the following locations, starting on the second Sunday of the month and lasting for two weeks: Kokugikan in **Tokyo** (Jan, May & Sept); Ōsaka Furitsu Taiiku Kaikan in **Osaka** (March); Aichi-ken Taiiku-kan in **Nagoya** (July); and the Fukuoka Kokusai Centre, **Fukuoka** (Nov).

Despite sumo's declining popularity, it's still difficult to book the prime ringside **seats** (around ¥45,000 for four seats in a tatami-mat block) but quite feasible to bag reserved seats in the balconies (starting around ¥3200). The cheapest unreserved seats (¥2100) go on sale on the door on the day of the tournament at 9am. To be assured of a ticket, you'll generally need to be there before 11am, though tickets only ever sell out on the last day of a *basho*. Matches start at 9am for the lower-ranked wrestlers, and at this time of day it's OK to sneak into any vacant ringside seats to watch the action close up; when the rightful owners turn up, play the dumb-foreigner card and return to your own seat. The sumo superstars come on around 4pm, and the day finishes at 6pm on the dot.

Full details in English about **ticket sales** can be found on the sumo association's website (ⓦ sumo.or.jp), and it's also possible to buy online at ⓦ buysumotickets.com. Also note that NHK televises each *basho* daily from 3.30pm (as does the sumo association's website), and you can tune in to FEN on 810 KHz for a simultaneous English commentary.

there's **aikido** – half-sport, half-religion, its name translates as "the way of harmonious spirit", and the code blends elements of judo, karate and kendo into a form of non-body-contact self-defence. It's one of the newer martial arts, having only been created in Japan in the twentieth century and, as a rule, is performed without weapons. For a painfully enlightening and humorous take on the rigours of aikido training, read Robert Twigger's *Angry White Pyjamas*.

Karate has its roots in China and was only introduced into Japan via the southern islands of Okinawa in 1922. Since then, the sport has developed many different styles, several with governing bodies and federations based in Tokyo.

Lastly, there's **kendo**; meaning "the way of the sword", this is Japanese fencing where players either use a long bamboo weapon, the *shinai*, or a lethal metal *katana* blade. This martial art has the longest pedigree in Japan, dating from the Muromachi period (1392–1573); it developed as a sport during the Edo period.

Skiing and snowboarding

Japan is a **ski and snowboard paradise**; even on the shortest trip to the country it's easy to arrange a day-trip to the slopes, since many major resorts on Honshū are within a couple of hours' train ride of Tokyo, Nagoya or Osaka. Serious skiers will want to head to the northern island of Hokkaidō, which has some of the country's best ski resorts.

The **cost** of a ski trip needn't be too expensive. Lift passes are typically ¥4000 per day, or less if you ski for several days in a row; equipment rental averages around ¥4000 for the skis, boots and poles per day, while accommodation at a family-run minshuku compares favourably to that of many European and American resorts.

Transport to the slopes is fast and efficient; at one resort (Gala Yuzawa in Niigata; ⓦ galaresort.jp) you can step straight off the Shinkansen onto the ski lifts. Ski maps and signs are often in English, and you're sure to find some English-speakers and, at the major resorts, *gaijin* staff, if you run into difficulties.

Top **resorts** can get very crowded, especially at weekends and holidays; if you don't want to ski in rush-hour conditions, plan your trip for midweek. In addition, the runs are, on the whole, much shorter than in Europe and the US. Compensating factors, however, are fast ski lifts, beautiful scenery – especially in the Japan Alps – and the opportunity to soak in onsen hot springs at night.

Recommended for beginners is either Gala Yuzawa (see above) or Naeba (ⓦ princehotels.co.jp/ski/naeba), both reached in under two hours from Tokyo by Shinkansen. Nozawa Onsen (see p.350) also has good beginners' runs, but its off-the-beaten-track location makes it a better bet for more experienced skiers. Appi Kōgen and Zaō in northern Honshū (see p.226) and Hakuba in Nagano (see p.351) are considered the Holy Trinity of Japanese ski resorts. Shiga Kōgen (see p.353) is another mammoth resort in Nagano. If you're after the best powder-snow skiing without the crowds, head north to Hokkaidō, to the world-class resorts of Furano (see p.320) and Niseko (see p.302). There are also many slopes easily accessible on a day-trip from Sapporo (see box, p.293).

All the major travel agents offer **ski packages**, which are worth considering. Hakuba-based Ski Japan Holiday (W japanspecialists.com) and Niseko-based SkiJapan.com (W skijapan.com) both have plenty of experience setting up deals for the expat community. **Youth hostels** near ski areas also often have excellent-value packages, including accommodation, meals and lift passes, and can arrange competitive equipment rental.

The most current and comprehensive English-language guide to Japan's ski resorts is *Snow-search Japan* (W wsg-media.com) which has details of over seventy resorts.

Mountaineering and hiking

Until the twentieth century, few Japanese would have considered climbing one of their often sacred mountains for anything other than religious reasons. These days, prime high and beauty spots such as Kamikōchi are very popular with day **hikers** and serious **mountaineers**, so much so that they risk being overrun. In addition, there are scores of national parks and other protected areas (see p.822), and exploring these and other picturesque parts of the countryside on foot is one of the great pleasures of a trip to Japan. Nevertheless, bear in mind that those areas close to cities can get very busy at weekends and holidays. If you can, go midweek or out of season when the trails are less crowded.

Hiking trails, especially in the national parks, are well marked. Campsites and mountain huts open during the climbing season, which runs from June to the end of August. The efficient train network means that even from sprawling conurbations like Tokyo, you can be in beautiful countryside in just over an hour. Top hiking destinations from the capital include the lakes, mountains and rugged coastline of the Fuji-Hakone-Izu National Park (see p.197) to the southwest and Nikkō (see p.164) to the north. Also west of the capital is the Chichibu-Tama National Park and the sacred mountain Takao-san, particularly lovely when the leaves change colour each autumn. The website W outdoorjapan .com has useful ideas and information if you plan to go hiking or camping in Japan.

Rafting, canoeing and kayaking

All the snow that gets dumped on Japan's mountains in winter eventually melts, swelling the country's numerous rivers. Although the vast majority of these have been tamed by dams and concrete walls along the riverbanks, there are stretches that provide the ideal conditions for **whitewater rafting**, **canoeing** and **kayaking**. Prime spots for these activities are Minakami in Gunma-ken (see p.173), Hakuba in Nagano-ken (see p.351), the Iya Valley (see p.642) and Shimanto-gawa (see p.652), both in Shikoku, and Niseko (see p.320) in Hokkaidō. A reputable firm to contact to find out more is Canyons (W canyons.jp).

Golf

One of Japan's premier pro-golfing events is the **Japan Open Golf Championship** (W www.jga .or.jp), held each October. If you fancy a round yourself, you'll find details of 2349 courses of eighteen holes or more at **Golf in Japan** (W golf-in-japan.com). Course fees vary widely from ¥3000 at the cheapest places to over ¥40,000 for a round at the most exclusive links.

Beaches, surfing and diving

Given that Japan is an archipelago, you'd be forgiven for thinking that it would be blessed with some pleasant beaches. The truth is that industrialization has blighted much of the coastline and that many of the country's beaches are covered with litter and/or polluted. The best **beaches** are those furthest away from the main island of Honshū, which means those or the islands of Okinawa, or the Izu and Ogasawara islands south of Tokyo.

Incredibly, Japan's market for surf goods is the world's largest, and when the surfers aren't hauling their boards off to Hawaii and Australia, they can be found braving the waves at various home locations. Top spots include the southern coasts of Shikoku and Kyūshū (see box, p.729). Closer to Tokyo, pros head for the rocky east Kujūkuri coast of the Chiba peninsula, while the beaches around Shōnan, near Kamakura, are fine for perfecting your style and hanging out with the trendiest surfers. A useful website is W japansurf.com.

The best places to head for **diving** are Okinawa (see box p.756), around the island of Sado-ga-shima, near Niigata (see p.274), and off the Izu Peninsula, close to Tokyo (see p.206). Those with walrus-like hides may fancy braving ice diving in the frozen far northern reaches of Hokkaidō (see p.330). Check out W divejapan.com for more information.

Culture and etiquette

Japan is famous for its complex web of social conventions and rules of behaviour. Fortunately, allowances are made for befuddled foreigners, but it will be greatly appreciated – and even draw gasps of astonishment – if you show a grasp of the basic principles. We provide a few tips for eating and drinking etiquette which are sure to come in handy (see p.47 and box p.51), but the two main danger areas are to do with footwear and bathing, which, if you get them wrong, can cause great offence.

Some general pointers

Japan is a strictly hierarchical society where men generally take precedence over women, so women shouldn't expect doors to be held open or seats vacated. **Sexual discrimination** remains widespread, and foreign women working in Japan can find the predominantly male business culture hard going.

Pushing and shoving on crowded trains or buses is not uncommon. Never respond by getting angry or showing **aggression**, as this is considered a complete loss of face. By the same token, don't make your **opinions** known too forcefully or contradict people outright; it's more polite to say "maybe" than a direct "no".

The meaning of "yes" and "no" can in themselves be a problem, particularly when **asking questions**. For example, if you say "Don't you like it?", a positive answer means "Yes, I agree with you, I don't like it", and "No" means "No, I don't agree with you, I *do* like it". To avoid confusion, try not to ask negative questions – stick to "Do you like it?" And if someone seems to be giving vague answers, don't push too hard unless it's important. There's a good chance they don't want to offend you by disagreeing or revealing a problem.

Note that it's particularly unwise to criticize any aspect of Japanese society, however small, to a local; in a land where people tend to describe themselves as a "we", it's often taken as a personal insult.

Blowing your nose in public is also considered rude – just keep sniffing until you find somewhere private (following the changes of season, you'll hear locals doing this for hours on end). Finally, you'll be excused for not **sitting** on your knees, Japanese-style, on tatami mats. It's agony for people who aren't used to it, and many young Japanese now find it uncomfortable. If you're wearing trousers, sitting cross-legged is fine; otherwise, tuck your legs to one side.

Meetings and greetings

Some visitors to Japan complain that it's difficult to **meet local people**; in fact, the Japanese famously have problems meeting each other, as evidenced by regular pay-for-company stories in the international press, and the legion of "snack" bars where local men essentially pay to have their egos massaged. It's also true that many Japanese are shy of foreigners, mainly through a fear of being unable to communicate. A few words of Japanese will help enormously, and there are various opportunities for fairly formal contact, such as through the Goodwill Guides (see p.74). Otherwise, try popping into a local bar, a *yakitori* joint or suchlike; with everyone crammed in like sardines, and emboldened by alcohol, it's far easier to strike up a conversation.

Whenever Japanese meet, express thanks or say goodbye, there's a flurry of **bowing**. The precise depth of the bow and the length of time it's held for depend on the relative status of the two individuals. Foreigners aren't expected to bow, but it's terribly infectious and you'll soon find yourself bobbing with the best of them. The usual compromise is a slight nod or a quick half-bow. Japanese more familiar with Western customs might offer you a hand to shake, in which case treat it gently – they won't be expecting a firm grip.

Japanese **names** are traditionally written with the family name first, followed by a given name, which is the practice used throughout this book (except where the Western version has become famous, such as Issey Miyake). When dealing with foreigners, however, they may well write their name the other way round. Check if you're not sure because, when **addressing people**, it's normal to use the family name plus *-san;* for example, Suzuki-san. *San* is an honorific term applied to others, so you do not use it when introducing yourself or your family. As a foreigner, you can choose whichever of your names you feel comfortable with; you'll usually have a *-san* tacked onto the end of your given name. You'll also often hear *-chan* or *-kun* as a form of address; these are diminutives reserved for very good friends, young children and pets. The suffix *-sama* is the most polite form of address.

Japanese people tend to **dress** smartly, especially in Tokyo. Tourists don't have to go overboard, but will be better received if they look neat and tidy, while for anyone hoping to do business, or even teach English to kindergarten kids, a snappy suit is all but essential. It's also important to be **punctual** for social and business appointments – remember that this is the land of the Shinkansen.

Business meetings invariably go on much longer than you'd expect, and rarely result in decisions. They are partly for building up the all-important feeling of trust between the two parties (as is the after-hours entertainment in a restaurant or karaoke bar). An essential part of any business meeting is the swapping of *meishi* (**name cards**). Always carry a copious supply, since you'll be expected to exchange a card with everyone present. If you're doing business here, it's a very good idea to have them printed in Japanese as well as English. *Meishi* are offered with both hands, held so that the recipient can read the writing. It's polite to read the card and then place it on the table beside you, face up. Never write on a *meishi*, at least not in the owner's presence, and never shove it in a pocket – pop it in your wallet, a dedicated card-holder, or somewhere suitably respectful.

Hospitality, gifts and tips

Entertaining, whether it's business or purely social, usually takes place in bars and restaurants. The host generally orders and, if it's a Japanese-style meal, will keep passing you different things to try. You'll also find your glass continually topped up. It's polite to return the gesture, but if you don't drink, or don't want any more, leave it full.

It's a rare honour to be invited to someone's home in Japan, and if this happens you should always take a **gift**, which should always be wrapped, using plenty of fancy paper and ribbon if possible. Most shops gift-wrap purchases automatically and anything swathed in paper from a big department store has extra cachet.

Japanese people love giving gifts, and you should never refuse one if offered, though it's good manners to protest at their generosity first. Again, it's polite to give and receive with both hands, and to belittle your humble donation while giving profuse thanks for the gift you receive. However, it's not the custom to open gifts in front of the donor, thus avoiding potential embarrassment.

Tipping is not expected in Japan. If someone's been particularly helpful, the best approach is to give a small present, or offer some money discreetly in an envelope.

Shoes and slippers

It's customary to change into **slippers** when entering a Japanese home or a ryokan, and not uncommon in traditional restaurants, temples and, occasionally, in museums and art galleries. If you come across a slightly raised floor and a row of slippers, then use them; leave your shoes either on the lower floor (the *genkan*) or on the shelves (sometimes lockers) provided. Also try not to step on the *genkan* with bare or stockinged feet. Once inside, remove your slippers before stepping onto tatami, the rice-straw flooring, and remember to change into the special **toilet slippers** kept inside the bathroom when you go to the toilet.

Toilets

Although you'll still come across traditional Japanese squat-style **toilets** (*toire* or *otearai*, トイレ／お手洗い), Western sit-down toilets are becoming the norm. Look out for nifty enhancements such as a heated seat and those that flush automatically as you walk away. Another handy device plays the sound of flushing water to cover embarrassing noises.

Hi-tech toilets, with a control panel to one side, are very common. Finding the flush button can be a challenge – in the process you may hit the temperature control, hot-air dryer or, worst of all, the bidet nozzle, resulting in a long metal arm extending out of the toilet bowl and spraying you with warm water.

There are lots of public lavatories on the street or at train and subway stations; department stores and big shops also have bathroom facilities for general use. Note that public toilets rarely provide paper.

Bathing

Taking a traditional Japanese **bath**, whether in an onsen, a *sentō* or a ryokan, is a ritual that's definitely worth mastering. Key points to remember are that everyone uses the same water, that the bathtub is only for soaking and to never pull out the plug. It's therefore essential to wash and rinse the soap off thoroughly – showers and bowls are provided, as well as soap and shampoo in most cases – before stepping into the bath. Ryokan and the more upmarket public bathhouses provide small towels (bring your own or buy one on the door if using a cheaper *sentō*), though no one minds full nudity. Baths are typically **segregated**, so memorize the kanji for female (女), which looks a little like a woman; and male (男), which looks like a chap with a box on his head.

Shopping

Even if you're not an inveterate shopper, cruising Japan's gargantuan department stores or rummaging around its vibrant discount outlets is an integral part of local life that shouldn't be missed. Japan also has some truly enticing souvenirs, from lacquered chopsticks and delicate handmade paper to the latest electronic gadgets.

All prices are fixed, except in flea markets and some discount electrical stores where bargaining is acceptable. Though it's always worth asking, surprisingly few shops take **credit cards** and fewer still accept cards issued abroad, so make sure you have plenty of cash.

In general, shop **opening hours** are from 10am or 11am to 7pm or 8pm. Most shops close one day a week, not always on Sunday, and smaller places tend to shut on public holidays. If you need anything **after hours**, you'll find late-opening convenience stores in even the smallest towns, and stores that are open 24 hours in most towns and cities, often near the train station.

Arts and crafts

Many of Japan's **arts** and **crafts** date back thousands of years and have been handed down from generation to generation. Though the best can be phenomenally expensive, there are plenty of items at more manageable prices that make wonderful **souvenirs**. Most department stores have at least a small crafts section, but it's far more enjoyable to trawl Japan's specialist shops. Kyoto is renowned for its traditional crafts, and in Tokyo you'll find a number of artisans still plying their trade, while most regions have a vibrant local crafts industry turning out products for the tourists.

Some of Japan's most beautiful traditional products stem from **folk crafts** (*mingei*), ranging from elegant, inexpensive bamboo-ware to woodcarvings, toys, masks, kites and a whole host of delightful dolls (*ningyō*). Peg-shaped *kokeshi* dolls from northern Honshū are among the most appealing, with their bright colours and sweet, simple faces. Look out, too, for the rotund, round-eyed *daruma* dolls, made of papier-mâché, and fine clay *Hakata-ningyō* dolls from northern Kyūshū.

Ceramics

Japan's most famous craft is its **ceramics** (*tōjiki*). Of several distinct regional styles, *Imari-ware* (from Arita in Kyūshū) is best known for its colourful, ornate designs, while the iron-brown unglazed *Bizen-ware* (from near Okayama, box p.549) and Mashiko's simple folk-pottery (see p.173) are satisfyingly rustic. Other famous names include *Satsuma-yaki* (from Kagoshima), *Kasama-yaki* (from Ibaraki), Kanazawa's highly elaborate *Kutani-yaki* and Kyoto's *Kyō-yaki*. Any decent department store will stock a full range of styles, or you can visit local showrooms. Traditional tea bowls, sake sets and vases are popular souvenirs.

Lacquerware

Originally devised as a means of making everyday utensils more durable, **lacquerware** (*shikki* or *urushi*) has developed over the centuries into a unique art form. Items such as trays, tables, boxes, chopsticks and bowls are typically covered with reddish-brown or black lacquer and either left plain or decorated with paintings, carvings, sprinkled with eggshell or given a dusting of gold or silver leaf. Though top-quality lacquer can be hugely expensive, you'll still find very beautiful pieces at reasonable prices. Lacquer needs a humid atmosphere, especially the cheaper pieces which are made on a base of low-quality wood that cracks in dry conditions, though inexpensive plastic bases won't be affected. Wajima (see p.388) is one of the most famous places for lacquerware in Japan.

DUTY-FREE SHOPPING

Foreigners can buy **duty-free** items (that is, without the eight percent consumption tax – see box, p.65), but only in certain tourist shops and the larger department stores. Perishable goods, such as food, drinks, tobacco, cosmetics and film, are exempt from the scheme, and most stores only offer duty-free if the total bill exceeds ¥10,000. The shop will either give you a duty-free price immediately or, in department stores in particular, you pay the full price first and then apply for a refund at their "tax-exemption" counter. The shop will attach a copy of the customs document (*wariin*) to your passport, to be removed by customs officers when you leave Japan. Note, however, that you can often find the same goods elsewhere at a better price, including tax, so shop around first.

ANTIQUE AND FLEA MARKETS

The regular outdoor **antique** and **flea markets** of Tokyo and Kyoto, usually held at shrines and temples (see individual city accounts for details), are great fun to attend. You need to get there early for the best deals, but you're likely to find some gorgeous secondhand kimono, satin-smooth lacquerware or rustic pottery, among a good deal of tat. Flea markets are also great for stocking up on inexpensive clothes and household items.

Paper products and woodblock prints

Traditional Japanese **paper** (*washi*), made from mulberry or other natural fibres, is fashioned into any number of tempting souvenirs. You can buy purses, boxes, fans, oiled umbrellas, lampshades and toys all made from paper, as well as wonderful stationery.

Original **woodblock prints**, *ukiyo-e*, by world-famous artists such as Utamaro, Hokusai and Hiroshige, have long been collectors' items fetching thousands of pounds. However, you can buy copies of these "pictures of the floating world", often depicting Mount Fuji, willowy geisha or lusty heroes of the kabuki stage, at tourist shops for more modest sums. Alternatively, note that some art shops specialize in originals, both modern and antique.

Textiles, metalwork and pearls

Japan has a long history of making attractive **textiles**, particularly the silks used in kimono (see box, p.64). Other interesting uses of textiles include *noren*, a split curtain hanging in the entrance to a restaurant or bar; cotton *tenugui* (small hand towels), decorated with cute designs; and the *furoshiki*, a square, versatile wrapping cloth that comes in a variety of sizes.

While the chunky iron kettles from Morioka in northern Honshū are rather unwieldy mementos, the area also produces delicate *fūrin*, or **wind chimes**, in a variety of designs. **Damascene** is also more portable, though a bit fussy for some tastes. This metal inlay-work, with gold and silver threads on black steel, was originally used to fix the family crest on sword hilts and helmets, though nowadays you can buy all sorts of jewellery and trinket boxes decorated with birds, flowers and other intricate designs.

Pearls, however, are undoubtedly Japan's most famous jewellery item, ever since Mikimoto Kōkichi first succeeded in growing cultured pearls in Toba in 1893. Toba (see p.521) is still the centre of production, though you'll find specialist shops in all major cities, selling pearls at fairly competitive prices.

Food and drink

Edible souvenirs include various types of rice crackers (*sembei*), both sweet and savoury, vacuum-packed bags of pickles (*tsukemono*), and Japanese sweets (*okashi*) such as the eye-catching *wagashi*. Made of sweet, red-bean paste in various colours and designs, *wagashi* are the traditional accompaniment to the tea ceremony. Tea itself (*ocha*) comes in a variety of grades, often in attractive canisters, while sake (see p.51), premium *shōchū* or Japanese whiskey are other great gift options, and often come in interesting-shaped bottles with beautiful labels.

Books and music

Imported foreign-language **books** are expensive and only available in major cities. However, some locally produced English-language books are cheaper here than at home, if you can find them at all outside Japan. The best bookstores are Kinokuniya, Tower Books (part of Tower Records), Maruzen, Yūrindō and Junkudō, all of which stock imported newspapers and magazines as well as a variable selection of foreign-language books. Most top-class hotels have a small bookstore with a range of titles on Japan and a limited choice of imported fiction and journals.

Imported **CDs and records** are a lot easier to get hold of, alongside a mammoth local output of pop and rock. Major record stores such as Tower Records and HMV have a tremendous selection. Imported CDs typically cost under ¥2000, while CDs of foreign artists produced for the Japanese market, with translated lyrics and extra tracks generally start in the region of ¥2300.

Department stores

Japan's most prestigious **department stores** are Isetan, Mitsukoshi and Takashimaya, followed by the more workaday Seibu, Tōbu and Matsuzakaya. All of these big names have branches throughout Japan, and sell almost everything, from fashion, crafts and household items to stationery and toys. One floor is usually devoted to restaurants, while bigger stores may also have an art gallery, travel bureau, ticket agent and a currency-exchange desk, as well as

English-speaking staff and a duty-free service. Seasonal sales, particularly those at New Year and early July, can offer great bargains.

Electrical and electronic goods

Japan is a well-known producer of high-quality and innovative **electrical** and **electronic goods**. New designs are tested on the local market before going into export production, so this is the best place to check out the latest technological advances. The majority of hi-tech goods are sold in discount stores, where prices may be up to forty percent cheaper than at a conventional store. Akihabara, in Tokyo (see p.90), is the country's foremost area for electronic goods, but in every major city you can buy audio equipment, computers, software and any number of ingenious gadgets at competitive prices.

Similarly, Japanese **cameras** and other photographic equipment are among the best in the world. Shinjuku, in Tokyo, is the main centre, where you can pick up the latest models and find discontinued and secondhand cameras at decent prices.

Before buying anything, compare prices – many shops are open to **bargaining** – and make sure the items come with the appropriate voltage switch (Japanese power supply is 100V). It's also important to check that whatever you buy will be compatible with equipment you have at home, if necessary. For English-language instructions, after-sales service and guarantees, stick to export models, which you'll find mostly in the stores' duty-free sections, but bear in mind that they may not be any cheaper than you would pay at home.

Contemporary fashion

Top **Japanese labels** such as Issey Miyake, Yohji Yamamoto, Comme des Garçons and Evisu jeans are worn by fashionistas around the world, but there are also plenty of up-and-coming designers and streetwear labels to discover in Japan. The epicentre of chic is Tokyo's Omotesandō and the surrounding Aoyama and Harajuku areas. If you want to check out the latest designers and labels, such as Jun Takahashi, Tsumori Chisato and Yanagawa Arashi, then head to the boutiques here and in trendy Daikan'yama and Naka-Meguro, or hit town during Tokyo Fashion Week (Ⓦjfw.jp) held twice a year. Kyoto also has an interesting fashion scene (see p.452).

Finding **clothes** that fit is becoming easier as young Japanese are, on average, substantially

---

THE COMEBACK OF THE KIMONO

In Japan, **kimono** are still worn by both sexes on special occasions, such as weddings and festival visits to a shrine. But as the demand for high-class kimono, such as those made by the craftspeople of Kyoto, declines – a result of the falling birth rate and Japan's ageing population – the one bright spot for the industry is the trend to adapt old kimono to new uses. Increasing numbers of fashion-conscious young women have taken to wearing a kimono like a coat over Western clothes or coordinating it with coloured rather than white *tabi* (traditional split-toed socks). At the same time, fashion designers are turning to kimono fabrics and styles for contemporary creations.

Few visitors to Japan fail to be impressed by the beauty and variety of kimono available, and every department store has a corner devoted to ready-made or tailored kimono. Ready-made versions can easily cost ¥100,000, while ¥1 million for the best made-to-measure kimono is not uncommon. Much more affordable secondhand or antique kimono can be found in tourist shops, flea markets or in the kimono sales held by department stores, usually in spring and autumn. Prices can start as low as ¥1000, but you'll pay more for the sumptuous, highly decorated wedding kimono (they make striking wall hangings), as well as the most beautifully patterned **obi**, the broad, silk sash worn with a kimono. A cheaper, more practical alternative is the light cotton **yukata**, popular with both sexes as a dressing gown; you'll find them in all department stores and many speciality stores, along with **happi coats** – the loose jackets that just cover the upper body. To complete the outfit, you could pick up a pair of **zōri**, traditional straw sandals, or their wooden counterpart, **geta**.

If you want to try the full kimono look, you'll find that most of the big hotels have a studio where you can dress up and have your photo taken (typically around ¥10,000–15,000), while some guesthouses also offer the opportunity. The most popular place to don kimono is, of course, Kyoto (see p.452). Men can get in on the act, too, dressing up in what is called "samurai" style (around ¥5000), though the male kimono is much less florid in design than the female version, and is usually in muted colours such as black, greys and browns.

bigger-built than their parents, and foreign chains tend to carry larger sizes. **Shoes**, however, are more of a problem. While stores stock larger sizes nowadays the range is still pretty limited – your best bet is to try a large department store, or the ubiquitous branches of ABC Mart.

Travelling with children

With high standards of health, hygiene and safety, and lots of interesting things to do, Japan is a great place to travel with children. At museums and other sights, school-age kids usually get reduced rates, which may be up to half the adult price. Children under age 6 ride free on trains, subways and buses, while those aged 6 to 11 pay half fare.

It's a good idea to bring a lightweight, easily collapsible **pushchair**. You'll find yourself walking long distances in cities and, while many subway and train stations now have lifts, there are still plenty of stairs.

Finding **hotels** offering **family rooms** that fit more than three people is tough: international chain hotels are your best bet. A great alternative is a Japanese-style ryokan or minshuku where you can share a big tatami room. Only at the more upmarket Western-style hotels will you be able to arrange **babysitting**.

All the products you need – such as **nappies** and **baby food** – are easily available in shops and department stores, though not necessarily imported varieties. If you need a particular brand, it would be wise to bring it with you. Although **breastfeeding** in public is generally accepted, it's best to be as discreet as possible. Most Japanese women who breastfeed use the private rooms provided in department stores, public buildings and in many shops, or find a quiet corner.

Although it's rather dated, Kodansha's *Japan for Kids* still contains a lot of useful general information; it's also worth checking out ⓦtokyowithkids.com.

Travel essentials

Costs

Despite its reputation as being an outrageously expensive country, prices in Japan have dropped,

CONSUMPTION TAX

A **consumption tax** (*shōhizei*) of eight percent is levied on virtually all goods and services in Japan, including restaurant meals and accommodation. This is supposed to be included in the advertised price, though you'll occasionally come across hotels that haven't quite got round to it yet; double-check to be on the safe side. Note that at the time of writing, the rate was five percent many prices listed here, particularly those at restaurants and hotels, are likely to have been increased marginally by the time you read this.

or at least stabilized, in recent years. With a little planning, it is a manageable destination even for those on an absolute minimum **daily budget** of ¥5000–10,000. By the time you've added in some transport costs, a few entry tickets, meals in classier restaurants and one or two nights in a ryokan or business hotel, ¥10,000–15,000 per day is more realistic.

If you plan to travel around the country, it's a good idea to buy a **Japan Rail Pass** (see p.35) before departure, though it's also worth investigating special deals on internal flights. Within the country, all sorts of discount fares and excursion tickets are available, while overnight ferries and buses are an economical way of getting around (see p.37 & p.38).

Holders of the **International Student Identity Card** (ISIC, ⓦisiccard.com) are eligible for discounts on some transport and admission fees, as are children. A **Hostelling International card** (ⓦhihostels.com) qualifies you for a reduction of ¥600 on the rates of official youth hostels, though these days most of the best are privately run (see p.44).

It's also worth checking JNTO's website (ⓦjnto .go.jp) for further tips on how to save money. **Welcome Card** schemes, for example, operate in some areas of the country, which entitle you to discounts at certain museums, sights, shops, restaurants and transport services. At the time of writing, there were ten Welcome Card schemes in operation, including in the Tōhoku area (see p.223) and the Tokyo museum pass (see p.130).

Crime and personal safety

Japan boasts one of the lowest crime rates in the world. Nonetheless, it always pays to be careful in crowds and to keep money and important documents stowed in an inside pocket or money belt, or in your hotel safe.

The presence of **police boxes** (*kōban*) in every neighbourhood helps to discourage petty crime, and the local police seem to spend the majority of their time dealing with stolen bikes (bicycle theft is rife) and helping people find addresses. This benevolent image is misleading, however, as the Japanese police are notorious for forcing confessions and holding suspects for weeks without access to a lawyer. Amnesty International have consistently criticized Japan for its treatment of illegal immigrants and other foreigners held in jail.

It's best to carry your **passport** or ID at all times; the police have the right to arrest anyone who fails to do so. In practice, however, they rarely stop foreigners. If you're found without your ID, the usual procedure is to escort you back to your hotel or apartment to collect it. Anyone found **taking drugs** will be treated less leniently; if you're lucky, you'll simply be fined and deported, rather than sent to prison.

The generally low status of women in Japan is reflected in the amount of **groping** that goes on in crowded commuter trains – there are even pornographic films and comics aimed at gropers. If you do have the misfortune to be groped, the best solution is to grab the offending hand, yank it high in the air and embarrass the guy as much as possible. More violent **sexual abuse** is rare, though harassment, stalking and rape are seriously under-reported. Women should exercise the same caution about being alone with a man as they would anywhere. Violent crimes against women are rare, but they do occur.

In **emergencies**, phone ☎110 for the police or ☎119 for an ambulance or fire engine. You can call these numbers free from any public phone by pressing the red button before dialling. If possible, ask someone to call for you, since few police speak English, though Tokyo Metropolitan Police do run an English-language hotline on ☎03 3501 0110 (Mon–Fri 8.30am–5.15pm). Two other useful options are Tokyo English Language Lifeline (TELL; ☎03 5774 0992, Ⓦtelljp.com; daily 9am–11pm) and Japan Helpline (☎0570 000 911, Ⓦjhelp.com; 24hr).

Each prefecture also has a Foreign Advisory Service, with a variety of foreign-language speakers who can be contacted as a last resort (see individual region or city Directory sections for details).

Earthquakes

Japan is home to one-tenth of the world's active volcanoes; it's also the site of one-tenth of the planet's major **earthquakes** (over magnitude 7 on the Richter scale). At least one quake is recorded every day somewhere in the country, though fortunately the vast majority consist of minor tremors that you probably won't even notice. One that the whole world noticed occurred off the country's east coast in March 2011 (see p.805). The fifth most-powerful earthquake in recorded history, it unleashed a tsunami

---

EARTHQUAKE SAFETY PROCEDURES

If you do have the misfortune to experience more than a minor rumble, follow the safety procedures listed below:

- Extinguish any **fires** and turn off **electrical appliances**.
- Open any **doors** leading out of the room you're in, as they often get jammed shut, blocking your exit.
- Stay away from **windows** because of splintering glass. If you have time, draw the curtains to contain the glass.
- Don't rush outside (many people are injured by falling masonry), but get under something solid, such as a ground-floor **doorway**, or a **desk**.
- If you are outside when the quake hits, head for the nearest **park** or other **open space**.
- If the earthquake occurs at night, make sure you've got a **torch** (all hotels, ryokan, etc provide flashlights in the rooms).
- When the tremors have died down, go to the nearest open space, taking your documents and other valuables with you. It's also a good idea to take a cushion or pillow to protect your head against **falling glass**.
- Eventually, make your way to the designated **neighbourhood emergency centre** and get in touch with your **embassy**.

of prodigious force; the combined effect killed almost 16,000 people, and caused a meltdown at the nuclear power plant in Fukushima, where the effects will be felt for decades. Do note, however, that since the 1980s, buildings have been designed to withstand even the most powerful 'quakes. Tokyo is equipped with some of the world's most sophisticated sensors, and architects employ mind-boggling techniques to try to ensure the city's new high-rises remain upright.

Nevertheless, earthquakes are notoriously difficult to predict, and it's worth taking note of a few basic **safety procedures** (see box below). Aftershocks may go on for a long time, and can topple structures that are already weakened. That said, most casualties are caused by fire and traffic accidents, rather than collapsing buildings.

Electricity

The **electrical current** is 100v, 50Hz AC in Japan east of Mt Fuji, including Tokyo; and 100v, 60Hz AC in western Japan, including Nagoya, Kyoto and Osaka. Japanese plugs have either two flat pins or, less commonly, three pins (two flat and one rounded, earth pin). If you are coming from North America, Canada, the UK or Europe, the voltage difference should cause no problems with computers, digital cameras, cell phones and the like, most of which can handle between 100V and 240V. Larger appliances such as hairdryers, curling irons and travel kettles should work, but not quite as efficiently, in which case you may need a converter. And, while Japanese plugs look identical to North American plugs, there are subtle differences, so you may also need an adaptor; you certainly will if coming from the UK or Europe.

Entry requirements

All visitors must have a passport valid for the duration of their stay. Citizens of Ireland, the UK and certain other European countries can stay for up to **ninety days** without a visa, providing they are visiting Japan for tourism or business purposes. This stay can be extended for another three months (see below). Citizens of Australia, Canada, New Zealand and the US can also stay for up to ninety days without a visa, though this is not extendable and you are required to be in possession of a return air ticket. Anyone from these countries wishing to stay longer will have to leave Japan and then re-enter.

Citizens of certain other countries must apply for a **visa** in advance in their own country. Visas are

usually free, though in certain circumstances you may be charged a fee of around ¥3000 for a single-entry visa. The rules on visas change from time to time, so check first with the nearest Japanese embassy or consulate, or on the Japanese Ministry of Foreign Affairs website (Ⓦ mofa.go.jp).

If eligible for a **visa extension**, you'll need to fill in two copies of an "Application for Extension of Stay", available from immigration bureaus (see individual city Directory sections for details). These must be returned along with passport photos, a letter explaining your reasons for wanting to extend your stay, and a fee of ¥4000. In addition, you may be asked to show proof of sufficient funds to support your stay, and a valid onward ticket out of the country. If you're not a national of one of the few countries with six-month reciprocal visa exemptions (these include Ireland and the UK), expect a thorough grilling from the immigration officials. An easier option – and the only alternative available to nationals of those countries who are not eligible for an extension – is a short trip out of the country, say to South Korea or Hong Kong, though you'll still have to run the gauntlet of immigration officials on your return.

Citizens of the UK, Ireland, Canada, Australia, New Zealand, South Korea, France, Germany, Denmark, Taiwan and Hong Kong aged between 18 and 30 can apply for a **working holiday visa**, which grants a stay of up to one year and entitles the holder to take paid employment as long as your stay is "primarily deemed to be a holiday" – full details of the scheme can be found at Ⓦ http://tinyurl.com/c2zwhx.

British nationals are also eligible for the **volunteer visa scheme**, which allows holders to undertake voluntary work for charitable organizations in Japan for up to one year. Your application must include a letter from the host organization confirming details of the voluntary work to be undertaken and the treatment the volunteer will receive (pocket money and board and lodging are allowed, but formal remuneration is not). You must also be able to show evidence of sufficient funds for your stay in Japan.

Foreigners staying in Japan for more than ninety days must obtain a **Residence Card** (在留カード, Zairyū Kādo), which you can apply for at an immigration bureau (see individual city Directory sections for details). The card includes your photograph and must be carried at all times. In addition, if you're on any sort of working visa and you leave Japan temporarily, you must get a **re-entry visa** before you leave if you wish to continue working on your return. Re-entry visas are available from local immigration bureaus.

JAPANESE EMBASSIES AND CONSULATES

You'll find a full list of **embassies and consulates** on ⓦ mofa.go.jp/about.

Australia 112 Empire Circuit, Yarralumla, Canberra (☎ 02 6273 3244, ⓦ au.emb-japan.go.jp); 17th Floor, Comalco Place, 12 Creek St, Brisbane (☎ 07 3221 5188, ⓦ brisbane.au.emb-japan.go.jp); Level 15, Cairns Corporate Tower, 15 Lake St, Cairns (☎ 07 4051 5177); 45F Melbourne Central Tower, 360 Elizabeth St, Melbourne (☎ 03 9639 3244); 21F The Forrest Centre, 221 St George's Terrace, Perth (☎ 08 9480 1800); Level 34, Colonial Centre, 52 Martin Place, Sydney (☎ 02 9231 3455).

Canada 255 Sussex Drive, Ottawa (☎ 613 241 8541, ⓦ ca.emb-japan.go.jp); 2300 Trans Canada Tower, 450-1st Street SW, Calgary (☎ 403 294 0782); 600 Rue de la Gauchetière West, Suite 2120, Montreal (☎ 514 866 3429); Suite 3300, Royal Trust Tower, 77 King St West, Toronto (☎ 416 363 7038); 900-1177 West Hastings St, Vancouver (☎ 604 684 5868).

China 7 Ri Tan Rd, Jian Guo Men Wai, Beijing (☎ 010 6532 2361, ⓦ cn.emb-japan.go.jp); 37F Metropolitan Tower, 68 Zourong Rd, Central District, Chongqing (☎ 023 6373 3585); Garden Tower, 368 Huanshi Dong Lu, Guangzhou (☎ 020 8334 3009); 46–47F One Exchange Square, 8 Connaught Place, Central, Hong Kong (☎ 2522 1184, ⓦ hk.emb-japan.go.jp); 8 Wan Shan Rd, Shanghai (☎ 021 5257 4766).

Ireland Nutley Building, Merrion Centre, Nutley Lane, Dublin (☎ 01 202 8300, ⓦ ie.emb-japan.go.jp).

New Zealand Level 18, Majestic Centre, 100 Willis St, Wellington (☎ 04 473 1540, ⓦ nz.emb-japan.go.jp); Level 12, ASB Bank Centre, 135 Albert St, Auckland (☎ 09 303 4106); Level 5, Forsyth Barr House, 764 Colombo St, Christchurch (☎ 03 366 5680).

South Africa 259 Baines St, Groenkloof, Pretoria (☎ 012 452 1500, ⓦ japan.org.za); 2100 Main Tower, Standard Bank Centre, Heerengracht, Cape Town (☎ 021 425 1693).

South Korea 18-11 Junghak-dong, Jongno-gu, Seoul (☎ 02 2170 5200, ⓦ kr.emb-japan.go.jp); 1147-11, Choryang-3-dong, Dong-ku, Busan (☎ 051 465 5101).

UK 101–104 Piccadilly, London (☎ 020 7465 6500, ⓦ uk.emb-japan.go.jp); 2 Melville Crescent, Edinburgh (☎ 0131 225 4777, ⓦ edinburgh.uk.emb-japan.go.jp).

US 2520 Massachusetts Ave NW, Washington DC (☎ 202 238 6700, ⓦ us.emb-japan.go.jp); One Alliance Center, Suite 1600, 3500 Lenox Rd, Atlanta (☎ 404 240 4300); Federal Reserve Plaza, 14th Floor, 600 Atlantic Ave, Boston (☎ 617 973 9774); Olympia Centre, Suite 1100, 737 North Michigan Ave, Chicago (☎ 312 280 0400); 1225 17th Street, Suite 3000, Denver (☎ 303 534 1151); 1742 Nuuanu Ave, Honolulu (☎ 808 543 3111); 2 Houston Center, 909 Fannin, Suite 3000, Houston (☎ 713 652 2977); 350 South Grand Ave, Suite 1700, Los Angeles (☎ 213 617 6700); Brickell Bay View Centre, Suite 3200, 80 SW 8th St, Miami (☎ 305 530 9090); 299 Park Ave, New York (☎ 212 371 8222); 50 Fremont St, Suite 2300, San Francisco (☎ 415 777 3533); 601 Union St, Suite 500, Seattle (☎ 206 682 9107).

Gay and lesbian travellers

Homosexual travellers should encounter few problems in Japan – it's highly unlikely for eyebrows to be raised if a **same-sex couple** check into the same room, for example. There are no laws against homosexual activity, though it can hardly be said Japan is an out-and-proud gay-supporting nation. Marriage remains an almost essential step on the career ladder at many corporations, and such expectations keep many Japanese gays in the closet, often leading double lives; outside the main cities, the gay scene is all but invisible. That said, in recent times, homosexuality and other alternative forms of sexuality have become more acceptable and there are a few openly gay public figures (although mainly media celebrities).

Useful online English sources of information on the city's gay life include Fridae (ⓦ fridae.com); GayNet Japan (ⓦ gnj.or.jp); Utopia (ⓦ utopia-asia .com); and the tri-lingual lesbian-focused Tokyo Wrestling (ⓦ tokyowrestling.com).

Health

Japan has high standards of health and hygiene, and there are no significant diseases worth worrying about. There are no immunizations or health certificates needed to enter the country.

Medical treatment and **drugs** are of a high quality, but can be expensive – if possible you should bring any medicines you might need with you, especially prescription drugs. Also bring a copy of your prescription and make sure you know what the generic name of the drug is, rather than its brand name. Some common drugs widely available throughout the US and Europe are generally not available in Japan. The contraceptive pill is available, but only on prescription.

Although mosquitoes buzz across Japan in the warmer months, **malaria** is not endemic, so there's no need to take any tablets. It's a good idea to pack mosquito repellent, however, and to burn coils in your room at night, or to use a plug-in repellent.

Tap **water** is safe to drink throughout Japan, but you should avoid drinking directly from streams or rivers. It's also not a good idea to walk barefoot through flooded paddy fields, due to the danger of water-borne parasites. Food-wise, you should have no fears about eating raw seafood or sea fish, including the notorious *fugu* (blowfish). However, raw meat and river fish are best avoided.

In the case of an **emergency**, the first port of call should be to ask your hotel to phone for a doctor or ambulance. You could also head for, or call, the nearest tourist information office or international centre (in major cities only), which should be able to provide a list of local doctors and hospitals with English-speaking staff. Alternatively, you could call the toll-free 24-hour Japan Helpline ☎0570 000 911, ⓦjhelp.com) or, in a last resort, contact the Prefecture's Foreign Advisory Service (see "Emergencies" in individual city Directory sections in the Guide).

If you need to call an **ambulance** on your own, dial ☎119 and speak slowly when you're asked to give an address. Ambulance staff are not trained paramedics, but will take you to the nearest appropriate hospital. Unless you're dangerously ill when you go to hospital, you'll have to wait your turn in a clinic before you see a doctor, and you'll need to be persistent if you want to get full details of your condition: some doctors are notorious for withholding information from patients.

For minor ailments and advice, you can go to a **pharmacy**, which you'll find in most shopping areas. There are also numerous smaller private **clinics**, where you'll pay in the region of ¥10,000 to see a doctor. You could also try **Asian medical remedies**, such as acupuncture (*hari*) and pressure point massage (*shiatsu*), though it's worth trying to get a personal recommendation to find a reputable practitioner.

Insurance

It's essential to take out a good **travel insurance** policy, particularly one with comprehensive medical coverage, due to the high cost of hospital treatment in Japan (see box below).

Internet

Many visitors soon realize that Japan doesn't quite live up to its tech-savvy reputation – some locals are still surprised to hear that one can book flights or tickets online. Some local websites are laughably bad – with italicized Times New Roman fonts and copious Clipart characters, many seem to have been ported directly from the mid-1990s. However, things are finally starting to improve, and **wi-fi** access is becoming more widespread; most big-city cafés offer it for free, though at some you have to register (often elsewhere, on another wi-fi connection, which is rather inconvenient; Starbucks, take a bow). In addition, it's par for the course at privately run hostels, though at hotels you still can't be sure – and, at the too end, you may well have to pay a daily fee (typically ¥1000). More offer free **broadband** in the rooms and should be able to supply a cable if necessary. Others may provide at least one terminal for guests travelling without their own computer, generally also for free.

Cybercafés can be found across Japan, often as part of a 24-hour computer-game and manga centre. Free access is sometimes available (usually in cultural exchange centres, or regular cafés looking to boost business); otherwise, expect to pay around ¥200–400 per hour. Cybercafés come and go fairly swiftly, although the copyshop Kinko's is pretty reliable and has branches (some 24hr) across Japan; check ⓦkinkos.co.jp to find the one nearest you. Also see the Directory sections of town and city accounts in the Guide for internet availability.

Laundry

All hotels provide either a **laundry service** or, at the lower end, **coin-operated machines**. These typically cost ¥100–300 for a wash (powder ¥30–50) and ¥100 for ten minutes in the drier. You'll also find coin-operated laundries (*koin randorii*) in nearly all Japanese neighbourhoods, often open long hours. Virtually all Japanese washing machines use cold water.

Living in Japan

Overall **employment opportunities** for foreigners have shrunk since the Japanese economy took a nosedive in the early 1990s, though finding employment is far from impossible, especially if you have the right qualifications (a degree is essential) and appropriate visa. In fact, the number of well-qualified, Japanese-speaking *gaijin* in the country employed in specialist jobs has increased over the last decade.

Working holiday visas, for which you don't need a job in advance, are available to citizens of a handful of countries – see p.67 for more details. All other foreigners must have sponsorship papers from a prospective employer in place before applying for a work visa, which need not be obtained in your home country (but must be applied for outside of Japan). A few employers may be willing to hire you before the proper papers are sorted out, but you shouldn't rely on this, and if you arrive without a job make sure you have plenty of funds to live on until you find one. Anyone staying in Japan more than ninety days must also apply for a Residence Card (see p.67). For tips on finding long-term **accommodation**, see p.45.

The most common job available to foreigners is **teaching English**. Some of the smaller schools are far from professional operations (and even the biggies get lots of complaints), so before signing any contract, it's a good idea to talk to other teachers and, if possible, attend a class and find out what will be expected of you. If you have a professional teaching qualification, plus experience, or if you also speak another language such as French or Italian, your chances of getting one of the better jobs will be higher.

Another option is to get a place on the government-run **Japan Exchange and Teaching Programme** (JET; Ⓦ jetprogramme.org), aimed at improving foreign-language teaching in schools and promoting international understanding. The scheme is open to graduates aged under 40, preferably holding some sort of language-teaching qualification. Benefits include a generous salary, help with accommodation, return air travel to Japan and paid holidays. Applying for the JET programme is a lengthy process for which you need to be well prepared. Application forms for the following year's quota are available from late September, the deadline for submission being early December. Interviews are held in January and February, with decisions made in March. After health checks and orientation meetings, JETs head off to their posts in late July on year-long contracts, which can be renewed for up to two more years by mutual consent. JET also offer some local government positions to Japanese-speaking foreigners.

A much more limited job option for *gaijin* is **rewriting** or **editing** English **translations** of Japanese text for technical documents, manuals, magazines and so on. For such jobs, it's a great help if you know at least a little Japanese. These days, there are also good opportunities for *gaijin* with **ski instructor** or **adventure sports** experience to work on the ski slopes, particularly in resorts such as Niseko, Furano and Hakuba which target overseas visitors. Other options include **modelling**, for which it will be an asset to have a professional portfolio of photographs, and **bar work** and **hostessing**, with the usual warnings about the dangers inherent in this type of work. Whatever work you're looking for – or if you're doing any sort of business in Japan – a smart set of clothes will give you an advantage, as will following other general rules of social etiquette (see p.60).

Apart from the websites listed below, the main places to look for **job adverts** are the free weekly magazines *Metropolis* and *Tokyo Notice Board* (see p.130).

EMPLOYMENT RESOURCES

GaijinPot Ⓦ gaijinpot.com. Classifieds focused on English-language teaching.

Japan Association for Working Holiday Makers Ⓦ jawhm.or.jp. Job referrals for people on working holiday visas.

Jobs in Japan Ⓦ jobsinjapan.com. Broad range of classified ads.

Work in Japan Ⓦ daijob.com/wij. Japan's largest bilingual jobs website.

WWOOF (Willing Workers on Organic Farms) Ⓦ wwoofjapan.com. Opportunities to work and live on organic farms across Japan, plus a few hotels and resorts.

Studying Japanese language and culture

There are all sorts of opportunities to study Japanese language and culture. In order to get a **student** or **cultural visa**, you'll need various documents from the institution where you plan to study and proof that you have sufficient funds to support yourself, among other things. Full-time courses are expensive, but once you have your visa, you may be allowed to undertake a minimal amount of paid work.

Japan's Ministry of Education, Culture, Sports, Science and Technology (MEXT; Ⓦ mext.go.jp) offers various **scholarships** to foreign students wishing to further their knowledge of Japanese or Japanese studies, undertake an undergraduate degree, or become a research student at a Japanese university. You'll find further information on the informative Study in Japan website (W studyjapan.go.jp), run by the Ministry of Foreign Affairs, or by contacting your nearest Japanese embassy or consulate.

Tokyo, Osaka, Kyoto and other major cities have numerous **Japanese language schools** offering intensive and part-time courses. Among the most established are Berlitz (W berlitz.co.jp), with branches nationwide, and Tokyo Kogakuin Japanese Language School (5-30-16 Sendagaya, Shibuya-ku; ☎03 3352 3851, W technos-jpschool.ac.jp). The monthly bilingual magazine Hiragana Times (W hiraganatimes.com) and the listings magazines Metropolis and Tokyo Journal also carry adverts for schools, or check out the Association for the Promotion of Japanese Language Education (2F Ishiyama Building, 1-58-1 Yoyogi, Shinjuku-ku; ☎03 4304 7815, W nisshinkyo.org), whose website lists accredited institutions.

Mail

Japan's **mail** service is highly efficient and fast, with post offices (yūbinkyoku) all over the country, easily identified by their red-and-white signs – a T with a parallel bar across the top, the same symbol that you'll find on the red letterboxes. All post can be addressed in Western script (rōmaji), provided it's clearly printed.

In urban post offices there are separate counters, with English signs, for postal and banking services; in central post offices you can also exchange money at rates comparable to those in banks. If you need to send bulkier items or **parcels** back home, you can get reasonably priced special envelopes and boxes for packaging from any post office. The maximum weight for an overseas parcel is 30kg (less for some destinations). A good compromise between expensive airmail and slow sea mail is Surface Air Lifted (SAL) mail which takes around three weeks to reach most destinations, and costs somewhere between the two. For English-language information about postal services, including postal fees, see the Post Office website W post.japanpost.jp.

Central **post offices** generally open Monday–Friday 9am–7pm, Saturday 9am–5pm and Sunday 9am–12.30pm, with most other branches opening Monday–Friday 9am–5pm only. A few larger branches may also open on a Saturday from 9am to 3pm, and may operate after-hours services for parcels and express mail. Major post offices that are open daily 24 hours can be found in Shinjuku (see map, pp.118–119) and Shibuya (see map, p.114)

among other city areas. For sending parcels and baggage around Japan, take advantage of the excellent, inexpensive takuhaibin (or takkyūbin, as it's more commonly known) or **courier delivery services**, which can be arranged at most convenience stores, hotels and some youth hostels. These services – which typically cost under ¥2000 – are especially handy if you want to send luggage (usually up to 20kg) on to places where you'll be staying later in your journey or to the airport to be picked up prior to your departure.

Maps

The Japan National Tourist Organization publishes **tourist maps** covering Tokyo, Kansai, Kyoto and the whole country. These are available for free at JNTO offices abroad and at the TICs in Japan, and are fine for most purposes. Tourist offices in other areas usually provide local maps, often dual-language. If you need anything more detailed, note that most bookshops sell maps, though you'll only find English-language maps in the big cities. If you're **hiking**, the best maps are those in the Yama-to-kōgen series, published by Shōbunsha but in Japanese only.

Note that **maps on signboards** in Japan, such as a map of footpaths in a national park, are usually oriented the way you are facing. So, if you're facing southeast, for example, as you look at the map, the top will be southeast and the bottom northwest.

There are also decent maps and map apps **online**. Google's is typically excellent, while with a little hunting you'll be able to find apps offering (offline-friendly) maps of certain cities; most useful, however, are apps portraying the Tokyo and Osaka subway networks, since such maps are not visible anywhere once you're on the trains themselves.

Money

The **Japanese currency** is the yen (¥; en in Japanese). Notes are available in denominations of

¥1000, ¥2000, ¥5000 and ¥10,000, while coins come in values of ¥1, ¥5, ¥10, ¥50, ¥100 and ¥500. Apart from the ¥5 piece, a copper-coloured coin with a hole in the centre, all other notes and coins indicate their value in Western numerals. At the time of writing, the exchange rates were £1 to ¥170, US $1 to ¥105, €1 to ¥140, Can1 to ¥95, Aus1 to ¥91, NZ$1 to ¥87 and R1 to ¥10; for up-to-date **rates** see Ⓦxe.com.

Though **credit and debit cards** are becoming more widely accepted, Japan remains very much a cash society. The most useful cards to carry are Visa and American Express, followed closely by Master-Card, then Diners Club; you should be able to use these in hotels, restaurants, shops and travel agencies accustomed to serving foreigners. However, many retailers only accept locally issued cards.

ATMs

The simplest way of obtaining cash in Japan is by making an **ATM** withdrawal on a credit or debit card. Both the **post office** and Seven Bank (whose machines are located in **7-Eleven** stores) operate ATMs which accept foreign-issued cards. Post office machines accept Visa, PLUS, MasterCard, Maestro, Cirrus and American Express, with instructions provided in English; 7-Eleven ATMs accept all of these, too, except overseas-issued MasterCard brand cash cards and credit cards (including Cirrus and Maestro cards). Withdrawal limits will depend on the card issuer and your credit limit. If the machine doesn't allow you to withdraw money in the first instance, try again with a smaller amount.

Seven Bank ATMs are often accessible 24 hours. You'll also find post office ATMs not only in post offices, but also in stations, department stores and the like throughout the main cities – they're identi-fied with a sticker saying "International ATM Service". Their ATMs have more restricted hours than the Seven Bank machines, but the ones in major post offices can be accessed at weekends and after the counters have closed, though none is open round the clock. You can also try **Citibank** (Ⓦcitibank. co.jp), which operates a number of ATMs in Tokyo, Sapporo, Nagoya, Osaka, Kyoto and Fukuoka. Most are accessible outside normal banking hours, and some are open 24 hours. If you're having problems, pick up the phone beside the ATM and ask to speak to someone in English.

Changing money

You can change cash and travellers' cheques at the exchange counters, or *ryōgae-jo* (両替所), of main **post offices** and certain **banks**. The post office

handles cash and travellers' cheques in six major currencies, including American, Canadian and Australian dollars, sterling and euros; the most widely accepted brands of cheque are American Express, Visa, Thomas Cook and MasterCard. There's little variation in rates between banks and the post office and there are no commission fees. Post office exchange counters have slightly longer opening hours (generally Mon–Fri 9am–4pm); banks open Monday to Friday from 9am to 3pm, but some don't open their exchange desks until 10.30am or 11am. Big **department stores** often have an exchange desk, which can be useful at other times, though most only handle dollars or a limited range of currencies and might charge a small fee. **Hotels** are only supposed to change money for guests, but some might be persuaded to help in an emergency. Remember to take your passport along in case it's needed, and allow plenty of time, since even a simple transaction can take twenty minutes or more. Finally, when changing money, ask for a few ¥10,000 notes to be broken into lower denomina-tions; these come in handy for ticket machines and small purchases.

Opening hours and public holidays

Business hours are generally Monday to Friday 9am–5pm, though private companies often close much later in the evening and may also open on Saturday mornings. Department stores and bigger

> ### PUBLIC HOLIDAYS
>
> If one of the holidays listed below falls on a Sunday, then the following Monday is also a holiday.
>
> **New Year's Day** Jan 1
> **Coming of Age Day** Second Mon in Jan
> **National Foundation Day** Feb 11
> **Spring Equinox** March 20/21
> **Shōwa Day** April 29
> **Constitution Memorial Day** May 3
> **Greenery Day** May 4
> **Children's Day** May 5
> **Marine Day** Third Mon in July
> **Respect the Aged Day** Third Mon in Sept
> **Autumn Equinox** Sept 23/24
> **Health and Sports Day** Second Mon in Oct
> **Culture Day** Nov 3
> **Labour Thanksgiving Day** Nov 23
> **Emperor's Birthday** Dec 23

shops tend to open around 10am and shut at 7pm or 8pm. Local shops, however, will generally stay open later, while many convenience stores are open 24 hours. Most shops take one day off a week, not necessarily on a Sunday.

The majority of **museums** close on a Monday, but stay open on Sundays and national holidays (closing the following day instead); last entry is normally thirty minutes before closing. However, during the New Year festival (January 1–3), Golden Week (April 29–May 5) and Obon (the week around August 15), almost everything shuts down. Around these periods, all transport and accommodation is booked out weeks in advance, and all major tourist spots get overrun.

Phones

You're rarely far from a payphone in Japan, but only at certain ones – usually grey or metallic silver and bronze colour, with a sign in English – can you make **international calls**. These phones can be difficult to find; try a major hotel or international centre.

The vast majority of payphones take both coins (¥10 and ¥100) and **phonecards** (*terefon kādo;テレフォンカード*). The latter come in ¥500 (50-unit) and ¥1000 (105-unit) versions and can be bought in department and convenience stores and at station kiosks. Virtually every tourist attraction sells specially decorated phonecards, though you'll pay a premium for these, with a ¥1000 card only giving ¥500 worth of calls.

Payphones don't give change, but do return unused coins, so for local calls use ¥10 rather than ¥100 coins. For international calls, it's best to use a phonecard and to call between 7pm and 8am Monday to Friday, or at any time at weekends or holidays, when rates are cheaper. Alternatively, use a **prepaid calling card**, such as KDDI's Super World card (w kddi.com), Primus (w primusel.co.jp), or Brastel (w brastel.com); all are available at convenience stores.

Everywhere in Japan has an **area code**, which can be omitted if the call is a local one. Area codes are given for all telephone numbers throughout this Guide. Toll-free numbers begin with either 0120 or 0088; in a few cases you may come across codes such as 0570, which are non-geographical and should always be included with the main number wherever you're calling from. Numbers starting with 080 or 090 are to mobile phones. For operator assistance for overseas calls, dial 0051.

PHONING JAPAN FROM ABROAD

To **call Japan** from abroad, dial your international access code (UK and Ireland 00; US 011; Canada 011; Australia 0011; New Zealand 00), plus the country code (81), then the area code minus the initial zero, then the number.

Mobile phones

Practically everyone in Japan has a **mobile phone**, or *keitai-denwa* (携帯電話), sometimes shortened to *keitai*, many of which can be used like a prepaid travel card on trains, subways and in shops.

The only foreign phones that reliably work in Japan are some **3G and 4G models** – contact your mobile phone service provider before leaving your home country to check on the current situation. If your phone isn't compatible with Japan's transmission technology, the solution for short-term visitors is to **rent** a Japan-compatible mobile phone (buying a prepaid phone in Japan generally requires you to show proof of local residency). Phones can be rented at the major international airports or online. Options include **GoMobile** (w gomobile.co.jp), who will deliver your phone to a nominated address in Japan such as your hotel, and **PuPuRu** (w pupuru .com/en) who also rent out data cards for internet access on your laptop. Other mobile phone operators include industry-biggie **DoCoMo** (w nttdocomo.co.jp) and **Softbank** (w softbank .jp/en), both of which have rental booths at Narita Airport (3G handsets should work with either of these networks).

Phoning abroad from Japan

The main companies in Japan offering **international phone calls** are KDDI (001), Softbank Telecom (0041), Cable & Wireless IDC (0061) and NTT (0033). If you want to call abroad from Japan from any type of phone, choose a company (there's little difference between them all as far as rates are concerned) and dial the relevant access code, then the country code (UK 44; Ireland 353; US and Canada 01; Australia 61; New Zealand 64; South Africa 27), then the area code minus the initial zero, then the number.

For operator assistance for overseas calls, dial 0051. You can make international operator-assisted calls by calling 0051 via KDDI.

Smoking

Many visitors to Japan are quite taken aback by how much smoke they're forced to inhale on a daily basis – notoriously conservative at the best of times, the country has, so far, failed to move with developed-nation norms in such regards. **Smoking** is banned on nearly all public transport (you'll find smoking rooms and carriages on some trains, though) and in most public buildings, shops and offices; in restaurants, bars, *izakaya*, cafés and even some hotel lobbies, however, you're likely to be inhaling smoke. An increasing number of cities are clamping down on smoking in the street, though smokers can light up in designated areas – look for the smoke-swathed huddle around the pavement ashtrays. Fines for smoking where it's prohibited typically start at ¥2000, though at the moment you are more likely to get away with a warning.

Time

The whole of Japan is nine hours ahead of Greenwich Mean Time, so at noon in London it's 9pm in Tokyo. Japan is fourteen hours ahead of Eastern Standard Time in the US. There is no daylight saving, so during British Summer Time, for example, the difference drops to eight hours.

Tourist information

The **Japan National Tourism Organization** (JNTO; Ⓦ jnto.go.jp) maintains a number of overseas offices (see p.33). Within Japan, JNTO operates **Tourist Information Centres** (TIC), all of which have English-speaking staff, in central Tokyo (see p.130), Tokyo's Narita Airport (see p.130) and Kansai International Airport (see p.498). Though staff will help sort out routes and timetables, they can't make travel reservations, nor usually sell tickets to theatres, cinemas and so on; instead, they'll direct you to the nearest appropriate outlet.

There is a network of government-run **tourist information offices** (観光案内所; *kankō annaijo*), many with English-speaking staff, in all major towns and cities and in the prime tourist destinations; you'll find a full list on the JNTO website. These offices are usually located in or close to the main train station or in the city centre, and are indicated by a sign with a red question mark in a white circle against a black background and the word "information". In practice, the amount of English information available – whether written or spoken – is a bit hit and miss, but staff should be able to assist with local maps, hotel reservations and simple queries. There are also ordinary local tourist information offices: practically every town has these, as do villages though there's only a slim chance of getting English-language assistance.

Another useful source of English-language information is the **Goodwill Guides**, groups of volunteer guides mostly in central and western Japan who offer their services free – although you're expected to pay for their transport, entry tickets and any meals you have together. Their language abilities vary, but they do provide a great opportunity to learn more about Japanese culture and to visit local restaurants, shops and so forth with a Japanese-speaker. Again, you'll find the groups listed on the JNTO website. Otherwise, tourist information offices can usually provide contact details of local groups and may be willing to help with arrangements; try to give at least two days' notice.

JNTO OFFICES ABROAD

Australia Suite 1, Level 4, 56 Clarence St, Sydney (☎ 02 9279 2177, Ⓦ jnto.org.au).

Canada 481 University Ave, Suite 306, Toronto (☎ 416 366 7140, Ⓦ ilovejapan.ca).

UK 5th Floor, 12/13 Nicholas Lane, London (☎ 020 7398 5670, Ⓦ seejapan.co.uk).

US 11 West 42nd St, 19th Floor, New York (☎ 212 757 5640, Ⓦ japantravelinfo.com); 340 E. 2nd St, Little Tokyo Plaza, Suite 302, Los Angeles (☎ 213 623 1952).

Travellers with disabilities

Disability has always been something of an uncomfortable topic in Japan, with disabled people generally hidden from public view. In recent years, however, there has been a certain shift in public opinion, particularly in the wake of the bestseller *No One's Perfect* by Ototake Hirotada, the upbeat, forthright autobiography of a 23-year-old student born without arms or legs.

The government is spearheading a drive to provide more accessible hotels and other facilities (referred to as "barrier-free" in Japan). Most train and subway **stations** now have an extra-wide manned ticket gate and an increasing number have escalators or lifts. Some **trains**, such as the Narita Express from Narita International Airport into Tokyo, have spaces for wheelchair users, but you should reserve well in advance. For travelling short distances, **taxis** are an obvious solution, though none is specially adapted and few drivers will offer passengers help getting in or out of the car.

New **hotels** are required to provide accessible facilities and several older ones are making them available, too. Your best bet is one of the international chains or modern Western-style business hotels, which are most likely to provide fully adapted rooms, ramps and lifts; check ahead to ensure the facilities meet your requirements. Similarly, most modern shopping complexes, museums and other public buildings are equipped with ramps, wide doors and accessible toilets.

But although things are improving, Japan is not an easy place to get around for anyone using a wheelchair, or for those who find it difficult to negotiate stairs or walk long distances. In cities, the sheer crush of people can also be a problem at times. Although it's usually possible to organize assistance at stations, you'll need a Japanese-speaker to phone ahead and make the arrangements. For further information and help, contact the Japanese Red Cross Language Service Volunteers (c/o Volunteers Division. Japanese Red Cross Society. 1-1-3 Shiba Daimon, Minato-ku, Tokyo 105-8521). You'll find useful, if slightly outdated, information on their website, ⊙ accessible. p.org

Tokyo

東京

SUMIDA RIVER CRUISE, TOKYO

1

Tokyo

With its sushi and sumo, pop culture and age-old tradition, serene gardens and traffic hell, Tokyo bombards the senses like no other city. Ordered yet bewildering, Japan's pulsating capital will lead you a merry dance – but being lost has never been so much fun. The planet's largest metropolis is Asia at its weirdest, straightest, prettiest, sleaziest and coolest, all at the same time.

Caught up in an untidy web of overhead cables, plagued by seemingly incessant noise, the concrete and steel conurbation may seem the stereotypical urban nightmare. Yet step back from the frenetic main roads and chances are you'll find yourself in tranquil backstreets, where dinky **wooden houses** are fronted by neatly clipped bonsai trees. Wander beyond the hi-tech emporia, and you'll discover charming fragments of the old city such as **temples** and **shrines** wreathed in wisps of smoking incense.

Centuries of organizing itself around the daily demands of millions of inhabitants have made Tokyo something of a **model metropolitan environment**. Trains run on time and to practically every corner of the city, **crime** is hardly worth worrying about, and shops and vending machines provide everything you could need (and many things you never thought you did) 24 hours a day.

With so much going on, just walking the streets of this hyperactive city can be an energizing experience. It need not be an expensive one, either. You'll be pleasantly surprised by how **affordable** many things are. Cheap-and-cheerful *izakaya* – bars that serve food – and casual cafés serving noodles and rice dishes are plentiful, the metro is a bargain, and tickets for a sumo tournament or a kabuki play can be bought for the price of a few drinks.

Browsing the **shops** and marvelling at the passing parade is mesmerizing – the next best thing to having a ringside seat at the hippest of catwalk shows. The city's great wealth and relative lack of planning restrictions have given **architects** almost unparalleled freedom to realize their wildest dreams. Likewise, in über-chic bars, restaurants and clubs you'll see today what the rest of the world will get tomorrow. You may not figure out exactly what makes Tokyo tick – and you're sure to get a little confused while trying – but the conclusion is inescapable: Japan's powerhouse capital is a seductive and addictive experience.

KABUKICHŌ, SHINJUKU

Highlights

❶ Ueno You could spend a whole day in this enjoyable district, which boasts parkland, manicured gardens, museums aplenty and a good zoo. **See p.92**

❷ Asakusa Bustling Sensō-ji temple is at the heart of Tokyo's most colourful and evocative district, packed with craft shops, traditional inns and restaurants. **See p.96**

❸ Meiji-jingū Escape the urban clamour amid the verdant grounds of the city's most venerable Shintō shrine. **See p.113**

❹ Harajuku Packed with boutiques, cafés and trendy brunch spots, this youthful area is a breeding ground for the Japanese fashions of tomorrow – and those too strange to ever hit the mainstream. **See p.115**

❺ Shinjuku Tokyo in microcosm, from the tiny bars of Golden Gai to the Gotham City-like Tokyo Metropolitan Government Building. **See p.117**

❻ Robot Restaurant Like nothing you've ever seen before, this wacky show constitutes the city's newest attraction. **See box, p.151**

HIGHLIGHTS ARE MARKED ON THE MAP ON PP.80–81

SEE 'ASAKUSA AND AROUND' MAP FOR DETAILS

▲ Tokyo Skytree

Fukagawa Edo Museum ▲

◀ Narita Airport

GREATER TOKYO

HIGHLIGHTS

1. Ueno
2. Asakusa
3. Meiji-jingū
4. Harajuku
5. Shinjuku
6. Robot Restaurant

1

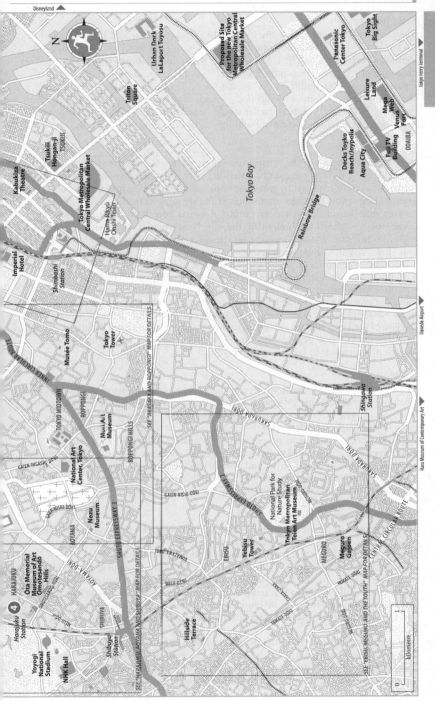

Disneyland

Tokyo Ferry Terminal

Haneda Airport

Hara Museum of Contemporary Art

Proposed Site for the new Tokyo Metropolitan Central Wholesale Market

Urban Dock LaLaport Toyosu

Panasonic Center Tokyo

Tokyo Big Sight

Leisure Land

Mega Web

Venus Fort

Fuji TV Building

Decks Toyko Beach/Joypolis

Aqua City

ODAIBA

Triton Square

Tsukiji Honganji
TSUKIJI

Kabukiza Theatre

Tokyo Metropolitan Central Wholesale Market

Hama-Rikyū Onshi Teien

Imperial Hotel

Shimbashi Station

Tokyo Bay

Rainbow Bridge

Musée Tomo

Tokyo Tower

INNER CIRCULAR ROUTE

TOKYO MIDTOWN

ROPPONGI

Mori Art Museum

ROPPONGI HILLS

National Art Center, Tokyo

SEE 'AKASAKA AND ROPPONGI' MAP FOR DETAILS

Shinagawa Station

SAKURADA DORI

GAIEN-HIGASHI-DORI

Nezu Museum

GAIEN-NISHI-DORI

AOYAMA

AOYAMA-DORI

SHUTO EXPRESSWAY 3

SAKURADA DORI

MEGURO-DORI

MEGURO-DORI

MEGURO-DORI

Ota Memorial Museum of Art

Omotesando Hills

OMOTESANDO

HARAJUKU

Harajuku Station

OMOTESANDO-DORI

MEIJI-DORI

KOMAZAWA-DORI

National Park for Nature Study

Tokyo Metropolitan Teien Art Museum

Meguro Gajoen

CENTRAL CIRCULAR ROUTE

Yoyogi National Stadium

NHK Hall

Shibuya Station

SEE 'HARAJUKU, AOYAMA AND SHIBUYA' MAP FOR DETAILS

MEIJI-DORI

KOMAZAWA-DORI

SHUTO EXPRESSWAY

EBISU

Yebisu Tower

MEGURO

Hillside Terrace

YAMATE-DORI

YAMATE-DORI

SEE 'EBISU, MEGURO AND THE SOUTH' MAP FOR DETAILS

0   kilometre   1

1

Brief history

The city's founding date is usually given as 1457, when minor lord Ōta Dōkan built his castle on a bluff overlooking the Sumida-gawa and the bay. However, a far more significant event occurred in 1590, when the feudal lord **Tokugawa Ieyasu** (see p.797) chose the obscure castle town for his power base. He seized control of the whole of Japan ten years later, reuniting the country's warring clans and taking the title of **shogun** – effectively a military dictator. Though the emperor continued to hold court in Kyoto, Japan's real centre of power would henceforth lie in Edo, at this point still little more than a small huddle of buildings at the edge of the Hibiya inlet.

The Edo era

By 1640 **Edo Castle** was the most imposing in all Japan, complete with a five-storey central keep, a double moat and a spiralling network of canals. The *daimyō* (feudal lords), who were required by the shogun to spend part of each year in Edo, were granted large plots for their estates on the higher ground to the west of the castle, an area that became known as **Yamanote**. Artisans, merchants and other lower classes were confined to **Shitamachi** (literally, "low town"), a low-lying, overcrowded region to the east. Though growing less distinct, this division between the "high" and "low" city is still apparent today.

During two centuries of peace, when Edo grew to be the most populous city in the world, life down in the Shitamachi buzzed with a wealthy merchant class and a vigorous, often bawdy, subculture of geisha and kabuki, of summer days on the Sumida-gawa, moon-viewing parties and picnics under the spring blossom. Inevitably, there was also squalor, poverty and violence, as well as frequent fires; in January 1657, the **Fire of the Long Sleeves** laid waste to three-quarters of the city's buildings and killed an estimated 100,000 people. This came just after Japan adopted a policy of national seclusion, which was to last for over 200 years.

The Meiji era

In 1853, Commodore Matthew Perry of the US Navy landed just west of Tokyo with a small fleet of **"black ships"**, demanding that Japan open at least some of its ports to foreigners. A year after the subsequent **Meiji Restoration**, in 1868 (see p.799), the emperor took up permanent residence in the city, now renamed **Tokyo** (Eastern Capital) in recognition of its proper status. As Japan quickly embraced Western technologies, the face of Tokyo gradually changed: the castle lost much of its grounds, canals were filled in or built over, and Shitamachi's wealthier merchants decamped to more desirable Yamanote. In addition, brick buildings, electric lights, trams, trains and then cars all made their first appearance in Tokyo around this time.

The twentieth century

The city remained disaster-prone: in 1923 the **Great Kantō Earthquake** devastated half of Tokyo and another 100,000 people perished. More trauma was to come during **World War II**. In just three days of sustained incendiary bombing in March 1945, hundreds of thousands were killed and great swathes of the city burnt down, including Meiji-jingū, Sensō-ji, Edo Castle and most of Shitamachi. From a prewar population of nearly seven million, Tokyo was reduced to around three million people in a state of near-starvation. This time, regeneration was fuelled by an influx of American dollars and food aid under the Allied Occupation, plus a manufacturing boom sparked by the Korean War in 1950.

By the time Emperor Hirohito opened the Tokyo **Olympic Games** in October 1964, Tokyo was truly back on its feet and visitors were wowed by the stunning new Shinkansen trains running west to Osaka. The economy boomed well into the late 1980s, when Tokyo land prices reached dizzying heights, matched by excesses of every conceivable sort.

TOKYO ORIENTATION

Tokyo is even bigger than you might think – technically, it spreads from the mountains in the north and west to a chain of tropical islands some 1300km away in the south. However, as a visitor you're unlikely to stray beyond its most central municipalities, or wards (*ku* in Japanese); a useful reference point is the **Yamanote line**, an elongated overland train loop that encloses the city centre and connects most places of interest to visitors.

At the very centre of Tokyo sits the **Imperial Palace** (see p.83), the city's spiritual heart. East of here, the wider **Ginza** district (see p.86) forms the heart of downtown Tokyo, functioning as its main shopping and financial centre. Just to the north lies **Akihabara** (see p.90), a tech-lover's paradise and home to most of the city's famed maid cafés; north again, the parks, museums and zoo in **Ueno** (see p.92) make for a great day out. East towards the river, spellbinding **Asakusa** (see p.96) is, Tokyo's most traditional district, with temples and craft shops at every turn. A boat ride down the Sumida-gawa will bring you to **Bayside Tokyo** (see p.100), where skyscraper-filled islands rise from the sea. Back inland are the neighbouring districts of **Akasaka** (see p.105) and **Roppongi** (see p.108), the latter particularly notable for its galleries and nightlife. South of central Tokyo, **Ebisu** (see p.109) is the hub of the city's main hipster hangouts; north of here the action takes a turn for the hectic in **Harajuku**, **Aoyama** and **Shibuya** (see p.113), before going altogether *Blade Runner* in **Shinjuku** (see p.117), the very epitome of rushed-off-its-feet Tokyo. Lastly, north of the centre is the busy **Ikebukuro** district (see p.121), with some diverting nearby sights.

In 1991, **the financial bubble** burst. This, along with revelations of political corruption, financial mismanagement and the release of deadly Sarin gas on Tokyo commuter trains by the AUM cult in 1995 (see p.803) led to a more sober Tokyo in the late 1990s.

In the new millennium, as the economy recovered, so did the city's vitality. Events such as the 2002 World Cup, growing interest in Japanese **pop culture** and the thriving food scene have contributed to more curious overseas visitors heading to Tokyo, with some staying on, making the capital feel more cosmopolitan than ever before. District after district has undergone structural makeover, starting with Roppongi and Shiodome back in 2003. The latest mega-development is at Oshiage east of the Sumida-gawa, where the **Tokyo Skytree** (see p.98) is Japan's tallest structure; expect another great glut of building in the run-up to the **2020 Olympic Games**.

The Imperial Palace and around

A vast chunk of central Tokyo is occupied by the **Imperial Palace**, home to the emperor and his family. The surrounding public gardens provide a gentle introduction to the city, giving a glimpse of its origins as a castle town. The most attractive is **Higashi Gyoen** where remnants of the seventeenth-century Edo Castle still stand amid formal gardens, while to its north **Kitanomaru-kōen** is a more natural park containing the excellent **National Museum of Modern Art**. Just outside the park's northern perimeter, the nation's war dead are remembered at the controversial shrine of **Yasukuni-jinja**.

The Imperial Palace

皇居, Kōkyo • Entrance off Uchibori-dōri • Access by official tour only; see details and apply online at ⓦ sankan.kunaicho.go.jp • Mon–Fri 10am & 1.30pm; 75min • Free • ☏ 03 3213 1111 • Sakuradamon Station

Huge and windswept, the Imperial Plaza forms a protective island in front of the modern **Imperial Palace**. Follow the groups of local tourists straggling across the broad avenues to **Nijūbashi**, where two bridges span the moat and a jaunty little watchtower

1

perches on its grey stone pedestal beyond. Though this double bridge is a late nineteenth-century embellishment, the tower dates back to the seventeenth century and is one of the castle's few original structures. Outside the two days a year on which Nijūbashi can be crossed (on December 23 – the emperor's birthday – and on January 2), the general public is only admitted to the palace grounds on pre-arranged **official tours**, conducted in Japanese but with English-language brochures and audio guides available.

Higashi Gyoen

東御苑 • East entrance off Uchibori-dōri • Tues–Thurs, Sat & Sun 9am–4pm (closed occasionally for court functions) • Free token available at park entrances; hand back on exit • Ōtemachi or Takebashi Stations

Though there's little to evoke the former glory of the shogunate's castle beyond some formidable gates and towering granite walls, **Higashi Gyoen** (East Garden) is a good place for a stroll. You'll likely enter via **Ōte-mon**, the eastern gate to the garden – and

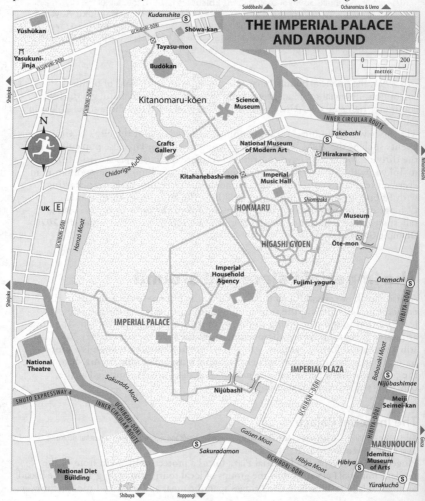

THE IMPERIAL PALACE
AND AROUND

DESCENDANTS OF THE SUN GODDESS

Emperor Akihito, the 125th incumbent of the Chrysanthemum Throne, traces his ancestry back to 660 BC and Emperor Jimmu, great-great-grandson of the mythological Sun Goddess Amaterasu. Most scholars, however, acknowledge that the first emperor for whom there is any historical evidence is the fifth-century Emperor Ojin.

Until the twentieth century, emperors were regarded as living deities whom ordinary folk were forbidden to set eyes on, or even hear. Japan's defeat in **World War II** ended all that, and today the emperor is a symbolic figure, a head of state with no governmental power. While he was crown prince, Emperor Akihito had an American tutor and studied at Tokyo's elite Gakushūin University, followed by a stint at Oxford University. In 1959 he broke further with tradition by marrying a commoner, **Shōda Michiko**.

Following in his father's footsteps, **Crown Prince Naruhito** married high-flying Harvard-educated diplomat Owada Masako in 1993. The intense press scrutiny that the couple came under when they failed to produce a male heir (current laws prohibit a female succession) has been cited as one of the reasons for the princess's miscarriage in 1999. Two years later the crown princess gave birth to a baby girl, **Aiko**, but the mother has barely been seen in public since, suffering from a variety of stress-related illnesses. One piece of good news for the royal succession is that Princess Kiko, wife of Naruhito's younger brother, gave birth to Hisahito in 2006 – allaying fears of a succession crisis in a royal family that had no male heirs, the young prince is third in line for the throne after his uncle and father.

formerly to Edo Castle itself. At the southern end of the garden lies its finest remaining watchtower, the three-tiered **Fujimi-yagura**, built in 1659 to protect the citadel's southern flank. From here, a path winds gently up, beneath the walls of the main citadel, and then climbs more steeply towards **Shiomizaka**, the "Tide-Viewing Slope", from where it was once possible to gaze out over Edo Bay. You emerge on a flat grassy area, empty apart from the stone foundations of **Honmaru** (the "inner citadel"), with fine views from the top, and a scattering of modern edifices, among them the pretty, mosaic-clad **Imperial Music Hall**.

Kitanomaru-kōen

北の丸公園 • North entrance off Yasukuri-dōri • 24hr • Free • Kudanshita or Takebashi stations

Edo Castle's old northern citadel is now occupied by the park of **Kitanomaru-kōen**. With its ninety-odd cherry trees, it's a popular viewing spot come *hanami* time, while rowing boats can be rented in warmer months on **Chidoriga-fuchi**, an ancient pond once incorporated into Edo Castle's moat. These natural pleasures aside, the park is also home to a couple of interesting museums and the Budōkan arena (see p.160).

National Museum of Modern Art

国立近代美術館, Kokuritsu Kindai Bijutsukan • Tues–Sun 10am–5pm, Fri until 8pm • ¥420 • ☎ 03 5777 8600, Ⓦ www.momat.go.jp

Located on the southern perimeter of the park is the **National Museum of Modern Art**. Its excellent collection showcases Japanese art since 1900, including Gyokudo Kawai's magnificent screen painting *Parting Spring* and works by Kishida Ryūsei, Fujita Tsuguharu and postwar artists such as Yoshihara Jirō.

Crafts Gallery

工芸館, Kōgeikan • Daily 10am–5pm • ¥200; usually ¥500 for special exhibitions • ☎ 03 5777 8600, Ⓦ www.momat.go.jp

Tucked away on the west side of Kitanomaru-kōen, the **Crafts Gallery** exhibits a selection of top-quality traditional Japanese craft works, many by modern masters. Erected in 1910 as the headquarters of the Imperial Guards, this neo-Gothic red-brick pile is one of very few Tokyo buildings dating from before the Great Earthquake of 1923.

1

THE PROBLEM WITH YASUKUNI

Ever since its foundation as part of a Shintō revival promoting the new emperor, Yasukuni-jinja has been a place of **high controversy**. In its early years the shrine became a natural focus for the increasingly aggressive nationalism that ultimately took Japan to war in 1941. Then, in 1978, General Tōjō, prime minister during World War II, and thirteen other "Class A" war criminals were enshrined here, to be honoured along with all the other military dead. Japan's neighbours, still smarting from their treatment by the Japanese during the war, were outraged.

This has not stopped **top politicians** from visiting Yasukuni on the anniversary of Japan's defeat in World War II (August 15). Because Japan's postwar constitution requires the separation of state and religion, ministers have usually maintained that they attend as private individuals, but in 1985 Nakasone, in typically uncompromising mood, caused uproar when he signed the visitors' book as "Prime Minister". Recent PMs have continued to visit Yasukuni every year – always in an "unofficial" capacity – despite continued protests both at home and abroad.

For many **ordinary Japanese**, however, Yasukuni is simply a place to remember family and friends who died in the last, troubled century.

Yasukuni-jinja

靖国神社 • Entrance off Yasukuni-dōri • 24hr • Free • ⓦ www.yasukuni.or.jp • Kudanshita Station

A monumental red steel *torii*, claimed to be Japan's tallest, marks the entrance to **Yasukuni-jinja**. This shrine, whose name means "for the repose of the country", was founded in 1869 to worship supporters of the emperor killed in the run-up to the Meiji Restoration. Since then it has expanded to include the legions sacrificed in subsequent wars, in total nearly 2.5 million souls, of whom some two million died in the Pacific War alone; the parting words of kamikaze pilots were said to be "see you at Yasukuni".

Every year some eight million Japanese visit this controversial shrine (see box above). Standing at the end of a long avenue lined with cherry and ginkgo trees and accessed through a simple wooden gate, the architecture is classic Shintō styling, solid and unadorned except for two gold imperial chrysanthemums embossed on the main doors.

Yūshūkan

Daily 9am–5pm • ¥800 • ⓣ 03 3261 8326

To the right of the inner shrine you'll find the **Yūshūkan**, a military museum established in 1882. The displays are well presented, and include plentiful information in English, but the intrigue lies as much in what is left out as in what is included. Events such as the Nanking Massacre ("Incident" in Japanese) and other atrocities by Japanese troops are glossed over, while the Pacific War is presented as a war of liberation, freeing the peoples of Southeast Asia from Western colonialism. The most moving displays are the ranks of faded photographs and the "bride dolls" donated by the families of young soldiers who died before they were married. You exit through a hall full of military hardware, including a replica of the glider used by kamikaze pilots on their suicide missions, its nose elongated to carry a 1200kg bomb, while a spine-chilling, black *kaiten* (manned torpedo) lours to one side.

Ginza and around

East of the palace, the city really gets into its stride. The districts of **Ginza**, **Marunouchi** and **Nihombashi** form the heart of downtown Tokyo, with the city's most stylish shopping street, its financial centre, principal train station, and enough bars and restaurants to last a lifetime. The best approach is simply to wander, but there are several specific sights, notably a clutch of **art museums**.

Ginza

銀座

1

GINZA, the "place where silver is minted", took its name after Shogun Tokugawa Ieyasu started making coins here in the early 1600s. It was a happy association – Ginza's Chūō-dōri grew to become Tokyo's most stylish shopping street. Though some of its shine has faded and cutting-edge fashion has moved elsewhere, Ginza still retains much of its elegance and undoubted snob appeal. Here you'll find the greatest concentration of exclusive shops and restaurants in the city, the most theatres and cinemas, branches of major department stores and a fair number of art galleries (see box below).

Sony Building

ソニービル • 5-3-1 Ginza, Chūō-ku • Daily 11am–7pm • Free • ⓦ sonybuilding.jp • Ginza Station

With four of its eleven storeys showcasing the latest Sony gadgets, and any number of products in development, the **Sony Building** is a must for techno-freaks. There's a tax-free shop on the fourth floor and restaurants on most levels, but even if you're a technophobe it's worth popping along to see just what all the fuss is about.

Kabukiza Theatre

歌舞伎座 • 4-12-15 Ginza, Chūō-ku • Gallery open daily 11am–7pm • Free • ⓦ kabuki-za.co.jp • Higashi-Ginza Station

Tokyo rejoiced when the famed **Kabukiza Theatre**, one of Ginza's most iconic buildings, reopened its doors in early 2013. First opened in 1889, the theatre has been rebuilt several times, a victim of fires and war damage. Kengo Kuma, the architect responsible for the Nezu Museum's (see p.116) new building, is behind its most recent incarnation and he has reinstated the elaborate facade of the original, which burned down in 1921. Backed by a 29-storey office block, this is classic "city of contrasts" territory. Even if

---

ON THE ART TRAIL IN GINZA

Though a little short on tourist sights, Ginza is the bastion of Tokyo's commercial galleries – there are enough of them here to keep you busy for a full day. Just to the north, and also highly recommended, is the Bridgestone Museum of Art (see p.89).

Creation Gallery G8 Recruit GINZA8 Building 1F, 8-4-17 Ginza, Chūō-ku ☏ 03 3578 6918; Shimbashi Station. Inside one of HR company Recruit's many Ginza buildings, this gallery hosts group shows, including occasional collaborations with the Ginza Graphic Gallery. Tues–Sat 11am–7pm.

Design Gallery 3-6-1 Ginza, Chūō-ku ☏ 03 3571 5206; Ginza Station. Hidden up on the seventh floor of the Matsuya Ginza department store, the Japan Design Committee's Design Gallery may be tiny, but shows are usually curated by Japan's top designers. Mon & Tues 10am–7.30pm, Thurs–Sun 10am–8pm, (Fri until 9pm).

Gallery Koyanagi 8F 1-7-5 Ginza, Chūō-ku ☏ 03 3561 1896, ⓦ gallerykoyanagi.com; Ginza-itchōme Station. Innovative gallery representing a varied group of Japanese and international artists. Exhibitions change monthly. Tues–Sat 11am–7pm.

Gallery Tsubaki 3-3-10 Kyōbashi, Chūō-ku ☏ 03 3281 7808, ⓦ gallery-tsubaki.jp; Kyōbashi Station. Representing about forty artists, mostly Japanese, this interesting little place is tucked down a side street just west of Chūō-dōri. Daily 11am–6.30pm.

Ginza Graphic Gallery 7-7-2 Ginza, Chūō-ku ☏ 03 3571 5206, ⓦ www.dnp.co.jp/gallery/ggg; Ginza Station. Presents monthly exhibitions, usually covering graphic design work from the best of Japan's creators. Mon–Fri 11am–7pm, Sat 11am–6pm.

Maison Hermès 8F 5-4-1 Ginza, Chūō-ku ☏ 03 3569 3611; Ginza Station. Home to Hermès' Tokyo boutique, this gallery hosts themed shows of Japanese and international art. Daily 11am–7pm.

Shiseidō Gallery B1F 8-8-3 Ginza, Chūō-ku ☏ 03 3572 3901. ⓦ group.shiseido.co.jp/gallery; Ginza or Shimbashi Stations. Located in the distinctive red showroom of Japanese cosmetics giant Shiseidō, this basement gallery hosts group and solo shows. Tues–Sat 11am–7pm, Sun 11am–6pm.

Tokyo Gallery + BTAP 7F 8-10-5 Ginza, Chūō-ku ☏ 03 3571 1808, ⓦ tokyo-gallery.com; Shimbashi Station. Shows cutting-edge work from the Chinese and Korean contemporary art scenes. Tues–Fri 11am–7pm, Sat 11am–5pm.

1

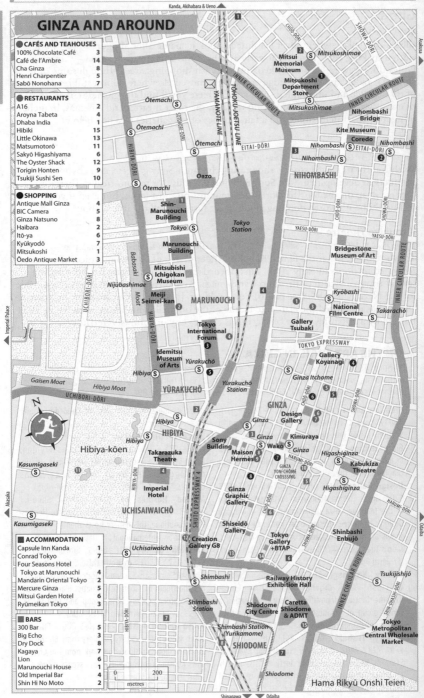

GINZA AND AROUND

● CAFÉS AND TEAHOUSES
100% Chocolate Café	3
Café de l'Ambre	14
Cha Ginza	8
Henri Charpentier	5
Sabō Nonohana	7

● RESTAURANTS
A16	2
Aroyna Tabeta	4
Dhaba India	1
Hibiki	15
Little Okinawa	13
Matsumotorō	11
Sakyō Higashiyama	6
The Oyster Shack	12
Torigin Honten	9
Tsukiji Sushi Sen	10

● SHOPPING
Antique Mall Ginza	4
BIC Camera	5
Ginza Natsuno	8
Haibara	2
Itō-ya	6
Kyūkyōdō	7
Mitsukoshi	1
Ōedo Antique Market	3

■ ACCOMMODATION
Capsule Inn Kanda	1
Conrad Tokyo	7
Four Seasons Hotel Tokyo at Marunouchi	4
Mandarin Oriental Tokyo	2
Mercure Ginza	5
Mitsui Garden Hotel	6
Ryūmeikan Tokyo	3

■ BARS
300 Bar	5
Big Echo	3
Dry Dock	8
Kagaya	7
Lion	6
Marunouchi House	1
Old Imperial Bar	4
Shin Hi No Moto	2

Kanda, Akihabara & Ueno

Akihabara

Mitsui Memorial Museum

Mitsukoshimae

Mitsukoshimae

Mitsukoshi Department Store

INNER CIRCULAR ROUTE

Nihombashi Bridge

Kite Museum

Coredo

Nihombashi

Nihombashi

Nihombashi

Nihombashi

NIHOMBASHI

Ōtemachi

Ōtemachi

Ōtemachi

Oazo

Ōtemachi

Shin-Marunouchi Building

Tokyo

Tokyo Station

YAESU-DŌRI

YAESU-DŌRI

Marunouchi Building

Bridgestone Museum of Art

Mitsubishi Ichigokan Museum

Meiji Seimei-kan

MARUNOUCHI

Kyōbashi

National Film Centre

Takarachō

Nijūbashimae

Tokyo International Forum

Gallery Tsubaki

Idemitsu Museum of Arts

Yūrakuchō

TOKYO EXPRESSWAY

Gallery Koyanagi

Hibiya

YŪRAKUCHŌ

Yūrakuchō Station

Ginza Itchome

GINZA

Hibiya

Ginza

Design Gallery

Hibiya

HIBIYA

Ginza

Ginza

Kimuraya

Hibiya

Sony Building

Ginza

Wakō

Higashiginza

Hibiya-kōen

Maison Hermès

GINZA YON-CHŌME CROSSING

Kabukiza Theatre

Kasumigaseki

Takarazuka Theatre

Ginza Graphic Gallery

Higashiginza

Imperial Hotel

Kasumigaseki

UCHISAIWAICHŌ

Shiseidō Gallery

Tokyo Gallery +BTAP

Shinbashi Enbujō

Creation Gallery G8

Uchisaiwaichō

Tsukijishijō

Shimbashi

Railway History Exhibition Hall

Shimbashi Station

Shiodome City Centre

Caretta Shiodome & ADMT

Tokyo Metropolitan Central Wholesale Market

Shimbashi Station (Yurikamome)

SHIODOME

Shiodome

Hama Rikyū Onshi Teien

Imperial Palace

UCHIBORI-DŌRI

Gaisen Moat

Hibiya Moat

UCHIBORI-DŌRI

Babasaki Moat

HIBIYA-DŌRI

SOTOBORI-DŌRI

HIBIYA-DŌRI

YAMANOTE LINE

TOHOKU-JOETSU LINE

INNER CIRCULAR ROUTE

CHŪŌ-DŌRI

SHOWA-DŌRI

EITAI-DŌRI

EITAI-DŌRI

CHŪŌ-DŌRI

SHOWA-DŌRI

INNER CIRCULAR ROUTE

HARUMI-DŌRI

HARUMI-DŌRI

SHIN-ŌHASHI-DŌRI

SHŪTO EXPRESSWAY

HIBIYA-DŌRI

N

0   200
metres

Shinagawa ▼   ▼ Odaiba

Asakusa

Akasaka

Odaiba

you're not here to catch a play (see p.151), check out the fifth-floor gallery, with its wonderful display of kabuki costumes.

Marunouchi

丸の内

Due north of Ginza, the business-focused **MARUNOUCHI** district has lately been transformed from a dull stretch of offices to a dynamic, tourist-friendly location. A major programme of construction and development – including the restoration of Tokyo Station's original handsome red-brick structure, has added swish shopping plazas, restaurants and cafés to the area.

Mitsubishi Ichigōkan Museum

三菱一号館美術館, Mitsubishi Ichigōkan Bijutsukan • 2-6-2 Marunouchi, Chiyoda-ku • Daily 10am–6pm, Fri till 8pm • Price depends on exhibition • ☎ 03 5405 8686, Ⓦ mimt.jp • Tokyo or Nijūbashimae stations

A relatively new addition to the area is the **Mitsubishi Ichigokan Museum**, focusing on nineteenth-century European art. It's housed in a meticulous reconstruction of a red-brick office block by British architect Josiah Conder; the original was erected on the same site in 1894, only to be demolished in 1968. The museum fronts Marunouchi Brick Square, where shops and restaurants overlook a lovely landscaped garden.

Idemitsu Museum of Arts

出光美術館, Idemitsu Bijutsukan • 9F Teigeki Building, 3-1-1 Marunouchi, Chiyoda-ku • Tues–Sun 10am–5pm, Fri until 7pm • ¥1000 • ☎ 03 5777 8600, Ⓦ idemitsu.com/museum • Hibiya or Yūrakuchō stations

Sitting above the Imperial Theatre, the **Idemitsu Museum of Arts** houses a magnificent collection of mostly Japanese art, though only a tiny proportion is on show at any one time. Its historically important pieces range from early Jōmon (10,000 BC–300 BC) pottery to late seventeenth-century *ukiyo-e* paintings.

Nihombashi

日本橋

North of Marunouchi, **NIHOMBASHI** was once the heart of Edo's teeming Shitamachi (see p.82), growing from a cluster of riverside markets in the early seventeenth century to become the city's chief financial district. The early warehouses and moneylenders subsequently evolved into the banks, brokers and trading companies that line the streets today. Other than the bridge at its heart – Japan's kilometre zero – the area's museums are the main reason to visit.

Bridgestone Museum of Art

ブリヂストン美術館, Burijisuton Bijutsukan • 1-10-1 Kyōbashi, Chūō-ku • Tues–Sun 10am–6pm • ¥800 • ☎ 03 3563 0241, Ⓦ bridgestone-museum.gr.jp • Tokyo, Kyōbashi or Nihombashi stations

Despite the presence of Van Gogh, Renoir, Degas, Monet, Manet, Miró and a whole room of Picasso, the superb **Bridgestone Museum of Art** is usually pretty quiet – all the more reason to visit. As the heavyweight names listed suggest, the collection focuses on Impressionism, but you can also enjoy many luminaries of early twentieth-century European art and a highly rated sampler of Meiji-era Japanese paintings in Western style.

Mitsui Memorial Museum

三井記念美術館, Mitsui Kinen Bijutsukan • 7F Mitsui Main Building, 2-1-1 Nihombashi Muromachi, Chūō-ku • Tues–Sun 10am–5pm • ¥1000; ¥1200 for special exhibitions • ☎ 03 5777 8600, Ⓦ mitsui-museum.jp • Mitsukoshimae Station

Just north of the main branch of Mitsukoshi (see p.157) is the **Mitsui Memorial Museum**, where a superb collection spanning three hundred years of Japanese and Asian art is on display. Changing exhibitions follow a seasonal theme, but are usually aimed at the connoisseur.

1

Akihabara and around

秋葉原

Up the tracks from the Ginza area, a blaze of adverts and a cacophony of competing audio systems announce **AKIHABARA**. Akiba, as it's popularly known, is renowned as Tokyo's foremost discount shopping area for electrical and electronic goods of all kinds; but it's also a hotspot for fans of anime and manga and is famed as the spawning ground for the decidedly surreal "maid cafés" (see box, p.143). There are a fair few sights to the west, including the lively Shintō shrine of **Kanda Myōjin**, and an austere monument to Confucius at **Yushima Seidō**. Across the Sumida-gawa to the east lies sumo central, **Ryogoku**.

Tōkyō Radio Depāto

東京ラジオデパート • 1-10-11 Sotokanda, Chiyoda-ku • Daily 11am–7pm • Akihabara Station

Today's electronic stores are direct descendants of a postwar black market in radios and radio parts that took place around Akihabara Station. You can recapture some of the atmosphere in the narrow passages under the tracks just west of the station in the tiny stalls of **Tōkyō Radio Depāto** – four floors stuffed with plugs, wires, boards and tools for making or repairing audio-visual equipment.

3331 Arts Chiyoda

6-11-14 Sotokanda, Chiyoda-ku • Wed–Mon noon–7pm • Price varies by exhibition; often free • ☎ 03 6803 2441, ⓦ 3331.jp • Suehirochō Station

Down a side street a little north of Suehirochō Station is the landscaped entrance to the **3331 Arts Chiyoda** complex. Based inside a renovated school, the centre hosts close to twenty galleries, where you'll find a revolving mix of exhibitions, interactive installations and workshops.

Kanda Myōjin

神田明神 • 2-16-2 Sotokanda, Chiyoda-ku • Daily 9am–4pm • Free • Ochanomizu and Marunouchi stations

A vermilion gate marks the entrance to **Kanda Myōjin**, one of the city's oldest shrines and host to one of its top three festivals, the **Kanda Matsuri** (see box, p.153). Founded in 730 AD, the shrine originally stood in front of Edo Castle, where it was dedicated to the gods of farming and fishing (Daikoku and Ebisu). Later, the tenth-century rebel Taira no Masakado – who was beheaded after declaring himself emperor – was also enshrined here. When Shogun Tokugawa Ieyasu was strengthening the castle's fortifications in 1616, he took the opportunity to move the shrine, but mollified Masakado's supporters by declaring him a guardian deity of the city. If you exit the shrine to the south, past the large, copper *torii*, you can pick up some *amazake* (sweet, non-alcoholic sake) at *Amanoya* (see p.141).

Yushima Seidō

湯島聖堂 • 1-4-25 Yushima, Bunkyō-ku • Daily: May–Oct 9.30am–5pm; Nov–April 9.30am–4pm • Free • Ochanomizu and Marunouchi stations

A copse of woodland hides **Yushima Seidō**, which was founded in 1632 as an academy for the study of the ancient classics. Today, the quiet compound contains an eighteenth-century wooden gate and, at the top of broad steps, the imposing, black-lacquered Taisen-den, or "Hall of Accomplishments", where a shrine to Confucius is located; look up to see panther-like guardians poised on the roof tiles.

AKIHABARA AND AROUND

■ ACCOMMODATION	
Anne Hostel	2
Nui Hostel & Bar Lounge	1
Ochanomizu Hotel Juraku	3

● SHOPPING	
Comic Tora-no-Ana	1
Laox	2
Radio Kaikan	3
Village Vanguard	4

● CAFÉS AND TEAHOUSES	
Amanoya	2
Gundam Café	4
Maidreamin	3
Maïlish	1
Mu'u Mu'u Diner	6
Saboru	7

● RESTAURANTS	
Go Go Curry	5
Hachimaki	8
Tomoegata	9

Edo-Tokyo Museum

National Sumo Stadium

RYŌGOKU

SHUTO EXPRESSWAY 7

SHUTO EXPRESSWAY 6

Sumida-gawa

Ryōgoku Station

KEIYŌ-DŌRI

(S) Kuramae

KURAMAE

Kuramae

EDO-DŌRI

Asakusabashi

(S) Asakusabashi Station

SŌBU LINE

Rad-ium von Röntgenwerke AG

BAKUROCHŌ

(S) Bakuroyokoyama

Taro Nasu Gallery

(S) Kodemmachō

EDO-DŌRI

Kanda-gawa

Iwamotochō (S)

(S) Akihabara

YASUKUNI-DŌRI

SHOWA-DŌRI

Nihombashi

ASAKUSA-DŌRI

Asakusa

(S) Naka Okachimachi

SHŌWA-DŌRI

Yodobashi Camera

Akihabara Station

YAMANOTE LINE

TOHOKU JŌETSU LINE

Ginza

Ueno

Matsuzakaya

(S) Okachimachi Station

(S) Yushima

(S) Suehirochō

CHŪŌ-DŌRI

Tokyo Anime Center

UDX Building

3331 Arts Chiyoda

Soldering Café

Tōkyō Daibiru

Radio Depato

Awajichō

KANDA

Kanda (S)

Kanda Station

SOTOBORI-DŌRI

(S) Hongo Sanchome

(S) Yushima

Kanda Myōjin

Yushima Seidō

YUSHIMA-ZAKA

SOTOBORI-DŌRI

Ochanomizu

Ochanomizu Station

Shinobazu-dōri (S)

Oginwanuchi (S)

Tokyo Station

CHŌ LINE

HONGŌ-DŌRI

Meiji University Museum

Meiji University

Nikolai Cathedral

MEIDAI-DŌRI

HONGŌ-DŌRI

Jimbōchō (S)

HAKUSAN-DŌRI

INNER CIRCULAR ROUTE

Takebashi ▼

YASUKUNI-DŌRI

Ikebukuro ▼

Shinjuku ▼

N

0 200 metres

1

1

Ryōgoku

両国

The **RYŌGOKU** area has just two sights – and one of those is only accessible for six weeks of the year. But even if your visit does not coincide with a **sumo** tournament, it's still worth coming along to see the fantastic **Edo-Tokyo Museum**, or to take a stroll down the banks of the Sumida-gawa.

National Sumo Stadium and museum

両国国技館, Ryogoku Kokugikan • 1-3-28 Yokoami, Sumida-ku • **Museum** Mon–Fri 10am–4.30pm; closed during tournaments • Free • Ryōgoku Station; west exit

Three times a year major sumo tournaments fill the **National Sumo Stadium** with a two-week pageant of thigh-slapping, foot-stamping and arcane ritual (see p.56). The one-room historical **museum** beside the stadium is for die-hard fans only; better to simply wander the streets immediately south of the train tracks, which until recently housed many of the major "stables" where wrestlers lived and trained. Though rising land prices have forced most of them out, there's still a good chance of bumping into some junior wrestlers, with slicked-back hair and wearing their *yukata* and wooden *geta*. Some are popping out for a quick snack of *chanko-nabe* (a bulk-building meat and vegetable stew). If you're feeling peckish yourself, one of the best places to sample the stew is *Tomoegata* restaurant (see p.136).

Edo-Tokyo Museum

江戸東京博物館 • 1-4-1 Yokoami, Sumida-ku • Tues–Fri & Sun 9.30am–5.30pm, Sat 9.30am–7.30pm • ¥600 • ☎ 03 3626 9974, ⓦ edo-tokyo-museum.or.jp • Ryōgoku Station

You'll need plenty of stamina for the extensive **Edo-Tokyo Museum**, housed in a colossal building behind the Sumo Stadium; the ticket lasts a whole day, so you can come and go. The museum tells the history of Tokyo from the days of the Tokugawa shogunate to postwar reconstruction, using life-sized replicas, models and holograms, as well as more conventional screen paintings, ancient maps and documents, with plenty of information in English, including a free audio guide. The museum's display about life in Edo's Shitamachi, with its pleasure quarters, festivals and vibrant popular culture, is particularly good.

Ueno and around

上野

Most people visit **UENO** for its park, **Ueno Kōen**, which is home to a host of good museums, including the prestigious **Tokyo National Museum**, plus a few relics from Kan'ei-ji, a vast temple complex that once occupied this hilltop. But Ueno also has proletarian, Shitamachi roots, and much of its eastern district has a rough-and-ready feel, which is best experienced in the market area of **Ameyokochō** (see box, p.95). The west side of central Ueno, just southeast of Tokyo University, boasts appealing **Kyū Iwasaki-tei Gardens**.

Ueno Kōen

上野公園 • Various entrances; information desk by east gate • Daily 9am–5pm • Ueno Station; use "Park Exit" for east gate and "Shinobazu Exit" for south gate

Although it's far from being the city's most attractive park, **Ueno Kōen** is where all Tokyo seems to flock during spring's cherry blossom season. Outside this brief period, however, the park only gets busy at weekends, and during the week it can be a pleasant place for a stroll, particularly around Shinobazu Pond. The sights below follow a rough route from the south of the park.

Shitamachi Museum

下町風俗資料館, Shitamachi Fuzoku Shiryōkan • 2-1 Ueno Kōen, Taitō-ku • Tues–Sun 9.30am–4.30pm • ¥300 • ☎ 03 3823 7451,
Ⓦ www.taitocity.net/taito/shitamachi • Ueno or Ueno-Hirokōji stations

At the southern end of the park, the **Shitamachi Museum** occupies a partly traditional-style building beside Shinobazu Pond. A reconstructed merchant's shophouse and a 1920s tenement row, complete with sweet shop and coppersmith's workroom, fill the ground floor. The upper floor is devoted to rotating exhibitions focusing on articles of daily life. All the museum's exhibits – most of which you can handle – have been donated by local residents; take your shoes off to explore the shop interiors.

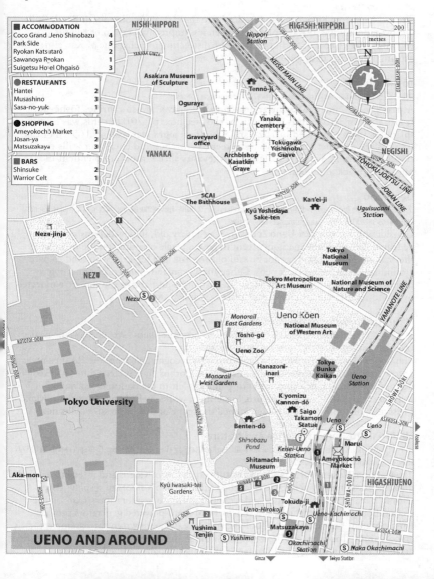

1

Shinobazu Pond

不忍池

Glorious **Shinobazu Pond**, once an inlet of Tokyo Bay, is now a wildlife protection area hosting a permanent colony of wild black cormorants as well as temporary populations of migrating waterfowl. A causeway leads out across its reeds and lotus beds to a small, leafy island occupied by an octagonal-roofed temple, **Benten-dō**, dedicated to the goddess of good fortune, water and music (among other things). Inside, the ceiling sports a snarling dragon.

Kiyomizu Kannon-dō

清水観音堂 • 24hr • Free

The red-lacquered **Kiyomizu Kannon-dō** sits to the east of the Shinobazu Pond. Built out over the hillside, this temple is a smaller, less impressive version of Kyoto's Kiyomizu-dera (see p.425), but has the rare distinction of being one of Kan'ei-ji's few existing remnants, dating from 1631.

Tōshō-gū

東照宮 • 9-88 Ueno, Taitō-ku • Daily 9am–sunset • ¥200 • Nezu or Ueno stations

A tree-lined avenue marks the approach to Tokugawa Ieyasu's shrine, **Tōshō-gū**. Ieyasu died in 1616 and is buried in Nikkō (see box, p.170), but this was his main shrine in Tokyo, founded in 1627 and rebuilt on a grander scale in 1651. For once it's possible to penetrate beyond the screened entrance and enclosing walls to take a closer look inside, where the highlight is Ieyasu's shrine room, resplendent in burnished black and gold.

Ueno Zoo

上野動物園, Ueno Dōbutsuen • 9-83 Ueno Kōen, Taitō-ku • Tues–Sun 9.30am–4pm • ¥600, free for children 12 and under; monorail ¥150 • ☎ 03 3828 5171, ⓦ www.tokyo-zoo.net • Ueno Station

Considering the fact that **Ueno Zoo** is over a century old, it's less depressing than might be feared. Yet while the macaques seem to have a whale of a time on the rocky crag they call home, the same cannot be said of the bears and big cats, who tend to pace around small corners of their pens. Other animals include rare gorillas and pygmy hippos, as well as a couple of pandas. The east and west parts of the zoo are connected by monorail, though a walking path plies the same route.

National Museum of Western Art

国立西洋美術館, Kokuritsu Seiyō Bijutsukan • 7-7 Ueno Kōen, Taitō-ku • Tues–Sun 9.30am–5.30pm, Fri till 8pm • ¥420; more for special exhibitions • ☎ 03 3828 5131, ⓦ www.nmwa.go.jp • Ueno Station

The **National Museum of Western Art** is instantly recognizable from the Rodin statues on the forecourt. The museum, designed by Le Corbusier, was erected in 1959 to house the mostly French Impressionist paintings left to the nation by Kawasaki shipping magnate Matsukata Kōjirō. Since then, works by Rubens, Tintoretto, Max Ernst and Jackson Pollock have broadened the scope of this impressive collection.

National Museum of Science and Nature

国立科学博物館, Kokuritsu Kagaku Hakubutsukan • 7-20 Ueno Kōen, Taitō-ku • Tues–Sun 9am–5pm, Fri to 8pm • ¥600 • ☎ 03 5777 8600, ⓦ www.kahaku.go.jp • Ueno Station

The **National Museum of Science and Nature** offers lots of videos and interactive displays, though sadly very little is labelled in English. Six floors of displays cover natural history as well as science and technology. In the "exploration space" on the second floor, pendulums, magnets, mirrors and hand-powered generators provide entertainment for the mainly school-age audience, while down in the basement there's an aquarium. The highlight, however, is on the second floor: sitting amid other stuffed animals, with surprisingly little fanfare, is Hachikō, Japan's canine hero (see p.117).

AMEYOKOCHŌ

The bustling **market** area south of Ueno Station, **Ameyokochō** (アメ横丁), extends nearly half a kilometre along the west side of the elevated JR train lines down to Okachimachi Station. The name is an abbreviation of "Ameya Yokochō", or "Candy Sellers' Alley", dating from the immediate postwar days when sweets were a luxury and the hundreds of stalls here mostly peddled sweet potatoes coated in sugar syrup (*daigakuimo*). Since rationing was in force, **black marketeers** joined the candy sellers, dealing in rice and other foodstuffs, household goods and personal possessions. Later, **American imports** also found their way from army stores onto the streets here, especially during the early 1950s during the Korean War, which is when the market was legalized. Today, Ameyokochō still retains a flavour of those early days: gruff men with sandpaper voices shout out their wares; stalls specializing in everything from bulk tea to jewellery and fish line the street; and there's a clutch of *yakitori* bars under the arches.

Almost all visitors, even the locals, walk past without a second glance, unaware that this is the real one – a rather sad end for the country's most famous hound.

Tokyo National Museum

東京国立博物, Tōkyō Kokuritsu Hakubutsukan • 13-9 Ueno Kōen, Taitō-ku • Jan–March Tues–Sun 9.30am–5pm; April–Sept Tues–Thurs 9.30am–5pm, Fri 9.30am–8pm, Sat & Sun 9.30am–6pm; Oct–Dec Tues–Sun 9.30am–5pm, Fri till 8pm • ¥600 • ☎ 03 5405 8685, ⓦ www.tnm.go.jp • Ueno Station

Dominating the northern reaches of Ueno Park is the **Tokyo National Museum**, containing the world's largest collection of Japanese art, plus an extensive collection of Oriental antiquities. The museum style tends towards old-fashioned reverential dryness, but among such a vast collection there's something to excite everyone's imagination. Displays are rotated every few months from a collection of 110,000 pieces, and the special exhibitions are usually also worth seeing if you can stand the crowds.

Hon-kan 本館

The **Hon-kan**, the museum's central building, presents the sweep of Japanese art, from Jōmon-period pottery (pre-fourth century BC) to early twentieth-century painting, via theatrical costume for kabuki, nō and *bunraku*, colourful Buddhist mandalas, *ukiyo-e* prints, exquisite lacquerware and even seventeenth-century Christian art from southern Japan.

Heisei-kan 平成館

In the **Heisei-kan**, you'll find the splendid Japanese Archeology Gallery containing important recent finds. Highlights include the chunky, flame-shaped Jōmon pots and a collection of super-heated Sue stoneware, made using a technique introduced from Korea in the fifth century.

Hōryū-ji Hōmotsu-kan 法隆寺宝物館

In the southwest corner of the compound lurks the **Hōryū-ji Hōmotsu-kan**, containing a selection of priceless treasures donated over the centuries to Nara's Hōryū-ji temple (p.480). The most eye-catching display comprises 48 gilt-bronze Buddhist statues in various poses, each an island of light in the inky darkness, while there's also an eighth-century inkstand, water container and other items said to have been used by Prince Shōtoku (p.471) when annotating the Lotus Sutra.

Tōyō-kan 東洋間

The museum's final gallery is the **Tōyō-kan**, housing a delightful hotchpotch of Asian antiquities: Javanese textiles and nineteenth-century Indian prints rub shoulders with Egyptian mummies and a wonderful collection of Southeast Asian bronze Buddhas.

1

Kyū Iwasaki-tei Gardens

旧岩崎邸庭園, Kyū Iwasaki-tei Teien • 1-3-45 Ikenohata, Taito-ku • Daily 9am–5pm • ¥400; tea ¥500 • ☎ 03 3823 8340 • Ueno-Hirokōji Station

The west side of central Ueno is dominated by seedy love hotels and dubious bars. A short walk past Yushima Station, however, is a remnant of a much more genteel past. The **Kyū Iwasaki-tei Gardens** date from 1896 and surround an elegant **house**, designed by British architect Josiah Conder, which combines a Western-style two-storey mansion with a traditional single-storey Japanese residence. The wooden Jacobean and Moorish-style arabesque interiors of the Western-style mansion are in fantastic condition – in stark contrast to the severely faded screen paintings of the Japanese rooms. The lack of furniture in both houses makes them a little lifeless, but it's nonetheless an impressive artefact in a city where such buildings are increasingly rare. You can take tea in the Japanese section, or sit outside and admire the gardens, which also combine Eastern and Western influences.

Asakusa and around

浅草

ASAKUSA is best known as the site of Tokyo's most venerable Buddhist temple, **Sensō-ji**, whose towering worship hall is filled with a continual throng of petitioners and holiday-makers. Stalls before the temple cater to the crowds, peddling trinkets and keepsakes as they have done for centuries; old-fashioned craftshops display exquisite hair combs, paper fans and calligraphy brushes; and all around is the inevitable array of restaurants, drinking places and fast-food stands. It's the infectious carnival atmosphere that makes Asakusa so appealing. The biggest festival here is the Sanja Matsuri (see box, p.153), but there are numerous smaller celebrations; ask at the **information centre** in front of Sensō-ji's main gate if there's anything on.

A more futuristic side of Tokyo is on view across the Sumida-gawa to the east, where the soaring **Tokyo Skytree** dominates the skyline. The river itself defines Asakusa almost as much as the temple, and ferries (see box below) are a lovely way to get in or out of the area.

Sensō-ji

浅草寺 • North end of Nakamise-dōri • 24hr; Sutra chants 6.30am, 10am & 2pm • Free • Asakusa Station

The great **Kaminari-mon**, or "Thunder Gate", named after its two vigorous guardian gods of thunder and wind (Raijin and Fūjin), marks the southern entrance to **Sensō-ji**. This magnificent temple, also known as Asakusa Kannon, was founded in the mid-seventh century to enshrine a tiny golden image of Kannon, the goddess of mercy, which, legend has it, was ensnared in the nets of two local fishermen.

ASAKUSA FERRIES

Though you can easily reach Asakusa by subway, a more pleasant way of getting here – or away – is **by river**. The ferry terminal is under Azuma-bashi bridge, opposite the Philippe Starck-designed Asahi Beer Hall, which is replete with what's supposed to be a stylized flame, but is known to all and sundry as the "Golden Turd" (金のうんこ, kin no unko). There are downriver departures roughly every 30–40min (daily 10am–6.30pm; ¥720 to Hama-Rikyū Onshi Teien, ¥760 to Hinode Pier); note that 3.40pm is usually the last departure that stops at Hama-Rikyū Onshi Teien (see p.101).

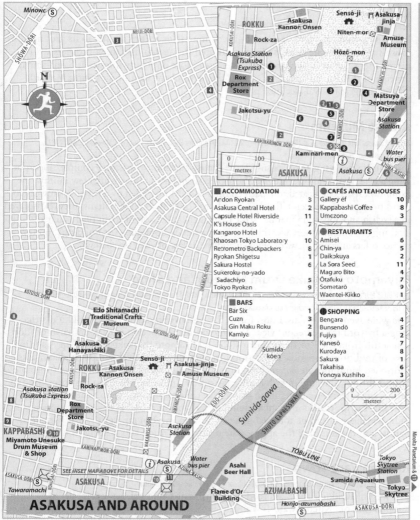

ACCOMMODATION

Ardon Ryokan	3
Asakusa Central Hotel	2
Capsule Hotel Riverside	11
K's House Oasis	7
Kangaroo Hotel	4
Khaosan Tokyo Laboratory	10
Retrometro Backpackers	8
Ryokan Shigetsu	1
Sakura Hostel	6
Sukeroku-no-yado Sadachiyo	5
Tokyo Ryokan	9

BARS

Bar Six	1
Cuzn	3
Gin Maku Roku	2
Kamiya	4

CAFÉS AND TEAHOUSES

Gallery éf	10
Kappabashi Coffee	8
Umezono	3

RESTAURANTS

Amisei	6
Chin-ya	5
Daikokuya	2
La Sora Seed	11
Maguro Bito	4
Otafuku	7
Sometarō	9
Waentei-Kikko	1

SHOPPING

Bengara	4
Bunsendō	5
Fujiya	2
Kanesō	7
Kurodaya	8
Sakura	1
Takahisa	6
Yonoya Kushiho	3

The main hall

There's a great sense of atmosphere as you approach the main hall, with its sweeping, tiled roofs, from **Nakamise-dōri**, a colourful parade of small shops selling all manner of souvenirs. The double-storeyed treasure gate, **Hōzō-mon**, stands astride the entrance to the main temple complex; the treasures, fourteenth-century Chinese sutras, are locked away on the upper floor. The two protective gods – *Niō*, the traditional guardians of Buddhist temples – are even more imposing than those at Kaminari-mon. Beyond, the crowd clustered around a large, bronze incense bowl waft the pungent smoke – breath of the gods – over themselves for its supposed curative powers before approaching the temple's inner sanctum where the little Kannon is a *hibutsu*, a hidden image considered too holy to be on view. Three times a day, drums echo through the hall into the courtyard as priests chant sutras beneath the altar's gilded canopy.

1

Asakusa-jinja

浅草神社

Like many Buddhist temples, Sensō-ji accommodates Shintō shrines in its grounds, the most important being **Asakusa-jinja**, dedicated to the two fishermen brothers who netted the Kannon image, and their overlord. More popularly known as Sanja-sama, "Shrine of the Three Guardians", this is the focus of the tumultuous **Sanja Matsuri**, Tokyo's biggest festival (see box, p.153).

Amuse Museum

2-34-3 Asakusa, Taitō-ku • Tues–Sun 10am–6pm; café daily 10am–7pm; *Bar Six* daily 6pm–2am • ¥1000 • ☎ 03 5806 1181, ⓦ amusemuseum.com • Asakusa Station

Just outside the east gate of Sensō-ji is the **Amuse Museum**, a six-storey complex incorporating a café, shop and bar, bridging the gap between old and new with a few quirky exhibition spaces dedicated to Japan's cultural past. Mostly filled by a rotating showcase of items from private collector Tanaka Chuzaburo's more than 30,000 items, they're displayed in a stylish and appealing manner – the permanent collection of traditional patched clothing (*boro*) looks more like the interior of a trendy boutique. The building's rooftop terrace offers amazing views of Sensō-ji and the Tokyo Skytree (see below).

Miyamoto Unosuke Drum Museum and Shop

宮本卯之助商店, Miyamoto Unosuke Shōten • 2-1-1 Nishiasakusa • Wed–Sun 10am–5pm; shop daily 9am–6pm • ¥300 • ☎ 03 3842 5622, ⓦ miyamoto-unosuke.co.jp • Asakusa Station

The wide avenue of Kokusai-dōri forms the western boundary of the Rokku district, long a byword for sleaze and vice. Near its southerly junction with Kaminarimon-dōri, just south from the Rox department store, is **Miyamoto Unosuke Shōten**, an Aladdin's cave of traditional Japanese percussion instruments and festival paraphernalia: masks, shortened kimono-style *happi* coats, flutes, cymbals and all kinds of *mikoshi* (portable Shintō shrine), the largest with a price tag over ¥3 million. The shop has specialized in drums since 1861, resulting in an impressive collection from around the world that now fills the fourth-floor **Drum Museum**. A red dot on the label of an instrument indicates those not to be touched; blue dots mean you can tap lightly, just with your hands; and the rest have the appropriate drumsticks ready and waiting.

Kitchenware Town

かっぱ橋道具街, Kappabashi Dōgu-gai • ⓦ kappabashi.or.jp • Many shops closed Sunday

Just west of Rokku is the main road of Kappabashi-Dōgu-gai, known locally as **Kappabashi**, or "Kitchenware Town": this is the best-known of several wholesale markets in northeast Tokyo where you can kit out a whole restaurant. You don't have to be a bulk buyer, however, and this is a great place to pick up unusual souvenirs (see p.155), such as the plastic food displayed outside restaurants to tempt the customer. This practice, originally using wax, dates from the nineteenth century but came into its own about forty years ago when foreign foods were being introduced to a puzzled Japanese market.

Tokyo Skytree

1-1-2 Oshiage, Sumida-ku • ☎ 03 6658 8012, ⓦ tokyo-skytree.jp • Oshiage or Tokyo Skytree stations

Across the river, the **Tokyo Skytree** is the city's newest star attraction, and the world's tallest tower at 634m in height – the only structure to beat it, at the time of writing, was Dubai's mighty Burj Khalifa. The main rationale behind the project was to replace

1

the comparatively puny Tokyo Tower (see p.108) as the city's digital broadcasting beacon, although the sightseeing potential of the structure is being fully exploited, with the Skytree offering the city's highest public observatory – a dizzying 450m above the ground – as well as an aquarium and planetarium at its base, plus tourist shops, restaurants and landscaped public spaces.

The observation decks

Daily 8am–10pm • 350m deck ¥2000, or ¥2500 booked online with time assigned (currently in Japanese only); 450m deck ¥1000 extra, no advance purchase possible

On sunny days and weekends, prepare for mammoth queues – first for the tickets, then for the lifts, and then for the return trip. The wait, however, is just about worthwhile, and there's a certain tingly excitement to be had in watching the numbers on the lift panel getting higher and higher – even the **lower deck** is marked as "Floor 350". The views from here are, predictably, fantastic: giant touch-screen displays show precisely what you're looking at, and also let you see how your view would appear at night (or by day, if you're visiting in the evening). Mount Fuji is, in theory, within visible range, but the unfortunate reality is that mist often blocks the view even in sunny weather, and it's usually only visible a couple of times per month.

Those who choose to head on to the **upper deck** (note: more queuing involved) will see more or less the same thing, although its space-age interior design is rather lovely – the inclined walkway wraps around the building, giving you the impression that you're climbing to the top.

Sumida Aquarium

5F & 6F Tokyo Solamachi West Yard • Daily 9am–9pm • ¥2000 • ☏ 03 5619 1821, ⓦ sumida-aquarium.com

Every major tower in Tokyo seems to have an **aquarium** attached, and the Skytree is no exception. It's a pretty good one, though, with a 350,000-litre tank (the largest in Japan) at its centre; clever design of the glass walls mean that you can see the whole tank from almost any angle.

Minolta Planetarium

7F Tokyo Solamachi East Yard • Hourly shows daily 10am–9pm • ¥1300 • ☏ 03 5610 3043

Part planetarium, part 4-D cinema, here the delights of the cosmos are relayed, for the sake of superfluous technology, in glorious smell-o-vision. Science has yet to capture the true scent of the stars, and though it's probably fair to assume that Finnish forests and Asian aromatherapy oils might be a bit wide of the mark, it's a fun experience nonetheless.

Bayside Tokyo

Several of the city's prime attractions are to be found around Tokyo Bay. The teeming fish market of **Tsukiji** provides a rowdy early-morning antidote to the serenity of the nearby traditional gardens, **Hama-Rikyū Onshi Teien**. Across the Rainbow Bridge lies the modern waterfront suburb of **Odaiba**, built on vast islands of reclaimed land and home to **Miraikan**, Tokyo's best science museum, as well as huge shopping malls.

On the north side of the bay, **Kasai Rinkai-kōen** is a good place to catch the sea breeze and has a fine **aquarium**. From the park, the Cinderella spires of **Tokyo Disneyland** are clearly visible to the west. Though you probably won't have time to visit both in one day, these places are at adjacent stops on the JR Keiyō line from Tokyo Station. Coming from Odaiba, you can pick up the Keiyō line at Shin-Kiba Station.

1

TSUKIJI TROUBLES

It's been dubbed the "fish market at the centre of the world" for its influence on world seafood prices. Tsukiji is undoubtedly big business, but during recent years the market's volume of trade has been dropping, along with the number of wholesalers and middlemen who work there.

Uppermost on merchants' minds is the Tokyo Metropolitan Government's plan to shift the market to **Toyosu**, 2km across the bay. The site was previously used by Tokyo Gas and the highly toxic ground must be thoroughly cleaned up before any construction starts on the new complex, where tourists are likely to be kept at arm's length from the action, restricted to walkways overlooking the wholesale fish section. This will help solve the problems caused in recent years by increasingly large groups of tourists disrupting the key tuna auctions: on a couple of occasions the authorities have had to put a temporary ban on visitor attendance. **Rules** now stipulate a maximum of 120 visitors, split into two groups with separate viewing times in a cordoned off area; registration for a place starts at 5am, though in warmer months the queues are such that you'd really have to be in line at 3am to get a place.

Tsukiji

築地 • Mon–Sat 4am–2pm; check website for occasional holidays • ⓦ tsukiji-market.or.jp/tukiji_e.htm • Tsukiji or Tsukiji-Shijō stations

A dawn visit to the vast **Tokyo Metropolitan Central Wholesale Market** (東京都中央卸売市場, Tōkyō-to Chūō Oroshiuri Shijō), more popularly known as **TSUKIJI**, is one of Tokyo's undisputed highlights. The site on which the market is located dates back to 1657, when Tokugawa Ieyasu had the debris from the Furisode (Long Sleeves) Fire shovelled into the marshes at the edge of Ginza, thus creating "reclaimed land" – which is what **Tsukiji** means. The market relocated to this area from Nihombashi following the 1923 earthquake, the current complex starting operations in 1935. Note, however, that by the time you read this operations may have shifted east to Toyosu (see box above) – contact the tourist offices (see p.130) for the latest developments.

Jōnai-Shijō

場内市場 **Tuna auctions** 5.25am–5.50am & 5.50am–6.15am; registration from 5am, earlier if queue is long • **Guided tours** Nakamura Nacto ⓦ homepage3.nifty.com/tokyoworks/TsukijiTour/newtsukijitour.html • Tsukiji or Tsukiji-Shijō stations

Tsukiji's main action is centred on its **Jōnai-Shijō** (main market), which lies closest to the water in the crescent-shaped hangar. The headline **tuna auctions** happen between 5am and 6.15am, and viewing, when allowed, is from within one of two cordoned-off areas, each accommodating around 60 people (see box above). It's well worth getting up early to witness sales of these rock-solid frozen fish, looking like steel torpedoes, all labelled with yellow stickers indicating their weight and country of origin. Depending on the quality, each tuna sells for between ¥600,000 and ¥1 million.

There are plenty of other things to see later in the day, including auctions for other seafood, meat, fruit and vegetables. From around 6am, restaurateurs and food retailers pick their way through the day's catch, which is put on sale at 1600 different wholesalers' stalls. Afterwards, head to one of the area's plentiful sushi stalls and noodle bars servicing the sixty thousand people who pass through here each day. One good choice, in one of the rows of sushi stalls directly opposite the market's fish section, is *Sushi Bun* (see p.137).

Hama Rikyū Onshi Teien

浜離宮恩賜庭園 • 1-1 HamaRikyūTeien, Chūō-ku • Daily 9am–4.30pm • ¥300 • Shiodome Station or ferry from Asakusa (see box, p.96)

The contrast between bustling Tsukiji and the traditional garden of **Hama Rikyū Onshi Teien**, less than a ten-minute walk west, couldn't be more acute. This beautifully designed park once belonged to the shogunate, who hunted ducks here. These days the ducks, protected inside the garden's nature reserve, are no longer used for target practice and only have to watch out for the large number of cats that

1

wander the idly twisting pathways. There are three ponds, the largest spanned by a trellis-covered bridge that leads to a floating teahouse, *Nakajima-no-Chaya*. One of the best times of year to come here is in early spring, when lilac wisteria hangs in fluffy bunches from trellises around the central pond. From the Tokyo Bay side of the garden, you'll get a view across to the Rainbow Bridge (see p.104), and can see the floodgate which regulates how much sea water flows in and out of this pond with the tides.

By far the nicest way of approaching the gardens is to take a ferry from Asakusa, down the Sumida-gawa (see box, p.96).

Odaiba

お台場

ODAIBA is an island of reclaimed land in Tokyo Bay. The name means "cannon emplacements", referring to the defences set up in the bay by the shogun in 1853 to protect the city from Commodore Perry's threatening Black Ships (see p.789). The remains of the two cannon emplacements, one now a public park, are these days dwarfed by the huge landfill site Rinkai Fukutoshin, of which Odaiba is a part. Here the Metropolitan Government set about constructing a brand-new urban development, fit for the twenty-first century, in 1988. The subsequent economic slump and spiralling development costs slowed the project down and, when the **Rainbow Bridge** linking Odaiba to the city opened in 1993, the area was still a series of empty lots. Odaiba has since filled out and is most appreciated by locals for its seaside location and sense of space – so rare in Tokyo. At night, the illuminated Rainbow Bridge, giant technicolour Ferris wheel and twinkling towers of the Tokyo skyline make Odaiba a romantic date location.

While you're here, consider going for a dip at Ōedo Onsen Monogatari (see box, p.159), one of Tokyo's largest hot-spring resorts.

Panasonic Center Tokyo

3-5-1 Ariake, Kōtō-ku • Tues–Sun 10am–6pm • Free; Risupia ¥500 • ☎ 03 3599 2600, ⓦ panasonic.net/center/tokyo • Ariake or Kokusai Tenjijō Seimon stations

At the **Panasonic Center Tokyo**, the electronics group's showcase, you can try out the latest Nintendo games on a large-screen plasma display or high-resolution projector, as well as check out the company's technologies of tomorrow. The centre includes the fun "digital network museum" Risupia, at which you're issued with an electronic tag upon entering the hi-tech display hall; as you learn about science and mathematics from the computer games and simulations within, the tag keeps track of how well you're doing.

GETTING TO AND FROM ODAIBA

The simplest way of reaching Odaiba is to hop on the **Yurikamome monorail** (ⓦ yurikamome.co.jp), which starts at Shimbashi Station and arcs up to the Rainbow Bridge on a splendid circular line, stopping at all the area's major sites before terminating at Toyosu. A one-day ticket for the monorail (¥800) is a good idea if you intend to see all of the island – walking across Odaiba can be a long slog. In addition, trains on the Rinkai line, linked with the JR Saikyō line and the Yūrakuchō subway line, run to the central Tokyo-Teleport Station on Odaiba. **Buses** from Shinagawa Station, southwest of the bay, cross the Rainbow Bridge and run as far as the Maritime Museum, stopping at Odaiba Kaihin-kōen on the way. There is also a variety of bus services (some free) to the Ōedo Onsen Monogatari. Finally, **ferries** shuttle from the pier at Hinode (日の出) to either Ariake pier on Odaiba or the Maritime Museum via Harumi and Odaiba Kaihin-kōen – the journey costs just ¥520 and doubles as a Tokyo Bay cruise.

Palette Town

パレットタウン • 1-3-15 Aomi, Kōtō-ku • Aomi Station

Aomi Station is the stop for the vast **Palette Town** shopping and entertainment complex, which offers something for almost everyone – test-drive a Toyota, go for a spin on a giant Ferris wheel, or sip coffee on a faux-Italian piazza at Venus Fort. Outside Harajuku (see box p.115), this is the most popular place in Tokyo for *cosplay* costume-wearing youngsters.

Mega Web

メガウェブ • Daily 11am–9pm • Free; virtual-reality drive ¥500, electric-vehicle drive ¥200, Toyota test drive ¥300 • ☎ 03 3599 0808, Ⓦ megaweb.gr.jp

On Palette Town's east side, **Mega Web** is a design showcase for Toyota's range of cars. Give them a call to sign up for various activities, such as designing your own auto using CAD technology, taking a virtual-reality drive or a spin in an electric vehicle, or even selecting a Toyota model and taking it for a test drive.

Wonder Wheel

ワンダーウィール • Daily 10am–10pm • ¥900

Just behind the Mega Web showroom are some more hi-tech diversions, the best of which is the **Wonder Wheel**, a candy-coloured, 115m-diameter Ferris wheel, which takes sixteen minutes to make a full circuit. If heights hold no fear then plump for one of the wheel's four fully transparent gondolas, which enable you to see down through the floor; they cost no extra, though you may have to queue.

Venus Fort

ヴィナスフォート • Daily 11am–9pm • Ⓦ www.venusfort.co.jp

The west side of Palette Town is dominated by **Venus Fort**, one of Tokyo's most original shopping and factory outlet malls. It's partly designed as a mock Italian city, complete with piazza, fountains and Roman-style statues – even the ceiling is painted and lit to resemble a perfect Mediterranean sky from dawn to dusk.

Miraikan

日本科学未来館, Nihon Kagaku Miraikan • 2-3-6 Aomi, Kōtō-ku • Daily except Tues 10am–5pm • ¥600 • ☎ 03 3570 9151. Ⓦ www. miraikan.jst.go.jp • Telecom Center Station

West of Palette Town is Tokyo's best science museum, the **National Museum of Emerging Science and Innovation**, also known as the **Miraikan**. Here you can learn about the latest in robot technology, superconductivity (including Maglev trains), space exploration and much more, as well as check out the weather around the world by looking up at a giant sphere covered with one million light-emitting diodes showing the globe as it appears from space that day. All displays have English explanations and there are also plenty of English-speaking volunteer guides on hand.

Museum of Maritime Science

船の科学館, Fune-no-kagakukan • 3-1 Higashiyashio, Shinagawa-ku • Mon–Fri 10am–5pm. Sat & Sun 10am–6pm • ¥700; canoeing ¥600 • ☎ 03 5550 1111, Ⓦ funenokagakukan.or.jp • Fune-no-kagakukan Station

The excellent **Museum of Maritime Science** is housed in a concrete reproduction of a 60,000-tonne cruise ship, where exhibits include many detailed model boats and the engines of a giant ship. Docked outside are a couple of real boats: the *Sōya*, which undertook scientific missions to the South Pole, and the *Yōtei Marine*, a ferry refitted as an exhibition space. Within the museum grounds you'll also find a couple of lighthouses, submarines, a flying boat and, from April to October, the opportunity to practise canoeing.

1

Odaiba beach

お台場浜, Odaiba hama · **Aqua City** Ⓦ aquacity.jp · **Decks Tokyo Beach** Ⓦ odaiba-decks.com · **Joypolis** ☎ 03 5500 1801, Ⓦ sega.jp/
joypolis/tokyo · Daiba Station

On the north side of the island, Odaiba's man-made **beach** boasts a fantastic view of
the Rainbow Bridge (see below), as well as an unexpected scale copy of the Statue of
Liberty. It's a wonderful place to be in the evening, looking at the bridge and twinkly
lights beyond, especially if you take off your shoes and dip your feet into the river.
Fronting the beach are a couple of linked shopping malls, **Aqua City** and **Decks Tokyo
Beach**. Apart from plenty of shops and restaurants (see p.137), the former includes the
Mediage multiplex cinema, while the latter has **Joypolis**, a multistorey arcade filled
with Sega's interactive entertainment technology.

Fuji TV Building

富士テレビビル · 2-4-8 Daiba, Minato-ku · Viewing platform Tues–Sun 10am–8pm · ¥500 · Daiba Station

A surreal, sci-fi aura hangs over Tange Kenzō's **Fuji TV Building** – with a huge metal
sphere suspended in its middle, it looks as if it's been made from a giant Meccano set.
You can pay to head up to the 25th-floor **viewing platform**, or save the cash for a drink
in the *Sky Lounge* at the top of the neighbouring *Grand Pacific Le Daiba* hotel, where
the view is thrown in for free.

Rainbow Bridge

レインボーブリッジ · Observation rooms daily: Jan–March, Nov & Dec 10am–6pm; April–Oct 10am–9pm · ¥300 · Shibaura Futō Station

From Odaiba you can cross back to mainland Tokyo along the **Rainbow Bridge**,
a 918m-long, single-span suspension bridge in two levels: the lower bears the
waterfront road and the monorail, the upper the Metropolitan Expressway. On
both sides is a pedestrian promenade linking the **observation rooms** in the
anchorages at either end of the bridge. The walk along the bridge takes about
forty minutes and provides good views across the bay, even as far as Mount Fuji if
the sky is clear.

Kasai Rinkai-kōen

葛西臨海公園 · 6-2-1 Rinkai-chō, Edogawa-ku · 24hr · Free · Ferry from Hamamatsuchō via Ariake (Odaiba) and Hinode Pier; 55min;
¥800; last boat back around 5pm · Kasai Rinkai-kōen Station; from Odaiba, take the Rinkai line and transfer at Shin-Kiba

An enjoyable way to experience Tokyo Bay is to head out to **Kasai Rinkai-kōen**, some
7km east of Odaiba. This park is a favourite weekend spot for many families who visit
to picnic, cycle or paddle off its small, crescent-shaped beach. Bird enthusiasts also
come to ogle water birds and waders in the well-designed sanctuary. The park's biggest
draw is its superb aquarium, the **Tokyo Sea Life Park**.

TOKYO FOR KIDS

Tokyo is a fantastic city for **kids**. For starters, there's a whole swathe of **museums**, the best
ones being Miraikan (see p.103), the National Science Museum (see p.94) and Edo-Tokyo
Museum (see p.92). For animal lovers, there's the fabulous aquarium at Kasai Rinkai-kōen (see
above) and Ueno zoo (see p.94).

The city also boasts Tokyo Disneyland (see opposite), of course, and the thrill of the rides at
Tokyo Dome (see p.124) as well as the wonderful Ghibli Museum (see p.121), based on the
popular anime films produced by the Ghibli studio. If your children are six or under, the
National Children's Castle (5-53-1 Jingumae, Shibuya; Tues–Fri 12.30–5.30pm, Sat, Sun & hols
from 10am; adults ¥500, children ¥400; ☎ 03 3797 5666, Ⓦ kodomono-shiro.jp) will keep them
occupied for hours.

Don't forget the myriad **shops** (see p.154) featuring the latest hit toys and crazes. For
older, tech-savvy kids, the electronic emporia of Akihabara will be a must (see p.90).

Tokyo Sea Life Park

葛西臨海公園, Kasai Rinkai Suizokuen • 6-2-3 Rinkai-chō, Edogawa-ku • Thurs–Tues 9.30am–5pm, last entry 4pm • ¥700, children free • ☎ 03 3869 5152, ⓦ www.tokyo-zoo.net

Set under a glass-and-steel dome overlooking the sea, the highlight at **Tokyo Sea Life Park** are the pair of vast tanks filled with tuna and sharks, where silver shoals race round you at dizzying speeds. Smaller tanks elsewhere showcase sea life from around the world, from flashy tropical butterfly fish and paper-thin seahorses to the lumpy mudskippers of Tokyo Bay.

Tokyo Disney Resort

東京ディズニーリゾート • Daily 8am or 9am to 10pm • ☎ 0570 008 632 • One-day passport ¥5800, two-day passport to both parks ¥10,000 • Maihama Station

Some 10km east of Odaiba lies big daddy of Tokyo's theme parks, **Tokyo Disney Resort**, which comprises two separate but adjacent attractions: **Tokyo Disneyland**, a close copy of the Californian original, and **DisneySea Park**, a water- and world-travel-themed area. You'll need to devote a day to each park to get your money's worth; expect long queues.

Akasaka and Roppongi

AKASAKA and **ROPPONGI** are famed nightlife zones, but both also have sights worth visiting during the daytime. In the former you'll find **Hie-jinja**, one of Tokyo's most historic shrines, while in the latter an "Art Triangle" has been formed by the **Suntory Museum of Art** in the huge **Tokyo Midtown** complex, the **National Art Center Tokyo**, and the **Mori Art Museum** in the equally enormous **Roppongi Hills** development. **Tokyo Tower** remains the area's retro landmark and nearby is the venerable temple **Zōjō-ji**.

Hie-jinja

日枝神社 • 2-10-15 Nagatachō, Chiyoda-ku • 24hr • Free • Akasaka, Akasaka-mitsuke or Tameike-sannō stations

At the southern end of Akasaka's main thoroughfare, Sotobori-dōri, stands a huge stone *torii*, beyond which is a picturesque avenue of red *torii* leading up the hill to the **Hie-jinja**, a Shintō shrine dedicated to the god Ōyamakui-no-kami, who is believed to protect against evil. Hie-jinja's history stretches back to 830, when it was first established on the outskirts of what would become Edo. The shrine's location shifted a couple more times before Shogun Tokugawa Ietsuna placed it here in the seventeenth century as a source of protection for his castle (now the site of the Imperial Palace), with the current buildings dating from the 1950s.

From the main entrance through the large stone torii on the east side of the hill, 51 steps lead up to a spacious enclosed courtyard, in which roosters roam freely. To the left of the main shrine, look for the carving of a female monkey cradling her baby, a symbol that has come to signify protection for pregnant women. In June, Hie-jinja hosts one of Tokyo's most important festivals, the **Sannō Matsuri** (see box, p.153).

Tokyo Midtown

東京ミッドタウン • 9-7-1 Akasaka, Minato-ku • ⓦ www.tokyo-midtown.com • Roppongi or Nagizaka stations

Tokyo Midtown is an enormous mixed-use complex of offices, shops, apartments, a convention centre, two museums and other public facilities, plus the small park Hinokichō-kōen, all revolving around the 248m **Midtown Tower**.

The complex's design and visual influences come from traditional Japanese architecture and art: look out for the *torii* in the rectangular archway entrance to the Galleria shopping mall, for instance.

1

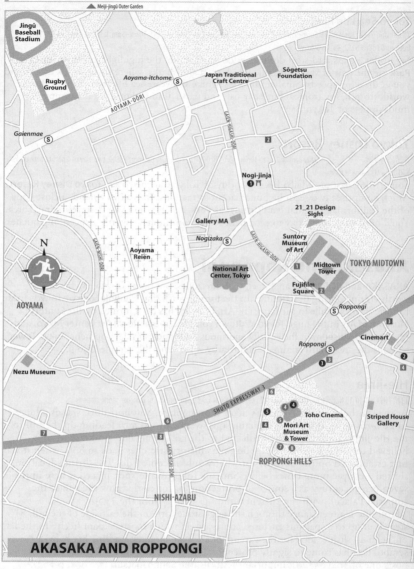

AKASAKA AND ROPPONGI

Suntory Museum of Art

サントリー美術館, Santorii Bijubukan • 3F Galleria, Tokyo Midtown • Mon & Sun 10am–6pm, Wed–Sat 10am–8pm • ¥1000 • ☎ 03 3470 1073, ⓦ www.suntory.co.jp/sma

Landscaped gardens planted with 140 trees nestle behind and along the west side of the complex, where you'll find the **Suntory Museum of Art**. This elegant Kuma Kengo-designed building hosts changing exhibitions of ceramics, lacquerware, paintings and textiles. There's also an on-site café serving tasty nibbles from Kanazawa, the capital of Ishikawa prefecture.

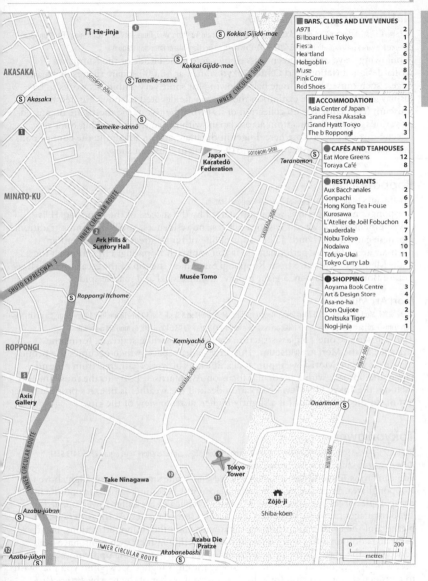

21_21 Design Sight

9-7-6 Akasaka, Minato-ku • Daily 11am–8.30pm • ¥1000 • ☎ 03 3475 2121, ⓦ 2121designsight.jp

Two giant triangular planes of steel, concrete and glass peeking out of a green lawn are part of the **21_21 Design Sight**, a fascinating collaboration between architect Andō Tadao and fashion designer Issey Miyake. The building's seamless shape was inspired by Miyake's A-POC ("A Piece Of Cloth") line, and the main gallery digs one floor into the ground to provide an elevated, airy space in which to view the various design exhibitions.

1

National Art Center, Tokyo

国立新美術館, Kokuritsu Shin-Bijutsukan • 7-22-2 Roppongi, Minato-ku • Mon, Wed, Thurs, Sat & Sun 10am–6pm, Fri 10am–8pm • Entrance fee varies with exhibition • ☎ 03 6812 9900, ⓦ www.nact.jp • Nogizaka or Roppongi stations

A billowing wave of pale-green glass ripples across the facade of the Kurokawa Kisha-designed **National Art Center, Tokyo** which, at 48,000 square metres, is Japan's largest such museum, the huge halls allowing for some very ambitious works to be displayed. Of the twelve exhibition rooms, two are devoted to shows curated by the museum (the centre has no collection of its own); the rest of the rooms are organized by various art associations from across Japan, with the sum total making for a very eclectic mix. While you are here, linger in the main atrium to admire the conical pods that soar up three storeys, and explore the excellent museum shop.

Roppongi Hills

8-11-27 Akasaka, Minato-ku • ⓦ roppongihills.com • Roppongi Station

Roppongi's metamorphosis was jump-started by the success of the **Roppongi Hills** development where, amid the shops, offices and residences, you'll also find a traditional Japanese garden and pond, a liberal sprinkling of funky street sculptures and an open-air arena for free performances. If you approach Roppongi Hills through the main Metro Hat entrance from Roppongi Station, at the top of the escalators you'll see Louise Bourgeois' **Maman**, a giant bronze, stainless steel and marble spider.

Mori Art Museum

森美術館, Mori Bijutsukan • 53F Mori Tower, Roppongi Hills • Museum Mon & Wed–Sun 10am–10pm, Tues 10am–5pm; Tokyo City View daily 9am–1am, last entry midnight • ¥1500; access to the roof ¥300 extra • ☎ 03 6406 6100, ⓦ mori.art.museum

The "Museum Cone", a glass structure enclosing a swirling staircase, forms the entrance to the **Mori Art Museum**. This large gallery space, which occupies the prime top floors of the Mori Tower, puts on exhibitions of works gathered from around Japan and abroad, with a particular focus on Asian artists. Entry to the museum also includes the **Tokyo City View** observation deck; if the weather is fine, it's possible to get out on to the tower's roof for a slightly higher, alfresco view of the city.

Tokyo Tower

東京タワー • 4-2-8 Shiba-kōen • Daily 9am–10pm • Main observatory ¥820, top observatory ¥600 extra • ☎ 03 3433 5111, ⓦ tokyotower.co.jp • Akabanebashi or Kamiyachō stations

You can't miss **Tokyo Tower**, a distinctive red-and-white structure rising high above the Roppongi area. Built during an era when Japan was becoming famous for producing cheap copies of foreign goods, this 333m-high replica of the Eiffel Tower, opened in 1958, manages to top its Parisian role model by several metres. At the tower's base a plethora of the usual souvenir shops, restaurants and other minor attractions, most incurring additional fees and none really worth seeing in their own right, have been added over the years. There are good views of Tokyo Bay from the uppermost observation deck but, at 250m, it's no longer the city's highest viewpoint; you may wish to consider saving your cash for a drink at the rooftop bar of the nearby *Prince Park Tower Tokyo* hotel, which is less crowded, less tacky, and also has great views.

Zōjō-ji

増上寺 • 4-7-35 Shiba-kōen • 24hr • Free • Akabanebashi, Onarimon or Shiba-kōen stations

The main point of interest at **Shiba-kōen** park (芝公園) is **Zōjō-ji**, the family temple of the Tokugawa clan, which dates from 1393. Zōjō-ji was moved to this site in 1598 by Tokugawa Ieyasu (the first Tokugawa shogun) in order to protect southeast Edo spiritually and provide a waystation for pilgrims approaching the capital from the

Tōkaidō road. This was once the city's largest holy site, with 48 sub-temples and over a hundred other buildings. Since the fall of the Tokugawa, however, Zōjō-ji has been razed to the ground by fire three times, and virtually all the current buildings date from the mid-1970s. Though some find it all rather lacking in charm, the imposing **San-gadatsu-mon**, a 21m-high gateway dating from 1612, is, nonetheless, Tokyo's oldest wooden structure and classed as an Important Cultural Property.

Ebisu, Meguro and the south

Named after the Shintō god of good fortune, **Ebisu** is home to hundreds of buzzing bars, many stylish restaurants and the huge, multipurpose **Yebisu Garden Place** development. Uphill to the west of Ebisu lies **Daikanyama**, one of Tokyo's classiest districts, and a great place to chill out at a pavement café or cruise boutiques. Dip downhill again to browse a rather earthier version of the same in **Nakameguro**, whose cherry-tree-lined riverbanks are prime strolling territory. **Meguro**, south along the river from here, is home to the tranquil **National Park for Nature Study**. Lastly, in the transport and hotel hub of **Shinagawa** you'll find the historic temple **Sengaku-ji**, a key location in Tokyo's bloodiest true-life samurai saga, and the wide-ranging **Hara Museum of Contemporary Art**.

Ebisu

恵比寿 • Ebisu Station

The focus of **EBISU** is **Yebisu Garden Place** (恵比寿ガーデンプレイス), a shopping, office and entertainment complex built on the site of the nineteenth-century brewery that was the source of the area's fortunes. For visitors, the main draw here is the excellent **Tokyo Metropolitan Museum of Photography**.

Tokyo Metropolitan Museum of Photography

東京都写真美術館, Tōkyō to Shashin Bijutsukan • Yebisu Garden Place • Tues–Sun 10am–6pm, Thurs & Fri until 8pm • Admission charges vary • ☎ 03 3280 0031, ⓦ syabi.com • Ebisu Station

The **Tokyo Metropolitan Museum of Photography** features regularly changing exhibitions of works by major Japanese and Western photographers. Be sure to check out the basement, which showcases the history of optical trickery. Afterwards, head for the 38th and 39th floors of the adjacent **Yebisu Tower**; you don't need to eat or drink here to enjoy the spectacular free views of the city.

Daikanyama

代官山 • Daikanyama Station

A ten-minute stroll west along Komazawa-dōri from Ebisu Station, or one stop from Shibuya on the Tōkyū Tōyoko line, is **DAIKANYAMA**. Home to some of the city's classiest homes, shops and watering holes, the village-like, laidback vibe makes a refreshing break from the frenzy of nearby Shibuya. The area is most notable for its many boutiques (see p.154) and cafés, but even if you're not in the market for clothing or caffeine it's worth a visit for the relaxed atmosphere.

Nakameguro

中目黒 • Nakameguro Station

Immediately southwest of Daikanyama is bohemian **NAKAMEGURO**, liberally sprinkled with eclectic boutiques and small cafés and bars. The district hugs the banks of the Meguro-gawa, a particularly lovely spot to head during cherry-blossom season and in the height of summer, when the waterway provides some natural air conditioning.

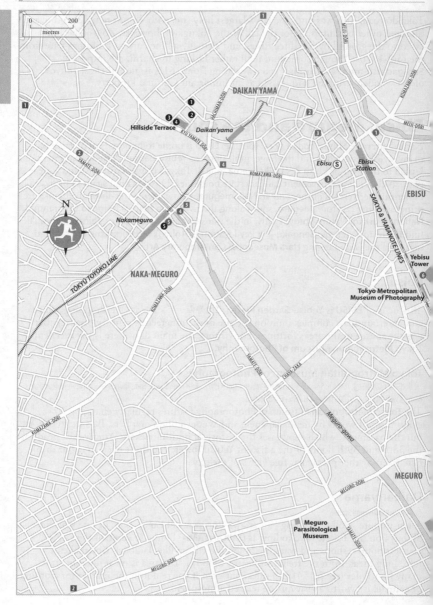

Meguro

目黒 • Meguro Station

Within walking distance of Nakameguro or Ebisu, **MEGURO** is decidedly less appealing than its neighbouring areas – the atmosphere here is rather more city than village. Nevertheless, there are a few interesting things to see, even if they're frustratingly spread out.

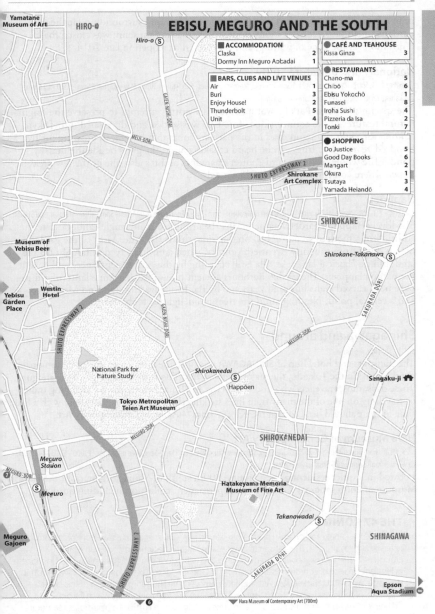

EBISU, MEGURO AND THE SOUTH

■ ACCOMMODATION	
Claska	2
Dormy Inn Meguro Aobadai	1

■ BARS, CLUBS AND LIVE VENUES	
Air	1
Buri	3
Enjoy House!	2
Thunderbolt	5
Unit	4

● CAFÉ AND TEAHOUSE	
Kissa Ginza	3

● RESTAURANTS	
Chano-ma	5
Chibō	6
Ebisu Yokochō	1
Funasei	8
Iroha Sushi	4
Pizzeria da Isa	2
Tonki	7

● SHOPPING	
Do Justice	5
Good Day Books	6
Mangart	2
Okura	1
Tsutaya	3
Yamada Heiandō	4

Tokyo Metropolitan Teien Art Museum

東京都庭園美術館, Tōkyō-to Teien Bijutsukan • 5-21-9 Shirokanedai, Meguro-ku • ☎ 03 3443 0201, ⓦ www.teien-art-museum.ne.jp • Meguro or Shirokanedai stations

The elegant, Art Deco **Tokyo Metropolitan Teien Art Museum** is the former home of Prince Asaka Yasuhiko, Emperor Hirohito's uncle, who lived in Paris for three years during the 1920s, where he developed a taste for the European style. It's worth popping

1

in to admire the gorgeous interior decoration and tranquil surrounding Japanese **gardens**, including a tea-ceremony house. Note that the museum was closed for renovations at the time of writing, and is expected to reopen in late 2014.

National Park for Nature Study

自然教育園, Shizen Kyōiku-en • 5-21-5 Shirokanedai, Meguro-ku • Tues–Sun 9am–4.30pm, May–Aug until 5pm • ¥300 • ⓦ www .ins.kahaku.go.jp • Meguro or Shirokanedai stations

The spacious **National Park for Nature Study** is a worthy attempt to preserve the original natural features of the countryside before Edo was settled and developed into Tokyo. Among the eight thousand trees in the park are some that have been growing for five hundred years, while frogs can be heard croaking amid the grass beside the marshy ponds. The whole place is a bird-spotter's paradise, and it's also one of the few areas in Tokyo where you can really escape the crowds.

Happōen

八芳園 • 1-1-1 Shirokanedai, Meguro-ku • **Garden** Daily 10am–5pm • Free • **Teahouse** Daily 11am–5pm • ¥800 • Shirokanedai Station

The lovely **Happōen** garden's name means "beautiful from any angle" and, despite the addition of a modern wedding hall on one side, this is still true. Most of the garden's design dates from the early twentieth century, when a business tycoon bought up the land, built a classical Japanese villa (still standing by the garden's entrance) and gave it the name Happōen. The garden harbours ancient bonsai trees, a stone lantern said to have been carved eight hundred years ago by the Heike warrior Taira-no Munekiyo, and a central pond. Nestling amid the trees is a delightful **teahouse**.

Shinagawa and around

品川 • Shinagawa Station

The transport and hotel hub of **SHINAGAWA** was once the location of one of the original checkpoints on the Tōkaidō, the major highway into Edo during the reign of the shoguns. These days, most travellers who find themselves in Shinagawa are merely changing trains or travelling on one of the many train lines snaking through the area, but those with a little time to spare should head to visit the eclectic **Hara Museum of Contemporary Art**.

Hara Museum of Contemporary Art

原美術館, Hara Bijutsukan • 4-7-25 Kitashinagawa, Shinagawa-ku • Tues–Sun 11am–5pm, Wed until 8pm • ¥1000 • ☎ 03 3445 0651, ⓦ www.haramuseum.or.jp • Shinagawa Station

Located in a quiet residential area around 800m south of Shinagawa Station, the **Hara Museum of Contemporary Art** has a small permanent collection including quirky

---

THE 47 RŌNIN

Celebrated in kabuki and *bunraku* plays, as well as on film, *Chūshingura* is a true story of honour, revenge and loyalty. In 1701, a young *daimyō*, Asano Takumi, became embroiled in a fatal argument in the shogun's court with his teacher and fellow lord Kira Yoshinaka. Asano had lost face in his performance of court rituals and, blaming his mentor for his lax tuition, drew his sword within the castle walls and attacked Kira. Although Kira survived, the shogun, on hearing of this breach of etiquette, ordered Asano to commit *seppuku*, the traditional form of suicide, which he did.

Their lord having been disgraced, Asano's loyal retainers, the **rōnin** – or masterless samurai – vowed revenge. On December 14, 1702, the 47 *rōnin*, lead by **Oishi Kuranosuke**, stormed Kira's villa, cut off his head and paraded it through Edo in triumph before placing it on Asano's grave in Sengaku-ji. The shogun ordered the *rōnin's* deaths, but instead all 47 committed *seppuku* on February 14, 1703, including Oishi's 15-year-old son. They were buried with Asano in Sengaku-ji, and today their graves are still wreathed in the smoke from the bundles of incense placed by their gravestones.

installations, such as *Rondo*, by Morimura Yasumasa, whose self-portrait occupies the downstairs toilet. The building itself, a 1938 Bauhaus-style house designed by Watanabe Jin, the architect responsible for Ueno's Tokyo National Museum and the Wakō department store in Ginza, is worth a look, as are the tranquil sculpture gardens overlooked by the museum's pleasant café.

Sengaku-ji

泉岳寺 • 2-11-1 Akanawa, Minato-ku • Temple Daily 7am–5pm; April–Sept to 6pm • Free • ☎ 03 3441 5560, ⓦ sengakuji.or.jp • **Museum** Daily 9am–4pm; April–Sept to 4.30pm • ¥200 • Sengaku-ji Station

Around a kilometre north of Shinagawa is **Sengaku-ji**, home to the graves of **Asano Takumi** and his **47 rōnin** (see box opposite). Most of what you see now was rebuilt after World War II, but a striking gate decorated with a metalwork dragon dates back to 1836. The statue and grave of **Oishi Kuranosuke**, the avenging leader of the 47 *rōnin*, are in the temple grounds, while a **museum** to the left of the main building contains the personal belongings of the *rōnin* and their master Asano, as well as a receipt for the severed head of Kira.

Harajuku, Aoyama and Shibuya

The trendsetting trio of **Harajuku**, **Aoyama** and **Shibuya** showcase contemporary Japanese fashion, style and architecture. Consumer culture reigns supreme in these streets, which are packed with smart cafés, designer boutiques and hip young spenders. Youthful and creative, Harajuku and Shibuya both cater to the funky, adventurous fashionista, while those with gilt-edged credit cards will feel more at home among the antique shops of Aoyama and the big-brand boutiques along **Omotesandō**, the area's key tree-lined boulevard, often referred to as Tokyo's Champs-Elysées.

Meiji-jingū

明治神宮 • ⓦ meijijingu.or.jp

Covering parts of both Aoyama and Harajuku are the grounds of **Meiji-jingū**, Tokyo's premier Shintō shrine, a memorial to Emperor Meiji and his empress Shōken. Together with the neighbouring shrines to General Nogi and Admiral Tōgō, Meiji-jingū was created as a symbol of imperial power and Japanese racial superiority. Rebuilt in 1958 after being destroyed during World War II, the shrine is the focus of several annual **festivals** (see box, p.153). Apart from the festivals, Meiji-jingū is best visited midweek, when its calm serenity can be appreciated without the crowds.

The shrine's grounds are split into two distinct parts. The **Outer Garden**, between and south of Sendagaya and Shinanomachi stations, contains the Meiji Memorial Picture Gallery and several sporting arenas, while about a kilometre west the more important **Inner Garden**, beside Harajuku Station, includes the emperor's shrine, the empress's iris gardens, the Treasure House and extensive wooded grounds.

The Inner Garden

御苑 • Harajuku or Meiji-jingū-mae stations

The most impressive way to approach the **Inner Garden** is through the southern gate next to Jingū-bashi, the bridge across from Harajuku's mock-Tudor station building. From the gateway, a wide gravel path runs through densely forested grounds to the 12m-high **Ō-torii**, the largest Myōjin-style gate in Japan, made from 1500-year-old cypress pine trees from Taiwan.

1

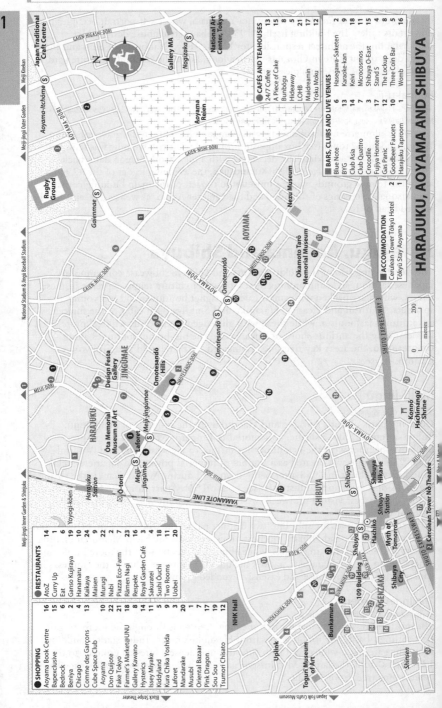

HARAJUKU, AOYAMA AND SHIBUYA

● CAFÉS AND TEAHOUSES

24/7 Coffee	13
A Piece of Cake	15
Bunbōgu	8
Hideaway	5
LOHB	21
Maidreamin	17
Yoku Moku	12

Hasegawa-Saketen	2
Karaoke-kan	9
Keivi	18
Microcosmos	11
Shibuya O-East	15
Stand S	4
The Lockup	8
Three Coin Bar	5
Womb	16

■ BARS, CLUBS AND LIVE VENUES

Blue Note	6
BYG	13
Club Asia	14
Club Quattro	7
Crocodile	3
Fujiya Honten	12
Gas Panic	10
Goodbeer Faucets	1
Harajuku Taproom	

■ ACCOMMODATION

Cerulean Tower Tōkyū Hotel	2
Tōkyū Stay Aoyama	1

● SHOPPING

Aoyama Book Centre	16
Bapexclusive	15
Bedrock	6
Beniya	2
Chicago	4
Comme des Garçons	13
Cube Space Club	
Aoyama	10
Don Quijote	22
Fake Tokyo	2
Farmer's Market@UNU	21
Gallery Kawano	8
Hysterics	14
Issey Miyake	11
Kiddyland	5
Kura Chika Yoshida	9
Laforet	3
Mandarake	20
Musubi	1
Oriental Bazaar	17
Pink Dragon	19
Sou Sou	12
Tsumori Chisato	

● RESTAURANTS

AtoZ	14
Curry Up	1
Eat	6
Ganso Kujiraya	19
Hanamaru	10
Kaikaya	24
Maisen	9
Murugi	22
Nabi	2
Piazza Eco-Farm	7
Rāmen Nagi	23
Respekt	16
Royal Garden Café	3
Sakuratei	4
Sushi Ouchi	18
Two Rooms	11
Uobei	20

Jingū Naien

神宮内苑 • Daily 8.30am–5pm • ¥500

To the left of the Ō-torii is one entrance to the **Jingū Naien**, a traditional garden said to have been designed by the Emperor Meiji for his wife. The garden is at its most beautiful (and most crowded) in June, when over one hundred varieties of irises, the empress's favourite flowers, pepper the lush greenery with their purple and white blooms. From the garden's main entrance, the gravel path turns right and passes through a second wooden *torii*, **Kita-mon** (north gate), leading to the impressive **Honden** (central hall). With their Japanese cypress wood and green copper roofs, the Honden and its surrounding buildings are a fine example of how Shintō architecture can blend seamlessly with nature.

Harajuku

原宿

As well as the wooded grounds of Meiji-jingū Inner Garden, **HARAJUKU** is also blessed with Tokyo's largest park, **Yoyogi-kōen**. However, ask Tokyoites what Harajuku means to them and they won't be talking about trees or shrines – this is one of the city's most important fashion centres (see box below), and there are reams of appealing places in which to reflect on your purchases over a coffee (see p.143).

Yoyogi-kōen

Once an imperial army training ground, **Yoyogi-kōen** was dubbed "Washington Heights" after World War II, when it was used to house US military personnel. In 1964 the land was used for the Olympic athletes' village, after which it became Yoyogi-kōen. Two of the stadia built for the Olympics remain the park's most famous architectural features. The ship-like steel suspension roof of Tange Kenzō's **Yoyogi National Stadium** was a structural engineering marvel at the time and is still used for sporting events and concerts. The smaller stadium, which looks like the sharp end of a giant swirling seashell, is used for basketball.

Ōta Memorial Museum of Art

太田記念美術館, Ōta Kinen Bijutsukan • 1-10-10 Jingū-mae, Shibuya-ku • Tues–Sun 10.30am–5pm • Fee varies with exhibition • ☎ 03 3403 0880, ⓦ ukiyoe-ota-muse.jp • Harajuku or Meiji-Jingū-mae stations

Near the crossing of Meiji-dōri and Omotesandō, look out for **Laforet**, another trendy boutique complex behind which is the excellent **Ōta Memorial Museum of Art**. Put on slippers to wander the small galleries, set over on two levels, which feature *ukiyo-e* paintings and prints from the private collection of the late Ōta Seizō, an insurance

---

HARAJUKU STYLE

With its name immortalized in several Western songs, Harajuku is better known abroad for its zany **youth culture** than it is for shopping, and with very good reason. Swing by the Harajuku Station area on a weekend and you'll see crowds of youngsters, mainly female, dressed up to the nines in a series of bizarre costumes – the epicentre is Jingū-bashi, a small bridge heading towards Meiji-Jingū shrine (see p.113) from Harajuku Station.

There are a number of interesting styles to look out for. **Cosplay** is probably the most familiar to outsiders: it involves dressing up as an anime, manga or game character, with occasionally startling results. Also easy to spot is **Gothic Lolita**, a mix of the gothic and the girlie; this itself is split into subgenres including punk, black, white (as in the hues), and country style. There are plenty more, including a whole host of smaller genres: **Visual Kei** adherents go for crazy make-up and hairstyles; **Decora** is a bright, flamboyant style often featuring myriad toys, pieces of jewellery and other accessories; **Kawaii**, which means "cute" in Japanese, usually involves clothing more appropriate to children. More styles are born every year, of course – be sure to go along and take a look.

tycoon. The art displayed comes from a collection of twelve thousand pieces, including masterpieces by Utamaro, Hokusai and Hiroshige.

Design Festa Gallery

デザイン・フェスタ・ギャラリー • 3-20-18 Jingū-mae, Shibuya-ku • Daily 11am–8pm • Free • ☎ 03 3479 1442, ⓦ designfesta.com • Harajuku or Meiji-jingū-mae stations

An anything-goes arts space sprouting out of Harajuku's backstreets, the **Design Festa Gallery** is an offshoot of the Design Festa, Japan's biggest art and design event. Behind the Day-Glo paintings, graffiti, sculptures and red scaffolding swarming over the building's front like some alien metal creeper, the interior features eclectic displays ranging from quirky sculpture to video installations – even the toilet is plastered from floor to ceiling with artwork.

Aoyama

青山

Harajuku's chaotic creativity finally gives way to **AOYAMA**'s sleek sophistication, as Omotesandō crosses Aoyama-dōri and narrows to a two-lane street lined with the boutiques of many of Japan's top designers (see p.154).

Aoyama Reien

青山霊園 • 2-32-2 Minami-Aoyama, Minato-ku • Aoyama-itchōme, Gaienmae or Nogizaka stations

Tokyo's most important graveyard is officially entitled **Aoyama Reien**, but most know it as **Aoyama Bochi**. Everyone who was anyone is buried here, and the graves, many decorated with elaborate calligraphy, are interesting to browse. Look out for the section where foreigners are buried: their tombstones provide a history of early *gaijin* involvement in Japan. Many locals enjoy partying here during the *hanami* season, under the candyfloss bunches of pink cherry blossoms.

Nezu Museum

根津美術館, Nezu Bijutsukan • 6-5-1 Minami-aoyama, Minato-ku • Tues–Sun 10am–5pm • ¥1000 • ☎ 03 3400 2536, ⓦ www.nezu-muse.or.jp • Omotesandō or Nogizaka stations

The prestigious **Nezu Museum** sits at the far eastern end of Omotesandō, in an elegant building designed by Kuma Kengo. The museum houses a classy collection of Oriental treasures, including the celebrated *Irises* screens, traditionally displayed for a month from the end of each April – expect big crowds for this popular exhibition. The museum's best feature, enjoyable any time of year and fully justifying the entrance fee, is its extensive garden, which slopes gently away around an ornamental pond. Dotted through it are several traditional teahouses, and mossy stone and bronze sculptures.

Okamoto Tarō Memorial Museum

岡本太郎記念館, Okamoto Tarō Kinenkan • 6-1-19 Minami-aoyama, Minato-ku • Wed–Mon 10am–5.30pm • ¥600 • ⓦ taro-okamoto.or.jp • Omotesandō Station

The quirky **Okamoto Tarō Memorial Museum** once functioned as the studio of the avant-garde artist; it now houses examples of his intriguing, often whimsical work, as well as a pleasant café (see p.143). If this has whetted your appetite, you might consider heading to the largest Okamoto Taro Museum of Art in Kawasaki, between Tokyo and Yokohama (ⓦ www.taromuseum.jp).

Shibuya

渋谷

It's hard to beat **SHIBUYA**, birthplace of a million-and-one consumer crazes, as a mind-blowing introduction to contemporary Tokyo. Here teens and twenty-somethings

HACHIKŌ

A statue just outside Shibuya Station marks the famous waiting spot of **Hachikō** (1923–35), an Akita dog who would come to greet his master every day as he returned home from work at the station – a practice that continued for almost a decade after the professor's death, with the dog arriving on time every day to greet the train. Locals were so touched by Hachikō's devotion that a **bronze statue** was cast of the dog. During World War II, the original Hachikō statue was melted down for weapons, but a replacement was reinstated beside the station in 1948 – it remains one of Tokyo's most famous rendezvous spots. If the statue's not enough for you, you can see the real Hachikō who lives on in stuffed form in the National Science Museum (see p.94), and there's a memorial in Aoyama Cemetery (map opposite).

throng **Centre Gai** (センター街), the shopping precinct that runs between the district's massive department stores. Centre Gai is bookended to the south by Shibuya station, visible across the hordes of people navigating the famously busy Shibuya crossing. Although there are a few interesting sights in the area, Shibuya, with a wealth of bars and clubs (see pp.144–150), is primarily an after-dark destination.

Shibuya Hikarie Building

渋谷ヒカリエ • 2-21-1 Shibuya, Shibuya-ku • Creative Space 8 daily 11am–8pm • ⓦ hikarie.jp • Shibuya Station

A 34-storey tower rising just east of Shibuya Station, **Shibuya Hikarie** is one of the city's more inventive recent constructions. Designed like a stack of mismatching building blocks, this complex contains offices, shops, restaurants and various cultural facilities, including a 2000-seat theatre whose lobby provides a sweeping view of the skyline. For regular visitors, the prime attraction is **Creative Space 8** on the eighth floor, a quirky mix of gallery space and shops.

Japan Folk Crafts Museum

日本民芸館, Nihon Mingeikan • Tues–Sun 10am–5pm • ¥1000 • ☎ 03 3467 4527, ⓦ mingeikan.or.jp • Komaba-Tōdaimae Station

Just two stops down the Keiō Inokashira line from Shibuya Station is the excellent **Japan Folk Crafts Museum**, a must-see for lovers of handcrafted pottery, textiles and lacquerware. The gift shop is a fine source of souvenirs. Opposite the museum stands a nineteenth-century **nagayamon** (long gate house), brought here from Tochigi-ken by the museum's founder, Yanagi Sōetsu (see p.813).

Shinjuku and the west

Some 4km due west of the Imperial Palace, **SHINJUKU** (新宿) is the modern heart of Tokyo. From the love hotels and hostess bars of **Kabukichō** to shop-till-you-drop department stores and hi-tech towers, the district offers a tantalizing microcosm of the city. Vast **Shinjuku Station**, a messy combination of three train terminals and connecting subway lines, splits the area into two. There's also the separate **Seibu-Shinjuku Station**, north of the JR Station. At least two million commuters are fed into these stations every day and spun out of sixty exits. If you get lost here (it's easily done), head immediately for street level and get your bearings by looking out for the skyscrapers of the **Nishi-Shinjuku** (西新宿) area to the west.

Tokyo Metropolitan Government Building

東京都庁舎, Tōkyō-to Chōsha • 2-8-1 Nishi-Shinjuku, Shinjuku-ku; both observation rooms 45F • Tours Mon–Fri 10am–3pm; observation rooms Mon–Fri 9.30am–10pm, Sat & Sun 9.30am–7pm • Free • Tochōmae Station

Some 13,000 city bureaucrats clock in each day at the Gotham City-like **Tokyo Metropolitan Government Building** (TMGB), a 400,000-square-metre complex

1

designed by Tange Kenzō. The complex includes twin 48-storey towers, an adjacent tower block, the Metropolitan Assembly Hall (where the city's councillors meet) and a sweeping, statue-lined and colonnaded plaza.

On the ground floor of the north tower you'll find the excellent Tokyo Tourist Information Centre (see p.130); free **tours** of the complex depart from here. Both the towers have **observation rooms**; the southern one is quieter and has a pleasant café, while the northern one is usually open later, and features a shopping area and (overpriced) restaurant. It's worth timing your visit for dusk, so you can see the multicoloured lights of Shinjuku spark into action as the setting sun turns the sky a deep photochemical orange.

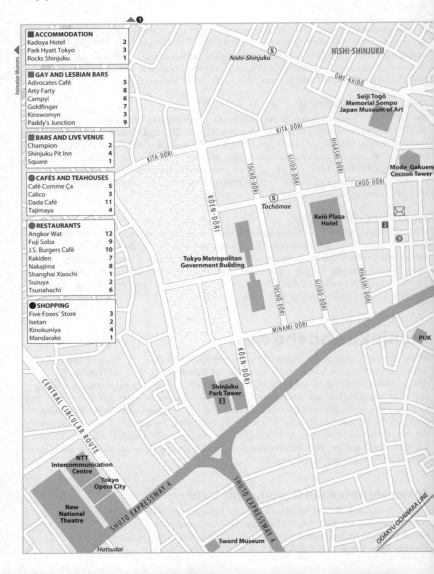

■ **ACCOMMODATION**
Kadoya Hotel 2
Park Hyatt Tokyo 3
Rocks Shinjuku 1

■ **GAY AND LESBIAN BARS**
Advocates Café 5
Arty Farty 8
Campy! 6
Goldfinger 7
Kinswomyn 3
Paddy's Junction 9

■ **BARS AND LIVE VENUE**
Champion 2
Shinjuku Pit Inn 4
Square 1

● **CAFÉS AND TEAHOUSES**
Café Comme Ça 5
Calico 3
Dada Café 11
Tajimaya 4

● **RESTAURANTS**
Angkor Wat 12
Fuji Soba 9
J.S. Burgers Café 10
Kakiden 7
Nakajima 8
Shanghai Xiaochi 1
Suzuya 2
Tsunahachi 6

● **SHOPPING**
Five Foxes' Store 3
Isetan 2
Kinokuniya 4
Mandarake 1

Animation Museums

Nishi-Shinjuku

NISHI-SHINJUKU

ŌME-KAIDŌ

Seiji Tōgō
Memorial Sompo
Japan Museum of Art

KITA-DŌRI

HIGASHI-DŌRI

GIJIDO-DŌRI

Mode Gakuen
Cocoon Tower

KITA-DŌRI

TOCHŌ-DŌRI

CHŪŌ-DŌRI

KŌEN-DŌRI

Tochōmae

Keiō Plaza
Hotel

Tokyo Metropolitan
Government Building

HIGASHI-DŌRI

TOCHŌ-DŌRI

GIJIDO-DŌRI

HIGASHI-DŌRI

MINAMI-DŌRI

PUK

KŌEN-DŌRI

CENTRAL CIRCULAR ROUTE

Shinjuku
Park Tower

NTT
Intercommunication
Centre

Tokyo
Opera City

SHUTO EXPRESSWAY 4

SHUTO EXPRESSWAY 4

New
National
Theatre

ODAKYU ODAWARA LINE

Hatsudai

Sword Museum

Omoide Yokochō

思い出横丁

Squashed up against the train tracks running north from the Odakyū department store is **Omoide Yokochō** (Memories Alley). Lit by hundreds of *akachochin* (red lanterns), it's also known as Shomben Yokochō (しょんべん横丁, Piss Alley), a reference to the time when patrons of the area's many cramped *yakitori* joints and bars relieved themselves in the street, for want of other facilities. Don't be put off: the alley remains a cheap and atmospheric place to eat and drink (and there are toilets these days). Enjoy it while you can, too, as there's talk of redeveloping the area. A pedestrian tunnel at the southern end of the alleys, just to the right of the cheap clothes outlets, provides a short cut to the east side of Shinjuku Station.

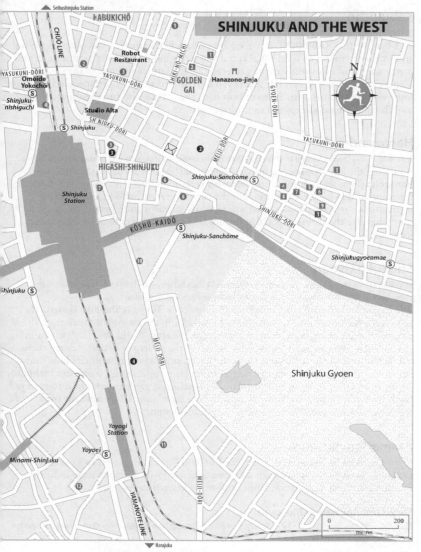

> ## GOLDEN GAI RENAISSANCE
>
> Intellectuals and artists have rubbed shoulders with Kabukichō's demimonde since just after World War II in the tiny bars of **Golden Gai** (ゴールデン街). For decades, this hugely atmospheric warren of around 150 drinking dens (see p.148) has teetered on the brink of oblivion, the cinderblock buildings under threat from both property developers and from their own shoddy construction.
>
> Recently, though, Golden Gai seems to be undergoing a mini-renaissance as a new generation of bar masters and mistresses takes over some of the shoebox establishments. Most bars continue to welcome regulars only (and charge exorbitant prices to anyone else), but with several places now posting their table and drink charges outside the door, *gaijin* visitors don't need to risk being fleeced rotten.

Kabukichō

歌舞伎町 • Northeast of Shinjuku Station

Red-light district **KABUKICHŌ** is named after a kabuki theatre that was planned for the area in the aftermath of World War II but was never built. For casual wanderers it's all pretty safe thanks to street security cameras, but at heart it's still one of the seediest corners of the city. In its grid of streets you'll see self-consciously primped and preening touts who fish women into the male host bars; the *yakuza* who run the show are there, too, though generally keeping a much lower profile.

Hanazono-jinja

花園神社 • 5-17-3 Shinjuku, Shinjuku-ku • 24hr • Free • Shinjuku, Higashi-shinjuku, Seibu-Shinjuku or Shinjuku-Sanchōme stations

Bordering the atmospheric bar quarter **Golden Gai** (see box above) is the attractive **Hanazono-jinja**, set in grounds studded with vermillion *torii*. This shrine pre-dates the founding of Edo by the Tokugawa, but the current granite buildings are modern re-creations – it was originally sited where the department store Isetan now is. At night, spotlights give the shrine a special ambience, and every Sunday there's a flea market in its grounds.

Shinjuku Gyoen

新宿御苑 • 11 Naitomachi, Shinjuku-ku • **Garden** Tues–Sun 9am–4.30pm, last entry 4pm • Entry ¥200 • **Rakū-tei** Tues–Sun 10am–4pm • Tea ¥700 • Main entrance Shinjuku-gyoenmae Station; west gate Sendagaya Station

The largest and arguably the most beautiful garden in Tokyo is **Shinjuku Gyoen**. The grounds, which once held the mansion of Lord Naitō, the *daimyō* of Tsuruga on the coast of the Sea of Japan, were opened to the public after World War II. Apart from spaciousness, the gardens' most notable feature is the variety of design. The southern half is traditionally Japanese, with winding paths, stone lanterns, artificial hills, and islands in ponds linked by zigzag bridges, and is home to *Rakū-tei*, a pleasant **teahouse**. At the northern end of the park are formal, French-style gardens, with neat rows of tall birch trees and hedge-lined flowerbeds. Clipped, broad lawns dominate the middle of the park, which is modelled on English landscape design.

Animation museums

From Shinjuku Station, you can take the JR Chūō line six stops west to Ogikubo (荻窪), the closest station to **Suginami**, an area long associated with the animation industry, location for several production houses and many key artists resident.

Suginami Animation Museum

杉並アニメーションミュージアム • 3-29-5 Kamiogi, Suginami-ku • Tues–Sun 10am–5.30pm • Free • ⓦ www.sam.or.jp • 5min bus journey from Ogikubo Station, platform 0 or 1

At the engaging **Suginami Animation Museum**, colourful displays trace the history of animation in Japan, interactive computer games allow you to create your own animations, a small theatre screens anime, and there's a library packed with manga and DVDs (some with English subtitles).

Ghibli Museum

三鷹の森ジブリ美術館, Mitaka no Mori Jiburi Bijutsukan · 1-1-83 Shimorenjaku, Mitaka-ku · Wed–Mon 10am–6pm · ¥1000, reductions for children; advance booking necessary as the museum can be booked out for weeks at a time; 2400 tickets per day; timed tickets available online or from Lawson convenience stores · ☎ 0570 055777, ⓦ ghibli-museum.jp · Short walk (follow signs) or bus ride (¥200) from south exit of Mitaka Station

Three stops further west along the Chūō line from the Suginami Animation Museum is **Mitaka**, location for the charming **Mitaka no Mori Ghibli Museum**, found at the southwest corner of leafy Inokashira Park. Beautifully designed throughout, the museum celebrates the work of the Ghibli animation studio, responsible for blockbuster movies including *My Neighbour Totoro*, *Princess Mononoke* and the Oscar-winning *Spirited Away*. Visitors gain an insight not only into Ghibli's films but also the animator's art in general. There's also a small cinema where original short animated features, exclusive to the museum, are screened.

Ikebukuro and the north

Northern Tokyo's main commercial hub is **IKEBUKURO** (池袋). Cheap accommodation and good transport links have attracted an increasing number of expatriates, typically Chinese and Taiwanese, but including a broad sweep of other nationalities, to settle around here, which lends Ikebukuro a faintly cosmopolitan air. Either side of the hectic station (around one million passengers pass through each day), the massive department stores Tōbu and Seibu square off against each other. Bar the Frank Lloyd Wright-designed **Myōnichikan** and some raucous nightlife, there's not all that much to see in the area; it is, however, useful as a springboard to interesting sights such as **Rikugi-en**, a wonderful old stroll-garden.

Myōnichikan

明日館 · 2-31-3 Nishi-Ikebukuro, Toshima-ku · Tues–Sun 10am–4pm, closed during functions · ¥400, ¥600 including coffee or Japanese tea and sweets · ☎ 03 3971 7535, ⓦ jiyu.jp · Ikebukuro Station

The distinctive **Myōnichikan** ("House of Tomorrow") is a former school designed by Frank Lloyd Wright and his assistant Endō Arata. The geometric windows and low-slung roofs are trademark Wright features, but the buildings are best appreciated

---

TOKYO'S LAST TRAMLINE

Early twentieth-century Tokyo boasted a number of tramlines, or *chin chin densha* ('ding ding trains', from the sound of the trams' bells), of which only the 12km-long **Toden-Arakawa Line** (都電荒川線) remains, running north from Waseda to Minowa-bashi. The most interesting section lies along a short stretch from **Kōshinzuka Station**, a 15min walk northwest of Sugamo Station, from where the line heads southwest towards Higashi-Ikebukuro, rocking and rolling along narrow streets and through Tokyo backyards.

Most of the original tramlines were private enterprises and have gradually been replaced with subways. The Arakawa Line, built purely to take people to the spring blossoms in Asukayama Park, will probably survive for its nostalgia value if nothing else, and recent replacements of all the cars have some sporting a retro look.

PASMO, Suica and SF Metro cards can be used on the system, as can Toei day tickets. Ordinary tickets cost ¥160, however far you travel. You pay as you enter and note that station signs and announcements are in Japanese and English.

1

from inside, where you get the full effect of the clean, bold lines, echoed in the hexagonal chairs, light fittings and other original furnishings.

Rikugi-en

六義園 • 6 Honkomagome, Bunkyō-ku • Daily 9am–5pm • ¥300 • Entrance on Hongō-dōri, 5min south of Komagome Station

Tokyo's best surviving example of a classical, Edo-period stroll-garden, **Rikugi-en** was designed in the early eighteenth century by high-ranking feudal lord **Yanagisawa**

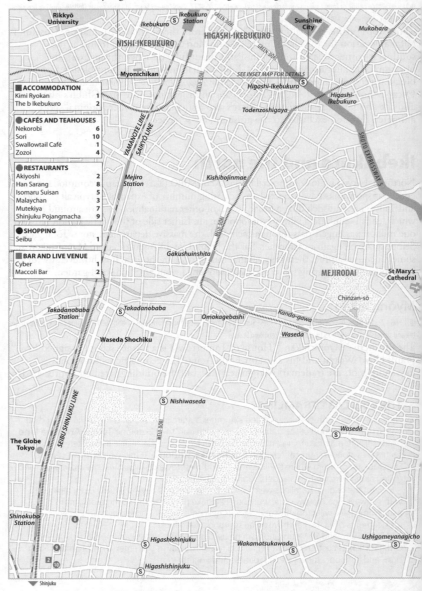

■ ACCOMMODATION	
Kimi Ryokan	1
The b Ikebukuro	2

● CAFÉS AND TEAHOUSES	
Nekorobi	6
Sori	10
Swallowtail Café	1
Zozoi	4

● RESTAURANTS	
Akiyoshi	2
Han Sarang	8
Isomaru Suisan	5
Malaychan	3
Mutekiya	7
Shinjuku Pojangmacha	9

● SHOPPING	
Seibu	1

■ BAR AND LIVE VENUE	
Cyber	1
Maccoli Bar	2

Yoshiyasu. A perfectionist and literary scholar, Yanagisawa took seven years to create this celebrated garden – with its 88 allusions to famous scenes, real or imaginary, from ancient Japanese poetry – and then named it Rikugi-en, "garden of the six principles of poetry", in reference to the rules for composing *waka* (poems of 31 syllables). Few of the 88 landscapes have survived – the guide map issued at the entrance identifies a mere eighteen – but Rikugi-en still retains its rhythm and beauty, beginning as you enter with an ancient, spreading cherry tree, then slowly unfolding along paths that meander past secluded arbours and around the indented

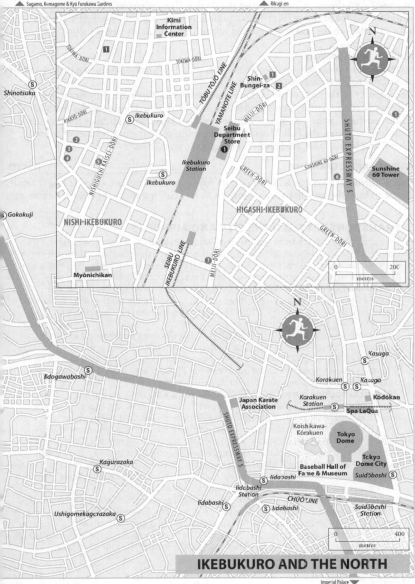

IKEBUKURO AND THE NORTH

1

shoreline of an islet-speckled lake. There are also areas of more natural woodland and a hillock from which to admire the whole scene.

Suidōbashi

水道橋

East of Ikebukuro and west of Akihabara lies the district of **SUIDŌBASHI**, where the stadium, shopping centres and amusement-park thrill rides of **Tokyo Dome City** (ⓦwww.tokyo-dome.co.jp) punctuate the skyline. The centrepiece is the plump, white-roofed **Tokyo Dome** (東京ドーム), popularly known as the "Big Egg", Tokyo's major baseball venue and home ground of the Yomiuri Giants (see p.159).

Koishikawa-Kōrakuen

小石川後楽園 • 1-6-6 Kōraku, Bunkyō-ku • Daily 9am–5pm • ¥300 • ⓣ 03 3811 3015, ⓦ tokyo-park.or.jp • Main entrance in southwest corner of garden, between Suidōbashi and Kōrakuen stations

Immediately to the west of Tokyo Dome is **Koishikawa-Kōrakuen**, a fine example of an early seventeenth-century **stroll-garden**. Zhu Shun Shui, a refugee scholar from Ming China, advised on the design, so Chinese as well as Japanese landscapes feature, the most obvious being the Full-Moon Bridge, echoing ancient stone bridges of western China, and Seiko Lake, modelled on Hangzhou's West Lake.

ARRIVAL AND DEPARTURE   **TOKYO**

If you're **arriving** in Tokyo from abroad, you'll touch down at Narita International Airport or Haneda Airport. If you're coming to the capital from elsewhere in Japan, it's more likely that you'll arrive at one of the main train

---

TRANSPORT BETWEEN THE CITY AND AIRPORTS

The fastest way into Tokyo **from Narita** is on the **New Skyliner** (36–44min; ¥2400) express train operated by Keisei (ⓦkeisei.co.jp), who also offer the cheapest connection into town in the form of the *tokkyū* (limited express) service, which costs ¥1000 to Ueno (every 30min; 1hr 11min). Both trains stop at Nippori where it's easy to transfer to the Yamanote or the Keihin Tōhoku lines.

JR's **Narita Express (N'EX**; ⓦwww.jreast.co.jp/e/nex) runs to several city stations. The cheapest fare is ¥2940 to Tokyo station (every 30min; 1hr), and there are also direct services to Shinjuku (hourly; 1hr 20min) for ¥3110. N'EX services to Ikebukuro (¥3110) and Yokohama (¥4180) via Shinagawa are much less frequent.

If you have a non-Japanese passport, JR offers a great **discount package**: for ¥3500 you can get a ticket on the N'EX to any Tokyo Stations it serves, or Yokohama, plus a Suica card (see box, p.126) to the value of ¥2000 (comprising a ¥500 deposit plus ¥1500 of train and subway travel). This makes travelling on the N'EX a much better deal than the JR *kaisoku* (rapid) trains which chug slowly into Tokyo Station (hourly; 1hr 20min) for ¥1280.

Airport Limousine buses (ⓣ03 3665 7220, ⓦlimousinebus.co.jp) are prone to traffic delays, but can be useful if you're weighed down by luggage and staying at or near a major hotel. Tickets are sold in each of the arrival lobbies; the buses depart directly outside (check which platform you need) and stop at many major hotels and train stations around the city. Journeys to central Tokyo cost around ¥3000 and take at least ninety minutes. Once you factor in the cost of a taxi from one of the train stations to your hotel, these buses can be a good deal. The ¥3100 **Limousine & Metro Pass** combines a one-way bus trip from Narita to central Tokyo and a one-day metro pass valid on nine of Tokyo's thirteen subway lines. **Taxis** to the city centre cost at least ¥20,000, and are no faster than going by bus.

From Haneda Airport, it's a twenty-minute monorail journey to Hamamatsuchō Station on the Yamanote line (daily 5.20am–11.15pm; every 5–10min; ¥460). Alternatively, you can board a Keihin-Kūkō-line train to Shinagawa or Sengakuji and connect directly with other rail and subway lines. A taxi from Haneda to central Tokyo costs ¥6000; a limousine bus to Tokyo Station is ¥900.

Lastly, there are frequent direct bus (1hr 20min; ¥3000) and train (1hr 10min; ¥1580) connections **between Narita and Haneda**.

stations (Tokyo, Ueno, Shinagawa or Shinjuku) or the long-distance bus terminals, the main ones being at Tokyo and Shinjuku stations.

BY PLANE

Narita International Airport (新東京国際空港), better known as Narita (成田; ☎0476 348000, Ⓦnarita-airport.jp), is around 66km east of the city centre. There are two terminals, both of which have tourist information and Welcome Inn Reservation Centres for accommodation bookings. If you have a Japan Rail Pass exchange order (see p.35) you can arrange to use your pass either immediately or at a later date at the JR travel agencies in the basement.

Destinations Nagoya Centrair (4 daily; 1hr).

Haneda Airport Located on a spit of land jutting into Tokyo Bay 20km south of the Imperial Palace, Haneda Airport (羽田空港; ☎03 5757 8111, Ⓦtokyo-airport-building.co.jp) is where most domestic flights and a few international services touch down. The opening of a third terminal and a fourth runway at the end of 2010 has seen more international routes offered from the airport.

Destinations Akita (7 daily; 1hr); Asahikawa (13 daily; 1hr 35min); Fukuoka (2–4 hourly; 1hr 45min–2hr); Hakodate (9 daily; 1hr 15min); Hiroshima (14 daily; 1hr 25min); Kagoshima (hourly; 1hr 50min); Kansai International (19 daily; 1hr 15min); Kōchi (8 daily; 1hr 50min); Komatsu (for Kanazawa; 11 daily; 1hr); Kumamoto (hourly; 1hr 50min); Kushiro (5 daily; 1hr 35min); Matsuyama (11 daily; 1hr 15min); Memanbetsu (7 daily; 1hr 40min); Miyazaki (hourly; 1hr 45min); Nagasaki (16 daily; 1hr 55min); Noto (2 daily; 1hr); Ōita (11 daily; 1hr 30min); Okayama (4 daily; 1hr 20min); Okinawa (Naha; 1–4 hourly; 2hr 30min); Osaka (Itami; 1–2 hourly; 1hr); Ōshima (daily; 30min); Sapporo (Chitose; every 30min; 1hr 30min); Takamatsu (10 daily; 1hr 10min); Tokushima (6 daily; 1hr 15min); Toyama (6 daily; 1hr); Wakkanai (2 daily; 1hr 45min); Yamagata (daily; 55min).

BY TRAIN

Shinkansen trains Most Shinkansen trains pull into Tokyo Station (東京駅), close to the Imperial Palace, or Shinagawa Station (品川駅), around 6km southwest. A few Shinkansen from the north go only as far as Ueno Station (上野駅), some 4km northeast of the Imperial Palace. All three stations are on the Yamanote line and are connected to several subway lines. Other long-distance JR services stop at Tokyo and Ueno stations, Shinjuku Station on Tokyo's west side and Ikebukuro Station in the city's northwest corner.

Non-JR trains Non-JR trains terminate at different stations: the Tōkyū Tōyoko line from Yokohama ends at Shibuya Station (渋谷駅); the Tōbu Nikkō line runs from Nikkō to Asakusa Station (浅草駅), east of Ueno; and the Odakyū line from Hakone finishes at Shinjuku Station (新宿駅), which is also the terminus for the Seibu-Shinjuku line from Kawagoe. All these stations have subway connections and (apart from Asakusa) are on the Yamanote rail line.

Destinations Asakusa Station Nikkō (14 daily; 1hr 55min).

Destinations Shibuya Station Yokohama (every 5min; 30min).

Destinations Shinjuku Station Hakone (hourly; 1hr 30min); Kamakura (every 10–20min; 1hr); Matsumoto (18 daily; 2hr 35min); Nikkō (daily; 1hr 55min); Shimoda (daily; 2hr 45min); Yokohama (every 20–30min; 30min).

Destinations Tokyo Station Fukuoka (Hakata Station; 2 hourly; 5hr); Hiroshima (hourly; 4–5hr); Kamakura (every 10–20min; 1hr); Karuizawa (hourly; 1hr 20min); Kyoto (every 15–30min; 2hr 15min–3hr 40min); Morioka (3 hourly; 2hr 20min–3hr 30min); Nagano (every 30min–1hr; 1hr 40min–2hr); Nagoya (every 15–30min; 1hr 40min–3hr); Niigata (1–3 hourly; 2hr–2hr 20min); Okayama (every 30min–1hr; 3hr 15min–4hr); Sendai (every 10–15min; 1hr 40min–2hr 20min); Shimoda (hourly; 2hr 40min–3hr); Shin-Kōbe (every 30min–1hr; 3hr 15min); Shin-Osaka (every 15–30min; 2hr 30min–4hr 10min); Yokohama (every 5–10min; 40min).

BY BUS

Long-distance buses pull in at several major stations around the city. The main overnight services from Kyoto and Osaka arrive beside the eastern Yaesu exit of Tokyo station; other buses arrive at Ikebukuro, Shibuya, Shinagawa and Shinjuku.

Destinations Ikebukuro Station Ise (3 daily; 8hr); Kanazawa (4 daily; 7hr 30min); Nagano (4 daily; 4hr 10min); Niigata (hourly; 5hr 30min); Osaka (1 daily; 8hr); Toyama (3 daily; 6hr 50min).

Destinations Shibuya Station Himeji (1 daily; 9hr); Kōbe (1 daily; 8hr 40min).

Destinations Shinagawa Station Hirosaki (1 daily; 9hr 15min); Imabari (1 daily; 12hr 10min); Kurashiki (1 daily; 11hr); Tokushima (1 daily; 9hr 20min).

Destinations Shinjuku Station Akita (1 daily; 8hr 30min); Fuji Yoshida (14 daily; 1hr 50min); Fukuoka (1 daily; 14hr 20min); Hakone-Tōgendai (14 daily; 2hr 10min); Kawaguchi-ko (14 daily; 1hr 45min); Kurashiki (2 daily; 11hr); Matsumoto (16 daily; 3hr 10min); Nagano (4 daily; 3hr 40min); Nagoya (2 daily; 7hr 10min); Okayama (2 daily; 10hr 30min); Osaka (4 daily; 7hr 40min); Sendai (8 daily; 5hr 30min–6hr 30min); Takayama (2 daily; 5hr 30min).

Destinations Tokyo Station Aomori (2 daily; 9hr 30min); Fukui (1 daily; 8hr); Hiroshima (1 daily; 12hr); Kōbe (1 daily; 8hr 45min); Kōchi (1 daily; 11hr 35min); Kyoto (hourly; 8hr); Matsuyama (2 daily; 11hr 55min); Morioka (2 daily; 7hr 30min); Nagoya (16 daily; 5hr 20min); Nara (1 daily; 9hr 30min); Osaka (hourly; 8hr 20min); Sendai (1 daily; 5hr

1

30min); Shimonoseki (2 daily; 14hr 20min); Takamatsu (1 daily; 10hr 15min); Yamagata (4 daily; 5hr 30min–8hr).

BY FERRY

Long-distance ferries from Tokushima (see p.635), Kita-Kyūshū and the Okinawan islands arrive at Tokyo Ferry Terminal (東京フェリーターミナル) at Ariake, on the man-made island of Odaiba (see p.102) in Tokyo Bay. For details see Ocean Tokyū Ferry (☎03 5148 0109, ⓦotf.jp) and

Maruei Ferry/A Lione (☎03 5643 6170, ⓦaline-ferry .com). Buses run from the port to Shin-Kiba Station, from which you can catch a subway train or the overland JR Keiyō line. A taxi to central Tokyo costs around ¥2000.

Destinations Takeshiba Ferry Terminal Ōshima jetfoil (3–5 daily; 1hr 45min–2hr); ferry (3 weekly; 8hr).

Destinations Tokyo Ferry Terminal Kita-Kyūshū (1 daily; 35hr); Naha (June–Sept 5 weekly; 3 days); Tokushima (1 daily; 18hr 40min).

GETTING AROUND

Getting around Tokyo is easy thanks to the city's super-efficient **trains** and **subways**, and there are also a couple of monorails, one tramline, and many buses. Walking and cycling are great ways to explore.

SUBWAY

Its colourful map (see pp.128–129) may look daunting, but Tokyo's subway is relatively easy to negotiate. The simple colour coding on trains and maps, as well as clear signposts (many in English), directional arrows and alpha-numeric codes for all central subway stations, make this by far the most *gaijin*-friendly form of transport. Avoid travelling at rush hour (7.30–9am & 5.30–7.30pm), and you'll have a much less crowded journey.

Essentials There are two systems, the nine-line Tokyo Metro (ⓦtokyometro.jp) and the four-line Toei (ⓦkotsu .metro.tokyo.jp). The systems share some stations, but unless you buy a special ticket from the vending machines that specifies your route from one system to the other, or you have a pass (see box below), you cannot switch mid-journey between the two sets of lines without paying extra at the ticket barrier. Subways have connecting passageways to overland train lines, such as the Yamanote.

Tickets You'll generally pay for your ticket at the vending machines beside the electronic ticket gates. There are no ticket sales windows other than at major stations. Most trips across central Tokyo cost no more than ¥190, but if in doubt, buy the cheapest ticket (¥160) and sort out the difference with the gatekeeper at the other end.

Running times Trains run from around 5am to just after midnight daily, and during peak daytime hours as frequently as every 5min (and at least every 15min at other times). Leaving a station can be complicated by the number of exits, but there are maps close to the ticket barriers and on the platforms indicating where the exits emerge, and strips of yellow tiles on the floor mark the routes to the ticket barriers.

TRAINS

JR East trains (ⓦjreast.co.jp) are another handy way of getting around the city. The main lines you'll find useful are the circular Yamanote (coloured lime green on the transport map); the Chūō line (deep orange), which starts at Tokyo Station and runs west to Shinjuku and the suburbs beyond; the Sōbu line (yellow) from Chiba in the east to Mitaka in the west, which runs parallel to the Chūō line in the centre of Tokyo; and the Keihin Tōhoku line (blue) from Ōmiya in the north, through Tokyo Station, to Yokohama and beyond. It's fine to transfer between JR lines on the same ticket, but you'll have to buy a new ticket if you transfer to a subway line, unless you have a PASMO or Suica card (see box below).

Tickets and passes The lowest fare on JR lines is ¥130. Like the subways, JR offers prepaid cards and *kaisūken* (carnet) deals on tickets. One of the handiest is the Suica (see box below). Also a good deal is the one-day Tokunai Pass (¥730), which gives unlimited travel within the Tokyo Metropolitan District Area.

TOKYO TRANSPORT PASSES

If you need to ride Tokyo's metro and trains a lot in the space of a day, you'll find both Tokyo Metro and Toei have day tickets for use exclusively on their own subway systems (¥710 and ¥700 respectively), the Toei pass also covering the city's buses and one tramline. However, it's far more convenient to get a one-day **economy pass** covering both systems for ¥1000.

Although they don't save you any money, the most convenient way to travel is to use a **PASMO** (ⓦpasmo.co.jp) or a JR **Suica** stored-value card. Both can be used on all subways, many buses and both JR and private trains in the wider Tokyo area. The card can be recharged at ticket machines and ticket offices. To get either card, you have to spend a minimum of ¥2000, of which ¥500 is a deposit, which will be returned to you, plus any remaining value (minus a small processing fee) when you cash in the card before leaving Tokyo.

BUSES

Once you've got a feel for the city, buses can be a good way of cutting across the few areas not served by a subway or train line. Only a small number of the buses or routes are labelled in English. The final destination is on the front of the bus, along with the route number.

Tickets You pay on entry, by dropping the flat rate (usually ¥200) into the fare box by the driver (there's a machine in the box for changing notes).

Maps The Transport Bureau of Tokyo Metropolitan Government issues a useful English pamphlet and map of all the bus routes; pick one up from one of the tourist information centres (see p.130).

BIKE

Rental The cheapest option is Sumida Park Bicycle Parking, based in an underground space beside the bridge in Asakusa (daily 6am–8pm; ¥200 for 24hr, ¥500 for 7 days; ☎03 5246 1305), but they only have a limited number of bikes available. Other rental outfits are listed on ⓦ cycle-tokyo.cycling.jp, as well as lots of useful information about cycling in the city.

Tours Guided cycling tours are offered by Tokyo Great Cycling Tour (☎03 4590 2995, ⓦ tokyocycling.jp), which has a few 6hr routes for ¥10,000 including lunch, reservations required; and Tokyo Bicycle Tours (ⓦ tokyobicycletours.com), which has a neat range of tours, including fun night-time options, from ¥4000.

FERRIES

Suijō basu The Tokyo Cruise Ship Company (☎0120 977311, ⓦ suijobus.co.jp) runs several ferry services, known as *suijō basu* (water buses), in and around Tokyo Bay. They can be a great-value way to cruise Tokyo's waterfront. The most popular is the double-decker service plying the 35min route (daily 10am–6.30pm; every 40min; ¥760) between the Sumida-gawa River Cruise Stations at Asakusa, northeast of the city centre, and Hinode Sanbashi, on Tokyo Bay. The river and bayside views of the city are reason enough for hopping aboard, especially if you want to visit Asakusa and the gardens at Hama Rikyū on the same day, and then walk into Ginza. The ferries stop at the gardens en route, and you can buy a combination ticket for the ferry and park entrance for around ¥1020.

Himiko For a few extra hundred yen you can travel on Himiko, a space-age ferry (4 daily between Asakusa and Odaiba via Hinode), designed by Matsumoto Leiji, a famous manga artist. From Thursday to Saturday (8–11pm) the ferry changes its name to Jicoo (☎0120 049490, ⓦ jicoofloating bar.com) and morphs into a floating bar shuttling from Hinode, under the Rainbow Bridge, to Odaiba and back.

Cruises Hinode Sanbashi (close to Hinode Station on the Yurikamome monorail or a 10min walk from Hamamatsuchō Station on the Yamanote line) is also the jumping-off point for several good daily cruises around Tokyo Bay, and for

ferries to various points around the island of Odaiba, or across to Kasai Rinkai-kōen on the east side of the bay.

TAXIS

For short hops around the centre of Tokyo, **taxis** are often the best option, though heavy traffic can slow them down. The basic rate is ¥710 for the first 2km, after which the meter racks up ¥80 every 274m, plus a time charge when the taxi is moving at less than 10km per hour. Between 11pm and 5am, rates are twenty percent higher. When flagging down a taxi, note that a red light next to the driver means the cab is free; green means it's occupied. There are designated stands in the busiest parts of town, but be prepared for long queues after the trains stop at night, especially in areas such as Roppongi and Shinjuku.

TOURS

There are the usual **bus** tours and some interesting **walking** options but, if these are not your cup of tea, then try a **cycling** (see left) or **gastronomic** (see p.134) tour, or a sightseeing **ferry** (see box, p.95 or opposite).

BUS TOURS

Established operations such as Hato Bus Tours (ⓦ hatobus .com) and Japan Grey Line (ⓦ www.jgl.co.jp/inbound) offer a wide variety of tours, from half-day jaunts around the central sights (¥5000) to visits out to Kamakura, Nikkō and Hakone (from ¥14,000).

Sky Bus ☎03 3215 0008, ⓦ skybus.jp. Offers four routes, most in open-top double-decker buses: choose from a route around the Imperial Palace grounds and through Ginza and Marunouchi (¥1500; 50min); from Tokyo Tower to the Rainbow Bridge (¥1700; 1hr); or an Odaiba night course (¥2000; 2hr). Their Omotesandō–Shibuya course is in a trolley-style bus (¥1200 1hr 10min).

WALKING TOURS

Otaku2 Akiba Tour ⓦ otaku2.com. Anime and manga scholar Patrick Galbraith (narrator of the Tokyo Realtime Akihabara tour, see below) or one of his equally knowledgeable colleagues, leads a 2hr 30min tour of Akihabara on Sundays including a visit to a maid café (¥3000).

Tokyo Realtime ⓦ tokyorealtime.com. These excellent self-guided audio-tours are a fine option for independent types. The 1hr walks cover Kabukichō and Akihabara and can be downloaded online (US$5.99 and US$3.99 respectively) or bought in local bookshops (¥1200; see p.156).

Tokyo Tour Guide Services ⓦ gotokyo.org. Ten walking tours – a few free, most for a fee – accompanied by volunteer guides under the auspices of Tokyo Metropolitan Government. Tours last about 3hr, departing from the tourist information centre in the Metropolitan Government Building in Shinjuku (see p.130). Reserve in advance online.

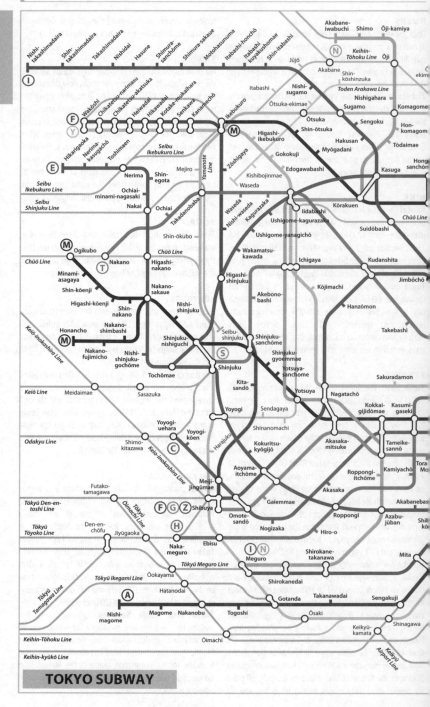

TOKYO SUBWAY

1

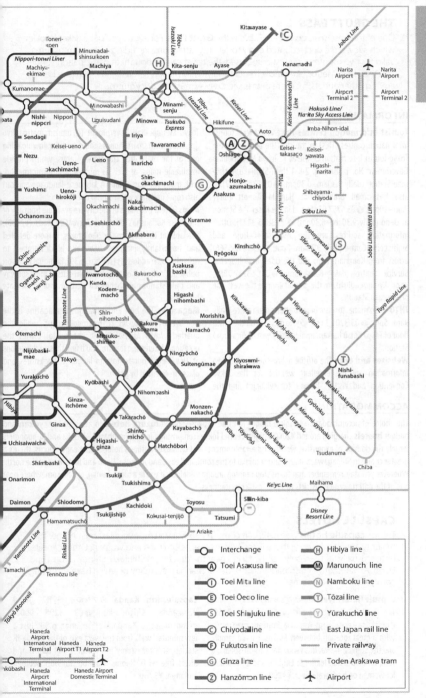

Interchange		Hibiya line
(A) Toei Asakusa line		(M) Marunouchi line
(I) Toei Mita line		(N) Namboku line
(E) Toei Ōedo line		(T) Tōzai line
(S) Toei Shinjuku line		(Y) Yūrakuchō line
(C) Chiyoda line		East Japan rail line
(F) Fukutoshin line		Private railway
(G) Ginza line		Toden Arakawa tram
(Z) Hanzōmon line		Airport

1

THE GRUTT PASS

One of the best deals on offer in Tokyo is the **Grutt Pass**. For ¥2000 you get a ticket booklet which allows free or discounted entry to seventy attractions, including all major museums. Valid for two months after first being used, the ticket can be bought at participating venues and the Tokyo Metropolitan Government tourist information centre in Shinjuku (see below), among other outlets; for more details see ⓦ www.museum.or.jp/grutto.

INFORMATION

Tourist information centres There are several tourist information centres (TICs) in the city, the best being the Tokyo Tourist Information Centre at 1F Tokyo Metropolitan Government No. 1 Building, 2-8-1 Nishi-Shinjuku, Tochō-mae Station (daily 9.30am–6.30pm; ☎ 03 5321 3077). It also has small branches at Haneda Airport (daily 9am–10pm; ☎ 03 5757 9345) and in the Kesei line Station at Ueno (daily 9.30am–6.30pm; ☎ 03 3836 3471). Other information sources are the Asakusa Culture and Sightseeing Centre (daily 9.30am–8pm; ☎ 03 3842 5566) across from Kaminari-mon; and the Odakyū Sightseeing Service Centre (daily 8am–6pm; ☎ 03 5321 7887, ⓦ odakyu.jp/english), on the ground floor on the west side of Shinjuku Station.

JNTO The national tourism organization's main office (daily 9am–5pm; ☎ 03 3201 3331, ⓦ jnto.go.jp) is on the tenth floor of Tokyo Kōtsū Kaikan, immediately east of Yūrakuchō Station.

Websites and apps The official online sources for Tokyo information are the excellent websites of the Tokyo Convention and Visitors Bureau (ⓦ tcvb.or.jp) and the Tokyo Metropolitan Government (ⓦ tourism.metro.tokyo .jp). Those with smartphones should consider downloading one of the many free city subway apps, which provide invaluable maps, as well as route and fare information, with many working offline. A Japanese-language app can also come in handy when dining out.

Maps Decent free maps of the city are available from any of the TICs. Kodansha's bilingual *Tokyo City Atlas* (¥2100), available at the city's major bookstores, is more detailed and, importantly, includes *chōme* and block numbers to help pin down addresses (see box, p.39). Bilingual maps on public notice boards outside the main exits to most subway and train stations are handy for getting your immediate bearings.

Magazines The best English-language magazine is the free weekly *Metropolis* (ⓦ metropolis.co.jp), while the quarterly *Tokyo Journal* (¥600; ⓦ tokyo.to) carries the occasional interesting feature. You'll find these publications at TICs, larger hotels, foreign-language bookstores and places frequented by *gaijin*.

ACCOMMODATION

The choice of accommodation in Tokyo ranges from no-expense-spared **luxury hotels** to atmospheric **ryokan** and budget **hostels** charging around ¥2000 a night. Central Tokyo (comprising Ginza, Nihombashi, Akasaka and Roppongi) is largely the domain of expensive, world-class establishments and upmarket business hotels. For cheaper rooms, there's a greater choice in Shinagawa, Shibuya and Shinjuku to the south and east, and Asakusa, Ueno and Ikebukuro in the north. Wherever you stay, remember that trains stop running around midnight; if you're a night animal, opt for somewhere near one of the entertainment districts to avoid costly taxi journeys.

CAPSULE HOTELS

Tokyo's **capsule hotels** (see p.42) can come in handy if you miss your last train home. The majority are for men only; those listed below accept both men and women. Other capsule hotels, usually for men only, can be found near the dtations in Shinjuku, Shibuya, Ebisu and Ueno. An alternative crash pad is an internet or manga café, many of which have surprisingly comfy semi-private rooms.

Capsule Hotel Riverside カプセルホテルリバーサイド 2-20-4 Kaminarimon ☎ 03 3844 1155, ⓦ asakusa-capsule.jp; Asakusa Station; map p.97. With a great location between Asakusa's main temple and the Sumida-gawa, this venue has English-speaking staff, an instruction leaflet in English, and 21 capsules for women on a separate floor. **¥3000**

Capsule Inn Kanda カプセルイン神田 1-8-9 Uchikanda, Chiyoda-ku ☎ 03 3295 9000, ⓦ copsule.com; Kanda Station; map p.88. Just a few minutes' walk from the west exit of the Kanda JR station, this ten-storey inn features 144 rooms and offers free wi-fi. Rooms available for both women and men. **¥3700**

HOSTELS

Until fairly recently, hostelling in Tokyo meant staying in one of the two municipal-run youth hostels. Now, however, you can forget about evening curfews and three-night maximum stays, since a glut of excellent privately run hostels have come on the scene, driving prices down and standards up. The majority are in, or near, the Asakusa area – another plus.

★**Anne Hostel** 庵ホステル 2-21-14 Yanagibashi, Taitō-ku ☎03 5829 9090, ⓦj-hostel.com; Asakusabashi or Kuramae Stations; map p.91. Now this is a lovely little place: part hostel, part traditional minshuku (see p.43), it's tremendously popular with international guests. Most rooms, even a couple of the dorms, boast tatami flooring, and prices include a decent little breakfast. Dorm ¥2600, twin ¥6800

Kangaroo Hotel カンガルーホテル 1-21-11 Nihonzutsumi, Taitō-ku ☎03 3872 8573, ⓦkangaroohotel.jp; Minami-Senju Station; map p.97. Although this contemporary-design, smoke-free place bills itself as a ('small stay') hotel the shared bathrooms and kitchen offer a mix of a hostel and capsule-like environment. Rates include things like hand towels and slippers, but it's ¥200 extra for a bath towel. Tiny rooms – both tatami and Western-style – have a small TV and free internet. Single ¥3300, twin ¥5000

★**Khaosan Tokyo Laboratory** カオサン東京ラボラトリー 2-1-4 Nishi-Asakusa, Taitō-ku ☎03 6479 1041, ⓦkhaosan-tokyo.com; Asakusa Station; map p.97. The most eye-catching Khaosan option – there's nary a dull surface in sight, with dorms and common areas alike decorated to within an inch of their lives, mostly along a retro-futuristic scheme. The "power nap" area is a nice touch, and all rooms are en suite. Dorm ¥3400

★**K's House Oasis** ケイズハウスオアシス 2-14-10 Asakusa-Nichōme, Taitō-ku ☎03 3844 4447, ⓦkshouse.jp/tokyo-oasis-e; Asakusa Station; map p.97. This one's a real winner, with Zen-like stylings, facilities galore, charming common areas, comfy dorm beds and en-suite private rooms. Dorm ¥2800, twins ¥8800

Nui Hostel & Bar Lounge ヌイホステルバーラウンジ 2-14-13 Kuramae, Taitō-ku ☎03 6240 9854, ⓦbackpackersjapan.co.jp/nui; Kuramae Station; map p.91. Just 15min on foot from Asakusa, this is an excellent recent addition to Tokyo's hostel scene. The funky common area features a bar that's hugely popular with locals, and a great mingling spot; the pine beds in the dorms aren't quite as fancy, but they do the job. Dorm ¥2700, double ¥6500

Retrometro Backpackers レトロメトロバックパッカーズ 2-19-1 Nishi-Asakusa, Taitō-ku ☎03 6322 7447, ⓦretrometrobackpackers.com; Tawaramachi or Asakusa Stations; map p.97. As far as backpackers go, it takes one to know one, and the owner of this tiny, two-dorm hostel certainly knows her stuff. Balinese and Thai stylings betray her favourite former travel destinations, and there's a sense of cosiness here absent from some of Tokyo's larger hostels. Dorm ¥2600

Sakura Hostel サクラホステル 2-24-2 Asakusa, Taitō-ku ☎03 3847 8111, ⓦsakura-hostel.co.jp; Asakusa Station; map p.97. This friendly, well-run hostel occupies a cherry-pink building a couple of minutes' walk northwest of Sensō-ji. Each floor has its own shower and toilet area and there's a good kitchen and TV lounge. They also operate a hotel near Jimbōchō Station, with similar prices. Dorm ¥2940, twin ¥8300

Reservations Whatever your budget, it's wise to reserve your first few nights' accommodation before arrival. A good local booking site is ⓦtravel.rakuten.com, while ⓦryokan.or.jp also has a list of good places to stay (mostly ryokan) in Tokyo and beyond. Otherwise, the international standbys have plenty of Tokyo options: try ⓦtrivago.com for hotels or ⓦhostelworld.com for hostels.

Taxes In addition to the standard hotel taxes (see p.41) there's an extra charge of ¥100 per person per night on rooms costing over ¥10,000 per night, and ¥200 for those costing ¥15,000 or above.

GINZA AND AROUND

★**Conrad Tokyo** コンラッド東京 1-9-1 Higashi-Shimbashi, Minato-ku ☎3 6388 8000, ⓦconradtokyo .co.jp; Shiodome Station map p.88. This luxury hotel easily holds its own when it comes to cutting-edge contemporary design and five-star facilities. But it's the views that really steal the show – from the lobby and bayside rooms feast your eyes on what are arguably the best vistas in Tokyo, taking in Hama Rikyū Gardens, Odaiba and the Rainbow Bridge. It's absolutely magical at night. ¥40,000

Four Seasons Hotel Tokyo at Marunouchi フォーシーズンズホテル丸の内 Pacific Century Place, 1-11-1 Marunouchi, Chiyoda-ku ☎03 5222 7222, ⓦfourseasons.com/tokyo; Tokyo Station; map p.88. Chic interior design and superb service are two selling points for this luxury hotel. With only 57 rooms, there's a personal touch which keeps it a top choice – let them know your arrival time and someone will be there on the platform to greet you at nearby Tokyo Station. Facilities include a spa, fitness centre, and a stylish bar and grill. **¥39,000**

Mandarin Oriental Tokyo マンダリンオリエンタル東京 2-1-1 Nihombashi-Muromachi, Chūō-ku ☎03 3270 8800, ⓦmandarinoriental.com/tokyo; Mitsukoshi-mae Station; map p.88. No expense has been spared in this branch of the *Mandarin Oriental*, from the dramatic 37th-floor lobby to some of the biggest standard-size rooms in Tokyo, where picture windows make the most of the stunning cityscapes. There's no pool, but guests can take advantage of a fabulous (and very pricey) spa, a fitness centre and seven restaurants. **¥49,000**

Mercure Ginza メルキュールホテル銀座東京 2-9-4 Ginza, Chūō-ku ☎03 4335 1111, ⓦmercureginza.jp; Ginza-itchōme Station; map p.88. French flair lends a delicate appeal to this mid-range hotel, on a quiet backstreet in the heart of Ginza. Rooms are reasonably spacious and the bathrooms a cut above the average for this price range. Their *L'Echanson* bistro serves very tasty French food. **¥22,400**

★Mitsui Garden Hotel 三井ガーデンホテル銀座 8-13-1 Ginza, Chūō-ku ☎03 3543 1131, ⓦwww.gardenhotels.co.jp; Shimmbashi Station; map p.88. Italian designer Piero Rissoni's chic design for Mitsui's flagship hotel helps it stand out from the crowd. Rooms are decorated in earthy tones with great attention to detail, but it's the bird's-eye views of the city and bay that grab the attention. **¥25,200**

Ryumeikan Tokyo ホテル龍名館東京 1-3-22 Yaesu, Chūō-ku ☎03 3271 0971, ⓦryumeikan-tokyo.jp; Tokyo Station; map p.88. This long-standing traditional inn has transformed into a stylish hotel, each room mixing Western comfort with attractive Japanese touches, accented in Edo-period purple (*edomurasaki*). Big discounts on offer for those who book in advance. **¥28,000**

AKIHABARA AND AROUND

Ochanomizu Hotel Juraku お茶の水ホテルジュラク 2-9 Kanda-Awajichō, Chiyoda-ku ☎03 3271 7222, ⓦhotel-juraku.co.jp/ocha; Ochanomizu or Akihabara Stations; map p.91. Okay, so the exterior of this hotel is far from fancy. The rooms, however, are superbly designed for the price, thanks to a well-considered recent refurbishment; throw in free internet access, a convenient location and cheery staff, and you can't really go wrong. **¥13,000**

UENO AND AROUND

Coco Grand Ueno Shinobazu ココグラン上野不忍ホテル 2-12-14 Ueno, Taitō-ku ☎03 3834 6221, ⓦcocogrand.co.jp; Yushima Station; map p.93. Newly refurbished hotel with friendly staff and a choice of Western- or Japanese-style accommodation, the latter quite spacious but a bit more expensive. Many rooms have great views across Shinobazu pond. **¥16,800**

Park Side ホテルパークサイド 2-11-18 Ueno, Taitō-ku ☎03 3836 5711, ⓦparkside.co.jp; Ueno Station; map p.93. One of the only non-sleazy hotels in the Ueno area where you'll still get change from ¥10,000 – the prices are, indeed, comparable with the love motels just to the west. Although there are few services, the rooms are kept in good nick, and some have lovely park views. **¥8800**

Ryokan Katsutarō 旅館勝太郎 4-16-8 Ikenohata, Taitō-ku ☎03 3821 9808, ⓦkatsutaro.com; Nezu Station; map p.93. Handily located within walking distance of Ueno Park, this homely place has just seven slightly faded tatami rooms, plus coin laundry and internet access. They also run a newer annexe in Yanaka (☎03 3828 2500). A good alternative if *Sawanoya* (see below) is full. Single **¥5200**, double **¥8400**

★Sawanoya Ryokan 旅館澤の屋 2-3-11 Yanaka, Taitō-ku ☎03 3822 2251, ⓦsawanoya.com; Nezu Station, map p.93. This welcoming family-run inn is a real home from home in a very convivial neighbourhood within walking distance of Ueno Park. Though nothing fancy, it offers good-value tatami rooms, all with washbasin, TV, telephone and a/c. Few are en suite, but the two lovely Japanese-style baths more than compensate. Facilities also include free internet access, bike hire (¥200 per day), coin laundry and complimentary tea and coffee. Single **¥5000**, double **¥9500**

Suigetsu Hotel Ohgaisō 水月ホテル鴎外荘 3-3-21 Ikenohata, Taitō-ku ☎03 3822 4611, ⓦohgai.co.jp; Nezu Station; map p.93. One of very few mid-range hotels with a Japanese flavour, this is built around the Meiji-period house and traditional garden of novelist Mori Ōgai. The three wings contain a mix of Western and tatami rooms; the latter offer more atmosphere, but at double the price. Rates with or without meals available. **¥13,600**

ASAKUSA AND AROUND

★Andon Ryokan 行燈旅館 2-34-10 Nihonzutsumi, Taitō-ku ☎03 3873 8611, ⓦandon.co.jp; Minowa Station; map p.97. An architectural gem that fuses traditional ryokan design with modern materials. The dimly lit tatami rooms share bathrooms and are tiny, but sport DVD players and very comfortable futon. Other pluses include a top-floor jacuzzi spa, and super-friendly, helpful English-speaking staff. Single **¥6300**, double **¥7450**

Asakusa Central Hotel 浅草セントラルホテル 1-5-3 Asakusa, Taitō-ku ☎03 3847 2222, ⓦpelican.co.jp/asakusacentralhotel; Asakusa Station; map p.97. Modest business cheapie which rises above the competition thanks to its convenient location on Asakusa's main street, its English-speaking staff and its small but well-appointed rooms, all with TV, telephone and internet access. **¥7000**

Ryokan Shigetsu 旅館指月 1-31-11 Asakusa, Taitō-ku

☎ 03 3843 2345, ⊛ shigetsu.com; Asakusa Station; map p.97. Just off bustling Nakamise-dōri, this smart little ryokan is a haven of kimono-clad receptionists and tinkling *shamisen* (Japanese lute) music, with a choice of small Western- or Japanese-style rooms, all en suite. There's a Japanese bath on the top floor, with views over temple roofs. Western singles **¥6700**, Japanese rooms **¥16,800**

★ **Sukeroku-no-yado Sadachiyo** 助六の宿 貞千代 2-20-1 Asakusa, Taitō-ku ☎ 03 3842 6431, ⊛ sadachiyo. co.jp; Asakusa or Tawaramachi Stations; map p.97. Step back into Edo-era Asakusa in this delightful old inn marked by a willow tree and stone lanterns, northwest of Sensō-ji temple. The elegant tatami rooms are all en suite, though you can also use the traditional Japanese-style baths. Meals are available and they can also arrange performances of traditional arts, including geisha dances. **¥19,000**

★ **Tokyo Ryokan** 東京旅館 2-4-8 Nishi-Asakusa, Taitō-ku ☎ 090 8879 3599, ⊛ www.tokyoryokan.com; Tawaramachi Station; map p.97. Beautifully rendered traditional design elements and attention to detail make this modern establishment stand out from the crowd. With just three tatami rooms (including one triple; ¥10,500) above a communal lounge area and a shared bathroom, it feels like you're staying in someone's home. **¥7000**

BAYSIDE TOKYO

Nikkō Tokyo ホテル日航東京 1-9-1 Daiba, Minato-ku ☎ 03 5500 5500, ⊛ www.hnt.co.jp; Daiba Station. The most pleasant of Odaiba's hotels has a light-filled lobby, walls peppered with contemporary art and great views of the Rainbow Bridge and the city across Tokyo Bay. Rooms are spacious and have small balconies, while staff are helpful to a tee – they even hand out jogging maps of the local area. **¥42,000**

AKASAKA AND ROPPONGI

Asia Center of Japan ホテルアジア会館 8-10-32 Akasaka, Minato-ku ☎ 03 3402 6111, ⊛ asiacenter. or.jp; Aoyama-Itchōme or Nogizaka Stations; map pp.106–107 A long-established place with a solid reputation. Rooms are small and unflashy but have everything you need. Book online for discounts. **¥12,390**

★ **Grand Fresa Akasaka** グランフレザ赤坂ホテル 6-3-17 Akasaka, Minato-ku ☎ 03 5572 7788, ⊛ solarehotels. com; Akasaka Station; map pp.106–107. The flagship of the good-value Chisun chain of business hotels is a real step up from rivals in quality. The appealing rooms, split over two wings and decorated in warm browns and reds, include spacious bathrooms. Breakfast is served in the attached *Organic House Deli & Café*. **¥9500**

★ **Grand Hyatt Tokyo** グランドハイアットホテル東京 6-10-3 Roppongi, Minato-ku ☎ 03 4333 1234, ⊛ tokyo.grand.hyatt.jp; Roppongi Station; map pp.106–107. Glamour is the order of the day at the

Grand Hyatt. The rooms' appealing design uses wood and earthy-toned fabrics, and restaurants and bars are all very chic, particularly *The Oak Door* and the slick sushi bar Roku Roku. **¥49,500**

The b Roppongi ザ b 六本木 3-9-8 Roppongi, Minato-ku ☎ 03 5412 0451, ⊛ www.theb-hotels .com; Roppongi Station; map pp.106–107. A boutique-style hotel that won't break the bank or offend the eyes even if uninspiring plastic-unit bathrooms are the norm throughout. A light breakfast is included in the rate. There's another equally appealing *b* in Ikebukuro (see p.134). **¥22,000**

EBISU, MEGURO AND THE SOUTH

★ **Claska** クラスカホテル 1-3-18 Chūō-chō, Meguro-ku ☎ 03 3719 8121, ⊛ claska.com; Meguro Station; map pp.110–111. This oversized Rubik's Cube is a real hipster's choice. A 10min bus or taxi ride from the station, the *Claska* makes up for its relatively remote location with an abundance of contemporary Tokyo style. Some rooms have been individually decorated by different local artists – worth considering, although they're not the largest or most practical in the hotel. There are cheaper rates for weekly stays, a stylish lobby café/bar and very classy gift shop, Do. **¥20,000**

Dormy Inn Meguro Aobadai ドーミーイン目黒青葉 台 3-21-8 Aobadai, Meguro-ku ☎ 03 3760 2211; Naka-Meguro Station; map pp.110–111. Within walking distance of trendy Naka-Meguro and a stone's throw from the delightful Meguro-gawa (see p.109), this functional business hotel is a good deal. Each room has a hotplate and small fridge, so it's feasible to self-cater. There's also a large communal bathroom and sauna. **¥11,000**

HARAJUKU, SHIBUYA AND AOYAMA

Cerulean Tower Tōkyū Hotel セルリアンタワー東急ホ テル 26-1 Sakuragaoka-chō, Shibuya-ku ☎ 03 3476 3000, ⊛ ceruleantower-hotel.com; Shibuya Station; map p.114. Shibuya's ritziest accommodation, with a range of intriguingly designed rooms. Some have bathrooms with a glittering view of the city, while also on site are a pool and gym (free to guests on the executive floor), several restaurants, a jazz club and even a nō theatre in the basement. **¥60,500**

★ **Tōkyū Stay Aoyama** 東急ステイホテル青山 2-27-18 Minami-Aoyama, Shibuya-ku ☎ 03 3497 0109, ⊛ tokyustay.co.jp; map p.114. Designed for long-staying guests, but open to short-stay visitors too, this high-rise hotel and apartment complex scores for facilities, location and slick décor. There's a women-only floor, wonderful views and rates include breakfast. There are thirteen other *Tōkyū Stays* around the city. **¥24,500**

1

SHINJUKU AND THE WEST

Kadoya Hotel かどやホテル 1-23-1 Nishi-Shinjuku, Shinjuku-ku ☎03 3346 2561, ⓦkadoya-hotel.co.jp; Shinjuku Station; map pp.118–119. This efficient business hotel is a little charmer. Single rooms (from ¥7560) are a bargain for such a handy location, and the doubles won't break the bank either. A major plus is the lively *izakaya* in the basement. **¥14,700**

★Park Hyatt Tokyo パークハイアット東京 3-7-1-2 Nishi-Shinjuku, Shinjuku-ku ☎03 5322 1234, ⓦtokyo .park.hyatt.jp; Tochōmae Station; map pp.118–119. Occupying the upper section of Tange Kenzō's Shinjuku Park Tower, this is the epitome of sophistication and holding up very well to newer rivals. All the huge rooms have breathtaking views, as do the restaurants and spa, pool and fitness centre at the pinnacle of the tower. **¥44,200**

Rocks Shinjuku ロックス新宿 2-10-4 Shinjuku, Shinjuku-ku ☎03 5367 6969, ⓦrocks-shinjuku.jp; Shinjuku Station; map pp.118–119. Safe and clean, this cheapie sits right in the heart of Tokyo's main gay area – a fun place to hang whatever your sexual orientation. Though rooms are often rented in two-hour slots, it actually makes a decent place to stay; you'll save ¥1000 if you check in after 10pm. **¥8400**

IKEBUKURO AND THE NORTH

Kimi Ryokan 貴美旅館 2-36-8 Ikebukuro, Toshima-ku ☎03 3971 3766, ⓦkimi-ryokan.jp; Ikebukuro Station; map pp.122–123. A great-value institution on Tokyo's budget scene, and a good place to meet fellow travellers – make sure you book well ahead. Rooms are compact but clean, access to a kitchen helps keep eating costs down and staff are friendly and speak English. There is a 1am curfew, and the place is a bit tricky to find, in the backstreets of west Ikebukuro. Single **¥4500**, double **¥6500**

The b Ikebukuro ザb池袋 1-39-4 Higashi-Ikebukuro, Toshima-ku ☎03 3980 1911, ⓦwww.theb-hotels.com; Ikebukuro Station; map pp.122–123. Located on the east side of the Station – just down the road from the Bic Camera store – the *b* offers a surprisingly stylish twist on the dreary ambience of most business hotels, with funky carpets leading to rooms decorated with pleasant colours and occasional wood panelling. **¥15,000**

EATING

When it comes to **gastronomic experiences**, few places can compare to Tokyo. The number, range and quality of restaurants are breathtaking, with practically any world cuisine you can think of available alongside all the usual (and many unusual) Japanese dishes.

Prices There's no need to panic. Even Michelin-starred restaurants offer good-value set-meal specials, particularly for lunch. There's an abundance of fast-food options (see below) and cafés (see p.141) offering light meals. Many *izakaya* (see p.47) and live music venues (see p.150) serve decent food, too.

Information Check out the free weekly magazine *Metropolis* (see p.130), the excellent Tokyo Food Page (ⓦbento.com), Gourmet Navigator (ⓦgnavi.co.jp) and Eatpia (ⓦeatpia.com).

Tours and classes Food writer Elizabeth Andoh (☎03 5716 5751, ⓦtasteofculture.com) leads highly popular trips around Japanese markets helping you to identify Japanese products and runs cooking classes. You'll need to book well in advance.

GINZA AND AROUND

A16 Brick Square, 2-6-1 Marunouchi, Chiyoda-ku ☎03 3212 5215, ⓦgiraud.co.jp/a16; Tokyo Station; map p.88. Californian-Italian cuisine served at indoor and outdoor tables facing the lovely garden at Brick Square – a great place to chill over a glass of wine and a crisp pizza (try the funghi, ¥1900) in between browsing through Marunouchi's boutiques. Mon–Sat 11am–11pm, Sun 11am–10pm.

TOKYO FOR VEGETARIANS

It may be the capital of a historically Buddhist nation, but Tokyo is a surprisingly bad place in which to be **vegetarian**. The problem stems from the fact that, although the average Japanese eats far less meat than the average Westerner, vegetarianism is extremely rare here: you might ask for a vegetarian (*saishoku*) dish in a restaurant, and still be served something with meat or fish in it. For example, the popular tofu dish *hiya yakko* (a small slab of chilled tofu topped with grated ginger, spring onions and soy sauce) is usually sprinkled with flakes of *bonito* (dried tuna). If you're a committed vegetarian, things to watch out for include *dashi* stock, which contains *bonito*; breads and cakes, as these can contain lard; and omelettes, which can contain chicken stock.

The good news is that places specializing in vegetarian and vegan food in Tokyo are on the rise. *Eat More Greens* (see p.142) serves high quality meat-free dishes, and you can find many more vegetarian, vegan and macrobiotic options on the useful **Vege-Navi** website (ⓦvege-navi.jp).

DINING ON THE WATER

Lunch and dinner cruises on **yakatabune**, low-slung traditional boats lit up with paper lanterns, are a charming Tokyo eating institution, dating back to the Edo period. The boats accommodate anything from sixteen to a hundred people on trips along the Sumida-gawa and out on Tokyo Bay. For a bar-like alternative, see *Jicoo* (see p.147).

Amisei あみ清 **⊕** 03 3844 1869, **Ⓦ** amisei.com; map p.97. Amisei boats set off from the southwest side of Azumabashi bridge, Asakusa. Two-hour evening cruises cost ¥8000, including all the tempura you can eat. More lavish menus can be ordered and, naturally, charges skyrocket for cruises on the night when Asakusa holds its annual fireworks extravaganza in July.

Funasei 船清 **⊕** 03 5479 2731, **Ⓦ** www.funasei .com; map pp.110–111. Cruises run out of Kita-Shinagawa and offer a choice of Japanese- and Western-style menus for around ¥10,500 per person.

Aroyna Tabeta あろいなたべた 3-7-11 Marunouchi, Chiyoda-ku **⊕** 03 5219 6099; Yūrakuchō Station; map p.88. Note the big ¥630 sign – that's the price you'll pay for every single plate listed, including set meals, at this basic Thai place under the tracks between Yūrakuchō and Shimbashi. The cooking is heavy on the chilli (a surprise in Tokyo) but tasty, and great value. Daily 11am–11pm.

★**Dhaba India** ダバインディア 2-7-9 Yaesu, Chūō-ku **⊕** 03 3272 7160, **Ⓦ** dhabaindia.com; Kyōbashi Station; map p.88. Give your taste buds a workout at this bustling South Indian restaurant, one of the best of its kind in Tokyo. The colourful decor avoids the usual clichés and the specialities include a potent chicken and black pepper curry, and a sweet-and-sour fish curry. There's also a wide selection of good-value set meals (the daily curry is ¥800) and they do a mean dosa. Mon–Fri 11.15am–3pm & 5–11pm, Sat & Sun noon–3pm & 5–10pm.

Hibiki 響 46F Caretta Shiodome Building, 1-8-1 Higashi-Shimbashi, Minato-ku **⊕** 03 6215 8051, **Ⓦ** www.dynac-japan.com/hibiki/; Shiodome Station; map p.88. Admire the breathtaking views from the windows of this modern *izakaya*, which serves contemporary Japanese cuisine in sleek surroundings. The lunch sets (from ¥1200) are particularly good value; count on around ¥6000 a head in the evening. Mon–Fri 11am–3pm & 5–11.30pm, Sat & Sun 11am–4pm & 5–11pm.

★**Little Okinawa** リトル沖縄 8-7-10 Ginza, Chūō-ku **⊕** 03 3572 2930; Shimbashi Station; map p.88. The welcome at this cosy Okinawan restaurant is as warm as it would be in the southern islands. Try Ryūkyū dishes such as *goya champuru* (noodles with stir-fried bitter melon, ¥880), and the strong rice liquor *awamori*. There's an English menu, but the Japanese one has photos. Bookings recommended. Mon–Fri 5pm–3am, Sat & Sun 4pm–midnight.

Matsumotorō 松本楼 1-2 Hibiya-kōen, Chiyoda-ku **⊕** 03 3503 1451, **Ⓦ** matsumotoro.co.jp; Hibiya Station; map p.88. On a sunny day it's a pleasure to sit on the terrace of this venerable restaurant, as old as Tokyo's first Western-style park in which it's located. The food is pretty standard, along the lines of *omu-raisu* (rice-filled omelette, ¥1050), hamburgers, *croques* and other Western "favourites". Daily 10am–9pm.

Sakyō Higashiyama 左京ひがしやま B1F Oak Ginza, 3-7-2 Ginza Chūō-ku **⊕** 03 3535 3577, **Ⓦ** sakyohigashiyama.com; Ginza Station; map p.88. Refined kyō-ryori (Kyoto-style cuisine) is served at this rustic basement space, decorated with bamboo and with an open kitchen that feels a million miles from Ginza's bustle. The lunch set (¥2100) includes six delicious, seasonal courses. Mon–Sat 11am–2pm & 5.30–9pm.

The Oyster Shack かき小屋 1-6-1 Uchisaiwai-chō, Chiyoda-ku **⊕** 03 6205 4328, **Ⓦ** jack-pot.co.jp; Shimbashi Station; map p.88. One of the city's most atmospheric oyster bars, snuggled under the train track arches north of Shimbashi Station. They've an all-you-can-eat oyster special for ¥2980, and a whole aquarium's worth of other stuff to slurp down – scallops from ¥250, or huge *sazae* (snail-like turban shells) for ¥350. Mon–Fri 4–11.30pm, Sat & Sun noon–11pm.

Torigin Honten 鳥ぎん本店 5-5-7 Ginza, Chūō-ku **⊕** 03 3571 3333, **Ⓦ** torigin-ginza.co.jp; Ginza Station; map p.88. Bright, popular restaurant hidden away on a side street – look for the red sign. They serve snacks like *yakitori* (from ¥150 per stick) and *kamameshi* (kettle-cooked rice with a choice of toppings). Their ¥800 weekday lunch sets are best if you want a full meal. Daily 11.30am–10pm.

Tsukiji Sushi Sen 築地 すし鮮 2F 5-9-1 Ginza, Chūō-ku **⊕** 03 5337 2878, **Ⓦ** sakanaya-group.com; Higashi-Ginza Station; map p.88. This outpost of the well-known *Tsukiji Sushi* restaurant is a bright and breezy place, serving up a good choice of well-priced sushi (from ¥100 to ¥500 per piece) and sashimi sets, as well as à la carte food from a picture menu with some English explanations. Daily 24hr.

AKIHABARA AND AROUND

Go Go Curry ゴーゴーカレー 1-16-1 Kanda-Sakumachō, Chiyoda-ku **⊕** 03 5256 5525, **Ⓦ** www.gogocurry.com; Akihabara Station; map p.91. No doubt about it, the official

1

meal of Akihabara regulars is *tonkatsu* curry (fried pork cutlet on rice, smothered in curry sauce), and one of the heartiest is at the growing *Go Go Curry* chain, whose *honten* (main branch) is, of course, in Akihabara. *Tonkatsu* curry plates start at ¥700. Daily 9.55am–9.55pm.

Hachimaki はちまき 1-19 Kanda-Jimbōchō, Chiyoda-ku ☎03 3291 6222; Jimbōchō Station; map p.91. Sat-Here since 1931, this tempura specialist is one of Tokyo's best time-warp restaurants – ageing posters, yellowing paper messages from the 1950s, and nary a sign that you're in the twenty-first century. Have a crack at their delectable *tendon*, which gets you four freshly made tempura on rice (¥800). Daily noon–9pm.

Tomoegata 巴潟 2-17-6 Ryōgoku, Sumida-ku ☎03 3632 5600, ⊛tomoegata.com; Ryōgoku Station; map p.91. In the heart of sumo territory, and a grand place to head if you're off to a tournament, this is a good place to sample *chanko-nabe*, the wrestlers' protein-packed meat, seafood and vegetable stew. For around ¥3000 you can have the full-blown meal cooked at your table, though most people will find the smaller lunch set (¥1260; lunch only) more than enough. It's easy to spot from its parade of colourful flags. Daily 11.30am–2pm & 5–11pm.

UENO AND AROUND

Hantei はん亭 2-12-15 Nezu, Bunkyō-ku ☎03 3828 1440, ⊛hantei.co.jp; Nezu Station; map p.93. Stylish dining in a beautiful, three-storey wooden house. There's only one dish, *kushiage* (deep-fried pieces of meat, fish and vegetables skewered on sticks), served in combination plates, six at a time: ¥2900 for the first plate (plus two appetizers); ¥1400 thereafter, until you say stop. Tues–Sat noon–2.30pm & 5–10pm, Sun 11.30am–2.30pm & 4–9.30pm.

Musashino 武蔵野 2-8-1 Ueno, Taitō-ku ☎03 3831 1672; Ueno-Hirokōji Station; map p.93. One of Ueno's few remaining old-style restaurants serving *tonkatsu*, for which the area was once famed. They come in big, thick, melt-in-the-mouth slabs. Choose between standard *rōsu* (fatty belly meat) and the leaner *hire* (loin fillet), both at ¥1000 including soup, rice and pickles. Daily 11.30am–9pm.

★**Sasa-no-yuki** 笹乃雪 2-15-10 Negishi, Taitō-ku ☎03 3873 1145, ⊛sasanoyuki.com; Uguisudani Station; map p.93. Three centuries ago, the chef here was said to make tofu like "snow lying on bamboo leaves", and both the name and the quality have survived, though the old wooden house is now marooned among flyovers. Calm prevails over the tatami mats as you feast on delicately flavoured silk-strained tofu. Prices are reasonable, with most tofu plates priced at around ¥600, and full courses starting at ¥2600 (or ¥2000 for lunch). Tues–Sun 11.30am–9pm.

ASAKUSA AND AROUND

Chin-ya ちんや 1-3-4 Asakusa, Taitō-ku ☎03 3841 0010, ⊛www.chinya.co.jp; Asakusa Station; map p.97. Founded in 1880, this famous *shabu-shabu* and *sukiyaki* (styles of Japanese hot pots) restaurant offers basic lunch sets from ¥3800, and dinner for another ¥1000 or so. The place occupies seven floors, with more casual, and slightly cheaper, dining in the basement. Mon & Wed–Fri noon–3.30pm & 4.30–9.30pm, Sat & Sun 11.30am–9pm.

Daikokuya 大黒家 1-38-10 Asakusa, Taitō-ku ☎03 3844 1111 & 1-31-9 Asakusa ☎03 3844 2222; ⊛tempura. co.jp; Asakusa Station; map p.97. There's always a lunchtime queue at this venerable tempura restaurant, set in an attractive old building. The speciality is *tendon* – shrimp, fish and prawn fritters on a bowl of rice (from ¥1470). If the main branch is too busy or closed, head for the annexe around the corner. Daily 11.10am–8.30pm (Sat till 9pm).

La Sora Seed ラソラシド 31F Solamachi, 1-1-2 Oshiage, Sumida-ku ☎03 5414 0581, ⊛kurkku.jp; Meiji-jingūmae Station; map p.97. Ecologically sound operation boasting one of the best possible views of the huge Skytree tower (see p.98). The company leans on European flavours, including great meatballs made with organic pork. Lunch sets go from ¥2800, dinner for around three times that. Daily 11am–4pm & 6–11pm.

Maguro Bito まぐろ人 1-21-8 Asakusa, Taitō-ku ☎03 3844 8736, ⊛magurobito.com; Asakusa Station; map p.97. Fuji TV viewers voted this the top *kaiten-zushi* shop in Japan, and it's easy to see why: the quality of fish and other ingredients is excellent, the turnover fast and the decor on the ritzy side. Expect a queue (but it moves fast). Electronically price-coded plates range from ¥140 to ¥700. Daily 11.30am–9.30pm, closed Tues or Sun each week.

Ōtafuku 大多福 1-6-2 Senzoku, Taitō-ku ☎03 3871 2521, ⊛otafuku.ne.jp; Iriya Station; map p.97. Customers have been coming to this charming restaurant for over eighty years to sample its delicious selection of *oden* boiled in a soy and *dashi* broth. Wash it all down with a glass of pine-scented *tarozake* (sake). There's a picture menu (individual pieces ¥110–530) or you can sit at the counter and point at what you want in the bubbling brass vats. Mon–Sat 5–11pm, Sun 5–10pm.

Sometarō 染太郎 2-2-2 Nishi-Asakusa, Taitō-ku ☎03 3844 9502; Tawaramachi Station; map p.97. Rambling, wooden restaurant specializing in *okonomiyaki*. An "introductory set" of three varieties (¥1575) is enough to feed two. Alternatively, try your hand at *yakisoba* (fried soba, from ¥610). There are English instructions and plenty of people to offer advice. Look for a bamboo-fenced garden and lantern halfway up the street. Daily noon–10.30pm.

★**Waentei-Kikko** 和えん亭 吉幸 2-2-13 Asakusa, Taitō-ku, ☎03 5828 8833, ⊛waentei-kikko.com; Asakusa Station; map p.97. A rare chance to see an excellent live performance of the *shamisen* in a delightful wooden house transported to Asakusa from Takayama. The lunch bentō is beautifully presented *kaiseki*-style food for ¥2500 (dinner starts at ¥6825). There are five performances daily; see the website for schedule. Daily except Wed 11.30am–1 30pm & 5–9.30pm.

BAYSIDE TOKYO

Ramen Kokugikan ラーメン国技館 5F Aqua City, 1-7-1 Daiba, Minato-ku ☎ 03 3599 4700; Odaiba Kaihin-kōen Station. Six top ramen noodle chefs from around Japan square off against each other in this cartoon-like section of Aqua City's restaurant floor. A bowl will cost you around ¥800 (the Hakata variety, from Fukuoka city, is well worth trying). Their outdoor balcony boasts fantastic views across the bay towards Tokyo's twinkling lights. Daily 11am–11pm.

★ **Sushi Bun** 鮨文 5 Tsukiji, Chūo-ku ☎ 03 3541 3860; Tsukijishijō Station. One of the most *gaijin*-friendly options among the rows of sushi stalls within Tsukiji fish market. They have an English menu with sets at ¥2625, though you won't regret spending ¥3675 for their top-quality ten-piece selection including creamy *uni* (sea urchin). Mon–Sat 6am–2.30pm, but closed during occasional market holidays.

Sushi-zanmai Honten すしざんまい本店 4-11-9 Tsukiji, Chūo-ku ☎ 03 3541 1117; Tsukiji Station. This is the main branch of a popular chain of sushi restaurants run by Kimura Kyoshi, the self-proclaimed "King of Tuna". It's the best *kaiten-zushi* operation in the area, with plates of sushi from around ¥1000, and is open around the clock. Daily 24hr.

AKASAKA AND ROPPONGI

Aux Bacchanales オーバッカナル 2F Ark Mori Building, 1-12-32 Akasaka, Minato-ku ☎ 03 3582 2225, ⓦ auxbacchanales.com; Roppongi-Itchōme Station; map pp.106–107. Tucked away in the Ark Hills complex, this is one of Tokyo's most authentic Parisian-style brasseries – their steak frites is the real thing – and it's a pleasant spot to hang out sipping coffee or red wine. Pastries start at ¥210, while daily lunch specials of both meat and fish dishes go for under ¥1300. Daily 10am–midnight.

Gonpachi 権八 1-13-11 Nishi-Azabu, Minato-ku ☎ 03 5771 0170, ⓦ gonpachi.jp; Roppongi Station; map pp.106–107. A faux-Edo-period storehouse is home to this atmospheric Japanese restaurant. Take your pick between reasonably priced soba (from ¥800) and grilled items (from ¥180) on the ground and second floors, while on the third it's sushi – a full meal will set you back around ¥3000. There's a wonderful samurai drama atmosphere, and it's easy to see how the place inspired the climactic scenes of Quentin Tarantino's *Kill Bill Vol. 1*. Daily 11.30am–5pm.

Hong Kong Tea House 香港茶樓 2F Roppongi Hills Hillside, 6-10-2 Roppongi, Minato-ku ☎ 03 5413 9588; Roppongi Station; map pp.106–107. One of the cheaper places in the Roppongi Hills complex, serving decent dim sum from ¥200 a plate, and mains for under ¥1000. The interior is surprisingly fancy-looking for a budget place. Daily 11am–10.30pm, Thurs–Sun till 3am.

★ **Kurosawa** 黒澤 2-7-9 Nagatachō, Chiyoda-ku ☎ 03 3580 9638; Tameike-sannō Station; map pp.106–107. Quality soba (from ¥735) and pork dishes (from around ¥5000) are the speciality of this atmospheric restaurant, whose design was inspired by the sets from Akira Kurosawa's movies *Yojimbo* and *Red Beard*. Mon–Fri 11.30am–3pm & 5–10pm, Sat noon–9pm.

L'Atelier de Joël Robuchon 2F Roppongi Hills Hillside, 6-10-1 Roppongi, Minato-ku ☎ 03 5772 7500, ⓦ robuchon.jp; Roppongi Station; map pp.106–107. The French masterchef has six Tokyo outposts, this one in Roppongi Hills is the best, offering *degustation* menus starting at ¥2950 for lunch, ¥4800 for dinner. There's a no-bookings policy, so you may have to wait to get a seat at the long counter, facing the open kitchen where black-garbed chefs create culinary mini-masterpieces before your very eyes. Daily 11.30am–2.30pm & 6–10pm.

Lauderdale ローダデール 6-15-1 Roppongi, Minato-ku ☎ 03 3405 5533, ⓦ lauderdale.co.jp; Roppongi Station; map pp.106–107. Top hotels aside there aren't too many places in Tokyo where you can get as good a Western-style gourmet breakfast as at this super casual place, which successfully conjures up the stylish South Beach vibe in the midst of Roppongi Hills; try the eggs benedict for ¥1800. Later in the day it's just as good a spot for bistro favourites on the outdoor terrace; their made-to-order soufflés are well worth trying. Daily 7am–10pm.

Nobu Tokyo NOBU東京 Toranomon Towers Office, 4-1-28 Toranomon, Minato-ku ☎ 03 5733 0070, ⓦ nobutokyo.com; Kamiyachō Station; map pp.106–107. There's a dramatic Japanese-style design for Nobu Matsuhisa's Tokyo operation, where you can sample the famous black-cod dinner (Robert de Niro's favourite) for ¥3500. For something a bit different, try *tiradito*, Nobu's South American twist on sashimi. Mon–Fri 11.30am–2pm & 6–10.30pm, Sat & Sun 6–10.30pm.

★ **Nodaiwa** 野田岩 1-5-4 Higashi-Azabu, Minato-ku ☎ 03 3583 7852, ⓦ nodaiwa.com/en; Kamiyachō Station; map pp.106–107. Kimono-clad waitresses shuffle around this 160-year-old *kura*, converted into one of Tokyo's best eel restaurants; a set meal will cost around ¥5000. The private rooms upstairs can only be booked by parties of four or more; if it's busy, they may guide you to the annexe around the corner, which has an almost identical interior. Mon–Sat 11am–1.30pm & 5–8pm.

★ **Tōfuya-Ukai** とうふ屋うかい 4-4-13 Shiba-kōen, Minato-ku ☎ 03 3436 1028, ⓦ ukai.co.jp; Akabanebashi

1

Station; map pp.106–107. At the foot of Tokyo Tower, this stunning re-creation of an Edo-era mansion, incorporating huge beams from an old sake brewery, serves unforgettable tofu-based *kaiseki*-style cuisine. Book well ahead, especially for dinner (at least a month in advance). Set meals only, with lunch from ¥5500 and dinner from ¥8400. Daily 11am–8pm.

Tokyo Curry Lab 4-2-8 Shiba-kōen, Minato-ku ☎03 5425 2900, ⓦtokyocurrylab.jp; Kamiyachō Station; map pp.106–107. Whether you choose to go up Tokyo Tower or not, this super slick operation at its base is worth checking out for a taste of *tonkatsu kare*, the quintessential local comfort food. Most curries clock in at around ¥1000. Plates are shaped so that you can easily get every last grain of rice. Daily 11am–10pm.

EBISU, MEGURO AND THE SOUTH

Chano-ma チャノマ 6F Naka-Meguro Kangyō Building, 1-22-4 Kami-Meguro, Meguro-ku ☎03 3792 9898; Naka-Meguro Station; map pp.110–111. Slip off your shoes and relax on the huge, padded, bed-like platform overlooking the river at this super-casual operation. They serve some very tasty rustic-style Japanese fusion dishes (under ¥1000), as well as a great selection of teas and flavoured lattes. Mon–Thurs & Sun noon–2am, Fri & Sat noon–4am.

Chibō 千房 38F Yebisu Garden Palace Tower, Shibuya-ku ☎03 5424 1011; Ebisu Station; map pp.110–111. Of the several restaurants housed in the top two levels of this tower, this is the most appealing – not to mention the cheapest. Tasty *okonomiyaki* goes from ¥680, and the views are predictably superb. Mon–Fri 11.30am–3pm & 5–10pm; Sat & Sun 11.30am–10pm.

★**Ebisu Yokochō** 千惠比寿横丁 Ebisu, Minato-ku; Ebisu Station; map pp.110–111. Not a restaurant, but a whole clutch of them, crammed into a hugely atmospheric covered arcade east of Ebisu Station. Come in the evening and take your pick – there's a curry stand, several noodle joints, places specializing in seafood, and even a miniature karaoke bar. In addition, the venues and the tables in them are arranged in a way that encourages mingling. Daily 5pm–late.

★**Iroha Sushi** いろは寿司 1-5-13 Kami-Meguro, Meguro-ku ☎03 5722 3560, ⓦirohasushi.com; Nakameguro Station; map pp.110–111. Relaxed sushi den that's the diametric opposite of most diners in this fancy part of town – you won't see any hipsters or bohos here, just salaryfolk and older locals. Every single piece is freshly made, yet the place remains cheaper than any *kaiten-zushiya*, especially at lunchtime, when huge sets go from just ¥680. Daily 11.30am–2.30pm & 5–10.30pm.

Pizzeria da Isa ピッツェリアダイーサ 1-28-9 Aobadai, Minato-ku ☎03 5768 3739, ⓦda-isa.jp; Naka-Meguro Station; map pp.110–111. The Japanese head chef at this authentically Italian-style pizzeria scooped a clutch of awards in Napoli – if he made his mark in the very home of pizza, you can be sure that this is the best you'll find in all Japan. Pizzas go from ¥1450, though note that every diner needs to order one dish and a drink; service is also notoriously uppity. Tues–Sun 11.30am–2pm & 5.30–11pm.

★**Tonki** とんき 1-1-2 Shimo-Meguro, Meguro-ku ☎03 3491 9928; Meguro Station; map pp.110–111. This minimalist, sharp-looking, family-run restaurant, where a seemingly telepathic team create order out of chaos, is the most famous place in town for *tonkatsu*. Expect to have to queue up for a seat at mealtimes. Sets from ¥1800, cutlet alone ¥1250. Daily except Tues 4–10.45pm.

HARAJUKU, AOYAMA AND SHIBUYA

AtoZ 5F 5-8-3 Minami Aoyama, Shibuya-ku ☎03 5464 0281; Omotesandō Station; map p.114. Enter the offbeat world of artist Yoshitomo Nara, whose pieces decorate this impressive café – part art installation, part kindergarten for the art-school set. The food includes tasty salads, noodle and rice dishes – all the kind of things a Japanese mum might cook up – for around ¥1000 a meal. Try the brown sugar coconut pudding for dessert. Daily 11.30am–11.30pm.

Curry Up 2-35-9 Jingūmae, Shibuya-ku ☎03 5775 5446, ⓦcurryup.jp; Meiji-jingūmae Station; map p.114. Punning name aside, there's not much to dislike about this stylish new curry canteen where they keep the menu simple and the food hot and spicy. Try their butter chicken (¥800–1200 depending on the size of the portion). Daily 11.30am–9pm, Sun to 8pm.

★**Eat** 2-12-27 Kita-Aoyama, Minato-ku ☎03 6459 2432; Gaienmae Station; map p.114. The top-quality Kōbe beef burger (¥1050, or ¥1470 for a double-decker) headlines at this fab little diner, but they also do an equally delicious lamb version and classy renditions of American faves such as seafood gumbo and burritos. Owner Michi, a top chef in LA for 24 years, speaks fluent English and loves to chat with the customers. Mon–Sat 11.30am–3.30pm & 6–10.30pm, Sun 11.30am–3pm.

Ganso Kujiraya 元祖くじら屋 2-9-22 Dōgenzaka, Shibuya-ku ☎03 3461 9145; Shibuya Station; map p.114. Like it or not, the Japanese have eaten whale meat for centuries, and this smart venue is a good option if you'd like to see what the fuss is about. You may not be able to make head or tail of the menu (though it does feature pictures of the latter), so take a Japanese-speaker along if possible; most dishes are ¥780–980. Mon–Fri 11am–2pm & 5–10.30pm, Sat & Sun 11.30am–11.30pm.

Hanamaru はなまる B1, 2-1 Udagawa-chō, Shibuya-ku ☎03 5428 0870; Shibuya Station; map p.114. Simple noodle restaurant which is a touch classier, and certainly makes tastier food, than the bigger chains. Their cheapest udon is ¥280, and though nothing's in English, picture menus help out somewhat. Daily 9am–10pm.

Kaikaya 開花屋 23-7 Maruyama-chō, Shibuya-ku ☎ 03 3770 0878, ⓦ kaikaya.com; Shinsen Station; map p.114. This convivial, smoky *izakaya*, specializing in fish, is plastered with snaps of carousing customers. There's an English menu and the friendly staff are happy to advise on what to order – most dishes are around the ¥1000 mark, though you'll need more than one per person to fill up. Daily 11.30am–2pm & 5.30–11.30pm.

Maisen まい泉 4-8-5 Jingūmae, Shibuya-ku ☎ 03 3470 0071; Omotesandō Station; map p.114. Located in an old bathhouse, this long-running *tonkatsu* restaurant serves up great-value set meals from ¥1580. The actual bathhouse bit is the smoking section of the restaurant. Daily 11am–10pm.

Murugi ムルギ 2-19-1 Dōgenzaka, Shibuya-ku ☎ 03 3462 0241; Shibuya Station; map p.114. In the heart of Shibuya's sleazeland, this curry restaurant has been going since 1951, perhaps thanks to their distinctive Fuji-shaped rice mounds (actually more like the Matterhorn, but whatever). The curries will set you back ¥1000, and taste just fine; the only problem is that they're only open for lunch. Daily except Fri 11.30am–3pm.

Nabi なび B1F Accorder Jingūmae, 2-31-20 Jingūmae, Shibuya-ku ☎ 03 5771 0071; Meiji-jingūmae Station; map p.114. Stylish Korean restaurant using mainly organic ingredients for dishes such as *bulgogi* (marinated beef) salad. Plenty of dishes are under ¥2000. Mon–Fri 11.30am–1am, Sat 6pm–1am, Sun 6pm–midnight.

Piazza Eco-Farm 4-27-2 Jingūmae, Shibuya-ku ☎ 03 3479 0039; Meiji-jingūmae Station; map p.114. Grand little place that's hidden well enough away to avoid the maddening queues typical of the surrounding area. Lunch sets, mainly Italian in nature, go for ¥900; the menu varies but expect pasta, salad, mashed potato and grilled veggies to be among the choices, along with a free coffee. Daily 10am–9pm.

★ Rāmen Nagi ラーメン凪 1-3-1 Higashi, Shibuya-ku ☎ 03 3499 0390; Shibuya Station; map p.114. At this crazy-busy gourmet ramen joint, the waiter will give you a choice of how soft or hard you'd like their superb noodles cooked. There are a few interesting selections available on the fun cross-section menu, including the "Midorio", made with basil and cheese – weird, but it works. More regular varieties are served in a rich pork broth, topped with delicious pork slices and a heap of chopped spring onions. A bargain at ¥850 a bowl. Mon–Sat 11.30am–4pm & 5pm–4am, Sun noon–2am.

Respekt レスペクト 2F 1-11-1 Shibuya, Shibuya-ku ☎ 03 6418 8144, ⓦ cafecompany.co.jp; Shibuya Station; map p.114. Apart from offering filling, attractive café-style dishes, such as nachos, falafel and roast chicken (most for ¥1000 or less), this hipster's hangout has tons of English style, plus fashion mags to browse and internet access. Mon–Thurs 11.30am–2am, Fri & Sat

11.30am–5am, Sun 11.30am–midnight.

Royal Garden Café 2-1-19 Kita Aoyama, Minato-ku ☎ 03 5414 6170; Gaienmae Station; map p.114. With its spacious, reclaimed-wood interior, bakery and wraparound terrace sheltered by leafy trees, this organic food café at the entrance to Meiji-jingū outer garden strikes all the right notes. Good set lunches including pasta or salad as a main are ¥1000 during the week and around ¥2000 for the weekend brunch. Daily 11am–11pm.

Sakuratei さくら亭 3-20-1 Jingūmae, Shibuya-ku ☎ 03 3479 0039; Meiji-jingūmae Station; map p.114. Funky cook-your-own *okonomiyaki*, *monjayaki* and *yakisoba* joint behind the weird and wonderful Design Festa Gallery (see p.116). From 11.30am to 3pm you can eat as much as you like within 90min for ¥980, and it's just as good value at night. Daily 11.30am–11pm.

Sushi Ōuchi 鮨大内 2-8-4 Shibuya, Shibuya-ku, ☎ 03 3407 3543; Shibuya Station; map p.114. Few Tokyo *sushi-ya* ensure they use the best organic produce and fish caught only from the wild. This one does, and the pleasant surprise is that it's very affordable, with a set platter of sushi for as little as ¥2100, although you can easily spend more. The interior presents a warm, farmhouse feel. Mon–Sat noon–1.30pm & 5.30–9.30pm.

Two Rooms 5F AO Building, 3-11-7 Kita-Aoyama, Minato-ku ☎ 03 3498 0002, ⓦ tworooms.jp; Omotesandō Station; map p.114. A sophisticated addition to the city's high-end dining scene, *Two Rooms* is a formal restaurant and a relaxed bar with a spacious outdoor terrace that provides one of the best views in Tokyo. Perfectly cooked European food using top-quality Japanese ingredients is enhanced by wonderfully polite service. On Sunday they do a brunch for ¥2950; otherwise lunch sets start at ¥1850, dinner tasting menus at ¥7500. Restaurant daily 11.30am–2.30pm, 6–10pm; bar 11.30am–2am (Sun until 10pm).

Uobei 魚べい 2-29-1 Dōgenzaka, Shibuya-ku ☎ 03 3462 0241; Shibuya Station; map p.114. Searingly bright restaurant in which your sushi is ordered by touch screen, then delivered by rail on automated plates – the only humans you see are those who point you to your table and take your cash. Gimmicky, yes, but it's a lot of fun – not to mention cheap, since it's a set ¥105 per plate. Daily 11am–midnight.

SHINJUKU AND THE WEST

Angkor Wat アンコールワット 1-38-13 Yoyogi, Shibuya-ku ☎ 03 3370 3019; Yoyogi Station; map pp.118–119. Tokyo's best Cambodian restaurant offers set meals, but you can also tell the waiters your budget and let them bring you a suitable selection of dishes (allow ¥2000 per head). The sweetly spicy salads, soups and vegetable rolls are all excellent. It's on a side street just off the main road; look out for the elephant. Mon–Fri 11am–2pm & 5–11pm, Sat & Sun 5–11pm.

1

Fuji Soba 富士そば 3-14-25 Shinjuku, Shinjuku-ku; Shinjuku Station; map pp.118–119. Filling, super-cheap meals from this round-the-clock joint. Their *curry katsudon* (¥530) and ramen are particularly good value; study the pictures then purchase your meal ticket from the machine. Daily 24hr.

J.S. Burgers Café 3F 4-1-7 Shinjuku, Shinjuku-ku ☎03 5367 0185, ⓦjsb-cafe.jp; Shinjuku Station; map pp.118–119. A fab range of home-made chunky burgers, hot dogs and sandwiches are served at this retro-styled café atop the Journal Standard boutique. Lunch deals (¥880–980) include a self-serve salad bar. Mon–Fri 11.30am–10pm, Sat & Sun 11am–9pm.

Kakiden 柿傳 8F Yasuyo Building, 3-37-11 Shinjuku, Shinjuku-ku ☎03 3352 5121, ⓦkakiden.com; Shinjuku Station; map pp.118–119. One of the best places in Tokyo to sample *kaiseki-ryōri* (a set menu of beautifully presented small dishes using seasonal produce and different cooking techniques). There's a lunch for ¥4000, but you won't regret investing in the eighteen-course dinner for ¥8000. They also conduct *kaiseki* appreciation classes. Daily 11am–9pm.

Nakajima 中嶋 3-32-5 Shinjuku, Shinjuku-ku ☎03 3356 4534; Shinjuku Station; map pp.118–119. At lunch all the delicious dishes served here are made with sardines – they're a bargain at around ¥1000 each, though you'll need at least a couple. For dinner it's worth the expense (over ¥8000 per person) to sample the chef's Kansai *kapo* style of cooking, similar to *kaiseki-ryōri* cuisine – after all, it's earned him a Michelin star. Mon–Sat 11.30am–1.45pm & 5.30–8.30pm.

Shanghai Xiaochi 上海小吃 1-3-10 Kabukichō, Shinjuku-ku ☎03 3232 5909; Shinjuku Station; map pp.118–119. Don't be scared of entering this dingy alley, parallel to and just south of the main road – it's home to one of the area's best Chinese restaurants. The authentic dishes here, such as clams in soy sauce with *age-pan* (fried bread), really hit the spot – they're around ¥1500 each. Mon–Sat 6pm–5am, Sun until 2am.

Suzuya すずや Kabukichō Ichibangai-iriguchi, Shinjuku-ku ☎03 3209 4408; Shinjuku Station; map pp.118–119. Little appears to have changed at this famous *tonkatsu* restaurant since it opened just after World War II. Their twist on the breaded pork cutlet dish (which costs around ¥1000 depending on the cut of meat) is to serve it *ochazuke* style – you pour green tea over the meat and rice to make a kind of savoury porridge. The bill will be around ¥2000. Daily 11am–10.30pm.

★**Tsunahachi** つな八 3-31-8 Shinjuku, Shinjuku-ku ☎03 3352 1012; Shinjuku Station; map pp.118–119. The main branch of the famous tempura restaurant almost always has a queue outside, though you're likely to get seated quickly if you settle for the upstairs rooms away from the frying action (or ask for the non-smoking section). Everything is freshly

made, and even the ¥1300 set (including soup, rice and pickles) will fill you up. Daily 11.15am–10pm.

IKEBUKURO AND THE NORTH

Akiyoshi 秋吉 3-30-4 Nishi-Ikebukuro, Toshima-ku ☎03 3982 0601; Ikebukuro Station; map pp.122–123. Unusually large *yakitori* bar with a good atmosphere and a helpful picture menu. You might have to queue at peak times for the tables, but there's generally space at the counter. Most dishes are around ¥400 for five skewers. Daily 5pm–midnight (Sun until 11pm).

Han Sarang ハンサラン 1-16-15 Ōkubo, Shinjuku-ku ☎03 5292 1161; Shin-Ōkubo Station; map pp.122–123. On the second floor above the Korean Culture Center in Koreatown, and designed like a Korean farmhouse, with wooden beams and intimate booths, this restaurant offers various set courses (from ¥1500), served with multiple side dishes (*banchan*). Daily 11am–midnight.

★**Isomaru Suisan** 磯丸水産 3-25-10 Nishi-Ikebukuro, Toshima-ku ☎03 5953 2585; Ikebukuro Station; map pp.122–123. This fantastic seafood *izakaya* is heaving all evening, every evening – it's so popular that it never shuts. There's no English menu, but there are plenty of pictures and live sea creatures to point at – try their colossal *sazae* (sea snails). Daily 24hr.

Malaychan 3-22-6 Nishi-Ikebukuro, Toshima-ku ☎03 5391 7638, ⓦmalaychan.jp; Ikebukuro Station; map pp.122–123. Tiny, unpretentious Malay restaurant dishing up decent food, from grilled fish on a banana leaf and *mee goreng* (fried noodles) to winter steamboats (the Malay equivalent of *sukiyaki*). Weekday lunch menus start at ¥850, and in general you'll eat well for under ¥2000. Mon 5–11pm, Tues–Sat 11am–2.30pm & 5–11pm, Sun 11am–11pm.

★**Mutekiya** 無敵家 1-7-1 Minami-Ikebukuro, Toshima-ku ☎03 3982 7565; ⓦmutekiya.com; Ikebukuro Station; map pp.122–123. Ramen fans should head straight to this joint, where the queue often stretches a full 40m from the door – don't worry, since it moves along fairly quickly. While you wait you can decide on the size of your helping (bowls start at ¥680), its flavour, and whether you want extra toppings and so forth. It's all delicious. Daily 10.30am–4am.

Shinjuku Pojangmacha 新宿ポジャンマチャ 1-2-3 Hyakunin-chō, Shinjuku-ku, ☎03 3200 8683; Shin-Ōkubo Station; map pp.122–123. Also known simply as "Pocha" this rustic *yakiniku* (grilled meat) restaurant is painted with colourful cartoon scenes of Korean life and has featured on Japanese TV. It serves the rice beer *makgeolli* the traditional way, in big wooden bowls with a ladle. If you like the drink, also check out the bar *Maccoli* (see p.148) further down the same street. Mon–Thurs noon–midnight, Fri–Sun until 3am.

TOKYO TEAHOUSES

Tokyo's **teahouses** are becoming more popular as the health benefits of tea are promoted. Other than the places listed below, you might also try the tea ceremony at *Andon Ryokan* (see p.97; guests/non-guests ¥500/1000) where the whole process is properly explained in English and you get to practise making tea yourself. There are also teahouses with pretty settings in Hama-Rikyū Onshi Teien (see p.101), Shinjuku Gyoen (see p.120) and Happōen (see p.112).

Cha Ginza 茶銀座 5-5-6 Ginza, Chiyoda-ku ☎ 03 3571 1211; Ginza Station map p.88. This teahouse, run by a tea wholesaler, offers a modern take on the business of sipping *sencha*. Iron walls add a contemporary touch, and the rooftop area, where they serve *matcha*, is the place to hang out with those Tokyo ladies who seem to have made a career of shopping ¥500 gets you two cups of the refreshing green stuff plus a traditional sweet. Tues–Sun 11am–7pm.

Sabō Nonohana 茶房 野の花 3-7-21 Ginza Chūō-ku ☎ 03 5250 9025; Ginza Station; map p.88 Lovely tearoom on the second floor of Nonohana Tsukasa, a shop that specializes in traditional flower arrangements and crafts. The *teisyoku* (set meal) lunches – starting at ¥800 – are beautifully presented and the green-tea ice cream (¥750, hard to turn down Mon–Sat 11am–7pm Sun 11.30am–6pm.

Sori ソリ B1 TK Bldg, 1-1-4 Hyakunin-chō ☎ 03 6233 9200; Shin-Ōkubo Station; map pp.122–123. Korean tearoom occupying a spacious basement plastered with giant posters of women in national dress and K-pop boy bands. Sample fruit and herbal infusions

including lemony sweet *yuja-cha*, gingery, winter-warmer *saenggang-cha*, and the tangy, shocking pink "five-flavoured" *omija-cha*; they'll set you back around ¥800. Daily 10am–11pm.

Toraya Café トラヤカフェ Keyakizaka-dōri, 6-12-2 Roppongi, Minato-ku ☎ 03 5789 9811; Roppongi Station; pp.106–107. Stylish café specializing in Japanese teas and sweets made from azuki beans; figure on over ¥1000 for both the former and the latter. It's usually busy with ladies lunching or sipping tea between boutique visits. Daily 10am–10pm.

Umezono 梅園 1-31-12 Asakusa, Taitō-ku ☎ 03 3841 7580; Asakusa Station; map p.97. This traditional teashop in the heart of Asakusa is famous for its *awa-zenzai*, millet flour cakes wrapped in sweet azuki bean paste, served with seeds of Japanese basil for contrast. Alternatively, choose a bowl of *anmitsu* from the window display: a colourful concoction of agar jelly, azuki beans and sticky rice topped with a variety of fruits (and, if you're really hungry, whipped cream or ice cream); it goes from ¥756. Daily except Wed 10am–8pm.

CAFÉS AND TEAHOUSES

You can hardly walk a block of central Tokyo without passing a chain **café** – as often as not a *Starbucks*, although local operations, such as *Doutor* and *Tully's*, are also pretty common. For all the convenience and keen prices of these operations, don't miss sampling at least one of the many other individual cafés, sometimes called **kissaten**, where the emphasis is on service and creating an interesting, relaxing, highly individual space.

At traditional **teahouses** (*sabō*; see box above) you can sample Japanese sweets made from compounded sugar or pounded rice cake (*mochi*) and red bean paste, the sweetness of which balances the bitterness of the tea. It's worth noting that while cafés often keep late hours, teahouses are generally a daytime affair.

GINZA AND AROUND

100% Chocolate Café 100%チョコレートカフェー 2-4-16 Kyōbashi, Chūō-ku ☎ 03 3273 3184, ⚲ choco -cafe.jp; Kyōbashi Station map p.88. Indulgence is taken to new heights at this trendy café, which boasts a choice of 56 chocolate varieties –make your selection at the bar or from the "chocolate library" lining one wall. This wall and the chocolate-bar-styled ceiling were dreamed up by Masamichi Katayama, one of Tokyo's hottest designers; go for a regular hot chocolate (¥420), or their wonderful range of slurp-worthy desserts. Mon–Fri 8am–3pm, Sat & Sun 11am–7pm

Café de l'Ambre カフェードランブル 8-10-15 Ginza, Chūō-ku ☎ 03 3571 1551; Shimbashi Station;

map p.88. One of Tokyo's best coffee venues – at least for those who don't mind the semi-permanent cloud of cigarette smoke. This old-school Ginza *kissaten* has been roasting up 300g batches of beans since the 1950s, achieving something approaching coffee perfection in the intervening years. Most cups are made with a cotton-felt filter – the process is quite mesmeric. Daily 8am–10pm.

Henri Charpentier アンリシャルペンティエール 2-8-20 Ginza, Chūō-ku ☎ 03 3562 2721, ⚲ henri -charpentier.com; Ginza-Itchōme Station; map p.88. This deep-pink boutique offers the ultimate in Tokyo patisserie on the ground floor and a *salon de thé* below. Here you can enjoy crêpe suzette (¥1575), flambéed at your table, as well as a range of gold-flecked chocolate morsels

1

and seasonal specialities, to go with a choice of coffees, teas and infusions (¥735 and up). Don't leave before checking out the cleverly hidden toilets. Daily 11am–9pm.

AKIHABARA AND AROUND

★**Amanoya** 天野屋 2-18-15 Soto-Kanda, Chiyoda-ku ☎03 3251 7911; Ochanomizu or Marunouchi Stations; map p.91. Charming little venue which makes a great place to drop by after visiting the nearby Kanda Myōjin shrine (see p.90). Most are here for the desserts, but don't pass up the opportunity to try their *amazake* – this sweet, ginger-laced, non-alcoholic sake is a by-product of the soya beans fermented in the on-site "mould rooms", a practice that has taken place here since 1904. Mon–Fri 10am–6pm, Sun 10am–5pm.

Gundam Café ガンダムカフェー 1-1 Kanda-Hanaokachō, Chiyoda-ku ☎03 3251 0078, ⓦg-cafe.jp; Akihabara Station; map p.91. Experience what a pilot from the incredibly popular anime series *Mobile Suit Gundam* would eat – or at least our terrestial equivalent – in a suitably sci-fi interior. Café time and bar time (from 5pm) have different menus. Coffee from ¥340. Mon–Fri 10am–10pm, Sat 8.30am–11pm, Sun 8.30am–9.20pm.

Maidreamin メイドリーミング 2F 1-8-10 Soto-Kanda, Chiyoda-ku ☎03 6252 3263, ⓦmaidreamin.com; Akihabara Station; map p.91. The *Maidreamin* maid café chain (see box opposite) has really taken off in recent years, and their spangly, anime-like Akiba branch draws a small stream of foreigners thanks to English-speaking staff – they'll let you know exactly which cute poses to make, which cute sounds to mimic and so on. It's all rather fun, and charged at ¥500 per hour, with an order from the menu mandatory: drinks run ¥500–1000, with meals a little dearer. There's another good one in Shibuya (see opposite). Daily 10am–11pm.

Mai:lish マイリシ 2F FH Kowa Square, 3-6-2 Soto-Kanda, Chiyoda-ku ☎03 5289 7310, ⓦmailish.jp; Suehirochō Station; map p.91. Akiba's famed maid cafés come in all sorts of shapes, sizes and styles; this is one of the originals, a relaxed venue in which costumed girls pander to their customers' every whim. It's ¥500 per hour, and you're obliged to order something from the menu: drinks cost from ¥550. Daily 11am–10pm.

Mu'u Mu'u Diner ムームーダイナー 3-14-3 Kanda-Ogawamachi, Chiyoda-ku ☎03 3518 6787; Jimbōchō Station; map p.91. Swap the dusty books of Jimbōchō for a sunny Hawaiian vibe at this café-restaurant, decked out with surfboards and hibiscus garlands. Besides Hawaiian Kona coffee, it also serves Kona beer as well as a few dishes, such as deep-fried octopus (¥880), hamburgers and pizza (¥980). Daily 11am–11pm.

Saboru サボール 1-11 Kanda-Jimbōchō, Chiyoda-ku ☎03 3291 8404; Jimbōchō Station; map p.91. Appealingly rustic *kissaten* tucked away on the alley

running parallel to Yasukuni-dōri. Once a popular hideaway for school kids skipping lessons (the nearby bookshops presumably functioned as an excuse), this three-level, tree-house-like establishment now attracts an older, more cosmopolitan clientele. You may hear crickets singing by the entrance, raised here for over two decades by the owner of a nearby hardware store. Coffee from ¥400. Mon–Sat 9am–11pm.

ASAKUSA AND AROUND

★**Gallery éf** ガラリーエフ 2-19-18 Kaminarimon, Taitō-ku ☎03 3841 0442, ⓦgallery-ef.com; Asakusa Station; map p.97. The *kura* at the back of this appealing café provides an intimate venue for an eclectic mix of concerts, performance art, and exhibitions that cover most of the space – the rest is taken up by the café's collection of retro goods. Drinks, meals (mostly Western-style, like chilli beans and spaghetti), and desserts are served using vintage tableware, and they carry a few import beers as well. Choose from four different types of blended coffee (¥550), or plump for a tasty fruit juice (¥630). Daily except Tues: café and gallery 11am–7pm; bar 6pm–midnight.

Kappabashi Coffee 合羽橋コーヒー 3-25-11 Nishi-Asakusa, Taitō-ku ☎03 5828 0308, ⓦkappabashi-coffee .com; Iriya or Tawaramachi Stations; map p.97. Chunky wooden furniture offset against white walls lends a sophisticated air to this café, which serves a wide range of coffees (from ¥450), teas (from ¥600), infusions and juices, as well as cakes and light meals. Mon–Fri 8am–9pm, Sat & Sun until 8pm.

BAYSIDE TOKYO

Starbucks スターバックス Venus Fort, Kōtō-ku ☎03 5500 5090; Aomi Station. Recommending a *Starbucks* might be terribly uncool, but while the coffee here's the same old same old, this Venus Fort branch is nestled into a faux-Italian piazza, sitting under a permanently twilit "sky" like something out of *The Truman Show* – twee, but somehow rather satisfying, especially on a rainy day. Daily 9.30am–9pm.

AKASAKA AND ROPPONGI

★**Eat More Greens** イートモアグリーンズ 2-2-5 Azabu-Jūban, Minato-ku ☎03 3798 3191, ⓦeatmore greens.jp; Azabu-Jūban Station; map pp.106–107. Taking its inspiration from urban US vegetarian cafés and bakeries, this appealing place mixes random pieces of wood furniture, good organic food (¥1000 for a set meal) and a street-side terrace, along with seriously good donuts (from ¥220). Mon–Fri 11am–11pm, Sat & Sun 9am–11pm.

EBISU, MEGURO AND THE SOUTH

Kissa Ginza 喫茶銀座 1-3-9 Ebisu-Minami, Shibuya-ku ☎03 3710 7320; Ebisu Station; map pp.110–111. Serving standard café dishes and drinks, the draw here is the retro-cool 1960s-style decor. By day it's a café (coffees from ¥450), and popular with a slightly older crowd, but in the evening it morphs into a DJ bar complete with glitter ball. Daily 10am–late.

HARAJUKU, AOYAMA AND SHIBUYA

24/7 Coffee 24／7コーヒー 1-19-8 Jin'nan, Shibuya-ku ☎03 3463 3323; Shibuya Station; map p.114. Artists and art lovers hang out at this trendy café, which is decorated with work from an adjoining gallery. Coffees (from ¥500) are professionally made and served in delightful vessels; come evening they offer beers, including a nice stout. Snacks and tasty cakes also available. Daily 10am–midnight.

A Piece of Cake アピースオヴケーキ 6-1-19 Minami-Aoyama, Minato-ku ☎03 5466 0686; Omotesandō Station; map p.114. Looking out onto the small sculpture garden in front of the Okamoto Tarō Memorial Museum (see p.116) this laidback place has some interesting options, including traditional Indian *chai* (¥650). Daily except Tues 10am–6pm.

Bunbougu ブンボーグ B1 4-8-1 Jingūmae, Shibuya-ku ☎03 3470 6420; Omotesandō Station; map p.114. This quirky space is part-café, part-library and part-stationery store. Those who like to doodle while they sup should note that for a one-off membership fee of ¥700 you'll be given a key that opens the stationery drawers tucked under the tables. Daily 10am–11.30am.

★**Hideaway** ハイダウェーィ 202 3-20-1 Jingūmae, Shibuya-ku ☎03 5410 2343, ⦿treehouse.jp/hideaway;

Harajuku or Meiji-Jingūmae Stations; map p.114. A cool travellers' vibe pervades this café-bar tucked away in a quiet corner of Harajuku near Design Festa. There's a tree growing through it and you can climb up to their tree house to enjoy drinks or their tasty curries; during lunch hours (noon–4pm), you can get curry and a drink for ¥1000. Daily except Wed 11am–10pm.

LOHB 4F Likes Bldg, 2-3-1 Dōgenzaka, Shibuya-ku ☎03 3464 1919; Shibuya Station; map p.114. The rather meaningless acronym stands for Likes Oriental Health and Beauty – all you need know is that this café-bar provides a first-class view across the mesmerizing Shibuya crossing, and serves coffees, cocktails and light snacks. The latter are mostly Italian-style, with lunch sets around ¥1100. Daily 11.30am–midnight.

★**Maidreamin** メイドリーミング B1 30-1 Udagawachō, Shibuya-ku ☎03 6427 8938, ⦿maidreamin.com; Shibuya Station; map p.114. Like its sister establishment in Akihabara (see opposite), this sci-fi-style maid café is an all-out cuteness assault, its glammed-up staff sporting inch-long fake eyelashes and umpteen petticoat layers. The food follows suit – think curry served in heart-shaped rice mounds and burgers cut up to look like teddy bears – and there's also a range of soft and alcoholic drinks. Entry ¥500 per hour, plus you have to make one order from the menu. Mon–Thurs 3pm–11pm, Fri 3pm–5am, Sat 11.30am–5am, Sun 11.30am–11pm.

Yoku Moku ヨックモック 5-3-3 Minami-Aoyama, Minato-ku ☎03 5485 3330, ⦿www.yokumoku.co.jp; Omotesandō Station; map p.114. Hushed café with

---

MAIDS, BUTLERS AND CATS: TOKYO'S QUIRKY CAFÉS

Japan in general, and Tokyo in particular, has long been famed for offering its own quirky variations on Western standards. So it should come as no surprise to find that the city has a few different takes on the humble café, and all are certainly worth trying at least once.

The most famous café reincarnations by far are Tokyo's weird and wonderful **maid cafés**, which come in a wide range of styles from seedy to sci-fi, via the unashamedly kitsch. Most maid cafés are clustered amongst the electronics outlets to the west of Akihabara Station; head there after sunset and you'll see lines of girls clamouring for custom. Once you've been persuaded to visit one, the deal is usually the same: girls in costumes (sometimes guys too) serving food and drink in an almost excruciatingly cute manner, their voices screeching a full two octaves above their natural pitch. There's usually an hourly fee, and in addition you're expected to order some food or drink from the menu. Recommended places to go include *Mai:lish* (see opposite) and *Maidreamin* (see opposite & above).

The success of maid cafés spawned an inevitable female-centric equivalent: the equally interesting **butler cafés**, where handsome, dressed-up young chaps (often Westerners) serve coffee, cake and wine to their entirely female clientele. Though the format is essentially the same as that for maid cafés, butler cafés tend to be fancier and are often rather more expensive; a good one to try is *Swallowtail Café* (see p.144).

Lastly, the latest hit formula in Tokyo's polymorphous *kissaten* culture is **cat cafés**. Offering quality time with pedigree cats, these are particularly popular among young women and dating couples, and it's easy to understand the appeal: they are relaxing places, offering the pleasures of pet ownership without the commitment. Two recommended cat cafés are *Calico* (see p.144), and *Nekorobi* (see p.144).

courtyard tables, in tune with the elegant sensibilities of the designer boutiques of Omotesandō. There's also a shop selling nicely packaged cakes, chocolates and confectionery, including its famous "cigar" wafer-thin rolled biscuits. Daily 10am–7pm.

SHINJUKU AND THE WEST

Café Comme Ça カフェーコムサ 5F Five Foxes Building, 3-26-6 Shinjuku, Shinjuku-ku ☎03 5367 5551; Shinjuku Station; map pp.118–119. On an upper floor of the trendy Five Foxes store, this ideal Shinjuku pit stop serves delicious cakes (around ¥800) against a background of stark concrete surfaces enlivened by paintings of Buddhist deities. Daily noon–8pm.

Calico キャリコ 6F, 1-16-2 Kabukichō, Shinjuku-ku, ☎03 6457 6387; Shinjuku Station; map pp.118–119. A great place to experience the cat café phenomenon (see box, p.143); ¥600 gets you thirty minutes of quality time with some fifty gorgeous kitties. With instructions and menu in English, it's very foreigner-friendly, and offers inexpensive drinks and food starting at ¥150 for coffee and ¥300 for a delicious fondant chocolate biscuit. Daily 11am–6.30am.

★Dada Café ダダカフェー 5-23-10 Yoyogi, Shibuya-ku ☎03 3350 2245, ⍟religare.biz; Yoyogi Station; map pp.118–119. In an artfully renovated old Japanese house tucked off the main street – and very easy to miss – this delightful café-bar and gallery is a quiet refuge for drinks or simple meals including interesting salads, rice dishes and desserts. As always, lunch sets (¥850) are the best value, served noon–3pm. Mon–Thurs

11.30am–10pm, Fri & Sat until 10.30pm.

Tajimaya 但馬屋 Omoide Yokochō, Shinjuku-ku ☎03 3342 0881; Shinjuku Station; map pp.118–119. Surprisingly genteel for this ragged area of dining and drinking alleys (see p.119), this elegant café serves quality drinks and cakes on a pretty assortment of china. Coffees from ¥580. Daily 10am–10.30pm.

IKEBUKURO AND THE NORTH

Nekorobi ねころび 3F Tact TO Bldg, 1-28-1 Higashi-Ikebukuro, Toshima-ku ☎03 6228 0646, ⍟nekorobi.jp; Ikebukuro Station; map pp.122–123. This cat café (see box, p.143) has a minimum ¥1000 cover charge for the first hour, which gets you unlimited drinks and use of internet, Wii or DVD terminals – a useful bait for luring non-cat-loving partners to join you in a visit. Daily 11am–11pm.

Swallowtail Café スヲローテール B1F 3-12-12 Higashi-Ikebukuro, Toshima-ku ⍟butlers-cafe.jp; Ikebukuro Station; map pp.122–123. A "butler café" where young guys dressed like Jeeves are the solicitous waiters in a room hung with chandeliers and antique-style furniture. Booking through the (mostly Japanese) website is essential. Expect to spend at least ¥2500 per head. Daily 10.30am–9pm.

Zozoi ゾゾイ 3-22-6 Nishi-Ikebukuro, Toshima-ku ☎03 5396 6676; Ikebukuro Station; map pp.122–123. Sheepskin-covered stools and a Beefeater statue are part of the eclectic decor at this small, amiable café offering good coffee (from ¥450), home-made cakes and biscuits, and a pleasant view onto the park. Daily except Tues noon–8pm.

DRINKING AND NIGHTLIFE

Tokyo's **nightlife** options run the gamut from *izakaya* to live music venues (known as "live houses"). The distinction between restaurants, bars and clubs in the city's *sakariba* ("lively places"), such as Ginza, Shibuya or Shinjuku, is hazy, with many places offering a range of entertainment depending on the evening or customers' spirits.

BARS AND IZAKAYA

Tokyo is a drinkers' paradise with a vast range of venues serving practically any brand of booze from around the world as well as local tipples such as sake, shōchū (a vodka-like spirit) and award-winning Japanese whisky. Roppongi easily has Tokyo's greatest concentration of **foreigner-friendly gaijin bars**, but note that many are closed on Sunday. If there's live music anywhere you'll often pay for it through higher drinks prices or a cover charge. Some regular bars also have cover charges and *izakaya* (bars that serve food) almost always do, though you'll usually get a small snack served with your first drink. There's plenty of choice among those that don't, though, so always check the deal before buying your drink. For **bars with a view**, towering major hotels such as the *Park Hyatt* (see p.134) and the *Cerulean Tower Tōkyū Hotel* (see p.133) are hard to beat, though you'll need to dress up.

GINZA AND AROUND

300 Bar 300円バー B1 Fazenda Building, 5-9-11 Ginza, Chūō-ku ☎03 3572 6300; Ginza Station; map p.88. The bargain-basement face of Ginza is this unusually large standing-only bar, where all food and drinks are ¥315; although you have to buy two food/drink tickets to enter, it'd be cheap by the standards of rural Japan, let alone Ginza. Daily 5pm–2am, Sun until 11pm.

Dry Dock ドライドック 3-25-10 Shimbashi, Minato-ku ☎03 5777 4755; Shimbashi Station; map p.88. Cosy craft-beer bar with a nautical theme nestling beneath the train tracks. Its no-smoking policy is a welcome change, and patrons often spill outside to enjoy the regularly changing menu of Japanese and overseas microbrews. Note there's no food served on Saturday. Mon–Fri 5pm–midnight, Sat until 10pm.

1

KARAOKE BARS AND BOXES

Legend has it that **karaoke**, literally translated as "empty orchestra", was invented by an Osaka record-store manager in the early 1970s. Today the mainstay of this ¥1 trillion-a-year business are **karaoke boxes** – buildings packed with comfy booths kitted out with a karaoke system. Rental of these boxes is by the hour and they have proved particularly popular with youngsters, women and families who prefer them to the smoky bars frequented by salarymen that were the original preserve of karaoke. You'll find branches of the biggest chains – *Karaoke-kan*, *Shidax* and *Big Echo* – all over the city; the charge is typically ¥800 per person per hour, but some independent bars are cheaper. There are always plenty of English-language songs to butcher, although it certainly helps to have a Japanese-speaker on hand to operate the karaoke system. Almost all venues serve alcohol, and many have drink-all-you-can (*nomi-hōdai*) specials; two hours of booze usually costs ¥3000 or so, plus the actual singing fee. If you're a first-timer, alcohol certainly helps to ease things along – those who are too shy to sing at the beginning of a session often end up hogging the microphone all night long.

Big Echo ビッグエコ 4-2-14 Ginza, Chūo-ku ☎ 03 3563 5100; Roppongi Station; map p.88. The most appealing branch of this major chain, with a few interesting themed rooms – try the Hello Kitty one. From ¥800 per person, with a minimum order of one drink. Daily 24hr.

Fiesta フィエスタ B1 6-2-35 Roppongi, Minato-ku ☎ 03 5410 3008, ⓦ fiesta-roppongi.com; Roppongi Station; map pp.106–107. A particularly good karaoke bar for newbie *gaijin*, offering thousands of songs in English, as well as several other languages. ¥3500 including three drinks. Mon 7pm–midnight, Tues–Sat until 5am.

Karaoke-kan カラオケ館 30-8 Udagawachō, Shibuya-ku ☎ 03 3462 0785; Shibuya Station; map p.114. Japan's premier karaoke-box operator has branches liberally peppered across the capital. Rooms 601 and 602 in their Udagawachō branch were featured in the movie *Lost in Translation*. An hour of karaoke here costs from ¥800 per person, with a minimum order of one drink. Daily 24hr.

★**Kagaya** かがや B1F Hanasada Building, 2-15-12 Shimbashi, Minato-ku ☎ 03 3591 2347; Shimbashi Station; map p.88. English-speaking Mark runs this simple basement bar as if he's hosting an 8-year-old's birthday party with alcohol. Around ¥3000 will get you plenty of drink and food; you're also welcome to don one of the frog or teddy bear costumes. Reservations recommended. Mon–Sat 5pm–midnight, though times vary.

Lion ライオン 7-9-20 Ginza, Chūo-ku ☎ 03 3571 2590; Ginza Station; map p.88. Opened in 1934, this flagship beer hall of the Sapporo chain is a rather baronial place, with dark tiles and mock wood panelling. As well as good draught beer (from ¥630), there are sausages, sauerkraut and other German snacks on offer alongside international pub grub, and a restaurant upstairs. You'll find other branches scattered around Tokyo, all using the same formula. Daily 11.30am–11pm, Sun until 10.30pm.

Marunouchi House 丸の内ハウス 7F Shin-Marunouchi Bldg, 1-5-1 Maranouchi, Chiyoda-ku ☎ 03 5218 5100; Tokyo Station; map p.88. The best thing about the open-plan space here, with its seven different restaurants and bars, is that you can take your drinks out on to the broad wraparound terrace for great views of Tokyo Station and towards the Imperial Palace. Check out *Limelight*, a kitsch place presided over by a transsexual bar keeper that pays homage to typical neighbourhood "snack" bars. Cover charge at night. Daily 11am–4am, Sun until 11pm.

Old Imperial Bar Imperial Hotel, 1-1-1 Uchisaiwaichō, Chiyoda-ku ☎ 03 3539 8088; Hibiya Station; map p.88. All that remains in Tokyo of Frank Lloyd Wright's Art Deco *Imperial Hotel* is this recreated bar. Try their signature Mount Fuji cocktail (¥1470), a wickedly sweet blend of gin, cream, egg white and sugar syrup with a cherry on top, which was invented here in 1924. And while you sup it, ask to see the photo albums of how the hotel once looked. Smart attire recommended. Daily 11.30am–midnight.

★**Shin Hi No Moto** 新日の基 2-4-4 Yūrakuchō, Chiyoda-ku ☎ 03 3214 8021; Yūrakuchō or Hibiya Stations; map p.88. Known to all and sundry as "Andy's", this is a lively English-owned *izakaya* under the tracks just south of Yūrakuchō Station. It's one of the few places you can try the excellent Sapporo Red Star beer, or go for the cheap, strong shōchū. The seafood and vegetables come fresh from Tsukiji. Reservations essential. Mon–Sat 5pm–midnight.

UENO AND AROUND

Shinsuke シンスケ 3-31-5 Yushima, Bunkyō-ku ☎ 03 3832 0469; Yushima Station; map p.93. Bookings are essential for this venerable *izakaya* where they serve only one brand of sake – Ryōzeki, a tiny brewer from way up north in Akita province. Simply choose between sweet or dry, and hot or cold. The sashimi is excellent (platters go for ¥2900), as are their famous *iwashi no gansekiage* sardine rissoles (¥1050). Mon–Sat 5–9.30pm.

Warrior Celt ウオリアーケルト 3F Ito Building, 6-9-22 Ueno ☎03 3836 8588, ⍵warriorcelt.jp; Ueno Station; map p.93. Things can get pretty raucous at this good-time bar in the thick of Ueno. Key ingredients include a fine range of beers, good food, a nightly happy hour (5–7pm), live bands and, last but not least, "Ladies Night" on Thursdays (cocktails ¥500 for female customers). Mon–Fri 5pm–midnight, Fri & Sat until 5am.

ASAKUSA AND AROUND

Bar Six バー6 6F 2-34-3 Asakusa, Taitō-ku ☎03 5806 5106; Asakusa Station; map p.97. Sophisticated watering hole on the sixth floor of the Amuse Museum complex (see p.98). The Asakusa views are amazing, especially of Sensō-ji, which is illuminated at night. A standing-only outdoor terrace surrounds the bar. Tues–Sun 6pm–2am.

Cuzn カズン 3F Wakaden Building, 1-2-6 Hanakawado, Taitō-ku ☎03 3842 3899; Asakusa Station; map p.97. This friendly bar has a comfy sofa area, free internet access and sometimes shows football games on its big screen. The food's not bad, either, and the same goes for the coffee. Daily noon–11pm.

★**Gin Maku Roku** 銀幕ロック 2F 1-41-5 Asakusa ☎03 5828 6969; Asakusa or Tawaramachi Stations; map p.97. The Asakusa spirit is alive and kicking in this intimate, backstreet bar full of colourful characters and festooned with homely bric-a-brac. A stage is squeezed in for the occasional gig (around ¥1000), which could feature anything from owner Hosayou's rockabilly band (he plays double bass), to Balkan gypsy music. Daily 9pm–5am.

★**Kamiya** 神谷 1-1-1 Asakusa, Taitō-ku ☎03 3841 5400; Asakusa Station; map p.97. Established in 1880, this was Tokyo's first Western-style bar. It's famous for its Denki Bran ("electric brandy" – a mix of gin, wine, Curaçao and brandy), invented in 1883. It's a potent tipple, though they also make a "weaker" version at 15 percent alcohol. The ground floor is the liveliest and most informal; pay for your first round of food and drinks at the cash desk as you enter. Daily except Tues 11.30am–9.30pm.

BAYSIDE TOKYO

Jicoo ジコー ☎0120 049490, ⍵jicoofloatingbar.com; Hinode Station. This night-time persona of the futuristic ferry *Himiko* (see p.127) shuttles between Hinode, under the Rainbow Bridge, and Odaiba. To board costs ¥2500, drinks run from ¥700 and there's a DJ playing so you can take to the illuminated dancefloor and show off your best John Travolta moves. Thurs–Sat 8am–11pm.

AKASAKA AND ROPPONGI

A971 Tokyo Midtown, 9-7-3 Akasaka, Minato-ku ☎03 5413 3210; Roppongi Station; map pp.106–107. This relaxed café-bar and restaurant at the front of the Midtown complex, with mid-twentieth-century modernist

furnishings, has proved itself a popular hangout with the area's many expats. Mon–Thurs 10am–2am, Fri & Sat 10am–5am, Sun 10am–midnight.

Heartland ハートランド 1F Roppongi Hills West Walk, 6-10-1 Roppongi, Minato-ku ☎03 5772 7600; Roppongi Station; map pp.106–107. It's often standing-room only at this trendy but friendly bar in the northwest corner of Roppongi Hills. Sink one of their trademark green-bottled beers and watch arty videos on the panoramic plasma screen behind the bar. Daily 5pm–4am.

Hobgoblin ホップゴブリン Aoba Roppongi Building, 3-16-33 Roppongi, Minato-ku ☎03 3568 1280, ⍵hobgoblin.jp; Roppongi Station; map pp.106–107. British microbrewery Wychwood serves up its fine ales at this spacious bar where you'll be part of a very boozy, noisy crowd of *gaijin* at weekends and on nights when there are major sports matches on the big-screen TVs. A plus is the very comforting English pub-style food, including shepherd's pie (¥1200) and fish and chips (¥1500). Daily 5pm–late, Sat & Sun from noon.

Pink Cow ピンクカーウ B1 5-5-1 Roppongi, Minato-ku ☎03 6434 5773, ⍵thepinkcow.com; Roppongi Station; map pp.106–107. There's always something interesting going on – book readings, art classes, comedy improv nights – at this funky haven for local artists and writers, run by the convivial Tracey. It stocks a good range of imported wines and has tasty Tex-Mex-style food; mains start at ¥1180. Daily 5pm–late.

EBISU, MEGURO AND THE SOUTH

★**Buri** ぶり 1-14-1 Ebisu-Nishi, Shibuya-ku ☎03 3496 7744, ⍵buri-group.com; Ebisu Station; map pp.110–111. A great range of chilled "one-cup sake" (a sealed glass, the size of a small can, ready filled with sake that you just pull the top off; ¥750) is the speciality at this trendy *tachinomiya* that's one of the best in town. They serve a good range of *yakitori* and other tasty nibbles. Daily 3pm–midnight.

Enjoy House! エンジョイハウス 2F Crystal Square Building, 2-9-9 Ebisu-Nishi, Shibuya-ku ☎03 5489 1591; Ebisu Station; map pp.110–111. The unique look here consists of zebra print, low velour sofas, red lace curtains and tons of shiny disco balls. The master is likely to be wearing shorts and Jackie Onassis-style sunglasses. It gets busy at weekends, with a suitably young and attitude-free crowd. Daily noon–late.

★**Thunderbolt** サンダーボルト 2F 1-3-19 Kami-Meguro, Meguro-ku ☎03 6666 6773; Naka-Meguro Station; map pp.110–111. Night after night, a cast of occasionally oddball regulars are lined up drinking spirits (most ¥700) at this immensely characterful bar – it's one of those places that few people remember leaving. Daily 5pm–late.

1

HARAJUKU, AOYAMA AND SHIBUYA

Fujiya Honten 富士屋本店 2-3 Sakuragaoka-chō, Shibuya-ku ☎03 3461 2128; Shibuya Station; map p.114. No-frills, good-value standing bar with some fifty different wines on offer from as little as ¥1600 a bottle, and a dozen by the glass at ¥400. Daily noon–midnight.

★Goodbeer Faucets グッドビアフォーセツ 2F 1-29-1 Shoto, Shibuya-ku ☎03 3770 5544; Shibuya Station; map p.114. An excellent place for craft beer, selling over forty varieties on draught – some are made by the Goodbeer brewery, and others from across Japan and abroad. Large glasses of the good stuff run ¥700–1300, with ¥200 off in the 5–8pm happy hour. Daily 5pm–midnight, Fri until 3am.

★Harajuku Taproom 原宿タップルーム 2F 1-20-13 Jingūmae, Shibuya-ku ☎03 6438 0450, ⓦbairdbeer .com; Harajuku Station; map p.114. Tucked away just off teen-scene Takeshita-dori is this real ale nirvana serving beers from Baird Brewing Company in Numazu (¥1000); its interior feels like a country pub. Mon–Fri 5pm–midnight, Sat & Sun noon–midnight.

Hasegawa-Saketen はせがわ酒店 3F Omotesandō Hills, 4-12-10 Jingūmae Shibuya-ku ☎03 5785 0833, ⓦhasegawasaketen.com; Omotesandō Station; map p.114. The standing bar at this classy retail sake shop allows you to sample various rice wines from boutique breweries around the country before buying a bottle. Daily 11am–10pm.

★The Lockup ザロックアップ B1 33-1 Udagawachō, Shibuya-ku ☎03 5728 7731; Shibuya Station; map p.114. The house of horrors-style entrance is so dark it's a trip merely walking into this bar, the best of a small chain of prison-themed establishments. Make it through and you'll be handcuffed then led to a cell-like room where you can take your pick of weird cocktails: some arrive in test tubes; others have fake eyeballs inside. Periodically, the lights dim and staff try their best to terrify customers – brilliant fun, believe it or not. Daily 5pm–1am, Fri & Sat until 5am, Sun until midnight.

Stand S スタンドS 37-16 Udagawa chō, Shibuya-ku ☎03 5452 0277; Shibuya Station; map p.114. Going for the bar-meets-Swedish-sauna look in a big pine-clad way is this groovy *tachinomiya* with a DJ and curious drink options such as Mojito Beer (tastier than it sounds). Daily 5pm–midnight.

Three Coin Bar 3コインバー B1 Noa Shibuya Building, 36-2 Udagawa chō, Shibuya-ku ☎03 3463 3039; Shibuya Station; map p.114. No need to ask about the prices at this spacious, stylish basement bar – it's ¥315 for any drink or plate of food, making this a top choice if you're on a budget. Music is usually hip-hop and R&B, despite the soul vinyl covers dotting the place; they also bring in DJs most weekends. Daily 4pm–12.30am, later at weekends.

SHINJUKU AND THE WEST

Champion チャンピオン Golden Gai, off Shiki-no-michi; Shinjuku-Sanchōme Station; map pp.118–119. At the western entrance to the Golden Gai stretch, this is the largest bar in the area. There's no cover charge and all drinks are a bargain ¥500. The catch? You have to endure tone-deaf patrons crooning karaoke for ¥100 a song. Mon–Sat 6pm–6am.

Square スクエーア 2F 3rd Street, Golden Gai; Shinjuku-Sanchōme Station; map pp.118–119. Cute, squashed little upper-floor bar with cheery staff, cheery customers, decent drinks, and some dangerous-looking bras on the wall. Look out for the blue sign, which is, ironically, a circle. Cover charge ¥500. Mon–Sat 6pm–4am.

IKEBUKURO AND THE NORTH

Maccoli Bar マコリバー 1-5-24 Hyakunin-chō, Shinjuku-ku ☎03 6380 3487; Shin-Ōkubo Station; map pp.122–123. *Makgeolli*, incorrectly Romanized in this bar's name, is a milky-coloured Korean rice beer with a growing following in Japan – it tastes like drinking yoghurt with a mild alcoholic kick. At this friendly and stylish Koreatown bar, you can sample it straight or mixed with various fruits. Daily 6pm–late.

CLUBS

A few **clubs** seem to weather the vagaries of fashion, but generally the ever-eclectic Tokyo scene seems to be moving away from major events in big spaces to more intimate nights in smaller bars where a DJ may have a particular following. **Cover charges** are typically ¥2500–3000, including your first drink, though you'll generally pay around ¥500 less if you book in advance. Most clubs don't really get going until after 11pm, especially at weekends, and the majority stay open until around 4am.

Ageha アゲハ Studio Coast, 2-2-10 Shin-kiba, Kōtō-ku ☎03 5534 2525, ⓦageha.com; Shin-Kiba Station. Ultra-cool mega-club with an outdoor pool, body-trembling sound system and roster of high-profile events. It's out by Tokyo Bay, but there's a free shuttle bus here from Shibuya – check the website for details and make sure you turn up at least half an hour before you want to depart to get a ticket to board the bus. Men ¥3500, women ¥3000. Usually Fri & Sat only.

Air エーア B1 Hikawa Building, 2-11 Sarugaku-chō, Shibuya-ku ☎03 5784 3386, ⓦair-tokyo.com; Shibuya Station; map pp.110–111. South of Shibuya Station on the way to Daikanyama, this eclectic club has a great sound system and gets big name DJs. Enter through *Nomad* restaurant, itself a decent place to eat. Entry ¥2500 or more. Daily except Wed.

Club Asia クラブアシア 1-8 Maruyamachō, Shibuya-ku ☎03 5458 2551, ⓦclubasia.co.jp; Shibuya Station; map p.114. A mainstay of the clubbing scene, with the

PECHAKUCHA NIGHT

It started in 2003 as an idea to bring people to a new "creative art" basement venue called *SuperDeluxe* (W super-deluxe.com) in the then pre-Roppongi Art Triangle days, but in a few short years **PechaKucha Night** (W pechakucha.org) became a worldwide **phenomenon** – it has now spread to over 300 cities and counting. Co-created by Tokyo-based architects Astrid Klein and Mark Dytham (KDa), the presentation format – 20 images shown for 20 seconds each – keeps participants on their toes, often forcing funny ad-lib moments due to the high pace. More importantly it acts as a platform for these creators to share their ideas. PechaKucha ("chit-chat") has ended up being the perfect platform for Tokyo's **young, up-and-coming creators** who would never previously have had a place to share their works in front of a large audience. Similar forums – events that manage to bring together a good mix of Japanese and non-Japanese participants – are a feature of both *Café Pause* (W cafepause.jp) and the *Pink Cow* (see p.147); the original PechaKucha usually takes place at *SuperDeluxe* on the last Wednesday of each month.

emphasis on techno and trance nights, though they occasionally wander into other territories such as reggae and new wave. It's in the heart of the Dōgenzaka love hotel district, and a popular place for one-off gigs by visiting DJs. Entry usually ¥3000 plus a drink. Open Fri & Sat, and sometimes Sun & Thurs.

Gas Panic ガスパニック B1 21-7 Udagawachō, Shibuya-ku T 03 3462 9099, W gaspanic.co.jp; Shibuya Station; map p.114. For many a year, the various *Gas Panic* clubs have, between them, constituted Tokyo's meat markets, with this one now the biggie. Free entry, cheap drinks, and lots of youngsters (both Japanese and foreign) doing things their parents wouldn't be proud of. Free entry. Daily 6pm–late.

Microcosmos ミックロコスモス 2-23-12 Dōgenzaka, Shibuya-ku T 03 5784 5496, W microcosmos-tokyo .com; Shibuya Station; map p.114. A good example of the new breed of Tokyo club, this chic dance space has a relaxed vibe and tends to draw a sophisticated crowd. Music ranges across the spectrum from reggae and hip-hop to electro and techno. Usually ¥2500 with a drink. Open Fri, Sat & sometimes Sun.

Muse ミューズ B1 4-1-1 Nishi-Azabu, Minato-ku T 03 5467 1188, W muse-web.com; Roppongi Station; map p.106–107. A pick-up joint, but an imaginatively designed one, with lots of interesting little rooms to explore or canoodle in. The dancefloor at the back gets packed at weekends, when they mostly play r'n'b. Free entry weekdays, weekends ¥3000; women usually free. Closed Mon.

★**Unit** ユーニット Za-house Bldg, 1-34-17 Ebisu-Nishi, Shibuya-ku T 03 5459 8630, W unit-tokyo.com; Ebisu or Daikanyama stations; map pp.110–111. DJ events and gigs from an interesting mix of artists and bands at this cool three-floor club, café and lounge bar. Events most nights.

Womb ウーム 2-16 Maruyama chō, Shibuya-ku T 03 5459 0039, W womb.co.jp; Shibuya Station; map

p.114. Mega-club with a spacious dancefloor, enormous glitter ball and a pleasant chill-out space. Top DJs work the decks, but be warned that at big events it can get ridiculously crowded. Usually ¥3000 with a drink; discount before midnight. Events most nights.

GAY BARS AND CLUBS

With over 150 bars and clubs, **Shinjuku Nichōme** (新宿 二丁目) is the most densely packed area of gay and lesbian (see p.68) venues in Japan, but clubbing events are held around the city. Check websites for regular monthly standbys such as Shangri-la at *Ageha* (see opposite), Goldfinger (W goldfingerparty.com) and Diamond Cutter (W diamondcutter.jp), all of which will have a cover charge of around ¥3000.

★**Advocates Café** アドボケイツ カフェ 7th Tenka Building, 2-18-1 Shinjuku, Shinjuku-ku T 03 3358 3988, W advocates-cafe.com; Shinjuku-Sanchōme Station; map pp.118–119. It's a rare night in Nichōme that doesn't include drinks here. The bar itself is barely big enough for ten people, which is why scores of patrons hang out on the street corner outside, creating a block party atmosphere. Daily 6pm–4am, Sun to 1am.

★**Arty Farty** アーティファーティ 2F Dai 33 Kyutei Building, 2-11-7 Shinjuku, Shinjuku-ku T 03 5362 9720, W arty-farty.net; Shinjuku-Sanchōme Station; map pp.118–119. As the night draws on, this pumping bar with a small dancefloor gets packed with an up-for-fun crowd. Their annexe bar, within staggering distance, hits its stride later in the evening and draws a younger clientele. Daily 6pm–1am.

Campy! カンピー! 2-13-10 Shinjuku, Shinjuku-ku T 03 6273 2154; Shinjuku-Sanchōme Station; map pp.118–119. This highly colourful venue is perhaps the tiniest of the area's many minuscule gay bars, but what it lacks in size it makes up for in pizzazz – the drag queen staff sure help. One of the better local venues for straight folk. Daily 6pm–2am, Fri & Sat to 4am.

1

Goldfinger ゴールドフィンガー 2-12-11 Shinjuku, Shinjuku-ku ⓣ03 6383 4649; Shinjuku-Sanchōme Station; map pp.118–119. Fun, female-only bar which throws wild parties from time to time (see box, p.150). Daily 6pm–2am, Fri & Sat until 4am.

★**Keivi** ケイヴィ 4F Yoshino Bldg, 17-10 Sakuragaoka chō, Shibuya-ku ⓣ090 3462 9200, ⓦkeivi.com; map p.114. This friendly bar is worth a look if only to enjoy its extraordinary decor that includes deer antlers, fairy lights, Japanese dolls and tropical fish. There's a map on the wall (and on their website) detailing other gay and lesbian bars in the area. The small cover charge gets you a choice of snack to go with reasonably priced drinks. Daily 6pm–late.

Kinswomyn キンズウイメン 3F Dai-ichi Tenka Building, 2-15-10 Shinjuku, Shinjuku-ku ⓣ03 3354 8720; Shinjuku-Sanchōme Station; map pp.118–119. Relaxed, women-only bar where there's no cover charge, and drinks are priced reasonably at around ¥700. Daily 8pm–4am.

★**Paddy's Junction** パッディーズジャンクション 2-13-16, Shinjuku, Shinjuku-ku ⓣ03 3355 7833, ⓦpaddys-junction.com; Shinjuku-Sanchōme Station; map pp.118–119. With its foreign and English-speaking staff, this Irish-style pub is a great addition to the area. They've cheap food (including excellent fish and chips), lots of imported beers, and cocktails are just ¥300 during the 5–7pm happy hour. Daily 5pm–1am.

LIVE MUSIC

Pop and **rock** acts usually play in "**live houses**", many of which are little more than a pub with a small stage, although some clubs such as *SuperDeluxe* and *Unit* also have live music events. **Jazz** and **blues** are also incredibly popular in Tokyo, with scores of clubs across the city. There are several larger venues where top local and international acts do their thing, most notably the cavernous Tokyo Dome (see p.124), and the Nippon Budōkan (see p.160). Tickets for concerts can be bought through ticket agencies.

Billboard Live Tokyo ビルボードライブ東京 4F Tokyo Midtown 9-7-4 Akasaka, Minato-ku ⓣ03 3405 1133, ⓦbillboard-live.com; Roppongi Station; map pp.106–107. A relatively intimate space at which everyone on the three levels gets a great view of the stage. Mainstream pop, rock and lounge artists. Tickets usually from ¥5800. Events most nights.

Blue Note ブルーノート 6-3-16 Minami-Aoyama, Minato-ku ⓣ03 5485 0088, ⓦbluenote.co.jp; Omotesandō Station; map p.114. Tokyo's premier jazz venue, part of the international chain, attracts world-class performers. Entry for shows is ¥6000–10,000 (including one drink), depending on the acts. Shows Mon–Sat 7pm & 9pm.

BYG 2-19-14 Dōgenzaka, Shibuya-ku, ⓦwww.byg .co.jp; Shibuya Station; map p.114. Tiny rock venue which has been around since the late 1960s – the acts often play music of a similar vintage. Tickets ¥1500–3500. Usually a few events each week, 5.30pm–2am.

Club Quattro クラブクアットロ 5F Quattro Building, 32-13 Udagawa-chō, Shibuya-ku ⓣ03 3477 8750, ⓦclub-quattro.com; Shibuya Station; map p.114. Intimate rock music venue which tends to showcase up-and-coming bands and artists, though it also plays host to well-known local and international acts. Tickets ¥2000–4500. One or two events per week.

Crocodile クロコダイル 6-18-8 Jingūmae, Shibuya-ku ⓣ03 3499 5205; Meiji-jingūmae or Shibuya Stations; map p.114. You'll find everything from samba to blues and reggae at this long-running basement space on Meiji-dōri, between Harajuku and Shibuya. Tickets ¥3000–4000. Events most nights.

Cyber サイバー B1, 1-43-14 Higashi-Ikebukuro ⓣ03 3985 5844, ⓦikebukuro-cyber.com; Ikebukuro Station; map pp.122–123. Dark, throbbing rock dive among the soaplands and love hotels north of Ikebukuro Station. The bands are of variable quality, so keep those fingers crossed. Usually Sat only; gigs start as early as 4.30pm.

Red Shoes レッドシューズ B1F Chigau Aoyama Bldg, 6-7-14 Minami-Aoyama, Minato-ku ⓣ03 3486 1169, ⓦredshoes.jp; Roppongi Station; map pp.106–107. A little uphill from the Nishi-Azabu crossing towards Shibuya, this is where fledgling bands try out their stuff. Worth a look. Tickets free–¥3000. Events most nights.

Shibuya O-East 2-14-8 Dōgenzaka, Shibuya-ku ⓣ03 5458 4681, ⓦshibuya-o.com; Shibuya Station; map p.114. This complex has several venues, all hosting live music events, ranging from J-pop to hard rock. International bands also play here. Tickets from ¥2500. Events most nights.

Shinjuku Pit Inn 新宿ピットイン B1F Accord Shinjuku Building, 2-12-4 Shinjuku, Shinjuku-ku ☎03 3354 2024, ✆pit-inn.com; Shinjuku Station; map pp.118–119. Serious, long-standing jazz club which has been the launch platform for many top Japanese performers and which also attracts overseas acts. Shows 2.30–5pm, ¥1300; from 8pm, ¥3000.

ENTERTAINMENT AND THE ARTS

Tokyo has all the **entertainment** options you'd expect of a major city, plus a couple of local ones. Here you can sample all of Japan's major performing arts, from **theatre** to **contemporary dance** (see below). Grab any chance you have to see a concert of **traditional Japanese music** (see p.152).

Essentials Information about performances is available in the English-language press and from the TICs (see p.130). Tickets are available from theatres and ticket agencies (see p.161).

TRADITIONAL THEATRE

The easiest of Japan's traditional performance arts for foreigners to enjoy are **kabuki** and the puppet theatre of **bunraku**, which predates kabuki but whose plays share many of the same storylines. If you don't want to sit through a full performance, which can last up to four hours, note that single-act tickets are often available. With its highly stylized, painfully slow movements and archaic language, **nō**, the country's oldest form of theatre, isn't as appealing, though some find the rarefied style incredibly powerful.

Practicalities Take advantage of hiring recorded commentaries in English at the theatre to gain a better understanding of what's happening on stage. Subtitles displayed on a screen beside the performers (or, at the National Theatre, on the back of each seat) are also sometimes used.

Cerulean Tower Nō Theatre セルリアンタワー能楽堂 26-1 Sakuragaoka-chō, Shibuya-ku ☎03 3477 6412; Shibuya Station. In the basement of the luxury *Cerulean Tower* hotel, this theatre provides an elegant setting for both professional and amateur nō and *kyōgen* performances (tickets typically ¥3500 and up).

★**Kabukiza** 歌舞伎座 6-18-2 Ginza, Chūō-ku ☎03 3541 2600, ✆kabuki-bito.jp. 2013 saw the long-awaited reopening of Tokyo's oldest and largest kabuki theatre, and it's the best place to head if you're at all interested in catching a performance. Getting a ticket (¥4000–22,000), on the other hand, can be tricky; they usually become easier to buy after the fifteenth of each month. Single-act tickets (¥800–2000) are available on the door for those who don't want to commit to a whole performance.

National Nō Theatre 国立能楽堂 4-18-1 Sendagaya, Shibuya-ku ☎03 3230 3000, ✆www.ntj.jac.go.jp; Sendagaya Station. Hosts nō performances several times a month, with tickets starting at around ¥2500. Printed English explanations of the plot help make some sense of what's going on.

National Theatre 国立劇場 4-1 Hayabusachō, Chiyoda-ku ☎03 3230 3000, ✆www.ntj.jac.go.jp; Hanzōmon Station. In its two auditoria, Tokyo's National Theatre puts on a varied programme of traditional theatre and music, including kabuki, *bunraku*, court music and dance. English-language earphones and programmes are available. Tickets start at around ¥1500 for kabuki and ¥4500 for *bunraku*.

Shimbashi Enbujō 新橋演舞場 6-18-2 Ginza, Chūō-ku ☎03 3541 2600; Higashi-Ginza Station. This large theatre stages a range of traditional dance, music and theatre, including the "Super-kabuki" (kabuki with all the bells and whistles of modern musical theatre). Single-act tickets for regular kabuki performances range from ¥800 to ¥1500 depending on the length of the act.

THE ROBOT RESTAURANT

Opened in 2012, the *Robot Restaurant* (ロボットレストラン; 1-7-1 Kabukichō, Shinjuku-ku ☎03 3200 5500, ✆shinjuku-robot.com; Shinjuku Station; map pp.118–119) is Tokyo's newest and zaniest attraction, and provides a little trip back to the wild days before Japan's financial bubble burst. It all starts at the entrance foyer, where there's nary an inch of regular, boring space – everything glistens, shines, flashes or reflects. There's far more of the same heading down the stairs to the trippy, video-screen-lined hall where you'll be sat with other excited tourists and locals, and given a bentō set to scoff before the carnage commences. Though the website, and plenty of YouTube clips, will give you a great idea what to expect, the performances are far more fun if you have no idea what's coming – for now, suffice it to say that dozens of robots, scantily dressed girls, more LEDs than anyone could ever count, and a wall of roaring music are on the cards. At around ¥5000 per head (including a light meal), it's not cheap, but most find it worth every yen. Performances daily 7pm & 8.30pm, Mon–Sat also 10pm.

1

CONTEMPORARY AND INTERNATIONAL THEATRE

Camp as a row of tents, the most unique theatrical experience you can have in Tokyo is **Takarazuka** (see box, below), the all-singing, all-dancing, all-female revue which appears occasionally at the Takarazuka Theatre (see below). If your Japanese is up to it, there are plenty of modern Japanese dramas to enjoy: look out for productions by **chelfitsch** (see below), or anything by the director **Ninogawa Yukio** who's famous for his reinterpretations of **Shakespeare**. Overseas theatre companies often appear at the Tokyo Globe or Shinjuku's New National Theatre, though seats sell out months in advance for the bigger names.

Black Stripe Theater B1 Sangubashi Guesthouse, 4-50-8 Yoyogi, Shibuya-ku ☎080 4184 0848, ⓦblackstripetheater.com; Sangubashi Station. A relatively recent addition to the expat theatre scene, this company has staged plays by Harold Pinter and David Mamet. Tickets ¥3500 on the door, ¥3000 in advance.

chelfitsch ⓦchelfitsch.net. Founded by award-winning writer Toshiki Okada, this internationally acclaimed group put on excellent shows in Tokyo when they're not busy touring the globe. They can usually be relied on for one new performance each year, although the venues and prices vary.

The Globe Tokyo 東京グローブ座 3-1-2 Hyakunin-chō, Shinjuku ☎03 3366 4020; Shin-Ōkubo Station. A variety of works, including Shakespearean plays and Western-style operas, are performed in this modern-day replica of the famous Elizabethan stage in London. Tickets from ¥4500.

New National Theatre 新国立劇場 1-20 Honmachi, Shinjuku-ku ☎03 5352 9999, ⓦnntt.jac.go.jp; Hatsudai Station. Just behind Tokyo Opera City, the New National Theatre comprises three stages specially designed for Western performing arts, including opera, ballet, dance and drama.

PUK 2-12-3 Yoyogi, Shibuya-ku, ☎03 3370 5128; Shinjuku Station. This charming puppet theatre was founded in 1929 as La Pupa Klubo. It's home to a resident group of puppeteers, as well as visiting troupes, and puts on shows that both young and old can enjoy.

Setagaya Public Theatre 世田谷パブリックシアター 4-1-1 Tasihido, Setagaya-ku ☎03 5432 1526, ⓦsetagaya-pt.jp; Sangenjaya Station. One of Tokyo's most watchable contemporary theatre companies specializing in contemporary drama and dance. There are two auditoria: one seats 600 and the other 218.

Takarazuka Theatre 宝塚劇場 1-1-3 Yūrakuchō, Chūō-ku ☎03 5251 2001; Hibiya Station. Mostly stages musicals, punched out by a huge cast in fabulous costumes. The theatre also stages regular Takarazuka performances (see box below). Tickets start at ¥3500.

Za Kōenji 座高円寺 2-1-2 Kōenji-Kita, Suginami-ku ☎03 3223 7300, ⓦza-koenji.jp; Kōenji Station. Managed by the non-profit Creative Theater Network, this new venue – in a suitably dramatic building designed by leading architect Toyo Ito – presents a high-quality programme of drama, dance and music performances.

BUTŌ

The highly expressive avant-garde dance form of **butō** (or butoh), which originates from Japan, shouldn't be missed if you're interested in **modern dance**. It can be minimalist, introspective, and often violent or sexually explicit.

Azabu Die Pratze 麻布ディープラッツ 2F 1-26-6 Higashi-Azabu, Minato-ku ☎03 5545 1385; Akabanebashi Station. Small but highly important venue for butō, experimental dance and theatre, located in an office block near Tokyo Tower.

Dairakudakan Kochūten 大駱駝艦壺中天 B1 2-1-18 Kichijōji-Kitamachi, Musashinoshi, ☎0422 214982, ⓦdairakudakan.com; Kichijōji Station. The studio of legendary butō troupe Dairakudakan; sometimes there are joint productions here with visiting foreign dancers.

TAKARAZUKA

There's a long tradition of men performing female roles in Japanese theatre, acting out a male fantasy of how women are supposed to behave. It's not so strange, then, that actresses playing idealized men have struck such a chord with contemporary female audiences. Along with glitzy productions, this has been the successful formula of the all-female **Takarazuka Revue Company** (ⓦkageki.hankyu.co.jp/english/index.html), founded in 1914 in Takarazuka, a town 20km northwest of Osaka. Western-style dance revues and musicals are their speciality, but Takarazuka also act out classical Japanese plays and have developed shows from Western novels, including *Gone with the Wind* and *War and Peace*.

Thousands of young girls apply annually to join the troupe at the age of 16, and devote themselves to a punishing routine of classes that will enable them to embody the "modesty, fairness and grace" (the company's motto) expected of a Takarazuka member. They must also forsake boyfriends, but in return are guaranteed the slavish adoration of an almost exclusively female audience, who go particularly crazy for the male impersonators or *otoko-yaku*.

MAJOR TOKYO FESTIVALS

Whenever you visit Tokyo, the chances are there'll be a **festival** (*matsuri*) taking place somewhere in the city. The tourist information centres can provide comprehensive lists of events in and around Tokyo, or check in the English press for what's on. Below is a review of the city's biggest festivals. Note that dates may change, so be sure to double-check before setting out.

January 1: Ganjitsu (or Gantan) The first shrine visit of the year (*hatsu-mōde*) draws the crowds to Meiji-jingū, Hie-jinja, Kanda Myōjin and other city shrines. Performances of traditional dance and music take place at Yasukuni-jinja. National holiday.

January 6: Dezomeshiki At Tokyo Big Sight in Odaiba, firemen in Edo-period costume pull off dazzling stunts atop long bamboo ladders.

Second Monday in January: Momoteshiki Archery contest and other ancient rituals at Meiji-jingū to celebrate "Coming-of-Age Day". It's a good time to spot colourful kimono, here and at other shrines.

Febuary 3 or 4: Setsubun The last day of winter is celebrated with a bean-scattering ceremony to drive away evil. The liveliest festivities take place at Sensō-ji, Kanda Myōjin, Zōjō-ji and Hie-jinja.

Early April: Hanami Cherry-blossom-viewing parties get into their stride. The best displays are at Chidoriga-fuchi Park and nearby Yasukuni-jinja, Aoyama Cemetery, Ueno-kōen and Sumida-kōen.

Mid-May: Kanda Matsuri One of Tokyo's top three festivals, taking place in odd-numbered years at Kanda Myōjin, during which people in Heian-period costume escort eighty gilded *mikoshi* (portable shrines) through the streets.

Third weekend in May: Sanja Matsuri Tokyo's most rumbustious annual bash, when over one hundred *mikoshi* are jostled through the streets of Asakusa, accompanied by lion dancers, geisha and musicians.

Mid-June: Sannō Matsuri The last of the big three festivals (after Kanda and Sanja), this takes place in even-numbered years, focusing on colourful processions of *mikoshi* through Akasaka.

Early July: Yasukuni Matsuri The four-night summer festival at Tokyo's most controversial shrine is well worth attending for its jovial parades, *Obon* dances and festoons of lanterns.

Late July and August: Hanabi Taikai The summer skies explode with thousands of fireworks, harking back to traditional "river opening" ceremonies. The Sumida-gawa display is the most spectacular (view it from riverboats or Asakusa's Sumida-kōen on the last Sat in July), but those in Edogawa, Tamagawa, Arakawa and Harumi come close.

Mid-August: Fukagawa Matsuri Every three years Tomioka Hachiman-gū, a shrine in Fukagawa, east across the Sumida-gawa from central Tokyo, hosts the city's wettest festival, when spectators throw buckets of water over a hundred *mikoshi* being carried through the streets.

Mid-November: Tori-no-ichi Fairs selling *kumade*, bamboo rakes decorated with lucky charms, are held at shrines on "rooster days", according to the zodiacal calendar. The main fair is at Ōtori-jinja (Iriya Station; map pp.128–129).

November 15: Shichi-go-san Children aged 3, 5 and 7 don traditional garb to visit the shrines, particularly Meiji-jingū, Hie-jinja and Yasukuni-jinja.

Late November: Tokyo International Film Festival One of the world's top competitive film festivals (w tiff-jp.net), with a focus on Japanese and Asian releases. The main venues for the week-long event are the cinemas in Roppongi Hills and Shibuya's Bunkamura (map p.114), though screenings take place at halls and cinemas throughout the city.

December 17–19: Hagoita-ichi The build-up to New Year begins with a battledore fair outside Asakusa's Sensō-ji temple.

CLASSICAL MUSIC & OPERA

The city is well stocked with **Western classical music** venues, and there are usually one or two concerts every week, either by one of Tokyo's several resident symphony orchestras or by a visiting group, as well as occasional performances of **opera**. Concerts of **traditional Japanese music**, played on instruments such as the *shakuhachi* (flute), the *shamisen* (a kind of lute that is laid on the ground), and the *taiko* (drum), are much rarer; one place that has excellent *shamisen* performances is the restaurant *Waentei Kikko* (see p.136).

NHK Hall NHKホール 2-2-1 Jinnan, Shibuya-ku

t 03 3465 1751, w www.nhk-sc.or.jp/nhk_hall; Harajuku or Shibuya Stations. One of Tokyo's older auditoria for classical concerts, but still well thought of and home to the highly rated NHK Symphony Orchestra. It's next to the NHK Broadcasting Centre, south of Yoyogi-kōen. Tickets from ¥1500–2500, depending on the performance.

Suntory Hall Ark Hills サントリーホール 1-13-1 Akasaka, Minato-ku t 03 3505 1001, w www.suntory .co.jp/suntoryhall; Roppongi-Itchōme Station. Reputed to have the best acoustics in the city, this elegant concert hall has one of the world's largest pipe organs, sometimes

1

used for free lunchtime recitals; check the website for details of this and other events. Prices vary by performance.
Tokyo Bunka Kaikan 東京文化会館 5-45 Ueno, Taitô-ku ☎03 3828 2111, ⌨t-bunka.jp; Ueno Station. Tokyo's largest classical music venue, with a main hall that seats over 2300. It has a busy and varied schedule of performances and a marvellous interior dating back to the 1960s, while ticket prices tend to be cheap. Classical music buffs should enquire about joining their music library, which holds over 100,000 recordings, books and scores.
Tokyo International Forum 東京国際フォーラム 3-5-1 Marunouchi, Chiyoda-ku ☎03 5221 9000, ⌨www.t-i-forum.co.jp; Yūrakuchō Station. The Forum's four multipurpose halls (including one of the world's largest auditoria, with over five thousand seats) host an eclectic mix of performing arts, including classical music and opera.
Tokyo Opera City 東京オペラシティ 3-20-2 Nishi-Shinjuku, Shinjuku-ku ☎03 5353 9999, ⌨operacity.jp; Hatsudai Station. This stunningly designed concert hall, with a giant pipe organ, seats over 1600 and has excellent acoustics – though despite its name it hosts only music concerts, not full-blown opera. There's a more intimate recital hall too.

CINEMA
On **Cinema Day**, generally the first day of the month, all tickets cost ¥1000, as opposed to the regular price of around ¥1800, or ¥2500 for a reserved seat (*shitei-seki*). Women can also get discounted tickets (¥1000) on **Ladies Day**, usually Wednesday. Otherwise, you can buy slightly reduced tickets in advance from a **ticket agency** (see p.161). Note that the **last screening** of the day is generally around 7 or 8pm. **Listings** are published on Friday in *The Japan Times* and *Metropolis*, which also have maps locating all the major cinemas.
Cinemart シネマート 3-8-15 Roppongi, Minato-ku ☎03 5413 7711; Roppongi Station; map pp.106–107. In its Global Recognition Series this small art-house cinema screens Japanese movies that have gained kudos at overseas festivals (with English subtitles).
National Film Centre 東京国立近代美術館フィルムセンター 3-7-6 Kyōbashi, Chūō-ku ☎03 3272 8600, ⌨www.momat.go.jp; Kyōbashi Station. A treasure-trove for cinephiles, with a small gallery on the seventh floor for film-related exhibitions and two small cinemas screening retrospectives from their vast movie archive. Most are Japanese classics, though they occasionally dust off their collection of foreign movies.
Shin-Bungei-za 新文芸坐 3F Maruhan-Ikebukuro Building, 1-43-5 Higashi-Ikebukuro, Toshima-ku ☎03 3971 9422, ⌨shin-bungeiza.com; Ikebukuro Station. Amid the game parlours and sex venues ("soaplands") of Ikebukuro is this theatre specializing in classic reruns and art-house movies. All-night screenings on Saturdays.
Toho Cinemas Roppongi Hills TOHOシネマズ六本木ヒルズ Roppongi Hills, Roppongi, Minato-ku ☎03 5775 6090; Roppongi Station. Ultra-modern multiplex cinema with bookable seats (no more rushing to grab the best spot), late-night screenings and popular Japanese movies with English subtitles.
Uplink アップリンク 37-18 Udagawachō, Shibuya-ku ☎03 6825 5502; Shibuya Station. World cinema is a staple at this arts centre, which combines a couple of cinemas, with a gallery, live music, bar and various workshops.

SHOPPING

Cruising the boutiques and fashion malls while toting a couple of designer-label carrier bags is such a part of Tokyo life that it's hard not to get caught up in the general enthusiasm. There are shops to suit every taste and budget, from funky **fashion boutiques** and swanky **department stores** to some great **crafts shops** and wonderfully quirky **souvenir** and **novelty stores**. Antique and bargain hunters shouldn't miss out on a visit to one of the city's **flea markets**, which if nothing else can turn up some unusual curios.

Essentials In general, opening hours are from 10am or 11am to 7pm or 8pm. Most shops close one day a week, not always on Sunday, and smaller places often shut on public holidays. Credit cards are becoming more widely accepted but make sure you have plenty of cash. Further information can be found at ⌨tokyo-bazaar.com.

TOKYO'S WHOLESALE DISTRICTS
Tokyo's **wholesale districts** can be fun to poke around. Best known to visitors are the fish and fresh produce market **Tsukiji** (see p.101) and the "Kitchenware Town" **Kappabashi** (see p.98). Other ones to search out include the area around **Edo-dōri**, north of Asakusabashi Station, east of Akihabara Station (see p.90), which specializes in traditional Japanese dolls. Further north along Edo-dōri, the area called **Kuramae** is, "Toy Town", where shops sell fireworks, fancy goods and decorations, as well as cheap plastic toys. South of here along Edo-dōri you'll find **Bakurochō**, a textile district with shops selling cheap clothes.

ANIME AND MANGA

In Japan all types of cartoons, from comic strips to magazines, are known as manga, while animation is called anime. Manga are available just about everywhere, from train-station kiosks to bookstores – at the latter and in CD shops you'll also find anime DVDs. Akihabara, Ikebukuro and Nakano are the key areas for anime, manga and associated character goods.

Comic Tora-no-ana コミックとらのあな 4-3-1 Soto-Kanda, Chiyoda-ku ☎ 03 3526 5330; Akihabara Station; map p.91. Seven floors of manga and related products, including self-published works and secondhand comics on the top floor. There are several other branches across the city. Daily 10am–10pm.

Mandarake まんだらけ 5-52-15 Nakano, Nakano-ku ☎ 03 3228 0007, ⓦ mancarake.co.jp; Nakano Station; map p.114. If you're into character dolls and plastic figures (*figua*) based on anime and manga, this multiple outlet operation in the Broadway shopping centre is the place to head. They also have a wide range of secondhand manga as well as posters, cards and even costumes. There's another branch in Shibuya (map p.114). Daily noon–8pm.

Radio Kaikan ラジオ会館 1-15-16 Soto-Kanda, Taitō-ku; Akihabara Station; map p.91. Nirvana for otaku in this one-time electronics shopping complex that now caters to a rich and varied set of anime and manga tastes – everything from the lifelike dolls, figurines and model kits of Volks to the fantasy and sexually charged items of the rental gallery Treasure Market Place. Mon–Sat 10.30–8pm, Sun until 7.30pm.

ANTIQUE AND FLEA MARKETS

There's at least one flea market in Tokyo every weekend, though you'll need to arrive early for any bargains.

Antique Mall Ginza アンティークモール銀座 1-13-1 Ginza, Chūō-ku ⓦ antiques-jp.com; Ginza-Itchōme Station; map p.88. Upmarket collection of classy antiques spread across three floors, including a good selection of kimono, though few bargains. Daily except Wed 11am–7pm.

Nogi-jinja 乃木神社 8-11-27 Akasaka, Minato-ku; Nogizaka Station; map p.106–107. Around thirty vendors gather at this lively flea market offering the usual assortment of old kimono, bric-a-brac and the like. Second Sun of month, dawn to dusk.

★Ōedo Antique Market 大江戸骨董市 Tokyo International Forum, 3-5-1 Marunouchi, Chiyoda-ku ⓦ antique-market.jp; Yūrakuchō Station; map p.88. One of the largest regular flea markets in Tokyo, with some 250 vendors offering real antiques and interesting curios. Don't expect any bargains, though. First and third Sun of month 9am–4pm.

ARTS AND CRAFTS

Tokyo has a wealth of specialist arts and crafts shops with the largest concentration in and around Asakusa. All the following outlets are good places to hunt for souvenirs, including paper products, satin-smooth lacquerware and sumptuous textiles. Also check out the splendid gift shop at the **Japan Folk Crafts Museum** (see p.117) for folk craft items and the ones in the basement of the **National Art Center Tokyo** (see p.108) for great contemporary gift products.

Art & Design Store 3F Roppongi Hills Mori Tower, 6-10-1 Roppongi, Minato-ku ☎ 03 6406 6654; Roppongi Station; map pp.106–107. A wonderful store near the entrance to Roppongi Hills' City View. The selection is ever-changing, but often features products from some of Japan's most famous contemporary designers; look out for the polka-dot-splashed produce of Yayoi Kusama. There's also a small gallery space here. Daily 11am–9pm.

Asa-no-ha 麻の葉 1-5-24 Azabu-Jūban, Minato-ku ☎ 03 3405 0161; Azabu-Jūban Station; map pp.106–107. Small shop selling some wonderful handkerchiefs, fans and other implements. All designs feature, or at least reference, traditional Japanese styles and patterns. Daily 10.30am–7pm.

Bengara べんがら 1-35-6 Asakusa, Taitō-ku ☎ 03 3841 6613; Asakusa Station; map p.97. This tiny store is crammed with a wide variety of noren, the split curtain seen hanging outside every traditional shop or restaurant. Even if you don't own a shop or restaurant, there'll be somewhere suitable in your own home – the toilet door is a (surprisingly) popular choice. Daily 10am–6pm, closed third Sun of month.

★Beniya べにや民芸店 2-7-1 Minami-Aoyama, Minato-ku ☎ 03 5875 3261; Aoyama-Itchōme Station; map p.114. Stocks one of Tokyo's best ranges of folk crafts (*mingei*). They also stage craft exhibitions at which you may get to meet the artist. Daily except Thurs 10am–7pm.

Bunsendō 文扇堂 1-30-1 Asakusa, Taitō-ku ☎ 03 3841 0088; Asakusa Station; map p.97. Shops selling paper fans are ten-a-penny in Asakusa, but this is one of the higher-grade offerings. They have two stores here, almost side by side. Daily 10.30am–6pm.

Fujiya ふじ屋 2-2-15 Asakusa, Taitō-ku ☎ 03 3841 2283; Asakusa Station; map p.97. Hand-printed cotton towels (*tenugui*) designed by the Kawakami family; some end up becoming collectors' items, so choose carefully. Daily except Thurs 10am–6pm.

★Ginza Natsuno 夏野 6-7-4 Ginza, Chūō-ku ☎ 03 3569 0952; Ginza Station; map p.88; 4-2-17 Jingūmae, Shibuya-ku, ☎ 03 3403 6033. Stuffed to the rafters with an incredible collection of over 1000 types of chopstick, plus chopstick rests and rice bowls. Prices range from ¥200 up to ¥35,000 or more for a pair made from ivory. Mon–Sat 10am–8pm, Sun 10am–7pm.

1

Haibara はいばら 2-8-11 Nihombashi, Chūō-ku ☎03 3272 3801; Nihombashi Station; map p.88. This shop has been selling traditional *washi* paper – and everything made from it – since 1806. Unfortunately, they upped sticks from their gorgeous original location in 2012, moving down the road to this less appealing one, but their products are just as great. Mon–Fri 10am–6.30pm, Sat & Sun 10am–5pm.

★**Itō-ya** 伊東屋 2-7-15 Ginza, Chūō-ku ☎03 3561 8311; Shibuya Station; map p.88. This fabulous stationery store comprising 11 floors and two annexes (Itō-ya 2 & 3), is a treasure-trove full of packable souvenirs such as traditional *washi* paper, calligraphy brushes, inks and so on. There are several other branches around the city, including one in Ginza Station. Mon–Sat 10.30am–8pm, Sun until 7pm.

Jūsan-ya 十三や 2-12-21 Ueno, Taitō-ku ☎03 3831 3238; Ueno-Hirokōji Station; map p.93. Tiny shop across the road from Shinobazu Pond, where a craftsman sits making beautiful boxwood combs – just as successive generations have done since 1736. Mon–Sat 10am–6.30pm.

Kanesō かね惣 1-18-12 Asakusa, Taitō-ku ☎03 3844 1379; Asakusa Station; map p.97. A mind-boggling array of knives, scissors, shears and files, crafted by the Hirano family over five generations. Daily 11am–7pm.

★**Kyūkyodō** 鳩居堂 5-7-4 Ginza, Chūō-ku ☎03 3571 4429; Ginza Station; map p.88. Filled with the dusty smell of *sumi-e* ink, this venerable shop has been selling traditional paper, calligraphy brushes and inkstones since 1800. During Edo times, they provided incense to the emperor but the shop's history actually goes back even longer – it was first founded in Kyoto in 1663 and, amazingly, the same family still runs it. Daily 10am–7pm.

Kurodaya 黒田屋 1-2-5 Asakusa, Taitō-ku ☎03 3844 7511; Asakusa Station; map p.97. Kurodaya has been selling woodblock prints and items made of traditional *washi* paper since 1856. Tues–Sun 11am–7pm.

Musubi むす美 2-31-8 Jingūmae, Shibuya-ku ☎03 5414 5678; Meiji-jingūmae Station; map p.114. Pick up the beautifully printed fabric *furoshiki* here to use instead of wrapping paper – they're also great gifts in themselves. The origami design prints are particularly unusual. Note that there's no obvious sign on the shop – look for the dangling handbags on the ground level of a silver building. Daily except Wed 11am–7pm.

★**Oriental Bazaar** オリエンタルバザー 5-9-13 Jingūmae, Shibuya-ku ☎03 3400 3933, ⓦorientalbazaar.co.jp; Meiji-jingūmae Station; map p.114. Although it may seem like a tourist trap, this very popular, one-stop souvenir emporium, selling everything from secondhand kimono to origami paper and top-class antiques, offers great deals and an almost unbeatable

selection. Daily except Thurs 10am–7pm.

Takahisa 高久 1-21-7 Asakusa, Taitō-ku ☎03 3844 1257; Asakusa Station; map p.97. Shop selling row upon row of richly decorated *hagoita*: battledores which are traditionally used by young girls playing shuttlecock at New Year. You wouldn't want to be playing sport with these fancy, lacquered versions, but they make great souvenirs. Daily 10am–8pm.

Yamada Heiandō 山田平安堂 2F Hillside Terrace, 18-12 Sarugaku-chō, Shibuya-ku ☎03 3464 5541, ⓦheiando.com; Daikanyama Station; map p.110–111. Hunt down this store for lacquerware – both traditional and contemporary – found on tables no less distinguished than those of the imperial household and Japan's embassies. Mon–Sat 10.30am–7pm, Sun until 6.30pm.

Yonoya Kushiho よのや櫛舗 1-37-10 Asakusa, Taitō-ku ☎03 3844 1755; Asakusa Station; map p.97. Tokyo's finest hand-crafted boxwood combs and hair decorations; much of the wood used here is sourced from forest land south of Kagoshima, and it's reputed to be particularly suitable for hair. Daily except Wed 10.30am–6pm.

BOOKS AND MAGAZINES

Most big hotels have a shop stocking English-language books on Japan, as well as imported newspapers and magazines.

Aoyama Book Centre 青山本屋 Garden Floor 2BF Cosmos Aoyama, 5-53-67, Jingūmae, Shibuya-ku ☎03 5485 5511; Omotesandō Station; map p.114. Innovative bookshop with a fine collection of titles related to design, architecture and photography. Also carries lots of foreign magazines. There's also a branch in Roppongi (map pp.106–107). Daily 10am–10pm.

★**Good Day Books** 3F Big B Shoes Building, 2-4-2 Nishi-Gotanda, Shinagawa-ku ☎03 6303 9116, ⓦgooddaybooks.com; Gotanda Station; map pp.110–111. One of Tokyo's best selections of secondhand books. Their monthly author talks and book club are popular with expats – see the website for details. Mon–Sat 11am–8pm, Sun until 6pm.

Kinokuniya 紀伊國屋 Takashimaya Times Square, Annex Building, 5-24-2 Sendagaya, Shinjuku-ku ☎03 5361 3301; Shinjuku Station; map pp.118–119. The sixth floor of Kinokuniya's seven-storey outlet offers Tokyo's widest selection of foreign-language books and magazines. Daily 10am–8pm, closed one Wed each month.

★**Tsutaya** つたや 17-5 Sakuragachō, Shibuya-ku ☎03 3770 2525, ⓦtsite.jp; Daikanyama Station; map pp.110–111. This award-winning bookshop, filled with a young, hip crowd, is a wonderful new addition to the Daikanyama area. As well as the CDs and DVDs that the chain's regular stores provide, this one has a tremendous selection of English-language books, as well as a café and lounge bar. Daily 7am–2am.

CAMERAS AND ELECTRONIC GOODS

Akihabara boasts Tokyo's biggest concentration of stores selling **electronic goods**. Shinjuku is Tokyo's prime area for **cameras** and photographic equipment, though Ikebukuro also has a solid reputation for new and **secondhand** deals at reasonable prices. Compare prices – many shops are open to bargaining – and make sure there's the appropriate **voltage** switch (the Japanese power supply is 100V). It's also important to check that whatever you buy will be **compatible** with equipment you have at home.

BIC Camera ビックカメラ 1-11-1 Yūrakuchō, Chiyoda-ku ☏ 03 5221 1111; Yūrakuchō Station; map p.88. The main branch of BIC offers hard-to-beat prices for cameras and audio and electronic goods – practically any gizmo you want can be found here, plus (strangely enough) discounted wine and liquor. You'll find other branches scattered around Tokyo's main shopping centres, including several in Ikebukuro, Shinjuku and Shibuya. Daily 10am–10pm.

Laox ラオクス 1-2-9 Soto-Kanda, Chiyoda-ku ☏ 03 3255 9041; Akihabara Station; map p.91. One of the most prominent names in Akiba and probably the best place to start browsing: they have a well-established duty-free section with English-speaking staff, and nine stores where you can buy everything from pocket calculators to plasma-screen TVs. Daily 10am–8pm, Fri & Sat until 9pm.

DEPARTMENT STORES

Although they're not as popular as they once were, Tokyo's massive **department stores** are likely to have almost anything you're looking for. They're also more likely to have English-speaking staff and a duty-free service than smaller shops, though prices tend to be slightly above average. Seasonal sales can offer great bargains.

★**Isetan** 伊勢丹 3-14-1 Shinjuku, Shinjuku-ku ☏ 03 3352 1111; ⓦ www.isetan.co.jp; Shinjuku-Sanchōme Station; map pp.118–119. One of the city's best department stores, with an emphasis on well-designed local goods and a reputation for promoting up-and-coming fashion designers. Their annexe, housing men's clothing and accessories, is particularly chic. The daily opening ceremony, with all staff bowing as you walk through the store, is worth attending. Daily 10am–8pm.

Matsuzakaya 松坂屋 3-29-5 Ueno, Taitō-ku ☏ 03 3832 1111; ⓦ www.matsuzakaya.co.jp/ueno/; Ueno-Hirokōji Station; map p.93. This 300-year-old store is based in Ueno, where its main outlet barely shows its age thanks to an updated look. Daily 10am–7.30pm.

Mitsukoshi 三越 1-4-1 Nihombashi-Muromachi, Chūō-ku ☏ 03 3241 3311; Mitsukoshimae Station; map p.88. Tokyo's most prestigious and oldest department store is elegant, spacious and renowned for its high-quality merchandise. Designer boutiques and more contemporary fashions are concentrated in the southerly shin-kan ("new building"). Daily 10am–7pm.

Seibu 西武 1-28-1 Minami-Ikebukuro, Toshima-ku ☏ 03 3981 0111; Ikebukuro Station; map pp.122–123. Sprawling department store with a reputation for innovation, especially in its homeware store "Loft" and clothing and lifestyle offshoot "Parco". There's also a cluster of Seibu, Loft and "Parco" stores in Shibuya. Mon–Sat 10am–9pm, Sun 10am–8pm.

FASHION

The city's epicentre of clothing chic is Omotesandō, where dazzlingly designed **boutiques** for famed brands such as Chanel, Ralph Lauren and Louis Vuitton vie to outdo each other in extravagance, alongside top **Japanese labels** such as Issey Miyake and Comme des Garçons. Daikanyama, Naka-Meguro and Shimo-Kitazawa are also worth browsing around – the fashion shops in the last two areas are slightly **cheaper**. For shoes, ubiquitous ABC-Mart stores are usually your best bet.

★**Bapexclusive** 5-5-8 Minami-Aoyama, Minato-ku ☏ 03 3407 2145; ⓦ bape.com; Omotesandō Station; map p.114. A Bathing Ape, the streetwear brand of designer Nigo, has a string of boutiques all over Aoyama and Harajuku, of which this is the main showroom. One of their T-shirts will set you back at least ¥6000. Daily 11am–8pm.

Bedrock ベッドロック B1 Omotesandō Hills West Wing, 4-12-10 Jingūmae, Shibuya-ku ☏ 03 3423 6969; Omotesandō Station; map p.114. Enter the Forbidden Fruit juice café at street level and take the stairs down to this darkly glamorous shop that stocks hip Harajuku fashions. Daily 11am–8pm.

Comme des Garçons 5-2-1 Minami-Aoyama, Minato-ku ☏ 03 3406 3951; Omotesandō Station; map p.114. More like an art gallery than a clothes shop, this beautiful store is a suitable setting for the high fashion menswear and womenswear by renowned designer Rei Kawakubo. Daily 11am–8pm.

Fake Tokyo フェーク東京 18-4 Udagawa-chō, Shibuya-ku ☏ 03 5456 9892; ⓦ faketokyo.com; Shibuya Station; map p.114. Hidden away near the Loft mall, this two-level store is great for contemporary female fashion. Candy, on the ground level, caters to younger tastes, while Sister up above is a fair bit more elegant. Daily noon–2am.

Five Foxes' Store 3-26-6 Shinjuku, Shinjuku-ku ☏ 03 5367 5551; Shinjuku Station; map pp.118–119. Stylish showcase for Comme ça du Mode, a bright and affordable unisex clothing brand. Mon–Sat 11am–11pm, Sun until 8pm.

1

★**Hysterics** 5-5-3 Minami-Aoyama, Minato-ku ☎03 6419 3899, ⓦhystericglamour.jp; Omotesandō Station; map p.114. The premier outlet for Hysteric Glamour, a fun, retro-kitsch Americana label which is one of Japan's leading youth brands. Daily noon–8pm.

Issey Miyake 三宅一生 3-18-11 Minami-Aoyama, Minato-ku ☎03 3423 1407, ⓦisseymiyake.co.jp; Omotesandō Station; map p.114. One of the top names in world fashion, famous for his elegant, eminently wearable designs. This flagship store, a pink building with Art Deco touches, is suitably fancy. Daily 11am–8pm.

★**Kura Chika Yoshida** クラチカヨシダ 5-6-8 Jingūmae, Shibuya-ku ☎03 5464 1766, ⓦwww .yoshidakaban.com; Omotesandō Station; map p.114. Access the full range of bags, wallets and luggage at this shrine to the hip Japanese brand Porter. It's just off Omotesandō, behind Tokyo Union Church. Daily except Wed noon–8pm.

Laforet ラフォーレ 1-11-6 Jingūmae, Shibuya-ku ☎03 3475 0411, ⓦlaforet.ne.jp; Meiji-jingūmae Station; map p.114. This pioneering "fashion building" is packed with boutiques catering to the fickle tastes of Harajuku's teenage shopping mavens. Wander through and catch the zeitgeist. Daily 11am–8pm.

★**Okura** オクラ 20-11 Sarugaku-chō, Shibuya-ku ☎03 3461 8511; Daikanyama Station; map pp.110–111. Youthful boutique specializing in indigo-dyed traditional and contemporary Japanese fashions, from jeans and T-shirts to kimono and *tabi* socks. Look for a wooden-style building with white lanterns outside. Daily 11am–8pm.

Onitsuka Tiger おにつかタイガー Westwalk 4F Roppongi Hills, 6-10-1 Roppongi, Minato-ku ☎03 5772 2660, ⓦonitsukatiger.com; Roppongi Station; map pp.106–107. Selling sneakers as seen on the most fashionable feet, this Japanese brand started business back in 1949. Other branches across the city. Daily 11am–9pm.

Pink Dragon ピンクドラゴン 1-23-23 Shibuya, Shibuya-ku ☎03 3498 2577; Shibuya Station; map p.114. You can't miss this Art Deco building adorned with a giant golden egg. Inside there are 1950s-with-a-twist rock'n'roll threads for guys and gals. Daily 11am–8pm.

★**Sou Sou** 5-4-24 Minami-Aoyama, Minato-ku ☎03 3407 7877, ⓦsousou.co.jp; Omotesandō Station; map p.114. After the Japanese saying sō sō, meaning "I agree with you", this range of modern design shoes and clothes based on traditional forms, such as split toe *tabi* (socks), is eminently agreeable. Their plimsolls are an ideal match for jeans. There's also an outlet in Venus Fort (see p.114). Daily 11am–8pm.

★**Tsumori Chisato** 津森千里 4-21-25 Minami-Aoyama, Minato-ku ☎03 3423 5170; Omotesandō Station; map p.114. Girlish streetwear that captures the Harajuku look but with better tailoring, materials and attention to detail. Daily 11am–8pm.

KIMONO AND YUKATA

Japan's national costume, the kimono is still worn by both sexes for special occasions, such as weddings and festival visits to a shrine. Ready-made kimono can easily cost ¥100,000, while ¥1 million is not uncommon for the best made-to-measure garments. Secondhand or **antique kimono**, with prices as low as ¥1000, can be found at tourist shops, flea markets or in the kimono sales held by department stores, usually in spring and autumn; *Oriental Bazaar* (see p.156) also offers a good selection of pre-loved kimono. You'll pay more for the highly decorated **wedding kimono** (they make striking wall hangings), as well as for the most beautifully patterned *obi*, the broad, silk sash worn with a kimono. Light cotton **yukata** are popular with both sexes as dressing gowns; you'll find them in all department stores and many speciality stores, along with *happi* coats – the loose jackets that just cover the upper body. To complete the outfit, pick up a pair of traditional wooden sandals (*geta*).

Chicago シカゴ 6-31-21 Jingūmae, Shibuya-ku ☎03 3409 5017; Meiji-jingūmae Station; map p.114. There's a fine selection of kimono, *obi* and so on at this large thrift store, as well as rack upon rack of good used clothes. Daily 11am–8pm.

Do Justice 1-23-1 Kami-Meguro, Meguro-ku ☎03 5724 3223, ⓦwww.dojustice.jp; Naka-Meguro Station; map pp.110–111. Antique kimono and *obi* fabric is used to decorate jeans and create ties, shirts and other fashion items. It's not cheap but each one-off item is utterly original. Daily 11am–10pm.

Gallery Kawano ギャラリー　川野 102 Flats-Omotesandō, 4-4-9 Jingūmae, Shibuya-ku ☎03 3470 3305; Omotesandō Station; map p.114. Excellent selection of vintage kimono, *yukata* and *obi*, with swatches of gorgeous kimono fabric available too. Daily 11am–6pm.

Sakura 桜 2-41-8 Asakusa, Taitō-ku ☎03 5826 5622; Asakusa Station; map p.97. Not your regular kimono shop – this tiny store sells Gothic-style clothing made with patches of old kimono fabric. Their pantaloons, which morph from skirt to trousers by way of hidden buttons, are fantastic. Daily 12.30–9.30pm.

TOYS, GAMES AND NOVELTIES

The land that gave the world Super Mario Brothers, the Tamagotchi and Hello Kitty is forever throwing up new must-have toys, games and novelties. Tokyo's top toy and novelty stores are prime hunting grounds for the **next big craze** before it hits the world market. For more **traditional playthings**, poke around the craft stalls of Asakusa's Nakamise-dōri. Also keep an eye out for the ubiquitous "¥100 Shops" (everything at ¥105, including tax), which can yield a crop of **bargain souvenirs**.

Don Quijote ドンキホーテ 1-16-5 Kabukichō, Shinjuku-ku ☎03 5291 9211, ⓦdonki.com; Shinjuku Station; map pp.106–107. Fancy some sushi-print socks? A

mind-boggling array of stuff is piled high and sold cheap here – everything from liquor to sex toys, as well as gadgets galore. A national institution, it's worth visiting just for the gawp factor. Several branches around the city. Daily 24hr.
Kiddyland キッディランド 6-1-9 Jingūmae, Shibuya-ku ☏ 03 3409 3431, ⓦ www.kiddyland.co.jp; Meiji-jingūmae Station; map p.114. Flagship store boasting six full floors of toys, stationery, sweets and other

souvenirs. Daily 10am–8pm, closed every third Tues.
Village Vanguard ヴィレジヴァンガード B1F 3-14 Kanda-Ogawamachi, Chiyoda-ku ☏ 03 5281 5535; Jimbōchō or Ogawamachi Stations; map p.91. This "exciting bookstore" stocks an amazing hotchpotch of toys and novelties, from inflatable bananas to Batman accessories – and a few fun books and CDs. You'll find quite a few branches around the city. Daily 10am–11pm.

SPORTS AND ACTIVITIES

For tickets to a tournament at the **National Sumo Stadium** (see p.93), go to a ticket agency (see p.161) or queue up early – before 8am – outside the stadium box office for one of the **unreserved tickets** sold on the day (¥2100); note that tickets are particularly hard to come by on the first and last days. Dates of tournaments, as well as other useful information, are posted on the **Nihon Sumō Kyōkai** website (ⓦ sumo.or.jp).

Baseball Tokyo's big baseball teams are the Yomiuri Giants and the Yakult Swallows, with the former playing at Tokyo Dome (1-3 Koraku, Bunkyō-ku; ☏ 03 5800 9999, ⓦ tokyo -dome.co.jp/e/dome) near Suidōbashi Station, and the Swallows based at Jingū Stadium (13 Kasumigaoka, Shinjuku-ku ☏ 03 3404 8999) near Gaienmae Station. Tickets start from around ¥1500.
Football You can watch FC Tokyo (ⓦ fctokyo.co.jp) or Tokyo Verdy 1969 (ⓦ verdy.co.jp) play at the Ajinomoto Stadium (376-3 Nishimachi, Chōfu; ☏ 0424 400555, ⓦ ajinomotostadium.com), near Tobitakyū Station on the Keiō Line from Shinjuku.

MARTIAL ARTS

From judo and karate to aikido and kendo (see p.58),

Tokyo is the best place in Japan to sate any martial arts cravings you may have. The TICs (see p.130) can provide a list of *dōjō* that allow visitors to watch practice sessions for free.

All Japan Kendo Federation 全日本剣道連盟 Nippon Budōkan, 2-3 Kitanomaru-kōen, Chiyoda-ku ☏ 03 3211 5804; Kudanshita Station. Nippon Budōkan (see p.160) is the venue for the All-Japan Championships each autumn, and the children's kendo competition in the summer.
International Aikido Federation 国際合気道連盟 17-18 Wakamatsuchō, Shinjuku-ku ☏ 03 3203 9236, ⓦ aikido-international.org; Wakamatsu-Kawada Station. You can learn more about the sport by heading here – if you like what you see and are in Tokyo for a while, it's quite possible to participate in their classes.

PUBLIC BATHS AND ONSEN

Until a few decades ago life in Tokyo's residential neighbourhoods focused round the **sentō**, the public bath. A surprising number of *sentō* survive, many fed by natural onsen waters. Then there are the larger hot-spring resorts – good fun, though not a patch on the smaller onsen facilities found elsewhere in the city. Wherever you head, note that it's hugely important to observe local bathing etiquette (see p.61).

Asakusa Kannon Onsen 浅草観音温泉 2-7-26 Asakusa, Taitō-ku; Asakusa Station; map p.97. Dating back to 1957, this large, ivy-covered bathhouse has segregated facilities and a winning location right next to Sensō-ji. ¥700. Daily except Thurs 6.30am–6pm.
Jakotsu-yu 蛇骨湯 1-11-11 Asakusa, Taitō-ku; Asakusa Station; map p.97. Located down a back alley just south of Rox department store. "black", mineral-rich hot-spring water is the thing here. One bath is designed to give you a mild but stimulating electric shock and it also offers small open-air bath (*rotemburo*). ¥450. Daily except Tues 1pm–midnight.
Ōedo Onsen Monogatari 大江戸温泉物語 2-6-3 Aomi, Kōtō-ku; free shuttle buses from Shinagawa

and Tokyo Stations. More of a theme park than a bathhouse, this giant onsen goes in for nostalgic kitsch in a big way. Extra fees are charged for massages, hot sand and stone baths and a separate footbath in which tiny fish nibble the dead skin from your feet – more pleasant than it sounds. Mon–Fri ¥2000, or ¥1500 after 6pm, Sat/Sun ¥2200/1700. Daily 11am–9pm.
Spa LaQua 6F 1-1-1 Kasuga, Bunkyō-ku; Suidōbashi or Korakuen Stations; map pp.122–123. Spread over five floors, this is by far the most sophisticated of Tokyo's bathing complexes, and is fed by onsen water pumped from 1700m underground. Access to the Healing Baden set of special therapeutic saunas costs ¥525 extra. ¥2565, Sat & Sun ¥2880, ¥1890 surcharge 1am–6am. Daily 11am–9am.

1

Japan Karate Association 日本空手協会 2-23-15 Koraku, Bunkyō-ku ☎03 5800 3091, ⓦjka.or.jp; Iidabashi or Kōrakuen Stations; map pp.122–123. Home of the world's largest karate association teaching the Shokotan tradition. You can apply to train here, but it's best to call or email first.

Kōdōkan 講道館 1-16-30 Kasuga, Bunkyō-ku ☎03 3818 4172, ⓦkodokan.org; Kasuga or Kōrakuen Stations; map pp.122–123. This *dōjō* has a spectators' gallery open to visitors free of charge, with classes held most evenings. There's also a hostel here where you can stay if you have an introduction from an authorized judo body or an approved Japanese sponsor. Classes Mon–Fri 5–8pm, Sat 5–7.30pm.

Nippon Budōkan 日本武道館 2-3 Kitanomaru-kōen, Chiyoda-ku ☎03 3216 5143, ⓦnipponbudokan.or.jp; Kudanshita Station; map p.84. Around fifty free martial-arts exhibition matches are held annually at this large, octagonal arena, an important centre for all martial arts, as well as judo.

DIRECTORY

Banks and exchange As with the rest of Japan, bigger branches of Tokyo-Mitsubishi UFJ (ⓦbk.mufg.jp) and SMBC (Sumitomo Mitsubishi Banking Corporation; ⓦsmbcgroup.com) are your best bets for changing cash or travellers' cheques. The only ATMs accepting foreign cards (see p.72) are in post offices, 7-Eleven stores and Citibank (ⓦcitibank.co.jp) machines.

Embassies Australia, 2-1-14 Mita, Minato-ku (☎03 5232 4111, ⓦaustralia.or.jp); Canada, 7-3-38 Akasaka, Minato-ku (☎03 5412 6200, ⓦcanadainternational .gc.ca); China, 3-4-33 Moto-Azabu, Minato-ku (☎03 3403 3380, ⓦwww.china-embassy.or.jp); Ireland, 2-10-7 Kōjimachi, Chiyoda-ku (☎03 3263 0695, ⓦirishembassy. jp); New Zealand, 20-40 Kamiyamachō, Shibuya-ku (☎03 3467 2271, ⓦnzembassy.com/japan); Russian Federation, 2-1-1 Azabudai, Minato-ku (☎03 3583 4445, ⓦrusconsul .jp); South Africa, 4F 1-4 Kōjimachi, Chiyoda-ku (☎03 3265 3366, ⓦsajapan.org); South Korea, 1-2-5 Minami-Azabu, Minato-ku (☎03 3452 7611); UK, 1 Ichibanchō, Chiyoda-ku (☎03 5211 1100, ⓦgov.uk); US, 1-10-5 Akasaka, Minato-ku (☎03 3224 5000, ⓦjapan.usembassy.gov).

Emergencies The Tokyo Metropolitan Police has an English-language hotline on ☎03 3501 0110 (Mon–Fri 8.30am–5.15pm). Japan Helpline (☎0570 000911, ⓦjhelp.com/en/jhlp.html) provides 24hr advice in English. Tokyo English Life Line (☎03 5774 0992, ⓦteljp.com) provides telephone counselling (daily 9am–11pm). Numbers for the emergency services are listed in Basics (see p.66).

Hospitals and clinics To find an English-speaking doctor and the hospital or clinic best suited to your needs, phone the Tokyo Medical Information Service (Mon–Fri 9am–8pm; ☎03 5285 8181, ⓦhimawari.metro.tokyo .jp); they can also provide emergency medical translation services over the phone. Two major hospitals with English-speaking doctors are St Luke's International Hospital at 9-1 Akashichō, Chūō-ku (☎03 3541 5151, ⓦluke.or.jp) and Tokyo Adventist Hospital at 3-17-3 Amanuma, Suginami-ku (☎03 3392 6151, ⓦtokyoeisei .com); their reception desks are open Monday to Friday 8.30–11am for non-emergency cases. Among several private clinics with English-speaking staff, try Tokyo Medical and Surgical Clinic at 32 Shiba-kōen Building, 3-4-30 Shiba-kōen, Minato-ku (by appointment only Mon–Fri 8.30am–5.30pm, Sat 8.30am–noon; ☎03 3436 3028, ⓦtmsc.jp).

Immigration To renew visas, apply to the Tokyo Regional Immigration Bureau at 5-5-30 Konan, Minato-ku (Mon–Fri 9am–noon & 1–4pm; ☎03 5796 7112, ⓦwww.immi -moj.go.jp). To reach it, take the Konan exit from Shinagawa Station and then bus #99 from bus stop 8. Go early in the day since the process takes forever.

Internet Internet access can be found across Tokyo, often as part of 24hr computer game and manga cafés. Connection charges are around ¥200–400 per hour. There's also internet access at branches of Kinko's throughout Tokyo; call their free number ☎0120 001966 or check ⓦwww.kinkos.co.jp to find the one nearest you. Most hotels offer broadband access (via cable, wi-fi or both) in every room, often for free or for a daily fee (typically ¥1000). Others may provide at least one terminal for guests travelling without their own computer, generally for free, though a nominal rate may apply at budget hotels and hostels. Many of Tokyo's cafés also have wi-fi access, though it's not always free.

Left luggage Most hotels will keep luggage for a few days. Also, the baggage room (daily 8am–8pm) at Tokyo Station takes bags for up to 15 days at a daily rate of ¥410 for the first five days and ¥820 per day thereafter. Note that coin-operated lockers (¥300–800 depending on the size) can only be used for a maximum of three days.

Lost property If you've lost something, try the local police box (*kōban*). Alternatively, ask your hotel to help call the following offices to reclaim lost property: taxis ☎03 3648 0300; JR ☎03 3231 1880; Tokyo Metro ☎03 3834 5577; Toei bus and subway ☎03 3812 2011. If all else fails, contact the Metropolitan Police Lost and Found Office on ☎03 3501 0110.

Pharmacies The American Pharmacy in the Marunouchi Building at 2-4-1 Marunouchi, Chiyoda-ku (Mon–Fri 9am–9pm, Sat 10am–9pm, Sun 10am–8pm; ☎03 5220 7716) has English-speaking pharmacists and a good range of drugs and general medical supplies. Alternatively, try

1

the National Azabu Pharmacy (☎ 03 3442 3495), above the National Azabu supermarket (nearest subway Station Hiro-o). Major hotels usually stock a limited array of common medicines.

Post offices Tokyo's Central Post Office is on the west side of Tokyo Station. Major post offices that are open daily 24 hours can be found in Shinjuku and Shibuya among other city areas.

Taxis Major taxi firms include Hinomaru Limousine (☎ 03 3212 0505, ⓦ hinomaru.co.jp); and Nippon Kōtsū (☎ 03 3799 9220, ⓦ www.nihon-kotsu.co.jp/en).

Ticket agencies To buy tickets for theatre performances, concerts and sporting events, use one of the major advance ticket agencies: Ticket Pia (ⓦ t.pia.co.jp), branches of which can be found in all main city areas; Lawson (ⓦ l-tike.com), which has thousands of convenience stores across the city; or CN Playguide (ⓦ cnplayguide.com). Major events sell out quickly; don't expect to be able to buy tickets at the venue door.

Around Tokyo

YŌMEI-MON, TŌSHŌ-GŪ SHRINE

Around Tokyo

Tokyo has more than enough sights to keep you busy, but it doesn't take long to get to some great places from the capital, and it's well worth the effort. The single best reason for venturing out is Nikkō, around 130km to the north, famed for its World Heritage-listed, mountain-based shrine complex. West of Tokyo there's the scenic Fuji Fives Lakes area, from where you'll be able to tackle Japan's highest and most majestic peak, or simply relax in the beautiful countryside; and Hakone, a mix of sulphur-seeping moonscapes, thrilling cable-car rides and hot springs.

2

The temple complex of **Naritasan Shinshō-ji**, with its lovely pagoda, extensive gardens, woods and ornamental ponds, is the highlight of the pilgrim town of **Narita**, some 60km northeast of Tokyo. Around 40km north of Tokyo, meanwhile, is **Kawagoe**, a great place to wander through nostalgic nineteenth-century streetscapes, poke around ancient temples and shrines, and indulge in some serious souvenir shopping.

Sacred **Mount Takao**, just an hour west of the capital, provides a more verdant escape for the casual walker and is the starting point for serious hikes northwest to the **Chichibu-Tama National Park**. Further west lie the inviting landscapes of the **Fuji-Hakone-Izu National Park**, particularly around **Hakone** and south through **Izu Hantō**, which warrant a couple of days' exploration. Off the coast here, **Ōshima** pokes its smouldering head out of the ocean, its laidback way of life providing a beguiling excursion for those on a more leisurely schedule.

Closer to Tokyo, **Kamakura** is one of Japan's major historical sights, home to several imposing Zen temples and the country's second-largest bronze Buddha, the magnificent **Daibutsu**. There are also hiking trails through the surrounding hills, and an enjoyable train ride further along the coast to the sacred island of **Enoshima**. Just north of Kamakura you're back into the urban sprawl where Tokyo merges with **Yokohama**, Japan's second-largest and most cosmopolitan city.

Nikkō and around

日光

"**NIKKŌ** is Nippon", goes the town's slogan. It's only half-correct, though: visitors to Japan come expecting a mix of the ancient and the modern, but this town, 128km north of the capital, is up there with the most traditional in the country. It certainly lives up to its billing better than Kyoto, the vaunted dynastic capital way out west.

Most come here to see the World Heritage-listed **Tōshō-gū** shrine complex, which sits amid mountains crisscrossed by the outstanding hiking trails of **Nikkō National Park**. It's

OWAKUDANI, HAKONE

Highlights

① Nikkō The dazzling shrine Tōshō-gū is the star turn of this cosy mountain town, and is surrounded by a beautiful national park and lakes. **See p.164**

② Kawagoe Discover a little slice of old Edo, with the temples, shrines and *kura-lined* streets of this historic town. **See p.175**

③ Chinatown, Yokohama Yokohama's Chinatown – the largest in Japan – is a blast of bright colours, pungent smells and frenetic commercial life, all focused around the lively Kantei-byō shrine. **See p.179**

④ Kamakura Japan's ancient seaside capital offers woodland walks between peaceful temples and bustling shrines, not to mention a giant bronze Buddha with a secretive smile. **See p.185**

⑤ Mount Fuji You don't need to climb Fuji to admire its snowcapped form, but reaching the summit is a rewarding, once-in-a-lifetime challenge. **See p.197**

⑥ Hakone This premier onsen resort has traditional ryokan, a funicular and ropeway ride, plus a lovely lake you can sail across in a seventeenth-century-style galleon. **See p.199**

HIGHLIGHTS ARE MARKED ON THE MAP ON P.166

NIIGATA

FUKUSHIMA

NIKKŌ
NATIONAL PARK

Yumoto **1** TOCHIGI
Ryuzu Falls **Kegon**
Falls Nikkō
Chūzenji-ko Chūzenji Imaichi

Utsunomiya

GUNMA

Asama-yama
(2568m)

NAGANO SHINKANSEN Maebashi Mashiko

Karuizawa Takasaki Mito

JŌETSU SHINKANSEN

Shimodate

NAGANO Oyama

IBARAKI

KASHIMA
NADA
SEA

Chichibu SAITAMA

Kasumiga-ura
Lake

CHICHIBU-TAMA
NATIONAL PARK

Kawagoe **2** Omiya

YAMANASHI

Mitake **Ghibli** Narita

Museum Narita
Airport

Kōfu *Mt Takao* Mitaka TŌKYŌ

HIGASHI KANTŌ EXPRESSWAY

TOKYO-TO **Disneyland**

Ōtsuki *Haneda*
Airport

Kawaguchi-
ko
Shōji-ko KANAGAWA Kawasaki Ichihara

Sai-ko Fuji-Yoshida **3**

Motosu-ko *Yamanaka-ko* Yokohama *Tōkyō-*
wan

5 *Mt Fuji* HAKONE Kisarazu

Gotemba Kamakura

TŌMEI EXPRESSWAY *Enoshima* **4**

FUJI-HAKONE-IZU **6** Odawara Yokosuka
NATIONAL PARK Hakone- CHIBA
Yumoto

Fuji *Ashino-ko* Miura *Sagami-* Ōhara
wan

SHIZUOKA Atami

Numazu Katsuura

Shūzen-ji Itō Kamogawa

Izu-hantō

Shizuoka *Ōshima*

Suruga-wan Motomachi Tateyama

Shimoda Habu

Irō-zaki

To-shima *PACIFIC OCEAN*

Nii-jima

N

Shikine-jima

Kōzu-shima **HIGHLIGHTS**

Izu Shotō Islands **1** Nikkō
Miyake-jima **2** Kawagoe
3 Chinatown, Yokohama
0 50 **4** Kamakura
kilometres **5** Mount Fuji

AROUND TOKYO *Mikura-jima* **6** Hakone

also worth investigating the far less crowded **Nikkō Tōshō-gū Museum of Art**, and the **Nikkō Tamozawa Imperial Villa Memorial Park**, before crossing the Daiya-gawa to explore the dramatically named **Ganman-ga-fuchi abyss**, which is in fact a tranquil riverside walk. The most beautiful parts of the national park are around the lake, **Chūzenji-ko**, some 17km west of Nikkō, and the quieter resort of **Yumoto**, higher in the mountains.

With a very early start it's possible to see both Tōshō-gū and Chūzenji-ko in a long day-trip from Tokyo, but to get the most out of the journey it's best to stay **overnight**; cramming both places into one day during the peak summer and autumn seasons is impossible.

Brief history

Although Nikkō has been a holy place in both the Buddhist and Shintō religions for over a thousand years, its fortunes only took off with the death of **Tokugawa Ieyasu** in 1616. In his will, the shogun requested that a shrine be built here in his honour. However, the complex, completed in 1617, was deemed not nearly impressive enough by Ieyasu's grandson, **Tokugawa Iemitsu**, who ordered work to begin on the elaborate decorative mausoleum seen today.

Iemitsu's dazzling vision had an underlying purpose. The shogun wanted to stop rival lords amassing money of their own, so he ordered the *daimyō* to supply the materials for the shrine, and to pay the thousands of craftsmen. The mausoleum, Tōshō-gū, was completed in 1634 and the jury has been out on its over-the-top design ever since. Whatever you make of it, Tōshō-gū – along with the slightly more restrained Taiyūin-byō mausoleum of Iemitsu – is entirely successful at conveying the immense power and wealth of the Tokugawa dynasty.

Despite its popularity as a tourist destination today, barely a century ago Nikkō, in the wake of the Meiji Restoration, was running to seed. It was foreign diplomats and business people who began to favour it as a highland retreat from the heat of the Tokyo summer in the 1870s.

Shin-kyō

神橋 • Off Nihon Romantic Highway • Daily: April–Sept 8am–5pm; Oct to mid-Nov 8am–4pm; mid-Nov to March 9am–4pm • ¥500

At the top of Nikkō's main street is the red-lacquered **Shin-kyō**, a bridge that is one of the town's most famous landmarks. Legend has it that when the Buddhist priest Shōdō Shōnin visited Nikkō in the eighth century, he was helped across the Daiya-gawa at this very spot by the timely appearance of two snakes, which formed a bridge and then vanished. The original arched wooden structure first went up in 1636, but has been reconstructed many times since, most recently in 2005. Unless you must have a close-up shot of the bridge, there's no need to pay the entrance fee, as the structure is clearly visible from the road.

Rinnō-ji

輪王寺 • Daily: April–Oct 8am–5pm; Nov–March 8am–4pm • ¥400; ¥900 including Taiyūin-byō (see p.169); Treasure House ¥300

North of Shin-kyō, an uphill pedestrian path works through gorgeous woodland; follow it up and you'll soon emerge in front of the main compound of **Rinnō-ji**, a Tendai Buddhist temple founded in 766 by Shōdō Shōnin, whose statue stands on a rock at the entrance. The large, red-painted hall, **Sanbutsu-dō**, houses three giant gilded statues: the thousand-handed Kannon, the Amida Buddha and the fearsome horse-headed Kannon. It's worth the entry fee to view these awe-inspiring figures from directly beneath their lotus-flower perches. Note that this hall will remain under protective housing until 2020, as part of a mammoth restoration programme.

Rinnō-ji's **Treasure House** (宝物殿, Hōmotsuden), opposite the Sanbutsu-dō, has some interesting items on display, but its nicest feature is the attached Shōyō-en, an elegant garden with a strolling route around a small pond.

2

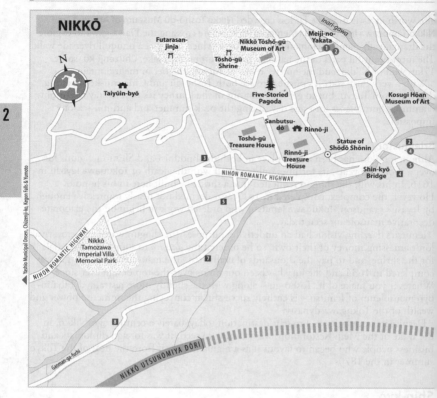

Yashio Municipal Onsen, Chūzenji-ko, Kegon Falls & Yumoto

Tōshō-gū

東照宮 • Daily: April–Oct 8am–5pm; Nov–March 8am–4pm • ¥1300

Broad, tree-lined Omotesandō leads up to the main entrance to **Tōshō-gū**, just to the west of Rinnō-ji. You'll pass under a giant stone *torii* (one of the few remaining features of the original 1617 shrine), while on the left is an impressive red and green five-storey pagoda, an 1819 reconstruction of a 1650 original, which burned down. Ahead is the Omote-mon gate, the entrance to the main shrine precincts.

Once inside, turn left to reach the **Three Sacred Storehouses** (*Sanjinko*) on the right and the **Sacred Stables** (*Shinkyūsha*) on the left, where you'll spot Tōshō-gū's most famous painted woodcarvings – the "hear no evil, see no evil, speak no evil" **monkeys**, which represent the three major principles of Tendai Buddhism. The route leads to the steps up to the dazzling **Yōmei-mon** (Sun Blaze Gate), with its wildly ornate carvings, gilt and intricate decoration. A belfry and drum tower stand alone in front of the gate. Behind the drum tower is the **Honji-dō**. This small hall is part of Rinnō-ji temple and contains a ceiling painting of a "roaring dragon"; a priest will demonstrate how to make the dragon roar by standing beneath its head and clapping to create an echo.

There's also a less impressive **sleeping cat** (*nemuri neko*) carving beyond the Yōmei-mon; you'd easily miss this minute animal, just above the Sakashita-mon to the right of the inner precinct, were it not for the gawping crowd. Two hundred stone steps lead uphill from the gate to the surprisingly unostentatious **tomb of Ieyasu**, which is set amid a glade of pines, and about the only corner of the shrine where tourists are generally absent.

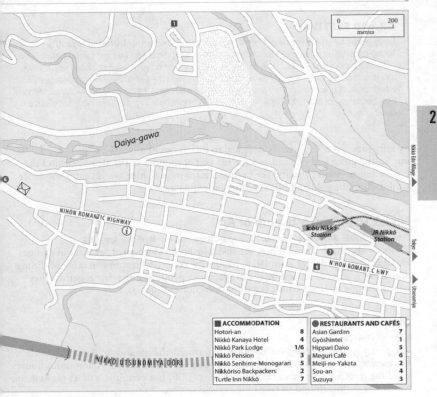

2

Nikkō Edo Village ▶

Tokyo ▶

Utsunomiya ▶

■ ACCOMMODATION		● RESTAURANTS AND CAFÉS	
Hotori-an	8	Asian Garden	7
Nikkō Kanaya Hotel	4	Gyōshintei	1
Nikkō Park Lodge	1/6	Hippari Dako	5
Nikkō Pension	3	Meguri Café	6
Nikkō Senhime-Monogatari	5	Meiji-no-Yakata	2
Nikkōriso Backpackers	2	Sou-an	4
Turtle Inn Nikkō	7	Suzuya	3

Directly in front of the Yōmei-mon is the serene white and gold gate of **Kara-mon**, beyond which is the **Haiden**, or hall of worship. The side entrance to the hall is to the right of the gate; you'll need to remove your shoes and stop taking photographs. Inside, you can walk down into the Honden, the shrine's central hall, which is still decorated with its beautiful original paintwork.

Futarasan-jinja

二荒山神社 · Daily: April–Oct 8am–4.30pm; Nov–March 9am–3.30pm · Free; garden ¥200

After Tōshō-gū, the simple design of **Futarasan-jinja** comes as a relief to the senses. This shrine, originally established by the priest Shōdō Shōnin in 782, is the main one dedicated to the deity of Mount Nantai, the volcano whose eruption created nearby Chūzenji-ko. There are some good paintings of animals and birds on votive plaques in the shrine's main hall, while the attached garden offers a quiet retreat, with a small teahouse serving *matcha* green tea and sweets. You can also inspect the *bakemono tōrō*, a "phantom lantern" made of bronze in 1292 and said to be possessed by demons.

Taiyūin-byō

大猷院霊廟 · Daily: April–Oct 8am–5pm; Nov–March 8am–4pm · ¥550; ¥900 including Rinnō-ji (see p.167)

The charming **Taiyūin-Reibyō** contains the mausoleum of the third shogun, Tokugawa Iemitsu, who died in 1651. This complex, hidden away on a hillside and surrounded

2

GRAND FESTIVAL

Every year, on May 18, the Grand Festival re-stages the spectacular **burial of Ieyasu** at Tōshō-gū, with a cast of over one thousand costumed priests and warriors taking part in a colourful procession through the shrine grounds, topped off with horseback archery. It's well worth attending, as is its smaller-scale cousin (also called the Grand Festival) on October 17, which doesn't have the archery and only lasts half a day, and the "Light Up Nikkō" event (end of Oct, beginning of Nov), during which the major temple buildings are illuminated at night to great effect.

by lofty pines, was deliberately designed to be less ostentatious than Tōshō-gū. Look out for the green god of wind and the red god of thunder in the alcoves behind the Futatsuten-no-mon gate, and the beautiful Kara-mon (Chinese-style gate) and fence surrounding the gold and black lacquer inner precincts.

Nikkō Tōshō-gū Museum of Art

日光東照宮美術館 Nikkō Tōshō-gū Bijutsukan • Daily: April–Oct 8am–5pm; Nov–March 8am–4pm • ¥800

Formerly the shrine's head office, the **Nikkō Tōshō-gū Museum of Art** is set in a huge wooden mansion dating from 1928. Inside, the collection features an array of sliding doors and screens decorated by the top Japanese painters of the day; together, they constitute one of Japan's most beautiful collections of such art.

Meiji-no-Yakata

明治の館 • Daily 24hr • Free

The pretty gardens of **Meiji-no-Yakata** were formerly the grounds of American trade representative F.W. Horne's early twentieth-century holiday home. The various houses amid the trees are now fancy restaurants (see p.172), but even if you don't eat here, it's worth wandering around to take in the sylvan setting.

Nikkō Tamozawa Imperial Villa

日光田母沢御用邸記念公園 Nikkō Tamozawa royotei kinen Kōen • Daily except Tues 9am–4.30pm • ¥500

In stark contrast to Nikkō's temples and shrines is the Zen-like simplicity of the beautifully restored **Nikkō Tamozawa Imperial Villa**. This 106-room residence, surrounded by manicured gardens (including a 400-year-old weeping cherry tree), combines buildings of widely different heritage, some parts dating back to 1632. Three emperors have lived in it, including Akihito, who was evacuated here during World War II. As you stroll the corridors, take time to appreciate the intricate details and the gorgeous screen paintings.

Ganman-ga-fuchi abyss

含満ヶ淵

The wonderfully named **Ganman-ga-fuchi abyss** is an easy stroll along the path which hugs the south side of the rocky river valley; the waterway itself can be a roaring beast after the rains. Part of this restful walk is lined by the Narabi-jizō, some fifty decaying stone statues of Jizō, the Buddhist saint of travellers and children.

ARRIVAL AND DEPARTURE NIKKŌ

Nikkō is accessible on two lines from Tokyo, which serve stations sitting almost side-by-side in the east of the town (the JR station is a real beauty, a historic wooden building designed by Frank Lloyd Wright). In general, the Tōbu line is more convenient.

2

TŌBU TRAVEL PASSES

Tōbu offers travel passes covering the return trip from Tokyo and transport around the Nikkō area. These tickets, which can only be bought at Tōbu stations, include the fare from Asakusa to Nikkō (express train surcharges for the Spacia still apply, though you get a twenty-percent discount), unlimited use of local buses, and discounts on entrance charges at many of the area's attractions, including the cable-cars and boat trips at Chūzenji-ko. It's not worth buying the pass if you only intend to visit Tōshō-gū, but if you're planning a trip out to Chūzenji-ko, the most useful ticket is the two-day All Nikkō Pass (¥4400).

BY TŌBU TRAIN

The Tōbu-Nikkō line (@www.tobu.co.jp) runs from the station in the basement of the Matsuya department store in Asakusa, Tokyo; it is connected by tunnel to Asakusa subway station. An alternative access point for this line is Kita-Senju Station. Note that on some trains you'll need to change at Shimo-Imaichi, while some direct trains split on the way, so be sure to board the right carriage. There are two types of train to choose from: the regular "Kaisoku" ones (2hr 20min; ¥1320), or

the fancier limited express "Spacia" (1hr 50min; ¥2740).

BY JR TRAIN

You can also reach Nikkō on JR trains but the fares are higher, so travelling with JR only makes sense if you have a rail pass from them. The fastest route (around 2hr total) is by Shinkansen from either Tokyo or Ueno to Utsunomiya (宇都宮), where you change to the JR Nikkō line for a local train to the JR Nikkō terminus, a minute's walk east of the Tōbu station.

GETTING AROUND

Buses to Chūzenji-ko and on to Yumoto run 1–2 times per hour from the train stations between 6am and 6pm. If you haven't bought a Tōbu pass (see box above), it's still possible to save money on transport by buying a two-day bus pass at either train station. For unlimited return trips to Chūzenji-ko the cost is ¥2000, while to Yumoto it's ¥3000.

INFORMATION

Nikkō Kyōdo Centre The main tourist office is the Nikkō Kyōdo Centre on the main road from the station to the Tōshō-gū complex (daily 9am–5pm; @0288 542496, @nikko-jp.org). If you're planning on walking in the area, you can pick up the free *Tourist Guide of Nikkō*, which shows you all the hiking trails found within Nikkō National Park.

Tōbu Nikkō Station There's another excellent

information desk at this station (daily 8.30am–5pm; @0288 534511).

ATMs The main post office (Mon–Thurs 8.45am–6pm, Fri 8.45am–7pm, Sat & Sun 9am–5pm) on the approach road to Tōshō-gū has an ATM which accepts foreign-issued cards, as do the ones in the post offices opposite Tōbu Station and up at Chūzenji; otherwise, it's near impossible to use credit cards in the town.

ACCOMMODATION

There's plenty of accommodation covering all categories in Nikkō and the surrounding area. However, in peak holiday seasons and autumn advance reservations are essential. Rates at virtually all places are slightly higher in August, October to early November, and during major holidays.

Hotori-an ほとり庵 8-23 Takumi-chō @0288 533663, @turtle-nikko.com. The modern annexe to the *Turtle Inn* (see p.172) is set in a tranquil location beside the path to the Ganman-ga-fuchi abyss and has good-value en-suite tatami rooms. There's a pottery shop on site, as well as a bath with forest views. Dinner is served at the *Turtle Inn*. **¥12,400**

Nikkō Kanaya Hotel 日光金谷ホテル 1300 Kami-Hatsuishi-machi @0288 540001, @kanayahotel.co.jp. This charming heritage property, practically a museum piece, remains Nikkō's top Western-style hotel, harking back to the glamorous days of early twentieth-century travel. There are some cheaper rooms with en-suite shower

or just a toilet (the hotel has a communal bath) but for the full effect, splash out on the deluxe grade. **¥17325**

Nikkō Park Lodge 日光パークロッジ 11-6 Matsubara-chō & 2828-5 Tokorono @0288 531201, @nikkoparklodge.com. This hostel has two locations in town: one right by the Tōbu station, and the other in a lovely spot high up on the north bank of the river – not terribly convenient, but it makes for a memorable stay. Vegan dinners available. Dorm **¥2990**, double **¥9980**

Nikkō Pension 日光ペンション 10-9 Nishi-sandō @0288 533636, @nikko-pension.jp. Eccentric decorations (including an organ, stained-glass windows and mock-Tudor facade) enliven this small Western-style

2

hotel close to Tōshō-gū. The rooms are comfy and excellent value, and there's also French-influenced cooking and an onsen. ¥11,600

Nikkō Senhime-Monogatari 日光千姫物語 6-48 Yasukawa-chō ☎0288 541010. Highly comfortable option in the calm western side of town, boasting a mix of tatami and Western-style rooms, and charming bathing facilities. Their meals are also quite superb. ¥15,750

★**Nikkorisō Backpackers** にっこり荘バックパカーズ 1107 Naka-Hatsuishi-machi ☎0288 540535,

Ⓦnikkorisou.com. Housed in a building which looks like a giant school carpentry experiment, this amiable hostel is delightfully set near the river. Rooms are small but cosy. Dorm ¥2500

Turtle Inn Nikkō タートルイン日光 2-16 Takumi-chō ☎0288 533168, Ⓦturtle-nikko.com. Popular pension run by an English-speaking family in a quiet location next to the Daiya-gawa. There are small, plain tatami rooms with common bathrooms, and en-suite Western-style rooms, plus a cosy lounge. Add ¥1050 for breakfast, and ¥2100 for the evening meal. ¥9000

EATING

Most restaurants shut around 8pm but your hotel, ryokan or minshuku may serve you Nikkō's speciality of *yuba-ryōri* – milky, thin strips of tofu, usually rolled into tubes and cooked in various stews. The dark and cosy hotel bar at the *Nikkō Kanaya Hotel* is Nikkō's best spot for a nightcap – outside the hotels there are almost no bars in town.

Asian Garden アジアン ガーデン Opposite Tobu Nikkō Station ☎0288 542801. Indian restaurant with a good vegetarian set menu (¥950) and reasonably priced meat-based set meals from ¥1200. Lunch sets are also a bargain at ¥840. Daily 10am–11pm.

Gyōshintei 尭心亭 2339-1 Sannai ☎0288 533751. Sample exquisitely prepared *shōjin-ryōri* vegetarian food (bentō ¥3230, course menu from ¥4050) in a traditional tatami room, served by kimono-clad waitresses. Part of the Meiji-no-Yakata complex (see p.170). Gaze out on a lovely garden as you eat. Daily except Thurs 11.30am–7pm.

Hippari Dako ひっぱり凧 1011 Kamihatsuishimachi ☎0288 532933. Classic *yakitori* and noodle café popular with just about every *gaijin* who has ever set foot in Nikkō, as the written recommendations and *meishi* (business cards) that plaster the walls testify. Five sticks will cost you ¥500, though the menu also has plenty of vegetarian options, plus beer and sake. Daily 11am–7pm.

★**Meguri Café** Café 廻 909-1 Nakahatsuishimachi ☎0288 253122. Run by a husband-and-wife team, this true vegan café has a great laidback atmosphere. Meals use vegetables grown in their own garden, as well as local organic

produce. You'll also find some yummy dessert choices, mostly Western style (such as cakes), and plenty of fresh fruits. Try to get there between Monday and Wednesday for lunch (until 2pm) for a set meal (¥1050), when vegetable ramen is served every other day (¥945). Daily 11.30am–6pm.

Meiji-no-Yakata 明治の館 2339-1 Sannai ☎0288 533751. The dishes, such as curry rice (¥1575, with other mains running to ¥3000), may well be simple, but the charming stone villa, once a Meiji-era holiday home, is a nostalgic treat. It's nice to enjoy coffee and cakes on their terrace. Daily 11am–7.30pm.

★**Sou-an** 草庵 915 Nakahatsuishimachi ☎0288 530534. The shop by traditional sweets maker Nisshōdo – specializing in *yōkan*, a Japanese sweet primarily made of azuki red beans – includes this lovely café and garden in the back. A drink (*matcha*, tea or coffee) and dessert will set you back ¥800. Daily 9am–6pm.

Suzuya 鈴家 2315-1 Sannai ☎0288 536117. Just before you cross over the bridge up the slope from the Kosugi Hōan Museum of Art. This standalone restaurant is a good place to sample *yuba-ryōri*; the set lunch costs ¥1400 and includes tempura, rice, noodles and rolled tofu. Daily 11am–3pm.

Chūzenji-ko

中禅寺湖

Some 10km west of Nikkō lies the tranquil lake of **CHŪZENJI-KO**, most famed for the dramatic **Kegon Falls** that flow from it. Buses from Nikkō run east along Route 120 and up the twisting, one-way road to reach **Chūzenji**, the lakeside resort. Both the lake and waterfalls were created thousands of years ago, when nearby **Mount Nantai** (男体山; 2486m) erupted, its lava plugging the valley.

Kegon Falls

華厳の滝 Kegon on Taki • Daily: Jan, Feb & Dec 9am–4.30pm; March, April & Nov 8am–5pm; May–Sept 7.30am–6pm; Oct 7.30am–5pm • ¥530 • Ⓦkegon.jp

The best view of the **Kegon Falls** is to be had from the viewing platform at their base. The lift to this vantage point lies east across the car park behind the Chūzenji bus

MINAKAMI AND ADVENTURE SPORTS

The sprawling township of **MINAKAMI** (水上), buried deep in the mountains of Gunma-ken, about 65km west of Nikkō, has become one of the hottest spots in Japan for adventure sports. No fewer than ten whitewater rafting companies, including **Canyons** (①0278 722811, ⑩canyons.jp), offer trips down the Tone-gawa. Other activities include paragliding, canyoning, abseiling, rock-climbing and a wide variety of treks, including the ascent to the summit of **Tanigawa-dake** (谷川岳; 1977m). To relax after all this, you can head to **Takaragawa onsen** (宝川温泉; daily 9am–5pm; ¥1500 before 4pm, ¥1000 after 4pm; ⑩takaragawa.com), famous for its mixed-sex bathing (though it also has separated baths) and its four huge rotemburo.

To reach Minakami, take the Shinkansen to **Jōmō-Kōgen** (上毛高原), from where the town is a 20min bus ride. The **tourist office** (daily 9am–5.15pm; ①0278 722611) is opposite the station. **Places to stay** include the Canyons-run *Alpine Lodge* (from ¥4000 per person), which offers private rooms and tatami dorms plus a lively bar.

station – don't be put off by the queues of tour groups since a shorter line is reserved for independent travellers. The lift drops 100m through the rock to the base of the falls, where you can see over a tonne of water per second cascading from the Ojiri River, which flows from the lake.

Futarasan-jinja

二荒山神社 · 24hr · Second Futarasan-jinja free; third Futarasan-jinja ¥500 to access peak

This colourful shrine, around 1km west along the shore of Chūzenji-ko from the falls, is the second **Futarasan-jinja** of the Nikkō area. It once bore the name Chūzenji and has a pretty view of the lake, but is nothing extraordinary. There's also a third Futarasan-jinja, on the actual summit of the volcano; to reach it you'll have to pay to climb the peak, which is owned by the shrine. The hike up is beautiful but takes around four hours, and should only be attempted in good weather; the tourist offices (see p.171) can provide you with maps.

ARRIVAL AND DEPARTURE CHŪZENJI-KO

Local buses from both of Nikkō's train stations (1–2 hourly; ¥1100 one-way) usually take 45min to get here, though travelling times can easily double – or even triple – during *kōyō* in mid-October, the prime time for viewing the changing autumn leaves, when traffic is bumper-to-bumper.

Mashiko

益子

Some 30km south of Nikkō is the village of **MASHIKO**, home to a major pottery museum, numerous pottery shops and over three hundred working kilns spread out around the surrounding paddy fields. **Mashiko-yaki**, the distinctive country-style earthenware pottery, has been made in this area since the Nara period (710–84), although the village only achieved nationwide fame in the 1930s, when potter Hamada Shōji (1894–1978) built a kiln here and promoted Mashiko-yaki pottery throughout Japan.

Tōgei Messe

陶芸メッセ · Tues–Sun: Feb–Dec 9.30am–5pm; Nov–Jan 9.30am–4pm · ¥600 · ①0285 727555

Hamada's former residence has since been restored and relocated – along with his traditional-style kiln – to the impressive **Tōgei Messe** complex. The building contains a pottery studio and a **museum** featuring works by Hamada and Bernard Leach, the renowned English potter who lived in the village for a short time.

By train The easiest way to get to Mashiko is by Shinkansen (50min; ¥4290) from Tokyo to Utsunomiya (宇都宮駅), where you transfer to a bus (1hr; ¥1100)

that leaves from stop 14, to the left of Miyano-hashi, the bridge on the west side of the station.

Narita

成田

Thanks to its international airport, **NARITA** is the first place most people hit when arriving in Japan. While the overwhelming majority of visitors scoot straight off to Tokyo without a second glance, it's actually a nice little town, a temporary or permanent home to many flight crews. For the casual visitor, there's one fantastic sight: the enormous temple complex of **Naritasan Shinshō-ji**, which attracts more than ten million pilgrims each year. It's located at the end of the town's main shopping street, Omotesandō, which is lined with souvenir stalls and the *unagi* (eel) restaurants for which the town is famous.

Naritasan Shinshō-ji

成田山新勝寺 • Daily 24hr • Free

It's well worth visiting the thousand-year-old temple of **Naritasan Shinshō-ji**, an important landmark in the Shingon sect of Buddhism. As long as you're not here on one of the main festival days (New Year, and Setsubun on Feb 3 or 4), you'll find that it doesn't get crowded, such is its vast size. The site feels special right from its ornate Niō-mon. The colourful three-storey pagoda in front of the Great Main Hall dates from the eighteenth century and is decorated with fearsome gilded dragon heads snarling from under brightly painted rafters. Behind the main hall, the temple's pretty gardens include a calligraphy museum, small forests and ornamental ponds.

By train Narita is connected both to Ueno in Tokyo (every 30min; 1hr) and the airport (every 15min; 7min) by JR and Keisei trains, which arrive at separate stations about one minute's walk from each other and around fifteen minutes' walk from the temple.

Tourist information There's a tourist information desk next to the JR station and at the Narita Tourist Pavilion (Jan–May & Oct–Dec 9am–5pm; June–Sept 10am–6pm; closed Mon; ⓦnrtk.jp), on Omotesandō, where internet access is available.

ACCOMMODATION

★**Azure Guesthouse** ゲストハウス アズール 10min walk southwest of the train stations ☎0476 915708, ⓦwww.azure-guesthouse.com. A friendly, surprisingly stylish place with English-speaking staff and good facilities. Book online for the best rates. Dorm <u>¥3000</u>, double <u>¥7900</u>

Kirinoya Ryokan 桐之家旅館 Five minutes east of

the main entrance to Naritasan Shinshō-ji ☎0476 220724, ⓦnaritakanko.jp/kirinoya. This spotless if somewhat worn establishment has tatami- and Western-style rooms, and is crammed full with heirlooms, including gold-plated suits of armour, swords and muskets. Breakfast (¥525–735) and dinner (¥1050–1365) available. <u>¥9000</u>

EATING AND DRINKING

Jet Lag Club 508 Kamichō. Lively British-style pub popular with local expats and visiting flight crews. Cocktails are just ¥400 during the 3–8pm happy hour. Daily 10am–2am.

Kikuya 385 Nakamachi, opposite the tourist pavilion. Moderately fancy-looking place, serving reasonably priced *unagi*, though it's still far costlier than regular fish at around ¥2400 per portion. Daily 10am–9pm.

Kawagoe

川越

The interesting old castle town of **KAWAGOE** lies just 40km north of Tokyo. Although it doesn't look promising on arrival, Kawagoe's compact area of sights, around 1km north of the main station, is aptly described as a "Little Edo", and once you've browsed the many traditional craft shops and paused to sample the town's culinary delights, you'll probably find the day has flown by. This would certainly be the case on the third Saturday and Sunday of October, when Kawagoe grand **matsuri** holds its, one of the most lively festivals in the Tokyo area, involving some 25 ornate floats (called *dashi*) and hundreds of costumed celebrants.

Kita-in

喜多院 • Palace daily 9am–4.30pm • ¥400 • ☎ 049 222 0859

Kawagoe's major highlight, around 500m east of Hon-Kawagoe station, is **Kita-in**, the main temple complex of the Tendai Buddhist sect. There's been a temple on these grounds since 830, and it gained fame when the first Tōkugawa shogun, Ieyasu, declared the head priest Tenkai Sōjō a "living Buddha". Such was the reverence in which the priests here were held that, when the temple burnt down in 1638, the third shogun, Iemitsu, donated a secondary palace from Edo Castle (on the site of Tokyo's present-day Imperial Palace) as a replacement building. This was dismantled and moved here piece by piece, and is now the only remaining structure from Edo Castle which survives anywhere. You have to pay an entry fee to view the palace part of the temple, but it's well worth it. The room with a painted floral ceiling is believed to be where Iemitsu was born. Serene gardens surround the palace and a covered wooden bridge leads across into the temple's inner sanctum, which is decorated with a dazzling golden chandelier.

The entry fee also includes access to the **Gohyaku Rakan**, a remarkable grove of stone statues. Although the name translates as "500 Rakans", there are actually 538 of these enigmatic dwarf disciples of Buddha and no two are alike: it is said that if you feel them all at night, one will be warm to the touch; come back the next day and you'll find it is the one that most resembles you. Since the gates are closed at night these days it's hard to put this to the test, but should you know your Chinese birth sign, it's fun to search the ranks for it, as twelve of the statues include the zodiac symbols of animals and mythical beasts.

Yamazaki Art Museum

山崎美術館 Yamazaki Bijutsukan • Daily except Wed 9.30am–5pm, closed last two days of the month • ¥500 • ☎ 049 224 7114

Housed in the old Kameya *okashi* (sweet) shop, warehouse and factory, the **Yamazaki Art Museum** is dedicated

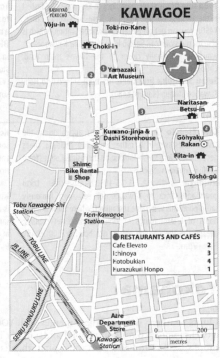

KAWAGOE

KASHIYAO YOKOCHO

Yōju-in

Toki-no-Kane

N

Choki-in

❶ Yamazaki Art Museum

❷

❸

Naritasan Betsu-in

Kumano-jinja & Dashi Storehouse

CHUO-DORI

❹

Gohyaku Rakan ⊙

Kita-in

Shimo Bike Rental Shop

Tōshō-gū

Tōbu Kawagoe-Shi Station

Hon-Kawagoe Station

TOBU LINE

JR LINE

RESTAURANTS AND CAFÉS
Cafe Elevato	2
Ichinoya	3
Kotobukian	4
Kurazukuri Honpo	1

SEIBU SHINJUKU LINE

Atre Department Store

Kawagoe Station

0   200
metres

2

KURAZUKURI

Kawagoe's fortunes owe everything to its strategic position on the Shingashi River and Kawagoe-kaidō, the ancient highway to the capital. If you wanted to get goods to Tokyo – then called Edo – they more than likely had to go via Kawagoe, and the town's merchants prospered as a result, accumulating the cash to build fireproof **kurazukuri**, the black, two-storey shophouses for which the town is now famous. At one time there were over two hundred of these houses, but their earthen walls didn't prove quite so effective against fire as hoped (nor were they much use in the face of Japan's headlong rush to modernization). Even so, some thirty remain, with sixteen prime examples clustered together along Chūō-dōri, around 1km north of the JR and Tōbu stations.

---

to the works of Meiji-era artist Hashimoto Gahō. Some of his elegant screen paintings hang in the main gallery, while there are artistic examples of the sugary confections once made here in the converted *kura* (storehouses); entry includes a cup of tea and *okashi*.

Toki-no-Kane

時の鐘 · Just off Chūō-dōri

The **Toki-no-Kane** is a wooden bell tower (rebuilt in 1894) that was used to raise the alarm when fires broke out. An electric motor now powers the bell, which is rung four times daily. It's backed by a tiny shrine believed to heal certain diseases (and a set of swings that, though devoid of curative powers, will at least put you in a better mood).

ARRIVAL AND INFORMATION   KAWAGOE

Tōbu line Of the three train lines to Kawagoe, the fastest is the express on the Tōbu line from Ikebukuro (32min; ¥450); you can get off either at Kawagoe Station (which is also on the slower JR Saikyō line) or at Tōbu Kawagoe-shi, which is marginally closer to the town's main road, Chūō-dōri.

Seibu Shinjuku line Trains run from Shinjuku to Hon-Kawagoe Station (43min; ¥480).

Tourist office The staff at Kawagoe Station's tourist office (daily 9am–4.30pm; ☏ 049 2225556) can provide you with a map of the town and an English pamphlet on the sights.

Bike rental Immediately northwest of the main square, in front of the Seibu line terminus, is the Shimo bicycle store (daily 10am–7pm), where you can rent bicycles (¥700/day) – handy if you plan to see all of Kawagoe's somewhat scattered sights.

EATING

Cafe Elevato Chūō-dōri. The most appealing of the town's cafés, set in a rather imposing building that's nevertheless very swish-looking on the inside. Coffees from ¥500. Daily 9am–9pm.

Ichinoya いちのや 1-18-10 Matsue-chō. Local gourmands flock to Kawagoe for eel, most famously sampled at this venerable restaurant, where there are two floors of tatami rooms in which to scoff set courses; cheapest is the *unadon* eel-on-rice bowl (¥2100). Daily 9am–7pm.

Kotobukian 寿庵 Beside Kita-in. This is a great place for soba with many types available, but the green *seirosoba* variety (¥650) is particularly notable. They also sell eel-on-rice (¥1300, or ¥2300 with soba). Daily except Wed 9am–1pm & 4–8pm.

Kurazukuri Honpo くらづくり本舗 Chūō-dōri. The area is also known for its *satsumaimo* (sweet potato) dishes; sample some at this confectionery shop and café, set in one of the town's famous kurazukuri (see box above). Daily 9am–6pm.

Yokohama

横浜

On its southern borders Tokyo merges with **YOKOHAMA**, Japan's second most populous city (home to 3.6 million people) and a major international port. Yokohama feels far more spacious and airy than the capital, thanks to its open harbour frontage and

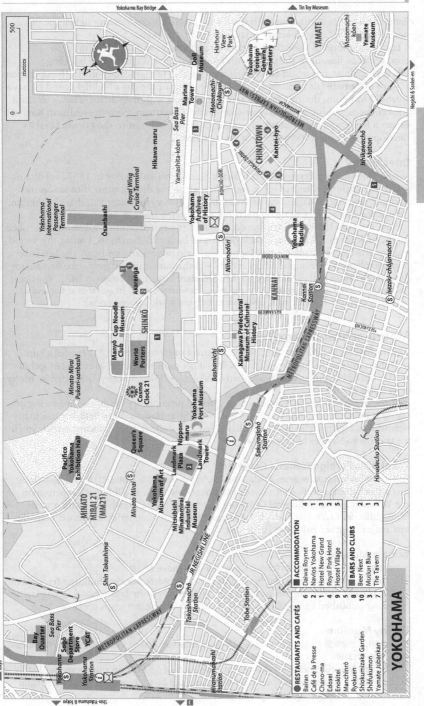

YOKOHAMA

Yokohama Bay Bridge

Tin Toy Museum

YAMATE

Motomachi-kōen

Yamate Museum

Harbour View Park

Yokohama Foreign General Cemetery

Doll Museum

Sea Bass Pier

Marine Tower

Motomachi-Chūkagai (S)

Ishikawachō Station

Hikawa-maru

Yamashita-kōen

CHINATOWN

Kantei-byō

Royal Wing Cruise Terminal

Yokohama International Passenger Terminal

Ōsanbashi

Yokohama Archives of History

HONCHŌ-DŌRI

Minato Mirai Pukari-sanbashi

Akarenga

SHINKŌ

Manyō Club

Cup Noodle Museum

World Porters

Cosmo Clock 21

NIHONDŌRI

MINATO-ŌDŌRI

Yokohama Stadium

KANNAI

Kanagawa Prefectural Museum of Cultural History

Kannai Station (S)

TAKASHIMACHI

Bashamichi (S)

Isezaki-chōjamachi (S)

METROPOLITAN EXPRESSWAY

ISEZAKICHŌ

Pacifico Yokohama Exhibition Hall

Queen's Square

Landmark Plaza

Nippon-maru

Yokohama Port Museum

Landmark Tower

Sakuragichō Station (S)

MINATO MIRAI 21 (MM21)

Minato Mirai (S)

Yokohama Museum of Art

Mitsubishi Minatomirai Industrial Museum

Hinodechō Station

JR NEGISHI LINE

Shin Takashima (S)

Takashimachō Station (S)

Tobe Station

Hiranumabashi Station

Bay Quarter

Sea Bass Pier

Sōgō Department Store

YCAT

Yokohama Station (S)

Shin-Yokohama & Tokyo

Negishi & Sankei-en

2

RESTAURANTS AND CAFÉS	
Bairan	6
Café de la Presse	2
Chano-ma	4
Edosei	5
Enokitei	9
Manchinrō	5
Ryokuen	8
Shiokumizaka Garden	10
Shōfukumon	3
Yamate Jūbankan	7

ACCOMMODATION	
Daiwa Roynet	4
Navios Yokohama	1
Hotel New Grand	3
Royal Park Hotel	2
Hostel Village	5

BARS AND CLUBS	
Beer Next	2
Mōtun Blue	1
The Tavern	3

500 metres
0

generally low-rise skyline, and though it can't claim any outstanding sights, the place has enough of interest to justify a day's outing from Tokyo.

Locals are proud of their city's international heritage, and there's definitely a cosmopolitan flavour to the place, with its scattering of Western-style buildings, Chinese temples and world cuisines, and its sizeable foreign community. The upmarket suburb of **Yamate** (also known as "the Bluff") is one of the city's highlights and boasts a splendid museum; the area forms a pleasant contrast with the vibrant alleys, colourful trinket shops and bustling restaurants of nearby **Chinatown**. Near the seafront, **Kannai** boasts a few grand old Western edifices, in complete contrast to the **Minato Mirai 21** development's hi-tech skyscrapers in the distance.

Brief history

When Commodore Perry sailed his "Black Ships" into Tokyo Bay in 1853, Yokohama was a mere fishing village of some eighty houses on the distant shore. But it was this harbour, well out of harm's way as far as the Japanese were concerned, that the shogun designated one of the five **treaty ports** open to foreign trade in 1858.

From the early 1860s until the first decades of the twentieth century, Yokohama flourished on the back of raw silk exports, a trade dominated by British merchants. During this period the city provided the main conduit for new ideas and inventions into Japan: the first bakery, photographers', ice-cream shop, brewery and – perhaps most importantly – the first railway line, which linked today's Sakuragichō with Shimbashi in central Tokyo in 1872. The **Great Earthquake** levelled the city in 1923, and it was devastated again in air raids at the end of World War II; the rebuilt city is, however, among the world's largest ports.

Motomachi and Yamate

The narrow, semi-pedestrianized shopping street of **Motomachi** (元町) exudes a faint retro flavour with its European facades. You'll get more of the old Motomachi feel in the two streets to either side, particularly Naka-dōri (仲通), to the south, with its funky cafés and galleries.

At the northeast end of Motomachi, a wooded promontory marks the beginning of the **Yamate** (山手) district. The panoramic view from **Harbour View Park** is particularly beautiful at night; if you look really hard, just left of the double chimney stacks, you'll see the Tokyo Skytree blinking away.

Yokohama Foreign General Cemetery

外国人墓地 Gaikokujin Bochi • 96 Yamate-chō • March–Dec Sat & Sun noon–4pm • ¥200 • ☎ 045 622 1311, ⓦ yfgc-japan.com

Just a few minutes' walk south of the Harbour View Park, you'll likely happen upon the **Yokohama Foreign General Cemetery** (Gaikokujin Bochi), which sits on a west-facing hillside. Over 4500 people from more than forty countries are buried here, the vast majority either British or American.

Yamate Museum

山手博物館 Yamate Hakubutsukan • 254 Yamate-chō • Daily 11am–4pm • ¥200 • ☎ 045 622 1188

The stunning **Yamate Museum**, housed in the city's oldest wooden building (erected in 1909), is most interesting for its collection of cartoons from *Japan Punch*, a satirical magazine published in Yokohama for a while in the late nineteenth century.

Tin Toy Museum

ブリキのおもちゃ博物館 Buriki no cinocha Hakubutsukan • Behind Christ Church • Mon–Fri 9.30am–6pm, Sat & Sun 9.30am–7pm • ¥200 • ☎ 045 621 8710

The **Tin Toy Museum** houses a wonderful collection of 13,000 tin toys from the 1890s to the 1960s – in a separate shop next door, you can buy a huge variety of Christmas decorations and stocking fillers at any time of year.

Chinatown

中華街, Chūkagai

Founded in 1863, Yokohama's **Chinatown** is the largest in Japan: its streets contain roughly two hundred restaurants and over three hundred shops, while some eighteen million tourists pass through its narrow alleyways every year; few leave without tasting what's on offer, from steaming savoury dumplings to a full-blown meal in one of the famous speciality restaurants (see p.184).

Kantei-byō

関帝廟 • 140 Yamashita-chō • Daily 9am–7pm • Free; ¥500 to see main altar

The focus of community life is **Kantei-byō**, a shrine dedicated to Guan Yu, a former general and guardian deity of Chinatown. The building is a bit cramped, but impressive nonetheless, with a colourful ornamental gateway and writhing dragons wherever you look. You can pay to enter the main building to see the red-faced, long-haired Guan Yu, but it's not really worth it.

The harbour

From the eastern edge of Chinatown it's a short hop down to the harbour, which is fronted by **Yamashita-kōen**, a pleasant park – more grass than trees – created as a memorial to victims of the Great Earthquake. Here you can pick up a *Sea Bass* ferry (see p.182) or take a harbour cruise (see box, p.182) from the pier beside the **Hikawa-maru**.

Marine Tower

横浜マリンタワー • 15 Yamashita-chō • Daily 10am–10.30pm • ¥750 • W marinetower.jp

Still the focal point of the area after all these years, the 106m-high **Marine Tower** was built in 1961 to celebrate the port's centenary. Though it's supposedly the world's tallest lighthouse, it's better to save your money for the Landmark Tower's much higher observation deck (see p.180).

Doll Museum

人形の家, Ningyōno Ie • South end of Yamashita-kōen • Tues–Sun 10am–6.30pm • ¥500 • T 045 671 9361, W yokohama-doll-museum.com

The **Doll Museum** offers a diverting display of dolls from around the world. The vast collection ranges from American "blue-eyed friendship dolls" – sent to Japan in the 1920s at a time of increasing tension between the two countries – to Japanese folk and classical dolls.

Hikawa-maru Museum

日本郵船氷川丸, Nihon Yūsen Hikowe maru • Off Yamashita-kōen • Tues–Sun 10am–5pm • ¥200 • T 045 641 4362, W nyk.com/rekishi

The *Hikawa-maru*, a retired passenger liner also known as the *Queen of the Pacific*, was built in 1930 for the NYK line Yokohama–Seattle service, though it was later commandeered as a hospital ship during World War II. It now serves as the **Hikawa-maru Museum**, with the ship done up to look as it did in its prime.

Ōsanbashi

大さん橋 • Opposite the Hikawu-maru Museum

The **Ōsanbashi** pier is where cruise ships pull up to berth at Yokohama's International Passenger Terminal. Originally dating from the late nineteenth century, the pier was rebuilt in 2002 to a beautifully fluid, low-slung design inspired by ocean waves – a skateboarder's dream come true. There are "proper" cafés inside, but the snack shacks on the park-like roof area are the best place to grab a drink; even if the coffee's not great, the superb view makes this one of the nicest spots in the whole city.

Administrative district and around

Between Chinatown and the Kannai area sits Yokohama's administrative district, where several European-style facades still survive – most attractive are the biscuit-coloured **Customs House**, topped by a distinguished, copper-clad dome, and the graceful **Port Opening Memorial Hall**, a red-brick neo-Renaissance building erected in 1918.

Yokohama Archives of History

横浜開港資料館 Yokohama Kaikō Shiryōkan • Just west of Silk Museum • Tues–Sun 9.30am–5pm • ¥200 • ⓦ www.kaikou.city.yokohama.jp

A modern, windowless building near the seafront houses the **Yokohama Archives of History**, a museum detailing the opening of Yokohama (and Japan) to the outside world after 1853. It features an impressive collection of photos, artefacts and documents, including contemporary newspaper reports from London, helped by an unusual amount of English translation.

Kanagawa Prefectural Museum of Cultural History

神奈川県立歴史博物館 Kanagawa Kenritsu Rekishi Hakubutsukan • 5-60 Minaminakadori • Tues–Sun 9.30am–5pm • ¥300 • ⓣ 045 201 0926, ⓦ ch.kanagawa-museum.jp

Recognizable by its Neoclassical flourishes, this building was completed in 1904 as the headquarters of a Yokohama bank, and then later converted into the **Kanagawa Prefectural Museum of Cultural History**. Though much of the material is devoted to Yokohama, including woodblock prints of the Black Ships and big-nosed, red-haired foreigners, exhibits also cover Kamakura's Zen temples and local folk culture. Although short on printed information in English, enthusiastic, English-speaking guides are on hand to answer questions.

Minato Mirai 21 (MM21)

みなとみらい21 • ⓦ www.minatomirai21.com

In a bid to beat Tokyo at its own game, Yokohama boasts Japan's second-tallest building and is creating a mini-city of apartment blocks, offices, recreational and cultural facilities: **Minato Mirai 21**, or **MM21**, a growing development that occupies over two square kilometres of reclaimed land and disused dockyards.

The Yokohama Port Museum

横浜みなと博物館 Yokohama Minato Hakubutsukan • 2-1-1 Minatomirai • Tues–Sun 10am–5pm • ¥600 • ⓦ nippon-maru.or.jp

Built in 1930, the **Nippon-maru** training sail ship saw service up until 1984 (during which time she sailed the equivalent of 45 times round the world) and now forms part of the enjoyable **Yokohama Port Museum**. You can explore the entire vessel, which has plenty of English labelling throughout, and alternating Japanese and English commentary over the loudspeakers.

Landmark Tower

横浜ランドマークタワー • 2-2-1 Minatomirai • **Observation deck** 69F • Mon–Fri & Sun 10am–9pm, Sat 10am–10pm • ¥1000 • ⓦ yokohama-landmark.jp

You can't miss the awesome, 296m **Landmark Tower** – Yokohama's tallest building by far, and still the second-tallest in the country. The **Sky Garden observation deck** is on its 69th floor, and on clear days, when Fuji is flaunting her beauty, the superb views more than justify the entry fee. You can also enjoy a coffee for about the same price in the opulent *Sirius Sky Lounge*, another floor up in the *Royal Park Hotel*, or splash out on an early evening cocktail as the city lights spread their magic.

The Yokohama Museum of Art

横浜美術館 Yokohama Bijutsukan • 3-4-1 Minatomirai • Daily except Thurs 10am–6pm • ¥500; varying prices for special exhibitions • ⓣ 045 221 0300, ⓦ www.yaf.or.jp/yma

The highlight of the MM21 area is the splendid **Yokohama Museum of Art**, which is filled with mostly twentieth-century works of Japanese and Western art. Such refinement is set off to fine effect by designer Tange Kenzo's cool, grey space, which grabs your attention as much as the exhibits.

Mitsubishi Minatomirai Industrial Museum

三菱みなとみらい技術館 Mitsubishi Minatomirai Gijutsu-Kan · Tues–Sun 10am–5pm · ¥300 · ⓦ mhi.co.jp/museum

Kids will be in their element at the **Mitsubishi Minatomirai Industrial Museum**. Six well-laid-out zones illustrate technological developments, from today's power generators, oil platforms and deep-sea probes to the space stations of tomorrow, with plenty of models and interactive displays, and English-speaking staff on hand if needed.

Shinkō island

新港

Between MM21 and Ōsanbashi is **Shinkō** island, which was reclaimed about a hundred years ago as part of Yokohama's then state-of-the-art port facilities. There are a few interesting things to see here, including a huge Ferris wheel, an even huger spa complex and some restaurant-filled buildings from the early twentieth century.

Cosmo Clock 21

コスモクロック21 · 2-8-1 Shinkō · Mon–Fri 11am–9pm, Sat & Sun 11am–10pm; occasionally closed on Thurs · ¥700

The slowly revolving **Cosmo Clock 21** is one of the world's largest Ferris wheels, with a diameter of 112m; one circuit takes around fifteen minutes, allowing plenty of time to enjoy the view, which is particularly spectacular at night. The clock's changing colours provide a night-time spectacle in their own right.

Manyō Club

万葉倶楽部 Manyō Kaiabu · 2-7-1 Shinkō · Daily 10am–9pm · ¥2620, plus ¥1680 after 3am · ☎ 045 663 4126

Spread over five floors, the **Manyō Club** spa complex offers a variety of hot-spring baths – the water is trucked in from Atami onsen down the coast – in addition to massages and treatments, restaurants and relaxation rooms. The rooftop is one of the best places from which to admire the night-time colour display of the Cosmo Clock.

Akarenga

赤レンガ

On the eastern side of Shinkō island, two handsome red-brick warehouses dating from 1911 now form the attractive **Akarenga** shopping, dining and entertainment complex. Live music concerts and other events often take place in summer and at weekends in the plaza, which transforms into a skating rink in winter.

Cup Noodle Museum

カップヌードルミュージアム · 2-3-4 Shinkō · Wed–Mon 10am–6pm · ¥500 · ☎ 045 345 0825, ⓦ cupnoodles-museum.jp

Instant noodles are one of Asia's most important snacks, and the contribution made since 1971 by the Japanese Cup Noodle brand is traced in the fun, beautifully designed **Cup Noodle Museum**. There are all sorts of interactive displays, though for many the main sources of enjoyment are sampling some of the many Cup Noodle varieties, and purchasing quirky branded souvenirs.

ARRIVAL AND DEPARTURE   **YOKOHAMA**

Located on the northwest side of town, **Yokohama Station** functions as the city's main transport hub, offering train, subway, bus and even ferry connections, and featuring several gargantuan department stores.

BY TRAIN

From Shibuya The fast Tōkyū-Tōyoko line (every 5min;

30min; ¥260) runs via Naka-Meguro, calling at Yokohama Station before heading off underground to Minato Mirai

2

YOKOHAMA SIGHTSEEING CRUISES

From Yamashita-kōen you can join the *Marine Shuttle* or *Marine Rouge* for a variety of **sightseeing cruises** round the harbour (from ¥1000 for 40min; ⓦyokohama-cruising.jp); the *Marine Rouge* also offers lunch and dinner cruises (¥2520 plus ¥5500–11,000 for food). In addition, the bigger and more luxurious *Royal Wing* cruise ship (☏045 662 6125, ⓦroyalwing .co.jp) runs lunch, tea and dinner cruises from Ōsanbashi pier (¥2000–2400 plus food options starting at ¥2100).

and terminating at Motomachi-Chūkagai Station.

From Tokyo Station You can choose from the Tōkaidō or Yokosuka lines (both every 5–10min; 30min; ¥450), or the Keihin-Tōhoku line (every 5–10min; 40min; ¥450). All three are JR lines; the first two terminate at Yokohama Station, while the latter continues to Sakuragichō, Kannai and Ishikawachō.

From Shinjuku JR's Shōnan-Shinjuku line brings you into Yokohama Station (every 20–30min; 30min; ¥540).

From Narita Airport Services on JR's Narita Express (N'EX) depart for Yokohama Station (hourly; 1hr 30min; ¥4180), but not all N'EX trains go to Yokohama and some divide at Tokyo Station, so check before you get on. Otherwise, get on the cheaper rapid train (JR, "Airport Narita"; 2hr; ¥1890).

From Handea Airport The choice is a Keihin-Kyūkō line train (every 10min; 40min; ¥470) to Yokohama Station or a limousine bus (every 10min; 30min; ¥560), which drops you at YCAT (Yokohama City Air Terminal), just east of Yokohama Station.

From Shin-Yokohama Shinkansen trains from Kyoto, Osaka and points south pause briefly at Shin-Yokohama, 5km north of the centre. From here there's a subway link to the main Yokohama Station (¥230), Sakuragichō and Kannai, but it's cheaper and usually quicker to get the first passing JR Yokohama-line train and change at Higashi-Kanagawa Station onto the Keihin-Tōhoku line (¥160).

BY FERRY

Ferries from Ōshima (Fri & Sat 1 daily; 6hr 30min) call at Ōsanbashi pier, a short walk from the city centre.

BY BUS

Services head around the country from the depot at Yokohama train station.

Destinations Hirosaki (1 daily; 9hr 45min); Hiroshima (1 daily; 12hr); Kyoto (2 daily; 6hr 30min–9hr); Nagoya (1 daily; 6hr 30min); Nara (1 daily; 8hr); Osaka (3 daily; 7hr 15min–8hr).

GETTING AROUND

By train Getting around central Yokohama is easy on either the Tōkyū-Tōyoko line or the JR Negishi line (the local name for Keihin-Tōhoku trains). Trains on both lines run every 5min; the minimum fare is ¥180.

By subway A single subway line connects Kannai and stations north to Shin-Yokohama, on the Shinkansen line; services run every 5–15min and the minimum fare is ¥200.

By Akai Kutsu sightseeing bus A retro-style sightseeing bus runs from outside Sakuragichō Station's east exit via Minato Mirai, Akarenga complex, Chinatown

and Yamashita-kōen to Harbour View Park, then loops back via Ōsanbashi pier. Services run every 10–15min (¥100 per hop, or ¥300 for a day-pass).

By ferry Perhaps the most enjoyable way of getting about the city is on the *Sea Bass* ferries (ⓦyokohama-cruising.jp) that shuttle between Yokohama Station (from a pier in the Bay Quarter shopping complex) and southerly Yamashita-kōen, with some services stopping at Minato Mirai and Akarenga on route. There are departures every 15min (10am–7.30pm; ¥700).

INFORMATION

The most useful centre (daily: April–Nov 9am–6pm; Dec–March 9am–7pm; ☏045 211 0111) is immediately outside Sakuragichō Station's east entrance, but there's another in the harbour-front Sanbo Centre (Mon–Fri 9am–5pm; ☏045 641 4759), east of Kannai Station. There's also a booth in the underground concourse at Yokohama Station (daily 9am–7pm; ☏045 441 7300).

ACCOMMODATION

Yokohama's luxury hotels, all located in the Minato Mirai 21 district, are a tourist attraction in their own right. You'll need a reservation at the weekend (when premium rates also usually apply), though weekdays shouldn't be a problem. Lower down the scale, there are a few reasonable business hotels scattered round the city centre and some welcome new budget options.

FROM TOP ONSEN (P.61); JIZŌ STATUES, NIKKŌ (P.170) >

2

★**Daiwa Roynet** ダイワロイネットホテル 204-1 Yamashita-chō, Naka-ku ☎045 664 3745, ⓦdaiwaroynet.jp. An astonishingly good-value business hotel, where rooms are both cheaper and more stylish than anything else in this category. Secure, clean and with a good location, it also has a convenience store downstairs, and ¥300 happy-hour cocktails in the bar. **¥7500**

Navios Yokohama ナヴィオス横浜 Shinkō-chō, Naka-ku ☎045 633 6000, ⓦnavios-yokohama.com. One of the best-value options in Yokohama; ask for a room facing the Landmark for terrific night-time views. Western-style double **¥15,000**; Japanese-style **¥19,000**

Hotel New Grand ホテルニューグランド 10 Yamashita-chō, Naka-ku ☎045 681 1841, ⓦhotel-newgrand .co.jp/english. Built in the late 1920s in European style, the main building retains some of its original elegance, while many rooms in the newer tower offer bay views. **¥38,000**

Royal Park Hotel ローヤルパークホテル 2-2-1-3 Minato Mirai, Nishi-ku ☎045 221 1111, ⓦyrph.com. Occupies the 52nd to 67th floors of the Landmark Tower, so spectacular views are guaranteed. Rooms are fairly spacious and come with good-sized bathrooms. As well as a fitness club and swimming pool (¥2100–5250), facilities include a tea ceremony room (¥1500) and the *Sirius Sky Lounge*. **¥30,000**

Hostel Village ホステルヴィレッジ 3-11-2 Matsukage-chō, Naka-ku ☎045 663 3696, ⓦyokohama .hostelvillage.com. As the name suggests, this hostel is spread across various buildings; the main location is nice and clean, has a fun rooftop area, and holds regular parties and other themed nights. They also do good weekly and monthly deals for those who'll be in Yokohama a while. Dorm **¥2250**, double **¥4600**

EATING

One of Yokohama's highlights is sampling the enormous variety of restaurants and snack-food outlets cramming the streets of Chinatown. In fine weather, the casual little eating places on the ground floor of Akarenga (see p.181) are a good option, if only because you can take your food to the tables outside.

CHINATOWN

Bairan 梅蘭 133-10 Yamashita-chō ☎045 651 6695. Small, unpretentious restaurant tucked in the backstreets and known for its Bairan *yakisoba*, stir-fried noodles served like a sort of pancake, crispy on the outside and with a juicy pork or beef stuffing (¥900 and ¥1260, respectively) – one serving is big enough for two. Mon–Fri 11.30am–3pm & 5–10pm, Sat & Sun 11am–10pm.

Edosei 江戸清 192 Yamashita-chō ☎045 681 3133. Mega-size steamed dumplings are the speciality here, stuffed with interesting ingredients including black bean and walnut, onion and seafood, shrimp and chilli, plus the usual barbecued pork. Prices vary, but one dumpling can be as much as ¥500. Mon–Fri 9am–8pm, Sat & Sun 9am–9pm.

Manchinrō 萬珍樓 153 Yamashita-chō ☎045 681 4004, ⓦmanchinro.com. This famous restaurant has been serving tasty Cantonese cuisine since 1892. Though prices are on the high side, the portions are generous. Noodle and fried-rice dishes start at around ¥1100, lunch sets at ¥2500, and evening course menus at ¥5000. The branch behind serves a full range of dim sum. Daily 11am–10pm.

Ryokuen 緑苑 220 Yamashita-chō ☎045 651 5651. Simple, stylish Chinese teashop with some thirty types of tea on the menu, from ¥800 for a pot serving up to six small cups. Daily except Thurs 11.30am–6.30pm.

Shōfukumon 招福門 81-3 Yamashita-chō ☎045 664 4141. Multistorey restaurant offering all-you-can-eat dim sum deals for ¥2625, plus fried rice and soup. Mon–Fri 11.30am–10pm, Sat & Sun 11am–10pm.

THE REST OF THE CITY

Café de la Presse カフェーデラプレッス 2F Media Centre Building, 11 Nihon-dōri ☎045 222 3348. Viennese-style café in the corner of one of Yokohama's grand old buildings, with a smarter restaurant attached. The speciality is macaroons, though they also serve cakes, sandwiches and light meals (set lunch ¥1100). Tues–Sun 10am–9pm.

Chano-ma チャノマ 3F Akarenga 2, 1-1-2 Shinkō, Naka-ku ☎045 650 8228. Sit back with a cocktail and nibble modern Japanese dishes at this large, relaxed restaurant-cum-tearoom – a sister of the one in Tokyo (see p.138) – with a very contemporary vibe. Lunch sets from ¥1000. Mon–Thurs & Sun 11am–11pm, Fri & Sat 11am–5am.

Enokitei えの木てい 89-6 Yamate-chō ☎045 6232 288. Set in a venerable Yamate former residence, this cute English-style café serves dainty sandwiches and home-made cakes. Tues–Fri 11am–7pm.

Shiokumizaka Garden 汐汲坂ガーデン 3-145 Motomachi, Naka-ku ☎045 641 5310. A café-restaurant with a slightly bohemian air, serving nicely presented dishes with an Italian twist, plus a big range of scrumptious home-made cakes. Set lunches from ¥1260; around ¥2500 at night. Mon 11am–6pm, Tues–Thurs & Sun 11am–10pm, Fri & Sat 11am–10.30pm.

Yamate Jūbankan 山手十番館 247 Yamate-chō ☎045 621 4466. Pleasant French restaurant in a pretty clapboard house opposite the Foreigners' Cemetery. Although the upstairs is on the formal side (set lunches from ¥3500), the more casual ground floor includes sandwiches and *croques* (¥800), or a more filling lunch platter (¥2000). In July and August they run a popular beer garden. Daily 11am–9pm.

BARS AND NIGHTLIFE

Though it's generally less boisterous than Tokyo, Yokohama has no shortage of lively drinking holes. The west side of Yokohama Station is the nightlife hub, but the area around Chinatown and across to Kanna Station also has a sprinkling of bars.

Beer Next ビールネキスと 3F Akarenga 2, 1-1-2 Shinkō, Naka-ku ☎ 045 226 1961 Stylish beer hall and restaurant with its refreshing own-brew, Spring Valley beer (¥550). They also have Guinness or tap. Daily 11am–11pm.
Motion Blue モーションブルー 3F Akarenga 2, 1-1-2 Shinkō, Naka-ku ☎ 045 226 1919. This cool jazz club attracts top acts – for which you'll pay top prices. There's no charge, though, to park yourself at the attached *Bar Tune*'s long counter and soak up the ambience. Also hosts several

free performances each month. Mon–Fri 5pm–midnight, Sat & Sun 11am–1.30pm & 5pm–midnight.
The Tavern ザタヴァーン B1F 2-14 Minami Saiwai-chō ☎ 045 322 9727, ⌨ the-tavern.com. British-style pub is popular with local expats, and serves the sort of bar food that will appeal to homesick Brits, including Sunday roast lunch (¥1300). Mon & Tues 6pm–midnight, Wed & Thurs 6pm–1am, Fri 6pm–5am, Sat 5pm–5am, Sun noon–midnight.

Kamakura

鎌倉

The small, relaxed town of **KAMAKURA**, lies an hour's train ride south of Tokyo trapped between the sea and a circle of wooded hills. The town is steeped in history, and many of its 65 temples and 19 shrines date back some eight centuries, when, for a brief and tumultuous period, it was Japan's political and military centre. Its most famous sight is the **Daibutsu**, a glorious bronze Buddha surrounded by trees, but the town's ancient **Zen temples** are equally compelling. The town is also well known for its **spring blossoms** and **autumn colours**, and many temple gardens are famous for a particular flower – Japanese apricot at Zuisen-ji and Tōkei-ji in February, and hydrangea at Meigetsu-in in mid-June.

Kamakura's prime sights can be covered on a day-trip from Tokyo, but the town more than justifies a two-day visit, allowing you time to explore the enchanting temples of **east Kamakura** or to follow one of the gentle "hiking courses" up into the hills.

Brief history

In 1185 the warlord **Minamoto Yoritomo** became the first permanent shogun and the effective ruler of Japan. Seven years later he established his military government – known as the bakufu, or "tent government" – in Kamakura. Over the next century, dozens of grand monuments were built here, notably the great Zen temples founded by monks fleeing Song-dynasty China. Zen Buddhism flourished under the patronage of a warrior class who shared similar ideals of single-minded devotion to duty and rigorous self-discipline.

The Minamoto rule was brief and violent. Almost immediately, Yoritomo turned against his valiant younger brother, **Yoshitsune**, who had led the clan's armies, and hounded him until Yoshitsune committed ritual suicide (*seppuku*) – a favourite tale of kabuki theatre. Both the second and third Minamoto shoguns were murdered,

KAMAKURA FESTIVALS

Kamakura's *matsuri* take place in early April (second Sun to third or fourth Sun) and mid-September, and include displays of horseback archery and costume parades, though the summer fireworks display (second Tues in Aug) over Sugami Bay is the most spectacular event.

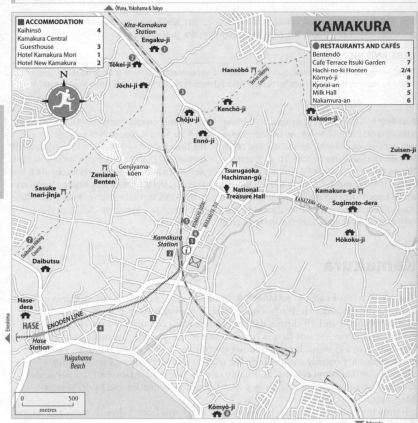

KAMAKURA

■ ACCOMMODATION

Kaihinsō	4
Kamakura Central Guesthouse	3
Hotel Kamakura Mori	1
Hotel New Kamakura	2

● RESTAURANTS AND CAFÉS

Bentendō	1
Cafe Terrace Itsuki Garden	7
Hachi-no-ki Honten	2/4
Kōmyō-ji	8
Kyorai-an	3
Milk Hall	5
Nakamura-an	6

and in 1219 power passed to the Hōjō clan, who ruled as fairly able regents behind puppet shoguns. Their downfall followed the Mongol invasions in the late thirteenth century, and in 1333 Emperor Go-Daigo wrested power back to Kyoto; as the imperial armies approached Kamakura, the last Hōjō regent and an estimated eight hundred retainers committed *seppuku*. Kamakura remained an important military centre before fading into obscurity in the late fifteenth century. Its **temples**, however, continued to attract religious pilgrims until Kamakura was "rediscovered" in the last century as a tourist destination and a desirable residential area within commuting distance of Tokyo.

Kita-Kamakura

北鎌倉

As the Tokyo train nears **Kita-Kamakura** Station, urban sprawl gradually gives way to gentle, forested hills which provide the backdrop for some of Kamakura's greatest Zen temples. Chief among these are **Kenchō-ji** and the wonderfully atmospheric **Engaku-ji**. It takes over an hour to cover the prime sights, walking south along the main road, the Kamakura-kaidō, to the edge of central Kamakura. If you have more time, follow the Daibutsu Hiking Course up into the western hills to improve your finances by washing your yen at an alluring temple dedicated to **Zeniarai Benten**.

Engaku-ji

円覚寺 • 409 Yama-no-uchi • Daily: April–Oct 8am–5pm; Nov–March 8am–4pm • ¥300; Butsunichi-an ¥100; tea including entrance ¥500

The second most important – but most satisfying – of Kamakura's major Zen temples, **Engaku-ji** lies buried among ancient cedars just two minutes' walk east of Kita-Kamakura Station. It was founded in 1282 to honour victims (on both sides) of the ultimately unsuccessful Mongolian invasions in 1274 and 1281. The layout follows a traditional Chinese Zen formula – a pond and bridge (now cut off by the train tracks), followed by a succession of somewhat austere buildings – but the encroaching trees and secretive gardens add a gentler touch.

The first building inside the compound is Engaku-ji's two-storey main gate, **San-mon**, a magnificent structure rebuilt in 1783, and beneath which the well-worn flagstones bear witness to generations of pilgrims. Beyond, the modern **Butsuden** (Buddha Hall) houses the temple's primary Buddha image, haloed in soft light, while behind it the charming **Shari-den** lies tucked off to the left past an oblong pond. This small reliquary, usually closed to visitors, is said to contain a tooth of the Buddha brought here from China in the early thirteenth century. It's also considered Japan's finest example of Song-dynasty Zen architecture, albeit a sixteenth-century replica. The main path continues gently uphill to another pretty thatched building, **Butsunichi-an**, where regent Hōjō Tokimune was buried in 1284; in fine weather green tea is served in its attractive garden. Finally, you'll come to tiny **Ōbai-in**, which enshrines a pale-yellow Kannon statue, but its best attribute is a nicely informal garden with a grove of Japanese apricot.

On the way out, follow signs up a steep flight of steps to the left of San-mon to find Kamakura's biggest bell, **Ōgane**, forged in 1301 and an impressive 2.5m tall; the adjacent teahouse, *Bentendō* (see p.192), is a great place to relax.

Tōkei-ji

東慶寺 • 1367 Yama-no-uchi • Daily: March–Oct 8.30am–5pm; Nov–Feb 8.30am–4pm • ¥100 • **Treasure House** Tues–Sun 9.30am–3.30pm • ¥300 • Ⓦ tokeiji.com

The intimate **Tōkei-ji** was founded as a nunnery in 1285 by the young widow of Hōjō Tokimune. The temple boasts a pleasing cluster of buildings and a profusion of flowers at almost any time of year: Japanese apricot in February, magnolia and peach in late March, followed by peonies and then irises in early June; September is the season for cascades of bush clover. The start of the wonderful Daibutsu Hiking Course (see box, p.188) is nearby.

Kenchō-ji

建長寺 • 8 Yama-no-uchi • Daily 8.30am–4.30pm • ¥300 • Ⓦ kenchoji.com

The greatest of Kamakura's Zen temples is **Kenchō-ji**, headquarters of the Rinzai sect and Japan's oldest Zen training monastery. More formal than Engaku-ji and a lot less peaceful, largely because of the neighbouring high school, Kenchō-ji contains several important buildings, most of which have been relocated here from Tokyo and Kyoto to

---

ZAZEN

Zazen, or sitting meditation, is a crucial aspect of Zen Buddhist training, particularly among followers of the Rinzai sect. Several temples in Kamakura hold public *zazen* sessions at various levels, of which the most accessible are those at Engaku-ji (daily: April–Oct 5.30am; Nov–March 6am in the Butsuden; second and fourth Sun of month at 10am in the Hōjō, or Abbot's hall; ☎ 046 722 0478) and Kenchō-ji (Fri & Sat 5pm in the Hōjō; ☎ 046 722 0981). These hour-long sessions are free and no reservations are required, though it's best to check the current schedule with the temple or Kamakura Information office (see p.191) before setting out, and you should get there at least fifteen minutes early. Though non-Japanese speakers are welcome, you'll get much more out of it if you have someone with you who can translate.

2

DAIBUTSU HIKING COURSE

Past **Tōkei-ji** (東慶寺) and along the main valley is Jōchi-ji (浄智寺), beside which you'll find steps which mark the start of the **Daibutsu Hiking Course** (大仏ハイキングコース). This meandering ridge-path (2.2km) makes an enjoyable approach to Hase's Great Buddha (see p.191), but in any case it's well worth taking a diversion as far as the captivating cave-shrine dedicated to the goddess **Zeniarai Benten** (銭洗弁天), the "Money-Washing Benten", an incarnation of the goddess of good fortune, music and water. Follow the somewhat erratic signs from **Genjiyama-kōen** (源氏山公園) along a trail heading vaguely south through the park, to a road junction where the main trail turns right. Here, you'll pick up signs pointing steeply downhill to where a *torii* and banners mark the Zeniarai Benten shrine entrance. Duck under the tunnel to emerge in a natural amphitheatre filled with a forest of *torii* wreathed in incense and candle smoke.

If you're following the Daibutsu Hiking Course all the way to **Hase**, then rather than retracing your steps, take the path heading south under a tunnel of tightly packed *torii*, zigzagging down to the valley bottom. Turn right at a T-junction to find another avenue of vermilion *torii* leading uphill deep into the cryptomeria forest. At the end lies a simple shrine, **Sasuke Inari-jinja** (佐助稲荷神社), which dates from before the twelfth century and is dedicated to the god of harvests. His messenger is the fox; as you head up the steep path behind, to the left of the shrine buildings, climbing over tangled roots, you'll find fox statues of all shapes and sizes peering out of the surrounding gloom. At the top, turn right and then left at a white signboard to pick up the hiking course for the final 1500m to the Daibutsu (see p.191).

---

replace those lost since the temple's foundation in 1253. Again, the design of the layout shows a strong Chinese influence; the founding abbot was another Song Chinese émigré, in this case working under the patronage of Hōjō Tokiyori, the devout fifth regent and father of Engaku-ji's Tokumine.

The main complex

The **main complex** begins with the towering, copper-roofed **San-mon**, an eighteenth-century reconstruction, to the right of which hangs the original temple bell, cast in 1255 and considered one of Japan's most beautiful. Beyond San-mon, a grove of gnarled and twisted juniper trees hides the dainty, nicely dilapidated **Butsu-den**. The main image is, unusually, of Jizō (the guardian deity of children) seated on a lotus throne, his bright, half-closed eyes piercing the gloom. Behind is the **Hattō**, or lecture hall, one of Japan's largest wooden Buddhist buildings. The curvaceous Chinese-style gate, **Kara-mon**, and the **Hōjō** hall beyond are much more attractive structures. Walk round the latter's balcony to find a **pond-garden** generally attributed to a thirteenth-century monk, making it Japan's oldest-surviving Zen garden, though it's been spruced up considerably.

The Ten'en Hiking Course

天園ハイキングコース

Behind the Hōjō, a path heads up the steep steps past **Hansōbō**, a shrine guarded by statues of long-nosed, mythical *tengu*: this is the start of the **Ten'en Hiking Course**. It takes roughly one and a half hours to complete the 5km trail from Kenchō-ji, which loops round the town's northeast outskirts to Zuisen-ji (see p.190); for a shorter walk (2.5km), you can cut down earlier to Kamakura-gū (see p.190).

From Kenchō-ji it's only another five minutes through the tunnel and downhill to the side entrance of Tsurugaoka Hachiman-gū (see opposite).

Central Kamakura

Modern Kamakura revolves around its **central train station** and a couple of touristy streets leading to the town's most important shrine, Tsurugaoka Hachiman-gū. The traditional approach to this grand edifice lies along **Wakamiya-ōji**, which runs straight from the sea to the shrine entrance. Shops here peddle a motley collection of souvenirs and crafts, the most famous of which is *kamakura-bori*, an 800-year-old method of laying lacquer over carved wood. More popular, however, is *hato*, a pigeon-shaped French-style biscuit first made by Toshimaya bakers a century ago. Shadowing Wakamiya-ōji to the west is **Komachi-dōri**, a narrow, pedestrian-only shopping street, packed with more souvenir shops, restaurants and, increasingly, trendy boutiques.

Tsurugaoka Hachiman-gū

鶴岡八幡宮 • 2-1-31 Yuki-no-shita • Daily 6am–8.30pm • Free

A majestic, vermilion-lacquered *torii* marks the front entrance to **Tsurugaoka Hachiman-gū**, the Minamoto clan's guardian shrine since 1063. Hachiman-gū, as it's popularly known, was moved to its present site in 1191, since when it has witnessed some of the more unsavoury episodes of Kamakura history. Most of the present buildings date from the early nineteenth century, and their striking red paintwork, combined with the parade of souvenir stalls and the constant bustle of people, creates a festive atmosphere in sharp contrast to that of Kamakura's more secluded Zen temples.

Three humpback bridges lead into the shrine compound between two connected ponds known as **Genpei-ike**. These were designed by Minamoto Yoritomo's wife, Hōjō Masako, and are full of heavy, complicated symbolism, anticipating the longed-for victory of her husband's clan over their bitter enemies, the Taira; strangely, the bloodthirsty Masako was of Taira stock.

The Mai-den

The **Mai-den**, an open-sided stage at the end of a broad avenue, was the scene of an unhappy event in 1186, when Yoritomo forced his brother's mistress, Shizuka, to dance for the assembled samurai. Yoritomo wanted his popular brother, Yoshitsune, killed and was holding Shizuka prisoner in the hope of discovering his whereabouts; instead, she made a defiant declaration of love and only narrowly escaped death herself, though her newborn son was murdered soon after. Her bravery is commemorated with classical dances and nō plays during the shrine **festival** (Sept 14–16), which also features demonstrations of horseback archery on the final day.

The main shrine

Beyond the Mai-den, a long flight of steps leads up beside a knobbly, ancient ginkgo tree, reputedly 1000 years old and scene of the third shogun's murder by his vengeful nephew, to the **main shrine**. It's an attractive collection of buildings set among trees, though, as with all Shintō shrines, you can only peer in. Appropriately, the principal deity, Hachiman, is the God of War.

Kamakura National Treasure Hall

鎌倉国宝館 Kamakura Kakunō-kan • 2-1-2 Yuki-no-shita • Tues–Sun 9am–4.30pm • ¥400; English-language leaflet ¥250

The one-room **Kamakura National Treasure Hall** is noted for its collection of Kamakura- and Muromachi-period art (1192–1573), mostly gathered from local Zen temples. Unfortunately, only a few of the priceless pieces are on display at any one time.

East Kamakura

The eastern side of Kamakura contains a scattering of less-visited shrines and temples, including two of the town's most enchanting corners. Though it's possible to cover the area on foot in a half-day (less if you hop on a bus for the return journey), by far the best way to explore these scattered locations is to rent a bicycle (see p.192).

2

Hōkoku-ji

報国寺 • 2-7-4 Jomyoji • Daily 9am–4pm • Bamboo gardens ¥200

The well-tended gardens and simple wooden buildings of **Hōkoku-ji**, or Take-dera – the "Bamboo Temple" – are attractive in themselves, but the temple is best known for a grove of evergreen bamboo protected by the encircling cliffs. This dappled forest of thick, gently curved stems, where tinkling water spouts and the soft creaking of the wind-rocked canes muffle the outside world, would seem the perfect place for the monks' meditation. Too soon, though, the path emerges beside the manicured rear garden, which was created by the temple's founding priest in the thirteenth century.

Sugimoto-dera

杉本寺 • 903 Nikaido • Daily 8am–4.30pm • ¥200

One of Kamakura's oldest temples, **Sugimoto-dera** is set at the top of a steep, foot-worn staircase lined with fluttering white flags. Standing in a woodland clearing, the small, thatched temple, founded in 734, exudes a real sense of history. Inside its smoke-blackened hall, spattered with pilgrims' prayer stickers, you can slip off your shoes and take a look behind the altar at the three wooden statues of Jūichimen Kannon, the eleven-faced Goddess of Mercy. The images were carved at different times by famous monks, but all three are at least 1000 years old. According to legend, they survived a devastating fire in 1189 by taking shelter – all by themselves – behind a giant tree; since then the temple has been known as Sugimoto ("Under the Cedar").

Kamakura-gū

鎌倉宮 • 154 Nikaido • Daily 9am–4pm • ¥300

Mainly of interest for its history and torchlight nō dramas in early October, **Kamakura-gū** was founded by Emperor Meiji in 1869 to encourage support for his new imperial regime. The shrine is dedicated to Prince Morinaga, a forgotten fourteenth-century hero who helped restore his father, Emperor Go-Daigo, briefly to the throne. The prince was soon denounced, however, by power-hungry rivals and held for nine months in a Kamakura cave before being executed. The small cave and a desultory treasure house lie to the rear of the classically styled shrine, but don't really justify the entry fee.

Zuisen-ji

瑞泉寺 • 710 Nikaido • Daily 9am–4.30pm • ¥200

A road heading north from Kamakura-gū marks the beginning – or end – of the short cut to the Ten'en Hiking Course (see p.188), though the main trail starts 900m further east, near **Zuisen-ji**. The temple's fourteenth-century Zen garden, to the rear of the main building, is rather dilapidated, but the quiet, wooded location and luxuriant gardens in front of the temple make it an attractive spot.

Hase

長谷

The west side of Kamakura, an area known as **Hase**, is home to the town's most famous sight, the **Daibutsu** (Great Buddha), cast in bronze nearly 750 years ago. On the way, it's worth visiting **Hase-dera** to see an image of Kannon, the Goddess of Mercy, which is said to be Japan's largest wooden statue. Both these sights are within walking distance of Hase Station, three stops from Kamakura Station (¥190) on the private Enoden line.

Hase-dera

長谷寺 • Daily: March–Sept 8am–5pm; Oct–Feb 8am–4.30pm • Free • **Treasure hall** Daily except Tues 9am–4pm • ¥300 • Hase Station • ⓦ hasedera.jp

Hase-dera stands high on the hillside a few minutes' walk north of Hase Station, with good views of Kamakura and across Yuigahama beach to the Miura peninsula beyond.

Though the temple's present layout dates from the mid-thirteenth century, according to legend it was founded in 736, when a wooden eleven-faced Kannon was washed ashore nearby. The statue is supposedly one of a pair carved from a single camphor tree in 721 by a monk in the original Hase, near Nara; he placed one Kannon in a local temple and pushed the other out to sea.

Nowadays the **Kamakura Kannon** – just over 9m tall and gleaming with gold leaf (a fourteenth-century embellishment) – resides in an attractive, chocolate-brown and cream building at the top of the temple steps. This central hall is flanked by two smaller buildings: the right hall houses a large Amidha Buddha carved in 1189 for Minamoto Yoritomo's 42nd birthday to ward off the bad luck traditionally associated with that age; the one on the left shelters a copy of an early fifteenth-century statue of Daikoku-ten, the cheerful God of Wealth. The real one is in the small **treasure hall** immediately behind, alongside the original temple bell, cast in 1264. The next building along is the Sutra Repository, where a revolving drum contains a complete set of Buddhist scriptures – one turn of the wheel is equivalent to reading the whole lot. Ranks of jizō statues are a common sight in Hase-dera, some clutching sweets or "windmills" and wrapped in tiny woollen mufflers; these sad little figures commemorate stillborn or aborted children. Finally, a cave in the far northern corner of the complex contains statues of the goddess Benten and her sixteen children, or disciples, though it can't compete with the atmospheric setting of the Zeniarai Benten cave-shrine (see box, p.188).

The Daibutsu

大仏 • 4-2-28 Hase • Daily: April–Sept 7am–6pm; Oct–March 7am–5.30pm • ¥200 • **Entering statue** Daily 8am–4.30pm • ¥20

After all the hype, the **Daibutsu**, in the grounds of Kōtoku-in temple, can seem a little disappointing at first sight. But as you approach, and the Great Buddha's serene, rather aloof face comes more clearly into view, the magic begins to take hold. He sits on a stone pedestal, a broad-shouldered figure lost in deep meditation, with his head slightly bowed, his face and robes streaked grey-green by centuries of sun, wind and rain. The 13m-tall image represents Amida Nyorai, the future Buddha who receives souls into the Western Paradise, and was built under the orders of Minamoto Yoritomo to rival the larger Nara Buddha, near Kyoto. Completed in 1252, the statue is constructed of bronze plates bolted together around a hollow frame – you can climb inside for a fee – and evidence suggests that, at some time, it was covered in gold leaf. Amazingly, it has withstood fires, typhoons, tidal waves and even the Great Earthquake of 1923.

ARRIVAL AND INFORMATION   KAMAKURA

By train You can take either the JR Yokosuka line from Tokyo Station via Yokohama, or the JR Shōnan-Shinjuku line from Shinjuku via Shibuya and Yokohama (both 1hr; ¥890); from Tokyo Station, make sure you board a Yokosuka- or Kurihama-bound train to avoid changing at Ōfuna. Trains stop at Kita-Kamakura before pulling into the main Kamakura Station a few minutes later. Enoshima (see p.193) is just a short way away (every 10–15min; 25min) on the Enoden line from Kamakura Station.
Travel pass For a two-day outing it's worth considering

the Kamakura-Enoshima Free Kippu, a discount ticket (¥1970) covering the return trip by JR services from Tokyo, and unlimited travel on the Enoden line and Shōnan monorail.
Tourist information Outside the main, eastern exit of Kamakura Station, and immediately to the right, there's a small tourist information window (daily: April–Sept 9am–5.30pm; Oct–March 9am–5pm; ☎046 723 3050) with English-speaking staff.

GETTING AROUND

Local buses depart from the main station concourse. Given the narrow roads and amount of traffic, however, it's usually quicker to use the trains as far as possible and then walk.

By bus The only time a bus might come in handy is for the more far-flung restaurants or the eastern sites; in the latter case you want stand 4 for Kamakura-gū and stand 5 for

Sugimoto-dera (¥190 minimum fare). To make three or more journeys by bus, you'll save money by buying a Kamakura Free Kippu, a day-pass (¥550) available from the

2

JR ticket office. The pass also covers JR trains from Kamakura to Kita-Kamakura and Enoden line services as far as Hase.

By train On the west side of Kamakura Station are ticket machines and platforms for the private Enoden line (ⓦ enoden.co.jp) to Hase and Enoshima (every 12min; daily 6am–11pm). If you plan to hop on and off the Enoden line a lot and haven't got any other form of discount ticket, it's worth investing in the "One Day Free Ticket" (¥580),

which entitles you to unlimited travel on this line.

By bike A better option is to rent a bike from the outfit (daily 8.30am–5pm; ☎ 046 724 2319) outside the station's east exit: turn right as you emerge and it's up the slope on the south side of the square. Rates range from ¥500 for the first hour to ¥1500 for a day on weekdays and ¥550 or ¥1600 respectively on weekends and national holidays, when you should try to get there early. You'll need to show a passport and give the name of your hotel.

ACCOMMODATION

Central Kamakura offers little budget accommodation, but a fair choice of mid-range hotels. Another option is to stay on **Enoshima** (see opposite) and enjoy the island when the crowds have gone. Many places charge more at weekends and during peak holiday periods, when it's harder to get a room anyway.

Kaihinsō かいひん荘 4-8-14 Yuigahama ☎ 046 722 0960, ⓦ kaihinso.jp. Nestled by the beach, this is one for the romantics: the surrounding area is placid, and the interior furnishings are elegant and beautiful. The building went up in 1924 as a private residence; though added to since, the Western-style section is now protected property. You can stay in one of the two rooms here, or in tatami rooms in the newer Japanese section; some of the latter have views onto the garden. **¥38,000**

Kamakura Central Guesthouse かいひん荘 2-22-1 Yuigahama ☎ 046 722 4529. The most conveniently located hostel in town, just 10min on foot from Kamakura station, and 3min from the beach – you don't even need to don your flip-flops. The rooms are fine enough, though the common areas can feel rather

crowded. Dorm **¥3000**

Hotel Kamakura Mori Hotel 鎌倉mori 3F, 1-5-21 Komachi ☎ 046 722 5868. A short walk up Wakamiya-ōji from the station, the *Mori* offers clean, decent-sized twin or triple rooms with TV and en-suite bathrooms, though rates are expensive. **¥16,000**

★**Hotel New Kamakura** ホテルニューカマクラ 13-2 Onarimachi ☎ 046 722 2230, ⓦ newkamakura .com. The best-value place to stay in Kamakura is this welcoming hotel in an early twentieth-century, Western-style building, a minute's walk north of Kamakura Station – take the west exit and follow the train tracks. Don't be put off by the car park out front: inside the rooms are light and airy, with a choice of Western or Japanese style. **¥10,000**

EATING AND DRINKING

Kamakura is famous for its beautifully presented **Buddhist vegetarian cuisine**, known as *shōjin ryōri*, though there's plenty more casual dining on offer at local restaurants. Kinokuniya has a good food hall on the west side of Kamakura Station, handy for picnic food, or try Union Store on Wakamiya-ōji. In summer, **wooden bars** line the beaches from Kamakura to Enoshima.

Bentendō 弁天堂 1-7-6 Komachi ☎ 046 725 3500. At this wonderful teahouse in the grounds of Engaku-ji temple (see p.187), you can enjoy a cup of *matcha* (¥600) while admiring the view across the valley to Tōkei-ji (see p.187). Daily 11am–4pm.

★**Cafe Terrace Itsuki Garden** カフェテラス樹ガーデ ン On Daibutsu Hiking Course. A fantastic place to get your breath back if you're panting your way along the Daibutsu Hiking Course (see box, p.188). There are seats inside, but in warmer months everyone's out on the steeply arrayed outdoor terraces. Coffees and teas around ¥600, alcoholic drinks a little more. Daily 10am–7pm.

Hachi-no-ki Honten 鉢の木本店 7 Yamanouchi ☎ 0467 228719; also two other branches side by side, opposite Tōkei-ji in Kita-Kamakura ☎ 046 723 3722. Reservations are recommended for this famous *shōjin ryōri*

restaurant beside the entrance to Kenchō-ji, though it's easier to get a table at their newer Kita-Kamakura branches. Whichever you opt for, prices start at around ¥3500. Kenchō-ji branch Tues–Fri 11.30am–2.30pm, Sat & Sun 11am–3pm; main Kita-Kamakura branch daily except Wed 11am–2.30pm & 5–7pm.

Kōmyō-ji 光明寺 6-1-19 Zaimokuza ☎ 046 722 0603. Enjoy the full *shōjin ryōri* experience in this temple set in beautiful gardens on the coast in southern Kamakura. Prices start at ¥4000 for a minimum of two people. Reservations required at least a day in advance. Open daily for lunch only.

★**Kyorai-an** 去耒庵 157 Yamanouchi ☎ 046 724 9835. Beef stew prepared in a demi-glace sauce has a long history in Japan, and *Kyorai-an* has one of the tastiest. The restaurant itself is inside a traditional Shōwa-era Japanese house. The set (¥2600) with toast or rice, salad and coffee is the best value. Mon–Thurs 11am–3pm Sat & Sun 11am–5pm

Milk Hall ミルクホール 2-3-8 Komachi ☎ 046 722 1179, ⓦ milkhall.co.jp. Relaxed, jazz-playing coffee house-cum-antique shop buried in the backstreets west of Komachi-dōri. Best for a coffee and cake, or an evening

beer, rather than as a place to eat. Occasional live music. Daily 11am–10.30pm.

Nakamura-an なかむら庵 1-7-6 Komachi ☎ 046 725 3500. A homely restaurant that has them queuing up outside at weekends for the handmade soba (¥700). To find it, walk up Wakamiya-ōji and take the first left after the Union Store. Wed–Mon 11am–4.30pm.

2

Enoshima

江の島 • Escalators ¥350 for all three; ticket covering escalators and all sights listed here ¥900 • 15min walk southwest from Enoshima Station, via a bridge

Tied to the mainland by a 600m-long bridge, and easily reached from Kamakura, the tiny, sacred island of **Enoshima** has a few sights – some shrines, a botanical garden and a couple of missable caves – but its prime attraction is as a pleasant place to walk, away from motor traffic. Enoshima's eastern side shelters a yacht harbour and car parks, but otherwise the knuckle of rock – less than 1km from end to end – is largely covered with woods and a network of well-marked paths. From the Enoshima end of the bridge, walk straight ahead under the bronze *torii* and uphill past restaurants and souvenir shops to where the steps begin; though the climb's easy enough, there are three escalators tunnelled through the hillside.

Enoshima-jinja

江の島神社 • Daily 9am–4.30pm • ¥150

The island features a wide-ranging shrine area – **Enoshima-jinja** – with three separate components, founded in the thirteenth century and dedicated to the guardian of sailors and fisherfolk. Inside one, Hatsu-no-miya, sits Enoshima's most famous relic – a naked **statue of Benten**, housed in an octagonal hall halfway up the hill. The statue has been here since the days of Minamoto Yoritomo (1147–99) of the Kamakura Shogunate, who prayed to it for victory over the contemporary Fujiwara clan. Although ranked among Japan's top three Benten images, it's a little hard to see what all the fuss is about.

Samuel Cocking Park

サムエル・コッキング苑, Samyueru Cokkingu-en • April–June, Sept & Oct Mon–Fri 9am–6pm, Sat & Sun 9am–8pm; July & Aug daily 9am–8pm; Nov–March Mon–Fri 9am–5pm, Sat & Sun 9am–8pm • ¥200; lighthouse ¥300

This nicely laid-out botanical garden is known as the **Samuel Cocking Park** after the English merchant and horticulturalist who built Japan's first greenhouse here in 1880. If it's a clear day, you'll get good views south to Ōshima's smoking volcano and west to Fuji from the lighthouse inside the garden.

ARRIVAL AND INFORMATION   **ENOSHIMA**

By train Enoshima is 25min west of Kamakura Station on the Enoden line (¥250); a helpful travel pass (see p.191) is also available. The most straightforward route back to Tokyo is the Odakyū-Enoshima line direct to Shinjuku, though note that weekday services are limited. The trains depart from Katase-Enoshima Station (二瀬江ノ島駅): from the island causeway, turn left across the river to find the station with its distinctive Chinese-style facade.

Another option is to hop on the Enocen line west to its terminal in Fujisawa, then change stations for JR services to central Tokyo.

Tourist information You can pick up an English-language map of the island at the small tourist office (daily 10am–5pm; ☎ 045 626 3544, ⓦ fujisawa-kanko.jp), on the left as you come off the bridge.

2

MOUNT TAKAO

An hour west of Shinjuku, **Mount Takao** (高尾山; 600m), also referred to as Takao-san, is a particularly pleasant place for a quick escape from Tokyo, and a starting point for longer trails into the mountains in the **Chichibu-Tama National Park** (秩父多摩国立公園). The Keiō line from Shinjuku provides the simplest and cheapest way of reaching the terminus of Takao-san-guchi (1hr; ¥370), where the spectacular **Hiwatarisai** fire ritual is held on the second Sunday in March, featuring priests, pilgrims and hardy tourists marching across hot coals. After a hike up or a ride on the cable-car or chairlifts from Takao-san-guchi, you'll get to **Yakuo-in** (薬王院; ⓦ takaosan.or.jp/index.html), a temple founded in the eighth century and notable for the ornate polychromatic carvings that decorate its main hall.

At the base of the mountain you'll find the delightful *Ukai Toriyama* (うかい鳥山; Mon–Fri 11am–9.30pm, Sat 11am–8pm, Sun 11am–7pm; ☎042 661 0739, ⓦ ukai.co.jp/toriyama), a traditional restaurant specializing in charcoal-grilled chicken and Hida beef. The food is served in small tatami rooms, with set menus starting at ¥4730. Above the upper cable-car terminus there's *Takao Beer Mount* (late June to early Oct: daily 3–9.30pm, Sat & Sun 2.30–9.30pm), which serves an all to you-can-eat-and-drink buffet (men/women ¥3500/3300) and provides a twinkling night view of the city.

ACCOMMODATION AND EATING

Ebisuya 恵比寿屋 1-4-16 Enoshima ☎046 622 4105, ⓦ ebisuyaryokan.jp. This good-value ryokan offers well-maintained Western and tatami rooms, plus traditional baths and excellent meals. From the distinctive bronze *torii* on the main road, head down the alley and the ryokan will be on your left. Rate includes two meals. **¥13,650** per person.

Kinokuniya 紀伊国屋 Enoshima ☎046 622 4247. Heading towards Enoshima from the station, you'll pass this simple ryokan-cum-restaurant on your right. It's highly popular with locals on account of the cheap sets; try the *kin-me-dai* (a delicious local red fish, served in soy), which costs ¥1000 for the set, including coffee. Daily 11am–4pm.

Shōnan Burger 湘南バーガー Enoshima ☎046 629 0688. Fun little burger bar, just over the Enoshima bridge and on the right. Their eponymous burger (¥400) is a real treat: a fish-cake patty served with ground radish, perilla leaf, and a miniature shoal of tiny sardines – look inside before you bite. Daily 11am–7pm.

Fuji Five Lakes

The best reason for heading 100km west from Tokyo towards the area known as **FUJI FIVE LAKES** is to climb **Mount Fuji** (富士山), Japan's most sacred volcano and, at 3776m, its highest mountain. Fuji-san, as it's respectfully known by the Japanese, has long been worshipped for its latent power (it last erupted in 1707) and near-perfect symmetry; it is most beautiful from October to May, when the summit is crowned with snow. The climbing season is basically July and August; even if you don't fancy the rather daunting ascent, just getting up close to Japan's most famous national symbol is a memorable experience. Apart from Fuji-san, don't miss the wonderfully atmospheric shrine **Fuji Sengen-jinja**, in the area's transport hub of **Fuji-Yoshida**.

During the summer, the **five lakes** in the area are packed with urbanites fleeing the city. **Kawaguchi-ko** is not only a popular starting point for climbing Mount Fuji, but also features a kimono museum and the easily climbable Mount Tenjō, which has outstanding views of Fuji-san and the surrounding lakes. The smallest of the other four lakes, horseshoe-shaped **Shōji-ko** (精進湖), 2km west of Kawaguchi-ko, is by far the prettiest. The largest lake, **Yamanaka-ko** (山中湖), southeast of Fuji-Yoshida, is just as developed as Kawaguchi-ko and has fewer attractions, while **Motosu-ko** (本栖湖) and **Sai-ko** (西湖) – the best for swimming and camping – are fine, but not so extraordinary that they're worth the trouble of visiting if you're on a short trip.

2

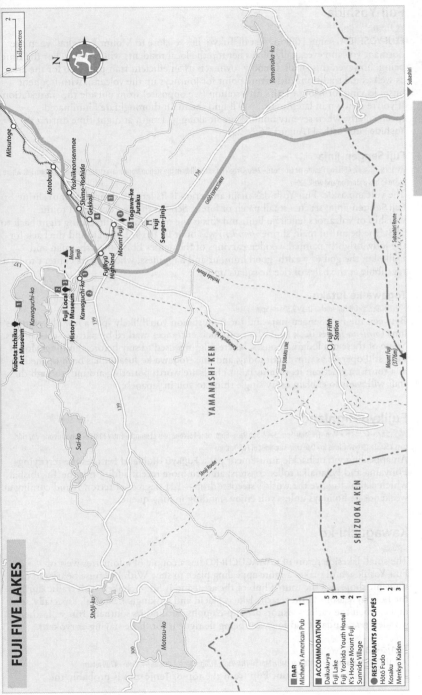

FUJI FIVE LAKES

Subashiri

Mitsutoge

Kotobuki

Yoshiikeonsenmae

Shimo-Yoshida

Gekkoi

Yamanaka ko

Mount Fuji

Togawa-ke Jutaku

Fuji Sengen-Jinja

Fujikyu Highland

Mount Tenjō

Kawaguchi-ko

Kubota Itchiku Art Museum

Fuji Local History Museum

Kawaguchi-ko

137

139

138

139

139

Sai-ko

Sho ji-ko

300

Motosu-ko

YAMANASHI-KEN

SHIZUOKA-KEN

Fuji Fifth Station

Mount Fuji (3776m)

Subashiri Route

Yoshida Route

Kawaguchi-ko Route

FUJI SUBARU LINE

Shoji Route

0   2

kilometres

N

■ **BAR**
| Michael's American Pub | 1 |

■ **ACCOMMODATION**
Daikokurya	5
Fuji Lake	3
Fuji Yoshida Youth Hostel	4
K's House Mount Fuji	2
Sunnide Village	1

● **RESTAURANTS AND CAFÉS**
Hōtō Fudo	1
Kosaku	2
Menkyo Kaiden	3

Fuji-Yoshida

富士吉田

FUJI-YOSHIDA, some 100km west of Tokyo, lies so close to Mount Fuji that when the dormant volcano eventually blows her top the local residents will be toast. For the time being, however, this small, friendly town acts as an efficient transport hub for the area, as well as the traditional departure point for journeys up the volcano, with frequent buses leaving for Mount Fuji's fifth station (see opposite) from outside the train station. If you're in town in late August, you'll find the main thoroughfare illuminated spectacularly, when seventy bonfires are lit along its length at night-time during the **Yoshida Fire Festival** (August 26 & 27).

Fuji Sengen-jinja

富士浅間神社 • Off Fuji Panorama Line road • 24hr • Free • Head uphill from the station along main street towards Fuji; turn left where the road hits a junction and walk 200m

The volcano aside, Fuji-Yoshida's main attraction is its large, colourful Shintō shrine, **Fuji Sengen-jinja**, set in a small patch of forest. Sengen shrines, dedicated to the worship of volcanoes, encircle Fuji, and this is the most important, dating right back to 788. The beautiful main shrine (*honden*) was built in 1615. Look around the back for the jolly, brightly painted wooden carvings of the deities Ebisu the fisherman and Daikoku, the god of wealth, good humour and happiness, who appears content to let a rat nibble at the bales of rice he squats upon.

Togawa-ke Jutaku

戸川家受託 • Off Fuji-michi • Daily 9.30am–5pm • ¥100

Between the Fuji Sengen-jinja and the train station you'll likely spot a few old **pilgrims' inns** (*oshi-no-ie*) set back from the road, their entrances marked by narrow stone pillars. Some of these old lodging houses, where pilgrims used to stay before climbing Mount Fuji, still operate as minshuku today, and one, **Togawa-ke Jutaku**, has been opened up as a tourist attraction; its various tatami halls are worth pottering around, though the staff will want to explain every single thing to you in Japanese.

Fujikyū Highland

富士急ハイランド • Mon–Fri 9am–5pm, Sat & Sun 9am–6pm, closed second Tues of month • Entry ¥1300; entry plus one-day ride pass ¥5000 • Ⓦ www.fujiq.jp • One train stop west of Fuji-Yoshida

An appealingly ramshackle amusement park, **Fujikyū Highland** features the terrifying Fujiyama and Eejanaika roller coasters; an even more recent addition is the Takabisha, which claims to have the world's steepest drop – 121 degrees of terror. Avoid coming at weekends or holidays unless you enjoy standing in long queues.

Kawaguchi-ko

河口湖

The small lakeside resort of **KAWAGUCHI-KO** lies a couple of kilometres west of Fuji-Yoshida, and makes a more appealing place to stay. With its cruise boats and crass souvenir shops, it's the tourist hub of the area, and is often choked with traffic during the holiday season. However, the lake is placid and strikingly beautiful, especially at night, when the various visitors are clip-clopping around its southern fringes in their wooden *geta* sandals (said footwear being de rigueur for those staying at ryokan).

Tenjō-zan

天上山 • Off Misaka-michi • **Cable-car** Daily: March–Nov 9am–5.20pm; Dec–Feb 9am–4.40pm • ¥700 return

The fabulous view of Mount Fuji from the top of **Tenjō-zan** is probably the highlight of a trip to Kawaguchi-ko; of course, you'll also get a great view of the lake from here, since it's right next door. You can either take a three-minute cable-car ride up to the lookout, or get some exercise by hiking up, which takes around 45 minutes.

Kubota Itchiku Art Museum

久保田一竹美術館 Kubota Itchiku Bijutsukan • 2255 Guchiko, 4km northwest of Kawaguchi-ko • April–Nov daily 9.30am–5.30pm; Dec–March daily except Wed 10am–4.30pm • ¥1300 • ☏ 0555 768811, ⓦ itchiku-museum.com • 25min by bus from Kawaguchi-ko station

One of the highlights of Kawaguchi-ko is the **Kubota Itchiku Art Museum**, on the northern shore of the lake. This small museum, housed in a Gaudí-esque building, showcases the work of Kubota Itchiku, who refined the traditional *tsujigahana* textile-patterning technique and applied it to kimono. Inside the pyramid-shaped building are pieces from the artist's *Symphony of Light* series, a continuous mountain landscape through the seasons, formed when the kimono are placed side by side.

Mount Fuji

富士山

"A wise man climbs Fuji once. A fool climbs it twice", says the Japanese proverb. Don't let the sight of children and grannies trudging up lull you into a false sense of security: this is a tough climb. There are several **routes** up the volcano, with the ascent divided into sections known as **stations**. Most people take a bus to the Kawaguchi-ko fifth station (*go-gōme*), about halfway up the volcano, where a Swiss-chalet-style gift shop marks the end of the road. The traditional hike, though, begins at Fuji-Yoshida; walking from here to the fifth station takes around five hours, and it's another six hours before you reach the summit. The shortest route is from the Fujinomiya-guchi fifth station to the south, accessible by bus from Shin-Fuji Station, on the Shinkansen route; these pass Fujinomiya JR station en route.

Many climbers choose to ascend the mountain at night in order to reach the summit by dawn; during the season, the lights of climbers' torches resemble a line of fireflies trailing up the volcanic scree. Essential items to carry include at least one litre of water and some food, a torch and batteries, a raincoat and extra clothes. However hot it might be at the start of the climb, the closer you get to the summit the colder it becomes, with temperatures dropping to well below freezing, and sudden rain and lightning strikes are not uncommon.

Mount Fuji's official **climbing season**, when all the facilities on the mountain are open, including lodging huts and phones at the summit, runs from July 1 to the end of August. You can climb outside these dates, but don't expect all, or indeed any, of the facilities to be in operation, and be prepared for snow and extreme cold towards the summit.

Once you're at the summit, it will take around an hour to make a circuit of the crater. Otherwise you can take part in the time-honoured tradition of making a phone call or mailing a letter from the post office.

ACCOMMODATION ON MOUNT FUJI

There are seventeen **huts** on Fuji, most of which provide dorm accommodation from around ¥5000 per night (add ¥1000 on weekends) for just a bed (no need for a sleeping bag), with an option to add meals for ¥1000 each. It's essential to book in advance during the official climbing season (July & Aug). The huts also sell snacks and stamina-building dishes, such as curry rice. For a full list of the huts, with contact numbers, see the Fuji-Yoshida city website (ⓦ www.city.fujiyoshida.yamanashi.jp).

2

ARRIVAL AND DEPARTURE

By bus The easiest way to reach the Fuji Five Lakes area is to take the bus (¥1700; 1hr 45min in good traffic) from the Shinjuku bus terminal in Tokyo, on the west side of the train station; during the climbing season there are frequent services, including at least three a day that run directly to the fifth station on Mount Fuji.

By train The train journey from Shinjuku Station involves transferring from the JR Chūō line to the Fuji

Kyūkō line at Ōtsuki, from where local trains (some with Thomas the Tank Engine decoration) chug first to Mount Fuji Station (the old name, Fuji-Yoshida, is still commonly used) and then on to Kawaguchi-ko; the whole process will take at least 2 hours (¥2390). On weekends, the early-morning *Holiday Rapid* train from Shinjuku does the trip directly; ironically, it takes longer (2hr 20min; also ¥2390).

GETTING AROUND

By bus A comprehensive system of buses will help you get around once you've arrived at either Fuji-Yoshida or Kawaguchi-ko.

Travel pass The two-day Retrobus pass (¥1000 or ¥1300,

depending on the route) allows travel around the Five Lakes area, while the Fuji Hakone Pass allows you to combine the Fuji Five Lakes area with a trip around Hakone (see box, p.205).

INFORMATION

If you're here to climb Fuji, pick up a free copy of the *Mount Fuji Climber's Guide Map*, available at both local tourist offices; there's similar information on the Fuji-Yoshida tourist office website (see below).

Fuji-Yoshida tourist office On the left as you exit Mount Fuji Station (daily 9am–5pm; ☎0555 227000, ⓦwww .city.fujiyoshida.yamanashi.jp), with tons of information, in English.

Kawaguchi-ko tourist office Outside Kawaguchi-ko station, this branch (daily 8.30am–5.30pm; ☎0555 72 6700) is just as useful as its counterpart in Fuji-Yoshida.

ACCOMMODATION

Fuji-Yoshida and Kawaguchi-ko have plenty of good places to stay, including youth hostels and hotels. Fuji **climbers** could consider overnighting in one of the mountain huts (see box, p.197), but the claustrophobic should stick to the roomier accommodation at the base of the mountain. There are also several **campsites** around the lakes.

FUJI-YOSHIDA

Daikoku-ya 大国屋 Honchō-dōri, Fuji-Yoshida ☎0555 223778. This original pilgrims' inn on the main road still takes guests in its very traditional and beautifully decorated tatami rooms (though the owner prefers guests who can speak some Japanese). Rate includes two meals. Closed Oct–April. **¥14,000**

Fuji-Yoshida Youth Hostel 富士吉田ユースホステル 2-339 Shimo Yoshida Hon-chō, Fuji-Yoshida-shi ☎0555 220533, ⓦjyh.or.jp. Small, appealing hostel with tatami rooms in a family home. It's a 20min walk from Fuji-Yoshida Station, less from Shimo-Yoshida, the preceding station. English is spoken and meals are available. Closed Jan. Dorm **¥3885**

KAWAGUCHI-KO

★**Fuji Lake** 富士レーク 1 Funatsu, Kawaguchi-ko-machi ☎0555 722209, ⓦfujilake.co.jp. Large lakeside hotel that dates back to the 1930s, making it one of Japan's oldest such facilities. Its rooms are all large and very stylish, and feature charming wash-rooms into which onsen water is piped. There's another fantastic onsen downstairs. **¥14,700**

★**K's House Mount Fuji** ケイズハウス富士山 6713-108 Funatsu, Kawaguchi-ko-machi ☎0555 835556, ⓦkshouse.jp. Super-friendly hostel with a choice of either bunk-bed dorms or private tatami-style rooms, some en suite. Also on offer are a well-equipped kitchen, comfy lounge, internet access, laundry and bike rental, as well as

FUJI-NOODLES

Both Fuji-Yoshida and Kawaguchi-ko are renowned for their thick *teuchi* (handmade) **udon noodles**. *Fuji-Yoshida udon* comes topped with shredded cabbage and carrot, and is usually prepared and served in people's homes at lunchtime only; the tourist office can provide a Japanese list and map of the best homes and restaurants serving it. Most places serve just three types of dishes: *yumori*, noodles in a soup; *zaru*, cold noodles; and *sara*, warm noodles dipped in hot soup. In Kawaguchi-ko, be sure to try *hōtō*, a hearty broth served piping hot; fillings vary, but sweet pumpkin is the local favourite.

small bar. They'll even pick up from the station for free 8am–7.30pm). Dorm ¥2500, double ¥6800

Sunnide Village サンニデヴィレッジ Kawaguchi-ko ☎0555 765004, ⓦsunnide.com. This attractive complex of hotel and holiday cottages offers spectacular

views across the lake towards Mount Fuji. They have lovely public baths too. It's on the north side of the lake, towards the Itchiku Kubota Art Museum. Double ¥12,600, cottage ¥16,000

EATING AND DRINKING

FUJI-YOSHIDA

★**Menkyo Kaiden** 麺許皆伝 849-1 Kami-Yoshida ☎0555 238306. Though a little bit of a hike from the station, this is the undisputed *udon* favourite with lunching locals; you may have to wait for a seat. The menu can be a little confusing, but staff recommend the *yokubari*, which comes in a miso-base soup (¥550). Mon–Sat 11am–2pm.

Michael's American Pub マイクルズアメリカンパップ 3-21-37 Shimo-yoshida ☎0555 243917, ⓦmfi.or.jp/ michael. If you're staying overnight in Fuji-Yoshida, a warm welcome here is guaranteed. The atmosphere can be surprisingly *genki* ("energetic" is the closest English word) given the location; simple snacks are on offer alongside a modest range of drinks. Daily except Thurs 7pm–2am, lunch 11.30am–4pm except Sat.

KAWAGUCHI-KO

Hōtō Fudo ほうとう不動 Train station plaza ☎0120 410457. Right in front of the train station in a building whose outside has been given a wooden panelling, this small restaurant serves decent *hōtō* (¥1050) and a range of tasty Japanese food; try the *basashi* (raw horse meat; ¥1050). Daily 11am–9pm.

★**Kosaku** 小作 1638-1 Kawaguchiko-chō ☎0555 721181. Though it's not very conveniently located, it's well worth hunting down this large, cabin-like restaurant if you're staying the night in Kawaguchi-ko. This serves the best *hōtō* in town (from ¥1100); fillings include duck, mushroom, seafood and even bear, but traditional types favour the sweet pumpkin. Daily 11am–9pm.

Hakone

箱根

South of Mount Fuji and 90km west of Tokyo is the lakeland, mountain and onsen area known as **HAKONE**, always busy at weekends and holidays. Most visitors follow the well-established day-trip route, which is good fun and combines rides on several trains or buses, a funicular, a cable-car and a sightseeing ship, styled as a seventeenth-century galleon, across the Ashino **lake**. However, the scenery is so pretty, and there's so much else to do – such as seeing great **art** at the Hakone Open-Air Museum and the Pola Museum of Art, not to mention soaking in numerous **onsen** – that an overnight stay is encouraged. Weather permitting you'll also get great views of nearby Mount Fuji.

The traditional day-trip itinerary, described below, runs anticlockwise from **Hakone-Yumoto**, gateway to the **Fuji-Hakone-Izu National Park**, then over **Mount Sōun**, across the length of **Ashino-ko** to **Moto-Hakone**, and back to the start. Approaching Hakone from the west, you can follow a similar route clockwise from Hakone-machi, on the southern shore of Ashino-ko, to Hakone-Yumoto.

Hakone-Yumoto

箱根湯元

HAKONE-YUMOTO, the small town nestling in the valley at the gateway to the national park, is marred by scores of concrete-block hotels and *bessō*, vacation villas for company workers – not to mention the usual cacophony of souvenir shops. It does, however, have some good **onsen** which are ideal for unwinding after a day's sightseeing around the park.

Tenzan Notemburo

天山野天鳳呂 • Off Hakoneshindō in Oku-Yumoto, 2km southwest of town • Daily 9am–11pm • ¥1200; wooden baths ¥200 weekdays; ¥1000 weekends • Free shuttle bus from bridge north of Hakone-Yumoto Station

The most stylish bathhouse in the area is **Tenzan Notemburo**, a luxurious public onsen complex. The main building has outdoor baths for men and women, including

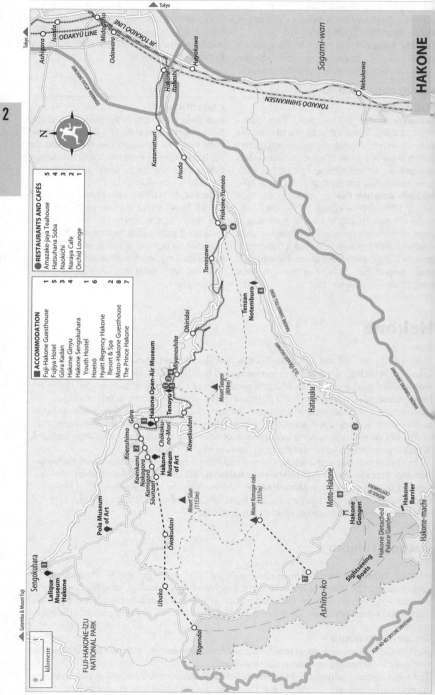

RESTAURANTS AND CAFÉS

Amazake-jaya Teahouse	5
Hatsuhana Soba	4
Naokichi	3
Naraya Cafe	2
Orchid Lounge	1

■ ACCOMMODATION

Fuji-Hakone Guesthouse	1
Fujiya Hotel	5
Gōra Kadan	3
Hakone Ginyu	4
Hakone Sengokuhara Youth Hostel	1
Hoeisō	6
Hyatt Regency Hakone Resort & Spa	2
Moto-Hakone Guesthouse	8
The Prince Hakone	7

waterfalls and jacuzzis in a series of rocky pools. There's also a clay-hut sauna for men, and for an extra charge both men and women can use the wooden baths in the building across the car park.

Miyanoshita

宮ノ下

Rising up into the mountains, the Hakone-Tozan switchback railway zigzags for nearly 9km alongside a ravine from Hakone-Yumoto to the village of Gōra. There are small traditional inns and temples at several of the stations along the way, but the single best place to alight is the village onsen resort of **MIYANOSHITA**. Interesting antique and craft shops are dotted along its main road, and there are several hiking routes up **Mount Sengen** (804m) on the eastern flank of the railway – one path begins just beside the station. At the top you'll get a great view of the gorge below. Back down in Miyanoshita is the historic *Fujiya* hotel (see p.205), which opened for business in 1878 and is well worth a look.

Hakone Open-Air Museum

彫刻の森美術館, Chōkoku no Mori Bijutsukan • 1121 Ninotaira • Daily 9am–5pm • ¥1600 • ⓦ hakone-oam.or.jp

Travelling two stops uphill from Miyanoshita on the Hakone-Tozan railway brings you to Chōkoku no Mori (彫刻の森), where you should alight if you want to visit the nearby **Hakone Open-Air Museum**. This worthwhile museum is packed with sculptures, ranging from works by Rodin and Giacometti to Michelangelo reproductions and bizarre modern formations scattered across the landscaped grounds, which have lovely views across the mountains to the sea. You can rest between galleries at several restaurants or cafés, and there's also a traditional Japanese teahouse here.

Gōra to Ashino-ko

Funicular tram Every 10–15min • ¥410 one-way • **Cable-car** Every 1–2min • ¥1330 one-way

The Hakone-Tozan railway terminates at **GŌRA** (強羅), another possible place to stay overnight or have lunch. Continuing west on the day-trip route, you'll transfer to a **funicular tram**, which takes ten minutes to cover the short but steep distance to **Sōunzan**, the start of the cable-car ride. From here, the **cable-car** floats like a balloon on its 30min journey high above the mountain to the Tōgendai terminal beside **Ashino-ko**, stopping at a couple of points along the way.

Hakone Museum of Art

箱根美術館, Hakone Bijutsukan • 1300 Gōra • Daily except Thurs 9am–4pm • ¥900 • ⓦ mcaart.or.jp

En route to Sōunzan, you might want to stop at Kōen-kami (公園上), a couple of stops from Gōra, for the **Hakone Museum of Art**. Its collection of ancient ceramics is likely to appeal to experts only, but the delicate moss gardens and the view from the traditional teahouse across the verdant hills is captivating.

Ōwakudani

大涌谷

If the weather is playing ball, you should get a good glimpse of Mount Fuji in the distance as you pop over the hill at the first cable-car stop, **ŌWAKUDANI**. This is the site of a constantly bubbling and steaming valley formed by a volcanic eruption three thousand years ago. You can hike up the valley through the lava formations to the bubbling pools where eggs are boiled until they are black and scoffed religiously by every tourist, for no better reason than it's the done thing when visiting Ōwakudani.

North from Gōra

If volcanic activity and cable-cars aren't your thing, there are a couple of worthy museums north of Gōra you could check out the splendid **Pola Museum of Art**, and the quirky **Lalique Museum Hakone**, both accessible by bus. The latter is in the pleasant village of **SENGOKUHARA** (仙石原), another good place to stay the night.

Pola Museum of Art

ポーラ美術館, Pōra Bijutsukan • 1285 Sengokuhara • Daily 9am–5pm • ¥1800 • ⓦ polamuseum.or.jp • Bus from Gōra Station (15min; ¥290)

The superb **Pola Museum of Art** boasts a diverse and eclectic collection of Western art, predominantly from French Impressionists and École de Paris artists. When you've had your fill of checking out pieces by the likes of Renoir, Monet, Picasso, Van Gogh, Cezanne and Gallé, hunt down the glasswork section, and the Japanese paintings and ceramics. The artworks are all displayed in modern galleries in a stunning building that blends beautifully with the surrounding forest, and there's a café and restaurant on site too.

Lalique Museum Hakone

箱根ラリック美術館, Hakone Rarikku Bijutsukan • 186-1 Sengokuhara • Daily 9am–5pm • ¥1500; train carriage (reservation necessary) ¥2100 including drinks and dessert • ☎ 0406 84 2225, ⓦ lalique-museum.com • Bus from Hakone-Yumoto station (30min; ¥540)

Perhaps the most interesting – and certainly the most beautifully situated – of Sengokuhara's museums is the **Lalique Museum Hakone**, dedicated to the delicate glass pieces of the French artist René Lalique. At the entrance is a parked Orient Express Pullman train carriage, kitted out with a Lalique glass panel, which is a great place for tea.

Ashino-ko and around

Sightseeing boats Tōgendai to Moto-Hakone or Hakonenomachi-ko ¥970 • ⓦ hakone-kankosen.co.jp • **Komaga-take cable-car** ¥1050

From **Tōgendai** (桃原台), a shoreline trail winds along the western side of **Ashino-ko** (芦ノ湖) to the small resort of **Hakone-machi** some 8km south, taking around three hours to cover. The western lakeshore, forming part of the *Prince* empire of hotels and resorts, is not covered by the Hakone Free Pass (see box, p.205) and so is somewhat marginalized – and all the more peaceful for it. Most visitors, however, hop straight from the cable-car on to one of the colourful sightseeing ships, modelled after the seventeenth-century man-o'-war *The Sovereign of the Seas*, that regularly sail the length of the lake in around thirty minutes. A cluster of upmarket hotels and ryokan can be found at Hakone-machi, where the sightseeing boats dock. Boats also run from Tōgendai to the *Prince* hotel resort at **Hakone-en**, midway down the east side of the lake, where there's a cable-car up the 1357m **Komaga-take** (駒ヶ岳), from where there's a fabulous view.

THE HAKONE SEKISHO

In 1618 the second shogun, Tokugawa Hidetada, put up the **Hakone Barrier** (Sekisho) – actually more of a large compound than a single gate – which stood at Hakone-machi until 1869. The shogun decreed that all his lords' wives and their families live in Edo (now Tokyo) and that the lords themselves make expensive formal visits to the capital every other year, a strategy designed to ensure that no one attempted a rebellion. The Tōkaidō, on which the barrier stands, was one of the major routes in and out of the capital, and it was here that travellers were carefully checked to see how many guns they were taking into the Edo area, and that the lords' families were stopped from escaping. Any man caught trying to dodge the barrier was crucified and then beheaded, while accompanying women had their heads shaved and were, according to contemporary statute, "given to anyone who wants them".

2

Hakone Barrier

箱根関所, Hakone Sekisho • Daily: March–Nov 9am–5pm; Dec–Feb 9am–4.30 • ¥500

The southern end of the lake is the location of the **Hakone Barrier**, through which all traffic on the **Tōkaidō**, the ancient road linking Kyoto and Edo, once had to pass (see box, p.202). What stands here today is a reproduction, enlivened by waxwork displays which provide the historical background. There's nothing much to keep you here, though; instead, stroll north of the barrier around the wooded promontory, past the bland reconstruction of the Emperor Meiji's Hakone Detached Palace, and take in the views of the lake.

Moto-Hakone

元箱根

Part of the Tōkaidō ancient road – shaded by 420 lofty cryptomeria trees planted in 1618, and now designated "Natural Treasures" – runs for around 1km beside the road leading from the Hakone Barrier to the lakeside **MOTO-HAKONE** tourist village. The prettiest spot around here is the vermilion *torii* (gate), standing in the water just north of Moto-Hakone – a scene celebrated in many an *ukiyo-e* print and modern postcard. The gate belongs to the **Hakone Gongen** (箱根権現) and is the best thing about this small Shintō shrine, set back in the trees, where samurai once came to pray.

Back to Hakone-Yumoto

From either Hakone-machi or Moto-Hakone you can take a **bus** back to Hakone-Yumoto or Odawara (see below). Far more rewarding, however, is the 11km **hike** along part of the Tōkaidō, which begins five minutes up the hill from the Hakone-Tozan bus station in Moto-Hakone; watch for the spot where large paving stones are laid through the shady forests. After the first 2km the route is all downhill and takes around four hours. When the path comes out of the trees and hits the main road, you'll see the **Amazake-jaya Teahouse** (see p.206). From the teahouse, the path shadows the main road to the small village of **HATAJUKU** (畑宿), where since the ninth century craftsmen have perfected the art of *yosegi-zaiku*, or marquetry. The wooden boxes, toys and other objects inlaid with elaborate mosaic patterns make great souvenirs and there are workshops throughout the village, including one right where the path emerges onto the main road. Hatajuku is a good place to pick up the bus the rest of the way to Hakone-Yumoto if you don't fancy hiking any further.

ARRIVAL AND INFORMATION   HAKONE

By train Most people visit Hakone aboard the Odakyū-line train from Shinjuku, using one of the company's excellent-value travel passes (see box opposite). The basic trains terminate in Odawara (小田原), but for ¥870 extra one-way you can take the more comfortable "Romance Car", which goes directly from Shinjuku through to Hakone-Yumoto (1hr 30min). If you're using a JR Pass (see p.35), the fastest route is to take a Shinkansen to Odawara, from where you should transfer to an Odakyū train or bus into the national park area.

By bus The Odakyū express bus (¥1950) from Shinjuku bus terminal will get you to Hakone in a couple of hours.

Buses stop first at Hakone-Yumoto, then Moto-Hakone, then the *Prince* hotel (see opposite) and finally Tōgendai. It's also possible to visit by bus from the Fuji Five Lakes area, in which case you'll enter Hakone through Sengokuhara to the north, passing through the major town of Gotemba; passes will save you money (see box opposite).

Tourist information You can pick up a map of the area and plenty of other information at the very friendly Hakone tourist office (daily 9am–5.45pm; ☎0460 855700, ⊛ hakone.or.jp) in the buildings at the bus terminal across the street from Hakone-Yumoto Station.

ACCOMMODATION

With excellent transportation links you can stay pretty much anywhere in the national park and get everywhere else easily. There's a good range of budget options and some top-grade ryokan.

2

HAKONE TRAVEL PASSES

Touring the Hakone area is great fun, but the various train, funicular, cable-car and boat tickets can add up quickly. One way to prevent this, and save a bundle of cash, is to invest in one of the many **travel passes** covering the area. As well as covering almost all transport, they can be used to lop a little off entry prices to some sights. You can buy passes at the **Odakyū Sightseeing Service Centre** at the west exit of Shinjuku Station (daily 8am–6pm; ☎03 5321 7887, ✆www.odakyu.jp/english); the English-speaking staff here can also make reservations for tours and hotels.

Hakone Freepass If you plan to follow the traditional Hakone route, invest in this pass, which comes in either two- or three-day versions; from Shinjuku, it costs ¥5000/¥5500 (2/3 days); from Odawara or Gotemba it costs ¥3900/¥4400 (2/3 days). The pass covers a return journey on the Odakyū line from Shinjuku to Odawara, and unlimited use of the Hakone-Tozan line, Hakone-Tozan funicular railway, cable-car, boats across the lake and most local buses.

Hakone One-day Pass If you're already in Odawara or Gotemba you can buy a special one-day pass for ¥2000. It doesn't cover the journeys to or from Tokyo, nor the cable-car and boat.

Fuji Hakone Pass If you're going directly from Hakone to the neighbouring Fuji Five Lakes area (or vice versa) then the three-day Fuji Hakone Pass (¥7200) is the way to go. This offers the same deal as a Hakone Freepass but also covers a one-way express bus trip between Hakone-Yumoto and Kawaguchi-ko.

ASHINO-KO

Moto-Hakone Guesthouse 元箱根ゲストハウス 103 Moto-Hakone ☎0460 837880, ✆hakone.syuriken.jp/hakone. Simple guesthouse a short bus ride (get off at Ashinokoen-mae) or stiff 10min walk uphill from Moto-Hakone village. The reward for the journey is spotless Japanese-style rooms and extremely friendly service – a cup of coffee will be plonked in front of you in no time at all. Surcharge of ¥1000 at weekends; breakfast costs ¥840 per person. **¥6250** per person

The Prince Hakone ザプリンス箱根 144 Moto-hakone ☎0460 831 111, ✆princehotels.com. This hotel boasts a prime location on the Komaga-take side of Ashino-ko and a multitude of facilities, including access to an outdoor hot bath with a view of the lake. Renovations have seen all rooms modernized, with the addition of new suite rooms. **¥20,000**

GORA

Gōra Kadan 強羅花壇 1300 Gōra ☎0460 823331, ✆gorakadan.com. One of Hakone's most exclusive ryokans is the stuff of legend, which means you might have to wait an eternity to secure a reservation. Expect beautiful tatami rooms, antiques, exquisite meals and a serene atmosphere. Rates include two meals. **¥100 000**

Hyatt Regency Hakone Resort & Spa ハイアット リージェンシー箱根 1320 Gōra ☎0460 822000, ✆hakone.regency.hyatt.com. This slickly designed hotel is a treat, offering some of the largest rooms in Hakone and elegant facilities, including lounge, two restaurants and the Izumi onsen spa. For those who can't bear to be parted from their pooch, there are even dog-friendly stone-floored rooms. **¥30,000**

HAKONE-YUMOTO

★**Hoeiso** 豊栄荘 227 Moto-hakone ☎0460 831111, ✆hoeiso.jp. Hugely atmospheric ryokan that's by far the best place to stay in the Moto-Hakone area. It's also almost next door to the Tenzan Notemburo (see p.199), but you won't need it since there are excellent bathing facilities on site, including outdoor pools with a river view. Pheasant often features in the superlative evening meals, which are taken in their large and strikingly beautiful rooms. **¥37,000**

MIYANOSHITA

Fujiya Hotel 富士屋ホテル 359 Miyanoshita ☎0460 822211, ✆fujiyahotel.co.jp. The first Western-style hotel in Japan, the *Fujiya* is a living monument to a more glamorous era of travel, and boasts lots of Japanese touches, including traditional gardens and decorative gables like those you find in temples. The plush 1950s-style decor is retro-chic and the rooms are good value. **¥16,000**

Hakone Ginyu 箱根吟遊 100-1 Miyanoshita ☎0460 823355, ✆hakoneginyu.co.jp. Outstanding luxury ryokan, where guests are assured maximum comfort. The views across the valley are stunning and the interiors are a tasteful blend of old and new. Huge *hinoki* wood tubs on private verandas are a major plus. Rates include two meals. **¥68,000**

SENGOKUHARA

Fuji-Hakone Guesthouse 富士箱根ゲストハウス 912 Sengokuhara ☎0460 846577, ✆hakone.syuriken.jp/hakone. This convivial guesthouse, run by the friendly, English-speaking Takahashi-san and his family, has tatami rooms and onsen water piped into a communal bath; only breakfast is available. **¥10,500**

Hakone Sengokuhara Youth Hostel 箱根仙石原ユ
ースホステル 912 Sengokuhara ☎0460 848966,
ⓦjyh.or.jp. Directly behind the *Fuji-Hakone Guesthouse*,
and run by the same family, this hostel offers good dorm
accommodation in a lovely wooden building. The on-site
hot spring is a nice bonus if you've been hiking. Dorm
¥3360

EATING AND DRINKING

HAKONE-YUMOTO

Hakone-Yumoto is stacked with good places to eat. There
are also three good-value restaurants at the Tenzan
Notemburo, serving rice, *shabu-shabu* and *yakiniku* (grilled
meat) dishes.

★**Hatsuhana Soba** はつ花そば 635 Hakone-Yumoto
☎0460 858287. The Hakone area is famed for its soba, on
account of purity of the local water, and this is the best
place to try it. Several options are available, including
tempura and curry bowls, but you can't go wrong with the
teijo soba, served with grated yam and raw egg (¥950). To
get here from the station, follow the riverbank into town,
then turn left at the first bridge – it's right on the other
side, overlooking the river. Daily 10am–7pm.

★**Naokichi** 直吉 696 Hakone-Yumoto ☎0460
855148. Excellent, elegant restaurant serving the
scrumptious local speciality, *yubadon* – soy milk skin in fish
broth, served on rice (¥980) or soba (¥1100). Not sold yet?
There's a free onsen footbath just outside. To find it, head
into town along the riverbank; you'll soon spot the place on
your right. Daily except Tues 11am–6pm.

HATAJUKU

Amazake-jaya 甘酒茶屋 Hatajuku. Rest at this
charming teahouse, just as travellers did hundreds of years
ago, and sip a restorative cup of the milky, sweet rice drink
amazake, with some pickles, for ¥400. Daily 7am–5.30pm.

MIYANOSHITA

Naraya Café ならやカフェー 404-13 Miyanoshita.
There's one major draw at this lovely café, just down the
road from Miyanoshita Station – the footbath which runs
under the table in the outdoor section, making it possible
to bathe your tootsies while sipping a latte (¥400). There's
also a gallery on the top level, and hot dogs and other
snacks on the menu. Daily 10.30am–6pm.

Orchid Lounge 359 Miyanoshita ☎0460 822211,
ⓦfujiyahotel.co.jp. At the wonderful *Fujiya* hotel (see
p.205), this is a grand place for coffee (¥1600 with cake) or
afternoon tea (¥1000); it's a pleasure to sit down and relax
with a view over the garden and carp-filled pond. Daily
9am–9pm.

Izu Hantō

伊豆半島

Formed by Mount Fuji's ancient lava flows, **Izu Hantō** protrudes like an arrowhead into
the ocean southwest of Tokyo, a mountainous spine whose tortured coastline features
some superb scenery and a couple of decent beaches. It takes at least two days to make
a complete circuit of this region, taking in some intriguing historical sights and
stopping at a few of the peninsula's estimated 2300 hot springs.

Direct train services from Tokyo run down Izu's more developed east coast, passing
through **Atami**, with its stylish art museum, to the harbour town of **Shimoda**, a good
base for exploring southern Izu and one of the places Commodore Perry parked his
"Black Ships" in 1854, as well as the site of Japan's first American consulate. Over on
west Izu, **Dōgashima** is another famous beauty spot, with a crop of picturesque islands
set in clear, tropical-blue water. The only settlement of any size in central Izu is
Shuzenji, whose nearby **onsen** resort has long been associated with novelists such as
Kawabata Yasunari and Natsume Sōseki (see p.837).

Izu's mild climate makes it a possible excursion even in winter, though it's close
enough to Tokyo to be crowded at weekends, and is best avoided during the summer
holidays.

ARRIVAL AND GETTING AROUND   IZU HANTŌ

Before making your Izu plans, check out the various discount tickets available, of which the most useful is the four-day "Izu
Free Q Kippu" (¥13,190), which covers the Shinkansen from Tokyo as well as local transport by train and bus. Renting a car
is a good idea, as public transport is slow and only really covers the main coastal settlements; you'll find rental companies
in Atami, Shimoda and Shuzenji.

Atami

熱海

The hot-spring resort of **ATAMI** serves as the eastern gateway to Izu, and also functions as one of the jumping-off points for Ōshima (see p.214). This has not always been the case, for in the 1970s the town was one of Japan's most popular honeymoon destinations but, since the advent of cheap package holidays to Guam, Saipan and the like, Atami has been stuck in a slow, spiralling decline, and those who take a night-time walk along its pleasant beach may feel as though they're stirring up ghosts of the past. However, and partly because of this best-days-behind-it air, the town remains a pleasant place; it's certainly worth popping by on your way to or from other places in Izu.

MOA Museum of Art

MOA美術館 • Daily except Thurs 9.30am–4.30pm • ¥1600; you can buy tickets for ¥1300 at Atami tourist office (see below) • Ⓦ moaart.or.jp • Bus from Atami station (5min; ¥160)

Carved into a hillside above the town, the stunning **MOA Museum of Art** takes a bit of effort to get to, though its remarkable architecture and collection of mostly ancient eastern art easily justify a visit. Buses drop you outside the museum's lower entrance, from where you ride four escalators that cut through the rock to the main exhibition halls. Each room contains just a few pieces, of which the most famous – only put on show in February of each year – is a dramatic folding screen entitled *Red and White Plum Blossoms* by the innovative Ogata Kōrin (1658–1716). The most eye-catching exhibit is a full-size replica of a golden tearoom, lined with gold leaf and equipped with utensils made of gold, and built in 1586. The museum's well-tended gardens contain teahouses serving *matcha* and sweet cakes.

ARRIVAL AND INFORMATION

ATAMI

By train Atami is on the Shinkansen line from Tokyo, meaning that you can be there in a flash (every 30min; 35min); slower trains run here too (every 15min; 2hr 10min). There are also services west, and slower ones south to Shimoda (every 30min; 1hr–1hr 25min).

By boat There are jetfoil services to and from Ōshima (2–3 daily; 45min).

Tourist information Just by the ticket booth in Atami station (daily: April–Sept 9am–5.30pm; Oct–March 9am–5pm; ☎ 0557 852222).

Shimoda and around

下田

At Atami trains peel off down the east coast of Izu, cutting through craggy headlands and running high above bays ringed with fishing villages or resort hotels.

WILL ADAMS

In 1600 a Dutch ship washed up on east Kyūshū, the sole survivor of five vessels that had set sail from Europe two years previously; three-quarters of the crew had perished from starvation and the remaining 24 were close to death.

One of those rescued was the navigator, an Englishman called **Will Adams** (1564–1620). He was summoned by Tokugawa Ieyasu, the future shogun, who quizzed Adams about European affairs, religion and various scientific matters. Ieyasu liked what he heard and made Adams his personal adviser on mathematics, navigation and armaments. Adams, known locally as Anjin ("pilot"), later served as the shoguns interpreter and as a diplomat, brokering trade treaties with both Holland and Britain. In return he was granted **samurai status**, the first and last foreigner to be so honoured, along with a Japanese wife and an estate near Yokosuka on the Miura Peninsula.

Adams' main task, however, was to oversee the construction of Japan's first Western-style sailing ships. In 1605 he set up a shipyard at **Itō**, on the east coast of Izu, where he built at least two ocean-going vessels over the next five years. His fascinating life story is told in Giles Milton's *Samurai William* and also forms the basis for James Clavell's novel, *Shogun*. Each August, Itō's Anjin Matsuri celebrates Adams.

2

Nearly halfway down the peninsula is Itō (伊東), the port where Will Adams launched Japan's first Western-style sailing ships (see box, p.207), but there's nothing really to stop for until you reach **SHIMODA**. Off season, this small, amiable town, with its attractive scenery and sprinkling of temples and museums, makes a good base for a couple of days' exploring. Its sights revolve around the arrival of Commodore Perry's so-called Black Ships (*Kurofune*) in 1854, making it one of Japan's first ports to open to foreign trade. The people of Shimoda are immensely proud of their part in Japanese history and you'll find Black Ships everywhere; there's even a **Black Ships Festival** (around the third Friday to Sunday in May), when American and Japanese naval bands parade through the streets, followed by the inevitable fireworks.

Central Shimoda lies on the northwestern shore of a well-sheltered harbour, surrounded by steep hills. Most of its sights are in the older, southerly district, where you'll find a number of attractive grey-and-white latticed walls near the original fishing harbour; this style of architecture (known as *namako-kabe*), found throughout Izu, is resistant to fire, earthquakes and corrosive sea air.

Brief history

Having signed an initial treaty in Yokohama, which granted America trading rights in Shimoda and Hakodate (on Hokkaidō) and consular representation, Commodore Perry (see above) sailed his Black Ships down to Izu. Here, in Shimoda's Ryōsen-ji, he

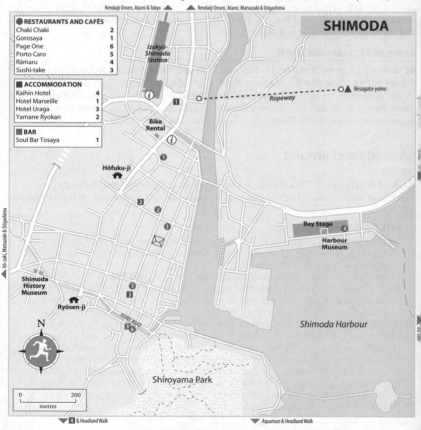

SHIMODA

RESTAURANTS AND CAFÉS
Chaki Chaki	2
Gorosaya	1
Page One	6
Porto Caro	5
Rāmaru	4
Sushi-take	3

ACCOMMODATION
Kaihin Hotel	4
Hotel Marseille	1
Hotel Uraga	3
Yamane Ryokan	2

BAR
Soul Bar Tosaya	1

Rendaiji Onsen, Atami & Tokyo — Rendaiji Onsen, Atami, Matsuzaki & Dōgashima

Izukyū-Shimoda Station

Nesugata-yama
Ropeway

Bike Rental

Hōfuku-ji

Shimoda History Museum

Ryōsen-ji

PERRY ROAD

Bay Stage

Harbour Museum

Shimoda Harbour

Irō-zaki, Matsuzaki & Dōgashima

N

Shiroyama Park

0   200
metres

4 & Headland Walk   Aquarium & Headland Walk

concluded a supplementary **Treaty of Friendship** in 1854. Russian, British and Dutch merchants were granted similar rights soon after, and in 1856 **Townsend Harris** arrived in Shimoda as the first American Consul. By now, however, it was obvious Shimoda was too isolated as a trading post and Harris began negotiating for a revised treaty, which was eventually signed (again in Shimoda) in July 1858, with Kanagawa replacing Shimoda as an open port, so the burgeoning foreign community decamped north to Yokohama.

Ryōsen-ji

了仙寺 • Museum daily 8.30am–5pm • ¥500 • ⓦ www.izu.co.jp/~ryosenji

Your first stop in Shimoda should be **Ryōsen-ji**, where Perry signed the Treaty of Friendship, though this small but elaborate temple, founded in 1635, is less interesting than its attached **museum**, which is full of fascinating historical documents and wood-block prints, many of them original, from the 1850s. Delightful portraits of Perry and his devilish crew, penned by Japanese artists, contrast with the European view of Japan – embellished with Chinese touches – from contemporary editions of the *Illustrated London News* and other European journals. Many exhibits relate to the tragic Saitō Okichi, the servant of Consul Harris, who earned the nickname of Tōjin ("foreigner's concubine"), while a second room contains a somewhat incongruous display of sex in religious art, including some beautiful pieces from India, Nepal and Japan's Shintō shrines.

Shimoda History Museum

下田開国博物館 Shimoda Kaikoku Hakabutsukep • Daily 8.30am–5.30pm • ¥1000

From Ryōsen-ji, **Perry Road** leads east along a small river lined with willows and picturesque old houses, some now converted into cafés and antique shops. Heading back west past Ryōsen-ji, you'll soon come to the **Shimoda History Museum**, housed in two *namako-kabe* buildings on opposite sides of the street. Alongside more caricatures of big-nosed foreigners, Harris and Okichi are again much in evidence, and the museum also includes plenty of information, much of it in English, about local life, including the area's distinctive architecture and festivals.

Hōfuku-ji

宝福寺 • Temple museum daily 8am–5pm • ¥300

When Okichi (see above) died in 1890, none of her family came forward to claim her body, so it was left to a local priest to bring her back to the family temple for burial. Her grave now lies behind the otherwise unremarkable **Hōfuku-ji**, where there's another small museum dedicated to her memory.

Nesugata-yama

寝姿山 • Ropeway daily 9am–5pm, departures every 10–15min • ¥1000 return

The east side of Shimoda is dominated by the 200m peak of **Nesugata-yama**. On a clear day it's worth taking the ropeway from beside the train station up to the summit for dramatic views of the harbour and out to the Izu islands on the eastern horizon.

Harbour Museum

Daily except Tues 9am–5pm • ¥500

Nesugata-yama's south face drops steeply to the harbour, where there's a string of resort hotels and the Bay Stage building, with its **Harbour Museum** on the second floor. Here, the story of Shimoda's brief spell in the limelight is enlivened by holograms re-enacting the 1854 arrival of Perry, as well as that of a Russian Admiral who pitched up here the same year. From the tourist wharf outside you can take a short **harbour cruise**, or set off on longer excursions to Irō-zaki (see p.211).

2

Townsend Harris Museum

Daily 8am–5pm • ¥300

Along the promenade at the far, eastern, side of the bay is **Gyokusen-ji** (玉泉寺), where Townsend Harris established Japan's first American consulate in 1856 – he lived and worked there for about fifteen months, accompanied by his Dutch interpreter, Chinese servants and, possibly, Okichi. On entering the **Townsend Harris Museum**, to the right of the temple, you're greeted by a startling, life-size model of Harris, complete with splendid handlebar moustache, relaxing in his rocking chair in full evening dress while Okichi offers him a glass of milk. Heading back to town, you can then retrace your steps to Perry Road and follow the coast road south around the Shiroyama headland; alternatively, climb the hill you've been walking round for good views over the town and harbour. It's particularly spectacular in June, when over a million hydrangea blooms colour the slopes.

ARRIVAL AND DEPARTURE   SHIMODA

By train JR express trains run direct from Tokyo Station to Izukyū-Shimoda Station on the north side of town (hourly; 2hr 40min–3hr); there's also the daily *Super View Odoriko* service from Ikebukuro and Shinjuku to Shimoda and back, which has extra-wide windows to take in the spectacular coastal views; reservations are essential. Some trains divide at Atami for Shuzenji, so check you're on the right section. JR passes are only valid for the journey as far as Itō; beyond Itō it's a private line down to Shimoda. All trains pass via Rendaiji.

By bus There are buses from in front of Shimoda station to Izu locations unreachable by train; these include Irō-zaki (1–2 hourly; 40min) and Shuzenji (1 daily; 2hr). If you're exploring the southern area up to Dōgashima and Irō-zaki (see opposite), it's worth buying the two-day "Minami Izu Free Pass" (¥2790); you'll make a saving on these two day-trips alone, and their buses also serve Rendaiji. The pass is available from the Tōkai Bus office (daily 8.30am–5.30pm; ☎0558 22 2511) on the other side of the bus terminal from the station, under the *Hotel Marseille*.

GETTING AROUND

Car rental Car rental is available from Nippon Rent-a-Car (☎0558 22 5711), Nissan (☎0558 23-4123) and Toyota (☎0558 27 0100), all with outlets close to the station.

Bike rental You can rent bikes at Noguchi Rentacycle (daily 9.30am–6pm; ¥500/hr, ¥2000/day; ☎0558 22 1099), one block south of the station.

INFORMATION AND TOURS

Tourist information There's an information desk inside the front exit of the station (daily 9am–5pm; ☎0558 22 3200); they usually sell discounted tickets to the town's sights. The Shimoda Tourist Association (daily 10am–5pm; ☎0558 23 5593, ⍟shimoda-city.info) is to the left of the station beside the main crossroads; both places can help with town maps and accommodation.

Tours You can get to Irō-zaki on one of the tourist boats which depart from Shimoda's tourist wharf during peak season (3 daily: March 25–31; April 29–May 6; July 29–Aug 20; Dec 30–Jan 5; rest of year 3 daily Mon, Sat & Sun; 40min; ¥1530). From here you can also take a short 20min harbour cruise (daily 9.10am–4pm, every 30min–1hr; ¥1100) on a replica Black Ship.

ACCOMMODATION

Much of the town's accommodation consists of either pricey resort **hotels** on the harbour-front or rather run-down minshuku. However, there are a few appealing options around the station and among the older streets to the south. Other possibilities in the area include Rendaiji's more stylish ryokan and a beach-side hotel at Kisami-Ōhama.

Kaihin Hotel 下田海浜ホテル 3-26-7 Shimoda-shi, a 10min walk from Perry Rd ☎0558 22 2065, ⍟itoenhotel .com/hotel/shimoda. Not the prettiest building, but the location on a quiet bay and the reasonable rates (including two meals) are a plus. Rooms are mostly Japanese-style, with balconies and sea views, and there are two onsen baths, one with sea views, plus a rotemburo. **¥18,000**

Hotel Marseille ホテルマルセーユ 3F, 1-1-5 Higashi-Hongo ☎0558 23 8000. Modest but well-kept business

hotel beside the station with a cheerful French theme. The single rooms (around ¥8000) are small but the doubles and twins are a decent size and nicely decorated. **¥12,000**

Hotel Uraga ホテルウラガ 3-3-10 Shimoda-shi ☎0558 23 6600. Clean, bright business hotel in the south part of town. It's worth paying a little extra for the larger twin rooms, but all are comfortable, and the coffee shop serves Japanese and Western breakfasts. Some English spoken. **¥10,500**

Yamane Ryokan やまね旅館 1-19-15 Shimoda-shi ☎0558 22 0482. One of the better budget minshuku in central Shimoda – the simple tatami rooms and communal bathrooms are clean and well kept. **¥9000**

EATING AND DRINKING

Shimoda has a number of affordable *izakaya* and sushi **restaurants**; as with the rest of Izu, the town is justly proud of its *kin-me-dai*, a red-scaled fish with a silver, coin-like eye, and the rather magnificent English name of "Splendid Alfonsino". There are also a few good **coffee shops** scattered around town and along Perry Road, some of which double as antiques showrooms.

Chaki Chaki 茶気茶気 1-20-10 Shimoda-shi ☎0558 27 1331. This surprisingly sophisticated café-bar serves tasty light meals along the lines of cajun chicken, pasta and bagels. Lunch sets from around ¥1100. Tues–Sun noon–2pm & 6–11pm.

★**Gorosaya** ごろさや 1-5-25 Shimoda-shi ☎0558 23 5638. Relaxed and popular fish restaurant which apparently predates the arrival of the Black Ships. Their standard *teishoku* (around ¥1600) includes a choice of sashimi, tempura or grilled *kin-me-dai* – almost everyone's here for the latter, and rightly so. English menu. Daily except Thurs 11.30am–2pm & 5–9pm.

Page One 3-14-30 Shimoda-shi. The best of Perry Road's many places for coffee. Though the brew's not all that great, it's the only one with an outdoor table, set on a bridge over the stream. Daily except Thurs 11am–8pm.

Porto Caro 2F, 3-3-7 Shimoda-shi ☎0553 22 5514. This cute Mediterranean restaurant turns out pretty authentic-tasting pizza, pasta and paella, among other dishes. The lunchtime deals are good value from around ¥1200; in the evening count on at least ¥2000/person. English menu. Daily except Wed 11.30am–2pm & 6–10pm.

★**Ramaru** ラーマル 1-1 Shimoda-shi ☎0558 27 2510. This retro-style American burger bar was nothing special until they started selling their wonderful Shimoda burger (¥1000), a real beast with a giant slab of *kin-me-dai* as a filling. Absolutely wonderful. Daily 10am–5pm.

Soul Bar Tosaya 3-14-30 Shimoda-shi ☎0558 27 0587. One of a few quirky places to drink in the Perry Road area, selling drinks from ¥500. The music's pretty cool, and generally in keeping with the establishment's name. Daily 6pm–midnight.

Sushi-take 寿司竹 2-4-6 Shimoda-shi ☎0558 22 2026. Choose from the picture menu or counter display at this sushi outlet, or simply opt for one of the well-priced sushi sets (from ¥1500). They also serve *donburi* dishes, including *aji-don* (local horse mackerel). Daily except Thurs 11.30am–3pm & 5–11pm.

South to Irō-zaki

In summer, Izu's beaches are packed, but out of season they're usually fairly deserted. The major resort is just north of Shimoda, at Shirahama, but there are a couple of smaller, more attractive bays southwest of the town on the bus route to Izu's southern cape, **Irō-zaki** (石廊崎); you'll find a range of places to sleep and eat at all of them.

RENDAIJI ONSEN

Set in a narrow valley just west of National Highway 414, **RENDAIJI ONSEN** (蓮台寺温泉) is a quiet, one-street village consisting mostly of exclusive ryokan that tap into the area's abundant supply of hot water. It's these onsen baths that make it worth a visit, though there are also a few meandering back lanes to explore, and you might want to splash out on a night of luxury after your dip. Two or three **trains** an hour (3–4min; ¥160) run between Shimoda – roughly 3km to the south – and Rendaiji Station, from where it's a short walk west across the river and highway to the village. Local **buses** are slightly less frequent, but most drop you right on the main street (1–2 hourly; 10min; ¥160).

Kanaya Ryokan 金谷旅館 ☎0558 22 0325. Set in a beautiful, traditional building, this ryokan features the most appealing of Rendaiji's many onsen – a big wooden public bath (¥700) in a cavernous hall. There are several other pools here too, including a rotemburo, where many of your fellow bathers will be local families. The ryokan also has an observatory for stargazing, and a tea ceremony room. It's located on the main highway, just north of the village turning. Rates include two meals. **¥20,000**

Ishibashi Ryokan 石橋旅館 ☎0558 22 2222. Also known as the *Kur hotel*, this beautiful and welcoming place has several attractive baths (non-guests ¥1050) including a little rotemburo. It's in Rendaiji proper, tucked under a small hill on the right as you walk from the highway. Rates include two meals. **¥23,500**

2

Around 4km southwest of Shimoda, Highway 136 passes through the village of **Kisami** (吉佐美) where a road forks left across a river towards the coast. **Kisami-Ōhama** (吉佐美大浜), the name of Kisami's sandy bay, is one of south Izu's more attractive beaches – marred slightly by a factory on the far horizon – and a popular surfing spot.

A little further along the coast, **Yumigahama** (弓ヶ浜) is a larger, more developed resort, but has the advantage that the bus takes you all the way down to the wide horseshoe bay, which is ringed with pines and casuarina.

Continuing round the coast, the road climbs through lush vegetation to emerge in an expanse of car parks that cap the headland. Fortunately, **Irō-Zaki** improves dramatically as you walk out along the promontory for about 500m, past souvenir shops and a lighthouse, to a minuscule **shrine** balanced on the cliff edge. The views here are superb: on either side the sea has cut deep-blue gashes into the coastline, leaving behind a sprinkling of rocky islets between which colourful **tourist boats** bob and weave.

ARRIVAL AND GETTING AROUND   SOUTH TO IRŌ-ZAKI

By bus From Izukyū-Shimoda Station, buses depart for Irō-zaki roughly every 30min, but check before boarding as some buses skip certain stops.

Boat tours Another scenic way of getting here – or returning to Shimoda – is to take one of the tourist boats

that ply between Shimoda and Irō-zaki port (see p.211). Depending on the weather and the season, there are one or two trips per hour around the Irō-zaki headland and back (25min; ¥1200). In addition, on certain days boats sail from here back to Shimoda (see p.207).

Shūzenji Onsen
修善寺町 温泉

Not to be confused with the modern town of **Shuzenji**, 3km to the northwest, **SHŪZEN-JI ONSEN** consists of little more than one road and a string of riverside hotels and souvenir shops along a narrow valley. Follow the main street west and you'll soon reach an open area with some pleasant older buildings and a succession of red-lacquered bridges over the tumbling Katsura-gawa. Here, on a rocky outcrop beside the river, Shūzen-ji's first and most famous **onsen**, *Tokko-no-yu*, is now considered too public to be used for bathing, though you can soak your feet. According to legend, the onsen was "created" in 807 by Kōbō Daishi, the founder of Shingon Buddhism (see p.793), when he found a boy washing his ailing father in the river; the priest struck the rock with his *tokko* (the short, metal rod carried by Shingon priests), and out gushed hot water with curative powers.

Shūzen-ji
修善寺

Kōbō Daishi is also credited with founding the temple, **Shūzen-ji**, close to the original onsen, from which the town gets its name. The present temple, which stands at the top

---

SHŪZEN-JI'S SHOGUNS

During the Kamakura period (1185–1333), Shūzen-ji was a favourite place of exile for the shoguns' potential rivals. In 1193 Minamoto Noriyori, the younger brother of Shogun Yoritomo, committed suicide – some say he was murdered – after being banished here on suspicion of treason. A more famous death occurred soon after when **Minamoto Yoriie** was murdered in the bath. Yoriie was the son of Yoritomo and had succeeded to the title of Shogun in 1199, aged only 18. Four years later his mother, Hōjō Masako, and grandfather seized power and sent Yoriie packing to Shūzen-ji, where he started planning his revenge. Yet the plot was discovered in 1204 and not long after Yoriie was found dead, supposedly killed by bathing in poisoned water.

of the steps on the river's north bank, was rebuilt in 1883 and its now quiet halls belie a violent history (see box opposite).

Shūzen-ji museum

Daily: April–Sept 8.30am–4.30pm; Oct–March 8.30am–4pm • ¥300

Opposite the Shūzen-ji temple office you'll find a small **museum** full of temple treasures, including possessions allegedly belonging to Kōbō Daishi and Minamoto Yoriie, and what is said to be Yoriie's death mask, all red and swollen. There's also information, some of it in English, about the many novels and plays inspired by these dramatic events, including Okamoto Kidō's famous modern kabuki play *Shūzen-ji Monogatari*, written in 1911.

Shigetsu-den
指月殿

Minamoto Yoriie's unassuming grave lies on the hillside directly across the valley from Shūzen-ji, beside a smaller temple, **Shigetsu-den**, which a repentant Hōjō Masako built to appease the soul of her son. Though not a dramatic building, it's the oldest in Shuzenji and has a fine Buddha statue inside accompanied by two guardians.

The onsen

Hako-yu Daily noon–9pm • ¥350 • Yu-no-sato-mura Daily 9am–10pm • ¥700 for 1hr, ¥950 no time limit

Although you can only bathe your feet in *Tokko-no-yu*, the town's most famous onsen, there are others just a short walk away. The old-style building nearby with a watchtower offers a lovely cedarwood **onsen bath**, *Hako-yu* (筥湯). Alternatively, follow the path west along the river, meandering across pretty bridges and through bamboo groves, and 400m later you'll emerge near a modern bathhouse, *Yu-no-sato-mura* (湯の里村), complete with both rotemburo and sauna. The bathhouse marks the western outskirts of Shūzenji village; turn right and you're back on the main street.

ARRIVAL AND INFORMATION   SHŪZEN-JI ONSEN

By train Travelling to Shūzenji from Tokyo, the best option is an Odoriko-gō Limited Express train direct from Tokyo Station (2 daily; 2hr 10min); the trains divide at Atami, so make sure you're in the right carriage. Alternatively, hop on any of the regular Shinkansen services to Mishima (every 30min; 40min), from where the private Izu-Hakone Railway runs south to Shūzenji (¥500).

By bus Buses depart from outside Shūzenji Station to Shūzen-ji Onsen (every 10–20min; ¥210), dropping you at a terminal east of the village centre, and also to Shimoda, Dōgashima and other destinations around the peninsula.

Tourist information Shūzenji's tourist information office (daily 9am–5pm; ☎0558 72 2501, ☻shuzenji.info) is in the city hall, on the main road coming into Shūzen-ji Onsen, a short walk east of the bus terminus.

Car rental Try Nissan (☎0558 72 2332) or Toyota (☎0558 74 0100) – both have branches near Shūzenji Station.

ACCOMMODATION

It's best to stay in Shūzen-ji Onsen rather than in Shūzenji itself. Prices for accommodation get cheaper the further away you get from the river.

Fukui 民宿福井 ☎0558 72 0558. Of a group of minshuku on the northern hillside, this is one of the few that welcomes non-Japanese speakers. None of the rooms has its own bathroom, but it's got a lovely little rotemburo perched on the hillside. Rates include two meals. **¥13,000** or **¥9000** without meals.

Goyōkan 五葉館 ☎0558 72 2066, ☻goyokan.co.jp. Located a few doors down to the east of *Yukairō Kikuya* and behind a latticework facade. The lack of en-suite facilities at this comfortable ryokan is compensated for by large onsen baths, cool, colour-coded rooms, and an affable, English-speaking owner. **¥17,000** or **¥12,000** without meals

Yukairō Kikuya 湯回廊菊屋 ☎0558 72 2000. One of the nicest options hereabouts, this elegant ryokan – patronized most famously by the writer Natsume Sōseki (see p.837) – sits under a high-peaked roof immediately opposite the bus station. Two meals included. **¥36,000**

EATING AND DRINKING

Nanaban な>番 On the main road east of the Shūzen-ji Onsen bus terminal ☏ 0558 72 0007. You'll find plenty of atmosphere at this rustic soba restaurant. Though they serve reasonably priced rice and noodle dishes, their speciality is *Zen-dera* soba, in which you dip cold soba in an eye-watering, do-it-yourself sauce of sesame and freshly grated horseradish – it's said to bring you the blessings of Buddha, so is surely a bargain at ¥1260. Daily except Thurs 10am–4pm.

Okura おくら Opposite Nanaban ☏ 0558 73 2266. In the evening, head to this friendly little *izakaya*, with an English menu and well-priced set meals from around ¥1300. Tues–Sun 11.30am–2pm & 5.30–9pm.

Izu-Ōshima

伊豆大島

Some 110km south of Tokyo, **IZU-ŌSHIMA**, or simply Ōshima, is the nearest and largest, at 52km in circumference, of the **Izu-Shotō**, a chain of seven volcanic islands stretching over 300km of ocean. While the others are now dormant, Ōshima's **Mihara-yama** (764m) has the dubious distinction of being the world's third most active volcano after Italy's Stromboli and Kilauea in Hawaii. It's probably better known, however, as the location for the *Godzilla* films (see p.828), for which the barren lava fields provide a fittingly apocalyptic backdrop. Mihara-yama's most recent major eruption took place in 1986, when the island was evacuated, but, fortunately, for much of the time it simply steams away. Do note, though, that the island was struck by a catastrophic typhoon in October 2013: 35 people died and many buildings were destroyed, with damage still much in evidence at the time of writing.

Other than the volcano, Ōshima's main draws are forests of **camellia**, and its status as a summer party spot: some Tokyoites refer to the place as "Sex Island". If you're here to party, pick any summer weekend; for the forests, springtime is best, since the blossoms of an estimated three million trees colour the lower slopes a dusky red, an event celebrated with a month-long **festival** (Feb–March) of folk dances and other events. Whenever you visit, try to stay at least one night, to experience the slow pace of island life.

ARRIVAL AND DEPARTURE IZU-ŌSHIMA

By plane ANA has a daily morning flight to Ōshima from Haneda Airport (30min; from ¥13,100), though by the time you've included travelling to the airport and check-in time, the jetfoils are just as quick.

By jetfoil The best way of getting to Ōshima is on one of the jetfoils (2 daily; 1hr 45min–2hr 10min; ¥7660) operated by Tōkai Kisen (☏ 03 5472 9999, ⊕ www.tokaikisen.co.jp) that depart from Tokyo's Takeshiba pier, two stops from Shimbashi on the Yurikamome monorail. They dock either at Motomachi or at the tiny port of Okata (岡田), 7km away on the more sheltered north coast, depending on the weather. Remember to check which port

it's leaving from for the return journey, either by going to the port terminal in Motomachi or phoning Tōkai Kisen (☏ 04992 25522).

By ferry The same company also runs a ferry service (1 daily July & Aug; 1 daily except Tues Sept–June; 4hr 20min–8hr; from ¥4720). Outward sailings leave from Takeshiba pier at 10pm or 11pm, arriving in Motomachi on the west side of the island early the next morning, while the return boat departs early afternoon, getting back to Tokyo the same evening; times vary, so check locally for the current schedule. Other options include jetfoils from Atami (2–3 daily; 45min; ¥4870), also operated by Tōkai Kisen.

GETTING AROUND

By bus There are at least nine services daily on the main route running north from Motomachi to Okata (20min; ¥350) and Ōshima Park (35min; ¥540). These buses stop on the road by the entrance to the airport (10min; ¥210), but there's also one bus a day to the airport terminal at 8.45am (8min; ¥250). The second main route takes you south from Motomachi to Habu (9–11 daily; 35min; ¥660) on the

island's southeastern tip, while other routes head up Mihara-yama (see opposite). If you anticipate using the bus a lot, you could consider buying a one-day "free ticket" for ¥2000; you can only use this for travel between 10am and 4pm. Although there are designated bus stops, you can flag down a passing bus anywhere.

By car By far the best way of getting around the island

is with your own transport. There are a number of car rental outfits, including Nissan Rent-a-Car (☎04992 22693) and Toyota (☎04992 21611), as well as local company Ōshima Rent-a-Car Association (☎04992 21043). Rates start at around ¥5000 for the smallest car for up to six hours, and the car will be delivered to the port if you book in advance.

By bike and motorbike You can rent motorbikes from Tōma garage (当馬; 2hr ¥3000, 1 day ¥6000; ☎04992 21515) on the main road in Motomachi near the post office,

and mountain bikes (2hr ¥1000, 1 day from ¥1800) from Marukyu (丸久; ☎04992 23317), on the road heading east from Motomachi port, or from Ranburu (らんぶる; ☎04992 23398), beside *Pension Minamoto* (see below). The most popular route is to cycle round the is and (44km), which takes five to six hours and is best tackled anticlockwise to reduce the number of climbs.

Taxis A taxi from Motomachi to Okata will cost around ¥3000 and around ¥1500 to the airport; call Ōshima Kankō Jidōsha on ☎04992 21051.

Motomachi

元町

Ōshima's main town, **MOTOMACHI**, is generally a sleepy little place which only springs into action when a ferry docks. It is, however, the hub of island life, where you'll find most of the facilities, and it makes a good base for exploring the island; it also boasts a couple of moderately interesting sights of its own.

Museum of Volcanoes

火山博物館, Kazan Hakubutsukan • Around 600m from the port • Daily 9am–5pm • ¥500 • ☎04992 24103

The rather grand **Museum of Volcanoes** on the town's southern outskirts, was built after the 1986 eruption partly to lure tourists back to the island. Nothing much is labelled in English, though few things – lumps of volcanic rocks, video footage of eruptions, and the like – really need explaining.

Camellia-oil factory

高田製油所, Takata Seiyu-jo • In a backstreet just north of the *Akamon* • Daily 10am–5pm; closes occasionally • Free • ☎04992 21125

It's worth dropping by the **camellia-oil factory** to see if the presses are in action. The factory uses traditional methods to dry, steam and press the nuts to produce the pure, golden oil which can be used for everything from cooking to hair care. Nothing is wasted: the remaining pressed cake is burnt in local pottery kilns and the ash used in the glaze

Hama-no-yu

浜の湯 • 300m north of the ferry terminal • Daily July & Aug 11am–7pm; Sept–June 1–7pm • ¥400

The best of Motomachi's several **onsen** baths is **Hama-no-yu**, a big public rotemburo on the cliff edge. It's the perfect spot for watching the sun go down – particularly on clear days when Mount Fuji's silhouette adds a poetic touch. Note that you'll need to bring a swimming costume.

ARRIVAL AND INFORMATION   **MOTOMACHI**

By plane Ōshima Airport is about 4km north of Motomachi.

By ferry and jetfoil Regular services arrive from Tokyo (see p.126).

Tourist information The tourist office (daily

8.30am–5pm; ☎04992 22177, ⌂izu-oshima.or.jp) lies across the road from the ferry terminal. They provide maps, bus timetables and a wealth of other information, though very little in English. You can also pick up basic maps at the bus ticket office in Okata.

ACCOMMODATION

Akamon ホテル赤門 ☎04992 21213. One of the smartest sleeps in central Motomachi, with a choice of tatami or Western-style rooms (the latter in separate chalet-style cottages), an attractive rotemburo and onsen bath, and excellent seafood meals. To find it, walk up the

road heading inland (east) from the ferry terminal, then take the first left where you'll see its distinctive red gates at the end of the lane. Rates include two meals. **¥29,000**
Pension Minamoto ペンションみなもと ☎04992 21142. On the same lane as the *Akamon*, this family-run

affair is equally welcoming, with simpler Japanese and Western-style rooms, none of which are en suite. They serve great food, the bulk of it made with local produce. Rates include two meals. **¥16,000**

EATING

In the evening you're best off eating in your hotel, but Motomachi does have a reasonable choice of restaurants in among the ramen and soba joints.

Otomodachi ペンションみなもと ☎ 04992 20061. A reliable bet among a row of little places opposite the port, serving a broad range of reasonably priced set meals (dishes from ¥700). Daily 7am–3pm & 5–10pm.

Sushikō 寿し光 ☎ 04992 20888. Upstairs in a modern building just south of the ferry terminal and on the left, this moderately swanky venue has sushi and sashimi sets from ¥1000, as well as pizzas, salads, *donburi* and the like. Daily 11am–2pm & 5–11pm.

Umisachi 魚味幸 ☎ 04992 22942. The friendly *izakaya* on the east side of town is worth seeking out: from the port walk east up to the main north–south road, go straight across at the traffic lights and you'll find it on the left where the road makes a right-hand bend. Mon–Sat 5–11pm.

Mihara-yama

三原山 · **Ōshima Onsen rotemburo** Daily 1–9pm · ¥800

From Motomachi the road climbs steeply up the mostly grassy slopes of **Mihara-yama**, affording good views over Motomachi and the island's west coast and, if you're lucky, northwest across Izu Hantō to Mount Fuji. At the top, a clutch of souvenir shops sits on the rim of a much older crater, from where you get your first sight of the smouldering new summit, its flanks streaked with black ribbons left by the 1986 lava flows. A path leads 2.2km across the floor of the old crater, where grasses are gradually recolonizing the black, volcanic soils, and up to the new summit, from where you can peek down into the new crater's sulphurous pit. You can then continue for another 2.5km round the rim and either return to the car park or walk down the northern slopes to rejoin the road 3km further down, but still 500m above sea level, near the *Ōshima Onsen Hotel* (大島温泉ホテル;). The hotel itself is rather dilapidated and overpriced, but its rotemburo offers a great view of the volcano. Another option is to walk all the way down to the coast from the volcano; a popular trail heads northeast to bring you out near Ōshima-kōen (see below) in a couple of hours.

ARRIVAL AND DEPARTURE
MIHARA-YAMA

By bus Mihara-yama can be reached by bus from both Motomachi (5 daily; 25min; ¥860) and Ōshima-kōen (2 daily; 25min; ¥840). Buses on both routes also call at the hotel on the way down.

Tsubaki-en botanical garden

椿園 · East side of island · Garden and museum daily 8.30am–5pm · Free

The **Tsubaki-en botanical garden**, part of the larger **Ōshima-kōen** (大島公園) municipal park, has dozens of different varieties of the camellia, or *tsubaki* as the tree is known locally. The tree's flower is the symbol of the island, and is best viewed in spring (Jan–March) when the blossoms are at their peak. Outside the flowering season, when the garden is closed, you get some idea of what all the fuss is about in the one-room **museum** across the road from the garden.

Habu-Minato

波浮港

The road south of Ōshima-kōen and all the way round to Motomachi takes you along through the most beautiful and least populated part of the island. On the southeast tip, **HABU-MINATO**, sitting on a perfect horseshoe-shaped bay – an ancient, flooded caldera –

makes a pleasant place to stop. It's hard to imagine now that in the early twentieth century this one-street village, with its row of old wooden fishermen's houses, was one of Japan's most important fishing ports.

Chisō-setsu-danmen

地層切断面 • 8km west of Habu

When they were building the island road in 1953, workmen uncovered the perfect, 1km-long geological cross section through the rock strata known as **Chisō-setsu-danmen**. The successive layers reveal at least one hundred volcanic eruptions stretching back over 15,000 years. Locals call it the *baumkuchen* – German layer cake. From here it's another 7km back to Motomachi.

2

Northern Honshū

Northern Honshū

When the famous poet Matsuo Bashō set out on his travels along the "narrow road to the deep north" in 1689, he commented, somewhat despondently, "I might as well be going to the ends of the earth." Even today, many urban Japanese regard the harsh, mountainous provinces of Northern Honshū as irredeemably backward. Not that it's all thatched farmhouses and timeless agricultural vistas, but certainly rural traditions have survived here longer than in many other parts of the country. However, it doesn't take long to discover the region's huge array of festivals; nor do you have to delve very deep to discover the rich heritage of folk tales and traces of ancient religious practices that give northern Honshū a deliciously mysterious tang.

Northern Honshū, or **Tōhoku** as much of the area is known, was the last part of Japan's main island to be brought under central control. As such, it boasts more in the way of military sights – ruined castles, samurai towns and aristocratic tombs – than great temples or religious foundations. The one glorious exception is north of **Sendai** at the seemingly insignificant town **Hiraizumi**, whose opulent Golden Hall (Konjiki-dō) is a highlight of any tour of the region. In contrast, the archetypal north-country town lies not far away at **Tōno**, often referred to as the birthplace of Japanese folklore, where goblin-like *kappa* inhabit local rivers and fairy children scamper through old farmhouses. Much of this is now commercialized, but it's still worth exploring Tōno's more secretive shrines, with their references to primitive cults. Darker forces are also at work further north where souls in purgatory haunt **Osore-zan**'s volcanic wasteland on the hammer-head peninsula of **Shimokita Hantō**. In summer, pilgrims come here to consult blind mediums, while in the west of the region, the holy mountain range of **Dewa-sanzan** is home to *yamabushi*, ascetic priests endowed with mystical powers.

The region is also characterized by its splendid scenery, ranging from prolific rice fields and cosseted orchards to wild, rugged coastlines and the pine-crusted islands of **Matsushima Bay**. The central spine of magnificent mountains provides excellent opportunities for hiking and skiing, notably around **Zaō Onsen** in **Yamagata-ken** and the more northerly **Towada-Hachimantai** area. Both are noted for their flora and fauna, including black bears in remoter districts, while **Towada-ko** itself is a massive crater lake

YAMABUSHI WATERFALL PURIFICATION, DEWA-SANZAN

Highlights

❶ Kinkazan Roam the steeply wooded slopes of this island with its views, framed by wind-whipped pines, of Matsushima Bay and Oshika Hantō. **See p.236**

❷ Cycling in the Tōno valley This flat valley, with an evocative landscape of rice paddies and traditional farms surrounded by wooded hills, is perfect for a pedal. **See p.240**

❸ Ja-ja men These udon-like noodles, served with a generous dollop of brown miso paste, are one of the north's most distinctive culinary flavours. Try them in Morioka along with other regional specialities. **See box, p.247**

❹ Kakunodate Discover the samurai heritage of this appealing town, including streets of gloriously preserved grand houses with extensive, impeccably maintained gardens. **See p.263**

❺ Dewa-sanzan Visit one of Japan's most sacred mountains and spend a day or two with the legendary *yamabushi* priests. **See p.265**

❻ Sado-ga-shima Dance to the rhythmic global beat at the annual Earth Celebration hosted by international drumming sensation Kodo. **See p.274**

HIGHLIGHTS ARE MARKED ON THE MAP ON P.222

accessed via the picturesque **Oirase valley**. The World Heritage-listed **Shirakami-Sanchi** mountains, on the border between Aomori and Akita prefectures, are equally beautiful, and remote enough to remain undeveloped. In **Sado-ga-shima**, a large island lying off Niigata, dramatic mountain and coastal scenery provides the backdrop for a surprisingly rich culture – a legacy of its isolation and the infamous characters once exiled to the island.

NORTHERN HONSHŪ

HIGHLIGHTS

1. Kinkazan
2. Cycling in the Tōno valley
3. Ja-ja men
4. Kakunodate
5. Dewa-sanzan
6. Sado-ga-shima

N

Otaru | *Hakodate & Sapporo*
Hokkaidō
Fukushima | Ōma
Tsugaru Straits
Osore-zan | Ōhata
Tsugaru Hantō | Mutsu
Shimokita
Kanita-machi | *Mutsu Bay* | *Shimokita-Hantō*
Aomori
Iwaki-san | **AOMORI** | Noheji
Hirosaki | *Hakkōda-san* | Misawa
Ōdate | Yakeyama | Hachinoh
Towada-ko | Yasumiya
Towada-Minami

SEA OF JAPAN
TOWADA-HACHIMANTAI NATIONAL PARK
AKITA | Ōbuke
Akita | *Tazawa-ko* | **IWATE**
Iwate-san
④ Kakunodate | Morioka
Ōmagari | ③ | Miyako
Tobishima | Hanamaki
Shin-Hanamaki
Sakata | *Kitakami* | ② Tōno
Tsuruoka | Shinjō | Kamaishi | RIKUCHI KAIGAN NATIONAL PARK
Awashima | Hiraizumi | *Geibikei*
⑤ *Dewa-sanzan* | Ichinoseki | Ōfunato
YAMAGATA | **MIYAGI**
⑥ Aikawa | *Sado-ga-shima*
Ryōtsu | Yamadera | Ishinomaki
Ogi | Akadomari | Yamagata | Matsushima | Onagawa
Zaō Onsen | Sendai | Shiogama | *Oshika Hantō*
Niigata | *Zaō-san* | Ayukawa | Kinkazan
Nagauka | Yonezawa | *Matsushima Bay* | ①
NIIGATA | BANDAI-ASAHI NATIONAL PARK | *Sendai Bay*
Kitakata | *BANDAI KŌGEN*
Kōide | Tadami | Aizu-Wakamatsu | Fukushima
Urasa | *Inawashiro-ko* | *PACIFIC OCEAN*
FUKUSHIMA | Kōriyama
Nikkō
Imaichi
Maebashi & Tokyo | *Utsunomiya & Tokyo* | *Mito & Tokyo* | *Tokyo & Nagoya*

0 ————— 50
kilometres

TRAVELLING IN POST-QUAKE TŌHOKU

The **3/11 earthquake and tsunami** of 2011 hit Fukushima, Miyagi and Iwate prefectures hardest. Matsushima (see p.232), protected by its bay of islands, emerged relatively unscathed, but Ishinomaki and Ayukawa (see p.236) were devastated and recovery efforts are still ongoing. Elsewhere in Tōhoku major transport networks, including highways, train routes and airports are back up and running. A 20km exclusion zone surrounds the stricken **Fukushima 1 Nuclear Power Plant** (no sights in Fukushima-ken are covered in this chapter) and the removal of fuel rods began in autumn 2013 – a complex, risky and long-term undertaking. However, the World Health Organization has categorized the risks to public health, outside the exclusion zone, as low, and radioactivity in food and water is constantly monitored (for the latest information, see ⓦ www.jnto.go.jp/eq/eng/04_recovery.html).

In general, the **best time to visit** is either spring or autumn, before it gets too busy and while the scenery is at its finest, though the uplands also provide welcome relief from summer's sweltering heat. Note, however, that early August sees thousands of people flocking to Tōhoku's big four **festivals** in Sendai, Aomori, Hirosaki and Akita. If you're travelling at this time, make sure to sort out transport and accommodation well in advance. Apart from ski resorts, many tourist facilities outside the major cities shut down from early November to late April.

GETTING AROUND	NORTHERN HONSHŪ

By plane There are a number of international flight connections to Northern Honshū, mainly from Russia, Korea and China, coming into Akita, Aomori, Fukushima, Niigata and Sendai airports. Domestic flights also service these airports, plus Yamagata and Iwatehanamaki, with services to and from Narita, Osaka, Sapporo and Tokyo airports.

By train JR offers a variety of special rail tickets covering the Tōhoku region (ⓦ japanrailpass.net). Although there are good transport links between the main cities (including a recently extended Shinkansen service to Aomori), allow plenty of time to explore the more remote areas.

By bus Public buses can be sporadic at the best of times, with many services stopping completely in winter, when heavy snowfalls close the mountain roads. Make sure to check services and connections with local tourist offices before setting off.

By car This is one place where car rental (see p.225 and p.231) is definitely worth considering as public transport is patchy, especially in the more rural areas.

Yamagata

山形

Few tourists make it to **YAMAGATA**, a large, workaday city ringed by high mountains, and those that do are usually just passing through. Apart from a couple of engaging museums, Yamagata's main attraction is as a base for visiting nearby **Yamadera**'s atmospheric temples, and **Zaō Onsen**, an excellent spot for summer hiking and winter skiing, known for its beguiling "snow monsters" (*juhyō*) – fir trees engulfed in wind-sculpted ice and snow. One time of year when it is worth staying

NORTHERN TŌHOKU WELCOME CARD

If you're spending any time in Akita-ken, Aomori-ken or Iwate-ken, make sure you get a **Northern Tōhoku Welcome Card**. This free card, valid for a year, provides discounts of up to fifty percent (though mostly ten to twenty percent) on hotels, restaurants, museums, car rental and other facilities in the three prefectures. Eligibility is restricted to overseas visitors staying in Japan for a year or less. The cards are available from the Tokyo TIC (see p.130) and local tourist offices, or online at ⓦ www.northern-Tōhoku.gr.jp/welcome; you'll need to take along your passport. The card comes with an English booklet listing participating organizations and businesses.

3

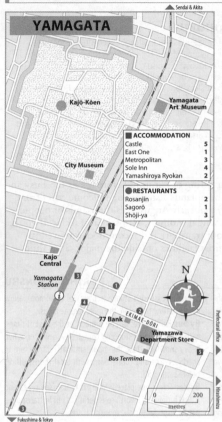

YAMAGATA

▲ Sendai & Akita

Kajō-Kōen

Yamagata Art Museum

City Museum

▉ ACCOMMODATION	
Castle	5
East One	1
Metropolitan	3
Sole Inn	4
Yamashiroya Ryokan	2

● RESTAURANTS	
Rosanjin	2
Sagorō	1
Shōji-ya	3

Kajo Central

Yamagata Station

EKIMAE-DŌRI

77 Bank

Yamazawa Department Store

Bus Terminal

N

0 — 200 metres

Prefectural office

Hitakinoto

▼ Fukushima & Tokyo

for longer is early August when the city's major festival, the **Hanagasa Matsuri** (see box below), brings the streets alive.

Central Yamagata occupies a grid of streets lying northeast of the train station. Its southern boundary is **Ekimae-dōri**, a broad avenue leading straight from the station as far as the *Castle hotel*, from where the main shopping street, **Nanokamachi-dōri**, runs perpendicular. **Yamagata Art Museum** is about a kilometre north along the train line, while the city's biggest park, **Kajō-kōen** is northwest of the central station.

Prefectural Office

文翔館, Bunshō-kan • 3-4-51 Hatagomachi • Daily 9am–4.30pm, closed first and third Mon every month • Free • ☎ 023 635 5500, ⓦ gakushubunka.jp • Roughly 20min walk from the station

Yamagata's **Prefectural Office** is an imposing, European-style building of stone and ornate stucco that dominates the north end of Nanokamachi-dōri. Originally built in 1911, the interior has been magnificently restored, particularly the third floor with its parquet-floored dining room and elegant Assembly Hall.

City Museum

郷土館, Kyōdo-kan • 1-1 Kajyomachi • Tues–Sun 9am–4.30pm • ¥200 • ☎ 023 644 0253

Yamagata's biggest park, **Kajō-kōen** (霞城公園), houses the **City Museum**, or *Kyōdokan*. In a multicoloured clapboard building in the park's southeast corner, the museum, built in 1878, was originally the town's main hospital. Exhibits include a gruesome collection of early medical equipment and anatomical drawings, including, notably, a pregnancy guide rendered as woodblock prints. Another attraction in the park worth checking out is the only remnant of Yamagata's castle, the beautifully restored **East Gate**.

ARRIVAL AND DEPARTURE ⁣ **YAMAGATA**

By plane Yamagata's airport, a 30min ride by local train north of the city, offers domestic flights to Osaka (Itami; 3 daily; 1hr 20min) and Tokyo (daily; 1hr).

By train Yamagata is a stop on a spur of the Tōhoku Shinkansen from Tokyo to Fukushima and is on the very scenic Senzan line from Sendai (1hr 20min; ¥1100).

HANAGASA MATSURI

During Yamagata's main **festival**, held annually from August 5 to 7, this normally sedate city bursts into life. The event involves a procession of more than ten thousand **dancers** accompanied by brightly decorated floats and Taiko drums. Traditionally, *yukata*-clad women wearing flowery hats perform slow, graceful dances in unison, but in recent years there has been a much greater variety of dance groups. Members of the crowd can also join in during several circle-dancing sessions.

HIRASHIMIZU KILNS

The pretty pottery village of **Hirashimizu** (平清水) has a surprisingly rural atmosphere, despite its location in Yamagata's southeastern outskirts. There's just one main street and a small river running down from the surrounding hills, providing local potters with their distinctive, speckled clay. If you explore a little, you'll find several family **potteries** with showrooms (generally daily 9am–5pm; till 6pm in high season). To reach Hirashimizu, take a bus from Yamagata Station (hourly; 15min; ¥460).

POTTERIES

Shichiemon-gama 七右衛門窯 153 Hirashimizu ☎ 023 642 7777. The largest pottery in the area, Shichiemon-gama offers visitors the chance to throw a pot or two. The pots go for around ¥800–2000. Daily 9am–3pm.

Seiryū-gama 精龍窯 50-1 Hirashimizu ☎ 023 631 2828. This is one of the many long-established workshop in the area, offering a variety of short courses from ¥1800. Daily 9am–5pm.

Destinations: Sendai (hourly; 1hr 15min–1hr 30min); Tokyo (hourly; 2hr 50min); Yamadera (hourly; 20min).

By bus Limousine buses (45min; ¥740) run between the airport and central Yamagata, stopping outside the train station and at the central bus terminal in the Yamakō building (山交ビル), behind Ekimae-dōri's Yamazawa

department store. All long-distance buses use this terminal, while most city buses depart from outside the station's east exit.

Destinations: Niigata (2 daily; 3hr 40min); Sendai (every 30min; 1hr 10min); Tokyo (4 daily; 6hr 20min–8hr 30min); Tsuruoka (9 daily; 1hr 50min).

INFORMATION

Tourist information The main tourist office (daily 9am–5.30pm; ☎ 023 647 2266) is in the train station, immediately to the right as you exit the turnstiles, where you'll find helpful English-speaking staff and some English-

language information (ⓦ yamagatakanko.com).

Banks There are branches of Yamagata Bank and 77 Bank near the station, on Ekimae-dōri.

GETTING AROUND

By bus A circular bus runs every 10min between the station and major sights (daily 9.30am–6.30pm; ¥100 flat fare).

By bike The city is fairly easy to navigate on foot, but you can also pick up (and drop off) a free rental bike at seven locations around the city, including the central station

tourist office (see above) – ask there for details of the rental system.

Car rental There are several car rental companies clustered around the Kajō Central Building; try Eki Rent-a-Car (☎ 023 646 6322) or Toyota (☎ 023 625 0100).

ACCOMMODATION

Yamagata has a reasonable choice of accommodation within easy walking distance of the train station. However, for more atmospheric lodging, you're better off staying in nearby Zaō Onsen (see p.226) or Yamadera (see p.227).

Castle ホテルキャッスル 4-2-7 Tōka-machi ☎ 0236 31 3311, ⓦ hotelcastle.co.jp. Just over 5mins walk from the station on Ekimae-dōri, this large hotel has a range of well-sized, contemporary Western-style rooms and a modern bistro serving Italian cuisine with menus for ¥5000. Breakfast is ¥1800 per person. **¥13,860**

East One イーストワン 1-18-12 Kasumi-chō ☎ 023 635 0303. A 3min walk from the station, this business hotel is a little dated but offers the cheapest rooms in town. It also has a ground-floor restaurant serving cheap noodle dishes and a basement shot bar. **¥5720**

Metropolitan ホテルメトロポリタン 1-1-1 Kasumi-chō ☎ 023 28 1111, ⓦ metro-yamagata.jp. This is a smart, modern hotel conveniently located above the station. If you're travelling on a JR rail pass, you can enjoy

substantial discounts; it's also worth looking online for deals. **¥19,635**

Sole Inn ソーレイン 1-1 Saiwa-chō ☎ 023 642 2111, ☏ 642 2114, ⓦ sole-inn.com. Well placed on Ekimae-dōri, directly opposite the *Metropolitan*. Rates for the small but spick-and-span rooms include a light breakfast and free internet access in the lobby. Rates drop by ¥800 (single) or ¥1800 (twin/double) on weekdays. **¥8600**

Yamashiroya Ryokan 山城屋旅館 1-18-20 Sawai-machi ☎ 023 622 3007, ☏ info@e-yamashiroya.jp. Located in the backstreets just to the north of the station, this ryokan has basic but adequate tatami rooms. Breakfast costs ¥1000. **¥4800**

EATING

Yamagata's **speciality foods** include marbled Yonezawa beef, similar to the more famous Matsuzaka variety, and *imoni*, a warming winter stew of potato, meat, onions and *konnyaku* (a jelly-like food made from the root of the devil's tongue plant) served in a slightly sweet sauce.

Rosanjin ロサンジン 2-2-34 Ekimae-dōri ☎ 023 615 2650. This cosy restaurant which has a wood-burning oven in its window, serves very authentic Italian pizzas (from ¥1000) and the owner even speaks to you in a mixture of French and Italian. You can also order set menus, which start at ¥2000. Daily noon–2.30pm & 5.30–11pm, Sun till 10pm.

Sagorō 佐五郎 1-6-10 Kasumi-chō ☎ 023 631 3560. A second-floor restaurant above its own butcher store, this refined restaurant is a good place to sample the local beef

sukiyaki and *Shabu-shabu* (set menus start from ¥4200) 11.30am–3pm & 5–10pm, closed Sun.

Shōji-ya 庄司屋 14-28 Sawai-machi ☎ 023 622 1380. Turn right out of the station, heading south, for about 400m until you see a level crossing; turn away from the tracks and you'll find Yamagata's oldest soba restaurant 50m on the left. Here you can try handmade soba in all its various forms (¥750–1500), and you might even be able to see the chefs rolling your noodles in the attached workshop. Tues–Sun 11am–8pm.

Zaō Onsen

蔵王温泉

Roughly 20km southeast of Yamagata city, **ZAŌ ONSEN** is the main focus of activity in the Zaō Quasi-National Park, an attractive region of volcanoes, crater lakes and hot springs. In winter (Dec to late March), the resort offers some of Japan's best **skiing**, with a dozen or so runs to choose from, as well as night skiing and onsen baths to soak away the aches and pains.

Non-skiers can enjoy the ropeway (cable-car) ride over **Juhyō Kōgen**, where a thick covering of snow and hoarfrost transform the plateau's fir trees into giant "snow monsters" (*juhyō*).

Juhyō Kōgen

Zaō Sanroku Ropeway (蔵王山麓ロープウェイ) daily 8.30am–4.45pm, every 10min (closed irregularly May and Sept); Sancho ropeway (サンチョロープウエ) daily 8.30am–4.30pm • One-way: ¥750, Zaō Sanroku only, ¥1400 both; return: ¥1400 Zaō Sanroku only, ¥2500 both • ☎ 023 694 9518 • Walk southeast from the bus station for 10min to reach the base station

The **Zaō Sanroku Ropeway** (cable-car) takes visitors up to the mountains to see the Juhyō Kōgen, which are at their best in February. From the base station you can see photos of the ghostly frozen formations in the **Juhyō Museum** (open same times as lifts; free). The **Sanchō Ropeway** continues up from the Juhyō Kōgen station to Zaō Jizō Sanchō Station at 1661m. This top station lies between Sampō Kōjin-san (1703m) and Jizō-san (1736m), just two of the peaks that make up the ragged profile of **Zaō-san**. In the summer hiking season (May–Oct), you can follow the right-hand (southeasterly) path over Jizō-san and Kumano-dake (1841m) for spectacular views and a fairly rugged hour's walk to the desolate, chemical-blue **Okama crater lake** (御釜火口湖, Okama Kakōko).

Dai-rotemburo onsen

大露天風呂 • Daily: April & Nov 9am–sunset; May–Oct 6am–7pm • ¥450 • ☎ 023 694 9417 • A 20min walk uphill from the bus station; many ryokans provide a bus shuttle for guests

Zaō Onsen village has plenty of public baths where you can recover from skiing or hiking with a good, long soak. The unforgettable **Dai-rotemburo onsen**, overflowing with steamy sulphur-laden water, can accommodate two hundred bathers, though it is only open during summer.

ARRIVAL AND INFORMATION

ZAŌ ONSEN

By bus Buses run approximately every hour from Yamagata Station to the Zaō Onsen bus terminal (40min; ¥980), at the

bottom of the village, and one bus per day goes all the way to Okama lake at 9.30am; the only return to Yamagata Station

SKIING IN ZAŌ ONSEN

Zaō is one of Japan's largest **ski areas**, covering 305 hectares with 41 lifts accessing slopes suited to all levels. Its northerly position ensures a large annual snowfall of dry, high-quality, powder snow. A shuttle bus (Mid-Dec to late March; ¥100) moves skiers and snowboarders between the base lifts. Lift passes are ¥4800 per day, ¥21,000 for seven days (plus ¥500 pass deposit; equipment and clothing hire is available from a number of shops near the base stations (prices around ¥3000 per day for ski set, ¥3000 for clothing). Pick up the English guide to Zaō at the tourist information offices for more details (see below).

leaves Okama at 1pm (May–Oct; 1hr 30min; one-way Yamagata–Okama ¥1990, Okama–Yamagata ¥1430). During ski season, highway buses run between Zaō Onsen and Sendai on weekends and holidays (mid-Dec to late March; leaving Sendai at 8am and returning at 4.30pm; 1hr 40min; ¥1500 one-way; reservations advisable, see ⓦj-bus.co.jp or phone ☎022 261 5333).

Tourist information The tourist office (daily 9am–6pm; ☎023 694 9328) is right as you exit the bus terminal and has English maps and pamphlets including a guide to the skiing area which comes with a piste map. English-speaking staff are available at the main office, a 10min walk from the bus station near Zaō gym (103 Zaō Onsen; daily 9am–6pm; ☎023 694 9005, ⓦzao-spa.cr.jp).

ACCOMMODATION AND EATING

Gokan-no-yu Tsuruya 五感の湯つるや 710 Zaō Onsen ☎023 694 9112, ⓦwww.tsuruyahotel.co.jp/english. Opposite the bus station, this high-end option offers an authentic ryokan experience with lavish *kaiseki* meals and a choice of indoor, open-air and private hot-spring baths. Discounts are available for hotel guests on lift passes and equipment hire. Two meals a day for guests will add ¥7350 to the room rate, per person. **¥10,800**

Izakaya Robata 居酒屋炉端 42-7 Zaō Onsen ☎023 694 9565. There's usually a good atmosphere at this small,

popular *izakaya* near the river, well known for its lamb barbeque skewers and other flame-grilled dishes. 11am–10pm, closed Thurs.

Lodge Chitoseya ロッジちとせや 954 Zaō Onsen ☎023 694 9145, ⓦlodge-chitoseya.com. Located after the first bridge on the road to right of the station, this reasonable and comfortable lodging has a youth hostel atmosphere and an English-speaking manager. For an extra ¥2100 per person, you can have two meals a day included in your stay. **¥7980**

Yamadera

山寺

The temple complex of Risshaku-ji, or **YAMADERA** as it's more popularly known, is one of Tōhoku's most holy places. It was founded in 860 by a Zen priest of the Tendai sect and reached its peak in the Kamakura period (1185–1333). Today around forty temple buildings still stand scattered among the ancient cedars on a steep, rocky hillside.

Kompon Chūdō

根本中堂 • Daily 8am–5pm • ¥200

Yamadera's main hall, **Kompon Chūdō**, lies at the foot of the mountain temple complex. This impressive building, dating from 1356, shelters a flame brought 1100 years ago from Enryaku-ji, the centre of Tendai Buddhism near Kyoto (see p.462), and which has supposedly been burning ever since – it's the hanging lantern on the left-hand side which you'll see if you peer inside.

Risshaku-ji temple walk

立石寺 • Daily 6am–6pm • ¥300 • Takes about 40min to walk up the steps to the highest temple

Entering Yamadera's **San-mon gate** (山門) takes you to the start of the **Risshaku-ji temple walk**. Over 1100 steps meander past moss-covered *Jizō* statues, lanterns and prayer wheels, and squeeze between looming rocks carved with prayers and pitted with caves. At the highest temple, **Okuno-in**, breathless pilgrims tie prayer papers around a mammoth lantern and light small bunches of incense sticks. Before setting off downhill, don't miss the views over Yamadera from the terrace of **Godai-dō**, perched on the cliff-face just beyond the distinctive red **Nōkyō-dō** pavilion.

Yamadera Bashō Memorial Museum

山寺芭蕉記念館, Yamadera Bashō Kinenkar • 4223 Nanin • Daily 9am–4.30pm • ¥400 • ☎ 023 695 2221, ⓦ yamadera-basho.jp

Located on a hilltop behind Yamadera Station, with a panoramic view of the Risshaku-ji temple, the modern **Yamadera Bashō Memorial Museum** commemorates famous poet Bashō's visit to Yamadera. Travelling before the days of coach parties, he penned a characteristically pithy ode to Yamadera: "In the utter silence of a temple, a cicada's voice alone penetrates the rocks." Exhibits include original haiku poems and Edo-period art works.

ARRIVAL AND DEPARTURE   YAMADERA

By train The temple lies close to Yamadera Station, which is on the JR Senzan line between Yamagata and Sendai. Trains run hourly to both Yamagata (¥230) and Sendai (¥820). To get to the temple from the station, cross the river and follow the road right, passing a row of shops selling souvenirs and snacks.

ACCOMMODATION AND EATING

Yamadera village consists mainly of expensive **ryokans** and souvenir shops; some of the latter have boiling vats of **konnyaku balls** outside, good for a warming snack (¥100 skewer).

Yamadera Pension 山寺ペンション 4273-1 Yamadera ☎ 023 695 2134. Located in a half-timbered building in front of the station, this is the most attractive accommodation option in town. The Western-style rooms are comfortable and tastefully decorated; rates include two meals in the decent restaurant downstairs that specializes in handmade soba. **¥17,800**

Sendai

仙台

The largest city in the Tōhoku region, **SENDAI** is a sprawling but pleasant place, with broad, tree-lined avenues and a lively downtown district. Though often regarded as a staging post on the way to Matsushima Bay (see p.232), the city's **castle ruins**, with their local history museum, and the ornate mausoleum of Sendai's revered founder, the *daimyō* **Date Masamune**, are worth a brief stop.

There are a number of colourful festivals in early August, including the **Tanabata**, or Star Festival, which features an impressive fireworks display over the Hirosegawa River (see box below). A month later, the city-centre streets turn into an urban music festival venue for the **Jorenji Street Jazz Festival** (second weekend in Sept; ⓦ j-streetjazz.com).

Though central Sendai was rebuilt after World War II, its streets follow the original grid pattern laid out by Date Masamune in the seventeenth century. The main downtown area, a high-rise district of offices, banks and shopping malls, lies on the east

STAR FESTIVAL

Over two million people make it to Sendai during the three-day festival of **Sendai Tanabata** (仙台七夕祭; Star Festival; Aug 6–8; ⓦ sendaitanabata.com/en), when the city centre is awash with thousands of bamboo poles festooned with colourful paper tassels, poems and prayers. The festivities celebrate the only day in the year when – weather permitting – the two astral lovers Vega, the weaver, and Altair, the cowherd, can meet.

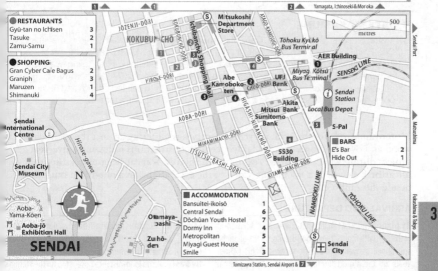

bank of the **Hirose-gawa**. Its principal thoroughfare, Aoba-dōri, runs west from the train station to the far side of the river, where the city's main sights are located.

Aoba-jō

青葉城 • 1 Kawauchi-ku • ☎ ℂ22 214 8259, ⓦ www.sendaijyo.com • Free • Buses run from Sendai Station (bus stop #9) to Aobajōshi-mae (20min), from where you can walk south up the hill to the park and castle

The wooded hilltop park, **Aobayama-kōen** (青葉山公園), was once the site of the magnificent **Sendai Castle**, popularly known as **Aoba-jō**. Only a few stretches of wall and a reconstructed gateway remain, but the site is impeccable, protected by the river to the east and a deep ravine on its south side. At the top of the hill is the **statue of Masamune** (see box p.230) astride his horse, surveying the city below. You can get a good idea of Sendai Castle's former glory at the **Aoba-jō Exhibition Hall** (青葉城資料展示館; daily 9am–5pm; ¥700; ☎022 222 0218) located above the park's souvenir shops, where a short computer-generated film takes you "inside" the castle.

Sendai City Museum

仙台市博物館, Sendaī-shi Hakubutsukan • 26 Kawauchi, Aoba-ku • Tues–Sun 9am–4.45pm • ¥400, extra for special exhibitions • ☎ 022 225 3074, ⓦ www.city.sendai.jp/kyouiku/museum/English • A 10min walk north of Aobayama-kōen

The modern, well-laid-out **Sendai City Museum** traces the city's history from the early Stone Age to the present day. The main emphasis, however, is on the glory days under Date Masamune, the "One-Eyed Dragon" (see box, p.230) and his successors. The second floor has displays of his armour, with the distinctive crescent moon on the helmet, his sword and various portraits – always with two eyes.

Zuihō-den mausoleum

瑞鳳殿 • 23-2 Otamayashita, Aoba-ku • Mausoleum and museum daily 9am–4.30pm, Dec & Jan till 4pm • ¥550, including entry to museum • ☎ 022 262 6250 • ⓦ zuihoden.com • A 20min walk from Aoba-jō; from Sendai Station take bus from stop #11 to Otamaya-bashi

When Date died in 1636, aged 70, he was buried in the **Zuihō-den** on a wooded hillside just along the river from Aoba-jō. Eventually his two successors joined him, and their three **mausoleums** now stand at the top of broad, stone steps. The opulent,

DATE MASAMUNE

Missing one eye since childhood, **Date Masamune** was a fearsome warrior, nicknamed the "One-Eyed Dragon". Heir to a long line of powerful *daimyō* in the Tōhoku region, he established the city of Sendai after being granted the fiefdom in return for helping bring Tokugawa Ieyasu to power in 1603. His Date clan continued to rule Sendai for the next 270 years, constructing their castle (see p.229) in a highly ornate Momoyama style, with painted ceilings and huge rooms divided by glorious screens, more like a luxurious palace than a fortress.

Momoyama-style tombs, with polychrome carvings glittering against the plain dark wood and overhanging eaves, are fairly recent reconstructions following a five-year project during which researchers exhumed the graves. You can see the treasures they unearthed, as well as a fascinating video of the excavations, in a one-room **museum** beside the Zuihō-den.

3

ARRIVAL AND DEPARTURE

By plane Sendai has an international airport, 18km south of the city, with flights from Seoul, Beijing, Guam, Shanghai and Taipei, as well as domestic services; trains (25min; ¥630) on the airport line and limousine buses (40min; ¥910) run from the airport to Sendai Station.

Destinations (domestic): Fukuoka (5 daily; 2hr); Dalian (2 weekly; 3hr 10min); Guam (2 weekly; 3hr 45min); Hiroshima (daily; 1hr 35min); Nagoya (6 daily; 1hr 10min); Naha (Okinawa; daily; 2hr 55min); Narita (2 daily; 1hr 10min); Osaka (Itami; 14 daily; 1hr 20min); Sapporo (11 daily; 1hr 10min).

Destinations (international): Beijing, China (6 weekly; 5–7hr); Seoul, South Korea (daily; 2hr 30min); Shanghai, China (3 weekly; 3hr 30min); Taipei, Taiwan (2 weekly; 3hr 40min).

By train The majority of visitors to Sendai arrive at the main JR station on the east side of town. The Tōhoku Shinkansen line links Sendai to Tokyo in the south and Morioka and Aomori in the north. Local JR lines run west to Yamagata and east to Matsushima.

Destinations: Hon-Shiogama (every 30min; 20–30min); Matsushima-kaigan (every 30min; 30–40min); Ichinoseki (hourly; 30min); Ishinomaki (every 30min; 55min–1hr 20min); Morioka (hourly; 45min); Tokyo (every 20min; 1hr 35min–2hr 30min); Yamadera (hourly; 50min–1hr 5min).

By bus Local and long-distance buses stop on the station's west side. Long-distance JR buses (❏ 022 256 6646) for Niigata and Tokyo (Shinjuku) leave from the east side of Sendai Station. Express buses go to Kyoto, Osaka, Nagoya and destinations around Tōhoku from the Miyagi Kōtsū (❏ 022 261 5333) bus terminal at the west end of Hirose-dōri, as does the JR bus to Akita. On the opposite side of the road, buses from Tōhoku Kyūkō (❏ 022 262 7031) leave for Tokyo Station.

Destinations: Akita (10 daily; 3hr 50min); Aomori (6 daily; 4hr 50min); Hirosaki (9 daily; 4hr 20min); Morioka (hourly; 2hr 40min); Nagoya (daily; 10hr 30min); Niigata (8 daily; 4hr); Osaka (daily; 12hr 20min); Tokyo (daily; 6hr 30min); Tokyo (Shinjuku; 3 daily; 5hr 30min); Tsuruoka (10 daily; 2hr 20min); Yamagata (every 30min; 1hr 10min).

By ferry Ferries from Nagoya and Hokkaidō (Tomakomai) dock at Sendai Port, northwest of the city, which is served by local buses from the main station (40min; ¥490).

Destinations: Nagoya (3 weekly; 21hr); Tomakomai (Hokkaidō; 6 weekly; 15hr).

INFORMATION

Tourist information Sendai's main tourist office (daily 8.30am–7pm; ❏ 022 222 4069) is located on the train station's second floor; the very helpful English-speaking staff can help with city maps and hotel bookings.

Listings A good website for information in English on accommodation, restaurants, events and travel is ❼ sentabi.jp/en.

GETTING AROUND

By train Sendai has one subway line, running north–south, which is particularly useful for *Dōchūan Youth Hostel* (see p.230). To reach the subway from Sendai's JR station, follow the signs through the basement of the Seibu store.

By bus The best way of getting around Sendai is by the local tourist bus, Loople Sendai, which stops at most of the city's sights – ask the tourist office for a route map. The flat fare is ¥250, payable to the driver as you exit, or there's a one-day pass (¥600). If you're heading beyond the city centre consider getting the Marugoto Pass (¥2600), sold at View Plaza, JTB and the station ticket office, which covers two days of unlimited travel on inner-city buses (including Loople) and subways, plus the JR lines that service Yamadera, Matsushima and Sendai Airport.

By car There are several car rental places outside the east exit of Sendai Station, including Eki Rent-a-Car (☎ 022 292 6501), Times (☎ 022 293 1021) and Nippon (☎ 022 297 1919).

Taxis There are plenty of taxis outside the main station exit or ring Kojin (☎ 022 252 1385) or Teisan Cabs (☎ 022 231 5151).

ACCOMMODATION

Sendai has plenty of mid-range and expensive **business hotels** within walking distance of the train station, with branches of most of the large chains in the streets east and south of the station. **Budget accommodation** is more limited, though there are a few options available a bit further from the central area.

★ **Bansuitei-ikoisō** 晩翠亭いこい荘 5-6 Kimachi-dōri, Aoba-ku ☎ 022 222 7885, ⓦ ikoisouryokan.co.jp. An excellent ryokan just outside the downtown area but easily accessible by bus (take the bus from stop #29 to the end), and subway (stop: Kita-Yonbanchō). Rooms are impeccably clean and nicely decorated. Two meals will cost you an extra ¥2625 per person; discounts are available online. **¥9450**

Central Sendai ホテルセントラル仙台 4-2-6 Chūō, Aoba-ku ☎ 022 711 4111, ⓦ hotel-central.co.jp. The highlight of this quintessential business hotel is the location – less than 5min from the JR train station. Most of the flowery rooms are singles, though there are a few twins. Single **¥7140**

Dōchūan Youth Hostel 道中庵ユースホステル 31 Onoda-Kitayashiki, Taihaku-ku ☎ 022 247 0511, ⓦ jyh.or.jp. The best of three youth hostels in Sendai, built among trees in traditional farmhouse style. Accommodation is in small tatami dormitories; there's also a cedar bath and excellent food – the English-speaking warden grows his own rice and vegetables. The only downside is the location: it's 15min by subway from central Sendai to Tomizawa Station (¥290), then a 10min walk due east. Dorm **¥3540**, double **¥10,230**

Dormy Inn ドーミーイン 2-10-17 Chūō, Aoba-ku ☎ 022 715 7077, ☎ 715 7078. About 5min from the station, near Hirose-dōri subway station, this budget business hotel has a range of boxy but adequate en-suite rooms. **¥13,000**

Metropolitan ホテルメトロポリタン 1-1-1 Chūō, Aoba-ku ☎ 022 268 2525, ⓦ www.s-metro.stbl.co.jp. Big, swish hotel next door to Sendai Station, with a range of comfortable Western- and Japanese-style rooms. Facilities include a choice of restaurants, a bar, gym and indoor pool. **¥20,790**

Miyagi Guest House 宮城ゲストハウス 2-1-35 Kakyō-in, Aoba-ku ☎ 022 778 8965 ⓦ ve.cat-v.ne.jp/miyagi-gh. A 10min journey north on foot from the JR station, this friendly hostel has clean but small dorms, a communal tatami lounge space and a private tatami room available. Dorm **¥2500**, double **¥6500**

Smile スマイルホテル 3F, 4-3-22 Ichiban-chō, Aoba-ku ☎ 022 26 7711, ⓦ smile-hotels.com. This is a simple but smart and modern business hotel in the heart of the busy Ichiban-chō shopping mall. Free internet access is available. **¥8000**

EATING

Sendai's **speciality foods** include *gyū-tan* (grilled, smoked or salted calf's tongue) and, in winter (Dec–March), oysters from Matsushima Bay. *Sasa-kamaboko*, a leaf-shaped cake of rather rubbery white-fish paste, is a popular local snack, which you can sample in *Abe Kamaboko-ten*, a famous shop in the Chūō-dōri shopping mall. Chūō-dōri and the connecting Ichiban-chō arcades are good places to look for **restaurants and cafés**, while S-Pal, at the south end of Sendai Station, also has a decent selection.

Gyū-tan no Ichisen 牛タンの一仙 4-3-3, Ichiban-chō ☎ 022 265 1935. A good alternative if *Tasuke* (see below) is closed, this no-frills basement *gyū-tan* restaurant, just off the Ichiban-chō arcade, has all sorts of tongue dishes (from ¥1000), including a deliciously rich stew. Daily 11am–midnight.

Tasuke 太助 4-4-13, Ichiban-chō ☎ 022 225 4641. One of Sendai's best-known *gyū-tan* restaurants, where you can eat tongue in all its forms including salted or in tare sauce. Dishes start at around ¥1000. 11.30am–10pm, closed Tues.

Zamu-Samu ザムサム 2F, 17-19 Futsukamachi-chō ☎ 22 22? 4326. In an ideal location for guests at *Bansuitei-ikoisō*, this tasty Indian buffet (¥830) brings in the crowds at lunchtime; the evening menu is more refined, with a range of curries and other dishes from ¥2100. Daily 11.30am–2.30pm & 5.30–10pm.

DRINKING AND ENTERTAINMENT

Kokubun-chō, just west of the Ichiban-chō shopping mall, is Sendai's main entertainment district, filled with bars, clubs and restaurants.

E's bar 日記 B1 2-12-19 Kokubu-chō, Aoba-ku ☎ 022 399 8439 ⓦ ezbar.jp. A small and convivial shot bar in the basement of the Daisankycuritsu building, E's offers a good range of drinks, small art exhibitions and a range of candles for sale which are handmade by the owner. Tues–Sun 8pm–4am.

Hide Out ハイドアウト2F 2-8-11 Kokubun-chō, Aoba-ku ☎022 268 6776. This small second-floor bar and "information exchange centre" is a shrine to bourbon, whisky, football and blues. Its genial host, late opening times and the contents of the 1000 bottles of spirits covering every surface of the place will ensure you exchange information till the small, or even not so small, hours. ¥600 cover, drinks from ¥600. Daily 8pm–8am, closed irregularly.

SHOPPING

The main shopping streets are the covered malls of Chūō-dōri and Ichiban-chō. Also worth checking out are the small alleys which run off Ichiban-chō, including Toichi Ichiba and Iroha Yokochō, which have a range of small independent, curio shops and small bars and restaurants.

Gran Cyber Cafe Bagus Clis Rd (Chūō-dōri) shopping arcade ☎022 217 7051, ⓦbagus-99.com. Covering three floors, this internet café features pool tables, darts and a space to read comic books, magazines and play games (¥200/30min; deals are available for longer periods). Also check the five-storey Taito Station arcade opposite to see more of Japanese gaming culture in action (2-3-25 Chuō; daily 9am–midnight; ☎022 262 2541). 24hr.

Graniph 3-3-26 Ichiban-chō ☎022 212 5565, ⓦwww .graniph.com. In the Ichiban-chō shopping arcade, this shop sells limited edition T-shirts (for around ¥2000) and clothes with fun designs from leading contemporary artists. Daily 11am–8pm.

Maruzen 1-3-1 Chūō-dōri ☎022 264 0151. This is the best place in town for foreign-language books and magazines; you'll find it on the first floor of the AER Building. Daily 10am–9pm.

Shimanuki 1-1-1 Chūō-dōri ☎022 267 4021, ⓦshimanuki.co.jp. Towards the west end of Chūō-dōri, this traditional crafts shop sells a good range of *kokeshi* dolls, wooden toys, *ittōbori* carved birds, fabrics, ironware and lacquer goods. There's another branch in Sendai station. Daily 10.30am–8.30pm.

DIRECTORY

Banks and exchange There are branches of major foreign exchange banks, such as Akita, Mitsubishi Sumitomo Bank and UFJ, at the east end of Aoba-dōri, near Sendai Station.

Emergencies The main police station is at 3-79 Itsutsubashi Aoba-ku (☎022 222 7171). In an absolute emergency, contact the English Hotline on ☎022 224 1919.

Hospitals Sendai City Hospital, 3-1 Shimizu-kōji (☎022 266 7111), has a 24hr emergency clinic; otherwise, ring the English Hotline (daily 9am–8pm; ☎022 224 1919) for advice on clinics with English-speaking doctors.

Internet Net-U (5F, AER building; ☎022 724 1200), near the west exit of the station, offers 30min internet access free of charge (daily 10am–8pm). The Sendai International Centre (daily 9am–8pm; ☎022 265 2450, ⓦsira.or.jp), near the castle, also offers free internet access.

Post office Sendai Central Post Office, 1-7 Kitame-machi, Aoba-ku, has a 24hr service for stamps and international mail (Mon–Sat).

Matsushima Bay

松島湾, Matsushima-wan

The jumble of wooded islands dotting **Matsushima Bay**, a short train ride northeast of Sendai, is officially designated one of Japan's top three scenic areas, along with Miyajima (see p.537) and Amanohashidate (see p.464). Roughly 12km by 14km, the bay contains over **260 islands** of every conceivable shape and size, many supposedly taking on familiar shapes such as tortoises, whales, or even human profiles, and each with scraggy fringes of contorted pine trees protruding out of the white rock faces. In between, the shallower parts of the bay have been used for farming oysters for around three hundred years.

Bashō, travelling through in 1689, commented that "much praise had already been lavished upon the wonders of the islands of Matsushima", but many visitors today find the bay slightly disappointing. Nevertheless, a **boat trip** among the islands makes an enjoyable outing, though it's best to avoid weekends and holidays when hordes of sightseers descend on the area. **Matsushima town** has a couple of less-frequented

picturesque spots, and a venerable temple, **Zuigan-ji**, with an impressive collection of art treasures. Most people visit Matsushima on a day-trip from Sendai, but there are some reasonable accommodation options in the area that are worth considering if you're heading on up the coast to Kinkazan (see p.236).

Matsushima

松島

These days, the modern town of **MATSUSHIMA** is little more than a strip of resort hotels and souvenir shops, but its origins go back to 828, when a Zen priest called Jikaku Daishi Enrin founded the temple of **Zuigan-ji**, which is set back from the bay. The entrance to the temple is marked by a suitably grand grove of four-hundred-year-old cedar trees halfway between (and a five-minute walk from) the central tourist pier, where boats from Shiogama dock, and the train station (Matsushima-kaigan).

Zuigan-ji

瑞巖寺 • 91 Matsushima Chōnai • Daily: April–Sept 8am–5pm; Oct & March 8am–4.30pm; Nov & Feb 8am–4pm; Dec & Jan 8am–3.30pm • ¥700, including guardhouse and Seiryū-den • ☎ 022 354 2023, ⓦ zuiganji.or.jp • Main building closed for renovations till 2016

Zuigan-ji has been rebuilt many times since its foundation, but retains a compelling sense of history. Though deceptively plain from the outside, the buildings bear the unmistakeable stamp of Date Masamune (see box, p.230), the first lord of Sendai, who oversaw Zuigan-ji's reconstruction in the early seventeenth century. He employed the best craftsmen and the highest-quality materials to create a splendid monument of intricately carved doors and transoms, wood-panelled ceilings and gilded screens lavishly painted with hawks, chrysanthemums, peacocks and pines. What would ordinarily be the highlight of a visit to the temple, the main building, is off limits to visitors until 2016 while it undergoes a renovation. However, you can still get a taste for Masamune's style with a walk around the neighbouring guardhouse and the modern **Seiryū-den**. Alongside the normal array of temple treasures, this museum has a statues of a squinting Masamune, in full armour and in an uncompromising mood, alongside statues of his angelic-looking wife and eldest daughter. This statue of Masamune is a rarity in that it makes clear his right eye is missing.

Godai-dō

五大堂 • 111 Matsushima Chonai • Daily till sunset • Free • ☎ 022 354 2618

These two tiny islands, just north of the ferry pier in front of Zuigan-ji, are linked via two vermilion bridges. No one knows why the bridges were built with precarious gaps between the planks, but one suggestion is that it kept women (who were forbidden) from crossing and sullying the sacred ground, because of their awkward traditional shoes and kimono. The object of their curiosity was the **Godai-dō**, a picturesque pavilion built by order of Masamune in the early 1600s. It houses statues of five Buddhist deities, which can only be seen every 33 years – the next viewing is 2039. Meanwhile, you'll have to make do with the charming carvings of the twelve animals of the zodiac that decorate the eaves.

MATSUSHIMA PANORAMAS

The hills around Matsushima town provide plenty of opportunities for panoramic views of the bay. Of the four main lookout points, southerly **Sōkanzan** (双観山) is reckoned to offer the best all-round views, including both Shiogama and Matsushima itself; take a taxi (¥2500 return fare) to avoid the thirty-minute climb on a busy road. Alternatively, try **Saigyō Modoshi-no-matsu** (西行戻しの松), which is a more pleasant, fifteen-minute scramble west of the station.

Fukuura-jima

福浦島 • Daily 8am–5pm • ¥200

This island of **Fukuura-jima** lies north of Godai-dō across a 252m-long bridge. A natural botanical garden, it's home to more than 250 native plant species, and you can enjoy some peaceful time in nature even on the busiest tourist days. Walking around the island, which is filled with great picnic spots, takes about an hour.

ARRIVAL AND INFORMATION

MATSUSHIMA

By train The fastest approach to Matsushima town is the JR Senseki line from the basement of Sendai Station to Matsushima Kaigan station (松島海岸駅; 30–40min; ¥400). Destinations Hon-Shiogama (every 30min; 10min); Ishinomaki (every 30min 30–45min); Sendai (every 30min; 30–40min).

By boat You can travel across the bay by boat from Shiogama (塩釜), if you leave the train from Sendai at Hon-shiogama. From there, the Marine Gate ferry pier (マリンゲート) is a 10min walk east. Tourist boats take a leisurely trip through Matsushima Bay before dropping you in Matsushima town. In high season (late April to Nov) boats run every 30min (daily 8.30am–4pm; 50min; ¥1400,

or ¥2200 for the upper deck), and there's also the option of a longer voyage into the northern reaches of the bay (daily; 60min; by group reservation only). From Dec to March, there are sailings every hour only on the shorter course. It's also possible to take a cruise round the bay from Matsushima tourist pier (Daily, roughly every hour: April–Oct 9am–4pm; Nov–March 9am–3pm; 50min; ¥1400), though they tend to be more crowded than the boats from Shiogama.

Information A good first stop if you arrive by train is the tourist office outside Matsushima Kaigan Station (Mon–Fri 9.30am–4.30pm, Sat & Sun 9am–5pm; ☎022 354 2263, ⓦ matsushima-kanko.com).

ACCOMMODATION AND EATING

While Matsushima is a very easy day-trip from Sendai (see p.228), the area also has a number of smart but expensive **hotels**; prices are more reasonable on weekdays and in winter (Dec to early April). Most of Matsushima's **restaurants** lining the main road cater to tourists, but there are a couple of attractive smaller places along the road between the station and the main street which serve reasonably priced seafood dishes.

Century Hotel センチュリーホテル 8 Senzui ☎022 354 4111 ⓦ centuryhotel.co.jp. On the waterfront, this modern hotel has a choice of Western or tatami en-suite rooms, plus seafront balconies at the higher end and a huge onsen bath with panoramic windows looking over the bay. Rates include two meals. **¥36,000**

Donjiki Chaya どんじき茶屋 89 Chōnai ☎022 354 5855. In a thatched building surrounded by gardens in the woods south of Zuigan-ji, this restaurant is great for lunch or a light snack. The menu offers soba, *dango* (rice dumplings) and drinks. Bowls of noodles start at around ¥400. Daily 9am–5pm, till 4pm winter.

Resort Inn Matsushima リゾートイン松島 17 Sanjukari ☎022 355 0888 ⓔ info@resort-inn.jp. A bright hotel with modern en-suite rooms. To reach it, turn

right from the station and follow the road leading under the tracks and up the hill about 700m. **¥13,000**

Santori Chaya さんとり茶屋 24-4-1 Senzui ☎022 353 2622. A small, simple restaurant on the seafront north of the Godai-dō, serving a range of reasonable *teishoku* (traditional set menu) as well as sashimi, sushi and rice dishes. Head upstairs for great sea views. Main dishes cost around ¥1000. 11.30am–3pm & 5.30–10pm, closed Wed.

Taritsuan 田里津庵 132-2 Idoriji ☎022 366 3328, ⓦ ichinobo.com/taritsuan. With minimalist decoration, this stylish restaurant serves seasonal seafood including oysters and abalone in *kaiseki* cuisine. Lunch is from ¥2800 and dinner from ¥3600. The breathtaking view of the bay alone is worth the 10min taxi ride from Kaigan station. Daily 11am–4pm.

Oshika Hantō

牡鹿半島

North of Sendai, Honshū's coastal plain gives way to a fractured shoreline of deep bays and knobbly peninsulas. The first of these is the **Oshika Hantō**, a rugged spine on the eastern edge of Sendai Bay, whose broken tip forms the tiny island of **Kinkazan**. This has been a sacred place since ancient times, but its prime attractions these days are its isolation and the hiking trails through forests inhabited by semi-wild deer and monkeys. This was one of the areas most badly affected by the

3/11 tsunami; the widespread destruction left a permanent scar on the physical landscape as well as on the psyche of the local population. Understandably, dealing with foreign tourists is not the priority, but there are some signs of a rebirth, with new businesses opening up.

Ishinomaki

石巻

With many now buildings flattened or empty, **Ishinomaki**, the main gateway to the area, has a forlorn air to it and many visitor facilities have closed down permanently. However, transport is running, and buses run down the peninsula to **Ayukawa** (鮎川), a former whaling port with connecting ferries to Kinkazan. What tourist infrastructure remains often closes in winter (Nov–March), so check the schedules first at the information offices in Sendai (see p.230) or Matsushima (see p.235), where you can also find out about any new businesses that have opened up.

Ishinomori Mangattan Museum

石ノ森萬画館, Ishinomori Manga-kan • 2-7 Nakaze, Ishinomaki • March–Nov daily 9am–6pm (closed every third Tues of the month); Dec–Feb daily except Tues 9am–5pm • ¥800 • ☎ 022 596 5055, ⓦ man-bow.com/manga

Manga-lovers will want to visit the entertaining **Ishinomori Mangattan Museum**, housed in a flying-saucer-style building across the river from the main shopping strip. The museum provided a ray of hope after the 2011 tsunami, remaining standing while all around was flattened, and acting as a centre for relief efforts.

ARRIVAL AND DEPARTURE   **ISHINOMAKI**

By train Connections at Ishinomaki can be quite poor, with waits of up to an hour for an onward bus or train. Check at Matsushima train station for the latest information. Note that passengers have to take a bus between Kaigan and Yamoto due to damage to that section of the train line.

Destinations: Kogota (11 daily; 45min); Sendai (every 30min; 55min–1hr 20min).

By bus The main bus stops are directly in front of Ishinomaki Station, with local and long-distance services. Services can be intermittent, so check for the latest timetables.

Destinations: Ayukawa (7 daily; 1hr 30min); Tokyo (Shinjuku) (daily; 7hr 10min).

Kinkazan

金華山

The first inhabitants of **KINKAZAN** ("Mountain of the Gold Flowers"), a conical island lying 1km off the tip of Oshika Hantō, were gold prospectors. Though the seams were exhausted long ago, Kinkazan is still associated with wealth and good fortune, and its prime sight, the shrine of **Koganeyama-jinja** (黄金山神社), is dedicated to the twin gods of prosperity, Ebisu and Daikoku. The shrine stands in a clearing, cropped by hungry deer, on the west slope of Kinkazan, fifteen minutes' walk from the ferry pier – turn left from the pier and follow the road steeply uphill. From behind the shrine buildings, a rough path leads to a stiff 2km hike up Kinkazan (445m), where the effort is rewarded with truly magnificent views along the peninsula and west towards distant Matsushima.

Various other **hiking trails** are indicated on the small green map you'll be given on the ferry to Kinkazan, which you can also pick up from the Ayukawa tourist office (see p.237). However, the paths themselves are poorly signed and may well be overgrown, so check the route before setting out. Additionally, the northern part of the island has been deemed too dangerous for hiking – the maps indicate the areas that are off limits. Remember also to take plenty of food and water. If you do get lost, head down to the rough track that circumnavigates the island; the whole place is less than 25km around, so you can't go too far wrong.

By train and bus The best way of getting to Kinkazan is to take the JR Senseki line from Sendai (or Matsushima) to Ishinomaki (石巻) and then hop on a bus south to Ayukawa (1hr 25min; ¥1460). Buses depart seven times a day (three times on weekends and hols) from bus stop #2 outside Ishinomaki Station.

By ferry Ferries only run at weekends.

Destinations: Ayukawa (Sat & Sun 3–10 daily; 25min).

Tourist information There's a small tourist office (daily 9am–6pm; ☎ 022 593 6448) at Ishinomaki Station, though its main focus is on recovery efforts; information for foreign tourists is very limited. Hiking trail maps for Kinkazan are available from the Ayukawa tourist office (daily 8.30am–5pm, Jan–March & Nov–Dec closed Sun; ☎ 022 545 3456).

Services Car rental is available at Ishinomaki through Eki Rent-a-Car (☎ 022 593 1665).

Kinkazan is best done as a day-trip, though there are some limited options to stay overnight, for which it's essential to book ahead. Note that there are no restaurants on the island, so bring something along to eat for lunch.

Koganeyama-jinja 黄金山神社 ☎ 022 545 2301 ✉ kinkasan@cocoa.ocn.ne.jp. The most atmospheric accommodation on Kinkazan is this pilgrims' lodge where you can attend the shrine's early-morning prayer sessions. Rates include two meals. D▪rm **¥9000**

Shiokaze 潮風 ☎ 022 545 2666. A fairy rundown minshuku a few hundred metres down the dirt road leading away from the right of the ferry pier. Rates include two meals. **¥13,650**

Hiraizumi and around

For a brief period in the eleventh century, the temples of **Hiraizumi**, around 120km north of Sendai and now a quiet backwater, rivalled even Kyoto in their magnificence. Though the majority of monasteries and palaces have since been lost, the gloriously extravagant **Konjiki-dō** and the other treasures of **Chūson-ji** bear witness to the area's former wealth and level of artistic accomplishment. Hiraizumi also boasts one of Japan's best-preserved Heian-period gardens at **Mōtsu-ji**, while a boat ride between the towering cliffs of the nearby **Geibikei** or **Gembikei** gorges (see box, p.240) provides a scenic contrast and offers especially spectacular views in autumn.

Hiraizumi

平泉

Nowadays it's hard to imagine **HIRAIZUMI** as the resplendent capital of the **Fujiwara** clan, who chose this spot on the banks of the Kitakami-gawa for their "paradise on earth". At first sight it's a rather dozy little town on a busy main road, but the low western hills conceal one of the most important sights in northern Honshū, the gilded **Konjiki-dō**, which has somehow survived war, fire and natural decay for nearly nine hundred years. You can easily cover this and the nearby gardens of **Mōtsu-ji** in a day, staying either in Hiraizumi or Ichinoseki, or even as a half-day stopover while travelling between Sendai and Morioka.

Brief history

In the early twelfth century, **Fujiwara Kiyohira**, the clan's first lord, began building a vast complex of Buddhist temples and palaces, lavishly decorated with gold from the local mines, in what is now Hiraizumi. Eventually, the Fujiwara's wealth and military might started to worry the southern warlord **Minamoto Yoritomo** (see p.794), who was in the throes of establishing the Kamakura shogunate. Yoritomo's valiant brother, **Yoshitsune**, had previously trained with the warrior monks of Hiraizumi, so when Yoritomo turned against him, Yoshitsune fled north. Though at first protected by the Fujiwara, the clan soon betrayed him on the promise of a sizeable reward, and in 1189 Yoshitsune committed suicide (although according to one legend he escaped to Mongolia, where

HIRAIZUMI FESTIVALS

The flight of Yoshitsune to Hiraizumi (see p.237) is commemorated with a costume parade during the town's main spring **festival** (May 1–5), which also features open-air nō performances at Chūson-ji. Other important events include an ancient **sacred dance**, Ennen-no-Mai, held by torchlight at Mōtsū-ji on January 20, May 5 and during the autumn festival (Nov 1–3).

he resurfaced as Genghis Khan). Meanwhile, Yoritomo attacked the Fujiwara, destroying their temples and leaving the town to crumble into ruin. **Bashō**, passing through Hiraizumi five hundred years after Yoshitsune's death, caught the mood in one of his famous haiku: "The summer grass, 'tis all that's left of ancient warriors' dreams."

Chūson-ji

中尊寺 • 202 Koromonoseki • Daily: April–Oct 8am–5pm; Nov–March 8.30am–4.30pm • ¥800 including Konjiki-dō, Kyōzō and Sankōzō • ☏ 019 146 2211 • On the main bus routes north from Ichinoseki (20min) and Hiraizumi (5min) stations

The Fujiwara's first building projects concentrated on the temple of **Chūson-ji**, which had been founded by a Tendai priest from Kyoto in the mid-ninth century. Of the forty original buildings that were built on the forested hillside, only two remain: Konjiki-dō (the Golden Hall) and the nearby sutra repository, Kyōzō. From the main road, a broad avenue leads uphill past minor temples sheltering under towering cryptomeria trees, until you reach the first building of any size, the Hondō, on the right-hand side. Chūson-ji's greatest treasure, the Konjiki-dō, is a little further up on the left in a concrete hall.

Konjiki-dō

金色堂

The **Konjiki-dō** is tiny – only 5.5 square metres – and protected behind plate glass, but it's still an extraordinary sight. The whole structure gleams with thick gold leaf, while the altar inside is smothered in mother-of-pearl inlay and delicate, gilded copper friezes set against dark, burnished lacquer. The altar's central image is of Amida Nyorai, flanked by a host of Buddhas, Bodhisattvas and guardian kings, all swathed in gold. Unveiled in 1124, this extravagant gesture of faith and power took fifteen years to complete and the bodies of all four generations of the Fujiwara lords still rest under its altar.

Kyōzō

恭三

Set behind the Konjiki-dō, the second of Chūson-ji's original buildings, the **Kyōzō**, is not nearly so dramatic. This small, plain hall, erected in 1108, used to house more than five thousand Buddhist sutras written in gold or silver characters on rich, indigo paper. The hall next door was built in 1288 to shelter the Konjiki-dō – and now houses an eclectic collection of oil paintings – while, across the way, there's a much more recent nō stage where outdoor performances are held in summer by firelight (Aug 14), and during Hiraizumi's two major festivals in spring and autumn (see box above).

Sankōzō

讚衡蔵

The road beside the entrance to the Konjiki-dō leads to the modern **Sankōzō**, a museum containing what remains of Chūson-ji's treasures. The most valuable items are a statue of the Senju Kannon (Thousand-Armed Goddess of Mercy), a number of sutra scrolls, and a unique collection of lacy metalwork decorations (*kalavinkas*), which originally hung in the Konjiki-dō.

Mōtsū-ji

毛越寺 • Aza Osawa 58 • Museum & castle daily: April–Oct 8am–5pm; Nov–March 8.30am–4.30pm • ¥500, including access to the museum • ☎0191 46 2331 • Poetry-writing contest held on the last Sun in May • 8min walk west from Hiraizumi Station

Hiraizumi's other main sight, apart from Chūson-ji, is the Heian-period gardens of Mōtsū-ji, a pleasant place for a stroll. In the twelfth century, the Fujiwara added to this temple, originally founded in 850, until it was the largest in northern Honshū. Only a few foundation stones of the original temple remain, along with Japan's best-preserved Heian garden, the **Jōdo-teien**. The garden's main feature is a large lake, speckled with symbolic "islands", in the midst of velvet lawns. You'll find flowers in bloom almost every season, including cherry blossom, lotus, bush clover and azaleas, but the most spectacular display is in late June, when thirty thousand irises burst into colour. There is a small **museum** on the left of the entrance, with photos of Mōtsū-ji's colourful festivals (see box opposite). The annual **poetry competition** recreates a pastime from a bygone era. Participants, dressed in traditional clothes, sit writing by a stream, under umbrellas. As they compose their poems, cups of sake are floated to them on the water and their completed works are read aloud by a master of ceremonies.

3

ARRIVAL AND INFORMATION

HIRAIZUMI

By train Hiraizumi is on the Tōhoku main line; change at Ichinoseki for Shinkansen services.

Destinations Hanamaki (hourly; 45min); Ichinoseki (hourly; 8min) Kitakami (hourly; 30min); Morioka (hourly; 1hr 20min); Sendai (hourly; 45min–1hr).

Tourist information There is a tourist office (daily 8.30am–5pm; ☎0191 46 2110, ⊛hiraizumi.or.jp/en) in the small building to the right of the station exit, with English maps and leaflets.

Services Hiraizumi has a post office and foreign exchange bank in the backstreets west of the station.

GETTING AROUND

By bus Buses for Mōtsū-ji and Chūson-ji (both ¥140), as well as Ichinoseki (¥310), depart from in front of the tourist office.

By bike Swallow Tours, next to the information office, rent bikes (April–Nov 8am–5pm, Dec–March 9am–4pm; ¥500/3hr, ¥1000/day; ☎070 5324 0611).

ACCOMMODATION

Accommodation options in Hiraizumi are fairly limited, though there are a number of onsen hotels and small inns. It's a good idea to book in advance, especially in peak season.

Daimonjiyama Camp-jō Nangashima 大文字山キャンプ城 51-651 Yamada ☎0191 46 5564. Located 10km east of the station, this campsite is a bargain option in summer and spring. Your best bet to get here is by taxi from the station. Pitch ¥200, tent hire ¥300 per person

Hiraizumi Hotel Masashi-bō 平泉ホテル武蔵坊 15 Osawa ☎0191 46 2241, ⊛www.musasibou.co.jp. This large hotel on the hill on route to Chūson-ji features

spacious and elegant tatami rooms and large onsen baths with panoramic views. Rates include two meals. **¥21,000**

Shirayama Ryokan 志羅山旅館 139-5 Shirayama ☎0191 46 2883. Located in the side streets west of the station, this is a clean and comfortable traditional inn. You'll need to call ahead to let them know when you plan to arrive. Rates include two meals. **¥13,000**

EATING

There are a couple of small restaurants lining the road from the station to Mōtsū-ji temple. There are also several near Chūson-ji serving noodles and classic dishes, albeit at slightly inflated prices. If you fancy a picnic, head for the small supermarket on the road to Mōtsū-ji.

Gokusui-tei 曲水亭 145-9 Shirayama ☎0191 46 3650. A refined restaurant on the main road running west from the station, serving traditional Japanese meals. Noon–3pm & 5–9pm, closed Wed.

Izumiya 泉屋 75 Izumiya ☎0191 46 2038. On the north side of the station, just before the crossroads, this

small and simple place serves good-value *soba teishoku* (traditional set menu) from ¥530. 9am–5pm, closed Wed.

Seoul Shokudō ソウル食堂 115-6 Shirayama ☎0191 46 5199. A *yakiniku* (Korean barbecue) restaurant that has set meals, an English menu and a good range of vegetarian choices. Dishes start at ¥650. Tues–Sun, evenings only.

GEIBIKEI GORGE

The Hiraizumi area boasts two river **gorges** with confusingly similar names. **Geibikei** (猊鼻渓), as opposed to **Genbikei** (厳美渓), is the more impressive of the two, a narrow defile best viewed by boat, some 20km east of Hiraizumi. You can get there by bus (stop #7; 45min; ¥620) or train (JR Ōfunato line to Geibikei Station; 30min) from Ichinoseki Station – an attractive ride either way. From the bus stop, turn left at the main road and then take the first right; from the train station, turn right and walk for five minutes, following the road under the tracks to find the dock.

Though not cheap, the Geibikei **boat trip** (daily: April–Oct 8.30–4.30pm, Nov–March 9am–3pm, hourly; 90min; ¥1500; ☎0191 47 2341) is a lot of fun. Despite poling fairly sizeable wooden punts upstream for 2km, the boatmen still find breath to regale their passengers with local legends, details of the passing flora and endless statistics about the gorge. It's all in Japanese, of course, but the general mirth is infectious.

3

Ichinoseki

一関

If you're travelling north to Hiraizumi by train it's necessary to change to a local train at **ICHINOSEKI**, a small town eight kilometres south. There are no particular attractions in the town itself worth visiting, but with good transport connections it is a convenient overnight base for visiting Hiraizumi and the Geibikei and Gembikei gorges (see box above), with reasonable business hotels, bars and restaurants near the station.

ARRIVAL AND INFORMATION   ICHINOSEKI

By train Ichinoseki is on the Tōhoku Shinkansen and Tōhoku main lines, and is the terminal for Geibikei trains. Destinations: Geibikei (11 daily; 30min); Hiraizumi (hourly; 8min); Kogota (hourly; 50min); Morioka (hourly; 40min); Sendai (every 30min; 30min); Shin-Hanamaki (every 30min; 25min).

By bus There are frequent local buses from Ichinoseki to Hiraizumi, departing from outside the station. Note

that the last Hiraizumi bus leaves around 7pm (6.30pm Sun).
Destinations: Chūson-ji (every 15–20min; 25min); Geibikei (9–11 daily; 30–40min); Hiraizumi (every 15–20min; 20min).
Tourist information The information office (1 Ekimae, daily 9am–5pm; ☎0191 23 2350) outside the main exit of Ichinoseki Station has English maps and brochures.

The Tōno valley

遠野バレー, Tōno bērē

The town of **Tōno** is set in a bowl of low mountains in the heart of one of Japan's poorest regions, surrounded by the flat **Tōno valley**. The people of Tōno and the farmers of the valley take pride in their living legacy of farming and folk traditions, embodied by the district's **magariya** – large, L-shaped farmhouses – and a number of museums devoted to the old ways. But the area is most famous for its wealth of **folk tales**, known as *Tōno Monogatari* (see box, p.242); there are references to these legends and traces of primitive cults throughout the valley, alongside ancient shrines and rock carvings, all of which lends the area a mysterious undercurrent.

The flat, tranquil roads and slow, rural pace of life here make the region a perfect place to explore by **bike**. There are a number of cycle paths and routes which guide you round the main sights in the valley and can easily be covered in a day's leisurely riding. The eastern part of the valley is especially lovely, and you can pass through some areas where you really feel as if you've stepped back in time.

GETTING AROUND   THE TŌNO VALLEY

By bus There are some local buses that run from outside Tōno Station, but the only really useful routes are those

heading northeast to Denshō-en and Furusato-mura (see p.244). These buses also stop near *Tōno Youth Hostel* (see p.242). Check with the tourist office (see below) for schedules.

By car and bike To make the most of the Tōno valley you really need your own transport – head to Tōno to hire cars or bikes (see p.242).

Tōno

遠野

TŌNO itself is a small town set among flat rice lands, with orchards and pine forests cloaking the surrounding hills. Although it's mainly a place to make use of for its hotels, banks and other facilities, there are a couple of museums to see before you set off round the valley. Allow a couple of days to do the area justice.

Tōno Municipal Museum

遠野市立博物館, Tōno Shiritsu Hakubutsukan • 3-9 Higashidate-chō • Daily 9am–5pm, closed last day of the month • ¥300 • ☎ 0198 62 2340 • 8min walk from Tōno Station straight across town and over the river

Some 700m directly south of the station, at the back of a red-brick building which doubles as the library, is **Tōno Municipal Museum**. The entertaining exhibitions and videos give information about the local environment and a good overview of Tōno's festivals, crafts and agricultural traditions.

Tōno Folktale Museum

とおの昔話村, Tōno Mukashi-banashi-mura • 2-11 Chuō-dōri • Daily 9am–5pm • ¥500 combined entrance • ☎ 0198 62 7837

Newly renovated in 2013, the **Tōno Folktale Museum** brings Tōno folk tales alive in a variety of interactive multimedia displays which are still interesting, even if most of the information is in Japanese. On-site is a "village" consisting of several buildings, including the inn where Yanagita Kunio (see box, p.242) stayed while researching his legends. Included in the ticket is entrance to the **Tōno Castle Town Materials Museum** (遠野城下町資料館; daily 9am–5pm; ☎0198 62 2502) across the road on a newly renovated pedestrian street; it exhibits historical artefacts, including amour, weapons, tableware, textiles and paintings.

ARRIVAL AND INFORMATION
TŌNO

By train If you travel to Tōno by train, you can enjoy an attractive journey east on the JR Kamaishi line from Hanamaki, or from Shin-Hanamaki for the Shinkansen.
Destinations Hanamaki (12 daily; 55min–1hr 10min); Morioka (3 daily; 1hr 25min); Shin-Hanamaki (12 daily; 45min–1hr).

Tourist information Tōno's tourist office (daily 8.30am–5.30pm; ☎ 0198 62 1333, ⓦTōnojikan.jp) is on the right as you exit the station. Though the staff don't speak much English, they have English-language maps and brochures, and a larger-scale Japanese map which is useful for navigating around the valley. The attached

shop stocks copies of *The Legends of Tōno* (see box, p.242; ¥2100).

Picnics If you plan on spending the day cycling in the valley, you can stock up on picnic supplies at the Tōno shopping mall, a block from the station (遠野ショッピングセンター とぴあ; Topia building, 1-11 Shinkoku-chō); daily 9.30am–8pm; ☎ 0198 62 277, ⓦtopia-Tōno.com). The ground floor has a well-stocked supermarket and a small farmers' market with fresh and cheap fruit and vegetables, complete with photographs and notes on the farmers who produced them.

THE LEGENDS OF TŌNO

When the far-sighted folklorist **Yanagita Kunio** visited Tōno in 1909, he found a world still populated with the shadowy figures of demons and other usually malevolent spirits which the farmers strove to placate using ancient rituals. The following year, he published **Tōno Monogatari** (published in English as *The Legends of Tōno*), the first book to tap the rich oral traditions of rural Japan. The 118 tales were told to him by Kyōseki Sasaki (or Kizen), the educated son of a Tōno peasant, to whom goblins, ghosts and gods were part of everyday life.

People in Tōno still talk about **Zashiki Warashi**, a mischievous child spirit (either male or female) who can be heard running at night and is said to bring prosperity to the household. Another popular tale tells of a farmer's beautiful daughter who fell in love with the family horse. When the farmer heard that his child had married the horse, he hanged it from a mulberry tree, but his grieving daughter was whisked off to heaven clinging to her lover.

Probably the most popular character from the legends, however, is the **kappa**, an ugly water creature which, while not being unique to Tōno, seems to exist here in large numbers. You'll find *kappa* images everywhere in town – on postboxes, outside the station; even the police box is *kappa*-esque. The traditional *kappa* has long skinny limbs, webbed hands and feet, a sharp beak, and a hollow on the top of his head that must be kept full of water. He's usually green, sometimes with a red face, and his main pastime seems to be pulling young children into ponds and rivers. Should you happen to meet a real *kappa*, remember to bow – on returning your bow, the water will run out of the hollow on his head and he'll have to hurry off to replenish it.

GETTING AROUND

By car Tōno Kankō Rent-a-Car (☏ 0198 62 1375) is inside the station, and a Mitsubishi Rent-a-Car (☏ 0198 62 3154) place is nearby, where vehicles can be hired in 3hr or 6hr increments (from around ¥4000).

By bike Most people opt to cycle; you can rent bikes from the information office and other outlets on the station concourse (¥500/2hr; up to ¥1000/day), or from *Tōno Youth Hostel* (see below) for ¥800 per day. Tōno maps show three recommended cycling routes (also possible by car), of around 4hr each, which cover the main sights – they're reasonably well signposted, though not always in English.

ACCOMMODATION

Folklore Tōno フォルクローロ遠野 5-7 Shinkoku-chō ☏ 0198 62 0700. A small JR-owned hotel inside the station building, with comfortable but rather unexciting Western-style rooms. Rates include a simple breakfast. **¥13,600**

Minshuku Rindō 民宿りんどう 2-34 Daiku-chō ☏ 0198 62 5726, ✉ rindou@crocus.ocn.ne.jp, ⊕ www.v-toono .jp/rindou. A simple, homely minshuku on an attractive street roughly 5min walk west from the station. Rates include two meals. **¥13,000**

Minshuku Tōno 民宿とおの 2-17 Zaimoku-chō ☏ 0198 62 4395, ⊕ minshuku-Tōno.com. Small, friendly family-run minshuku, on the north side of the railway tracks. The rooms have seen better days, but the dining room, with its open hearth and excellent rustic food, compensates. Two meals are included in the rates, and single rooms are available. **¥11,600**

Tōno Youth Hostel 遠野ユースホステル 13-39-5 Tsuchibuchi-chō, 10km northeast of the city ☏ 0198 62 8736, ⊕ jyh.or.jp. Delightful modern hostel with dorms, family rooms and excellent home cooking. It's set among rice fields outside Tōno city; take a bus from in front of Tōno station to Nitagi then it's a 10min walk (¥200, check timetable at tourist information office as buses can be infrequent). There are basic bikes for hire, and the genial manager speaks good English and can advise on local cycling routes. It is advisable to eat the tasty meals on offer (¥1700 for two meals), as there are few other options nearby. Dorm **¥3300**

EATING

Local **speciality foods** include *hitsuko soba*, small bowls of rough, handmade noodles eaten with a mix of chicken, raw egg, onion and mushrooms, and the regional dish, *nambu hitssumi* (or *suiton*), a soup laced with seasonal vegetables and dumplings. You can try these, along with other specialities, at many of the area's minshuku. The folk village restaurants (same opening times as villages) are a good place to try local delicacies such as *ayu* (river fish) and *jingisukan* (barbecued lamb).

Korean Kitchen 韓国のキッチン 10-13 Chūō Dōri ☏ 0198 62 2655. Next to the post office, this modern restaurant has lunches from ¥880, including barbecued meat sets and noodles, and a range of meaty and spicy *yakiniku* (Korean BBQ) dishes at night. 11.30am–2pm & 5.30–11pm, closed Tues.

Taigetsu 待月 3-1 Shinkoku-Chō ☎0198 62 4933. Located on the street running south from the station, this cosy café serves good cake and coffee along with small dishes such as cheese on toast, pizza, curry, and pasta ramen dishes. A coffee with cake costs around ¥450. Daily 10am–10pm.

Ume-no-ya うめのや 2-2 Shinkoku Chō ☎0198 62 2622. Directly opposite Taigestru, this simple place offers good portions of curry rice, *ebi-fry* (fried prawns), omelettes from ¥500 and set meals from ¥950. 11.30am–8pm, closed Tues.

West of Tōno

West of Tōno, the main valley narrows, funnelling the road and railway along beside the Sarugaishi-gawa. The wooded southern hillside hides some unusual **shrines** and an appealing group of **Buddha images**, which makes one of the best short trips out of Tōno. Further up the valley, an imposing *magariya* farmhouse attracts a lot of attention, but if you are short on time it's better to save your energy for more accessible examples on the east side of town.

Unedori-jinja

卯子西神社 • 2.5km southwest of Tōno Station • Accessible during daylight hours • Free

Head west out of Tōno on the south side of the river for 2.5km, on the old Route 283, and look out for a stone staircase on the left. At the bottom of the steps, past the house, you'll find a tree festooned with red and white ribbons and, behind it, **Unedori-jinja**. This tiny shrine is dedicated to the god in charge of matrimonial affairs; if you want to get married, tie a red ribbon onto the tree with your left hand.

Gohyaku Rakan

五百羅漢 • 2.8km southwest of Tōno Station

Climb the stone staircase by Unedori-jinja, cross a lane and follow the path into a narrow, wooded valley filled with mossy stones. Keep looking closely at these stones: at first you won't see anything, but gradually faint outlines appear, then full faces and rounded bodies, until you're seeing little figures everywhere. Known as the **Gohyaku Rakan**, there are supposedly five hundred of these Buddhist "disciples", which were carved by a local monk in the late eighteenth century to pacify the spirits of the victims of a terrible famine in 1754.

Chiba Magariya

千葉家の曲り家 • 1-14 Aya-ori-chō kamiayori • Daily: April–Oct 8.30am–5pm; Nov–March 9am–4pm • ¥350 • ☎0198 62 9529 • 11km west of Tōno Station

The thatch-roofed **Chiba Magariya** stands high above Tōno, north of the main valley up a steep side road. Once home to the Chiba family, fifteen labourers and twenty horses, this two-hundred-year-old farmhouse was restored as an important example of a *magariya*, an L-shaped building with the stables in the shorter wing. Also look at the **Tsuzuki Stone** (続石), in the woods 500m from the house. No one knows if the enormous, rounded boulder balanced on a smaller stone is natural or man-made, though many believe it is an ancient tomb.

Northeast of Tōno

The broad valley northeast of Tōno is home to a number of somewhat touristy "folk villages" aimed at preserving the old crafts. The best one to visit is **Furusato-mura**, though the smaller **Denshō-en** and **Sui-kōen** are slightly more accessible. Other sights to aim for include a *kappa* pool, an old watermill and a temple housing Japan's tallest Kannon statue. However, the area's chief highlight is its scenery – rice fields and rolling hills dotted with the occasional thatched farmhouse. The best way to explore is to hire a bike and slowly pedal your way through the country lanes.

Denshō-en

伝承園 • 6-5-1 Tsuchibuchi • Daily 9am–5pm, last entry 4pm • ¥310 • ☎ 0198 62 8655 • 5km northeast of Tōno station on route 340; buses depart from Tōno Station around every hour and stop at either end of the village (15–20min; ¥290)

The museum village of Denshō-en contains various buildings relocated from around Tōno, including a waterwheel, storehouses and a *magariya* (see p.240), where local folk demonstrate weaving, rope-making and other crafts. At the back of the *magariya* is a small shrine room filled with brightly dressed dolls. These are images of **Oshira-sama**, an agricultural deity worshipped throughout northern Honshū. According to legend, Tōno's original Oshira-sama came from the same tree on which the horse-husband died (see box, p.242). The deities, often used by blind mediums, are also supposed to predict the future – hence all the prayer papers tied around the shrine.

Jōken-ji

常堅寺 • 7-50 Tsuchibuchi • 24hr • Free

A short distance east along the main road from Denshō-en, a signposted right-turn leads to the **Jōken-ji** temple. Founded in 1490, the temple is mainly of interest for its statue of **Obinzuru-sama**, a little figure in a cloak and hat with a very shiny anatomy – the deity is supposed to cure illnesses if rubbed in the appropriate place. Behind the temple there's a **kappa pool**, home to a particularly helpful *kappa* credited with dousing a fire in Jōken-ji. An eccentric local has also built a small shrine to himself beside the pool and, if he is around, will probably regale you with incomprehensible but good-natured stories.

Fukusen-ji

福泉寺 • 7-57 Matsuzaki-chō, Komagi • April–Nov daily 8am–5pm • ¥300 • ☎ 0198 62 3822

From Tōno, a road branches north just before Denshō-en, following the main valley for another 2km to **Fukusen-ji**, a temple founded in 1912 and famous for its 17m-tall image of **Kannon**, the Goddess of Mercy. The slender, gilded statue with a blue hairdo is apparently the largest wooden statue in the country and, carved from a single tree trunk, took twelve years to make. It stands in an attractive temple at the top of the hill, where the artist's tools and photos of the huge tree being brought to Tōno by train are also on display.

If you want to cycle to Tōno after Fukusen-ji, follow the road back towards Denshō-en for about one minute and take the Tōno-Towa Bicycle Path indicated by the happy *kappa* sign to the right. This 8km-long path winds through rice fields and along streams before joining Route 396 for the final two kilometres.

Furusato-mura

ふるさと村 • Tukimoushi-chō, Kamitukimoushi 5-89-1 • Daily 9am–5pm, last entry 4pm • ¥520, workshops ¥600–1000 • ☎ 0198 64 2300 • Some Denshō-en buses continue up the valley, though service is sporadic (every 1–2hr; 25min; ¥500)

Some 3km further northwest from Denshō-en is **Furusato-mura**, the biggest and most attractive of Tōno's folk museums. It resembles a working village, with rice fields, vegetable plots and duck ponds. There are five refurbished *magariya* on the hillside dating from the eighteenth and nineteenth centuries, where pensioners sit beside smoking hearths, busily making souvenirs such as straw slippers, wooden *kappa* and bamboo baskets – the old folk run a number of workshops, including how to make straw horses and bamboo dragonflies, as well as soba making and *mochi* pounding, should you want to have a go. You can also buy their handiwork in the museum shop, where there's a small restaurant with some good-value lunch sets.

East of Denshō-en

The most beautiful part of the Tōno valley lies **east of Denshō-en**, though to appreciate it you'll have to get off onto the side roads. One attractive ride takes you out to an old watermill and then loops back past the third folk village. To find the turning, follow

Route 340 for 3km east from Denshō-en and then fork right immediately after crossing a red-lacquered bridge. The lane climbs gently uphill, past a number of old farms to a small, thatched **watermill** (山口の水車). On the way you pass the **house of Kyōseki Sasaki** (see box, p.242), opposite which there's a path signed to **Dan-no-hana** (ダンノハナ), a place where in the not-so-distant past all people over 60 were sent to die. However, here the elderly residents got bored waiting, so they came down to work the fields during the day and returned to their hill at night.

When you head back down to the main road, look out on the left for a turning signed to **Denderano** (デンデラ野). Follow this lane west for nearly 2km and you'll come to the last of the folk villages, **Takamuro Sui-kōen** (たかむろ水光園; 7-175-2 Tsuchibuchi-chō; daily 10am–4pm, closed every fourth Mon; ¥310; ☎0198 62 2834), which has a *magariya*, a *kappa* pool, displays of antique farm implements and a solar-powered sauna and steam bath.

Morioka

盛岡

A former castle town on the confluence of three rivers, the small, congenial city of **MORIOKA** has no outstanding sights, but the combination of an attractive setting, a good range of accommodation, interesting local cuisine and entertainment makes it a good stop on the journey through northern Honshū. Additionally, Morioka is one of the main access points for hikes around the nearby **Hachimantai plateau**.

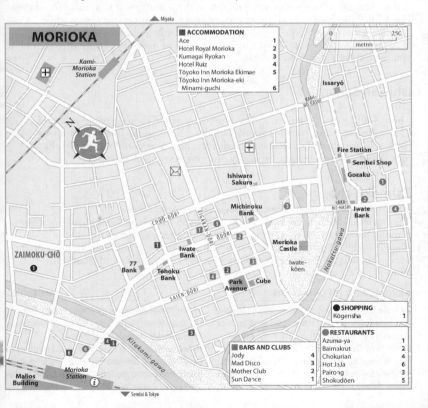

MORIOKA FESTIVALS

The city has two major summer festivals. At the end of the rice-planting season, the **Chagu-Chagu Umakko** (チャグチャグ馬コ; second Sat in June) features a 15km procession of richly caparisoned horses, ending at the city's Hachiman-gū shrine. Then, in early August (1–3), thousands of dancers parade through town during the **Sansa Odori** (さんさ踊), accompanied by flutes and drums and followed by a general knees-up.

Iwate-kōen and around

岩手公園 • 1-37 Uchimaru • 24hr • Free • A 20min walk east of the station through the main shopping area

With a couple of hours to spare in Morioka, you can wander around the castle ruins and some of the older neighbourhoods. **Iwate-kōen**, Morioka castle park, was once the seat of the Nambu lords; it took 36 years to complete (1597–1633), only for it to be destroyed in the battles of the Meiji Restoration. Only some high stone walls and ramparts remain of the castle, but the surrounding park is a peaceful space for a stroll, with a variety of plants, trees and water features. To the east of the old castle walls is a pleasant riverside path along the bank of **Nakatsu-gawa**, and at the northeast corner of the park you can cross the river via the **Naka-no-hashi** bridge (中ノ橋).

Immediately over the river is the ornate red-brick and grey-slate facade of Iwate Bank, which dates from 1911, and to the left is a row of traditional Meiji-era buildings known as **Gozaku** (こざ九), now housing stores selling local crafts such as brushes, straw and wicker goods. Stores opposite specialize in the region's most famous crafts – heavy iron kettles and eye-catching cotton textiles dyed with intricate patterns – while appetizing odours greet you at the top of the street, where a *sembei* shop turns out local-style rice crackers sprinkled with sesame seeds or nuts; walk round the side and you can see the bakers hard at work.

Ishiwari Sakura

石割桜

About 400m west of the river, a three-hundred-year-old cherry tree bulges out of a 15m-wide fissure in a rounded granite boulder. Known as the **Ishiwari Sakura**, or "rock-splitting cherry", no one knows whether the centuries-old tree really split the rock, but it's a startling sight, especially in spring when in blossom.

Zaimoku-chō

材木町 盛岡 • A 5min walk northeast of the station on the opposite bank of the Kitakami-gawa

The small neighbourhood known as **Zaimoku-chō** has a traditional shopping street running parallel to the river. Among small boutiques, there are a number of craft shops, notably **Kōgensha** (see p.248), which sells local specialities including pottery, heavy iron kettles, cotton textiles dyed with intricate patterns and colourful hand-painted paper kites.

ARRIVAL AND INFORMATION
MORIOKA

By train The Tōhoku Shinkansen line splits in Morioka, with connections north to Aomori and west to Akita. Morioka Station is on the west side of the city centre.
Destinations Akita (hourly; 1hr 30min); Aomori (hourly; 1hr 45min); Hanamaki (every 30min; 20–35min); Kakunodate (hourly; 50min); Kitakami (every 30min; 50min); Noheji (hourly; 1hr 15min); Sendai (every 30min;

45min); Shin-Hanamaki (every 30min; 12min); Tazawako (15 daily; 40min); Tokyo (every 30min; 2hr 20min–3hr 30min); Towada-Minami (7 daily; 2hr).
By bus Local and long-distance buses depart from the east side of Morioka Station, with services running to Tokyo, the Hachimantai plateau and Towada-ko. Note that many bus services only operate from late April to late Nov.

Destinations Aomori (4 daily; 3hr 15min); Hirosaki (hourly; 2hr 15min); Sendai (hourly; 2hr 40min); Tokyo (2 daily; 7hr 30min).
Tourist information Morioka's Northern Tōhoku information centre (daily 9am–5.30pm; ☎019 625 2090) is located on the train station's second floor, near the southern entrance to the Shinkansen tracks. The helpful English-speaking staff can provide maps and information about the region, and there's also a JR information desk in the same office. The official tourism office site ⓦwww.japan-iwate.info is a useful source of info on the Iwate region.

GETTING AROUND

By bus There is an "¥100 loop bus" that runs between the station and various central locations.
By bike Central Morioka can easily be covered on foot, but another option is to rent a bike. Sasaki Bicycles (¥200/hr, ¥1000/day; ☎019 624 2692), by *Hotel Ruiz* (see below), is one of several bicycle rental places.

By car Nippon Rent-a-Car (☎019 635 6605), Nissan (☎019 654 5825), Toyota (☎019 622 0100) and Eki Rent-a-Car (☎019 624 5212) all have offices in or near the station. To book a taxi, call the station's central booking office on ☎019 622 5240 (daily 9am–5am).

ACCOMMODATION

Ace ホテルニース 2-11-35 Chūō-dōri ☎019 654 3811. Just north of Ōdōri, this is a good choice if you want to stay in the downtown area. The rooms are comfortable, although it's worth paying a little extra to stay in the new wing. Breakfast is included in the rates. **¥8000**
★**Kumagai Ryokan** 熊ヶ井旅館 3-2-5 Ōsakawara ☎019 651 3020, ⓦkumagairyokan.com. An 8min walk from the station, this ryokan is one of the best options in town, with a welcoming English-speaking owner, attractive tatami rooms and well-priced meals available (breakfast ¥1000, dinner ¥2000). **¥8400**
Hotel Royal Morioka ホテルロイヤル盛岡 11-11 Saien-dōri ☎019 653 1331, ⓦhotelroyalmorioka .co.jp. A high-end hotel in the heart of the city's main entertainment area. The Western-style rooms are elegantly furnished and spacious. There are two in-house restaurants, serving *Shabu-shabu* and Korean barbecue, as well as a ground-floor café. Breakfast is available for ¥1260. **¥16,275**
Hotel Ruiz ホテルルイズ 7-15 Ekimae-dōri ☎019 625 2611, ⓦhotel-ruiz.jp. Located near the station, just before the river, this mid-range business hotel has a choice of Western- or Japanese-style rooms and two unexciting in-house restaurants. Breakfast is included in the rates. **¥8800**
Tōyoko Inn Morioka Ekimae 東横INN盛岡駅前 14-5 Ekimae-dōri ☎019 625 1045, ⓦtoyoko-inn.com. Opposite the station, this *Tōyoko Inn* branch has smart and clean rooms, and rates include a light Japanese breakfast. Also has free internet access. Breakfast included in the rates. **¥7140**
Tōyoko Inn Morioka Ekimae 東横INN南口駅前 3-60 Ekimae-dōri ☎019 604 1045, ⓦtoyoko-inn .com. Another branch of the dependable hotel chain, situated next to *Hotel Ruiz*. Breakfast included in the rates. **¥7140**

3

MORIOKA CUISINE

One highlight of visiting Morioka is its cuisine, the city's most famous speciality being **wanko-soba**, named after the small bowls that the thin, flat buckwheat noodles are served in. They're often eaten as a contest, during which diners don an apron and shovel down as many bowls as possible while a waitress relentlessly dishes up more; to stop, you have to get the top on to your emptied bowl – easier said than done. Another rather odd Morioka concoction, **reimen**, is originally a summer dish, though you can easily find it year-round in the city as well as in other parts of the country. This consists of a large bowl of cold, semi-transparent, slightly chewy egg noodles eaten with Korean *kimchi* (spicy pickled vegetables) and a variety of garnishes that might include boiled egg, sesame seeds and slices of apple or cold meat.

The final local speciality is another unusual noodle dish; **ja-ja men**, a bowl of thick, white noodles (a bit like udon) that comes with a few slices of cucumber, red pickles and a slab of brown miso paste. You'll find *ja-ja men* in many of the city's noodle shops; mix up the miso paste and noodles once you are served and, if you're still hungry when you've finished, crack open and beat up a raw egg in your bowl and hand it to your server, who will pour broth over it: to make *chii tantan*, a palate-cleansing soup. A little bland if eaten straight, most locals mix in either grated ginger or miso paste to give it a bit more flavour.

EATING AND DRINKING

Azuma-ya 東家 1-8-3 Nakanohashi-dōri ☎019 622 2252. Across the street from the Nakachan department store, this is a good place to head to for *wanko-soba* if *Chokurian* (see below) is full; *wanko* course menus start at ¥2625. Daily 11am–8pm.

Baimakrut バイマックルー 1-4-22 Nakanohashi-dōri ☎019 622 8109. Against a backdrop of unrelenting Thai pop music, the chef at this welcoming and popular restaurant whips up great curries at lunch (set menus from ¥840) and all sorts of Thai specialities at night. Daily 11.30am–2.30pm & 6–11pm.

Chokurian 直利庵 1-12-13 Nakanohashi-dōri ☎019 624 0441. Opened in 1884, this is the best-known restaurant in town for *wanko-soba*. Expect to pay ¥2625–5200, although they also serve reasonably priced standard noodle dishes in an adjoining room. 11am–8pm, closed Wed.

Hot JaJa ホットジャジャ 9-5 Ekimae-dōri ☎019 606 1068. If you can't get into *Pairong* (see below), head to this *ja-ja men* place near the station. The noodles are good, and they also serve the good local Baeren Beer, which is inspired by German brewing traditions. *Ja-ja men* starts at ¥450, with sets from ¥750. Daily 10am–11.30pm.

★**Pairong** 白龍 5-15 Uchimaru ☎019 624 2247. Just off Ōdōri, across from Iwate-kōen; walk under the big *torii* and look on the left side. One of the most popular places for *ja-ja men*, with huge but cheap portions. The portions are so filling that the staff advise new customers to try the regular (*futsū*; ¥500) size first; the egg soup costs another ¥50. Expect queues during peak lunch and dinner hours. Mon–Sat 11.30am–9pm.

Shokudōen 食道苑 1-8-2 Ōdōri ☎019 651 4590. Nestled in the backstreets of Morioka's drinking area, you can try *reimen*, served to your required level of spiciness, or *yakiniku* (Korean BBQ) dishes, starting from ¥850. Daily 11.30am–midnight, closed first and third Tues of the month.

NIGHTLIFE AND ENTERTAINMENT

Considering its size, Morioka has a surprisingly bustling nightlife with a thriving **club** scene and plenty of lively **bars**. The main areas for drinking and entertainment are in the streets on either side of the covered Ōdōri shopping arcade.

Mad Disco マッド・ディスコー B1 1-6-3 Hinoshita ☎019 681 6660, ⓦ ameblo.jp/maddisco. The place to go for hip-hop and R&B Japanese style, with the cream of the region's DJs and MCs providing the tunes. Entry varies from ¥1000 to ¥2000, usually including two drinks; ladies get in free on some nights. Tues–Sun 10pm till late.

Mother Club モザー・クラブ 3F Plaza Tiger Bld, 1-6-17 Ōdōri ☎019 651 0530 ⓦ mother-morioka.com. Attracting top Japanese and international DJs, there's an eclectic mix of music at this small and friendly club with a big reputation. Open till late, often closed Sun & Mon; check site for weekly schedule.

Soul Bar Jody ソール・バー・ジョーディー 2-23 Saien-dōri ☎019 651 8108. This long-running intimate bar in the basement of the Vent Vert Building plays funk, R&B and soul and attracts a friendly crowd. Drinks start from ¥700, and there is a ¥1000 table charge. Daily 7.30pm–3am.

Sun Dance サンダンス 2-4-22 Daitsū ☎019 652 6526. This busy Irish bar is popular with expats and serves Tex-Mex dishes and other pub grub. It has a good range of imported beers, including Guinness on tap as well as specials on jugs of cocktails. Daily till late.

SHOPPING

Ōdōri and Saien-dōri are Morioka's two major shopping streets, with a good selection of large department stores including Park Avenue and Cube II, as well as smaller independent retailers. Nambu ironware, dyed cotton textiles and plain wooden *kokeshi* dolls are the representative crafts of this region.

Kōgensha 光原社 2-18 Zaimoku-chō ☎019 622 2894. Centred around a lovely courtyard, this craftshop sells a range of modern and traditional pottery, ironware, paper and bamboo designs. It also has a café at the back. Daily 10am–6pm.

DIRECTORY

Banks Iwate Bank, Tōhoku Bank, Michinoku Bank and 77 Bank all have branches with foreign-exchange desks on Ōdōri. Iwate Bank also has a branch outside the train station.

Hospitals The two main central hospitals are Iwate Medical University Hospital, 19-1 Uchi-maru (☎019 651 5111), and the Prefectural Hospital, 1-4-1 Ueda (☎019 653 1151).

Internet access There is free internet access at the Iwate International Association, 5F AIINA (☎019 654 8900, ⓦ iwate-ia.or.jp). Located next to Malios at the East–West Passage of Morioka Station, this is the local forum for international exchange; they can also offer help and advice to any foreigner in difficulties.

HIKES AROUND MORIOKA

Tōhoku's highest peak, **Iwate-san** (岩手山; 2041m), dominates Morioka's northern horizon and marks the eastern edge of the **Hachimantai plateau**, a beautiful area for hiking among marshes and pine forests. At present the volcanic peak is off limits, but you can spend a day walking around the plateau to the north of Iwate-san, from where it's an easy stroll to the less daunting summit of **Hachimantai** (八幡平; 1613m). From the Hachimantai Chōjō bus stop, a well-marked path leads to the summit (40min), across Hachiman-numa marshes. Afterwards, you can follow a variety of tracks wandering across the plateau with views south to the barren slopes of Iwate-san.

There are a couple of infrequent bus routes from Morioka to Hachmantai Chōjō, taking between two and two and half hours (one-way around ¥1300). The timetables, however, change annually and services are limited to summer months. Contact the tourist office in Morioka station (see p.247) for full details.

Post office The Central Post Office, just north of Chūō-dōri, has the best hours (daily 9am–7pm, Sat till 5pm, Sun till 12.30pm, ATM Mon–Fri 7am–11pm, Sat 9am–9pm, Sun 9am–7pm). There is also a sub-post office in the blocks in front of the station.

3

Aomori

青森

Honshū's most northerly city, **AOMORI**, sits at the bottom of Mutsu Bay, sheltered by the two claws of the Tsugaru and Shimokita peninsulas. It's a small and rather characterless port city, though it comes to life during the **Nebuta Matsuri** (Aug 2–7), one of Japan's biggest and rowdiest festivals (see box, p.251). The redeveloped harbourside, a few minutes walk from the station, is home to an eye-catching modern museum dedicated to the *nebuta*, displaying floats and giving visitors the chance to see, and try their own hand at, the traditional festive drumming performances.

ASPAM

青森県観光物産館, Aomori-kan Karko Bussan-kan • 1-1-40 Yasukata • Daily 9am–10pm (most shops close at 6pm) • **Slide show** Daily 10am–5pm, hourly • ¥600 • **Observation lounge** Daily 9am–10pm • ¥400, or ¥800 with slide show • ☎ 017 735 5311, ⓦ aomori-kanko.or.jp • 10min walk northeast of the station

The harbour-front **ASPAM** (Aomori Prefectural Centre for Tourism and Industry) building – a fourteen-storey glass pyramid – is a good place to start exploring Aomori. There's usually a video of the Nubeta Matsuri festival playing in, the entrance hall twenty-minute panoramic slide show of the region, including its festivals and scenery on the second floor. It's not really worth forking out for the thirteenth-floor observation lounge, but take a look at the second floor, where they are occasional demonstrations of local crafts.

Wa Rasse

ワ・ラッセ • 1-1-1 Yasukata • Daily 9am–7pm, Sept–April till 6pm; Nebuta Matsuri screenings and dance performances hourly • ¥600 • ☎ 017 752 1311, ⓦ www.nebuta.jp/warasse

Opened in 2011, it's difficult to miss the harbour-side museum and cultural centre, **Wa Rasse**, its angular exterior cloaked in strips of red and black metal. Celebrating the Nebuta Matsuri (see box, p.251), the darkened halls of the centre house five of the large illuminated floats from the latest festival, dramatic explosions of colour filled with menacing figures. There are regular performances of the festival dances and drumming in the main hall, during which visitors can try on masks and play the drums or other instruments. The auditorium holds screenings of footage from the event.

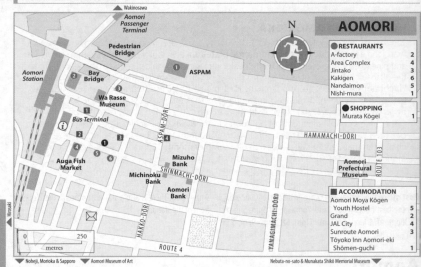

Aomori Prefectural Folk Museum

青森県立郷土館, Aomori Kenritsu Kyōdo-kan • 2-8-14 Honcho • Tues–Sun: May–Oct 9.30am–6pm; Nov–April 9am–5pm • Jan & Feb ¥250, March–Dec ¥310 • ☎ 017 777 1585, ⊛ bit.ly/1gGQrN0 • A 15min walk southeast of ASPAM

The **Aomori Prefectural Museum** takes a look at the region's history, culture and natural environment. Archeological digs have revealed evidence of human occupation in the area since at least 3000 BC, and the museum kicks off with Jōmon-period earthenware pots, replica thatched huts and the beautiful, insect-eyed *dogū* figurines whose ritualistic purpose is still unclear. The top-floor gallery devoted to local folk culture is the best starting point for visitors; here you'll find vine-woven baskets and rice-straw raincoats rubbing shoulders with fertility dolls and the distinctive agricultural deity Oshira-sama (see p.244).

Auga fish market

アウガ新鮮市場, Auga Shinshen Ichiba • 1-3-7 Shinmachi • Mon–Sat 5am–6.30pm (closed some Wed) • ☎ 017 721 8000, ⊛ auga.co.jp/shinsen.html

At the west end of Aomori's main shopping street is **Auga fish market**, an old-fashioned market in the basement of the Auga building (アウガ). Most of the stalls are loaded with iridescent fish, hairy crabs, scallops and squids, but among them you'll also find neat pyramids of Aomori's other staple product: juicy, oversized apples. You can buy bowls of rice and choose fish fresh from the stalls to eat with it.

Nebuta-no-sato

ねぶたの里 • 1-Yaegiku • Daily: April 1–April 20 10am–4pm; April 21–Nov 9am–5.30pm, Dec–March 10am–5pm • April–Nov ¥630, Dec–March ¥420 • ☎ 017 738 1230, ⊛ nebutanosato.co.jp • JR and Shiei buses (1–2 hourly; 30min; ¥450) drop you on the main road, from where it's a short walk to the entrance

Even if you visit the Wa Rasse museum (see p.249), it's still worth a trip to Aomori's southern suburbs, to see the "village" of festival floats at **Nebuta-no-sato**, which is set in lovely wooded countryside. Among the displays, you can see several of today's magnificent *nebuta* in a darkened hall on the hillside to the left of the site, alongside photos of construction techniques and early festivals.

Munakata Shikō Memorial Museum

棟方志功記念館, Munakata Shiko Kinenkan • 2-1-2 Matsubara • Tues–Sun 9.30am–5pm • ¥500 • ☎ 017 777 4567,
ⓦ munakatashiko-museum.jp • Buses from Aomori Station bound for Koyanagi stop at Munakata Shikō Kinenkan-dōri-mae (15min;
¥190), from where it's a 4min walk west to the museum, in front of the NTT building

One of Aomori's most famous citizens, a woodblock artist inspired by Van Gogh, is honoured in the **Munakata Shikō Memorial Museum**. The small museum shows rotating exhibitions of Shikō's bold, almost abstract, scenes of local festivals and Aomori people. Though best known for his black-and-white prints, Shikō also dabbled in oils, painted screens and calligraphy.

Aomori Museum of Art

青森県立美術館, Aomori Kenritsu Bijutsukan • 185 Chikano, Yasuta • June–Sept 9am–6pm; Oct–May 9.30am–5pm, closed every
second Mon • ¥500; temporary exhibits extra • ☎ 017 783 3000, ⓦ aomori-museum.jp/en/index.html • Take bus #6 from Aomori Station
bound for Mer kyo Centre and get off at Kenritsu-bijutsukan-mae (20min; ¥330)

The **Aomori Museum of Art** is well worth a visit, and is itself a marvel to admire, its stark white rectangular building seemingly an extension of the snowy landscape that surrounds it for much of the year. The collection includes over 120 works by Hirosaki-born artist Nara Yoshimoto, famous for his depictions of wide-eyed children and white dogs; a few pieces by woodblock printmaker Munakata Shikō; a chilling photography exhibit on the Vietnam War; and three enormous murals by Marc Chagall.

ARRIVAL AND DEPARTURE · AOMORI

By plane Aomori airport (☎ 017 773 2135, ⓦ aomori-airport.co.jp) has domestic services to major Japanese cities as well as to South Korea. There are regular limousine buses to Aomori Station (13 daily; 40min; ¥680).
Destinations Nagoya (2 daily; 1hr 25min); Osaka (Itami) 2 daily; 1hr 35min); Sapporo (2 daily; 45min); Seoul, South Korea (4 weekly; 2hr 50min); Tokyo (6 daily; 1hr 15min).
By train The recently extended Tōhoku Shinkansen from Tokyo, which passes through Sendai, Ichinoseki, Morioka and Hachinohe, arrives at Shin-Aomori Station, 5min by JR Ōu line from Aomori Station. The station lies on the west side of the city centre, just inland from the Bay Bridge and Aomori passenger terminal.
Destinations Akita (3 daily; 2hr 25min); Hakodate (hourly; 2hr); Hirosaki (hourly; 30min–1hr); Morioka (hourly; 1hr

45min); Noheji (1–2 hourly; 30–45min); Sendai (hourly; 2hr 30min); Tokyo (hourly; 3hr 24min).
By bus Long-distance buses terminate by the train station.
Destinations Morioka (4 daily; 3hr 15min); Sendai (6 daily; 4hr 50min); Tokyo (daily; 9hr 30min–10hr); Towada-ko (April–Oct, 6–8 daily; 3hr 15min).
By ferry Higashi-Nihon Ferry Co. (☎ 017 782 3631) operates daily ferries to Hokkaidō (Hakodate) from the car ferry wharf, 20min by bus from Aomori Station (20min; ¥300). Passenger ferries for Wakinosawa, on the coast of Shimokita Hantō, leave from the passenger terminal beside Bay Bridge, a short walk to the station (call Shimokita Kisen on ☎ 017 722 4545).
Destination Hakodate (8 daily; 4hr); Wakinosawa (2 daily; 2hr 20min).

INFORMATION

Tourist information There are several places where you can get information, but the most useful tourist office is the City Tourism Office (daily 8.30am–7pm; ☎ 017 723 4670), located next to the JR Bus terminal to the left-hand side of the station exit, which has English-speaking staff.

NEBUTA MATSURI

The **Nebuta Matsuri** (Aug 2–7) is one of Japan's biggest and rowdiest festivals, featuring giant illuminated floats and energetic dancing on the streets of Aomori. The festival takes its name from the gigantic bamboo-framed paper **lanterns** (*nebuta*) which take the form of kabuki actors, samurai or even sumo wrestlers in dramatic poses. The features are painted by well-known local artists, and the lanterns – lit nowadays by electricity rather than candles – are mounted on wheeled carts and paraded through the night-time streets of Aomori. According to the most popular local legend, the lanterns originated in 800, when local rebels were lured out of hiding by an imaginative general who had his men construct an eye-catching lantern and play festive music.

3

GETTING AROUND

By bus Most of central Aomori is manageable on foot, but you'll need local buses to reach the southern sights. Both the green Shiei buses and the less frequent blue-and-white JR buses run out to Nebuta-no-sato from Aomori Station; rail passes are valid on these JR services.
By car Eki Rent-a-Car (☎017 722 3930), Toyota (☎017 734 0100) and Nippon (☎017 722 2369) all have branches near the station. For cabs, try Aomori Taxi (☎017 738 6000) or Miyago Kankō Taxi (☎0177 43 0385).
By bike You can rent fixed-gear bikes (May–Oct daily 10am–5pm) for ¥300 a day from the bicycle parking lot to the left of the station. You'll need to show photo ID.

ACCOMMODATION

It's a good idea to book accommodation in advance in Aomori especially during the Nebuta Matsuri (Aug 2–7). Though there's a decent range of chain business hotels in the city centre, it's short on budget places and ryokan.

Aomori Moya Kōgen Youth Hostel 青森雲谷高原ユースホステル 9-5 Aza Yamabuki Ōaza Moya ☎017 764 2888, ⓦjyh.or.jp. Relaxed youth hostel nestled at the foot of the Moya plateau. You can't beat the clean shared tatami rooms, herbal tea and Guinness, although it gets a little cramped when busy. There's also an onsen next door. Take the bus from Aomori Station going towards Moya Hills (last bus 6.30pm) and get off at the Moya Kōgen stop (40min). **¥2500** per person
Grand Hotel グランドホテル 1-1-23 Shinmachi ☎017 723 1011, ⓔinfo2@agh.co.jp, ⓦagh.co.jp. This old-fashioned hotel on the main street offers a range of comfortable, well-furnished rooms, some with sea views. Add ¥1100 for breakfast. **¥10,000**
JAL City ホテルJALシティ 2-4-12 Yasukata ☎017 732 2580, ⓦaomori.jalcity.co.jp. The smart rooms at this popular hotel are well priced, and there's a decent in-house restaurant. It's about a 6min walk east of the station. Breakfast costs ¥1300; online discounts are available. **¥16,100**
Sunroute Aomori ホテルサンルート 1-9-8 Shinmachi ☎017 775 2321, ⓔpost@sunroute-aomori.com, ⓦwww.sunroute.jp. This is a good business hotel with large, en-suite Western-style rooms and a choice of restaurants. Breakfast is ¥1155 extra; lower prices are available in winter. **¥12,960**
Tōyoko Inn Aomori-eki Shōmen-guchi 東横INN青森駅正面口 1-3-5 Yasukata ☎017 735 1045, ⓦtoyoko-inn.co.jp. This modern business hotel is in a great spot opposite the station. The no-nonsense rooms are clean, bright and come with free wi-fi. Breakfast is included, and they knock ¥500 off the rates in winter. **¥6480**

EATING

Seafood, apples and apple products fill Aomori's food halls and souvenir shops. Among the local **speciality foods** worth a try are *hotate kai-yaki*, fresh scallops from Mutsu Bay grilled in their shells and served with a dash of miso sauce, and *jappa-jiru*, a winter cod-fish stew.

A-Factory A-工場 1-4-2 Yanagigawa ☎017 752 1890, ⓦjre-abc.com. Opposite the Wa Rasse museum and part of the new harbourside development; there's a host of good eating places in this bright, modern food gallery. Apple-based products feature highly – look out for the cider brewed on site and the French-style patisseries. Daily 9am–9pm (individual businesses vary).
Area Complex エリアコンプレックス B1 Auga Bldg ☎017 721 4499. This collection of small stalls and restaurants, attached to the market in the basement of the Auga building, is a great place to sample the local seafood. They have sushi, sashimi, grilled scallops and seafood *donburi*, and you can also get ramen and *teishoku* (traditional set menu) here. Daily 10am–9pm.
Jintako 甚太古 1-6 Yasukata ☎017 722 7727. Cosy restaurant with evening dinner concerts by some of Aomori's famous *shamisen* players. Reservations are essential. A set menu featuring a variety of regional dishes accompanied by a concert costs ¥6000. Daily 6–11pm
(last orders 9.30pm), closed first and third Sun of the month.
Kakigen 柿源 1-8-9 Shin-chō ☎017 722 2933. Small, casual restaurant specializing in *hotate* and other seafood, though also serving *tonkatsu*, *donburi* and noodle dishes at reasonable prices (from ¥600). Look for its moss-green *noren* (hanging curtain) just east of the Sunroute Aomori on Shinmachi-dōri. Daily 10.30am–9pm.
Nandaimon 南大門 1-8-3 Shinmachi ☎0177 77 2377, ⓦnandaimon.tv. This cheap and cheerful Chinese–Korean eatery serves good-value *yakiniku* (Korean BBQ), grilled *hotate* and other seafood. Lunch sets start at ¥725. English menus are available. Daily 11am–midnight.
Nishi-mura 西村 10F ASPAM, 1-1-40 Yasukata ☎017 734 5353. Choose from a broad range of inexpensive local cuisine including *hotate* and *jappa-jiru*, or set meals from ¥1260. Reservations recommended in summer. Daily 10.30am–9.30pm, Sun till 8pm.

SHOPPING

Murata Kōgei むらた工芸 1–9–18 Shinmachi-dōri ☎0177 23 3451, ⓦmkougei.jp. Apart from ASPAM's souvenir and craft shops, Shinmachi-dōri is good for browsing along, and Murata Kōgei stocks a good range of local kites, embroidery, lacquerware, brightly painted horses, and *Tsugaru kokeshi* dolls at reasonable prices. Mon–Fri 9.30am–7pm, Sat 10am–7pm, Sun 10am–6pm.

DIRECTORY

Banks Dai-ichi Kangyō, Michinoku and Aomori banks are all located on Shinmachi-dōri, around the junction with ASPAM-dōri.

Emergencies The main police station is at 2-15 Yasukata Aomori-shi ☎017 723 0110). For other emergency numbers, see p.66.

Hospital Aomori City Hospital, 1-14-20 Katsuda (☎017 734 2171).

Internet access The I-plaza (daily 10am–9pm), on the fourth floor of the Auga building (1-3-7 Shinmachi), offers an hour's free internet access.

Post office Aomori Central Post Office is located on the west side of town, at 1-7-24 Tsutsumi-machi.

3

Shimokita Hantō

The **Shimokita Hantō** protrudes into the ocean northeast of Aomori like a great axe-head. Its jagged blade is covered with low, forested peaks, of which the most notorious is **Osore-zan**, the "terrible mountain" where Buddhists believe the spirits of the dead linger on their way to paradise. Despite its growing commercialization, Osore-zan's bleak crater lake, surrounded by a sulphurous desert where pathetic statues huddle against the bitter winds, is a compelling, slightly spine-tingling place; an eerie wasteland where souls hover between life and death.

Osorezan-bodaiji

恐山菩提寺 • May–Oct daily 6am–6pm; festival July 20–24 • ¥500 • ☎0175 22 3825 • May–Oct four buses a day run from Mutsu (40min; ¥1500 return); last bus leaves Osore-zan at 5.30pm (3.50pm in Oct)

The main focus of **Osore-zan** (恐山), an extinct volcano consisting of several peaks, lies about halfway up its eastern slopes, where the fearsome **Osorezan-bodaiji** temple sits on the shore of a silvery crater lake. Though the temple was founded in the ninth century, Osore-zan was already revered in ancient folk religion as a place where dead souls gather, and it's easy to see why – the desolate volcanic landscape, with its yellow- and red-stained soil, multicoloured pools and bubbling, malodorous streams, makes for an unearthly scene. The temple also receives a steady trickle of non-spectral visitors, while during the summer **festival** in July, people arrive in force to contact their ancestors or the recently deceased through the mediation of *itako*, usually blind, elderly women who turn a profitable trade.

From **Mutsu**, the road to Osorezan-bodaiji winds through pine forests, past a succession of stone monuments and a spring where it's customary to stop for a sip of purifying water. At the top, you emerge by a large **lake** beside which a small humped bridge represents the journey souls make between this world and the next; it's said that those who led an evil life find it impossible to cross over. After a quick look round the temple, take any path leading over the hummock towards the lake's barren foreshore. The little heaps of **stones** all around are said to be the work of children who died before their parents. They have to wait here, building stupas, which demons gleefully knock over during the night – most people add a pebble or two in passing. Sad little statues, touchingly wrapped in towels and bibs, add an even more melancholy note to the scene. Many have offerings piled in front of them: bunches of flowers, furry toys – faded and rain-sodden by the end of summer – and plastic windmills whispering to each other in the wind.

By train The easiest access route is via JR train from Noheji Station (野辺駅), on the main Tōhoku line, to Shimokita Station (下北駅) in the southern suburbs of Mutsu (むつ), a workaday town on the southern edge of Shimokita Hantō and the main base for Osore-zan.

Destinations Noheji (9 daily; 45min–1hr).

By bus Local buses to Osore-zan stop at Shimokita Station on their way to the central Mutsu bus terminal, so you can go up to the mountain straight off the JR train and get off in the centre of Mutsu on the way back down if you plan to

stay the night. Alternatively, blue-and-white JR buses (for which rail passes are valid) run from Ōminato Station, the last stop on the local JR line, to the JR bus terminal, which is confusingly called Tanabu Station (田名部駅), on the east side of Mutsu town centre.

Tourist information Mutsu's tourist office (daily 10am–5pm; ☎0175 22 0909) is in the ground-floor lobby of Masakari Plaza (まさかりプラザ), a pink building northwest of the JR bus terminal. Staff can provide English-language maps and bus timetables.

Murai Ryokan むら井旅館 9-30 Tanabe-chō, Mutsu ☎0175 22 5581. Just in front of Masakari Plaza, this is one of the nicest places to stay in Mutsu. Although none of the tatami rooms are en suite, everything's extremely clean and the food is excellent value. Two meals are included in the rates, but room only is available for ¥4300 per person. **¥14,000**

Hotel New Green ホテルニューグリーン 1-4 Honmachi ☎0175 22 6121. With a choice of Western- or Japanese-style rooms, this business hotel is reasonably priced and convenient for the station and restaurants. It's 5min walk west from the JR bus terminal; past the private bus terminal and Matsukiya department store, then left at the T-junction. Single rooms are also available. **¥9500**

Masakari Plaza マサカリプラザ 2-46 Shimokita-chō ☎0175 23 7111. A second-floor restaurant in the *Plaza* hotel, *Masakari* serves a decent range of Japanese-style set meals from ¥1500, and noodle dishes for as little as ¥450. Daily 5pm–midnight, Sun till 11pm.

Nankō 楠こう2-5 Tanabe-chō ☎0175 22 7377. This smart restaurant near the *Hotel New Green* (see above), has good deals on *teishoku* (from ¥1200), and serves a range of seafood, steaks and stews starting at around ¥1000 per dish. Daily 11.30am–9.30pm.

Hirosaki

弘前

Behind its modern facade, **HIROSAKI**, former seat of the Tsugaru clan, still retains remnants of its feudal past. The older and more interesting parts of the town are around the park **Hirosaki-kōen**, on the west side of the Tsuchibuchi-gawa and the modern city centre. Here, picturesque turrets and moats mark the site of Hirosaki-jō, the once magnificent castle. Nearby, you'll find **Fujita Kinen Teien**, a well-preserved Japanese garden, and a collection of Meiji-era Western-style buildings, contrasting with the traditional samurai houses to the north of the castle grounds.

Hirosaki's summer lantern festival, the **Neputa Matsuri** (Aug 1–7), has its own museum, and there's also a district of dignified **Zen temples** in the west of the town. Though its sights can be covered in a day-trip from Aomori, Hirosaki is a pleasant place to stay and is worth considering as a base for the area.

Fujita Kinen Teien

藤田記念庭園 • 1-1 Shimishirogane-chō • Mid-April to mid-Nov Tues–Sun 9am–5pm • ¥300 • ☎0172 33 8733

A beautiful and unusually varied Japanese garden, **Fujita Kinen Teien** was commissioned in 1919 by local entrepreneur Ken'ichi Fujita. The garden consists of three distinct sections spread over a steep hillside. At the top, beside Fujita's elegant residence, dark pines frame the distant peak of Iwaki-san – a classic example of "borrowed scenery". Paths head downward to a tumbling waterfall from where a perfect, red-lacquer bridge leads to another flat area of lawns and ponds at the bottom.

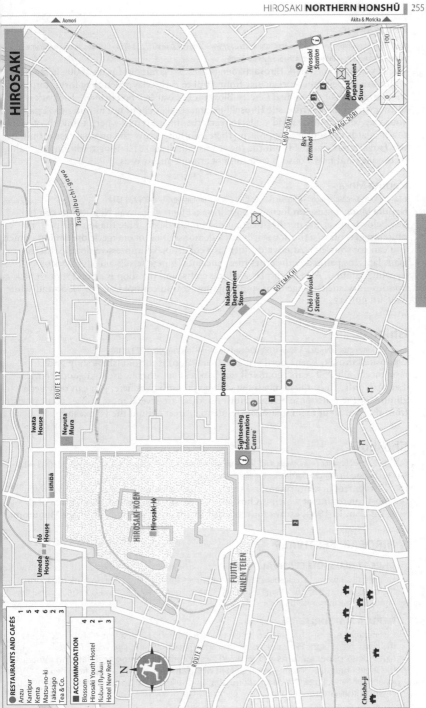

HIROSAKI

3

● RESTAURANTS AND CAFÉS

Anzu	1
Kantipur	5
Kenta	4
Matsu-no-ki	6
Jakasago	2
Tea & Co.	3

■ ACCOMMODATION

Blossom	4
Hirosaki Youth Hostel	2
Ikubui Ryokan	1
Hotel New Rest	3

Tsuchibuchi-gawo

ROUTE 112

Iwata House

Neputa Mura

Ishibā

Umeda House

Itō House

HIROSAKI-KŌEN

Hirosaki-jo

FUJITA KINEN TEIEN

ROUTE 3

N

Chōshō-ji

Hirosaki Station

Jeppal Department Store

CHŪŌ-DŌRI

KARAGI-DŌRI

Bus Terminal

Nakasan Department Store

DOTEMACHI

Chūō Hirosaki Station

Dotemachi

Sightseeing Information Centre

0   100

metres

Hirosaki-jō

弘前城 • Shimoshirogane-chō • Tower April to mid-Nov daily 9am–5pm • ¥300 • ☎ 0172 33 8739 • Ōte-mon, the main entrance to Hirosaki park lies across the road from the Sightseeing Centre

The large landscaped park **Hirosaki-kōen** (弘前公園) is famous for its 2600 cherry trees which are at their most spectacular from April to early May when they form, forming the centrepiece of the annual Cherry Blossom Festival (see box below). The park is the former site of the town's castle **Hirosaki-jō**, and it takes about ten minutes to zigzag your way between moats and walls, to reach the inner keep of where a tiny, three-storey tower guards the southern approach. There's nothing left of the original castle, built by the Tsugaru lords in 1611, but the tower was rebuilt in 1810 using traditional techniques and now houses a collection of armour and swords.

Neputa Mura

ねぷた村 • 61 Kamenokō-machi • Daily 9am–5.30pm, Dec–March till 4pm • ¥500 • ☎ 0172 39 1511

Neputa Mura, a museum focusing on Hirosaki's lantern festival, **Neputa Matsuri** (see box below), lies at the northeast corner of Hirosaki-kōen. Like the festival itself, the museum gets off to a rousing start with a demonstration of energetic **drumming** (which you can try yourself). Afterwards, there is a collection of impressive floats, with the giant lanterns painted with scenes from ancient Chinese scrolls and the faces of scowling samurai. Also on display are local crafts, and the shop is a good spot to pick up souvenirs, such as ingenious spinning tops, cotton embroideries or black-and-white Tsugaru pottery.

Ishiba

石破 • 88 Kamenokōmachi • Daily 8.30am–7.30pm, closed irregularly • Tour ¥100 • ☎ 0172 32 1488

Opposite Hirosaki-kōen's northern gate (Kita-mon) is the old **Ishiba** shop and residence, built 250 years ago to sell rice baskets and other household goods to the Tsugaru lords. Since the family (now selling sake) still lives here, you can only get a glimpse of the warehouse behind. However, there are several more houses you can visit from this era, all of them in a smart residential street behind the Ishiba shop.

Chōshō-ji

長勝寺 • 23-8 Nishishigemori • Jan–March, Nov & Dec by appointment only; April–Oct daily 9am–4.30pm • ☎ 0172 32 0813 • ¥300 • Bus #3 for Shigemori (¥200); get off at the Chōshō-ji Iriguchi stop

In the seventeenth century, around thirty temples were relocated to a "temple town", the most interesting of which is **Chōshō-ji**, the family temple and burial place of the Tsugaru clan. In 1954, excavations revealed the mummified body of **Prince Tsugutomi**,

---

HIROSAKI FESTIVALS

CHERRY BLOSSOM FESTIVAL (桜まつり)

From April 23 to May 5, Hirosaki-jō's little white turret, floodlit and framed in **pink blossom**, is the focus of the Cherry Blossom Festival, as Hirosaki-kōen's two-thousand-odd trees signal the end of the harsh northern winter.

NEPUTA MATSURI (弘前ねぷたまつり)

Lasting from August 1 to 7 and similar in style to the Aomori Nebuta Matsuri (see box, p.251), the centrepiece of the Hirosaki Neputa festival is a parade of large, illuminated three-dimensional **paper lanterns** accompanied by energetic **drumming and dancing** through the streets. Here, the lanterns are fan-shaped with pictures depicting scenes from heroic legends of Sangokushi ("Three Kingdom Saga") and Suikoden or ("Outlaws of the Marsh"), both of which originated from China.

son of the eleventh lord, who had died about a century before – his death was variously blamed on assassination, poisoning or eating peaches with imported sugar. During the Cherry Blossom Festival (see box opposite) the **mummy** is on display, but usually you'll have to make do with a photo in the mortuary room behind the main altar, where it's rather overshadowed by a life-like statue of **Tsugaru Tamenobu**, the founder of the clan.

ARRIVAL AND INFORMATION
HIROSAKI

By train Hirosaki is served by trains on the JR Ōu line between Aomori and Akita.

By bus Long-distance buses arrive at the terminal immediately west of the train station.

Destinations Morioka (hourly; 2hr 15min); Sendai (9 daily; 4hr 20min); Tokyo (daily; 10hr); Towada-ko (late April to late Oct 3 daily; 3hr 15min–4hr); Yokohama (daily; 11hr).

Tourist information Hirosaki has two tourist offices with English-speaking staff and town guides: a big one in the station (daily 8.45am–6pm; ☎0172 26 3600), which has free internet access, plus the main Hirosaki Municipal Tourist Centre (2-1 Shiomoshirogane-chō; daily 9am–6pm; ☎0172 37 5501), beside the southern entrance to Hirosaki-kōen, which also houses an exhibition area including *neputal* floats and displays on local culture.

GETTING AROUND

By bus Local buses stop outside the station for destinations around town, including a "¥100 loop bus" which loops between the station and the Sightseeing Information Centre outside the castle grounds.

By bike The best way to see the sights is to take advantage of the town's free bicycle rental system.

Between 9am and 4pm (mid May to late Nov) you can pop into any one of the town's four bike stations, which are marked by a spoked wheel inside an apple and include one in the underground passage in front of Hirosaki Station. Full details are available at the station tourist office (see above).

ACCOMMODATION

Blossom ブロッサムホテル弘前 7-3 Ekimaechō ☎0172 32 4151, ☻blossom@aiorcs.ocn.ne.jp. This smallish and brightly decorated hotel offers discounts for women travelling alone and families. A simple breakfast is included in the rates, and discounts are available from ⓦtravel. rakuten.com. **¥9960**

Hirosaki Youth Hostel 弘前ユースホステル 11 Morimachi ☎0172 33 7066, ⓦjyh.or.jp. An old but welcoming hostel in a prime location for exploring the castle area. Take a bus from the station to Daigaku Byōin-mae (20min; ¥100), from where it's a 5min walk further

west. Dorm **¥3045**

Kobori Ryokan 小掘旅館 89 Hon-chō ☎0172 32 5111, ☻kobori_ryokan@hiroyado.com. This old wooden ryokan near the castle offers a choice of smart tatami rooms, some with private bathrooms, as well as two Western-style rooms. **¥9500**

Hotel New Rest ホテルニューレスト 14-2 Ekimae-chō ☎0172 33 5300. A basic business hotel near the train station, with bright, simple rooms, most of which are singles, though there are some doubles. Single **¥3500**, double **¥5700**

EATING AND ENTERTAINMENT

Like Aomori, Hirosaki has a fine tradition of **folk music**, played on the *Tsugaru jamisen*, which has a thicker neck than the ordinary *shamisen* stringed instrument and is struck harder. You can hear dinner concerts at *Anzu* (see below) and many other places in town.

Anzu 杏 1-44 Oyakata-machi ☎0172 32 6684. Opposite the Asahi bowling alley, on a side street at the west end of Dotemachi, this cosy restaurant has two evening *jamsen* concerts at 7.30pm and 9.30pm – reservations are recommended. With lots of seafood, the menu features traditional Japanese cuisine and unusual regional dishes with specialities such as whole red snapper sashimi. Set meals range from ¥3000 to ¥6000. Mon–Sat 5–11pm.

Kantipur カンティプル Ekimae-chō ☎0172 55 0371. A friendly restaurant serving a range of good Indian and Thai curries and other dishes. Set lunch menus start at ¥750,

and expect to pay around ¥2000 per person for dinner. It's on the ground floor of the same building as the *Tōyoko Inn*, just to the right as you exit the station. Daily 11am–3pm & 5pm–midnight.

Kenta けん太 3 Okeya-chō ☎0172 35 9614. Cheap and popular *izakaya* that specializes in grilled food such as *yakitori*; prices for individual dishes start at ¥550. It fills up quickly on the weekends – if you can't get a seat here, try the branch around the corner. Daily 5pm–2am.

Matsu-no-ki 松ノ木 Ekimae-chō ☎0172 34 2521. This small *izakaya*, with aged-wooden interiors and retro posters, is across the pedestrian mall from *Blossom* hotel. It does a range of *teishoku* (traditional set menu) lunches from ¥850 and has dinner sets from ¥2100 including a drink. Daily 11.30am–2.30pm & 5pm–midnight.

Takasago 高砂 1-2 Oyakata machi. An inexpensive soba restaurant in an attractive old wooden house southeast of the castle grounds. The limited menu includes tempura

soba, *zaru* soba and curry soba. Prices start at ¥650. Tues–Sun 11am–6pm.

Tea & Co. ティー&カンパニー Dotemachi ☎ 0172 39 1717. Relaxed coffee shop inside a store across the river from the Nakasan department store, with a great range of teas and coffees and some luscious home-made cakes. Daily 10am–8pm.

South to Towada-ko

十和田湖

Japan's third-largest lake, **Towada-ko**, fills a 300m-deep volcanic crater in the northern portion of the Towada-Hachimantai National Park. The steep-sided, crystal-clear lake rates as one of northern Honshū's top tourist attractions, but for many visitors the real highlight is the approach over high passes and along deep, wooded valleys. Though there are four main access roads, the most attractive route is south from Aomori via the Hakkōda mountains, Sukayu Onsen and the picturesque **Oirase valley**. For this last stretch it's the done thing to walk the final few kilometres beside the tumbling Oirase-gawa, and then hop on a cruise boat across to the lake's main tourist centre, **Yasumiya**. Note that many roads around Towada-ko are closed in winter, and public buses only operate from April to November.

Hakkōda-san

八甲田さん • Ropeway daily 9am–4.20pm, mid-Nov to Feb till 3.40pm • Return ¥1800 • ☎ 0177 38 0343, ⓦ hakkoda-ropeway.jp

South from Aomori, Route 103 climbs steeply onto the Kayano plateau before reaching the flanks of **Hakkōda-san**. Every winter, up to 8m of snow falls on these mountains, transforming the fir trees into "snow monsters" (*juhyō*) and maintaining a flourishing ski industry. In summer, this beautiful spot offers excellent walking among Hakkōda-san's old volcanic peaks, of which the tallest is Ōdake (1584m). To ease the climb, the **Hakkōda Ropeway** (cable-car) can whisk you to the top of nearby Tamoyachi-dake (1326m), from where you can walk down to Sukayu Onsen, both of which are stops on the bus route from Aomori to Towada-ko.

Sukayu Onsen

酸ヶ湯温泉 • 50 Sukayuzawa • Bath 7am–6pm • ¥600 • ☎ 0177 38 6400, ⓦ sukayu.jp • Take a bus from Aomori, direction Towada-ko

The most famous of several onsen resorts in the Aomori region, **Sukayu Onsen** consists of just one **ryokan**, which has a "thousand-person" cedar-wood bath. Heavy with sulphur, Sukayu's healing waters have been popular since the late seventeenth century, and this is one of very few onsen left in Japan which is not segregated.

ACCOMMODATION   **SUKAYU ONSEN**

Sukayu Onsen Ryokan 酸ヶ湯温泉旅館 50 Sukayuzawa, Minami Arakawasan Kokuyurin ☎ 0177 38 6400. The only ryokan in the resort, in business for over 300 years, offers a variety of traditional tatami

rooms in the large building, with the most expensive ones having private baths. Two meals are included in the rates, though rooms without meals are available from ¥3000 per person. **¥14,000**

The Oirase valley

奥入瀬渓流, Oirase Keiryu

South of Sukayu, the road crosses another pass and then starts descending through pretty, deciduous woodlands – spectacular in autumn – to **YAKEYAMA** (焼山) village, the start of the **Oirase valley** walk, but it's better to join the path 5km further down the road at **ISHIGEDO** (石ヶ戸). From here it takes less than three hours to walk the 9km to Towada-ko following a well-trodden path running gently upstream, marred slightly by the fairly busy main road which you have to join for short stretches. But for the most part you're walking beside the Oirase-gawa as it tumbles among ferns and moss-covered rocks through a narrow, tree-filled valley punctuated by ice-white waterfalls. You'll emerge at lakeside **NENOKUCHI** (子ノ口), where you can either pick up a passing bus or take a scenic cruise across Towada-ko to Yasumiya (see below).

Towada-ko

十和田湖

Two knobbly peninsulas break the regular outline of **Towada-ko**, a massive crater lake trapped in a rim of pine-forested hills within the Towada-Hachimantai National Park. The westerly protuberance shelters the lake's only major settlement, **YASUMIYA** (休屋), which is also known somewhat confusingly as Towada-ko. Though this small town consists almost entirely of hotels and souvenir shops, its shady lakeside setting makes it a pleasant overnight stop. Roughly 44km in circumference, the lake is famous for its spectacularly clear water, with visibility down to 17m, and best appreciated from one of several **boat trips** available (see below).

Maidens by the Lake

おとめの像, Otome no Zō

Once you've navigated the lake, the other thing to do in Towada-ko is pay a visit to the famous statue of the **Maidens by the Lake**, which stands on the shore fifteen minutes' walk north of central Yasumiya. The two identical bronze women, roughcast and naked, seem to be circling each other with hands almost touching. They were created in 1953 by the poet and sculptor **Takamura Kōtarō**, then 70 years old, and are said to be of his wife, a native of Tōhoku, who suffered from schizophrenia and died tragically young.

ARRIVAL AND DEPARTURE

TOWADA-KO

By train During the tourist season (April–Nov) there are regular services to Towada-minami, which is on the line between Ōdate and Morioka, and to the southwest of the lake. From there it's necessary to take a bus to Yasumiya. It's best to buy tickets in advance on all these routes. Japan Rail passes (not Japan East rail passes) are valid, but you should still reserve a seat in advance.

Destinations Morioka (7 daily; 2hr); Ōdate (9 daily; 30–40min).

By bus Public buses only travel to and from Towada-ko April–Nov. Yasumiya's town centre is dominated by two bus terminals opposite each other on a T-junction just inland

from the boat pier; the more northerly is for JR buses. Buses to Towada-minami and Aomori leave from the JR bus terminal; other services to Hirosaki and Hachimantai use the Towada-ko terminal, opposite. If you're heading to Akita, take a bus south to Towada-minami (十和田南) and then a local train to Ōdate (大館) on the main JR line between Aomori and Akita.

Destinations Aomori (April–Oct 6–8 daily; 3hr 15min); Hachimantai (late April to Nov daily; 2hr 30min); Hirosaki (late April to late Oct 3 daily; 3hr 15min–4hr); Ōdate (April to early Nov daily; 1hr 30min); Towada-minami (April to early Nov 4 daily; 1hr).

INFORMATION AND TOURS

Tourist information The information office (daily 8am–5pm; ☎0176 75 2425), in a building immediately right (north) of the Yasumiya JR bus terminal. has town maps and can help with accommodation.

Boat trips From early April to the end of Jan. boat trips run on the lake, though sailings are fairly limited in winter.

The most interesting route is from Yasumiya to Nenokuchi (April to early Nov; hourly; 50min; ¥1400); or there is also a less frequent service that starts and finishes at Yasumiya (Dec to late March; 4 daily; 1hr; ¥1100).

Bike hire You can hire bicycles (¥630/2hr) at Yasumiya and drop them off at Nenokuchi (or vice versa).

ACCOMMODATION

It's advisable to book accommodation in advance from July through to Oct, when people come for the autumn leaves.

Oide Camp-jō 生出キャンプ場 486 Yasumiya ☎0176 75 2368 ⓦwww.bes.or.jp/towada/camp.html. In summer, the patches of flat land around Towada-ko fill with tents; this is the closest campsite to Yasumiya, some 3km southwest. There is a shop on site selling food and hiring camping equipment. Late April to Oct. **¥200** per pitch per night plus **¥300** per person

Sansō Kuriyama 山荘くりやま 62 Towadako ☎0176 75 2932. A small rustic minshuku near the centre of Yasumiya with a homely atmosphere and serving up tasty local specialities. Rates include two meals. **¥12,900**

Shunzan-sō 春山荘 5-1 Kyu-ya ☎0176 75 2607. In a traditional old building, this inn is a few minutes' walk from the pier, with tatami rooms and communal bathroom. Two meals are included in the rates, though room only is available for ¥4200 per person. **¥11,400**

Towada-ko Grand Hotel 十和田湖グランドホテル 48 Towada-ko Hanyasumiya, Okuse ☎0176 75 1111 ⓦitoenhotel.com. To the south of the ferry pier, this large resort hotel on the lake is a popular choice among busloads of Japanese seniors. It offers a choice of large and luxurious Western or tatami rooms, a number of onsen baths, and amenities include a bar, café and souvenir shop. Rates include meals, and discounts are available online. **¥16,800**

Kirisuto No Haka

キリストの墓 • 33-1 Nozuki • Museum 9am–5pm, closed Wed • ¥200 • ☎0178 78 3741

About 20km east of Towada-ko along Route 454, the town of **SHINGŌ** is home to **Kirisuto No Haka** (Christ's Grave), a grave with a huge wooden cross built in 1935 to commemorate an unusual local myth. The story goes that Jesus came to Japan as a 21-year-old and learned from a great master, before returning to Judea to spread the wonders of "sacred Japan". According to the tale, it was these revolutionary teachings that lead Jesus to the cross, but another twist from the traditional version saw Jesus's brother crucified, while Christ himself escaped to Shingō, where he married, had several children and lived until the age of 106. A small **museum** displays a scripture corroborating the story, though it doesn't give much detail about the nationalist historian, Banzan Toya, who "discovered" the tale in the 1930s – a time when Japan was funnelling substantial resources into demonstrating Japanese racial superiority.

Ōishigami Pyramids

大石神ピラミッド

Just a few minutes' walk west of Kirisuto No Haka lie the **Ōishigami Pyramids** which, according to other ancient writings unearthed by Toya, prove that the Japanese built pyramids tens of thousands of years before the Egyptians and Mexicans. Both pyramids seem little more than a pile of huge boulders, but the top of the second pyramid makes a great picnic spot.

Akita

秋田

One of the few large cities on the northwest coast of Japan, modern **AKITA** is an important port and industrial centre with access to some of the country's few domestic oil reserves. Though it was founded in the eighth century, almost nothing of the old city remains, and Akita's few central sites – three contrasting museums – can easily be covered on foot in half a day. With its airport and Shinkansen services, Akita makes a convenient regional base.

KANTŌ MATSURI

The city of Akita is home to one of the great Tōhoku summer festivals, the **Kantō Matsuri** (Aug 3–6) – though it's a pleasantly low-key affair compared to events in Sendai (see p.228) and Aomori (see p.251). During the festival, men parade through the streets balancing tall bamboo poles strung with **paper lanterns**, which they transfer from their hip to head, hand or shoulder while somehow managing to keep the swaying, top-heavy structure upright.

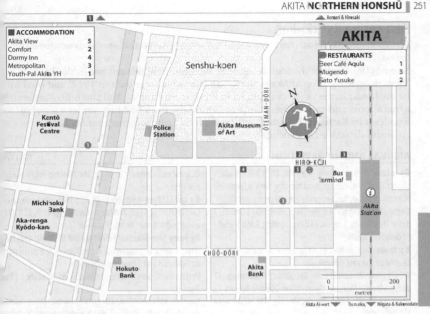

Senshū-kōen

千秋公園 • 1-1 Senshū-kōen • ☎ 0188 32 5893 • A 5min walk from the station along Hiro-kōji

The centre of modern-day Akita is bounded to the east by its smart train station, and to the north by the willow-lined moats of its former castle, **Kubota-jō**. This was Akita's second castle, founded in 1604 by the Satake clan who, unusually for northerners, backed the emperor rather than the shogun during the Meiji Restoration. Despite their loyalty, the castle was abandoned by the late nineteenth century and the site is now a park, **Senshū-kōen**.

Akita Museum of Art

秋田県立美術館, Akita Kenritsu Bijutsukan • 1-4-2 Nakadori • Daily 10am–6pm • ¥300 • ☎ 0188 53 3636, ⓦ common.pref.akita .lg.jp/art-museum

Directly in front of Senshū-kōen is the striking triangular building of the **Akita Museum of Art**, opened in September 2013. On display are works from the collection of the Masakichi Hirano art foundation, especially local artist Tsuguharu Foujita, the most memorable of which is *Events in Akita*, a 3.65m by 20.5m canvas depicting Akita's annual festivals and taking up an entire wall of the museum. It was completed in an incredible fifteen days in 1937, after which the wall of Foujita's studio had to be knocked down to get it out.

Kantō Festival Centre

ねぶり流し館, Neburi-Nagashi-kan • 1-3-30 Omachi • Daily 9.30am–4.30pm • ¥100, or ¥250 with Aka-renga Kyōdo-kan • ☎ 0188 66 7091

You can learn about local festivals and celebrations at the **Kantō Festival Centre**, located to the west of Senshū-kōen and across a small river. There are videos of recent Kantō Matsuri and sample *kantō* to try out. The *kantō* is a bamboo pole, up to 10m tall and weighing perhaps 60kg, to which dozens of paper lanterns are attached on crossbars. During the festival, as many as two hundred poles are carried through the streets in celebration of the coming harvest, as teams of men and young boys show their skill in balancing and manipulating the hefty poles.

Aka-renga Kyōdo-kan

赤れんが郷土館 • 3-3-21 Omachi • Daily 9.30am–4.30pm • ¥200, or ¥250 with Kantō Festival Centre / Folklore and Performing Arts Centre • ☎ 0188 64 6851

Some 500m south of the festival centre is, the unmistakeable red-and-white-brick Western-style building of **Aka-renga Kyōdo-kan**, which was built in 1912, and used to be the headquarters of Akita Bank. Its well-preserved banking hall and offices are worth a quick look, and the modern extension behind the main building houses a series of woodcuts by **Katsuhira Tokushi**, a self-taught local artist acclaimed for his bold, colourful depictions of rural life.

ARRIVAL AND INFORMATION

By plane Akita's airport (☎ 0188 86 3366, ⓦ akita-airport.com) is 40min south of the city, with a limousine bus service taking passengers to the city centre (¥900).
Destinations Nagoya (4 daily; 1hr 10min); Osaka (Itami) (2 daily; 1hr 20min); Sapporo (3 daily; 55min); Tokyo Haneda (9 daily; 1hr 10min).

By train Most visitors to Akita arrive at the JR station, located on the east side of town.
Destinations Aomori (3 daily; 2hr 30min); Kakunodate (17 daily; 50min); Morioka (hourly; 1hr 30min); Niigata (3 daily; 3hr 40min); Tokyo (hourly; 4hr–4hr 30min); Tsuruoka (15 daily; 2hr).

By bus Long-distance buses to Tokyo and Sendai stop outside Akita Station.

AKITA
Destinations: Sendai (10 daily; 3hr 50min); Tokyo (daily; 8hr 30min).

By car Eki Rent-a-Car (☎ 0188 33 9308), Nissan Rent-a-Car (☎ 0188 24 4123) and Toyota Rentals (☎ 0188 33 0100) are all located near Akita's JR station.

By ferry Shin-Nihonkai Ferry (☎ 0188 80 2600) sails five times a week to Tomakomai (11hr 20min), the main port on Hokkaidō and a gateway to Sapporo.
Destinations: Tomakomai, Hokkaidō (5 weekly; 11hr 20min).

Tourist information The city's tourist office (daily 9am–6/7pm; ☎ 018 832 7941) is directly across from the main JR ticket gates and stocks English-language maps and other printed information.

ACCOMMODATION

Akita View 秋田ビューホテル 6-1-2 Naka-dōri ☎ 0188 32 1111, ⓦ akitaviewhotel.jp. This large, upscale hotel has smart, spacious rooms as well as a range of restaurants and even a pool in the fitness centre. Singles are also available and all rates include breakfast. **¥19,000**

Comfort コンフォートホテル 3-23 Senshūkubota-machi ☎ 0188 25 5611, ⓦ choice-hotels.jp. A well-placed modern business hotel with bright rooms, just a 2min walk from Akita Station. All rates include a light buffet breakfast. **¥12,000**

Dormy Inn ドーミーイン 2-3-1 Naka-dōri ☎ 0188 35 6777. This business hotel has contemporary monochrome interiors, spacious singles and a good range of facilities. It also has a nice public bath on the eleventh floor and free wi-fi. Single **¥5800**, double **¥14990**

Metropolitan ホテルメトロポリタン 7-2-1 Naka-dōri ☎ 0188 31 2222, ⓦ metro-akita.jp. Immediately outside the station, this classy hotel is part of the JR East collection, which means JR Pass holders can enjoy an almost twenty percent discount on standard rooms. Rooms are tastefully decorated, and there is a stylish cocktail bar and elegant Japanese restaurant. Breakfast costs ¥1500. **¥20,500**

Youth-Pal Akita YH ユースパルあきた 3-1 Kamiyashiki ☎ 0188 80 2303, ⓔ youthpal@tkcnet.ne.jp. This youth hostel is a good bargain, with spacious rooms and decent meals. To get here, take a bus to the Akita Seishōnen Center (bus stop #6; every 30min; ¥160), then walk west for 5min and it's on the right. Dorm **¥3255**

EATING AND DRINKING

The region's most famous **speciality food** is *kiritampo*, a substantial stew of chicken, mushrooms, onions, glass noodles, seasonal vegetables and the key ingredient, *mochi* (rice cakes), made of pounded, newly harvested rice and shaped round a cedar-wood stick before grilling over a charcoal fire. *Shottsuru* is more of an acquired taste – a strong-tasting stew made with a broth of fermented, salted fish. Akita's main bar and restaurant area is one block southeast of the Aka-renga Kyōdo-kan museum.

Beer Cafe Aqula アックーウーラー 1-2-40 Omachi ☎ 0188 64 0141 ⓦ aqula.co.jp/english. This modern bar in the Aqula foursquare building serves a range of craft beers from its own microbrewery and hearty, largely meat-based food to accompany them, such as tongue, generous spare ribs and German würst. Main courses start at ¥700. Daily 11.30am–2pm & 5–11pm.

Mugendo 無限堂 2-4-12 Naka-dōri ☎0188 25 0800 ⓦmugendo.jp. With its dark-wood interior and stained-glass lamps, this popular restaurant near the station is a great place to sample local specialities and traditional regional dishes. Look for the red curtain around the wooden entrance. Lunch dishes such as noodles start at ¥800; expect to pay around ¥3500 a

head for dinner. Daily 11am–2pm & 5–10pm.
Sato Yosuke 佐藤洋介 2-6-1 Naka-dōri ☎0188 34 1720 ⓦsato-yoske.co.jp/akitaten.htm. Very reasonable Udon and Inaiwa restaurant in basement of the Seibu department store near the station area. It also has a shop attached to the restaurant selling delicacies. Daily 11am–9pm.

DIRECTORY

Banks and exchange For foreign exchange, try Akita Bank or Hokuto Bank on Chūō-dōri, running parallel to Hiro-kōji two blocks further south, or the Michinoku Bank near the Akarenga-kan.
Emergencies The main police station is at 1-9 Meitoku-chō, Senshū Akita-shi (☎0188 35 1111). In an absolute emergency contact the Akita International Association

on ☎0188 64 1181. For other emergency numbers, see p.66.
Hospitals The biggest central hospital is the Red Cross Hospital, 222-1 Kamikitade Saruta-Nawashirusawa (☎0188 29 5000).
Post office The Central Post Office is located at 5 Hodōno Teppo-machi, Akita-shi.

3

Kakunodate

角館
While Akita City has lost nearly all of its historical relics, nearby **KAKUNODATE** still has the air of a feudal town, with its strictly delineated samurai and merchants' quarters. Kakunodate was established as a military outpost in 1620 by the lords of Akita, with a castle on a hill to the north, a **samurai town** of around eighty residences, and 350 merchants' homes in a cramped district to the south. This basic layout and a handful of the two-hundred-year-old samurai houses have survived here, as have several hundred of the weeping cherry trees brought from Kyoto three centuries ago. It's still an atmospheric place, and although you can visit on a day-trip from either Akita or Morioka, it also merits an overnight stay in its own right.

The samurai quarter is a fifteen-minute walk northwest, its wide avenues of spacious mansions behind neatly fenced gardens making a dramatic contrast to the packed streets of the modern and rather run-down commercial district.

Aoyagi-ke

青柳家 • 3 Omote-machi • Daily 9am–5pm, Dec–March till 4pm • ¥500 • ☎0187 55 3257, ⓦsamuraiworld.com
The most interesting samurai house in Kakunodate is **Aoyagi-ke**, a large thatched house towards the northern end of the quarter, easily identified by its unusually grand entrance gate. Aoyagi-ke was built in 1890 and occupied until 1985; it now contains an eclectic mix of galleries, combining samurai armour, agricultural implements and memorabilia from the Sino-Japanese and Pacific wars, together with a wonderful display of antique gramophones and cameras.

Ishiguro-ke

石黒家 • 1 Omote-machi • Daily 9am–5pm • ¥300 • ☎0187 55 1496 • ⓦwww.hana.or.jp/~bukeishi
Dating back to 1809, the impressive **Ishiguro-ke** is one of the oldest of Kakunodate's samurai houses, and part of the building is still occupied by a descendant of the Ishiguro family – the original occupant and the *daimyō*'s financial adviser. Its main features are two large fireproof warehouses (*kura*) used for storing rice, miso and other valuables, along with exhibits include that of armour, weapons and old maps.

Hirafuku Memorial Art Museum

平福記念美術館, Hirafuku Kinen Bijutsukan • 4-4 Omotemachi • Daily 9am–4.30pm, Dec–March till 4pm • ¥300, or ¥510 combined entrance to the Denshōkan • ☎ 0187 54 3888

Behind its sterile, green concrete exterior, the **Hirafuku Memorial Art Museum** houses a small but decent collection of traditional Japanese art. Built in honour of father and son Hirafuku Suian and Hirafuku Hiyasui, the museum features the work of Naotake Odano and other painters from Kakunodate.

Denshōkan

伝承館 • 10-1 Omote-machi • Daily 9am–4.30pm, Dec–March till 4pm • ¥300, or ¥510 with Hirafuku Memorial Art Museum • ☎ 0187 54 1700

To the south of the Samurai district, the **Denshōkan** museum holds various Satake-clan treasures. The attractive red-brick building also doubles as a training school for *kaba-zaiku*, the local craft in which boxes, tables and tea caddies are coated with a thin veneer of cherry bark. Developed in the late eighteenth century to supplement the income of impoverished samurai, *kaba-zaiku* is now Kakunodate's trademark souvenir. If you prefer your bark still on the trees, turn right outside Denshōkan, where there's a 2km tunnel of cherry trees along the Hinokinai-gawa embankment.

ARRIVAL AND INFORMATION
KAKUNODATE

By train Kakunodate is best reached by train from either Akita or Morioka. The station lies on the southeast side of town.

Tourist information the main tourist office (daily 9am–6pm; ☎ 0187 54 2700) is in a *kura*-style building to the right as you exit the station. You can get English-language maps and other printed information here, and they also have bike rental (¥300/hr). Useful English maps and information can be found online at ⊕ kakunodate-kanko.jp.

ACCOMMODATION

Folkloro Kakunodate フォルクローロ角館 14 Nakasuga-sawa ☎ 0187 53 2070. Located right beside the station, this is your best bet if you want a simple, modern Western-style room. There is a ten percent discount for JR Pass holders, and rates include a basic breakfast. **¥12,600**

Ishikawa Ryokan 石川旅館 32 Iwase-machi ☎ 0187 54 2030. This old roykan offers comfortable tatami rooms, some en suite. To get here from the station, take a left one block before the post office. Room only **¥13,000**, with 2 meals **¥27,000**

Tamachi Bukeyashiki Hotel 田町武家屋敷ホテル 23 Tamachi Shimo-chō ☎ 0187 52 1700, ⊕ bukeyashiki.jp. Housed in a stunning Meiji-style building, this traditional inn provides equally attractive and luxurious tatami rooms. There are also smart Western-style rooms available. It's four blocks south of Inaho (see below). Breakfast is included in the rates; add ¥5250 per person for dinner. **¥25,200**

EATING AND DRINKING

Aoyagi-ke 青柳家 3 Omote-machi ☎ 0187 55 5241. This samurai house (see p.263) has a decent restaurant serving *inaniwa udon* – long, slippery noodles in a thin soup of mushrooms, onion and bamboo shoots. Daily 9am–5pm, Dec–March till 4pm.

Hyakusui-en 百穂苑 23 Kawahara-chō ☎ 0187 55 5715, ⊕ hyakusuien.com. A hundred-year-old inn in the merchant's quarter, popular for its hearty meals and traditional interiors, including sunken *irori* fireplaces. . Dishes start at ¥2100, and course menus cost ¥9870. Reservations essential for dinner. Daily 11am–3pm & 7–11pm.

Inaho 食堂いなほ 4-1 Tamachikami-chō ☎ 0187 54 3311, ⊕ ryotei-inaho.com. A very elegant restaurant in the centre of town that specializes in *kiritanpo* – rice balls grilled on cedar skewers. Nine-course *kaiseki* lunch menus from ¥2310, and dinner starts at ¥4620. 11am–4pm & 6–8pm, closed Thurs.

Kosendō 古泉洞 9 Higashi-Katsuraku-chō ☎ 0187 53 2902. Set in an old schoolhouse in the middle of the samurai quarter, this is a popular lunch spot. Speciality dishes include soba noodles served with bamboo, with prices starting at around ¥1000. Daily 9am–4.30pm.

Nyūtō Onsen

乳頭温泉 • 10km northeast of Tazawa-ko • **Tsurunoyu Onsen** (鶴の湯温泉) • Daily 10am–3pm • ¥500 • ☎ 0187 46 2139, ⊕ tsurunoyu.com • **Ganiba Onsen rotemburo** (蟹場温泉) • Daily 9am–4.30pm • ¥500 • ☎ 0187 46 2021, ⊕ nyuto-onsenkyo.com

On the southeastern fringes of the Towada Hachimantai National Park are numerous ski resorts and a hot-spring area called **Nyūtō Onsen**. This is made up of seven different onsen and adjoining ryokans, the most famous and quaint being the **Tsurunoyu Onsen**, a 350-year-old establishment with eight separate baths and three rotemburo, each fed by a different source. It's a fifteen-minute walk from Nyūtō Onsen baths to **Ganiba Onsen**, whose rotemburo (open to non-guests; see below) nestles quietly next to a small brook and forest – an ideal place to get rid of travelling stress.

ARRIVAL AND DEPARTURE
NYŪTŌ ONSEN

By train The nearest train station for Nyūtō Onsen is Tazawako, 20km northeast of Kakunodate on the Shinkansen line between Morioka (40min; ¥1780) and Akita (1hr; ¥3080). From the station, take a bus going towards the

Tazawa Kōgen Ski-jō (every 70–90min; 50min) and get off at the Tazawa Kōgen Onsen bus stop. Call *Tsurunoyu* or *Ganiba* onsens (see below) beforehand, and someone will pick you up at the Tazawa Kōgen Onsen bus stop.

ACCOMMODATION

Ganiba Onsen 蟹場温泉 Sendatsu ☎ 0187 46 2021. In a peaceful setting surrounded by nature, this traditional ryokan offers a choice of spacious Western or well-kept tatami rooms which look out onto the surrounding woods, with some adjoining the wraparound veranda. The big draw, though, is the wonderful outdoor bath set in natural rocks amid the forest (see above). Rates include two meals. **¥21,000**

Tsurunoyu Onsen 鶴の湯温泉 50 Sendatsu ☎ 0187 46 2139. ⓦ tsurunoyu.com. The ancient wooden building

of this ryokan is full of rustic and picturesque charm, though amenities are on the basic side. The cosy, tatami rooms come with a small *irori* or fire pit. There is a choice of various mixed and single-sex onsen (see above). Rates include two meals. **¥17,100**

Yamanoyado Inn 山の宿 1-1 Sawayunotai ☎ 0187 46 2100. Housed in a newer building, *Tsurunoyu's* slightly less traditional sister has more spacious rooms with modern amenities. Rates include two meals. **¥27,600**

Dewa-sanzan

出羽三山 • Best to visit July–late Sept

A lumpy extinct volcano with three peaks, **Dewa-sanzan** faces the Sea of Japan across the prolific rice fields of the Shōnai plain. **Dewa-san**, as it is also known, is one of Japan's most sacred mountains, with **pilgrims** trekking up its slopes for more than a thousand years. It's an arduous, rather than difficult climb, taking in ancient cedar woods, alpine meadows and three intriguing shrines where *yamabushi* (mountain ascetics) continue to practise a series of ancient rites which combine Tendai Buddhism with Taoism and Shintō elements.

Though it's possible to complete the circuit in a long day, it's more enjoyable to spread it over two or three days and spend a couple of nights in the *shukubō* (temple lodgings) scattered over the mountain or in the village of **Haguro-machi** (羽黒町), the traditional start of the pilgrimage.

Alternatively, **Tsuruoka** (鶴岡) town, a short bus ride to the northwest, provides a convenient base and has a few moderately interesting historical sights of its own.

The route

It's best to visit Dewa-san in summer, when all three shrines are open, but at any time of year you'll find white-clothed pilgrims climbing the well-worn 2446 steps on the summit of **Haguro-san** (羽黒山; 414m) where the first shrine, the thatch-roofed **Gosaiden**, pays homage to the deities of each of the three mountains.

From here, the path follows a ridge to Dewa-san's middle shrine which perches atop **Gassan** (月山; 1984m), the highest peak in the range. There are spectacular views in clear weather, though otherwise it's the least interesting of the three mountain shrines. The descent on the other side leads you to the final shrine, **Yudono-jinja** (湯殿山神社), an ochre-coloured rock washed by a hot spring, and you can visit a couple of rather grisly mummified monks en route at the village of **Ōami** (大網).

3

DEWA-SAN AND THE YAMABUSHI

Today Dewa-san and its three shrines fall under the Shintō banner, but the mountain was originally home to one of the colourful offshoots of Esoteric Buddhism, later unified as **Shugendō**. The worship of Dewa-san dates from the seventh century, when an imperial prince fled to this area following the death of his father. In a vision, a three-legged crow led him to Haguro-san (Black Wing Mountain), where he lived to the ripe old age of 90, developing his unique blend of Shintō, Buddhism and ancient folk religion. Later, the **yamabushi**, the sect's itinerant mountain priests (literally "the ones who sleep in the mountains"), became famous for their mystic powers and extreme asceticism – one route to enlightenment consisted of living in caves off a diet of nuts and wild garlic. Though once fairly widespread, the sect dwindled after the mid-nineteenth century, when Shintō reclaimed Japanese mountains for its own. Nevertheless, you'll still find a flourishing community of *yamabushi* around Dewa-san, kitted out in natty checked jackets, white knickerbockers and tiny, black pillbox hats. They also carry a huge conch-shell horn, the haunting cry of which summons the gods.

The best time to see *yamabushi* in action is during the area's various **festivals**. The biggest annual bash is the Hassaku Matsuri (Aug 24–31), when pilgrims take part in a fire festival on Haguro-san to ensure a bountiful harvest. At New Year, Haguro-san is also the venue for a festival of purification, known as the Shōreisai, which combines fire and acrobatic dancing with ascetic rituals.

The ascent

There are various ways of tackling Dewa-san, depending on the time of year and how much walking you want to do. The recommended **route** (see p.265) involves climbing Haguro-san on the first day and then continuing via Gassan to Yudono-jinja on the second. From there, you can either head straight back to Tsuruoka or spend the night in a *shukubō* and visit the Ōami temples the next day. However, note that Gassan-jinja (July to mid-Sept) and Yudono-jinja (May to early Nov) are only open in summer, although the path itself stays open longer.

Ideha Bunka Kinenkan

いでは文化記念館 • 72 Injuminami • Daily except Tues 9am–4pm, 9.30am–4.30pm in low season • ¥400 • ☎ 0235 62 4727 • Buses from Tsuruoka (8–15 daily; 40min; ¥680) serve Haguro-machi – get off at the Haguro Centre stop

The village of **HAGURO-MACHI** (羽黒町) is the start of the trail. Before heading off along the track, take a look at the **Ideha Bunka Kinenkan** museum if you're interested in the *yamabushi*. This surprisingly hi-tech exhibitions contain examples of *yamabushi* clothes and foodstuffs, as well as holograms of various rituals.

The Haguro-san trail

羽黒山トレイル • The 1.7km trail takes roughly 1hr • Buses from Tsuruoka (8–15 daily; 40min; ¥680) serve Haguro-machi; get off at the Haguro Centre stop – the road kinks left from here to the start of the path

A weather-beaten, red-lacquered gate marks the start of the **Haguro-san trail**, which consists of three long staircases built by a monk in the early seventeenth century. The first stretch is a deceptively gentle amble beside a river among stately cedar trees, where pilgrims purify themselves. After passing a magnificent five-storey pagoda, last rebuilt in the fourteenth century, it's uphill all the way, past a little **teashop** (late April to early Nov daily 8.30am–5pm) with superb views, until a large red *torii* indicates you've made it.

Gōsaiden shrine

三神合祭殿, San-jin Gōsaiden • Museum mid-April to late Nov daily 8.30am–4pm • ¥300 • The shrine is at the top of the Haguro-san walking trail; to return, follow the paved road exiting the compound's south side and you'll find the Haguro-sanchō bus stop among restaurants and souvenir shops – buses depart from here for Tsuruoka (6–12 daily; 50min; ¥990) via Haguro-machi (15min; ¥530), and also to Gassan Hachigōme (see opposite)

The **Gosaiden shrine** compound at the top of the Haguro-san trail contains a collection of unmistakeably Buddhist buildings. At the centre stands a monumental vermilion hall, the **Gosaiden**, where the mountain's three deities are enshrined behind gilded doors under an immaculate thatch. In front of the hall, the lily-covered **Kagami-ike** is said to mirror the spirits of the gods. However, it's better known for its treasure-trove of over five hundred antique polished-metal hand mirrors; in the days before women were allowed onto Dewa-san, their male relatives would consign one of their mirrors into the pond. The best of these are now on display in the shrine **museum**. There's also a useful relief map of Dewa-san here.

Gassan

月山 • Buses only run here daily in July & Aug and weekends in Sept, from Tsuruoka via Haguro-machi (4 daily; 1hr 20min) and from Haguro-san (4 daily; 55min)

It's a long 20km hike along the ridge from Haguro-san to **Gassan**, so it really is worth taking a bus as far as the "Eighth Station", **Gassan Hachigōme**. Even from there it takes over two hours to cover the final 5km along the ridge to Gassan (1900m), though it's a beautiful walk across the marshy Mida-ga-hara meadows, renowned for the explosion of rare alpine plants in late June.

Gassan-jinja

月山神社 • July to mid-Sept daily 6am–5pm • ¥500

The final few metres of the ridge walk to Gas-san are a bit of a scramble onto the rocky peak, where the **Gassan-jinja** shrine huddles behind stout stone walls. There's not a lot to the shrine, but you need to be purified before venturing inside; bow your head while a priest waves his paper wand over you and chants a quick prayer; then rub the paper cut-out person (which he gives you) over your head and shoulders before placing it in the water.

Yudonosan-jinja

湯殿山神社 • May to early Nov daily 8am–5pm • ¥500 • A shuttle bus runs from the *torii* in Yudono-san to Yudono-jinja (5min; ¥100), or it's a steep 20min walk; May to early Nov there's a bus from Tsuruoka (3 daily; 1hr 20min; ¥1480)

From Gassan, the trail drops more steeply to **Yudonosan-jinja**, located in a narrow valley on the mountain's west flank (9km). For the final descent you have to negotiate a series of iron ladders strapped to the valley side where the path has been washed away. Once at the river, it's only a short walk to the inner sanctum of Dewa-san, which occupies another walled area. Inside, take off your shoes and socks before receiving another purification and then enter the second compound. Having bowed to the steaming orange boulder, you can then haul yourself over it using ropes to reach another little shrine on the far side. It's then just a ten-minute trot down the road to the **Yudono-san** (湯殿山) bus stop.

Ōami

大網 • All buses from Yudono-san to Tsuruoka stop at Ōami (approximately every 2 hours; 27min; ¥780)

On the way back to Tsuruoka from Yudono-jinja, the hamlet of **ŌAMI** is worth a stop for its two "living Buddhas", the naturally mummified bodies of ascetic Buddhist monks who starved themselves to death. The mummies, or *miira*, are on display in two competing temples, **Dainichibō** and **Chūren-ji**, on either side of the village, each around ten minutes' walk from the bus stop next to the general store.

Dainichibō

大日坊 • Daily 8am–5pm • ¥500 • From Ōami bus stop, follow red signs of a little bowing monk, then take a left in front of the post office and walk for 10min

Dainichibō is the more accessible of the two temples on the east side of Ōami. The temple is thought to have been founded in 807 by Kōbō Daishi (see box, p.510) – after a brief purification ceremony and introductory talk, the head priest will show you the hard-working saint's staff, a handprint of Tokugawa Ieyasu and other temple treasures, before taking you to the **mummy**. The tiny figure sits slumped on an altar, dressed in rich, red brocades from which his hands and skull protrude, sheathed in a dark, glossy, parchment-thin layer of skin. He's said to have died in 1782 at the age of 96, which is quite extraordinary when you learn that he lived on a diet of nuts, seeds and water. As the end drew closer, the monk took himself off to a cave to meditate and eventually stopped eating all together. Finally, he was buried alive with a breathing straw until he expired completely. This process of self-mummification as a path to enlightenment, known as **sokushimbutsu**, was relatively common prior to the nineteenth century, when the practice was banned.

Chūren-ji

注連寺 • Daily 8am–5pm • ¥500 • Head north from Ōami bus stop on a country road and follow the signs until you reach a fork; take the left fork and walk past a graveyard

Though it's a bit of a walk from Ōami (2km), **Chūren-ji** is slightly less commercialized and more atmospheric than Dainichibō. As before, you receive a short talk and a purification ceremony before entering the side hall, where the *miira* rests in a glass case. It is thought that this living Buddha, Hommyokai Shonin, was a criminal before he saw the error of his ways and devoted himself to the ascetic life.

ARRIVAL AND DEPARTURE   DEWA-SANZAN

By bus Two bus services run from Tsuruoka: one via Haguro-machi to the Haguro-sanchō stop at the top of Haguro-san, with onward services to Gassan Hachigōme (see p.267) from July to Sept; the second operates May to early Nov, looping round from Tsuruoka to Yudono-jinja. For details see ⓦ japan-guide.com/e/e7901.html.

INFORMATION AND ACTIVITIES

Tourist information Bus services are few and far between, so make sure you pick up a map and timetable at Tsuruoka's information centre (see opposite), where they can also help book accommodation. The website ⓦ hagurokanko.jp has lots of useful regional information.

Yamabushi courses If you'd like to try your hand at being a *yamabushi*, there are several two- and three-day taster courses available in which you get to stand under waterfalls, leap over fires and take part in a pilgrimage. Prices start from around ¥25,000; contact the Tsuruoka tourist office for information (see opposite).

ACCOMMODATION

If possible, try to spend at least one night at a **shukubō** (temple lodging) while visiting Dewa-san. There are over thirty in Haguro-machi's Tōge district, including a number of traditional thatch-roofed inns, each run by a *yamabushi*; you may well be invited to attend a prayer service, involving a lot of conch-blowing and a ritual fire. Prices don't vary much (typically ¥7000–7500 per person, with meals) and they all serve the exquisitely prepared *shōjin-ryōri* (Buddhist vegetarian cuisine) favoured by *yamabushi*. If you have problems booking directly, the Haguro Town Office (☎ 0235 62 2111) may be able to assist with reservations. All rates listed below include two meals

Ōrimbō 桜林坊 ☎ 0235 62 2322. Near to *Sankō-in* in the centre of the village, this thatched *shukubō* is an atmospheric place to stay. **¥14,000**

Saikan 斎館 ☎ 0235 62 2357. On Haguro-san itself is an impressive old *shukubō* with great views over the Shōnai plain, where you can also get excellent vegetarian lunches, available to non-residents as well (from ¥1500; reservations recommended). It's at the conclusion of the Haguro-san trail (see p.266), on the left at the end of a mossy path, just before you duck under the *torii*. **¥14,000**

Sankō-in 三光院 ☎ 0235 62 2302. A lovely old thatched place near the centre of Haguro, this authentic temple

lodging serves vegetarian cuisine. **¥14,000**

Sanrōjo 参籠所 ☎ 0235 54 6131. Only open from May to early Nov, *Sanrōjo* occupies a wonderful setting beside the Yudono-jinja bus terminal. They also serve delicious lunches here to both residents and non-residents (from ¥1500; reservations recommended). **¥14,000**

Tamon-Kan 多聞館 115, Touge, Haguro-machi ☎ 0235 62 2201, ⓦ tamonkan.hiciao.com. This ryokan, in a large 300-year-old building in the centre of Haguro-machi, is open all year round, offering more comfortable accommodation than the *shukubōs*, and, has excellent *shōjin-ryōri* cuisine. **¥16,800**

Tsuruoka

鶴岡

A former castle town with a handful of attractive, willow-lined streets in its old centre, **TSURUOKA** is mainly useful as a staging post on the pilgrimage to Dewa-san. Its few sights are located in and around **Tsuruoka-kōen**, the town's park and site of the castle, and include an eclectic local museum and an unusual Edo-period school for samurai.

The old centre of Tsuruoka lies on the banks of the Uchi-gawa, some 2km southwest of the station, which is surrounded by business hotels, department stores and bus terminals.

Chidō Hakubutsukan

致道博物館 · 10-18 Kachū-Shinmachi · Daily 9am–4.30pm · ¥700 · ☎ 0235 22 1199

It takes about twenty minutes to walk from the station, partly along the river, to reach Tsuruoka-kōen, and Tsuruoka's prime sight, the **Chidō Hakubutsukan**. Once a retirement home for lords of the ruling Sakai clan, the compound now contains a number of striking buildings, beginning with the **Nishitagawa District Office**, built in 1881 in Western style. The **Goinden**, the lords' residence, was constructed only two decades earlier but to a classic Japanese design, and now houses a few Sakai family heirlooms as well as a beautiful collection of bamboo fishing rods made by trainee samurai. Local folk culture is well represented in a massive thatched farmhouse and in a modern building packed with old fishing tackle, sake barrels, lacquerware and huge wooden mortars.

Chidō-kan

致道館 · 11-45 Baba-chō · Tues–Sun 9am–4.30pm · Free · ☎ 0235 23 4572

The Confucian school, **Chidō-kan**, was founded in 1805 by the ninth Sakai lord, who wanted to restore order among his restless clan and educate young samurai. Inside there are still a few of the original buildings, including a shrine to Confucius, and the main auditorium, where you can see the old textbooks and printing blocks as well as some marvellous photos of the school when it was still in use (it closed in 1873).

ARRIVAL AND DEPARTURE   TSURUOKA

By plane Limousine buses serving the local Shōnai Airport run to and from outside Tsuruoka train station (40min; ¥760).

Destinations Tokyo Haneda (4 daily; 1hr).

By train Tsuruoka's train station is located on the northeast side of town.

Destinations Akita (7 daily; 2hr); Niigata (7 daily; 1hr 50min).

By bus The Shōkō Mall bus centre lies a few minutes' walk west from the train station along the tracks under the *Dai-ichi Hotel* (第一ホテル), where most long-distance buses start. The majority of buses also stop in front of the train

station, including services to and from the airport.

Destinations Sendai (7 daily; 2hr 35min); Tokyo (2 daily; 8–9hr); Yamagata (11 daily; 2hr).

Tourist information The town's information office (daily: March–Oct 9.30am–5.30pm, Nov–Feb 10am–5pm; ☎ 0235 25 2111, ⓦ www.city.tsuruoka.yamagata.jp) is to the right as you exit the station building; you can pick up a bicycle for the day free of charge here.

Services Car rental is available at Eki Rent-a-Car (☎ 0235 24 2670; daily 8.30am–6.30pm), next to the information office.

ACCOMMODATION

Narakan 奈良館 2-35 Hiyoshi-chō ☎ 0235 22 1202. A small, friendly inn that provides good-value tatami rooms and serves traditional food. Go left from the station for 5min, then turn right at *Hotel Alpha One*, walk another 5min and it's on the left after the traffic lights. Two meals

are included in the rates and various meal plans are available.‾**¥10,600**

Tsuruoka Youth Hostel 鶴岡ユースホステル 1-1 Miyanomae ☎ 0235 73 3205, ⓦ jyh.or.jp. Off the beaten track, in the village of Sanze, this place makes for a welcoming rest if you fancy a day off from your travels and the idea of macrobiotic vegetarian food and 1950s jazz appeals. It's a 15min walk from Sanze Station, three stops out of town on the local line. Get directions (and a map) at the tourist office in Tsuruoka (see p.269). Dorm **¥2625**

Washington Hotel ワシントンホテル 5-20 Suehiro-chō

☎0235 25 0111, ⊛en.washington-hotels.jp. A good choice for somewhere convenient to stay near the station, offering cheerful rooms with modern stylish decor. It fills up quickly with business travellers midweek, so check availability in advance and look for online promotions. **¥10,972**

EATING

In addition to the restaurants below, you'll also find several well-priced places serving staples, such as soba, udon and *izakaya* fare, just outside the station.

Pizzeria Gozaya ピッツェリア・ゴザヤ 5-38 Baba-chō ☎0235 24 1105. This bright and modern Italian restaurant does authentic pizzas from a wood-burning oven along with pastas and other European dishes. Main courses start at ¥1000. Daily except Tues 11.30am–2pm

& 6pm–late (Thurs lunch only).

Sanmai-an 三昧庵 10-18 Kachushinmachi ☎0235 24 3632. A decent udon restaurant, beside the Chidō Hakubutsukan (see p.269). Set menus start at around ¥1000. Daily 9am–4.30pm.

Niigata

新潟

Most visitors to **NIIGATA**, the largest port-city on the Sea of Japan coast, are either on their way to Sado-ga-shima (see p.274) or making use of the ferry and air connections to Korea, China and Russia. It's a likeable but unexciting city, sitting on the banks of Shinano-gawa, with few specific sights beyond a well-presented local history museum. In 1964, a tidal wave devastated much of east Niigata, though the area on the west side of the river retains some attractive streets of older houses.

Hakusan-kōen

白山公園 • 1-2 Ichiban Hori-dōri-chō, Chūō-ku • **Park** 24hr • Free • **Enkikan teahouse** (燕喜館) Daily 9am–5pm, closed first and third Mon of the month • Tea ¥300 • ☎025 228 1000 • From the station, take a bus for Irefune-chō and get off at the Assembly Hall

On the southwestern edge of the city centre, the pleasant park of **Hakusan-kōen** contains a shrine to the God of Marriage and various stone monuments, including one to the happiness of pine trees. There are also a couple of manicured lily-pad-covered ponds around which wisteria trellises bloom into life in late spring.

In the northwest corner of the park, **Enkikan**, a Meiji-era teahouse transplanted from Kyoto with its pristine tatami rooms and overlooking a peaceful garden, provides great atmosphere for a rest; tea is served in the room of your choice.

Former Prefectural Assembly Hall

新潟県記念館, Nii gata-ken Kinenkan • 3-3 Ichiban Hori-dori-chō, Chuo-ku • Tues–Sun 9am–4.30pm • Free • ☎025 228 3607

The gingerbread building next to Hakusan-kōen is the **Former Prefectural Assembly Hall**, which was built in 1883, and in which local representatives continued to meet until 1932. Inside, there is an exhibition telling the story of Japan's young democracy in action, with a display of archive sepia photos.

Next 21

6-866 Nishibori-dōri, Chūō-ku • Daily 8am–11.30pm • Free • ☎025 226 5021 • From the Assembly Hall, get a bus bound for Irefune-chō or Furumachi; on foot; head northwest along Nishibori-dōri for 1km

At 125m high, with 21 floors above ground and three below, the landmark **Next 21** building is Niigata's second-highest building. The **Laforet** department store occupies floors

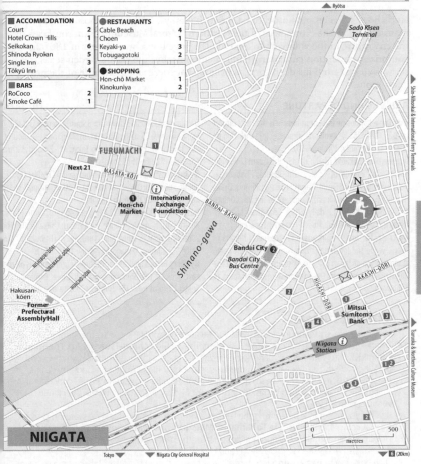

■ **ACCOMMODATION**			● **RESTAURANTS**	
Court		2	Cable Beach	4
Hotel Crown Hills		1	Choen	1
Seikokan		6	Keyaki-ya	3
Shinoda Ryokan		5	Tobugagotoki	2
Single Inn		3		
Tōkyū Inn		4	● **SHOPPING**	
			Hon-chō Market	1
■ **BARS**			Kinokuniya	2
RoCoco		2		
Smoke Café		1		

B1 to 5, with a wealth of boutiques from Japanese and international fashion labels big and small. Head up to the nineteenth-floor observation lounge for a free view of the city.

Hon-chō Market

本町市場, Hon-chō Ichiba • Daily 8am–5pm, closed three days a month, usually on Sun

If you want to get a glimpse into an older Niigata, check out the **Hon-chō Market**, which spread over a few pedestrianized streets to the south of Masaya-kōji survives as a relic of the past. This fresh-produce and seafood market is a lively place to mix with locals, find cheap places to eat, and try out your bargaining skills.

Northern Cultural Museum

北方文化博物館, Happō Bunka Hakubutsukan • 2-15-25 Somi, Yokogoshi village • Daily 9am–5pm, Dec–March till 4.30pm • ¥800 • ☎ 025 385 2001 ⓦ hoppou-bunka.com • Take the express bus from Bandai City or Eki-mae terminal (10 daily; ¥490 one-way); last bus back leaves at 5pm

The fertile plains around Niigata supported a number of wealthy landowners who lived in considerable luxury until the Land Reform Act of 1946 forced them to sell all rice land above 7.5 acres per household. One such family was the Itō, whose superb mansion is now the centrepiece of the **Northern Cultural Museum**, 12km southeast of the city centre in the village of Yokogoshi. The huge house was erected in 1887 and comprises sixty rooms containing family heirlooms, but the classic garden steals the show – viewed from inside, it forms a magnificent frieze along one side of the principal guest room.

ARRIVAL AND DEPARTURE   NIIGATA

By plane Limousine buses run between the city's airport (☎025 275 2633, ⊛niigata-airport.gr.jp) and Niigata Station (2–3 hourly; 30min; ¥400).
Destinations Fukuoka (daily; 1hr 45min); Guam (2 weekly; 4hr 45min); Harbin (4 weekly; 2hr 30min); Khabarovsk, Russia (weekly; 1hr 55min); Nagoya (4 daily; 55min); Osaka (Itami) (10 daily; 1hr 10min); Sapporo (3 daily; 1hr 10min); Seoul, South Korea (2 daily; 2hr); Shanghai, China (2 weekly; 4hr); Vladivostok, Russia (weekly; 1hr 20min).
By train The Joetsu Shinkansen line connects Niigata to Tokyo, while the local Inaho and Tsugaru lines run north along the Sea of Japan coast to Akita and Aomori, and the Hakutaka, Hokuetsu and Ohayo express lines head south to Kanazawa.

Destinations Akita (3 daily; 3hr 35min); Aomori (3 daily; 7 hr); Kanazawa (5 daily; 3hr 40min); Nagano (1–2 hourly; 2hr 15min, with one transfer); Tokyo (1–2 hourly; 2hr); Tsuruoka (7 daily; 1hr 55min).
By bus Most express buses use the Bandai City Bus Centre, about 500m northwest of Niigata Station, though some also stop outside the train station.
Destinations Kanazawa (2 daily; 4hr 40min); Kyoto (daily; 8hr 10min); Nagano (4 daily; 3hr 15min); Osaka (daily; 9hr 20min); Sendai (8 daily; 4hr 5min); Tokyo (Ikebukuro) (16 daily; 5hr 20min); Yamagata (2 daily; 3hr 40min).
By ferry Ferries dock at one of three ferry terminals on the east bank of the Shinano-gawa. All three terminals are linked by local bus (15–30min; ¥200) to Niigata Station;

ECHIGO-TSUMARI

Every three years, the mountainous, rural and relatively unspoilt Echigo-Tsumari region of Niigata-ken hosts a spectacular international art festival, the **Echigo-Tsumari Art Triennial**, from mid-July to early September (the next edition is in 2015). Artists from all over the world are invited to exhibit their work, with previous standouts being Cai Guo Quiang from China, who reconstructed an old Chinese climbing kiln, and Rina Banerjee, who, inspired by the Taj Mahal, converted a school gymnasium into a giant bird cage. For more details check out ⊛echigo-tsumari.jp/eng.

Even if you're not in Japan during the festival, a visit to this region is still a rewarding journey. The main places to head for are **Tokamachi**, **Matsudai** and **Matsunoyama**, all of which have fascinating permanent exhibition facilities built for the past triennials and plenty of sculptures and other artworks sited in paddy fields and on hillsides.

The best way to **get around** is to hire a car, although during the festival there are also free bikes available at all the main sites. Otherwise you can travel here by local train from either Echigo-Yuzawa on the Niigata Shinkansen route or Saigata on the Joetsu line.

ACCOMMODATION

A memorable lodging experience is to spend a night in one of the **artworks**, which are either newly commissioned pieces or renovated abandoned buildings such as old farms or schools. There are five artworks to choose from; the two listed below are short taxi rides from Tokamachi Station and are open from April to December. See ⊛echigo-tsumari.jp/eng/facility/ for details on booking or phone ☎025 761 7767 for enquiries.

Dream House 夢の家 643 Yumoto ☎025 596 3134, ⊛tsumari-artfield.com/dreamhouse. Serbian artist Marina Abramovic's refurbished century-old farmhouse merges tradition and modern elements in a simple and elegant building. Breakfast is available from ¥500, dinner from ¥2000. ¥6300 per person
House of Light 光の館 2891 Ueno-ko, Tokamachi ☎025 761 1090, ⊛www11.ocn.ne.jp/~jthikari/e/.

This meditation house which stands on stilts 2.7m above ground, was designed by James Turrell designed in a traditional, local style. It features a retractable roof, a slick, modern interior and media installations, as well as combining natural and artificial light to stunning effect. The house sleeps up to twelve people, though different groups can share the accommodation. ¥20,000 plus ¥3500 per person taxis cost around ¥1200. Sado Kisen (☎025 245 1234) operates ferries and jetfoil services to Ryōtsu (Sado) from the Sado Kisen Terminal. Ferries to Otaru (Hokkaidō) are run by Shin-Nihonkai Ferry (☎025 273 2171) and leave from the Shin-Nihonkai Ferry Terminal; take a bus from the station for Rinkō Nichōme and get off at the Suehiro-bashi stop (20min).

Destinations Otaru, Hokkaidō (1–2 daily; 18hr); Ryōtsu, Sado (10–19 daily; 1hr–2hr 30min).

INFORMATION

Tourist information The tourist office (daily 9am–6pm; ☎025 241 7914) is outside the station's central (Bandai) exit. You can also get English-language maps and information here, and the staff can help with hotel reservations and ferry tickets to Sado. Online, ⓦenjoyniigata.com/English and ⓦvisit-niigata.com have good information in English.

GETTING AROUND

By bus Local buses depart from the station terminal and may stop outside Banda City depending on the route. Within the central district there's a flat fare of ¥200, which you pay on exit; on most buses you need to take a ticket as you enter.

By bike A good way to get around is using the city's great bike rental system; you can get and drop off bikes at a number of locations around the city, including the station (from ¥100/3hr). Full details are available at the tourist office.

By car Try Eki Rent-a-Car ☎025 245 4292; Nippon ☎025 245 3221; or Nissan ☎025 243 5523.

Taxis Try Fuji ☎025 244 5166; Hato ☎025 287 1121; or Miyakō ☎025 222 0611.

ACCOMMODATION

Court こーとホテル 2-3-35 Benten ☎025 247 0505, ⓔinnniigata.info@court-hotels.co.jp. A smart, mid-range business hotel located halfway between the station and busy shopping area of Bandai City. Singles are available as well as doubles. **¥12,735**

Hotel Crown Hills 金寿 8-1429 Higashibori-dōri ☎025 229 1695. A good choice downtown, in an interesting area of old streets surrounded by decent restaurants and bars. Most of the simple Western-style rooms are singles, but there are some twins available. Single **¥3280**, double **¥7160**

Seikokan 清廣館 802 Deyu Agano-shi, Deyu Onsen ☎025 062 3833 ⓦseikokan.jp. This wonderful old family-run inn in the hamlet of Deyu Onsen, 20km from Niigata city, is perfect for a relaxing ryokan experience. The rooms in the wooden building are spacious and comfortable, there's an atmospheric hundred-year-old bath, and the public areas include tasteful modern design touches. Rates include two meals including vegetables fresh from the garden. To get here, take the train from Niigata to Shibata or Suibara (takes 20min–1hr) and the friendly English-speaking owners will usually be happy to pick you up. **¥21,300**

Shinoda Ryokan 篠田旅館 1-2-8 Benten ☎025 245 5501. A nice old ryokan just past the *Tōkyū Inn* and just north of the station. Rates include two meals, but only the more expensive rooms are en suite. **¥16,500**

Single Inn シングルイン 1-6-1 Hanazono ☎025 290 7112. This basic but adequate business hotel, in a side street three minutes east of station, has the cheapest rooms around. There are plenty of places to get a bite to eat or a drink in the surrounding streets. Rooms are small but clean, with the majority singles. Single **¥3150**, double **¥5250**

Tōkyū Inn 東急イン 1-2-4 Benten ☎025 243 0109, ⓦwww.tokyuhotelsjapan.com. This big hotel opposite the station has a range of good-sized en-suite rooms, and free wi-fi. **¥13400**

EATING AND DRINKING

Niigata is famous for its fresh fish and fragrant rice, which means excellent **sushi**. Glutinous rice is used to make *sasa-dango*, a sweet snack of bean paste and rice wrapped in bamboo leaves, while in winter, *noppe* combines taro, ginkgo nuts, salmon roe and vegetables in a colourful stew that is commonly served as a side dish. Niigata-ken's most famous product, however, is its **sake**. You can sample it at many of the numerous **restaurants** and **bars** in the streets near the station and around Furumachi.

Cable Beach ケーブルビーチ 1-2-15 Yoneyama ☎025 245 1055. An intimate Italian restaurant on the quiet side of Niigata Station. Bowls of classic pasta dishes such as spaghetti carbonara start around ¥700. Follow the main road outside the south exit; it's down a side street just beyond *Keyaki-ya* (see p.274). 11am–2pm & 6pm–1am, closed Tues.

Choen 張園 1-5-2 Higashi-Ōdōri ☎025 241 7620. Cheap and cheerful Chinese restaurant serving good-value lunch sets from ¥700. At night, you'll eat well for around

¥2000 per head. Daily 11am–3pm & 5–11pm.

Keyaki-ya 欅屋 1-1-2 Yoneyama ☎ 25 246 7302. Lively *izakaya* facing the south side of the station, with lots of snack foods and small meat dishes on the menu (from ¥700), attracting crowds of enthusiastic twenty-somethings who fill the two floors of funky booths and long tables. Daily 5pm–1am, Sun till midnight.

RoCoco ロココ 3-1-15 Yoneyama ☎025 290 6699. Extremely popular restaurant with eclectic furnishings that match the randomness of its menu, where spring rolls and pad Thai mingle with spicy cheese pizza and chicken wings (dishes from ¥350). It also serves cheap but delicious cakes. On the block after *Cable Beach* (see above) as you walk away from the station. Daily 11am–12.30am.

Smoke Café スモークカフェ 1-18-4 Sasaguchi ☎025 246 0250, ⓦsmokecafe.jp. This friendly, trendy bar specializes in international beers (pints from ¥800), including Guinness and Belgium Trappist beers, and also does good pizza and pasta. It's just south of the station, on the second floor of a modern building in the backstreets behind the *Chisun Hotel* and a Bic Camera store. Daily 11.30am–2pm & 6pm–3am, Fri & Sat till 4am.

Tobugagotoki 翔ぶが如 2nd Floor, 1-18-4 Sasaguchi ☎ 025 244 0899. Next door to *Smoke Café* and run by the same company is this atmospheric *izakaya* specializing in regional dishes (mains ¥1500) from places as far as Kochi and Kagoshima. The dark, natural decor gives off an old European ambience that matches the Euro-inspired local microbrewed beers (around ¥800). They also serve local sake. Daily 5pm–1am, Fri & Sat till 2am.

SHOPPING

Niigata's foremost shopping district is **Furumachi** (古町), 2km northwest of the station on the west side of the Shinano-gawa. The area is centred around the covered shopping mall of Furumachi-dōri and extends north to Hiro-kōji and south to Niitsuya-kōji. You can catch a glimpse of an older Niigata in the surrounding backstreets and at Hon-chō market on the eastern edge of the area (see p.271). On the opposite side of the river, the Bandai City (ⓦbandaicity.com) district features large, modern department stores, cinemas and restaurants.

Hon-chō Ichiba 本町市場. Spread over a few streets to the south of Masaya-kōji, this fresh-produce market is a great place to look for cheap places to eat and to try out your bargaining skills (see p.271). Daily 10am–5pm, closed three days a month, usually on Sun.

Kinokuniya 紀伊國屋書店 1-5-1 Bandai ☎025 241 5281. On the sixth floor of the LoveLa department store in the Bandai City complex, this has Niigata's best selection of foreign-language books. Daily 10am–8pm.

DIRECTORY

Banks and exchange You'll find foreign exchange banks near the station on Akashi-dōri and along Masaya-kōji on the west side of the river.

Hospitals The largest central hospital is Niigata University Hospital, 1-754 Asahimachi-dōri (☎025 227 2478).

Post office Niigata Central Post Office, 2-6-26 Higashi-ōdōri, is located a few minutes' walk north of the station.

Sado-ga-shima

佐渡島

For centuries, the rugged, S-shaped island of **SADO-GA-SHIMA** was a place of exile for criminals and political undesirables; and even today it continues to exude a unique atmosphere born of its isolation and a distinct cultural heritage that encompasses haunting folk songs, nō theatre and puppetry, as well as the more recently established Kodō drummers. It's a deceptively large island, consisting of two parallel mountain chains linked by a fertile central plain that shelters most of Sado's historical relics. These include several important **temples**, such as Kompon-ji, founded by the exiled Buddhist

---

SADO FESTIVALS

Sado has a packed calendar of **festivals** from April to November. Many of these involve *okesa* folk songs and the demon-drumming known as *ondeko* (or *oni-daiko*), both of which are performed nightly during the tourist season in Ogi and Aikawa. Throughout June, nō groups perform in shrines around the central plain, while the island's biggest event nowadays is the Kodō drummers' International Earth Celebration, held in Ogi (see box, p.279).

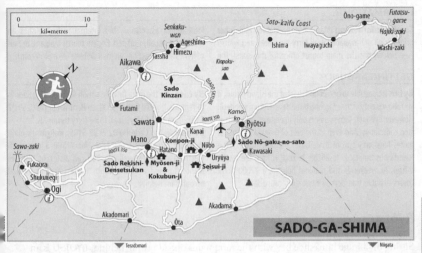

monk Nichiren, and a couple of bizarre, hi-tech **museums** where robots narrate local history. The Edo-period gold mines of **Aikawa**, on Sado's northwest coast, make another interesting excursion, but the island's greatest attractions are its **coastal scenery** and glimpses of an older Japan. It is becoming increasing popular as a location for trekking, biking, canoeing and other **outdoor activities** and it hosts a number of international competitions including an annual triathlon in September which attracts more than 17,000 entrants.

Brief history

Prior to the twelfth century, the powers-that-be viewed Sado as a suitably remote place to banish their enemies and unwanted elements of society. The most illustrious exile was the ex-emperor **Juntoku** (reigned 1211–21) who, after trying to wrestle power back from Kamakura, was condemned to spend the last twenty years of his life on the island. A few decades later, **Nichiren**, the founder of the eponymous Buddhist sect (see p.808), found himself on the island for a couple of years; he wasted no time in erecting temples and converting the local populace. Then there was **Zeami**, a famous actor and playwright credited with formalizing nō theatre, who was sent here in 1434 and spent eight years in exile at the end of his life.

In 1601, rich seams of gold and silver were discovered in the mountains above Aikawa. From then on, criminals were sent to work in the **mines**, supplemented by "homeless" workers from Edo (now Tokyo), who dug some 400km of tunnels down to 600m below sea level – all by hand. In 1896, Mitsubishi took the mines over from the imperial household, and today they're owned by the Sado Gold Mining Co. which continued to extract small quantities of gold up until 1989.

ARRIVAL AND DEPARTURE
SADO-GA-SHIMA

BY FERRY

From Niigata The main gateway to Sado is Ryōtsu town, on the east coast, which is best reached by ferry from Niigata. Sado Kisen (Niigata ☎ 0252 45 1234, Ryōtsu ☎ 0259 27 5614) operates car ferries (5–7 daily; 2hr 30min; from ¥2320) and jetfoil services (5–12 daily; 1hr; one-way ¥6220, 5-day return ticket ¥11250) from Niigata's Sado Kisen Terminal (see p.272). Reservations are required for the jetfoil and recommended for

all crossings in the summer season.
From elsewhere Sado Kisen ferries also operate between Naoetsu port, south of Niigata (20min by bus from Naoetsu Station), and Ogi on the island's south coast (1–4 daily; 2hr 40min; ¥2530). There's also a ferry service from Teradomari (寺泊) to Akadomari (赤泊) on Sado's southeast coast (1–3 daily, closed Jan 23–Feb 6; 1hr; from ¥2760).

INFORMATION

Tourist information Maps, bus timetables and other information are available at all ferry terminals, and Ryōtsu (see below) has the main tourist office for the island. The local tourist association, MIJ International, publishes an excellent, annually updated, English tourist map and details of ferries and attractions on their website (ⓦmijintl.com).

GETTING AROUND

By bus It's possible to get around most of the island by bus, if you allow plenty of time (around three days is recommended). However, in winter some services only operate at weekends or stop completely. And even at the best of times, a number of routes have only two or three buses per day, so check the island's bus timetable (available in English from the tourist office). At weekends and national holidays a ¥2000 ticket covers all public transport over two consecutive days.

By car By far the most flexible option for exploring Sado is to rent a car; you'll find Sado Kisen Rent-a-Car (ⓣ0259 27 5195; from ¥5775/day) at all three ferry terminals.

By bike Nakao Cycle (ⓣ0259 23 5195) in Ryōtsu's main shopping street rents out bikes for ¥1500 a day, with electric-assist bikes available. You can also rent bikes in Mano, Ogi and at some youth hostels (see individual accounts for details).

Ryōtsu
両津

Sitting on a huge horseshoe bay with the mountains of Sado rising behind, **RYŌTSU** is an appealing place that makes a good base for a night. The town revolves around its modern ferry pier (両津埠頭) and bus terminal, at the south end, while there's still a flavour of the original fishing community among the rickety wooden houses with their coiled nets and fishy odours in the older backstreets to the north. Much of the town occupies a thin strip of land between the sea and a large salt-water lake, **Kamo-ko**, which is now used for oyster farming.

INFORMATION   RYŌTSU

Tourist information The main Sado-ga-shima tourist office (daily 8.30am–6pm, Aug till 6.30pm, Nov–March till 5.30pm; ⓣ0259 23 3300, ⓦwww.visitsado.com/en) is located in a row of shops opposite the ferry terminal building. Buses depart from the bus terminal under the ferry building, where you'll also find car rental agencies and taxis.

Services There's a post office on the north side of the channel leading from the lake, near the middle bridge, and foreign-exchange banks further along this high street.

ACCOMMODATION AND EATING

Kagetsu Hotel 花月ホテル 262 Ryōtsu-Ebisu ⓣ0259 27 3131, ⓦwww5.ocn.ne.jp/~kagetsu. A smart place, with elegant tatami rooms, a garden running down to the lake and onsen baths. Rates include two meals; deduct around ¥3000 per head for room only. **¥21,000**

Tenkuni 天国 206 Minato ⓣ0259 23 2714. This popular local restaurant specializes in fresh seafood, offering moderately priced (around ¥1000) sashimi, tempura and *donburi* dishes. Daily 11am–3pm & 6–10pm.

Yoshidaya 吉田家 261-1 Ryōtsu-Ebisu ⓣ0259 27 2151, ⓦyosidaya.com. Large ryokan on the lake with spacious tatami rooms, most of which have balconies with stunning views over the water. It also features an outdoor rotemburo bath on the rooftop. Rates include two meals; deduct around ¥2000 per head for room only. **¥16,800**

Central Sado
国仲佐渡

Sado's **central plain** is the most heavily populated part of the island, accommodating the majority of the 70,000 islanders. A flat, fertile landscape filled with rice fields, the region is also home to a number of impressive temples, some dating back to the eighth century, built with the wealth brought in during Sado's boom periods from the gold and rice trades.

Kompon-ji
根本寺 • 1837 Niibo-ono • Daily 9am–4.30pm • ¥300 • ⓣ0259 22 3751 • Take the Minamisen line bus from Ryōtsu

Sado's most accessible and important temple, **Kompon-ji**, marks the spot where the exiled **Nichiren** (see p.275) lived in 1271, though the temple itself was founded some years later. If you can get there before the coach parties, it's a pleasant stroll round the mossy garden with its thatched temple buildings filled with elaborate gilded canopies, presided over by a statue of Nichiren in his characteristic monk's robes.

Mano and around

真野

On the southwest corner of Sado's central valley, coastal **MANO** was once Sado's provincial capital. The area around has a number of historical sights that are worth checking out, including some impressive temple complexes that were built during the island's prosperous past.

Myōsen-ji

妙宣寺 • 29 Abutsubō • Dawn–dusk • Free • ☎ 0259 55 2061 • A 15min walk from the nearest bus stop, Takeda-bashi, on the Minamisen line

The **Myōsen-ji** temple complex was founded by one of Nichiren's first disciples, the retired Samurai Tamemori Endo, in the late thirteenth century and includes a graceful five-storey wooden pagoda that took over thirty years to build, a large thatched-roof building and elegantly sculptured gardens.

Kokubun-ji

国分寺 • 113 Kokubun-ji • Dawn–dusk • Free • ☎ 0259 55 3589 • A 35min walk from the nearest bus stop, Takeda-bashi, on the Minamisen line

Sado's oldest temple, **Kokubun-ji**, dates from 741, though the temple's present buildings were constructed in the late seventeenth century. Dotted around the site, a few remains, including foundation stones and the central and south gates, give you an idea how vast the original complex once was.

Sado Rekishi-Densetsukan

佐渡歴史伝説館 • 655 Mano • Daily 8am–5pm, mid-Nov to March till 4.30pm • ¥700 • ☎ 0259 55 2525, ☒ www.3.ocn.ne.jp/~srdk • 30min walk southeast from central Mano; 10min from the nearest bus stop, Mano goryō-iriguchi, on route #4 from Sawata south to Ogi

The interesting museum, **Sado Rekishi-Densetsukan**, next door to a simple shrine dedicated to Emperor Juntoku, has a number of multimedia displays bringing local history and folk tales to life via full-sized robots and holograms representing Juntoku, Nichiren and other notable characters.

Sawata

佐和田

A few kilometres north along the coast from Mano, **SAWATA** serves as Sado's main administrative centre. The town is not the most alluring of places, but if you happen to be passing through around lunchtime, pop along to the **Silver Village** resort, on Sawata's northern outskirts.

ARRIVAL AND INFORMATION	CENTRAL SADO

By bus Sawata's bus terminal is located on the north side of town.

Tourist information Mano's tourist office (488-8 Mano-shinmachi; April–July & Sept–Oct Mon, Tues & Thurs–Sat 9am–6pm, Aug daily 9am–6pm, Nov–March Mon–Fri 9am–6pm; ☎ 0259 55 3589, ☒ www.visitsado.com) is a few doors south of the main junction between Route 350 and the Niibo road.

GETTING AROUND

By bus Two routes cross Sado's central plain linking Ryōtsu to towns on the west coast: the main highway cuts southwest from Kamo-ko to Sado Airport and on to Sawata, served by buses on the Hon-sen route (line 1), while the quieter, southerly route takes you through Niibo (新穂), Hatano (畑野) and Mano (真野) along the Minamisen bus route (line 2).

By car and bike The majority of historical sites lie scattered across the southern district – for many of them you'll need your own transport (see opposite) or be prepared to walk a fair distance. One solution is to rent a bike at Mano's tourist office for only ¥1100 a day.

ACCOMMODATION AND EATING

Green Village Patio House グリーンヴィレッジパティ オハウス 750-4 Niibo-Uryūya ☎0259 22 2719. A homely guesthouse east of Niibo village – take the Ogi Port Minamnisen line and ask the bus driver to let you off at the correct turning. As well as good-value meals, laundry facilities and free wi-fi, they have bikes for rent and can suggest cycling routes. Two meals a day are available for ¥2415 per head. Dorm **¥3360**

Ryokan Urashima 浦島 978-3 Kubota ☎0259 57 3751. This modern inn designed by architect Kitayama Koh overlooks the beach at Mano bay just west of Sawata and features stylishly minimalistic Western and Japanese-style rooms. For two meals, add ¥4730 per person. **¥11,540**

Shimafūmi シマフウミ 105-4 Daishō ☎0259 55 4545, ⓦprimosado.jp/shimafumi.html. It's well worth making the trip to this chic café on the coast for the stunning sea views from its outside decking. With its own bakery on site, you can get great bread, pastry and sandwiches. Mon, Tues & Fri–Sun 10am–5pm.

Ogi

小木

Sado's second port is tiny **OGI**, situated near the island's southern tip. This sleepy fishing town is split in two by a small headland, with the original harbour to the west and modern ferry terminal on its east side. It is best known for its **tub boats**, once fishing crafts, which now bob around in the harbour for tourists, and the annual **Earth Celebration** hosted by the locally based Kodō drummers (see box opposite), during which the village's population almost doubles. But the area's principal attraction is the picturesque indented coastline to the west of town; you can explore the headland on a bike, take boat trips round it, or cycle over the top to **Shukunegi**, a traditional fishing village huddled behind a wooden palisade.

ARRIVAL AND INFORMATION

By bus Local buses use the station behind Ogi post office, just inland from the tourist-boat pier and run west along the coast as far as Sawasaki (line 11).
Destination Sawasaki (5 daily; 25min).

By ferry Ogi links to the mainland by sea to Naoetsu (¥2530), the port of Joetsu town and a major train junction for lines along the Sea of Japan coast and south to Nagano, Nagoya and Tokyo; see ⓦmijintl.com for details.
Destination Naoetsu (1–4 daily; 2hr 40min).

Tourist information The town's tourist office (1935-26 Ogi-machi, Mon–Sat 8.30am–5.30pm, June & Aug till 6pm, Dec–Feb till 5.15pm; ☎0259 86 3200, ⓦ visitsado.com) occupies the ground floor of the Marine Plaza building, one block west of the post office, where you can get maps, book accommodation and arrange car and bike rental (see below). This building is also used for evening performances of *okesa odori* folk singing (April– Oct; ¥500).

GETTING AROUND

By bike The ideal way to explore the headland is to rent an electric bicycle from the tourist office (¥500/2hr, ¥200 each extra hour or ¥2000/24hr).

ACCOMMODATION

It's a good idea to book accommodation well ahead in summer, but during the rest of the year you shouldn't have any problem.

Hananoki 花の木 78-1 Shukunegi ☎0259 86 2331, ⓦsado-hananoki.com. Set in a renovated 150-year-old house, this traditional inn features a beautiful dining room complete with open hearth and organically shaped

---

BOAT TRIPS FROM OGI

The **tub boats**, or *tarai-bune*, were originally used for collecting seaweed, abalone and other shellfish from the rocky coves. Today they're made of fibreglass, but still resemble the cutaway wooden barrels from which they were traditionally made. If you fancy a shot at rowing one of these awkward vessels, go to the small jetty west of the ferry pier, where women will take you out for a ten-minute spin round the harbour (daily 8.20am–5pm; ¥450 per person). The jetty is also the departure point for **sightseeing boats** (April–Nov 6–18 daily; 40min; return trip ¥1400) which sail along the coast past caves and dainty islets as far as Sawa-zaki lighthouse.

CHILDREN OF THE DRUM

In the early 1970s a group of students came to the seclusion of Sado-ga-shima to pursue their study of traditional *Taiko* drumming and to experiment with its potent music. A decade later, the **Kodō Drummers** unleashed their primal rhythms on the world and have since continued to stun audiences with their electrifying performances. The name Kodō can mean both "heartbeat" and "children of the drum" – despite its crashing sound, the beat of their trademark giant *Ōdaiko* is said to resemble the heart heard from inside the womb.

The drummers are now based in Kodō village, a few kilometres north of Ogi, where they have set up the **Sado Island Taiko Centre** (see p.280). Apart from a two-year apprenticeship programme, the drummers take workshops for tourists. Each year, usually the third week of August, they also host the three-day **Earth Celebration** arts festival when percussionists from all over the world and a friendly multinational audience of several thousand stir up the sleepy air of Ogi. Details of Kodō scheduled tours and the next Earth Celebration are posted on their website (Ⓦ kodo.or.jp).

3

tree-trunk tables. The tranquil guest rooms are set amidst a pretty traditional garden in a row of separate cabins with views over the surrounding paddy fields. Two meals a day are available for ¥4000 per person. **¥11,000**

Minshuku Sakaya 民宿さかや 1991 Ogimachi ☏ 0259 86 2535. In central Ogi, a 5min walk east of the ferry terminal, this popular seafront inn offers clean tatami rooms and tasty food, but unfortunately its sea views are

blocked by the harbour wall. Rates include two meals. **¥14,000**

Ogi Sakuma-sō Youth Hostel 小木佐久間荘ユースホステル 1562 Ogimachi ☏ 0259 86 2565; Ⓦ jyh.or.jp. A cheap but basic hostel in the countryside outside town, a 20min walk uphill from the ferry; take the road heading west for Shukunegi, then turn right beside the Shell fuel station. Dorm **¥3600**

EATING

Sakae-zushi 栄寿司 66-1 Ogi ☏ 0259 86 3898. In the block behind the Marine Plaza, where they serve sea-fresh sushi and sashimi at reasonable prices. Expect to pay between ¥1000 and ¥2000 per head. Daily 11am–2pm & 5–10pm.

Shichiemon 七右衛門 643-1 Ogi ☏ 0259 86 2046. At the top of the shopping street curving behind the western harbour, this restaurant dishes up just one variety of delicious, handmade soba (¥480). 11am–2pm, closed Thurs.

Around Ogi

In the southwest corner of Sado, the coastline west of Ogi is perfect to explore by bike, with rocky inlets, isolated fishing villages and quiet, undulating roads. After a tough uphill pedal out of the port on the road west to Shukunegi, turn right towards a concrete *jizō* standing above the trees. From here, continue another 300m along this side road and you'll find a short flight of steps leading up to the **Iwaya cave** – the old trees and tiny, crumbling temple surrounded by *jizō* statues make a good place to catch your breath. Return to the coast and follow the road round the peninsula for stunning sea views.

Sadokoku Ogi Folk Culture Museum

佐渡国小木民俗博物館, Sadokoku Ogi Minzoku Hakubutsukan・270-2 Shukunegi・Daily 8.30am–5pm・¥500・☏ 0259 86 2604

On the road from Ogi to Shukunegi, next to a still-functioning boatyard, **Sadokoku Ogi Folk Culture** is worth a brief stop. It contains a delightful, dusty jumble of old photos, paper-cuts, tofu presses, straw raincoats and other remnants of local life. Behind, in a newer building, there's a relief map of the area and beautiful examples of the ingenious traps used by Ogi fisherfolk.

Shukunegi

宿根木

Tucked in a fold of the hills beside a little harbour full of jagged black rocks is the **SHUKUNEGI** fishing village, a registered national historic site. As the home of skilful ship builders, the village was an important port at the peak of Sado's gold trade between the seventeenth and nineteenth centuries. The village itself is hardly visible behind its high wooden fence – protection against the fierce winds – where its old wooden houses, two of which are open to the public in summer (June–Aug daily 10am–5pm; ¥400 each), are all jumbled together, in a tangle of odd-shaped corners and narrow, stone-flagged alleys.

Sado Island Taiko Centre

佐渡太鼓体験交流館, Sado Taiko Taiken Kōryu-kan• 150-3 Ogikaneta Shinden, Kodō • Tues–Sun 9am–5pm • ¥2000 for 1hr 30m in drumming lesson (advance reservations preferred); contact the centre for details of a longer workshop, *Kodō juku*, which takes place once a year • ☎ 0259 86 2320, ⓦ sadotaiken.jp

Housed on the top of a hill above the Kodō village, with stunning views out to the coast, is the smart **Sado Island Taiko Centre**. Visitors can learn drumming from Kodō drummers in fun and energetic lessons in the spacious practice room on the ground floor. The drums come in a variety of sizes, up to giant ones some 3m in diameter, and you use sticks weighing up to 5Kg, so come prepared for a workout.

North Sado

北佐渡

Sado's northern promontory contains the island's highest mountains and some of its best coastal scenery. **Aikawa**, the only settlement of any size in this area, was once a lively mining town whose gold and silver ores filled the shoguns' coffers. The mines are no longer working, but a section of tunnel has been converted into a museum, **Sado Kinzan**, where yet more computerized robots show how things were done in olden times. North of Aikawa, there's the rather overrated **Senkaku-wan** (尖閣湾), a small stretch of picturesque cliffs; it's better to head on up the wild Soto-kaifu coast to **Hajiki-zaki** (弾崎) on the island's northern tip. Not surprisingly, this area isn't well served by public transport, particularly in winter when snow blocks the mountain passes; to explore this part of the island you really need to rent a car or be prepared for hard cycling.

Aikawa

相川

After gold and silver were discovered in 1601, the population of **AIKAWA** rocketed from a hamlet of just ten families to 100,000 people, including many who were convict labourers. Now a mere tenth of that size, there's nothing specific to see in Aikawa beyond the **mine museum** a few kilometres out of town. Nevertheless, it's not an unattractive place for an overnight stay once you get off the main road and delve among the temples, shrines and wooden houses pressed up against the hillside.

Sado Kinzan

日本最大の金銀山 • 1305 Shimo-Aikawa • Daily: April–Oct 8am–5.30pm; Nov–March 8am–5.30pm • ¥800 • ☎ 0259 74 2389 • ⓦ sado-kinzan.com/en • 10min by bus from Aikawa on the Sado Kinzan Nanaura-kaigan line (4 daily)

North of Aikawa, a steep, narrow valley leads to the old gold mines of **Sado Kinzan**. The Sōdayū tunnel, one of the mine's richest veins, is now a museum showing working conditions during the Edo period, complete with sound effects and life-size mechanical models, followed by a smaller exhibition with equally imaginative models of the miners at work.

INFORMATION   **AIKAWA**

Tourist information Aikawa's tourist office (daily 8.30am–6pm, Nov–April till 5.15pm) ☎ 0259 74 2220) is located outside the bus terminal's seaward side.

ACCOMMODATION AND EATING

With a fair number of tourists, Aikawa has several large **hotels** as well as smaller **ryokans** to choose from, though little in the way of budget accommodation. The best place to look for somewhere to **eat** in Aikawa is in the main shopping street north of *Dōyū Ryokan*.

Dōyū Ryokan 道遊旅館 333-1 Aikawa-Kabuse ☏0259 74 3381, ⓦdouyuu.com. Located on a quiet street one block inland from the bus terminal, this small traditional inn comes highly recommended. Rates include two meals. **¥16,800**

Hotel Ōsado ホテル大佐渡 288-1 Aikawa-Kabuse ☏0259 74 3300, ⓦoosado.com. This large and luxurious seafront hotel, built on the Kasugazaki Point headland, offers both Japanese and Western-style rooms. Onsen addicts will love its glorious large rotemburo. Rates include two meals. **¥18,900**

The northern cape

Five kilometres north of Aikawa, the road skirts round the edge of a bay where jagged cliffs crumble away into clusters of **little islands**. You get a pretty good view of the bay of **Senkaku-wan** from the road itself or from the observatory in **Ageshima-yūen** (揚島遊園; 1561 Kitaebisu; daily 8am–5.30pm; ¥500; ☏0259 75 2311), a park on the bay's north side. You can get closer: a variety of **tour boats** regularly set sail during the summer season (April–Nov) from **Tassha** village (達者), 2km further south; expect to pay around ¥800 for a thirty-minute trip in either a glass-bottomed "shark" boat or ordinary sightseeing (*yūransen*) boats.

As you continue north, the settlements gradually peter out and the scenery becomes wilder as you approach **Ōno-game** (大野亀), a 167m rock rising up from the ocean. From here, a pretty coastal pathway leads around to the island of **Futatsu-game** (二つ亀), linked to the mainland by a thin strip of black-sand beach; along the path is an intriguing cave, **Sai-no-Kawara** (賽の河原), housing hundreds of *jizō* statues. In summer this area is popular for swimming and camping, but it's worth doing at any time of year for the journey alone, especially if you return to Ryōtsu down the east coast, where you're treated to further precariously twisting roads clinging to the base of the mountains as they plummet into the sea.

ARRIVAL AND DEPARTURE — THE NORTHERN CAPE

By bus Tassha and Ageshima-Yūen are both stops on the Kaifu-sen bus route (line 3) from Aikawa to Iwayaguchi, with services roughly every hour.

ACCOMMODATION

Kokuminshukusha Senkaku-sō 国民宿舎尖閣荘 1431-2 Himezu ☏0259 75 2226, ⓦsenkakusou.com. A plush, if slightly dated, government-run hotel featuring elegant tatami rooms and communal baths overlooking the bay. Rates include two meals, though lodging without meals is possible for a reduced rate. **¥14,700**

Sado Belle Mer 佐渡ベルメールユースホステル 369-4 Himezu ☏0259 75 2011, ⓦsado.bellemer.jp. In a modern building on the hilltop near Ageshima-yūen, this good youth hostel has stunning views out over Senkaku Bay. Private rooms are available for an extra ¥500 per person. Dorm **¥3360**

WALKING THE CEDAR FORESTS

Sado's northern Ōsado mountain range contains primeval forests of giant, ancient **cedar trees**. These are protected areas, but a newly constructed **walkway** near Ishina, midway along the northern coast, takes you into prime wooded areas. The circuit is fairly gentle and takes around an hour, but, given the elevation of more than 900m, high winds and temperatures 5°C below those at the coast, come prepared for changeable weather. **Trekkers** wanting to go further afield need to hire a guide, as access is strictly limited. Sado's tourism information office in Ryōtsu (see p.276) arranges **tours** to a prime cluster of great cedars at weekends from June to October (limited to 16 people per day; ¥5,000, including transport from Ryōtsu; ☏0259 27 5000, ⓦhttp://bit.ly/1c5vzla).

Hokkaidō

北海道

SAPPORO SNOW FESTIVAL, YUKI MATSURI

Hokkaidō

An unspoiled frontier, an escape from industrialized Japan and a chance to connect with nature – although this vision of Hokkaidō is rose-tinted, Japan's main northern island certainly has an untamed and remote quality. Over seventy percent of it is covered by forest, and wildlife is ubiquitous, both in and out of the enormous national parks, where you'll also find snow-covered slopes, active volcanoes and bubbling onsen. This is Japan's second-largest island, with twenty-two percent of the nation's landmass, yet a mere five percent of the population lives here. Even so, cities such as the stylish capital Sapporo and historically important Hakodate are just as sophisticated and packed with facilities as their southern cousins.

Only colonized by the Japanese in the last 150 years, Hokkaidō is devoid of ancient temples, shrines and monuments over 200 years old. What it does have is a fascinating cultural history, defined by its dwindling **Ainu** population (see box, p.289). From spring till autumn is the ideal time to explore the island's six major national parks and countryside. Apart from the highlights listed opposite, other attraction include **Shikotsu-Tōya National Park**, which has two beautiful lakes and a volcano that only started sprouting in 1943, while the countryside around **Furano** bursts in colour with fields of lavender and other flowers. Come winter, Hokkaidō takes on a special quality; you can ski at some of Japan's best – and least crowded – ski resorts or view many snow and ice festivals, of which Sapporo's giant **Yuki Matsuri** is the most famous.

ARRIVAL AND DEPARTURE

By plane Hokkaidō's main gateway is New Chitose Airport, 40km south of Sapporo, where you can pick up connecting flights to other places on the island.

By train The Shinkansen line is currently being extended to Hakodate and is likely to be completed by March 2016. For now, the fastest way from Tokyo by train is by Shinkansen to Shin-Aomori and then limited express to Hakodate. There are also nightly direct sleeper trains from Tokyo to Sapporo, via Hakodate, and several a week from Ōsaka; if you're using a rail pass, you'll need to pay a supplement for these (see box, p.288).

By ferry There are overnight ferry services from Honshū. MOL Ferry Co (⬭sunflower.co.jp) offers a service from Tokyo to Sapporo via the ports of Oarai (for Tokyo) and Tomakomai (for Sapporo), from ¥8500 (see p.294). You'll need to take local buses for city transfer at either end.

CRABS AT A HAKODATE MARKET STALL

Highlights

❶ **Sapporo** Hokkaidō's fun capital city is home to Japan's largest Snow Festival, a park designed by the artist and landscape architect Noguchi Isamu and the eponymous freshly brewed beer. See p.288

❷ **Niseko** Superb powder snow, great scenery and chic accommodation and dining add up to Japan's best ski resort. See p.302

❸ **Hakodate** Travel by rickety old trams around this historic port, with its gentrified harbourside district and deservedly famous seafood. See p.304

❹ **Noboribetsu Onsen** Explore the steaming, sulphurous volcanic landscape, then enjoy a

traditional ryokan experience complete with relaxing onsen. See p.313

❺ **Daisetsu-zan National Park** Home to Asahi-dake, Hokkaidō's highest mountain, the spectacular Sōunkyō Gorge and a choice of onsen. See p.318

❻ **Rishiri-tō and Rebun-tō** These beautiful, far northern islands are sprinkled with wild flowers and perfect for hiking. See p.323

❼ **Shiretoko National Park** Nature is in all her glory at this UNESCO World Heritage Site, which offers challenging treks and abundant wildlife – including bears. See p.330

HIGHLIGHTS ARE MARKED ON THE MAP ON PP.286–287

HOKKAIDO

Niigata & Maizuru
Akita, Niigata & Tsuruga
Aomori
Hachinohe, Sendai, Oarai & Nagoya

SEA OF JAPAN

Korsakov (Sakhalin)
Sōya Misaki
Rebun-tō
Wakkanai
RISHIRI-REBUN-SAROBETSU NATIONAL PARK
Wakkanai Airport
Kafuka
6
Oshidomari
Kutsugata
Rishiri-zan
Rishiri-tō
Sarobetsu Natural Flower Garden

SŌYA LINE

Kami
Asahikawa
Sōunk
Asahikawa Airport
Biei
Asahi-dake Onsen
Takikawa
Bibaushi
Kami-furano
Shakotan Peninsula
Yoichi
Otaru
Okadama Airport
Tokachi-dake
DA
NA
Furano
Furano-dake
Sapporo
1
H o k k
Sahoro-dake
Niseko Annupuri
Yōtei-zan
Shikotsu-ko
Shikotsu Kohan
2
Niseko
New Chitose Airport
SHIKOTSU-TŌYA NATIONAL PARK
Tarumae-zan
Tōya-ko
Noboribetsu Onsen
Shiraoi
Nibutani
Oshamambe
Usu-zan
Tōya
Shōwa Shin-zan
4
Tomakomai
MURORAN LINE
HIDA
SANMYAKU QUASI-NAT PARK
Noboribetsu
HIDAKA LINE
Uchiura-wan Bay
Muroran
HAKODATE LINE
ŌNUMA QUASI-NATIONAL PARK
Komaga-take
Ōnuma
3
Hakodate Airport
Hakodate
TSUGARU-KAIKYŌ LINE
Fukushima
Seikan Tunnel
Ōma

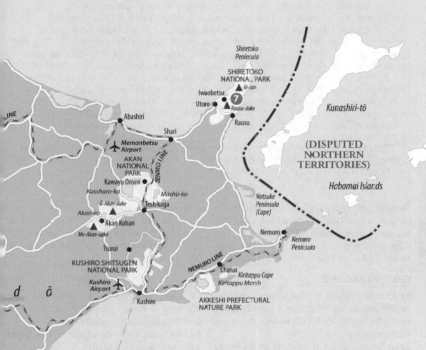

SEA OF OKHOTSK

Shiretoko Peninsula

SHIRETOKO NATIONAL PARK

▲ *Iō-zan*

Iwaobetsu

Utoro   **7**

▲ *Rausu-dake*

Rausu

Abashiri

Shari

Memanbetsu Airport

AKAN NATIONAL PARK

Kawayu Onsen

Kussharo-ko

Mashū-ko

Ō-Akan-dake ▲

Akan-ko ▲ Akan Kohan

Teshikaga

Me-Akan-dake ▲

Tsurui

KUSHIRO SHITSUGEN NATIONAL PARK

Kushiro Airport

Kushiro

Kunashiri-tō

(DISPUTED NORTHERN TERRITORIES)

Habomai Islands

Notsuke Peninsula (Cape)

Nemuro

Nemuro Peninsula

NEMURO LINE

Chanai

Kiritappu Cape

Kiritappu Marsh

AKKESHI PREFECTURAL NATURE PARK

SENMO LINE

LINE

d   *ō*

● Hirō

PACIFIC OCEAN

Misaki

▼ Tokyo

HIGHLIGHTS

1 Sapporo

2 Niseko

3 Hakodate

4 Noboribetsu Onsen

5 Daisetsu-zan National Park

6 Rishiri-tō and Rebun-tō

7 Shiretoko National Park

SLEEPER TRAINS TO HOKKAIDŌ

There are several **overnight sleeper** options for getting to Hokkaidō, which combine the convenience of overnight long-distance travel with the old-style glamour of dining cars, first-class hospitality and the chance to have a shower on a moving train. JR Pass holders can use these sleepers, but have to pay additional berth and limited express charges.

The deluxe version from Tokyo is the **Cassiopeioa**, which runs three times a week in each direction (カシオペア; ⓦbit.ly/1a21UbZ). On this most luxurious train in Japan, all sleeper compartments are private twin rooms, and there are a limited number of much sought-after suites. It generally departs at 4.20pm on Sundays, Tuesdays and Fridays from Ueno Station in Tokyo, arriving in Sapporo at 9.32am the next morning; and at 4.12pm on Mondays, Wednesdays and Saturdays from Sapporo Station, arriving in Ueno at 9.25am next day.

The second option from Tokyo is the daily **Hokutosei** (北斗星; ⓦbit.ly/1gzMVV3), which departs at 7.03pm from Ueno Station and arrives in Sapporo at 11.15am the next morning. The reverse journey departs Sapporo at 5.12pm, arriving in Ueno at 10.05pm. This train has suites, twin berths and solo compartments, so is more convenient for those travelling on their own.

If you're travelling from **Osaka** and you're not in any hurry, then you could consider the Twilight Express (トワイライトエクスプレス; ⓦbit.ly/1eOxkzT), which leaves Osaka Station at 11.50am four times a week, on Mondays, Wednesdays, Fridays and Saturdays, and arrives in Sapporo at 9.52am the following day. For the return journey, the train departs Sapporo at 2.05pm on Tuesdays, Thursdays, Saturdays and Sundays, arriving back in Osaka at 12.53pm the next day.

Tickets go on sale one calendar month from date of travel, and you're advised to book as far in advance as possible, particularly in the summer months and at peak ski season. Bookings can be made at any JR ticket counter or travel agency, but can't be made online or from overseas.

4

Shin Nihonkai Ferry (ⓦsnf.jp) runs services from Otaru to Maizuru, north of Kyoto, and Niigata (see p.272). They also run overnight services from Tomakomai to Akita (12hr; daily), Niigata (20hr; daily) and Tsuruga (34hr; weekly) in Fukui-ken. Taiheiyo Ferry Co (ⓦtaiheiyo-ferry. co.jp/english) runs a service from Tomakomai to Sendai (daily; 15hr) and Nagoya (every 2 days; 39hr 30min). Silver Ferry (ⓦsilverferry.jp) operates a four-times daily service from Tomakomai to Hachinohe in Aomori-ken (7hr 15min).

GETTING AROUND

By train The Hokkaidō Rail Pass (ⓦwww2.jrhokkaido .co.jp/global), costing ¥15,000 for a three-day ticket, ¥19,500 for five days and ¥22,000 for seven days, is well worth considering.

By car To reach more remote corners of the island, hiring a car is best. Useful websites for general and driving information include ⓦen.visit-hokkaido.jp and ⓦnorthern-road.jp/navi/eng/index.htm.

By bike Cycling is also very popular on Hokkaidō (see individual accounts for rental info).

Sapporo

札幌

With a population of nearly two million, Hokkaidō's vibrant capital **SAPPORO** is the fifth-largest city in Japan. As the transport hub of the island, you're almost bound to pass through here. It's worth lingering, as Sapporo is generously endowed with parks and gardens. The mountains that attract skiers and snowboarders rise up to its south, and the dramatic coastline around the Shakotan Peninsula is less than thirty minutes away.

Sapporo is also synonymous with its beer, which has been brewed here since 1891; a visit to the handsome, late nineteenth-century **Sapporo Bier Garten and Beer Museum** is a must, as is a stroll through the grounds and museums of the **Botanical Gardens**, which date from the same era. Seeing central Sapporo's main sights will fill a day; after dark, the bars and restaurants of **Susukino** (pronounced "suskino") spark to life, and you'd be hard pressed to find a livelier nightlife district outside of Tokyo or Ōsaka. South of Susukino, **Nakajima-kōen** (中島公園) is another of central Sapporo's large-scale green spots and is worth visiting to see the **Hasso-an**, an early Edo-period teahouse.

Head out of the city centre to see the **Historical Village of Hokkaidō**, a huge landscaped park featuring more than sixty restored buildings from the island's frontier days. **Moerenuma**, a park designed by the late Japanese-American sculptor Noguchi Isamu, also makes for a pleasant half-day trip, as does the entertaining **Sapporo Winter Sports Museum**.

Pleasantly cool temperatures tempt many visitors to Sapporo's **Summer Festival** (usually July 21–Aug 20), which features outdoor beer gardens and other events in **Ōdōri-kōen**, the swathe of parkland that cuts through the city centre. This park is also the focus of activity during the fabulous **Yuki Matsuri**, a snow festival held every February (see box, p 291).

Brief history

Sapporo's name comes from the Ainu word for the area, *Sari-poro-betsu*, meaning "a river which runs along a plain filled with reeds". The city's easy-to-follow grid-plan layout was designed in the 1870s by a team of European and American experts engaged by the government to advise on Hokkaidō's development. Statues of these advisers can be found around Sapporo; the most famous (overlooking the city from atop Hitsujigaoka hill in the south) is the one of the American **Dr William S. Clark**, who set

---

THE AINU

…they are uncivilizable and altogether irreclaimable savages, yet they are attractive … I hope I shall never forget the music of their low sweet voices, the soft light of their mild, brown eyes and the wonderful sweetness of their smile.

Isabella Bird, *Unbeaten Tracks in Japan*, 1880

Victorian traveller Isabella Bird had some misconceived notions about the **Ainu**, but anyone who has ever listened to their hauntingly beautiful music will agree that they are a people not easily forgotten. The Ainu's roots are uncertain – some believe they come from Siberia or Central Asia, and they are thought to have lived on Hokkaidō, the Kuril Islands, Sakhalin and northern Honshū since the seventh century. The early Ainu were hairy, wide-eyed (even today you can notice such characteristics in full-blooded Ainu) and lived a hunter-gatherer existence, but their culture – revolving around powerful **animist** beliefs – was sophisticated, as shown by their unique clothing and epic songs and stories in a language quite unlike Japanese.

Up until the Meiji Restoration, Japanese contact with the Ainu in Hokkaidō, then called Ezochi, was limited to trade, and the people were largely left alone in the north of the island. However, when the Japanese sought to fully **colonize** Hokkaidō, the impact on the Ainu was disastrous. Their culture was suppressed, they were kicked off ancestral lands, saw forests cleared where they had hunted and suffered epidemics of diseases from which they had no natural immunity. Their way of life went into seemingly terminal decline and assimilation seemed inevitable after a law of 1899 labelled the Ainu as former aborigines, obliging them to take on Japanese citizenship.

Over a century later, against all odds, fragments of Ainu culture and society remain. Around 25,000 people admit to being full- and part-blooded Ainu (although the actual number is thought to be closer to 200,000). A tiny piece of political power was gained when Kayano Shigeru (1926–2006), an Ainu, was elected to the House of Councillors – the second house of Japan's parliament – in 1994. A landmark legal verdict in 1997 recognized Ainu rights over the land and led to the New Ainu Law of 1997 which aimed to protect what is left of Ainu culture and ensure it is passed on to generations to come. In 2008, Japan's Diet also passed a resolution recognizing Ainu, for the first time in 140 years, as "an indigenous people with a distinct language, religion and culture". Generally, there is now more interest in and sensitivity towards this ethnic group from the Japanese who visit tourist villages such as **Poroto Kotan** (see box, p.314) and **Akan-kohan** (see p.333). The best place to get an accurate idea of how Ainu live today is at **Nibutani** (see p.314).

Worth seeking out for a broader understanding of the Ainu and their relationship to similar ethnic groups are the museums of Northern Peoples in Hakodate (see p.307) and Abashiri (see p.328).

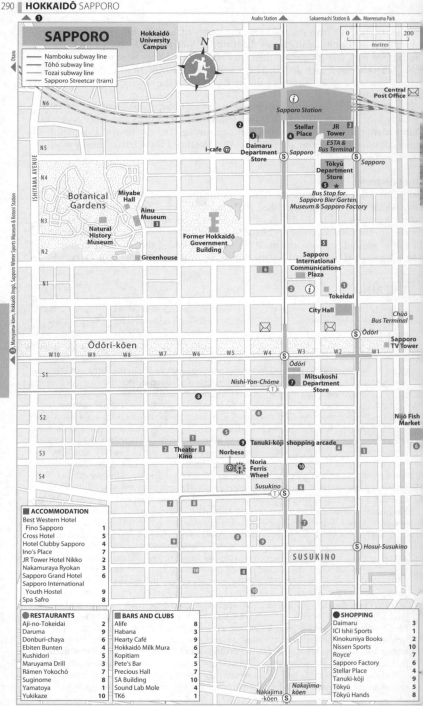

SAPPORO

— Namboku subway line
— Tōhō subway line
— Tozai subway line
— Sapporo Streetcar (tram)

Asabu Station ▲ Sakaemachi Station & ▲ Moerenuma Park

0 — 200 metres

Hokkaidō University Campus

N

Otaru ▲

Central Post Office ✉

N6

Sapporo Station

N5

i-cafe @

Daimaru Department Store

S Sapporo

Stellar Place

JR Tower

ESTA & Bus Terminal

S Sapporo

N4

Tōkyū Department Store

★

Bus Stop for Sapporo Bier Garten Museum & Sapporo Factory

ISHIYAMA AVENUE

Botanical Gardens

Miyabe Hall

Ainu Museum

N3

Natural History Museum

N2

Greenhouse

Former Hokkaidō Government Building

Sapporo International Communications Plaza

Tokeidai

N1

City Hall

Chūō Bus Terminal

✉

✉

S Ōdōri

Sapporo TV Tower

Ōdōri-kōen

W10 W9 W8 W7 W6 W5 W4 W3 W2 W1

S Ōdōri

S1

Nishi-Yon-Chōme T

Mitsukoshi Department Store

S2

Nijō Fish Market

S3

Theater Kino

Norbesa

Tanuki-kōji shopping arcade

Noria Ferris Wheel

S4

Susukino T S

SUSUKINO

S Hosui-Susukino

Nakajima-kōen

Nakajima-kōen

Maruyama-kōen, Hokkaidō Jingū, Sapporo Winter Sports Museum & Kotoni Station

Maruyama-kōen

4

■ ACCOMMODATION
Best Western Hotel Fino Sapporo	1
Cross Hotel	5
Hotel Clubby Sapporo	4
Ino's Place	7
JR Tower Hotel Nikko	2
Nakamuraya Ryokan	3
Sapporo Grand Hotel	6
Sapporo International Youth Hostel	9
Spa Safro	8

● RESTAURANTS
Aji-no-Tokeidai	2
Daruma	9
Donburi-chaya	6
Ebiten Bunten	4
Kushidori	5
Maruyama Drill	3
Rāmen Yokochō	7
Suginome	8
Yamatoya	1
Yukikaze	10

■ BARS AND CLUBS
Alife	8
Habana	3
Hearty Café	9
Hokkaidō Milk Mura	6
Kopitiam	2
Pete's Bar	5
Precious Hall	7
SA Building	10
Sound Lab Mole	4
TK6	1

● SHOPPING
Daimaru	3
ICI Ishii Sports	1
Kinokuniya Books	2
Nissen Sports	10
Royce'	7
Sapporo Factory	6
Stellar Place	4
Tanuki-kōji	9
Tōkyū	5
Tōkyū Hands	8

Sapporo Concert Hall Kitara ▼

Makomanai Station ▼

THE YUKI MATSURI AND OTHER SNOW FESTIVALS

Sapporo's famous snow festival, the **Yuki Matsuri** (ⓦ snowfes.com /english), has its origins in the winter of 1950, when six small snow statues were created by high-school children in Ōdōri-kōen, the city's main park. The idea caught on, and by 1955 the Self Defence Force (the Japanese military) was pitching in to help build gigantic **snow sculptures**, which included intricately detailed copies of world landmarks such as the Taj Mahal.

Running from around February 5–11 and spread across three sites (Ōdōri-kōen, Susukino and Sapporo Tsudome), the festival now includes an international snow sculpture competition and many other events, such as snowboard jumping and nightly music performances in the park. Arrive one week in advance and you'll be able to see the statues being made, as well as take part in the construction, since at least one giant statue in Ōdōri-kōen is a community effort – all you need do is turn up and offer your services. Book **transport and accommodation** well ahead of time: with two million visitors flooding into Sapporo during the *matsuri*, finding last-minute options for both can be a challenge.

If you don't make it to Sapporo's snow festival, note that there are several others around Hokkaidō that take place in January and February, including at Abashiri (see box, p.330), Asahikawa (see box, p.317), Otaru (see p.299), Shikotsu-ko (see p.315), and Sōunkyō (see p.319).

up Hokkaidō University and whose invocation to his students – "Boys, be ambitious!" – has been adopted as the city's motto.

Botanical Gardens

植物園, Shokubutsu-en • Kita 3, Nishi 8 • **Gardens & museums** April 29–Nov 3 Tues–Sun 9am–4pm • ¥400 • **Greenhouse** Nov 4–April 28 Mon–Fri 10am–3.30pm, Sat 10am–12.30pm • ¥110 • ⓦ hokudai.ac.jp/fsc/bg

A ten-minute walk southwest of Sapporo Station is the compact and pretty **Botanical Gardens**. Immediately to the right as you enter is the small but interesting **Ainu Museum**, known as the "Batchelor Kinen-kan" in memory of the Reverend John Batchelor, a British priest and author of *The Ainu of Japan*, considered to be the definitive work on Hokkaidō's indigenous people. The museum has a collection of around 2500 Ainu artefacts (though only a fraction is displayed at any time), ranging from clothes made of bird skins from the Kuril Islands to a sacred altar for performing the ritual slaughter of a bear cub – there are English-language captions. The gardens themselves are very attractive, with a long pond, a greenhouse, a rockery, shaded forest walks and neat flower gardens, including a collection which shows the plants and flowers used by the Ainu in their daily lives. In the centre of it all stands the **Natural History Museum**, housed in a pale green wooden building dating from 1882. Inside you'll find a staggering collection of bizarre stuffed animals, such as snarling wolves and huge sea lions, as well as other curiosities including a dog sled from Sakhalin. Following the red-gravel pathway around to the right of the museum leads you to **Miyabe Hall**, where you'll find intriguing displays of letters and journals belonging to Professor Miyabe Kingo, the first director of Hokkaidō University, who established the gardens in 1886. Miyabe's descriptions of his travels abroad, written in English and illustrated with photographs, make fascinating reading.

Former Hokkaidō Government Building

赤れんが, Akarenga • Kita 3, Nishi 6 • Daily 8.45am–6pm • Free • ☎ 0112 31 4111

On your way to or from the Botanical Gardens, swing by the **Former Hokkaidō Government Building**. This palatial red-brick building (nicknamed *akarenga*, or "red-brick building"), dating to 1888, is a fine example of the local architecture that fused the late nineteenth-century European and New World influences flooding into the country with Japanese traditions. Inside, the wood-panelled interiors have been nicely maintained and hung with large-scale historical paintings.

Tokeidai

時計台 • Kita 1, Nishi 2 • Daily 8.45am–5pm; closed fourth Monday of the month • ¥200 • ⓦ bit.ly/1i3jYBF

Five blocks south of Sapporo Station, opposite the Sapporo International Communication Plaza, is the **Tokeidai**, a wooden clock tower that's one of the city's key landmarks. You'd be right in thinking that this wood-clad building would look more at home somewhere like Boston, because that's where it was made in 1878; inside is an uninspiring exhibition on the building's history.

Sapporo TV Tower

さっぽろテレビ塔, Sapporo Terebi-tō • Ōdōri Nishi 1 • Daily: April 9.30am–10pm; May–Oct 9am–10pm; Nov–March 9.30am–9.30pm • ¥700 • ⓦ tv-tower.co.jp

One block south of the Tokeidai lies Ōdōri-kōen and the contrasting 147m red steel **Sapporo TV Tower**. During the snow festival, the viewing platform provides a lovely vista down the park, particularly at night. On a clear day, you can see the surrounding mountains and even the sea.

Susukino

すすきの

The neon-illuminated excess of **Susukino**, the largest area of bars, restaurants and nightclubs north of Tokyo, begins on the southern side of Ōdōri-kōen, and is best explored at night. If you're here during the day, you could follow the covered shopping arcade **Tanuki-kōji Shōtengai** (狸小路商店街) to its eastern end, where you'll find the lively **Nijō Fish Market** (二条市場; daily 7am –6pm), ideal for lunch or a fresh sushi breakfast (see p.296).

Sapporo Bier Garten and Beer Museum

サッポロビール園, Sapporo Biiru-en • サッポロビール博物館, Sapporo Biiru Hakubutsukan • Kita 7 Higashi 9 • **Museum** Daily 10.30am– 6pm • Free; one beer sample ¥200, three for ¥400 • ⓦ sapporobeer.jp • **Bier Garten** Daily 11.30am–10pm; Free; BBQ lamb ¥3370 • ⓦ www .sapporo-bier-garten.jp • Bus #88 runs every 20min directly to the complex (¥200) from behind Tōkyū department store, near Sapporo Station

The hugely popular **Sapporo Bier Garten and Beer Museum** stands just east of the city centre. It was an American adviser to Hokkaidō who noted the hops growing locally and realized that with its abundant winter ice, Sapporo was the ideal location for a commercial **brewery**. When the first brewery opened in 1876, locals didn't touch beer, so for years Sapporo exported to the foreign community in Tokyo, which is where the company's headquarters are now.

Built in 1891, this grand red-brick complex was originally the factory of the Sapporo Sugar Company; it's now Sapporo's smallest brewery, since much of the building has been turned over to an **exhibition** on the brewing process and the history of the company, not to mention several restaurants, pubs and souvenir shops. At the end of the exhibition, while sipping beer samples, you can admire a wall coated with a century's worth of colourful ad posters.

After you've learned all about the making of the beer, you can enjoy it at your leisure, along with a huge plate of Genghis Khan barbecued lamb, in the Bier Garten next door.

The bus that goes here from near Sapporo Station passes the **Sapporo Factory**, the first of Sapporo's breweries in the city, converted in 1993 into a shopping and entertainment complex (see p.298).

Hokkaidō Jingū

北海道神宮 • 474 Miyagaoka, Chuo-ku • 24hr • Free • ⓦ hokkaidojingu.or.jp • 15min from Maruyama-kōen Station on the Tōzai line

The upscale suburb of Maruyama-kōen is where you'll find the island's principal Shintō shrine, **Hokkaidō Jingū**, amid a leafy park where 1400 cherry trees break into pectacular blossom each May. See the website for details of annual major **festivals**, ncluding the main Festival June 14–16, when four *mikoshi*, or portable shrines, are paraded through the streets of Sapporo.

Sapporo Winter Sports Museum

札幌ウィンタースポーツミュージアム • Daily: May–Oct 9am–6pm, June–Sept Fri & Sat till 9pm; Nov–April 9.30am–5pm • ¥600: ski jump lift ¥500 return • Ⓦ sapporo-dc.co.jp • Bus #14 from Maruyama-kōen subway station to Ōkurayama Kyōgijō Iriguchi bus stop 10min), and then a 10min walk uphill; a taxi from Maruyama-kōen station is around ¥1000

The highlight of the fun **Sapporo Winter Sports Museum** which occupies the Ski Jump Stadium at Ōkurayama (大倉山), built for the 1972 Winter Olympics, is a ski jump simulator that gives you an idea of what it's like to participate in this daring winter sport. There are also simulations for bobslighing, cross-country skiing and speed skating, among other things – it's all a hoot, and afterwards you can ride the passenger lift to the top of the ski jump to see the view for real.

Historical Village of Hokkaidō

北海道開拓の村, Hokkaidō Kaitaku no Mura • 50-1 Konopporo, Atsubetsu-chō • May–Sept daily 9am–5pm; Oct–April Tues–Sun 9am–4.30pm • May–Sept ¥830, Oct–April ¥680; trolley car ¥270 • Ⓦ www.kaitaku.or.jp • Buses run directly to the Historical Village (Kaitaku no Mura) each morning from stop #3 at the south exit of Sapporo Station (around 1hr), or there are more frequent buses from platform 10 at the terminus beneath Shin Sapporo Station, connected to the city centre by both train and subway; you can also take a train from Sapporo Station to Shinrin-kōen Station (¥260; 15min) and then a bus from there to the park (¥200, 12min), or a taxi from Shin-Sapporo for ¥1000

The **Historical Village of Hokkaidō** is one of Hokkaidō's highlights. Laid out across spacious grounds in Nopporo Forest Park, this impressive outdoor museum contains some sixty buildings constructed between the mid-nineteenth and early twentieth centuries, as large-scale immigration from Honshū cranked up. Wandering around the village's four main areas, representing town, farm, mountain and fishing communities, will give you a strong impression of what Hokkaidō looked like before prefabricated buildings and concrete expressways became the norm.

The buildings have been **restored** as beautifully inside as out and spruced up with displays related to their former use, be it sweet shop, silkworm house or woodcutter's shanty. There are guides in some houses (Japanese-speaking only) and written English explanations in all. It's a good idea to wear slip-on shoes, as you'll be taking them off a lot to explore the interiors. In summer, you can hop aboard the horse-drawn trolley car that plies the main street – in winter this is replaced by a sleigh. Some of the houses are shut from December to April (hence the reduced admission fee), but the village is worth visiting even then for its special atmosphere when blanketed in snow.

4

WINTER SPORTS IN SAPPORO

As you'd expect for the location of the 1972 Winter Olympics, there are several good ski hills with in easy reach of Sapporo including **Teine** (Ⓦ sapporo-teine.com; 10–15min from Sapporo Station to Teine Station, then 15min by bus), **Kokusai** (Ⓦ sapporo-kokusai.jp/en; 1hr 30min from Sapporo Station by bus) and **Takino Snow World** (Ⓦ takinopark.com; subway to Makomanai Station on the Namboku line, then 35min on the bus to Suzuran-kōen Higashi-guchi), which offers six cross-country ski courses from 1–16km long, in addition to ski and snowboard slopes, snowshoe treks and sledding.

At **Snowmobile Land** (Ⓣ 0116 61 5355, Ⓦ snowmobileland.jp), you can take a ride on one of the eponymous machines over a 90km course that winds through the forests to viewpoints looking out over the city and, most dramatically, into the base of a quarry. Rates start at ¥10,000 for 60 minutes, or ¥13,500 for 90 minutes, including all protective gear. Women riders may drive single-seaters, but not the heavier double-seaters, which they may only ride pillion. To reach the course (usually open Dec to end March), take the subway to Hassamu Minami Station on the Tōzai line, then bus #41 to Fuku Entei-mae, which is the final stop.

To cover the whole site will take you at least half a day; either bring a picnic or try one of the inexpensive **restaurants** or refreshment stops within the village.

Historical Museum of Hokkaidō

北海道開拓記念館, Hokkaidō Kaitaku Kinenkan • 53-2 Konopporo, Atsubetsu-chō • Tues–Sun 9.30am–4.30pm • ¥500 • ⑩ www .hmh.pref.hokkaido.jp • Same travel details as for Historical Village of Hokkaidō (see p.293), but get off the bus one stop earlier at Kinenkan Iriguchi

As well as the Historical Village of Hokkaidō, the grounds of Nopporo Forest Park are also home to the mildly interesting **Historical Museum of Hokkaidō**, which contains over four thousand items showing the history of Hokkaidō from a million years ago to the present day. There are separate displays on the island's ancient times, Ainu history, colonization, the postwar period and the Hokkaidō of tomorrow.

Moerenuma Park

モエレ沼公園, Moerenuma Kōen • Park daily 7am–10pm; beach June 1–Sept 23 daily except Thurs 10am–4pm • Free • ⑩ sapporo-park.or.jp/moere • Subway to Kanjō-dōri Station on the Tōhō line, then from the bus terminal above the station take bus #69 or #79 (¥320) and get off at Moere-kōen Higashiguchi (combined journey around 40min) from where the park is a 5min walk

About 10km northeast of the city centre, **Moerenuma Park** is part playground, part sculpture garden, displaying the works of internationally renowned artist and landscape architect **Noguchi Isamu**. In the giant glass pyramid, with observation decks and a library/lounge, you can peruse English-language books about the artist, who died shortly after completing the masterplan for the park in 1988. With its massed plantings of cherry trees, wide lawns, the spectacular Sea Fountain water sculpture and a shallow pebbled bathing beach, the park is popular with local families and is a convivial spot for a picnic.

ARRIVAL AND DEPARTURE

SAPPORO

By plane New Chitose airport (新千歳空港; ☎0123 23 0111, ⑩new-chitose-airport.jp/en) is 40km southeast of Sapporo. From here, the fastest way to Sapporo is on the frequent JR train (35min; ¥1040); the bus is marginally cheaper (¥1000) but takes at least twice as long to arrive at the same point. There are also a few flights from Tokyo and Sendai to Okadama A irport (札幌丘珠空港, ☎0117 81 4161, ⑩okadama-Airport.co.jp/eng), 8km northeast of Sapporo, but it's mainly for services within Hokkaidō. A regular bus (30min; ¥400) runs from here to opposite the JR Sapporo station; the same journey by taxi costs around ¥3000.

Destinations from New Chitose (domestic) Akita (5 daily; 1hr); Aomori (3 daily; 50 min); Fukuoka (5 daily; 2hr 40min); Hakodate (2 daily; 40min); Hiroshima (2 daily; 2hr 15min); Kansai International (9 daily; 2hr); Kushiro (3 daily; 45min); Memanbetsu (6 daily; 45min); Nagoya (15 daily; 1hr 50min); Naha (daily; 4hr); Osaka (2hr 15 min); Sendai (18 daily; 1hr 10min); Tokyo (46 daily; 1hr 30min); Wakkanai (2 daily; 55min).

Destinations from New Chitose (international) China (Shanghai, Beijing, Hong Kong), South Korea (Seoul, Busan), Thailand (Bangkok), Hawaii (Honolulu), Taiwan (Taipei) and Guam.

Destinations from Okadama Hakodate (5 daily; 45min); Kushiro (4 daily; 45min); Rishiri (daily; 1 hr); Misawa (2 daily; 1hr).

By train Arriving by train, you'll pull in at busy JR Sapporo Station, six blocks north of Ōdōri-kōen, the park that bisects Sapporo from east to west.

Destinations: Abashiri (5 daily; 5hr 15min); Asahikawa (35 daily; 1hr 30min); Hakodate (11 daily; 3hr 30min); Kushiro (7 daily; 3hr 35min); New Chitose Airport (55 daily; 40min); Noboribetsu (15 daily; 1hr 10min); Osaka (daily; 22–23hr); Otaru (27 daily; 30min); Tokyo (6 daily; 9 hr 30min; overnight daily; 16–17hr); Tomakomai (16 daily; 40min); Wakkanai (3 daily; 5hr).

By bus Long-distance buses terminate at Chūō Bus Terminal just northeast of Ōdōri-kōen and Sapporo Station Bus Terminal on the south side of the train station beneath the Esta shopping complex.

Destinations Abashiri (9 daily; 6hr); Furano (11 daily; 2hr 30min); Kushiro (2 daily; 6hr 30min); Niseko (3 daily; 3hr); Noboribetsu (2 daily; 1hr 40min); Tōya-ko (daily; 3hr); Wakkanai (6 daily; 6hr).

By ferry The closest ferry port to Sapporo is Otaru (see p.298), 40km to the northwest; ferries arrive here from Maizuru (1 daily; 20hr–21hr 30min) and Niigata (1 daily except Mon; 18hr–19hr 30min). Ferries from Tokyo (Oarai port) arrive at Tomakomai, 70km to the south (daily, 18hr), as do ferries from Akita (daily, 10hr 30min–12hr); Hachinohe (4 daily, 7–9hr); Nagoya (3 or 4 per week, 40hr); Niigata (daily, 18hr–20hr); Sendai (daily, 15 hr); and Tsuruga (daily, 32–34 hr).

INFORMATION

Tourist information Sapporo has several excellent tourist information facilities, all staffed by English-speakers. Start your visit at the Hokkaidō-Sapporo Food and Tourism Information Centre (daily 8.30am–8pm; ☎0112 13 5088, ⓦ www.city.sapporo.jp) inside Sapporo Station. You can sort out train tickets and rail passes here, as well as access the internet and do some food souvenir shopping. More leaflets, along with English books, magazines, free internet access

and a jobs and events noticeboard, are available at the Sapporo International Communications Plaza "i" (Mon–Sat 9am–5.30pm; ☎012 11 3678, ⓦ plaza-sapporo.or.jp), on the 3rd floor of the MN Building, opposite the Tokeidai, the city's famous clock tower.

Listings Look out for the monthly free listings newsletter *What's on in Sapporo*, available at the tourist offices around town.

GETTING AROUND

Most of Sapporo's sights are within easy **walking distance** of each other, but the efficient network of **subways** and **buses** can be useful if you get tired. Public transport stops running at around 11.30pm, after which you can hail one of the many taxis that roam Sapporo's streets.

Passes There are all-day passes for the subway (¥800) or a combined all-day pass covering the subway, tram and the city routes of the JR, Jotetsu and Chūō bus lines for ¥1000 (¥500 on Sat, Sun and holidays). For long-term visitors, the "With You" pre-paid travel card, which gives ten percent extra travel for free and is valid on all types of transport, is useful.

By subway There are three subway lines: the green Namboku line (南北線) and the blue Tōhō line (東豊線) run from north to south through Sapporo Station, while the orange Tōzai line (東西線) intersects them both, running east to west under Ōdōri-kōen. The lowest fare is ¥200, which covers all the stops in the city centre between Sapporo Station in the north and Nakajima-kōen in the

south, and Maruyama-kōen in the west and Higashi Sapporo in the east.

By tram There's a purple tram line, which for a flat fare of ¥170 runs from Nishi-Yon-Chōme, just south of Ōdōri-kōen, out to Mount Moiwa, south of the city, and back to Susukino.

By bus Buses depart from in front of the Esta building next to Sapporo Station, or nearby; fares start at ¥200.

By car Car rental companies include: Eki Rent-a-Car ☎0112 41 0931; Nippon Rent-a-Car, Sapporo Station north exit branch ☎0117 46 0919; and Orix Rent-a-Car ☎0117 26 0543.

By taxi Call the Taxi Association (☎0118 92 6000; Japanese only) to book a cab.

ACCOMMODATION

Even though Sapporo has plenty of accommodation, places get booked up well in advance of the summer season and the snow festival in Feb. There can be great bargains to be had at the upmarket hotels in winter when rates are slashed.

Best Western Hotel Fino Sapporo ベストウェスタンホテルフィーノ札幌 Kita 8, Nishi 4-15 ☎0117 29 4055, ⓦ bwjapan.co.jp/finosapporo. The stylish design in a natural palette of colours helps this business hotel stand out from the crowd around the station. Bathrooms include massage showers, and there's a pleasant café next to the lobby where the buffet breakfast is served. **¥18,900**

Hotel Clubby Sapporo ホテルクラビーサッポロ Kita 2, Higashi 3 ☎0112 42 1111 ⓦ sapporofactory.jp/clubby/english. This smart hotel is part of the Sapporo Factory redevelopment. Leather and wood fittings lend an

old-fashioned air to the lobby and restaurant, but the rooms are modern, spacious and elegantly decorated. **¥25,410**

★**Cross Hotel** クロスホテル札幌 2-23 Kita, Nishi 2 ☎0112 72 0010, ⓦ crosshotel.com/eng_sapporo. The city's best boutique-style hotel offers rooms in three appealing decorative styles (natural, urban and hip), a relaxing rooftop pool and bath, and a cool lounge bar. **¥22,600**

★**Ino's Place** イノーズプレイス 4-6-5 3-Higashi-Sapporo, Shiroishi-ku ☎0118 32 1828, ⓦ inos-place .com. Few – if any – hostels have a juggling shop, but there's one at this cosy, welcoming place run by the

---

SAPPORO ADDRESSES

Finding your way around central Sapporo is easy compared to many other Japanese cities because every address has a precise location within the city's **grid plan**. The city blocks are named and numbered according to the compass points, the apex being the **TV Tower** in Ōdōri-kōen. Sapporo Station, for example, is six blocks north of the TV Tower and three blocks west, so its address is Kita 6 (North Six), Nishi 3 (West Three), while **Nijō Fish Market** is Minami 3 (South Three), Higashi 1-2 (East One-Two).

wonderfully friendly Eiji and Miwa (who both speak fluent English). It's a 5min walk from Shiroishi subway station on the Tōzai line. Dorm **¥2900**, single **¥3800**

JR Tower Hotel Nikkō Sapporo JRタワーホテル日航 札幌 Kita 5, Nishi 2-5 ☎0112 51 2222, ⓦwww.jrhotels .co.jp. Dazzling views are guaranteed from the smallish rooms and the 35th-floor bar and restaurant of this luxury hotel, which occupies the top dozen floors of the JR Tower atop Sapporo Station. Facilities include a spa on the 22nd floor which has real onsen water pumped in. Twenty percent off with a JR rail card. **¥29,000**

★**Nakamuraya Ryokan** 中村屋旅館 Kita 3, Nishi 7 ☎0112 41 2111, ⓦwww.nakamura-ya.com/English. html. This high-quality Japanese inn is a wonderful choice. The tatami rooms are spacious, the maids wear kimono and there's a café in the lobby. **¥14,700**

Sapporo Grand Hotel 札幌グランドホテル Kita 1, Nishi 4 ☎0112 61 3311, ⓦgrand1934.com. Dating back to 1934, the city's first European-style hotel has some very nicely remodelled rooms, and there's an unbeatable range of facilities, including a spa and small display area on the hotel and city's history. **¥21,000**

Sapporo International Youth Hostel 札幌国際ユー スホステル Toyohira 6-5-35 6jō ☎0118 25 3120, ⓦyouthhostel.or.jp/kokusai. Just east of Exit 2 of Gakuen-mae Station on the Tōhō-line, this large modern hostel has dorm rooms, tatami rooms for families, and twins for married couples. English is spoken. Dorm **¥3200**, double **¥7600**

Spa Safro スパ サフロ Minami 6, Nishi 5 ☎0115 31 2233, ⓦwww.safro.org. Amazingly luxurious and excellent-value capsule hotel in the heart of Susukino. Facilities include ornamental baths, massage and treatments and a mini-cinema. There's also a floor of capsules for women. Check-in is from 5pm. Add ¥500 to prices on weekends. Women **¥4100**, men **¥3800**

EATING

Sapporo is renowned for its **ramen** – try the version called *batā-kōn*, which is a noodle broth laden with butter and corn. Another local speciality is the lamb *jingisukan* BBQ (see box below).

Aji-no-Tokeidai 味の時計台 Kita 1, Nishi 3 ☎0112 21 3330. A dependable and inexpensive noodle chain, serving large tasty bowls of ramen – ¥950 for the Sapporo speciality of butter-corn noodles. You'll be asked whether you want your soup flavoured with miso, *shōyu* (soy sauce) or *shio* (salt). Daily 11am–1am.

Daruma だるま Minami 5, Nishi 4 ☎0115 52 6013. This is the original cosy fifteen-seater branch of this *jingisukan* chain, tucked away on a narrow street in the midst of Susukino; look for the red lantern and scowling bald Genghis on the sign outside. One plate of meat costs ¥735. If it's full, you could try the larger places at Minami 6, Nishi 4 and Minami 4, Nishi 4 (all with same opening hours). Daily 5pm–2.30am, Fri & Sat till 4.30am, Sun till 12.30am.

Donburi-chaya どんぶり茶屋 Nijō Ichiba, Minami 3, Higashi 1-2, within Nijō Fish Market ☎0112 00 2223. There's often a queue of people waiting here for the rice bowls topped with a selection of fresh seafood, which go for around ¥1500. The miso soup comes with crab, and they also do a *jingisukan* and scallop rice bowl combo. 7am–5.30pm, closed Wed.

Ebiten Bunten 蛯天分店 Minami 2, Nishi 4 ☎0112 71 2867 ⓦebiten.co.jp. Great-value tempura restaurant, with a stuffed brown bear for decoration. You can get a meal of rice topped by plump batter-covered prawns for under ¥1000. Daily 11.30am–10pm.

Kushidori 串鳥 Minami 2, Nishi 5 ☎0112 22 1231. A row of red lanterns dangles from the front of this busy *yakitori* joint. Sit at the counter to take in the full atmosphere of the place. An English menu eases ordering from a wide range of skewered delights, starting at around ¥115 a serving. Daily 4.30pm–12.30am.

Maruyama Drill マルヤマドリル Kita 1, Nishi 27 ☎0112 13 7374. A cute café-bar serving an appealing range of inexpensive curry rice dishes as well as huge

---

MEAL FIT FOR A KHAN

Lamb is an uncommon meat on Japanese menus, but not in Sapporo, home of the *jingisukan*, or "Genghis Khan" BBQ. This delicious feast of flame-grilled meat and vegetables gets its name from the convex table grill on which it's cooked, said to resemble the Mongolian-warrior's helmet. All of the restaurants at the **Sapporo Bier Garten** (see p.292) next to the Sapporo Beer Museum (see p.292) offer the dish, as does the rival beer garden **Kirin Biiru-en**. At either, you can pig out on as much BBQ and beer as you can within one hundred minutes, for a set price of around ¥3700. You'll be provided with a plastic bib to protect against dribbles from the dipping sauce, but it's still best to dress down, since the smell of sizzled mutton lingers long after you've left. The big beer gardens, packed with tourists, have a boisterous Germanic quality; for a more intimate *jingisukan* experience, try *Daruma* (see above).

gourmet burgers for about ¥1000 and home-made apple, orange and tomato juice. It's a block west of Maruyama-kōen subway station, behind the bus station. Daily 11.30am–midnight.

Rāmen Yokochō ラーメン横丁 Minami 5, Nishi 3. A huge bowl of freshly cooked noodles at any of the busy ramen joints in Rāmen Yokochō ("Ramen Alley") costs under ¥1000 Daily around 11am–2am.

Suginome 杉ノ目 Minami 5, Nishi 5 ☎ 0115 21 0888. Housed in a historic stone building, this traditionally decorated place is a good spot in which to sample

kaiseki-style course meals made using local produce from ¥7350. Mon–Sat 5–11pm.

Yamatoya 大和家 Kita 1, Nishi 2 ☎ 0112 41 6353. Reasonably priced, unassuming sushi and tempura shop behind the clock tower that gets the nod from local foodies. A tempura-*teishoku* set lunch costs ¥1050. Mon–Sat 11am–3pm & 5–10pm.

Yukikaze 雪風 Minami 7, Nishi 4. Customers eagerly queue up at this convivial, late-night ramen shop where the noodle dish (¥1000) is made with loving care and better-than-average ingredients. Daily 9pm–3am.

DRINKING AND NIGHTLIFE

Amid the myriad hostess clubs and sex joints of the neon-drenched party district of **Susukino**, there are plenty of reputable bars and restaurants, making it easy to avoid the sleazy places. The covered shopping arcade **Tanuki-kōji** also has a good selection of bars. In the summer, outdoor **beer gardens** sprout across the city, including in Ōdōri-kōen.

BARS

Habana ハバナ Minami 3, Nishi 6. On the second and third floors along Tanuki-kōji shopping arcade, this Cuban-styled café-bar offers spicy chicken, rice entrées and lively Latin American music, plus occasional salsa parties. Daily 6pm–3am.

Hokkaidō Milk Mura 北海道ミルク村 6F New Hokusai Building, Minami 4, Nishi 3 ☎ 0112 19 6455. Hokkaidō is famous in Japan for the quality of its milk products, and in this quirkily decorated bar, all sorts of flavours of ice cream are paired with liqueurs to make original cocktails. Daily noon–midnight.

Kopitiam コピティアム Minami 3, Nishi 7 ☎ 0112 19 7773. Take an instant holiday from Japan at this fairly authentic Singaporean café-bar at the far west end of Tanuki-kōji shopping arcade. It's a relaxed place for a drink or light bite to eat. 6pm–2am, closed Tues.

Pete's Bar ピーツ・バー Minami 3, Nishi 1 ☎ petesbar .jp. Offering a similar formula to *TK6* (see below), this is another convivial *gaijin* bar with reasonable pub grub and committed regulars. There's live acoustic music on the last Thursday of the month. Mon–Fri 5pm–late, Sat & Sun noon–late.

TK6 ティ・ケイ・シックス Minami 2, Nishi 6 ☎ tk6.jp. At the western end of the Tanuki-kōji arcade, this spacious and relaxed *gaijin*-run café-bar serves Aussie meat pies, salads and burgers (around ¥800) with their draught ales. Daily 4pm–late.

CLUBS

Alife エーライフ Minami 4, Nishi 5 ☎ alife.jp. One of the larger clubs in Sapporo, with a variety of DJ events, theme parties and special shows. Price varies depending on the night; Fri & Sat women pay ¥2500, men pay ¥3000; there's one drink included in entry. Daily 8pm–5am.

Precious Hall プレシャスホール No 9 Green Building Basement, Minami 4, Nishi 7 ☎ precioushall.com. This venue has an amazing sound system and is a great place for live shows and visiting DJs. Entry prices vary. Thurs–Sat and other days on ad hoc basis depending on event.

Sound Lab Mole Sound Lab モール Nikō Building Basement, Minami 3, Nishi 6 ☎ mole-sapporo.jp. You'll find this club in a basement off the Tanuki-kōji arcade. It's open most days, either for live bands or club nights. Entry prices vary depending on what's on. Most days; hours vary depending on event.

ENTERTAINMENT

Sapporo Concert Hall Kitara 札幌コンサートホールキタラ Kitara 1-15 Nakajima-kōen ☎ 0115 20 2000, ☎ kitara-sapporo.or.jp. This concert hall in Nakajima Park hosts regular classical and other popular music concerts by Japanese and

visiting overseas musicians; see website for listings.

Theater Kino シアターキノ 2F Grand Building, Minami 2, Nishi 6 ☎ 0112 31 9355, ☎ theaterkino.net. A two-screen cinema showing mainly art-house films, with subtitles.

GAY AND LESBIAN SAPPORO

Next to Tokyo, Sapporo has Japan's most visible gay and lesbian bar scene and used to trump the capital with its **Rainbow March**, Japan's longest-running lesbian, gay and transgender parade, held every Sept in Susukino since 1996, though the march in 2013 was rumoured to be its last. Although it's dated, the web document **Queer Hokkaidō** (☎ hajet.org/lifearticles/Queer_Hokkaido.pdf) is also a useful reference with some recommendations for outside of Sapporo, too. *Sound Lab Mole* (see above) and *Precious Hall* (see above) sometimes host gay dance nights.

4

NORIA FERRIS WHEEL

A popular date spot in Sapporo is the fluorescent multicoloured **Noria Ferris wheel** (Mon–Thurs & Sun 11am–11pm, Fri & Sat 11am–3am; ¥600), atop the Norbesa shopping mall at Minami 3, Nishi 5. There's a wonderful view of the city lights from the top.

BARS

Hearty Café ハーティ・カフェ 2F Dai-ichi Family Building, Minami 5, Nishi 7 ☎ 0115 30 6022. A relatively spacious bar where *gaijin* should receive a friendly welcome. Admission of ¥1500 includes one drink. Daily 8pm–3am, Fri & Sat till 4am.

SA Building SAビル Minami 6, Nishi 6. The SA Building is home to twenty-plus tiny gay bars, seating ten to twenty people in each. Opening hours vary.

SHOPPING

Daimaru 大丸 Kita 5, Nishi 4 ⓦ daimaru.co.jp. Located at the west end of Sapporo Station complex, with eight floors of top-end products. Daily 10am–8pm.

ICI Ishii Sports ICI石井スポーツ Kita 11, Nishi 15 ⓦ ici-sports.com. A well-equipped outdoor gear shop, away from the city centre. Daily 10am–8pm.

Kinokuniya Books 紀伊國屋 Kita 5, Nishi 5 ⓦ www .kinokuniya.co.jp. Just west of Sapporo Station, this has the best selection of English-language books and magazines. Daily 10am–9pm.

Royce ロイス Minami 1, Nishi 3 ⓦ royce.com. Chocolate from the city's top confectioners, Royce', is a good souvenir to get in Sapporo. You can find it in the food courts of most department stores, including Mitsukoshi's. Daily 10am–8pm.

Nissen Sports ニッセンスポーツ Minami 3, Nishi 3 ⓦ xc-nissen.com. This sports shop is a great place to come for cross-country skis and gear. Daily 10am–8pm.

Sapporo Factory サッポロファクトリー Kita 2, Higashi 4 ⓦ sapporofactory.jp. This was the first of Sapporo's breweries in the city, converted in 1993 into a shopping and entertainment complex. It now has dozens of outlets, with a huge selection of outdoor clothing and camping gear in the block furthest back from the street. Daily 10am–8pm.

Stellar Place ステラプレイス Kita 5, Nishi 2 ⓦ stellarplace.net. This seven-floor shopping mall is located next to Sapporo Station. Daily 10am–9pm.

Tanuki-kōji 狸小路商店街 Minami 3 ⓦ tanukikoji .or.jp. The oldest shopping street in Hokkaidō, this covered shopping arcade stretches for six blocks across Minami 3 and is well worth exploring.

Tōkyū 東急 Kita 4, Nishi 2 ⓦ tokyu-dept.co.jp. Just across from Sapporo Station, this department store has 11 floors to choose from. Daily 10am–8pm.

Tōkyū Hands 東急ハンズ Minami 1, Nishi 6 ⓦ tokyu-hands.co.jp. A great place for souvenir shopping, with seven floors of hobby, DIY and lifestyle products. Daily 10am–8pm.

DIRECTORY

Banks The Bank of Tokyo Mitsubishi, Ōdōri, Nishi 3, changes all major currencies, as does the Ōdōri post office (one block west), the Central Post Office and Hokkaidō Bank, Minami 1, Nishi 3.

Consulates Australia (Kita 5, Nishi 6; ☎ 0112 42 4381); China (Minami 13, Nishi 23; ☎ 0115 63 6191); South Korea (Kita 2, Nishi 12; ☎ 0116 21 0288); Russia (Minami 14, Nishi 12; ☎ 0115 61 3171); US (Kita 1, Nishi 28; ☎ 0116 41 1115).

Emergencies The main police station is at Kita 1, Nishi 5 (☎ 0112 42 0110). In an absolute emergency, contact the Foreign Advisory Service on ☎ 0112 41 9110. For other emergency numbers, see p.66.

Hospital Sapporo City General Hospital is at Kita 11, Nishi 13 (☎ 0117 26 2211).

Internet Terminals are available at both main tourist offices (see p.295). Alternatively, there are plenty of internet cafés and manga cafés offering facilities; try the *i-café* with branches at Norbesa, Minami 3, Nishi 5, and Sapporo Century Royal Hotel, Kita 5, Nishi 5, near Sapporo Station. Rates start at ¥200 for 30min.

Laundry Sukatto (Kita 4, Nishi 12-1).

Post office The Central Post Office is at Kita 6, Higashi 1 (daily 9am–7pm, Sat till 5pm, Sun till 12.30pm). There's also a branch in the Paseo shopping centre in the JR Sapporo station complex (daily 10am–7pm, Sat & Sun till 5pm).

Otaru and around

小樽

The attractive port of **OTARU**, some 40km northwest of Sapporo, grew rich at the turn of the nineteenth century on the back of herring fishing and as a base for the modern development of Hokkaidō. Reminders of this wealth remain in the shape of scores of handsome, heritage-listed Meiji-era buildings. Parts of town are touristy, but to escape the crowds just hop on a bus to **Shukutsu**, where you'll find a couple of the best architectural examples from Otaru's glory days. In summer, take a **canal cruise** from Asakusa-bashi bridge to see the town from the water (see p.301). In Februrary, Otaru hosts its **Snow Light Path Festival** at the same time as Sapporo, though on a much smaller scale, with small snow sculptures and lanterns running along the canal and the old train line.

If you have trouble finding somewhere to stay in Sapporo, Otaru makes an easy base for excursions back to Sapporo, or on to **Yoichi** if you're interested in the whisky distillery. However, it's also a pleasant place to spend a day or two in its own right. Otaru's romantic, antique atmosphere is best experienced beside the **Otaru Unga** (小樽運河), the portside canal lined with brick warehouses, particularly the section between Chūō-dōri, the main street heading towards the harbour from the train station, and parallel Nichigin-dōri. **Sakai-machi Hon-dōri** (堺町本通り), which shadows the canal to the south, is a street worth exploring, particularly for its many-cut and blown-glass shops.

Bank of Japan Otaru Museum

日本銀行旧小樽支店金融資料館, Nihon Ginkō Kū-Otaru Shiten Kinyū Shiryōkan • Nichigin-dōri, 1-11-16 Ironai • Tues–Sun 9.30am–5pm • Free

The **Bank of Japan Otaru Museum**, a stone and brick structure dating from 1912, was designed by Kingo Tatsuno, the architect of the original red-brick Tokyo Station. Look for the striped owl keystones decorating the exterior – the birds are guardian deities of

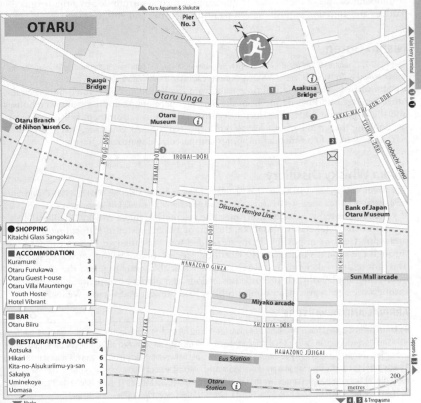

the Ainu. Inside, the 10.5m-high ceiling of the main banking hall looks as impressive today as it must have to Otaru's citizens back in the early twentieth century.

Tenguyama

天狗山 • **Ropeway** Daily 9am–9pm • Return ¥1100 • **Ski lift** Dec–Feb 9am–8pm; March 9am–5pm • Day-ticket ¥3100 • ⓦ bit.ly/IVv5jF • Buses (¥210) run to the cable-car from platform #3 outside Otaru Station (15min)

For a wonderful view of Otaru and the bay, ride the ropeway (cable-car) up **Tenguyama**, southwest of the station, where the panoramic view has been designated one of the top three in Hokkaidō. There's a restaurant, an interesting archive outlining the history of ski materials and a free exhibition of more than seven hundred Tengu masks from all over Japan (Tengu is the long-nosed goblin after whom the mountain is named). There's also good skiing in winter with half a dozen runs varying in difficulty.

Nishin Goten Otaru Kihinkan Villa

にしん御殿小樽貴賓館 • 3-63 Shukutsu • Daily: 9am–5pm, Jan–March till 4pm • ¥1000 • Bus #11 from Otaru Station heads to Shukutsu (20min); in summer (April 1– Oct 14), a great alternative is to hop on the Otaru Aquarium-bound boats from Otaru's Pier no. 3

From Otaru, it's about 6km to **Shukutsu** (祝津), home of the area's best sight: the spectacular traditional Japanese villa **Nishin Goten Otaru Kihinkan Villa**. The Aoyama family, herring tycoons of the early twentieth century, spared little expense when they commissioned this beautiful wooden building, which is surrounded by ornamental gardens and contains exquisite screen paintings, fixtures and antique pieces.

Nishin Goten

鰊御殿 • 3-228 Shukutsu • Daily: April–Oct 9am–5pm; Nov 9am–4pm • ¥300 • Bus #11 from Otaru Station heads to Shukutsu (20min); in summer (April 1– Oct 14), a great alternative is to hop on the Otaru Aquarium-bound boats from Otaru's Pier no. 3

By Shukutsu Harbour, a ten-minute walk from the Kihinkan Villa, you'll find several other heritage buildings dating from the herring boom era, including stone warehouses and the large-scale fishermen's dormitory **Nishin Goten** in a prominent hillside position overlooking the small harbour – look out for its red roof. As you'll see, this area is refreshingly free of commercial trappings compared to downtown Otaru.

Nikka Whisky Distillery

余市蒸溜所, Yoichi Jōryūsho • 7-6 Kurokawa-chō, Yoichi • Daily 9am–5pm; regular tours (1hr) • Free • ☎ 0135 23 3131, ⓦ nikka.com/eng/distilleries • Yoichi is one stop west of Otaru on the train line, and the distillery is a 1min walk from the station

If you're interested in whisky, don't miss the fascinating **Nikka Whisky Distillery**. This was founded by **Taketsuru Masataka**, the son of a sake brewer in Hiroshima prefecture (see box opposite). There are guided **tours** in Japanese, or you can wander through the grounds following the distilling process, before trying some free samples. The film telling Taketsuru and Rita's story is particularly moving, and there's an interesting display of their personal possessions and Nikka advertising materials through the ages featuring, amongst others, Rod Stewart and Orson Welles.

ARRIVAL AND DEPARTURE
OTARU

By train Limited express trains (¥620) from Sapporo take 30–45min to reach Otaru JR Station. Local trains are slower and slightly cheaper (roughly every 15min).

By bus Buses to the city from Sapporo are slower (55min; every 10min) and marginally less expensive than trains.

By ferry Ferries (☎ 0134 22 6191) from Niigata (see p.270) and Maizuru (north of Kyoto) dock at the ferry terminal, some 5km east of the train station. Regular buses run between the ferry terminal and the train station; a taxi will cost around ¥1000.

Destinations Maizuru (1 daily; 20hr–21hr 30min); Niigata (1 daily except Mon; 18hr–19hr 30min).

THE WHISKY OF YOICHI

Having studied the painstaking art of sake brewing, **Taketsuru Masataka** developed a passion for Scotch whisky, and went to study the techniques of whisky-making in Scotland in 1918. While there he met and married a young Scottish girl, Rita Cowan, despite the objections of her parents, and took her back with him when he returned to Japan two years later.

Taketsuru and Rita eventually established a **whisky distillery** (see opposite) in 1934 in Yoichi, which Taketsuru rightly realized had the necessary climate and conditions for whisky production. The distillery came under the control of the military in 1940 shortly after the release of its first distilled whisky, and for the duration of the war it made cheap **military ration whisky**. After the war, the company's investors insisted he focus the distillery's efforts on producing cheap, low-quality whisky, believing the Japanese population couldn't afford the luxury of high-class spirits. But Taketsuru continued to improve his methods on the side, and in 1964 was able to sell three grades of whisky for the first time. In 2008, Yoichi 20 Year Old was voted best **single malt** at the World Whisky Awards.

INFORMATION AND CRUISES

Tourist information There's a helpful tourist office inside the train station (daily 9am–6pm; ☎ 0134 29 1333, ⓦ www.city.otaru.lg.jp), plus a couple of other tourist offices up by the canal – a larger one next to the Otaru Museum (daily 9am–6pm; ☎ 0134 33 1661), and a tiny one by Asakusa Bridge (daily 9am–6pm; ☎ 0134 23 7740).

Canal cruise In the warmer months, you can get a good perspective of the town on a cruise from Asakusa-bashi bridge (April–Oct, 40min loop; day cruise ¥1200, night cruise ¥1500; ☎ 0134 31 1733).

ACCOMMODATION

★**Kuramure** 蔵群 2-685 Asarigawa Onsen ☎ 0134 51 5151, ⓞ kuramure.com/en. Nestling in a valley bubbling with hot springs, 20min drive from Otaru Chikko Station, this elegant modern ryokan combines contemporary design with traditional architectural touches. Basic rates include breakfast, or you can have two meals included in the price. **¥42,000**; with 2 meals **¥63,000**

Otaru Furukawa 小樽ふる川 2-15-1 Ironai ☎ 0134 29 2345, ⓦ otaru-furukawa.com/english. A pleasing mix of a traditional Japanese inn and Western-style hotel, offering great extras such as the opportunity to hire a private bath (¥2100 for 50min) with a view of the Otaru canal. Rates include two meals. **¥36,000**

Otaru Guest House 小樽ゲストハウス 3-9-5 Midori ☎ 0134 22 4162. This delightful guesthouse occupies a 1927 building combining Western and Japanese influences. There are three rooms in the main building and one in the attached *kura* (storehouse). Take bus #19 from Otaru Station to Shōgyō Gakkō-mae. **¥11,600**

Otaru Villa Mauntengu Youth Hostel 小樽ヴィラ・マウンテングYH 2-13-1 Mogami ☎ 0134 33 7080, ⓦ tengu.co.jp. There are great views of Otaru from this pleasant pension-style hostel near the cable-car up Tenguyama – take bus #9 from the station to the final stop. Dorm **¥3350**, double **¥7600**

Hotel Vibrant ホテル ヴィブラント 1-3-1 Ironai ☎ 0134 31 3939, ⓦ vibrant-otaru.jp. Occupying a former bank, the *Vibrant* offers good-value rooms with wooden floors. Rates include breakfast served in the soaring ex-banking hall. **¥6500**

EATING AND DRINKING

Otaru is renowned for its sushi and sashimi restaurants. If unusual ice-cream flavours are more your thing, then Otaru may offer your only chance to tick off such flavours as sea urchin and *nattō* (fermented soyabeans), amongst others.

Aotsuka 青塚 Opposite the harbour, Shukutsu ☎ 0134 22 8034. Drop by this simple waterside café, below the fishermen's dormitory, for super-fresh fish dishes (around ¥1000). Herring, the fish that made the areas fortunes, are grilled outside. Daily 10am–7pm.

Hikari 光 Miyako-dōri Arcade ☎ 0134 22 0933. Good for a cup of coffee and cake for under ¥1000, this hushed café, open since 1933 and packed to the rafters with antique glass lamps and china, is a rare treat and generally unmobbed by the tourist throng. 10.30am–6pm, closed Wed.

Kita-no-Aisukuriimu-ya-san 北のアイスクリーム屋さん 1-2-18 Ironai ☎ 0134 23 8983. Popular ice-cream parlour offering unique flavours such as squid, sea urchin and *nattō*, alongside more common ones. ¥300 for a single scoop, ¥450 for a double. Daily 10am–7pm (Oct–April till 4pm).

4

SAPPORO-OTARU WELCOME PASS

JR Hokkaidō's good-value **Sapporo-Otaru Welcome Pass** (¥1500), available to overseas visitors, includes a return train ticket and a one-day Sapporo subway ticket. There's also the **Otaru Furii Kippu** (¥1900) which combines return train travel from Sapporo with a Chūō bus one-day pass (¥750 if bought separately) to get around town. This is valid on the three **Stroller Bus** lines which are otherwise ¥210/ride, and will take you out to Shukutsu, up to Tenguyama or to the sights around town.

Otaru Biiru 小樽ビール 5-4 Minato-machi ☎0134 21 2323 🌐otarubeer.com. This microbrewery beside the Otaru Canal turns out quaffable German-style ales, and you can take a free 20min guided tour in English if you want to see behind the scenes. Wurst sausage plates are ¥500, and pizzas are less than ¥1000. Daily 11am–11pm.

Sakaiya さかい家 4-4 Sakai-machi ☎0134 29 0105. Occupying a handsome 1907 wooden building, this café is a charming place to sample green tea and traditional sweets. April–Oct 10am–5pm, Nov–March 10am–6pm.

Uminekoya 海猫屋 2-2-14 Ironai ☎0134 34 8222, 🌐uminekoya.com. In an old warehouse covered in ivy, one block back from the canal, this is a cosy, atmospheric place for a drink or a light meal of Western or Japanese food. Pasta dishes are under ¥2000, pork curry is ¥840 and clam chowder soup is ¥650. Free wi-fi is available. 11.30am–2pm & 5.30–9pm, closed Tues.

★**Uomasa** 魚真 2-5-11 Inaho ☎0134 29 0259. You'll find scores of touristy sushi restaurants on Sakai-machi Hon-dōri, but this one on a side street closer to Otaru Station is a winner. Their fifteen-piece sushi set is great value at ¥2500. Mon–Sat noon–2pm & 4–10pm.

SHOPPING

Kitaichi Glass Sangokan 北一硝子三号館 7-26 Sakaimachi ☎0134 33 1993, 🌐kitaichiglass.co.jp. This is a good place to shop for the glass souvenirs Otaru is famous for. Daily 9am–6pm.

Niseko

ニセコ

Around 70km south of Otaru is **NISEKO**, Japan's premier **winter resort**, with awesome amounts of perfect powder snow and top-class, interlinked ski fields. The resort hugs Mount Niseko Annupuri and faces the dormant volcano Mount Yōtei-san (also known as the Ezo Fuji for its resemblance to its more famous southern cousin). The village of **Hirafu** (比羅夫), close to the area's main town of **Kutchan** (倶知安), has seen the brunt of development, much of it through foreign investment and not all of it particularly sympathetic to the magnificent natural surroundings.

During the ski season (Dec–April) the *gaijin* population of Hirafu booms as skiers jet in from as far afield as Melbourne, Hong Kong and London to take advantage of a fantastic range of facilities, including stylish accommodation and dining options. Situated within the Niseko-Shakotan-Otaru Quasi National Park, the area also makes a good **summer base** when it's far less crowded and becomes the focal point for many **adventure sports** including whitewater rafting, mountain biking and kayaking.

ARRIVAL AND GETTING AROUND

In summer, public transport is scaled back and it gets a whole lot trickier (but not impossible) to get here – and to get around – without your own **car**.

By train Alight from the train at Kutchan and connect to Hirafu by bus (15min; free). Various return packages offered by JR from either Sapporo or Otaru make things really simple and can be unbeatable deals: for example, train, bus, ski-lift ticket and ski or snowboard rental for ¥5500 for the day – check with tourist information in Sapporo (see p.295) for what's available.

By bus Many buses run directly to the ski slopes from Sapporo and New Chitose Airport (from around ¥2300 one-way). Good access information is available at 🌐nisekotourism.com.

By car Peak Niseko Car Rental in Kutchan (🌐nisekocarrental.com) rent out 4WDs and can deliver to your accommodation.

By bike You can rent bikes from The Bicycle Corner in Niseko (walkthe-bicycle-corner.com) and Rhythm Tours in Kutchan (wnisekocycles.com), who can arrange tours and provide advice on your cycling plans.

INFORMATION

Tourist information Both Kutchan (9am–6pm; ☎0136 22 3344) and Niseko stations (daily 9am–6pm; ☎0136 44 2468) have small tourist information booths where you might find English-speaking assistants. There's also a welcome centre at the Grand Hirafu Parking Lot No. 1 (8.30am–6pm), where the bus from Kutchan terminates. More information is available at wnisekotourism.com.

ACCOMMODATION

Niseko's best selection of **hotels** and **pensions** is clustered at Hirafu. If you're looking for somewhere more peaceful, consider the options at Annupuri, Hanazono and Higashiyama, all of which are nearby. There are plenty of **self-catering** apartments and chalets; apart from those listed below, try Hokkaido Tracks (☎0136 23 3503, whokkaidotracks.com). Unless otherwise mentioned, all rates below include breakfast.

HIRAFU

Grand Papa グランパパ 163 Yamada ☎0136 23 2244, wniseko-grandpapa.com. Largish, convivial pension with an alpine theme: they even offer fondue dinners. Japanese culture classes are also held here. Add ¥1000/person for en suite. **¥13,000**

★**Hirafutei** ひらふ亭 204 Yamada ☎0136 23 2239, whirafute.info/en. This large hotel is handily located for the ski lifts, with all-you-can-eat buffet meals and great onsen baths. **¥26,250**

J-Sekka ジェイセッカ 167-3 Aza-Yamada ☎0136 21 6133, wj-sekka.com. A set of spacious self-catering apartments is attached to this fab restaurant/deli complex (see p.304). The decor successfully mixes Japanese antique rusticity with icy-white smoothness, and they also have a gym. Minimum stay is three nights. **¥33,000**

★**Kimamaya by Odin** ペンション気まま舎 170-248 Aza-Yamada ☎0136 23 2603, wkimamaya.com. French expat Nicolas Gontard has created a charming, modern pension from the bones of an old minshuku, preserving the beams and cosy atmosphere. Meals are taken in the glass-sided *Barn* restaurant next door, which looks spectacular when lit up at night. **¥26,000**

The Vale Niseko ザ・ヴェール・ニセコ 194-5 Aza-Yamada ☎0136 22 0038, wthevaleniseko.com. Ski-in, ski-out self-catering apartments and hotel rooms are available at this well-designed contemporary complex with a lively restaurant/bar, relaxing onsen and tiny lap pool. **¥26,400**

ANNUPURI, HANAZONO AND HIGASHIYAMA

Black Diamond Lodge ブラックダイヤモンドロッジ 24-3 Higashiyama ☎0136 44 1144, wbdlodge.com. One of Niseko's best backpacker lodges, this comfortable place includes breakfast in its rates and has a lively restaurant and bar. They also arrange various ski tours and packages as well as equipment rental and car hire. Dorm **¥6300**; tatami room **¥13,200**

Hilton Niseko Village ヒルトンニセコビレッジ Higashiyama ☎0136 44 1111, whilton.com. There are fantastic views of Mount Yōtei from this tower, which sports a glitzy lobby area and an excellent range of food

4

SKIING IN NISEKO

Niseko United (wniseko.ne.jp/en) is the umbrella name for three separate ski resorts: **Niseko Grand Hirafu/Hanazono** (ニセコ グラン・ヒラフ/花園), **Niseko Village** (ニセコ町) and **Niseko Annupuri** (ニセコアンヌプリ). You can buy individual lift tickets from each of the resorts, but the smartest deal is to go for one of the All Mountain Passes (from ¥5200 for an 8hr ticket), which is issued as an electronic tag – you'll need to wave it at the barrier by each of the lifts – with a ¥1000 refundable deposit.

If you're looking to ski Niseko's **backcountry**, then hire a guide from either Niseko Adventure Centre (NAC; ☎0136 23 2093, wnac-web.com) or Niseko Outdoor Adventure Sports Club (NOASC; ☎0136 23 1688, wnoasc.com), both in Hirafu; each employs English-speaking guides and also offers snowboarding, telemark skiing and ice climbing in winter, and activities such as kayaking and whitewater rafting in summer. Other reputable and local ski tour operators include Black Diamond Tours (☎090 2054 8687, wblackdiamondtours.com) and Ski Japan (☎0136 22 4611, wskijapan.com).

Soaking in an **onsen** is a fine way to wind down after a day on the slopes. Try the baths at *Hirafutei* (daily 1–11pm; ¥800) on Hirafu-zaka Street, or *Yukoro* (ゆころ; daily 2–10pm, ¥600) at the southeastern end of Hirafu village.

and drink options – just as well, as there's little else around here. Rooms are fine but lack the pizzazz of other Niseko options. ¥33,150

Hotel Kanro no Mori ホテル甘露の森 415 Aza-Niseko ☏ 0136 58 3800, ⓦ kanronomori.com. A 10min walk from the Annupuri Kokusai ski lifts, and surrounded by greenery, this appealing 78-room ryokan combines Japanese- and Western-style rooms. There's a large rotemburo, and rates include two meals. ¥15,600

Niseko Annupuri Youth Hostel ニセコアンヌプリYH 479-4 Aza-Niseko ☏ 0136 58 2084, ⓦ youthhostel .or.jp. This charming European-style log-cabin pension with a roaring fire is the most convenient youth hostel for

the slopes, located at Annupuri. Dorm ¥3360

Niseko Northern Resort Annupuri ニセコノーザンリ ゾート・アンヌプリ 480-1 Aza-Niseko ☏ 0136 58 3311, ⓦ niseko-northern.com. A good upmarket choice next to the ski lifts offering spacious "Scandinavian chic" rooms with white-wood and red-brick accents. Fine facilities include a rotemburo and classy bar area. ¥35,000

Niseko Weiss ニセコワイスホテル Hanazono ☏ 0136 23 3311, ⓦ niseko-weiss.com. Discover the quieter side of Niseko resort before Hanazono gets overdeveloped with a stay at this stylish boutique hotel. There are both Japanese- and Western-style rooms, and a great set of onsen baths. ¥12,960

EATING AND DRINKING

All of Niseko's hotels and pensions offer meals, but the area has such a good range of **restaurants**, **cafés** and **bars** that you can easily opt for a room only. Unless mentioned, the places below are only open during the ski season. At busier times, it's a good idea to book, particularly at weekends.

Abucha 2 阿武茶 2 Suiboku complex, Hirafu ☏ 0136 22 5620. At the main intersection in the village, this popular bakery, café and bar is a good option for breakfast or lunch away from the slopes. It can get busy in the evenings, when a good range of standard Japanese dishes, including *nabe* stews (around ¥2500), is offered. Open year-round. Daily 7am–4pm & 6pm–2am.

Bang-Bang バンバン Hirafu ☏ 0136 22 4292, ⓦ niseko. or.jp/bangbang. Set back from the main drag, this convivial restaurant specializes in local fish dishes and *yakitori* (over thirty different types; ¥160–450). It's one of the few places where you're likely to be surrounded by more Japanese than *gaijin*. In addition to the ski season, it's also open between Aug and mid-Oct. 5.30–11.30pm, closed Wed.

★**Dragon Restaurant and Wine Bar** レストラン&ワ インバー「ドラゴン」 Hirafu ☏ 0136 55 5157, ⓦ dragon-nf.com. Delicious Japanese–Italian fusion restaurant using the freshest Hokkaidō produce, with lunchtime pasta dishes from ¥1000. There's also the stylish *Dragon Bar Lohas* with an open fire. Daily: restaurant 7am–3pm & 6–11pm; bar 4pm–2am.

Gentem café 玄天 Hirafu ☏ 0136 23 3154. How's this for cultural fusion – a Mongolian yurt in a Japanese ski village serving vaguely Southeast Asian dishes (around ¥2000/meal including a ¥400 cover charge). It's a fun, unusual atmosphere, and, if you make a booking – which is advisable – they will pick you up and drop you back to your lodgings after. It's located just off the main road midway

between Hirafu and Higashiyama. Daily 6–11.30pm.

★**Graubünden** グラウビュンデン Hirafu ☏ 0136 23 3371. This fantastic bakery-café is located on the way out of Hirafu towards Kutchan. They do a scrumptious selection of breakfasts, sandwiches and cakes (all for under ¥1000), with leaf tea served in tea-cosy-covered pots. 8am–8pm (April–Dec till 7pm), closed Thurs.

Gyu+Bar ギュータス Hirafu ☏ 0136 23 1432. On the right head downhill from the main intersection, you'll find the entrance to this funky DJ bar as you go through a Coca-Cola vending-machine-turned door. Daily 6pm–1am.

Kamimura 上村 Shiki Hotel, Hirafu ☏ 0136 21 2288, ⓦ kamimura-niseko.com/en. The full white tablecloth experience from the eponymous Michelin-starred chef who brings out the best from local produce. Set menus, which may include dishes such as a snow crab and avocado salad and roasted *wagyu* beef with pureed local potato, kick off at ¥6500. Reservations essential. Mon–Sat 6–11pm.

Niseko Pizza ニセコピザ Hirafu ☏ 0136 55 5553. In the basement of the J-Sekka complex, offering over twenty types of pizza and delicious home-made pasta – try the lasagne at ¥1700. Mon, Thurs & Fri 5–11pm, Sat & Sun 11am–11pm.

Tsubara Tsubara つばらつばら Hirafu ☏ 0136 23 1116. Soup curry is a Hokkaidō speciality and this friendly, relaxed bistro is a great place to try it – the heat rating runs from a bland zero to an on-fire twenty. It's good value too, with a meal under ¥1500. Daily 11.30am–3pm, Sat & Sun 6–9.30pm.

Hakodate

函館

If you travel to Hokkaidō by train, the first major city you'll come to after emerging from the Seikan Tunnel connecting Hokkaidō to Honshū is **HAKODATE**, 260km southwest of Sapporo. This attractive **port** was one of the first to open to foreign traders following the Japan–US amity treaty of 1854. Over the next few years, ten countries including Britain, Russia and the US established consulates in Hakodate, with both foreigners and rich Japanese building fancy wooden homes and elaborate churches on the steep hillsides. Many of these late nineteenth- and early twentieth-century buildings have been preserved, particularly in the **Motomachi** area, which is Hakodate's highlight.

Among the city's other draws are the lively fish and fresh produce market **Asa-ichi**; an outstanding exhibition on **Ainu** culture at the Hakodate City Museum of Northern Peoples; and the night view from the top of **Hakodate-yama**. The **Ōnuma Quasi National Park**, a beautiful lakeland and mountain area with good hiking trails, is an easy day-trip. Try to time your visit for the **Hakodate Port Festival** (Aug 1–5), when twenty thousand people parade through town performing the "squid dance", an entertaining jig where hands are flapped and clapped in time to rhythmic drumming.

Hakodate-yama

函館山 • **Trails** May–Oct • Free • **Ropeway** (函館山ロープウェイ) Daily 10am–10pm, Oct 16–April 24 till 9pm • ¥640 one-way, ¥1160 return • W 334.co.jp/eng • The ropeway is a 7min uphill walk from the Jūjigai tram stop, and direct buses to the top of the mountain run from Hakodate Station (April 12–Nov 8 daily 6–9pm, Sat & Sun also 1.15pm; 30min; ¥350); the serpentine road up the mountain is open April 25–Oct 15, but closed to private vehicles 5–10pm

Lording it over Hakodate is the 334m **Hakodate-yama**. On a clear day, the view from the summit is spectacular, but best of all is the night-time panorama, when the twinkling lights of the port and the boats fishing for squid just off the coast create a magical scene. The energetic can climb to the summit along various trails, but most people opt for the ropeway (cable-car).

Motomachi

元町

Heading downhill from Hakodate-yama, you'll find yourself in **Motomachi**. With its Western-style, late nineteenth-century architecture, combined with the steeply raked streets, it's easy when you're here to see why Hakodate is known as the San Francisco of Japan. The best thing to do is simply wander about, stopping to explore some of the **churches**, which are mainly free, though some ask for a suggested donation (few of the other buildings merit their entrance charges).

Churches

The most striking church in Motomachi is the white **Russian Orthodox Church** of 1919, seven minutes' walk uphill from Jūjigai tram stop, complete with green copper-clad onion domes and spires (daily 10am–5pm, Sat till 4pm; suggested donation ¥200). Inside, there's an impressive icon-festooned carved-wood altarpiece, and piped Russian choral music adds to the atmosphere. Nearby, you can admire the unusual modern architecture of the **Episcopal Church** from the outside (not open to the public), while, slightly downhill, the Gothic-style **Motomachi Roman Catholic Church** (daily 10am–4pm, Sat & Sun from noon; free) is worth a look for its decoration, which is based on the Stations of the Cross.

Old Public Hall of Hakodate Ward

旧函館区公会堂, Kyū Hakodate-ku Kōkaidō • 11-13 Motomachi • Daily 9am–5pm, April–Oct till 7pm • ¥300, or ¥720 including the Old British Consulate of Hakodate and Hakodate City Museum of Northern Peoples • W www.zaidan-hakodate.com/koukaidou

A couple of hundred metres west of the cluster of churches across the hillside streets of Motomachi will bring you to the extraordinary **Old Public Hall of Hakodate Ward**, a sky-blue and lemon confection with pillars, verandas and fancy wrought-iron and plaster decoration. This replacement was completed in 1910 after a fire destroyed the original hall, and is now used as a concert hall.

4

HAKODATE

Hakodate-yama

Hakodate Harbour

Tsugaru-Kaikyō Strait

0   250   metres

MOTOMACHI

Hakodate-eki-mae

City Hall

HAKODATE STREETCAR

HAKODATE STREETCAR

Shiyakusho-mae

Uoichiba-dōri

Jūjigai

Hōrai-chō

Suehiro-chō

Aka-renga Warehouses

Museum of Photographic History & Information

Old Public Hall of Hakodate Ward

Motomachi-kōen

Hakodate City Museum of Northern Peoples

Old British Consulate of Hakodate

Motomachi Roman Catholic Church

Episcopal Church

Russian Orthodox Church

Cable car station

Asa-ichi

Hakodate Station & Bus Station

MOTOI-ZAKA
HACHIMAN-ZAKA
DAISAN-ZAKA
NIJUKKEN-ZAKA
MANBE-ZAKA
YACHI-ZAKA
GOKOKU-JINJA-ZAKA

Goryōkaku & Yunokawa

Ōnuma Quasi National Park, Seikan Tunnel & Hakodate-kō Port

Hakodate-Dokku-mae

Hakodate-yama

ACCOMMODATION
Hotel & Spa Resort La Vista	4
Nagashima	8
Niceday Inn	5
Pension Hakodate-Mura	7
Pension Jyo-Kura	1
Toyoko Inn Eki-mae Asa-ichi	2
Toyoko Inn Eki-mae Daimon	6
Winning Hotel	3

RESTAURANTS AND CAFÉS
Aji-no-ichiban	1
Asari	9
Café Tutu	4
Daimon Yokochō	2
Hakodate Bay Bishoku Club	5
Hishii	8
Lucky Pierrot	6
Nihombashi	3
Ton'etsu	7

BARS
Bar Shares Hishii	2
Hakodate Beer	1

Old British Consulate of Hakodate

函館市旧イギリス領事館 Hakodate-shi Kyū Igirisu Ryōjikan • 33-14 Motomachi • Daily 9am–5pm (April–Oct till 7pm) • ¥300, or ¥720 including the Old Public Hall of Hakodate Ward and Hakodate City Museum of Northern Peoples • ⓦ hakodate-kankou.com/british

In front of the Old Public Hall of Hakodate Ward is the small Motomachi Park, beneath which is the **Old British Consulate of Hakodate**, from where the Empire's affairs in Hokkaidō were looked after from 1859 to 1934. The cream-and-blue building now houses a ho-hum museum, the twee *Victorian Rose Tea Restaurant* and a gift shop.

Hakodate City Museum of Northern Peoples

函館市北方民族資料館, Hakodate-shi Hoppō Minzoku Shiryōkan • 21-7 Suehiro-chō • Daily 9am–5pm, April–Oct till 7pm • ¥300, or ¥720 including the Old Public Hall of Hakodate Ward and the Old British Consulate of Hakodate • ⓦ www.zaidan-hakodate.com/hoppomirzoku

The **Hakodate City Museum of Northern Peoples** is in an old bank down Motoi-zaka, which leads away from the consulate. The museum's superb collection of artefacts relating to the Ainu and other races across Eastern Siberia and the Alaskan islands has clear, English captioning and is well worth the entrance fee. Some of the clothes on display are simply amazing – look out for the Chinese silk robe embroidered with dragons, an example of the types of items traded between China, the islanders of Sakhalin and the Ainu.

Asa-ichi

朝市 • Daily 5am–noon (May–Dec from 5am) • ⓦ hakodate-asaichi.com

No visit to Hakodate is complete without dropping by the atmospheric **Asa-ichi**, the morning market immediately to the west of the train station. Even if you arrive at the relatively late hour of 9am, there's still plenty to see at the hundreds of tightly packed stalls lining the streets in this waterside location. Old ladies in headscarves squat amid piles of vegetables and flowers in the central hall, and huge, alien-like red crabs, squid, sea urchin and musk melons are the local specialities. Be sure to sample seafood atop a bowl of ramen or rice before you leave (see p.308).

Goryōkaku

五稜郭 • 43-9 Goryōkaku-chō • **Viewing tower** Daily: April 21–Oct 20 8am–7pm; Oct 21–April 20 9am–6pm • ¥840 • ⓦ goryokaku-tower.co.jp • **Open-air theatre** Late July to mid-Aug • Check website for performance schedules and tickets • ⓦ yagaigeki.com/en/index. html • Around a 10min walk north of the Goryōkaku-kōen-mae tram stop

The remains of **Goryōkaku**, a late nineteenth-century Western-style fort, lie some 3km northeast of the station. The star-shaped fort was built to protect Hokkaidō against attack from Russia. In the event, however, it was used by Tokugawa Yoshinobu's naval forces in a last-ditch battle to uphold the shogun against the emperor in the short-lived civil war that ushered in the Meiji Restoration of 1869. The Emperor's victory is celebrated each year in mid-May with a period costume **parade**.

What's left of the fort today – a leafy park planted with 1500 cherry trees, the moat and outer walls – looks best 90m up from the inelegant **viewing tower** by the main entrance. On weekend evenings in the summer, open-air plays about Hakodate's history are performed enthusiastically by five hundred amateurs.

ARRIVAL AND INFORMATION HAKODATE

By plane Hakodate's airport (☎0138 57 8881) lies 8km north of the city; buses ¥400) take roughly 20min from there to Hakodate Station.
Destinations Kansai International (2 daily; 1hr 45min); Nagoya (1 daily; 1hr 20min); Sapporo (2 daily; 40min); Tokyo (8 daily; 1hr 15min).
By train The central Hakodate Station, on the eastern side of the harbour, is where trains terminate. The Shinkansen extension linking Hokkaidō to Tokyo will arrive in 2016. Destinations Aomori (10 daily; 2hr); Hachinohe (9 daily; 3hr); Ōnuma-kōen (7 daily; 20min); Sapporo (11 daily; 3hr 30min); Tokyo (9 daily; 6hr; 2 overnight sleeper; 12hr 40min).
By bus The bus station is in front of the train station. Destinations Ōnuma-kōen (3 daily; 1hr 20min); Sapporo (8 daily; 5hr 30min).
By ferry Ferries dock at Hakodate-kō Port, some 4km

4

north of Hakodate Station. Catch either bus #101 or #111 to Hakodate Station (¥230 or ¥250, depending on which ferry you alight from); a taxi from the port to the city centre is around ¥2000.

Destinations Aomori (9 daily; 3hr 40min); Ōma (2 daily; 1hr 30min).

Tourist information The helpful Hakodate tourist office (daily 9am–7pm, Nov–March till 5pm; ☎ 0138 23 5440, ⓦ hakodate-kankou.com/en, ⓦ hakodate.travel/en) is inside Hakodate Station.

GETTING AROUND

By tram Hakodate's sights are quite spread out. There's a good tram system with two lines, both starting at the onsen resort of Yunokawa (湯の川), east of the city. Each runs past Goryōkaku and the train station before diverging at the Jūjigai stop in Motomachi. From here, tram #5 heads west to Hakodate Dokku-mae (函館どっく前), while tram #2 continues further south to Yachigashira (谷地頭) on the eastern side of Hakodate-yama. Trams run 7am–10pm.

By bus There are a number of useful buses. A shuttle bus departing from Hakodate Station will take you to the Hakodate-yama ropeway and the Goryōkaku Tower. The "LCSA (Lexa) Motomachi" bus, which operates on a continuous loop between Hakodate Station and the Bay Area/Motomachi, is another convenient option.

Tickets One-day (¥1000) and two-day passes (¥1700) can be bought from the tourist office for unlimited use of both the trams and most city buses. These passes, only worth buying if you plan to tour extensively around town, also cover the bus service up Hakodate-yama. The ¥600 all-day tram ticket is better value; individual tram trips cost ¥200–250.

Car rental Eki Rent-a-Car (☎ 0138 22 7864) is next to Hakodate Station.

ACCOMMODATION

Hotels are busiest during the summer, when you'll need to book ahead. Prices at most places drop considerably in winter, and many have good deals for online bookings, so it's worth shopping around.

★ **Hotel & Spa Resort La Vista** ラビスタ函館ベイ 12-6 Toyokawa-chō ☎ 0138 23 6111, ⓦ hotespa.net/hotels/lahakodate. With great views of the harbour and Hakodate-yama, Hakodate's newest luxury hotel offers elegantly designed rooms and a fantastic set of rooftop baths. Good internet deals and very affordable rates out of season. ¥21,800

★ **Nagashima** 長島 18-5 Hōrai-chō ☎ 0138 26 2101, ⓦ www5b.biglobe.ne.jp/~m-naga. Good-value, spotless minshuku near Hakodate-yama, offering mainly tatami rooms, plus a couple of Western-style ones. The shared bathroom has a *hinoki* (a type of pine) tub. Rates include two meals. ¥14,280

Niceday Inn ナイスデイ・イン 9-11 Ōtemachi ☎ 0138 22 5919. A friendly hostel in a convenient location between the station and Motomachi. All the rooms have two bunk beds and are very small, but if it's quiet you may get one to yourself. The owners speak English, and there's free tea and coffee. Dorm ¥3000

Pension Hakodate-Mura B&B ペンション はこだて村 16-12 Suehiro-chō ☎ 0138 22 8105, ⓦ bb-hakodatemura .com. Appealing B&B just off the waterfront at the start of Motomachi, offering both Western- and Japanese-style rooms, with most sharing a common bathroom. Breakfast is ¥800. ¥8960

Pension Jyō-Kura じょう蔵 9-8 Ōmachi ☎ 0138 27 6453, ⓦ j-kura.com. This is a twee pension with a facade styled like a *kura* (storehouse). There's a homely common area where breakfast is served (¥800) and a choice of Western- or Japanese-style rooms. ¥9600

Tōyoko Inn Hakodate Eki-mae Asa-ichi 東横INN函館 駅前朝市 22-7 Ōtemachi ☎ 0138 23 1045, ⓦ toyoko-inn .com. Only a 2min walk from the station, this branch of the handy chain is right next to the Asa-ichi morning market. If this one is full, try the other (see below). ¥8480

Tōyoko Inn Hakodate Eki-mae Daimon 東横INN函 館駅前大門 5-1 Matsukaze-chō ☎ 0138 24 1045, ⓦ toyoko-inn.com. A 4min walk from the station, this *Tōyoko Inn* branch is close to City Hall. ¥8480

Winning Hotel ウイニングホテル 22-11 Suehiro-chō ☎ 0138 26 1111, ⓦ hotel-winning.jp. Located in a modern but Art Deco-styled building facing the harbour; the rooms are pleasantly decorated, large, and some have lovely views. ¥13,000

EATING AND DRINKING

The best places to feast on fresh seafood are the sushi and *donburi* restaurants scattered around the morning market near Hakodate Station). **Local specialities** include crab (*kani*), squid (*ika*) and ramen noodles in a salty soup topped with seafood. Goryōkaku is the city's main **drinking** area although you'll also find several bars around the converted warehouses in Motomachi.

Aji-no-ichiban 味の一番 11-13 Wakamatsu-chō ☎ 0138 26 5587. Set at the back of the market. They serve a lovely *donburi* topped with creamy sea urchin, salmon roe and fresh crab for ¥1700, as well as delicious, freshly squeezed melon juice. May–Oct daily 7am–2pm

★ **Asari** 阿佐利 10-11 Hōrai-chō ☎ 0138 23 0421. The old wooden building and tatami-floor dining rooms of this restaurant are just part of the pleasure – the rest is in the quality of the *sukiyaki*, their speciality dish, using meat fresh from the butchers downstairs. Lunch is a bargain at ¥1200–1400; set menus at other times start at ¥2300. 11.30am–9.30pm. closed Wed.

Bar Shares Hishii バーシェアーズヒシイ 27-1 Motomachi ☎ 0138 22 5584. Brought to you by the same owners as *Hishii*, this small but elegant bar is a relaxing place for an evening drink. Mon–Sat 8pm–1am

Café Tutu カフェトゥトゥ 13-5 Suehiro-chō ☎ 0138 27 9199. This trendy café-bar, to the rear of one of the renovated brick warehouses by the harbour is a nice place to relax over gourmet coffee and cake. Daily 11.30am–11pm, closed Thurs Nov–April.

Daimon Yokochō 大門横丁 7-5 Matsukaze-chō. Choose from 26 *yatai* (stalls) serving everything from *oden* and sushi to ramen and *yakitori*. It's an atmospheric place and a good spot to drop by for a beer and small plate of food. Daily 5pm–midnight.

Hakodate Bay Bishoku Club 函館ベイ美食倶楽部 12-7 Toyakawa-chō. Adjoining the converted brick warehouses by the waterfront is this attractive complex of seven restaurants set around a free outdoor foot spa. Take your pick between seafood *donburi* (around ¥2500) at *Kikuyo*, Hakodate-style *shio* (salt) ramen (¥700) at

Ajisai, soup curry at *Mecumi* (¥1000) or a *jingisukan* lamb BBQ at *Mei Mei Tei* (¥2000). Daily 11am–10.30pm.

Hakodate Beer はこだてビール 12-12 Toyokawa-machi ☎ 0138 23 8000. This cavernous brewery pub/restaurant where there's sometimes live music, serves the local *ji-biiru* – sample four of their brews for ¥1200. Daily 11am–3pm & 5–10pm.

★ **Hishii** ひし伊 9-4 Hōrai-chō ☎ 0138 27 3300. Near the Hōrai-chō tram stop, this elegant ivy-draped 1920s wooden building houses a serene teashop and antique kimono shop, plus there's a tatami area on the second floor. They also run the nearby *Bar Shares Hishii* (see above). Daily 10am–6pm.

Lucky Pierrot ラッキーピエロ 8-11 Suehiro-chō ☎ 0138 26 2300. For something a little unusual, head to the hamburger and curry chain *Lucky Pierrot*. There are ten branches in the city, including this one just west of the Jūjigai tram stop, which is heavily Christmas-themed. There are other branches next to the Aka-renga brick warehouses and by the Goryōkaku Tower. Daily 10.30am–midnight.

Nihombashi 日本橋 7-9 Motomachi ☎ 0138 26 0480. Good-value Japanese restaurant serving huge set meals and bowls of noodles in a relaxing atmosphere amid the old houses of Motomachi. Daily 11.30am–6pm.

Ton'etsu とん悦 22-2 Hōrai-chō ☎ 0133 22 2448. Convivial *tonkatsu* restaurant with tatami seating and a good range of reasonably priced set meals from ¥1000, including free coffee. Daily 11.30am–9pm.

DIRECTORY

Banks There's an ATM upstairs at Hakodate Station and several banks nearby that can change cash and travellers' cheques (Mon–Fri 9am–2.30pm).

Hospital Hakodate City Hospital, 1-10-1 Minato-chō (☎ 0138 43 2000).

Internet HotWeb Café, 1-8-1 TMO Building, Wakamatsu-chō (10am–8pm, closed Tues; ¥400/hr including one soft drink), is on the main road leading from Hakodate Station. I-Café, 2nd floor, Pabot Bldg, 9-3 Yanagawa-chō, is open

24hr and charges ¥300/hour.

Laundry *Aqua Garden Hotel*, 19-13 Ōtemachi, 5min walk south of the station, has a coin laundry (daily 7am–midnight).

Police The main police station is on the western side of Goryōkaku-kōen. For emergency numbers, see p.66.

Post office The Central Post Office, 1-6 Shinkawa-chō, is a 10min walk east of Hakodate Station (Mon–Fri 9am–7pm, Sat & Sun 9am–5pm).

Ōnuma Quasi National Park

大沼国定公園, Ōnuma Kokutei Kōen

Just 29km north of Hakodate, the serene **Ōnuma Quasi National Park** can easily be visited in a day but is worth considering as an overnight stop. Of the park's three **lakes**, the largest and most beautiful is **Ōnuma**, carpeted with water lilies and containing more than one hundred tiny islands, many linked by humpback bridges. The view from the lake towards the 1133m jagged peak of the dormant volcano of **Komaga-take** (駒ヶ岳) is rightly considered to be one of the most breathtaking in Japan.

Ōnuma is popular with tour groups, but they are usually herded into sightseeing boats, leaving the walking paths around the lake and islands quiet for strolls. **Cycling** is another good way of exploring. **Hikers** can also tackle the **volcano**, which has two main routes, both taking around two and a half hours to complete.

ARRIVAL AND INFORMATION ŌNUMA QUASI NATIONAL PARK

By train Local trains from Hakodate to Ōnuma-kōen Station take 50min (¥530), while limited express trains take 20min (¥1130).

By bus There are three daily buses from Hakodate (1hr 20min, one-way/return ¥1200/2400).

Tourist information Information is available from Ōnuma International Communication Plaza (daily 8.30am–5.30pm; ☎ 0138 67 2170, ⓦ onuma-guide.com) next to the train station.

Bike rental Bikes can be rented (around ¥500/hr or ¥1500/day) from numerous shops around the station.

ACCOMMODATION

Crawford Inn Ōnuma クロフォード・イン大沼 85-9 Ōnuma ☎ 0138 67 2964, ⓦ crawford.jp/en/index.html. This Western-style hotel next to Ōnuma-kōen Station is the upmarket choice. It's named after Professor Joseph Crawford who introduced the railways to Hokkaidō. **¥11,000**

Higashi-Ōnuma Yaeijō campsite 東大沼野営場 Higashi-Ōnuma ☎ 0138 67 347. This free campsite on the eastern shore of Ōnuma Lake has toilets, running water and

firepits. The nearest station is Chōshi-guchi, around 6km east of Ōnuma-kōen Station. Open late April to Oct. Free

Ōnuma Kōen Youth Hostel 大沼公園YH 4-3 Ikusagawa ☎ 0138 67 4126, ⓦ youthhostel.or.jp. This friendly hostel, a 3min walk from Ikedaen Station, offers bunk-bed dorms, good breakfasts and dinners and activities such as canoeing, cross-country skiing and ice fishing, depending on the season. Dorm **¥3960**

4 Shikotsu-Tōya National Park

支笏洞爺国立公園, Shikotsu-Tōya Kokuritsu Kōen

Follow the coastal road or rail line around Uchiura-wan from Hakodate and you'll reach the eastern side of the **SHIKOTSU-TŌYA NATIONAL PARK**, one of Hokkaidō's prettiest lakeland and mountain areas, but also the most developed, thanks to its proximity to Sapporo, some 80km to the north. Both the park's two main caldera lakes – **Tōya-ko** to the west and **Shikotsu-ko** to the east – are active volcanoes and surrounded by excellent hiking trails. Between the two lakes lies **Noboribetsu Onsen**, Hokkaidō's largest hot-spring resort, worth visiting to soak up the otherworldly landscape of bubbling and steaming **Jigokudani** (Hell Valley).

Tōya-ko

洞爺湖

The beautiful caldera lake of **Tōya-ko** is punctuated dead centre by the conical island of **Nakajima**. Its southern shore is home to the tired-looking resort **Tōya-ko Onsen** (洞爺湖温泉), where you'll find most accommodation and local transport connections. Between April 28 and October 31, spectacular fireworks (nightly 8.45–9.05pm) illuminate the lake. Pretty as the location is, the best reason for visiting Tōya-ko is to see the nearby active volcano **Usu-zan**, around 2km south, and its steaming "parasite volcano" **Shōwa Shin-zan** (昭和新山; see box, p.313).

Usu-zan

有珠山 • Ropeway (有珠山ロープウェイ) daily: April–Oct 8.15am–5.30pm; Nov–March 9am–4pm • ¥1450 return • The ropeway station is at the end of the row of tourist shops by Shōwa Shin-zan; buses run from the bus station at Tōya-ko Onsen to Shōwa Shin-zan (4/day; 15min; ¥330)

Usu-zan remains frighteningly active; the last eruption, on March 31, 2000, coated Tōya-ko Onsen with volcanic dust and forced a three-month evacuation. To look directly into the beast, ride the ropeway to a viewing platform 300m from the crater, which also provides stunning vistas over Shōwa Shin-zan, Tōya-ko and out to sea.

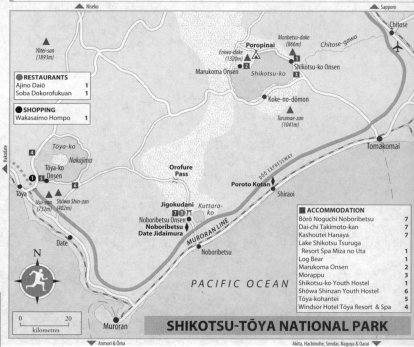

RESTAURANTS
| Ajino Daiō | 1 |
| Soba Dokorofukuan | 1 |

SHOPPING
| Wakasaimo Hompo | 1 |

ACCOMMODATION
Bōrō Noguchi Noboribetsu	7
Dai-chi Takimoto-kan	7
Kashoutei Hanaya	7
Lake Shikotsu Tsuruga	
Resort Spa Miza no Uta	1
Log Bear	1
Marukoma Onsen	2
Morappu	3
Shikotsu-ko Youth Hostel	1
Shōwa Shinzan Youth Hostel	6
Tōya-kohantei	5
Windsor Hotel Tōya Resort & Spa	4

SHIKOTSU-TŌYA NATIONAL PARK

Tōyako Visitor Centre and Volcanic Science Museum

洞爺湖ビジターセンター, Tōya-ko Bijitā Sentā・火山科学館, Kazan Kagaku-kan・142-5 Tōyako Onsen・Daily 9am–5pm・Visitor centre free; museum ¥600・ⓦ toyako-vc.jp

The area damaged by the eruptions – known as the **Konpira Promenade** (daily April 20–Nov 10; free) – is nerve-shreddingly close to town. In front of it, in the newly built **Tōyako Visitor Centre** building, which houses the **Volcanic Science Museum**, you can watch a seat-tremblingly loud film about that eruption and other explosions on the mountain. You can also walk or take a three-minute bus ride (¥160) to the **Nishiyama Crater Promenade** (西山火口散策路洞爺; daily April 20–Nov 10; free), a 1.3km boardwalk across the recent break in the earth's crust.

The onsen

The best way to enjoy the positive side of volcanic activity is to take an **onsen** dip. Most of the lakeside hotels allow day visitors – try the *Tōya Sun Palace* (洞爺サンパレス; 7-1 Tōyako-onsen; daily 10am–3pm; ¥800), which features two floors with more than twenty different soaking pools, some with lake views, and a large swimming pool with artificial waves and a water slide, for which you'll need your bathing costume. There are also nice rooftop baths at the *Tōya-kohantei* (see opposite; daily 11.30am–5pm; ¥700), which is closer to the bus station.

ARRIVAL AND DEPARTURE   TŌYA-KO

By train Trains run to Tōya Station, on the coast, from where you can get a bus (20min; ¥320) up the hill to Tōya-ko Onsen.

By bus There are seven daily buses to Tōya-ko Onsen from Sapporo (2hr 50min; one-way/return

¥2700/4790). Buses pull in at the Dōnan bus station, 2min walk from the shore of Tōya-ko. From April to Oct, four buses (15min, ¥330) run daily from Tōya-ko Onsen to Shōwa Shin-zan.

BIRTH OF A VOLCANO

On December 28, 1943, severe earthquakes began shaking the area around Usu-zan and continued to do so until September 1945. In the intervening period, a new lava dome rose out of the ground, sometimes at the rate of 1.5m a day. By the time it had stopped growing, **Shōwa Shin-zan**, the "new mountain" named after the reigning emperor, stood 405m above sea level. The wartime authorities were desperate to hush up this extraordinary event for fear that the fledgling mountain would serve as a beacon for US bomber planes.

Fortunately, Shōwa Shin-zan's daily growth was carefully documented by local postmaster and amateur volcanologist Mimatsu Masao. After the war, Mimatsu bought the land on which the mountain stood, declaring, "I purchased the volcano to continue my research uninterrupted. I did not buy it to make money. Nor did I buy it for tourists to gawk at." His efforts were rewarded in 1958 when Shōwa Shin-zan was made a Special Natural Treasure by the government.

Nevertheless, Mimatsu never turned away tourists – but nor did he charge them admission, a practice still upheld. The **Mimatsu Masao Memorial Hall** (三松正夫記念館; daily 8am–5pm; ¥300), tucked behind the ghastly row of gift shops at the base of the volcano, contains an interesting collection of exhibits on the history of the fledgling volcano.

INFORMATION AND ACTIVITIES

Tourist information The tourist office (daily 9am–5pm; ☎0142 75 2446, ⓦ laketoya.com) is above the bus station.
Lake cruises For a cruise on the lake, hop aboard the kitsch castle-styled ferry *Espoir* (daily: April–Oct 8am–4pm, sailings every 30min; Nov–March 9am–4pm, sailings every hour; ¥1320; ⓦ toyakokisen.com). Only the summer cruises stop at Nakajima, where you can see Ezo deer grazing in the forests. There are also nightly fireworks cruises in summer (8.30pm; ¥1500).
Horseriding Animal lovers can arrange horseriding at Lake Toya Ranch (☎0142 73 2455, ⓦ www.dioce.co.jp/toya; from ¥4725/40min) on the west side of the lake.

ACCOMMODATION AND EATING

Shōwa Shinzan Youth Hostel 昭和新山YH 103 Sōbetsu-onsen ☎0142 75 2283, ⓦ youthhostel.or.jp. At the turn-off to Shōwa Shin-zan, and a 10m n bus or taxi ride (¥1300) from Tōya-ko Onsen, this hostel has bunk-bed dorms, shared tatami rooms and its own onsen, plus rents out bikes (¥1000/day). Dorm **¥3750**

Tōya-kohantei 洞爺湖畔亭 7-8 Tōya-ko Onsen ☎0142 75 2211, ⓦ toya-kohantei.com. This is a good upmarket option, with fabulous lake views and delicious meals. **¥24,450**

Wakasaimo Hompo わかさいも本舗 144 Tōya-ko Onsen ☎0142 75 4111. This red-roofed restaurant with lake views is a good place for lunch – try the *sansai-soba* (mountain vegetable noodles) for ¥880. Afterwards, sample their various baked goods in the shop downstairs for dessert or takeaway presents. Daily 11am–7pm.

Windsor Hotel Tōya Resort & Spa ザ・ウィンザーホテル洞爺リゾート&スパ Shimizu Tōyako-chō ☎0142 73 1111, ⓦ windsor-hotels.co.jp. If it's unfettered luxury you're after, head to the west side of the lake to this stylish hotel, which hosted the G8 summit in 2008. **¥36,960**

Noboribetsu Onsen

登別温泉

East around the coast from Tōya-ko, and nestling amid lush green mountain slopes ripped through by a bubbling cauldron of volcanic activity, is **NOBORIBETSU ONSEN**. Hokkaidō's top hot-spring resort may be peppered with lumpen hotel buildings and tacky souvenir shops, but its dramatic landscape is definitely worth seeing, and there's ample opportunity for some serious onsen relaxation.

Jigokudani

地獄谷 • Hell Valley • A 10min walk from the bus station up Gokuraku-dōri

Noboribetsu's main street leads up to a roadside **shrine** guarded by two brightly painted statues of demons. A bit further up the street, you will find the entrance to **Jigokudani**, a steaming, lunar-like valley created by an ancient volcanic eruption. It takes less than an hour to explore the area, wandering along wooden pathways through a landscape of rusty red rocks, streaked green and white by mineral deposits, ending up at **Ōyu-numa** (大湯沼), a malevolent-looking hot-water lake. Along the way you can soothe your feet in a natural footbath.

All the hotels draw water from Jigokudani (ten thousand tonnes are pumped out daily), and many have built elaborate **baths** so that guests can enjoy the water's therapeutic benefits. The tourist offices (see below) provide a list of the baths open to the public.

Noboribetsu Date Jidai-mura

登別伊達時代村 • 53-1 Naka Noboribetsu-chō • Daily: April–Oct 9am–5pm; Nov–March 10am–4pm • ¥2900 • ⓦ edo-trip.jp

If you have time, skip the village's deplorable bear park and visit the whacky Edo-era theme park **Noboribetsu Date Jidai-mura** to step back in time and watch costumed *oiran* (top-ranked courtesans) theatre shows, ninja performances and Samurai shows.

ARRIVAL AND INFORMATION — NOBORIBETSU ONSEN

By train Trains run to Noboribetsu Station from where the resort is a 13min bus ride (¥330).

By bus There are direct buses to Noboribetsu Onsen from Sapporo's New Chitose Airport (1hr 5 min; ¥1330) and the nearby ports of Tomakomai to the north (1hr 10 min) and Muroran to the south (1hr 40 min).

Tourist information At the resort's bus terminal you'll find one of Noboribetsu's trio of tourist offices (daily 9am–6pm; ☎ 0143 84 3311, ⓦ noboribetsu-spa.jp).

ACCOMMODATION AND EATING

Rates at all of the onsen's hotels typically include two meals. The town makes a good place to treat yourself to the full ryokan experience, where you're served course upon course of immaculately presented delicacies, each as beautiful to look at as to taste, before relaxing in the healing baths.

Ajino Daiō 味の大王 Gokuraku-dōri ☎ 0143 84 2415. A great little noodle shop a couple of doors up from *Soba Dokorofukuan* – try the spicy *jigoku ramen* (¥800). Daily noon–2pm & 9pm–2am.

Bōrō Noguchi Noboribetsu 望楼NOGUCHI登別 203 Noboribetsu Onsen-chō ☎ 0143 84 3939 ⓦ bourou.com/en. A masterclass in contemporary chic, featuring Western-style suites, each with their own private spa bath. ¥66,300

Dai-ichi Takimoto-kan 第一滝本館 55 Noboribetsu Onsen-chō ☎ 0143 84 3322, ⓦ takimotokan.co.jp. It's worth checking internet deals for this traditional inn, which has seven different types of hot springs and a swimming pool. ¥23,100

★**Kashoutei Hanaya** 花鐘亭はなや 134 Noboribetsu Onsen-chō ☎ 0143 84 2521, ⓦ kashoutei-hanaya.co.jp. Just below the Kōseinenkin Byōin-mae bus stop, or a 5min walk downhill from the main bus terminal, this modest-sized, modern ryokan is an excellent choice, with exquisite meals, Japanese-

---

EXPERIENCING THE AINU

The re-created Ainu village of **Poroto Kotan** (ポロトコタン; daily 8.45am–5pm; ¥750, ☎ 0144 82 3914, ⓦ ainu-museum.or.jp) is on the shore of Lake Poroto in the southern coastal town of Shiraoi, on the train line between Sapporo and Hakodate, a few stops northeast of Noboribetsu. Admittedly, it's a very touristy experience; you can see traditionally dressed Ainu men and women perform the ritual dance, *Iyomante Rimse*, and listen to the haunting music of the *mukkur*, a mouth harp made of bamboo and thread.

For a more accurate idea of how Ainu live today, head to **Nibutani** (二風谷), some 50km due east of the port of Tomakomai on Route 237 – the only place in Japan where they form a majority of the community. A fascinating personal collection of Ainu artefacts is on display in the charming **Kayano Shigeru Nibutani Ainu Museum** (萱野茂二風谷アイヌ資料館; 79 Nibutani; April–Nov daily 9am–5pm; Dec–March by appointment only; ☎ 0145 72 3215; ¥400, or ¥700 with the Nibutani Ainu Culture Museum). The **Nibutani Ainu Culture Museum** (二風谷アイヌ文化博物館; 61 Nibutani; daily 9am–4.30pm; ¥400 or ¥700 with the Kayano Shigeru Ainu Memorial Museum), on the opposite side of the village main road, is also worth a look. To reach Nibutani, take a train south from Tomakomai to Tomikawa Station (富川), from where buses run to the village.

style rooms and a lovely rotemburo. **¥25,500**

Soba Dokorofukuan そば処福庵 Gokuraku-dōri

☎0143 84 2758. Serves delicious buckwheat noodles and set meals for under ¥1000. Daily 11.30am–2pm & 5–10pm.

Shikotsu-ko

支笏湖

Tourist development around the beautiful lake of **Shikotsu-ko** is remarkably low key, despite this being the closest part of the park to Sapporo. At 363m, this is Japan's second-deepest lake (after Tazawa-ko in Akita-ken), and its blue waters never freeze over. All buses stop at the tiny village of **SHIKOTSU-KO ONSEN** (支笏湖温泉), nestled in the woods beside the mouth of the Chitose-gawa on the east side of the lake, and mercifully free of the multistorey hotels present at Tōya-ko.

Just behind the visitor centre, the **Chitose-Shikotsu-ko Ice Festival** is held from the end of January to the third week of February – it's well worth coming to see the ice sculptures and caves which are particularly dramatic when illuminated at night.

ARRIVAL AND INFORMATION   SHIKOTSU-KO

By train If you're coming from Sapporo, take a train to Chitose (the town, not the airport; 30min, ¥1110) then take the bus from the station (45min; ¥900).

By bus Daily buses run to Shikotsu-ko Onsen from New Chitose Airport (1hr; ¥1020 one-way), via Chitose Station.

Tourist information The visitor centre (Apr 1–Nov daily 9am–5.30pm; Dec–March 9.30am–4.30pm, closed Tues; ☎0123 25 2404), next to the bus terminal, has displays in Japanese on the area's nature and geology, and puts on a good slide show of the lake through the seasons – you can also pick up a free area map here.

GETTING AROUND AND ACTIVITIES

Bike rental Getting around the lake is best with your own transport, as there are no local buses. You can rent a bike from the youth hostel in Shikotsu-ko Onsen for ¥1800 a day (or ¥1200 if you're staying at the hostel).

Boat rides The usual boat rides are available on the lake (30min; ¥1200).

Walks You can opt for a gentle, self-guided nature walk if hiking uphill isn't your thing (see box, p.316) lasting about 2hr, over the old red-painted railway bridge across the Chitose-gawa and along the lakeshore to the campsite at Morappu (モラップ), 7km south.

ACCOMMODATION

★ **Lake Shikotsu Tsuruga Resort Spa Mizu no Uta** し こつ湖鶴雅リゾートスパ水の謌 Shikotsuko-onsen ☎0123 25 2211 ⓦmizunouta.com. A gorgeous contemporary-styled ryokan where the most expensive rooms have their own private onsen baths. Two meals included. **¥31,500**

Log Bear ログベアー Shikotsuko-onsen ☎0123 25 2738. This charming log cabin and café amid the tourist shops next to the bus terminal is a cosy budget option, where the owner speaks English. All rooms have shared bathrooms, and the rate includes breakfast. **¥10,000**

Marukoma Onsen 丸駒温泉 7 Poropinai ☎0123 25 2341. On the west side of the lake is this plush ryokan with

wonderful rotemburo (open to non-residents daily 10am–3pm; ¥1000) and stunning views across Shikotsu-ko to Tarumae-zan. Rates include two meals. **¥20,000**

Morappu Campsite モラップキャンプ場 Morappu ☎0123 25 2439. About 7km south of Shikotsu-ko Onsen, this is the largest campsite on the lake and is in an attractive location, open May to mid-Oct. **¥700** per person

Shikotsu-ko Youth Hostel 支笏湖ユースホステル Shikotsuko-onsen ☎0123 25 2311, ⓦyouthhostel .or.jp. This youth hostel has reasonable bunk-bed and tatami rooms and friendly management; they offer bike hire, too. **¥3645**

Asahikawa

旭川

Mainly a place for business, **ASAHIKAWA**, 136km northeast of Sapporo, straddles the confluence of the Ishikari, Biei, Chubetsu and Ushibetsu rivers and is surrounded by mountains. It's the access point for the Daisetsu-zan National Park (see p.318),

---

SHIKOTSU-KO HIKING ROUTES

One of the easiest trails starts at the northern end of the village and leads up **Monbestu-dake** (紋別岳; 866m), which takes around one hour and twenty minutes to climb. The hike up **Eniwa-dake** (恵庭岳; 1320m), on the north side of the lake above the *Poropinai* campsite, is more challenging and takes at least two and a half hours; staff at the visitors' centre advise only climbing to the Miharashi-dai, beneath the summit, because the trail to the top can be dangerous. After this climb, you could unwind beside the lake at the foot of the mountain in the lovely rotemburo at **Marukoma Onsen** (see p.315).

Most people, however, opt to climb **Tarumae-zan** (樽前山; 1041m), an active volcano (the last eruption was in 1951) south of the lake. The hike begins at the seventh "station", three-quarters of the way up the volcano at the end of a dirt road; the easiest way of reaching the start is to hitch a ride from Shikotsu-ko. The walk from the seventh station up to the summit shouldn't take more than an hour. At the top, the pungent aroma from the steaming crater discourages lingering. Following the northwest trail down from Tarumae-zan towards the lake leads, after a couple of hours, to the moss-covered gorge of **Koke-no-dōmon** (苔の洞門); sadly, erosion at this site means that you'll only be able to view the soft green velvet rock walls from a distance. From here it's a 14km hike back to Shikotsu-ko Onsen.

---

some 40km east, and worth considering as a base for park activities or, in winter, the various nearby ski slopes, including Furano (see p.320). Asahikawa's February **Winter Festival** (see box opposite), is as impressive as Sapporo's Yuki Matsuri (see box, p.291).

GETTING AROUND ASAHIKAWA

By bus Asahikawa's main tourist attractions are spread out, and getting to them by public transport involves shuttling from the city centre on a variety of buses, all leaving from around the JR Station.

Asahiyama Zoo

旭山動物園, Asahiyama Dōbutsuen • Higashi Asahikawa-chō Kuranuma • Daily: late April–Oct 9.30am–5.15pm; Nov–mid April 10.30am–3.30pm • ¥800 • bit.ly/1oWTCWL • Buses leave from stop 5 in front of the JR station (20 min; ¥400)

Most locals will recommend that you visit **Asahiyama Zoo**, about 10km east of the city centre. The penguins, polar bears, seals, amur leopards and others that live here are cute and appear well cared for at what, thanks to skilful marketing, is Japan's most popular zoo.

Hokkaidō Folk Arts and Crafts Village

北海道伝統美術工芸村, Hokkaidō Dentō Bijutsu Kōgei-mura • 3-1-1 Minamigaoka • **International Dyeing and Weaving Art Museum** Daily: April–Oct 9am–5.30pm; Nov 9am–5pm • ¥550 • **Yukara Ori Folk Craft Museum** April–Oct daily 9am–5.30pm; Nov–March 9am–5pm, closed Mon • ¥450 • **Snow Crystals Museum** April–Oct daily 9am–5.30pm; Nov–March 9am–5pm, closed Mon • ¥650, joint entry all three ¥1200 • ☎ 0166 62 8811, ⓦ yukaraori.co.jp • Buses leave from platforms 6, 7, 11 and 13 in front of the JR station

West of the city centre is a trio of museums that comprise the **Hokkaidō Folk Arts and Crafts Village**. The most interesting of the three is the **International Dyeing and Weaving Art Museum**, which exhibits a diverse collection of handwoven fabrics from around the world, from sixteenth-century Belgian tapestries to beautiful kimono. The **Yukara Ori Folk Craft Museum** displays the colourful local style of textile, and you can watch weavers at work. Least appealing is the kitsch **Snow Crystals Museum**; the displays on the myriad shapes of snow crystals are pretty but dwarfed by the castle-like complex with turrets, an ice corridor and a two-hundred-seat concert hall with a sky-painted ceiling.

Kawamura Kaneto Ainu Memorial Hall

川村カ子トアイヌ記念館 • Hokumon-chō 11 chōme • Daily 9am–5pm, July & Aug till 6pm; ☎ 0166 51 2461 • ¥500 • Buses #24 and #23 run to the hall from platform 14 in front of the JR station

Asahikawa was once a major Ainu settlement. There's a modest collection of Ainu-related artefacts on display at the **Kawamura Kaneto Ainu Memorial Hall**, which celebrates the Ainu chief Kaneto who worked as a surveyor with Hokkaidō's railways. Occasionally, Ainu dance performances and events take place – call ahead to check. The **Ainu Kotan Matsuri** (アイヌコタン祭), an Ainu festival, is held each September, beside the Ishikari-gawa, around 10km south of Asahikawa.

ARRIVAL AND DEPARTURE ASAHIKAWA

By plane Asahikawa Airport (☎ 0166 83 3939, ⬥ aapb .co.jp) is 18km to the east of the city, towards Biei (see p.320); regular buses head into town from here (30min; ¥570).
Destinations Kansai International (daily; 2hr); Nagoya (daily; 1hr 50min); Tokyo (7 daily; 1hr 45min).

By train Trains arrive at the JR station, at the southern end of Heiwa-dōri, the city's main shopping street.
Destinations Abashiri (4 daily; 3hr 44min); Furano (11

daily; 1hr 10min); Sapporo (35 daily; 1hr 30min); Wakkanai (3 daily; 3hr 30min).

By bus Buses leave in front of the train station.
Destinations Asahidake Onsen (2 daily; 1hr 30min); Furano (5 daily; 1hr 55min); Kushiro (2 daily; 6hr 30min); Sapporo (every 20–40min; 2hr 30min); Sōunkyō Onsen (5 daily; 1hr 45min); Tenninkyō Onsen (2 daily; 1hr); Wakkanai (daily; 4hr 40min).

INFORMATION

Tourist information There's a helpful tourist office (daily 8am–7.30pm; ☎ 0166 22 6704, ⬥ www.asahikawa-daisetsu.jp/e) inside the station, to the right as you exit the ticket barrier. Tourist information is also available from the international department in the Asahikawa Government Office, 3F City Hall, 10-chōme, Rokujo-dōri (Mon–Fri 9am–5pm).

Services The Asahikawa Government Office has free internet access. Alternatively, to get online try *Comic Buster Compa 3.7* (daily 11am–3am; ¥500/hr), six blocks north of the station along Heiwa-dōri and to the left. There's an ATM within the JR station and at the Central Post Office, next to the *Loisir Hotel Asahikawa* (see below).

ACCOMMODATION

Loisir Hotel Asahikawa ロワジールホテル旭川 6-7 Jo-dōri ☎ 0166 25 8811, ⬥ solarehotels.com. Right outside the station, with good online discounts, this classy hotel has free wi-fi in the rooms and a spa/gym in the basement. **¥10,000**

Tōyoko Inn Asahikawa Ekimae Ichijo-dōri 東横INN旭川駅前一条道 9-164-1, Ichijo-dōri ☎ 0166 27 1045, ⬥ toyoko-inn.com. This branch of the reliable chain is a few

minutes' walk from the station; there's wi-fi in the rooms and lobby, and breakfast is included in the rate. **¥8480**

Tōyoko Inn Asahikawa Ekimae Miyashita-dōri 東横INN旭川駅前宮下通 11-176, Miyashita-dōri ☎ 0166 25 2045, ⬥ toyoko-inn.com. The second branch of the *Tōyoko Inn* is a few blocks east of the station, and marginally cheaper than the other branch (see above). It also has free wi-fi and breakfast included. **¥7480**

EATING AND DRINKING

There are plenty of places to eat around Heiwa-dōri and, one block west, the Sanroku entertainment district, where you'll find lively *izakaya* and sushi bars.

Baikōken 梅光軒 8-chōme, 2-jo-dōri ☎ 0166 24 4575. Asahikawa is renowned for its *shōyu*-style ramen: sample it at this basement restaurant a few blocks down from the

station, where a large bowl will set you back less than ¥1000. Daily 11am–9pm.
Hachiya ラーメンの蜂屋 7 chōme, 5-jo-dōri

ASAHIKAWA'S WINTER FESTIVAL

The spectacular Winter Festival takes place over five days in the second week of February. The giant stage for the festival's opening and closing events holds the world record for the **largest snow sculpture**. The festival's many other snow and ice sculptures are displayed in Tokiwa-kōen, a fifteen-minute walk north of the station, and along pedestrianized Shōwa-dōri, among other places.

☎0166 23 3729. One of several good ramen shops on the atmospheric alleyway Furariito (ふらりーと), a 10min walk from the station. You'll get a large bowl of ramen for less than ¥1000. Daily 11am–11pm.

Machibar マチバル Heiwa-dōri, 8 chōme, 2-jo-dōri ☎0166 23 5977. This stylish café-bar runs over two floors and serves pasta, pizza and gratin from ¥680. Fresh fruit cocktails are ¥800. Daily 11.30am–midnight.

Osteria Nacon ナコン Mitsui Dai-ichi Building, 7-chōme, 5-jo-dōri ☎0166 25 1900. Tasty Italian-style bistro food made with organic local ingredients is served up at this cute basement space, opposite Furariito alley, for around ¥3000. Mon–Sat 6pm–1am.

Taisetsu Ji Beer 大雪地ビール館 11-1604 Miyashita-dōri ☎0166 25 0400. Asahikawa has a couple of *gaijin* bars, but they're lacklustre; instead, sample the local beer here, a couple of blocks east of the JR station along Miyashita-dōri. The food menu includes a *jingisukan* lunch for ¥1000 and hamburgers for ¥790. Daily 11.30am–10pm.

Daisetsu-zan National Park

大雪山国立公園, Daisetsuzan Kokuritsukōen

The 2309-square-kilometre **Daisetsu-zan National Park** offers a spectacular range of gorges, hot springs and mountains – including **Asahi-dake**, the island's tallest peak – crisscrossed by hiking trails which could keep you happily occupied for days. Tourism in the park is generally low-key, especially at the wooded and remote **Asahi-dake Onsen**. **Sōunkyō Onsen**, on the northeast edge of the park, hosts the bulk of tourists, though a tasteful redevelopment has made it much more attractive than most hot-spring resorts. The highlight here is the **gorge**, a 20km corridor of jagged cliffs, 150m high in places. In July, the mountain slopes are covered with alpine flowers, while September and October see the landscape painted in vivid autumnal colours; these are the best months for hiking. During the winter, both Asahi-dake and **Kuro-dake** in Sōunkyō are popular skiing spots, enjoying the longest ski season in Japan (usually Oct–June).

Asahi-dake Onsen

旭岳温泉

Quiet and uncommercialized, **ASAHI-DAKE ONSEN** is little more than a handful of hotels and pensions dotted along a road that snakes up to the cable-car station, from where hikers in the summer and skiers in the winter are whisked to within striking distance of the 2291m summit of **Asahi-dake** (旭岳). The area's remoteness means that it remains a delightful and relatively little-visited destination. Cross-country skiers in particular will appreciate the kilometres of groomed trails, some of the best in Japan, which wind through beautiful forests of white birch and Hokkaidō spruce.

ASAHIKAWA'S SAKE BREWERIES

The pure waters flowing off Daisetsu-zan are one reason that Asahikawa has long had a flourishing sake industry. To sample some of the local product, head to the **Takasago Sake Brewery** (高砂酒造; Miyashita-dōri 17-chōme; daily 9am–5.30pm, Sun till 5pm; ☎0166 23 2251; ⊛takasagoshuzo.com), set in a traditional wooden building around ten minutes' walk east of Asahikawa Station. They've been making sake here since 1899, and from late January to early March they have a tradition of building an ice dome in which some of their sakes are fermented. If you have more time, head 6km north of the city centre to the **Otokoyama Sake Brewery and Museum** (男山酒造り資料館; 2-7 Nagayama; daily 9am–5pm; ☎0166 48 1931, ⊛otokoyama.com), where there's a fascinating history of Otokoyama sake told through *ukiyo-e* woodblock prints, and you can also taste the award-winning rice wines for free. Buses #67, #70, #71 and #667 from platform 18 in front of the JR station will get you here.

Walk to Tenninkyō Onsen

天人峡温泉 • From the main car park at Tenninkyō Onsen, you can catch the bus to Asahikawa (¥1180) or back to Asahi-dake Onsen (¥730)

There's a good two-hour walk, mainly downhill and through forests, from the campsite in Asahidake Onsen to **Tenninkyō Onsen**, where a gaggle of tourist hotels stands at the mouth of a dramatic gorge which terminates in two spectacular **waterfalls**.

Asahi-dake

旭岳 • Ropeway daily: March–May 9am–5pm; June & Oct 8am–5pm; July–Sept 6am–6pm; Nov–Feb 9am–4pm, closed Nov 11–Dec 10; check the website for more detailed running times, as they vary greatly by month • June 15–Oct 10 one-way ¥1500, return ¥2800; Oct 11–June 14 one-way ¥1000, return ¥1800 • ⓦ wakasarescrt.com/eng

It's a fifteen-minute **ropeway** (cable-car) ride to **Asahi-dake**'s top station, worth visiting for its ethereal landscape of steaming pools and rocky outcrops, even if you're not planning to hike to the top of Asahi-dake. There's a 2km strolling course from the ropeway station which takes around an hour.

Asahi-dake's peak is an arduous ninety-minute to two-hour slog over slippery volcanic rock from the ropeway station, but the view from the summit is fantastic. From here you can hike across to Sōunkyō (see below).

ARRIVAL AND INFORMATION

ASAHI-DAKE ONSEN

By bus There are 2–4 buses daily from Asahikawa Station (platform 4) to Asahi-dake Onsen (1hr 40min; ¥1320), all stopping at Tenninkyō Onsen en route; check with the tourist office at Asahikawa Station for the timetable.

Tourist information Near the ropeway station, the tourist office (daily: June–Oct 9am–5pm; Nov–May 10am–4pm; ⓦ bit.ly/1jNatra) has nature displays (all in Japanese), information on weather conditions on the mountain and hiking maps.

ACCOMMODATION AND EATING

Asahi-dake Seishōnen Yaeijō Camp Area 旭岳青少年野営場 Yukomanbetsu ☎0166 97 2544. Daisetsu-zan's campsite is open June 20–Sept 20; tent rental (¥520) and other camping equipment is available. **¥210** per person

Hotel Bearmonte ホテルベアモンテ Asahi-dake Onsen ☎0166 97 2321. These upmarket but unremarkable lodgings, opposite the visitor centre, offer mainly Western-style rooms. In its favour are the nicely designed onsen baths, including rotemburo, and small gym. **¥20,000**

★**Daisetsuzan Shirakaba-sō Hotel and Youth Hostel** 大雪山白樺荘 Asahi-dake Onsen ☎0166 97 2246, ⓦ park19.wakwak.com/~shirakaba. There's both hotel and hostel-style lodgings at this lovely wooden building, opposite the campsite bus stop and next to a running stream; the attached log house has a convivial communal lounge and there's a rotemburo (¥500 for non-guests). Evening meals are excellent (there's a ¥2020 surcharge for dinner and breakfast), and the hostel staff can provide all you need to climb Asahi-dake, including a bell to warn off bears. Dorm **¥4870**, double **¥11,840**

La Vista Daisetsuzan ラビスタ大雪山 Asahi-dake Onsen ☎0166 97 2323; ⓦ tinyurl.com/25erlmn. In the style of a large alpine chalet, the resort's newest hotel offers pleasant, spacious accommodation, lovely views and well-designed onsen baths. **¥24,000**

Lodge Nutapu-Kaushipe ロッジヌタプカウシペ Asahi-dake Onsen ☎&ⓕ0166 97 2150. Next to the youth hostel (see below) and equally appealing is this attractive wooden cabin with six comfortable, Japanese-style rooms – all non-smoking. They also run a noodle café. Two meals are included. **¥15,000**

Sōunkyō Onsen

層雲峡温泉

On the northeastern edge of Daisetsu-zan, 70km east of Asahikawa, is **SŌUNKYŌ ONSEN**, the park's main resort and ideal base for viewing the astonishing **Sōunkyō gorge**, its jagged rock walls carved out by the Ishikari-gawa.

The village's main street is lined with small hotels, shops and a large bathing complex, **Kurodake-no-yu** (黒岳の湯; daily 10am–9pm, Nov–Jan closed Wed; ¥600). From January to the end of March, it's also possible to enjoy the **Hyōbaku Matsuri** (Ice Waterfall Festival; ¥100), a park of giant ice sculptures which are lit spectacularly every night from 5pm to 10pm.

Sōunkyō gorge

層雲峡 Sōunkyō-Kai

Cycling to **Sōunkyō gorge** is a pleasant way of getting there – rent a bike from the *Northern Lodge* (see below) and follow the riverside route for 8km to Ōbako. About 3km east of the resort, pause to view the **Ginga ("Milky Way")** and **Ryūsei ("Shooting Star")** waterfalls. A twenty-minute climb up the opposite hill will lead to a viewpoint from where you'll get a fabulous view of the two cascades of white water tumbling down the cliffs. Continuing along the cycling and walking path, you'll eventually arrive at **Ōbako** ("Big Box"), a touristy spot where visitors line up to be photographed in front of the river that gushes through the narrow gap in the perpendicular cliffs.

ARRIVAL AND INFORMATION

SŌUNKYŌ ONSEN

By train The closest train station to Sōunkyō Onsen is Kamikawa (上川), 20km north; buses (¥800) take 30min from here to reach the resort.

By bus Some of the buses passing through Kamikawa and on to Sōunkyō originate in Asahikawa (¥1950); some also go on to Akan Kohan. See ⊚ dohokubus.com for the schedule.

Tourist information There's a small tourist office (daily 10am–5.30pm; ☎ 01658 5 3350, ⊚ sounkyo.net) in the bus terminal building, while the Sōunkyō Visitor Centre next to the cable car station (daily June–Oct 8am–5.30pm; Nov–May 9am–5pm; ☎ 01658 9 4400) has excellent nature displays.

ACCOMMODATION AND EATING

Beer Grill Canyon ビアグリル・キャニオン ☎ 0165 85 3361. In the same complex as Kurodake-no-yu, this place serves tasty thin-crust pizza, pasta and creative dishes such as Ezo venison stroganoff (¥1500). Daily 11.30am–3.30pm & 5.30–8.30pm; Nov–April closed Wed.

Midori 民宿みどり ☎ 0165 85 3315. Within the village itself, you can get basic tatami rooms here between May and Oct, two meals included. There's a friendly manager who may be found at the souvenir shop downstairs. **¥14,000**

Northern Lodge ホテル・ノーザンロッジ ☎ 01658 5 3231, ⊚ h-northernlodge.com. If you crave a bit of luxury, this is a good choice, offering both tatami and Western-style rooms, with two meals included. Bikes are available to rent for ¥1000 per day. **¥21,000**

Sōunkyō Youth Hostel 層雲峡YH ☎ 0165 85 3418, ⊚ youthhostel.or.jp/sounkyo. This budget hostel is a 10min walk uphill from the bus terminal, near the *Prince Hotel*. The dorms here have bunk beds, meals are served in a rustic lounge area and you can get information – mainly in Japanese – on hiking in the park. Closed Nov–May. Dorm **¥3150**, double **¥9800**

Furano and around

富良野

Surrounded by beautiful countryside, **FURANO** is famous in Japan as the location of a popular soap opera *Kita no Kuni Kara* (*From the Northern Country*), about a Tokyo family adapting to life in Hokkaidō. The landscape evokes Provençal France, with bales of hay lying around and lone poplars etched against the peaks of Daisetsu-zan National Park. The busiest season is June and July, when vast fields of lavender and other flowers bloom, drawing visitors to the gently undulating countryside – ideal for walks, cycling and photography; the most scenic farmlands surround the tranquil settlements of **Kami-Furano** (上富良野), **Biei** (美瑛) and **Bibaushi** (美馬牛), each with its own train station. In winter, Furano is known for its **skiing**.

Further afield, if you need goals for your perambulations, head to Kami-Furano where the **Goto Sumio Museum of Art** (後藤純男美術館; Higashi 4-sen Kita 26-go; daily 9am–5pm, Nov–March till 4pm; ¥1000; ⊚ gotosumiomuseum.com) contains dreamy landscape paintings from one of Japan's major contemporary artists, or to Furano's wine and cheese factories (see box, p.323). Furano and the outlying towns in the area can also be used as a base for a hike up the 2077m active volcano of **Tokachi-dake**, some 20km southwest and within the Daisetsu-zan National Park.

HIKING ACROSS THE PARK

You can start the **Daisetsu-zan hike** across the park's central mountain range either from the top of the ropeway (cable-car) at Asahi-dake Onsen (see p.319) or from Sōunkyō Onsen where there's also a **ropeway** (@rinyu.cc.jp; one-way/return ¥1000/1850), followed by a **chairlift** (one-way/return ¥400/600) up to within one hour's hike of the 1984m **Kuro-dake** (Black Mountain); check the website for running times, which vary month by month. From the summit capped by a small shrine and giving marvellous views of the park, there's a choice of two trails to **Asahi-dake** – the southern route via Hokkai-dake (2149m) is the more scenic.

By the time you reach Asahi-dake's summit, you'll have spent around six hours walking, so returning on foot to Sōunkyō Onsen the same day is only possible if you set out at the crack of dawn. There are **overnight huts** on the mountain, but the more comfortable option is to continue down to Asahi-dake Onsen and rest there for the night. If you don't want to backtrack for your luggage, consider having it sent on by *takkyūbin* (see p.71). Also make sure you're well prepared for the hike with food, topographical maps, and bells to scare away the odd bear, even though they're not that common (see box, p.332).

ARRIVAL AND INFORMATION

FURANO AND AROUND

By train In summer, and sometimes in winter, there are direct trains from Sapporo, but usually the fastest way is to take a limited express to Takikawa then change to the local train along the Furano line. From Asahikawa, the train takes 1hr 15min (¥1040), passing through Biei, Bibaushi and Kami-Furano.

By bus Furano is connected by direct bus with Sapporo (around 2hr 30min; ¥2200); if you're coming to ski, ask to be dropped at Kitanomine-iriguchi (the hub of the ski village)

rather than getting off in the centre of town. Regular buses also run from Asahikawa station via the airport, Furano train station, and various other stations en route, to the *New Furano Prince Hotel* (8 daily; 1hr 55min, ¥1000); a taxi to the hotel from Furano Station costs around ¥2300.

Tourist information The Furano tourist office (@0167 23 3388, @furanotourism.com/en; daily 9am–6pm) has operations both next to Furano Station and at the Kitanomine gondola station.

ACCOMMODATION

If you've come to ski, it's most convenient to stay in either the *Prince* hotels or at Kitanomine village, from where you can walk to the lifts. Furano town itself isn't too far away and is connected to the slopes by regular buses. In summer, the countryside around Bibaushi and Biei draws visitors with its displays of lavender, tulips, iris, cosmos and sunflowers, amongst others.

Alpine Backpackers アルパインバックパッカーズ 14-6 Kitanomine-chō @0167 22 1311, @alpn.co.jp. A 5min walk from the Kitanomine ski lifts, this great lodge has bunk-bed dorms or twins, a kitchen, a bakery-café, free wi-fi and young, enthusiastic staff. They also organize balloon trips year-round, plus fishing and adventure sports such as rafting, mountain biking and horseriding in summer. Dorm ¥2700, twin ¥5400

Bibaushi Liberty Youth Hostel 美馬牛リバティYH Bibaushi-shigaichi @0166 95 2141, @youthhostel .or.jp. Next to the Bibaushi JR station, this stylish hostel offers comfy bunk-bed dorms and private rooms; excellent, inexpensive meals are also available. Dorm ¥4580, twin ¥10,160

Furano Fresh Powder フレッシュパウダー・アパートメント 14-26 Kitanomine-chō @0167 23 4738, @freshpowder.com. These six well-equipped self-catering units are opposite the Kitanomine ski slopes, and sleep between four and eight people. There's a three- to seven-day minimum during ski season. ¥25,000

★ **Furano Guest House Phytoncide Mori no Kaori** フィトンチッド森の香り 17-2 Kitanomine-chō @0167 39 1551, @woodlandfarm.co.jp. This is one of Furano's most original accommodation options. The charming owners, who bake their own bread and serve foods grown on their organic farm, have an amazing collection of antique cash registers. Each of the six Western-style rooms has its own bathroom, and one is wheelchair-accessible. Rates include breakfast. ¥29,700

Natulux Hotel ナチュラクスホテル 1-35 Asahi-chō @0167 22 7777, @natulux.com. Next to Furano Station, this tasteful boutique property sports a minimalist design contrasting concrete walls with black or brown wooden fixtures. The English-speaking management are very obliging and guests can use the neighbouring sports complex with swimming pool for free. ¥14,700

New Furano Prince Hotel 新富良野プリンスホテル Nakagoryo @0167 22 1111, @princehotels.co.jp/ newfurano. A few kilometres south of Kitanomine village, this 400-bed oval-shaped tower block is a world

---

FURANO CULTURAL PERFORMANCES

The local tourism office is working hard to ensure that the Japanese character and charm of the Furano area aren't lost or overlooked by visiting *gaijin*. During the ski season, a free **cultural performance** is held every Sunday night at the restaurant at the Kitanomine gondola station. This includes a presentation of the town's "belly button dance", the highlight of Furano's **Heso Matsuri** (Navel Festival), held every July 28–29 and celebrating the town's position at the centre of Hokkaidō.

---

unto itself, featuring everything from several restaurants and bars, ski rental and a coin laundry to a sophisticated onsen (guests/non-guests ¥750/¥1500) and a twee log-cabin shopping village. Families will love their Snow Land winter amusement park. In winter there are package deals with meals and ski-lift tickets. The *Prince* group has a second smaller hotel in Furano that's mainly used by groups. **¥36,400**

EATING AND DRINKING

Furano Brewery Yama no Doxon 山の独尊 20-29 Kitanomine-chō ☎0167 22 5599. A rustic microbrewery where they make their own very palatable beers, sausages, smoked meats and curries. Tues–Sun 5.30–9.30pm; Fri–Sun also 11.30am–2.30pm.

★**Kuma Gera** くまげら 3-22 Hinode-machi ☎0167 39 2345, ⊕www.furano.ne.jp/kumagera. A lively place in the midst of Furano town where they serve the meat-laden *sanzoku nabe* (bandits' stew), full of duck, venison and chicken – a pot for two costs ¥3300. Daily 11.30am–midnight.

Soh's Bar ソーズ・バー Nakagoryo ☎0167 22 1111. A good place for a nightcap, in a log-and-stone cabin in the forest near the *New Furano Prince Hotel* (see p.321), where you can admire the collection of cigarette packets whether you're a "miserable smoker" or not. On the way there, you can go gift shopping in the attractive log-house complex Ningle Terrace. Daily 7pm–midnight.

Wakkanai

稚内

The windswept port of **WAKKANAI**, 320km from Sapporo, is the gateway to the **Rishiri-Rebun-Sarobetsu National Park** (see p.323) and, in particular, the lovely islands of Rebun-tō and Rishiri-tō. There's little reason to linger in town, but there are a few places of minor interest in the area, should you find yourself killing time waiting for a ferry.

A short stroll from Wakkanai Station is the impressive **North Breakwater Dome**, a 427m-long arched corridor supported by seventy concrete pillars, inspired by the arches of Rome's Colosseum. For a longer walk (around 1hr, round-trip), head west of the train station to **Wakkanai-kōen** (稚内公園), a grassy park from where, on a clear day, you can see the island of **Sakhalin**, some 60km northwest; it's now part of Russia, but before World War II it was occupied by the Japanese.

Wakkanai is the access point for the desolate cape **Sōya Misaki** (宗谷岬), 32km east of Wakkanai and the northernmost point of Japan (7 buses daily; 50min; ¥2430 return). A couple of monuments, including "Tower of Prayer", a memorial to the Korean Airlines plane shot down by the Soviet Union just north of the cape, mark this dull spot.

A quirky reason for heading here out of season is to attend the **Japan Cup National Dogsled Races**, held the last weekend of February.

SKIING IN FURANO

Furano's winter focus is its **ski resort** (⊕snowfurano.com, ⊕princehotels.co.jp/ski/furano; day ticket ¥4500) on the slopes of Mount Kitanomine, a popular option with those seeking to escape the crowded foreigner scene at Niseko (see p.302). The slopes are challenging, but not as varied or as long as Niseko's; to go off-piste, or try backcountry skiing with qualified English-speaking guides, contact **Hokkaidō Powder Guides** (☎0167 22 5655, ⊕hokkaidopowderguides.com).

FERTILE FURANO

It's not just flowers that thrive in Furano's fertile soil. The area is also known for its melons, potatoes, onions, milk and grapes. At **Chateau Furano** (ふらのワイン; Shimizuyama; daily 9am–4.30pm, June & Aug till 6pm; free; ☎0167 22 3242, ☻furanowine.jp), around 4km northwest of Furano Station, you can sip from a range of eighteen different wines; some of them are fairly palatable. The obvious accompaniment is cheese, and this can be sampled at the **Furano Cheese Factory** (富良野チーズ工房; Nakagoku; daily 9am–5pm, Nov–March till 4pm; free; ☎0167 23 1156, ☻www.furano.ne.jp/furano-cheese), about 1km east of the *New Furano Prince Hotel* (see p.321). Apart from selling concoctions such as a brie turned black with squid ink, this fun facility also allows you to practise milking a fake cow (¥100) and sign up for bread-, butter, cheese- and ice cream-making workshops (¥680–350): ring ahead to book.

ARRIVAL AND DEPARTURE

WAKKANAI

By plane A bus from Wakkanai's airport (☎0162 27 2121), 10km east of the port, costs ¥590 for the 30min journey, and a taxi ¥3500.

Destinations Sapporo (daily; 50min); Tokyo (daily; 1hr 45min).

By train Wakkanai Station (the northernmost train station on Hokkaidō) is close by both the ferry terminal and the new combined bus terminal and cinema.

Destinations Asahikawa (5 daily; 4hr); Sapporo (3 daily; 5hr).

By bus There are six buses from Sapporo, including one overnight (¥6000).

Destinations Asahikawa (daily; 4hr 40min); Sapporo (6 daily; 6–7hr).

By ferry Wakkanai is the jumping-off point for the islands of Rebun-tō and Rishiri-tō.

Destinations Rebun-tō (2–4 daily; 1hr 40min); Rishiri-tō (2–4 daily; 1hr 45min).

INFORMATION

Tourist information Inside the train station is a helpful tourist office (daily May–Sept 10am–6pm; ☎0162 24 1216, ☻welcome.wakkanai.hokkaido.jp).

Services If you're heading on to Rishiri-tō and Rebun-tō, stock up on cash in Wakkanai, as there are no foreign

exchange facilities on either of the islands. There's an ATM that accepts overseas cards at the post office, five blocks west of the JR station (ATM hours Mon–Fri 8.45am–7pm, Sat & Sun 9am–5pm).

ACCOMMODATION

ANA Hotel Wakkanai 稚内全日空ホテル 1-2-2 Kaiun ☎0162 23 8111, ☻ana-hotel-wakkanai.co.jp. The most luxurious option in Wakkanai, directly in front of the ferry terminal. Prices here drop dramatically in the off-season. **¥21,000**

Wakkanai Moshiripa Youth Hostel 稚内モシリパ ユースホステル Chuo 2-9-5 ☎0162 24 0180, ☻youthhostel.or.jp. The most convenient youth hostel

for the port is a 5min walk north from the train station and east of the ferry terminal; guests must check in before 8pm. Note that it's closed Oct 15–Dec 15. Dorm **¥3960**

Wakkanai Youth Hostel 稚内ユースホステル Koma-dōri 3-9-1 ☎0162 23 7162, ☻youthhostel.or.jp. Better equipped than Wakkanai's other hostel and open year-round, this is a 10min walk south from JR Minami Wakkanai Station. Dorm **¥3960**

EATING

Takechan 竹ちゃん Chuo 2-8 ☎0162 22 7130. Definitely sample some seafood while you're in town; this place is particularly convivial, specializing in sushi and *tako-shabu* (octopus stew; ¥1500). Daily 11.30am–2pm & 5–10pm.

Wakkanai Fukukō Ichiba 稚内副港市場 1-6-28

Minato. A 15min walk south of the JR station, you can combine a seafood meal at several inexpensive restaurants in the market with a dip in the spacious onsen baths of Minato no Yu (港の゜; daily 10am–10pm; ¥700 plus ¥150 for a towel).

Rishiri-Rebun-Sarobetsu National Park

利尻礼文サロベツ国立公園, Rishiri-Rebun-Sarobetsu Kokuritsu Kōen

The two islands that make up the bulk of the **Rishiri-Rebun-Sarobetsu National Park** are quite different: slender **Rebun-tō** is low-lying, its gentle hills sprinkled with alpine

---

THE RUSSIAN CONNECTION

There's a monument in Wakkanai-kōen to nine female **telephone operators** who committed suicide in Sakhalin's post office at the end of World War II, rather than be captured by the Russians. Russo–Japanese relations are now much improved, and there's steady trade between Wakkanai and its northern neighbour, as witnessed by the many signs in Russian around town. From mid-May to October a **ferry** runs between Wakkanai and the town of **Korsakov** on Sakhalin (5hr 30min; economy class ¥22,500 one-way, ¥35,000 return); see ⓦ www.kaiferry.co.jp for details.

---

flowers, while **Rishiri-tō** is a Fuji-like volcano rising from the sea. Offering lovely scenery and mild weather, both islands are exceptionally popular with Japanese tourists from June to September, when accommodation should be booked well in advance. At other times you're likely to have the islands to yourself, although they pretty much close down entirely between November and March. In order to get the most out of a stay here it's worth scheduling a couple of nights on each island.

Rishiri-tō

利尻島

Most people come to **RISHIRI-TŌ** to hike up the central 1721m volcano **Rishiri-zan** (利尻山). The island is sometimes called Rishiri-Fuji because its shape is said to resemble the famous southern volcano; in reality, it's spikier and a lot less symmetrical. Even if the weather is unpromising, it's still worth making the ascent (which takes 10–12hr) to break through the clouds on the upper slopes and be rewarded with panoramic views from the summit, which is crowned with a small shrine.

The most straightforward ascent of Rishiri-zan starts some 3km south of the main port of **Oshidomari** (鴛泊), at the Rishiri Hokuroku campsite. Information and maps for the climb are available from the island's tourist office (see below). Around fifteen minutes' climb from the peak of Chōkan-zan (長官山), the eighth station up the volcano, there's a basic hut where you can take shelter en route. Take plenty of water, as there's none available on the mountain.

ARRIVAL AND DEPARTURE

RISHIRI-TŌ

By plane There's a daily flight to Rishiri-tō from New Chitose; the airport (☏ 0163 82 1770) is a few kilometres west of Oshidomari.

By ferry Most visitors come by ferry from Wakkanai to Oshidomari (1hr 40min; ¥2280 one-way); May–Sept there are four services daily, then three daily in Oct, dropping to two Nov–March before increasing to three again in April.

INFORMATION

Tourist information The tourist office (mid-April to mid-Oct daily 8am–5.40pm; ☏ 0163 82 2201, ⓦ kankou.rishiri .jp/eng), inside the ferry terminal at Oshidomari, has maps and English notes on the hikes to Rishiri-zan and Himenuma.

GETTING AROUND

By bus Buses run in both directions around the island (a circuit which takes 1hr 45min; ¥2200). If you arrive by ferry at Kutsugata on the western side of Rishiri, you'll need to get a bus north to Oshidomari (30min; ¥730).

By bike Bicycles are a good way to get around and can be rented from near the ferry terminal for around ¥2000 a day.

ACCOMMODATION

Island Inn Rishiri アイランド・イン・リシリ Kutsugata ☏ 0163 84 3002. Located in Kutsugata on the island's west coast, the large, modern Western-style rooms here have views of either the port or the mountains. There's a public bath and rates include two meals. **¥21,300**

Kitaguni Grand Hotel 北国グランドホテル Oshidomari ☏ 0163 82 1362, ☐ 82 2556. Rishiri-tō's most upmarket accommodation is found in an unsightly

RISHIRI-REBUN-SAROBETSU NATIONAL PARK

Korsakov (Sakhalin)

SEA OF JAPAN

Sukoton Misaki

Funadomari

Noshappu Misaki

Wakkanai

Rebun-dake (490m)

Rebun-tō

Minami-Wakkanai

HACHI JIKAN COURSE

Naioro

Uennai

Motochi   Kafuka

Bakkai

Rebun-kaikyō Strait

Motochi Tōdai

Yūchi

■ ACCOMMODATION

Field Inn Seikan-sō	1
Hana Rebun	3
Island Inn Rishiri	6
Kitugani Grand Hotel	4
Kutsugata Misaki-kōen	
Campsite	6
Minshuku Kaidō	1
Momoiwa Youth Hostel	2
Pension Hera-san-no-ie	4
Rishiri Hokuroku Forest	
Park Campsite	5

Rishiri Airport

Oshidomari

Himenuma

Rishiri-tō

Rishiri-kaikyō Strait

Kutsugata

Rishiri-zan (1721m)

0   10
kilometres

Sarobetsu Natural
Flower Garden

---

red-brick tower that sticks out like a sore thumb amid the surrounding houses. Rates include two meals and drop significantly in the off season. **¥33,900**

Kutsugata Misaki-kōen Campsite 沓形岬公園キャンプ場 Kutsugata-misaki ☎0163 84 2345. Much quieter than *Rishiri Hokuroku* campsite (see below), this free site is located in the park just south of Kutsugata port. Open May–Oct. **Free**

Pension Hera-san-no-ie ペンションへらさんの家 Oshidomari ☎&℻0163 82 2361. Located near the ferry terminal, next to the path leading up the rock that looms over the harbour, this pension has nice tatami rooms and a couple of Western-style bedrooms. **¥21,300**

Rishiri Hokuroku Forest Park campsite 利尻北麓野営場 Sakae-machi Oshidomari-aza ☎0163 82 2394. This campground is 3km south of the port and on the main route up the volcano. Alternatively, you can kip in one of the wooden cabins, which sleep four people (¥3000/person). Open mid-May to mid-Oct. **¥300** per person

Rebun-tō

礼文島

Shaped like a crab's claw adrift in the Sea of Japan, **REBUN-TŌ** is most famous for its wild flowers – from May to September the island's rolling green slopes are said to bloom with three hundred different types of alpine plants. At the island's southern end is its main port, the small and attractive settlement of **Kafuka** (香深), which spreads uphill from the coast. In the north is the small fishing village of **Funadomari**

THE ROAD TO HIMENUMA

A less strenuous alternative to climbing Rishiri-zan is the three-hour hiking trail which starts at pretty **Himenuma** pond (姫沼) and continues across the slopes of two smaller mountains, **Kopon-zan** and **Pon-zan**, to the *Rishiri Hokuroku* campsite (see above). To get to Himenuma from Oshidomari, follow the coastal road 1km or so west until you reach a junction going up into the hills. The walk to the pond is quite steep – you might be able to hitch a lift – and takes around an hour.

(船泊), which makes a good base for hikes out to the northern cape, Sukoton Misaki (スコトン岬).

The whole island is fabulous **hiking** territory. The longest and most popular hike is the 32km **Hachi-jikan** (8hr) down the west coast from Sukoton Misaki, the island's northernmost point, to Motochi (元地) in the south. The cliffs at the end of this hike can be slippery and sometimes dangerous; easier is the **Yo-jikan** (4hr) course, which omits the difficult coastal section of the Hachi-jikan course from Uennai to Motochi. The youth hostel (see below) arranges walking groups for the two hikes and holds briefings the night before. Stock up on food and drink before you start, as there are no refreshment stops along the way, and it's not safe to drink river water on the island.

ARRIVAL AND DEPARTURE
REBUN-TŌ

By ferry Rebun-tō is only accessible by ferry. From May to Sept, five ferries daily go from Wakkanai to Kafuka (1hr 55min; ¥2200), and there are at least a couple each day during the rest of the year. Daily ferries also sail between Kafuka on

Rebun-tō and Oshidomari and Kutsugata on Rishiri-tō (40min; ¥930 one-way). Hostels and most minshuku will pick you up from the ferry terminals, if you book in advance. For full details of the ferries go to ⊚ heartlandferry.jp.

INFORMATION AND TOURS

Tourist information Rebun's tourist office (April–Oct daily 8am–5.30pm; ☎0163 86 2655, ⓦwww .rebun-island.jp/en), in the ferry terminal at Kafuka, has a good map of the island marked with the main hiking routes including ones up Rebun-dake and to the Momo-iwa ("Peach-Shaped Rock") on the west coast. Staff can also help with booking accommodation.

Bike rental Bike rental is available from several shops near the ferry terminal for ¥50/hr, or ¥2000/day.
Bus tours If time is limited, consider taking one of the three bus tours (¥3300–4000), which cover all the scenic highlights and are timed to connect with the ferries; details are available from the tourist office.

ACCOMMODATION

Field Inn Seikan-sō 星観荘 Funadomari 5 ☎0163 87 2818. This comfortable minshuku in Funadomari occupies a Scandinavian-style wooden cottage with great views. Rooms have bunk beds and rates include two meals. **¥12,000**
Hana Rebun 花れぶん Kafuka ☎0163 86 1177. Next to the ferry terminal, this is the luxury option, with its appealing traditional-style rooms combining Western and Japanese interior design. The most expensive suites sport outdoor tubs on balconies. Rates include two meals. **¥36,000**
Minshuku Kaidō 民宿海憧 Ō-aza, Funadomari-mura ☎0163 87 2717, ☻87 2183. Larger than the *Field Inn Seikan-sō*, this establishment next to the beach campsite

has tatami rooms and some cheaper dorm accommodation (under 35s only). Rates include two meals. Dorm **¥6000**, double **¥15,000**
Momo-iwa-sō Youth Hostel 桃岩荘ユースホステル Aza Motochi, Kafuka ☎0163 86 1421, ⓦyouthhostel .or.jp. Occupying a dramatic location on the rocky western coast south of Motochi and a 15min bus ride from Kafuka, this hostel makes a good base for the Hachi-jikan hiking course it's situated at the end of the walk, but staff can organize transport to the start. It gets packed in peak season and the atmosphere becomes akin to a summer camp, featuring lots of singing and dancing from the high-spirited staff. Closed Jan–May. Dorm **¥3850**

Eastern Hokkaidō

With three major national parks, **eastern Hokkaidō** will be a high priority for those interested in Japan's natural environment. **Abashiri** is known throughout Japan for its old maximum-security **prison** (now a museum), and for winter boat tours through the drift ice on the Sea of Okhotsk. Jutting into these inhospitable waters northeast of Abashiri is **Shiretoko National Park**, a UNESCO World Heritage Site and one of Japan's most naturally unspoiled areas. Inland, south of the peninsula, is the **Akan National Park**, which also stunning, with hot springs and three scenic lakes. More eco-tourist delights await at **Kushiro Shitsugen National Park** and **Kiritappu Marsh**, where you can spot regal red-crested cranes among many other fauna and flora.

By car Public transport is sparse, so consider renting a car to get around. Nippon Rent-A-Car has offices throughout Hokkaidō, a user-friendly website and an English phone line open Mon–Fri 9am–5pm (☎03 3485 7196; ⓦ nipponrentacar.co.jp).

Abashiri

網走

Bordered by a couple of pretty lakes, the fishing port of **ABASHIRI**, 350km from Sapporo, is best visited in the dead of winter, when snow covers the less appealing modern parts of the town, whooper swans fly in to stay for the winter at Lake Tofutsu, a few kilometres east of the harbour, and drift ice (*ryūhyō*) floats across the Sea of Okhotsk (see opposite).

An excellent vantage point from which to take in Abashiri's coastal location is the summit of **Tento-zan**, directly behind the train station, where you'll also find several enjoyable **museums**. Check with the tourist office (see opposite) for coupons to get discounted entry to all these museums and for information on a bus service that runs a circuit around them.

Okhotsk Ryūhyō Museum

オホーツク流氷館, • 245-1 Tentozan • Daily: April–Oct 8am–6pm; Nov–March 9am–4.30pm • ¥520 • ⓦ ryuhyokan.com

At the informative **Okhotsk Ryūhyō Museum**, you can touch huge lumps of ice in a room where the temperature is kept at -15°C; coats are provided for warmth. A panoramic film of the drift ice is screened regularly throughout the day, and the observatory provides a 360° panoramic view of the Sea of Okhotsk.

Hokkaidō Museum of Northern Peoples

北海道立北方民族博物館, Hokkaidō-ritsu Hoppō Minzoku Hakubutsukan • 309-1 Shiomi • 9.30am–4.30pm, closed Mon • ¥450 • ⓦ hoppohm.org/english

The **Hokkaidō Museum of Northern Peoples** has interesting displays on the native peoples of northern Eurasia and America, prompting comparisons between the different cultures. A colour-coded chart at the start of the exhibition will help you identify which artefacts belong to which races; look out for the Inuit cagoules, fascinating garments made of seal intestines.

By plane Memanbetsu (女満別) Airport (ⓦmmb-airport.co.jp) is 20km south of Abashiri and 30min from town by bus (¥880).

Destinations Kansai (daily; 2hr 10min); Nagoya (daily;

CRANES, SWANS AND EAGLES

Birdwatchers will be thrilled by eastern Hokkaidō. The area is home to three of Japan's top four ornithological spectacles: red-crested white cranes (*tanchō-zuru*) in the Kushiro and Kiritappu regions (see p.335); whooper swans, also in the Kushiro region, and near Abashiri and Odaito towards the Notsuke Peninsula; and Steller's sea eagles at Rausu on the Shiretoko Peninsula. The fourth must-see is the cranes at Arasaki in Kyūshū. The best months to view all of these are January, February and March.

The **red-crested white cranes**, commonly called *tanchō*, are a symbol of Japan and were once found all over the country. However, they became so rare in the twentieth century that they were thought to be almost extinct. Fortunately, the birds – designated a "Special Natural Monument" in 1952 – have survived, and their population, living exclusively in eastern Hokkaidō, now numbers around one thousand. Thanks to feeding programmes at several sites around the Kushiro Shitsugen National Park (see p.335), it's possible to see these grand but shy birds; with a 2m wingspan they are the largest in Japan.

VIEWING THE DRIFT ICE

Global warming has impacted on the drift ice off the coast of Abashiri and the Shiretoko Peninsula, and both its volume and the season for its sighting – typically February to late March – are shrinking. Should the conditions be right, the ideal way to witness this astonishing phenomenon is to hop aboard the *Aurora*, an **ice-breaking sightseeing boat**, for a one-hour tour (Jan 20 to end March daily; ¥3300; ⓣ0152 43 6000, ⓦms-aurora.com), which departs from Abashiri four to six times a day, depending on the month and weather. The boat cracks through the ice sheets, throwing up huge chunks, some more than 1m thick. An alternative is to take the slow-moving sightseeing train **Ryūhyō Norokko-go** (流氷ノロッコ号; ¥810), which chugs along the coast between Abashiri and Shiretoko-Shari twice a day between the end of January and mid-March; if that's not available, there's also the regular *futsū* train that runs into Akan National Park (see p.332). **Gojiraiwa-Kankō** (ゴジラ岩観光; ⓣ0152 24 3060, ⓦkamuiwakka.jp/driftice) in Utoro (see p.330) offers walking trips across the ice and the chance to get in the frozen water, comfortably attired in a dry suit (¥5000).

2hr); Sapporo (6 daily; 50min); Tokyo (6 daily; 1hr 40min).

By train By train, the fastest option is the limited express from Sapporo via Asahikawa (5hr 15min). There's also a plodding local train on the Senmō line from the port of Kushiro (see p.335), 146km south.

Destinations Asahikawa (4 daily; 3hr 44min); Kushiro (4 daily; 3hr); Sapporo (5 daily; 5hr 14min); Shiretoko-Shari (9 daily; 45min).

By bus Buses from Sapporo (¥6210; ⓦj-bus.co.jp) to Abashiri take 6hr.

Destinations Sapporo (9 daily; 6hr); Shari (5 daily; 1hr).

INFORMATION

Tourist information Inside the JR station is the helpful tourist office (Mon–Fri 12–5pm, Sat & Sun 9am–5pm; ⓣ0152 44 5849, ⓦcity.abashiri.hokkaido.jp/english).

Services There's free internet access at the Ekō Centre (エコーセンター 9am–7pm, closed Mon), on the north bank of the Abashiri-gawa across the bridge near the *Abashiri Central Hotel* (see below).

ACCOMMODATION

Abashiri Central Hotel 網走セントラルホテル Minami 2 Nishi 3 ⓣ0152 44 5151, ⓦabashirich.com. The town's top overnight choice offers a classy selection of rooms, a good restaurant (serving a buffet lunch for ¥1200) and is convenient for the shopping district. **¥15,750**

Abashiri Ryūhyō-no-Oka Youth Hostel 網走流氷の丘ユースホステル Aza Meiji 22-6 ⓣ0152 43 8558, ⓦyouthhostel.or.jp. This modern hostel overlooks the Sea of Okhotsk. It's a long, steep walk up here, so catch a taxi (around ¥1000), or request the station pick-up service. Bike rental is available. Dorm **¥3850**

Auberge Kita-no-dan-dan 北の暖援 Omagari 39-17 ⓣ0152 45 5963. This engagingly rustic retreat atop a hill and surrounded by greenery is a 5min taxi ride from the JR station. There's a rotemburo, and rates include two European-style meals. **¥40,000**

Shimbashi ホテルしんばし Shin-machi 1-2-12 ⓣ0152 43 4307 ⓕ45 2091. This old-style hotel, directly opposite the JR station, has decent tatami and Western-style rooms. Its restaurant serves good-value set meals and cheap noodle dishes. **¥6300**

Tōyoko Inn Okhotsk Abashiri Ekimae 東横INNオホーツク・網走駅前 1-3-3 Shin-machi ⓣ0152 45 1043, ⓦtoyoko-inn.com. This branch of the dependable hotel chain is handily located directly opposite the station. **¥7980**

EATING AND DRINKING

Abashiri specializes in fresh seafood – don't leave town without trying some of the freshly caught succulent crabs. It's also home to a microbrewery, which is worth a visit to sample the local infusion.

Sushiyasu 寿し安 Minami 5 Nishi 2 ⓣ0152 43 4121. Reliable and inexpensive, this place is a couple of blocks behind the *Abashiri Central Hotel* (see above): sushi sets cost as little as ¥900 for lunch and ¥1550 for dinner. Daily 11am–11pm.

Yakiniku Abashiri Biirukan Yakiniku 網走ビール館 Minami 2 Nishi 4, ⓣ0152 41 0008. Sample locally brewed Abashiri beer and grilled beef here, a 5min walk from the station towards the port; the *yakiniku* set menu is ¥2480. Mon–Sat 5–11pm, Fri & Sat also 11.30am–3pm.

4

> ### ABASHIRI-KO WINTER ACTIVITIES
>
> From late January to early March, fun winter activities take place on frozen Abashiri-ko, on the town's western flank. You can take a **snowmobile** for a spin around a 7km course over the lake (daily 9am–4.30pm; ¥3000), or be dragged around the ice sitting inside a raft or astride an inflatable banana. This site, along with the quay at Abashiri Port, is also the location for the town's mini **snow festival**, which takes place in the second week of February each year. Buses run to the lake from outside Abashiri Station. If none of that feels cold enough, then try **diving beneath the ice** (¥30,000 for two dives; ☎0152 61 5102).

Shiretoko National Park

知床国立公園, Shiretoko Kokuritsu Kōen

Since 176,000 acres of the Shiretoko Peninsula, including the **SHIRETOKO NATIONAL PARK**, gained UNESCO World Heritage Site status in 2005, there's been an increasing amount of investment in, as well as visitors to, this magnificent ecosystem, 42km east of Abashiri. Even so, by any standards the park, which covers about half the 70km-long peninsula thrusting into the Sea of Okhotsk, remains virtually untouched by signs of human development: there are few roads or tourist facilities and **wildlife** is abundant – you're almost guaranteed to encounter wild deer, foxes and even brown bears (see box, p.332). Peak season is from June to September, the best period for hiking and viewing the five small lakes at Shiretoko Go-ko, most easily reached from the peninsula's main town, **Utoro**. In the winter, drift ice litters the shore, and some two thousand Steller's sea eagles can be observed near **RAUSU** (羅臼; ⓦrausu-shiretoko.com/en) on the peninsula's southeast coast. This remote fishing village can be used as a base for the park and is the only place offering winter cruises (see opposite).

Utoro

ウトロ

Roads stop halfway up both sides of the Shiretoko Peninsula, so the only way you'll get to see the rocky cape, with its unmanned lighthouse and waterfalls plunging over sheer cliffs into the sea, is to take one of the sightseeing boats from **UTORO** (see opposite). Near the town's tiny harbour are several large rocks, one of which is nicknamed "Godzilla", for reasons that become obvious when you see it.

Shiretoko World Heritage Conservation Centre

知床世界遺産センター, Shiretoko Seikaiisan Sentā • 186-10 Utoro Nishi • April 20–Oct 20 8.30am–5.30pm; Oct 21–April 19 9am–4.30pm; closed Tues • Free • ⓦ shiretoko-whc.jp

While in Utoro, drop by the excellent Shiretoko **World Heritage Conservation Centre** to learn about Shiretoko National Park and its vegetation and wildlife. They have separate displays on the animals of the mountain, forest, river and sea, and a scale relief map of the area.

Shiretoko Shizen Centre

知床自然センター, Shiretoko Sekai Isan Santa • 531 Iwaobetsu, Shari-chō • Daily: April 20–Oct 20 8am–5.40pm, Oct 21–April 19 9am–4pm • Free; film ¥500 • ⓦ centre.shiretoko.or.jp

Based outside Utoro, en route to the Five Lakes, is the **Shiretoko Shizen Centre**, which shows a twenty-minute giant-screen film throughout the day, with swooping aerial shots of the mountains and rugged coastline. Behind the centre, a few well-marked nature trails lead through forests and heathland to cliffs, down which a waterfall cascades.

Shiretoko Go-ko

知床五湖 • Late April to early Nov 7.30am–sunset • Short route: free; long route: ¥5000 with mandatory guide in Active Bear Season (May 10–July 31), ¥250 in Ecosystem Aware Season (late April–May 10 & Aug 1–Oct 20), free Oct 21 to early Nov • ⓦ goko.go.jp/english • A bus from Utoro runs to the lakes seven times a day (¥690; 25min); hitching is another option

Fourteen kilometres north of Utoro, past the *Iwaobetsu Youth Hostel* (see p.332), lies the **Shiretoko Go-ko**, where five jewel-like lakes are linked by wooden walkways and sinuous forest paths. In fine weather, some of the lakes reflect the mountains, and a lookout point west of the car park provides a sweeping view across the heathland to the sea. The further you walk around the 2.4km circuit, the more serene the landscape becomes Note that in the Active Bear Season, you're only able to walk the full route as part of a guided tour. There is a shorter elevated walkway which is free throughout the park's open months. Allow at least an hour to see all five lakes.

Kamuiwakka-no-taki
カムイワッカの滝

Coming from Utoro, just before the turn-off to the Shiretoko Go-ko lakes, a dirt road continues up the peninsula. Following this track for about twenty minutes by car, as it rises uphill, will bring you to **Kamuiwakka-no-taki**, a cascading warm-water river and series of waterfalls, creating three levels of natural rotemburo, although these days only the lowest pool is accessible, due to the risk of falling rocks. To reach the bathing pool (bring your bathing costume) you'll have to climb up the river – be careful on the slippery rocks. The water is mildly acidic, so be warned that if you have any cuts it's going to sting, and bring a water bottle to rinse off with afterwards.

ARRIVAL AND DEPARTURE SHIRETOKO NATIONAL PARK

By train The gateway to the Shiretoko peninsula is Shari (斜里), where there's a JR station (Shiretoko-Shari) on the Senmō line

Destinations Abashiri (9 daily; 45min); Kushiro (5 daily; 3hr).

By bus From the bus terminal opposite the station, frequent services run to Utoro (50min; ¥1600) and less frequently to Rausu (1hr; ¥1600). Between May and October, services continue up to Iwaobetsu for the youth hostel (see p.332) and as far as Kamuiwakka-no-taki. In the same time period there are services to Rausu (¥2590) via the Shiretoko Pass; note this road is closed to traffic Nov to late April. For more details check ⓦ sharibus.co.jp. Rausu is also connected by bus with JR Nemuro Station on the Nemuro line.

INFORMATION AND TOURS

Tourist information There's a tourist office in the road station on the way into Utoro (daily 8am–7.30pm; ☎ 0152 24 2639, ⓦ www.town.shari.hokkaido.jp/sh), or and, on the other side of the peninsula, there's the Rausu Visitor Center (羅臼ビジターセンター; 6-27 Yunosawa, Rausu-chō; May–Oct 9am–5pm; Nov–April 10am–4pm; closed Mon; ☎ 0153 87 2828) about 1km or so out of Rausu, near the Kuma-no-yu hot springs.

Cruises There are several sightseeing boats that leave from Utoro. Trips on the largest boat, the Aurora (☎ 0152 24 2147, ⓦ ms-aurora.com) run to Kamuiwakka-no-taki waterfall and Mount Iō (end April–Oct daily, 1hr 30min; ¥3100) and out to the cape (June–Sept daily, 3hr 45min;

HIKING IN THE SHIRETOKO NATIONAL PARK

The peak of **Rausu-dake** (羅臼岳), the tallest mountain in Shiretoko at 1661m, can be reached in around four-and-a-half hours from the *Iwaobetsu Youth Hostel* (see p.332), passing a natural rotemburo on the way. From the summit, there are spectacular views along the whole peninsula, and to the east you should be able to see Kunashiri-tō, one of the disputed Kuril Islands, or "Northern Territories" as they are known in Japan (see box, p.333). It takes a full day to continue across Rausu-dake to Rausu

Iō-zan (硫黄山), the active volcano that produces hot water for the Kamuiwakka-no-taki waterfalls, is a more difficult climb. The trail begins beside the Shiretoko Ōhashi, the bridge just beyond the entrance to the falls. A hike to the 1562m summit and back takes at least eight hours and can be combined with a visit to the hot waterfall.

You'll need to be a serious mountaineer to tackle the difficult ridge trail linking Iō-zan and Rausu-dake; bring a topographical map, take precautions against bears (see box, p.332) and plan to stay one or two nights at the campsites along the way. The **Rusa Field House** (ルサフィールドハウス; May–Oct Wed–Sun 9am–5pm, Feb–April same days 10am–6pm; ☎0153 89 2722), about 10km north along the coast from Rausu, can provide rules and current information to mountaineers and sea kayakers.

¥6500); you'll get closer to the coastline on one of the smaller boats run by any of a number of different operators. Gojiraiwa-Kankō (ゴジラ岩観光; ☎0152 24 3060, ⓦkamuiwakka.jp) run cruises out to the cape (3hr–3hr 30 min; ¥8000), and shorter cruises up to Kamuiwakka-no-taki and Mount Iō (1hr; ¥3000). Rausu is the place to go for winter cruises – try Hamanasu Kankō (☎0153 87 3830; from ¥6000/person).

ACCOMMODATION AND EATING

Utoro has the best range of accommodation and good access to the peninsula. The more remote **Rausu** is another option if you have more time. Unless mentioned otherwise, rates include two meals.

Ikkyuya 一休屋 13 Utoro-higashi ☎0152 24 2557. Just north of the bus station, there's a varied menu here, with a delicious salmon *oyako-don* (parent-child rice bowl, with salmon sashimi and roe) for less than ¥1000. Daily 11am–10pm.

Iwaobetsu Youth Hostel 知床岩尾別ユースホステル Aza Iwaobetsu ☎0152 24 2311, ⓦyouthhostel.or.jp. Nestling in a valley beside the Iwaobetsu-gawa, this hostel is large and well managed, with welcoming staff and good food. Closed March 26–April 28 & Nov 26–Dec 23. Meals extra. Dorm ¥3900

Mine-no-yu 峰の湯 Yunosawa-chō 7-3, Rausu ☎0153 87 3001, ⓦrausu-minenoyu.com. The least shabby of Rausu's three large onsen hotels, the majority of rooms here are Japanese-style but have attached Western-style toilets and baths. ¥19,200

Minshuku Maruman 民宿マルマン Rausu ☎0153 87 2479. Probably the best deal in Rausu, but don't expect anything luxurious. ¥14,000

Shiretoko Grand Hotel 知床グランドホテル 172 Utoro-higashi ☎0152 24 2021, ⓦshiretoko.co.jp. This opulent hotel has both Western- and Japanese-style rooms, as well as a rooftop onsen bath and rotemburo with views across the harbour. ¥33,600

Shiretoko Yaei-jō 知床野営場 Utoro-kagawa ☎0152 24 2722. On the hill overlooking Utoro, this well-maintained campsite is open June–Sept. ¥500 per person

Akan National Park

阿寒国立公園, Akan Kokuritsu Kōen

Some 50km south of the Shiretoko Peninsula is the densely forested **AKAN NATIONAL PARK**, its 905 square kilometres harbouring three major **lakes** – Mashū-ko, Kussharo-ko and Akan-ko – and the **volcanic peaks** of Me-Akan and Ō-Akan. Patchy public transport makes this a difficult area to tour unless you have your own car or don't mind hitching. Nevertheless, the park is a haven for birdwatchers and walkers and has some pleasant lakeside onsen, while in **Akan Kohan** you can see traditional Ainu dancing, as well as the rare balls of algae known as *marimo*.

ARRIVAL AND INFORMATION   AKAN NATIONAL PARK

By bus Buses run to Akan Kohan (see.oposite) from Asahikawa (2 daily; 5hr; ¥4580) via Sōunkyō (see p.319; 3hr 30min; ¥3260). There are services from Kushiro (釧路; 4 daily; 2hr; ¥2650) and, between Jan 25 and March 3, Abashiri (daily; 6hr 30min; ¥4500) via Kawayu Onsen (see p.334) and Mashū-ko, where it pauses for a 15min sightseeing break. You can also pick up this bus from outside JR Mashū Station; check ⓦakanbus.co.jp for the latest schedule.

BEWARE BEARS

The **brown bear** (*ezo higuma*) is common to wilderness areas of Hokkaidō, with around 200 thought to be living in the Shiretoko-hantō (see p.330). The bears, which can grow to a height of 2m and weigh up to 400kg, can be dangerous if surprised. If you're planning a **hiking** trip in these parts, it is important to be alert for bears and take appropriate precautions so you don't disturb them. Carrying a **bell** that jangles as you walk is a good idea as this will warn bears of your approach and hopefully keep them away. It's also vital, if carrying **food**, that you take great care to keep this away from bears. Don't discard food scraps around where you camp – leave them until you reach a river or stream where they can be washed away. If you do encounter a bear, don't run away – this will be an invitation for them to chase you – and don't make any sudden movements or look them directly in the eyes. Try to remain as still as possible until the bear gets bored and moves on.

> ## THE DISPUTED KURIL ISLANDS
>
> A protracted territorial dispute over the **Kuril Islands**, some of which can be seen clearly from the Shiretoko Peninsula, means that technically Japan and Russia are still fighting World War II. A peace accord has yet to be signed because of Russia's continued occupation of these volcanic islands, which are strung across the Sea of Okhotsk between the Kamchatka Peninsula and northeastern Hokkaidō.
>
> Known in Japan as the **Northern Territories**, or *Chishima* (Thousand Islands), and in Russia as the Kurils, only five of the islands are permanently inhabited. Japan demands the return of the four southernmost islands, the closest of which is less than 20km off Hokkaidō's coast. The islands themselves are fairly desolate; it is their strategic importance, **rich mineral resources** and the surrounding fishing grounds that make them so desirable.

Tourist information There's free internet access and plenty of information on local activities, including hiking trails, at the tourist office (daily 9am–6pm; ☎ 0154 67 3200, ⓦ lake-akan .com/en, ⓦ kam-kankouken.jp/tourism/en), opposite the *New Akan Hotel Shangriia* about a 5min walk from the bus terminal towards the lake. You can hire bikes from here for ¥500/day.

Akan Kohan

阿寒湖畔

The compact onsen resort of **AKAN KOHAN** on the southern shore of the lake is the most commercialized part of the Akan National Park, with no shortage of tacky gift shops down its main street. However, it can be used as a base for hikes up the nearby peaks of **Me-Akan-dake** (雌阿寒岳; 1499m) and **O-Akan-dake** (雄阿寒岳; 1371m). Many of the hotels allow day visitors into their onsen baths, usually between 11am and 3pm, for around ¥1500.

Ainu Kotan Village

アイヌコタン • **Folklore Museum** Daily 10am–10pm • ¥300 • **Ikor dance and music performances** Evenings; times vary • ¥1000

At the western end of town, is the **Ainu Kotan**, a contrived Ainu "village" which is little more than a short road of gift shops selling identical carved wood figures. Some two hundred Ainu are said to live in the town. Traditional dance and music performances are staged in the thatched *chise* (house) at the top of the shopping parade, and there's a tiny **folklore museum** in a hut beside the *chise* with some interesting traditional Ainu costumes. There are also regular evening performances of puppet plays and traditional Ainu dancing in the impressive Ainu Theatre Ikor (イコロ).

Akan Kohan Eco Museum Centre

阿寒湖畔エコミュージアムセンター • 1-1 Akanko Onsen 1-chōme • 9am–5pm; closed Tues • Free • ☎ 0154 67 3263

At the eastern end of Akan Kohan is the **Akan Kohan Eco Museum Centre**, where you can find out how the Akan caldera was formed and view *marimo* up close. These velvety green balls of algae are native to Akan-ko, which is one of the few places in the world where you'll find this nationally designated "special natural treasure". Despite their rarity and the fact that it can take two hundred years for the *marimo* to grow to the size of baseballs, it's possible to buy bottled baby *marimo* in all of Akan's gift shops – although, in recent years, these souvenirs are more likely to be hand-rolled algae from other lakes. From the Eco Museum, pleasant woodland trails lead to the **Bokke** (ボッケ), a small area of bubbling mud pools beside the lake.

ACCOMMODATION   AKAN KOHAN

Akan-kohan Campground 阿寒湖畔キャンプ場 5-1 Akanko Onsen ☎ 0154 67 3263. This decent wooded campsite is a 5min walk beyond the Ainu Kotan village (see above). Open June–Sept. **¥630** per person

Hinanoza 邸の座 2-3-1 Akanko Onsen ☎ 0154 67 5500 ⓦ hinanoza.com. To see how amazing Ainu carving can be, take a peek – or better yet stay – at this beautifully designed hotel, the most luxurious of the Tsuruga group's three properties by the lake. Rooms have terraces with private onsen baths. **¥69,300**

Kiri 桐 4-3-26 Akanko Onsen ☎ 0154 67 2755. Meals aren't included at this good-value minshuku above a souvenir shop, but you can bathe in a beautiful handmade Sakhalin fir bathtub. **¥8400**

4

Mashū-ko
摩周湖

Some 35km east of Akan-ko, just outside the Akan National Park boundaries, is the famed lake **MASHŪ-KO**, lying at the bottom of sheer cliffs that keep tourists at bay and the waters pristine. There are three lookout points over the 212m-deep caldera lake, which on rare occasions sparkles a brilliant blue. Usually, though, the view is obscured by swirling mists and thick cloud, creating a mysterious atmosphere which led the Ainu to christen Mashū-ko "The Devil's Lake".

ARRIVAL AND DEPARTURE
MASHŪ-KO

By bus Between April 20 and October 6, two buses a day run from JR Mashū Station in Teshikaga (弟子屈) to Mashū-ko (¥540); they pause at the lookout for 20min before continuing on to Kawayu Onsen (see below). Similarly, two buses daily run from Kawayu Onsen and pause at Mashū-ko en route to JR Mashū. Between July 13 and October 6, four buses a day do a round trip from JR Mashū Station to the lookout, where it pauses for 15min before returning. Four buses a day also do a round-trip from Kawayu Onsen, pause for 40min, and return.

ACCOMMODATION AND EATING

The Great Bear ザ・グレートベア Genya 883, Teshikaga-chō ☏ 0154 82 3830 ⓦ www2.ocn .ne.jp/~gbear/access.htm. Next door to *Mashū-ko Youth Hostel*, this restaurant serves delicious meals using local ingredients – set menus range from ¥1575 to ¥2625. Daily 8am–9pm.

Mashū-ko Youth Hostel 摩周湖ユースホステル Genya 883, Teshikaga-chō ☏ 0154 82 3098, ⓦ masyuko .jp. This large and modern hostel halfway to the lake from Teshikaga runs a number of reasonably priced guided tours of the area. Meals are served next door in the good-value *Great Bear* restaurant. Dorm **¥3900**, double **¥9000**

Kussharo-ko
屈斜路湖

West of Mashū-ko is Akan National Park's largest lake, picturesque **Kussharo-ko**, which at eighty square kilometres is the biggest **crater lake** in Japan. It's also said to be the home of Kusshi, Japan's answer to the Loch Ness Monster. Whether it has a monster or not, Kussharo-ko is special because it is fed by onsen water, creating a warm temperature and several natural rotemburo around its edge, such as the piping-hot pools at **Wakoto Hantō** (和琴半島), a mini-promontory on the lake's southern shore. You can hop into another lakeside rotemburo at **Kotan Onsen** (コタン温泉), an easy cycle ride from the *Kussharo-Gen'ya Youth Guesthouse* (see opposite). Here you'll find the **Museum of Ainu Folklore** (アイヌ民俗資料館; mid-April to Oct daily 9am–5pm; ¥400), in a strikingly modern concrete building, but it's only worth a visit if you've not checked out any of the other collections around Hokkaidō.

A strong whiff of sulphur from the hot springs drifts over the area's main village, **KAWAYU ONSEN** (川湯温泉), 3km from the lake, where there are several hotels and minshuku and free *ashiyu* (foot baths). The bus terminal is located here, which makes the village a good base for touring the park.

ARRIVAL AND INFORMATION
KUSSHARO-KO

By train Kawayu Onsen's train station is on the Senmō line and is a 10min bus journey (¥280) south of the village; buses are timed to meet the trains, with the last bus to the onsen leaving at 6.30pm.

Tourist information There's a good tourist office (daily 9am–5pm; ☏ 0154 83 2670) with lots of information. The Kawayu Eco-Museum Center (川湯エコミュージアム センター; 2-2-6 Kawayu Onsen; April–Oct 8am–5pm, closed Wed in April; Nov–March 9am–4pm, closed Wed) has plenty of information on the park, but it's virtually all in Japanese.

Tours The Kawayu Eco-Museum Center (see above) can provide information on the several hiking trails around the village, one of which is wheelchair-accessible, and rent out cross-country skis and snowshoes in winter. Contact River & Field (☏ 080 6648 4288) if you're interested in taking a guided canoe tour of the Kushiro River (from ¥5000/ person, min two people).

Bike hire You can rent bikes from Sun Energy near the Sumo Memorial Hall (April–Oct daily 8am–5pm; ¥500 for first hour, ¥100 for every additional hour).

Services There's free internet access at the town hall.

ACCOMMODATION AND EATING

Hotel Kitafukurou オテルきたふくろう 1-9-15 Kawayu-orsen ☎0154 83 2960. This is the nicest place to stay in Kawayu Onsen, with both pleasant Japanese- and Western-style rooms and onsen baths (open to non-guests noon–6pm; ¥600). Two meals included. **¥13,000**

★**Kussharo-Gen'ya Youth Guesthouse** 屈斜路原野ユースホステル 443-1 Kussharo-genya ☎0154 84 2609, ⓦ www.gogogenya.com. In a tent-like wooden building some 30min walk from the southern shore of Kussharo-ko, the rooms here are Western-style, and superb Japanese meals are available. You can rent mountain bikes (¥1500/day) or take advantage of the various tours on offer, which include cross-country skiing in winter. In the evening, the staff will also take you to a natural rotem-buro beside the lake. Dorm **¥3000**, double **¥9800**

San San Go Go 三三五五 1-4-10 Kawayu-onsen ☎0154 83 3355. On the main shopping street in Kawayu Onsen, this friendly establishment serves tasty set meals, including their speciality, fried chicken, or *jingisukan* (barbecued mutton), for around ¥1200. Tues–Sun 11.30am–2pm & 6–10pm.

Orchard Grass オーチャードグラス 1-1-18 Kawayu-eki-mae ☎0154 83 3787. This cute café at JR Kawayu Station serves excellent curry rice (¥330). Daily 10am–6pm, Oct–June closed Tues.

Wakoto-Hantō Kohan Camp Area 和琴半島湖畔キャンプ場 Wakoto-hantō ☎0154 84 2350. At the Wakoto Hantō Peninsula on the southern shores of Kussharo-ko, you can enjoy canoeing, fishing and the natural rotemburo by the lake. Open Apri–Oct. **¥450** per person

Kushiro Shitsugen National Park

釧路湿原国立公園, Kushiro Shitsugen Kokuritsu Kōen

Japan's largest protected wetland, at 45,200 acres, is the **Kushiro Shitsugen National Park**. Birdwatchers flock here in winter to see **tanchō cranes** (see box, p.328), but the wetlands are home to many other birds and animals, including deer, grey herons, whooper swans and eagles. One of the best places to observe the cranes is actually just north of the park, in the fields near the village of **TSURUI** (鶴居), an hour's drive north of Kushiro, at the **Tsurui Itō Japanese Crane Sanctuary** (鶴居・伊藤タンチョウサンクチュアリ; Aza Nakasetsuri Minami; Nov–March Mon & Thurs–Sun 9am–4.30pm; ☎0154 64 2620). Half an hour further north of here towards Akan is the **Akan International Crane Centre** (daily 9am–5pm, April–Oct closed Mon; ¥400) at **GRUS**, which has breeding facilities and an interesting exhibition hall.

ARRIVAL AND INFORMATION

By bus The industrial port of Kushiro (釧路) is the southern gateway to the park, which is best toured by car, but the Akan Kohan-bound bus from Kushiro Station also passes several of the facilities; get details from Kushiro's tourist office.

Tourist information There's a helpful tourist office (daily 9am–5.30pm; ☎0154 22 8294, ⓦ www.kushiro-kankou.or.jp/english) in Kushiro Station; ask for the very useful *Kushiro Wetland Teku-Teku Map*.

ACCOMMODATION

Hickory Wind ヒッコリーウィンド Tsurui ☎0154 64 2956, ⓦ bit.ly/1h9DXP2. There's excellent accommodation and a friendly welcome in this rustic location overlooking the crane sanctuary. Call ahead to be picked up at the airport or Tsurui bus station. Guide facilities also available from ¥7500/day. Rates include two meals. **¥21,000**

Kushiro Shitsugen Tōro Youth Hostel 釧路湿原とうろユースホステル Tōro 7, Shibecha-chō ☎0154 87 2510, ⓦ youthhostel.or.jp. At Tōro, on the east side of the park, this cosy hostel is only moments from the train station. **¥3960**

4

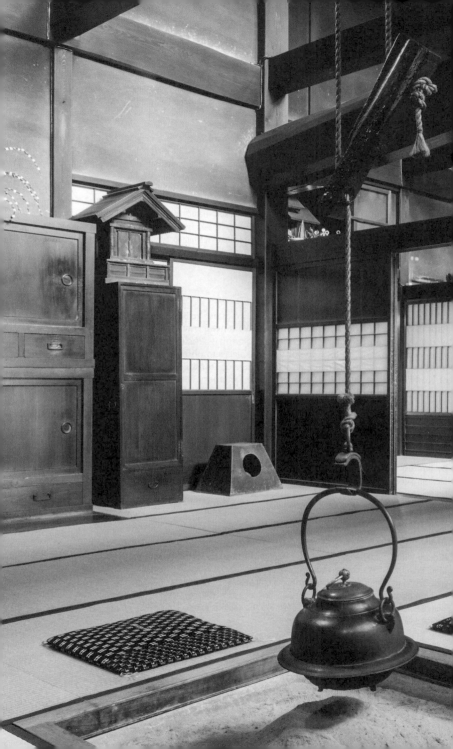

Central Honshū

本州中部

MERCHANT HOUSE, TAKAYAMA

5

Central Honshū

Dominated by the magnificent Japan Alps, peppered with top onsen and ski resorts, old castle- and temple-towns and quaint old-fashioned villages in remote valleys, Central Honshū offers a fantastic choice of terrain and travel possibilities. If all you want to do is admire the grand scenery – even for a day – that's easily done, thanks to the Shinkansen line that zips from Tokyo to Nagano, where you should pause long enough to visit the venerable and atmospheric temple, Zenkō-ji.

Other places worth seeing in the region, known locally as Chūbu, include the summer resort of **Karuizawa** and the charming village of **Nozawa Onsen**, northeast of Nagano, where you'll find excellent ski slopes and free hot-spring baths. **Hakuba** is another popular skiing and outdoor activities destination, while in the southern half of Nagano-ken it's possible to explore several immaculately preserved post towns along the old Nakasendō route from Kyoto to Tokyo, even hiking for a day between the best of them – **Tsumago** and **Magome**.

On the west side of the Alps, there's the convivial town of **Takayama** and the unusual A-frame thatched houses of the **Shirakawa-gō** and **Gokayama** valleys, where three villages – **Ogimachi**, **Suganuma** and **Ainokura** – have been designated UNESCO World Heritage Sites. This area can also be accessed from the Sea of Japan, where the elegant, historic city of **Kanazawa** is an ideal base. The tranquil fishing villages dotted around the rugged coastline of the **Noto Hantō** peninsula, northeast of Kanazawa, are also worth searching out to let you experience a Japan far away from the modern metropolises.

Along the southern Pacific Ocean side of Chūbu run the main expressways and train lines that link Tokyo with the Kansai region. Ugly vistas of rampant industrialization bracket these transportation links, yet even here there are places worth stopping to see, including Japan's fourth main city, **Nagoya**, home to the region's main airport. This enjoyable and easily negotiated metropolis is a good base for day-trips to the attractive castle town of **Inuyama**, where you can see summertime displays of the ancient skill of *ukai* (cormorant fishing), or to **Meiji Mura**, an impressive outdoor museum of architecture dating from the beginning of the twentieth century.

GETTING AROUND

By train and bus A couple of train lines cut across from the southern to the northern coasts, but many places in the mountains are only served by buses, which can be infrequent and pricey. The trains between the major cities

Highlights

❶ Obuse Enjoy gourmet treats, sake, traditional architecture and art in this rural town – a model of sensitive tourist development. **See p.346**

❷ Japan Alps skiing Ride Japan's legendary powder snow at the ski resorts dotted around Nagano. **See p.350**

❸ Matsumoto Survey the mountains surrounding this friendly city from the donjon of Japan's oldest wooden castle. **See p.357**

❹ Kamikōchi Climb Japan's magnificent Alps from this beguiling alpine resort that's only accessible from April to November. **See p.361**

❺ Kiso Valley Follow in the footsteps of the Samurai with a hike through the atmospheric post towns. **See p.365**

❻ Takayama Famous for its skilled carpenters, whose craftsmanship is evident in the town's attractive merchant houses, shrines and temples. **See p.368**

❼ Kanazawa Refined city that's home to verdant Kenroku-en and the cutting-edge vision of the 21st Century Museum of Contemporary Art. **See p.378**

❽ Gujō Hachiman The August Obon holidays are a great time to visit this charming castle town and dance the night away. **See p.404**

HIGHLIGHTS ARE MARKED ON THE MAP ON P.340

5

listed in this chapter are the fastest direct services, but there are also frequent slower services covering the same destinations. Changing between services will often be faster, especially on long-distance routes.

By car Renting a car will sometimes be your best bet,

although some of the most scenic routes – such as the Skyline Drive across the Alps from Gifu-ken to Nagano-ken – are closed in winter because of deep snow. The mountain resort of Kamikōchi and the Tateyama-Kurobe Alpine route are similarly off limits Nov–April.

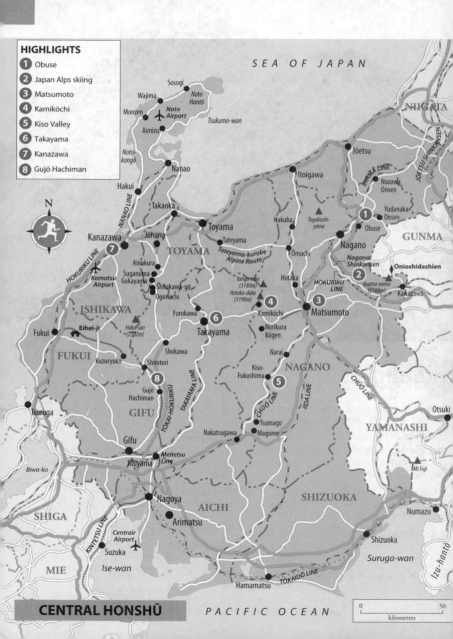

HIGHLIGHTS

1 Obuse
2 Japan Alps skiing
3 Matsumoto
4 Kamikōchi
5 Kiso Valley
6 Takayama
7 Kanazawa
8 Gujō Hachiman

SEA OF JAPAN

CENTRAL HONSHŪ

PACIFIC OCEAN

0   50
kilometres

Nagano

長野

Surrounded by fruit orchards and snowcapped peaks, **NAGANO**, capital of Nagano-ken, had its moment in the international spotlight back in 1998 when it hosted the Winter Olympics. For the Japanese, however, this modern, compact city some 200km northwest of Tokyo has been on the tourist map for centuries. Every year, millions of pilgrims descend on Nagano to pay homage at **Zenkō-ji**, home of a legendary sixth-century image of Buddha.

This temple aside, there's little else special to see in the city itself, although it's a very handy base for trips to surrounding destinations such as Karuizawa, Togakush, Obuse, Nozawa Onsen, Hakuba, and Kanbayashi Onsen, home to Japan's famed snow monkeys.

Zenkō-ji

善光寺 • 49 Motoyoshi-chō • Daily 9am–4pm; morning service starts 1hr before sunrise; see website for details • ¥500 to enter inner sanctuary • ☎ 026 234 3591, ⓦ zenkoji.jp

Zenkō-ji's popularity is linked to the fact that the temple has traditionally welcomed believers of all Buddhist sects, has never barred women and is run alternately by an abbot of the Tendai sect and an abbess of the Jōdo sect. Visitors can join the hundreds of daily petitioners searching for the "key to paradise" which lies beneath Zenkō-ji's main temple building; find it, and you'll have earned eternal salvation.

The traditional way to approach the temple is on foot. Passing through the impressive 13.6m-tall gate, **Niō-mon** (仁王門), and a short precinct lined with souvenir stalls and lodgings, you'll see the **Rokujizō** (六地蔵) on the right, a row of six large metal statues symbolizing the guardians of the six worlds through which Buddhists believe the soul must pass: hell, starvation, beasts, carnage, human beings and heavenly beings. On the left is **Daikanjin** (大勧進), the home of the high priest, which is reached by crossing an attractive arched bridge.

The central courtyard

At the top of the precinct stands the **San-mon** (山門), a double-storey wooden gateway into Zenkō-ji's **central courtyard**. In the middle of the courtyard is a large metal cauldron decorated with a lion whose mouth exhales the perfumed smoke of incense sticks. A charm for health and good fortune, pilgrims waft the smoke around their bodies before moving on to the vast, imposing main hall, the Hondō, which dates from 1707.

Hondō

本堂

As you enter the outer sanctuary, look straight ahead for the worn-out statue of Binzuru, a physician and fallen follower of Buddha; pilgrims rub the statue in the hope of cures to their ailments. Just beyond is the awe-inspiring worshipper's hall, the **Hondō**, a vast space with golden ornaments dangling from the high ceiling, where pilgrims used to bed down for the night.

5

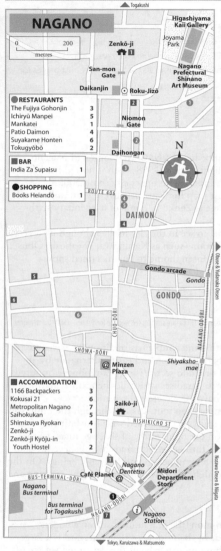

▲ Togakushi

NAGANO

0   200
metres

Zenkō-ji
♨ ❶

Higashiyama
Kaii Gallery

Joyama
Park

San-mon
Gate

Nagano
Prefectural
Shinano
Art Museum

Daikanjin

⊙ Roku-Jizō

● **RESTAURANTS**
The Fujiya Gohonjin   3
Ichiryū Manpei   5
Mankatei   1
Patio Daimon   4
Suyakame Honten   6
Tokugyōbō   2

2

■ **BAR**
India Za Supaisu   1

● **SHOPPING**
Books Heiandō   1

Niomon
Gate

2

Daihongan

ROUTE 406

3

DAIMON

4

N

Gondo arcade

Gondo

GONDO

5

6

6

SHŌWA-DŌRI

✉

@ Minzen
Plaza

Shiyaksho-
mae

■ **ACCOMMODATION**
1166 Backpackers   3
Kokusai 21   6
Metropolitan Nagano   7
Saihokukan   5
Shimizuya Ryokan   4
Zenkō-ji   1
Zenkō-ji Kyōju-in
Youth Hostel   2

Saikō-ji
♨

NISHIKICHO ST

BUS-TERMINAL-DŌRI

Nagano
Dentetsu
@
Café Planet

Midori
Department
Store

Nagano
Bus terminal

Bus terminal
for Togakushi

ℹ Nagano
Station

NAGANO-DŌRI

▼ Tokyo, Karuizawa & Matsumoto

CHŪŌ-DŌRI

NAGANO-ODŌRI

Ōsuze & Yudanaka Onsen

Nozawa Onsen & Niigata

People traditionally come for the **morning service**, which starts around 5.30am; it's worth making the effort to attend in order to witness Zenkō-ji at its most mystical, with the priests wailing, drums pounding and hundreds of pilgrims joined in fervent prayer. Afterwards, the O-juzu Chōdai ceremony takes place in the courtyard in front of the Hondō. Pilgrims kneel while the high priest or priestess rustles by in their colourful robes, shaded by a giant red paper umbrella; as they pass, they bless the pilgrims by tapping them on the head with prayer beads.

O-kaidan

お戒壇 • ¥500; buy a ticket from the machines to the right of Binzuru's statue

If you're at all uncomfortable in the dark, don't enter the **O-kaidan**, a pitch-black passage that runs beneath the Hondō's innermost sanctum. This is the resting place of the revered **Ikkō Sanzon Amida Nyorai** (see box opposite), and pilgrims come down here to grope around in the dark tunnel for the metaphorical "key to paradise". Follow the crowds plunging into the darkness; once you're in, keep your right hand on the wall, and chances are you'll find the key (it actually feels more like a door knob) towards the end of the passage.

Daihongan

大本願

Located to the left of the southern entrance, the **Daihongan** is the nunnery and residence of the high priestess of Zenkō-ji, who is usually a member of the imperial family. In the courtyard, look out for the fountain with a statue of Mizuko Jizō, the patron saint of aborted and stillborn babies – little dolls and toys are left as offerings around the base.

Saikō-ji

西光寺 • 1398-1 Kitaishidocho • Sunrise to sunset • Free; guided tours from ¥300 • ☎ 026 226 8436

North along Chūō-dōri, west of the JR station, is **Saikō-ji**, a small temple tucked away in a quiet courtyard. Also known as Karukaya-san, after the Buddhist saint who founded it in 1199, the main temple building contains two wooden statues of Jizō, the guardian of children, one carved by Karukaya, and the other by his son Ishidō.

THE IKKŌ SANZON AMIDA NYORAI

Zenkō-ji's most sacred object is the **Ikkō Sanzon Amida Nyorai**, a triad of Amida Buddha images sharing one halo. This golden statue is believed to have been made by Buddha himself in the sixth century BC and is said to have arrived in Japan some 1200 years later as a gift from Korea to the emperor. For a while, the image was kept in a specially built temple near Ōsaka, where it became the focus of a clan feud. The temple was eventually destroyed and the statue dumped in a nearby canal, from where it was later rescued by **Honda Yoshimitsu**, a poor man who was passing by and apparently heard Buddha call. Honda brought the image back to his home in Nagano (then called Shinano). When news of its recovery reached Empress Kōgyoku, she ordered a temple to be built in its honour and called it Zenkō-ji after the Chinese reading of Honda's name. The empress also ordered that the image should never be publicly viewed again, so a copy was made, and it is this that is displayed once every six years in the grand **Gokaichō festival**, held from early April to late May. The next festival is in 2016.

Nagano Prefectural Shinano Art Museum

長野県信濃美術館, Nagano-Ken Shinano Bijutsukan • 1-4-4 Hakoshimizu • 9am–5pm; closed Wed • ¥500 • ☎ 026 232 0052, ⓦnpsam.com/english

A couple of minutes east of Zenkō-ji, across Joyama-kōen, is the **Prefectural Shinano Art Museum**, worth popping into mainly for the modern gallery devoted to the vivid, dreamy landscape paintings of celebrated local artist Higashiyama Kaii (1908–99).

ARRIVAL AND INFORMATION

By train Nagano's JR station is the terminus for trains on the Nagano Shinkansen line from Tokyo, and also the hub for services around the prefecture and up to the Sea of Japan. The local Nagano Dentetsu, a private railway with trains to Obuse and Yudanaka Onsen, has its terminus beneath the Midori department store.

Destinations Matsumoto (hourly; 50min); Nagoya (hourly; 2hr 50min); Niigata (2 daily; 3hr); Obuse (9 daily; 24min); Osaka (daily; 4hr 50min); Tokyo (every 30min; 1hr 30min); Yudanaka (8 daily; 45min).

NAGANO

By bus Long-distance buses pull in at the Nagano Bus Terminal on Basu Tāminaru-dōri, west of the JR station.

Destinations Hakuba (10 daily; 1hr); Matsumoto (hourly; 1hr 20min); Nozawa Onsen (5 daily; 1hr 15min); Togakushi (5 daily; 1hr 30min); Tokyo (hourly; 3hr 40min).

Tourist information The excellent tourist information centre (daily 9am–6pm; ☎ 026 226 5626) is inside the station's main concourse. Also check out the city website: ⓦ www.city.nagano.nagano.jp; and Go! Nagano (ⓦ go -nagano.net), the prefecture's official online tourism guide.

GETTING AROUND

By bus You can hop on a bus that goes up the main street, Chūō Dōri, to Zenkō-ji from platform one on the west side of the JR station (one-way ¥150).

By car Car rental is available from Eki Rent-a-Car (☎ 026

227 8500), beside the Zenkō-ji exit of the JR station.

On foot The best way to get around is on foot – walking the 2km up to Zenkō-ji is an especially good way of taking in the city.

ACCOMMODATION

Nagano has plenty of accommodation, with several business hotels clustered close to the station including a branch of *Tōyoko Inn*. For a better ambience, it's best to stay near Zenkō-ji – also handy if you want to join the early morning services.

1166 Backpackers 1166 バックパッカーズ 1048 Nishimachi ☎ 026 217 2816, ⓦ 1166bp.com. Some 5min walk from Zenkō-ji, the staff at this sociable hostel are happy to share their knowledge of the local area. The place has a retro design vibe about it, with a comfortable lounge centred round a large dining/work table. Most of the rooms are dorms, though a private double room is also available; a snack breakfast is on offer for ¥400. Dorm **¥2600**, double **¥5600**
Kokusai 21 ホテル国際21 576 Agata-machi ☎ 026 234 1111, ⓦ kokusai21.jp Battling it out with the

Saihokukan (see p.344) as Nagano's top hotel, *Kokusai 21* has a more contemporary look. Rooms are spacious and well appointed, but slightly dull. It has a good selection of restaurants and great views from its sixteenth-floor bar. Deals are available online. **¥14,600**
Metropolitan Nagano メトロポリタン長野 1346 Minami-Ishido-chō ☎ 026 291 7000, ⓦ metro-n.co.jp. Beside the west exit of the JR station, this good-value upmarket hotel offers high-standard Western-style rooms, a stylish lobby and chic restaurants. Breakfast is

5

an additional ¥1600 per person. **¥18,480**

Saihokukan サイホクカン 528-1 Agata-machi ☎026 235 3333, ⓦsaihokukan.com. This venerable hotel has been in business since 1890, although the current building is of a much more modern vintage. There are economy rooms here, but you're better off going for the larger and far plusher regular rooms. Online deals are a good bet. **¥15,750**

Shimizuya Ryokan 清水屋旅館 49 Daimon-chō ☎026 232 2580, ⓔshimizuya.ryokan@gmail.com. Service able, foreigner-friendly ryokan in a very handy location on the approach to Zenkō-ji. All rooms are tatami and bathrooms are shared. Breakfast is available for ¥840 and dinner for ¥2100. **¥9720**

Zenkō-ji 善光寺 491 Motoyoshi-cho ☎026 234 3591, ⓦzenkoji.jp. There are a few lodgings (*shukubō*) at Zenkō-ji itself (see p.341), open only to genuine Zen Buddhist students. Call for bookings. Rates include two vegetarian meals. **¥10,500** per person

Zenkō-ji Kyōju-in Youth Hostel 善光寺教授院ユースホステル 479 Motoyoshi-chō ☎026 232 2768, ⓕ232 2767. This is an ideal place to stay if you're planning an early-morning visit to Zenkō-ji (see p.341), which is just a minute's walk away. The hostel is housed in an atmospheric old temple building, of which the management are understandably very protective; you have to leave your belongings in lockers in the entrance hall. Closed irregularly; it's best to reserve by phone. **¥4000**

EATING AND DRINKING

You'll find plenty of places to **eat** on or around Chūo-dōri, with handmade soba being a popular local dish. To sample *shōjin ryōri*, the vegetarian cuisine prepared for the monks, head for the area around Zenkō-ji. There are many small **bars** around Gondō, as well as a beer garden in summer on top of the Nagano Dentetsu building, at the eastern end of the Gondō arcade.

★The Fujiya Gohonjin 藤屋御本陳 80 Daimon-chō ☎026 232 1241. The Meiji-era elegance of this one-time hotel has been spruced up with a snazzy contemporary design to become a very sophisticated Italian restaurant. The food is pretty authentic with *al dente* pasta and rustic meat and fish dishes on the menu. Expect to pay around ¥5000 per head for dinner. Their café-bar overlooking traditional gardens is a lovely place to relax with a drink. Mon–Fri 11.30am–3pm & 6–9.30pm, Sat & Sun 7–10.30pm.

Ichiryū Manpei 一粒万平 52 Daimon-chō ☎026 234 8255. Lots of fresh, locally produced veggies figure in the wholesome meals prepared at this small place, popular with locals and tourists. The lunchtime buffet clocks in at a reasonable ¥1300. 11.30am–6.30pm; closed Tues.

India Za Supaisu INDIA ザすぱいす 1418 Minamiishido-chō ☎02 2266136. A funky beer and curry joint serving organic food near the unexpected London-double-decker-bus-turned-hot-dog-café at the southern end of Chūo-dōri. There is a generous happy "hour" from 4.30pm to 8.30pm, with half-price drinks. Daily noon–midnight.

Mankatei 萬佳亭 2502 Higashinomon-chō ☎026 232 2326, ⓦmankatei.com. Enjoy the fine dishes, including sashimi, tempura, delicate noodles, the waitresses in kimono, and the twinkling cityscape views at this classy restaurant east of Zenkō-ji, on the edge of Joyama-kōen, overlooking the downtown area. Course menus starts at ¥5000. Daily 11am–2pm & 5–9pm.

Patio Daimon ぱてぃお大門 54 Daimoncho ⓦpatio-daimon.com. On the corner of Chūo-dōri and Route 406, this complex of restaurants and shops is styled like traditional white-walled *kura* (storehouses). Most tastes and budgets are catered for here, from a cheerful café specializing in tofu-based sweets to the private dining room (Fri & Sat only; ¥15,000 per head). Hours vary.

Suyakame Honten すや亀本店 625 Nishi-go-chō ☎026 35 4022, ⓦsuyakame.co.jp. Café and shop specializing in miso – they even serve miso ice cream, something of an acquired taste. From 11.30am to 2.30pm they offer a set menu of rice balls topped with different types of miso sauce (¥410). Daily 9am–6pm.

Tokugyōbō 徳行坊 448 Motoyoshi ☎026 232 0264. This old pilgrim's inn is a good place to sample *shōjin ryōri*. Prices start from ¥3000 per person and reservations are recommended a week in advance; the owner speaks a little English. Daily 9am–5pm; closed Aug 12–17 & Dec 30–Jan 3.

SHOPPING

Books Heiandō 平安堂 1355-5 Suehiro-chō ☎026 224 4545. Opposite the west exit of the station, the city's biggest bookshop has a selection of English-language books. Daily 10am–7.30pm.

DIRECTORY

Banks and exchange There are several branches of Hachijū Ni ("82") Ginkō around the city offering foreign exchange, including one about 5min walk west of JR Nagano Station.

Emergencies The main Prefectural Police Office is at 692-2 Habashita (☎ 026 244 0110). For other emergency numbers, see p.66.

Hospital Nagano's main hospital is Nagano Sekijūji Byōin, 5-22-1 Wakasato ☎ 026 226 4131.

Internet There's free access at the tourist information centre and on the third floor of Minzer Plaza on the corner of Chūō-dōri and Shōwa-dōri, in the International Exchange Plaza (daily 10am–7pm, except first and third Wed of month). *Café Planet* is a 24-hour internet and manga café, a few minutes' walk west of the JR station.

Post office The Central Post Office is at 1085-4 Minami-Agata (daily 9am–7pm).

Around Nagano

In the heart of the Japan Alps, and often dubbed "the rooftop of Japan", the area around Nagano boasts dramatic scenery which provides a perfect location for visitors in search of nature-based activities. It is also worth taking time to visit some of the area's small towns for their distinctive attractions. **Togakushi**, the training ground for the legendary ninja warriors, makes an enjoyable trip, while the pleasant town of **Obuse** is a centre for refined culture and cuisine.

Togakushi

戸隠

Famous for its ninjas, the alpine area of **Togakushi**, 20km northwest of Nagano, lies within the jagged ridge of Togakushi-yama and Iizuna-Yama. As well as great scenery, there's a decent **museum** and a legendary **shrine** worth visiting. In winter, there's good **skiing**.

Togakushi Minzoku-kan

戸隠民族館 • 3688-12 Togakushi • Daily 9am–5pm, closed irregularly Nov–mid April • ¥500 • ☎ 026 254 2395

The **Togakushi Minzoku-kan** is a museum complex of traditional farm buildings, some of which have exhibits on the **Ninja warriors** who once trained here (see box, p.346). Within the complex, the Togakure-ryū Ninpō Shiryōkan displays some amazing photographs of the stealthy fighters in action and examples of their lethal weapons. The Ninja House next door is great fun, with a maze of hidden doors and staircases that is fiendishly difficult to find your way out of.

Togakushi Okusha

戸隠奥社 • 3690 Togakushi • Daily 9.30am–5pm • Free • ☎ 026 254 2001

Opposite Togakushi Minzoku-kan is the entrance to **Togakushi Okusha**, the innermost of the three main sanctuaries of the **Togakushi Shrine**. According to ancient Shintō belief, Togakushi-Yama was created when the god Ame-no-Tajikarao tossed away the rock door of the cave where the Sun Goddess Amaterasu had been hiding (see box, p.716). A 2km-long corridor of soaring **cedar trees** takes you to the shrine – a collection of small wooden and stone buildings under the rocks. The adventurous can continue up the sharp ridge to the summit; but take food, water and appropriate clothing, as it's a strenuous route, and log your name in the book at the start of the trail.

Chūsha

中社

Heading downhill from Togakushi Okusha along pleasant woodland trails through the Togakushi Omine Recreational Forest, you reach the attractive village of **CHŪSHA**, a good base for skiing in winter (see ☉togakusi.com). Here you find the outer sanctuary of the **Hōkōsha** shrine (宝光社; 24hr; free) decorated with intricate wooden carvings, along with shops selling baskets and woven bamboo goods: the best one (where you can see basket weavers working) is downhill, opposite the Spar store.

5

NINJA: THE SHADOW WARRIORS

Long before their ancient martial art was nabbed by a bunch of cartoon turtles, the **Ninja** were Japan's most feared warriors, employed by lords as assassins and spies. They practised **Ninjutsu**, "the art of stealth", which emphasized non-confrontational methods of combat. Dressed in black, Ninja moved like fleeting shadows and used weapons such as *shuriken* (projectile metal stars) and *kusarikama* (a missile with a razor-sharp sickle on one end of a chain), examples of which are displayed in the Togakushi Minzoku-kan (see p.345).

According to legend, Ninjutsu was developed in the twelfth century, when the warrior Togakure Daisuke retreated to the mountain forests of Iga, near Nara, and met Kain Dōshi, a monk on the run from political upheaval in China. Togakure studied Dōshi's fighting ways and it was his descendants who developed them into the **Togakure-ryū school** of Ninjutsu. By the fifteenth century, there were some fifty family-based Ninjutsu schools across Japan, each jealously guarding their techniques.

Although the need for Ninja declined while Japan was under the peaceful rule of the Shogunate, the Tokugawa had their own force of Ninjutsu-trained warriors for protection. One Ninja, Sawamura Yasusuke, even sneaked into the "black ship" of Commodore Perry in 1853 to spy on the foreign barbarians. Today, the Togakure-ryū school of Ninjutsu, emphasizing defence rather than offence, is taught by the 34th master, **Hatsumi Masaaki**, in Noda, Chiba-ken, just north of Tokyo.

ARRIVAL AND DEPARTURE   TOGAKUSHI

By bus Buses (¥2400 return) leave from outside Books Heiandō, opposite Nagano train station, and run along the vertiginous Bird-line Driveway, giving panoramic views of the city as they wind up the mountain around a series of hairpin bends. Stay on the bus through Chūsha, about an hour from Nagano, and get off a couple of stops later when you reach the entrance to the Togakushi Okusha.

ACCOMMODATION AND EATING

Togakushi Kōgen Yokokura Youth Hostel 戸隠高原 横倉ユースホステル 3347 Nakayashiro ☎ 026 254 2030. This excellent-value hostel offers tatami dorms in a thatched, 150-year-old pilgrim's lodge, a 5min walk south of the shrine near Chūsha ski resort. There's a quaint log-cabin café, and the owner is a hospitable woman who speaks some English. Dorm **¥3000**

Uzuraya うずらや 3229 Togakushi ☎ 026 254 2219. On the main road in the thatched farmhouse opposite the Hōkōsha shrine, this is Chūsha's top restaurant for freshly made soba and tempura. Dishes start at around ¥600. Daily 10.30am–4pm.

Yamabōshi やまぼうし 3511-18 Togakushi ☎ 026 254 2624. The excellent Italian cuisine and home-made desserts at this cosy restaurant, on the way up to the Hōkōsha shrine, are almost worth making the journey for on their own. Daily 10.30am–8.30pm, closed Wed.

Obuse

小布施

Famous for its connection with the artist Hokusai and for its production of chestnuts, **OBUSE**, some 20km northeast of Nagano, is one of Japan's most attractive small towns. The streets around the venerable **Masuichi-Ichimura** estate and brewery in the centre of town (see box, p.349) have been beautified and many residents take part in an open garden scheme. Pavements have been relaid with blocks of chestnut wood, and old buildings have been spruced up and turned into excellent restaurants, bars and a super-stylish hotel. Casually exploring Obuse, which is surrounded by **orchards and vineyards** and dotted with traditional houses, temples, small museums and craft galleries, makes a wonderful day-trip; even better is to stay overnight and use Obuse as a base for trips around the area, including to nearby Yudanaka Onsen (see p.350).

FROM TOP A BABY SNOW MONKEY AT JIGOKUDANI MONKEY PARK (P.352); SHIROYONE NO SENMAIDA RICE FIELDS NEAR WAJIMA (P.388) >

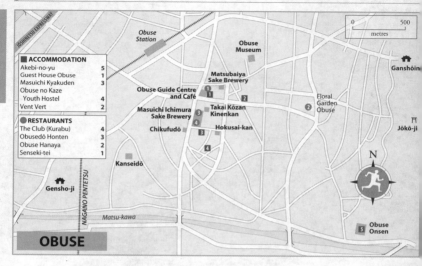

Hokusai-kan

北斎館 • 485 Obuse • Daily: March–Sept 9am–6pm; Oct–Feb 9am–5pm; ¥500 • ☎ 026 247 5206 • About a 10min walk southeast of the station

The **Hokusai-kan** is devoted to the master of *ukiyo-e* woodblock prints, **Katsushika Hokusai**. In 1842, the 83-year-old artist was invited to live and work in Obuse by Takai Kōzan, the town's leading merchant and art lover. The thatched-roofed **Hekiiken**, a special studio, was built for Hokusai, and it was here that he completed four paintings for the ceilings of two large festival floats and a giant mural of a phoenix for the ceiling of **Ganshōin** (岩松院), a red-roofed temple 1km to the east (403 Obuse; 9am–5pm; ¥300). The beautiful floats, decorated with dragons, seascapes and intricate carvings, are displayed in the museum along with forty other works, including painted scrolls, delicate watercolours and woodblock prints.

Takai Kōzan Kinenkan

高井鴻山記念館 • 805-1 Ōaza • Daily: March–Sept 9am–6pm; Oct–Feb 9am–5pm; ¥300 • ☎ 026 247 4049

Near the Hokusai-kan, amid the Masuichi-Ichimura compound, is the **Takai Kōzan Kinenkan**, the atmospheric home of Hokusai's patron, who was also an accomplished artist and calligrapher himself. His drawings of ghosts and goblins are meant as ironic comments on the turbulent early Meiji-era years and are intriguing. In one of the rooms you can see long banners inscribed with *kanji* characters as well as the 2.5m-long brush used to paint them.

Obuse Museum

おぶせミュージアム • 595 Obuse • Daily: March–Sept 9am–6pm; Oct–Feb 9am–5pm; ¥500 • ☎ 026 247 6111

The delightful **Obuse Museum**, which includes the Nakajima Chinami Gallery, houses an exhibition of this highly regarded artist's colourful works. Also on display are five more of the town's traditional festival floats, along with regularly changing art exhibitions.

ARRIVAL AND INFORMATION

OBUSE

By train Obuse is 20min by train (¥650 or ¥750 on the limited express) from Nagano on the Nagano–Dentetsu line.

Tourist information Pick up an English map of the town at Nagano's tourist information centre (see p.343), or at the Obuse Guide Centre & Café (daily 9am–6pm; ☎ 026 247 5050), about a 5min walk southeast of the station, where there's also free internet access.

SAKE AND CHESTNUTS

You can sample the four excellent **sakes** of Masuichi-Ichimura brewery (桝一市村...); Ⓦ masuichi.com), and a few others, at the *teppa* counter in the brewery's shop (807 Obuse; daily 9am–7pm; ¥150–320). Try *Hakkin*, the only sake in Japan to be brewed in huge cedar barrels the old-fashioned, labour-intensive way – hence its high price. Around the corner, you can also sip some award-winning sake for free at Obuse's other brewery, Matsubaya (松葉屋本店; 778 Nakamachi; daily 8am–6.30pm; ☎026 247 201, Ⓦ matsubaya-honten.co.jp).

Masuichi's sister company, Obusedō (小布施堂; 808 Obuse; daily 11am–3pm; Ⓦ obusedo.com), is just one of several **chestnut confectioners** in town battling it out for the public's sweet tooth. Others are Chikufudō (竹風堂; 973 Obuse; daily 10am–6.30pm, winter till 5.30pm; ☎026 247 2569, ☎026 247 2569; Ⓦ chikufudo.com) and Kanseidō (桜井甘精堂 2460 Obuse; daily 11am–7.30pm; ☎026 247 2132; Ⓦ kanseido.co.jp), both of which have restaurants serving meals featuring the sweet nut.

GETTING AROUND

By bus From March to Nov, an hourly shuttle bus makes a circuit of the town's sights – an all-day ticket costs ¥300.

By bike The best way of getting around is to rent a bicycle from one of several places, including the station and the youth hostel (see below) for around ¥400 per day.

ACCOMMODATION

Akebi-no-yu あけびの湯 1311 Obuse-chō ☎026 247 4800, Ⓦ akebinoyu.com. This modern ryokan complex's hillside position on the east of town grants the rooms splendid mountain views. Guests can relax in the adjoining onsen baths for free (daily 6–8.30am & 10am–10pm; ¥500 for non-guests). Rates include two meals. **¥20,780**

Guest House Obuse ゲストハウス小布施 789-1 Ōaza ☎026 247 5050, Ⓦ ala-obuse.net/gesthouse/index .html. Behind the Obuse Guide Centre & Café, this charming guesthouse offers three Western-style rooms and, in a converted *kura*, a two-storey family-style place sleeping up to four for ¥23,100. Add ¥800 per person for breakfast. **¥16,800**

★**Masuichi Kyakuden** 桝一客殿 815 Obuse-machi ☎026 247 1111, Ⓦ kyakuden.jp/english. John Morford, the interior designer of Tokyo's celebrated *Park Hyatt*, is also

responsible for the chic contemporary style of this luxury hotel, which incorporates three *kura* moved from Nagano city and a central koi-filled pond. There are several great restaurants and bars to choose from. Rates include breakfast. **¥28,000**

Obuse no Kaze Youth Hostel おぶせの風ユースホステル 475-2 Higashimachi ☎026 247 4489, Ⓦ homepage2.nifty.com/obusenokaze. A great budget choice, this youth hostel is run by a hospitable family; it's close to the Hokusai-kan, with a choice of Western-style dorms or tatami rooms, as well as private rooms. Dorm **¥3600**

Vent Vert ヴァンヴェール 34-8 Obuse-chō ☎026 247 5512, Ⓦ www.obusenoyado.com. Located above a cute French brasserie, this small hotel has four nicely designed en-suite Western-style rooms. Rates rise by ¥1000 at weekends and public hols. **¥12600**

EATING AND DRINKING

The Club 蔵部 815 Obuse-machi ☎026 247 5300. The most animated and convivial of *Masuichi Kyakuden's* (see box, p.349) three restaurants, with an open kitchen where you can watch the chefs at work preparing a good range of local meat and fish dishes to complement their sakes. Dinner with drinks will cost around ¥3500 per head. Daily 11 30am–2.30pm & 5.30–9pm.

Obuse Hanaya 花屋 506-1 Obuse-chō ☎026 247 1187. On the east side of town overlooking the Floral Garden is this delightful restaurant and café offering Western-style meals (lunch ¥1000, dinner ¥3000) using fresh local produce. 11am–9pm, closed Thurs.

Obusedō Honten 小布施堂本店 815 Obuse-machi ☎026 247 2027. Part of the *Masuichi Kyakuden* business, and behind the confectionery shop of the same name is this Zen-calm restaurant, offering a *kaiseki ryōri*-style menu of local delicacies (from ¥2630) – especially chestnuts – that changes monthly. Drinks and chestnut sweets are also available. Daily 10am–5pm.

Senseki-tei 泉石亭 779 Obuse-chō ☎026 247 5166, Ⓦ kanseido.co.jp. Chestnuts figure large in the wide range of set menus (starting around ¥1000) at this appealing restaurant overlooking an exquisite ornamental garden. 11am–7.30pm, closed Tues.

5

The Nagano-ken mountains

Nagano-ken's mountains are home to several ski resorts and onsen villages, including the delightful **Nozawa Onsen**, self-proclaimed home of Japanese skiing; **Hakuba**, a valley with seven different ski resorts; and **Shiga Kōgen**, Japan's biggest skiing area, which lies within the Jōshinetsu Kōgen National Park. The park is also home to **Yudanaka Onsen**, famous for its snow monkeys, which splash about in their own rotemburo.

Nozawa Onsen

野沢温泉

Even though international word is out on how great the skiing is at **NOZAWA ONSEN**, this village of four thousand people, nestled at the base of Kenashi-yama (1650m), 50km northeast of Nagano, maintains a traditional atmosphere. The **ski resort** (late Nov to early May; one-day lift pass ¥4600; ⓦnozawaski.com) is family-friendly, has lots of English signs and offers varied terrain that will put all levels through their paces. Time your visit to coincide with the spectacular **Dōso-jin fire festival**, held every January 15.

Ō-yu bathhouse

大湯 • 9328 Toyosato • Daily 5am–11pm • Free

Dotted along the narrow, twisting streets of Nozawa, you'll find fourteen free bathhouses, all lovingly tended by the locals. Most impressive is **Ō-yu bathhouse**, housed in a temple-like wooden building in the centre of the village, complete with a trio of statues of the Buddha of Healing and his two attendant Bodhisattvas. Each side of the building has two pools, one of which is so hot that it's almost impossible to get into.

Japan Ski Museum

日本スキー博物館, Nihon Sukii Hakubutsukan • 8270 Toyosato • 9am–4pm; closed Tues • ¥300 • ☏ 0269 85 3418

Nozawa claims to be the birthplace of Japanese skiing, since it was here, in 1930, that Hannes Schneider – an Austrian who popularized the two-pole technique – gave skiing demonstrations to awestruck crowds. One of the resort's most tricky runs is named after Schneider, and photos of the man in action, impeccably dressed in suit and tie, can be seen in the **Japan Ski Museum**, a white, church-like building at the bottom of the Hikage slope.

ARRIVAL AND INFORMATION

NOZAWA ONSEN

By train JR Iiyama line runs from Nagano to Togari-Nozawa-Onsen (1hr; ¥740); from there, Nozawa Onsen is a 20min bus (¥300) or taxi ride (¥3000).

By bus There's a direct bus from Nagano (1hr 15min; ¥1400); for timetables, check with the information offices at Nagano or Nozawa Onsen.

Tourist information Nozawa Onsen's tourist information centre (daily 7.30am–6pm; ☏ 0269 85 3155, ⓦnozawakanko.jp) is opposite the central bus terminal. English information on skiing is available at ⓦnozawaski.com.

Bathhouses All public baths are free and open daily 5am–11pm.

ACCOMMODATION

Hotel Garni Haus St Anton ハウスセントアントン 9515 Toyosato ☏ 0269 85 3597, ⓦst-anton.jp/eng. A cute little piece of Switzerland transplanted to the heart of the village, near the restaurants and bars. Hotel facilities include a restaurant, bar, onsen baths and ski hire, plus they do their own range of home-made jams. Rates include breakfast and dinner, with the restaurant serving fine cuisine blending European and Japanese cooking. **¥25,200**

Pension Schnee ペンションシュネー 8276 Toyosato ☏ 0269 85 2012, ⓦpensionschnee.com. Pretty European-style chalet in a ski-in, ski-out location on the mountainside. It's run by a friendly couple who were Olympic competitors, and rooms are named after resorts which have hosted the winter games. Rates include breakfast and dinner. **¥20,800**

Ryokan Sakaya 旅館さかや 9329 Toyosato ☏ 0269 85 3118, ⓦryokan-sakaya.co.jp. This elegant luxury ryokan, behind the Ōyu bathhouse, has its own spacious indoor and outdoor baths and a choice of Western- or Japanese-style rooms. The service is attentive and warm. Rates include breakfast and dinner. **¥33,000**

★ **Villa Nozawa** 別荘野沢 6631 Toyosato ☎ 0269 85

3272, ⓦ nozawaholidays.com. Savvy foreigner-friendly operation offering several excellent accommodation options around the village, including self-catering cottages sleeping eight. Breakfast is included in the room rates. Double **¥14,000**, cottage **¥32,000**

EATING AND DRINKING

For a **snack**, try the local speciality *onsen manjū*, deliciously plump dumplings with different fillings; buy them from the street vendors with wooden steam-boxes. Nozawa Onsen has more in the way of **après-ski** than many Japanese ski resorts, with a few decent laidback bars, but don't expect Euro-style nightlife.

Bar Heaven カラオケヘベン Ō-yu ☎ 0269 85 4349. A karaoke bar in the centre of town, with private singing rooms available for ¥600 per hour, but you can grab the mic for free in the main bar. There's a happy hour (5–7pm), with drinks for ¥450 and free karaoke booths and snacks. Daily 5pm–2am.

Foot フット Ō-yu ☎ 0269 85 4004. This sports bar, situated on the main street, is good for an après-ski drink, with friendly staff, a table football and free wi-fi. Daily 3pm–11.30pm

Panorama House Buna パノラマハウスぶな Shimotakai-gun ⓦ panoramahouse-buna.com. With great panoramic views, this slope-side restaurant serves a

curry udon for ¥950 that's worth going up the mountain for even if you don't ski. Daily when lifts are running.

Stay ステイ Ō-yu. A long-running convivial basement bar next to *Foot* (see above) which often has live music. Drinks cost around ¥500, and their burgers and desserts come highly recommended. There's a happy hour, too (4–6pm). Daily 3pm–midnight.

Yoshimi Shokudō 良味食堂 8757 Toyosato ☎ 0269 85 2497. A fine place to sample the local noodles, and the menu features a range of hearty stews and curries to build you up for the next day on the slopes. Most dishes are around ¥1000. Daily 11am–3pm & 5–10pm.

Hakuba

白馬

Situated in the dramatic northern Japan Alps, 60km northwest of Nagano, **HAKUBA** is one of Japan's top ski destinations, with a variety of terrain spread across the valley in seven main ski areas and plenty of fun après-ski. The largest and most popular is **Happō-one** (八方尾根; ⓦ hakuba-happo.or.jp), site of the 1998 Nagano Olympics downhill course. Meanwhile, **Hakuba 47** (hakuba47.co.jp), which links to the **Goryū** (五竜; ⓦ hakubagoryu.com) and **Limori** (飯森) areas, is good for snowboarding and freestyle skiing with a terrain park, halfpipe and tree-skiing zone.

With two very pretty **lakes** – Aoki and Kizaki – the Hakuba valley also makes a fine base for a whole range of outdoor pursuits in summer.

ARRIVAL AND DEPARTURE   HAKUBA

By train The best way to get here by train is from Matsumoto along the JR Ōito line; by express it's about an hour's journey. There are also a few direct trains to Shinjuku in Tokyo.

By bus There are plenty of buses from Nagano to Hakuba (1hr; ¥1500) as well as four daily direct buses from

Shinjuku, Tokyo (4hr 30min; ¥4700), and a direct service from Narita Airport (see ⓦ hakubus.com; ¥9800). During winter, check ⓦ hakuba47.co.jp for details about the free bus service that's sometimes available (put on by the Hakuba 47 ski area) from Nagano.

INFORMATION AND ACTIVITIES

Tourist information The tourist information centre (daily 8.30am–5pm; ☎ 0261 72 2279, ⓦ vill.hakuba. nagano.jp) is to the left as you exit JR Hakuba Station; you can leave your bags here for ¥300. The Nippon Ski Resort Development Office (6329-1 Hokujyo; ☎ 0261 72 6900, ⓦ hakuba1.com), 20m on the right on the street running from the station, can help with accommodation, lift passes, equipment hire and resort information. A good website in English with information on ski areas,

accommodation, nightlife and more is ⓦ hakubaconnect .com.

Activities Locally based Ski Japan Holidays (☎ 0261 72 6663, ⓦ japanspecialists.com) can arrange ski trips here as well as tours to other attractions in the area. The reliable Evergreen Outdoor Centre (☎ 0261 72 5150, ⓦ evergreen-outdoors .com) offers everything from rafting and mountain biking in summer to backcountry ski expeditions and avalanche-awareness courses in winter.

5

ACCOMMODATION

New places to stay keep appearing every year. In addition to those listed below, check out the chalets and backpacker lodge deals offered by Snowbeds Travel (☏ 03 9555 4839, ⓦ skijapantravel.com).

Azekura Sansō あぜくら山荘 Wadano ☏ 0261 72 5238, ⓦ en.azekura.com. Smart, modern log house, in the Happō ski area, offering a calm, comfortable retreat and its own rotemburo, a few kilometres away from the base station. If you work at the lodge for five hours, your day's lodging and meals are covered. Breakfast is ¥1200, dinner ¥3500; discounts are available for long stays. **¥15,600**

K's House Hakuba Alps ケイズハウス白馬アルプス 22201-36 Kamishiro ☏ 0261 75 4445, ⓦ kshouse.jp/hakuba-e. This appealing Kamishiro budget option replicates the successful formula of the Kyoto and Tokyo hostel operations. It's only a short walk from Goryū. Dorm **¥2800**

Hakuba Alps Backpackers 白馬アルプスバックパッカーズ 22407-4 Kamishiro ☏ 0261 75 4038, ⓦ hakubabackpackers.com. In Kamishiro, two stops down the train line from Hakuba, this relaxed hostel, topped by a windmill, is run by a very friendly Kiwi–Japanese couple. It's a little scruffy, but the price and location is ideal for the Goryū ski field. Dorm **¥2500**, double **¥6000**

★Maison de Sasagawa めぞん・ど・ささがわ 4620 Hokujo Hakubamura ☏ 261 72 2386, ⓦ maisondesasagawa.net/english. You become part of the family at this friendly lodge in the woods of Wadano – the Happō-one base station is 4min walk. The owners, locals who grew up skiing in the area, make you very welcome, and will pick you up from the station and take you to the supermarket. There are cosy communal dining and lounge areas, a well-equipped kitchen and the Japanese or Western-style rooms are basic but comfortable. Discounts are available for long stays. Dorm **¥3400**, double **¥8400**

Morino Lodge 森のロッヂ 4692-3 Wadano ☏ 0261 85 9098, ⓦ morinolodge.com. A smart lodge in Wadano, about a 15min walk to the Happō-one base station, run by Scottish and Canadian owners. Featuring modern and stylish Western rooms and a large open-plan lounge area complete with sofas and pleasing design touches. This clued-up operation also runs several other lodges; check the website for more options. Rates go up by ¥2000 per person in peak holiday weeks in Jan and Feb. Dorm spaces are also available. Dorm **¥4000**, double **¥18,000**

Phoenix Hotel フェニックスホテル 4690-2 Hokujo ☏ 0261 72 4060, ⓦ phoenixhotel.jp. This elegant boutique-style hotel next to the *Hakuba Tōkyu Hotel* and chalet operation, is about a kilometre from the Happō-one base station. It's surprisingly reasonably priced – especially if you go for the rooms with shared showers (there's also an onsen bath). Note that the hotel only operates during winter, but the chalets are open all year. Discounts are available for longer stays. **¥11,500**

EATING AND DRINKING

Places to **eat** and **bars** are scattered along the valley, but during the winter season a night shuttle-bus services (mid-Dec to early March; ¥200) make it easy to get to most of them from wherever you're staying. For après-ski and evening drinks, the Echoland strip between Hakuba Ski Jumping Stadium and Hakuba 47 is the most popular area.

Gravity Worx グラヴィティー ワークス 6305 Hokujo ☏ 0261 72 5434. In a big log cabin, a minute's walk right from Hakuba Station, this long-running café-bar is run by welcoming English-speaking staff and serves excellent home-made pizza, pasta, salads and desserts. Daily 10am–8pm, closed Tues out of ski season.

Mangetsu-do 満月堂 3020-682 Hokujo ☏ 0261 75 1707. On the Echoland strip, this cool *izakaya* has good food and a choice of forty *umeshu* (plum wines). Daily 5pm–3am.

Master Braster マスターブラスター B1 3020-351 Echoland ☏ 0261 72 2679, ⓦ masterbraster .homepagelife.jp. A basement reggae bar that can get lively, with suitably chilled music and bongo playing encouraged. The menu includes curry, steaks, and bar snacks starting from ¥700. Draught beers are ¥500. Daily 8pm–2am.

Mimi's ミミさん 4690-2 Hokujo ☏ 0261 72 4060. Hakuba's fine dining option is this excellent restaurant in the *Phoenix Hotel*. The menu combines modern European cuisine with local produce, such as Akou oysters and Shinshu pork. Australian wines feature highly in the extensive list, and you can choose from à la carte or the five-course tasting menu. Daily 6.30pm–12pm; ski season only.

Pizzakaya Country Road カントリーロード 22404-1 Kamishiro ☏ 0261 75 2889. Near Kamishiro Station, this friendly, relaxed place offers a range of tasty pizzas and pasta dishes incorporating local ingredients such as mountain vegetables, seaweed and spicy cod roe. Daily 5.30–11.30pm, closed 5, 15 and 25 of the month.

Shōya Maruhachi 庄屋丸八 11032-1 Hokujo ☏ 0261 75 5008. In this handsome merchant's house, originally built in 1854, you can enjoy traditional Japanese dishes at reasonable prices during the ski season. If you want a break from the mountain activities, you can take free Japanese culture courses, including how to make soba. It's a short walk from Shinano Morue Station towards the Hakuba Iwatake ski area. Tues–Sun 11am–2pm & 5–9pm.

Tracks Bar 22200-7 Kamishiro ☎0261 75 4366, ⓦtracksbar.info. Popular with foreigners, this long-running bar in Kamishiro features live music, DJs, pool tables and sports on a large screen. Daily 11am–2am.

Uncle Steven's アンクルスティーブンズ Happō Gondola Rd ☎0261 72 7569, ⓦunclestevenshakuba .com. Located near the base of Happō-one, this Tex-Mex restaurant is good for an après-ski bite, serving pretty authentic burrito, *chimichanga* and enchiladas as well as pizzas and risottos. There's a festive atmosphere, with daily specials, generous portions and a big selection of tequila and imported beers. Daily 11.30am–midnight, irregular out of ski season.

Shiga Kōgen

志賀高原

The complaint that Japanese ski resorts are too small certainly doesn't apply to mammoth **SHIGA KŌGEN**, eighteen resorts strung out along the Shiga plateau in the Jōshinetsu Kōgen National Park, 20km northeast of Nagano. The huge variety of terrain makes the one-day lift pass (¥4800), which covers the entire lift network, terrific value. It takes several days to ski the whole area; if you're short of time, head for the northern end of the mountain range to the resorts at **Okushiga-kōgen** (奥志賀高原) and **Yakebitai-yama** (焼額山), where the slalom events of the 1998 Olympics were held.

ARRIVAL AND INFORMATION

SHIGA KŌGEN

By bus The closest train station to Shiga is Yudanaka (湯田中) – the ski resorts are a 30min bus ride away from here up a stunning mountain pass.

By bus There are direct buses from the east exit of Nagano Station (1hr 15min; ¥1900) and an overnight service during

ski season from Ikebukuro in Tokyo (9hr; one-way/round-trip ¥4000/7500; ⓦtravex.co.jp).

Tourist information For more advice on lodgings, contact the Shiga Tourism Association (☎0269 34 2404, ⓦshigakogen.gr.jp).

ACCOMMODATION

Okushiga Kōgen Hotel 奥志賀高原ホテル ☎0269 34 2034, ⓦokushiga-kougen.com/eng. This sizeable hotel in front of the ski slopes offers Western-style rooms. Amenities include a restaurant serving a buffet dinner and breakfast, cocktail lounge with an open fireplace, big public baths and on-site ski hire. Rates include breakfast and dinner. ¥30,000

Shiga Kōgen Prince Hotel 志賀高原プリンスホテル

Yakebitai-yama ☎0269 34 3111, ⓦprincehotels.com/ en/shiga. A large resort hotel offering three separate wings at the foot of Yakebitai-yama: the eastern part sports retro 1980s glamour while the slightly cheaper west wing, with a big outdoor bath, is geared to families and groups. Online deals are available, with good discounts on basic rooms. Breakfast is included. ¥49,200

Jigokudani Monkey Park

地獄谷野猿公苑, Jigokudani Yaen-kōen • 6845 Yamanouchi-machi • Daily 8am–5pm • ¥500 • ⓦjigokudani-yaenkoen.co.jp • The Nagano–Dentetsu train line from Nagano terminates in Yudanaka (express 40min; ¥1230; local 1hr; ¥1130), from where it's a 15min bus journey (¥210) to Kanbayashi Onsen – there's also a direct bus from Nagano to Kanbayashi Onsen (40min; ¥1300); to get to the Monkey Park, walk uphill from the bus stop till you find a sign for a trail leading through the woods for around 2km

KANBAYASHI ONSEN's (上林温泉) star attraction is a troupe of some two hundred Japanese long-tailed monkeys (*nihon-zaru*) that like to bathe in the rotemburo at the **Jigokudani Monkey Park**, a twenty-minute walk from the town. Legend has it that they started to take dips in the hot pools during the 1960s, when a local ryokan owner took pity on them and left food out in winter. A special rotemburo was eventually built for the "snow monkeys", as *Life* magazine named them, even though they live beside the onsen year-round. It's curiously addictive watching these primates fooling around by the pool; get a preview via webcam on the park website. The monkeys are so used to humans now that they feign dignified nonchalance at the paparazzi-style snapping from the tourist hordes.

5

ACCOMMODATION

Kanbayashi Hotel Senjukaku 上林ホテル仙壽閣 1410 Hirao, Yamanouchi ☎ 0269 33 3551, ⓦ senjukaku .com/en. This elegant, traditional inn, set amid the trees in Kanbayashi Onsen, is a place to indulge yourself. The tatami rooms are spacious and luxurious, and the outdoor baths are set amid bamboo and rocks. Rates include two meals, and local produce, including Shinshu beef from apple-fed cows, features high on the menu. **¥52,000**

Kōrakukan 後楽館 Yamanouchi ☎ 0269 33 4376, ⓦ www.kanbayashi-onsen.com/kourakukan.htm. Beside the monkey park, this rambling wooden ryokan set on the hillside offers homely Japanese-style accommodation, where rates include two meals. There's a selection of indoor and outdoor onsens, including private family baths; non-residents can take a dip in the rotemburo for ¥500. **¥20,000**

Togura Kamiyamada Onsen

戸倉上山田温泉

Some 20km southwest of Nagano towards Matsumoto, straddling the Chikuma river and surrounded by mountains, lies **TOGURA KAMIYAMADA ONSEN**. The town was traditionally a stop-off point for pilgrimages after visiting Zenkō-ji Temple and it is proud of its strong geisha heritage that continues today, though it is now somewhat urbanized as an agglomeration of the small workaday city **Chikuma** (千曲). Offering more entertainment options than the average onsen resort, with its lively bar and restaurant district, public footbaths and unique shops, as well as easy access to surrounding nature, Togura Kamiyamada makes an enjoyable overnight stay.

ARRIVAL AND DEPARTURE

By train Togura Station lies on the local Shinano railway, 15min from Nagano. if you are coming from the south, change from the JR line at Shinonoi Station, from where it's a 10min ride. The Onsen district is on the opposite side of the river, 2km from the station. Most hotels provide a shuttle bus; otherwise, hop in a taxi (¥1000).

Destination Nagano (every 30min; 15min; ¥360).

ACCOMMODATION, EATING AND DRINKING

With more than forty **ryokans**, ranging from the traditional to Western, there are no shortage of onsen hotels here, but it's better to avoid the large, old-style government ryokans in favour of more characterful options. Eating and drinking options are similarly wide, with lots of good places to choose from, serving local specialities including *Oshibori Udon*, noodles with a spicy *daikon* radish sauce.

Daikokuya 大黒屋 2-24-1 Kamiyamada Onsen ☎ 026 275 0768. This small noodle shop is a local institution – there's often a queue at lunchtimes, but it's worth the wait. The garlic sauce pork fillet "*nintare tonkatsu*" is a local favourite. Bowls of noodles start at ¥600. Daily 11.30–4.30pm.

Kamesei 亀清 2-15-1 Kamiyamada Onsen, ☎ 026 275 1032, ⓦ kamesei.jp/english/kannai.html. An excellent small ryokan run by a very friendly Japanese–American couple. The old building's passageways wind around small inner gardens and ponds, tatami rooms feature modern en-suite bathrooms, and there is a "hundred-year-old" outdoor bath, as well as a private family onsen. For an extra ¥5000 per head, two meals are included in the rate. **¥11,000**

Yakitori Yumi's やきとり裕味 2-18-22 Kamiyamada Onsen ☎ 026 276 1258. The ex-geisha owner hasn't lost her ability to entertain, and will make you very welcome, even if her English is limited. *Yakitori* skewers are ¥300 for two; beer and *Yakotori* set menus are available from ¥2000. 6–10pm, closed Thurs.

Karuizawa and around

軽井沢

At Nagako-ken's eastern edge, on the slopes of Asama-yama, is the ritzy resort of **KARUIZAWA** where Crown Prince Akihito (now the emperor) met his future wife, Michiko, on the tennis courts in the 1950s, and where John Lennon and Yoko Ono vacationed in the late 1960s and 1970s. Decades of such superstar patronage have lent this small town a fashionable reputation, and the place can get very hectic in summer as Tokyoites descend to relax in the cooler mountain air and spend up a storm at the giant outlet mall and tacky tourist-shop strip either side of the main station. It's pretty easy to escape this commercial frenzy and enjoy Karuizawa's natural tranquillity on easy trekking and cycling routes into the forested hills that are dotted with charming wooden villas and heritage buildings.

Kyū-Karuizawa

旧軽井沢 • About 1km north of the station • Frequent buses run here from in front of Karuizawa Station (¥160)

The scenic part of Karuizawa begins a kilometre or so from the station, in the **Kyū-Karuizawa** district. Work your way past the tourists jamming the pedestrianized, rather tacky, shopping street dubbed "Little Ginza", to emerge into a forest. Here you'll find the quaint wooden **Anglican Chapel** (daily 9am–5pm; free), which is fronted by a bust of the Canadian missionary Alexander Croft Shaw, who helped popularize the area as a retreat. A short walk southeast is the historic *Mampei Hotel* (see p.356), which has a small museum of memorabilia.

North of Karuizawa

Frequent buses run from in front of Karuizawa Station northbound to the Old Mikasa Hotel (¥270) via Kyū-Karuizawa

Head northwest along the main road, Mikasa-dōri, and it's a pleasant 2km cycle ride or hike to the secluded **Old Mikasa Hotel** (旧三笠ホテル; daily 9am–4.30pm; ¥400), an elegant wooden building built in 1906 that's now a national monument. Follow the road past the camping ground to **Kose** (小瀬), where a 10km hike gets you to the scenic **Shiraito Falls** (白糸の滝). Afterwards, head west to **Mine-no-chaya** (峰の茶屋), from where buses head back to Karuizawa.

Hoshino Resort

星野リゾート • **Onsen** Daily 10am–10pm • ¥1200 • **Nature tours** Daily 10am & 1.30pm; night tours available at varying times – call ☎ 0267 45 7777 for prices and to book • ☎ 0267 45 3853, ⓦ hoshino-area.jp • A free bus runs here from the south side of Karuizawa Station; ask for the schedule at the tourist office (see p.357)

A 6km pedal (or free bus ride) west of Karuizawa is **Naka-Karuizawa** (中軽井沢), another beautiful area for cycling, hiking and relaxing. The main focus is the **Hoshino Resort**, where you'll find the luxury hotel *Hoshinoya Karuizawa* (see p.356), an excellent onsen, **Tonbo-no-yu** (トンボの湯), a forest of chestnut and larch trees where you can take guided nature tours, and a stylish, low-key shopping and dining complex, **Harunire Terrace**.

Onioshidashien

鬼押出し園 • 21km northwest of Karuizawa • Mid-March to early Dec daily 8am–5pm • ¥400 (low), ¥600 (high) • Regular buses run here from outside Karuizawa Station (50min; ¥1180)

Looming ominously over Karuizawa is 2568m **Asama-yama** (浅間山), Japan's highest triple-cratered active volcano, which last erupted in 2004. The closest you can get to the crater is on its north side at **Onioshidashien**. Onioshidashien was the scene of a cataclysmic eruption on August 5, 1783, when ashes from the blowout were said to have darkened the sky as far as Europe, and a 7km-wide lava flow swept away Kanbara village. When the lava cooled, it solidified into an extraordinary landscape of black boulders and bizarre rock shapes, where alpine plants now sprout and across which twisting pathways have been laid. To see the scale of the place, head up to the observation floor in the gift shop and restaurant complex at the entrance. Most of the crowds head for the central temple, **Kannon-dō**, which stands on a raised red

5

platform amid the black rocks, but you can easily escape them by continuing past to the quieter area behind.

ARRIVAL AND INFORMATION

By train The fastest route to Karuizawa is by train on the Shinkansen from either Tokyo (1hr 7min; every 30min) or Nagano (32min; every 30min). Regular train services only go as far as Yokokawa Station, from where you have to travel up to Karuizawa by bus (¥500) from the valley below.

By bus There are direct buses from Ikebukuro in Tokyo, as well as Osaka and Kyoto.

Tourist information Karuizawa's sights are widely scattered, so it's best to pick up the good English map of the area from the tourist information office (daily 9am–5.30pm, ☎0267 42 2491, ⊕karuizawa-kankokyokai.jp) at the station. However, the staff at the information office outside the west side of the station are more equipped to deal with English-speaking visitors.

GETTING AROUND

By bus Local buses depart from outside Karuizawa train station, serving the main attractions in the surrounding area.

By bike The most enjoyable way of exploring is by bicycle; you can rent one from the many outlets near the train station (around ¥1000 a day).

ACCOMMODATION

Karuizawa is not a cheap place to stay, so if you are on a budget a day-trip is probably best. Prices in the summer high season can be up to triple those in low season; those given here are for high season. During holidays it's best to reserve in advance, as rooms fill up fast.

APA Hotel Karuizawa-Ekimae ホテル軽井沢駅前 1178-1135 Karuizawa ☎0267 42 0665, ⊕tinyurl .com/2b7olct. Handily located beside the JR station, this dependable business hotel chain charges reasonable rates (for Karuizawa) for functional rooms. A bonus is their restaurant's open-air terrace, where you eat breakfast. Rates are less than a third in low season. **¥33,000**

★**Hoshinoya Karuizawa** 星のや軽井沢 Hoshino, Karuizawa-machi ☎0267 45 6000, ⊕tinyurl.com/ nhproz6. Outstandingly beautiful, luxury onsen hotel, which blends with the forest and is 75 percent energy self-sufficient thanks to hydro-power generators. Choose between garden, river and mountainside villas, each equally gorgeous and all sporting cypress-wood bathtubs. There's a two-night minimum. Rates halve in low season. **¥108,000**

Karuizawa Prince Hotel East 軽井沢プリンスホテルイ ースト Kitasaku-gun ☎0267 42 1111, ⊕princehotels. co.jp/karuizawa-east. This is the best deal of several *Prince* properties located on a sprawling site south of the station. It offers a mammoth shopping plaza, spa and onsen, tennis, golf and, in winter, direct access to a small ski field. Choose between stylish, large hotel rooms or log cabins. Low-season rates are around a third of high. **¥60,000**

Mampei Hotel 万平ホテル 925 Kitasaku-gun ☎0267 42 1234, ⊕mampei.co.jp. This hotel, the area's grand dame, established in 1894, is where Lennon stayed when he was in town. Surrounded by the forest, it has a quirky, rambling elegance, although the cheapest rooms are a little dowdy. Rates halve in low season. **¥39,000**

Hotel Wellies ホテル・ウェリーズ 2350-160 Nagakura ☎0267 46 1670, ⊕www.hotelwellies.jp. Run by a British–Japanese couple, this small hotel is one of the most affordable options in town. Named after the Duke of Wellington, it is a little patch of England in the East, with some quirky design features and an eclectic mix of decor combining the modern and traditional. There's a lovely granite-tiled family bathroom as well as an indoor garden. Low-season rates are just over half of high. **¥17,000**

EATING AND DRINKING

Many restaurants are closed Wed and Thurs in winter.

Kawakamian 川上庵 6-10 Kyū-Karuizawa ☎0267 42 009, ⊕kawakamian.com. This is a smart place in the woods with a fantastic terrace when it is sunny. The handmade soba and tempura set meals cost around ¥1785. Daily 11am–9pm.

Sekireibashi Kawakami-an せきれい橋川上庵 2145-5 Nagakura-asa, Yokobuki ☎0267 31 0266. Another branch of *Kawakamain* (see above) in a lovely setting overlooking a babbling river in Hoshino's Harunire Terrace, where you'll also find several other appealing dining options. Daily 11am–10pm.

Kastanie カスターニエ 2-3-2 karaizawa-east ☎0267 42 3081, ⊕kastanie.co.jp. A 7min walk north of Karuizawa Station, this reliable restaurant offers Western dishes including its speciality slow-roasted chicken, fine pizzas and grilled meat dishes. Set lunch menus start at ¥1200. Daily 11am–3pm & 5–10pm, closed Tues.

Matsumoto

公本

Some 50km southwest of Nagano across the Hijiri Kōgen mountains is
MATSUMOTO, gateway to the Japan Alps. Attracted by the slower pace of life and
surrounding nature, many former urbanites are moving to Matsumoto and setting
up a new generation of small, artsy shops, cafés, bars and other businesses. This
attractive city, Nagano-ken's second largest, is famous for its splendid castle,

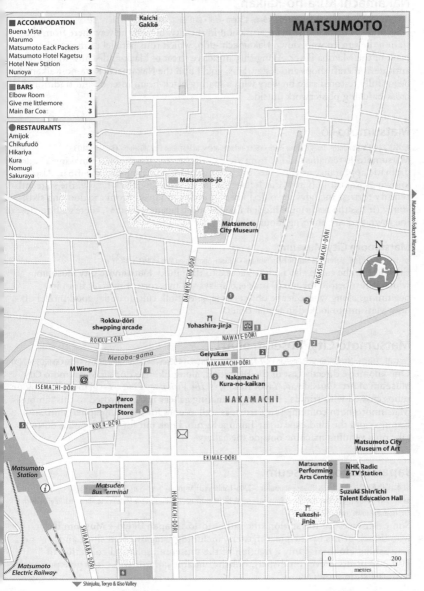

ACCOMMODATION	
Buena Vista	6
Marumo	2
Matsumoto Back Packers	4
Matsumoto Hotel Kagetsu	1
Hotel New Station	5
Nunoya	3

BARS	
Elbow Room	1
Give me littlemore	2
Main Bar Coat	3

RESTAURANTS	
Amijok	3
Chikufudō	4
Hikariya	2
Kura	6
Nomugi	5
Sakuraya	1

MATSUMOTO

5

5

Matsumoto-jō, and **Nakamachi**, an area of traditional white-walled houses, several of which have been renovated into ryokan, cafés and craft shops. Art lovers can enjoy traditional prints at the **Japan Ukiyo-e Museum** and the contemporary work of native-child Yayoi Kusama at the **Matsumoto City Museum of Art**. If you're here for the last weekend in May, it's worth checking out the **Crafts Fair Matsumoto** (ⓦmatsumoto-crafts.com).

Nakamachi Kura-no-Kaikan

中町蔵の会館 • 9-15 Nakamachi-dōri • Daily 9am–4.30pm • Free • ☏ 0263 36 3053

Matsumoto's castle is the main attraction in the city, but on the way there from the station, be sure to walk down **Nakamachi-dōri**, which runs parallel to the southern bank of the Metoba River. Along this attractive street of black-and-white-walled inns, antique and craft shops and restaurants, you'll find the **Nakamachi Kura-no-Kaikan**, a beautifully restored sake brewery with a soaring black-beam interior and traditional cross-hatching plasterwork outside.

Matsumoto-jō

松本城 • 4-1 Marunouchi • Daily 8.30am–5pm • ¥600; includes access to Matsumo City Museum • ☏ 0263 32 0133

Matsumoto-jō remains hidden from view until the very last moment, making a sudden dramatic appearance as you enter the outer grounds and approach the moat. Also known as Karasu-jō (Crow Castle) because of its brooding black facade, the sixteenth-century fortress includes the oldest **keep** (donjon) in Japan. From the donjon's sixth storey (it has the traditional hidden floor of most Japanese castles), there's a fine view of the town and surrounding mountains.

Matsumoto City Museum

松本市立博物館, Matsumoto Shiritsu Hakubutsukan • 8.30am–5pm; closed Mon • ⓦbit.ly/1fCdYfw

Entrance to the castle also includes access to the quirky **Matsumoto City Museum**, which is just before the moat. Inside, displays tell the story of the city from its beginnings along with eclectic objects of Japanese folk culture and a good model of how Matsumoto looked in feudal times.

Matsumoto City Museum of Art

松本市美術館, Matsumoto-Shi Bijutsukan • 4-2-22 Chūō • Tues–Sun 9am–4.30pm • ¥400, special exhibitions ¥1000 • ☏ 0263 39 7400

One kilometre directly east of the JR station, along Ekimae-dōri, is **Matsumoto City Museum of Art**. Outside are Yayoi Kusama's *The Visionary Flowers* – giant technicolour tulips crossed with triffids. There's a fascinating gallery inside devoted to this famous, Matsumoto-born contemporary artist, as well as ones for the calligrapher Shinzan Kamijyo and the landscape artist Tamura Kazuo. Look out for Yayoi's polka-dotted take on a vending machine outside the gallery.

Japan Ukiyo-e Museum

日本浮世絵美術館, Nihon Ukiyo-e Bijutsukan • 2206-1 Shimadate Koshiba • Tues–Sun 10am–5pm • ¥1200 •
☏ 0263 47 4440 • The closest station, a 15min walk south of the museum, is Ōniwa on the Matsumoto–Dentetsu line; or catch a taxi from the town centre (¥1500)

Some 3km west of the station, the rather forlorn **Japan Ukiyo-e Museum** has woodblock prints by the great masters, including Utagawa Hiroshige and Katsushika Hokusai. Only a fraction of the museum's splendid collection of 100,000 prints is ever on display, but the amiable curator will often give personally narrated slide shows.

Matsumoto Folkcraft Museum

松本民芸館 Matsumoto Mingai-Kan • Tues–Sun 9am–5pm • ¥300 • ☎0263 33 1569 • Catch a bus out of the city towards Utsukushigahara Onsen and get off at Shimogana Mingeikanguchi (¥290; 15min)

If you've an interest in Japanese folk crafts, head to the worthwhile **Matsumoto Folkcraft Museum**, in the outskirts of the city. Set in a traditional-style building, the museum contains some exquisite objects, including giant pottery urns, lacquerware inlaid with mother of pearl and wooden chests.

ARRIVAL AND DEPARTURE | MATSUMOTO

By plane Matsumoto's small airport (☎0263 57 8818) is 8km southwest of the town centre; buses to the city centre meet all flights (25min; local bus ¥540, direct service ¥600).
Destinations Fukuoka (daily; 1hr 30min); Sapporo (daily; 1hr 30min).

By train Matsumoto is connected by direct trains with Nagano, Nagoya and Tokyo from the latter, the fastest train is the Azusa limited express service from Shinjuku (2hr 30min)

Destinations Hakuba (11 daily; 1hr 45min); Nagano (every 30min; 45min); Nagoya (hourly; 2hr); Osaka (daily; 4hr); Tokyo (Shinjuku Station; hourly; 2hr 30min).

By bus All long-distance buses stop in front of the train station.
Destinations Kanazawa (April–Nov 2 daily; 4hr 50min); Nagano (hourly; 1hr 20min); Osaka (2 daily; 6hr 50min); Takayama (4 daily; 2hr 30min); Tokyo (Shinjuku Station; hourly; 3hr 10min).

INFORMATION

Tourist information The helpful tourist information office (daily 9am–5.45pm; ☎0263 32 2814) is inside Matsumoto Station. An irreverent but good website with local info on the city is ☻welcome.city.matsumoto.nagano.jp.

Services There's free internet access at the community centre M Wing building (daily 9am–9pm; 0263 48 7000) on Isemachi-dōri, a 5min walk north of the station.

GETTING AROUND

By bus Convenient Town Sneaker minibuses run along four circular routes from the JR station. One ride costs ¥190, or you can buy a ¥500 day pass on the bus; the tourist office has a map of the routes. Regular buses leave from the Matsuden Bus Terminal, under the ESPA department store opposite Matsumoto Station.

By bike You can borrow one of the free bikes from various locations around the city – ask the tourist office for a map with them marked.
On foot The main sights are within easy walking distance of the train station.

ACCOMMODATION

Buena Vista ブエナ・ビスタ 1-2-1 Honjo ☎0263 37 0111, ☻buena-vista.co.jp. With a recent stylish contemporary makeover, this is Matsumoto's most opulent Western-style accommodation. The cheaper rooms are pretty cramped, so pay up for the premier rooms if you want to experience real luxury. Online booking deals are available. **¥19,635**

Marumo まるも 3-3-10 Chūō ☎0263 32 0115, ☻www. avis.ne.jp/~marumo/index.html. Set in a whitewashed house and Meiji-era wooden building on the banks of the Metoba River this small ryokan is an appealing mix of old and new, with tatami rooms, a wooden bath, a small enclosed bamboo garden and a nice café where breakfast (¥1000) is served to classical music. Note there is an 11pm curfew. **¥10,000**

★Matsumoto Back Packers 松本バックパッカーズ 1-1-6 Shirata ☎0263 31 5848, ☻matsumotobp. com/en. This friendly hostel is 5min walk from the station in a quiet riverside location, and it's owned by an enthusiastic Irish–Japanese couple happy to share their

wealth of local knowledge. The tatami dorms, shared bathrooms and small kitchen are immaculately clean, and the communal lounge s very sociable. Single rooms and twins are also available. Dorm **¥3000**, double **¥7000**

Matsumoto Hotel Kagetsu 松本ホテル花月 4-8-9 Ōte ☎0263 32 0114, ☻hotel-kagetsu.jp. Although it's showing some wear and tear this handsome old-fashioned hotel, close to the castle, has some stylish touches and makes use of the local dark-wood furniture. The tatami rooms are good and the same price as the Western-style ones. **¥10,000**

Hotel New Station ホテルニューステーション 1-1-11 Chūō ☎0263 35 3850, ☻www.hotel-ns.co.jp. Good-value and friendly business hotel, with an excellent top-floor public bath and a men-only sauna. On the ground floor, their lively izakaya serves traditional local dishes including basashi (raw horse meat). **¥8600**

Nunoya ぬのや 3-5-7 Nakamachi ☎0263 32 0545, ☻www.mcci.or.jp/www/nunoya/en. This delightful

5

ryokan, in a charming wooden building in the middle of Nakamachi-dōri, has attractive tatami rooms (which all share a communal Japanese-style bathroom) as well as a pleasant lounge and dining room. **¥9000**

EATING AND DRINKING

Soba, best eaten cold (ask for *zaru-soba*), is the local speciality. Unique to the area is *sasamushi*, eel steamed inside rice wrapped in bamboo leaves. The adventurous may also want to try horsemeat served in a variety of ways, including raw (*basashi*). Another local speciality is *Sanzuko Yaki*, spicy fried chicken. Note that several of the best **places to eat** in Matsumoto are closed on Wed.

Amijok アミジョク 3-4-14 Chūō ☎ 0263 88 6238. A cute, friendly café with a retro vibe, just off the eastern end of Nakamachi-dōri. The house speciality is muffins, with five different types baked fresh each day along with other home-made cakes, breads and savoury snacks. There are regular exhibitions by local artists and modern craft items from local makers for sale. A coffee and cake costs around ¥500. Daily 10am–8pm, closed Thurs.

Chikufudō 竹風堂 3-4-20 Nakamachi ☎ 0263 36 1102, ⓦ chikufudo.com. Local rice dishes and sweets made with chestnuts are served at this restaurant in one of the old whitewashed houses on Nakamachi-dōri. Set meals start at ¥900. 10am–7pm, closed Wed.

Hikariya ヒカリヤ 4-7-14 Ōte ☎ 0263 38 0186. An elegant 120-year-*old machiya* (townhouse) has been beautifully restored and converted into this very stylish complex of two restaurants: *Higashi*, serving an austere but masterful *kaiseki* menu, and *Nishi*, specializing in French cuisine. Lunch starts at ¥3800, dinner ¥5700.

11.30am–1.30pm & 6.30–9.30pm, closed Wed.

★**Kura** 蔵 1-10-22 Chūō. The building might be a reproduction of a white-walled storehouse (*kura*), but the food – top-notch sushi and tempura – is the real deal. Also on the English menu are local specialities including *basashi* (horsemeat sashimi) and their own brand of sake. Expect to pay around ¥4000 per head for dinner. 11.45am–2pm & 5.30–10pm, closed Wed.

Nomugi 野麦 2-9-11 Chūō ☎ 0263 36 3753. Another celebrated soba noodle shop; you may have to queue for one of the few seats here, and they close up when sold out. Bowls of noodles cost around ¥1000. Mon & Thurs–Sun 11.30am–2pm.

Sakuraya 桜家 4-9-1 Ōte ☎ 0263 33 2660, ⓦ sakuraya .ne.jp. This traditional restaurant, with waitresses in kimono, specializes in eel dishes, including *sasamushi*. A variety of set meals, from around ¥1800, are described on the English menu. Tues–Sun 11.30am–2pm and 5–9pm.

NIGHTLIFE

★**Elbow Room** エルボー・ルーム 4-3-3 Nawate Yokochō ☎ 0263 39 3017. One of the tiny drinking dens in the lanes off Nawate-dori, this cosmically themed bar is lively at weekends, with an eclectic mix of electronic and psychedelic sounds attracting a young crowd of skaters and partiers. Drinks around ¥500, with a range of cocktails and daily food specials for ¥600. Mon–Sat 8pm till late.

Give me little more ギブミーリトルモア 3-11-7 Chūō ☎ 080 5117 0059, ⓦ givemelittlemore.blogspot.jp.

Attracting an arty crowd, this tiny wooden bar next to the river hosts regular DIY art exhibitions, film screenings and music performances in its adjoining event space. It also offers daily food specials, usually curry (¥800). Drinks from ¥500. Wed–Sun 8pm till late.

Main Bar Coat イン・バー・コート ☎ 0263 34 7133 Miwa Bldg, 2-3-5 Chūō. This stylish bar serves a wide range of cocktails and has a good whiskey collection. Cocktails start at ¥800, and there's an ¥800 cover charge. Daily 6pm–2am; closed Mon.

CLASSICAL MUSIC IN MATSUMOTO

Matsumoto has a reputation as a centre for classical music. It was here that **Dr Suzuki Shin'ichi**, an internationally famous music teacher, encouraged children to learn to play instruments using their natural gift for mimicry. His "Suzuki Method" is taught in the town's Suzuki Shin'ichi Talent Education Hall, around 1km east of Matsumoto Station. The **Saitō Kinen** (ⓦ saito-kinen.com) is a major classical music festival held from mid-August to early September in memory of another local talent, Saitō Hideo, celebrated conductor and mentor to many famous musicians, including the festival's director, conductor Ozawa Seiji.

If you are in town on a Sunday, it's well worth checking out the weekly performances of the classical Japanese string instrument, the *shamisen*, at Geiyūkan (芸游館; Nakamachi; Sun 1.30pm and 3pm; ¥700 including tea and cake; ☎ 0263 32 1107).

Around Matsumoto

It's all about the mountains around Matsumoto. To the north is the ski centre of **Hakuba** (see p.351), while to the west is the serene lake and mountain resort of **Kamikōchi** (see below) – a place that gets so much snow that it is inaccessible all winter. A generally less crowded alternative is the nearby onsen and ski resort of **Norikura Kōgen**.

(see p.351)

GETTING AROUND   AROUND MATSUMOTO

By car The fabulous Skyline Road runs through the mountainous area around Matsumoto, across to Takayama in neighbouring Gifu-ken (see p.368); drive along it, and you'll see why Nagano-ken is known as the "roof of Japan".

By bus If you don't have your own wheels, look into the bus company Alpico's three-day ticket (¥6400; ⓦ www .alpico.co.jp) for use of all its services in the area.

(see p.368)

Hotaka
穂高

A thirty-minute train ride north of Matsumoto lies the quiet country town of **Hotaka**, well known for its production of the *wasabi* paste which accompanies sushi and sashimi. The best way to explore this tranquil area is to pick up a map from the **tourist information office** at the station and rent a bicycle from one of the many outlets around here. Keep an eye open along the country roads for *dōsojin*, small stones on which guardian deity couples have been carved.

Dai-ō Wasabi Farm
大王わさび農場, Dai-ō Wasabi Nōjō • 1692 Hotaka • Daily 9am–5pm • Free • ⓣ 0263 82 2118, ⓦ www.daiowasabi.co.jp • A 15min bike ride from Hokata station

Set in pleasant countryside, the enjoyably touristy **Dai-ō Wasabi Farm**, one of the largest in Japan, has vast fields of the fiery green horseradish growing in wide, waterlogged gravel trenches. Inside, you can sample all types of *wasabi*-flavoured food, including surprisingly tasty ice cream and even beer.

Rokuzan Art Museum
碌山美術館, Rokuzan Bijutsukan • 5095-1 Hotaka • Tues–Sun 9am–5.10pm, Nov–Feb till 4.10pm • ¥700 • ⓦ rokuzan.jp • A 7min walk from Hotaka station

The serene **Rokuzan Art Museum**, comprising an ivy-covered, church-like building and a couple of modern galleries, houses the sculptures of **Ogiwara Rokuzan**, known in Japan as the "Rodin of the Orient", whose career was cut short with his death in 1910 from tuberculosis, aged 32.

ARRIVAL AND INFORMATION   HOTAKA

By train Hotaka is connected by direct trains with Matsumoto on the JR Ōito line (hourly; 30min; ¥320)
Tourist information The Hotaka tourist office (daily: April–Nov 9am–5pm, Dec–March 10am–4pm; ⓣ 0263 82

9363, ⓦ azumino-e-tabi.net/en) is on the left as you exit the station; there are English-speaking staff and information available here.

Kamikōchi
上高地

Tucked away in the Azusa valley at an altitude of 1500m is the beautiful mountaineering and hiking resort of **KAMIKŌCHI**. Little more than a bus station and a handful of hotels scattered along the Azusa-gawa, Kamikōchi has some stunning alpine scenery, which can only be viewed between April 27 and November 15 before heavy snow blocks off the narrow roads and the resort shuts down for winter. As a result, the place buzzes with tourists during the season, and the prices at its hotels and restaurants can be as steep as the surrounding mountains.

5

WALTER WESTON

Born in Derbyshire, England, in 1861, the missionary **Walter Weston** was 29 years old when he first set foot in the mountains of Nagano-ken. The phrase "Japan Alps" was actually coined by another Englishman, William Gowland, whose *Japan Guide* was published in 1888, but it was Weston's *Climbing and Exploring in the Japan Alps*, which appeared eight years later, that really put the peaks on mountaineers' radar. Previously, these mountains, considered **sacred**, were only climbed by Shintō and Buddhist priests, but in fast-modernizing Japan alpinism caught on as a **sport** and Weston became its acknowledged guru. Weston favoured Kamikōchi as a base from which to climb what he called "the grandest mountains in Japan", and he frequently visited the tiny village from his home in Kōbe. Although he is honoured in Kamikōchi with a monument and a festival in his name on the first Sunday in June (the start of the climbing season), Weston is said to have wept at the prospect of mass tourism ruining his beloved mountains. His ghost can take comfort from the fact that the area's beauty survives largely intact, despite Kamikōchi's popularity.

Kamikōchi owes its fortunes to the late nineteenth-century British missionary **Walter Weston** (see box above), who helped popularize the area as a base for climbing the Northern Alps. The highest mountain here is the 3190m **Hotaka-dake** (also known as Oku-Hotaka-dake), followed by **Yari-ga-take** (3180m). Both are extremely popular climbs; one trail up Yari-ga-take has been dubbed the Ginza Jūsō ("Ginza Traverse") after Tokyo's busy shopping area. However, the congestion on the mountain is nothing compared to that found at its base, where, at the height of the season, thousands of day-trippers tramp through the well-marked trails along the **Azusa valley**. With an early start, the scenic spots of the valley can be covered in a day's hike, but the best way to appreciate Kamikōchi is to stay overnight so you can experience the valley in the evening and early morning minus the day-trippers. Alternatively, visit in June, when frequent showers deter fair-weather walkers. Pick up the English *Kamikōchi Pocket Guide* from the information office at the bus stop for a map of the main trails.

Azusa valley

梓川谷

At the entrance to the **Azusa valley**, the **Taishō-ike** (大正池) is a glass-like pond that reflects the snowcapped peaks. From here, an hour-long amble starts along the pebbly riverbank and splits after the Tashiro bridge, one leg continuing beside the Azusa-gawa, the other following a nature trail along wooden walkways, over chocolatey marshes. The Taishō-ike was formed when the Azusa-gawa was naturally dammed following a 1915 eruption of the nearby volcano, Yake-dake – dead tree trunks still poke out of the water. Rowing boats can be rented from the *Taishō-ike Hotel* (¥800/30min).

Returning the way you came, cross over the Tashiro bridge to the opposite bank of the river, where the path leads past some of Kamikōchi's hotels and a rock-embedded relief statue of Walter Weston. In the centre of the village, a very photogenic wooden suspension bridge, **Kappa-bashi** (河童橋), crosses the river. A few minutes' walk from here is a good national park **visitor centre** (see opposite), where there are some stunning photographs of the mountains.

The crowds fall away on the hike north from the visitor centre to the picturesque pond, **Myōjin-ike** (明神池, ¥300), with its tiny shrine and mallard ducks; the 7km return trip will take you around two hours at a leisurely pace. Myōjin-ike is the location of a festival on October 8 when two boats, their prows decorated with the head of a dragon and a legendary bird, float on the sacred pond. From here, really keen hikers can follow a six-hour course up the valley to the **Tokusawa campsite** (徳沢) and the Shinmura suspension bridge, named after a famous climber, Shinmura Shōichi.

The hike to Yari-ga-take

Beyond Tokusawa, the serious hiking begins. The steep hike up the "Matterhorn of Japan" (so called because of its craggy appearance) to the mountain huts at Ichinomata on the lower slopes of **Yari-ga-take** (槍ヶ岳) takes around five hours, and can be done in a long day from Kamikōchi. There are basic huts on the mountain for overnight stays; a futon and two meals cost around ¥8000 per person, but it can get very crowded.

Reaching the summit of Yari-ga-take may well give you a taste for mountaineering. The popular route to follow is due south across the alpine ridge to **Hotaka-dake** (穂高岳), the third-highest peak in Japan, a three-day loop that will bring you back to Kamikōchi.

ARRIVAL AND DEPARTURE

KAMIKŌCHI

By train To get here from Matsumoto, take a 30min train journey on the Matsumoto Dentetsu line to Shin-Shimashima Station (新島々; ¥680), then transfer to a bus to Kamikōchi (1hr 15min; ¥2000).

By bus There are also a few direct buses in summer from Matsumoto bus terminal ¥2600 one-way, ¥4600 return). From Takayama there are a couple of direct buses daily (¥2200), but it's quicker to hop on the more frequent bus to Hirayu Onsen (¥1530), then transfer to the Kamikōchi bus (¥1050). There's also a daily bus between Norikura Kōgen

(see p.364) and Kamikōchi Once you've arrived, make sure you reserve your seat on a bus out of Kamikōchi – the sheer number of visitors often leaves many people at the mercy of the taxi drivers.

By car Private vehicles are banned from the valley. If you're driving, park your car in the village of Naka-no-yu (中の湯), 8km outside Kamikōchi. From here buses (¥1000 one-way, ¥1800 return) and taxis (¥4500 for up to four passengers) make regular runs to and from Kamikōchi, passing through narrow rock tunnels.

INFORMATION AND ACTIVITIES

Tourist information There's an information centre (daily 8am–5pm; ☎0263 95 2433, ⓦkamikochi.or.jp/english) at the bus terminal where you can pick up a good English map showing the main hiking trails. The assistants don't speak much English, so if you need more information or want to arrange accommodation, do this at the Matsumoto tourist office (see p.359) before setting out. The Sacred Highland Kamikōchi site is another good source of information (ⓦkamikochi.org).

Hiking Even for day walks, make sure you pack warm, waterproof clothing, as the weather can change rapidly. Even at the height of summer, temperatures on the peaks can be freezing, especially in early morning. The staff at the national park visitor centre (daily 8am–5pm; ☎0263 95 2606), just past Kappa-bashi, can give some description in English of the local flora and fauna.

Services There is no ATM or bank in Kamikōchi, so bring plenty of cash.

ACCOMMODATION

Kamikōchi is not a cheap place to stay. If the options listed below are beyond your budget, another option is to stay at the youth hostel in *Norikura Kōgen* (see p.355) and travel in for the day.

Kamikōchi Gosenjaku Lodge 五千尺ロッヂ ☎0263 95 2221, ⓦgosenjaku.co.jp. In the main village, this is the less expensive of the two very comfortable *Gosenjaku* properties, with private tatami rooms and a bunk dorm available. Two meals are included in the rates. Dorm **¥1000**, double **¥35,700**

Kamikōchi Imperial Hotel 上高地帝国ホテル ☎0263 95 2001, ⓦwww.imperialhotel.co.jp. Built in

1933, this historic top-end hotel has the delightful spookiness of a grand old hotel in a wilderness setting. The Western-style rooms, restaurant and bar ooze quality, as does the attentive service of the staff. **¥32,550**

Konashidaira 小梨平 ☎0263 95 2321, ⓦnihonalpskankou.co.jp. This campsite is set in a serene location just beyond Kappa-bashi and the visitor centre. Showers are available, as are self-catering cabins. Camping

---

CABLE-CAR TO THE ROOF OF JAPAN

An adventurous option for approaching Kamikōchi across the mountains from the west is to take the **cable-car** (one-way ¥1500, return ¥2800; ⓦwww.okuhi.jp) up from Shin-Hotaka Onsen (新穂高温泉) in **Gifu-ken**. This onsen resort, best reached by bus from Takayama (see p.368), is reputed to have one of the longest cable-car rides in Asia (3200m), which takes you halfway to the 2908m summit of Nishi-Hotaka-dake; from here, Kamikōchi is a three-hour hike southeast.

(per person) ¥700, 2-person cabin ¥7000
Nishi-itoya Sansō 西糸屋山荘 ☎0263 95 2206,
ⓦwww.nishiitoya.com. The best budget option in
Kamikōchi, with both bunk beds and shared tatami areas.
The rates here include two meals – a good deal for the
area. Dorm **¥7700**

Yamanohidaya 山のひだや ☎0263 95 2211, ⓦi-sk
.com/yh. To escape the crowds, head for this delightfully
rustic lodge next to Myōjin-ike (see p.362), complete
with stuffed animals as decoration. Two meals, cooked
on an ancient iron range, are included in the rates.
¥16,000

EATING AND DRINKING

Eating options include standard soba and curry rice at inflated prices from the hotels, where fancier set meals are also
served. If you're visiting for the day or are planning a hike into the mountains, bring a picnic.

Kamonjigoya 嘉門次小屋 ☎0263 95 2418,
ⓦkamonjigoya.wordpress.com. Located beside Myōjin-
ike (see p.362), it is worth stopping here for the *iwana* (river

trout) lunch at ¥1500. The fish are roasted on sticks beside an
irori (charcoal fire), making this an ideal refuge if the weather
turns nasty. Daily 8.30am–4.30pm, closed in winter.

Norikura Kōgen

乗鞍高原

Much like Kamikōchi, **NORIKURA KŌGEN**, an alpine village some 30km southwest of
Matsumoto, offers splendid mountain scenery, hiking trails and onsen. The closest
thing to a centre in this straggle of a village is the modern onsen complex,
Yukemurikan, (湯けむり館; daily except Tues 9.30am–8pm); ¥700) which has both
indoor wooden baths and a rotemburo with mountain views.

In winter, ski lifts shoot up the lower slopes of **Norikura-dake**, while in summer the
hike to the peak can be done in ninety minutes from the car park, where the Echo Line
road leaves Nagano-ken and becomes the **Skyline Road** in Gifu-ken. This is the highest
road in Japan, providing spectacular mountain-top views (the upper section is closed
from Nov to end May). The car park is an hour's drive from Norikura Kōgen.

Walks around Norikura Kōgen

Near to Yukemurikan onsen are the ski lifts and an hour-long trail east to **Sanbon-daki**
(三本滝), where three waterfalls converge in one pool. An alternative hiking route from
the ski lifts is south for twenty minutes to another beautiful waterfall, **Zengorō-no-taki**
(善五郎の滝), reached along a clearly marked nature trail, with signs in English – a
rainbow often forms in the spray across this impressive fall during the morning. Twenty
minutes' walk further south of Zengorō, a small reflecting pond, **Ushidome-ike** (牛留
池), provides a perfect view of the mountains. Continuing downhill from the pond,
you can walk towards another small water hole, **Azami-ike** (あざみ池), or to the main
picnic area, **Ichinose** (一の瀬), a picturesque spot at the confluence of two streams.

ARRIVAL AND INFORMATION
NORIKURA KŌGEN

By bus Norikura Kōgen can be reached by infrequent buses
from both Shin-Shimashima train station, on the
Matsumoto Dentetsu line, and Takayama (see p.368), with
a change of buses at Tatamidaira and Hirayu Onsen. From
June to Oct there's also one daily bus between Norikura

Kōgen and Kamikōchi. Check with local tourist offices for
the current timetables.
Tourist information There's a tourist information office
(daily 9.30am–4.30pm; ☎0263 93 2952, ⓦnorikura.gr.jp)
opposite the Yukemurikan onsen complex.

ACCOMMODATION

BELL Suzurangoya BELL 鈴蘭小屋 4284-1 Azumi
☎0263 93 2001, ⓦbit.ly/1fY8mP5. This large and
friendly European-style chalet near the tourist
information office features cosy rooms, large onsen
baths and tasty home-cooked food. Two meals are
included in the rates. **¥15,000**

Kyūkamura Norikura Kōgen 休暇村乗鞍高原 4307
Azumi ☎0263 93 2304, ⓦqkamura.or.jp/en/norikura.
This modern hotel near the Ushidome pond has fine tatami
rooms or fairly standard Western ones. There are large
outdoor and indoor onsen and rates that include two buffet
meals; an extra heating charge applies in winter. **¥22,000**

Norikura Kōgen Youth Hostel 乗鞍高原ユースホステ
ル 4275 Azum Suzuran ☏ 0263 93 2748. Some 10min walk
north from the bus stop and next to the ski lifts, this hostel is
ideally placed for quick access to the slopes. The young,
friendly staff can arrange ski rental and point out the most
interesting hikes during the summer. Dorm **¥3500**

The Kiso valley

木曽谷

The densely forested river valley of **Kiso**, southwest of Matsumoto, between the Central and
Northern Alps, provides a glimpse of what Japan looked like before concrete and neon became
the norm. Running through this valley was part of the route for the 550km Nakasendō, one
of the five main highways spanning out from Edo (present-day Tokyo). Eleven post towns
(*juku*) lined the Kiso-ji (Kiso road) section of the Nakasendō, and three of them – **Narai**,
Tsumago and **Magome** – have been preserved as virtual museums of the feudal past, the latter
two linked by an easy two-hour hiking trail. Another *juku*, **Kiso-Fukushima**, looks less like a
samurai film set than the others, but still has attractive areas and is useful as a transport hub.

Narai

奈良井

Attractive **NARAI**, 30km southwest of Matsumoto, can easily be visited in half a day
and is generally less infested with tour groups than Tsumago and Magome. This was
the most prosperous of the Kiso-ji *juku*, a fact evident in the village's beautifully
preserved wooden buildings, with their overhanging second floors and *renji-gōshi*
latticework. The conservation area runs for 1km south from the train station, where
only the occasional passing cars remind you which century you're in.

In the Kamimachi area stands **Nakamura House** (中村邸; daily 9am–4.30pm; ¥200),
dates which back to the 1830s and was once the home of a merchant who made his
fortune in combs, still one of the area's specialities. Side streets lead off to pretty
temples and shrines in the foothills and **Kiso-no-Ōhashi**, an arched wooden bridge,
takes you to the rocky banks of the Narai-gawa.

Look out for the shop selling *kashira ningyō*, colourfully painted traditional dolls and
toys made of wood and plaster, as well as the sake brewery Sugi-no-Mori (杉の森), both
in the Nakamachi area of town.

ARRIVAL AND INFORMATION
NARAI

By train Narai is a 45min local train journey from
Matsumoto.
Tourist information The tourist office (daily

10am–5pm; ☏ 0264 34 3048, ⓦ naraijyuku.com) is in the
Nakamachi area of town. The informative website
ⓦ nakasendoway.com is good for historical background.

ACCOMMODATION AND EATING

Iseya 伊勢屋 388 Narai ☏ 0264 34 3051, ⓦ oyado-
iseya.jp. This lovely minshuku in one of the traditional
wooden post inns on the main street has cosy tatami
rooms and a peaceful inner garden. Rates include two
meals. **¥18,000**

Kokoro-ne こころ音 368 Narai ☏ 0264 34 3345. On the
main street, this appealing café has soaring wooden-
beamed ceilings and *irori* (a central charcoal fire) that serves
soba noodles and other local dishes. Expect to pay around
¥1350 for a bowl of soba. 11am–3pm, closed Wed.

Kiso-Fukushima

木曽福島

Four train stations south of Narai is **KISO-FUKUSHIMA**, a much more developed town
than the other *juku* – hence it being a stop for the express train between Matsumoto
and Nagoya. Pick up a map at the tourist office (see p.366) to point you towards the
hilltop **Ue-no-dan** (上の段) conservation area and the serene temple **Kōzen-ji** (興禅寺).

By train Kiso-Fukushima is on the JR Shinano line running from Matsumoto to Nagoya. Make sure to check the return journey, as services finish fairly early.
Destinations Matsumoto (30min); Nagoya (hourly; 1hr 22min).

By bus Highway buses run from Tokyo Shinjuku (4hr 10min).
Tourist information The tourist office (2012-10 Kiso-Fukushima ☎0264 22 4000, ⓦkankou-kiso.com) is opposite the train station.

ACCOMMODATION

Kiso-Ryojōan Youth Hostel 木曽旅情庵ユースホステル 634 Shinkai, Kiso-machi ☎0264 23 7716. In a large traditional building in the peaceful mountain village of Ōhara, this hostel is a cheap base to explore the valley's post towns. A 25min bus ride from Kiso-Fukushima. Breakfast is available for ¥700, and a ¥200 heating charge

applies Jan– March. Dorm **¥3000**
Tsutaya つたや 2012-4 Fukushima ☎0264 22 2145, ⓦkisoji-tutaya.com. A pleasant ryokan opposite the station which combines traditional decor with some modern design touches. Rates include two meals. **¥33,600**

Tsumago

妻籠

Given the number of tourists it now attracts, it's hard to believe that, back in the 1960s, **TSUMAGO**, 80km south of Matsumoto, was virtually a ghost town, with most of its traditional Edo-era houses on the verge of collapse. The locals banded together to restore the village's buildings, eventually earning Tsumago protected status and helping to spark the idea of cultural preservation across Japan. Telegraph poles and TV aerials are banished from sight, so that the scene that greets you on the pedestrian-only streets is probably very similar to that encountered by lords and their retinues passing through here hundreds of years ago. You can get a bird's-eye view of Tsumago from the former site of **Tsumago castle**, destroyed in the late sixteenth century. To get there, follow the path north out of the village on the hiking route to Nagiso (see box opposite).

Nagiso-machi Museum

南木曽町博物館, Nagiso-machi Hakubutsukan • 2190 Azuma • Daily 9am–4.45pm • ¥600 • ☎0264 57 3322

The **Nagiso-machi Museum** consists of two sections, the main one of which is the **Waki Honjin Okuya** (脇本陣奥谷), a finely constructed two-storey mansion dating from 1877 and one of the village's designated post inns for government officials. Attached is the **Historical Museum** (歴史博物館, Rekishi Hakubutsukan), including photographs showing just how dilapidated Tsumago once was.

Kisojikan

木曽路館 • Daily 10am–8pm • ¥700, soba-making classes ¥1050 (30min) or ¥2100 (1hr) • ☎0264 58 1126, ⓦhotelkisoji.jp

A good way to relax if you've done the Magome to Tsumago hike (see box opposite) is to hop on the free shuttle bus from the village's northern car park to the onsen and tourist complex **Kisojikan**. There are fine views of the valley from its rotemburo, and you can learn how to make soba in group classes.

ARRIVAL AND INFORMATION

TSUMAGO

By train The closest train station to Tsumago is Nagiso (南木曽), from where the village is an hour's walk south or a 10min bus ride.
Tourist information Tsumago's helpful tourist

information office (daily 8.30am–5pm; ☎0264 57 3123, ⓦtumago.jp/english) is in the centre of the village; here you can arrange to have your bag forwarded if you're planning to hike to Magome.

ACCOMMODATION AND EATING

There's no shortage of lunchtime restaurants and cafés in Tsumago; however, evening eating options are limited, so all the inns listed below include two meals in their prices. Local specialities include *sansai soba* (buckwheat noodles with mountain vegetables) and *gohei-mochi* (balls of pounded rice coated in a sweet nut sauce).

Daikichi 大吉 902-1 Nagiso-chō ☎0264 57 2595. A small minshuku at the northern end of the village, serving authentic local mountain dishes and wines. **¥18,000**

Fujioto 藤乙 Nagiso-machi ☎0264 57 2239 ✉fujioto@takenet.or.jp. This charming traditional inn, with friendly English-speaking owners, is set in a beautiful Japanese garden. **¥23,000**

Matsushiro-ya 松代屋 807 Nagiso-chō ☎0264 57 3022. An upmarket, 140-year-old ryokan that has been run by the same family for nine generations. Speciality dishes include carp sashimi, grilled river fish, and *tora soba* (soba noodles with yams). Note that the inn closes on Thurs. **¥21,000**

Magome

馬籠

With its buildings perched on a steep slope, **MAGOME**, 5km south of Tsumago, stands 800m high, in the hills above the Kiso valley. Magome means "horse basket", because this *juku* was where travellers were forced to leave their nags before tackling the mountainous stretch of road ahead. Plaster and wooden buildings line either side of the stone-flagged path – many of the wooden roofs are still held down by stone. Despite appearances, most buildings date from the twentieth century; the village suffered a history of fires, the most recent being in 1915, when 42 houses burnt down.

Tōson Kinenkan

藤村記念館 • 4256-1 Magome • Daily 8.30am–4.45pm • ¥500 • ☎0573 69 2047, ⓦtoson.jp

In the middle of the village, the **Tōson Kinenkan** museum is dedicated to Magome's famous native son, **Shimazaki Tōson** (1872–1943), who put the town on Japan's literary map with his historical novel *Yoake Mae* (*Before the Dawn*). Note that the artefacts are all labelled in Japanese.

ARRIVAL AND INFORMATION   MAGOME

By train The closest train station to Magome is in Nakatsugawa (中津川), a 55min journey northeast of Nagoya (see p.390) by limited express.

By bus Buses to Nakatsugawa also run from Nagoya and the spa town of Gero (下呂) on the JR Takayama Line. Buses to Magome run from platform three outside

---

HIKING THE KISO-JI

It's traditional to hike the Kiso-ji from Magome to Tsumago to experience the supposedly tough initial climb into the mountains – though it's actually not that difficult. The 7.7km route has English signs, but it's best to pick up a map from the tourist information offices.

There's a **baggage-forwarding** service (weekends and national holidays late March to July & Sept to Nov; daily late July to late Aug; ¥500 per piece) to and from the tourist information offices in both Tsumago and Magome. Get your bag to the offices before 11.30am and they will be delivered at the other end by 5pm.

MAGOME–TSUMAGO

To start the hike in **Magome**, continue up the hill, past the *kōsatsu*, the old town noticeboard on which the shogunate posted rules and regulations, including the death penalty for anyone found illegally logging the forests' trees. The steepest part of the hike is over once you've reached the Magome-tōge (pass), where there's an old teahouse beside the road and a stone monument engraved with a lyrical verse by the haiku master Masaoka Shiki (see box, p.562). From here, the route enters the forest and later passes two **waterfalls** O-dake and Me-dake.

TSUMAGO–MAGOME

If you choose to walk in the opposite direction, start at **Nagiso Station** on the Chūō line, from where Tsumago is less than an hour south through picturesque fields and small villages. Set aside a day to explore both post towns and to complete the hike. You'll enjoy the experience all the more if you stay in either Tsumago or Magome overnight.

5

Nakatsugawa Station (30min; ¥540).

Tourist information Magome's tourist information office (daily 8.30am–5pm; ☎0264 59 2336, ⓦkiso-magome.com), opposite the Tōson Kinenkan, has an English map of the area; staff speak Japanese only and can help with accommodation bookings at the village's numerous minshuku.

ACCOMMODATION

Magome-chaya 馬籠茶屋 4296 Magome ☎0264 59 2038, ⓦmagomechaya.com/English. Close to the tourist office, this is a well-maintained old ryokan. The Filipino owners speak some English and also run a restaurant attached to the hotel. Two meals are included in the rates. **¥15,960**

Tajimaya 但馬屋 4266 Magome ☎0264 59 2048. A little further downhill from *Magome-chaya*, this atmospheric inn has been in the same family for eight generations. Accommodation is in tatami rooms, and bathrooms and toilets are shared. Dinner, which is included in the rate (along with breakfast) is served around an irori fireplace. **¥16,000**

Takayama

高山

On the Gifu-ken side of the Central Alps, in an area known as Hida, the busy tourist town of **TAKAYAMA**, 110km northeast of Nagoya, was once an enclave of skilled carpenters employed by the emperors to build palaces and temples in Kyoto and Nara. Takayama's appeal today lies in its old merchant houses, small museums, and its tranquil temples and shrines, all clustered into a compact area. The main tourist draw is the **San-machi Suji**, but for those with more time, there are also worthwhile attractions west of the train station, in particular the **Hida Folk Village**.

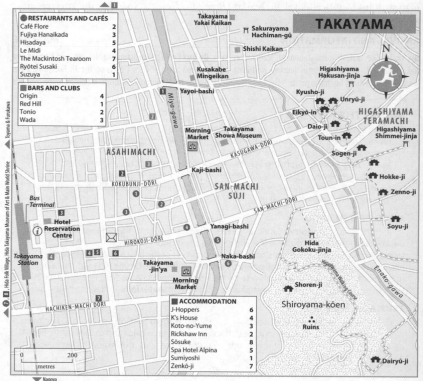

San-machi Suji

三町筋 • Around a 10min walk from the station

On the east bank of the Miya-gawa lies the **San-machi Suji** area, full of dark wooden merchant houses dating from the mid-nineteenth century. The quarter's main three narrow streets are most evocative at dusk, when the crowds have thinned. During the day, you'll have to negotiate your way through rickshaws and tourists pottering in and out of craft shops, cafés and sake breweries (see box, p.371).

Takayama-jin'ya

高山陣屋 • 1-5 Hachiken-machi • Daily: April–Oct 8.45am–5pm; Nov–March 8.45am–4.30pm • ¥420; English-language tours free • ☎ 0577 32 0643 • A 5min walk southeast of the station

Before you cross the Miya-gawa, drop by the town's feudal-era government complex, **Takayama-jin'ya**, at the end of Hachikenmachi-dōri. This small-scale palace, built in 1615 and the only building of its kind left in Japan, was the seat of power for the Hida area's governor. Most of the buildings seen today, including a torture chamber and a rice storehouse, date from a reconstruction in 1816. The best way to explore them is to go on one of the guided tours in English.

Takayama Shōwa Museum

高山昭和館 Takayama Shōwa-Kan • 6 Shimoichinomachi • Daily 9am–5pm • ¥500 • ☎ 0577 33 7836 • ⓦ shouwakan.hida.vc

The fascinating **Takayama Showa Museum** gives an insight into everyday life during the boom years of the Shōwa period. Inside is a warren of narrow lanes recreating street life from that fast-moving era in Japanese history, with a cinema, classroom, barber's and many shops filled with mid-twentieth-century memorabilia.

Sakurayama Hachiman-gū

桜山八幡宮 • 178 Sakura-machi • 24hr • Free • ☎ 0577 32 0240

In the northeast of the city is **Sakurayama Hachiman-gū**, Takayama's main shrine, dating back to the fourth century. Here you'll find the **Takayama Yatai Kaikan** (see box below), the entrance charge to which includes the **Sakurayama-Nikkō-kan**, a hall displaying a dazzling one-tenth-scale replica of 28 buildings from Nikkō's Tōshōgū shrine, where a computer controls the lighting to reproduce sunrise and sunset.

Shishi Kaikan

獅子会館 • 53-1 Sakura-machi • Daily: mid-April to mid-Nov 8.30am–5.30pm; mid-Nov to mid-April 9am–5pm • ¥600 • ☎ 0577 320 881, ⓦ www.hida-kakuri.com

It's worth checking out the enjoyable demonstration of automated *karakuri* puppets in the **Shishi Kaikan**, on the south side of the Sakurayama Hachiman-gū. A video of a *shishi* (mythical lion) dance, common to festivals in the Takayama area, is screened at

---

TAKAYAMA'S FESTIVALS AND YATAI

Takayama's two famous festivals are the **Sannō Matsuri** (April 14–15) and the **Hachiman Matsuri** (Oct 9–10), when eleven huge elaborate *yatai* (floats), adorned with mechanical dolls (*karakuri*), are paraded around town, a spectacle that attracts hundreds of thousands of visitors. If you're not in town for the festivals, you can still view four of the *yatai* at the **Takayama Yatai Kaikan** (高山屋台会館; daily: March–Nov 8.30am–5.30pm; Dec–Feb 9am–4.30pm; ¥820), a large exhibition hall within the grounds of the shrine **Sakurayama Hachiman-gū** (see above). At least once a year, all eleven floats and the golden *mikoshi* (portable shrine) are displayed inside a huge glass case that you wind your way around at different levels so you can see all of the decoration closely. Many of the floats date from the seventeenth century and are usually stored in the tall storehouses (*yatai-gura*) that you'll notice around Takayama.

5

regular intervals during the day, and you can also see many lion masks and musical instruments used in these dances.

Higashiyama Teramachi

東山寺町

Following the narrow Enako-gawa southeast from the Sakurayama Hachiman-gū, towards the hills, will bring you to the tranquil **Higashiyama Teramachi** area, where thirteen temples and five shrines are dotted among the soaring pine trees and linked by a pleasant walk that goes over the river to **Shiroyama-kōen**. This wooded park stands on the remains of Lord Kanamori's castle, destroyed over three hundred years ago; you can still trace the donjon's foundations on the top of the hill. The route is signposted and you can pick up a map from the tourist information office (see below).

Hida Folk Village

飛驒民俗村, Hida Minzoku-mura · 1-590 Kamikamoto-chō · Daily 8.30am–5pm · ¥700; Hida-no-Sato discount ticket (¥900) includes return bus · ☎ 0577 34 4711, ⓦ hidanosato-tpo.jp/english12.htm · 30min by foot from the station or bus #1 (¥900 return)

In a lovely hillside location overlooking the mountains, the **Hida Folk Village** is an outdoor museum of over twenty traditional buildings gathered from the Hida area, including the *gasshō-zukuri* thatched houses of the Shirakawa-gō and Gokayama districts (see p.347).

You're free to explore inside the houses, many of which have displays of farm implements and folk crafts of their former owners. You can see real artists working at traditional crafts such as lacquering and woodcarving in the four old houses next to the ticket gate.

Hida Takayama Museum of Art

飛驒高山美術館, Hida Takayama Bijutsukan · 1-124-1 Kamikamoto-chō · Daily 9am–5pm · ¥1300 · ☎ 0577 35 3535, ⓦ htm-museum.co.jp

Near the Hida Folk Village, the **Hida Takayama Museum of Art** is an elegant and modern museum containing wonderful Art Nouveau and Art Deco collections. A beautiful glass fountain by René Lalique, which once stood in the Paris Lido, greets you at the entrance; further on, the collection includes lustrous objets d'art by Gallè, Tiffany glass lamps, and the interior designs of Charles Rennie Mackintosh and the Vienna Secessionists.

ARRIVAL AND INFORMATION
TAKAYAMA

By train Takayama is connected by train to both Toyama (see p.377) in the north and Nagoya (see p.390) in the south.

Destinations Kyoto (daily; 4hr 20min); Nagoya (10 daily; 2hr 10min); Osaka (daily; 5hr); Toyama (4 daily; 1hr 20min).

By bus The long-distance bus terminal is next to JR Takayama Station, a 10min walk west of the San-machi Suji district, where many of the town's main sights can be found.

Destinations Gifu (4 daily; 2hr); Gujō Hachiman (11 daily; 1hr 10min); Kanazawa (2 daily; 2hr 15min); Kyoto (2 daily; 4hr); Matsumoto (4 daily; 2hr 20min); Nagoya (9 daily; 2hr 35min); Ogimachi (7 daily; 50min); Osaka (2 daily; 5hr); Tokyo (5 daily; 5hr 30min); Toyama (4 daily; 2hr 30min).

Tourist information The Hida tourist information office (daily: 8.30am–6.30pm, Nov–March till 5pm; ☎ 0577 32 5328, ⓦ www.hida.jp), immediately in front of the JR station, has clued-up, English-speaking staff. The Hotel Reservation Centre opposite the station will make reservations for visitors. A useful website on all things Hida is ⓦ hida-kankou.jp/kanko/foreign/en.

Services Kankakokan Community Centre, 40-4 Kamininomachi (daily 10am–5pm; ☎ 0577 33 5055), has a couple of internet terminals (¥100/30min); you can also quickly access the internet at the tourist office for free.

GETTING AROUND

By bike Takayama is best explored on foot or by bicycle, which can be rented from the car park to the right of the station

(¥200/hr, ¥1200/day). There are several bike hubs around the city and a number of bike shops around the city centre.

TAKAYAMA'S MORNING MARKETS

Every day, from 7am (6am in summer) until around noon, Takayama has two **morning markets** (*asa ichi*), which are well worth getting up early to attend. The fruit and veg market is held in front of the *jin'ya* (see p.369), while the larger, more tourist-orientated market is strung out along the east bank of the Miya-gawa, between the Kaji-bashi and Yayoi-bashi bridges. Here, apart from pickles and flowers, you can buy local handicrafts, (including *sarubobo*, the little fabric baby monkeys seen all over Takayama), grab a coffee or locally brewed beer or you can and sample the sweet marshmallow snack *tamaten*.

ACCOMMODATION

If you're planning on staying in Takayama during its festivals (see box, p.369), book well ahead, and note that prices are likely to be higher than usual. In addition to the places listed below, there are several inexpensive business hotels near the train station.

J-Hoppers ジェイ・ホパーズ 5-52 Nada-machi ☎0577 32 3278, ⓦtakayama.j-hoppers.com. This modern, friendly hostel is a slick affair. They offer dorms and private rooms, organize trips, have bike rental, wi-fi and a shared PC and even provide wellies for sloshing through the winter snow. Dorm **¥2500**

K's House ケイズ・ハウス 4-45-1 Tenman-chō ☎0577 34 4410, ⓦkshouse.jp. This modern backpacker's hostel is 3min walk from station. It features bunk dormitories or tatami private rooms, all with their own private bathrooms. There's a comfortable lounge downstairs with beanbags and internet terminals and a newly fitted kitchen to prepare meals. Bikes are available for hire for ¥150 per hour and the English-speaking staff are happy to help. Dorm **¥2800**, double **¥6800**

★**Koto-no-Yume** 古都の夢 6-11 Hanasato-chō, ☎0577 32 0427, ⓦkotoyume.com. This small-scale ryokan blends traditional style with contemporary design touches, and guests get to choose from a number of colourful modern *yukatas*. Both indoor and outdoor onsen baths are available. Rates include two meals. **¥27,600**

★**Rickshaw Inn** 旅籠 力車イン 54 Suehiro-chō ☎0577 32 2890, ⓦrickshawinn.com. With friendly, English-speaking owners, this relaxing place has well-furnished tatami (shared or private bathrooms) or Western rooms (private bathrooms only). There's a comfy lounge with sofas, English newspapers, magazines and art books as well as a small kitchen for self-catering. The stylish ground-floor suite, sleeping up to six, is great

value for a family or group. Add ¥700 per person for breakfast. **¥8900**

Sōsuke 惣助 1-64 Okamoto-machi ☎0577 32 0818, ⓦirori-sosuke.com. Good-value traditional minshuku, about 10min walk west of the station, opposite the *Takayama Green Hotel*. The building is 170 years old and has a traditional *irori* hearth. Breakfast is ¥700, and dinner is also available from ¥2000. **¥10,000**

Spa Hotel Alpina スパホテルアルピナ 5-41 Nada-machi ☎0577 33 0033, ⓦspa-hotel-alpina.com. The pleasant, smallish rooms here offer slightly more contemporary design than your average business hotel. It also has the advantage of rooftop spa baths with a decent view. **¥10,500**

Sumiyoshi 寿美吉 21-4 Honmachi ☎0577 32 0228, ⓦsumiyoshi-ryokan.com. This is a delightful *gaijin*-friendly ryokan, offering en-suite or shared Japanese-style rooms in a building dating back to 1912, with a great riverside location. The staff are very friendly and the place is chock-full of interesting antiques and knick-knacks. Breakfast costs an additional ¥1050, and dinner ¥3150. **¥14,700**

Zenkō-ji 善光寺 4-3 Tenman-chō ☎0577 32 8470, ⓦtakayamahostelzenkoji.com. Buddha is watching you, but in the nicest way possible at this appealing hostel attached to a temple. The tatami-mat rooms, some with views of a pleasant rock garden, are a steal. Like its Nagano namesake, the temple has a dark underground corridor hiding the "key to paradise". Private rooms are available for just an extra ¥500 per person. Dorm **¥2500**

SAKE BREWERIES

The Hida area has been well known for its **sake** for over 400 years; at one time there were some 56 **breweries** in Takayama. Now there are just six functioning ones in San-machi Suji – Hirata (平田), Harada (原田), Kawashiri (川尻), Niki (二木), Hirase (平瀬) and Tanabe (田邊), all easily spotted by the balls of cedar leaves hanging above their entrances. Each brewery takes it in turns to provide free tours (10am–noon, 1–4pm) of their facilities – check with the tourist office for details.

5

EATING AND DRINKING

The best thing to sample at Takayama's numerous **restaurants** is the area's speciality, *sansai ryōri*, dishes of local mountain vegetables, ferns and wild plants. Also look out for *sansai soba*, buckwheat noodles topped with greens, and *hōba miso*, vegetables mixed with miso paste and roasted on a magnolia leaf above a charcoal brazier (a beef version is also served). In addition, the local Hida beef is excellent, and a delicious snack sold around town is *mitarashi-dango* – pounded rice balls dipped in soy sauce and roasted on skewers. Note that many of the San-machi Suji tourist restaurants are only open at lunch, when they can get very busy. The Asahimachi area between the station and the Miya-gawa is packed with small **bars**.

RESTAURANTS AND CAFÉS

Café Flore カフェフロール 37 Aioi-chō ☎ 0577 35 0099. There's a cycling theme and a laidback jazz soundtrack at this small French café which offers a range of European dishes, most of which are under ¥1000. It also has a wider range of vegetarian options than many places. 11am–4.30pm & 6.30–10pm, closed Wed.

Fujiya Hanaikada 富士屋花筏 46 Hanakawa-chō ☎ 0577 36 0339. This stylish café with an outdoor deck is a good place for a break from sightseeing. It specializes in *wagashi* (traditional Japanese sweets) and is also a showroom for locally made wooden furniture. Snacks start at ¥500. 10am–6pm, closed Thurs.

Hisadaya 久田屋 11-3 Kamisanno-machi ☎ 0577 32 0216. Excellent set lunches of *sansai ryōri* (from ¥1400 per person) are served in the tatami rooms of one of the San-machi Suji's old merchants' houses. 11am–3pm, closed Wed.

Le Midi ル・ミディ 2-2 Honmachi ☎ 0577 36 6386, ⓦ le-midi.jp. Sample top-quality Hida beef and other local meat and fish at this sophisticated bistro that feels like a slice of Paris. There are two branches on opposite sides of the road – one serving Hida beef and Italian dishes, the other French cuisine. It also has a takeaway booth for its speciality pumpkin pudding. Lunch menus start at ¥1800 and dinner from ¥4800. 11.30am–2.30pm & 6–9.30pm, closed Thurs.

The Mackintosh Tearoom マキントッシュ・ティールーム 1-124-1 Kamiokamoto-cho ☎ 0577 35 3535, ⓦ htm-museum.co.jp. Attached to the Hida Takayama Museum of Art (see p.370), *The Makintosh* is modelled on the famous tearooms in Glasgow, designed by Charles Rennie Mackintosh, and offers specially blended tea and cakes, as well as light meals from around ¥1000. The view across the mountains is lovely, and you can eat outside. 9am–5.30pm, closed Tues.

★**Ryōtei Susaki** 料亭洲さき 4-14 Shinmei-machi ☎ 0577 32 0023, ⓦ ryoutei-susaki.com. This memorable *ryōtei* has been run by the same family since 1794 and serves *honzen* cuisine, which is similar to *kaiseki* in style and presentation. *Ryōtei* are famously exclusive places, but here the service is friendly, the setting serene and atmospheric, and the food worth every last yen. Lunch courses start at ¥6300, dinner ¥12,750; reservations essential. Daily 11.30am–2pm & 5–9pm.

★**Suzuya** 寿々や 24 Hanakawa-machi ☎ 0577 32 2484. Beamed, family-run restaurant that's a great place to sample *sansai ryōri*, and especially *hōba miso*. There's an English menu with pictures, friendly waitresses to assist you, and you can either sit at tables or on tatami. Expect to pay around ¥2500 per head, and note that it can get really busy at night with tour groups. 11am–2.30pm & 5–8pm, closed Tues.

BARS AND IZAKAYA

Orijin おりじん 4-108 Hanasato-chō ☎ 0577 36 4655. You can sample three local sakes for ¥525 at this rustic *izakaya*, as well as a good range of *sōchū*. The food, including sashimi and sushi, is tasty and affordable. Daily 5pm–midnight.

Red Hill レッド・ヒル 2-4 Sowa-chō ☎ 0577 33 8139. You'll get a warm welcome at this small bar, which serves a good range of bottled beer from around the world and appealing food that borrows from a global menu. Tues–Sun 7pm–midnight.

Tonio トニオ 4-65 Honmachi ☎ 0577 32 1677. This self-styled "Western bar", plastered with old film posters and other memorabilia, is a quiet place for a beer and snack. It has a good range of drinks and European-style pub-grub dishes for around ¥1000. Daily 5pm–1am.

★**Wada** 和田 Ichiban-gai ☎ 0577 33 4850. If you're wondering where the locals choose to drink and nibble on snacks in this very touristy town, search no further. Don't be put off by the menu, which features fried chicken bowels with miso, and grilled pig's trotters – there are plenty of things to try here, and it's all good value. Dishes start at ¥500. Daily 5pm–1am.

Furukawa

古川

With its old white-walled storehouses by the canal, sake breweries and temples decorated with intricate woodcarvings, charming **FURUKAWA**, in the Hida province, is like a compact version of Takayama, minus the crowds. The sleepy riverside town comes alive during its annual spring *matsuri* (see box below) and is an easy day-trip from Takayama.

Hida Furukawa Matsuri Kaikan

飛騨古川まつり会館 • 14-15 Ichino-machi • Daily 9am–5pm, Dec–Feb till 4.30pm • ¥800, or ¥1000 combined with Hida Craftsmens Cultural Hall • ☎ 0577 73 3511, ⓦ okosidaiko.com • A 5min walk west of the station

You can get a taste of the Furukawa Matsuri festival at the **Hida Furukawa Matsuri Kaikan**, west of the station. Here you can inspect three of the nine *yatai*, as well as watch a 3-D film of the festival and a computer-controlled performance by one of the puppets decorating the *yatai*. Local craftsmen work here, too. The drums used in the festival are in an open hall on the square in front of the main hall.

Hida Craftsmens Cultural Hall

飛騨の匠文化館, Hida no Takumi Bunkakan • 10-1 Ichino-machi • March–Nov daily 9am–5pm; Dec–Feb 9am–4.30pm, closed Tues • ¥300, or ¥1000 combined with Hida Furukawa Matsuri Kaikan • ☎ 0577 73 3321

The skill of Hida craftsmen was revered for centuries, and they were employed to build many of Japan's most famous temples in Kyoto and Nara. The **Hida Craftsmens Cultural Hall** highlights the local woodworkers' traditional techniques, skills and tools, with displays showing how buildings – including the museum itself – are made from wooden beams without using nails; visitors can try for themselves on scale models.

Shirakabe-dozō

白壁土蔵

Immediately south of the square at Matsuri Kaikan is the **Shirakabe-dozō** district, where a row of traditional storehouses stands beside a narrow, gently flowing canal packed with carp. From here, a five-minute walk east along the canal will take you to **Honkō-ji** (本光寺), an attractive temple decorated with the intricate carving and carpentry for which the town is famous. From the temple, return to the town centre along Ichino-machi-dōri, where you'll find the two-hundred-year-old **candle shop** Mishima (三嶋; 3-12 Ichino-machi; 9am–5pm, closed Wed; ☎0577 73 4109); a candle-maker gives regular demonstrations. On this street, you'll also find two of Furukawa's three **sake breweries** – Kaba (蒲; 6-6 Ichino-machi; daily 9am–5pm) and Watanabe (渡辺; 7-7 Ichino-machi; daily 9am–5pm); both will happily let you sample their products whether you buy or not.

ARRIVAL AND INFORMATION FURUKAWA

By train There are frequent local trains to Furukawa from Takayama (15min; ¥230). The JR station is called Hida-Furukawa (飛騨古川).

By bus Buses (¥360) take at most 30min to reach the town from Takayama.

Tourist information The Kita-Hida tourist

FURUKAWA MATSURI

One of the region's liveliest annual festivals, the **Furukawa Matsuri** (April 19 & 20) celebrates the arrival of spring with grand parades of wonderfully decorated floats (*yatai*). The highlight is the **Okoshi Daiko** procession, which starts at 9pm on April 19 and runs until about 2am: led by over a thousand people carrying lanterns, hundreds of men, clad only in baggy white underpants and belly bands, compete to place small drums (tied to long poles) atop a portable stage that bears the huge main drum, which is all the while being solemnly thumped. The men also balance atop poles and spin around on their stomachs. Extra late-night trains and buses run on festival days between Takayama and Furukawa. The *yatai* and *mikoshi* processions happen during the day. For more information see ⓦ bit.ly/NmHpMv.

5

information booth (daily 9am–5pm; ☏ 0577 73 3180) is located just outside Hida-Furukawa Station – the helpful staff can assist you in finding accommodation.

Try ⓦ hida-kankou.jp/kanko/foreign/en for maps, accommodation and information on things to do in Furukawa.

ACCOMMODATION AND EATING

With Takayama so close, there's little reason to stay in Furukawa itself unless you're planning on hiking into the surrounding mountains.

Hida Furukawa Youth Hostel 飛騨古川ユースホステル 180 Nobuka ☏0577 75 2979, ⓦwww.d2.dion .ne.jp/~hidafyh. A good base for hikers, this modern hostel is housed in a homely wooden cabin amid rice fields. Take a bus to Shinrin-kōen from Hida-Furukawa Station (15min); check times at the tourist information booth. Rates include two meals. Dorm ¥5600

Katsumi 克己 5-19 Furukawacho ☏0577 73 7888. In a grey building a minute's walk west of the station, this

is a great spot for lunch. The lunchtime *wagamama teishoku* (¥950) is a feast of delicious vegetable, tofu and fish dishes, while in the evening you can try their fish specialities (¥2000/head). Mon–Sat 11.30am–1pm & 5.30–10pm.

Maeda まえだ 11-10 Furukawachō ☏0577 73 2852. On the right-hand corner of the junction with the road from the station, *Maeda* has set meals starting at ¥2100 and beef curry for under ¥1000. 11.30am–9pm, closed Thurs.

Shirakawa-gō and Gokayama

白川郷・五箇山

Designated a World Heritage Site in 1995, the picturesque villages of the **Shirakawa-gō** and **Gokayama** areas, northwest of Takayama, were among the many fabled bolt holes of the Taira clan after their defeat at the battle of Dannoura (see p.566). Until the mid-twentieth century, these communities, with their distinctive, thatched A-frame houses, were almost entirely cut off from fast-modernizing Japan. The damming of the Shō-kawa in the 1960s, together with the drift of population away from the countryside, threatened the survival of this rare form of architecture called *gasshō-zukuri* (see box below). In 1971, local residents began a preservation movement, which has been so successful that the trio of villages – **Ogimachi** in Gifu-ken, and **Suganuma** and **Ainokura** in neighbouring Toyama-ken – is now in danger of being swamped by visitors. It is still worth braving the crowds to see these remarkable thatched buildings, set in idyllic valleys surrounded by forests and mountains. To feel the full magic of the place, arrange to stay overnight in a minshuku in a *gasshō-zukuri* house.

PRAYING-HANDS HOUSES

Gasshō-zukuri means "praying hands", because the sixty-degree slope of the thatched gable roofs is said to recall two hands joined in prayer. The sharp angle is a way of coping with the heavy snowfall in this area and the size of the houses is the result of multi-generational family living. The upper-storeys of the home were used for industries such as making gunpowder and cultivating silkworms. The **thatched roofs** – often with a surface area of around six hundred square metres – are made of *susuki* grass, native to the northern part of the Hida region (wooden shingles were used in the south), and have to be replaced every 25 to 35 years.

Since it can cost ¥20 million to rethatch an entire roof, many of the houses fell into disrepair until the government stepped in with grants in 1976, enabling the local building traditions to continue. The local preservation society decides which buildings are most in need of repair each year and helps organize the **yui**, a two-hundred-strong team who work together to rethatch a roof in just one day. Despite these initiatives, however, there are now fewer than 200 *gasshō-zukuri* houses left.

Ogimachi

荻町

In the shadow of the sacred mountain Hakusan, **OGIMACHI** is home to 114 **gasshō-zukuri** houses, the largest collection within the Shirakawa-gō area of the Shō-kawa valley. Many of the thatched houses were moved here when threatened by the damming of the Shō-kawa leading to a somewhat contrived landscape, not helped by the main road which cuts through the village centre, bringing a daily overdose of tourists. Even so, this is a real working village, with most of the houses still populated by families who farm rice in the surrounding fields. Start your explorations by hiking up to the Shirakawa lookout (*zenbōdai*) at the north end of the village, from where you can get a good view of Ogimachi's layout.

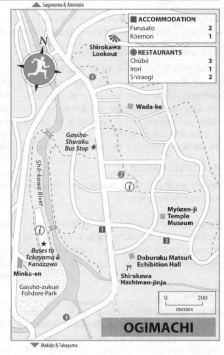

Wada-ke

和田家 • 997 Ogimachi • Daily 9am–5pm • ¥300 • ☎ 0576 96 1058

The thatched-roofed **Wada-ke** with a lily pond in front, is the one of several "museum" houses and one of the best examples of local architecture. The home of the wealthy Wada family for generations, it contains fine lacquerware, decorations and furniture passed down through the generations for over two hundred years.

Myōzen-ji Temple Museum

明善寺郷土館, Myōzen-ji Kyodo-Kan • 679 Ogimachi • Daily: April–Nov 9am–5pm; Dec–March 9am–4pm • ¥300 • ☎ 0576 96 1009

The huge five-storey **Myōzen-ji Temple Museum** was once the living quarters for the priests and monks from the attached temple; on its upper floors you can see where over a tonne of silk cocoons were cultivated each year. Gaps in the floorboards allowed the smoke from the *irori* fire to permeate the whole building, preserving the wood and thatch. A narrow passageway connects the main house to the thatched temple next door.

Doburoku Matsuri Exhibition Hall

どぶろく祭りの館, Doburoku Matsuri no Kan • April–Nov daily 9am–5pm • ¥300 • ☎ 0576 96 1655

Next to the village's main shrine, **Shirakawa Hachiman-jinja** (白川八幡神社) stands the **Doburoku Matsuri Exhibition Hall**, devoted to the annual festival (Oct 14–19), which involves the making of *doburoku*, a rough, milky sake. The exhibition itself is small, but you can watch a good video in Japanese about life in the village and try a drop of the potent alcohol.

Gasshō-zukuri Folklore Park

合掌造り民家園, Gasshō-zukuri Minka-en • 2499 Ogimachi • April–July & Sept–Nov daily except Thurs 8.40am–5pm; Aug daily 8am–5.30pm; Dec–March daily except Thurs 9am–4pm • ¥500 • ☎ 0576 96 1231

On the west side of the Shō-kawa, reached by a footbridge, is the **Gasshō-zukuri Folklore Park**, an open-air museum of some 25 buildings gathered together from the region. Enjoy a rest and a free cup of tea in the Nakano Chōjirō family house near the entrance. Just outside the park is the village hall where you can learn how to make soba noodles (April–Oct daily 10am & 1.30pm; advance booking recommended; ¥1800; ☎0576 96 1231).

ARRIVAL AND INFORMATION OGIMACHI

By bus Seven direct buses connect Takayama to Ogimachi (50min; ¥2400 one way, ¥4300 return), with two continuing on to Kanazawa; reserve your seat in advance. Four daily buses head north from Ogimachi to Suganuma (¥840) and Ainokura (¥1250), terminating at Takaoka (¥2350) on the JR Hokuriku line.

By car Touring the region by car is recommended; try

Toyota Rent-a-Car opposite Takayama Station (☎0577 36 6110; daily 8am–8pm).

Tourist information The main tourist information office (daily 9am–5pm; ☎05769 6 1013; ⊛shirakawa-go.gr.jp) is in the car park beside the Gasshō-zukuri Folklore Park, where the buses stop. There's a second smaller office in the village centre (same details).

ACCOMMODATION

The only way of seeing Ogimachi without the crowds is to stay overnight. There are several nice minshuku in the thatched-roof houses to choose from.

Furusato ふるさと 588 Ogimachi ☎0576 96 1033. Just south of Myōzen-ji, this thatched farmhouse has endearing decorative touches throughout its tatami rooms. Rates include two meals. **¥17,600**

Kōemon 幸エ門 456 Ogimachi ☎0576 96 1446. A short walk from the bus terminal, this 200-year-old thatched farmhouse is full of charm and has a friendly English-speaking owner. The modern bathrooms are shared. Rates include two meals. **¥16800**

EATING

Chūbe 忠兵衛 3065 Ogimachi ☎0576 96 1435. In a picturesque location overlooking the river at Ogimachi's south end, you'll eat well here with feasts of mountain vegetable cuisine, *sansai ryōri*. Dishes cost around ¥1300. Daily, lunchtimes only.

Irori いろり 374-1 Ogimachi ☎0576 96 1737. You can eat around the raised hearth at this busy restaurant on the main road, at the north end of the village. The set lunches which include fish, noodles or tofu are good value at ¥1000.

Daily, lunchtimes only.

Shiraogi しらおぎ 155 Ogimachi ☎0576 96 1106, ⊛j47.jp/shiraogi. In the village centre opposite the tourist office, this traditional building with lots of painted wooden signs outside has an English menu and offers a set menu of local delicacies (ask for the *shiraogi-setto*), including trout and miso bean paste, for ¥2600 a head. Daily, lunchtimes only.

Suganuma

菅沼

Route 156, along the Shō-kawa valley, tunnels through the mountains, running for the most part alongside the frequently dammed river as it meanders north. Some 10km from Ogimachi, the road passes the quaint hamlet of **SUGANUMA**, featuring nine *gasshō-zukuri*, beside a sharp bend in the river.

Gokayama Minzoku-kan

五箇山民俗館 · 436 Suganuma · Daily 9am–4pm · ¥300 · ☎0763 67 3652

It's worth popping into the **Gokayama Minzoku-kan**, a folklore museum made up of two houses. One displays artefacts from daily life, the other details the production of gunpowder, made here because Suganuma's remote location allowed the ruling Kaga clan to keep it secret.

Murakami-ke

村上家 · 742 Kaminashi · Daily except Wed 8.30am–5pm · ¥300 · ☎0763 66 2711, ⊛murakamike.jp

Some 4km from Suganuma, the modern village of **KAMINASHI** is home to the **Murakami-ke**, one of the oldest houses in the valley, dating from 1578. The owner gives guided tours around the tatami rooms, pointing out the sunken pit beside the entrance where gunpowder was once made, and finishing with spirited singing of folk tunes accompanied by a performance of the *bin-zasara*, a rattle made of wooden strips.

Ainokura

相倉 • ⓦ g-ainokura.com

The last of the three World Heritage Site villages, and perhaps the loveliest, is **AINOKURA**, 4km north of Kaminashi. The bus will drop you on the main road, a five-minute walk from the village, which nestles on a hillside and will not take you more than an hour to look around. Make sure you hike up the hill behind the main car park for a great view, and you could also while away a little more time in the **Ainokura Minzoku-kan** (相倉民俗館; daily 8.30am–5pm; ¥200; ⓣ 0763 66 2732), a tiny museum of daily life, including examples of the area's handmade paper and toys.

Appealing as it is, Ainokura's charms can be all but obscured as you battle past yet another group of camera-toting day-trippers. To experience the village at its best, stay overnight.

ARRIVAL AND DEPARTURE   AINOKURA

By train If you're heading to Ainokura from the Sea of Japan coast, take a train from Takaoka to Jōhana (城端; 53min), where you can pick up the bus to the Gokayama area (28min). See ⓦ japan-guide.com/bus/gokayama.

html for details.

By bus Ainokura is a stop on the bus line between Ogimachi and Takaoka. There are four buses a day from Ogimachi to Ainokura (45 min; ¥1250).

ACCOMMODATION AND EATING

Make sure you reserve accommodation well in advance – they don't like people just showing up here. Seven of the *gasshō-zukuri* offer lodging, including the two listed below, and it's advisable to take dinner in-house, as there are few other eating options in the evenings.

Goyomon 五ヨ門 438 Ainokura ⓣ 0763 66 2154, ⓦ www.goyomon.burari.biz. A recommended *gasshō* that has been run by the same family for several generations. The food here is hearty and plentiful. Rates include two meals; room only is available for ¥4200 per person. **¥16,000**

Matsuya まつや 445 Ainokura ⓣ 0763 66 2631, ⓦ gokayama-matsuya.com. Serving soba, tempura and

sweets, this restaurant-cum-souvenir shop is a friendly place for lunch. They'll even look after your bags while you wander around. Dishes start at around ¥1000. Daily 8am–5pm.

Nakaya なかや 231 Ainokura ⓣ 0763 66 2555. The friendly owners speak a little English at this tranquil *gasshō* which offers very tasty home-cooked traditional meals around the *irori* fireplace. Rates include two meals. **¥17,600**

Toyama

富山

Northeast of the Gokayama valley is the coastal city of **Takaoka** and, further west, the prefectural capital of **TOYAMA** (富山). Neither city particularly warrants an overnight stop, and you'd do well to press on south along coast to Kanazawa and the more scenic Noto Hantō peninsula (see p.383). That said, Toyama has a some interesting sights and is a start or finish for excursions along the famous Alpine Route (see box, p.379) to Nagano-ken.

Toyama Municipal Folkcraft Village

富山市民俗民芸村, Toyama Minzoku Mingei Mura • 1118-8, Anyobo • Daily 9am–4.30pm • ¥500 • ⓣ 076 433 8270 • A free shuttle bus runs on the hour (daily10am–4pm); catch it from the Excel Tokyo hotel opposite the station

Gathered together at the foot of the Kureha hills is the **Toyama Municipal Folkcraft Village** offering eight museums highlighting local arts, crafts and industries, as well as the atmospheric temple **Chōkei-ji** (長慶寺) – its Gohyaku Rakan terraces, contain over five hundred miniature stone statues of the Buddha's disciples.

5

ARRIVAL AND DEPARTURE   TOYAMA

By plane Toyama Airport for, international flights to China and Korea and domestic flights to major cities, is 15km south of the city centre. There are regular shuttle buses to the centre (☎076 495 3101, ⊛toyama-airport .co.jp/english).

Destinations Fukuoka (daily; 1hr 20min); Hakodate (daily; 1hr 50min); Kansai International (daily; 1hr 15min); Nagoya (2 daily; 55min); Sapporo (daily; 1hr 20min); Tokyo (6 daily; 1hr 5min).

By train Toyama is on the main JR lines running along the Sea of Japan Coast and south to Nagoya. The station is in the centre of the city.

Destinations Kanazawa (hourly; 40min); Nagoya (4 daily; 3hr 40min); Niigata (5 daily; 3hr); Osaka (hourly; 3hr 15min); Takayama (4 daily; 1hr 30min); Tateyama (hourly; 1hr); Tokyo (Ueno; daily; 5hr 40min).

By bus Express buses connect Toyama with Tokyo, Osaka, Nagoya and Niigata, arriving and departing from Toyama station.

Destinations Kanazawa (16 daily; 1hr 15min); Nagoya (2–4 daily; 4hr 30min); Niigata (2 daily; 3hr 20min); Osaka (2 daily; 7hr 40min); Tokyo, (Ikebukuro, 4 daily; 6hr 30min).

INFORMATION

Tourist information The tourist information booth (daily 8.30am–8pm; ☎076 432 9751, ⊛visit-toyama. com), to the left of the central exit at Toyama Station, has a good selection of leaflets and English-speaking staff. There's also free bike hire March–Nov. The Toyama

International Centre Foundation's newsletter *What's Happening* (⊛tic-toyama.or.jp) provides events listings in English.

Services The post office, main banks and shops are close to the station.

ACCOMMODATION AND EATING

There are several good **business hotels** near the station. Toyama is known for the quality of its **sushi** and **sashimi**, getting fresh fish from the Sea of Japan coast

Minamoto Masu-no Sushi Museum 源ますのすしミュージアム 37-6 Nano-chō ☎076 429 7400, ⊛www .minamoto.co.jp. A 130-year-old restaurant and sushi factory, the house speciality trout sushi comes wrapped in bamboo leaves. Visitors can see traditional and modern sushi manufacturing processes and take part in workshops. It's 10min walk from Anjoji bus stop on the route from Toyama Station to Chitestu. Daily 9am–5pm.

Sushitama すし玉 5-8 Kakeosakaemachi ☎076 491 1897, ⊛sushitama.com. Locals highly recommend this *kaitenzushi* (conveyor belt sushi restaurant) operation, though it is a 15min bus or taxi ride south of the station. Daily 11am–9.30pm.

Tōyoko Inn 東横INN 5-1 Takaramachi & 4-5 Sakuramachi ☎076 405 1045, ⊛toyoko-inn.com. There are two branches of this reliable chain of business hotels close to the station. ¥5206

Kanazawa

金沢

Back in the mid-nineteenth century **KANAZAWA**, meaning "golden marsh", was Japan's fourth-largest city, it was built around a grand castle and the beautiful garden **Kenroku-en**. Today, the capital of Ishikawa-ken continues to cultivate the arts enthusiastically and contains attractive historic areas. Its modern face is ably represented by the impressive **21st Century Museum of Contemporary Art, Kanazawa** – all in all, this is the one place you shouldn't miss on the Sea of Japan coast.

Kanazawa is a city that rewards a leisurely pace, so set aside at least a couple of days. Having escaped bombing during World War II, traditional inner-city areas, such as **Nagamachi**, with its samurai houses, and the charming geisha teahouse district of **Higashi Chaya**, remain intact and are a joy to wander around.

Brief history

Kanazawa's heyday was in the late fifteenth century, when a collective of farmers and Buddhist monks overthrew the ruling Togashi family, and the area, known as **Kaga** (a name still applied to the city's exquisite crafts, such as silk dyeing and lacquerware, and

TATEYAMA–KUROBE ALPINE ROUTE

A dramatic and memorable way to travel from the Sea of Japan coast across the Alps to Nagano-ken or vice versa, is to follow the **Tateyama–Kurobe Alpine Route** (立山黒部アルペンルート; ⊕alpen-route.com), using a combination of buses, trains, funicular and cable-cars. The 90km route is only open from mid-April to mid-November, depending on the snow, and is at its busiest between August and October, when you may have to wait a while for a seat or a spot on the cable-car. It takes about six hours to traverse the roof of Japan, so start early so you have some time to wander around along the way. The spectacular views justify the ¥10,560 one-way ticket.

TATEYAMA TO MURODŌ

Starting from Toyama, take the Toyama Chihō Tetsudō line to the village of **Tateyama** (立山) at the base of Mount Tateyama (45min; ¥1170), one of the most sacred mountains in Japan. Board the Tateyama Cable Railway for the seven-minute journey (¥700 up to the small resort of **Bijo-daira** (美女平), meaning "beautiful lady plateau". One of the best parts of the journey follows, taking the Tateyama Kōgen bus (55min; ¥1660) up the twisting alpine road, which early in the season is still piled high with snow on either side, to the terminal at **Murodō** (室堂). There are several places to stay here. Five minutes walk north of the bus terminal is the **Mikuriga-ike** (みくりが池), an alpine lake in a 15m-deep volcanic crater and, twenty minutes' further on, **Jigokudani** (地獄谷; Hell Valley), an area of boiling hot springs. There are also several longer hikes that you can do around Murodō, which is the best place to end your journey along the Alpine Route, if you're short of time or money.

Tateyama Murodō Sansō 立山室堂山荘 14 Ashikuraji, Murodō ☎076 465 5763. Being at such altitude, the accommodation at this mountain hotel is rather basic, but it is comfortable and clean. There are public baths, one of which has a great panoramic view over the mountains. It is also a good place to head for lunch, if you are passing through; the curry dishes are very reasonable. Two meals are included in the rates. **¥20,000**

MURODŌ TO KUROBE-KO

The next section of the journey – a ten-minute bus ride to **Daikanbō** (大観峰) along a tunnel cut through Mount Tateyama – is the most expensive (¥2100). The view from Daikanbō across the mountains is spectacular, and you'll be able to admire it further as you take the Tateyama Ropeway cable-car (¥1260) down to the Kurobe Cable Railway (¥840) for a five-minute journey to the edge of the Kurobe lake formed by the huge **Kurobe dam** (黒部ダム; ⊕kurobe-dam .com). There are boat trips across the lake (30min; ¥930) and some excellent hiking. An easy thirty-minute walk south of the lake gets you to a campsite; and if you have the right gear and the Tateyama topographical map, you can hike for days along some of Japan's most spectacular trails.

KUROBE-KO TO SHINANO-ŌMACHI

From the cable railway, you'll have to walk 800m across the dam to catch the trolley bus (¥1260) for a sixteen-minute journey through tunnels under Harinoki-dake to the village of **Ōgisawa** (扇沢), across in Nagano-ken. Here you'll transfer to a bus (40min; ¥1330) down to the station at **Shinano-Ōmachi** (信濃大町), where you can catch trains to Matsumoto (see p.357) or Hakuba (see p.351). You can buy a ticket covering the whole trip at either end (¥10,560).

its refined cuisine), became Japan's only independent Buddhist state. Autonomy ended in 1583 when the *daimyō* Maeda Toshiie was installed as ruler by the warlord Oda Nobunaga, but Kanazawa continued to thrive as the nation's richest province, churning out five million bushels of rice a year.

Kenroku-en

兼六園 • Kenroku-machi • Daily: March to mid-Oct 7am–6pm; mid-Oct to Feb 8am–5pm • ¥300 • ☎076 234 3800, ⊕bit.ly/1dBG5uB

Early morning or late afternoon are the best times for experiencing Kanazawa's star attraction, **Kenroku-en**, at its most tranquil. Otherwise, you're bound to have your thoughts interrupted by a megaphone-toting guide and party of tourists – such is the

5

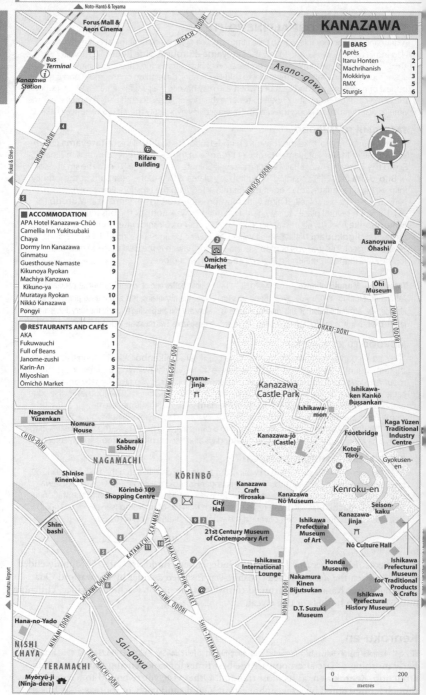

Noto-Hantō & Toyama

KANAZAWA

Forus Mall & Aeon Cinema

Bus Terminal

Kanazawa Station

HIGASHI- ŌDŌRI

Asano-gawa

Rifare Building

HIKOSO-ŌDŌRI

BARS
Après	4
Itaru Honten	2
Machrihanish	1
Mokkiriya	3
RMX	5
Sturgis	6

N

Asanoyuwa Ōhashi

Ōhi Museum

JŌHOKU-ŌDŌRI

Ōmichō Market

OHARI-DŌRI

ACCOMMODATION
APA Hotel Kanazawa-Chūō	11
Camellia Inn Yukitsubaki	8
Chaya	3
Dormy Inn Kanazawa	1
Ginmatsu	6
Guesthouse Namaste	2
Kikunoya Ryokan	9
Machiya Kanzawa Kikuno-ya	7
Murataya Ryokan	10
Nikkō Kanazawa	4
Pongyi	5

RESTAURANTS AND CAFÉS
AKA	5
Fukuwauchi	1
Full of Beans	7
Janome-zushi	6
Karin-An	3
Miyoshian	4
Ōmichō Market	2

HYAKUMANGOKU-DŌRI

Oyama-jinja

Kanazawa Castle Park

Ishikawa-mon

Ishikawa-ken Kankō Bussankan

Nagamachi Yūzenkan

Nomura House

CHŪŌ-DŌRI

Kaburaki Shōho

NAGAMACHI

Shinise Kinenkan

Kōrinbō 109 Shopping Centre

KŌRINBŌ

Kanazawa-jō (Castle)

Kanazawa Craft Hirosaka

Kanazawa Nō Museum

Footbridge

Kaga Yūzen Traditional Industry Centre

Kotoji Tōrō

Gyokusen-en

Kenroku-en

Seison-kaku

Shin-bashi

City Hall

Kanazawa-jinja

Komatsu Airport

KATAMACHI

TATEMACHI SHOPPING STREET

SCRAMBLE

21st Century Museum of Contemporary Art

Ishikawa Prefectural Museum of Art

Nō Culture Hall

Ishikawa International Lounge

Honda Museum

Ishikawa Prefectural Museum for Traditional Products & Crafts

SAIGAWA-ŌHASHI

SAI-GAWA-ŌDŌRI

SHIN-TATEMACHI

HONDA-DŌRI

Nakamura Kinen Bijutsukan

D.T. Suzuki Museum

Ishikawa Prefectural History Museum

Hana-no-Yado

MINAMI-ŌDŌRI

Sai-gawa

TERA-MACHI-DŌRI

NISHI CHAYA

TERAMACHI

Myōryū-ji (Ninja-dera)

0		200

metres

Fukui & Eihei-ji

price of visiting one of the official top three gardens in Japan (Kairaku-en in Mito and Kōraku-en in Okayama are the other two; see p.545). Kenroku-en – developed over two centuries from the 1670s – is rightly regarded as the best.

Originally the outer grounds of Kanazawa castle, and thus the **private garden** of the ruling Maeda clan, Kenroku-en opened to the public in 1871. Its name, which means "combined six garden", refers to the six horticultural graces that the garden embraces: spaciousness, seclusion, artificiality, antiquity, water and panoramic views. It's a lovely place to stroll around, with an ingenious pumping system that keeps the hillside pools full of water and the fountains working. There are many carefully pruned and sculpted pine trees and sweeping views across towards Kanazawa's geisha district Higashi Chaya.

Seison-kaku

成巽閣 • Daily except Wed 9am–5pm • ¥700 • ☎ 076 221 0580, ⓦ seisonkaku.com

In the garden's northeast corner is the elegant **Seison-kaku**, a two-storey shingle-roofed mansion built in 1863 by the *daimyō* Maeda Nariyasu as a retirement home for his mother. Look out for paintings of fish, shellfish and turtles on the wainscots of the *shōji* sliding screens in the formal guest rooms downstairs. The view from the Tsukushi-no-rōka (Horsetail Corridor) across the mansion's own raked-gravel garden is particularly enchanting, while upstairs the decorative style is more adventurous, using a range of striking colours and materials including, unusually for a traditional Japanese house, glass windows, imported from the Netherlands. These were installed so that the occupants could look out in winter at the falling snow.

21st Century Museum of Contemporary Art

金沢21世紀美術館, Kanazawa Ni-ju Seiki Bijutsukan • 1-2-1 HirOsaka • Public spaces daily 9am–10pm, exhibits Tues–Sun 10am–6pm • Collection ¥350, special exhibits vary • ☎ 076 220 2800, ⓦ kanazawa21.jp

The excellent **21st Century Museum of Contemporary Art**, opposite Kenroku-en's southwest entrance, highlighting a forward-thinking attitude that had previously been obscured by the city's love of the traditional arts.

The hyper-modern design by the architectural practice SANAA – a circle of glass embracing a series of galleries, a library and a free crèche – is like a giant geometry puzzle and perfectly suited to the multiple uses of the facility. Exhibitions frequently change, although there are some specially commissioned works on permanent display. James Turrell's *Blue Planet Sky* is a great place to relax and watch the clouds float by, while Leandro Erlich's *Swimming Pool* encourages fun interaction between viewers around the pool's edge and those walking beneath. The twelve tuba-shaped tubes that sprout out of the lawns surrounding the gallery are by the German artist Florian Claar; if you speak into one, sound comes out of another.

Kanazawa Nō Museum

金沢能楽美術館, Kanazawa Ni-jū Seiki Bijutsukan • 1-2-25 HirOsaka • Tues–Sun 10am–6pm • ¥300 • ☎ 076 220 2790, ⓦ www.kanazawa-noh-museum.gr.jp

The **Kanazawa Nō Museum** shines light on the most refined of Japan's dramatic arts. On the ground floor is a virtual nō stage where you can try on a nō costume and get your picture taken. Upstairs are prime examples of nō's ornate costumes and eerie masks, as well as videos and displays of performances.

Kanazawa-jō

金沢城 • Marunouchi • Daily March to mid-Oct 7am–6pm; mid-Oct to Feb 8am–5pm • Grounds free, castle interior ¥300 • ☎ 076 234 3800

The footbridge from Kenroku-en's northernmost exit leads to the **Ishikawa-mon**, a towering eighteenth-century gateway to the castle, **Kanazawa-jō**. There's been a

5

fortification on the Kodatsuno plateau since 1546, but the castle in its present form dates back mainly to the early seventeenth century. In 2001, part of the inner enclosure was rebuilt using traditional methods and plans from the Edo period. These included the three-storey, diamond-shaped Hishi Yagura and Hashizume-mon Tsuzuki Yagura watchtowers, the Gojukken Nagaya corridor linking them, and the Hashizume bridge and gate leading to the enclosure. Inside the buildings, you can see the intricate joinery and inspect the scale model carpenters used to master the complexities of their task.

Parts of the original castle are within the grounds, as well as an attractive modern garden with traditional elements – an interesting contrast to Kenroku-en.

Gyokusen-en

玉泉園 • 8-3 Kosho-machi • April–Nov daily 9am–4pm • ¥500, tea ¥500 • ☎ 076 221 0181

The small traditional garden **Gyokusen-en** runs along Kenroku-en's eastern flank. Built on two levels on a steep slope, this quiet garden has many lovely features, including mossy stone paths leading past two ponds and a mini waterfall. The main villa's tearoom serves green tea and sweets.

Kaga Yūzen Traditional Industry Centre

加賀友禅伝統産業会館, Kaga Yūzen Dentō-Sangyō Kaikan • 8-8 Kosho-machi • Daily except Wed 9am–5pm • ¥300, silk dyeing ¥1575, kimono fittings ¥2000 (reservations required) • ☎ 076 224 5511, ⓦ kagayuzen.or.jp/english.html

Next to Gyokusen-en is the **Kaga Yūzen Traditional Industry Centre** where you can watch artists painting beautiful designs on silk, following a 500-year-old dyeing method. You can then try your own hand at this traditional Kanazawa craft, or dress in a kimono made from the dyed material.

D.T. Suzuki Museum

鈴木大拙館, Suzuki Daisetsu Kan • 3-4-20 Honda-machi • Tues–Sun 9.30am–5pm • ¥300 • ☎ 076 221 8011, ⓦ kanazawa-museum .jp/daisetz/english

The impressive **D.T. Suzuki Museum**, opened in 2012, is dedicated to a native son of Kanazawa, Daisetz Teitarō Suzuki, the philosopher and writer who largely introduced Zen Buddhism to the Western world. The highlight of the stylish contemporary building is its inner courtyard "contemplation zone". This serene space, built around a shallow pool and blending minimal architecture, simple materials, plants and natural light, is a great place to spend some peaceful moments of reflection.

Nagamachi

長町

Scenic **Nagamachi**, west of Kōrinbō, is a compact area of twisting cobbled streets, gurgling streams and old houses, protected by thick mustard-coloured earthen walls, topped with ceramic tiles. This is where samurai and rich merchants once lived; many of the traditional buildings remain private homes.

Nomura House

野村家, Nomura-ke • 1-3-32 Nagamachi • Daily 8.30am–5.30pm, Oct–March till 4.30pm • ¥500 • ☎ 076 221 3553

A former Samurai home, **Nomura House** is worth visiting for its compact but beautiful garden with its flowing carp-filled stream, waterfall and stone lanterns. The rich, but unflashy, materials used to decorate the house reveal the wealth of the former patrons and, in keeping with the culture of the time, there is a simple teahouse where you can enjoy *matcha* and a sweet.

Higashi Chaya

東茶屋 • A 15min walk northeast from Kenroku-en

Kanazawa is the only place outside of Kyoto to support the old-style training of geisha. Of the three districts where this happens, **Higashi Chaya** is the largest and most scenic (the others are Kazue-machi Chaya and Nishi Chaya; see below).

Several old teahouses are open to the public. The **Ochaya Shima** (お茶屋志摩; 1-13-21 Higashiyama; daily 9am–6pm; ¥400; ☎076 252 5675, ⓦochaya-shima.com) is the most traditional, while opposite **Kaikarō** (懐華樓; 1-14-8 Higashiyama; daily except Tues 9am–6pm; ¥700), decorated in a more modern style, has an unusual Zen rock garden made of broken glass and a tearoom with gilded tatami mats. You can take tea at both (without geisha, unfortunately) for a small extra fee.

Tea is also part of the deal at the venerable **Shamisen-no-Fukushima** (三味線の福島; 1-1-18 Higashiyama; Mon–Sat 10am–4pm, closed second & fourth Sat of the month; ¥300; ☎076 2523703), where you can learn to pluck the Japanese stringed instrument, the *shamisen*.

Nishi Chaya

西茶屋 • A 10min walk from Sai-gawa Ohashi, a distinct iron bridge

The third of Kanazawa's pretty geisha districts, **Nishi Chaya**, is on the south side of the Sai-gawa. It's less commercial than Higashi Chaya – to see inside the beautifully decorated teahouse **Hana-no-Yado** (華の宿; 2-24-3 Ichinomachi; daily 9am–5pm) you need only buy a coffee (¥300) or *matcha* (¥500).

Myōryū-ji

妙立寺 • 2-12 Nomachi • Daily 9am–4pm, March–Oct till 4.30pm • ¥800 (including guided tour) • ☎076 241 0888 • A 5min walk east of Nishi Chaya

In the temple-packed **Teramachi** (寺町) district, you'll find **Myōryū-ji**, also known as Ninja-dera. Completed in 1643 and belonging to the Nichiren sect of Buddhism, this temple is associated with the Ninja assassins (see box, p.346) because of its many secret passages, trick doors and concealed chambers, including a lookout tower that commanded a sweeping view of the surrounding mountains and coast. It's necessary to book a tour to look around the temple.

Ishikawa Prefectural Museum for Traditional Products and Crafts

石川県立伝統産業工芸館, Ishikawa Kenritsu Dentō Sangyō Kōgeikan • 1-1 Kenrokumachi • Daily 9am–5pm, Dec–March closed Thurs, rest of year closed third Thurs of the month • ¥250 • ☎076 262 2020

The informative **Ishikawa Prefectural Museum for Traditional Products and Crafts** displays prime contemporary examples of Kanazawa's rich artistic heritage, including lacquerware, dyed silk, pottery, musical instruments and fireworks that the city is famous for. None of the articles is for sale but all have a price tag, so if you take a fancy to one of the gold leaf and lacquer Buddhist family altars, for example, you'll know that it costs ¥4.5 million.

Ishikawa Prefectural Museum of Art

石川県立美術館, Ishikawa Kenritsu Bijutsukan • 2-1 Dewa-machi • Daily 9.30am–7pm • ¥350, special exhibitions extra • ☎076 231 7580 • ⓦishibi.pref.ishikawa.jp

The **Ishikawa Prefectural Museum of Art** has beautiful examples of calligraphy, kimono, pottery, lacquerware and other relics of the Maeda clan, displayed along with a more eclectic collection of contemporary local art. There are also regular special exhibitions showcasing local and national art.

ARRIVAL AND DEPARTURE

By plane Komatsu Airport (☎076 121 9803, ⓦkomatsuairport.jp), 30km southwest of the city, is connected to Kanazawa Station by bus (40min; ¥1100). The bus stops first in the Katamachi district, close to many hotels. Destinations Fukuoka (2 daily; 1hr 15min); Izumo (6 weekly; 1hr 5min); Kagoshima (5 weekly; 1hr 40min); Naha (daily; 2hr 15min); Narita (daily; 1hr); Okayama (2 daily; 55min); Sapporo (daily; 1hr 35min); Sendai (daily; 1hr 5min); Tokyo (11 daily; 1hr).

By train The Shinkansen is set to streak into town in 2015; until then, take the bullet train from Tokyo to Nagaoka and change to an express train. There's also a daily direct limited express train (6hr) from Tokyo's Ueno Station. If you're coming from the Kansai area, take the Thunderbird express from

Ōsaka, via Kyoto which, does the journey in 2hr 30min; there's also a direct express service from Kyoto and Nagoya. Destinations Echigo-Yuzawa (10 daily; 2hr 30min); Fukui (every 15min; 50min); Kyoto (every 30min; 2hr 20min); Niigata (5 daily; 3hr 40min); Nagoya (8 daily; 2hr 50min); Osaka (every 30min; 2hr 45min); Tokyo (Ueno Station; daily; 6hr 5min); Toyama (every 45min; 40min).

By bus Long-distance buses pull up at the bus terminal on the east side of the train station. Destinations Kyoto (5 daily; 3hr 50min); Matsumoto (2 daily; 4hr 50min); Nagoya (10 daily; 3hr); Niigata (2 daily; 4hr 40min); Osaka (2 daily; 3hr 40min); Sendai (daily; 8hr 30min); Takayama (2 daily; 3hr); Tokyo, Shinjuku (8 daily; 7hr 30min); Toyama (16 daily; 1hr 15min); Wajima (4 daily; 2hr).

INFORMATION

Tourist information Providing assistance to foreign visitors is one of Kanazawa's strengths. In the JR station is an excellent tourist information office (daily 9am–7pm; ☎076 232 3933, ⓦkanazawa-tourism.com) with English-speaking staff (daily 9.30am–6.30pm) who can arrange for a guide to show you around town for free. Look out for the free quarterly English tourist paper *Eye on Kanazawa* (ⓦeyeon.jp) and the Japanese-language mini-magazine *Kanazawa Soraaruki* (¥330; ⓦsoraaruki.com).

International exchange foundations A 5min walk southeast of the station in the Rifare Building (1-5-3,

Hon-machi), The Ishikawa Foundation for International Exchange (国際交流石川財団; 3/F; Mon–Fri 9am–6pm, Sat 9am–5pm; ☎076 262 5931, ⓦifie.or.jp) and The Kanazawa International Exchange Foundation (KIEF; 金沢国際交流財団; 2F; Mon–Fri 9am–5.45pm; ☎076 220 2522, ⓦkief.jp) are good places to meet locals who want to practise English. Near Kenroku-en, the Ishikawa International Lounge (石川国際交流ラウンジ; 1-8-10 Hirosaka; Mon–Fri 10am–5pm, Sat 10am–4pm; ☎076 221 9901), offers free cultural and Japanese-language courses.

GETTING AROUND

By bus Buses leave frequently from stops #7, #8 and #9 at the train station for both Kōrinbō and Katamachi (¥200). The Kanazawa Loop Bus (daily 8.30am–6pm; ¥200, or ¥500 for a one-day pass) is a useful service that runs in a clockwise direction around the city from the train station and back again, covering all the main sights.

By car Toyota Rent-a-Car (☎076 223 0100) and Nippon Rent-a-Car (☎076 263 0919) are both close by Kanazawa Station.

By bike For hopping around the city, you can hire *Machinori* bikes from hubs dotted around the city for ¥200 a day. Register at the station (individual rides limited to 30min).

On foot Getting around is easy enough by foot. Most sights are clustered within walking distance of Kōrinbō and Katamachi, the neighbouring downtown areas, 10min by bus from outside the east exit of Kanazawa Station.

ACCOMMODATION

There's a host of hotels near the train station, but it's handier to stay in the central **Kōrinbō** district, within easy walking distance of Kenroku-en and other sights. On the east side of the city, **Higashi Chaya** is also a pleasant area to stay overnight; for details of other ryokan, see ⓦyadotime.jp/english.

APA Hotel Kanazawa Chūō アパホテル〈金沢中央〉1-5-24 Katamachi ☎076 235 2111, ⓦapahotel .com. There are several branches of this classy business chain in Kanazawa including this central one. The rooms offer business-hotel-style comfort, but adding a little luxury is a top-floor onsen and sauna, with outdoor and hot stone baths that guests can use for free (non-guests Mon–Fri ¥500, Sat & Sun ¥1000). **¥15,444**

★**Camellia Inn Yukitsubaki** カメリアイン雪椿 4-17 Kosho-machi ☎076 223 5725, ⓦwww.camellia.jp.

Laura Ashley meets traditional Japan at this charming guesthouse that offers spacious Western-style rooms and a lounge set in a *kura*. Rates include breakfast; add ¥4000 for a dinner of French cuisine served on Kutani pottery. **¥24,000**

Chaya 茶屋 2-17-21 Honmachi ☎076 231 2225, ⓦchayaryokan.co.jp. This is a good choice if you want to splash out on a small, high-end hotel and fine dining near the station. A slick modern take on a ryokan, the design and decor of the tatami rooms is minimal and luxurious, and the food in its highly rated restaurant similarly updates the traditional *Kaiseki*-course menu. Two meals are included in the rates, but room only is available from ¥8500 per person. **¥58,800**

Dormy Inn Kanazawa ドーミーイン金沢 2-25 Horai-kawa Shin-machi ☎ 076 263 9888. Opposite the slick Forus shopping mall is this stylish business hotel, offering full and half tatami rooms, a rooftop spa, internet terminals and a pleasant lounge area where a big buffet breakfast (¥950) is served. **¥6390**

Ginmatsu 銀松 1-17-18 Higashi Chaya ☎ 076 252 3577, @ ginmatsu@nifty.com. This pleasant, good-value minshuku is in the lovely Higashi Chaya district there's; a friendly welcome and they have neat tatami rooms. There's a communal bathroom with shower, and they also provide free tickets for the local *sentō*. **¥7000**

Guesthouse Namaste ゲストハウスナマステ 6-14 Kasaichi-machi ☎ 076 255 1057, @ guesthouse-namaste.com. Conveniently located in a calm side street 5min walk from the station, this is possibly the best value accommodation in town, with impeccably clean tatami dorm rooms, a communal bathroom, kitchen and lounge. The relaxed English-speaking owner will give you good tips on where to go and rents bikes for ¥500 a day. Dorm **¥2600**, double **¥6000**

Kikunoya Ryokan きくのや旅館 1-1-27 Hirosaka ☎ 076 231 3547, @ kikunoya.ninja-web.net. This centrally located ryokan is meticulously maintained by its friendly elderly owners. Even with rates boosted by ¥750 per person for Sat-night stays, it remains very good value. **¥9000**

Machiya Kanazawa Kikuno-ya 町屋金沢菊乃や 3-22 Kazue-machi ☎ 076 287 0834, @ machiya-kanazawa .jp. In the heart of the atmospheric geisha district of Kazue-machi, this renovated teahouse sleeps up to five people. The building dates to 1898, but has modern amenities including wi-fi. Breakfast and tickets to the public bath are included; cultural programmes are extra. three people **¥54,000**, five people **¥72,000**

Murataya Ryokan 村田屋旅館 1-5-2 Katamachi ☎ 076 263 0455, @ murataya-ryokan.com/eng. Set in an old building, this central ryokan has some stylish touches and is run by a welcoming family well used to foreign guests. Internet access, laundry and a handy map of local restaurants are available. **¥9000**

Nikkō Kanazawa 日航金沢 2-15-1 Honmachi ☎ 076 234 1111, @ hnkanazawa.co.jp. Good views are guaranteed from the rooms in this thirty-storey luxury hotel opposite Kanazawa Station, which sports a sophisticated modern European design. Breakfast is included in the rates. **¥38,400**

★**Pongyi** ポンギー 2-22 Rokumai-machi ☎ 076 225 7369, @ pongyi.com. A 5min walk from the JR station, behind the old sake shop Ichimura Magotaro, is this convivial budget guesthouse beside a gurgling stream. The cosy dorms are in a converted *kura*, and there's one spruce tatami room that sleeps up to four people, though none of the rooms is very spacious. The very hospitable English-speaking owner donates ¥100 of each night's accommodation charge to a charity that helps poor children in Asia. Dorm **¥2700**, double **¥6000**

EATING

Kanazawa's refined local cuisine, *kaga ryōri*, includes many special **seafood dishes** including steamed bream, snow crab and prawns. Sushi is also great – you'll find the freshest slices of fish at the lively market, **Ōmichō** (see p.386). Another typical Kanazawa dish is *jibuni*, boiled duck or chicken and vegetables in a viscous broth spiced up with a dab of wasabi.

★**AKA** アーカ RENN Building, 2-10-42 Kata-machi ☎ 076 231 3233, @ shiki-inc.com/aka. *Atelier Kitchen for Artisans* (*AKA*) offers outstandingly good modern Japanese food served in a chic yet casual setting by very friendly young staff. Their short-course menu (¥3500) is brilliant value for this standard of cooking. There's some wonderful local sake to drink here, too, as well as rustic pottery for sale. Tues–Sun 6pm–midnight.

Fukuwauchi 福わ家 1-9-31 Hikoso-machi ☎ 076 264 8780. There's a warm welcome and equally warming udon, soba and *nabe* (stew) at this rustic complex of four restaurants in a 120-year-old building next to the Ko-bashi. Set lunch menus start at ¥980 and dinner from ¥1800. Mon–Fri 11.30am–2.30pm & 5–9pm, Sat & Sun 11.30am–9pm.

Full of Beans フルオブビーンズ 41-1 Satomi-chō ☎ 076 222 3315, @ fullofbeans.jp. Cute café, just off the Tatemachi shopping street, specializing in onigiri (rice balls) in a wide variety of flavours. Their lunch sets, including several different curries, are a great deal starting at ¥900; upstairs there's an art gallery and bookshop you are free to browse. Mon–Fri 11.30am–3.30pm & 5–10pm (closed Tues evenings), Sat & Sun 11am–10pm.

Janome-zushi 蛇の目寿司 1-12 Katamachi ☎ 076 231 0093. Set in an attractive building by a gurgling stream, this excellent sushi restaurant has reasonably priced set menus and also does some *kaga ryōri* dishes. Expect to pay around ¥1200 per head for lunch and ¥5000 for dinner. Sit at the counter to admire the chefs at work. 11am–2pm & 5–10pm, closed Wed.

Karin-An かりん庵 2-23 Hashiba-chō ☎ 076 224 2467, @ kinjohro.co.jp. Part of the venerable *ryotei* *Kinjohro*, this less formal restaurant allows you to enjoy

5

the same quality of cooking in comfort at a table or the counter, where you can watch the chefs create their beautiful dishes. Lunch courses start at ¥2625. 11am–2.30pm & 5–9pm, closed Tues.

Miyoshian 三芳庵 1-11 Kenroku-machi ☎076 221 0127. Atmospheric 100-year-old restaurant in Kenroku-en, just past the row of shops at the north entrance. Specializes in *kaga ryōri*; try the bentō boxed lunches (from ¥1575) or come for a cup of *matcha* tea and sweets (¥525), overlooking the ornamental pond. 9am–4pm; closed Wed, (dinner by reservation till 8.30pm).

Ōmichō Market 近江町市場 88 Aokusa-machi ☎076 231 3323. Kanazawa's lively central market is well worth a visit. In and around it are many small sushi bars and restaurants serving rice-bowl dishes (*donburi*) – there are usually several open daily. Try the *kaitenzushi* operation *Mori Mori Sushi* (もりもり寿し; Mon–Fri 10am–4pm, Sat & Sun until 8pm) or go upstairs to find the cute French patisserie and restaurant *La Cook Mignon* (10am–9.30pm, closed Wed). Daily 8am–6pm.

DRINKING AND ENTERTAINMENT

Nightlife revolves around buzzing Katamachi Scramble, the neon-lit drag connecting the Sai-gawa to Kōrinbō. The warren of streets around here is chock-full of **bars**. The city's geisha put on free **concerts** throughout the year and perform at various festivals: check with the tourist office for details. Also check at the same offices for the latest on nō plays (enthusiastically nurtured by Kanazawa's arty citizens) and classical music performances.

BARS

Après アプレズ 2-3-7 Katamachi ☎076 221 0002. This long-running *gaijin* bar with a pool table is now found on the seventh floor of the Space Building, while its Thai restaurant is on the ninth. From July to Sept they also run a popular beach bar out at Uchinada, on the coast a few kilometres north of the city. Tues–Sun: bar 10pm–2am; restaurant 6–11pm.

Itaru Honten いたる本店 3-8 Kakinobatake ☎076 221 4194. Locals tip this as Kanazawa's best *izakaya* – it's a great place to get acquainted with the area's excellent sakes and enjoy some sashimi or grilled fish. Mon–Sat 5.30–11.30pm.

★Machrihanish マクリハニッシュ 2F Nishino Bldg, 2-4 Kigura-machi ☎076 233 0072. Haba-san used to work at the Royal St Andrew's Golf Club and continues to communicate his passion for Scotch whisky and golf at this convivial bar stocking some 170 different single malts and blends. Mon–Sat 6.30pm–2am.

Mokkiriya もっきりや 3-6 Kakinokibatake ☎076 231 0096, 🌐 spacelan.ne.jp/~mokkiriya. *Mokkiriya* is a legendary jazz café that's been running for over 30 years, with live music on most nights. It has a good range of well-priced coffee, drinks and snacks. There is a charge for some evening performances, and advance booking is advisable for bigger acts. Daily noon–midnight.

RMX レミックス 2-30-2 Katamachi ☎076 262 0881. There's a friendly welcome at this relatively spacious gay bar that's pronounced "remix". The cover charge is ¥1500 including one drink. Mon–Sat 8pm–2am.

Sturgis スタージス 4F Kirin Bldg, 1-7-15 Katamachi ☎76 262 9577. Like stumbling into a New Year's Eve party, circa 1975, this silver-streamer-festooned bar is the domain of rocker Nitta-san who, if things are quiet, takes to the stage to play a live set or two. There's a ¥1000 cover charge. Daily 8pm–6am.

SHOPPING

Kanazawa is a fantastic place to shop for souvenirs and lovely objets d'art. The austerely rustic *Ōhi* and highly elaborate *Kutani* pottery can be bought at many shops around the city; several good options line Hirozaka, the street leading up to Kenroku-en from Kōrinbō. For unusual modern design gifts, browse the shop in the 21st Century Museum of Contemporary Art (see p.381). Also check out the **Tatemachi shopping street** (タテマチストリート) for quirky design shops and individual independent retailers.

Hakuza 箔座 1-26-7 Higashiyama. Kanazawa produces 98 percent of Japan's gold leaf. At this specialist shop in the heart of Higashi Chaya, you can buy all kinds of gold-leaf-decorated products, including chocolate cake. It's worth popping in just to take a look at their gilded *kura* (storehouse). 10am–5.30pm, closed Wed.

Ishikawa-ken Kankō Bussankan 石川県観光物産館 Kenroku-en-shita ☎076 222 7788. This three-storey tourist shop has a good selection of everything from food products to *washi* paper and pottery. A variety of craft classes are also held. on the second-and third-floor workshops. 10am–6pm, closed Tues.

Kaburaki Shōho 鏑木商舗 1-3-16 Nagamachi 🌐 kaburaki.jp. This *Kutani* pottery shop and restaurant-cum-bar in the heart of Nagamachi occupies an elegant old house surrounded by pleasant gardens. They also have a small museum, which houses gorgeous pieces of pottery and is worth a browse. Daily 9am–10pm.

Kanazawa Craft Hirosaka 金沢クラフト広坂 1-2-25 Hirosaka. Exquisite examples of Kanazawa's traditional crafts are sold here, and the shop hosts special exhibitions of work on its second floor. Tues–Sun 10.30am–5pm.

TEMPLE OF ETERNAL PEACE

A complex of over seventy buildings blending seamlessly with the forest **Eihei-ji** (永平寺; ☎077 663 3640; daily 9am–5pm, Nov–April till 4.30pm; ¥500) is home to some two hundred shaven-headed monks. Established by the Zen master Dōgen Zenji in 1244, this serene temple in cedar-covered mountains is one of the two headquarters of **Sōtō Zen Buddhism**.

It's easy to make a day-trip to the temple which is 10km northeast of Fukui (福井), less than an hour's train ride south of Kanazawa. Eihei-ji is closed periodically for special services, so it's wise to check first with **Fukui City Sightseeing Information** (daily 9am–6pm; ☎0776 21 6492, ⊕fuku-e.com) or with the temple before setting off. Also make an advance reservation if you'd like to enjoy a vegetarian *shōjin-ryōri* meal as part of your visit

From JR Fukui Station, the easiest way to reach Eihei-ji is by direct bus (¥720; 35min). Alternatively, hop on the local train to Eihei-ji Guchi Station, then either walk uphill for five minutes or take a bus or taxi.

Affiliates of a Sōtō Zen Buddhist organization can arrange to stay overnight here (¥8000) and participate in the monks' daily routine, including cleaning duties and pre-dawn prayers and meditation; for serious devotees a four-day/three-night course (¥12,000) is also available. Details of how to apply can be found at ⊕bit.ly/1dT3tow.

Sakuda さくだ 1-3-27 Higashiyama ☎076 251 6777. A dazzling shop that specializes in gold-leaf products, from beautiful screens to gilded golf balls. You can see the making of gold leaf in action, and staff are happy to explain the process. Daily 9am–6pm.

DIRECTORY

Banks and exchange Several banks can be found along the main road leading southeast from Kanazawa Station, as well as around Kōrinbō.

Hospital Kanazawa University Hospital, 13-1 Takaramachi (☎076 265 2000), is around 1km southeast of Kenroku-en.

Internet access There's free access at the library on the third floor of the Rifare building.

Police The Police Help Line (☎076 225 0555) operates from 9am–5pm Mon–Fri.

Post office There are branches at Kōrinbō as well as the JR station.

Noto Hantō

能登半島

Jutting out like a gnarled finger into the Sea of Japan is **Noto Hantō** peninsula, the name of which is said to derive from an Ainu word, *nopo*, meaning "set apart". The peninsula's rural way of life, tied to agriculture and fishery, is certainly worlds away from fast-paced, urban Japan – there's little public transport here, so the area is best explored by car or bicycle. The rugged and windswept west coast has the bulk of what constitutes the Noto Hantō's low-key attractions, while the calmer, indented east coast harbours several sleepy fishing villages, where only the lapping of waves and the phut-phut of boat engines breaks the silence.

Cosmo Isle Hakui

コスモアイル羽咋 • 25 Menda • 9am–4.30pm, closed Tues • ¥300

If you're travelling up the peninsula's **west coast** from Kanazawa, drive past the wide, sandy beach Chiri-hama (千里浜), cluttered with day-trippers and their litter, and head briefly inland to the alleged UFO-hotspot of **HAKUI** (羽咋). In a suitably saucerish hall near Hakui Station, you'll find **Cosmo Isle Hakui**, a fascinating museum devoted to space exploration which houses a great deal of authentic paraphernalia, most impressively the Vostok craft that launched Yuri Gagarin into space in 1961 – it looks like a giant cannonball.

5

Keta-taisha

気多大社 • Daily 8.30am–4.30pm • Free • ⓦ keta.jp

Set in a wooded grove near the sea is **Keta-taisha**, Noto's most important shrine. The complex dates from the 1650s, although it is believed that the shrine was founded in the eighth century. It's attractive but the atmosphere is spoilt by the modern-day commercialization of the place, catering to young lovers who come to seek the blessing of the spirits.

Myōjō-ji

妙成寺 • 1 Takidanimachi • Daily 8am–4.30pm • Temple free, pagoda ¥300

A few kilometres further up the coast from Keta-taisha, **Myōjō-ji** is a seventeenth-century temple with an impressive five-storey pagoda. The surrounding area is pretty striking, too – millennia of poundings from the Sea of Japan have created fascinating rock formations and cliffs along this coastline.

Wajima

輪島

Midway up Noto's west coast is **WAJIMA**, the peninsula's main tourist centre and an appealing fishing port, straddling the mouth of the Kawarada-gawa. Wajima hosts the **Asa Ichi** (daily 8am–noon, except second & fouth Wed of the month; ☏076 822 7653), a touristy, yet colourful morning market, where around two hundred vendors set up stalls along the town's main street selling fish, vegetables and other local products. It's a good place to pick up lacquerware at reasonable prices, but buy from the shops rather than the stalls on the street.

Gō Nagai Wonderland Museum

永井豪記念館 • 123-banchi (asa ichi-dōri-zoi) • Daily 9am–5pm • ¥500 • ☏ 076 823 0715, ⓦ www.go-wonderland.jp

Anime and manga fans will enjoy the **Gō Nagai Wonderland Museum**, which celebrates the locally born creator of series such as *Mazinger Z*, *Devilman* and *Cutie Honey*. In one section you can draw your own manga character on a computer and get a printout as a souvenir.

Kiriko-kaikan

キリコ会館 • 22-2 Tsukadamachi • Daily 8am–5pm • ¥600 • ☏ 076 822 7100

Well worth a visit is the **Kiriko-kaikan**, on the east side of town by the coast. This exhibition hall houses the enormous colourful paper lanterns that are paraded around town in Wajima's lively summer and autumn festivals, videos of which are shown.

Sosogi and around

曽々木

The scenic coastline between Wajima and the cape **Rokkō-zaki** (禄剛崎) is scattered with many strange rock formations – look out for **Godzilla Rock** (ゴジラ岩) and, near the village of **Sosogi**, the **Shiroyone no Senmaida** (白米の千枚田) rice paddies, which make a stunning view. Just south of the cape, a winding road leads down to the "secret onsen" inn of *Lamp-no-Yado* (see p.390).

Shiroyone no Senmaida

白米の千枚田 • Shiroyone-machi • LED light display mid-Nov to March daily 6–8pm • ☏ 0768 23 1146 • The bus from Wajima takes 20min (¥500 return)

It's worth taking the trip to **Shiroyone no Senmaida** to see the dramatic coastal landscape. Covering 1.2 hectares, over two thousand rice paddies in small shelves cling to the mountainside as it plunges towards the sea. The fields have to be tended by hand

---

WAJIMA LACQUERWARE

Wajima is renowned for its high-quality lacquerware (know locally as *wajima nuri*), and you'll find many shops around town selling it. Below are some of the best places to see high-quality products and get involved in workshops:

Ishikawa Wajima Urushi Art Museum (石川県輪島漆芸美術館; 11 Shijukari Mitomori-machi; daily 9am–5pm; ¥600; ☎768 22 9783) On the southwest side of town, this is where the best collection of pieces can be viewed.

Nuritaro (塗太郎; 95-banchi (asaichi-dōri); daily 8am–5pm; classes from ¥1000; ☎0768 22 6040, ⊕nuritaro.com) Visitors at this traditional workshop can take acquerware classes and see craftsmen at work. It's located in a side street off where the morning market is held.

Wajima Kōbō Nagaya (輪島工房長屋; 4-66-1 Kawai-machi; 9am–6pm (Nov–Feb till 5pm), closed Wed; free; ☎076 823 0011) More modern styles of lacquerware can be seen at this complex of traditional-style wooden buildings close to the sea, in the centre of town, where you can also see the artists creating it. If you make an advance booking, it's possible to engrave lacquerware yourself.

---

as the land is too steep to allow access by machine. Every night in winter, when no rice is grown, the hillside becomes the world's largest display of solar-panelled LEDs – in total, 21,000 lights line the fields, making the hillside sparkle with colour.

The Tokikuni houses

Kami Tokikuni-ke 上時國家 • 13-4 Machinomachi • Daily 8.30am–5pm, April–Nov till 6pm • ¥500 • ☎076 832 0171 • **Shimo Tokikuni-ke** 下時國家 • 2-1 Machinomachi • Daily: Jan–March & Dec 8.30am–4pm; April–Nov 8.30am–5pm • ¥250 • ☎076 832 0075

Head inland towards Iwakura-yama, a steep 357m mountain, to visit two traditional thatched-roof houses that once belonged to the wealthy Tokikuni family, supposed descendants of the vanquished Taira clan (see p.566). The family split in the sixteenth century, with one contingent staying in the **Kami Tokikuni-ke**; the other building, the smaller **Shimo Tokikuni-ke**, with its attractive attached garden, is only a short walk away.

ARRIVAL AND INFORMATION   NOTO HANTŌ

By plane Noto Airport (☎076 826 2000), 25min south of Wajima, has two flights daily to and from Tokyo's Haneda Airport.

By train Trains from Kanazawa terminate at the uninteresting east-coast resort town of Wakura Onsen (和倉温泉), which can also be reached from Toyama, with a change of trains at Tsubata.

By bus More convenient than trains are the buses (2hr 15min; ¥2200) that cruise up the peninsula's central highway from Kanazawa to Wajima.

Tourist information There's a tourist information office (daily 8am–7pm; ☎076 822 1503, ⊕wajimaonsen.com) in Wajima Bus Station. A useful website on the area is ⊕notohantou.net.

GETTING AROUND

By bus Local buses connect most other places of interest, but they're infrequent and you might want to try cycling or renting a car instead. There are also several daily tour buses (¥7200) from Kanazawa which take in all the sights, with an unrelenting Japanese commentary.

By car Renting a car is the best option for getting around the peninsular. If you're coming from Kanazawa, the main tourist office in the station can advise.

By bike You can rent bicycles (¥800/8hr) from the tourist information office in Wajima Bus Station.

ACCOMMODATION AND EATING

Wajima has the widest choice of places to stay on the peninsular and is a good base for day-trips around the area. Eating options are limited in many of the parts of Noto, so it is advisable to book accommodation with meals included.

Flatt's by the Sea 海のそばの元ふらっと27-26-3 Otoritama Yanami, Hanami ☎076 862 1900, ⊕flatts.jp. In the town of Hanami (花見) at the northern tip of the Noto Hantō is this cute seaside minshuku, restaurant and bakery run by an Australian–Japanese couple, using local seafood and produce for their innovative menu. The restaurant is closed Wed and Thurs. Rates include two meals. **¥29,400**

5

Fukasan ふかさん 4-4 Kawai-machi, Wajima ☎076 822 9933 ⊛wajima-minsyuku.com/fukasan/fukasan.html. There's a friendly welcome at this newly restored minshuku that has views over the Wajima coast. The four tatami-style rooms are simply furnished and share a large onsen bathtub. Includes two meals, with plenty of delicious local seafood. **¥15,600**

Kagaya 加賀屋 80 Yobu, Wakura-machi, Wakura ☎076 762 1111, ⊛www.kagaya.co.jp/en. An army of kimono-clad staff greet you outside this large resort hotel, regularly voted the number one onsen resort in Japan, which combines Japanese elegance with Vegas-esque opulent kitsch. The attentive, though slightly overbearing service continues as you negotiate between the host of restaurants, bars, karaoke, cabaret shows and souvenir shops designed to keep you – and your wallet – occupied. There are a host of different onsen spread over three floors, with spectacular views over the bay – it's an experience to remember, if you can afford it. Rates include two meals. **¥58,800**

Lamp-no-Yado ランプの宿 10-11 Misakimachijike, Suzu ☎076 886 8000, ⊛lampnoyado.co.jp. One of the peninsula's most famous ryokan, this fourteen-room place offers rooms that each have their own rotemburo, and a spectacular cliffside location in Suzu (珠洲). **¥38,100**

Noto Isaribi Youth Hostel 能登漁火ユースホステル 51-6 Ogi-yo, Ogi ☎076 874 0150, ⊛www2.plala.or.jp/isaribi0150. Facing onto Tsukumo-wan in the sleepy village of Ogi (小木), this hostel has good-quality tatami dorms and is run by a friendly man who rustles up local seafood feasts. The bus from Kanazawa will drop you at Ogi-kō, an 8min walk from the hostel. Dorm **¥3800**

Wajima Minshuku 輪島民宿 2-5-1 Futatsuyamachi, Wajima ☎076 822 4243. Next to the river and a 10min walk west of Wajima Station, this small minshuku has good-sized and well-priced tatami rooms. There are tasty rustic home-cooked meals available, featuring rice and vegetables grown by the owners. **¥9500**

Nagoya

名古屋

Completely rebuilt after a wartime drubbing, **NAGOYA** is a modern metropolis of high-rise buildings, wide boulevards, multilane highways and flyovers, where business takes precedence over tourism. Here you'll find the headquarters of industrial powerhouse Toyota (see box, p.393) as well as numerous other companies that exploit the local skill of *monozukuri* (making things) to the hilt.

Less overwhelming than Tokyo or Osaka, the capital of Aichi-ken and Japan's fourth-largest city provides an easily accessible introduction to urban Japan and all its contemporary delights, one of the highlights of which is its **food scene**. The grand **Tokugawa Art Museum** and attached gardens display possessions of the powerful family who once ruled Japan and who built Nagoya's original castle back in 1610. In the city centre, the cutting-edge **Nagoya City Science Museum** boasts the largest planetarium in the world and a host of immersive displays to entertain and educate kids of all ages. Another highlight is the **Toyota Commemorative Museum of Industry and Technology**, an appropriate tribute to Nagoya's industrial heritage.

Nagoya's sights are quite spread out, but walking from the main hub of train stations to Sakae and around, even down to Ozu, is quite feasible. Excellent transport links, including an international airport, also make Nagoya an ideal base from which to tour the region. Day-trip possibilities include the castle towns of **Inuyama** (see p.400) and **Gifu** (see p.404), both places where you can view the ancient skill of *ukai* – fishing with cormorants. The Shima Hantō (see p.517) can easily be visited from Nagoya, too.

Tokugawa Art Museum and Tokugawa-en

Museum 徳川美術館 • 1017 Tokugawa-chō • Tues–Sun 10am–5pm • ¥1200, or ¥1350 including the garden • **Tokugawa-en** 徳川園 • Daily 9.30am–5.30pm • ¥300, or ¥640 combined ticket with Nagoya-jō • ☎052 935 6262, ⊛tokugawa-art-museum.jp/english

Nagoya's single best sight is the **Tokugawa Art Museum** and its lovely attached garden **Tokugawa-en**, which was laid out in the late seventeenth century. The museum, around 4km east of the stations, houses heirlooms from the Owari branch of the Tokugawa family who once ruled Nagoya, and includes items inherited by the first Tokugawa

5

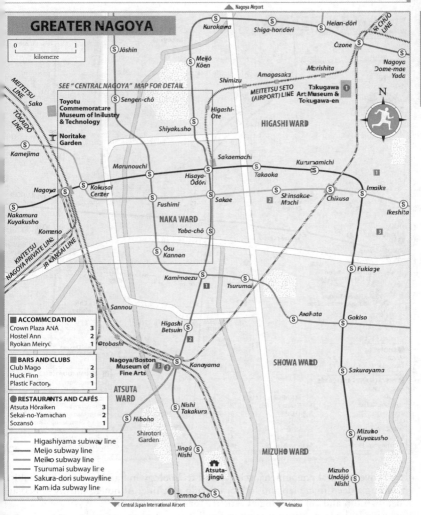

GREATER NAGOYA

Nagoya Airport

0   1
kilometre

SEE "CENTRAL NAGOYA" MAP FOR DETAIL

Toyota Commemorative Museum of Industry & Technology

Noritake Garden

Kamejima

Nagoya

Nakamura Kuyakusho

Komeno

MEITETSU LINE
TOKAIDO LINE
KINTETSU NAGOYA PRIVATE LINE
JR KANSAI LINE

Sako

Jōshin

Sengen-chō

Marunouchi

Kokusai Center

Fushimi

NAKA WARD

Yaba-chō

Ōsu Kannon

Kurokawa

Shiga-hon-dōri

Meijō Kōen

Shimizu

Amagasaka

Shiyakusho

Sakaemachi

Hisaya-Ōdōri

Sakae

Higashi-Ōte

Takaoka

Shinsakae-Machi

Kamimaezu

Tsurumai

Heian-dōri

Ōzone

Morishita

MEITETSU SETO
(AIRPORT) LINE

HIGASHI WARD

Kurumamichi

Imaike

Chikusa

Fukiage

Anakata

Nagoya Dome-mae Yada

Tokugawa Art Museum & Tokugawa-en

JR CHŪŌ LINE

N

Ikeshita

Gokiso

Sannou

Higashi Betsuin

Otobashi

Nagoya/Boston Museum of Fine Arts

ATSUTA WARD

Kanayama

Hiboho

Nishi Takakura

Shirotori Garden

Jingū Nishi

Atsuta-jingū

Temma-Chō

SHOWA WARD

Sakurayama

Mizuho Kuyakusho

MIZUHO WARD

Mizuho Undōjō Nishi

Higashiyama subway line
Meijō subway line
Meikō subway line
Tsurumai subway line
Sakura-dori subway line
Kamiida subway line

Central Japan International Airport   Arimatsu

shogun, Ieyasu, reconstructions of the formal chambers of the *daimyō*'s residence, and a nō stage all of which provides around which beautiful traditional costumes are arranged, which enables you to get a sense of the rich and cultured life led by the Tokugawas. The museum's most treasured piece is the twelfth-century painted scroll *The Tale of Genji* (see p.837); it's so fragile, it's only displayed for a month each year from November 10 – the rest of the time you can see reproduced panels and video programmes about this priceless relic.

Nagoya City Science Museum

名古屋市科学館, Nagoya-shi Ragaku-Kan · 2-17-1 Sakae · Daily 9.30am–5pm · ¥400, or ¥300 including planetarium; primary school children free, high-school and university students ¥200, or ¥500 including planetarium · ☏ 052 201 4486, ⓦ ns.ncsm.city.nagoya.jp/en

You can't miss the newly renovated **Nagoya City Science Museum**, with the **Hayabusa** space rocket out front and its 35m diameter spherical planetarium. Inside, nineteen

5

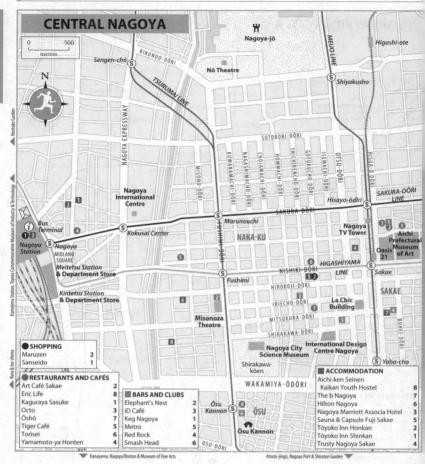

CENTRAL NAGOYA

0 — 500
metres

N

Nortake Garden
Noa & Ike-shima
Kamejima Station, Toyota Commemorative Museum of Industry & Technology

Nagoya-jō

Higashi-ote

KIKUNOO-DŌRI

Sengen-chō

Nō Theatre

Shiyakusho

TSURUMAI LINE

MEIJO LINE

NAGOYA EXPRESSWAY

SOTOBORI-DŌRI

KUWANAMACHI-DŌRI
NAGASHIMACHO-DŌRI
CHOMACHI-DŌRI
HOMMACHI-DŌRI
SHICHIKENCHO-DŌRI
GOFUKUCHO-DŌRI
ISEMACHI-DŌRI
ŌTSU-DŌRI

MISONO-DŌRI

SHICHIKENCHŌ-DŌRI

SAKURA-DŌRI LINE

Nagoya International Centre

Hisayo-ōdlri

Bus Terminal

Kokusai Center

Marunouchi

SAKURA-DŌRI

NAKA-KU

Nagoya TV Tower

Aichi Prefectural Museum of Art

Oasis 21

Nagoya Station

Nagoya MIDLAND SQUARE

Meitetsu Station & Department Store

Kintetsu Station & Department Store

FUSHIMI-DŌRI

Fushimi

NISHIKI-DŌRI

HIGASHIYAMA LINE

Sakae

SAKAE

HIROKOJI-DŌRI

IRIECHO-DŌRI

La Chic Building

BUHEI-DŌRI

Misonoza Theatre

MITSUKURA-DŌRI

SHIRAKAWA-DŌRI

Nagoya City Science Museum

International Design Centre Nagoya

Yaba-cho

Shirakawa-kōen

WAKAMIYA-ŌDŌRI

Ōsu Kannon

ŌSU

Ōsu Kannon

ŌSU-DŌRI

Kanayama, Nagoya/Boston & Museum of Fine Arts

Atsuta-jingū, Nagoya Port & Shiraton Garden

● SHOPPING
Maruzen	2
Sanseido	1

■ RESTAURANTS AND CAFÉS
Art Café Sakae	2
Eric Life	8
Kaguraya Sasuke	1
Octo	3
Ōshō	7
Tiger Café	5
Torisei	6
Yamamoto-ya Honten	4

■ BARS AND CLUBS
Elephant's Nest	2
iD Café	3
Keg Nagoya	4
Metro	5
Red Rock	1
Smash Head	6

■ ACCOMMODATION
Aichi-ken Seinen Kaikan Youth Hostel	8
The b Nagoya	7
Hilton Nagoya	6
Nagoya Marriott Associa Hotel	3
Sauna & Capsule Fuji Sakae	5
Tōyoko Inn Honkan	2
Tōyoko Inn Shinkan	1
Trusty Nagoya Sakae	4

floors cover natural phenomena, science and technology in hands-on, active exhibits including a deep-freeze lab and indoor tornado machine. Although mostly aimed at kids, it's a fun and enlightening experience for all ages, but one downside is the lack of information in English, and, unless you understand Japanese, it's probably not worth paying for the 50-minute projection shows in the planetarium.

Nagoya-jō

名古屋城 • 1-1 Honmaru • Daily 9am–4.30pm • ¥500, or ¥640 including Tokugawa-en • ☎ 052 231 1700, ⓦ www.nagoyajo.city. nagoya.jp • Honmaru Goten under reconstruction until 2018

The moated **Nagoya-jō** lies around 1km east of the Nagoya stations. Tokugawa Ieyasu started to build this fortress in 1610, but the original was largely destroyed during World War II – all that survived were three turrets, three gates and sequestered screen paintings. A handsome concrete replica was completed in 1959, the central donjon topped by huge gold-plated *shachi*, the mythical dolphins that are one of the symbols of Nagoya. The **Honmaru Goten** (本丸御殿), the palace that once stood at the foot of the donjon, is currently under reconstruction; eventually it will house Edo-era painted screens including the famous bamboo grove, leopard and tiger scenes.

Midland Square

ミッドランドスクエア • **Main building** 11am–8pm (restaurants till 11pm) • Free • **Sky Promenade** Daily 11am–10pm • ¥700 • ☎ 052 527 8877, ⓦ midland-square.com

The area around Nagoya's trio of train stations is a mini-Manhattan with a clutch of tower blocks including **Midland Square**, Toyota's headquarters. Here you'll find shops, restaurants and a multiplex cinema, as well as the **Sky Promenade** (スカイ・プロメナード), a partially open walkway that descends from the building's 46th to 44th floors and gives a panoramic view of the city.

Noritake Garden

ノリタケの森, Noritake no Mori • 3-1-36 Noritake Shinmachi • Daily 10am–5pm • Free; craft centre ¥500 (plate painting ¥1600), joint entry with Toyota Commemorative Museum of Industry and Technology ¥800; Morimura-Okura Museum Canvas free • ☎ 052 561 7114 , ⓦ www.noritake.co.jp/eng/mori

Ten minutes' walk north of Nagoya Station, the grounds around the former china factory have been transformed into a very pleasant park, **Noritake Garden**, where you'll find a **craft centre**. Visitors can watch pottery being created and try their own hand at painting a plate. Elsewhere on the spacious green site, you'll find a good café, a restaurant, a gallery of modern pottery and showrooms where you can buy Noritake products.

In a 1904 vintage brick building, the **Morimura-Okura Museum Canvas** reveals the history and science involved in the ceramics technologies of the Morimura group (of which Noritake is a member).

Toyota Commemorative Museum of Industry and Technology

産業技術記念館 • 1-35 Noritake shinmachi • Tues–Sun 9.30am–5pm • ¥500 • ☎ 052 551 6115, ⓦ www.tcmit.org/english

Ten minutes' walk northwest of Noritake Garden and close to Sakō Station (on the Meitetsu Nagoya line), the **Toyota Commemorative Museum of Industry and Technology** is housed in one of the car manufacturer's old red-brick factories. There are two pavilions, one housing cars, the other textile machinery (Toyota began life as a textile producer). In the first space, rows of early twentieth-century looms make an incredible racket; in contrast, a computer-controlled air-jet loom at the end of the display purrs like a kitten. In the automobile area, it's the car-making robots, resembling giant, menacing aliens, that grab the attention.

THE TOYOTA WAY

No business is more closely associated with Nagoya than **Toyota**, whose 47-floor headquarters are based in the Midland Square Tower (see above) opposite Nagoya Station. The automobile company was started in 1937 by Kiichiro Toyoda as a spin-off from Toyoda Automatic Loom Works, founded by his father Sakichi, who invented the **wooden handloom** in 1890; the company diversified into car manufacturing in 1933. You can learn much about this huge company's history at the Toyota Commemorative Museum of Industry and Technology (see above). Devoted **auto enthusiasts** will also want to visit one of Toyota's factories to see its famous production processes in action. The one-hour tours round the Kaikan factory are free but reservations are needed – call ☎ 056 529 3355 or check ⓦ bit.ly/1cwN8p8.

5

Nagoya TV Tower

名古屋テレビ塔, Nagoya Terebi-tō · 3-6-15 Nishiki · Viewing deck daily 10am–10pm · ¥600 · ☎ 052 971 8546, ⓦ nagoya-tv-tower.co.jp

Sakae (栄) is Nagoya's central shopping and entertainment playground. Hisaya ōdōri-kōen, a swathe of parkland splitting the area, is punctuated more or less in the centre by the 180m **Nagoya TV Tower**. This handsome silver-painted structure, Japan's first TV signal transmission tower, built in 1954, has been designated a National Tangible Cultural Property. In summer, the ground-floor café and beer garden are good for a drink or snack in the sun. Also worth visiting is the UFO-shaped complex opposite, which is the bus station **Oasis 21** (ⓦ sakaepark.co.jp); its oval-shaped roof, covered with a pool of water, provides a great view of the surrounding cityscape.

Aichi Prefectural Museum of Art

愛知県美術館, Aichi-Ken Bijutsukan · 1-13-2 Higashisakura · Tues–Sun 10am–5.30pm, Fri till 7.30pm · ¥500 · ☎ 052 971 551, ⓦ www.aac.pref.aichi.jp

Immediately behind Oasis 21 is the **Aichi Arts Centre**, housing a major concert hall, theatre and the excellent **Aichi Prefectural Museum of Art**; its permanent collection provides a brisk romp through superstars of the post nineteenth-century art scene, includes pieces by Picasso, Klimt, Matisse and Modigliani, as well as Japanese painters such as Kishida Ryūsei and Takahashi Yuichi. The large galleries here also host good temporary exhibitions, and the museum is the focus of the Aichi Triennale international arts festival (ⓦ aichitriennale.jp/english), which has been going since 2010.

International Design Centre Nagoya

国際デザインセンター · 4F 3-18-1 Sakae · 11am–8pm, closed Tues · ¥300 · ☎ 052 265 2105, ⓦ idcn.jp/e

Within the glass and exposed girders of the spectacular Nadya Park Building is the engrossing **International Design Centre Nagoya**. Charting the story of commercial design, the collection includes iconic landmarks in product design, including the museum's unique collection of American Art Deco items.

Ōsu

大須

Five minutes' walk southwest of Nadya Park, and beside the Ōsu Kannon stop on the Tsurumai subway line, is **Ōsu Kannon** (大須観音), a vermilion-painted temple bustling with a steady stream of petitioners. A lively antiques and flea market is held in the temple's precincts on the 18th and 28th of the month; at other times it's still worth heading here to explore the bargain-hunters' district of **Ōsu**, where old-style arcades are lined with shops selling discount electronic goods, cheap clothes and used kimono – it's an area that's popular with Nagoya's youth, and you'll find several funky clothing and gift shops around here, including the mega-retailer *Komehyo* (ⓦ www.komehyo.co.jp), sells everything from electronics to used clothing priced by weight. It's also a good area for small, hip bars and restaurants.

Nagoya/Boston Museum of Fine Arts

名古屋ボストン美術館, Nagoya Bosutan Bijutsukan · 1-1-1 Kanayama-chō · Mon–Fri 10am–7pm, Sat & Sun till 5pm · ¥1200, after 5pm ¥1000 · ☎ 052 684 0101, ⓦ nagoya-boston.or.jp/english

This excellent branch of the respected US gallery 2km south of Ōsu, next to the busy **Kanayama** (金山) station is At any one time the **Nagoya/Boston Museum of fine Arts** will usually have on several exhibitions, and the plaza in front of the building is a favourite spot for buskers and impromptu dance performances.

FROM TOP TATEYAMA–KUROBE ALPINE ROUTE (P.379); NAGOYA CITY SCIENCE MUSEUM (P.391)>

5

WORLD COSPLAY SUMMIT

Short for "costume play", **cosplay** is when fans dress up as their favourite character from anime, manga, video games or Japanese rock (J-rock) bands. It's said the word was coined by Japanese journalist Nobuyuki Takahashi in 1984, when he wrote a feature about US fans dressing up for a masquerade (a combination of a skit show and fashion parade for people in *cosplay* costumes) at a science fiction convention in Los Angeles. Since then, the term has caught on and it's now inconceivable for an anime convention anywhere in the world not to have a substantial *cosplay* element to it. At the ultimate level there's the **World Cosplay Summit** (ⓦ www.tv-aichi.co.jp/wcs/what), held annually in early August since 2003 by the Aichi Broadcasting Company in Nagoya, with participants from up to fourteen countries. The main events are a *cosplay* parade in the Ōsu district and the championship show itself, held in the public areas of Oasis 21 (see p.394).

Atsuta-jingū

熱田神宮 • 1-1-1 Atsuta-jingū • Daily 9am–4.30pm, closed last Wed & Thurs of the month • ¥300 (including museum) • ☎ 052 671 4151
• 20min by Meijō line subway from Nagoya Station to Jingū-Nishi

The ancient shrine of **Atsuta-jingū** is 5km south of central Nagoya, amid extensive wooded grounds. Its prized possession is the *kusanagi-no-tsurugi*, or "grass-cutting sword", which is one of the three sacred treasures that symbolize the Imperial throne, along with jewels in Tokyo's Imperial Palace and the mirror at Ise-jingū (see p.521).

Look out in the shrine grounds for the giant camphor tree, said to have been planted by the Buddhist saint Kōbō Daishi (see box, p.510) 1300 years ago. There's a small **museum** also in the grounds, where you can see many other swords offered to the Shintō gods at Atsuta-jingū, including a ferocious 2m-long blade in the entrance hall.

Arimatsu

有松 • Direct trains run from Meitetsu Nagoya Station (20min; ¥310)

Dating back to 1608, **Arimatsu**, once a town on the Tokaidō highway but now a suburb 11km southeast of central Nagoya, is famous for **shibori**, an intricate and time-consuming traditional method of tie-dyeing cotton that is still practised. Kimono made using this method takes up to six months each to complete, which accounts for the high price they command. You'll find many shops selling them along the very picturesque street that lies just south of Meitetsu Arimatsu Station. If not for the utility poles and power lines, it could be a scene from a woodblock print: the old wooden houses with intricate tiled roofs provide the perfect backdrop to spring and autumn festivals (held on the third Sun in March and first Sun in Oct) when ornate floats are paraded down the street. You can find out about the tie-dyeing industry at the **Arimatsu-Namuri Shibori Kaikan** (有松鳴海絞会館; daily except Wed 9.30am–4.30pm; ¥300; ⓦ shibori-kaikan.com).

The ticket collector at Meitetsu Arimatsu can give you an English map of the area, although the houses are clearly visible from the station exit. One of the first of the old wooden houses you'll pass after you turn left into the conservation area is Kaihantei, which is also home to the delicious bakery-café *Dasenka* (ダーシェンカ蔵; 106 Oukankita; Wed–Sun 10am–6.30pm; ☎ 052 624 0050).

ARRIVAL AND DEPARTURE
NAGOYA

By plane All international and some domestic flights arrive at Central Japan International Airport (☎ 056 538 (20min; ¥700), ⓦ www.centrair.jp), commonly known as Centrair, on a man-made island in Isewan Bay, some 30km south of Nagoya. The airport has become something of a tourist attraction in its own right – locals visit just to sample its restaurants and bathe in its giant onsen with a view of the runways. The high-speed Meitetsu Airport line connects Centrair with the city (28min; ¥1200), while a taxi will set you back around ¥10,000. Nagoya Airport (☎ 056 828 5633, ⓦ www.nagoya-airport-bldg.co.jp), 12km north of the city, serves nine domestic destinations. Buses run from the airport to Midland Square opposite the train stations (20min; ¥700).

Destinations (Centrair) Akita (daily; 1hr 10min); Aomori (2 daily; 1hr 20min); Asahikawa (daily; 1hr 40min); Fukuoka (hourly; 1hr 15min); Fukushima (daily; 1hr 5min); Hakodate (daily; 1hr 25min); Kagoshima (8 daily; 1hr 20min); Kōchi (2 daily; 55min); Kumamoto (4 daily; 1hr 15min); Matsuyama (3 daily; 1hr 5min); Miyazaki (3 daily; 1hr 15min); Nagasaki (2 daily; 1hr 20min); Narita (3 daily; 1hr); Niigata (3 daily; 55min); Ōita (2 daily; 1hr 10min); Okinawa (5 daily; 2hr 10min); Sapporo (12 daily; 1hr 35min); Sendai (5 daily; 1hr 5min); Takamatsu (2 daily; 1hr 5min); Tokushima (2 daily; 1hr); Toyama (2 daily; 55min); Yonago (2 daily; 1hr 10min).

Destinations (Nagoya) Akita (2 daily; 1hr 10min); Fukuoka (5 daily; 1hr 20min); Kōchi (2 daily; 1hr); Kumamoto (2 daily; 1hr 20min); Matsuyama (2 daily; 1hr); Nagasaki (2 daily; 1hr 25min); Niigata (2 daily; 50min); Tokachi-Obihiro (daily; 1hr 40min); Yamagata (daily; 1hr).

By train The lines of three train companies converge on Nagoya, and their stations are all close to each other on the west side of the city. The main station, belonging to JR, is where you'll alight from Shinkansen and regular JR services. Immediately south of the JR station, beneath the Meitetsu department store, is the Meitetsu line terminus for trains to and from Inuyama and Gifu, while next door is the Kintetsu line terminus for services to Nara (see p.470) and the Shima Hantō region (see p.517).

Destinations Fukui (8 daily; 2hr 5min); Fukuoka (Hakata Station; every 30min; 3hr 25min); Gifu (every 30min; 30min); Hiroshima (every 30min; 2hr 20min); Inuyama (every 30min; 35min); Kanazawa (8 daily; 2hr 55min); Kii-Katsuura (4 daily; 3hr 20min); Kyoto (every 10min; 45min); Matsumoto (hourly; 2hr); Nagano (hourly; 2hr 50min); Okayama (every 30min; 2hr); Osaka (every 10min; 1hr); Takayama (9 daily; 2hr 35min); Toba (8 daily; 1hr 30min); Tokyo (every 10min; 1hr 50min); Toyama (11 daily; 3hr 40min).

By bus Long-distance buses pull in at the terminal at the north end of the JR station as well as at the Oasis 21 terminal in Sakae.

Destinations Gujō Hachiman (2 daily; 2hr); Kanazawa (8 daily; 3hr); Kyoto (every 30min; 2hr 15min); Magome (daily; 2hr); Ogimachi (daily; 4hr); Osaka (2 daily; 3hr 20min); Takayama (9 daily; 2hr 45min); Tokyo (hourly; 6hr).

By ferry Ferries arrive and depart Nagoya-kō port, 10km south of the train stations. To reach the city from the port, hop on the Meitetsu bus (35min; ¥500).

Destinations Sendai (3–4 weekly; 21hr); Tomakomai (3–4 weekly; 38hr 45min).

INFORMATION

Tourist information The clued-up Nagoya Station Tourist Information Centre (daily 9am–7pm; ☎ 052 541 4301; ⓦ ncvb.or.jp/en) is found on the central concourse of the JR station. The Nagoya International Centre (名古屋国際センター; 1-47-1 Nagono, Nakamura-ku; Tues–Sun 9am–7pm; ☎ 052 581 0100, ⓦ nic-nagoya.or.jp) is a 7min walk east of the JR station and has a library, internet access and the opportunity to meet English-speaking locals.

Listings A local English-language publication to look out for entertainment, arts and events listings is *Ran* (ⓦ ranmagazine.co), with a regularly updated website and a free bimonthly print edition.

GETTING AROUND

By subway The easiest way to get around is on the subway; the four lines you'll use the most are: Higashiyama (yellow on the subway map), Meijō (purple), Sakura-dōri (red) and Tsurumai (blue). Both the Sakura-dōri and Higashiyama lines connect with the train stations.

By bus The extensive bus system is handy: Me-guru (メーグル; ⓦ ncvb.or.jp/en/routebus) is a convenient service that runs Tues–Sun around Nagoya's central sights, which you can hop on and off all day for ¥500.

Tickets Single journeys by subway or bus start at ¥200; if you plan to travel a lot, consider buying one of the day tickets (¥740 for subway only; ¥600 for buses only; ¥850 for subway and buses). There's also the Weekend Eco Pass (¥600), a one-day pass valid on buses and subways and available on weekends, national holidays and the 8th of the month. For full details of the city's public transport systems, see ⓦ tinyurl.com/23godyf.

By car You can rent a car from Eki Rent-a-Car ☎ 052 581 0882 or Nissan Rent-a-Car ☎ 052 451 2300.

ACCOMMODATION

Nagoya has a good range of accommodation, with many places situated near the train stations. However, the city's excellent public transport system means you can stay pretty much anywhere and get around quickly; choose **Sakae** or **Kanayama** if you're after lively nightlife. If you are planning to stay at the weekend or around holiday time, make sure to book a few days in advance as the more reasonable places tend to get booked up.

Aichi-ken Senen Kaikan Youth Hostel 愛知県青年会館ユースホステル 1-18-8 Sakae, Naka-ku ☎ 052 221 6001; map p.392. In a great location, this hostel is very good value since it's more like a hotel, with big rooms and a huge top-floor communal bath. The downside is the 11pm curfew. Dorm ¥2992, Double ¥8190

5

The b Nagoya ビー 名古屋 4-15-23 Sakae, Naka-ku ☎052 241 1500, ⓦwww.heb-hotels.com/the-b-nagoya/en; map p.392. A stylish makeover pushes this business hotel into boutique territory, with modern rooms and free wi-fi and coffee in the lobby. Lower rates are available at weekends, and it's worth looking for online deals. **¥13,000**

Crown Plaza ANA クラウンプラザホテル 1-1-1 Kanayama-chō, Naka-ku ☎052 683 4111, ⓦwww .anacrowneplaza-nagoya.jp/english; map p.391. This fine hotel in groovy Kanayama is a handy base for southern Nagoya. There's a good choice of restaurants and a selection of four different pillows for your bed. **¥40,000**

Hostel Ann 名古屋ゲストハウス Hostel Ann 2-4-2 Kanayama-chō, Naka-ku ☎052 253 7710, ⓦhostelann. comPages/english.aspx; map p.391. A 10min walk northeast of Kanayama Station is this relaxed hostel you ll find in a small old house. They have a kitchen, football table in the lounge, bike rental for ¥500 per day and no curfew. Dorm **¥2500**, double **¥7000**

Nagoya Marriott Associa Hotel 名古屋マリオットアソシアホテル 1-1-4 Meieki, Nakamura-ku ☎052 584 1113, ⓦassocia.com/nma; map p.392. These luxurious lodgings, high above the mammoth station and twin towers complex, offer comfortable rooms with a chintzy old European look and wonderful views. There's an excellent range of restaurants and a fitness club with a 20m pool. **¥48,000**

Ryokan Meiryū 旅館名龍 2-4-21 Kamimaezu, Naka-ku ☎052 331 8686, ⓦwww.japan-net .ne.jp/~meiryu; map p.391. Friendly English-speaking owners run this ryokan. The tatami rooms have a/c and TV, bathrooms are communal and there's a little café for breakfast and dinner. Take exit three at Kamimaezu subway station and walk a couple of minutes east. **¥10,500**

Sauna & Capsule Fuji Sakae サウナ&カプセル フジ栄 3-22-31 Sakae, Naka-Ku ☎052 962 5711; map p.392. Nagoya's largest capsule hotel (men only) is a snazzy affair, with its own restaurant, comfortable lounge area, sauna and a huge communal bathing area. If you just want to use the sauna and bath, it's ¥1000 for 15min. Rates rise by ¥500 on Fri and Sat. **¥3000**

Tōyōko Inn 東横 INN Honkan: 3-16-1 Meieki, Nakamura-ku ☎052 571 1045; Shinkan: 3-9-16 Meieki, Nakamura-ku ☎052 562 1045, ⓦtoyoko-inn.com; map p.392. Two branches of this reliable business chain hotel face off against each other, about a 5min walk northeast of the station. The smaller, newer Honkan building is a bit cheaper than the larger Shinkan. Check the website for deals. **¥6980**

Trusty Nagoya Sakae ホテルトラスティ名古屋栄 3-15-21 Sakae, Naka-ku ☎052 968 5111, ⓦtrusty.jp; map p.392. There's an old European feel to this pleasant, small, mid-range hotel in the heart of the city. Nice touches include William Morris-inspired duvets and handsome inlaid wood furniture and fixtures. **¥13,500**

EATING AND DRINKING

Nagoya has many food **specialities**, including the flat, floury noodles *kishimen*, and the succulent chicken dishes made from *Nagoya kochin* birds. Foodies should consult the schedule of the excellent local **farmers' market** (ⓦwww.marche-japon .org/area/2301), held most weekends in a different part of the city and attracting vendors from the surrounding region. Sakae is packed with lively **restaurants**, and Ōsu is a calmer place to dine.

Art Café Sakae アートカフェ栄 1-10-18 Higashi Sakura, Higashi-ku ☎052 971 0456; map p.392. Tucked away in the corner of a car park and behind a grove of bamboo is this old-world gallery and café where you can admire the traditional-themed art of Morimura-san, including a lovely ceiling painting. Wed–Sun 10am–5pm.

★**Atsuta Hōraiken** あつた蓬莱軒 503 Gōdo, Atsuta-ku ☎052 671 8686; map p.391. *Hitsumabushi* is a famous Nagoya *unagi* (eel) dish, and this is the best place to eat it. There's another branch next to the southern entrance of Atsuta-jingū, but it's worth heading to this main restaurant, set in a traditional mansion with tatami rooms. A set meal costs ¥2520: you can eat the eel dish plain on top of rice; with dried seaweed, spring onion and *wasabi*; or with added soup. Tues–Sun 11.30am–2pm & 4.30–8.30pm.

Eric Life エリック-ライフ 2-11-8 Ōsu, Naka-ku ☎052 222 1555; map p.392. There's a mid-century retro look at this hipsters' café behind Ōsu Kannon, where you can lounge on green velvet chairs enjoying *yōshoku*

(Western-style) dishes such as *omu-raisu* (rice omelette) or nursing a cappuccino. Prices for drinks start at ¥350 and main dishes from ¥750. Noon–midnight, closed Wed.

★**Kaguraya Sasuke** 神楽家左助 1-10-6 Higashi Sakura, Higashi-ku ☎052 971 6203; map p.392. It feels incredible to find this charming old building overlooking lovely gardens in the heart of modern Nagoya – even better is that they serve delicious, beautifully presented traditional food. Enjoy a course lunch from ¥3000 and dinner from ¥5000. Daily 11.30am–2pm & 5–10pm.

Octo 東桜 1-9-22 Higashi Sakura, Higashi-ku ☎052 971 1088; map p.392. A modern restaurant with Art Nouveau design touches, run by the same owners as *Tiger Café* (see below). Dishes include French and European-inspired cuisine such as duck confit or squid ink risotto. Main courses range from ¥1000 to ¥2000. Daily 11am–3am Sun till midnight.

Ōshō 王将 3-91-1 Sakae, Naka-ku; map p.392. This cheap and cheerful Chinese ramen joint in the heart of

Sakae is nearly always full, but you don't normally have to queue for too long and it's worth the wait. It has an English menu and pictures of set meals, which rarely cost over ¥1000. Daily 11am–midnight Sun till 10.30pm.

Sekai-no-Yamachan 世界の山ちゃん 2-4-16 Kanayama-chō, Naka-ku ☎052 259 2782 ⓦwww. yamachan.co.jp; map p.391. This fun *izakaya* serves addictively spicy chicken wings and other cheap, tasty dishes. Popularly known as *Yamachan*, it's a local phenomenon, with scores of branches across the city and more around Japan. Set meals start from ¥2300. Daily 5–11.30pm Sun till 10.30pm.

Sozansō 蘇山荘 1001 Tokugawa-chō, Higashi-ku ☎052 932 7887; map p.391. Attached to a fancy French restaurant overlooking the beautiful Tokugawa Gardens, this chic café-bar in a reconstructed VIP guesthouse dating from 1937 is more affordable than its neighbour. During the day, sip premium teas or coffee and nibble on *temmusu*, Nagoya's own style of *onigiri* rice balls embedded with shrimp tempura. In the evening, drop by to drink in sophisticated surroundings. Expect to pay around ¥3000 a head for dinner. Daily: café-bar noon–5pm & 7pm–

midnight; restaurant 11am–2pm & 5–10pm.

Tiger Café タイガーカフェ 1-8-26 Nishiki, Naka-ku ☎052 220 0031 ⓦtiger-cafe-nagoya.com; map p.392. This 1930s-style French café-bistro is good for a sandwich (¥800), an espresso (¥500) or a leisurely after-dinner *digestif*. There's another similar café, *Octo*, run by the same owners (see above). Daily 11am–3am Sun till, midnight.

Torisei 鳥勢 3-19-24 Sakae, Naka-ku ☎052 951 7337, ⓦtorisei.jp; map p.392. You'll need to book ahead, especially at weekends, to enjoy the excellent *yakitori* and other chicken dishes at this restaurant, which has counter seating downstairs and tatami rooms upstairs. Lunch specials and *yakitori* meals are ¥880. Mon–Sat 11.30am–1.30pm & 5–10.30pm.

Yamamoto-ya Honten 山本屋本店 B1, Horiuchi Building, Meieki ☎052 565 0278; map p.392. The chief outlet of this noodle café chain is on Sakura-dōri, a few minutes' walk from the JR station. The specialties are *miso nikomi* (thick udon noodles in a bean paste), locally reared *Nagoya kochin* (chicken) and Berkshire pork. Bet on around ¥2000 per head. Daily 11am–7.30pm.

NIGHTLIFE AND ENTERTAINMENT

Sakae is the place to go for busy, upbeat bars, clubs and karaoke boxes, or head to Ōsu for a quieter, hipper evening out. Drinking and dining options are plentiful around Nagoya Station, south in Kanayama or east in Imaike and Ikeshita, two districts with relaxed **bars** and **clubs**. Traditional **performing arts** are well supported in Nagoya, with a splendid nō theatre opposite the castle and the grand kabuki theatre, Misono-za, in the downtown area of Fushimi. There are also plenty of **cinemas**, including a modern multiplex in Midland Square. You could also try your hand at a game of **pachinko** – Nagoya is where the noisy pinball pastime really took off in the 1950s. Nagoya also has an enthusiastically supported **live music** scene.

Club Mago マーゴ 2-1-9 Shin-Sakae, Naka-ku ☎052 243 1818, ⓦclub-mago.co.jp; map p.391. Big-name DJs front up at this friendly and nicely decorated club, which also hosts a recovery party every Sun from 5am. The same building is home to the live house venues *Diamond Hall* and *Apollo Theatre* (ⓦdiamond-apollo.sf.ag.co.jp). Opening hours vary, check site for details; club nights generally 10pm–late.

Elephant's Nest エレファントネスト 1-4-3 Sakae, Naka-ku ☎052 232 4360, ⓦe-nest.jp; map p.392. This British pub next to the *Hilton* hotel is a good bet if you want *gaijin* company. There's free darts, English football on the telly, draught Guinness and staple British pub-grub dishes. Happy hour runs from 5.30–8pm with ¥100 knocked off beers on weekdays and any whiskey for ¥500 on Sun. Daily 5.30pm–1am Fri & Sat till 2am.

Huck Finn ハックフィン 5-19-7 Imaike ☎052 733 8347, ⓦhuckfinn.co.jp; map p.391. A long-running punky club in the basement of the Ishii building, hosting regular live music nights of local and international bands. The entrance charge is usually between ¥1000 and ¥2000 and is cheaper if you buy in advance; drinks are ¥500. Opening hours vary (check website for schedule.

iD Café iDカフェ 3-1-15 Sakae, Naka-ku ☎052 251 0382, ⓦidcafe.info; map p.392. Hip-hop, reggae and r'n'b can all be heard at this long-running bastion of the Nagoya club scene. Entrance is ¥2000 including four drinks. Thurs–Sun 9pm–4am.

Keg Nagoya ケグナゴヤ 1-10-13 Higashi Sakura, Higashi-ku ☎052 971 8211; map p.392. Sample a great range of Japanese craft beers on tap at this appealing real-ale bar. On the food menu they do special types of curry rice and a range of pizzas. Daily 11.30am–1.30pm & 5–11pm Sun till 10pm.

Metro メトロ Lover:z (club), 1-2-8 Shin-ei, Nakaku ☎090 4194 9722, ⓦthenagoyametroclub.com; map p.392. The fabulous Madame Matty hosts this long-running *gaijin*-friendly gay and lesbian club event, a guaranteed fun time for all, held monthly at *Lover:z club*, in the basement next to *Tōyōko Inn*. Entry is ¥2500 including two drinks. Second Sat of the month 10pm–6am.

Plastic Factory プラスチックファクトリー 32-13 Kanda-chō, Chikusa-ku ☎090 9894 9242, ⓦplasticfactory.jp; map p.391. Hosting an eclectic range of events in – guess what? – an old plastic factory, three blocks north of Imaike

5

Station. Expect anything from progressive techno to live rock. Fri–Sun normally 8pm–2am (check website for schedule).

Red Rock レッドロック 2F Aster Plaza Building, 4-14-6 Sakae, Naka-ku ☎ 052 262 7893, ⓦ theredrock.jp; map p.392. There's an Aussie theme to this spacious, centrally located bar serving beers such as Coopers, VB and Cascade, as well as traditional pub grub like shepherd's pie and fish and chips. Mon–Thurs 5.30pm–2am, Fri & Sat 5.30pm–6am, Sun 11.30am–2am.

Smash Head スマッシュヘッド 2 -21-90 Ōsu ☎ 052 201 2790, ⓦ smashhead.com; map p.392. With "Zen and the Art of Maintenance" emblazoned above the entrance, this bar-cum-motorbike repair shop is one chilled spot, with exposed brick walls, retro furniture an extensive library of motorcycling, art and counterculture books. There's Guinness and Hoegarden on tap and a good selection of bottled Belgium beers and spirits to choose from. Locals swear by the tasty handmade burgers, and daily lunch specials cost ¥850. Noon–midnight, closed Tues.

DIRECTORY

Banks and exchange Several major bank branches can be found around the stations, along Sakura-dōri and Nishiki-dōri in Sakae. These include Citibank, whose ATMs accept some foreign-issued cards.

Consulates Australia, 13F, Amnat Building, 1-3-3 Sakae, Naka-ku ☎ 052 211 0630; Canada, 6F, Nakatō Marunouchi Building, 3-17-6 Marunouchi ☎ 052 972 0450; USA, 6F, International Centre Building, 1-47-1 Nagono, Nakamura-ku ☎ 052 581 4501.

Emergencies The Prefectural Police Office is at 2-1-1 Sannomaru (☎ 052 951 1611). In an absolute emergency, contact the International Centre (☎ 052 581 0100). For other emergency numbers, see p.66.

Hospital The main hospital is the Nagoya Medical Centre, 4-1-1 Sannomaru, Naku-ku (☎ 052 951 1111), but it's best to first call the International Centre (☎ 052 581 0100) and they'll tell you the most appropriate place to go.

Internet access The Nagoya International Centre (see above) has internet terminals. Each of the four Kinkos – at Chiyogaoka, Ikeshita, Sakae and Meikei Minami – offers internet access.

Post office There's a post office (Mon–Fri 9am–7pm, Sat 9am–5pm, Sun 9am–12.30pm) at 1-1-1 Meieki, a minute's walk north of the JR station, as well as one in the station itself.

Inuyama

犬山

The appealing castle town of **INUYAMA**, 25km north of Nagoya, lies beside the Kiso-gawa. From May to October the river is the stage for the centuries-old practice of *ukai* (see box, p.402), to which the castle's floodlit exterior provides a dramatic backdrop. Other highlights of this picturesque area are the **Meiji Mura** architectural museum which showcases buildings designed by Frank Lloyd Wright and the privately owned castle, **Inuyama-jō**.

Inuyama Artefacts Museum

犬山市文化史料館, Inuyama-Shi Bunka Shiryōkan • 8 Kitakoken • Daily 9am–5pm; karuki-making demos Fri & Sat throughout the day • ¥100 • ☎ 056 862 4802

Some ten minutes walk west of Inuyama Station is an area dotted with old wooden houses and craft galleries, culminating in the small **Inuyama Artefacts Museum**. Here you can see two of the thirteen towering, ornate floats (*yatai*) that are paraded around Inuyama during the major festival on the first weekend of April. Two days a week, you can also see a craftsman demonstrating the art of making *karakuri*, the mechanical wooden puppets that perform on the *yatai*. The museum is just in front of **Haritsuna-jinja**, the shrine at which the colourful festival takes place.

Inuyama-jō

犬山城 • 65-2 Kitakoken • Daily 9am–4.30pm • ¥500, joint ticket with Uraku-en ¥1200 • ☎ 056 861 1711

On the hill behind the **Artefacts Museum** is the entrance of the only privately owned castle in Japan, **Inuyama-jō**. This toy-like fortress was built in 1537, making it the oldest in Japan (although parts have been extensively renovated), and it has belonged to the Naruse family since 1618. Inside, the donjon is nothing special, but there's a pretty view of the river and surrounding countryside from the top, where you can appreciate the defensive role that this white castle played.

Uraku-en

有楽苑 • 1 Gomonsaki • Daily 9am–5pm, mid-July to Aug till 6pm, Dec–Feb till 4pm • ¥1000, combined garden & tea ¥1300, tea only ¥500; joint ticket with Inuyama-jō ¥1200 • ☎ 056 861 4608

A five-minute walk east of Inuyama-jō, within the grounds of the luxury *Meitetsu Inuyama Hotel* (名鉄犬山ホテル), is the serene garden of **Uraku-en**. The mossy lawns and stone pathways act as a verdant frame for the subdued **Jo-an**, a traditional teahouse. Originally built in Kyoto by Oda Uraku, the younger brother of the warlord Oda Nobunaga, the yellow-walled teahouse has floor space for just over three tatami mats, though it can only be viewed from the outside. Tea is served in one of the garden's larger modern teahouses.

Meiji Mura

明治村 • 1 Uchiyama • Daily 9.30am–5pm, Nov–Feb till 4pm • ¥1600, extra for trains & buses • ☎ 056 867 0314, ⓦ meijimura.com/english • Regular buses leave from the east side of Inuyama Station (20min; ¥410)

One of Japan's best open-air architectural museums, **Meiji Mura**, is 7km east of Inuyama. Dotted around a huge park are 67 structures, including churches, banks, a kabuki theatre, a lighthouse and a telephone exchange (from Sapporo). All the structures date from around the Meiji era (see p.799) when Western influences were flooding into Japan, a development that resulted in some unique hybrid architecture. A highlight is the front of the original **Imperial Hotel**, designed by Frank Lloyd Wright (see box below).

Allow at least half a day to see the park fully. If you don't fancy walking, take the electric bus that beetles from one end of the park to the other, or you could hop on an old Kyoto tram and steam locomotive, though these only go part of the way. There are several places to snack or eat lunch within the park, including inside the *Imperial Hotel* itself.

ARRIVAL AND INFORMATION   INUYAMA

By train Inuyama is roughly 30min from both Nagoya (¥540) and Gifu (¥440) on the Meitetsu railway.
Tourist information There's a tourist information booth

(daily 9am–5pm; ☎ 056 861 6000, ⓦ ml.inuyama.gr.jp/en) beside the central exit of Inuyama Station.

ACCOMMODATION AND EATING

Inuyama International Youth Hostel 犬山国際ユー スホステル 152-1 Himuro, Tsugao ☎ 056 861 1111, ⓦ inuyama-hostel.com/en. This is a modern hostel that's

like a hotel as it features private rooms – either Western- or Japanese-style. It also has a good restaurant, with dinner available from ¥1500. It is, however, a couple of kilometres

---

WRIGHT IN JAPAN

Frank Lloyd Wright's fame in Japan has much to do with the fact that his grand **Imperial Hotel** in Tokyo (part of which now stands in Meiji Mura) survived the Great Kantō Earthquake, which hit Tokyo the day after the hotel opened in 1923. The US-born architect first visited Japan in 1905 and was so enamoured of the country that he pursued and eventually received the commission to build the hotel. He moved to the city to live and work on this and thirteen other projects between 1917 and 1923. Of these, only seven were built, and today just five survive in total or partially: the front lobby of the *Imperial Hotel* in **Meiji Mura** (see above); the school **Jiyū Gakuen Myonichikan** (ⓦ jiyu.jp) and a portion of the **Aisaku Hayashi House**, both in Tokyo; JR Nikkō Station (see p.170); and Tazaemon Yamamura House (ⓦ www.yodoko .co.jp/geminkan) in Ashiya, near Kōbe. For more information see ⓦ wrightinjapan.org.

5

from town; take the monorail from Inuyama-Yūen Station to the Monkey Park (¥150) and walk north for 10min past the park and up the hill on your left. **¥6600**
Narita なり田 395 Higashikoken ☏056 865 2447, ⓦf-narita.com. Set in a former kimono-weaving factory and mansion with lovely traditional gardens, this upmarket French restaurant offers a five-course set lunch for ¥2940. It's a 5min walk north of Inuyama station. Daily 11am–9pm (closed first Mon of the month).

Gifu

岐阜

On the other side of the Kiso-gawa from Inuyama is Gifu-ken, whose capital, **GIFU**, lies 20km further west. Like Inuyama, Gifu offers *ukai* on a meandering river overlooked by a hilltop castle (see box below), but is otherwise a bigger and more modern city, rebuilt after the double whammy of an earthquake in 1891 and blanket bombings during World War II. The boat office is in the picturesque riverside area of old wooden houses known as **Kawaramachi** (川原町); you'll find some good places to eat, interesting small galleries and craft shops here.

Gifu is also renowned for its high-quality **paper crafts**, including umbrellas, lanterns, fans and the painted rice-paper fish you see flying off poles like flags. The tourist

---

UKAI

Inuyama and Gifu are two of the main locations for **ukai**, or night-time fishing with **cormorants**, a skill developed back in the seventh century; other *ukai* spots include Kyoto, Iwakuni and Ōzu in Shikoku. The specially trained, slender-necked birds are used to catch *ayu*, a sweet fresh-water fish, which is in season between May and September. Traditionally dressed fishermen handle up to twelve cormorants on long leashes, which are attached at the birds' throats with a ring to prevent them from swallowing the fish. The birds dive into the water, hunting the *ayu*, which are attracted to the light of the fire blazing in the metal braziers hanging from the bows of the narrow fishing boats.

The fast-moving show usually only lasts around thirty minutes, but an *ukai* jaunt is not just about fishing. Around two hours before the start of the fishing, the audience boards long, canopied boats, decorated with paper lanterns, which sail upriver and then moor to allow a pre-show picnic. Unless you pay extra you'll have to bring your own food and drink, but sometimes a boat will drift by selling beer, snacks and fireworks – another essential *ukai* component. Although you can watch the show for free from the riverbank, if you do so you won't experience the thrill of racing alongside the **fishing boats**, the birds splashing furiously in the reflected light of the pine wood burning in the brazier hanging from the boats' prows.

If you are not around in season to see the fishing in action, the brand-spanking-new **Nagara River Ukai Museum** in Gifu (長良川うかいミュージアム; 51-2 Choryo; May–Oct daily 9am–6.30pm; mid-Oct to April 9am–4.30pm, closed Tues; ¥500; ☏058 210 1555, ⓦukaimuseum.jp) can teach you all about the art of *ukai* through its practical demonstrations and high-tech displays.

WATCHING UKAI IN INUYAMA

Boats sail from the dock beside the Inuyama-bashi bridge, five minutes' walk north of Inuyama Yūen Station. From May to August, the boats depart at 6pm and the fishing show begins at 7.45pm, while in September and October the start time is 5.30pm, with the *ukai* kicking off at 7.15pm. In May, June, September and October the cost is ¥2500, rising to ¥2800 during the peak months of July and August, when it's best to make a reservation (☏056 861 0057). There's no *ukai* on August 10 when Inuyama stages its riverside fireworks display.

WATCHING UKAI IN GIFU

Displays run each year from May 11 to October 15 on the Nagara-gawa (長良川), around 2km north of the town's two train stations. To book a seat on a boat, go to the boat office (☏058 262 0104; ¥3000–3300) beside the Nagara-bashi, reached on buses from stands 11 and 12 (¥200) outside the JR station – take care not to get on an express (快速) bus, though.

information office has a map of workshops which sell these products, and you can watch craftsmen at work.

Gifu-jō

岐阜城 • 1近 Tenshukaku • **Castle** Daily: mid-March to mid-May 9.30am–5.30pm; mid-May to mid-Oct 8.30am–5.30pm; mid-Oct to mid-March 9.30am–4.30pm • ¥200 • **Ropeway** Closes 30min after castle • ¥600 one-way, ¥1050 return • ☎ 058 263 4853, ⓦ www.city.gifu .lg.jp • The park from which you can walk or cable-car it up to the castle is reached by buses from platform 11 or 12 from JR Gifu Station or from platform 4 from Meitetsu Gifu Station

Perched 329m up on Mount Kinka-zan, the small white castle of **Gifu-jō** is nothing special in itself but does command a panoramic view of the city. A ropeway (cable-car) saves you having to slog up the densely forested hill from the base of **Gifu-kōen** (岐阜公園), a lovely city park, otherwise it takes around an hour to hike.

Shōhō-ji

正法寺 • 8 Daibutsu-chō • Daily 9am–5pm • ¥200 • ☎ 058 264 2760

Shōhō-ji, a weatherworn temple opposite the verdant Gifu-kōen, houses an imposing 13.7m-tall sculpture of Buddha, the Gifu Great Buddha (岐阜大仏), made of lacquered bamboo and papier mâchié, and one of the three biggest Buddhas in Japan. The statue was built in the nineteenth century to remember those who perished in earthquakes and epidemics, and took 38 years to complete.

ARRIVAL AND INFORMATION | GIFU

By train Gifu's two train stations – JR and Meitetsu – are 5min from one another at the south end of the city's commercial district.

Tourist information The tourist information office (daily 9am–7pm, Dec–Feb till 6pm; ☎ 058 262 4415, ⓦ gifucvb .or.jp) is inside JR Gifu Station.

ACCOMMODATION

Jūhachirō 十八楼 10 Minato-machi ☎ 058 265 1551. A very pleasant large ryokan overlooking the Nagara-gawa river, *Jūhachirō* famously hosted the poet Bashō. The luxurious indoor and outdoor onsen baths have great panoramic views. Rates include two meals. **¥34,000**

Weekly Sho Gifu Daiichi Hotel ウィークリー翔岐阜第一 ホテル 2-5 Fukuzumi-chō ☎ 058 251 2111, ⓦ weekly-sho .jp. There's nothing very special about this basic hotel, two blocks northwest of the station, but it is really good value. There are some twin rooms but, geared towards business travellers, most of the rooms are singles; discounts are available for bookings of over seven days. Rates include breakfast. Single **¥1900**

EATING AND DRINKING

There are plenty of restaurants and bars on the roads heading north from the JR station; check out the lively *yakitori* stands around the bar *Bier Hall*. Other good places to eat can be found in Kawaramachi.

Bunkaya 文化屋 35 Motohamachō ☎ 058 212 0132. Facing on to the Nagara-gawa, this place is particularly lovely, with a traditional wooden interior, panoramic windows and innovative menu. Bookings are essential for its course meal (¥2940). Daily 11.30am–3pm & 5.30–10pm.

Kawaramachi Izumiya 泉屋 20 Motohamachō ☎ 058 263 6788. Specializes in *ayu*, serving the sweet river fish in a range of dishes, especially grilled with salt, on skewers. Main dishes are around ¥1000. 11.30am–2pm & 5–7.30pm, closed Wed.

Kawaramachiya 川原町屋 28 Tamachō ☎ 058 266 5144. This pleasant café/gallery, serving bowls of udon noodles for around ¥1000, is easily spotted by the old-fashioned red post box outside. Daily 10am–6pm.

Natural Café & Gallery ナチュラルカフェアンドギャラリー 一蔵) 2-14 Honmachi ☎ 058 269 5788, ⓦ natural-group .com. This convivial café and gallery based in an old storehouse is close to the Hon-machi San-chōme bus stop. There's a bohemium atmosphere with live regular live jazz in the evenings, a menu featuring meze-style sharing plates and a good selection of cocktails and wine. Mains are around ¥800, sharing plates from ¥1200. Daily 11am–midnight, closed first & third Tues of the month.

Tamaiya-honpo 玉井屋本舗 42 Minatomachi ☎ 058 262 6893, ⓦ www.tamaiya-honpo.com. Relax over a *matcha* and sweet cake at this venerable traditional confectionery shop opposite the ryokan *Jūhachirō* in Kawaramachi. 8am–8pm, closed Wed.

5

Gujō Hachiman

郡上八幡

It is a town of low, dark, wood-and-plaster buildings, paved lanes, and running water. The windows of the buildings are narrow and slatted. The lanes, too, are narrow, steeply walled, and end in dimly lanterned eating places or in small stone bridges that arch over splashing streams. It was like an Edo-era stage set.

Alan Booth, *Looking for the Lost*, 1995

Booth's romantic description captures **GUJŌ HACHIMAN**'s bygone-days atmosphere and mountain-bound location perfectly. Tucked in a valley on an old trade route that once led to the Sea of Japan, the town lies around 55km north of Gifu. Two pristine rivers, the Yoshida and Nagara, running through its centre, lend it great appeal; the town's close link to water is represented by the **Fountain of Youth** (宗祇水), the town's natural spring, dubbed the Sōgi-sui.

It's worth visiting year-round, but the best time is during the **Gujō Odori** (see box below), one of Japan's top three dance festivals. In summer, you might be tempted to take a swim in the sparkling river. **Anglers** with long poles and tall straw hats can be seen along both of the town's rivers trying their luck for the *ayu* (sweet fish) and trout for which the region is famous.

Hakurankan

博覧館 • 50 Tonomachi • Daily 9.30am–5pm; during Gujō Odori 9am–6pm • ¥500 • ☎ 057 565 3215, ⓦ gujohachiman.com

The excellent **Hakurankan** museum, on the northern side of the Yoshida River, is a ten-minute stroll from the tourist office. The exhibitions are split into four sections, detailing the town's history; arts and crafts; connection with water; folk dancing, and the Gujō Odori festival.

Gujō-Hachiman-jō

郡上八幡城 • Yanagimachi • Daily: March–May 9am–5pm; June–Aug 8am–6pm; Nov–Feb 9am–4.30pm • ¥300 • ☎ 0575 67 1819, ⓦ gujohachiman.com/siro

The photogenic replica of the old castle, **Gujō-Hachiman-jō**, was built in 1934 on the stone foundations of the less elaborate original structure. From its ramparts you'll see that the town resembles the shape of a fish, the elegant concrete span of the motorway accenting the tail.

GUJŌ ODORI

Bon-odori festivals are common across Japan, but nowhere is the dance so firmly rooted in the life of the community as at Gujō Hachiman, where the **Gujō Odori** has been going since the 1590s. Nearly every night from mid-July to early September, from about 8pm to 10.30pm (the tourist information centre can tell you exactly when and where), the locals don their *yukata* and *geta* and dance in the streets.

People dance in circles around a tall wood-and-bamboo structure from which a singer, drummers, flute player and a chorus call the tune. There are ten kinds of **dances** and the singer will announce them before each one commences. Watch the hand and feet movements of those in the inner circle, as these are the people who learned these steps as children – and try to follow along.

During the **Obon holiday** in mid-August, dancing goes on all night, and thousands crowd into the town. Don't worry if you can't find a bed, since there's always a place for revellers to rest during the festivities – check with the tourist office.

ARRIVAL, TOURS AND INFORMATION

By train By train, take the JR line to Mino-Ōta then transfer to the private Nagaragawa line (1hr 20min; one-way ¥1320, day return ¥2000).

By bus Gujō Hachiman has direct bus connections with Nagoya (2hr) and Gifu (1hr 10min; ¥1480). Buses also stop at the highway intersection for Gifu Hachiman, around 30min west of the town centre, for services to and from Takayama 1hr 15min; ¥1600), Kyoto (2hr 30min; ¥3300) and Osaka 3hr 30min; ¥4450).

Tourist information The tourist information office (daily 8.30am–5.15pm; ☎ 057 567 0002, ⓦ gujohachiman.com/kanko) is set in a handsome Western-style building in the town centre, about 1km north of the train station. They sell a ¥1500 ticket providing access to nine places of interest around town.

Tours Rafting trips are available year-round downriver at Minami with Outdoor Support Systems (☎ 058 248 4711).

ACCOMMODATION

Gujō-Tōsen-ji Youth Hostel 郡上洞泉寺ユースホステル 417 Ozaki-machi ☎ 057 567 0290. In the grounds of the Tosen-ji temple along the river east of the station, this is the best budget accommodation option in Gujō Hachiman, with clean but basic rooms and amenities. Dorm **¥3300**

Nakashimaya 中嶋屋 940 Shinmachi ☎ 057 565 2191, ⓦ nakashimaya.net/English1.html. This is a good

traditional ryokan right on Shinmachi, the main shopping street where all-night Obon dancing takes place. The rooms are meticulously maintained and dinner is available for ¥1550. **¥11,600**

Hotel Sekisuien ホテル積翠園 511-2 Hachiman ☎ 057 565 3101. Halfway uphill to the castle, this modern hotel offers large, bright tatami rooms, excellent meals and a big public bath. Rates include two meals. **¥24,000**

EATING

One curiosity about Gujō Hachiman is that around eighty percent of the plastic food samples displayed in restaurant windows in Japan are made here. For somewhere to eat real food, try the following:

Hanamura 花むら Shinmachi ☎ 057 567 0056. Around the corner from *Nakashimaya* is this rustic, friendly place where the set dinner of local dishes (*oraikase*) is a great deal at ¥2500. Daily 11.30am–1.30pm & 5–10.30pm.

Ristorante Suzume no Iori 雀の庵 Takiwachō ☎ 057 567 2355. An upmarket option, in an elegant house behind the tourist office, this restaurant offers set menus of Italian dishes, and the menu is especially big on seafood. Prices start at ¥2800 for lunch and ¥4500 for dinner. 11.30am–2pm & 5–9pm, closed Tues.

Soba-no-Hirajin そば乃平甚 Honmachi ☎ 057 565 2004. Expect to have to wait for a table at this popular noodle restaurant on the north side of the Yoshida River, close to the Fountain of Youth. A bowl of noodles costs around ¥700. Daily 11.30am–5pm.

Uotora 魚寅 Shinmachi ☎ 057 565 3195. Located on the main shopping street, this is where to come for tasty fish and *unagi* (eel) dishes: a set meal is around ¥2000. 11am–2.30pm & 5–8pm, closed Wed.

Kyoto and Nara

KINKAKU-JI, KYOTO

Kyoto and Nara

The former imperial capitals of Kyoto and Nara are home to a sublime collection of temples, palaces, shrines and gardens. Both cities are deeply revered by the Japanese for their imperial history, their highly developed traditional arts and centuries-old festivals. Yet each has its own distinct personality. Kyoto is notoriously exclusive, whereas Nara has a relaxed dignity; as a result, the two cities complement each other well, with Nara displaying the foundations of traditional Japanese culture, which reached its zenith in Kyoto.

Until Emporer Meji decamped for the bright lights of Tokyo in 1868, **Kyoto** was Japan's imperial capital, and despite modern trappings the city still represents a more traditional version of the country than the current capital. Kyoto maintains its reputation for cultural finesse – with its cuisine and traditional crafts – while fusing tradition with contemporary innovation. It's a delight to explore the exquisite **temples** and **gardens**, as well as designer shops and stylish cafés. It's also rewarding to spend at least a day in the surrounding districts; meander through rice fields in **Ohara**, tea fields in **Uji** or view the city from atop **Hiei-zan**, where the temples of Enryaku-ji are nestled in a cedar forest.

Before Kyoto even existed, the monks of **Nara** were busily erecting their great Buddhist monuments under the patronage of an earlier group of princes and nobles. In 2010, this relaxed, appealing town celebrated the thirteen-hundredth anniversary of **Heijō-kyō**, the site close to the centre of modern-day Nara city, where Japan's first permanent capital was founded in the early eighth century. A surprising number of buildings survive – notably the great **Tōdai-ji** with its colossal bronze Buddha – but Nara's real glory lies in its wealth of statues. Nowhere is this more evident than at the nearby temple complex of **Hōryū-ji**, a treasure-trove of early Japanese art. Kyoto and Nara house the bulk of Japan's sixteen UNESCO World Heritage Sites – a truly impressive collection that make a visit to both cities a valuable experience.

Kyoto

京都

The capital of Japan for more than a thousand years, **KYOTO** is endowed with an almost overwhelming legacy of ancient Buddhist temples, majestic palaces and

NISHIKI-KŌJI STREET MARKET

Highlights

❶ Kyoto International Manga Museum
Kyoto gets into "Cool Japan" with the first
museum in the world devoted to Japanese
comics. **See p.418**

❷ Kinkaku-ji Kyoto's most elaborate Zen temple,
the Golden Pavilion, was built as a retirement
home for a fourteenth-century shogun and is a
beautiful sight in any season. **See p.434**

❸ Kyō-ryōri Experience the city's sophisticated
food culture by touring "Kyoto's kitchen" – as
Nishiki market is known – and then dining on the
ultimate *kaiseki* multicourse banquet. **See p.445**

❹ Green tea Visit the tea fields of Uji and
harvest your own green tea. Later enjoy the
sophisticated *matcha* salons of Kyoto and a
traditional tea ceremony. **See p.448 & p.460**

❺ Ine fishing village Enjoy superb water views
and fresh seafood in this picturesque fishing
village on the northern coast of Kyoto
prefecture. **See p.467**

❻ Tōdai-ji In the ancient capital city of Nara, the
world's largest wooden building houses a
monumental bronze Buddha. **See p.474**

HIGHLIGHTS ARE MARKED ON THE MAP ON P.410 & PP.412–413

gardens of every size and description, not to mention some of the country's most important works of art, its richest culture and most refined cuisine. For many people the very name Kyoto conjures up the classic image of Japan: streets of traditional wooden houses, the click-clack of *geta* (traditional wooden sandals) on the paving stones, geisha passing in a flourish of brightly coloured silks, and temple pagodas surrounded by cherry blossom trees.

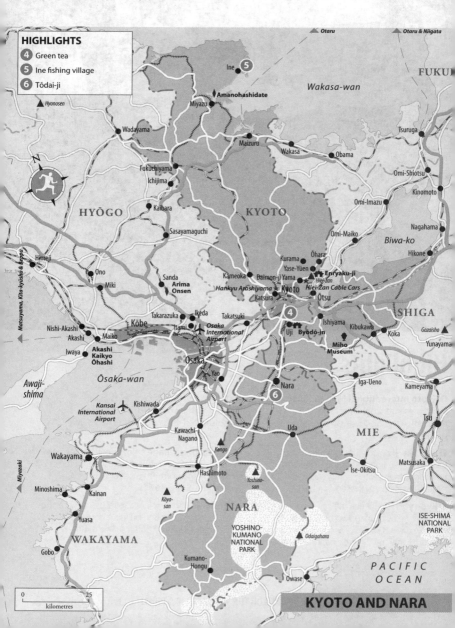

HIGHLIGHTS

4 Green tea
5 Ine fishing village
6 Tōdai-ji

KYOTO AND NARA

While you can still find all these things, and much more, first impressions of Kyoto can be disappointing. Decades of haphazard urban development and a conspicuous industrial sector have affected the city, eroding the distinctive characteristics of the townscape. However current regulations limiting the height of new buildings and banning rooftop advertising indicate that more serious thought is being given to preserving Kyoto's visual environment.

The vast amount of culture and history in Kyoto is mind-boggling, yet it's possible to get a good feel for the city with in a couple of days. Top priority should go to the eastern, Higashiyama, district, where the walk north from famous **Kiyomizu-dera** to **Ginkaku-ji** takes in a whole raft of fascinating temples, gardens and museums. It's also worth heading for the northwestern hills to contemplate the superb Zen gardens of **Daitoku-ji** and **Ryōan-ji**, before taking in the wildly extravagant Golden Pavilion, **Kinkaku-ji**. The highlight of the central sights is **Nijō-jō**, a lavishly decorated seventeenth-century palace, while nearby **Nijō-jin'ya** is an intriguing place riddled with secret passages and hidey-holes. Also worth seeing are the imperial villas of **Shūgaku-in Rikyū** and **Katsura Rikyū**, and the sensuous moss gardens of **Saihō-ji**, in the outer districts. Take time to walk around the city's old merchant quarters; one of the best is found in the **central district**, behind the department stores and modern shopping arcades north of **Shijō-dōri**, and across the river in **Gion** you'll find the traditional **crafts shops**, selling everything from handmade bamboo blinds to geisha hair accessories, and beautiful old **ryokan** for which the city is justifiably famous. However, the city is not all temples and tradition: the **Kyoto International Manga Museum**, alongside an increasing number of innovative **designer shops** and **stylish cafés**, are examples of Kyoto's modern spirit, showing how the city manages to combine its heritage with contemporary culture.

Spring and autumn are undoubtedly the **best times to visit** Kyoto, though also the busiest; after a chilly winter, the cherry trees put on their finery in early April, while the hot, oppressive summer months (June–Aug) are followed in October by a delightful period of clear, dry weather when the maple trees erupt into fiery reds.

Brief history

Kyoto became the **imperial capital** in the late eighth century when Emperor Kammu relocated the court from Nara (see p.470). His first choice was Nagaoka, southwest of today's Kyoto, but a few inauspicious events led the emperor to move again in 794AD. This time he settled on what was to be known as **Heian-kyō**, "Capital of Peace and Tranquillity". Like Nara, the city was modelled on the Chinese Tang-dynasty capital Chang'an (today's Xi'an), with a symmetrical north–south axis. By the late ninth

---

APPLICATIONS TO VISIT RESTRICTED SIGHTS

To visit some of Kyoto's most famous palaces and gardens it's necessary to apply in advance. Usually, this is a simple procedure and well worth the effort. Tours of the **Imperial Palace**, **Sentō Gosho**, **Katsura Rikyū** and **Shūgaku-in Rikyū** are all handled at the **Imperial Household Agency** office, 3 Kyotogyoen, Kamigyō-ku (IHA; Mon–Fri 8.45am–noon & 1–4pm; ☎075 211 1215, ⊛sankan.kunaicho.go.jp/english), on the west side of the Imperial Park, near Imadegawa subway station. It's best to book your tour two days in advance, though it is possible to visit the Imperial Palace itself on the same day that you make a booking, provided that you get to the IHA at least 30 minutes in advance. You can apply online up to three months in advance. All tours are free and conducted in Japanese, with the exception of the Imperial Palace, where there are tours in English at 10am and 2pm. Note that anyone under 20 years old (still a minor in Japanese law) has to be accompanied by an adult when visiting the Sentō Gosho, Katsura Rikyū or Shūgaku-in Rikyū. Don't forget to take your passport with you to the office and also for the tour itself.

Other sights in Kyoto that require reservations in advance are **Nijō-jin'ya** (see p.417) and **Saihō-ji** (see p.436).

6

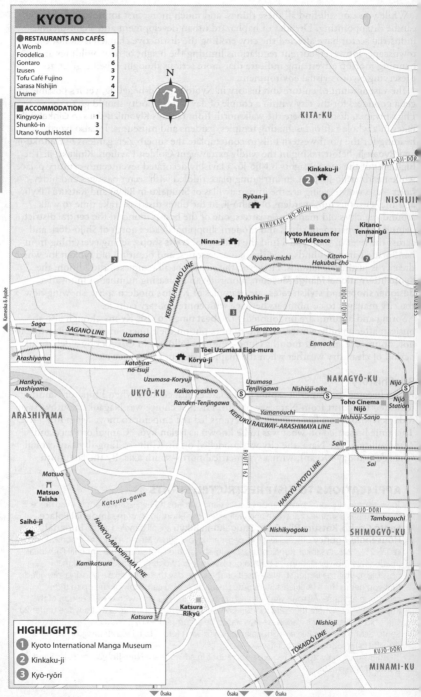

KYOTO

RESTAURANTS AND CAFÉS

A Womb	5
Foodelica	1
Gontaro	6
Izusen	3
Tofu Café Fujino	7
Sarasa Nishijin	4
Urume	2

■ ACCOMMODATION

Kingyoya	1
Shunkō-in	3
Utano Youth Hostel	2

N

KITA-KU

Kinkaku-ji

Ryōan-ji

NISHIJIN

KINUKAKE-NO-MICHI

Kitano-Tenmangū

Ninna-ji

Kyoto Museum for World Peace

Ryōanji-michi

Kitano-Hakubai-chō

Myōshin-ji

Saga

SAGANO LINE   Uzumasa   Hanazono

Arashiyama

Enmachi

Katabira-nō-tsuji

Tōei Uzumasa Eiga-mura

Kōryū-ji

NAKAGYŌ-KU

Uzumasa-Koryuji

Nijō

Hankyū-Arashiyama

UKYŌ-KU   Kaikonoyashiro

Uzumasa Tenjingawa   Nishiōji-oike

Toho Cinema Nijō

Nijō Station

Randen-Tenjingawa

Yamanouchi

Nishiōji-Sanjo

ARASHIYAMA

Saiin

Sai

Matsuo

Matsuo Taisha

Katsura-gawa

ROUTE 162

Saihō-ji

Nishikyogoku

GOJŌ-DŌRI

Tambaguchi

SHIMOGYŌ-KU

Kamikatsura

Katsura

Katsura Rikyū

Nishioji

TOKAIDŌ LINE

KUJŌ-DŌRI

MINAMI-KU

HIGHLIGHTS

1 Kyoto International Manga Museum

2 Kinkaku-ji

3 Kyō-ryōri

Kameoka & Ayabe

KITA-ŌJI-DŌR.

SENBON-DŌRI

NISHIŌJI-DŌRI

KEIFUKU-KITANO LINE

KEIFUKU RAILWAY–ARASHIMAYA LINE

HANKYŪ-KYOTO LINE

HANKYŪ-ARASHIYAMA LINE

Ōsaka   Ōsaka   Ōsaka

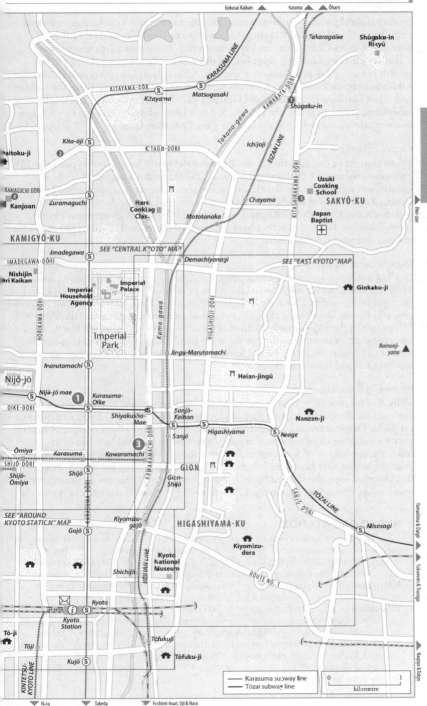

century **Heian-kyō** was overflowing onto the eastern hills and soon had an estimated population of 500,000. In 894, imperial missions to China ceased and earlier borrowings from Chinese culture began to develop into distinct Japanese forms.

The city's history from this point is something of a roller-coaster ride. In the late twelfth century a fire practically destroyed the whole place, but two centuries later the **Ashikaga shoguns** built some of the city's finest monuments, among them the Golden and Silver Pavilions (Kinkaku-ji and Ginkaku-ji). Many of the great Zen temples were established at this time and the arts reached new levels of sophistication. Once again, however, almost everything was lost during the **Ōnin Wars** from 1467–78 (see p.795).

Kyoto's golden era

Kyoto's knight in shining armour was **Toyotomi Hideyoshi**, who came to power in 1582 and sponsored a vast rebuilding programme. The **Momoyama period**, as it's now known, was a golden era of artistic and architectural ostentation, epitomized by Kyoto's famous **Kanō school of artists**, who decorated the temples and palaces with sumptuous gilded screens. Even when **Tokugawa Ieyasu** moved the seat of government to Edo (now Tokyo) in 1603, Kyoto remained the imperial capital and stood its ground as the nation's foremost cultural centre.

Meiji modernization

In 1788 another huge conflagration swept through the city, but worse was to come; in 1869 the new **Emperor Meiji** moved the court to Tokyo. Kyoto went into shock, and the economy foundered for a while. In the 1890s a canal was built from Biwa-ko to the city, and Kyoto, like the rest of Japan, embarked on a process of industrialization. Miraculously, the city narrowly escaped devastation at the end of **World War II**, when it was considered a potential target for the atom bomb. Kyoto was famously spared by American Defence Secretary Henry Stimson, who recognized the city's supreme architectural and historical importance.

Preserving Kyoto's heritage

Sadly, Kyoto's own citizens were not so mindful and post-World War II many of the city's old buildings were sold for their land value and replaced by concrete structures or car parks. Despite continued modernization, however, a more enthusiastic approach to strengthening the city's traditional heritage is now being adopted by some of its residents, not least in efforts towards attracting foreign visitors. In particular, many younger Japanese are becoming interested in not only preserving but also developing this historical legacy, evidenced by the growing number of businesses set in traditional townhouses, or *machiya* (see box, p.429) and taking traditional arts and crafts into the

---

KYOTO ORIENTATION

Kyoto is contained within a wide basin valley surrounded by hills on three sides and flanked by two rivers – the Katsura-gawa to the west and the smaller Kamo-gawa to the east. A grid street system makes this one of Japan's easier cities to find your way around. The **central district** of banks, shops and the main tourist facilities lies between the Imperial Palace in the north and **Kyoto Station** to the south. Nijō-jō and Horikawa-dōri define the district's western extent, while the Kamo-gawa provides a natural boundary to the east. Within this core, the **downtown** area is concentrated around Shijō-dōri and north along Kawaramachi-dōri to Oike-dōri. Shijō-dōri leads east over the Kamo-gawa into **Gion**, the city's major entertainment district, and to the eastern hills, **Higashiyama**, which shelter many of Kyoto's most famous temples. Much of this central area is best tackled on foot, but the city's other sights are widely scattered. To the northwest, **Kinkaku-ji** and **Ryōan-ji** provide the focus for a second group of temples, while tucked away in the southwestern suburbs are the superb gardens of **Saihō-ji** and the **Katsura Rikyū**.

KYOTO ADDRESSES

In general, Kyoto **addresses** follow the same pattern as for the rest of Japan (see p.39). There are, however, a few additional subtleties worth mastering. Unusually, most of the city's main roads are named and the location of a place is generally described by reference to the nearest major junction. Since the land slopes gently south, the most usual indicator is whether a place lies north (*agaru*, "above") or south (*sagaru*, "below") of a particular east–west road. For example, Kawaramachi Sanjō simply means the place is near the intersection of Kawaramachi-dōri and Sanjō-dōri; Kawaramachi Sanjō-agaru tells you it's north of Sanjō-dōri; Kawaramachi Sanjō-sagaru, that it's to the south. At a higher level of sophistication, the address might also indicate whether a place lies east (*higashi-iri*) or west (*nishi-iri*) of the north–south road.

6

twenty-first century (see box, p.453). The disasters of March 2011 in northern Japan did not damage Kyoto physically, but its economy was badly affected. Kyoto relies heavily on tourism, receiving millions of visitors a year, and the industry was almost decimated for much of 2011. Some businesses closed while others were forced to dramatically reduce prices, though visitor numbers have since slowly returned to pre-2011 levels.

Central Kyoto

The **Imperial Palace** is at the core of central Kyoto, just a short walk north of **Nijō-jō**, with its magnificent screen paintings, and the intriguing **Nijō-jin'ya**. Nearby, Kyoto's **downtown** district is contained within the grid of streets bounded by Oike-dōri to the north, Shijō-dōri to the south, Karasuma-dōri to the west and the Kamo-gawa in the east. While there are few specific sights here, the backstreets still hide a number of traditional wooden buildings, including some of Kyoto's best ryokan (see p.440). You'll also come across fine old craft shops (see p.450) among the boutiques and department stores, while the colourful shopping arcades of **Teramachi-dōri** and neighbouring **Shinkyōgoku** are worth a browse.

The Imperial Park and Palace

京都御苑, Kyōtogyōen and 京都御所, Kyōto Gosho • Park open 24 hours a day • Palace tours in English Mon–Fri 10am & 2pm; 1hr • Free, guidebook ¥200 • Book tours at the IHA office, Kamigyō-ku (Mon–Fri 8.45am–noon & 1–4pm; ☏ 075 211 1215, ⊛ sankan.kunaicho .go.jp/english) at least 30min in advance or online up to three months in advance • The nearest subway station is Imadegawa, or take a bus to Karasuma Imadegawa

Dun-coloured earth walls enclose the verdant **Imperial Park**, or Kyoto Gyoen, inside which wide expanses of gravel and clipped lawns have replaced most of the former palaces and subsidiary buildings. It's a popular spot for locals to picnic, exercise or walk the dog. The **Imperial Palace**, was the nation's physical and spiritual centre before the emperor moved to Tokyo in 1868. Today's palace is by no means a high priority among Kyoto's wealth of sights, but it's a good idea to come here early in your stay to visit the **Imperial Household Agency** (IHA), in the park's northwest corner, to make arrangements for visiting the city's more rewarding imperial villas and gardens (see box, p.411).

The **English-language tour** of the palace is quite detailed, though it's still worth investing in the English-language guidebook for the photos of some of the interior sections that you won't be able to access. The palace originally stood about 2km further west, at Nijō-jō, but was relocated to its present site in the late twelfth century. However, nearly all of the buildings date from the mid-nineteenth century and the overwhelming impression is rather monotonous – wide spaces of pure white gravel, set against austere Meiji-period replicas of Heian-style (794–1185) architecture. The most important building is the ceremonial **Shishin-den** (紫宸殿), flanked by two cherry and citrus trees, where the Meiji, Taishō and Shōwa emperors were all enthroned. Further on, you can peer inside the **Seiryō-den** (清涼殿), which was once the emperor's private residence, while beyond there's a tantalizing glimpse of a pond-filled stroll-garden designed by the landscape gardener Kobori Enshū (1579–1647).

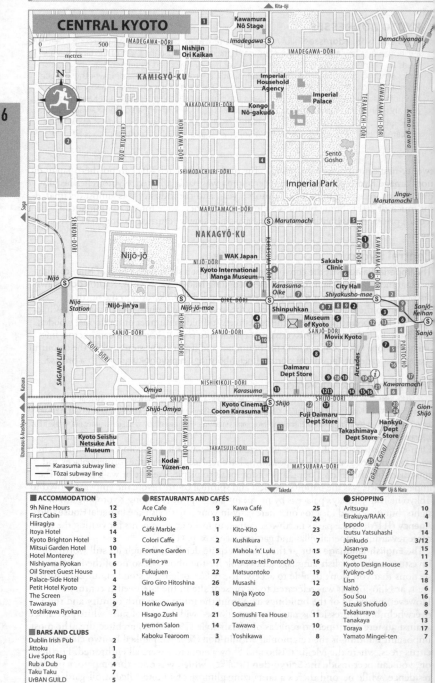

ACCOMMODATION
9h Nine Hours	12
First Cabin	13
Hiiragiya	8
Itoya Hotel	14
Kyoto Brighton Hotel	3
Mitsui Garden Hotel	10
Hotel Monterey	11
Nishiyama Ryokan	6
Oil Street Guest House	1
Palace-Side Hotel	4
Petit Hotel Kyoto	5
The Screen	5
Tawaraya	9
Yoshikawa Ryokan	7

BARS AND CLUBS
Dublin Irish Pub	2
Jittoku	1
Live Spot Rag	3
Rub a Dub	4
Taku Taku	7
UrBAN GUILD	5
World	6

RESTAURANTS AND CAFÉS
Ace Cafe	9	Kawa Café	25
Anzukko	13	Kiln	24
Café Marble	1	Kito-Kito	23
Colori Caffe	2	Kushikura	7
Fortune Garden	5	Mahola 'n' Lulu	15
Fujino-ya	17	Manzara-tei Pontochō	16
Fukujuen	22	Matsuontoko	19
Giro Giro Hitoshina	26	Musashi	12
Hale	18	Ninja Kyoto	20
Honke Owariya	4	Obanzai	6
Hisago Zushi	21	Somushi Tea House	11
Iyemon Salon	14	Tawawa	10
Kaboku Tearoom	3	Yoshikawa	8

SHOPPING
Aritsugu	10
Eirakuya/RAAK	4
Ippodo	1
Izutsu Yatsuhashi	14
Junkudo	3/12
Jūsan-ya	15
Kogetsu	11
Kyoto Design House	5
Kyūkyo-dō	2
Lisn	18
Naitō	6
Sou Sou	16
Suzuki Shofudō	9
Takakuraya	8
Tanakaya	13
Toraya	17
Yamato Mingei-ten	7

Sentō Gosho

仙洞御所 • In the southeast quadrant of the Imperial Park • Tours Mon–Fri 11am & 1.30pm; 1hr • Free

A fine example of Kobori Enshū's landscape design can be seen by taking a (compulsory) guided tour of the **Sentō Gosho** garden – though the tour is all in Japanese. Originally built as a retirement home for former emperors, the palace here burnt down in 1854 and now only the peaceful garden remains. Apart from several graceful pavilions, its main features are a zigzag bridge – stunning when its wisteria trellis is in full bloom – and a cobbled "seashore", which lends the garden an extra grandeur.

6

Nijō-jō

二条城 • 541 Nijō-jō-chō, 1km southwest of the Imperial Park • Daily 8.45am–4pm, closed Tues in Jan, July, Aug & Dec • ¥600; gallery ¥100 • ☎ 075 841 0096, ⓦ www.city.kyoto.jp/bunshi/nijojo/english • The main entrance is the East Gate on Horikawa-dōri, near the Nijō-jō-mae subway station and bus stop.

Nijo Castle

The swaggering opulence of **Nijō-jō** provides a complete contrast to imperial understatement. Built as the Kyoto residence of Shogun Tokugawa Ieyasu (1543–16), the castle's double moats, massive walls and watchtowers demonstrate the supreme confidence of his new, Tokyo-based military government. Inside, the finest artists of the day filled the palace with sumptuous gilded screens and carvings, the epitome of Momoyama style (see p.812), leaving the increasingly impoverished emperor in no doubt as to where power really lay. The castle took 23 years to complete, paid for by local *daimyō*, but Nijō-jō was never used in defence and was rarely visited by a shogun after the mid-1600s.

After entering through the East Gate, head to the **Ninomaru Palace** (二の丸御殿), whose five buildings face onto a lake-garden and run in a staggered line connected by covered corridors. Look out for the "nightingale floors" which squeak when trodden on and were specially designed to detect intruders. Each room is lavishly decorated with replicas of **screen paintings** by the brilliant Kanō school of artists, notably Kanō Tanyū and Naonobu. You can view the actual screens in a separate **gallery** to north of the main gate.

Nijō-jin'ya

二条陣屋 • 137 Sanbō Ōmiya-chō • Tours in Japanese daily except Wed at 10am, 11am, 2pm & 3pm; 1hr • ¥1000 • ☎ 075 841 0972, ⓦ nijyojinya.net/English.html • Advance reservations only – book by phone (in Japanese) a day before; non-Japanese-speakers must bring an interpreter

The mysterious **Nijō-jin'ya** was built in the early seventeenth century as an inn for feudal lords who came to pay homage to the emperor. As these were days of intrigue and treachery, it is riddled with trap doors, false walls and ceilings, "nightingale floors", escape hatches, disguised staircases and confusing dead ends to trap intruders. It is owned by the Ogawa family and is a private residence, hence the strict rules for touring the house, and the rather frosty reception. After years of extensive restoration work, it reopened in 2013 and is a fascinating example of traditional craftsmanship – it's worth organizing an

---

THE KAMO-GAWA

Running through central Kyoto, the **Kamo-gawa** (鴨川) is a much-loved hangout for Kyoto's inhabitants, who flock to its banks for exercise and relaxation, such as t'ai chi and picnics. The **Sanjō bridge** area is very popular with the city's youth, and buskers often perform here to large crowds. From late spring the river's western bank between **Shijō bridge** and **Ōike bridge** is covered with *yuka* (wooden platforms that extend out from the restaurants of Pontochō), which catch the cooling river breezes during humid summers. The river has an eventful history: **Kabuki** theatre began in 1603 and in 1619 the "Martyrs of Kyoto", more than fifty **Christians** including women and children, were burnt alive on the riverbank. The river was also used for hundreds of years to rinse out **kimono** fabric that had been dyed using the *kyō-yūzen* hand-dyeing technique. It's no surprise, then, that by the early 1990s it was very polluted. However, at the end of the decade the city government undertook a rejuvenation programme and now all 35 kilometres of the river and its surroundings support an abundance of bird and plant life.

interpreter for the tour (details on website) so that you can learn more about Nijō-jin'ya's clever safeguards against intruders.

Kyoto International Manga Museum

京都国際マンガミュージアム, Kyōto Jokusai Manga Myujiamu • Kanafuki-chō • 10am–5.30pm, closed Wed • ¥800 • ☎ 075 254 7414, Ⓦ kyotomm.jp/english

The excellent **Kyoto International Manga Museum** is the world's first museum entirely devoted to **Japanese comics**. A joint project between Kyoto City and Seika University, it's housed in an old elementary school, which has been remodelled to accommodate the huge, all-encompassing collection of popular manga (see p.813), as well as provide plenty of space for art workshops (held at weekends) to teach the techniques of manga, and international conferences to discuss research. The great thing about the museum is that most of the manga can be taken outside and read on the lawn, and there is also an international section with some English-language manga.

Museum of Kyoto

京都文化博物館 Kyōto Bunka Hakubutsukan • 623-1 Higashikata-machi • Tues–Sun 10am–7.30pm; special exhibitions usually close at 6pm; screenings of Japanese classic movies Tues–Fri 1.30pm & 5pm • ¥500, including film screenings • ☎ 075 222 0888, Ⓦ bunpaku.or.jp

In a trendy area of galleries and cafés, the **Museum of Kyoto** incorporates a Meiji-era bank building and a replica Edo-period shopping street with craft shops and some reasonable restaurants. The museum's exhibits focus mainly on local history, culture and modern crafts, with some interesting historical dioramas, though there is little detailed explanation about the exhibits in Japanese or English – ask for one of the museum's volunteer guides if you want an English-language explanation. Check out the small section on Kyoto's film industry, which is enlivened by screenings of classic movies (in Japanese).

Pontochō

先斗町

Running parallel to the west side of the Kamo-gawa between Sanjō and Shijō bridges, the geisha district of **Pontochō** is packed with teahouses, restaurants, and bars – many of which are built in traditional wooden *machiya*. It's best at night, when lantern-light fills the district's narrow lanes and you can often catch a glimpse of a geisha or trainee maiko on her way to an appointment. In July and August, Pontochō restaurants open wooden *yuka* terraces over the cooling Kamo-gawa, making Kyoto's sweltering summer nights a little more bearable.

Nishiki-kōji street market

錦小路通 • Parallel to Shijō-dori, one block north • Daily 9am–7pm, but varies from shop to shop • Ⓦ kyoto-nishiki.or.jp

Known as "Kyoto's kitchen", **Nishiki-kōji street market** has been one of the city's main fish and vegetable markets since the early seventeenth century. The tantalizing smells of fresh tofu, grilled fish and all kinds of pickled, fermented and dried Kyō-yasai (Kyoto vegetables) will greet you in this narrow covered alley. There are more than a hundred small shops here, many offering samples to taste, as well as plenty of restaurants. The Haru Cooking School offers a fun and informative one-hour **tour** of the market (see p.440).

Kyoto Seishū Netsuke Art Museum

京都清宗根付け • 46-1 Mibukayōgosho-chō • April, July, Sept, Nov & Feb daily 10am–4.30pm • ¥1000 • ☎ 075 802 7000, Ⓦ netsukekan.jp • 10min walk southwest of Hankyu Ōmiya Station or Keifuku Shijō-Ōmiya Station

The fascinating **Kyoto Seishū Netsuke Art Museum** is home to a private collection of *netsuke* – hand-carved objects traditionally used for hanging pouches from *obi* sashes. These miniature pieces of art were originally made from ivory and mainly depict people and animals, as well as natural objects such as fruit and flowers. The antique and contemporary *netsuke* are displayed here over two floors of an old samurai mansion that has been beautifully restored.

Around Kyoto Station

Historically, the principal entrance to Kyoto lay through its great southern gate, so it's only fitting that this district, south of the city centre, should be home to the monumental **Kyoto Station**, the entry point for most visitors to the city. Opposite the station is the **Kyoto Tower,** which can clearly be seen throughout the city and makes a useful landmark when walking around. This area is also home to some of the city's more venerable temples – in their day, when their massive wooden halls were filled with shimmering gold, **Nishi-Hongan-ji** and **Higashi-Hongan-ji** were probably just as awe-inspiring as the modern train station. Across the tracks, **Tō-ji** boasts Japan's tallest original wooden pagoda and some of the city's oldest surviving buildings.

Kyoto Station

京都駅, Kyoto-eki • Karasuma Shichijō-sagaru

The city's main transport hub – where the JR, Kintetsu and Kyoto subway lines meet – **Kyoto Station** was rebuilt and enlarged in the 1990s by Tokyo architect Hara Hiroshi. The new building was initially the source of much local controversy, but over time many people have come to appreciate its shiny black bulk. Uncompromisingly modern, with its marble exterior and giant central archway, the station building also houses the Isetan department store, restaurants and underground shopping malls, plus a hotel and theatre.

Kyoto Tower

京都タワー • Karasuma Shichijō-sagaru • Observatory daily 9am–8.40pm • ¥770 • ☎ 075 361 3215, ⓦ kyoto-tower.co.jp

The tallest structure in Kyoto, the 131m-high **Kyoto Tower** was built in the 1960s and

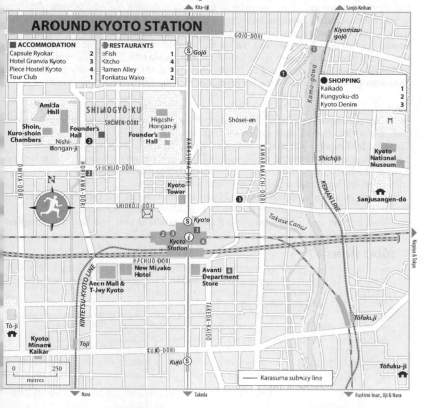

caused controversy at the time for its modern design. Though still considered by many to be rather unsightly, the tower's observatory does provide fantastic panoramic views, which give you a good understanding of the city's geography – on a clear day you can even see parts of Ōsaka. The tower houses a hotel, restaurants, bars and even a public *sentō* bath.

Nishi-Hongan-ji

西本願寺 • Hanaya-chō sagaru • Daily Sept–April 5.30am–5.30pm; May–Aug 5.30am–6pm • Free • ☎ 075 371 5181, ⓦ www.hongwanji.or.jp/English • A 5min walk from Kyoto Station, on the west side of Horikawa-dōri

The vast temple complex of **Nishi-Hongan-ji** is the headquarters of the **Jōdo Shinshū** sect (see box below). Compared to other Kyoto temples, Nishi-Hongan-ji is relatively crowd-free and has a pleasant atmosphere. The gravel courtyard contains two huge halls, the oldest of which is the Founder's Hall, **Goeidō** (御影堂), built in 1636, and located on the left as you enter through the gate. The temple is dedicated to Shinran and was recently restored. The **Amida Hall** (阿弥陀堂) dates from 1760. Both are decked with gold, including screens by Kanō artists in the Amida Hall. The temple's real highlights, the even more ornate **Shoin** (書院) and **Kuro-shoin Chambers** (黒書院), are only open to guided tours – ask in the green-roofed building, to the left of the Founder's Hall.

Higashi-Hongan-ji

東本願寺 Karasuma Shichijō sagaru • **Temple** daily March–Oct 5.50am–5.30pm; Nov–Feb 6.20am–4.30pm • Free • **Garden** daily 9am–3.30pm • ¥500 • ☎ 075 371 9181, ⓦ higashihonganji.or.jp/english • West side of Karasuma-dōri, 5min walk from Kyoto Station

Though **Higashi-Hongan-ji** was constructed in a similar style to its neighbour and rival, Nishi-Hongan-ji (see p.420), it had to be completely rebuilt after a fire in 1864, and today only the two main halls are open to the public. The first hall, the **Goeidō** (御影堂), is one of Japan's largest wooden buildings – when it was built, ordinary ropes proved too weak to lift the massive roof beams, so female devotees from around the country sent in enough hair to plait 53 ropes. You can see an example of these black ropes preserved in the open corridor that connects the Goeidō to the **Amida Hall** (阿弥陀堂), with its image of Amida on an elaborate altar. Two blocks further east, the temple's shady garden, **Shōsei-en** (渉成園) provides a welcome respite from the surrounding city blocks.

Tō-ji

東寺 • 1 Kujō-chō • Daily: mid-March to mid-Sept 8.30am–5.30pm; mid-Sept to mid-March 8.30am–4.30pm • Flea market 21st of each month • ☎ 075 691 3325, ⓦ toji.or.jp • 10min walk southwest of Kyoto Station

Founded by Emperor Kammu in 794, the historic temple of **Tō-ji** contains some of Japan's finest esoteric Buddhist sculpture and its lovely **pagoda** is one of the symbols of Kyoto. The best time to visit is during the **monthly flea market**, when Tō-ji is thronged with pilgrims, hustlers and bargain hunters.

The main entrance to eighth-century Heian-kyō lay through the great south gate, Rashō-mon, which stood at the junction of Kujō-dōri and Senbon-dōri. After the problems in Nara (see p.471), Emperor Kammu permitted only two Buddhist temples

---

JŌDO SHINSHŪ

One of Japan's most popular and wealthy Buddhist sects, the **Jōdo Shinshū** (True Pure Land) was founded by the Kyoto-born priest **Shonin Shinran** (1173–1262). His simple creed, which at the time was regarded as heresy, asserts that merely chanting the *nembutsu*, "Praise to Amida Buddha", can lead to **salvation**. Not surprisingly, the sect grew rapidly, despite opposition from the established hierarchy, until eventually Toyotomi Hideyoshi granted them a plot of land in southern Kyoto in 1591 – today, this is the Nishi-Hongan-ji. By 1602, Shogun Tokugawa Ieyasu was sufficiently alarmed at the sect's power to sponsor a splinter group, Higashi-Hongan-ji, now based just a few hundred metres to the east of the Nishi-Hongan-ji. Even today, the two groups continue to differ over doctrinal affairs.

within the city walls: Tō-ji and Sai-ji, the East and West temples. Standing either side of Rashō-mon, they were charged with the young capital's spiritual wellbeing. While Sai-ji eventually faded in the thirteenth century, Tō-ji prospered under **Kōbō Daishi**, the founder of Shingon Buddhism (see box, p.510), who was granted the stewardship of the temple in 823. Over the centuries, the temple gathered a treasure-trove of calligraphy, paintings and Buddhist statuary, the oldest of which were supposedly brought from China by the Daishi himself.

Gojū-no-tō

五重塔 • In the temple's southwest corner • Daily 9am–4.30pm • ¥800

Tō-ji's most distinctive feature is the five-storey **Gojū-no-tō**, Japan's tallest pagoda. Erected in 826 and last rebuilt in the mid-seventeenth century, it now stands in an enclosure alongside Tō-ji's greatest treasures, the **Kō-dō** (講堂) and more southerly **Kon-dō** (金堂). These solid, confident buildings both date from the early seventeenth century, but it's the images inside, such as Heian-period Buddhist statues, that are the focus.

Miei-dō

御影堂 • In the temple's northwest corner • Daily 8.30am–4.30pm • Statue can be seen on 21st of each month

The **Miei-dō**, or Founder's Hall, is said to be where Kōbō Daishi lived. The present building, erected in 1380, houses a thirteenth-century statue of him, which can be seen monthly, on the day that marks the entry of the Daishi into Nirvana, when hundreds of pilgrims queue up to pay their respects.

Hōmotsu-kan

東宝物館 • In the temple's northern section • Approx mid-March to late May & mid-Sept to late Nov daily 9am–4.30pm, but check the temple's website for exact dates • ¥500

Beyond the Miei-dō, the modern **Hōmotsu-kan** contains Tō-ji's remaining treasures, including priceless mandala, portraits of Kōbō Daishi and a 6m-tall Senju Kannon (thousand-armed Buddhist Goddess of Mercy), carved in 877. The museum opens for two seasons (spring and autumn) with different exhibitions each time.

East Kyoto

If you only have one day in Kyoto, it's best to concentrate on the wealth of temples and museums lining the eastern hills. Not only does this district include many of Kyoto's more rewarding sights, but it's also fairly compact and contains areas of attractive lanes and traditional houses set against the wooded slopes behind. If you're pushed for time head straight for **Kiyomizu-dera**, with its distinctive wooden terrace, and then follow cobbled **Sannen-zaka** north. **Gion**, the famous entertainment district traditionally associated with geisha and teahouses, has retained a surprising number of wooden facades and photogenic corners, though its seductive charms are best savoured after dark. Garden lovers should also arrange to visit **Shūgaku-in Rikyū** on the northeast edge of Kyoto, for its inspired use of borrowed scenery on a grand scale – you'll need to allow a half-day for this.

Fushimi-Inari Taisha

伏見稲荷大社 • 68 Yabunochi-chō • Daily 24 hours • Free • ☎ 075 641 7331, ⓦ inari.jp • From Kyoto Station take either the JR Nara line to Inari Station or the Keihan line to Fushimi-Inari Station; from eastern Kyoto, take a #202, #207 or #208 bus to Tōfuku-ji Station and get a train from there to JR Inari or Keihan Fushimi-Inari Station; it's a short walk east from either station to the shrine

The spectacularly photogenic **Fushimi-Inari Taisha**, about 2.5km southeast of Kyoto Station, is the head shrine of the Inari cult, dedicated to the god of rice and sake. In 711, the local Hata clan established a shrine on top of Inari-san, the mountain, although this was eventually moved in the ninth century to the site of the current sanctuary at the foot of the mountain. Don't linger here too long though – the real highlight is the **4km maze of paths** that wind their way up through the deep forest to

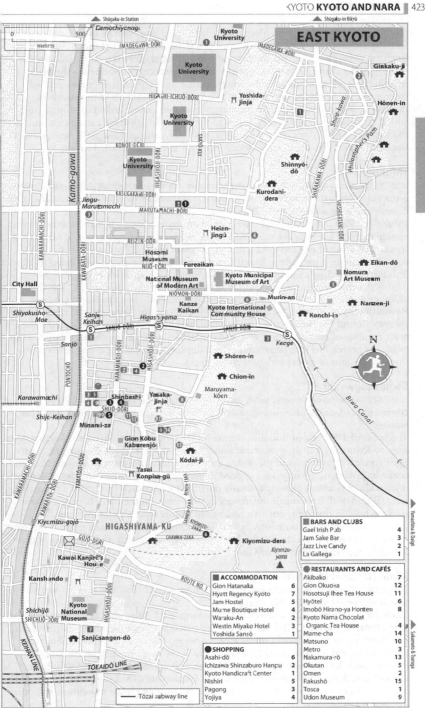

EAST KYOTO

BARS AND CLUBS

Gael Irish Pub	4
Jam Sake Bar	3
Jazz Live Candy	2
La Gallega	1

RESTAURANTS AND CAFÉS

Akibako	7
Gion Okuoka	12
Hosotsuji Ihee Tea House	11
Hyōtei	6
Imobō Hirano-ya Honten	8
Kyoto Nama Chocolat	
Organic Tea House	4
Mame-cha	14
Matsuno	10
Metro	3
Nakamura-rō	13
Okutan	5
Omen	2
Pakushō	15
Tosca	1
Udon Museum	9

ACCOMMODATION

Gion Hatanaka	6
Hyatt Regency Kyoto	7
Jam Hostel	5
Mume Boutique Hotel	4
Waraku-An	2
Westin Miyako Hotel	3
Yoshida Sansō	1

SHOPPING

Asahi-dō	6
Ichizawa Shinzaburo Hanpu	2
Kyoto Handicraft Center	1
Nishiri	3
Pagong	3
Yojiya	4

the summit of the mountain. More than 10,000 vermilion *torii* gates frame the paths, forming a mysterious tunnel that in some places cuts out most light, even on the brightest days. These painted wooden gates are replaced every ten years, each one an offering by local and national companies asking for success in business – the black lettering on each gate indicates the company that has donated it. At times you will emerge out of the gloom into bright sub-shrines, with hundreds of thousands of miniature wooden gates hanging from every available space, flanked by stone foxes, which are believed to be the messengers of the rice gods. It's quite a steep climb up to the top, but you'll be rewarded with great views of Kyoto, and along the way you can stop for tea and grab some *inari-zushi* – rice balls in pockets of fried tofu.

Tōfuku-ji

東福寺 • 778 Honmachi• Daily: April–Oct 9am–4pm, Nov & Dec 8.30am–4pm, late Dec to March 9am–3.30pm • ¥400 • ⓦ tofukuji .jp • Catch a #202, #207 or #208 bus from central or eastern Kyoto or a train from Kyoto Station on the JR Nara line to Tōfuku-ji Station; the temple is a short walk east from the station, across a busy road

Tōfuku-ji, a Zen temple, is most often visited during autumn, when the colours of the *momiji* (maple) leaves in the man-made mini valley in the temple grounds turn a spectacular array of red and gold – though it is well worth a visit at other times of the year. The temple is part of the Rinzai sect of Zen Buddhism and was founded in 1236. This large, sprawling complex with 23 sub-temples is significant not only for its medieval temple architecture – the two-storey San-mon gate, built in 1425, is the oldest example of Zen gate architecture still in existence – but also for its gardens. Revolutionary twentieth-century gardener Mirei Shigemori designed and installed the gardens around the **Hōjō** (main hall) in 1939, and his work here is considered to be a great example of **contemporary Japanese garden** design, creating abstract shapes with moss and gravel. His interpretation of the traditional Zen raked gravel garden is also interesting – lots of extra swirls and coned peaks.

Sanjūsangen-dō

三十三間堂 • 657 Sanjūsangendōmawari-chō • Daily: April–Oct 8am–4.40pm; Nov–March 9am–3.30pm • ¥600 • ☎ 075 525 0033, ⓦ sanjusangendo.jp • Sanjūsangen-dō lies south of Shichijō-dōri; to get here, take Raku bus #100, or city buses #206 and #208 from Kyoto Station

The ranks of 1001 gilded Buddhist statues inside **Sanjūsangen-dō**, on the southeastern edge of Kyoto, are a truly memorable sight. After passing through the turnstiles, turn right and leave your shoes in the porch; a short corridor takes you to the northern end of the hall. At first, the impassive, haloed figures appear as identical **images of Kannon**, the Buddhist Goddess of Mercy, usually portrayed with eleven heads and a thousand arms. But they all have subtle differences in their faces, clothes, jewellery and in the symbols held in their tiny, outstretched hands. Rather than a thousand arms, the statues have been given only forty apiece (excluding the two hands in prayer), but each of these can save 25 worlds. In addition, every figure represents 33 incarnations, giving a total of 33,033 Kannon to help save mankind.

Kyoto National Museum

京都国立博物館, Kyōto Kokuritsu Hakubutsukan • 527 Chaya-machi • 9am–4.30pm, Fri until 7.30pm, closed Mon • ¥500, plus extra for special exhibitions • ☎ 075 531 7509, ⓦ kyohaku.go.jp

Immediately across Shichijō-dōri from Sanjūsangen-dō is the southern entrance to the **Kyoto National Museum**. The vast permanent collection, covering Kyoto culture from prehistory up to 1868, is held in the modern wing, while the original hall, built in 1895, is reserved for special exhibitions. Many of the items on display are national treasures and the museum is a manageable size, though the displays and lighting are somewhat lacking. The permanent collection is currently closed for restoration and the construction of a new hall (due to reopen late 2014), though the museum is still open for special exhibitions.

1001 BUDDHIST STATUES

Commissioned by the devout former emperor Go-Shirakawa in 1164, during the bloody Genpei Wars, the rows of gilded wooden statues in **Sanjūsangen-dō** were carved by some seventy craftsmen under the direction of the renowned sculptor **Tankei** (c.1173–1256). He completed the central, seated Kannon at the age of 82 and is also attributed with several of the superb images along the front row. Of these, 28 are disciples of Kannon, while Fujin and Kanjin, the muscular gods of Wind and Thunder, bring up the two ends. Unfortunately, many of the original satues were lost in a fire in 1249, but 156 Kannon and the head of the main image were saved, and by 1266 a replica hall had been completed with the Kannon back up to full strength. In the early seventeenth century, the west veranda of the 188m-long hall became a popular place for samurai to practise their **archery**. This developed into a competition, **Tōshiya**, in which archers had to fire arrows from a squatting position along the length of the building without hitting a pillar. Nowadays, the event is commemorated with an archery display outside the hall on or around January 15.

Kawai Kanjirō's House

河井寛次郎記念館, Kawai Kanjirō Kinen-Kan • 569 Kanei-chō • Daily 10am–5pm, closed Mon, Aug 11–20 & Dec 24–Jan 7 • ¥900 • ☎ 075 561 3585, ⓦ kanjiro.jp • Turn west off Higashiōji-dōri shortly before the Gojō-dōri flyover

If you are interested in Japanese folk crafts, then drop in at **Kawai Kanjirō's House**, the tastefully rustic home of the innovative potter Kawai Kanjirō (1890–1966), who helped revive *mingei* (folk crafts) in the 1930s. The house is as he left it, beautifully furnished with ceramics and sculptures from his long career, including the kilns where many of these pieces were made, as well as personal items, such as his opium pipe.

Kiyomizu-dera

清水寺 • 294-1 Kiyomizu • Daily 6am–6pm • ¥300 • ⓦ kiyomizudera.or.jp • The closest bus stops are Kiyomizu-michi or Gojō-zaka on Higashiōji-dōri served by buses #100 (Raku bus), #202, #206 & #207

With its trademark wooden platform overhanging the valley, **Kiyomizu-dera** is one of Kyoto's defining sights. There's been a temple here since 778, when a visionary priest came across its fount of clear water (*kiyo-mizu*); however, nearly all the buildings you see today date from 1633. Just north of the Gojō-dōri flyover a right fork brings you to **Chawan-zaka** (茶わん坂), a quiet lane lined with shops selling local pottery. If you'd rather use the traditional approach, continue on to **Kiyomizu-zaka** (清水坂), where you'll find a colourful, crowded parade of souvenir shops and craft galleries – though the street is currently undergoing an extensive renovation project that is expected to last for a couple of years, so some of its buildings may well be covered in scaffolding.

Hon-dō

本堂

Beyond the three-storey pagoda, you can step for a moment into the monumental **Hon-dō** (Main Hall) to enjoy its surprisingly peaceful interior. There's little to actually see in here – its principal image, an eleven-headed Kannon, only goes on show every 33 years (next time will be 2033), so head for the wide terrace in front, originally a stage for sacred dances, to soak up the famous view over the wooded gorge and Kyoto beyond.

Jishu-jinja

地主神社主 • Daily 9am–5pm

On the hill behind the Hon-dō a jumble of shrine buildings competes for the attention of people looking for luck in love. **Jishu-jinja** is dedicated to several Shintō gods, of whom the most popular is Okuninushi-no-mikoto, an ancient deity in charge of love and good marriages; his messenger is a rabbit. To test your current love life, try walking in a straight line between the two "blind stones", set 18m apart, with your eyes closed and intoning your partner's name. If you arrive at the other stone without erring, all is well. If not, well, it's time for a new relationship.

Otowa waterfall

音羽の瀧, Otoma no Taki

At the base of the wooden terrace, the **Otowa-no-yaki** waterfall is reputed to have magical powers if you drink its waters. There are three separate streams, each of which grants a different wish – success, health or beauty – though it's considered bad luck to sip from more than one. From the waterfall you can follow a short path up the opposite hillside from where you get the best views of Kiyomizu-dera.

Kōdai-ji

高台寺 • Shimokawara-chō • Daily 9am–5pm • ¥600 • W kodaiji.com

At the north end of the cobbled lanes of Ninen-zaka (see box below), walk straight ahead up the steps and through the car park to find the entrance to the peaceful gardens of **Kōdai-ji**. This temple was granted to Kita-no-Mandokoro, the wife of Toyotomi Hideyoshi, when she became a nun after his death in 1598. Kōdai-ji owes its finery, however, to the generosity of Hideyoshi's successor, Tokugawa Ieyasu, who donated buildings from his own castles and financed paintings by Kanō artists, before he wiped out the Toyotomi dynasty at Osaka in 1615. Nowadays, the temple buildings blend beautifully into their attractive hillside garden, its two ponds graced by a moon-viewing pavilion and the aptly named "Reclining Dragon Corridor". Between the ponds, check out the ceilings of the pretty **Kaisan-dō** hall which are made from recycled panels from Ieyasu's ship and from the carriage of Kita-no-Mandokoro. But the temple's most important building lies at the top of the **Reclining Dragon Corridor** – you have to walk round by path – where statues of Hideyoshi and his widow are enshrined. The exquisite gold-inlay lacquer work is among the finest of its kind in Japan.

Chion-in

知恩院 • 400 Rinka-cho • Daily: March–Nov 9am–3.30pm; Dec–Feb 9am–4pm • Gardens ¥500 • ☎ 075 531 2111, W chion-in.or.jp

On the northern edge of Maruyama-kōen public park, is the temple of **Chion-in**, a big, busy complex where everything is built on a monumental scale. Founded in 1175 by the priest Hōnen, it is the headquarters of his popular Jōdo (Pure Land) sect of Buddhism. On entering via the huge **San-mon** (三門) gate, look up to the right and you'll see the colossal **Daishō-rō** (大鐘楼) bell, the biggest in Japan, hanging in its belfry; at New Year it takes seventeen priests to ring this 67-tonne monster. Behind the cavernous **Miei-dō** (御影堂) main hall – all dark wood and sumptuous gold – red arrows lead to the entrance of the **Ōhōjō** and **Kohōjō** halls and gardens representing Amida's paradise. The main feature of both halls is the Momoyama-period screens that fill them; since you can only peer in, they've placed replicas of the screens in a room behind the ticket desk – the most famous features a cat with uncannily lifelike eyes. The Miei-do is currently undergoing extensive restoration work and will be closed to the public until 2017.

SANNEN-ZAKA AND NINEN-ZAKA

Two charming cobbled lanes connect Kiyomizu-dera with Kōdai-ji. Known as **Sannen-zaka** (三年坂; "Three-Year Slope") and **Ninen-zaka** (二年坂; "Two-Year Slope"), these lanes preserve some of the last vestiges of the old Kyoto townscape (see box, p.429). There has been a path here since the ninth century, while the two-storey wooden **townhouses** date from the late 1800s. Many of these buildings still cater to passing pilgrims and souvenir hunters in time-honoured fashion, peddling Kiyomizu pottery, bamboo-ware, pickles and refreshments – look out for Hyōtan-ya, at the bottom of the steps at the Kiyomizu-dera end, which has been selling gourd flasks (hyōtan) for two hundred years. Be careful walking along these two lanes, though: according to popular belief, a fall here brings two or three years of bad luck.

THE GEISHA OF KYOTO

Often mistakenly considered by foreigners to be high-class prostitutes, **geisha** (which means "practitioner of the arts"), are in fact refined women who entertain affluent men with their various accomplishments, such as singing, dancing, conversation and playing a traditional instrument such as a *shamisen* (three-string banjo). In Kyoto, geisha are called **geiko**, which literally means "child of the arts". English conversation skills are also becoming important, as a result of the international attention generated by the Hollywood film of *Memoirs of a Geisha* (see p.833), which has brought overseas visitors into the teahouses of the *hanamachi* ("flower towns"), where geisha live and work.

It takes five years for an apprentice geisha – known as **maiko** – to master her art, training with the same focus and dedication as an Olympic athlete in the various arts, and living according to a strict code of dress and deportment. The world of the geisha is shrinking, however: from a pre–World War II peak of eighty thousand there are now reckoned to be no more than a few thousand geisha left, the majority concentrated in Kyoto, the centre of the tradition. Though few fifteen-year-olds are tempted to sign up as apprentices, the internet is beginning to change this – some geisha houses have established websites to recruit apprentices, with successful results. Geisha have also started blogging; one Kyoto maiko has even translated her musings on life in a *hanamachi* into English (Wichi-kyoto.jp).

It's also becoming more common to be able to meet and talk to geisha and maiko in person. Many hotels and ryokan now offer exclusive **dinner shows** (see p.449), where it is possible to experience a little of the elegant yet fun entertainment that has until recently been the exclusive playground of wealthy male customers. There are also **walking tours** (see p.440) that provide a chance to learn more about geisha culture. Don't be fooled by daylight groups of "geisha" in Kyoto tourist spots: they are likely to be visitors who have paid for the chance to wear the distinctive make-up, wig and costume for a couple of hours.

Shōren-in

青蓮院 • 69-1 Sanjobo-cho • Daily 9am–4.30pm • ¥500 • ☎ 075 561 2345, Ⓦ shorenin.com

North of the bustling Chion-in, **Shōren-in** is a quiet little place surrounded by pleasant gardens and ancient camphor trees. The temple started life in the ninth century as lodgings for Tendai-sect priests from Enryaku-ji (see p.461) and later served as a residence for members of the imperial family. After seeing the collection of painted screens, the main reason to come here is to stroll along the paths that wind through the beautifully landscaped hillside garden.

Yasaka-jinja

八坂神社 • 625 Gion machi Kitagawa • Daily 24hr • Free • ☎ 075 561 6155, Ⓦ yasaka-jinja.or.jp

The main entrance to the lively shrine of **Yasaka-jinja** faces west onto the intersection of Higashiōji-dōri and Shijō-dōri. Instead of the usual *torii*, you enter through a brightly coloured Buddhist-style gate – a legacy of the days before 1868 when Buddhism and Shintō often cohabited. Located on the southern edge of Maruyama-kōen and the eastern edge of Gion, Yasaka-jinja is at the heart of many Kyoto cultural events – from cherry blossom viewing in spring, which brings thousands to the park, to the spectacular Gion Matsuri in July (see box, p.428). Because of its role as the guardian shrine of Gion, many geisha-related ceremonies are conducted here too.

Gion Entertainment District

祇園花街, Gion Hammadi

The area around Shijō-dōri, east of the Kamo-gawa and west of Yasaka-jinja, is known as the **Gion entertainment district**. Its narrow lanes, which lead off to the north and south of Shijōdōri, contain dozens of traditional teahouses and geisha houses, as well as modern bars and nightclubs. Historically, the area grew into a vibrant **pleasure quarter** as the teahouses, kabuki theatres and geisha performers flourished. By the middle of the eighteenth century, Gion was Kyoto's largest "floating world" (as the urban, pleasure-seeking culture of the Edo period was referred to), and you can still get a flavour of this

6

if you walk south along picturesque Hanamikōji-dōri, where many of the lovely wooden buildings function as exclusive teahouses with geisha holding court. It's best after dark when red lanterns hang outside each secretive doorway, allowing the occasional glimpse down a stone-flagged entranceway; early evening is also a good time to spot geisha and trainee maiko arriving at the teahouses for an appointment.

Gion Kōbu Kaburenjō

祇園甲部歌舞練場 • Near the south end of the Hanamikoji-dōri • Gion Corner performances March–Nov daily at 6pm & 7pm • ¥3150 • ☎ 075 561 1119, ⓦ kyoto-gioncorner.com

The **Gion Kōbu Kaburenjō** theatre is the nightly venue for a touristy sampler of traditional arts known as **Gion Corner** (ギオンコーナー), which includes maiko dancing. Though it's far better to spend a little extra to see the real thing, this is an easy opportunity to watch brief extracts of court dance, *bunraku* puppet theatre, slapstick *kyōgen*, and demonstrations of ikebana (flower arranging) and a tea ceremony. English-language guided commentary is available to rent at the entrance. During April's Miyako Odori (都をどり), the theatre also hosts local geisha giving performances of traditional dance (see p.449).

Shinbashi

新橋

Gion north of Shijō-dōri consists mainly of high-rise blocks packed with clubs, bars and restaurants. But walk up Kiritoshi, one block west of Hanamikōji-dōri, on the other side of Shijō-dōri, and you eventually emerge into another area of teahouses, known as **Shinbashi**. Although it comprises just two short streets, the row of slatted facades reflected in the willow-lined Shirakawa Canal makes a delightful scene, day or night.

Minami-za

南座 • Shijō-Ōhashi Higashi-zume • Opening times depend on the performance schedule; tickets can be bought at the box office or website • ☎ 075 561 1155, ⓦ shochiku.co.jp/play/minamiza

One of the most distinctive buildings in Gion, on the corner overlooking the Kamo-gawa, is the **Minami-za**. This famous kabuki theatre, the oldest in Japan, was established in the early seventeenth century, though last rebuilt in 1929. Kabuki has been an integral part of Gion life since the late sixteenth century when a female troupe started performing religious dances on the riverbanks. Eventually this evolved into an equally popular, all-male theatre, patronized by an increasingly wealthy merchant class. In contemporary Japan, kabuki still has a popular following, and each December Minami-za is the venue for a major kabuki festival featuring Japan's most celebrated actors (see p.451).

Heian-jingū

平安神宮 • Nishi Tenno-chō • Daily: March–Sept 6am–6pm; Oct 6am–5.30pm; Nov–Feb 6am–5pm • Free • ☎ 075 761 0221, ⓦ heianjingu.or.jp • The shrine lies about a 10min walk north of Higashiyama subway station, or you can take one of the many buses that run along Higashiōji-dōri

In the late nineteenth century, after Emperor Meiji moved his imperial court to Tokyo, Kyoto authorities felt the need to reaffirm their city's illustrious past. The result was

---

GION MATSURI

祇園祭

Each July, Yasaka-jinja hosts one of Kyoto's biggest spectacles, the **Gion Matsuri** (ⓦ gionfestival.com). This festival is one of the oldest in the world and, except for wars and one case of interference from the shogunate, it has been held annually since 970. Lasting from to July 1 to July 29, Gion Matsuri is more like a series of mini-festivals, with the highlight being the July 17 Yamahoko Junkō – a grand procession of 32 floats decorated with Silk Road treasures. The procession's traditional, ancient route, however, has had to be altered in the postwar era to avoid present-day obstacles such as power lines.

MACHIYA

Kyoto's traditional townhouses, *machiya*, were built in a unique architectural style and remain an enduring symbol of the city's **cultural heritage**. These long wooden houses are made up of a succession of rooms, connected by a single corridor, sometimes stretching as far back as 100m from the front. Their design is a result of the taxes that were levied on buildings during the Edo period according to the size of their street frontage. *Machiya* were generally built by merchants, encompassing a front shop space, living quarters in the middle and a warehouse at the rear. A courtyard garden was also included to aid the flow of light and air through the centre. Their long, thin shape lead to their colloquial name, *unagi no nedoko*, or "bedroom of eels".

Machiya were built almost entirely out of wood, which means that because of fire and earthquakes few that remain today are more than a century old. Some of the best examples are protected by law, but this has not stopped others being demolished at an alarming rate (some figures estimate by more than ten percent a year) since the end of World War II, as land values increased and modern development was encouraged. However, you can still walk along **Sannen-zaka** (see box, p.426), **Shinbashi** (see opposite) or through the **Nishijin** weaving district in Western Kyoto and find some almost complete rows of these beautiful old houses, each dark facade showing subtle variations on the same overall design. Note the distinctive gutter-guards made of curved bamboo, and the narrow-slatted ground-floor windows, which keep out both the summer heat and prying eyes.

Encouragingly, though some continue to be demolished, many *machiya* now seem to be experiencing a period of revitalization, having been remodelled as restaurants, guesthouses, boutiques and galleries, particulary in the central area north of Shijō and west of Kawaramachi. You can find a selection of the best of these in the accommodation and restaurant listings (see pp.440–443 & pp.443–447).

6

Heian-jingū, an impressive though rather garish shrine that was modelled on a scaled-down version of the original eighth-century emperor's Hall of State. Completed in 1895 to commemorate the 1100th anniversary of the founding of the city, it was dedicated to emperors Kammu and Komei (1846–67), Kyoto's first and last imperial residents. The present buildings are reconstructions from 1979, but this is still one of Kyoto's most famous landmarks.

The shrine's bright orange and white halls have an unmistakably Chinese air. Two wings embrace a huge, gravelled courtyard, at the north end of which sits the main worship hall flanked by a couple of pretty two-storey towers representing the protective "Blue Dragon" and "White Tiger".

The gardens

Daily: March–Sept 8.30am–5.30pm; Oct 8.30am–5pm; Nov–Feb 8.30am–4.30pm • ¥600

More interesting than the actual shrine are the **gardens** behind, which were also designed in Heian style. They're divided into four sections, starting in the southwest corner and ending beside a large pond in the east. The south garden features a collection of plants mentioned in Heian literature, while the middle (third) garden is famous for a row of stepping stones made from the columns of two sixteenth-century bridges. The more spacious east garden boasts the shrine's most attractive buildings – the graceful Taihei-kaku pavilion and its covered bridge.

Fureaikan

ふれあい館 • 9-1 Seishoji-chō • Daily 9am–4.30pm • Free • ☎ 075 762 2670, ⓦ miyakomesse.jp/fureaika

Heian-jingū faces south towards a large vermilion *torii* across a park dotted with museums and other municipal buildings. The most rewarding of these is the **Fureaikan**, a museum of traditional crafts in the basement of the modern Miyako Messe exhibition building. Well designed and informative, the museum provides an excellent introduction to the whole range of Kyoto crafts, from roof tiles and metalwork to textiles, confectionery and ornamental hairpins. You can also watch the craftsmen and women at work here, or join a Yuzen dyeing class (weekends only).

Hosomi Museum

細見美術館, Hosomi Bijutsukan • 6-3 Saishōji-chō • 10am–6pm; closed Mon; café 10am–6pm; tearoom 11am–5pm • ¥1000 • ☎ 075 752 5555, ⓦ emuseum.or.jp

The cube-shaped **Hosomi Museum** is a private establishment whose inspiring collection includes Japanese painting, sculpture and decorative art from all major historical periods. It hosts seasonal exhibitions that are curated from the museum's collection. On the top floor is a traditional tearoom, while downstairs the *Café Cube* serves tasty Italian dishes. The museum's Artcube shop is also worth a visit for its excellent selection of contemporary crafts.

National Museum of Modern Art

京都国立近代美術館, Kyōto kokuritsu Kindai Bijutsukan • Enshoji-chō • Tues–Sun 9.30am–4.30pm, until 7.30pm on Fri • ¥430, special exhibitions ¥1300 • ☎ 075 761 4111, ⓦ momak.go.jp

The **National Museum of Modern Art** focuses on local and international twentieth-century artists. On display in this smart modern building are paintings, sculptures, ceramics, crafts and photos. The museum also has an excellent collection of contemporary *nihonga* (Japanese-style painting) and *yōga* (Western-style painting). From the fourth floor, there are good views over the large red *torii* gate in front of the museum.

Kyoto Municipal Museum of Art

京都市美術館 Kyoto-shi Bijutsukan • Enshōji-chō • 9am–4.30pm; closed Mon • Free, prices vary for special exhibitions • ☎ 075 771 4107, ⓦ www.city.kyoto.jp/bunshi/kmma/en

The brick-built **Kyoto Municipal Museum of Art**, inaugurated in 1933, hosts special exhibitions from its vast collection of post-1868 fine arts. On display are Japanese and foreign artists, and it's also possible to see visiting exhibitions of Baroque treasures or painters such as Van Gogh. Check the museum's website for the exhibition schedule.

Murin-an

無鄰庵 • Kusakawa-chō • Daily 9am–4.30pm • ¥400 • ☎ 075 771 3909, ⓦ www.city.kyoto.jp/bunshi/bunka/murin_an/murin_an_top .html • Walk east along the canal from the large *torii* between the Municipal Museum of Art and the Museum of Modern Art

At the same time that Heian-jingū was being built, Marshal Yamagata Aritomo, a leading member of the Meiji government, was creating his villa, **Murin-an**, a delightful haven beside the Biwa Canal. Even today, as you look east from the garden to the Higashiyama hills beyond, it's hard to believe that you're in the middle of a busy city. Designed by Yamagata himself, the unusually naturalistic garden incorporates a meandering stream, pond and lawns in a surprisingly small space. There are also three buildings: take a look upstairs in the two-storey brick house, where parquet floors and wood panelling blend beautifully with Kanō-school painted screens.

Nanzen-ji

南禅寺 • Fukuchi-chō • Daily March–Nov 8.40am–5pm; Dec–Feb 8.40am–4.30pm • Free • ☎ 075 771 0365, ⓦ nanzen.net • A 10min walk from Keage subway station, or #5 bus to Nanzenji/Eikandō-michi

Nestled in the eastern hills near the Biwa Canal, is the stately **Nanzen-ji**. This large, active temple complex belongs to the Rinzai sect of Zen Buddhism and is one of the most important in Kyoto. Nanzen-ji is also famous for its **shōjin-ryōri** (Buddhist vegetarian cuisine) and **yūdōfu** (simmered tofu), which can be sampled in a number of its sub-temples.

Konchi-in

金地院 • ¥400

Before entering the main Nanzen-ji compound, it's worth exploring its quiet sub-temple, **Konchi-in**, on the right in front of the first gate. An arched gate leads straight into one of Kyoto's most beautiful dry gardens – one of the rare works by famed landscape gardener

Kobori Enshū, with documents to prove it. Its centrepiece is a large rectangle of raked gravel with two groups of rocks set against a bank of clipped shrubs. The right-hand, vertical rock group represents a crane, in balance with the horizontal "tortoise"-shaped rock topped by a twisted pine, on the left; both these animals symbolize longevity.

San-mon
三門 • ¥500

Erected in 1628 to commemorate the soldiers killed during the siege of Osaka Castle (see p.491), the looming bulk of **San-mon**, the main gate to Nanzen-ji, seems excessively monumental after Konchi-in. Aside from the pleasant views from the gate, the main reason to come here is to see the fabulous ceiling of birds and celestial beings painted by Tosa- and Kanō-school artists.

The Hōjō
方丈 • ¥500

Nanzen-ji's prize treasures can be found in the **Hōjō**, up to the right behind the San-mon. These include a series of beautiful screens painted by Kanō Tanyū that depict tigers in a bamboo grove, and the "Leaping Tiger" garden, also attributed to Enshū, though the space in worked here is much more confined than that of Konchi-in.

Nomura Art Museum
野村美術館 Namura Bijutsukan • 61 Shimokawara-chō • March–June & Sept–Dec Tues–Sun 10am–4pm • ¥700, tea ¥600 • ☎ 075 751 0374, ⓦ nomura-museum.or.jp

A short walk north of Nanzen-ji, before the start of the Philosopher's Path, lies the small and extremely esoteric **Nomura Art Museum**. It's only open twice a year and holds exhibitions of tea-ceremony utensils and related paraphernalia from the collection of wealthy businessman Nomura Tokushiki (1878–1945). Nomura was also a nō theatre enthusiast and there are some interesting masks and costumes in the collection. The museum also has a pleasant tearoom where you can take a break with a bowl of green tea.

Eikan-dō
永観堂 • 48 Eikandō-chō • Daily 9am–4pm; maple-leaf viewing Nov daily 8.30am–5pm & 5.30–8.30pm • ¥600 • ☎ 075 761 0007, ⓦ eikando.or.jp

Also known as Zenrin-ji due to its unusual Amida statue, the temple of **Eikan-dō** was founded in the ninth century by a disciple of Kōbō Daishi (see p.510), but later became the headquarters of a sub-sect of Jōdoshū (Pure Land Buddhism). In 1082 the then head priest, Eikan, was circling the altar and chanting the *nembutsu*, "Praise to Amida Buddha", when the Amida statue stepped down and started walking in front of him. When Eikan stopped in his tracks, Amida turned to encourage him. Soon after, the priest commissioned the statue you see today of Amida looking over his left shoulder. Eikan-dō is also a popular location for **maple-leaf viewing** during November. Viewing the floodlit leaves in the evening is quite magical, if you don't mind sharing the experience with big crowds; weekends during this period are best avoided.

Hōnen-in
法然院 • 30 Goshonodan-chō • Daily 7am–4pm • Free • ☎ 075 771 2400, ⓦ honen-in.jp

Restored in 1680 by the then head priest of Chion-in, **Hōnen-in** is a tranquil place with a pleasing carp pond and small garden, which is especially attractive in autumn when the leaves of the maples turn red and orange. Occasional events and exhibitions are held here in a converted *kura* (storehouse) in the temple grounds.

Ginkaku-ji
銀閣寺 • 2 Ginkaku-ji-chō • Daily March–Nov 8.30am–5pm; Dec–Feb 9am–4.30pm • ¥500 • ☎ 075 771 5725, ⓦ shokoku-ji.jp

The Temple of the Silver Pavilion, **Ginkaku-ji**, is one of Kyoto's most celebrated sights.

Though modelled on its ostentatious forebear, the golden Kinkaku-ji (see p.434), this simple building sits quietly in the wings while the garden takes centre stage, dominated by a truncated cone of white sand whose severity offsets the soft greens of the surrounding stroll-garden.

Ginkaku-ji originally formed part of a much larger villa built in the fifteenth century for Shogun **Ashikaga Yoshimasa** (1436–90), the grandson of Kinkaku's Ashikaga Yoshimitsu. Interrupted by the Ōnin Wars (1467–77) and plagued by lack of funds, the work continued for thirty years, until Yoshimasa's death in 1490. During that time, however, it became the focal point of Japanese cultural life. Yoshimasa may have been a weak and incompetent ruler, but under his patronage the arts reached new heights of aesthetic refinement; in this mountainside retreat, significantly turned away from the city, he indulged his love of the tea ceremony, poetry and moon-viewing parties while Kyoto succumbed to war. After 1490, the villa became a Rinzai Zen temple, **Jishō-ji**, and eventually fires razed all except two buildings, one of which was the famous pavilion.

The garden

The approach to Ginkaku-ji creates a wonderful sense of anticipation as you're funnelled between tall, thick hedges down an apparently dead-end lane. Turning the corner, a high wall blocks the view except for one small, low window that offers a teasing glimpse. Inside, you're directed first to the **dry garden**, comprising a raised, rippled "Sea of Silver Sand" – designed to reflect moonlight – and a large "moon-facing" cone of sand. The jury's out on whether these enhance the garden or intrude, but it's almost certain that they weren't in the original design, and were probably added in the early seventeenth century. Behind the cone to the west, the small, dark two-storey building with the phoenix topknot is **Ginkaku-ji**, or "Silver Pavilion", despite its lack of silver plating.

Shūgaku-in Rikyū

修学院離宮 • Shūgaku-in • Guided tours Mon–Sat at 9am, 10am, 11am, 1.30pm & 3pm • Free • Tours are in Japanese, though the English-language pamphlet provided gives a basic overview, and must be booked well in advance at the IHA office, 3 Kyōtogyōen, Kamigyō-ku (Mon–Fri 8.45am–noon & 1–4pm; ✆ 075 211 1215, ⓦ sankan.kunaicho.go.jp/english) • City Bus #5 to the Shūgaku-in Rikyū-michi stop on Shirakawa-dōri, from where the villa is a signed ten-minute walk to the east; alternatively, take a train on the private Eizan line from Demachiyanagi Station (in northeast Kyoto) to Shūgaku-in Station (10min), located a couple of minutes west of Shirakawa-dōri

In the foothills of Hiei-zan (see p.460) in the far northeast of Kyoto, the imperial villa of **Shūgaku-in Rikyū** boasts one of Japan's finest examples of garden design using "borrowed scenery"; a technique which incorporates the existing landscape to give the impression of a much larger space. Emperor Go-mizuno'o, who reigned between 1611 and 1629, built Shūgaku-in Rikyū in the late 1650s as a pleasure garden rather than a residence. Just fifteen years old when he ascended the throne, the artistic and highly cultured Go-mizuno'o fiercely resented the new shogunate's constant meddling in imperial affairs – not least being forced to marry the shogun's daughter. After

---

THE PHILOSOPHER'S PATH

One of the prettiest walks in Kyoto, especially during cherry blossom season, is the 2km-long **Philosopher's Path** (哲学の道) which starts just north of Nanzen-ji (see p.430) and leads to Ginkaku-ji (see above). Its name refers to a respected philosopher, **Nishida Kitarō** (1870–1945), who took his daily constitutional along the path through the wooded hillside on his way to Kyoto University. Every so often stone bridges link it to the tempting residential lanes on either side, while the occasional souvenir shop or quaint teashop provides an additional distraction. You can reach the southern end of the path by exiting Eikan-dō (see p.431), and taking the first right turn, then you'll emerge beside the Ginkaku-ji bridge about thirty minutes later. From here you can pick up bus routes #5, #203 and #204, and Raku buses #100, #102, which stop nearby at Ginkaku-ji-michi.

Go-mizuno'o abdicated in 1630, however, the shogun encouraged him to establish an imperial villa. He eventually settled on the site of a ruined temple, Shūgaku-in, and set about designing a series of gardens, which survived more than a century of neglect before the government rescued them in the 1820s. Though some of the original pavilions have been lost, Go-mizuno'o's overall design remains – a delightfully naturalistic garden that blends seamlessly into the wooded hills.

The gardens

Shūgaku-in Rikyū is made up of three separate **gardens**, each in their own enclosure among the terraced rice fields. Of these, the top lake-garden is the star attraction. Climbing up the path towards the upper villa, you pass between tall, clipped hedges before suddenly emerging at the compound's highest point. An airy pavilion, **Rin-un-Tei**, occupies the little promontory, with views over the lake, the forested, rolling hills in the middle distance and the mountains beyond. As you walk back down through the garden, the grand vistas continue with every twist and turn of the path, passing the intricate Chitose bridge, intimate tea-ceremony pavilions and rustic boathouses.

West Kyoto

Compared to east Kyoto, sights in the city's **western districts** are more dispersed, but it is worth devoting a day to this area, particularly the northwest fringes, where the city meets the encircling hills. The extravagant **Kinkaku-ji**, the Golden Pavilion, the enigmatic Zen garden of **Ryōan-ji** and the dry gardens of **Daitoku-ji**, should not be missed, while the **Nishijin** weaving district is an interesting area to explore with its streets of *machiya* and the sounds of the silk-weaving looms.

Nishijin Ori Kaikan

西陣織会館 • Horikawa-dōri Imadegawa Minami-iri • Daily 9am–5pm; kimono shows hourly 10–4pm • Free • ☎ 075 451 9231, ⓦ nishijin.or.jp/kaikan • Raku Bus #101 & #102 or City Bus #9 & #12

Kyoto has long been famous for the high quality of its **weaving** of kimono and *obi* sashes, and the centre of the city's textile industry is the Nishijin district, to the west of the Imperial Palace. The number of weaving businesses has decreased rapidly in recent years, from more than twelve hundred in 1980 to fewer than six hundred now, due to the economic conditions and reduced local demand. However, as you walk through the area today you'll still hear the clatter of looms in dozens of family-run workshops, and you can watch demonstrations of Nishijin weaving at the **Nishijin Ori Kaikan**. Their display rooms have examples of exquisite silk kimono and *obi* and you can also watch the **kimono shows**, which, although touristy, are a good basic introduction to the different types of kimono.

Daitoku-ji

大徳寺 • 53 Daitokuji-chō • Daily 24hr • Free • ☎ 075 491 0019, ⓦ zen.rinnou.net/head_temples/07daitoku.html • Roughly 1500m west of Kita-ōji subway station (on the Karasuma line), or can be reached by City Bus #101, #102, #205 and #206 – get off at Daitoku-ji-mae

Lying halfway between the Kamo-gawa and the Kitayama hills, **Daitoku-ji** is one of Kyoto's largest Zen temple complexes, with over twenty sub-temples in its large, walled compound. Of these only four are open to the public, but within them you'll find a representative sampler of the dry gardens (*kare-sansui*) for which Japanese Zen Buddhism is renowned. Daitoku-ji is also an excellent place to sample top-quality **shōjin-ryōri**, Buddhist vegetarian cuisine.

Daisen-in

大仙院 • Daily: March–Nov 9am–5pm; Dec–Feb 9am–4.30pm • ¥400 • ☎ 075 491 8346, ⓦ b-model.net/daisen-in/index.htm

Entering Daitoku-ji from the east, head through the huge San-mon gate to the sub-temple of **Daisen-in** in the north of the compound: if you can, it pays to visit early in the day before the crowds arrive. Of the temple's two gardens, the most famous is on the right as you enter the main hall – it replicates a Chinese landscape painting and uses carefully selected rocks, pebbles and a few scaled-down plants to conjure up jagged mountains.

Ryōgen-in

龍源院 • Daily 9am–4.30pm • ¥350 • ☎ 075 491 7635

Founded in the early sixteenth century, **Ryōgen-in** is home to Japan's smallest Zen rock garden. The minuscule Tōtekiko garden, on your right-hand side as you continue along the corridor from the entrance, consists of waves of sand round a rock, symbolizing a Zen saying that the harder a stone is thrown, the bigger the ripples. This sub-temple also contains four other gardens, including the mossy Ryugin-tei, which claims to be the oldest garden in the compound.

Kinkaku-ji

金閣寺 • 1 Kinkakuji-chō • Daily 9am–5pm • ¥400 • ☎ 075 461 0013, ⊛ shokoku-ji.jp • Kinkaku-ji lies on several bus routes, of which the most convenient are City Bus #101, #102, #205 & #206

West of Daitoku-ji, the wooded hills of Kitayama are home to **Kinkaku-ji**, the famous Temple of the Golden Pavilion. The pavilion originally formed part of a larger retirement villa built by the former Shogun Ashikaga Yoshimitsu (1358–1408) on the site of an earlier aristocratic residence; it was converted into a Zen temple on his death. A noted scholar of Chinese culture, Yoshimitsu incorporated various Chinese motifs into the pavilion and its surrounding garden, the focus of which is a lake studded with rocks and pine-covered islets.

Even the crowds can't diminish the impact of seeing the temple for the first time – a hint of gold glimpsed though the trees, and then the whole, gleaming apparition floating above the aptly named **Kyōko-chi** (Mirror Pond). If you're lucky enough to see it against the autumn leaves, or on a sunny winter's day after a dusting of snow, the effect is doubly striking. Note the different architectural styles of the pavilion's three floors and the phoenix standing on the shingle roof. It's an appropriate symbol: having survived all these years, Kinkaku-ji was torched in 1950 by an unhappy monk. The replica was finished in just five years, and in 1987 the building was gilded again, at vast expense.

Kyoto Museum for World Peace

国際平和ミュージアム, Kokusai Heiwa Myūjiamu • 56-1 Kita-machi • 9.30am–4pm; closed Mon • ¥400 • ☎ 075 465 8151, ⊛ www .ritsumei.ac.jp/mng/mng/er/wp-museum/english • On the campus of Ritsumeikan University, halfway between Kinkaku-ji and Ryōan-ji

The **Kyoto Museum for World Peace** unflinchingly examines the roots of Japan's twentieth-century militarization and its devastating effects on other Asian countries, as well as considering what could have happened if the US plan to drop an atomic bomb on Kyoto had not been abandoned in favour of Nagasaki. The displays in the main exhibition room have English-language descriptions and include a replica of a wartime-era house, showing blacked-out windows and other precautions. The two large reliefs on the wall of the entrance hall depicting the mythical phoenix were painted by noted manga artist Tezuka Osamu and symbolize the living energy of all creatures on earth.

Ryōan-ji

龍安寺 • 13 Goryōnoshita-machi • Daily: March–Nov 8am–5pm; Dec–Feb 8.30am–4.30pm • ¥500 • ☎ 075 463 2216, ⊛ ryoanji.jp • Take bus #12 or #59 from Kinkaku-ji, or walk southwest along Kitsuji-dōri for about twenty minutes

While Kinkaku-ji is all about displays of wealth and power, the dry garden of **Ryōan-ji** hides infinite truths within its riddle of rocks and sand. Thought to date back to the late fifteenth century, and said by some to be the work of Sōami, the most famous artist, landscape gardener and tea ceremony master of the time, it was largely unknown until the 1930s. Now it's probably Japan's most famous garden, which means you're unlikely to be able to appreciate the Zen experience thanks to intrusive loudspeaker announcements and almost constant crowds, though very early morning tends to be better.

The garden

The **garden** consists of a long, walled rectangle of off-white gravel, in which fifteen stones of various sizes are arranged in five groups, some rising up from the raked sand and others almost completely lost. In fact, the stones are placed so that wherever you stand one of them is always hidden from view. The only colour is provided by electric-green patches of moss around some stones, making this the simplest and most abstract of all Japan's Zen gardens. It's thought that the layout is a *kōan*, or riddle, set by Zen masters to test their students, and there's endless debate about its "meaning". Popular theories range from tigers crossing a river to islands floating in a sea of infinity. Fortunately, it's possible to enjoy the garden's perfect harmony and in-built tension without worrying too much about the meaning. Walk round the veranda of the main hall and you'll find a stone water basin inscribed with a helpful thought from the Zen tradition: "I learn only to be contented".

Kyoyō-chi

鏡容池

Leaving the main hall, it's worth strolling round **Kyoyō-chi**, Ryōan-ji's refreshingly quiet lake-garden. It dates back to the twelfth century, when a noble of the Fujiwara clan built his villa here, before the estate was donated to the Rinzai Buddhist sect in the fifteenth century. Kyoyō-chi is particularly scenic in the autumn when the fiery colours of the maple leaves frame its edges.

Kōryū-ji

広隆寺 • 32 Hachioka-chō • Daily 9am–5pm • ¥700 • ☎ 075 861 1461 • The easiest way to get here is to take a train on the private Keifuku Arashiyama line from Shijō-Ōmiya Station in central Kyoto to Uzumasa Station. Alternatively, it's 10min walk from Uzumasa Tenjingawa Subway Station. Coming from central Kyoto, City Bus #11 and Kyoto Bus #71, #72, #73 and #74 all stop outside Kōryū-ji.

In the Uzumasa district, due south of Ryōan-ji, **Kōryū-ji** is said to have been founded in the early seventh century by Nara's Prince Shōtoku (see p.471), making it one of Japan's oldest temples. Some scholars believe that the real founder was actually a friend of the prince's by the name of Hata no Kawakatsu, who had a lineage that stretched back to Korea, and possibly all the way to Turkestan.

The **Kōdō** (Lecture Hall) – straight ahead once you've entered the compound from the Heian-period gate – dates from 1165 and is one of the oldest buildings in Kyoto. The three Buddhas inside are imposing enough, but Kōryū-ji's main attractions are the statues kept in the modern **Reihōden** (霊宝殿) Treasure House at the back of the compound. The "newest" of these images is a thirteenth-century statue of Prince Shōtoku aged 16, his sweet face framed by bun-shaped pigtails. The oldest is the exquisite **Miroku Bosatsu** (弥勒菩薩), the Future Buddha rendered as a Bodhisattva pondering how to save mankind. Originally, it was probably gilded and it is thought to have been a gift to Shōtoku from the Korean court in the early seventh century; its soft, delicate features are certainly unlike any other Japanese images from the time. The small, slim figure sits, elbow on knee, leaning forward slightly and head tilted in a pose of utter concentration.

Tōei Uzumasa Eiga-mura

東映太秦映画村 • 10 Higashi Hachioka-chō • Daily: March–Nov 9am–4pm; Dec–Feb 9.30am–3.30pm • ¥2200, plus extra charges for some attractions; ¥1100 for children • ☎ 075 864 7716, ⚲ toei-eigamura.com • The easiest way to get here is to take a train on the private Keifuku Arashiyama line from Shijō-Ōmiya Station in central Kyoto to Uzumasa Station. Alternatively, it's 10min walk from Uzumasa Tenjingawa Subway Station. Coming from central Kyoto, City Bus #11 and Kyoto Bus #71, #72, #73 and #74 all stop outside Kōryū-ji, from where it's a short walk to Eiga-mura

In western Kyoto, **Tōei Uzumasa Eiga-mura** is a functioning film studio that doubles as a theme park. Run by one of Japan's major film companies, the Tōei **studios** opens its sets to the public, who can look round the location where directors such as **Kurosawa Akira** filmed their classics. One of the indoor studios is usually in action, nowadays mostly making

6

historical TV dramas, while the outdoor sets – an Edo-period street, thatched farmhouses, Meiji-era Western-style buildings and so on – are enlivened by roaming geisha and sword-fighting samurai. You can also rent a costume and stroll around as a geisha, samurai or ninja (from ¥11,000 with professional photos). More recent attractions include The Ninja Mystery House (¥500), the Toei Anime Museum and the Trick Art Museum.

Katsura Rikyū

桂離宮 • Katsura • Guided tours of the gardens (in Japanese only) Mon–Fri (and occasionally Sat) at 9am, 10am, 11am, 1.30pm, 2.30pm & 3.30pm • Free • Applications to visit must be made through the Imperial Household Agency at 3 Kyōtogyoen, Kamigyo-ku (Mon–Fri 8.45am–noon & 1–4pm; ☎ 075 211 1215, ⓦ kunaicho.go.jp) • It's a 20min walk from Katsura Station, on the private Hankyū line from central Kyoto. Alternatively, City Bus #33 will drop you at Katsura Rikyū-mae, the first stop after crossing the river, from where it's a 5min walk north to the gate – this bus stop lies just outside the bus-pass zones, so if you want to save a few yen, get off before the river and walk over

Located on the west bank of the Katsura-gawa, **Katsura Rikyū** is a former imperial villa that was built in the early seventeenth century as a residence for the imperial Prince Toshihito, and then expanded by his son, Toshitada, in the 1650s. Toshihito was a highly cultured man, who filled his villa and garden with references to *The Tale of Genji* and other literary classics, while also creating what is considered to be Japan's first **stroll-garden**. As the name suggests, these gardens were to be enjoyed on foot – rather than from a boat or from a fixed viewpoint – and designed to look "natural". In fact they were planned in minute detail so that scenes unfold in a particular order as the viewer progresses. Focused on a large, indented lake, the Katsura garden is famed for its variety of footpaths and stone pavings, and for its stone lanterns, all of which helped create the desired mood of relaxation. Several tea pavilions occupy prime spots around the lake, the most attractive of which is **Shokin-tei** (松琴亭). But perhaps the most interesting aspect of the garden is the sheer ingenuity of the designer – Toshihito managed to wrestle a splendidly harmonious, seemingly spacious garden out of an unexciting bit of flood plain.

Saihō-ji

西芳寺 • 56 Jingatani-chō • Daily, visiting time at the discretion of the temple • ¥3000 • ☎ 075 391 3631 • To visit the temple, you need to reserve via a special postal application. Write to Saihō-ji, 56 Jingatani-chō, Matsuo, Nishikyō-ku, Kyoto-shi, 615-8286, giving your name, address, age (you must be over 18), number of visitors, and proposed date of visit (with 1 or 2 alternative dates). Note that you must apply with a Japanese address (a hotel address is fine). Allow two weeks' notice, and your request has to be at least 7 days before the day you desire to visit. You must enclose a stamped self-addressed postcard for a reply. Japanese post offices sell special reply-paid "double postcards", or *ōfuku hagaki* (往復はがき), for this type of application. Once your reservation has been approved the date cannot be changed • From Arashiyama or Kyoto Station, take City Bus #28 to Matsuo Taisha-mae (松尾大社前), just west of the river, and walk for 15min

Three kilometres northwest of Katsura Rikyū, in a narrow, tree-filled valley, you'll find the voluptuous and tranquil moss gardens of **Saihō-ji**, also known as Koke-dera (苔寺), or the "Moss Temple". A visit to Saihō-ji needs planning, but don't be put off by the application process (see above) or the distance from Kyoto – this temple is well worth visiting and a memorable experience. All visitors are required to attend a short Zen service during which you'll chant a sutra, trace the sutra's characters in *sumi-e* ink and finally write your name, address and "wish" before placing the paper in front of the altar. After that you're free to explore the garden at your leisure.

Like Kōryū-ji (see p.435), the temple started life in the seventh century as one of Prince Shōtoku's villas. Soon after, Jōdo Buddhists adopted the site for one of their "paradise gardens", after which the gifted Zen monk, **Musō Kokushi**, was invited to take over the temple in 1338. The present layout dates mostly from his time, though the lakeside pavilion – the inspiration for Kinkaku-ji (see p.434) – and nearly all Saihō-ji's other buildings burnt down during the Ōnin Wars (1467–77). In fact, given the temple's history of fire, flooding and periods of neglect, it seems unlikely that today's garden bears much resemblance to Musō's. Saihō-ji was in complete ruins by the eighteenth century and some sources even attribute the famous mosses to accident, arguing that they spread naturally as the garden reverted to damp, shady woodland.

Whatever their origin, the swathes of soft, dappled moss – some 120 varieties in all – are a magical sight, especially after the rains of May and June, when the greens take on an extra intensity.

ARRIVAL AND DEPARTURE

KYOTO

BY PLANE

The nearest airports to Kyoto are **Kansai International Airport** (KIX and T2), which handles both international and domestic flights, and **Osaka International Aiport** (also known as Itami Airport) which, despite the name, only handles domestic flights.

KANSAI AIRPORT

Kansai International Airport (KIX; 関西国際空港; ☎072 455 2500, ⓦkansa-airport.or.jp) is on a man-made island in Osaka Bay, some 35km south of Osaka city centre, and approximately 100km from Kyoto. The international departure lounge is on the fourth floor and domestic departures are on the second floor. In 2012, KIX Terminal 2 (KIX; 第2 ターミナル; ☎072 455 2911, ⓦkansai-airport.or.jp/t2) opened, though it is currently only used by Peach Aviation for Asian and some domestic destinations. Shuttle buses connect Teminal 2 with the main building, Kansai International Airport Terminal 1.

Destinations Fukuoka (10 daily; 1hr); Kagoshima (3 daily; 1hr 10min); Nagasaki (2 daily; 1hr 10min); Naha (13 daily; 1hr 15min); Sapporo (13 daily; 2hr); Sendai (3 daily; 1hr 10min); Tokyo Haneda (9 daily; 1hr); and Tokyo Narita (8 daily; 1hr 15min).

By train If you're coming direct from Kansai International Airport, the quickest and easiest option is a JR Haruka Limited Express train, which whisks you direct to Kyoto in just over an hour (¥3490 reserved; ¥2980 unreserved); JR passes are valid on this service for unreserved seats. JR West sells a ICOCA+HARUKA prepaid card for tourists which includes a good discount on the Haruka ticket (see ⓦwestjr.co.jp/global/en/travel-information/pass/icoca-haruka for more details). For those not travelling with a JR Pass, a cheaper option is to take an express from the airport to Osaka Station, changing there to an express train on the JR Kyoto line; this takes a little under 2hr and costs about ¥1830.

By bus Comfortable airport limousine buses do the journey into Kyoto in under 2hr, traffic permitting, and terminate on the south (Hachijō-guchi) side of Kyoto Station (1–2 hourly 6am–3pm; ¥2300). If you're heading from Kyoto direct to Kansai Airport, it's a good idea to reserve your transport in advance. Buses depart (hourly 6am–8pm; 1hr 45min; ¥2300; ☎075 682 4400) from outside the New Miyako Hotel and the Avanti department store. Tickets are available from the ground floor of the nearby Keihan Hotel.

By taxi shuttle Another option for getting from and to the airport is to take a "door-to-door" taxi shuttle bus (¥3500): the MK Skygate shuttle (☎075 702 5849, ⓦmktaxi-japan.com)

or the Yasaka Kansai Airport Shuttle (☎075 803 4800, ⓦwww.yasaka.jp/english/shuttle/index.html). The ride time varies, depending on the traffic, but will be calculated to get you there on time for check-in. Reservations for both services must be made at least 2 days in advance.

OSAKA INTERNATIONAL AIRPORT

Osaka International Airport (大阪国際空港; ☎06 6856 6781, ⓦOsaka-airport.co.jp) lies 10km north of Osaka city centre, and around 50km southwest of Kyoto.

Destinations Akita (6 daily; 1hr 30min); Aomori (3 daily; 1hr 40min); Fukuoka (19 daily; 1hr); Kagoshima (15 daily; 1hr 10min); Kumamoto (12 daily; 1hr 5min); Miyazaki (12 daily; 1hr 5min); Nagasaki (7 daily; 1hr 10min); Naha (6 daily; 1hr 15min); Niigata (10 daily; 1hr 10min); Ōita (7 daily; 1hr); Sapporo (5 daily; 2hr); Sendai (19 daily; 1hr 10min); Tokyo Haneda (32 daily; 1hr); Tokyo Narita (4 daily; 1hr 15min); and Yamagata (3 daily; 1hr 20min).

By train The easiest way to get to Kyoto by train from Osaka International Airport is to ride the monorail to Hankyū Hotarugaike Station, then take a train to Juso Station where you can change to a Kyoto-bound train. From here you can catch an express train to Kyoto (72min; ¥650). JR Pass holders will need to take the Hankyū line to its terminus in Umeda and then walk to JR Osaka Station for a Kyoto-bound express train.

By bus Direct limousine buses run between the airport and Kyoto Station (every 20min 5.50am–6.55pm; 55min; ¥1280; ☎06 6844 1124).

By taxi shuttle The MK Skygate shuttle (☎075 702 5849, ⓦmktaxi-japan.com; ¥2300) has services between Kyoto and Osaka International Airport. Reservations must be made more than 2 days in advance.

BY TRAIN

Kyoto Station Most visitors arrive in Kyoto at the JR Station. The JR local lines all converge here, and Kyoto is also linked by Shinkansen to Tokyo and Nagoya in the east, and Ōsaka, Hiroshima and Fukuoka, to the west. The terminus for the Kintetsu Kyoto line which links the city to Nara, Kōya-san and Ise is also located here, next to the Shinkansen station.

Destinations Amanohashidate (7 daily; 2hr 30min); Fukuoka (Hakata Station; 1–2 hourly; 2hr 50min); Hikone (every hour; 50min); Himeji (1–3 hourly; 50min); Hiroshima (1–2 hourly; 1hr 40min); Ise (hourly; 2hr); Kanazawa (1–2 hourly; 2hr); Kansai International (every 30min; 1hr 15min); Kashikojima (hourly; 2hr 45min); Kōbe (& Shin-Kōbe) (1–3 hourly; 30min); Nagoya (every 15min;

40min); Nara (every 15–20min; 40min); Osaka (& Shin-Ōsaka) (every 15min; 17min); Toba (hourly; 2hr 20min); Tokyo (every 15min; 2hr 10min); Toyama (hourly; 2hr 40min); and Uji (every 10–15min; 20min).

BY BUS

Long-distance buses Long-distance buses arrive at and depart from terminals either side of Kyoto Station. JR Highway buses (ⓦ nishinihonjrbus.co.jp) to Tokyo, Nagoya and Kanazawa depart from a stand on the north side of the station, while Keihan Bus (ⓦ keihanbus.jp) uses a terminal on the south side, outside the *Keihan Hotel*. Keihan services cover Nagasaki, Kumamoto, Fukuoka, Tokyo and Kanazawa. Willer Bus (ⓦ willerexpress.com) departs from the Hachijō exit on the south side and from in front of Hotel New Hankyū on the north side of the station.

Destinations Amanohashidate (2 daily; 2hr 40min); Fukuoka (1 daily; 11hr); Hiroshima (4 daily; 6hr 45min); Kanazawa (5 daily; 4hr); Kumamoto (1 daily; 11hr); Matsuyama (1 daily; 9hr 35min); Nagasaki (1 daily; 11hr); Nagoya (16 daily; 2hr 30min); Tokyo (6 daily; 8hr); Tottori (3 daily; 4hr); and Yokohama (1 daily; 7hr 30min).

INFORMATION

Tourist information Kyoto's main source of information is the Kyoto Tourist Information Centre (daily 8.30am–7pm; ☎ 075 343 0548), on the second floor of Kyoto Station next to the main entrance of Isetan department store. In the city centre, there's a small tourist information office on the west side of Kawaramachi, between Shijō and Sanjō. In eastern Kyoto, near Nanzen-ji, Kyoto International Community House (9am–9pm; closed Mon; ☎ 075 752 3010, ⓦ kcif.or.jp/en) is aimed primarily at foreign students and longer-term residents, but will happily assist tourists where possible. Also in eastern Kyoto, the Kyoto Handicraft Center (10am–6pm; ☎ 075 761 8001, ⓦ kyotohandicraftcenter.com) on Marutamachi has a tourist information office.

Maps Detailed bilingual maps of Kyoto are available free from the Kyoto Tourist Information Centre (see above).

Listings The free monthly tourist magazine, *Kyoto Visitor's Guide* (ⓦ kyotoguide.com), is the best source of information regarding what's on in Kyoto and also has useful maps for sightseeing. It includes details of festivals and cultural events; you can usually pick it up in tourist information offices, major hotels and other tourist haunts. The free monthly *Kansai Scene* (ⓦ kansaiscene.com) magazine also has a good listings section, with the latest on Kyoto events and exhibitions.

Websites Some useful online resources for general Kyoto travel and cultural information are Kyoto Travel Guide (ⓦ kyoto.travel) and Mago-no-Te (ⓦ kyoto-magonote .jp/en).

GETTING AROUND

BY SUBWAY

The lines Kyoto's two subway lines (5.29am–11.49pm; ¥210–340) are the quickest way to scoot around the city. The Karasuma line runs from southerly Takeda (where it connects with the Kintetsu line), via Kyoto Station and Kita-ōji, to Kokusai Kaikan in the north, while the Tōzai line starts at Uzumasa Tenjingawa in the west and cuts east through Sanjō-Keihan and Higashiyama to Rokujizō in the southeast suburbs; the two lines intersect at Karasuma-Oike Station.

Tickets and passes As well as single tickets (minimum fare ¥210), you can buy the Kyoto Sightseeing Pass (one-day ¥1200; two-day ¥2000) for use on City Buses, the subway and one section of the Kyoto Bus route. Alternatively, the *Torafika Kyoto Card* is a stored-fare card (¥1000 or ¥3000) that can be used to buy subway tickets and tickets on City Bus services. These cards are both available from the Kyoto Bus Information Center in front of Kyoto Station, as well as from train and subway stations. The Kyoto Sightseeing Pass can also be purchased from bus drivers. Another option is the Surutto Kansai Miyako Card, which can be used on city buses, the subway, and the Keihan and Hankyū train lines; it's available in ¥1000, ¥2000, ¥3000 and ¥5000 denominations from station vending machines and bus information centres. If you are planning day-trips from Kyoto to other parts of Kansai, the Kansai Thru Pass (two days ¥3800; three days ¥5000; ⓦ surutto.com/tickets/kansai_thru_english.html) is a good option for tourists, as it allows you to use almost any bus, subway or private railway in the region. It can be purchased from major tourist information centres and bus information centres by showing your passport.

BY TRAIN

Hankyū railway Trains on Hankyū railway's Kyoto line for Osaka (Umeda) run beneath the city centre from Kawaramachi Station west along Shijō-dōri. A branch line heads northwest from Katsura Station in west Kyoto to Arashiyama, where it's a short walk across the Togetsu-kyō bridge to the main part of town.

JR The JR Sagano line runs from Kyoto Station to Saga-Arashiyama Station. The JR Nara line runs south through the southern Kyoto suburbs and Uji, and the JR Biwako line runs east through Yamashima, Otsu and Hakone.

Keifuku Railway Also known as Randen, the Keifuku Railway services Arashiyama from Shijō-Ōmiya Station, and Kitano-Hakubai-chō Station in northwest Kyoto.

Eizan line In northeast Kyoto, Demachiyanagi is the terminus for the Eizan line, which covers Shūgaku-in Rikyū and Yase-yūen, one of the routes up Hiei-zan (see p.460).

Keihan mainline services Keihan mainline services start from a separate station in Demachiyanagi and then head south via Sanjō-Keihan to Osaka (Yodoyabashi and Nakanoshima).

Kintetsu-Kyoto line Trains on the Kintetsu Kyoto line depart from the south side of Kyoto Station, from where they link into the main Kintetsu network, with services to Nara, Kōya-san and Ise.

BY BUS

Kyoto's excellent bus system is relatively easy to use. The buses are colour-coded, the majority show their route numbers on the front and the most important stops are announced in English, either on the electronic display or over the internal speakers. Within the city there's a flat fare of ¥220, which you pay on leaving the bus. You enter via the back door, where you may need to take a numbered ticket if the bus is going into the suburbs, though the flat fare still applies within the central zone. Most services stop running around 11pm, or earlier on less popular routes.

Bus maps Before leaping on board, get hold of the English-language Bus Nav route map from the Kyoto Tourist Information Centre, or the Bus Information Center in front of Kyoto Station. This map shows the central zone boundary and routes operated by both Kyoto City Bus and the far less comprehensive Kyoto Bus. You'll need to use Kyoto Bus services for Ōhara and Shugakuin, but otherwise you can stick to City Bus for the central districts, including Arashiyama.

Bus terminals The main bus terminal is outside Kyoto Station's Karasuma exit. Most routes loop around the city; the most useful is #206, with stops near the National Museum, Gion, Heian-ingū, Daitoku-ji and Nijō-jō. Buses running clockwise leave from boarding platform B, and anticlockwise from boarding platform A. The other major terminals are at Sanjō-Keihan, in east Kyoto, and Kita-ōji in the north. Many routes also converge centrally at Shijō Kawaramachi.

Raku bus routes The Raku bus routes are tourist buses that stop at major sightseeing spots and have English-language commentary, and are ideal if you want to cover a lot of sights in a short amount of time. Buses #100 and #101 start from Kyoto Station, with Raku #100 travelling up the east side of Kyoto from Kiyomizu-dera to Ginkakuji, and Raku #101 heading towards Nijo and then Kinkakuji. Raku #102 starts from Kinrin Shako-mae, on Kitashirakawa-dōri, goes towards Ginkakuji and then across to Kinkakuji, where it terminates. The buses operate 9am–5pm, with route #100 buses running every 10min, but #101 and #102 only running once an hour. You can use any of the prepaid card systems on the Raku buses or it's ¥220 per ride.

Tickets and passes The bus companies offer a range of discount tickets. The simplest, *kaisūken*, are booklets of five ¥220 tickets available for ¥1000 at the bus terminals, and valid on all buses. Next up are the one-day passes (*shi-basu*

ichi-nichi jyōshaken; ¥500), which allow unlimited travel on City Bus services within the central zone; available at information centres, hotels, bus terminals and from the bus driver. To validate the pass, put it through the machine beside the driver when you get off the first bus – after that, just show it as you exit. Finally, there's the Kyoto Sightseeing Pass, a combined subway and bus pass available for one day (*shi-basu chikatetsu icai-nichi jyōshaken*; ¥1200) or two days (*shi-basu chikatetsu futsuka jyōshaken*; ¥2000), covering unlimited travel on the subways, City Bus and Kyoto Bus within a wider area marked on the bus maps in white. They're sold at hotels, tourist information offices, bus terminals, subway information windows or travel agents.

ON FOOT

Walking is the best way to explore Kyoto so that you can avoid using the bus network which can get very congested during spring and autumn's peak visitor seasons. It's also easier to wander the narrow back lanes on foot.

BY BIKE

Renting a bike is a viable option for exploring central Kyoto, though not much use along the eastern hills, where you're better off walking. The following bike rental outlets have terminals near Kyoto Station: Kyoto eco-trip (daily 9am–6pm; ☎075 691 0794, ⓦ kyoto-option.com), charges ¥800/day for the most basic bicycle, and electric bicycles are ¥2000/day. Fuune Rental Cycles (daily 8.30am–7pm; ☎075 371 7800, ⓦfuune.jp) offers half-day and night-time rentals (summer only), with a good range of electric (¥1800/day) and non-electric bicycles (¥1000/day). Kyoto Cycling Tour Project (daily 9am–7pm; ☎075 354 3636, ⓦ kctp.net) rents various kinds of bikes from ¥1000/day and also arranges tours (see p.440). Be aware that Kyoto City regularly impounds bicycles parked in prohibited zones, such as in front of train and subway stations, and it costs ¥2300 and a lot of effort, to recover them check ⓦ kyochari-navi.jp/churin/index.html for official bicycle parks.

BY CAR

Car rental outlets with offices near Kyoto Station include Nippon Rent-a-Car (☎075 661 6680; ⓦ nipponrentacar.co.jp), Nissan Rent-a-Car (☎075 661 4123 ⓦnissan-rentacar.com/english) and Eki Rent-a-Car (ⓦ www.ekiren.cc.jp, ☎075 681 3020), and Europcar (☎075 681 7779, ⓦeuropcar.jp).

BY TAXI

Taxis are useful for hopping short distances – the minimum fare is ¥580 for 2km. In Kyoto, MK Taxi (☎075 778 4141, ⓦ mktaxi-japan.com) and Yasaka Taxi (☎075 842 1212, ⓦ www.yasaka.jp) are both reliable services. Since drivers don't always speak English, it's useful to have your destination written down in Japanese.

TOURS

Bus tours The Kyoto World Heritage Tour Bus takes passengers around Kyoto's major historical sites (¥2000/person; Sat, Sun & national holidays 8.40am–5.30pm; ☎075 672 2100, ⍟kyoto-lab.jp/hirubus). It's a hop-on-hop-off service that runs approx hourly, with audio commentary (¥500 extra) on the bus between sites. You can do the same route in the evening on the Kyoto Night Cruise Bus Tour (¥1600/person; Thurs–Sat 7.50pm–9.25pm; ☎075 662 7100, ⍟kyoto-lab.jp/nc/rve.php) and see the sights illuminated, though it's not a hop-on-hop-off service.

Cycling tours If you'd rather travel around on two wheels, try the Kyoto Cycling Tour Project (☎075 354 3636, ⍟kctp.net) which offers daily guided English tours of Kyoto's backstreets and hidden alleyways (3hr; from ¥5500/person for groups of four), as well as a World Heritage Site tour (8hr; ¥12,000/person for groups of four). The cost includes bicycle rental and any admission fees. Reservations must be made three days in advance.

Food tours The Haru Cooking School guides small groups on a 90min tour through Nishiki-kōji street market (see p.418) in conjunction with their cooking classes (weekly from noon; ¥4000/person; ☎090 4284 7176, ⍟kyoto-cooking-class.com). As well as learning about the essential ingredients of Kyoto cuisine, you'll have plenty of chance to sample an array of pickles, dried fish and traditional sweets.

Geisha tours In collaboration with Kyoto City Tourism Association, Waraido runs the Gion Night Walking Tour (March–Nov, Mon, Wed & Fri, 6pm–7.45pm; Dec–Feb, 5pm–6.40pm; ¥1000/person; reservations not required; ☎075 752 7070, ⍟waraido.com/walking/gion.html) from Shinbashi to Gion Corner. The tour offers a basic introduction to Kyoto geisha culture and points of interest, though groups tend to be large and obtrusive. Alternatively, long-term resident Peter Macintosh offers a 90-minute Geisha Culture Walking Lecture to small groups. Winding through the backstreets of Gion and Miyagawa-chō districts, it provides a chance to learn about where geisha live, study and entertain, accompanied by Macintosh's entertaining anecdotes (¥3000/person; call from noon–3pm to reserve; ☎090 5169 1654, ⍟kyotosightsandnights.com).

Walking tours Waraido's Daytime Walking Tour take small groups on a slow amble through southern Kyoto from Higashi-Hongan-ji to the eastern hills (March–Nov Mon, Wed & Fri, except national holidays, 10am to mid-afternoon; ¥2000/person; ☎075 257 7676, ⍟waraido.com/walking/index.html). The Deepest Kyoto Tour (second & fourth Wed of every month, 1–3pm; ¥3000/person; ⍟deepestkyototour.com) takes small groups on a tour of *machiya* townhouse architecture and Kiyomizu pottery artisans. They also occasionally conduct more specialized artisan tours – check the website for details. For a theatrical-style exploration of Kyoto on foot, the Cool Kyoto Walking Tour (Saturday 10am–3pm; ¥3000/person; ☎077 377 5514, ⍟cool-kyoto.net) with "last samurai" Joe Okada is a fun stroll from Teramachi to the Imperial Park area.

ACCOMMODATION

Kyoto's accommodation options range from basic guesthouses, capsule hotels, youth hostels and temple lodgings (*shukubō*) to luxurious international **hotels** and top-class **ryokan**. One night in a full-blown Kyoto ryokan, enjoying the world's most meticulous service, is an experience not to be missed. The ongoing recession has made many establishments that were previously difficult to access more affordable and welcoming. Increasingly, old Kyoto houses (*machiya*) are being developed into **guesthouses**, offering visitors the chance to experience traditional Kyoto life. It's essential to make **reservations** at these places as far in advance as possible, but all accommodation in Kyoto gets pretty busy in spring and autumn, at holiday weekends and around the major festivals (see box, p.451); room rates may rise considerably during these times. In terms of

JINRIKISHA

Jinrikisha (人力車), which means "man-powered vehicle", were a common form of transportation in Kyoto from the 1880s until the early twentieth century, when it became more fashionable to use bicycles, automobiles and street trams. A local company is now producing two-seater Meiji-period-style *jinrikisha*, and has revived this form of transport for tourists. It's a fun way to see the main tourist sites in any season – they all have hoods to protect passengers from sun and rain.

There are *jinrikisha* stations in front of Heian-jingū, near Nanzen-ji (☎075 533 0444) and at Arashiyama (☎075 864 4444) on the northwest side of Togetsu-kyō bridge, covering three routes: Kiyomizu-dera to Yasaka-jinja, Heian-jingū to Ginkaku-ji and around Arashiyama. Tours (daily 10am–sunset) last from ten minutes (¥2000 for one person, ¥3000 for two) to two hours (¥18,000 for one, ¥30,000 for two), depending on the route and whether you want to stop and take photos. Some of the *jinrikisha*-pullers speak English and will be able to give you a commentary on the sights.

districts, Central Kyoto is a popular choice, with its easy access to the main shops and nightlife as well as good transport links to sights around the city, while the area around the station may not be as pleasant as other parts of Kyoto but it's undoubtedly convenient, with an abundance of inexpensive accommodation. It's also worth considering east Kyoto, where many places are in quieter, more attractive surroundings but also within walking distance of Gion and the city centre.

CENTRAL KYOTO

9h Nine Hours ナインアワーズ Teramachi-dōri Shijō-sagaru ☎075 353 9005, ⓦninehours.co.jp; map p.416. The design of this capsule hotel is minimalist bordering on sci-fi, and the capsules are actually quite spacious sleeping pods. After check-in, female and male guests take separate elevators to pods and shower rooms. Impeccably clean and comfortable and in a convenient central location. Capsule pod for one **¥4900**

First Cabin ファーストキャビン 4F 331 Kamiyanagi-chō ☎075 361 1113, ⓦfirst-cabin.jp; map p.416. First-class air-travel themed capsule hotel, for both men and women, close to Karasuma-Shijō, with good facilities and friendly staff. Cabins are bigger than the business capsules and all have their own TV and internet connections. Clean bathrooms and comfortable café/bar facilities. First-class cabin **¥4100**

Hiiragiya 柊家旅館 Fuyachō Anekoji-agaru ☎075 221 1136, ⓦhiiragiya.co.jp/en; map p.416. One of the city's most famous ryokan, since the mid-nineteenth century it has hosted the rich and famous, including Elizabeth Taylor and Charlie Chaplin. You need to book well in advance, but it's worth it for a quintessential Kyoto experience. Choose between the charming traditional wing and the stylish modern wing. Rates include meals. **¥90,000**

Itoya Hotel 糸屋ホテル Karasuma Matsubara-agaru ☎075 365 1221, ⓦitoyahotel.com/en; map p.416. Pleasant boutique hotel, opened in 2013, in a nice central location with friendly staff. The stylish rooms are cosy yet comfortable. Free wi-fi. **¥12,800**

Kyoto Brighton Hotel 京都ブライトンホテル Shinmachi Nakadachiuri-dōri ☎075 441 4411, ⓦkyotobrighton.com; map p.416. Top-end hotel a stone's throw from the Imperial Palace with spacious and comfortable rooms. It was completely renovated in 2011, and the service is efficient and friendly. The only downside is the rather pricey in-house restaurant. **¥28,000**

Mitsui Garden Hotel Kyoto Sanjō 三井ガーデンホテル京都三条 80 Mikura-chō, Sanjō Karasuma Nishi-iru, Nakagyō-ku ☎075 256 3331, ⓦgardenhotels.co.jp/en/kyoto-sanjo; map p.416. Conveniently located very close to Karasuma-Oike shopping area, this reasonable mid-range hotel is surprisingly good value. All rooms have free wi-fi and there's also an onsen bath that is open to guests in the morning and evening. **¥19,000**

Hotel Monterey ホテルモントレ京都 Karasuma Sanjō-sagaru ☎075 251 7111, ⓦhotelmonterey.co.jp/en/htl/kyoto; map p.416. With a stylish, classic European interior, Japanese and French restaurants, as well as a wedding

chapel and a "British Library" themed café, this hotel is a good choice for location and convenience. Free wi-fi. **¥22,000**

Nishiyama Ryokan 西山旅館 433 Yamamoto-chō ☎075 222 1166, ⓦwww.ryokan-kyoto.com; map p.416. More a hotel than a ryokan, with Japanese and western-style rooms, the *Nishiyama* is comfortable, good-value and close to all the downtown shopping and sightseeing areas. There's an onsen bath in the basement and free monthly cultural events (tea ceremony, calligraphy) held in the lobby. **¥32,000**

★Palace-Side Hotel ザ・パレスサイドホテル Karasuma Shimodachiuri-agaru ☎075 415 8887, ⓦpalacesidehotel.co.jp; map p.416. Large hotel overlooking the Imperial Palace, with good views from the higher, more expensive rooms. Nothing fancy, and the rooms are small, but it's excellent value for the location, just 3min north of Marutamachi subway station. There are substantial discounts if you stay six days or more. **¥10,200**

The Screen ザ・スクリーン Teramachi-dōri Marutamachi-sagaru ☎075 252 1113, ⓦscreen-hotel.jp/en; map p.416. Kyoto's first major boutique hotel is tastefully decorated with contemporary designs of traditional Kyoto crafts – from the lamps to the upholstery. Rooms are spacious and equipped with espresso machines. The in-house French restaurant uses local ingredients and the champagne terrace has great views over the Imperial Park. **¥38,600**

★Tawaraya 俵屋旅館 Fuyachō Anekoji-agaru ☎075 211 5566, ⓕ221 2201; map p.416. The epitome of Kyoto elegance and refinement, from the impeccable service to the gorgeous interior gardens, this exquisite ryokan is so traditional that it doesn't even have a website. Rates include breakfast and dinner. **¥116,000**

Yoshikawa Ryokan 吉川旅館 Tominokoji Oike-sagaru ☎075 221 5544, ⓦkyoto-yoshikawa.co.jp; map p.416. Intimate, traditional inn that's renowned for its tempura *kaiseki* cuisine. Cypress-wood baths, an immaculate garden and all the understated luxury you could want in a traditional setting. Rates include two meals. **¥60,000**

AROUND THE STATION

★Capsule Ryokan カプセル旅館京都 204 Tsuchihashi-chō ☎075 344 1510, ⓦcapsule-ryokan-kyoto.com; map p.419. Modern-style budget ryokan that boasts the world's first tatami capsules with futon (and mini-TVs) and en-suite rooms for two. Free internet, security lockers and tea/coffee. Managed by the same friendly and efficient team who run *Tour Club* (see below). Capsules **¥3500**, en-suite double **¥7980**

6

★**Hotel Granvia Kyoto** ホテルグランヴィア京都 657 Higashi-Shiokoji-chō ☎075 344 8888, ⊛granviakyoto .com; map p.419. Deluxe hotel incorporated into the Kyoto Station building, with rooms on the upper floors overlooking southern Kyoto, and decorated with artworks by local artists. Facilities include a good range of restaurants and bars, an indoor swimming pool, boutiques and business suites. Free wi-fi. **¥28,000**

★**Piece Hostel Kyoto** ピースホステル京都 21-1 Higashi Kujō Higashisanno-chō ☎075 693 7077, ⊛piecehostel.com; map p.419. Sleek new backpacker hostel on the southside of Kyoto Station. Dorms and private rooms are functional, clean and well equipped. Shared spaces include a BBQ terrace and lounge with a library of art books. Free wi-fi and breakfast. Dorm **¥3000**, double **¥7600**

Tour Club ツアークラブ 362 Momiji-chō ☎075 353 6968, ⊛kyotojp.com; map p.419. Conveniently located, this popular backpacker hostel has a solid reputation and is a great source of sightseeing information. Dorms and en-suite double, twin and triple rooms are available. Facilities include a Japanese-style communal living room, internet access, coin laundry, showers, money-changing facilities, the chance to try on a kimono and very reasonable bicycle rentals. Rates get cheaper the longer you stay. Dorm **¥2450**, double **¥6980**

EAST KYOTO

Gion Hatanaka 祇園畑中 Yasaka-jinja Minamimon-mae ☎075 541 5315, ⊛www.thehatanaka.co.jp; map p.423. Elegant ryokan in a fabulous location near Yasaka-jinja with quiet, spacious rooms. It effortlessly blends traditional service with modern style – don't miss their Kyoto cuisine and maiko evening (eee p.423). Free wi-fi. **¥44,200**

★**Hyatt Regency Kyoto** ハイアットリージェンシー京都 644-2 Sanjūsangendo-mawari ☎075 541 1234, ⊛kyoto.regency.hyatt.com; map p.423. Right next to Sanjūsangen-dō, this is Kyoto's top modern luxury hotel with an emphasis on contemporary Japanese style. Guest-room interiors are sleekly decorated with traditional Kyoto fabrics. There are three in-house restaurants to choose from and the spa specializes in traditional Japanese therapies. **¥33,000**

★**Jam Hostel** ジャムホステ 170 Tokiwa-cho ☎ 075 201 3374, ⊛jamhostel.com; map p.423. This modern hostel has a prime location in Gion overlooking the Kamo-gawa. Dorms and private rooms are clean and comfortable, with shared bathing facilities. Free wi-fi and in-house sake bar and café. Dorm **¥2300**, double **¥5500**

★**Mume Boutique Hotel** ホテルムメ 261 Uemoto-cho ☎075 525 8787 ⊛hotelmume.jp; map p.423. This delightful boutique hotel is tucked away on a street of antique shops in Gion and overlooks the Shirakawa canal. The rooms are tastefully decorated with antique furniture. Staff are both discrete and attentive, and you also get complimentary cappuccinos and cocktails. **¥28,350**

Waraku-An 和楽庵 19-2 Sannō-cho ☎075 771 5575, ⊛kyotoguesthouse.net; map p.423. Nicely restored *machiya* (see p.423) guesthouse, conveniently located to the northwest of Heian-jingū. All the rooms are traditional in style and have shared bathing facilities. The deluxe room next to the garden is recommended for its pleasant outlook and can sleep up to four. Dorm **¥2700**, double **¥6480**

Westin Miyako Hotel ウェスティン都ホテル Sanjō Keage ☎075 771 7111, ⊛miyakohotels.ne.jp/westinkyoto/ english; map p.423. Huge, efficient, top-class hotel complete with landscaped gardens, bird sanctuary and a range of restaurants. There's a choice of elegant Japanese-style rooms, some in the garden annexe, or Western-style accommodation, where higher rates get you balconies with views over the city. Free shuttle buses operate between the hotel, Sanjō-dōri and Kyoto Station. **¥33,000**

Yoshida Sansō 吉田山荘 59-1 Shimo Ōji-chō ☎075 771 6125, ⊛yoshidasanso.com; map p.423. Located on Mt Yoshida, this high-class ryokan is the former second residence of the current emperor's uncle. With such imperial associations, don't be surprised if your room has a historical connection, not to mention a lovely garden view. *Kaiseki* cuisine is served and there's also an in-house tea salon. **¥60,374**

NORTH AND NORTHWEST KYOTO

Kingyoya 金魚家 243 Kanki-chō ☎075 411 1128, ⊛kingyoya-kyoto.com; map pp.412–413. Small and friendly guesthouse in a tastefully restored *machiya* located in the heart of Nishijin, the weaving district. Dorm rooms and private rooms have traditional interiors, and dinner and breakfast are also served. Dorm **¥2700**, double **¥7560**

Oil Street Guest House 87-2 Mizuochi-chō ☎075 432 8867, ⊛oilstreetkyoto.com; map p.416. This large *machiya* on a quiet street in Nishijin has been nicely renovated into a guest house and event space. There are two rooms with en-suite bathrooms which can both sleep up to four guests on futons. Free wi-fi and use of the kitchen. Book well in advance. **¥20,000**

Petit Hotel Kyoto プチホテル京都 281 Motosa-chō ☎075 431 5136, ⊛ph-kyoto.co.jp; see map, pp.412–413. Small, friendly hotel on busy Imadegawa-dōri in Nishijin that's convenient for exploring the north and west. The traditional Kyoto breakfast wth fresh tofu is excellent (¥700). Bicycle rental is available. **¥12,000**

Shunkō-in 春光院 42 Myōshinji-chō ☎075 462 5488, ⊛shunkoin.com; see map, pp.412–413. Welcoming and peaceful temple lodging in the historic Myōshinji temple complex, run by a young American-educated Zen priest. All

rooms are tatami-style with futon and private bath. Free wi-fi and shared kitchen facilities. Zen meditation class daily at 9am (¥500). **¥11,000**
Utano Youth Hostel 宇多野ユースホステル 9 Nakayama-chō Uzumasa **⊕** 075 462 2288, **⊛** yh-kyoto .or.jp/utano/ ndex.html; see map, pp.412–413.

Award-winning modern hostel with a good atmosphere and helpful, English-speaking staff. Set in its own grounds on Kyoto's western outskirts, it has an excellent range of facilities. The dorms are very clean and comfortable and there are also Japanese and Western-style double rooms with private bath. Dorm **¥3300**, double **¥8000**

EATING

It's worth treating yourself to a meal in a traditional *Kyō-ryōri* (Kyoto cuisine) restaurant, such as **kaiseki** (a multi-course banquet of seasonal delicacies), **obanzai** (Kyoto home-style cooking), **shōjin-ryōri** (Buddhist vegetarian cuisine) or **yūdōfu** (simmered tofu). **Nishin soba**, a big bowl of soba noodles with a part-dried piece of herring on top, and **saba-zushi**, made with mackerel, are two of the more everyday Kyoto dishes. **Reservations** are nearly always essential at top-end *kaiseki* restaurants in the evening; elsewhere it's not a bad idea to book ahead at weekends and during peak holiday times.

CENTRAL KYOTO

★**Anzukko** 杏っ子 2F Le Shisenmme Building Ebisu-chō **⊕** 075 211 3801, **⊛** anzukko.com; map p.416. This is the place to go for gourmet-style *gyōza* in Kyoto. Mouthwatering variations on fried, grilled and steamed dumplings. The pan-grilled 12 *gyōza* set (¥980) and the boiled shrimp dumplings dribbled with spicy oil (¥840) are highly recommended. 6–11 30pm, closed Mon.

Fortune Garden フォーチュンガーデン Kawaramachi Oike-agaru **⊕** 075 254 8830, **⊛** fortunegarden.com/en; map p.416. This elegant restaurant and bar in a Shōwa-period building is located behind Kyoto City Hall. The menu is French bistro-style using local ingredients. Weekday lunch sets (¥1000) are good value. The best tables are at the rear next to the carp pond. 11am–10pm; closed Mon.

Fujino-ya 藤の家 Pontochō Shijō-agaru **⊕** 075 221 2446, **⊛** kyoto-fujinoya.com; map p.416. One of Pontochō's more affordable restaurants, with the added attraction of a river view. The simple menu (in English) offers either tempura or *kushi-katsu* (deep-fried pork skewers), with standard sets from around ¥2500. In the summer you can eat on the *yuka* (riverside terrace), but the price of dinner increases to ¥3800 for the minimum set. 5–10pm, closed Wed.

★**Giro Giro Hitoshina** 枝魯枝魯ひとしな Nishi Kiyamachi Matsubara-sagaru **⊕** 075 343 7070, **⊛** guiloguilc.com; map p.416. This is the hippest place in Kyoto for an innovative ten-course meal at the unbelievable price of ¥3680. Dishes are a superb fusion of traditional Japanese and European cuisine, making this a fun and unforgettable dining experience. Reservations are essential well in advance. Daily 5.30–11pm.

Hale 晴 Nishiki-koji Fuyachō Nishi-iru **⊕** 075 231 2516; map p.416. Organic and vegan restaurant in a quaint *machiya* with a garden, down a narrow entrance off Nishiki food market. *Hale* is good for a healthy and relaxing meal; lunch sets are very reasonable at ¥1000, and six-course dinner sets (¥2200), with deliciously fresh tofu and steamed vegetables, can be shared between two. 11.30am–2pm & 6–9pm, closed Mon.

Honke Owariya 本家尾張屋 Nishiki-koji Fuyachō Nishi-iru **⊕** 075 231 2516, **⊛** honke-owariya.co.jp/english; map p.416. Lovely old soba restaurant in business since 1465. There's a wide variety of hot and cold soba and udon noodle dishes on the menu. The local favourite Nishin soba is ¥1155, and the simple Seiro soba set (served cold in summer) is just ¥840. Daily 11am–6.30pm.

Hisago Zushi ひさご寿し Kawaramachi Shijō-agaru **⊕** 075 221 5409, **⊛** hisagozushi.com; map p.416. Top-quality Kyoto-style sushi conveniently located in the central shopping area. Superbly presented lunch (¥2400) and dinner sets (¥5250), as well as takeaway bentō (¥2205). Counter seating downstairs and table seating upstairs. Daily 9.30am–8.30pm.

Kawa Café かわカフェ Kiyamachi Matsubara-agaru **⊕** 075 341 0115, **⊛** kawa-cafe.com; map p.416. This bistro-style café overlooks the Kamo-gawa and has an interesting collection of historical photos of geisha, maiko and Gion life on its walls. They serve brunch (¥1200) at weekends from 10.30am–4pm. Daily 9am–midnight.

★**Kiln** キルン Kiyamachi Shijō-sagaru **⊕** 075 353 3555, **⊛** kilnrestaurant.jp; map p.416. Stylish new modern restaurant overlooking the Takase-gawa with shared table seating. The menu is fusion-style using local ingredients – *sake lees* (compacted rice left over from the brewing process) and cured foie gras (¥1850) and Kawachi duck with a shot of *umeshū* (plum wine) (¥2500) are two excellent choices. Crusty fresh bread served with all meals. Noon–2pm & 5–11pm, closed Wed.

Kito-Kito 喜人来人 Shijō-sagaru Ohashi Nishi-iru **⊕** 075 351 5110; map p.416. Small restaurant (with counter and table seating) serving dishes of fresh seafood from Kanazawa – fried fish (¥1600) and seasonal salads (¥890). English menu available. Daily 6pm–2am.

Kushikura 串くら Takakura-dōri Oike-agaru **⊕** 075 213 2211, **⊛** fukunaga-tf.com/kushikura; map p.416. Premium *yakitori* and other skewer foods in a nicely restored old Kyoto house. Sit at the counter and watch the chefs grill your food over charcoal, or enjoy the privacy of

6

6

the small dining rooms. Sets start at ¥1600, or you can order by skewers separately from ¥160. Daily 11.30am–2pm & 5–9.45pm.

Mahola 'n' LuLu マホランルル Rokkaku Tominokōji Higashi-iru ☎075 222 0634; map p.416. This comfy Hawaiian café on the second floor of a *machiya* is one of the few places in Kyoto with free accessible wi-fi. The menu is mainly local variations of the Loco Moco Hawaiian hamburger (from ¥1050). Daily noon–11am.

Manzara-tei Pontochō まんざら亭先斗町 Pontochō Shijō-agaru ☎075 212 0028, ⓦmanzara.co.jp/pont; map p.416. Elegant *izakaya* with a welcoming atmosphere and English menu. Serves seasonal dishes as well as local specialities such as Kyoto's favourite midnight snack of rice, pickle and tea – *ochazuke* ((¥600). Also stocks local beers, sake and shōchū (from ¥650). Table seating downstairs and tatami rooms upstairs. Reservations advised. Daily 5pm–12am.

★**Matsuontoko** まつおんとこ Shinkyōgoku Shijō-agaru ☎075 251 1876, ⓦthinkagain.jp/cafe/matsuontoko; map p.416. Vegan café off the busy Shinkyōgoku shopping arcade with cosy seating and lunchtime anime screenings. The yummy vegan burger set (¥850) and the Kyoto veggie curry (¥780) are good choices for lunch. In the evenings they serve vegan pizza (¥700). Daily 11am–11pm.

Musashi むさし Kawaramachi Sanjō-agaru ☎075 222 0634, ⓦsushinomusashi.com; map p.416. The original branch of the reliable, region-wide *kaitenzushi* (conveyor-belt sushi) chain. Located right on the junction, it also does a brisk trade in takeaway bentō. Unless you're ravenous, lunch – or dinner – shouldn't set you back more than ¥1000, and the cheapest dishes are just ¥137. Daily 11am–9.50pm.

Ninja Kyoto 忍者京都 Shinkyōgoku Shijō-agaru ☎075 253 0150, ⓦninja-kyoto.com; map p.416. This ninja theme restaurant, with its labyrinth of basement dining booths and costume-clad staff, is a lot of fun and the food's not bad either. There's an à la carte menu but given the level of theatrics it's better to go with a course menu (from ¥2800) and watch your food metamorphose with magic tricks performed by the staff. Daily 5–10pm.

Obanzai おばんざい Koromonotana-dōri Oike-agaru ☎075 223 6623; map p.416. It's well worth searching out this very popular buffet-style restaurant east of Nijō-jō for their excellent-value vegetarian buffets (¥840–1050 for lunch, ¥2100 in the evening). They also serve good organic coffee and cakes. 11am–2pm & 5–8.30pm, closed Wed eve.

Tawawa タワワ 3F Shinpukhan, Karasuma-dōri Anekōji-sagaru ☎075 257 8058, ⓦkyo-tawawa.co.jp; map p.416. All-you-can-eat buffet of dishes based on Kyoto vegetables. Pasta, salads, bread and fresh fruit desserts also served. The 90min lunch buffet

(11am–2.30pm; ¥1200) is a great deal. Dinner is à la carte only with a good selection of vegetable pizzas (from ¥700) and salads (from ¥750) on offer. They serve coffee and cake in the afternoon. Daily 11am–10pm.

★**Yoshikawa** 吉川 Tominokōji Ōike-sagaru ☎075 221 5544, ⓦkyoto-yoshikawa.co.jp; map p.416. The best tempura restaurant in Kyoto is located inside this eponymous ryokan. Definitely worth sitting at the counter to watch the chefs expertly deep-fry your meal. Lunch sets (¥3000) include hearty portions of seafood and vegetables. In the evenings, the tempura supper (¥6000) or tempura *kaiseki* course (¥12,000) are both recommended. 11am–2pm & 5–8.30pm; closed Sun.

AROUND THE STATION

efish エフィッシュ Nishi-Hashizumi-chō ☎075 361 3069, ⓦshinproducts.com/efish/cafe.php; map p.419. Riverside café east of the station near Gojo bridge, serving chunky bread sandwich sets (¥800–900), cheesecake (¥580) and coffee (¥450) in a very stylish interior, designed by the owner. A good place to gaze out at the river and eastern hills from a comfortable chair. Daily 11am–10pm.

Kitcho 吉兆 3F Granvia Hotel, Kyoto Station ☎075 342 0808, ⓦkitcho.com/kyoto; map p.419. The Kyoto Station branch of this famous *kaiseki* restaurant (see p.419) serves bentō boxes (¥6930) and *kaiseki* courses (¥11,550) for lunch and dinner. It lacks the extravagance and sublime decor of its sister branch in Arashiyama (see p.419), but the food is excellent. Daily 11am–2pm & 5–8.30pm.

★**Ramen Alley** 京都拉麺小路 10F Isetan, Kyoto Station ☎075 361 4401; map p.419. Eight ramen noodle shops, serving Kyoto, Ōsaka, Hakata, Sapporo and other varieties, are tucked into this "alley" on the tenth floor of Kyoto Station's Isetan department store. Some of the shops display English menus outside. When you've chosen, buy a ticket from the vending machine outside (from ¥500) and hand it to the staff when you are seated. Daily 10am–10pm.

Tonkatsu Wako とんかつ和幸 11F Eat Paradise, Isetan, Kyoto Station ☎075 342 0024; map p.419. The Kyoto Station branch of this well-known *tonkatsu* (fried pork cutlet) restaurant serves good-value lunch and dinner sets. All sets come with rice, cabbage salad and miso soup – try the Hirekatsu Gohan set (¥1155). Daily 11am–9.15pm.

EAST KYOTO

If you want to treat yourself to traditional Kyoto cuisine, the city's eastern districts are a good place to head. One or two of the more affordable restaurants are recommended below, and these still offer a glimpse into the world of kimono-clad waitresses, elegant tatami rooms, carp ponds and tinkling bamboo water spouts. There are also some pleasant cafés in this part of Kyoto serving healthy, organic food.

★A Womb アウーム 35-2 Ichijōji Hinokuchi-chō ☎075 721 1357, ⓦawomb.com map pp.412–413. Ultra-modern cavernous concrete space with a restaurant and small clothing shop a street back from Shirakawa-dōri, *A Womb* serves contemporary interpretations of *kaiseki*, sushi and *donburi* rice bowls, which you can order à la carte. The lunch set is ¥2700 and dinner courses start from ¥7000. Noon–2pm & 6–8pm, closed Tues & Wed.

★Foodelica フーデリカ Kitayama-dōri Shirakawa ☎075 703 5208, ⓦfoodelica.com; map pp.412–413. Retro fusion café serving home-made pasta and delicious sweets. The lunch *plat du jour* (¥1100), with organic vegetables, includes coffee. If you are visiting Shūgaku-in Rikyū, this is a great place to stop for a meal or a snack: it's just a few steps east of the Eiden Station. 11.30am–8pm, Thurs closes at 5pm, closed Tues & fourth Wed of the month.

★Gion Okuoka 祇園おくおか 44-66 Bishamon-chō Higashiōji-dōri ☎075 531 5155; map p.423. At this friendly restaurant specializing in Kyoto cuisine you can make fresh *yuba* (tofu skin) at your table (¥2500). In the evening, Okuoka serve *kaiseki* courses from ¥5000 and a *yuba* pot course (¥3500). English menu available. Daily 11.30am–2.30pm & 5–9.30pm.

Hyōtei 瓢亭 35 Kusagawa-chō Nanzen-ji ☎075 771 4116, ⓦhyotei.co.jp/en; map p.423. Next to Murin-an garden, this sublime thatch-roofed garden-restaurant started serving *kaiseki* cuisine in 1837. Their specialities are *asagayu*, a summer breakfast (served July & Aug 8am–10am; ¥6000), and *uzuragayu* (rice gruel with quail eggs) in winter (¥12,100). Prices are lower in the new annexe, but even here expect to pay ¥4500 for the cheapest meal. Reservations are essential and English is spoken. 11am–7pm, closed second & fourth Tues of the month.

KYOTO FOOD & TEA CULTURE

It's possible to study Kyoto's culinary arts and tea culture at venues around the city. The main advantage of taking a class is to gain some insights into Kyoto's enduring food and tea traditions and special techniques, and to spend time with local people.

COOKING

Haru Cooking Class Shimogamo Miyazaki-chō ☎090 4284 7176, ⓦkyoto-cooking-class.com. Fun and friendly cooking class run by a charming young couple out of their home kitchen. They offer vegetarian and non-vegetarian (including Kobe Beef) courses, and give useful explanations of essential ingredients and the fundamentals of Japanese cuisine such as dashi (stock) making (¥5900–10,900/person). Classes are held 3–4 times a week at 2pm.

Uzuki Cooking School Shirakawa-dōri Imadegawa-agaru ⓦkyotouzuki.com. This cooking school in northeastern Kyoto holds classes for 2–4 people in seasonal Kyoto cuisine, mostly on weekday afternoons. The enthusiastic instructor brings you into her own kitchen and takes you through the steps of creating a delicious three or four-course meal (¥4500–5000/person).

TEA CEREMONY

Kanjoan 緩徐庵 Nishijin ☎075 200 7653, ⓦkanjoan.com. At this beautifully restored teahouse in the heart of Nishijin you can experience a 2hr introduction to the tea ceremony with a Swiss-born tea master (¥3000–11,000/person depending on group size). As well as getting insider information on Kyoto tea culture you can learn to make your own bowl of *matcha* and enjoy a traditional sweet. Day and time by appointment.

WAK Japan ワックジャパン Takakura Nijō-agaru ☎075 212 9993, ⓦwakjapan.com. WAK Japan is a cultural organization which offers a 45-minute morning tea ceremony experience (¥2500/person) in their traditional *machiya* townhouse classroom. Reservations must be made 2 days in advance. Mon–Fri 9.30am–10.15am.

SWEET MAKING

Izutsu Yatsuhashi 井筒八つ橋 Teramachi Shijō-agaru ☎075 255 2121, ⓦyatsuhashi.co.jp. Learn how to mix and bake Kyoto's famous cinnamon-flavoured biscuits in a 40min class (¥1050/person). You can take home a special tin with 32 biscuits. It's best to make a telephone reservation in advance. Daily 10am–8pm.

Kanshundo 甘春堂 Kawabata Shomen Higashi-iru ☎075 561 1318, ⓦkanshundo.co.jp. At this traditional Kyoto confectioner you can learn how to handcraft four different kinds of kyō-gashi (traditional Kyoto sweets made with pounded rice and bean paste) in a 1hr 15min class (¥2000/person). Reservations must be made on the website at least 3 days in advance. Classes daily at 11am, 1pm and 3pm.

6

Imobō Hirano-ya Honten いもぼう平野屋本店 Maruyama-kōen-uchi ☎075 561 1603, ⓦimobou.net/ english.html; map p.423. Quaint three-hundred-year-old restaurant located inside the north entrance to Maruyama park. Their speciality is *imobō* (dried cod stew) incorporating an unusual type of potato (*ebi-imo*), and finding ingenious ways to make preserved fish taste superb. Try an *imobō* set for ¥2520, but expect to pay upwards of ¥7000 for a wonderful *kaiseki* experience. Daily 10.30am–8pm.

★**Mame-cha** 豆ちゃ Yasaka-jinja Nanmon-sagaru Ishibekōji ☎075 532 2788, ⓦcommercial-art.net/wp/ kansai/mamecha_kyoto; map p.423. Elegant *obanzai* (Kyoto-style home cooking) restaurant in a modern-designed *machiya* up one of Kyoto's most scenic alleyways, just south of Yasaka-jinja. The ¥4000 eleven-course dinner has a wonderful combination of flavours and is beautifully presented. Counter seating or tatami rooms upstairs, plus English-speaking staff and menu. Reservations are essential. Daily 5–11pm.

Matsuno 松乃 Shijō-dōri ☎075 561 2786, ⓦmatsuno-co.jp; map p.423. This century-old *unagi* (eel) shop is family-run and very friendly. Eels are traditionally eaten in the hot summer months to revive one's stamina, and the menu here has delicious variations on eel cuisine. Standard sets start at ¥2800 and there's an English menu. Open 11.30am–9pm.

Nakamura-rō 中村楼 Gion-machi Minami-gawa ☎075 561 0016, ⓦnakamurarou.com; map p.423. A wonderful four-hundred-year-old restaurant adjacent to the south gate of Yasaka-jinja serving exquisite Kyoto cuisine. It's surprisingly relaxed and informal, with tatami rooms overlooking a lush garden and a modern room with counter seating. However, even just a lunchtime bentō will set you back ¥5250. Full *kaiseki* dinners start at ¥13,000. Reservations are essential. Daily 11.30am–2pm & 5–7pm.

Okutan 奥丹 Fukuchi-chō, Nanzen-ji ☎075 771 8709; map p.423. This small restaurant has been serving *yūdōfu* (simmered tofu) since the fourteenth century. It's half hidden in a bamboo grove on the east side of the Chōshō-in garden, just outside Nanzen-ji. The *yūdōfu* sets start at ¥3150. 11am–4.30pm, closed Thurs.

★**Omen** おめん Jōdo-ji Shibashi-chō ☎075 771 8994; ⓦomen.co.jp; map p.423. Excellent udon restaurant near Ginkaku-ji, serving bowls of thick white noodles topped with the nutritious combination of fresh ginger, sesame seeds and pickled *daikon* radish (from ¥1100). The tempura prawn and vegetables side dish (¥1500) is also delicious. Daily 11am–8.30pm.

Tosca トスカ Kitashirakawa Oiwake-chō ☎075 721 7779, ⓦtosca-kyoto.com; map p.423. Vegetarian café in light, breezy space opposite Kyoto University. It's run by English-speaking Tomoka and Asuka (hence the name), and the menu is healthy and delicious. Lunch courses of soup, curry or burgers from ¥1000, and tasty dinner courses

of seasonal vegetables from ¥1980. There's also an à la carte menu. Lunch Tues–Sat 11.30am–2.30pm; dinner Thurs–Sat 5.30–9pm.

Udon Museum うどん博物館 238-2 Gion-machi ☎075 531 0888, ⓦudon.mu; map p.423. A new addition to the Kyoto food scene, this is less of a museum (the small display looks like an afterthought) than a theme restaurant, that serves more than forty different regional kinds of thick white noodles. Bowls start at ¥690 and sets (with rice) from ¥970. If you're keen to sample a few, note that half-size portions are available on weekdays from 3pm, and 5pm at the weekend. Daily 11am–10pm.

NORTHWEST KYOTO

Cafe Marble カフェマーブル Chiekōin-dōri Imadegawa-sagaru ☎075 451 8777, ⓦcafe-marble .com; map p.416. This retro-style Nishijin café has yummy cakes (try the seasonal fruit tart ¥450) and Kyoto's best quiche plate – served with soup and salad (¥950). A great place to grab lunch if you are sightseeing in Kyoto's northwest. 11.30am–10pm, Fri & Sat until midnight, Sun closes at 8pm; closed Wed.

★**Colori Caffe** コロリカフェ Senbon-dōri Demizu-sagaru ☎075 801 5634, ⓦcoloricaffe.com; map p.416. Kyoto's only LGBT hangout – look for the rainbow flag flying on Senbon-dōri. The charming English-speaking owner/chef serves delicious pasta dishes (from ¥1000), great coffee (from ¥450), and gives a warm welcome to all. Check the website for events. Noon–10pm, closed Mon.

Gontaro 権太呂 Kinukake-no-michi ☎075 463 1039, ⓦgontaro.co.jp/english/kyoto/kinkakuji.html; map pp.412–413. Suburban branch of the Shijō soba shop in an old house just a few minutes' walk west of Kinkaku-ji. Fresh, reasonably priced noodle dishes (Nishin soba ¥1100) and welcoming atmosphere. 11am–9pm, closed Wed.

★**Izusen** 泉仙 Daitoku-ji ☎075 491 6665, ⓦkyoto-izusen.com/html/store_daijin.html; map, pp.412–413. Located in the gardens of Daiji-in, a sub-temple of Daitoku-ji, this is one of the nicest places to sample vegetarian *shōjin-ryōri* at an affordable price, though it's still around ¥3150 for the simplest lunch. Reservations are recommended in spring and autumn. Daily 11am–4pm.

Sarasa Nishijin さらさ西陣 Kuramaguchi-dōri ☎075 432 5075, ⓦcafe-sarasa.com/shop_nishijin; map, pp.412–413. This café and bar in a converted *sentō* (public bathhouse) in the Nishijin weaving district still has its lovely original tiled interior. The food is, unfortunately, woeful but it's a really nice place for a drink – coffee costs ¥350. Monthly live music performances. Noon–11pm, closed Wed.

★**Tofu Café Fujino** とうふカフェ藤野 Imadegawa-dōri ☎075 463 1028, ⓦkyotofu.co.jp/shoplist/cafe; map pp.412–413. A little west of Kitano Tenmangū shrine, this modern café serves innovative soy bean cuisine. The healthy *obanzai* lunch plate (¥1250) is very filling.

Extremely busy on the 25th of the month, when the shrine market is held. Daily 11am–6pm.

Urume うるめ 51 Ōno-chō Kitaōji-dōri ☎ 075 495 9831; see map, p.412–413. This pleasant soba restaurant in a lovely old *machiya* (see box, p.429) is run by a young couple and makes a good stop for a generous lunch while sightseeing: the menu includes dishes such as *Zaru-soba* from ¥740 and tempura with soba from ¥1680. The private room at the back has a nice garden view. Northside of Kitaōji-dōri between Shinmachi and Horikawa. 11am–5pm, closed Tues.

DRINKING AND NIGHTLIFE

Kyoto has plenty of **teahouses**, **coffee shops** and cosy **bars** as well as a decent late-night scene with a small range of **clubs** and **live music** venues. It may not compete with the likes of Osaka and Tokyo, but the prime entertainment districts of **Kiyamachi** and **Gion** are both stuffed with bars and clubs. However, even fairly innocuous-looking establishments can be astronomically expensive (many have a "seating" fee of over ¥1000), so check first to make sure you know exactly what you're letting yourself in for. Some of the more upmarket establishments used to require an introduction by a regular customer before you could even set foot inside, but the ongoing recession has loosened the formalities to some extent.

BARS, CLUBS AND LIVE MUSIC

With boisterous *izakaya* and trendy wine **bars**, the epicentre of the city's nightlife can be found either side of the Kamo-gawa in downtown Kyoto, in the two traditional pleasure quarters of Gion and Pontochō. In the evening you might be lucky enough to see a maiko or a geisha as she hurries between teahouse assignations. The Kiyamachi area between Sanjō and Shijō is where most of the clubs are and is brimming with buskers, fortune-tellers and bar touts at weekends. In summer, look out for rooftop **beer gardens** on top of the big hotels and department stores.

CENTRAL KYOTO AND PONTOCHŌ

Ace Café エースカフェ 10F Empire Biru Kiyamachi Sanjō-agaru ⓦ ace-cafe.com; see map, p.416. Enjoy a cocktail (¥730) while sitting on a comfortable sofa with fabulous panoramic views over the Kamo-gawa and eastern hills from this popular tenth floor bar and café. Also serves pasta and pizza (from ¥850). Daily 6pm–2am.

Dublin Irish Pub ダブリン Oike-dōri Kawaramachi higashi-iru ☎ 075 241 9155, ⓦ dublin.kyoto-pontocho .jp; see map, p.416. Right next to the *Kyoto Hotel Okura*, this popular Irish pub has Kilkenny and Guinness on tap (¥900 a pint), voluminous portions of hearty Irish food (Irish Stew ¥1000, fish & chips ¥900), and an enjoyable atmosphere, especially on the live music nights. Happy hour 5–7pm. Mon–Sat 5pm–2am, Sun 4pm–1am.

Jittoku 拾得 Ōmiya Marutamachi-agaru ☎ 075 841 1691, ⓦ odnune.jp/jittoku; see map, p.416. It's a little bit out of the way, north of Nijō-jō, but this wonderful old *kura* (storehouse) has good acoustics and hosts regular rock and blues band performances. Cover charge ¥1000–3000. Daily 5.30pm–midnight.

Live Spot Rag 京都ライブスポトラグ 5F Empire Biru Kiyamachi Sanjō-agaru ☎ 075 255 7273, ⓦ www.ragnet .co.jp; see map, p.416. Well-established musicians' hangout (they have rehearsal rooms and recording studios here as well) which hosts local and international bands, mainly playing jazz. Entry from ¥1600. 7pm until late, closed Sun.

Rub a Dub ラバダブ B1 Tsujita Biru, Kiyamachi Sanjō-sagaru ☎ 075 256 3122, ⓦ rubadub.org; see map, p.416. Sip a piña colada (¥600) in this compact reggae beach bar decked out with fairy lights, palm trees and plastic fruit. DJ nights occur occasionally. It's at the north end of canalside Kiyamachi-dōri – look out for a small signboard on the pavement. Daily 7pm until late.

Taku Taku 磔磔 Tominokōji Bukkōji-sagaru ☎ 075 351 1321, ⓦ geisya.or.jp/~takutaku; see map, p.416. In the blocks southwest of Takashimaya department store, this converted *kura* makes a great live venue. The music's pretty varied but tends towards rock and blues, including the occasional international artist. Cover charge from ¥1500 (depending on performer), including one drink. Daily 7pm until late.

UrBAN GUILD アバンギルド 3F New Kyoto Biru, Kiyamachi Sanjō-sagaru ☎ 075 212 1125, ⓦ urbanguild.net; see map, p.416. Avant-garde club with a good reputation for hosting interesting underground local and international acts playing psych-rock, acid folk and lo-fi electronica. Occasional butō dance performances. Entry ¥1800–3000. Daily 6.30pm–midnight.

World ワールド京都 B1-B2 Imagium Building ☎ 075 213 4119, ⓦ world-kyoto.com; see map, p.416. Cavernous basement club attracting big-name house, hip-hop and techno DJs from Japan and abroad. Weekday nights are quieter, but the place heaves at the weekend. Average entry is ¥1500–2500 (including one drink). Open most nights from around 9pm.

GION AND EAST KYOTO

Akibako 空き箱 103-1 Sueyoshi-chō ☎ 075 708 2332; see map, p.423. Classy wine bar in the heart of Gion with surprisingly reasonable prices – wine by the bottle from ¥3000. Aim for the relaxing window seat with a superb view over the Shirakawa canal. Mon–Sat 2pm–midnight.

The Gael Irish Pub ゲールアイリッシュパブ 2F Ōto Bldg, Keihan Shijō Station ☎ 075 525 0680, ⓦ irishpubkyoto .com; see map, p.423. Popular expat hangout with a warm

6

THE TEAHOUSES OF KYOTO

The world of **tea** tends to have a reputation for rigidity and rules, but fortunately there are now some innovative and modern ways in which to experience this quintessential **Japanese drink**. Whether you want just a relaxing cuppa or a tea ceremony, both are easily accessible in these elegant Kyoto teahouses.

Fukujuen 福寿園 Shijō Tominokōji ☏075 221 6174, ⓦfukujuen-kyotohonten.com; map p.416. The flagship store of this tea company has five floors of tea-related activities – from the tea-making workshop in the basement (¥1575) to a 30-minute tea ceremony experience in the elegant fourth-floor tearoom (¥2625). There are also two tea-inspired restaurants and a ground-floor shop. Daily 10am–6.30pm.

Hosotsuji Ihee Tea House ほそつじいへえティーハ ウス Gion Shijlh ☏075 551 3534, ⓦeirakuya.jp; map p.423. Modern teahouse tucked away at the back of the Enveraak tenugui shop on Shijō serving Kyoto blends of Ceylon tea. Royal Milk tea lattes (hot/cold) are a pricey ¥1260. It's open late and also serves tea cocktails – try the brandy-based "Gion Nocturne" (¥1680). Daily 11am–10.30pm.

Iyemon Salon 伊右衛門サロン Sanjō Karasuma Nishi-iri ☏075 221 1500, ⓦiyemonsalon.jp; map p.416. This large bustling teahouse, on Sanjō-dōri just west of Karasuma, is aiming to be Kyoto's trendiest teahouse – it has an internet café, bookshop, tea counter and a kitchen serving tea-inspired cuisine. *Mactha* from ¥750. Daily 8am–11pm.

Kaboku Tearoom 喫茶室嘉木 Teramachi Nijō-agaru ☏075 211 3421, ⓦippodo-tea.co.jp/en/index.html; map p.416. The *Kaboku Tearoom*, in the historic Ippodo teashop, is a wonderful place to sample different types and grades of green tea (¥683–1155). The tearoom has a hushed atmosphere but the staff are friendly and happy to guide you through the extensive menu (in English). Daily 11am–5pm.

Somushō Kochaya 素夢古茶屋 Sanjō Karasuma Nishi-iri ☏075 253 1456, ⓦsomushi.com; map p.416. Just across from the Iyemon Salon is an artfully rustic Korean teahouse that's an incredibly calm space to try a variety of medicinal teas, such as ginseng and jujube (from ¥500), as well as healthy vegetarian Korean dishes. 10am–8pm, closed Wed.

Rakushō 洛匠 Kōdaiji Kitamonmae-dōri ☏075 561 6892, ⓦwww.rakusyou.co.jp; map p.423. In eastern Kyoto, don't miss *Rakushō*, a charming old teahouse between Kōdai-ji and Yasaka-jinja. Enjoy a bowl of *matcha* and *warabi mochi* (jelly-like cakes rolled in sweet soybean flour) for ¥840 while gazing out over the pond of enormous carp. Daily 9am–5pm.

Kyoto Nama Chocolat Organic Tea House 76-15 Tenno-chō ☏075 751 2678, ⓦkyoto-namachocolat .com; map p.423. East of the Heian-jingū is the tranquil *Kyoto Nama Chocolat Organic Teahouse* in an elegant old house with a rambling garden. They serve a variety of teas and coffee (¥550), as well as their own brand of delectable fresh soft chocolate, which is made on the premises (¥550 for 4 pieces). Daily noon–5pm.

---

friendly atmosphere. There's good-quality food (try The Gael Burger ¥900) and a decent range of beers (from ¥650). Weekly live music and other events. Daily 5pm–1am.

Jam Sake Bar ジャムサケバー *Jam Hostel* 170 Tokiwa-chō ☏075 201 3374, ⓦsakebar.jp; map p.423. At this casual sake bar in the *Jam Hostel*, you can sample a selection of sake from all over Japan. The English-speaking bartender will help you make a selection. The tasting set (of three) is ¥1000, or you can have one shot for ¥400. Beers are ¥500. Daily 5pm–midnight.

Jazz Live Candy ジャズライブキャンディ B1 Hanamikōji Shinmonzen-agaru ☏075 531 2148, ⓦh3.dion .ne.jp/~candy-h; map p.423. Well-established jazz bar with top, mostly local, live acts every night. Serious yet friendly atmosphere. Seating charge of ¥735, plus cover charge (¥1500–2500). Daily 7.30pm–1am.

La Gallega ラガジェガ Kyouen Complex, Keihan Sanjō Station ☏075 533 7206, ⓦla-gallega.jp; map p.423. Spacious Spanish tapas and standing bar which looks out onto a Zen-style rock garden: tapas from ¥300. It hosts occasional flamenco shows, and is excellent value at happy hour (6–8pm). Daily 11am–10pm.

Metro メトロ Keihan Marutamachi Station ☏075 752 4765, ⓦmetro.ne.jp; map p.423. In the depths of the train station (take exit 2), this progressive club offers an eclectic selection of music, from local guitar bands and big-name foreign techno DJs to drag shows and hardcore dub reggae parties. It's small, loud and very popular. Entrance ¥1000–2200 (more for foreign DJs or bands), including one drink. Daily, but opening hours vary.

DANCE, THEATRE AND CINEMA

Kyoto is famous for its traditional **geisha dance** shows. Performances of kabuki and nō plays are more sporadic but worth attending if you happen to be in town when they are on. The **Kyoto Art Center** (☏075 213 1000, ⓦkac.or.jp/en) hosts a range of exhibitions and art performances as well as lectures, field trips and a well-regarded series of "Traditional Theatre Training" workshops (held every July) for those who want to learn more about nō and other Japanese performing arts.

GEISHA ODORI

Geisha (or *geiko*, as they are known locally) and maiko (trainee geisha) from each of the city's former pleasure quarters (see p.427) have been putting on *Odori* (dance performances) in spring and autumn since the late nineteenth century, though the music and choreography are much older. By turns demure and coquettish, they glide round the stage in the most gorgeous kimono, straight out of an Edo-period woodblock print of Japan's seductive "floating world". If you're in Kyoto during these seasonal dances, it's well worth going along, but note that the autumn dances are more like recitals, and not as extravagant as the spring dances. Performances take place several times a day, so it's usually possible to get hold of tickets; you can buy them from the theatre box offices and major hotels. At all of the *Odori*, you can also buy tickets that combine the show with a tea ceremony conducted by geisha and maiko, which is well worth the extra cost (¥3800–6000, depending on the district). Make sure you get there early enough to enjoy your bowl of *matcha* (powdered green tea).

Kitano Odori 北野をどり ☏075 461 0148, ⊚maiko3 .com/index.html; tickets from ¥4000. Kyoto's northern geisha district holds their Odori in early spring (March 25– April 7) at the Kami-shichiken Kaburenjō, near Kitano Tenmangū shrine.

Miyako Odori 都をどり ☏075 541 3391, ⊚miyako-odori.jp; tickets from ¥2000. The annual dance performances in the geisha districts kick off with the Miyako Odori (April 1–30) performed at Gion Kōbu Kaburenjō (see p.428) by the geisha and maiko of Gion. This is the most prestigious and well known of the *Odori*, mainly because it is the oldest, having started in 1872. The dances are based on a seasonal theme and have lavish sets and costumes. Live musicians playing *shamisen*, flutes and drums, as well as singers, perform in alcoves at each side of the stage.

Kyo Odori 京おどり ☏075 561 1151, ⊚miyagawacho .jp; tickets from ¥2500 with tea. The smaller-scale Kyo Odori is held in the Miyagawa-chō district, south of Gion from April 7–22. This is a more intimate production than Miyako Odori though just as opulent.

Kamo-gawa Odori 鴨川をどり ☏075 221 2025, ⊚www1.odn.ne.jp/~adw58490; tickets from ¥2000. The geisha and maiko of Pontochō stage their Kamo-gawa Odori once a year (May 1–24) in Pontochō Kaburenjō, at the north end of Pontochō-dōri.

Onshūkai 温習会 ☏075 541 3391, ⊚miyako-odori .jp/onsyukai; tickets from ¥4000. The Onshūkai dances are held during the first week in Oct at the Gion Kōbu Kaburenjō.

Kotobukikai 寿会 ☏075 461 0148, ⊚maiko3.com/ event/ev-8.html; tickets from ¥4000. The Kotobukikai dances (around Oct 8–12) are held in northwest Kyoto's

Kami-shichiken Kaburenjō, close to Kitano Tenmangū shrine.

Mizuekai みずえ会 ☏075 561 1151, ⊚miyagawacho .jp/mizuekai; tickets from ¥4000. Miyagawa-chō's Mizuekai recital is usually held in mid-Oct at the Miyagawa-chō Kaburenjō.

Gion Odori 祇園をどり ☏075 561 0160, ⊚gionkaikan .jp; tickets from ¥3300. The Gion Odori, performed by the maiko and geisha of the smaller Gion Higashi district, wraps things up in early Nov (Nov 1–10) at the Gion Kaikan theatre near Yasaka-jinja.

GEISHA SHOWS

If your visit doesn't coincide with any of the seasonal Geisha performances there are several opportunities to see Kyoto's geisha and maiko dance.

Fureaikan ふれあい館 On Sundays you can see a free 15min dance performance by maiko at the Fureaikan Museum of Traditional Crafts in the basement of Miyako Messe Exhibition Hall (see p.429). Performances are at 2pm, 2.30pm and 3pm.

Gion Corner ギオンコーナー As part of Gion Corner's sampler of traditional performance arts, maiko perform *kyō-mai* (Kyoto-style) dances at the Gion Kōbu Kaburenjō (see p.428). Performances are at 6pm and 7pm (¥3150).

Gion Hatanaka 祇園畑中旅館 The *Gion Hatanaka* ryokan (see p.442) holds Kyoto Cuisine and Maiko Evening events (Mon, Wed, Fri & Sat at 6pm; ☏075 541 5315; ⊚kyoto-maiko.jp; ¥18,000; reservations essential) which non-guests are welcome to attend. This is a great chance to see maiko performing at close range and to take photos.

KABUKI AND NŌ

Colourful and dramatic, kabuki theatre originated in Kyoto, though performances are, unfortunately, fairly sporadic these days. Nō theatre is a far more stately affair; though it is often incomprehensible, even to the Japanese, it can also be incredibly powerful to watch.

KABUKI 歌舞伎

Minami-za 南座 Shijō-Ōhashi Higashi-zume ☏075 561 1155, ⊚shochiku.co.jp/play/minamiza. This theatre is the main venue to see a kabuki performance in Kyoto. Throughout December there's a major kabuki-fest here known as *kaomise*, or "face-showing" (Dec 1–25), when big-name actors perform snippets from their most successful roles.

NŌ 能

Kanze Kaikan 観世会館 South of Heian-jingū ☏075 771 6114, ⊚www.kyoto-kanze.jp. This is Kyoto's main

6

venue for nō, with performances (including *kyōgen*), slapstick most weekends (tickets from ¥3500, occasional free performances).

Kawamura Nō Stage 河村能舞台 On Karasuma-dōri near Dōshisha University ☎075 722 8716, ⓦwww .kid97.co.jp/kawamur. Lovely old theatre run by the Kawamura family, a long line of famous nō actors (tickets from ¥4000).

Kongo Nō-gakudō 金剛能楽堂 On Karasuma-dōri on the west side of the Imperial Park ☎075 441 7222, ⓦkongou-net.com. Large modern theatre holding regular performances of nō classics (tickets from ¥3500).

CINEMA

Kyoto Cinema Karasuma Shijō-sagaru ☎075 353 4723, ⓦkyotocinema.jp. On the third floor of the Cocon Karasuma shopping complex, this cinema has three screens and mainly shows local and foreign art-house films and documentaries. Daily 11am–7pm.

Movix Kyoto 400 Sakurano-chō ☎075 254 3215, ⓦmovix.co.jp/kyoto/index.html. Located at the top end of Shinkyōgoku, just south of Sanjō, this is Kyoto's largest cinema complex with an annexe. It screens the latest Japanese and Hollywood blockbusters. Daily 9.30am–11pm.

Minami Kaikan 79 Higashi Hieijō-chō ☎ 075 661 3993, ⓦkyoto-minamikaikan.jp. Small cinema near the junction of Ōmiya and Kujō, southeast of Kyoto Station, showing an interesting mix of alternative and mainstream films. Daily 10.30am–9.40pm.

T-Joy Kyoto 1 Toriiguchi-machi ⓦt-joy.net/site/ Kyoto/index.html. Cinema complex on the fifth floor of the Aeon Shopping Mall near Kyoto Station showing Japanese and mainstream Hollywood movies. Daily 9am–midnight.

Toho Cinema Nijō 1-6 Togano-chō ☎075 813 2410, ⓦtohotheater.jp/theater/nijo/index.html. Large complex next to Nijō Station showing all the mainstream Japanese and Hollywood blockbusters including late-night screenings. Look out for the funky bamboo walls and Zen rock garden perspex floor in the theatre hallway. Daily 9.30am–1.30am.

SHOPPING

Kyoto's main shopping district is focused around the junction of **Shijō-dōri** and **Kawaramachi-dōri**, and spreads north of Shijō along the **Teramachi** and **Shinkyōgoku** covered arcades. You'll find the big-name department stores, notably Takashimaya, Hankyū and Daimaru, all on Shijō. Souvenir shops, smart boutiques and even a few traditional craft shops are mostly situated on **Sanjō-dōri**, just west of the river. Beneath Oike-dori, between Teramachi and Kawaramachi, is the Zest underground shopping mall. As well as more than a hundred eating options, the **station** area is home to the huge Isetan department store and an underground shopping mall, Porta, beneath the northern bus terminal. East Kyoto is best known for its wealth of shops around **Kiyomizu-dera**, which sell the local pottery, while nearby **Sannen-zaka** hosts a lovely parade of traditional craft shops. Further north, Gion's **Shinmonzen-dōri** specializes in antiques – prices are predictably high, but it's a good area to browse.

Shopping complexes The Aeon Mall near Kyoto Station is Kyoto's newest shopping complex housing popular fashion stores and restaurant chains. There are two stylish shopping complexes on Karasuma-dōri: Shinpuhkan, just south of Oike, consists of four levels of boutiques, restaurants and a variety of goods shops, built around an inner courtyard, while Cocon Karasuma, south of Shijō, has designer furniture and contemporary Japanese craft shops, as well as restaurants and cafés. On Kawaramachi, the trendy Mina shopping complex houses fashion boutiques, cafés and the Loft department store. In northeastern Kyoto, the Qanat shopping complex at Takano has fashion boutiques, chain stores and a large basement supermarket and food hall.

BOOKS

Junkudō ジュンク堂 ⓦjunkudo.co.jp. The BAL building on Kawaramachi-dōri, which usually houses Kyoto's main Junkudō branch, is currently being rebuilt and is due to reopen in autumn 2015. Until then, there's a branch on Shijō-dōri and a small outlet in the Asahi-kaikan on Kawaramachi-dōri north of Sanjō which both have a small selection of English books and magazines. Daily 10am–8pm.

Kyoto Handicraft Center 京都ハンディクラフトセンタ —Marutamachi-dōri ☎075 761 8001, ⓦkyoto handicraftcenter.com; map p.423. On the fifth floor, there's a good range of cultural books on Japan, including photography books and guidebooks. Daily 10am–6pm.

FOOD

Kyoto is as famous for its beautiful foodstuffs as it is for crafts, all made with the same attention to detail and love of refinement. You can see this in even the most modest restaurant, but also in the confectionery shops, where the window displays look more like art galleries. A popular local delicacy is pickled vegetables (*tsukemono*), which accompany most meals. If you take a walk down Nishiki-kōji market street (see p.418), you'll notice that pickles predominate among all the vegetables, tofu and dried fish. The shops listed below sell souvenir packaging of their famous products.

Ippodō 一保堂 Teramachi Nijō-agaru ☎075 211 3421, ⓦippodo-tea.co.jp; map p.416. This historic tea-seller has

MAJOR KYOTO FESTIVALS AND ANNUAL EVENTS

Thanks to its central role in Japanese history, Kyoto is home to a number of important **festivals**; the major celebrations are listed below. The **cherry-blossom** season hits Kyoto in early April – famous viewing spots include the Imperial Park, Yasaka-jinja and Arashiyama – while early November brings dramatic **autumn colours**. Many temples hold special **openings** in October and November to air their inner rooms during the fine, dry weather. This is a marvellous opportunity to see paintings, statues and other treasures not normally on public display; details are available in the free *Kyoto Visitors' Guide*. Kyoto gets pretty busy during major festivals and national holidays, especially Golden Week (April 29–May 5).

Febuary 2–4 Setsubun 節分 Annual bean-throwing festival celebrated at shrines throughout the city. At Yasaka-jinja, "ogres" scatter beans and pray for good harvests, while Heian-jingū hosts performances of traditional *kyōgen* theatre (see p.815) on Feb 3.

April 1–30 Miyako Odori 都をどり Performances of traditional geisha dances in Gion (see p.449).

April 7–22 Kyo Odori 京おどり Performances by the geisha and maiko of the Miyagawa-chō district (see p.449).

May 15 Aoi Matsuri 葵祭 The "Hollyhock Festival" dates back to the days when this plant was believed to ward off earthquakes and thunder. Now it's an occasion for a gorgeous, yet slow, procession of people dressed in Heian-period costume (794–1185). They accompany the imperial messenger and an ox cart decked in hollyhock leaves from the Imperial Palace to the Shimo-gamo and Kami-gamo shrines, in north Kyoto.

May 1–24 Kamo-gawa Odori 鴨川をどり Performances of traditional dances by geisha in Pontochō (see p.418).

June 1–2 Takigi Nō 薪能 Nō plays performed by torchlight at Heian-jingū.

July 1–31 Gion Matsuri 祇園祭 One of Kyoto's great festivals dates back to Heian times, when ceremonies were held to drive away epidemics of the plague. The festivities focus on Yasaka-jinja and culminate on July 17, with a grand parade through central Kyoto of tall, pointy *yama-boko* floats, richly decorated with local Nishijin silk. Night festivals are held three days prior to the parade, when the floats are lit with lanterns. Some can be viewed inside for a few hundred yen.

August 16 Daimonji Gozan Okuribi 大文字五山送り火 Five huge bonfires etch *kanji* characters on five hills around Kyoto; the most famous is the character for *dai* (big) on Daimonji-yama, northeast of the city. The practice originated from lighting fires after Obon (see p.55).

October 22 Jidai Matsuri 時代祭 This "Festival of the Ages" was introduced in 1895 to mark Kyoto's 1100th anniversary. More than two thousand people, wearing costumes representing all the intervening historical periods, parade from the Imperial Palace to Heian-jingū.

October 22 Kurama-no-Himatsuri 鞍馬の火祭 After the Jidai parade, hop on a train north to see Kurama's more boisterous Fire Festival. Villagers light bonfires outside their houses and local lads carry giant, flaming torches (the biggest weighing up to 100kg) to the shrine. Events climax around 8pm with a mad dash up the steps with a *mikoshi* (portable shrine), after which there's heavy-duty drinking, drumming and chanting till dawn. To get there, take the Eizan line from Kyoto's Demachiyanagi Station (30min); it's best to arrive early and leave around 10pm.

December 1–25 Kabuki Kaomise 顔見世 Grand kabuki festival.

December 31 Okera Mairi 白朮詣り The best place to see in the New Year is at Gion's Yasaka-jinja. Locals come here to light a flame from the sacred fire, with which to rekindle their hearths back home. As well as general good luck, this supposedly prevents illness in the coming year.

been in business since 1717. The shop sells all grades of Japanese green teas, locally grown in Uji – from top-quality *matcha* to the earthy roasted *hōjicha*. Daily 9am–7pm.

Izutsu Yatsuhashi 井筒八つ橋 Teramachi Shijō-agaru ☎075 255 2121, ⓦ yatsuhashi.co.jp; map p.416. Yatsuhashi sweet cinnamon-flavoured biscuits and soft rice

cakes are Kyoto favourites and make great souvenirs. At this Izutsu branch store you can also try your hand at baking the famous Yatsuhashi biscuits (see p.416). Daily 10am–8pm.

Kogetsu 鼓月 681 Takanna-chō ☎075 221 1641, ⓦ kogetsu.com; map p.416. This elegant confectioner is famous for its *senju-sembei* – a waffle biscuit filled with

6

bean jam. The chrysanthemum-shaped Hana soft cakes with white bean fillings are also delicious. Daily 9am–7pm.

Nishiri 西利 Shijō-dōri, Gion ☎075 541 8181, ⓦnishiri.co.jp; map p.423. This renowned Kyoto *tsukemono* (pickle) company is popular for their crispy *nasu* (aubergine) pickles, while the kyūri (cucumber) pickles are also excellent. Daily 10am–9pm.

Takakuraya 高倉屋 Nishiki-kōji ☎075 231 0032, ⓦtakakuraya.jp; map p.416. Takakuraya is famous for its thinly sliced daikon (white radish) pickles which are expertly prepared and have a fresh and flavoursome taste. Daily 10am–6.30pm.

Toraya とらや Gokomachi Nishi-iru Shijō-dōri ☎075 221 3027, ⓦtoraya-group.co.jp; map p.416. Toraya has been in business since the sixteenth century. It produces superbly artistic creations of seasonal sweets made from *mochi* (pounded rice) and sweet red or white beans. Daily 10am–7pm.

TEXTILES AND FASHION

Kyoto has long been famous for its high-quality kimono silk weaving and dyeing, with the Nishijin district (see p.433), located northwest of the Imperial Palace, being the centre of city's textile industry. Some of the wonderful traditional techniques have been revitalized by young Kyoto fashion designers in recent years. The shops listed below offer top-quality locally designed and made clothes and accessories.

Pagong パゴン 373 Kiyomoto-chō Gion ☎075 541 3155, ⓦpagong.jp/en; map p.423. Traditional Yūzen dyer now producing aloha shirts, camisoles, dresses, scarves and T-shirts with traditional patterns and designs. Look out for sister brand Sanjō by Pagong on Sanjō-dōri between Fuyachō and Tominokōji. Daily 11.30am–8pm.

Eirakuya/RAAK 永楽屋 Muromachi Sanjō-agaru ☎075 256 7811, ⓦeirakuya.jp; map p.416. The main store of this traditional *tenugui* (cotton hand-cloth) manufacturer, which now reproduces stylish Taishō designs from the 1920s, can be found on Muromachi, which runs parallel to the west of Karasuma. The *tenugui* can be worn

as a scarf or framed and hung on the wall, while modern styles are produced through the RAAK label. There are also smaller branches on Shijō, on both sides of the bridge. Daily 11am–7pm.

Kyoto Denim 京都デニム 79-3 Koinari-chō ☎075 352 1053, ⓦkyoto-denim.jp; map p.419. Fashionable denim jeans and clothing incorporating local fabrics, such as cotton, silk and brocade. Look out for their denim kimono range. Daily 10am–8pm.

Sou Sou ソウソウ 565-72 Nakano-chō ☎075 212 8005, ⓦsousou.co.jp; map p.416. A winning combination of traditional footwear and modern style, this local label designs and produces *jikatabi*, split-toe workmen's shoes, in funky fabrics and styles. Also sells sportswear and kimono. Daily 11am–8pm.

TRADITIONAL ARTS AND CRAFTS SHOPS

You can still find shops in Kyoto producing crafts in the traditional way, using skills passed down through the generations; these offer superb, if often pricey, souvenirs of the city. There's also no shortage of innovative shops and galleries that expertly fuse time-honoured traditional techniques with modern design.

Aritsugu 有次 Nishiki-kōji Goko-machi Nishi-iru ☎075 221 1091; map p.416. This top-end knife shop has been in business since the sixteenth century, when they specialized in sword production. Now they do a roaring trade in sashimi knives and other hand-crafted kitchen implements. Daily 9am–5.30pm.

Asahi-dō 朝日堂 1-280 Kiyomizu ☎075 531 2181, ⓦasahido.co.jp; map p.423. The best and most famous of several pottery shops on the road up to Kiyomizu-dera, established in the Edo period and selling a wide variety of locally produced *Kiyomizu-yaki*. Daily 9am–6pm.

Ichizawa Shinzaburo Hanpu 一澤信三郎帆布 602 Takabatake-chō ☎075 541 0436, ⓦichizawa.co.jp; map p.423. Long-established canvas-bag manufacturer on Higashiōji-dōri producing beautifully hand-stitched rucksacks, tote bags and purses in functional designs and a variety of colours. Prices start at around ¥5000. Arrive early to beat the crowds. 9am–6pm; closed Sun.

TEMPLE AND SHRINE FLEA MARKETS

If you're in Kyoto towards the end of the month, don't miss its two big **flea markets**. On the 21st, Kōbō-san (in honour of the founder) is held at **Tō-ji** temple (see p.420), and on the 25th, Tenjin-san (in honour of the enshrined deity) is held at **Kitano Tenmangū**, a large shrine in northwest Kyoto (entrance on Imadegawa-dōri). Both kick off before 7am and it's worth getting there early if you're looking for special treasures. There's a fantastic carnival atmosphere at these markets, where stalls sell everything from used kimono to dried fruit and manga. Tō-ji has an antiques market on the first Sunday of every month.

A monthly market is also held at **Chion-ji** on the 15th of every month (16th if raining), which focuses more on crafts and other handmade goods. Chion-ji sits on the corner of Imadegawa-dōri and Higashiōji-dōri, close to Kyoto University.

KYOTO HANDMADE

Kyoto has a rich heritage of **arts and crafts** though you'll often hear laments about vanishing traditions and the lack of interest by young Japanese in continuing these highly specialized handmade skills. A new government-sponsored initiative called **Japan Handmade** (ⓦ japan-handmade.com) is attempting to revive traditional Kyoto crafts in a sustainable way by promoting new products made by local artisans. These traditional craftsmen are actually the sons of established Kyoto craft families – some of which have been in business for centuries. In collaboration with the Danish design studio OeO, six young Kyoto men who have inherited their family's artisanal heritage of kimono weaving, ceramics, metalwork, woodcraft, and bamboo work are taking their stylish **modern designs** to new domestic and international markets.

Jūsan-ya 十三や 13 Shijō Teramachi Higashi-iru ☏ 075 211 0498; map p.416. This little shop on Shijō-dōri is crammed with exquisite combs and hair ornaments in plain boxwood or covered in lacquer that are usually worn by geisha and apprentice maiko. All the items are handcrafted using traditional techniques. Daily 11am–8.30pm.

Kaikadō 開化堂 84-1 Umeminato-chō ☏ 075 351 5788, ⓦ kaikado.jp/english; map p.419. This traditional Kyoto tea caddy manufacturer has branched out into modern design (see box above). Using centuries-old techniques, Kaikadō is now producing stylish teapots, water pitchers, milk jugs, trays and boxes. Mon–Sat 9am–6pm.

Kungyoku-dō 薫玉堂 Horikawa-dōri, Nishi-Hongan-ji-mae ☏ 075 371 0162, ⓦ kungyokudo.co.jp/english; map p.419. Though you wouldn't guess it from its modern, grey-stone frontage, this shop has been selling incense since 1594 – the original customers were Buddhist temples and court nobles indulging in incense parties (players had to guess the ingredients from the perfume). The shop lies opposite the west gate of Nishi-Hongan-ji. Daily 9am–5.30pm; closed first and third Sun of the month.

Kyoto Design House 京都デザインハウス 105 Fukunaga-chō ☏ 075 221 0200, ⓦ kyoto-dh.com/en; map p.416. Premium selection of contemporary local designs – from sleek tableware to functional leather purses and wallets. The craftsmanship is excellent and this is a great place to buy sophisticated souvenirs. Daily 11am–8pm.

Kyoto Handicraft Center 京都ハンディクラフトセンタ ー Marutamachi-dōri, ☏ 075 761 8001, ⓦ kyotohandicraftcenter.com; map p.423. Five floors packed with a surprisingly decent range of traditional Kyoto crafts, souvenirs from all over Japan, and even antique ukiyo-e prints. There are tax-free prices for goods over ¥10,502 (see p.62). Located near the northwest corner of Heian-jingū. Daily 10am–6pm.

Kyūkyo-dō 鳩居堂玉堂 520 Teramachi ☏ 075 231 0510, ⓦ kyukyodo.co.jp; map p.416. This wonderful old shop on Teramachi shopping arcade smells great thanks to all the incense on sale, but it's also a good place to purchase handmade cards and other stationery items, as well as uchiwa fans and calligraphy goods. Mon–Sat 10am–6pm.

Lisn リスン Karasuma-dōri Shijō-sagaru ☏ 075 353 6466, ⓦ www2.lisn.co.jp; map p.416. This stylish incense shop on the ground floor of Cocon Karasuma shopping complex has the decor of an exclusive nightclub. Choose from a wide range of modern seasonal blends. Daily 11am–8pm.

Naitō 内藤 Sanjō-ōhashi Nishizume ☏ 075 221 3018; map p.416. You might not be in the market for a broom, but take a look at this old shop just west of the Sanjō bridge, which is a treasure-trove of beautifully made palm hemp brushes of every size and description (from ¥700). Daily 8am–8pm.

Suzuki Shofudō 鈴木松風堂 409 Izutsuya-chō ☏ 075 231 5003, ⓦ shofudo-shop.jp; map p.416. Wonderful traditional paper shop selling a creative array of paper crafts such as boxes, trays and sugar pots with wooden spoons attached (¥1260). Daily 10am–7pm.

Tanakaya 田中彌 Shijō Yanaginobanba ☏ 075 221 1959; map p.416. This stately old shop on Shijō-dōri is one of the best places to shop for Kyō-ningyō – traditional Kyoto dolls – in all shapes and sizes. There's also a gallery upstairs with changing exhibitions of antique dolls. 10am–6pm, closed Wed.

Yamato Mingei-ten やまと民芸店 Kawaramachi Takoyakushi-agaru ☏ 075 221 2641; map p.416. The best place in Kyoto to buy folk crafts. The main shop has two floors stuffed full of tempting items from all over Japan, while the annexe round the corner displays furniture and more modern designs. Daily 11am–7pm, closed Tues.

Yojiya よーじや Shijō-dōri, Gion ⓦ yojiya.co.jp/english; map p.423. Traditional Kyoto aburatori-gami (face oil blotting paper) manufacturer with branches all over the city. Powders, lipsticks and brushes, just like those used by geisha, as well as cute make-up pouches and hand-mirrors are also on sale. There is another central branch on Sanjō, which has an excellent in-house Italian café. Daily 10am–8pm.

DIRECTORY

Banks and exchange The main banking district is around the Karasuma Shijō junction, where Sumitomo Mitsui Banking Corporation, Citibank and Bank of Tokyo Mitsubishi UFJ (MUFG) banks all have foreign-exchange facilities. At the station, the Central Post Office (Mon–Fri 9.30am–6pm), and the Tokai Ticket shop (10am–8pm) in Kyoto Tower both handle foreign exchange. The Kyoto Handicraft Centre (10am–6pm) in eastern Kyoto can change major foreign currencies. Post office ATMs and ATMs at Seven-Eleven convenience stores throughout Kyoto take international cards. Note that some machines are not accessible to foreign-issued cards outside regular banking hours (9am–3pm).

Emergencies The main police station is at 85-3 Yabunouchi-chō, Shimodachiuri-dōri, Kamanza Higashi-iru, Kamigyō-ku (☎075 451 9111). In an absolute emergency, call 110 where you will be transferred to an English-speaker.

Hospitals and clinics The best Kyoto hospital with English-speaking doctors is the Japan Baptist Hospital, 47 Yamanomoto-chō, Kitashirakawa, Sakyō-ku (☎075 781 5191, ⓦjbh.or.jp). Sakabe International Clinic, 435 Yamamoto-chō, Gokomachi Nijō-sagaru (closed Thurs & Sat afternoons and all day Sun; ☎075 231 1624, ⓦsakabeclinic.com), is run by English-speaking staff. For more information about medical facilities with English-speaking staff in Kyoto or throughout the region, call the AMDA International Medical Information Centre (☎06 4395 0555).

Immigration To renew your tourist or student visa, apply to the Immigration Bureau, 4F, 34-12 Higashi Marutamachi, Kawabata Higashi-iru, near Keihan Marutamachi Station (☎075 752 5997).

Internet The Kyoto Tourist Information Center on the second floor of Kyoto Station next to the Isetan department store charges ¥100/10min. Kyoto International Community House has free wi-fi and PC rental (¥200/30min). Downtown, you can use PCs or Macs (¥210/10min) at Kinkos on Karasuma-dōri (☎075 213 6802). The free Kyoto WiFi (ⓦkanko.city.kyoto.lg.jp/wifi/en) service is available at bus stops, subway stations and Seven-Eleven stores. You must register online in advance and it is limited to three hours per log-in.

Language courses Kyoto Japanese Language School, Ichijō-dōri Muromachi-nishi, Kamigyō-ku (☎075 414 0449, ⓦkjls.or.jp); Kyoto Institute of Culture and Language, 21 Kamihate-chō, Kitashirakawa, Sakyō-ku (☎075 722 5066, ⓦkicl.ac.jp); Kyoto YMCA Japanese Language School, Sanjō Yanaginobanba (☎075 255 3287, ⓦkyotoymca.or.jp); and Kyoto International Academy, Kitano Tenmangū (☎075 466 4881, ⓦkia-ac.jp); The Kyoto International Community House, 2-1 Torii-chō Awataguchi, Sakyō-ku (☎075 752 3010, ⓦkcif.or.jp); and Trademark, 15 Naginomiya-chō, Nakagyō-ku (☎075 201 6139, ⓦj-space.sakura.ne.jp).

Mobile phone rental Kyoto-based company Rentafone Japan (☎075 752 5997, ⓦrentafonejapan.com) rents out mobile phones for ¥3900 a week and will deliver to your accommodation in Kyoto. Incoming calls are free and outgoing calls are charged at ¥35/minute.

Post office The Central Post Office, 843-12 Higashi Shiokōji-chō, Shimogyō-ku, Kyoto-shi, is located in front of Kyoto Station. Downtown, the Nakagyō Ward Post Office, 30 Hishiya-chō, Nakagyō-ku, is near the Museum of Kyoto. Both have a 24hr window for stamps and express mail.

Around Kyoto

There's so much to see in Kyoto itself that most people don't explore the surrounding area. First priority should probably go to **Arashiyama**, to the west of Kyoto, which is famous for its gardens and temples, as well as the Hozu-gawa gorge boat ride and the monkey park. **Uji**, to the south of Kyoto, is another quiet pocket of history and home to the magnificent **Byōdō-in**, whose graceful Phoenix Hall is a masterpiece of Japanese architecture, as well as the tea fields which support Kyoto's cultural traditions. In the northeast of Kyoto is **Hiei-zan**, atop a mountain overlooking the city, where age-old cedars shelter the venerable temple complex of **Enryaku-ji**. Below Hiei-zan, **Ōhara** contains a scattering of beguiling temples in a rustic valley.

Slightly further afield, but definitely worth the effort, are **Amanohashidate**, the "Bridge to Heaven", on the northern coast of Kyoto prefecture and the picturesque fishing village of **Ine**. The attractive castle town of **Hikone** on Biwa-ko, Japan's largest lake, and the architecturally stunning **Miho Museum**, nestled in the Shigaraki mountains, are also both worth visiting.

Arashiyama

嵐山

Western Kyoto ends in the pleasant, leafy suburb of **ARASHIYAMA**. Set beside the Hozu-gawa, Arashiyama, literally "storm mountain", was originally a place for imperial relaxation, away from the main court in central Kyoto, where aristocrats indulged in pursuits such as poetry-writing and hunting. The palaces were later converted into Buddhist temples and monasteries, the most famous of which is **Tenryū-ji**, noted for its garden, while the smaller, quieter temples have a more intimate appeal. In contrast with Tenryū-ji's somewhat introspective garden, that of **Ōkōchi Sansō** – the home of a 1920s movie actor – is by turns secretive and dramatic, with winding paths and sudden views over Kyoto. For a break from temples and gardens, take the Torokko train up the scenic Hozu valley to **Kameoka**, from where boats ferry you back down the fairly gentle **Hozu rapids**.

The town's most interesting sights, as well as the majority of its shops, restaurants and transport facilities, lie north of the Hozu-gawa. Note that central Arashiyama can get unbearably crowded, particularly on spring and autumn weekends; however, if you head north along the hillside you'll soon begin to leave the crowds behind. A good way to explore the area is to rent a bike (see p.458) and spend a day pottering around the lanes and through magnificent bamboo forests; alternatively, it is possible to see some of the main sights by *jinrikisha* (rickshaw).

Togetsu-kyō

渡月橋 • A 3min walk south of Keifuku Arashiyama Station

Arashiyama is centred on the long **Togetsu-kyō** bridge, which spans the Hozu-gawa (known as the Katsura-gawa east of the bridge). This is a famous spot for viewing cherry blossoms in spring, maples in autumn, and *ukai* (cormorant fishing) in the summer. In September 2013 a very powerful typhoon caused severe flooding of the Hozu-gawa and many businesses near the bridge and on the nearby river park of Nakanoshima were damaged.

Tenryū-ji

天龍寺 • 68 Susukinobaba-chō • Daily 8.30am–5pm • ¥600 • ☎ 075 881 1235, ⓦ tenryuji.org

The first major sight in Arashiyama is the Zen temple of **Tenryū-ji**, which started life as the country retreat of Emperor Kameyama (1260–74), grandfather of the more famous **Emperor Go-Daigo** (1318–39). Go-Daigo overthrew the Kamakura shogunate (see p.795) and wrested power back to Kyoto in 1333 with the help of a defector from the enemy camp, **Ashikaga Takauji**. The ambitious Ashikaga soon grew exasperated by Go-Daigo's incompetence and staged a counter-coup. He placed a puppet emperor on the throne and declared himself shogun, thus also gaining the Arashiyama palace, while Go-Daigo fled south to set up a rival court in Yoshino, south of Nara. After Go-Daigo died in 1339, however, a series of bad omens convinced Ashikaga to convert the palace into a temple to appease Go-Daigo's restless soul.

The garden

The temple buildings are nearly all twentieth-century reproductions, but the **garden** behind dates back to the thirteenth century. It's best viewed from inside the temple, from where you get the full impact of the pond and its artfully placed rock groupings against the tree-covered hillside. The present layout of the garden is the work of **Musō Kokushi**, the fourteenth-century Zen monk also responsible for Saihō-ji (see p.436), who incorporated Zen and Chinese motifs into the existing garden. There's still an argument, however, over who created the garden's most admired feature, the dry, Dragon Gate waterfall on the far side of the pond. Apparently inspired by Chinese Sung-dynasty landscape paintings, the waterfall's height and bold vertical composition are extremely unusual in Japanese garden design.

Ōkōchi Sansō

大河内山荘 • 8 Tabuchiyama-chō • Daily 9am–5pm • ¥1000, including green tea • ☏ 075 872 2233 • A 10min walk west of Keifuku Arashiyama Station

On the hillside at the edge of Arashiyama's iconic bamboo grove you'll find the entrance to the very attractive **Ōkōchi Sansō**. Once the home of Ōkōchi Denjirō, a silent-film idol of the 1920s, this traditional Japanese villa has a spectacular location. The path through the villa's expansive grounds takes you winding all over the hillside, past tea-ceremony pavilions, a moss garden, a dry garden and stone benches, up to a ridge with views over Kyoto on one side and the Hozu gorge on the other. Finally, you drop down to a small museum devoted to the actor.

Seiryō-ji

清凉寺 • 45 Fujinoki-chō • Daily 9am–4pm • ¥400 • ☏ 075 861 0343 • A 15min walk north from JR Saga-Arashiyama Station

The main reason to visit the temple of **Seiryō-ji** is to see its wonderful statue of Shaka Nyorai (the Historical Buddha), though the compound itself is a pleasant place to wander around, too, and it's usually not crowded. The statue is currently on public display in April, May, October and November; at other times, a donation of ¥1000 will enable you to view it. The image was carved in China in 985 AD and is a copy of a much older Indian statue, which in turn was said to have been modelled on the Buddha while he was alive. The rest of the time you'll only be able to see the statue's "internal organs" – when it was opened in 1953 several little silk bags in the shape of a heart, kidneys and liver were found, and these are now on display in the temple museum.

Daikaku-ji

大覚寺 • 4 Osawa-chō • Daily 9am–4.30pm • ¥500 • ☏ 075 871 0071, ⓦ daikakuji.or.jp • A 25min walk north from JR Saga-Arashiyama Station

The palatial-looking **Daikaku-ji** was founded in 876, when Emperor Saga ordered that his country villa be converted to a Shingon-sect temple. The main Shin-den hall was moved here from Kyoto's Imperial Palace in the late sixteenth century and still contains some fine screens painted by renowned artists of the Kanō school. Behind this building is the Shoshin-den, also noted for its panels of a hawk and an endearing group of rabbits. Afterwards you can wander along the banks of the picturesque Osawa-ike, Emperor Saga's boating lake and a popular spot for viewing the autumn Harvest Moon.

Arashiyama Monkey Park Iwatayama

嵐山モンキーパークいわたやま • 8 Genryōzan-chō • Daily: mid-March to mid-Nov 9am–5.30pm; mid-Nov to mid-March 9am–4.30pm • ¥550 • ☏ 075 872 0950, ⓦ kmpi.○.jp • Enter through the *torii* (shrine gate) near the southern end of Togetsu-kyō

Located on the side of Mount Arashiyama, the **Arashiyama Monkey Park Iwatayama** is home to more than 130 Japanese macaque monkeys. The park is also a research centre, and is well worth a visit for a break away from the crowds. A steep path winds up Mount Arashiyama to the observation deck, where the monkeys are fed, and from here you can enjoy excellent views of Arashiyama, the Hozu-gawa and Kyoto city.

ARRIVAL AND DEPARTURE   ARASHIYAMA

By train Three train lines connect Arashiyama with central Kyoto. The quickest and most pleasant way to get here is to take a train on the private Keifuku Electric Railway (nicknamed "Randen") from Kyoto's Shijō-Ōmiya Station (every 10min; 20min; ¥200) into the main Arashiyama Station in the centre of town. The "Randen All-Day Ticket" (¥500) allows unlimited travel on this Arashiyama line, as well as the Keifuku Kitano line, which connects with Kitano Hakubaichō Station in northwest Kyoto. Alternatively, the JR Sagano line runs from Kyoto Station to Saga-Arashiyama

Station (every 20min; 15min; ¥230), which is handy for the Torokko trains, but it's roughly a 15min walk to central Arashiyama from here; make sure you get on a local JR train from Kyoto and not the express, which shoots straight through. Finally, there's the less convenient Hankyū Electric Railway; from central Kyoto you have to change at Katsura Station, and you end up in the Hankyū Arashiyama Station on the south side of the river (every 20min; 15min; ¥220).
By bus Buses are slightly more expensive than trains and take longer, especially when the traffic's bad. However,

Arashiyama is on the main Kyoto bus network and falls within the limits for the combined bus and subway pass (see p.438). City Bus routes #11, #28 and #93 all pass through central Arashiyama.

INFORMATION AND TOURS

Tourist information There's a tourist information booth (daily 9am–5pm) inside the Keifuku Arashiyama Station where you can pick up a free tourist map. There's also a small information office at JR Arashiyama Station (daily 9am–4.30pm).

Tours The Kyoto Sagano Walk (Tues & Thurs at 10am; 3hr; ¥2000; ⓦkyotosaganowalk.main.jp) is a good way to discover some of Arashiyama's lesser-known sites in the Sagano area on foot. Reservations, on the website, at least one day in advance are essential.

GETTING AROUND

By bike If you plan to do more than just the central sights, it's worth considering bike rental. There are rental outlets at each of the train stations (¥500–1000 per day).

ACCOMMODATION

Arashiyama Benkei Ryokan 嵐山辨慶旅館 34 Susukinobaba-chō ⓣ075 872 3355, ⓦbenkei.biz. This high-class ryokan sits elegantly on the northern bank of the Hozu-gawa with Tenryū-ji at its rear. Located on the estate of a Heian court noble, the ryokan and its beautiful gardens have a special atmosphere. Rates include meals. **¥60,000**

Hoshinoya Kyoto 星のや 11-2 Genryokuzan-chō ⓣ075 871 0001, ⓦglobal.hoshinoresort.com/hoshinoya_kyoto. This luxury ryokan has become popular with celebrity visitors to Kyoto because of its secretive location on the southern bank of the Hozu-gawa. Guests are transported upriver by boat from a special jetty near Togetsu-kyō. **¥96,000**

EATING

Arashiyama is famous for its Buddhist vegetarian cuisine, *shōjin-ryōri*, and particularly for *yūdōfu* (simmered tofu), which is closely associated with the Zen tradition. Some of the top-end places are very pricey but Arashiyama also has plenty of cheaper places to eat, mostly clustered around the main station.

★ **Arashiyama Yoshimura** 嵐山よしむら Togetsukyō Kitazume ⓣ075 863 5700, ⓦarashiyama-yoshimura.com. This traditonal soba restaurant, near the Togetsu-kyō bridge has fantastic views of the Hozu-gawa and Mt Arashiyama from its second-floor dining area. Tasty soba set lunches start from ¥1575. English menu available. Daily 10.30am–5pm.

Kitcho 吉兆 58 Susukinobaba-chō ⓣ075 881 1101, ⓦkitcho.com/kyoto. One of the most expensive restaurants in Japan, if not the world (science fiction writer Arthur C. Clarke described it as "frighteningly expensive"), *Kitcho* has a world-famous reputation for offering the best in culinary artistry, hospitality and decor. Each meal is uniquely designed to include the best produce of the season, with preparations beginning days in advance – infinite care is taken over everything from the garnish to the antique ceramic plates on which the dishes are served. Set *kaiseki* lunches start at ¥36,750 and dinner courses are from ¥42,000. 11.30am–1pm & 4.30–7pm, closed Wed.

Nishiki 錦 Nakanoshima Kōen ⓣ075 871 8888, ⓦkyoto-nishiki.com. One of the best-known restaurants in Kyoto, *Nishiki* is on the eastern end of Nakanoshima, the low island in the middle of the Hozu-gawa. Specializing in Kyoto cuisine, it serves exquisite eight- to thirteen-course meals, starting at ¥4600. Reservations essential at weekends. 11am–7.30pm, closed Tues.

Sagano 嵯峨野 45 Susukinobaba-chō ⓣ075 871 6946. In a graceful bamboo grove south of Tenryū-ji, Sagano is a tranquil place for lunch or an early dinner of Tofu-based cuisine. The walls are lined with Imari chinaware, and their *yūdōfu* set meal is superb, accompanied by lots of sauces and vegetarian side dishes (¥3800). Daily 11am–7pm.

★ **Shigetsu** 天龍寺篩月 68 Susukinobaba-chō ⓣ075 882 9725, ⓦtenryuji.com/shigetsu. Located within Tenryū-ji, this is a truly authentic *shōjin-ryōri* experience in a lovely setting. There's a choice of three courses (from ¥3000) and reservations are recommended; note that if you're eating in the restaurant you have to pay the ¥500 entry fee for the garden. Daily 11am–2pm.

Uji
宇治

The town of **UJI**, thirty minutes' train ride south of Kyoto, has a long and illustrious past and boasts one of Japan's most fabulous buildings, the **Byōdō-in** – for a preview, look at the reverse side of a ¥10 coin. Somehow this eleventh-century hall, with its glorious statue of Amida Buddha, survived war, fire and years of neglect, and today preserves a stunning display of Heian-period art at its most majestic. Uji is also famous for being the setting of the final chapters of *The Tale of Genji*, and there is now a museum entirely devoted to this aspect of the town's past. While you're here, see the tea fields and sample some of Uji's famous green tea: since the fourteenth century, this area's tea leaves have been rated among the best in the country, and you'll find plenty of teashops where you can sample it on the way from the train station to Byōdō-in. Uji can easily be visited on a half-day excursion from Kyoto, and it's only a little bit further from Nara (see p.740).

Byōdō-in

平等院 • 116 Uji Renge • Daily 8.30am–5.30pm • ¥600 • ☎ 0774 21 2861, �🖾 byodoin.or.jp • A 10min walk from JR Uji Station

One of the nicest places to visit in western Japan, the elegant temple of **Byōdō-in** boasts a remarkable collection of Heian-period art , some impressive buildings and a tranquil atmosphere. After the imperial capital moved to Kyoto in 794, Uji became a popular location for aristocratic country retreats. One such villa was taken over in the late tenth century by the emperor's chief adviser, **Fujiwara Michinaga**, when the Fujiwara clan was at its peak (see p.793). His son, Yorimichi, continued developing the gardens and pavilions until they were the envy of the court. Those pavilions have long gone, but you can still catch a flavour of this golden age through the great literary masterpiece, *The Tale of Genji* (see p.837), written in the early eleventh century. In 1052, some years after *The Tale of Genji* was completed, Yorimichi decided to convert the villa into a temple dedicated to Amida, the Buddha of the Western Paradise. By the following year, the great Amida Hall, popularly known as the Phoenix Hall, was completed. Miraculously, it's the only building from the original temple to have survived.

Phoenix Hall

宇鳳凰 • Daily 9.30am–4.10pm • ¥300

The best place to view the **Phoenix Hall** (*Hōō-dō*) is from the far side of the pond, where it sits on a small island. The hall itself is surprisingly small, but the architect added two completely ornamental wings that extend in a broad U, like a pair of open arms. Inside, the gilded statue of **Amida** dominates. It was created by a sculptor-priest called Jōchō, using a new method of slotting together carved blocks of wood, and is in remarkably fine condition. At one time the hall must have been a riot of colour, but now only a few traces of the **wall paintings** remain, most of which are reproductions. If you look very carefully, you can just make out faded images of Amida and a host of heavenly beings descending on billowing clouds to receive the faithful. Meanwhile the white, upper walls are decorated with a unique collection of 52 carved Bodhisattvas, which were also originally painted. The original wall paintings, as well as the temple bell and two phoenixes, are now preserved in the excellent modern **treasure hall**, *Hōmotsu-kan,* partially submerged into a hill behind the Phoenix Hall. It's worth seeing them up close, especially as these are now the oldest examples of the *Yamato-e* style of painting (see p.812) still in existence.

The Tale of Genji Museum

源氏物語ミュージアム, Genji Monogatari Myujiamu • 45-26 Higashiuchi • 9am–4.30pm; closed Mon • ¥500 • ☎ 0774 39 9300, ⍉ uji-genji.jp/en • To get to the museum, cross Uji bridge, north of Byōdō-in, head towards Keihan Uji Station, and take a right turn up the hill

The small but engaging **The Tale of Genji Museum** is a delightful place to connect with Japan's literary history. *The Tale of Genji* (see p.837) was written in the early eleventh century by Murasaki Shikibu, the daughter of an official of the Imperial Court in Kyoto, and is regarded as the world's first novel. It is an epic saga of love affairs, court intrigues and political machinations, centring on Genji, the Shining Prince, the beautiful son of an emperor and his concubine. The book's finale is set in Uji, which Murasaki Shikibu would have known intimately – she was a distant relative of Fujiwara Michinaga and she served as lady-in-waiting to his daughter, Empress Akiko. At the

6

THE TEA PLANTATION TOUR

The area around Uji is the second-biggest **tea-growing** region in Japan (the largest is Shizuoka in the east of the country) and the fields here have supplied Kyoto's tea culture since the fourteenth century, when seeds brought over from China were first planted. Uji tea is considered the finest in Japan and it is also the most expensive. The best times to visit Uji's tea fields and processing factories are in late spring, when the first leaves of the season, later drunk as *shin-cha* ("new tea"), are being picked, and in early autumn for the next harvest.

InsideJapan Tours organizes a one-day tea picking, roasting and tasting tour of the **Obubu Tea Farm** in Wazuka (**ⓦ** obubutea.com), approximately 40 minutes south of Uji by train. The staff here (including foreign interns) are full of passion and energy for crafting tea and warmly welcome foreign visitors. The visit begins in Obubu's tea fields where you'll be taught how to pick the best leaves; next you'll learn about the roasting processes, roast your own leaves and have a chance to make Hōji-cha and *matcha*. A delicious bentō lunch of tea cuisine is included. The tour is only available at certain times of the year and requires advance reservations: contact InsideJapan for details (**ⓦ** insidejapantours.com, **ⓔ** info@insidejapantours.com).

---

museum, you can learn about the fictional world of Genji in 3-D format, which includes a reproduction of a Heian-period home and an animated film based on the heroine of the Uji chapters, Ukifune. Pick up one of the English-language pamphlets which explain the basics of the museum at the entrance.

ARRIVAL AND INFORMATION UJI

By train Uji lies on the JR Nara line between Kyoto and Nara, with trains running roughly every 15min from Kyoto (¥230; 15–30min) and every 20min from Nara (¥480; 30–50min). The Keihan line, which runs between Kyoto and Ōsaka, stops at Chushojima where you can change for the Keihan Uji line (¥320; 30min).

Tourist information There's a tourist information office at JR Uji Station (daily 9am–5pm; **☎** 0774 24 8783) near the south exit. It's a good place to pick up a map in English before heading to the sights. The Uji City Tourist Information Centre (daily 9am–5pm; **☎** 0774 23 3334) is further along the riverbank from Byōdō-in.

Fishing demonstrations On summer evenings the river at Uji is used for demonstrations of *ukai* (cormorant fishing (see box, p.402); it's best experienced from one of the fishing boats (mid-June to early Sept daily 7–8.30pm; **☎** 077 421 2328; ¥1500).

EATING AND DRINKING

Magozaemon 孫左エ門 21 Uji Renge **☎** 0774 22 4068. Just opposite the entrance to Byōdō-in, this popular restaurant serves especially good and inexpensive handmade noodle dishes. The Uji green-tea udon sets, either hot or cold (¥860), are delicious. 11am–3pm, closed Thurs.

Mitsuboshien Kanbayashi 三星園上林 27-2 Uji Renge **☎** 0774 21 2636, **ⓦ** ujicha-kanbayashi.co.jp. Long-established tea-seller with a tearoom and a reference library on the history and culture of Uji tea. You can join a class here and learn to make your own *matcha* (¥840 with a sweet). Reservations are essential. Daily 9am–6pm.

Taihou-an 対鳳庵 2 Tokawa **☎** 0774 23 3334. This traditional teahouse is a lovely place to take a break and enjoy a fresh bowl of Uji's famous green tea with a seasonal sweet (¥500). Tickets to enter the teahouse and have tea can be purchased at the Uji City Tourist Information Center next door. Daily 10am–4pm; closed Dec 20–Jan 10.

Tsuen-jaya 通園 1 Higashiuchi **☎** 0774 21 2243, **ⓦ** tsuentea.com. Proudly claiming to be Japan's oldest teashop, *Tsūen-jaya* has been run by the same family for over 800 years. The current building, near to the Keihan Uji Station, dates back to the seventeenth century and is full of historical tea paraphernalia. Fresh *matcha* with a sweet is ¥630. Daily 9.30am–5pm.

Hiei-zan

比叡山

Protecting Kyoto's northeastern flank (traditionally considered the source of evil spirits threatening the capital), the sacred mountain of **Hiei-zan** is the home of Tendai Buddhism (see box, p.462). Its headquarters are housed in an atmospheric collection of buildings, **Enryaku-ji**, a pleasant place to meander along ancient paths through cedar forests. The route up to Enryaku-ji from Kyoto wriggles up the mountainside, then follows a ridge road north and, on a clear day, you'll be rewarded with huge views west over **Biwa-ko**, Japan's largest lake and the second-oldest fresh-water lake in the world after Lake Baikal in Siberia.

Enryaku-ji

延暦寺 • 4220 Honmachi • Daily 9am–4pm • ¥550 covering the main compounds • ☎ 077 578 0001, ⓦ hieizan.or.jp

The top of Hiei-zan consists of a narrow ridge, at the south end of which stand the central halls of **Enryaku-ji**. From this core area, known as the **Tō-tō** (Eastern Pagoda), the ridge slopes gently northwest down to the **Sai-tō** (Western Pagoda). A third compound, **Yokawa**, lies further north again, but this was a later addition and contains little of immediate interest. Buses from Kyoto loop around the rather uninteresting **Garden Museum Hiei**, an outdoor museum devoted to re-creating garden scenes from famous paintings by Monet and Renoir, and then stop at the Enryaku-ji Bus Centre, where the main entrance is. To find the ticket office, walk behind the car park and souvenir shop.

Tō-tō

東塔 • Kokuhō-den • ¥450

Enryaku-ji's most important buildings are concentrated in the southerly **Tō-tō** compound. Immediately inside the entrance you'll find a modern treasure hall, the **Kokuhō-den** (国宝殿). Its most interesting exhibits are a fine array of statues, including a delicate, thirteenth-century Amida Buddha and a lovely Senjū Kannon (Thousand-Armed Kannon) of the ninth century. You can also see a scroll apparently recording Saichō's trip to China in 804 AD. Up the hill from the Kokuhō-den, the first building on your left is the **Daikō-dō** (大講堂), the Great Lecture Hall, where monks attend lectures on the sutras and discuss doctrinal subtleties. Keeping an eye on them are life-size statues of Nichiren, Eisai, Hōnen, Shinran and other great names from the past – a sort of Tendai Hall of Fame.

Konpon Chū-dō

根本中堂

Enryaku-ji's most sacred hall is the **Konpon Chū-dō**, located in the Tō-tō compound. This powerful, faded building marks the spot where Saichō built his first hut; his statue of Yakushi Nyorai is kept inside, though hidden from view. Despite the crowds, the atmosphere in the dark, cavernous hall is absolutely compelling. Unusually, the altars are in a sunken area below the worship floor, where they seem to float in a swirling haze of incense smoke lit by low-burning lamps. It's said that the three big lanterns in front of the main altar have been burning ever since Saichō himself lit them 1200 years ago. Some sources hold that the lanterns did go out after Nobunaga's attack, and that a monk was sent up to Yamadera, in northern Honshū, to bring back a light from their sacred flame, which had itself originally come from Enryaku-ji. Monks tending the flames nowadays wear a mask in case they sneeze and accidentally blow the flame out.

Kaidan-in and Amica-dō

戒壇院 • 阿弥陀堂

The pretty **Kaidan-in**, the Ordination Hall, and the recently reconstructed **Amida-dō** and its two-storey pagoda are surrounded by cherry blossoms in the spring, and colourful maple trees in the autumn. Kaidan-in houses some important Buddhist images which are not on display to the public, while the bright-red Amida-dō is used for memorial services. Behind here, a path leads off through the woods to the Sai-tō compound.

Sai-tō

西塔

Located to the north of the Tō-tō compound, the **Sai-tō** compound has a peaceful atmosphere and is one of the highlights of a visit to Enryaku-ji. It houses some important buildings, including the **Jōdo-in** (浄土院), which you'll come to after about ten minutes on the path through the misty woods at the bottom of a lantern-lined staircase. Inside the temple's courtyard, behind the main hall, is **Saichō's mausoleum** (伝教大師御廟), a red-lacquered building that stands in a carefully tended gravel enclosure and is one of Enryaku-ji's most sacred sites.

Ninai-dō
にない堂

Two identical square halls standing on a raised area in the Sai-tō compound are commonly known as **Ninai-dō**, which roughly translates as "shoulder-carrying hall"; this refers to the legendary strength of a certain Benkei, who's said to have hoisted the two buildings onto his shoulders like a yoke. Their official names are Jōgyō-dō (常行堂), the Hall of Perpetual Practice, and the Hokke-dō (法華堂), or Lotus Hall. They're used for different types of meditation practice: in the former, monks walk round the altar for days reciting the Buddha's name, in the latter they alternate between walking and sitting meditation while studying the Lotus Sutra.

Shaka-dō
釈迦堂

The centre of the Sai-tō area is marked by the **Shaka-dō**, another imposing hall. Though smaller and not so atmospheric as Konpon Chū-dō, this building is much older. It was originally erected in the thirteenth century on the shores of Biwa-ko, but was moved here in 1595 to replace the earlier hall destroyed by Nobunaga's armies. It enshrines an image of Shaka Nyorai (Sakyamuni, the Historical Buddha), which is attributed to Saichō, but unfortunately you can't see it. Otherwise, the Shaka-dō is similar to the Tō-tō, with its sunken centre and three lanterns. It's a lovely, quiet place to rest before you start heading back.

ARRIVAL AND DEPARTURE

HIEI-ZAN

By bus The quickest and simplest way of getting to Enryaku-ji is to take a direct bus (1hr; ¥800) from either Kyoto Station or Sanjō-Keihan Station in east Kyoto. The timetable varies according to the season, so check in Kyoto for the latest schedule and note that in winter the road is sometimes closed by snow. Enryaku-ji lies about 800m above sea level and can get pretty chilly in winter; even in summer you'll find it noticeably cooler than Kyoto.

ENRYAKU-JI AND THE TENDAI SECT

The mountain temple complex of **Enryaku-ji** was founded in 788 AD by a young Buddhist monk called Saichō (767–822), who was later sanctified as **Dengyō Daishi.** Saichō built himself a small hut on the mountain and a temple to house an image of Yakushi Nyorai (the Buddha of Healing), which he carved from a fallen tree. He then went to China for a year to study Buddhism; on his return to Hiei-zan in 805 AD he founded the Japanese **Tendai sect.** Based on the Lotus Sutra, Tendai doctrine holds that anyone can achieve enlightenment through studying the sacred texts and following extremely rigorous practices. Its followers went on to establish a whole host of splinter groups: Hōnen (who founded the Jōdo sect), Shinran (Jōdo Shinshū), Eisai (Rinzai Zen) and Nichiren all started out as Tendai priests.

In the early days, Enryaku-ji received generous imperial funding and court officials were sent up the mountain for a twelve-year education programme. As the sect expanded it became enormously rich and politically powerful, until there were three thousand buildings on the mountain. It owned vast areas of land and even maintained an army of several hundred well-trained **warrior monks** – many of whom were not really monks at all. They spent a good deal of time fighting other Buddhist sects, notably their great rivals at Nara's Kōfuku-ji (see p.472). In 1571, the warlord **Oda Nobunaga** (see p.769) put a stop to all this, leading 30,000 troops up Hiei-zan to lay waste to the complex, including the monks and their families. Nobunaga died eleven years later and his successor, Toyotomi Hideyoshi, was more kindly disposed to the Tendai sect, encouraging the monks to rebuild.

MARATHON MONKS

Followers of the Buddhist **Tendai sect** (see box opposite) believe that the route to enlightenment lies through chanting, esoteric ritual and extreme physical endurance. The most rigorous of these practices is the "thousand-day ascetic mountain pilgrimage", in which **marathon monks**, as they're popularly known, are required to walk 40,000km through the mountains and streets of Kyoto in a thousand days – the equivalent of nearly a thousand marathons. The thousand days are split into hundred-day periods over seven years; during each period the monk has to go out every day in all weathers, regardless of his physical condition. He must adhere to a strict vegetarian diet and, at one point during the seven years, go on a week-long fast with no food, water or sleep, just for good measure.

Not surprisingly, many monks don't make it – in the old days they were expected to commit ritual suicide if they had to give up. Those that do finish (nowadays, about one person every five years) are rewarded with enlightenment and become "living Buddhas". Apparently, the advice of modern marathon monks is much sought after by national baseball coaches and others involved in endurance training.

Sakamoto Cable Car The alternative is to take one of two cable-cars up the mountain. The most convenient of these is the eastern Sakamoto Cable (坂本ケーブル; every 30min; 11min; ¥840, or ¥1570 return), which has the added benefit of views over Biwa-ko. To reach the cable car, take a JR Kosei line train from Kyoto Station to Hiei-zan Sakamoto Station (比叡山坂本駅; every 15min; 20min; ¥320), then a bus (¥220). From the top station it's a 700m-walk north to the central Tō-tō area along a quiet road.

Eizan Cable Car The main disadvantage of the western Eizan Cable (叡山ケーブル; every 30min; 20min; ¥840 one-way, or ¥1640 return) is that it dumps you at the Sanchō Station (山頂駅), about 1.5km from the Tō-tō: from the station you can catch a shuttle bus (see below), or walk along a footpath behind the Garden Museum Hiei. Eizan Cable leaves from near Yase-Hiei-zan-guchi Station (八瀬比叡山口駅) on the private Eizan line; to get there, either take a train from Kyoto's Demachiyanagi Station (every 12min; 14min; ¥260) or a Kyoto Bus headed for Ōhara from Kyoto Station (#17 and #18) or Sanjō-Keihan Station (#16 and #17).

GETTING AROUND

By bus Once you've arrived on the mountain, the best way to get around is on foot. If you're in a hurry, however, you can take the shuttle bus (late March to Nov; every 30min), which runs from Sanchō via the central Tō-tō car park to Sai-tō and Yokawa. The whole journey only takes about 20min and costs ¥740. A one-day pass (*hiei-zan-nai ichi-nichi jyōshaken*; ¥800) is available from the bus driver or at the Tō-tō bus terminal; this allows unlimited travel and also entitles you to a ¥100 discount on entrance to Enryaku-ji.

Ōhara

大原

Though only a short bus ride north from Kyoto, the collection of temples that make up **ŌHARA** is almost in a different world. All are sub-temples of Enryaku-ji (see p.461), but the atmosphere here is quite different: instead of stately cedar forests, these little temples are surrounded by maples and flower-filled gardens that are fed by tumbling streams. The sights are divided into two sections: the easterly **Sanzen-in** and the melancholy **Jakkō-in** across the rice fields.

Sanzen-in

三千院 • 540 Raigōin-chō • Daily March–Nov 8 30am–5pm & Dec–Feb 8.30am–4.30am • ¥700 • ☎075 744 2531 • A 10min walk up the hill from the bus terminal

A fortress-like wall contains Ōhara's most important temple, **Sanzen-in**. The temple is said to have been founded by Saichō, the founder of Tendai Buddhism, but its main point of interest is the twelfth-century **Hon-dō**, a small but splendid building standing on its own in a mossy garden. Inside is an astonishingly well-preserved tenth-century Amida Buddha flanked by smaller statues of Kannon (on the right as you face them) and Seishi, which were added later.

Shōrin-in

勝林院 • 187 Shōrinin-chō • Daily 9am–5pm • ¥300 • ☎ 075 744 2537

With its thatched roof, the main hall of **Shōrin-in** is a very pretty sight in June when the surrounding hydrangea bushes are in bloom. Reconstructed in the 1770s and containing another image of Amida, the temple is used for studying *shōmyō*, the Buddhist incantations practised by followers of Tendai. *Shōmyō* were first introduced from China in the eighth century and have had a profound influence on music in Japan such as *gagaku* (court music); press the button in the booth on the left side of the altar and you can hear a short recitation.

Hōsen-in

宝泉院 • 187 Shōrinin-chō • Daily 9am–5pm • ¥800, including green tea • ☎ 075 744 2409

The main reason to visit the temple of **Hōsen-in** is for its intriguing garden, whose highlight is a magnificent pine that is almost seven hundred years old. The temple's ceiling is made from planks that were originally in Fushimi Castle in southern Kyoto, where more than three hundred samurai committed *seppuku* (ritual suicide) after losing a battle in 1600. If you look carefully, traces of blood are still visible.

Jakkō-in

寂光院 • 676 Kusao-chō • Daily 9am–5pm • ¥600 • ☎ 075 744 2545 • A 15min walk west from Ōhara bus station across the river

Situated in a quiet garden which was landscaped in the late Edo period and is fringed by a row of tufted pines, the main hall of the **Jakkō-in** temple had to be rebuilt after it was destroyed in an arson attack in May 2000. This unfortunately damaged its Jizō Bodhisattva and also its one-thousand-year-old pine tree, mentioned in the *Tale of Heike*, which withered and died in 2004. The hall has now been completely rebuilt, and the temple and its surrounding area have been reinvigorated by the restoration work: photos of the devastating fire are on display in the Homotsuden.

ARRIVAL AND DEPARTURE   ŌHARA

By bus To reach Ōhara from central Kyoto, take a cream-and-red Kyoto Bus either from Kyoto Station (#17 and #18), Sanjō-Keihan Station (#16 and #17) or Kita-ōji Station (#15). The journey takes 30–50min and costs a maximum of ¥580, or you can use the Kyoto-wide subway and bus pass (see p.438). The route takes you past Yase-yūen, the starting point of the Eizan cable-car up Hiei-zan (see p.460), making it possible to visit both places in one rather hectic day. Note that in autumn buses are very crowded and there are frequent traffic jams on the road to Ōhara. Visiting on a weekend during this time is best avoided.

ACCOMMODATION AND EATING

Seryo 芹生 22 Shōrinin-chō ☎ 075 744 2301. This is one of the nicest places to eat in Ōhara. They serve a beautifully presented bentō of seasonal vegetables (¥2756) as well as more expensive *kaiseki* meals (from ¥3307). In good weather you can eat outside on a riverside terrace. Daily 11am–4pm.

Seryo Chaya 芹生茶屋 Sanzenin-mae ☎ 075 744 2301. At the top of the steps, just before the entrance to Sanzen-in, *Seryo Chaya* is a cheap option for lunch – their tasty soba lunch set with rice and pickles costs just ¥1200. Daily 9am–5pm.

Seryo 芹生 22 Shōrinin-chō ☎ 075 744 2301, ⓦ seryo .co.jp/english/index.html. This fine ryokan has a choice of comfortable tatami or Western-style rooms as well as open-air and indoor onsen baths. It was refurbished in 2012 and is worth considering if you want to enjoy Ōhara once the crowds have gone. Rates include dinner and breakfast. **¥44,000**

Amanohashidate

天橋立

At the northern tip of Kyoto-fu (Kyoto prefecture), the stubby peninsula of **Tango-Hantō** (丹後半島) leans protectively over Wakasa Bay, shielding the sand spit of **AMANOHASHIDATE**, the "Bridge to Heaven". As one of the trio of top scenic views in Japan (the other two are Matsushima and Miyajima), Amanohashidate has a lot to live up to. The "bridge" is actually a 3.6km ribbon of white sand and pine trees slinking its way between the villages of **Monju** (文珠) near the train station, and **Fuchū** (府中) across the bay.

Monju is the main tourist hub of Amanohashidate, and has an attractive wooden temple, **Chion-ji**, standing on the brink of the sand bar – a lovely area for a quiet stroll or cycle ride, or simply lazing on the beach. To reach the sand bar itself, cross the red bridge, Kaisenkyō, which swings around to allow boats through the narrow channel to the open sea. The sandy, crescent-shaped beaches on the east side of the pine-forested spit are at their busiest from July to August. Above Fuchū there are fantastic views over the bay and along the coast from the touristy sightseeing park of **Kasamatsu-kōen**. Beyond the park on the upper slopes of Mount Nariai, is the splendidly

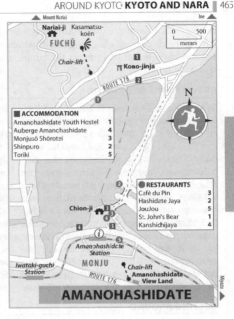

atmospheric **Nariai-ji**, one of the 33 temples on the Saigoku Kannon pilgrimage route.

Chion-ji

智恩寺 · 466 Jimonju · Daily 8am–5pm · Free · ☎ 0772 22 2553, ⓦ monjudo-chionji.jp · A 5min walk north of Amanohashidate Station, at the end of a shopping street leading towards the sand spit

The attractive temple of **Chion-ji** is dedicated to the Buddhist saint of wisdom and intellect, Chie-no-Monju. Between the main gate and the hall (Monju-dō), which houses a revered image of the saint, stands the Tahoto, an unusual squat wooden pagoda dating from 1500. In the temple precincts, near the ferry jetty, you'll also see the Chie-no-wa Torō, a granite ring monument symbolizing wisdom, which has been adopted as an emblem of the town.

Kono-jinja

籠神社 · 43 Jiōgaki · Daily 8am–5pm · Free · ☎ 0772 27 0006, ⓦ motoise.jp · A 3min walk north of the Fuchu ferry jetty.

At the Fuchū end of Amanohashidate, **Kono-jinja** is the oldest shrine in the area, and is guarded by a pair of stone dogs dating from the Kamakura era (1185–1333). Note that the roofs of the shrine buildings are reminiscent of the architecture of Ise-jingu (see p.518).

Kasamatsu-kōen

傘松公園 · Funicular and chairlift daily 8am–5.30pm · ¥640 return

On the lower slopes of Mount Nariai is **Kasamatsu-kōen**, the principal lookout point over Amanohashidate, where tourists gather for official group photos in rather amusing poses. Signs demonstrate how best to do the "mata-nozoki": turn your back to Amanohashidate and bend over with your head between your legs, so that the view of the sand spit seems to float in midair like a bridge to heaven.

Nariai-ji

成相寺 · Fuchū · Daily 8am–5pm · ¥500 · From the Kasamatsu-kōen you can either catch a bus (¥700 return) or walk for 20min further up the mountain to the gate to Nariai-ji

Founded in 704 AD and dedicated to Kannon, the Buddhist goddess of mercy, **Nariai-ji** is a charming rustic temple surrounded by lofty pines. It is one of the 33 temples on the Saigoku Kannon pilgrim route, and so attracts a steady stream of visitors, many of whom clutch elaborate hanging scrolls which are specially inscribed at each temple. Legend has it that if you pray at the temple and make a vow to Kannon, your prayer will be granted.

ARRIVAL AND INFORMATION

AMANOHASHIDATE

By train Trains to Amanohashidate Station (天橋立駅) in Monju run along the scenic Kita-kinki Tango Tetsudō line (北近畿丹後鉄道). When taking the express service from Osaka (2hr; ¥5590; hourly) and Kyoto (2hr; ¥4710; hourly) in the Kansai region, you may be required to switch in Fukuchiyama. There are a few direct JR trains from Amagasaki, Kyoto and Ōsaka, which take around two hours and 30min, but you'll have to pay for the Kita-kinki Tango Tetsudō portion of the journey if you're using a JR Pass (¥1520 for the express service). Alternatively, international visitors who hold a Japan Rail Pass or JR West Rail Pass can buy one of three types of "Kyoto Sea Area Pass": the Amanohashidate Pass (¥1600) and the Ine Pass (¥1600) are both valid for one day and are a significant saving on travel and sightseeing costs, while the Wide Pass (¥2600) is valid

for two days and combines the above two passes. All passes can be purchased in cash on board express trains from Kyoto. Check the JR West website for more details (ⓦwestjr.co.jp).

By bus Buses from both Kyoto Station (¥2700; two daily) and Shin-Osaka Station (¥2600; three daily) take around 2hr 40min.

Tourist information The assistants at the tourist information office (daily 9am–6pm; ☎0772 22 8030) inside Amanohashidate Station are helpful but don't speak much English, although they can provide English-language pamphlets on the area and help with accommodation bookings. There's also free wi-fi access here.

Essentials The Post Office ATM, opposite the station, takes international cards (Mon–Fri 9am–5.30pm).

GETTING AROUND

By bus Buses across the bay to Fuchū (15 daily; 20min; ¥400) and around the Tango-hantō leave from outside Amanohashidate Station until 7pm.

By ferry Ferries run between Monju and Fuchū (18 daily; 12min; ¥520; last ferry at 4.45pm) from the jetty beside Chion-ji, 5min walk from the station, to the Fuchū-side jetty at Ichinomiya.

By chairlift A 5min walk over the rail tracks and up the hill behind Amanohashidate Station brings you to the chair

lift (daily 8.30am–5pm; ¥850 return), which takes 6min to reach the touristy Amanohashidate View Land, a mini-amusement park where loudspeakers pump out a 1950s musical soundtrack.

By bike and on foot If you fancy some exercise, bicycles can be rented from various shops close to Amanohashidate station and near the jetty (¥400–500 for 2hr), or you could stroll the 2.4km across the sand bar, which takes about 50 minutes.

ACCOMMODATION

Monju has the widest range of accommodation, including several inexpensive minshuku near the station and a couple of top-class ryokan. The youth hostel is across the bay in Fuchū. The tourist information desk at the station can help with accommodation but it's best to book in advance, especially if you arrive late in the day. Note that businesses in the area close early, especially in winter, so it's best to eat meals at your accommodation.

Amanohashidate Youth Hostel 天橋立ユースホステル Fuchū ☎0772 27 0121, ⓦhashidate-yh.jp. This hostel is a 15min hike uphill to the right from the ferry and bus stop at Ichinomiya, but it's worth it for the pleasant location and wonderful views. It has bunk-bed dorms, a comfy lounge, wi-fi, helpful English-speaking staff and cheap bike rental (¥500/day). Dorm **¥2950**

Auberge Amanohashidate オーベルジュ天橋立 Eki-dōri ☎0772 22 0650. Scruffy Western-style business hotel near the station with a surprisingly decent in-house French restaurant. The cheaper rooms are without bathrooms but all guests have access to the public bath in the hotel next door. **¥8400**

★ **Monjusō Shōrotei** 文殊荘松露亭 Monju ☎0772 22 2151, ⓦshourotei.com. Exquisite high-end ryokan behind Chion-ji temple, set amidst private gardens at the

tip of a mini-peninsula overlooking the sand bar. Shorotei's cuisine and hospitality are both excellent. Rates vary depending on the room and your choice of meals. **¥79,800**

Shinpūrō 神風楼 Fuchū ☎0772 27 0007, ⓦshinpuro .com. Pleasant ryokan in Fuchū near the Ichinomiya jetty with a smart, modern interior and serving delicious fresh seafood meals. The elegant rooms have garden or Wakasa Bay views, and there's a choice of futons or beds. Guests may use the in-house hot-spring bath. Rates include meals. **¥46,200**

★ **Toriki** 鳥喜 Monju ☎0772 22 0010, ⓦtoriki.jp. This ryōri ryokan (cuisine inn) doesn't look very fancy but it's well-known for serving top-class local cuisine. All the rooms are tatami-style and there's also an onsen bath in the garden. The convenient location and friendly atmosphere make this an excellent choice. Rates include meals. **¥31,500**

EATING AND DRINKING

★**Café du Fin** カフェドパン 468 Jimonju ☎0772 22 1313. One of the nicest places to take a break in Monju. It's just near the bridge to the sand spit and serves curry and rice (¥1000), sandwiches (¥750), cake sets (¥800), good coffee and the award-winning local wine. Daily 9am–5.30pm.

Hashidatejaya はしだて茶屋 Monju ☎0772 22 3363, ⓦhashidate-chaya.jp. Nestling amid the pines at the Monju end of the sand spit this traditional restaurant serves good-value meals and snacks, including hearty bowls of *asari-don* (small shellfish and green vegetables on rice) for ¥1000. 9am–5pm, closed Thurs.

St John's Bear セントジョンズベア Fuchū ☎0772 27 1317, ⓦwww8.plala.or.jp/bear. This friendly Western-style café-bar at the water's edge down from the chairlift station is a good place for lunch or a snack. The Ebichan

shrimp lunch set with salad, rice and soup is ¥1302, and they also serve a variety of meaty-topped pizzas (from ¥1260). Daily 9am–8pm, closed on irregular days.

Pain de JouJou パンデジュジュ 640-6 Monju ☎0772 25 2518. This trendy new bakery café is a good place to grab some bread for a picnic or the train journey. There's also table seating. Sandwich and coffee sets are ¥1000. 10am–6pm, closed Fri.

Kanshichijaya 勘七茶屋 471-1 Monju ☎0772 22 2105. In front of the main gate of Chion-ji is a row of traditional teashops all serving the same local speciality – *Chie-no-mochi*. These small rice cakes are topped with a sweet red bean paste and served here with *matcha* (¥500) – they are freshly made on site and the locals say you'll get wise if you eat them. Daily 8am–5pm.

Ine

伊根

The charming fishing hamlet of **INE**, sheltering in a hook-like inlet towards the eastern end of the Tango-hantō, is a wonderful place to experience peaceful village life by the sea and eat deliciously fresh fish. The picturesque rows of funaya wooden boat houses, some of which date from the Edo period, are the main tourist attraction here. There are some 230 traditional houses built over the water, with space beneath for fishing boats to be stored – from a distance they appear to be floating on water. The funaya rim the shores of Ine Bay creating a unique water landscape, so much so that many films and television dramas have been filmed here, including the *Tora-san* series (see box, p.829).

ARRIVAL, INFORMATION AND GETTING AROUND INE

By bus Buses depart from in front of Amanohashidate station in Monju (15 daily; ¥400) and take around 50min.

By bike You can borrow bikes for free 24hr a day (no deposit necessary) from the bus stop near the Ine Bay boat cruise jetty, with several drop-off/pick-up "ports" around the village.

Tourist information The Ine tourist information office (daily 9am–5pm; ☎0772 32 0277, ⓦine-kankou.jp) is located in Fuya-no-Sato Park on the hill overlooking Ine. The staff speak a little English and can help with accommodation and sea taxi reservations.

EATING AND ACCOMMODATION

★**Kagiya** 鍵屋 ☎0772 32 0356, ⓦine-kagiya.net. This comfortable modern funaya has a living and dining space on the first floor with sublime views of the bay. Upstairs there are two stylish bedrooms that can sleep up to eight guests. Rates include an excellent dinner and breakfast. Guests can also take Kagiya's private sea taxi tours of Ine Bay for ¥1000 per person. **¥40,200**

Shibatasō しばた荘 ☎0772 32 0254, ⓦshibata-sou. com. Located along the coast north of Ine, this large traditional-style minshuku serves excellent *kaiseki* cuisine as well as crab and yellowtail when in season. There are six

tatami rooms which can sleep up to 20 guests. The owner can pick up guests by car from the boat cruise jetty. **¥19,000**

Kamome かもめ ☎0772 32 0025. This small restaurant and coffee shop is above a souvenir shop on the main road leading into Ine and has wonderful views of the bay. Tasty lunch sets with fresh local fish, miso soup and pickles are ¥1500. 9am–6pm, closed Thurs.

Yoshimura よしむら ☎0772 32 0062. Serving super-fresh fish cuisine this is a great place for lunch right in the centre of Ine. Multicourse lunch sets of various fish dishes including sashimi are ¥2000. 11.30am–2pm, closed Wed.

Hikone

彦根

On the northeastern shore of Biwa-ko, Japan's largest lake, lies the stately castle town of **HIKONE**, an easy day-trip or a pleasant overnight stay from Kyoto. This attractive town

6

INE BAY BOAT TRIPS

Sightseeing boats daily 9am–4pm every 30min; closed Jan & Feb · 30min tour ¥660 · ☎ 0772 32 0009, ⊛ tankai.jp · **Sea taxis** ¥1000 per person for 30 minutes (minimum two passengers)

The calm waters of **Ine Bay** (伊根湾, Ine-wan are so clear that various types of fish, eels and even shrimp can be seen from the regular **cruise boats** (伊根湾めぐり遊覧船, Ine-wan Megun Yuransen) that circle the bay providing a comprehensive but brief view of the unusual architecture of the funaya. A more satisfying experience, though more expensive, is to rent a **sea taxi** from one of the funaya and tour the bay at your leisure. The taxi driver will take you much closer than the boat cruise and point out some of the more unusual funaya.

---

not unreasonably claims that it has retained the look and feel of the Edo period more than any other place in the country. The town's castle is one of the few in Japan to have remained intact since the early seventeenth century, and is well worth a visit. Hikone is also known for its *butsudan* (Buddhist altar) industry and the town has an abundance of shops with elaborate altars on display. Hikone's main attractions can all be seen on foot and, except during the cherry blossom season when the castle is engulfed by hordes of tourists, the town can be enjoyed at a leisurely and crowd-free pace.

Hikone-jō

彦根城 · 1-1 Konki-chō · Daily 8.30am–5pm · ¥600 including access to Genkyū-en; combined pass including museum and Genkyū-en ¥1000 · ☎ 0749 22 2742

Very little has changed in the 400 years and more that **Hikone-jō** has stood on the hill looking out onto the town and the lake. One of the most authentic castles remaining in Japan, it is also one of only four designated as a National Treasure. There are spectacular views of Biwa-ko from the donjon on a clear day, and with very few modern buildings and little pollution to obscure the panorama it is possible to imagine something of what people in the Edo period may have seen.

Hikone-jō was built between 1602 and 1622 by the Ii family from the ruins of other castles in the area, including one on the original site. If you look at the stone walls as you climb up the hill, you can see that the style is inconsistent. The lower levels were constructed by untrained labourers while the upper levels have been assembled using the patchwork-like *gobo-zumi* masonry technique. Although the walls look rather precarious, they have successfully protected the castle from earthquake damage since their construction. The fortress is double-moated and also features many *yagura* or turrets. In particular, the *tenbin-yagura*, in the unique shape of a *tenbin* (Japanese scales), and the *taikomon-yagura*, so called because a *taiko* or Japanese drum was kept there to send warnings, are both architecturally significant.

Hikone-jō Museum

彦根城博物館, Hikone-jō Hakubutsukan · Daily 9am–4.30pm · ¥500; combined pass including Hikone-jō and Genkyū-en ¥1000 · ☎ 0749 22 6100

Just inside the main gate of the castle, the **Hikone-jō Museum** was reconstructed in 1987 and is an exact copy of the Edo-period official quarter of the castle. Inside you can see how the Ii family lived. Their nō stage, tearoom and living area have been re-created, and there are a large number of artefacts on display including nō costumes, weaponry, calligraphy manuscripts and other artworks.

Genkyū-en

玄宮園 · Daily 8.30am–5pm · ¥200; free entry with Hikone-jō ticket, or combined pass for Hikone-jō and museum ¥1000 · ☎ 0749 22 2742

On the northeast side of Hikone-jō is the **Genkyū-en**. Built in 1677, the garden is modelled on the ancient Chinese palace of Tang dynasty emperor Genso and features a large pond full of carp. Genkyū-en has many imitation scenes of the region and the pond is Biwa-ko in miniature. The *Hoshō-dai* teahouse, where the Ii Lords entertained, is a good place to stop for a bowl of *matcha* and a sweet (¥500) while enjoying pleasant views of the garden and castle.

Yume-Kyōbashi Castle Road

夢京橋キャッスルロード • South of Hikone-jō • ⓦ yumekyobashi.jp

The **Yume-Kyōbashi Castle Road** is a charming imitation of a bustling Edo-period merchant area. The 350m stretch has modern reconstructions of traditional Japanese shops on both sides, housing a variety of cafés, restaurants, bars and souvenir shops. At the end of the road farthest from the castle, turn left into **Yonban-chō**, another reconstructed shopping and dining area. Here, dozens of small shops and restaurants have been built in a style reminiscent of the Taishō era of the 1920s.

Ryōtanji

龍潭寺 • 1104 Furusawa-chō • Daily 9am–5pm • ¥400 • ⓣ 0749 22 2777 • A 10min taxi ride north of Hikone JR station

The Zen temple **Ryōtanji**, located on the eastern edge of the town, was founded in 733 and was the family temple of the Ii Lords. The temple's gardens were designed by monks in training and it was once an important centre for Zen gardening. The Fudaraku stone garden, dating from 1670, is considered to be a fine example of the genre.

Tennei-ji

天寧寺 • 232 Satone-chō • Daily 8am–5pm • ¥400 • ⓣ 0749 22 5313 • A 30min walk from Hikone Station

East of Hikone-jō, at the Zen temple of **Tennei-ji**, 500 Buddhist disciples who reached Nirvana are enshrined as *Gohyaku Rakan* wooden statues. It is said that you should be able to find a face that resembles someone you know among the statues.

ARRIVAL AND INFORMATION
HIKONE

By train Express JR trains take 1hr 30min from Osaka (¥1890) and 50min from Kyoto (¥1100). On the Shinkansen Tokaido line, get off at Maibara Station (25min from Kyoto; ¥3300) and change for the JR Biwako line to Hikone Station (5min; ¥180). From here, it's about a 10min walk to the castle area.

Tourist information There's a helpful tourist office (daily 9am–5.30pm; ⓣ 0749 22 2954) with English-speaking staff at JR Hikone Station, on your left-hand side as you exit: you can also pick up English pamphlets on Hikone here.

ACCOMMODATION

Hikone Castle Hotel 彦根キャッスルホテル 1-8 Sawa-chō ⓣ 0749 21 2001, ⓦ hch.jp. The best place to stay in Hikone, this hotel is situated right on the northeast corner of the castle moat and was refurbished in late 2013. The rooms are clean, spacious and most have clear views of the castle. The in-house restaurant serves local Ōmi beef lunch and dinner courses. **¥16,000**

Comfort Hotel Hikone コンフォートホテル彦根 155 Furusawa-chō ⓣ 074 927 8211, ⓦ comfortinn.com, hotel-hione-japan-JP079. Hikone's newest business hotel

is clean and functional but the service can be surly. The location is convenient to the JR station but the area is currently under development. Free breakfast and wi-fi. **¥9000**

Hotel Estacion Hikone ホテルエスタシオンひこね 8-31 Asahimachi ⓣ 0749 22 1500, ⓦ www.estacion-hikone.com. This friendly and efficient business hotel is conveniently located near the JR station and shopping area. Rooms are on the small side but are clean and well appointed. Free internet and breakfast. **¥11,000**

EATING AND DRINKING

Hokkoriya ほっこりや ⓣ 0749 21 3567. This popular *izakaya* on the Yume Kyōbashi Castle Road is in an atmospheric traditional-style house serving a variety of local chicken dishes, such as *yakitori* (¥350 per stick) and chicken with rice *donburi* (¥1200). 11.30am–2.30pm & 5.30–11pm, closed Wed.

Ton Ton とんとん ⓣ 0749 23 0359. *Yōshoku* (western-style) steak restaurant serving the local Ōmi beef on the Yume

Kyōbashi Castle Road. *Toku toku* lunch sets are excellent value (¥1980) and in the evening the Ton Ton dinner course (¥2530) is also a good choice 11.30am–9pm, closed Wed.

Yabuya やぶや ⓣ 0749 20 4330. This Spanish bar is one of Hikone's most popular drinking spots and attracts a lively crowd on Friday and Saturday nights. Tapas plates are ¥350 each and cocktails and wine by the glass cost ¥500. Mon–Thurs 5–11.30pm; Fri & Sat 5pm–1.30am.

Miho Museum

ミホミュージアム • 300 Tashiro Momodani, Shigaraki, Shiga-ken • Tues–Fri & Sun 10am–5pm; only open for a few months every year – exact dates vary; check the website for details • ¥1000 • ☎ 0748 82 3411, ⓦ miho.jp/english

Around 50km south of Kyoto, the I.M. Pei-designed **Miho Museum** is one of the architectural highlights of the Kansai region, although it's only open at certain times of the year. Located in a rural, mountainous part of Shiga Prefecture, which is best known for its Shigaraki pottery, this stunning museum houses an incredible collection of artworks belonging to the late Koyama Mihoko and her daughter Hiroko. Koyama, whom the museum is named after, founded Shinji Shūmeikai, one of Japan's so-called "new religions" in 1970. There are an estimated 300,000 followers worldwide, hundreds of whom live and work here at the museum. The central tenet of Shinji Shūmeikai's philosophy is that spiritual fulfilment lies in art and nature, hence the setting.

From the entrance and restaurant, access to the museum proper is by an electric shuttle bus through a tunnel that opens onto a beautiful valley spanned by a 120m-high bridge; alternatively, you can walk – it takes about ten minutes on foot. Inside the museum, which is built into the mountainside, a continually shifting pattern of light and shadow is created by the innovative use of skylights, pyramid-shaped wall lights and ever-so-slightly uneven corridors which look out – through windows fitted with aluminium screens – onto bamboo gardens and tranquil green landscapes.

The collection

The museum has two wings. The **north wing** houses Japanese art, including priceless porcelain, scrolls, screens and Buddhist relics; the **south wing** has antiquities from the rest of the world, including jewellery, frescoes, textiles and statues produced by a range of civilizations, from ancient Egyptian to classical Chinese. Among the numerous treasures are a three-thousand-year-old silver-and-gold cult figure of a falcon-headed deity from Egypt's nineteenth dynasty, a fourth century AD Roman floor mosaic and a statue dating from the second century AD of a Gandhara Buddha. Each artwork is labelled in English and Japanese and there are explanatory leaflets in some of the galleries, but the overall effect is one of art that is meant to be experienced for its intrinsic beauty rather than its historical or cultural import.

ARRIVAL AND DEPARTURE   MIHO MUSEUM

By train There are tours available to the museum from Kyoto but it is better (and very much cheaper) to make the journey there by yourself. From JR Kyoto Station, take a local train on the JR Biwako line (for Nagahama or Maibara) two stops to JR Ishiyama Station (every 10–15min; 13min; ¥230). From here it's a 50min bus (or an expensive taxi) ride to the museum (see below).

By bus Buses run by the Teisan Bus Company

(ⓦ teisan-konan-kotsu.co.jp) leave for the museum from outside Ishiyama Station's south exit (50min; ¥800). On weekdays, buses leave at ten minutes past the hour between 9.10am and 1.10pm. If you miss the last bus, you'll have to take a taxi, which is quite expensive (¥6000). On Sat, Sun and national holidays, the weekday timetable is supplemented by buses at 9.50am and 2.10pm.

EATING AND DRINKING

Peach Valley Miho Museum reception area ☎ 0748 82 3411. This excellent vegetarian organic restaurant is extremely popular with museum visitors. The lunch menu is seasonal and all dishes are made from locally grown ingredients. The Onigiri-zen (rice ball set menu) is beautifully presented (¥1600) and the soba and udon lunch sets, served hot or cold (from ¥700) are also delicious. Arrive early to avoid disappointment. Daily 11.30am–2pm.

Nara

奈良

Before Kyoto became the capital of Japan in 794 AD, this honour was held by **NARA**, a town some 35km further south in an area that is regarded as the birthplace of Japanese civilization. During this period, particularly the seventh and eighth centuries, Buddhism became firmly established within Japan under the patronage of court nobles, who sponsored magnificent temples and works of art, many of which have survived to this day. Fortunately, history subsequently left Nara largely to its own devices and it remains today a relaxed, attractive place set against a backdrop of wooded hills.

Nara's grid-street system is well signposted in English and the main sights, four of which are designated as UNESCO World Heritage Sites, are all gathered on the city's eastern edge in the green expanse of **Nara-kōen**. Its greatest draws are undoubtedly the monumental bronze Buddha of **Tōdai-ji**, and Nara's holiest shrine, **Kasuga Taisha** with its rows of lanterns, while **Kōfuku-ji**, **Sangatsu-dō** and **Shin-Yakushi-ji** all boast outstanding collections of Buddhist statuary. The town also retains the well-preserved traditional merchants quarter of **Nara-machi**, where some attractive old shophouses have been converted into museums and craft shops.

All Nara's sights are packed into a fairly compact space, and the central area is easily explored on foot. It can just about be covered in a day-trip from Kyoto, though if you want to visit the more distant temples (see p.479) you'll need to stay overnight – this gives you the added advantage of being able to enjoy the peaceful atmosphere once the crowds have left. If at all possible, try to avoid Nara on Sundays and holidays when it can become exceptionally crowded.

Brief history

During the fifth and sixth centuries a sophisticated culture evolved in the plains east of Ōsaka, an area known as **Yamato**. Close contact between Japan, Korea and China saw the introduction of Chinese script, technology and the Buddhist religion, as well as Chinese ideas on law and administration. Under these influences, the regent **Prince Shōtoku** (574–622) established a strictly hierarchical system of government. However, he's probably best remembered as a devout Buddhist who founded numerous temples, among them the great **Hōryū-ji** (see p.480). Though Shōtoku's successors continued the process of centralization, they were hampered by the practice of relocating the court after each emperor died, in line with purification rites. In 710 AD, therefore, it was decided to establish a permanent capital modelled on China's imperial city, Chang'an (today's Xi'an). The name chosen for this new city was **Heijō-kyō**, "Citadel of Peace", today known as **Nara**. In fact, Heijō-kyō lasted little more than seventy years, but it was a glorious period in which Japanese culture began to take shape. A frenzy of building and artistic creativity during this period culminated in the unveiling of the great bronze Buddha in **Tōdai-ji** temple by **Emperor Shōmu** in 752 AD. But beneath the surface things were starting to unravel. As the temples became increasingly powerful, so the monks began to dabble in politics, until one, Dōkyō, seduced a former empress and tried to seize the throne in 769. In an attempt to escape such shenanigans Emperor Kammu decided to move the court out of Nara in 784, and eventually founded Kyoto.

Nara-kōen

奈良公園

The ancient forested parklands on the eastern side of Nara are known as **Nara-kōen** and house many of the town's most important historical and religious sites. The park is also home to more than a thousand semi-wild deer, which were originally regarded as divine messengers of the Shintō gods, and anyone who killed a deer was liable to be dispatched shortly afterwards. Vendors sell *shika sembei* (deer crackers) for feeding the deer throughout the park, which can either be an enjoyable or hazardous experience. The most pleasant route into the park is along Sanjō-dōri, which cuts across the central district and brings you out near the pond of **Sarusawa-ike** (猿沢池).

Kōfuku-ji

興福寺 • 48 Noboriōji-chō • Daily 9am–5pm • Tōkondō ¥300; Kokuhōkan ¥800 • ☎ 0742 22 4096, ⓦ kohfukuji.com

The picturesque **Five-Storey Pagoda** which rises from the trees on the northern edge of Sarusawa-ike belongs to **Kōfuku-ji**, which in the eighth century was one of Nara's great temples. Founded in 669 by a member of the Fujiwara clan, it was moved to its present location when Nara became the new capital in 710. The prime draw here is the fine collection of **Buddhist statues** contained in the **Tōkon-dō** and the **Kokuhōkan**. At the moment almost half of Kōfuku-ji is a building site as a new **Chukon-dō** (Central Hall) is being built in the temple grounds: completion is expected in 2018.

Tōkon-dō

東金堂

The **Tōkon-dō**, a fifteenth-century hall to the north of the Five-Storey Pagoda, is dominated by a large image of Yakushi Nyorai, the Buddha of Healing. He's flanked by three Bodhisattvas, the Four Heavenly Kings and the Twelve Heavenly Generals, all beady-eyed guardians of the faith, some of which date from the eighth century. Perhaps the most interesting statue, though, is the seated figure of Yuima Koji to the left of Yakushi Nyorai; depicting an ordinary mortal rather than a celestial being, it's a touchingly realistic portrait.

NARA FESTIVALS AND ANNUAL EVENTS

Several of Nara's **festivals** have been celebrated for well over a thousand years. Many of these are dignified court dances, though the fire rituals are more lively affairs. In spring and autumn the New Public Hall (☎ 0742 27 2630, ⓦ pref.nara.jp/koukaido-e) in Nara-kōen stages a series of **nō dramas**, while the biggest cultural event of the year is undoubtedly the autumn exhibition of Shōsō-in's treasures.

January Yama-yaki (若草山焼き; grass-burning festival). On the fourth Saturday evening of January at 6pm, priests from Kōfuku-ji set fire to the grass on Wakakusa-yama – supervised by a few hundred firemen. The festival commemorates the settlement of a boundary dispute between Nara's warrior monks.

February 3 Lantern Festival (万燈籠 Mantōrō). To mark *setsubun*, the beginning of spring, three thousand stone and bronze lanterns are lit at Kasuga Taisha (from 6pm).

March 1–14 O-Taimatsu and O-Mizutori (お松明 & お水取り Torch-lighting and water drawing). A 1200-year-old ceremony that commemorates a priest's dream about the goddess Kannon drawing water from a holy well. The climax is on the night of March 13 when, at around 6.30pm, priests on the second-floor veranda of Nigatsu-dō light huge torches and scatter sparks over the assembled crowds to protect them from evil spirits. At 2am the priests collect water from the well, after which they whirl more lit flares round in a frenzied dance.

Mid-May Takigi Nō 薪御能 Outdoor performances of nō dramas by firelight at Kōfuku-ji and Kasuga Taisha: check at any of Nara's tourist offices (see p.477) or ⓦ narashikanko.or.jp/en for exact dates.

August 14–15 Chugen Mantoro (中元万燈籠). To celebrate Obon, the festival of souls, Kasuga Taisha's lanterns are spectacularly lit.

September Uneme Matsuri (采女祭). On the night of the harvest moon, this festival takes place at the Sarusawa-ike Pond as a dedication to Uneme, a court lady who drowned herself here after losing the favour of the emperor. At around 7pm two dragon-bowed boats bearing costumed participants and *gagaku* musicians commemorate the lady's death in multicoloured splendour. The festival lasts until 9.30pm.

Early to mid-October Shika-no-Tsunokiri (鹿の角きり; antler cutting). This is the season when the deer in Nara-kōen are wrestled to the ground and have their antlers sawn off by Shintō priests. It all takes place in the Roku-en deer pen, near Kasuga Taisha. Check at any of Nara's tourist offices (see p.477) or ⓦ narashikanko.or.jp/en for exact dates.

Late Oct–early Nov Shōsō-in Treasures (正倉院) At the National Museum (see box, p.475).

December 15–18 On-matsuri (おん祭). At around midday a grand costume parade sets off from the prefectural offices to Kasuga Wakamiya-jinja, stopping on the way for various ceremonies. It ends with outdoor performances of nō and courtly dances.

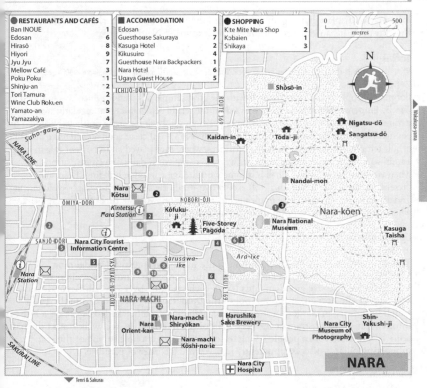

Kokuhōkan

国宝館

The modern **Kokuhōkan** is a veritable treasure-trove of early Buddhist statues. The most famous image is the standing figure of **Ashura**, one of Buddha's eight protectors, instantly recognizable from his three red-tinted heads and six spindly arms. Look out, too, for his companion Karura (Garuda) with his beaked head. Though they're not all on display at the same time, these eight protectors are considered to be the finest dry-lacquer images of the Nara period. The large **bronze Buddha head**, with its fine, crisp features, comes from an even earlier period. Apart from a crumpled left ear, the head is in remarkably good condition considering that the original statue was stolen from another temple by Kōfuku-ji's warrior priests sometime during the Heian period (794–1185). Then, after a fire destroyed its body, the head was buried beneath the replacement Buddha, only to be rediscovered in 1937 during renovation work.

Nara National Museum

奈良国立博物館, Nara Kokuritsu Hakubutkan • 50 Noboriōji-chō • 9am–5pm; closed Mon and late Oct to early Nov for Shōsō-in Treasures festival • ¥500; ¥1000 for special exhibitions • ☎ 050 5542 8600, ⓦ narahaku.go.jp

The **Nara National Museum** holds a superb collection of centuries-old Buddhist art, of which only a small part is on display at any one time. The exhibits are arranged chronologically, so you can trace the development of the various styles, and there's plenty of English-language information available. The main Western-style building houses the sculpture collection, while the modern annexe is where the museum's collection of treasures from Tōdai-ji are shown once a year (see below). In the lower-level passageway between the original building and the annexe you'll find an informative display that explains the forms, techniques and other characteristics of Buddhist art. It's an excellent primer before exploring Nara's temples.

Tōdai-ji

東大寺 • 406-1 Zoshi-chō • Daily: mid-March to mid-Sept 8.30am–5pm; mid-Sept to mid-March 8.30am–4pm • ¥500 • ☎ 0742 22 5511, ⓦ todaiji.or.jp

For many people Nara is synonymous with the great temple of **Tōdai-ji**, which was founded in 745 by **Emperor Shōmu**, ostensibly to ward off the terrible epidemics that regularly swept the nation, but also as a means of cementing imperial power. In doing so he nearly bankrupted his young nation, but the political message came across loud and clear; soon an extensive network of sub-temples spread throughout the provinces, where they played an important role in local administration. It took more than fifteen years to complete Tōdai-ji, which isn't surprising when you learn that the main hall is still the world's largest wooden building. Even so, the present structure (last rebuilt in 1709) is only two-thirds the size of the original. Avoid visiting Tōdai-ji at weekends, especially in spring and autumn, the two peak times for visiting Nara, when the temple is overrun with thousands of tourists and school groups.

Daibutsu-den

大仏殿

The main entrance to Tōdai-ji lies through the suitably impressive **Nandai-mon** (南大門), or Great Southern Gate. Rebuilt in the thirteenth century, it shelters two wonderfully expressive guardian gods (*Niō*), each standing over 7m tall. Beyond, you begin to see the horned, sweeping roof of the **Daibutsu-den**, the Great Buddha Hall, which houses Japan's largest bronze statue, a giant 15m-tall blackened figure on a lotus throne, that seems to strain at the very walls of the building. As you walk round the hall, don't be surprised to see people trying to squeeze through a hole in one of the rear supporting pillars – success apparently reserves you a corner of paradise.

Kaidan-in

戒壇院 • Daily 8am–4.30pm • ¥500

West of the Daibutsu-den compound, you'll find the more modest **Kaidan-in**, which was established in 754 as Japan's first, and foremost, ordination hall. It was founded by the Chinese high priest, Ganjin, who Emperor Shōmu hoped would instil some discipline into the rapidly expanding Buddhist priesthood. He had to be patient, however; poor Ganjin's ship took six attempts to arrive here, by which time the priest was 67 years old and completely blind. His ordination hall was rebuilt in the Edo period, but the statues inside include eighth-century representations of the Four Heavenly Kings (*Shi-Tennō*), crafted in clay.

Nigatsu-dō

二月堂 • 406-1 Zoshi-chō • Daily 8am–4.30pm • Free

Built on the slopes of Wakakusa-yama, which forms Nara's eastern boundary, **Nigatsu-dō** is a sub-temple of Tōdai-ji. It's well worth a visit to enjoy the expansive views over the city from its second-floor wooden terrace, where dozens of lanterns hang and are lit everyday at dusk – a rather beautiful sight. Next to the terrace, a rest area for pilgrims serves tea. Nigatsu-dō is the site of the O-Taimatsu and O-Mizutori ceremonies held in March every year (see box, p.472).

Sangatsu-dō

三月堂 • 406-1 Zoshi-chō • Daily 8am–5pm • ¥500

Another sub-temple of Tōdai-ji, the single-storey **Sangatsu-dō** was completed in 729, making it Nara's oldest building. Also known as Hokke-dō, it contains another rare collection of eighth-century dry-lacquer statues. The main image is a dimly lit, gilded figure of Kannon, bearing a silver Amida in its crown, while all around stand gods, guardians, Bodhisattvas and other protectors of the faith.

SHŌSŌ-IN TREASURES

Each autumn (late Oct to early Nov), the Nara National Museum is closed for two weeks while an exhibition of the **Shōsō-in Treasures** (正倉院) takes place in the annexe. This priceless collection was donated to Tōdai-ji in 756 by Empress Kōmyō, on the death of her husband Emperor Shōmu, and then added to with more treasures in 950. It contains unique examples of Buddhist art and ritual objects, musical instruments, household utensils, glassware and games, not only from eighth-century Japan but also from the countries of the Silk Road – China, Korea, India and Persia. The exhibition takes a different theme each year; check ⓦ narahaku.go.jp for details.

Kasuga Taisha

春日大社 • 160 Kasugano-chō • Daily dawn to dusk • Free; Inner shrine ¥500; Treasure House ¥400 • ☎ 0742 22 7788, ⓦ kasugataisha.or.jp

Some two thousand stone lanterns line the approach to **Kasuga Taisha** (Kasuga Grand Shrine), which is nestled in the hillside of Wakakusa-yama. It was founded in 768AD as the tutelary shrine of the Fujiwara family and, for a while, held an important place in Shintō worship; indeed, the emperor still sends a messenger here to participate in shrine rituals. The four sanctuaries are just visible in the inner compound, while the thousand beautifully crafted bronze **lanterns** hanging round the outer eaves are easier to admire. Donated over the years by supplicants, they bear intricate designs of deer, wisteria blooms, leaves or geometric patterns. The best time to see them is when they are lit up twice a year for the Mantoro ("Ten-thousand lantern") festivals – on February 3 marking *setsubun*, the beginning of spring, and during Obon, the festival of souls, in mid-August (Aug 14–15) for the Chugen Mantoro festival. Alternatively, try to visit in the early morning or dusk, when the stone lanterns are lit.

Kasuga Taisha Shin-en garden

春日大社神苑 • Daily 9am–4.30pm • ¥500

Just before the entrance to the inner shrine of Kasuga Taisha is the **Kasuga Taisha Shin-en garden**, especially charming in early May when the dozens of varieties of wisteria are in bloom. The garden is also a living museum of over nine hundred flowers, herbs and other plants mentioned in the verses of the *Manyōshū* ("Collection of Ten Thousand Leaves") poetry anthology, compiled in the Nara and early Heian periods.

Shin-Yakushi-ji

新薬師寺 • 1352 Takabatake-chō • Daily 9am–5pm • ¥600 • ☎ 0742 22 3737, ⓦ k5.dion.ne.jp/~shinyaku • Continuing south through the woods from Kasuga Taisha, cross over the main road into a quiet residential area; 5min further on you'll come to Shin-Yakushi-ji

The temple of **Shin-Yakushi-ji** was founded by Empress Kōmyō to pray for Emperor Shōmu's recovery from an eye infection; she apparently had some success since he lived for another decade. Inside the temple's quiet precincts, a modest-looking hall houses a stunning collection of eighth-century Buddhist statues. The central image is a placid-looking, slightly cross-eyed Yakushi Nyorai (the Buddha of Healing), carved from one block of cinnamon wood. He's surrounded by a ring of clay statues of the Twelve Heavenly Generals; it's worth visiting just to see their wonderful manga-like expressions and poses.

Nara City Museum of Photography

奈良市写真美術館, Nara-shi Shashin Bijutsukan • 600-1 Takabatake-chō • 9.30am–4.30pm, closed Mon • ¥500 • ☎ 0742 22 9811, ⓦ www1.kcn.re.jp/~naracmp

The **Nara City Museum of Photography** houses a superb collection of some eighty thousand photographs by the late Irie Taikichi, who spent most of his life capturing the town of Nara and its temples throughout the seasons on film. Housed in a sleek,

6

THE GREAT BUDDHA

Housed in the Daibutsu-den, the **great Buddha** (*Daibutsu*) depicts Rushana (later known as Dainichi Nyorai), the Cosmic Buddha who presides over all levels of the Buddhist universe, and was a phenomenal achievement for the time. Not surprisingly, several attempts at casting the Buddha failed, but finally in 752 the gilded statue was officially dedicated by symbolically "**opening**" its eyes. To achieve this, an Indian priest stood on a special platform and "painted" the eyes with a huge brush, from which coloured strings trailed down to the assembled dignitaries, enabling them to participate in the ceremony. Not only were there hundreds of local monks present, but also ambassadors from China, India and further afield, bearing an amazing array of gifts, many of which have been preserved in the Shōsō-in treasury – as has the original paintbrush.

The Buddha has had a rough time of it since then. As early as the ninth century an **earthquake** toppled his head, then it and his right hand were melted in a **fire** in 1180 and again in 1567. As a result, only tiny fragments of the original statue remain intact, the rest being made up of patchwork parts put together over the centuries. Nonetheless, the remodelled giant is definitely large, and it's hard not to be impressed by the **technological triumph** involved in re-creating it.

modern and almost completely underground building just to the west of Shin-Yakushi-ji, the museum also holds regular exhibitions of other photographers who have also focused on the city and its ancient culture.

Nara-machi

ならまち

The southern district of central Nara is known as **Nara-machi**. It's a quaint area of narrow streets, worth exploring for its traditional shops and lattice-front houses. The best approach is to start by the southwest corner of willow-fringed Sarusawa-ike, a good spot for views of the Five-Storey Pagoda, and then head south.

Nara-machi Shiryōkan

奈良町資料館 • 14-2 Nishonoshinya-chō • Daily 10am–4pm • Free • ☎ 0742 22 5509, ⓦ naramachi.co.jp

Strings of red-cloth monkeys (good-luck charms) hang outside the **Nara-machi Shiryōkan**, a small museum which occupies the former warehouse of a mosquito-net manufacturer. It houses a wonderful jumble of antique household utensils, shop signboards, Buddhist statues, pots and other folkloric objects from the local area.

Nara-machi Kōshi-no-ie

ならまち格子の家 • 44 Gangōji-chō • 9am–5pm, closed Mon • Free • ☎ 0742 23 4820

One of Nara-machi's best-preserved traditional houses, **Nara-machi Kōshi-no-ie** is an Edo-period merchant's dwelling with a long and narrow interior, including an inner courtyard garden. You can explore the house at will, but the staff will also happily demonstrate various features, such as the clever operating mechanism of the front door and kitchen skylights.

Harushika Sake Brewery

春鹿酒造元 • Jōzō Moto 24-1 Fukuchi-in-chō • Daily 8.15am–5.15pm, closed Obon and New Year holidays • Free • ☎ 0742 23 2255, ⓦ harushika.com

Producing high-quality sake since 1884, the **Harushika Sake Brewery** is a wonderfully atmospheric place to try rice wine produced in Nara. The front of the traditional premises has been remodelled into a comfortable tasting area where, for the very reasonable price of ¥400, you can sample five different kinds of sake and take the glass home. The staff will explain the dry and sweet flavours of Harushika's sake as you sip each one, and Narazuke pickles are served at the end of the tasting. You can also sample the brewery's surprisingly refreshing sake ice cream (¥350).

ARRIVAL AND DEPARTURE

BY TRAIN

Nara has two competing train stations: the JR Nara Station, on the west side of the town centre, and the private Kintetsu-Nara Station which is close to the main sights.

From Kyoto The quickest option is a Limited Express train on the private Kintetsu–Kyoto line (every 30min; 35min; ¥1110); the ordinary express takes a little longer and you have to change at Yamato-Saidaiji (1–2 hourly; 45min; ¥610). JR also has a choice of express trains (8 daily; 45min; ¥690) and regular trains (every 30min; 1hr 20min; ¥690) from Kyoto.

From Osaka Trains on the private Kintetsu–Nara line (from Ōsaka's Kintetsu-Namba Station) arrive at the Kintetsu-Nara Station (every 15min; 30–40min; ¥540–1040). Alternatively, take a JR line train from Osaka Station (every 20min; 40min; ¥780) or from JR Namba Station (every 20min; 30–40min; ¥740) to JR Nara Station.

From Kansai International Airport You can go into central Osaka to pick up a train (see p.489) or hop on a limousine bus (hourly; 1hr 35min; ¥2000), which stops at both of Nara's train stations.

BY BUS

Long-distance buses Services from Tokyo (Shinjuku; 1 daily; 8hr) and Yokohama (1 daily; 9hr) stop outside both the Kintetsu and JR Nara train stations.

GETTING AROUND

By bus You'll need to use local buses for some of Nara's more far-flung sights—the main termini for these are outside the JR and Kintetsu-Nara train stations. The standard fare is ¥200 within the city centre, which you usually pay as you get on, though buses going out of central Nara employ a ticket system –take a numbered ticket as you board and pay the appropriate fare on exit. The one-day Nara Tourist Local Bus Free Pass (¥500) covers buses in central Nara, but the Kansai Thru Pass does not cover bus services in and around Nara.

By car Rental outlets include Eki Rent-a-Car (☏0742 26 3929), next door to JR Nara Station. Toyota (☏0742 22 0100) and Nippon Rent-a-Car (☏0742 24 5701) have branches near the Kintetsu Station.

By bike Another option for central Nara is bike rental. You'll find Eki Rent-a-Cycle (daily 9am–5pm; ¥1000/day) outside the JR Station, and Nara Rent-a-Cycle (daily 9am–5pm; ¥1000–1200/day, or ¥2000 for two days), outside exit 7 of the Kintetsu Station.

INFORMATION AND TOURS

Tourist information Nara is well provided with information offices. The most useful of these is the Nara City Tourist Centre (daily 9am–9pm; ☏0742 22 3900, ⓦnarashikanko.or.jp/en), located on Sanjō-dōri. There's also an office next to the JR Station (daily 9am–9pm; ☏0742 27 2223), one in Kintetsu Station (daily 9am–5pm; ☏0742 24 4358) and another at Sarusawa pond (daily 9am–5pm), at the eastern end of Sanjō-dōri.

Listings magazines The free bilingual newspaper called *nara nara* (ⓦnaranara.jp) has features on local dining, shopping and sightseeing. It can be picked up at one of the tourist offices. The free monthly *Kansai Scene* also carries the latest information about what's on in Nara.

Tours There are a number of bus tours which take in some of the World Heritage Sites in and around Nara (ⓦwww .narakotsu.co.jp/teikan/index.html), but the best way is to walk and take public transport when needed. The Nara SCG Club (ⓦnarakanko.jp/sgg/jap.html) and the Nara YMCA EGG (ⓦsites.google.com/site/eggnaragg/home) both offer free guided walking tours in English, with interesting historical anecdotes. Reservations are required at least a day in advance.

ACCOMMODATION

★**Edosan** 江戸三 1167 Takabatake-chō ☏0742 26 2662, ⓦedosan.jp. Located within Nara-kōen, this is the most exquisite place to spend the night in any season. All guests stay in their own private rustic cottage, from where deer can be seen wandering past as you dine on artistically presented top-class *kaiseki*. Despite Edosan's exclusivity, the service is warm and down to earth. The bathhouse is separate and can be used individually. Rates include dinner and breakfast. **¥53,000**

Guesthouse Nara Backpackers 奈良バックパッカーズ 31 Yurugi-chō ☏0742 22 4557, ⓦnara-backpackers.com. In a charming 100-year-old mansion just 10 minutes walk northeast of the Kintetsu Station, this budget guesthouse is a quiet and convenient place to stay. Retaining all the features of a traditional Japanese home, it has shared bathing and kitchen facilities, as well as a communal lounge overlooking the large internal garden. Private rooms, including a tea ceremony room, are very comfortable and there are also dorm rooms with bunk beds. Dorm **¥2400**, double **¥6,900**

★**Guesthouse Sakuraya** ゲストハウス桜舎 1 Narukawa-chō ☏0742 24 1490, ⓦguesthouse-sakuraya .com. This stylish guesthouse, located in historic Nara-machi, has been tastefully restored with three clean and comfortable tatami rooms and a lovely garden. The multilingual owner is very helpful and hospitable, and there's free wi-fi as well as tea-and coffee-making facilities. **¥14,000**

Kasuga Hotel 春日ホテル 40 Noborioji-chō ☏0742 22 4031, ⓦkasuga-hotel.cc.jp. A short walk from

6

Kintetsu-Nara Station, this luxurious ryokan-like hotel has both Japanese and Western-style rooms, some of which have their own private outdoor baths. Locally sourced *kaiseki* cuisine is served for the evening meal. The staff speak a little English and service is polite and efficient. **¥22,050**

Kikusuirō 菊水楼 1130 Takabatake-chō ☎0742 23 2001, ⊛kikusuiro.com. Conveniently located near Nara-kōen, this stately old three-storey ryokan serves highly rated French and Japanese *kaiseki* cuisine. The rooms are quaintly decorated and spacious. Only a little English is spoken but the service is friendly and charmingly old-fashioned. Rates include dinner and breakfast. **¥54,000**

★ **Nara Hotel** 奈良ホテル 1096 Takabatake-chō ☎0742 26 3300, ⊛narahotel.co.jp. Oozing with nostalgia, the *Nara Hotel* is one of Japan's most historic hotels. Its staff will gladly point out the hotel's unusual architectural features and tell stories of its famous guests, such as Albert Einstein, Audrey Hepburn and the Dalai Lama. The rooms in the newer wing are smart and comfortable, but the Meiji-era ambience of the original rooms with their high ceilings and period furniture is recommended. The hotel is set in its own gardens on the edge of Nara-kōen and has two restaurants serving French and Japanese cuisine, as well as a bar (see below) and a tea lounge. **¥29,700**

Ugaya Guest House 奈良ウガヤゲストハウス 4-1 Okukomori-chō ☎0742 95 7739, ⊛ugaya.net. Formerly a pharmacy, this friendly guesthouse, located between the JR and Kintetsu stations, is a good place to make new friends and enjoy Nara's nightlife. It has women-only and mixed dorms with bunk beds as well as private rooms – all with shared shower facilities. There's also wi-fi, an in-house library and an organic coffee shop. Dorm **¥2500**, double **¥6000**

EATING AND DRINKING

Like Kyoto, Nara has its own brand of *kaiseki*, the elaborate meals that originally accompanied the tea ceremony, but local specialities also include some rather bland dishes. *Cha-ga-yu* may have evolved from the breakfast of poor people into a fairly expensive delicacy, but there's no escaping the fact that it's basically a thin rice gruel, boiled up with soya beans, sweet potatoes and green tea leaves. It's best as part of a set meal, when the accompaniments such as pickles add a bit of flavour. *Tororo* is pretty similar: thickened grated yam mixed with soy sauce, seaweed and barley, then poured over a bowl of rice – full of protein and rather sticky. Less of an acquired taste is *kakinoha-zushi*, sushi wrapped in persimmon leaves, and *Nara-zuke*, vegetables pickled in sake.

Ban INOUE 幡 • INOUE 16 Kasugano-chō ☎0742 27 1010, ⊛asa-ban.com/ban-inoue-todaiji.html. Locally grown vegetables, as well as soy sauce and miso produced in Nara, are part of the macrobiotic-style meals served in this cheerful café and craft shop in the Yume-Kaze Plaza shopping complex. The Healthy Lunch Set (¥1200) includes three seasonal vegetable dishes, soup and rice. Daily 10am–6.30pm, closed irregularly.

★ **Edosan** 江戸三 1167 Takabatake-chō ☎0742 26 2662, ⊛edosan.jp. If you can't stay at this gourmet ryokan, located within Nara-kōen, having a meal here is just as memorable. *Edosan* serves wonderful *kaiseki* meals to non-guests. The Mahoroba kaiseki lunch (¥5500) is a good example of their seasonal creations. Full *kaiseki* courses are priced from ¥8400. Reservations are required. Daily 11.30am–2.30pm & 5pm–9pm.

Hirasō 平宗 30-1 Imanikadō-chō ☎0742 22 0866, ⊛kakinoha.co.jp/naramise. *Hirasō* specializes in *kakinoha-zushi*, though you'll also find all sorts of other tasty local delicacies on the menu. Sushi sets start at ¥920, with multicourse meals including *kakinoha-zushi* and *cha-ga-yu* from around ¥3680. Tues–Sun 11am–8.30pm.

Hiyori ひより 26 Nakanoshinya-chō ☎0742 24 1470, ⊛narakko.com/hiyori. *Yamato-yasai*, the vegetable cuisine of Nara, is the speciality here but it's not strictly vegetarian – there are also meat and fish dishes. Delicious and healthy *Yasai-biyori* lunch sets are ¥1575 and Hiyori's *kaiseki* dinner course, with seven vegetable dishes and one main dish, is just ¥3675. 11.30am–2pm & 5–9pm, closed Tues.

Jyu Jyu 樹樹 27-1 Mochiidono-chō ☎0742 27 6121, ⊛jyujyunara.com. Up a narrow alleyway off the arcade south of Sanjō-dōri, this friendly *izakaya* is in an old geisha house and serves Japanese home-style cooking. Try their avocado and anchovy pizza (¥780), tofu with miso sauce (¥570) or Korean *chijimi* pancake (¥730). Wine by the glass is ¥520 and draught beer is ¥630. 5–11pm; closed Mon and every first and third Tues of the month.

Mellow Café Axe Unit, 1-8 Konishi-chō ☎0742 27 9099, ⊛mellowcafe.jp. This large, spacious Italian café-restaurant, specializing in oven-fired pizza, is up a lane off the Konishi Sakuradōri shopping street. The most adventurous topping on the menu is the Narazuke (pickles) and *sake lees* pizza (¥900). The daily Mellow lunch plate is ¥900 and the dinner course with pasta, meat and fish dishes is ¥3600. English menu available. Daily 11am–1pm.

Poku Poku ぼくぼく 23 Shonami-chō ☎0742 31 2537. Down a quiet street on the northern edge of Nara-machi, this is the place to come for fried pork cutlets. As well as *tonkatsu* and *katsu* with curry, they serve ginger pork and *tonteki* (garlic) pork in regular or large portions (¥1200–2000). All sets come with shredded cabbage, rice, soup and a small side dish. There's an English menu and they also serve lunch all afternoon. 11am–8pm, closed Tues.

Shinju-an 心樹庵 22 Nishishinya-chō ☎0742 27 3083, ⊛homepage3.nifty.com/shinjyuan. High-quality Yamato-cha teas are served in this quaint teashop located in an 85-year old *machiya* in Nara-machi. The daily tea set with sweets is ¥750, or you can just enjoy a cup (choose from 100 ifferent kinds of tea) for ¥500. Noon–4.30pm, closed Sun, Mon & National holidays.

'ori Tamura 鳥田村 2-19 Aburasaka-chō ☎0742 26 '739, ⓦtori-tamura.com. This bustling restaurant, not ar from the JR station, offers 30 different kinds of *yakitori* from ¥120 a skewer), served with locally brewed sake. There's a good value set-menu for ¥2500 which includes the chef's pick of the day and one drink. English menu available. Tues–Sun 5–11pm.

★**Wine Club Rokuen** ワイン倶楽部鹿宴 1 Hashimoto-machi ☎0742 22 1991. Tucked away off the Mochiidono shopping arcade is this sophisticated little wine bar run by young sommelier, Namika-san. There's a nice selection of international and local wines from ¥600–1000 a glass, or bottles from ¥5600. Nibbles on offer include cheese, fresh ham and salami (from ¥400). Mon–Sat 3–11.30pm.

★**Yamato-an** やまと庵 495-1 Sanjō-machi ☎0742 26 3585. Nara-produced beef, chicken and pork are the main ingredients in the scrumptious dishes served here. The Yamato chicken tempura (¥680) and the simmered Yamato pork are very popular (¥787). Vegetarians are also catered for – the tofu dishes are excellent (from ¥504). English menu available. Daily 11.30am–2.30pm & 5–11pm.

Yamazakiya 山崎屋 5 Higashimuki-chō ☎0742 27 3715, ⓦajiyama.com. Located at the back of the eponymously named pickle shop, this traditional restaurant has a good range of set meals to choose from. The Hana-Gozen chirashi-zushi set is ¥880, the Tempura-Gozen set with Nara pickles is ¥2000, and *kaiseki* courses start at ¥3990. The staff are welcoming but don't speak English. It's easiest to check the window display first and then order from the English menu. Tues–Sun 11.15am–8.30pm.

6

SHOPPING

Kite Mite Nara Shop きてみてならショップ 1F Nara Commerce & Tourism Bldg ☎0742 26 8828, ⓦnara-shop.jp. Conveniently located just 2 minutes east of the Kintetsu Station, this shop sells a wide variety of Nara crafts, arts and food, and is a good place for last-minute souvenir shopping. Tues–Sun 10am–6pm.

Kobaien Calligraphy Goods 古梅園 1-11-40 Obiyamachi ☎0742 22 2646, ⓦkajisyouten.com. Nara is renowned for its high-quality *sumi-e* ink, calligraphy brushes (*fude*), tea whisks (*chasen*) and bleached hemp cloth (*sarashi*). At the foot of Wakakusa-yama, this

traditional shop stocks the full range of top-quality calligraphy goods, plus various tea ceremony utensils. Calligraphy sets start from ¥5000. Daily 9am–5pm.

Shikaya 鹿屋 23 Kasugano-chō ☎0742 22 3181, ⓦsikaya.co.jp. Rather tacky but fun souvenir shop catering to pop culture tastes. The large collection of Hello Kitty goods contrasts sharply with the fierce range of ninja costumes and weapons, as well samurai swords and armour. They also sell kimono and the friendly staff will help you get kitted out. Daily 10am–5pm, closed irregularly.

DIRECTORY

Banks and exchange Kinki Osaka Bank, Mizuho Bank and Nara Bank, all on Sanjō-dōri, have foreign exchange desks. The ATM in the post office opposite the JR station accepts international cards.

Hospital Nara's central hospital is the Nara City Hospital (市立奈良病院), 1-5-1 Higashi Kidera-chō (☎0742 24 1251), with a 24hr emergency department It's located

south of Nara-kōen on Route 169.

Internet Nara City Tourist Centre and the Nara City Tourist Information Center next to the JR station both have free wi-fi.

Post offices Nara's Central Post Office is on Ōmiya-dōri, a fair walk west of the centre. It has 24hr mail services, but for other purposes the sub-post offices opposite the JR station and in the centre of town (see map, p.473) are more convenient.

Around Nara

Even before Nara was founded, the surrounding plains were sprinkled with burial mounds, palaces and temples. A few of these still survive, of which the most

NARA'S MASCOT

Many towns in Japan, as well as companies and even restaurants, have their own mascot – usually a cute manga-style character. As part of Nara's 1300th anniversary celebrations in 2010, a strange half-deer/half-boy monk called **Sento-kun** appeared as Nara's official mascot. Sento-kun received a lot of criticism from both the media and the public for being "creepy" and a waste of ¥5 million of taxpayers' money. Religious organizations were also not happy about his distinctive Buddhist appearance combined with deer antlers, and called the mascot "sacreligious". However, Sento-kun has endured and can be found in different forms all over the city.

6

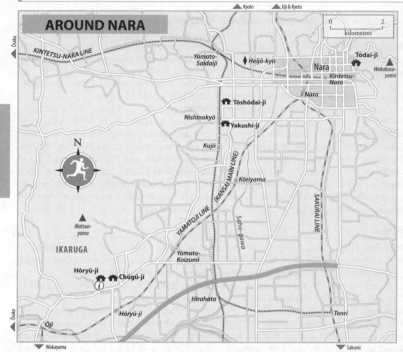

remarkable is the historic temple of **Hōryū-ji**, home to some impressive artworks and the world's oldest wooden building. Around 10km southwest of Nara in Ikaruga district, it also houses the tranquil **Chūgū-ji** nunnery. Closer to Nara, the two temples of Nishinokyō district, **Yakushi-ji** and **Tōshōdai-ji**, contain yet more early masterpieces of Japanese art and architecture, with some stunning examples on display. The route described below starts at Hōryū-ji and then works back towards Nara.

Hōryū-ji

法隆寺 • Temple complex daily: mid-Feb to early Nov 8am–5pm; early Nov to mid-Feb 8am–4.30pm • ¥1000 • ⓦ www.horyuji.or.jp
As you walk round the UNESCO World Heritage Site of **Hōryū-ji**, which was completed in 607 AD, it's worth bearing in mind that Buddhism had only really got going in Japan some fifty years earlier. The confident scale of Hōryū-ji and its superb array of Buddhist statues amply illustrate how quickly this imported faith took hold. One of its strongest proponents was Prince Shōtoku (574–622), the then-regent, who founded Hōryū-ji in accordance with the dying wish of his father, Emperor Yōmei. Though the complex burnt down in 670, it was soon rebuilt, making this Japan's oldest-surviving Buddhist temple.

The main approach to Hōryū-ji is from the south, which takes you past the helpful information centre (see opposite). Walk north from here along a wide, tree-lined avenue to **Nandai-mon** (Great South Gate), which marks the outer enclosure. Inside lies a second, walled compound known as the **Sai-in Garan**, or Western Precinct. Within the Sai-in Garan's cloister-gallery, the **Five-Storey Pagoda** will inevitably catch your eye first. This is Japan's oldest five-tier pagoda, and inside you can see the early eighth-century clay images of Buddha entering nirvana. However, it's actually the right-hand building, the **Kon-dō** (Golden Hall), which is Hōryū-ji's star attraction. This is the world's oldest wooden structure, dating from the late seventh century, and although it's not very large, the building's multilayered roofs and sweeping eaves are extremely striking.

Kon-dō
金堂

Entering the east door of the **Kon-dō**, you're greeted by a bronze image of Shaka Nyorai (Historical Buddha) flanked by two Bodhisattvas still bearing a few touches of the original gold leaf that they were once covered in; this **Shaka triad** was cast in 623 AD in memory of Prince Shōtoku, who died the previous year. To its right stands **Yakushi Nyorai**, the Buddha of Healing, to which Hōryū-ji was dedicated, and to the left a twelfth-century **Amida Buddha** commemorating the Prince's mother.

Daihōzō-in
大宝蔵院

Exiting the Sai-in compound, walk east past two long, narrow halls, to the **Daihōzō-in** (Hall of Temple Treasures), which houses Hōryū-ji's priceless collection of more than 2300 national treasures in two halls. Look out for the bronze **Yume-chigae Kannon**. This "Dream-Changing" Kannon is credited with turning bad dreams into good, and has a soft, secretive smile.

Kudara Kannon-dō
百済観音堂

Connecting the two museum halls is the **Kudara Kannon-dō**, which houses the wooden **Kudara Kannon** (Kudara Goddess of Mercy) statue, thought to date from the seventh century. Not much is known about this unusually tall, willowy figure, but it has long been recognized as one of the finest Buddhist works of art in Japan. Kudara refers to an ancient province in Korea and subsequently there has been some debate as to whether the statue came from there.

Chūgū-ji
中宮寺 • Daily: Oct to mid-March 9am–3.45pm; mid-March to Sept 9am–4.15pm • ¥500 • ☎ 0745 75 2106, ⓦ chuguji.jp

A gate in the northeast corner of the Tō-in Garan leads directly into **Chūgū-ji**. This intimate, peaceful nunnery was originally the residence of Prince Shōtoku's mother, which he converted into a temple on her death in 621. The main reason for coming here, however, sits inside a modern hall facing south over a pond. If you've already visited Kyoto's Kōryū-ji (see p.435), you'll recognize the central image of a pensive, boy-like **Miroku Bosatsu** (Future Buddha) absorbed in his task of trying to save mankind from suffering. Here, the statue is of camphor wood, burnished black with age, and is thought to have been carved by a Korean craftsman in the early seventh century.

Chūgū-ji marks the eastern extent of the Hōryū-ji complex. If you exit from here it's about an eight-minute walk south down to the main road and the Chūgū-ji-mae bus stop, one stop east of the Hōryū-ji-mae stop; alternatively, trek back and exit from the Nandai-mon, which will take you down to the Hōryū-ji bus depot.

ARRIVAL AND INFORMATION   HŌRYŪ-JI

By bus The simplest way of getting to Hōryū-ji from Nara is by #52 or #97 bus (hourly; 50–60min; ¥760) from Nara's JR or Kintetsu stations; get off at the Hōryū-i-mae stop.

By train Ōsaka-bound trains from JR Nara stop at Hōryū-ji Station (every 10min; 15min; ¥210), from where it's a good 20min walk to the temple on a fairly busy road, or you can catch a #72 bus (weekdays 2–3 hourly, weekends every 10min; 10min; ¥170).

Tourist information The Information Centre (daily 8.30am–5pm; ☎0745 74 6800, ⓦwww4.kcn.ne.jp/~ikaru-i) is across the road from the Hōryū-ji-mae bus stop.

6

> ## THE HIDDEN BUDDHA OF HŌRYŪ-JI
>
> **Tō-in Garan** is the eastern precinct of Hōryū-ji, which was added in 739. At its centrepiece is the octagonal **Yume-dono** (Hall of Dreams), with its magnificent statue, the **Kuze Kannon**. Until the late nineteenth century, this gilded wooden figure, said to be the same height as Prince Shōtoku (perhaps even modelled on him in the early seventh century), was a *hibutsu*, a hidden image, which no one had seen for centuries. Somewhat surprisingly, it was an American art historian, Ernest Fenellosa, who in the 1880s was given permission by the Meiji government, against the wishes of the temple, to unwrap the Kannon from the bundle of white cloth in which it had been kept. He revealed a dazzling statue in an almost perfect state of repair, carrying a sacred jewel and wearing an elaborate crown, with the famous enigmatic smile of the Kon-dō's Shaka Nyorai on its youthful lips. Unfortunately, the Kannon is still kept hidden for most of the year, except for brief spells in spring and autumn (usually April 11–May 15 & Oct 22–Nov 22).

Yakushi-ji

薬師寺 • Nishinokyō, 6km northwest of Hōryū-ji • Daily 8.30am–5pm • ¥1000 • ☎ 0742 33 6001, ⍟ nara-yakushiji.com

The Nishinokyō area is home to two great temples that are also famed for their age and wealth of statuary – Yakushi-ji and Tōshōdai-ji (see opposite). The older of the pair is southerly **Yakushi-ji**. Emperor Tenmu first ordered its construction sometime around 680 AD when his wife was seriously ill. Although she recovered, Tenmu himself died eight years later, leaving the empress to dedicate Yakushi-ji herself in 697. Over the centuries, fires have destroyed all but one of the original buildings, the **East Pagoda**, though Yakushi-ji's amazing collection of statues has fared better. **Major restoration work** is currently underway on the **East Pagoda** and is expected to continue until 2018. A special exhibition hall has been built to explain the restoration process and to display the pagoda's beautiful metal rooftop ornaments.

The inner compound

The only building of historical note in Yakushi-ji's inner compound is the three-storey **East Pagoda**, which was famously described as "frozen music" by Ernest Fenellosa (see box above). He was referring to the rhythmical progression of the smaller double roofs that punctuate the pagoda's upward flow. It's the sole surviving remnant of the original temple and contrasts strongly with the spanking red lacquer of the new West Pagoda, the **Daikō-dō** (Great Lecture Hall) and the **Kon-dō** (Golden Hall), all of which have been rebuilt during the last thirty years. However, inside the Kon-dō the temple's original seventh-century bronze **Yakushi triad** sits unperturbed. Past fires have removed most of the gold and given the statues a rich black sheen, but otherwise they are remarkably fine condition.

The outer compound

Continuing through the outer compound you come to a long, low wooden hall on your left, the **Tōin-dō**. Rebuilt around 1285, the hall houses a bronze image of **Shō-Kannon**, an incarnation of the goddess of mercy, which dates from the early Nara period. This graceful, erect statue, framed against a golden aureole, shows distinctly Indian influences in its diaphanous robes, double necklace and the strands of hair falling over its shoulders.

ARRIVAL AND DEPARTURE
YAKUSHI-JI

By train Kintetsu-line trains run from Nara to Nishinokyō Station (¥250) with a change at Saidai-ji; Yakushi-ji's north gate is a 3min walk east of the station.

By bus Arriving by #97 or #98 bus from Hōryū-ji (35min; ¥560) or #52 bus from Nara (20min; ¥240) – get off at the Yakushi-ji Chūsha-jo stop, from where it's a short walk to the temple's south gate.

On foot After exiting from Yakushi-ji's north gate, go straight ahead for five minutes and you'll find the front entrance to Tōshōdai-ji.

Tōshōdai-ji

唐招提寺 • Nishinokyō • Daily 8.30am–4.30pm • ¥600 • ☎ 0742 33 7900, ⍟ toshodaiji.jp

The weathered, wooden halls of **Tōshōdai-ji** in their pleasant shady compound are superb examples of late eighth-century architecture. The temple was founded in 759 by the eminent Chinese monk Ganjin – he of Nara's Kaidan-in (see p.474) – when he was granted permission to move from the city to somewhere more peaceful.

The first thing you'll see on entering the south gate is the stately Chinese-style **Kon-dō** (Main Hall), which has been masterfully restored in recent years. Craftsmen who accompanied Ganjin from the mainland are responsible for the three superb dry-lacquer statues displayed here. The **Kō-dō** (Lecture Hall) behind the Kon-dō also dates from the late eighth century, and is more Japanese in styling. During the Nara period, this hall was a major centre of learning and religious training.

Shin-Hōzō

新宝蔵 • Daily March–May & Sept–Nov 8.30am–4pm • ¥100

On the compound's east side is the rather modern-looking concrete **Shin-Hōzō**, where, each spring and autumn, Tōshōdai-ji's stunning collection of treasures go on display. These are mostly statues, of which the most celebrated is a headless wooden Buddha known as the "Venus of the Orient" – the voluptuousness of the statue contrasts with the more sculptural styles of the surrounding artworks. The exhibits are mostly labelled in English but staff also provide an explanation book in English to use as you view the treasures.

Just once a year – on June 6, the anniversary of Ganjin's death – the doors of the **Miei-dō** (Founder's Hall), in the northern section of the compound, are opened to reveal a lacquered image which was carved just before Ganjin died in 763 at the grand age of 76. He's buried next door, in the far northeast corner of the compound, in a simple grave within a clay-walled enclosure.

ARRIVAL AND DEPARTURE   TŌSHŌDAI-JI

By train Kintetsu-line trains run from Nara to Nishinokyō Station (every 10min; 15min; ¥250) with a change at Saidai-ji; the main gate is 1km walk northeast of the station.
By bus Buses #52 and #97 from Nara (every 30min; 20min;

¥240) drop you at the Tōshōdaiji Higashi-guchi bus stop on the main road, a 5min walk west of Tōshōdai-ji's main gate.
On foot From Tōshōdai-ji's main gate it's a short walk south to Yakushi-ji.

Kansai

関西

VIEW FROM FLOATING GARDEN
OBSERVATORY, OSAKA

Kansai

In a country so devoid of flat land, the great rice-growing plains of Kansai, the district around Osaka and Kyoto, are imbued with an almost mystical significance. This was where the nation first began to take root, in the region known as Yamato, and where a distinct Japanese civilization evolved from the strong cultural influences of China and Korea. Kansai people are tremendously proud of their pivotal role in Japanese history and tend to look down on Tokyo, which they regard as an uncivilized upstart. The former imperial capitals of Kyoto and Nara (see p.406–483), with their enduring historical and cultural importance, are naturally a major part of the region's appeal. Today, Kansai's diverse legacy of temples, shrines and castles, combined with an increasing array of exciting modern architecture, makes it one of Japan's top tourist destinations.

Although **Osaka** has been much maligned as an "ugly" and "chaotic" city, it is not short of attractions and easily makes up for its aesthetic shortcomings with an excess of commercial spirit – the source of its long-established wealth – and an enthusiastic love of eating, drinking and its own style of comedy.

South of Osaka, the temples of **Kōya-san** provide a tranquil glimpse into contemporary religious practice in Japan. This mountain-top retreat – the headquarters of the Shingon school of Buddhism – has been an active centre of pilgrimage since the ninth century. People of all faiths are welcome to stay in the quiet old temples and join in the morning prayer service.

Shintō, Japan's native religion, also has deep spiritual roots in Kansai. Not far from **Kōya-san** is the **Kumano Kodō**, an ancient pilgrimage route through the "Land of the Gods", where for centuries both emperors and peasants sought purification and healing at sacred sites and hot springs. Over on the far eastern side of the region is **Ise-jingū**, one of the country's most important Shintō shrines, dedicated to Amaterasu, the Sun Goddess, from whom all Japan's emperors are descended. **Ise** itself is the gateway to the attractive peninsula of **Shima Hantō**. Here, *ama* women divers still use traditional fishing methods to collect seafood. The unspoiled scenery of **Agō-wan**, the bay at the southern tip of the peninsula, is a rewarding destination for scenic boat rides which give a bird's-eye view of the cultured pearl industry.

The port of **Kōbe**, now fully recovered from 1995's devastating earthquake, is less than thirty minutes west of Osaka in a dramatic location on the edge of Osaka Bay. Kōbe's sights are less of a draw than its relaxed cosmopolitan atmosphere, best

KOBE BEEF COWS, TAJIMA

Highlights

❶ **Osaka nightlife** Enjoy the neon-lit buzz of streets of Japan's third-largest city and sample some typical Osakan street food, such as *takoyaki* – grilled octopus dumplings **See p.503**

❷ **Takarazuka** See the popular all-female revue troupe gender-bend their way through lavish musical productions of Hollywood movies and traditional Japanese plays. **See p.505**

❸ **Kōya-san** Spend an atmospheric night in temple lodgings atop a sacred mountain and participate in a dawn *gomataki* fire ritual. **See p.507**

❹ **Kumano Kodō** Wander the pilgrimage route through ancient forests, discover sacred

mountain shrines and soak in the healing waters of isolated hot springs. **See p.514**

❺ **Shima Hantō** Visit the Grand Shrine at Ise, Japan's spiritual heartland, and later eat fresh seafood with the *ama* women divers of Osatsu and hear their stories of the sea. **See p.517**

❻ **Arima Onsen** Spend a day dipping in the mineral-rich gold and silver waters of this historical onsen town. **See p.531**

❼ **Kōbe Beef** Visit a beef farm and learn about how this top-quality meat is produced, then enjoy a meal in one of Kōbe city's sophisticated restaurants. **See p.531**

HIGHLIGHTS ARE MARKED ON THE MAP ON P.488

experienced with a stroll around its harbourside and an evening in one its jazz clubs. Close by is the ancient hot-spring resort **Arima Onsen**, which has managed to retain some old-world hospitality in its elegant ryokan.

Wherever you choose to stay in Kansai, don't miss **Himeji**, on the area's western edge, and **Himeji-jō**, Japan's most impressive castle (though closed for renovations until early 2015). Himeji also has a couple of intriguing museums in buildings designed by top contemporary architects, and the lovely **Himeji Kōko-en**, nine connected gardens laid out according to traditional principles.

KANSAI

HIGHLIGHTS
1. Osaka nightlife
2. Takarazuka
3. Kōya-san
4. Kumano Kodō
5. Shima Hantō
6. Arima Onsen
7. Kōbe Beef

GETTING AROUND

KANSAI

BY TRAIN

The most convenient way of getting around the Kansai district is by train. The area is crisscrossed by competing JR and private rail lines, while the Tōkaidō Shinkansen provides a high-speed service between Ōsaka, Kyoto, Kōbe and Himeji.

Kansai Area Pass If you plan to travel intensively around the region, you might want to buy JR West's Kansai Area Pass. Valid for between one and four consecutive days (¥2000–6000, the pass allows unlimited travel on all local services operated by JR West, apart from the Shinkansen. It also offers discounts on admission to various cultural and tourist sights including art museums and amusement parks along JR lines.

San'yō Area Pass For those travelling on to Fukuoka, the San'yō Area Pass covers JR services from Kansai Airport via Ōsaka, Kōbe and Himeji, including the Shinkansen (four consecutive days; ¥20,000 eight consecutive days; ¥30,000).

Kansai Thru Pass A convenient and economical way to access the region's private railway lines, subway networks and bus companies is with the Kansai Thru Pass (two-day ticket, ¥3800; three-day ticket, ¥5000), which enables travellers to ride on almost any bus, subway or private railway in the region. Even if you have a JR Pass this pass is handy, as it saves the hassle of buying tickets each time you jump on a bus or ride the subway.

Kintetsu Rail Pass The Kintetsu Rail Pass (three-day pass; ¥3800, five-day pass; ¥5700) covers the whole of the extensive Kintetsu network, including three rides on limited express trains. The five-day pass includes a return trip from the airport and good discounts on entry to major sights.

7

Osaka

大阪

Japan's third-largest city after Tokyo and Yokohama, the vibrant metropolis of **OSAKA** is inhabited by famously easy-going citizens with a taste for the good things in life. It may lack the pockets of beauty and refinement found in nearby Kyoto, but having received a bad rap as a tourist destination for many years, Osaka has attempted to re-brand itself and improve its image over the last decade. Urban revitalization, ambitious architectural projects and schemes such as offering free wi-fi hotspots throughout the city are combining to make it a more attractive destination for tourists.

Osakans speak one of Japan's more earthy dialects, Ōsaka-ben, and are as friendly as Kyoto folk can be frosty. They may greet each other saying "Mō kari-makka?" ("Are you making any money?"), but Osakans also know how to enjoy themselves once work has stopped. There are large entertainment districts in the north and south of the city, and the Osaka live music scene showcases eclectic local talent as well as international acts. In a city that cultivated high **arts**, such as *bunraku* puppetry, the locals also have a gift for bawdy comedy; Takeshi "Beat" Kitano, the internationally famous film director, started his career as a comedian here. The city continues to produce successful comedy duos who dominate national TV variety shows, and Osakans are very proud that their dialect has now become popular as the language of comedians. Osaka is also one of Japan's great **food** cities, though the residents are not snobby about their cuisine – a typical local dish is *takoyaki*, grilled octopus dumplings, usually sold as a street snack.

OSAKA ORIENTATION

Like all big Japanese cities, Osaka is divided into wards (*ku*), but you'll often hear locals talking of Kita (north) and Minami (south). the split being along Chūō-dōri. **Kita** covers the areas of **Umeda**, where all the main railway companies have stations, and **Shin-Osaka**, north of the Yodo-gawa River and location of the Shinkansen station. On the east side of this area is **Ōsaka-jō**, the castle. The shopping and entertainment districts of Shinsaibashi, Dōtombori, Amerika-mura and Namba are all part of **Minami**.

Slightly further south is **Tennōji**, where you'll find Tennōji-kōen and the temple Shitennō-ji and, further south again, the ancient shrine Sumiyoshi Taisha. West of these districts lies the patchwork of landfill islands edging Osaka Bay the Osaka Aquarium Kaiyūkan is at **Tempozan Harbour Village** while the Kansai area's tallest building, the WTC Cosmotower, is further south at **Nankō**.

7

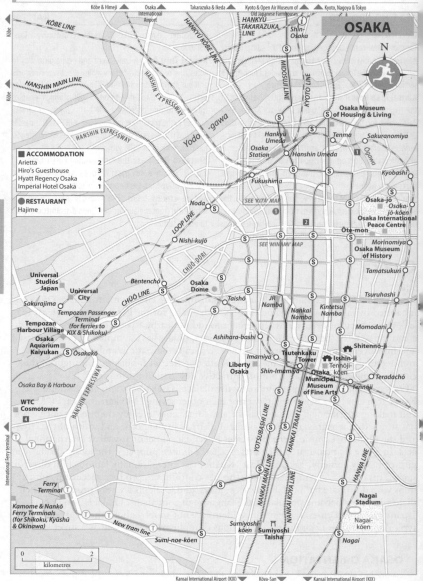

ACCOMMODATION
Arietta 2
Hiro's Guesthouse 3
Hyatt Regency Osaka 4
Imperial Hotel Osaka 1

RESTAURANT
Hajime 1

Brief history

Osaka's history stretches back to the fifth century AD, when it was known as **Naniwa** and its port served as a gateway to the more advanced cultures of Korea and China. For a short period, from the middle of the seventh century, the thriving city served as Japan's capital, but in the turbulent centuries that followed it lost its status, changed its name to Osaka and developed as a temple town. It was on the site of the temple Ishiyama Hongan-ji that the warlord **Toyotomi Hideyoshi** decided to build his castle in 1583 (see box opposite) and it became a key bastion in his campaign to unite the country.

With Toyotomi's death in 1598, another period of political instability loomed in Osaka for his supporters, as rival **Tokugawa Ieyasu** shifted the capital to Edo. The shogun's troops besieged the castle in 1614 and destroyed it a year later. With Japan firmly under their control, the Tokugawa shoguns were happy to allow the castle to be rebuilt and for Osaka to continue developing as an economic and commercial centre. The wealth of what became known as the "kitchen of Japan" led to patronage of the arts, such as kabuki and *bunraku*, and a deep appreciation of gourmet pursuits (the expression "kuidaore", to eat oneself bankrupt) that still exists today.

Despite having a gross domestic product comparable to that of Canada, plus the city's extensive commercial activity, the local government has been in the red for nearly two decades. Since his election in 2008, the current mayor, and former governor, **Hashimoto Tōru** has initiated severe cost-cutting measures affecting education and community programmes. A controversial figure, lawyer and TV celebrity, Hashimoto launched the right-wing national political party **Ishin-no-kai** (Japan Restoration Party) in 2012, and made several damaging comments regarding prostitution and sexual slavery during World War II. He has also argued that Osaka should become the "back-up" capital in case Tokyo is affected by a disaster.

Ōsaka-jō

大阪城 • 1-1 Ōsaka-jo • Daily 9am–4.30pm • Park free; Ōsaka-jōkoen Castle ¥600 • ☎ 06 6941 3044, ⓦ Ōsakacastle.net • Ōte-mon gate is a 2min walk northeast of the Tanimachi 4-chōme subway station; alternatively, take the JR loop line to Ōsaka-jo Koen Station

Some cynics suggest that the only reason the castle **Ōsaka-jō** is the single most-visited attraction in Japan – outdoing the country's best fortress Himeji-jō (see p.535) and even Mount Fuji – is because it's the only thing to see in the city. In fact, Osaka has plenty to see, but the castle is the main focus, and justly so.

There are several entrances to the park surrounding the castle, but the most impressive is through the **Ōte-mon** (Main Gate), dating from 1629, on the west side. As you head up towards the donjon through the southern Sakura-mon gate, keep an eye out for the 130-tonne **Tako-ishi** ("Octopus Stone"): with a surface area of sixty square metres, this is the largest rock used in the original construction of the castle walls.

THE INDOMITABLE FORTRESS

Despite being largely a concrete reconstruction, **Ōsaka-jō** can be counted a great survivor, a tangible link with the city's illustrious past as Japan's one-time seat of power. The castle's roots go back to the early sixteenth century, when an influential Buddhist sect built its fortified temple headquarters **Ishiyama Hongan-ji** beside the confluence of the Ōgawa and Neya-gawa rivers. For a decade the monks held out against warlord Oda Nobunaga (see p.796), before handing their fortress over in 1580. Nobunaga's successor, **Toyotomi Hideyoshi**, decided to build the grandest castle in Japan on the temple site. For three years from 1583, tens of thousands of men laboured on the enormous castle, and craftsmen were drafted in from around Japan to give the eight-storey central donjon the finest gold-leaf decoration.

Hideyoshi died in 1598, and his son and heir Hideyori was immediately under threat from rival **Tokugawa Ieyasu**. In 1614, the would-be shogun laid siege to the castle, even though his favourite granddaughter Senhime, wife of Hideyori, was inside. A year later he breached the castle and reduced it to ruins. Hideyori and his mother committed suicide rather than surrender, but Senhime survived and went on to become mistress of Himeji-jō (see p.535). When Ieyasu allowed the castle to be rebuilt in the 1620s, he made sure it was not on the same scale as his own residence in Edo. In 1665, the donjon was again burnt to the ground after being struck by lightning. It was not rebuilt until the 1840s and then only lasted another thirty years before the Tokugawa troops set fire to it during the civil war that briefly raged before the Meiji Restoration of 1868. Osaka's citizens, however, had grown fond of their castle, so the donjon was rebuilt once more in 1931 – this time from concrete – and it has remained standing despite the heavy bombing of the city during World War II.

7

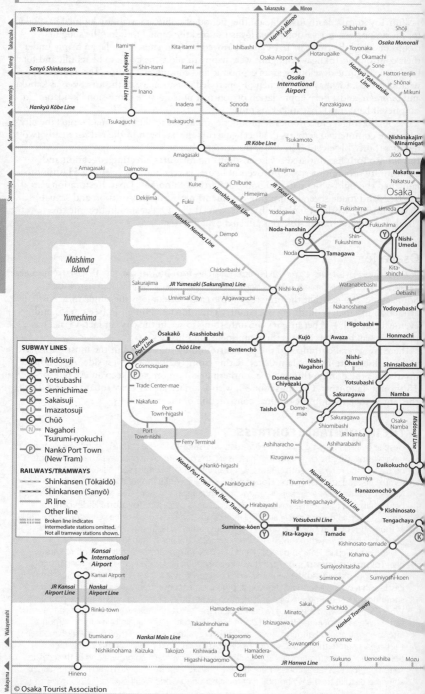

© Osaka Tourist Association

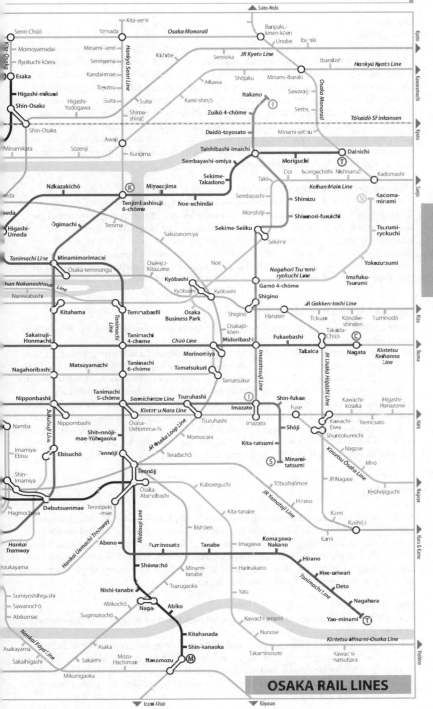

OSAKA RAIL LINES

Donjon

天守閣, Tenshukaku

It's long been a point of amusement that Ōsaka-jō's main tower, or **donjon**, has its own elevator inside, as well as one outside, so that the elderly and those in wheelchairs can avoid the steps to the entrance. Head up to the eighth floor for a panoramic view of the city and castle grounds; the orchards you can see between the moats on the castle's eastern flank are a riot of plum blossom in March. Working your way down the floors you'll be guided through the life of Toyotomi Hideyoshi (see box, p.491) and the castle's colourful history. The displays include the highly detailed folding screen painting *Summer War of Osaka* and a full-scale re-creation of Toyotomi's famous golden tearoom. On the first floor, it's worth dropping by the mini-theatre to see the free history videos with English subtitles.

Osaka International Peace Centre

大阪国際平和センター, Ōsaka Kokusai Heiwa Senta • Tues–Sun 9.30am–4.30pm • ¥250 • ☎ 06 6947 7208, ⓦ peace-osaka.or.jp

The sobering **Osaka International Peace Centre** is located in the southern corner of the Ōsaka-jō park. As at similar museums in Hiroshima and Nagasaki, the worthy but heavy-going displays attempt to explain Japan's provocative actions before and during World War II, as well as the devastation caused by the atomic bombings of Hiroshima and Nagasaki. Osaka was heavily bombed during the war and the displays detailing life during that time emphasize the misery of war. Visitors are asked to leave a message of peace.

Osaka Museum of History

大阪歴史博物館, Ōsaka Rekishi Hakubutsukan • 4-1-32 Otemae • 9.30am–4.30pm, Fri until 8pm, closed Tues • ¥600 • ☎ 06 6946 5728, ⓦ mus-his.city.osaka.jp

To the southwest of Ōsaka-jō, the stunning **Osaka Museum of History** is housed in a twelve-storey concrete and glass structure shaped like a giant ship's funnel – the "edge" pointing towards the castle is made of glass and offers excellent views. One of the city's premier attractions, the museum is built on the site of the Asuka period Naniwa-no-Miya Palace, remains of which have been preserved in the museum's basement. Above that are four storeys of interesting displays featuring antique manuscripts and intricate scale models of street scenes and long-vanished buildings which once played important roles in Osaka's cultural and social life. English explanations are limited so it's worth renting an audio guide (¥400) to get more out of your visit.

Umeda

梅田

In the north of Osaka, the meeting point of the JR, Hankyū and Hanshin railway lines, plus the Midosuji, Yotsubashi and Tanimachi subway lines, is the **Umeda** area, home to some interesting modern architecture. Even if you don't plan to take a train, the baroque entrance hall of the **Hankyū Umeda Station** (阪急梅田駅) is worth a look. JR Osaka Station has recently been upgraded and now boasts two large department stores, as well as a shopping mall and cinema complex.

Hep Five

ヘップファイブ大阪 • Shops daily 11am–9pm • Restaurants daily 11am–10pm • Ferris Wheel daily 11am–11pm • Ferris wheel ¥700 • ⓦ hepfive.jp

The eleven-storey **HEP Five** shopping and dining extravaganza is one of northern Osaka's landmark buildings. The huge red Ferris wheel on its roof offers excellent vistas of the city and, inside, you'll find more than 150 shops and restaurants. Outside the main entrance, Osaka's trendy urban youth congregate, making it a great place to observe the latest fashions.

Umeda Sky Building

梅田スカイビル・1-1-88 Oyoconaka・Floating Garden Observatory: daily 10am–10.30pm・¥700・☎ 06 6440 3855, ⓦ skybldg.co.jp

Immediately west of Umeda Station, a tunnel leads beneath the railway sidings to the twin towers of the **Umeda Sky Building**, a striking skyscraper, where you can take a glass elevator up to the **Floating Garden Observatory**, 170m above the ground, and enjoy 360-degree views of north Osaka. The Shōwa-period **Takimi-koji** (滝見小路) restaurant street at the base of the building has a nice retro atmosphere and is a good place for a drink or a snack.

Osaka Museum of Housing and Living

大阪くらしの今昔館, Ōsaka Kusashi Konjyaku-Kan・8F-10F 6-4-20 Tenjinbashi・Daily 10am–4.30pm; closed Tues・¥600・Take Tanimachi subway line to Tenjinbashisuji 6-chome, and the museum is a 2min walk from exit 3・☎ 06 6242 1170, ⓦ konjyakukan.com

The Osaka Museum of Housing and Living is a great place to get a sense of Naniwa, as the city was called in the Edo period. On one floor there's a complete replica of an 1830s neighbourhood with streets of shops, homes and other urban features of the time. Models and images showing how modern Osaka developed from the Meiji period to the post-World War II era take up the other floor of the museum.

Open-Air Museum of Old Japanese Farmhouses

日本民家集落博物館, Nihon Minka Shuraku Hakubutsukan・Tues–Sun 9.30am–4.30pm・¥500・Take the Midosuji subway line to Ryokuchi-koen from here, it's a 30min walk from the west exit・☎ 06 6862 3137, ⓦ www.occh.or.jp./minka

The **Open-Air Museum of Old Japanese Farmhouses** in Ryokuchi-kōen is an outdoor

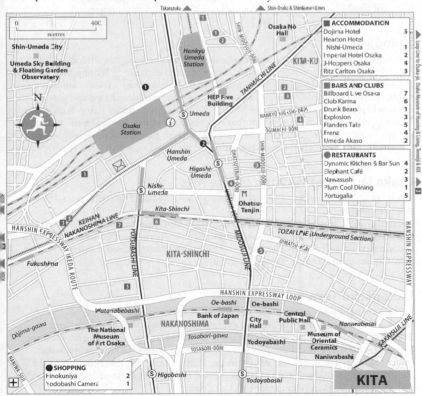

architectural museum with a wonderful collection of eleven thatched roof *minka*, or traditional Japanese farmhouses. The original buildings have been transported here from all over Kansai, as well as from Kyūshū and Kantō, and immaculately reconstructed in the park. Many were built during the Edo period and were still in use up until the 1960s. The park is especially nice to visit during spring and autumn.

Museum of Oriental Ceramics

東洋陶磁美術館, Tōyō Tōji Bijutsukan • 1-1-26 Nakanoshima • Tues–Sun 9.30am–4.30pm • ¥500 • ☎ 06 6223 0055, ⓦ moco.or.jp

Sandwiched between the Dōjima and Tosabori rivers, southeast of Umeda, the thin island of **Nakanoshima** (中之島) is home to Ōsaka's impressive **Museum of Oriental Ceramics**. Housing an exemplary collection of ancient Chinese and Korean pottery, the museum has a hushed, reverential atmosphere that is a world away from the bustling city outside. The exhibits are well-displayed and regular special exhibitions offer fascinating insights into the ancient flow of arts and crafts between China, Korea and Japan.

The National Museum of Art Osaka

国立国際美術館 • 4-2-55 Nakanoshima • Tues–Sun 10am–4.30pm, until 8pm on Friday • ¥420 • ☎ 06 4860 8600, ⓦ nmao.go.jp

At the western end of the island of Nakanoshima, **The National Museum of Art Osaka** holds engaging exhibitions of contemporary Japanese and international art. The museum's entrance is above ground – look out for a large steel structure which is supposed to represent bamboo – while the galleries are housed in two floors underground.

Tennōji-kōen

天王寺公園 • 1-108 Chausuyama-cho • Tues–Sun 9.30am–5pm; May–Sept Sat & Sun closes at 7.30pm • ¥150 • ☎ 06 6771 8401

South of the downtown area of Osaka, the large green expanse of **Tennōji-kōen** opened as a botanical garden in 1909 on a historic site that includes an ancient tumulus (burial mound). The park is also home to **Keitakuen**, a pretty, traditional Japanese garden arranged around a central pond, which was donated to the city by Baron Sumitomo, whose family owned the trading company of the same name. As well as the modern Great Conservatory, a giant glasshouse brimming with plants and flowers from around the world, Tennōji-kōen also houses a rather depressing zoo, which isn't worth visiting.

Osaka Municipal Museum of Fine Arts

大阪市立美術館 Ōsaka Shiritsu Bijutsukan • 1-82 Chausuyama-chō • Tues–Sun 9.30am–4.30pm • ¥300 • ☎ 06 6771 4874, ⓦ osaka-art-museum.jp

Located within Tennōji-kōen's gardens, the **Osaka Municipal Museum of Fine Arts** is a grand building with an old-fashioned atmosphere. Its permanent collection is spread over numerous galleries, and includes fine examples of ancient and modern Oriental painting, sculpture, ceramics and calligraphy.

Tsūtenkaku Tower

通天閣 • 1-18-6 Ebisu-higashi • Daily 9am–8.30pm • ¥600 • ☎ 06 6641 9555, ⓦ www.tsutenkaku.co.jp

On the western side of Tennōji-kōen, near the zoo, is the rather run-down area of **Shin-Sekai** ("New World"; 新世界), a raffish district of narrow shopping arcades, cheap bars, restaurants and pachinko parlours. At its centre stands the retro **Tsūtenkaku Tower**. This city landmark was rebuilt in the 1950s after it was destroyed in World War II, though at just 103m it's long been surpassed by Umeda's skyscrapers to the north and the 256m WTC Cosmotower by Osaka Bay.

Shitennō-ji

四天王寺 • 1-11-18 Shitennōji • **Temple** Daily 8.30am–4.30pm • ¥300 • **Treasure house** Tues–Sun 8.30am–4pm • ¥200 • ☎ 06 6771 0066, ⊕ shitennoji.or.jp • The main entrance to the temple is a 5min walk south of Shitennō-ji-mae subway station and 15min north of the Tennōji overground station

One of the first Buddhist temples in Japan, **Shitennō-ji** lies just outside Tennōji-kōen, on its northern edge, some 2km southeast of Namba. The temple has retained its classical layout but contains none of the buildings originally erected in 593 AD; the oldest feature of this windswept, concrete complex, with turtle ponds and a five-storey pagoda at its centre, is the late thirteenth-century *torii* at the main entrance gate. The **treasure house**, in the modern white building behind the central courtyard, contains gorgeous orange costumes and enormous mandalas, carved with fantastic birds and dragons, which are used for the ceremonial *bugaku* dances held at the temple three times a year (check the website for dates).

Liberty Osaka

リバティ大阪 • 3-6-36 Naniwanishi • Tues–Fri 10am–3.30pm, Sat 1–4.30pm • ¥500 • ☎ 06 6561 5891, ⊕ liberty.or.jp • An 8min walk south of Ashiharabashi Station on the JR Loop line

Popularly known as **Liberty Osaka**, the Osaka Museum of Human Rights contains remarkable exhibits that tackle Japan's most taboo subjects. There's an English-language leaflet and a portable audio guide that explains the displays, which include the untouchable caste (the Burakumin), Japan's ethnic minorities, the disabled, the sexist treatment of women, and the effects of pollution, most tragically seen in the exhibition about Minamata disease (see p.824). Unfortunately, the Osaka City government has cut funding to the museum and its future is currently in doubt.

Sumiyoshi Taisha

住吉大社 • 2-9-89 Sumiyoshi • Dawn to dusk • ☎ 06 6672 0753, ⊕ sumiyoshitaisha.net • A 15min subway or tram ride south from Ebisuchō Station, immediately north of Shin-Sekai

Built in 211 AD, Osaka's grandest shrine is **Sumiyoshi Taisha**, home of the Shintō gods of the sea. According to legend, the grateful Empress Jingō ordered its construction after returning safely from a voyage to Korea. With logs jutting out at angles from the thatched roofs, its buildings exemplify *sumiyoshi zukuri*, one of Japan's oldest styles of shrine architecture. Unlike similar complexes at Ise (see p.518) and Izumo Taisha (see p.602), Sumiyoshi Taisha is painted bright red, in sharp contrast with its wooded surrounding. The approach to the complex takes you over the elegant humpbacked Sori-hashi (arched bridge), donated to the shrine by Yodogimi, the warlord Toyotomi Hideyoshi's lover.

Osaka Bay

大阪湾, Ōsaka-wan • To reach the Osaka Bay area take the JR Loop line to Bentenchō Station (弁天町), then take the Chūō line subway to Ōsaka-kō Station and walk north towards the huge Ferris wheel beside Tempozan Harbour Village. Alternatively, you can get the subway directly to Ōsaka-kō Station from other parts of the city

The **Osaka Bay** area consists of man-made islands and reclaimed waterfront areas such as Sakishima, home to the city's tallest building, the WTC Cosmotower, and Sakurajima, where Universal Studios Japan is based. The waterfront **Tempozan Harbour Village** (天保山ハーバービレッジ) district features Osaka's largest Ferris Wheel and an excellent aquarium.

Osaka Aquarium Kaiyukan

大阪海遊館, Ōsaka Kaiyūkan • 1-1-10 Kaigan-dōri • Daily 10am–7pm • ¥2300 • ☎ 06 6576 5501, ⊕ kaiyukan.com

Inside an exotic butterfly-shaped building, decorated with a giant fish-tank mosaic, is the fabulous **Osaka Aquarium Kaiyukan**. It's constructed so that you wind down, floor by floor between fourteen elongated tanks, each representing a different aquatic environment, from Antarctica to the Aleutian Islands. The beauty of the design means you can, for example, watch seals basking on the rocks at the top of the tank and see them swimming, torpedo-like, through the lower depths later. The huge central tank represents the Pacific Ocean and is home to a couple of whale sharks and several manta rays, among many other fish. The giant spider crabs, looking like alien invaders from *War of the Worlds*, provide a fitting climax to Japan's best aquarium.

Universal Studios Japan

ユニバーサル・スタジオ・ジャパン • 2-1-33 Sakurajima • Mon–Fri 10am–5pm, Sat & Sun 10am–6pm, longer hours during summer • Day pass ¥6790 • ☎ 06 6465 3000, ⊛ usj.co.jp/e • Direct express trains run from JR Osaka Station to Universal City Station on the JR Yumesaki line (every 10min; 14min). From other stations on the JR Loop line, change at Nishi-kujō Station

Covering some 140 acres on Osaka's western waterfront, **Universal Studios Japan** is one of the nation's leading theme parks and is hugely popular amongst young Japanese. Its attractions are based on Hollywood movies, and there are a huge variety of rides, live shows and restaurants in the park.

7

ARRIVAL AND DEPARTURE   OSAKA

Served by two airports, numerous ferries and buses, not to mention a slew of railway companies, Osaka is accessible from almost any point in Japan and, via Kansai International Airport, from many places overseas, too. There's also a weekly ferry service between Osaka and Shanghai in China.

BY PLANE

KANSAI INTERNATIONAL AIRPORT

On a man-made island in Osaka Bay, some 35km south of the Osaka city centre, and approximately 100km from Kyoto, Kansai International Airport (KIX; 関西国際空港; ☎072 455 2500, ⊛kansai-airport.or.jp) handles both international and domestic flights. The international departure lounge is on the fourth floor and domestic departures are on the second floor. In 2012, KIX Terminal 2 (KIX第2ターミナル; ☎072 455 2911, ⊛kansai-airport.or.jp/t2) opened for budget airlines, but is currently only used by Peach Aviation for Asian and some domestic destinations. Shuttle buses connect Terminal 2 with the main building, Kansai International Airport Terminal 1.

Destinations Fukuoka (10 daily; 1hr); Kagoshima (3 daily; 1hr 10min); Nagasaki (2 daily; 1hr 10min); Naha (13 daily; 1hr 15min); Sapporo (13 daily; 2hr); Sendai (3 daily; 1hr 10min); Tokyo Haneda (9 daily; 1hr); and Tokyo Narita (8 daily; 1hr 15min).

GETTING INTO TOWN FROM KANSAI

By train The fastest way into the city is by train, from the station connected to the second floor of the passenger terminal building. The regular Nankai Express, or *kyūkō* (急行; ¥890), takes 47min to reach Nankai Namba Station (南海難波駅), although it's hard to resist the chic Rapi:t, designed like a train from a sci-fi comic, which costs ¥1390 and does the journey in 38min. From Nankai Namba Station you can take a subway or taxi to other parts of the city. JR also runs trains directly to several stations in and around Osaka from KIX, and if you have a rail pass voucher you can exchange it at Kansai Airport Station. After that, you can

either take a train with your pass to JR Namba Station (難波駅; 1hr; ¥1010), where it's easy to transfer to the subway, or take a taxi. Alternatively, JR Pass holders can also ride the Haruka limited express which stops at Tennōji Station (天王寺駅; 30min; ¥2300) and Shin-Osaka Station (新大阪駅; 45min; ¥3000), before you can catch the Shinkansen, before continuing on to Kyoto (1hr 15min; ¥3490). If you're in no hurry, the regular JR express trains to Tennōji Station (45min; ¥1030) and Osaka Station (70min; ¥1160), in the Umeda area of the city, are worth considering.

By limousine To avoid the hassle of dragging your luggage on and off trains, limousine buses and taxis to various locations around Ōsaka, including several hotels, depart from international arrivals. All central city locations take 40min–1hr to reach, depending on the traffic, and cost ¥1500.

By taxi Taxis to central Osaka are expensive (from ¥10,000), and no faster than the buses.

ITAMI AIRPORT

Osaka International Aiport, also known as Itami Airport (大阪国際空港; ☎06 6856 6781, ⊛Ōsaka-airport.or.jp) is 10km north of the city centre and, despite the name, only handles domestic flights.

Destinations Akita (6 daily; 1hr 30min); Aomori (3 daily; 1hr 40min); Fukuoka (19 daily; 1hr); Kagoshima (15 daily; 1hr 10min); Kumamoto (12 daily; 1hr 5min); Miyazaki (12 daily; 1hr 5min); Nagasaki (7 daily; 1hr 10min); Naha (6 daily; 1hr 15min); Niigata (10 daily; 1hr 10min); Ōita (7 daily; 1hr); Sapporo (5 daily; 2hr); Sendai (19 daily; 1hr 10min); Tokyo Haneda (32 daily; 1hr); Tokyo Narita (4 daily; 1hr 15min); and Yamagata (3 daily; 1hr 20min).

GETTING INTO TOWN FROM ITAMI

By bus From the airport there are regular buses into the city (25–50min depending on destination; ¥340–680) and also to Shin-Ōsaka Station (25min; ¥480), where you can connect to the Shinkansen.

By limousine Direct limousine buses run to Osaka Station (1hr 20min; ¥2000) and on to Kyoto and Kōbe.

By monorail A monorail (tickets from ¥190) links the airport with parts of north Ōsaka, connecting at various points to the city subway system and both the Hankyū and Keihan private railways.

By taxi A taxi to Umeda in central Osaka costs ¥5000.

BY TRAIN

Shin-Ōsaka Station Shinkansen pull into Shin-Ōsaka Station (新大阪駅), north of the city centre. You can transfer here to other JR services around the area or to the city's subway lines.

Destinations Fukuoka (Hakata Station; every 30min; 2hr 20min); Himeji (every 20min; 35min); Hiroshima (every 15min; 1hr 15min); Kansai International (every 30min; 45min); Kōbe (every 5min; 15min); Kyoto (every 15min; 20min); Nagoya (every 15min; 1hr 10min); Okayama (every 15min; 1hr 5min); and Tokyo (every 15min; 2hr 30min).

Osaka Station JR services along the Tōkaidō line, connecting Nagoya, Kyoto and Kōbe with Ōsaka, arrive at the central Osaka Station (大阪駅) in Umeda, where you'll also find the termini for the Hankyū (阪急) and Hanshin (阪神) lines: these both provide cheaper connections to Kyoto and Kōbe than JR, if you don't have a rail pass.

Destinations Akita (daily; 12hr); Aomori (daily; 15hr); Kanazawa (24 daily; 2hr 30min); Kii-Tanabe (hourly; 2hr); Kōbe Sannomiya (every 15min; 22min); Kyoto (every 10min; 28–46min); Matsumoto (daily; 4hr); Nagano (daily; 4hr 50min); Nagoya (every 30min; 2hr 42min); Takarazuka (every 30min; 30min); and Toyama (14 daily; 3hr 5min).

Hankyu Umeda Station The Hankyū line services from Kyoto, Kōbe Sannomiya and Takarazuka arrive at Hankyū Umeda Station (阪急梅田駅) in the north of the city.

Destinations Kōbe Sannomiya (every 15min; 30min); Kyoto (every 15min; 50min); and Takarazuka (every 30min; 30min).

Hanshin Umeda Station The Hanshin line connects Kōbe Sannomiya with Osaka at Hanshin Umeda Station (阪神梅田; every 15min; 30min).

Keihan Yodoyabashi Station The Keihan line connects Osaka with Kyoto at Yodoyabashi Station (京阪 淀屋橋駅).

Destinations Kyoto Demachiyanagi (every 15min; 47min).

Kintetsu Namba Station Services from Nara and outer Osaka on the Kintetsu line arrive at Kintetsu Ōsaka-Namba Station (近鉄難波駅), in the heart of the Minami district.

Destinations Nara (every 15min; 30min).

Kintetsu Uehonmachi Station Services from Ise (see p.520) arrive at Uehonmachi, on the Kintetsu network.

Destinations Ise (every 15min; 1hr 45min); Kashikojima (1–2 hourly; 2hr 20min); and Toba (every 20–30min; 2hr).

Nankai Namba Station Services from KIX and Kōya-San on the Nankai line arrive at Nankai Namba Station (南海 難波駅), in the heart of the Minami district.

Destinations Kansai International Airport (every 30min; 35min); and Kōya-san (every 20–30min; 1hr 15min).

BY BUS

Osaka has various long-distance bus stations with services mainly operated by Willer Express (@ willerexpress.com) and JR Highway Buses (@ nishinihorjrbus.co.jp). There are stations located beside the JR Osaka Station in Umeda; at the Namba Kaisoku Bus Terminal and Osaka City Air Terminal in Namba; at Kintetsu Uehonmachi, south of the castle; and at Abenobashi near Tennōji, 1km further south of the castle. All are beside or near subway and train stations for connections around the city. If you plan to depart from Osaka by bus, check first with one of the tourist information centres (see p.500) for timetables and which station to go to.

Destinations: Beppu (daily; 9hr); Fukuoka (daily; 9hr 30min); Hagi (daily; 12hr); Hiroshima (5 daily; 6hr); Kagoshima (daily; 12hr); Kansai International (every 15min; 40min); Kumamoto (daily; 11hr); Miyazaki (daily; 12hr); Nagano (daily; 8hr); Nagasaki (1 daily; 10hr); Niigata (daily; 9hr); Osaka (Itami; every 20–30min; 50min); Tokyo (30 daily; 8hr 50min); Tottori (20 daily; 4hr); Wakayama (8 daily; 3hr); and Yonago (18 daily; 5hr).

BY FERRY

Osaka is a major port of call for many of the ferries plying routes around Japan, and sailing into Osaka Bay is a memorable way of approaching the city. The port is west of the city centre and has good transport links via the subway and train network.

Ōsaka Nankō Terminal Most domestic and international ferries use the Ōsaka Nankō Terminal (大阪南港フェリ ーターミナル), close to Ferry Terminal Station on the New Tram monorail, which connects to the city's subway network.

Tempozan East Wharf Ferries to and from Shikoku and Kansai International Airport arrive and depart from the less busy Tempozan East Wharf (天保山東岸壁); the nearest station to here is Ōsaka-kō (大阪港) on the Chūō subway line, a 10min walk away.

Ferry companies The main ferry operators are A Line Ferry (@ aline-ferry.com), Ferry Sunflower (@ ferry-sunflower.co.jp), and Hankyū Ferry (@ han9f.co.jp). Services to Shanghai, China are run by Xin Jian Zhen (@ shinganjin.com) and The Shanghai Ferry Company

7

(@ shanghai-ferry.co.jp), while Pan Star (@ panstar.co.kr) runs ferries to Busan, in South Korea.

Destinations Ashizuri (daily; 9hr 20min); Beppu (daily; 11hr 30min); Busan, South Korea (weekly; 18hr 50min); Kannoura (daily; 5hr); Matsuyama (daily; 9hr 20min); Miyazaki (daily; 12hr 50min); Naha (weekly; 39hr); Shanghai, China (2 weekly; 23hr); Shibushi (daily; 14hr 40min); and Shinmoji (daily; 12hr).

GETTING AROUND

By subway and train Like Tokyo, Osaka has an extensive subway and train system as well as a JR Loop line (see map, pp.492–493). The latter is handy if you're using a rail pass, but most of the time you'll find the subway more convenient and quicker for getting around the city. You can transfer between the nine subways and the New Tram line on the same ticket, but if you switch to any of the railway lines at a connecting station you'll need to either buy another ticket or a special transfer ticket when you start your journey. Most journeys across central Osaka cost ¥230.

Tickets and passes Because Osaka's attractions are widely scattered, investing in a one-day Osaka Visitors' Ticket (¥550) is worth considering if you're up for a hectic round of the sights. The pass is valid on all the subway lines and buses, and will be date-stamped when you first pass through the gate machines. You could also buy a one- or two-day Osaka Unlimited Pass (¥2000–2700), valid for both trains and buses, and including free admission to 26 popular tourist sites. These can be bought at subway-ticket vending machines as well as station kiosks.

By bus There are plenty of buses, but you'll find the subways and trains with their English signs and maps much easier to use.

Car rental Several major car rental firms can be found at both Shin-Osaka and Osaka stations (both daily 8am–8pm) including Eki Rent-a-Car (Shin-Osaka ☎ 06 6303 0181, Osaka ☎ 06 6341 3388; @ ekiren.co.jp) and Nippon Rent-a-Car (Osaka Reservation Center ☎ 06 6344 0919; @ nipponrentacar.co.jp).

INFORMATION

The Osaka Tourist Association is very helpful, with information offices all over the city, as well as at Kansai International Airport. All the tourist offices have English-speaking staff and can help with accommodation and transport.

TOURIST OFFICES

JR Osaka Station 1F north central gate, JR Osaka Station, houses the main tourist information centre on the central concourse (daily 9am–8pm; ☎ 06 6345 2189).

JR Shin-Osaka Station 3F JR Shin-Osaka Station, has a new tourist office next to the Shinkansen central ticket gates (daily 9am–6pm; ☎ 06 6305 3311) .

JR Tennōji Station 1F JR Tennō ji Station, has a small office (daily 9am–6pm; ☎ 06 6774 3077).

Nankai Namba Station 1F Nankai Terminal Building, has a tourist information centre near the Nankai and Midosuji lines (daily 9am–8pm; ☎ 06 6631 9100).

Kansai International Airport 1F South Arrivals, has a tourist information counter (daily 9am–9pm; ☎ 072 456 6025) along with a separate desk where you can make hotel reservations, and several bureaux de change.

LISTINGS

Information on events is listed in the free monthly *Kansai Scene* (@ kansaiscene.com), an English-language magazine that also has interesting features, and includes information on the Osaka club scene. It's available from tourist offices, as well as main bookstores and pubs.

ACCOMMODATION

Osaka's accommodation is predominantly Western-style hotels. The **Umeda** area hosts the bulk of the city's luxury hotels, while the shopping and nightlife districts of **Shinsaibashi** and **Namba** have a greater range of accommodation, catering to all budgets. Local transport is so efficient, however, that it's no great problem to be based outside the central area.

KITA

★ **Dōjima** 堂島ホテル 2-1-31 Dōjimahama ☎ 06 6341 3000, @ dojima-hotel.com; map p.495. Osaka's first boutique hotel, with starkly elegant decor, an in-house patisserie and an all-day diner. The comfortable rooms have wide-screen TVs and large designer bathtubs. **¥27500**

Hearton Hotel Nishi-Umeda ハートンホテル西梅田 3-3-55 Umeda ☎ 06 6342 1111, @ www.heartonhotel.com/nis; map p.495. Popular business hotel just behind the main post office next to JR Osaka Station. It's not the newest hotel in Umeda but the rooms are smart, clean and functional, and

come with cable TV and internet access. **¥18, 500**

Imperial Hotel Osaka 帝国ホテル大阪 1-8-50 Tenmabashi ☎ 06 6881 1111, @ www.imperialhotel .co.jp/e/osaka; map p.495. This opulent hotel, overlooking the Ōkawa River, is just as luxurious as its famous Tokyo parent. Purified air, a golf driving range and a choice of elegant restaurants and bars are all part of the experience. Free wi-fi. **¥24900**

J-Hoppers Osaka ジェイホッパーズ大阪 7-4-22 Fukushima ☎ 06 6453 6669, @ osaka.j-hoppers.com; map p.495. This is Kita's best budget option, in a handy

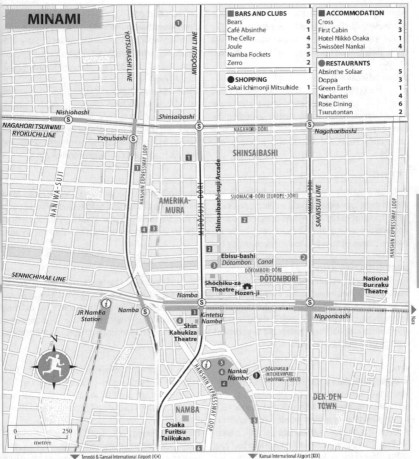

MINAMI

■ BARS AND CLUBS	
Bears	6
Café Absinthe	1
The Cellar	4
Joule	3
Namba Rockets	5
Zerro	2

● SHOPPING	
Sakai Ichimonji Mitsuhide	1

■ ACCOMMODATION	
Cross	2
First Cabin	3
Hotel Nikkō Osaka	1
Swissôtel Nankai	4

● RESTAURANTS	
Absinthe Solaar	5
Doppa	3
Green Earth	1
Nanbantei	4
Rose Dining	6
Tsurutontan	2

7

▼ Tennōji & Kansai International Airport (KK) ▼ Kansai International Airport (KIX)

location for exploring Osaka. Rooms are clean, the staff are happy to help with travel information, and the breezy rooftop garden is very popular. Free PC usage and wi-fi. Bicycle rental (¥500/day) also available. **Dorm ¥2500, double ¥6000**

Ritz Carlton Osaka リッツカールトン大阪 2-5-25 Umeda ☎06 6343 7000, ⓦritzcarlton.com; map p.495. Luxury hotel with the intimate feel of a European country house, liberally sprinkled with antiques, Japanese objets d'art and there's also live piano music. Rooms have fantastic views across the city, there's a great range of restaurants and the pool and gym are free to guests. **¥27600**

MINAMI

Arietta アリエッタホテル 3-2-6 Azuchimachi ☎06 6267 2787, ⓦthehotel.co.jp/en/arietta_osaka; map p.490. Clean and smart business hotel conveniently located close to three subway lines with friendly English-speaking staff. There's a coin laundry, and breakfast and LAN internet access are free. **¥10500**

★**Cross Hotel Osaka** クロスホテル大阪 2-5-15 Shinsaibashi ☎06 6213 8281, ⓦcrosshotel.com/ eng_osaka; map p.501. A stylish hotel with efficient service, just minutes away from the Minami shopping and nightlife scene. The decently sized rooms are tastefully decorated and include internet access. **¥17500**

★**First Cabin** ファーストキャビン 4-2-1 Namba ☎06 6631 8090, ⓦfirst-cabin.jp; map p.501. Smart capsule hotel for both men and women in the heart of Namba, with a first-class air travel theme. Cabins, for single occupancy, are bigger than the business capsules but all have their own TV and internet connection. Excellent bath, café/bar and communal lounge facilities. **¥3500**

Hotel Nikkō Osaka ホテル日航大阪 1-3-3 Nishi-Shinsaibashi ☎06 6244 1281, ⓦhno.co.jp;

map p.501. Deluxe hotel close to nightlife and shopping arcades, with spacious and comfortable rooms, attentive service and a good range of restaurants, including a coffee shop that serves an excellent buffet breakfast. ¥15500

Swissôtel Nankai Osaka スイスホテル南海大阪 5-1-60 Namba ☎ 06 6646 1111, ⓦ swissotel-osaka.co.jp; map p.501. Large international hotel located above Nankai Station which makes it ultra-convenient for direct airport access. Rooms are fresh and modern with comfortable beds, and the service is impeccable. ¥22500

OTHER AREAS

Hiro's Guesthouse ヒロゲストハウス 4-9-7 Momodani ☎ 06 7897 6608, ⓦ hirosguesthouse.com; map p.490. Stylish and modern guesthouse in Korea Town. Rooms are clean, with air conditioning. Free wi-fi. Dorm ¥2500, double ¥7000

Hyatt Regency Osaka ハイアットリージェンシー大阪 1-13-11 Nankō-Kita ☎ 06 6612 1234, ⓦ hyattregencyosaka.com; map p.490. Good luxury choice near the port area, offering well-equipped rooms with a minimalist design, elegant public areas and restaurants, and indoor and outdoor pools. ¥23800

EATING

Osaka has a reputation as a foodies' paradise, and it boasts many excellent local specialities. You shouldn't leave town without going to an **okonomiyaki** restaurant, preferably one where you can fry the thick pancakes yourself, or just grab some piping hot **takoyaki** (octopus dumplings) from a street stall. Osaka's own style of **sushi** is oshizushi, layers of vinegared rice, seaweed and fish cut into bite-size chunks, and the city also has a particular way of cooking chunky udon noodles, simmering them in a veggie, seafood or meat broth.

RESTAURANTS AND CAFÉS

The best choice of **restaurants** and **cafés** is around the Kita areas of Umeda and Chayama, and the Minami areas of Shinsaibashi, Dōtombori and Namba, while Tsuruhashi, on the JR Loop line to the east, is the main place to head for Korean food. Strolling around the narrow streets dotted with stand-up noodle and takoyaki bars, and restaurants with flickering neon signs and crazy displays – especially along Dōtombori (道頓堀), with its redeveloped promenade – is an appetizing experience in itself. The major **hotels** and **department stores** are also worth checking out, especially at lunchtime, when many restaurants offer special deals.

KITA

★**Dynamic Kitchen & Bar Sun** 燦 27F 4-5-10 Nishi-Tenma ☎ 06 6367 5512, ⓦ dynac-japan.com/sun; map p.495. With stunning night views over the Kita area, this is a great place to enjoy modern Japanese cuisine. You can choose to sit at either ozashiki floor tables, or at the counter. Excellent-value dinner courses of Kōbe and Nara beef from ¥8000. Mon–Sat 11.30am–2pm & 5–10pm, Sun 11.30am–2pm & 5–9.30pm.

Elephant Café エレファントカフェ 2-28 Chayamachi ☎ 06 6359 0136, ⓦ ug-gu.co.jp/restaurant/elephant/elephant.html; map p.495. International cuisine restaurant in the Chayama area with an exotically decorated interior of hanging lamps and fabrics, serving curries, noodles, pasta, dumplings, tapas and salads. The weekend set lunch (¥1200) is good value. Mon–Fri 5–11.30pm, Sat & Sun 11.30am–11.30pm.

★**Hajime** ハジメ 1-9-11-1 Edobori ☎ 06 6447 6688, ⓦ hajime-artistes.com; map p.490. Michelin-starred gourmet restaurant with a fabulous seasonal tasting menu (¥26,250) that fuses Japanese and French cuisine into a work of gastronomic art. There's also a shorter, and slightly less expensive, tasting menu (¥21,600). Reservations must be made in advance and there's a strict dress code and cancellation policy. Daily 11.30am–2pm & 5.30–8pm.

Nawasushi 縄寿司 2-14-1 Sonezaki ☎ 06 6312 9891; map p.495. Generous servings of super-fresh sushi (from ¥400/plate) and sashimi platters (from ¥1050) in a no-frills traditional setting. Don't be shy about yelling out your order. Daily noon–1am; closed first and second Mon of the month.

Plum Cool Dining プラム3F 4-6 Chayamachi ☎ 06 6377 0701, ⓦ plum.co.jp/chayamachi.html; map p.495. Everything on the menu here is intended to be paired with umeshu (sweet plum wine). Try the delicious tofu and avocado salad (¥780) or their "plum-style" rice (from ¥800); there's also an extensive umeshu list, from ¥400 a glass. Daily 5.30–11.30pm.

Portugalia ポルトガリア 14-12-11 Nishi-tenma ☎ 06 6362 6668, ⓦ portugalia.jp; map p.495. Authentic Portuguese cuisine near the American Consulate. Their ¥990 lunch sets (fish, chicken or pork) are excellent value, but the evening menu can be a little pricey. Good selection of wine and port (from ¥600/glass). Mon–Sat 11.30am–10.30pm.

MINAMI

Absinthe Solaar アブサンソラー Namba Dining Maison 8F, 5-1-18 Namba ☎ 06 6633 1445, ⓦ absinthe-jp.com; map p.501. Rooftop restaurant with outdoor lounge area, great for enjoying the evening breeze during the hot summer months. The Mediterranean menu includes Greek salad (¥1000) and Moroccan-style lamb chops (¥2300).

Daily 11am–11.30pm, closed Wed.

Doppa ドッパ 2F 1-6-9 Dōtombori ☎06 6212 0530; map p.501. A friendly restaurant that's a good mix of Italian and Osakan – hearty portions served without fuss. There are thirty kinds of pasta dish on offer (from ¥980), as well as pizza (¥850). Daily noon–9pm.

Green Earth グリーンアース 4-2-2 Kitakyūhōji-machi ☎06 6251 1245, ⊛osaka-vegetarian-ge.com/english; map p.501. This narrow café is one of the city's most popular vegetarian establishments. They serve jumbo sandwiches (from ¥500), good pasta (¥580) and filling veggie pizza (¥800). Mon–Sat 11.30am–4.30pm.

Nanbantei 南蛮亭 4-5-7 Nanba ☎06 6631 6178; map p.501. In the alleyway behind the Shin Kabukiza Theatre, this popular *yakitori-ya* has a huge range of skewer food (from ¥110), an English menu and a friendly atmosphere. Because of its popularity, dining time is limited to 2hr. Daily 5pm–midnight.

Rose Dining ローズダイニング Namba Dining Maison 9F, 5-1-18 Namba ☎06 6633 1034, ⊛uoman-group .com/28_rose_dining.html; map p.501. Elegant restaurant in the dining complex on top of the Takashimaya department store, serving an eclectic range of Japanese, Chinese and Western dishes, including dim sum, sushi and pasta. The lunch menu starts at ¥1580 and there are good-value set dinner courses from ¥1980. Daily 11am–9pm.

★**Tsurutontan** つるとんたん 3-17 Soemon-chō ☎06 6211 0021, ⊛tsurutontan.co.jp/shop/soemoncho-udon; map p.501. Fabulous udon restaurant that serves an amazing range of traditional and modern fusion dishes in extremely large bowls. The *umeboshi* (pickled plum) udon is unbeatable for its classic home-style cooking taste (¥880), while the carbonara udon (¥1800) really pushes the fusion boundaries by serving the thick white noodles with creamy seafood. Daily 11am–7.30pm.

NIGHTLIFE

The epicentre of Osaka's frenetic nightlife is **Ebisu-bashi**, a dazzling area to wander around, if only to check out the wild youth fashions on view, and pose for a photo with locals in front of the landmark Glico Man sign. Don't miss out on strolling through **Amerika-mura**, immediately west of Shinsaibashi, a street crowded with extremely cool shops and bars. In contrast, the **Hozen-ji Yokochō** area, around the paper-lantern-festooned temple Hozen-ji, is old-time Osaka, a narrow alley of tiny watering holes. The city's **gay scene** is much smaller than that in Tokyo, and historically it's tended to be in the Doyama-chō area of Kita rather than Minami. Check the free magazine *Kansai Scene* for the latest info on clubs, bars and one-off dance events.

BARS AND CLUBS

Bears ライブハウスベアーズ B1 Shin-Nihon Namba Building, 3-14-5 Namba-naka ☎06 6649 5564, ⊛namba-bears.main.jp; map p.501 The heart of the city's underground music scene, with a diverse range of local experimental and avant-garde acts playing every night. Daily 5 30–11.30pm

Billboard Live Osaka ビルボードライブ大阪 B2 Herbis Plaza Ent Building, 2-2-2 Umeda ☎06 6342 7722, ⊛billboard-live.com/club/o_index.html; map p.495. Top-class jazz, soul, R&B and folk performers regularly play at this small-scale supper club. It's pricey though, with tickets often in excess of ¥6000. Still, the sound system is excellent and the food's tasty and reasonably priced (from ¥1580). Mon–Fri 5.30pm–10pm & Sat-Sun 3.30pm–10pm.

★**Café Absinthe** カフェアブサン 1-2-27 Kita-Horie ☎06 6534 6635, ⊛www.absinthe-jp.com map p.501. Mediterranean-style bar with live music, DJs and photography exhibitions. Tabbouleh and hummus (¥800) are on the menu, and they serve absinthe drinks (from ¥800). Mon–Thurs 11.30am–3am, Fri & Sat 11.30am–5am, Sun 2pm–3am.

The Cellar ザセラー B1 Shin-Sumiya Building, 2-17-13 Nishi-Shinsaibashi ☎06 6212 6437, ⊛ip.tosp.co.jp/i. asp?i=thecellar; map p.501. Comfortable neighbourhood bar with reasonably priced drinks and a daily happy hour (6–8pm), plus live music on Wed, Fri and Sat, and a popular jam session on Sun afternoons. Tues–Thurs 6pm–2am, Fri & Sat 6pm–4am, Sun 6pm–midnight.

Club Karma カーマ B1 Zero Building, 1-5-18 Sonezaki-Shinchi ☎06 6344 6181, ⊛club-karma.com; map p.495. Stark yet roomy bar and club that hosts a range of up-to-the-minute music and dance nights, with the added bonus of a good menu and a happy hour until 9pm. The all-night techno and house events are usually held on Fri and Sat, when there's a cover charge of ¥2500 (more if big-name foreign DJs are in town). *Karma* is the most gay-friendly of the mainstream clubs and stages occasional gay or lesbian events. Daily 5pm–2am.

★**Drunk Bears** ドランクベアーズ B1 10-12 Chayamachi ☎06 6372 7275; map p.495. Friendly tapas bar (from ¥480) in the NU Chayamachi shopping centre. Belgian beers on tap (from ¥850). Mon–Thurs 11am–11.30pm, Fri & Sat 11am–2am & Sun 11am–11.30pm.

Explosion エクスプロージョン B1 Sanyo Kaikan, 8-23 Doyama-chō ⊛ex-osaka.com; map p.495. This club hosts men only, women only and mixed nights, with drag shows and films. ¥2000 cover charge, with two drinks for Japanese and three drinks for non-Japanese customers. Daily 8pm–4am.

Flanders Tale フランダーステイル B2 2-5-25 Umeda ☎06 6344 5258, ⊛flanders-tale.com; map p.495. Spacious Belgian beer house with a good selection of premium draught and bottled beers. Excellent food

7

selection too, including steamed mussels (¥1350) and "blooms" – onions fried in flower shapes (¥750). Unusually for this area, last order is at 10.30pm. Daily 5–11.30pm.

Frenz フレンズ 1F 8-14 Kamiyama-cho ☎06 6311 1386, ⊛frenz-frenzy.jp; map p.495. The first gay bar in Japan to be run by a non-Japanese, *Frenz* has firmly established itself at the centre of the Kansai gay community. It's a relaxed and friendly place where you can drop by on your own or with friends, especially if you enjoy retro disco music. Sister bar *Frenzy*, which has hosted celebrities such as Lady Gaga, is in the same building but only open at weekends. Daily 8pm–2am.

Joule ジュール 2,3,4F Minami-sumiyamachi Building, 2-11-7 Nishi-Shinsaibashi, chō ☎06 6214 1223, ⊛club-joule.jp; map p.501. This very popular Shinsaibashi club has a fairly mainstream music policy and a laidback atmosphere. There's a third-floor lounge for relaxing in when the dancefloor gets too full. Entrance ¥1500–3000. Daily 8pm–late.

Namba Rockets 難波ロケッツ 2-11-1 Nambanaka ☎06 6649 3919, ⊛namba-rockets.musicstuff-pro.com; map p.501. Alternative club nestling under the railway tracks running south from Namba Station. DJs spin everything from drum 'n' bass to reggae and punk, depending on the night of the week. It's best to phone in advance as it's not open every night. Entrance ¥2500 including one drink. Daily 7pm–late.

★**Umeda Akaso** 梅田アカソ16-3 Doyama-chō ☎06 7897 2450, ⊛www.akaso.jp; map p.495. By local standards, this live music venue is surprisingly large. Akaso regularly hosts well-known domestic and international acts – everything from folk to heavy metal. Depending on who's performing, entrance fees range from free to ¥8500 (including one drink). Daily 5pm–late.

Zerro ゼロ 2-3-2 Shinsaibashi ☎06 6211 0439; map p.501. Popular bar with foreign and Japanese staff, that hosts DJ events on Sat nights. Drinks are rather pricey but there's no extra charge for enjoying the music and dance on weekends. Daily 8pm–late.

SHOPPING

While Umeda, Shinsaibashi and Namba attract hordes of shoppers to their covered **malls**, there are other places in Osaka where window-shopping is just as interesting as picking up a **bargain**. In the Minami area, **Den Den Town** (でんでんタウン), south of Nipponbashi Station, has long been the focus for electronic. Increasingly, this is a handy place to pick up "character goods" for all your favourite manga and anime heroes. If you are keen on Japanese cuisine, **Dōguyasuji** (道具屋筋), just west of Nankai Namba Station, is the place to pick up an interesting souvenir – it's an entire street of kitchen and tableware shops, all stocked full with every kind of pot, pan, dish, knife and chopstick required for Japanese cooking.

Books Kinokuniya 紀伊国屋 1-1-3 Noda ☎06 6372 5821, ⊛kinokuniya.co.jp; map p.495. Located behind the main entrance to Hankyū Umeda Station, this branch of the nationwide chain has a good range of books and magazines in English. Daily 10am–10pm, except the third Wed of the month.

TRADITIONAL PERFORMING ARTS

Traditional performing arts have flourished in Osaka since the Tokugawa Shoguns in the seventeenth century. Full details of **performances** appear in the free monthly *Kansai Scene*, which you can pick up from tourist offices, pubs and large bookstores.

BUNRAKU

Osaka is where **bunraku** puppetry flourished during the seventeenth century and performances are still held weekly at 11am and 4pm at Namba's **National Bunraku Theatre** (国立文楽劇場; ☎06 6212 2531, ⊛ntj.jac.go.jp/english.html) in January, April, June–August and November. Tickets (price depends on performance) sell out quickly, but you can try at the theatre box office, a 3min walk from exit seven of Nipponbashi Station.

KABUKI

The place to catch **kabuki** plays is the handsomely restored **Ōsaka Shōchiku-za Theatre** (大阪松竹座; ☎06 6214 2211, ⊛shochiku.co.jp/play/shochikuza; tickets from ¥4000), a 5min walk north of Namba Station, beside the Dōtombori canal.

NŌ

If you're interested in sampling the more difficult **nō** plays head to the **Ōsaka Nō Hall** (大阪能楽会館; ☎06 6373 1726, ⊛nougaku.wix.com/nougaku; tickets from ¥5500), near Nakazakichō Station on the Tanimachi line, or a short walk east of Hankyū Umeda Station, which often puts on free performances at weekends and on national holidays.

Sakai Ichimonji Mitsuhide 堺一文字光秀 Dōguyasuji ☎06 6633 9353, ⓦ ichimonji.co.jp; map p.5C1. This shop specializes in Sakai knives which are manufactured by veteran craftsmen in southern Osaka. It also stocks a huge range of blades for every type of culinary need. Daily 10am–7pm.

Yodobashi Camera ヨドバシカメラ 1 Ofuka-chō ☎06 4802 1010, ⓦ yodobashi.com; map p.495. Directly across the street from the north exit of Osaka Station, this large electronics emporium has five floors of the latest camera, computer and other electronic equipment – there's an overwhelming range of choice and you can bargain here for a good deal. Daily 9.30am–9pm.

SPORTS

Osakans are mostly huge fans of the Hanshin Tigers baseball team and tend to get very excited when their team wins, often jumping into the Dōtombori canal to celebrate. Things are no less enthusiastic at Sumo bouts, where female fans tend to be the most vocal in cheering on their favourite wrestler.

Sumo Osaka's fifteen-day sumo tournament is held mid-March at Ōsaka Furitsu Taiikukan (ⓦ sumo.or.jp), a 10min walk from exit 5 of Namba Station. Seats for the bouts, which begin at 10am and run through to 6pm, sell out quickly, and you'll need to arrive early to snag one of the standing-room tickets (¥1500), which go on sale each day at 9am.

Baseball The Hanshin Tigers play at the huge Osaka Dome during the professional baseball season, but the highlight of the city's sporting summer is the All-Japan High School Baseball Championship, held at Kōshien Stadium, a 5min walk from Kōshien Station on the Hanshin line. For ticket availability, check first with tourist information at JR Osaka Station (daily 9am–8pm; ☎06 6345 2189).

DIRECTORY

Banks and exchange There are plenty of banks around Umeda, Shinsaibashi and Namba. Major department stores also have foreign exchange desks, as does the Central Post Office, beside JR Osaka Station. The ATM at the Central Post Office is open Mon–Fri 7am–11.30pm, Sat 8am–11.30pm and Sun 8am–9pm.

Consulates Australia, 29F, Twin 21 MID Tower, 2-1-61 Shiromi, Chūō-ku (☎06 6941 9448); China, 3-9-2 Utsubohommachi, Nishi-ku (☎06 6445 9431); Russia, 1-2-2 Nishimidorigaoka, Toyonaka-shi (☎06 5848 3451); South Korea, 2-3-4 Nishi-Shinsaibashi Chūō-ku (☎06 6213 1401); UK, 19F Epson Osaka Building, 3-5-1 Bakuromachi, Chūō-ku (☎06 6120 5600); USA, 2-11-5 Nishitemma, Kita-ku (☎06 6315 5900).

Emergencies The main police station is at 3-1-16 Otemae, Chūō-ku (Mon–Fri 9.15am–5.30pm; ☎06 6943 1234). In an absolute emergency, contact the Foreign Advisory Service on ☎06 773 6533. For other emergency numbers, see p.66.

Hospitals and medical advice Yodogawa Christian Hospital, 2-9-26 Awaji, Higashi-Yodogawa-ku (☎06 6322 2250, ⓦ ych.or.jp/en) or the more central Sumitomo Hospital, 5-2-2 Nakanoshima, Kita-ku (☎06 6443 1261, ⓦ sumitomo-hp.or.jp). Otherwise contact one of the tourist information counters (see p.500).

Immigration Osaka's immigration bureau at 1-29-53 Nankō Kita, Suminoe-ku (☎06 4703 2100).

Internet The Osaka Free Wi-Fi Project (ⓦ osaka-info.jp/en/wifi) provides free access points all over the city including at train stations, hotels, restaurants and sightseeing spots. If you use a PC, there are four branches of Kinko's around the city offering internet access (¥200/10min). The Umeda branch is 5min from the Sakurabashi exit of JR Osaka, opposite the Herbis Plaza. Other branches can be found in Minami-Morimachi, Shinsaibashi, Shin-Osaka and on Sakaisuji-Honmachi.

Lost property The lost and found department for Osaka's buses and subways is at 1-17 Motomachi (☎06 6633 9151).

Post office The Central Post Office (3-2-4 Umeda; ☎06 6347 8097) is immediately southwest of JR Osaka Station and open daily 7am–midnight.

Takarazuka

宝塚

When the Hankyū railway tycoon Kobayashi Ichizō laid a line out to the tiny spa town of **TAKARAZUKA**, 20km northwest of Osaka, in 1911, he had an entertainment vision that extended way beyond soothing onsen dips. By 1924 he'd built the **Takurazuka Grand Theatre** (宝塚大劇場), which has been home ever since to the all-female musical drama troupe the **Takarazuka Revue** (see box, p.506). Almost two million people – mainly women – flock to the town each year to watch the theatre's lavish musical productions, while the Revue itself has become an enduring part of Japanese popular culture, having just celebrated its hundredth anniversary. Takarazuka is also the childhood home of the "God of Manga", **Tezuka Osamu**, and a **memorial museum** here celebrates his life and work. Visitors rarely stay overnight in Takarazuka, since accommodation is expensive and it's perfectly possible to see a performance and visit the museum in a day-trip from Osaka, Kōbe or Kyoto.

Tezuka Osamu Manga Museum

手塚治虫記念館, Tezuka Osamu Kinenkan • 7-65 Mukogawa-chō • Daily except Wed 9.30am–5pm; check in advance for temporary closures • Animation workshops 40min session; 10am–4pm • ¥700 • ☎ 0797 81 2970, ⓦ tezukaosamu.net

The **Tezuka Osamu Manga Museum**, just beyond the Grand Theatre, celebrates the comic-book genius **Tezuka Osamu** (1928–89), creator of *Astro Boy* and *Kimba the White Lion* among many other famous manga and anime series. Tezuka was raised in Takarazuka, and as his mother was a big fan of the Revue, he saw dozens of its performances as a child. This apparently led him to create the romantic tale of the cross-dressing Princess Knight, and the Revue has subsequently adapted manga by Tezuka into its popular productions. This colourful museum charts his career, displays art from his books, comics and animated films, screens cartoons and gives you the chance to become an animator in the workshop.

ARRIVAL AND INFORMATION   TAKARAZUKA

By train The fastest train on the Hankyū Takarazuka line from Osaka's Umeda Station takes less than 30min to reach Takarazuka Station (¥270). There are also direct trains on the JR Fukuchiyama line, taking a few minutes more from JR Osaka Station to JR Takarazuka Station, next to the Hankyū terminus and department store.

Tourist information The town's tourist information office (daily 9am–5pm; ☎ 0797 81 5344) is in front of the second-floor Hankyū Station entrance; you can pick up a map of the town here.

THE WONDERFUL WORLD OF TAKARAZUKA

The **Takarazuka Revue Company** (宝塚歌劇団) has been thrilling audiences with their Broadway-style shows since 1914. The company's founder, **Kobayashi Ichizō**, was impressed by cabaret shows he'd seen in Paris, and sensed that Japanese audiences were ripe for lively Western musical dramas, but he also wanted to preserve something of Japan's traditional theatre. So, as well as performing dance reviews and musicals, Takarazuka also act out **classical Japanese plays** and have developed **shows** from Western literature, including *Gone with the Wind* and *War and Peace*, and Hollywood movies, the most recent adaption being Oceans 11. Even manga has been adapted, with *The Rose of Versailles* still one of Takarazuka's most successful and enduring productions. The dramatizations tend to be heavy on romance, allowing the otoko-yaku (male role) and musume-yaku (daughter or female role) stars to shine on stage as they sing, dance and act out epic love stories.

The Revue has **five troupes** – Hana (flower), Tsuki (moon), Hoshi (star), Yuki (snow) and Sora (cosmos) – with approximately 400 members in total. It is thought that the overwhelmingly female audiences come to see the Revue to escape the frustrations of their daily lives, and that they enjoy seeing the idealized gender performances of the otoko-yaku. Thousands of young girls apply annually to join the troupe at the age of 16, and devote themselves to a punishing routine of classes that will enable them to embody the "modesty, fairness and grace" (the company's motto) expected of a Takarasienne, as Takarazuka members are called.

Takurazuka Grand Theatre (宝塚大劇場) 1-1-57 Sakaemachi ⓦ kageki.hankyu.co.jp/english/index.html. Shows are also staged regularly in Tokyo (see box, p.152), but most fans prefer to see the troupe on their home ground, and perhaps glimpse one of the stars on her way to and from the theatre. There are daily shows (except Wed) at 11am and 3pm, and tickets cost ¥3500–11,000. Reservations should be made up to a month in advance via the ticket office (daily 10am–5pm except for four-day closures between performances; ☎ 0570 00 5100, ⓦ kageki.hankyu.co.jp/ticket; no English spoken, but tourist offices can often check availability on your behalf). Alternatively, tickets can be purchased from Ticket Pia outlets (ⓦ t.pia.jp) or at Lawson convenience stores. The theatre is a 10min walk southeast of the train stations, along the Hana-no-michi, or Flower Road, an elevated platform along an avenue of cherry trees, which is supposed to be like a passage leading onto the stage. At the theatre, there's a vast complex of shops and cafés where you can easily pick up a bentō lunch or sandwiches.

7

Kōya-san

高野山

Ever since the Buddhist monk Kōbō Daishi founded a temple here in the early ninth century, **KŌYA-SAN** has been one of Japan's holiest mountains. The town itself is in a high, cedar-filled valley near the top of the mountain, 800m above sea level, where more than one hundred monasteries cluster round the head temple of the Shingon school of Buddhism, **Kongōbu-ji**. This isolated community is protected by two concentric mountain chains of eight peaks, which are said to resemble an eight-petalled lotus blossom.

Whatever your religious persuasion, there's a highly charged, slightly surreal atmosphere about this group of temples suspended among the clouds. The journey alone, a dramatic ride by train and cable-car, is spectacular, and Kōya-san is also a good place to step out of Japan's hectic city life for a day or two. One of its great delights is to stay in a *shukubō*, or **temple lodging**, and attend a dawn prayer service. Afterwards, head for the **Garan**, the mountains spiritual centre, or wander among the thousands of ancient tombs and memorials which populate the **Okunoin cemetery**, where Kōbō Daishi's mausoleum is honoured with a blaze of ten thousand oil-fuelled brass lanterns.

Kōya-san may be remote but it is not unpopulated. Some six thousand people live in the valley and each year thousands of pilgrims visit the monasteries. In 2004 it became a UNESCO World Heritage Site, which has resulted in an increase in the number of overseas visitors. Life still moves at a fairly slow pace on Kōya-san and the town only recently got its first convenience store. By early evening, the shops are shuttered and the streets almost deserted. Be aware that while the mountain can be pleasantly cool in summer, winter temperatures often fall below freezing.

Brief history

The first monastery on Kōya-san was founded in the early ninth century by the monk Kūkai (774–835), known after his death as **Kōbō Daishi** (see p.510). As a young monk, Kūkai travelled to China to study Esoteric Buddhism for two years. On his return in 806 he established a temple in Hakata (now Fukuoka) before moving to Takao-san

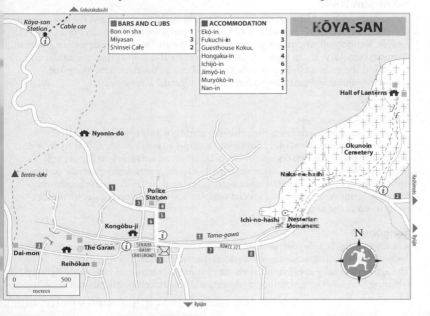

■ BARS AND CLUBS	
Bon on sha	1
Miyasan	3
Shinsei Cafe	2

■ ACCOMMODATION	
Ekō-in	8
Fukuchi-in	3
Guesthouse Kokuu	2
Hongaku-in	4
Ichijō-in	6
Jimyō-in	7
Muryōkō-in	5
Nan-in	1

KŌYA-SAN

KŌYA-SAN FESTIVALS

Kōya-san's biggest **festival** takes place on March 21, when all the monks gather for a service at the **Mie-dō**, which is fully opened to the public, and worshippers make flower and candle offerings. Everyone's out in force again for the **street parade** on Kōbō Daishi's birthday (June 15), while during Obon several thousand lanterns light the route through Okunoin cemetery as part of Japan's **festival for the dead** (Aug 13).

near Kyoto, where his ardent prayers for the peace and prosperity of the nation won him powerful supporters. Kūkai was soon granted permission to found the **Shingon** school which, in a break from contemporary belief, held that enlightenment could be achieved in one lifetime (see box, p.510). But city life was too disruptive for serious meditation, so Kūkai set off round Japan to find a suitable mountain retreat.

According to legend, when Kūkai left China he prayed for guidance on where to establish his monastery. At the same time he flung his three-pronged *vajra* (the ritual implement of Shingon monks) clear across the ocean. Later, as he drew near **Kōya-san**, he met a giant, red-faced hunter, who gave him a two-headed dog. The dog led Kūkai to the top of the mountain where, of course, he found his *vajra* hanging in a pine tree. In any event, the historical records show that Kūkai first came to Kōya-san in 816 and returned in 819 to consecrate the first temple. For a while after 823 he presided over Kyoto's Tō-ji (East Temple; (see p.420), but eventually returned to Kōya-san, where he died in 835. Even without his religious work it seems that Kūkai was a remarkable man (see box, p.510). After his death, Kūkai's disciple **Shinzen** continued developing the monasteries, then collectively known as **Kongōbu-ji**, until there were more than 1500 monasteries and several thousand monks on the mountain top. The sect then had its ups and downs, of which the most serious was during the anti-Buddhist movement following the 1868 Meiji Restoration. Today there are 117 temples atop Kōya-san and it is once again a major centre of pilgrimage.

Kōya-san town

The secular centre of Kōya-san lies at the **Senjuin-bashi** junction, and the town's main sights are located either side of this crossroads: head west for Kōya-san's principal temple, **Kongōbu-ji**, and its religious centre, the **Garan**, or east for the mossy graves of **Okunoin cemetery**. Buses from the cable-car station also stop at the crossroads, and you'll find the tourist office, post office and police station all nearby, alongside restaurants and shops peddling souvenirs and pilgrims' accessories.

Nyonin-dō

女人堂 • Daily 8.30am–5pm • Free

The road into Kōya-san from the cable-car station winds through cool, dark cryptomeria forests for about 2km before passing a small temple called **Nyonin-dō**. This "Women's Hall" marks one of the original seven entrances to the sacred precincts, beyond which women weren't allowed to proceed; the practice continued until 1906 despite an imperial edict against it issued in 1872. In the meantime, female pilgrims worshipped in special temples built beside each gate, of which Nyonin-dō is the last remaining.

Kongōbu-ji

金剛峯寺 • Daily: May–Oct 8.30am–5pm; Nov–April 8.30am–4.30pm • ¥500, or a two-day combination ticket covering the six major sites ¥2000 • ☎ 0736 56 2011, ⌾ koyasan.or.jp • A 3min walk west of the central crossroads

Though it originally applied to the whole mountain community, the name **Kongōbu-ji**, meaning "Temple of the Diamond Mountain", now refers specifically to the Shingon

school's chief monastic and administrative offices. In fact, this temple was a late addition to the complex, founded in 1592 by the ruler Toyotomi Hideyoshi in honour of his mother. It only later became Shingon's headquarters.

Rebuilt in 1861 in the original style, the graceful building is famous largely for its late sixteenth-century **screen paintings** by Kyoto's Kanō school of artists. The best of these are the cranes and pine trees by Kanō Tanyū decorating the Great Hall, and Kanō Tansai's *Willows in Four Seasons* two rooms further along. Beside the temple's front entrance, the **Rokuji-no-kane** (六時の鐘) or "Six O'Clock Bell", cast in 1535, sits on a castle-like foundation; a monk comes out to ring it every even hour (6am–10pm).

The Garan

伽藍 • Daily 8.30am–5pm • Free • ☎ 0736 56 3215, ⓦ koyasan.or.jp • A 5min walk west of the central crossroads

Kōya-san's most sacred precinct, the **Garan** is a large sandy compound, filled with cryptomeria trees, lanterns and wooden halls wreathed in incense. It is the spot where Kōbō Daishi's three-pronged *vajra* landed and where he founded his original monastery (see box below).

Konpon Daitō

根本大塔 • Daily 8.30am–5pm • ¥200

The Garan's most important building is the monumental **Konpon Daitō**, the Fundamental Great Stupa, which is covered in strident, orange lacquer. The original stupa was established in 816, but the current building dates from the 1930s. A statue of the Dainichi Nyorai (Cosmic Buddha) and images of four Buddhist deities are enshrined inside.

Kon-dō

金堂 • Daily 8.30am–5pm • ¥200

South of the Konpon Daitō stupa, the more restrained **Kon-dō**, also rebuilt in the 1930s, marks the spot in the Garan where Kūkai gave his first lectures. Buddhist services are still held here today, and the Asuku Nyorai, or Buddha of Medicine, is enshrined here.

Kūkai reputedly lived where the **Miei-dō** (御影堂) now stands, just to the west, which is regarded as one of the mountain's most holy places. Note the two sacred pines in front which are said to be offspring of the tree in which Kūkai's *vajra* (ritual implements) landed.

KŌBŌ DAISHI

Kōbō Daishi (known during his lifetime as Kūkai) was born in 774 AD in the town of Zentsūji, 30km from Takamatsu on the island of Shikoku. This pious man walked all over Shikoku as an itinerant priest and spent two years in Tang dynasty China studying Esoteric Buddhism, before apparently gaining enlightenment at Muroto Misaki in Kōchi-ken and founding the **Shingon** ("True Word") school of Buddhism. Shingon was influenced by the Tibetan and Central Asian tantric Buddhist traditions and this is reflected in the Shikoku temples, with their exotic decor and atmosphere.

In addition to his significant efforts in the development of **Japanese Buddhism**, Kōbō Daishi is often referred to as the father of Japanese culture; in many ways, he was the Japanese Leonardo da Vinci. He is credited with a phenomenal number of cultural and technological **achievements**: devising the kana syllabary, opening the first public school, inventing pond irrigation, discovering mercury, and compiling the first dictionary. In addition, he was also renowned as a master calligrapher, poet, sculptor and healer.

Kōbō Daishi died on April 22, 835, the exact day he predicted he would. For his achievements, he was posthumously awarded the title Daishi ("Great Saint") by the imperial court. Soon after his death, his disciples began a tour around the temples of Shikoku associated with the Daishi, thus establishing the **pilgrimage** as it is known today (see box, p.613).

Dai-mon

大門

The main road in front of the Garan eventually leads to the **Dai-mon**, or Great Gate, which was Kōya-san's main entrance until the cable-car was built in the 1930s. The huge, rust-red gate sits on the mountain's western edge, where on a clear day you can see right out to sea.

Reihōkan

霊宝館 • Daily 8.30am–4.30pm • ¥600, or two-day combination ticket for all six major sites ¥2000 • ☎ 0736 56 2029, ⓦ reihokan.or.jp

Kōya-san's greatest treasures are in the **Reihōkan**. Though the old buildings don't really do the exhibits justice, this collection includes a number of priceless works of esoteric Buddhist art including Heian-and Kamakura-period wooden sculptures. The displays are changed every few months, but look out for a triptych of Amida welcoming souls to the Western Paradise, painted in 965, and a Heian-era silk painting of Buddha entering nirvana. Unfortunately, due to their fragile nature they are only on display every three years. However there are plenty of other impressive works on display in the museum throughout the year.

Okunoin

奥の院

About 1km east of Kōya-san's central crossroads, **Okunoin** is Kōya-san's vast forest cemetery. Stretching from Ichi-no-hashi to the cemetery's spiritual centre, Kōbō Daishi's mausoleum, a 2km forest path winds through more than 200,000 stone stupas of all shapes and sizes. A large number of historical characters are buried here, among them the great general Oda Nobunaga. You'll also find numerous jizō statues and the occasional war memorial. It's best to walk through Okunoin in the early morning or around dusk, when lamps light up the path; at these times the only other people you're likely to meet are the occasional white-garbed pilgrims with their tinkling bells.

Kōbō Daishi mausoleum

Once across the bridge over the Tama-gawa, the approach to the **mausoleum of Kōbō Daishi** begins. First comes the **Hall of Lanterns**, where ten thousand oil lamps donated by the faithful are kept constantly alight. Two of them are said to have been burning since the eleventh century, one donated by the former Emperor Shirakawa and another by an anonymous poor woman. After this blaze of light and colour, the **tomb** itself is surprisingly restrained. Indeed, it's only just visible within a gated enclosure behind the hall, sheltered by lofty cryptomeria trees and clouds of incense.

According to Shingon tradition, the Great Master, Daishi, did not die in 835 but rather entered "eternal meditation". He's now waiting to return as Miroku, the Future Buddha, when he will help lead the faithful to salvation – which is one reason why so many Japanese wish to have their ashes buried on Kōya-san. Next to the Daishi's tomb you'll see the octagonal ossuary where ashes are collected.

The modern cemetery

Okunoin's **modern cemetery** lies south of the Tama-gawa bridge on a short cut back to the main road. It contrasts sharply with the atmospheric and ancient forested area leading up to Kōbō Daishi's mausoleum. Here, large companies maintain plots for past employees with some unusual memorials – the space rocket and UCC's coffee cup are two that stand out. Also note the "letter boxes" on some monuments for company employees to leave their *meishi* (business cards). The cemetery ends at Naka-no-hashi (中の橋), on the main road beside a clutch of restaurants and a bus park.

ARRIVAL AND DEPARTURE   **KŌYA-SAN**

By train Direct express and super-express trains do the 50km journey south on the private Nankai line from Osaka's Namba Station (every 20–30min; 1hr 15min–1hr 40min; ¥1230; ¥760 limited express train supplement), to

7

A VICTORIAN LADY ON KŌYA-SAN

Elizabeth Anna Gordon was a Victorian aristocrat and religious scholar who not only made an important contribution to the western study of Buddhism but is one of the few foreigners to be buried in Okunoin. Born in 1851, she was a lady-in-waiting to Queen Victoria and an Oxford University graduate with a strong interest in Japan. She was responsible for erecting a replica of the **Nestorian Monument**, a kind of Rosetta Stone of world religions discovered in China in around 1625, on Kōya-san in 1911. For Gordon, the monument was a symbol of the common roots of Buddhism and Christianity. Her activities on the mountain are remarkable for the time – women were banned until 1868, but only really began visiting in the early twentieth century. The monks welcomed this intrepid woman and the monument as a means of promoting Koya-san around the world. Gordon died in a Kyoto hotel in 1925 and her grave is on the right side of the Nestorian monument, close to the Ichi-no-hashi entrance to Okunoin.

Gokurakubashi Station, where they connect with the cable-car to Kōya-san (price included in the ticket); note that reservations are required on the limited express. From Nara and Kyoto you can either travel via Osaka or use the JR network as far as Shin-Imamiya (新今宮) or Hashimoto (橋本) and then change onto the Nankai line.

Destinations Hashimoto (every 20–30min; 45min); Nara (every 15–20min; 3hr); and Osaka (every 20–30min; 1hr 15min–1hr 40min).

By cable-car Most visitors access Kōya-san's mountain-top hideaway via a ropeway (cable-car) which departs every 30min from Gokurakubashi Station (極楽橋駅), arriving at Kōya-san Station 5min later. Nankai trains usually arrive in time for cable-car departures, and the price is included in the train ticket.

By bus At the top cable-car station you'll find buses waiting for the 10min ride into town (every 20–30min; ¥280). If you plan on doing a lot of bus journeys, you can buy a one-day

pass, or *ichi-nichi furii kippu* (¥800) at the cable-car station. All buses stop at the central Senjuin-bashi crossroads (千手院橋), where the routes then divide, with the majority of services running east to Okunoin and fewer heading past Kongōbu-ji to the western gate, Dia-mon. If you are travelling on from Kōya-san to Kumano Kodō, from April 1 to Nov 30 there are buses between Kōya-san and Tanabe (¥4430) at weekends and during peak seasons only. Check the Tourism Bureau website (🌐 tb-kumano.jp/en/transport) for the latest information.

By taxi Taxis also wait outside the cable-car station, or call Kōya-san Taxi (☎ 0736 56 2628).

Koya-san World Heritage Ticket This ticket (¥3310) is valid for two days and covers a return trip from Namba to Kōya-san (limited express train), bus travel from the cable-car station and around the mountain top, and a twenty percent discount on admission to Kongōbu-ji, Kon-dō, Konpon Daitō and Reihōkan.

GETTING AROUND

On foot/by bike Kōya-san's major sights are within walking distance of each other, and it's more pleasant to explore on

foot. Alternatively, you can rent bikes from the Kōya-san Tourist Association office (see below) for ¥400/1hr.

INFORMATION AND TOURS

Tourist information The Kōya-san Tourist Association office (daily 8.30am–5pm; ☎ 0736 56 2616, 🌐 shukubo .jp) is beside the Senjuin-bashi junction. You can book accommodation here, or in advance through their English website. The Kōya-san Visitor Information Center (April–Nov, Mon, Wed & Fri 10am–4pm; ☎ 0736 56 2270, 🌐 koyasan-ccn.com) near Kongōbu-ji also has helpful staff and free internet access. They also offer a free interpreter service if you get stuck (☎ 090 1486 2588, or ☎ 090 3263 5184).

Tours The tourist office offers the Kōya-san Audio Guide (daily 8.30am–4.30pm; ¥500), which has a commentary in

English of Kōya-san's places of interest, corresponding to numbered sixes throughout the town. A better way to learn the stories and the secrets of this sacred site is with the Kōya-san Interpreter Guide Club (☎ 0736 56 2270, 📧 mail@koyasan-ccn.com), whose walking tours include Okunoin, as well as Kongōbuji and the Garan. Reservations must be made at least a day in advance (April–Oct, Wed only; ¥1000 plus transportation). You can also do night tours of Okunoin, which is a great way to soak up the nocturnal spiritual atmosphere with a local English-speaking guide (🌐 okunoin-night-tour.jp): the 1hr tour starts at Eko-in at 7.15pm (¥1500).

ACCOMMODATION

More than fifty monasteries on Kōya-san offer **accommodation** in *shukubō* – temple lodgings run by monks, and occasionally also by nuns (see box, opposite). The rooms are all Japanese-style and usually look out over beautiful gardens or are decorated with painted screens or antique hanging scrolls; most have communal washing facilities. In recent years, some of the temples have upgraded rooms to include private bathing facilities, Western-style toilets, mini-refrigerators, TVs and internet connections. Note that accommodation is very hard to find during Kōya-san's festivals (see box, p.508), so if you plan to visit during any of these, book well in advance.

Ekō-in 惠光院 ☎0736 56 2514, ☯ekoin.jp/en. This friendly temple has simple but comfortable rooms overlooking a garden. There's also a meditation hall for after-dinner sessions, as well as a *goma-taki* fire ceremony at dawn, which anyone can attend. Internet available. **¥10,000**

Fukuchi-in 福智院 ☎0736 56 2021, ☯fukuchiin.com/en. This temple is famous for its modern dry landscape garden by Mirei Shigemori, who controversially used concrete and avant-garde shapes in the design. Even if you're not staying here, it's worth a visit to see the garden. The temple also has Kōya-san's only onsen hot-spring bath. **¥27,300**

★**Guesthouse Kokuu** ゲストハウスコクウ ☎0736 26 7216, ☯koyasanguesthouse.com. This guesthouse is in an impressively designed modern building, and run by an English-speaking young couple. The space's compact (rather than dorms they have capsules) but light and airy. In winter there's a cosy wood stove. Capsules **¥3500**, double **¥9000**

★**Hongaku-in** 本覚院 ☎0736 56 2711, ☯hongakuin.jp. One of the nicest. Temples to stay in Kōya-san, there's a quiet atmosphere here, some interesting Buddhist art and they serve excellent *shōjir-ryōri*. The prayer hall has recently been restored and the morning prayer service is

welcoming and inclusive – listen out for your name. **¥27,300**

Ichijō-in 一乗院 ☎0736 56 2214, ☯itijyoin.or.jp. Elegant and modern lodgings; all rooms have internet connection, TV and some have en-suite facilities. The *shōjin-ryōri* meals here are especially good. **¥30,000**

Jimyō-in 持明院 ☎0736 56 2222, ☯koyasan-jimyoin .com. This peaceful temple is surrounded by a large garden and some of the rooms have nice views. It's not as swish as some of the other temples but the monks are friendly and welcoming. The morning prayer service is at 6.30am. **¥21,000**

Muryōkō-in 無量光院 ☎0736 56 2104, ☯muryokoin .org. This large, rambling temple is known for its international atmosphere – a few of the monks and nuns are foreigners. The rooms are spacious and have the basic comforts. The morning service here, including a fire ceremony (see p.507), is well worth rising at dawn for. **¥20,000**

★**Nan-in** 南院 ☎0736 56 2534, ☯sea.sannet .ne.jp/namikiri-nanin. This stately temple is adjacent to the Tokugawa Mausoleum, northwest of the Senjuin-bashi junction, and has a friendly atmosphere. The rooms are decorated with historic artworks and the bathing facilities are clean and modern. **¥19,000**

EATING AND DRINKING

★**Bon On Sha** 梵恩舎 ☎0736 56 5535. Welcoming café and art gallery run by a young Japanese and French couple, serving organic vegetarian lunch sets (¥1200) as well as delicious cake and coffee sets (¥550). It's east of the Senjuin-bashi intersection. Wed–Sun 9.30am–5.30pm.

Miyasan みやさん ☎0736 56 2827. Just south of Senjuin-bashi this cheap and friendly *izakaya* serves up

fried chicken (¥600). potato salad (¥300) and locally distilled plum wine (¥450). Mon–Sat 4.30–10pm.

Shinsei Café みやさん ☎0736 56 5535. Newly-opened café with Koya-san's first espresso machine, making cappuccino and café latte (¥380). They also serve breakfast sets of toast (¥450) and sandwiches (¥700). 7.30am–7pm, closed Wed.

STAYING IN A SHUKUBŌ

Shukubo are primarily **places of worship**, so you'll be asked to keep to fairly strict meal and bath times, and you shouldn't expect hotel-style service. Guests are usually welcome to attend the early-morning prayers (around 6am). At some temples this also includes a *goma-taki* fire ceremony – the burning of 108 pieces of wood which are said to represent the number of "defilements" that need to be overcome in order to gain enlightenment. All *shukubo* offer excellent vegetarian meals (*shōjin-ryōri*), which consist of seasonal vegetable and tofu-based dishes cooked without meat, fish, onion or garlic seasoning. Due to the number of foreign tourists making the journey to Kōya-san, there is usually someone at the temples who can speak English. It's a good idea to make **reservations** in advance, either through the Kōya-san Tourist Association (see opposite) or by approaching the temples recommended below directly. **Prices** generally start at around ¥9500 per person per night, including two meals.

Kumano Kodō

熊野古道

Set amongst the isolated mountain ranges of the **Kii Hantō** (紀伊半島) peninsula, in southern Wakayama prefecture, southeast of Osaka, is a network of ancient pilgrimage routes known as the **Kumano Kodō**. In 2004, Kumano Kodō, literally the "Kumano ancient road", became a UNESCO World Heritage Site. An area of stunning natural beauty – old-growth forests, charming mountain tea fields, magnificent waterfalls and healing hot springs – it is also the spiritual heartland of Japanese mythology and religion, and unique for its synthesis of Shintōism and Buddhism, in which indigenous Japanese deities were accepted as manifestations of Buddhist deities. This is where the mountain-worshipping Buddhist-Shintō practice of Shugendō evolved and is still active today. The Kumano Kodō is a special place to visit both for its serene natural beauty and its ancient spiritual atmosphere. Despite its remoteness from modern, hi-tech Japan, it is an incredibly friendly place, with good transport and accommodation that caters well to international visitors.

7

Brief history

Though mentioned in the eighth-century *Kojiki* historical record as the "Land of the Dead", where the spirits of the gods reside, Kumano Kodō became popular from the tenth century mainly through Imperial pilgrimages by retired emperors and aristocrats, who made the trek from Kyoto to worship at the **Kumano Sanzan** (熊野三山), a set of three important Grand Shrines of **Kumano Hongū Taisha**, **Kumano Hayatama Taisha** and **Kumano Nachi Taisha**, and to perform rites of purification in the surrounding rivers and waterfalls. The working classes were also attracted to worshipping here, so, by the fourteenth century pilgrims from all over the country had forged routes here from other parts of the county. Unlike Kōya-san, some seventy kilometres away, female pilgrims have always been welcomed in Kumano from its earliest history.

Another reason for the historical popularity and significance of the Kumano Kodō is the number of excellent **hot springs**, many in remote villages, which since ancient times have been known for their healing and restorative powers. The area boasts Japan's only hot spring to be recognized as a UNESCO World Heritage Site – the 1800-year-old **Tsuboyu** at **Yunomine Onsen**.

Kumano Hongū Taisha

熊野本宮大社 • Hongū • Daily 8am–5pm • Free; Treasure Hall ¥300 • ☎ 0735 42 0009, ⊛ hongutaisha.jp • Buses from Tanabe to Hongū stop at the shrine (2hr; ¥2000)

The four pilgrimage routes converge at the stately **Kumano Hongū Taisha**, making it both the geographical and sacred centre of the Kumano Kodō. The most important of the three Grand Shrines of Kumano, it's similar in style to the architecture of Ise-jingū – note the thatched rooves and decorated gables. The shrine was moved to its current, and slightly more elevated, location after a massive flood in 1889 almost completely destroyed it at nearby Oyunohara, a sandbank on the Kumano-gawa, and where a gigantic *torii* now stands. In 2011, the area flooded again when a powerful typhoon ripped through the region, but the shrine was safe from damage this time. Look out for the *yatagarasu* black crow symbol at the shrine – the sacred three-legged bird is believed to be both a heavenly messenger and a supernatural guide. Amongst the many pilgrims who visit the shrine are the Japanese national soccer team, who use the *yatagarasu* symbol as part of their official emblem.

Kumano Hongū Heritage Center

世界遺産熊野本宮館, Sekai Isan Kumano Hongū-kan • Hongū • Daily 9am–5pm • Free • ☎ 0735 42 0751, ⊛ city.tanabe.lg.jp/hongukan/en • Buses from Tanabe to Hongū stop at the Heritage Center (2hr; ¥2000)

Just across the road from the entrance to the Kumano Hongū Taisha, the **Kumano Hongū Heritage Center** is a large modern building where you can learn more about the

THE NAKAHECHI PILGRIMAGE ROUTE

The Kumano Kodō is actually a rubric for the network of four pilgrimage routes: the **Imperial Nakahechi** route, the mountainous **Kohechi** route, the coastal **Ohechi** route and the eastern **Iseji** route. The Kohechi and Iseji routes link up Kumano with Kōya-san and Ise-jingū, respectively. Detailed information on all the routes, as well as suggested itineraries, are available in English (see p.512)

The Nakahechi is the most popular route to the Grand Shrines. Beginning in Tanabe, it traverses the **mountains** eastwards towards Hongū, where it splits into a river route to Shingū and a mountain route to Nachi. The Nakahechi passes through some remote villages but has excellent accommodation facilities for **multi-day walks**. This route has many *oji*, small roadside shrines for worshipping various deities, hence many of the villages are named accordingly. Most pilgrims take a bus from Kii-Tanabe station to Takijiri-oji, a major trailhead, and walk to Chikatsuyu (6–7hr) on the first day, stopping at Takahara Kumano-jinja to see the wonderful vista of clouds and mountains. The second full-day walk leads to Hongū and its onsen. Many pilgrims continue on the trail for another few days, also taking in **Kumano Nachi Taisha** and its amazing waterfall, before arriving at the final destination in Shingū.

It is also possible to use a combination of buses and selected trail walks to experience the Nakahechi route – either way, it takes in some of the most tranquil natural scenes in western Japan, and is a great way to visit the **Kumano Sanzan Grand Shrines**. Remember that this is a mountainous area and the weather can change quickly – be prepared for different temperatures.

7

history of the area. Its informative and multilingual displays provide a deeper understanding of the culture and religion of the Kumano Kodō, and you can also see photos and models of the shrine before the 1889 flood. In the more recent 2011 flood, the Heritage Center was almost washed away and has since been fully restored.

Nachi-Katsuura

Nachi-Katsuura marks the confluence of the Nakahechi and Ohechi pilgrimage routes. The sacred mountain of **Nachisan**, with its Grand Shrine and ancient Buddhist temple, is just a few kilometres inland from the fishing port of **Katsuura**, famous for its tuna industry and hot springs.

Kumano Nachi Taisha and Seiganto-ji

熊野那智大社 and 青岸渡寺 • Nachisan • **Kumano Nachi Taisha** daily 8.30am–4.30pm • Free • ☎ 0735 55 0321, ⓦ www .kumanonachitaisha.or.jp • **Seiganto-ji** daily 8.30am–4pm • Free • ☎ 0735 55 0401 • Take a bus from JR Kii-Katsuura Station (25min; ¥600)

Just outside the town of Katsuura is the Grand Shrine of **Kumano Nachi Taisha** and the adjacent Buddhist temple of **Seiganto-ji**. Perched on the side of Nachisan mountain, they are fine examples of the interconnectivity of Shintō and Buddhist faiths in the Kumano region, given that they have been situated next to each other for centuries and attract large numbers of pilgrims, especially from the western pilgrimage routes.

Nachi-no-Ōtaki

那智の大滝 • Nachisan • Daily 7am–5pm • Free; viewing platform ¥300 • ☎ 0735 55 0321 • Take a bus from JR Kii-Katsuura Station (25min; ¥600)

Nachi-no-Ōtaki is said to be the tallest waterfall in Japan. The water comes pounding out of a primeval forest and spectacularly drops 133m into the valley. The nearby Kumano Nachi Taisha shrine is dedicated to the god of the waterfall and it's also an important place of nature worship for Shugendō followers. If you don't have time to trek down to the waterfall, you can still enjoy the superb view from Seiganto-ji.

Daimonzaka-chaya

大門坂茶屋 • Nachisan • Daily 9am–4pm • Reservations necessary during high season • ☎ 0735 55 024-, ⓦ nachikan.jp • Take a bus from JR Kii-Katsuura Station (25min; ¥600)

If you've wondered what it felt like to walk the Kumano Kodō in Heian times, the

7

Daimonzaka-chaya costume rental shop is a great place to find out. Here, you can dress up in a ninth-century-style kimono, *zori* shoes and veiled headwear (¥2000/1hr; ¥3000/2hr), and walk a little on Daimon-zaka – a cobblestone staircase set amongst towering ancient trees that's part of the pilgrimage route up to Kumano Nachi Taisha and Seiganto-ji. Female and male costumes are available, as well as children's.

ARRIVAL AND INFORMATION

By train The main access point for the Kumano Kodō is the city of Tanabe (田辺); its JR station is Kii-Tanabe (紀伊田辺). Express train services run here from Kyoto and Osaka. From eastern Japan, trains from Nagoya go to Shingū (新宮). Otherwise, you can get a train from Kōya-san, changing at Hashimoto for services towards Wakayama city and Tanabe.

By bus JR Nishi-Nihon and Meiko buses run from Osaka to Tanabe (10 daily; ¥2600) and from Kyoto to Tanabe (2 daily; ¥3200). From April to Nov, buses run between Kōya-san and Tanabe (¥4430) at weekends and during peak seasons only. Check the Tourism Bureau website (ⓦ tb-kumano.jp/en/transport) for the latest information.

Tourist information The newly built Tanabe Tourist Information Center (daily 9am–6pm; ☎ 0739 26 9025, ⓦ tb-kumano.jp/en) next to JR Kii-Tanabe Station is an excellent place to pick up English-language pamphlets and maps of the ancient routes. Their website is also the best source for up-to-date information on the Kumano Kodō, translated into English, including transport timetables and an accommodation reservation system. There are also visitor information centres at Takijiri-oji, the spiritual entrance to the sacred Kumano mountains, and also at the Kumano Hongū Heritage Center, near Kumano Hongū Taisha (see p.514).

GETTING AROUND

By bus Pilgrims are usually intent on walking the Kumano Kodō, but there is also a good network of fairly regular bus services, depending on the season, which connect the main sights of the pilgrim routes and the surrounding areas; see the Tourism Bureau website (ⓦ tb-kumano.jp/en/transport) for route details and timetables.

By bike Bike rental is available at Kii-Tanabe Station (9am–6pm; ¥500/1 day) and also from the Kumano Hongū Heritage Center (100 Hongū; 8.30am–5pm; ¥1500/day).

ACCOMMODATION

Along the Kumano Kodō there is a range of good-quality accommodation options for all budgets. Many ryokan or minshuku have their own onsen, or are close to one, and most places can provide dinner and breakfast, as well as a boxed lunch to take on the trail the next day. All the accommodation listed below can be booked through the Kumano Tourism Bureau reservation system (ⓦ kumano-travel.com).

KUMANO'S ONSEN

The Kumano region is blessed with some of western Japan's best **onsen** towns, which can be easily visited while walking the Kumano Kodō.

Yunomine Onsen 湯の峰温泉 near Hongū. In this 1800-year-old onsen (daily 6am–9.30pm; ¥750) town, the main attraction is Tsuboyu (つぼ湯) – the only hot spring in Japan to be registered as a UNESCO World Heritage Site. A small cloudy-coloured spring, built out of the narrow stream that runs through the town, Tsuboyu is covered by a wooden cabin that you can use privately for thirty minutes.

Kawayu Onsen 川湯温泉 near Hongū. In winter, the river here is transformed into a piping-hot giant outdoor bath called the Sennin-buro (仙人風呂), literally a bath for one thousand people (6.30am–10pm; free). Given it's very public, outdoor location it's one of the few hot springs where

swimwear is acceptable. It's also fine to dig your own spring in the river.

Wataze Onsen 渡瀬温泉 near Hongū. The main claim to fame of this onsen town is having the largest rotemburo (outdoor bath) in western Japan (6am–9.30pm; ¥700). It may not be as historic as the other two onsen in Hongū, but its garden setting is just as picturesque.

Ryūjin Onsen 龍神温泉. Slightly outside Hongū, in a remote mountain area, Ryūjin Onsen is worth considering for a visit if you are travelling from Kōya-san towards Hongū. Its waters are well known for their beautifying effects on the skin, and the views from the outdoor baths in spring and autumn are sublime.

TANABE

Altier アルティエホテル Tanabe ☎0739 81 1111, ⓦaltierhotel.com. If you are starting your journey in Tanabe, this comfortable business hotel near the station, with free breakfast and internet, is a good choice. **¥13,000**

★**Konyamachiya Townhouse** 紺屋町家 Tanabe ☎0739 26 9025, ⓦkumano-travel.com. This nicely restored townhouse in Tanabe city sleeps up to six guests, and it's a lovely place to experience living in a traditional Japanese house. It's fully equipped for self-catering and also has a washing machine. Check-in is at the Kishifuan-En souvenir shop at Kii-Tanabe Station. **¥10,800**

THE NAKAHECHI ROUTE

Kiri no Sato Takahara 霧の郷たかはら Takahara ☎0739 64 1900, ⓦkirinosato-takahara.com. Friendly mountain lodge in Takahara village on the Nakahechi route. The comfortable Japanese and Western-style rooms (with toilets) have stunning views looking directly out over the valley. Bathing facilities are shared. **¥22,736**

Minshuku Chikatsuyu 民宿ちかつゆ Chikatsuyu ☎0739 65 0617. This minshuku on the Nakahechi route has comfortable private and shared tatami rooms, as well as its own orsen with water as smooth as silk. Rates include breakfast and dinner. **¥18,800**

HONGŪ AND AROUND

Blue Sky Guesthouse 蒼空げすとはうす Hongū ☎0735 42 0800, ⓦkumano-guesthouse.com. A spacious modern building in a pleasant natural setting, this guesthouse has tatami rooms and excellent facilities. There's a friendly and international atmosphere. **¥12,000**

Minshuku Ōmuraya 民宿大村屋 Kawayu Onsen ☎0735 42 1066, ⓦoomuraya.net At Kawayu Onsen, near Hongū, this family-run inn is steps away from the Sennin-buro river bath, and offers a delicious evening meal, as well as a hearty breakfast and gourmet boxed lunch the next day. The clean and spacious tatami rooms all have their own WC. **¥21,000**

Kamigoten Ryokan 上御殿 Ryūjin Onsen ☎0739 79 0005, ⓦkamigoten.jp. High-class ryokan at Ryūjin Onsen in an exquisite Edo-period building, serving multi course dinners of hearty mountain cuisine. The onsen facilities are modern, with superb river valley views. **¥31,800**

Yoshinoya よしのや Yunomine ☎0735 42 0101, ⓦyunomine.com. This friendly inn right on the narrow stream near the ancient Tsuboyu, has clean and comfortable rooms, as well as its own pleasant outdoor bath. It also serves delicious local cuisine. **¥11,500**

NACHI-KATSUURA

Hotel Nakanoshima ホテル中の島 Nachi-Katsuura ☎0735 52 1111, ⓦhotel-nakanoshima.jp. Situated on an island a few minutes by boat from Katsuura port, this large hotel is like the set of a James Bond movie – there are internal tunnels, lookout points and hot-spring baths close to the ocean with wonderful views. **¥24,000**

EATING

TANABE

★**Kanteki** かんてき Tanabe ☎0739 26 1031. Friendly, and sometimes raucous, *izakaya* in the Ajikokoji area near the station with a fantastic menu of local fish and seafood dishes and *ume-shu* (plum wine). For around ¥3000 you can feast like a king. 5pm–11pm, closed Wed.

★**Shinbe** しんべ Tanabe ☎0739 24 8845, ⓦjpcenter .co.jp/shinbe. *Shinbe* serves delicious sashimi, sushi and fish dishes at very reasonable prices – top-quality sashimi platters are just ¥1800. The cheery chef will happily make recommendations from the menu for the best of the season. Mon–Sat 5pm–10.30pm.

THE NAKAHECHI ROUTE

Bocu 朴 Chikatsuyu ☎0739 65 0694. Macrobiotic restaurant and bakery in a charming old farmhouse on the Nakahechi route. Delicious lunch sets, made with vegetables grown in the neighbouring field, are ¥1500. Wed–Sat 10am–4pm.

HONGŪ

Sangenjaya 三軒茶屋 Hongu ☎0735 43 0513, ⓦsangendyaya.com At this small shop next to the Post Office, you can buy takeaway lunch packs of 5 fresh pieces of *mehari-zushi* for ¥600. Tues–Sun 11am–2pm & 5–8pm.

NACHI-KATSUURA

★**Bodai** 母大 Nachi-Katsuura ☎0735 52 0039. Stylish restaurant directly opposite Kii-Katsuura Station serving super-fresh maguro tuna dishes. The *maguro chūtoro katsu teishoku* lunch set (¥1500), with tuna pieces delicately fried in breadcrumbs, is highly recommended. 11am–2pm & 5–11pm, closed Tues.

Shima Hantō

志摩半島

East of the Kii Hantō mountain ranges, on the far side of the Kii Peninsula, a small knuckle of land sticks out into the ocean. Known as **Shima Hantō**, this peninsula has been designated a national park, partly for its natural beauty but also because it contains Japan's spiritual heartland, **Ise-jingū**. Since the fourth century the Grand Shrine of Ise, on the edge of **Ise** town, has been venerated as the terrestrial home of the Sun Goddess Amaterasu, from whom it was once believed all Japanese emperors were descended. Beyond Ise it's **pearl** country. The world-famous Mikimoto company started up in **Toba** when an enterprising restaurant owner discovered the art of cultivating pearls, and now there's a whole island dedicated to his memory, **Mikimoto Pearl Island**. Today, most of the pearls are raised further east in **Ago-wan**, where hundreds of rafts are tethered in a beautiful, island-speckled bay. The **Ama women divers** of the peninsula have been diving for seafood, and pearls, for centuries and it's possible to meet them at **Osatsu** and hear their stories of the sea.

Ise

伊勢

The town of **ISE** wears its sanctity lightly, and many visitors find the town a disappointingly ordinary place. However, the main reason to come here is to visit the two sanctuaries of **Ise-jingū**, Japan's most sacred Shintō shrine, and even non-Japanese visitors will appreciate the spiritual atmosphere here. Apart from their historical importance, there is a sense of awe and mystery about these simple buildings, with their unusual architecture, deep in the cedar forests.

Ise-jingū

伊勢神宮 · ☎ 0596 24 1111, ⓦ isejingu.or.jp

The two sacred sanctuaries of **Ise-jingū** are in separate locations in the town of Ise. The **Naikū**, or inner shrine, is some 6km to the southeast of town – you'll need to take a bus (see p.520) – while the southwestern quarter of Ise is taken up by a large expanse of woodland (which accounts for a full third of the town's area), in the midst of which lies the **Gekū**, or outer shrine. The two shrines follow roughly the same layout, so if you're pushed for time, head straight for the more interesting Naikū.

Naikū

内宮 · 1 Ujitachi-chō · Sunrise to sunset · Free · Take bus #51 or #55 from JR Ise-shi Station, Kintetsu Uji-Yamada Station, or from the stop outside the Gekū (every 10–15min; ¥410)

The **Naikū**, Ise-jingū's inner shrine, is Japan's most sacred shrine and was established sometime in the fourth century. Dedicated to **Amaterasu Ōmikami**, the ancestress of the imperial family, the shine houses a **mirror** that Amaterasu gave her grandson Ninigi-no-Mikoto when she sent him to rule Japan. At first the mirror was stored in the Imperial Palace, along with the sacred sword and beads (these are now held in Nagoya's Atsuta-jingū and Tokyo's Imperial Palace), but the goddess gave instructions to move her mirror to somewhere more remote. Eventually they settled on a wooded spot beside Ise's Isuzu-gawa, which has been the mirror's home ever since.

After crossing the Uji-bashi, turn right and walk through a small, formal garden to reach the purification fountain just in front of the first sacred *torii*. A little further on, the path goes down to the river where, traditionally, pilgrims would purify themselves. The path loops round to approach the **inner sanctum** from the south. The main building is contained within four increasingly sacred enclosures, with the inner sanctum the furthest from view, making it difficult to see the details. Nevertheless, the architecture's pure, strong lines hold the same mystical power. Only members of the imperial family and head priests can enter the inner sanctuary where Amaterasu's **sacred mirror** is enshrined. It's wrapped in layers of cloth and, according to the records, no one has laid eyes on it for more than a thousand years.

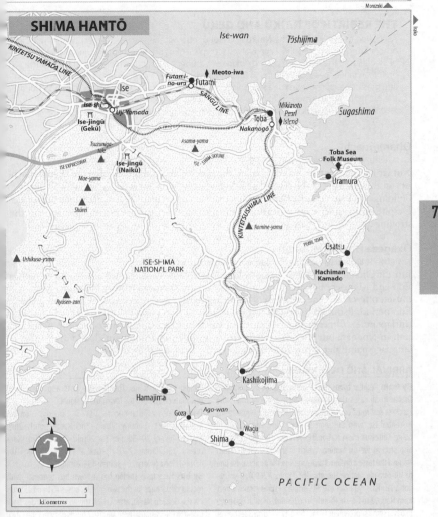

Gekū

外宮 • Toyokawa-machi • Sunrise to sunset • Free • A 15–20min walk from from JR Ise-shi and Kintetsu Uji-Yamada stations, or buses #55 or #51 from the Naikū (every 10–15min; ¥410) drop you at the bus stop on the main road opposite the Gekū's main entrance

The **Gekū**, or outer shrine, is located close to the southern edge of the modern business district of Ise city, and is much smaller, with fewer crowds, than Naikū. Its entrance lies over a small humped bridge and along a gravel path leading into the woods. It was constructed in the fifth century to honour the goddess **Toyouke-no-Ōmikami**, who was sent by Amaterasu to look after the all-important rice harvests. Another of her duties is to provide Amaterasu with sacred food, so twice a day priests make offerings to Toyouke in a small hall at the back of the compound. Having paid their respects to Toyouke by bowing deeply twice, clapping and bowing deeply a third time, most people hurry off to visit the Naikū.

THE REBIRTH OF NAIKŪ AND GEKŪ

According to custom, both the **Naikū** and **Gekū** (outer shrine) are rebuilt every twenty years in order to re-purify the ground. Each is an exact replica of its predecessor, following a unique style of architecture that has been passed down over the centuries and is free of any of the Chinese or Korean influences usually found in Buddhist architecture. Only plain *hinoki* (Japanese cypress) and grass thatch are used, plus a few gold embellishments. When the buildings are dismantled, the old timbers are passed on to other shrines around the country to be recycled. The most recent rebuilding was completed in 2013, and the next one will be in 2033.

Oharai-machi

おはらい町 • 48 Ujinakanokiri-chō • ☎ 0596 28 3705

Not far from the entrance to the Naikū, the pedestrianized shopping street of **Oharai-machi** sits on the exact site of the town's late Edo-and early Meiji-era merchants' quarter. The buildings here are reproductions of those that existed in that time, but they look authentic. Despite being rather touristy, it's one of the nicest streetscapes in western Japan and worth strolling around, and there are also some decent places to eat local cusine (see opposite).

Okageza History Museum

おかげ座 • 52 Ujinakanokiri-chō • Daily 9am–4.30pm • ¥300 • ☎ 0596 23 8844

Just off Oharai-machi, the Okage-Yokochō (おかげ横町) square is home to more replica Edo and Meiji-era buildings, including the quaint **Okageza History Museum**. The museum re-creates the encounters between pilgrims and the people of Ise during the Edo period, using scale models and recordings of Edo-period stories and street sounds (in Japanese). On entering the museum, you'll be given a short introduction by the staff in Japanese but after that you're free to wander un accompained, and an English-language pamphlet is provided that adequately explains the exhibits.

ARRIVAL AND DEPARTURE   ISE

By train Regular trains run to Ise from Nagoya, Kyoto and Osaka: in all cases the private Kintetsu network offers the quickest and most convenient service. There are two stations in central Ise, with the more easterly, Uji-Yamada Station, being Kintetsu's main station. However, some Kintetsu trains also stop at Ise-shi Station, which is shared with JR. From Nagoya the fastest option is an express on the Kintetsu-Ise line to Uji-Yamada Station (hourly; 1hr 25min; ¥2690). If you've got a JR Pass, you can use JR's limited express trains direct from Nagoya to Ise-shi (hourly; 1hr 30min), though you have to pay a small supplement (¥440) for travelling on a section of Kintetsu track. Kintetsu also runs direct trains from Osaka's Namba and Tsuruhashi stations (every 15min; 1hr 45min; ¥3030) and from Kyoto (hourly; 2hr; ¥3520). If you are spending a few days in the area, note that the ¥3800 three-day or ¥5700 five-day Kintetsu Rail Pass covers the whole of the extensive Kintetsu network, including three rides on limited express trains. The five-day pass also gives good discounts on entry to the town's major sights.

Destinations Futaminoura (1–3 hourly; 6min); Kashikojima (1–3 hourly; 50min–1hr); Kyoto (hourly; 2hr); Nagoya (every 20–30min; 1hr 20min–1hr 35min); Nara (every 15–20min; 2–3hr); Osaka (every 15min; 1hr 45min); Toba (every 20–30min; 15–20min).

By bus Each train station has its own bus terminal, with regular departures for the two shrines; buses #51 and #55 run via the Gekū to Naikū, after which the #51 route circles back round to the stations. There are also 7 buses daily to Toba (1hr).

By car Car rental is available through Kinki Nippon Rent-a-Car (☎ 0596 28 0295), at Uji-Yamada Station, and Eki Rent-a-Car (☎ 0596 25 5019), at Ise-shi Station.

By bike Bike rental is available at Ise-shi Station (9am–5pm; ¥1030 per day) and from the *Hoshidekan* (see below) for ¥300 per day.

INFORMATION AND TOURS

Tourist information Ise's main tourist information office (daily 8.30am–5pm; ☎ 0596 23 3323, ⓦ ise-kanko .jp/english) is located opposite the entrance to the Gekū, with a smaller office opposite the bus stop at the Naikū (daily 8.30am–4.30pm; ☎ 0596 24 3501). At Uji-Yamada Station there is a helpful office with English-speaking staff (daily 9am–5.30pm; ☎ 0596 23 9655), who can help arrange accommodation throughout the Shima Hantō area.

Tours Tours of both Ise-jingu sanctuaries with English-speaking guides can be arranged in advance through the local volunteer guide organization (ⓔ kk_sta@kanko-pro.co.jp).

Services Ise's main shopping area lies south of Ise-shi

Station. For foreign exchange, try the Daisan Bank opposite the JR Station or walk down the pleasant, lantern-lined street leading from the station to the Gekū, where you'll find the Bank of Tokyo-Mitsubishi UFJ.

ACCOMMODATION

Hoshidekan 星出館 2-15-2 Kawasaki ☎ 0596 28 2377, ⓦ www.hosh dekan.jp. This eccentric, rambly old ryokan has tatami rooms centred around a garden, all with shared bath and toilet facilities. They serve macrobiotic food in their restaurant for breakfast and dinner. **¥14,000**

Ise City Hotel 伊勢シティホテル 1-11-31 Fukiage ☎ 0596 28 2111, ⓦ greens.co.jp. Fairly bland business hotel with English-speaking staff, rather small rooms and an in-house steak restaurant. They have a slightly more expensive annexe just along the road towards the Kawasaki district. **¥11,230**

★ **Ise Guesthouse Kazami** 風見荘 1-6-36 Fukiage ☎ 0596 64 8565, ⓦ ise-guesthouse.com. Newly opened backpacker hostel in a former ryokan with clean and comfortable rooms. Run by a punk rocker, it's a friendly, vibrant place with occasional live music performances. There's free wi-fi and unlimited tea and coffee, too. Dorm **¥2600**, double **¥6000**

Town Hotel Ise タウンホテル伊勢 1-8-18 Fukiage ☎ 0596 23 4621. Small and reasonably priced business hotel right next to the train tracks. The rooms are functional and, thankfully, double-glazed. There's no in-house restaurant or food available here so you'll definitely have to eat out. **¥9450**

EATING

Ise's **speciality foods** include lobster (*Ise-ebi*) and the rather salty *Ise udon*, which consists of thick, handmade noodles served in a thin soy sauce. Matsuzaka beef, marbled and fatty like its Kōbe cousin, is another local favourite. Oharai-machi near the Naikū is a better, and more interesting, choice for lunch than the Gekū area.

Akafuku 赤福本店 26 Uji-nakanokiri-chō ☎ 0596 22 7000, ⓦ akafuku.co.jp. A 300-year-old sweet shop near the Shinbashi bridge that serves the local speciality – *akafuku mochi*, deliciously fresh pounded rice cakes covered with red bean paste (¥280 for three pieces including tea, or ¥530 with matcha). Daily 9am–5pm.

★ **Daiki** 大喜 2-1-48 Iwabuchi ☎ 0596 28 0281, ⓦ ise .ne.jp/daiki. Touted as "Japan's most famous restaurant", *Daiki* has made its name catering to the imperial family. It's located in a traditional building near Uji-Yamada Station that has recently been renovated, and serves great bentō lunch sets (¥1000), while their *kaiseki* and *Ise-ebi* sets (both from ¥5000), are also excellent value. Daily 9am–10pm.

Okadaya 岡田屋 31 Ujimazaike-chō ☎ 0596 22 4554. Very popular *Ise udon* restaurant in the main part of Oharai-machi. Their lunch sets (¥1250) are good value. Arrive early to avoid the long queues. 10.30am–5pm, closed Thurs.

Toramaru 虎丸 2-13-6 Kawasaki ☎ 0596 22 9298. Friendly, non-smoking *izakaya* in a restored *kura* (warehouse) in the Kawasaki merchant area, serving sashimi (¥1100–1680) lotus root tempura (¥580) and deep-fried oysters (from ¥780). 5–10pm, closed Thurs and irregularly.

Yamaguchi-ya 山口屋 1-1-18 Miyajiri ☎ 0596 28 3856, ⓦ iseudon.jp. Very friendly *Ise udon* restaurant down a shopping street across from the JR station, serving excellent, tasty udon noodles (¥500). They also offer soba (¥550) and tempura (¥800). 10am–7pm, closed Thurs.

Toba

鳥羽

East of Ise, the ragged Shima Peninsula juts out into the Pacific Ocean. Most of this mountainous area belongs to the Ise-Shima National Park, whose largest settlement is the port of **TOBA**, home to the birthplace of cultured pearls, the famous **Mikimoto Pearl Island**. Although it's sited on an attractive bay, Toba's seafront is mostly a strip of car parks, ferry terminals and shopping arcades, behind which run the main road and train tracks. However, there are a number of interesting museums, a decent **aquarium** and an abundance of excellent seafood restaurants.

ISE-JINGŪ EVENTS AND CEREMONIES

Ise-jingū is a top choice for the **first shrine visit** of the New Year (*hatsu-mōde*) on January 1. This is followed by more than 1500 annual **ceremonies** in honour of Ise's gods. The most important of these revolve around the agricultural cycle, culminating in offerings of sacred rice (Oct 15–17). In spring (April 5–6) and during the autumn equinox (Sept 22 or 23), ancient Shintō dances and a moon-viewing party take place at the inner shrine.

Mikimoto Pearl Island

ミキモト真珠島, Mikimoto Shinju-Shima • Daily: April–Oct 8.30am–5.30pm; Nov–March 9am–4.30pm • ¥1500 • ☏ 0599 25 2028 • A 5min walk south of Toba's train and bus stations

In 1893, **Mikimoto Kokichi** (1858–1954), the son of a Toba noodle-maker, produced the world's first cultivated pearl using tools developed by a dentist friend. Just six years later he opened his first shop in Tokyo's fashionable Ginza shopping district, from where the Mikimoto empire spread worldwide. His life's work is commemorated – and minutely detailed – on **Mikimoto Pearl Island**, a complex of shops, restaurants and exhibition rooms, that is connected to the mainland by a short bridge. Devoted to the history and cultivation of pearls, the exhibitions are extremely well put together, with masses of information in English describing the whole process from seeding the oyster to grading and stringing the pearls. There's also a section devoted to Mikimoto's extraordinary pearl artworks and jewellery collection. The highlight of the visit are the **ama women divers** (see box opposite) who stoically come out every hour in all weathers to demonstrate their diving skills.

Toba Aquarium

鳥羽水族館, Toba Suizokukan • 3-3-6 Toba • Daily: April–Oct 9am–5pm; Nov–March 9am–4.30pm • ¥2400 • ☏ 0599, ⓦ aquarium.co.jp

Right on Toba seafront, next to Mikimoto Pearl Island, the **Toba Aquarium** is one of only two places in the world where you can see a captive dugong. This large aquarium is divided into twelve zones and has finless porpoises and sea otters on display, as well as sea lion and walrus shows.

Meito-iwa

夫婦岩, Umi no Hakubutsukan • 575 Futami-chō • Daily dawn to dusk • ¥2400 • ☏ 0596 43 2020 • 15min walk northeast of JR Futami-no-ura Station

Between Ise and Toba, the coastal town of Futami (二見) is famous for its "wedded rocks", **Meoto-iwa**. Joined by a hefty, sacred rope, this pair of "male" and "female" rocks lies just offshore from the Okitama shrine. They're revered as representations of Izanagi and Izanami, the two gods who created Japan, and it's the done thing to see the sun rise between them – the best season to do this is from May to August. On a clear day, you can also see Mount Fuji in the distance from above the rocks.

Toba Sea Folk Museum

海の博物館 • Uramura-chō • Daily: mid-March–Nov 9am–5pm; Dec to mid-March 9am–4.30pm • ¥800 • ☏ 0599 32 6006, ⓦ umihaku.com • The museum is on the Pearl Road driveway; take the Kamome bus for Ijika (石鏡) from the bus terminal in front of Toba Station, and get off at the Umi-hakubutsukan-mae (海博物館前) bus stop, from where it's a 7min walk down the hill

The excellent **Toba Sea Folk Museum**, located 10km south of Toba in Uramura, is housed in an award-winning wooden building overlooking the ocean. The museum, both inside and out, has been constructed to resemble the upturned hull of a wooden fishing boat. It has some informative 3-D exhibits on the historical relationship between the people of Toba and the sea, as well as a short film and some comprehensive displays providing more historical background on the *ama* women divers (see opposite).

ARRIVAL AND DEPARTURE — TOBA

By train Kintetsu (¥290) and JR (¥230) trains both run east from Ise to Toba. JR services are less frequent and terminate at Toba, while the Kintetsu line continues south to Kashikojima, for Ago-Wan. Toba's JR and Kintetsu stations and the bus terminal are all located next door to each other in the centre of town.

Destinations Kashikojima (every 30min; 30–40min); Kyoto (hourly; 2hr 20min); Nagoya (every 20–30min; 1hr 45min); Osaka (every 20–30min; 2hr).

By bus From Ise, the best option is the "Canbus" bus service (Mon–Fri hourly, Sat & Sun every 30min), which departs from Uji-Yamada Station and stops at all the major sights and train stations between Ise and Toba, including the inner and outer shrines, and Mikimoto Pearl Island. One-day (¥1000) and two-day (¥1600) passes for the "Canbus" can be bought at major train stations, the Geku tourist information office, Mikimoto Pearl Island and on the bus; both passes come with a book of coupons offering further discounts to attractions.

By ferry Isewan Ferry (☏ 0599 25 2880, ⓦ isewanferry .co.jp) connects Toba with Irago, on the other side of Ise Bay in Aichi Prefecture (¥1500; 8 daily; 50min).

INFORMATION AND TOURS

Tourist information There's a very helpful tourist information office with English-speaking staff (daily 9am–5pm; ☎0599 25 2844 in the Kintetsu station. The entire station area is also a free wi-fi zone: tourist office staff can give you the password.

Tours The Kaito Yumin Club (☎0599 25 2844, ⓦoz-group.jp/english) is run by a friendly all-female crew who lead eco-tours in and around the Toba area. They offer lunch trips to fishing villages by boat (¥3300), kayaking day-trips (¥6500) and snorkelling tours (¥4200), as well as night-walking tours of Toba (¥4500). Their office is next to the *Kaigetsu Inn*, a 3min walk from Toba Station.

ACCOMMODATION

Kaigetsu Inn 海月 1-10-52 Toba ☎0599 26 2056, ⓦkaigetsu.co.jp. This friendly ryokan serves excellent gourmet meals and is the best place to stay in Toba in terms of convenience and value for money. The tatami rooms are spacious and comfortable. Rates include breakfast and dinner. **¥23,000**

Road Inn Toba ロードイン鳥羽 1-63-11 Toba ☎0599 26 5678, ⓦgreens.co.jp/toba. This standard business hotel is located on a hill behind the station. The rooms are basic but clean. It has free internet, and the sauna and swimming pool next door can be used by guests. **¥9270**

Toba International Hotel 鳥羽国際ホテル 1-23-1 Toba ☎0599 25 3121, ⓦtobahotel.co.jp. Pricey resort-style hotel in a fine position on the headland overlooking Toba Bay. Rooms are well appointed with marvellous views and the in-house restaurant serves French cuisine. It takes about 10min to walk from the station. **¥40,200**

EATING

Tenbinya Honten てんびん屋本店 1-4-61 Toba ☎0599 25 2223. Located in the streets just inland from Mikimoto Pearl Island, *Tenbinya* makes a great choice for a very reasonably priced *kaiseki* seafood dinner that can cost as little as ¥3150. There's also a branch in the Ichibangai building opposite Toba Station. Tues–Sun 11.30am–2pm & 5–10.30pm.

Kippei 吉平 Ichibangai building, opposite Toba station ☎0599 26 2085. This small noodle restaurant does a hearty bowl of *asari* (shellfish) *soba* for ¥850, and also serves the local speciality *Ise udon* (¥700). Daily 10am–5pm.

Nagatokan 長門館 1-10-45 Toba ☎0599 25 2006, ⓦnagatokan.co.jp. Popular seafood restaurant with slightly more expensive but hearty lunch (from ¥1680) and dinner (from ¥3150) set meals. They specialize in *awabi* (abalone) and *Ise-ebi* lobster dishes. 11am–7pm, closed Tues.

Grand Blue グランブルー Ichibangai building, opposite Toba station ☎0599 26 3129. Café specializing in "Tobarger" (Toba burgers), which are made with lobster, octopus and other seafood patties (¥600). It's also a pleasant place to sit and look out onto the harbour. Daily 10am–5pm.

Ōsatsu

鳥羽

The coastal village of **ŌSATSU** is home to one of Japan's largest communities of **ama women divers**, with more than 150 women still practising this 2000-year old tradition. Ōsatsu is one of the few places that you can meet the women in their amagoya huts where they grill freshly-caught seafood and are happy to chat with visitors.

THE AMA WOMEN DIVERS

The female diving culture of Ise-shima dates back to the earliest annals of Japanese history. Known as *ama* (海女, literally "sea woman"), the women **free-dive** for shellfish, such as oysters and abalone, as well as harvesting seaweed. On average they'll spend three to four hours a day in the water, going down to a depth of 10–15m without any breathing apparatus, and some are still diving past the age of 70. *Ama* usually dive year-round either in small groups, or from boats skippered by their husbands. The reason for women-only divers is that they can hold their breath longer than men and are blessed with an extra layer of insulating fat, which protects them from the freezing waters.

Traditionally, *ama* harvested seafood in Ise Bay and transported it to Ise-jingū where they presented their catch as an offering. The women played a major role in the development of the **cultured pearl industry** in the nineteenth century, helping to gather the *akoya* pearl oysters. Today, there are approximately 1300 *ama* in the Toba area; they still wear the customary white outfits, which apparently scare off sharks, and which are also marked with special protective star-shaped charms to ward off bad luck.

Osatsu Ama Bunka Shiryōkan

相差海女文化資料館 • 1238 Osatsu-chō • Daily 9am–5pm • Free • ☎ 0599 33 7453

The small museum of **Osatsu Ama Bunka Shiryokan** details the history and culture of the *ama* women divers in the Shima-Hantō area. It's a good first stop to gain some insight into the history and traditions of the practice, and some of the exhibits have English explanations. There's also quite a bit of diving equipment on display, and seasonal exhibitions of *ama*-inspired artworks.

Ishigami Shrine

石神さん, Ishigami-san • 1385 Osatsu-chō • Dawn to dusk • Free

Located within Shinmei-jinja (神明神社), the small **Ishigami Shrine** is dedicated to Ishigami-san, the female deity who is the guardian of the *ama* divers. The shrine is also known for its mystical powers, and can apparently grant special wishes to women. Not only *ama*, but women from all over Japan visit the shrine to pray for safety and happiness, and on 5 May each year, hundreds of *ama* gather here for a special festival. You can buy special protective amulets from the shrine for ¥800.

Hachiman Kamado

はちまんかまど • 1094 Osatsu-chō • Daily by appointment • From ¥3500 (including seafood snack) • ☎ 0599 33 6145, ⓦ amakoya.com

The highlight of a visit to Ōsatsu is meeting the ama divers, and the star of the show at Hachiman Kamado is 80-year old Nomura Reiko, a veteran diver. Nomura-san and her ama friends are very welcoming and as they grill freshly caught seafood, they will tell you their stories of the sea and the *ama* lifestyle. Unless you speak Japanese, however, it's best to come with an interpreter to help you chat with the women.

ARRIVAL AND INFORMATION

ŌSATSU

By bus To get ōsatsu, take the Kamome bus from Toba Station (10 daily; 50min; ¥600).

Tourist information There's an information desk in the Ōsatsu Ama Bunka Shiryōkan, 1238 Ōsastu-chō (Daily 9am–5pm; ☎ 0599 33 7453) which can help with

accommodation and transport information for the area.

Tours The Kaito Yumin Club (☎ 0599 25 2844, ⓦ oz-group. jp/english) runs "Land of Ama Divers" tours from Toba to Ōsatsu including a visit to the Ishigami shrine and an *amagoya* hut (¥5500/3hr).

Ago-wan

あご湾

The Shima Hantō ends in a bay of islands known as **Ago-wan**. With myriad coves and deep inlets, this huge, sheltered bay is scattered with wooded islands between which float banks of oyster rafts. For centuries, divers have been collecting natural pearls from its warm, shallow waters, but things really took off when Mikimoto (see p.522) started producing his cultured pearls in Ago-wan early in the twentieth

---

BOAT TRIPS FROM AGO-WAN BAY

A choice of **sightseeing boats and ferries** leave from the tiny Kashikojima (賢島) harbour at the end of the Kintetsu train line. For ¥1500 you can cruise in the Esperanza, a very tacky mock-Spanish galleon (50min; every 30min; 9am–4.30pm) which stops off at a pearl farm. There are also **small boats** called *yūransen* (遊覧船), which take you further in among the islands (50–60min; from ¥1400). The cheapest option is one of the infrequent passenger **ferries** called *teikisen* (定期船). There are two ferry routes: across to **Goza** (御座), on the long arm forming the bay's southern edge, and back via **Hamajima** (浜島) to the west of Kashikojima (1hr 15min; ¥1800 for the round-trip); or via Masaki island (間崎) in the middle of the bay to **Wagu** (和具), a village east of Goza (25min; ¥600 one-way). You can get tickets and information about the ferries and Spanish cruise boats from an office beside the harbour – on the right as you walk down from the station – or buy *yūransen* tickets from one of the small booths opposite.

century. Nowadays, hundreds of rafts moored between the islands trace strangely attractive patterns on the water, while, in the nets beneath, thousands of oysters busily work their magic.

The main reason to visit Ago-wan is to take a **boat trip** round the scenic bay (see box opposite) and see the modern pearl industry at work, including a visit to a pearl farm.

ARRIVAL AND INFORMATION   AGO-WAN

By train The Kintetsu line from Ise runs through Toba and terminates at Kashikojima Station, just one-minute's walk north of the harbour for boats to Ago-wan. Trains from Toba to Kashikojima take 40min and cost ¥460.

Destinations Ise (1–3 hourly; 50min–1hr); Kyoto (hourly; 2hr 45min); Nagoya (hourly; 2hr 15min); and Osaka

(hourly; 2hr 20min).

Tourist information For local maps and general information, head to the *Kashikojima Ryokan Annaijo* (賢島旅館案内所; Tues, Wed & Fri–Sun 9am–4.30pm; ☏0599 43 3061), on the right-hand side as you come down the escalator leading from the station to the pier.

ACCOMMODATION

★**Prime Resort Kashikojima** プライムリゾート賢島 3618-33 Ago-chō ☏0599 43 7211, ⓦmiyakohotels .ne.jp/prime.english. Spanish-style resort villa hotel in a lovely setting overlooking a cove. The rooms are spacious and have balconies, and the in-house French and Japanese restaurants are excellent. **¥15,000**

Ryokan Ishiyama-sō 旅館石山荘 Yokoyama-jima ☏0599 52 1527, ⓦlosmen.info. A great place to spend the night on the small island of Yokoyama-jima (横山島). The English-speaking owner will come and collect you in

his boat from a jetty near Kashikojima pier for the 2min trip to the island. After dining on a scrumptious feast of fresh seafood in their restaurant you can watch the sun go down over Ago-wan. **¥18,000**

Shima Kankō Hotel 志摩観光ホテル 731 Ago-chō ☏0599 43 1211, ⓦmiyakohotels.ne.jp/shima. This classic luxury hotel is starting to look a bit worn, despite a refurbishment in recent years. However, it's in a magnificent position overlooking the bay, has spacious rooms with wonderful views, and quaint old-fashioned service. **¥23,000**

Kōbe

神戸

A historic port and distinct city in its own right, **KŌBE**, the capital of Hyōgo-ken, now seems more like a fashionable western suburb of sprawling Osaka. Kōbe's cosmopolitan atmosphere, eclectic food scene, jazz clubs and dramatic location on a sliver of land between the sea and Rokkō-san are the main reasons to visit this friendly harbourside city.

Although it's nearly twenty years since the 1995 **earthquake**, Kōbe has far from forgotten this horrific event – the oddly named **Disaster Reduction and Human Renovation Institution** documents the quake and its aftermath, while the **Tetsujin** robot monument is a reminder of the spirit and effort of Kōbe citizens in rebuilding their city. The **Kōbe City Museum**, covering the port's earlier illustrious history, is also worth a look, as is the space-age-looking **Fashion Museum** on the man-made Rokkō Island, east of the city harbour. For the best view of the whole city and the Inland Sea, take the **Shin-Kōbe Ropeway** up Rokkō-san to the Nunobiki Herb Garden, where you might also be lucky enough to see one of the many wild boars that roam the city's mountainous northern districts.

Brief history

Kōbe's history is dominated by two important events; the opening of Japan's ports to foreign trade in 1868 and the Great Hanshin Earthquake of 1995. Although it had been a port as long ago as the eighth century, Kōbe's fortunes really took off when **foreign traders** set up shop in the city in the latter part of the nineteenth century, bringing their new ways and styles of living with them. Japan got its first taste of beef and football in 1871 in Kōbe, the first cinema film was shown here in 1896, and the first golf course was laid down close to the city in 1903, designed by Arthur Gloom, a Brit. This trendsetting nature and booming trade made Kōbe a very popular place and,

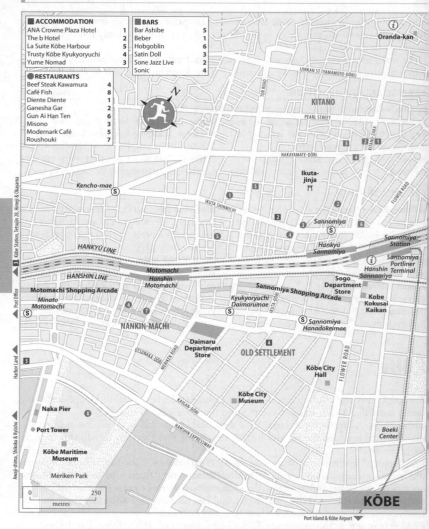

Port Island & Kōbe Airport ▼

despite suffering heavy bombing during World War II, by the 1960s the city was bursting out of its narrow stretch of land between the mountains and the sea. A solution was found by levelling the hills and dumping the rubble in the sea to create Port Island and Rokkō Island in the bay.

All this came to a sudden halt, though, at 5.46am, January 17, 1995, when a devastating **earthquake** struck the city and surrounding area. As dawn broke, Kōbe resembled a war zone, with buildings and highways toppled, whole neighbourhoods in flames, some 6500 people dead and tens of thousands homeless. While the authorities were criticized for not responding promptly to the disaster, Kōbe recovered well and today the city bears little physical sign of the tragedy. Lessons learnt from this experience helped with relief efforts in Tōhoku after the 2011 tsunami (see p.805), and groups of Kōbe volunteers have also been active in assisting affected communities in Tōhoku.

Kōbe City Museum

神戸市博物館, Kobe-shi Hakubutsukan • 24 Kyomachi • Tues–Sun 9.30am–4.30pm • ¥200 • ☎ ⑺ 3 391 0035, ⓦ city.kobe.lg.jp/culture/culture/institution/museum/main.html • A 10min walk south of either Sannomiya or Motomachi stations

Around a century ago, the area south of Sannomiya Station (三宮駅) was Kōbe's principal foreign settlement, although there's little evidence of it today. To get a better idea of what it once looked like, head for the **Kōbe City Museum**, which contains a finely detailed scale model of early twentieth-century Kōbe and many woodblock prints from the same era. The highlight of the museum, however, is its collection of *Narab-an* (southern barbarian) art. These paintings, prints and screens – some of extraordinary detail and beauty – by Japanese artists of the late sixteenth and seventeenth centuries, show how they were influenced by the art of the first Europeans, or "southern barbarians", to come to Japan. Due to their fragile nature, however, only a few of these artworks are on display at any one time.

Nankin-machi

南京町 • South of JR Motomachi Station • ⓦ nankinmachi.or.jp

Kōbe's Chinatown is called **Nankin-machi** and is packed with restaurants, shops and colourful street stalls which are all fairly touristy but add to Kōbe's international atmosphere. The entrance is marked by the ornate Choan-mon gate opposite the Daimaru department store. It's better to visit during the day as most businesses are closed by mid-evening.

Kitano

北野 • 1km north of Sannomiya Station • Daily 9am–5pm • Free, or ¥300–1000 • ⓦ kobeijinkan.com

Of primary interest to the hordes of Japanese visitors to Kōbe are the *ijinkan*, the foreign residences of **Kitano**. After Kobe opened as an international port in 1868, dozens of Western-style brick and clapboard houses were built on the hillside. Less than thirty now remain, however, as virtually all the *ijinkan* had to be reconstructed after the 1995 earthquake and most are now fairly tacky reconstructions heavily focused on souvenir sales. The most popular *ijinkan* is the **Oranda-kan**, the former home of the Dutch consul-general. The area also has some fashionable cafés, restaurants and shops, and is a pleasant place to explore, occasionally throwing up the odd surprise such as a mosque and a Jain temple.

Shin-Kōbe Ropeway and Nunobiki Herb Garden

Ropeway 新神戸ロープウニー • Daily: mid-March to mid-July & Sept–Nov Mon–Fri 9.30am–4.45pm, Sat & Sun 9.30am–8.30pm; mid-July to Aug 9.30am–8.15pm; Dec to mid-March 10am–5pm • ¥900 one-way, ¥1400 return (includes garden admission) • **Garden** 布引ハーブ園, Nunobiki Habu-en • Daily 10am–5pm • ¥200 • ☎ 078 271 1160, ⓦ kobeherb.com

From the top of Kitano, it's a short walk across to the **Shin-Kōbe Ropeway** near Shin-Kōbe Station. The cable-car provides sweeping views of the bay on the way up to the restful **Nunobiki Herb Garden**, a flower garden with a field of lavender and glasshouses stocked with more exotic blooms. Hiking up the hill along the course, starting behind Shin-Kōbe Station, takes around thirty minutes.

Meriken Park and Kobe Harborland

メリケンパーク・@ kobe-meriken.or.jp・神戸ハーバーランド・@ harborland.co.jp

Kōbe's **port** lies directly south of Nankin-machi and is marked by the waterfront **Meriken Park** and **Kōbe Harbor Land**. The park houses the Kōbe Port Tower, the Kōbe Maritime Museum (see below) and an unusual memorial to the victims of the Great Hanshin Earthquake, which is partly submerged in the harbour. Directly across the bay is the **Kōbe Harbor Land** development, where spruced-up brick wharf buildings are joined by modern shopping malls, a cinema complex and a huge Ferris wheel.

Kōbe Maritime Museum

神戸海洋博物館, Kōbe Kaiyō hakubutsukan・2-2 Hatoba-chō・Tues–Sun 10am–4.30pm・¥500・☎ 078 327 8983, @ kobe-meriken .or.jp/maritime-museum

The filigree roof of the **Kōbe Maritime Museum**, a swooping white framework symbolizing waves and sails is the city's most striking architectural feature. The museum itself contains detailed models of a wide range of ships and intriguing audiovisual displays, and has good English explanations, although it lacks the impact of its exterior.

Kōbe Fashion Museum

神戸ファッション美術館, Kōbe Fasshon Bijutsukan・2-9-1 Koyochonaka・Daily except Wed 10am–5.30pm・¥500・☎ 078 858 0050, @ fashionmuseum.or.jp・Take the Rokkō Line monorail from JR Sumiyoshi or Hanshin Uozaki stations to Island Centre Station (¥240), and the museum is a couple of minutes' walk from the southeast exit

East of the city centre, on the artificially built Rokkō Island (六甲アイランド), the main attraction is the **Kōbe Fashion Museum**. Housed inside what looks like a docked *Starship Enterprise*, this museum is a must for fashionistas, with regular special exhibitions that mainly focus on historical developments and classic couture collections. There's also an extensive multilingual library of fashion magazines.

Disaster Reduction and Human Renovation Institution

人と防災未来センター, Hito to Bōsai Mirai Senta・1-5-2 Kaigan-dōri・Tues–Sun 9.30am–4.30pm, Fri & Sat 9.30am–6pm・¥600 for both museums・☎ 078 262 5050, @ dri.ne.jp・About a 10min walk from Hanshin Iwaya or JR Nada stations' south exits

The **Disaster Reduction and Human Renovation Institution** consists of two conjoined museums dedicated to the **Great Hanshin-Awaji Earthquake**. The Disaster Reduction Museum is the more interesting of the two, and its hi-tech multimedia facilities, interactive exhibits and film screenings devoted to the 1995 disaster make this one of Kōbe's highlights. Queue in the lobby and you'll be led up to the fourth floor, where you'll see two short films, and experience the sensation of a tremor, before proceeding to the incredibly detailed exhibits. Audio guides are available, and there are often English-speaking volunteers on hand, some of them quake survivors, who are happy to answer questions.

Hyōgō Prefectural Museum of Art

兵庫県立美術館, Hyōgō Kenritsu Bijutsukan・1-1-1 Kaigan-dōri・Tues–Sun 10am–5.30pm・¥500, special exhibitions ¥1200・☎ 078 262 0901, @ artm.pref.hyogo.jp・Adjacent to the Disaster Reduction and Human Renovation Institution

The Andō Tadao-designed **Hyogo Prefectural Museum of Art** is highly recommended. Exhibitions tend to focus on artists from the prefecture, but as this includes the postwar Gutai – a controversial group of loosely aligned 1950s artists who went very much against the local grain with their stunts and visceral visual art – the quality is extremely high.

Kōbe Tetsujin Project

神戸鉄人プロジェクト・Wakamatsu Kōen・Daily 24hr・Free・ⓦ kobe-tetsujin.com・Take the JR line from Sannomiya to Shin-Nagata Station

In Wakamatsu Park, one of the areas of Kōbe that was hardest hit by the 1995 earthquake, stands an impressive 18m-tall, fifty-tonne replica of the famous manga and anime robot **Tetsujin 28,** known as Gigantor outside Japan. The citizens of Kōbe raised $1.4 million to build the giant-sized statue of this fictional robot as a symbol of the city's revival after the earthquake The manga artist who created Tetsujin 28, Mitsuteru Yokoyama, was a native of Kōbe. His Tetsujin, literally "iron man", was the first giant robot to appear in manga, in 1956. Later, the manga was adapted into an animated television series, which was first broadcast in 1963. The full-scale robot has now become a popular hub for manga and anime-related events in Kōbe.

ARRIVAL AND INFORMATION
KŌBE

By plane The nearest airports to Kōbe are Kōbe Airport on Port Island (神戸空港ターミナル; ☏078 304 7777,ⓦ kairport.co.jp/eng), which only handles domestic flights, and Kansai International Airport (関西国際空港; ☏072 455 2500, ⓦ kansai-airport.o.jp) where international flights arrive. To get from Kobe Airport to Sannomiya, take the Port Liner monorail (18min; ¥320). The most convenient way of getting directly to Kōbe from Kansai International Airport is by limousine bus (1hr; ¥1900/¥1750), which drops passengers at Sannomiya Station and the *Kōbe Bay Sheraton Hotel*.

Destinations from Kōbe Airport Ibaraki (2 daily; 1hr 15min); Ishigaki (1 daily; 2hr 50min); Kagoshima (1 daily; 1hr10min); Nagasaki (4 daily; 1hr 15min); Naha (2 daily; 2hr 15min); Sapporo (5 daily; 1hr 50min); Tokyo Haneda (8 daily; 1hr 15min); and Yonago (2 daily; 40min).

By train Shinkansen trains stop at Shin-Kōbe Station at the foot of Rokkō-san, around 1km north of Sannomiya Station in downtown Kōbe As well as JR trains, those on the Hankyū and Hanshin lines also stop at Sannomiya Station, and are the cheaper way of connecting with Osaka and Kyoto if you're not using a JR Pass.

Shinkansen destinations Fukuoka (Hakata Station; every 15min; 2hr 10min); Himeji (every 30min; 20min); Hiroshima (every 30min; 1hr 10min); Kyoto (every 10min;

30min); Nagoya (every 10min; 1hr 10min); Okayama (every 30min; 35min); Shin Osaka (every 10min; 15min); Tokyo (every 10min; 2hr 50min).

By bus Long distance buses operated by JR Highway Buses (ⓦ nishinihonjrbus.co.jp) depart from Sannomiya.

Destinations Fukuoka (daily; 10hr); Kagoshima (daily; 12hr); Kumamoto (daily; 9hr); Tokyo (30 daily; 8hr); Tottori (7 daily; 3hr 10min); Uwajima (2 daily; 7hr 30min); Yokohama (8 daily; 9hr); and Yonago (6 daily; 4hr).

By ferry Ferries (ⓦ orange-ferry.co.jp and ⓦ han9f.co.jp) from Shikoku, Kyūshū and Awaji-shima arrive at Naka Pier next to the Port Tower, a 10min walk south of Motomachi Station, and at Rokkō Island Ferry Terminal, east of the city. From here you can take the Rokkō Liner monorail to JR Sumiyoshi or Hanshin Uozaki stations, from where it's 10min to either JR Sannomiya or Hanshin Sannomiya stations.

Destinations Imabari (daily; 6hr 40min); Matsuyama (2 daily; 8hr); Ōita (daily; 12hr); Shinmoji (daily; 12hr); and Takamatsu (5 daily; 3hr 30min).

Tourist information The main tourist information office (daily 9am–7pm; ☏078 322 0220), is at the eastern side of the south exit of JR Sannomiya Station, but there's a much more helpful information counter inside Shin-Kōbe Station near the main Shinkansen gate (daily 9am–6pm; ☏078 241 9550).

GETTING AROUND

By bus If you feel like taking things easy, hop on the city loop tourist bus (¥200 per ride, or ¥600 for a day pass, with substantial discounts to many of the city's major sights), which runs a regular circuit around Kōbe's main sights.

Car rental Nippon Rent-a-Car (☏078 231 0067), Kōbe Rent-a-Car (☏078 241 5151) and Eki Rent-a-Car (☏078 241 2995) all have branches near Sannomiya Station.

ACCOMMODATION

ANA Crowne Plaza Hotel Kōbe ANAクラウンプラザ ホテル神戸 1-7-14 Kitano-chō ☏078 291 1121, ⓦ anacrowneplaza-kobe.jp. This upmarket hotel occupies a soaring skyscraper next to Shin-Kōbe Station, with fantastic views from all rooms, great service and a good range of restaurants both in the hotel and the connected shopping plaza. ¥14,500

The b Hotel ザ・ビー神戸 21-5 Shimoyamate-dōri

☏078 333 4480, ⓦ theb-hotels.com/the-b-kobe/en. An excellent mid-range choice right in the middle of Sannomiya. Their stylish rooms are comfortable though on the small side. Internet is free, and there's a coffee lounge in the lobby. ¥7800

La Suite Kōbe Harborland ホテルラ・スイート神戸ハーバーランド 7-2 Hatoba-chō ☏078 371 1111, ⓦ l-s.jp/eng. A luxury hotel with great harbour views from its sweeping

7

7

terraces and balconies. The rooms are lavishly decorated in a classic modern style with comfortable lounges. The in-house French and *teppanyaki* restaurants emphasize local produce but are very pricey. ¥45,000

★**Trusty Kōbe Kyūkyoryūchi** ホテルトラスティ神戸旧居留地 63 Naniwamachi ☏078 330 9111, ⍟trusty .jp/kobe. Located in the Motomachi district, not far from Chinatown, this stylish hotel is a good mid-range option. The rooms are clean but rather pokey. On the second floor

there's a pleasant outdoor terrace café with a good breakfast buffet. ¥8700

★**Yume Nomad** ユメノマド 1-2-2 Shinkaichi ☏078 576 1818, ⍟yumenomad.com. Friendly new backpacker hostel in a converted ryokan with a stylish café and bar, as well as an art gallery a thats double as an occasional cinema. All rooms, both shared and private, have an attached shower/toilet. There's also a well-equipped kitchen for self-catering. Dorm ¥2600, double ¥6400

EATING

Kōbe's long history of international exchange has given it a reputation for having the best Western-style and ethnic cuisine **restaurants**, all aimed at Japanese palates. Despite the density of restaurants catering to Chinese and Indian cuisine, it can be difficult to find a good curry or authentic dim sum. The most cosmopolitan dining area is between Sannomiya Station and Kitano-zaka, where you can also find the local delicacy, Kōbe beef – expensive slices of meat heavily marbled with fat.

RESTAURANTS AND CAFÉS

Beef Steak Kawamura ビーフステーキカワムラ6F 1-10-6 Kitanagasa-dōri ☏078 335 0708, ⍟bifteck .co.jp/en. Kawamura serves award-wining local beef in an opulent setting complete with Greco-Roman statues and chandeliers. The deluxe Kōbe beef lunch sets start at ¥9240, while set dinner courses are from ¥18,000. It's also possible to order à la carte. Daily 11.30am–3pm & 5–9.30pm.

★**Café Fish** カフェフィッシュ 2-8 Hatoba-chō ☏078 334 1820, ⍟cafe-fish.com. Easily recognizable by the giant metal fish outside, this funky warehouse-style café in the Harbor Land development serves tasty fish and seafood burgers (¥1050) and is a relaxing place to while away a few hours gazing out on the harbour. Daily 11am–10pm.

Diente Diente ディエンテディエンテ 3-12-2 Kitanagasa-dōri ☏078 332 3131. Trendy Spanish café and restaurant with an excellent wine list and a good tapas menu (dishes from ¥550). A fun place for an evening with friends. Daily 5pm–5am.

Ganesha Ghar ガネーシャガル 4F 1-6-21 Nakayamate-dōri ☏078 391 9060, ⍟jin.ne.jp/ganesha. Popular Indian restaurant serving fresh naan bread and delicious lunch (¥850) and dinner sets (¥3000). Call ahead to reserve. There's also a branch in Kitano. Tues–Sun 11am–10.30pm.

Gun Ai Han Ten 群愛飯店 2-4-3 Motomachi-dōri

☏078 332 5203, ⍟gunai.com. In the heart of Nankin-machi, this no-frills Chinese restaurant has great lunch deals which include dim sum and tasty beef and chicken dishes (¥900). Mon, Wed–Fri 11.30am–2pm & 5–8.30pm, Sat & Sun 11.30am–8.30pm.

★**Misono** みその 7F&8F 1-1-2 Shimoyamate-dōri ☏078 331 2890, ⍟misono.org. This restaurant proudly boasts that it is the originator of the *teppanyaki* grilling technique, but it also has a reputation for serving top-quality local beef. Locals flock here for the 150g fillet (¥8715), grilled expertly on the counter hotplates. Daily noon–9.30pm.

Modernark Cafe モダナークカフェ3-11-15 Kitanagasa-dōri ☏078 391 3060, ⍟chronicle.co.jp/ shop/shop_MODcafe.html. This vegetarian restaurant is spacious, light and bursting with indoor plants. The veggie brown rice curry and wrap sandwiches (¥1050), and the chilli bean burrito (¥1100) are great choices. Also recommended are the organic fresh juices and scrumptious desserts. Daily 11.30am–10pm.

Roushouki 老祥記 2-1-14 Motomachi-dōri ☏078 331 7714, ⍟roushouki.com. Extremely popular *buta-man* (steamed pork bun) restaurant that's been in business since 1915. Buns are just ¥90 each. The line snakes out the door down Nankin-machi. Daily 10am–6.30pm.

DRINKING AND NIGHTLIFE

While Kōbe doesn't have as strong a club scene as neighbouring Osaka, it does have a good range of **bars**, most clustered around Sannomiya and Motomachi, and all within easy walking distance of each other. As Kōbe is the birthplace of Japanese Jazz, it's worth spending an evening on one of the city's **jazz clubs**.

BARS AND CLUBS

Bar Ashibe バーあしべ 2-12-21 Shimoyamate-dōri ☏078 391 2039. Dark and moody bar with lots of intimate seating space plus an extensive cocktail menu. Popular with both locals and the expat crowd. Daily 6pm–3am.

Beber ベベル B1 & 6F 1-22-10 Nakayamate-dōri

☏078 231 6262, ⍟beber-kobe.com. This club specializes in r'n'b, hip-hop and reggae. Events are held simultaneously on both floors (cover charge from ¥2500 each floor), and attract large crowds of fashionable Kōbe youth. Fri & Sat 9pm–5am.

Hobgoblin ホブゴブリン 4-3-2 Kano-chō ☏078 325 0830, ⍟hobgoblin.jp. Bustling British pub with live music and sports broadcasts. There's a range of local and imported draught beers (from ¥900 a pint) as well as a large bar-food menu that includes fish & chips (¥1500) and chilli beef nachos (¥800). Free wi-fi. Mon–Sat 5pm til late.

Satin Doll サテンドール 1-26-1 Nakayamate-dōri ☎078 242 0100, ☻satindollkobe.jp. Cosy, relaxing live jazz club serving French cuisine (from ¥3800). The acts are mostly local amateurs and there are usually only one or two acts a night. Cover charge ¥500. Tues–Sun 2–11pm.

★**Sone Jazz Live & Restaurant Kitano-zaka** ソネ Kitano-zaka ☎078 221 2055, ☻kobe-sone.com. The birthplace of Japanese jazz, attracting many top international artists as well as local talent. The first live set starts around 7pm and there are four performances a night; cover charge from ¥1200. Daily from 5pm.

Sonic B1 1-13-7 Nakayamate-dōri ☎078 391 6641. During the week it's a sports bar but at weekends *Sonic* hosts popular DJ and dance music events, mixing house, world music and hip-hop (cover charge from ¥1500; foreigners are free at some events). Daily 8pm–5am.

DIRECTORY

Banks and exchange MUFJ Bank and Sumitomo-Mitsubishi Bank are 5min walk south of Sannomiya Station, just off Flower Road. There's also a City Bank branch northwest of Kōbe City Hall.

Emergencies The main police station is at 5-4-1 Shinoyamate-dōri (☎078 341 7441). There's also a police box opposite the information centre at the Sannomiya Station south exit. In an emergency, contact the Foreign Advisory Service on ☎078 291 8441.

Hospital and medical advice Kōbe Adventist Hospital, at 8-4-1 Arinodai, Kita-ku (☎078 981 0161; ☻kahns.org), has many English-speaking staff, but is a 30min drive north of the city. Kōbe Kaisei Hospital, at 3-11-15 Shinohara Kitamachi, Nada-ku (☎078 871 5201; ☻kobe-kaisei.org),

has an international division with many English-speaking staff, but, like the Adventist Hospital, is a little awkward to reach, being a 15min walk uphill from Hankyū Rokkō Station. Kōbe University Hospital, at 7-5-2 Kusunoki-chō (☎078 382 5111; ☻hosp.kobe-u.ac.jp/e), is a 10min walk north of Kōbe Station.

Internet Netsquare, beneath the tracks of JR Sannomiya Station, close to Flower Road, has both Mac and Windows terminals (7am–9pm; ¥100 for 10min).

Post office Kōbe Central Post Office is a 2min walk northeast of JR Kōbe Station. There's also a convenient branch in the Kōbe Kokusai Kaikan Building, directly south of Sannomiya Station, as well as a small postage-only branch beneath JR Sannomiya Station.

7

Arima Onsen

有馬温泉

On the northern slopes of Rokkō-san, northeast of Kōbe, is one of Japan's oldest hot-spring resorts, **ARIMA ONSEN**. Since the seventh century, Arima has been famous for attracting emperors, shoguns and, in more modern times, the literati, all of whom have come to bathe in its healing gold and silver waters. It's even mentioned in the ancient chronicle the *Nihonshoki*. Toyotomi Hideyoshi brought the tea master Sen no

---

KŌBE BEEF FARM TOUR

Despite stories of being fed beer and getting massages, the production of **wagyū**, or Japanese beef is actually all about the careful monitoring of breeding and bloodlines. To produce the famous fat-marbled meat, the wagyū cattle are fed the best quality feed, given clean water and kept in a stress-free environment. Only a limited number of wagyū cows are slaughtered every year. **Kobe Beef**, produced from cattle with the purest bloodlines (Tajima-gyū), is considered to be the best and most flavoursome meat and commands high prices.

InsideJapan Tours (☻insidejapantours.com) can organize a day-trip to the **Takami Beef Farm** (☻takamibeef.com) for a tour of the farm and a chance to enjoy a meal in the scenic countryside of Hyōgo Prefecture. The farm is in Ichijima, approximately two hours north of Kōbe by train, and has won many awards for their premium beef production. After seeing how the cattle, some of which weigh more than 300kg, are raised there's a chance to eat lunch at the farm's excellent and very reasonably priced Gurumeria Tajima restaurant (Daily 11am–8.30pm; closed Wed, ☎079 585 2612, ☻gourmetria.com). InsideJapan also provides an interpreter guide, and requires reservations in advance: contact them for dates and prices (info@insidejapantours.com).

SAKE BREWING

The Nada (灘) sake-brewing district is home to more than forty breweries. Take the Rokkō Liner train to Minami Uozaki Station and walk five minutes east to the Uozaki-Gō area (魚崎郷). Here you can visit two **breweries** and see the production of sake, as well as sample a few free thimblefuls.

Hamafukutsuru 浜副鶴 4-4-6 Uozaki Minami-machi ☎078 411 8339, ⓦhamafukutsuru.co.jp. There are simple explanations in English of the brewing process, which you can observe from decks overlooking the production area. You can sample some of Hamafukutsuru's sake after you have toured the brewery. Tues–Sun 10am–5pm.

Sakuramasamune 櫻正宗 Uozaki Minami-machi ☎078 436 3030, ⓦsakuramasamune.co.jp. Check out the historical exhibits and the in-house restaurant, *Sakuraen*, where you can enjoy lunch (from ¥1500) and dinner (from ¥4000) with the house brews, there's also a counter bar, *Sanbaiya*, where you can sample different grades of sake by the cup (from ¥300). 10am–10pm, closed Tues.

Rikyū here in the sixteenth century to perform a tea ceremony, an event commemorated annually in November with the Arima Great Tea Ceremony.

Arima has two kinds of **mineral-rich hot springs**, both recognized for their numerous health benefits, as well as some top-class ryokan, where you can soak yourself in luxury on an overnight trip. If you are only here for the day, you can either take a dip in the **public baths**, or (more expensively) visit the spas of some of Arima's ryokan and hotels: the tourist information office can tell which private spas accept non-residents.

Kin no Yu

金の湯 · 833 Arima-chō · Daily 8am–9.30pm, closed second and fourth Tues of the month · ¥650 · ☎ 078 904 0680 · A 5min walk uphill from the train station, close to the bus station and tourist information office

At the large **Kin no Yu** public bath, you can soak in the sludgy brown *kinsen* (gold spring) waters, at their source, and get relief for a wide variety of common health complaints, including some forms of rheumatism and sensitive skin. Don't be put off by the colour – after bathing here your skin will feel wonderfully soft, and the *kinsen* waters also have a relaxing effect. Outside the bathhouse there is a free *ashi-yu* footbath, as well as a fountain of drinkable spa water.

Gin no Yu

銀の湯 · 1039-1 Arima-chō · Daily 9am–8.30pm, closed first and third Tues of the month · ¥550 · ☎ 078 904 0256 · Gin no Yu is at the top of Negai-zaka slope past Nembutsu-ji temple

The **Gin no Yu** public bath is much quieter than Kin no Yu and has a high ceiling with skylights; the light streaming in through the steam is quite spectacular. The clear *ginsen* (silver spring) waters are believed to be effective for curbing high blood pressure and improving blood ciculation, and drinking these waters is reputedly good for your digestive system.

ARRIVAL AND INFORMATION ARIMA ONSEN

By train To reach the resort by train from Kōbe, take the subway from Sannomiya to Tanigami, then transfer to the Kōbe Dentetsu line to Arima Guchi (有馬口), where you may have to change again (same platform) to reach the terminus at Arima Onsen. The journey takes around 40min and costs ¥900. If you're coming from Osaka, take a local JR train to Sanda (JR Fukuchiyama line), where you can change to the Kōbe Dentetsu line. The journey costs ¥1290 and takes about 80min.

By cable-car and ropeway A more scenic route from Kōbe to Arima Onsen, though a little more time-consuming and expensive than the train, is to take a cable-car via Rokkō-san. Take the Hankyū line to Rokkō Station and then transfer to the Rokkō cable-car, from where it's a 10min (¥570) trip to the Rokkō Arima Ropeway. From here, it's another 10min to Arima Onsen (¥980).

By bus There are also direct buses from Sannomiya (50min; ¥680) via Shin-Kōbe Station to Arima, as well as JR West Japan

RIGHT DAIMON-ZAKA ON THE KUMANO KODŌ PILGRIMAGE ROUTE (P.515) >

By bus There are also direct buses from Sannomiya (50min; ¥680) via Shin-Kōbe Station to Arima, as well as JR West Japan highway buses from Shin-Kōbe Station (50min; ¥750) via Sannomiya. Alternatively, note that comfortable air-conditioned coaches from Ōsaka's Hankyū Bus Station beneath Hankyū Umeda Station cost ¥1330 and take just over an hour.

Tourist information The Arima Onsen Tourist Information Center (daily 9am–7pm; ☎078 904 0708, ⓦ arima-onsen.com) is located uphill from the train station. You can pick up a handy English map of the town here, and arrange accommodation, though it's best to book in advance.

ACCOMMODATION

★**Tosen Goshobō** 陶漣御所坊 858 Arima-chō ☎078 904 0551, ⓦgoshoboh.com/en. This is the top place to stay in Arima – there have been lodgings in this exact location since the twelfth century, and its current incarnation – a fusion of Japanese and Western styles – is the height of onsen sophistication. Fortunately, they serve lunch to non-guests (daily 11am–2pm; from ¥2950), and accept day visitors to their stylish baths (Daily 11am–2pm/¥1575); both great opportunities to experience the tasteful surroundings. **¥27,500**

Nakanobō Zui-en 中の坊瑞苑 808 Arima-chō ☎078 904 0787, ⓦzuien.jp/english. A superb Arima resort, which has hosted the likes of Princess Grace of Monaco as well as other international celebrities. Both the rooms and bathing areas look out onto carefully manicured gardens. Non-residents are allowed to visit the bathhouse with the option of a private room (daily 11.30am–3.30pm; ¥7320). **¥23,092**

Kami-ō-bō 上大坊 1175 Arima-chō ☎078 904 0531, ⓦkamiobo.com. Small and friendly inn just up the main street from Kin no Yu which serves delicious seasonal kaiseki ryōri. The tatami rooms are compact but comfortable. Rates include two meals. Non-residents can bathe here too (Daily 3–6pm; ¥1000). **¥25,200**

Himeji

姫路

Of Japan's twelve surviving feudal-era fortresses, by far the most impressive is the one in **HIMEJI**, 55km west of Kōbe. The fortress, **Himeji-jō**, made the memorable backdrop to the Bond adventure *You Only Live Twice*, as well as countless feudal-era dramas and the Tom Cruise film, *The Last Samurai*, part of which was also filmed here and around the city. The splendid gabled donjons of Himeji-jō – also known as Shirasagi-jō, or "white egret castle", since the complex is supposed to resemble the shape of the bird in flight – miraculously survived the World War II bombings that laid waste to much of the city, and in 1993 it was added to UNESCO's World Heritage list.

Major renovation work is currently taking place at Himeji-jō on the central donjon, which is due for completion in early 2015: until then, visitors can still enter the castle grounds, and some buildings, but not the donjon. Despite this, Himeji is a pleasant place and it's worth visiting the beautiful **Himeji Kōko-en**, nine linked traditional-style gardens; there are also a couple of interesting **museums** around the fortress walls.

THE WORLD'S LONGEST SUSPENSION BRIDGE

The **Akashi Straits Suspension Bridge** (明石海峡大橋), at 3.91km, is the longest suspension bridge in the world, linking mainland Hyōgo-ken to Awaji-shima, the largest island in the Inland Sea after Shikoku. The bridge was still under construction when the 1995 earthquake hit (Awaji-shima was the epicentre), which caused the bridge to lengthen by an extra metre. Since opening in 1998, this commanding concrete-and-steel engineering feat, with a central span of 1.99km, has become a tourist draw in its own right, with fishermen and artists gathering on the promenades around its imposing base. You can enter one of the bridge's pylons and wander out 150m along the undercarriage of the structure. If you're a serious bridge-spotter, though, you might want to bus across the bridge to Iwaya on Awaji-shima and take a ferry back in order to fully comprehend the structure in its entirety. For more facts and figures on this marvel of civil engineering, visit the **Bridge Exhibition Centre** (Daily 9.15am–4.30pm; ¥300; ⓦhashinokagakukan.jp) near Maiko Station, twenty minutes west of Kōbe by train.

Himeji-jō

姫路城 • 68 Honmachi • Daily 9am–4pm, April 27–Aug till 5pm • ¥400, or ¥720 combined ticket with Kōko-en • Free tours 1hr 30min • ☎ 079 285 1146, ⓦ himeji-castle.gr.jp • Tours are in English, and guides are usually waiting at the main castle gate, but it's best to ask about the start time of the next tour when buying your ticket; if you don't have a guide, finding your way around the castle is no problem, since the route is clearly marked and there are English explanations on plaques at many points of interest.

Around 1km directly north of Himeji Station lies the main gateway to **Himeji-jō**. The present complex of moats, thick defensive walls, keeps and connecting corridors dates from the early seventeenth century, although there has been a fortress in the town since around 1346. By the time Tokugawa Ieyasu's son-in-law, Ikeda Terumasa, took control of the area in 1600, the country was at peace and so when he set about rebuilding Himeji-jō, adding the central five-storey donjon and three smaller donjons, the aim was to create something visually impressive. Even so, the castle incorporates many cunning defensive features, only really appreciated if you go on one of the **free guided tours** in English.

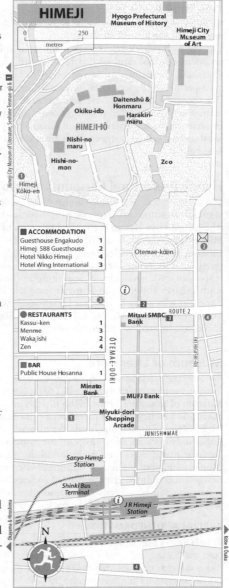

HIMEJI

Hyogo Prefectural Museum of History

Himeji City Museum of Art

Daitenshū & Honmaru

Okiku-ido

HIMEJI-JŌ

Harakiri-maru

Nishi-no-maru

Hishi-no-mon

Zoo

Himeji Kōko-en

■ **ACCOMMODATION**

Guesthouse Engakudo	1
Himeji 588 Guesthouse	2
Hotel Nikko Himeji	4
Hotel Wing International	3

● **RESTAURANTS**

Kassui-ken	1
Menme	3
Wakaishi	2
Zen	4

■ **BAR**

| Public House Hosanna | 1 |

Otemae-kōen

Mitsui SMBC Bank
ROUTE 2

ŌTEMAE-DŌRI

Minato Bank

MUFJ Bank

Miyuki-dori Shopping Arcade

JUNISHIMAE

Sanyo Himeji Station

Shinki Bus Terminal

ⓘ JR Himeji Station

N

7

Nishi-no-maru

西の丸

To the west of the main gateway, the Hishi-no-mon, are the open grounds of the **Nishi-no-maru** (western citadel), where the *daimyō* and his family lived; the central donjon was only used in times of war. All that remains of the original palace are the outer corridor and "cosmetic tower", where Princess Sen adjusted her kimono and powdered her nose in the mid-seventeenth century. It was Sen's dowry that enabled the castle to be built in its present form.

Honmaru

本丸

A zigzag path through more gates and past turrets and walls from which defending soldiers could fire arrows, shoot muskets and drop stones and boiling liquids leads up to the **Honmaru** (inner citadel), which is dominated by the magnificent central donjon, **Tenshū** (天守). There are six levels within the dark and chilly keep, supported by a framework of huge wooden pillars, one of which is made from a 780-year-old cypress tree; touch it and it's said you'll have long life. On the top level, where the lord and his family would have committed suicide if the castle was captured (which it never was), you can usually look out across the city and see as far as the Inland Sea on clear days.

Himeji-jō Kōko-en

姫路城好古園 • 68 Honmachi • Daily: Jan–April & Sept–Dec 9am–4.30pm; May–Aug 9am–5.30pm; ¥300, or ¥720 combined ticket with the castle • Tea ceremony ¥500 • ☎ 079 289 4120

On the west side of Himeji-jō's moat is the splendid **Himeji-jō Kōko-en**, a reconstruction of samurai quarters built in 1992 on the former site of the Nishi Oyashiki, the *daimyō's* west residence for his samurai. The nine connected Edo-period-style gardens are separated by rustic mud walls topped with roof-tiles, like those which would have stood around each samurai villa. In the gardens are mini-forests, carp-filled pools, rockeries and an elegant teahouse where you can experience the tea ceremony. The Kassui-ken restaurant, which specializes in the local *anago* (grilled conger eel) cuisine, is located in a teahouse in the gardens (see below).

Hyōgo Prefectural Museum of History

兵庫県立歴史博物館, Himeji Bungaku-Kan, Hyogo Kenritsu Rekishi Hakubatsuken • 68 Honmachi • Tues–Sun 10am–4.30pm • ¥200 • ☎ 079 288 9011, ⊕ hyogo-c.ed.jp/~rekihaku-bo/english/about.html

The informative **Hyōgo Prefectural Museum of History** on the northeast side of Himeji-jō's moat, is in a striking building designed by the founding father of modern Japanese architecture, Tange Kenzō. Inside are detailed scale models of the twelve castle donjons across Japan that survive in their original form, as well as a display of children's culture, beginning in the Edo period, and an interesting multimedia exhibition on Himeji's festivals. The museum also provides three opportunities a day to try on a Heian-style twelve-layered court kimono and samurai armour (at 10.30am, 1.30pm & 3.30pm): apply at reception on arrival as spaces are limited to one visitor per session.

Museum of Literature

姫路文学館 路文 • 84 Yamanoi-chō • Tues–Sun 10am–4.30pm • ¥300 • ☎ 079 293 8228, ⊕ city.himeji.lg.jp/bungaku

Tange's contemporary rival, Andō Tadao, has made his mark on Himeji at the city's **Museum of Literature**, some 600m directly west of the Museum of History across the moat and just beyond the entrance to Princess Sen's shrine, **Senhime Tenman-gū** (千姫天満宮). The exhibits inside the museum are all in Japanese (the English-language leaflet only outlines the concept of the museum), but the displays are imaginative and Japanese literature enthusiasts will find the novelist Shiba Ryōtaro's (see box, p.662) Memorial Hall of interest. If nothing else, come here to admire Andō's ultra-modern design – a disjointed arrangement of squares, circles and walkways made from rough concrete – which also respects traditional principles, such as the *shakkei* (borrowed scenery) of the castle behind the museum and the use of water.

ARRIVAL AND INFORMATION   **HIMEJI**

By train Himeji is a stop on the Shinkansen line between Osaka and Okayama, and is also served by slower but cheaper *shinkaisoku* trains, which take 40min from Kōbe or an hour from Osaka. The train station is around 1km south of the castle at the end of Ōtemae-dōri (大手前通り), the main boulevard.

Destinations Fukuoka (Hakata Station; hourly; 2hr 15min); Hiroshima (every 30min; 1hr); Kōbe (every 30min; 20min); Kyoto (every 30min; 1hr); Nagoya (30 daily; 1hr 50min); Okayama (every 30min; 20min); Osaka (every 30min; 30min); and Tokyo (hourly; 3hr 40min).

By bus Long-distance highway buses from Tokyo (Shinjuku; daily; 9hr) stop at the southside of the JR Himeji train station. Buses from Osaka and Kōbe also pull in here, though it's much easier and quicker to travel from these destinations by train.

Tourist information Pick up a map from the excellent Himeji Kanko Navi Port (daily 9am–7pm; ☎ 079 287 0003, ⊕ himeji-kanko.jp) on the west side of the central entrance to the station, which is staffed by English-speakers between 10am and 3.30pm. They can also make accommodation bookings here, and lend out free bikes (see below).

GETTING AROUND

Loop bus Himeji's major sights are within easy walking distance of the station, but if you are pushed for time, take the convenient retro-styled city "loop bus" (ループバス; daily: March–Nov Mon–Fri 9am–4.30pm every 30min; Jan–Dec Sat & Sun 9am–5pm every 15–30min), which starts from the Shinki Bus Terminal outside Himeji Station and stops at all the major tourist attractions. Rides cost ¥100, though the one-day pass (¥300) offers good value as it includes a twenty percent discount on entry to a number of the city's major sights, including the castle and some of the museums.

Bicycle rental Himeji has a convenient free bicycle loan service for tourists. Bikes can be picked up between 9am and 4pm, from outside the station, and must be returned by 6pm. Apply and register at Himeji Kankō Navi Port.

ACCOMMODATION

Guesthouse Engakudou 緑楽堂 8-2 Yanagi-machi ☎ 079 260 7373, ⓦ engakudou.com. Tucked away in a residential area on the western side of the castle, this guesthouse is in a rambling 100-year-old house with lots of character – the owner has decorated the interior with a Tibetan theme. The tatami rooms with futon are clean and comfortable, and there's a shared kitchen and bathroom. Dorm **¥2500** double **¥6000**

★**Himeji 538 Guesthouse** ガハハゲストハウス 68 Honmachi ☎ 079 283 2588, ⓦ himeji588.com. This super-friendly guesthouse is conveniently located at the castle end of the shopping arcade that runs from the train station. Run with great care by the lovely Kyoko-san, it has been nicely renovated and has good facilities. It's a great place to get insider information on Himeji and meet fellow travellers. Dorm beds **¥2700**, double **¥6000**

Hotel Nikkō Himeji ホテル日航姫路 100 Minami-eki-mae ☎ 079 222 2231, ⓦ hotelnikkohimeji.co.jp. This is Himeji's best upmarket option and is conveniently located close to the station. The rooms are fairly spacious and some of the higher floors have good views of the castle. There are four in-house restaurants and a gym. **¥20,700**

Hotel Wing International ホテルウィングインタナーショナル 132 Watamachi ☎ 079 287 2111, ⓦ himeji .hotelwingjapan.com. Stylish budget hotel with castle views from some floors. The rooms are compact yet comfortable and have good amenities. Breakfast is optional (¥800). **¥12,000**

EATING AND DRINKING

The Miyuki-dōri covered shopping arcade (みゆき通り), one street east of Ōtemae-dōri, is a good place to stop for a snack or pick up a bentō to enjoy within the castle grounds. There are also several good lunch options closer to the castle.

Kassui-ken 活水軒 68 Honmachi ☎ 079 289 4131. Classic teahouse within Himeji Kōko-en serving the local specialty *anago* (grilled conger eel) cuisine. The *anago-don* set lunch (¥1300) is the best deal here and is also served with tempura, pickles and miso soup. Daily 10am–4.30pm.

Menme めんめ 68 Honmachi ☎ 079 225 0118. A specialist udon shop with noodles made on the premises throughout the day and a variety of healthy toppings such as tofu and vegetables to choose from. Bowls of noodles start at ¥550. 11.30am–7pm, closed Wed.

Public House Hosanna パブリックハウスホサンナ 9 Tatemachi ☎ 079 288 3289, ⓦ pub-hosanna.com. British-style pub-restaurant with a cosy and authentic interior that's heated by a wood-fired stove. There are eight kinds of local and imported draught beer on tap, and a wine bar. The food is a mishmash of typical *izakaya* fare, British fish and chips (¥1350), and Italian pizza (¥1050). 5pm–midnight; closed Mon.

Wakajishi 若獅子 195-2 Soshahonmachi ☎ 079 282 5676. This family-run restaurant serves delicious home-style *teishoku* meal sets with generous portions from ¥600. The friendly English-speaking waitress will explain the day's specials. Daily 11am–1pm & 5–9pm.

★**Zen** ぜん 96 Motoshio-machi ☎ 079 288 1039. Ramen noodle restaurant serving top-quality fusion Japanese and Asian fare at reasonable prices. The spring roll lunch set (¥800) is excellent value, and the evening à la carte menu offers some tasty stir-fries with seasonal ingredients (¥950). There's no English menu but the staff are helpful. 11am–2pm & 6–11pm, closed Wed.

Western Honshū

TOMONOURA PORT

Western Honshū

Also known as *Chūgoku*, meaning "middle country" – and spelled with the same kanji which designates "China" in Japanese – western Honshū used to be at the centre of the Japanese nation, lying between the country's earliest settlements in Kyūshū and the imperial city of Kyoto. The region is split geographically into two distinct areas. The southern San'yō coast is blighted by heavy industry but borders the enchanting Inland Sea, while the rugged and sparsely populated northern San'in coast boasts some delightful small towns and a generally pristine landscape. The southern coast is easy to travel around, with Shinkansen lines, good local railway services and highways, while the northern coast takes more planning to tour by public transport, but easily repays the effort with some properly remote destinations.

Though western Honshū is rich in history, with burial mounds on both coasts dating from the first century, it's a more contemporary event that brings most visitors to the region. Lying midway along the San'yō coast, **Hiroshima**, site of the first atomic bomb attack and the region's largest city, is the one place you'll definitely want to stop off en route to or from Kyūshū. At the eastern end of the San'yō coast, **Okayama** has one of Japan's most famous gardens, **Kōrakuen**, and with great hotel offerings and a solid nightlife makes a good base for visiting the beautifully preserved Edo-era town of **Kurashiki** or the island art project on **Inujima**. Head west along the coast, and one of the treasures of Hiroshima-ken is the laconic fishing village of **Tomonoura** with its gorgeous views across the Inland Sea. The port of **Onomichi**, just to the north, is also the jumping-off point for the Shimanami Kaidō, or Sea Road, which connects Honshū via a series of breathtaking bridges and islands to Imabari on Shikoku, taking in the laidback island of **Ikuchi-jima** en route.

The one island of the Inland Sea you won't want to miss is **Miyajima**, just west of Hiroshima and site of the ancient shrine **Itsukushima-jinja**. (Note that those Inland Sea islands not covered here are discussed in chapter 9). On the southern coast of neighbouring Yamaguchi-ken, pause to admire the elegant Kintai-kyō bridge at **Iwakuni** and the spectacular view across the narrow Kanmon Straits to Kyūshū from Hino-yama in the port of **Shimonoseki**, at the tip of Honshū. Inland, the highlights of the prefecture's small capital, **Yamaguchi**, are an impressive pagoda and classic Zen rock and moss garden.

East along the frequently deserted San'in coast, the old castle town of **Hagi** is, which boasts a lovely cluster of samurai houses and atmospheric temples. Perhaps even more beautiful is **Tsuwano**, another small castle settlement nestling in a tranquil valley inland, further east in Shimane-ken. This prefecture is the heartland of Japan's eight million Shintō deities, who are believed to gather each year in November at the ancient

8

PEACE MEMORIAL PARK, HIROSHIMA

Highlights

❶ Washū-zan Climb Washū-zan and watch the sun set over the Seto Ōhashi bridge and the islands of the Inland Sea. **See p.555**

❷ Tomonoura Wander the narrow, twisting streets of this picturesque port with a famous view of the Inland Sea. **See p.556**

❸ Ikuchi-jima Make a day-trip to this easy-going island for a peek at Japan's craziest temple, Kōsan-ji, and the wonderful collection of Hirayama Ikuo's paintings. **See p.563**

❹ Miyajima Watch the summer fireworks explode over Itsukushima-jinja's magnificent

torii, or view the island's spectacular autumn foliage. **See p.573**

❺ Tsuwano Explore this picturesque old castle town by bicycle, then climb up to the Taikodani Inari-jinja through a tunnel of over a thousand red *torii*. **See p.596**

❻ Adachi Museum of Art Enjoy the museum's exquisite gardens, ranked the best in Japan by the *Journal of Japanese Gardening* every year since 2003. **See p.602**

HIGHLIGHTS ARE MARKED ON THE MAP ON P.542

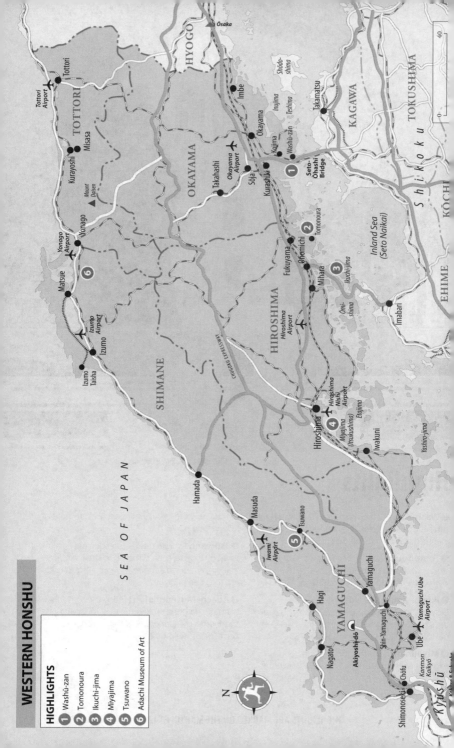

WESTERN HONSHU

HIGHLIGHTS

1. Washū-zan
2. Tomonoura
3. Ikuchi-jima
4. Miyajima
5. Tsuwano
6. Adachi Museum of Art

SEA OF JAPAN

Shikoku

Inland Sea (Seto Naikai)

HYOGO

TOTTORI

OKAYAMA

HIROSHIMA

SHIMANE

YAMAGUCHI

KAGAWA

TOKUSHIMA

KŌCHI

EHIME

Kyūshū

Ōsaka

Tottori
Tottori Airport

Misasa
Kurayoshi

Yonago
Yonago Airport
Matsue

Izumo
Izumo Airport
Izumo Taisha

Mount Daisen

Imbe
Okayama
Washū-zan
Takahashi
Okayama Airport
Sōja
Kurashiki
Kojima

Seto-Ōhashi Bridge

Inujima
Tejima
Shōdo-shima

Takamatsu

Tomonoura
Onomichi
Fukuyama
Mihara
Ikuchi-jima
Ōmi-shima
Imabari

Hiroshima
Hiroshima Airport
Hiroshima Nishi Airport
Etajima
Miyajima (Itsukushima)
Iwakuni

Yoshima-jima

Hamada
Masuda
Iwami Airport
Tsuwano
Yamaguchi

Hagi
Shin-Yamaguchi
Yamaguchi Ube Airport
Ube

Nagato
Akiyoshi-dō

Shimonoseki
Chōfu
Kanmon Kaikyō

CHŪGOKU EXPRESSWAY

N

0   40

THE INLAND SEA

"They rise gracefully from this protected, stormless sea, as if they had just emerged their beaches, piers,
harbors all intact … Wherever one turns there is a wide and restful view, one island behind the other, each
soft shape melting into the next until the last dim outline is lost in the distance."

Donald Richie, *The Inland Sea*

It's difficult to improve on Richie's sublime description of the **Inland Sea** (Seto Naikai), written
in 1993, and, despite his fears that it would all be ruined in Japan's rush to the twenty-first
century, this priceless panorama has changed remarkably little since. Boxed in by the islands of
Honshū, Kyūshū and Shikoku, and dotted with more than three thousand other islands, the sea
is one of Japan's scenic gems, often likened to the Aegean in its beauty.

Several islands are now connected by bridges and fast ferries to the mainland, reducing their
isolation and much of their charm, but on many others you'll be struck by the more leisurely pace
of life and the relative lack of modern-day blight. The best islands to head for are **Naoshima**
(p.627), **Inujima** (p.630), **Ikuchi-jima** (p.563), **Ōmi-shima** (p.565), **Miyajima** (p.573) and
Shōdo-shima (p.633), all popular for their relaxed atmosphere and beautiful scenery.

If you don't have time to linger, consider a **boat trip** across the sea or heading to a vantage
point such as Washū-zan (p.555) or Yashima (p.620) to look out over the islands. There are also
several sightseeing cruises, though these are expensive for what they offer; you're better off
putting together your own itinerary using individual ferry services.

shrine Izumo Taisha, near the appealing capital of **Matsue**. Matsue has the region's only
original castle tower, as well as some old samurai houses and interesting museums. In
neighbouring Tottori-ken, you'll find **Mount Daisen**, the highest peak in the Chūgoku
region, with great hiking in the summer and skiing in winter.

If you only have a matter of days, aim to take in Kurashiki and Matsue, as well as
Hiroshima and Miyajima. In a couple of weeks, you could make a circuit of both coasts
taking in most of the region's highlights.

8

GETTING AROUND
WESTERN HONSHŪ

By plane For quick access to the region there are several
airports, including two near Hiroshima, plus those at
Okayama, Ube (close to Shimonoseki), Yonago (near
Matsue) and Tottori.

By train A regular JR Pass is the most convenient way of
getting around the region, but if you plan to stick only to
the San'yō coast, consider the cheaper JR West San'yō Area
Pass. Trains between the region's major cities are the fastest
direct services.

By bus Though trains are quicker (especially when it

comes to shorter journeys), buses are also an option —
though rarely a less expensive one. Long-distance bus
services often travel overnight between the major cities.

By car Renting a car is a good idea, especially if you're
planning to tour the quieter San'in coast, as you can make
good use of the fast Chūgoku Expressway, which threads its
way through the region's central mountainous spine, from
where you can branch off to sights on either coast.

By ferry If time isn't an issue, then schedule a leisurely
ferry ride across the Inland Sea (see box above).

Okayama

岡山

The main reason for stopping off in the capital of Okayama-ken, **OKAYAMA**, 730km
west of Tokyo, is to stretch your legs in its famous garden, **Kōrakuen**, considered one of
Japan's top three, overlooked by the castle, **Okayama-jō**, around which the city
developed in the Edo period. A short walk from the station along the main street,
Momotarō-dōri, takes you across the tree-lined **Nishigawa Greenway Canal**, a pleasant
spot for a stroll. The city is not a bad place to be based for trips out to attractions in the
surrounding towns and areas, though aside from the intriguing **Okayama Orient
Museum** there's little else of note in this modern town.

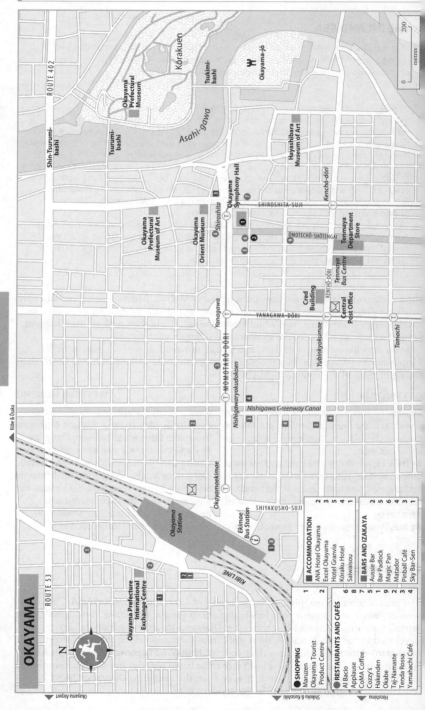

OKAYAMA

Kōrakuen

Okayama-jō

Okayama Prefectural Museum

ROUTE 402

Shin-Tsurumi-bashi

Tsurumi-bashi

Tsurumi-bashi

Tsukimi-bashi

Asahi-gawa

Hayashibara Museum of Art

Okayama Symphony Hall

Kenchō-dōri

SHIROSHITA-SUJI

Shiroshita

Okayama Prefectural Museum of Art

Okayama Orient Museum

ŌMOTECHŌ-SHŌTENGAI

Tenmaya Department Store

Yanagawa

Tenmaya Bus Centre

KENCHŌ-DŌRI

Cred Building

Central Post Office

YANAGAWA-DŌRI

Yubinkyokumae

MOMOTARŌ-DŌRI

Tamachi

Nishigawaryokudōkōen

Nishigawa Greenway Canal

Okayamaekimae

Kōbe & Ōsaka

Okayama Station

Ekimae Bus Station

SHIYAKUSHO-SUJI

KIBI LINE

Okayama Prefecture International Exchange Centre

ROUTE 53

N

Okayama Airport

Hiroshima

Shikoku & Kurashiki

8

0   200
metres

SHOPPING
Maruzen	1
Okayama Tourist Product Centre	2

RESTAURANTS AND CAFÉS
Al Bacio	6
Applause	8
CoMA Coffee	7
Cozzy's	5
Hakenden	9
Okabe	3
Taj-Namaste	2
Tenda Rossa	3
Yamahachi Café	4

ACCOMMODATION
ANA Hotel Okayama	2
Excel Okayama	3
Hotel Granvia	5
Kōraku Hotel	4
Saiwaisou	1

BARS AND IZAKAYA
Aussie Bar	2
Bar Padlock	5
Magic Pan	6
Matador	4
Pinball Café	3
Sky Bar-Sen	1

Okayama Orient Museum

岡山市立オリエント美術館, Okayama Shiritsu Bijutsukan • 9-31 Tenjin-chō • Tues–Sun 9am–5pm • ¥300 • ☎ 0862 32 3636, Ⓦ www.orientmuseum.jp

Set in an award-winning modernist building, the atmospheric **Okayama Orient Museum** gives, in chronological order, an unusual and well-presented collection of Near Eastern antiquities, ranging from Mesopotamian pottery and Syrian mosaics to Roman sculptures.

Okayama Prefectural Museum of Art

岡山県立美術館, Okayama Kenritsu Bijutsukan • 8-48 Tenjin-chō • Tues–Sun 9am–5pm • ¥350, special exhibitions extra; combined ticket with Kōrakuen ¥520 • ☎ 0862 25 4800, Ⓦ www.pref.okayama.jp/seikatsu/kenbi

The **Okayama Prefectural Museum of Art**, just north of the Okayama Orient Museum, holds a collection of contemporary local art. As well as dreamy ink paintings by the fifteenth-century artist and priest Sesshū Tōyō, there are examples of the local pottery style, *Bizen-yaki*, and regularly changing special exhibitions.

Kōrakuen

後楽園 • 1-5 Kōrakuen Daily: late March to Sept 7.30am–6pm; Oct to late March 8am–5pm • ¥400; combined ticket with Okayama Prefectural Museum ¥520, or with Okayama-jō ¥560 • ☎ 0862 72 1148, Ⓦ okayama-korakuen.jp • Buses from Okayama Station (12min) depart from terminal 4, headed for Fujiwara Danchi; Higashi-yama tram stop Shiroshita (¥140) is the closest to Kōrakuen, or it's a 20min walk east of the JR station

Okayama's star attraction is the **Kōrakuen**, at the northern end of the comma-shaped island, Nakanoshima, in the bend of the Ashi-gawa. Founded in 1686 by Lord Ikeda Tsunamasa, this **landscaped garden** is notable for its wide, lush lawns, which are highly unusual in Japanese garden design. Otherwise, all the traditional elements, including teahouses, artificial lakes, islands and hills, are present, and the black keep of Okayama-jō has been nicely incorporated into the scenery. The strange bleating sound you'll hear on entering the garden comes from a flock of caged **red-crested cranes**. Fortunately, Kōrakuen is large enough to soak up the kinds of crowds that deluge other famous gardens, such as Kenroku-en in Kanazawa and Ritsurin-kōen in Takamatsu.

Okayama-jō

岡山城 • 2-3-1 Marunouchi • Daily 9am–5pm • ¥300; combined ticket with Kōrakuen ¥560 • ☎ 0862 25 2096, Ⓦ okayama-kanko.net/ujo

South of Kōrakuen, accessible via the Tsukimi-bashi ("Moon-viewing Bridge"), is the smartly restored castle of **Okayama-jō**. Its nickname, U-jō ("Crow Castle"), refers to the black wood cladding of the donjon, from the top of which you get an excellent view of the surrounding area. Founded in 1573 by Lord Ukita Hideie, the adopted son of the great warlord Toyotomi Hideyoshi, the castle fell foul of both the Meiji restoration and World War II bombings, with the only original bit of the building now being the **Tsukimi Yagura** ("Moon-Viewing Turret"), at the western corner of the compound. You can pick up a good English-language leaflet from the ticket desk at the entrance to the donjon, and inside there's the chance to dress up in kimono as a samurai lord or lady for no extra charge.

Hayashibara Museum of Art

林原美術館 Hayashibara Bijutsukan • 2-7-15 Marunouchi • Tues–Sun 10am–4.30pm • ¥500 • ☎ 0862 23 1733, Ⓦ hayashibara-museumofart.jp

One of Okayama's smallest collections of artefacts is held at the **Hayashibara Museum of Art**, just southwest of Okayama-jō, which displays selections from the Asian art collection of local businessman Hayashibara Ichirō. There are some beautiful items kept here, including armor, paintings, ceramics, metalwork, delicate ink scroll paintings and exquisite nō theatre robes from the sixteenth century, but

KIBI PLAIN BICYCLE ROAD

The 17km-long **Kibi Plain bicycle road** (吉備路サイクリングロード), accessed from either Okayama or Kurashiki (see p.549), is an enjoyable way to see a visually rich area of countryside studded with ancient burial grounds, shrines and temples. Running from Bizen-Ichinomiya Station in the east to Sōja Station in the west, the route takes about four hours to cycle, or a full day to walk. Bikes can be rented at either station (¥200/hr, or ¥1000/day) and dropped off at the other end.

In the fourth century this area, known as Kibi-no-kuni, was the centre of early Japanese civilization. Lords were buried in giant keyhole-shaped mounds known as *kofun*, one of which can be visited along the cycle route. Starting from **Bizen-Ichinomiya Station** (備前一宮駅), three stops from Okayama on the JR Kibi line, cross the tracks and follow the cycle path to **Kibitsuhiko-jinja** (吉備津彦神社; daily 5am–6pm; free), an ordinary shrine beside a pond notable only for its huge stone lantern, one of the largest in Japan. Around 300m further southwest is the much more impressive **Kibitsu-jinja** (吉備津神社; daily 5am–6pm; free), dating from 1425 and dedicated to Kibitsu-no-mikoto, the valiant prince who served as the inspiration for the legend of **Momotarō**, the boy who popped out of the centre of a giant peach rescued from a river by a childless farmer's wife. This shrine nestles at the foot of Mount Naka and has a magnificently roofed outer sanctum, with twin gables.

Several kilometres further west is the **Tsukuriyama-kofun** (造山古墳), a burial mound constructed in the fifth century in the characteristic keyhole-shape (only really appreciated from the air). Measuring 350m in length and 30m at its highest point, this wooded mound in the midst of rice fields is the fourth-largest *kofun* in Japan. Around 1km east of here is a cluster of sights, including the foundation stones of Bitchū Kokubun-niji, an eighth-century convent, another burial mound and the five-storey pagoda of **Bitchū Kokubun-ji** (備中国分寺; daily 10am–4pm; free), a temple dating from the seventeenth century.

It's another couple of kilometres to the train station at **Sōja** (総社), from where you can return to either Okayama or to Kurashiki. Before leaving, check out **Iyama Hōfuku-ji** (井山宝福寺; daily 5am–5pm; free), a pretty Zen Buddhist temple, 1km north of Sōja Station along a footpath that follows the railway line. The celebrated artist and landscape gardener Sesshū Tōyō (1420–1506) trained here as a priest.

they're not always on display, so take a moment to leaf through the catalogue while sipping a free cup of green tea in the lounge.

ARRIVAL AND INFORMATION OKAYAMA

By plane Okayama Airport is 20km northwest of the train station; regular buses run from the airport into the city (¥740; 30min).
Destination Beijing (China) (3 weekly; 4hr 30min); Kagoshima (2 daily; 1hr 15min); Okinawa (2 daily; 2hr); Sapporo (daily; 2hr); Seoul (daily; 1hr 30min); Shanghai (China) (daily; 2hr 10min); Tokyo (9 daily; 1hr 20min).
By train Shinkansen and regular trains stop at Okayama Station, just over 1km west of Kōrakuen. If you're heading across to Shikoku, change here from the Shinkansen to the JR Seto Ōhashi line.
Destinations Kurashiki (every 15min; 15 min); Hiroshima (every 15min; 35min); Matsue (hourly; 2hr 20min); Shin-Ōsaka (every 30min; 45min); Takamatsu (3 hourly; 1hr); Tokyo (every 20min; 3hr 53min); Yonago (hourly; 2hr).
By bus Long-distance buses arrive either at the Ekimae bus station on the east side of Okayama Station or the Tenmaya Bus Centre, in the heart of the city's shopping district.
Destinations Chiba (1 daily; 10hr 55min); Fukuoka (1 daily; 9hr); Kōbe (2 daily; 2hr 50min); Kōchi (8 daily; 2hr

30min); Matsue (7 daily; 3hr 50min); Matsuyama (6 daily; 2hr 40min); Osaka (2 daily; 4hr); Tokyo (2 daily; 10hr 20min); Yonago (6 daily; 2hr 10min).
By ferry Ferries arrive at Shin-Okayama Port, 10km south of the city; from the port, buses go to Tenmaya Bus Centre every hour or so (30min).
Destination Shōdo-shima (hourly; 1hr 10min).
Tourist information You'll find tourist information at the Momotarō Kankō Sentā (daily 9am–8pm; ☏ 0862 22 2912) in the shopping mall beneath the station, near the *Hotel Granvia* exit on the east side of the building. The Okayama Prefecture International Exchange Centre, 2-2-1 Hokan-chō (information centre Tues–Sun 9am–5pm; library Mon–Sat 10am–7pm; ☏ 0862 56 2914, ⌨ www.pief.or.jp), a 2min walk from the west exit of the station, has English-speaking staff, a good library and information centre, plus free internet access. There is also a small tourist information counter (daily 9am–6pm) inside the train station, located near the departure area for the Shinkansen.

GETTING AROUND

By tram Kōrakuen and the city's other main sights are clustered around the Asahi-gawa, a 20min walk down Momotarō-dōri, the main road heading east from Okayama Station, along which trams run.

By bus Buses operate throughout the city, within which trips never cost more than a few hundred Yen.

By car Car rental is available from Nippon Rent-a-Car ☎ 0862 35 0919, Toyota Rent-a-Car ☎ 0862 54 0100 or Eki Rent-a-Car ☎ 0862 24 1363.

By bike If you don't fancy walking, you can rent bicycles from several outlets by the station, behind *Hotel Granvia* (see below), from ¥300 a day.

ACCOMMODATION

ANA Hotel Okayama 全日空ホテル 15-1 Ekimoto-chō ☎ 0868 98 1111, ⓦ anahotel-okayama.com. This plush hotel, ideally located next to the train station and attached to the Okayama Convention Centre, offers 217 spacious, elegant rooms, two restaurants and superb views from the twentieth-floor bar, *Sky Bar-Sen* (see p.548). Ask for one of the corner rooms, which have especially large windows, or a room facing south, which offers views of the station and downtown just beyond. Big with business travellers. **¥24,000**

Excel Okayama エクセル岡山 5-1 Ishiseki-chō ☎ 0862 24 0505, ⓦ www.excel-okayama.com. Good-value mid-range hotel, smartly decorated and conveniently located near Kōrakuen and Okayama's shopping arcades. **¥9000**

Hotel Granvia ホテルグランヴィア 1-5 Ekimoto-chō

☎ 0862 34 7000, ⓦ granvia-oka.co.jp. A close second to *ANA Hotel Okayama* in terms of luxury, this tall tower block alongside the station features large, tastefully furnished rooms and several restaurants, bars and shops. **¥27,720**

Kōraku Hotel 後楽ホテル 5-1 Heiwa-machi ☎ 0862 21 7111, ⓦ hotel.kooraku.co.jp. This hotel offers big, simple and stylish boutique rooms. There's a Japanese restaurant on the second floor, two computers in the lobby and a business centre, plus wi-fi in all rooms (for which there is sometimes a charge). **¥11,000**

Saiwaisou 幸荘 24-8 Ekimoto-chō ☎ 0120 254 080, ⓦ w150.j.fiw-web.net. A small, good-value business hotel with tatami and Western rooms – the cheaper ones share a bathroom. **¥7600**

8

EATING AND DRINKING

Okayama has the widest range of **eating** and **drinking** options between Kōbe and Hiroshima. The main districts to head for are immediately east of Okayama Station, where you'll find all the usual fast-food outlets and many other restaurants, and along Omotechō-shōtengai, the lengthy covered shopping street closer to the river. Local dishes include *somen*, handmade noodles dried in the sun and often served cold in summer, and *Okayama barazushi* (festival sushi), a mound of vinegared rice covered with seafood and regional vegetables.

Al Bacio アルバーチョ Omotechō-shōtengai ☎ 0862 23 1722, ⓦ al-bacio.com. Stock up on carbs at this upscale Italian eatery with modern art on the walls and a rather bourgeois feel. They serve a small selection of antipasti (from ¥420), while mains start at ¥1260. Alternatively, try the four-course set menu (¥3820). Daily 11am–9.30pm

Applause アプローズ Hotel Granvia, 1-5 Ekimoto-chō ☎ 0862 34 7000, ⓦ granvia-oka.co.jp/english/dining. With seating for a hundred, the main lounge bar on the nineteenth floor of this upmarket hotel (see above) does good-value buffet lunches (¥1890) until 2.30pm. But its cityscape view especially at night, is unbeatable, making it a very popular stop for late-night cocktails. Mon–Fri 11.30am–2.30pm & 5.30pm–midnight, Sat & Sun 11.30am–midnight.

CoMA Coffee コマ コーヒー 1-1-5 Marunouchi ☎ 0862 25 5530, ⓦ coma-coffee.com. A dainty little second-floor coffee joint opposite the Symphony Hall with excellent views all the way down Momotarō-dōri. In addition to very good freshly brewed coffee (¥400), they sell sandwiches (peanut butter and jam, for example), plus various coffee paraphernalia and their own bagged blends of beans.

Service can lag, but its so calm and relaxing here you'll probably not notice. Daily 9am–8pm, Sun till 7pm.

Cozzy's コージーズ 1-1-40 Omotechō ☎ 0862 25 1803. A rival to the myriad coffee chairs in the Omotechō area, this chic little café-grill has espresso drinks, sandwiches and a wide range of gourmet hamburgers (from ¥650) including bacon cheese, avocado and *teriyaki* versions Lunchtime sets are around ¥900. Daily 11.30am–9.30pm

Hakenden 八剣伝 2-19-18 ☎ 0862 54 2969. This mid-sized *izakaya* standby is presided over by something of a hard rocking chef, which accounts for the endless selection of pop and rock music streaming here. You can eat a full meal for around ¥1000, with dishes including *tamago harumaki* (spring rolls filled with egg; ¥230), *tsukune* (pork meatballs; ¥120) and *gyōza* (¥280). Daily 5pm–1am.

Okabe おかべ 1-10-1 Omotechō ☎ 0862 32 9167. All forms of tofu are celebrated in this small, no-nonsense restaurant on a side street off the shopping arcade. There's no menu per se; recommended dishes are daily *teishoku* (¥700) and the *yuba* (tofu skin) *donburi* (¥750). Mon–Sat 11.30am–2pm.

Tenda Rossa テンダロッサ 1-7-15 Nodaya-chō ☎ 0862 27 9011, ⓦ www2.oninet.ne.jp/tenda-r. Plaid tablecloths and rustic decor complement the pseudo-traditional Italian menu at this large pink restaurant. The menu includes pastas, pizzas and grilled meats and fish from ¥1200, and Italian specialities such as chicken cacciatori (¥1380). Set menus start at ¥2800. Tues–Sun 11.30am–2pm & 5.30–9.30pm.

Taj-Namaste タージ ナマステ Misawa building, 30-10 Ekimoto-chō ☎ 0862 52 5006. Great little Nepali-run curry house, painted a just-bearable orange colour, serving good-value lunch and dinner specials (from ¥900) ranging from tandoori keema to fish biryani. Daily 11am–3pm & 5–10pm.

Yamahachi Café ヤマハチカフェ 1-19 Tenjin-chō ☎ 0862 24 1719, ⓦ yamahachicafe.com. Sporting a spot-on Muji aesthetic, this quaint little upstairs hideaway, sometimes known as *Waffle*, serves a dozen or so great waffle plates (from ¥480), with toppings such as roasted almonds, green tea ice cream and chicken salad. Also serves beer. It's so popular that a queue to get in often forms down the stairwell outside. Daily noon– 9pm.

NIGHTLIFE

There's not a huge variety of nightlife in Okayama, but several jolly **izakaya** cater to a mainly younger crowd. Towards the southern end of the arcade, several **cinemas** screen mainstream films.

Aussie Bar オーヅーバー 1-10-21 Ekimae-chō ☎ 0862 23 5930. By the Nishigawa Greenway Canal, north of Momotarō-dōri, this smokey, divey spot with various flags on the ceiling and US licence plates on the walls is popular with foreigners and busiest on weekends – though you won't find any Fosters here. Look for the inevitable Australian yellow road sign hanging outside. Daily 7pm– around 3am.

Bar Padlock バー パドロック 8-23 Saiwai-chō ☎ 0862 22 4155 ⓦ padlock1986.com. Cool, classy and very laidback cocktail bar that has a hushed, speakeasy feel to it, with barmen in tuxes, jazzy vibes and a great selection of whiskys from ¥840. Cover charge is ¥500. 7pm–3am, Sun till 2am, closed Mon.

Magic Pan ハワイアンバー マジックパン Saiwai-chō 3-10 Hazime Tomozawa Building ☎ 0862 34 2121 ⓦ magicpan.net. This small Hawaiian-themed bar and restaurant does a decent trade in various colourful tropical cocktails, doled out by energetic bartenders who may have seen *Cocktail* one too many times – bottles of Blue Curaçao on fire and so on. Occasional ¥300 cover charge applies. Daily 7pm–3am, Fri & Sat till 5am, Sun till 1am.

Matador マタドール 3-8 Nishikimachi, ☎ 0862 32 7219. Spanish-themed bar with a menu of burritos, buffalo wings (from ¥650) and pizzas (from ¥1200). Show up after midnight and you're likely to hear some pretty dire karaoke renditions. Tues–Fri & Sun 5.30pm–4am, Sat 5.30pm–6am.

Pinball Café ピンボール カフ 4-18 Honmachi ☎ 0862 22 6966. Pinball's not on the menu in this casual, American-themed café which turns bar in the evenings, though Guinness and live music acts are, and a foreign crowd regularly shows up to hold session by the draught heads. Take the escalators up from the ground level. Daily 11.30am–3pm & 5pm–2am.

Sky Bar-Sen スカイバー「SEN」 ANA Hotel Okayama 15-1 Ekimoto-chō ☎ 0868 98 1111, ⓦ anahotel-okayama.com. Intimate bar on the twentieth floor of this upscale hotel (see p.547), with white leather seating and stupendous views of the city and the surrounding hills. Cocktails from ¥1000 and an all-you-can-drink happy hour from 5–7pm (¥3000). Daily 5pm–midnight, Sat & Sun till 11pm.

SHOPPING

Maruzen 丸善 Okayama Symphony Hall, 1-5-1 Omote-chō ☎ 0862 33 4640. In the Omotechō-shōtengai entrance of the hall, this bookshop has a good selection of English books and magazines and Japanese language learning materials on the basement level, down the escalators. Daily 10am–8pm.

Okayama Tourist Product Centre 岡山県観光プロダクトセンター 1-2-2 Omote-chō ☎ 0862 34 2270. Opposite Okayama Symphony Hall, this is a good place for local foods and crafts, including *Bizen-yaki* pottery, masks and weaving. Daily 10am–8pm.

DIRECTORY

Banks and exchange There are several banks along Momotarō-dōri, and you can also change money at the Central Post Office (see below).

Hospital Okayama University Medical Research Hospital, 2-5-1 Shikata-chō ☎ 0862 23 7151.

Internet You can get 30min free at the Okayama Prefecture International Exchange Centre, 2-2-1 Hokan-chō (Mon–Sat 9am–5pm ☎ 0862 56 2914).

Police Okayama Prefectural Police HQ, 2-4-6 Uchisange ☎ 0862 34 0110.

Post office Central Post Office, 2-1-1 Naka-sange (daily 9am–7pm, Sat till 5pm, Sun till 12.30pm).

POTTERY IN IMBE

Only dedicated lovers of ceramics will want to linger in drab **IMBE** (伊部), 30km east of Okayama and home of *Bizen-yaki*, Japan's oldest method of making pottery, developed here over a thousand years ago. The ceramics' distinctive earthy colour and texture are achieved without the use of glazes by firing in wood-fuelled kilns, whose brick chimneys you'll see dotted around Imbe Station. Beside the station is a **tourist information** counter (daily 9am–6pm, closed Tues; ☏0869 64 1100), where you can pick up an English leaflet about *Bizen-yaki* and get directions to the local pottery museums, the best being the **Bizen Pottery Traditional and Contemporary Art Museum** (備前陶芸美術館; 1659-6 Inbe; Tues–Sun 9.30am–5pm; ¥700; ☏0869 64 1001). in the grey concrete block immediately north of the station; it displays both old and new examples of the ceramics, providing an overview of the pottery's style and development. There are plenty of kilns with attached shops in which you can mooch around, and at some there are studios where you can sculpt your own blob of clay, for around ¥3000. This is then fired and shipped to your home (for overseas deliveries you'll need to pay extra). The most convenient place to try your hand at making pottery is the **Bizen-yaki Traditional Pottery Centre** (備前焼伝統産業会館、☏0869 64 1001), on the third floor of Imbe Station, where workshops are held each weekend and on holidays.

Kurashiki
倉敷

At first sight, **KURASHIKI**, 26km west of Okayama, looks like just another bland identikit Japanese town. But ten minutes' walk south of the station, the modern buildings and shops are replaced by an atmospheric, well-preserved enclave of picturesque, black-and-white walled merchants' homes (*machiya*), storehouses (*kura*) and canals dating from the town's Edo-era heyday, when it was an important centre for trade in rice and rush reeds. The compact **Bikan** historical area (美観地区), cut through by a narrow, willow-fringed canal, in which swans drift and carp swim, is full of museums and galleries, the best of which is the excellent **Ōhara Museum of Art**, containing four separate halls for Western art, contemporary Japanese art and local crafts.

Kurashiki is hugely popular with tourists and can get very busy during the day; to really appreciate the town's charm it's best to stay overnight and take an early-morning or evening stroll through the Bikan district.

Ōhashi House

大橋家住宅, Ōhashi-ke Jūtake • 3-21-31 Achi • Tues–Sun 9am–5pm • ¥500 • ⓦ ohashi-ke.com

Heading along Kurashiki Chūō-dōri from Kurashiki Station, peel off west after the fourth set of traffic lights to check out **Ōhashi House**. A rich merchant family, the Ōhashi prospered through salt production and land holdings. When they built their home in 1796, it was designed like those of the high-ranking samurai class, indicating how wealth was beginning to break down previously rigid social barriers. After passing through a gatehouse and small courtyard, and listening to a recorded history of the house (in Japanese), you're free to wander through the spacious, unfurnished tatami rooms.

Bikan

美観

It's a 1km walk from southeast from Kurashiki Station to the **Bikan** district of seventeenth-century granaries and merchant houses, the start of which is marked by the inevitable cluster of shops and dawdling tourists. Either side of the willow-lined canal are beautifully

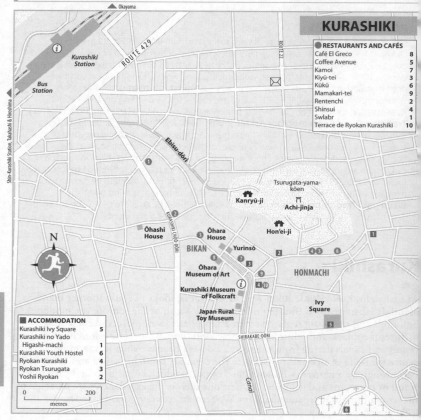

▲ Okayama

KURASHIKI

● **RESTAURANTS AND CAFÉS**
Café El Greco	8
Coffee Avenue	5
Kamoi	7
Kiyū-tei	3
Kūkū	6
Mamakari-tei	9
Rentenchi	2
Shinsui	4
Swlabr	1
Terrace de Ryokan Kurashiki	10

■ **ACCOMMODATION**
Kurashiki Ivy Square	5
Kurashiki no Yado Higashi-machi	1
Kurashiki Youth Hostel	6
Ryokan Kurashiki	4
Ryokan Tsurugata	3
Yoshii Ryokan	2

0 _____ 200
metres

preserved houses and warehouses, including the **Ōhashi House** (大橋家住宅), with its typical wooden lattice windows, and the adjacent **Yūrinsō** 有隣荘, the Ōhara family guesthouse with its distinctive green roof tiles (neither house open to the public).

Ōhara Museum of Art

大原美術館, Ōhara Bijutsukan • 1-1-15 Chūō • Daily 9am–5pm, Sept–May closed Mon • ¥1300 • ☎ 0864 22 0005, ⓦ ohara.or.jp

Located across a stone bridge decorated with carved dragons, the impressive **Ōhara Museum of Art**, the best of Kurashiki's many galleries and museums, is easily spotted by its creamy Neoclassical facade. This is the entrance to the original gallery, established in 1930 by local textile tycoon **Ōhara Magosaburō** to house his collection of **Western art**, including works by Cézanne, El Greco, Matisse, Monet, Picasso and Rodin, hand-picked by his friend, the painter Kojima Torajirō, in Europe in the 1920s. The first gallery to exhibit Western art in Japan, it was a roaring success and has been continually expanded ever since, with Magosaburō's heirs adding contemporary Western and Japanese art to the collection, as well as ancient Chinese artworks and an excellent range of top-class Japanese folkcrafts.

Main gallery

The entrance to the **main gallery** is flanked by bronze sculptures of St John the Baptist and the Burghers of Calais by Rodin – both were nearly melted down to make armaments during World War II. Starting with Ōhara's nineteenth-century purchases, he paintings are displayed in roughly chronological order, with works by Kandinsky, Pollock, Rothko and Warhol included in the twentieth-century and contemporary art sections. Despite the impressive range of artists displayed, however, there are few truly memorable works in this collection.

Craft Art Gallery

In contrast to the main gallery, the **Craft Art Gallery**, housed in an attractive quadrangle of converted wooden-beamed storehouses, leaves a much stronger impression. The **ceramics rooms** display beautiful and unusual works by four potters who were prime movers in the resurgence of interest in Japanese folk arts (*mingei*) earlier last century: Hamada Shōji, Kawai Kanjirō, Tomimoto Kenkichi and Bernard Leach, the British potter who worked with Hamada both in Japan, at Mashiko (see p.173), and in England at St Ives. A room filled with the strikingly colourful and sometimes abstract **woodblock prints** of Munakata Shikō follows, with the last section devoted to Serizawa Keisuke, a textile dyer and painter whose exquisite work features on kimono, curtains and fans, and who designed the gallery and the adjoining Asian Art Gallery.

Asian Art Gallery and Annex

The small collection in the **Asian Art Gallery**, on two levels, features displays of ancient East Asian art, including seventh-century Tang Dynasty ceramics and sculptures and serene Buddhas. The ground floor of the **Annex**, in a separate building behind the main gallery, displays unmemorable pastiches of modern Western-style art by Japanese artists, while downstairs you'll find bizarre contemporary works, made from Day-Glo perspex and the like.

8

Kurashiki Museum of Folkcraft

倉敷民芸館, Kurashiki Mingei-kan • 1-4-11 Chūō • Tues–Sun 9am–5pm, Dec–Feb till 4.15pm • ¥700 • ☏ 0864 22 1637, Ⓦ kurashiki-mingeikan.com

Located in a handsomely restored granary around a canal bend, the engaging **Kurashiki Museum of Folkcraft** is set adjacent to a stylish Meiji-era wooden building that houses the tourist information centre (see p.552). The museum displays a wide range of crafts, including *Bizen-yaki* pottery, baskets and traditional clothes, and has a small shop selling souvenirs a cut above those found in most of Kurashiki's other gift shops.

Japan Rural Toy Museum

日本郷土玩具館, Nihon Kyōdo Gangu-kan • 1-4-16 Chūō • Daily 9am–5pm • ¥400 • ☏ 0864 22 8058, Ⓦ gangukan.jp

A few doors down from the folkcraft museum, there's another excellent gift shop attached to the **Japan Rural Toy Museum**, which sells colourful new versions of the traditional playthings on display in the museum. Among a vast collection of dolls, spinning tops, animals and suchlike – most faded and tatty with age and use – the best displays in the museum are of huge kites and masks in the hall across the garden, at the back of the shop. The large top in the corner put the museum's owner, **Ohga Hiroyuki**, into the Guinness World Book of Records in 1985 after he spun it for 1 hour, 8 minutes, and 57 seconds.

Honmachi

本町

The seventeenth-century merchant houses in the district of **Honmachi** are a great spot for an afternoon amble. Here, you'll find some artsy craft shops, or stroll up the hillside towards **Tsurugata-yama Park** (鶴形山公園; 24hr), which includes the grounds of the simple **Achi-jinja** (阿智神社; 24hr; free; ☏0864 25 4898) shrine and **Hon'ei-ji** (本栄寺; 24hr; free) and **Kanryū-ji** (観龍寺; daily 6am–5pm; free; ☏0864 22 0357) temples. Another option is to potter around **Ivy Square**, east of the canal, where the ivy-covered late nineteenth-century **Kurashiki Cotton Mill** has been redeveloped into a shopping, museum and hotel complex. There's another good craft shop here, as well as an atelier where you can try your hand at pottery (¥2100).

ARRIVAL AND INFORMATION

By train Local trains arrive at Kurashiki Station, 15min west of Okayama on the San'yō line (¥320). Kodama Shinkansen stop at Shin-Kurashiki, from where you can change to a local train (¥190).

By bus Regular buses from Okayama and Kojima (see p.554) stop in front of Kurashiki Station.

Destinations Osaka (2 daily; 5hr); Tokyo (daily; 11hr).

Tourist information The tourist office (daily 9am–7pm ☎ 0864 26 8681) is on the second floor of the brow building attached to the southwest corner of Kurashik Station. There's another helpful tourist information office i the Bikan district (1-4-8 Chūō; daily 9am–6pm; ☎ 0864 2 0542), beside the canal.

ACCOMMODATION

Kurashiki is an excellent place to stay if you want to experience a traditional ryokan or minshuku, the best of which are in the Bikan district. The town is also fairly well served with upmarket Western-style hotels. Rates at most hotels rise by a couple of thousand yen at weekends and during holidays.

Kurashiki Ivy Square 倉敷アイビースクエアホテル 7-2 Honmachi ☎ 0864 22 0011, ⓦivysquare.co.jp. Part of a renovated factory complex at the southern corner of the Bikan district, this is a good mid-range stay with pleasantly decorated rooms, a couple of restaurants, a bar and shops. **¥21,000**

Kurashiki no Yado Higashi-machi 倉敷の宿東町 2-7 Higashi-machi ☎ 0864 24 1111. The out-of-the-way location keeps prices affordable without sacrificing comfort or impressive service at this top-notch ryokan. The mood inside is bright and airy, the rooms clean and comfortable. **¥25,920**

Kurashiki Youth Hostel 倉敷ユースホステル 1537-1 Mukōyama ☎ 0864 22 7355, ⓦjyh.gr.jp/kurashiki. This homely hostel is set beside a cemetery, atop a hill overlooking the Bikan district at the southern end of Kurashiki. It has bunk-bed dorms, excellent food, a self-catering kitchen and a comfortable lounge area with fireplace, bilingual TV and a piano. Rates almost half in off season. Dorm **¥4200**

Ryokan Kurashiki 旅館倉敷 4-1 Honmachi

☎ 0864 22 0730, ⓦwww.ryokan-kurashiki.jp/en. A recently renovated swanky ryokan housed in three converted rice and sugar storehouses in the middle of the Bikan district. Each individual suite has a Western-style bedroom and Japanese living room full of antiques, with women in blue kimono ministering to every need. The rates include extravagant *kaiseki* meals – exhorbitant, but the genuine article. **¥113,850**

Ryokan Tsurugata 旅館鶴形 1-3-15 Chūō ☎ 0864 22 1635, ⓦgambo-ad.com/english. A good deal cheaper than *Ryokan Kurashiki* (see above) and set in a 250-year-old canal-side merchant's house with atmospheric tatami rooms overlooking a traditional rock garden. Guests are served top-class *kaiseki ryōri* meals, which are also available to non-residents. **¥12,600**

Yoshii Ryokan 吉井旅館 1-29 Honmachi ☎ 0864 22 0118, ⓦyoshii-ryokan.com. Set back from the canal, this peaceful little abode has eight big rooms peering out over either beautifully manicured gardens or a courtyard. **¥50,000**

EATING, DRINKING AND NIGHTLIFE

There's a bewildering choice of **restaurants** in Kurashiki, with the Bikan district being the place to head to for excellent-value set-lunch deals. In the evenings, many places are closed, and you may be best off heading towards the station area. The town's signature dish is *mamakari-zushi*, a vinegared sardine-like fish on top of sushi rice. Though there are one or two places that hold late-night sessions, **bars and evening entertainment** aren't exactly Kurashiki's strong point – for that you'll want to head to Okayama (see p.543). In July and August you can chill out at the beer garden in the inner courtyard of the red-brick, ivy-clad complex of Ivy Square (daily 6–9.30pm).

Café El Greco カフェエルグレコ 1-1-11 Chūō ☎ 0864 22 0297, ⓦwww.elgreco.co.jp. Next to the Ōhara Museum of Art (see p.550), this classic Bikan café in an ivy-clad building facing the canal is run by a delightful team of older ladies and is a popular pit stop for tea and cake. Seating is at shared tables and a coffee will set you back ¥500. Tues–Sun 10am–5pm.

Coffee Avenue アベニュー 11-30 Honmachi

☎ 0864 24 8043. This coffee shop, on a street of old merchant houses, transforms come evening time into *Robert Brown Jazz Avenue* bar, which features live jazz from 8pm (cover ¥500). Daily noon–11pm.

Kamoi カモ井 1-3-17 Chūō ☎ 0864 22 0606, ⓦwww .kamoi-net.co.jp. Good-value sushi shop in an old granary facing the canal, with meals from ¥1050. Choose from the plastic food display in the restaurant window and cabinet utside. Tues–Sun 10am–6pm.

Kiyū-tei 亀遊亭 1-2-20 Chūō ☎0864 22 5140. At the head of the car al that runs through the Bikan district, this rustic steak restaurant offers curry rice for ¥1100, or there's a three-course lunch or dinner menu for ¥3150. Tues–Sun 11am–3pm & 5–9pm.

Kūkū 空空 11-19 Honmachi ☎0864 24 3075. This quaint restaurant, located away from the bustle of the tourist track, serves up great Indian and Thai curries from ¥650. 11.30am–7.30pm, closed Wed.

Mamakari-tei ままかり亭 3-12 Honmachi ☎0864 27 7112. This is a good place to try the local speciality *mamakari-zushi*; a set lunch including the sushi, alongside baked fish, tofu and soup, is ¥2625. Tues–Sun 11am–2pm & 5–10pm.

Rentenchi 東天地 2-19-18 Achi ☎0864 21 7858, ⓦrentenchi.com. Intimate, dimly lit Italian restaurant done up in brick and tile with pasta and pizza meals for around ¥1500, with wines starting at ¥600 a glass. Look for the green awning marked "Enoteca Osteria Rentenchi". 12.30–4pm & 6–10pm, closed Tues.

Shinsui 新粋 11-35 Honmachi ☎0864 22 5171, ⓦk-suiraitei.com/shinsui. This is a delightful restaurant with atmospheric lighting and a range of meals which you can have at the bar or in proper seats. Food includes *oden* (from ¥160), conger eel (¥1200) and a handful of creamy, crunchy croquettes (¥800). Jazz piano is often the soundtrack of the day. Daily 5–10pm.

Swlabr スーラバー 2-18-2 Achi ☎0864 34 3099. Bearing a resemblance to your cool great uncle's living room, this vibey café-bar has great old worn seating, collections of (Japanese) books and Neil Young (among other kindred sounds) on the radio. It serves snacks such as BLTs and pasta (from ¥800) and smoothies, lassi and floats. Daily noon–3am, Thurs from 3pm.

★**Terrace de Ryokan Kurashiki** テラスデ旅館くらしき 4-1 Honmachi ☎0864 22 0730, ⓦwww.ryokan-kurashiki.jp/en. This elegant café inside the *Ryokan Kurashiki* (see opposite) opens out onto a beautiful traditional garden complete with moss-covered rocks, gnarled pines and stone lanterns. Indulge in tea and biscuits for ¥800. Daily 2–5pm.

Takahashi

高梁

Some 40km northwest of Okayama, in the foothills of the mountain range that divides western Honshū, **TAKAHASHI** is a small and charming time-warped castle town. Few visitors venture here, despite the fine old buildings and temples in the **Ishibiya-chō Furusato Mura** ("Hometown Village") area, a name evoking images of a long-lost Japan. The temples, ranged attractively at staggered levels along the hillside on the eastern side of the train tracks, extend north towards Furusato Mura. They can best be viewed from above; the steep hike up to **Bitchū Matsuyama-jō** – Japan's highest castle – rewards visitors with excellent panoramas over the temples and town.

The castle aside, almost all of Takahashi's sights are within easy walking distance of Bitchū Takahashi Station and can be covered in half a day. Finding your way around is simple, since there are plenty of direction signs in English.

Raikyū-ji

頼久寺 • 18 Raikyūji-chō • Daily 9am–5pm • ¥300

The single most impressive temple in Takahashi is **Raikyū-ji**, ten minutes' walk from the train station, with its serenely beautiful raked-gravel **garden**. The exact date of the temple's construction is uncertain, though it is known that in 1604, Kobori Enshū, governor of the province and expert gardener, lived here. The Zen garden he designed is maintained today exactly as he left it, with its islands of stones, plants and trimmed azalea hedges carefully placed to resemble a crane and a tortoise in the "well-wishing garden" style, and featuring the distant borrowed scenery of Mount Atago.

Bitchū Matsuyama-jō

備中松山城 • Yamashita • Donjon daily 9am–5.30pm, Oct–March till 4.30pm • ¥300 • ☎0866 22 1487 • Take a taxi (¥1300) from the station then walk 15min up a steep hill, or it's an hour's walk from the station; note that no local buses go to anywhere near the castle

Rest by Raikyū-ji's garden before tackling the strenuous hour-long hike up to the castle,

Bitchū Matsuyama-jō, following a shaded track through the hillside forest. Takahashi's fortunes prospered from the mid-thirteenth century, when warlord Akiba Saburō Shigenobu built the original fortress on top of nearby Mount Gagyū. Don't bother paying to go into the **donjon**, restored this century, since there are few relics inside and not much of a view from its narrow windows. At 480m, it's the highest altitude castle in Japan, and the vistas on the walk back downhill make the effort of hiking up worthwhile.

Ishibiya-chō Furusato Mura

石火矢町ふるさと村

You can easily kill a good hour or two by exploring the **Ishibiya-chō Furusato Mura** area of old houses and buildings, sandwiched between the rail tracks and the Takahashi-gawa, and cut through by a stream crossed by stone bridges topped with miniature shrines.

Buke-yashiki-kan samurai houses

武家屋敷館 • Nishi 95 • Daily 9am–5pm • ¥400 for both • ☎ 0795 52 6933

Of the several buildings in the Ishibiya-chō Furusato Mura which have been turned into museums, the most interesting are the two **Buké-yashiki-kan samurai houses**. Here you can explore the residence's various living spaces and have a wander around the gardens.

Takahashi Museum of History

高梁市郷土資料館, Takahashi-shi Kyoda Shiryōkan • Uchisange 1 • Daily 9am–5pm • ¥300 • ☎ 0866 21 0180

The clapboard Meiji-era Takahashi Elementary School is now the **Takahashi Museum of History**, a small Western-style Meiji-era building 500m south of the station housing a jumble of items running from *mikoshi* (portable shrines) to a morse code machine. At the back of the ground floor are some evocative black-and-white photos of the town, while on the second floor, look out for the dancing doll models made from old cigarette packets – a nod to Japan Tobacco, which has a factory in Takahashi.

ARRIVAL AND INFORMATION   TAKAHASHI

By train Takahashi's train station, Bitchū-Takahashi (備中高 梁駅), is on the JR Hakubi line, around an hour from Okayama (¥820) or half that on the express train from Kurashiki (¥520). Destinations Kurashiki (hourly; 33min); Okayama (hourly;

50–55min)

Tourist information You can pick up a Japanese map of the town from the tiny information office (daily 9am–3pm; ☎ 0866 21 0461) at the bus terminal, next to the station.

ACCOMMODATION AND EATING

Jūjū-tei じゅうじゅう亭 20-3 Omotezaki-chō ☎ 0184 24 1626. Inexpensive restaurant near the *Takahashi Kokusai Hotel* (see below), serving a range of Japanese plates, including various steak (¥350) and soup (¥320) dishes. Daily 11am–11.30pm, closed Thurs.

Kōzō Sushi 浩三 1965-1 Masamune-chō ☎ 0866 22 5207. Take-away sushi shop ideal for a picnic at the castle,

with good-sized seafood plates from ¥500. Daily 11am–7pm.
Takahashi Kokusai Hotel 高梁国際ホテル 2033 Masamune-chō ☎ 0866 21 0080. Good spot just 3min north of the station that serves as the closest thing to a reasonable business hotel. Rooms are sizeable, as are the breakfasts, served in a decent on-site restaurant. Ask for a room on the opposite side of the train station. <u>12,000</u>

Kojima and around

児島

About 25km south of Okayama, **KOJIMA**, with its sprawling shopping centres and newly laid roads, has boomed since the opening in 1988 of the nearby 12.3km-long **Seto Ōhashi** (Great Seto Bridge), a series of six bridges and four viaducts hopping from island to island across the Inland Sea to Shikoku. The summit of **Washū-zan** on the prefecture's southern tip offers fantastic views, and outdoor lovers might want to explore fragments of the area's ancient history by taking the leisurely and fairly flat **Kibi Plain** bicycle route, which runs past fifth-century burial mounds and rustic temples and shrines; it takes about four hours to cycle in its entirety.

Seto Ōhashi

瀬戸大橋 • Boat tours daily 9am–3pm, Dec–Feb Sat & Sun only • 45min • ¥1550 • To see the bridge by land, you can get regular buses to the lookout point from Kojima station; stay on the bus past the fishing hamlet of Shimotsui (下津井) and Washū-zan Highland (鷲羽山ハイランド), a tacky amusement park, and get off at the car park by the official lookout spot – from here you can climb to Washū-zan's summit

One of the most memorable ways to view the series of bridges that make up the epic **Seto Ōhashi** and the islands of the Inland Sea is to take a boat tour from the sightseeing pier immediately to the east of Kojima Station. If you'd prefer to view it all from dry land, head 4km south of Kojima to **Washū-zan** (鷲羽山), a 134m-high hill jutting out into the Inland Sea. From Washū-zan's summit, you can take in what has to be one of Japan's most glorious panoramas.

Bridge Museum

瀬戸大橋記念館, Seto Ōhashi Kinenkan • 1-2 Tanora • Tues–Sun 9am–10pm • Free • ☎ 0864 74 5111 • A 15min walk west of the train station.

The **Bridge Museum** is one of the more unusual attractions in Kojima, displaying scale models of bridges from around the world. You can actually walk over the arched museum building, inspired by a *taiko-bashi* (drum bridge), and enjoy the small **park** over the road containing eleven amusingly miniature bridges, a chessboard-like square decorated with bizarre silver statues (supposedly symbolizing the seasons) and a model of Stephenson's famous steam engine, the *Rocket*. Inside the museum, the eye is drawn immediately to the **ceiling**, which is painted with a lively mural of Edo-era travelling performers, craftsmen, merchants and priests.

Shimotsui

下津井

A quick taxi ride south of Kojima is the "textile city" of Shimotsui, which is home to the interesting **Mukashi Shimotsui Kaisendonya** (むかし下津井回船問屋; 9am–5pm, closed Tues; free; ☎0864 72 1289), a museum of fisherfolk life. It's also worth having a wander around the old streets, taking in the castle ruins, the covered wells from which passing boats stocked up on fresh water, and the Gion shrine.

ARRIVAL AND INFORMATION

KOJIMA

By train Kojima is on the Seto Ōhashi line, 20min by express train from Okayama (¥480).

Tourist information The tourist office (daily 9am–5.30pm; ☎0864 72 1289) in Kojima Station can provide you with an English map and booklet on the area.

ACCOMMODATION

Washū-zan Youth Hostel 鷲羽山ユースホステル Obatake 1666-1 ☎0864 79 9280. Bunk-bed dorms and good food (breakfast ¥525, dinner ¥945), as well as impressive views of the Seto Ōhashi and the Inland Sea from its location at the tip of a promontory, make this a choice stay for Kojima. It takes 20min to reach the hostel on one of the hourly buses (last bus is at 5.30pm) leaving for Washū-zan from platform #4 outside Kojima Station. Dorm **¥2100**

Fukuyama

福山

Some 65km west of Okayama, along the industrialized Sanyō coast, is the old castle town of **Fukuyama**, now the key industrial city of Hiroshima-ken's Bingo district and a place known for its hundreds of thousands of rose blossoms in the summer months. For those travelling it's more often used as a jumping-off point for the lovely seaside town of **Tomonoura** (see below).

Hiroshima Prefectural Museum of History

広島県立歴史博物館, Hiroshima Kenritsu Rekishi Hakubutsnkan • 2-4-1 Nishimachi • Tues–Sun 9am–5pm • ¥290 • ☎ 0849 31 2513

The memorable **Hiroshima Prefectural Museum of History**, just west of the station, was designed around the excavation of the ruins of **Kusado Sengen** (草戸千軒), a medieval town buried in the nearby riverbed of the Ashida-gawa. The museum has some imaginatively displayed artefacts and haunting background music, as well as a reconstructed village street from the old settlement, lit to re-create twilight in May.

Fukuyama Museum of Art

ふくやま美術館, Fukuyama Bijutsukan • 2-4-3 Nishimachi • Tues–Sun 9.30am–5pm • ¥300 • ☎ 0849 32 2345

Opened in 1988, the **Fukuyama Museum of Art** holds a permanent collection of Japanese art, focusing on contemporary works by local artists, as well as some European works. The most striking pieces of sculpture are in the surrounding gardens.

ARRIVAL AND INFORMATION FUKUYAMA

By train Fukuyama Station is on both the Shinkansen and JR San'yō train lines.
Destinations Tomonoura (every 30min; 40min).
By bus The bus terminus is beside the station's south exit.
Destination Tomonoura (hourly; 30min).

Tourist information Inside the station, beside the north exit, is the tourist information desk (daily 9am–5.30pm; ☎ 0849 22 2869), which has English maps and leaflets on Fukuyama and Tomonoura.

ACCOMMODATION AND EATING

There are plenty of **hotels** just north of the station. **Restaurants** are in abundance along the south side of the JR station. Tenmaya Department store, 2min walk south, also has restaurants on the seventh floor.

Cafe Estancia カフェエスタンシア Fukuyama Station. Located just next to the Shinkansen entrance inside the station, this brightly lit café, done up in pale woods, is a fine place to await your bullet train out of town. A selection of coffees (from ¥390), plus pancakes, ice cream and a few more substantive noodle dishes (from ¥750) are served at diner-style booth seating. Daily 7am–8pm.
Fukuyama Oriental Hotel 福山オリエンタルホテル 1-Marunouchi ☎ 0849 27 0888, ⊛ oriental-web.co.jp/ fukuyama. This smart, mid-brow business hotel just behind the train station offers modern en-suite rooms with design features that include stylish desk chairs and

futuristic phones. There is also an indoor onsen bath. **¥11,000**
Marunouchi Hotel 丸の内ホテル 1-3-3 Marunouchi ☎ 0849 23 2277. At the park north of the station, this mid-level property has some of the cheapest accommodation in town. The plain, Western-style rooms tend to be on the small side, but most have views straight up to the castle. **¥8600**
Zucchero e Sale ズッケロサーレ 1-1 Sannomaru-chō ☎ 0849 28 3543. A great basement trattoria just outside the station serving Italian standby dishes (from ¥650) such as aubergine parmigiana and spaghetti di fungi. Daily 11.30am–3pm & 5.30–10pm.

Tomonoura

鞆の浦

There are few more pleasant ways to spend half a day or more in Japan than exploring the enchanting fishing port of **TOMONOURA**, at the tip of the Numakuma Peninsula, 14km south of Fukuyama, and the inspiration for Hayao Miyazaki's 2008 film *Ponyo*. The town has one of the most beautiful locations on the Inland Sea, and its narrow, twisting streets

RIGHT LIVING PICTURE SCROLLS VIEW, ADACHI MUSEUM OF ART (P.602) >

and surrounding hills are easily explored on foot or by bicycle. Boats unload their catch daily beside the horseshoe-shaped **harbour**, which has hardly changed since the town's Edo-era heyday, when trading vessels waited here for the tides to change direction or rested en route to mainland Asia. Today, you're just as likely to see locals dreaming the day away on the sea walls, rod in hand, waiting for the fish (especially *sakura dai*, or sea bream) to bite, or selling catches of prawns, squirming crabs and other seafood on the streets.

Get your bearings by climbing up to the ruins of **Taigashima-jō** on the headland immediately above the ferry landing, where you'll find a small monument to the celebrated haiku poet Bashō and great views from Empuku-ji. To the west, you can see the gentle sweep of the harbour and the temple-studded slopes of Taishiden hill, while to the east is tiny **Benten-jima**, an outsized rock crowned with a temple to the Buddhist deity, and the larger island **Sensui-jima** (仙酔島), incidentally, one of the better places to stay the night (see opposite).

Tomonoura Museum of History

鞆の浦歴史民俗資料館, Tomonoura Rekishi Minzoku Shiryokan・536-1 Ushiroji・Tues–Sun 9am–5pm・¥150・☎ 0849 82 1121

You'll find a few mildly diverting exhibits at the **Tomonoura Museum of History**, including a miniature model of the sea bream-netting show held at the harbour every

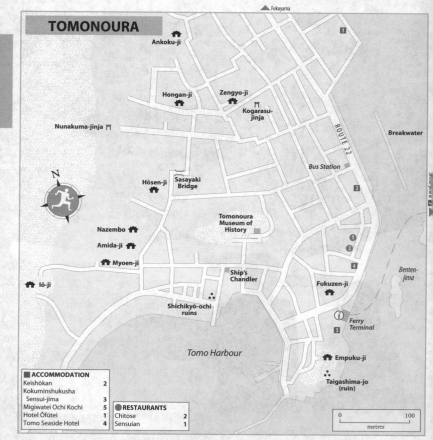

ACCOMMODATION

Keishōkan	2
Kokuminshukusha Sensui-jima	3
Migiwatei Ochi Kochi	5
Hotel Ōfūtei	1
Tomo Seaside Hotel	4

RESTAURANTS

Chitose	2
Sensuian	1

day in May, when the local fishermen use age-old methods to herd the fish into their nets. The **view** from the museum's hilltop location in the middle of the town, across a patchwork of grey and blue tiled roofs dropping away to the harbour, is one of Tomonoura's most pleasant.

Shichikyō-ochi Ruins

七卿落ち・8-4-2 Tomochō・10am–5pm; closed Tues・¥400・☎ 0849 82 3553

Located on a street lined with one-time wood-and-plaster eighteenth- and nineteenth-century warehouses, now turned into gift and coffee shops, are the **Shichikyō-ochi Ruins** (the ruins of the exile of the seven nobles), a perfectly intact old sake brewery that briefly sheltered a band of anti-shogun rebels in the turbulent times prior to the Meiji Restoration.

Shrines

A dozen odd **temples** are set in and around the town centre. The pretty **Iō-ji** (医王寺; 13-97 Ushiroji; 24hr; free) is located down a narrow pedestrian alley, up Taishiden hill. If you're cycling there, it's best to leave your bike on the main road before hiking up to the temple, one of many founded by the revered Buddhist priest **Kōbō Daishi** (see p.510). About 300m away is **Hōsen-ji** (法宣寺; 11-94-3 Ushiroji; 24hr; free), set at the bottom of a small hill on a site where a 14.3m-wide Tengai pine tree once stood (now only a truncated stump remains). **Nunakuma-jinja** (沼名前神社; 12-25 Ushiroji; 24hr; free), a few minutes' walk northwest, is a large shrine which, although ancient, was recently rebuilt in concrete. More impressive than the building is the traditional wooden nō stage that used to be taken around battlefields to entertain warlord Toyotomi Hideyoshi.

Fukuzen-ji

福禅寺・6-2-9 Tomocho・Daily 9.30am–5pm・Taichōrō ¥200・☎ 0849 82 2705

The airy tatami space of the **Taichōrō** reception hall of the tenth-century **Fukuzen-ji**, by the ferry port, features paper screens that open to reveal a striking panorama of the Inland Sea, a view which has changed little since 1711, when a visiting Korean envoy hailed it "the most beautiful scenery in Japan".

ARRIVAL AND INFORMATION   TOMONOURA

By bus Buses leave platform 15 at Fukuyama bus terminus roughly every 20min, and take around 30min to reach Tomonoura (¥510). They stop just down the road from the tiny ferry terminal.

Tourist information Inside the ferry terminal is an information desk (daily 9am–5.30pm; ☎ 0849 82 3200), where you can pick up an English map of the town.
Services Bikes can be rented from the car park adjoining the ferry terminal (¥300/2hr, plus ¥500 deposit).

ACCOMMODATION

Keishōkan 景勝館 421 Tomochō ☎ 0849 82 2121, ⓦ keishokan.com. It's worth shelling out a few thousand more Yen for a sea-view room or one with private onsen at this once-luxurious but now dated tatami-style seafront accommodation. A selection of indoor and outdoor baths make it slightly more appealing. **¥15,750**

★ **Kokuminshukusha Sensui-jima** 国民宿舎仙酔島 3373-2 Tomochoushiroji, Sensui-jima ☎ 0849 70 5050, ⓦ kokumin-shukusha.or.jp. One of the most enjoyable options for a night's accommodation is on

Sensui-jima, the island that's a 5min ferry ride (¥240 return) east of Tomonoura. It has superior-quality tatami rooms and a relaxing set of public baths, including an outdoor rooftop pool. Unusually for a Japanese hotel, there are no TVs in the rooms; instead, you'll find pens and paper and a note encouraging guests to write a letter or even a poem. **¥15,600**

★ **Migiwatei Ochi Kochi** 汀邸遠音近音 6-2-9 Tomochotomo ☎ 0849 82 1575, ⓦ ochikochi.co.jp. Set right at the edge of the sea, this top-notch ryokan, built into an expanded 250-year-old building, is Tomonoura's

8

best. The rooms here feature understated decor with ultra modern amenities – think Jacob Jensen telephones, large flat screens and hand-powered coffee mills with beans. Every room has its own black bamboo onsen set on a large balcony offering views straight out to the water, and there's also a roof terrace. Hugh Jackman stayed here when filming a Samurai sequence from *X-Men*. **¥54,600**.

Hotel Ōfūtei ホテル鴎風亭 136 Tomochō ☎0849 82 1123. One of the more upmarket choices in town, with a large wooden deck along the waterfront for dining,

spacious tatami-style rooms and the highlight: its collection of huge roofop baths. Thankfully, at least, the strikingly ugly hotel building is safely out of view at the north end of the town. **¥42,000**

Tomo Seaside Hotel 鞆シーサイドホテル 555 Tomochō ☎0849 83 5111, ☺tomonoura.co.jp/tomo. This "modern" Seventies-style hotel offers traditional tatami rooms with sea views at reasonable prices, though the whole place is looking a bit frayed around the edges. **¥16,200**

EATING

Chitose 千とせ 552-7 Tomochō ☎0849 82 3165. A friendly place just behind the car park on the town's eastern waterfront, this spot is low on atmosphere but big on taste and value. A delicious set meal of many dishes, including the trademark catch of *tai* (sea bream), costs ¥1890, though more affordable is the tempura dinner (¥945) with shrimp, octopus, squid and whitefish.

Cash only. 11.30am–2.30pm & 6–9pm, closed Tues.
Sensuian 仙酔庵 3373-2 Ushiroji Tomochō ☎0849 70 5050. This charming café serves *matcha* and *dango* rice balls in winter and shaved ice desserts in the summer. Their hot *taiyagi* (¥390) is worth a try. Daily 9am–8.30pm.

Onomichi

尾道

Twenty kilometres west of Fukuyama lies the enchanting port of **ONOMICHI**, overlooked by the houses and temples that tumble down the steep face of the wooded hill, Senkōji-san. Many Japanese come here to linger along the town's vertiginous byways, imagining scenes from their favourite films by local director Ōbayashi Nobuhiko. Onomichi is also a gateway to some of the islands of the Inland Sea,

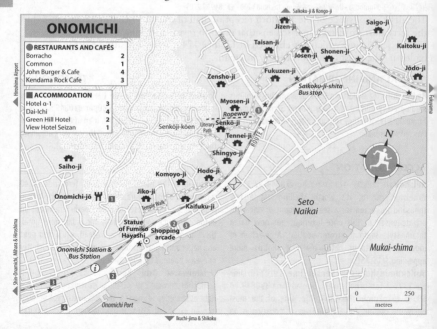

ONOMICHI

RESTAURANTS AND CAFÉS
Borracho	2
Common	1
John Burger & Cafe	4
Kendama Rock Cafe	3

ACCOMMODATION
Hotel α-1	3
Dai-Ichi	4
Green Hill Hotel	2
View Hotel Seizan	1

including **Ikuchi-jima** and **Ōmi-shima** (see p.565), and to Shikoku via ferry or by road along the Shimanami Kaidō Expressway.

The temple walk

古寺めぐり, Koji Meguri • Ropeway daily 9am–5.15pm • ¥280 one-way, ¥440 return • Skip the first temples by catching the regular bus from stand 1 at Onomichi Bus Station and heading east for 5min to the Nagaeguchi stop (¥140), then taking the ropeway up to Senkōji-kōen

There's a pleasant **temple walk** from Onomichi Station past most of the town's 25 temples; to complete the full course takes the better part of a day, by which time you'll be sick of temples. You might want to skip those at the start by hopping on a bus from ousitde the train station and then catching the **ropeway** (cable-car) up to **Senkōji-kōen** (千光寺公園), which blooms with cherry blossom and azaleas each spring and from which point you can rejoin the walk from the southeast corner of the park. The views from the park's hilltop observatory across the town and narrow sea channel to the nearest island, Mukai-shima, are impressive.

Senkō-ji

千光寺 • Daily 8.30am–5pm • Free • ⓣ 0848 23 2310

The most colourful temple on the Senkōji-kōen park hill is the scarlet-painted **Senkō-ji**, packed with *jizō* statues and doing a lively trade in devotional trinkets, particularly heart-shaped placards on which visitors scribble a wish; these are then left dangling in the temple for good luck.

Literary path

文学のこみち, Bungaku no komichi

Heading back downhill from Senkō-ji, you can follow the section of the temple walk known as the "**literary path**", so called because famous writers' words are inscribed on stone monuments along the way. The most celebrated of the local writers is **Hayashi Fumiko**, a female poet who lived in Onomichi from 1917 and whose bronze statue can be found crouching pensively beside a wicker suitcase and umbrella at the entrance to the shopping arcade a minute east of the station.

Fukuzen-ji

福善寺 • Daily 9am–5pm • Free

Fukuzen-ji, which dates from 1573, has a vast spreading pine tree in its grounds, said to be shaped like an eagle, and its main gate is decorated with beautiful woodcarvings of cranes and dragons. On the steps up to the temple, look out for **Tile-ko-michi** (Little Tile Street), a narrow alley back down the hill which has been plastered over the last 25 years with ceramic slabs inscribed by visitors.

Saikoku-ji

西国寺 • Daily 9am–5pm • Free • ⓣ 0848 37 0321, ⓦ saikokuji.jp

Saikoku-ji, thought to have been built around 739, is one of the largest temple complexes in western Japan and easily spotted by the giant straw sandals which hang either side of its imposing entrance gate; pray here and it's said that you'll find the strength to continue your journey.

Jōdo-ji

浄土寺 • Daily 9am–5pm • Temple free, garden ¥500 • ⓣ 0848 37 2361

The last temple worth visiting on Onomichi's temple walk is **Jōdo-ji**, at the eastern end of the route. Pigeons flock around its squat two-storey pagoda, and there's an elegant Zen garden, with a tea-ceremony room transported from Kyoto's Fushimi castle, hidden behind the main hall of worship.

8

ARRIVAL AND INFORMATION

By train Trains on the JR San'yō line take 20min from Fukuyama to Onomichi Station (¥400), a minute's walk from the waterfront. Shinkansen take 9min to Shin-Onomichi (¥400), 3km north of the town; from here a regular bus (¥180) takes 15min to reach Onomichi Station.

Destinations Fukuyama (every 30min; 20min); Okayama (hourly; 1hr 25min).

By bus Buses leave from outside Onomichi Station for Ikuchi-jima (see p.565, 1hr; ¥1000) and Hiroshima Airport (1–2hr; ¥1100; see p.570), 30min west. Ferries to Setoda on Ikuchi-jima leave from the jetty immediately in front of

Onomichi Station (40min; ¥800 one-way).

Destinations Imabari, Shikoku (10 daily; 1hr 30min); Matsuyama, Shikoku (2 daily; 2hr 50min); Ōmi-shima (1 daily; 55min).

Tourist information A helpful, English-speaking information counter greets those arriving by train just inside the station (daily 9am–6pm; ☎ 0848 20 0005). Here you can pick up an English map showing the walking route around the town's temples, get suggestions on places to eat and find out about transport schedules. You can hire cycles from just across the road at the *Green Hill Hotel* (see below) for ¥500 per day.

ACCOMMODATION

Hotel α-1 アルファ・ワン 1-1 Nishigosho-chō ☎ 0848 25 5600, ⓦ alpha-1.co.jp. The contemporary Western-style rooms at this affordable place a few minutes' walk from the station are presentable enough, if not entirely up to date in terms of amenities. Ask for one on the south side; those on the north catch noise from the train tracks just below. **¥9900**

Dai-Ichi Hotel 第一ホテル 4-7 Nishigoshōch ☎ 0848 23 4567. A few metres from the port, this dated old hotel nevertheless has affordable small rooms, all with views of the water and furnished with half-fridges, plus some of the twin rooms even have small couches in them. **¥9450**

Green Hill Hotel グリーンヒルホテル Onomichi 9-1 Higashigosho-chō, ☎ 0848 24 0100,

ⓦ shimanami-gho.co.jp. Pay no attention to the sore thumb of a building this Western-style hotel is set in. The rooms, done in beige and pale woods, are bright, decently sized and relatively cheap. Next to the lobby, which is on the first floor, is a spacious café with floor-to-ceiling windows out to the port. Best of all, boats to Ikuchi-jima depart from just outside the back door and the train station is just outside the front. **¥16,800**

View Hotel Seizan ビュウホテルセイザン 16-21 Nishitsuchidō-chō ☎ 0848 23 3313, ⓦ onomichi-viewhotel.co.jp. This friendly place up by the castle has great views out over the Inland Sea and discounted off-peak rates. Rooms are simple and many have bathtubs; there's also a small restaurant serving dinner. **¥7000**

EATING AND DRINKING

Onomichi fancies itself as something of a gourmet destination, and the tourist office produces a map in Japanese detailing an impressive range of eating options. Being a port, fresh seafood is the thing to go for, especially at the sushi restaurants clustered along the harbour-front east of the station. There are plenty of bars and late-night restaurants in the entertainment district, Saikoku-ji-shita, south of the bus stop, in the narrow streets between the railway line and the waterfront.

Borracho ボラーチョ 1-4-14 Tsuchido 1-chōme ☎ 0848 23 8951. In the arcade near the station, this Spanish-influenced place offers drinks and tapas (from ¥240), salads and a variety of South American *cazuela* dishes. Tues–Sun 6pm–midnight.

Common 茶房こもん 1-2-2 Nagae ☎ 0848 37 2905. Located at the base of the ropeway, this spot specializes in freshly made Belgian waffles (around ¥500). Daily 10am–5pm.

John Burger & Cafe ジョンバーガーアンドカフェ 3-25 Gosho-chō ☎ 0848 25 2688, ⓦ john-burger.com. Cosy,

casual spot by the station that serves up a solid selection of burgers, including fish (¥500) and teriyaki (¥400) versions. 11am–9pm, closed Wed.

Kendama Rock Cafe ケンダマロックカフェ 1-17-13 Tsuchidō ☎ 848 24 8180. A very cute, very tiny coffee spot with rickety floorboards and half a dozen seats. Run by a gregarious professional kendama player and awash in the sport's paraphernalia. They serve good fresh brewed Americano (¥500) and a few snacks. Daily 11am–6pm.

Ikuchi-jima and Ōmi-shima

生口島・大三島

Among the Geiyo archipelago of islands clogging the Inland Sea between Onomichi and the northwest coast of Shikoku, **IKUCHI-JIMA** and **ŌMI-SHIMA** are both worth a

THE SHIMANAMI CYCLING ROAD

Onomichi is the gateway to the **Shimanami Kaidō**, which connects Honshū with Shikoku via the 65km **Nishi-Seto Expressway**. This ties together nine islands of the Inland Sea via a series of ten bridges, including the Tatara Ōhashi between Ikuchi-jima and Ōmi-shima, and at 1480m the world's longest cable-stayed suspension bridge. These are the only bridges between Honshū and Shikoku over which cyclists are allowed to ride, and the route makes a stunning way to explore the islands of the Inland Sea. If you're a keen cyclist, it's possible to do the whole thing in a day, although staying overnight in Ikuchi-jima (see p.365) allows you to enjoy the scenery in more leisurely fashion. The final section takes in the 4km-long **Kurushima-Kaikyō** between Ōshima and Imabari on Shikoku, the longest three-span suspension bridge in the world.

You can **rent bikes** from the car park attached to the ferry terminal in Onomichi, and from a dozen other locations between here and Imabari; they all provide maps of the route, which is clearly signposted in English along the way. Bridge cycle tolls range from ¥50 to ¥200. Bike rental along the route is ¥500/day, plus a ¥1000 deposit, refundable only if you return your bike to the place where you hired it.

visit. Of the two, Ikuchi-jima is the place to stay and has the best attractions, including **Kōsan-ji**, a dazzling, kaleidoscopic temple complex, and the exquisite **Hirayama Ikuo Museum of Art**.

While part of the fun of visiting these islands is the ferry ride there (see p.564), you can also get to Ikuchi-jima by bus or bicycle from Onomichi along the Shimanami Kaidō (see box above). Both islands are best explored by bicycle.

Ikuchi-jima

生口島

Sun-kissed **IKUCHI-JIMA**, covered with citrus groves, attracts plenty of tourists each summer to its palm-fringed beaches, in particular the sweeping man-made Sunset Beach on the west coast. The island can comfortably be toured by bicycle in a day, as can the islet Kōne-shima, which is linked by bridge to Ikuchi-jima's main settlement, the quaint **Setoda** (瀬戸田) on the island's northwest coast. Around the island, look out for the fourteen bizarre contemporary outdoor sculptures, including a giant saxophone and a stack of yellow buckets, which form part of Ikuchi-jima's "Biennale" modern art project.

Kōsan-ji

耕三寺 • 553-2 Setoda • Daily 9am–5pm • ¥1200 • ☎ 0845 70 800, ⓦ kousanji.or.jp

It's an unmistakeably gaudy entrance that leads visitors to Ikuchi-jima's most famous attraction – the technicolour temple complex of **Kōsan-ji**. The temple was the creation of steel-tube manufacturer **Kanemoto Kozo**, who made much of his fortune from the arms trade. When his mother died, the bereft Kanemoto decided to build a temple in her honour, so bought a priesthood from Nishi-Hongan-ji temple in Kyoto and took over the name of a minor-league temple, Kōsan-ji, in Niigata. He resigned from his company, grew his hair, changed his name to **Kōsanji Kozo**, and began drawing up plans for the new Kōsan-ji – a collection of copies of the most splendid examples of Japanese temple buildings – which includes about ten halls, three towers, four gates, an underground cave and an enormous statue of Kannon, the Goddess of Mercy. Although many of the re-creations are smaller than the originals, Kanemoto cut no corners when it came to detail, even adding his own embellishments – most famously to the already over-the-top replica of the Yōmei-mon from Nikkō's Tōshō-gū, earning Kōsan-ji its nickname Nishi-Nikkō, the "Nikkō of the west".

Senbutsudō and the Hill of Hope

千仏洞・未来心の丘, Mirai Kokoro no Oka

The entrance gate, reached from a gift-shop-lined street off the waterfront just west of Setoda's ferry landing, is modelled on one from the imperial palace in Kyoto. To the right of the main temple building is the entrance to the **Senbutsudō** ("Cave of a Thousand Buddhas") and the Valley of Hell. An underground passage leads past miniature colourful tableaux showing the horrors of damnation, followed by the raptures of a heavenly host of Buddhas. You then wind your way up to emerge beneath the beatific gaze of a 15m-tall statue of Kannon (観音), the Buddhist goddess of mercy. From here you can walk up to the **Hill of Hope**, a collection of unusual modern marble sculptures with names like "Flame of the Future" and "Stage of the Noble Turtle", and where you'll have access to some of the best views available over Setoda.

Chōseikaku and the gallery

潮聲閣・アートギャラリー

Kōsan-ji's five-storey pagoda, modelled on the one at Murō-ji in Nara, is the last resting place of Kanemoto's beloved mother, whose holiday home, **Chōseikaku**, is right by the exit. The building is a fascinating combination of Western and traditional styles – two of the rooms have beautiful painted panels on their ceilings and a Buddha-like model of Mrs Kanemoto resting in one of the alcoves. Opposite the mother's retreat is Kōsan-ji's **art gallery**, a plain building housing sober displays of mainly religious paintings and statues.

8

Hirayama Ikuo Museum of Art

平山郁夫美術館, Hirayama Ikuo Bijutsukan • 200-2 Sawa • Daily 9am–5pm • ¥800 • ☎ 0845 27 3800, ⓦ hirayama-museum.or.jp

Topping Kōsan-ji's treasures takes some doing, but the **Hirayama Ikuo Museum of Art**, next door to the temple's art gallery, eclipses it with a superior calibre of paintings. **Hirayama Ikuo** (1930–2009), born in Setoda, was a junior-high-school student in Hiroshima when the bomb dropped – his famous painting *Holocaust at Hiroshima* can be seen in the Hiroshima Prefectural Museum of Art (see p.570). Despite travelling the world and becoming famous for his series of paintings on the Silk Road, he continually returned to the Inland Sea for inspiration. Hirayama used a traditional Japanese painting technique for his giant canvases, working very quickly with fast-drying paint – the resultant swift brush strokes give the finished paintings a distinctively **dreamy quality**. Because the special paint (*iwaenogu*) needed for this method is much less flexible and dries faster than oil paint, each picture has its own series of preparatory sketches. These full-sized blueprints for the final painting are known as **oshitazu**, and this museum contains many such sketches of Hirayama's most celebrated works, as well as original paintings and watercolours.

Kōjō-ji

向上寺

After the Hirayama museum, you can take in the view that inspired one of the artist's most beautiful paintings by hiking up to the summit of the hill behind Setoda. A small park here overlooks the attractive three-storey pagoda of **Kōjō-ji**, breaking out of the pine trees below, with the coloured tiled roofs of the village and the islands of the Inland Sea beyond.

ARRIVAL AND INFORMATION | **IKUCHI-JIMA**

By ferry There are ferries to Ikuchi-jima from Onomichi (40min; ¥800 one-way) and Mihara, further west along the coast, which is on both the San'yō rail line and Shinkansen (25min; ¥800 one-way).

By bus The bus from Onomichi (1hr; ¥1000) leaves from platform 7 in front of Onomichi Station and terminates at the southern end of Setoda; you have to change buses at the terminus on Inno-shima along the way. There's also a bus back to Onomichi from Inokuchi (¥1000 one-way, with a change at Inno-shima), or you can catch a bus on to Imabari (¥1180 one-way).

Destinations Onomichi via Inno-shima (several daily; 2hr).

Tourist information The tourist information booth (daily 9am–5pm; ☎0845 27 0051), across from the Hirayama Ikuo Museum of Art, has maps of Ikuchi-jima and a well-illustrated brochure on the island's attractions, partly in English.

Bike hire Bikes can be rented from the tourist information booth (¥500/day, plus ¥1000 deposit).

ACCOMMODATION AND EATING

Most of Setoda's eating options are along the Shiomachi-shōtengai (shopping street) leading up to the temple, but almost everything in this area is closed on Wednesdays. If you're cycling around the island, pack a picnic from Setoda's shops.

Chidori ちどり 530-2 Setoda-chō ☎0845 27 0231. Nicely kitted out but casual seafood place with soups (from ¥320) and larger dishes (from ¥500), including catch of the day. 10am–4pm, closed Tues.

Ikuchi-jima Shimanami Youth Hostel 生口島しまなみユースホステル 50-8 Setoda-chō ☎0845 27 3137. A slightly run-down spot beside Sunset Beach, a couple of kilometres south of Setoda, this is the cheapest accommodation option on the island. You can eat meals and rent bikes here, and the hosts will pick you up from the ferry port. Dorm **¥3000**

Keima 桂馬 2-5-1 Setoda-chō ☎0845 27 1989. Brilliant little sushi spot at (relatively) down-to-earth prices. Their sizeable dishes go from ¥1400. 10am–9pm, closed Thurs.

Mansaku 万作 530-1 Setoda-chō ☎0845 27 3028.

Located opposite Kōsan-ji, this smart fish restaurant serves pricey set lunches (¥1000–2500) of local cuisine. Daily 10am–3pm.

★ **Ryokan Tsutsui** 旅館つつ井 216 Setoda-chō ☎0845 27 2221. This traditional establishment, placed just next to the ferry terminal, is run by a charming man and his wife. They feature recently refurbished spacious tatami rooms and a deliciously invigorating lemon bath (many of Japan's lemons come from the trees on Ikuchi-jima). The lobby features comfy seating and an upright, well-tuned piano. Rates include half board. **¥24,000**

Sazanami さざなみ 181-5 Setoda-chō ☎0845 27 3373. Just off the main approach to the Kōsan-ji, a couple of blocks from the waterfront, this down-at-heel ryokan is one of the cheapest in town. **¥13,000**

Ōmi-shima

大三島

While Ikuchi-jima's top attraction is a temple, the big draw of neighbouring **ŌMI-SHIMA** is one of the oldest shrines in the country, **Ōyamazumi-jinja**. The shrine is around a fifteen-minute walk from the small, undistinguished port of **Miyaura**, on the west side of the island. The coast around here makes for pleasant explorations – most effectively by bike, which should occupy the better part of half a day. The interior tends to be quite hilly, but there is a decent 5km, mainly downhill, cycle track from **Inokuchi**, the ferry port closest to Ikuchi-jima, across the island from Miyaura. Alternatively, if you're just looking to kick back, you could linger on some of Ōmi-shima's (rather average) beaches.

Ōyamazumi-jinja

大山祇神社 • Miyaura 3327 • Daily 8.30am–5pm • Free • ☎0897 82 0032

The **Ōyamazumi-jinja**, which dates back to the end of the Kamakura era (1192–1333), is dedicated to Ōyamazumi, the elder brother of the Shintō deity Amaterasu. Between the twelfth and sixteenth centuries, it used to be a place of worship for pirates – among its deities is one who protects sailors – who used the island as a base before being brought to heel by the warlord Toyotomi Hideyoshi. The present structure dates from the late fourteenth century, and features a pleasant garden courtyard.

Ōyamazumi-jinja museum

大山祇神社宝物館, Ōyamazumi-jinja Homotsukan • 3327 Omishimacho Miyaura • Daily 8.30am–5pm • ¥1000, including entrance to the Kaiji Museum • ☎0897 82 003

To the right of the main shrine grounds, you'll find three modern buildings comprising the **Ōyamazumi-jinja museum**. The Shiyōden hall and connected Kokuhō-kan are reputed to contain the largest collection of armour in Japan – over two-thirds of the country's national treasures in weaponry – but unless you're a samurai freak you probably won't find the dry displays all that interesting.

8

Kaiji Museum

絵事比屓, Kaiji Hiken • 3327 Ōmishimachō Miyaura • ¥1000, including entrance to the Ōyamazumi-jinja museum • Daily 8.30am–4.30pm • ☎ 0897 82 0032

The intriguing **Kaiji Museum** houses the Hayama-maru, the boat built for Emperor Hirohito so he could undertake marine biology research. Beside the boat are some meticulously catalogued displays of fish, birds and rocks; some of the sea life looks like pickled aliens.

ARRIVAL AND DEPARTURE — ŌMI-SHIMA

By ferry Ferries run from Miyaura (宮浦) to Imabari (今治) on Shikoku (7 daily; 1hr–1hr 30min).

By bus You can reach Miyaura by local bus from the ferry port of Inokuchi (hourly; 15min) – the bus station is located just below the Tatara Ōhashi (the bridge linking Ōmi-shima with Ikuchi-jima).

Hiroshima

広島

Western Honshū's largest city needs little introduction. Since August 6, 1945, **HIROSHIMA** has become a byword for the devastating effects of the atomic bomb, and for this reason alone millions visit the city every year to pay their respects at the Peace Memorial Park and museum. But more than either of these formal monuments, the reconstructed city – bigger, brighter and more vibrant than ever – is an eloquent testimony to the power of life over destruction. Where once there was nothing but ashes as far as the eye could see, there now stands a modern city that still retains an old-world feel with its trundling trams and sunny disposition.

Poised on the coast at the western end of the Inland Sea, Hiroshima is also the jumping-off point for several offshore islands, including **Miyajima**, home of the handsome shrine **Itsukushima-jinja**.

Brief history

During the twelfth century, the delta of the Ōta-gawa on which Hiroshima now stands was known as **Gokamura** ("Five Villages"). The delta was ruled by Taira no Kiyomori, a scion of the Taira clan who was for a while the power behind the emperor's throne in Kyoto and who commissioned the Ikutsushima shrine on Miyajima. All this ended when the Taira were vanquished by the Minamoto clan (or Genji) at the Battle of Dannoura in 1185. However, Gokamura continued to grow and became crucial during warlord **Mōri Motonari**'s campaign to take control of Chūgoku during the latter half of the fifteenth century. When Motonari's grandson Terumoto built his castle, the city was renamed **Hiroshima** ("Wide Island"), and by the Meiji era the city had become an important base for the imperial army, a role that placed it firmly on the path to its terrible destiny.

A-bomb Dome

原爆ドーム, Genbaku Dōmu • 1-10 Ōtemachi • Entry to the dome itself is prohibited, but you can admire it from the outside

The most appropriate place to start exploring Hiroshima is beside the twisted shell of the Industrial Promotion Hall, built in 1914 and now better known as the **A-bomb**

HIROSHIMA ORIENTATION

Many of Hiroshima's top attractions – the **Peace Memorial Park and Museum**, and the **A-bomb Dome** – are all within walking distance of the Genbaku Dōmu-mae tram stop. **Hiroshima-jō**, **Hiroshima Prefectural Museum of Art** and **Shukkei-en** lie north of the Hondōri Arcade and Shintenchi district, where there is a high concentration of hotels, restaurants and bars. The **Hiroshima City Museum of Contemporary Art**, the most far-flung point of interest, is best explored on foot from the station or by public transport.

▲ 2 , MAZDA Zoom Zoom Stadium Hiroshima & Fukuyama

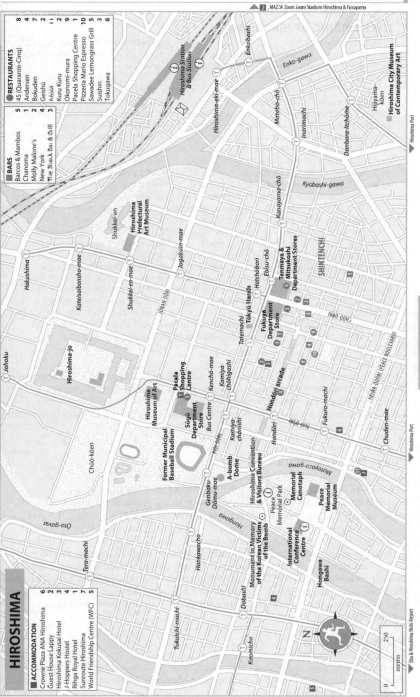

HIROSHIMA

■ ACCOMMODATION

Crowne Plaza ANA Hiroshima	6
Guest House Lappy	3
Hiroshima Kokusai Hotel	2
J-Hoppers Hostel	4
Rihga Royal Hotel	1
Sunroute Hiroshima	7
World Friendship Centre (WFC)	5

■ BARS

Barcos & Mambos	5
Chanoma	1
Molly Malone's	2
New York	4
The Shack Bar & Grill	3

● RESTAURANTS

45 (Quarante-Cinq)	8
Andersen	4
Bokuden	7
Geishū	2
Kissui	1
Kuru Kuru	2
Okonomi-mura	9
Pacela Shopping Centre	2
Pizzeria Mario Espresso	10
Sawadee Lemongrass Grill	5
Suishin	3
Tokugawa	6

8

▼ Koi & Miyajima-guchi

▼ Eba & Hiroshima Nishi Airport

▶ Hiroshima Nishi Airport

▶ Hiroshima Port

▶ Hiroshima Port

N

0   250
metres

THE BOMBING OF HIROSHIMA

As a garrison town, Hiroshima was an obvious target during **World War II**, but until August 6, 1945, it had been spared **Allied bombing**. It's speculated that this was an intentional strategy by the US military so that the effects of the **atom bomb**, when exploded, could be fully understood. Even so, when the B29 bomber *Enola Gay* set off on its mission, Hiroshima was one of three possible targets (the others being Nagasaki and Kokura) whose fate was sealed by reconnaissance planes above the city reporting clear skies.

When "**Little Boy**", as the bomb was nicknamed, exploded 580m above the city at 8.15am it unleashed the equivalent of the destructive power of **15,000 tonnes of TNT**. Beneath, some 350,000 people looked up and saw what must have looked like the sun falling to the earth. In less than a second a kilometre-wide radioactive fireball consumed the city. The heat was so intense that all that remained of some victims were their outlines seared onto the rubble. Immediately, some 70,000 buildings were destroyed and **80,000 people** killed. By the end of the year, **60,000** more had died from burns, wounds and radiation sickness. The final death toll is still unknown, the figure offered by the Hiroshima Peace Memorial Museum being "140,000 (plus or minus 10,000)". (For all Hiroshima's symbolic significance, it's important to put the number of those killed into context – in Tokyo, close to 20,000 died in a single night of bombing in 1945.)

Many survivors despaired of anything growing again for decades in the city's poisoned earth, but their hopes were raised on seeing fresh buds and blossom on the trees less than a year after the blast. Since then, the city has been reconstructed to an astounding degree, and many of the traditional buildings that were levelled, such as the turreted **Hiroshima-jō** and its five-floor donjon (広島城; 21-1 Motomachi; daily 9am–6pm, Dec–Feb till 5pm Mon–Fri; ¥360; ☎0822 21 7512, ⓦwww.rijo-castle.jp), were rebuilt a decade or two later. The reborn Hiroshima, with its population of more than a million, is now a self-proclaimed "city of international peace and culture", and one of the most memorable and moving days to visit the city is August 6, when a **memorial service** is held in the Peace Park and ten thousand lanterns for the souls of the dead are set adrift on the Ōta-gawa delta.

8

Dome, or *Genbaku Dōmu*. Almost at the hypocentre of the blast, the hall was one of the few structures in the surrounding 3km that remained standing. It's been maintained ever since in its distressed state as a historical witness to Hiroshima's suffering and packs a powerful punch as you emerge from the modern-day hustle and bustle of the Hondōri arcade.

Peace Memorial Park

平和記念公園, Heiwa Kinen-kōen • 1 Nakajimachō • 24hr • Free • ☎0825 04 2390

The verdant **Peace Memorial Park** is set on the banks of the Motoyasu gawa and dotted with dozens of statues and monuments to the A-bomb victims. One of the most touching is the **Children's Peace Monument**, a statue of a young girl standing atop an elongated dome and holding aloft a giant origami crane – the symbol of health and longevity. The monument's base is eternally festooned in multicoloured garlands of origami cranes, folded by schoolchildren from all over Japan and many other countries, a tradition that originated when radiation victim Sasaki Sadako fell ill with leukaemia in 1955. The 12-year-old started to fold cranes on her sick bed in the hope that if she reached a thousand she'd be cured; she died before reaching her goal, but her classmates continued after her death and went on to build this monument.

Memorial Cenotaph

原爆死没者慰霊碑, Genbaku Shibotsu-sha Irai Ijibumi

The main monument in the Peace Memorial Park – a smooth concrete and granite arch aligned with the A-bomb Dome and the Peace Memorial Museum – is the **Memorial Cenotaph**, designed by architect Kenzō Tange in the style of protective objects found in ancient Japanese burial mounds. Underneath the arch lies a stone coffin holding the names of all the direct and indirect A-bomb victims, and beside it burns the **Flame of Peace**, which will be put out once the last nuclear weapon on earth has been destroyed. It is before this monument that a memorial service is held every August 6, when white doves are released.

Monument in Memory of the Korean Victims of the Bomb

韓国人原爆犠牲者慰霊碑 Kankaku-jin Genbaltn Giseisha Irei Ijibum

Set on the eastern bank of the Hongawa, inside the Peace Memorial Park and just north of the Hongawa-bashi, the **Monument in Memory of the Korean Victims of the Bomb** is a worthy stop. Some two thousand forced labourers from Korea, a Japanese colony at the time of the war, died anonymously in the A-bomb blast, but it took decades before this monolith, mounted on the back of a turtle, was erected in their memory.

Peace Memorial Museum

平和記念資料館, Heiwa Kinen-Shiryōkan • Daily 8.30am–6pm, Aug till 7pm, Dec–Feb till 5pm • ¥50, taped commentary ¥300 • ☎0822 41 4004, ⓦ www.pcf.city.hiroshima.jp

The **Peace Memorial Museum** deserves to be seen by every visitor to Hiroshima; it presents a balanced picture of why the atrocity took place, as well as of its harrowing effects. The newer displays in the **east building** revolve around two models of the city before and after the explosion, and explain the lead-up to the bombing, including Japan's militarism. A watch in one case is forever frozen at 8.15am. There's a video theatre showing two short documentary films in English; in one, a doctor's voice breaks as he recalls his realization that vast numbers of childhood leukaemia cases were caused by radiation. Unfortunately, the melodramatic soundtrack from the video on perpetual repeat at the building entrance resonates loudly throughout the entire floor's exhibits, disturbing the contemplative atmosphere of the place.

On the third floor, after displays on the nuclear age post-Hiroshima, a connecting corridor leads to the old museum in the **west building**. You can rent a taped commentary in one of sixteen different languages – worth doing, although the appalling injuries shown in photographs and re-created by models need no translation, shirking none of the horror of the bomb's aftermath. At the end, you'll walk along a corridor overlooking the Peace Memorial Park and the resurrected city, providing a chance for contemplation on the bomb that once wiped it all out.

THE HIBAKUSHA

I saw, or rather felt, an enormous bluish white flash of light, as when a photographer lights a dish of magnesium. Off to my right, the sky split open over the city of Hiroshima.

Ogura Toyofumi, *Letters from the End of the World*

As of March 2013 there were 201,779 **hibakusha** (A-bomb survivors, though literally "explosion-affected people") alive who, like Ogura, lived through the A-bomb, including around 70,000 still living in Hiroshima. Ogura's poignant account – a series of letters penned to his dead wife in the immediate aftermath of the war – stands alongside many others, many of which are the videotaped testimonies of survivors, which can be viewed at the Peace Memorial Museum.

Through the museum it's also possible to meet a *hibakusha*. To do this, you need to make a request in writing to the Heiwa Bunka Center (☎0822 41 5246 ⓦwww.pcf.city .hiroshima.jp/hpcf) stating the dates you'd prefer and whether you'll need an interpreter. You'll be asked to cover their taxi costs of ¥8000–10,000. The World Friendship Centre (see p.571) also arranges meetings and occasionally hosts discussions with experts and visiting scholars.

Shukkei-en

縮景園 • 2-11 Kaminoborichō • Daily 9am–6pm, Oct–March till 5pm • ¥250 • ☎ 0822 21 3620, ⓦ shukkeien.jp • Tram #9 from the Hatchōbori stop; get off at Shukkei-en-mae (縮景園前)

A fetching post-bomb reconstruction, **Shukkei-en** comprises a beautiful stroll-garden with a central pond and several teahouses. Built originally by Asano Nagaakira after he had been made *daimyō* of Hiroshima in 1619, the garden aims to present in miniature the Xihu lake from Hangzhou, China, and its name literally means "shrunk scenery garden".

Hiroshima Prefectural Art Museum

広島県立美術館, Hiroshima Kenritsu Bijutsukan • 2-22 Kaminoboricho • Tues–Fri & Sun 9am–5pm, Sat 9am–7pm (April to mid-Oct Fri till 8pm) • ¥500, temporary exhibitions extra, combined ticket for museum and garden ¥600 • ⓦ hpam.jp

Adjacent to Shukkei-en is **Hiroshima Prefectural Art Museum**, an impressive modern facility worth visiting to see two paintings alone: the fiery, awe-inspiring *Holocaust at Hiroshima* by Hirayama Ikuo (see p.564), who was in the city when the bomb dropped, and the floppy watches of Salvador Dalí's surreal piece *Dreams of Venus*. The temporary exhibition area is often worth checking out, too.

Hiroshima City Museum of Contemporary Art

広島市現代美術館 • 1-1 Hijiyamakoen • Tues–Sun 10am–5pm • ¥360 • ⓦ hiroshima-moca.jp • Trams #1, #3 or #5 to Hijiyama-shita and hike up the hill; on Sat, Sun and hols, there's a free shuttle from the Bus Centre to the museum

Around 1km south of Hiroshima Station, on the crest of Hiji-yama, is the thought-provoking **Hiroshima City Museum of Contemporary Art**, one of the best art collections in the region thanks to its ultra-modern collection of art inspired in part by the atomic bombing. The surrounding leafy **Hijiyama-kōen** is dotted with more modern sculptures, including some by Henry Moore, and provides splendid views across the city.

ARRIVAL AND DEPARTURE
HIROSHIMA

By plane Two airports serve the city, the closest being Hiroshima Nishi, on the bay around 4km southwest of the centre, which handles services to smaller regional airports, such as Niigata and Miyazaki; buses from the airport to the city centre leave roughly every 40min (30min; ¥240); a taxi will set you back around ¥3000. Flights from Tokyo Haneda airport and several other cities arrive at Hiroshima Airport, some 40km east of the city; regular buses run from here to Hiroshima Station and the central Bus Centre (50min; ¥1300), or you can take a bus to nearby Shiraichi Station and transfer to a local train to the city.

Destinations (Hiroshima) Beijing (China) (4 weekly; 3hr 15min); Dalian (China) (4 weekly; 1hr); Okinawa (2 daily; 1hr 50min); Sapporo (2 daily; 2hr); Sendai (daily; 1hr 20min); Seoul (daily; 1hr 35min); Tokyo Haneda (15 daily; 1hr 15min); Tokyo Narita (daily; 1hr 20min).

Destinations (Hiroshima Nishi) Kagoshima (3 daily; 1hr); Miyazaki (daily; 1hr); Iwami (Hagi) to: Osaka (daily; 1hr); Tokyo (daily; 1hr 30min).

By train Hiroshima Station, on the east side of the city, is where local trains and Shinkansen arrive.

Destinations Fukuoka, Hakata Station (every 15min; 1hr 10min); Kyoto (every 15min; 1hr 50min); Matsue, via Okayama (1 hourly; 4hr); Okayama (every 15min; 40min); Shin-Osaka (every 15min; 1hr 30min); Tokyo (at least 25 daily; 4hr 50min).

By bus Long-distance buses arrive beside Hiroshima Station, although some also terminate at the Bus Centre (ⓦ h-buscenter.com) on the third floor of Sogō department store in the city centre.

Destinations Hagi (4 daily; 4hr); Izumo (8 daily; 3hr 30min); Kyoto (daily; 8hr); Matsue (14 daily; 3hr 30min); Osaka (daily; 7hr 30min); Tokyo (daily; 12hr).

By ferry Ferries from Imabari and Matsuyama in Shikoku, and various other locations around the Inland Sea, arrive at Hiroshima Port, 4km south of Hiroshima Station and connected to the city by regular trams (¥150).

Destinations Beppu (daily; 3hr 10min); Matsuyama (25 daily; ferry 2hr 40min, hydrofoil 1hr 10min); Miyajima (every 20min; 10min).

GETTING AROUND

The city is well served by public transport, with nine tramlines, an extensive network of city buses and the zippy Astram monorail line which transforms into a subway in the city centre, terminating beneath the Hondōri arcade. In practice, however, traffic can make catching a bus or a tram a frustratingly slow business; to get around the central sights quickly, you're often better off walking. Within the city centre the minimum tram and city bus fares are ¥150.

Tram routes From the station, trams #1 and #5 head south to Hiroshima Port past Hijiyama-kōen, while #2 and #6 head west to the Peace Park and beyond. Tram #9 shuttles back and forth from Hatchōbori past the Shukkei-en garden. If you need to transfer from one tram to another to get to your destination, ask for a *norikae-kippu* from the driver; drop this in the fare box when you leave the second tram. If you need to transfer again, a second *norikae-kippu* costs ¥60.

Travel cards With fares so cheap, neither of the one-day tram tickets is worth buying. A better option is the prepaid travel card, which can be used on the buses, trams and monorail/subway – the ¥1000 card gets you ¥1100-worth of travel. These cards can only be bought at the tram terminus at Hiroshima Station. the Bus Centre and the main JTB office on Rijo-dōri Kamiya-chō Biru, 2-2-2 Kamiya-chō (☎0825 42 5005).

Car rental Eki Rent-a-Car is at Hiroshima Station (☎0822 63 5933). Otherwise, try local branches of Avis (☎0120 390 784) and Budget (☎0822 62 4455).

INFORMATION

Tourist information There are two small tourist information booths in Hiroshima Station; one in the concourse at the south (*minemi*) entrance and one on the second floor of the north (*kita*) Shinkansen entrance (both daily 9am–5.30pm). Hiroshima's main tourist office, the Hiroshima Convention & Visitors Bureau (daily: April–Sept 9.30am–6pm, Oct–March 8.30am–5pm; ☎0822 47 6738, ⊚www.hiroshima-navi.or.jp), is in the *Hiroshima Rest*

House beside the Motoyasu bridge in the Peace Park. It has the best range of tourist literature, including information on other areas of Hiroshima-ken, and a small souvenir shop. The International Exchange Lounge (see below) also has information on local events and an excellent library and reading area with magazines and newspapers, plus 30min free internet access.

ACCOMMODATION

Hiroshima has plenty of inexpensive accommodation, and the only time of year you might have a problem finding somewhere to stay is Aug 6, when the annual peace ceremony is held. Although there are many business hotels in the charmless area around Hiroshima Station, it's better to stay closer to the Peace Park, west of which are more business hotels, minshuku and, if all else fails, love hotels.

★**Crowne Plaza ANA Hiroshima** ANAクラウンプラザ ホテル広島 7-20 Nakamachi ☎0822 41 1111 ⊚anacrowneplaza-hiroshima.jp. Placed right in the centre of the action on Peace Boulevard, across the water from the memorial, these whopping 409 guest rooms make the ANA one of the city's largest hotels. Service here is top notch, too. **¥33,200**

Guest House Lappy ゲストハウスラッピー 1-7 Wakakusa-chō ☎0825 69 7939 ⊚lappy.jp. A 10min walk north of the station is this very sociable little hostel known for its group *okonomiyaki* dinners (¥300) put on by the friendly owner. Private tatami rooms are very small but perfectly acceptable, and they also have laundry facilities on the roof (¥200, but only a clothesline for drying) and cycle rental. Dorm **¥2200**, double **¥4400**

Hiroshima Kokusai Hotel 広島国際ホテル 3-13 Tatemachi, Naka-ku ☎0822 48 2323, ⊚kokusai.gr.jp. Good-value mid-range hotel in a great location just off the Hondōri shopping arcade. It's showing a bit of wear, but has economy singles (from ¥8085), plus a fourteenth-floor revolving restaurant (see p.573) and a decent Japanese restaurant (see p.572). **¥11,780**

J-Hoppers Hostel ジェイホッパーズ 5-16 Dobashi-chō, Naka-ku ☎0822 33 1360, ⊚hiroshima.j-hoppers.com.

A great little hostel west of the Peace Park with dorms and tatami rooms, wi-fi access and internet terminals, self-catering kitchen and laundry facilities. If it's full, try the *Hana Hostel* near Hiroshima Station (☎0822 63 2980; ⊚hiroshimahostel.jp), run by the same management. Dorm **¥2300**

Rihga Royal Hotel リーガロイヤルホテル 6-78 Motomachi, Naka-ku ☎0825 02 1121, ⊚rihga.com/hiroshima. Hiroshima's grandest hotel soars 33 floors and was designed in the image of its neighbour, the reconstructed castle. It has spacious rooms, six restaurants, a pool, a gym and a stunning painting of Itsukushima-jinja by Hirayama Ikuo (see opposite) in the plush lobby. Breakfast is included. **¥23,000**

Sunroute Hiroshima ホテルサンルート 3-3-1 Ōtemachi, Naka-ku ☎0822 49 3600, ⊚www.sunroute .jp/hiroshima. This is one of the more upmarket branches of this nationwide chain of business hotels, with two good restaurants (the Italian *Viale* and the Japanese *Kissui*; see p.572), rooms specially equipped for disabled guests and decent prices. **¥12,600**

World Friendship Centre (WFC) ワールドフレンドシップセンター 8-10 Higashi-Kannonmachi, Nishi-ku

📞 0825 03 3191, 🌐 www.wfchiroshima.net. This small and homely non-smoking B&B has tatami rooms and is run by a friendly American couple who can also arrange meetings with A-bomb survivors and guided tours around the Peace Memorial Park for non-guests. Breakfast is included. ¥7800

EATING

Hiroshima's excellent selection of restaurants is the best you'll find in western Honshū. **Local specialities** are fresh seafood from the Inland Sea, in particular oysters, which are cultivated on thousands of rafts in Hiroshima Bay, and *okonomiyaki*. The local tradition is to make these delicious batter pancakes with the diner's choice of separate layers of cabbage, bean sprouts, meat, fish and noodles, unlike in Osaka, where all the ingredients are mixed up – don't leave Hiroshima without sampling one. Where the reviews below list a telephone number, it's a good idea to book.

45 (Quarante-Cinq) キャラントサンク Fukuromachi 📞 0505 868 5183. Swish, European-spot spot with bourgeois flair filled with young would-be VIPs sipping champagne and looking gorgeous. The white tablecloth restaurant serves various seafood dishes, while the *yakitori* bar is crowded with people drinking cocktails and munching on hot skewers. Daily 11.30am–2pm & 6–11pm.

Andersen 広島アンデルセン 7-1 Hondōri 📞 0822 47 2403 🌐 www.andersen.co.jp. With its ground-floor deli full of quality imports, top-notch bakery and café, and second-floor restaurants (European, Chinese and pizzeria), this homage (in name, at least) to Hans Christian Andersen is a true gourmet foodie's paradise – even if it feels vaguely like an office cafeteria. Worth the visit for their Danish pastries alone, which you can pick up at the counter downstairs from 7.30am. Daily 11am–9.30pm.

★**Bokuden** ボクデン Takata Arei Biiru, 4-20 Horikawa-chō, on the covered arcade just behind Tenmaya department store 📞 0822 40 1000 🌐 www.bokuden .co.jp. The glossy, postmodern decor of this trendy Korean restaurant is an interesting contrast to the sizzling barbecue meat skewers (from ¥360), fiery *chijimi* (a kind of omelette with leeks, meat and chilli; ¥790) and sprawling sashimi plates (from ¥890). Daily 5pm–midnight.

Geishū 芸州 Hiroshima Kokusai Hotel, 3-13 Tatemachi 📞 0822 48 2323, 🌐 kokusai.gr.jp. Expect pricey but beautifully presented local seafood dishes (¥800–¥5000), such as the *shingozen* sashimi plate (¥1500), here at the *Hiroshima Kokusai Hotel*'s Japanese restaurant. Mon–Sat 11am–2.30pm, 5–11pm, Sun until 10pm.

Kissui 吉水 15F Sunroute Hiroshima, 3-3-1 Ōtemachi 📞 0822 49 5657. Elegant *shabu-shabu* (beef) restaurant overlooking the Peace Park, where the waitresses wear pale-green kimono. Dinner is pricey, but the ¥1800 lunch is much more affordable. Daily 11.30am–3pm & 5–9.30pm.

★**Okonomi-mura** お好み村 5-13 Shin-tenchi 📞 0822 41 2210, 🌐 okonomimura.jp. This building behind the Parco department store, in the heart of the lively entertainment district, has 28 small *okonomiyaki* stalls crammed into three floors. *Hasshō* on the second floor and *Itsukushima*, the first stall you see on emerging from the elevator on the fourth floor, are two of the best in town.

Meals are around ¥780. Daily 11am–9pm.

Pacela Shopping Centre パセーラ 6-78 Motomachi 📞 0825 02 3515. This shopping complex connecting the *Rihga Royal Hotel* and Sogō department store has four floors of restaurants and a food court in the basement, mostly made up of fast-food places and cafés. Daily 10am–8pm.

Pizzeria Mario Espresso ピッツエリア マリオエスプレッソ 7-9 Fukuro-machi 📞 0862 41 4956, 🌐 sanmario.com. A lively pizzeria set across three floors of cerulean-painted wood, with red-and-white checkered tablecloths, distressed rickety wooden chairs and various rustic accoutrements. A few outside tables overlook a small park. This is a nice spot to chill out over a coffee and dessert if you don't fancy a full meal. Lunch pastas and pizzas are around ¥900, dinner mains around ¥1500. Daily 11am–11pm.

Sawadee Lemongrass Grill サワディー レモングラスグリル 4F Mozart House Building, Chūō-dōri 📞 0822 41 0066. Authentic casual Thai restaurant above the posh *Mozart* cake shop and café (take the elevator at the back of the shop). The chef's most popular requests are *tom yam kung* soup (¥1260), massaman (¥1050) and green (¥1050) curries. Portions tend towards the small side and the dishes aren't overly spicy, but this is the real deal. Daily 11am–2pm & 5–11pm.

Suishin 酔心 6-7 Tatemachi 📞 0822 47 2331. This long-established fish restaurant serves dishes in the local style; it's set across two separate spaces – sushi downstairs and *kamameshi* (rice casseroles) upstairs. The crab, eel, oyster, shrimp and *chirimen* (boiled, dried local fish) *kamameshi* (from ¥735) are particularly good, and there is a set menu from ¥1300. It's fairly limited in seating options, however, and often very busy. 11.30am–9pm, closed Wed.

Tokugawa 徳川 2F Tohgeki Building, Ebisu-chō 📞 0822 41 7100. Cook your own *okonomiyaki* for around ¥800 at this large *teppanyaki/okonoimiyaki* restaurant, halfway down the covered arcade running behind Tenmaya department store. Also serves "Hawaiian" pancakes with bacon and savory toppings (¥350). Expect a bright, family-oriented atmosphere, though no English menu. Daily 11am–3am.

DRINKING

Come sundown, the thousands of bars crammed into the Nagarekawa and Shin-tenchi areas of the city, at the east end of the Hondōri arcade, fling open their doors. In summer, several beer gardens sprout on city rooftops, including one at the *ANA Hotel* (see p.571).

Barcos & Mambos バルコス & マンボス 2F, 3F, Sanwa Building 2, Yagenbori 7-9 ☎0822 46 5800. This is the place to come if you want to mingle with an international crowd; head to *Mambos* (closed Sun) on the third floor for some Latin vibes and salsa dancing. ¥1000 cover gets you one drink, and *Barcos* has a food menu too. Daily 9pm–5am, Fri & Sat from 8pm.

Chano-ma チャノマ 2F, 2-19 Honden, above the Cine Twin Cinema ☎0827 30 0035. This unusual and swish but unpretentious café-bar of soft mattresses is swathed in whites and off-whites and offers a wide range of cocktails and Asian-fusion food menu. The rice and pasta dishes include an excellent avocado and tuna with spicy cod roe, and they serve a range of coffees. Lunch set menus from ¥1000. Tends to be extremely popular among teenage girls. Daily noon–2am.

Kuru Kuru クルクル Hiroshima Kokusai Hotel, 3-13 Tatemachi ☎0822 40 7556, ⨁kokusai.gr.jp. The American-themed revolving restaurant on the top floor of the *Hiroshima Kokusai Hotel* is worth dropping by for a romantic evening cocktail (¥500). Daily 11.30am–11pm.

Molly Malone's モーリー・マロンズ 4F Teigeki Building, Chūō-dōri ☎0822 44 2554. This popular Irish bar is a good place to meet local expats, and the Irish chef rustles up generous-sized portions of tasty Irish food – try the Jameson chicken or Galway mussels (¥1000). Pints of Guinness go for ¥900. Mon–Thurs 5pm–1am, Fri 5pm–2am, Sat 11.30am–2.30am, Sun 11.30am–midnight.

New York ニューヨーク カフェ 7-2 Fukuro-machi ☎0825 41 7000. Industrial-style but with hints of traditional Japan; this all-day *izakaya* has dim lighting and comfortable seats, with jazz often playing on the tubes and Woody Allen films often shown on the tube. You can find just about anything on the expansive cocktail menu (all ¥500), and the food includes pastas, pizzas and snacks, from around ¥800. Daily 11am–midnight.

Shack The Bar & Grill ザ シャック バー アンド グリル 6F Takarazuka Building, Chūō-dōri ☎0505 841 9133. Popular for its beers, burgers, sausages and Tex-Mex food (such as quesadillas and nachos, ¥890), *this place* has a pool table and dartboards for when you're pining for a bit of pub-style entertainment. A DJ is often found spinning later into the night. Daily 5pm–1am, Fri & Sat till 3am.

DIRECTORY

Banks and exchange There are several banks clustered around the Hondōri arcade as it crosses Rijo-dōri, including Hiroshima Bank, Sumitomo Bank and Tokyo Mitsubishi Bank. You can make cash withdrawals with cards including Visa and Mastercard at the Tokyo Mitsubishi Bank (Mon–Fri 9am–3pm). Foreign exchange is also available at the Central Post Office (see below) and Higashi post office next to Hiroshima Station.

Bookshops There's a small selection of English-language books and magazines at Kinokuniya, on the 6th floor of Sogō department store. The Book Nook Global Lounge, 2F Nakano Building, 1-5-17 Kamiya-chō, Naka-ku, near the *Hiroshima Kokusai Hotel* (see p.571), has an excellent selection of secondhand books in English and internet available at ¥200/15min.

Emergencies The main police station is at 9-48 Moto-machi (☎0822 24 0110). In an absolute emergency, contact the Foreign Advisory Service on ☎0822 47 8007. For other emergency numbers, see p.66.

Hospital Hiroshima Municipal Hospital, 7-33 Moto-machi ☎0822 21 2291.

Post office The main Central Post Office is on Rijo-dōri near the Shiyakusho-mae tram stop (daily 9am–7pm, Sat till 5pm, Sun till 12.30pm). Other convenient branches are the Higashi post office beside the south exit of Hiroshima Station (also open Sat until noon) and the Miru Paruku post office next to Sogō department store.

Miyajima

宮島

The most famous attraction on MIYAJIMA, officially known as Itsukushima, is the venerable shrine of Itsukushima-jinja, where the vermilion Ō-torii gate rising grandly out of the shallows (and seemingly floating on the sea) is considered to be one of Japan's most beautiful views. In the right light, when the tide is high and the many day-trippers have left, you may be tempted to agree. The peaceful **Daishō-in** keeps a

8

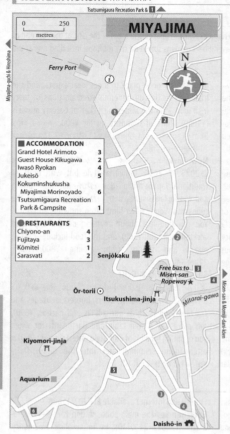

Tsutsumigaura Recreation Park & 1

MIYAJIMA

0   250
metres

Ferry Port

N

Miyajima-guchi & Hiroshima

ACCOMMODATION
Grand Hotel Arimoto   3
Guest House Kikugawa   2
Iwasō Ryokan   4
Jukeisō   5
Kokuminshukusha
  Miyajima Morinoyado   6
Tsutsumigaura Recreation
  Park & Campsite   1

RESTAURANTS
Chiyono-an   4
Fujitaya   3
Kōmitei   1
Sarasvati   2

Senjōkaku

Free bus to
Misen-san
Ropeway ★

Ōr-torii

Itsukushima-jinja

Mitarai-gawa

Misen-san & Momiji-dani-kōen

Kiyomori-jinja

Aquarium

Daishō-in

watchful eye from its perch on the hill above. Although the island is often swamped by visitors, it's a delightful place to spend the night.

The shrine and temples clustered around Miyajima's only village at the northern tip of this long, mountainous island can comfortably be seen in a half-day trip from Hiroshima. For those with have more time, there are plenty of other attractions, including beaches to laze on and hikes over **Mount Misen**, which makes a pleasant afternoon hike and whose summit provides panoramic views across the Inland Sea. Several kilometres north of the ferry landing is the **Tsutsumigaura Recreation Park** (包ケ浦自然公園), which has a long stretch of sandy beach and shallow waters ideal for paddling in. Further north still, you'll find beautiful empty beaches with crystal-clear water and fantastic views.

Consider splashing out on a night's accommodation at one of the island's classy ryokan so that you can enjoy the after-hours atmosphere with only tame deer and a few other guests for company. Autumn is a particularly beautiful time to visit, when the myriad maple trees turn a glorious red and gold, perfectly complementing Itsukushima-jinja. The main town centre is a stretch of restaurants and souvenir shops, many selling various versions of the lute-shaped Miyajima dipper (*kijakushi*, locally), the famed spatula made from local trees.

Itsukushima-jinja

厳島神社 • 1 Miyajima-chō • Daily 6.30am–6pm, mid-Oct to Feb till 5pm • ¥300 • ☎ 0829 44 2020 • A 10min walk south of the ferry landing; either walk along the seafront (home to many tame deer) or amble through the parallel shopping arcade – there's only one way to walk through the shrine itself, however: from its most northern entrance to its southern exit beside the Nishi-matsubara sand spit

Ancient records tell that a sea deity has been worshipped on Miyajima since the sixth century, but it wasn't until 1168 that **Itsukushima-jinja** took on its present splendid form, courtesy of the warlord Taira-no-Kiyomori. When the sea is lapping beneath its low-slung halls and red-colonnaded, lantern-fringed corridors, you can see why it's called the "floating shrine". More than likely, though, the tide will be out and the muddy sea bed revealed. Still, the classical beauty of the architectural ensemble, modelled after the *shinden*-style villas of the Heian period, endures, although the shrine is at its most enchanting come dusk, when the lights of the surrounding stone lanterns flicker on.

Most of the attached halls are closed, but in the centre, 200m ahead of the projecting stage for nō plays, you'll see the famed 16m-tall **Ō-torii**, dating from 1875. This is the

MIYAJIMA FESTIVALS

As well as the regular celebrations, such as New Year, there are special **festivals** held most months on Miyajima at both the Itsukushima-jinja shrine and the main temple, Daishō-in. From time to time, *bugaku* (traditional court dancing) is also performed on the shrine's nō stage; check with the main tourist information offices in Hiroshima (see p.571) for details.

Kaki Matsuri (second Sat in Feb): Free oysters, an island speciality, are served to sightseers.
Spring and Autumn festivals (April 15 & Nov 15): At Daishō-in, including firewalking displays by the resident monks.
Jin-Nō (April 16–18): Sacred nō plays, first performed for the *daimyō* Mōri Motonari in 1568, are re-enacted on the shrine's stage as part of the spring peach-blossom festival.
Kangensai (June 16): Itsukushima-jinja's main annual festival includes an atmospheric night-boat parade, accompanied by traditional music.
Hanabi Matsuri (Aug 14): The largest fireworks display in western Japan explodes in front of Itsukushima-jinja.
Chinkasai (Dec 31): Huge pine torches, blazing in front of Itsukushima-jinja, are fought over by groups of young men.

seventeenth incarnation since the original gate was erected by Taira-no-Kiyomori; its position in the sea indicates that the entire island is a Shintō holy place.

Senjōkaku

千畳閣 • 1-1 Miyajima-chō • Daily 8.30am–4.30pm • ¥100 • ☎ 0829 44 2020

Just north of Itsukushima-jinja, head up the hill towards the red-painted five-storey pagoda that you'll see poking through the trees. Beside this is the "hall of a thousand tatami", **Senjōkaku**, part of Hokoku-jinja, a shrine started by Toyotomi Hideyoshi but left unfinished when the warlord died. Votive plaques decorate the inside of the large, airy hall, which was originally a library for Buddhist sutras.

Daishō-in

大聖院 • 210 Miyajima-chō • Daily 8am–5pm • Free • ☎ 0829 44 0111 • Around a 10min walk south of Itsukushima-jinja

Miyajima's main temple, **Daishō-in**, is located on the hillside south of Itsukushima-jinja. This attractive complex, with ornate wooden pavilions, arched bridges across lily-pad-dotted ponds and stone lanterns, belongs to the Shingon sect of Buddhism associated with the revered Kōbō Daishi, who blessed the island with a visit in the ninth century. Look out for the "universally illuminating cave" towards the back of the complex, which is hung with hundreds of lanterns and packed with mini-Buddhas laden down with lucky talismans.

Misen-san

弥山 • Ropeway daily 9am–5pm, Nov–Feb till 4pm • One-way ¥1000, return ¥1800 • ☎ 0829 44 0111 • The ropeway base station is beside Momiji-dani-kōen (紅葉谷公園), a leafy hillside park around a 20min hike from the ferry terminal; a free minibus runs here from opposite the Iwasō Ryokan

If you're feeling energetic, the 530m **Misen-san**, Miyajima's sacred mountain, be you could climb in a couple of hours. Otherwise, a two-stage **ropeway** (cable-car) provides a thrilling and somewhat scary 1.7km ride up to within easy walking distance of the summit.

Around the Shishiwa station on top of the mountain, you'll see a colony of wild monkeys as well as more deer. Cute as they may look, it's important to keep your distance from the monkeys, which can occasionally become aggressive. There's an excellent lookout spot across the Inland Sea near the station, but the actual summit is a good twenty minutes further on. The path initially drops down but then starts to climb past various small temples built in honour of Kōbō Daishi. Opposite the Misen Hondō, the main hall of worship on the mountain, is the **Kiezu-no-Reikadō**, in which a sacred fire said to be originally lit by the Daishi has burnt for over 1200 years. Legend has it that if you drink tea made from the boiling water in the suitably blackened iron pot which hangs over the fire, all your ills will be cured.

Five more minutes' climb will take you past mysterious giant boulders to the resthouse at the summit; if you haven't packed refreshments, you can buy them here, but at accordingly high prices. The main route down passes more small temples and provides stunning views over Itsukushima-jinja, especially as you near Daishō-in.

ARRIVAL AND INFORMATION

By train and ferry The train-plus-ferry route from Hiroshima is only worth considering if you have a rail pass or special excursion ticket that will cover the cost of both the 30min journey from Hiroshima to Miyajima-guchi Station and the crossing on the JR-run ferry.

By ferry High-speed ferries (¥1800) from Hiroshima's port – connected by tram #5 to Hiroshima Station and tram #3 to the city centre – take 20min.

By tram and ferry Tram #2, which you can hop on at the A-bomb Dome in downtown Hiroshima, will take you to the ferry terminal at Miyajima-guchi (55min). A one-way trip costs ¥270, and the 10min ferry fare is

¥170 (it is covered by the JR Pass). If you pla to return to Hiroshima the same day and travel a b around the city, you'll save money buying a ¥840 one day ticket.

Tourist information There's a booth (daily 9am–6pm ☎ 0829 44 2011) inside the island's ferry termina where you can pick up a basic map and boo accommodation.

Bike hire There is no cycle hire available on Miyajima, so you want to head to the northern beaches, you'll need t plan for a 40min walk (one-way) – everything else within easy walking distance of the ferry.

ACCOMMODATION

There is reasonably cheap accommodation on Miyajima, but if you can afford it you should splash out on one of the mor upmarket ryokan or the excellent Western-style pension. Also try and visit midweek, since at weekends and during pea holiday seasons rates at many of the hotels rise.

★ **Grand Hotel Arimoto** グランドホテル有もと364 Minamimachi ☎ 0829 44 2411, ⊛ miyajima-arimoto .co.jp. The closest of the island's hotels to the shrine, the rooms at this sprawling complex come either in tatami or Western style (or both) and some have water views and/or private outdoor onsen. Several excellent dining options are on offer, and they put on regular classical music concerts and storytelling evenings in the lobby, as well as offering free guided tours (in Japanese only). **¥18,360**

Guest House Kikugawa ゲストハウス菊川 796 Miyajima-chō ☎ 0829 44 0039, ⊛ kikugawa.ne.jp. Set back in the village a couple of minutes from the ferry, this delightful pension offering Western- and Japanese-style rooms is clean and comfortable. The staff speak decent English and the owner, Kikugawa-san, is an excellent chef. Prices include two meals. **¥12,600**

★ **Iwasō Ryokan** 岩惣旅館 Momiji-dani ☎ 0829 44 2233, ⊛ iwaso.com. The most famous ryokan on the island, and by far the most luxurious, with immaculate tatami rooms and sumptuous meals. Rooms overlooking the gorge behind the building are booked solid throughout

autumn when the view transforms into a sea of red, yellow and orange. Rates include two meals. **¥52,140**

Jukeisō 聚景荘 50 Miyajima-chō ☎ 0829 44 0300. Thi ryokan has an excellent hillside location south o Itsukushima-jinja, overlooking the shrine. There's a choic of Western and tatami rooms, and prices include tw meals. **¥40,000**

Kokuminshukusha Miyajima Morinoyado 国民名 舎みやじま杜の宿 Omoto-Kōen, Miyajima-chō ☎ 0829 44 0430, ⊛ morinoyado.jp. This minshuku, o the island's quiet southern end, is the best deal o Miyajima, but you'll have to book well in advance, a rooms are almost consistently sold out. There are bot Western and Japanese rooms. Prices include two meals **¥19,110**

Tsutsumigaura Recreation Park and Campsite 宮 島包ヶ浦自然公園キャンプ場＋ Miyajima-chō ☎ 0829 44 2903. The only real budget accommodation option or the island is at its northern end. It has fairly plush cabin with air conditioning, kitchen and bathroom, as well a tent space (tent rental available). Camping **¥300** pe person, 4-person cabin **¥15,000**

EATING AND DRINKING

Because most people dine at their hotels, non-lunch eating options on the island are limited, and the town, while it is properly bustling during the day, virtually shuts down at dusk. Besides oysters, which you can taste fried or grilled at the stalls lining the road south of the ferry terminal, another local speciality is *anago*, a long eel-like fish, cooked and served sliced on top of rice (*anagoburi*).

Chiyono-an 千代乃庵 215-1 Takimachi ☎ 0829 44 0234. On the first floor of the *Auberge Watanabe*, this small *hotel place* offers *anago* set lunches for ¥1600, as well as rice bowls and noodle soups for about half the price. Daily 10.30am–5pm.

Fujitaya ふじたや 125-2 Miyajima ☎ 0829 44 0151. The most famous place to sample *anago* is this refined, busy restaurant a couple of minutes' walk northwest of Daishō-in. A large serving of *anagoburi*, accompanied by soup and pickles, costs ¥2300. Daily 11am–3.30 pm.

Kōmitei 好み亭 1162-1 Minatomachi ☎ 0829 44 0177. Of the arcade of tourist shops and restaurants leading to the shrine along the seafront close to the ferry terminal, this is one of the most esteemed. They serve *okonomiyaki* (¥708), have an English menu and feature a pretty ornamental garden at the back. You can have your *okonomiyaki* Hiroshima-style (layered and cooked for you) or Kansai-style (cook it yourself). 5–9pm, closed Wed.

Sarasvati サラスパティ 407 Miyajima-chō ☎ 0829 44 2266, ⓦ sarasvati.jp. Of all the town's cafés, this posh atmospheric spot, set in a former granary, is the cosiest and has the best coffee. Brimming with bags of coffee and grinders, the place nails the industrial-rustic look, with dark woods and brushed cobalt walls, and is a great place to kick back for an hour or so over their excellent blended coffees (¥550; ¥250 to take away). They also serve sandwiches, scones and pasta lunches (¥1280). Daily 8.30am–7.30pm.

Iwakuni

岩国

Heading south along the coast from Miyajima, you'll soon cross the border into western Honshū's last prefecture, Yamaguchi-ken. The first place to pause briefly is the pleasant old castle town of **IWAKUNI**, 40km southwest of Hiroshima and home to an American military base, as well as one of Japan's top three bridges, a scattering of samurai houses and a mildly interesting museum; it's also one of the best places in the country to watch the ancient practice of **cormorant fishing**. In any event, all Iwakuni's sights can be comfortably seen in a couple of hours.

Kintai-kyō

錦帯橋 • ¥300, or combined ticket for the bridge, the return ropeway up Shiro-yama and the castle (see p.578) ¥930

Two kilometres west of the present Iwakuni town centre and roughly between the Shinkansen and local train stations, is one of the country's top three bridges, **Kintai-kyō**, an elegant five-arched structure, spanning the rocky Nishiki-gawa like a tossed pebble skipping across the water. It was *daimyō* Kikkawa Hiroyoshi who ordered the bridge's construction in 1673 to solve the problem of crossing the Nishiki-gawa every time it flooded. The first bridge was quickly washed away during the rainy season of 1674, but the second attempt – a 210m-long structure built without a single nail and bound together with clamps and wires – survived until Typhoon Kijiya swept it away in 1950. What you see today is the **1953 reconstruction**, no less impressive for that. For once, the hordes of tourists add something to the bridge's attraction, as they parade across the steep arches like figures in an *ukiyo-e* print.

Out of regular office hours, you either drop the bridge toll in the box beside the ticket office, or avoid it altogether by crossing the river on the nearby modern concrete span, the Kinjō-kyō, a good vantage point for a photo. It's also worth checking out the bridge at night, when it's glamorously floodlit.

8

Kikkō-kōen

吉香公園 • Park 24hr, Chōko-kan (徴古館) Tues–Sun 9am–5pm • Free

Adjoining Kintai-kyō on the west bank of the Nishiki-gawa is a landscaped park, **Kikkō-kōen**, once the estate of the ruling Kikkawa clan. With its grass lawns and cooling fountains, the park preserves some of the layout and buildings of the former estate. Immediately ahead from the bridge, on the right, is the **Nagaya-mon** (長屋門), the wooden gate to the home of the Kagawa family, samurai to the Kikkawa *daimyō*; there are also several other samurai houses you can wander around in the same area. There's a mildly interesting collection of old maps and plans from feudal times, photos and prints featuring the bridge through the centuries, as well as craftwork from Iwakuni's past, on display at the **Chōko-kan**, at the north end of the park.

Kikkawa Historical Museum

吉川史料館, Kikkawa Shiryōn • 9-3 Nichome • 9am–5pm, closed Wed • ¥500 • ☎ 0827 41 1010

The **Kikkawa Historical Museum** holds various artefacts from the family collection of the Kikkawa warlords. The weapons on display include a multitude of swords, and you can also peer at samurai armour, jewellery and hanging scrolls. However, the explanations are all in Japanese.

Shiro-yama

Ropeway daily 9am–5pm • ¥320 one-way, ¥540 return; combined ticket for Kintai-kyō, the return ropeway and the castle ¥930 • Marked "tram" on town maps

Located at the northern edge of Kikkō-kōen park, the **ropeway** (cable-car) saves a forty-minute hike up **Shiro-yama** – the walking route begins beside the youth hostel (see below). An impressive view of the meandering river, town and Inland Sea from the summit makes the effort of hiking up worthwhile. Unless you're interested in displays of armour, swords and a miniature wooden model of the Kintai-kyō, however, **Iwakuni castle** (daily 9am–4.45pm; ¥260; ☎ 827 41 1477) isn't worth entering.

ARRIVAL AND INFORMATION   IWAKUNI

By train and bus Shinkansen stop at Shin-Iwakuni Station, 10min by bus west of the bridge, while trains on the JR San'yō line stop at Iwakuni Station, a 15min bus journey east of the centre. Buses operate from both stations; the fare to Iwakuni is ¥240, to Shin-Iwakuni, ¥280.

Tourist information There's a tourist office by the bridge with some English-language leaflets (8.30am–5pm; ☎ 0827 41 2037).

ACCOMMODATION AND EATING

Iwakuni Kokusai Kankō Hotel 岩国国際観光ホテル 1-1-7 Iwakuni ☎ 0827 43 1111, ⓦ iwakunikankohotel .co.jp. With branches on both sides of the river, this large property is popular with groups, and offers Japanese-style rooms as well as public indoor/outdoor onsens, and a gift shop. **¥31,900**

Iwakuni Youth Hostel 岩国ユースホステル 1-10-46 Yokoyama ☎ 0827 43 1092. The cheapest place to stay on the island is in the peaceful southwest corner of the Kikkō-kōen, a 10min walk from the bus stop by the bridge; it has shared Japanese-style rooms with TVs. Dorm **¥2835**

Shiratame Ryokan 白為旅館 1-5-16 ☎ 0827 41 0074, ⓦ Shiratame.justhpbs.jp/. This pretty spot is Iwakuni's best ryokan, with rooms overlooking the bridge; even if you can't afford to stay, try to go for lunch, where you can get great sushi as well as noodle soup with tofu and *kamaboko* (fish cake). **¥23,100**

CORMORANT FISHING

If you are in Iwakuni overnight between June 1 and August 31, don't miss the **cormorant fishing** (*ukai*), which takes place on the Nishiki-gawa beside the bridge between 6.30pm and 9pm. This colourful and exciting method of fishing with birds (see box, p.402) can be watched for free from the pebbly riverbank.

Yoshida よしだ本店 1-16-9 Iwakuni ☎ 0827 41 0373. A good place to try the local fish dishes (from ¥550), such as *iwakuni-zushi*, a block of vinegared rice topped with bits of cooked fish and vegetables. It's on the east side of the bridge just beyond some interesting antique shops leading up to the Kintai-kyō. Daily 9am–5pm.

Yamaguchi

山口

The coastal route west of Iwakuni is blighted by heavy industry, but head inland to the hills and you'll find an old-world atmosphere hanging over the sleepy prefectural capital, **YAMAGUCHI**. It's a modern city, but one can see why it's also known as the "Kyoto of western Japan". Highlights are the beguiling temple garden of **Jōei-ji**, designed by the fifteenth-century artist and priest Sesshū, the handsome five-storey pagoda at **Rurikō-ji**, and **St Francis Xavier Memorial Cathedral**, an ultra-contemporary church commemorating the first Christian missionary to Japan.

The city's commercial heart is where Ekimae-dōri, the main street heading northwest towards the hills from the station, crosses the Komeya-chō shopping arcade; all the main sights are north of here. Surrounding attractions in the city include the hot-spring resort neighbourhood **Yuda Onsen**, just one train stop to the west of Yamaguchi, and the intriguing caverns and rocky plateau of **Akiyoshi-dai** Quasi National Park, some 20km northwest.

Brief history

Many of the temples spread around Yamaguchi, not to mention its artistic sensibilities, date from the late fifteenth century, when war raged around Kyoto, and the city

8

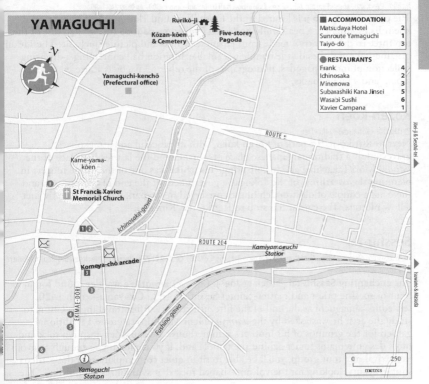

YAMAGUCHI

Rurikō-ji
Kōzan-kōen & Cemetery
Five-storey Pagoda

Yamaguchi-kenchō (Prefectural office)

Kame-yama-kōen

St Francis Xavier Memorial Church

Ichinosaka-gawa

ROUTE 9

ROUTE 204

Kamiyamaguchi Station

Komeya-chō arcade

EKIMAE-DŌRI

Fushino-gawa

Yamaguchi Station

■ ACCOMMODATION	
Matsudaya Hotel	2
Sunroute Yamaguchi	1
Taiyō-dō	3

● RESTAURANTS	
Frank	4
Ichinosaka	2
Minenowa	3
Subarashiki Kana Jinsei	5
Wasabi Sushi	6
Xavier Campana	1

Jōei-ji & Sesshū-tei

Iwakuni & Masuda

0 ——— 250
metres

became an alternative capital for fleeing noblemen and their retinues. The tolerant ruling family of **Ōuchi Hiroyo**, who settled in the area in 1360, allowed the missionary Francis Xavier to stay in Yamaguchi in 1549. By the Edo period, the **Mōri** clan had gained power over the whole of western Japan, and several of the Mōri lords are buried in Kōzan-kōen, including Mōri Takachika, who was a key figure in the overthrow of the Tokugawa government in 1867.

St Francis Xavier Memorial Church

サビエル記念聖堂, Zabieru Kinen Seidō • 4-1 Kameyama-chō • 9am–5pm, closed Wed • ¥100 • ⓦ www.xavier.jp

The twin towers of the modern **St Francis Xavier Memorial Church** are easily spotted atop Kame-yama-kōen, on the northwest side of the city. The church was named after the pioneering Spanish missionary Francis Xavier who, having already had success in Goa and Malacca, landed in Japan on August 15, 1549, and in the following year was granted leave to preach in Yamaguchi. When he left, the city had a community of more than five hundred Christians, many of whom later died for their beliefs under the less tolerant Tokugawa government. In 1991, the original church (built in 1952 to commemorate the four-hundredth anniversary of Xavier's visit) burnt down, but was replaced in 1998 by a striking contemporary structure incorporating a pyramid-like main building, and **twin square towers** topped by metallic sculptures, one hung with nine bells.

Rurikō-ji

瑠璃光寺 • Kōzan-kōen • **Temple** 24hr • Free • **Exhibition hall** Daily 9am–5pm • ¥300 • ☎ 0839 249 1399

The charming **Rurikō-ji** is located in the foothills around 1km north of Kame-yama-kōen. Its highlight is a beautifully preserved **five-storey pagoda** (designated one of the top three in the country), made from Japanese cypress and picturesquely sited beside an ornamental pond. Beside the temple is a small exhibition hall containing a diverting collection of model pagodas, photographs of the other 53 pagodas scattered around Japan, and strange masks.

Kōzan-kōen

香山公園 • Kōzan-chō • 24hr • Free

Next to Rurikō-ji, the park of **Kōzan-kōen**, with its peaceful and atmospheric graveyard, is a traditional Japanese place of worship and the last resting place of the *daimyō* Mōri Takachika and his offspring. Takachika was one of the prime movers in planning the overthrow of the Tokugawa government at the end of the Edo era, and there are a couple of old wooden houses preserved in the park where he secretly met fellow plotters. The closest bus stop to Rurikō-ji is Kimachi.

Sesshū-tei

雪舟庭 • 2001 Miyano-shimo • Garden and temple daily 8am–5pm • ¥300 • ☎ 0839 22 272 • Orimoto is the closest bus stop, from where it's a 10min walk north

The enchanting **Sesshū-tei** garden at **Jōei-ji** (常榮寺) is worth a wander round for an hour or so. The priest and master-painter Sesshū, born in Okayama-ken in 1420, settled in Yamaguchi at the end of the fifteenth century. After travelling to China to study the arts, he was asked by the *daimyō* Ōuchi Masahiro to create a traditional garden for the grounds of his mother's summerhouse. Sesshū's Zen-inspired rock and moss design remains intact behind the temple and, if you're fortunate enough to avoid the arrival of a tour group, you'll be able to sit in quiet contemplation of the garden's simple beauty, looking for the volcano-shaped rock that symbolizes Mount Fuji. The urrounding forest and the lily-pad pond add brilliant splashes of colour, particularly in autumn, when the maple trees flame red and gold.

Yuda Onsen

湯田温泉

One train stop west of Yamaguchi, or a short bus ride south of the city centre, is **Yuda Onsen**, easily spotted by the cluster of large (and not particularly attractive) hotels. A cute legend about a white fox curing its injured leg in the natural spring water explains both how the onsen and the town's mascot, immortalized by an 8m-high cartoon-like fox statue beside the station, developed. Take a left at the intersection in front of Yuda Onsen Station, then your first right and follow the road for about 10min to **Onsen no Mori** (温泉の森; 4-7-17 Yuda Onsen; daily 10am–midnight; ¥1000), a modern spa complex with several different jacuzzi baths, a sauna and a rotemburo; you're given a small towel to use when you enter. The *Kamefuku Hotel* (かめ福ホテル; 4-5 Yuda Onsen; daily 11.30am–10pm; ¥800; ⓦ kamefuku.com) along Route 204 also has good spa facilities, with individual turtle-shaped baths outside.

ARRIVAL AND INFORMATION
YAMAGUCHI

By plane Yamaguchi Ube Airport lies some 40km south, near the coastal city of Ube. There's a shuttle bus to Shin-Yamaguchi Station (8 daily; 35min).
Destinations Tokyo Haneda (7 daily; 1hr 30min).

By train Yamaguchi is 20min by train from Shin-Yamaguchi (¥230) on the branch JR Yamaguchi line, which runs between Shin-Yamaguchi (新山口) on the southern coast (a Shinkansen stop) and the north-coast town of Masuda in Shimane-ken.
Destinations Shin-Yamaguchi (every 20min; 20min); Tsuwano (17 daily; 50min–1hr 20min)

By bus Regular bus services run to the city from Hagi, 40km north. All buses stop in front of Yamaguchi Station. Destinations Akiyoshi-dai (19 daily; 55min); Hagi (11 daily; 1hr 15min); Shin-Yamaguchi to: Akiyoshi-dai (12 daily; 40min); Hagi (6 daily; 1hr 26min).

Tourist information The tourist office (daily 9am–6pm; ☎ 0839 330 090) is on the second floor of Yamaguchi Station. English maps and leaflets are available and there is free wi-fi. There's also an information counter at Shin-Yamaguchi Station beside the exit from the Shinkansen tracks, where you can get English leaflets on most attractions in Yamaguchi-ken.

GETTING AROUND

By bike Yamaguchi might be the smallest of Japan's prefectural capitals, but its main sights are too widely spread out to walk between them. There are plenty of local buses, but the easiest way to get around is to rent a bicycle from the shop across the street from the station (¥300/2hr, ¥700/day).

ACCOMMODATION

★**Matsudaya Hotel** 松田屋ホテル 3-6-7 Yuda Onsen ☎ 0839 22 0125, ⓦ matsudayahotel.co.jp. Set one train stop south of Yamaguchi centre, this is easily the pick of accommodation in the west of *Chūgoku*. The historic 300-year-old ryokan, cocooned by high walls, is on the main road running through the onsen resort. Ignore the modern high-rise extension and go for elegant, sprawling tatami rooms, delicious meals and lovely traditional garden. Well worth the expense (rates include breakfast and dinner). **¥42,000**

Sunroute Yamaguchi ホテルサンルート 1-1 Nakagawara-chō ☎ 0839 23 3610, ⓦ www.sunroute .jp Modern business chain hotel set in a convenient location, 15min walk from the station. The spiffy rooms have smart decor and typical amenities, and there's a Japanese restaurant, *IchinŌsaka* (see p.582). **¥12,180**

Taiyō-dō 太陽堂 2-3 Komeya-chō ☎ 0839 22 0897. With a small central garden and tatami rooms with shared bathrooms, this surprisingly large ryokan is good value. The entrance is on the east side of Komeya-chō arcade. **¥7000**

EATING

There's a limited range of **restaurants** in Yamaguchi, with most options clustered along Ekimae-dōri and the Komeya-chō arcade, and a few cafés along the riverside beyond the arcade. Many **shops** also sell the local speciality, *uirō*, a glutinous sweet made from pounded rice, a supposed favourite of the ruling Ōuchi clan six hundred years ago.

Frank フランク 2-4-19 Ekimae-dōri 2F ☎ 0839 32 5166. Spacious hipster-chic, artsy café with a very relaxed vibe, a small art gallery upstairs and a tiny veranda out back with one table. It offers staple Japanese café food including curry rice and pilaf, with lunch mains for around ¥800–1000. The entrance to the stairway is off the side street. 11.30am–1am, closed Tues.

Ichinōsaka いちの坂 1-1 Nakagawara-chō ☎ 0839 23 3610, ⓦ www.sunroute.jp. Handy restaurant in the *Sunroute Yamaguchi* hotel (see p.581) serving good-value set meals from around ¥1000. Daily 10am–10pm.

Subarashiki Kana Jinsei 素晴らしきかな人生 Ekimae-dōri ☎ 0839 28 6770. Lively, modern little spot with various rooms, decked out in dark woods, branching off a labrynthine corridor. The hip waiters here serve all the usual *izakaya* staples from around ¥500. Dail 5am–7pm.

Wasabi Sushi 和さび 2-1 Ekidori ☎ 0839 21 6535 Cheap and cheerful conveyor-belt sushi stop near th station with decent cuts of fish starting at ¥280. Daily ti 8.30pm.

Xavier Campana サビエル・カンパーナ 5-. Kameyama ☎ 0839 23 6222. This mouthwaterin bakery and restaurant serves a wide range of breads cakes, salads and a mixture of European meals, includin German-style dishes, fondue and pasta. The baker downstairs, in addition to all its baked fare, such as udo cake (¥200), also sells sausages with mustard in a bu (¥230). Daily 7.30am–7pm.

Akiyoshi-dō

秋芳洞 • Daily 8.30am–4.30pm • ¥1200 • ☎ 0834 62 0018, ⓦ english.karusuto.com

Midway between Yamaguchi and the northern coast city of Hagi are the vast caverns and rock-strewn tablelands of **AKIYOSHI-DAI** (秋吉台). The main attraction of this bleak landscape is **Akiyoshi-dō**, the largest limestone cave in Japan, stretching around 10km underground, although only about a tenth of it is open to the public. The cave's main entrance is located a few minutes from Akiyoshi-dō bus station.

A raised walkway through a copse of lofty, moss-covered pine trees provides an atmospheric introduction to the gaping cavern mouth. Inside, however, the booming loudspeakers of competing tour-group leaders, combined with unimaginative lighting, detract from the huge cave's potential impact. It took more than 300,000 years of steady erosion and dripping to create some of the rock walls and formations, which have since been given names like "Big Mushroom" and "Straw-Wrapped Persimmon".

From the bowels of the earth, an elevator whisks you up to the alternative cave entrance **Yano-ana**, a short walk from Akiyoshi-dai, Japan's largest karst plateau. A lookout point commands an impressive view of rolling hills, and there is a range of hikes you can follow across the 130 square kilometres of the plateau.

ARRIVAL AND INFORMATION　　　　　　　　　　　　　　　　AKIYOSHI-DŌ

By bus Buses run to Akiyoshi-dō from Higashi-Hagi (¥1760), Shin-Yamaguchi (¥1140), Shimonoseki (¥1730) and Yamaguchi (¥1130). The fastest connection is from Shin-Yamaguchi Station, a Shinkansen stop (43min). If you have a JR Rail Pass, it's best to take the JR bus service from Yamaguchi. The main entrance is a 5min walk from

Akiyoshi-dō bus station along a pedestrianized street of gift shops; if you return to the cave in the elevator, you'll be charged ¥100, but you can just as easily walk down the hill or catch a bus back to Akiyoshi-dō Station.

Tourist information There is an information counter inside the bus centre (daily 9am–6pm; ☎ 0837 62 1620).

Shimonoseki and around

Most travellers pass through the port of **SHIMONOSEKI** (下関) at the southern tip of Honshū, 65km west of Yamaguchi, as quickly as possible en route to Kyūshū, or to Pusan in South Korea on the daily ferry. However, this unpretentious city is not without its attractions. The narrow **Kanmon Channel**, which separates Honshū from Kyūshū, is best viewed from **Hino-yama**, the mountain park that rises above the port. The channel was the scene of the battle of Dannoura, the decisive clash between the

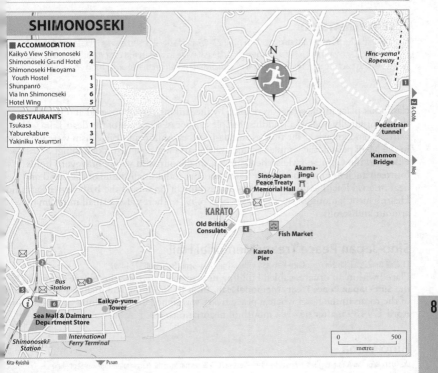

SHIMONOSEKI

■ ACCOMMODATION	
Kaikyō View Shimonoseki	2
Shimonoseki Grand Hotel	4
Shimonoseki Hinoyama Youth Hostel	1
Shunpanrō	3
Via Inn Shimonoseki	6
Hotel Wing	5

● RESTAURANTS	
Tsukasa	1
Yaburekabure	3
Yakiniku Yasumori	2

Taira and Minamoto clans in 1185, and the colourful shrine **Akama-jingū** is dedicated to the defeated Taira.

Kaikyō-yume Tower

海峡ゆめタフー • 3-3-1 Buzendachō • Daily 9.30am–9.30pm • ¥600 • ☎ 0832 31 5600, ☒ kaikyomesse.jp

You'll find good views of the city and surrounding area some ten minutes' walk east of Shimonoseki Station from the top of **Kaikyō-yume Tower**, a 153m-high observation tower made of glass which looks like a giant golf tee with a ball resting on top. The tower is at its most striking at night, when the interior glows green and points of light dot the spherical observation deck, which also has a restaurant.

Karato

唐戸

Karato, the early twentieth-century port area that lies between Hino-yama and Shimonoseki Station, still has a handful of handsome brick and stone buildings, including the former British Consulate. On the waterfront is the **Karato Fish Market** (唐戸市場; 5-50 Karato-machi; daily 4am–noon; ☎ 0832 31 0001), a lively place early in the morning.

Akama-jingū

赤間神宮 • 4-1 Amidaiji-chō • 24hr • Free; museum ¥100 suggested donation • ☎ 0832 31 4138

The **Akama-jingū** shrine is dedicated to Antoku, an 8-year-old emperor who drowned along with the Taira clan when they were routed in the naval battle of Dannoura. The clash took place in the straits overlooked by the striking vermilion, gold and pale-green shrine, originally built as a Buddhist temple to appease the souls of the dead Taira warriors, and known at the time as Amida-ji. When Shintō and Buddhism were separated in the Meiji period, the temple became a shrine and was renamed Akama-jingū.

Beyond the Chinese-style arched gate is a small courtyard whose **graveyard** holds fourteen ancient graves of notable Taira warriors and a small statue of the blind and deaf priest, Hōichi Miminashi – the "earless Hōichi" in one of the Irish writer Lafcadio Hearn's most famous ghost stories (see box, p.599). There's also a small **museum** of armour and scrolls.

Sino-Japan Peace Treaty Memorial Hall

日清講和記念館, Nisshin Kowa Kinen-Kan • 454 Ayalagi • Daily 9am–5pm • Free • ☎ 0832 54 4697

Placed within an ornate, gabled building next to the *Shunpanrō* hotel (see opposite) is the **Sino-Japan Peace Treaty Memorial Hall**. Built in 1936, the hall includes a re-creation of the room in the hotel where a peace treaty was signed between China and Japan on April 17, 1895, after nearly a month of negotiations.

Hino-yama

火の山 • Ropeway (cable-car) July & Aug daily 10am–5pm • ¥200 • Buses run from the station to the ropeway Sept–June 9.15am–6.15pm (hourly)

Just beside the Kanmon Bridge is a kilometre-long pedestrian tunnel (daily 6am–10pm) through which you can walk under the straits to Moji, on Kyūshū. Uphill from the bridge is **Hino-yama**, with a number of trails leading up to the 268m summit. The view from the top of the mountain takes in the whole of the Kanmon Straits and the islands to the west of Shimonoseki – particularly memorable towards sunset. Over a thousand ships a day sail through this narrow waterway, making it one of Asia's busiest maritime crossroads.

ARRIVAL AND DEPARTURE
SHIMONOSEKI

The fastest way of getting between Shimonoseki and Kyūshū is by train or road across Kanmon suspension bridge; traditionalists can still make the short ferry hop (¥390) between Karato Pier, around 1.5km east of Shimonoseki Station, and Moji on Kyūshū's northwest tip.

By train If you're travelling by Shinkansen, you'll need to change trains at Shin-Shimonoseki Station and go two stops on the San'yō line to Shimonoseki Station.
Destinations Fukuoka Airport (hourly; 1hr); Hiroshima (hourly; 1hr 20min); Tokyo (hourly; 4hr 20min–5hr 40min); Yamaguchi (hourly; 1hr 45min).

By bus Long-distance buses arrive at the bus station in front of Shimonoseki Station.

Destinations Osaka (1 daily 10hr); Tokyo (1 daily; 15hr 30min).

By ferry If you arrive by ferry from South Korea, you'll come in at the Shimonoseki Port International Terminal (see box, p.586).
Destinations Pusan (daily; 13hr 30min); Shanghai (China) (weekly; 39hr); Qingdao (China) (2 weekly; 16hr).

INFORMATION

Tourist information Maps and local sightseeing literature in English are available from the tourist information booth (daily 9am–7pm; ☎ 0832 56 3422) in Shin-Shimonoseki Station by the Shinkansen exit.

here's another tourist office (daily 9am–7pm; ☎0832 82 8383) on the concourse of Shimonoseki Station. The Yamaguchi International Exchange Association

(Tues–Sun 9am–5.30pm), on the second floor of the Kaikyō-yume Tower complex, also has information in English.

GETTING AROUND

By bus Shimonoseki's main sights don't take long to see, but are spread out several kilometres east along the waterfront from the station, so it's best to use the local buses to get around. The buses departing from platforms 1 and 2 outside Shimonoseki Station are the most

convenient, passing Akama-jingū and Hino-yama on their way to Chōfu (¥340).

By bike If you're staying at the youth hostel (see below) you can hire a bike from there (¥300/day).

ACCOMMODATION

Kaikyō View Shimonoseki 海峡ビューしものせき 3-58 Mimosusogawa-chō ☎0832 29 0117. This low-rise concrete block has a fantastic view across the Kanmon Channel and a choice of spacious tatami rooms or Western-style suites. **¥19,890**

Shimonoseki Grand Hotel 下関グランドホテル 31-2 Nabe-chō ☎0832 31 5000, ⊛sgh.co.jp. A comfortable upmarket hotel beside Karato Pier with Western-style rooms and a couple of restaurants – one French, one Japanese. **¥16,170**

★**Shimonoseki Hinoyama Youth Hostel** 下関火の山 ユースホステル 3-47 Mimosusogawa-chō ☎0832 22 3753, ⊛e-yh.net/shimonoseki. Fine hostel with bunk-bed dorms, views across the Kanmon Bridge and free wi-fi. The friendly English-speaking manager is a reasonable cook. From Shimonoseki Station, take the bus from platform 1 to the Hino-yama ropeway, from where the hostel is a 2min walk downhill. More buses stop at the base of Hino-yama at Mimosuso-gawa; it's a 10min hike up to the hostel from here.

Note there's a 9.30pm curfew. **¥3200**

Shunpanrō 春帆楼 4-2 Amida-dera ☎0832 23 7181. Top-notch hotel near the Akama-jingū, with large suites of Western-style bedrooms and tatami sitting rooms overlooking the Kanmon Channel. The meals include lavish fugu dishes. **¥22,000**

Via Inn Shimonoseki ヴィアイン下関 4-2-33 Takezaki-chō ☎0832 22 6111, ⊛viainn.co.jp. One of the newest of the many business hotels close to the station, this one has mostly characterless rooms, many of which look out onto the chapel cupola next door. The rooms are done out in beiges and off-beiges and have wide, comfortable beds. **¥6385**

Hotel Wing ホテルウィング下関 3-11-2 Takezakicho ☎0832 35 2111, ⊛hotelwing.co.jp/shimonoseki. Amenable, fairly chassy Western-style rooms are on offer at this super central spot a 2min walk from the station. Rooms are done up with twee floral wallpaper, designer couches and comfy beds. **¥11,340**

EATING

Shimonoseki is packed with restaurants specializing in fugu (see box below), but the daily ferry connection with Pusan means Korean cuisine is almost as popular. Several restaurants around the Green Mall near the station specialize in Korean barbecue dishes, called yakiniku, while for fugu head for the parade running parallel to Route 9, northwest of the Kaikyō-yume Tower, and for fish restaurants try Karato. The area around the station has plenty of fast-food options, while the seventh floor of Daimaru department store has a variety of inexpensive restaurants.

FUGU

Shimonoseki revels in its role as Japan's centre for **fugu**, the potentially deadly blowfish or globefish, which provides inspiration for many local sculptures and souvenirs of spiky, balloon-shaped fish. It is known in Shimonoseki as *fuku*, homonymous with the character for fortune and wealth, in order to attract good luck and happiness. About half the entire national catch (3000 tonnes a year) passes through Haedomari, the main market for fugu, at the tip of the island of Hiko-shima, some 3km west of Shimonoseki Station.

Champing on the translucent slivers of the fish, which are practically tasteless, you may wonder what all the fuss is about. However, it is the presence of **tetrodotoxin** – a poison more lethal than potassium cyanide – found in the fugu's ovaries, liver and a few other internal organs, that make this culinary adventure both dangerous and appealing. Fugu chefs spend up to seven years in training before they can obtain a government licence to prepare the fish. Even so, a small number of people do die, the most famous fatality being kabuki actor **Bandō Mitsugorō** – a national treasure – who dropped dead after a globefish banquet in Kyoto in January 1975.

8

THE KAMPU FERRY TO SOUTH KOREA

The Kampu Ferry service to Busan in South Korea (ⓦkampuferry.co.jp) leaves daily at 7pm from the **Shimonoseki Port International Terminal**, five minutes' walk from Shimonoseki Station. The ticket booking office is on the second floor of the terminal building (daily 9am–5pm; ☎0832 24 3000); the cheapest one-way ticket is ¥9000 (¥7200 student fare) for the tatami resting areas, or ¥12,000 for beds. Although there's a ten percent discount on a return ticket, it's still cheaper to buy another one-way ticket in Pusan.

The ferry is one of the cheapest routes in and out of Japan, and is often used by people working illegally who need to renew their tourist visas. For this reason, the immigration officials at Shimonoseki have a reputation for being tough on new arrivals. Note also that if you need a **visa** for South Korea, you must arrange it before arriving in Shimonoseki; the nearest consulate is in Hiroshima.

There is also a twice-weekly ferry service to Qingdao (Orient Ferry ☎0832 32 6615) and a weekly ferry service to Shanghai (Shanghai-Shimonoseki Ferry).

Tsukasa つか佐 4-6 Akama-chō, Karato ☎0832 31 4129, ⓦtsukasa-shimonoseki.com. In this excellent fish restaurant, set back from the road, a team of motherly waitresses serves hearty set lunches for around ¥1890. The *fugu* course is ¥8400 at dinner. 11.30am–3pm & 5.30–10pm, closed Wed.

Yaburekabure やぶれかぶれ 2-2-5 Buzenda-chō ☎0832 34 3711. Look out for the large plastic *fugu* and red signs hanging outside this restaurant on the shopping parade east of the station. The speciality is a mea including seven different *fugu* dishes (¥6500). Daily 11am–10pm.

Yakiniku Yasumori 焼肉やすもり 2-1-13 Takezaki-chō ☎0382 22 6542. One of Shimonoseki's best *yakiniku* restaurants: order plates of raw meat and vegetables to sizzle on a tabletop cooker (from ¥1150). Also try *pivinpa*, a traditional mix of rice and vegetables in a stone bowl. 11am–midnight, closed Thurs.

Chōfu

長府

If you have enough time, make the short trip from Shimonoseki to neighbouring **CHŌFU**, an old castle town of the Mōri family, with its authentic enclave of samurai houses and streets, sleepy temples and lovely garden. One of the joys of Chōfu is its relative lack of tourist development, making it easy to feel you have slipped back several centuries while wandering round the samurai district.

Head east along Route 9 from Hino-yama for around 3km, ignoring the lacklustre aquarium and amusement park in favour of the elegant garden **Chōfu-teien** (長府庭園; 8-11 Kuromo; daily 9am–5pm; ¥200; ☎0832 46 4120), which makes a civilized introduction to Chōfu. Built for the ruler of a Mori clan, the garden dates from the Taishō era and has several teahouses dotted around an ornamental pond and babbling river. After the garden, branch off from the main road at the next turning and head inland towards a compact enclave of old **samurai houses**, shielded by wooden gates and crumbling earthen walls, topped with glazed tiles, with the roads bordered by narrow water channels. Further up the hill in a leafy glade approached by a broad flight of stone steps is **Kōzan-ji** (功山寺; 1-2-3 Chofukawabata; daily 9.30am–4.30pm; free; ☎0832 45 0258), the Mōri family temple dating from the fourteenth century and the oldest zen temple in the country. Next to the temple, you'll see the small **Chōfu Museum** (長府博物館; 1-2-5 Chōfukawabata; Tues–Sun 9.30am–5pm; ¥200; ☎0832 45 0555), which displays beautiful scrolls decorated with calligraphy and intriguing old maps.

ARRIVAL AND DEPARTURE · CHŌFU

By bus Buses to Chōfu (25min; ¥340) run from platforms 1 and 2 at Shimonoseki Station, every 15min or so. For Chōfu-teien get off at Shiritsu Bijutsukan-mae (市立美術館前) bus stop; for the samurai district, get off at Jōkamachi (城下町) bus stop and head uphill.

EATING

★**Chayashō** 茶屋祥 2-1-6 Chōfukawabata ☎ 083 245 0080. Delightful café-cum-shop in a kimono emporium, where the gracious hosts serve tea and coffee with cakes for ¥500. The delicious chocolate cake comes on indigo china plates and is decorated with a gold maple leaf. They also sell kimono, pottery and other colourful knick-knacks. Look for the large red-paper umbrella by the entrance to the century-old house, downhill from Kozan-ji. Daily 9am–6pm.

Hagi

萩

As you head east from Shimonoseki along the San'in coast, the landscape becomes much more rugged and sparsely populated. Here the savage Sea of Japan has eroded the rocks into jagged shapes, and if you take the train you'll see some marvellously bleak shorelines. The next town of any consequence is **HAGI**, some 70km northeast of Shimonoseki, which dates back to 1604 when warlord Mōri Terumoto built his castle at the tip of an island between the Hashimoto and Matsumoto rivers. Hagi's castle is long ruined, but the atmospheric graveyards of the Mōri *daimyō*, the layouts of the samurai and merchants' quarters – **Horiuchi** (堀内) and **Jōkamachi** (城下町) – and the temple district of **Teramachi** district (*tera* means "temple") remain, with several significant buildings intact. Much of Hagi's charm is as a place for meandering strolls and bike rides along these attractive plaster-walled streets. The town is known for its pottery. **Hagi-yaki**, considered Japan's next-best style of ceramics after Kyoto's *raku-yaki* – you can hardly move here without coming across a shop selling the pastel-glazed wares. Hagi is also famous for the role that some of its citizens played in the Meiji Restoration, such as Yoshida Shōin (see box below), who was executed by the Tokugawa Shogunate for his radical beliefs and is now enshrined at **Shōin-jinja**.

Sharing the relaxed, friendly atmosphere of other Yamaguchi-ken towns, Hagi is certainly worth visiting. If you rent a bike (see p.592), you can easily take in the most important sights in a day and still have time to crash out on **Kikugahama** (菊ヶ浜), a fine stretch of beach beside the castle ruins, officially open for swimming only from mid-July to mid-August, after which you'll have to watch out for jellyfish.

8

YOSHIDA SHŌIN

Born into a Hagi **samurai** family in 1830, the charismatic **Yoshida Shōin** believed that the only way self-isolated, military-ruled Japan could face up to the industrialized world – knocking at the country's door in the insistent form of Commodore Perry (see p.789) – was to ditch the Tokugawa government, reinstate the emperor and rapidly emulate the ways of the West. To this end, he tried to leave Japan in 1854 on one of Perry's ships, together with a fellow samurai, but was handed over to the authorities who imprisoned him in Edo (Tokyo) before banishing him back to Hagi.

Once at home, Yoshida didn't let up in his revolutionary campaign to "**revere the emperor, expel the barbarians**". From 1857, he was kept under house arrest in the Shōka Sonjuku (now within the shrine grounds of Shōin-jinja; see p.589), where he taught many young disciples, including the future Meiji-era prime minister Itō Hirobumi. Eventually, Yoshida became too big a thorn in the shogunate's side and he was executed in 1860, aged 29, for plotting to assassinate an official.

Five years later, samurai and peasants joined forces in Hagi to bring down the local Tokugawa government. This, and similar **revolts** in western Japan (see p.798), led to Yoshida's aim being achieved in 1868 – the restoration of the emperor to power.

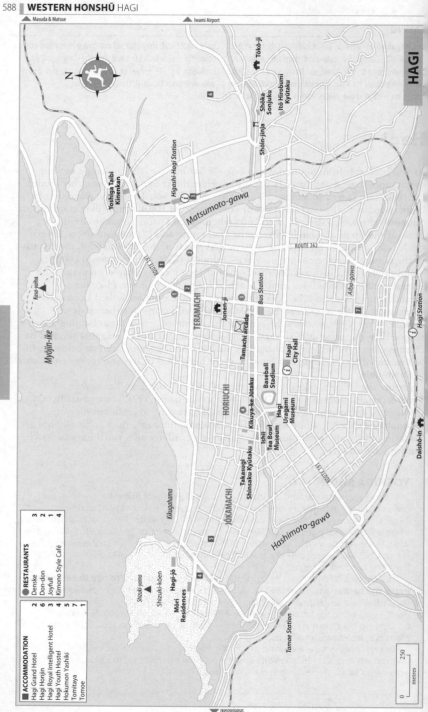

HAGI

▲ Masuda & Matsue

▲ Iwami Airport

Tōkō-ji

Shōka
Sonjuku
Itō Hirobumi
Kyūtaku

Shōin-jinja

Higashi-Hagi Station

Yoshiga Taibi
Kinenkan

Matsumoto-gawa

ROUTE 191

ROUTE 262

Aiba-gawa

Myōjin-ike

Kasa-yama ▲

Bus Station

TERAMACHI

Jōnen-ji

Tamachi Arcade

Hagi Station

ROUTE 191

Baseball
Stadium

Hagi
City Hall

HORIUCHI

Kikuya-ke Jūtaku

Ishii
Tea Bowl
Museum

Hagi
Uragami
Museum

Daishō-in

Takasugi
Shinsaku Kyūtaku

Kikugahama

JŌKAMACHI

Hashimoto-gawa

Shizuki-yama ▲

Shizuki-kōen

Mōri
Residences

Hagi-jō

Tamae Station

▼ Shimonoseki

■ ACCOMMODATION	
Hagi Grand Hotel	2
Hagi Honjin	6
Hagi Royal Intelligent Hotel	3
Hagi Youth Hostel	4
Hokumon Yashiki	5
Tomitaya	7
Tomoe	1

● RESTAURANTS	
Denske	3
Don-don	2
Joyfull	1
Kimono Style Café	4

0   250
metres

Shizuki-kōen

指月公園・Horiuchi・Daily: March 8.30am–6pm; April–Oct 8am–6.30pm; Nov–Feb 8.30am–4.30pm・¥210, including entry to Mōri soldiers' residence; tea at teahouse ¥500・ ☏ 0835 25 1826

Shizuki-kōen, on Hagi's western tip, is home to the rustic *Hananoe* teahouse, an atmospheric shrine, and the moat and sloping stone walls of **Hagi-jō** (萩城), all that remains of the castle destroyed in 1874 when Mōri Takachika shifted court to Yamaguchi (see p.579). The park is towered over by Shizuki-yama, a 143m-high hill that takes twenty minutes to hike up. Alternatively, you can relax beside the quiet cove with modern sculptures on the west side of the park.

Mōri residences

Immediately south of Shizuki-kōen are several large pottery factories with showrooms and a long wood-and-plaster tenement building, which contains **Mōri residences** where soldiers of the clan once lived. Though you can't go inside, as you walk the path outside the building you can look into the various rooms and imagine life here two centuries ago.

Horiuchi

堀内

The picturesque **Horiuchi** quarter is typified by narrow lanes lined by whitewashed buildings decorated with distinctive black-and-white lattice plasterwork. High- and low-ranking samurai, along with rich merchants, once lived in this area – in season you'll notice the *natsu mikan* (summer orange) trees heavily laden with fruit behind the high stone and mud walls; these were planted in 1876 as a way for the redundant samurai to earn some money.

Kikuya-ke Jūtaku

菊屋家住宅・1-1 Gofuku・Daily 9am–5pm・¥500・ ☏ 0838 25 8282

Several of Horiuchi's old houses are open to the public, the most interesting being the **Kikuya-ke Jūtaku**, built in 1604 for a wealthy merchant family. It has a particularly lovely garden, which you can see from the main tatami guest room, as well as displays of several thousand household items.

Takasugi Shinsaku Kyūtaku

高杉晋作旧宅・2-9-3 Minami Furuhagi Machi・Daily: April–Oct 8am–5pm, Nov–March 9am–4pm・¥100・ ☏ 0838 22 3078

Takasugi Shinsaku Kyūtaku, home to Takasugi Shinsaku, a leading figure in the fight to restore the emperor to power, is worth a stop. Like his mentor, Yoshida Shōin (see box, p.587), Takasugi died tragically young at 29, a year before the Meiji Restoration in 1867.

Hagi Uragami Museum

萩浦上記念館, Hagi Uragami Kinen-kan・586-1 Hiyako・Tues–Sun 9am–5pm; 525-4 Emukai; ¥300; ☏ 0838 25 6447

The **Hagi Uragami Museum** shows off some of the works that Hagi has produced over several centuries. It houses a collection of several thousand *ukiyo-e* prints and oriental ceramics, as well as a display of the tools and processes employed in *ukiyo-e* printmaking.

Shōin-jinja

松陰神社・**Temple** Daily 8am–5pm・Free・**Yoshida Shōin History Museum** (吉田松陰歴史館) Daily 9am–5pm・¥500・
Residence Daily 9am–5pm・Free・ ☏ 0838 292 4543

One kilometre southeast of Higashi-Hagi Station, on the mountain side of the Mastumoto-gawa, is **Shōin-jinja**, Hagi's largest shrine, dedicated to the

8

nineteenth-century scholar and revolutionary figure Yoshida Shōin (see box, p.587). Within the shrine grounds is **Shōka Sonjuku** (松下村塾), the small academy where Yoshida lived and taught during the final years of his life, the **Yoshida Shōin History Museum**, illustrating various scenes from Yoshida's life and also the **residence** where he was held under house arrest following his attempt to leave Japan in 1854.

Tōkō-ji

東光寺 • 1647 Chintō • Daily 8.30am–5pm • ¥300 • ☏ 0838 26 1052, ⍈ toukouji.net

Following the riverside cycle path uphill from the Shōin-jinja shrine leads you to one of the family temples of the Mōri clan, **Tōkō-ji**, where there's an atmospheric graveyard packed with neat rows of more than five hundred moss-covered stone lanterns. The temple, founded in 1691, has a Chinese flavour to its many handsome buildings and gates. Look out for the giant wooden carp gong hanging in the courtyard as you walk behind the main hall towards the graveyard. Here you'll find the **tombs** of five Mōri lords, all odd-numbered generations, save the first lord buried with the even-numbered generations in nearby Daishō-in (see below), guarded by an army of lanterns. During the **Obon** (Aug 15), the lanterns are lit to send off the souls of the dead.

Cycling up the hill behind the temple will bring you to **Tanjōchi** (誕生地), the birthplace of Yoshida Shōin, marked by a bronze statue of the samurai revolutionary and one of his followers. Take in the view of the town before heading back downhill, past the small thatched home of **Itō Hirobumi** (伊藤博文旧宅), another Yoshida disciple who later became prime minister and drafted the Meiji constitution.

Daishō-in

大照院 • 4132 Oazatsubaki Oumi • Daily 8am–5pm • ¥200 • ☏ 0838 22 2124 • Around a 10min bike ride from the Aiba-gawa, west of Hagi Station on the south bank of the Hashimoto-gawa

Daishō-in was built after the death of Mōri Hidenari, the first lord of the Hagi branch of the Mōri clan. A rickety gate at the temple entrance leads to another lantern-filled graveyard, where you'll find the tombs of all the even-numbered generations of Mōri lords, as well as Hidenari's and those of eight samurai who committed *seppuku* (ritual suicide) on his death.

Yoshiga Taibi Kinen-kan

吉賀大眉記念館 • 425-1 Chinto • Daily 9am–5pm • ¥500, pottery-making ¥2000 (call well in advance) • ☏ 0838 26 5180

Along the coastal route Highway 191, directly north of Higashi-Hagi Station, is **Yoshiga Taibi Kinen-kan**, one of Hagi's most respected pottery kilns, with an attached museum displaying an outstanding collection of *Hagi-yaki*. If you book ahead you can make your own pottery, which will be fired and sent to you for an extra fee after a couple of months. Unlike some other kilns, this one will post pottery abroad.

Kasa-yama

笠山

Some 10km or so north of Hagi station along the indented coast will take you past several fishing villages, where drying squid hang on lines like wet underwear. Set out along a narrow peninsula is a small, extinct volcano, known as **Kasa-yama**. Set back from the **Myōjin-ike** (明神池), a salt-water pond teeming with fish, beside a small shrine, is an interesting natural phenomenon: the **Kazeana**, a shaded glade cooled by

FROM TOP TOTTORI SAND DUNES (P.606); CAVE TUNNEL IN SHIMANE-KEN (P.596) >

8

cold air rushing from cracks in the lava. At the summit, there are panoramic views along the coast and you can inspect the 30m crater, one of the smallest in the world.

ARRIVAL AND DEPARTURE
HAGI

By plane Iwami Airport (☎ 0856 24 0010), an hour east along the coast, is served only by flights from Tokyo and Osaka; a connecting bus (80min; ¥1560) runs to Hagi bus station.

Destinations Osaka (daily; 1hr); Tokyo (daily; 1hr 30min).

By train There are three train stations around Hagi. The main train station, close to the modern side of town, is Higashi-Hagi (東萩駅). If you're staying near the remains of Hagi-jō, then Tamae Station (玉江駅) two stops west

of Higashi-Hagi, is more convenient. Hagi Station (萩駅), between Higashi-Hagi and Tamae, is the least useful of the three unless you're staying at *Tomitaya* (see below).

Destinations Masuda (7 daily; 1hr 20min).

By bus Long-distance buses all stop in the centre of town at the bus station, near the Tamachi shopping arcade, a short walk east of Jōkamachi.

Destinations Akiyoshi-dai (2 daily; 1hr 10min); Osaka (daily; 12hr); Tokyo (daily; 14hr 30min).

INFORMATION

Tourist information There are tourist information booths at Higashi-Hagi (daily 9am–5pm, April–Nov till 5.45pm; ☎ 0838 25 3145) and Hagi (same hours as Higashi-Haji; ☎ 0838 25 1750) stations, to the left as you leave the station buildings. Both provide bilingual maps

and pamphlets, although they don't get updated very often. If you have detailed enquiries, contact the tourism section (desk 14) at Hagi City Office (Mon–Fri 8.30am–5.15pm; ☎ 0838 25 3131) in the City Hall, where there's a helpful English-speaking assistant.

GETTING AROUND

Hagi's sights are spread over a wide area. From Higashi-Hagi Station, the samurai district of Jōkamachi and the remains of Hagi-jō in Shizuki-kōen are a good 30min walk west, while other major temples and shrines are similar distances to the east and south.

By bus There are two bus routes – *nishi mawari* (西回り; west) and *higashi mawari* (東回り; east) – that cover the entire town and its attractions in a circular route. Buses run twice hourly and cost ¥100 per ride.

By bike The best way of getting around is by bicycle; there

are plenty of rental shops at Higashi-Hagi Station (from ¥150/ hr). The cheapest day rentals (¥800/day) are available from the outfit next to the station. The tourist map available from the information office (see above) suggests several cycling routes, and there is no shortage of English direction signs.

ACCOMMODATION

Hagi Grand Hotel 萩グランドホテル 25 Furuhagi-chō ☎ 0838 25 1211, ⊛ hagi-gh.com. Large Western-style hotel close to the modern heart of town, with dated decor but spacious and well-furnished rooms. **¥26,300**

★ **Hagi Honjin** 萩本陣 385-8 Chintō ☎ 0838 22 5252, ⊛ hagihonjin.co.jp. Though slightly out of the way, this upscale hotel features fabulous rotemburo baths, a monorail up to a viewpoint over the city, beautiful tatami rooms and exquisite meals. Definitely the place to get away from it all. Prices include half-board. **¥26,000**

Hagi Royal Intelligent Hotel 萩ロイヤルインテリジェン トホテル 3000-5 Chintō ☎ 0838 21 4589. A dated business hotel, next to Higashi-Hagi Station, with an onsen, a rotemburo and a large art gallery and fitness centre adjacent to the lobby. Rates include breakfast. **¥8000**

Hagi Youth Hostel 萩ユースホステル 109-22 Horiuchi ☎ 0838 22 0733. This hostel has bunk-bed dorms placed around a central open courtyard. It's not a modern place, but staff are helpful and bike rental is available (¥500/day). From Tamae Station, walk 15min north across the Hashimoto-gawa. Closed mid-Jan to mid-Feb. Dorm **¥2940**

Hokumon Yashiki 北門屋敷 210 Horiuchi ☎ 0838 22 7521, ⊛ hokumon.co.jp. Set in a picturesque area close to the castle ruins, Hagi's most luxurious ryokan combines traditional Japanese rooms, gardens and cuisine with a Western-style lobby backed by an English garden. **¥50,000**

Tomitaya 冨田屋 Hashimoto-chō 61 ☎ 0838 22 0025. Friendly ryokan with spotless rooms, each with an alcove featuring a suitably seasonal hanging scroll as well as a sitting room. Breakfast, served in front of the big-screen television in the communal dining room, is beautifully presented; you can opt out of dinner for a cheaper rate. **¥12,600**

★ **Tomoe** 常茂恵 Hijiwara ☎ 0838 22 0150, ⊛ tomoehagi.jp. This is Hagi's best place to stay and a great place to enjoy traditional, personalized Japanese hospitality and cuisine, all presided over by Keiko, a charming local who speaks good English. The entire place exudes a cool Zen minimalism throughout. The 25 extremely well kitted out suites overlook the surrounding raked-gravel gardens. **¥40,000**

EATING AND DRINKING

You'll find many of Hagi's restaurants around the central Tamachi shopping arcade and the main cross street, Route 262. There's not a huge choice, but you won't go wrong if you opt for a cheap noodle bar or fish restaurant. The local speciality is *shirasu* (whitebait), and in spring you'll see fishermen on the Matsumoto-gawa sifting the water with giant nets hung from their narrow boats.

Denske デンスケ 14-3 Higashitamachi ☎0838 25 3983. A familial dining spot that sports a half-diner, half-traditional Japanese look and feel, with both booth and tatami seating. They do a delicious breaded, deep-fried pork tonkatsu ¥800). Daily 11am–8pm, Thurs till 5pm.

Don-don どんどん 177 Hijiwara 3-ku ☎0838 22 0751. Bustling inexpensive noodle joint near the Hagi-bashi across the Matsumoto-gawa. A bowl of udon noodles plus *taki-kome gohan* (vegetable rice) and pickles costs ¥700. Order at the counter, and point at the plastic dishes in the window if you can't read the menu. Daily 8am–8pm.

Joyfull ジョイフル 2-39 Gofuku-machi, Jōkamachi ☎0838 24 1065. A diner in the middle of Hagi might seem out of place, but this inviting Western spot is very big among locals. Dishes include hamburgers (from ¥430) and pasta plates (¥400). 24hr.

Kimono Style Café キモノスタイルカフェ 2-39 Gofuku-machi, Jōkamachi ☎0838 21 7000, ✺kimono-raison-d-etre.com. Café, shop and

kimono experience all in one: delicious cake and coffee sets for ¥700, soup and toast from ¥650 and kimono rental experience from ¥4000. Alternatively, you can admire the mini-garden and enjoy your tea and sweets served by waitresses in kimono. 9am–6pm, closed Thurs.

Tsuwano

津和野

Some 80km east of Hagi, in the neighbouring prefecture of Shimane-ken, is the older and even more picturesque castle town of **TSUWANO**. Nestling in the shadow of the 908m-high extinct volcano, **Aono-yama**, around which mists swirl moodily each autumn, this is yet another small town that touts itself as a "Little Kyoto". Thankfully (for once), there really is an air of courtly affluence along the tourist-jammed streets of **Tonomachi**, the well-preserved central area of samurai houses, with their distinctive cross-hatched black-and-white plaster walls. Each July 20–27, at the **Yasaka-jinja** shrine (八坂神社; 625 Gionmachi; 24hr; free; ☎075 561 6155), the ancient *Sagi-Mai* ("Heron Dance") is performed by men dressed as the white birds, complete with flapping wings and long-necked hats.

TSUWANO

- Mesuda
- Tsuwano Station
- Otonetōge Maria Seidō
- Katsushika Hokusai Museum of Art
- TONOMACHI
- Kakuōzan Yōmei-ji
- Catholic Church
- Yōrōkan
- Bus Station
- Yasaka-jinja
- Taikodani Inari-jinja
- Musée de Morijuku
- Chairlift
- Tsuwano-jō (Ruin)
- Tsuwano-kawa

■ ACCOMMODATION	
Hoshi Ryokan	1
Meigetsu	2
Wakasaginoyado	3

● RESTAURANTS	
Furusato	1
Kureha	3
Saranoki Shōintei	4
Yūki	2

- Mori Ōgai Kyūtaku & Mori Ōgai Memorial Museum
- Washibari-Hachimangū

0 | 250
metres

▼ Yamaguchi & Ogōri

It's also well worth braving the crowds on the second Sunday in April to see the annual Yabusame Horseback Archery Competition held at **Washibaria Hachimangū** shrine 鷲原八幡宮; 6322 Washibara; 24hr; free; ☎856 72 0650).

Tonomachi

殿町

The streets of **Tonomachi**, southeast of the station, are bordered by narrow, carp-filled canals; the fish (which outnumber the town's nine thousand residents by more than ten to one) were originally bred as emergency food supplies in the event of famine. The town's prosperity, born of peace and enlightened rule by local *daimyō*, is evident from the handsome buildings, among them the town's ornate **Catholic Church** (667 Ushiroda; daily 9am–5.30pm; free; ☎0856 72 0251), built in 1931, which combines a stately copper spire, stained-glass windows and an organ with tatami flooring. Look out for sake breweries and shops selling traditional sweets, including *genji-maki*, a soft sponge filled with sweet red-bean paste.

Katsushika Hokusai Museum of Art

葛飾北斎美術館, Katsushika Hokusai Bijutsukan • 254 Ushiroda • Daily 9.30am–5pm • ¥500 • ⓦ katsushikahokusai.org

At the north end of the main pedestrian thoroughfare, Tonomachi-dōri, pause at the small **Katsushika Hokusai Museum of Art** to view its refined collection of woodblock prints, illustrations and paintings by Japan's best-known (if its least Japanese) visual artist, Katsushika Hokusai, who lived in the nineteenth-century.

Musée de Morijuku

杜塾美術館, Morijunku Bijutsukan • 542 Oazamori-mura • Daily 9am–5pm • ¥500 • ☎0856 72 3200

A restored farmhouse fronted by raked-gravel gardens, the **Musée de Morijuku** has been converted into a smart modern gallery showing works by local contemporary artists, plus a small collection of etchings by Goya. Upstairs, the attendant will show you the pinhole camera in the *shōji* screen, capturing an image of the garden outside.

Taikodani Inari-jinja

太鼓谷稲成神社 • Goda 409 • 24hr • Free • ☎0856 72 0219 • It's around a 20min walk from Tsuwano Station to the stairway which leads up to the shrine, and from there another 15min to climb up to the shrine grounds

The **Taikodani Inari-jinja**, one of the five largest Inari shrines in Japan, is set uphill from a path covered by a tunnel of over a thousand red *torii*. There are some decent views over Tsuwano from the bright-red and gold shrine, built in the mid-eighteenth century, which bustles with tourists saying prayers to the local Shintō deities outside the splendid main hall.

Tsuwano-jō

津和野城 • Chairlift daily 9am–5pm, Dec–Feb irregular hours • ¥450 return

The town's castle, **Tsuwano-jō**, was built in 1295 by Lord Yoshimi Yoriyuki as protection against potential Mongol invaders. It was dismantled at the start of the Meiji era, but you can still walk around the remnants of the walls and catch some excellent town panoramas from the top of the hill. If you fancy an energetic hike, follow the pathway leading up to the old castle grounds (around a 30min walk), otherwise take the **chairlift**.

Mori Ōgai Memorial Museum

森鴎外記念館, Mori Ōgai Kinen-kan • 238 Machida • Tues–Sun 9am–5pm • ¥600 • ☎0856 72 3210

The preserved wood-and-mustard-plaster home of a famed Meiji-era novelist, translator, poet and surgeon, **Mori Ōgai** (Mori Ōgai Kyūtaku 森鷗外旧宅; daily 9am–5pm; ¥100) is worth a stop. Personal effects of the writer, and his death mask, are displayed next door in the modern **Mori Ōgai Memorial Museum**.

Otometōge Maria Seidō

乙女峠マリア聖堂 • 717-3 Ushiroda • 24hr • Free

If you have some time to spare, you can take pleasant woodland hike in the hills behind Tsuwano Station. Head southwest and cross the train tracks at the first opportunity, then double back and continue to the car park, from where a footpath leads up to the cosy chapel of **Otometōge Maria Seidō**, nestling in a leafy glade. In 1865, the Tokugawa shogunate transported some 150 Christians from Nagasaki to Tsuwano; 36 were eventually put to death for their beliefs before the new Meiji government bowed to international pressure, lifting the ban on the religion in 1874. This chapel was built in 1951 to commemorate the martyrs, and the quaint wooden building is the scene of the **Otometōge festival** on May 3.

Kakuōzan Yōmei-ji

覚皇山永明寺 • Daily 8.30am–5pm • ¥300 • ☎ 0856 72 0137 • A 5min walk south from Tsuwano Station

Inside the charming temple of **Kakuōzan Yōmei-ji**, stone steps lead up to an elegant collection of thatched wooden buildings, used by generations of Tsuwano lords since 1420. Inside, look out for the lovely screen paintings decorating some of the tatami rooms and take a moment to sit and admire the verdant traditional garden. The temple is located just downhill from a forest footpath.

8

ARRIVAL AND INFORMATION TSUWANO

By train By train, Tsuwano is reached on the cross-country JR Yamaguchi line. From Shin-Yamaguchi, where the Shinkansen stops, the fastest journey takes just over an hour, while from Masuda (near Iwami Airport; see p.592), on the San'in coast, express trains take 30min, just 10min faster than the local service. Tsuwano Station is also the terminus for the SL Yamaguchi-gō steam-train service. Note that at the time of writing, due to severe floods in mid-2013, JR and steam trains from Yamaguchi were terminating at Jifuku (50min), from where replacement buses continued on to Tsuwano.

By bus There are direct bus services to Tsuwano from Hagi (5 daily; ¥2080, 1hr 45min); JR passes are not valid on this service as it is run by Bochō Bus. The bus station is a few minutes' walk from Tonomachi, the heart of the old samurai district.

Tourist information The tourist office is to the right of the train station (daily 9am–5pm; ☎ 0856 72 1771).

GETTING AROUND

By bike Tsuwano's sights are somewhat spread out, so if you intend to explore beyond Tonomachi, rent a bicycle from one of the many operations around the station (¥500/2hr, ¥800/day).

ACCOMMODATION

There's little more than a day's leisurely sightseeing and walks around Tsuwano, but an overnight stay is recommended if you want to sample a traditional ryokan or minshuku, of which the town has several. Rates mostly start at a reasonable ¥7000 per person including two meals, and the tourist office by Tsuwano Station can help you find a place if the ones below are full.

Hoshi Ryokan 星旅館 53-6 Ushiroda ☎ 0856 72 0136. Slightly ramshackle but charming and friendly ryokan near the station that calls to mind the weathered home of an elderly aunt. Insulation is not the best, so if you're here in winter be sure the heater works. Add on ¥1,000 per person per meal. **¥10,000**

Meigetsu 明月 7-21-10 Minamisenju ☎ 0856 72 0685.

Tsuwano's most charming ryokan, with an attractive flower display at the front door, plenty of polished wood fittings, spacious tatami rooms and a small traditional garden. Rates include two meals, which feature seasonal mountain vegetables and carp. **¥21,000**

Wakasaginoyado 若さぎの宿 93-6 Morimura Russia ☎ 0856 72 1146. This homely, vaguely kitschy minshuku has an English-speaking owner and offers good tatami rooms with TV and a/c. Rates include breakfast and dinner but you can also pay ¥4500 per person without meals **¥15,600**

EATING

Tsuwano isn't short of restaurants, with several *shokudō* and noodle shops close to the station and around the sceni Tonomachi area. Finding an evening meal can be tricky, since most visitors who stop over eat in their ryokan or minshuku *Uzume-meshi*, the traditional local dish of rice in a broth with shredded green mountain vegetables, pieces of tofu anc mushrooms, is worth trying, as is the carp.

Furusato ふる里 277-6 Ushiroda ☎ 0856 72 0403. This small restaurant, in a traditional plaster house, specializes in *uzume-meshi*, served as part of a set meal (¥1500) with slices of white root-vegetable jelly coated in lemon sauce and pickles. Daily 11am–3pm.

Kureha 紅葉 201 Ushiroda ☎ 0856 72 1006. Cakes and omelettes are the speciality at this cute little coffee house with tatami and Western seating, English menu and English-speaking staff. You can pick up coffee and a cake (such as yummy cheesecake with tofu, or apricot tart) for ¥700, while a beef curry will cost you ¥1000. Avoid the lunch rush at noon. Tues–Fri 9am–6pm.

Saranoki Shōintei 沙羅の木松韻亭 70 Ushiroda

☎ 0856 72 1661. From the large tatami room you car gaze out on a lovely traditional garden while eating a se meal (¥2625 or ¥5250) of *kaiseki ryōri* haute cuisine slightly cheaper are their bowls of udon (¥1000) or soba (¥850). There's an attached *omiyage* shop and café that overlooks the main street. Daily 9am–3pm.

Yūki 遊亀 271-4 Ushiroda ☎ 0856 72 0162. This famous restaurant has some real atmosphere, with tatami booths pottery and porcelain on the walls and a carp-filled stream running right through the dining room. Some of the fish end up on the plate as sashimi or in the miso soup. Try the ¥2000 *Tsuwano teishoku*, a set meal of local dishes. Reservations recommended. 10.30am–7pm, closed Fri.

Matsue

松江

Straddling the strip of land between the lagoons of Nakaumi and Shinji-ko is **MATSUE**, the appealing prefectural capital of Shimane-ken, 180km east of Tsuwano, and one of the highlights of the San'in coast. The lakes, rivers and castle moat lend this modern city a soothing, faintly Venetian atmosphere, and it's still possible to catch glimpses of the old Japan that so enchanted Hearn a century ago, such as fishermen casting their nets in **Shinji-ko**, or prodding the lake bed with poles, searching out shellfish. A more modern phenomenon, however, is the mass of photographers often gathered to capture the golden sunset behind Yomegashima, a tiny pine-studded island in the lake. Clustered together around **Jōzan-kōen** and **Shiomi Nawate**, the latter a parade of samurai residences, are Matsue's finest attractions: **Matsue-jō**, one of Japan's few original castles and the **Matsue Historical Museum**, a handsome samurai district and the museum and former residence of **Lafcadio Hearn** (see box, p.599). Although the city's main sights are so closely grouped together that they can all easily be seen in half a day, it's well worth lingering here. What's more, the city has a fairly buzzing nightlife, with several neighbourhoods packed with bars and small restaurants.

Matsue-jō

松江城 • 1-5 Tonomachi • Daily 8.30am–6.30pm, Oct–March till 5pm • ¥550, foreign visitors ¥225 • ☎ 0852 21 4030 • English-speaking guides are available at weekends, and on weekdays if you book at the tourist information office (see p.600) • If you're taking a bus from Matsue Station to the castle, get off at Kenchō-mae and you'll see the castle grounds dead ahead

The brooding, five-storey donjon of **Matsue-jō**, standing on top of the hill, Oshiro-yama, is still the focal point of the city, as it was when the *daimyō* Horio Yoshiharu first built his castle in 1611. Compared to Himeji-jō's donjon (see p.535), this one looks as if it's been squashed, but it is, in fact, the largest of the twelve remaining original castle towers scattered around Japan – its sinister aspect is enhanced by the black-painted

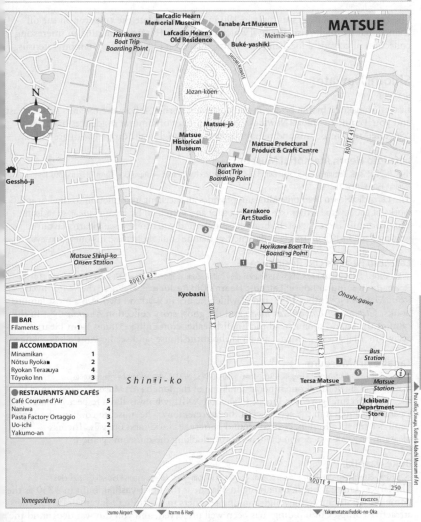

MATSUE

Lafcadio Hearn
Memorial Museum
Lafcadio Hearn's
Old Residence
Horikawa
Boat Trip
Boarding Point
Tanabe Art Museum
Meimei-an
Buké-yashiki
SHIOMINATE
Jōzan-kōen
Matsue-jō
Matsue
Historical
Museum
Matsue Prefectural
Product & Craft Centre
Horikawa
Boat Trip
Boarding Point
ROUTE 431
Gesshō-ji
Karakoro
Art Studio
Matsue Shinji-ko
Onsen Station
ROUTE 43
Horikawa Boat Trip
Boarding Point
Kyobashi
ROUTE 37
Ohashi-gawa
ROUTE 27
Bus
Station
Shinji-ko
Tersa Matsue
Matsue
Station
Ichibata
Department
Store
Yomegashima

BAR	
Filaments	1

ACCOMMODATION	
Minamikan	1
Nōtsu Ryokan	2
Ryokan Terazuya	4
Tōyoko Inn	3

RESTAURANTS AND CAFÉS	
Café Courant d'Air	5
Naniwa	4
Pasta Factory Ortaggio	3
Uo-ichi	2
Yakumo-an	1

8

Izumo Airport ▼   ▼ Izumo & Hagi   ▼ Yakumotatsu Fudoki-no-Oka

0   250
metres

wood decorating the walls. The castle was extensively renovated in the 1950s, and the surrounding grounds, defined by the inner moat, have been turned into a pleasant park, **Jōzan-kōen** (城山公園).

Leave your shoes at the entrance to the donjon, and climb the slippy wooden stairs to the fifth-floor *Tengu* ("Long-Nosed Goblin") room in your socks. This is where the lords would have commanded their armies from if there had been any battles (which there weren't). On the second floor there are displays of armour, weapons and other artefacts, including the original *shachi* (mythical dolphins) that topped the roof. The views across the city towards the lake and sea are splendid.

Matsue History Museum

松江郷土館, Matsue Kyōdo-kan • Tonomachi 279 • Daily 8.30am–6.30pm, Oct–March till 5pm • Free • ☎ 0852 32 1607
The elegant whitewashed wooden **Matsue Historical Museum** is built of a combination of pillars, verandas and ornate gabled roof typical of the hybrid style of the Meiji era.

The two-storey mansion was built in 1903 to accommodate the emperor on the off chance that he might visit the city, which he never did. It now contains an interesting collection of colourful local arts and crafts, including plenty of tea ceremony utensils.

Shiomi Nawate
塩見縄手

Leave Jōzan-kōen by the bridge in the northwest corner, follow the moat as it turns east and you'll come to **Shiomi Nawate**, where a number of samurai residences have been converted into museums and remain protected by high walls capped with grey tiles.

Lafcadio Hearn Memorial Museum
小泉八雲記念館, Koizumi Yakumo Kinen-kan • 322-4 Okudani-chō • Daily 8.30am–6.30pm, Oct–March till 5pm • ¥300, foreign visitors ¥150 • ☎ 0852 21 2147

The **Lafcadio Hearn Memorial Museum** provides an excellent introduction to the life and works of the revered writer (see box opposite) and is curated by Hearn's great-grandson, Bon Koizumi. There are lots of English captions and you can also see Hearn's favourite writing desk and chair, specially designed so that he could better use his one good eye.

Lafcadio Hearn's Old Residence
小泉八雲旧居, Koizumi Yakumo Kyūkyo • 315 Kitahori-chō • Daily 8.30am–6.30pm, Oct–March till 5pm • ¥350 • ☎ 0852 23 0714

A small old samurai house, **Lafcadio Hearn's Old Residence**, is where the writer lived from May to November 1891 and in which he began work on two of his most famous books, *Glimpses of Unfamiliar Japan* and the ghost story collection *Kwaidan*. Sit in the calm of the tatami rooms, read the English leaflet containing extracts from Hearn's essay, "In a Japanese Garden", which is about the house, and see how little has changed.

Tanabe Art Museum
田部美術館 • 310-5 Kitahoricho • Tues–Sun 9am–5pm • ¥600 • ☎ 0852 26 2211, ⓦ www.tanabe-museum.or.jp

A high wall shields the contemporary building of the **Tanabe Art Museum**, established by the late prefectural governor Tanabe Chōemon XXIII, who was also a respected artist with a particular interest in the aesthetics of the tea ceremony. The museum contains the Tanabe family's refined collection, centred around pottery tea bowls and utensils. There's a pleasant, airy café where you can have tea overlooking the museum's garden.

Buke-yashiki
武家屋敷 • 305 Kitahori-chō • Daily 8.30am–6.30pm, Oct–March till 5pm • ¥300, foreign visitors ¥150 • ☎ 0852 22 2243

The largest samurai house remaining in Matsue is the **Buke-yashiki**, built in 1730 as the home of the Shiomi family, high-ranking retainers to the ruling Matsudaira clan. The attractive complex of buildings has been well preserved, and you can wander round the exterior, looking into tatami and wood rooms, which give some sense of what eighteenth-century samurai life was like.

Meimei-an teahouse
明々庵 • 278 Kitahori-chō • Grounds daily 9am–5pm • ¥400 • ☎ 0852 21 9863

The dusty grounds of the Buké-yashiki are a contrast to the precise Zen beauty of the raked gravel and artfully positioned stones around the **Meimei-an teahouse**, a short walk up the hill directly behind Shiomi Nawate. Originally designed by the *daimyō* Matsudaira Fumai to exact tea-ceremony principles, the tiny cottage has creamy beige plaster walls which hardly look capable of holding up the heavily thatched roof. In 1966, to celebrate its 150th anniversary, Meimei-an was restored and moved to this spot beside an existing samurai mansion with a good prospect of the castle. You can't enter the teahouse itself, but it's still worth taking time to admire it from the veranda of the adjoining mansion.

LAFCADIO HEARN

"There is some charm unutterable in the morning air, cool with the coolness of Japanese spring and wind-waves from the snowy cone of Fuji …"

Lafcadio Hearn, *My First Day in the Orient*

The journalist **Lafcadio Hearn** was enchanted by Japan, and of all expat writers is by far the most respected by the Japanese. Celebrated by the people of Matsue as an adopted son, his books, including *Glimpses of Unfamiliar Japan* and *Kwaidan*, are considered classics.

The offspring of a passionate but doomed liaison between an Anglo-Irish army surgeon and a Greek girl, and named after the Greek island of Lefkada on which he was born on June 27, 1850, Hearn grew up in Dublin, a contemporary of Bram Stoker and Oscar Wilde. A schoolyard accident in 1866 left him permanently **blind** in his left eye, and in 1869, young and penniless, he decided to chance his fortune in the United States. Over the course of the next fourteen years, Hearn worked as a reporter and writer in Cincinatti, New Orleans and the West Indian island of Martinique (where he penned his first novel, *Chita*), with a brief marriage to an African-American girl along the way.

Commissioned by *Harper's Monthly* to write about Japan, Hearn arrived in **Yokohama** on April 4, 1890. By the end of the day, he had decided to stay, get a teaching job and write a book. The teaching post brought Hearn to Matsue, where he met and married Koizumi Setsu, the daughter of an impoverished samurai family.

Hearn would happily have stayed in Matsue, but the freezing winter weather made him ill, and in 1891 they moved south to Kumamoto, in Kyūshū, closer to Koizumi's relatives. The couple had four children, and in 1896 he adopted the name **Koizumi Yakumo** (Eight Clouds) and secured Japanese nationality. By the turn of the century, Hearn's novels and articles had become a great success; he had started teaching at Tokyo's prestigious Waseda University, and was invited to give a series of lectures at London University and in the United States. But on September 30, 1904, at the age of 54, Hearn suffered a series of heart attacks and died. His gravestone in Zoshigaya cemetery, near Ikebukuro in Tokyo, proclaims him a "man of faith, similar to the undefiled flower blooming like eight rising clouds who dwells in the mansion of right enlightenment".

Hearn's **books** stand as paeans to the beauty and mystery of old Japan, something he believed worth recording, as it seemed to be fast disappearing in the nonstop modernization of the early Meiji years.

8

Karakoro Art Studio

カラコロ工房, Karakoro Kōbō • 43 Tonomachi • Daily: complex 9.30am–6.30pm, some shops close at 5pm; restaurant 11am–10pm; bakery-café 11am–6pm • Free • ☎ 0852 20 7000

Near the Kyobashi is the **Karakoro Art Studio**, housed in a stately former bank building. The complex contains a small gallery exhibiting locally produced glass art, kimono and fabric, and a number of **craft shops** selling jewellery, clothing and stained glass. There's also a classy restaurant with affordable lunchtime specials, and a bakery-café serving cappuccino and mouthwatering Italian ice cream that can be enjoyed in the breezy courtyard.

ARRIVAL AND INFORMATION   MATSUE

By plane The closest airport is Izumo Airport, 35km west, although Yonago Airport to the east is also an option. Direct buses run from Izumo to Matsue Station (25min; ¥1000), while from Yonago you can catch a train on the JR airport link for Yonago Station, then change for Matsue (1hr 10min; ¥740).

Destinations Nagoya (daily; 1hr 10min); Tokyo Haneda (5 daily; 1hr 15min); Seoul (3 weekly; 1hr 30min).

By train JR trains arrive at Matsue Station, south of the Ōhashi-gawa, while Matsue Shinji-ko Onsen Station (complete with public hot-spring footbath outside), just north

of where the river flows into Lake Shinji, is the terminus for Ichibata trains from Izumo Taisha (see p.602). The most convenient Shinkansen stop is Okayama, from where local trains run to Matsue (the fastest takes 2hr 20min). There are also sleeper train services from Tokyo via Yonago, the main San'in coast railway junction some 25km east of Matsue.

Destinations Izumo Taisha (10 daily; 1hr); Shin-Yamaguchi (3 daily; 3hr 45min); Okayama (14 daily; 2hr 20min); Tottori (5 daily; 1hr 30min); Tokyo (daily; 13hr); Tsuwano (3 daily; 2hr 30min).

By bus Most long-distance buses arrive beside Matsue Station; the rest go to Matsue Shinji-ko Onsen Station. There are overnight services from Tokyo (¥11,550) and Fukuoka (¥8800) and daily services from Osaka (¥5100) and Hiroshima (¥4000).

Destinations Fukuoka (1 daily; 12hr); Hiroshima (hourly; 4hr 20min); Kyoto (hourly; 5hr); Okayama (hourly; 3hr); Nagoya (1 daily; 8hr); Osaka (several daily; 4hr 30min–7hr 45min); Tokyo (1 daily; 12hr).

GETTING AROUND

By bus Regular buses connect Matsue Shinji-ko Onsen with Matsue Station, from where you can catch buses to other parts of the city and surrounding area. From outside both stations you can also pick up the Lakeside Line bus service, a motorized red trolley bus that makes a leisurely circuit of Matsue's sights (¥200/trip). The day-pass for ¥500 is hardly worth it, since it's far quicker to walk parts of the route. However, if you're planning to visit Izumo Taisha (see p.602) the same day, you might save money if you buy the one-day L&R Free Kippu ticket (¥1500), which covers the Lakeside bus and one leg of the round-trip to Izumo on the Ichibata train – you'll have to pay for the return journey (¥790).

By bike Cycling is the best mode of transport in pedal-friendly Matsue. Bikes can be rented from the Times Car Rental office (daily 8am–6.30pm; ¥300/day, or ¥500/day for electric-assisted) over the road from Matsue Station.

On foot If you're not pressed for time, Matsue is not impossible to navigate on foot; indeed many of the pedestrian only areas are what gives the city some of its charm.

INFORMATION AND TOURS

Tourist information The tourist office (daily 9am–6pm; ☎ 0852 21 4034), just outside the north exit of Matsue Station, is competent in English, has plenty of leaflets and maps and can help with accommodation bookings. Note that if you plan to visit all the main sights, it's best to buy the Universal Pass (¥920) at the first of the sights you visit; it's valid for three days, will save you money on the separate entrance fees and get you discounts at other attractions around the city.

Boat tours If you visit Matsue between March and Nov, an ideal way to appreciate the city's watery charms is to take a 30- or 50min-long boat trip (¥800 for foreigners) around the castle moat and canals. There are departures between 9am and 5pm (July & Aug till 6pm) from any of the three Horikawa Boat Trip Boarding Points: near Karakoro Art Studio, southeast of Matsue-jō and on the northwest side of the Jōzan-kōen.

ACCOMMODATION

Accommodation options in Matsue are split across two main areas: there's the usual cluster of business hotels around Matsue Station, while on the lake south of Matsue Shinji-ko Onsen Station are the upmarket, expensive hotels catering to the hot-spring crowd.

Minamikan 皆実館 14 Suetsugu-Honmachi ☎ 0852 21 5131, ⊚ www.minami-g.co.jp/minamikan. Matsue's top ryokan is in a recently renovated modern complex but has a distinctly traditional feel, from the courteous service to the neatly clipped pines in the gravel garden. Huge suites of tatami rooms and the best local cuisine push up the prices. **¥60,000**

★ **Nōtsu Ryokan** 野津旅館 555 Isemiya-chō ☎ 0852 21 1525. Smart, well turned out ryokan on the banks of the Ōhashi-gawa with rooms overlooking the river, a rooftop rotemburo, friendly service and excellent meals included in the price. Prices drop by well over half off season. **¥54,000**

Ryokan Terazuya 旅館寺津屋 60-3 Tenjin-machi ☎ 0852 21 3480, ⊚ mable.ne.jp/~terazuya. Set in a quiet location above a sushi restaurant, this quaint, excellent-value ryokan is run by a friendly couple who speak a bit of English, it and has well-kept Japanese-style rooms with a/c and TV. **¥14,400**

Tōyoko Inn 東横INN 498-10 Asahi-machi ☎ 0852 60 1045, ⊚ toyoko-inn.com. This budget, fairly characterless

---

KYŌDO RYŌRI IN MATSUE

Epicureans flock to Matsue for its **Kyōdo ryōri**, seven types of dishes using **fish and seafood** from Shinji-ko. The dishes, best sampled in winter when all the fish are available and tasting their freshest, are: *amasagi*, smelt either cooked as tempura or marinated in teriyaki sauce; *koi*, carp baked in a rich, sweet sauce; *moroge-ebi*, steamed prawns; *shijimi*, small shellfish usually served in miso soup; *shirauo*, whitebait eaten raw as sashimi or cooked as tempura; *suzuki*, bass wrapped in paper and steam-baked over hot coals; and *unagi*, grilled freshwater eel. To sample the full seven courses, make an advance reservation with one of the top ryokan, such as *Minamikan* (see above), and be ready to part with at least ¥10,000.

accommodation is nevertheless clean, reliable, near the station and offers in-room internet access and complimentary Japanese breakfast. ¥6480

EATING AND DRINKING

Matsue's range of **restaurants** isn't wide, but they are of a high standard and reasonably priced; a good place to head for is the Suetsugu Honmachi area beside the canal just south of the castle. If you're on a budget, pack a picnic to enjoy in the castle grounds or at Meimei-an. You'll find a gaggle of **drinking** options in the Isemiya district near Matsue Station and the side streets of Tohonchō between the canal and the Ōhashi-gawa.

Café Courant d'Air カフェ クーラン デ エール 494-13 Asahi-machi ☎0852 27 8577. This sophisticated café, with subdued lighting, classical music and classy decor, offers thick slices of creamy sponge and strawberry short cake (from ¥380) and fancy coffees (cappuccino ¥690). Mon–Sat 11am–11pm.

Filaments フィラメンツ 5 Hakkenya-chō ☎0852 24 8984. Gaijin-friendly corner bar that can get a little expensive, with drinks at around ¥700. Still, if it's not to your liking, there are several dozen other drinking establishments within a few blocks of this one. Daily 7pm–1am.

★ **Naniwa** なにわ 21 Suetsugu-Honmachi ☎0852 21 2835, ⓦhorten.naniwa-i.com. Popular, classy restaurant perched on the edge of Shinji-ko that serves beautiful *kaiseki* meals and more modest "ladies'set" dinners. It's also one of the best places to try *Kyōdo ryōri* (see box below), with prices for multicourse meals from ¥5250 and up depending on the size. Daily 11am–2pm & 5–9pm.

Pasta Factory Ortaggio パスタファクトリー オルタッジョ ョ 82 Suetsugu-Honmachi ☎0852 28 0701. Rather good Italian staple dishes are the name of the game at this fun,

casual restaurant, including pomodoro and *crema* pastas (from ¥800) and small pizzas (¥880). Also has a decent wine list (from ¥350/glass). Mon–Fri 11.30am–2.30pm & 5.30–10.30pm, Sat & Sun 11.30am–3pm & 5.30–9pm.

Uo-ichi 魚一 78 Katahara-chō ☎0852 22 2935, ⓦuoichi.net. This is a good place to try some of the *Kyōdo ryōri* fish dishes (see box, beow). The set menu, with an English translation, costs ¥4200, but there are cheaper meals, such as *joten don*, rice topped with deep-fried shrimp, smelt, conger eel, green pepper and perilla teaf tempura (¥1280). Friendly staff will serve you either at the counter or at tables on tatami. 11.30am–2pm & 5.30–10pm, closed Tues.

Yakumo-an 八雲庵 308 Kitabori-chō, Shiomi Nawate ☎0852 22 2400, ⓦyakumoan.jp. Popular, picturesque restaurant in a former samurai residence, with a central garden, teahouse and carp-filled pond, specializing in good-value soba and udon noodles, including *warigo soba* (cold seaweed-seasoned buckwheat noodles, served in three-layer dishes, over which you pour stock). Daily 10am–4.30pm.

8

Around Matsue

The area around Matsue, once known as **Izumo**, is one of the longest settled in Japan, with a written history dating back to the seventh century *Izumo-no-Kuni Fudoki* (*The Topography of Izumo*). There's plenty to see here, including the stunning landscapes at the **Adachi Museum of Art**, the shrines and burial mounds at **Fudoki-no-Oka**, and **Izumo Taisha**, one of Japan's most important shrines, holiday home of the Shintō pantheon of deities, and the reason that Matsue was dubbed "chief city of the province of the gods" by Hearn.

Yakumotatsu Fudoki-no-Oka

八雲立つ風土記の丘 • 456 Oba-chō • **Park** 24hr • Free • **Museum** Daily 9am–5pm, closed Tues • ¥200 • ☎0852 23 2485, ⓦyakumotatu-fudokinooka.jp • Take #21 or #22 bus from Matsue Station towards Oba/Yakumo and gett off at Oba Shako

Keyhole-shaped burial mounds (*kofun*) from the earliest-recorded settlers around Matsuo can be seen in the rice-field-dotted countryside at **Yakumotatsu Fudoki-no-Oka**, a museum and park. The **museum** will mainly be of interest to archeology and history buffs, with its small display of finds from nearby excavations, including impressive pottery horses and some first- and second-century bronze daggers and bells. The park has several pleasant forest and nature walks, plus the **Izumo Kanbe-no-sato** (出雲かんべの里; 9am–4pm, closed Tues; ¥200; ☎0852 28 0040, ⓦkanbenosato. com), a couple of buildings promoting local culture where you can watch woodworkers, basket-makers, weavers, potters and a specialist in *temari*, the art of making colourful thread-decorated balls.

Kamosu-jinja

神魂神社 • 563 Oba-chō • 24hr • Free • ☎ 0852 21 6379 • Take #21 or #22 bus from Matsue Station towards Oba/Yakumo and get off at Oba Shako, or take the bus for Kanbe-no-Sato and get off at the last stop

An impressive site, 8km south of Matsue, is the fourteenth-century shrine, **Kamosu-jinja**, dedicated to the Shintō mother deity Izanami. The handsome raised wooden structure, in a glade of soaring pines reached via stone steps lined by cherry trees, is said to be the oldest remaining example of *Taisha-zukuri* or "Grand shrine style" left in Japan.

Adachi Museum of Art

足立美術館, Adachi Bijutsukan • 320 Furukawachō • Daily 9am–5.30pm, Oct–March till 5pm • ¥2300, foreign visitors ¥1150 • ☎ 0854 28 7111, ⓦ adachi-museum.or.jp • You can take a train to Yasugi (安来市; ¥400 from Matsue, ¥190 from Yonago), 20min from the museum by free shuttle bus (11 daily) – the tourist information offices in Matsue (see p.600) and Yasugi Station (daily 9am–6pm; ☎ 0859 22 6317) can provide timetables; direct buses from Matsue's and Yonago's JR stations take around 50min to reach the museum (get off at Saginoyu Onsen)

Don't miss the stunning **Adachi Museum of Art**, some 20km east of Matsue, near the village of Yasugi, en route to Yonago. The large collection of Japanese artworks, dating from 1870 to the present day, includes masterpieces by Yokoyama Taikan and Uemura Shoen. The surrounding gardens are also exquisite, covering 43,000 square metres.

The gardens

The museum's founder, Adachi Zenkō, was an enthusiastic gardener, and his passion for the artform shows through in the six separate gardens comprising beautiful landscapes (165,000 square metres in all) that envelop the galleries and steal your attention at every turn. The museum is designed so that as you move around, the views of the Dry Landscape Garden, the White Gravel and Pine Garden, the Moss Garden and the Pond Garden appear like living picture scrolls when viewed through carefully placed windows. A couple of the gardens have traditional teahouses where you can take *matcha* and sweets (from ¥1500). *Juryū-an* is a copy of a teahouse in the former Imperial Palace, Katsura Rikyū, in Kyoto, and looks over a peaceful moss-covered garden; in the smaller *Juraku-an*, visitors are served a bowl of green tea made with water boiled in a kettle of pure gold, said to aid longevity. The two coffee shops in the museum are less atmospheric but cheaper, and the views just as fine.

The museum

Give yourself plenty of time here because, once you've dragged yourself away from the gardens, the art itself isn't bad either. The museum has the largest collection of paintings by **Yokoyama Taikan**, whose delicate ink drawings and deep colour screens set the standard for modern Japanese art. There is also a section on kitsch art from children's books, and a ceramics hall which includes works by Kawai Kanjirō – a brilliant local potter who participated actively in the *mingei* (folk art) movement begun by Yanagi Sōetsu – and Kitaōji Rosanjin, a potter and cook, whose pieces were designed to complement and enhance the food served on them.

Izumo Taisha

出雲大社 • 195 Kizukihigashi • Daily 6am–6pm • Free • ☎ 0853 53 3100

The grand, graceful shrine of Izumo Ōyashiro, second only in importance to that at Ise, is better known as **Izumo Taisha**, after the town it's situated in, 33km west of Matsue.

Although most of the current buildings date from the nineteenth century, the original shrine was built – if you believe the legend – by Amaterasu, the Sun Goddess, and is still visited each November by all eight million Shintō deities for their annual get-together (see box opposite). In this region, the tenth month of the lunar calendar is traditionally known as the "month with gods", while in all other parts of Japan it's known as the "month without gods". Since the shrine is dedicated to Okuninushi-no-mikoto, the God of Happy Marriage, many couples visit in the hope that they will live happily ever after; visitors to the shrine clap their hands four times to summon the deity rather than the usual two.

The shrine

A giant concrete *torii* stands at the southern end of Shinmon-dōri, the main approach to the shrine. More in keeping with the shrine's natural grace is the wooden *torii* that marks the entrance to the forested grounds at the foot of Yakumo-yama. Closer to the central compound, to the right of the Seki-no-Baba, an avenue of gnarled pine trees leaning at odd angles, is a large modern statue of the deity Okuninushi. The branches of the trees surrounding the shrine, on which visitors tie *omikuji* (fortune-telling) papers for good luck, are so heavily laden they look as if they have been coated with snow.

Straight ahead, beyond a bronze *torii*, is the shrine's central compound, the **Oracle Hall**, in front of which hangs a giant *shimenawa*, the traditional twist of straw rope. Legend has it that good fortune shall befall those who can successfully toss a coin that lodges in the cut ends of the ropes. Inside the hall, Shintō ceremonies take place all day, with accompanying drumming and flute playing. Leaving the shrine by the west exit (the closest to the bus station and main car park), you'll see a large modern hall, where more daily ceremonies take place and which is also used for the sacred *kagura* dances performed on festival days. In front of the hall hangs another *shimenawa* into which people fling coins, hoping they will stick and bring them luck.

Treasure hall

宝院 • Daily 8am–4.30pm • ¥50

To the right of the Oracle Hall is a modern building containing a small museum of historical artefacts, the **treasure hall**, on the second floor of which you'll find a small collection of swords, statues, armour, painted screens and a map of the shrine, dating from 1248, painted on silk and in remarkably good condition. There's also an illustration of the shrine as it was supposed to have been in the Middle Ages, when it was 48m tall, with projecting rafters that shoot out from the roof. It's now 24m, but still the country's highest wooden structure, topping Nara's Tōdai-ji, home of the great statue of Buddha (see p.474).

Honden

本殿 • Not generally open to the public

The inner shrine, or **Honden**, is well worth a visit. As the shrine is completely closed off to the general public, you'll have to stand outside the **Eight-Legged East Gate** entrance,

---

IZUMO TAISHA FESTIVALS

Apart from the usual Shintō festival days (see pp.54–55), the important festivals at Izumo Taisha are:

Imperial Grand Festival (May 14–16): The welcome mat is rolled out for an envoy from the imperial family.

Kamiari-sai (A week between Oct and Nov): Celebration for the annual gathering of some eight million Shintō gods. During the festival, the gods are carried into the Honden, where they hold a conference to discuss, among other things, wedding matches between Japanese people.

decorated with beautiful unpainted wooden carvings, and peer through to the inner courtyard. Even pilgrims are not allowed anywhere near the central Holy of Holies hall, buried deep within the **Honden** – only the head priest can enter. In the woods behind the Honden is the **Shōkōkan** (7am–5pm; ¥200), the former treasure house, which displays many jolly statues of Daikoku (one of the guises of Okuninushi), and his bon viveur son Ebisu, who usually has a fish tucked under his arm.

ARRIVAL AND INFORMATION   IZUMO TAISHA

By plane A regular bus leaves Izumo Airport for Izumo Taisha daily (35min; ¥850).

Destinations Fukuoka (2 daily; 1hr 15min); Osaka (7 daily; 1hr); Tokyo (5 daily; 1hr 20min).

By train From Matsue, the easiest way to reach Izumo Taisha is by train on the Ichibata line from Matsue Shinji-ko Onsen Station (松江しんじ湖温泉駅) – you'll have to change at Kawato for the final leg to Izumo Taisha (total 1hr; ¥790). If you're travelling round both Matsue and Izumo Taisha in the same day, you can save some money by buying the ¥1000 L&R Free Kippu (see p.600). JR trains stop at Izumo-shi Station, from where you'll have to transfer to

the Ichibata line, changing again at Kawato. The Izumo-Taisha-mae terminus is a 5min walk south of the shrine.

By bus There's a direct Ichibata bus from Izumo-shi Station (¥510; 25min). The Izumo Taisha bus station, from where you can catch buses to Hinomisaki (see below), is a minute's walk west of the shrine.

By bike It's only worth hiring bicycles, available to rent from the station, if you plan on making the journey to Hinomisaki, about 10km from Izumo Taisha (see p.602).

Tourist information The tourist office (daily 9am–5.30pm; ☎ 0853 53 2298) is in the train station and has English leaflets.

ACCOMMODATION AND EATING

With Matsue so close, there's no pressing reason to stay overnight in Izumo Taisha, though if need be you can grab a bite at any number of restaurants around the bus station near the shrine.

Arakiya 荒木屋 409-2 Kizukihigashi ☎ 0853 53 2352. A hospitable outfit about a 5min walk south of the main throng of tourist canteens. This is a good place to try the local speciality, *warigo soba* (¥780), cold buckwheat noodles seasoned with seaweed flakes, served in three-layer dishes, over which you pour *dashi* (stock); you can also try one layer of noodles for just ¥250. Both are served with a cup of hot soba-water soup, which you can flavour with *dashi*. 11am–5pm, closed Wed.

Hinode-kan 日の出館 776 Kizukinishi ☎ 0853 53 3311. Several minutes from the train station and shrine, this quaint spot offers Japanese-style air-conditioned rooms and a public bath. **¥29,000**

Takenoya 竹野屋 857 Kizukiminami ☎ 0853 53 3131. Better-kept than nearby *Hinode-kan* (see above) but slightly more expensive, this is an attractive, friendly place to stay on the main Shinmon-dōri approach to the shrine. **¥32,000**

Hinomisaki-jinja

日御碕神社 • 455 Hinomisaki • **Shrine** Daily 8am–5pm • Free • **Lighthouse** Daily 9am–4.30pm • ¥150 • A 20min bus ride (¥530) from Izumo Taisha bus station; you can rent a bicycle at Izumo Taisha Station (¥500/3hr, ¥800/day) and cycle out to Hinomisaki (30min)

About 10km northwest of Izumo Taisho is the scenic cape of **Hinomisaki** (日御碕), where you'll find a quieter shrine complex, **Hinomisaki-jinja**, built in 1644 under the shogun Tokugawa Ieyasu but since given a full restoration and a brand new coat of bright orange paint. The complex boasts a 44m-tall white stone **lighthouse** dating from 1903. Climb the more than 150 steps of the steep spiral staircase to the top of the lighthouse for a splendid view out to the nearby islands (though you can't go up in bad weather). Around the cape are several bathing beaches, and the rocky cliffs around the lighthouse are good for exploring.

Mount Daisen

大山

The main rail and road routes along the coast east of Matsue cross into the neighbouring prefecture of Tottori-ken and through the uninteresting industrial city of **Yonago** (米子); trains from Okayama on the JR Hakubi line terminate here. Yonago s the gateway to **Mount Daisen**, at 1711m the highest mountain in the Chūgoku region, and home to beautiful beech forests and ancient temples. Daisen has the largest **ski slopes** in western Japan and sees heavy snowfall from November to April; it's also known for the **Daisen Ice and Snow Festival**, which takes place over three days at the end of January, with fireworks lighting up the night sky and an amazing display of ice sculptures.

ARRIVAL AND INFORMATION   MOUNT DAISEN

By bus Buses (9 daily) depart from bus stop 4 outside Yonago Station for the village of Daisen-ji (大山寺; 8–9 daily; 50min; ¥720), the main hub for accommodation on Mt Daisen, with access to the ski slopes in winter and hiking paths in summer.

Tourist information A couple of minutes' walk east from the bus stop, the tourist information booth (daily 8.30am–5pm; ✆ 0859 52 2502) has plenty of maps of the area and staff can help book accommodation.

Kurayoshi

倉吉

Set just in and from the coast, **KURAYOSHI** is a small town in central Tottori-ken and the jumping-off point for the hot-spring resort of **Misasa** and the temple hike up to **Nageire-dō** on Mount Mitoku. The town offers some pleasant architecture and is home to *Bokoro*, a gorgeous ryokan at which it's well worth a night or two spending (see below).

Akagawara

赤瓦 · A 20min cycle ride from Kurayoshi Station (follow signs for Shirokabe-dozō-gun, 白壁土蔵群)

If you have an hour or two to spare in Kurayoshi, head for the picturesque **Akagawara** area, where a number of refurbished Edo- and Meiji-era black-and-white storehouses stand next to the shallow Tama-gawa. These are now home to various souvenir and craft shops selling local goods including beautiful *Kurayoshi-gasuri* items made from the locally woven, indigo-dyed cloth.

ARRIVAL AND INFORMATION   KURAYOSHI

By train Kurayoshi is connected to Yonago (to the west) and Tottori (to the east) on the JR San'in Line.
Tourist information The booth (daily 8.30am–5pm; ✆ 0858 24 5024), to the left outside Kurayoshi station at

the end of the bus stands, has maps and information (in Japanese) on the surrounding area, as well as free bikes with which to explore the town.

ACCOMMODATION AND EATING

Bokoro 望湖楼 4-25 Hawai Onsen, Yurihama-chō ✆ 0858 35 2221, ✆ bokoro.com. Located on the western shores of Lake Togo, a few minutes' drive north of Kurayoshi Station, this is one of the region's best spots for bedding down. The large Japanese- and Western-style rooms are plenty accommodating, but the real reason to come is for the fresh seafood dinners – crab is a local speciality – and the public baths, which are set out on a raised structure in the middle of

the lake and offer 360-degree views. ¥25,200
Café Mela カフェ メーラ 2-2453 Shinmachi ✆ 0858 22 6445. On the second floor of the Sadar Chowk (サダル チョーク) crafts shop, opposite the storehouses, this charming café serves up authentic Indian curry (from ¥800), lassi and chai in a large open room of exposed woods, with Indian fashion sold below. 10am–7pm, closed Thurs.

Misasa and around

The hot-spring resort **MISASA** (三朝) is situated in the mountains south of Kurayoshi. While here you could see some of the contemporary woodblock prints at the **Misasa Museum of Art** (みさき美術館; 199-1 Misasa; daily 10am–6pm, closed Tues;

8

free; ☎0858 43 3111), or take advantage of the free **rotemburo** (24hr) in the river if you're passing through and feeling brave. There are bamboo screens by the pools, but as onlookers from the nearby bridge have a bird's-eye view of proceedings, this is one communal bathing experience that's not for the shrinking violet.

Nageire-dō

投入堂 • 1010 Mitoku • April–Dec 8am–5pm • ¥400 • ☎0858 43 2666 • Bus from Misasa (15min; ¥370)

While in the area south of Kurayoshi, it's worth taking the bus from Misasa 8km up the road to **Mount Mitoku** (三徳山) to visit the famous shrine of **Nageire-dō**, part of **Sanbutsu-ji** (山佛寺); the main Sanbutsu-ji temple complex is just over the road from the bus stop. From here, it's an hour's climb up a rugged path (there are chains in places to help you scramble over the massive boulders) past a belfry and a number of smaller temple buildings, including **Monju-dō** (文殊堂), **Jizō-dō** (地蔵堂) and – at the very top – Nageire-dō, all spectacularly perched on a precipice and with marvellous views. Nageire-dō, nestling under an overhanging rock and balanced precariously on stilts which grip the cliff face below, is an incredible feat of engineering, and no one knows quite how it was built. Legend has it that it was thrown into place by an ascetic priest named Ennogyoja; certainly Sanbutsu-ji has been a centre for Buddhism since the eighth century, and Nageire-dō is thought to date back to the eleventh or twelfth.

On your way down, try the local speciality of *sansai-ryōri*, mountain vegetables and tofu, at one of the **restaurants** at the foot of the main temple complex, near the bus stop.

8

ARRIVAL AND DEPARTURE MISASA

By bus Buses from Kurayoshi Station (¥460) depart from platform 3 and take 20min; get off at the Daigaku Byoin-mae stop. Be sure to check bus times for the return trip, however, or you could end up with a long wait for the next bus back to Misasa.

ACCOMMODATION

Misasa is a picturesque place to spend the night, and you'll come across *yukata*-clad visitors wandering through the streets from inn to rotemburo or bar and back again.

Kiya Ryokan 木屋旅館 895 Miyasa ☎0858 43 0521, ⓦmisasa.co.jp. A friendly place with fine food and a choice of baths, located on the narrow street dotted with craft shops and tearooms east of the river. You'll be able to spot its mint-green roofs from the bus stop. **¥26,000**

Tottori

鳥取

An hour's train ride east from Kurayoshi lies the provincial capital of **TOTTORI**, famous in Japan for the 16km-long **sand dunes**, part of the **San'in Coast National Park**, at nearby Hamasaka. The coastline around here is blessed with some particularly fetching beaches and headlands, bedecked with pretty flora and interesting geological formations.

Tottori sand dunes

鳥取砂丘, Tottori Sakyū • Chairlift daily 8am–5pm • ¥200 • Buses to Sakyū Kaikan and the Sakyū Centre leave from platform 4 at the bus station next to Tottori train station (¥360; 20min)

Designated a national monument, the **Tottori sand dunes** are quite atmospheric and come complete with imported camels for would-be Lawrence of Arabias to pose on.

Buses to the dunes pass through the city centre on the way to either Sakyū Kaikan, beside the dunes, or the Sakyū Centre, overlooking them from a hill. The centre is nothing more than a souvenir and food stop for the tour buses that pile in daily. There's a **chairlift**, which runs between the centre and the edge of the dunes, but you can just as easily walk between the two.

The Uradome coastline

浦富海岸, Uradome kaigan • If you have a car, you can drive along the coast from the sand dunes on Route 178, stopping at any of the many parking places along the way to enjoy the views from the cliff top, or follow one of the many paths down to the secluded beaches below; if using public transport, take the bus bound for Iwai-onsen (岩井温泉) and get off at Uradome-kaigan-guchi ((浦富海岸口)

The **Uradome coastline** covers the 15km between the edge of the Tottori sand dunes and the eastern edge of the prefecture, and which, together with the dunes, forms part of the **San'in Coast National Park**. The shore is fringed with strangely shaped rocks and islands jutting out of the water, some topped with pine trees, and many sculpted with wave-carved tunnels, caves and openings. Taking a sightseeing boat is a popular way to enjoy the scenery (see below).

The **views** from the clifftop paths along much of the pine-covered coastline looking out over the blue-green Sea of Japan are also stunning, and if you follow one of the steep paths down through the trees to the shore, you'll find numerous sandy **bays** and bathing **beaches**.

ARRIVAL AND INFORMATION

TOTTORI

By plane Tottori Airport (☎0857 28 1150), 10km northwest of the city, has daily flights to Tokyo. A bus to the city from the airport takes 20min and costs ¥450.
Destination Tokyo Haneda (4 daily; 1hr 10min).

By train Tottori Station, on the San'in line, is the terminal of the JR Tsuyama line from Okayama.
Destinations Okayama (5 daily; 1hr 25min); Osaka (15 daily; 2hr 20min); Yonago (7 daily; 1hr 40min).

By bus The bus terminus next to the train station is where

long-distance buses from Tokyo, Himeji, Hiroshima, Kyoto, Kōbe and Osaka stop.
Destinations Hiroshima (5 daily; 4hr 50min); Kyoto (3 daily; 4hr); Osaka (13 daily; 3hr 30min); Tokyo (daily; 10hr 30min).

Tourist information The tourist information booth (daily 8.30am–7pm; ☎0857 22 3318) by the north exit of Tottori Station has English leaflets and maps of the city and prefecture.

TOURS

Sightseeing boats Boats (daily March–Nov 9.10am–4.10pm; ¥1200; ☎0857 73 1212) depart for 40min tours of the coastline. The journeys depart every 30min, but don't sail in bad weather. To get there, take a bus

(40min; ¥620) bound for Iwai-onsen (岩井温泉) from platform 4 outside Tottori Station and get off at Shimameguri Yuronsen-noriba (島巡り 湯論戦-のりば).

ACCOMMODATION AND EATING

Although there is a handful of **restaurants** at the sand dunes, you'll be better served by those in the shopping arcades that run north of Tottori Station, or those under the train tracks, most of which have plastic food displays.

Hotel New Otani Tottori ホテルニューオータニ鳥取 2-153 Imamachi ☎0857 23 1111, ⓦnewotani.co.jp. This upscale business chain next to the Daimaru department store has elegant standard and luxury contemporary rooms. Rates include breakfast. **¥22,660**

Sakyū Centre Hotel 砂丘センターホテル 2083 Yuyama ☎0357 22 2111. This hotel offers old-fashioned, good-value Japanese-style rooms on a hillside overlooking the coast, with two meals included in the rates and, in summer, an outdoor pool. To get there, take any bus from platform 0 at the station to the last stop. **¥14,700**

Tottori Green Hotel Morris 鳥取グリーンホテルモーリス 1-107 Imamachi ☎0857 22 2331 ⓦhotel-morris.co.jp/tottori. Set behind the Daimaru department store, across from the station, this good-value business hotel has a swanky lobby that leads to only slightly less swanky rooms, many of which look onto an alleyway. The economy doubles have slightly smaller beds in them but are otherwise the same as the pricier versions. A Western-style breakfast is available for ¥550. **¥8190**

8

Shikoku

四国

TESHIMA ART MUSEUM

9

Shikoku

With beautiful scenery, a laidback atmosphere, friendly people and several notable sights, it is perhaps surprising that Shikoku , Japan's fourth main island, is the least visited by international tourists. This tranquil island, nestling in the crook between Honshū and Kyūshū, offers elements of traditional Japan that are often hard to find elsewhere, making it an excellent destination. An ancient Buddhist pilgrimage, original castles and distinctive arts and crafts are some of Shikoku's attractions – but equally appealing are the island's rural pace of life and little-visited villages and smaller surrounding islands. Set aside at least a week to get around all Shikoku's four prefectures. If you only have a day or two, though, head straight for Matsuyama's splendid castle and the hot springs at nearby Dōgo; or pay a visit to the landscape gardens of Ritsurin-kōen in Takamatsu, before hopping on a ferry over to the idyllic, contemporary art-filled islands of the Seto-Naikai (Inland Sea).

According to legend, Shikoku was the second island (after Awaji-shima) born to Izanagi and Izanami, the gods who are considered to be Japan's parents. Its ancient name was Iyo-no-futana, and it was divided into four main prefectures: **Awa** (now Tokushima-ken), **Iyo** (Ehime-ken), **Sanuki** (Kagawa-ken) and **Tosa** (Kōchi-ken). These epithets are still used today when referring to the different prefectures' cuisines and traditional arts. Apart from being the scene of a decisive battle between the Taira and Minamoto clans in the twelfth century (see p.794), Shikoku has had a relatively peaceful history, due in part to its isolation from the rest of Japan. The physical separation ended with the opening of the **Seto Ōhashi** in 1989, a series of six bridges that leapfrog the islands of the Inland Sea, carrying both trains and cars. It has since been joined by the **Akashi Kaikyō Ōhashi suspension bridge** (see p.534), connecting Shikoku to Honshū via Awaji-shima, the island to the west of Tokushima, and the **Nishi Seto Expressway**, running along ten bridges spanning nine islands on Shikoku's northern coast (see p.963).

Most of Shikoku's population of just over four million lives in one of the island's four prefectural capitals: **Takamatsu**, **Tokushima**, **Kōchi** and **Matsuyama**. The island is split by a vast mountain range that runs from Tsurugi-san in the east to Ishizuchi-san, Shikoku's tallest peak, in the west. The northern coast, facing the Inland Sea, is heavily developed, in contrast to the predominantly rural south, where the unimpeded *kuroshio* (black current) of the Pacific Ocean has carved a rugged coastline of sheer cliffs and

RITSURIN-KŌEN

Highlights

❶ Ritsurin-kōen Enjoy a peaceful bowl of *matcha* tea in the elegant teahouse of Takamatsu's beautifully landscaped garden, a century in the making. **See p.615**

❷ Sanuki udon Enjoy a tasty bowl of hand-made thick white noodles served with tempura and mountain vegetables throughout Kagawa, known as the Udon Prefecture. **See p.618**

❸ Art Islands of the Inland Sea Exciting contemporary art and architecture combined with friendly fishing villages on the islands of Naoshima, Teshima, Inujima and Shōdoshima in the Inland Sea. **See p.625**

❹ Awa Odori Over a million revellers let their hair down at Tokushima's annual summer dance festival as the city's streets sway with dancers in colourful cotton kimono. **See p.635**

❺ Iya Valley Go whitewater rafting on the crystal-clear Yoshino River and explore remote villages in this spectacular gorge hidden away in the island's central mountains. **See p.642**

❻ Matsuyama This easy-going castle city boasts good nightlife, an important literary history, a famous hot-spring resort and a very unusual temple. **See p.662**

HIGHLIGHTS ARE MARKED ON THE MAP ON P.612

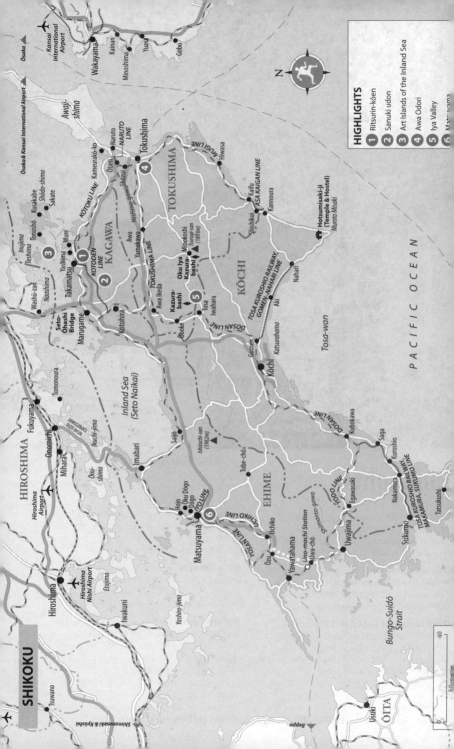

THE SHIKOKU PILGRIMAGE

Wherever you are in Shikoku, you'll seldom be far from Japan's longest and most famous **pilgrimage**, established by disciples of the Buddhist saint **Kōbō Daishi**, founder of Shingon Buddhism (see box, p.510). It usually takes over two months to walk the 1400km between the 88 temples on the prescribed route, and plenty of pilgrims, known as *henro-san*, still complete the journey this way, though far more follow the route by bicycle, motorbike, car, train or on bus tours. The number of temples represents the 88 evils that, according to Shingon Buddhism, bedevil human life.

HENRO-SAN

Henro-san are easy to spot, since they usually dress in traditional short white cotton coats, coloured shoulder bands and broad-rimmed straw hats, and generally clutch rosaries, brass bells and long wooden staffs (for support on the steep ascents to many of the temples). The characters on their robes and staffs translate as "Daishi and I go together". Many of the 150,000 annual pilgrims are past retirement age, but younger Japanese and even foreign visitors are increasingly experiencing this religious journey.

THE ROUTE

The present-day headquarters of the Shingon sect is **Kōya-san**, in Wakayama-ken (see p.507), and this is the traditional start of the pilgrimage. The first temple visited on Shikoku is **Ryōzen-ji**, near Naruto in Tokushima-ken. Pilgrims then follow a circular route that winds its way clockwise around the island, stopping at all the temples en route to the 88th, **Ōkubo-ji**, in Kagawa-ken. Many temples allow pilgrims to stay for around ¥4000 per person including meals. It's a lucrative business: you'll see many pilgrims dropping coins by the thousands of Buddhas along the way, and they fork out again at the temples, where an official stamp costs around ¥300.

BOOKS AND INFO

For frequently updated online information, check out ⓦ shikokuhenrotrail.com, created by the American *henro* David Turkington. Several books in English describe the 88-temple hike – we've listed a few below:

Miyazaki Tateki *Shikoku Japan 88 Route Guide*. This guide, currently in its third edition, is an excellent choice. It has maps, accommodation and other information essential for a pilgrimage, whether you go on foot, or use transport.

Amy Chavez *Running the Shikoku Pilgrimage: 900 Miles to Enlightenment*. A recently published book by *Japan Times* columnist Chavez who ran the route (almost a marathon a day) and recounts the experience with humour and humility.

---

outsized boulders. The climate throughout the island is generally mild, although the coasts can be lashed by typhoons, and the mountains see snow in the winter.

Apart from the chapter highlights (see p.611), other places to consider building into a trip to this part of Japan include the lovely Inland Sea island of **Shōdoshima**, the whirlpools at **Naruto Hiwasa**, where turtles come to lay their eggs each summer, and the surfing spots of **Kaifu** and **Shishikui**. With more time, you could hit Shikoku's southern coast for the dramatically rocky capes at **Ashizuri** and **Muroto**, and explore the **Shimantogawa**, one of Japan's most beautiful rivers.

In the prefectural capitals, you'll find a wide range of hotels, restaurants and bars, as well as international centres and tourist information offices, while the island's famous 88-temple **pilgrimage** (see box above) means that even in the countryside, you're unlikely to be stuck for accommodation.

GETTING AROUND
SHIKOKU

By train Getting around by train is easy enough, but will require planning and coordination. JR Shikoku runs regular express trains, though local train services are not as frequent as on the mainland. There are also five small private railway companies. The All Shikoku Rail Pass, which must be purchased outside Japan by tourist visa holders, allows travel on JR and the private lines for two days (¥5300), three days (¥7200), four days (¥7900), or five days (¥9700). The Shikoku Free Kippu (¥15,700) is available to residents and is valid on all JR trains and buses on the island for three days.

9

TAKAMATSU

0 — 250
metres

Sunport

Takamatsu
Symbol Tower
& Maritme Plaza
Bus Station

TIC

Kotoden
Takamatsu
Chikkō Station

MIZUKI-DŌRI

Takamatsu-jō

Takamatsu
Station

Tamamo-
kōen

Kagawa
Museum

SETO O-HASHI-DŌRI

Mitsukoshi
Department
Store

Hyogo-machi Arcade

Kotoden
Katahara-
machi
Station

Takamatsu City
Museum of Art

Marugame-machi Arcade

Lion-dōri Arcade

FERRY-DŌRI

I-PAL

ROUTE 11

Black Pumpkin
Sculpture

Tenmaya
Department
Store

ROUTE 11

Chūō-
kōen

Tokiwashimmachi Arcade

Kotoden
Kawaramachi
Station

Police

KIKUCHIKAN-DŌRI

NAGAO LINE

CHŪŌ-DŌRI

Minami-Shimmachi Arcade

Tokiwa-gai
Arcade

KANKO-DŌRI

KANKO-DŌRI

Ritsurin-kōen
Kita-guchi Station

JR KOTOKU LINE

North
Gate

Ritsurin
Station

Ritsurin-
kōen

KOTOHIRA LINE

Sanuki Folkcraft
Museum

Mt Shiun

East
Gate

Kotoden
Ritsurin-kōen
Station

Takamatsu Airport

Kotohira

■ ACCOMMODATION		● RESTAURANTS AND CAFÉS	
JR Hotel Clement		Gowariyasu	7
Takamatsu	1	Kanaizumi	5
Guesthouse		Merikenya	3
Chottoco-Ma	2	Okageya	8
Hotel Kawaroku	5	Ramjhan	9
Takamatsu Terminal Hotel	3	Shigi China Kitchen	6
Takamatsu Tōkyū Inn	4	Szechwan Restaurant Chin	1
		Tenkatsu	
		Tokiwa Saryō	10
■ BARS AND CLUBS		Umie	2
Amazon	2	● SHOPPING	
Bar & Flair Recommend	1	Mingei Fukuda	2
King's Yawd	3	Miyawaki	3
Ruff House	4	Shikoku Shop 88	1

By car Renting a car (see p.617) will give you more
flexibility than public transport and really is the best
option if you want to get to the villages of the Iya Valley
or explore western Kōchi-ken and the Shimantogawa
area. Major car rental companies all have offices in
Shikoku's main cities.

Takamatsu and around

Even before the Seto Ōhashi connected
Shikoku's rail network with Honshū,
the port of **TAKAMATSU** (高松), capital
of **Kagawa-ken**, was a major gateway
into the island. Warlord Chikamasa
Ikoma built his castle here in 1588, but
the city and surrounding area's history
go back a long way before that. The
priest and mystic Kōbō Daishi (see box,
p.510) was born in the prefecture, the
banished Emperor Sutoku was
murdered here in 1164 and, 21 years
later, the Taira and Minamoto clans
clashed at nearby **Yashima**. In air raids
during World War II, Chikamasa's
castle was virtually destroyed, along
with most of the city.

Today, Takamatsu is a sprawling but
attractive cosmopolitan city of close to
420,000 inhabitants, peppered with
covered shopping arcades and chic
boutiques. Next to Takamatsu JR
station, you can't miss the thirty-storey
Takamatsu Symbol Tower. The city's
tallest building anchors the **Sunport**
complex of offices, shops, convention
halls and ferry piers. Northwest of here,
the red-glass brick lighthouse at the end
of the Tamamo breakwater is a good
place to aim for if you're out for a
seaside stroll or want to join local
runners for a jog. Further east is the
trendy **Kitahama Alley** (北浜アリー), a
small area of brick warehouses and old
buildings that have been converted into
appealing cafés (see p.618) and
boutiques. As twenty-first-century as all
this is, the city's star attraction remains
Ritsurin-kōen, one of Japan's most
classical, spacious and beautifully
designed gardens. The gardens are easily
accessible on a day-trip from Honshū,

out it's well worth staying longer so you can also take in **Shikoku Mura**, the open-air museum of traditional houses at Yashima, or **Kotohira-gū** (see p.622), the ancient shrine an hour's train ride west of the city. Takamatsu is also a gateway to two of the most appealing islands in the Inland Sea: **Shōdoshima**, a mini-Shikoku with its own temple circuit and scenic attractions; and delightful **Naoshima**, a must for contemporary art and architecture fans with several outstanding galleries designed by Andō Tadao (see p.627).

Ritsurin-kōen

栗林公園 • Chūō-dōri • Daily, opening hours vary but usually 5.30am–7pm in summer and 7am–5pm in winter • ¥400 • ☎ 087 833 7411 • ⓦ ritsuringarden.jp • The East Gate is the garden's main entrance, but JR trains stop at least every hour at Ritsurin-kōen Kita-guchi 栗林公園北口), close by the North Gate; at either entrance you can buy tickets and pick up a free English map of the gardens

Takamatsu's one must-see sight, **Ritsurin-kōen**, is 2.5km south down Chūō-dōri from the JR station. The formal garden, Japan's largest at 750,000 square metres, lies at the foot of Mount Shiun. Its construction began in the early seventeenth century and took several feudal lords over one hundred years to complete. The gardens were designed to present magnificent vistas throughout the seasons, from an arched red bridge amid a snowy landscape in winter, to ponds full of purple and white irises in early summer.

From the East Gate main entrance you can either follow a route through the **Nantei**, South Garden, to the left or **Hokutei**, North Garden, to the right. It's possible to enter or exit the garden at the North Gate, but the route from the East Gate makes for a more pleasant meander.

Nantei

南庭 • **Kikugetsu-tei teahouse** (掬月亭) Daily 9am–4.30pm • Free, *sencha* or matcha ¥510/¥710 • **Higurashi-tei teahouse** (日暮亭) Sat & Sun 9am–4.30pm • Free, matcha ¥500

The more stylized of the two gardens, **Nantei** has paths around three lakes, dotted with islands with carefully pruned pine trees. The highlight here is a visit to the delightful *Kikugetsu-tei* (or "Scooping the Moon") teahouse overlooking the South Lake; the experience is all the better if you stop in for a cup of *sencha* or *matcha*. Dating from around 1640 and named after a Tang-dynasty Chinese poem, the teahouse exudes tranquility, with its screens pulled back to reveal perfect garden vistas. Viewed from across the lake it's just as impressive, swaddled in trees that cast a shimmering reflection over the water. The Nantei also has the less elaborate but more secluded *Higurashi-tei* teahouse, set in a shady grove, where you can also enjoy a cup of *matcha*.

Hokutei

北庭

Hokutei has a more natural appearance than the South Garden and is based around two ponds – Fuyosho-ike, dotted with lotus flowers, and Gunochi-ike, where feudal lords once hunted ducks and which now blooms with irises in June. Keep an eye out for the Tsuru Kame no Matsu, just to the left of the main park building, a black pine tree shaped like a crane spreading its wings and considered to be the most beautiful of the 29,190 trees in the gardens. Behind this is a line of pines called the "Byōbu-matsu", after the folding-screen painting (*byōbu*) they are supposed to resemble.

Sanuki Folkcraft Museum

讃岐民芸館 • Sanuki Mingeikan • Daily 8.45am–4.30pm • Free

After you've viewed the gardens, head towards the East Gate, where you'll find the **Sanuki Folkcraft Museum**, displaying beautiful examples of local basketwork, ceramics, furniture and huge, brightly painted banners and kites. Though some of the pieces are over 100 years old, the designs are surprisingly modern. Also of interest are some pieces by twentieth-century Japanese-American architect and furniture designer George Nakashima.

9

Takamatsu-jō

高松城 • Ferry-dōri • Daily, opening hours vary but usually 5.30am–7pm in summer and 7am–5pm in winter • ¥200 • ☎ 087 851 1521,
ⓦ www.tamamokoen.com • Restoration work on the castle ruins is scheduled for completion in 2015

A couple of minutes' walk east of the JR station is **Tamamo-kōen** (玉藻公園), a small
but pleasant park which contains the ruins of the city's castle, **Takamatsu-jō**. Four
hundred years ago, the stronghold was one of the three major Japanese fortresses
protected by sea, with three rings of moats surrounding the central keep. Like many of
Japan's castles, Takamatsu-jō was decommissioned in 1869 following the Meiji
Restoration (see p.799); all that remains today are a couple of turrets, parts of the
moat, and grounds that are only a ninth of their original size. Unfortunately, you can't
currently enter the main keep due to restoration works. Still, the castle grounds host a
fantastic display of blossom on the cherry trees in spring, and there are great views out
across the Inland Sea. At the park's east end, you can also look around the very
traditional **Hiunkaku**, a sprawling wooden mansion surrounded by stunted pines.
Rebuilt in 1917, it's now used as a public event space.

The Kagawa Museum

香川県立ミュージアム, Kagawa Kenritsu Myújimu • Ferry-dōri • Tues–Sun 9am–4.30pm • ¥400 • ☎ 087 822 0002, ⓦ www.pref
.kagawa.lg.jp/USERS/s12730/kmuseum/

Immediately east of Tamamo-kōen is **The Kagawa Museum**, built on part of the old
castle grounds. This museum is housed in a modern building and combines displays
of historical information and fine art. Head to the third floor to see the main
exhibition, which has lots of hi-tech displays as well as some impressive relics and
life-size replicas of local landmarks, such as the 7m-tall copper lantern from
Marogame. There is also a special section relating to Kōbō Daishi (see box, p.510),
with some amazing giant mandala paintings and ancient statues. On the ground
floor, you can try on a multilayered kimono or a samurai warrior's armour and have
your photo taken.

Takamatsu City Museum of Art

高松市美術館, Takamatsu-shi Bijutsukan • Chūō-dōri • Tues–Sun 9.30am–5pm • ¥200 • ☎ 087 823 1711 • ⓦ www.city.takamatsu
.kagawa.jp/12754.html

Just off Chūō-dōri on Bijutsukan-dōri is the modern **Takamatsu City Museum of Art**.
The small but impressive permanent collection includes a large variety of Sanuki
lacquerware, as well as a superb display of Western and Japanese contemporary art. The
Western art collection is almost entirely made up of works by major artists such as
Pablo Picasso, Jasper Johns, Andy Warhol, David Hockney and Henri Matisse, making
the entrance ticket a real bargain. There's also a library where you are free to browse art
books and videos – some in English – and the spacious entrance hall is used for dance
and music performances.

Shōtengai (shopping arcades)

East of Chūō-dōri are Takamatsu's main commercial and entertainment districts, which
are connected by covered **shōtengai (shopping arcades)**. This is a lively area to wander
around, both day and night, with a seemingly endless array of shops and restaurants.
The longest *shōtengai* – comprised of the **Marugame-machi**, **Minami Shin-machi** and
Tamachi arcades – stretches for 2.7km and is said to be the longest in Japan. Running
parallel is **Lion-dōri**, which leads from Katahara-machi arcade into the Tokiwa
Shin-machi and then Tokiwa-gai arcades. The southern end of the Marugame-machi
arcade has recently been updated and boasts one of Yayoi Kusama's pumpkin
sculptures, the *Black Pumpkin*.

ARRIVAL AND DEPARTURE

TAKAMATSU

By plane Takamatsu Airport (@C87 335 8110, @takamatsu-airport.com) lies 16km south of the city, 45min away by bus (¥740) or taxi (¥4700).

Destinations Naha (daily; 1hr 55min); Seoul (3 weekly; 1hr 50min); Shanghai (3 weekly; 55min); Taipei (2 weekly; 1hr); Tokyo Haneda (12 daily; 1hr 15min).

By train The JR train station is at the northern, seaside end of the central thoroughfare, Chūō-dōri, and a 10min walk from the heart of the city.

Destinations Kōchi (16 daily; 2hr 5min); Kotohira (24 daily; 55min); Matsuyama (hourly; 2hr 30min); Okayama (every 30min; 1hr); Tokushima (17 daily; 1hr 5min); Uwajima (15 daily; 4hr).

By bus Long-distance and most local buses pull in nearby to the JR train station, at the north end of Chūō-dōri.

Destinations Kōbe (17 daily; 2hr 35min); Kōchi (13 daily; 2hr 10min); Matsuyama (15 daily; 2hr 40min); Osaka (32 daily; 3hr 25min); Tokyo (daily; 11hr); Yokohama (daily; 10hr 30min).

By ferry Ferries from Kōbe (¥1800 one-way, ¥3300 return; @ferry.co.jp) dock a 10min bus ride from the city centre at Takamatsu-East; a free shuttle bus transports passengers to JR Takamatsu Station. Ferry connections with Shōdoshima and Naoshima are at the Sunport ferry terminal, a 5min walk east of the train station.

Destinations Kōbe (4 daily; 3hr 40min); Naoshima (8 daily; 1hr); Shōdoshima (hydrofoil: 21 daily; 35min; ferry: 28 daily; 1hr); Uno (22 daily; 1hr).

GETTING AROUND

Laid out on a grid plan, Takamatsu is an easy city to walk or cycle around. Otherwise, you'll find trains and buses perfectly user-friendly, and good for getting to sights outside the city.

By train As well as JR, Takamatsu has the Kotoden network whose trains run to Yashima or Kotohira. Kawaramachi Station (瓦町), where the Kotoden's three main lines intersect, is beside the Tenmaya department store at the end of the Tokiwa arcade, while Kotoden Takamatsu Chikkō Station (高松築港) is next to Tamamo-kōen, a few minutes' walk from JR Takamatsu Station. If you're heading from Takamatsu Chikkō Station to Yashima, you'll need to change at Kawaramachi.

By bus Buses for Ritsurin-kōen and Yashima run from the stops outside Chikkō Station at the top of Chūō-dōri.

By bike You can rent bikes from the cavernous rent-a-cycle offices and parking lot beneath JR Takamatsu Station. At ¥100 for 24 hours this is an absolute steal and the best way to see the city. You need to register first, but it's a very quick and simple process; the paperwork can be done in English. Make sure to park your bicycle in designated areas otherwise it could be impounded and incur a ¥1500 retrieval fee.

Car rental Eki Rent-a-Car (@087 821 1341) and Toyota Rent-a-Car (@087/851-0100) both have offices at Takamatsu JR Station.

INFORMATION

Tourist information office There's a helpful tourist office (daily 9am–6pm; @087 851 2009) with friendly English-speaking staff on the east side of the plaza outside the train station.

I-PAL The Kagawa International Exchange Centre, better known as I-PAL (Tues–Sun 9am–6pm; @087 837 5908, @i-pal.or.jp), is a convenient facility with a library of foreign-language books, magazines and newspapers and free internet access (30min). Here you can pick up the free information sheet *Takamatsu Information Board* (*TiA*), which carries details of what's on in town. I-PAL is at the northwest corner of Chūō-kōen, 750m south of Takamatsu Station.

ACCOMMODATION

Takamatsu has many business hotels, with plenty near the station – the better ones are listed below and have single rooms from around ¥6000. More upmarket options can be found around Chūō-dōri.

★JR Hotel Clement Takamatsu JRホテルクレメント 高松 1-1 Hamanchō @087 811 1111, @www.jrhotelgroup.com. With great Inland Sea views, stylish, spacious rooms and plenty of top-notch facilities including six bars and restaurants, this remains the city's swankiest hotel, right next to JR Takamatsu Station. From May to Aug it also has a beer garden on the fifth floor. **¥20,790**

Guesthouse Chottoco-Ma ちょっとこま 3-7-5 Ogimachi; @090 6548 8735, @chottoco-ma.com. Small recently opened guesthouse with friendly and helpful owners, this is one of the very few budget options in Takamatsu. It's just one stop from JR Takamatsu Station. All facilities are shared and there's free internet access. Dorm **¥2500**; double **¥46,000**

Hotel Kawaroku ホテル川六エルステージ 1-2 Hyakken-machi @087 821 5666, @kawaroku.co.jp/english. Centrally located business hotel that has been designed to appeal to female visitors with on-site spa facilities and a women-only floor. The excellent tatami rooms are the same price as the standard Western-style

9

ones, and are clean and functional. Breakfast and internet access are available for an additional charge, and there's also a large public bath. **¥11,750**

Takamatsu Terminal Hotel 高松ターミナルホテル 10-17 Nishinomaru-chō ☎087 822 3731, ⓦwww .webterminal.co.jp. There are both Western- and Japanese-style rooms at this welcoming business hotel, just a short walk from the JR station. The rooms are clean, though rather pokey, and some double rooms have a sofa that can be turned into a bed if you want to

share a room between three and bring the cost down There's free internet access in the lobby and a coi laundry. **¥11,550**

Takamatsu Tōkyū Inn 高松東急イン 9-9 Hyogo-mach ☎087 821 0109, ⓦtokyuhotelsjapan.com. Nothin fancy, but the rooms at this well-placed chain hotel are modern, very reasonably priced and have a good range o facilities. There are non-smoking floors and internet access is free. **¥10,000**

EATING

Takamatsu has a wide range of **restaurants** and **cafés**, many conveniently concentrated around the central arcade district, jus off Chūō-dōri. Like Shikoku's other seaside cities, this is a great place to sample fresh and delicious **fish** and **seafood**. The othe local speciality is **sanuki udon**, thick white noodles usually served with a separate flask of stock and a variety of condiments.

Gowariyasu 吾割安 6-3 Fukudamachi ☎087 851 5030. This atmospheric *izakaya*, decorated with old film posters, record covers and other memorabilia, offers a wide range of tasty inexpensive dishes such as *yakitori* (from ¥120), ramen noodle soup (¥400) and gyōza dumplings (¥380). Daily 6pm–3am (Sun till midnight).

Kanaizumi かな泉 9-3 Konyamachi ☎087 822 0123. This busy branch of a noted *sanuki udon* chain is a great place to fill up if you're on a budget – just ¥500 for a generous medium-sized bowl of udon with a topping. It's self-service, but the chefs are happy to help you choose from the wide choice of noodle toppings such as prawn tempura, deep-fried sardines or freshly grated mountain yam. Daily 9.30am–5pm.

Merikenya めりけんや 6-20 Nishinomaru-chō ☎087 811 6358, ⓦmerikenya.com. Located just opposite the plaza in front of the JR station, this branch of the Merikenya chain has high-quality udon noodles, hence the long queues at lunchtime. Meat-topped *niku-bukkake* noodles and mountain vegetable *yama-bukkake* noodles start at ¥380 for the smallest size. Daily 7am–8pm.

★**Okageya** おかげや Tamura Building, 1-12-1 Kawara-chō ☎087 862 6004. This place, specializing in fish and country-style cuisine, serves gourmet standard dishes at very reasonable prices. A beautifully presented sashimi platter for two is ¥2400, and there are many tasty side dishes to choose from such as mountain potato tempura (¥430), grilled ika (¥570) and tofu salad (¥520). You can opt for counter or private tatami room seating. Mon–Sat 5–11.30pm, Tues–Thurs also 11.30am–1pm.

Ramjham ラムジャム Minami Building, 2-3 Tamachi ☎087 834 8505. Friendly, Indian-run place serving thirty different kinds of Indian and Nepali curries, tandoori-cooked meats (from ¥650) and six types of naan (from ¥300). Dinner shouldn't cost more than ¥2000, and if you really want to indulge there's an all-you-can-eat-and-drink

deal for ¥4000. Lunch sets are available from ¥600. Daily 11am–3pm & 5–10pm.

★**Shigi China Kitchen** シギチャイナキチン Kitajima Building, 1-11 Furubaba-chō ☎087 823 7377. It's easy to spot this dining bar with its distinctive orange sign. Shigi, the friendly chef, cooks a wide variety of Chinese-style dishes using local seasonal ingredients. The *mabo-dōfu* (tofu in spicy sauce; ¥700), and fish and vegetable *itame* stir-fries (from ¥600) are highly recommended. Counter seating only. Daily 6pm–1am.

Szechwan Restaurant Chin スーツアンレストラン陳 29th floor Maritime Plaza, 2-1 Sunport ☎087 811 0477, ⓦbit.ly/1aJJQnh. The most appealing and certainly the most welcoming of Sunport's top-of-the-tower trio of upmarket restaurants. The Chinese cuisine is authentically spicy, the decor chic and the views spectacular. The menu is mostly seasonal courses, but you can order à la carte dishes such as swallow nest soup (¥3000) and sauteed lobster with chilli sauce (¥ 3500). Expect to pay around ¥5000 for dinner and from ¥1500 for lunch. Daily 11am–2pm & 5–9pm.

Tenkatsu 天勝 7-8 Hyogo-machi ☎087 821 5380. The interior of this reputable fish restaurant is dominated by a central sunken tank around which you can sit either at the jet-black counter bar or in tatami booths. Kimono-clad waitresses will bring you your pick of the fish served raw, as part of a sus hi platter (from ¥3800 per person), or cooked in a *nabe* stew (¥3465 per person). Set lunches start from as little as ¥1575. Mon–Fri 11am–2pm & 5–9.40pm, Sat & Sun 11am–9pm.

Tokiwa Saryō ときわ茶寮 1-8-2 Tokiwa-chō ☎087 861 5577, ⓦtrs1515.com/~saryou/top.html. Much of the lovely interior decoration of this old ryokan has remained intact in its transformation into a restaurant. Set courses of local delicacies (mainly fish, seafood and vegetables) start at as little as ¥1800 for lunch and ¥5250 for dinner. It can be difficult to find, so look out for the giant white lantern hanging outside. Daily 11am–2pm & 6–9pm.

★**Umie** ウミエ Kitahama Alley, 3-2 Kitahama-chō ⊕087 811 7455, ⓦumie.info. Relax over great coffee (¥600) or tasty meals such as hearty beef stew (¥1200), bagels (¥600) and pizza (¥1000) at this cool joint decorated with retro furniture and stacks of art books, magazines and LP records. Sometimes there are live music events here, and within the same complex are a gift and stationery shop, gallery and secondhand furniture store. Mon–Fri 11am–11.30pm, Sat 10am–11.30pm, Sun 10am–9pm; closed Wed.

BARS

Takamatsu has a large nightlife scene for a provincial city. There is a surprisingly good range of bars to explore in the lanes off the central shōtengai (shopping arcades).

Amazon アマゾン 3F One Foot Building, 4-21 Kajiyamachi ⊕087 851 4360. Lively international bar playing 80s and 90s pop and rock, with dancing and retro video games. Shin-san, the owner, speaks fluent English and will mix any cocktail you desire from ¥500–¥700. Shots are ¥300 each and there's a variety of bar snacks such as pizza (¥700) and hot dogs (¥600) to nibble on. Daily 8pm–5am; closed first Mon of the month.

★**Bar & Flair Recommend** レコメンド 2F Shincho Building, 8-52 Furubaba-chō ⊕087 823 3757.Takamatsu seems an unlikely place to find an Asia-Pacific Flair champion bartender, but Komoda-san's nightly performances are not to be missed. This bar has low lighting, plush sofas and smart counter seating, attracting a smartly dressed local crowd. Prices range from ¥800 for a standard mix and from ¥1000 for a tropical cocktail. Mon–Sat 8pm–5am.

King's Yawd キングスヤード 1-2-2 Tokiwa-chō, ⊕087 837 2660, ⓦblog.livedoor.jp/kingsyawd. This laid-back Jamaican bar has a friendly atmosphere and is presided over by the dreadlocked Satoko-san, who knows how to whip up a tasty plate of Ackee and Saltfish (¥1200) or a rum dessert (¥400). Drinks are reasonably priced (beer ¥500) and cocktails (¥600) are poured generously. There are regular DJ, hip-hop and reggae events. Mon–Sat 5pm–2am.

Ruff House ラッフハウス B1F Minami Building, 2-3 Tamachi ⊕087 835 9550, ⓦbarruffhouse.com. A relaxed basement bar with nightly musical performances by young and upcoming local musicians. The schedule is eclectic – anything from Okinawan *shamisen* banjo to punk acoustic guitar – and the audience is enthusiastic. Beer from ¥600 and cocktails from ¥700. Arrive early to get a seat. Daily 7pm–midnight.

SHOPPING

Sanuki lacquerware and papier-mâché dolls are the main local crafts in Takamatsu. The **gift shops** in Ritsurin-kōen (see p.615) and The Kagawa Museum (see p.616), as well as **shops** in the shōtengai (arcades) are good places to hunt for souvenirs.

Mingei Fukuda 民芸福田 9-7 Hyakken-machi; ⊕087 821 3237 ⓦmingei-fukuda.com. A fine emporium of locally produced folk crafts, pottery, glassware and paper goods. Look out for their beautiful hand-painted traditional paper kites (¥8000). Tues–Sun 10am–6pm.

Miyawaki 宮脇書店 4-8 Marugame-chō ⓦmiyawakishoten.com. Has a small selection of English-language mass-market paperbacks and books about Japan on the sixth floor. Daily 9am–10pm.

Shikoku Shop 88 四国ショップ88 Maritime Plaza ⊕087 822 0459, ⓦshikokushop88.com. This shop sells different types of well-known food and crafts produced in all of Shikoku's prefectures. It's a great place to pick up packaged *sanuki udon* noodles (from ¥300) or senbei rice crackers (¥580). Daily 10am–9pm.

ISAMU NOGUCHI

Born in Los Angeles in 1904 to an Irish-American mother and a Japanese father, **Isamu Noguchi** spent part of his childhood in Japan before returning to the States, aged 13. In his late 20s he settled in New York, where his main studio (also a museum) can be found. It was here that he began to establish his reputation through his **iconic designs** for paper lanterns and furniture, as well as high-profile commissions for sculptures and landscape works around the world. Noguchi travelled widely prior to World War II, studying art in Paris, Kyoto and Beijing. He returned to Japan after the war, creating numerous site-specific pieces such as the two bridges in the Hiroshima Peace Park (1952) and the lobby of the Sōgetsu Kaikan in Tokyo (1977). Noguchi had many love affairs with famous twentieth-century women such as French writer Anaïs Nin and Mexican artist Frida Kahlo, and he was married to Chinese-born Japanese actress Ōtaka Yoshiko for five years. In 1988, the year of his death, he completed his design for Moerenuma Park in Sapporo (see p.294). Apart from the work at his studio in Mure, another of Noguchi's sculptures, *Time and Space*, stands at Takamatsu Airport.

9

DIRECTORY

Banks and exchange The main branch of Hyakujūshi Bank is at 5-1 Kameichō; Kagawa Bank is at 6-1 Kameichō; and Sumitomo Mitsui Bank is at 10 Hyōgo-machi. The main post office (see below) and most smaller branches have ATMs that accept foreign cards; the ATM at the main branch of the post office is accessible Mon–Fri 7am–11pm, Sat 9am–9pm, Sun & public hols 9am–7pm.

Hospital Kagawa Kenritsu Chūō Byōin (Prefectural Central Hospital) is at 5-4-16 Banchō (☎087 835 2222).

Internet There are free terminals at I-PAL (see p.617) and free wi-fi spots at Kagawa Plaza (3F Symbol Tower, daily 10am–6pm), Ritsurin-kōen and The Kagawa Museum. Right next door to the *Tokyū Inn* (see p.618) there is also Planet Media Café (24hr), where access starts at ¥250/30min.

Police The main police station is at 4-1-10 Banchō (☎087 833 0110). Emergency numbers are listed on p.66.

Post office The main post office (Mon–Fri 9am–7pm, Sat 9am–5pm, Sun 9am–12.30pm) is at the north end of the Marugame arcade, opposite the Mitsukoshi department store.

Yashima
屋島

Literally meaning "rooftop island" (which thousands of years ago it was), the plateau **YASHIMA** lies 6km east of Takamatsu's city centre. It was at Yashima that, in 1185, the Taira and Minamoto clans famously battled to determine who ruled Japan (see p.794). A small detachment of Minamoto forces surprised the Taira by attacking from the land side of the peninsula – the Taira had expected the attack to come from the sea. Within a month the Taira were defeated at the Battle of Dannoura and forced to flee to the mountainous hinterland of Shikoku.

Buses run to the top of the 293m-high volcanic lava plateau (see opposite), or you can spend an hour hiking up a steep, winding path starting to the west of the decommissioned cable car. Once at the top, you might be a little disappointed, as on the southern ridge of the plateau is a massive car park, some rather dingy tourist hotels, souvenir shops and an aquarium. However, the expansive views out over the Inland Sea and the stone workshops of Mure make the trek worthwhile.

Yashima-ji
屋島寺 • **Temple** Daily, dawn till dusk • Free • **Treasure House** Daily 9am–5pm • ¥500 • ☎087 841 9418

Supposedly founded in 754 by the Chinese monk Ganjin (see p.474), **Yashima-ji** temple is number 84 on the Shikoku pilgrimage. Look out for the saucy granite carvings of raccoons next to the temple's main hall, and elephants carved into the eaves of the smaller halls near the front gate. Yashima-ji's **Treasure House** is worth popping into for its collection of screens, pottery and a mixed bag of relics from the battle between the Taira and Minamoto. There's also a traditional garden near the front gate, with the distinctly unbloody "Pond of Blood", believed to be the spot where the Minamoto soldiers cleansed their swords after the Battle of Yashima.

Shikoku Mura
四国村 • 91 Yashima Nakamachi • Daily 8.30am–5pm (Nov–March till 4.30pm) • ¥800, or ¥1000 including Shikoku Mura Gallery • ☎087 843 3111 • ⊕ www.shikokumura.or.jp • A 5min walk north of Kotoden Yashima station

At the base of the Yashima plateau is the outdoor architectural museum of **Shikoku Mura**. More than thirty traditional houses and buildings from across the island and Inland Sea were relocated here in an imaginatively landscaped park rising up the hill. The route around the park, which takes about an hour, starts with a small and slightly dilapidated replica of the Iya Valley's Kazura-bashi (see p.644), a bridge made of vines and bamboo which crosses a pond to an impressive thatched-roof kabuki theatre from Shōdoshima. Plays are occasionally performed here – check with the tourist information office in Takamatsu (see p.617). Look out also for the circular Sato Shime Goya (Sugarcane Press Hut) with a conical roof – a unique feature in Japanese architecture. Each of the houses has an excellent English explanation of its history.

Shikoku Mura Gallery

四国村ギャラリー • 91 Yashima Nakamachi • Daily 8.30am–5pm (Nov–March till 4.30pm) • ¥500, or ¥1000 including Shikoku Mura • ☎ 087 843 311 • ⓦ www.shikokumura.or.jp

Near the top of the Shikoku Mura park is the Andō Tadao-designed **Shikoku Mura Gallery**. Inside the polished concrete building is a single long gallery featuring original paintings by the likes of Marc Chagall and Pablo Picasso, and sculpture by Auguste Rodin, as well as regularly changing themed exhibitions of contemporary art.

ARRIVAL AND DEPARTURE   YASHIMA

By train From Takamatsu JR, trains run at least every hour to Yashima Station (15min; ¥210), from where it's a 15min walk north to the base of the plateau. More convenient is the Kotoden line (every 20min; 20min; ¥310 from Kotoden Takamatsu Chikkō Station), as

Kotoden Yashima Station is only a 5min walk from Shikoku Mura.
By bus Between 9am and 5pm there's a shuttle bus every hour from outside both the JR and Kotoden stations running to the top of the plateau (10min; ¥100).

EATING

Ikkaku 一鶴 220-1 Yashima Nakamachi ☎ 087 844 3711. A short walk east of Kotoden Station, this cavernous beer hall-style restaurant specializes in *honetsukidori*, local chicken cuisine. Dishes start at ¥980. Mon–Fri 11am–2pm & 4–10pm, Sat & Sun 11am–10pm.

Waraya わら家 Shikoku Mura 91 Yashima Nakamachi

☎ 087 843 3115. This branch of a famous udon chain is beside the entrance to Shikoku Mura, in a building with a thatched roof and water wheel. You can sit and slurp a variety of delicious udon dishes (from ¥410); they also serve tempura (¥210). Admission to Shikoku Mura gives you a ¥100 discount coupon here. Daily 10am–6.30pm.

Mure

A few kilometres east of Yashima in **Mure**, the streets resound to the clack of hammer on granite and are lined with fantastic stone sculptures and designs – everything from traditional lanterns to pot-bellied Buddhas and long-necked giraffes. It was in this long-established stonemasons' town that the celebrated American-Japanese sculptor **Isamu Noguchi** (see box, p.619) created a traditional-style home and sculpture studio during the latter part of his life.

Isamu Noguchi Garden Museum Japan

イサムノグチ庭園美術館 Isamu Noguchi Teien Bijatsukan • 3519 Mure-chō • Tues, Thurs & Sat 10am, 1pm & 3pm • ¥2100; preferably book two weeks in advance by email • ☎ 087 870 1500, ⓔ museum@isamunoguchi.or.jp • Take the Kotoden train either in Takamatsu or at Kotoden Yashima Station, alighting at Yakuri Station (八栗駅) from where the museum is a 20min walk northeast

Although you must make an appointment and the entrance fee is more expensive than most museums, a visit to the **Isamu Noguchi Garden Museum Japan** is highly recommended. The lovely traditional house Noguchi lived in, filled with his signature paper lanterns, the inspiring stone sculpture gardens and his large studio (where you can still see all his tools) have been left exactly as they were when he died. You can see more than 150 of Noguchi's sculptures, some only partly finished, including the signature pieces *Energy Void*, a 3.6m-tall work that looks more like a giant rubber tube than solid black granite, and the two-coloured stone ring *Sun at Midnight*. Exactly an hour is granted to wander the studio and grounds soaking up the singular atmosphere. No photography is allowed but there are some excellent books in English for sale at the reception area.

Kotohira

琴平

Approximately 30km southwest of Takamatsu, **KOTOHIRA** is home to the ancient shrine Kotohira-gū, popularly called **Kompira-san**. Along with the Grand Shrines of Ise and Izumo Taisha, Kotohira is one of the major Shintō pilgrimage sites, attracting

9

some four million visitors a year. Despite the crowds, it is still one of Shikoku's highlights. The town itself is pleasantly located, straddling the Kanakura-gawa at the foot of the mountain Zozu-san, so called because it is said to resemble an elephant's head (*zozu*). Kotohira can easily be visited on a day-trip from Takamatsu, one hour away by train, or en route to Kōchi or the mountainous interior. However, it has a number of enjoyable attractions as well as traditional atmosphere, making it a worthwhile overnight stay.

Kotohira-gū

琴平宮 • 892-1 Kotohira-chō • Daily 8.30am–5pm • Free • ⓣ 087 775 2121, ⓦ konpira.or.jp

Kotohira-gū, Kotohira's star attraction, is usually known as **Kompira-san** (see box opposite). It's a venerable shrine, dating back to at least the tenth century, and the mainly wooden hillside complex can only be accessed via a long staircase ascent. It's a total of 1368 steps to reach the Oku-sha inner shrine at the top. You'll see many people huffing and puffing on the slopes, and some even hire traditional *kago* (palanquins) to carry them to the top. Depending on weather and crowd conditions, it will take about an hour to make your climb at a leisurely pace.

Kompira-san is one of the only two places in Japan where you can see the ancient sport of *kemari* performed. Deemed an Intangible Cultural Property, this ninth-century forerunner of soccer is played by the shrine's monks on May 5, July 7 and in late December.

The museums

All daily 8.30am–4.30pm • ¥800 each

The Kompira-san shrine grounds begin at the Ō-mon (大門), a stone gateway just beyond which you'll pass the Gonin Byakushō (五人百姓) – five red-painted stalls shaded by large white umbrellas. The souvenir sellers here stand in for the five farmers who were once allowed to hawk their wares in the shrine precincts. Further along to the right of the main walkway, lined with stone lanterns, are three small museums housing different collections of the shrine's artistic treasures: the **Hōmotsukan** (宝物館), the **Gakugei Sankō-kan** (学芸参考館) and the **Takahashi Yuichi-kan** 高橋由一館). Only the latter, displaying the striking paintings of the nineteenth-century artist Takahashi Yuichi, is really worth the entrance fee.

KOMPIRA'S BUDDHIST CONNECTION

Kompira-san, the unofficial but more commonly used name for Kotohira-gū, comes from the nickname for Omono-nushi-no-Mikoto, the spiritual **guardian of seafarers**. Kompira was originally Kumbhira, the Hindu crocodile god of the River Ganges, and was imported as a deity from India well before the ninth century, when Kōbō Daishi chose the shrine as the spot for one of his Buddhist temples. For a thousand years Kompira-san served as both a **Buddhist** and **Shinto** holy place and was so popular that those who could not afford to make the pilgrimage themselves either dispatched their pet dogs, with pouches of coins as a gift to the gods, or tossed barrels of rice and money into the sea, in the hope that they would be picked up by sailors who would take the offering to Kompira-san on their behalf.

When the **Meiji Restoration** began, Shinto took precedence, and the Buddhas were removed from the shrine, along with Kompira, who was seen as too closely associated with the rival religion. While there are no representations of Kompira at the shrine today, an open-air gallery decorated with pictures and models of ships (see below) serves as a reminder of the shrine's original purpose, and the Chinese architectural style of some of the buildings hints at the former Buddhist connection.

Omote Shoin

表書院 • Daily 8.30am–4.30pm • ¥800

Before climbing to the shrine's next stage, look left of the steps to see a giant gold ship's propeller, a gift from a local shipbuilder. To the right is the entrance to the serene reception hall **Omote Shoin**, built in 1659. Delicate screen paintings and decorated door panels by the celebrated artist Maruyama Okyo (1733–95) are classified as Important Cultural Assets; they're so precious you have to peer through glass into the dim interiors to see them.

Asahi-no-Yashiro and the Hon-gū

朝日の社 • 本宮

Return and to the main ascent, the next major building reach you after the Omote Shoin is the grand **Asahi-no-Yashiro**, the Rising Sun Shrine. Dedicated to the sun goddess Amaterasu, the shrine is decorated with intricate woodcarvings of flora and fauna, and topped with a green copper roof. Two flights of steep steps lead from here to the thatched-roof **Hon-gū**, the main shrine, built in 1879 and the centre of Kompira-san's daily activities. Priests and their acolytes in traditional robes rustle by along a raised wooden corridor linking the shrine buildings.

Oku-sha

奥社

Many visitors stop at **Hon-gū**, but the hardy, and truly faithful, trudge on up the last 583 steps to the **Oku-sha** following a path to the left of the main shrine. When you reach this inner shrine, located almost at the top of Zozu-san, look up at the rocks on the left to see two rather cartoonish stone carvings of the demon Tengu.

Ema-dō gallery

絵馬堂

From the main shrine area, head to the wooden platforms for magnificent views of the surrounding countryside – on a clear day you can see as far as the Inland Sea. To the left of the main shrine is the open-air **Ema-dō gallery**, which displays votive plaques, paintings and models of ships. These are from sailors who hope to be granted good favour on the seas. The offerings extend to one from Japan's first cosmonaut, a TV journalist who was a paying passenger on a Russian Soyuz launch in 1990.

9

Kinryō Sake Museum

金陵の郷, Kinryō noSato • 623 Kotohira-chō • Mon, Tues, Thurs & Fri 9am–4pm, Sat & Sun 9am–6pm • ¥310 • ☎ 087 773 4133, ⓦ nishino-kinryo.co.jp

The **Kinryō Sake Museum**, at the start of the main approach to Kompira-san, is also well worth a visit. There has been a sake brewery on this spot since 1616, and the buildings arranged around a large courtyard have changed little over the centuries. Inside, the well-presented exhibition runs step by step through the sake-making process, using life-size displays and recordings of traditional brewers' songs. At the end of the displays there is an informative video in English that you can enjoy while sampling Kinryō's high-quality sake.

Kanamaru-za

金丸座 • 817-10 Enoi Kotohira-chō • Daily 9am–5pm; plays April only • ¥500 • ☎ 087 773 3846, ⓦ konpirakabuki.jp

On the hill to the left of the lower shrine steps of Kompira-san is **Kanamaru-za**. This performance hall, built in 1835, is said to be the oldest-surviving kabuki theatre in Japan and was fully restored when it was moved to this location from the centre of Kotohira in 1975. Plays are only performed here one month of the year, but the theatre itself merits a visit, especially for its impressive wooden-beamed and lantern-lit auditorium, and intriguing trapdoors and tunnels.

Nakano Udon School

中野うどん学校, Nakano Udon Gakkō • 720 Kotohira-chō • Daily 9am–3pm; classes 40min–1hr • ¥1575; reservations are required in advance • ☎ 087 775 0001, ⓦ nakanoya.net

Kagawa Prefecture is full of udon noodle restaurants, but there aren't so many places where you can actually learn how to make them. On the second floor of a hundred-year old udon noodle shop, on the left side of the shrine approach, is the **Nakano Udon School** that will teach you these special skills. The class is a fun experience, and though the teachers don't speak much English, they are welcoming and the demonstrations are easy to follow. You can eat your noodles on site, or take them home.

ARRIVAL AND INFORMATION

By train JR Kotohira Station is a 10min walk northeast of the town centre. Left of the exit are coin lockers (24hr; ¥400/bag). If you've travelled by Kotoden train from Takamatsu, you'll arrive at the smaller station closer to the town centre on the banks of the Kanekura-gawa.

Tourist information The tourist information office (☎ 087 775 6710; daily 10am–7pm) is next to the JR station. No English is spoken here, and there's only one English-language pamphlet about the town. If possible, it's better to get the latest information from the Takamatsu tourist information centre (see p.617).

ACCOMMODATION

Accommodation in Kotohira is always in high demand, and prices can rise substantially on weekends and public holidays. The town is famed for its top-notch **ryokan**; unless mentioned, rates include breakfast and dinner, usually of high quality.

Kōbaitei 紅梅亭 556-1 Kotohira-chō ☎ 087 775 1111, ⓦ koubaitei.jp. Charming ryokan with lovely public areas including a tea lounge, traditional garden, small swimming pool and public onsen bath. There's a choice of tatami and Western-style rooms. **¥54,600**

★**Kotobuki Ryokan** ことぶき旅館 Kotohira-chō ☎&ℱ 087 773 3872, ℯ kotobukiryokan@hotmail .co.jp. The best deal in Kotohira, this small and attractive ryokan is run by a friendly couple and has a quaint traditional interior. Rooms and bathing facilities are spotless, and it's conveniently located by the river and shopping arcade. The price includes dinner and breakfast, as well as wi-fi access. **¥12,600**

Kotohira Riverside Hotel 琴平リバーサイドホテル 246-1 Kotohira-chō ☎ 087 775 1880, ⓦ hananoyu .co.jp/river. This small Western-style hotel, shōdoshima located on the west bank of the Kanekura-gawa, is a good mid-range option, where the modern rooms are clean and fairly spacious. There's free wi-fi and PC use in the lobby. **¥14,900**

Mi Casa Su Casa Guesthouse ミカサスカサ・ゲストハウス 1230-1 Konzoji-chō ☎087 763 1353, ⊚micasasucasa.jp. This small budget guesthouse is two stops east on JR from Kotohira Station and right next to Konzoji Station. Rooms are simple but very clean, and there's also a shared kitchen area. The friendly English-speaking owner is on hand to give travel advice. Dorm **¥2500**, Single **¥3000**, Double **¥5000**

Sakura-no-Shō 桜の抄 977-1 Kotohira-chō ☎087 775 3218, ⊚sakuranosho.jp. At the foot of the steps leading up to Kompira-san, this large modern ryokan has comfortable Japanese and Western-style rooms and some nice public baths. If you fancy a splurge, it's also worth visiting for the beautifully presented mix of traditional and contemporary Japanese dishes at its main restaurant, *Ikiri* (いきり), a large, sleek affair with an open kitchen in its centre and romantic views out over the illuminated Ō-mon at night. **¥18,300**

EATING

Henkotsu-ya へんこつ屋 240 Shin-machi Kotohira-chō ☎0877 75 2343. This traditional *manju* (baked rice flour cakes with sweet bean filling) shop is worth stopping at for a refreshing cup of *matcha* and some *manju* (set ¥650) after climbing Kompira-san. The unusual tearoom, decorated with calligraphy, is at the end of a narrow hallway stacked with samurai armour and other antiques. You'll find it on the same street as the *Kotobuki Ryokan* (see opposite). Daily 8.30am–6.30pm.

Kamitsubaki 神椿 892-1 Kotohira-chō ☎087 773 0202 ⊚kamitsubaki.com. Located in the Kompira-san grounds, this elegant restaurant and café has a tranquil atmosphere and pleasant views. The restaurant serves pricey Western-style courses – expect to pay more than ¥2500 for lunch and from ¥5000 for dinner. The café, with a beautifully tiled feature wall, serves snacks such as sandwiches (¥600) and curry (¥900), as well as tea

(¥400) and coffee (¥450). Restaurant Tues–Sun 11.30am–2.30pm & 5pm–9pm; café daily 9am–5pm.

★**Kompira Udon** 金比羅うどん 810-3 Kotohira-chō ☎087 773 5785, ⊚konpira.co.jp. Large, bustling restaurant closest to the Kompira-san steps serving all types of delicious *sanuki udon*. A bowl topped with tempura is ¥650, while sets with noodles, tempura, rice and a tofu side dish are good value at ¥850. Daily 8am–5pm.

New Green ニューグリーン 722-1 Kotohira-chō ☎087 773 3451, ⊚new-green.sakura.ne.jp. If you're looking for somewhere to eat after 5pm, this friendly café at the shrine end of the shopping arcade is a cheap and cheerful choice. It serves Japanese and Western food including hearty set meals (from ¥900), pasta (¥750) and curry (¥630). English menu available. 8am–8.30pm; closed Thurs.

Naoshima and the Art Islands of the Inland Sea

The islands of the Seto Inland Sea, between Shikoku and the main island of Honshū, are some of the most scenic and friendly places in Japan. For centuries, they were at the crossroads of maritime transportation, including piracy, and developed their own unique culture and ecological lifestyle. In Japan's rapid economic growth period, despite the islands becoming Japan's first **national park**, natural resources were exploited and illegal industrial waste dumping was rampant, destroying forests and polluting the waters. After the collapse of the "bubble" economy in the late eighties, the islands suffered from depopulation and neglect. However, the cultural foundation of publishing company Benesse has been a major force for revitalizing these island communities through ambitious **art and architectural projects** and **sustainable tourism**. The main focus was originally **Naoshima**, but there are currently eleven other Inland Sea islands being developed as art sites and attracting thousands of visitors for the **Setouchi Triennale**, an international art festival featuring exciting contemporary artworks (see box, p.627).

The islands described below can be visited in a loop from either Naoshima or Shōdoshima on day-trips, both of which are easily accessed from Takamatsu or Okayama. Note that nearly all the museums and art sites on the islands are closed on Mondays, or Tuesdays if a public holiday falls on the Monday.

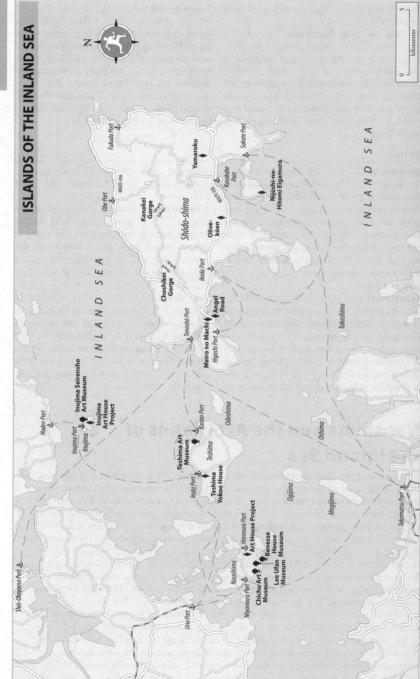

ISLANDS OF THE INLAND SEA

Naoshima

直島

The dynamic hub for Benesse's ongoing "community revitalization through art" project, idyllic **NAOSHIMA**, 13km north of Takamatsu, is now home to six stunning Andō Tadao-designed galleries as well as several large-scale installations and outdoor sculptures from major international and Japanese talent. In the island's main town and ferry port, **Miyanoura** (宮浦), is an amazing public bathhouse, while around the southern Gotanji area there are sheltered beaches with glorious Inland Sea views – all making Naoshima a blissful escape.

Benesse House Museum

ベネッセハウスミュジアム • Gotanji • Daily 8am–9pm, last entry 8pm • ¥1000 • ⓣ 087 892 3233, ⓦ benesse-artsite.jp/en

Overlooking the Inland Sea, the spacious contemporary art gallery and hotel **Benesse House Museum**, 2km southeast of Miyanoura, is home to some stunning art including works by Bruce Nauman, Jasper Johns, Andy Warhol, David Hockney and Frank Stella. Scattered around the museum are seventeen outdoor sculptural works ranging from Yayoi Kusama's *Pumpkin*, an icon for the island, to Cai Gui Quang's witty and practical *Cultural Melting Bath*, an open-air jacuzzi in a glade surrounded by 36 jagged limestone rocks imported from China. Guests of *Benesse House* (see p.629) can book to use the jacuzzi (Wed, Fri & Sun 4–5pm, closed Dec–Feb; ¥1000).

Chichū Art Museum

地中美術館, Chichū Bijutsukan • 3449-1 Naoshima • Tues–Sun 10am–5pm (Oct–Feb till 4pm) • Museum ¥2000; garden free • ⓣ 087 892 3755, ⓦ benesse-artsite.jp/en/chichu/ • A 20min walk northwest around the coast from Benesse House

The serene hill-top **Chichū Art Museum** is a naturally lit gallery housing five of Monet's *Water Lily* series paintings. The artworks are the climax of a wonderful winding tour through towering corridors of polished concrete connecting spaces dedicated to a dazzling installation by Walter De Maria and three signature "playing with light" pieces by James Turrell. The museum's lovely café offers a spectacular panorama of the Inland Sea. On the approach to the museum, the picturesque, and free, **Chichū Garden** has been planted with flowers and plants similar to those cultivated by Monet at his famous garden in Giverny.

Lee Ufan Museum

李禹煥美術館, Li Ūfan Bijutsukan • 1390 Azakuraura • Tues–Sun 10am–5.30pm (Oct–Feb till 4.30pm) • ¥1000 • ⓣ 087 892 3754, ⓦ benesse-artsite.jp/en/lee-ufan/

Situated between the Benesse House Museum and the Chichū Art Museum is the **Lee Ufan Museum.** This minimalist three-room gallery and courtyard garden, also designed by Andō Tadao, showcases the work of major Korean artist **Lee Ufan**, a major force in the contemporary Japanese art movement of the 1970s. At the entrance to the gallery is a pole sculpture by Lee, and as you go through the angular corridors of the museum you'll pass several of his sculpture works, culminating in the hushed atmosphere of the final gallery where you must take your shoes off before entering.

SETOUCHI TRIENNALE INTERNATIONAL ART FESTIVAL

The attractive islands of the Inland Sea are the exhibition spaces for the **Setouchi Triennale**, the Setouchi Triennale (瀬戸内国際芸術祭, Setouchi Kokusai Geijutsusai ⓦ setouchi-artfest.jp), a **contemporary art festival** held every three years. Japanese and international artists are invited to exhibit their works on the eleven participating islands, and many collabarote with the local community to produce fantastic sculptures, installations and audiovisual works. Local people are enthusiastic about the festival, and there are pop-up restaurants and cafés near the art sites. First held in 2010, the 2013 festival exhibited more than 150 pieces. Visiting the islands to see the festival sites is relatively easy thanks to well-organized ferry services and detailed information available in English. The next Triennale is expected to be held in 2016.

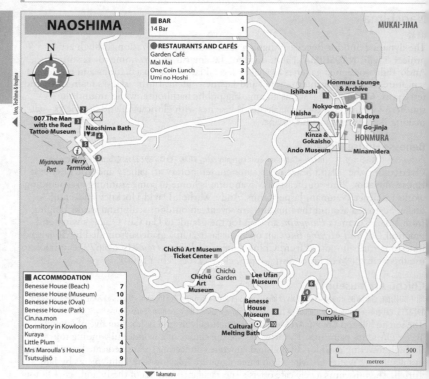

NAOSHIMA

MUKAI-JIMA

Uno, Teshima & Inujima

■ BAR	
14 Bar	1

● RESTAURANTS AND CAFÉS	
Garden Café	1
Mai Mai	2
One Coin Lunch	3
Umi no Hoshi	4

007 The Man with the Red Tattoo Museum
Naoshima Bath

Miyanoura Port
Ferry Terminal

Ishibashi
Haisha
Nokyo-mae
Kinza & Gokaisho
Ando Museum

Honmura Lounge & Archive
Kadoya
Go-jinja
HONMURA
Minamidera

Chichū Art Museum Ticket Center
Chichū Garden
Chichū Art Museum
Lee Ufan Museum
Benesse House Museum
Cultural Melting Bath
Pumpkin

■ ACCOMMODATION	
Benesse House (Beach)	7
Benesse House (Museum)	10
Benesse House (Oval)	8
Benesse House (Park)	6
Cin.na.mon	2
Dormitory in Kowloon	5
Kuraya	1
Little Plum	4
Mrs Maroulla's House	3
Tsutsujisō	9

0 — 500 metres

Takamatsu

Art House Project

家プロジェクト, Ie purojekuto • Honmura • Tues–Sun 10am–4.30pm • General admission ¥1000 (not including Kinza) or ¥400 per site (Kinza ¥500, prior booking essential); tickets and information are available from Honmura Lounge and Archive (same hours), around the corner from the Nokyo-mae bus stop • ☎ 087 892 3233, Ⓦ benesse-artsite.jp/en/arthouse/

The charming fishing village of **Honmura** (本村), located midway down Naoshima's east coast, is the base for the **Art House Project**, in which five old wooden houses, a temple and a shrine have been transformed into artworks.

Kadoya (角屋), an art house close to two hundred years old, is the forum for a trio of works by Miyajima Tatsuo, including the beguiling light-and-water installation *Sea of Time '98*. On the small hill to the east stands the Edo-era shrine **Go-ō-jinja** (護王神社), renovated to include a stone chamber and a glass staircase. **Minamidera** (南寺) is a collaboration between Andō Tadao and American artist James Turrell. Andō designed the stark building that stands on the site of a long-since-demolished temple and incorporates the charred wooden walls that are typical of the village. As you enter you'll be plunged into darkness (staff are on hand to assist) and Turrell's artwork will be revealed after some fumbling around. A former dental clinic now houses the scrapbook-style **Haisha** (はいしゃ) by Ōtake Shinrō, which includes a partial life-size copy of the Statue of Liberty; the **Ishibashi** (石橋) building is decorated with beautiful waterfall paintings by Senju Hiroshi; and **Gokaisho** (碁会所) displays amazingly realistic wooden sculptures of camellias by Suda Yoshihiro in tatami rooms. You must book in advance to visit **Kinza** (きんざ), where the collections of small wood, glass and stone objects slowly reveal themselves out of the darkness.

Andō Museum

安藤ミュージアム • 736-2 Naoshima • Tues–Sun 10am–4.30pm • ¥500 • ☎ 087 892 3754, ⓦ benesse-artsite.jp/en/ando-museum/

Opened in 2013 in Honmura, the latest addition to Naoshima's art sites is the **Andō Museum**, a tribute to renowned Japanese architect **Andō Tadao**, one of the key participants in revitalizing the island. The museum was designed by Andō himself and displays models of projects and other work that has connected the artist to the island. However, it is the construction and design of the building, using his signature materials of concrete, glass, steel and wood, which really showcase Andō's talent. From the outside, the museum looks deceptively like a typical Honmura house. The completely new concrete interior, including a basement, uses natural light and the hundred-year-old house's original wooden beams to great effect. It's a wonderful example of creating something modern in a traditional space.

Naoshima Bath "I♥湯"

直島銭湯 • 2252-2 Naoshima • Tues–Fri 2–9pm, Sat & Sun 10am–9pm • ¥500; ofuro sets ¥1000 • ☎ 087 892 2626, ⓦ benesse-artsite .jp/en/naoshimasento • A 1min walk from the ferry terminal

Ōtake Shinrō collaborated with design studio Graf on the incredible *sentō* **Naoshima Bath "I♥湯"**, 150m or so from Miyanoura's sleek SANAA-designed Naoshima ferry terminal. As with his Haisha (see opposite), there's a wealth of detail both inside and out this public bath ("I♥湯" is a pun on the Japanese word *yu*, meaning hot water), including recycled ceramic tile mosaics, pop art paintings and photo collages, video, erotica and a small elephant perched on the divide between the male and female baths. The reception area sells special "I♥湯" *ofuro* sets including towels, soap and shampoo.

007 The Man with the Red Tattoo Museum

007赤い刺青青の男記念館, 007 Akai Seisei no Otoko Kinenkam • Miyanoura • Daily 9am–5pm • Free • ☎ 087 892 2299

James Bond fans will want to drop by Miyanoura's tiny **007 The Man with the Red Tattoo Museum**. Plastered with posters, photos and other memorabilia, it feels like a shrine created by an obsessive teenage fan and is part of the island's campaign to feature as a location in a future Bond film – not too big a stretch, since Raymond Benson set his 007 novel *The Man With The Red Tattoo* on Naoshima. Don't miss watching the locally produced video that introduces the island – James Bond style.

ARRIVAL AND INFORMATION

NAOSHIMA

By ferry Regular ferries sail to Miyanoura from Takamatsu (1hr; ¥510) and from Uno on Honshū (20min; ¥280). 1hr by train from Okayama (see 543). Timetables are regularly updated on the Benesse website ⓦ benesse-artsite.jp/en/ access. There are irregular/summertime or Triennale-time only ferries from Honmura. However, it's much easier and more convenient to depart from Miyanoura.

Tourist information The information desk in the ferry terminal (daily 8.30am–6pm; ☎ 087 892 2299) has an excellent English map and guide to the island.

GETTING AROUND

By bus There's a regular minibus (¥100) that runs between Miyanoura and the Chichū Art Museum via Honmura and *Benesse House*. The bus timetable is available from the tourist information desk in the ferry terminal. Benesse also have their own shuttle service on the same route which is free for guests.

By bike Cycle rental is available from *Café Ogiya* in the ferry terminal and from the TVC bike shop opposite the terminal (both ¥500/day). TVC also have electric-powered cycles for ¥1500. Some of the guesthouses (see below) also rent out bicycles.

ACCOMMODATION

During Japanese holidays and the Setouchi Triennale, **accommodation** is almost impossible to find on Naoshima. Even outside these periods, the island is a very popular destination. Book well in advance, if you can; note that some places will charge higher rates on arrival if you don't.

★ **Benesse House** ベネッセハウス Gotanji ☎ 087 892 3223, ⓦ benesse-artsite.jp/en/benesse-house/. This is a fine hotel offering comfortable, spacious rooms in four separate blocks: one in the museum (see p.627), one in the adjoining Oval and two within the hotel's newer complex, *Benesse House Park and Beach*. These two are closer to the water and have a Scandinavian feel to the decor, as well as a spa, library and guest lounge. In all properties, guests get to see artworks that aren't on view to the general public. **¥35,000**

Cin.na.mon シナモン Miyanoura ☎087 840 8133, ⓦwww.cin-na-mon.jp. This stylishly renovated wooden house has three basic tatami bedrooms that all share a bathroom, and a trendy café-bar (Tues–Sun 11am–10pm) decorated with a collection of colourful plastic models of characters from *Star Wars*, *Dragon Ball* and the like. They offer a selection of curry dishes (¥900) and have a 1hr 30min all-you-can-drink deal for ¥2000. Rates include breakfast, and bicycle rental is also available. **¥8000**

Dormitory in Kowloon ドミトリーin九龍 Miyanoura ☎090 7974 2424, ⓦdomi-kowloon.com. This friendly, simple hostel is the cheapest place to stay on Naoshima and is a solid choice. It's just steps from the ferry terminal, with clean and comfortable rooms, self-catering facilities, a lounge area and free internet access. Dorm **¥2800**

★**Kuraya** くらや Honmura ☎087 892 2253, ⓦkuraya-naoshima.net. Set in a traditional Naoshima house with central courtyard, this charming B&B is run by a friendly English-speaking artist. *Kuraya* is also a gallery, and it's

possible to stay in the exhibition space. Rate includes a hearty breakfast. **¥9000**

Little Plum リトルプラム Miyanoura ☎087 892 3751, ⓦlittleplum.net. Behind the bathhouse (see p.629) is a cute hostel and café-bar (Tues–Sun 11am–9.30pm) made out of shipping containers. *Little Plum* offers four comfortable bunk beds in each of the crates and a shared bathroom/shower between them all. Wi-fi and bicycle rental is also available. Dorm **¥3000**

★**Mrs. Maroulla's House** マローラおばさんの家 Miyanoura ☎090 7979 3025, ⓦyado-sevenbeach.com. This recently opened self-catering cottage is a riot of colour both inside and out; no other house on Naoshima is painted in hot pink. It's comfortably furnished, the dining-kitchen area and shower room have all the mod cons, and the place can sleep up to five guests. **¥15,000**

Tsutsujisō つつじ荘 Gotanji ☎087 892 2838, ⓦtsutsujiso.com. Choose between chalets with tatami floors, caravans or "*pao*", spacious Mongolian circular tents with four beds, table and chairs at this great seaside-facing camp. There's a small café (daily 11am–2.30pm) selling drinks and snacks, and the BBQ cooking area and shower rooms have recently been upgraded. **¥4200** per person

EATING AND DRINKING

CAFES AND RESTAURANTS

Garden Café ガーデンカフェ Honmura ☎087 892 3301. Look out over Honmura port at this curry restaurant which is in an old house and has friendly staff. Meat or vegetarian curries are served with a side salad and start at ¥800. The fresh orange juice (¥500) and apple cake (¥350) are delicious. You can also rent bikes here. Tues–Sun 11.30am–5pm.

Mai Mai マイマイ Honmura ☎090 8286 7039, ⓦmaimaipj.exblog.jp/. Operating out of a garage with courtyard seating, this burger café sells the popular Naoshima Burger (¥640) and the RocoMoco burger plate (¥680), which you can wash down with fresh juice (¥400) or draft beer (¥300). Daily 10am–5pm.

One Coin Lunch ワンコインランチ Miyanoura ☎090 7143 0500. This outdoor café serves tasty Chinese food and *izakaya*-style one-plate snacks – all for ¥500. Locally brewed Naoshima Monogatari ales are ¥700 a bottle. In the same space is the *Hana to Tsuki* café

selling a variety of cakes and coffee. 11am–8.30pm; closed Thurs.

★**Umi no Hoshi** 海の星 Benesse Park, Gotanji ☎087 892 3223, ⓦbenesse-artsite.jp/en/benessehouse/restaurant_cafe.html. Offering wonderful Inland Sea views, the *Umi no Hoshi* restaurant serves superb Mediterranean-style cuisine featuring fresh local produce. The breakfast buffet is ¥2500 and dinner courses range from ¥7500–10,000. Daily 7.30am–9.30am and 6–9pm.

BAR

14 Bar イシバー Honmura ☎080 4550 8459 ⓦ14bar.web.fc2.com. Tucked away near Honmura port, this lively bar is one of the few places open in the evening on the island. There's a 2hr all-you-can-drink deal for ¥2000 and bar meals including moussaka (¥800) and *nasi goreng* (¥700). Sports matches are shown on a large screen, and there's also a darts board if you fancy some intercultural communication. Mon–Sat 6pm–2am.

Inujima
犬島

The tiny island of **INUJIMA** is home to the dramatic Inujima Seirensho Art Museum and the ongoing Inujima Art House Project. These two sites are another excellent example of how the history, traditional architecture, and natural environment of the Inland Sea have been skilfully combined with contemporary art. Currently, the

island has a population of fifty, and it's likely you'll meet at least half the residents as you wander around the sites. It's probably worth setting aside two or three hours to visit the island.

Inujima Seirensho Art Museum

犬島精錬所美術館, Inujima Seirensho Bijutsukan • 327-5 Inujima • **Museum** March–Nov daily except Tues 10am–4pm; Dec–Feb Mon & Fri–Sun • ¥2000 (combined ticket with Inujima Art House Project) • **Café** Daily 10.30am-4pm • Bentō seafood lunches ¥1000 • ☎ 086 947 1112, ⓦ benesse-artsite.jp/en/seirensho/

The industrial-looking **Inujima Seirensho Art Museum** has been built into the ruins of a copper refinery constructed in 1909. Using local granite and waste products from the smelting process, architect **Sambuichi Hiroshi** has transformed the abandoned buildings and smokestacks into a fantastic eco-building and art space, with solar power and geothermal cooling creating a naturally air-conditioned environment. The museum displays the work of **Yanagi Yukinori** who has used parts of the dismantled home of controversial writer **Mishima Yukio** to explore the contradictions of Japanese modernization. The museum's café serves delicious *bentō* lunches of local seafood.

Inujima Art House Project

犬島家プロジェクト, Inujima Ie purojeckuto • Inujima • March–Nov daily except Tues 10am–4pm; Dec–Feb Mon & Fri–Sun • ¥2000 (combined ticket with Seirensho Art Museum) • ☎ 086 947 1112, ⓦ benesse-artsite.jp/en/inujima-arthouse/

The vibrant **Inujima Art House Project** opened in 2010. Given that Inujima only has a small land mass, the project has taken over the entire village, and the local residents live amongst the five Art House galleries and other installation spaces. Of note is Kojin Haruka's *Contact Lens* – distortions of the surrounding environment through different lenses, and Jun Nguyen-Hatsushiba's *The Master and the Slave: Inujima Monogatari*, a video installation on the theme of stonecutting, once a major industry on the island.

ARRIVAL AND GETTING AROUND   INUJIMA

By ferry Ferries sail to Inujima port from Miyanoura (¥1800; 45min), and Teshima (¥1200; 25min). There's also a ferry to Inujima from Hoden port in Okayama (¥300; 10mins). Timetables are regularly updated on the Benesse website (ⓦ benesse-artsite.jp/en/access).

On foot There's no transport once you're on the island, so you'll need to walk between the sights.

INFORMATION

Tourist information The Inujima Ticket Center is in the same building as the Seaside Inujima Gallery and is on your left as you exit the port (March–Nov daily except Tues 10am–4pm; Dec–Feb Mon & Fri–Sun plus all national hols; ☎ 0876 947 1112, ⓦ benesse-artsite.jp/en/inujima). You can buy museum and ferry tickets here, as well as pick up a map to the sites. There's also a small café (daily 10am–4.30pm) and coin lockers.

Teshima

豊島

The lush island of **TESHIMA** is home to prosperous fishing and dairy-farming industries. Amongst this verdant environment are many magical art sites – all of which you can see in a single day-trip – located between the island's two ports, Ieura and Karato, the notable standouts being **Teshima Art Museum** and **Teshima Yokoo House**.

Teshima Art Museum

豊島美術館, Teshima Bijutsukan • 607 Karato • March–Sept 10am–5pm, closed Tues; Oct–Nov 10.30am–4pm, closed Tues; Dec–Feb Mon & Fri–Sun 10.30am–4pm • ¥1500 • ☎ 087 968 3555, ⓦ benesse-artsite.jp/en/teshima-artmuseum

The splendid **Teshima Art Museum**, a collaboration between architect **Nishizawa Ryūe** and artist **Naito Rei**, is a concrete shell open to the elements on the edge of a rice terrace. From the outside, the museum looks something like a UFO, and once inside you'll feel even more like you've entered another world. You must take your shoes off to enter the hushed interior space, where small springs of water spontaneously erupt from the floor and then travel around, fascinating visitors who lie all over the floor to observe them. It's recommended that you spend at least thirty minutes sitting here, observing the mobile puddles of water, and listening to the wind whistle through the roof openings. The museum's café (same as museum hours) is a smaller version of the museum with a white carpet lounge and glass roof.

The Teshima Yokoo House

豊島横尾館 · 2359 Ieura Teshima Yokookan · March–Sept 10am–5pm, closed Tues; Oct–Nov 10am–4pm, closed Tues; Dec–Feb Mon & Fri–Sun 10am–4pm · ¥500 · ☎ 087 968 3555, ⊕ benesse-artsite.jp/en/teshima-yokoohouse

Compared to the serenity of the Teshima Art Museum, the **Teshima Yokoo House** is a rude shock of pop culture collage. Exploring the themes of life and death, the house is a collaboration between architect **Nagayama Yuko** and artist **Yokoo Tadanori**, whose works are exhibited throughout. Yokoo's style is eccentric and provocative: a carp pond flows under the persplex floors of the main house; nine hundred postcards of waterfalls are displayed on the walls of a 14m-high tower; and the amazing "outhouse" installations are definitely worth a look, whether nature calls or not.

ARRIVAL AND INFORMATION

TESHIMA

By ferry Ferries sail to Ieura port from Miyanoura (¥1800; 55min), Inujima (¥1200; 25min), Uno (¥750; 25min) and Tonosho (¥750; 40min), as well as to Karato port from Uno (¥1000; 35min) and Tonosho (¥750; 30min). Timetables are regularly updated on the

Benesse website (⊕ benesse-artsite.jp/en/access).
Tourist information The desk in the ferry terminal (daily 8.30am–5pm; ☎ 080 2850 7330) has an English map and guide to the island.

GETTING AROUND

By bus A regular bus (¥200) runs between Ieura and Karato, stopping at some art sites and the Teshima Art Museum along the way.
By bike The best way to get around is by bicycle, and you

can hire bikes from both Ieura and Karato ports (¥100/1hr). The island is quite hilly, so it's advisable to rent an electric-powered bicycle if possible (¥1000/4hr). The rental shops will also mind your luggage for a small fee (¥300–500).

Shōdoshima

小豆島

It may not have quite the same idyllic appeal as its smaller Inland Sea neighbours such as Naoshima (see p.627) and Teshima (see opposite), but thanks to its splendid natural scenery and a collection of worthwhile sights, **Shōdoshima** should still be high on any list of places to visit in Shikoku. The mountainous, forested island styles itself as a Mediterranean retreat, and has a whitewashed windmill and mock-Grecian ruins strategically placed in its terraced olive groves. But local culture also gets a look-in, since Shōdoshima – which translates as "island of small beans" – promotes its own version of Shikoku's 88-temple pilgrimage and its connection with the classic Japanese book and film *Nijūshi-no-Hitomi* (*24 Eyes*). This tear-jerking tale of a teacher and her twelve young charges, set on Shōdoshima between the 1920s and 1950s, was written by local author **Tsuboi Sakae**. In recent years, Shōdoshima has become part of the Setouchi Triennale International Art Festival (see box, p.627), and there are now several interesting art installations on the island.

Though most of the main sights can be covered in a day, it's a bit of a rush if you don't have your own transport, in which case it's better to spend at least one night on the island.

Meiro no Machi 迷路のまち

The town of Tonoshō was originally built during the Edo period in a complicated **maze** (*meiro*) pattern to protect the inhabitants from pirate attack; it was believed that pirates

9

wouldn't enter if they couldn't retreat quickly. The maze of narrow streets, some less than 2m wide, is known as **Meiro no Machi**. Having survived the centuries, the area has an intriguing atmosphere and is worth a wander. There are a considerable number of Taishō and Shōwa-era houses in the streets, some of which have started to be used for the Setouchi Triennale International Art Festival (see box, p.627). Check the festival information office for details of the latest exhibitions.

Olive-kōen

オリーブ公園 • Park & museum daily 8.30am–5pm • Free; onsen ¥700 • ☎ 087 982 2200, ⓦ olive-pk.jp

Along the main Highway 436 heading east from Tonoshō and around the south of Shōdoshima lies **Olive-kōen**, a pleasant but touristy hillside park of olive groves and fake Grecian ruins where, among other things, you can buy green-olive chocolate or take an onsen bath followed by a moisturizing session with olive-oil creams. There's also an interesting small **museum** in the park that explains the history of olive growing on the island.

Nijūshi no Hitomi Eigamura

二十四の瞳映画村 • Tanoura • Daily 9am–5pm • ¥790 (including entry to the old school in Tanoura) • ☎ 087 982 2455, ⓦ 24hitomi.or.jp

Just a little further along the southern coast of Shōdoshima than Olive-kōen is **Nijūshi no Hitomi Eigamura**, a mini-theme park dedicated to the 1954 film *24 Eyes*. This fake village, which was used in the 1980s remake, has some charming old buildings. If you're not familiar with the film, you can watch it on-site. Also in the park you'll find a museum dedicated to the prolific author Tsuboi Sakae, best known for the novel on which the film was based, and the very stylish *Café Shinema Kurabu*, a good place for lunch and part of a display devoted to classic Japanese films of the 1950s and 1960s. Just before reaching Eigamura, as you come along the road from Sakate, is the rustic fishing village of **Tanoura** (田の浦), where the original schoolhouse that served as an inspiration for the book is also open to visitors (daily 9am–5pm; ¥200).

Yamaroku

ヤマロク醤油, Yamaroku shōyu • 1607 Yasuda-ko • Daily 9am–5pm • Free • ☎ 087 982 0666, ⓦ yama-roku.net

Scattered around the southeastern part of Shōdo-shima, between Eigamura and the youth hostel, you'll find several **soy sauce** factories, the most worthwhile of which is **Yamaroku**. Here, each batch of the local sauce is fermented for two years in hundred-year-old, 2m-high wooden barrels, and carefully watched over by a fifth-generation soy master. The staff don't speak much English, but are happy to show visitors around and let you climb up and peer into the pungent, bacteria-coated barrels. They also have a small souvenir shop where you can sample their different sauces.

ARRIVAL AND INFORMATION   SHŌDOSHIMA

By boat and ferry Shōdoshima is best reached by ferries from Takamatsu (1hr; ¥670) and high-speed boats (35min; ¥1140) that depart daily for several ports on the island. If you're coming from Honshū, there are also ferries from Himeji (1hr 40min; ¥1480), Hinase (1hr; ¥1000), Okayama (1hr; ¥1000), Uno (1hr 30min; ¥1200) and Osaka (3hr 25min; ¥3900) to Sakate. The island's main port of Tonoshō, on the west coast, is served by the most services. If you

intend to stay at the youth hostel (see opposite), take a ferry from Takamatsu to Kusakabe.

Tourist information There's a helpful tourist information desk (daily 9am–5pm; ☎ 0879 62 0649) inside Tonoshō's ferry terminal, but if you're coming from Takamatsu, you can easily pick up information on the island from the tourist information centre there (see p.617).

GETTING AROUND

By bus Buses for main points around the island depart from the terminal next to the Tonoshō Port building. Here you can buy a one-day ticket for ¥2000 or a two-day ticket for ¥2500 – only worthwhile if you intend to do a lot of sightseeing by bus. Note that the frequency of the bus

services changes seasonally, and some routes around the island don't operate in Jan, Feb or June; check with the tourist information desk before setting off.

By bike Rental bicycles are available at both Tonoshō port, where the high-speed passenger boats arrive (¥500; daily

10am–5.30pm; ☎ 087 962 0162) and also the youth hostel (¥200/day). Other transportation can also be easily arranged in Tonoshō – for cars, try Naikai Ferry Rentacar (☎ 087 982 1080) at the port, and Ishii Rent-a-bike on Olive-dōri (☎ 087 962 1866) for scooters.

ACCOMMODATION AND EATING

Tonoshō offers plenty of business and tourist hotels that charge around ¥8000 per person, including two meals. Shōdoshima doesn't have many good places to eat, so it's best to plan on having dinner and breakfast at your hotel.

Celeste Shodōshima チェレステ小豆島 1462 Kashima-ko ☎ 087 962 5015, ⓦ celesteshodoshima.com; map p.626. This is a smart new hotel with spacious, well-appointed Japanese-style rooms with excellent views of the bay and "Angel Road", a slinky sandbar linking three tiny islands. Rates include meals in the hotel's Italian restaurant, and there's also an in-house art gallery and rooftop jacuzzi. **¥36,000**

Minshuku Maruse 民宿マルセ Tonoshō-ko ☎ 087 962 2385, ⓦ new-port.biz/maruse/Honkan.htm; map p.626. Next to the Tonoshō post office, this is a small, clean minshuku with Japanese and Western-style rooms and a coin laundry for guests. Breakfast is ¥520, and dinner can be arranged in advance for ¥750–1580. **¥5760**

New Port ニューポートTonoshō-ko ☎ 087 962 6310, ⓦ new-port.biz; map p.626. A friendly business hotel run by the same management as *Minshuku Maruse*, here you'll find Japanese and Western-style rooms with private bathrooms, TV and wi-fi. Rates include breakfast, and dinner can also be arranged in advance. **¥7960**

Shōdoshima International Hotel 小豆島国際ホテル 24-67 Tonoshōmachi-ko ☎ 087 962 2111, ⓦ shodoshima-kh.jp; map p.626. A big resort-style hotel in a beautiful location on the south side of Tonoshō next to "Angel Road". Rooms are quite luxurious, and if you aren't lucky enough to get your own outdoor onsen bath, you can always use the hotel's own spa. **¥42,525**

Shōdoshima Olive Youth Hostel 小豆島オーリブユ ースホステル 1072 Nishimura ☎ 087 982 6161, ⓦ shodoshima-oliveyh-en.tumblr.com; map p.626. Just a 10min walk west of Kusakabe port, this hostel has clean dorms and private tatami rooms for two. The friendly, English-speaking manager whips up a good *teishoku* dinner (set meal including a main dish, rice, miso soup and pickles ¥1050), and a filling breakfast for ¥630. **¥6510**

Tokushima

徳島

Built on the delta of the Yoshinogawa – Shikoku's longest river – and bisected by the Shinmachi-gawa, **TOKUSHIMA**, the capital of Tokushima-ken, is known across Japan for its fantastic summer dance festival, the **Awa Odori**, which is attended every year by over one million people (see box below). If you're not among them, then don't worry, as Tokushima does its best to provide a flavour of the Awa Odori experience year-round at the Awa Odori Kaikan, at the foot of **Mount Bizan**, a parkland area providing sweeping views of the city.

THE DANCING FOOLS

Every year in mid-August, many Japanese return to their family homes for **Obon** (Festival of the Dead), which is as much a celebration as a remembrance of the deceased. Towns all over the country hold *bon* dances, but none can compare to Tokushima's **Awa Odori** – the "Great Dance of Awa" – a four-day festival that runs every year from August 12 to 15. Over a million spectators come to watch the eighty thousand participants, dressed in colourful *yukata* (summer kimono) and half-moon-shaped straw hats, who parade through the city, waving their hands and tapping their feet to an insistent two-beat rhythm, played on *taiko* drums, flutes and *shamisen* (traditional stringed instruments). With plenty of **street parties** and sideshows, this is as close as Japan gets to Rio's Mardi Gras, and there's plenty of fun to be had mingling with the dancers, who famously chant, "The dancing fool and the watching fool are equally foolish. So why not dance?"

If you plan to attend the festival, book **accommodation** well in advance or arrange to stay in one of the nearby towns and travel in for the dances, which start at 6pm and finish at 10.30pm (though street parties continue well into the night). To take part as a dancer, contact the Tokushima International Association or Tokushima Prefecture International Exchange Association (see p.638), who organize dance groups on one of the festival nights.

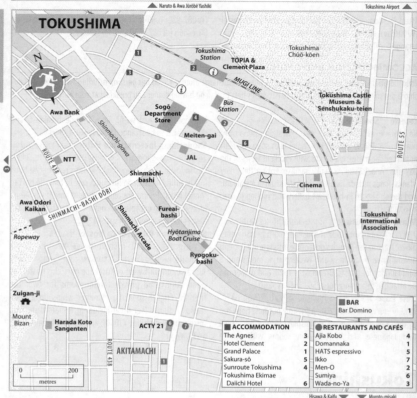

▲ Naruto & Awa Jūrōbē Yashiki   Tokushima Airport ▲

TOKUSHIMA

■ ACCOMMODATION		● RESTAURANTS AND CAFÉS	
The Agnes	3	Ajia Kobo	4
Hotel Clement	2	Domannaka	1
Grand Palace	1	HATS espressivo	5
Sakura-sō	5	Ikko	7
Sunroute Tokushima	4	Men-O	2
Tokushima Ekimae		Sumiya	6
Daiichi Hotel	6	Wada-no-Ya	3

■ BAR	
Bar Domino	1

Hisawa & Kaifu ▼▼   ▼ Muroto-misaki

Home to the first temple of the Shikoku pilgrimage, Tokushima has a long history of welcoming visitors, and you'll find it a noticeably friendly and relaxed place, as well as a good base from which to explore the rest of the prefecture. The city's sights are all within easy walking distance of Clement Plaza.

Mount Bizan

眉山 · **Ropeway** Daily: April–Oct 9am–9pm, Nov–March 9am–5.30pm · One way ¥600, return ¥1000 (including museum) · ☎ 088 652 3617 **Museum** Daily 9.30am–5pm · ¥200, or free for ropeway ticket holders ☎ 088 623 5342 · If you take the ropeway, the entrance to the station is on the fifth floor of the Awa Odori Kaikan (see opposite)

On a clear day, it's worth ascending the 280m-high **Mount Bizan** for the panoramic view, and it's not too difficult a hike if you want to save on the ropeway fee or fancy the exercise; a route starts from the temple to the left of the *kaikan* (hall) at the end of Shinmachibashi-dōri. At the summit, there's a park with a stupa, called **Tokushima Pagoda**, in memory of the Japanese soldiers who served in Burma during World War II, and the interesting **Moraesu-kan** (モラエス館), a tiny museum dedicated to Wenceslao de Morães, a Portuguese naval officer and former consul-general in Kōbe. Morães lived in Tokushima for sixteen years until his death in 1929 and wrote many books on Japan.

Zuigan-ji

瑞巖寺 · 3-18 Higashi Yamate-chō · Daily 8am–5pm · Free · ☎ 088 692 5968

Walk east around the base of Mount Bizan and you'll come to the delightful Buddhist emple, **Zuigan-ji**. Built in the Momoyama-style, Zuigan-ji dates from 1614 and has an elegant traditional garden with carp-filled pools, a waterfall and rock paths across mossy lawns leading up to a picturesque red pagoda. Look out for one of the lamps in the garden which, during the Edo period when Christianity was forbidden in Japan, the image of the Virgin Mary was engraved on it. While here, drop by the small music shop, Harada Koto Sangenten (daily 10am–6pm; ☎088 652 5625).

Awa Odori Kaikan

阿波踊り会館 · 2-20 Shinmachi-bashi · Higashi Yamate · **Complex** Daily 9am–6pm · Free · **Museum** Daily 9am–5pm · ¥300
Awa Odori Hall Performances Mon–Fri 2pm, 3pm, 4pm & 8pm, Sat & Sun also 11am · ¥500, evening dance ¥700 · If you plan to do the lot, buy the ¥1500 ticket which covers the daytime dance performance, museum, and ropeway; the ¥700 ticket covers the museum and day performance ☎ 088 611 1611, ⊕ awaodori-kaikan.jp

Five minutes' walk southeast of the river, at the base of Mount Bizan, is the **Awa Odori Kaikan**. The complex is dedicated to the city's famous dance (see p.635) and houses a good souvenir shop on the ground floor, a **ropeway** on the fifth floor that goes to the top of Mount Bizan (see opposite), a museum dedicated to the history of the dance on the third floor, and the **Awa Odori Hall**, where there are at least four live dance performances daily. The daytime performances are explanatory and highly interactive – don't be surprised if you end up on stage – and the evening performances showcase Tokushima's most distinguished dance troupes.

Awa Jūrōbē Yashiki

阿波十郎兵衛屋敷 · 184 Kawauchi-chō Miyajima Motoura (4km north of Tokushima Station) · Daily 9.30am–5pm; check website for performance times · ¥400 · ☎ 088 665 2202, ⊕ joruri.info/jurobe · A 20min bus journey from stop number 7 at the bus terminal

Traditional Japanese puppetry, *bunraku*, is a highly skilled performance art which takes years of training to master and is one of Tokushima's enduring traditions. At the historic premises of the Jūrōbei family, **Awa Jūrōbē Yashiki**, you can immerse yourself in the world of *ningyō jōruri*, as it's called locally. This former samurai residence, with an enclosed garden and display room of beautifully made antique puppets, was once the home of the tragic figure Jūrōbē, immortalized in *Keisei Awa no Naruto*, the epic eighteenth-century play by Chikamatsu. The theatre has recently been completely rebuilt in the traditional manner, and you can see part of the play performed here, usually the classic scene where Jūrōbē's wife, Oyumi, turns away their daughter Otsuru as a stranger. Live performances are held regularly, and a video of the play is also shown inside a large tatami hall. The theatre staff are welcoming and there's a helpful English pamphlet.

Tokushima Chūō-kōen

徳島中央公園 · **Senshūkaku-teien** 千秋閣庭園 · Daily 9am–5pm · ¥50 · **Tokushima Castle museum** 徳島城博物館 · Tues–Sun 9am–5pm · ¥300 · ☎ 088 656 2525 · A 5min walk east of the JR station

The attractive park of **Tokushima Chūō-kōen** lies on the site of *daimyō* Hachisuka Iemasa's fortress. From 1586, Hachisuka's clan lived in the castle for 280 years, creating

---

HYŌTANJIMA BOAT CRUISE

Central Tokushima city is encircled by two rivers, the Shinmachi-gawa and the Suketo-gawa, in the shape of a hyōtan, or gourd. A relaxing thirty-minute **Hyōtanjima Boat Cruise** (ひょうたん島クルーズ; daily 1–3.40pm, July & Aug also 5–7.40pm; every 40min; ¥100; ☎088 621 5232) takes in all **fifteen bridges** – some of the bridges are decorated with sculpture and art related to Awa Odori – that connect this urban island, called Hyōtanjima, to the rest of the city. The cruises leave from the boathouse in front of the Shinmachi-gawa Riverside Park (新町川公園), at the northern end of the Ryōgoku-bridge (両国橋).

9

the town that is now Tokushima. All that remains of the castle, which was destroyed in 1896, are a few stone walls, part of the moat and the **Senshūkaku-teien**, a beautiful formal garden. Beside the garden is the small **Tokushima Castle Museum**, with informative, modern displays explaining the history of the Hachisuka clan and a large model that gives a good idea of what the fortress and its surrounding compound once looked like.

ARRIVAL AND DEPARTURE

TOKUSHIMA

By plane Tokushima's airport (☎088 699 2831, ⑳tokushima-airport.co.jp) lies 8km north of the city centre; there are buses from here to Clement Plaza (30min; ¥430).
Destinations Fukuoka (2 daily; 1hr 40min); Tokyo (11 daily; 1hr 15min).

By train Trains pull in at JR Tokushima Station, next to the Clement Plaza shopping centre, at the head of Shinmachibashi-dōri, the main thoroughfare.
Destinations Awa Ikeda (6 daily; 1hr 20min); Kaifu (3 daily; 1hr 40min); Naruto (14 daily; 40min); Takamatsu (17 daily; 1hr).

By bus Long-distance buses come and go from the bus station in front of the JR train station.
Destinations Awaji-shima IC (4 daily; 45min); Matsuyama (7 daily; 3hr 10min); Osaka (every 30min; 2hr 40min); Takamatsu (12 daily; 1hr 35min); Tokyo (3 daily; 10hr 40min).

By ferry Ferries arrive at Okinosu port, 3km east of the centre.
Destinations Kita-Kyūshū/Kokura (daily; 17hr); Tokyo (daily; 17hr 30min); Wakayama (8 daily; hydrofoil 1hr, ferry 2hr).

Car rental Eki Rent-a-Car (☎088 622 1014) is situated in front of Tokushima Station, while Nippon Rent-a-Car (☎088 699 6170) is at the airport.

INFORMATION

Tourist information Although there is a tourist information booth outside Clement Plaza, it's better to go to Tokushima Prefecture International Exchange Association (TOPIA), on the plaza's sixth floor (daily 10am–6pm; ☎088 656 3303, ⑳topia.ne.jp), where the English-speaking staff are very helpful. There's also a small library of English books and magazines, as well as free internet access. The Tokushima International Association (Mon–Fri 10am–5.30pm; ☎088 622 6066, ⑳www.nmt.ne.jp/~tia81717, one block beyond the city hall to the east of the JR station, offers similar services and, for longer-term visitors, both facilities offer Japanese classes.

ACCOMMODATION

Tokushima has a decent range of **accommodation**, most of it of a high standard and conveniently located around the JR station. Book well in advance if you plan to visit during the Awa Odori in Aug. If you're having problems finding somewhere to stay, pop into TOPIA (see above), where staff can make enquiries for you.

★**The Agnes** アグネスホテル徳島 1-28 Terashima Honchō Nishi ☎088 626 2222, ⑳agneshotel.jp. West of the JR station, this hip, monochrome hotel has decent-sized, well-equipped rooms and a trendy patisserie on the ground floor. The in-house café is open from breakfast until late evening serving sandwiches, pasta and other Western-style food. There's also a coin laundry and free wi-fi. **¥12,600**

Hotel Clement ホテルクルメント徳島 1-61 Terashima Honchō Nishi ☎088 656 3111, ⑳hotelclement.co.jp. Upmarket hotel next to the station with spacious, tastefully furnished rooms, and polite and friendly staff. There's an eighteenth-floor Sky bar and Japanese restaurant with a fabulous view of Mount Bizan. Wi-fi access is free, and there's also an in-house spa. **¥19,700**

Grand Palace ザ・グランドパレス 1-60-1 Terashima Honchō Nishi ☎088 626 1111, ⑳gphotel.jp. Going for the shiny and sleek black look in a big way, this boutiquish hotel offers larger than average rooms, with very comfortable beds, and an excellent breakfast buffet. The staff don't speak much English but they do make an effort to ensure your stay is enjoyable. **¥13,600**

Sakura-sō さくら荘 1-25 Terashima Honchō Higashi ☎088 652 9575, ☏652 2220. Don't be put off by the drab exterior – this minshuku is the best budget choice in Tokushima and is conveniently located a few blocks east of the station. Rooms are simple but clean and spacious, with shared bathing facilities. The friendly owner speaks a little English and is very welcoming. **¥6600**

★**Sunroute Tokushima** サンルート徳島 1-5-1 Moto-machi ☎088 653 8111, ⑳www.sunroute.jp. Reception for this slick modern hotel is on the third floor of the Meiten-gai block right opposite Tokushima Station. The comfortable rooms are decorated in monochrome hues and each one has its own personal computer. There's also free access to the rooftop onsen bath, jacuzzi and sauna (¥700 for non-guests). **¥14,490**

okushima **Ikimae Daiichi Hotel** 徳島駅前第一ホ
テル 2-21 Ichibanchō ☎088 655 5005, ⍰www
.tokushima-daiichihotel.co.jp. You'll find tiny but
clean rooms at this convenient and modern business

hotel. Rates are lower for online bookings and eco-plans (room cleaning every second day). Breakfast is extra (continental ¥380, Japanese ¥680) but there are non-smoking rooms and free internet access. **¥17,360**

EATING AND DRINKING

okushima has a good choice of **restaurants** and no shortage of **bars**, with the densest concentration in Akitamachi, okushima's lively entertainment area. Rooftop beer gardens open during the summer at several hotels, including the *lement* (see opposite).

★**Ajia Kobo** 亜細亜香房 1-7 Higashi Daikumachi ☎088 655 2581. An Asian restaurant set back off the street in a leafy garden, where dishes are reasonably priced and there are lots of spicy cuisines to choose from - *nasi goreng* is ¥850 and Okinawan-style taco rice is ¥800. Drinks such as beer, cocktails and tea are all ¥500. The friendly English-speaking manager will help you order from the Japanese menu. 6pm–midnight, closed Tues.

Bar Domino どみの 1-33 Akitamachi ☎088 655 5556. This sophisticated and intimate mood-lit cocktail and whiskey bar is located in a 50-year old traditional house with a modern interior. Cocktails are priced from ¥800, whiskey shots from ¥1000, and the snack menu includes pizza (¥900) and fried octopus (¥700). You can opt for counter or table seating. Daily 7pm–4am.

★**Domannaka** どまん中 1-47 Honmachi Nishi ☎088 623 3293, ⍰wa-domannaka.jp. This stylish *izakaya* serves delicious local fish, chicken and vegetable cuisine (English menu available). There are grilled dishes such as *yakitori* (from ¥150) and *robata-yaki* (from ¥400), as well as sashimi platters (from ¥1500) and *nabe* hot-pots. The hearty chicken dumpling *nabe* for two (¥1000) is especially tasty. Daily 11.30am–2pm & 5pm–10pm.

HATS espressivo ハッツエスプレッシーヴォ1-16-5 Higashi-shinmachi ☎088 635 4698, ⍰whats-espressivo.com. Trendy café-bar on two levels in the city's central covered arcade that's a popular hangout and a good lunch spot. Their take on the Tokushima burger (¥600), a local burger that ditches ketchup in favour of a sweetish sauce containing thin strips of beef, comes highly recommended. Smoking is allowed in all

areas. Daily 11am–midnight.

★**Ikko** 一鴻 2F Acty Annex ☎088 623 2311. ⍰i-kko. com. *Ikko* is the place to fully sample all the different ways Tokushima chicken can be cooked. Specializing in *honetsuki* cuisine, you can enjoy superbly grilled chicken breasts (¥1100) or chicken sashimi (¥720) with a fresh salad of locally grown vegetables (¥550). Wash it all down with a draft beer (¥520) or locally brewed *sudachi-shu*, a kind of citrus vodka (¥580). Daily 5pm–11.30pm.

Men-O 麺王 240-1 Kawauchi-chō ☎088 623 4116, ⍰7-men.com. Arrive here early to sample Tokushima ramen, because the queues are often out the door and along the street. This local ramen style is distinguished by noodles in a salty-sweet pork belly soup and topped with roast pork and a raw egg. Regular size bowls are ¥480; buy a ticket from the vending machine at the entrance. Daily 11am–midnight.

Sumiya 炭や 2F Acty 21 ☎088 622 3300, ⍰sumiya .sub.jp. This *sumibiyaki* charcoal grill restaurant has a lively atmosphere and serves a wide range of grilled food, mostly with an international flavour. Popular dishes on the menu are their home-made pork sausages (¥780), roast ham sandwiches (¥880) and spicy chicken drumsticks (¥180 for two). Daily 6pm–1am.

Wada-no-Ya 和田の屋 5-3 Otakiyama ☎088 652 8414, ⍰wadanoya.com. A delightful teahouse at the foot of Bizan with a view onto a rock garden. *Matcha* and Tokushima's signature *yaki-mochi* (small, lightly toasted patties of pounded rice and red beans) cost ¥650. There's also a small branch in the Awa Odori Kaikan. 10am–5pm, closed Thurs (both stores).

DIRECTORY

Banks and exchange The main branch of Awa Bank, beside the Kazuga-bashi, only cashes US and Australian dollars. There's an ATM accepting foreign cash cards at the post office (see right).
Hospital Tokushima Prefectural Central Hospital (Kenritsu Chūō Byōin), 1-10-3 Kuramoto-chō ☎088 631 7151.
Internet Available free at TOPIA (see opposite).
Laundry There's a Laundry Queen at 1-19-1 Ryogoku

Honmachi, open 24 hours.
Police The main police station is close to Kachidoki-bashi ☎088 622 3101. Emergency numbers are listed on p.66.
Post office The Central Post Office is just south of the JR station at 1-2 Yaoya-chō (Mon–Fri 9am–7pm, Sat 9am–5pm & Sun 9am–12.30pm).

9

Around Tokushima

North of Tokushima are the whirlpools of **Naruto**, and to the south there's the pretty coastal village of **Hiwasa** (where turtles lay their eggs on the beach each summer), popular surf beaches, and, across the border in Kōchi-ken, the jagged cape at **Muroto**. Inland, the best place to head is the spectacular **Iya Valley**, including the river gorge at **Ōboke**.

Naruto

鳴門 • **Cruise boats** Daily 9am–4.20pm; around 30min • ¥2200 • ⓦ uzusio.com • **Uzu-no-Michi walkway** (渦の道) • Daily Jan–March & Oct–Dec 9.30am–4.30pm; April–Sept 9.30am–5.30pm • ¥500 • ⓦ uzunomichi.jp • Although there are several trains daily from Tokushima to Naruto, the Naruto-Ōhashi bridge is a fair way from the station; it's more convenient to hop on the regular direct bus from Clement Plaza (around 1hr; ¥690)

The 88-temple pilgrimage (see p.613) begins in Shikoku at **NARUTO**, around 13km north of Tokushima. However, the town is more famous for the **whirlpools** that form as the tides change and water is forced through the narrow straits between Shikoku and Awajishima. This is one of Tokushima's most heavily hyped attractions, but it's not a consistently reliable phenomenon. The whirlpools are at their most dramatic on days of the full and new moon; to avoid a wasted journey, check first on the tidal schedule with tourist information in Tokushima (see p.638).

One way to see the whirlpools up close is to hop on a tourist cruise boat from Kameurakankō-ko. There are two options for viewing the whirlpools on foot: you can traverse the Uzu-no-Michi, a walkway under Naruto bridge, which puts you 45m directly above the maelstrom, or go for the cheaper alternative – a bird's-eye view from Naruto-kōen, the park on Oge Island, just to the north of Naruto town.

Hiwasa

日和佐

Picturesque **HIWASA**, 55km south of Tokushima, is worth pausing at for its intriguing temple, quaint harbour and pretty beach. Facing the Pacific Ocean, this coastal area has some of the best surfing spots in Japan, and attracts wave-seekers all year round. From November to February, it's also a well-known spot for viewing the sunrise as it emerges from the ocean horizon.

Yakuō-ji

薬王寺 • 285-1 Okugawauchi Teramae • Pagoda basement ¥100 • ☎ 0884 77 0023, ⓦ yakuouji.net

Yakuō-ji, the 23rd temple on the Shikoku pilgrimage, is on the hillside as you pull into Hiwasa train station. It's particularly popular as a temple with powers to ward off bad luck. Climbing the steps to the main temple, you can't fail to notice lots of ¥1 coins on the ground: some pilgrims place a coin on each step for luck as they head up. At the top of the steps is the main temple area, where the buildings date from 815 and there's a striking

---

SURFING AROUND HIWASA

Big waves and warm currents from the Pacific make the southern part of Tokushima prefecture one of the best places for surfing in Western Japan. The popular surfing spot of **Kaifu** (海部), 26km south of Hiwasa, is where the JR train line ends and is replaced with the private Asa Kaigan railway. You'll nearly always have to change trains here to continue south (simply cross over to the opposite platform). There's a ¥270 extra charge to travel the remaining two stops – the first is **Shishikui** (宍喰), Tokushima's top surf beach, where there's a good range of accommodation and surf shops that rent out boards (from ¥2000 per day). The end of the line is **Kannoura** (甲浦), a sleepy village with another popular surfing beach, **Ikumi** (生見), located just over the border in Kōchi prefecture. Even if you're not an avid surfer, it's fun to experience the laid-back atmosphere and beach culture of these pleasant seaside towns.

statue of a goddess carrying a basket of fish and flanked by lotus blooms. Off to the right is a more recently built single-storey **pagoda**. There's a good view of Hiwasa's harbour from the platform, but the highlight here is to descend into the pagoda's darkened basement, where you can fumble your way around a pitch-black circular corridor to a central gallery containing Brueghel-like painted depictions of all the tortures of hell. In a second gallery is a creepy long scroll showing the steady decay of a beautiful, but dead, young woman.

Hiwasa-jō

日和佐城 • 445-1 Hiwasaura • Daily 10am–4pm • ¥200 • ☎ 0884 77 1166

About 1km south of Hiwasa harbour, the reconstructed castle **Hiwasa-jō** sits atop Shiroyama and has impressive views of the town and coastline. Aside from that, there's not a lot to see on display but the grounds are very pleasant during March and April when the cherry blossoms bloom.

Sea Turtle Museum

うみがめ博物館カレッタ, Umigame Hakubutsukan Karetto • 374-4 Hiwasaura • Tues–Sun 9am–5pm • ¥600 • ☎ 088 477 1110

Ōhama beach (大浜), north of the harbour, is where **turtles** lay their eggs between May and August. During this time, the beach is roped off and spectators must watch the action from a distance. For a closer look at the turtles, make your way to the **Sea Turtle Museum**, beside the beach. The displays are mainly in Japanese, but are very visual, with step-by-step photos of turtles laying eggs. You can also see some turtles swimming in indoor and outdoor pools. In mid-July there's a turtle festival involving ceremonies on Ōhama beach, and some events at the museum.

ARRIVAL AND INFORMATION   HIWASA

By train Limited express and local trains link Hiwasa to Tokushima (50min; ¥2520).

Tourist information There's a left-luggage service (¥200 per bag) at the small tourist information office at the Hiwasa station (daily 9am–5pm, ☎ 088 477 0768), where you can also pick up an English map of the town. There is also a tourist information desk (daily 9am–5pm, ☎ 088 4 77 2121) in the Michi-no-eki rest stop on the other side of the station, which has a free wi-fi spot.

GETTING AROUND

By bike Renting a bicycle for the day is a good idea, as the town's sights are spread out. The tourist information desk at the Michi-no-eki rest stop (see above) rents bicycles for ¥500 per day; these must be returned by 5pm.

ACCOMMODATION

Business Hotel Cairns ビジネスホテルケアンズ 75-17 Okugawauchi Benzaiten ☎ 088 477 1211, ⓦ hotel-cairns.net. This no-frills business hotel is conveniently located right across from the station – particularly useful if you arrive in Hiwasa late in the day. It's clean and friendly but facilities are minimal. All rooms have futons on bed-like tatami platforms. **¥8500**

Umigamesō うみがめ荘 370 Hiwasaura ☎ 0884 77 1166, ⓦ umigamesou.com. This large minshuku is close to the turtle museum and beach, with tatami-style rooms and free wi-fi. Guests use the public bath, which has stunning sea views. If you want to eat dinner or breakfast here (not included in the room price) you must reserve in advance. **¥7800**

White Lighthouse ホテル白い燈台 455 Hiwasaura ☎ 088 477 1170, ⓦ shiroitodai.jp. Situated on the edge of a rocky cliff, this is the most scenic place to stay in Hiwasa. Choose from Western or Japanese-style rooms, all with gorgeous ocean views. Rates include two meals, including a beautifully presented seafood dinner. **¥18900**

EATING

Hiwasaya ひわさ屋 122 Okugawauchi Teramae ☎ 088 477 3528. This popular restaurant is a good lunch spot and serves a variety of chicken dishes. The tasty oyakodon ("parent-and-child bowl", a bowl of rice topped with soy-sauce-flavoured chicken and egg (¥1000), is highly recommended. 11.30am–2pm & 5.30pm–9pm, closed Wed.

Murakami むらかみ 68-1 Okugawauchi Benzaiten ☎ 088 477 0083. *Murakami* serves locally fished aori-ika (reef squid). The super-fresh sashimi on rice aori-ika-don sets, served with soup and pickles, are great value at ¥1500. 11am–2.30pm & 5–9pm, closed Tues.

9

Muroto Misaki
室戸岬

From Kannoura, buses continue south to the black-sand beaches and rugged cape of **MUROTO MISAKI**, an important stop on the pilgrimage route. On the way, look out for **Meotoiwa** (夫婦岩) – two huge rock outcrops between which a ceremonial rope has been strung, creating a natural shrine. Virtually at the cape, a towering white **statue of Kōbō Daishi** commemorates the spot where the priest gained enlightenment when he had a vision of the Buddhist deity Kokūzō in a nearby cavern.

Apart from experiencing deep-sea water at **Searest Muroto**, there's not much else to do at Muroto Misaki other than take in the spectuacular views and follow a series of paths along the shore and up the mountainside to the rustic temple.

Searest Muroto
シレストむろと • 3795-1 Muroto Misaki-chō • Daily except every second Wed 10am–9pm • ¥1300 • ☎ 088 22 6610, ⊛ searest.co.jp

In recent years, Muroto Misaki has attracted pilgrims of a different ilk to those hiking the *henro* trail. Unusual currents off the cape push pure and mineral-rich sea water from as deep as 1000m closer to the surface. Near the Kōbō Daishi statue this deep-sea water is pumped into **Searest Muroto**, a state-of-the-art bathing complex where you can be pummelled by high-pressure water jets, relax in a spa bath or follow a workout video on a pool-side touch-controlled screen.

Hotsumisaki-ji
最御崎寺 • 4058-1 Muroto Misaki-chō • 24hr • Free

Pilgrims pay their respects at the Kōbō Daishi statue before tackling the stiff climb up to a glade of lush vegetation swaddling **Hotsumisaki-ji**. This appealingly shabby Buddhist temple, known locally as **Higashi-dera** (East Temple), is the 24th on the pilgrimage circuit.

ARRIVAL AND INFORMATION
MUROTO MISAKI

By train Most trains run from Nahari all the way to Kōchi, though the Gomen to Kōchi stretch is on JR lines. From Nahari, it costs ¥1040 to get to Gomen and takes about an hour. With an early start from Tokushima, it's possible to visit the cape and make it all the way to Kōchi in a day (and vice versa), but you should allow two days if you plan to linger en route. If you are coming from Tokushima, you'll have to take a bus from Kannoura Station, where the Asa Kaigan line ends.

Tourist information The Muroto Geopark Information Centre (daily 8.30am–5pm; ☎ 0887 22 5161, ⊛ muroto-geo.jp), beneath the wooden lookout platform close to the bus stop, has maps in English and will be able to assist if you're stuck for somewhere to stay.

ACCOMMODATION

Hoshino Resort Utoco Aberge & Spa 星野リゾートウトコオーベルジュ＆スパ 6969-1 Muroto Misaka-chō ☎ 0887 22 1811, ⊛ utocods.co.jp. This hotel and spa resort, next door to Searest Muroto, is housed in a series of striking circular buildings. English-speaking staff glide around in white coats administering high-end beauty treatments (packages from ¥16,000) designed by the renowned Japanese cosmetics artist Shu Uemura. The attached hotel has seventeen chic rooms, all with unimpeded views of the Pacific. Meals using local seafood and deep-sea-water products can be enjoyed at the hotel's classy *Bonne Peche* restaurant, where a set lunch starts at ¥1500. **¥33,600**

Hotsumisaki-ji Youth Hostel 最御崎寺ユースホステル 4058-1 Muroto Misaka-chō ☎ 088 23 0024, ☎ 22 0055. Just behind Hotsumisaki-ji, this friendly temple-lodging facility offers spacious, clean tatami rooms with separate bathrooms and toilets. The food here is excellent, but you must order your meals when you book (¥2100 extra per head for two meals), or bring your own pre-prepared food, because there's nothing else around up here. Dorm **¥3885**

Ōboke Gorge and Iya Valley
大歩危・祖谷

Inland from Tokushima, Highway 192 shadows the JR Tokushima line for around 70km to the railway junction at **AWA IKEDA** (阿波池田), also easily reached from Kotohira (see p.621).

From Awa Ikeda, the road and railway enter the spectacular **Ōboke Gorge**, cut through by the sparkling Yoshino-gawa. The vertiginous mountains here and in the adjacent **Iya Valley** can be coated in snow during the winter, while less than one hour south, the palms of Kōchi sway in the sunshine. This remoteness from the rest of the island made the gorge an ideal bolt hole for the Taira clan after their defeat at Yashima in 1185. Here the warriors traded their swords for farm implements and built distinctive thatched-roof cottages on the steep mountainsides. The valley continues to retain a special atmosphere, reminiscent of old Japan, though decades of ugly construction projects and depopulation have disrupted the traditional lifestyle of the region. Today, there is more awareness of conserving Iya's cultural heritage, and it's definitely worth spending time to explore this mountainous heart of Shikoku, often referred to as the Tibet of Japan.

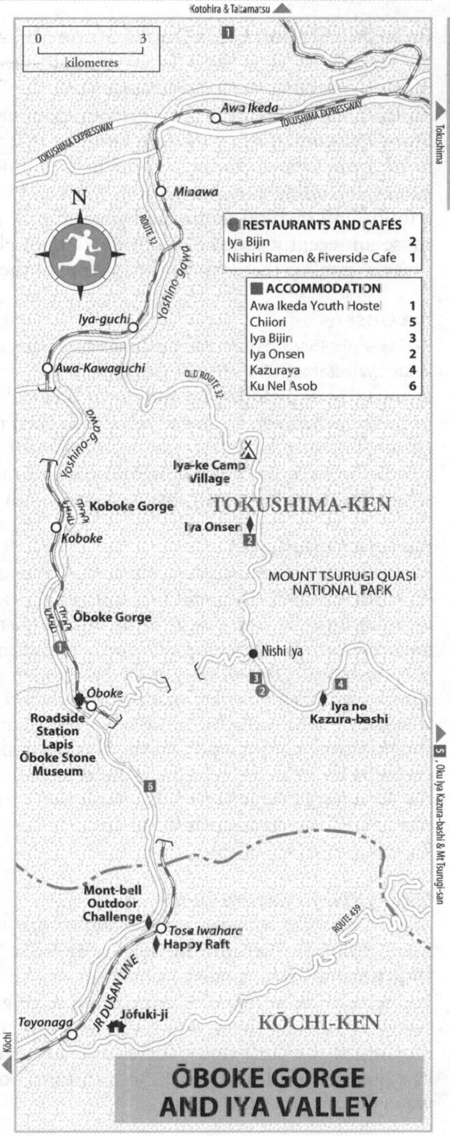
Kotohira & Takamatsu
0 3
kilometres
Awa Ikeda
TOKUSHIMA EXPRESSWAY
TOKUSHIMA EXPRESSWAY
Tokushima
N
Miyawa
ROUTE 32
Yoshino-gawa
RESTAURANTS AND CAFÉS
Iya Bijin 2
Nishiri Ramen & Riverside Cafe 1
ACCOMMODATION
Awa Ikeda Youth Hostel 1
Chiiori 5
Iya Bijin 3
Iya Onsen 2
Kazuraya 4
Ku Nel Asob 6
Iya-guchi
Awa-Kawaguchi
OLD ROUTE 32
Yoshino-gawa
Iya-ke Camp Village
Koboke Gorge
TOKUSHIMA-KEN
Iya Onsen
Koboke
MOUNT TSURUGI QUASI NATIONAL PARK
Ōboke Gorge
Nishi Iya
Ōboke
Iya no Kazura-bashi
Roadside Station Lapis Ōboke Stone Museum
Oku Iya Kazura-bashi & Mt Tsurugi-san
Mont-bell Outdoor Challenge
Tosa Iwahara
Happy Raft
ROUTE 439
JR DOSAN LINE
Jōfuki-ji
Toyonaga
KŌCHI-KEN
Kōchi
ŌBOKE GORGE AND IYA VALLEY

Chiiori

篪庵 • 209 Tsurui Higashi Iya • Day visit by appointment only • ¥500 • ☎ 088 388 5120, ⓦ chiiori.org

High up in the Iya Valley, in the village of **Tsurui** (釣井), is a beautifully restored 300-year-old thatched cottage called **Chiiori**, meaning the "house of the flute". The story of how American writer **Alex Kerr** saved Chiiori from the elements and spent decades restoring it is an unforgettable part of his award-winning book, *Lost Japan* (see p.834). The cottage retains the traditional features of Iya architecture, such as wooden floors and an *irori* floor hearth, yet has been decorated in a minimalist manner using traditional Japanese crafts and design. A modern kitchen and bathroom have also been recently installed, and the overall result is exceptional. As part of Kerr's vision to revive rural areas through sustainable tourism based on **cultural heritage**, it's possible to stay at Chiiori (see p.645). Getting away from the noise, clutter and pollution of contemporary urban life to such an idyllic retreat, where you can enjoy inspiring views out over the misty valleys, is a unique experience.

The Chiiori Trust is also helping to restore other **thatched cottages** in the area, and three of these are now also available to visitors for short-term stays – see ⓦ tougenkyo-iya.jp for more details.

9

Roadside Station Lapis Ōboke Stone Museum

道の駅大歩危石の博物館, Michi no Eki Ōbake Ishi no Hakubutsukan • 1553-1 Kamimyo Yamashiro-chō • Daily 9am–5pm (Dec–Feb closed Mon) • ¥500 • ☎ 088 384 489, ⊛ yamashiro-info.jp/lapis

To learn more about the area's geology, pop into the **Roadside Station Lapis Ōboke Stone Museum**, it's in a modern building that's situated across the river and about 1km north from Ōboke Station. Inside there's a model of the gorge and all manner of stones, including a meteorite from Mars and various glittering gems. It also doubles as a **tourist information centre**, and you can pick up pamphlets in English here too. The museum recently added a colourful *yōkai*, or ghost, exhibition featuring all the different types of goblins that exist in the folklore of the area.

Iya Onsen

祖谷温泉 • Old Route 32, between the Iya-guchi and Nishi Iya junctions • Daily 7.30am–5pm • ¥1500, or free if you're staying at the attached *Iya Onsen* hotel • ☎ 088 375 2311, ⊛ iyaonsen.co.jp

If you've been peddling up and down Iya's valleys or whitewater rafting (see box opposite), then you'll want to relax your tired muscles in the sulphurous waters of **Iya Onsen**. Guests take a short funicular train ride down a ravine to the hot spring right beside the river, with its panoramic views of the river valley. The bath water is a murky white but that's just proof that it's loaded with minerals.

Iya no Kazura-bashi

祖谷のかずら橋 • 162-2 Zentoku Nishi Iya • Daily 7am–5pm • ¥500 • ☎ 0120 404 344, ⊛ miyoshinavi.jp

At **Nishi Iya** (西祖谷), you'll find a shocking example of inappropriate development surrounding the vine bridge attraction of **Iya no Kazura-bashi**, with a monstrous concrete car park lurching out over a ravine and rows of tacky tourist shops. Iya no Kazura-bashi is one of only three bridges left in the area whose style dates from Taira times, when bridges were made out of *shirakuchi* (mountain vines) and bamboo so that they could easily be cut down to block an enemy. The Taira would have a tougher time chopping down the Kazura-bashi today, since it's strengthened with carefully concealed steel cables. There are often hordes of tourists lining up to cross the **45m-long bridge**, which is rebuilt every three years. If possible, avoid spending time here. The recommended alternative is to visit the vine bridges at Oku Iya Ni-jū Kazura-bashi (see below).

Oku Iya Ni-jū Kazura-bashi

奥祖谷二重かずら橋 • 620 Yamason Higashi Iya • Daily 7am–5pm • ¥500 • ☎ 0120 404 344

Some 30km further into the Iya Valley from Nishi Iya is the picturesque **Oku Iya Ni-jū Kazura-bashi**, a pair of vine bridges also known as the "Fufu-bashi" (husband and wife bridges) in a pleasant natural setting in Higashi Iya. The bridges tend to sway as you cross them, and it can be a little unnerving if there are many others crossing at the same time. There's also a human-powered three-seater wooden cable cart, another traditional form of transportation in the area and another entertaining way you can cross the river.

Mount Tsurugi

剣山, Tsurugi-san • Ropeway daily 9am–4.45pm • ¥1800 return • ☎ 088 387 2800

At 1955m, **Mount Tsurugi** is Shikoku's second-highest mountain and is worth visiting for its magical forest paths and pure mountain springs. As a sacred site of mountain workship, it was off limits to women until the early twentieth century. A special festival is held at the peak every August 1 and attracts large numbers of worshippers. However, most visitors come to Tsurugi-san on a day hike. It's a four-hour round-trip starting at **Minokoshi** (見ノ越), from where there's a ropeway part of the way up the mountain, useful if you want to save time and effort and get to the peak quickly.

RIDING ŌBOKE'S RAPIDS

With thrilling rapids and spectacular rocky scenery, a **boat trip** (daily 9am–5pm unless there is heavy rain or strong wind; 30min; ¥1050) down the Yoshino-gawa is the best way to view the Ōboke Gorge. Boats leave from the *Manaka* restaurant (☎088 384 1211), a five-minute walk past the Lapis Ōboke Stone Museum.

More exciting **rafting and canyoning trips** on the Yoshino-gawa are offered between March and October by the Australian-run *Happy Raft* (☎088 775 0500, ⊛en.happyraft.com) further upriver near Tosa Iwahara Station; half-day trips start at ¥5000, full day at ¥9000. Mon:Bell Outdoor Challenge (☎088 775 0898) also offers whitewater rafting trips (April–Nov, from ¥5000).

ARRIVAL AND DEPARTURE

By train Regular express trains from Okayama and Kōchi stop at Awa Ikeda (most also stop at Ōboke). Several daily local trains ply the route through the Iya Valley between Awa Ikeda and Ōboke, but they are infrequent, as are buses. The Miyoshi City Tourist Information Centre (daily 9am–5pm, ☎088 376 0877) beside Awa Ikeda Station has details, and they're also available from Ōboke Station

and at Lapis Ōboke 9 (☎0883 84 489, ⊛yamashiro-info.jp/lapis), which doubles as a tourist information centre for the area.

Car rental It's possible to rent a car for as little as ¥5000 for three hours from the *Manaka* restaurant (☎088 384 1211, ⊛mannaka.co.jp/restaurant/rentacar/rentacar.html).

ŌBOKE GORGE AND IYA VALLEY

GETTING AROUND

By car and bike To get to Chiiori and many of the area's other attractions, you're best off using your own transport – either a car or bicycle (though pedalling up and down these valleys is tough work). This way you'll

have the choice of taking the quieter old Route 32 through the Iya Valley.

By taxi Without your own transport, you can get around by taxi (Ōboke Taxi; ☎088 384 1225).

TOURS

Bus tours The Shikoku Transit Information Bureau (☎0883 72 1231) runs "Bonnet Bus" tours from March to the end of Nov, starting and finishing in Awa Ikeda and

taking in most of the area's sights for ¥5200 or ¥6300, depending on the route.

ACCOMMODATION

With its rustic onsen and river-rafting possibilities, the Iya Valley is a popular tourist spot that offers a good range of accommodation in beautiful natural settings.

Awa Ikeda Youth Hostel 阿波池田ユースホステル 3798 Nishiyamasako, Ikeda-chō ☎088 372 5277, ⊛jyh.or.jp/English. Part of a temple, this hostel is in a spectacular location on the side of the mountain overlooking the town. The manager will pick you up at the station if you call. Accommodation is in high-standard tatami rooms with shared bathroom. There's a cosy lounge with TV, and the meals (breakfast ¥530, dinner ¥1050) are excellent. Dorm ¥3000

Chiiori 篪庵 209 Tsurui Higashi Iya; reservations through the Chiiori Trust ☎088 388 5120, ⊛chiiori.org. The Chiiori traditional mountain lodge (see p.643) can sleep up to ten guests on futons; price per head increases for smaller groups. The Chiiori Trust can help organize some meals, but you'll mostly have to self-cater. If you don't have your own transportation to get to Chiiori, you will need to organize a taxi from Ōboke station (Ōboke Taxi; ☎0883 84 1225), as there is no shuttle service for guests. ¥32,000

★**Iya Bijin** 祖谷美人 9-3 Zentoku Nishi Iya ☎088 387 2009, ⊛iyabijin.jp. Housed in a modern building with traditional style, this hotel and restaurant (see p.646) is in a lovely setting overlooking the river gorge. The luxurious tatami rooms are spacious and elegantly decorated, and the more expensive rooms have their own onsen baths. ¥37,800

Iya Onsen ホテル祖谷温泉 Old Route 32 Nishi Iya ☎088 375 2311, ⊛iyaonsen.co.jp. One of the most stylish ryokan in Shikoku, *Iya Onsen* makes the most of its spectacular location. It's highly recommended for its fine food and luxurious traditional-style rooms with beautiful riverside views. Meals are included in the rate. ¥45,240

Kazuraya かずらや 78 Kanjo Nishi Iya ☎088 387 2831, ⊛www.ctm.ne.jp/~kazuraya. This smart ryokan-style hotel is close to the Iya no Kazura-bashi vine bridge. Rooms are tatami-style and have wonderful valley views. The hotel's indoor and outdoor onsen bathing areas are nicely

9

situated and very clean. Rates include delicious country-style meals. **¥28,000**

Ku Nel Asob 空音遊 442 Enoki Nishi Iya ☎090 9778 7135, ⊚k-n-a.com. Three kilometres' walk south of JR Ōboke Station (call and someone will come and pick you up), this casual guesthouse, also known as *K & A*, offers large tatami dorms in a ninety-year-old house by the river. There's no shower, but the friendly owners will take you to the local onsen. Rates include macrobiotic breakfast or dinner. Dorm **¥6500**

EATING

Several tourist restaurants around the Iya no Kazura-bashi serve *yakisakana* – fish roasted on sticks over hot coals; set meals start at around ¥1000.

Iya Bijin 祖谷美人 9-3 Zentoku Nishi Iya ☎088 387 2009, ⊚iyabijin.jp/soba. This restaurant serves Iya soba noodles and has both indoor and outdoor seating with stunning views of the river below. The noodles are made from locally grown buckwheat and fresh mountain spring water, giving them a rich flavour. Try the Genpei soba with beef and egg (¥1300), or the Sansei mountain vegetable soba (¥900). Daily 8am–5pm.

Nishiri Ramen & Riverside Cafe にし利ラーメン 1468-1 Yamashiro-chō ☎088 384 1117, ⊚west-west .com. Located in the River Station West-West complex, this friendly ramen restaurant and café is a great place to stop for a snack. Bowls of Tokushima ramen are ¥680, and *gyōza* dumplings are just ¥300 a plate. They also serve a small range of fresh juices including *yuzu* citrus juice (¥400) as well as coffee (from ¥300). Daily 10am–6pm.

Kōchi and around

高知

Sun-kissed **KŌCHI** lies dead in the centre of the arch-shaped southern prefecture of Shikoku. With its palm-lined avenues, network of rivers, enjoyable shopping arcades and gently trundling trams, it's a pleasant town to explore. The area's old name of **Tosa** is still used by people today, particularly when referring to the local cuisine. It wasn't until 1603, when ruling *daimyō* Yamauchi Katsutoyo named his castle Kōchiyama (now Kōchi-jō), that the city adopted its present name.

The **castle** remains Kōchi's highlight. To see other places of interest requires a short journey out of the city centre. The most immediately rewarding trip is to **Godai-san-kōen**, a mountain-top park overlooking the city, and the nearby **Chikurin-ji**, the 31st temple on the pilgrimage circuit. South of the city lies **Katsurahama**, with its over-hyped beach, and the **Sakamoto Ryōma Memorial Museum**, dedicated to a local hero of the Meiji Restoration (see box, p.648). In the right season, Kōchi can be a base from which to take a whale-watching tour (see box, p.652). The weekly **Sunday market** (7am–5pm) on Kōchi's Otesuji-dōri, when farmers from all over the prefecture bring their produce to town, is worth attending, as is the colourful **Yosakoi Matsuri** (around Aug 9–12), when fourteen thousand dancers parade along the city's streets.

Kōchi-jō

高知城 • 1-2-1 Marunouchi • Daily 9am–4.30pm • ¥400 to enter the donjon • ☎088 824 5701, ⊚kochipark.jp/kochijyo

Follow the covered Obiya-machi shopping arcade west of Harimaya-bashi to reach the hilltop castle of **Kōchi-jō**. The feudal lord Yamauchi Katsutoyo began construction in 1601, but what you see today dates mainly from 1748, when reconstruction of the donjon turrets and gates was completed following a major fire 21 years earlier.

The main approach is through the **Ōte-mon**, an impressive gateway flanked by high stone walls at the end of Otesuji-dōri. In the anti-feudal fervour that heralded the start of the Meiji era, almost all the castle's buildings were demolished, leaving the steeply sloping walls surrounding empty courtyards. The exception was the three-storey donjon, within the inner citadel (*honmaru*). To the left of the entrance, there's an exhibition of old samurai armour and a scroll from 1852 showing the English

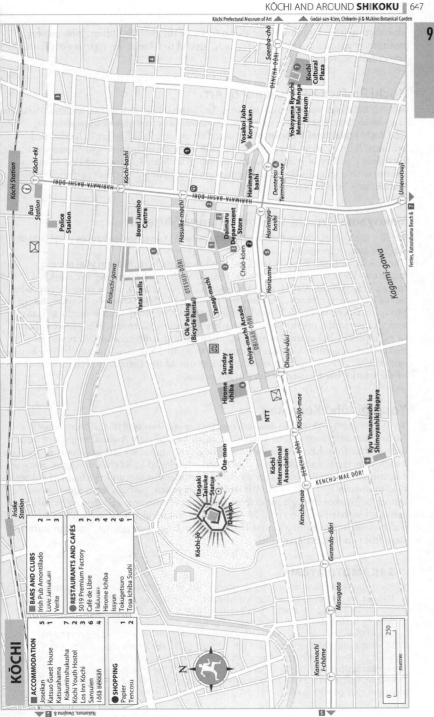

Kōchi Prefectural Museum of Art ▲ | ▲ Godai-san-kōen, Chikurin-ji & Makino Botanical Garden

Nakamura, Uwajima & 2 ◀▼

Ferries, Katsurahama Beach & 7 ▶

KŌCHI

■ ACCOMMODATION
Joseikan	5
Katsuo Guest House	1
Katsurahama	7
Kokuminshukusha	2
Kōchi Youth Hostel	3
Los Inn Kōchi	6
Sansuien	4
Tōsā Bekkan	

● SHOPPING
Papier	1
Tencosu	2

■ BARS AND CLUBS
Irish Pub Amontillado	2
Love Jamaican	1
Verite	3

● RESTAURANTS AND CAFÉS
5019 Premium Factory	3
Café de Libre	7
IaiJuzau	5
Hirome Ichiba	4
Issyun	2
Tokugetsuro	6
Tosa Ichiba Sushi	1

Kōchi-eki

Kōchi Station

Bus Station

Police Station

Bowl Jumbo Centre

Hasuike-machi

Yatai stalls

Enokuchi-gawa

HARIMAYA-BASHI-DŌRI

Kōchi-bashi

Yosakoi Jōhō Koryukan

Yokoyama Ryuichi Memorial Manga Museum

Kōchi Cultural Plaza

Sōenba-chō

DENCHŌ-DŌRI

Umenotsuji

Dentetsu Terminal-mae

Harimaya-bashi

Kagami-gawa

Horizume

Harimaya-bashi

Daimaru Department Store

Chūō-kōen

OTESUJI-DŌRI

OK Parking (Bicycle Rental)

Yanagi-machi

Ohya-machi Arcade

OBISAN-DŌRI

Sunday Market

Hirome Ichiba

NTT

Kōchi International Association

Ote-mon

Itagaki Taisuke Statue

Donjon

Kōchi-jō

Kōchijō-mae

Otesuji-dōri

Kyu Yamanouchi ke Shimoyashiki Nagaya

Kenchō-mae

DENCHŌ-DŌRI

KENCHŌ-MAE DŌRI

Kencho-mae

Gurando-dōri

Masugata

Kamimachi I-chōme

Iriake Station

N

0   250   metres

9

alphabet, written by John Mung (see p.654). In the main building, look out for a beautifully painted palanquin before you ascend to take in the superb view from the uppermost storey.

Kōchi Prefectural Museum of Art

高知県立美術館, Kōchi Keuritsu Bijutsukan • 353-2 Takasu • Tues–Sun 9am–4.30pm • ¥350 • ☎ 088 866 8000, ⊛ kochi-bunkazaidan .or.jp/~museum/index.html • A 15min tram journey east of Harimaya-bashi – ask to get off at Kenritsu Bijutsukan-dōri

The **Kōchi Prefectural Museum of Art**, a stylish modern building set in landscaped grounds, is home to an impressive collection of modern Japanese and Western art including a gallery of lithographs and paintings by Marc Chagall and Paul Klee and a theatre with a specially designed stage for nō plays. Films and other performances are occasionally held here too.

Yokoyama Ryūichi Memorial Manga Museum

横山隆一記念まんが館, Yokoyama Ryūichi inex Memorial Manga-Kan • 2-1 Kutanda • Tues–Sun 9am–6pm • ¥400 • ☎ 088 883 5029, ⊛ bunkaplaza.or.jp/mangakan

The Kōchi Cultural Plaza is home to the **Yokoyama Ryūichi Memorial Manga Museum**. Though Tezuka Osamu is credited with revolutionizing the world of manga after World War II, it was Yokoyama (1909–2001), a native of Kōchi, who paved the way for Tezuka's success by founding the *Shinmanga-ha Shudan* manga group in Tokyo in 1932. It was the members of this group who brought a freshness and vitality to the previously staid world of Japanese cartoons. The museum is full of examples of Yokoyama's work, including his signature creation, "Eternal Boy" Fuku-chan, a comic strip that clocked up a record 5534 serializations before bowing out in 1971. There's also an exact replica of one of his ateliers, as well as a mock-up of the quirky bar he used to have in his house.

Yosakōi Jōhō Kōryukan

よさこい情報交流館 • 1-10-1 Harimaya-machi • Daily except Wed 10am–6pm • Free • ☎ 088 880 4351, ⊛ honke-yosakoi.jp

Kōchi's famous dance festival Yosakoi Matsuri, held in early August, might not be as historical as Tokushima's Awa Odori (see box, p.635), but it's just as colourful. Yosakoi, a highly energetic and fast-paced dance form, developed in Kōchi during the postwar era, combining traditional dance moves with modern music, and the first festival was held in the city in 1954. At the **Yosakoi Jōhō Kōryukan**, you can learn more about the history of Yosakoi through the colourful displays of costumes and the use of *naruko*, the small wooden clappers held by each dancer. There's also a theatre where you can watch dance teams from previous festivals and a dance studio where you can learn the steps from an instructional video.

SAKAMOTO RYŌMA

You'd have to be blind to miss the scowling features of Kōchi's favourite son, **Sakamoto Ryōma**, on posters and other memorabilia around Kōchi. Born in 1835 to a mixed samurai and farming family, Sakamoto directly challenged the rigid class structure of the Shogunate years by leaving the city to start a trading company in Nagasaki (samurai never normally dirtied their hands in business). In his travels around Japan, he gathered support for his pro-Imperial views, eventually forcing the shogun, Tokugawa Yoshinobu, to agree to give supreme power back to the emperor. But one month later, on November 15, 1867, Sakamoto was **assassinated** in Kyoto. Although he was just 33 at the time, his writings included an enlightened plan for a new political system for Japan, aspects of which were later embraced by the Meiji government.

Godai-san-kōen

五台山公園 • On weekends and public holidays a bus runs directly to the park from Kōchi Station and continues on to Katsurahama (one-day pass ¥700); buses also run daily from Harimaya-bashi to Aoyogi-bashi Higashi-zume (around 20min), from where it's a 30min walk up the hill

Perched on the wooded mountain top overlooking Kōchi's harbour, 2km south of the city centre, is the attractive park of **Godai-san-kōen**. The park is famous for its beautiful cherry blossom trees which explode into masses of pink each spring. It's a pleasant place to stroll around or take a picnic lunch.

Chikurin-ji

竹林寺 • 3577 Godaisan • **Temple** Daily 8.30am–5pm • Free • **Treasure House** Daily 8.30am–4.30pm • ¥400 • ☎ 088 882 3085, Ⓦ chikurinji.com

Alongside Godai-san-kōen lie the equally pleasant grounds of the **Chikurin-ji**. This was founded in 724, making it one of the oldest temples in the prefecture, and its atmospheric main building, decorated with intricate carvings of animals, dates from the Muromachi period. The pagoda, built in the 1970s, is said to contain a bone of the Buddha from Bodh Gaya in India, but there's no way of verifying this since the tower is closed to the public. The **Treasure House**, to the right of the temple's main entrance gate, is worth a visit for its tranquil traditional gardens, overlooked by an Edo-era villa, and small collection of Tantric statues and Buddhas.

Makino Botanical Garden

牧野植物園, Makino Shokubutsuen • 4200-6 Godaisan • Daily 9am–5pm • ¥700 • ☎ 088 882 2601, Ⓦ makino.or.jp

Opposite Chikurin-ji lies the large **Makino Botanical Garden**, a pleasant parkland which has lovely views out to the coast and is dedicated to celebrated local botanist Dr Makino Tomitarō, who died in 1957 aged 95. The large greenhouse and fossil gallery, easily spotted since it has a giant model of a tyrannosaurus rex outside, are blots on an otherwise peaceful landscape. The rather more tasteful **Makino Museum of Plants and People** is designed to harmonize with the environment.

Katsurahama

桂浜 • 13km south of Kōchi • Frequent buses head to Katsurahama from Kōchi's Harimaya-bashi (¥610; 40min); buses also leave from beside Kōchi Station

Katsurahama is famous for two things: its beach and the Tosa fighting dogs that compete in mock sumo tournaments. The crescent-shaped beach, though capped off at one end with a picturesque clifftop shrine, is rather pebbly and swimming isn't allowed because of strong currents. Equally, animal lovers will want to give the vicious canine bouts a wide berth. The main reason to come here is to learn more about Kōchi's hero, Sakamoto Ryōma.

Sakamoto Ryōma Memorial Museum

高知県立坂本龍馬記念館, Kochi Kenritsu Sakamoto Ryōma Kinenkan • 830 Urado-shiroyama • Daily 9am–5pm • ¥500 • ☎ 088 841 0001, Ⓦ www.ryoma-kinenkan.jp

The architecturally stunning building which houses the **Sakamoto Ryōma Memorial Museum** is on the headland above Katsurahama beach. Dedicated to local hero Sakamoto (see box opposite), the building uses bold colours and a radical freestanding design for the main exhibition halls. There's a good English pamphlet which helps guide you through the exhibition spaces. Inside, there are state-of-the-art displays using touch screens, as well as many artefacts such as the blood-spotted screen from the room in which Sakamoto was assassinated in Kyoto. If the weather is good, you can walk out onto the top of the building for spectacular views of the Pacific. Down on the beach, there's a large statue of Sakamoto, in an intense pose gazing out to the ocean.

9

ARRIVAL AND INFORMATION

By plane Kōchi Ryoma Airport (☎ 088 863 2906, ⊛ kochiap. co.jp) is a 40min drive east of the city; a bus (¥700) runs at least hourly from the airport to opposite Kōchi Station, while a taxi into the city will cost around ¥4500.

Destinations Fukuoka (3 daily; 50min); Nagoya (2 daily; 1hr); Osaka Itami (8 daily; 40min); Tokyo (8 daily; 1hr 25min).

By train All trains and most buses arrive at Kōchi Station, at the head of Harimaya-bashi-dōri, around 500m north of the city centre.

Destinations Awa Ikeda (14 daily; 1hr 5min); Kotohira (16 daily; 1hr 30min); Nakamura (9 daily; 1hr 50min); Okayama (hourly; 2hr 25min); Takamatsu (5 daily; 2hr 15min).

By bus Most buses arrive at Kōchi Station, just by the train station.

Destinations Okayama (9 daily; 2hr 30min); Osaka (21 daily; 5hr 35min); Takamatsu (14 daily; 2hr 10min); Tokyo (daily; 11hr 40min).

Tourist information Just outside the south exit of Kōchi Station, in a swanky wooden building called the Tosa Terrace, you'll find Kōchi's excellent tourist information centre (daily 8.30am–6pm, hotel information by phone till 7.30pm; ☎ 088 879 5489). Also helpful is the Kōchi International Association (KIA), close to the castle on the second floor of the Marunouchi Biru, 4-1-37 Honmachi (Mon–Sat 8.30am–5.15pm; ☎ 088 875 0022, ⊛ kochi-f.co.jp/kia), which also has a small library of English books and magazines as well as free internet access.

GETTING AROUND

While central Kōchi is easily negotiated on foot, the distances between the major sights make catching a tram or bus a sensible option.

By tram The tram terminus is immediately outside the south exit of Kōchi Station. The system consists of two lines, one running north to south from the station to the port, crossing the east–west tracks at Harimaya-bashi. To travel within the city costs a flat ¥190, paid to the driver on leaving the tram; you'll need to ask for a transfer ticket (*norikae-ken*) when you switch lines at Harimaya-bashi. A one-day ticket covering the central city area costs ¥500; an ¥800 ticket gives you access to everywhere on both lines.

By bus The My-Yu tourist bus leaves from Kōchi station and takes a circular route to Katsurahama and Godai-san. A one-day pass costs ¥1000 and can be purchased from the My-Yu bus ticket office at Tosa Terrace, in front of the station.

Bike rental Bikes are available for ¥500/day from OK Parking (OKパーキング; ☎ 088 871 4689) 100m east of the Sun market site along Otesuji-dōri.

Car rental Try Eki Rent-a-Car ☎ 088 882 3022; Toyota Rent-a-Car ☎ 088 823 0100; or Nissan ☎ 088 883 6444.

ACCOMMODATION

There's the usual cluster of identikit business **hotels** close to the train station. More convenient for the shopping and entertainment districts are the hotels between Dencha-dōri and the city's principal river, Kagami-gawa. If you want to stay by the beach, head for the good *kokuminshukusha* (national lodging house) at Katsurahama (see below).

Joseikan 城西館 2-5-34 Kamimachi ☎ 088 875 0111, ⊛ jyoseikan.co.jp. This elegant ryokan may be housed in a large modern building, but it has a long history and offers top-grade, spacious tatami rooms with service fit for an emperor – which is why he stays here when he visits town. Its public bath is open to non-guests (12–4pm; ¥1000). They also run night "*ozashiki-asobi*" tours introducing traditional entertainment and popular night food stands. Rates include two meals. **¥35,700**

★**Katsuo Guest House** かつおゲストハウス 4-7-28 Kitajima ☎ 070 5352 1167, ⊛ katuo-gh.com. Run by an energetic mother-and-daughter team, this friendly new guesthouse has comfortable rooms (with futons) decorated creatively with the *katsuo* fish (local tuna) theme. There's a share kitchen and lounge area for guests, including free internet access. **¥5000**

Katsurahama-so Kokuminshukusha 桂浜荘国民宿舎 830-25 Urato Shiroyama ☎ 088 841 2201, ⊛ katsurahama.jp. Located 13km south of central

Kōchi, this modern hotel has spectacular views across the beach from its clifftop location and good-value, high-standard tatami rooms. Rate includes two meals. **¥21,420**

Kōchi Youth Hostel 高知ユースホステル 4-5 Fukui Higashi-machi ☎ 088 823 0858, ⊛ kyh-sakenokuni .com. One of Shikoku's best youth hostels, in a modern but rustic-styled building with lots of character. The friendly English-speaking manager used to work in a sake brewery and offers sake-tasting courses after dinner each evening (¥500). You can stay in single rooms or dorms, and the nearest train station is Engyōji, two stops west of Kōchi Station, then a 5min walk. Dorm **¥3885**

Los Inn Kōchi ロスイン高知 2-4-8 Kitahonmachi ☎ 088 884 1110, ⊛ losinn.co.jp. Close to the station, this friendly place has kitsch decor (a mixture of reproduction antiques, heavy leather sofas and 1970s-style chandeliers), an English-speaking manager and comfortable Western- and Japanese-style rooms. Guests may use bicycles for free. ¥6930

Sansuien 三翠園 1-3-35 Takajō-machi ☎088 822 0131, ⓦsansuien.co.jp. Don't judge it by the modern exterior; this ryokan has a refined interior, while the attached traditional gardens and buildings beside the Kagami-gawa add some atmosphere. They also have some slightly cheaper Western-style rooms. The onsen bath complex is also open to non-residents (10am–4pm; ¥900). **¥32,550**

Tosa Bekkan とさ別館 1-11-34 Sakurai-chō ☎088 883 5685. Friendly and relaxed budget minshuku-style hotel. The clean tatami rooms have TV, a/c and toilet, though bathrooms are communal. Meals are available, and there's a coin-operated laundry outside. **¥7600**

EATING AND DRINKING

The best area for **eating** in Kōchi is around the Obiya-machi arcade, although on Wed you find several places closed. The warm weather and a convivial atmosphere mean locals tend to favour the many cheap **yatai** (street stalls) around town, serving oden, ramen, gyōza and beer – a good location on a balmy night is beside the Enokuchi-gawa near the Bowl Jumbo centre. If you want to splash out, try sawachi-ryōri, Kōchi's most refined style of cuisine, featuring lots of fresh seafood dishes, including the famous local tuna, katsuo.

5019 Premium Factory 1-10-21 Obiya-machi ☎088 872 5019, ⓦ5019.co.jp/premium. This laid-back café and wine bar is a great spot to grab a midnight snack. Try the Ryōma Burgers – grilled katsuo patties with Kōchi vegetable salad (¥790), Glasses of wine start at ¥500. 11am–3am Sun till 1am), closed Thurs.

Café de Libro 3F Kōchi Cultural Plaza, 2-1 Kutanda ☎088 882 7750. In the same building as the Yokoyama Ryūichi Memorial Manga Museum (see p.648), this stylish and spacious café serves a good range of light meals, such as pasta and quiche, for around ¥1000, as well as some very tasty desserts and cakes. Tues–Sun 9am–6.30pm.

Habotan 葉牡丹 2-21 Sakaia-machi ☎088 823 8686, ⓦhabotan.jp. Cheerful izakaya serving good local food, such as sashimi-moriawase platters (¥1050) and "stamina" tofu (¥280). Probably the only izakaya in Shikoku that opens for lunch – tuna rice bowls are ¥630 and grilled chicken lunch sets go for ¥750. Daily 11am–11pm.

★ **Hirome Ichiba** ひろめ市場 2-3-1 Obiya-machi ☎088 822 5287. At the end of the Obiya-machi arcade, this lively indoor market has over sixty stalls selling a range of Japanese food, as well as Indian, and Chinese food and even toasted sandwiches. You'll eat well for under ¥1000, and the cheap beer and lively atmosphere mean you may even make a lot of new friends. Daily 8am–11pm, (Sun from 7am).

Issyun 一旬 2-1-3 Harimaya-chō ☎088 824 2030, ⓦissyun.jp. Appealing contemporary izakaya with a long counter bar and discreet nooks. It specializes in sake from around Shikoku as well as local beers and nicely presented seasonal food. Katsuo tuna dishes start at ¥1000, and lunchtime set meals are good value (from ¥340). Daily 11.30am–11pm, Sat & Sun till midnight.

Tokugetsuro 得月楼 1-17-3 Minami Harimaya-chō ☎088 882 0101, ⓦtogetsukyo.jp. This highly traditional restaurant with kimono-clad waitresses and tatami rooms is the place to sample a sawachi-ryōri meal (lunch from ¥6300, dinner ¥8400). The lunch bentō (from ¥2635) are a more affordable option. Bookings essential. Daily 11am–2pm & 5–10pm.

Tosa Ichiba Sushi 土佐市場寿し 5-1 Nijudai-machi ☎088 823 01130. This sushi restaurant is an excellent place to sample the local favourite, katsuo no tataki – seared bonito tuna (¥1200). It's served with salt or ponzu vinegar dipping sauce. Out the front of the restaurant is a BBQ, and you can choose any type of seafood or fish you'd like grilled. Daily 5pm–2am.

BARS AND CLUBS

As the largest city on Shikoku's southern coast, Kōchi attracts many people looking for a night on the town, so it's not short of a **bar** or ten and has a lively atmosphere, especially at weekends. The city's famous drinking street is **Yanagi-machi**, which runs parallel to the Obiya-machi arcade. During summer Kōchi's many yatai and rooftop beer gardens are the ideal places to relax with a cold brew on a sultry night.

Irish Pub Amontillado 1-1-17 Obiya-machi ☎088 875 0599. Owner Shimai-san's fascinating tale of how this Irish bar ended up with a Spanish name trundles on for at least a couple of pints of Guinness or Kilkenny (¥900 a pint). There's decent fish 'n' chips and Irish stew (both ¥800) and occasional live music. Happy Hour runs from 5–8pm. Daily 5pm–1am.

Love Jamaican 3F 1-5-5 Obiya-machi ☎088 872 0447. If you feel like dancing, this hip-hop and reggae bar is the place to mix it up with the locals. The door charge is usually ¥1000. Tues–Sun 10pm–5am.

Verite 2F 1-7-19 Obiyamachi ☎088 873 5560. This cosy cocktail bar offers both standard and original drinks from ¥600, as well as a large range of Belgian Beers from ¥800. Also available are tasty bar snacks from ¥300. 6pm–2am, closed Wed.

SHOPPING

Kōchi is well known as a centre for handmade paper production. The shops listed below are good places to pick up top-quality paper products.

Papier パピエ 2-8-11 Harimaya-chō ☎ 088 880 9185. Kōchi is well-known for its handmade *tosa washi* paper. Papier has a lovely selection of wrapping papers, cards and small paper goods. You can also buy metres of plain or dyed paper. 9am–6pm; closed Tues.

Tencosu てんこす 1-11-40 Obiya-machi ☎ 088 855 5411. This large emporium of Kōchi crafts and food is a great place to pick up souvenirs. Prices are reasonable and there's a good range of cute *tenugui* hand towels and rustic local pottery. Daily 9am–9pm.

DIRECTORY

Banks and exchange Shikoku Bank is on the corner at Harimaya-bashi; there's a branch of Kōchi Bank further west, along Dencha-dōri. Foreign cards can be used in the ATM at the post office next to the JR station (Mon–Fri 7am–11pm, Sat 9am–9pm, Sun 9am–7pm).

Hospital The Red Cross Hospital (☎ 088 822 1202) is behind Kōchi Station.

Internet There's free internet access at the Kōchi

International Association (see p.650). Otherwise, try the *Book Off* café in front of Kōchi station.

Laundry There are coin-operated machines outside the *Tosa Bekkan* (see p.651).

Police The main police station is opposite Kōchi Station. Emergency numbers are listed on p.66.

Post office The main post office is just to the west of Kōchi Station (Mon–Fri 9am–7pm, Sat till 5pm, Sun till 12.30pm).

Western Kōchi-ken

Some of Shikoku's best scenery is in western Kōchi-ken. Inland, you can raft or kayak down the beautiful **Shimantogawa**, while along the indented coast, carved by the savage Pacific Ocean, there are several fishing communities, including **Kuroshio** (黒潮), from where you can take **whale-watching tours** (see box below). The rocky cape at **Ashizuri Misaki**, 180km southwest of Kōchi, with its twisting scenic roads, temple and lush foliage, is well worth the journey.

Shimantogawa

四万十川 • Western Kochi Prefecture

Often claimed to be the last free-flowing river in Japan, the **Shimantogawa** actually has one small dam along its 196km length, though this doesn't detract from the wide river's beauty, winding as it does through green countryside, past pine-clad slopes and terraced rice fields. This is the place to head for tranquil boating, canoeing and fishing.

WHALE-WATCHING TOURS

It's said that the **whaling industry** in Kōchi dates from 1591, when the local *daimyō* Chōsokabe Motochika gifted the warlord Toyotomi Hideyoshi in Osaka a whale and in return received eight hundred bags of rice. Japan and whales have, in recent times, become a **controversial** combination, but along Kōchi-ken's coast few are complaining, as whale-watching tours are replacing the old way of making a living. The best time to see whales is May and August, though the season runs from spring through to autumn. Nothing's guaranteed, but with a good skipper expect to see the large **Bryde's whales** and medium-sized **false killer whales**, as well as schools of white-sided and Risso's **dolphins**.

TOURS

Ōgata Town Leisure Fishing Boats Owners' Association 3573-5 Ukibuchi Kuroshio-chō; ☎ 0880 43 1058, ⊕ nitarikujira.com. Tours typically last 3hr and cost around ¥5000 per person in small boats holding eight to ten people.

SHIMANTOGAWA CANOE TOURS

The best way to enjoy the beautiful **Shimantogawa** is to paddle along its gentle azure-blue waters. There are a number of **boat cruises**, including in the traditional white-sailed Senba boats, which take large groups up and down the river. However, joining a **canoe tour** is both fun and relaxing, and the young Japanese guides are very enthusiastic and helpful for beginners. Depending on weather conditions, tours usually run from April until November. Both full-day and half-day canoeing courses are available, and all equipment is provided. For more details, see Soramil Outdoor Tours (W soramil.co.jp), Canoe Kan (W canoekan.com) and Kawarakko (W kawarakko.com).

ARRIVAL AND INFORMATION
SHIMANTO-GAWA

By train The nearest train station is Ekawasaki (江川崎) on JR's plodding Yodo line, which runs from Kubokawa (窪川) on the bay side of Kōchi-ken, to Uwajima along a very scenic route. In Aug and most weekends March–Nov, you can ride part of the line in open-air carriages (*torroko ressha*).
By bus There are also a few buses (Mon–Sat) to Kuchiyanai from Nakamura on the Tosa Kuroshio train line.

Tourist information The Shimanto City Tourist Information Centre is a 5min walk south of the JR station (daily 8.30am–5.30pm, ☎ 0880 35 4171). The English-speaking staff are very helpful, and there's also a good selection of maps and pamphlets in English.

ACCOMMODATION

Hotel Seira Shimanto ホテル星羅四万十 ☎ 0880 52 2225, W se rashimanto.com. The views from this modern, elegant hotel, located on a hill overlooking the Shimantogawa, are superb. The hotel's relaxing hot spring spa also has great views, and the Japanese and Western-style rooms are tastefully decorated. The in-house restaurant serves sweetfish and shrimp from the river. **¥25,400**

Ashizuri Misaki and around

足摺岬

The tourist trail has beaten a steady path to **ASHIZURI MISAKI**, a friendly village spread thinly around the cape that makes up Shikoku's most southerly point. Pilgrims have long been coming here to pay their respects at picturesque **Kongōfuku-ji** (金剛福寺), the 38th temple on the sacred circuit. Dedicated to the Buddhist deity Kannon, who symbolizes infinite compassion, the temple has a two-storey pagoda and is situated amid a palm grove at the eastern end of the village. Ashizuri's white-painted lighthouse stands atop 80m-high cliffs, while at shore level there's a natural rock arch, crowned by a small shrine. Also at the cape is a stern-looking bronze statue of **John Mung** (see box, p.645), which is a popular photo spot with local tourists. All these sights are within easy walking distance of each other, along clifftop pathways that burst forth with crimson camellia blossoms each February.

John Mung Museum

ジョン万次郎資料館, John Manjirō Shiryōkan • Umi no Eki Ashizuri, Tosa Shimizu (18km from Ashizuri) • Daily 8.30am–5pm • ¥400 • ☎ 0880 82 3155, W johnmung.info • Buses bound for Nakamura or Ashizuri stop at Tosa Shimizu

Nakahama Manjirō, also known as **John Mung** (see box, p.654), was a local lad who travelled the world and pioneered relations between Japan and the USA in the early years of the Meiji Restoration. The interesting John Mung Museum, recently relocated from Ashizuri Misaki to the nearby town of Tosa Shimizu, includes some of Mung's personal possessions, including a recreation of his study in the United States and some fascinating displays on the whaling industry he was once part of.

ARRIVAL AND INFORMATION
ASHIZURI MISAKI

By public transport To reach the cape by public transport, take a train to Nakamura (中村), then transfer to a bus (7 daily; ¥1900; 1hr 45min) directly outside the station. The bus journey becomes progressively more spectacular the closer to the cape you get, the driver whipping the bus around the narrow, cliff-hugging road. The buses all go to Kongōfuku-ji, but most accommodation is closer to Ashizuri's tiny bus station.

9

JOHN MUNG

In the normal course of life, **Nakahama Manjirō**, born in 1827 into a poor family living in Tosa Shimizu, near Ashizuri Misaki, would have lived and died a fisherman. His fortunes changed when he was marooned on an uninhabited volcanic island some 580km south of Tokyo, along with five shipmates. After nearly five months, they were saved by a landing party from a passing US whaling ship, who had come to the island in search of fresh water.

John Mung, as he was nicknamed, ended up serving with the American crew for four years, before returning with the captain, **John Whitfield**, to his home in Bedford, Massachusetts. A bright student, Mung mastered English, mathematics, surveying and navigation, and undertook journeys to Africa, Australia and around southeast Asia. After making some money in the California Gold Rush of 1849, Mung returned to Japan in 1851, where he soon found himself serving as an advisor to the feudal lord of Tosa. Two years later Mung was summoned to Tokyo to assist with the drawing up of international trade treaties, and in 1860 he returned to the US as part of a national delegation.

Before his death in 1898 he taught at the **Kaisei School for Western Learning** in Tokyo (later to become part of the prestigious Tokyo University), sharing the knowledge he had accumulated during a period when Japan was still living in self-imposed isolation from the rest of the world.

By car In your own car, you can opt for the less hair-raising but equally scenic Skyline Rd which runs down the middle of the peninsula to the cape.

Tourist information There's a small information counter at the Ashizuri bus station which can deal with accommodation enquiries, though foreign visitors will most likely be directed to the youth hostel or one of the large hotels.

Services The post office opposite Ashizuri's bus station has an ATM (Mon–Fri 7am–11pm, Sat 9am–9pm, Sun 9am–7pm).

ACCOMMODATION AND EATING

On the second floor of the souvenir shops opposite Kongōfuku-ji there are a few *shokudō* (cafeterias) serving **lunch** as well as tea and coffee. In the evening, it's advisable to organize **dinner** where you are staying.

Ashizuri Kokusai Hotel 足摺国際ホテル 662 Ashizuri Misaki ☎0880 88 0201, ⓦashizuri.co.jp. This fairly standard-looking hotel has fabulous ocean views and plenty of facilities, such as a spa, karaoke room and coin laundry. The Japanese-style rooms are clean and spacious. The food is excellent, and it's worth splashing out on an Ashizuri seafood supper (from ¥8400). **¥58,800**

Ashizuri Thermae 足摺テルメ1433-3 Higashihata Ashizuri Misaki ☎0880 88 0301, ⓦterume.com. This large hotel and spa resort complex offers Western and Japanese-style rooms of a good standard, and has a stylish French restaurant. The hotel has a number of terraces and observation decks designed to help you enjoy the panoramic views of the Pacific. **¥16,700**

Ashizuri Youth Hostel あしずりユースホステル 1351-3 Ashizuri Misaki ☎0880 88 0324. This basic but friendly and relaxed hostel is next to a small shrine, and it's the best budget option for the area. Accommodation is in small, clean tatami dorms and meals are available if you reserve in advance. Dorm **¥3360**

Uwajima and around
宇和島

From Sukumo, Route 56 continues through countryside before emerging on the coast. The cliff-side road, passing though small fishing communities, provides unforgettable

WAREI TAISAI

The major festival of **Warei Taisai**, held at the shrine of **Warei-jinja** from the evening of July 22 to July 24, involves huge models of devil bulls (*ushi-oni*) being paraded in the streets, along with ornate portable shrines, the aim being to dispel evil. The bulls, like giant pantomime horses, eventually do battle in the river, while at the shrine there's much banging of *taiko*, bonfire burning and a fireworks finale.

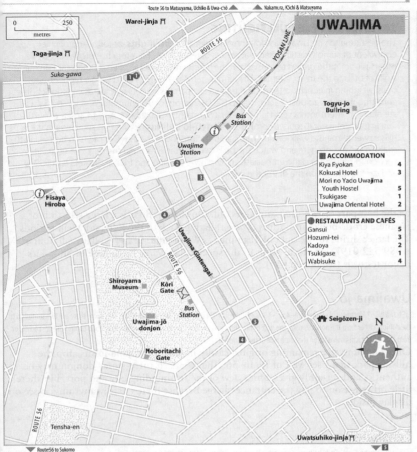

UWAJIMA

Route 56 to Matsuyama, Uchiko & Uwa-chō ▲   ▲ Nakamura, Kōchi & Matsuyama

Warei-jinja 🛕

ROUTE 56

YOSAN LINE

Taga-jinja 🛕

Suka-gawa

Togyu-jo
Bullring

Bus
Station

Uwajima
Station

Hisaya
Hiroba

Uwajima Gintengai

ROUTE 56

Shiroyama
Museum

Kōri
Gate

Bus
Station

Uwajima-jō
donjon

Seigōzen-ji

Noboritachi
Gate

ROUTE 56

Tensha-en

Uwatsuhiko-jinja 🛕

Route 56 to Sukomo ▼   ▼ 5

ACCOMMODATION	
Kiya Ryokan	4
Kokusai Hotel	3
Mori no Yado Uwajima	
Youth Hostel	5
Tsukigase	1
Uwajima Oriental Hotel	2

RESTAURANTS AND CAFÉS	
Gansui	5
Hozumi-tei	3
Kadoya	2
Tsukigase	1
Wabisuke	4

views of the deep-blue sea, carpeted with nets held up by a crisscross network of buoys. Pearls are cultivated here, and at the port of **UWAJIMA**, 67km north of Sukomo, there are plenty of shops selling them. The town's main sights – which include a **castle** and a **fertility shrine** – can be seen easily in half a day, though it's worth staying a night and using Uwajima as a base from which to explore the small country town of Uwa-chō (see p.658) to the north.

Taga-jinja

多賀神社 • 1340 Fujie • Sex museum daily 8am–5pm • ¥800 • ☎ 089 522 3444, ☞ www3.ocn.ne.jp/~dekoboko • A 10min walk north of the JR station, across the Suka-gawa

Uwajima's most provocative attraction, the fertility shrine **Taga-jinja**, is set back from the Suka-gawa in a small compound packed with various statues, most of which are stone or log phalluses. The attached **sex museum**, spread over three floors of a bland modern building, is wall-to-wall erotica, with display cases packed with all manner of sexual objects, literature and art. On the ground floor is a collection of Japanese fertility symbols and figurines dating back centuries, including an ivory *netsuke* collection. The first floor holds similar objects from around the world, including displays devoted to Tibet, India, Europe and elsewhere; some exhibits are claimed to

9

JAPANESE-STYLE BULLFIGHTING

The best time to visit Uwajima is for one of its bloodless **bullfights**, or *tōgyū*, the bovine equivalent of sumo wrestling. Some accounts date the sport back four hundred years, while others pinpoint the origins to an event in the nineteenth century, when a Dutch captain made a gift of bulls to the town, after local fishermen came to his ship's aid during a typhoon. The bulls, weighing in at up to a tonne and treated like pampered pets by their owners, lock horns and struggle either to push each other to the floor or out of the tournament ring. The fights are held five afternoons a year (Jan 2, the first Sunday in April, July 24, Aug 14 and the fourth Sun in Oct; details at ⓦ tougyu.com) at the **Tōgyū-jō Bullring**, a white-walled arena in the hills a twenty-minute walk east of the JR train station, above the city. Get there an hour early to soak up the atmosphere and watch the bulls being paraded around the ring. The bouts are very good-natured and the enthusiastic crowd is welcoming and friendly. Tickets cost ¥3000 and can be bought on the day at the arena.

be the best part of two thousand years old. On the top floor is a large selection of Japanese erotic books and prints (*shunga*) dating back to the Edo and Meiji periods. The larger shrine to the right of Taga-jinja is **Warei-jinja** (和霊神社; daily, all hours; ☎089 522 0197), the focal point of the spectacular Warei Taisai, one of Shikoku's major festivals (see box, p.654).

Uwajima-jō

宇和島城 • 1 Marunouchi • Daily 9am–4pm • ¥200 • ☎089 524 1111 • A 15min walk south of the JR station; there are two routes up to the donjon, either from the north through the gate of the Kōri samurai family, tucked back from the main road behind the post office, or from the Noboritachi-mon gate on the south side of the castle hill

Only one of twelve remaining original castles in Japan, **Uwajima-jō** sits atop the hillside park that rises west of Route 56. The compact, three-storey donjon may be authentic, and certainly gives a fine view of the surrounding city and port, but there's little other reason to pay the entrance charge because there's hardly anything to see on display inside.

Tensha-en

天赦園 • Tensha Kōen • Daily 8.30am–5pm, July–March till 4.30pm • ¥300 • ☎089 525 2709

A short walk south of the castle park is the small formal garden of **Tensha-en**. Dating from 1866, the pretty garden is laid out in circular style with a feature made of a wisteria trellis over a pond. Nearby, you can also explore the narrow residential streets immediately southeast of the centre. Here shrines, temples and graveyards are huddled on the slopes leading up to the *Mori no Yado Uwajima Youth Hostel* (see opposite). Even if you're not staying at the hostel, the hill is worth climbing for sweeping views of the town.

ARRIVAL AND INFORMATION
UWAJIMA

By train Uwajima Station is the terminus for both the JR Yodo line running from Kubokawa and the JR Yosan line from Matsuyama.
Destinations Kubokawa (6 daily; 2hr 20min); Matsuyama (14 daily; 1hr 25min).

By bus Buses to and from Sukumo stop in front of Uwajima Station as well as at the main bus centre at the foot of the castle hill on Route 56.
Destinations Matsuyama (15 daily; 2hr 20min); Sukumo (11 daily; 2hr).

Tourist information Inside the JR station is a small tourist information booth (daily 9am–6pm). The Uwajima Sightseeing Information Centre at Kisaya Hiroba, near the port, is staffed with English-speakers and has English maps and pamphlets for the area (9am–5pm; ☎089 522 3934).

Services You can change money at Iyo Bank just off the Gintengai, and there's an ATM at the main post office near the Kōri Gate to the castle. Out of hours, the convenience store next to the Uwajima Oriental Hotel has a 24-hour ATM.

GETTING AROUND

By bike Renting a bike to get around is a good idea; the information booth at the station (see opposite) can help arrange bicycle rental (¥100/hr).

ACCOMMODATION

There are several **hotels** near the station and even more towards the port area; the **youth hostel** is a little further away, in Atago Park.

★**Kiya Ryokan** 木屋旅館 2-8-2 Oute-Honmachi ☏089 522 0101, ⊛kiyaryokan.com. The chance to spend the night in the stylishly restored Meiji-era Kiya Ryokan is a good reason to stay in Uwajima. More of a boutique hotel than a traditional ryokan, you'll have the place to yourself, and the staff only appear at breakfast time. There are three gorgeous guest rooms, sleeping up to eight in total between them, as well as a library and living room. **¥26,250**

Kokusai Hotel 国際ホテル 4-1 Nishiki-machi ☏089 525 0111, ⊛uwajima-kokusaihotel.jp. Close to the station, this friendly and traditional hotel offers large, well-appointed Japanese rooms, as well as some Western-style rooms with outlandish 1970s decor. **¥14,600**

Mori no Yado Uwajima Youth Hostel 森の宿宇和島ユースホステル Atago-kōen ☏089 522 7177, ⊛www2 .odn.ne.jp/~cfm91130. The building's a bit dreary, but the views on the way up the hill and the friendly reception from the young, English-speaking couple who run the place make the hike worth the effort. There's a pool table, a treehouse and free bike rental. The hostel is at the top of a steep hill, a 20min walk south of the JR station. If you're carrying heavy luggage, it's best to take a taxi there (around ¥1000) or ask the manager to pick you up. Dorm **¥2100**, double **¥7000**

Tsukigase 月ヶ瀬 1-5-6 Miyukimachi ☏089 522 4788, ⊛sanyukai.sakura.ne.jp/tsukigase.html. This old-fashioned ryokan is a little quirky, but the rooms are spacious and well kept, and there's a fine attached restaurant, Tsukigase (see below), and a rooftop communal bath. Rates are substantially cheaper on weekdays and include two meals. **¥16,700**

Uwajima Oriental Hotel 宇和島オリエンタルホテル 6-10 Tsurushima-chō ☏089 523 2828, ⊛oriental-web.co.jp/uwajima This stylish business hotel, a few minutes' walk from the station, has comfortable rooms and discount rates. At check-in, you'll be offered the luxury of a pillow menu. There's a decent restaurant, internet access, and they offer free use of a bicycle for three hours. Rates are slightly cheaper at the weekend. **¥10,500**

EATING AND DRINKING

Not surprisingly for a port, Uwajima offers ample opportunity to eat **fresh fish** – two popular dishes are *taimeshi* (sashimi of sea bream on top of hot rice) and *satsuma-jiru* (strips of fish mixed with a white miso sauce and eaten with rice). For cheap lunch options and cafés, explore Uwajima Gintengai shopping arcade.

CAFÉS AND RESTAURANTS

Gansui 丸水 2-3-10 Honmachi Ote ☏089 522 3636, ⊛gansui.jp. *Gansui* is an upmarket *izakaya* east of the Gintengai, with a picture menu and daily set dishes from as little as ¥1000. It's known for its *taimeshi*. 11am–2pm & 5–8.30pm; closed Tues.

Hozumi-tei ほづみ亭 2-3-8 Shin-machi ☏089 522 0041, ⊛hozumitei.com. An appealingly rustic fish restaurant with tables and tatami seating areas overlooking a stream. An evening meal will cost around ¥2000. Mon–Sat 11am–1 30pm & 5–9.40pm.

★**Kadoya** かどや Tsurushi-machi ☏089 522 1543, ⊛kadoya-ta meshi.com. With reasonable prices and friendly service, this is one of the best places in town to sample seafood dishes, including *taimeshi*, with various set menus for around ¥1500. There's also a useful picture menu. Mon–Sat 11am–2.30pm & 5–9pm, Sun 11am–9pm.

Tsukigase 月ヶ瀬 1-5-6 Miyuki-machi ☏089 522 4788. Bamboo grows in the centre of this restaurant specializing in *fugu* (in winter) and tempura. Set lunch starts from as low as ¥790, and their *satsuma-jiru* meal is ¥1500. Daily 11am–10.30pm.

Wabisuke 和日輔 1-2-6 Ebisu-chō ☏089 524 0028. This large restaurant near the castle combines traditional decor with a friendly welcome and a range of set meals, including sashimi sets, soba, udon and *kamameshi* (a kind of pilaf). Lunches are available from ¥840. Mon–Sat 11am–2pm & 5–9.30pm, Sun 11am–9.30pm.

North of Uwajima

Between Uwajima and Matsuyama are three appealing small towns – **Uwa-chō**, **Ozu** and **Uchiko**. They are interesting places to explore, mainly for their preserved streetscapes which evoke Edo-and-Meiji period Japan. All three places can easily be visited in a day via train.

Uwa-chō

宇和町

Less than 20km north of Uwajima, the small country town of **UWA-CHŌ** with its lovely traditional townscape and excellent museum makes a very pleasant half-day trip from Uwajima. As a plus, large tour groups don't stop here, so there are few crowds.

Museum of Ehime History and Culture

愛媛県歴史文化博物館, Ehime-Kan Rekishi Sunkd Hakubutsukan • 4-11-2 Uno-machi • Tues–Sun 9am–5.30pm • ¥500, English audio guide ¥200 • ⓣ 089 562 6222, ⓦ i-rekihaku.jp • The museum can be reached by an infrequent bus (¥150) from the stop about a 5min walk south of the JR Uno-machi Station, along Route 56; to walk up the hill to the museum takes around 20min

Uwa-chō's highlight is the outstanding **Museum of Ehime History and Culture**. Inside this ultra-modern building that sticks out from the hillside is ample space for the spectacular and informative displays inside, which include full-sized **replicas of buildings**, including a Yayoi-era (330 BC to 300 AD) hut, a street of Meiji-era shops and a small wooden temple. In the centre of the museum is a **folklore exhibit**, which includes examples of the fabulous portable shrines, costumes and other decorations used in local festivals, such as Uwajima's Warei Taisai (see box, p.654). There's also an interesting display on the Shikoku Pilgrimage. The audioguide in English is essential, as all the display explanations are in Japanese. The museum's café is a good place to have lunch.

Kaimei School

開明学校, Kaimei Gattō • 3-106 Uno-machi • Tues–Sun 9am–5pm • ¥200 (or ¥400 combined ticket with Uwa Folkcraft Museum, Rice Museum and Memorial Museum of Great Predecessors) • ⓣ 089 462 4292

Uwa-chō's street of well-preserved, white-walled houses is known as **Naka-chō**, which is also the name given to this part of town. Some of the buildings date from the Edo the period and most have been maintained in top condition, making it another reason to visit the town. Along here is the **Kaimei School**, a lovely example of a Meiji-period school and one of the oldest remaining in western Japan. Founded in 1882, the architectural style is considered to be Western-influenced. Inside, there's a fascinating collection of antique textbooks and education posters.

Uwa Folkcraft Museum

宇和町民具館, Uwa-machi Mingu-kan • Uwa-chō Mingu-kan • Tues–Sun 9am–5pm • ¥200 (or ¥400 combined ticket with Kaimei School, Rice Museum and Memorial Museum of Great Predecessors) • ⓣ 089 362 1334

Opposite the old schoolhouse is the **Uwa Folkcraft Museum**, with a well-organized exhibition that contains a wide range of interesting items that were once in daily use in the town. There are bamboo swords and deer costumes used in local festivals, as well as old record players and dioramas depicting life during the Edo period.

ARRIVAL AND INFORMATION — UWA-CHŌ

By train The JR train station for Uwa-chō is Uno-machi (卯之町), less than 20min from Uwajima by the hourly limited express.

Tourist information You can pick up a simple map-cum-guide to the town's sites in English from the Uwa Folkcraft Museum (see above).

Ōzu

大洲

Further north along the Yosan line from Uwa-chō the train hits the coast at **Yawatahama** (八幡浜), before turning inland to reach **ŌZU** on the banks of the

9

Hiji-kawa. The town's billing as a mini-Kyoto is exaggerated and inaccurate; Ōzu has its own charms and unique townscape. From June 1 to September 20, the river is the location for **ukai** – fishing with cormorants (see box, p.402). To view the display from a boat costs ¥3000; for bookings call Ōzu tourist office (see below).

Ōzu-jō

大洲城 • 903 Ōzu • Daily 9am–4.30pm • ¥500, or ¥800 with entry to Garyū Sansō • ☏ 089 324 1146

The picturesque **Ōzu jō** is in a commanding position overlooking the town and river. Destroyed in 1888, the four-storey donjon of this fortress was rebuilt in 2004 to its original sixteenth-century specifications. Apart from getting a more elevated view, the other reason to go inside is to admire the authentic reconstruction. The grounds are a riot of pink in cherry-blossom season, and locals flock here for picnics, day and night.

Garyū Sansō

臥龍山荘 • 411-2 Ōzu • Daily 9am–4.30pm • ¥500 or ¥800 with entry to Ōzu jō • ☏ 089 324 3759

Along the river from Ōzu jō, on the other side of the town is the **Garyū Sansō**, a beautiful example of a traditional villa built in the *sukiya kenchiku* architectural style with a triangular thatched roof. Exquisitely detailed woodcarvings and fixtures inside are matched by a lovely moss-and-stone garden outside leading to a teahouse and a separate moon-viewing platform overlooking the river.

Ōzu Aka-renga-kan

おおず赤煉瓦館 • 60 Ōzu • Daily 9am–5pm • Free • ☏ 089 324 2664

Worth a look before leaving the town is the gallery, gift shop and café in the **Ōzu Aka-renga-kan**, a handsome red-brick complex dating from 1901 and once used as a bank. The architectural style is significant because it combines Western-style brickwork with a Japanese-style tiled roof. Inside, the high ceilings and large windows contrast markedly with the traditional Japanese interiors.

ARRIVAL AND INFORMATION   ŌZU

By train Ōzu is 40min by express train from either Uwajima or Mastuyama. The town's train station, Iyo Ōzu (伊予大洲), is around 2km northwest of the Hiji-kawa and the castle.

By ferry At Yawatahama (八幡浜) there are ferries to Beppu (6 daily; 2hr 50min) and Usuki in Kyūshū (7 daily; 2hr 25min).

Tourist information The tourist information centre (daily 8.30am–5pm, though sometimes open earlier till later; ☏ 0893 24 2664) is in the Michi no Eki Asamoya complex on the south side of Ōzu. You can pick up an excellent local guide-cum-map in English from here, as well as rent bicycles between 9am and 5pm (¥400/2hr). You can also buy a bentō lunchbox and other snacks here.

Uchiko

内子

A trip to Ōzu can easily be combined with a visit to the appealing small town of **UCHIKO**, about 15km northeast. Uchiko was once an important centre for the production of Japanese **wax** (*moku-rō*), made from the crushed berries of the sumac tree. The wax is still used in candles, polishes, crayons, cosmetics, food and even computer disks. The wealth generated by the industry has left Uchiko with many fine houses preserved in the picturesque **Yōkaichi** (八日市) district of the town, where craftsmen can still be seen making candles by hand. Recently, Uchiko has become a popular destination for both domestic and international visitors, mainly due to its handsome streetscapes, which are reminiscent of old Japan.

Uchiko-za

内子座 • 2102 Uchiko • Tues–Sun 9am–4.30pm • ¥300 (or ¥720 combined ticket for all museums in town) • ☎ 089 344 2840

The best place to start your tour of Uchiko – which is easily explored on foot – is at the handsomely restored kabuki theatre **Uchiko-za**, which lies around 500m northeast of the train station. Performances are held once or twice a week at the theatre, which was built in 1916 to celebrate the accession of the Emperor Taishō; during the day you can wander around the auditorium and stage.

Museum of Commercial and Domestic Life

商いと暮らし博物館, Akinai-to-Kurashi Hakubutsukan • Daily 9am–4.30pm • ¥200 (or ¥720 combined ticket for all museums in town)
• ☎ 089 344 5220

The **Museum of Commercial and Domestic Life** is set in a charmingly converted merchant's house, with mechanical talking wax dummies that help show the daily life of a shopkeeper during the Taishō era (1912–26). The mannequins, electronically activated to start speaking (in Japanese), include a moaning pharmacist in the upstairs storeroom. Make sure to pick up an English pamphlet at the door.

Takahashi Residence

高橋邸, Takahashi-bei • 2403 Uchiko • Daily except Tues 9am–4.30pm • Free • ☎ 089 344 2354

If you're planning on heading northwest uphill into the **Yōkaichi** district, take a detour towards the Oda-gawa to admire the venerable **Takahashi Residence**, the birthplace of Takahashi Ryūtarō, a politician and founder of the Asahi Beer company. The elegant two-storey building with castle-like stone walls has a lovely garden which you can admire from the café inside.

Omura and Hon-Haga Residences

大村家 • 本芳我邸 • South end of Yōkaichi historical district • Free • Both residences can only be viewed from outside

The two most picturesque buildings in the town are the **Ōmura Residence**, the Edo-era home of a dye-house merchant, and the neighbouring **Hon-Haga Residence**, home of the main family behind Uchiko's wax industry. The Hon-Haga residence is more elaborate than the other houses in the district, with ornate gables, a facade decorated with intricate plaster sculptures, and a small, attractive garden.

ARRIVAL AND INFORMATION   UCHIKO

By train Uchiko is 10min by express train north along the Yosan line from Ōzu. The fastest train to Uchiko from Uwajima takes 1hr and from Matsuyama takes 25min. JR offers a handy ¥2700 day-pass ticket covering Matsuyama, Uchiko and Ōzu.

By bus Several buses a day run from Matsuyama (1hr), Ōzu (20min) and Uwajima (50min), stopping a couple of hundred metres to the east of Yōkaichi.

Tourist information There's a tourist information centre at the train station (☎ 089 343 1450) with English maps and pamphlets. The Uchiko Visitor Centre (daily except Thurs 9am–5.30pm, Oct–March till 4.30pm; ☎ 0893 44 3790, ⌘ we-love-uchiko.jp) is staffed by English-speakers and has more detailed information on the town.

GETTING AROUND

By bike Bicycle rental is available at the train station (daily 9.30am–5pm; ¥300/hr).

By bus An old-fashioned bus shuttles back and forth from the station to Yōkaichi (Fri–Sun; ¥300 a trip or ¥2000 for a one-day pass).

Information If you plan to enter all the buildings and museums around town, a small saving can be made by purchasing the ¥700 combination ticket from Uchiko-za, the Japanese Wax Museum and Kamihaga Residence (north end of Yōkaichi; ☎ 0893 44 2771) or the Museum of Commercial and Domestic Life.

9

Matsuyama and around

松山

Historic **MATSUYAMA**, with a population of over 450,000, is Shikoku's largest city and has a fascinating cultural heritage. Despite its size, Matsuyama is a convivial, friendly place that's easy to get around, thanks to a tram network that bestows an old-fashioned grace to a city that also proudly promotes its literary connections (see box below). Most points of interest are centred on the impressive castle, **Matsuyama-jō**, and the popular hot-spring suburb of **Dōgo**, 2km east of the centre, home to one of Japan's most magnificent bathhouses.

Local warlords from the **Kono clan** built a fortress in Dōgo in the fourteenth century, while Matsuyama was created in 1602 by *daimyō* Katō Yoshiakira when he built his castle on Katsuyama Hill. In 1635, the **Matsudaira clan** took charge of the castle and ruled the area until the **Meiji Restoration** in 1868. Rebuilt following the drubbing it received during **World War II**, this largely modern city is now the capital of Ehime-ken and has expanded to encompass the once separately administered Dōgo.

You can see Matsuyama's main sights in a day, but it's better to give yourself an extra day or two to savour the relaxed mood induced by Dōgo's onsen. The city is also a good base for day-trips to Uchiko, Ōzu and Uwajima.

Matsuyama-jō

松山城 • 1 Marunochi • Daily: March–July & Sept–Nov 9am–5pm; Aug 9am–5.30pm; Dec–Jan 9am–4.30pm • ¥500; ropeway and chairlift ¥260 each way, ¥500 return • ☎ 089 5921 4873, ⓦ matsuyamajo.jp

The 132m-high Katsuyama dominates the centre of Matsuyama, and on its summit stands the city's prime attraction, **Matsuyama-jō**. Warlord Katō Yoshiakira began building his fortress in 1602, but by the time it was finished, 26 years later, he had moved to Aizu in Tōhoku. Like many Japanese castles hailed as "original", this one has gone through several incarnations during its lifetime. The main five-storey donjon was destroyed by lightning on New Year's Day in 1784 and rebuilt two storeys shorter in 1820 – the three lesser donjons are all modern-day reconstructions. Despite this, the

---

MASAOKA SHIKI

Matsuyama heavily promotes its Japanese literary connections, and one of the most prominent is with the poet **Masaoka Shiki**, a rather tragic figure who died at 35 from tuberculosis. He took his pen name, Shiki, from that of a bird, which – according to legend – coughs blood as it sings. His life story can be traced at the **Shiki Kinen Museum** in Dōgo (see p.667) and there are two houses connected with the poet preserved as tourist attractions in Matsuyama, including the villa he shared for a short period with **Sōseki Natsume**, one of Japan's most famous authors, whose novel *Botchan* draws on his experiences as a young teacher working in Matsuyama in 1895.

Masaoka made his reputation by encouraging reforms to the then hidebound traditional poetic form **haiku**, which comprises just three lines of five, seven and five syllables and has a subject matter traditionally connected with the seasons. Famously criticizing the master of the genre, Bashō, Masaoka advocated that poets be allowed to use whatever words they wanted for haiku, on any subject matter, while striving to be more reflective of real life. Encapsulating his approach is one of his most famous poems: *"Kaki kueba kane-ga narunari Hōryū-ji"* ("I was eating a persimmon. Then, the bell of Hōryū-ji temple echoed far and wide").

Masaoka is also one of the principal characters in *Saka no Ue no Kumo* (*Clouds Over the Hill*) by Shiba Ryōtarō, a bestseller about Japan's destruction of the Baltic fleet during the Russo-Japanese War, and Japan's modernization. *Saka no Ue no Kumo* was recently filmed as an NHK TV drama series, and has been translated into English. The novel and its heroes are celebrated at the modern **Saka no Ue no Kumo Museum Kinen Museum** (see p.664).

9

▲ Dōgo

■ Prefectural Cultural Centre

EPIC (i)

Minami-machi

N

■ ACCOMMODATION	
Abis Inn	1
ANA Hotel Matsuyama	3
Check Inn Matsuyama	5
International Hotel Matsuyama	2
Hotel JAL City Matsuyama	4

■ BARS AND CLUBS	
Flankey Kobayashi	2
Underground Café	1

● RESTAURANTS AND CAFÉS	
Café Marinecco	3
Charlie's Vegetable	2
Everest Food	9
Fujiko Michael	5
Goshiki Sōmen Morikawa	10
Kawasemi	6
Kingyotei	7
Kushihide	8
Provence Dining	4
Sova Sova	1

● SHOPPING	
Ehimeism Lublu Matsuyama	1
Tobe-yaki Kankō Centre	2

Iyo Ichinoie

Keisatsuho-mae

Katsuyama-chō

KATSUYAMA-DŌRI

Heiwa-dōri 1-chōme

Sekijuji Byōin-mae

HEIWA-DŌRI

Teppō-chō

Shinonome-jinja

Ropeway & Chairlift Entrance

MAKANOKAWA-DŌRI

KATSUYAMA-DŌRI

ICHIBANCHŌ-DŌRI

Katsuyama-chō

Okaidō

NIBANCHŌ-DŌRI

SANBANCHŌ-DŌRI

Matsuyama-jō

Katsu-yama

Bansui-Sō

Saka-no-Ue-no-Kumo Museum

Ichiban-chō

OKAIDŌ

Okaidō Cinema Sunshine

NAKANOKAWA-DŌRI

▶ Tobe (13km)

Kenchō-mae

Ninomaru Shiseki Teien

Ehime Prefectural Office

NTT

Shiyakusho-mae

Matsuyama City Hall

Cinema Lunatic

HEIWA-DŌRI

Honmachi 4-chōme

Honmachi 3-chōme

Minami-Horibata

Gintengai Arcade

Shoshu-ji

Shiki-dō

Komachi

Nishi-Horibata

Matsuyama Shimin Kaikan

NHK

COMS Matsuyama International Centre & Internet

Matsuyama Shieki-mae

Matsuyama City Station trains & buses

RCUTE 56

Shieki & Takashimaya Department Store

RCUTE 56

▶ Uwajima

Miyata-chō

Ōtemachi

SANBANCHŌ-DŌRI

JR Ekimae

Matsuyama Station

MATSUYAMA

▶ Matsuyama Airport, Uchiko & Uwajima

▼ Okayama & Takamatsu

0 — 250 metres

▶ ② (13km) & Takamatsu

9

castle is one of Japan's more impressive fortresses, and its location certainly provides commanding views of the city and Inland Sea.

You can get up to the castle using the ropeway or rickety chairlift on the eastern flank of the hill. There are also several steep walking routes, the main one starting just beside the ropeway, at the steps up to **Shinonome-jinja** (東雲神社), also on Katsuyama's east side. This picturesque shrine is famous for its Takigi festival, held every April, when nō plays are performed by the light of fire torches. Other routes run up the west side of the hill, and can be combined with a visit to the Ninomaru Shiseki Teien (see below). Whichever route you take, you'll end up at the Tonashi-mon gateway to the castle, through which you emerge onto a long plateau surrounded by walls and turrets and planted with blossom trees. Inside the main donjon, climb up to the **top floor** for the view and, on the way down, pass through the **museum** which has displays of calligraphy, old maps, samurai armour and some gorgeously painted screens.

Ninomaru Shiseki Teien

二之丸史跡庭園 • 5 Marunouchi • Daily: Feb–July & Sept–Nov 9am–5pm; Aug 9am–5.30pm; Dec–Jan 9am–4.30pm • ¥100 • ☎ 089 921 2000

On the western side of the castle slope of Matsuyama-jō are the tranquil gardens of the **Ninomaru Shiseki Teien**. The gardens which look a bit like a giant geometry puzzle, are built on the site of the Ninomaru, the outer citadel of the castle. The pools and pathways at the front of the gardens represent the floor plan of the former structure, which succumbed to fire in 1872. To the rear, as the grounds climb Katsuyama, the design becomes more fluid, and there are rockeries, a waterfall and two teahouses, one of which serves tea and *wagashi* (a sweet cake) for ¥300.

Saka no Ue no Kumo Museum

坂の上の雲ミュージアム • 3-20 Ichiban-chō • Tues–Sun 9am–6pm • ¥400; English audioguide ¥200 • ☎ 089 915 2600, ⓦ www.sakanouenokumomuseum.jp

At the base of the south side of the castle hill is the modern **Saka no Ue no Kumo Museum**, devoted to the famous novel by Shiba Ryōtarō (see box, p.662). The museum is housed in a highly contemporary polished concrete-and-glass building designed by Andō Tadao. The displays, which focus on many fascinating aspects of the Meiji period and Shiba's novel, are all in Japanese. Thankfully, there is a superb **audio guide** in English which takes you through the museum's exhibition rooms, making this well worth a visit. Be aware that the gentleman in the Imperial military uniform who hangs around the front gate for photo opportunities is not officially employed by the museum.

Bansui-sō

萬翠荘 • 3-3-7 Ichiban-chō • Tues–Sun 9am–6pm • ¥300 • ☎ 089 921 3711

The Saka no Ue no Kumo Museum contrasts nicely with the striking French-style villa, **Bansui-sō**, a little further up the hill. Built in 1922 for Count Sadakoto Hisamatsu, the fifteenth lord of Matsuyama-jō, the villa now houses the **Annexe of the Prefectural Art Museum**. It's no longer possible to go inside, but it's the exterior of the building which is most impressive, particularly the juxtaposition of trees pruned like poodles and the wild palms in the forecourt.

Shiki-dō

子規堂 • 16-3 Suehiro-machi • Daily 8.30am–5pm • ¥50 • ☎ 089 945 0400

South of the Iyo Tetsudō rail line is the **Shiki-dō**, an evocative re-creation of the poet

Masaoka Shiki's (see box p.662) **childhood home** sandwiched between his family's local temple, Shoshu-ji, and the cemetery (where there's a memorial to the poet). Inside the tiny one-storey house, which you can enter, are some of his personal effects, his writing desk and examples of his calligraphy. It's rather dusty in places but, thanks to the photographs and other memorabilia, it's easy to imagine something of the life of the nineteenth-century poet.

Raikō-ji

来迎寺 • 1-525 Miyuki • Daily dawn till dusk • Free • Raiko-ji is a 15min walk northeast of the Takasago-chō tram stop

In the Yamagoe district lie a number of temples whose purpose it was to defend the area immediately to the north of the castle. The most worthy of a visit is **Raikō-ji**, originally located in Dōgo but reconstructed in its present location in the eighteenth century.

Russian Cemetery

ロシア人の墓地, Rashia-jin no Bochi • 1 Goko • Daily dawn till dusk

Beside Raikō-ji, up a steep incline, is the so-called **Russian Cemetery**. Some six thousand Russian prisoners were interned at the POW camp here during the Russo-Japanese War of 1904–5. The prisoners – being something of a novelty and having little chance of escaping back to Russia – were allowed a fair amount of freedom. Ninety-eight prisoners died from natural causes during their imprisonment, and their graves are still kept immaculate, with fresh flowers regularly placed in front of each of the crosses. An impressive commemorative bust of a fierce-looking, bearded Russian officer stands watch at the entrance to the cemetery.

Dōgo

道後 • 15min by tram from JR Matsuyama Station

Like many other places in Matsuyama, **DŌGO** onsen has a literary history and a reputation for high-quality hot-spring water. Like many other onsen towns in Japan, it has a seedy side, as well as an over-abundance of tacky souvenir shops. However,

---

DŌGO ONSEN'S CULTURAL HERITAGE

"If you went first class, for only 8 sen they lent you a bathrobe, an attendant washed you, and a girl served you tea in one of those elegant, shallow cups that they use in the tea ceremony. I always went first class."

Botchan, by Sōseki Natsume, 1906

It may no longer be so cheap, nor do the attendants scrub your back, but a bath at the grand **Dōgo Onsen Honkan** is still a treat, as Sōseki lovingly described in his classic novel, set in Matsuyama in the early twentieth century. This is the oldest **hot-spring** resort in Japan, and is mentioned in the 1300-year-old history book the Nihon-shoki. According to legend, a white **heron** dipped its injured leg into the hot water gushing out of the rocks and found that it had healing properties. By the sixth century, the onsen's fame reached the ears of Prince Shotoku, and his royal patronage cemented its reputation. By the seventeenth century, the local *daimyō* Matsudaira Sadayuki had **segregated** the baths into those for monks and samurai, and those for lower-class merchants and craftsmen. He also introduced women-only baths and created facilities for animals to soak away their ills (the animal baths were only closed in 1966).

The present architectural extravaganza was built in 1894 and the heron, which has become the symbol of the baths, is commemorated in a statue atop the three-story building's ornate roof. Inside, there are two types of bath, plus the Yushinden, a special bath built in 1899 for the Imperial family, but now drained of water.

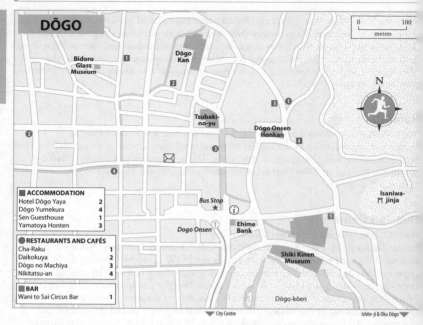

Dōgo's bathtime delights more than make up for this. Once you've sampled the **onsen**, there are also a couple of interesting museums to explore, along with the appealing **Isaniwa-jinja** shrine and over-the-top **Ishite-ji** temple.

Dōgo Onsen Honkan

道後温泉本館 • 5-6 Dōgo Yuno-machi • **Kami-no-yu bath** (神の湯) Daily 6am–10.30pm • ¥400; upgrade ¥800 **Tama-no-yu bath** (霊の湯) Daily 6am–9pm • ¥1200 **Private bath** Daily 6am–8.40pm • ¥1500 **Yushinden** (又新殿) Daily 6am–9pm • ¥250; the extra fee is waived if you've opted for the Tama-no-yu bath • ☎ 089 921 5141

The cheapest way to soak at **Dōgo Onsen Honkan** is to use the rather raucous **Kami-no-yu**, or "Hot Water of the Gods", a section with two identical baths, decorated with mosaics of the heron, on each side of the changing rooms. For an extra fee you can relax afterwards in the second-floor public room, where you'll be served green tea and rice crackers, and you also get to borrow a cotton *yukata* robe. The next level up is the **Tama-no-yu** or "Hot Water of the Spirits", a more exclusive bath at the back of the complex. There's a view of a small garden from the changing room, and you relax afterwards in a separate section on the second floor. The first-class experience recommended by the title character of *Botchan* entitles you to a **private room** on the third floor, where you'll be offered green tea and three-coloured *dango* (sweet rice-dough balls on a stick) after your dip.

Even if you opt for the no-frills bath, the staff will allow you to explore the rest of the building. On the second floor, look out for a display of tea-ceremony items and old calligraphy scrolls to the side of the large tatami resting-room with carved wooden verandas. On the third floor, the corner room has a small exhibition (all in Japanese) of items related to *Botchan* and his creator **Sōseki Natsume**.

You'll need to return to the second floor to gain entrance to the **Yushinden**, which has been empty since 1950 (it was only ever used ten times), but the imperial apartments, with their silver- and gilt-coated screens and ornamental gardens, have been preserved. You'll be guided around by one of the no-nonsense female attendants who'll explain, in Japanese, how the rooms were specially constructed to foil any would-be assassins.

Tsubaki-no-yu

椿の湯 • 19-22 Dōgo Yuno-machi • Daily 6am–10.30pm • ¥360 • ☎ 089 921 5141

A minute's walk along the arcade from the Dōgo Onsen Honkan is the separate modern bathhouse **Tsubaki-no-yu**, meaning "Hot Water of Camellia". The granite bath here is much larger than those at the Honkan and uses water from the same hot-spring source. You won't find so many tourists here; rather, elderly locals who take their bathing seriously.

Shiki Kinen Museum

子規記念博物館, Shiki Kinen Hateubutsukan • Tues–Sun 9am–4.30pm • ¥400 • ☎ 089 931 5566, ⓦ sikihaku.lesp.co.jp • Contact in advance to organize English-language tour

In the eastern corner of Dōgo Kōen park is the **Shiki Kinen Museum**, which houses some rather dry displays telling the life story of Masaoka Shiki (see box, p.662), and setting his literature in its cultural context. The displays have English translations, and it's also possible to book an English-language tour which provides more insight into the displays and Shiki's life.

Bidoro Glass Museum

瓶泥舎びいどろぎやまんグラス美術館, Bindeisha Bidoro Giyaman Garasu Dijuthukan • 7-21 Dōgo Midoridai • Mon & Thurs–Sun 10am–5pm • ¥1000 • ☎ 089 922 3771, ⓦ bindeisha.co.jp

Near the *Sen Guesthouse* and housed in a private home away from the bustle of downtown Dōgo is the charming **Bidoro Glass Museum**. Displaying exquisite Edo, Meiji and Taishō-period pieces of glass from the owner's private collection, the designs and colours are surprisingly modern. It's remarkable that so many fragile objects, such as a set of small glass plates made in 1788, have survived more than two hundred years of earthquakes and war. Don't be put off by the museum manager escorting you through the exhibition rooms – it's because of the fragile nature of the objects on display.

Ishite-ji

石手寺 • 2-29-21 Ishite • **Temple** Daily 8am–5pm • Free • **Museum** Daily 9am–4.30pm • ¥300 • Walk for 15min east of the Dōgo tram terminus along the main road or hop on the #3 or #52 bus (¥150) to Oku Dōgo from the tram terminus, which will drop you outside the temple gate • ☎ 089 977 0870

Eight of the 88 temples on Shikoku's sacred circuit are in Matsuyama, but the most famous – and without a doubt the most unusual – is the 51st, **Ishite-ji**. Unlike the pilgrimage's other 87 temples, Ishite-ji has used its accumulated wealth to branch out into **surreal forms** of religious expression. Tucked away behind the main temple buildings are dimly lit tunnels lined with hundreds of Buddhas and other icons. Condensation drips heavily from the tunnel ceiling if it's been raining, adding to the slightly foreboding atmosphere. Further on, in the tunnel which heads upwards, flashing fairy and strobe lights (activated as you approach) and the piped sound of a priest wailing mantras, create the impression that you've stumbled into an esoteric rave.

The main tunnel emerges from behind a rock on the hill above the temple, close to the crumbling entrance to a **park** containing more bizarre statues, at the centre of which is a squat, golden-domed 3-D **mandala**. Enter this dimly lit circular hall and you'll be confronted by a two-hundred-strong congregation of wooden *jizō*, between 1m and 3m high, carved with Buddhist sexual symbols, and arranged in tiered circles. Oddly, while the main temple is usually heaving with pilgrims, very few bother to head up to the park, making it a nice place to relax for a few minutes and take in your unusual surroundings. Climbing up the slope from the mandala will lead to a large graveyard and, on the summit of the adjoining hill, the looming statue of Buddhist saint Kōbō Daishi, founder of Shikoku's pilgrim trail (see p.510).

ARRIVAL

By plane Matsuyama's airport (**☎**089 972 5600, **ⓦ**matsuyama-airport.co.jp) lies 6km west of the centre; bus #52 from here takes about 15min to reach the JR station (¥330) and continues on to Dōgo; there's also a more comfortable, though less frequent, limousine bus (¥400). A taxi from the airport costs around ¥2500.

Destinations Fukuoka (4 daily; 45min); Kagoshima (daily; 1hr); Nagoya (4 daily; 1hr 10min); Naha (daily; 1hr 55min); Osaka (13 daily; 50min); Seoul (3 weekly; 1hr 40min); Shanghai (2 weekly; 50min); Tokyo (11 daily; 1hr 15min).

By train Trains pull in at the JR Matsuyama Station, just west of the city centre – from here it's roughly a 10min walk to the castle.

Destinations Okayama (hourly; 2hr 45min); Takamatsu (hourly; 2hr 30min); Uwajima (14 daily; 1hr 20min).

By bus Buses pull in just by the train station.

Destinations Kōbe (9 daily; 2hr 50min); Kōchi (11 daily;

2hr 30min); Kyoto (2 daily; 5hr 30min); Nagoya (daily; 10h 40min); Okayama (6 daily; 2hr 50min); Onomichi (2 daily 2hr 10min); Osaka (15 daily; 5hr 20min); Takamatsu (1 daily; 2hr 40min); Tokyo (daily; 11hr); Tokushima (7 daily 3hr 10min).

By ferry and hydrofoil Ferries from several ports i western Honshū and Kyūshū dock at Takahama an Matsuyama Kankō ports – both around 10km north o Matsuyama. The terminus of the Iyo Tetsudō train line i within walking distance of both ports, from where it's a 25min journey (¥400) into Shi-eki, just south of the castle The fastest connection with Honshū is the hydrofoil from Hiroshima (1hr; ¥6900).

Destinations Beppu (daily; 3hr 30min); Hiroshima (hydrofoil: 14 daily; 1hr 10min; ferry: 10 daily; 2hr 40min) Kita-kyushu/Kokura (daily; 7hr); Oita (daily; 3hr 45min) Osaka (daily; 9hr); Yanai (4 daily; 2hr 20min).

INFORMATION

Tourist information Tourist information is available all over Matsuyama, starting with booths at the train station and the airport. For more detailed help, head for EPIC – Ehime Prefectural International Centre (Mon–Sat 8.30am–5pm; **☎**089 917 5678, **ⓦ**epic.or.jp), a couple of minutes' walk from the Minami-machi tram stop. As well as a small library of English-language books, free internet access and bicycle rental (for up to two weeks), EPIC can arrange goodwill guides to show you around the city and also hosts classes on Japanese traditional arts. Another option for free volunteer guides is the Matsuyama

International Centre (Tues–Sun 9am–5.30pm; **☎**089 943 2025), on the ground floor of COMS, 6-4-20 Sanbanchō. They also publish the free monthly *What's Going On?* booklet (**ⓦ**home.e-catv.ne.jp/wgo), available here and at EPIC. The Dōgo tourist information office (daily 8am–9pm, Oct–March till 8pm; **☎**089 921 3708, **ⓦ**Dōgo.or.jp), across the road from the Dōgo tram terminus, has English maps and leaflets, as well as bicycle rental (¥300/day). *Sen Guesthouse* in Dōgo provides information in English about Matsuyama and the rest of Shikoku, especially the pilgrimage route, to guests and visitors to their café-bar.

GETTING AROUND

By tram Matsuyama's city centre is easily covered on foot, but to travel between here and Dōgo you'll most likely use the tram network. There are four tram routes: one loop line and three other routes all running through the city centre at Ichiban-chō, past the castle and ending at the delightfully old-fashioned Dōgo terminal. Fares are a flat ¥150 and must be paid to the driver on leaving the tram. A one-day ticket, offering unlimited travel on the trams and the Loop Bus, is a bargain at ¥400, and can be bought on the trams. A couple of special tram services are pulled by the Botchan Ressha, designed like the steam trains that ran through the city during the Meiji era; a single trip on these costs ¥300, a day pass ¥500.

By bus Retro-fans might want to experience the Madonna Bus (single trip ¥200, day pass ¥400), an old-fashioned bus named after the heroine of Botchan that runs a circuit of Matsuyama's main sights on weekends and national holidays. Regular buses, from the station, are most useful for reaching further-flung areas of the city, such as the airport and Oku Dōgo.

By car Budget Rent-a-Car has a branch at the airport (**☎**089 974 3733).

By bike Apart from the castle hill, Matsuyama is reasonably flat, making this a good city to cycle around. Bicycles can be rented from the cycle port in front of the station, the castle and Dōgo station for ¥300 a day.

ACCOMMODATION

With its baths and great range of accommodation, the most pleasant **place to stay** in Matsuyama is Dōgo. If you want to be based more centrally, you'll find plenty of cheap business hotels around the JR station as well as in the city centre – expect to pay around ¥5000 for a single room or ¥8000 for a double or twin.

MATSUYAMA

Abis Inn アビスイン 2-3-3 Katsuyamachō **☎**089 998

6000, **ⓦ**abis.ne.jp/dogo/index.html; map p.663. This standard business hotel is well positioned at the end of ori-Ichiban. Rooms are well maintained, and singles are good value. Rates include a light breakfast and internet access. **¥7980**

ANA Hotel Matsuyama 松山全日空ホテル 3-2-1 Ichiban-chō ☎089 933 5511, ⚑anahotelmatsuyama.com; map p.663. This smart hotel in the city centre offers a range of stylish rooms, several restaurants and a shopping arcade. Rates for the less flash rooms in the annexe are substantially cheaper, especially the singles. **¥30,000**

Check Inn Matsuyama チェックイン松山 2-7-3 Sanbanchō ☎089 998 7000, ⚑checkin.co.jp/matsuyama; map p.663. Emerald-green leather sofas, a Rococo-style grandfather clock and chandeliers in the lobby, plus even more chandeliers in the rooms, give this comfortable, well-priced business hotel in the centre of the city more than a touch of elegance. Rooftop onsen baths are also a plus. **¥7700**

Hotel JAL City Matsuyama ホテルJALシティ松山 1-10-10 ōtemachi ☎089 913 2580, ⚑jalhotels.com/matsuyama; map p.663. Surprisingly good value for the price and location. Rooms are super clean, comfortable and well appointed, and some have castle views. Staff are helpful and attentive, and there's both an Italian and Japanese restaurant in house. **¥19,000**

International Hotel Matsuyama 国際ホテル松 1-13 Ichiban-chō ☎089 932 5111, ⚑kokusai-h.jp; map p.663. Good-value mid-range hotel near the castle and shopping district, with comfortably furnished rooms and some striking interior design in its public areas and restaurants. The retro-to-the-max top-floor Chinese restaurant has to be seen to be believed. **¥12,000**

DŌGO

Dōgo Yumekura 道後夢蔵 4-5 Yugetsu-chō ☎089 931 1180, ⚑yume-kura.jp; map p.666. This fancy new ryokan is just behind the Hon-kan. The rooms are modern and luxurious with their own wooden bathtubs and deluxe amenities. The food is beautifully presented *kaiseki ryori*, served in your room. **¥52,500**

Hotel Dōgo Yaya 道後ややホテル 6-1 Dōgo Tako-chō ☎089 907 1181, ⚑yayahotel.jp; map p.666. Elegant new hotel decorated in a modern style with tatami and wood. Rooms are chic and comfortable. The in-house buffet restaurant serves up healthy vegetable and seafood dishes. **¥26,000**

★ Sen Guesthouse 泉ゲストハウス Dōgo Tako-chō ☎089 961 1513, ⚑senguesthouse-matsuyama.com; map p.666. This friendly, well-run guesthouse is the best budget option in Matsuyama, and it's also an excellent place to pick up information about further travels in Shikoku. The facility is spacious, with pleasant communal areas and a roof terrace. Rooms are stylish and well equipped with comfortable mattresses and lockers. Dorm **¥2700**, double **¥6000**

Yamatoya Honten 大和屋本店 20-8 Dōgo Yunomachi ☎089 935 8880, ⚑yamatoyahonten.com; map p.666. Hotels with their own nō stage are few and far between, but not only does the *Yamatoya Honten* have one, it also stages two short nightly performances (30min and 10min). The tatami rooms are well up to deluxe standard, but there are also more modest, slightly dated Western-style single rooms and a *rotemburo* in the basement. **¥30,000**

EATING AND DRINKING

As befits a big city, Matsuyama has a wide range of **restaurants**, **cafés** and **bars**. Local specialities include the sponge roly-poly cake called *taruto* (タルト), inspired by a Portuguese confection introduced to Japan 350 years ago through the port of Nagasaki; the three-coloured rice dumplings on sticks called *Botchan dango*, after the character's favourite sweet; and *goshiki sōmen*, thin noodles made in five colours.

MATSUYAMA

Café Marinecco カフェマリネコ 3-1-3 Ōkaidō ☎089 935 5896; map p.663. Convivial café-cum-wine bar with stylish wooden interiors and menus handwritten on chalkboards. Has a good selection of lunch dishes such as pasta (from ¥680), while the outdoor tables are the perfect place for watching the world go by with a pint of Guinness or Kilkenny (¥800) and a pizza (¥980). Daily 11.30am–3pm & 5pm–2am.

★ Charlie's Vegetable チャーリーズ・ベジタブル 2-3-16 Ōkaidō ☎089 935 6110, ⚑charlies-vegetable.com; map p.663. A new addition to the Matsuyama dining scene, this stylish restaurant is entirely devoted to vegetable cuisine. The first floor is the buffet area where you can choose from a huge array of fresh salads, soups, curries and even vegetable desserts. Table seating is

upstairs. Lunch from ¥1280 and dinner from ¥1750. Daily 11am–11pm.

Everest Food エベレスト・フード 2F 2-2-7 Ōkaidō ☎089 945 7577; map p.663. This is a popular Indian and Nepali restaurant serving twenty different types of curry (from ¥970), tandoori mixed grill (¥1590), momos (¥600), samosa (¥490) and nan (¥300). Indian and Nepali beers are also available (from ¥390). Daily 11am–4pm & 4–10.30pm.

★ Fujiko Michael 不二子マイケル 2-5-18 Niban-chō ☎089 943 0600; map p.663. Wildly popular *izakaya* with counter seating and small tatami booths. The menu is mostly fish and seafood dishes. The *kamameshi no dashi kake* (¥450), a rice and fish stew cooked in an iron pot, is highly recommended. Daily 5pm–1am, Sat & Sun till 3am.

9

Goshiki Sōmen Morikawa 五色そうめん森川 3-5-4 Sanban-chō ☎089 933 3838; map p.663. The most famous place in town to sample *somen*, the five-coloured noodles. In front of the restaurant is a shop where you can buy the noodles, packed as souvenir sets, for around ¥300. Lunchtime set menus start at ¥880; noodles on their own are cheaper. Daily 11am–10.30pm.

Kawasemi 川瀬見 2-5-18 Niban-chō ☎089 933 9697, ⓦkawasemi.ecnet.jp; map p.663. The portions in this stylish *kaiseki* (Japanese haute cuisine) restaurant are small, but your taste buds will be subtly challenged. Look for the world "club" in English on the mauve sign and go up to the second floor. You can get a *kaiseki*-style lunch/dinner from ¥2100/7000. Daily noon–2pm & 5–10pm.

Kingyūtei 金牛亭 2-5-18 Niban-chō ☎089 921 0007; map p.663. This Japanese take on Korean barbecue (*yakiniku*) in the heart of Niban-chō is worth seeking out if you fancy gorging on grilled beef and spicy Korean side dishes such as *kimchi*. You cook the beef yourself on grills at your table. Expect to pay around ¥4000 for a meal. Mon–Sat 5–11pm.

★Kushihide くし秀 3-2-8 Niban-chō ☎089 921 1587, ⓦshokunomori.co.jp; map p.663. This rustic restaurant is a top place to try a variety of chicken dishes which are made from local free-range Ehime fowls. The course and à la carte menu has a huge variety of *kushiyaki*, chicken and vegetables grilled on skewers. A meal will set you back around ¥3500, and there's an English menu available. Tues–Sun 5.30–11pm.

Provence Dining プロヴァンス ANA Hotel Matsuyama, 3-2-1 Ichiban-chō ☎089 933 5511, ⓦanahotelmatsuyama.com; map p.663. The best thing about the *ANA*'s top-floor restaurant is its grandstand view of Katsuyama Hill and the Bansui-sō villa, especially romantic when the buildings are spotlit at night. The lunch buffet (¥1980) offers a selection of Mediterranean dishes. Dinner courses start at ¥3000. Daily 6.30am–9pm.

Sova Sova ソバソバ 3-2-35 Ōkaidō ☎089 945 5252; map p.663. Chic, laidback café-bar serving a range of simple dishes such as cold soba and rice bowls for under ¥1000. It's also a pleasantly quiet place for a drink in the evening. Daily except Wed 11am–9pm, closes irregularly.

DŌGO

Cha-Raku 茶楽 5-13 Yugetsu-chō ☎089 921 5388, ⓦyamadayamanju.jp/charaku; map p.666. This elegant, modern tearoom serves a variety of traditional teas and their signature *manju* (baked rice flour cakes with sweet bean filling). A *matcha* and *manju* set is ¥735. Daily 10am–7pm.

Daikokuya 大黒屋 8-21 Dōgo Tako-chō ☎089 925 5005, ⓦdaikokuya-udon.co.jp; map p.666. An udon and *kamameshi* (rice dishes cooked in a traditional iron pot) restaurant serving reasonably priced set meals from ¥1850. There's also a 100min all-you-can-drink deal for ¥1500. Daily 11am–10pm, closed every third Wed of the month.

Dōgo no Machiya 道後の町家カフェ 14-26 Yunomachi ☎089 986 8886, ⓦdogonomachiya.com; map p.666. Burger (¥650) and sandwich (¥450) café in a traditional house with a lovely garden at the rear. The space is split into smoking and non-smoking areas. Hearty breakfast sets go for ¥630. Daily 9am–10pm, closed Tues and the third Wed of every month.

Nikitatsu-an にきたつ庵 3-18 Dōgo Kitamachi ☎089 924 6617; map p.666. This sake brewery and restaurant serves imaginative modern Japanese cooking with their superbly brewed sake and beers. Lunches start at ¥1470, dinners from ¥3150 and drinks from ¥450. There's also an outdoor deck for balmy nights. Tues–Sun 11am–2pm & 5–8.30pm.

NIGHTLIFE

MATSUYAMA

The tight grid of streets between Niban-chō and Sanban-chō in the city centre heaves with **bars** and, in the summer, beer gardens appear on the roofs of several hotels including the *ANA Hotel Matsuyama*.

★Flankey Kobayashi フランキー小林 2-3 Ichiban-chō; map p.663. Drinks are a bargain at this lively standing bar popular with an international crowd, with beers and sake starting at ¥300. There's also dirt-cheap but fairly decent food available, such as pasta and curry (from ¥300). Daily 5pm–3am.

Underground Café アンダーグラウンド・カフェ 3-3-6 Ōkaidō ☎089 998 7710; map p.663. Down a side street on the way to the castle chairlift, this retro-chic café-bar has a very laidback vibe. Look out for the large Union Jack flag hanging outside. The food is reasonable and there are occasional club events. Daily noon–4am, closed second and fourth Wed of every month.

DŌGO

Wani to Sai Circus Bar ワニとサイ 1-39 Yunomachi ☎080 3319 2765, ⓦwanitosai.untokosho.com; map p.666. Quirky "artspace" bar and café run by a musician serving Ehime sake (¥600) and noodles (¥800). It's located up near the steps to Isaniwa-jinja. Daily 8pm–late, closed irregularly.

CULTURE AND ENTERTAINMENT

MATSUYAMA

Cinema Lunatic シネマルナティック 2F Matsuaeki Building ☎089 933 9240, ⦿movie.geocities.jp/cine_una/kinjitu.html. This cinema shows independent foreign films. Closed Tues.

Matsuyama Shimin Kaikan 松山市民会館 Horinouchi ☎089 931 8181, ⦿cul-spo.or.jp/mcph/index.html. Theatre, dance and orchestral performances are held at this venue south of the city centre, close to the Tachibana-bashi

across the Ishite-gawa.

Ōkaido Cinema Sunshine シネマサンシャイン大街道 1-5-10 Ōkaidō ☎089 986 6633, ⦿cinemasunshine .co.jp/theater/okaido. Shows mainstream Hollywood and Japanese films. Daily.

Prefectural Cultural Centre 県民文化会館 2-5-1 Dōgo-machi ☎089 923 5111, ⦿ecf.or.jp/himegin_hall. Orchestral and other music performances are held at this venue.

SHOPPING

Local products that make good **souvenirs** include *iyo-gasuri*, an indigo-dyed cloth; *hime temari*, colourful thread-covered balls that bring good luck; and *Tobe-yaki*, distinctive blue-patterned pottery. Check out Ōkaicō and Gintengai **arcades** for souvenir shops. Tobe-yaki pottery is distinguished by its robust feel and simple blue-and-white glaze.

Ehimeism Lublu Matsuyama エヒメイズムルブリュ松山 3-2-45 Ōkaidō ☎089 993 7557; map p.663. This is one of Matsuyama's most stylish souvenir shops. All the locally produced art and craft objects for sale here are stylish, functional and well designed. They also sell citrus essential oils (¥1500), room fragrances and other aromatherapy goods manufactured in Ehime Prefecture. Daily 9am–7pm.

Tobe-yaki Kankō Centre 砥部町芸創作館 82 Gohonmatsu, Tobe ☎089 962 6145, ⦿www2.ocn .ne.jp/~sosaku; map p.663. The centre of the local pottery industry is Tobe, 13km from Matsuyama. Take a #18 or #19 bus here from Shi-eki (45min; ¥600) to visit the Tobe-yaki Kankō Centre, where you can watch pottery being made and make or decorate some pieces yourself. 9am–5pm, closed Thurs.

DIRECTORY

Banks and exchange Ehime Ginkō has several branches in downtown Matsuyama. There's also a branch by the Dōgo tram terminus.

Bookshop Junkudo (5-7-1 Chifune-machi; ☎089 915 0075) has English books and magazines on the fourth floor (daily 10am–7.30pm).

Hospital The central prefectural hospital, Ehime Kenritsu Chūō Byōin (☎089 947 1111), is in Kasuga-machi, south of Shi-eki.

Internet There's free internet access at EPIC and Matsuyama International Centre (see p.668).

Laundry Okaya Coir Laundry, 43 Minami-Mochida (daily 6am–10.30pm).

Police The main police station is at 2 Minami Horibata (☎089 941 0111). Emergency numbers are listed on p.66.

Post office Matsuyama's main post office is at 3 Sanban-chō (Mon–Fri 9am–7pm, Sat 9am–5pm & Sun 9am–12.30pm). There's also a branch in Dōgo (Mon–Fri 9am–5pm), to the west of the shopping arcade. Both have ATMs that accept credit cards.

Kyūshū

九州

VOLCANIC POOL AT BEPPU

Kyūshū

The spectacular array of natural attractions on KYŪSHŪ makes this, Japan's third-largest island, a feasible holiday destination on its own, providing a thrilling alternative to the regular Kantō and Kansai circuits. Here visitors can find themselves hiking the rim of the world's largest caldera, taking a lonesome onsen dip in the forest, surfing Japan's gnarliest waves, tracking down moss-coated cedar trees that predate Christianity or being showered with ash from a live volcano. It's perfectly possible to just scoot round the main cities in a week, but you'll need more like two to do the region justice, allowing time for the splendid mountainous interior and a few of the more far-flung islands.

Closer to Korea than Tokyo, Kyūshū has long had close links with the Asian mainland, and its chief city, **Fukuoka**, is an important regional hub. An energetic city on the island's heavily developed north coast, Fukuoka is worth a stop for its museums, modern architecture and vibrant nightlife. If you've only got a couple of days on Kyūshū, however, **Nagasaki** represents the best all-round destination. Though its prime draw is the A-Bomb museum and related sights, the city also has a picturesque harbour setting, a laidback, cosmopolitan air and a smattering of temples and historical museums. From here it's a short hop east to **Kumamoto**, famous for its castle and landscaped garden, and the spluttering, smouldering cone of **Aso-san**. This is great hiking country, while hot-spring enthusiasts will also be in their element – from **Kurokawa Onsen's** delightful rotemburo to the bawdy pleasures of **Beppu** on the east coast. The mountain village of **Takachiho** requires a fair detour, but it's worth it to see traditional dance performances depicting the antics of Japan's ancient gods. The island's southern districts contain more on the same theme – volcanoes, onsen and magnificent scenery. Highlights include **Sakurajima**, one of the world's most active volcanoes, which looms over the city of **Kagoshima**, while the lush island of **Yakushima**, roughly 100km south of Kyūshū, sports towering, thousand-year-old cedar trees.

Brief history

The ancient chronicles state that **Emperor Jimmu**, Japan's legendary first emperor, set out from southern Kyūshū to found the Japanese nation in 660 BC. Though the records are open to dispute, there's evidence of human habitation on Kyūshū from before the tenth century BC, and by the beginning of the Yayoi period (300 BC–300 AD) the small

YATAI STREET STALL, FUKUOKA

Highlights

❶ Fukuoka Slurp a bowl of ramen noodles at one of the open-air *yatai* stalls along the Tenjin River. **See p.684**

❷ Aso-san The peaks of this active volcano offer great hiking and superb views across the largest caldera in the world. **See p.710**

❸ Takachiho Go boating through a gorge on the emerald-green Gokase-gawa, then watch the gods cavort at a *kagura* performance in this beguiling mountain village. **See p.715**

❹ Beppu's hidden onsen Escape the Beppu crowds by hiking up to a secluded array of onsen in the western hills. **See p.720**

❺ Usuki Contemplate Japan's finest stone-carved Buddhas, sitting serenely in the r wooded valley for more than seven hundred years. **See p.724**

❻ Kagoshima's volcano onsen Yes, you really can take a hot-spring dip on a live volcano which erupts several times each day. **See p.740**

❼ Yakushima Go hiking in the rainiest place in Japan, through lush green forests up to the ancient *yaku-sugi* cedars, some of the oldest trees in the world. **See p.745**

HIGHLIGHTS ARE MARKED ON THE MAP ON P.676

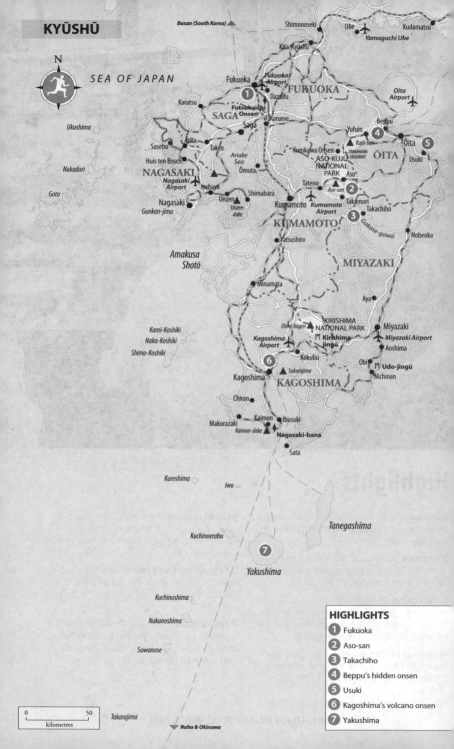

kingdom of **Na** (as it was then known) was trading with China and Korea. Local merchants brought rice-farming and bronze-making techniques back to Japan, while in the twelfth century monks introduced Zen Buddhism to northern Kyūshū. Less welcome visitors arrived in 1274 and 1281 during the **Mongol invasions** under Kublai Khan. The first ended in a narrow escape when the Mongols withdrew, and the shogun ordered a protective wall to be built around Hakata Bay. By 1281 the Japanese were far better prepared, but their real saviour was a typhoon, subsequently dubbed *kami kaze*, or "wind of the gods", which whipped up out of nowhere and scattered the Mongol fleet on the eve of their massed assault.

Three hundred years later, in 1543, the first **Europeans** to reach Japan pitched up on the island of Tanegashima, off southern Kyūshū. Finding an eager market for their guns among the local *dairayō*, the Portuguese sailors returned a few years later, bringing with them **missionaries**, among them the Jesuit priest Francis Xavier. Within fifty years the Catholic Church, now also represented by Spanish Franciscans and Dominicans, was claiming some 600,000 Christian converts. The centre of activity was **Nagasaki**, where Chinese, Dutch and British merchants swelled the throng. In the early 1600s, however, the government grew increasingly wary of the Europeans in general and Christians in particular. By fits and starts successive shoguns stamped down on the religion and restricted the movement of all foreigners, until eventually only two small communities of Dutch and Chinese merchants were left in Nagasaki.

This period of isolation lasted until the mid-1850s, when Nagasaki and Kagoshima in particular found themselves at the forefront of the modernizing revolution that swept Japan after the **Meiji Restoration**. Indeed, it was the armies of the Satsuma and Chōshū clans, both from Kyūshū, which helped restore the emperor to the throne, and many members of the new government hailed from the island. In 1877, however, Kagoshima's **Saigō Takamori** led a revolt against the Meiji government in what became

10

KYŪSHŪ'S TRAINS

Everyone knows that Japanese trains are among the best in the world – in Kyūshū, they go that little bit further. JR Kyūshū, the local division of Japan Rail, has won several international awards for the design of its trains, and some of them count as tourist sights in themselves. The bad news is that you'll have to pay extra for a ticket on the more interesting services; the good news is that they're all included on the island- and nation-wide rail passes (see p.678). Such refinement has also come at a price: you may notice, on your way around the island, that some of the tracks are a little bumpy, the result of investment being directed to the trains themselves.

Kyūshū Shinkansen Completed in 2011, the Fukuoka-Kagoshima route is Japan's newest major high-speed line. Though slower than many mainland trains, with a top speed of 260km/hr, they have had much attention lavished on their carriages – check out the stylish seat design, or the rope curtains on the way to the bathrooms.

Yufuin-no-mori A green beast reflecting the colour of the mountains it passes through on its Fukuoka-to-Beppu route (via Yufuin), this features cabin-like relaxation rooms whose large windows allow you to enjoy superb views over a coffee.

Kamome and **Sonic** Heading from Fukuoka to Nagasaki and down the east coast respectively, these passenger trains come with wonderfully comfy seating. If riding the Kamome, check out the backlit ink-brush paintings in between carriages – the only time you'll ever want to take a picture of a train's toilet area.

Huis ten Bosch Linking the eponymous sight (see p.691) to Fukuoka, this train's carriages have been designed to an appropriately European template.

Aso Boy! Rather like a rolling amusement park, this rides the rails from Aso to Kumamoto. The toy box and wooden ball pool are great ideas, as is the space-age white seating in the family car, and the cartoon-meets-hotel-lobby lounge car. What a pity that it only runs at weekends.

Ibusuki-no-tamatebako If you're heading from Kagoshima to Ibusuki, adjust your schedule to ride this train, which features ocean-facing seats and a pine-lined interior.

known as the **Satsuma Rebellion**. Saigō's army was routed, but he's still something of a local hero in Kyūshū.

GETTING AROUND

By train Fukuoka's Hakata Station receives Shinkansen from the mainland, and fires its own out on a new line heading south to Kagoshima. From Hakata, JR Kyūshū trains (ⓦ jrkyushu.co.jp) fan out to all the major cities; the vehicles are a cut above Japan's already sky-high standards (see box, p.677). The company offers its own three- and five-day rail passes (¥13,000 and ¥16,000) for travelling round the whole island, or just the north (everything north of Kumamoto; ¥7000 and ¥9000). There are more details on JR passes and discount tickets in Basics (see p.35).

By bus In the central uplands and southern Kyūshū, you'll be more reliant on a limited number of private train lines and on local buses. If you're on a whistle-stop tour, you might want to consider one of the three-day SunQ bus passes (ⓦ sunqpass.jp), which offer unlimited travel on most highway buses and local services throughout Kyūshū (¥10,000) or just the five northern prefectures (¥8000). Not all bus companies are covered, however, nor are some of the fastest express services between cities.

By car For exploring the more remote areas, car rental is an excellent option; there are car rental outlets in almost every town and in all the main tourist areas.

Fukuoka

福岡

Kyūshū's largest city, **FUKUOKA** is one of the most likeable places in Japan – indeed, despite the fact that it's not exactly a household name abroad, it regularly pops up on global best-places-to-live lists. While it boasts few actual sights, there's a certain Kyūshū-style joie de vivre here, best exemplified at the umpteen rustic street-side *yatai*, where locals slurp happily away on their ramen while knocking back beer, sake or whatever takes their fancy. Until recently, the city was an industrial nonentity, notable only for its transport connections to Korea and the rest of the island, but its renaissance has been remarkable. Visit today and you'll find a squeaky-clean metropolis that makes for a great introduction to Kyūshū, or indeed Japan as a whole; as such, it deserves a day or two of any traveller's time.

Highlights here include one or two excellent museums and ranks of eye-catching modern architecture – most notable in the latter category are **Canal City**, a self-contained cinema, hotel and shopping complex built around a semicircular strip of water, and **Hawks Town**, which forms part of a major seafront redevelopment incorporating venues for shopping, eating and entertainment. The city is also renowned for its festivals and folk crafts, which are presented at **Hakata Machiya Folk Museum**. As with any self-respecting Japanese city of this size, Fukuoka maintains a lively

---

FUKUOKA ORIENTATION

Even today the old cultural and economic divide between the original castle town, Fukuoka, and the former merchants' quarter of Hakata can be traced, albeit faintly, in the city's streets. Much of **Hakata** (博多) consists of dull office blocks, but the district is also home to the city's oldest **shrine** and its most rumbustious festival. You'll also still find the occasional wooden building, narrow lane or aged wall, while some of the unique Hakata culture is showcased in its well-presented **folk museum**. Not surprisingly, many **craft industries** originated in this area, most famously Hakata dolls and *ori* silks, while geisha still work the traditional **entertainment district** of Nakasu (though these days they're vastly outnumbered by the area's working girls). Hakata is also home to one of Fukuoka's most famous landmarks, the futuristic **Canal City** complex, a startling contrast to the rest of the district.

West of the Naka-gawa, **Tenjin** (天神) has upmarket boutiques, galleries, department stores and "fashion buildings", but there's little in the way of sights until you go further west to the ruins of Fukuoka castle in **Ōhori-kōen**. As well as an attractive lake, this park also contains an **art museum** with an important collection of twentieth-century works.

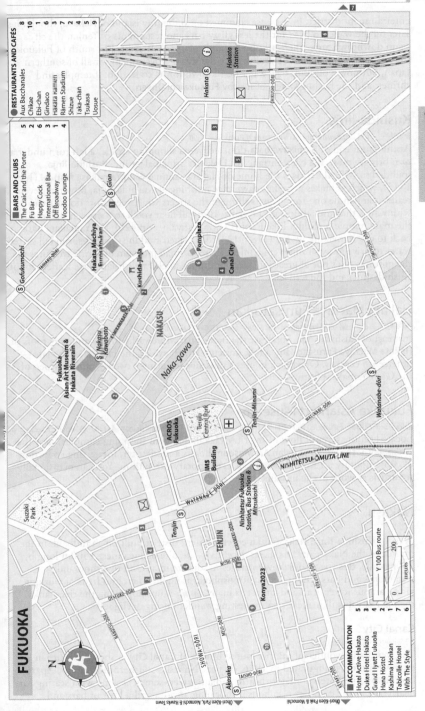

FUKUOKA

RESTAURANTS AND CAFÉS

Aux Bacchanales	8
Chikae	10
Ebi-chan	1
Gindaco	6
Hakata Ramen	3
Ramen Stadium	7
Shizue	2
Taka-chan	4
Tsukasa	5
Uosue	9

BARS AND CLUBS

The Craic and the Porter	5
Fu Bar	2
Happy Cock	6
International Bar	3
Off Broadway	1
Voodoo Lounge	4

ACCOMMODATION

Hotel Active Hakata	5
Dukes Hotel Hakata	3
Grand Iyett Fukuoka	2
Hana Hostel	1
Kashima Honkan	7
Tabicolle Hostel	4
With The Style	6

---- Y100 Bus route

0 — 200 metres

entertainment district, in this case crammed onto the tiny island of **Nakasu**, though it's safer on the wallet to head for the less glitzy bars and restaurants of **Tenjin**, the city's main downtown area. There are also a couple of excellent sights just south of Fukuoka: the ancient temple town of **Dazaifu**, once the seat of government for all of southern Japan, but now a pleasant backwater best known for its collection of temples and shrines; and the healing waters of nearby **Futsukaichi Onsen**.

10 Kushida-jinja

櫛田神社 • 1-41 Kamikawabatamachi • Museum daily 10am–5pm • ¥300

At the south end of **Kamikawabata-dōri**, a covered shopping arcade, a left turn under a *torii* brings you to the back entrance of Hakata's principal shrine, **Kushida-jinja**, founded in 757 AD. This is the home of Hakata's annual **Gion Yamakasa festival** (July 1–15), which climaxes in a 5km dawn race finishing at Kushida-jinja, in which seven teams manhandle one-tonne floats through the streets while spectators douse them with water; they use replicas of the giant, 10m-tall float you'll see between the *torii* and the main temple building. Like Kyoto's Gion festival (see p.428), the Yamakasa harks back to the Kamakura period (1185–1333 AD) when Buddhist priests sprinkled sacred water to drive away summer epidemics. There's a small **museum** of shrine treasures in the grounds – it's not of great interest, but it does stock English-language leaflets about Kushida-jinja and the festival.

Hakata Machiya Furusato-kan

博多町家ふるさと館 • 6-10 Reisenmachi • Daily 10am–6pm • ¥200 • Ⓦ hakatamachiya.com

Just east of Kushida-jinja, you'll see the traditional whitewashed walls and grey roofs of **Hakata Machiya Furusato-kan**, a folk museum which evokes the Hakata of the late nineteenth century. One block houses a museum featuring a twenty-minute video of the Gion Yamakasa festival.

Fukuoka Asian Art Museum

福岡アジア美術館, Fukuoka Ajia Bijutsukan • 7F 3-1 Shimokawabatamachi • 10am–8pm; closed Wed • ¥200 • Ⓦ faam.city.fukuoka.lg.jp

Located on the seventh floor of the ritzy Hakata Riverain shopping complex, near the Naka-gawa, the **Fukuoka Asian Art Museum** boasts a modest but interesting collection of contemporary art from Asia, as well as temporary exhibitions. You can occasionally see artists at work in the upstairs studio.

Nakasu

中洲

West of Kushida-jinja, **Nakasu** is an entertainment district built on a sandbank in the middle of the Naka-gawa. Its size is deceptive – despite being a mere 1500m long by 250m wide, this space somehow manages to squeeze in around two thousand restaurants and bars. Though most atmospheric at night, when hundreds of working girls clamour for custom and almost as many *yatai* set up shop along the riverbanks, the district can still make for an interesting wander during daylight.

Canal City

1-2 Sumiyoshi • Ⓦ canalcity.co.jp

The weird and wonderful multicoloured blocks of **Canal City**, a showpiece urban renewal project inaugurated in 1996, lie near Nakasu's southernmost point. Apart from two large hotels, a major theatre and a thirteen-screen cinema with seating for nearly 2600, the complex also houses shopping arcades and a host of bars and restaurants. The liveliest part, however, is the interior court, where the salmon-pink and turquoise buildings wrap round the "canal", which erupts on the hour with five-storey-high jets of water.

ACROS Fukuoka building

1-1 Tenjin • Step-garden daily 10am–dusk • Free

From Nakasu, a pedestrian bridge leads west across the Naka-gawa to Tenjin. Immediately over the river is the unusual **ACROS Fukuoka building**, meaning "Asian Crossroads Over the Sea", which was completed in 1995 as a cultural centre. Its terraced south side forms a "step garden", giving it the vague air of an Inca ruin, while inside there is a symphony hall, an information centre (see p.683) and an interesting prefectural crafts exhibition space, shops and restaurants.

10

Ōhori-kōen

大濠公園

In 1601, the Kuroda lords built their castle on a low hill sitting among coastal marshes to the west of the Naka-gawa. Today, just a few old stone walls and ruined watchtowers remain, but the castle grounds have been landscaped to form **Ōhori-kōen**, a large public park. It's most easily accessible from the subway; exit 3 of Ōhori-kōen Station brings you up beside a large lake spanned by a pleasing necklace of islets and bridges.

Fukuoka Art Museum

福岡市美術館, Fukuoka-shi Bijutsukan • 1-6 Ōhori-kōen • 9.30am–5.30pm; closed Mon • ¥200 • W fukuoka-art-museum.jp

The park's foremost attraction is the **Fukuoka Art Museum**, situated in its southeast corner. Its three ground-floor rooms contain a hotchpotch of early Japanese and Asian art, including the Kuroda family treasures and several eye-catching statues of Buddhism's twelve guardian generals (Jūni Jinshō), each crowned with his associated zodiacal beast. Upstairs you leap a few centuries to the likes of Dalí, Miró and Chagall in a great retrospective of twentieth-century Western art, displayed alongside contemporary Japanese works.

Momochi

モモチ

To the west of central Fukuoka, the **Momochi** district has only recently been reclaimed from the sea, and handed over to ambitious city planners. A fair proportion of international visitors to the area are English teachers on visa runs from Korea, while locals swing by for baseball games at the Fukuoka Dome and retail therapy at the district's several outlet malls. However, it's worth heading this way for a zip up the **Fukuoka Tower**, while the excellent **Fukuoka City Museum** also merits a visit.

Fukuoka Tower

福岡タワー • 2-3-26 Momochihama • Observation deck daily 9.30am–9pm • ¥800 • W fukuokatower.co.jp • 15min walk from Nishijin subway station, or bus #305 from Hakata and Tenjin

Momochi's most striking building by far is the 234m, pencil-thin **Fukuoka Tower**, which has become one of the city's most famous icons. Primarily a communications tower, its first section is an empty shell coated with 8000 sheets of mirror glass, while the top third bristles with radio transmitters. In between, at 123m, the architects slipped in an observation deck to capitalize on the spectacular views of Fukuoka and Hakata Bay.

10

Fukuoka City Museum

福岡市博物館, Fukuoka-shi Hakubatsukan · 3-1-1 Momochihama · July & Aug Tues–Sat 9.30am–7.30pm; Sun 9.30am–5.30pm; Sept–June 9.30am–5.30pm; closed Mon · ¥200 · ⓦ museum.city.fukuoka.jp

Five minutes' walk south of the Fukuoka Tower is the excellent **Fukuoka City Museum** which occupies an imposing, late-1980s structure of mirrored glass and grey stone. The museum's most famous exhibit is the two-centimetre-square **Kin-in gold seal**, ornamented with a dumpy, coiled snake. According to its inscription, the seal was presented by China's Han emperor to the King of Na (see p.677) in 57 AD – it was only rediscovered in 1784 in a grave on an island in Hakata Bay.

ARRIVAL AND DEPARTURE
FUKUOKA

By train Don't go looking for a Fukuoka station; the vast majority of trains to the city arrive at Hakata, a station to the east of the centre, its somewhat confusing name dating from before the two neighbouring towns of Fukuoka and Hakata merged. Hakata station is where the Tōkaidō and Kyūshū Shinkansen meet, and also the focal point of Kyūshū's local JR services. Further west, across the Naka-gawa, Nishitetsu-Fukuoka station serves Dazaifu and Futsukaichi Onsen.

Hakata destinations Beppu (1–3 hourly; 2hr–3hr 20min); Hiroshima (every 15min; 1hr 10min–1hr 50min); Huis ten Bosch (8 daily; 1hr 40min); Kagoshima (every 30min; 1hr 20min–2hr 30min); Kumamoto (every 30min; 40min–1hr 20min); Kyoto (every 30min; 2hr–2hr 45min); Miyazaki (2 daily; 5hr 35min–8hr); Nagasaki (every 30min–1hr; 2hr); Osaka (every 15–20min; 2hr 40min); Takeo (7 daily; 1hr); and Tokyo (every 30min; 5hr–5hr 20min).

Nishitetsu-Fukuoka destinations Dazaifu (every 30min; 30min); and Futsukaichi Onsen (every 10min; 10–20min).

By plane So close to the city centre that you could walk into town in half an hour, Fukuoka Airport (domestic terminal ☎ 092 621 6059, international ☎ 092 483 7007; ⓦ fuk-ab.co.jp) is handily located only two stops down the line from Hakata and five from Tenjin; the subway station is

located in the domestic terminal, which is linked to the international terminal by shuttle bus (10–15min; free). International destinations include Bangkok, Beijing, Ho Chi Minh City, Manila, Seoul, Shanghai, Singapore and Taipei. And yes, the airport's code really is "FUK".

Destinations Aomori (4 weekly; 2hr); Kagoshima (5 daily; 45min); Kansai International (4 daily; 1hr); Miyazaki (7 daily; 40min); Nagoya (1–2 hourly; 1hr 10min); Naha (1 hourly; 1hr 40min); Niigata (1 daily; 1hr 30min); Osaka (Itami; hourly; 1hr 10min); Sapporo (4 daily; 2hr 10min); Sendai (5 daily; 1hr 40min); Tokyo (2–4 hourly; 1hr 30min).

By ferry There are services from Fukuoka to the Korean city of Busan (see box below), as well as some surrounding Japanese islands. From the ferry terminals, take a Nishitetsu city bus for the ten-minute ride to either Tenjin (¥180) or Hakata Station (¥220).

By bus Long-distance buses call at a stop in the Nishitetsu-Fukuoka Station, before terminating at the Fukuoka Kōtsu Centre, immediately north of Hakata Station.

Destinations Beppu (every 30min–1hr; 2hr 30min); Kagoshima (every 30min–1hr; 3hr 40min); Kumamoto (every 10–20min; 2hr 20min); Kyoto (1 daily; 9hr 30min); Miyazaki (every 30min–1hr; 3hr 40min); Nagasaki (every 15–30min; 2hr); Osaka (2 daily; 9hr 40min).

GETTING AROUND

By subway The easiest way of getting around Fukuoka is on its fast and efficient subway system; most places of

interest fall within walking distance of a station. Trains run 5.30am–11.45pm, and the minimum fare is ¥200. If you

TO KOREA BY SEA

Fukuoka is connected by ferry and hydrofoil to Busan, Korea's second-largest city, which is less than three hours from Seoul by high-speed train. Most travel on one of Beetle's **hydrofoils** (☎ 092 281 2315, ⓦ jrbeetle.co.jp), which take just three hours. There are at least four daily services, costing ¥13,000 one-way; round-trips can be as low as ¥20,000, though booking the return leg in Korea will also save money. Some find the journey uncomfortable – it's a little like sitting on a washing machine for a few hours – but a more leisurely trip can be enjoyed on the daily Camellia Line **ferry** (☎ 092 262 2323, ⓦ camellia-line.co.jp), which costs from ¥9000 one-way. The ferry heads to Busan by day in under six hours, then back to Fukuoka overnight. With both ferry and hydrofoil, travellers must pay a ¥700 **departure tax** from a machine in the terminal, and around the same is added to the ticket price as a **fuel surcharge**. Korean tourist visas – ranging from one to six months in length, depending on nationality – are available on arrival.

xpect to make several journeys, it's worth buying a one-day subway card (¥600), which also gets you small discounts at several museums.

By bus For those places not within immediate striking distance of the subway, such as the Hawks Town area, you'll need to use Nishitetsu city buses, most of which funnel through the Hakata Station—Tenjin corridor. Look out for the handy "100-yen bus" – where you pay a flat fare of ¥100 – which loops round from Hakata Station to Nishitetsu-Fukuoka Station via Nakasu and Canal City.

Car rental Budget (☎092 473 0543), Eki Rent-a-Car (☎092 431 8775) and Toyota Rent-a-Car (☎092 441 0100) all have offices in or near Hakata Station.

INFORMATION

Information offices Fukuoka has a good sprinkling of information offices with English-speaking staff. There are desks in both airport terminals, but the main tourist office (daily 8am–8pm; ☎092 431 3003) is located on Hakata Station's central concourse. In Tenjin, there's an office on the ground floor of the Mitsukoshi store (daily 10.30am–6.30pm; ☎092 751 6904), above the Nishitetsu-Fukuoka Station. Staff at all these locations can help make hotel reservations but only for the same day. If you need more English-language assistance, try the Fukuoka International Association (daily 10am–8pm;

☎092 733 2220, ⊚rainbowfia.or.jp) which offers a broad range of information, plus English-language newspapers and free internet access; you'll find it in the Rainbow Plaza, on the eighth floor of Tenjin's IMS Building.

Listings magazines Though mostly full of adverts, the free monthly *Fukuoka Now* (⊚fukuoka-now.com) is worth a look for local events; you'll find it at tourist information offices and various hotels, shops and restaurants. In addition, tourist offices dish out the *Fukuoka City Visitor's Guide*, a handy booklet outlining the main sights.

ACCOMMODATION

Fukuoka has several modern, world-class **hotels** and a good selection of business hotels scattered around the city centre. The standard of budget accommodation has also improved recently; it's mostly located around Hakata Station. You can make hotel **reservations** at the Hakata Station and Tenjin information offices and at the airport, though only for the same day. Weekend rates tend to be slightly more expensive.

HOTELS

★**Hotel Active Hakata** 3-20-16 Hakata-ike-mae ☎092 452 0001, ⊚hotel-active.com. Fantastic new option between Nakasu and the train station. They've got the basics right and a lot more besides – witness the hot-drink vending machines by the lift on every floor, stylishly decorated corridors, great onsen-style facilities, and the excellent buffet breakfasts. Rooms are small, but that's a given at this price level. **¥8500**

★**Dukes Hotel Hakata** 2-3-9 Hakata-ike-mae ☎092 472 1800, ⊚dukes-hotel.com. A lobby heavy with the scent of flowers sets a suitable tone for this elegant business hotel, whose lovingly decorated rooms are excellent value for the price and location. **¥10,000**

Grand Hyatt Fukuoka 1-2-82 Sumiyoshi ☎092 282 1234, ⊚fukuoka.grand.hyatt.com. Can't-miss-it hotel occupying a large chunk of Canal City. The oval-shaped lobby and plunging atrium are worth a visit even if you're not staying, though the rooms don't disappoint – large and beautifully designed with Japanese touches, such as *shōji* screens and contemporary artwork. Find hefty discounts online. **¥34,000**

Kashima Honkan 鹿島本館 3-11 Reisen-machi ☎092 291 0746, ✉kashima-co@mx7.tiki.ne.jp. This homely, ninety-year-old ryokan is located on a pleasant backstreet, just round the corner from Gion subway station. The 27 tatami rooms are elegant, with antique screens and wall

hangings, though none is en suite. Rooms are available with or without meals. There's free internet access and English is spoken. **¥15,600**

With The Style 4-1-18 Hakataeki-minami ☎092 433 3900, ⊚withthestyle.com. So hip it hurts, this snazzy boutique hotel is a favourite with young, moneyed Japanese. It'll hit you in the wallet, but, when you're zoning out in the rooftop spa or sipping cocktails in the private penthouse bar you may find it worth the splurge. **¥40,000**

HOSTELS

★**Hana Hostel** 4-213 Kamimawabata-machi ☎092 282 5353, ⊚fukuoka.hanahostel.com. A recent addition to the city's hostel scene, but already up there with the best on the island; it has cheery staff and a fantastically central location, and the curtained-off dorms are surprisingly large, and the many private rooms well-appointed. Popular with travellers from other Asian countries, it regularly sells out at weekends. Dorm **¥2800**, double **¥6800**

Tabicolle Hostel 3-7-14 Hakataeki-minami ☎092 473 6767, ⊚tabicolle.com. Just a short walk east of Hakata Station in an earthy part of the city, this is a laidback place with a stylish common area that's the ideal place to meet some travel buddies. Dorms are more than adequate, while the rooftop is a lovely place for a relaxing coffee by day, or something stronger by night. Dorm **¥2400**

EATING

Not surprisingly for such a cosmopolitan city, Fukuoka boasts a range of international cuisines. For a cheap meal, however, try some of the city's characteristic **yatai kitchens** (see box below), many of which serve the miso-based ramen that the city is known for. **Tenjin** is a good bet for traditional restaurants, particularly the **Daimyō** district, immediately west of Tenjin Nishi-dōri, which is packed with little bars and funky designer boutiques. Finally, Fukuoka's most notorious **speciality food** is *fugu*, the poisonous blowfish eaten only in winter (Nov–March); though you'll find *fugu* throughout Japan, the best is said to come from the waters off northern Kyūshū.

10

Aux Bacchanales オーバカナル 1-4-1 Chūō ☎092 762 7373. A swanky, Frenchified café with windows looking out onto a covered arcade. Despite the charming decor, dickie-bow-wearing waiters and the fact that it's the in-place for local sophisticates, prices aren't all that high – coffees cost from ¥450, while petits plats such as saucisse frites start at around ¥600. Cheese and scrumptious cakes are on the menu, and all is served to a background of French radio. Daily 10am–10pm.

Chikae 稚加榮 2-2-17 Daimyō ☎092 721 4624. Famous fish restaurant where you sit at a counter overlooking the fish tanks, or at tables to the side. Kimono-clad staff bustle about bearing platters laden with ultra-fresh sashimi and sushi, adding to the spectacle. It's a good place to try the local speciality *karashi mentaiko* (spicy fish eggs), as well as *fugu*. Sashimi platters start at around ¥2000, sushi at ¥2700. Daily 11am–10pm.

Gindaco 銀だこ B1 Canal City ☎092 432 0123. Great little *takoyaki* joint which serves octopus balls in an intriguing range of flavours – Kansai folk may sneer at the pesto-and-cheese variety (¥600 for eight), but they're pretty darn tasty. It's right next to the Canal City fountains – grab your meal to take away and munch it while watching the show. Daily 10am–9pm.

Hakata Rāmen 博多ラーメン Kamikawabata-dōri. This round-the-clock operation is one of the cheapest noodle bars in town, with bowls going from just ¥290; surprisingly, they're not bad at all, and the same can be said for the ¥250 *gyōza*. Daily 24hr.

Rāmen Stadium ラーメンスタヂアム 5F Canal City ☎092 282 2525. A funny little place on the top floor of the Canal City complex, with no fewer than eight restaurants specializing in slurpworthy ramen; slightly tacky though it may seem, these are some of the city's (and therefore, the country's) best noodles. Bowls go from ¥700; take your pick from various picture menus. Daily 11am–11pm.

Uosue 魚末 2-1-30 Daimyō ☎092 713 7931. Small, traditional sashimi restaurant famous for having the freshest fish in town. Menus change daily and you should expect to pay at least ¥3000 for a satisfying meal – stick to items with a price tag (indicating the day's market price) to avoid any nasty shocks. Even on weekdays it pays to make a reservation, or get here at 6pm. Tues–Sun 6pm to late.

YATAI

Forget the sights – *this* is Fukuoka. Come evening, steam billows out from more than one hundred **mobile street-kitchens**, each cocooning a fascinating little world of its own. Customers push their way through a thin drape of plastic sheets to find a garrulous clutch of locals, crammed onto narrow benches and filling up on scrumptious food – pork-based **tonkotsu ramen** is the meal of choice (¥600 or so), usually accompanied by flasks of sake and a few new friends. Mobile in nature, none of these **yatai** has a fixed location, but this being Japan they rarely venture too far from their original mark, and you'll usually find them open from 7pm–3am. The greatest concentrations of *yatai* are around the intersection of Tenjin Nishi-dōri and Shōwa-dōri, and along the southwest bank of Nakasu Island. These are some of the most enjoyable places to eat in all Japan, and the focus on merry-making means that any noisy *yatai* is worth a go, but a few certainly stand out from the crowd.

Ebi-chan えびちゃん. All *yatai* have beer and sake, but this goes further – as well as Italian-themed food, its menu contains no fewer than fifty cocktails (from ¥700), while staff are dressed in dickie-bows and starched shirts. There's a ¥400 sit-down charge.

Shizue しずえ. The tricolour on the outside isn't just a decoration: amazingly, its menu is based upon French cuisine. Beef in red wine sauce at a *yatai*? Somehow, it works.

Taka-chan たかちゃん. *Kokin-chan* is a local institution, having dished out ramen for over four decades. But here's the secret – the place next door is just as good, and you won't have to queue for an hour to get in.

★ **Tsukasa** 司 ⓦyatai-tsukasa.com. The best of a clutch on the riverside (it even has a website), this shack specializes in *mentaiko* tempura – spicy cod roe fried in batter (¥900). *Fugu* (blowfish) tempura goes for the same price. Mmm ... *oishii*.

DRINKING

Fukuoka's famous **Nakasu** nightlife district is crammed full of clubs, restaurants and bars, as well as a whole clutch of seedier establishments aimed at Japanese businessmen. It's a great area to wander round, but most places are extortionately expensive and only take customers by recommendation, if they accept foreigners at all. A happier hunting ground lies around Tenjin's main crossroads, particularly **Oyafukō-dōri** and the streets immediately to the east, which are packed with bars and clubs; roughly translated, Oyafukō-dōri means "street of disobedient children", originally referring to a local school but nowadays more applicable to groups of drunken college kids who gather here at weekends under the blind eye of the *kōban* (neighborhood police) on the corner. Lastly, any *yatai* worth its salt serves booze, and they're certainly the city's most characterful and atmospheric drinking spots (see box opposite).

10

The Craic and the Porter 2F, 3-5-16 Tenjin ☎090 4514 9516. Still going strong thanks to a superb, ever-changing roster of draught beers and ales (¥900/pint), this tiny Irish pub makes a nice change from the norm, and is a good place for a chat. Mon–Wed 2pm–2am, Thurs–Sun 7pm–4am.

Fu Bar 4F, 3-6-12 Tenjin ☎092 722 3006. This DJ bar is popular with foreigners and locals alike, largely thanks to a winning cocktail of good music and cheap booze – drink all night for ¥3000 if you're a chap, ¥2000 if you're a lady. 9pm–late, closed Mon.

Happy Cock 9F, 2-1-51 Daimyō ☎092 734 2686. It's elbow room only at weekends in this large, laidback bar just off Tenjin Nishi-dōri. DJs, party nights and all-you-can-eat-and-drink deals pull a younger crowd. Cover charge Fri & Sat ¥1200 including two drinks. Wed–Thurs 7pm–1am, weekends to 5am.

International Bar 4F, 3-1-13 Tenjin ☎092 714 2179. This ordinary little bar is a good place to meet local *gaijin*. No cover charge and inexpensive bar food. Look out for the English sign on the main street opposite the Matsuya Ladies store, north of the main Tenjin crossroads. Daily from 6.30pm.

Off Broadway 2F, 1-8-40 Maizuru ☎092 724 5383. Imagine a processed chunk of New York – fries, burgers and buffalo wings fill up a sophisticated, multinational clientele, who find themselves serenaded by jazz and Latin music (live most weekends). 7.30pm–late, closed Mon.

Voodoo Lounge 3F, 3-2-13 Tenjin ☎092 732 4662. Boogie the night away or chill out among the jungle palms in this capacious bar tucked off Oyafukō-dōri. Stages an eclectic programme of DJs, live bands and other events. Entry charges and opening times vary.

ENTERTAINMENT

Fukuoka is large enough to be on the circuit for pop stars, musicals and major theatre productions. To find out what's on, consult the *Rainbow* newsletter and *Fukuoka Now* (see p.683) or ask at any of the tourist offices; tickets are available through PIA (☎092 708 9999), which has an outlet next to the tourist office on the second floor of the ACROS Building.

THEATRES AND MUSIC VENUES

Fukuoka City Theatre Canal City ☎092 271 1199, ⓦshiki.gr.jp. Major venue for imported plays and the like; pretty much everything is in Japanese, but you'll certainly be familiar with some of the stories.

Hakata-za Hakata Riverain ☎092 263 5858, ⓦhakataza .co.jp. Stages occasional kabuki performances, though it's imperative to book in advance. When you arrive, ask for an English-language leaflet to guide you through proceedings.

Zepp Hawks Town ☎092 832 6639, ⓦzepp.co.jp. A venue that hosts big-hitting musical artists and groups, including many international names, such as Avril Lavigne and Bruno Mars, as well as domestic acts.

CINEMA

United Cinemas 4F Canal City ☎092 291 0730, ⓦunitedcinemas.jp. Film fans should check the current week's showings at United Cinema's thirteen-screen

---

FUKUOKA FESTIVALS AND EVENTS

Hakata celebrates a whole host of **festivals**, of which the biggest are the **Gion Yamakasa** (July 1–15) and the **Hakata Dontaku**, now held during Golden Week (May 3 & 4). In feudal times, Hakata townspeople were permitted across the river once a year to convey New Year greetings to their lord. Today's festival centres on a parade along Meiji-dōri to the old castle (see p.581). On a similarly traditional theme, the sumo circus comes to town each November for Japan's last *basho* of the season, at Fukuoka's Kokusai Centre (ⓦsumo.or.jp). A much newer festival is the **Isla de Salsa** (ⓦtiempo.jp), a celebration of Latin music held mid-August on Nokonoshima island, a ten-minute ferry ride from Fukuoka.

multiplex. They also operate a ten-screen cinema in Hawks Town; at both locations, English-language films are shown with Japanese subtitles. ¥1800 all day Sat and before 9pm Sun–Fri, ¥1000 after 9pm Sun–Fri.

SHOPPING

Department stores Fukuoka's big department stores are grouped around the main crossroads in Tenjin and south along Watanabe-dōri, and around Hakata Station. They all sell a selection of local crafts, the most famous of which are Hakata *ningyō*, hand-painted, unglazed clay dolls fashioned as samurai, kabuki actors, or demure, kimono-clad women. *Champon* are long-stemmed, glass toys with a bowl at the end which make a clicking sound when you blow into them, while Hakata *ori* is far more transportable – slightly rough silk fabric traditionally used for *obi* (sashes worn with kimono), but now made into ties, wallets and bags.

Local souvenirs As well as at the large department stores, local souvenirs can be bought at Hakata Machiya Furusato-kan (p.680), the Kawabata-dōri arcades (p.680) or Hakata Station's underground arcades.

DIRECTORY

Banks and exchange There are ATMs in both airport terminals. You can change money at Fukuoka Bank in the international terminal. Fukuoka Bank also offers foreign exchange facilities at its branches outside the front west entrance of Hakata Station and next to the IMS Building in Tenjin. You can also change money at the two main post offices (see below).

Consulates Australia, 7F, 1-6-8 Tenjin ☎092 734 5055, ⓦconsular.australia.or.jp/fukuoka; China, 1-3-3 Jigyohama ☎092 713 1121, ⓔchinaconsul_fuk_jp@mfa.gov.cn; South Korea, 1-1-3 Jigyohama ☎092 771 0461, ⓔfukuoka@mofat.go.kr; US, 2-5-26 Ōhori ☎092 751 9331, ⓦjapan.usembassy.gov.

Emergencies The main police station is at 7-7 Higashikoen, Hakata-ku (☎092 641 4141). In an absolute emergency contact the Foreign Advisory Service on ☎092 733 2220. Other emergency numbers are listed in Basics (see p.66).

Hospitals The largest general hospital with English-speaking staff is National Kyūshū Medical Centre, 1-8-1 Jigyohama (☎092 852 0700), near Hawks Town. More centrally, there's Saiseikai Fukuoka General Hospital, 1-3-46 Tenjin (☎092 771 8151), south of the ACROS building.

Immigration For visa renewals, contact Fukuoka Regional Immigration Bureau, 1-22 Okihama-chō, Hakata-ku (☎092 281 7431).

Police ☎092 641 4141.

Post offices Fukuoka Central Post Office (4-3-1 Tenjin), just north of Tenjin subway station, offers foreign exchange and a 24hr mail service. There's another big branch beside the west exit of Hakata Station.

Travel agents For domestic travel, JTB (☎092 733 1300) has English-speaking staff; there are branches in the two train stations and another in the basement of Iwataya department store to the west of Nishitetsu Fukuoka Station. International travel can be arranged through H.I.S, 2F, 2-7-9 Tenjin (☎092 736 8661, ⓦhis-j.com), by the junction of Tenjin Nishi-dōri and Meiji-dōri, and No 1 Travel, 3F, ACROS Building, 1-1-1 Tenjin (☎092 761 9203, ⓦno1-travel.com/fuk).

Dazaifu

太宰府

Only 15km southeast of Fukuoka, **DAZAIFU** only just breaks free of the urban sprawl, but manages to retain a definite country air. The town is very much on Kyūshū's tourist map, thanks to the important **Kyūshū National Museum**. The crowd of art lovers and historians gets a boost in late February and March, when plum blossoms signal both the start of spring and the onset of the exam season, and anxious students descend on **Tenman-gū**, Japan's foremost shrine dedicated to the god of learning. Thankfully, the nearby **temples** and other historical relics remain surprisingly peaceful. Everything is within easy walking distance of the station, making it possible to cover the main sights in a day.

Brief history

Dazaifu rose to prominence in the late seventh century, when the emperor established a regional seat of government and military headquarters (known as the Dazaifu) here, responsible for defence, trade and diplomatic ties, particularly with China and Korea. For

CLOCKWISE FROM TOP LEFT GUNKANJIMA, "BATTLESHIP ISLAND" (P.699); KAGURA PERFORMANCE, TAKACHIHO (P.715); STONE BUDDHA, USUKI (P.724) >

more than five hundred years successive governor generals ruled Kyūshū from Dazaifu, protected by a series of ditches, embankments and hilltop fortresses, until political circumstances changed in the twelfth century and the town gradually fell into decline.

Tenman-gū

天満宮 • 4-7-1 Saifu • **Shrine** daily 7am–7pm • Free • **Museum** 9am–4.30pm; closed Tues • ¥200 • **Treasure house** 9am–4.20pm; closed Mon • ¥300 • ⓦ dazaifutenmangu.or.jp

From the train station, it's a short walk east up Tenjin-sama-dōri to Dazaifu's main historical sight, **Tenman-gū**, a tenth-century shrine dedicated to Tenjin, the guardian deity of scholars, also known as Sugawara-no-Michizane (see box below).

The approach to Tenman-gū lies over an allegorical stone bridge, **Taiko-bashi**; its first, steep arch represents the past, the present is flat, while the final, gentler hump indicates difficulties yet to come. While negotiating the bridge, take a close look at the second of the two little shrines on the right, which was constructed in 1458 – its intricate, Chinese-style roof shelters some particularly fine carving. Beyond, a two-storey gate leads into a courtyard dominated by the main **worship hall**, built in 1591 but resplendent in bright red and gold lacquer under its manicured thatch. A twisted plum tree stands immediately to the right (east) of the hall. Known as the "flying plum tree", it's said to be over a thousand years old and, according to legend, originally grew in Michizane's Kyoto garden. On the eve of his departure he wrote a farewell poem to the tree, but that night it upped roots and "flew" ahead of him to Dazaifu.

To the left and behind the worship hall, a modern building houses a small **museum** detailing the life of Michizane through a series of tableaux. And you can see a few older portraits, alongside a poem supposedly written by Michizane and other historical items, in the **treasure house**, set back to your left as you leave the main compound.

Kyūshū National Museum

九州国立博物館, Kyūshū Kokuritsu Hakubutsukan • 4-7-2 Ishizaka • 9.30am–5pm; closed Mon • ¥420 • ⓦ kyuhaku.com

A path beside the Tenman-gū treasure house leads to an escalator that tunnels through the rock to emerge beside a magnificent, wave-shaped building that houses the **Kyūshū National Museum**. Japan's fourth national museum after Tokyo, Kyoto and Nara, it focuses on the history of Japan's cultural trade with other Asian countries and illustrates the profound impact these interactions had on local art and culture. It's fascinating to see Chinese, Korean, Japanese and Egyptian ceramics side by side, and to compare Japanese Buddhist statues, musical instruments and lacquerware with those from neighbouring countries. The permanent exhibition hall, on the fourth floor, is beautifully laid out, comprising five themed spaces and auxiliary galleries covering prehistoric times to the Edo period; before going in,

---

THE STORY OF TENJIN

Tenjin is the divine name of **Sugawara-no-Michizane**, a brilliant scholar of the Heian period, who died in Dazaifu in 903 AD. By all accounts, Michizane was a precocious youngster – composing *waka* poems at five years old and Chinese poetry by the age of eleven – and went on to become a popular governor of Shikoku before rising to the second-highest position at court as "Minister of the Right". Not surprisingly, he found no favour with his powerful superior, Fujiwara Tokihira, who persuaded the emperor to banish Michizane. So, in 901 Michizane, accompanied by his son, daughter and a retainer, travelled south to take up a "post" as deputy governor of Dazaifu. He was kept under armed guard until he died in despair – though still loyal to the emperor – two years later. Soon after, a succession of national disasters was attributed to Michizane's restless spirit, so in 919 Tenman-gū was founded to pray for his repose. This was the first of an estimated 12,000 shrines dedicated to Tenjin in Japan.

make sure you pick up a free audio guide at the desk. The museum also hosts major temporary exhibitions.

Kōmyōzen-ji

光明禅寺 • 2-16-1 Saifu • Daily 8am–5pm • ¥200 donation

From Tenman-gū, it's about a 100m-walk south to the small, serene temple of **Kōmyōzer-ji**, founded in the mid-thirteenth century. It's an appealing collection of simple, wooden buildings whose tatami rooms contain Buddha figures or works of art. There's usually no one around, but you're welcome to explore – take your shoes off and follow the polished wooden corridors round to the rear, where there's a contemplative garden made up of a gravel sea swirling round moss-covered headlands and jutting rocks, caught against a wooded hillside. The stones in the garden at the front of the temple are arranged in the character for "light", referring to the halo of the Buddha.

Kanzeon-ji

観世音寺 • 1-1 Kanzeonji

Dazaifu's other major sights lie about twenty minutes' walk – or a short bicycle ride – west of the station; to avoid the main road, turn right in front of the post office to pick up a riverside path and then follow signs pointing you along a quiet lane. Take a left down a footpath just before a set of old foundation stones lying in the grass and the route brings you to the back of **Kanzeon-ji**. Founded in 746 AD by Emperor Tenji in honour of his mother, Empress Saimei, at one time Kanzeon-ji was the largest temple in all Kyūshū and even rated a mention in the great eleventh-century novel *The Tale of Genji* (see p.837). Only some Buddhist statues and the bronze **bell**, the oldest in Japan, remain from the original temple, while the present buildings – unadorned and nicely faded – date from the seventeenth century.

Treasure house

Daily 9am–5pm • ¥500

Kanzeon-ji's main hall holds a graceful standing Buddha, but you'll find its most magnificent statues in the modern **treasure house**, to the right as you face the hall. The immediate impression is of the sheer power of the huge wooden figures, of which even the newest is at least 750 years old. The oldest is Tobatsu-Bishamonten, standing second in line, which was sculpted from a single block of camphor wood in the eighth century. An informative English brochure provides further details, starting with the **jizō** figure facing you as you come up the stairs and working clockwise from there.

Kaidan-in

戒壇院 • 5-7-10 Kanzeonji • Daily 9am–5pm

A short walk west of the Kanzeon-ji treasure house (see above) is the two-tiered roof of **Kaidan-in** built in the late eighth century for the ordination of Buddhist priests. This is one of only three such ordination halls in Japan – the other two being in Tochigi and Nara – and again the statuary is of interest, in this case an eleven-headed Kannon from the Heian period, dressed in fading gold.

ARRIVAL AND INFORMATION   DAZAIFU

By train The easiest way of getting to Dazaifu is by train from Fukuoka's Nishitetsu-Fukuoka Station in Tenjin (3–4 hourly; 30min; ¥390).

Tourist information There's a tourist office outside Dazaifu Station (daily 9am–5.30pm; ☎ 092 925 1880),

with local maps and brochures in English.

Bike rental Ask at the train station ticket window if you'd like to rent a bike (from ¥300/3hr; 9am–6pm) to visit the western sights.

EATING

Ume-no-hana 梅の花 4-4-41 Saifu ☎0120 28 7787, ⓦumenohana.co.jp. This restaurant in the lanes east of Kōmyōzen-ji, is by far the best in Dazaifu, famed for its melt-in-the-mouth tofu creations. Served in tatami rooms overlooking a pretty garden, set meals start at ¥2500, or ¥3000 on Sundays; arrive before noon if you haven't got a reservation. Daily 11am–3.30pm & 4.30–9pm.

Yasutake やす武 Tenjin-sama-dōri ☎092 922 5079. This little place is popular for its inexpensive handmade soba dishes (from ¥750); it's on the right-hand side of Tenjin-sama-dōri, just beyond the first *torii*. Daily 10am–6pm.

Futsukaichi Onsen

二日市温泉

People have been coming to **Futsukaichi Onsen**, around 3km south of Dazaifu, since at least the eighth century to soothe muscle pain, skin complaints and digestive troubles in its healing waters. Despite being the closest hot spring to Fukuoka, the resort is still surprisingly undeveloped. There are three **public baths** (daily 9am–9pm), all grouped together in the centre of Futsukaichi, about ten minutes' walk south of JR Futsukaichi Station. The first, and easiest to spot by its English sign, is Baden House (¥460) – it's also the biggest, with a small rotemburo and sauna as well as a variety of other pools, though it is beginning to show its age. In the attractive, old-style building next door, Hakata-yu (博多湯; ¥300) is a small but spruce bathhouse favoured by Futsukaichi's senior citizens, while over the road Gozen-yu (御前湯; ¥200) with three large pools is another good option.

ARRIVAL AND INFORMATION

By train To get to the onsen from Fukuoka, take a train from JR Hakata Station to JR Futsukaichi Station (15–20min; ¥270). From Dazaifu, regular trains make the five-minute journey on the Nishitetsu line to Futsukaichi's Nishitetsu-Futsukaichi station, which is a 10min walk north of Futsukaichi Station.

Tourist information Futsukaichi's tourist office (daily 9am–6pm; ☎092 922 2421) is inside the JR station.

ACCOMMODATION AND EATING

★**Daimaru Bessō** 大丸別荘 1-20-1 Yumachi ☎092 924 3939. An atmospheric old ryokan on the south side of town, set round a traditional garden of pine trees and carp ponds. The price of the beautifully appointed tatami rooms includes two meals, and the use of their huge hot-spring bath; even if you're not staying here, it makes a grand place to eat a gourmet meal. ¥42,000

Ivy Hotel 1-14-3 Yumachi ☎092 920 2130. Ivy-clad business hotel next to the Baden House public bath (see above). Its functional Western- and Japanese-style rooms – two with their own private onsen bath – are a good option for those on a budget, while their buffet dinners are well worth splashing out on. ¥8800

Takeo

武雄

Squeezed into a narrow valley, the pleasant onsen resort of **TAKEO** makes a worthwhile stopover on your way between Fukuoka and Nagasaki. The bathing facilities are a ten-minute walk northwest of the station, behind a squat, Chinese-style gate. First on the left through the gate is Moto-yu (元湯; daily 6.30am–midnight; ¥300), the most traditional of the **public baths**. If you prefer outdoor bathing, note that the nearby Ryokan Kagetsu (旅館花月; daily 3–9pm; ¥700) has a beautiful rotemburo, and makes a good place to stay (see opposite). Takeo, indeed, often tempts its visitors to stay the night, and there are several ryokan gathered round the onsen.

ARRIVAL AND DEPARTURE

By train There are direct trains to Takeo from Fukuoka's Hataka Station (hourly; 1hr 10min; ¥2500). Getting here from Nagasaki is trickier; you'll have to change in Saga or Hizenyamaguchi (1hr 20min–3hr).

ACCOMMODATION

Mifuneyama Kankō 御船山観光 411 Takeo-chō ☎ 0954 23 3131, ⓦ mifuneyama.co.jp. Probably the best value in the area is to be had at this delightful place, whose tatami rooms have been designed with the attention to detail you'd expect at a higher-class venue. You're in Takeo for the onsen, though, and there are several gorgeous pools to choose from; the hillside-backed outdoor ones are best. **¥19,000**

Ryokan Kagetsu 旅館花月 7385 Takeo-chō ☎ 0954 26 8060. This large ryokan doesn't look that grand from the outside, but its tatami rooms are surprisingly elegant, and its onsen pools a joy to plunge into. **¥14,500**

Huis Ten Bosch
ハウステンボス

Opened in 1992 at a cost of ¥250 billion, the resort town of **HUIS TEN BOSCH** is a meticulously engineered replica of an old Dutch port. Part theme park, part serious experiment in urban living, it owes its existence to the drive and vision of **Kamichika Yoshikuni**, a local entrepreneur who was so impressed with Dutch land reclamation and environmental management that he persuaded his financiers it could work in Japan as a commercial venture. While the result may seem quaintly old world, it's equipped with the latest technology to manage its sophisticated heating systems, wave control, desalination, water recycling and security. All the pipes, cables and wires are hidden underground, and it's designed to be as environmentally benign as possible.

The attractions
Daily 9am–8.30pm · From ¥5900 · ⓦ english.huistenbosch.co.jp

The town is divided into an exclusive residential district, Wassenaar, and public areas where you'll find a raft of **museums and attractions**, plus dozens of souvenir shops and numerous restaurants. There's a wealth of themed rides and shows on site, of which three stand out – the **Great Voyage Theatre** screens a short film about the first Dutch ships to reach Japan, during which the whole seating area pitches and rolls; in **Mysterious Escher** you enter a topsy-turvy world to watch a sickly sweet but well-executed 3-D film based on Escher's famous graphics; and **Horizon Adventure** stages a real-life flood with 800 tonnes of water cascading into the theatre.

ARRIVAL AND DEPARTURE

By train The easiest way to get to the resort is on JR's special Huis ten Bosch Express direct from Fukuoka's Hakata Station (hourly; 1hr 45min; ¥2070) or on the Seaside Liner from Nagasaki (hourly; 90min; ¥1430).

By boat For those in a hurry, high-speed boats zip across Ōmura Bay direct to Huis ten Bosch from Nagasaki Airport (3 daily; 50min; ¥1600).

Nagasaki
長崎

Gathered in the tucks and crevices of steep hills rising from a long, narrow harbour, and spreading its tentacles along several tributary valleys, **NAGASAKI** is one of Japan's more picturesque cities, and one of the most popular with international visitors. This appeal is furthered by an easy-going attitude and an unusually cosmopolitan culture, resulting from over two centuries of contact with foreigners when the rest of Japan was closed to the world.

However, it does have to be said that "dark tourism" is Nagasaki's biggest draw. The city would probably have remained little more than a bustling harbour town had a chance break in the clouds on August 9, 1945, not seared it into the world's consciousness – within minutes, it became the target of the world's second **atomic**

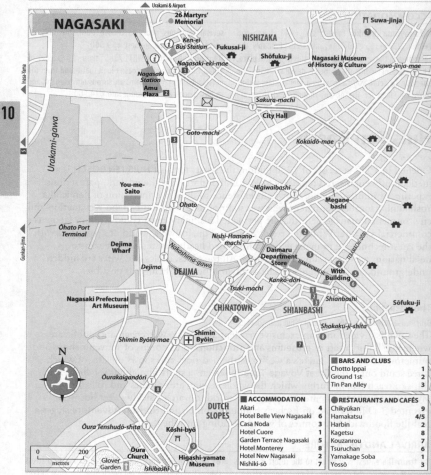

bomb. It's the A-Bomb hypocentre and nearby museum, as harrowing as that in Hiroshima, that brings most people to Nagasaki, yet the city has much else to offer. Successive communities of Chinese, Dutch, Portuguese and British have left their mark here, building colourful **Chinese temples**, Catholic **churches** and an array of European-style houses gathered in Glover Garden, as well as imported cuisines and festivals. Despite efforts to stamp out another European import, the Catholic faith, Nagasaki remains Japan's centre of **Christianity**, claiming one-sixth of the country's believers. It's possible to cover the two main areas – the Hypocentre and around Glover Garden – in a day, but Nagasaki deserves at least one extra night's stopover to explore its backstreets, soak up some atmosphere and sample a few of the city's culinary treats.

Brief history

Portuguese traders first sailed into Nagasaki in 1570, establishing a trading post and **Jesuit mission** in what was then a small fishing village of just 1500 inhabitants. For a brief period, Christianity was a major influence here, but in the late sixteenth century Toyotomi Hideyoshi, fearing the missionaries would be followed by military

AUGUST 9, 1945

In the early twentieth century, Nagasaki became an important naval base with huge munitions factories, making it an obvious target for America's second **atomic bomb** in 1945. Even so, it was only poor visibility at Kokura, near Kita-Kyūshū (see map, p.676) that forced the bomber, critically short of fuel, south to Nagasaki. The weather was bad there too, but as the B-29 bomber **Bock's Car** flew down the Urakami-gawa at 11am on August 9, a crack in the cloud revealed a sports stadium just north of the factories and shipyards. A few moments later "Fat Boy" exploded. It's estimated that over 70,000 people died in the first few seconds; 75,000 were injured and nearly forty percent of the city's houses were destroyed by the blast and its raging fires. By 1950, radiation exposure had increased the death toll to 140,000. Horrific though these figures are, they would have been higher had the valley walls not contained much of the blast; a spur of hills shielded southern Nagasaki from the worst of the damage. An American naval officer visiting the city a few weeks later described his awe at the "deadness, the absolute essence of death in the sense of finality without resurrection. It's everywhere and nothing has escaped its touch." But the city, at least, did rise again; like fellow bomb-victim Hiroshima, it's now a centre for anti-nuclear protest, and hosts many ardent campaigns for world peace.

10

intervention, started to move against the Church. Though the persecutions came in fits and starts, one of the more dramatic events occurred in Nagasaki in 1597 when Hideyoshi ordered the crucifixion of 26 Franciscans.

After 1616 the new shogun, Tokugawa Hidetada, gradually took control of all dealings with foreigners, and by the late 1630s only Chinese and Portuguese merchants continued to trade out of Nagasaki. The latter were initially confined to a tiny island enclave called **Dejima**, but in 1639 they too were expelled following a Christian-led rebellion in nearby Shimabara (see box, p.705). Two years later, their place on Dejima was filled by Dutch merchants who had endeared themselves to the shogun by sending a warship against the rebels. For the next two hundred years this tiny Dutch group, together with a slightly larger Chinese community, provided Japan's only link with the outside world. Dutch imports such as coffee, chocolate, billiards and badminton were introduced to Japan via Dejima.

Eventually, the restrictions began to ease, especially after the early seventeenth century, when technical books were allowed into Nagasaki, making the city once again Japan's main conduit for **Western learning**. Nevertheless, it wasn't until 1858 that five ports, including Nagasaki, opened for general trade. America, Britain and other nations established diplomatic missions as Nagasaki's foreign community mushroomed and its economy boomed. New inventions flooded in: the printing press, brick-making and modern shipbuilding techniques all made their Japanese debut in Nagasaki. Then came high-scale industrial development and, of course, the events of 1945 (see box above).

The Atomic Bomb Museum

長崎原爆資料館, Nagasaki Genbaku Shiryōkan • 7-8 Hiranomachi • Daily 8.30am–5.30pm; May–Aug open til 6.30pm • ¥200 • ⓦ city .nagasaki.lg.jp

Notable for its balanced approach to the events of 1945, Nagasaki's much-vaunted **Atomic Bomb Museum** is entered via a symbolic, spiralling descent. Views of prewar Nagasaki then lead abruptly into a darkened room full of twisted iron girders, blackened masonry and videos constantly scrolling through horrific photos of the dead and dying. It's strong stuff, occasionally too much for some, but the most moving exhibits are always those single fragments of an individual life – a charred lunchbox, twisted pair of glasses or the chilling shadow of a man etched on wooden planks.

The purpose of the museum isn't merely to shock, and the displays are packed with information, much of it in English, tracing the history of atomic weapons, the effects of the bomb and the heroic efforts of ill-equipped emergency teams who had little idea what they were facing. There's a fascinating video library of interviews with survivors, including

10

some of the foreigners present in Nagasaki at the time; figures vary, but probably more than 12,000 non-nationals were killed in the blast, mostly Korean forced labour working in the Mitsubishi shipyards, as well as Dutch, Australian and British prisoners of war. The museum then broadens out to examine the whole issue of nuclear weapons and ends with a depressing video about the arms race and test ban treaties.

Just outside the museum, in **Hypocentre Park**, an austere black pillar marks the precise spot where the bomb exploded 500m above the ground, while the **Peace Memorial Hall**, right by the museum, is another place for quiet reflection: its centrepiece is a remembrance hall where the names of victims are recorded in 141 volumes.

The Peace Park

平和公園, Heiwa Kōen

A short way north of the Atomic Bomb Museum, a long flight of steps leads up into the **Peace Park**, or *Heiwa-kōen*, as popular with young kids skateboarding among the donated plaques and memorials as it is with anti-nuclear lobbyists trawling for signatures. The park is watched over by sculptor Kitamura Seibō's muscular **Peace Statue**, unveiled in 1955: the figure's right hand points skyward at the threat of nuclear destruction, its left hand is extended to hold back the forces of evil. As Kazuo Ishiguro remarked in *A Pale View of Hills* from a distance the figure resembles a "policeman conducting traffic", but when an elderly person pauses on the way past, head bowed, it's not easy to remain cynical.

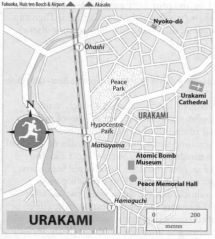

Urakami Cathedral

浦上大聖堂, Urakami Taiseidō • 1-79 Motomachi • Tues–Sun 9am–5pm • Free

From the Peace Park you can see the twin red-brick towers of **Urakami Cathedral**, dominating a small rise 400m to the east. The present building is a postwar replica of the original, which was completed in 1925 and destroyed when the atomic bomb exploded only 500m away. The blast left scorch marks on the statues now preserved at the top of the steps, and tore off huge chunks of masonry, including a section of the bell tower which still rests on the bank under the north wall. Inside the south door, a chapel is dedicated to the "Bombed Mary", from whose charred face stare sightless eyes.

26 Martyrs' Memorial

日本二十六聖人記念館, Bihon Nijūroku Seijin Kinenkan • 7-8 Mishizakamachi • Daily 9am–5pm • ¥250

In 1597, six foreign missionaries and twenty Japanese converts were the unlucky victims of the shogunate's growing unease at the power of the Church. They were marched from Kyoto and Osaka to Nagasaki, where they were crucified on February 2 as a warning to others. The group was canonized in 1862, and a century later the **26 Martyrs' Memorial**, a bizarre, mosaic-clad church, was erected on the site to commemorate Japan's first Christian martyrs, together with a small **museum** telling the history – mostly in Japanese – of the martyrs and of Christianity in Japan. A surprising amount survives, including tissue-thin prayer books hidden in bamboo and statues of the Virgin Mary disguised as the goddess Kannon. One document records the bounties offered to informers: 500 silver pieces per priest, down to 100 for a lowly catechist.

Fukusai-ji

福済寺 • 2-56 Chikugomachi • Daily 7am–4pm • ¥200

The original Zen temple, **Fukusai-ji**, was founded in 1628, destroyed in 1945 by the bomb, then replaced with a quirky, turtle-shaped building, topped by an 18m-tall, aluminium-alloy goddess and a circle of supplicating infants. Inside the temple, a 25m-long Foucault's pendulum represents a perpetual prayer for peace, oscillating over the remains of 16,500 Japanese war dead buried underneath. For the best views of the goddess, head up the hill to the graveyard behind the temple; with high-rise buildings stretching towards the ocean, it brings to mind Rio's Christ the Redeemer, and makes for a particularly beautiful view at sunset.

Shōfuku-ji

聖福寺 • 3-77 Tamazonomachi • Daily 24hr • Free

Showing its age somewhat, the Zen temple **Shōfuku-ji**, which originally dates from the early seventeenth century, was rebuilt in 1715 and survived the bomb. Inside the imposing gateway you'll find an attractive collection of aged wooden buildings surrounded by rustling bamboo stands and shady trees. Its main attributes are some detailed carving on the gates and unusual decorative features such as the red balustrade around the worship hall.

Nagasaki Museum of History and Culture

長崎歴史文化博物館, Nagasaki Rekishi Bunka Hakubutsukan • 1-1-1 Tateyama • Tues–Sun 8.30am–7pm; closed 3rd Tues of month • ¥900 • ⊕ nmhc.jp

The engaging **Nagasaki Museum of History and Culture** focuses on the city's role as a conduit for cultural exchange. It's set in a pretty building in a large, grassy compound that's worth visiting even if you don't fancy seeing the exhibits. Inside (be sure to pick up a free audio guide at the ticket desk), there are plenty of original materials, including an exquisite seventeenth-century folding screen depicting British and Dutch ships in Nagasaki harbour, and the first Japanese–English dictionary compiled by Dutch interpreters in 1814. Alongside scale models and videos, there's a room devoted to local crafts, some showing distinctly foreign influences, and you exit through a reconstruction of the Nagasaki Magistrate's office.

Suwa-jinja

諏訪神社 • 8-15 Kaminishiyamamachi • 24hr • Free

Accessed via a challenging flight of steep steps, **Suwa-jinja** is Nagasaki's major shrine. It was founded in 1625 when the shogunate was promoting Shintoism in opposition to

> ## KUNCHI MATSURI
>
> Each autumn, Suwa-jinja hosts the famous **Kunchi Matsuri** (Oct 7–9). This festival is believed to have originated in 1633 when two courtesans performing a nō dance attracted huge crowds during celebrations to mark the ninth day of the ninth lunar month. Gradually, European and Chinese elements were incorporated – this was one of the few occasions when Dutch merchants were allowed to leave Dejima – and the jollities now consist of dragon dances and heavy floats, some fashioned as Chinese and Dutch ships, being spun round outside the shrine.

10

the Christian Church. Its main hall, rebuilt in 1869, is fresh and simple, but for most foreigners its greatest attraction is the English-language fortune papers on sale beside the collecting box (¥200). The grounds are scattered with unusual subsidiary shrines, notably two *koma-inu* (guardian lions) known as the **stop lions**, where people vowing to give up unwanted habits fasten paper strings around the front legs, like plaster casts; you'll find them just around the corner from the main hall. Lastly, there's a good place to eat on site, *Yamakage Soba* (see p.701)

Along the Nakashima-gawa

Below Suwa-jinja, the **Nakashima-gawa** flows west through central Nagasaki under a succession of stone bridges linked by a pleasant riverside walk. The most noteworthy of these is the double-arched **Megane-bashi** (眼鏡橋), aptly named "Spectacles Bridge", which is Japan's oldest stone bridge, dating from 1634. Across **Megane-bashi**, Teramachi-dōri (Temple-town Street) parallels the river; in between this street and the river lies a lattice of quiet alleys that constitutes one of Nagasaki's most charming areas.

Chinatown

In the seventeenth century, Nagasaki's Chinese community comprised over fifteen percent of the population. Like the Europeans, they were restricted to a designated area that lay just inland from Dejima, near today's **Chinatown**. Four elaborate gates signpost this colourful grid of six blocks packed with shops and restaurants, while a bare earth park over on the south side houses an older wooden gate and a Chinese pavilion where old men sit and gossip over chess pieces.

Dejima

出島 • Dejimamachi • Daily 8am–6pm; grounds open until 7pm • ¥500

Immediately northwest of Chinatown, traces of **Dejima**, the Portuguese and (later) Dutch enclave, can still be found along a curve of the old sea wall. Created in 1636, this tiny artificial island provided Japan's only access to the Western world for over two hundred years (see p.797). The island was swallowed up in later land reclamations, but has recently been re-created in its original style. It's best to start at the far, west gate, where the **Chief Factor's residence** is one of the grandest buildings, its dining room laid out for a lavish and – to Japanese eyes – exotic Christmas dinner. In the charming garden area outside, keep your eyes peeled for a tree transported here from Jakarta (then Dutch territory) in the mid-nineteenth century.

Nagasaki Prefectural Art Museum

長崎県美術館, Nagasaki-ken Bijutsukan • 2-1 Dejimamachi • Daily 10am–8pm; closed second & fourth Mon of month • Free • ⓦ nagasaki-museum.jp

A couple of minutes' walk southwest of Dejima, the modern **Nagasaki Prefectural Art Museum** occupies a splendidly airy building on the waterfront. It's particularly strong on Spanish art, including works by Picasso, Dalí and Miró, and Meiji-era art from Nagasaki, though only part of the collection is on show at any one time.

Sōfuku-ji

崇福寺 • 7-5 Kajiyamachi • Daily 8am–5pm • ¥300

Some way east of Chinatown, at the southern end of a street lined with temples on one side and neighbourhood shops on the other, you'll see signs pointing left to **Sōfuku-ji**. This is Nagasaki's most important Chinese Zen temple, founded in 1629 by Fujian immigrants and containing rare examples of Ming-period Chinese architecture.

Ōura Catholic Church

大浦天主堂, Ōura Tenshudō 5-3 Minamiyamatemachi • Daily 8am–6pm • ¥300

In the south of the city, a parade of souvenir shops lines the road up to **Ōura Catholic Church**, Japan's oldest extant Christian place of worship. A pretty little white structure with nothing much to see inside, it was built by French missionaries in 1864 to serve Nagasaki's growing foreign community. A few months later Father Petitjean was astonished to find outside his door a few brave members of Nagasaki's "hidden Christians" who had secretly kept the faith for more than two centuries.

10

Glover Garden

グラバー園, Gumbā-en • Daily: April 27 to May 7 & July 15–Oct 9 8am–9.30pm; May 8 to July 14 & Oct 10–April 26 8am–6pm • ¥600 • ⓦ glover-garden.jp • From Ishibashi Station, take the elevator-like structure which whisks you diagonally to an upper vantage point, from where a more regular lift will take you up to the garden's upper entrance

Despite the crowds, and day-round piped music, pretty **Glover Garden** is well worth a visit. As well as offering some of Nagasaki's best views, it features seven late nineteenth-century, European-style buildings, each typically colonial with wide verandas, louvred shutters and high-ceilinged, spacious rooms. The houses also contain odds and ends of furniture and evocative photos of the pioneering inhabitants they once housed.

The best approach is to enter via the garden's upper entrance and work down. From here, the first building you'll come across is **Walker House**, a modest bungalow built in the 1870s for the British-born captain of a Japanese passenger ship after he helped provide transport for government troops in the Satsuma Rebellion (see p.706). On retiring from the sea in 1898 he joined Thomas Glover, the bluff's most colourful and illustrious resident (see box below), in setting up Japan's first soft drinks company, which produced a popular line in "Banzai Lemonade" and "Banzai Cider" and eventually became Kirin Brewery. Glover's old house is worth a look around, as are those formerly belonging to Frederick Ringer, founder of the Nagasaki Press, and tea merchant William Alt.

THOMAS GLOVER

Scotsman **Thomas Glover** arrived in Nagasaki from Shanghai in 1859, aged just 22, and became involved in various enterprises, including arms dealing. In the mid-1860s, rebels seeking to overthrow the shogun approached Glover for his assistance. Not only did he supply them with weapons, he also furthered their revolutionary cause by smuggling some of them abroad to study, including Ito Hirobumi, who eventually served as prime minister in the new Meiji government. For this, and his subsequent work in modernizing Japanese industry, Glover was awarded the Second Class Order of the Rising Sun – a rare honour – shortly before his death in Tokyo, aged 73.

Glover built the bungalow now known as **Glover House** in 1863, where he lived with his wife Tsuru, a former geisha, and his son from an earlier liaison, Tomisaburō. After his father's death, Tomisaburō was a valued member of both the Japanese and foreign business communities, but as Japan slid towards war in the mid-1930s his companies were closed and he came under suspicion as a potential spy. Forced to move out of Glover House, with its bird's-eye view of the harbour, and kept under virtual house arrest, he committed suicide two weeks after the atomic bomb flashed above Nagasaki.

The exit from Glover Garden takes you through the **Museum of Traditional Performing Arts** (same ticket), which displays the beautifully fashioned floats and other paraphernalia used during the Kunchi festivities (see box, p.696).

The Dutch Slopes

オランダ坂, Oranda-Saka

On the opposite bluff to Glover Garden, and divided from it by a small stream, is a prettified hillside district known as the **Dutch Slopes**. Though it's only a short walk from Glover Garden and the Catholic Church, few visitors bother to venture into this area, which is centred on the **Higashi-yamate** (東山手) clutch of blue, wooden Western-style buildings that have been preserved on roads still paved with their original flagstones. The first group of period wooden houses on the left consists of two neat rows: the lower row houses a **photography museum** (9am–5pm, closed Mon; ¥100) displaying fascinating early photos of Nagasaki. The second building in the upper row is the **Higashi-yamate Museum** (9am–5pm, closed Mon; free), which exhibits Japanese-language materials about the district and efforts to rescue the old buildings.

Kōshi-byō

孔子廟 • 10-36 Ouramachi • Daily 8.30am–5pm • ¥525

Walking along the Dutch slopes you can't miss the bright yellow roofs of **Kōshi-byō**, nestling at the foot of the hill within its stout, red-brick wall. Interestingly, the land beneath this **Confucian shrine**, completed in 1893, belongs to China and is administered by the embassy in Tokyo. Its present pristine state is due to an extensive 1980s rebuild using materials imported from China, from the glazed roof tiles to the glittering white marble flagstones and the statues of Confucius's 72 disciples that fill the courtyard.

Inasa-yama

稲佐山 • **Ropeway** daily: March–Nov 9am–10pm; mid-Dec to Feb 9am–9pm; closed early Dec • ¥700 one-way, ¥1200 return • Take Nagasaki Bus #3 or #4 from outside Nagasaki train station and get off across the river at Ropeway-mae bus stop, from where the entrance is up the steps in the grounds of a shrine

Nagasaki is not short of good viewpoints, but none can compare with the spectacular night-time panorama from **Inasa-yama**, a 333m-high hill to the west of the city. A **ropeway**, or cable-car, whisks you up there in just five minutes; cars run every twenty minutes. From the top, you get stunning views of the contorted local coastline, as well as the confetti of nearby islands and islets.

ARRIVAL AND INFORMATION
NAGASAKI

By plane Nagasaki Airport (☎ 095 752 5555) occupies an artificial island in Ōmura Bay, 40km from town and connected by limousine bus (40min–1hr; ¥800) to Nagasaki train station. It receives a few international flights from neighbouring Asian countries, including regular services from Seoul and Shanghai.
Destinations Nagoya (3 daily; 1hr 15min); Naha (1 daily; 1hr 35min); Osaka (Itami; 6 daily; 1hr 5min); and Tokyo (1–2 hourly; 1hr 30min).

By train The train station sits at the south end of the highway running into the city, roughly 1km north of the main downtown area.
Destinations Hakata, Fukuoka (every 30min–1hr; 2hr); Huis ten Bosch (1 hourly; 1hr 30min); and Isahaya

(1–2 hourly; 20min).

By bus Most long-distance buses either stop outside the train station, or pull into Ken-ei bus station on the opposite side of the road.
Destinations Beppu (7 daily; 3hr 10min–4hr 40min); Huis ten Bosch (1–2 hourly; 1hr 15min); Kumamoto (8 daily; 3hr); and Unzen (7 daily; 1hr 40min).

Tourist information The best source of information is the Nagasaki Prefectural Tourist Information Centre (daily 9am–5.30pm; ☎ 095 828 7875), located on the second floor above Ken-ei bus station. You can also pick up city maps and a few English pamphlets at Nagasaki City Tourist Information (daily 8am–8pm; ☎ 095 823 3631, ⓦ at-nagasaki.jp), inside the station by the ticket barrier.

BATTLESHIP ISLAND

Jutting out of the sea about 15km off Nagasaki lies the city's most fascinating attraction, and one that may well be familiar due to its appearance as a menacing location in the 2012 James Bond film *Skyfall*. Properly known as Hashima, it's more commonly referred to as **Gunkan-jima**, or "Battleship Island"; this may sound like a board game or pirate film, but the reality is far more interesting.

Gunkan-jima was once one of Japan's most important sources of coal, and from 1890 to 1974 it was inhabited by hundreds of miners and their families. This dense concentration of people gave Japan a sneak preview of what it has become today – Gunkan-jima boasted the country's first ever high-rise concrete buildings, which together with the island's high sea walls make it appear from a distance like some huge and rather monstrous ship, hence the name. For a time it functioned quite well, with just enough schools, shops and housing to keep its tiny population satisfied. However, development in mainland Japan soon raced ahead, giving this brave attempt at urban utopia a relatively improverished appearance. Its fate was sealed when the domestic coal industry collapsed in the mid-1970s; the island was abandoned and left to decay.

Gunkan-jima only opened to tourists in 2009, and it is now possible to visit on short trips. Interest has ballooned since the place was used as a set on *Skyfall* – if you look anything like Daniel Craig or Javier Bardem (in other words, male and white), you may well become photo-fodder for local tourists. Once on the island, you'll be taking plenty of pictures yourself, as it's rather unique, and quite spectacular–with a little imagination, you'll discern echoes of Cappadocian caves, Pompeii, or (suitably, given its proximity to Nagasaki) a nuclear disaster.

At least four companies run near-identical **tours**, though cut-throat competition means that prices yo-yo almost as fast as the ocean waves; your hotel or hostel should be able to book you a place, but if this fails try the tourist office (see opposite). It's wise to book at least a couple of days ahead, and note that trips can be cancelled in bad weather (this happens quite often). Tours cost from ¥3000 and last around 3hr; as well as a brief stop on Gunkan-jima (you're not allowed to wander off on your own), most include a visit to a small museum on a neighbouring island.

10

GETTING AROUND

By tram Given its elongated shape, Nagasaki's sights are all fairly spread out. However, it's one of the easier cities for getting around, thanks mainly to its cheap and easy tram system. There are four lines, numbered #1 to #5 (line #2 doesn't run for most of the day), each identified and colour-coded on the front. If transferring, ask for a transfer ticket (*norikae-kippu*). There's a flat fare of ¥120 which you feed into the driver's box on exit or you can buy a one-day pass (¥500) at the information centres and hotels. While you're clanking along, take a look around: some of these trolley cars are museum pieces – the oldest dates from 1911 – which were snapped up when other Japanese cities were merrily ripping up their tramlines.

By bus City buses are more complicated than trams, but the only time you're likely to need them is to get to the Inasa-yama Ropeway (see opposite).

Car rental Eki Rent-a-Car ☎ 095 826 0480; Nippon Rent-a-Car ☎ 095 821 0919; Nissan Rent-a-Car ☎ 095 825 1988; Toyota Rent-a-Car ☎ 095 825 0100.

ACCOMMODATION

Nagasaki offers a broad range of rooms, widely dispersed around the city. The main choice is whether to stay at the cheaper places near the station or in the southern, downtown district. There are also a few reasonable places near the A-Bomb Hypocentre, in the north of the city, but it's not that pleasant a place to stay.

Hotel Belle View Nagasaki 1-20 Edo-machi ☎ 095 826 5030, ⊛ hotel-belleview.com. Reasonably priced business hotel with friendly and efficient service plus a restaurant, bar and free internet access in all rooms. Rates include a buffet breakfast. **¥7000**

Hotel Cuore 7-3 Daikoku-machi ☎ 095 818 9000, ⊛ hotel-cuore.com. Spruce business hotel opposite the station. Everything you could possibly need, including trouser press and tea-making equipment, is squeezed into the smallest space imaginable in the single rooms, which aren't really worth the money; double and twins are slightly more spacious. Rates include a good buffet breakfast. **¥7000**

★**Garden Terrace Nagasaki** 1-20 Akizuki-machi ☎ 095 864 7777, ⊛ gt-nagasaki.jp. Imagine a giant Rubik's Cube made of pine, and you're halfway to visualizing award-winning architect Kuma Kengo's classy boutique hotel. Sitting halfway up a mountain on the other side of the bay, its various suites are decked out with

10

MADAME BUTTERFLY

Puccini's opera, written in the early twentieth century, tells the story of an American lieutenant stationed in Nagasaki who marries a Japanese woman known as **Madame Butterfly**. Whereas she has given up her religion and earned the wrath of her family to enter the marriage, Lt. Pinkerton treats the marriage far less seriously, and is soon posted back to the US. Unknown to Pinkerton, Butterfly has given birth to their son and is waiting faithfully for his return when he arrives back in Nagasaki three years later. Butterfly pretties up her house and prepares to present her child to the proud father. Pinkerton, meanwhile, has remarried in America and brings his new wife to meet the unsuspecting Butterfly. When he offers to adopt the child, poor Butterfly agrees and tells him to come back later. She then embraces her son and falls on her father's sword.

The opera was adapted from a play by David Belasco, though some attribute it to a book by Frenchman Pierre Loti who wrote *Madame Chrysanthème* after spending a month in Nagasaki in 1885 with a young Japanese woman called Kane. Whatever its origin, the opera was not well received at its debut and Puccini was forced to rewrite Pinkerton and his American wife in a more sympathetic light. Efforts to trace the real Pinkerton have led to a William B. Franklin, but there are many contenders; it was common practice in the late nineteenth century for Western males stationed in Japan to "marry" a geisha in order to secure their companion's faithfulness and reduce the spread of venereal disease. In return, they provided accommodation plus some remuneration. As soon as the posting ended, however, the agreement was considered null and void on both sides.

angular furniture, and each provides a wonderful city view – in some cases, even from the bathtub. **¥50,000**

Hotel Monterey 1-22 Ōura-machi ☎095 827 7111, ⓦhotelmonterey.co.jp. Good location, smartly designed rooms, attentive service and free internet connections – not bad, in other words. You can get big discounts by booking online. **¥22,500**

Hotel New Nagasaki 14-5 Daikoku-machi ☎095 826 8000, vnewnaga.com. Central Nagasaki's top hotel, conveniently placed just outside the station, has all the trimmings: grand marble lobby, shopping arcade, restaurants, bar and fitness centre with swimming pool. The rooms are mostly Western-style, some boasting harbour views. **¥24,500**

Nishiki-sō にしき荘 1-2-7 Nishiko-shima ☎095 826 6371. If you're after a bit of Japanese flavour, try this welcoming budget guesthouse on the far east side of town, up a short flight of steps. There's a choice of well-kept tatami rooms that come with or without views and en-suite facilities. **¥9000**

HOSTELS

★ **Akari** 2-2 Kojiya-machi ☎095 801 7900, ⓦnagasaki-hostel.com. Home to pretty much every backpacker who swings though, and rightly so – dorms and private rooms alike are cosy places to bunk down, there's a cool common room to relax in, and the canalside location is very pleasant. In addition, the clued-up, super-friendly staff are able – and, more importantly, willing – to advise on all things Nagasaki. Dorm **¥2500**, double **¥6300**

Casa Noda 2F 6-1 Motofuna-machi ☎095 800 2484, ⓦcasanoda.jp. Just a few minutes from the station, this laidback flophouse has a few spacious (if soulless) dorms, as well as some cheerier private rooms. What you'll get from the staff largely depends upon who's behind the desk at the time. Dorm **¥2300**, double **¥6000**

EATING

Nagasaki's most famous culinary **speciality** is *shippoku*, in which various European, Chinese and Japanese dishes are served almost like tapas at a lacquered round table. It's not cheap, starting at around ¥4000 per head; for the best *shippoku* you need to reserve the day before, although most of the big hotels also offer a less formal version. Nagasaki's other home-grown dishes include the cheap and cheerful *champon*, in which morsels of seafood, meat and vegetables are served with a dollop of thick noodles in piping-hot soup. *Sara udon* blends similar ingredients into a thicker sauce on a pile of crispy noodle strands—this tasty dish is an import from Hong Kong and southern China. One bizarre local dish is Toruko rice, an unwieldy fusion of spaghetti, rice, salad, breaded pork cutlet and curry sauce, all co-existing on the same plate; the first component of its name means "Turkish", possibly due an old, erroneous presumption that Turkish folk, being exotic, eat curry.

★ **Chikyūkan** 地球館 Higashi-yamate ☎095 822 7966. A fun little place in the delightful wooden buildings on the Dutch Slopes. On normal days it's a simple café serving Indian chai (¥500), English apple cake (¥300) and the like; at weekends, they dole out meals from a different country each week, usually cooked by international students from the city universities. Thurs, Fri & Mon 10am–5pm; Sat & Sun noon–3pm.

Hamakatsu 浜勝 1-14 Kajiya-chō. Popular restaurant on Teramachi-dōri specializing in juicy *tonkatsu* (pork cutlets). Though it looks smart, with its gold signboard and iron lantern, prices are reasonable (¥1000–1500) and you can eat all you want of the extras – soup, rice and salad. Daily 11am–midnight.

Hamakatsu 浜勝 6-50 Kajiya-chō ☎095 826 8321. This even smarter *Hamakatsu* offers good-value *shippoku* meals. You can try a mini-*shippoku* for ¥3800 or the real thing from ¥4800 up to over ¥10,000/person; it's best to reserve, and for a full *shippoku* they require a minimum of two people. Daily 11am–11pm.

Harbin ハルビン 2F, 4-13 Yorozuya-machi ☎095 824 5650. Above the *Doutor* café on Kankō-dōri pedestrian arcade, this Nagasaki institution has been serving French and Russian cuisine since 1959. Portions aren't huge, but the food's tasty and there's plenty of choice, from borscht to Russian-style *pot au feu*, and over 30 different vodkas. Lunchtime set menus from ¥1000; count on at least ¥3000 in the evening. 11.30am–2.30pm & 5–11pm, closed Wed.

Kagetsu 花月 2-1 Maruyama-machi ☎095 822 0191, ⊛ryoutei-kagetsu.co.jp. Set in an exquisite traditional garden, this lovely, 360-year-old restaurant is the best spot in town for *shippoku*. Lunchtime prices start at ¥5220 for a *shippoku* bentō or ¥10,000 for the full meal; in the evening you'll pay upwards of ¥13,900. Booking is essential and you need at least two people to order the full *shippoku*. Noon–3pm & 6–10pm, closed one day a week.

Kouzanrou 江山楼 12-2 Shinchi-machi ☎095 824 5000. Chinatown is packed with tempting restaurants, but this Fukien establishment is recommended for its reasonably priced *champon* and *sara udon* (both ¥840), as well as more mainstream Chinese dishes. Try to nab a table by the window. Daily 11am–9pm.

Tsuruchan ツル茶ん 2-4-7 Aburayamachi, ☎095 824 2679. This claims to be the restaurant where Toruko rice, Nagasaki's prime culinary oddity (see above), was invented: whether this should invoke pride or shame is anyone's guess. The "regular" variety of this irregular dish goes for ¥980, and the place doubles as a decent, atmospheric little café. Daily 9am–10.30pm.

Yamakage Soba 山陰そば Suwa-jinja. Part of the Suwa-jinja shrine complex, this is a very pleasant place for chow down soba (from ¥750) or other Japanese staples; their *katsu-kare* (¥760) is gigantic. Choose an outdoor seat if possible, so you can eat accompanied by views out over Nagasaki, and the sound of nearby trickling water. Mon, Tues, Wed & Thurs 10am–4pm; Sat & Sun 9am–5pm.

Yossō 吉宗 8-9 Hamano-machi ☎095 821 0075. Famous old restaurant specializing in *chawan-mushi*, a steamed egg custard laced with shrimp, shiitake mushroom, bamboo shoots and other goodies. You'll pay around ¥750 for a basic bowl, or ¥1260 with rice and pickles, while a *teishoku* will set you back ¥1800. Tinkling *shamisen* music sets the tone. Daily 11am–9pm.

DRINKING AND ENTERTAINMENT

Nagasaki's entertainment district, **Shianbashi** (思案橋), is sandwiched between Hamanomachi shopping district and Chinatown, in the south of the city. Ironically, *shi-an* translates as something like "peaceful contemplation", which is the last thing you'll find in this tangle of lanes, packed with bars, clubs, pachinko parlours, *izakaya* and "soaplands" (seedy massage parlours), where nothing really gets going until 10pm and ends at dawn. The choice is bewildering and prices can be astronomical, but a safe place to start is the With Building, on the east edge of the district on Kankō-dōri. It's a one-stop night out, starting in the basement and working upwards through a host of restaurants, bars and nightclubs.

Chotto Ippai 2-13 Motoshikkui-machi. Meaning "a little drunk" but also known as "Ken's Bar" on account of its affable American owner. It's a real rarity among foreign-owned bars, since it's just as likely to be filled with elderly locals as English teachers. A huge *shōchū* selection – mainly from Amami-Ōshima – keeps everyone entertained. Come after 10pm. Mon–Sat 6pm–late.

Ground 1st 4-10 Motoshikkui-machi. A cocktail-and-beer bar with English-speaking staff, a dartboard, graffiti all over the walls and a pleasantly scruffy atmosphere. It's popular with expats, the Japanese who want to meet them, and local shipyard workers. Mon–Sat 5pm–late.

Tin Pan Alley 4F, 5-10 Motoshikkui-machi ☎095 818 8277, ⊛tin-pan-alley.jp. The house band struts its stuff nightly with a playlist ranging from mellow groove to rock and pop classics. Entry charge ¥1500 for men, ¥1000 for women. Tues–Sun 7pm–3am.

SHOPPING

The main department stores, Daimaru and Hamaya, are in the Hamanomachi shopping arcades, while Amu Plaza and You-me-saito are the two biggest shopping malls. The most popular local souvenir is Castella (*kasutera*) sponge cake – the best-known Castella bakeries are Fukusaya and Bunmei-dō, both of which have outlets all over the city.

NAGASAKI FESTIVALS

Chinese New Year is celebrated in Chinatown with a Lantern Festival, dragon dances and acrobatic displays (late Jan to mid-Feb). **Dragon-boat races**, here called *Peiron*, were introduced by the Chinese in 1655 and still take place in Nagasaki harbour every summer (June–July). The last evening of **Obon** (Aug 15) is celebrated with a "spirit-boat" procession, when recently bereaved families lead lantern-lit floats down to the harbour. The biggest bash of the year occurs at the **Kunchi Matsuri** held in early Oct at Suwa-jinja (see box, p.696).

DIRECTORY

Banks and exchange The 18th Bank, next to the *New Nagasaki Hotel*, is the closest foreign exchange service to the train station; its main branch is at 1-11 Dōza, on the banks of the Nakashima-gawa just north of Chinatown. You can also change money at the Central Post Office.

Hospital Shimin Byōin, 6-39 Shinchi-machi (☎095 822 3251) is an emergency hospital on the western edge of Chinatown.

Police 6-13 Okeya-machi (☎095 822 0110). Emergency numbers are listed on p.66.

Post office Nagasaki Central Post Office is 300m east of the station at 1-1 Ebisu-machi.

Travel agencies For domestic travel, the main JTB office is on the ground floor of the *New Nagasaki Hotel* (☎095 824 5194). International tickets can be bought at H.I.S., 2F, 4-22 Tsuki-machi (☎095 820 6839, ⊛his .com), across the river from the north end of the Hamanomachi arcade.

Shimabara Hantō

East of Nagasaki, the **Shimabara Hantō** bulges out into the Ariake Sea, tethered to mainland Kyūshū by a neck of land just 5km wide. The peninsula owes its existence to the past volcanic fury of **Unzen-dake**, which still grumbles away, pumping out sulphurous steam, and occasionally spewing lava down its eastern flanks. Buddhist monks first came to the mountain in the eighth century, followed more than a millennium later by Europeans from nearby Nagasaki, attracted by the cool, upland summers and mild winters. Even today, **Unzen**, a small onsen resort surrounded by pine trees and billowing clouds of steam, draws holiday-makers to its hot springs, malodorous "hells" and scenic hiking trails. One of the most popular outings is to the lava dome of **Fugen-dake**, which roared back into life in 1990 after two centuries of inactivity, and now smoulders menacingly above the old castle town of **Shimabara** – this was protected from the worst of the eruption by an older lava block, but still suffered considerable damage to its southern suburbs. Previously, Shimabara was famous largely for its association with a Christian-led rebellion in the seventeenth century when 37,000 peasants and their families were massacred. Both towns can be covered on a long day's journey between Nagasaki and Kumamoto, but if time allows, Unzen makes a relaxing overnight stop.

Unzen

雲仙

Little more than a village, the lofty town of **UNZEN** sits contentedly on a plateau of the same name. Its name means "fairyland among the clouds", perhaps inspired by the pure mountain air and colourful flourishes of vegetation – azaleas in spring, and fiery-red leaves in the autumn. Competing for attention against this sumptuous backdrop are the town's **onsen**, renowned for their silky-smooth water, and the spitting, scalding **jigoku** (地獄), whose name translates as "hells". Unzen town consists largely of resort hotels and souvenir shops strung out along the main road, but fortunately there's plenty of space around and a variety of **walking trails** leads off into the surrounding national park. The best hikes explore the peaks of Unzen-dake; from the top of **Fugen-dake** you're rewarded with splendid views of the Ariake Sea and, if you're lucky, Aso-san's steaming cauldron.

Brief history

A Shingon Buddhist priest is credited with "founding" Unzen when he built a temple here in 701 AD; the area developed into a popular retreat where monks could contemplate the 84,000 tortures awaiting wrongdoers in the afterlife as they gazed at Unzen's bubbling mud pools. The first commercial onsen bath was opened in 1653, and two hundred years later Europeans arriving from Nagasaki, Hong Kong, Shanghai and east Russia prompted the development of a full-blown resort, complete with mock-Tudor hotels and one of Japan's first golf courses, laid out in 1913. The volcanic vents are less active nowadays but still emit evil, sulphurous streams and waft steam over a landscape of bilious-coloured clay. Only the hardiest of acid-tolerant plants can survive, and local hoteliers have added to the satanic scene by laying a mess of rusting, hissing pipes to feed water to their onsen baths.

10

The jigoku

The *jigoku* provide an interesting hour's diversion, particularly the more active eastern area. The paths are well signposted, with lots of maps and information along the way, and there's also a descriptive English-language brochure available free at the information centre (see p.704). **Daikyōkan Jigoku**, the highest and most active "hell", takes its name ("great shout") from the shrill noise produced as it emits hydrogen sulphide steam at 120°C. The noise is likened to the cries of souls descending to hell, but could well be the howls of the 33 Christian martyrs commemorated on a nearby monument, who were scalded to death here around 1630 by the Shimabara lords (see opposite). Another unhappy end is remembered at **Oito Jigoku**, which, according to legend, broke out the day a local adulteress, Oito, was executed for murdering her husband. The tiny, bursting bubbles of **Suzume Jigoku**, on the other hand, supposedly resemble the twittering of sparrows. Over in the western section, the main point of interest is **Mammyō-ji** temple, beside the Shimatetsu bus station. Founded nearly 1300 years ago, the temple is now home to a large gilded Shaka Buddha sporting a natty blue hairdo.

Fugen-dake

普賢岳 • Ropeway daily 8.50am–5.20pm • ¥1220 return • 6 buses daily run from Unzen's Ken-ei station (25min; ¥740 return) to the departure point for the Ropeway; the last bus back leaves at 5.20pm (4.30pm in Nov & Dec).

While Unzen-dake is the name of the whole volcanic mass, **Fugen-dake** (1488m) refers to a newer cone on its east side that now forms the highest of the Unzen peaks. Fugen-dake erupted suddenly in November 1990, reaching a crescendo in June 1991 when the dome collapsed, sending an avalanche of mud and rocks through Shimabara town. Forty-three people were killed and nearly 2000 homes destroyed. There have been some minor rumbles since, but the eruption officially ended in 1996 and for now Fugen-dake just steams away gently.

A **ropeway** takes visitors up from Nita Pass to an observation platform to the west of Fugen-dake. Cars run every twenty minutes, though not in bad weather or if the volcano is misbehaving. From the top station, you can walk up Fugen-dake (1347m) in about an hour for views of the 1990 lava dome, though check beforehand that the path is open.

UNZEN'S ONSEN

The nicest of Unzen's **public baths** is the old-style **Kojigoku Onsen** (小地獄温泉; daily 9am–9pm; ¥400), which occupies two octagonal wooden buildings roughly ten minutes' walk south of town; take the left turn just past the *Fukuda-ya* hotel. More central is **Shin-yu** (新湯; daily 10am–11pm; ¥100), a small but traditional bathhouse overlooking a car park at the southern entrance to the *jigoku*. Lastly, there's the rather glitzy **Unzen Spa House** (daily 10am–6pm; ¥800), which offers a sauna and a variety of baths, including a rotemburo, in a half-timbered building on the main road into town. In addition, most hotels also open their baths to non-residents during the day, for a fee.

10

By bus Without your own transport, the best way to get to Unzen is by bus. Direct services leave from Nagasaki's Ken-ei bus station (7 daily; 1hr 45min–2hr; ¥1900), or JR Pass holders can take the train to Isahaya Station (諫早) and pick up a Nagasaki Ken-ei bus from the other side of the road (¥1300; 9 daily; 1hr 20min). Unzen has two bus stations: Ken-ei buses from Nagasaki and Isahaya pull in at the far north end of town, while Shimatetsu buses for the onward journey to Shimabara

(6 daily; 45min) depart from a square a little furth back down the main road.

Tourist information For general information abo accommodation and transport, try Unzen Informatio Centre (daily 9am–5pm; ☎0957 73 3434, ⑳unzen.org located at the south end of town, next to Unzen Spa House **Services** The post office opposite has an ATM tha accepts international cards (Mon–Fri 9am–5.30pm, Sa 9am–12.30pm).

ACCOMMODATION AND EATING

Fukuda-ya 福田屋 380-2 Obama-chō ☎0957 73 2151, ⑳fukudaya.co.jp. A modern hotel with good-sized rooms decked out in warm ochre colours and a choice of rotemburo (non-residents noon–9pm; ¥700). Even if you're not staying, try the sizzling plates of *yōgan* (lava) soba noodles big enough for two, as well as delicious sweet-potato ice cream, among other inexpensive dishes (daily 11am–10pm). **¥24,000**

Kaseya かせや 315 Obama-chō ☎0957 73 3321. The pleasingly-worn-around-the-edges tatami rooms of this

ryokan have been housing guests for decade Reservations are recommended, as are the deliciou meals. **¥14,500**

Unzen Kankō Hotel 雲仙観光ホテル 320 Obama-ch ☎0957 73 3263, ⑳unzenkankohotel.com. With wonderful garden setting, this is one of the origina European-style hotels, built in 1935, with lots of dark highly polished wood and spacious public areas. The cheaper rooms are all Western-style; small but comfortable and equipped with large, old-fashioned bathtubs. **¥36,00**

Shimabara
島原

With its superb castle and the brooding, volcanic backdrop of Fugen-dake, the small port town of **SHIMABARA** makes for a pleasingly relaxed stay, or a day-trip from Nagasaki or Kumamoto. Its quiet streets, which give no inkling of the town's chequered history, straggle along the coast for more than 2km from the southerly Shimabara-kō ferry terminal to the main centre, Ōte, just below the castle. Following the ructions of the **Shimabara Rebellion** (see box opposite), the place was decimated when Unzen-dake erupted in 1792, sending rock and hot ash tumbling into Shimabara Bay. An estimated 15,000 people died in the disaster, mostly from huge tidal waves that swept the Ariake Sea. The volcano then lay dormant until Fugen-dake burst into life again in 1990 (see p.703) and cut a swathe through the town's southern reaches. To the outsider, there's little visible evidence of the devastation wreaked by the mud flows, beyond some heavy-duty retaining walls aimed at channelling any future flows directly down to the sea.

Shimabara-jō
島原城 • April–Oct daily 9am–5.30pm • Grounds free; museum ¥520

Completed in 1625, **Shimabara-jō** castle took seven years to build – it was partly the taxes and hard labour demanded for its construction that provoked the Shimabara Rebellion. The grounds make for pleasant walking, and the reconstructed turrets contain a **museum**, spread among three buildings – most interesting are the main keep's local history exhibits, including relics of clandestine Christian worship. The modern building in the northwest corner shows a short film about Fugen-dake, while fans of Nagasaki's Peace Statue (see p.694) will be interested in the Kitamura Seibō Memorial Museum located in the southeast turret. Kitamura, a local sculptor who died in 1987, specialized in powerful bronzes, the best of them gripped by a restless, pent-up energy.

Bukeyashiki
武家屋敷 • Houses daily 9am–5pm • Free

A few remnants of the old castle-town still exist. A couple of minutes' walk northwest of the castle, **Bukeyashiki** is a pretty little street of samurai houses. You can wander round the gardens and peek inside three of the grander, thatched houses at the street's northern end. Those willing to pay the price of a drink or snack can poke their noses into another old house, **Mizuyashiki** (see p.706).

Mount Unzen Disaster Memorial Hall

雲仙岳災害記念館, Unzen-dake Saigai Kinenkan • Highway 251, 5km south of central Shimabara • Daily 9am–6pm • ¥1000 • ⓦ udmh or.jp • Take Shimatetsu bus south from Ōte via Shimabara-kō ferry terminal, and get off at Arena-iriguchi stop (hourly; 15min; ¥240)

A kilometre north of the Mizunashi River, the **Mount Unzen Disaster Memorial Hall** contains a moderately interesting museum commemorating the eruption. English-speaking staff are on hand to guide you through the exhibits, of which the most accessible are videos of the disaster and a technologically impressive but ultimately rather tacky Great Eruption Theatre which places you in the middle of the pyroclastic flows.

Suffer House Preservation Park

土石流被災家屋保存公園, Dosekiryū Hisai Kaoku Hozon Kōen • Daily 9am–5pm • Free • Same bus as Memorial Hall (see above), or rent a bike from Shimabara's tourist office (see below)

A solemn memorial to the dead from 1792, this is a small area of **half-buried houses**, signed as the "Suffer House Preservation Park". The houses are preserved beneath two plastic domes about ten minutes' walk across the river from the Disaster Memorial Hall; don't go expecting Pompeii, but the area is certainly worth the effort to get to.

ARRIVAL AND INFORMATION   SHIMABARA

By train Trains running south from Isahaya (1–2 hourly; 1hr 10min) on the private Shimabara line stop at the main Shimabara Station, a couple of minutes' walk east of Ōte, and then continue three more stops to Shimabara-Gaikō Station near the ferry port.

By bus Buses from Unzer (6 daily; 45min) call at the Shimabara-kō Station before proceeding into town, where they either terminate at the Shimatetsu bus station or stop a little further on in Ōte.

By ferry There's a choice of a high-speed ferry (6–7 daily; 30min; ¥800) or regular services (10 daily; 1hr; ¥680) to and from Kumamoto-kō (see p.709).

Tourist information Shimabara's tourist office (daily 8am–5.30pm; ☎0957 62 3986, ⓦshimabaraonsen.com) is inside the Shimabara-kō station building. It provides good English-language maps and brochures, and also rents out bikes (¥150/hr; ¥750/5hr), which are handy for scooting into town or out to the southern sights.

ACCOMMODATION

Business Hotel Toraya 1-4 Minatomachi ☎0957 63 3332. Cheap and cheerful business hotel next to the ferry terminal, offering either Western- or tatami-style rooms, and views out towards Kumamoto if you crane your head to the left. There's a decent restaurant on site. **¥7000**

Hanamizuki 花みずき 548 Nakamachi ☎0957 62 1000. Bright business hotel, 5min walk southwest from

Shimabara Station. The on-site spa is delightful, as are the breakfasts – rise early to savour them both. Single go for ¥5000. **¥10,000**

Shimabara Youth Hostel 7938 Shimokawashirimachi ☎0957 62 4451. There's something delightful about a youth hostel with an onsen – just what's on offer at this chalet-like building behind Shimabara-Gaikō Station. Dorm **¥2850**

THE SHIMABARA REBELLION

In 1637 exorbitant taxes and the oppressive cruelty of two local *daimyō* sparked off a large-scale **peasant revolt** in the Shimabara area, though the underlying motive was anger at the **Christian persecutions** taking place at the time. Many of the rebels were Christian, including their leader, a 16-year-old boy known as Amakusa Shirō, who was supposedly able to perform miracles. His motley army of 37,000, which included women and children, eventually sought refuge in abandoned Hara castle, roughly 30km south of Shimabara town. For three months they held off far-superior government forces, but even Shirō couldn't save them when Hara was stormed in April 1638 and, so it's said, all 37,000 were massacred. Rightly or wrongly, Portuguese missionaries were implicated in the rebellion and soon after all foreigners were banished from Japan as the country closed its doors.

EATING

★Aoi Rihatsu-kan 青い理髪館 888-2 Uenomachi. Eighty-year-old venue immediately east of the castle (look out for the blue building) that's part barber shop, part coffee shop. They serve a limited range of set lunches and delightful home-baked cakes and cookies. 10.30am–7pm, closed Wed.

Himematsu-ya 姫松屋 1-1208-3 Jonai, opposite the entrance to Shimabara-jō. Popular restaurant that serves Shimabara's speciality food, *guzōni* – a delicious clam broth packed with rice cakes, fish, pork, lotus root, tofu and egg – at ¥980 for a regular portion or ¥1180 for large. It also offers a choice of well-priced sets and mainstream Japanese dishes. Daily 10am–7pm.

Hōjū ほうじゅう 2-243 Shinmachi, a couple of blocks east of the shopping arcade. An attractive and welcoming little place beside a carp stream; try th Shimabara *teishoku* (¥1350) for a sampler of loca delicacies, or go for their tasty *fugu* (blowfish) sush (¥1200). Daily 11am–11pm.

Shimabara Mizuyashiki しまばら水屋敷 51: Yorozumachi, in the shopping arcade southeast of th castle. One of several Meiji-era houses in the area (se p.705), this place serves drinks and snacks above delightful garden. Daily 11am–5pm.

Kumamoto

熊本

A fair proportion of travellers to Kyūshū find themselves in **KUMAMOTO** at some point. Not only is the city handily located between Fukuoka in the north and Kagoshima down south, but it also lies within striking distance of Aso to the east and Unzen to the west; it's possible to pop by and tick off the main sights on a day-trip from any of these places, but the city itself is reasonably attractive and rewards an overnight stay. Chief among its sights is the fearsome, fairy-tale **castle** dominating the town centre, and **Suizenji-jōjuen**, one of Japan's most highly rated gardens, in the eastern suburbs. Wars and development have meant that little else of particular note survives, though you've got to admire a city which invented the endearingly offbeat "Kobori-style" swimming which "involves the art of swimming in a standing posture attired in armour and helmet".

Brief history

Kumamoto owes its existence to the Katō clan, who were given the fiefdom in the late sixteenth century in return for supporting Tokugawa Ieyasu during his rise to power. **Katō Kiyomasa**, first of the feudal lords, not only built a magnificent fortress but is also remembered for his public works, such as flood control and land reclamation. However, political intrigue resulted in the Katō being ousted in 1632 in favour of the **Hosokawa** clan, who had previously held Kokura. Thirteen generations of Hosokawa lords ruled Kumamoto for more than two centuries, during which time the city thrived as Kyūshū's major government stronghold, until feudal holdings were abolished in 1871. Six years later, the final drama of the Meiji Restoration was played out here when Saigō Takamori's rebel army was defeated by government troops, but not before destroying much of Kumamoto's previously impregnable castle.

Kumamoto-jō

熊本城 • Daily: April–Oct 8.30am–5.30pm; Nov–March 8.30am–4.30pm • ¥500

Completed in 1607 after only seven years' work, **Kumamoto-jō** is Japan's third-largest castle (after Osaka and Nagoya) and one of its most formidable. It was designed by lord **Katō Kiyomasa**, a brilliant military architect who combined superb fortifications with exquisitely graceful flourishes – as Alan Booth observed in *The Roads to Sata* (see p.836), the main keep seems like "a fragile bird poised for flight". At its peak, Kumamoto-jō had an outer perimeter of 13km and over 5km of inner wall built in what's called *musha-gaeshi* style, meaning that no invading warrior could scale their smooth, gently concave surfaces. In case of prolonged attack, 120 wells were sunk, while camphor and ginkgo trees provided firewood and edible nuts. These defences were severely tested during the 1877 **Satsuma**

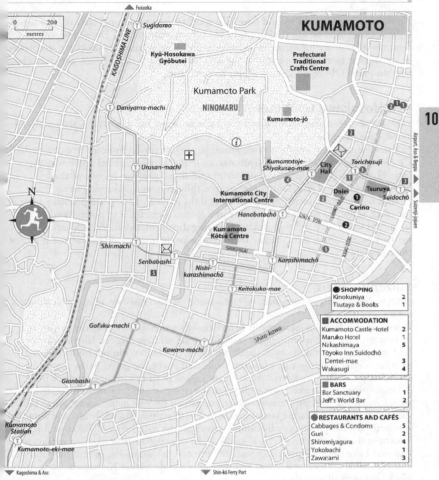

KUMAMOTO

Fukuoka

Sugidomo

Kyū-Hosokawa
Gyōbutei

Prefectural
Traditional
Crafts Centre

Kumamoto Park

NINOMARU

Daniyama-machi

Kumamoto-jō

Urusan-machi

Kumamotoje-
Shiyakusao-mae

City
Hall

Torichosuji

Kumamoto City
International Centre

Daiei

Tsuruya
Suidochō

Hanabatachō

Carino

GINZA-DORI

Kumamoto
Kōtsū Centre

SHINSHIGAI

Shinmachi

Senbabashi

Nishi-
karashimachō

Karashimachō

Keitokuko-mae

● SHOPPING

| Kinokuniya | 2 |
| Tsutaya & Books | 1 |

Gofuku-machi

■ ACCOMMODATION

Kumamoto Castle Hotel	2
Maruko Hotel	1
Nakashimaya	5
Tōyoko Inn Suidochō	
Dentei-mae	3
Wakasugi	4

Kawara-machi

Shira-kawa

Gionbashi

■ BARS

| Bar Sanctuary | 1 |
| Jeff's World Bar | 2 |

Kumamoto
Station

Kumamoto-eki-mae

● RESTAURANTS AND CAFÉS

Cabbages & Condoms	5
Guri	2
Shiromiyagura	4
Yokobachi	1
Zawatami	3

Kagoshima & Aso

Shin-kō Ferry Port

Rebellion (see box, p.734), when Saigō Takamori's army besieged Kumamoto-jō for fifty days. Government reinforcements eventually relieved the garrison, soon after trouncing the rebels. Though the castle held, most of its surrounding buildings were burnt to the ground and left in ruins until 1960, when the main keep was magnificently restored around a concrete shell; turrets and various other buildings are now also in good shape.

The best approach to the castle is from its south side, which brings you up into the grassy expanse of **Ninomaru** and the main, west, gate into the **inner citadel**. Inside to the left, **Uto Yagura** was the only turret to survive the 1877 battle, while straight on, a high-sided defile leads to the imposing central keep, which hosts an excellent historical **museum** about the castle and the Hosokawa lords. Immediately south of the keep, the low-lying **Go-ten Ōhiroma** – the main reception hall – is resplendent after its recent restoration.

Prefectural Traditional Crafts Centre

熊本県伝統工芸館, Kumamoto-ken Dentō Kōgeikan • 3-35 Chibajomachi • 9am–5pm; closed Mon • Kumamoto craft display ¥200

Opposite the castle's northeastern gate (Akazu-no-mon), the **Prefectural Traditional Crafts Centre** hosts free exhibitions promoting local artists and an excellent display of

Kumamoto crafts on the second floor. The most famous traditional craft is *Higo zogan*, a painstaking method of inlaying gold and silver in a metal base. Developed in the seventeenth century for ornamenting sword hilts, it's now used for jewellery, decorative boxes and the like. Look out among the toys for a little red-faced fellow with a black hat, the ghost Obake-no-kinta – try pulling the string.

Kyū-Hosokawa Gyōbutei

旧細川刑部邸 • 3-1 Furukyomachi • Daily: April–Oct 8.30am–5.30pm; Nov–March 8.30am–4.30pm • ¥300, or ¥640 including entry to the castle • Sugidomo tram stop

In the northwest corner of the castle grounds, roughly fifteen minutes' walk from the Crafts Centre, is **Kyū-Hosokawa Gyōbutei**, an immaculately restored and unusually large high-ranking samurai residence set in traditional gardens. It's one of the few buildings of its kind remaining in Japan, and though it won't take long to squeak around its wooden floors, and crunch around the garden paths, you'll probably have the place almost to yourself. There are some gorgeous examples of pottery and lacquered wood here and there, many featuring the distinctive nine-circle motif used by the house's former inhabitants. There's also a lovely tearoom on the northern side of the complex.

Suizenji-jōjuen

水前寺成趣園 • 8-1 Suizenji-kōen • Daily: March–Nov 7.30am–6pm; Dec–Feb 8am–5.30pm • ¥400 • W suizenji.or.jp • Suizenji-kōen tram stop

It pays to visit **Suizenji-jōjuen** early, before crowds arrive. In any case, the garden is at its best with an early-morning mist over the crystal-clear, spring-fed lake, its surface broken by jumping minnows or the darting beak of a heron. Plump, multicoloured carp laze under willow-pattern bridges, while staff sweep the gravel paths or snip back an errant pine tuft. Considered to be one of Japan's most beautiful stroll-gardens, Suizenji-jōjuen was created over eighty years, starting in 1632, by three successive Hosokawa lords. The temple from which the garden took its name is long gone, but the immaculate, undulating landscape, dotted with artfully placed shrubs and trees, has survived. The design supposedly mimics scenes on the road between Tokyo and Kyoto, known as the "53 stations of the Tōkaidō" – the ones you're most likely to recognize are Fuji and Lake Biwa. Considering Suizenji's prestige, it's surprising to find the garden cluttered with souvenir stalls; many of the items on sale feature Kumamon, the cartoon black bear seen all over the city.

Teahouse

March–Nov 9am–5.30pm; Dec–Feb 9am–5pm • Tea outside ¥500, in ceremony room ¥600

On the southern side of the complex is the Izumi shrine, dedicated to the Hosokawa lords, and a four-hundred-year-old **teahouse** overlooking the lake. If it's not too early, you can drink a cup of green tea on the benches outside or in the tea ceremony room, while admiring one of the best views of the garden; the price includes an *izayoi*, a white, moon-shaped cake made using egg white.

ARRIVAL AND INFORMATION   **KUMAMOTO**

By plane From Kumamoto Airport (☎ 096 232 2810), roughly 15km northwest, limousine buses shuttle into town (approx 1hr; ¥670), stopping at Shimo-tōri and the Kumamoto Kōtsū Centre before ending up at the train station.
Destinations Nagoya (5 daily; 1hr 15min); Naha (1 daily; 1hr 30min); Osaka (Itami; 8 daily; 1hr 5min); Seoul

(3 weekly; 1hr 40min); and Tokyo (1–2 hourly; 1hr 35min).
By train The main train station lies some 2km to the south of the city centre, and now receives Shinkansen services from Fukuoka's Hakata station.
Destinations Aso (1 hourly; 1hr 30min); Beppu (4 daily; 3hr); Fukuoka (every 30min; 40min–1hr 20min); Kagoshima (every 30min; 40min–1hr 15min).

By bus Kumamoto Kōtsū Centre (熊本交通センター) is the city's central bus station, and most long-distance buses terminate here though a few continue through to the train station; in addition, most buses from the ferry port, Kumamoto-kō (熊本港), stop at the train station first.

Destinations Aso (1 hourly; 1hr 30min); Beppu (4 daily; 5hr 40min); Fukuoka (every 10–20min; 2hr 20min); Kagoshima (11 daily; 3hr 10min); Kumamoto-kō (1–3 hourly; 30min); Miyazaki (1 hourly; 3hr); Nagasaki (8 daily; 3hr); and Takachiho (3 daily; 2hr 50min).

By ferry Kumamoto Ferry (☎096 311 4100, ⊚kumamotoferry.co.jp) operates high-speed ferries from

Kumamoto-kō to Shimabara (6–7 daily; 30min; ¥800), while Kyūshū Shōsen (☎096 329 6111, ⊚kyusho.co.jp) also runs a regular service to Shimabara (10 daily; 1hr; ¥680). To get to the port, take a bus from Kumamoto Station (1–3 hourly; 30min; ¥420).

Tourist information Kumamoto's helpful tourist information service (daily 8.30am–7pm; ☎096 352 3743, ⊚kumamoto-icb.or.jp) occupies a desk inside the train station's central exit. There are also branches at the airport (daily 6.50am–9pm) and beside the main entrance to the castle (April–Oct 8.30am–6pm; Nov–March 8.30am–5pm; ☎096 322 5060).

GETTING AROUND

By tram Getting around central Kumamoto is fairly straightforward thanks to the tram system, which covers most sights. There are just two lines (A and B), both of which run from the eastern suburbs through the city centre before splitting near the Kōtsū Centre. Line A then heads off south to Kumamoto Station, while Line B loops north round the castle. You can change from one line to another at Karashimachō where the lines split; ask for a transfer ticket

(norikae-kippu) to avoid paying twice. Trams run every 5–10min from 6.30am–11pm, with a flat fare of ¥150. Alternatively, if you're moving about a lot, you can buy a one-day pass (ichi-nichi jōshaken; ¥500), which also entitles you to discounted tickets to various sights.

Car rental Nippon Rent-a-Car (☎096 359 0919), Toyota Rent-a-Car (☎096 311 0100) and Eki Rent-a-Car (☎096 352 4313) all have branches near Kumamoto Station.

ACCOMMODATION

★**Kumamoto Castle Hotel** 熊本ホテルキャッスル 1-20 Joto-machi ☎096 326 3311, ⊚hotel-castle.co.jp. One of the few places in Kumamoto boasting views of the city's most famous sight – despite this, and the high quality of the rooms and service, it's not that expensive. Repair to the top-floor bar for evening drinks and wonderful castle views. **¥12,000**

Maruko Hotel 丸小ホテル 11-10 Kamitōri-chō ☎096 353 1241, ⊚maruko-hotel.jp. A modern hotel in an interesting area to the north of the centre; don't let the unappealing reception area and bare corridors put you off. The rooms are mostly Japanese-style and all en suite, and there's a Japanese bath with views on the top floor. Discounts off the official rates are often offered if you ask. **¥15,000**

★**Nakashimaya** 中島屋 2-11-6 Shin-machi

☎096 202 2020, ⊚nakashimaya.ikidane.com. A wonderful hostel: cheap, friendly, decorated with traditional flourishes, free internet ... and you can try your hand at dyeing your own shoes or T-shirts. If you bring your own sleeping bag, tatami berths coast as little as ¥2000. Tatami Dorm **¥2500**

Tōyoko Inn Suidochō Dentei-mae 東横INN水道町 電亭前 1-1 Suidō-chō ☎096 325 1045, ⊚toyoko-inn .com. Typically good-value option from the business hotel chain, handily located on Kumamoto's main shopping street, right beside the Suidochō tram stop. There's another branch next to the train station. **¥6480**

Wakasugi 若杉 1-14 Hanabatachō ☎096 352 2668. Rooms here won't win any prizes for design, though they're cheap and do the job, and some have views of the castle walls. Breakfast included at the ground-floor café. **¥6000**

EATING, DRINKING AND NIGHTLIFE

Local **specialty foods** include horsemeat sashimi (basashi) eaten with lots of garlic, and karashi renkon, which consists of lotus-root slices stuffed with a mustard and bean paste, dipped in batter and deep-fried. In addition to the restaurants listed below, you'll find a good variety on the seventh floor of Tsuruya department store's main building.

CAFÉS AND RESTAURANTS

★**Cabbages & Condoms** 1-11-13 Shimotōri-chō ☎096 356 3337. Delicious, fairly priced Thai cuisine – it's around ¥1100 for a tom yum or pad thai. Ah yes, the name – apparently a share of the profits go to Thailand in the form of prophylactics. Daily noon–3pm & 6pm–midnight.

Guri 11-3 Kamitōri-chō. Artistic café with a soothing, semi-European atmosphere, serving a global range of

coffees. As a little bonus, you get to choose your own cup from a delightful selection. Mon–Sat 11am–10pm, Sun 11am–7pm.

★**Shiromiyagura** 城見櫓 1-10 Hanabata-chō ☎096 356 1146. One of the few Kumamoto restaurants with castle views – they are especially good from the uppermost of its four levels. Though costly in the evening, lunch set menus are fairly priced; it's ¥2100 for a filling meal, or

¥2625 for one including *basashi* (raw horsemeat). The entrance is a little hard to spot, but the building stands out: it's by the river, topped with a green-tiled oriental roof. Daily 11.30am–2pm & 5–10pm.

Yokobachi 11-40 Kamitorōri-chō ☏ 096 351 4581. Enjoy *karashi renkon* or *basashi* at this bustling *izakaya* around the corner from the *Maruko Hotel*. The tatami-mat rooms overlook a pretty Japanese garden. Daily 5pm–midnight.

Zawatami 坐和民 2F 1-22 Kamitorōri-chō ☏ 096 312 1810. On the second floor of a covered arcade, this restaurant serves a mix of Western and Japanese dishes. There's only one real reason to come here, though: the all-you-can-eat-and-drink specials (¥2980), which allow you unlimited food and booze for three full hours. Daily 5pm–1am, Fri & Sat to 3am.

BARS AND CLUBS

Bar Sanctuary 4-16 Tetori-honmachi. Kumamoto's one-stop party venue, with a dance club on the ground floor (entry charge ¥1500 Fri & Sat) and a bar as well a dart room, karaoke and pool. Daily 8pm–6am.

Jeff's World Bar 2F, 1-4-3 Shimo-dōri. A foreigners' favourite, it's good for a pint or cocktail and some friendly conversation. You can drink as much as you like for ¥3000. Daily 8pm–late.

SHOPPING

Arcades The main covered shopping arcades, Shimo-dōri and Kami-dōri, are in Central Kumamoto on the north bank of the Shira-kawa, between the river and the castle: this area is also home to most of the city's major hotels, banks and restaurants.

Bookshops Kinokuniya, on Shimo-dōri, near the corner with Ginza-dōri, and Tsutaya & Books, in the Carino Building on Sannenzaka-dōri, east of the Daiei store, both have small selections of English-language books.

DIRECTORY

Banks and foreign exchange The best bet for foreign-exchange services is Higo Bank and Kumamoto Family Bank, both of which have branches on the main road near Tsuruya department store.

Festivals Kumamoto's main events are the Hinokuni Festival (Aug 11–13), celebrated with folk dances, a city-centre parade and fireworks, and the Fujisaki Hachiman-gū autumn festival (Sept 11–15). On the final day, there are two processions, morning and afternoon, when some twenty thousand people parade through the streets in historical garb.

Hospital Kumamoto National Hospital (☏ 096 353 6501) is immediately south of Ninomaru Park.

Police Kumamoto Prefectural Police Headquarters, 6-18-1 Suizenji ☏ 096 381 0110.

Aso and the central highlands

Central Kyūshū is dominated by sparsely populated, grassy highlands, in places rising to substantial peaks, which offer some of the island's most magnificent scenery and best walking country. These mountains are relics of ancient volcanic upheavals and explosions of such incredible force that they collapsed one gigantic volcano to create the **Aso caldera**, the world's largest crater. Today the floor of the caldera is a patchwork of fields like many tatami mats, and the surrounding uplands form a popular summer playground, but the peaks of Aso-san at its centre provide a potent reminder that the volcano is still very much alive. Most people come here to peer inside its steaming crater, eruptions permitting, and then scale some of the neighbouring peaks or walk over the lush green meadows at its base.

All this subterranean activity naturally means a wealth of hot springs to wallow in, mostly within the caldera itself, although there are a few gems hidden deep in the highlands. One is the picturesque village of **Kurokawa Onsen**, squeezed in a narrow gorge on the Senomoto plateau, which makes a great overnight stop on the road to Beppu. The village lies a few kilometres off the **Yamanami Highway**, the main route between Aso and Beppu, providing a spectacular mountain ride through the **Aso-Kujū National Park**. In the opposite direction, another dramatic road climbs over the crater wall and heads southeast to **Takachiho**. Perched above an attractive gorge of angular basalt columns, this is where the mythical Sun Goddess Amaterasu hid, according to legends about the birth of the Japanese nation. A riverside cave and its neighbouring hrine make an easy excursion, but a more compelling reason to stop here is to catch a night-time performance of the story told through traditional folk dances.

GETTING AROUND   ASO AND THE CENTRAL HIGHLANDS

The Aso region is one place where having your own transport is a definite advantage (see p.714 for rental info); it's perfectly feasible to get around by public transport, but everything takes a lot longer. It's possible to visit Aso-san on a day-trip from Kumamoto or Beppu, or to break the journey here en route between the two.

By bus If you're heading between Aso and Beppu, the Yamanami Highway (see p.714) offers the most scenic option, with several buses plying the route daily (see p.714).
By train Trains stop at Aso on their way between

Kumamoto and Beppu, and are a good alternative for JR Pass holders, providing a magnificent journey through lush green forest deep in the mountains before dropping down to the coast.

10

The Aso Caldera

The ancient crater of **Aso Caldera**, measuring 18km from east to west, 24km north to south and over 120km in circumference, was formed about 100,000 years ago when a vast volcano collapsed. As the rock cooled, a lake formed, but the eruptions continued, pushing up five smaller cones, today known collectively as **Aso-san**. Eventually the lake drained and the area became inhabited; local people attribute their fortune to the god Takeiwatatsu-no-mikoto, grandson of Emperor Jimmu, who kicked a gap in the western wall – the same gap the train uses – to give them rice land. Now some 70,000 people live within the crater, working the rich volcanic soils, while cattle and horses graze the higher meadows in summer. **Aso Town** (阿蘇市) is a grandiose name for a scattered group of villages located in the northern caldera, including a tourist area around Aso Station, which represents the centre of local life.

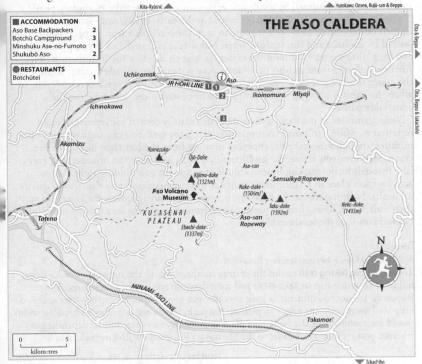

Aso-san

阿蘇山 • 7 daily buses from Aso station (40min; ¥540); last bus up leaves at 3.20pm.

The five peaks of **Aso-san** line up across the caldera. At the eastern end of the chain lies the distinctively craggy Neko-dake (1433m), while the next peak west is Taka-dake (1592m), the highest of the five summits, and its volcanic offshoot Naka-dake (1506m). West of here lie Eboshi-dake (1337m) and Kijima-dake (1321m).

As the road climbs up to the pass between Kijima-dake and Eboshi-dake, you look down on the perfect cone of **Komezuka**, the "hill of rice" – its dimpled top is said to have been created when Takeiwatatsu-no-mikoto scooped up a handful of rice to feed his starving people. Unfortunately, it's off limits. Turning the other way, you get your first glimpse of Naka-dake's gaping mouth across the grassy bowl of **Kusasenri plateau**, which is speckled with shallow crater lakes.

Kijima-dake

杵島岳

On the plateau, the bus stops outside the missable Aso Volcano Museum, and it is here that you'll need to get off to climb **Kijima-dake** (1321m), which rises behind the museum. The paved path from the far northeast corner of the car park takes you on an easy thirty-minute climb, rewarded with more views over the caldera, and then down into Kijima-dake's extinct crater. From here, you can descend via a ski slope to join a path alongside the road to Naka-dake; the whole walk should take under ninety minutes.

Naka-dake

中岳 • Ropeway daily 9am–5pm • Every 15min or so • ¥410

Of the five volcanic cones, only **Naka-dake** is still active; it's really just a gash on the side of Taka-dake, formed by a volcanic explosion which created a secondary peak. Naka-dake's most recent eruptions occurred in the early 1990s, since when it has calmed down considerably, but it's wise to treat the mountain with respect. Notices are posted in the train and bus stations when Naka-dake is closed, but if you plan to do any long-distance walks around the crater it's wise to check at the information office. Anyone suffering from asthma or other respiratory problems is advised not to approach the crater rim because of strong sulphur emissions; when these reach certain levels, or when the wind is blowing in the wrong direction, staff come out and close the crater-side paths.

Buses terminate at the foot of **Naka-dake** in a scruffy area of souvenir shops and restaurants, while a toll road continues to the top for cars. You can walk up in twenty minutes, though most take the **ropeway** running from the bus terminus up to the crater. However you arrive, the multicoloured rocks and glimpses of a seething grey lake through turbulent, sulphurous clouds of steam are a forbidding sight. Most activity takes place in a 100m-deep crater at the northern end, and this area is strictly off limits. Near the top of the ropeway, however, you can approach the crater lip and then walk south beside barren, dormant craters and across the lava fields – mercifully out of earshot of the loudspeakers.

Taka-dake

高岳 • Sansuikyō Ropeway daily 9am–5pm; every 25min • ¥750

There's a great **hiking trail** round the crater's southern rim to the summit of Naka-dake, followed by a side trip to **Taka-dake** and then down to the northeastern Sansuikyō Ropeway. It's not too difficult as long as you've got good boots, plenty of water and you keep well away from the edge. To pick up the path, follow the boardwalks heading south round the crater across the Sunasenri plateau. Allow two to three hours, depending on whether you include Taka-dake, to the Sansuikyō Ropeway. With any luck, you'll

coincide with a cable-car down, but from the bottom you'll have to hitch a ride or set off on the ninety-minute downhill trot to Miyaji Station (宮地駅), two stops east of Aso.

ARRIVAL AND INFORMATION

ASO-SAN

By train From Kumamoto (1 hourly; 50min–1hr 10min), the JR Hōhi line heads to Aso across the caldera floor. This is a great journey in its own right, but for an added bit of fun, at weekends you can ride on the *Aso Boy!*, one of Japan's most interesting trains (see box, p.677); be sure to reserve a seat in advance (¥1100). There are also direct services to Aso from Beppu (4 daily; 2hr); if you miss these, you may have to change in Ōita.

By bus Aso bus station is to the right as you exit the train station.

Destinations Beppu (5 daily; 3hr); Kumamoto (1 hourly; 1hr 30min); Kurokawa Onsen (6 daily; daily 9am–6pm); and Senomoto Kōgen (5 daily; 45min–1hr).

By car There's a car rental desk in the same building as the tourist office (T 096 734 1001; same hours).

Tourist information To the left of the bus station is a well-organized tourist office (daily 9am–6pm; T 096 735 5077, W aso-denku.jp), with helpful, English-speaking staff and a wealth of information on local transport, walks and accommodation.

ACCOMMODATION AND EATING

★ **Aso Base Backpackers** 1498 Kurokawa T 0967 34 0408, W aso-backpackers.com. A short walk south of the train station, this squeaky-clean, pine-lined venue is a great place, its comfy beds augmented by a pleasing, lodge-style atmosphere. Dorm **¥2800**, double **¥6000**

Botchū Campground 坊中キャンプ場 1440-1 Kurokawa T 0967 34 0351. About 1km south of the station – just within comfortable walking distance. You can rent tents, blankets and cooking equipment here, and there are some great hiking trails up to Aso-san. Open April–Nov. Tent plus two people **¥930**

Botchūtei 坊中亭 Aso train station. Surprisingly good restaurant inside the train station. The fantastically warming *dangojiru* stew (see box, p.722) costs ¥550, or try the huge curry rice (¥800). Fri–Wed 9am–5pm.

Minshuku Aso-no-Fumoto 民宿阿蘇のふもと 64 Kurokawa T 0967 34 0624. Welcoming option offering bed and breakfast. The owners speak English and will pick you up at the station. **¥6000**

Shukubō Aso 宿坊あそ 1076 Kurokawa T 0967 34 0194. By far the fanciest place to stay in Aso, this minshuku has beautiful, traditional rooms in a wonderful old farmhouse. Good meals are also available, and the English-speaking owner will collect you from the station. **¥24,000**

Kurokawa Onsen

黒川温泉

One of the most popular hot-spring resorts in Japan, **KUROKAWA ONSEN** is made up of twenty-odd ryokan, which lie higgledy-piggledy at the bottom of a steep-sided, tree-filled valley scoured into the **Senomoto Kōgen** plateau (瀬の本高原), some 6km west of the Yamanami Highway. The village is completely devoted to hot-spring bathing and most of its buildings are at least traditional in design, if not genuinely

THE YAMANAMI HIGHWAY

From Aso, the **Yamanami Highway** heads north over the Kujū mountains to Beppu. The road breaches the caldera wall at Ichinomiya, from where the classic profile of Aso-san's five peaks supposedly conjures up a sleeping Buddha with head to the east and Naka-dake's steaming vent at his navel, although it's a little more convincing from Daikambō lookout further west. North of here, **Kurokawa Onsen** (see above) offers a choice of rotemburo along a picturesque valley. The highway then climbs again through the Kujū range, which for some reason receives far less attention than Aso-san or Ebino-Kōgen (see p.733), although it offers good hiking and the Kyūshū mainland's highest peaks. The tallest, Kujū-san (1787m), is no longer active, but even here wisps of steam mark vents high on the north slopes. More spa towns lie strung along the route from here, and then start again at **Yufuin** (see p.723) before the road makes its final descent into Beppu. While the Yamanami Highway is best avoided during peak holiday periods, for the most part it's fairly traffic free. Every day, four buses ply the route between Kumamoto and Beppu, stopping at Aso, Kurokawa Onsen, Senomoto, Yufuin and a few other places en route.

KUROKAWA'S BATHS

All the baths in town are attached to ryokan and you can either buy tickets at the reception of each individual ryokan (from ¥500), or get a day pass (¥1200) from the tourist office (see below) or the ryokan allowing entry to any three; the tourist office provides a good English map showing the location of all the public rotemburo with a key indicating whether they're mixed or segregated. If you only have time for one, try the central *Okyaku-ya Ryokan* (see below) for all-round atmosphere, or *Yamabiko Ryokan* (see below) for its unusually large rotemburo, though the latter is both mixed-gender and has a no-clothes policy. *Yumotoso* (湯本荘) has a gorgeous little rotemburo, and women can bathe in old-fashioned iron tubs. If you have your own transport, it's worth travelling a few kilometres out of central Kurokawa to try the riverside baths at *Yamamizuki* (山みず木) or *Hozantei* (帆山亭), set in wooded hills away from the crowds.

10

old, while *yukata*-clad figures wandering the lanes add to its slightly quaint atmosphere. The village is particularly famous for its rotemburo: there are 24 different locations in total, offering rocky pools of all shapes and sizes. Out of the main tourist season, when the crowds have gone, it's well worth making the effort to get here, and Kurokawa makes an excellent overnight stop, if you don't mind paying a little extra for accommodation.

ARRIVAL AND INFORMATION

KUROKAWA ONSEN

By bus Though it helps if you have your own transport, it's possible to reach Kurokawa Onsen from Aso Town (5 daily; 1hr; ¥940). The first bus from Aso departs at 10.28am and the last bus back leaves Kurokawa at 5.26pm, so there is time to explore a few of the ryokan baths in a day, though it's wise to check current bus times locally before setting off. There are also buses to

and from Beppu (2 daily; 2hr 30min), but get to the stop at least ten minutes early since they occasionally run ahead of schedule.

Tourist information The tourist office (daily 9am–6pm; ☎ 0967 44 0076, ⊛ kurokawaonsen.or.jp) is beside a car park and taxi rank on the north side of the river, just uphill from the bus stop.

ACCOMMODATION AND EATING

Aso Kujū-kōgen Youth Hostel 阿蘇くじゅう高原ユースホステル 〒332 Manganji ☎ 0967 44 0157. The closest acceptable budget accommodation lies 5km away, near the Senomoto Kōgen junction; buses bound for Kurokawa stop at the end of the drive. Meals are available and staff can provide good hiking information. Dorm **¥2800**

Okyaku-ya Ryokan 御客屋旅館 6546 Manganji ☎ 0967 440454. Founded in 1603, this ryokan occupies a lovely wooden building right in the centre of things, and (trinket shop aside) maintains a pleasant Edo-era atmosphere. The on-site baths are nothing short of spectacular, particularly as evening encroaches. The rates quoted here include two meals. **¥26,000**

Warokuya わろく屋 6600-1 Manganji. Amiable, cosy place by the river, serving a mix of light meals. The emphasis is on quirky curry dishes (¥900–1200); try the *yakikare* (baked with mozzarella), or the *kurokare* (made with black pork and a viscous black sauce). The chocolate cakes are rather tempting, too. Tues–Sun 9.30am–5pm.

★**Yamabiko Ryokan** やまびこ旅館 6704 Manganji ☎ 0967 44 0311, ⊛ yamabiko-ryokan.com. Grand riverside ryokan set in spacious grounds – the place for a splurge. The meals are simply delectable, and the outdoor rotemburo make heavenly places for a relaxing bathe. The rates quoted here include two meals. **¥32,000**

Takachiho

高千穂

The small town of **TAKACHIHO** lies on the border between Kumamoto and Miyazaki prefectures, where the Gokase-gawa has sliced a narrow channel through layers of ancient lava. In winter, when night temperatures fall below freezing, local villagers perform time-honoured **Yokagura dances** in the old farmhouses, bringing back to life the gods and goddesses who once inhabited these mountains (see p.716). The main reason for visiting Takachiho is to see a few excerpts from this dance-cycle, but combine that with **Takachiho gorge**, a pretty spot whose strange rock formations are woven into local myths, plus a dramatic journey from whichever direction you arrive, and Takachiho becomes somewhere to include on any Kyūshū tour.

Takachiho sits on the north bank of the **Gokase-gawa**, grouped around the central Honmachi crossroads. Both the gorge and Takachiho-jinja, where nightly Yokagura dances are held, are on the southwest edge of town, within easy walking distance, while its other main sight, a mildly interesting riverside cave, lies a short bus ride to the east. It's possible to cover both areas in a day, see a Yokagura performance in the evening and travel on the next morning.

10

Takachiho-jinja

高千穂神社 • Yokagura dances at 8pm • ¥500

The road southwest to the gorge first passes **Takachiho-jinja**, at the top of mossy steps roughly 800m from the Honmachi crossing. It's a simple wooden building, engulfed in ancient cryptomeria trees and mainly of interest for a high-relief carving of the guardian deity dispatching a demon; to find the carving, facing the shrine, walk round to the right of the building. The wooden **Kagura-den** next door is where the nightly **Yokagura** dances are held (see box below).

Takachiho gorge

高千穂峡 • Rowing boat hire daily 8.30am–4.20pm • ¥1500 for 30min; three people per boat

Corkscrew down from town for just over 1km on a series of hairpin bends, and you'll emerge at the south end of **Takachiho gorge**. At its narrowest point the gorge is just 3m wide and plunges 100m between cliffs of basalt columns, which in one place fan out like a giant cockleshell. If you want to see what the gorge looks like from below you can hire rowing boats at the southern end – it's particularly impressive when viewed from the emerald-green river. Otherwise, follow the path along the east bank, which takes you along the gorge's most scenic stretch, crossing and recrossing the river. Six hundred metres later you come out at an old stone bridge and the main road back into Takachiho, which soars high above. Before tackling the climb, you might want to stop off at *Araragi-no-chaya* restaurant (see opposite).

MYTHS AND DANCE IN TAKACHIHO

Takachiho's famous **traditional dances** have their roots in local legend. The story goes that the Storm God, Susano-ō, once destroyed the rice fields of his sister, the Sun Goddess **Amaterasu**, and desecrated her sacred palace. Understandably offended by these actions, Amaterasu hid in a cave and plunged the world into darkness. The other gods tried to entice her out with prayers and chants, but nothing worked until, finally, a goddess named Ama-no-uzume broke into a provocative dance. The general merriment was too much for Amaterasu, who peeped out to see the fun, at which point the crowd grabbed her and hauled her back into the world. Takachiho locals also claim that nearby mountain Takachiho-no-mine – not the mountain of Ebino Kōgen (see p.733) – is where Amaterasu's grandson, Ninigi-no-mikoto, descended to earth with his mirror, sword and jewel to become Japan's first emperor.

A visit to Takachiho is not complete without viewing a sample of this dance at the Kagura-den (see above). In one hour you see three or four extracts from the full cycle, typically including the story of Amaterasu and her cave, and ending with an explicit rendition of the birth of the Japanese nation in which the two "gods" leave the stage to cavort with members of the audience – to the great delight of all concerned. The performers are drawn from a pool of around 550 local residents, aged from 5 to 80 years, who also dance in the annual **Yokagura festival** (mid-Nov to mid-Feb). In a combination of harvest thanksgiving and spring festival, 24 troupes perform all 33 dances in sequence in private homes and village halls, lasting through the night and into the next day.

Amano Iwato-jinja

天岩戸神社 •Buses leave Takachiho hourly (15min; ¥300).

From Takachiho's central station, buses make the attractive ride 8km east along the Iwato-gawa to **Amano Iwato-jinja**. The shrine buildings are closed to the public, but it's an attractive setting among venerable cedars, and from behind the shrine it's just possible to make out Amaterasu's cave on the river's far bank. Unfortunately, you can't reach it, but, when her fellow gods were deciding their strategy, they convened in the more accessible **Amano Yasugawara**, which is on the same side as the shrine. It's about a fifteen-minute walk east, down some steps and beside the river, to find the cave with its diminutive shrine beneath a sacred rope.

10

ARRIVAL AND INFORMATION

TAKACHIHO

By bus and train Takachiho bus station lies about 100m south of the central Honmachi crossroads. To get here from Aso Town and points west, you need to take a private Minami-Aso line train from Tateno (立野), three stops west of Aso on the JR line, round the caldera's south side as far as Takamori (高森; 3 daily; 32min; ¥470), from where three buses a day continue to Takachiho (1hr; ¥1280); check the connection times locally before setting off. There are also buses from Kumamoto (3 daily; 2hr 40min). The east coast, however, is the main access route; Miyazaki Kōtsu buses track the Gokase valley from Nobeoka (延岡; 1–2 hourly; 1hr–1hr 30min), on the JR line between Beppu and Miyazaki, up to Takachiho (hourly; 1hr 10min–1hr 30min; ¥1710). Sadly, the spectacular JR Takachiho line between Nobeoka and Takachiho was closed after a typhoon washed away parts of the track in 2005. There are tentative plans to reopen the line; check with the local ryokan (see below) for up-to-date information.

Tourist information Staff at the bus station ticket window can provide sketch maps of the town, which is just as well since the tourist office (daily 9.30am–5pm; ☎0982 73 1213, ⓦtakachiho-kankc.jp) is inconveniently located on the bypass a good kilometre northwest of town. And, since none of the staff speaks English, you're best off in any case talking to the owners at one of the two ryokan mentioned below for information in English.

Services There's an international ATM at the post office, buried in the backstreets to the northeast of the Honmachi crossing. Local shops are full of dried mushrooms, sweet potatoes, shōchū and other local produce alongside *kagura* dolls and locally crafted camphor-wood masks, which make unusual souvenirs.

ACCOMMODATION

★**Kamino-ya** かみの家 806-5 Mitai ☎0982 72 2111, ⓦkaminoya.jp. Homely ryokan with a nice, rustic atmosphere, and rooms decorated with original ink paintings. None is en suite, but you can use the lovely traditional baths. The price includes good-value meals, though you can opt for room only. **¥14,700**

Hotel Takachiho 1037-4 Mitai ☎0982 72 3255. On a promontory overlooking the gorge, just beyond Takachiho-jinja, this grand hotel is a good option if you want to sleep in a bed. It has spick-and-span Western-style en-suite rooms; if you phone ahead they'll collect you from the bus station. The price includes meals. **¥23,200**

Takachiho Youth Hostel 高千穂ユースホステル 5899-2 Mitai ☎0982 72 3021. About 3km out of town to the east, and run by a wonderfully friendly woman who will happily pick you up and take you back out for the Yokagura dances. Dorm **¥2800**

EATING

Araragi-no-chaya あらうぎ乃茶屋 1245 Oshikata. Restaurant-cum-souvenir shop beside the stone bridge near Takachiho gorge; stop here for a light meal or a taste of the local speciality, *kappo saké* – sake heated in a pipe of fresh green bamboo. Daily 8.30am–5pm.

Hatsu-e 初栄 10 Mitai ☎0982 72 3965. Up towards the post office, this restaurant provides a warm welcome on cold evenings with its table-top braziers for cooking *yakiniku*; set menus start at ¥1200. Tues–Sun 11am–2pm & 5–9pm.

Kenchan けんちゃん 796-2 Mitai ☎0982 72 5224. Cosy *yakitori* bar opposite *Kamino-ya* (see above). A good meal, excluding drinks, will set you back about ¥2000/person. 5pm–midnight, closed Sun.

★**Ten-an** 天庵 1180-25 Mitai ☎0982 72 3023. Rustic noodle joint serving excellent home-made soba – for just ¥850, the *Ten-an* soba set meal is a real feast. To find it, walk southwest from the Honmachi junction, straight over the next set of lights (the Shiroyama crossing) and take the first right. 11am–8pm, closed Sun.

Tentsukuten てんつくてん 805 Mitai ☎0982 72 3858. This popular *izakaya* is hidden behind a shack-like door just south round the corner from the bus station. You can sample some of Takachiho's well-rated shōchū, and eat well. 5pm–midnight, closed Sun.

10

Beppu
別府

Walking around the relaxed, coastal city of **BEPPU**, it is at times tempting to think that the place was built atop the den of some giant dragon – spirals of steam billow skywards from a thousand holes, lending certain streets a magical, otherworldly air. However, this is no myth or fairy tale, simply one of the world's most geothermically active regions. Over one hundred million litres of near-boiling water gush out of more than three thousand springs each day, harnessed for use by local homes and swimming pools, for heating and medicinal purposes, or to fill the dozens of public and private baths that make this one of Japan's most popular **onsen** resorts. The place is unashamedly commercial in nature, yet despite receiving over ten million visitors per year, it manages to feel like a town in decline – largely built during the domestic tourism boom of the 1970s, it seems half-forgotten by modern Japan. Still, the humble, throwback air that this creates enhances the city's pleasure, and it's easy to escape from the crowds.

There's not a lot more to do in Beppu than soak in a tub or be buried in hot sand. The most popular attractions are the **jigoku**, which spew out steaming, sulphurous mud and form simmering lakes in lurid hues; they're named after the Japanese word for the Buddhist notion of hell. Beppu's *jigoku* are located in three distinct clusters: seven in the northern district of **Kannawa** – these are of the most interest – one on Kannawa's western edge and two in Shibaseki Onsen, 3km further north. If you're feeling adventurous, however, you'd do better to head for a clutch of **secret onsen** hiding away in the western hills (see box, p.720). Beppu is also one of only two places in Japan where you can take a real, ocean-side **sand bath**, or *suna-yu*. Alternatively, you can ride the ropeway to the top of **Tsurumi-dake** for superb views over Beppu bay and inland to the Kujū mountains.

Takegawara Onsen

竹瓦温泉 • 16-23 Motomachi • **Bath** daily 6.30am–10.30pm • ¥100 • **Sand bath** daily 8am–9.30pm • ¥1000

Takegawara Onsen is a grand old Meiji-era edifice in the backstreets south of Ekimae-dōri. Its ordinary bath is nicely traditional, but try the **sand bath** first. After rinsing in hot water, you lie face up – take a towel to cover your front – on a bed of coarse, black

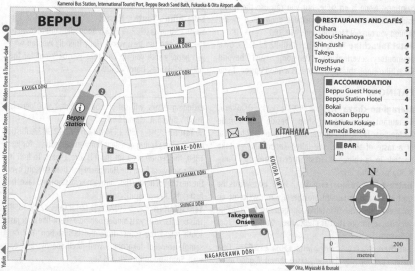

Kamenoi Bus Station, International Tourist Port, Beppu Beach Sand Bath, Fukuoka & Oita Airport ▲

BEPPU

NAKAMA DORI

KASUGA DORI

KASUGA DORI

Beppu Station

Tokiwa

KÎTAHAMA

EKIMAE-DÔRI

KITAHAMA DÔRI

SHINGU DÔRI

Takegawara Onsen

NAGAREKAWA DÔRI

KOKURA HWY

Global Tower, Kannawa Onsen, Shibaseki Onsen, Kankaiis Onsen,   ◄ Hidden Onsen & Tsurumi-dake

Yōtōin ◄

▼ Oita, Miyazaki & Ibusuki

● **RESTAURANTS AND CAFÉS**
Chihara	3
Sabou-Shinanoya	1
Shin-zushi	4
Takeya	6
Toyotsune	2
Ureshi-ya	5

■ **ACCOMMODATION**
Beppu Guest House	6
Beppu Station Hotel	4
Bokai	1
Khaosan Beppu	2
Minshuku Kokage	5
Yamada Bessō	3

■ **BAR**
Jin	1

N

0   200
metres

sand while an attendant gently piles sand on to you – a heavy, warm cocoon (around 42°C) that comes up to your neck. Then just relax as the heat soaks in for the recommended ten minutes, before another rinse and then a soak in the hot tub.

Beppu Beach Sand Bath

別府海浜砂湯, Bappu Kaihei Sunaba• On Shoningahama beach, near Beppu Daigaku Station • Daily 8.30am–5pm • ¥1000 • Bus #20 or #26 from central Beppu to Rollushoen stop (20min; ¥230)

On a fine day, the seaside location of **Beppu Beach Sand Bath** may seem preferable to Takegawara, but it's slightly marred by the busy main road behind and a concrete breakwater that dominates the view. The end result after a bath here, however, is still an overall sense of wellbeing. You'll need a swimsuit, but they provide *yukata* to wear in the "bath".

Global Tower

Daily: March–Nov 9am–9pm; Dec–Feb 9am–7pm • ¥300

On the way up to Kankaiji, you pass the pencil-thin **Global Tower**, which serves as both viewing platform and a landmark for **B-Con Plaza**, Beppu's lavish convention centre and concert hall. The 100m-high, open observation deck provides giddying views, but if you've got time you'll get a better all-round panorama from the western hills.

Kannawa Onsen

鉄輪温泉 • Buses #2, #5, #7 or #41 from Beppu Station (20min; ¥320)

The charming area of **Kannawa Onsen** is the focal point of many visitors to Beppu, but it's also a spa in its own right with a beautiful garden rotemburo. Most people are here to see the **jigoku**, but only those recommended below are really worth it – any more and you'll tire of the tacky commercialism, loudspeakers and tour groups. A **day-pass** for ¥2000 covers all the *jigoku* except Hon-Bōzu Jigoku and Kinryu Jigoku, but you'd have to visit several to make it worthwhile. If you visit any of the district's **public baths**, it's a good idea to bring a towel, though you can always buy one on the spot for a couple of hundred yen.

Umi Jigoku

海地獄 • Daily 8am–5pm • ¥400 • Bus #2, #5, #7 or #41 from Beppu Station to Umijigoku-mae stop (25min; ¥360)

The most attractive of Beppu's *jigoku* is **Umi Jigoku**, set in a bowl of hills among well-tended gardens. Its main feature is a sea-blue pool – 120m deep and, at 90°C, hot enough to cook eggs – set off by a bright-red humped bridge and *torii* swathed in clouds of roaring steam. Walking around the manicured grounds, you'll also find a small, onsen steam-fed greenhouse, and a delightful footbath.

Oniishi-Bōzu Jigoku

鬼石坊主地獄 • Daily 8am–5pm • ¥400 • Bus #2, #5, #7 or #41 from Beppu Station to Umijigoku-mae stop (25min; ¥360)

An easy walk from Umi Jigoku, the speciality of **Oniishi-Bōzu Jigoku** is mud – boiling, smelly, steaming, hiccuping pools of it. Indeed, the place takes its

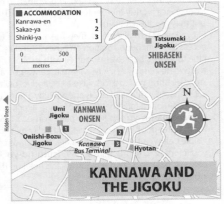

ACCOMMODATION
Kannawa-en	1
Sakae-ya	2
Shinki-ya	3

0   500
metres

Tatsumaki Jigoku

SHIBASEKI ONSEN

N

Umi Jigoku — KANNAWA ONSEN

Hidden Onsen

Oniishi-Bōzu Jigoku

Kannawa Bus Terminal

Hyotan

KANNAWA AND THE JIGOKU

name from the belief that the largest mud bubbles look like the bald pate of a Buddhist monk, a *bōzu* – and, in fact, the resemblance is quite uncanny.

Kannawa-en ryokan

神和苑 • 6-kumi Miyuki • Daily 10am–2.30pm • ¥800

If you fancy an onsen, it's definitely worth heading for the **Kannawa-en ryokan**, whose picturesque, milky-white rotemburo are open to the public (see p.722). Built on a hillside to the east of Umi Jigoku, the ryokan has a beautiful, classic garden enclosing a small lake and hidden rocky pools reached by winding paths.

Hyōtan Onsen

ひょうたん温泉 • Daily 9am–1am • ¥700; ¥550 after 6pm; Yukata rental ¥200 • ☎ 0977 66 0572, ⊕ hyotan-onsen.com

Hyōtan Onsen is a modern bath complex at the bottom of the hill, offering a rotemburo, sauna, a range of indoor pools and a sand bath. Should you feel peckish, you can even buy *jigoku mushi* to snack on.

Shibaseki Onsen

柴石温泉 • 4-1 Noda • Daily 7am–8pm • ¥210 • ☎ 0977 67 4100 • Bus #16 from Beppu or Kannawa Onsen

There are two *jigoku* in **Shibaseki Onsen**, a five-minute bus ride north of Kannawa. **Chi-no-ike Jigoku** (血の池地獄), "Blood Pond", is the better of the two, a huge bubbling pool whose vermilion fringes result from a high iron-oxide content. Fifty metres down the road, **Tatsumaki Jigoku** (龍巻地獄) consists of an unimpressive geyser that spouts around 5m into the air roughly every half-hour; it used to reach 50m until a stone block was placed over it for safety.

Kankaiji Onsen

観海寺温泉 • 1 Kankaiji • Tana-yu & Acquabeat daily 9am–10.30pm • ¥2000, free to hotel guests • ☎ 0977 24 1141, ⊕ suginoi-hotel.com • Bus #8 from Beppu Station (every 15min; 30min; ¥210)

Kankaiji Onsen spews out its hot water high up on a hill overlooking western Beppu, where it feeds the multifarious baths of *Suginoi Hotel*'s **Tana-yu**. This is Beppu's foremost bathing extravaganza, with an enormous terraced outdoor bath boasting

---

BEPPU'S HIDDEN ONSEN

If you're looking for something less commercial than the Beppu onsen, a few "hidden" baths lurk in the western hills – they are not exactly holes in the ground, but close enough. However, they are pretty isolated, and women in particular should think twice about going alone. Since a grisly murder took place here in 2010, the onsen have officially been off limits, but they are still accessible.

If you want to make the journey, the first step is to get to Myoban (明礬), an onsen area accessible from Beppu Station on buses #5 and #41 (25min; ¥360). From here directions are a little tough; it's best to arm yourself with a suitably rough map from the tourist office, or one of the two hostels (p.721). A twenty-minute walk on a road heading up and left from Myoban bus stop will bring you to a fork. Take a left, and follow the road around to **Hebin-yu** (へびん湯), a valley-based cascade of pools attended by a ramshackle hut. Turning right instead at the aforementioned fork, then scrambling up a rock path at the second gate, will bring you to **Nabeyama-no-yu** (鍋山の湯), a pair of onsen sitting in a forest-like setting. The first is a black-water pool, the second filled with clay that you can use for a free mud bath. Beppu is visible below, yet all one can hear are the sounds of nature – there isn't even a place to put your clothes. To hit the third spring, **Tsuru-no-yu** (鶴の湯), you'll have to get off the bus just before it passes under the highway, and head up the dirt track alongside a graveyard. Not easy – but it's Beppu at its purest.

fantastic views over the city and Beppu Bay, plus a separate spa complex and the Acquabeat resort, a huge indoor pool with a spiral water slide.

Tsurumi-dake

鶴見岳 • Ropeway daily 9am–5.30pm • ¥1400 return; ¥700 one way • ⓦ beppu-ropeway.co.jp • Buses #36 or #37 from Beppu Station drop you at the ropeway's lower terminus (every 30min; 40min; ¥510).

There are spectacular views from the top of **Tsurumi-dake** (1375m) mountain – it's even possible to see Shikoku in the distance on a clear day. Though it's perfectly climbable, the majority of visitors use the **ropeway** instead to get to the summit. Buses here from Beppu pass near Kankaiji Onsen en route, meaning that you could combine the two sights to make a pleasant half-day trip from Beppu.

10

ARRIVAL AND INFORMATION

BEPPU

By plane Beppu is served by Ōita airport (ⓣ 0978 67 1174), 40km away on the north side of the bay; frequent airport buses run south to Ōita city, stopping at Kitahama on the way (40min; ¥1450), and a few terminate at Beppu Station.

Destinations Nagoya (2 daily; 1hr 5min); Naha (1 daily; 1hr 45min); Ōsaka (Itami; 5 daily; 55min); and Tokyo (10 daily; 1hr 30min).

By train Beppu's main station is conveniently located right in the centre of town, an easy walk from most accommodation and restaurants.

Destinations Aso (4 daily; 2hr); Fukuoka (1–3 hourly; 2hr–3hr 20min); Kumamoto (4 daily; 3hr–3hr 20min); Miyazaki (1 hourly; 3hr 30min); Ōita (2–4 hourly; 10min); and Usuki (1–3 hourly; 30min–1hr 15min).

By bus Long-distance buses mostly stop at the Kamenoi bus station, in Kitahama, although some services terminate at Beppu train station.

Destinations Aso (5 daily; 3hr); Fukuoka (hourly; 2hr 30min); Hiroshima (2 daily; 5hr 15min); Kumamoto (4 daily; 4hr 40min); Nagasaki (7 daily; 3hr 40min); Nagoya (1 daily; 11hr); and Ōita (frequent; 20min).

By ferry Ferries from Honshū and Shikoku dock a couple of kilometres north of the centre at the International Tourist Port. To reach the port from Beppu train station, take bus #20 or #26 and get off at Kansai Kisen-mae.

Destinations Ōsaka (1 daily; 13hr; from ¥9100), via Matsuyama (4hr; from ¥3300) with Kansai Kisen (ⓣ 0977 22 2181, ⓦ ferry-sunflower.co.jp); Yawatahama on Shikoku (6 daily; 2hr 50min; ¥3020) with Uwajima Unyu Ferry (ⓣ 0977 21 2364).

Tourist information The town's main tourist office (daily 9am–5pm; ⓣ 0977 21 1119) lies just inside the central east exit of Beppu Station and has maps, brochures and information on local bus routes. The English-speaking staff can also assist with hotel reservations and there's a computer you can use to access the internet (free for ten minutes).

GETTING AROUND

By bus Local buses are the best way of getting around Beppu. Fortunately, they're not too complicated and there's a fair amount of information in English for the major routes. Most routes start at Beppu Station, but could leave from either the west or east sides – ask to make sure you're waiting in the right place.

Bus passes It may be worth buying a one-day "Mini Free Pass" (¥900), available at the station information desk or

the Kamenoi bus station in Kitahama. The pass includes all buses within the city centre, which covers the *jigoku*, Suginoi Palace, sand baths and even the ropeway. It also entitles you to a ten percent discount on entry to the main sights, including the *jigoku* day-pass (see opposite).

Car rental Eki Rent-a-Car (ⓣ 0977 24 4423), Nippon Rent-a-Car (ⓣ 0977 22 6181) and Toyota Rent-a-Car (ⓣ 0977 22 7171) all have offices near Beppu Station.

ACCOMMODATION

The most convenient place to look for **accommodation** is around Beppu Station, where you'll find a clutch of business hotels, a couple of appealing ryokan and some good-value budget options. Though less central, the **Kannawa** area offers a few atmospheric alternatives buried among its old streets. Prices tend to go up at weekends, when it can be hard to find a room anywhere in Beppu – make sure you book ahead.

AROUND THE STATION

Beppu Guest House 1-12 Ekimae-chō ⓣ 080 4642 9044, ⓦ beppu-e.cloud-line.com. Perfectly acceptable hostel just a stone's throw from the station. There's free laundry and internet access, as well as a communal

kitchen; though it can be a fun place with the right crowd, it can feel a little sterile at other times. Dorm **¥1500**, double **¥5000**

Beppu Station Hotel 別府ステーションホテル 12-8 Ekimae-chō ⓣ 0977 24 5252. Rooms here are pretty

10

sharp for a business hotel, and as the name suggests, it's right next to the station. The cheapest singles (¥3900) are a little tight, but regular singles, twins and triples are a decent size. There's also an onsen bath. **¥8000**

Bokai 望海 3-8-7 Kitahama ☎ 0977 22 1241, ⓦ bokai .jp. Excellent ryokan facing the beach – ask for a room with a view, if possible. Rooms are all en suite and extremely comfortable (there's a choice of tatami or Western styles), and there are onsen facilities on the rooftop. Meals are exquisite, with dinners often featuring *fugu* (blowfish). **¥18,000**

★**Khaosan Beppu** 3-3-10 Kitahama ☎ 0977 23 3939, Ⓦkhaosan-tokyo.com. Now here's something you don't see every day: a hostel with a hot spring, and one which is open throughout the night to boot. There's a comfy lounge area to chill or cook in, while the welcoming staff are great sources of local advice. Dorm **¥2500**, double **¥7000**

Minshuku Kokage 国際民宿こかげ 8-9 Ekimae-chō ☎ 0977 23 1753, ⓦ ww6.tiki.ne.jp/~kokage. Popular cheapie with a choice of tatami or Western rooms, with or without bath, and an onsen downstairs. Internet access, washing machines and bike rental are thrown in for free, though there is a midnight curfew. **¥6000**

★**Yamada Bessō** 山田別荘 3-2-18 Kitahama ☎ 0977 24 2121, ⓦ yamadabessou.jp. Welcoming ryokan occupying a nicely faded seventy-year-old wooden building, set in gardens a couple of blocks north of Ekimae-dōri. Cheaper rooms have no en-suite facilities, but the onsen and gorgeous outdoor rotemburo more than compensate; non-guests can use these facilities for just ¥500. Meals are available on request, though prices almost double if you go for the full dinner-and-breakfast deal. **¥10,800**

KANNAWA

Kannawa-en 神和苑 6-kumi Miyuki ☎ 0977 66 2111, ⓦ kannawaen.jp. This beautiful old ryokan boasts nineteen lovely tatami rooms, some in individual buildings, set in a classic, hillside garden with beautiful rotemburo. Rates include breakfast and an evening meal. **¥40,000**

★**Sakae-ya** サカエ家 2-kumi Ida ☎ 0977 66 6234. The century-old *Sakae-ya* is an elegant ryokan hidden in the eastern, less touristy part of Kannawa. They offer twelve rooms at either minshuku rates (¥12,000), with optional meals, or in the more upmarket ryokan including two meals. There are ovens for steaming *jigoku mushi* (see below) at the back – order in advance if you'd like to try it. **¥20,000**

★**Shinki-ya** しんき屋 2-kumi Furimoto ☎ 0977 66 0962, ⓦ shinkiya.jp. Five minutes' walk downhill from the bus terminal, tucked up a small lane on the right, this little ryokan has been beautifully renovated with gleaming tatami rooms (none en suite), *hinoki* onsen baths and a rotemburo. Meals are offered on request (for much higher rates), including home-steamed *jigoku mushi*. **¥11,100**

EATING AND DRINKING

Beppu has a pleasing range of **speciality foods** to look out for (see box below). When it comes to finding a **restaurant**, you're best off in the downtown area, while ramen joints are everywhere you look. The town's **bars** tend to be of the seedy variety, and some of the naughtier ones do not accept foreigners (a good thing, since their prices can be sky-high).

Chihara ちはら 1-11-2 Kitahama ☎ 0977 27 1129. Fun place serving Korean-style barbecued meat. Their set lunches are a bargain: *reimen*, meat, salad, coffee and side-dishes for just ¥798. In the evening, meat starts at ¥740 a portion, and there's lots of cheap shōchū to enjoy. Daily 11am–2pm & 5pm–midnight.

Jin 仁 1-15-7 Kitahama ☎ 0977 21 1768. Lively joint at the east end of Ekimae-dōri with an English menu listing a good range of fish, vegetable and tofu dishes, as well as *yakitori* skewers (¥320 for three) and local specialities such as *toriten* (¥500). Also note that local shōchū starts at just ¥280 per glass … insane. Daily 5pm–midnight.

★**Sabou-Shinanoya** 尾信濃屋 6-32 Nishinoguchi ☎ 0977 21 1395. Set in a delightful old Shōwa-era holiday home, now featuring classy-looking furniture and lighting, this is the place to head for *dango-jiru*, Beppu's tasty local noodle soup (see box below). Thurs–Mon 9am–10pm; Tues & Wed 9am–6pm.

BEPPU'S CULINARY SPECIALITIES

Beppu's **speciality foods** include *fugu* (blowfish) and *karei* (flounder), which are traditionally winter dishes, though they're often available year-round. Far cheaper are the piping-hot *dango-jiru*, a cheap, filling soup which comes with thick white noodles, assorted vegetables and chunks of either chicken or pork; *toriten*, a local chicken tempura; and reimen, buckwheat noodles in a cold soup. You might also like to try *jigoku mushi*, a name given to a whole assortment of comestibles (vegetables and eggs are most prominent) slow-cooked in steam from Beppu's hells; you'll find it on sale at stalls and supermarkets in the Kannawa area, where it also often features in ryokan meals (see p.43).

Shin-zushi 新鮨し 8-15 Ekimae-chō ☎ 0977 25 0005. Sushi fans should head to this pristine sushi-ya round the corner from *Minshuku Kokage* (see opposite). It has a good choice of sushi, sashimi and tempura set dishes from ¥1500, while individual sushi start at ¥200. 2pm–midnight, closed Sun.

Takeya 竹屋 15-7 Gen-chō. Sweet café with a bamboo theme (hence the name) and tasty coffee, more or less opposite the Takegawara baths (see p.718). A good place to meet local artists. Opening times vary.

Toyotsune とよ常 3-7 Ekimae-chō ☎ 0977 22 3274. Unpretentious restaurant opposite Beppu Station

specializing in *fugu*, either as sashimi (¥2625/person) or a full, two-hour-long meal (from ¥5250). Less exotic dishes include well-priced tendon, tempura or sashimi sets (from ¥750), and a good range of local shōchū. 11am–2pm & 5–10pm; closed Thurs.

★ **Ureshi-ya** うれしや 7-12 Ekimae-chō ☎ 0977 22 0767. At some time or other, almost every foreign visitor to Beppu ends up eating at this unassuming little place, where you can choose from a tempting display of ready-prepared dishes, such as vegetable tempura, sashimi, salads and fried fish. They also serve up standard rice and noodle dishes, all at very reasonable prices. 5.30pm–2am, closed Mon.

DIRECTORY

Banks and exchange Ōita Bank, on Ekimae-dōri, accepts the widest range of currencies in cash and travellers' cheques.

Hospital Beppu National Hospital (☎ 0977 67 1111) is in north Beppu's Kamegawa district, inland from Kamegawa Station.

Police The main police station (☎ 0977 21 2131) is opposite the post office on Route 10.

Post office The most convenient post office is on Ekimae-dōri.

Shopping The Beppu region is famed for its bamboo handicrafts, which you'll find in the station malls and department stores on Ekimae-dōri. Another popular souvenir, which is on sale all over town, is *yu-no-hana*, natural bath salts to create that instant hot-spring feel back home.

Yufuin

湯布院

The small resort town of **YUFUIN** sits in a mountain-surrounded hollow just 25km inland from Beppu. It's perfect day-trip distance so hordes of tourists converge here each day, reaching their peak at weekends and holiday times. However, Yufuin has made great efforts to protect its original character, and if you stay overnight, you'll better appreciate its charming, thatched-roof-lined alleyways augmented by silence and streetlights rather than the *souvenir* frenzy of the daytime.

Yufuin's appeal centres around tripping from one **onsen** to the next, though they are frustratingly rather spread out. Head in a straight line from the station towards the mountains, and after thirty minutes or so you'll be by beautiful **Kinrin Lake** (金鱗湖), surrounded by trees, trinket shops and camera-toting visitors. Right by the lake, you'll find the tiny **Shitan-yu** (下ん湯), a mixed-gender onsen with rustic thatched roofing.

There are few other sights as such, though Yufuin boasts a number of picturesque temples, as well as the opportunity to climb **Yufu-dake**, the double-headed volcano that rears up above town.

ARRIVAL AND DEPARTURE   YUFUIN

By train Most visitors arrive by train on the Yufuin-no-mori limited express service from Hakata (2hr 10min; ¥4600; see box, p.677). You can get trains from Beppu too, though you're more likely to have to break your journey in Ōita.

Tourist information Don't expect too much from the

booth in the station (daily 9am–7pm; ☎ 0974 84 2446), though they're fantastic at handing out maps.

Services A post office, with an ATM that accepts international cards, can be found just along from the information booth.

ACCOMMODATION

Country Road Youth Hostel カントリーロードユースホステル ☎ 0977 84 3734. The town's budget choice, a superb place with its own onsen and a rarified location on a hillside above town – try to arrange pick-up from the station in advance. Dorm **¥3435**, double **¥8000**

Makiba-no-ie 牧場の家 ☎ 0977 84 2138. Almost exactly in the middle of the station and Kinrin Lake, this is the most atmospheric option in town, with thatched-roof huts set around a charming rotemburo. Their meals are fantastic. **¥29,700**

EATING

Cafe la Roche カフェラロシュ ☎0977 84 3348. It's hard to beat the stunning setting here, right next to Kinrin Lake. Coffees go from ¥400, and they serve a range of snacks and small meals. Daily 9am–6pm.

Izumi 泉 ☎0977 85 5262. Right next to *Cafe la Roche*, this beautiful venue is the best place in the area for a meal. It sells tasty handmade soba (¥1260) – you can even watch the noodles being pounded and whacked out in an open area at the front of the restaurant. Daily 9am–6pm.

Usuki

臼杵

The small and attractive castle town of **USUKI**, some 40km to the south of Beppu, offers a reminder of the spiritual side of life, and makes a pleasant stop on the coastal route to or from Miyazaki. Between the twelfth and fourteenth centuries, in a little valley around 5km southwest of town, skilled craftsmen sculpted some sixty **Buddha statues** in the soft lava tuff. The weather has taken its toll since then, but restoration work has saved several of these serene statues, which continue their vigil unperturbed.

Seki Butsu

石仏 • Daily 6.30am–6pm • ¥530 • Bus from train station (7 daily; 20min; ¥300); 30min by bicycle (hire from station, ¥200/hr); or ¥1400 by taxi

The stone Buddhas, or **Seki Butsu**, are grouped around the sides of a narrow north–south valley and divided into four clusters, of which the first and last are the most interesting. Following the path anticlockwise, you'll reach the Hoki Second Cluster first of all; it's dominated by a 3m-tall figure of **Amitabha Buddha** and his two attendants, each individually expressed. The path then takes you round via the Hoki First Cluster – comprising over twenty statues – and the rather worn Sannōsan trinity of Buddhas, to the Furuzono Cluster. Here, the central **Dainichi Nyorai** is considered one of Japan's finest stone-carved Buddhas. While the lower body has partly rotted away, the Buddha's face, picked out with faded pigment, is still sublime.

The old town

After you've walked round the Buddhas, which won't take much over thirty minutes, it's worth taking a quick stroll through the **old centre** of Usuki on the way back to the station; if you're travelling by bus (see below), ask to get off at the *Hirasōzu* stop on the west side of town. From here, a stone-paved street leads northeast between high mossy walls and past temples and samurai houses. You'll eventually come out on a traditional shopping street, where the local speciality, *fugu*, is much in evidence, either for sale dried in shops or on restaurant menus. Where you come to the big red *torii* on the far east side of town, turn right and you'll be back at the station.

ARRIVAL AND DEPARTURE

USUKI

By train Usuki is a stop on the JR Nippō Line, forty minutes south of Beppu by express train, with services roughly every hour; make sure you get a train which stops at Usuki.

Destinations Beppu (1–3 hourly; 30min–1hr 15min); Miyazaki (hourly; 3hr); and Nobeoka (1 hourly; 1hr 30min).

Tourist information Staff at the station hand out basic sketch maps, but for anything more complicated, you'll need to walk into the centre of town (around ten minutes) to the tourist office (daily 9am–7pm; ☎0972 64 7271) on the main shopping street.

Miyazaki

宮崎

There's a relaxed, summery feel to the breezy city of **MIYAZAKI**, with its palm trees, flower-lined streets and the longest sunshine hours in Japan. While the city itself has few draws bar the odd shrine, park and museum, it makes a good base for exploring the **Nichinan coast**, which is particularly appealing to the **surfers** who head here in droves in warmer months (see box, p.729).

Though they won't appear on anyone's must-see list, the city's sights are sufficiently interesting to fill a leisurely day. **Heiwadai-kōen** in the northern suburbs, is a hilltop park with a delightful collection of clay *haniwa* figurines – replicas of statues found in ancient burial mounds. The grounds of nearby **Miyazaki-jingū**, the city's foremost shrine, contain a good municipal museum, while Miyazaki's sleek **art museum** lies nearby, and there's an entertaining **Science Centre** in the city centre, near Miyazaki Station. Further south, much is made of the riverside **Tachibana Park**; by day it's just a narrow strip of green with a few tables and chairs, but at dusk it comes into its own, when the palm trees glitter with fairy lights.

10

Science Centre

科学技術館, Kagaku Gijitsukan • 1-2-2 Miyazakiekihigashi • 9am–4.30pm; closed Mon • Planetarium shows Tues–Sat 3 daily, Sun 4 daily • ¥520, or ¥730 including planetarium

In the city centre there's little to see bar the excellent **Science Centre**, which covers everything from microorganisms, wind power and pulleys to robots and satellite imagery, making use where possible of examples from Kyūshū. The museum also boasts one of the world's largest **planetariums** – 27m in diameter – which is well worth the extra expense. The shows give you a superb fifty-minute ride through the heavens.

Heiwadai-kōen

平和台公園 • Bus from Depāto-mae stop #1, outside Bon Belta department store (10–20min; ¥270)

Low hills rise to the north of Miyazaki, where the rather Stalinist "Tower of Peace" dominates a large public park, **Heiwadai-kōen**. Behind the tower you'll find the **Haniwa Garden**, where dozens of clay statues of houses, animals and people populate a mossy wood. Look out for the charming warriors with elaborate uniforms and the pop-eyed, open-mouthed dancers. These are copies of the *haniwa* figures discovered in fourth-century burial mounds at nearby Saitobaru; it's believed the statues were used to "protect" aristocratic tombs.

Miyazaki Prefectural Museum of Nature and History

宮崎県総合博物館, Miyazaki-ken Sōgō Hakubutsukan • 2-4-4 Jingū • **Museum** 9am–5pm, closed Tues • **Minka-en** daily 10am–4.30pm • Free

Around 1km southeast of Heiwadai-kōen, and close to Miyazaki-jingū Station, the **Miyazaki Prefectural Museum of Nature and History** is worth visiting for its displays of local folklore. The same complex includes an archeological centre, where you can watch people patiently glueing together pottery shards, and the **Minka-en**, a collection of four thatched farmhouses from around the area. Don't miss the two traditional stone baths; the water was heated by lighting a fire underneath, like giant cauldrons.

Miyazaki-jingū

宮崎神宮, Miyazaki Kenritsu Bijutsukan • 2 Jingū • 24hr • Free

Extensive woodlands surround **Miyazaki-jingū**, a shrine dedicated to Japan's first emperor, Jimmu Tennō. An unusually large shrine at the end of an imposing avenue, the sanctuary itself is typically understated, though if you're lucky you'll catch a festive ceremony, or at least spot some of the colourful, semi-wild chickens scurrying round the raked-gravel compound.

Prefectural Art Museum

宮崎県立美術館 • 10am–6pm; closed Mon • Free

Five minutes' walk west of Miyazaki-jingū is the aptly named Culture Park, a complex of public buildings, including a theatre, a library and a concert hall that contains Japan's largest pipe organ. It is also home to the monumental **Prefectural Art Museum**, which hosts temporary exhibitions of twentieth-century Japanese and Western painting.

ARRIVAL AND INFORMATION   **MIYAZAKI**

By plane The airport (☏ 0985 51 5114) is 5km south of the city centre and connected to Miyazaki Station by both train (1–3 hourly; 10min; ¥340) and bus (every 30min; 30min; ¥400).

Destinations Fukuoka (7 daily; 45min); Nagoya (3 daily; 1hr 10min); Naha (1 daily; 1hr 25min); Osaka (Itami; 6 daily; 1hr); Seoul (3 weekly; 1hr 40min); and Tokyo (1–2 hourly; 1hr 30min).

By train Miyazaki's main station is right in the centre of the city, opposite the main bus station.

Destinations Aoshima (1 hourly; 30min); Beppu (1 hourly; 3hr 10min–3hr 30min); Fukuoka (2 daily; 5hr 35min–6hr 30min); Kagoshima (7 daily; 2hr–2hr 10min); Nobeoka (1 hourly; 1hr); Obi (1 hourly; 1hr 15min); and Usuki (hourly; 3hr).

By bus Long-distance buses tend to stop at the Miyazaki Eki-mae Bus Centre just across the road from the train station, though some arrive at Miyakō City terminal, south of the river near JR Minami-Miyazaki Station.

Destinations Aoshima (1 hourly; 50min); Aya (every 30min; 50min); Fukuoka (1–2 hourly; 4hr–4hr 15min); Kagoshima (9 daily; 2hr 40min); Kumamoto (1 hourly; 3hr); and Udo-jingū (1 hourly; 1hr 30min).

By ferry Ferries from Osaka (1 daily; 12hr; from ¥11,600) dock at Miyazaki Port Ferry Terminal, east of the city centre: buses to Miyazaki train station (15–20min; ¥240) wait outside the terminal buildings. Ferry tickets can be bought from Miyazaki Car Ferry (☏ 0985 29 5566, ⊛ miyazakicarferry.com), or local travel agents (see p.728).

Tourist information Miyazaki is well provided with English-language information at both the main tourist office inside Miyazaki Station (daily 9am–6pm; ☎ 0985 22 5469) and the desk at the airport (daily 7am–9pm; ☎ 0985 51 5114). The International Plaza on the eighth floor of the Carino shopping mall (Tues–Sat 10am–7pm; ☎ 0985 32 8457, ⓦ mif.or.jp) is another useful resource, aimed primarily at long-term residents.

GETTING AROUND

By bus Local buses depart from either the Miyazaki Eki-mae Bus Centre or from the Miyakō City terminal, south of the river. However, since almost all buses call at stops around the city's central crossroads, Depāto-mae, the best thing is to head for this junction and ask which stop you need; the minimum fare is ¥150. If you're doing a lot of bus travel, you can buy a one-day bus pass (¥1000), which covers all Miyazaki Kōtsū buses throughout the prefecture, as far afield as Obi. You can buy it at the train station, or the Miyazaki Eki-mae Bus Centre across the road.

By bike The city provides free bikes to reduce the number of cars on the roads. You can pick up a bike at the Wheels outlet (daily 9am–6pm) to the west of the station on Hiroshima-dōri, and at Yotten Plaza (よってんプラザ; daily 11am–6.30pm) on Tachibana-dōri beside the APA Hotel. There's a ¥500 deposit and the first three hours are free – the cost for the rest of the day is ¥200.

Car rental Eki Rent-a-Car (☎ 0985 24 7206) and Nippon Rent-a-Car (☎ 0985 25 0919) have outlets near the station. The latter has an airport outlet (☎ 0935 56 5007).

ACCOMMODATION

APA Hotel APAホテル 3-4-4 Tachibanadōri-higashi ☎ 0985 20 5500. South of Miyazaki's central crossroads, this smartish business hotel features English-style facilities, and boasts a few twin and double rooms. Cheaper rooms lack windows, but they're all equipped with phone, TV and en-suite bath. **¥9000**

Green Rich Hotel グリーンリチホテル 1-5-8 Kawaramachi ☎ 0985 26 7411. This excellent value business hotel is indeed green in hue. It's near the river, and has spick-and-span rooms which are equipped with wi-fi. **¥5600**

Guesthouse Heiwa ホテルゲストハウス平和 1041-4 Oaza ☎ 0985 48 1880. The closest thing Miyazaki has to a youth hostel is located some way north of the centre, though this makes it pretty convenient for Miyazaki-jingū and some of its surrounding sights. The owner speaks little English, but goes out of her way to make guests feel welcome. Dorm **¥2000**

Miyazaki Kankō Hotel 宮崎観光ホテル 1-1-1 Matsuyama ☎ 0985 27 1212, ⓦ miyakan-h.com. Central

Miyazaki's poshest hotel boasts a riverside location, shopping mall, choice of restaurants and onsen spa complete with a rotemburo. Rooms are smarter – and considerably more expensive – in the newer east wing, but all are very comfortable. Ask for a river view. **¥24,600**

Sheraton Grande シェラトングランドオーシャンリゾート Hamayama, Yamasaki-chō ☎ 0985 21 1111, ⓦ starwoodhotels.com. Housed in a distinctive 154m-tall skyscraper forming part of the Phoenix Seagaia Resort complex (which also features a golf range, onsen and a Banyan Tree spa), this is Miyazaki's most luxurious accommodation, with large, bright rooms – try to bag one with an ocean view – and facilities including tennis courts and several pools. Book online for the cheapest rates. **¥17,000**

Tōyoko Inn Miyazaki Eki-mae 東横INN宮崎駅前 2-2-31 Oimatsu ☎ 0985 32 1045, ⓦ toyoko-inn.com. This business hotel boasts the low prices and excellent location typical of the chain – it's right outside Miyazaki Station's west entrance. **¥5960**

EATING, DRINKING AND ENTERTAINMENT

The best choice of **restaurants** is in the streets either side of Tachibana-dōri and particularly those behind the Bon Belta department store, which is also where you'll find Miyazaki's energetic **nightlife** district. **Local specialities** include beef, wild boar, *ayu* (sweet fish), shiitake mushrooms from the mountains, clams, flying fish and citrus fruits. There's also good local sushi – *retasu-maki* – containing shrimp, lettuce and mayonnaise; chicken *Namban* – deep-fried, succulent chicken morsels with tartar sauce; and, in summer, *hiyajiru*, an aromatic soup of fish, tofu, cucumber and sesame, served ice-cold and then poured over hot rice. A popular local snack is cheese *manju*, consisting of a small, sweet almond butter-cake bun filled with melt-in-the-mouth cream cheese.

CAFÉS AND RESTAURANTS

★**Gunkei** ぐんけい 8-12 Chūō-dōri ☎ 0985 28 4365, ⓦ gunkei.jp. Tender *jidori* chicken seared over coals and brought sizzling to the table is the order of the day in this great restaurant, decorated in traditional rustic style. There's no English menu, but ask for the *jidori* set (¥2600)

and you won't be disappointed. Reservations strongly recommended. Daily 5–11.30pm.

Hidaka Honten 日高本店 3-10-24 Tachibanadōri-nishi ☎ 0985 26 101. This shop is the best place to sample Miyazaki's delectable cheese *manju* (see above). While you're at it, try their *Nanjya-kora Daifuku* – a chilled

10

package of soft white rice-flour, filled with red-bean paste, a strawberry, a chestnut and cream cheese; it's absolutely divine. Daily 10.30am–8pm.

Kokoro 心 6-24 Chūō-dōri. Behind a low, wooden door and a bit tricky to spot, this is a stylish vegetarian *izakaya* where the friendly English-speaking owner will guide you through the extensive menu. Portions aren't huge but the food is lovingly prepared and presented. The ¥2000 "course menu" represents good value. 5pm–2am, closed Mon.

★ **Ogura** おぐら 3-4-24 Tachibanadōri-higashi ☎0985 27 7333. A diner-style restaurant offering good, cheap food, which has hardly changed since they invented chicken *Namban* (¥950) here in 1968. They also serve burgers, fried pork cutlets, curry rice and other comfort food in generous portions. 11am–3pm & 5–8.30pm, closed Tues.

Sangam サンガム 1-2-25 Tachibanadōri-nishi ☎0985 31 6639. Decent curries on offer at this local favourite, and

they'll add extra spices if you like it fiery. Lunch set menu from ¥1000, dinner around ¥2000. Daily noon–2pm & 6.30–11pm.

Suginoko 杉の子 2-1-4 Tachibanadōri-nishi ☎0985 22 5798. One of the city's most famous restaurants, at the southern end of Tachibana-dōri, serving tasty country cooking in elegant surroundings. Try their lunchtime *Kuroshio teishoku* or *Shokado bentō* sampler (both ¥1600). Evening set menus start at ¥4200. Daily 11.30am–2pm & 4–10.30pm, closed for lunch once a week, usually Mon; phone to check.

BARS AND LIVE MUSIC

The Bar ザバー 3-7-15 Tachibanadōri-higashi ☎0985 71 0423. Popular expat drinking hole, and a good base from which to organize further drinking. As well as laying on pool and Wii games, the owner is also an expert source of advice regarding the region's surf-spots. Tues–Sun 7pm–3am.

DIRECTORY

Banks and exchange Mizuho Bank and Fukuoka City Bank, both on Tachibana-dōri, just north of the central crossroads, have foreign exchange desks. As with any city in Japan, if you want to get money from an international card, hunt down a post office or 7-Eleven.

Hospitals and medical care The Prefectural Hospital 1, 5-30 Kita-takamatsu-chō (☎0985 24 4181), is on Takachiho-dōri, west of the central crossroads. Staff at the International Plaza should be able to help find English-speaking doctors.

Police Miyazaki-Kita Police Station, 2-10-1 Higashi, Tachibana-dōri Miyazaki (☎0985 27 0110).

Post office Miyazaki Central Post Office, 1-1-34 Takachiho-dōri, is on the main road east of the Tachibana junction. They operate a 24hr service for express mail.

Travel agents For domestic travel arrangements, try JTB (☎0985 29 2111) in Miyazaki Station. For international tickets, contact H.I.S. (☎0985 31 6686) on Tachibana-dōri south of the main crossroads.

Around Miyazaki

South of Miyazaki, the hills close in as road and railway follow the coast down to **Aoshima**, a small island surrounded by peculiar rock formations; further along the coast, **Udo-jingū**'s main shrine nestles in a sacred cave. As you head down the Nichinan coast to **Cape Toi**, famed for its wild horses, there are more sandy coves and picturesque islands, as well as the castle remains and old samurai houses of **Obi**, a small, attractive town lying 6km inland.

Aoshima

青島

Fourteen kilometres south of Miyazaki, the tiny island of **AOSHIMA**, just 1500m in circumference, is little more than a heap of sand capped by a dense forest of betel palms and other subtropical plants. The island lies a five-minute walk across a causeway from the neighbouring town, also known as Aoshima. The town itself has no other sights worth stopping for, though the **botanical garden** (daily 8.30am–5pm; free), beside the causeway, is worth a quick browse while you're waiting for onward transport.

Aoshima-jinja

Aoshima island is at its best at low tide when you can explore the rock pools trapped on the surrounding "devil's washboard" shelf of rocks, scored into deep grooves as if by a giant's comb. After that, the only other thing to do is walk round the island – it takes all of fifteen minutes – and drop in at its small attractive shrine, **Aoshima-jinja**. Swathed in vegetation, the shrine is dedicated to Yamasachi Hiko, a god of mountain products. Each year he's honoured with a couple of lively festivals: on the last weekend in July portable shrines are paraded round the island on boats and then manhandled back to Aoshima, while mid-January sees men rushing semi-naked into the sea. Come warmer weather, countless souls do likewise, though armed with surfboards – Aoshima is a prime base for the surfing fraternity (see box below).

ARRIVAL AND DEPARTURE   AOSHIMA

By train You can take the JR Nichinan Line train from Miyazaki Station (hourly; 30min; ¥360) to Aoshima Station, from where it's an 800m walk east to the island; the map outside the station will point the way.

By bus Buses depart from Miyazaki's Eki-mae Bus Centre (hourly; 50min; ¥670), with a stop at Depāto-mae, and drop you beside the west entrance to the botanical garden.

ACCOMMODATION

Aoshima Guesthouse Hooju 青島ゲストハウス風樹 ☏ 090 5945 5303, ⓦ hoojuaoshima.web.fc2.com. Worthy hostel on the mainland side of the island, just a few minutes' walk from the causeway. Dorms are tatami in style, rather pretty, and perfectly comfortable. Dorm **¥2500**

Udo-jingū

鵜戸神宮 • Free • Five *undama* ¥100

Eighteen kilometres south of Aoshima, a cleft in the rock hides one of this area's most famous sights, **Udo-jingū**. The main **shrine** fills the mouth of a large, low cave halfway down the cliff face, its striking, vermilion *torii* and arched bridges vivid against the dark rock. According to legend, Udo-jingū was founded in the first century BC and marks the spot where Emperor Jimmu's father was born. The rounded boulders in front of the cave are said to represent his mother's breasts – expectant women come here to pray for an easy birth and newlyweds for a happy marriage. It's also supposed to be lucky if you land a small clay pebble (*undama*) in the hollow in the top of the nearest "breast"; women throw with their right hand, men with their left.

ARRIVAL AND DEPARTURE   UDO-JINGŪ

By train The shrine is only accessible by road, though those seeking to eke out the most from their JR Pass should note that the closest station is Aburatsu, accessible from both Miyazaki and Aoshima. From Aburatsu Station, it's a

---

SURFIN' MIYAZAKI

To scores of adventurous young Japanese, Miyazaki prefecture is inextricably linked to **surfing**. These are Japan's best and warmest waters, and though few foreigners get in on the action, this makes a trip here all the more appealing. The peak season runs from August to October, when most weekends will have a surfing event of some description.

There's decent surfing in the waters immediately west of Aoshima (see above) – protected by the island, these smaller swells are perfect for beginners. **Nagisa Store** (☏ 0985 65 1070), between Kodomonokuni Station and *Grand Hotel Qingdao*, rents boards (¥3000) and wetsuits (¥2000), while a few minutes' walk north of the same station similar prices are on offer at **Wellybird** (☏ 0985 65 1468). A little further towards Miyazaki is Kisaki-hama (木崎浜), a decent beach popular with surfers, and a ten-minute walk from Undōkōen Station. Equipment here can be rented at **Blast Surf World** (☏ 0985 58 2038), located behind the Mos Burger just about visible from the station exit.

Experienced surfers with their own equipment should head to the reefs and reef breaks south of Aoshima, though these can be hard to get to without a local friend. Far to the north of Miyazaki, there are similarly ferocious waters surrounding **Hyūga** (日句), just south of Nobeoka.

20min (¥460) bus ride to the shrine.

By bus Direct buses run from Miyazaki (hourly; 1hr 30min; ¥1440) or Aoshima (hourly; 40min; ¥990). Buses on towards Obi (6 daily; 40min; ¥880) are less frequent – check the schedules in Miyazaki. If you're coming here from Miyazaki, it's better value to buy the day-pass (see p.727).

Obi

飫肥

An old **castle town** 45km south of Miyazaki, **OBI** is a pristine little place with a number of samurai houses and a fine collection of traditional whitewashed warehouses, many of them immaculately restored, clustered under the castle walls. Obi's heyday was under the Itō family, who were granted the fiefdom in 1588 and then spent much of their time feuding with the neighbouring Shimazu clan of Kagoshima. Only the walls of their once formidable castle remain, though the main gate and lord's residence have been rebuilt in the original style.

Central Obi lies in a loop of the Sakatani-gawa, with its historic core concentrated north of the main east–west highway.

Obi-jō

飫肥城 · Daily 9.30am–4.30pm · ¥600 ticket includes entry to all the sights within the castle

Here you'll find a few streets of **samurai houses** and carp streams, as well as the castle, **Obi-jō** on the low hill behind. Walk north up Ōte-mon-dōri to enter the castle via its great southern gate and follow the path round to the right to find a white-walled **history museum**, which has a small but impressive collection of Itō family heirlooms.

Matsu-no-maru

松の丸

On the hill heading up from the main entrance stands the **Matsu-no-maru**, an exact replica of the rambling Edo-period buildings where the lords once lived, including the reception rooms, women's quarters, tea-ceremony room and a lovely "cooling-off" tower, where the lord could catch the summer breezes after his steam bath.

Yoshōkan

豫章館

The rest of the castle grounds are now just grass and trees, but on the way out take a quick look at Obi's largest samurai house, the **Yoshōkan**, immediately west of Ōte-mon gate. When the Meiji reforms abolished feudal holdings in the late nineteenth century, the Itō family moved to this more modest villa, which had previously belonged to their chief retainer. Though you can't go in, the house is a lovely, airy building surrounded by a spacious garden that's looking a bit worse for wear.

Komura Memorial Hall

小村記念館, Komura Kinentan

On the opposite side of Ōte-mon-dōri from the Yoshōkan, the **Komura Memorial Hall** commemorates a famous Meiji-era diplomat who was born in Obi in 1855. He's best remembered for his part in concluding the 1905 peace treaty following the Russo-Japanese War; the museum's most interesting material, much of it in English, revolves around this period.

ARRIVAL AND DEPARTURE

OBI

By train The quickest way to reach Obi is by train on the JR Nichinan line from Miyazaki (hourly; 1hr 15min; ¥910) via Aoshima. Obi Station lies on the east side of town, about 15min walk across the river from the castle – staff at the ticket office can provide a sketch map.

By bus Buses from Aoshima (6 daily; 1hr 30min; ¥1680) and Udo-jingū (6 daily; 40min; ¥880) stop on the main road five minutes' walk south of the castle; ask for "Obi-jō".

EATING

Obi-ten Chaya おび天茶屋 4-2-15 Obi. A nicely rustic restaurant in a garden immediately south of the Komura Memorial Hall. They sell good-value obi-ten *teishoku* (a local speciality of minced flying fish mixed with tofu, miso and sugar, rolled into a leaf shape and deep-fried), including rice, soup and pickles, for ¥950. Daily 9am–5pm.

Kirishima National Park

10

On the border between Kagoshima and Miyazaki prefectures, **Kirishima National Park** is Japan's oldest and comprises no fewer than 23 volcanic mountains, ten crater lakes and numerous hot springs. The park's main centre is the plateau village of **Ebino Kōgen**, a cluster of shops, hotels and a campsite, from where it's a short scramble up the park's highest peak, Karakuni-dake (1700m). The park's easternmost peak, Takachiho-no-mine, however, holds greater significance, since according to legend this is where Ninigi-no-mikoto, grandson of the Sun Goddess Amaterasu (see p.85) and legendary founder of the Japanese imperial line, descended to earth. The traditional approach to Takachiho is from the park's southern gateway, **Kirishima Jingū**, stopping first at a shrine shrouded in cryptomeria trees. The peaks are linked by a skein of **hiking** trails – it's worth scaling at least one of them for superb views over jagged craters filled with perfectly round, cobalt-blue lakes and Sakurajima puffing angrily on the southern horizon.

GETTING AROUND **KIRISHIMA NATIONAL PARK**

By bus The Kirishima range is best tackled by car, since public transport is patchy, however there is a daily sightseeing bus from Kirishima Jingū Station a 9.55am (3hr; ¥2220), that calls at Maruo and Hayashida Onsen on the way up to Ebino Kōgen. A better option if you want to see much on the plateau is to visit on a Saturday or Sunday, when a "Trekking Bus" departs at 8am and 10.20am from Kirishima-jingū Station for Takachiho-gawara and Ebino Kōgen (1hr; ¥740). Coming down, buses leave the plateau at 1pm and 3.30pm, but make sure you double-check bus times locally before setting off.

Kirishima

霧島

The small town of **KIRISHIMA**, built on the southern slopes of Takachiho-no-mine, makes a possible alternative base to Ebino Kōgen. The town is named after the beautiful shrine of Kirishima-jingū, at its top end, an appealingly village-like area partly enveloped in cedar forests and focused around a cheerful, red-lacquer bridge. Kirishima also boasts a number of reasonable accommodation options and a couple of mildly interesting sights.

Kirishima Tengu-kan

霧島天狗館 · Daily 9am–5pm · ¥350

The first sight of any interest in Kirishima-jingū is Kirishima Tengu-kan at the top of the central square – look for the building sprouting long-nosed goblin-like creatures. These are *tengu*, supernatural mountain spirits that often

appear in folk tales, nō plays and, more recently, manga and video games. Inside, some 1600 masks are on display, including a monster over 2m in length carved from local camphor wood.

Kirishima-jingū

霧島神宮 • 24hr • Free

A short walk from Kirishima Tengu-kan – head over a lacquered bridge, beneath the bright vermilion *torii* and up a steep flight of steps – is the shrine of **Kirishima-jingū** after which the town is named. A surprisingly imposing complex, it's dedicated to Ninigi-no-mikoto and his fellow gods who first set foot in Kirishima at the dawn of Japan's creation. It also provides some fine views over Kagoshima Bay.

Takachiho-no-mine

高千穂峰 • Visitors' Centre Daily 9am–5pm • ☎ 0995 57 2505

The summit of **Takachiho-no-mine** (1574m) is a good three-hour walk to the northeast of Kirishima, but rewards the effort with some fantastic views over the bay of Kagoshima. With your own transport you can halve the walking time by driving 7km up the road to **Takachiho-gawara** (高千穂河原). It's then a steady climb on a well-marked path, ending in a short scramble on scree to the crater rim where a replica of Ninigi's sacred sword points skywards. Takachiho last erupted in 1913, and now only faint wisps of steam indicate that it's still active. Before setting off from Takachiho-gawara, you might want to take a brief look at the displays in the **visitors' centre**, where you can also get local maps and other tourist information.

ARRIVAL AND INFORMATION

KIRISHIMA JINGŪ

By train The best way to reach Kirishima-jingū is by train to Kirishima-jingū Station, in the valley 7km to the south of the town. Buses from the station (7–11 daily; 15min; ¥240) coincide with train arrivals, and will drop you in the main square at the top of the town, just below the red-lacquer bridge.

Destinations Kagoshima (10 daily; 40–50min); and Miyazaki (4 daily; 1hr 20min).

By bus Most buses to the area drop off first at the train station, and then in the main square at the top of the town,

a journey of a further 15 minutes or so. The journey times quoted below are from the station.

Destinations Ebino Kōgen (Sat & Sun 2 daily; 1hr 10min), and Hayashida Onsen (7–9 daily; 35min).

Tourist information There's a small tourist office (daily: April–Sept 9am–6pm; Oct–March 9am–5pm; ☎ 0995 57 1588, ✉ info@kirishimacho.com) beside the big *torii* at the south end of the main square.

Services The main square has convenience stores and a post office.

ACCOMMODATION AND EATING

If you want to stay overnight, head to the top end of Kirishima Jingū, where you will find a cluster of minshuku and a smattering of restaurants, though most of the latter stop serving by 7pm – there's also a convenience store here. There are some excellent accommodation options in the surrounding area, though these can be hard to get to on public transport.

★**Sakura Sakura Onsen** さくらさくら温泉 3km west of Kirishima Jingū ☎ 0995 57 1227. This quality hotel has several rotemburo, but its speciality is volcanic mud – especially popular with young women for its skin-softening effects. The stunning baths are open to non-residents (daily 10am–8pm; ¥700): a taxi from the centre of town will cost around ¥720. **¥19,000**

Tenkuno Mori 天空の森 3389 Kirishima ☎ 0995 76 0777, ⊕ tenkunomori.net. Perfection at a price – the room rates are jaw-dropping. With superb mountain views, all-pervasive scents and sounds of the outdoors

and pampering at every turn, it would be hard to come away from this swish, remote resort feeling anything but a state of Zen-like bliss. Until, at least, you get your credit card bill. **¥200,000**

Tozan-guchi Onsen 登山口温泉 2459-83 Kirishimataguchi ☎ 0995 57 0127. Spruce little minshuku tucked just off the square – take the road heading east from the roundabout. It has a rooftop rotemburo and also doubles as a youth hostel (¥3500/ person, or ¥5000 including meals), with accommodation in shared tatami rooms. **¥10,000**

Ebino Kōgen

えびの高原

At 1200m above sea level, the views from **EBINO KŌGEN** are stunning. Temperatures here on the plateau rarely exceed 20°C in summer and dip well below freezing in winter when the peaks boast a dusting of snow and hoarfrost and the tennis courts morph into an ice-skating rink. This is the best time to appreciate the local **onsen** – Kirishima is Japan's highest hot-spring resort – while spring and autumn provide perfect hiking weather. Despite the natural beauty, the epicentre of Ebino Kōgen consists of a large, bleak car park, around which all tourism activity is based.

10

Karakuni-dake

韓国岳

If it's a clear day, the hike up to **Karakuni-dake** is worth tackling: it's not a difficult climb, taking under two hours, though you'll want good footwear on the loose stones. The trails are signposted from the car park, heading northeast, with the quickest trail running beside a steaming, sulphurous scar known as Sai-no-kawara and then climbing steeply along a heavily eroded ridge. From here, you can extend the hike by circling south to Ōnami-no-ike (大波の池), Japan's largest crater lake, and then back to Ebino Kōgen, which will take about another three and a half hours. The classic walk, however, is east along Kirishima's magnificent volcanic peaks from Karakuni-dake to Takachiho-gawara – allow about five hours for the hike and remember to carry plenty of water. The path leads over Shishiko-dake (獅子戸岳; 1428m), the still-active Shinmoe-dake (新燃岳; 1421m) and Naka-dake (中岳; 1345m) with its two grassy hollows, and then descends to Takachiho-gawara. From here it's a 7km trot down to the comforts of Kirishima Jingū (see opposite), though if you time it right, at weekends you may be able to catch the bus (see opposite).

Hiking the Ebino plateau

There are also more gentle ambles across the Ebino plateau. The most rewarding is a 4km walk starting from behind the Visitor Centre, where you can use the free hot-spring footbath to ease your aching feet. The walk wends through forests of white fir and maple, and past three beautiful **crater lakes** before emerging beside Sai-no-kawara. If you are here in May or June, head southeast to where wild azaleas give the hillsides a dusty-pink tinge.

ARRIVAL AND INFORMATION   EBINO KŌGEN

By bus Buses stop outside a souvenir shop to the south of the large car park which forms Ebino Kōgen's tourism centre.

Tourist information You can get information at the Visitor Centre (9am–5pm; closed Mon; ☎ 0984 33 3002) to the northeast of the car park. The centre also provides local sketch maps and sometimes has more detailed trekking maps, though it's safer to bring one with you if you're doing the longer hikes, just in case they've run out. While you're here, take a look at the 3-D model of the area – it's handy for getting the lie of the land.

ACCOMMODATION AND EATING

In Ebino Kōgen itself there are just two **hotels**. If you're not staying, it's a good idea to bring food with you to the plateau, since the few shops sell little more than souvenirs, snacks and drinks.

Ebino-Kōgen Campground えびの高原キャンプ村 ☎ 0984 33 0800. Open from April–Oct, this campground has tents and cheap wooden cabins among the pine forests. Prices start at around ¥980 per person for a cabin sleeping up to four, but by the time you've added on extra fees for blankets and heating (almost essential, outside the summer), it'll be more like ¥1500–2000 per head.

Ebino-kōgen-sō えびの高原荘 ☎ 0984 33 0161. A couple of minutes' walk west of the central car park, this is by far the swisher of the two hotels, with comfortable Western and Japanese rooms and a decent restaurant. Non-residents can also use the smart rotemburo here (daily 11.30am–8pm; ¥500). **¥17,600**

Karakuni-sō からくに荘 ☎ 0984 33 0650. A 5min walk north of the visitor centre, comprising mostly Japanese rooms, including one in the annexe with a private onsen and mountain views. **¥13,000**

Visitor Centre Northeast of the car park. The area's only non-hotel option for a warm meal, unless you're doing the

cooking yourself. They serve ramen and bentō downstair and an array of set lunches in the restaurant upstairs. Dai 8am–5pm, last orders 4.30pm.

Kagoshima

10

鹿児島

KAGOSHIMA's most obvious and compelling attraction is the smouldering cone of **Sakurajima**, one of the most active volcanoes on earth. On the other side of the bay from the city – just fifteen minutes away by ferry – it frequently billows an enormous cloud of ash into the southern Kyūshū sky. Local weather forecasts show which direction the plume is heading; if it's coming your way, ash will get in your eyes, hair and teeth, while cars end up covered in a sheet of dust. In fact, given Sakurajima's recent heightened activity – it has erupted almost every day since 2009 – the dirt never really leaves Kagoshima, with rich, black dust on every street.

Aside from the volcano, Kagoshima contains a few sights of its own which justify a day's exploration. They're mainly gathered around the informative **Reimeikan** museum at the foot of Shiroyama; from here, you can either walk or take a tram south to the banks of the Kōtsuki-gawa and the gimmicky but entertaining **Museum of the Meiji Restoration**.

Brief history

Originally known as **Satsuma**, the Kagoshima region was ruled by the powerful **Shimazu** clan for nearly seven centuries until the Meiji reforms put an end to such fiefdoms in 1871. The area has a long tradition of overseas contact and it was here that Japan's first Christian missionary, the Spanish-born Jesuit **Francis Xavier**, arrived in 1549. Welcomed by the Shimazu lords – who were primarily interested in trade and acquiring new technologies – he spent ten months working in Kagoshima, where he found the poorer classes particularly receptive to Christian teachings. After just a few months Xavier declared "it seems to me that we shall never find among heathens another race to equal the Japanese".

Soon after, Japan was closed to foreigners and remained so for the next two hundred years. As central control crumbled in the mid-nineteenth century, however, the far-sighted **Shimazu Nariakira** began introducing Western technology, such as spinning machines, the printing press and weapons manufacture, and it was Kagoshima that saw Japan's first gas light, steamships, electric lights, photographs

---

SAIGŌ TAKAMORI

Born in 1827, **Saigō Takamori** made his name as one of the leading figures in the **Meiji Restoration**. Though aware of the need for Japan to modernize, he grew increasingly alarmed at the loss of traditional values and eventually left the government to set up a military academy in Kagoshima. He soon became a focus for opposition forces – mainly disaffected samurai but also peasants protesting at punitive taxes. Things came to a head in January 1877 when Saigō led an army of forty thousand against the government stronghold in Kumamoto, in what came to be known as the **Satsuma Rebellion**. After besieging the castle for nearly two months, the rebels were forced to withdraw before the sixty-thousand-strong Imperial Army. They retreated to Kagoshima where they were gradually pinned down on Shiroyama. On September 24, the imperial forces closed in and Saigō, severely wounded, asked one of his comrades to kill him. His courage, idealism and heroic death earned Saigō enormous popular support – so much so that he was officially pardoned by imperial decree in 1891.

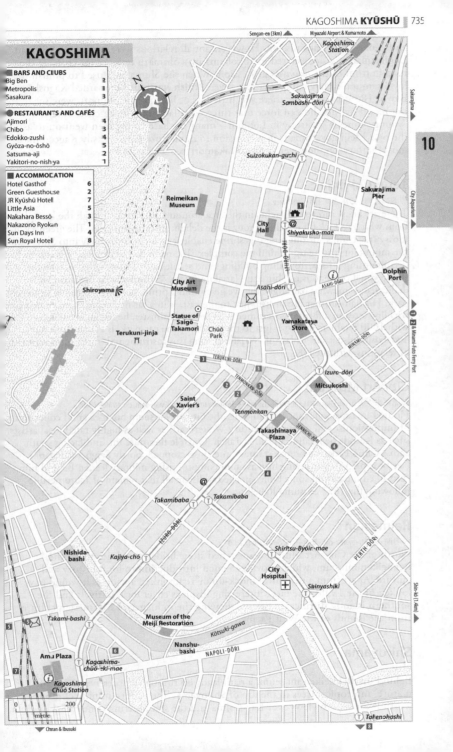

KAGOSHIMA

BARS AND CLUBS
Big Ben	2
Metropolis	1
Sasakura	3

RESTAURANTS AND CAFÉS
Ajimori	4
Chibo	3
Edokko-zushi	4
Gyōza-no-ōshō	5
Satsuma-aji	2
Yakitori-no-nishiya	1

ACCOMMODATION
Hotel Gasthof	6
Green Guesthouse	2
JR Kyūshū Hotel	7
Little Asia	5
Nakahara Bessō	3
Nakazono Ryokan	1
Sun Days Inn	4
Sun Royal Hotel	8

Sengan-en (3km)

Miyazaki Airport & Kumamoto

Kagoshima Station

Sakurajima

City Aquarium

10

Sakurajima Sambashi-dōri

Suizokukan-guchi

Sakurajima Pier

Reimeikan Museum

City Hall

Shiyakusho-mae

Dolphin Port

Shiroyama

City Art Museum

Asahi-dōri

ASAHI-DŌRI

& Minami-Futo Ferry Port

Statue of Saigō Takamori

Chūō Park

Yamakataya Store

Terukuni-jinja

MINAMI-DŌRI

TERUKUNI-DŌRI

Izuro-dōri

Mitsukoshi

TENMONKAN-DŌRI

Saint Xavier's

Tenmonkan

SENMICHI-DŌRI

Takashimaya Plaza

Takamibaba

ISURO-DŌRI

Takamibaba

Shiritsu-Byōin-mae

Nishida-bashi

Kajiya-chō

PERTH-DŌRI

City Hospital

Shinyashiki

Shin-kō (1.4km)

Takami-bashi

Museum of the Meiji Restoration

Kōtsuki-gawa

Nanshu-bashi

NAPOLI-DŌRI

Amu Plaza

Kagoshima-chūō-eki-mae

Kagoshima Chūō Station

0   200
metre

Takenohashi

Chiran & Ibusuki

and Morse code transmission. However, not all relations were cordial. In 1862 an Englishman was decapitated in Yokohama by a Shimazu retainer for crossing the road in front of the *daimyō*'s procession. When the Shimazu refused to punish the loyal samurai or pay compensation, seven **British warships** bombarded Kagoshima Bay in 1863. Fortunately there was little loss of life and the Shimazu were so impressed by this show of force that three years later they dispatched nineteen "young pioneers" to study in London – many of these young men went on to assist the new Meiji government in its mission to modernize Japan. Easily Kagoshima's most famous son, however, is **Saigō Takamori** (see box, p.734).

Terukuni-jinja

照国神社 • 19-35 Terukuni-chō • 24hr • Free

There are a few interesting sights in the area around Chūō Park, though the best place from which to kick off a walking tour is the delightful **Terukuni-jinja**. The greenery and mossy tree trunks surrounding this shrine enable it to blend seamlessly into Shiroyama, the mountain rearing up behind the complex. The main hall of the shrine is somewhat disappointing – its surrounding buildings and statues are of more interest. The first statue you'll come to is of Shimazu Nariakira (see p.734), to whom the shrine is dedicated; somewhat bafflingly, they've given him a prime position overlooking the car park. His half-brother Hisamitsu, just to the east, is in a far nicer spot, surrounded by a trickling stream; a former government advisor and minister, he led an excursion to Edo with 1000 retainers in 1862. Just to the south, by the car-park, is Hisamitsu's son Tadayoshi (also a son-in-law of Nariakira), who was instrumental in the improvement of relations with the UK.

City Art Museum

鹿児島市立美術館, Kagashima Shiritsu Bijutsukan • 4-36 Shiroyama-chō • 9.30am–6pm, closed Mon • ¥200

Housed in a spacious modern building, the **City Art Museum** boasts a good collection of Impressionist and twentieth-century Western art, as well as highly rated local artists such as Kuroda Seiki and Fujishima Takeji. Outside the museum, and facing south across Chūō Park, is a bronze statue of the close-cropped, portly Saigō Takamori (see box, p.734), portraying him as an uncompromising military leader. Behind him, carp-filled moats and some bullet-pocked walls are all that remain of **Tsurumaru-jō** following the 1877 Satsuma Rebellion.

Reimeikan

黎明館 • 7-2 Shiroyama-chō • 9am–5pm, closed Mon • ¥300

North of the City Art Museum, an arched stone bridge that leads up to the **Reimeikan** museum, which provides a good introduction to local history and culture. Apart from a delightful mock-up of Tenmonkan arcade as it would have looked in the 1930s, the most interesting displays cover local festivals and the southern islands' distinct traditions, showing the influence of Melanesian culture from the islands of the West Pacific.

Shiroyama

城山

Behind the Reimeikan museum, a path leads up through impressive stands of mature, subtropical trees to the top of **Shiroyama**. The twenty-minute climb is worth it for superb views over Kagoshima and the smouldering cone of Sakurajima.

Museum of the Meiji Restoration

維新ふるさと館, Ishiu Furusato-kan・ Daily 9am–5pm ・¥300 ・ Sound and light show hourly 9.15am–4.30pm

The engaging **Museum of the Meiji Restoration** sits beside the tranquil Kōtsuki-gawa. No expense has been spared to re-create the "golden age" of Kagoshima, when Saigō and other local luminaries were instrumental in returning power to the emperor and then spearheading the Meiji reforms. The highlight is a 25-minute sound and light show in which robots – including a wild-eyed Saigō – re-enact scenes from the restoration. The show takes place in the basement theatre and headsets are available for an English-language translation. Upstairs, don't miss the original version of the Japanese national anthem, recorded by the Satsuma Military Band in 1870, composed two years earlier by Irish bandmaster, John William Fenton.

City Aquarium

かごしま水族館, Kagoshima Suizokukan ・ 3-1 Honkoshinmachi ・ Daily 9.30am–6pm ・¥1500 ・ ⓦ .ioworld.jp

A ten-minute walk southeast from the Reimeikan museum, the **City Aquarium** sits on a man-made island in the harbour. Thanks to the warm Kuroshio Current sweeping across from the East China Sea, the waters around Kagoshima's southern islands are rich in temperate and subtropical aquatic life, a broad range of which is on show in this well-designed installation, from Sakurajima's unique tube worm to colourful sea anemones.

Sengan-en

仙巌園 ・ Daily 3.30am–5.30pm ・ Garden tour ¥1000, or ¥1500 including entry to the villa, plus tea and sweet ・ ⓦ www.senganen.jp ・ City View touristbus, or regular bus from Kagoshima Chūō Station or Tenmonkan (every 30min; 15–20min; ¥130)

When their base at Tsurumaru-jō was destroyed during the Satsuma Rebellion, the Shimazu lords set up residence in their lovely garden-villa Iso Tei-en, now known as **Sengan-en**, 3km east of the city centre. Though the villa itself is beautiful, the main points of interest are the garden, with its views of Sakurajima, and the neighbouring history museum that celebrates the modernizing zeal of the enterprising Shimazu lords.

ARRIVAL AND DEPARTURE
KAGOSHIMA

By plane Kagoshima Airport (ⓣ 099 558 2740), served by flights to Seoul and Shanghai as well as domestic routes, is located some 30km north of the city, near the Kirishima National Park (see p.731). Buses leave the airport every ten or twenty minutes for town (¥1200); express services (40min) head straight to Kagoshima Chūō Station, while regular services (1hr) stop at central Kagoshima's Tenmonkan crossroads en route.

Destinations Fukuoka (5 daily; 50min); Nagoya (7 daily; 1hr 15min); Naha (3 daily; 1hr 25min); Osaka (Itami, hourly; 1hr 10min); Seoul (3 weekly; 1hr 40min); Shanghai (2 weekly; 1hr 20min); Tokyo (1–2 hourly; 1hr 35min); and Yakushima (5 daily; 35min).

By train The new Shinkansen line connects Kagoshima Chūō Station with Kumamoto and Hakata; local trains use the same station (and sometimes Kagoshima Station, east of the city centre).

Destinations Fukuoka (every 30min; 1hr 20min–2hr 30min); Ibusuki (1–2 hourly; 50min–1hr 20min); Kirishima-Jingū (10 daily; 40–50min); Kumamoto (every

30min; 40min–1hr 15min); Miyazaki (7 daily; 2hr–2hr 15min); and Shin-Yatsushiro (2 hourly; 30–40min).

By bus Most bus services to Kagoshima stop at Kagoshima Chūō Station, or the central Kagoshima's Tenmonkan crossroads, or both.

Destinations Chiran (7–8 daily; 1hr 20min); Fukuoka (every 30min–1hr; 3hr 40min); Ibusuki (6–7 daily; 1hr 30min); Kumamoto (10 daily; 3hr 10min); and Miyazaki (9 daily; 3hr); Osaka (1 daily; 12hr).

By ferry A Line (ⓣ 099 226 4141) and Marix Line (ⓣ 099 225 1551, ⓦ marix-line.cc.jp) ferries currently sail to Naha, Okinawa from Kagoshima Shin-kō, the city's southern port (4–6 weekly; 25hr; ¥14,200). Services to Yakushima and Ibusuki use the more central Minami-Futō (South Pier): Toppy (ⓣ 099 256 7771, ⓦ tykousoku.jp) operates hydrofoils to both Yakushima (2hr–2hr 40min; ¥8500) and Ibusuki (1 daily; 40min; ¥2400); Cosmc Line (ⓣ 099 223 1011, ⓦ cosmoline. jp) also runs hydrofoils to Yakushima for the same price. Regular ferries also run to Yakushima from Minami-Futō (1 daily; 4hr; ¥4600); buy tickets at the terminal.

10

INFORMATION

Tourist office Kagoshima's main tourist office (daily 8.30am–7pm; ☎099 253 2500, ⓦcity.kagoshima.lg.jp), inside Kagoshima Chūō Station, has copies of the useful *Kagoshima Course Guide*, which comprises a city map and recommended itineraries; they can also assist with accommodation and provide information about Kirishima (see p.731) and Yakushima (p.745).

GETTING AROUND

By tram Moving around central Kagoshima is simplified by a highly efficient two-line tram system that has been in operation since 1912 – some of the original cars are still used. There's a flat fare of ¥160, which you pay on exit; trams run roughly every eight minutes from 6.30am–10.30pm.

By bus The local bus system is a lot more complicated, with services run by five different companies. However, easily recognizable, retro-style City View tourist buses depart every half-hour (9am–5pm) on a circuit of the main sights from Kagoshima Chūō Station (stand #9) via the Museum of the Meiji Restoration, Reimeikan and Shiroyama observatory to Sengan-en, before returning via Dolphin Port and Tenmonkan. You can buy individual tickets (¥180) or a one-day pass (¥600), which also covers the trams; it's available at the tourist information centre, or on board the buses and trams, and entitles you to discount tickets to various sights.

By ferry Local ferries to Sakurajima depart from a pier to the east of the city centre. The nearby Minami-Futō (South Pier) is used by services to Yakushima and Ibusuki, while those to Okinawa currently operate out of the more southerly Shin-kō, though it's possible they may move at some point to Kita-Futō (North Pier), which lies between Minami-Futō and the Sakurajima pier.

ACCOMMODATION

★**Hotel Gasthof** ホテルガストフ 7-1 Chūō-chō ☎099 252 1401, ⓦgasthof.jp. Remodelled in an eclectic mix of foreign styles, this hotel is excellent value. The attention to detail is admirable – think bathrooms lined with pearlescent tiling, chunky beds and tartan frills – while there are some superb restaurants in the same building. ¥8900

★**Green Guesthouse** グリーンゲストハウス 5-7 Sumiyoshi-chō ☎099 802 4301, ⓦgreen-guesthouse .com. Excellent new hostel just a hop and a skip from the ferry terminals – great if you've got an early morning departure. There's a lovely little bar downstairs selling local booze (see box,opposite); for a mere ¥500 above the regular dorm price, you can sleep in a capsule-like private cabin. Dorm ¥1800

JR Kyūshū Hotel JR九州ホテル鹿児島 Kagoshima Chūō Station ☎099 213 8029, ⓦjrhotelgroup.com. Rooms in the new north wing of this station hotel have been designed along the lines of the award-winning JR Kyūshū trains – sleek contours, soft lighting and dark wood. Perfect for the style-conscious, or those with an early train to catch. ¥12,000

Little Asia リトルアジア 2-20-8 Nishida ☎099 251 8166, ⓦcheaphotelasia.com. Clean, cheap and within spitting distance of the train station, this is a decent backpacker base; the somewhat surly staff, however, usually commandeer the common room, to the detriment of those actually paying to stay here. Dorm ¥2000

Nakahara Bessō 中原別荘 15-19 Higashi-Sengoku chō ☎099 225 2800, ⓦnakahara-bessou.co.jp. Nicely decorated onsen hotel in the city centre overlooking Chūō Park. The Japanese-style rooms are the best value and while you can opt for room-only rates, the meals are highly recommended. ¥14,600

Nakazono Ryokan 1-18 Yasui-chō ☎099 226 5125, ⓦnakazonoryokan.wix.com/nakazonoryokan. There's always service with a smile at this homely ryokan, tucked behind a temple opposite Kagoshima City Hall. The tatami rooms are clean and large enough, though facilities are shared. ¥8400

Sun Days Inn サンデイズイン 9-8 Yamanokuchi-chō ☎099 227 5151 ⓦsundaysinn.com. Stylish rooms, friendly staff and low prices make this nicely contemporary business hotel a real treat. You can often get hefty discounts by booking online – staff have been known to let guests use the lobby computer for this purpose – but try to get a room with views of Sakurajima. ¥8300

★**Sun Royal Hotel** サンロイヤルホテル 1-8-10 Yojiro ☎099 253 2020, ⓦsunroyal.co.jp. Kagoshima's top hotel, set in a slightly inconvenient location southeast of the centre, though connected to the train station and Tenmonkan by free shuttle buses. The meals are excellent (especially the breakfast buffet), and all rooms are exceedingly comfortable; ask for one with a Sakurajima view, and watch out for volcanic explosions. ¥20,800

EATING AND DRINKING

Central Kagoshima is chock-full of **restaurants**, with the classiest establishments in a tight, semi-pedestrianized area west of Tenmonkan-dōri. Its most popular **speciality foods** are *Satsuma-age*, a deep-fried, slightly sweet patty of minced fish and sake, eaten with ginger and soy sauce, and steaks of succulent *kurobuta* pork. The prettiest local dish is *kibinago sashimi*, in which slices of a silvery, sardine-like fish are arranged in an eye-catching flower head. *Keihan* mixes shredded chicken with rrot, egg, mushroom and spring onions over a bowl of rice in a hot, tasty broth, while *sake-zushi* consists of sushi with a top of sake. For snacks, there's *Satsuma-imo* ice cream (made with sweet potato) and *jambo mochi* – rice cakes smothered in sweet sauce and impaled on a pair of bamboo skewers. A good place to sample shōchū (see box below) is in the city's pleasantly sleazy **nightlife district**, in the lanes either side of the Sennichi arcade, east of Izuro-dōri.

RESTAURANTS

Ajimori あぢもり 13-21 Sennichi-chō ☎099 224 7634. This nicely informal restaurant, specializing in *tonkatsu* and *shabu-shabu*, has a good choice of set meals from around ¥700, or ¥3200 for shabu shabu. Noon–2.30pm & 5.30–9.30pm, closed Wed.

Chibo 千房 15-4 Higashisengoku-chō ☎099 255 7001 ⌐ chibo.com. This excellent okonomiyaki chain started in Kansai, but has gone down well in southern Kyūshū too. Prices are very reasonable, with the savoury pancakes going from just ¥680. Daily 11.30am–10pm.

Jidokko-zushi 江戸ッ子寿司 13-21 Sennichi-chō ☎099 225 1890. Long-established and justifiably popular sushi bar right next to Ajimori. Prices are reasonable, with sushi sets starting at around ¥1100. It also does sashimi and tempura; an English menu is available. Daily 11.30am–midnight.

★**Gyōza-no-ōshō** 餃子の王将 1-4 Chūō-chō ☎099 253 4728. Good, cheap Chinese-style food near the main station, served up by cheery staff. Mains on the English menu start at just ¥320 – try the spicy *tantanmen* noodles (¥530), the crispier *agesoba* variety (¥480) or the delectable *gyōza* dumplings (¥200). Daily noon–11pm.

Satsuma-aji さつま路 6-29 Higashi-Sengoku-chō ⌐ satumaji.co.jp ☎099 226 0525. Elegantly rustic restaurant in the heart of Kagoshima's trendiest area, serving fairly pricey but top-quality local food. Lunch deals start at ¥1575, or try *Satsum-age* (¥630) or *kibinago sashimi* (¥735) from the picture-menu. Daily 11.30am–2.30pm & 5.30–10pm.

★**Yakitori-no-nishiya** 焼鳥の西屋 Dolphin Port, 5-4 Honkōshin-machi ☎099 224 0850. All the Kagoshima specialities (see opposite) are available in this lovely-looking restaurant near the ferry terminal; there's no English-language sign, so just look for the red one. Try the satsuma-age (¥380), keihan (¥550) or kibingo-zushi (¥680), plus some yakitori sticks (from ¥80), and wash the lot down with some local shōchū. Daily 5–10pm.

BARS

Big Ben ビッグベン B1 8-23 Higashisengoku-chō ☎099 226 4470. From the name you'd expect a British-style pub, but in reality it's a regular-looking Japanese bar. Nevertheless, it's a hit with local expats, and also popular with locals (in part due to its imported booze) – all in all, it's a great place to meet people and the city's best venue for watching international sports. Daily 5.30pm–3am.

★**Metropolis** メトロポリス 3F 16-18 Higashisengoku-chō ☎099 225 0020. Visually appealing venue with

KAGOSHIMA SHŌCHŪ

Kagoshima prefecture is Japan's biggest producer and consumer of shōchū and the Japanese are in near-unanimous agreement that Kagoshima's **shōchū** is the best in the land. There are more than 800 local varieties available, and these are usually made from **sweet potato** rather than rice, which makes for a heavier flavour and a higher alcohol content – 25 percent, rather than the national norm of 20 percent. As is the case elsewhere, one can have the hooch served straight, with soda, heated, mixed with hot water, or on the rocks. Like wine, each variety has its own specific taste – here are a few top picks to get you started.

Kaidō 海童 Served in a distinctive red bottle, this is perhaps the best low- to mid-range choice, and has a clean, crisp taste that works best on the rocks.

Kojika 小鹿 Cheap but high-quality option, whose slightly dry taste is magnified when served heated.

Kuro 黒 Popular with young and old alike, this tasty cheapie is available in pretty much every izakaya and convenience store across the prefecture. Best served heated.

Maō 魔王 Running Mori Izō a close second for quality, this slightly sweet variety is a favourite with Kagoshima connoisseurs.

Mori Izō 森伊蔵 The king of local shōchū, this high-roller favourite can cost over ¥70,000 per bottle in a Tokyo izakaya, but is usually available here for a fraction of the price. Have it neat, or with hot water.

Nofū 野風 A rarity in Kagoshima shōchū terms, in that it's made from corn rather than sweet potato. Though, being 35 percent alcohol by volume, you may not notice.

Shiranami 白波 The most famed variety in Kagoshima city itself, this is available in over a dozen different grades, including the somewhat hazardous 37 percent-alcohol Genshū variety.

colourful chandeliers, bright red walls, comfy floor-cushions and bizarre egg-like lights. Various all-you-can-drink deals make it possible to select your desired level of inebriation; the cheapest, at ¥1500, gets you 90 minutes. Daily 6pm–3am.

Sasakura 酒々蔵 9-17 Yamanokuchi-chō ☎099 22 1356. There are over 150 different types of Kagoshima shōchū available in this traditionally styled *izakaya*. Price start at a very reasonable ¥300 per glass, and there's goo inexpensive food to soak it up with. Daily 6.30pm–3am.

DIRECTORY

Banks and exchange There are banks offering foreign exchange along Izuro-dōri. The Central Post Office has international ATMs, and there's another in the Amu Plaza.

Bookshops Kinokuniya, on Amu Plaza's fourth floor, has the largest selection of English-language books and magazines.

Car rental Eki Rent-a-Car (☎099 258 1412), Budget (☎099 250 0543) and Japaren (☎099 257 3900) all have offices near Kagoshima Chūō Station.

Hospital The most central hospital with English-speakin staff is the Kagoshima City Hospital, 20-17 Kajiya-chō (☎09 224 2101), near the Shiritsu Byōin-mae tram stop (line #1).

Police Kagoshima-Chūō Police Station, 13-1 Yamashita chō ☎099 222 0110.

Post office Kagoshima Central Post Office is right next t Kagoshima Chūō Station. There's also a handy sub-office o Asahi-dōri near Chūō-kōen. Both have ATMs which tak international bank cards.

Sakurajima

桜島

Kagoshima's most stirring sight is the volcanic cone of **SAKURAJIMA**, which grumbles away just 4km from the city centre, pouring a column of dense black ash into the air. It is home to some of Japan's most exciting **onsen** and the island's smouldering cone provides tangible proof of just how their waters have been heated This is one of the world's most active volcanoes, and hiking its peak has been prohibited since 1955 – adventurous sorts should note that security cameras have been installed around the mountain. A single road (40km) circles Sakurajima at sea level, past lava fields, onsen baths and a couple of observation points.

Yunohira Observatory

Sightseeing buses kick off their **tour** of the island with a tortuous route up the volcano's west flank to the **Yunohira Observatory** (373m). This is the closest you can get to the deeply creviced summit, which in fact comprises three cones, from the highest, northerly Kita-dake (1117m), to Minami-dake (1040m), the most active, in the south. Weather permitting, you'll also be treated to sweeping views of Kagoshima Bay.

Furusato Onsen

古里温泉 • Sakurajima Seaside Hotel, 1078-63 Furosato-chō • Rotemburo daily 8am–8pm • ¥500

On the south coast of the island at **Furusato Onsen**, a smattering of dowdy resort hotels capitalize on the abundant supplies of hot water. Unfortunately, the best of these, the

---

EXPLOSIVE ISLAND

Major **eruptions** of Sakurajima have been recorded from the early eighth century until as recently as 1947, though the most violent in living memory was that of 1914, during which enough lava spilled down the southeast slopes to fill the 400m-wide channel that previously separated Sakurajima from the mainland. Volcanic activity varies from year to year: there were just 18 eruptions in 2005, but this increased to an all-time record of more than two thousand eruptions in 2010 – around half-a-dozen every single day. During periods of high activity, the likely direction of the resultant **ash** forms part of the weather forecasts on TV – it usually heads northeast during colder months, and west (towards Kagoshima city centre) in the summer, when you may find yourself crunching granules of dust that were, just a few hours beforehand, several hundred metres below the surface of the earth, and considerably hotter. Sakurajima's prime **viewing point** is its eastern coast at night-time – if you're in luck, you may well see the faraway glow of molten lava.

10

urusato Kankō Hotel, closed in 2013, but it's worth checking to see if it has reopened. n the meantime, the next best option is the rotemburo at the otherwise poor akurajima Seaside Hotel, which overlooks the sea and has great views at sunset.

he rest of the island

s you continue along the south coast, Sakurajima's brooding presence becomes more pparent as you start to see the lava fields around the **Arimura Observatory**, barren since he devastating explosion of 1914 (see box opposite). A little further on, past the narrow eck of land, look out on the left for the buried *torii* of Kurokami-jinja. It was originally m tall, but now just the top crossbars protrude from a bed of ash and pumice. Along the orth coast, the slopes get gentler and you'll see plenty of crops growing in the fertile olcanic soils, which produce not only the world's largest radishes – up to 40kg in weight nd over 1m in diameter – but also its smallest mandarins, measuring a mere 3cm across.

ARRIVAL AND INFORMATION

SAKURAJIMA

y ferry Ferries from Kagoshima (15min; ¥150) dock at a mall pier on Sakurajima's west coast. The service operates 24 ours a day, with sailings every 10–15min, 7am–8pm; you ay at the Sakurajima end.

ourist information The information desk (daily 8.30am–5pm; ☏ 099 293 4333) is upstairs in the ferry terminal building, though there's a more useful visitor centre (daily 9am–5pm) a ten-minute walk away, just beyond the *Rainbow Sakurajima* hotel.

GETTING AROUND

y bus Most people get around using sightseeing buses, which depart twice daily from Kagoshima Chūō Station 9am & 1.40pm; ¥2200 including return ferry tickets); you an also pick them up from Sakurajima ferry terminal 9.40am & 2.20pm; ¥1700) Once on the island, you can lso use local buses which do shorter loops up to the Yunohira Observatory and back (8 daily; ¥500).

By car and bike The island is much too large to walk, ut Sakurajima Rent-a-Car (☏ 099 293 2162) rents cars ¥8500 for half a day) and bikes (¥300/hour) just outside the ferry terminal. The youth hostel will also let you on their rather old bike for the price of a coffee. Note that if you're cycling, it's best to go clockwise around the island (around 4hr); not only will you usually be on the outside of the road and thus more visible to cars, but the relaxing onsen will come nearer the end of your ride – just when you need it. If you're only planning a short ride, you'll find the north coast far nicer than the south, where most of the traffic pours through on the way to the ferries.

ACCOMMODATION

Moon Garam Masala 1722 Yokoyama-chō ☏ 090 9952 3513. Just around the corner from the ferry terminal and doubling as a café, this curious venue with just two dorms is something like a Thai beach hut transported to a Japanese car park. Run by an Okinawan musician, who pops by from time to time (but doesn't like talking much), it's presided over by a delightful former hippy whose travels took her across most of the world. Dorm **¥1300**

Rainbow Sakurajima レインボー桜島 1722-16 Yokoyama-chō ☏ 099 293 2323. This modern hotel on the seafront, less than 10min walk south round the harbour from the Sakurajima ferry terminal, makes a good base for exploring the island. It offers a mix of Japanese and Western rooms and a big onsen bath (¥300 for non-guests; 10am–10pm). **¥20,700**

Sakurajima Youth Hostel 桜島ユースホステル 189 Yokoyama-chō ☏ & ☏ 099 293 2150. This big, relaxed hostel with dorms and an onsen bath is a 10min walk uphill from the ferry terminal – just follow the signs. Meals available. Dorm **¥2650**

Ibusuki and around

指宿

Japan's third-largest hot-spring resort by volume of water, the small onsen town of **IBUSUKI** is a low-key, relaxed place, where hot-spring-goers clank around in their wooden sandals, wearing the different coloured *yukata* of competing ryokan. The town's main attributes are an attractive setting on a sweeping bay and a **sand bath** where you can be buried up to the neck in hot sand – a more enjoyable experience than

10

IBUSUKI

N

Nitanda-gawa

Central Post Office ✉

@

Bus Station Office ❶
CHŪO-DŌRI ❷
Footbath ❸

Ibusuki Station

Ferry Terminal

Kagoshima Bay

✉

❶

Moto-yu

❷
Sand baths Saraku
Surigahama Beach
❸

ROUTE 226

■ **ACCOMMODATION**	
Ginshō	3
Sennari-sō	1
Tamaya Youth Hostel	2

■ **RESTAURANTS AND CAFÉS**	
Aoba	1
Paddle	2

0 ——— 300
metres

Kaimon-dake & Makurazaki ▼ ▼ Kaimon Station & Makurazaki

it sounds. Once you've rinsed off the grains and strolled the promenade, however, there's nothing much to do except head off to visit the neighbouring sites of Nagasaki-bana and Kaimon-dake (see opposite).

Ibusuki town

Ibusuki's main north–south avenue, palm-tree-lined **Hibiscus-dori**, is shadowed a few hundred metres inland by a road passing in front of the JR station. **Chūō-dōri**, which counts as Ibusuki's prime shopping street, leads from the station to meet the sea at the bay's midpoint. Ten minutes' walk south of here, there's a second clutch of shops and restaurants gathered around the famous sand bath.

This southern stretch of beach is known as **Surigahama** (摺ヶ浜). Like much of Japan's coast, it is protected by concrete breakwaters, but a few stretches of black, volcanic sand remain, from which wisps of scalding steam mark the presence of hot springs.

The sand baths

Surigahama beach • Daily 8.30am–8.30pm • ¥900, including sand bath and *yukata* rental

It's the done thing in Ibusuki to take a **sand bath** (*suna-mushi*), which is best at low tide when you can be buried on the beach itself, leaving a just a row of heads visible beneath snazzy sunshades; at high tide a raised bed beside the sea wall is used. You can buy tickets and change into a *yukata* in the modern **Saraku** (砂楽) bathhouse immediately behind the beach. You then troop down to the beach and lie down – take a small towel to wrap round your head. At over 50°C, the sand temperature is much hotter than at Beppu (see p.719), and most people find it difficult to last the recommended ten minutes. All sorts of claims are made as to the sand bath's medical benefits, but if nothing else it leaves you feeling wonderfully invigorated.

Nagasaki-bana

長崎鼻 • **Flower Park Kagoshima** Daily 9am–5pm • ¥600 • ⓦ fp-k.org • **Parking Garden** Daily 8.20am–5pm • ¥1200 • Hourly bus from Ibusuki (35min; ¥510)

Some 13km southwest of Ibusuki, the Satsuma Peninsula comes to a halt at **Nagasaki-bana**. It's a popular tourist spot and it's worth walking past the souvenir stalls and out along the rocky promontory to enjoy the classic view of Kaimon-dake and, on clear days, the distant peaks of Yakushima.

Next to the bus stop and car park, **Flower Park Kagoshima** (フラワーパークかごしま) lives up to its name with nearly 2500 flowering species spread over 90 acres. Also here is the rather oddly named **Parking Garden** (長崎鼻パーキングガーデン), a moderately interesting subtropical garden where parrots, monkeys and flamingos roam free.

Kaimon-dake

開聞岳 • Daily: Feb–Oct 7.30am–5.30pm; Nov–Jan 7.30am–5pm • ¥350 • From Ibusuki take the JR line to Kaimon Station (6 daily; 35min)

Though rather small at 922m, the triangular peak of **Kaimon-dake** is known locally as "Satsuma Fuji". The volcano last erupted some 15,000 years ago and much of it is now a nature park inhabited by wild Tokara ponies. The classic route up Kaimon-dake is from Kaimon Station, the start of a 5km-long path which spirals round the cone. It takes about two hours and the effort is rewarded with views south to the Satsunan Islands of Yakushima and Tanegashima, and north beyond Sakurajima to Kirishima.

10

ARRIVAL AND INFORMATION

IBUSUKI

By train The easiest and quickest way to reach Ibusuki is on the JR line from Kagoshima Chūō (1–2 hourly; 50min–1hr 20min; ¥970); the station is on the west side of town, and features a lovely onsen footbath to use while waiting for your train. Sit on the west side of the train for sea views.

By hydrofoil The most pleasant way of arriving, if costly, is on the Toppy hydrofoil (1 daily; 40min; ¥2400) from Kagoshima, which offers good views across Kagoshima Bay to Sakurajima and the Sata Peninsula; reservations are a good idea, and given the schedules you may have to do one leg by train. The hydrofoil also heads on to Yakushima (1 daily; 1hr 15min; ¥7200). Return tickets are slightly cheaper outside high season.

By bus Buses stop on the road outside the station, and the Kagoshima Kōtsū bus office is across the road.

Tourist information There's a small tourist information desk inside the train station (daily 8am–8pm).

GETTING AROUND

By bike As Ibusuki is so spread out, it's worth renting a bike to get around the central district. Eki Rent-a-Car (daily 8am–5pm; ☎ 0993 23 3879), next to the station, rents out standard bikes (¥300/2hr, up to ¥900/day), as well as electric bikes and cars.

ACCOMMODATION AND EATING

Among the big, upmarket resort **hotels**, Ibusuki does have a number of reasonable and attractive places to stay in the town centre. In general, you're probably best off **eating** in your hotel, since the choice of restaurants in Ibusuki is pretty limited, and all the hotel prices given below include meals.

HOTELS AND HOSTELS

★**Ginshō** 吟松 5-6-29 Yunohana ☎ 0993 22 3231. On the seafront at the far south end of town, this is Ibusuki's nicest place to stay. Though the building itself is modern, inside it has a traditional Japanese atmosphere. Most of the tatami rooms have ocean views, many of them have balcony-style bathing facilities, and there's a wonderful little rotemburo perched on the rooftop. **¥36,000**

Sennari-sō 千成荘 5-10-9 Yunohana ☎ 0993 22 3379. Budget place 200m north of the sand bath on Hibiscus-dōri, with a home-like atmosphere, friendly staff and small but sparkling en-suite tatami rooms. **¥14,350**

Tamaya Youth Hostel 圭屋ユースホステル 5-27-8 Yunohana ☎ 0993 22 3553. Acceptable place to stay opposite the sand bath, about 15min walk from the station. Dorm **¥2720**

RESTAURANTS AND BARS

Aoba 青葉 1-2-11 Minato ☎ 0993 22 3356. One of the only restaurants in town, conveniently located on the main road just north of the station, and serving a broad range of inexpensive dishes and set meals – try the fish *keishoku* (¥1380). 11am–3pm & 5.30–10pm, closed Wed.

Paddle パドル 1-6-3 Minato. Nice *izakaya*-style venue that's just about the only non-seedy place to drink in town. They also do nice *kurobuta* (black pork) steak and several curry dishes, all around ¥1000. Daily 3pm–midnight.

Chiran

知覧

A small town lying in a broad valley, **CHIRAN** owes its fortune to the Shimazu lords of Kagoshima (see p.734). In the eighteenth century, the Shimazu's chief retainers, the Sata family, were permitted to build a semi-fortified village, and a number of their handsome **samurai houses** survive today. Two hundred years later, an airfield on the outskirts of Chiran became the base for Kamikaze suicide bombers during World War II. The site is now a **museum**, documenting the history of the kamikaze and commemorating the young pilots who died. The road to it is lined with stone lanterns, one for each pilot.

Special Attack Peace Hall

特攻平和会館, Tokko Hewa Kaikan • 17881 Chiranchokori • Daily 9am–5pm • ¥500, or ¥600 including Museum Chiran; audio guide ¥100 • The Hall is on the bus route from Kagoshima, or it's an easy walk from Chiran town centre

The **Special Attack Peace Hall** marks the site of a military airfield that was established in 1942. Two years later Chiran was chosen as the base for the "Special Attack Forces", known in the west as **Kamikaze** pilots. During the battle of Okinawa (see p.755), 1036 pilots died; before leaving, they were given a last cigarette, a drink of sake and a blessing, after which they donned their "rising sun" headband and set off on the lonely, one-way mission with enough fuel to last for two hours. It seems that many never reached their target: the toll was 56 American ships sunk, 107 crippled and 300 seriously damaged.

The hall, which was established in 1975, is essentially a memorial to the pilots' undoubted courage and makes little mention of the wider context or moral argument. That aside, the photos, farewell letters and the pilots' often childish mascots are tragic mementoes of the young lives wasted. Several pilots' letters reveal that, though they knew the war was lost, they were still willing to make the ultimate sacrifice – you'll see many older Japanese people walking round in tears and it's hard not to be moved, despite the chilling overtones. Since very little is translated into English, make sure you pick up an audio guide at the ticket desk.

Museum Chiran

ミュージアム知覧 • 17881 Chiranchokori • 9am–5pm; closed Wed • ¥300, or ¥600 including the Peace Hall

Beside the Peace Hall, you can visit the more cheerful **Museum Chiran**. Concentrating on local history and culture, its exhibits are beautifully displayed, with the most interesting showing the strong influence of Okinawan culture on Kagoshima's festivals and crafts.

Hotaru-kan

ホタル館 • 103-1 Chiranchokori • Daily 9am–5pm • ¥350 • Opposite the Nakagōri bus stop, 5min by bus from the Peace Hall, or around ¥700 by taxi

The main road runs roughly east–west through Chiran town centre: just before it crosses the river for the second time you'll find **Hotaru-kan**, a moving museum that commemorates the young Kamikaze pilots. During the war this old wooden house was a restaurant, run by a motherly figure called Torihama Tome, who saw hundreds of young pilots pass through on their way to certain death. Many left personal possessions and messages for their families with Tome-san, some of which are now on display, alongside deeply moving pictures, letters and personal effects. Unfortunately, there are no English-language translations.

The samurai houses

武家屋敷, Bukeya Shiki • Daily 9am–5pm • ¥500 • The houses are on the bus route from Kagoshima, or it's an easy walk from Chiran town centre

East of the town centre, across the river, several **samurai houses** – known as *buke yashiki* – are scattered along an attractive lane that runs parallel to and south of the main road, behind ancient stone walls topped by neatly clipped hedges. Since many of the houses are still occupied, you can't see inside, but the main interest lies in their small but ntricate **gardens**, some said to be the work of designers brought from Kyoto. Seven ardens, indicated by signs in English, are open to the public. Though each is different n its composition, they mostly use rock groupings and shrubs to represent a classic cene of mountains, valleys and waterfalls taken from Chinese landscape painting. In he best of them, such as the gardens of Hirayama Katsumi and Hirayama Ryōichi, the lesign also incorporates the hills behind as "borrowed scenery". Look out, too, for lefensive features such as solid, screened entry gates and latrines beside the front gate - apparently, this was so that the occupant could eavesdrop on passers-by.

10

ARRIVAL AND INFORMATION

CHIRAN

By bus Bus services to Chiran run more or less hourly from Kagoshima (1hr 20min), stopping at the samurai houses a few minutes before hitting the town centre, and the Peace Hall a few minutes after; the last bus back to Kagoshima is usually at 6.30pm.

By car Coming from Ibusuki, you arrive first on the southwest side of Chiran at an expanse of car parks and

souvenir shops that marks the entrance to the town's two museums.

Tourist information Near the museums, you'll also find the town's information office (daily 9am–4pm; ☎ 0993 83 2511), on the far side of the car parks, where you can pick up handy maps and bus timetables and arrange a taxi if needed.

EATING

Nagōmi 和 93 Chiranchokori ☎ 0993 83 1753. One of the nicest places to eat in Chiran, set in gardens on a lane behind the Hotaru-kan, this offers a range of well-priced set lunches from ¥780. Daily 10am–3pm.

Taki-an 高城庵 6329 Chiranchokori ☎ 0993 83 3186. In a thatched building set in a garden at the east end of the samurai street. Their speciality is soba and udon, or try the sweet *jambo-mochi* (pounded rice on bamboo skewers). Daily 10.30am–4pm.

Yakushima

屋久島

Craggy mountain peaks; wave after wave of dripping, subtropical rainforest; towering cedar trees which predate the Roman Empire; and the all-pervasive scent of moss and flowers – if this all sounds a little like the setting for an anime, rather than real-life Japan, you'd be half-right: Miyazaki Hayao was said to have taken his inspiration from Yakushima's lush forests when creating *Princess Mononoke* (see p.833). Logging companies worked **Yakushima's** forests until the early 1970s, but now much of the island is protected within the Kirishima-Yaku National Park, a UNESCO World Heritage Site. Climbing steeply from the sea some 60km off Kyūshū, this is one of the rainiest places in Japan, with an average annual rainfall of at least 4m on the coast and a staggering 8–10m in its mountainous interior.

Yakushima's population of around 13,600 is concentrated in the two main towns of **Miyanoura** and **Anbō** or scattered in small settlements around the coast. An increasingly popular tourist destination, Yakushima now boasts a number of swish resort hotels in addition to simpler accommodation. Most people, however, come to hike and camp among the peaks, where the older cedars are found. For the less adventurous, **Yaku-sugi Land** contains a few more accessible trees and can be reached by public bus. Otherwise, there are a couple of good **local museums**, a seaside **onsen** and several **beaches**, two of which – Isso and Nakama – offer decent snorkelling. There are no dry months here, but the best time to visit is May or during the autumn months of October and November. June sees by far the highest rainfall, though this is when the rhododendrons are at their best, followed by a steamy July and August. Winter brings snow to the peaks, although sea-level temperatures hover around 15°C.

Lastly, if you're in luck, you may get to see **rocket launches** from the nearby island of Tanegashima, the centre of the Japanese space agency.

10

Miyanoura

宮之浦

While first impressions of the little port of **MIYANOURA**, Yakushima's main town, aren't very favourable, the place soon grows on visitors. It's true that there are no real sights besides the environment and culture centre, but it's a delight to walk around the port (note that the river often runs in reverse when the tide's in), and simply appreciate the calm atmosphere. It's also the best place on the island to stay, with a number of lovely ryokan and minshuku, and even a couple of good places to eat.

Yakushima Environmental and Cultural Village Centre

屋久島環境文化村センター, Yakushima Kankyō Bunkamura Sentā • 9am–5pm, closed Mon • Film hourly; 25min • ¥500

The informative **Yakushima Environmental and Cultural Village Centre** is set in a modern building, just two minutes' walk up from the ferry pier. The exhibits are arranged in a spiral, proceeding from the ocean up through village life and the cedar forests to the mountain tops. Allow time to see the film, projected onto a huge screen, which takes you on a fabulous helicopter ride over the island – not recommended for anyone prone to motion sickness.

Yunoko-no-yu

ゆのこの湯 • Daily 8am–8pm • ¥400

From Miyanoura, there's a pleasant riverside walk away from town, towards the mountains, with paths bustling up the hillside all the way along. The first path leads up to an intriguing little shrine that has a cute *torii* made from plastic piping. Further up the stream is **Yunoko-no-yu**, a tiny, two-room onsen, a forty-minute walk in total from Miyanoura. If you finish your wash after sunset, bring a torch as the walk back to town is delightfully dark.

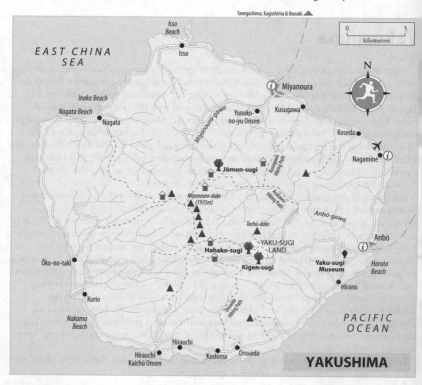

The interior

From Miyanoura, the main road leads east past the airport to the rather scruffy town of Anbō (安房), which is the best place from which to tackle the island's interior. Here, you turn inland for a wonderful forty-minute ride up into the mountains along a single-track road, in places almost washed away or blocked by fallen trees, that corkscrews up into a lost world wreathed in drifting cloud banks. Every so often there are glimpses of plunging, tree-filled valleys, the lush greens accentuated by cascading, ice-white torrents.

Yaku-sugi Museum

屋久杉自然館, Yaku-sugi Shizan-kan • Daily 9am–5pm • ¥600 • Bus stop Shizenkan-mae

Some 2km outside Anbō on the road up to the interior, the well-designed **Yaku-sugi Museum** or *Yaku-sugi Shizen-kan*, is full of fascinating displays about the cedar trees, including a stump and cross section of a 1660-year-old tree.

Yaku-sugi Land

屋久杉ランド • Daily 9am–5pm • ¥300

At around 1000m above sea level, a wooden resthouse marks the entrance to **YAKU-SUGI LAND**, a forest reserve that contains four **walking trails** varying in length from 800m (around 30min) to 3km (around 2hr 30min). The three shortest and most popular walks wind along an attractive river valley that is home to several thousand-year-old cedar trees, their gnarled roots clinging to the rock. For those with the time and energy, the longest course is by far the most interesting, taking you deeper into the forest and past another three ancient Yaku-sugi, of which the oldest is the 2600-year-old **Hahako-sugi**. Alternatively, continue up the paved road from the resthouse for about 6km to the **Kigen-sugi**, a grand old lady of 3000 years. Travelling by bus (see p.748), you can save yourself the walk by staying on the bus to the terminus, near Kigen-sugi, and then walk back down.

Jōmon-sugi

縄文杉

The trees in Yaku-sugi Land are mere saplings compared with the great **Jōmon-sugi**, whose mossy, tattered trunk, 16.4m in circumference, looks more like rock face than living tissue. The tree is at least 2300 years old, though some estimates go back 7200 years, which would make it pre-date Ancient Egypt – since its centre has rotted away it's impossible to tell exactly. Growing 1300m up and five hours' hike from the nearest road, the tree was only discovered in 1968, an event which sparked moves to protect the forests and also created the tourist industry that now accounts for over half the island's economy. The Jōmon-sugi stands on the north face of **Miyanoura-dake** (宮之浦岳; 1935m), the highest of Yakushima's seven peaks and the highest mountain in Kyūshū prefecture.

There are two main routes up to the tree: the **Kusugawa Hiking Path** from east of Miyanoura, and the eastern **Arakawa trail** starting at the Arakawa Dam. In both cases you can get a fair way up by road if you've got your own transport.

The south coast onsen

Hirauchi Kaichū 平内海中温泉 • Low tide only • Free • **Yudomari Onsen** 湯泊温泉 • Daily 8am–8pm • ¥100

On Yakushima's southern coast, the area around the tiny town of **Onoaida** (尾之間) is surrounded by orchards of tropical fruits, such as mango, papaya and lychee, which sit alongside the more traditional orange groves, while bright sprays of bougainvillea and bird-of-paradise flowers decorate the region's villages. A few kilometres west of Onoaida, **Hirauchi Kaichū Onsen** makes the perfect place to kick back with the locals in a hot rock pool overlooking the sea. You just have to get the timing right – the pool is only uncovered for two hours or so either side of low tide – though most locals and the tourist offices will be able to tell you the times each day. If the tide doesn't agree with your own schedule, head 500m west along the coast to **Yudomari Onsen**.

ARRIVAL AND DEPARTURE

By plane Yakushima's tiny airport (☎099 742 1200) lies on the island's northeast coast roughly midway between the two main towns, Miyanoura and Anbō, and is served by local buses and taxis. There are regular flights from Kagoshima (5 daily; 35min), though the hydrofoils that cover this route (see below) are almost as speedy, by the time you've included transport to and from the airport. There are also flights from Osaka's Itami airport (1 daily; 1hr 35min).

By hydrofoil Toppy hydrofoils run between Yakushima and Kagoshima (5 daily; 2hr–2hr 40min; ¥8400); you can buy tickets from their offices in Miyanoura (☎099 742 0034) or Anbō (☎099 746 3399). Some of these hydrofoils also stop at

Tanegashima or Ibusuki (p.741) en route and, while most doc at Miyanoura, one or two use Anbō port, so check beforehand Cosmo Line (☎099 223 1011, ⊚cosmoline.jp) runs three dail services from Kagoshima (1hr 50min–2hr 50min; ¥8400), tw via Tanegashima. Reservations are always required and can b made through a travel agent or with the ferry company, or yo can buy advance tickets at the terminal in Kagoshima. Bear i mind that hydrofoils stop running in bad weather.

By ferry Daily ferries also depart from Kagoshima (4h ¥3600). If you're not in a hurry, these ships are a great wa to travel; reservations are not required unless you want a private cabin.

GETTING AROUND

By bus Yakushima's road system consists of one quiet highway circumnavigating the island, plus a few spurs running up into the mountains. Buses depart from outside the Toppy terminal on Miyanoura ferry pier for Nagata (永田) in the west (7 daily; 30min; ¥890), or on the more useful route east via the airport and Anbō (hourly; 40min; ¥810) to terminate at the *Iwasaki Hotel* in Onoaida (hourly; 1hr; ¥1250), in Kurio (栗生; 8 daily; 1hr 30min; ¥1700), or a little further on at Ōko-no-taki (大川の滝; 2 daily; 1hr 35min; ¥1820). The last service from Miyanoura to Kurio leaves around 6pm, and 5pm from Kurio back to Miyanoura. The last bus is sometimes cancelled in low season and these buses regularly run ahead of schedule, so it pays to get to the stop at least ten minutes early. For most of the year (March–Nov) buses also operate twice daily from Anbō to Yaku-sugi Land (1hr; ¥720, or ¥910 to the terminal at Kigensugi). The timetable varies according to the season, so check locally, or grab a schedule from the information offices.

By car It's worth renting your own transport. A day's car rental costs ¥5000–10,000 for the smallest car, depending

on the season. Local companies are generally cheaper such as Suzuki Rent-a-Car in Miyanoura (☎099 742 1772 and Shinyama Rent-a-Car in Anbō (☎099 749 7277) while national companies such as Nippon Rent-a-Car (☎099 749 4189) have offices at the airport. Make sure you keep the tank topped up since there are no petro stations on west Yakushima between Hirauchi and Nagata those on the rest of the island close at 5pm or 6pm and many close on Sundays.

By motorbike Motorbikes are available for rent at Suzuki Rent-a-Car (see above) and at You Shop (April–Oct; ☎099 746 2705) on the main road in Anbō; count on around ¥4000 per day (up to 9hr) for a 125cc bike.

By bike You can rent mountain bikes (¥800/day) at the Yakushima Kankō Center (屋久島観光センター; daily: March–Oct 8am–7pm; Nov–Feb 8am–6pm), on the main road opposite the Miyanoura ferry terminal.

By taxi The three main taxi companies on the island are Yakushima Kōtsū Taxi (☎099 746 2321), Anbō Taxi (☎099 746 2311) and Matsubanda Kōtsū Taxi (☎099 742 0027).

INFORMATION

Tourist information Both of Yakushima's main towns have tourist offices. The most useful is in Miyanoura (daily 8.30am–5pm; ☎099 742 1019), in the circular white building at the end of the ferry pier, which has English-speaking staff. You can pick up bus timetables, hotel lists, maps and brochures here and they can book accommodation for you if you need it. Anbō's tiny tourist office (daily 8.30am–5pm; ☎099 746 2333) is located on the main crossroads in the centre of town just north of the river. There's also a small desk at the airport (daily 8.30am–5pm; ☎099 749 4010), while Yakumonkey (⊚yakumonkey.com) has good, up-to-date information.

Services Miyanoura is the largest centre for supermarkets and other facilities. The main post office is located in the town centre, just west of the river. Although it does have an international ATM (Mon–Fri 8.45am–6pm, Sat 9am–5pm, Sun 9am–3pm), it's best not to rely on it – stock up with cash in Kagoshima. Both Anbō and Onoaida have sub-post offices and small supermarkets. Internet access is available upstairs in the Yakushima Kankō Centre (屋久島観光センター), on the main road opposite Miyanoura ferry pier. A left-luggage service is also available here at the shop downstairs (¥300/bag/day).

TOURS AND ACTIVITIES

Equipment There are a number of dive and hiking shops on the island that rent gear; enquire at the Miyanoura tourist office for details.

Adventure tours The Yakushima Nature Activity Centre

(☎099 742 0944, ⊚ynac.com) on the main drag in Miyanoura offers various guided adventure tours, with a choice of walking, hiking, paddling, canyoning, kayaking and scuba diving.

ACCOMMODATION

Yakushima has a fair range of **accommodation**, but you still need to plan well ahead during holiday periods. Other than at hostels, the prices listed below include meals. Note that those hiking the interior can make use of mountain huts; ask at one of the island's tourist offices for advice.

MIYANOURA

Miyanoura Portside Youth Hostel 宮之浦ポートサイド YH ☎099 749 1316, ⓦyakushima-hostel.com. Conveniently located just 10min walk round the harbour from the ferry pier, this has simple but pleasing rooms, and a common area with good sea views. It's rather overpriced, but you can get discounts if you book online. Dorm **¥3800**

Seaside Hotel Yakushima シーサイドホテル屋久島 ☎099 742 0175, ⓦssh-yakushima.co.jp. In a convenient location, right on the promontory overlooking the ferry port. It's a comfortable place with spacious Western and tatami rooms, plus a pool and restaurant. **¥15,000**

Yakusugi-sō 屋久杉荘 ☎099 742 0023. On the east side of the river, this gorgeous ryokan has well-appointed rooms, which range from cosy to absolutely huge – you could fit a whole football team in some of them. **¥8500**

★**Yaman-kami** 山ん神 ☎099 742 0618. The cheapest minshuku in the area, and it's quite lovely – built in a sort of chalet-style, its tatami rooms are simple and have shared facilities, but are perfectly comfortable. It's on the west side of the river, backing up against the hillside. **¥5000**

ANBŌ

Minshuku Shiho 民宿志保 ☎099 746 3288. The best cheap option in the area – a white bungalow shaded by palm trees, it's the first building you come to on the road up from the pier, and provides spick-and-span, no-frills tatami rooms. No evening meals served. **¥10,500**

★**Sankara** 8km south of Anbo ☎099 747 3488, ⓦsankarahotel-spa.com. Yakushima's first boutique hotel opened in 2010, and is the island's most appealing accommodation; the rooms have been designed in keeping with Yakushima's natural vibe, and all have balconies with

a sea view. The attached spa is rather heavenly, while the on-site restaurant serves local ingredients in a distinctively French style. **¥60,000**

ONOAIDA

Chinryu-an 枕流庵 ☎099 747 3900, ⓦchinryu.com. Remote place, 2km west of Onoaida, offering dormitory bunks or private tatami rooms in a cedar-wood chalet buried amidst the trees. The English-speaking owner is a fount of local information and also provides hearty meals, though you can use the kitchen for a small fee. Kurio-bound buses will drop you at the entrance, beside the Yaishi stop, or you can take the more frequent service that terminates at the Iwasaki Hotel and walk west for a few minutes, keeping your eyes peeled for a sign on the right. It's a bit pricey, however, all things considered. Dorm **¥5100**, double **¥14,000**

Yakushima Youth Hostel 屋久島ユースホステル ☎099 747 3751, ⓦyakushima-yh.net. Despite being run along military lines, with a strict policy of lights out at 10pm, this hostel is popular, so make sure you book ahead. It's 5km west of Onoaida in Hirauchi, 5min walk east of the Hirauchi-irigichu stop, sign posted down a quiet lane. Dorm **¥3540**

INAKA BEACH

★**Sōyō-tei** 送陽邸 ☎099 745 2819. Located on Inaka Beach (いなか浜) in the northwest of the island, this tasteful, antique-decorated ryokan was painstakingly constructed using new materials and hundred-year-old beams. The best rooms boast verandas and stunning views of the finest beach in Yakushima, and there's also a rotemburo for a perfect sunset soak. The ryokan is located at the western tip of Inaka Beach next to the road leading to Nagata. **¥27,300**

EATING AND DRINKING

MIYANOURA

Coco ココ Miyanoura. Ramshackle yakitori joint, selling said chicken sticks from ¥100, and oden sets from ¥500. It's a good place for a drink too, situated on Miyanoura's nicest road, one block back from the river's west bank. Daily 5–11pm.

★**Naminohana** 波の華 Miyanoura. This is where the locals come to eat – don't expect an English-language menu, or speedy service. Do expect an exceedingly cheery atmosphere in the evenings, and delicious suppers of flying-fish (tori-uo), the local speciality (¥1000); the dish lands on your table with its wings still on, like a little fried angel. Daily 5pm–midnight.

Stax Cafe スタクスカフェー Miyanoura. The best of

Miyanoura's few cafés, it's easy to find on the corner, where the main road crosses the river. The coffees are okay, and it's a good place for an evening drink, all presided over by the picture of Steve McQueen behind the bar. Daily 10am–6pm & 8pm until the last customer leaves.

ANBŌ

Rengaya れんが屋 Anbo. Pleasantly rustic venue on the road down to the harbour. It offers a varied menu, including yakiniku (meat barbecued at your table) and tonkatsu (pork cutlets), with set meals from around ¥1500. Try the sashimi set which comes complete with deep-fried flying-fish "wings" at a jaunty angle. Daily 10am–2pm & 6–10pm.

Okinawa

沖縄

OKINAWA CHURAUMI AQUARIUM

Okinawa

Mention Okinawa to a mainland Japanese and you'll likely receive a wistful sigh in return. Perpetually warm weather, clear seas bursting with fish, fantastic food, gentle people, unspoilt beaches and jungle … the list could go on. More than one hundred subtropical islands, collectively known as the Ryūkyū Shotō, stretch over 700km of ocean from Kyūshū southwest to Yonaguni-jima, almost within sight of Taiwan, and provide one of Japan's favourite getaways. Getting here may be a little costly, but Okinawa's lush vegetation, vision-of-paradise beaches and superb coral reefs can charm the most jaded traveller – if you've had your fill of shrines and temples and want to check out some of Japan's best beaches and dive sites (see box, p.756), or simply fancy a spot of winter sun, then Okinawa is well worth a visit.

11

The largest island in the group, **Okinawa-Hontō**, usually referred to simply as Okinawa, is the region's transport hub and home to its prefectural capital, **Naha**. It's also the most heavily populated and developed of the Ryūkyū chain, thanks largely to the controversial presence of **American military bases** (see box, p.766). Okinawa-Hontō boasts a number of historical sights, many of them associated with the **Battle of Okinawa** at the end of the Pacific War (see p.755). But the island has more to offer than battlegrounds, particularly in its northern region, where the old way of life still survives among the isolated villages.

To see the best of the region, you'll have to hop on a plane or ferry and explore the dozens of **outer islands** away from Okinawa-Hontō, many of them uninhabited. One of the most accessible places to head for is **Zamami-jima**, part of the **Kerama Islands** and just a short ferry ride west of Naha, which offers great beaches and diving and has recently become a centre for whale-watching. For a real sense of escape, however, you need to head further south, to **Miyako-jima** and the **Yaeyama Islands**. The latter grouping includes mountainous **Ishigaki-jima**; **Taketomi-jima**, a tiny place with almost no traffic and a languid, end-of-the-line feel; and nearby **Iriomote-jima**, often described as Japan's last wilderness. In most of these islands, it's the scenery and watersports that provide the main attractions, but Iriomote has the added distinction of its unique wildlife population and lush, almost tropical rainforest; it's also home to the elusive Iriomote lynx.

With its subtropical **climate**, Okinawa stays warm throughout the year. Average annual temperatures are around 23°C, with a winter average of 17°C and a minimum of 10°C. Winter lasts from December to February, while the hot, humid summer can start as early as April, and continues into September. Temperatures at this time hover around 34°C, and the sun can be pretty intense, though the sea breezes help. The **best time to visit** is in spring or autumn (roughly March to early May and late Sept to Dec). The rainy season lasts from early May to early June, while typhoons can be a problem in July and August, and occasionally all the way into October.

Highlights

❶ Diving From the soft corals and tropical fish around the Kerama islands to the enigmatic rocks near Yonaguni-jima, Okinawa offers a wealth of outstanding diving experiences. See p.756

❷ Shuri-jō Perhaps the most distinctive of Japan's wonderful array of castles, this World Heritage-listed re-creation of the Ryūkyū kingdom's former base is Naha's crowning glory. See p.759

❸ Okinawa Churaumi Aquarium Get to grips with Okinawa's diverse sea life without the need to don diving gear at this fabulous aquarium. See p.770

❹ Zamami-jima This island has some of Japan's finest beaches, and it's just a short ferry-ride from Naha. See p.772

❺ Taketomi-jima Wave goodbye to the day-trippers and watch the stars come out at this tiny, beach-fringed island. See p.784

❻ Iriomote-jima An adventure paradise, with great kayaking and trekking opportunities – or just kick back on the serenely beautiful beach at Funauki. See p.785

HIGHLIGHTS ARE MARKED ON THE MAP ON P.754

RYŪKYŪ CULTURE

On Okinawa's outer islands, you'll find evidence of the much-vaunted **Ryūkyū culture**, borne of contact with Taiwan and China, as well as the rest of Japan. The most obvious expressions of this culture are found in the islands' cuisine and in a vibrant use of colour and bold tropical patterns, while the Chinese influence is clearly visible in the region's architecture, traditional dress and the martial art of karate – the Ryūkyū warriors' preferred mode of protection. Ancient religious beliefs are kept alive by shamen (called *yuta*) and, in central Okinawa-Hontō, there are sumo bouts between bulls. There's also a Ryūkyū dialect, with dozens of variations between the different islands, unique musical instruments, and a distinctive musical style that has reached an international audience through bands such as Nēnēs, Diamantes and Champloose (see p.764).

If you're lucky, you'll stumble on a **local festival**, such as giant rope tug-of-war contests or dragon-boat races, while the biggest annual event is the **Eisā festival** (the fifteenth day of the seventh lunar month, usually late Aug or early Sept), when everyone downs tools and dances to the incessant rhythms of drums, flutes and the three-stringed *sanshin*.

11

Brief history

In the fifteenth century, the islands that now make up Okinawa were united for the first time into the **Ryūkyū kingdom**, governed from Shuri Castle in present-day Naha. This period is seen as the golden era of Ryūkyū culture. Trade with China, the rest of Japan and other Southeast Asian countries flourished, while the traditionally non-militarized kingdom maintained its independence by paying **tribute to China**. But then, in 1609, the **Shimazu** clan of Kagoshima (southern Kyūshū) invaded. The Ryūkyū kings became **vassals** to the Shimazu, who imposed punitive taxes and ruled with an iron hand for the next two hundred years, using the islands as a gateway for trade with China when such contact was theoretically outlawed by the Togukawa Shogunate. When the Japanese feudal system was abolished in the 1870s, the islands were simply annexed to the mainland as **Okinawa Prefecture**. Against much local

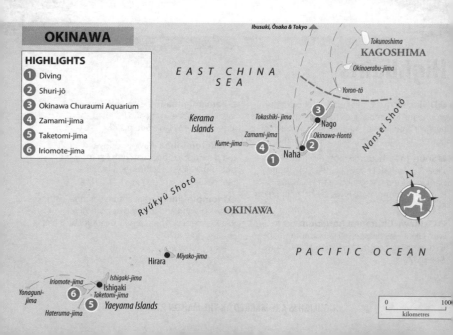

OKINAWA

HIGHLIGHTS

1 Diving
2 Shuri-jō
3 Okinawa Churaumi Aquarium
4 Zamami-jima
5 Taketomi-jima
6 Iriomote-jima

Ibusuki, Ōsaka & Tokyo

Tokunoshima
KAGOSHIMA
Okinoerabu-jima

EAST CHINA SEA

Yoron-tō

Kerama Islands
Tokashiki-jima
Zamami-jima
Kume-jima
Nago
Okinawa-Hontō
Naha

Nansei Shotō

Ryūkyū Shotō

OKINAWA

N

Hirara ● Miyako-jima

PACIFIC OCEAN

Iriomote-jima
Ishigaki-jima
Ishigaki
Yonaguni-jima
Taketomi-jima
Yaeyama Islands
Hateruma-jima

0   100
kilometres

opposition, the Meiji government established a military base and tried to eradicate local culture by forcing people to speak Japanese and swear allegiance to the emperor, forbidding schools to teach Ryūkyū history.

Battle of Okinawa

By the early twentieth century, Okinawa had been fairly successfully absorbed into Japan and became a key pawn in Japan's last line of defence during the **Pacific War**. Following the battle of Iwō-jima in March 1945, the American fleet advanced on Okinawa and, after an extensive preliminary bombardment, referred to locally as a "typhoon of steel", the Americans invaded on **April 1, 1945**. It took nearly three months of bitter fighting before General Ushijima, the Japanese commander, committed suicide and the island surrendered. The **Battle of Okinawa** left 12,500 American troops dead (plus 37,000 injured) and an estimated 250,000 on the Japanese side, nearly half of whom were local civilians.

American occupation

It's estimated that one third of the population of Okinawa died in the war, many in **mass suicides** that preceded the surrender, and others from disease and starvation. But the islanders' subsequent anger has been directed at the Japanese government rather than America. Most people feel Okinawa was sacrificed to save the mainland – this was the only major battle fought on Japanese soil – and that they were misled to believe they were luring the American fleet into a trap. Compounding this was the behaviour of Japanese troops, who are accused of denying locals shelter and medical treatment, and ultimately of abandoning them to the Americans.

By comparison, the American invaders were a welcome relief, despite the islanders' worst fears. They brought in much-needed food supplies – Spam was an instant hit, and a precursor of the processed luncheon meat found in pork *champurū* – and gradually helped restore the local economy. This wasn't wholly altruistic, of course, since Okinawa was ideally placed for monitoring events in Southeast Asia. As the 1950s Korean War merged into the Vietnam War, so the **American bases** became a permanent feature of the Okinawa landscape (see box, p.766).

Japanese sovereignty

Okinawa remained under **American jurisdiction** until 1972, when local protests led to the restoration of **Japanese sovereignty**. Since then, the two governments have colluded to maintain an American military presence on the island despite growing opposition, which reached a peak when three American servicemen were found guilty of raping a 12-year-old schoolgirl in 1995.

Okinawa has since borne witness to some curious political shifts. **Aiko Shimajiri** has been in power since the 2007 local elections, winning with a focus on the local

11

WILDLIFE IN OKINAWA

Besides Hokkaidō, Okinawa contains Japan's largest areas of unspoilt natural environment and its greatest biodiversity. Much of this wealth of **wildlife** is underwater, spawned by the warm Kuroshio Current that sweeps up the east coast and allows coral reefs to flourish. But there are a number of endemic species on land, too, including turtles, a crested eagle and the *noguchigera* (Pryer's woodpecker), in addition to Iriomote's wild cat, the *yamaneko*. A less welcome local resident is the highly venomous **habu snake**. It measures around 2m in length, is dark green with a yellow head, and usually lurks in dense vegetation or on roadsides; it rarely ventures into urban areas. As long as you're careful – especially during spring and autumn, when the snakes are more active – you should have no problems; if you are bitten, make for the nearest hospital, where they should have antivenin.

economy rather than military issues. However, these came to the fore in national elections two years down the line, with Yukio Hatayama elected Prime Minister on a pledge to remove, rather than relocate, the Futenma air base – his failure to do so saw him step down in disgrace less than a year later (see box, p.766).

ARRIVAL AND DEPARTURE

By plane By far the majority of visitors arrive by plane. Most come from the Japanese mainland, though there are international flights (see p.31). Domestic airlines operate between Naha and most major Japanese cities (see p.37); Naha acts as a hub for the rest of the islands, though there are direct services from the mainland to Ishigaki and Miyako. Though flying can be expensive, overseas visitors can take advantage of the air passes offered by JAL and ANA (see p.37). In addition, budget carriers (see p.37) fly to the islands: Solaseed to Naha from Kagoshima, Kōbe and Miyazaki; Vanilla to Naha from Tokyo (often the cheapest way from the capital); Peach to Naha and Ishigaki from Osaka; and Solaseed to Naha from Kagoshima, Kumamoto, Miyazaki and Kōbe.

By ferry The most pleasant way to get to Okinawa is by ferry: there are sailings to Naha from Tokyo, Osaka, Kōbe or one of several cities on Kyūshū.

GETTING AROUND

By plane These days, getting around between the island groups is almost entirely done by plane, since the ferry network has been scaled down in recent years. Using Naha as the main hub, inter-island flights are operated by Japan Transocean Air (JTA), Ryūkyū Air Commuter (RAC) and Air Nippon (ANK), with connections to all the major islands.

By ferry There are some services from Naha to Zamami-jima and other nearby islands, though you'll have to fly to head south to Miyako-jima or the Yaeyama Islands.

The Yaeyamas themselves are well connected by ferry services.

By bus Okinawa-Hontō has a fairly decent bus network; most smaller islands have bus services, though they can be very sparse indeed.

By car The lack of a strong bus network on the smaller islands is a good reason to rent a car: Okinawa is probably the most pleasant place to drive in Japan. Rental details are given in the individual accounts.

DIVING IN OKINAWA

With scores of dive sites around Okinawa-Hontō – and many more around the outer islands – one of the best reasons for visiting Okinawa is to go **diving**. There are plenty of dive shops, but only a few with English-speaking instructors. A useful website is ⓦdivejapan .com, which includes links to operators, articles, dive-site maps and photos. PADI courses are available on Okinawa-Hontō from *Maeda Misaki Divers House* (see p.768) and the American-run *Reef Encounters* (ⓦreefencounters.org). Once you have your certificate, the islands are yours for the taking. Prices vary, but equipment hire is generally ¥3000–5000, first dives ¥8000–11,000, and second dives usually a couple of thousand more. To rent equipment, you should know the metric readings of your height, weight and shoe size.

DIVE SITES

There are great diving opportunities every way you turn on the islands, but the following sites are particularly notable.

Zamami-jima (p.772) Fantastic hard corals, more reef fish than you could count in a week, and plenty of turtles.

Miyako-jima (p.774) Over fifty different dive spots to choose from, with cave dives being particularly popular.

Ishigaki-jima (p.778) As well as rare blue coral reefs off Shiraho-no-umi, species of fish you can expect to swim with are barracuda, butterfly fish, redfin fusiliers, spadefish and manta rays.

Iriomote-jima (p.785) There's easily accessible coral in the waters surrounding this enchanting island.

Yonaguni-jima (p.789) For the ultimate dive experience consider lugging your gear out here to see sea turtles and hammerhead sharks, and to explore the enigmatic rocks that some claim are the remains of a sunken civilization.

EAT YOUR WAY TO 100: OKINAWAN CUISINE

The Japanese have famously long average lifespans – the current **life expectancy** is just under 83 years, while 350 people in every million live to 100 years of age. These are both world ranking-toppers, yet in Okinawa those stats go through the roof; the tiny village of **Ōgimi**, on the main island's northwest coast (see map, p.754) is often said to be the oldest place on earth, since it boasts over a dozen centenarians. Such figures are put down to the fact that Okinawa has particularly low incidences of heart disease, cancer and other maladies, and this in turn is put down to the **diet** of the islanders – even more fish, tofu, grains, veggies and soy products than mainland Japan, with a fraction of the meat, sugar or dairy goods. Visiting Okinawa might just add a few weeks to your life; what follows are a few recommended culinary specialties to look out for on your way around.

Gōyachampurū A stir-fry featuring egg, pork and slices of *gōya* (bitter melon), this is the most famous Okinawan dish, and when done right it's extremely tasty. Variants include *fū champurū*, which is made with tofu instead of *gōya*.

Shimahata It almost seems a crime to eat such a beautiful fish – this local one's a big fella with gorgeous red and yellow stripes. Other sea goodies to look out for (then gobble) are *irabucha*, a blue parrotfish; *gurukun*, a small fish usually served fried; and *yakōgai*, a giant turban shell.

Sōki soba The local favourite, featuring yellow wheat noodles, spring onions and bonito flakes in a clear soup, with hunks of pork rib; still on the bone, they'll give your chopstick skills a thorough examination. The quality of the pork varies substantially; in some places it's mostly fat and gristle, while in better venues (such as those listed throughout this chapter) the meat is lean and tender. Variants include *Okinawa soba* and *Yaeyama soba*.

Sukugarasu Tiny pieces of tofu topped with a salted minnow. Often served with *awamori* (see below), it should be eaten in one bite.

Taco rice OK, so this one's not so healthy. It would be, if made with the other *tako* (octopus); instead, what we have here is a bed of rice topped with taco ingredients: egg, greens, minced meat, cheese and a little spice. As with most unhealthy food, it tastes great.

Umi budō Sold in Naha's market areas as "green caviar", this is actually a strange sort of seaweed, made up of poppable bubbles that do, indeed, resemble sturgeons' eggs. Yummy stuff, it's often served with local sashimi.

Awamori Also worth a mention is Okinawa's own variant on sake; it's anywhere from 30–50 percent alcohol, though even the "weak" stuff can give you a banging headache. Orion is the local beer of choice

11

Okinawa-Hontō

沖縄本島

Once the centre of the Ryūkyū kingdom, **Okinawa-Hontō**, or Okinawa Main Island, is a strangely ambivalent place. Locals are fiercely proud of their Ryūkyū heritage, and yet the competing cultures of Japan and America are far more prevalent. To some extent, the island still feels like occupied territory, especially central Okinawa-Hontō, where the **American bases** and the nearby "American" towns, with their drive-ins and shopping malls, have become a bizarre tourist attraction for mainland Japanese, who come to soak up a bit of American culture.

Fascinating though all this is, it doesn't make Okinawa-Hontō the most obvious holiday destination. However, if you're drawn by the more appealing outer islands (see p.772), the chances are you'll spend some time on the main island waiting for plane or ferry connections. Okinawa-Hontō's chief city and the former Ryūkyū capital is **Naha**, whose prime attraction is its reconstructed castle, **Shuri-jō**, the ruins of which were awarded World Heritage status in 2001. There are also some interesting market streets and a pottery village to explore, and you might want to take advantage of its banks – not to mention excellent bars and restaurants – before heading off to remoter regions.

Southern Okinawa-Hontō saw the worst fighting in 1945, and the scrubby hills are littered with **war memorials**, particularly around Mabuni Hill, where the final battles took place. North of Naha, the island's central district has little to recommend it, but

11

Tokyo, Osaka & Kagoshima

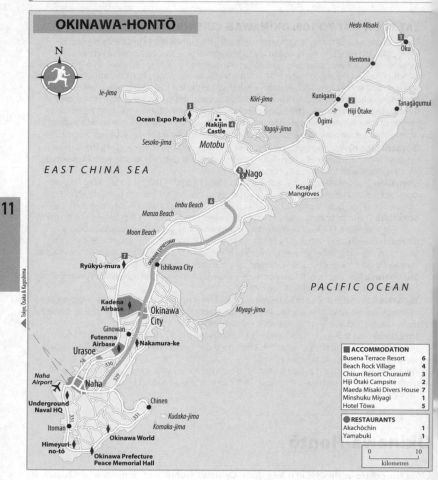

OKINAWA-HONTŌ

N

Hedo Misaki

Oku **1**

Hentona

Ie-jima

Kōri-jima

Kunigami

Tanagāgumui

Hiji Ōtake **2**

Ōgimi

3 Ocean Expo Park

Nakijin **4**
Castle

Yagaji-jima

Sesoko-jima

Motobu

70

Nago **1**
5

Kesaji
Mangroves

EAST CHINA SEA

Imbu Beach **6**

Manza Beach

Moon Beach

OKINAWA EXPRESSWAY

Ryūkyū-mura **7**

Ishikawa City

PACIFIC OCEAN

Kadena
Airbase

Okinawa
City

Miyagi-jima

Ginowan

Futenma
Airbase

Nakamura-ke

Urasoe

58

330

Naha
Airport

329

Naha

Chinen

Underground
Naval HQ

Kudaka-jima

331

Komaka-jima

Itoman

Okinawa World

Himeyuri-
no-tō

Okinawa Prefecture
Peace Memorial Hall

■ ACCOMMODATION	
Busena Terrace Resort	6
Beach Rock Village	4
Chisun Resort Churaumi	3
Hiji Ōtaki Campsite	2
Maeda Misaki Divers House	7
Minshuku Miyagi	1
Hotel Tōwa	5

● RESTAURANTS	
Akachōchin	1
Yamabuki	1

0   10
kilometres

beyond Kadena the buildings start to thin out. Here you'll find one of the better "Ryūkyū culture villages", **Ryūkyū-mura**, and the island's best beaches. The largest settlement in northern Okinawa-Hontō, **Nago** is an appealing town that provides a base for visiting the stunning Okinawa Churaumi Aquarium and exploring the scenic coastline and mountainous tip of the island, culminating in the dramatic cape of **Hedo Misaki**.

GETTING AROUND   OKINAWA-HONTŌ

By car Long and thin, Okinawa-Hontō measures just 135km from tip to toe, so you can drive the whole length in a matter of hours. The best way to get around is to rent your own car or motorbike, particularly if you want to explore the northern hills. But be warned – the speed limit on many of the narrow streets that wind around the island is 40 or 50kph, and the roads around the southern and central strip are gridlocked during rush hour, so allow plenty of time for your journey and take the expressway if you're in a hurry.

By bus Exploring by bus involves a lot of waiting for connections (see individual accounts for details), but an easy alternative is to join one of the organized bus tours out of Naha, which pack a lot into a short time at a reasonable price, and come with a practically nonstop Japanese commentary. Naha Bus (☎098 868 3750) runs three separate full-day tours from Naha's bus terminal (¥4700–5800). You can buy tickets at the bus terminal, or from their counter in the airport's domestic terminal.

Naha

那覇

The Okinawan capital of **NAHA** should, in fairness, be a place to get things done and be on one's way. This is the only large city in a region of Japan that leans heavily on nature – despite being capital of the Ryūkyū kingdom for over four hundred years, wartime destruction and rampant commercialization have colluded to ensure that there's precious little to see bar bland residential blocks and souvenir shops catering to a near-constant stream of Japanese holiday-makers. Yet, somehow, it's a great place to kick back – a fair proportion of the locals you meet will be mainland Japanese, here to trade in a hefty chunk of their previous salary, at least temporarily, for a relaxed lifestyle. Foreign travellers often end up staying far longer than they planned – the weather's great, the food's terrific, beaches and bars are never far away, and busting a gut to get somewhere else just wouldn't be in the Okinawan spirit of things.

There are, of course, a few things to see while you're here. The beautifully reconstructed **Shuri-jō**, the old Ryūkyū kings' small, solid castle, constitutes the city's major sight and is well worth visiting; the **Tsuboya** district, a pleasing area of little workshops and dusty galleries that is famous for its pottery kilns, is fun for a wander; and there's **Naminoue beach**, a short curl of sand that would boast grand sea views were it not for the roads firing across the waves a few dozen metres offshore. Domestic tourists make a beeline for **Kokusai-dōri** (国際通り), the city's main thoroughfare; nearly 2km long, it's lined with a strange mix of classy boutiques, souvenir stalls and army-surplus outlets selling American military leftovers. The **market** area to its south is charmingly ramshackle; within its several covered arcades you'll find some great souvenirs, as well as one of Japan's best fish markets.

Shuri-jō

首里城 • 1-2 Shurikinjocho • Daily: April–June & Oct–Nov 8.30am–7pm; July–Sept 8.30am–8pm; Dec–March 8.30am–6pm • ¥800 • Bus #1 from Kokusai-dōri or #17 from Naha Bus Terminal (every 15–20min; 30min); or a 10min walk from Shuri monorail station

Perched on a hill 3km northeast of central Naha, **Shuri-jō** served as the royal residence of the Ryūkyū kings from the early fifteenth century until 1879. Elaborate ceremonies took place in the castle's opulent throne room, on occasion attended by envoys from China and, later, from Kyūshū. Very little of the original remains, but the present buildings, painstakingly restored in the early 1990s, are certainly worth seeing for their distinctive blend of Chinese and Japanese architecture.

The castle's main entrance is the decorative **Shurei-mon**. This outer gate is a popular spot for group photos, but the inner **Kankai-mon** is a far more impressive structure, its no-nonsense guard tower flanked by sun-baked limestone walls. Inside, there's yet another defensive wall and no fewer than three more gates – the last now housing the ticket office – before you reach the central courtyard. Pride of place goes to the **Seiden**, a double-roofed palace with an immense, colourful porch and two throne halls. From the more elaborate upper throne room, the king, surrounded by gilded dragons writhing against lustrous red and black lacquer, would review his troops or watch ceremonies in the courtyard below. Other buildings house remnants of the dynasty and details of the restoration work, though with only a smattering of English explanations to bring them alive.

NAHA FESTIVALS

Shuri-jō is the venue for traditional **Ryūkyū New Year** celebrations (Jan 1–3) and the **Shuri-jō Festival** (Nov 1–3), featuring a parade of Ryūkyū-dynasty clothing, dance displays and other performing arts. The **Naha Dragon Boat Race** takes place on May 5, while **The Naha Festival** (Oct 10) includes the world's largest tug-of-war – using a rope 180m long and 1.5m in diameter – as well as a ten-thousand-strong Eisa folk dance parade down Kokusa-dōri.

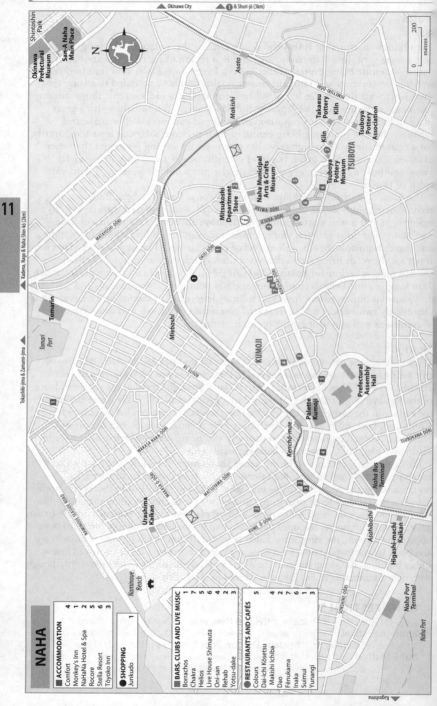

NAHA

◼ ACCOMMODATION

Comfort	4
Monkey's Inn	1
NaHaNa Hotel & Spa	2
Rocore	5
Stella Resort	6
Tōyoko Inn	3

● SHOPPING

Junkudo	1

◼ BARS, CLUBS AND LIVE MUSIC

Borrachos	1
Chakra	7
Helios	5
Live House Shimauta	6
Oni-san	4
Rehab	2
Yotsu-dake	3

● RESTAURANTS AND CAFES

Colours	5
Dai-ichi Kōsetsu	4
Makishi Ichiba	2
Dao	7
Fenukama	6
Inaka	1
Suimui	1
Yunangi	3

Shuri-jō Park

A quiet place featuring a stone-walled pond and old trees, **Shuri-jō Park** lies across the road from the Shuri-jō exit. The pond's pretty, island pavilion once belonged to Enkaku-ji, which was built in 1492 as the local headquarters of the Rinzai sect; it was said to have been the most impressive structure in the kingdom. Nowadays, only a few shell-pocked walls remain of the original temple, east of the pond.

Okinawa Prefectural Museum

沖縄県立博物館, Okinawa kenritsu Hakubutsukan • 3-1-1 Omoromachi • Daily 9am–6pm (Fri & Sat til 8pm) • ¥400; art section ¥300, extra for special exhibitions • 10min walk from Omoromachi monorail station • ☎ 098 941 8200

Sitting on the route between Shuri-jō and central Naha, the splendid **Okinawa Prefectural Museum** is worth popping into on your way to or from the castle. Designed to make visitors feel that they're stepping onto an island, this modern venue provides a good overview of local history, nature and culture; in addition, a separate wing focuses on local art and puts on diverting **exhibitions** several times per year.

Naha Municipal Arts and Crafts Museum

那覇市伝統工芸館, Naha-shi Dentoū Kōgei-kan • 3-2-10 Makishi • Daily 9am–6pm • ¥300 • Craft classes ¥1500–3000 • ☎ 098 868 7866

If you're interested in local crafts, drop by the **Naha Municipal Arts and Crafts Museum** on the second floor of the Tembusu building on Kokusai-dōri, near Mitsukoshi. The entrance fee will get you into a small gallery with prime examples of fabrics, ceramics, glass and lacquerware, but more interestingly (and without paying the entrance fee) you can watch artisans fashion these objects in the adjoining workshops and studios. You can try your hand at weaving, *bingata* dyeing, glass-blowing, pottery and lacquerware, and there's also a well-stocked gift shop.

Dai-ichi Kōsetsu Makishi Ichiba

第一公設牧志市場 • Daily 9am–8pm, closed fourth Sun of every month

Just south of Kokusai-dōri, the **Ichiba-dōri** and **Heiwa-dōri** shopping arcades are great places for a wander – 1960s architecture, cheap fruit and occasionally hilarious Okinawan novelty T-shirts are all on the agenda. Among the souvenir stalls and discount outlets, these covered streets host a number of lively **markets**, of which the best is Ichiba's food market, **Dai-ichi Kōsetsu Makishi Ichiba**. The ground-floor stalls are piled high with sweet-smelling tropical fruits, every conceivable part of pig and ice-packed arrays of multicoloured fish and mysterious, spiny crabs. You'll see fishmongers deftly slicing sashimi, some of it destined for the **food stalls** upstairs (see p.763).

Tsuboya

壺屋 • From Dai-ichi Kōsetsu Makishi Ichiba market, walk north onto Heiwa-dōri and follow it east for a few minutes

The pottery district of **Tsuboya** is a compact area that's been the centre of local ceramics production since 1682, when the government gathered a number of workshops together, of which around ten are still in operation. Traditionally, the potters here produced large jars for storing the local liquor (*awamori*) and miso paste, but nowadays they concentrate on smaller items for the tourist market, typically half-moon-shaped sake flasks and snarling *shiisā* lions.

Tsuboya Pottery Museum

壺屋焼物博物館, Tsuboya Yakimono Hakubutsukan • 1-9-32 Tsuboya • Tues–Sun 10am–6pm • ¥315 top-floor art exhibits free • ☎ 098 862 3761

To get an overview of the area's history, drop into the **Tsuboya Pottery Museum**, less than 100m from the end of the covered arcade. It's a decent enough place, though the exhibitions can feel a little repetitive. Head on up to the top floor to see the latest **art exhibition** (usually featuring the works of an Okinawan artist); exit through the back door, and you'll see the remains of an ancient kiln. There's another one – far larger and more interesting – on the neighbouring embankment, backing onto the excellent *Fēnukama* café (see opposite); a traditional climbing kiln dating from the late seventeenth century, it's one of the oldest still intact.

ARRIVAL AND DEPARTURE

By plane Naha Airport (那覇空港) occupies a promontory some 3km southwest of the city centre. One terminal handles flights from mainland Japan and to Okinawa's outer islands, while the adjacent building is for overseas flights. From the airport, you can either take a taxi (around ¥1500) or the monorail (¥230) for the short journey into central Naha, or one of several frequent local buses departing from outside the terminal buildings (¥200).

Destinations Beijing (2 weekly; 3hr); Fukuoka (17 daily; 1hr 40min); Hiroshima (1 daily; 1hr 40min); Hong Kong (1–2 daily; 2hr 40min); Ishigaki (1–3 hourly; 1hr); Kagoshima (3 daily; 1hr 15min); Kōbe (6 daily; 1hr 50min); Kumamoto (1 daily; 1hr 35min); Matsuyama (1 daily; 1hr 35min); Miyako (1–2 hourly; 45min); Miyazaki (1 daily; 1hr 35min); Nagasaki (1 daily; 1hr 35min); Nagoya (9 daily; 2hr); Osaka (15 daily; 1hr 50min); Okayama (2 daily; 1hr 50min); Sapporo (1 daily; 4hr); Sendai (1 daily; 2hr 30min); Seoul (2 daily; 2hr 20min); Shanghai (1 daily; 2hr); Shizuoka (1 daily; 2hr 10min); Taipei (3–4 daily; 1hr 30min); Takamatsu (1 daily; 1hr 50min); Tokyo (1–4 hourly; 2hr 30min); Yonaguni (2 daily; 1hr 15min).

By bus Services run around the island from the main bus terminal, just to the east of the Asahibashi monorail stop; see individual accounts through the island for details. This is also where most of the local bus tours start (see p.758).

By ferry The ferry port, Naha Shin-kō (那覇新港), lies 2km north of the city centre. Most ferries from mainland Japan dock here, while slow boats from Kagoshima pull in further south at the old Naha Port Terminal (那覇埠頭). Naha Shin-kō is on the #101 bus route (1–3 hourly; 25min; ¥200), while Naha Port is more conveniently located about a 15min walk from the main Naha Bus Terminal. Marix Line (☎098 868 9098) and Maru A Ferry (☎098 861 1886) have slow boats through the Satsunan islands to Kagoshima (2 daily; 25hr); the latter also has sailings to Kōbe (1–2 weekly; 42hr), Osaka (weekly; 41hr) and Tokyo (1–2 weekly; 54hr). From the Tomari Port, on the west side of the city centre, there are sailings to Zamami-jima and other islands due west; you'll have a choice of fast (at least 2 daily; 55min; ¥3140) or slow services (10am daily; 2hr; ¥2120).

GETTING AROUND

By monorail The smart monorail (daily 6am–11.30pm; ¥200 minimum fare) is a useful way to get around, linking the airport with Shuri, 13km away.

By bus There are plenty of local buses, though services can be confusing and traffic often gridlocks at peak times. There's a flat fare of ¥200 within the city, but on other buses take a numbered ticket on entry and pay at your destination. If you plan to use the buses a lot, pick up the island-wide Naha City Bus Route Map (in English) from the tourist information offices. Taxi fares start from around ¥500.

Bike rental You can rent motorbikes and scooters at Helmet Shop SEA, 3-15-50 Makishi (☎098 864 5116), west of Kokusai-dōri, from ¥1700 for 3hr; most hostels and some hotels also rent bikes out, though the prices vary.

Car rental Nippon Rent-a-Car (☎098 868 4554), Japaren (☎0120 413900) and Toyota (☎098 857 0100) all have representatives in both Naha Airport and the city centre.

Taxis Okitō Kōtsū (☎098 946 5654) has English-speaking drivers, and you can arrange sightseeing taxi tours with English-speaking driver-guides through Okinawa-ken Kojin Taxi ☎098 868 1145.

INFORMATION

Tourist information Naha's tourist information service has desks in both the domestic (daily 9am–9pm; ☎098 857 6884) and international (daily 10.30am–7.30pm; ☎098 859 0742) terminals at the airport. Both have

English-speaking staff, plentiful maps and brochures, and can help with hotel reservations. In downtown Naha, there's an office on Okiei-dōri (daily 8.30am–8pm; ☎098 862 1442).

ACCOMMODATION

Naha has a good range of accommodation, especially for backpackers – there are more than a dozen hostels charging just ¥1000–1500 for a dorm bed, making this the cheapest backpacker city in Japan. Rooms are hard to come by in the peak holiday seasons – Golden Week, August and New Year – when rates may rise by up to forty percent. Don't assume, however, that Naha is the only place on Okinawa-Hontō with accommodation, as there are some great alternatives around the island.

Comfort コンフォートホテル 1-3-11 Kumoji ☎098 941 7311, ⓦ choice-hotels.jp. Popular business hotel

within spitting distance of the monorail. Rooms have been decorated with gentle pastel colours, and you can sually score hefty discounts from the rack rates. **¥9000**

Monkey's Inn おさるのおやど 3-23-21 Wakasa ☏ 098 863 7252, ⊕ saruyado.com. The best of the city's backpacker joints, with decent dorm rooms and comfy privates – some are huge, yet can be sold as singles. Close to the Zamami ferries (see opposite) yet far from anything else, the atmosphere depends upon who's here; it's popular with students, and the kitchen area is a good place to drink. Dorm **¥1500**, single **¥3000**, double **¥5000**

NaHaNa Hotel & Spa ナハナホテル 2-1-5 Kume ☏ 098 866 0787, ⊕ ishinhotels.com. An appealingly retro exterior – replete with a edge that may have been envisioned as a hover-car parking space – conceals surprisingly swish rooms, each mixing modern design with Okinawan motifs. Guests get special rates at the attached spa. **¥14,000**

Rocore ホテルロコアナハ 1-1-2 Matsuo ☏ 098 868 6578, ⊕ roccre.jp. Sleek, well-located hotel designed along a pine, black and white tricolour. The tastefully decorated rooms, while not over-large, are extremely comfortable, right down to the complimentary pyjamas, while some of the third-floor rooms have enclosed balconies. Note that you can lop a full third off the rates by booking online. **¥19,000**

★**Stella Resort** ステラリゾート 3F 3-6-41 Kumoji ☏ 098 863 1330, ⊕ stella-cg.com. There is tremendous value to be had at this immaculate and superbly located guesthouse, sitting at the end of the charming covered arcades south of Kokusai-dōri. Fanning out from the fascinating, fake-forest lobby area are dorm rooms and some cosy privates. Dorm **¥1500**, single **¥3500**, double **¥5000**

Tōyoko Inn 東横イン那覇旭橋駅前 2-1-20 Kume ☏ 098 951-1045, ⊕ toyoko-inn.com. Obligatory branch of the ubiquitous budget hotel chain – most of the rooms are good-value singles. They have laundry facilities and free wi-fi. Single **¥6500**

EATING

Naha undoubtedly has Okinawa-Hontō's widest choice of restaurants, spanning the range from international cuisine to delectable **local dishes** (see box, p.757). One Naha speciality is *tundā-bun*: banquets once enjoyed by **Ryūkyū** kings, and today generally served with an accompanying show.

Colours カラーズ 3-6-5 Matsuo ☏ 098 927 6508. Appropriately colourful restaurant which has taken the taco rice theme and run with it; here you can have the minced meat, cheese and greens served in a meat curry, or in a *doria* (rice gratin), both for ¥580. It's located on Naha's artiest road – the clientele here is an odd mix of hipsters and grannies. Wed–Mon 11.30am–8pm.

★**Dai-ichi Kōsetsu Makishi Ichiba** 第一公設牧志市場 Matsuo 2-10-1. An absolute must for seafood fans, this is not one restaurant but several tiny ones, all set together atop the city's biggest and best fish market. All the Okinawan staple dishes are here, but it would be a crime not to go for some tasty fresh fish – choose from the menu, or for added fun pick your own sea creature from downstairs and pay an extra ¥500 to have it cooked for you. Simply wonderful. Daily 10am–8pm.

Dao ダーオ 2F, Matsuo 2-8-28 ☏ 093 867 3751. Head down Ichiba-dōri from the main road, and you'll soon spy this popular second-floor Vietnamese restaurant, where there's a good selection of authentic Vietnamese dishes, most in the ¥700–1200 bracket. The spring rolls are especially tasty. Daily 11am–11pm.

★**Fēnukama** 南窯 Tsuboya 1-9-29 ☏ 098 861 6404. This is Naha's best café, and a handy excuse to pop over to the Tsuboya pottery district (see p.761); it is, in fact, backed by the ruins of a kiln built more than 300 years ago, as seen from a couple of the cafés outdoor tables. Inside or out, the coffee's great (¥400); take it with a *chinbin*, a sort of local crepe (¥250). Daily 10am–7pm.

Inaka 田舎 Matsuo 2-9-5. This hard-to-find market den dates from just after Okinawa's handover to Japan and, amazingly, prices haven't changed since 1976: it's still just ¥350 for a bowl of *sōki soba*. If you're still in the retro mood, spider your way up any neighbouring staircase to drink in some throwback architecture. Daily 9am–9pm.

Suimui 首里杜 Suimuikan, Shuri-jō ☏ 098 886 2020. A surprisingly good restaurant in the Shuri-jō information centre (see p.759); not to be confused with the castle's noisy snack bar, it serves Okinawan dishes as well as mainstream Japanese and Western meals. If you fancy something local, try the taco rice and Okinawa soba set, a bargain at ¥850. Daily 9am–6.30pm.

Yūnangi ゆうなんぎい 3-3-3 Kumoji. Country-style restaurant, offering a warm welcome and serving Okinawa cuisine, including Okinawa soba, *champurū* and various pork dishes. Set meals go from around ¥1300, with free rice refills. Mon–Sat 9am–6pm.

DRINKING AND NIGHTLIFE

As you'd expect, with plenty of off-duty GIs and footloose young Japanese tourists and locals, Naha's **entertainment** scene is far from dull. Following orders from above, the grunts are only allowed into certain bars. The city is also a good place to catch performances of traditional **Ryūkyū court dance**; some performances are served with *tundā-bun* banquets.

BARS

Borrachos ボラチョス 1-3-31 Makishi ☎ 098 943 4488. Mexican bar which, it seems, only employs male staff with copious facial hair. Good Mexican beer (from ¥600) and food are on offer, and the atmosphere is as relaxed as Naha gets. Daily 5pm–midnight.

Helios ヘリオス 1-2-25 Makishi, Kokusai-dōri ☎ 098 863 7227. Stylish "craft beer pub" belonging to a local microbrewery and offering several types of home brew including pale ale, Weissen, Pilsner and porter. A small taste of three costs ¥700. Also serves bar snacks. Daily 5–11pm, Fri & Sat till midnight.

Oni-san 鬼さん B1, 3-12-4 Kumoji ☎ 098 861 5578. Noisy, upbeat *izakaya* with a grotto-style entrance leading down to a basement complete with devil masks and fake burning torches hanging off the walls. The food's good, prices are reasonable and there's always a free sweet on the way out. Daily 5pm–2am, Sat & Sun till 3am).

Rehab リーハブ 3F, 2-4-14 Makishi, Kokusai-dōri ☎ 098 864 0646, ⓦ rehabokinawabar.com. Follow the sign up the stairs to find this friendly little *gaijin* bar, whose staff have long been helping out foreign residents and visitors – it's a good place to ask about anything from scuba diving to teaching English in Naha. Beers start at around ¥500 (you'll pay more for international options). Daily 7pm–2am, Sat & Sun till 3am.

LIVE MUSIC

Chakra チャクラ 2F, 1-2-1 Makishi, Kokusai-dōri ☎ 09⬛ 869 0283. Owned by local music legend Kina Shoukich⬛ and often home to the nationally renowned Champloos⬛ collective, this is a fun place to hear some local sounds⬛ Okinawan dancing often forms part of the performance⬛ and guests sometimes get to join in. Entry is ¥2500⬛ 7pm–1am, closed Wed.

Live House Shimauta ライブハウス島唄 3F, 1-2-3⬛ Makishi, Kokusai-dōri ☎ 098 863 6040. Just up the roa⬛ from *Chakra*, above a gift shop, this venue is run by anothe⬛ local music luminary: China Sadao, who brought the all-female group Nēnēs to world attention, and the concert⬛ here get rave reviews. Entry is ¥2000. Tues–Sun⬛ 8pm–midnight.

TRADITIONAL DANCE

Yotsu-dake 四つ竹 2-22-1 Kume ☎ 098 866 3333, ⓦ yotsutake.co.jp. The best of Naha's umpteen dinner-and-dance venues and somewhat less touristy than the slew on Kokusai-dōri (where they've another venue). As well as watching a local court dance (40min), you can also get a *tundā-bun* – a set meal of beautifully presented royal hors d'oeuvres. The staff are friendly, and they have a printed English explanation of the food and dances. Entry is ¥1575, or from ¥6300 including a meal. Shows daily 6.30pm & 8.30pm.

DIRECTORY

Banks and exchange Ryūkyū Bank in the airport (Mon–Fri 9am–4pm) exchanges currencies. The post office cash machine (Mon–Fri 9am–9pm, Sat & Sun 9am–5pm) in the airport accepts foreign cash and cards, as do post offices across the city. Banks on Kokusai-dōri offer foreign exchange.
Consulates United States, 2564 Nishihara, Urasoe City (just north of Naha; ☎ 098 876 4211).

Hospitals and medical care Izumizaki Hospital, 1-11-2 Kumoji (☎ 098 867 2116). If you need an English-speaking doctor, your best bet is the Adventist Medical Centre, 4-11-1 Kohagura, on Route 29 northeast of Naha (☎ 098 946 2833).
Immigration office To renew your visa, apply to the Naha Immigration Office, 1-15-15 Hikawa (☎ 098 832 4185), southeast of Kokusai-dōri on Route 221.

OKINAWAN SOUVENIRS

Those in search of local **crafts** will find beautiful **bingata** textiles the most appealing. Originally reserved for court ladies, *bingata* fabrics are hand-dyed with natural pigments from hibiscus flowers and various vegetables, in simple but striking patterns. Also worth searching out are the fine **jōfu** cloths of Miyako-jima and the Yaeyama Islands, once gifted in tribute to the local monarchs. **Ceramics** are thought to have been introduced to the region from Spain and Portugal in the fifteenth century, but Ryūkyū potters concentrated on roof tiles and fairly rustic utensils. Nowadays, they churn out thousands of sake flasks and *shiisā*, the ferocious lion figures that glare down at you from every rooftop – there are plenty for sale around Naha's Tsuboya district. The exquisite local **lacquerware** has a long history in the islands, too, having been introduced over five hundred years ago from China, but the glassware you'll find is much more recent: it's said production took off in the postwar years when Okinawans set about recycling the drinks bottles of the occupying US forces. Lastly, there's plenty of cheap **food and clothing** in the covered arcades off Kokusai-dōri: hunt down some Okinawan-patterned underpants, Puma T-shirts with the panther replaced by a smiling *shiisā*, and all manner of other pleasing tat.

olice 1-2-9 Izumizaki (☎098 836 0110). See p.66 for emergency numbers.

Post offices Naha Central Post Office is located on the south side of town around 500m down Naha Higashi Bypass from the Meiji Bridge. For ordinary services, you'll find sub-post offices in every district around town.

Travel agents Okinawa Tourist (☎098 862 1111) can help with domestic or international tickets.

Southern Okinawa-Hontō

During the long, drawn-out Battle of Okinawa (see p.755), it was the area south of Naha that saw the worst fighting and received the heaviest bombardment. Not only were the **Japanese Naval Headquarters** dug deep into the hills here, but the region's many limestone caves also provided shelter for hundreds of Japanese troops and local civilians, many of whom committed suicide rather than be taken prisoner. One of these caves has been preserved as a memorial to the young Himeyuri nurses who died there, and the area is dotted with peace parks and prayer halls. It's not completely devoted to war sights, however. **Okinawa World**, over on the southeast coast, combines 890m of extraordinary stalactite-filled caves with a tourist village dedicated to Ryūkyū culture, and there's also the lovely **Komaka Island**, a great spot for snorkelling.

Underground Naval Headquarters

旧海軍司令部壕, Kyū Kaigun Shireibu Gō • 236 Tomigusuku • Daily 8.30am–5pm • ¥420 • Bus #33, #46 or #101 from central Naha to Tomigusuku Jōshi Kōen-mae stop (1–2 hourly; 25min; ¥240), then a 10min walk

For centuries, the castle of Tomigusuku-jō has stood on the low hills looking north over Naha. During the Pacific War, the spot was chosen for the headquarters of the Japanese navy, but, instead of using the old fortifications, they tunnelled 20m down into the soft limestone. The complex, consisting of Rear Admiral Ōta's command room and various operations rooms, is now preserved as the **Underground Naval Headquarters**. Inside, there are a few photos of the 1945 battle, but little else to see beyond holes gouged in the plaster walls; the cavities are said to be where Ōta and 175 of his men killed themselves with hand grenades on June 13 as the Americans closed in. Beside the tunnel entrance, there's a small museum and a monument to the four thousand Japanese troops who died in this area.

Himeyuri-no-tō

ひめゆりの塔 • 671-1 Ihara • Museum daily 9am–5pm • ¥300 • Bus #33 from Naha or naval headquarters to Itoman (1–2 hourly; 40min; ¥370), then #108 (runs mostly in morning and late afternoon; 20min; ¥200)

Heading south down the coast from the Underground Naval Headquarters, Highway 331 passes through **Itoman** town (糸満) and then cuts inland across the peninsula to **Himeyuri-no-tō**, a deeply moving war memorial dedicated to more than two hundred schoolgirls and their teachers who committed suicide here in a shallow cave.

The nearby **museum** describes in Japanese (though there are detailed English leaflets) how the high-school students, like many others on Okinawa, were conscripted as trainee nurses by the Japanese army in the spring of 1945. As the fighting became more desperate, the girls were sent to a field hospital, gradually retreating south from cave to cave, and were then abandoned altogether as the Japanese army disintegrated. Terrified that they would be raped and tortured by the Americans, the women and girls killed themselves rather than be captured.

Peace Memorial Hall

平和記念堂 • Heiwakinen Park, Itoman • Daily 9am–5.30pm (winter till 5pm) • ¥500 • Bus #82 from Itoman (9 daily; 30min; ¥220)

The final battle for Okinawa took place on **Mabuni Hill** (摩文仁の丘), on the island's southeast coast. The site is now occupied by a cemetery and park containing monuments (the "Cornerstone of Peace") to the more than 200,000 troops – both Japanese and American – and civilians who died on the islands during the war. A white tower crowns the **Peace Memorial Hall**, which contains a 12m-high lacquered Buddha.

11

11

THE AMERICAN QUESTION

Twenty percent of Okinawa-Hontō and a small number of outer islands are covered by **American military bases**, employing 27,000 American military personnel. This in itself has fuelled local anger, but what rankles most is that Okinawa makes up less than one percent of the Japanese landmass, yet contains 75 percent of the country's American bases. The issue is, however, far from black and white for the islanders, since the bases provide thousands of jobs and contribute vast sums to the local economy – rather important, given that Okinawa remains the poorest of Japan's prefectures. In addition, many younger Okinawans relish the peculiar hybrid cultural atmosphere that the large number of foreigners brings to the islands.

Opinion of the bases, both local and national, has yo-yoed in the past couple of decades. A 1995 poll revealed a majority of Okinawans in favour of a continued American presence, but with a more even distribution throughout Japan. At that time, only twenty percent of the population wanted a complete withdrawal, but by 1996 the figure had increased to a convincing ninety percent – partially the result of an incident that took place between the two polls, in which a twelve-year-old schoolgirl was raped by three American servicemen. Mass protests against American military presence were the inevitable result.

Manoeuvrings since then have been largely political in nature, and focused on **Futenma**, a large US Marine Corps air base just northeast of Naha. After years of half-hearted relocation plans, in 2009, **Hatoyama Yukio** was elected Prime Minister on a campaign promise to move the base outside Japan as the first step in a systematic removal of the American military presence. However, torn between Okinawa and Washington, Hatoyama reneged on his promise, and resigned just eight months after taking office. At the time of writing, a decision had still not been made; regardless of what happens with Futenma, the American issue is likely to rumble on for some time.

Okinawa Prefecture Peace Memorial Museum

沖縄県立平和記念資料館, Okinawa Kenritsu Heiwa Kinen Shiryōkan • 614-1 Mabuni, Heiwakinen Park, Itoman • Tues–Sun 9am–5pm, winter till 4.30pm • ¥300 • ⦿ www.peace-museum.pref.okinawa.jp • Bus #82 from Itoman (9 daily; 30min; ¥220)

You'll learn plenty (though not the full story) about the Battle of Okinawa if you visit the **Okinawa Prefecture Peace Memorial Museum**, very close to the Peace Memorial Hall, which has full English translations throughout. This interesting museum, planned under the anti-establishment regime of Governor Ōta, but completed by the more conservative Governor Inamine, doesn't shirk the uncomfortable fact that Japanese soldiers ruthlessly killed Okinawan civilians. Generally, however, the whole build-up to the war is treated in the usual euphemistic way, and the exhibition ends on an upbeat note with displays on the postwar history of Okinawa to the present day.

Okinawa World

おきなわワールド • 1336 Tamagusuku • Daily 9am–6pm, Eisā dances 10.30am, 12.30, 2.30 & 4pm, Snake show 11am, noon, 2, 3.30 & 4.30pm • Day pass ¥1600, village and cave ¥1200, village and snake exhibit ¥1100; craft workshops additional ¥100–200 • ☎ 098 949 7421 • Bus #83 or #54 from Naha (8 daily; 1hr; ¥490), or #82 from Itoman (9 daily; 30min; ¥220)

Okinawa World is a quirky "village" showcasing local crafts and culture, including *bingata* dyeing, *awamori* brewing and performances of Eisā dances. It's built over an 890m-long cave with an impressive array of rock formations along an underground river, but the most popular attraction is the **Habu Park**, where you can learn about the Okinawan venomous snake and pose for the cameras with a python wrapped around your shoulders. You can also try your hand at the various local crafts.

Komaka-jima

コマカ島 • Bus #38 to Chinen from Naha; speedboats run 9am–5pm from the Chinen Kaiyō Leisure Centre (知念海洋レジャーセンター) in Chinen village (知念村) to the island (every 30min; ¥2500 return)

If you just want to chill out, head to tiny **Komaka-jima**, 3km east of the Chinen Peninsula. An uninhabited islet surrounded by golden sands and a coral reef, it's an

Ideal snorkelling spot; alternatively, it's pleasant to simply muck around on a pristine, tourist-free beach. Plenty choose to camp here overnight, though be sure to bring all your own supplies if you plan to stay.

Central Okinawa-Hontō

North of Naha, traffic on Highway 58 crawls up the coast of central Okinawa-Hontō between a strip of *McDonald's, Shakey's Pizza* and used car lots on one side, and neat rows of artillery on the other. This is army country, with huge tracts of land occupied by the American military (see box, p.766). Camps and bases extend along the coast as far north as the Maeda peninsula, where beach resorts take over. You can avoid the coastal strip by taking the expressway or Highway 330 up the island's less crowded centre past Okinawa City – this is the best way to reach the north of the island quickly. A bizarre mix of American and Japanese life, Okinawa City is the region's main urban centre, but there's little reason to stop. North from here, though difficult to get to, is **Nakamura-ke** one of the few genuinely old buildings still standing on Okinawa-Hontō, and the nearby ruins of **Nakagusuku Castle** offer commanding views. On the district's northern fringes lies **Ryūkyū-mura**, a quieter, more interesting culture village than Okinawa World (see opposite).

11

Kita-Nakagusuku

北中城 • Bus from Naha to Okinawa City, getting off at Futenma junction, then bus #59 (hourly; 15min; ¥140) to the Nakamura-ke turning; a taxi from Futenma costs ¥1500 each way

About 10km north of Naha, Highway 330 skirts east of Futenma Airbase before hitting a major junction. A little further north, a road cuts east through the hills to **KITA-NAKAGUSUKU** village where, in the early fifteenth century, Nakamura Gashi served as a teacher to a local lord, Gosamaru.

Nakamura-ke

中村家 • 106 Ogusuku • Daily 9.30am–5.30pm • ¥300, including tea • ⓦ nakamura-ke.net

In the early eighteenth century, after a rocky patch, one of Gashi's descendants was appointed village leader and started building his family's large, beautifully solid residence, **Nakamura-ke**. Protected by limestone walls, a thick belt of trees and a growling *shiisā* perched on the red-tile roof, the house is typical of a wealthy landowner's residence, with its barns, a lovely grain store and the inevitable rows of pigsties. Inside, there are a few family heirlooms, and the enterprising owners have set up a small shop and restaurant next door.

Nakagusuku-jō

中城跡 • 503 Kitanakagusuku • Daily 8.30am–5pm (May–Sept till 6pm) • ¥400 • ☎ 098 935 5719, ⓦ nakagusuku-jo.jp/er

If you're in Kita-Nakagusuku, be sure to walk five minutes west – here, limestone cliffs merge into the crumbling walls of **Nakagusuku-jō**, designated a World Heritage Site in 2000. These impressive fortifications, consisting of six citadels on a spectacular promontory, were originally built in the early fifteenth century by Lord Gosamaru. However, they weren't enough to withstand his rival, Lord Amawari, who ransacked the castle in 1458 and then abandoned the site. Nowadays you can walk through the grassy, tree-filled park and scramble among the ruins to admire the views clear across the island. Taxis usually hang around the castle entrance to whisk visitors back down to Futenma.

Ryūkyū-mura

琉球村 • 1130 Yamada • Daily 8.30am–5.30pm • ¥840 • ⓦ ryukyumura.co.jp • Bus #120 or #20 from Naha (every 15–20min; 1hr 20min; ¥970); from Okinawa City, bus #62 to Kadena (every 15–30min; 30min; ¥400), then the #120 northbound

The final sight in Okinawa-Hontō's central region lies on the west coast, where **Ryūkyū-mura** preserves several old Okinawa farmhouses brought from all over the islands and reassembled here to showcase the remnants of Ryūkyū culture. Though some will find it too touristy, the village provides a hint of what Okinawa was like before the war. In addition to performances of Eisā dances and traditional music, you can see people weaving, dyeing textiles and milling sugar cane for molasses – try the freshly fried local doughnuts.

ACCOMMODATION

Maeda Misaki Divers House 真栄田岬ダイバーズハ ウス 357 Yamada, Onna village ☎098 965 6459; ⓦmaedamisaki.com. A 15min walk northwest of Ryūkyū-mura, this is a great place to stay, particularly if you've come to Okinawa to dive (see p.756). The building – an old youth hostel – is a bit run-down, but it's in a

quiet location, with walks along the cliffs and down to the white, sweeping curve of Moon Beach. Accommodation is in bunk beds, and they do good meals. The nearest bus stop is Kuraha, on bus route #120, from where the hostel is a 10min walk northwest. Dorm **¥2000**

ACTIVITIES

Diving and cycling The *Maeda Misaki Divers House* run diving trips, starting from ¥9500 for an introductory dive, including all equipment. Five-day PADI courses are ¥51,000, accommodation included. They also rent out bikes for ¥1000 per day.

Northern Okinawa-Hontō

North of Okinawa-Hontō's pinched waist, the scenery begins to improve, as classy resort hotels line the western beaches. Bleached-white, coral-fringed Moon Beach merges into Tiger Beach after which there's the rocky, wild Onna promontory before you rejoin the sands at Manza and up through Imbu Beach. Beyond this strip, **northern Okinawa-Hontō**'s only major settlement, **Nago**, sits at the base of the knobbly **Motobu peninsula**. A generally quiet, workaday place, there's not a lot to see in Nago, but the small city makes a good base for exploring the region's mountainous north and visiting the impressive **Okinawa Churaumi Aquarium** at the far western tip of the peninsula. The district boasts the island's most attractive scenery, particularly around **Hedo Misaki**, the northern cape, and on through sleepy **Oku** village down the rugged northeast coast. It's possible to travel up the west coast by slow local bus, but after Oku you're on your own.

Nago
名護

Apart from weekends, when off-duty soldiers come up from the bases, **NAGO** sees few foreigners. If the proposed relocation of the Futenma base goes ahead (see box, p.766) all this will change, but for the moment Nago is a slow-moving, fairly pleasant city – more a large town – best known for its huge **banyan tree** and a spectacular display of **spring cherry blossoms**. Its other sights consist of a marginally interesting local museum and views from the former castle hill.

Nago curves round a south-facing bay. Highway 58 runs along the seafront and then turns north again on the west side of town, while behind the harbour a road strikes inland to the central **Nago crossroads**, where it cuts across the city's main shopping street. There's little to actually see in the area, bar nearby **Nago Castle Hill**; nothing remains of the castle, but it does boast lovely views over Nago bay.

Busena Resort Underwater Observatory
ブセナ海中公園, Busena Kaichi Kōen • 1808 Kise • Daily 9am–6pm • ¥1000

Some 10km southeast of Nago, at the tip of the promontory occupied by the *Busena Terrace Beach Resort* (see p.770), there's an **Underwater Observatory** owned and operated by the hotel. It's a good way to see some of the area's marine life, if you're not going diving; though not a patch on Ocean Expo Park (see p.770), it's markedly less busy, and the location is almost as spectacular.

By bus Arriving by bus (including the #111 from Naha), most services stop near Nago's central crossing before terminating at the bus terminal on the main highway to the west of town. However, some stop on the seafront, notably the Express Bus from Naha Airport, via Naha Bus Terminal (hourly; 2hr; ¥2000), which ends up outside Nago's Lego-block City Hall, roughly 500m west of the central crossroads.

Tourist information You'll find the tourist informatic office (Mon–Fri 8.30am–5.30pm, Sat & Sun 10am–5pr ☎ 0980 53 7755) in Nago City Hall (1-1-1 Minato) whic has English-language maps and pamphlets on the area.
Services The Ryūkyū Bank, just north of the centr junction, can exchange dollar and sterling cash ar travellers' cheques, and there's a small post office with a ATM a couple of blocks to the west.

ACCOMMODATION

Busena Terrace Resort ブセナテラスリゾート 1808 Kise ☎ 0980 51 1333, ⓦ terrace.co.jp. Some way south of Nago, and still proudly displaying evidence of hosting the G8 Summit in 2000, this resort has simple but tastefully designed rooms, charming staff and impressive facilities, including six restaurants, an enormous landscaped pool and a pleasant beach. If you want to see what's going on under the waves, you can visit the Busena Resor Underwater Observatory (see p.768). **¥50,000**
Hotel Tōwa ホテル東和 1-13-10 Ohigashi ☎ 0980 5 3793. This reasonably priced hotel, situated in th backstreets northeast of Nago crossroads, offers amiabl service and surprisingly large rooms for the price. Walk eas along the main street and take the second left. **¥5550**

EATING AND DRINKING

Akachōchin 赤提灯 1-6-9 Ohigashi. Head down towards the harbour from *Hotel Tōwa* and you can't miss the cheerful red lanterns of this lively *izakaya* offering cheap, filling food on the far side of the shopping street. You'll fill up for under ¥2000. Daily 5pm–1am.

Yamabuki 山吹 1-7-19 Ohigashi ☎ 0980 52 2143. An upmarket restaurant in a grey, modern building one block eas of *Hotel Tōwa*, where they serve an Okinawa set mea *champurū* (¥800) and other local dishes. Prices are reasonable and there's a picture menu. Mon–Sat 11am–10pm.

Ocean Expo Park

海洋博公園, Kaiyō Haku-kōen • 424 Ishikawa • Daily 8am–7.30pm; Oceanic Culture Museum closed for renovations at time of writing • Electric bus day ticket ¥200, one ride ¥100 • Oceanic Culture Museum ¥170; Tropical Dream Centre ¥670 • ⓦ oki-park-jp • Bus #111 from Naha to Nago (2hr), then #65, #66 or #70 (1hr)

Sitting pretty on the northwestern tip of the hilly, mushroom-shaped Motobu peninsula, the **Ocean Expo Park** is up there with Okinawa's most famous attractions. The majority of visitors race to the fantastic, world-famous **aquarium** (see below) and head straight back to Naha, but the sprawling park boasts umpteen other attractions to help you make the most of the long trip here (and it is a long trip). These include dolphin shows, an ocean nursery, a manatee tank (if you haven't come across these creatures before, be prepared for some strange sights) and a good beach at the north end. Other minor highlights include an **Oceanic Culture Museum**, whcih contains a vast collection of boats and artefacts from Southeast Asia and the South Pacific, though it was closed for renovation at the time of writing; and the **Tropical Dream Centre**, containing two thousand types of orchids and flowers. All of the above are connected by electric bus.

Okinawa Churaumi Aquarium

沖縄美ら海水族館, Okinawa Churaumi Suizokukan • Daily 8.30am–6.30pm (March–Sept till 8pm) • ¥1800

The highlight of the park is the **Okinawa Churaumi Aquarium**, a spectacular facility showcasing the marine life of the Kuroshio Current. The main tank holds 7500 tonnes of water and is home to several whale sharks, the largest sharks in the world; there are plenty of manta ray here too, and the aquarium is justly proud of the fact that four have actually been born here. When the place opened in 2002, the glass panel at its front was the largest in the world, at a whopping 22.5m in length; though since surpassed by one in a Dubai shopping mall, the cinema-scope view will still hold you entranced, and it's de rigueur to step back from the action and take a photo of tiny humans silhouetted against a blue backdrop of giant sea beasts. Most explanations are in English, and there's an informative section on sharks that dispels many myths about these extraordinary creatures.

ACCOMMODATION

Beach Rock Village ☎0980 56 1126, ⓦshimapro om. A little artsy gem about 15km east of the park. Accommodation here is in tents, with rates depending upon your required level of luxury, while you can also drop by for coffee or tea, served on balconies with commanding views. Superb. **¥690–6000** per person

Chisun Resort Churaumi チサンリーゾト沖縄美ら海 ☎0980 48 3631, ⓦsolarehotels.com. This swanky hotel is ideally located for the aquarium, which is right next door. The decor in the rooms is a wee bit cheesy, but all of them have a sea view, and there's a fantastic on-site pool to splash around in. **¥16,000**

Hiji Ōtaki

比地大滝 • Daily sunrise–3.30pm • Trail ¥200

North of Nago, Highway 58 hugs the mountainside as the cliffs rise higher, and the only settlements are a few weather-beaten villages in sheltered coves. At the village of Kunigami (国頭), head inland along the road that follows the river to reach the start of the walk to **Hiji Ōtaki**, a picturesque 26m waterfall. About halfway along the 1.5km-long trail, you'll cross a 17m suspension bridge, with lovely views across the river; further up and at the falls themselves there are excellent swimming spots.

ACCOMMODATION

Hiji Ōtaki Campsite 比地大滝キャンプ 781-1 Kunigami ☎0980 41 3636. This is a rather beautiful campsite at the beginning of the Hiji Ōtaki walking trail. It

has good washing and cooking facilities, plus a small restaurant-cum-shop; it's possible to rent tents if you haven't brought your own. **¥2000** per person

Hedo Misaki

辺戸岬 • Bus #67 from Nago to Hentona (辺土名; 1–2 hourly; 1hr; ¥880), then the special "Oku" bus to Hedo Misaki Iriguchi (4 daily; 30min; ¥670) and a 20min walk

From Kunigami, it's another 20km to Okinawa-Hontō's northern cape, **Hedo Misaki**. The unsightly restaurant block and cigarette butts aside, this is a good spot to stretch your legs and wander over the headland's dimpled limestone rocks while the waves pound the cliffs below. On clear days, you can see northerly Yoron-tō, the first island in Kagoshima Prefecture, and lumpy Iheya-jima to the west, over a churning sea where the currents sweeping round Okinawa collide.

Oku

奥 • Take bus #67 from Nago to Hentona (辺土名; 1–2 hourly; 1hr; ¥880), then the special "Oku" bus the rest of the way (4 daily; 50min; ¥830)

About 8km east of Hedo Misaki, the bus terminates in a large fishing village, **OKU**, which features an attractive array of traditional Okinawan houses with low, tiled roofs. A quiet, seemingly deserted place, there's nothing to do but wander the lanes and peer at the neat, walled gardens protected to the seaward side by thick stands of trees. In January and February the surrounding hills are clothed in bright cherry blossoms – and in early April you can feast on the ripened fruit.

ACCOMMODATION

Minshuku Miyagi 民宿みやぎ ☎0930 41 8383. Most of Oku's inhabitants are elderly, but one young couple run this delightful minshuku beside the river mouth; there are only three rooms – two tatami and one Western – so make

sure you book early. From the bus terminus, outside the wonderful village shop, the minshuku's red roof is clearly visible beside the bridge, a few minutes' walk down a sandy track. Rates include two meals. **¥10,500**

Tanagāgumui and Kesaji mangrove forest

タナガーグムイ • 慶佐次マングローブ

Route 70 snakes its way along the east coast, through forests and pineapple groves with the occasional sea view, all of which makes for a pleasant drive. There are few sights here, but one place to aim for is **Tanagāgumui**, a gorgeous swimming hole and small waterfall in a glade reached by a perilous scramble down a 200m clay slope. There are ropes strung down the drop to help, but you still need to be sure-footed.

Further south, just beyond Tairawan Bay, is the **Kesaji mangrove forest**, where a boardwalk runs alongside the river. This is a good spot to arrange a kayak trip – ask at the tourist offices in Naha (see p.762).

Kerama Islands

慶良間諸島, Kerama Shotō

The **KERAMA ISLANDS** are the closest group to Naha, lying some 30km offshore. A knot of three large, inhabited islands and numerous pinpricks of sand and coral, the Keramas offer some of the most beautiful and unspoilt beaches in Okinawa and superb diving among the offshore reefs. **Zamami-jima** is a sleepy place home to mere hundreds of people, yet has recently become hugely popular with international tourists thanks to the recent boom in wintertime whale-watching, as well as the demise of ferries heading from Naha to Miyako and the Yaeyamas – many travellers are now choosing the Keramas over costly flights south

Zamami-jima

座間味島

A whale statue greets ferries pulling in to **Zamami-jima**'s harbour, behind which lies the tiny village of **ZAMAMI** (座間味村), the only settlement of any size on the island, with seven hundred inhabitants out of a total population of one thousand. They speak their own dialect and maintain a fierce rivalry with the people of the much larger island of Tokashiki-jima, a couple of kilometres away to the east. A fine place to get away from i all, Zamami-jima has spectacular **beaches**, both on the island itself or a short boat ride away. You can **dive** year-round, but the best time to visit is in autumn, when most of the beach bums have gone, but the whale-watchers are yet to appear; the water stays warm enough for swimming and snorkelling well into December.

Even allowing for stops, it only takes a couple of hours to explore every road on Zamami, after which there's nothing to do but head to the beach. Roughly 1km southeast of the village, **Furuzamami beach** (古座間味浜) is the best on the island, with excellent coral and shoals of multicoloured fish. In season, you can rent snorkels at the small shop, and there's also a restaurant and showers. As for diving, there are dozens of places offering trips and courses, but *Joy Joy* (see p.774) in Zamami are recommended for their friendly, reliable service.

Outer islands

The beaches on Zamami-jima are great, but things get even better on the tiny **outer islands**, such as **Gahi-jima** (嘉比島) and **Agenashiku-jima** (安慶名敷島), just south of

---

DOGS AND DOLPHINS

Zamami-jima has sourced much of its fame from the animal kingdom. The millions of fish enjoyed by divers (and diners at local restaurants) are an obvious draw, but dogs and whales have also made their mark. Historically, **whaling** was an important part of the local economy, but in the 1960s the whales disappeared and the industry died. Then, towards the end of the last century, the **humpbacks** started coming back to their winter breeding grounds – which the locals have been quick to exploit, though this time for tourism rather than hunting (see box opposite). In addition, most young Japanese associate the Keramas with the cutesy 1988 film **I Want to See Marilyn**. Based on a true story, it tells of a romance between two dogs on neighbouring islands: Shiro on Aka-jima, and Marilyn some 3km away on Zamami. They met when Shiro travelled to Zamami in his owner's boat, but the passion was such that he started swimming over every day to rendezvous with Marilyn on Zamami's Ama beach – or so the story goes. So enduring is this story that the pup's purported route is often featured on local maps.

WHALE-WATCHING

From late January through to April, Zamami is Okinawa's main centre for **whale-watching**. The Whale-Watching Association (☎ 098 896 4141, ⓦ www.vill.zamami.okinawa.jp) arranges **boat trips** from Zamami port every day at 10.30am and 12.30pm depending on the weather (2hr 30min; ¥5000). Reservations are essential, and you should bring rain gear, as you'll be out in the open sea. With a good pair of binoculars, you can even spot humpbacks spouting and cavorting off Zamami's north coast. There's a special **whale observatory** about 3.5km northwest of Zamami village, one of several lookout points scattered round the cliffs and on the island's highest peak, **Takatsuki-yama**.

Zamami. In summer, small boats take day-trippers out to these islands (see below); in addition, dozens of operators in Zamami offer trips and courses here (see below). There are also passenger services from Zamami to **Aka-jima** (阿嘉島), which has some spectacular beaches on its periphery and plentiful accommodation (see below); if you really want to get away from it all, bring along a bike and cycle over the bridge to **Geruma-jima** (慶留間島), home to yet more pristine stretches of sand.

ARRIVAL AND DEPARTURE　　　　　　　　　　　　　　　　KERAMA ISLANDS

By ferry The islands are served by ferry from Naha's Tomari Port. The high-speed Queen Zamami departs 2–3 times daily fo Zamami, calling at Aka-jima either on the outward or return journey (50min–1hr 15min; ¥3140 one-way/¥5970 return; ☎ 098 868 4567); it's best to reserve tickets at least a day ahead of time for these journeys. Alternatively, there's the slower Ferry Zamami (2hr 15min; ¥2120 one-way/¥4030 return; ☎ 098 868 4567) which leaves Naha at 10am and returns at 2pm;

this stops at Aka-jima too, and tickets almost never sell out. In bad weather, which is quite often, everyone gets bundled onto the slow services; cancellations, when they do take place, are announced daily at 8am (just ask at your accommodation).

By plane You may well see Kerama Airport on local maps. It does exist, on Fukaji-jima, an island connected to Geruma-jima, which is itself connected to Aka-jima; however, there have been no scheduled passenger services since 2006.

INFORMATION AND ACTIVITIES

Tourist information As you come off the ferry in Zamami, the first buildings you pass contain the ferry booking office; the tourist information office (daily 9am–5pm; ☎ 098 987 2277); and the Whale-Watching Association office. Be sure to pick up an English map of the island from the tourist office; all places to sleep and eat in town are on this, which is handy when local addresses are next to useless.

Diving There are dozens of operators around Zamami, but *Joy Joy* (see p.774) is recommended for its

knowledgeable service. Prices tend to be the same across the village; figure on ¥3000 for a simple snorkelling trip, plus ¥1000 for equipment rental.

Kayaking The Kerama Kayak Centre (☎ 098 868 4677), operating from a small office near *Cat's Inn*, offers kayaking excursions around the Zamami area, with prices heavily dependent on group size, trip duration and where you want to go.

Boat trips Operators around Zamami offer banana boat (¥1500) or glass-bottomed-boat rides (¥2000).

GETTING AROUND

By car Zamami Rent-a-Car (daily 9am–6pm; ☎ 098 987 3250) operate from the sandy lanes on the village's eastern edge; they only have a few vehicles, so it's good to reserve in advance.

By ferry In summer (June to mid-Sept) there are a few local services from Zamami to the uninhabited islets of Gahi-jima and Agenashiku-jima, just to the south; at these times they cost ¥1500 return, but out of season

you'll have to charter your own boat. There are also year-round passenger services from Zamami to Aka-jima for ¥300 each way.

By bike and moped There are plenty of places from which to hire a bike, but the main rental depot is in the very centre of Zamami, just along from the supermarket. It's ¥500 for an hour, or ¥2000 for the day. The same place rents mopeds for ¥1500 for an hour, or ¥4500 for the day.

ACCOMMODATION

Accommodation on Zamami comprises a reasonable choice of family-run minshuku with a few simple Japanese- and Western-style rooms. It's wise to book ahead at any time of year. Rates listed below include meals, though at all places you

can opt to go without for a (sometimes far lower) price. It's also possible to stay on Aka-jima, though it's a far le
interesting base than Zamami.

ZAMAMI

Joy Joy ジョイジョイ 434-2 Zamami ☎ 098 987 2445, ⌨ keramajoyjoy.com. Neat little place on the northwest edge of the village, with a handful of decent rooms and a small garden. They're also the people to go to if you're looking for a diving trip (see p.773). **¥10,500**

Shirahama Islands Resort シラハマアイランズリゾート 32 Zamami ☎ 098 987 2915. On the road out to Furuzamami, this is Zamami's biggest, smartest hotel. You'll chop a fair bit from the rates stipulated here if you go without meals, which are decent but not quite worth the extra fee. **¥18,000**

Okinawa Resort 沖縄リゾート 415 Zamami

☎ 098 987 2736, ⌨ bit.ly/LH6jpn. Just down the roa from *Joy Joy*, this is probably the friendliest place in th village, presided over by a delightful local couple who'll b more than willing to assist with diving trips. They offe some good-value rooms, as well as comfy chalet-styl accommodation. **¥7600**

Zamami Campsite 座間味キャンプ ☎ 098 987 3259 A 20min walk east along the coast road, this campsit offers several camping pitches and, for those who woul rather a sturdier roof over their head, some pleasing six berth cabins. You can rent tents (¥500) and othe equipment such as sleeping bags and BBQ sets. Campin **¥300** per person

EATING

It's generally best to arrange **meals** at your accommodation, though Zamami does have a couple of half-decent places to eat, as well as a well-stocked supermarket (daily 7am–10pm). Note that opening times can vary; those listed here should not be taken as gospel.

ZAMAMI

Cat's Inn キャッツイン 125 Zamami ☎ 098 987 2860. The only reliable place in the village for your morning coffee (from ¥350), with some nice outdoor seating and friendly service. Daily 11am–6pm.

La Toquee ラとけー 225 Zamami ☎ 098 987 3558. On the second floor opposite the bike rental depot, this is a smart place to eat local dishes such as taco rice (¥750) and Okinawa soba (¥700). It comes into its own in the evening, however, when a range of beer and spirits make this the village's best place to drink. 6pm–midnight, closed Tues.

Marumiya まるみや 432-2 Zamami ☎ 098 987 3166 Next door to *Joy Joy* (see above), this is the most reliable restaurant in town. They do a ¥680 lunch special, typically focusing on Japanese staples or Okinawan specialities, as well as reasonable evening meals. 11.30am–2pm & 6–11pm, closed Wed.

Urizun うりずん 31-3 Zamami ☎ 098 987 2432. Opposite the *Shirahama Islands Resort* (see above), this is the most appealing of a clutch of *izakaya*, with a sort of end-of-the-line atmosphere and cold draught beer. Their food is nice and cheap, too; try the *gōya champurū* (¥500). 11.30am–2pm & 6–11pm, closed Wed.

Miyako Islands

One has to feel sorry for the **MIYAKO ISLANDS**. Centred around **Miyako-jima**, the main island of the chain, this small cluster boasts some of the best beaches in all Japan, but these are graced by precious few international visitors. Long overshadowed by Zamami-jima and the Yaeyama group, its appeal took another knock with the closure of ferry services to Naha and Ishigaki, making Miyako an expensive add-on to an Okinawan tour. However, it remains a favourite with mainland Japanese, some of whom stay for weeks or months on end, chalking off beach after beach and dive after dive.

Miyako-jima

宮古島

The flat, triangular-shaped island of **Miyako-jima** is roughly 35km from tip to tip – its most immediately notable aspect is field after field of sugar cane. **HIRARA** (平良), the main town, lies on the island's northwest coast, from where roads fan out through the fields.

It won't take long to tick off Hirara's paltry collection of sights before scooting off to the beaches, and few bother. Most appealing is the newly tarted-up **Miyako Traditional Arts and Crafts Centre** (宮古伝統工芸品研究センター Miyako Dentō Kōgeihin Kenkyū Sentā; 3 Nishizato; Mon–Sat 9am–6pm; free), where you can watch women weaving the delicate Miyako-jōfu fabric, designated an Important Intangible Cultural Asset (see Okinawan souvenirs box, p.764).

Beaches

Hirara has its own beach, **Painagama** (パイナガマ浜), immediately south of the harbour, but there are much better ones around the island. Top of the list is **Maehama** (前浜), around 10km south of Hirara, a long and remarkably pristine strip of soft white sand that is hailed as Japan's best beach. Naturally, a prime chunk of it has been requisitioned by the swanky *Miyako-jima Tōkyū Resort* (see p.777).

The east coast

Way out by Miyako's eastern corner, and reached by a steep, twisting road from Route 390, is **Boragawa beach** (保良川浜). It's a good spot for snorkelling and kayaking, and equipment for both is available from the attractive beachside complex that includes a refreshment hut and a fresh-water swimming pool.

At the very eastern point of the island lies beautiful **Higashi Henna-zaki** (東平安名崎), a 2km-long peninsula renowned for its wild flowers and panoramic views. Head out to the lighthouse at the very tip (daily 9am–4.30pm; ¥150), where you can climb to the top and check out the views.

11

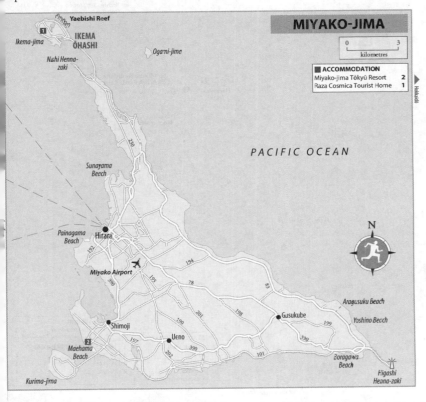

MIYAKO-JIMA

0   3
kilometres

■ ACCOMMODATION
Miyako-Jima Tōkyū Resort   2
Raza Cosmica Tourist Home   1

Yaebishi Reef
Ikema-jima
IKEMA
ŌHASHI
Ogami-jima
Nishi Henna-zaki

Hokkaido

PACIFIC OCEAN

Sunayama Beach

Painagama Beach
Hirara

Miyako Airport

N

Aragusuku Beach

Gusukube
Yoshino Beach

Shimoji
Ueno

Maehama Beach

Boragawa Beach

Kurima-jima

Higashi Heana-zaki

As you heading north up the east side of the island, duck off the coastal road to find the quiet beaches at **Yoshino** (吉野) and **Aragusuku** (新城), both excellent snorkelling spots with corals and a plethora of tropical fish.

Sunayama

砂山浜 • 2.5km north of Hirara • Accessed via a steep winding path through trees and over a large sand dune

On the northwestern corner of the island is another lovely beach, **Sunayama**, which some find the best of the lot. The beach, when you first catch sight of it, looks nothing short of heavenly. Western-facing, it's a good spot to come for sunset, which at certain times of year can be viewed through a naturally eroded stone arch.

Ikema-jima

池間島 • Glass boat rides 50min • ¥2000

At the far north of Miyako, a bridge connects the island with tiny **Ikema-jima**. Ikema has a lazy fishing port and more deserted beaches and good coral reefs, including the extensive Yaebishi reef, which is exposed annually during the low spring tides. You can take a glass-boat tour out there, too. The best reason for detouring here, however, is the *Raza Cosmica Tourist Home* (see opposite).

11

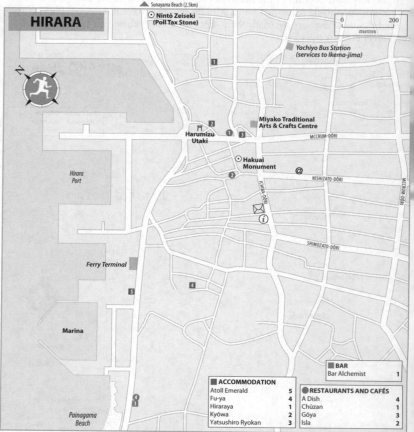

HIRARA

ARRIVAL AND DEPARTURE

By plane Most flights to Miyako come from Naha, though there are also a few direct services from the mainland. From Miyako Airport, there are only three buses per day into the main town of Hirara, meaning that you'll most likely have to get a taxi (¥1500), as it's too far to walk. However, if you arrange motorbike or scooter hire at the airport, the agents will ferry you to your hotel in Hirara for free first, before you pick up your chosen mode of transport.

Destinations Ishigaki (2 daily; 30min); Naha (1–2 hourly; 45min); Osaka Kansai (1 daily; 1hr 55min); Tokyo (2 daily; 2hr 35min).

By ferry It's important to note that there's currently no ferry service to Miyako-jima; the poor ferry terminal in Naha has to disappoint at least one foreign traveller every single day with this information. However, when planning your Okinawa trip it's certainly worth double-checking to see if services have resumed.

INFORMATION AND ACTIVITIES

Information There's a helpful information desk in the airport (daily 8am–5.30pm; ☎0980 72 0899).

Services An ATM accepting foreign cards is at Hirara's post office (Mon–Sat 8.45am–7pm, Sun 9am–5pm). Some local places also accept international card payments, but

it's still advisable to come with plenty of cash.

Diving Most hotels will be able to hook you up with a diver operator, though you could start off by contacting the *Good FellasClub* (☎0980 73 5483, ✉fellas@goodfellas.co.jp, ⓦgoodfellas.co.jp), just south of central Hirara.

11

GETTING AROUND

By bus In Hirara, irregular buses for the north of the island depart from Yachiyo bus station, a few blocks north of the Central Post Office, while buses south to Maehama and Higashi Henna-zaki leave from Miyako Kyoei bus station on

McCrum-dōri, around 1km east of the post office.

By car The airport has car-hire stands aplenty, and given the paucity of public transport this is by far the best way of getting to the beaches.

ACCOMMODATION

HIRARA

Atoll Emerald ホテルアトールエメラルド 108-7 Shimozato ☎0980 73 9800; map p.776. Right beside the ferry terminal, this upmarket option is the classiest place in downtown Hirara, with spacious rooms, a pool and a smart Japanese restaurant with waitresses in kimono. **¥18,000**

★ **Fu-ya** 風家 109-7 Shimozato ☎0980 75 4343; map p.776. Run by an impossibly cute family who have converted the ground floor of their house into a mini-hostel. They don't seem too concerned about turning a profit – they'll pick up from the airport for ¥500, let you in on their family dinner for the same price, and dorm beds are an absolute bargain. Superb. Dorm **¥1000**

Hiraraya ⓣららや 282-1 Higashinakasone ☎0980 75 3221; map p.776. Backpacker decadence – the bunk beds at this hostel are simply huge. Service is friendly and staff can help to organize trips, but the common areas may be too smoky for some. Dorm **¥2000**

Kyōwa ホテルキョウワ 7 Nishizato ☎0980 73 2288, ☎73 2285; map p.776. Tucked into a quiet area behind the Harumizu Utaki shrine, this hotel has a range of decent-value Western-style rooms. **¥9600**

Yatsushiro Ryokan 八城旅館 847-3 Shimojonaha ☎0980 72 1950, ☎73 1725; map p.776. This ryokan is nothing special, but solo travellers will find particularly good value in large tatami rooms featuring bathrooms. TV and a/c. Single **¥4000**

AROUND THE ISLAND

Miyako-jima Tōkyū Resort 宮古島東急リゾート 914 Shimoji ☎0980 75 2109, ⓦtokyuhotels.co.jp; map p.775. Top-class resort sitting pretty on delectable Maehama beach (see p.775, to which there's a free shuttle bus from the airport. Watersports enthusiasts won't be disappointed by the range of activities on offer. **¥34,000**

Raza Cosmica Tourist Home ラサコスミカツーリストホーム 309-1 Hiraramaezato ☎0980 75 2020; map p.775. There's a vaguely hippy feel to this delightful South Asian-themed adobe pension, perched above a secluded beach on Ikema-jima (see opposite). The five guest rooms are Western-style, rates include an organic vegetarian breakfast, and snorkelling equipment and bikes are available. It's popular, so booking well in advance is essential. **¥14,000**

EATING AND DRINKING

The best place to look for restaurants is in the streets immediately inland from the Hirara harbour, particularly Nishizato-dōri, which runs parallel to the main road, Highway 390, but two blocks west.

HIRARA

A Dish アディシュ 215-3 Shimozato ☎0980 72 7114; map p.776. The menu changes daily at this stylish and

relaxed restaurant 500m south of the ferry terminal. There's good pasta and fine thin-crust pizza for ¥800–1000, as well as local dishes with a contemporary spin. Tues–Sat

6pm–midnight, Sun 5–11pm.

Bar Alchemist バーアルケミスト 2F 215-3 Shimozato ☎090 4582 4278; map p.776. After finishing your meal at *A Dish* (see p.777), nip upstairs to this convivial bar, which is decorated with a telescope, piano and world globe. The owner organizes live events twice a month, including folk and classical music. Daily 6pm–2am.

Chūzan 中山 McCrum-dōri ☎0980 73 1959; map p.776. Authentic *izakaya*, specializing in fish and sushi as well as what they call "ethnic" food. A meal shouldn't cost more than ¥1000. Daily 4pm–midnight.

★**Gōya** 郷家 570-2 Nishizato ☎0980 74 2358; ma p.776. Friendly *izakaya* and *minyō* house further east alon Nishizato-dōri. Be warned – you may well end up dancin your way around the venue with the rest of the clientele 5.30pm–midnight, closed Thurs.

Isla イスラー 172 Nishizato ☎0980 74 3461; ma p.776. Hirara's obligatory reggae bar, a short stroll awa from the west end of Nishizato-dōri, is a cut above th average, conjuring an appropriately tropical vibe. Grea cocktails, weekly salsa nights and regular gigs make thi well worth a visit. Daily 8pm–5am.

Yaeyama Islands

八重山諸島, Yaeyama Shotō

Star-sand beaches to pad along, waterfalls tumbling down emerald mountains, and not a soldier in sight … it's no wonder that even Okinawans go misty-eyed when talking about the **YAEYAMA ISLANDS**. Japan finally fizzles out at this far-flung spray of semi-tropical islets, 430km south of Okinawa-Hontō and almost 3000km from northern Hokkaidō, and those lucky enough to make it this far are in for quite a finale. The bad news is that the Yaeyamas are no longer accessible by ferry, meaning that you'll have to take a flight from Naha or the mainland – but it's worth it, especially if you're into diving, hiking, kayaking or meeting "alternative" Japanese.

Most flights arrive at **Ishigaki-jima**, the most populous Yaeyama island by far. Travellers tend to base themselves here for convenience, but while Ishigaki has its charms, you'd be mad to come this far and not go that little bit further – a fifteen-minute ferry-ride away is tiny **Taketomi-jima**, essentially a freeze-frame of traditional Ryūkyū life, while a little further away is **Iriomote-jima**, almost entirely cloaked with jungle and about as wild as Japan gets. Even more remote are **Hateruma-jima**, to the south, and **Yonaguni-jima**, stuck out on its own between Ishigaki and Taiwan.

Ishigaki-jima 石垣島

Yaeyama life revolves around **Ishigaki-jima**, the islands' main transport hub and population centre. Most travellers base themselves here, making use of the excellent accommodation and dining options to be found in Ishigaki, the only Yaeyama settlement large enough to warrant description as a town. The rest of the island is a predominantly rural and mountainous landscape, fringed with rocky peninsulas, stunning beaches and easily accessible reefs, while its interior is scored with the gorgeous walls of hand-stacked stone which gave Ishigaki its name. Though the main town is nice enough, it may make you wonder why you came so far to enjoy yet more urban Japan; consider basing yourself up north in beautiful **Kabira Bay** instead.

Ishigaki town
石垣

ISHIGAKI is quite a nice little town; there are plenty of cool restaurants in the tight lattice of streets north of the bus and ferry terminals, as well as most of the mod cons of mainland Japan. However, apart from hosting the Yaeyamas' best range of tourist facilities, there's not too much to actually see – after your umpteenth walk through the **covered arcades**, or along the scruffy **portside**, you might start to feel a tiny bit bored. Following the airport's recent eastward relocation, and considering the island's irregular bus connections, it's perhaps best used as a first or last base if you've a late flight in or early one out.

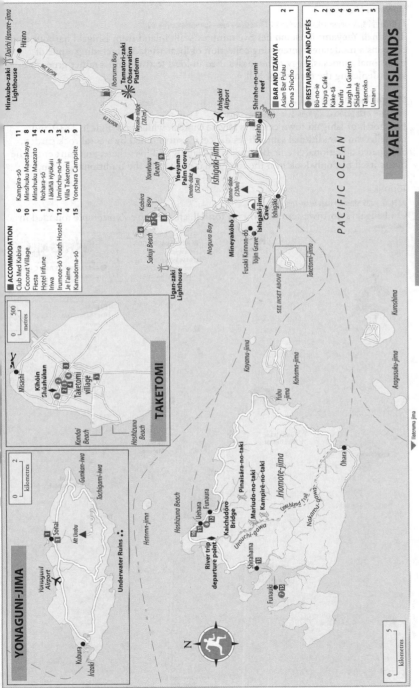

YAEYAMA ISLANDS

11

PACIFIC OCEAN

■ ACCOMMODATION

Club Med Kabira	6	Kampira-sō	11
Coconut Village	10	Minshuku Maetakaya	8
Fiesta	1	Minshuku Maezato	14
Hotel Irifune	1	Nohara-sō	2
Iriwa	7	Takana Ryōkan	3
Irumote-sō Youth Hostel	12	Uminchu-no-ie	13
Je t'aime	4	Villa Taketomi	5
Kamadoma-sō	15	Yonehara Campsite	9

■ BAR AND IZAKAYA

Asian Bar Pulau	2
Onna Shūcho	1

● RESTAURANTS AND CAFÉS

Bū-no-ie	7
Hoaya Café	2
Kake-tā	6
Kanifu	4
Laugh la Garden	3
Shidamē	1
Takenoko	5

TAKETOMI

Kōin Shūshūkan
Taketomi village
Kondai Beach
Hoshizuna Beach
Misashi

0 500 metres

YONAGUNI-JIMA

Yonaguni Airport
Sotai
Mt Urabu
Gunkan-iwa
Tachigami-iwa
Kubura
Irizaki
Underwater Ruins

0 2 kilometres

Hirakubo-zaki Lighthouse
Daichi Hanare-jima
Hirano
Ibaruma Bay
Tamatori-zaki Observation Platform
ROUTE 206
Nosoko-dáke (282m)
ROUTE 79
Ishigaki Airport
Shiraho-no-umi reef
Shiraho
Yaeyama Palm Grove
Omoto-dáke (525m)
Ishigaki-jima
Yonehara Beach
Kabira bay
Sukuji Beach
Nagura Bay
Banna-dáke (230m)
Mineyakōbo
Ishigaki-jima Cave
Fusaki Kannon-dō
Tōjin Grave
Ishigaki
Ugan-zaki Lighthouse

SEE INSET ABOVE

Taketomi-jima
Kuroshima
Kayama-jima
Kohama-jima
Yubu-jima
Aragusuku-jima
Hatoma-jima
Hoshizuna Beach
Funaura
Uehara
Pinaisāra-no-taki
Mariudo-no-taki
Kampire-no-taki
Kaichūdōro Bridge
Iriomote-jima
Cross Island Trail
Urauchi-gawa
Nakama-gawa
River trip departure point
Shirahama
Ōhara
Funauki

Hateruma-jima

N

0 5 kilometres

Yonaguni-jima (see inset top left)

Yaeyama Museum

八重山博物館, Yaeyama Hakubutsukan • 4-1 Tonoshiro • Tues–Sun 9am–5pm • ¥200

The small **Yaeyama Museum** lies five minutes' walk inland from Ishigaki harbour, and contains a moderately interesting collection of local artefacts, including a pile of traditional canoes, shaggy *shiisā* masks used in local festivals and a rather gruesome scroll depicting the tortures of hell.

Miyara Dunchi

宮良殿内 • 178 Okawa • Daily 9am–5pm; closed Tues • ¥200

Just north of Ishigaki town centre is **Miyara Dunchi**, which was built in 1819 and modelled on a traditional samurai residence; it's surrounded by a coral rock garden, designated a National Scenic Beauty. As the family still lives there, you can't enter the house itself but only look into the rooms that open onto the traditional garden.

Tōrin-ji

桃林寺 • 285 Ishigaki • Daily 9am–7pm • Free

On Ishigaki's northwestern outskirts is **Tōrin-ji**, an attractive Zen temple founded in

11

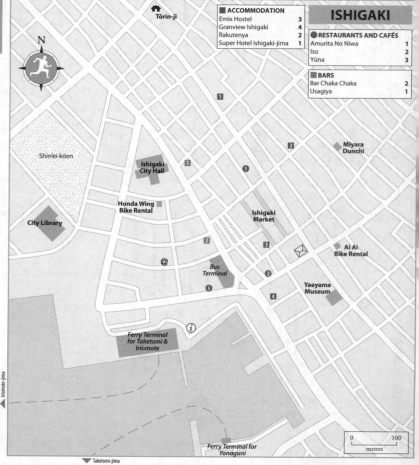

614. Meditation is still practised here, though you'll be lucky to see it. Interestingly, the temple's two Deva king statues (called *niōzo*) are now worshipped as the island's protectors.

Tōjin Grave
唐人墓

Around 2km northwest of Ishigaki town centre along the coastal road is the striking **Tōjin Grave**, or Tōjin-baka, a highly decorative monument erected in 1971 to the several hundred Chinese labourers who died off the shores of Ishigaki in 1852. Keep your eye out for a couple of colourful, sinuous Chinese dragons.

Fusaki Kannon-dō
冨崎観音堂・Fusaki・24hr・Free

Located close to the Tōjin Grave is the temple of **Fusaki Kannon-dō** which was originally built in 1701. It boasts good views of Taketomi and Iriomote from its hillside perch, though the paths around the temple are arrestingly beautiful too – shrouded by trees, some are lined with pretty stone lanterns.

Ugan-zaki Lighthouse
御神崎灯台, Uganzaki Tōdai

On the very northwestern tip of the island is the picturesque **Ugan-zaki Lighthouse**, or Ugan-zaki Tōdai, which commands an impressive view back across the island. Pack a picnic and enjoy it in peace here or at one of the secluded nearby beaches that are scattered with giant shells; the sunsets are often spectacular.

Kabira Bay
川平湾, Kabira-wan・Glass-bottom boat tours every 30min, 9am–5pm・¥1000

Locals and tourist literature will urge you to head straight to **KABIRA BAY**, or Kabira-wan, home of cultured black pearls and gorgeous emerald waters. Though a bit over-commercial in feel, it's still worth battling through the *omiyage* stands for superb views of the pearl farms and surrounding confetti of islands; with the place near-silent after the tourist hordes are safely tucked up back in Ishigaki town, it's almost up there with the best places to stay on the island. You can also head out on a glass-bottom boat tour for a fish-filled view, while north of the bay is **Sukuji Beach** (底地浜), one of the nicest on Ishigaki.

Yonehara beach and around
米原浜, Yonehara-hama

Ishigaki's most rewarding beach experience by far lies some 5km east of Kabira at **YONEHARA** (米原). Here you can wade out across a broad expanse of dead coral (make sure to wear foot protection), teeming with sea life, to the very edge of the reef, which drops off to the sea floor and is full of tropical fish. Be wary of jellyfish here, which can pack a potentially fatal sting. Snorkelling gear can be rented from shops on the main road (see p.782), and there's a good **campsite**, too (see p.783). You also won't fail to notice the colourfully painted giant *shīsā* statues outside *Yoneko Yaki Kōbō* (米子焼工房; daily 9am–6pm; free), a cottage industry factory and shop churning out the traditional Okinawan guardians in a range of cartoon-like styles.

Omoto-dake
於茂登岳

Behind Yonehara, Ishigaki's mountainous interior holds several **trekking** possibilities, including the hike up **Omoto-dake**; not far north of Yonehara is the turn-off to a grove of Yaeyama palms from where a trail runs up the slopes of the mountain to an observation platform.

Hirakubo-zaki and Tamatori-zaki Observation Platform

平久保岬・玉取崎展望台 • Infrequent buses #5 and #6 head up the east coast from Ishigaki bus terminal; they drop off at the foot of the hill at the Tamatori stop, before heading on to Hirakubo-zaki (you'll need to walk the rest of the way)

At **Ibaruma Bay**, Route 79 swings east to the opposite side of the island. At the fork you have a choice. Head north through a pastoral landscape and you'll eventually hit the pretty viewpoint of **Hirakubo-zaki**, the end of the line on Ishigaki-jima, punctuated by a dazzling white **lighthouse** overlooking the tiny island, Daichi Hanare-jima. Otherwise, turn south on Route 390 and take the turn-off for the **Tamatori-zaki Observation Platform**, or Tamatori-zaki Tembōdai. The views from here are splendid, and the landscaped grounds burst with crimson hibiscus blooms. Naturally, it's a favourite stop for tour buses.

Shiraho-no-umi

白保の海 • Boat trips from Shiraho around ¥2000

One of Ishigaki's main attractions lies off the southeast shore – **Shiraho-no-umi**, a patch of reef containing the rare Ao (blue) and Hama corals. The village of **Shiraho** (白保) has several minshuku where you can stay and arrange snorkelling boat trips at high tide.

11

ARRIVAL AND DEPARTURE

ISHIGAKI-JIMA

By plane Currently, the only way into the Yaeyamas is by plane. Ishigaki's sparkling new airport handles daily flights from Tokyo and a handful of other mainland cities, though far more arrive from Naha. Buses to Ishigaki town run every 20min or so (¥500), in fact, it's usually worth buying one of the island passes (see below).

Destinations Fukuoka (1 daily; 2hr); Kōbe (1 daily; 2hr 15min); Osaka Kansai (2 daily; 2hr 15min); Miyako (2 daily;

30min); Nagoya (1 daily; 2hr 40min); Naha (1–2 hourly, 1hr); Tokyo (3 daily; 3hr 15min); Yonaguni (2 daily; 30min)

By ferry The ferry terminal serving Taketomi-jima and Iriomote-jima is in the thick of things, just across the road from the bus terminal; a smaller wharf serving Yonaguni-jima is a 10min walk around the dock.

Destinations Ōhara, Iriomote-jima (every 30min; 45min); Uehara, Iriomote-jima (hourly; 50min); Yonaguni-jima (2 weekly; 4hr 30min).

INFORMATION AND ACTIVITIES

Tourist information There's a small information booth at the airport, though more useful are the staff at Hirata Tourism (daily 7.30am–6pm; ☎ 0980 82 6711, ⓦ hirata-group.co.jp), located in the main ferry terminal. There's also good, reasonably up-to-date information about the island online at ⓦ ishigaki-japan.com.

Diving There are dozens of dive operations itching to get visitors underwater; recommended are *Sea Friends* (☎ 0980 82 0863) in Ishigaki City, and *Umicoza* (☎ 0980 88 2434, ⓦ umicoza.com) in Kabira.

Snorkelling Equipment can be rented out from the shops on the main road by Yonehara beach for ¥1000.

GETTING AROUND

By bus If you're planning on getting around the island by bus, it's worth investing in one of the two Free Passes, available from the driver: a one-day pass costs ¥1000, and a five-day is ¥2000; both cover all of the island's buses. However, services are not all that regular. You could also try one of the guided bus tours (4hr 30min; ¥4350; Japanese

only), which visit all the island's main sights, departing from the bus terminal daily at 9am.

By car Car rental is easy to organize at the airport, or prior to arrival. On Sunday, most of the island's petrol stations are closed, except for those in Ishigaki; make sure you fill up before setting off around the island.

ACCOMMODATION

ISHIGAKI

Emix Hostel えみっくすホステル 117 Tonoshiro ☎ 0980 82 5236, ⓦ emix-ishigaki.com; map p.780. The best of several hostels in the town centre, with relatively spacious dorms, piping hot water in the showers, fun hosts and a great location in the covered arcade. Their private rooms are very good value. Dorm **¥1500**, double **¥3800**

Granview Ishigaki ホテルグランビュー石垣 1 Tonoshiro ☎ 0980 82 6161, ⓦ granview.co.jp; map

p.780. This is a smart hotel in a convenient location, with simple but elegantly furnished rooms. It also has a large communal bath and sauna. The official rates are fairly of high; it's worth asking about discounts. **¥22,000**

Rakutenya 楽天屋 291 Ōkawa ☎ 0980 83 8713; map p.780. English-speaking hosts Ren and Miyako have created a cosy guesthouse (actually two, next door to each other) with both tatami and Western-style rooms. Advanced booking is advised. **¥6000**

uper Hotel Ishigaki-jima スーパーホテル石垣島 36 shigaki ☏09E0 83 9000; map p.780. Smart business notel with single rooms only. All have TV, a/c and small bathrooms, and there's a great light breakfast served in the obby; great value. Single **¥4500**

KABIRA BAY

Club Med Kabira クラブメッドカビラ 1 Ishizaki ☏0980 84 4600, ⓦcubmed.com; map p.779. A good resort option, with all the creature comforts one might expect – all staff speak English or French and there are excellent facilities, including a trapeze artist on hand to teach you the ropes. Note that most guests book their rooms here as part of a tour; otherwise rates are even higher. **¥30,000**

★ Iriwa 島宿イリワ 599 Kabira ☏0980 88 2563, ⓦiriwa.org; map p.779. A fantastic addition to the area, this has swiftly become the best hostel in the Yaeyamas. The welcoming Korean–Japanese couple running the place are great sources of local information, while accommodation – from the dorms to the private cabins – is clean and comfy. It's hard to find by yourself, so call to be picked up from the nearby Kabira Rotari bus stop, or ask the

tourist office to let the owners know which bus you're taking. Dorm **¥2500**, double **¥8000**

Minshuku Maetakaya 民宿前高屋 934-32 Kabira ☏0980 88 2251; map p.779. Just south of the bay's main tourist area, this delightful minshuku offers good tatami rooms with shared facilities, tasty Asian meals and a beautiful view of the bay from its wooden deck. An extra ¥2300/head will get you two meals. **¥8000**

SHIRAHO

Minshuku Maezato 民宿まえざと 68 Shiraho ☏0980 86 8065; map p.779. The best minshuku option in the area, with amiable owners who are adept at organizing snorkelling trips. It's next to the post office; if you're coming here by bus, get off at the Shōgaku-mae stop. Rates include two meals. **¥8800**

YONEHARA BEACH

Yonehara Campsite 米原キャンプ場 446-1 Fukai; map p.779. Simple campground with basic toilet facilities, located in the copse of trees beside the beach. Open April– Dec. **¥400** per person

EATING

For self-catering and local colour, check out the market in the covered arcade in Ishigaki town, just north of the central Shiyakusho-Jōri.

ISHIGAKI

★ Amurita No Niwa あむりたの庭 Ōkawa 282 ⓦamuritanoniwa.com; map p.780. This smart yet laidback venue serves local dishes with a contemporary twist – perhaps the most delectable example is Yaeyama-soba in green curry soup (¥900), though their vegan specials are certainly worth a mention. Also good for coffee or an evening drink – they'll prove that the galaxy of Okinawan beer extends far beyond Orion. Note that it can close unpredictably, as the friendly young hosts take breaks and holidays when they feel like it. Daily 11am–midnight.

Iso 磯 9 Ōkawa ☏0980 82 7721; map p.780. Appealingly gloomy, this is one of the best places for traditional Yaeyama cuisine. There is a handy a photo-

menu, and dishes start at ¥700. Daily 11am–10.30pm.

Yūna ゆうな 3 Misaki-chō; map p.780. Some of the best Yaeyama-soba (similar to sōki soba) on the island, this place is highly convenient if you're waiting for a ferry or a bus. A bowl of noodles will come to ¥630, while a set with pickles and rice is ¥800. Daily 11am–11pm.

KABIRA BAY

Umaru うーまる 900 Kabira ☏0980 88 2841; map p.779. Small, simple joint whose okonomiyaki, for whatever reason, hits the spot every single time; prices are reasonable, starting at ¥650. It's just uphill from the Kabira bus stop, on the right-hand side of the road. Daily 5–10pm.

NIGHTLIFE

ISHIGAKI

Bar Chaka Chaka バーチャカチャカ 2-10 Misaki-chō; map p.780. Funky little bar on the second floor of an unassuming building. Cocktails go from ¥700, and in season the atmosphere can be electric. Daily 9pm–late.

★ Usagiya うさぎや 1-1 Ishigaki ☏0980 88 5014; map p.780. Every night's music night at this fun izakaya – performances of traditional sanshin music get going at 7pm, and songbook menus mean that, if you can read katakana (see p.840), you can join in the singalong. The food's great, with a mix of local dishes and izakaya

staples; it's best washed down with some three-year-old awamori. Daily 5pm–midnight.

KABIRA BAY

Asian Bar Pulau プラウ 852-2 Kabira ☏0980 88 2620; map p.779. Whatever an "Asian bar" should be, this one is very nice – strangely so, for such a remote location. Hammerheads, sharks and the like cavort in the aquarium (OK, it's a television, but one can pretend), while the cheery owners dole out cocktails, locally brewed sake and more. Daily 5pm–midnight.

11

DIRECTORY

Internet Internet cafés in Ishigaki come and go – an outlet of the popular *Gera Gera* chain lies on the street behind the bus station.

Post office The post office in Ishigaki (12 Okawa has cash machines (daily 9am–7pm) which accep foreign cards.

Taketomi-jima
竹富島

Just before six o'clock each evening, the tiny island of **Taketomi-jima** undergoes a profound, magical transformation. This is the time of the last ferry back to Ishigaki-jima – after that, you're marooned, but there are few better places to be stuck. Just over 1km wide and home to fewer than three hundred people, the island's population swells during the day with folk eager to see its traditional houses, ride on buffalo-drawn carts and search lovely sandy beaches for the famous minuscule star-shaped shells. When the day-trippers are safely back in Ishigaki, those who have chosen to stay on will have Taketomi almost to themselves – it's possible to walk its dirt paths at night for hours on end without seeing a single soul.

A great way to get around the island is by pedalling your way over the dusty paths and roads on a bike, which is also a good way to see the local butterflies.

Taketomi village
竹富

There's only one village on Taketomi – also called **TAKETOMI** – and it's a beauty. Practically all its houses are built in traditional bungalow style with low-slung terracotta-tiled roofs, crowned with bug-eyed *shiisā*. Surrounding them are rocky walls, draped with hibiscus and bougainvillea: these are the *ishigaki* that gave a certain neighbouring island its name, yet these days they're far more prevalent on Taketomi. There aren't too many traditional sights here bar a small **museum**; most domestic tourists make a beeline for a concrete lookout tower, set in a tiny landscaped garden a few blocks to its east, from which both Ishigaki and Iriomote can be seen. However, a lovelier ocean scene is provided from the pier on the west side of the village – the best spot from which to view sunset.

Kihōin Shūshūkan

喜宝院蒐集館 • 108 Taketomi • Daily 9am–5pm • ¥300

Apart from soaking up the atmosphere, the main thing to see in Taketomi village is the **Kihōin Shūshūkan**, a small museum with an attached gift shop. There are over two thousand items on display here, including old cigarette packets, rusting samurai swords, an ornate shrine and expressive festival masks.

Beaches

The star-sand beaches, **Kondoi** (コンドイ浜) and **Hoshizuna** (星砂浜), also known as **Kaiji** (カイジ浜), are a short pedal south of Taketomi, also on the west side of the island. Swimming is possible at both, but at low tide you'll have to wade a long way out. The best snorkelling spot is at **Misashi** (ミサシ), on the northern coast, where three rocky islets and their surrounding reefs provide a home to a multitude of colourful sea life.

ARRIVAL AND INFORMATION

TAKETOMI-JIMA

By ferry Ferries from Ishigaki (¥670 one-way; 15min) run regularly (daily 7.30am–5.30pm). There are two companies serving this route; you'll save a full ¥60 by purchasing a return ticket (enough for a can of coffee, if there are two of you), though this is slightly inconvenient, since you'll only be able to return with the same company. If you've booked accommodation anywhere but the

hostel and given advance warning of your arrival time, you'll be met at the terminal and taken to your room. Otherwise, it's a 10min walk to Taketomi village.

Tourist information There's a small information booth inside the ferry terminal, but more interesting is the adjacent visitor centre (ゆがふ館; daily 8am–5pm; free; ⓦ taketomijima.jp), which has displays and short films about the island's unique lifestyle. You can equip yourself with a "town" map from the ferry terminal, or just ask around if you can't find your way – these are some of the friendliest locals in Japan.

GETTING AROUND

By bike There are plenty of places in town to rent bicycles, with prices starting at ¥300/hr. Touts for the larger operations meet the ferries, and if you agree to rent a bike from them, they'll give you a free ride into town; they'll also take you back to the ferry at intervals on a pre-arranged schedule.

By suigyūsha Another way to get around is on buffalo-driven carts known as *suigyūsha* (¥1200 per person for 30min), while being serenaded by a *sanshin*-plucking local; it has to be said that these days, they're commonly not locals at all, but young mainlanders on a gap year. Local or no, the experience is fun but rather cheesy, and as with rickshaws or other similar forms of transport, it's hard not to feel like a bit of a plum once you actually get moving.

ACCOMMODATION

Taketomi has some great accommodation options, almost all of which are in the village. Rates at all except the youth hostel include breakfast and dinner.

Je l'aime ジュテーム 321-1 Taketomi ☎0930 85 2555, ⓦtaketomi net/jetaime. A little bit of Thailand transported to the Yaeyama, this rickety little hostel has bunk beds in a scruffy dorm and geckos patrolling the walls. Non-smokers may not like the common room very much; the chain-smoking owners make it reek, and some of your dorm-mates will doubtless join in the fun. Dorm **¥2500**

★**Nohara-sō** のはら荘 280 Taketomi ☎0980 85 2252. A fantastic place to stay, with a very laidback atmosphere, excellent food and free snorkelling gear. Come sundown, a bottle of *awamori* is likely to appear, the three-stringed *sanshin* comes out and an Okinawan singsong begins.

¥11,000

Takana Ryokan 高那旅館 499 Taketomi ☎0980 85 2151, ⓦjyh.or.jp/english/kyushu/takana. Well-run youth hostel with a mix of tatami dormitory and ryokan rooms – the ryokan side of the building is slightly fancier, and you get served better-quality meals (breakfast ¥550, dinner ¥850). Dorm **¥2900** double **¥8800**

Villa Taketomi ヴィラたけとみ 1493 Taketomi ☎0980 84 5600; ⓦwww.taketomi-v.com. There's a real sense of remoteness at this cluster of en-suite pine chalets, sitting in solitude to the west of the island, and perfect for those who want to unwind. They also run an excellent nearby restaurant. **¥23,000**

EATING AND DRINKING

The village offers a few eating options, but things can wind down early. A mini-market by the post office sells snacks until 7pm.

Haaya Café ハーヤカフェー 379 Taketomi ☎0980 85 2253. Set on the second floor of an abandoned guesthouse, this café is a nice recent addition to the island. The coffee's good, the atmosphere is a sort of modern South Sea style, and alcoholic drinks are available; from the front windows you'll also be able to see visitors scurrying up the adjacent concrete tower for their obligatory *keitai* (mobile phone) photos. Daily 10am–5pm & 7–10pm.

Kanifu かにふ 494 Taketomi ☎0980 85 2311. *Gōya champurū* (¥700), pork-and-ginger stir-fry (¥700) and local shrimp are the stars of the show at this excellent restaurant, while the sweet potato cheesecake (¥350) is great for dessert. Check out the cute tropically styled bar by the outdoor seating area. Daily 11am–5pm, 6.30–10.30pm, closed Thurs eve.

★**Shidamē** しだめー館 361 Taketomi ☎0980 85 2239. Right by the famed concrete tower (see opposite), this is the closest thing Taketomi has to an *izakaya*. The favoured drinking venue of visitors and locals alike, it has nice outdoor seating on which to imbibe a range of beer and Yaeyama *awamori*. They're no slouches in the kitchen department either – try the taco rice or *sōki soba* (both ¥800), or the *maguroage keishoku* (a set featuring fried, breaded tuna balls; ¥700). Daily 10am–11pm.

Takenoko 竹の子 206-1 Taketomi ☎0980 85 2009. This is a pleasing little noodle bar with the best *sōki soba* on the island (¥500), as well as good curry rice. Though the interior is pretty enough, in fair weather it's hard to resist the outdoor tables. Daily 10.30am–4pm, sometimes later in high season.

Iriomote-jima

西表島

Brooding darkly some 20km west of Ishigaki, **Iriomote-jima** is an extraordinarily wild place for Japan. Rising sharply out of the ocean, some ninety percent of its uncharted,

DIVING ON IRIOMOTE

Iriomote is a **divers' paradise**; the **Manta Way**, between the island's eastern coast and Kohama-jima, is particularly famous for its shoals of manta rays, which you're most likely to see between April and June. The youth hostels and all minshuku can put you in touch with the island's several dive operations (see p.788). **Snorkelling** is particularly good at **Hoshizuna Beach** (星砂の浜), around 4km northwest of Funaura, where you'll also find a **campsite** (¥300 per person), a decent restaurant and snorkelling gear for rent – all of which makes it popular. If you're looking to escape the crowds, head to **Funauki** (船浮), reached by three ferries a day (¥410) from **Shirahama** (白浜), at the far west end of the coastal road; the beach here, a short trek through the jungle, is one of the most beautiful in all of Japan.

mountainous interior is covered with dense subtropical rainforest, much of it protected as the **Iriomote National Park**. Yaeyama rumour would have it that Iriomote often – or even perpetually – plays host to disaffected Japanese, living rough in the jungle. A more substantiated inhabitant, though equally elusive, is one of the world's rarest species, the *yamaneko*, or **Iriomote lynx**, a nocturnal animal that looks something like a scruffy house cat. The island and its surrounding waters are also home to a splendid array of flora and coral reefs shimmering with tropical fish. There are also plenty of opportunities for snorkelling, diving, kayaking and hiking through the rainforest.

Although it's Okinawa's second-largest island, fewer than two thousand people live here, most of them along barely developed strips on the north and south coasts. Ferries from Ishigaki sail to two ports on the island: **Ōhara** (大原) in the south and **Uehara** in the north. The latter is the better place to head for since it's closer to Iriomote's main scenic attractions and offers the widest range of accommodation, but neither are very visually appealing. With more time on your hands, consider heading way out west to end-of-the-line **Shirahama** (白浜), or even further on by ferry to remote **Fukauki** (舟浮), which cannot be reached by road. It's certainly worth staying at least one night on the island, and it's best to opt for an accommodation deal that includes two meals, since eating options are thin on the ground.

Uehara
上原

It's hard to believe that **UEHARA** is Iriomote's main settlement – it's home to mere hundreds of souls, and you can traverse every single road in an hour or two. It's not terribly interesting or very attractive, but this is the main centre of affairs; if you want to kayak, hike or go diving, it's best to bite the bullet and use Uehara as a base. If you find yourself staying here and craving a little adventure, wander up any of the side streets heading uphill away from the main road. All eventually head to a charmingly bucolic plateau, full of farmyard sights and smells; if the moon's fat and the sky clear, head up at night to drink in some truly haunting beauty (and perhaps a little *awamori*).

Urauchi-gawa and the waterfalls
浦内川 · **Jungle cruise** 7 daily 9.30am–3.30pm; 1hr · ¥1800 · **Waterfall trip & hike** 6 daily 9.30am–2pm; 3hr · ¥1800 · **Waterfall & kayak tour** Daily 9.30am; 6hr · ¥8400 · **Kayak tour** Daily 10am & 1.30pm; 2hr · ¥4000 · **Waterfalls & jungle trek** Daily 10.30am; 5hr · ¥7000 · **Night tour** Daily 7pm; 2hr · ¥5000 · ☏ 0980 85 6154, ⓦ urauchigawa.com · Boat and kayaking tours can be arranged at the Urauchi-gawa centre (daily 8am–5pm) · Island bus to Urauchi-gawa stop

The vast majority of visitors to Iriomote-jima come only for the day, heading straight to the **Urauchi-gawa**, a broad, almost Amazon-like river reachable by island bus. Here they hop on one of various boat tours operated by the local visitor centre; the most popular terminate at a trail heading up to two scenic waterfalls: **Kampirē-no-taki** (カンピレーの滝) and **Mariudo-no-taki** (マリウドの滝). The touristy nature of this excursion is undeniable (almost anyone can easily negotiate the gentle 1.5km "trek" through the rainforest up to the falls), yet it's still enjoyable, and there are several more adventurous options. The truly hardy may wish to consider the 15km hike across the island from the head of the Kampirē falls to the **Nakama-gawa** (仲間川), Iriomote's second-largest waterway, and Ōhara; you'll need local advice and a guide before tackling this. It's also possible to paddle back from the falls in a **kayak**, which is a great way to view the rainforest at close quarters.

Pinaisāra-no-taki

ピナイサーラの滝

Operators in town (see p.788) can organize kayaking trips and treks up to **Pinaisāra-no-taki**, the tallest waterfall in Okinawa; the youth hostel can also provide details of hiking trails from **Funaura** (船浦), but even if you don't get too close, you can clearly see the cascade from the Kaichūdōro bridge that spans the bay immediately south of Funaura. At low tide, you may well find yourself dragging your kayak across the shallows to the Hinai-gawa before paddling to the start of the trek. This will give you a chance to inspect the mangrove forests closely and see armies of purple soldier crabs scuttling across the sandbanks. On the climb to the head of the falls, keep a lookout for snakes and be prepared for leeches, especially in the wet season. At the foot of the trail, you'll also pass many of the distinctive **sakishima suōnoki** trees, with huge, billowing buttress roots. You may notice lumps of coal sparkling in the ground – this was one of Iriomote's riches that Commodore Perry had his eye on when he forced the opening up of Japan in the mid-nineteenth century (see p.798).

Shirahama and Funauki

白浜・船浮 • Ferries between Shirahama and Funauki: 5 daily; 10min • ¥900 return

The road that snakes most of the way around Iriomote hits its western terminus in **Shirahama**; there is no lovelier, more relaxed place on the full 53km stretch than this. However, an even more pleasant and chilled out place lies not far away – **Funauki**, a tiny village off the road network, and only reachable by ferry. While there are no tourist sights as such in either place, they're Okinawan through and through.

In Shirahama, it won't take long to spot the **monument** to a geographical nicety: it's placed on the 123°45'6.789" line of longitude (the eagle-eyed will have seen another one on the way in from Uehara). Gorgeous Funauki has even less to see, its own focal point the hilariously oversized **school**; at the time of writing, this boasted a large, fully stocked gymnasium, a whole orchestra's worth of musical equipment, seven staff, one principal ... and two poor students. Pop by to say hello, and you'll make everyone's day. The real draw here, however, is a stretch of pristine **beach**, reachable after a fifteen-minute walk along a jungle path; this is one of the most splendid beaches in all Japan.

Yubu-jima

由布島 • Buffalo every 30min • ¥1300 per load • ⓦ yubujima.com/english

If schedules oblige you to use the Ōhara ferry terminal (which is quite often the case), you may care to stop by quirky little **Yubu-jima** on the way between here and Uehara; many buses working the route pause here awhile on their way around, but there's more to do than stretch your legs. The islet lies just offshore, and for much of the day it's basically possible to walk across with suitable footwear. A more enjoyable means of access – and useful if you don't have a pair of wellies with you – are the **buffalo** which trudge through the mud, carting wagons behind them. Amazingly, and in what may be the only such case worldwide, these sad-eyed beasts actually run to a schedule. Once on the island, walking paths allow you to see butterflies, warthogs and flowers aplenty, as well as part-submerged mangrove forests on the land-facing side.

ARRIVAL AND DEPARTURE | IRIOMOTE-JIMA

By ferry Yaeyama Kankō and Anei Kankō both run regular high-speed ferries from Ishigaki to Uehara (50min; ¥2300 one way, ¥4400 return) and Ōhara (40min; ¥1770 one-way, ¥3390 return). Inclement conditions (or a lack of demand) may force ferries to use Ōhara – check with your guesthouse owner when you're on your way back to Ishigaki.

11

GETTING AROUND

By bus Iriomote's only main road runs along the coast from Ōhara via Funaura and Uehara to Shirahama in the west; all these villages are linked by infrequent public buses. It's usually best to buy a pass, which will pay for itself if you take three or more rides; a one-day pass costs ¥1000, and a three-day one ¥1500.

By car and bike To really explore the island, you'll need to rent a bike or car; if your accommodation can't help, they'll be able to point the way to the nearest rental spot.

INFORMATION AND ACTIVITIES

Services The island's few post offices are usually able to accept international cards; that said, it's advisable to arrive with enough cash to cover your stay.

Diving Reef Encounters (see box, p.756), on Okinawa-Hontō, organizes excellent trips to this distant island. There are plenty of operators in the immediate environs of the Uehara ferry terminal; Marine Club Sa-Wes is a reliable option (☎0980 87 2311, ✉sawes@yonaguni.jp).

Kayaking You'll find a variety of places around the Uehara ferry terminal that hire out kayaks or arrange tours.

Hiking An excellent guide to arrange trips with is Murata Susumu (☎ & ☎0980 85 6425), aka Hige-san, a wildlife photographer who runs a variety of eco-trips through his company, Murata Shizenjuku (村田自然塾), based in Uehara.

ACCOMMODATION

UEHARA

Coconut Village ココナッツビレッジ 397-1Uehara ☎0980 85 6045. On the northwestern outskirts of Uehara, this modern beachside complex has small tatami and Western-style rooms (with very low beds), a restaurant and a fresh-water pool. **¥13,000**

★**Irumote-sō Youth Hostel** いるもて荘ユースホステル 870-95 Uehara ☎0980 85 6255. Great budget place with a hilltop location that makes it a little hard to walk to – no matter, since the friendly owners will pick you up from Uehara. Serves excellent meals, has bikes and scooters for rent, and organizes a daily drop-off at the Urauchi-gawa and Hoshizuna beach (see p.786). Dorm **¥3100**

★**Kampira-sō** カンピラ荘 545 Uehara ☎0980 85 6508, ⊕kanpira.com. Only a minute on foot from Uehara ferry terminal (turn right at the main road and you're already there), this is a lovely place with cosy, good-value rooms, both en-suite and otherwise. Little English is spoken, but they have a wealth of pamphlets, schedules and the like. **¥6000**

FUNAUKI AND SHIRAHAMA

Kamadoma-sō かまどま荘 By the port, Funauki ☎0980 85 6165. This basic minshuku is nothing special, but there's no other choice in Funauki; it's right next to a pleasant noodle bar and *izakaya*. **¥6000**

Uminchu-no-ie 海人の家 1499-57 Taketomi-chō ☎0980 85 6119. Simple Japanese-style accommodation in a large blue municipal building at Shirahama – useful if you want to get away from what constitutes crowds on Iriomote. Rates include a breakfast of coffee and bread. **¥8000**

EATING AND DRINKING

As with any small Okinawan island, don't take the stipulated restaurant opening times too seriously. There aren't too many **eating options** in Uehara; those who are not getting fed at their **accommodation** should note that there's also a small supermarket opposite the ferry terminal (daily 8am–8pm).

UEHARA

Kake-tā かけたー 564 Uehara ☎0980 85 8014. On Uehara's main "drag", though a bit hard to spot, this is good for pizza (from ¥800) or cocktails. 11.30am–2pm & 6.30pm–midnight, closed Wed.

Laugh la Garden ラフラガーデン 550-1 Uehara ☎0980 85 7088. On the other side of the main road from the ferry terminal, this second-floor venue is Uehara's most reliable restaurant by far (despite the odd name). The *gōya champurū* set meal (¥800) is big and tasty; they specialize in *oden*, and since you'll need to read Japanese to make sense of the menu, ask to see the offerings instead. Lastly, it's a nice drinking hole, too; there's plenty of *awamori* (from ¥400), as well as more regular Japanese tipples. Daily 6.30pm–midnight.

FUNAUKI

★**Bū-no-ie** ぶーの家. For a Funauki restaurant, this has its marketing cap on straight – you'll see signs for their curry (¥900) and coffee (¥400) all the way from Shirahama ferry terminal. They're both quite tasty, and best taken in the garden-like outdoor area. Daily 9am–5pm.

UNDERWATER YONAGUNI

Much more interesting than anything on Yonaguni's tiny landmass is what lies on the sea bed beneath. In 1986, local divers came across what looked like a giant rock-carved staircase, or possibly part of a pyramid, 80m long, 50m wide and 20m high. Researchers have flocked to what have been described as the **underwater ruins** (海底遺跡) ever since. Some claim the rocks are part of the legendary ancient civilization of Mu, an Asian Atlantis. Weather dictates whether diving is possible – when the wind's blowing from the south, it's too dangerous. Another diving highlight here is the sight of schools of hammerhead sharks, particularly in the winter months.

To organize diving, your best bet is *Hotel Irifune* (see below), whose owner actually discovered the ruins. They also offer snorkelling (¥5000). For kayaking, try your luck at *Guesthouse ADAN* (ゲストハウス阿檀; 136-1 Yonaguni; ☎0980 87 2947).

Yonaguni-jima

与那国島

11

Some 127km northwest of Ishigaki and 2000km from Tokyo, **Yonaguni-jima** is the furthest west you can go and still be in Japan; on a clear day, you can see Taiwan 111km away from Yonaguni's high point, **Mount Urabu**. It's just 11km long, so it won't take you long to tour this predominantly rural but hilly island. **SONAI** (祖納) on the north coast is the main community; ferries dock in its port, and the **airport** is a couple of kilometres west. A circuit of the island shouldn't take you more than half a day, although you'd be mad to pass up the chance to linger at some of the most deserted beaches in the Yaeyamas. Heading west from Sonai past the tiny port of **Kubura** (久部良) and out to **Irizaki** (西崎), you'll find a simple monument marking Japan's westernmost point, atop sheer cliffs.

Intriguing rock formations can be found above water on Yonaguni's east coast. **Gunkan-iwa** (軍艦岩) is said to resemble a battleship, although it actually looks more like a submarine rising to the surface. There's little debate over what the **Tachigami-iwa** (立神岩) outcrop resembles – it's worshipped by locals as a symbol of virility. On the nearby hillsides, wild Yonaguni horses roam.

ARRIVAL AND GETTING AROUND

YONAGUNI-JIMA

By plane Yonaguni is accessible on daily flights from Ishigaki (2 daily; 30min) and Naha (2 daily; 1hr). The planes are tiny, propeller-driven cuties.

By ferry Twice-weekly ferries run from Ishigaki (4hr; ¥3740) to Kubura port, on the west side of the island.

By bike and car The best way to get around is by rented bike or car, which can be arranged in town or at the airport.

ACCOMMODATION, EATING AND DRINKING

SONAI

Sonai has a handful of hotels, though not many places to eat – few places are open for more than a couple of hours a day.

Fiesta ホステルフィエスタ 1080 Yonaguni ☎0980 87 2339. Occasionally lively hostel, with dorm "beds" (futons on the floor) and a few private rooms, plus cooking facilities and free coffee. Dorm **¥2000**, private room **¥4500**

Hotel Irifune ホテル入船 59-6 Yonaguni ☎0980 87 2311. This is the classiest place in town, though that's not saying much – the rooms are overpriced for sure. However, it's run by Aratake Kihachiro, who discovered the nearby underwater ruins and runs glass-bottom boat tours, diving and fishing trips (see box above). **¥9000**

Onna Shūcho 女酋長 5-2 Yonaguni ☎0980 87 3282. Yonaguni's best *izakaya* by a long way, *Onna Shūcho* is a sometimes rowdy affair lassoing together the area's locals, divers and visitors. Try their delectable *gōya tempura*, a snip at ¥500. 5pm–1am closed Wed.

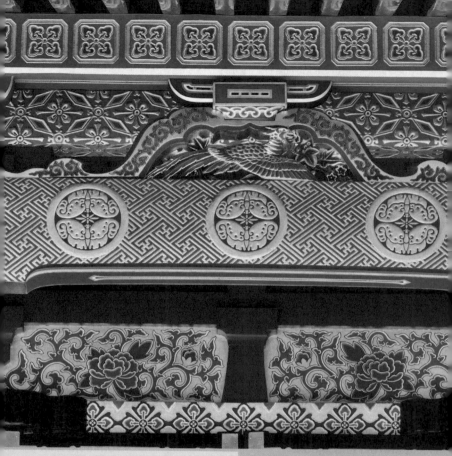

SHRINE DETAIL, NIKKŌ NATIONAL PARK

Contexts

History

Archeological evidence shows that humans settled in Japan more than 30,000 years ago; most probably migrants from mainland Asia as well as Polynesians who moved north along the east Asian coast. Living mainly by hunting, fishing and gathering, with some cultivation of plants, they spread through the Japanese archipelago. The Jōmon culture began about 10,000–15,000 years ago; in this age, the Japanese began to live in fixed communities composed of large wooden structures. The pottery they made was decorated with a rope pattern (jōmon). By about 1000 BC, these communities showed increasingly developed social structures and cultural practices.

The impetus for the change from a hunting, fishing and gathering culture to one based on **agriculture** was the arrival of large numbers of Korean immigrants to Japan, who brought with them the technologies for growing rice in irrigated fields and for making bronze implements. This process had begun at least by 400 BC, initiating what is called the **Yayoi period**, which was characterized by highly developed communities and lasted until about 300 AD. As the Yayoi communities developed socially and economically, **class divisions** appeared, and some families became rulers of small "countries". Chinese records indicate that Japan was composed of more than a hundred of these local states, which were often at war with each other.

The Kofun (Tomb) period

As the ruling families of the Yayoi era became more powerful and wealthy, they began to build large **burial mounds** (*kofun*) for their deceased leaders. This took place from the fourth to the seventh centuries AD, in what is known as the Kofun, or Tomb, period. These mounds, numbering in the thousands, can be found throughout Japan. The largest, attributed to the ruler **Nintoku**, was built in the mid-fifth century and is one of the three largest tombs in the world. In this period, many **technologies** were brought from Korea that improved upon existing methods, including new techniques for irrigating rice fields, making ceramics, metalworking, weaving and writing. At the

THE MAJOR HISTORICAL PERIODS

Jōmon	10,000–300 BC	Azuchi-Momoyama	1573–1500
Yayoi	300 BC–300 AD	Edo (or Tokugawa)	1600–1368
Kofun	300–710	Meiji	1868–1912
Nara	710–794	Taishō	1912–1926
Heian	794–1185	Shōwa	1926–1989
Kamakura	1185–1333	Heisei	1989–present
Muromachi (or Ashikaga)	1333–1573		day

c.35,000 BC	c.12,000 BC	c.400 BC	c.300 AD
Humans settle in Japan.	Jōmon era begins; people live in settlements and produce distinctive pottery.	Yayoi period sees the arrival of Koreans with new technologies.	Kofun period begins. Small local kingdoms gradually unite under the Yamato court.

same time, political organization spread throughout Japan, fuelling the increasing power of ruling families.

During the **Tomb period**, the numerous small local kingdoms gradually merged into one nation under the rule of the **Yamato** court, in central Japan. To consolidate their power, the Yamato rulers made use of Chinese political ideas, such as court rituals and Confucian philosophy. The introduction of **Buddhism** in around 550 (see p.808) provided another opportunity for the imperial family to strengthen its position. **Prince Shōtoku**, regent during the reign of Empress Suiko, emphasized both Confucian and Buddhist principles for governance in his Seventeen-article Constitution of 604, and he is traditionally associated with the founding of the Buddhist temples Hōryū-ji near Nara and Shitennō-ji in Osaka.

However, the ruling family was still weak and had been dominated by the **Soga** clan since the mid-sixth century. The Soga's power came to an end with the **Taika** ("great change") coup d'état in 645, followed by the Taika Reforms, which decreed that all agricultural land was state property and all persons were subject to the imperial government. **Emperor Tenmu** was the key figure in establishing the power of the imperial family and the building of a strong central government. Having obtained real power through his victory in the succession dispute known as the Jinshin War (672), he staffed his government with imperial relatives and brought other clan chieftains into the government at lower ranks. The concept of a **divine emperor**, descended from the gods, was established at this time. Tenmu put Amaterasu (the Sun Goddess), the ancestral deity of the imperial clan, ahead of all other ancestral deities.

The first permanent capital city, **Fujiwara-kyō**, was established in 694, with a layout similar to the Chinese capital city of Chang'an. Further, a number of penal and administrative codes were promulgated at this time, attempting to establish a government on the Chinese model, headed by the emperor and administered by a vast bureaucracy.

The Nara period

The city of **Nara**, originally named Heijō-kyō, was established in 710 as the capital city. It, too, was laid out in a checkerboard pattern on the model of Chang'an, and was built on a grand scale, a hint of which can be seen in the recent reconstructions of the Nara imperial palace. The government continued to issue **Chinese-style law codes**, expand the bureaucracy and attempt to establish control over the provinces. **Emperor Shōmu** sought to use the increasing popularity of Buddhism as an additional means of enhancing imperial power. He ordered the construction of the Great Buddha (*daibutsu*) statue depicting the cosmic Buddha Rushana (Vairocana), who presides over the universe; Shōmu sought to establish a parallel between Rushana's rule over the universe and the emperor's rule over the officials and the people.

The Nara period saw a tremendous flowering of the **arts**, remains of which can be seen in the city today (see p.470). In addition to great works of sculpture, painting and architecture, important literary works were produced. Japan's oldest surviving historical documents were transcribed in these years – the *Kojiki* (*Record of Ancient Matters*) and the *Nihon-shoki* (*Chronicles of Japan*) – establishing the legitimacy of the Imperial rulers through divine descent. Nara was the eastern terminus of the **Silk Road** trade route, and many objects from as far as Persia – now deposited in the Shōsō-in, the imperial

c.550	604	672	694
Buddhism is brought to Japan and gradually spreads throughout the country.	Prince Shōtoku issues his Seventeen Articles, based on both Confucian and Buddhist ideas.	The Jinshin War establishes the power of the imperial family.	Fujiwara-kyō, in present-day Nara Prefecture, is made the first permanent capital.

epository at Tōdai-ji – reached Japan this way. Finally, numerous advances in administrative procedures such as **taxation** and **census-taking** helped to establish the imperial government in Nara as the government of all Japan.

Beneath the surface however, imperial rule was far from stable. The **Fujiwara** family, descendants of a clan that aided the imperial family to escape from the control of the Soga clan in the Taika coup of 645, increasingly exerted control over the imperial family by marrying their daughters to princes, such as in the case of Emperor Shōmu, whose mother and wife were both Fujiwara women. There were even two armed rebellions against the imperial government led by members of the Fujiwara family. Struggles both within the imperial family itself and against the Fujiwara caused several temporary relocations of the capital during this period; finally, under Emperor Kammu, a new capital city was built at **Nagaoka-kyō** (near present-day Kyoto), and the government resided there from 784 until 794.

The Heian Period

In 794, the imperial palace moved once again, and a new capital was established at **Heian-kyō (Kyoto)**. This move served to strengthen Emperor Kammu's branch of the imperial family, weakening the other noble families at court because of the heavy cost of the move, and bringing the Buddhist clergy under stricter control. Again, the capital was laid out on the Chinese model in a checkerboard pattern, evidence of which remains to this day. The Heian Shrine, a modern replica on a smaller scale, gives some idea of the Chinese style of the original Great Hall of State. In contrast to the many relocations of the capital in the past, Kyoto was to remain the imperial capital of Japan for more than a thousand years, until 1869.

For much of the **Heian period**, the imperial court was dominated by the Fujiwara family, who continued their strategy of "marriage politics." Fujiwara Michinaga, whose villa in Uji became Byōdō-in, represented the high point of Fujiwara dominance, with four of his daughters married to emperors. However, the daughters of his son Yorimichi did not produce male heirs, so when **Go-Sanjō** ascended the throne in 1068, he was the first emperor in almost two centuries whose mother was not a Fujiwara. This competition between the imperial family and the Fujiwara continued throughout the Heian period, complicated by the increasing influence of the great Buddhist temples and the rising power of **warrior families**. These elite groups gradually usurped powers of taxation and administration, so that aspects of government began to be privatized, beginning with land. Noblemen sent as governors to the provinces formed ties with powerful local families and gradually established control over **land** that they treated as their private property and for which they paid no taxes. The great temples and shrines also held land that was tax exempt; the income from it was used to support religious activities. Finally, even the imperial family came to hold land privately. By the end of the Heian period, almost half of the land in the country was no longer public land.

The privatization of government functions was also reflected in the rise of the notorious military class of the **samurai** (see box, p.796). Chinese-style conscription, established in the mid-seventh century, proved both unnecessary and ineffective, and led the government gradually to rely on private military professionals, composed of provincial elites as well as aristocrats of lower rank: two of the leading warrior families,

710	794	806	c.1000
A new capital is established at Heijō-kyō present-day Nara.	The imperial capital is moved from Nagaoka-kyō to Heian-kyō, present-day Kyoto, which remains the capital until 1869.	The monk Kobo Daishi returns from China and founds the Shingon school of Buddhism.	Murasaki Shikibu writes *The Tale of Genji* – the world's first novel.

the **Taira** (Heike) and **Minamoto** (Genji), were descendants of emperors. Despite this, while the central government itself gradually lost political power as administrative and military functions were privatized, the imperial family and the aristocrats surrounding them continued to hold symbolic and sacerdotal authority. Just as the Fujiwara clan ruled by dominating the imperial family rather than replacing it, so too would the succeeding **military governments** rule in the emperor's name.

The struggle between the Taira and the Minamoto brought the Heian period to an end. Taking part in a succession dispute within the imperial family, these two clans fought each other in the late 1150s; the Taira, led by **Taira Kiyomori**, emerged the victors. Kiyomori sought to consolidate his power by adopting the same methods that the existing elite had used, taking high court posts and using "marriage politics" to become grandfather to an infant emperor.

In the meantime, **Minamoto Yoritomo**, who had been sent into exile in eastern Japan, spent several years building a strong military force from his headquarters at Kamakura, and in a civil war lasting from 1180 to 1185, the Minamoto defeated the Taira. The tragic figure in this story is **Minamoto Yoshitsune**, Yoritomo's half brother. His skill in battle did much to enable the Minamoto victory; however, jealous of Yoshitsune's popularity and suspicious of his loyalty, Yoritomo sent soldiers out to kill him. On the run for several years, Yoshitsune was eventually betrayed and forced to commit suicide; his head was sent, preserved in sake, to his brother.

The Kamakura period

The **Kamakura bakufu** (shogunate) was founded by Minamoto Yoritomo in 1185. It was legitimized by the imperial court, specifically by his appointment as shogun in 1192. However, it remained separate from the imperial establishment in Kyoto not only by maintaining headquarters in Kamakura (see p.185), but by creating a highly developed civil administration and code of government.

After Yoritomo's death, the *bakufu* was dominated by the **Hōjō** clan, the family of the late shogun's wife Masako, who by all accounts was one of the dominant personalities of this era. The Hōjō served as regents to the actual shogun, who were often aristocrats brought from Kyoto. Although the Kamakura *bakufu* increased its power over Kyoto to some extent, thirteenth-century Japan was basically a "dual polity" in which the imperial government in Kyoto ruled Japan in tandem with the military government in Kamakura.

The thirteenth century was marked by two great events: Japan was **invaded** twice by forces of the **Mongol Empire**, first in 1274 and again in 1281. The Japanese managed to fight off the Mongols, with the aid of typhoons ("divine winds" or kamikaze), from Hakata Bayin northern Kyushu, where the foreigners landed. Remains of the stone wall constructed around Hakata Bay after the first invasion as defensive fortifications can be seen to this day. Despite this victory, the invasions were a heavy blow to the *bakufu*. The basic relationship between the shogun and his vassals was the granting of land in return for service. Many vassals had been mobilized, at great expense to themselves, but after the defeat of the Mongols, there was no land available for distribution as rewards for service. This added to the economic hardships many vassals were already undergoing; the situation was ripe for revolt.

1185	1227	1274; 1281	1333
The Minamoto family destroys the Taira forces and Yoritomo founds the Kamakura *bakufu*; he is appointed shogun in 1192.	The monk Dōgen returns from China and establishes the Sōtō sect of Zen Buddhism.	Mongol forces attack Japan.	The Kamakura *bakufu* is destroyed and Emperor Go-Daigo asserts direct rule.

The Muromachi (or Ashika) period

The insurgency was led by **Emperor Go-Daigo** and aided by **Ashikaga Takauji** 1305–1358), head of an eastern warrior family that had become disaffected with the Kamakura *bakufu* and its Hōjō leaders. Kamakura was taken in 1333, and for the next three years Go-Daigo attempted to re-establish direct rule by the imperial family. However, by favouring court nobles and officials rather than the warriors who had supported him, he alienated Takeuji, who drove him from Kyoto in 1336 and threw his support behind a rival claimant to the throne, Kōmyō. Go-Daigo fled to the mountains of Yoshino, where he set up court at **Yoshimizu Shrine**. Until the end of the fourteenth century, two lines of the imperial family each claimed legitimacy. This occasioned much warfare, although the military tactics of the time relied on small groups of mounted **archers**, so the number of combatants was relatively small.

The Ashikaga (or **Muromachi**) *bakufu* began officially in 1338 when Takeuji was appointed shogun; he was the first of fifteen Ashikaga shogun who headed the *bakufu*, until it was destroyed in 1573. The *bakufu* headquarters was in Kyoto, which suggests how closely they were dependant on the imperial court for legitimacy. In fact, the Ashikaga shoguns' control over the military families in the provinces was quite weak.

The early Ashikaga shoguns are justly famous for their love of the **arts**. The nō theatre developed under their patronage; Kinkaku-ji and Ginkaku-ji temples were originally their villas. They also established a network of Zen temples throughout Japan, in an unsuccessful attempt to use Buddhism to strengthen their political power.

This Muromachi period saw a number of important **changes** in Japanese society: military force gradually replaced the imperial court and *bakufu* as the ultimate authority in settling disputes; the population grew; the economy developed significantly and became increasingly based on capital; international trade, both official and private, expanded significantly; and farmers became more economically powerful vis-à-vis their rulers. The shogunate itself relied less on income from land holdings and more from taxes on the commerce that flourished in Kyoto.

The beginning of the end for the Ashikaga *bakufu* was the **Ōnin War** (1467–77), which had its roots in succession disputes among the Ashikaga leadership. During this drawn-out struggle, much of Kyoto was destroyed. Many of the participants were troops led by provincial governors, who fought on one side or the other to secure recognition from the shogun to legitimize their authority in the provinces. But while they were engaged in this struggle at the centre, the very provinces the governors were trying to protect were being taken over by local warriors. Other governors remained in the provinces to consolidate their control by military force without much concern for court or *bakufu* appointments. This ushered in the century of warfare, the **Warring States** period from roughly the end of the Ōnin War until the unification of Japan in the late sixteenth century.

The "states" of this era were areas of land under the control of warlords called "*daimyō*" who held this land by virtue of their military strength, although they often sought prestige and legitimacy by seeking appointment by the shogun as provincial governor or even imperial court titles. *Daimyō* established formal governments and legal systems, tried various means to expand agricultural production, took control of local resources (such as metals) and stimulated the local economy by encouraging trade.

1336	1467–1477	1549	1573
Ashikaga Takeuji drives Go-Daigo from Kyoto and founds the Ashikaga *bakufu*.	The Ōnin War is fought in Kyoto, destroying much of the city.	Francis Xavier of the Society of Jesus lands in Kagoshima.	Oda Nobunaga drives the last Ashikaga shogun from Kyoto, ending the Muromachi *bakufu*.

Where they were successful, towns grew up around their castles. These ruling warlords were able to improve their military strength by creating large armies of **foot soldiers** equipped initially with pikes, and, after the Portuguese brought powerful new weapons to Japan in the 1540s, subsequently with firearms.

"State" instability caused **constant war** between them; in many cases the domains were nothing more than a coalition of alliances, not actual territory, so the *daimyō's* rule lasted only for as long as he could keep his vassals satisfied by grants of new land. To gain this land, the *daimyō* had to be perpetually engaged in warfare; this required more vassals, who in turn required more land as rewards, which led to a vicious circle from which most *daimyō* were unable to escape.

Reunification (Azuchi-Momoyama period)

The end of the **Warring States** period of political uncertainty and relentless warfare came in the late sixteenth century. First, **Oda Nobunaga** managed through military tactical skill and sheer ruthlessness to dominate first his local area to the east of Kyoto, and then to enter the capital at the head of fifty thousand troops in 1568. He established relationships with the *bakufu* and the court, and set about gaining control of central Japan. In 1573, he drove the last Ashikaga shogun out of Kyoto, thus bringing the *bakufu* of the Muromachi period to an end. He continued to expand and strengthen his hold over central and a portion of eastern Japan until he met his death by the treachery of a vassal in 1582.

Shortly afterwards, another Oda vassal, **Toyotomi Hideyoshi**, avenged Nobunaga's death, took over as leader of Nobunaga's forces and, by military might and skilful diplomacy, managed to bring all of Japan under his control by 1590. Hideyoshi sought legitimacy by supporting the imperial family and being rewarded with court rank. The

---

THE WAY OF THE WARRIOR

The origins of the **samurai**, Japan's warrior caste, go back to the ninth century, when the feudal lords began to maintain regular forces. Gradually, they evolved into an elite group of hereditary warriors, their lives governed by an unwritten code of behaviour and unquestioning loyalty that came to be known as *bushidō*, **the way of the warrior**.

According to *bushidō*, the samurai and his family were expected to die willingly to protect the life and honour of their feudal lord. If they failed in this duty, or were about to be taken prisoner on a battlefield, then suicide was the only fitting response. The traditional method of **ritual suicide** was disembowelment with a sword or dagger (*seppuku*), though in later years an accomplice would stand by to cut off the victim's head. The samurai creed reached full bloom in the early Tokugawa era when class distinctions were officially delineated. The samurai were deemed "the masters of the four classes" – above farmers, artisans and merchants – and they alone were permitted to carry swords. They even had the right to kill any member of the lower orders for disrespectful behaviour, real or imagined.

During the more peaceful seventeenth and eighteenth centuries, many samurai found themselves out of work as their lords were dispossessed and fiefdoms redistributed. Many became **rōnin**, or masterless samurai, whose lives were romanticized in such films as *The Seven Samurai* (see p.832).

1579	1582	1590	1600
Sen no Rikyū becomes tea master to Oda Nobunaga, establishing the core tenets of the tea ceremony.	Oda Nobunaga is assassinated by a vassal at Honnōji temple in Kyoto.	Toyotomi Hideyoshi completes the reunification of Japan.	Tokugawa Ieyasu defeats the Toyotomi forces at the Battle of Sekigahara.

political system he established, together with his social and economic policies, set the stage for the next two centuries. Politically, Hideyoshi dominated the central government, but most of Japan was ruled by local *daimyō* who served as Hideyoshi's vassals, and in turn were confirmed as the rulers of their domains. Farmers were tied to their land by means of land surveys, and their weapons confiscated. The local samurai in turn were cut off from their local bases of power and forced to move to the *daimyō's* castle town. Hideyoshi's economic policies included **freeing production and trade** by abolishing guilds, minting coins, standardizing weights and measures and taking control of international trade.

When he died in 1598, Hideyoshi's heir, Hideyori, was still a child, allowing **Tokugawa Ieyasu**, Hideyoshi's most powerful vassal, to take control. After defeating the Toyotomi forces at the **Battle of Sekigahara** in 1600, Ieyasu asserted his authority over the other *daimyō* and was appointed shogun by the emperor in 1603. This began the Tokugawa (or Edo) *bakufu*, headquartered at Edo Castle, the present-day site of the Imperial Palace in Tokyo.

Tokugawa shogunate (Edo period)

The basis for **Tokugawa rule** was the overwhelming military strength of the Tokugawa and their allies over the other *daimyō*. As liege lord, the shogun commanded the obedience of the 260 to 280 *daimyō*, who owed their loyalty to him in return for being confirmed in their domains. As shogun, the Tokugawa drew on the authority and legitimacy of the imperial court. Further, the *bakufu* held vast territories throughout Japan under its direct control; these included not only agricultural land but also important cities such as Kyoto and Osaka, as well as ports, mines and markets. The *daimyō* were required to reside part of the year in **Edo**, thus forcing them into expensive time-consuming journeys, and to surrender family hostages who lived in Edo permanently. The expense of these journeys, combined with the cost of maintaining a household in Edo, could cost the *daimyō* as much as one-half of their annual revenues. Further, a network of inspectors and spies was set up, and any significant rebuilding of local castles had to be reported.

Despite this successful control of the ruling elite, the Tokugawa *bakufu* never established a unified, centralized government. Its revenues came from its own lands; the *daimyō* domains were not taxed. Likewise, administrative and legal functions were not unified; each *daimyō* domain had its own administration and laws. This system of "centralized feudalism" lasted for more than 250 years, interrupted by only one major rebellion, at Shimabara in 1637–38 (see p.704), and numerous small-scale riots by farmers.

It is often said that Tokugawa Japan was isolated from the rest of the world, but in fact the *bakufu* maintained **trading relations** with several Asian countries, as well as the Dutch. Embassies from **Korea** and the **Netherlands** visited the shogun in Edo regularly, enhancing the government's prestige. Fearful of subversion, the shogunate outlawed Christianity, expelled the Portuguese merchants and missionaries and confined the Dutch traders to Deshima (Dejima) in Nagasaki in 1641. International trade declined from the late seventeenth century, as Japan mined less silver but produced more silk. Conversely, the demand for European scientific knowledge brought by the Dutch grew stronger.

1603	1637–38	1641	1703
Tokugawa Ieyasu is appointed shogun; the Tokugawa *bakufu* begins.	The Shimabara Rebellion, led by Japanese Catholics, takes place in Kyūshū. Christianity is outlawed until 1865.	The Dutch are confined to Deshima in Nagasaki.	The Forty-seven Rōnin Incident takes place in Edo.

Tokugawa society was dominated by the samurai class, whose main function was to serve as administrators in the *bakufu* and domain governments. In this way, the samurai were transformed from warriors into **bureaucrats**, and their study of the martial arts became more philosophical than practical. There were more samurai than administrative posts, however, so many were reduced to poverty.

A main characteristic of Tokugawa Japan was that it was a **highly urbanized society**, with more than thirty cities of over 25,000 residents; Edo itself was perhaps the largest city in the world in the eighteenth century with a population of one million. Most of these cities were castle towns, such as Himeji, Matsumoto, and Matsue. The *daimyō* lived in the castle, which was surrounded by the houses of their samurai retainers, and of the merchants and artisans who supplied their needs. The requirement that all *daimyō* travel regularly to Edo led to the construction of a nationwide network of highways, stimulated commerce in both Edo and the domains, and the creation of a national culture, including the kabuki and *bunraku* theatres and *ukiyo-e* prints.

The arrival of the Black Ships

British survey vessels and **Russian** envoys visited Japan in the early nineteenth century, but the greatest pressure came from the **US**, whose trading and whaling routes passed to the south of the country. In 1853, Commodore Matthew Perry of the US Navy arrived with a small fleet of "**black ships**", demanding that Japan open at least some ports to foreigners. Japan's ruling elite was thrown into turmoil. The shogunate was already fearful of foreign incursions following the British defeat of China in the Opium Wars. However, when the emperor demanded that the foreigners be rebuffed, it quickly became clear that Japan's military was not up to the task.

There followed a decade of jockeying for power among different factions, and for influence by the foreign envoys. The first of these was the American Townsend Harris, who managed to extract concessions in the form of the pioneering **Treaty of Commerce and Navigation** in 1858. This was followed by a flurry of similar **agreements** with other Western countries, which opened the treaty ports of Yokohama, Hakodate, Nagasaki and, later, Kōbe and Osaka to trade, forbade the Japanese to impose protective tariffs and allowed foreigners the right of residence and certain judicial rights in the enclaves.

Opponents of such shameful appeasement by the shogunate took up the slogan *sonnō jōi* (*Revere the emperor! Expel the barbarians!*). Other, less reactionary factions could see that Japan was in no state to do this, and their only hope of remaining independent was to learn from the more powerful nations. Eventually, the great **western domains** – Satsuma, Chōshū, Tosa, and Hizen, previously rivals – combined forces under the banner of the emperor to exact revenge against the Tokugawa, whom they had seen as usurpers of the throne's authority ever since the Battle of Sekigahara, two hundred and fifty years previously.

Evidence of the shift in power came in 1863, when Emperor Kōmei ordered the fourteenth shogun, **Tokugawa Iemochi**, to Kyoto to explain his conciliatory actions; it was the first visit by a shogun to the imperial capital since 1634. To add to the humiliation, Iemochi could only muster a mere three thousand retainers, compared with the three hundred thousand who had accompanied the third shogun, Tokugawa Iemitsu, to Kyoto on that earlier occasion.

1853	1858	1867	1869
Commodore Perry's ships arrive in Japan.	The US–Japan Treaty of Commerce and Navigation is signed.	The Tokugawa *bakufu* comes to an end and power is returned to the emperor.	Edo, renamed Tokyo, becomes the new capital of Japan.

In 1867, the fifteenth and final shogun, Tokugawa Yoshinobu, formally applied to the emperor to have imperial power restored. The shogunate was terminated, and in December of the same year, the **Imperial Restoration** was formally proclaimed, and the 15-year-old **Mutsuhito** acceded to the throne, ushering in a period dubbed **Meiji**, or "enlightened rule." In 1869, the young emperor moved his court from Kyoto to Edo, and renamed it **Tokyo** (Eastern Capital).

The Meiji period

The reign of **Emperor Meiji**, as Mutsuhito was posthumously known, saw vast changes in Japan. A policy of **modernization**, termed *fukoku kyōhei* ("enrich the country, strengthen the military"), was adopted. Railways were built, compulsory education and military service introduced, the solar calendar adopted, and the *daimyō* domains and the class system abolished. Such rapid changes created resistance, and in 1877, **Saigō Takamori**, a hero of the restoration, led an army of forty thousand in the **Satsuma Rebellion**, named after the area of Kyūshū in which it erupted (see p.678). His defeat demonstrated that an army of farmers trained as soldiers could overcome samurai.

In the 1880s, even more changes were imposed by the ruling oligarchy of **Meiji Restoration** leaders, who imported several thousand foreign advisers for assistance. Japan adopted a Western-style constitution in 1889, drawn up by **Itō Hirobumi** (1841–1909), who had spent time in Europe studying constitutions. The **Meiji Constitution** created a weak parliament (the Diet), the lower house of which less than two percent of the population were entitled to vote for. In effect, a small group of leaders known as the Meiji "oligarchs" dominated the government, a situation reinforced by the Imperial Rescript on Education in 1890, which enshrined almost as law loyalty to the emperor, family, and state. Shintō, which emphasized emperor-worship, became the state religion, while Buddhism, associated too closely with the previous order, was disestablished. Japan's rulers also began to copy the West's **territorial ambitions**. The island of Hokkaidō, previously left pretty much to the native Ainu, was actively colonized, partly to ward off a takeover by Russia. In 1894, territorial spats with an ailing China developed into the **Sino-Japanese War** over the Chinese tributary state of Korea. The fighting lasted less than a year, with a treaty being signed in Shimonoseki in 1895 that granted Korea independence, and indemnities, economic concessions and territory to Japan, including Taiwan, then called Formosa.

This unexpected victory brought Japan into conflict with Russia who had her eye on China's Liaodong peninsula for a naval base at Port Arthur. After cordial relations with Britain were cemented in the 1902 Anglo-Japanese Alliance, Japan declared war on Russia in 1904 and destroyed the Russian fleet in 1905. The land battles of the **Russo-Japanese War** were less decisive, but in a US-mediated treaty in 1905, Russia was forced to make some territorial concessions to Japan. In 1909, the assassination of Itō Hirobumi, the newly appointed "resident general" of Korea, provided Japan with an excuse to fully annex the country the following year. Thus, by the beginning of the twentieth century, Japan had not only "modernized" its government and society but had become a **colonial power** as well.

1871–73	**1877**	**1879**	**1889**
The Iwakura Mission travels in the USA and Europe to study Western civilization.	The Satsuma Rebellion fails to overhaul the Meiji government.	The Ryūkyū Islands are incorporated into Japan as Okinawa Prefecture.	The Meiji Constitution is promulgated on Feb 11.

The Taishō period

The sudden death of Emperor Meiji in 1912 ushered in the relatively brief **Taishō** (Great Righteousness) **era**. This period saw much political ferment and numerous popular protests, including the nationwide Rice Riots of 1918. This period is called the age of "Taishō Democracy" because of the rise of political parties and the growing prominence of elected politicians. Universal male suffrage became law in 1925.

During **World War I**, Japan allied itself with Britain. Despite gaining more territory in Asia after the war and being one of the "Big Five" at the Paris Peace Conference and a founding member of the League of Nations in 1920, Japan was frustrated by Australia, Britain, and the US in its attempts to get a declaration of racial equality inserted as part of the Charter of the League. This snub, however, didn't preclude continued friendly relations between Japan and the West. In 1921, Crown Prince Hirohito was a guest of King George V at Buckingham Palace, while the following year the Prince of Wales spent a month touring Japan.

Levelling Yokohama and much of Tokyo, and leaving over a hundred thousand dead or missing, the 1923 **Great Kantō earthquake** was a significant blow, but the country was quickly back on its feet and celebrating the enthronement of Emperor Hirohito in 1926, who chose the name **Shōwa** (Enlightened Peace) for his reign.

The slide to war

Economic and political turmoil in the early 1930s provided the military with the opportunity it needed to seize full control. In 1931, the **Manchurian Incident** saw army officers cook up an excuse for attacking and occupying the Manchurian region of northern China. Japan installed **P'u Yi**, the last emperor of China's Qing dynasty, as the head of their puppet state, Manchukuo, and responded to Western condemnation of its actions by withdrawing from the League of Nations in 1933.

At home, the military increased its grip on power in the wake of **assassinations** in 1932 of both the prime minister and the former finance minister, and a confused, short-lived **coup** by 1400 dissident army officers in February 1936. **Rapid industrialization** also laid the foundations for some of the most famous Japanese firms of the twentieth century, including the automobile makers Mazda, Toyota and Nissan, and the electronics giant Matsushita.

In 1936, Japan joined Nazi Germany (and later Fascist Italy) in the **Anti-Comintern Pact**, and the following year launched a full-scale invasion of China. From December 1937, the infamous **Rape of Nanking** took place over a six-week period, with appalling atrocities committed by the Japanese military. As **World War II** began in Europe, Japan initially held off attacking Allied colonies in the Far East, but when France and the Netherlands fell to Germany, Japan's qualms disappeared. Sanctions were imposed by Britain and the US as Japan's army moved into Indo-China, threatening Malaya and the East Indies.

The Pacific War

On December 7, 1941, the Japanese launched a surprise attack on the US naval base at Hawaii's **Pearl Harbor**, starting the **Pacific War**. In rapid succession, the Philippines,

1894–95	1904–05	1910	1912
Japan defeats China in the Sino-Japanese War, winning control over Taiwan.	Japan's victory in the Russo-Japanese War gives her exclusive rights in Korea.	Japan annexes Korea as a colony.	The Meiji emperor dies and the Taishō era begins.

ndonesia, Malaya, and Burma fell to Japanese forces. However, the tide was stemmed n New Guinea and, in June 1942, the US Navy won a decisive victory at the **Battle of Midway** by sinking four Japanese aircraft carriers. Although Japan had launched her ampaign to secure a "Greater East Asia Co-Prosperity Sphere" in which she would free er neighbours from colonization and help them develop like the West, the brutal, acist, and exploitative reality of Japanese occupation meant there was no support from these potential Southeast Asian allies. Nor was there a likelihood of military cooperation between Japan and Germany, who eyed each other suspiciously, despite their pact.

By 1944, with the US capture of the Pacific island of Saipan, Japan was heading for defeat. The country was now within range of US heavy bombers, but there was a determination to fight to the bitter end, as exemplified by suicidal "kamikaze" pilots and the defending forces on the islands of Iwo-jima and Okinawa who fought to the last man. In March 1945, Tokyo was in ashes, and a hundred thousand were dead following three days of fire bombings. The government insisted that the emperor system remain inviolate when they put down arms, but no such assurances were offered in July 1945 when the Allies called for Japan's unconditional surrender in the Potsdam Declaration. Japan failed to respond, providing the Allies with the excuse they needed to drop an **atomic bomb** on **Hiroshima** on August 6. Two days later, the USSR declared war on Japan, and the next day, August 9, the second A-bomb exploded over **Nagasaki**.

With millions homeless and starving, and the country brought to its knees, it was a breathtaking understatement for Emperor Hirohito to broadcast, on August 15, 1945, that the war had "developed not necessarily to Japan's advantage." For his subjects, gathered at wireless sets around the country, the realization of defeat was tempered by their amazement at hearing, for the first time, the voice of a living god.

The American occupation

Never having been occupied by a foreign power, Japan little knew what to expect from the arrival of the "American Shogun" **General Douglas MacArthur**, designated the Supreme Commander for the Allied Powers (SCAP). Some five hundred soldiers committed suicide, but for the rest of the population the **occupation** was a welcome relief from the privations of war and an opportunity to start again. MacArthur wasted no time in instituting **political and social reform**. The country was demilitarized, the bureaucracy purged of military supporters, and war crimes trials were held, resulting in seven hangings, including that of the ex-prime minister, Tōjō Hideki. The emperor, whose support for the new regime was seen as crucial, was spared, although he had to publicly renounce his divinity to become a symbolic head of state.

In 1946, the Americans took a week to draft a **new constitution**, which proclaimed that sovereignty resided in the Japanese people, and contained the unique provision renouncing war and "the threat or use of force as a means of settling international disputes". Land and education reforms followed.

The **peace treaty**, signed in San Francisco on September 8, 1951, resolved all issues with the Allies, except that the USSR refused to sign. The outbreak of the **Korean War** in 1950 gave a much needed boost to Japan's economy, as the country became an important supplier to the US forces.

1914	**1923**	**1931**	**1933**
Japan enters World War I on the British side and captures German possessions in China.	The Great Kantō Earthquake devastates the Tokyo area.	The Manchurian Incident serves as an excuse for Japan to occupy Manchuria.	Japan withdraws from the League of Nations.

The occupation officially ended on April 28, 1952, but with the Korean War continuing and the **Treaty of Mutual Cooperation and Security** guaranteeing the US the right to maintain bases on Japanese soil, a strong American presence remained. The island of Okinawa was returned to Japan in 1972, but a large American military presence remains there to this day.

The 1960s economic miracle

In 1955, the Democratic and the (conservative) Liberal parties joined forces to form the **Liberal Democratic Party** (LDP), a coalition of factions that governed Japan uninterruptedly for close to the next forty years, creating stable political conditions for an incredible economic recovery. The term "**Japan, Inc.**" was coined to show the close cooperation that developed among government, bureaucracy and business.

In 1959, **Crown Prince Akihito** married Shōda Michiko, a commoner he had met while playing tennis at the summer resort of Karuizawa. In 1964, Japan joined the **Organization for Economic Cooperation and Development** (OECD), inaugurated the high-speed bullet train, or **Shinkansen**, and hosted the Summer Olympic Games.

During the 1960s, Japanese exports grew twice as fast as world trade, while Japan protected its home markets by subjecting imports to quotas, a mass of regulations, or outright bans. Yet **rapid industrialization** physically scarred the country, and **pollution** wrecked lives. In 1971, Tokyo's metropolitan government officially declared that the capital's residents breathed polluted air, drank contaminated water, and were "subjected to noise levels that strain the nerves."

By the 1970s, the ingrained **corruption** festering at the heart of Japanese politics was also becoming clear. The conservative LDP had continued to hold power mainly by entering into cosy financial relationships with supporters in industry and commerce. Prime Minister **Tanaka Kakuei**, a self-made politician from Niigata, had already attracted criticism for pushing through the needless construction of a Shinkansen line to his home town, when his abuse of party funds in the Upper House elections of July 1974 caused fellow LDP grandees to quit the Cabinet in protest. Tanaka rode the scandal out, but couldn't survive the bribery charges, brought in February 1976, in connection with the purchase of aircraft from America's Lockheed Corporation.

The bubble economy

As the economy continued to grow in the 1980s, Japan's huge balance of payments surplus and restrictive trade practices set it at odds with the international community, and particularly the US. The tense situation wasn't eased as cash-rich Japanese companies snapped up American firms and assets, such as the Rockefeller Center in New York, and the trade surplus with the US totalled over $30 billion. This overseas spending spree was made possible by what would later be known as the **bubble economy** – a period when low interest rates fuelled booming land prices and a runaway stock market. The **Tokyo Stock Exchange** became the largest in the world, and by late

1936	1937	1941	1945
In February, a group of army troops attempts a coup, assassinating some government officials.	A skirmish at the Marco Polo Bridge near Beijing leads to full-scale war with China.	The attack on Pearl Harbor leads to war with the USA, Britain and Australia.	Japan surrenders after atomic bombs are dropped on Hiroshima and Nagasaki.

1987 the market value of Japan's land area came to almost three times that of the United States. Weak opposition parties and a continually rising standard of living across the country allowed the LDP to hold on to power, despite factional infighting within the party.

The Heisei period

When Emperor Hirohito died in January 1989, it wasn't just the Shōwa period coming to an end: the overheated bubble economy had also reached bursting point. The new Heisei (Accomplished Peace) period started, and Emperor Akihito took the throne in November 1990. In 1993, Crown Prince Naruhito married Owada Masako, a high-flying career diplomat (see box, p.85). In the same year, a successful no-confidence motion led to a hasty general election, with the result that the overall balance of power passed to a **coalition** of opposition parties, who formed the first non-LDP government in 38 years. The following year, the LDP was forced to form a coalition government with their rivals, the Japan Socialist Party. Finally, after a series of party realignments, the LDP managed to regain control with the assistance of coalition partners. In the meantime, the collapse of the bubble in both the stock market and real estate led to a period of **economic stagnation** and deflation lasting more than a decade.

The government earned much ignominy for its botched response to the massive **Great Hanshin Earthquake** of January 1995, which devastated Kōbe. Offers of foreign help were initially rebuffed, and the local *yakuza* (criminal gangs) further shamed the government by organizing food supplies to the thousands of homeless. The nation's self-confidence took a further battering two months later when members of a religious cult, **Aum Shinrikyō**, killed twelve people and poisoned a further 5500 in a nerve gas attack on the Tokyo subway.

In 1996, the LDP returned to full power, under the leadership of former tough-talking trade negotiator **Hashimoto Ryūtarō**, but economic woes continued. The official announcement of recession in June 1998, coupled with the plummeting value of the yen and rising unemployment, saw the LDP take a drubbing in the July 1998 upper-house elections. Hashimoto resigned and was replaced by the genial but lacklustre **Obuchi Keizō**. A major nuclear accident in September caused pause for thought, but no cancellation of Japan's increased form of reliance on this form of energy.

LDP defeated

Much hope for positive change was placed on reform-minded **Koizumi Jun'ichirō**, who became prime minister in April 2001. Exports began to recover in 2003, and the stock market headed for heights last seen in the 1980s, helping Koizumi win two general elections for the LDP. However, when he stepped down as prime minister in 2006, Koizumi's reputation as a maverick reformer was undermined by the fact that he had ultimately been unable to push through many structural changes to Japan's system of government and economy. He'd also angered pacifists at home by deploying Self-Defense Force troops in **Iraq** and – much to the ire of China and South Korea –

1951	1964	1966	1972
The San Francisco Peace Treaty is signed, bringing the Occupation of Japan to an end the following year.	The first Shinkausen (bullet train) service starts between Tokyo and Osaka. Japan hosts the Summer Olympics.	Japan's first commercial nuclear power plant begins operating at Tōkai, Ibaraki Prefecture.	Sovereignty of Okinawa is returned to Japan, but US military bases remain.

continuing to visit Tokyo's controversial **Yasukuni shrine** that honours the nation's war dead (see p.86).

Koizumi's successors didn't fare much better, and as Japan's economy was battered by the **global financial crisis of 2008**, voters signalled that they had finally had their fill of the LDP. After a nearly unbroken run of 54 years in power, the party lost almost two-thirds of its seats in the Diet's lower house in the general election of 2009. The LDP was replaced by the **Democratic Party of Japan** (**DPJ**), with **Hatoyama Yukio** as prime minister. The euphoria over this major political change quickly evaporated in 2010 when a series of events dented national pride. The national airline JAL declared bankruptcy, and Toyota was forced to recall millions of its cars from around the world in the light of possible product faults. In the political arena, too, the DPJ fumbled, and following more of the usual funding scandals and the breaking of a campaign promise to close a military base on the island of Okinawa, Hatoyama was forced to resign. His replacement, **Kan Naoto** – Japan's fifth prime minister in three years – saw his party lose badly in the upper-house elections in July 2010. Voters had been turned off by Kan's call for a sales tax hike to help deal with the nation's public debt, estimated to be twice the size of Japan's US$5 trillion economy. Kan raised the ire of right-wingers a month later, when his government issued an apology to Korea on the centenary of Japan's annexation of their country (see box below) and, along with his Cabinet, refrained from visiting Yasukuni shrine.

JAPANESE–KOREAN RELATIONS

For centuries, Japan has had close links with **Korea**, with a significant number of Japan's ruling class – including the imperial family – believed to have had Korean heritage. Despite this, relations between the two countries have frequently been far from neighbourly. Toyotomi Hideyoshi (see p.796) led two unsuccessful invasions of the peninsula in the late sixteenth century, before Japan annexed Korea in 1910. Japan's harsh colonial rule has impacted on relations with its neighbour ever since.

The successful co-hosting of the **2002 World Cup** and a Japanese taste for the country's soap operas, pop music and spicy food have helped mend relations with South Korea. There have also been several **official apologies** for Japan's colonial rule of the peninsula, the latest coming from PM Kan Naoto in August 2010, which also stated that various confiscated cultural artefacts would be returned to South Korea. In 2011, the Royal Archives were returned but South Korea is still waiting for tens of thousands of other artefacts.

Japan's latest apologies were specifically directed at South Korea, rather than **North Korea**, where relations remain decidedly frosty. In 2002, after decades of denials, North Korea came clean about how it had abducted thirteen Japanese citizens in the 1970s and 1980s and forced them to train North Korean spies in Japanese language and culture. Some of the kidnapped were eventually returned to Japan but others had died while in captivity. North Korea's nuclear weapons ambitions don't help, especially as the rogue state keeps launching test missiles in Japan's direction. More recently, during the 2013 escalation of tensions between North and South Korea, Japan was threatened by the North with a "nuclear catastrophe" and had its anti-ballistic missile defence system on full alert against a possible attack.

1989	1995	2009	2011
Emperor Hirohito dies and the Heisei era begins.	The Great Hanshin Earthquake in Jan is followed by the sarin gas attack on the Tokyo subway in March.	The LDP suffers a crushing defeat in the election for the lower house.	The Great East Japan Earthquake occurs on March 11, accompanied by a massive tsunami and serious nuclear accident.

Tōhoku earthquake

On March 11, 2011 a **magnitude nine earthquake** ripped up from the seabed, its epicentre 70km east of Tōhoku's Oshika Peninsula. The subsequent destruction brought by one of the most powerful seismic events to ever hit Japan, and the ensuing tsunami that smashed into the coast, left the country reeling under the weight of over 15,883 confirmed deaths, 6150 injured and 2651 missing people. Entire towns were swept away and millions more households were left without electricity and water. Wrecked highways, railways and airports hampered the immediate relief efforts, while the damaged **Fukushima nuclear plant**, 200km north of Tokyo, appeared to be heading for meltdown, necessitating the government to call a nuclear emergency and evacuate 140,000 people living within 20km of the facility.

At a televised news conference three days after the quake, Prime Minister Kan acknowledged the crisis as "the toughest and the most difficult" for Japan since the end of World War II, and called on the country's stunned but typically stoical and quietly heroic population to pull together and jointly shoulder the necessary sacrifices. On top of the financial toll, estimated to be in the range of ¥25 trillion (US$300 billion), there was the immediate effect of the need to assist some 300,000 refugees and a steep decline in electricity generation, leading to rolling blackouts throughout 2011. Reflecting the anxious mood of the population, the prime minister adopted an **anti-nuclear stance**, closing down the ageing Hamaoka nuclear power plant, 200km southwest of Tokyo, and saying he would freeze plans to build new reactors. However, facing mounting public dissatisfaction at his government's handling of the crisis, he was forced to **resign**, and at the end of August 2011 was replaced by Noda Yoshihiko, the country's sixth prime minister in five years.

Recent developments

In the lower-house election held in December 2012, the LDP made a strong comeback, and the party's head, **Abe Shinzō**, became Prime Minister for the second time (having previously held office in 2006–7). He carried out measures to stimulate the economy and led his party to another victory in the upper-house election in July 2013. He has also stated that it's time to amend Japan's "peace" constitution and allow for the **Self-Defense Forces** to be more active. This move has angered China and South Korea, and brought about claims that Abe's agenda is to remilitarize Japan. Meanwhile, Japan still faces many problems concerning the stagnant economy, an ageing population and the ongoing clean-up of the Fukushima nuclear plant. The public mood was lifted in September 2013 though, when the International Olympic Committee chose Tokyo as the site of the **2020 Olympic Games**, which remain a bright spot on the nation's horizon.

2012	2013
The LDP is returned to power in the lower-house election, and the government purchases the Senkaku islands, sparking territorial disputes with China and Taiwan.	In July, it is discovered that contaminated water from the Fukushima Daiichi Nuclear Power Plant has been leaking into the Pacific Ocean. In Sept, Tokyo is chosen as the site of the 2020 Summer Olympics.

Religion

Japan's indigenous religion is Shintō, and all Japanese belong to it by default. About half the population are also practising Buddhists and around one million are Christian. Combining religions may seem odd, but a mixture of philosophy, politics and a bit of creative interpretation has, over time, enabled this to happen.

It has helped that Shintō does not possess one all-powerful deity, sacred scriptures or a particular philosophy or moral code. Followers live their lives according to the way or mind of the **kami** (gods), who favour harmony and cooperation. In this way, Shintō tolerates its worshippers following other religions, and it's a fairly easy step to combine Shintō's nature worship with the worship of an almighty deity, such as that of Christianity, or with the philosophical moral code of Buddhism.

Religious festivals are common, and many Shintō customs are still manifest in everyday Japanese life, from marriage ceremonies to purifying building plots and new cars. Nevertheless, few Japanese today are aware of anything other than the basic tenets of either Shintō or Buddhism, and many would not consider themselves "religious" as such.

Shintō

Shintō, or "the way of the gods", only received its name in the sixth century to distinguish it from the newly arrived Buddhism. Gods are felt to be present in natural phenomena – mountains, for example, or trees, waterfalls, strangely shaped rocks and even in sounds. But Shintō is more than just a nature-worshipping faith; it is an amalgam of attitudes, ideas and ways of doing things that, over two thousand years, has become an integral part of what it is to be Japanese.

Shintō shrines

Shintō shrines are called **jinja** (*kami*-dwelling), although you will also see the suffixes *-jingū* and *-gū*. These terms, and the *torii* (see below), are the easiest ways to distinguish between Shintō shrines and Buddhist temples. The shrine provides a dwelling for the *kami*, who are felt to be present in the surrounding nature, and it is also a place to serve and worship them. Though there are many styles of **shrine architecture**, they are traditionally built from unpainted cypress wood with a grass-thatch roof. The best examples of such traditional architecture are the Grand Shrine of Ise (see p.518),

---

STATE SHINTŌ

Throughout most of Japanese history, Shintō did not play a particularly important role in state politics. This all changed, however, after the Meiji Restoration of 1868 (see p.799), when Shintō was declared the national faith, largely to re-establish the cult of the emperor. Most Buddhist elements were removed from Shintō shrines and destroyed, and Buddhism was suppressed. **State Shintō** ushered in a period of **extreme nationalism** that lasted from around 1890 to 1945. During this period, Japan's mythological origins were taught as historical fact and people were encouraged to believe that all Japanese were descended from the imperial line. At the same time, the traditional values of *bushidō* (see box, p.796) were promoted as desirable personal qualities. After World War II, Emperor Hirohito was forced to renounce his divinity, becoming a merely titular head of state, and the State branch of Shintō was abolished, returning freedom of religion to Japan.

umo Taisha (near Matsue; see p.502) and Tokyo's Meiji-jingū (see p.113). Later designs show Chinese or Korean influences, such as the use of red and white paint or other ornamentation.

The **torii** marks the gateway between the secular and the spiritual world. Traditionally, these were plain and simple wooden constructions consisting of two upright pillars and two crossbeams. Gradually, various styles, such as the distinctive ed paint, evolved on the same basic design until there were over twenty different types of *torii*. Nowadays, they are also made of stone, metal and concrete, in which case they tend to remain unpainted.

Inside the compound, you often find pairs of human or animal **statues** on the approach to the shrine building: austere dignitaries in ancient court costume laden with weapons are the traditional Japanese guardians, though you'll also find lion-dogs (*koma-inu*), or large, ferocious-looking *Niō*, the wooden guardians that usually guard the gates of Buddhist temples. Others may be animal-messengers of the *kami*, such as the fox-messenger of Inari, the deity of good harvests.

Somewhere in the compound, you'll often see a **sacred tree**, denoted by a twisted straw rope, *shimenawa*, sporting zigzags of white paper tied around it. In the past, these trees were believed to be the special abode of some *kami*. Now they're just an expression of divine consciousness which, like other aspects of the surrounding nature, helps to bring people's minds out of the mundane world and enter into that of the *kami*.

Finally, you come to the **shrine building** itself. At the entrance, there's a slotted box for donations and a rope with a bell or gong at the top. Some say the bell is rung as a purification rite to ward off evil spirits, others that it's to attract the *kami*'s attention. You'll also notice another *shimenawa* delineating the *kami*'s sacred dwelling place. Inside each shrine, there's an **inner chamber** containing the *shintai* (divine body). This is a sacred object which symbolizes the presence of the *kami* and is kept under lock and key – if ever seen, it loses its religious power.

A large shrine will also comprise many other buildings, such as subordinate shrines, an oratory, ablution pavilion, offering hall, shrine office and shop, priests' living quarters, treasure house and sometimes even a platform for **sacred dances**, a nō drama stage or a sumo arena. In some cases, there will be no shrine building as such, but simply a *torii* and a straw rope around a tree or rock to indicate a *kami*'s dwelling place.

Visiting a shrine

When **visiting a shrine**, try to fulfil at least three of the four elements of worship. Of these, **purification** is perhaps the most important, as it indicates respect for the *kami*. At the ablution pavilion (a water trough near the entrance), ladle some water over your fingertips and then pour a little into your cupped hand and rinse your mouth with it; afterwards, spit the water out into the gutter below. Now purified, proceed to the shrine itself and the **offering**. This normally consists of throwing a coin in the box – a five-or fifty-yen coin (the ones with holes in the middle) are considered luckiest – though a special service warrants a larger sum wrapped in formal paper. Depending on the occasion, food, drink, material goods or even sacred dances (*kagura*, performed by female shrine attendants) or sumo contests are offered to the *kami*.

The third element is **prayer**. Pull the rope to ring the bell, step back, bow twice and clap twice. Pray quietly, then bow again. The final element of worship is the **sacred feast**, which usually only follows a special service or a festival. It sometimes takes the form of consuming the food or drink offered to the *kami* – once the *kami*'s had its symbolic share.

At the shrine shop you can buy charms (*omamori*) against all manner of ills, fortune papers (*omikuji*), which people then twist round tree branches to make them come true, and wooden votive tablets (*ema*) – write your wishes on the tablet and tie it up alongside the others.

KNOW YOUR FOLK GODS

Adding spice to the Japanese religious pot is a legion of folk gods, guardians and demons. The ones to have on your side are the **Seven Lucky Gods** (*Shichi Fuku-jin*), often seen sailing in a boat on New Year greetings cards to wish good fortune for the coming year. Of these, the best-loved are **Ebisu**, the god of prosperity, identified by his fishing rod and sea bream; **Daikoku**, the god of wealth, who carries a treasure-sack over one shoulder and a lucky hammer; the squat **Fukurokuju**, god of longevity, marked by a bald, egg-shaped head; while the jovial god of happiness, **Hotei**, sports a generous belly and a beaming smile.

Characters to avoid, on the other hand, are the **oni**, a general term for demons and ogres, though *oni* aren't always bad. **Tengu** are mischievous mountain goblins with red faces and very long noses, while **kappa** are a bit like small trolls and live under bridges. If anything goes missing while you're hiking, you can probably blame one of these, as they both like to steal things. If it's your liver that's missing, however, it will definitely be a *kappa*; he likes to extract them from people's bodies through the anus, so watch out.

All shrines have at least one annual **festival**, during which the *kami* is symbolically transferred from the inner chamber to an ornate palanquin or portable shrine, called a *mikoshi*. This is its temporary home while young men hurtle around the local area with it so that the *kami* can bless the homes of the faithful. The passion with which they run, turning it this way and that, jostling it up and down shouting "*wasshoi, wasshoi*", has to be seen to be believed, especially in rural towns where festivals are usually conducted with more gusto. All this frantic action is said to make the *kami* happy, and it is highly contagious: long after the palanquin has returned to the shrine the merriment continues with the help of copious amounts of alcohol.

Buddhism

Buddhism, which originated in India, was introduced to Japan from China and Korea in the mid-sixth century. As with many things, Japan adapted this import to suit its own culture and values. The Buddha was accepted as a *kami* and, over the years, certain religious aspects were dropped or played down, for example celibacy and the emphasis on private contemplation.

But Buddhism did not travel alone to Japan; it brought with it Chinese culture. Over the next two centuries, monks, artists and scholars went to China to study religion, art, music, literature and politics, all of which brought great advances to Japanese culture. As a result, Buddhism became embroiled in the **political struggles** of the Nara and Heian eras, when weak emperors used Buddhist and Chinese culture to enhance their own power and level of sophistication and to reduce the influence of their Shintoist rivals. Buddhist temples were often built next to Shintō shrines, and statues and regalia placed on Shintō altars to help raise the *kami* to the level of the Buddha. Eventually, some *kami* became the guardians of temples, while the Buddha was regarded as the prime spiritual being.

Up until the end of the twelfth century, Japanese Buddhism was largely restricted to a small, generally aristocratic minority. However, at this time the dominant sect, **Tendai**, split into various **new sects**, notably Jōdo, Jōdo Shinshū, Nichiren and Zen Buddhism. The first two – simple forms of the faith – enabled Buddhism to evolve from a religion of the elite to one which also appealed to the population en masse. The Nichiren sect had a more scholastic approach, while Zen's concern for ritual, form and practice attracted the samurai classes and had a great influence on Japan's traditional arts. Almost all contemporary Japanese Buddhism developed from these sects, which are still very much in existence today.

uddhist temples and worship

s with Shintō shrines, **Buddhist temples** (called *-tera*, *-dera* or *-ji*) come in many
ifferent styles, depending on the sect and the date they were built, but the foremost
rchitectural influences are Chinese and Korean. The temple's **main hall** (the *kon-dō* or
on-dō) is where you will find the principal image of the Buddha, and a table for
fferings. Sometimes the entry gate (*San-mon*) is as imposing as the temple itself,
onsisting of a two-storey wooden structure with perhaps a pair of brightly coloured,
earsome guardians called *Niō*, or *Kongō Rikishi*. Despite their looks, *Niō* are actually
uite good-natured – except to evil spirits.

Some temples also have a **pagoda** in their compound – they are Chinese versions
f stupas, the Indian structures built to enshrine a relic of the Buddha, and were
nce the main focus of Buddhist worship. Depending on the temple's size, you
night also see other buildings such as a study hall (*kō-dō*), scripture or treasure
ouses and living quarters. Zen temples are also famous for their stunningly
eautiful rock and landscape gardens, which are designed to aid meditation. The
most important occasion in Japan's Buddhist calendar is **Obon**, in mid-August,
when spirits return to earth and families traditionally gather to welcome them back
o the ancestral home. *Ohigan*, which falls on the spring and autumn equinox
usually March 21 and Sept 23), is again a time to visit ancestors' graves. But
probably the biggest celebration is **Shōgatsu** (New Year), though it's as much a
Shintō event as a Buddhist one.

Christianity

Though churches can be found even in small rural towns, Christians represent less than
one percent of Japan's population. The religion arrived in Japan with the Jesuit
missionary **Saint Francis Xavier** in 1549 (see p.795). Initially, the local *daimyō* were
eager to convert, largely in order to acquire firearms and other advanced European
technologies, while the poor were attracted to the message of equality and social
programmes which helped raise their standard of living.

The port of **Nagasaki** soon became a centre of Jesuit missionary activity, from where
Catholicism spread rapidly throughout Kyūshū. Converts were tolerated, but by the
late sixteenth century the authorities considered that the Christian merchants'
increasing stranglehold on trade, coupled with a growing influence in secular affairs,
was beginning to pose a threat. **Persecution** began in 1587. Suspected Christians were
forced to trample on pictures of Christ or the Virgin Mary to prove their innocence. If
they refused, they were tortured, burnt at the stake or thrown into boiling sulphur;
over three thousand Japanese converts were martyred between 1597 and 1660.

Following the **Battle of Shimabara** of 1637 (see box, p.705), Christianity was
forbidden in Japan up until the late nineteenth century. Amazingly, the religion
endured, and when foreign missionaries again appeared in Nagasaki in the mid-1860s,
they were astonished to discover some twenty thousand "hidden Christians". Since
then, around 250 Japanese martyrs have either been recognized as saints or beatified by
the Catholic Church, including Nagasaki's 26 martyrs (see p.695).

SŌKA GAKKAI

Several **new religions** appeared in Japan during the nineteenth and twentieth centuries,
many of them offshoots of Shintō or Nichiren Buddhism. The most successful has been **Sōka
Gakkai** (Value Creation Society), founded in 1930 by schoolteacher Makiguchi Tsunesaburō,
who emphasized the importance of educational philosophy alongside the day-to-day benefits
of religion. With its proselytizing mission and broad appeal to people of all ages and classes,
Sōka Gakkai International (W sgi.o g) now claims around twelve million members. The
movement also endorses the political party New Kōmeitō (W www.komei.or.jp).

Japanese arts

One of the joys of visiting Japan is experiencing the ordinary ways in which the Japanese aesthetic enters into everyday life. The presentation of food, a window display or the simplest flower arrangement can convey, beyond the walls of any museum or gallery, the essential nature of Japanese art.

Periods of aristocratic rule, military supremacy and merchant wealth have all left their mark on **Japanese arts**, building on a rich legacy of religious art, folk traditions and the assimilated cultural influences of China and Korea. More recently, the West became a model for artists seeking to join the ranks of the avant-garde. Today, Japanese artists both draw on traditional sources and take their place among international trends.

Spanning the centuries is a love of nature, respect for the highest standards of craftsmanship and the potential for finding beauty in the simplest of things. These qualities pervade the visual arts of Japan but are also reflected in aspects of the performing arts, where the actor's craft, costume and make-up combine with the stage setting to unique dramatic effect. The official designation of valued objects and individuals as **National Treasures** and **Living National Treasures** acknowledges the extent to which the arts and artists of Japan are revered.

The religious influence

Shintō and Buddhism, Japan's two core religions, have both made vital contributions to its arts. **Shintō's** influence is extremely subtle, but apparent in the Japanese love of simplicity, understatement and a deep affinity with the natural environment. The plain wooden surfaces of Shintō shrines, for example, together with their human scale, is reflected in a native approach to architecture in which buildings strive to be in harmony with their surroundings (for more about Shintō shrines, see p.807).

Some of Japan's earliest **Buddhist sculptures** can be found at Hōryū-ji, near Nara (see p.480) and take their inspiration from Chinese and Korean sculpture of an earlier period. The temple's bronze Shaka (the Historic Buddha) Triad by Tori Bushii, a Korean–Chinese immigrant, dates back to 623 and reflects the stiff frontal poses, archaic smiles and waterfall drapery patterns of fourth-century Chinese sculpture. At

---

THE WAY OF THE FLOWER

Ikebana, or the art of flower arranging, has its roots in ancient Shintō rituals and Buddhist practice. The original emphasis was on creating flower displays that imitated their **natural state**. This gradually evolved into using just three leading sprays to represent heaven, earth and humankind, which are arranged to express the harmonious balance of these elements, with the use of empty space being as crucial as the sprays themselves. The container, setting and season influence the choice of materials, which can range from bare branches and withered leaves to fruits, moss and grass.

The art of *ikebana* reached its peak in the sixteenth century, largely on the coat tails of the **tea ceremony** (see p.52) in which the only decoration in the room is an *ikebana* display or hanging scroll. As it became more widely practised, several distinct styles evolved, broadly divided into the self-explanatory *shōka* (living flowers), the formal *rikka* (standing flowers), *moribana* (heaped flowers), and the more naturalistic *nage-ire* (thrown in). Each of these is further subdivided into different schools, dominated nowadays by Ikenobō (🆆 www.ikenobo .jp), Ohara (🆆 ohararyu.or.jp) and Sōgetsu (🆆 sogetsu.or.jp). To find out more, contact Ikebana International (🆆 ikebanahq.org), an umbrella organization with branches in sixty countries.

he same time, Hōryū-ji's standing wooden Kudara Kannon, depicting the most
compassionate of the Bodhisattvas, is delicately and sensitively carved to emphasize
its spirituality.

During the early years of Buddhism in Japan and the periods of closest contact with
China (the seventh to tenth centuries), Japanese styles of Buddhist art mimicked those
current in China or from its recent past. However, a gradual process of assimilation
took place in both painting and sculpture until during the Kamakura period (see
p.794), when the adaptation of a distinctly Japanese model can be observed in
Buddhist art.

The Heian Period

In 898, the Japanese stopped sending embassies to the Chinese T'ang court, ending
centuries of close relations with China. Gradually, the cloistered and leisured
lifestyle of the Heian period (794–1185) aristocracy spawned a uniquely Japanese
cultural identity.

Court life in Heian Japan revolved around worldly pleasures and aesthetic pastimes,
and the period is renowned for its artistic and cultural innovation. *Kana*, or the
phonetic syllabary, was developed and employed in the composition of one of Japan's
greatest literary masterpieces, **The Tale of Genji**, or *Genji Monogatari*. Lady Murasaki's
portrayal of the Heian-court nobility eloquently described the artistic pursuits which
dominated their daily life – poetry competitions, the arts of painting, calligraphy and
gardening and the elaborate rituals of court dress.

A new painting format, the **emaki**, ("picture scroll"), also evolved during the Heian
period. *Emaki* depicted romances, legends and historical tales, of which the most
famous is an illustrated edition of *The Tale of Genji*, published around 1130. The
painting technique used, known as *Yamato-e*, employs flat blocks of colour with a
strong linear focus and a unique boldness of style. The **decorative arts** reached a
similarly high level of sophistication. Inlaid lacquerware, using the *maki-e* technique
(sprinkling the surface with gold or silver powder) and finely crafted bronze mirrors
employed surface designs to equally dramatic effect.

The lavishness of Heian taste is reflected in **Buddhist painting and sculpture** of this
period. New sects of Buddhism gave rise to the diagrammatic mandalas, schematic
depictions of the Buddhist universe, while religious sculpture became more graceful
and sensual, with gilded, delicately featured deities marking the transition to an
aristocratic form of Buddhist art

Samurai culture

The establishment of the Kamakura Shogunate in 1185 (see p.794) generated an
alternative artistic taste more in keeping with the simplicity, discipline and rigour of
the military lifestyle This new **realism** made itself felt in the portrait painting and
picture scrolls of the **Kamakura era** (1185–1333), most graphically in the *Handbook on
Hungry Ghosts*, now in Tokyo's National Museum (see p.95). Highly individualized
portraits of military figures and Zen masters became popular. Kamakura sculpture
similarly combined a high degree of realism with a dynamic energy. The two giant
guardian figures at Nara's Tōdai-ji (see p.474), fashioned by the sculptors Unkei and
Kaikei in 1203, are outstanding examples of this vigorous new style.

However, samurai culture had a more direct impact on the development of the
decorative arts. By the Edo period (1600–1868), Edo and Osaka had become leading
centres of **sword-making**, where swordsmiths were noted for their skill in forging and
for the meticulousness of finish which they applied to the blades. Through the
peaceful years of the Edo era, however, sword fittings gradually came to be more
decorative than functional.

The arts of Zen

With the spread of **Zen Buddhism** in the thirteenth century, Japanese arts acquired a new focus. Meditation is at the centre of Zen practice and many Zen art forms can be seen as vehicles for inward reflection or as visualizations of the sudden and spontaneous nature of enlightenment.

Monochromatic **ink painting**, known as *suiboku-ga* or *sumi-e*, portrayed meditative landscapes and other subjects in a variety of formats including screens, hanging scrolls and hand-scrolls, with a free and expressive style of brushwork that was both speedily and skilfully rendered. *Haboku*, or "flung-ink" landscapes, took this technique to its logical extreme by building up (barely) recognizable imagery from the arbitrary patterns formed by wet ink splashed onto highly absorbent paper. **Sesshū** (1420–1506), a Zen priest, was Japan's foremost practitioner of this technique.

Zen **calligraphy** similarly can be so expressively rendered as to be almost unreadable except to the practised eye. One of the most striking examples, by the monk Ryōkan Daigu (1757–1831), is a hanging scroll with the intertwined symbols for heaven and earth. These qualities of abstraction and suggestion were also applied to the design of **Zen gardens**, while meditation techniques spawned the highly ritualized and almost mesmeric **tea ceremony** (see p.52).

The Momoyama and Edo Periods

Japanese art was most opulent during the **Momoyama period** (1573–1600). The scale of feudal architecture created a new demand for decorative **screen paintings**, which were placed on walls, sliding doors (*fusuma*) and folding screens (*byōbu*). From the late sixteenth century, the Kyoto-based **Kanō School** of artists came to dominate official taste. Subjects were mainly drawn from nature and from history and legend, while the extensive use of gold leaf added a shimmering brightness to the dark interior spaces of the great Momoyama castles, palaces and temples. Kanō Eitoku and his grandson, Kanō Tan'yū, were the school's most famous exponents, and their works can still be seen in Kyoto's Daitoku-ji and Nijō-jō.

During the **Edo-period** (1600–1868), the arts flourished under the patronage of a newly wealthy merchant class. Artists such as Tawaraya Sōtatsu and Ogata Kōrin stand out for reviving aspects of the *Yamato-e* tradition and injecting new decorative life into Japanese painting. Sōtatsu's famous golden screen paintings based on *The Tale of Genji* dramatically adapt the subject matter and style of Heian-era *emaki* to this larger format. Kōrin's most noted works include the "Irises" screens at Tokyo's Nezu Museum (see p.116).

PICTURES OF THE FLOATING WORLD

During the Edo era, the lively entertainment districts of Edo, Osaka and Kyoto, with their brothels, teahouses and kabuki theatres, provided inspiration for artists. This new genre of painting, **ukiyo-e**, or "pictures of the floating world", devoted itself to the hedonistic pastimes of the new rich. By the early eighteenth century, *ukiyo-e* were most commonly produced as hand-coloured woodblock prints which became more sophisticated in their subtle use of line and colour as mass-printing techniques developed.

Late eighteenth-century artists such as Harunobu, Utamaro and Sharaku portrayed famous beauties of the day and kabuki actors in dramatic poses. Explicitly erotic prints known as *shunga* (spring pictures) were also big sellers, as were humorous scenes of daily life (*manga*), the forerunners of today's comics. **Hokusai** (1760–1849), perhaps the most internationally famous *ukiyo-e* artist, was originally known for his *manga*, but went on to create one of the most enduring images of Japan, *The Great Wave*, as part of his series *Thirty-Six Views of Mount Fuji*. Followed by the equally popular *Fifty-Three Stages of the Tōkaidō*, by Hiroshige (1797–1858), these later landscape prints were instantly popular at a time when travel was both difficult and restricted.

MINGEI: THE FOLK CRAFT TRADITION

Japanese **folk crafts**, *mingei*, delight in the simplicity and utilitarian aspects of ordinary everyday objects. *Mingei* really is "people's art", the works of craftsmen from all regions of Japan that are revered for their natural and unpretentious qualities.

While Japanese folk crafts flourished during the Edo period, the mass production techniques of the machine age led to a fall in the quality of textiles, ceramics, lacquer and other craft forms. The art critic and philosopher Yanagi Sōetsu (1889–1961) worked from the 1920s to stem this tide and to preserve the craft products of the pre-industrial age. Yanagi established the **Mingei-kan**, or Japanese Folk Crafts Museum, in Tokyo in 1936 (see p.117). But the revival of the *mingei* tradition also celebrated works by living artist-craftsmen, as well as regional differences in style and technique. The potters Hamada Shōji, Kawai Kanjirō and the Englishman Bernard Leach were most famously associated with the *mingei* movement, as was the woodblock artist Munakata Shikō, and the textile designer Serizawa Kiesuke.

A wide range of **traditional handicrafts**, including pottery, lacquerware, wood, bamboo and handmade paper products, are still being produced today all over Japan. *Yūzen*-style kimono dyeing and *kumihimo* braid craft are associated with Kyoto; *shuri* weaving techniques with Okinawa; *Hakata ningyō*, or earthenware dolls, with Fukuoka; and Kumano brushes with Hiroshima.

The **decorative arts** reached new heights of elegance and craftsmanship. Varieties of Imari- and Kutani-ware **porcelain** were made in large quantities for domestic consumption and later for export. Inlaid **lacquerware** was executed in bold and simple designs. Hon'ami Kōetsu was a leading lacquer artist of the period, as well as a celebrated painter and calligrapher. One of Kōetsu's most famous lacquer works, an inkstone box in the Tokyo National Museum, reflects these combined talents with its inlaid-lead bridge and silver calligraphy forming integral parts of the overall design.

Western influences

The period of **modernization and westernization** which followed the fall of the Tokugawa Shogunate in 1867 transformed the face of Japanese visual arts. The opening of the treaty ports furnished a new subject matter for woodblock print artists who produced marvellous portraits of Westerners in Yokohama and other ports. The opening of the first railway, spinning factory and many other advances were also recorded for posterity.

In the early years of the Meiji period (1868–1912), traditional Japanese and Chinese styles of painting were rejected in favour of Western styles and techniques. Artists such as Kuroda Seiki and Fujishima Takeji studied in Paris and returned to become leaders of **Western-style painting** (*Yō-ga*) in Japan. Realism, Impressionism and other Western art movements were directly transplanted to the Tokyo art scene. More conservative painters, such as Yokoyama Taikan, worked to establish *Nihon-ga*, a modern style of Japanese painting, drawing on a mixture of Chinese, Japanese and Western techniques.

Western influence on the arts expanded greatly in the Taishō period (1912–26) with **sculpture**, as well as painting, closely following current trends. In the postwar period, Japanese artists looked again to Europe and America but more selectively took their inspiration from a range of avant-garde developments in the West.

Contemporary visual art

Visual art in Japan today blends Japanese and international currents, which at best interact to create innovative new styles. A prime example of such vigorous cross-fertilization is the development of **manga** as a sophisticated, internationally popular art form in which sources of tradition can no longer be identified purely with the East or the West.

CONTEMPORARY JAPANESE WOMEN ARTISTS

Over the last decade, Japanese women artists working in the contemporary visual field have been producing diverse and exciting works that challenge both their society and international perceptions of female identity in Japan. **Yanagi Miwa** (ⓦyanagimiwa.net) has explored the roles of women in Japanese society, from elevator girls to grandmothers in beautifully executed photographic series. **Sawada Tomoko** (ⓦwww.e-sawa.com) also looks at women's roles, usually with herself as the subject. The work of **Yamaguchi Ai** (ⓦninyu.com) is influenced by manga and anime, with references to Edo-period courtesans, and depicts young female prostitutes. **Ninagawa Mika** (ⓦninamika.com) is known for her colourful photographs of flowers and goldfish, while also branching into fashion and film. **Matsui Fuyuko** (ⓦmatsuifuyuko.com) is a *Nihon-ga* artist who skillfully uses the traditional ink-painting genre to depict disturbing gothic scenes.

The international success of artists such as **Nara Yoshitomo**, **Murakami Takashi** and **Yayoi Kusama** has shaped the world's perception of Japanese contemporary art during the last decade. The works of **Matsuura Hiroyuki** and **Nishizawa Chiharu** are also much in demand at international art fairs and auctions. Matsuura, a one-time manga character model maker, now produces ambiguous but dynamic canvases that have been described as "manga as fine art". Nishizawa's work uses the elevated point of view of traditional Japanese painting, but portrays the uneasy emptiness of modern life. The Damien Hirst-influenced **Nawa Kohei** creates installations and sculptures which reject the "culture of cute" which has become symbolic of Japanese pop culture art. **Ito Zon** is known for his delicate drawings, embroideries and video works that explore nature. The mystical paintings of **Yamaguchi Akira** are rooted in traditional Asian aesthetics and display a masterful technique. Artists who deal with more political themes include **Tomiyama Taeko**, who visually explores war and issues of social justice, and **Morimura Yasumasa**, who deals with gender and identity through photography and lithograph.

Manga

The word **manga** (meaning "whimsical pictures") is attributed to the great nineteenth-century artist Hokusai. Today, it covers comics, graphic novels, cartoon strips and even creations such as the character Hello Kitty. Japan's love of images is ingrained in the culture; **ukiyo-e**, woodblock prints, many of which depict lively scenes of daily life and imaginative renditions of fables and fantast, were as popular two centuries ago as manga is today. Indeed, Hokusai's erotic print *The Dream of the Fisherman's Wife* (1824), which depicts a naked woman being pleasured by a couple of rather randy octopuses, could be straight out of contemporary pornographic manga (*hentai*).

International reception of the medium can be clouded by the graphic sexual imagery and violence seen in some manga, compounded by the misconception that the subject matter is exclusively limited to sci-fi and fantasy. In reality, manga covers an enormous range of stories, from cooking to politics, and has many genres – for example, *manga-shi* (magazines) aimed at young people are split into *shōjo* (girls), *shōnen* (boys) and *seinen* (youth) categories.

Performing arts

The traditional theatre arts of **nō** (sometimes written Noh in English), **bunraku**, **kabuki** and **buyō** evolved in the context of broader cultural developments during different periods of Japan's history. The plays of each art form often draw on similar plots, but their presentation couldn't be more different.

Nō

The oldest – and most difficult to appreciate – type of Japanese theatre is **nō**. This form of masked drama has its roots in sacred Shintō dances, but was formalized six hundred years ago under the patronage of the Ashikaga shoguns and the aesthetic influence of Zen. The bare wooden stage with its painted backdrop of an ancient pine tree, the actors' stylized robes and the fixed expressions of the finely crafted masks create an atmosphere that is both understated and refined. The dramatic contrasts of stillness and sudden rushes of movement, and of periods of silence punctuated by sound, conjure up the essence of the Zen aesthetic.

The actor's skill lies in transcending the conventions of archaic language, mask and formalized costume to convey the dramatic tensions inherent in the play. Dance elements and musical effects aid directly in this process and draw on the folk entertainment tradition from which nō is derived.

The comic **kyōgen** interludes in a nō programme provide light relief. As in the main drama, *kyōgen* performers are all male and assume a variety of roles, some of which are completely independent of the nō play, while others comment on the development of the main story. The language used is colloquial (though of sixteenth-century origin) and, compared with the esoteric poetry of nō, far more accessible to a contemporary audience.

Kabuki

Colourful, exuberant and full of larger-than-life characters, **kabuki** is a highly stylized theatrical form which delights in flamboyant gestures and elaborate costumes, make-up and staging effects. While the language may still be incomprehensible to foreigner, the plots themselves deal with easily understood, often tragic themes of love and betrayal, commonly taken from famous historical episodes.

Kabuki originated in the early 1600s as rather **risqué dances** performed by all-female troupes. The shogun eventually banned women taking part, because of kabuki's association with prostitution, but their replacement – young men – were also available to customers as prostitutes. In the end, kabuki actors were predominantly older men, some of whom specialize in performing female roles (*onnagata*). Kabuki developed as a more serious form of theatre in the late sixteenth century when it was cultivated chiefly by the merchant class. It gave theatrical expression to the vitality of city life and to the class tensions between samurai, merchants and peasants that inform the plots of so many plays. To learn more about kabuki, go to Ⓦkabuki21.com and Ⓦkabuki-bito.jp/eng.

Bunraku

Japan's puppet theatre, **bunraku**, developed out of the *jōruri* storytelling tradition, in which travelling minstrels recited popular tales of famous heroes and legends, accompanied by the *biwa* (Japanese lute) or *shamisen* (three-stringed guitar). Adapted to the stage in the early seventeenth century, *bunraku* made use of stylized **puppets**, one-half to one-third the size of humans, to enact the various roles. The great Osaka

---

THE TEZUKA EFFECT

Many of anime and manga's stylistic traits – exaggerated facial features, episodic storytelling and the cinematic quality of presentation – are credited to the seminal manga artist **Tezuka Osamu** (1928–89) creator of **Astro Boy**, or Tetsuwan Atomu, as he's known in Japan. Astro is a boy robot with rockets for feet and a memory bank of human experiences who forever ponders his relationship to humans; such philosophical character traits and dark, complex themes are a prominent feature throughout the genre. Tezuka is credited with jump-starting anime in the 1960s, when he turned his comic Astro Boy into a TV series. The flat, two-dimensional look of anime, which is still common today, was a result of the need to keep production budgets low, using fewer images per second.

playwright **Chikamatsu Monzaemon** (1653–1724), often referred to as "the Shakespeare of Japan", is responsible for around one hundred *bunraku* plays, many of which are still performed today.

Puppets are worked by three operators, while a chanter, using a varied vocal range, tells the story to the accompaniment of *shamisen* music. The main puppeteer is in full view of the audience and uses his left hand to manipulate the face and head, with his right controlling the puppet's right arm. One assistant operates the left arm while another moves the puppet's legs. The skill of the puppeteers – the result of lengthy apprenticeships – contributes to the high degree of **realism** in the performance, and the stylized movements can result in great drama. Indeed, kabuki actors employ some puppet-like gestures from *bunraku* to enhance and enliven their own acting techniques. To learn more about *bunraku*, go to ⓦbunraku.or.jp.

Buyō

Classical Japanese dance is known as **buyō**, and elements of this art form intersect with other traditional performing arts traditions such as Nō and kabuki. Buyō originates from the folk and ritual dances of ancient Japan. It developed into a refined form of dance, to be performed on stage, around the time that kabuki began to flourish in the seventeenth century. Today, there are over 200 schools of buyō. Dancers usually wear kimono, and as a result their graceful movements are slow and restricted. The geisha of Kyoto continue the Kamigata style of buyō, which they perform throughout the year (see p.449).

Contemporary theatre and dance

Contemporary Japanese theatre and dance ranges from the all-female musical revues of **Takarazuka** (see box, p.152) and serious drama, to the abstract and improvisational dance form of **butō** (or Butoh), which draws on the traditions of kabuki and Nō as well as contemporary American dancers such as Martha Graham. Though it remains a marginal art form in Japan, butō's haunting beauty and eccentric expression has found greater appreciation in Europe and America.

In the 1970s, **Hideki Noda** became one of the most prominent figures in Japanese contemporary theatre and has since been involved in projects ranging from new kabuki writing and working with his theatre group, Noda Map (ⓦnodamap.com), to forays into opera. The director **Ninagawa Yukio** has also won a considerable following both inside and outside Japan for his traditional Japanese plays and productions of Shakespeare that bridge the theatrical conventions of East and West. Members of the **Setagaya Public Theatre** have also collaborated with foreign producers on international productions such as a stage adaptation of Haruki Murakami's collection of short stories, *The Elephant Vanishes*.

There are hundreds of other theatre groups throughout Japan creating original works. One of the most acclaimed and active both locally and abroad is **chelfitsch** (ⓦchelfitsch.net/en), the project of **Okada Toshiki**. The work of auteur/director Tanino Kurō, a specialist in the theatre of the absurd, is also worth looking out for.

ONLINE RESOURCES FOR THE ARTS

KIE (Kateigaho International Edition) ⓦint.kateigaho.com. This biannual magazine covers the range of Japanese arts and culture.

The Performing Arts Network ⓦperformingarts.jp. Presents the broad range of Japanese performing arts, with a focus on groups and artists active on the international scene.

Tokyo Art Beat ⓦtokyoartbeat.com and **Kansai Art Beat** ⓦkansaiartbeat.com. Excellent bilingual resource listing exhibitions and events in the Tokyo and Ōsaka/Kyoto areas.

The Virtual Museum of Japanese Arts ⓦweb-japan.org/museum. Useful overview of traditional Japanese arts and culture from the Ministry of Foreign Affairs.

Music

The arrival of eighty Korean musicians in 453 AD and the introduction of Buddhism in the mid-sixth century are key early events in the history of Japanese music. *Gagaku* (court orchestral music) and religious music survive from this period, and Buddhist chanting, *shōmyō*, can still be heard in temples today.

Similar to a chamber orchestra, *gagaku* ensembles include as many as twenty instruments, with flutes, oboes, zithers, lutes, gongs and drums. *Gagaku* is now played only as bugaku (dance music) or **kangen** (instrumental music), typically at the imperial court and at larger Shintō shrines and Buddhist temples. Unlike Western classical music, themes aren't stated and repeated. Instead, the rhythms are based on breathing and the result is a form that sounds sometimes discordant, sometimes meditative.

Distinctive musical styles also developed for the principal theatrical arts: Nō, *bunraku* and kabuki (see p.815). The sparse music of **nō** features solo singers, small choruses and an instrumental ensemble of *fue* (bamboo flute), two hourglass drums and a barrel drum. The **shamisen** (three-string lute) was added to the flute and drums for *bunraku*, leading to a more lively and popular musical style.

In the seventeenth and eighteenth centuries, during Japan's period of isolation from the outside world, instruments like the *koto* (a kind of zither) continued to develop a repertoire, as did the *shakuhachi* bamboo flute. The *nagauta shamisen* style for kabuki theatre also developed at this time, as did the *sankyoku*, the typical instrumental ensemble of the age – *koto*, *shamisen*, *shakuhachi* and *kokyū* (a bowed fiddle).

Min'yō (regional folk music)

Each region of Japan has its own style of **min'yō** (folk music), the most famous being the instrumental *shamisen* style from Tsugaru in Tōhoku. **Kinoshita Shin'ichi** has earned the nickname "the man with the divine hands" for his pioneering Tsugaru *shamisen* playing that marries the traditional northern *shamisen* style of fast plucking with jazz and rock. Kinoshita played a major part in the *shin-min'yo* (new *min'yō*) wave led by singer **Ito Takio**, well known for his passionate singing style and willingness to experiment. Since the millennium, Tsugaru *shamisen* has been experiencing a boom in popularity, helped by stand-out performers the **Yoshida Brothers** (⊚domomusicgroup .com) and **Agatsuma Hiromitsu** (⊚agatsuma.tv).

Traditional **drumming** from Sado-ga-shima (see p.279) has now become famous internationally. **Za Ondekoza** (⊚ondekoza.com), the original group of drummers, and its offshoot, **Kodō** (⊚kodo.or.jp), are capable of playing very powerful, theatrical gigs with just the various Japanese drums (from the big *daiko* to small hand-drums).

At Japan's northern extremity is the island of Hokkaidō, home to the indigenous Ainu. Their traditional music and instruments, including the skinny string instrument the *tonkori* and the *mukkuri* ("Jew's harp"), have been taken up by **Oki Kano**, a half-Ainu musician. Together with his Oki Dub Ainu Band (⊚tonkori.com), Oki has released several toe-tapping and soulful albums and has played at international music festivals including WOMAD in the UK.

Enka

Described as *Nihonjin no kokoro*, "the soul of the Japanese", **enka** (from *enzetsu*, "public speech", and *ka*, "a song") are songs about lost love, homesickness or simply drowning

> ### BEAUTIFUL SKYLARK
>
> A musical icon and the undisputed queen of *enka* is **Misora Hibari** ("beautiful skylark"). Born Kazue Katō, she made her debut as a singer in 1946, at the tender age of 9, and became an instant hit for her ability to memorize long poems and mimic adult singers. Her powerful, sobbing *kobushi* vocal technique created a highly charged atmosphere, but she was also talented enough to cover jazz, *min'yō*, Latin, chanson and torch songs in the thousand recordings and 166 films she made before her untimely death in 1989, aged 52. See ⓦ misorahibari.com for more information on this Japanese musical legend.

the sorrows of a broken heart with sake. Over one hundred years old, and still enormously popular, *enka* originally was a form of political dissent, disseminated by song sheets. However, in the early twentieth century it became the first style to truly synthesize Western scales and Japanese modes. Shimpei Nakayama and Koga Masao were the trailblazing composers. Koga's first hit in 1931, *Kage Wo Shitaite* (*Longing For Your Memory*), remains a much-loved classic.

It's difficult to escape *enka*. Television specials pump it out, and you'll hear it in restaurants and bars. And, of course, it received a major boost with the invention of karaoke, which helped to spread the genre's popularity both with younger Japanese and foreigners.

The classic image is of *enka* queen **Misora Hibari** (see box above) decked out in a kimono, tears streaming down her face as she sobs through Koga's *Kanashii Sake* (*Sad Sake*), with typically understated backing and single-line guitar. **Miyako Harumi** is also famed for her growling attack and the song *Sayonara*. Many *enka* stars have long careers, and veterans like Kitajima Saburō are still going strong today, as are Mori Shin'ichi, Yashiro Aki, Kobayashi Sachiko and Itsuki Hiroshi. More recent stars are **Hikawa Kiyoshi**, known as the prince of *enka*, and Pittsburgh native **Jero**, aka Jerome Charles White Jr, whose hip-hop attire gives a contemporary spin to the genre.

Rock and pop classics

By the late 1960s, musicians were starting to create **Japanese-language rock**. Seminal band **Happy End** were pioneers. Led by composer Hosono Haruomi (later a founding member of Yellow Magic Orchestra) and lyricist Matsumoto Takashi, the band meshed folk-rock with Japanese lyrics about love and politics. Their song *Kaze Wo Atsumete* featured on the soundtrack for the film *Lost in Translation*.

Okinawan musician **Kina Shōkichi** and his band named after the traditional Okinawan stir-fry, **Champloose** (ⓦchamploose.co.jp), gained acclaim in the 1970s, particularly with his song *Haisai Oji-san* (*Hey, Man*), which became so famous that it is used today as a drill song for high-school baseball games. **Southern All Stars** (ⓦsas-fan.net), whose way of singing Japanese as if it were English helped them to become Japan's biggest-selling band in the late 1980s, were another influential group; they're still going strong today.

Yellow Magic Orchestra (YMO; ⓦwww.ymo.org), formed in 1978 by Hosono Haruomi, Sakamoto Ryūchi and Takahashi Yukihiro, were heavily influenced by German technopop band Kraftwerk. Having gone their own ways in the mid-1980s – Sakamoto, in particular, developed a highly successful international career, both as a soloist and as an Oscar-winning film-score composer – the trio reformed in 2007 and still play together today.

The roots boom

The growing popularity of **world music** has had a significant effect in Japan. **Reggae**, for example, was considered "underground" for years, but is now part of the mainstream, as is ska, following the success of the **Tokyo Ska Paradise Orchestra** (Ⓦtokyoska.net). **Latin music** has also had a big effect, propelling salsa band **Orquesta de la Luz** (Ⓦlaluz.jp) to the top of the Billboard Latin chart in the early 1990s.

The Boom (Ⓦtheboom.jp), led by Miyazawa Kazufumi, helped to spawn the Okinawan music boom (see box below) in 1993 with their single *Shima Uta* (*Island Songs*). In the mid-1990s, they experimented with Brazilian music, opening up a new generation's ears to the South American melodies. In 2006, Miyazawa formed a new band, **Ganga Zumba**, with Brazilians Marcos Suzano and Fernando Moura, again playing a mix of Brazilian- and Latin-inspired pop.

The most significant development of the 1980s, however, was the rise of **roots-influenced** bands and singers such as **Shang Shang Typhoon** (Ⓦshangshang.jp), Rinken Band, Nenes and Daiku Tetsuhiro. Inspiration came from both within Japan (Okinawa and local popular culture) and outside (world music).

Foremost among the 1990s wave of bands plundering global music styles was **Soul Flower Union** (SFU), a seven-member outfit from Osaka led by Nakagawa Takashi. SFU also have an appealing alter ego, **Soul Flower Mononoke Summit** (SFMU), where the band blends acoustic guitars, Okinawan and *chindon* (street) music, which advertises products or shops, with drums and various brass instruments. Recent work has included gigs with the respected Irish musician and producer Donal Lunny who is married to SFU member Itami Hideko.

THE SOUND OF THE DEEP, DEEP SOUTH

Music has been integral to **Okinawa**'s culture and social life for centuries: it's said that peasants carried their musical instruments into the rice fields, ready for a jam session after work. The **folk tradition** is very much alive: in some villages, *umui* (religious songs) are still sung at festivals to honour ancestors; work songs that reflect communal agriculture techniques can still be heard; and various kinds of group and circle dances, some performed exclusively by women, can be found in the smaller islands.

Popular entertainment is known by the general term *zo odori* (common dance), though everyone calls these songs **shima uta** (island songs). The best-known style, one no wedding would be complete without, is called *katcharsee*. Set to lively rhythms laid down by the *sanshin* which plays both melody and rhythm, and various drums, the dance is performed with the upper body motionless and the lower body swaying sensuously, accompanied by graceful hand movements that echo similar dances in Thailand and Indonesia.

The Asian connection can be clearly seen in the history of the **sanshin**. This three-stringed lute began life in China as the long-necked *sanxian* and was introduced to Okinawa around 1392. Local materials were quickly exhausted, so that Thai snakeskin was used for the soundbox and Filipino hardwood for the shorter neck of the altered instrument, which became known as the *sanshin*. Once introduced to mainland Japan, the *sanshin* became bigger, produced a harder sound and was renamed the *shamisen*, one of the quintessential Japanese instruments.

A more recent influence on Okinawan music has come via the US military presence. Local musicians started to copy American pop styles in the 1950s, sometimes mixing in folk music. One major star whose music developed in this way was **Kina Shōkichi** who formed the band Champloose (see opposite) while still at high school, thus opening the way for a new generation of Okinawan rockers, including ex-band members **Nagama Takao**, famous for his fast-action *sanshin* playing, and **Hirayasu Takashi**.

Another legendary Okinawan musician is **Sadao China**, who records his own solo *min'yō*, as well as reggae-rock with an Okinawan flavour. As a producer, China brought the all-female group **Nenes** to international fame; the original four band members have since played with Ry Cooder and Michael Nyman among others. China has a club, *Shima Uta Live House*, in Naha, which is one of the best places in the islands to see Okinawan roots music. A good blog to find out more on the Okinawan music scene is Ⓦpowerofokinawa.wordpress.com.

INTERNET RESOURCES FOR JAPANESE MUSIC

CD Japan (ⓦcdjapan.co.jp) Online shop offering comprehensive selection of CDs, DVDs and other collectables released in Japan.

Far Side Music (ⓦwww.farsidemusic.com) A good place to buy CDs and DVDs, and for further explorations into Japanese and Okinawan music.

McClure Music (ⓦmccluremusic.com) All the latest music industry news from Japan and Asia. Updated regularly.

NEC Navigates Japan's Classical Music Artists (ⓦjapansclassic.com) Promoting not only top local musicians specializing in Western classical music but also those skilled at traditional Japanese instruments and forms.

Contemporary sounds

Among teenagers and young adults across Asia, it's **J-pop** (Japanese pop) that shifts the largest number of units. **Hamasaki Ayumi** (ⓦavexnet.or.jp/ayu/en) commonly known as Ayu, is J-pop's ruling empress. **SMAP** (ⓦwww.jvcmusic.co.jp/-/Artist/A002763. html), formed in 1991, has graduated from Japan's premier boy band to simply its top band. SMAP member **Kimura Takuya** is as big a star as you can get, his enduring celebrity bolstered by many acting roles on TV and in films. More appealing to goths, glam-rock and cyberpunk fans are the so-called **Visual kei**, bands such as Dir en Grey, X and Luna Sea.

Super **idol groups** such as **AKB48** (ⓦwww.akb48.co.jp), a singing and dancing ensemble with 89 girl members and their own theatre, plus love-balladeers **Arashi** (ⓦj-storm.co.jp), a group of five young men, are incredibly popular both at home and abroad and have active fan groups. The biggest J-pop sensation recently has been **Kyary Pamyu Pamyu** (ⓦkyary.asobisystem.com), a singer who has emerged from the Harajuku kawaii fashion scene. Her child-like super-sweet pop songs such as Pon Pon Pon and Fashion Monster have also found an enthusiastic international audience. She toured in Europe, the Asia-Pacific and North America in 2013.

Hip hop and **rap** have been enthusiastically adopted by musicians and spin-masters such as DJ Krush (aka Ishi Hideaki; ⓦsus81.jp/djkrush), the duo **m-flo** (ⓦm-flo.com) and rock band **Dragon Ash** (ⓦwww.dragonash.co.jp). Techno DJs **Ken Ishii** and **Ishino Takkyu** (of Denki Groove fame) and electronica outfits such as **Ryukyu Underground** (ⓦryukyu-underground.wwma.net), who mix up the sounds of Okinawa with dub beats and the occasional lounge-style tempo, are finding an audience outside Japan, too.

Indie bands and singers have a strong local following. The singer known as **UA** (ⓦuauaua.jp) has a unique style – part jazz, part avant-garde – and is one of Japan's most interesting contemporary singer-songwriters. **Ringo Sheena**'s 2003 *Karuki, Zamen, Kuri no Hana* (*Chlorine, Semen, Chestnut Flowers*) is an impressive concept album embracing everything from big-band swing to traditional *koto, shamisen* and flute music. Sheena has since gone on to form the band Tokyo Jihen, before going solo again to score the music for the period drama film *Sakuran*. She's also collaborated with explosive jazz combo **Soil & "Pimp" Sessions** (ⓦjvcmusic.co.jp/soilpimp) which is gaining international attention.

If you want to hear work by some of the artists mentioned above, check out the *Rough Guide to the Music of Japan* (available from World Music Network; ⓦwww. worldmusic.net) which offers a fine introduction to the nation's music scene, covering both traditional and contemporary classics.

The environment

In the words of one of Japan's leading environmental activists, Yamashita Hirofumi "Japan's postwar development has had a disastrous impact on the natural environment." In the wake of the March 2011 nuclear accident, this statement is truer than ever. There is now increased public debate over Japan's future energy use, and much concern over the damage which nuclear radiation has caused both humans and the environment. There's a growing awareness of the need to safeguard spectacular areas of unspoilt natural beauty that remain, and ensure that neither the government nor big business can exploit these areas. Japan also stands guilty of over-packaging products and wasteful use of disposable chopsticks, but at the same time, levels of recycling of items such as plastic, paper and metal cans are admirably high.

Fauna and flora

Generally speaking, the fauna and flora of the Japanese archipelago can be divided into three categories: the Southeast Asiatic tropical zone, the Korean and Chinese temperate zone and the Siberian subarctic zone.

The **Southeast Asiatic tropical zone** extends from Taiwan up into the Ryūkyū island chain (Okinawa). Wildlife typically associated with this zone includes the flying fox, crested serpent eagle, variable lizard and butterflies of the Danaidae family. Animals that belong to the **Korean and Chinese temperate zone** inhabit the deciduous forests of Honshū, Shikoku and Kyūshū, the most common of which are the racoon dog, sika deer and mandarin duck. If you're lucky, you'll see the rarer yellow marten, badger and flying squirrel, while in the seas around central Honshū you may also spot sea lions and fur seals. The **Siberian subarctic zone** covers the coniferous forests of Hokkaidō, inhabited by the brown bear, rabbit-like pika, hazel grouse, common lizard, arctic hare and nine-spined stickleback, among other species.

LAST CHANCE TO SEE …

According to the Mammalogical Society of Japan (wmammalogy.jp), over half of the country's **endangered animals** are close to extinction. Examples include the Iriomote wild cat, endemic to Iriomote-jima (p.785), of which probably fewer than one hundred remain, the short-tailed albatross and the Japanese otter of Shikoku, both of which were once thought to be extinct.

Conservation efforts come in the form of breeding and feeding programmes, habitat improvement and research projects. In an example of Russo–Japanese cooperation, researchers from both countries attached transmitters to fourteen sea eagles and tracked them by satellite to discover their migratory routes and feeding grounds. Unfortunately, however, many such **conservation programmes** fall far short of their goals, largely due to an ineffective government system.

One programme that has been successful has been that to protect the **red-crowned** or **Japanese crane** (*tanchō* in Japanese). This magnificent, tall-standing bird, highly celebrated in Japan for its grace and beauty and as a symbol of longevity, has benefited from volunteer-based feeding programmes and other conservation measures in its home territory of eastern Hokkaidō (see p.327).

In addition, the archipelago contains a number of **endemic species** such as the Japanese macaque, Japanese dormouse, copper pheasant, giant salamander, Pryer's woodpecker and Amami spiny mouse, all of which are now relatively rare. Japan is also home to a number of "living fossils", animals whose characteristics differ from more developed species, such as the critically endangered Amami rabbit and Iriomote wild cat (both native to the Ryūkyū Islands), the frilled shark and the horseshoe crab of Sagami Bay, off Kamakura.

You don't need to get off the beaten track to encounter wildlife in Japan. In urban areas **racoon dogs** (*tanuki*) come out at night to forage for food. These dogs are an integral part of Japanese folklore and are believed to have supernatural powers and cause all sorts of mischief; they are always depicted as big-bellied, with huge testicles and a bottle of sake. Foxes, too, are widespread and were believed to possess people – fox (or *inari*) shrines are found across the country.

Monkeys are also common in some areas, such as Wakinosawa and Shiga Kōgen, while **wild boar** occasionally make an appearance in outer urban areas, though fortunately these forbidding-looking creatures avoid human contact and are generally heard but not seen. Kites, cranes, herons, cormorants and migratory seagulls can often be seen around lakes and rivers, while the steamy summer brings an onslaught of insects, none more so than the **cicada** (*semi*), whose singing provides a constant background thrum.

Marine life

Japan's seas and rivers contain roughly three thousand species of fish. The waters around the Ryūkyū Islands are home to subtropical anemone fish, parrot fish, wrass and spiny lobster as well as numerous species of shark, turtle and whale. The ocean south of Shikoku and Honshū teems with life, from loggerhead turtles and butterfly fish to dugongs and porpoises, while the colder waters around Hokkaidō bring with them some of the larger whale species – humpback, grey and blue whale – from the Bering Sea and north Pacific.

Ocean currents play a crucial role in this diversity. Warm water flowing round Taiwan and up through the Ryūkyū island chain splits into two on reaching the island of

---

THE NATIONAL PARKS

In the early twentieth century, the growing popularity of recreational activities such as mountaineering provided the spur for the creation of Japan's first **national parks** (*kokuritsu-kōen*), the first of which were created in 1934 and are now under the control of the **Ministry of Environment** (Ⓦ www.env.go.jp). There are 29 national parks, covering around 5.4 percent of Japan's land mass, and 55 quasi-national parks (*kokutei-kōen*; 3.6 percent), which between them receive over 900 million visitors each year. In addition, prefectural natural parks cover a further 5.4 percent of Japan. While for the most part national parks are thought of in terms of recreation, their establishment has been a lifesaver for ecological preservation. Below are details of some of the most important.

Aso-Kujū National Park, Kyūshū (p.710). Includes the world's largest volcano crater (90km in circumference), part of which is still active.

Chichibu-Tama-Kai National Park, Honshū (p.000). Only three hours west of Tokyo, this is a haven for city dwellers. Its forested hills, gorges and valleys give rise to the Tama river that flows through Tokyo.

Iriomote National Park, Okinawa (p.785). Features lush, virgin jungle, cascading waterfalls, mangroves, white beaches and Japan's largest coral reef, with spectacular underwater life. The dense jungle, which has served to resist human encroachment, is home to the rare Iriomote wild cat.

Shiretoko National Park, Hokkaidō (p.330). Another UNESCO World Heritage Site, and utterly wild; it's home to brown bears, Blakiston's fish-owls and Steller's sea eagles.

Kyūshū. The branch flowing north into the Sea of Japan, between Japan and China, is known as the Tsushima-shio, while the Kuro-shio or "Black current" follows the more easterly route. Bearing down from the north, hitting Hokkaidō's northern and eastern shores, comes the cold, nutrient-rich Oya-shio or Kuril current. Where it meets the Kuro-shio off northeastern Honshū, abundant plankton and the mingling of cold- and warm-water species create one of the richest fishing grounds in the entire world.

Forests

Forests of beech, silver fir, broad-leaf evergreens and mangroves once carpeted Japan. However, development during the postwar economic boom – in particular the massive increase in construction and the rampant building of golf courses – led to the decimation of many of these natural forests. While nearly 67 percent of Japan is still forested, about half of this comprises commercial plantations of quick-growing Japanese cedar and cypress. Not only do these contain a fraction of the biodiversity found in natural forests, but when cheaper timber flooded in from Southeast Asia, Canada and South America in the 1970s and local demand slumped, a large proportion of Japan's domestic plantations were left unused and untended.

As a result, Japan has come precariously close to losing some of its most spectacular areas of natural forest. The old-growth **beech forests** – stands of ancient trees, but not necessarily untouched virgin forest – of the Shirakami Mountains in northwest Honshū, for example, came under direct threat in the 1980s from a government proposal to build a logging road right through them. Citizens' groups, together with the Nature Conservation Society of Japan (NCSJ), mounted a huge campaign to demonstrate the forest's immeasurable ecological and national value. The government reconsidered the plan and the forest is now designated a UNESCO World Heritage Site.

Environmental issues

Japan is forging ahead with measures to improve its environmental performance. The gradual shift from heavy to hi-tech industry has led to apparently cleaner rivers and air; anecdotal evidence points to an increase in birdlife and statistics show that Mount Fuji is visible more often these days from Tokyo. However, although there have been successes down the years, there remains a litany of **environmental issues** blotting Japan's ecological scorecard.

Waste and recycling

In 2009, Japan's Ministry of Environment announced plans to reduce the country's **total waste** from a staggering 52 million tons a year (as measured in 2007) to about 50 million tons in 2012, and to raise the waste **recycling rate** from 20 to 25 percent. This reduction in waste generation was intended to be achieved through raising awareness and promoting a charging system for waste disposal services.

Unfortunately, **illegal dumping** in the countryside has increased since people now have to pay for the disposal of large items. However, the Home Appliance Law, in effect since 2001, is reported to have resulted in an 85 percent recycling rate by 2012 for white goods such as refrigerators and air-conditioning units. Despite such moves, working out exactly what to do with all the waste still remains a logistical nightmare. Burning it releases poisonous dioxins, while using garbage for land reclamation and landfill has also resulted in significant contamination in some areas.

One positive sign has been the **Mottainai campaign** (ⓦmottainai.info/english), launched in 2005. The campaign, backed by the Mainichi newspapers and the Itochu Corporation, aims to cut all types of waste by reducing consumption and encouraging greater levels of recycling through education and awareness-raising activities.

Nuclear power

With hardly any natural resources of its own Japan has long been reliant on **fossil fuel** imports to meet its energy needs. Government tax incentives and subsidies supporting the use of solar power mean that Japan is now a world leader in photovoltaic production. It is also beginning to develop wind power, biomass and other **renewable energies**.

However, the main area of investment has been in **nuclear power**. Up until March 11, 2011 the country was meeting around a third of its electricity needs from 55 nuclear reactors, with a plan to increase this to sixty percent by 2050. The Tōhoku earthquake and the **ongoing crisis** at the Fukushima 1 Nuclear Power Plant confirmed the worst fears environmentalists and the public had about this strategy. The electricity companies have been conducting stress tests on all remaining nuclear power plants to evaluate their safety margins. The Fukushima plant is still undergoing delicate and dangerous shutdown operations, but there have been a number of worrying accidents during the clean-up operation, including the discovery that huge amounts of contaminated water have been leaking into the ocean.

As of late 2013, there were no nuclear power plants functioning in Japan. Polls now show that up to eighty percent of Japanese are anti-nuclear and distrust government information on radiation, with around fifty percent wanting nuclear power plants scrapped or the number of them reduced. Before his resignation, Prime Minister Kan called for a **new energy policy** with less reliance on nuclear power, a line of action that his successor Noda Yoshihiko also committed to follow. However, the return of the LDP, with Abe Shinzō as Prime Minister, signals the likelihood of continued reliance on nuclear energy in the future. The current government have included nuclear power in their basic energy policy, with the argument that it is still important for "energy security". Abe and his ministers are seeking to restart reactors once their safety has been confirmed, while concurrently there is a major ongoing campaign to stop the building of a nuclear reprocessing plant in Rokkasho in northeast Aomori prefecture (ⓦstop-rokkasho.org).

In the meantime, there remains the question of what to do with the growing stockpiles of **nuclear waste**, environmental contamination caused by radiation and Japan's increased carbon dioxide emissions from restarting coal power plants in order to meet energy needs.

Pollution

The Minamata tragedy of the 1950s, in which a Kyūshū community suffered the devastating effects of organic mercury poisoning, was a landmark case that brought to public attention the hazards of industrial pollution. Half a century later, **chemical pollution** – from agriculture and domestic use, as well as the industrial sector – remains a serious problem; one of the issues raised in the Oscar-winning documentary *The Cove* is about the off-the-scale toxicity levels of some types of seafood.

Citizens' movements have been active in tackling issues related to **air pollution** from factories, power plants and national highways, helping victims to win important lawsuits or reach out-of-court settlements against local authorities and industrial corporations. In November 2000, for example, the Nagoya District Court ordered the state and ten enterprises to pay a total of nearly 300 million yen in compensation to pollution victims and ordered that emissions along a stretch of national highway should be substantially reduced. The government subsequently imposed stricter emission limits and is gradually replacing its own transport fleets with "green" vehicles as well as working towards phasing out diesel buses and trucks in general.

A related issue is the widespread habit of drivers to keep their **engines running** – for the air-conditioning or heating – even when parked or in long traffic queues. You'll often see taxis parked up, for example, engine running and the driver sound asleep inside. Despite a number of public awareness campaigns, the message is slow getting across and, though some prefectures have even introduced "anti-idling" laws, there is little enforcement.

NUCLEAR RADIATION IN JAPAN

Apart from the exclusion zone surrounding the Fukushima nuclear power plant, Japan has been declared **safe** for both citizens and visitors. However, many environmental and human rights groups still have major concerns about the levels and extent of the **radioactive contamination** from the nuclear accident. Both agriculture and fishing industries have been affected by the disaster, and although the government has stated that it is conducting rigorous checks on food and water there is much debate over safe and acceptable levels of exposure. Citizen groups have also been conducting their own monitoring activities all over Japan. Below are some resources for checking the latest radiation levels.

Citizens' Nuclear Information Center (W www.cnic.co.jp/english) Information gathered by a network of citizens, scientists and activists.

Nuclear Regulation Authority (W radioactivity.nsr.go.jp/en) Government website with monitoring information of environmental radioactivity levels.

Safecast (W blog.safecast.org) Citizen group which collects radiation measurements from all over Japan and aims to strengthen the global information network.

Traveller's Guide to Avoid Radiation in Japan (W zerobqjapan.wordpress.com) Blog by activists with information on areas to avoid and safe places to eat.

Whaling

The Japanese have traditionally caught whales for oil and meat, and the country continues to catch hundreds of these mammals every year, despite an international ban, exploiting a loophole which allows a quota for "scientific research". Japan argues the research provides essential data on populations, feeding habits and distribution to allow the mammals to be properly monitored. Indeed, the government now claims that populations of minke, humpback and some other whale species have recovered sufficiently to support managed **commercial whaling**. In 2005, the national whaling fleet began hunting endangered fin whale for the first time and the following year added the vulnerable humpback to its quota, which now stands at a total of nearly 1300 whales a year.

All the major political parties support whaling, and it is often presented as a matter of **national pride** to preserve Japanese cultural identity in the face of Western, particularly American, imperialism. Opponents of whaling, on the other hand, accuse Japan of buying the votes of developing countries in order to overturn the 1986 ban imposed by the International Whaling Commission (IWC).

Ironically, less than thirty percent of the Japanese public are in favour of whaling; some surveys put the figure as low as ten percent. Consumption of **whale meat**, or *kujira*, has declined markedly since 1986, and the only way the government can now get rid of the meat its scientific fleet brings home is to sell it at highly subsidized prices. Even then, as revealed by Morikawa Jun in his book *Whaling in Japan: Power, Politics and Diplomacy*, a third of this meat remains unsold.

Japan's continued whaling has been an international public relations disaster. In recent years, the environmental rights organization **Sea Shepherd Conservation Society** (W seashepherd.org) have disrupted Japanese whaling with violent clashes in the Southern Oceans, which has been documented in the Animal Planet series *Whale Wars*. In 2013, the **International Court of Justice** tried a case brought by Australia against Japan over its research whaling (decision pending at the time of writing).

Scientists have also begun voicing their concerns over the high levels of toxins found in dolphin and whale meat available in Japanese stores. At the same time, interest in whale-watching has been on the increase, and it is becoming abundantly clear that there's more money to be made from whales through tourism than from killing them. For more information on whaling, see the **Whale and Dolphin Conservation Society** website (W uk.whales.org).

Over-fishing

To offset problems caused by **over-fishing**, the Japanese fishing fleet has been cut by a quarter in recent years and increasingly strict quotas are being imposed. This has not, however, stopped the import of fish into Japan from developing countries which, for their own economic reasons, are less concerned about protecting fish stocks.

Of particular concern is the **bluefin tuna** (*hon-maguro*), which is prized for sashimi and sushi, particularly the *toro* (the fatty belly meat). It's estimated that Japan consumes around eighty percent of the world's total bluefin tuna catch. At the same time, bluefin populations are decreasing at an alarming rate in the face of increasing demand worldwide. Conservationists argue that curbing Japanese consumption is a key to preventing total collapse. Japan's case was not helped when it admitted to exceeding its 6000-ton-quota of southern bluefin (which inhabit the southern hemisphere) by around 1800 tons in 2005. The **Commission for the Conservation of Southern Bluefin Tuna** (Ⓦ ccsbt.org) says the figure is probably much higher if you also include fish caught by other countries over and above their quotas and sold in Japan. As a punishment, Japan's quota was halved to 3000 tons a year. However, overfishing has continued, and it was reported that Japan caught more than 13,000 tons in 2011. In early 2014, it was estimated that Pacific bluefin tuna stocks had been depleted by 96.4 percent.

At the consumer's end, the rocketing price of bluefin tuna should put the breaks on consumption. Conservation bodies have started to mount awareness campaigns, encouraging people to opt for yellowfin tuna and other environmentally sustainable species instead.

Sustainable forestry

Japan has long been the world's largest consumer of **tropical timber**, and the activities of Japanese paper and timber companies in the old-growth and primary forests (those subjected to only minimal human disturbance) of neighbouring countries is a huge concern for environmentalists worldwide. Much of the timber is now imported in the

---

ENVIRONMENTAL CONTACTS AND RESOURCES

Bicycle for Everyone's Earth Ⓦ beejapan.org. Promotes environmental awareness and green living through direct action, including an annual bike tour from Hokkaidō to Kyūshū.

Earth Embassy Ⓦ earthembassy.org. Promoting environmentally sustainable lifestyles, Earth Embassy runs a guesthouse and café, organic farm and develops environmentally friendly technologies at its centre, run by international volunteers, near Mt Fuji.

Ecozzeria Ⓦ ecozzeria.jp. An environmental strategy centre, with an events and exhibition space, in Tokyo's Shin-Marunouchi Building.

Friends of the Earth Japan Ⓦ foejapan.org. Local branch of the international environmental organization.

Green Action Ⓦ greenaction-japan.org. Working for a nuclear-free Japan.

Greenpeace Japan Ⓦ greenpeace.org/japan. Local branch of the worldwide campaigning organization.

Japan Ecotourism Society Ⓦ ecotourism.gr.jp. Provides a forum for people involved in ecotourism and promotes good practice.

Japan Environmental Exchange Ⓦ jeeeco.org. Disseminates information on environmental issues and organizes international exchanges.

Japan for Sustainability Ⓦ japanfs.org. Information service for sustainability projects nationwide.

Japanese NGO Center for International Cooperation (JANIC) Ⓦ janic.org. Provides a rundown of NGOs working in Japan.

Nature Conservation Society of Japan Ⓦ www.nacsj.or.jp. NGO working in general environmental conservation.

Wild Bird Society of Japan Ⓦ wbsj.org. Organization concerned with monitoring and protecting Japan's wild bird populations.

WWF Japan Ⓦ wwf.or.jp. Local branch of World Wide Fund for Nature.

form of plywood, which is used in the construction industry to make moulds for pouring concrete and incinerated after it's been used a couple of times. Since the early 1990s, rainforest protection groups in Japan and abroad have had some success in persuading construction companies and local authorities to reduce their use of tropical wood.

Excessive packaging and **disposable wooden chopsticks** (*waribashi*) are other incredibly wasteful uses of resources. While "my chopsticks" awareness drives are having some impact in getting people to carry their own chopsticks with them, Japan still gets through a staggering 130 million *waribashi* daily, accounting for over 400,000 cubic metres of timber a year.

The role of Japanese companies in the Australian **woodchip industry** has also caused much criticism, both at home and abroad. One such company operates a wood-chipping mill that is fed by old-growth eucalyptus trees at a rate of several football fields a day under a twenty-year licence granted by the Australian government. Various Australian environmental groups, including Chipstop (@chipstop.forests.org.au) and The Wilderness Society (@wilderness.org.au), have joined forces with the Japan Tropical Forest Action Network (JATAN; @jatan.org), to petition the Australian government and the Japanese paper industry to use woodchips from sustainable sources instead. Again, the campaign seems to be paying off: due to public pressure, Japanese companies are increasingly sourcing woodchips from sustainable forests.

Film

Japan got its first taste of cinema at Kōbe's Shinko Club in 1896 – and since then, as in many other creative endeavours, the country has excelled at making films, producing many internationally recognized directors including Kurosawa Akira, Ozu Yasujirō, Itami Jūzō, Kitano Takeshi and Miyazaki Hayao. For more information, Midnight Eye (ⓦmidnighteye.com) provides an excellent introduction to the wealth of Japanese cinema, as does film scholar Donald Richie's book *A Hundred Years of Japanese Film*.

Pre-World War II

From the advent of **cinema** in Japan, theatrical embellishments were considered a vital part of the experience; one theatre had a mock-up of a valley in front of the screen, complete with fish-filled ponds, rocks and fan-generated breeze, to increase the sense of realism. Additionally, the story and dialogue were acted out to the audience by a *benshi* (narrator). Thus when "talkies" arrived in Japan they were less of a sensation, because sound had long been part of the film experience.

The **1930s** were the boom years for early Japanese cinema, with some five hundred features being churned out a year, second only in production to the United States. One of the era's top directors, though he didn't gain international recognition until the mid-1950s, was **Mizoguchi Kenji** (1898–1956). His initial speciality was melodramas based in Meiji-period Japan, but he is best known in the West for his later lyrical medieval samurai dramas, such as *Ugetsu Monogatari* (1954). During the 1920s and 1930s, however, Mizoguchi also turned his hand to detective, expressionist, war, ghost and comedy films. As Japan fell deeper into the ugliness of nationalism and war, Mizoguchi embraced traditional concepts of stylized beauty in films such as 1939's *The Story of the Last Chrysanthemums* (*Zangiku Monogatari*). Also honing his reputation during the pre-World War II period was director **Ozu Yasujirō**, whose *Tokyo Story* (see p.832) from 1954 is a classic.

The 1950s and 1960s

World War II and its immediate aftermath put the dampers on Japan's cinematic ambitions, but in 1950, the local industry produced **Kurosawa Akira**'s brilliant *Rashōmon* (see p.832) which subsequently won a Golden Lion at the following year's Venice Film Festival and an honorary Oscar. A string of Kurosawa-directed classics followed, including *The Seven Samurai* (*Schichinin no Samurai* 1954; see p.832), *Throne of Blood* (*Kumonosu-jō*; 1957) based on *Macbeth*; *Yōjimbō* (1961; see p.832); and *Ran* (1985; see p.832).

The 1950s also saw the birth of one of Japan's best-known cinema icons, **Godzilla** – or *Gojira* as he was known on initial release in 1954. Despite the monster being killed off in the grand finale, the film's success led to an American release, with added footage, in 1956, under the title *Godzilla, King of the Monsters*. Over the next four decades, in 28 movies, Godzilla survived to do battle with, among others, King Kong, giant shrimps, cockroaches and moths, and a smog monster.

Highly romanticized, violent **yakuza** flicks were also popular in the 1960s. These *ninkyō eiga* (chivalry films) often played like modern-day samurai sagas, the tough, fair *yakuza* being driven by a code of loyalty or honour. One of the major actors to emerge

TORA-SAN

Although hardly known outside of Japan, the country's most beloved – and financially successful – series of films are those featuring **Tora-san**, or Kuruma Torajirō, a loveable itinerant peddler from Tokyo's Shitamachi. The series began with *Otoko wa Tsurai yo* (*It's Tough Being a Man*) in 1969, and the lead character was played by Atsumi Kiyoshi in 48 films up until the actor's death in 1996. The format of the films is invariably the same, with Tora-san chasing after his latest love, or "Madonna", in various scenic areas of Japan, before returning to his exasperated family.

from these films is Takakura Ken, who has since starred in Western films including Ridley Scott's *Black Rain*. Try to check out the cult classics *Branded to Kill* (*Koroshi no Rakuin*) and *Tokyo Drifter* (*Tokyo Nagaremono*) by maverick director **Suzuki Seijun**, whose visual style and nihilistic cool was an inspiration to Kitano Takeshi and Quentin Tarantino among others.

The 1970s and 1980s

In 1976, *In the Realm of the Senses* (see p.832) by rebel film-maker **Ōshima Nagisa** created an international stir with its explicit sex scenes and violent content. Ōshima fought against Japan's censors, who demanded cuts, but ultimately lost. This was all the more galling for the director, whose film gathered critical plaudits abroad, but remained unseen in its full version at home, because at the same time major Japanese studios were making money from increasingly violent films and soft-core porn, called *roman poruno*.

By the **late 1970s**, Japanese cinema was in the doldrums. Entrance fees at the cinema were the highest in the world (they're still relatively expensive), leaving the public less willing to sample offbeat local films when they could see sure-fire Hollywood hits instead. Ōshima turned in the prisoner-of-war drama *Merry Christmas Mr Lawrence* in 1983 and the decidedly quirky *Max Mon Amour* (1986), in which Charlotte Rampling takes a chimp as a lover, before retiring from directing to build his reputation as a TV pundit. Instead of investing money at home, Japanese companies, like Sony, went on a spending spree in Hollywood, buying up major American studios and film rights, thus securing access to lucrative video releases.

Flying the flag for the local industry was **Itami Jūzō**, an actor who turned director with the mildly satirical *The Funeral* (see p.832) in 1984. His follow-up, *Tampopo* (1986; see p.832), a comedy set against the background of Japan's gourmet boom, was an international hit, as was his *A Taxing Woman* (*Marusa no Onna*) in 1988. The female star of Itami's films, which poke gentle fun at Japanese behaviour and society, was his wife, the comic actress Miyamoto Nobuko.

Anime

Japanese animation is known as **anime**, and it encompasses movies, television series and straight-to-video releases. It was developed from the early twentieth century and is considered to have a distinctive style, particularly in regards to its aesthetics and production. Around sixty percent of anime is based on previously published manga, while others, like *Pokémon*, are inspired by video games. Anime has been a staple of Japanese TV since the 1960s, with some series such as *Astro Boy* (see box, p.830) becoming popular overseas. However, it was the critical international success of **Ōtomo Katsuhiro**'s feature-length film *Akira* and the rise of **Studio Ghibli**, purveyors of some of the most successful anime of all time, including *Howl's Moving Castle* and the Oscar-winning *Spirited Away*, that has ignited the current global interest in all things anime.

ANIME ON THE BIG SCREEN

In 1958, Toei produced Japan's first full-length, full-colour animated feature *Hakujaden* (released as *Tale of the White Panda* in the US) and went on to make a series of increasingly sophisticated films, culminating in *Little Norse Prince* (*Taiyō no Ōji Horusu no Daibōken*) in 1968. This was the directorial debut of Takahata Isao who, in 1985, teamed up with Miyazaki Hayao to form **Studio Ghibli** (𝕨 ghibli.jp), the most successful of Japanese animation companies.

During the 1960s, TV anime came to fore with **Tezuka Osamu**'s *Tetsuwan Atomu* series, more popularly known as *Astro Boy*, a success both at home and abroad. Tezuka's *Kimba the White Lion* and Tatsuo Yoshida's *Mach Go Go Go* (*Speed Racer* in the US) were other hit TV series from this era, while in the 1970s it was space-based adventures, such as *Space Battleship Yamato* (*Star Blazers*) and *Kagaku Ninja tai Gatchaman* (*Battle of the Planets*), that had kids glued to the gogglebox.

By the 1980s, ambitious artists were pushing the boundaries of the genre into cinema-scale works with higher production values such as Ōtomo Katsuhiro's dark sci-fi fantasy **Akira** (see p.833). Miyazaki Hayao was also making his name, initially with his ecological man vs nature fantasy adventure *Nausicaä of the Valley of Wind* (1984), then with Studio Ghibli smashes such as *My Neighbour Totoro* (see p.833), *Princess Mononoke* (see p.833) and the Oscar-winning **Spirited Away** (see p.833). In 2013, Miyazaki announced his retirement. His last feature-length film, *The Wind Rises*, is based on the story of the man who designed of Zero fighter planes in World War II and attracted controversy due to its anti-war message.

Among other cinema anime directors to watch out for are: **Kon Satoshi**, whose films include the Hitchcockian psychological drama *Perfect Blue* (1997), *Tokyo Godfathers* (see p.833), and *Paprika* (2006), a visually splendid tale about the search for a stolen device that allows physical access to people's dreams; **Oshii Mamoru**, who has the seminal *Ghost in the Shell* (see p.833) and *The Sky Crawlers* (2008) to his credit; and **Hosoda Mamoru**, whose *The Girl Who Leapt Through Time* (*Toki o Kakeru Shōjo;* 2006) and *Summer Wars* (2009) have both garnered rave reviews. For an in-depth look at the medium, read *The Rough Guide to Anime*.

The 1990s

Itami Jūzō's 1992 satire *The Gentle Art of Japanese Extortion* (*Minbō-no-Onna*), which sent up the *yakuza*, led to the director suffering a knife attack by mob thugs. Undaunted, he recovered and went on to direct more challenging comedies, such as *Daibyōnin* (1993), about the way cancer is treated in Japanese hospitals, and *Sūpā-no-Onna* (1995), which revealed the shady practices of supermarkets. Itami committed suicide in 1997, prior to the publication of an exposé of his love life in a scandal magazine, leaving the field clear for **Kitano Takeshi** (see box opposite) to emerge as Japan's new cinema darling.

Kurosawa Akira, referred to respectfully as "Sensei" (teacher) by all in the industry, received a lifetime achievement Academy Award in 1990, the same year as he teamed up with George Lucas and Steven Spielberg to make the semi-autobiographical *Yume* (*Dreams*). His anti-war film *Rhapsody in August* (*Hachigatsu-no-Kyōshikyoku;* 1991), however, attracted criticism abroad for its somewhat one-sided treatment of the subject. Kurosawa's final film before his death, aged 88, on September 6, 1998, was the low-key drama *Mādadayo* (1993) about an elderly academic.

Meanwhile, the prolific **Kurosawa Kiyoshi** had begun to make waves with quirky genre pictures, such as *The Excitement of the Do-Re-Mi-Fa Girls* (1985), *The Serpent Path* (1998) and its sequel *Eyes of the Spider* (1998). **Tsukamoto Shin'ya** had an art-house hit with the sci-fi horror film *Tetsuo* about a man turning into a machine, a story inspired by the acclaimed anime *Akira* (see p.833). A much bigger hit, with both local and international audiences, was *Shall We Dance?*, a charming comedy-drama ballroom dancing about which swept up all thirteen of Japan's Academy Awards in 1996.

The new millennium

While Kitano continues to be one of Japan's most internationally popular film-makers, other directors are coming to the fore. Master of the gleeful splatterfest is the prolific **Miike Takashi**, who has jumped around from the stylized gangster violence of *Ichi the Killer* (see p.833) to the sci-fi action of his *Dead or Alive* trilogy, via the musical horror comedy of *The Happiness of the Katakuris*. In 2009 his *Yatterman*, based on a popular cartoon series from the 1970s, was a local hit.

Reinterpreting the horror genre has been **Nakata Hideo**, whose *Ring* (1998) and paranormal chiller *Dark Water* (2002) were both remade in English in Hollywood before Nakata himself went West in 2005 to direct his English-language debut *The Ring Two*, a new sequel to the Hollywood version of *Ring*. Fans will want to compare it to Nakata's original – and different – Japanese sequel *Ring 2* (1999). This trend of English-language remakes and new versions has continued with **Takashi Shimizu's** *Ju-on: The Grudge* (2000) and *Ju-on: The Grudge Two* (2003).

A decade into the new millennium, the film industry seemed to be thriving. In his 80s, **Suzuki Seijun** made a wonderful and surprising comeback in 2006 with the fairy-tale musical *Princess Racoon*. In 2007, *The Mourning Forest* scooped up the Grand Prix at Cannes for director **Kawase Naomi**, a decade after her debut film *Moe no Suzaku* had scored a prize at the same festival. Also scoring at Cannes and other awards ceremonies was Kurosawa Kiyoshi's satirical drama *Tokyo Sonata* (see p.833). And, in 2009, **Takita Yōjirō's** *Departures* (see p.832) took top honours as best foreign-language film at the Oscars.

Since the March 2011 earthquake and tsunami, there have been fewer major successes for Japanese films, both at home and abroad. In 2011, Kawase premiered another film at Cannes, *Hanezu*, to mixed reviews. In 2012, a considerable number of films released were based on manga and even video games. The film *A Letter to Momo* became the first anime to be screened at the Warsaw International Film Festival, and two Japanese films were screened at Cannes in 2012: *Ai to Makoto* (based on a manga series) and the drama *11.25 Jiketsu no Hi: Mishima Yukio to Wakamonotachi*, based on the suicide of the novelist. In 2013, **Kore'eda Hirokazu's** family drama *Like Father, Like Son* won the Prix du Jury at Cannes, making it the first Japanese film to win an award since Kawase's film in 2007.

FILMS/RECOMMENDATIONS

JAPANESE CLASSICS

Black Rain (Imamura Shōhei; 1989). Not to be confused with the US *yakuza* flick, this serious drama traces the strains put on family life in a country village after the atomic bomb is dropped on Hiroshima.

Godzilla, King of the Monsters (Honda Ishirō & Terry O Morse; 1956). Originally released two years earlier in Japan as *Gojira*, the film about a giant mutant lizard, born after a US

BEAT TAKESHI

Comedian, actor, director, writer, painter and video-game designer – is there anything that **Kitano Takeshi** (W kitanotakeshi.com) can't do? Known locally as Beat Takeshi after his old comedy double act, the Two Beats, Kitano, who was born in Tokyo in 1947, first came to international attention for his role as a brutal camp sergeant in Ōshima's *Merry Christmas Mr Lawrence*. His directorial debut *Violent Cop* (1989) saw him star as a police officer in the *Dirty Harry* mould. His next film, *Boiling Point (3-4 x 10 Gatsu)*, was an equally bloody outing, but it was his more reflective and comic *Sonatine* (see p.832), about a gang war in sunny Okinawa, that had foreign critics hailing him as Japan's Quentin Tarantino.

Kitano survived a near-fatal **motorbike accident** in 1994, and triumphed with *Hanabi* (see p.832), which scooped up a Golden Lion at the Venice Festival in 1997. In *Dolls* (2002) he collaborated with fashion designer Yohji Yamamoto in a visually ravishing but glacially slow film based on the plots of *bunraku* puppet plays. Far more fun is *Zatoichi* (see p.832), which saw a bleached-blonde Kitano play the blind swordsman of the title. For another side of Kitano, read *Boy*, an English translation, published by Vertical, of a trio of captivating short stories about adolescence.

hydrogen bomb test in the Bikini Atoll, was such a hit that previously cut scenes were added for the American market. Raymond Burr plays the journalist telling in flashback the event that led to Godzilla running amok in Tokyo.

In the Realm of the Senses (*Ai no Koriida*; Ōshima Nagisa; 1976). Based on the true story of servant girl Sada Abe and her intensely violent sexual relationship with her master Kichi – who ends up dead and minus his penis.

Kagemusha (Kurosawa Akira; 1980). Nominated for an Academy Award and co-winner of the Grand Prix at Cannes, Kurosawa showed he was still on form with this sweeping historical epic in which a poor criminal is recruited to impersonate a powerful warlord who has inconveniently died mid-campaign.

Ran (Kurosawa Akira; 1985). This much-lauded, loose adaptation of *King Lear* is a real epic, with thousands of extras and giant battle scenes. The daughters become sons, although the Regan and Goneril characters survive in the form of the gleefully vengeful wives Lady Kaede and Lady Sue.

★**Rashōmon** (Kurosawa Akira; 1950). The film that established Kurosawa's reputation in the West. A notorious bandit, the wife he perhaps rapes, the man he perhaps murders and the woodcutter who perhaps witnesses the events each tell their different story of what happened in the woods. Fascinatingly open-ended narrative and a memorable performance by Mifune Toshirō as the restless bandit make this a must-see film.

The Seven Samurai (*Shichinin no Samurai*; Kurosawa Akira; 1954). A small village in sixteenth-century Japan is fed up with being raided each year by bandits, so it hires a band of samurai warriors for protection. Kurosawa's entertaining period drama was later remade in Hollywood as *The Magnificent Seven*.

Tokyo Story (*Tōkyō Monogatari*; Ozu Yasujirō; 1954). An elderly couple travel to Tokyo to visit their children and grandchildren. The only person who has any time for them is Noriko, the widow of their son who was killed in the war. On their return, the mother falls ill and dies. Ozu's themes of loneliness and the breakdown of tradition are grim, but his simple approach and the sincerity of the acting make the film a genuine classic.

Twenty-Four Eyes (*Nijūshi no Hitomi*; Kinoshita Keisuke; 1954). This four-hankie weepy is one of Japan's most-loved films. Events leading up to, during and after World War II are seen through the eyes of a first-grade female teacher (a luminous performance by Takanime Hideko), on the island of Shōdo-shima. The twelve cute children in Ōishi-san's class make up the 24 eyes.

When a Woman Ascends the Stairs (*Onna ga Kaidan o Agaru Toki*; Naruse Mikio; 1960). Naruse ranks alongside Kurosawa and Ozu as one of Japan's great film directors. This film, about an ageing hostess in a Ginza bar, is from the latter end of his career and has a splendid central performance by Takamine Hideko.

Yōjimbō (Kurosawa Akira; 1961). Mifune Toshirō stars one of Kurosawa's best-known samurai sagas as a *rōn* who arrives in a dusty town, is greeted by a dog carrying human hand and discovers he's walked in on a bloody feu

ITAMI JŪZŌ AND KITANO TAKESHI

The Funeral (*Osōshiki*; Itami Jūzō; 1984). Itami directorial debut is a wry comedy about a grieving fami bumbling their way through the obscure conventions of proper Japanese funeral. The young couple learn the "rule by watching a video, and the Buddhist priest turns up in white Rolls-Royce.

★**Hanabi** (Kitano Takeshi; 1997). Venice Festival winne with Kitano directing himself as a detective pushed t breaking point by a stakeout that goes wrong, a seriously i wife and outstanding loans to the *yakuza*. Kitano als painted the artwork that appears in the film.

Sonatine (Kitano Takeshi; 1993). One of Kitano's mos accomplished films. He plays a tired gangster, hightailin it to the sunny isles of Okinawa and getting mixed up i mob feuds, before it all turns nasty on the beach.

★**Tampopo** (Itami Jūzō; 1985). Tampopo, th proprietress of a noodle bar, is taught how to prepare th perfect ramen, in this comedy about Japan's gourme boom. From the old woman squishing fruit in supermarket to the gangster and his moll passing a raw egg sexily between their mouths, this is a film packed witl memorable scenes.

★**Zatoichi** (Kitano Takeshi; 2003). A classic of Japanese TV remade with an assured, modern touch by Kitano, whc also stars as the eponymous hero, a blind master swordsman whom you really don't want to tangle with The film's finale has the cast doing a tap-dancing numbe in *geta* (wooden sandals).

CONTEMPORARY JAPANESE CINEMA

★**Campaign** (*Senkyo*; Sōda Kazuhiro; 2007) and **Campaign 2** (*Senkyo 2*; Sōda Kazuhiro; 2013). Fly-on-the-wall-style documentary following Yamauchi-san, a novice LDP candidate on the campaign trail during the Kawasaki municipal elections. The follow-up catches him as an independent candidate standing in local elections less than a month after the 2011 disaster; he was the only candidate mentioning the nuclear issue. Both films are a brilliant insight on Japanese politics and society.

Departures (*Okuribito*; Takita Yōjirō; 2008). Oscar-winning drama about an out-of-work cellist who winds up working at a funeral parlour in his home town in Yamagata prefecture. Because of the nature of this taboo profession, he at first keeps his new job secret from his family and friends.

From Ashes to Honey (Kamanaka Hitomi; 2010). Third in a trilogy on anti-nuclear activism in Japan. Kamanaka follows the residents of Iwaijima, in the Inland Sea, as they try to stop the construction of a nuclear power plant.

…hi the Killer [Miike Takashi; 2001). Stand by for graphic pictions of bodies sliced in half in this *yakuza* tale, set in …kyo's Kabukichō, as told by the *enfant terrible* of Japanese …nema. Not for the squeamish.

…he Mourning Forest (*Mogari no Mori*; Kawase Naomi; …007). This Cannes film festival prize-winner is a moving …le of a caretaker at a retirement home and one of the …sidents, both struggling with bereavement, who make a …ad trip into the forests around Nara.

…obody Knows (Kore'eda Hirokazu; 2004). Tragic story …f four children trying to survive after being abandoned …y their mother. Wonderful performance by the child …ctors which earned Yagira Yaya a best actor award at …annes in 2004.

…saka Story (*Ōsaka Monogatari*; Nakata Toichi; 1994). …akata Toichi ticks off many difficult contemporary …sues in this documentary, which follows the …omecoming of a gay, Korean–Japanese film student to …is Osaka-based family. His staunchly Korean father …xpects him to take over the business and get married, …ut the son has other ideas.

…ing (Nakata Hideo; 1998). Remade in Hollywood, this is …he original and far superior spine-chiller about a …ideotape that kills everyone who sees it exactly one week …fter viewing.

…hall We Dance? (Suo Masayuki; 1996). At turns touching …nd hilarious *Shall We Dance?* features Yakusho Kōji …laying a quietly frustrated middle-aged salaryman whose …spark returns when he takes up ballroom dancing, though …he must keep it secret from his family and work colleagues …o avoid social stigma.

Tokyo Sonata (Kurosawa Kiyoshi; 2008). When a father …decides not to tell his family he's lost his job as a salaryman …t has all kinds of repercussions. A bleak, satirical drama …reflective of contemporary Japanese society.

ESSENTIAL ANIME

Akira (Ōtomo Katsuhiro; 1988). Dynamic action sequences …drive forward this nihilistic sci-fi fantasy about biker gangs, terrorists, government plots and a telekinetic teenager mutating in Tokyo, 2019.

Ghost in the Shell (*Kokaku Kidōtai*; Oshii Mamoru; 1995). A sophisticated sci-fi thriller that's director Mamoru Oshii's finest work, together with its sequel *Innocence* and the fascinating TV series it spawned.

My Neighbour Totoro (*Tonari no Totoro*; Miyazaki Hayao; 1988). Charming kids' fable set in 1950s Japan about two little girls with a sick mother who make friends with the mythical creatures of the forest, including the giant cuddly character of the title.

Only Yesterday (*Omohide Poroporo*; Takahata Isao; 1988). Beautifully realized film about a woman, on a life-changing vacation in the countryside, recalling childhood episodes that shaped her personality.

★**Princess Mononoke** [*Mononoke Hime*; Miyazaki Hayao; 1997). Exciting period drama set in medieval Japan has an ecological message about saving the earth's resources.

Spirited Away (*Sen to Chihiro no Kamikaskushi*; Miyazaki Hayao; 2001). Oscar-winning Japanese *Alice in Wonderland*-style adventure. When her parents take a wrong turn into a mysteriously deserted theme park, Chihiro finds she has to negotiate her way around the strange creatures she meets at a huge bathhouse before finding a way home.

★**Tokyo Godfathers** (Kon Satoshi; 2003). This heart-warming Christmas fairy tale of redemption for three tramps and the baby they discover in the trash is pure anime magic.

FOREIGN FILMS FEATURING JAPAN

Black Rain (Ridley Scott; 1989). Gruff Michael Douglas and younger sidekick Andy Garcia team up with stoic Osaka policeman, played by Takakura Ken, to deal with the *yakuza*.

The Great Happiness Space (Jake Clennell; 2006). This riveting documentary on an Osaka host club has brutally honest interviews with the male hosts and their female customers.

The Last Samurai (Edward Zwick; 2003). Tom Cruise, Billy Connolly and some of Japan's top acting talent star in this tale of a US Civil War vet who comes to train the Emperor Meiji's troops in modern warfare, but finds much to learn himself in the samurai code of honour.

Letters from Iwo-jima (Clint Eastwood; 2006). Experience the bloody battle for the island of Iwo-jima at the end of World War II from the point of view of two Japanese soldiers played by Watanabe Ken and Ninomiya Kazunari.

Lost in Translation (Sofia Coppola; 2003). Memorable performances from Bill Murray and Scarlett Johansson in this stylish comedy-drama set in and around Shinjuku's Park Hyatt hotel. Brilliantly captures the urban experience for foreigners in Tokyo.

Memoirs of a Geisha (Rob Marshall; 2005). Epic-scale film which gallops through Arthur Golden's bestselling tale of the trials and tribulations of apprentice geisha Sayuri, played here by Chinese actor Zhang Ziyi, wearing uncommonly blue contact lenses. Gong Li chews up the scenery as her arch-rival, and Watanabe Ken, Hollywood's pin-up Japanese actor *de jour*, also puts in an appearance as Sayuri's saviour, the Chairman.

Ramen Girl (Robert Allen Ackerman; 2009). One of Brittany Murphy's last films where she does a charming job of learning to cook ramen at a neighbourhood Tokyo restaurant with no Japanese language skills. Heavily references the classic *Tampopo*.

Shugendo Now (Jean-Marc Abela; 2010). Poetic documentary on modern mountain ascetics in Japan as they perform shamanistic rituals and Tantric Buddhism. Shows the extraordinary contrast between urban life and ancient spirituality in Japan.

Books

The one thing the world is not short of is books about Japan; the followin‹
selection includes ones that provide a deeper understanding of what is
lazily assumed to be one of the world's most enigmatic countries. As
throughout this guide, for Japanese names we have given the family
name first. This may not always be the order in which it is printed on the
English translation.

The following publishers specialize in English-language books on Japan, as
well as translations of Japanese works: Kodansha (ⓦwww.kodanshausa.com);
Charles E. Tuttle (ⓦtuttlepublishing.com); Stonebridge Press (ⓦstonebridge.com);
and Vertical (ⓦvertical-inc.com), which publishes not only great manga titles
but also a series of fiction and non-fiction titles by lesser-known (outside of Japan)
talents.

HISTORY

Ian Buruma *Inventing Japan*. Focusing on the period
1853 to 1964, during which Japan went from a feudal,
isolated state to a powerhouse of the modern world
economy. Buruma's *The Wages of Guilt* also skilfully explains
how and why Germany and Japan have come to terms so
differently with their roles in World War II.

★**John Dougill** *In Search of Japan's Hidden Christians*.
Part historical narrative, part travelogue, the fascinating
and largely unknown history of Japan's hidden Christians is
told in an engaging way. The in-depth research reveals
some surprising stories of survival and belief.

John Dower *Embracing Defeat: Japan in the Aftermath of
World War II*. Accessible look by a Pulitzer prizewinner at
the impact of the American occupation on Japan. First-
person accounts and snappy writing bring the book alive.

Karl Friday *Japan Emerging: Premodern History to 1850*.
Incorporating the latest scholarship on premodern Japan,

this textbook is both comprehensive and highly readable.
Andrew Gordon *A Modern History of Japan: From
Tokugawa Times to the Present*. An excellent overview o‹
two centuries of history covering modernization an‹
militarism, as well as the postwar economic "miracle".

John Hersey *Hiroshima*. Classic account of the devastation
and suffering wrought by the first A-bomb to be used in war.

Giles Milton *Samurai William*. Will Adams was one of a
handful of shipwrecked sailors who arrived in Japan in
1600 and went on to become adviser to the shogun and the
only foreigner ever to be made a samurai. Milton tells the
tale with gusto.

★**William Tsutsui** *A Companion to Japanese History*. An
authoritative and in-depth text which includes the latest
research and current debates on Japanese history from
early civilization to popular culture, with both Japanese
and western viewpoints.

BUSINESS, ECONOMICS AND POLITICS

★**Alex Kerr** *Dogs and Demons*. A scathing and thought-
provoking attack on Japan's economic, environmental and
social policies of the past decades, by someone who first
came to Japan as a child in the 1960s and has been
fascinated by it ever since. Also worth reading is his earlier
book *Lost Japan*.

Laura J Kriska *Accidental Office Lady*. Kriska's account of
her two years working in Japan as a trainee for Honda in
the late 1980s is particularly good for its perspective on
gender in Japanese corporate life.

Miyamoto Masao *Straitjacket Society*. As the subtitle
hints, this "insider's irreverent view of bureaucratic Japan"
is quite an eye-opener. Unsurprisingly, Miyamoto was fired
from the Ministry of Health and Welfare, but his book sold

over 400,000 copies.

★**Niall Murtagh** *The Blue-eyed Salaryman*. Anyone who
has ever worked for a Japanese company will find much to
identify with in this honest, witty account by an Irish
computer programmer, who became a salaryman for
Mitsubishi.

Jacob M. Schlesinger *Shadow Shoguns*. Cracking crash
course in Japan's political scene, scandals and all, from *Wall
Street Journal* reporter Schlesinger, who spent five years at
the newspaper's Tokyo bureau.

★**Karel Van Wolferen** *The Enigma of Japanese Power*. A
weighty, thought-provoking tome, but one worth wading
through. This is the standard text on the triad of Japan's
bureaucracy, politicians and business.

TRADITIONAL ARTS, ARCHITECTURE AND GARDENS

Liza Dalby *Geisha*. In the 1970s, anthropologist Dalby immersed herself in the fast-dissolving life of the geisha. This is the fascinating account of her experience and those of her teachers and fellow pupils. *Kimono*, her history of that most Japanese of garments, is also worth reading.

Thomas F. Judge and **Tomita Hiroyuki** *Edo Craftsmen*. Beautifully produced portraits of some of Shitamachi's traditional craftsmen, who can still be found working in the backstreets of Tokyo. A timely insight into a disappearing world.

Joan Stanley-Baker *Japanese Art*. Highly readable introduction to the broad range of Japan's artistic traditions (though excluding theatre and music), tracing their development from prehistoric to modern times.

Itoh Teiji *The Gardens of Japan*. Splendid photos of all Japan's great historical gardens, including many not generally open to the public as well as contemporary examples.

Nakagawa Takeshi *The Japanese House*. Comprehensively illustrated book, which takes the reader step by step through the various elements of the traditional Japanese home, and is the essential manual on vernacular architecture.

CULTURE AND SOCIETY

Jake Adelstein *Tokyo Vice*. With forensic thoroughness and gallows humour, Adelstein documents his unsentimental education in crime reporting for the *Yomiuri Shimbun*, Japan's top-selling newspaper. Soon to made into a movie starring Daniel Radcliffe.

★**Anne Allison** *Precarious Japan*. A sobering look at modern Japanese society immediately before and after the 2011 disaster. Anthropologist Allison provides some fascinating insights into the many social ills which plague daily life and the stories of those who are affecting change.

Ruth Benedict *The Chrysanthemum and the Sword*. This classic study of the hierarchical order of Japanese society, first published in 1946, remains relevant (and controversial) for its conclusions on the psychology of a nation that had just suffered defeat in World War II.

★**Lucy Birmingham and David McNeill** *Strong in the Rain*. Tokyo-based journalists ponder their experiences in the aftermath of the 2011 disaster and closely follow the lives of six survivors who showed great courage and determination. A moving and well-written account.

Ian Buruma *A Japanese Mirror* and *The Missionary and the Libertine*. The first book is an intelligent, erudite examination of Japan's popular culture, while *The Missionary and the Libertine* collects together a range of essays including pieces on Japan-bashing, Hiroshima, Pearl Harbor, the authors Mishima Yukio and Tanizaki Juni'chirō and the film director Ōshima Nagisa.

Veronica Chambers *Kickboxing Geishas*. Based on interviews with a broad cross section of women, from Hokkaidō DJs to top executives, Chambers argues that modern Japanese women are not the submissive characters so often portrayed in the media, but in fact a strong force for change. A sympathetic and insightful book.

Edward Fowler *San'ya Blues*. Fowler's experiences living and working among the casual labourers of Tokyo's San'ya district make fascinating reading. He reveals the dark underbelly of Japan's economic miracle and blows apart a few myths and misconceptions on the way.

Saga Junichi *Confessions of a Yakuza*. This life story of a former *yakuza* boss, beautifully retold by a doctor whose clinic he just happened to walk into, gives a rare insight into

JAPAN THROUGH AN AMERICAN'S EYES

Donald Richie wrote intelligently about Japanese culture since he first arrived in the country in 1947 to work as a typist for the US occupying forces, until his death in 2013. Richie is best known as a scholar of Japanese cinema, but among his forty-odd books it's his essay collections – **Public People, Private People; A Lateral View; Partial Views** – that set a standard other expat commentators can only aspire to. *Public People* is a series of sketches of famous and unknown Japanese, including profiles of novelist Mishima Yukio and the actor Mifune Toshiro. In *A Lateral View* and *Partial Views*, Richie tackles Tokyo style, avant-garde theatre, pachinko, the Japanese kiss and the Zen rock garden at Kyoto's Ryōan-ji temple, among many other things.

His subtle, elegiac travelogue *The Inland Sea*, first published in 1971, captures the timeless beauty of the island-studded waterway and is a must read. In *Tokyo*, Richie captures the essence of the city he lived in for more than fifty years. Naturally, he also served as editor on *Lafcadio Hearn's Japan*, which includes sections from the classic *Glimpses of Unfamiliar Japan*, among Hearn's other works (see p.599). For an overview of the immense Richie oeuvre, dip into *The Donald Richie Reader: 50 Years of Writing on Japan* or his *Japan Journals 1947–2004*.

a secret world. Saga also wrote the award-winning *Memories of Silk and Straw*, a collection of reminiscences about village life in premodern Japan.

★**David Suzuki** and **Oiwa Keibo** *The Japan We Never Knew*. Canadian scientist, broadcaster and writer Suzuki teamed up with half-Japanese anthropologist Oiwa to tour the country and interview an extraordinary range of people, from the Ainu of Hokkaidō to descendants of the "untouchable" caste, the Burakumin. The result is an excellent riposte to the idea of a monocultural, conformist Japan.

Tendo Shoko *Yakuza Moon*. The daughter of a *yakuza*, Tendo lived her teens in a blur of violence, sex and drugs. By age 15, she was in a detention centre and then gradually

pulled her life together to write this searing account of li' in the underclass of Japanese society.

★**Mark Willacy** *Fukushima*. ABC Australia journali' Willacy goes back to the disaster-struck areas of northe' Japan which he covered in the aftermath of the 201 earthquake, and sympathetically reports on the ongoin' human drama. The harrowing interviews show bot' remarkable resilience and great loss.

Robert Whiting *Got to Have Wa*. Whiting's third book o' baseball and Japan follows the often hilarious exploits ' US baseball players in Japan. In the process, it reveals muc' about Japanese society. His *The Meaning of Ichiro* turns th' tables by focusing on the experiences of Ichiro Suzuki, a to' baseball star who now plays for the Seattle Mariners.

POP CULTURE

Apart from the following, also worth a read is *The Rough Guide to Anime* by Simon Richmond and *The Rough Guide to Manga* by Jason Yadao.

Patrick Galbraith *The Otoku Encyclopedia*. This is the insider's guide to *otaku* (geek or nerd) culture in Japan. It looks at the history of fandom of manga and anime and the associated cultural practices of maid cafés and cosplay.

★ **Hector Garcia** *A Geek in Japan*. An encyclopedic overview of "Cool Japan". This cultural guide has everything from tea ceremonies to TV Drama, covered in an engaging and visual style.

★**Roland Kelts** *Japanamerica*. Highly accessible,

personalized account of how Japanese pop culture – and i' particular manga and anime – has become such a hug' success in the US. Kelts, half Japanese, half American an' living in both countries, makes many intelligen' observations and digs up some fascinating tales.

Frederik L. Schodt *Dreamland Japan: Writings o' Modern Manga*. A series of entertaining and informativ' essays on the art of Japanese comic books, profiling th' top publications, artists, animated films and English-language manga. Also read Schodt's *The Astro Boy Essay:* for great insight into the life and times of Astro Boy': creator Tezuka Osamu.

FOOD AND DRINK

Shirley Booth *Food of Japan*. More than a series of recipes, this nicely illustrated book gives lots of background detail and history on Japanese food.

★**Nancy Singleton Hachisu** *Japanese Farm Food*. Recipes and life experiences from an American expat living in an 80-year-old farmhouse in rural Japan. Beautiful photography and healthy food.

Philip Harper *The Insider's Guide to Sake*. Handy pocket-sized guide that will tell you most of what you need to know about Japanese rice wine, from an English writer who brews his own sake near Nara. The listing of over one hundred different sakes, plus their labels, is very useful.

Kurihara Harumi *Harumi's Japanese Cooking*. An easy to follow guide from Japan's Martha Stewart, with a

down-to-earth approach to preparing typical dishes that Japanese eat at home.

★ **Barak Kushner** *Slurp! A Social and Culinary History o' Ramen*. A fun and informative history of Japan's favourite noodle soup, looking at its political identity (is it Chinese or Japanese food?) and its place in popular culture.

★**Jane Lawson** *Zenbu Zen*. The author spends a year in Kyoto soaking up the seasons and the food culture. Sumptuous photos, recipes and observations on life in the ancient capital.

Robb Satterwhite *What's What in Japanese Restaurants*. Written by a Tokyo-based epicure, this handy guide covers all the types of Japanese food and drink you're likely to encounter, and the menus annotated with Japanese characters are particularly useful.

TRAVEL WRITING

Isabella Bird *Unbeaten Tracks in Japan*. After a brief stop in Meiji-era Tokyo, intrepid Victorian adventurer Bird is determined to reach parts of Japan unexplored, as yet, by tourists. She heads north to Hokkaidō, taking the time to make acute, vivid observations along the way.

★**Alan Booth** *The Roads to Sata* and *Looking for the Lost*. Two classics by one of the most insightful and entertaining

modern writers on Japan, whose talents were tragically cut short by his death in 1993. The first book sees Booth, an avid long-distance walker, hike (with the aid of many a beer) from the far north of Hokkaidō to the southern tip of Kyūshū, while *Looking for the Lost*, a trio of walking tales, is by turns hilarious and heartbreakingly poignant.

Josie Drew *A Ride in the Neon Sun*. At nearly seven

undred pages this isn't a book to pop in your panniers, but full of useful tips for anyone planning to tour Japan by bike. Drew has subsequently put out an equally entertaining sequel, *The Sun In My Eyes*.

★ **Will Ferguson** *Hokkaido Highway Blues*. Humorist Ferguson decides to hitch from one end of Japan to the other, with the aim of travelling with the Japanese, not among them. He succeeds (despite everyone telling him – even those who stop to pick him up – that Japanese never stop for hitch-hikers), and in the process turns out a great book of travel writing about the country. Funny and ultimately moving.

Pico Iyer *The Lady and the Monk*. Devoted to a year Iyer spent studying Zen Buddhism and dallying with a married woman in Kyoto, who subsequently became his life partner. It's a rose-tinted, dreamy view of Japan, which he has since followed up, in a more realistic way, with his excellent and thought-provoking *The Global Soul*.

Karin Muller *Japanland*. Documentary film-maker and travel writer Muller heads to Japan in search of *wa* – the Japanese concept of harmony. The interesting cast of characters she meets in the year she spends there – part of the time living just south of Tokyo, the other travelling, including to Kyoto, Shikoku and northern Honshū – is what makes this book rise above similar efforts.

GUIDES AND REFERENCE BOOKS

John Dougill and **Joseph Cali** *Shinto Shrines: A Guide to the Sacred Sites of Japan's Ancient Religion*. An interesting introduction to the history and philosophy of Japan's native religion. This detailed and practical guide profiles more than sixty major Shintō shrines, many of which are World Heritage Sites.

Ed Readicker-Henderson *The Traveller's Guide to Japanese Pilgrimages*. A practical guide to Japan's top three

pilgrim routes: Hiei-zan (near Kyoto); the 33 Kannon of Saigoku (a broad sweep from the Kii peninsula to Lake Biwa); and following the steps of Kōbō Daishi round Shikoku's 88 temples.

Marc Treib and **Ron Herman** *A Guide to the Gardens of Kyoto*. Handy, pocket-sized guide to more than fifty of the city's gardens, with concise historical details and step-by-step descriptions of each garden.

CLASSIC LITERATURE

★ **Kawabata Yasunari** *Snow Country, The Izu Dancer* and other titles. Japan's first Nobel prizewinner for fiction writes intense tales of passion – usually about a sophisticated urban man falling for a simple country girl.

Matsuo Bashō *The Narrow Road to the Deep North*. The seventeenth-century haiku poetry master chronicles his journey through northern Japan, pausing to compose his thoughts along the way.

★ **Murasaki Shikibu** *The Tale of Genji*. Claimed as the world's first novel, this lyrical epic about the lives and loves of a nobleman was spun by a lady of the Heian court around 1000 AD.

Sōseki Natsume *Botchan, Kokoro* and *I am a Cat*. In his comic novel *Botchan*, Sōseki draws on his own experiences as an English teacher in early twentieth-century Matsuyama. The three volumes of *I am a Cat* see the humorist adopting a wry feline point of view on the world. *Kokoro* – about an ageing *sensei* (teacher) trying to come

---

HARUKI MURAKAMI

One of Japan's most entertaining and translated contemporary writers, **Haruki Murakami** has been hailed as a postwar successor to the great novelists Mishima, Kawabata and Tanizaki, and talked of as a future Nobel laureate.

Many of Murakami's books are set in Tokyo, drawing on his time studying at Waseda University in the early 1970s and running a jazz bar, a place that became a haunt for literary types and, no doubt, provided inspiration for his jazz-bar-running hero in the bittersweet novel *South of the Border, West of the Sun*. A good introduction to Murakami is **Norwegian Wood**, a book in two volumes about the tender coming-of-age love story of two students, which has sold over five million copies.

Considered among his best works are **The Wind-Up Bird Chronicle** a hefty yet dazzling cocktail of mystery, war reportage and philosophy, and the surreal **Kafka on the Shore**, a murder story in which cats talk to people and fish rain from the sky. *After Dark*, set in the dead of Tokyo night, has all the usual Murakami trademark flourishes, from quirky characters to metaphysical speculation. His latest mega-opus is *1Q84*, a complex tale of cults and assassins set in 1984 that unravels over more than 1000 pages.

For a wonderful insight into what makes this publicity-shy author tick, read his brief memoir about running marathons and writing, **What I Talk About When I Talk About Running**.

to terms with the modern era – is considered his best book.

Sei Shōnagon *The Pillow Book*. Fascinating insight into the daily life and artful thoughts of a tenth-century noblewoman.

Tanizaki Jun'ichirō *Some Prefer Nettles* and *The Makioka Sisters*. One of the great stylists of Japanese prose, Tanizaki finest book is often considered to be *Some Prefer Nettles* about a romantic liaison between a Japanese man and Eurasian woman. However, there's an epic sweep to *The Makioka Sisters*, which documents the decline of a wealthy merchant family in Osaka.

CONTEMPORARY FICTION

Natsuo Kirino *Out*. Four women working in a bentō factory just outside Tokyo discover that committing murder is both easier and much more complicated than they could ever have imagined, in this dark, superior thriller. Follow-up books include *Grotesque*, about the deaths of two Tokyo prostitutes, and *Real World*, a grim thriller about alienated Japanese teenagers.

Mishima Yukio *After the Banquet*, *Confessions of Mask*, *Forbidden Colours* and *The Sea of Fertility*. Novelist Mishima sealed his notoriety by committing ritual suicide after leading a failed military coup in 1970. He left behind a highly respectable, if at times melodramatic, body of literature, including some of Japan's finest postwar novels.

Mizumura Minae *A True Novel*. A wonderful reworking of *Wuthering Heights* in the context of postwar Japan and the high economic growth period. The heroine straddles east and west and suffers many trials and tribulations through her doomed romance with an angry young man.

★**Murakami Ryū** *Almost Transparent Blue*, *Sixty-nine* and *Coin Locker Babies*. Murakami burst onto Japan's literary scene in the mid-1980s with *Almost Transparent Blue*, a hip tale of student life mixing reality and fantasy. *Sixty-nine* is his semi-autobiographical account of a 17 year

old stirred by rebellion. *Coin Locker Babies* is his most ambitious work – a revenger's tragedy about the lives of two boys dumped in adjacent coin lockers as babies.

Ōe Kenzaburō *Nip the Buds*, *Shoot the Kids*, *A Personal Matter* and *A Healing Family*. Winner of Japan's second Nobel prize for literature in 1994. *Nip the Buds*, his first full-length novel, published in 1958, is a tale of lost innocence concerning fifteen reformatory schoolboys evacuated in wartime to a remote mountain village and left to fend for themselves when a threatening plague frightens away the villagers. *A Personal Matter* sees Ōe tackling the trauma of his handicapped son Hikari's birth, while *A Healing Family* catches up with Hikari thirty years later.

Shiba Ryōtarō *Clouds Above The Hill*. This best-selling epic novel of the modernization of Japan and the Russo-Japanese War has only recently been translated into English. The four-volume set is enthralling reading and shows the hope and vision of the Meiji reformers.

Tsujihara Noboru *Jasmine*. Nicely written adventure and suspense novel which explores the relationships between a Japanese man and a Chinese woman, linking the Tiananmen Massacre of 1989 to the 1995 Kōbe earthquake and the touchy issue of Sino–Japanese relations.

JAPAN IN FOREIGN FICTION

Ellis Avery *The Teahouse Fire*. Set in the tea ceremony world of Kyoto in the late nineteenth century, this elegantly written novel is told through the eyes of a young American woman who is orphaned and then adopted by a family of tea masters. A fascinating portrait of women's lives and the political upheavals of Meiji Japan.

Alan Brown *Audrey Hepburn's Neck*. Beneath this rib-tickling, acutely observed tale of a young guy from the sticks adrift in big-city Tokyo, Brown weaves several important themes, including the continuing impact of World War II and the confused relationships between the Japanese and *gaijin*.

William Gibson *Idoru*. Love in the age of the computer chip. Cyberpunk novelist Gibson's sci-fi vision of Tokyo's hi-tech future – a world of non-intrusive DNA checks at airports and computerized pop icons (the *idoru* of the title) – rings disturbingly true.

Arthur Golden *Memoirs of a Geisha*. Rags to riches potboiler following the progress of Chiyo from her humble beginnings in a Japanese fishing village through training as a geisha in Kyoto to moving to New York.

Mo Hayder *Tokyo*. Disturbing crime thriller set in 1990s Tokyo and Nanking during the Japanese invasion in 1937, weaving a frightening story around war atrocities, the *yakuza* and foreign women bar hostesses. Also recently re-published as *The Devil of Nanking*.

★**Barry Lancet** *Japantown*. Thriller set in San Francisco and Tokyo that follows an antique-dealer PI as he sets out to solve the murder of a Japanese family. Lots of detailed cultural references and interesting plot twists make this a fun and informative read.

★**David Mitchell** *Ghostwritten*, *number9dream* and *The Thousand Autumns of Jacob De Zoet*. Mitchell lived in Japan for several years, a fact that is reflected in three of his novels. *Ghostwritten* is a dazzling collection of interlocked short stories, a couple of which are based in Japan. *number9dream* conjures up a postmodern Japan of computer hackers, video games, gangsters and violence. His latest, *The Thousand Autumns of Jacob De Zoet*, is a fascinating historical novel focusing on life on Nagasaki's island enclave of Dejima – the only place Europeans were allowed to live in Japan during the Tokugawa era.

Japanese

Picking up a few words of Japanese is not difficult. Pronunciation is simple and standard and there are few exceptions to the straightforward grammar rules. With a just a little effort, you should be able to read the words spelled out in *hiragana* and *katakana*, Japanese phonetic characters, even if you can't understand them. And any time spent learning Japanese will be amply rewarded by delighted locals, who'll always politely comment on your fine linguistic ability.

That said, it does take a very great effort to master Japanese. The primary stumbling block is the thousands of **kanji** characters (Chinese ideograms) that need to be memorized, most of which have at least two pronunciations, depending on the sentence and their combination with other characters. Also tricky are the language's multiple levels of **politeness**, married with different sets of words used by men and women, as well as different **dialects** involving whole new vocabularies.

Japanese characters

Japanese is written in a combination of three systems. To be able to read a newspaper, you'll need to know around two thousand *kanji*, much more difficult than it sounds, since what each one means varies with its context.

The easier writing systems to pick up are the phonetic syllabaries, **hiragana** and **katakana** Both have 46 regular characters (see box, p.840) and can be learned within a couple of weeks. *Hiragana* is used for Japanese words, while *katakana*, with the squarer characters, is used mainly for "loan words" borrowed from other languages (especially English) and technical names. **Rōmaji** (see p.840), the roman script used to spell out Japanese words, is also used in advertisements and magazines.

The first five letters in *hiragana* and *katakana* (**a**, **i**, **u**, **e**, **o**) are the vowel sounds (see p.840). The remainder are a combination of a consonant and a vowel (eg **ka**, **ki**, **ku**, **ke**, **ko**), with the exception of **n**, the only consonant that exists on its own. While *hiragana* provides an exact phonetic reading of all Japanese words, *katakana* does not do the same for foreign loan words. Often words are abbreviated, hence television becomes *terebi* and sexual harassment *sekuhara*. Sometimes, they become almost unrecognizable, as with *kakuteru* (cocktail).

Traditionally, Japanese is written in vertical columns and read right to left. However, the Western way of writing from left to right, horizontally from top to bottom is increasingly common. In the media and on signs you'll see a mixture of the two ways of writing.

Grammar

In Japanese, **verbs** do not change according to the person or number, so that *ikimasu* can mean "I go", "he/she/it goes", or "we/they go". **Pronouns** are usually omitted, since it's generally clear from the context who or what the speaker is referring to. There are no **definite articles**, and **nouns** stay the same whether they refer to singular or plural words.

Compared to English grammar, Japanese **sentences** are structured back to front. An English-speaker would say "I am going to Tokyo" which in Japanese would translate directly as "Tokyo to going". Placing the sound "*ka*" at the end of a phrase indicates a

KATAKANA AND HIRAGANA

Katakana and *hiragana* are two phonetic syllabaries represented by the characters shown below. *Katakana*, the squarer characters in the first table, are generally used for writing foreign "loan words". The rounder characters in the bottom table, *hiragana*, are generally used for Japanese words, in combination with, or as substitutes for, *kanji*.

KATAKANA

a	ア	i	イ	u	ウ	e	エ	o	オ
ka	カ	ki	キ	ku	ク	ke	ケ	ko	コ
sa	サ	shi	シ	su	ス	se	セ	so	ソ
ta	タ	chi	チ	tsu	ツ	te	テ	to	ト
na	ナ	ni	ニ	nu	ヌ	ne	ネ	no	ノ
ha	ハ	hi	ヒ	fu	フ	he	ヘ	ho	ホ
ma	マ	mi	ミ	mu	ム	me	メ	mo	モ
ya	ヤ			yu	ユ			yo	ヨ
ra	ラ	ri	リ	ru	ル	re	レ	ro	ロ
wa	ワ							wo	ヲ
n	ン								

HIRAGANA

a	あ	i	い	u	う	e	え	o	お
ka	か	ki	き	ku	く	ke	け	ko	こ
sa	さ	shi	し	su	す	se	せ	so	そ
ta	た	chi	ち	tsu	つ	te	て	to	と
na	な	ni	に	nu	ぬ	ne	ね	no	の
ha	は	hi	ひ	fu	ふ	he	へ	ho	ほ
ma	ま	mi	み	mu	む	me	め	mo	も
ya	や			yu	ゆ			yo	よ
ra	ら	ri	り	ru	る	re	れ	ro	ろ
wa	わ							wo	を
n	ん								

question, hence *Tokyo e ikimasu-ka* means "Are you going to Tokyo?" There are also levels of **politeness** to contend with, which alter the way the verb is conjugated, and sometimes change the word entirely. Stick to the polite -*masu* form of verbs which we use in this chapter and you should be fine.

Japanese: A Rough Guide Phrasebook includes essential phrases and expressions and a dictionary section and menu reader. The phonetic translations in the phrasebook are rendered slightly differently from the standard way *rōmaji* is written in this book, as an aid to pronunciation.

Pronunciation

Japanese words in this book have been transliterated into the standard Hepburn system of romanization, called **rōmaji**. Pronunciation is as follows:

a as in cat
i as in macaroni, or **ee**
u as in put, or **oo**
e as in bed; e is always pronounced, even at the end of a word
o as in not
ae as in the two separate sounds, **ah-eh**

ai as in Thai
ei as in weight
ie as in two separate sounds, **ee-eh**
ue as in two separate sounds, **oo-eh**
g, a hard sound as in girl
s as in mass (never z)
y as in yet

A bar (macron) over a vowel or "ii" means that the vowel sound is twice as long as a vowel without a bar. Only where words are well known in English, such as Tokyo,

JAPANESE SCRIPT IN THE GUIDE

To help you find your way around, in the guide we've included **Japanese script** for all places covered, as well as sights, hotels, restaurants, cafés, bars and shops where there is no prominent English sign. Where the English name for a point of interest is very different from its Japanese name, we've also provided the *rōmaji* (see opposite), so you can pronounce the Japanese.

Kyoto, judo and shogun, have we not used a bar to indicate long vowel sounds. Sometimes, vowel sounds are shortened or softened; for example, the verb *desu* sounds more like *des* when pronounced, and *sukiyaki* like *skiyaki*. Some syllables are also softened or hardened by the addition of a small ° or ˝ above the character; for example, **ka** (か) becomes **ga** (が) and **ba** (ば) becomes **pa** (ぱ). Likewise a smaller case ya, yu or yo following a character alters its sound, such as **kya** (きゃ) and **kyu** (きゅ). All syllables are evenly stressed and pronounced in full. For example, Nagano is Na-ga-no, not Na-GA-no.

Wherever there's a double consonant (eg *tetsudatte*), pause for a moment before saying it. It's somewhat like a glottal stop, and, as always, the best way to learn it is to listen out for it. When you see "**tch**" (eg *matcha*), pronounce it as a double c.

USEFUL WORDS AND PHRASES

BASICS

Yes	hai	はい
No	iie/chigaimasu	いいえ／違います
OK	daijōbu/ōkē	大丈夫／オーケー
Please (offering something)	dōzo	どうぞ
Please (asking for something)	onegai shimasu	お願いします
Excuse me	sumimasen/shitsurei shimasu	すみません／失礼します
I'm sorry	gomen nasai/sumimasen	ごめんなさい／すみません
Thanks (informal)	dōmo	どうも
Thank you	arigatō	ありがとう
Thank you very much	dōmo arigatō gozaimasu	どうもありがとうございます
What?	nani?	なに
When?	itsu?	いつ
Where?	doko?	どこ
Who?	dare?	だれ
This	kore	これ
That	sore	それ
That (over there)	are	あれ
How many?	ikutsu?	いくつ
How much?	ikura?	いくら
I don't want/need (x)	Watashi wa (x) ga hoshii desu	私は(x)が欲しいです
I don't want (x)	Watashi wa (x) ga irimasen	私は(x)がいりません
Is it possible…?	…koto ga dekimasu ka	。。。ことができますか
It is not possible	…koto ga dekimasen	。。。ことができません
Is it…?	…desu ka	。。。ですか
Can you please help me?	Tetsudatte kuremasen ka	手伝ってくれませんか
I don't speak Japanese	Nihongo ga hanasemasen	日本語は話せません
I don't read Japanese	Nihongo ga yomemasen	日本語は読めません
Can you speak English?	Eigo ga dekimasu ka	英語ができますか
Is there someone who can interpret?	Tsūyaku wa imasu ka	通訳はいますか
Could you please speak more slowly?	Motto yukkuri hanashite kuremasen ka	もっとゆっくり話してくれませんか

Please say that again	Mō ichido yutte kuremasen ka	もう一度言ってくれませんか
I understand/I see	Wakarimasu/Naruhodo	わかります／なるほど
I don't understand	Wakarimasen	分かりません
What does this mean?	Kore wa dō iyu imi desu ka	これはどういう意味ですか
How do you say (x) in Japanese?	Nihongo de (x) o nan-to iimasu ka	日本語で(x) を何と言いますか
What's this called?	Kore wa nan-to iimasu ka	これは何と言いますか
How do you pronounce this character?	Kono kanji wa nan-to yomimasu ka	この漢字は何と読みますか
Please write in English/Japanese	Eigo/Nihongo de kaite kudasai	英語／日本語で書いてください

PERSONAL PRONOUNS

I	watashi	私
I (familiar, men only)	boku/ore	僕/俺
You	anata	あなた
You (familiar)	kimi	君
He	kare	彼
She	kanojo	彼女
We	watashi-tachi	私たち
You (plural)	anata-tachi	あなたたち
They (male/female)	karera/kanojo-tachi	彼ら／彼女たち
They (objects)	sorera	それら

GREETINGS AND BASIC COURTESIES

Hello/Good day	Konnichiwa	今日は
Good morning	Ohayô gozaimasu	おはようございます
Good evening	Konbanwa	今晩は
Good night (when leaving)	Osaki ni	お先に
Good night (when going to bed)	Oyasuminasai	おやすみなさい
How are you?	O-genki desu ka	お元気ですか
I'm fine (informal)	Genki desu	元気です
I'm fine, thanks	Okagesama de	おかげさまで
How do you do/Nice to meet you	Hajimemashite	はじめまして
Don't mention it/You're welcome	Dô itashimashite	どういたしまして
I'm sorry	Gomen nasai	ごめんなさい
Just a minute please	Chotto matte kudasai	ちょっと待ってください
Goodbye	Sayonara/sayônara	さよなら／さようなら
Goodbye (informal)	Dewa mata/Jâ ne	では又／じゃあね

CHITCHAT

What's your name?	Shitsurei desu ga o-namae wa	失礼ですがお名前は
My name is (x)	Watashi no namae wa (x) desu	私の名前は(x)です
Where are you from?	O-kuni wa doko desu ka	お国はどこですか
Britain	Eikoku/Igirisu	英国／イギリス
Ireland	Airurando	アイルランド
America	Amerika	アメリカ
Australia	Ôsutoraria	オーストラリア
Canada	Kanada	カナダ
France	Furansu	フランス
Germany	Doitsu	ドイツ
New Zealand	Nyū Jiirando	ニュージーランド
Japan	Nihon	日本
Outside Japan	Gaikoku	外国
How old are you?	O-ikutsu desu ka	おいくつですか

am (age)	(age) sai desu	(age)才です/ (age)歳です
re you married?	Kekkon shite imasu ka	結婚していますか
am married/not married	Kekkon shite imasu/imasen	結婚しています／いません
o you like…?	…suki desu ka	。。。好きですか
do like	…suki desu	。。。好きです
don't like	…suki dewa arimasen	。。。好きではありません
What's your job?	O-shigoto wa nan desu ka	お仕事は何ですか
'm a student	Gakusei desu	学生です
'm a teacher	Sensei desu	先生です
work for a company	Kaisha-in desu	会社員です
'm a tourist	Kankō kyaku desu	観光客です
Really?	Hontō/Hontō ni	本当/本当に
That's a shame	Zannen desu	残念です
It can't be helped (formal/informal)	Shikata ga nai/shō ga nai	仕方がない／しょうがない

NUMBERS

There are special ways of **counting** different things in Japanese. The most common first translation is used when counting time and quantities and measurements, with added qualifiers such as minutes (*pun/fun*) or yen (*en*). The second translations are sometimes used for counting objects. From ten, there is only one set of numbers. For zero, four and seven, alternatives to the first translation are used in some circumstances.

Zero	zero/rei		-	
One	ichi	hitotsu	一	ひとつ
Two	ni	futatsu	二	ふたつ
Three	san	mittsu	三	みっつ
Four	yon/shi	yottsu	四	よっつ
Five	go	itsutsu	五	いつつ
Six	roku	muttsu	六	むっつ
Seven	shichi/nana	nanatsu	七	ななつ
Eight	hachi	yattsu	八	やっつ
Nine	kyū	kokonotsu	九	ここのつ
Ten	jū	tō	十	とう
Eleven	jū-ichi		十一	
Twelve	jū-ni		十二	
Twenty	ni-jū		二十	
Twenty-one	ni-jū-ichi		二十一	
Thirty	san-jū		三十	
One hundred	hyaku		百	
Two hundred	ni-hyaku		二百	
Thousand	sen		千	
Ten thousand	ichi-man		一万	
One hundred thousand	jū-man		十万	
One million	hyaku-man		百万	
One hundred million	ichi-oku		一億	

TIME AND DATES

Now	ima	今
Today	kyō	今日
Morning	asa	朝
Evening	yūgata	夕方
Night	yoru/ban	夜/晩
Tomorrow	ashita	明日
The day after tomorrow	asatte	あさって
Yesterday	kinō	昨日

Week	shū	週
Month	gatsu/tsuki/getsu	月
Year	nen/toshi	年
Monday	Getsuyōbi	月曜日
Tuesday	Kayōbi	火曜日
Wednesday	Suiyōbi	水曜日
Thursday	Mokuyōbi	木曜日
Friday	Kin'yōbi	金曜日
Saturday	Doyōbi	土曜日
Sunday	Nichiyōbi	日曜日
What time is it?	Ima nan-ji desu ka	今何時ですか
It's 10 o'clock	Jū-ji desu	十時です
...10.20	Jū-ji ni-juppun	十時二十分
...10.30	Jū-ji han	十時半
...10.50	Jū-ichi-ji juppun mae	十一時十分前
AM	gozen	午前
PM	gogo	午後
January	Ichigatsu	一月
February	Nigatsu	二月
March	Sangatsu	三月
April	Shigatsu	四月
May	Gogatsu	五月
June	Rokugatsu	六月
July	Shichigatsu	七月
August	Hachigatsu	八月
September	Kugatsu	九月
October	Jūgatsu	十月
November	Jūichigatsu	十一月
December	Jūnigatsu	十二月
1st (day)	tsuitachi	一日
2nd (day)	futsuka	二日
3rd (day)	mikka	三日
4th (day)	yokka	四日
5th (day)	itsuka	五日
6th (day)	muika	六日
7th (day)	nanoka	七日
8th (day)	yōka	八日
9th (day)	kokonoka	九日
10th (day)	tōka	十日
11th (day)	jū-ichi-nichi	十一日
12th (day)	jū-ni-nichi	十二日
20th (day)	hatsuka	二十日
21st (day)	ni-jū-ichi nichi	二十一日
30th (day)	san-jū-nichi	三十日

GETTING AROUND

Aeroplane	hikōki	飛行機
Airport	kūkō	空港
Bus	basu	バス
Long-distance bus	chōkyori basu	長距離バス
Bus stop	basu tei	バス停
Train	densha	電車
Station	eki	駅
Subway	chikatetsu	地下鉄

erry	ferii	フェリー
eft-luggage office	azukarijo	預かり所
oin locker	koin rokkā	コインロッカー
icket office	kippu uriba	切符売り場
icket	kippu	切符
ne-way	kata-michi	片道
eturn	ōfuku	往復
on-smoking seat	kin'en seki	禁煙席
Window seat	mado-gawa no seki	窓側の席
latform	hōmu/purattofōmu	ホーム/プラットフォーム
icycle	jitensha	自転車
axi	takushii	タクシー
Map	chizu	地図
Where is (x)?	(x) wa doko desu ka	(x)はどこですか
traight ahead	massugu	まっすぐ
n front of	mae	前
ight	migi	右
eft	hidari	左
North	kita	北
South	minami	南
ast	higashi	東
West	nishi	西
Entrance	iriguchi	入口
Exit	deguchi/-guchi	出口/−口
Highway	kaidō	街道
Street	tōri/dōri/michi	通り/道

PLACES

Temple	otera/-dera/-ji/-in	お寺/−寺/−院
Shrine	jinja/jingū/-gū/-taisha	神社/神宮/−宮/−大社
Castle	shiro/-jō	城
Park	kōen	公園
River	kawa/gawa	川
Bridge	hashi/-bashi	橋
Museum	hakubutsukan	博物館
Art museum	bijutsukan	美術館
Garden	niwa/teien/-en	庭/庭園/−園
Island	shima/-jima/-tō	島
Slope	saka/-zaka	坂
Hill	oka	丘
Mountain	yama/-san/-take	山/岳
Hot spring spa	onsen	温泉
Lake	-ko	湖
Bay	-wan	湾
Peninsula	hantō	半島
Cape	misaki/saki	岬
Sea	umi/kai/nada	海/灘
Gorge	kyō	峡
Plateau	kōgen	高原
Prefecture	-ken/-fu	県/府
Ward	-ku	区
Shop	mise/-ten/-ya	店/屋

ACCOMMODATION

Hotel	hoteru	ホテル
Traditional-style inn	ryokan	旅館
Guesthouse	minshuku	民宿
Youth hostel	yūsu hosuteru	ユースホステル
Single room	shinguru rūmu	シングルルーム
Double room	daburu rūmu	ダブルルーム
Twin room	tsuin rūmu	ツインルーム
Dormitory	kyōdō/ōbeya	共同/大部屋
Japanese-style room	washitsu	和室
Western-style room	yōshitsu	洋室
Western-style bed	beddo	ベッド
Bath	o-furo	お風呂
Do you have any vacancies?	Kūshitsu wa arimasu ka	空室はありますか
I'd like to make a reservation	Yoyaku o shitai no desu ga	予約をしたいのですが
I have a reservation	Yoyaku shimashita	予約しました
I don't have a reservation	Yoyaku shimasen deshita	予約しませんでした
How much is it per person?	Hitori ikura desu ka	一人いくらですか
Does that include meals?	Shokuji wa tsuite imasu ka	食事はついていますか
I would like to stay one night / two nights	Hitoban/futaban tomaritai no desu ga	一晩/二晩泊まりたいのですが
I would like to see the room	Heya o misete kudasaimasen ka	部屋を見せてくださいませんか
Key	kagi	鍵
Passport	pasupōto	パスポート

SHOPPING, MONEY AND BANKS

Shop	mise/-ten/-ya	店/屋
How much is it?	Kore wa ikura desu ka	これはいくらですか
It's too expensive	Taka-sugimasu	高すぎます
Is there anything cheaper?	Mō sukoshi yasui mono wa arimasu ka	もう少し安いものはありますか
Do you accept credit cards?	Kurejitto kādo ga tsukaemasu ka	クレジットカードが使えますか
I'm just looking	Miru dake desu	見るだけです
Gift/souvenir	omiyage	お土産
Foreign exchange	gaikoku-kawase	外国為替
Bank	ginkō	銀行
Travellers' cheque	toraberāzu chekku	トラベラーズチェック

INTERNET, POST AND TELEPHONES

Internet	intānetto	インターネット
Post office	yūbinkyoku	郵便局
Envelope	fūtō	封筒
Letter	tegami	手紙
Postcard	hagaki/ehagaki	葉書/絵葉書
Stamp	kitte	切手
Airmail	kōkūbin	航空便
Telephone	denwa	電話
International telephone call	kokusai-denwa	国際電話
Reverse charge/collect call	korekuto-kōru	コレクトコール
Mobile phone	keitai-denwa/keitai	携帯電話/携帯
Fax	fakkusu	ファックス
Telephone card	terefon kādo	テレフォンカード
I would like to call (place)	(place) e denwa o kaketai no desu	(place) へ電話をかけたいのです
I would like to send a fax to (place)	(place) e fakkusu shitai no desu	(place) へファックスしたいのです

HEALTH

hospital	byōin	病院
pharmacy	yakkyoku	薬局
Medicine	kusuri	薬
Doctor	isha/o-isha-san	医者/お医者さん
Dentist	haisha	歯医者
Diarrhoea	geri	下痢
Fever	netsu	熱
Food poisoning	shoku chūdoku	食中毒
I'm ill	byōki desu	病気です
I've got a cold/flu	kaze o hikimashita	風邪を引きました
I'm allergic to (x)	(x) arerugii desu	(x) アレルギーです
Antibiotics	kōsei busshitsu	抗生物質
Antiseptic	shōdoku	消毒

FOOD AND DRINK

PLACES TO EAT AND DRINK

Bar	nomiya	飲み屋
Standing-only bar	tachinomiya	立ち飲み屋
Café/coffee shop	kissaten	喫茶店
Cafeteria	shokudō	食堂
Pub	pabu	パブ
Pub-style restaurant	izakaya	居酒屋
Restaurant	resutoran	レストラン
Restaurant specializing in charcoal-grilled foods	robatayaki	炉端焼
Street food stall	yatai	屋台

ORDERING

Breakfast	asa-gohan	朝ご飯
Lunch	hiru-gohan	昼ご飯
Dinner	ban-gohan/yūshoku	晩ご飯/夕食
Boxed meal	bentō	弁当
Chopsticks	hashi	はし
Fork	fōku	フォーク
Knife	naifu	ナイフ
Spoon	supūn	スプーン
Set meal	teishoku	定食
Daily special set meal	higawari-teishoku	日替り定食
Menu	menyū	メニュー
Do you have an English menu?	eigo no menyū ga arimasu ka	英語のメニューがありますか
How much is that?	ikura desu ka	いくらですか
I would like (a)…	(a) …o onegai shimasu	(a)をお願いします
May I have the bill?	okanjō o onegai shimasu	お勘定をお願いします

STAPLE FOODS

oil	abura	油
butter	batā	バター
rice	gohan	ご飯
pepper	koshō	こしょう
fermented soybean paste	miso	味噌
garlic	ninniku	にんにく
dried seaweed	nori	のり
bread	pan	パン

sugar	satō	砂糖
salt	shio	塩
soy sauce	shōyu	しょうゆ
egg	tamago	卵
bean curd tofu	tōfu	豆腐

FISH AND SEAFOOD DISHES

horse mackerel	aji	あじ
abalone	awabi	あわび
sweet fish	ayu	あゆ
yellowtail	buri	ぶり
sushi topped with fish, egg and vegetables	chirashi-zushi	ちらし寿司
prawn	ebi	えび
blowfish	fugu	ふぐ
squid	ika	いか
lobster	ise-ebi	伊勢海老
shellfish	kai	貝
oyster	kaki	かき
crab	kani	かに
tuna	maguro	まぐろ
sushi rolled in crisp seaweed	maki-zushi	まき寿司
bite-size portion of sushi rice with topping	nigiri-zushi	にぎり寿司
herring	nishin	にしん
fish	sakana	魚
raw fish	sashimi	さしみ
sushi	sushi	寿司
sea bream	tai	たい
octopus	tako	たこ/タコ
cod	tara	たら
eel	unagi	うなぎ
sea urchin	uni	うに

FRUIT

banana	banana	バナナ
grapes	budō	ぶどう
grapefruit	gurēpufurūtsu	グレープフルーツ
strawberry	ichigo	いちご
persimmon	kaki	柿
fruit	kudamono	果物
melon	meron	メロン
tangerine	mikan	みかん
peach	momo	桃
pear	nashi	なし
orange	orenji	オレンジ
pineapple	painappuru	パイナップル
lemon	remon	レモン
apple	ringo	りんご
watermelon	suika	すいか
Japanese plum	ume	うめ

VEGETABLES

radish	daikon	大根
cauliflower	karifurawā	カリフラワー
mushroom	kinoko	きのこ
sweetcorn	kōn	コーン
beans	mame	豆
beansprouts	moyashi	もやし
aubergine	nasu	なす
leek	negi	ねぎ
carrot	ninjin	にんじん
green pepper	piiman	ピーマン
potato	poteto/jagaimo	ポテト、じゃがいも
salad	sarada	サラダ
onion	tamanegi	たまねぎ
tomato	tomato	トマト
green horseradish	wasabi	わさび
vegetables	yasai	野菜

MEAT AND MEAT DISHES

pork	butaniku	豚肉
beef	gyūniku	牛肉
skewers of food dipped in breadcrumbs and deep-fried	kushiage	串揚げ
stew including meat (or seafood), vegetables and noodles	nabe	鍋
meat	niku	肉
lamb	ramu	ラム
thin beef slices cooked in broth	shabu-shabu	しゃぶしゃぶ
thin beef slices braised in a sauce	sukiyaki	すきやき
breaded, deep-fried slice of pork	tonkatsu	とんかつ
chicken	toriniku	鶏肉
grilled meat	yakiniku	焼肉
chicken, grilled on skewers	yakitori	焼き鳥

VEGETARIAN AND NOODLE DISHES

Chinese-style dumplings	gyōza	ぎょうざ
soba in a hot soup	kake-soba	かけそば
stewed chunks of vegetables and fish on skewers	oden	おでん
Chinese-style noodles	rāmen	ラーメン
Buddhist-style vegetarian cuisine	shōjin-ryōri	精進料理
thin buckwheat noodles	soba	そば
thick wheat noodles	udon	うどん
fried noodles	yakisoba/yakiudon	焼そば／焼うどん
cold soba served with a dipping sauce	zaru-soba/mori-soba	ざるそば／もりそば

OTHER DISHES

fried rice	chāhan	チャーハン
Chinese food	Chūka-/Chūgoku-ryōri	中華／中国料理
rice topped with fish, meat or vegetable	donburi	どんぶり
French food	Furansu-ryōri	フランス料理
Italian food	Itaria-ryōri	イタリア料理
Japanese haute cuisine	kaiseki-ryōri	懐石料理

Korean food	Kankoku-ryōri	韓国料理
curry served with rice	karē raisu	カレーライス
pounded rice cakes	mochi	もち
"no-nationality" food	mukokuseki-ryōri	無国籍料理
fermented soybeans	nattō	納豆
savoury pancakes	okonomiyaki	お好み焼き
rice triangles wrapped in crisp seaweed	onigiri	おにぎり
Thai food	Tai-ryōri	タイ料理
octopus in balls of batter	takoyaki	たこ焼き
lightly battered seafood and vegetables	tempura	天ぷら
meat, vegetable and fish cooked in soy sauce and sweet sake	teriyaki	照り焼き
Japanese-style food	washoku	和食
Western-style food	yōshoku	洋食

DRINKS

beer	biiru	ビール
fruit juice	jūsu	ジュース
black tea	kōcha	紅茶
coffee	kōhii	コーヒー
powdered green tea	matcha	抹茶
milk	miruku	ミルク
water	mizu	水
whisky and water	mizu-wari	水割り
sake (rice wine)	sake/nihon-shu	酒／日本酒
green tea	sencha	煎茶
distilled liquor	shōchū	焼酎
whisky	uisukii	ウイスキー
Oolong tea	ūron-cha	ウーロン茶
wine	wain	ワイン

Glossary

aikido A form of self-defence recognized as a sport.

ANA All Nippon Airways.

anime Japanese animation.

banzai Traditional cheer, meaning "10,000 years".

basho Sumo tournament.

benten or **benzai-ten** One of the most popular folk-goddesses, usually associated with water.

bentō Lunch box of rice, fish, vegetables, and pickles.

bodhisattva or **bosatsu** A Buddhist intermediary who has forsaken nirvana to work for the salvation of all humanity.

bunraku Traditional puppet theatre.

Butō or **Butoh** Highly expressive contemporary performance art.

cha-no-yu, chadō or **sadō** The tea ceremony. Ritual tea drinking raised to an art form.

-chō or **-machi** Subdivision of a city, smaller than a -ku.

-chōme Area of the city consisting of a few blocks.

daimyō Feudal lords.

Dainichi Nyorai or **Rushana Butsu** The Cosmic Buddha in whom all Buddhas are unified.

-dake Mountain peak, usually volcanic.

DPJ Democratic Party of Japan.

Edo Pre-1868 name for Tokyo.

ema Small wooden boards found at shrines, on which people write their wishes or thanks.

fusuma Paper-covered sliding doors, more substantial than shōji, used to separate rooms or for cupboards.

futon Padded quilt used for bedding.

gagaku Traditional Japanese music used for court ceremonies and religious rites.

gaikokujin or **gaijin** Foreigner.

geisha Traditional female entertainer accomplished in the arts.

genkan Foyer or entrance hall of a house, ryokan and so forth, for changing from outdoor shoes into slippers

genki Lively and/or healthy, friendly.

geta Traditional wooden sandals.

haiku Seventeen-syllable verse form, arranged in three lines of five, seven and five syllables.

hanami "Flower-viewing"; most commonly associated with spring outings to admire the cherry blossom.

-hashi or **-bashi** Bridge.

hiragana Phonetic script used for writing Japanese in combination with kanji.

ijinkan Western-style brick and clapboard houses.

ikebana Traditional art of flower arranging.

Inari Shintō god of harvests, often represented by his fox-messenger.

JAL Japan Airlines.

-ji Buddhist temple.

jigoku The word for Buddhist "hell", also applied to volcanic mud pools and steam vents.

-jinja or **-jingū** Shintō shrine.

Jizō Buddhist protector of children, travellers and the dead.

JNTO Japan National Tourist Organization.

-jō Castle.

JR Japan Railways.

kabuki Popular theatre of the Edo period.

kami Shintō deities residing in trees, rocks and other natural phenomena.

Kamikaze The "Divine Wind" which saved Japan from the Mongol invaders (see p.794). During World War II the name was applied to Japan's suicide bombers.

kanji Japanese script derived from Chinese characters.

Kannon Buddhist goddess of mercy. A bodhisattva who appears in many different forms.

katakana Phonetic script used mainly for writing foreign words in Japanese.

-kawa or **-gawa** River.

-ken Prefecture. The principal administrative region, similar to a state or county.

kendo Japan's oldest martial art, using wooden staves, with its roots in samurai training exercises.

kimono Literally "clothes", though usually referring to women's traditional dress.

-ko Lake.

kōban Neighbourhood police box.

kōen or **gyoen** Public park.

kōgen Plateau, or highlands.

-ku Principal administrative division of the city, usually translated as "ward".

konbini Convenience store.

kura Traditional storehouse built with thick mud walls as protection against fire, for keeping produce and family treasures.

kyōgen Short, satirical plays, providing comic interludes in nō drama.

LDP Liberal Democratic Party.

-machi Town or area of a city.

maiko Apprentice geisha.

manga Japanese comics.

matcha Powdered green tea used in the tea ceremony.

matsuri Festival.

Meiji Period named after Emperor Meiji (1868–1912), meaning "enlightened rule".

Meiji Restoration End of the Tokugawa Shogunate, when power was fully restored to the emperor.

mikoshi Portable shrine used in festivals.

minshuku Family-run lodgings which are cheaper than ryokan.

mon Gate, usually to a castle, temple or palace.

mura Village.

netsuke Small, intricately carved toggles for fastening the cords of cloth bags.

ningyō Japanese doll.

nō Highly stylized dance-drama, using masks and elaborate costumes.

noren Split curtain hanging in shop and restaurant doorways to indicate they're open.

notemburo Outdoor hot-spring pool, usually in natural surroundings.

obi Wide sash worn with kimono.

odori Traditional dances performed in the streets during the summer Obon festival.

onsen Hot spring, generally developed for bathing.

pachinko Vertical pinball machines.

pond-garden Classic form of garden design focused around a pond.

rōmaji System of transliterating Japanese words using the roman alphabet.

rōnin Masterless samurai.

rotemburo Outdoor hot-spring pool, often in the grounds of a ryokan.

ryokan Traditional Japanese inn.

salarymen Office workers who keep Japan's companies and ministries ticking over.

samurai Warrior class who were retainers of the *daimyō*.

SDF (Self-Defence Forces) Japan's army, navy and airforce.

sensei Teacher.

sentō Neighbourhood public bath.

seppuku Ritual suicide by disembowelment, also referred to as *harakiri*.

Shaka Nyorai The Historical Buddha, Sakyamuni.

shamisen Traditional, three-stringed instrument played with a plectrum.

-shima or **-jima** Island.

Shinkansen Bullet train.

Shintō Japan's indigenous animist religion.

Shitamachi Old working-class districts of east Tokyo.

shogun Japan's military rulers before 1868, nominally subordinate to the emperor.

shōji Paper-covered sliding screens used to divide rooms or cover windows.

shōjin ryōri Buddhist cuisine

shukubō Temple lodgings.

sumi-e Ink paintings, traditionally using black ink.

sumo A form of heavyweight wrestling which evolved from ancient Shintō divination rites.

taiko Drums.

tatami Rice-straw matting, the traditional covering for floors.

tokonoma Alcove in a room where flowers or a scroll are displayed.

torii Gate to a Shintō shrine.

ukiyo-e Colourful woodblock prints.

waka Thirty-one-syllable poem, arranged in five lines of five, seven, five, seven and seven syllables.

washi Traditional handmade paper.

Yakushi Nyorai The Buddha in charge of physical and spiritual healing.

yakuza Professional criminal gangs, somewhat akin to the Mafia.

yamabushi Ascetic mountain priests.

yokozuna Champion sumo wrestler.

yukata Cotton kimono usually worn in summer, and after a bath.

Small print and index

Rough Guide credits

Editor: Helen Abramson, Neil Mcquillian and Mandy Tomlin
Layout: Ankur Guha
Cartography: Katie Bennett and Ed Wright
Picture editor: Natascha Sturny
Proofreader: Susanne Hillen
Managing editor: Keith Drew
Assistant editor: Prema Dutta

Production: Charlotte Cade
Cover design: Nicole Newman and Ankur Guha
Photographer: Martin Richardson
Editorial assistant: Rebecca Hallett
Senior pre-press designer: Dan May
Programme manager: Helen Blount
Publisher: Joanna Kirby

Publishing information

This sixth edition published September 2014 by
Rough Guides Ltd,
80 Strand, London WC2R 0RL
11, Community Centre, Panchsheel Park,
New Delhi 110017, India
Distributed by Penguin Random House
Penguin Books Ltd,
80 Strand, London WC2R 0RL
Penguin Group (USA)
345 Hudson Street, NY 10014, USA
Penguin Group (Australia)
250 Camberwell Road, Camberwell,
Victoria 3124, Australia
Penguin Group (NZ)
67 Apollo Drive, Mairangi Bay, Auckland 1310,
New Zealand
Penguin Group (South Africa)
Block D, Rosebank Office Park, 181 Jan Smuts Avenue,
Parktown North, Gauteng, South Africa 2193
Rough Guides is represented in Canada by Tourmaline
Editions Inc. 662 King Street West, Suite 304, Toronto,
Ontario M5V 1M7
Printed in Singapore by Toppan Security Printing Pte. Ltd.

MIX
Paper from
responsible sources
FSC™ C018179
www.fsc.org

Help us update

We've gone to a lot of effort to ensure that the sixth edition of **The Rough Guide to Japan** is accurate and up-to-date. However, things change – places get "discovered", opening hours are notoriously fickle, restaurants and rooms raise prices or lower standards. If you feel we've got it wrong or left something out, we'd like to know, and if you can remember the address, the price, the hours, the phone number, so much the better.

Please send your comments with the subject line **"Rough Guide Japan Update"** to ✉ mail@uk.roughguides .com. We'll credit all contributions and send a copy of the next edition (or any other Rough Guide if you prefer) for the very best emails.

Find more travel information, connect with fellow travellers and plan your trip on Ⓦ roughguides.com

Acknowledgements

Sophie Branscombe Many thanks to: Kylie Clark and Mikami-san at JNTO London; Yoshimine Nakamura at Nikkanren; Genki Yasuoka at PuPuRu International; Inside Japan and North South Travel; and to Ed and Helen and the Rough Guides team. Thanks to Simon Richmond for the top tips and many happy years of RG collaboration, and to Nina Homma in Hakodate, for saving me from the typhoon. Huge thanks, as always, to Dom and Yuri for the soft landing, KC and family for the flying visit, and all my friends in Kurayoshi, especially Sumiyoshi B&B. Finally, to Enric and Xavier for mapping my travels from afar – thank you for letting me go on my Japanese adventures; next time I'll be taking both of you!

Neil Maclean I am very grateful to everybody who helped during my research, especially: Yoshimune Nakamura from the Japan Ryokan Association; Kylie Clark at JNTO; Takanori Ogasawara from Tohuku Tourist Promotion; Jamie Mundy and Karen Tomney from Inside Japan; and Genki Yasuoka from PuPuRu. And particular thanks for practical help during my trip to Chie Otsuka and Atsushi Sugeno from the Kodo Cultural Foundation on Sado-ga-shima; Yoshikazu Kitaguchi and Ayako Miyata from the Ishikawa Prefectural Government and Kazumori Yachi in Kanazawa and Noto Hanto; Hitomi Murayama from Nippon Ski Resort Development and Yoko Hirose in Hakuba. Finally, thanks to Raluca for introducing me to Japan and Mike, Lulu, Tim and Mayumi for welcoming me in Tokyo.

Sally McLaren A big arigato to the many people in Kansai and Shikoku who went out of their way to help me, especially: Kyoko in Himeji, Mari at Takamatsu TIC, Rie and Yoshino at Benesse, Ayako on Koya-san, Muruka in Amanohashidate, Kayoko in Nara, Matthew and Noriko in Dogo, Keiji Shimizu in Kyoto, and Brad Towle and the Kumano Tourism Bureau. To Kylie Clark & JNTO London and

Nakamura-san at the Japan Ryokan & Hotel Association, I'm very grateful for your generous cooperation. Thanks so much to friends in Kyoto for your kindness, especially Junko and Wang Li, Hiroki Tamai, Michael and Harumi, as well Prof. Bernard Susser for his historical expertise and generous help, and Prof. Juliet Winters Carpenter for her literary recommendations. Thank you to Buddhist scholar Dr. Elizabeth Tinsley for sharing her research on EA Gordon. Many thanks to Ed, Helen, and Mandy – it was a pleasure working with you. As always, thanks to Albie for love and support.

Roger Norum My utmost thanks go to my longstanding editors Helen and Ed for their patience, tenacity and honed, fine-toothed combs. In Japan, I am extremely grateful for the help and generosity of Genki Yasuoka, Yoshimune Nakamura, James Mundy, Daniel Robson, Takako Ushio, Sugiyama-San in Yamaguchi, Ishizu-San and Keiko-San in Hagi, Uratsmi-San and Miyashita-San in Tottori, Tsutsui-San in Setoda and Kawasaki-San on Miyajima. Thank you, too, to Raluca Nagy and Jamie Coates for sharing their insights and passions about everything Japan.

Martin Zatko I would like to thank the many wonderful people I met on my trip around Japan. Particular thanks to Thomas Clinard, the self-proclaimed mayor of Nakameguro; Andy Rowan, his willing deputy; Justin Frescott and the Sakura House team; Naoko Tabata and the Tokyo Convention & Visitors Bureau; Toshiko at Andon Ryokan; Nakamura-san at the Ryokan Association; Kylie Clark and the JNTO; James Mundy and the InsideAsia team; the jolly staff and management at Hana Hostel in Fukuoka and Kheosan in Beppu; Eluise Fu for helping to track down the Yakushima onsen; and the chefs at innumerable restaurants across the land for making research work so incredibly tasty.

Photo credits

All photos © Rough Guides except the following:

(Key: t-top; c-centre; b-bottom; l-left; r-right)
p.1 Corbis, Gavin Hellier/AWL Images
p.2 Tim Draper
p.4 Corbis, Norio Masuyama/Amana Images
p.5 Robert Harding Picture Library, Jose Fuste Raga
p.9 Alamy, Amana Images (t); Corbis, B.S.P.I. (br); Craig Lovell (bl)
p.10 Getty Images, MIXA
p.15 Alamy, David Cherepuschak (c); imageBROKER (b); Robert Harding Picture Library, Michael Boyny/Look (t)
p.16 Corbis, Peter Adams
p.17 Alamy, Hemis (c); Corbis, Aflo (t); Getty Images, AFP (b)
p.18 Alamy, Damon Coulter (tl); J Marshall, Tribaleye Images (c); JTB Media Creation (b); Robert Harding Picture Library, Lucas Vallecillos (tr)
p.19 Corbis, Aflo (b)
p.20 Alamy, David Kleyn (t); Corbis, Ocean (c); Robert Harding Picture Library, Lucas Vallecillos (b)
p.21 Alamy, Ivan Vdovin (br); Corbis, Kimimasa Mayama (tr); Tim Draper, (tl)
p.22 Alamy, JTB Media Creation (b); Tim Draper, (t); Robert Harding Picture Library, Gavin Hellier (c)

p.23 Alamy, JTB Media Creation (c); StockShot (t); Robert Harding Picture Library, Hauke Dressler/Look (b)
p.24 Alamy, John Lander Photography (b); JTB Media Creation (c); Robert Harding Picture Library, Gavin Hellier (t)
p.25 Corbis, B.S.P.I. (tr); Robert Harding Picture Library, Lucas Vallecillos (b)
p.26 Alamy, Age Fotostock (tr); Alamy, JTB Media Creation (tl)
p.29 Alamy, Jon Arnold Images Ltd
p.76–77 Corbis, Michihiko Kanegae/Amana Images
p.99 Alamy, Roussel Photography (b); Robert Harding Picture Library, Photo Japan (tl)
p.145 Tim Draper, (t); Robert Harding Picture Library, Nano Calvo (b)
p.162–163 Robert Harding Picture Library, Jochen Schlenker
p.165 Alamy, John Lander Photography
p.183 Alamy, JTB Media Creation (t); Robert Harding Picture Library, Julier Garcia (b)
p.203 Alamy, JTB Media Creation (t); Ross Kelly (b)
p.218–219 Robert Harding Picture Library, Tibor Bognar
p.221 Robert Harding Picture Library, Peter Essick/Aurora Photos

Index

Maps are marked in grey

Map symbols

The symbols below are used on maps throughout the book

✈	Airport	�335;	Viewpoint	════	JR line
✗	Airfield	※	Observation platform	━━━	Shinkansen line
Ⓢ	Subway station	🛕	Pagoda	⋯⋯⋯	Other rail line
♦	Place of interest	🏯	Shrine	━━━	Monorail
♆	Museum	🏯	Buddhist temple	—Ⓣ—	Tram
✉	Post office	👁	Lighthouse	----	Cable car
ⓘ	Tourist information	🏠	Mountain refuge	⋯⋯⋯	Funicular
@	Internet access	▲	Mountain peak	— · —	Ferry
✚	Hospital	🕳	Cave	----	Footpath
Ⓔ	Embassy	⟱	Waterfall	▪	Building
☉	Statue	⚓	Port	⚙ □	Market
🌴	Gardens	⌇⌇	Snorkelling	◯	Stadium
🌳	Tree	∴	Ruin	+	Cemetery
⊠	Gate	♙	Castle		Park
★	Bus stop	△	Campsite	□	Beach
⛽	Fuel station	✺	Ferris wheel		

Listings key

■ Accommodation

● Restaurant/café/teahouse

■ Bar/club/live venue/music

● Shopping

A ROUGH GUIDE TO
ROUGH GUIDES

Published in 1982, the first Rough Guide – to Greece – was a student scheme that became a publishing phenomenon. Mark Ellingham, a recent graduate in English from Bristol University, had been travelling in Greece the previous summer and couldn't find the right guidebook. With a small group of friends he wrote his own guide, combining a highly contemporary, journalistic style with a thoroughly practical approach to travellers' needs.

The immediate success of the book spawned a series that rapidly covered dozens of destinations. And, in addition to impecunious backpackers, Rough Guides soon acquired a much broader and older readership that relished the guides' wit and inquisitiveness as much as their enthusiastic, critical approach and value-for-money ethos.

These days, Rough Guides feature recommendations from shoestring to luxury and cover more than 120 destinations around the globe. Our ever-growing team of authors and photographers is spread all over the world, particularly in Europe, the US and Australia.

Rough Guides now number around 200 titles, including Pocket city guides, inspirational coffee-table books and comprehensive country and regional titles, plus technology guides from iPods to Android. As well as print books, we publish groundbreaking ebooks for every major digital device.

Visit Ⓦ roughguides.com to see our latest publications.

Rough Guide travel images are available for commercial licensing at Ⓦ roughguidespictures.com.

Japan Ryokan & Hotel Association

Looking for somewhere to stay in Japan? Visit our website, where you'll find around 3,200 ryokan and hotels all over Japan, in main cities, small towns and tourist spots.

We can offer you a variety of accommodation from budget places to luxury class. We have any type of lodging you could wish for. Come and visit Japan for sightseeing or on business. We're ready to welcome you.

We're waiting for you to visit us in the near future.

www.ryokan.or.jp/english/